WESTERN NEVADA COMMUNITY COLLEGE
3 1439 00043 8120

D0952692

Learning Resources
Western Nevada Community College
2201 West Nye Lane
Carson City, NV 89703
WITHDRAWN

OXFORD DICTIONARY OF CURRENT IDIOMATIC ENGLISH

Volume 2: Phrase, Clause & Sentence Idioms

A P COWIE
R MACKIN &
I R McCAIG

Oxford University Press

Oxford University Press, Walton Street, Oxford OX2 6DP
LONDON NEW YORK TORONTO
DELHI BOMBAY CALCUTTA MADRAS KARACHI
KUALA LUMPUR SINGAPORE HONG KONG TOKYO
NAIROBI DAR ES SALAAM CAPE TOWN
MELBOURNE AUCKLAND
and associated companies in
BEIRUT BERLIN IBADAN MEXICO CITY NICOSIA

ISBN 0 19 431150 3

OXFORD is a trade mark of Oxford University Press

First published 1983
Third impression 1984

Computer typeset in Times and Univers by
Oxford University Press and Filmtype Services Ltd.
Printed in Hong Kong

Contents

Foreword

The appearance of this volume marks the realization of a project started a long ago as 1958. It was in that year that, at the suggestion of Bill (Dr W R Lee, I began to compile a *Dictionary of Fixed (or Invariable) Phrases*,[1] of whic a major feature was to have been an indication of frequency of occurrence, a in Michael West's *A General Service List of English Words*.[2] Like that book the present dictionary was written primarily for the use of foreign learners o English, though for those at an advanced level. If native speakers find it a interesting as many have apparently found Volume 1 the authors will, o course, be delighted.

The collecting of idiomatic expressions quickly became obsessive. My read ing became more intensive and more varied; the collection grew more and mor formidable as I tried, in vain, to establish some meaningful order o 'frequency'. Somehow I did not seem to be able to find, in the curren 'literature' I was so diligently combing, even a couple of examples of ex pressions (other than of phrases like *in fact*, *of course* etc) that I knew to be bot current and used, or at least understood, by most native speakers.

About this time other researchers in related areas of lexis began to use othe techniques to establish native speakers' 'knowledge' of their mother tongue. I France Professor Gougenheim and his colleagues used the notion of 'availabil ity'[3] to elicit words from French schoolchildren in drawing up the vocabular of *Le Français Fondamental*.[4] Later, in Birmingham, an interesting piece o research[5] was carried out by Professor John Sinclair and his colleagues: th object was to listen out for and record any uses of the phrase *red herring* tha might crop up in their presence, in addition to numerous 'dissociated' uses o the two words. They had been struck by the fact that this idiomatic combina tion had not occurred a single time in the admittedly limited corpus of writte material that they had analysed. The small group of observers collected no les than 50 instances in 'a period of several months'. Yet in all my years o collecting from written sources I had not come across more than three or fou occurrences of this expression.

These two experiments, together with my own observations, convinced m that no useful statements could be made about the 'frequency' of the kind o idiomatic expression I was collecting. For most of the expressions likely t appear in the dictionary one or two authentic examples might be enough t qualify them for entry, provided they could be elicited with ease from nativ speakers. I have described this method, and its sometimes unexpected result in an article contributed to the commemorative volume in celebration of A Hornby's 80th birthday.[6] Briefly, the method was simply to supply severa

[1]An impracticable title, as it turned out. The dictionary as it now appears contains many idioms clause or sentence length, and provides ample evidence both of normal variation in idioms and 'nonce' variation for special effect.

[2]M West: 'A General Service List of English Words' in Faucett, Palmer, Thorndike and West: *Interi Report on Vocabulary Selection*, Part V, 1936; 2nd edn West: *A General Service List of Englis Words*, London, 1953.

[3]In French, *disponibilité*. (Professor Gougenheim visited Edinburgh University in 1959.)

[4]i e Basic French (for the foreign learner).

[5]See *English Lexical Studies* OSTI Report January 1967-September 1969, Birmingham, England.

[6]R Mackin: 'On collocations: "Words shall be known by the company they keep".' in: Strevens (e *In honour of A S Hornby*, Oxford, 1978.

people with an incomplete version of a particular expression; a prompt, complete phrase in the expected form in reply was sufficient evidence that it was 'available' to them and probably to other native speakers, or at least to members of the British 'speech community'. It was thus taken to be a part of current usage.

From 1958–63 the examples had mounted alarmingly day by day, and I became more and more aware of the dangers involved in accumulating an unmanageable corpus of material. This awareness became all the more acute as a result of my preparing a new edition of Henry Sweet's *The Practical Study of Languages*. On p 269 of that book,[7] Sweet writes:

> It should never be forgotten that it is much easier to heap up material than to utilize it. It is easy for the dictionary compiler to brag of the tons of material, the millions of slips that have been collected for him, but when it comes to sorting these slips according to the meanings of the words, and weighing the evidence of each, he often wishes he had started with a ton or two less.

With these words in mind I looked at my own accumulation of slips (still manageable though little short of a ton, it seemed) and, as Sweet put it, 'pausing to review my gains from a higher and freer point of view', sought a means of avoiding the possible fate described by him as 'sinking into a monomaniac machine incapable of any higher work'. Fortunately, I had for many years been aware of that most difficult area of English for the foreign learner: the so-called phrasal and prepositional verbs. If some hiving off were possible, here was a ready-made category of idiomatic expressions that called out for a more thorough description, clarification and illustration than it had hitherto received, numerous though the collections (in monolingual and bilingual books of reference) had been. They seemed to be worthy of a volume in their own right. Conscious that the description of these constructions was far from complete, I urged Tony Cowie, who was in 1963–64 a postgraduate student at the then School (now Department) of Applied Linguistics in the University of Edinburgh, to make this the subject of his Dissertation. He did so with enthusiasm and produced an analysis of the categories, though making use of a smaller corpus than I had gathered.[8] Subsequently, he joined me in the writing up and editing of the *Oxford Dictionary of Current Idiomatic English, Volume 1*. However, mindful of Professor J R Firth's[9] stress on 'collocation' as a means of determining meaning and indeed as part of the meaning of a word or phrase, I proposed that we should make 'collocation' a feature of this Dictionary. Thus it is that, for the first time I believe, there took shape an idiomatic dictionary that combined original up-to-date citations with discrete meanings enlightened if not almost 'defined' by listed collocations, all within a rigorously described grammatical system. This system was presented in a detailed Introduction, the work of Tony Cowie, who also wrote up over half of the entries.

While we were wrestling with Volume 1, I had to address myself to the problem of what was to be done with the huge number of expressions that I had collected which lay outside the broadest definition of *Verbs with Prepositions and Particles*, the title of Volume 1. My interest in linguistics, and in the founding and early development of The British Association for Applied Linguistics, led inevitably to my meeting Dr Peter Wexler, now Reader in the Department of Language and Linguistics at Essex University, but then work-

[7]H Sweet: *The Practical Study of Languages*, 1st edn, London, 1899; revised edn, London, 1964.

[8]At least one valuable study had already been made (T F Mitchell: 'Syntagmatic relations in linguistic analysis' in *Transactions of the Philological Society*, 1958, pp 101-18). Tony extended Professor Mitchell's basic categories of 'phrasal verb' from four to six.

[9]Professor Firth had been a colleague of mine for all too brief a period in 1958 at the School of Applied Linguistics.

ing at Manchester University on the application of computer technology to linguistic analysis and allied problems. He had access to the giant steam-age computer named Atlas and arranged for my endless examples to be programmed for sorting into alphabetical order – a case of taking a sledge-hammer to crack a nut if ever there was one. Nevertheless, it was an enormous relief to have this chore taken over by a machine, and I hereby record my thanks to Peter and his monster, Atlas. The complexities of dealing with the headphrases in this present Volume 2 have been dealt with by the umpteenth Son of Atlas and the sweat of brows other than mine!

In working out ways of presenting what we have now come to describe as *Phrase, Clause and Sentence Idioms*, the title of Volume 2, I considered many other possible groupings: grammatical categories; notions (as now featuring in *The Threshold Level*[10]); etymological groupings; proverbs; catchwords; clichés; and so on, including that proposed by Harold Palmer in the *Second Interim Report on English Collocations* (IRET, Tokyo, 1933). However, I eventually rejected them all in favour of an alphabetical ordering, to be supplemented by as comprehensive an Index as possible, containing not only an alphabetically-arranged list of other words in each headphrase, but also many of the collocates as well.

Prevented by *force majeure* from making any worthwhile progress on this volume, in 1969 I invited Isabel McCaig to undertake the writing up of the material, and she agreed, with the happy consequences that will soon become apparent to the reader. We were, of course, conscious that the entries could not be related as neatly as those of Volume 1 to a limited grammar that could be offered as an explanatory system in the Introduction: we were concerned with nothing less than the whole grammar of English. As we proceeded with the entries, providing collocational information similar to that of Volume 1, and some grammatical categorization, we realized that the problems relating to the latter were too complex to be dealt with by means of the improvised 'code' we were then using. So we were very glad at this point to press Tony Cowie back into service after a period of heavy commitments elsewhere. With his help the new system evolved quite quickly from 1976 on. During the years 1976 to 1980 Isabel McCaig patiently wrote and rewrote her earlier drafts of the entries, adapting them all to the changes that were agreed upon at numerous editorial meetings. While doing so her own reading led to an enormous increase in the number of quotations available to her: some more apposite than those I had already collected, others containing phrases for which I had provided her with no example at all. Her thoughtful, pithily expressed definitions and the cleverly constructed illustrations that she abundantly provided to supplement the 'authentic' quotations in order to cover additional meanings for which no suitable ones were available, will, I am convinced, add hugely to the user's enjoyment and satisfaction in reading through this wide-ranging collection of idiomatic expressions. The editor-in-charge at Oxford during this crucial period between 1976 and 1980 was Jonathan W Price.

In the course of our collaboration, the text was organized, amended and added to, notably by Tony Cowie. For a time Robin Laidlaw generously gave us his help, working on the details of entries for several letters, as well as attending editorial meetings at which his contributions were always helpful. But it is Tony Cowie's midnight oil that has burned longest of recent years. As in Volume 1, the Introduction has been prepared by him. In it he explains the coherent scheme of idiomaticity which he has developed from the happy combination of his own independent work in the field and the work done by Isabel McCaig and me.

[10]J A van Ek: *The Threshold Level*, Strasbourg, 1976.

Since 1981 the production of the Dictionary has been in the capable hands of Marion Strachan at Oxford. She has worked hard and single-mindedly to ensure that it did not gather dust. It has been for her a demanding but I hope a not unrewarding or too exhausting a task.

All three authors wish to record their thanks also to Simon Nugent, who dealt with Volume 2 in its early stages; to Christina Ruse, who, as editor of the Educational Reference section at OUP, for a time helped us with many valuable suggestions; and to Lesley Jeffries, Rosemary Sansome and Penny Willis, all of Leeds University, for their careful scrutiny of the Introduction.

I wish to record my personal thanks to all those mentioned above; to others in the Press whom I do not know, but of whose efforts I am always conscious; to innumerable friends and acquaintances who have wittingly or unwittingly contributed to the book; to members of my own family; but above all to my wife Marian, whose tolerance and help have been exemplary. She it is who has often reassured me by providing the missing words in an incomplete phrase at any time of the day or night.

Ronald Mackin — Colchester 1983

General Introduction

The accurate and appropriate use of English expressions which are in the broadest sense idiomatic is one distinguishing mark of a native command of the language and a reliable measure of the proficiency of foreign learners. We can go beyond simple observation of the usage of such students and ask them whether the noun in *a chequered career* or the verb in *catch someone's imagination* can be replaced. If they recognize *a chequered history* or *seize someone's imagination*, they have a sense of fine lexical tolerances which surpasses that of many British undergraduates.

However, such are the semantic and structural problems posed by idioms that many students view them with the trepidation of a man approaching a well-planted minefield. Of all the difficulties the most familiar is that of meaning: to the learner, idioms such as *fill the bill* or *spill the beans* do not mean what they appear to mean. The sense of the whole cannot be arrived at from a prior understanding of the parts. In those examples, a special meaning is attached to the whole expression. In others, one word may have a common, literal meaning, while the other has a specialized sense which may be difficult to grasp. Examples of such 'semi-idioms' are *foot the bill* and *sink one's differences* (where the first word in both cases has a figurative meaning).

The complexities can be formidable, so that the student needs precise guidance, often in considerable detail. It is with the aim of providing such information in depth that the *Oxford Dictionary of Current Idiomatic English* has been compiled. Work on the Dictionary, which is now completed by the publication of the second volume, extends over more than twenty years. Two volumes were decided on at an early stage. In the course of preparing Volume 2 we discussed many expressions that, because of their construction, we decided ought more properly to go into a second edition of Volume 1. Most of these had been considered at first to be simple prepositional phrases (e g *in the limelight*, *in the family way*, *(up) in the clouds*) but since their meanings depended on the presence of a verb – often the verb was *be*, or *get*, or some other equally common – we concluded that they should be held back. A revised edition of Volume 1 will appear and any expressions that have fallen between the two stools will be rescued and incorporated therein.

Uniformity of grammatical treatment in the first volume was made possible by limiting it to a small range of idiom-types (verbs with particles or prepositions). The present volume is grammatically heterogeneous (though there are certain dominant phrase and clause patterns); but the view of idiom which informs both volumes is the same; and users familiar with the layout and typography of Volume 1 will find few changes in the internal organization of entries.

An important feature of the whole Dictionary is that the grammatical and semantic description of idioms is supported by quotations from a variety of contemporary sources, both written and spoken. Most of the examples are drawn from an analysis of works of fiction, biography, history etc which was specially undertaken to provide illustrations for the Dictionary. As the drafting of entries proceeded, this collection of upwards of 30,000 recorded excerpts was added to from time to time, especially from such sources as the daily and weekly press, and radio and television broadcasts. Further substantial additions were made after 1971, when work began on the second volume.

The scope of the present volume is explained in some detail below (0.1). We set out some of the grammatical types represented here and discuss the nature of idiomaticity itself, showing how the criteria adopted are used to decide which entries to include. The second part of the Introduction (0.2) describes features of the entries which are specifically designed to help in the learning and teaching of idioms.

The scope of the dictionary

0.1 To turn from Volume 1 to Volume 2 is to be reminded of the enormous structural variety of English idioms. Those treated in the first volume could be allocated to six related clause patterns; those dealt with here are found in phrase patterns – *a bargain basement*, *easy on the eye*, *in the nick of time* – subject-less clause patterns – *cut one's losses*, *paint the town red*, *pay sb a compliment* – and simple or complex sentence patterns – *one swallow does not make a summer*, *give sb an inch and he'll take a mile*. This is to give but a small sample of the great range of construction types represented.

The spread is considerable, yet the majority of entries can be classified under two general headings – *phrase idioms* and *clause idioms*. Within these major groupings are several dominant sub-categories (each of which is given detailed tabular treatment in the front matter (⇨ *The content and arrangement of the entries*, 3.0)). The most common *clause* patterns spanned by idioms, for instance, are the following:

Verb + Complement	**go berserk**
Verb + Direct Object	**ease sb's conscience/mind**
Verb + Direct Object + Complement	**paint the town red**
Verb + Indirect Object + Direct Object	**do sb credit**
Verb + Direct Object + Adjunct	**take sth amiss**

while the most commonly occurring *phrase* patterns are these:

Noun Phrase	**a crashing bore**
Adjective Phrase	**free with one's money etc**
Prepositional Phrase	**in the nick of time**
Adverbial Phrase	**as often as not**

In this necessarily selective survey of the grammatical patterns in which expressions are found, the term 'idiom' has been applied without distinction as to pattern. The view taken here – as in Volume 1 – is that idiomaticity is largely a semantic matter, and that it is manifested in much the same way in expressions of different structural types. How then can idiomaticity itself be recognized and defined? Here it will be best to consider under separate headings the rather complex issues that face the analyst and the dictionary-maker.

1 How in practice do we decide whether a particular expression is idiomatic or not? We may sense that *fill the sink* as used in

She **filled the sink** *with hot water.*

is not idiomatic, while *fill the bill* ('be satisfactory or adequate for a purpose') as in

Sometimes solid food doesn't **fill the bill.**

is idiomatic. What kinds of criteria can be called upon in support of our intuitions?

2 Is the distinction between idioms and non-idioms clear-cut, or do the two categories shade off into each other?

3 What criteria in particular must expressions satisfy to merit inclusion in the Dictionary?

4 Finally, how do the conclusions we reach as to the idiomaticity of individual items affect the way they are categorized grammatically? If *fill the bill* is shown to be a unit of meaning in some ways comparable to a single word (c f *satisfy*, *suit*) why not simply classify it as 'verb', rather than as an instance of a Verb + Direct Object construction (the second of the clause patterns listed just above)?

In considering these questions, undue complication will be avoided if the discussion is limited to idioms of a few structural types. Here we shall confine ourselves to two: (i) noun phrases containing an adjective and a noun (e g *a chequered career*, *a blind alley*, *an eager beaver*); (ii) clauses consisting of a verb and a direct object (e g *catch sb's imagination*, *jog one's/sb's memory*, *blow the gaff*). We shall return later to the more complex cases and especially to those idioms which span whole sentences.

The best-known approach to the definition of idiomaticity, and one which linguists as well as dictionary-makers have helped to popularize, fastens on the difficulty of interpreting idioms in terms of the meanings of their constituent words. Definitions such as the following are representative of this approach:

> ... groups of words with set meanings that cannot be calculated by adding up the separate meanings of the parts.[1]

> ... peculiarity of phraseology ... having meaning not deducible from those of the separate words ...[2]

However, defining idioms in a way which throws emphasis on ease or difficulty of interpretation leaves a great deal unsaid. This characterization does, it is true, identify what is odd about an expression such as *blow the gaff* (or *kick the bucket*). Moreover, certain tests appear to bear out the appropriateness of the judgement in such cases. Thus it is impossible to find acceptable substitutes for the noun or verb in either of those expressions. Consider **puff the gaff* and **kick the pail*. In addition, the object noun cannot be replaced by a pronoun in a subsequent mention of the idiom:

?*I expected him to* **blow the gaff** *and* **blow it** *he did.*

This can be compared with the altogether acceptable:

I asked him to **fill the sink**, *but not to* **fill it** *to overflowing.*

However, an approach based simply on the semantic opaqueness (or transparency) of whole combinations yields a very small class of idioms. It leaves out of account, for example, an important group of expressions which have figurative meanings (in terms of the whole combination in each case) but which also keep a current literal interpretation. Among such 'figurative idioms' are *catch fire* and *close ranks*. There is other evidence, too, especially the fact that a small number of words can be substituted in expressions often regarded as opaque (consider *burn one's boats* or *bridges*), that idioms are not divided as a small water-tight category from non-idioms but are related to them along a scale or continuum (⇨ Volume 1, p x).

A view of idiomaticity which does full justice to the rich diversity of word-combinations in English must recognize that the meaning of a combination may be related to those of its components in a variety of ways, and must take account also of the possibility of internal variation, or substitution of part for part. The application of both criteria together produces a complex categorization.[3]

(i) *Pure idioms*. Though discussions of idiomaticity at both a technical and non-technical level are usually limited to the type illustrated by *blow the gaff* and *kick the bucket* (surely the most often quoted idiom of all), idioms in the strict sense comprise only one, and certainly not the largest, of a spectrum of related categories. Historically, pure idioms form the end-point of a process by which word-combinations first establish themselves through constant re-use, then undergo figurative extension and finally petrify or congeal.[4]

[1] D Bolinger: *Aspects of Language*, 2nd edn, New York, 1975.

[2] J B Sykes (ed): *The Concise Oxford Dictionary of Current English*, 7th edn, Oxford, 1982.

[3] For a more detailed treatment, see A P Cowie: 'The treatment of collocations and idioms in learners' dictionaries', in: *Applied Linguistics* 3/1981, pp 223-35.

[4] The term 'petrification' is aptly used of various types of meaning-development by Geoffrey Leech in: *Semantics*, 2nd edn, Harmondsworth, 1981.

(ii) *Figurative idioms*. This category has already been identified. It is idiomatic in the sense that variation is seldom found (though note *act the part* or *role*; *a close*, *narrow shave*) and pronoun substitution unlikely (though consider *Bill had* **a narrow shave** *and Fred* **an even narrower one**). The merging of this group into that of pure idioms is illustrated by such expressions as *beat one's breast* and (again) *burn one's boats*. The literal senses of these expressions do not survive alongside their figurative ones in normal, everyday use and for some speakers they may indeed be unrelatable. For such speakers the expressions fall into the category of pure idioms.

(iii) *Restricted collocations*. In such combinations, sometimes referred to as 'semi-idioms', one word (i e in the case of two-word expressions) has a figurative sense not found outside that limited context. The other element appears in a familiar, literal sense (c f the verb and noun, respectively, in *jog one's/sb's memory*) and the adjective and noun in *a blind alley*. Some members of this category allow a degree of lexical variation (consider, for instance, *a cardinal error*, *sin*, *virtue*, *grace*), and in this respect 'restricted' collocations resemble 'open' ones (see below). Another point of similarity is that the 'literal' element is sometimes replaced by a pronoun, or deleted altogether, in sentences where there is an earlier use of the full expression:

The Board didn't **entertain the idea**, *and the Senate wouldn't* **entertain it** *either*.
Bloggs had **a rather chequered career**, *and I've heard it said that Blenkinsop's was equally* **chequered** (or: **an** *equally* **chequered one**).

In other respects, however, restricted collocations are idiom-like. The particular sense which *jog* has in *jog one's/sb's memory* occurs in no other context, while that of *chequered* is limited to collocations with *career* and *history*. It is the determination of a special meaning by a limited context which argues for the inclusion of such expressions in an 'idiomatic' dictionary.

(iv) *Open collocations*. Most sharply and easily distinguished from idioms in the strict sense are combinations such as *fill the sink* (already referred to) and *a broken window*. The use of the terms 'open', 'free' or 'loose' to refer to such collocations reflects the fact that, in each case, both elements (verb and object, or adjective and noun) are freely recombinable, as for example in *fill*, *empty*, *drain the sink* and *fill the sink*; *basin*, *bucket*. Typically also, in open collocations, each element is used in a common literal sense.

What has been said of the relationship between idioms and non-idioms occurring in two types of pattern (verb + direct object and adjective + noun) holds true of other construction types. Clause patterns containing a complement in addition to an object, for example, subsume figurative idioms (*bleed sb white*) as well as restricted collocations (*catch sb red-handed*). So do prepositional phrases: compare *in a nutshell* (idiom) with *in the raw* (collocation).

We have discussed the nature of idiomaticity in some depth partly to throw light on the problem of deciding which word-combinations to include in a dictionary which has 'idiomatic' as part of its title. In the spectrum of categories set out earlier in this Introduction, two were identified as 'idiomatic'; clearly items belonging to those categories must be recorded. As regards the central area – the restricted collocations – we have suggested that there are strong arguments for covering that also. On the other hand, we have been careful to exclude open collocations as defined in section (iv). The Dictionary will not, for example, be found to include an entry for *on one's return* since *on* in the sense 'at the time of' can be combined with a number of other nouns: *arrival*, *departure*, *demise*, *death*, *dismissal*. There are, however, a number of borderline problems which are not so easily resolved. In doubtful cases we have tended to be accommodating, so that some combinations in which both or all the constituents are used in a straightforward sense have been included. The expression *a fair question* is listed, for example, because while both adjective and noun occur in several other contexts (*a fair settlement*, *a reasonable question*), *a fair question* is the collocation most often heard in debates or discussions. Regular users of the Dictionary will note also that we have been liberal in including expressions one or more of whose key elements is a 'grammatical' word – a modal verb, for example, or a subordinating conjunction. The entries *can't hear oneself think*, *can't help oneself*, *can't help doing sth* are among several introduced by modal auxiliaries. Finally, users will note that where a figurative idiom has a literal equivalent in current use, the latter is sometimes given an entry of its own, as in the following example:

do you mind?[1] an enquiry as to whether sb objects to some action or event
do you mind?[2] an expression of objection, sometimes aggressive, to sth which is occurring ...

We can now return to the question of grammatical classification that was raised earlier. If it is true that highly idiomatic expressions tend in some ways to resemble single words, should this unity be reflected in the way they are grammatically described in dictionary entries?

One answer would be to say they should, and to describe such idioms as *a red herring* and *a sacred cow* as nouns. This is the practice in certain general English dictionaries which, following well-established American precedents, treat idiomatic noun phrases as main entries.[5] However, the labelling (if not the separate listing) is open to criticism. As we have seen there is no clear dividing-line between idioms and non-idioms: they form the end-points of a continuum. That being so, the question is raised of how semi-idioms (restricted collocations) are to be designated. To call such combinations as *the cold war* or *a narrow escape* 'nouns' would not accord with the fact that *war* and *escape* can function with unchanged meaning in other, non-idiomatic, phrases (c f *a conventional war*, *a remarkable escape*) or that in certain noun phrase idioms, though not in all, the adjective has a comparative form (*an even narrower escape*). On balance it seems preferable to classify expressions of this structural type as noun phrases, drawing no distinction in doing so between the more and the less idiomatic cases. This approach has the advantage of enabling us to speak of *a sacred cow* as a unit of meaning (and the parts of *the simple life* as tightly bound together) while at the same time leaving us free to account for possible syntactic mobility or modification.

The same general principles govern the recognition of other syntactic patterns. Consider, for example, the case of *kick the bucket* and *blow the gaff*. One approach, taking account of the semantic fusion of the parts, would be to treat the expressions as intransitive verbs. To do so, however, would leave the lexicographer with no means of accounting for those pure idioms (such as *blow the gaff*) which allow a passive transformation (c f *the gaff was blown*), since the specification of this structural change requires the recognition of an independent direct object which, as shown in the example, moves forward to become the subject of the passive clause. An appropriate designation in such cases would be 'Verb (transitive) + Direct Object', and this labelling, in the abbreviated form [V + O], appears in the entries concerned.

Idioms of the types considered throughout this Introduction (phrases and subject-less clauses) occupy syntactic units longer than the word but smaller than a complete simple sentence. Indeed, many linguists would take the view that nothing more extensive should concern the student of idiomaticity. However, there are good grounds for treating as idiomatic certain expressions which span simple or complex sentences. Their claim to be included in a dictionary of idiomatic English merits careful consideration.

[5]See **red herring** *n*, **sacred cow** *n*, in: *Webster's Third New International Dictionary*, Springfield, Massachusetts, 1966.

We are concerned with combinations such as:

the early bird catches the worm
when/while the cat's away the mice will play
the buck stops here
if one believes that one will believe anything

One fact that calls for immediate comment is that the first two expressions have some of the hallmarks of figurative idioms, as identified earlier. Thus *the early bird catches the worm* is both metaphorical in origin and invariable in form (**the early cat catches the mouse* though recognizably a reworking of the original is clearly a nonce variation – of which more later). Moreover, when acceptable variation is found, as in *give sb an inch and he'll take a mile/a yard/an ell*, it is characteristically limited. The general class of sentence idioms also appears to include some items that have moved to total opaqueness. Many native speakers, for example, will be unable to trace the reference to 'a buck' (in *the buck stops here*) to the game of poker. For others, the precise literary origin of *the emperor has no clothes* will be equally obscure.

Most, if not all, of the examples already cited will be recognized by native speakers as falling within long-established functional categories. Thus *the early bird catches the worm* is a well-known saying or proverb, while *the buck stops here* is a somewhat less familiar catchphrase. No attempt is made in this volume to match in range or fullness of historical documentation the authoritative treatments of English sayings and catchphrases which already exist.[6] Our aim, rather, has been to focus on aspects of their structure and use in present-day English which will be of particular interest to advanced foreign students.

One such feature is that proverbs and catchphrases may be structurally shortened for a variety of reasons and with a number of effects. Traditional sayings of a given structural type tend to be used in a narrow and stereotyped set of functions. Thus *a stitch in time saves nine* and *the early bird catches the worm* are typically used to comment approvingly on timely or judicious action or to reinforce a recommendation. Often it will be felt sufficient to hint at the whole by the use of a part, as in such utterances as *'A stitch in time, you know!'* Sometimes, the fragment will take on a life of its own as a phrase idiom, as is the case with *an early bird*. This coexists in present-day usage alongside the saying from which it originated and is granted a separate entry in this volume.

Although individual sayings occasionally develop special functions, catchphrases characteristically do so. Catchphrases normally originate with a popular entertainer – when they serve much the same purpose as a signature tune – or with a well-known public figure. *The buck stops here* and *if you can't stand the heat, get out of the kitchen* were first spoken by the late President Truman; and their association with him, combined with the vigour and freshness of his language, ensured that they were taken up and repeated more widely. As in many similar cases, both the function and form of these catchphrases are varied from time to time, as the following quotation from an article on the Vietnam war makes clear:

The harsh truth is that **the buck** *started here* (i e in the US) *and that it* **stops here** *as well.*

This example of nonce variation in an expression whose original form is well-known brings us to a final point. Sentence idioms in particular are commonly refashioned by native speakers to achieve a variety of striking effects. The effect may be a pun, as when an element in a fixed expression is replaced

[6] See especially: W G Smith: *Oxford Dictionary of English Proverbs*, 3rd edn, Oxford, 1970; and E Partridge: *A Dictionary of Catch Phrases*, London 1977.

by a similar-sounding but semantically incongruous word:

(add to) the gaiety of nations (catchphrase) . . . (NONCE) *Whatever else he does he will surely* ***add to the gaiety of NATO.***

Or the device may be to take an existing semantic contrast – say between words of 'favourable' and 'unfavourable' meaning – and vary the words which carry that contrast:

The way ***one man's meat is another man's poison,*** *so* ***one woman's ideal husband is another woman's pain in the neck.***

The achievement of humorous effects by the manipulation of idioms normally regarded as fixed calls for a degree of cultural or literary awareness possessed only by mature native speakers of English.[7] But of course the advanced foreign student can be helped to use and vary idioms in ways which will be thought normal and regular. It is with design features which are intended to provide such help that the second part of this Introduction is concerned.

The dictionary and the practical needs of the learner

0.2 This Dictionary has been designed primarily for the foreign student, so it is chiefly his or her needs which we have had in mind when deciding what information about individual entries to include, and how to present it. Dictionaries for the foreign student must be organized to help with problems of production as well as interpretation, and both volumes of this work incorporate a number of special features which are intended to encourage the confident use of idiomatic expressions. Three features are singled out for special mention here: the use of special conventions in headphrases to show limited lexical choice; the inclusion in most entries of words with which the headphrase can co-occur, or collocate; and guidance about special kinds of idioms which can be used to link sentences, or exchanges between speakers, together.

As we explained in the first part of the Introduction, the vocabulary of English contains many expressions that are semi-fixed, or partially variable, in their form. Variability may mean the possibility of substituting one word or several words at one or more points – consider, for example, *a matter, problem* or *question of academic interest* or *concern.* Knowing how many words, and which words, to substitute is important for the learner, because failure to make the right choices may result in combinations that no native speaker would produce. (It is for this reason, among others, that many foreign learners steer clear of English idioms altogether.) The student therefore needs clear guidance on these fine points of lexical detail. Fortunately it is often possible to provide such information clearly and simply through the headphrase (the phrase or clause in bold print which introduces dictionary entries).

When the student has to deal with a 'restricted collocation' (a semi-idiomatic expression which allows internal variation) there may in fact be a choice between two words which are related in meaning. In such cases these words are divided by an oblique stroke:

(as) clever/smart as paint
take the biscuit/cake
in the long/short run

Or the choice may be wider, in which case **etc** is placed in the headphrase after the word for which others can be substituted, and the full range of possible alternatives appears lower down in the entry:

cut a fine etc figure . . . adj: fine, ⚠ handsome, neat; sorry, ridiculous, abject.

[7] See: R Mackin: 'On collocations: "Words shall be known by the company they keep"', in: P Strevens (ed): *In honour of A S Hornby*, Oxford, 1978.

These conventions may seem daunting at first, but time spent in learning them is time well spent, for they are the key to a central element in the control of idiomatic usage: the ability to make precise choices within permitted limits that are often very narrow (⇨ 1.1).

It is important to make clear that the kinds of choices – whether limited or more extensive – that have been illustrated so far concern variation *within the idiom itself*. But there is another kind of lexical choice – which is also either restricted or open– which helps to make up the context in which an idiom is used in sentences. This external aspect of lexical choice also constitutes a problem for the foreign learner. How can he be helped? The arrangement that we have decided on – which closely resembles that adopted for Volume 1 – is to list some of the words which combine acceptably with an idiom in the body of the entry, and to precede them with a letter which indicates where they function in a sentence. In this entry, for example:

the face of the earth [O/o (NP)] ... **V**: change, cover, disfigure, transform; disappear from; wipe sb/sth off/from ...

the letter **V** in bold print indicates that the words following it are verbs. All of these acceptably combine with the idiom used either as a direct object (**O**) or as the object of a preposition (**o**).

Indicating collocates in this way in fact serves a double purpose. The first, as we have said, is that the student can make up many sentences of his own on the basis of the collocates listed, adding to that list himself when it is shown to be relatively open (⇨ 1.2). The second is that the student is confronted, in a highly concentrated form, with many of the contexts in which, in the course of reading, he would normally meet the idiom in question. This helps to speed up the process by which the idiom is learnt.

The third feature which we have chosen to single out is new to this volume. Among the many short clause idioms which it lists are a considerable number used in structuring exchanges between speakers. They may refer back to a preceding statement or anticipate a following one, but in either case also indicate the speaker's attitude to what has been, or is to be, said. Idioms such as *you can say that again*, used to express emphatic, and often ironic, agreement, and *you could have fooled me*, used to indicate mocking dissent from a preceding assertion or judgement, fall into the first category. The exclamatory expression *do you know*, on the other hand, introduces a statement, especially one that may cause some surprise:

Do you know *that's the first time I've heard of burglars having children. Makes them quite human doesn't it?* DC

Expressions of this kind are often inadequately treated in general dictionaries, possibly because of pressure on space, but a specialized dictionary of idioms provides scope for detailed coverage. Not only can the exact function be explained, in each case, with stress and intonation patterns shown where appropriate (⇨ **do you mind?**[1,2]), but the role of such expressions in exchanges between speakers can be fully illustrated, as in the following example from the entry for *doesn't one know it*, a comment to the effect that one is very well aware, or too much aware, of something previously mentioned:

SARAH: *He knows he can go to her – she'll feed him.* CISSIE: *He's her son for God's sake.* SARAH; ***Don't I know it.*** CSWB

Functional idioms such as these are a further reminder of the range of information – stylistic and literary as well as simply structural – which the learner must capture in getting to grips with idiomatic usage. Mastery of such usage presupposes a competence which is not merely linguistic but cultural in the broadest sense.

The content and arrangement of the entries

In the following set of entries, the user is referred from a number of features which are often found in the dictionary itself to the detailed explanations provided in sections 1–9 of *The content and arrangement of the entries*.

alternative words in headphrase **1.1.1**

grammatical code **3**

headphrase picked out in illustrations **7.3**

air/parade one's knowledge [V + O pass] show, demonstrate, the (great) amount of knowledge that one has on a subject or subjects, often in a boastful and superior way □ *Why don't you go in for one of those TV quizzes? It'll give you a chance to* **air** *all* **that** *useless* **knowledge** *you've been cluttering your brain up with over the years!* □ *The author seldom misses an opportunity to* **parade his knowledge**; *we are meant to be impressed, but for every fact he gets right there are half a dozen he gets wrong.*

source of idiom **5.2(ii)**

source of quotation **7.2**

an Aladdin's cave [Comp/O (NP)] a place, a source, of riches and wealth of a material kind or (fig) of purely aesthetic value, which has to be, or has been, discovered and made use of (from the treasure cave in the story 'Aladdin and the Wonderful Lamp') V: be, find sth; discover, reveal □ *It is hard to believe it can be so difficult to make a home among the terraces of Glasgow's beautiful West End housing —* **a** *veritable* **Aladdin's cave** *of architectural treasure when you look below the grime.* SC □ *I was taking Susan not as Susan, but as a Grade A lovely, as the daughter of a factory-owner, as the means of obtaining the key to* **the Aladdin's cave** *of my ambitions.* RATT

cross-reference to synonym **5.3**

cross-reference to 'false friend' **9.1.1**

all at once[2] [A (PrepP)] suddenly and unexpectedly; all of a sudden (q v) □ ***All at once*** *she found herself telling them everything about the evening.* WI □ *I found myself* **all at once** *on the brink of panic.* DOP □ **All at once**, *with the diminishing of the pain in his eye, the cold and exhaustion came back.* PM □ front, middle or end position. ⇨ ⚠ at one (fell) swoop.

attitudinal marking **4.4**

a banana republic (derogatory) a state that is (considered to be) dependent on primary, agricultural products and that is, therefore, backward economically and politically, and subject to internal disorder □ *Until recently there was a tendency to dismiss whatever happened, good or bad, in South America as just the sort of thing one would expect of* **banana republics**; *but now such simple and derogatory attitudes no longer hold good.* □ (NONCE) *These projects* (in technology) *may properly be described as a lunge into the future, undertaken because of psychological pressures, to prove that we* (the UK) *are not yet* **a banana kingdom.** L □ formerly used of some Central and South American states.

nonce variation marking **7.3.4(iv)**

reference to set of verbs **1.1.3, 6.2**

grammatical function of collocates **6.2, 6.3**

beat etc one's brains [V + O] puzzle, think very hard, esp in order to solve a problem, find a way of doing sth **V:** beat, ⚠ cudgel, rack □ *I've been* **beating my brains** *all evening, trying to think of an excuse for not going to Martin's wedding.* □ *He greatly despised crossword puzzles. 'People should* **cudgel their brains** *to some better purpose,' he often said.* □ **Rack her brains** *as she would she could think of no way to raise the money.* □ *After several hours of* **brain-racking** *they were still no nearer to a solution.* □ n compound brain-racking.

footnote showing compound derived from headphrase **8.1**

register marking **4.3(i)**

break the bank [V + O] (gambling) win so much money that one's winnings cannot be paid; (fig) be more than one can afford **S:** gambler, punters; spending; week-end, party □ (partial source) *You can see them sigh and wish to die,/You can see them wink the other eye/At the man who* **broke the Bank** *at Monte Carlo.* SONG (F GILBERT 1850–1903) □ *I'm afraid we'll be staying in Britain this year. A European holiday would just about* **break the bank.**

open set of collocates **6.5**

optional word in headphrase **1.2.1**

(stone-)cold sober [Comp (AdjP)] (informal) completely sober, in the sense that one has either been drinking no alcohol or too little to be affected by it **V:** ⚠ be, become; make sb ▫ *He was smoking a cigar, emblem of the celebration of that night, but he had drunk little and was* ***cold sober****.* NM ▫ *Will you promise me something — now,* ***stone-cold sober*** *in broad daylight?* RATT ▫ (NONCE) *I'd like a drink first. I can't go to a show like that* ***stone sober****.* OMIH

restricted set of collocates **6.5**

definition **5**

damn with faint praise not condemn, but mention for praise only qualities of such slight merit as to imply that more valuable or important qualities are lacking ▫ (source) ***Damn with faint praise****, assent with civil leer,/And, without sneering, teach the rest to sneer.* EPISTLE TO DR ARBUTHNOT (A POPE 1688–1744) ▫ *'But your book wasn't so unkindly reviewed as you say.' '****Damned with faint praise****—I would rather it had been violently attacked, which arouses people's interest at least.'* ▫ used esp in literary or other forms of professional criticism.

source of idiom, showing original use and form **7.2**

footnote showing function of idiom **8.3**

numbered headphrase **1.5**

do you mind?[1] an enquiry as to whether sb objects to some action or event; if you don't mind[1] (q v) ▫ *I think I'll go along to the club this evening for a game of snooker.* ***Do you mind?*** ▫ stress pattern do you 'mind?; medium rising tone on mind?

footnote showing stress and intonation **8.2**

style marking **4.2**

easy on the eye [Comp (AdjP)] (informal) quite pretty, good-looking (in the opinion of the observer or speaker) **S:** girl, woman; nurse, secretary. **V:** ⚠ be, find sb. **adv:** very, rather ▫ *Peggy is not quite so good-looking as her sister but very* ***easy on the eye****, all the same.* ▫ used to describe a woman. ⇨ ⚠ next entry.

order of presentation of collocate lists **6.2.2**

finding is keeping (saying) if you find something, then it is rightfully your property ▫ (Colin has picked up a packet with two cigarettes in it, from the gutter.) *'Come on,' Bert said, cajoling, threatening, 'lets's 'ave* (= have) *one.' Colin stood firm.* ***Finding was keeping.*** *'I'm saving 'em for our dad.'* LLDR ▫ *'That's my ball! I lost it in the park yesterday!' 'I don't believe you. Anyway,* ***finders keepers.****'* ▫ said, esp by children, as a claim to ownership, of sth found; variants finders keepers, findings keepings.

functional marking **4.5**

explanatory note in illustration **7.4**

footnote showing structural variants of headphrase **8.1**

in private [A (PrepP) privately; when or where alone, or with one other person **V**: argue, fight; discuss, arrange, sth ▫ *It's when a man–or woman–starts to drink a lot* ***in private*** *that he's in danger of becoming an alcoholic.* ▫ *I could feel that he was waiting for Luke to leave. He had something to say to me* ***in private.*** NM ⇨ next entry.

internal arrangement of collocate list **6.4**

cross-reference to immediately adjacent antonym **9, 9.1.2(i)**

The headphrase

One recurrent problem faced by foreign learners wishing to use or understand English idioms is that while some are entirely fixed others allow the speaker a measure of choice. As was explained in the General Introduction, the learner's task is made more difficult by the fact that the choices open to him may vary both in kind and in degree. Faced with the idiom *burn one's boats*, for example, he must understand that while the verb *burn* can be used in many of the tenses associated with its non-idiomatic use, idiomatic *boats* can only occur in the plural form. Moreover, while *bridges* (also plural) can be substituted for *boats* with no change of meaning, *ships* can not. The extent to which the form of an idiom can be altered in these various ways is largely unpredictable, so that errors can easily be made, and clear guidance is essential.

Help in identifying different kinds and degrees of variation in idioms is given in this dictionary chiefly through the form of the *headphrase* (the phrase in bold print which introduces each entry), though in conjunction with other parts of the entry (⇨ also *Collocations*, 6; *Illustrations*, 7.3; *Footnotes*, 8.1). Four types of variation will be discussed here:

(i) *Obligatory vs optional choice*. In some idioms, one of a number of alternative words or phrases *must* be used to give a complete and acceptable expression (⇨ **can/could do no wrong**, where one of the modal verbs *can* or *could* must be used for the idiom to make sense). In other cases, alternatives shown need not be taken up (⇨ **(shed/weep) crocodile tears**, where there is an acceptable idiom whether a verb is chosen or not). (C f 1.1 and 1.2, below.)

(ii) *Limited vs open choice*. In certain idioms, only a very few words can be substituted for a noun, verb, adjective, etc which appears in the headphrase

(➪ **a wildcat scheme etc** where *venture* and *speculation* virtually exhaust the range of choice at *scheme*). In others, a great many appropriate words or phrases can be substituted (➪ **lead a busy etc life**, where there are many possible replacements for *busy*). (Note that in idioms where there is limited choice this may be obligatory or optional and that the same is true of open choice; cf the corresponding subsections in 1.1 and 1.2.)

(iii) '*Lexical' vs 'grammatical' choice*. Choice of both the above types can be between 'lexical' words – nouns, verbs, adjectives, adverbs – or 'grammatical' words – articles, pronouns, modal verbs. Compare with the above examples **leave much to be desired**, where a choice must be made from the determiners *much*, *a lot*, *a good deal*, etc, and **(one/another of) life's little ironies**, which contains optional alternative pronouns. (➪ also 1.1. 2.1)

(iv) *Choice of words vs choice of inflections*. All the above categories show alternation between *words*. It is also characteristic of idioms, however, that they should at times display restrictions in the choice of the grammatical endings (inflections) which indicate differences of tense in verbs, number in nouns, etc. Compare in this respect **pack a punch**, which has a normal plural *pack punches*, and **pass the buck**, which has not. (➪ also 1.3)

Obligatory choice of words and phrases

1.1 In each of the examples to be considered here, one of the alternative words or phrases shown *must* be chosen to make a full and acceptable idiom. In the following sub-sections, ways of showing more or less *limited* obligatory choice are explained and illustrated.

1.1.1 *Minimal choice*. Where a choice must be made between *two* nouns, verbs, adjectives, articles, etc, the alternatives are both given in the headphrase and marked off by an oblique:

a chink/crack in one's armour
I should say/think so etc(!)
in good/bad faith
the/one's daily dozen

1.1.2 *Limited choice*. When a choice must be made from a severely restricted set of nouns, verbs, etc (though from more than two) one word from the set (followed by *etc*) is included in the headphrase, and the same word, with possible alternatives, appears in the body of the entry. The 'danger sign' ⚠, which signals limited choice, is placed after the repeated word:

damn etc it (all) ... **V**: damn, ⚠ dash, hang

the call of the wild etc ... **o**: the wild, ⚠ the hills, the West, the prairie

Users will note that a limited choice of verbs in 'possessive' entries (➪ 3.2) is treated in the same way, and that the danger sign in the following entry covers the possessive prepositions (*with, without*) also:

give sb/sth etc one's blessing [possess] ... **V**: give sb/sth; ⚠ get, receive, have
prep: with, without

1.1.2.1 *Limited choice of 'grammatical' words*. A choice must often be made from a limited set of modal verbs (*can, could, may, might*), determiners (*the, that, some, any*) or indefinite pronouns (*nothing, something, anything*) to arrive at the correct form of an idiom. In the entry **can't do sth for love (n)or money**, for example, *couldn't*, *won't*, *wouldn't* are possible replacements for *can't* (though not *shan't*, *mightn't*). Variation of this kind is shown as follows (i e without *etc* in the headphrase, or ⚠ in the body of the entry):

can't do sth for love (n)or money ... **modal**: can't, couldn't; won't, wouldn't

1.1.3 *More open choice*. Sometimes the set of words (or phrases) from which a speaker must choose is more open. Here, one word (followed by *etc*) appears in the headphrase and is taken up below, though without the danger sign:

a day etc or two .. n: day, minute, week; inch; glass; word

play one's cards well etc ... A: well, right, properly, skilfully; badly, stupidly; with skill, cunning, forethought

In some idioms, matching choices at two points are involved:

like father etc, like son etc ... n: father...son; ⚠ mother...daughter; master/man...maid

Note that in all these examples, the lists of words given simply indicate areas in which *several* appropriate choices can be made (⇨ also *Collocations* 6).

Optional choice of words and phrases

.2 In the idioms to be discussed here, none of the alternative words or phrases shown need be selected to give an acceptable expression. They may be omitted altogether, or in some cases replaced by a pronoun or a verb such as *do*. In the sub-sections below, ways of indicating more or less *limited* optional choice are explained and illustrated.

.2.1 *Minimal choice*. When a single word or phrase is highly predictable in the context of an idiom and can be removed without making nonsense of the remainder it is given in parenthesis in the headphrase:

like a (hot) knife through butter/margarine
win etc the hand (and heart) of sb

Where optional choice is between two words or phrases, they are divided by an oblique and placed in parenthesis in the headphrase:

it/that (all/rather) depends
with etc (no) strings (attached/binding its use)

The use of parentheses and the oblique in the last example can be taken to mean that *with strings*, *with no strings*, *with strings attached*, *with no strings binding its use* are among possible variants of the headphrase.

.2.2 *Limited choice*. When one of a restricted set of words can combine with an idiom, though none is a necessary part of it, the limited set (preceded by ⚠) is given in the body of the entry. No member of the set, however, appears in the headphrase itself:

delusions of grandeur/power ... V: ⚠ have, develop, suffer from

a whipping boy ... V: ⚠ be, become; treat sb as

(For a treatment of more open optional choice ⇨ 6.)

Inflection

.3 This section is concerned with restrictions on the use in idioms of those grammatical word-endings (inflections) which indicate differences of *number* (singular/plural) in nouns and *tense* in verbs. These restrictions are shown through the headphrase in conjunction with example sentences and footnotes (⇨ also 8.1).

.3.1 *Nouns*. The learner should note especially the conventions used when a noun can be *only* singular or *only* plural. The various possibilities are shown as follows:

(i) When a noun (or nouns) forming part of an idiom can function in both singular and plural forms, the singular is given in the headphrase and the plural is either illustrated or indicated in a footnote:

lose one's shirt ... *George Macbeth* **loses his shirt**. L ▫ *Not many industries* ...

then proceed to **lose their shirts** *...*

(ii) When a noun can be used only in the singular or plural, it appears in tha fixed form in the headphrase and example sentences:

the penny drops ... *It was quite a time before* **the penny dropped.** ... ST □ **The penny** *is finally* **dropping** *for investors with matured National Savings Cer-tificates. ...*

pennies from heaven ... *the Church cannot bank on* **pennies from heaven.** L □ *Every time it rains, it rains* **pennies from heaven.** ...

1.3.2 *Verbs.* In most entries containing a verb, the form given in the headphrase is the 'base' form – the infinitive without *to*:

chance one's arm/luck
drive a hard bargain
go etc berserk

The use of this form indicates that the verb can function in its normal range of finite and non-finite forms (so that *drive a hard bargain, drove a hard bargain* and *to drive a hard bargain,* for instance, are all possible).

Exceptions to the general rule are as follows:

(i) When an idiom fits the pattern of a finite clause with a subject, the verb is given in the present simple tense. This convention also shows that the verb has a full range of tense forms in its idiomatic context (two or more usually being illustrated):

the coast is clear ... **The coast's clear.** *I've just heard you can go ahead.* ... SM □ ... *in the manner of people making sure that* **the coast was clear.** TST

(ii) In any expression in which a verb is restricted to a particular tense, non-finite form, etc (often the case with proverbs and sayings), the verb is shown in that form in the headphrase and examples:

curiosity killed the cat
every man has his price
love me, love my dog

Abbreviations

1.4 A number of abbreviations are used in headphrases as a means of indicating places at which fairly open sets of lexical and grammatical words can function. In the headphrase

a clear case of sth

for example, *sth* (*something*) indicates that a number of inanimate nouns can be used as the object of the preposition *of*. The abbreviations are of three types: (i) those which stand for nouns; (ii) those which stand for possessive adjectives; (iii) those which stand for verbs.

(i) The abbreviations *sb* (*somebody*) and *sth* (*something*) appear at places in headphrases where nouns (or pronouns) can be substituted. They thus occur in subject, object, indirect object and prepositional object positions. Note that the substitutable words do *not* form part of the idioms in question:

(and) what sb says goes	(*sb* = S)
pack sb like sardines	(*sb* = O)
get sth going	(*sth* = O)
give sb etc the benefit of one's advice etc	(*sb* = IO)
play fair (with sb)	(*sb* = o)
the cut and thrust (of sth)	(*sth* = o)

The abbreviations can represent alternatives:

play sb/sth false

(ii) The abbreviation *sb's* (and also *one's*, *his*) represent the possessive adjectives *my*, *his*, *her*, *our*, *your*, *one's* and *its* and are used to indicate differences in the way the possessive adjective in examples is related to other parts of the sentence. Consider:

call sb's bluff ... *he had* ***called our bluff*** *from the start* ...

In this headphrase, *sb's* is used because in the example the people referred to by the possessive pronoun (*our*) are different from the subject (*he*). Compare:

count one's blessings ... *I must* ***count my blessings.*** DPM □ ...

Here *one's* is used in the headphrase because the possessive in the illustration (*my*) refers to the same person as the subject (*I*). Note finally:

give sb his due ... *John Bayley does better than most in* ***giving*** *Byron* ***his due.*** L □ ...

Here *his* is used (rather than *sb's* or *one's*) because the possessive in the entry (*his*) refers to the same person as the object (*Byron*).

(iii) the 'dummy' verb *do* (also in the form *doing*) is commonly used in headphrases with *sth* to indicate an open choice of transitive *or* intransitive verbs. Compare the examples in the entry for:

have etc the grace etc to do sth ... ***have the grace to*** *accept the polite lie* ... □ ... ***have the grace to*** *feel a bit ashamed* ... □ ... ***had the courtesy to*** *explain why.*

– where *to do sth* is replaced by a number of more specific verbs.

Numbered entries

.5 Expressions which have the same form but quite different meanings are given separate, numbered, entries:

give sb etc a break[1] ... give sb etc a rest, respite, or change from work or activity

give sb etc a break[2] ... give sb etc an opening for his talents or abilities ...

Some expressions with two or more *related* meanings are treated in separate entries also, especially if the differences in meaning correspond to a contrast in grammatical pattern or function or to an important difference in use. The first of the following two numbered expressions, for instance, is an Adjunct – an expression which tells us when, how, why, where etc, the event referred to by a main verb takes place. The second phrase is a Conjunct – an expression used to introduce or conclude a stage in an argument or to join two stages together:

first of all[1] [A (AdvP)] before (doing) anything else ...

first of all[2] [Conj (AdvP)] (used to introduce what the speaker considers to be) the first or most important item in an argument or process ...

Order of headphrases

Headphrases in this volume have been arranged in strict alphabetical order to make the location of individual entries as easy as possible. According to common practice, certain words, abbreviations and punctuation marks are ignored for purposes of alphabetical arrangement, and users will find it useful to note these:

(i) Among words, only *a/an*, *the*, *and* and the particle *to* (as used in the *to*-infinitive – *to love, to listen*, and so on) are disregarded in determining the order of entries. Consider these sequences:

lucky at cards, unlucky in love
a lucky dip
(where *at* and *dip* determine order)

the dog days
dog ears/-eared
(where *the* is ignored)

change course
change and decay
(where *course* and *decay* decide the order)

born to command/rule
born in the gutter
(where *to* is discounted)

Note, however, that when an article etc serves to distinguish two headphrase which are in other respects the same, it is taken account of, the headphrase wit the article being placed second:

in future
in the future

(ii) The common abbreviations *sb* (= *somebody*), *sth* (= *something*) and *sb'* (also *one's* and *his* when they stand for one of the full set of possessive adjec tives *my*, *your*, *his*, *her*, *its*, *our*, *their*, as used in example sentences) are als ignored when determining the order of entries. Consider:

catch sb napping
catch a packet
catch sb red-handed
(where *napping*, *packet* and *red-handed* decide the order)

hold sb's hand
hold hands
(where *sb's* is ignored)

catch sb's attention
catch one's breath
(where both *sb's* and *one's* are discounted)

Note again, however, that when two headphrases are identical except for th presence of *sb's* etc, the one with the possessive is placed second:

heart and soul
one's heart and soul

In addition, when two headphrases are the same, except that *sb* occurs in on and *sth* in the other, the spelling of the abbreviations determines order:

according to sb
according to sth
according to/by one's lights

It should be noted that the non-abbreviated words *someone* and *something* ca form part of headphrases (thus, *someone or other*, *something like*). If so the are taken account of in the alphabetical arrangement of entries:

someone or other
something/nothing doing
something else again

The use of *etc* in a headphrase does not affect alphabetical arrangement:

make etc a decision
make do (with sth)
(where *decision* and *do* decide the order)

(iii) Words in parentheses or following an oblique do not affect the alphabetical order of the headphrases:

plain living and high thinking
(all) plain sailing

mad etc (at/with sb/sth)
mad etc about sb/sth
(in both these pairs of entries words in parentheses are ignored)
each and every
each/every man for himself
(where *every* is ignored in the second entry)

Where, however, one headphrase of two which are otherwise alike contains an item after an oblique or in parentheses, that headphrase is placed second:
get sb the sack
get/give sb the sack

A headphrase may have as its first main word a hyphenated compound (e g *rose-coloured*). For purposes of alphabetical arrangement the parts of such compounds are treated as separate words, except in the few cases where a part of the compound never appears as a separate word, e g *non-*. The sequence
a rose by any other name
rose-coloured/rose-tinted spectacles
a rose is a rose is a rose
is determined by the alphabetical ordering of *by*, *coloured* and *is*.

In this Dictionary, idioms are listed alphabetically according to the first word which forms an integral part of them. The success which a student has in locating an expression thus depends on how far he is able to recognize that key word in an idiom he is meeting for the first time. He may not always do so, believing for example that *through thick and thin* begins with *thick* or that *take the long view* is located via *long*. Moreover, possible variations in an idiom may result in the student being faced, at various times, with rearrangements beginning with a different word. Compare *catch sb's fancy*, *take sb's fancy* and *tickle sb's fancy* (all variants of the entry catch etc sb's fancy).

To help the student with these problems of location, an Index has been provided at the back of this volume of all prominent words other than those with which idioms begin. Thus a user wishing to retrieve the main entry *take the long view* via *long* or *view* can, by referring to those words in the Index, find his way to the correct entry in the Dictionary itself. He will also find in the Index an alphabetical listing of those words which can be substituted at one or more points in a headphrase and which at the same time represent *obligatory*, *limited*, *non-grammatical* choice. (For further clarification ⇨ *Index of headphrases*, explanatory notes.)

Grammatical patterns and codes

The second volume of *ODCIE*, like the first, contains a good deal of grammatical information. For the most part this is information about syntax. The student is helped to determine what kind of *pattern* an idiom corresponds to, how it can be broken down into elements smaller than itself, and what other elements precede, follow or interrupt it. A simple scheme has been devised to show, for instance, that the idiom *force sb's hand* matches a clause pattern – though without the subject – and that it consists of a verb and a direct object. The student can be shown, too, that an idiom such as *a damsel in distress* spans a unit smaller than a clause (a noun phrase), that it has a plural form *damsels in distress* and that it characteristically functions as the object of such verbs as *rescue* and *save*.

As these examples will perhaps make clear, information about syntax and grammar is essential for a variety of reasons. First, it enables the student to compare like with like and to build up a general categorization of idioms. Growing familiarity with the dictionary and with the scheme of grammatical abbreviations and codes will reveal that a fairly narrow range of clause and phrase types accounts for the great bulk of idioms treated here. Secondly it is important for the learner to be able to locate and identify the exact point or points in idioms at which lexical choice can operate. In the idiom *give sb etc a good hiding etc*, for instance, the user can substitute a limited number of items for the first word and the last, and this can be made clear; but the learner must be shown, too, that the first set of substituted words are verbs, while the second are direct objects, and this is done by means of conventional abbreviations (**V** and **O**). In this way the syntactic relationship of the parts to the whole is made explicit. Such guidance has the further advantage that it helps to explain structural changes, or *transformations*. A sentence such as

***Bill* gave *Fred* a good hiding**

is systematically related to a sentence containing *get*, thus:

Fred* got a good hiding *(from Bill)

and this can be shown by reference both to the sentence *patterns* and to the verbs which function in them.

How is guidance on these various points to be presented? This volume covers a much wider spread of grammatical types than Volume 1 – to the examples of phrases and clauses already given we can add idioms spanning complex sentences, such as *if one believes that, one will believe anything* – and it would be impossible to devise a scheme of labels or abbreviations for all those types that would not be forbiddingly difficult for the learner to handle. Moreover some idiom types, and especially those which fit complete sentences, allow very little lexical variation. (Sayings such as *if the cap fits, (wear it)* or *when/while the cat's away, the mice will play*, illustrate this point.) It is also the case that the structure of such idioms is normally fixed: there is no need for a mechanism to explain transformational possibilities. For these various reasons, there is seldom any need to provide a syntactic pattern in entries for sentence idioms (and thus for many sayings and catchphrases).

For the great majority of entries, i e most clause and phrase idioms, two complementary approaches are adopted. First, and as a cardinal editorial principle, entries are very broadly illustrated, to the extent that most common variants of each grammatical type are covered. Thus, even in entries with no explicit grammatical designation, grammatical variety will be recorded. Second, the commonest clause and phrase patterns and/or functions are identified by means of a grammatical *code*. This is set in square brackets after the headphrase, as follows:

brook no delay etc [V + O]

There are four main types of code, corresponding to the differences between

(i) clauses (i e simple sentences) containing objects and/or complements;

(ii) 'possessive' clauses – those introduced by one of the verbs *get*, *have*, *give*

(iii) phrases having a noun, adjective, preposition or adverb as the central or 'head' word;

(iv) phrases in which a particular class of word is repeated (thus, noun + noun).

The codes are illustrated and explained in a tabular treatment below and appear in dictionary entries as follows:

put sth right/straight [V + O + Comp pass]

have etc an idea of sth [possess]
out of the corner of one's eye [A (PrepP)]
fair and square [adj + adj non-rev]

It will be noted that, for the most part, codes consist of, or contain, abbreviations of familiar grammatical terms (O = direct object, adj = adjective). When referring to the tables, readers will also notice that the examples selected are taken from, or based closely on, examples in actual entries. They illustrate, too, in each table a spread from least idiomatic to most idiomatic (restricted collocations to idioms proper). Notes following each table explain various syntactic changes and show, where appropriate, how the grammar of an expression can be affected by how idiomatic it is.

Clause patterns

.1 The order in which the tables of clause patterns are set out below is as follows:
[V + Comp] verb + complement pattern.
[V + O] verb + direct object pattern.
[V + O + Comp] verb + direct object + complement pattern.
[V + IO + O] verb + indirect object + direct object pattern.
[V + O + A] verb + direct object + adjunct pattern.

When referring to the tables and notes, users will notice that the examples appear in the same typographical form as in the dictionary entries themselves, with the headphrase picked out in each illustration in ***bold italic.***

[V + Comp] verb + complement pattern

subject	(aux +)	verb	complement
			adj phrase/n phrase
1 *Your measurements*	*must*	***be***	***dead right.***
2 *A friend*	*would*	***be***	***good for*** *her*.
3 *You*	*would*	***get***	***high on*** *this stuff*.
4 *The oil market*	*has*	***gone***	***beserk.***
5 *The suspects*	*should*	***come***	***clean about*** *themselves*.
6 *Bill*	*would*	***get***	***even with*** *the gang*.
7 *Peter*		***was***	***a dab hand at*** *carpentry*.
8 *Their greatest explorer*	*had*	***gone***	***native.***

Notes

(a) The place of the complement in this pattern may be filled by an adjective phrase (examples 1-6) or a noun phrase (7 and 8).

(b) Some verb + complement expressions correspond to expressions which fit the [V + O + Comp] pattern and contain a transitive verb such as *get*, *drive* or *send*:

1 *Your measurements must* ***be dead right.***
You must ***get*** *your measurements* ***dead right.***
4 *The oil market has* ***gone berserk.***
These fluctuations have ***sent*** *the oil market* ***berserk.***

These variants are illustrated in the entries for **be dead right, go berserk** etc and the alternative verbs are listed as collocates there (⇨ 6.3).

(c) In some cases an adjective occurring as complement in this pattern may be used in the comparative form, as in

2 *A friend would* ***be better for*** *her*.

5 *The suspects should* **come** *a little* **cleaner** *about themselves.*

– where 2 contains a relatively unidiomatic and 5 a relatively idiomati example. Such variation is generally illustrated.

[V + O] verb + direct object pattern

subject	(aux +)	verb	direct object
1 *The police*	*have*	**cleared**	*all* **our characters.**
2 *An article*		**caught**	**his attention.**
3 *The state*	*should*	**foot**	**the bill.**
4 *The minister*	*can't*	**blink**	**the fact** *any longer.*
5 *You*		**led**	**a cat and dog life.**
6 *They*		**play**	**a** tiresome **cat-and-mouse game.**
7 *Fred*	*must have*	**dished**	**the dirt.**
8 *George*	*had*	**spilled**	**the beans.**

(a) Expressions of this structural type which undergo the passive transforma tion have the code [V + O pass]. The syntactic changes – with the direct objec of the active pattern becoming the subject of the passive one – are shown in

1 *The police have* **cleared** *all* **our characters.**
All **our characters** *have been* **cleared** *(by the police).*

There is no straightforward relationship between how idiomatic a [V + O expression is and whether it can be made passive. Thus example 8, which contains a highly idiomatic expression, allows the passive transformation while sentence 3 – containing a less idiomatic item – does not:

8 **The beans** *had been* **spilled** *by George.*
3 ***The bill** *should be* **footed** *by the state.*

(b) In some cases the nature of whatever is denoted by the direct object can b questioned:

6 *What sort of* **a cat-and-mouse game** *are they* **playing?**

Where however the meanings of verb and object are totally merged – as i examples 7 and 8 – such questions cannot be formed:

8 **What kind of* **beans** *had George* **spilled?**

[V + O + Comp] verb + direct object + complement pattern

subject	(aux +)	verb	direct object	complement adj phrase/n phrase
1 *The children*		**drive**	*their mother*	**mad**
2 *I*		**took**	*Martin*	**unawares.**
3 *David*		**counts**	**himself**	**fortunate.**
4 *The Chancellor*		**made**	*his strategy*	**plain.**
5 *The boss*		**caught**	*Steve*	**napping.**
6 *His demands*	*have*	**bled**	*the family*	**white.**
7 *The crew*	*had*	**painted**	**the town**	**red.**
8 *John*	*has*	**made**	*his colleagues*	**a laughing-stock.**
9 *The matron*		**made**	**their lives**	**a misery.**

Notes

(a) The place of the complement in this pattern may be filled by an adjectiv (phrase), as in examples 1-7 or a noun (phrase), as in examples 8 and 9.

(b) Some expressions with this pattern have corresponding intransitive forms. Compare:

8 *John has* **made** *his colleagues* **a laughing stock.**
His colleagues have **become a laughing stock.**

Such variant patterns are illustrated in the appropriate entries (here, **make etc (sb/sth) a laughing stock**) and the alternative intransitive verbs (*become, go, come* etc) listed as collocates (⇨ 6.3).

(c) Idioms in this pattern for which a passive transformation is possible have the code [V + O + Comp pass]. To form the passive pattern from the active, the direct object is moved to front position and the form of the verb phrase modified. Cf:

5 *The boss* **caught** *Steve* **napping.**
Steve was **caught napping** *(by the boss).*

The passive transformation is generally not possible when the direct object is an integral part of the idiom. However, in some cases where the object forms a continuous unit with the verb and complement the passive *is* found:

9 **Their lives** *were* **made a misery** *by the matron.*

(d) When the direct object does not form part of a larger idiom (for example, in 7 and 9 above, *the town* and *their lives* are necessary parts of their respective idioms) and is long relative to the complement, it may be possible to transpose these two elements:

4 *The chancellor* **made plain** *the strategy on which his Budget is based.*

Where the complement is a noun phrase after the verb *make*, a different pattern is found:

8 *John has* **made a laughing stock of** *his colleagues.*

(e) In some cases an adjective functioning as complement in this pattern can be compared:

3 *David* **counts himself** *even more* **fortunate.**

Generally, however, this is not possible when verb and complement are a highly idiomatic unit:

6 ?*His demands have* **bled** *the family even* **whiter.**

[V + IO + O] verb + indirect object + direct object pattern

subject	(aux +)	verb	indirect object	direct object
1 *This exhibition*	*doesn't*	**do**	*the artist*	**credit.**
2 *I*		**bore**	*Bolshaw*	**little ill-will.**
3 *You*	*had better*	**blow**	*daddy*	**a kiss.**
4 *The firm*	*has*	**sold**	*you*	**a real pup.**
5 *You*	*must*	**show**	*these guys*	**who's boss.**
6 *The old chap*		**paid**	*you*	**a great compliment.**
7 *Mary*		**sets**	*us all*	**a good example.**
8 *The salesman*		**spun**	*me*	**a terrific yarn.**

Notes

(a) Many expressions which fit this pattern can also be used in a construction without the indirect object. Consider:

3 *You had better* **blow a kiss.**
5 *You must* **show who's boss.**

In both these cases, however, the implication is still that the action is bein directed at *someone*: the indirect object is said to be 'ellipted'. In all instance where such ellipsis is possible, the expression is given the code [V + IO + O] – a at the top of the table – but the indirect object *in the headphrase* is placed i parentheses. Compare the following headphrase, code and examples:

pay (sb) a compliment [V + IO + O pass]
The old chap **paid** *you a great* **compliment.**
The old chap **paid a** *great* **compliment.**

(b) Two passive transforms are associated with this sentence pattern. Compare:
The postman handed me a letter.
I was handed a letter (by the postman).
A letter was handed me (by the postman).

However, when the direct object is part of an idiomatic expression, the secon passive transform (that in which the *direct* object of the active sentenc becomes the subject of a passive one) is rarer than the first (in which the *indirec* object becomes subject). Compare (as transforms of example 4):
You have been **sold a** *real* **pup.**
?**A** *real* **pup** *has been* **sold** *you*

– where *a pup* is idiomatically linked to the verb *sell*. For this reason, th reference to the passive which appears in the code for this entry (and simila entries) [V + IO + O pass] refers only to a transform involving the indirect objec When a transform involving the direct object can occur, it is generall illustrated.

(c) A common variant of the pattern illustrated in the table is one in which th indirect object is moved to the end, after the preposition *to*:

7 *Mary* **sets** *us all* **a good example.**
Mary **sets a good example to** *us all.*

This transform is not shown in the grammatical code, but it is commonl illustrated (as in the entry **bear sb no ill-will**).

(d) When the direct object can be modified, as *how much credit*, *how man kisses*, it is possible to form questions, thus:
1 *How much* **credit** *does this exhibition* **do** *the artist?*
3 *How many* **kisses** *did you* **blow** *daddy?*

[V + O + A] verb + direct object + adjunct pattern

subject	(aux +)	verb	direct object	adjunct adj/adv
1 *The neighbours*	*had*	**taken**	*our suggestion*	**amiss.**
2 *Janet*		**took**	*everything*	*too* **hard.**
3 *A doctor*	*has to*	**put**	*his patients*	**first.**
4 *You*	*have*	**cast**	**your net**	**wide.**
5 *The explanation*		**blows**	*the myth*	**sky-high.**
6 *The writer*		**sells**	*his characters*	**short.**
7 *The newspapers*	*won't*	**play**	**it**	**straight.**

Notes

(a) Idioms for which the passive transformation is possible have pass as part their code, thus: [V + O + A pass]. The syntactic changes are as follows:

5 *The explanation* **blows** *the myth* **sky-high.**
The myth is **blown sky-high** *(by the explanation).*

Note that idioms may become passive even when the object (as in examples 4 and 7) is part of a longer expression.

(b) When the direct object is relatively long and the adjunct relatively short, they can sometimes be transposed:

3 *A doctor has to* **put first** *his poorer patients and their families.*

When the object is itself part of the idiom, however, such transposition is usually not possible:

4 **You have* **cast wide your net.**

(c) In a few cases the final adjunct (whether adjective or adverb) can be moved into initial position in its own clause:

4 *How* **wide** *have you* **cast your net?**
I notice how **wide** *you have* **cast your net.**

2 *How* **hard** *did Janet* **take** *everything?*

Possessive clause patterns

.2 An important grouping of clause idioms is identified by the grammatical code [possess]. These are 'possessive' idioms in the sense that they make use of the same verbs (principally *get*, *give* and *have*) as ordinary non-idiomatic sentences concerned with ownership or change of ownership. Compare these two groups of sentences:

John got a brand-new bicycle.
Father gave John a brand-new bicycle.
John now has a brand-new bicycle.

John **got a** *good* **idea of** *the problems.*
Father **gave** *John* **a** *good* **idea of** *the problems.*
John now **has a** *good* **idea of** *the problems.*

Here, the second group closely parallels the first in structure and in the choice of verbs; the difference is that the second set contains an idiom:

get
give sb } **an idea of sth**
have

The purpose of the following two tables is to show the *patterns* which underlie the above examples, and to help the user understand how they are related. Reference will be made also to the information about *verbs* which all possessive entries contain (➪ also 1.1.2 and 6.3(ii)).

[possess] possessive clause pattern (i)

subject	(aux +)	verb	direct object
		get	
1 *The leaders*		**got**	**a taste of their own medicine.**
2 *Everybody*		**gets**	**a** *fair* **share of the cake.**
3 *That club*	*is*	**getting**	**a bad name.**
4 *The customer*	*was*	**getting**	**cold feet.**
5 *The economy*		**got**	**a** *quick* **shot in the arm.**

Notes

(a) The verb *get* (= 'receive', 'acquire') in possessive idioms can often be replaced by *have* (= 'possess'). There is also a closely similar pattern, for some idioms, containing the preposition *with*:

4 *The customer* **had cold feet.**
The customer **with cold feet** . . .

In all cases where these changes in vocabulary and pattern are possible in possessive idioms, the collocate lists at **V** and **prep** in the entries concerned wil contain the words which can be substituted.

(b) A corresponding possessive pattern which should be studied carefully i one containing the verb *give*, which takes an indirect as well as a direct object As the following table shows, the indirect object in this pattern, (ii), corres ponds to the subject of *get* (and of *have*) in pattern (i):

[possess] possessive clause pattern (ii)

subject	(aux +)	verb	indirect object	direct object
		give		
1 *The voters*		**gave**	*the leaders*	**a taste of their own medicine**
2 *The firm*		**gives**	*everyone*	*a fair* **share of the cake.**
3 *Drug pushers*	*are*	**giving**	*that club*	**a bad name.**
4 *The excess tariff*	*was*	**giving**	*the customer*	**cold feet.**
5 *The Chancellor*		**gave**	*the economy*	**a** *quick* **shot in the arm.**

Note

Most possessive idioms will be found in entries beginning with one of the verb *get*, *have* or *give*. If a choice of verbs is possible, as in the idioms shown above the verb given in the headphrase will be the one that occurs most often. (Thos in the tables all appear at *get*, with *have* and/or *give* listed as collocates.) B comparing the tables carefully, the student should be able to derive a *giv* pattern from a *get* pattern, and vice versa.

Phrase patterns

3.3 The following tables show the arrangement of constituent words (adjective nouns etc) in four types of phrase idiom. The notes do not deal with trans formations, as it is more generally the case with phrase idioms than with claus idioms that they are syntactically invariable (so ***a blue fit***, for instance, canno be changed to ****the fit*** *was* ***blue***). However, two features of the grammar o phrase idioms are of importance. The first is that the constituent elements int which they are broken down may mark the place at which items can be inserte or substituted (➪ 6.2). In the adjective phrase table, for example, it will be see that adverbial modifiers (*quite*, *absolutely*, etc) can often be inserted before th adjective, while in the case of

absolutely **mad about** *football*,

'adjective' marks the place of substitution of *crazy*, *wild* and *nuts* for *mad*.

It is also a point of some significance that all phrase idioms function in the turn as elements in clauses, the precise element varying both with the type o phrase and with particular instances. Thus the noun phrase idiom *a false alar* operates either as a complement or as an object:

It was **a false alarm.**

Such functions are always indicated in the grammatical code for the noun, or other, phrase

a false alarm [Comp/O (NP)] . . .

and are more fully explained in notes below the relevant tables. The student should also note that Comp, as indicated above, is the complement of clause patterns that have already been detailed. There is thus an implicit link between the codes for clause idioms and phrase idioms.

[NP] noun phrase

	determiner	adjective	noun	prep phrase/clause
1	***a***	***blue***	***fit***	
2	***his***	***blue-eyed***	***boy***	
3	***the***	***common***	***touch***	
4		***easy***	***terms***	
5		***either***	***way***	
6	***a***	***false***	***alarm***	
7	***a***		***feather***	***in one's cap***
8	***the***	***good***	***things***	***in life***

Functions of noun phrase idioms:

The commonest functions (with appropriate codes) are as follows:

[O (NP)] as the direct object of a clause:
3 *He lacks* ***the common touch.***

[Comp (NP)] as the complement of a clause:
7 *It's* ***a feather in your cap.***

[Comp/O] as either a complement or object:
2 *John's* ***his blue-eyed boy.***
They have ***their blue-eyed boys.***

[o (NP)] as the object of a preposition:
4 *You can buy the furniture on* ***easy terms.***

[AdjP] adjective phrase

	adv modifier	adjective	prep phrase/infinitive/clause
1	***all***	***right***	***by*** *me*
2	***all too***	***brief***	*for me*
3	***as***	***big***	***as saucers***
4	***as***	***happy***	***as the day is long***
5	*absolutely*	***mad***	***about*** *football*
6	***fast***	***asleep***	
7	*far too*	***full***	***of his own importance***
8	***not***	***fit***	***to wash his feet***

Functions of adjective phrase idioms:

The commonest function is:

[Comp (AdjP)] as complement of a clause:
4 *They were* ***as happy as the day is long.***
7 *He's far too* ***full of his own importance.***

Occasionally one finds

[Comp/A (AdjP)] as complement or adjunct:

3 *Her eyes were* **as big as saucers.**
Her eyes grew **as big as saucers.**

[PrepP] prepositional phrase

preposition	object of preposition		
	det	adj	noun
1 ***above***	***one's***		***station***
2 ***at***	***one's***	***own***	***discretion***
3 ***in***	***sb's***		***opinion***
4 ***in***	***the***	***ordinary***	***way***
5 ***in***	***the***	***same***	***way***
6 ***of***		***good***	***standing***
7 ***under***	***his***		***nose***
8 ***under***	***your***	***own***	***steam***

Functions of prepositional phrase idioms:

Prepositional phrases have very diverse functions:

[A (PrepP)] as an adjunct modifying a verb:

2 *The police could act* ***at their own discretion.***

[Comp/A (PrepP)] as a complement or adjunct:

1 *He'd got* ***above his station.***
They've educated him ***above his station.***

[Disj (PrepP)] as a disjunct (a phrase which indicates the speaker's judgement of the value of his statement):

3 ***In my opinion****, the vertebra is compressed.*

[Conj (PrepP)] as a conjunct – a connecting phrase:

5 *Young athletes need support.* ***In the same way*** (= similarly) *young artists need encouragement.*

[AdvP] adverbial phrase

adv modifier	adverb	prep phrase/clause
1 ***all too***	***briefly***	
2 ***as***	***fast***	***as his legs could carry him***
3 ***far***	***afield***	
4	***full***	***in the face***
5 ***none too***	***soon***	

Function of adverbial phrase idioms:

In almost every case adverbial phrases function as adjuncts (modifiers of a verb):

[A (AdvP)]

1 *The concert ended* ***all too briefly.***

3 *He travelled* ***far afield.***

Noun phrase pattern with repeated element

3.4 One sub-grouping of phrases contains a repeated element, which may be a noun, adjective, verb, determiner or adverb. Note, for example:

body and soul [n + n non-rev]
fair and square [adj + adj non-rev]
bow and scrape [v + v non-rev]
each and every [det + det non-rev]
hard and fast[2] [adv + adv non-rev]

The salient feature of these combinations is that, in most cases, they cannot be reversed: hence, in the above examples the code non-rev (non-reversible). The code rev is included in those instances where the nouns etc can be transposed:

day and night [... n + n rev]

Examples of the two commonest patterns are tabulated below, with some indication of their possible functions:

[n + n] noun + noun pattern

1 ***body and soul***
2 ***(the) deaf and dumb***
3 ***day and night***
4 ***head to tail***
5 ***death or glory***
6 ***airs and graces***

Functions

When such phrases have a wide range of functions (as subjects, objects and prepositional objects, for example) they are given the simple code [n + n ...]. Some phrases have a more limited function, and this is shown as follows:

[A (n + n non-rev)]
1 *She devotes herself to George* ***body and soul.***
3 *He plays that damned trumpet* ***day and night.***

[adj + adj adjective + adjective pattern

1 ***bright and early***
2 ***free and easy***
3 ***fair and square***
4 ***(all) hot and bothered***
5 ***slow but sure***

Functions

The normal function of adj + adj phrases is as the complement of a verb such as *be*; phrases with this function have the code [adj + adj], as above. When, however, a phrase functions as an adjunct, the coding is:

[A (adj + adj non-rev)]
1 *Don't forget to wake me* ***bright and early.***

Style, register and function

No lexicographer can be content with simply detailing the meanings and grammatical properties of idioms. As foreign students come to realize, many idioms are restricted to particular groups of *users* or particular occasions of *use*, or indicate the speaker's *attitude* to the persons of events denoted, or are used to perform special *functions* (for example, greetings or warnings). The native speaker knows for instance, that expressions such as *drive sb crazy* or *be no great shakes* are more likely to crop up during relaxed conversation between friends than in an official document or formal essay, while *stand easy* and *mark time* (in a non-figurative sense) suggest the specialized language, or register, of military commands.

Since the foreign student often finds it difficult to identify, or to use appropriately, expressions which are restricted in these various ways, guidance is clearly essential in a dictionary designed especially to meet his needs. This is provided in two ways. Where some degree of comment on the use of a given expression is called for, it is provided in a footnote (⇨ 8.3), thus:

a prize ass etc ... □ a prize ass/idiot mildly derogatory.

In most cases, however, a simple conventional marking, or label, is all that is needed, and an appropriate scheme has been devised for this dictionary. Users will note that where an entry calls for a marking of some kind, it is entered in parentheses after the grammatical code, thus:

a queer fish [Comp (NP)] (informal) ...
one with sb/sth [Comp (AdjP)] (formal) ...

Provenance and currency

4.1 The idioms in this dictionary represent the usage of educated British speakers in the latter half of the twentieth century.[1] This is not to say that the dictionary confines itself to idioms that are peculiarly British. Very many – if not most – of the expressions listed form part of a 'common core': they are readily understood, and commonly used, in other parts of the English-speaking world.

While no attempt has been made to describe expressions which are solely, or principally, American, the dictionary does include a few items – marked (US) or (esp US) – which have a marginal status in British English. These are idioms which though not fully established in British usage, and still regarded as 'American' by some speakers, are nonetheless used often enough to merit inclusion in a dictionary of this kind. Note, for example:

be a different etc ball-game ... (esp US)...

Though the expressions recorded here are drawn from texts published since the end of the Second World War (⇨ 7.1), a number are now confined to speakers in or beyond middle age, and will be thought dated by many now reaching adulthood. Informal idioms are particularly susceptible to shifts of fashion, and are sometimes revived, with some awareness of period flavour, as this example shows:

gee whizz(!) (dated US informal) ... can now be used humorously, with awareness that it is dated ...

(Note that where indications of currency and/or provenance accompany a style label, the order is currency, provenance, style – thus, (dated US informal).)

Style

4.2 For purposes of labelling entries in the dictionary, the *style* of an idiom is regarded as the reflection of certain variable factors in situations in which that idiom is normally used. Among the most significant of those factors are:

(i) The social relationship between the speakers or correspondents (which may be that of friend to friend, or employer to employee, etc).

(ii) The setting (communication may take place over a drink in a bar, or at an official reception).

(iii) The degree of seriousness, light-heartedness, etc adopted by the speakers – possibly as imposed or suggested by the setting (compare the pre-match banter in a changing-room with discussion at a board-meeting).

Idioms can be said to differ along a scale from *formal* to *informal* according to variation in these factors, considered together. Thus:

(i) An idiom marked (formal) will tend to reflect a distant rather than a close relationship; be more likely to be associated with an official setting; and tend to suggest a serious or elevated tone:

make answer/reply ... (formal) answer, reply ... *He presented an Address from the House of Commons to which Her Majesty was graciously pleased to* ***make reply***.

(the example is part of an account of the State Opening of Parliament)

(ii) An idiom marked (informal) reflects an intimate rather than a distant relationship; a domestic rather than an official occasion; an easy, relaxed attitude:

take it easy (informal) ... not become (so) flustered, angered, excited etc ... *You make a mistake in answering him back, though, mate. He doesn't like that, old Frank doesn't. Just* ***take it easy*** ... AITC □ ... *Myra, love, you'd better* ***take it easy***. EHOW ...

(here both examples are of reported conversations between close acquaintances; *mate* and *love* are indicators of intimacy)

Users should note that most idioms are stylistically *neutral* in the sense that they fall somewhere between the limits represented by the labels (formal) and (informal). They should bear in mind also that stylistic values are constantly shifting, and that the conventions observed by individual speakers and writers differ considerably. We can only attempt to give general guidance here.

Register and slang

4.3 The occupational or professional fields with which certain expressions are particularly associated are not ranged along a scale, and the labels shown below generally designate separate areas (though horse-racing, it will be noted, is a specific kind of sport). The examples show a selection of the register markings used in the dictionary. They are largely self-explanatory:

foul play[1] (sport)
even odds (horse-racing)
break even (commerce)
a closed shop (industrial relations)
grievous bodily harm (legal)
make (sth) fast (esp nautical)
give sb etc his marching orders (military)

The category *slang* is treated under the same general heading as register because while the use of slang signifies a close and informal relationship between speakers, its chief characteristic is its function in identifying and reinforcing membership of particular sub-groups in society (e g criminals, the police, students, the military etc). Once slang terms become widely known outside the groups with which they originate they no longer serve this essential purpose and tend to merge into the wider category of informal usage. Nonetheless, a considerable number of slang idioms retain their currency with 'insiders' despite their widespread use by 'outsiders', and this is the range which the dictionary attempts to capture. Consider:

a tail-end Charlie ... (dated RAF slang)
splice the mainbrace (nautical slang)
six of the best (dated school slang)

Emotive and attitudinal markings

4.4 Certain idioms serve to reflect the speaker's own emotional state and/or to convey an unfavourable or frivolous attitude towards the persons, events etc which they denote. Three categories are recognized here:

(i) Idioms which express the speaker's own irritation, anger, etc and/or a violently abusive or dismissive attitude to others. These are regarded as 'taboo' by some speakers because they include a reference to God, or to excretory or sexual organs and functions. For this reason they are generally avoided by educated male speakers in the presence of women and children (though conventions vary from one speaker, or social class, to another):

God damn (it) (taboo) damn (it), blast (it) ...
get stuffed (taboo) be quiet; go away ...

(ii) Idioms which connote a disparaging or contemptuous attitude towards the persons or thing denoted:

a flea pit (derogatory) a cheap theatre or cinema ...
the rag-tag and bobtail (of sth) ... (derogatory) the lower classes generally ...

(iii) Idioms which convey a lightly humorous or quietly mocking view of the persons or things they refer to. Note that some idioms marked facetious may have a quite separate formal use:

a shrinking violet (facetious) a timid, shy, unassertive person ...
the patter of little/tiny feet (facetious) (the sound of) young children in the home, around one ...
the object of one's affection(s) (formal) a person with whom one has fallen in love ...

One further label – cliché – concerns not the attitude of speakers to events but the judgements which discriminating users of the language make of the usage of others. A cliché is an expression of any structural type which has become, or is regarded as becoming, hackneyed through overuse by undiscriminating or unresourceful speakers. Examples include:

plough a lone/lonely furrow (cliché)
leave no/(not) any stone unturned (cliché)
an angry young man (cliché)

Functional idioms

4.5 A large number of dictionary entries are identified as *sayings* and *catchphrases*. What such expressions have in common is that they are idioms, generally of sentence length, and often long established in usage, which are used to perform communicative functions (speech acts) of various kinds. These features can be illustrated by considering the form of the following catchphrase and its explanatory gloss:

did he fall or was he pushed? (catchphrase) a humorous or ironic enquiry into the cause of some apparent injury or accident (originally a music-hall joke)

The two categories can be further distinguished as follows (for a fuller treatment ⇨ *General Introduction* and c f 5.2, 8.3).

(i) Sayings – whose form is often made striking and memorable by rhythm, assonance etc – are used to make comments and recommendations, or issue warnings and prohibitions, which enshrine traditional values and sanctions. In some entries the precise nature of the comment etc is elaborated in a footnote:

out of sight out of mind (saying) ... □ usu a comment on sb or sth that can easily be forgotten, or on sb of a forgetful nature.

(ii) Catchphrases are expressions often originating with a person prominent in public life, or in the world of entertainment etc, and which on passing into more general currency acquire other functions or are used with reference to other events:

diamonds are a girl's best friend (catchphrase) diamonds, or gifts with a lasting cash value, esp from a lover or succession of lovers, are an insurance or one's future □ . . . (from a song in the musical comedy GENTLEMEN PREFER BLONDES, 1949) . . .

Definitions

5 The definition is located after the headphrase, or if there is a grammatical code and/or style marking, after that code and/or marking:

one's native heath the country, district, town etc in which one was born, grew up, etc . . .

only too well [A (AdvP)] to a greater degree than is right, pleasant or good for oneself or others . . .

take a back seat [V + O] (informal) change to, or be relegated to, a less important role or function . . .

Definitions usually consist of a paraphrase of the idiom in question (thus of a phrase which is equivalent in meaning to it, and sometimes substitutable in context for it). This accords with standard lexicographical practice, and is reflected in the above examples. Entries with two or more senses will have a corresponding number of paraphrases, separated by semi-colons:

sell sth/sb short [V + O + A pass] (commerce) agree to sell sth one does not yet have in the hope of obtaining it quickly and cheaply enough to make a profit; cheat sb in value or quantity; belittle oneself or sb/sth else . . .

However, in a dictionary containing many complex idioms it is often necessary (i) to modify or extend definitions in a way which shows their relationship to other parts of the entry; (ii) to supplement the definition(s) proper by providing information about the *use* and *origin* of idioms. Users may find it helpful to familiarize themselves with the following conventions.

The form of definitions

5.1 Definitions can sometimes be made clearer by including words (in parentheses) which are not part of the paraphrase proper but which round out a complete sentence and so relate the idiom to its wider context:

let alone . . . how much less likely, less probable (is it that one would find, do etc this thing than the one just mentioned) □ *No hot drinks,* **let alone** *sandwiches, were available.* SC . . .

Since alternative words or phrases are often marked off by the oblique in headphrases, it is helpful to pick up such alternation in the definition(s) also:

say the right/wrong thing . . . say sth tactful/tactless, that pleases/displeases the listener . . .

In so-called 'possessive' entries (⇨ 3.2, 6.3) verbs shown to be alternatives by the use of the oblique correspond to contrastive grammatical patterns (cf *They* **gave him the boot***: He* **got the boot**). This is reflected in the definition, thus:

give sb/get the boot [possess] (informal) dismiss, or reject, sb from one's employment, company, favour etc/be dismissed, rejected etc . . .

definitions

Phrase idioms which have two grammatical functions, say as complement and adjunct, will have those differences reflected in their definitions:

at one's ease [Comp/A (PrepP)] comfortable/comfortably ...

in agreement (with) [Comp/A (PrepP)] (be) of the same opinion (as sb about sth); (do sth) as a result, or indication, of agreeing (with sb about sth) ...

Information about the use and origin of idioms

5.2 Supplementary glosses setting out the circumstances and conditions of *use* of an idiom, or the *source* of its current meaning etc are provided in parentheses after the definition proper (occasionally in place of the definition).

(i) When an idiom carries an implication which adds to, or departs from, its meaning, this is shown as follows:

as well etc as the next man/person ... in a way that is equally as good as the way other people do it (often with the implication that it is even better) ...

ride etc a/one's hobby-horse ... be active in promoting, try to promote, a cause, way of life, method of work etc (the implication usu being that most people don't think it is of great interest or importance; ...) ...

If an idiom is always or often used in a special setting and/or on a special occasion (e g in court when taking an oath) this is indicated thus:

so help me (God) ... as God helps me; with the help of God (esp concluding a solemn or legally sworn oath) ...

When an idiom is often or chiefly used to perform a particular function (such as making a comment or issuing a reminder) that function is normally indicated in a footnote (➪ 8.3), where it supplements the definition proper. In some entries, however, an indication of function stands in place of the definition, especially where an idiom's use is its most important feature;

I don't know what the world's coming to a complaint, serious or humorous, about (changes in) present-day conditions, morals etc ...

let them eat cake (catchphrase) unrealistic or flippant suggestion for remedying the lack of a basic necessity ...

(ii) A notable feature of this volume is the provision of detailed information on the sources of idioms (and especially of sayings and catchphrases). An idiom may be given in its original, generally written, context (and original form, if there have been later changes) as the first example sentence (➪ 7.2). Alternatively, a note is provided in parentheses at the end of the definition. This may explain the present meaning and/or use of the idiom by reference to the circumstances in which it was coined:

praise the Lord and pass the ammunition (catchphrase) (let us) be devout and prepared to fight, defend ourselves against enemies, too (from a comment attributed to a US naval Lieutenant (Howell Forgy) at the attack on Pearl Harbor, 1941 ...) ...

or the note may refer to an original in a language other than English:

other times etc other manners etc (saying) in other or different times, customs were different also (from the French expression *autre temps, autres moeurs*) ...

or it may refer to the origin of the idiom in the title of a book etc:

the hidden persuaders ... (from the title of a book by V PACKARD 1957) ...

Cross-references to synonyms

5.3 An entry for an idiom may contain a cross-reference to another *synonymous* idiom. This cross-reference is placed after the definition proper (and before any indication of functions or origins) and identified by the abbreviation (q v):

a saving grace . . . sth which prevents, saves, one from being altogether bad; a redeeming feature (q v) . . .

A corresponding cross-reference appears in the entry to which the user is referred:

a redeeming feature . . . a characteristic in sb/st that (partly) atones for other faults or shortcomings; a saving grace (q v) . . .

Many idioms which are explicitly linked in this way are *close* synonyms, in the sense that they are interchangeable in given sentences without the cognitive or emotive meanings of those sentences being thereby affected. It should be noted, however, that few idioms are *exactly* equivalent. Even when they share the same stylistic or emotive overtones, two synonymous idioms will be found to differ in one or more particulars. Thus while *a redeeming feature* usually denotes a characteristic of a person or thing, *a saving grace* normally refers only to a personal characteristic. The learner should be alert to these fine differences when comparing synonymous entries.

Three further conventions of arrangement should be noted. The first is that when reference is made to a synonym in Volume 1, the abbreviation (Vol 1) is inserted:

(not) bear stand close examination/inspection . . .; stand up (to)² (Vol 1) (q v) . . .

The second point to note is that where two meanings of an idiom are treated in distinct numbered entries, each may be cross-referred to a synonym. These will appear as follows:

in the last resort¹ . . . as the only thing left to try, do or accept in difficult circumstances; if nothing else succeeds; (as) a/one's last resort (q v) . . .

in the last resort² . . . as an examination of the facts, or a line of reasoning, finally makes clear; in the final/last analysis (q v) . . .

The third convention is that where an idiom (or one of its meanings) has two or more synonyms, these are grouped together after the appropriate definition:

backward(s) and forward(s) . . . (moving) from one place to another and back again, repeatedly and usu in a regular way; back and forth (q v); to and fro (q v) . . .

Note in a final example that the arrangement of cross-references is the same as in the entry just quoted but that the first cross-reference is to an immediately following entry:

odds and bobs/sods . . . a miscellaneous collection of articles or items, usu remnants or things of little value; next entry (q v); bits and bobs (q v); bits and pieces (q v) . . .

Collocations

Words which combine with other words, or with idioms, in particular grammatical constructions are said to *collocate* (to form *collocations*) with those words or idioms. So *utterly*, *totally* and *violently*, for instance, collocate as adverbs with the verb *disagree*, while *restore*, *retrieve* and *squander* are among the verb collocates of the idiom *the family fortune(s)*. However, not all collocations are of equal interest to the foreign learner, or to the user of this dictionary. Some idioms collocate within such broad limits that the learner needs very little guidance in order to use them acceptably. The expression *follow sb's lead*, for example, takes as its subject, or in place of the possessive *sb's*, a wide range of nouns referring to people and animals – compare *the clown*, *the elephant, the department, followed my lead.* In such cases, the learner needs only the briefest of indications to point him in the right direction, and these can usually be provided through example sentences.

There are circumstances, however, in which separate and perhaps detailed information about collocates is essential in a dictionary of this kind. One case is where a word selected from a particular set of collocates – the set may be long or short – forms an integral part of the idiom itself (⇨ also 1.1). In the expression *make a good etc showing*, for example, an adjective from a list which includes *good, splendid, poor, unsatisfactory*, must be chosen if the idiom is to be complete: **make a showing* is unacceptable.

A second case where information of this kind must be given is where the set of words which can combine with an idiom at a given point is *restricted* (⇨ also 1.2). An example is *catch etc sb's imagination*, where in addition to forming a set from which a selection must be made to give an acceptable idiom, the list *catch, capture, seize, grip, fire* virtually exhausts the possibilities of choice at *catch*.

The third type of entry in which explicit guidance on collocation needs to be provided is one in which the idiom, while collocating fairly freely with verbs, say, combines much more regularly and predictably with some than with others. Among the verb collocates of *at a glance*, for instance, *know, realize, see* and *tell* will suggest themselves most readily to native speakers, though *understand* and *gather* are not unacceptable and certainly make sense. In such cases, the dictionary must spell out the predictable collocates if the learner is to be encouraged to aim at a native-like standard of usage.

As has been explained, words collocate with idioms as the subjects, objects, verbs, etc of grammatical patterns. Information about collocates is set out below, and in the dictionary entries themselves, in a way which makes this relationship clear.

Position of the collocates in entries

6.1 Words or phrases which collocate with the headphrase of an entry are arranged in sets, each of which is preceded by a letter or other abbreviation in **bold type** indicating the grammatical function of the set (⇨ *Abbreviations and symbols used in the dictionary*, p lxiii). The set(s) follow the definition:

in time² ... eventually; gradually throughout a period of time **V**: disappear; be solved, resolved, healed □ ...

devoid of sth ... without, not having, sth desirable (as an undesirable condition) **V**: ⚠ be; seem, appear. **o**: quality, merit; intelligence, beauty; goodwill, generosity □ ...

The words listed may be repeated in the example sentences, but if the range of possible collocates is large, those used in one or more examples are often chosen to extend the list(s) already given:

make progress ... **S**: convoy, column; survey, project; patient, wounded (man) ... □ ... *But the general disarmament conversations seem to be* ***making*** *no* ***progress*** *and might as well be suspended now.* SC □ *Though not a brilliant scholar, James is* ***making*** *steady* ***progress*** *in most subjects.* □ *At the hospital, the two survivors were* ***making progress*** *but were not well enough to be questioned ...*

Abbreviations used to indicate grammatical functions of collocates

6.2 The abbreviations which introduce collocate lists represent (i) the subject, object, complement, etc of a small number of basic *clause* (simple sentence) patterns; (ii) the constituent words (adjectives, nouns etc) of various *phrase* patterns (⇨ also 3). The order in which those abbreviations are presented in entries always follows their arrangement in the patterns (usually as set out in the codes in square brackets at the head of entries).

6.2.1 *Clause elements and clause patterns.*

S = *subject* – all clause patterns.
V = *main verb, or verb phrase* – all clause patterns.
IO = *indirect object* – [V + IO + O] pattern.
O = *(direct) object* – [V + O], [V + IO + O], [V + O + Comp], [V + O + A] patterns.
Comp = *complement* – [V + Comp], [V + O + Comp] patterns.
A = *adjunct* – all clause patterns.

When **O** (say) introduces a set of collocates in an entry, this means that any of the words or phrases listed can function as the direct object in a simple sentence formed on the pattern given in the grammatical code for that entry. In the following entry, for instance, *it*, *his wife's death*, etc can occur as the object of *take* in a V(erb) + O(bject) + A(djunct) pattern – the pattern to which the whole idiom *take sth hard/lightly* conforms:

take sth hard/lightly [V + O + A pass] be greatly/little grieved, disturbed, disappointed or inconvenienced by sth **O**: it; his wife's death, her dismissal, the additional burdens; failing his exam ... □ *Try not to* **take** *it too* **hard** ... TGLY □ *She* **took** *everything too* **hard** ... TSMP □ ... *you can* **take** *losing £50 so* **lightly** ....

The grammatical patterns indicated in square brackets (as above) do not normally extend beyond the limits of the idiom dealt with in the entry concerned. Thus, when an expression is given the grammatical code [V + O], the subject of the sentence falls outside the idiom and also the pattern shown. If it is nonetheless helpful to show words which collocate as subjects (or as adjuncts) in such cases, they will be introduced in the normal way:

make the grade [V + O] ... reach a desired standard in ability, education, social or popular acceptance, etc **S**: manager, executive; husband, lover; athlete ... □ ... *Only those students who can pass through the finest sieve* **make the grade.** ST ...

take pains [V + O pass] be very careful; involve oneself in a great deal of work or trouble ... **A**: over her garden, over preparing a meal; to explain sth clearly, to make the guests comfortable; in getting his facts right, in cleaning the carpet □ *Her garden is her great passion – she* **takes** *more* **pains** *over it than she does over bringing up her children.* ...

The abbreviation **V** may introduce main verbs (*show*, *display*), verbs followed by particles or prepositions (*put on*, *go on*) or, occasionally, main verbs preceded by one or more auxiliaries (*must have been*):

a bold/brave front ... **V**: show, display; put on ...
a duty call ... **V**: make, pay; receive; go on ...
born under a lucky star **V**: ⚠ be, appear, seem; must have been ...

When it is important to list modal verbs (*may*, *might*, etc) separately from main verbs, they are introduced thus:

can do worse than ... **modal**: can, could; might ...

The order in which abbreviations (and collocate lists) are arranged in entries is the order in which they appear in clause patterns:

take etc sth as/for gospel etc [V + O + A pass] ... **V**: take, ⚠ accept, receive. **O**: it; what he says; their pronouncements ...

When a subject falls outside the pattern shown in square brackets, the subject collocates are normally listed first:

cause etc a stir [V + O pass] ... **S**: (sudden) entry, appearance; action, decision. **V**: cause, ⚠ create, make. ...

6.2.2 *Phrase constituents and phrase types.* Phrase idioms are of the following types: noun phrases [NP], adjective phrases [AdjP], prepositional phrases [PrepP] and adverbial phrases [AdvP] (⇨ 3.3). These can be broken down into the constituents (parts of speech in most cases) shown below. Note that the order of abbreviations given under each phrase heading is that in which collocate lists are presented in entries:

Noun phrase constituents:
det = *determiner*, e g the, a; this, that; some, any.
adj = *adjective*, e g green, blue; certain, total.
n = *noun*, e g door, house; feeling, uncertainty.
{ **cl** = *finite or non-finite clause*, e g that he would; how to do it.
{ **Inf** = *infinitive or infinitive phrase*, e g to go; to take a chance.
pron = *pronoun*, e g he, she; something, nothing (usually replacing a whole noun phrase).
Adjective phrase constituents:
adj = *adjective*, e g happy; unsure; undecided
{ **cl** = *finite or non-finite clause*, e g as to what would happen; whether to go.
{ **Inf** = *infinitive or infinitive phrase*, e g to go, to see you.

Preposition phrase constituents:
prep = *preposition*, e g at, into; with, without.
o = *object of preposition* (which may in turn be a noun phrase or clause – see above).

Adverbial phrase constituents:
adv mod = *adverbial (pre-)modifier*, e g very, so, somewhat, rather.
adv = *adverb*, e g happily; totally.

The arrangement of lists introduced by these abbreviations is as follows:

a fine etc kettle of fish . . . **det**: a; what, such a. **adj**: fine, ⚠ nice, pretty . .
a fat etc lot of good etc [Comp/o (NP)] . . . **adj**: fat, ⚠ damned, great, precious **o**: good, ⚠ help, sense, use . . .

(Note, incidentally, that whenever a word is followed by *etc* in a headphrase that word is repeated in the corresponding set of collocates below.)

6.2.3 *Collocates and patterns: some special cases.* In addition to the more straightforward possibilities illustrated above, adjectives, nouns etc may be listed in entries for clause idioms, and subjects, verbs etc in entries for phrase idioms. Moreover, a single set of collocates may be shown to function at two points in a single pattern, or in two distinct patterns:

(i) The clause idiom *make a beginning/start* has as its object a noun phrase (*a beginning/start*) which may in turn contain one of a small set of adjectives (*good, bad, small*). Since these occur commonly enough to be of interest to the learner, they are indicated, thus:

make a beginning/start [V + O pass] . . . **adj**: good, bad; small. . .

A more complex entry is the following, which contains sets of words which function as subjects, determiners and adjectives respectively:

carry conviction [V + O] . . . **S**: speaker; account, argument, lie. **det**: some, more, less. **adj**: total, absolute . . .

(ii) The whole of the noun phrase idiom *the last word (in sth)* functions as the complement of a clause – a possibility which is signalled by the grammatical code (⇨ 3.3). The verbs with which the idiom can combine in the clause are listed at **V** in the body of the entry:

the last word (in sth) [Comp (NP)] sb/sth that, of its kind, cannot be surpassed . . . **V**: ⚠ be; become, seem; make sth . . .

When in addition it is necessary to list words which can be inserted in the phrase idiom itself, they appear as follows:

every bit as bad etc (as) [Comp (AdjP)] . . . **V**: ⚠ be, look, sound. adj: bad, good; important, relevant, effective, useless . . .

(iii) Some headphrases contain two prepositions. Rather than separate the words which collocate with each into two lists, we present them as one, with the prepositions set in bold italic in front of their respective collocates:

born and bred (in/to sth) . . . **o**: ***(in)*** the country, Yorkshire; ***(to)*** the life of a farmer, the life of a fisherman . . .

(iv) When one part of a set of words (say adjectives) collocates exclusively with certain members of another (say nouns), the former set is kept together and the restrictions are shown as follows:

a matter of concern etc . . . **adj**: ***(concern, interest)*** national, general; some, considerable, the greatest; ***(indifference)*** complete, utter. **n**: concern, interest; indifference . . .

(v) A phrase idiom may have two functions – say as a complement and a direct object. Verbs given as collocates of the idiom in such cases are listed together, but separated into sub-groups by a semi-colon. The sub-group listed first always contains those verbs which fulfil the first of the alternative functions given in the grammatical code.

the lesser of two evils [Comp/O (NP)] . . . **V**: be, seem; choose, prefer . . .

Collocations and grammatical transforms

6.3 Collocates always have grammatical functions (as indicated above), and those functions may change when the pattern of a clause is transformed (e g from active to passive). Consider the example:

put sth right/straight [V + O + Comp pass] . . . **O**: it, this; the matter, things; these misunderstandings . . .

Here, the words *it*, *this* etc can function in the active clause pattern [V + O + Comp] as direct objects, as in the example:

We would have to **put this right** *at once.*

When the clause is transformed into the passive, however, the word *this* functions as subject:

This would have to be **put right** *at once.*

(Note that the passive clause is given as an example in the entry concerned.)

Other types of entry in which the grammatical function of collocates alters as the result of changes in syntactic pattern are as follows:

(i) In entries for noun phrase or adjective phrase idioms, the list introduced by **V** may include intransitive and transitive verbs. If so, the transitive verbs appear last, after a semi-colon, and are followed by *sb* and/or *sth*:

a decent/good sort [Comp (NP)] . . . a likeable person . . . **V**: ⚠ be; think, find, sb . . . *She was* ***a good sort*** . . .

(as) poor as a church mouse [Comp (AdjP)] . . . **V**: ⚠ be, look; leave sb □ *Miss Pilchester was* ***as poor as a church mouse;*** . . .

The arrangement of verb collocates in such entries should be taken to mean that an example sentence containing *be*, for instance, can be changed into one containing *think*, *find*, *leave* etc, with the subject of the former sentence becoming the object of the latter. Compare the examples just above with:

We found her **a good sort.**

Her father left Miss Pilchester **as poor as a church mouse.**

(ii) In possessive entries whose headphrases begin with *get*, the list introduced by **V** will often include verbs which take a direct object (including *get* itself) and others which take an indirect object in addition (especially *give*, but occasionally *grant* or *allow*). The two types are separated off by a semi-colon:

get etc a shot in the arm [possess] ... get etc sth that has a stimulating or restorative effect **S**: patient; institution, industry, economy; project, campaign. **V**: get, ⚠ have (got), give sb ... *The Chancellor's immediate problem is to* ***give*** *the economy* ***a*** *quick* ***shot in the arm.*** OBS

The whole arrangement of collocates here can be taken to mean that a sentence containing *get*, with *patient*, *institution*, *economy* etc as its subject, can be changed into one containing *give*, having a word from the *same* list of collocates as its indirect object (⇨ also 3.2, 7.3.4). Compare:

The economy ***gets a shot in the arm.***
The Chancellor ***gives*** *the economy* ***a shot in the arm.***

Corresponding conventions are used in entries introduced by *give*, so that a member of the collocate list appearing after **IO** in such entries can be assumed to function as the subject of a *get* sentence:

give sb/sth etc the (full) works [possess] ... do, say, provide etc everything one possibly can ... **V**: give sb/sth, ⚠ (formal) accord sb/sth; get. **IO**: audience; visitor, guest; house, car ...

Using this information, a sentence such as

We've ***given*** *the car* ***the full works.***

can be constructed, and changed to

The car has ***got the full works.***

Semantic groupings in lists of collocates

6.4 Apart from the conventions of arrangement in collocate lists discussed above, users should note the following:

(i) When collocates belong to different word-classes (parts of speech) the classes are separated off by a semi-colon:

money can't buy everything etc ... **O**: everything; happiness, health, peace of mind ...

shall be etc nameless ... **S**: my informant; who, that, which ...

(ii) Words, phrases and clauses are marked off in the same way:

a matter of sth ... **o**: patience, will-power, luck; economic viability; finding the right backers, adjusting the intake valve ...

(iii) Words, etc, which are closely related in meaning are grouped together and separated by a semi-colon from others which are more remote:

change course ... **S**: dog, fox; ship; industry, management ...

have etc enough luggage etc to sink a battleship ... **O**: luggage, money, food, drink; confidence, conceit ...

The purpose of these various types of sub-grouping is to mark out for the learner areas of the vocabulary from which other acceptable choices can be made. The nouns *dog*, *fox* in the *change course* entry, for example, may suggest *rabbit*, while *industry*, *management* may indicate *agriculture*, *leadership*.

Limited and open choice of collocates

6.5 The distinction between limited and open choice in sets of collocates was drawn at the beginning of this major section and fully discussed in 1.1 and 1.2.

Sets which represent a severely restricted range of options are marked with the 'danger sign' – ⚠. This precedes the set when *none* of its members is a part of the idiom in question, and follows the first word when that word or another is an integral element in the idiom:

the villain of the piece [Comp (NP)] ... V: ⚠ be; regard sb as, think sb ...
start etc a hare [V + O] ... V: start, ⚠ raise, put up ...

Sets marked in these ways do not altogether exhaust the speaker's options; he may choose other words, usually for special effect. Nonetheless, students should, for normal everyday purposes, confine themselves to the choices indicated.

Illustrations

Sources

7.1 Illustrative sentences in this volume (as in Volume 1) are of two kinds: *citations* from written or spoken texts and *made-up* examples.

In 1959, work began on the collection of idiomatic expressions of all types as a prelude to the writing of this dictionary. A substantial collection of excerpts from texts of various kinds, chiefly written, was thus available from which suitable illustrations for the dictionary entries could be selected. As the compilation and editing of Volume 1 (1964-74) proceeded, however, the material was added to from more up-to-date written and spoken sources. Further substantial additions were made during the preparation of the present volume (1971 onwards) and the range of publications surveyed was broadened to include several popular and serious magazines. (⇨ *List of Sources* pp lviii–lxii.) Taken together, the sources span the period from the end of the Second World War to almost the present day; they can thus be fairly said to represent English usage of the latter part of the twentieth century.

Position of illustrations in entries

7.2 Illustrations are placed after the collocations, or where there are no collocations, after the definition, and preceded by a box □, thus:

make sth work ... O: machine, car; scheme, arrangements; system □ *He found no faults in any of the parts but still couldn't* **make** *the wretched lamp* **work**.

Examples are divided from each other by a smaller box ▫.

the best/better part of sth ... □ *He ate* **the best part of** *a chicken, and gave the rest to the dog.* ▫ *The gourd must have held* **the best part of** *a gallon.*

The titles of books, newspapers etc from which citations are taken appear in abbreviated form, as follows:

earn/turn an honest penny etc ... □ *Soon Elliott was* **turning** *further* **honest coppers** *by giving poetry recitals as well as lectures.* L ▫ BLACK: *Look, give us a break – help me* **earn an honest coin** *– I'm not really a traveller in tombstones.* HSG

(where L = *The Listener* and HSG = *The Hamlet of Stepney Green*; ⇨ *List of Sources*, pp lviii–lxii.)

A number of expressions (and most of the catchphrases) recorded in the dictionary have a known source, whether literary or in the words of an individual speaker. In such cases, the expression is given in its original context (and in its original form if there have been later modifications) as the first example sentence:

by the skin of one's teeth . . . narrowly; by a small margin . . . □ (source) *And I am escaped* ***with the skin of my teeth.*** JOB XIX 20

accidents etc will happen in the best regulated families etc (saying) . . . □ (source) ***Accidents will occur in the best-regulated families*** *and in families not regulated they may be expected with confidence, and must be borne with philosophy.* DAVID COPPERFIELD (C DICKENS 1812-70)

Illustrations and the headphrase

7.3 Illustrations are printed in *italic*. To help the user to pick out the headphrase in example sentences, it is printed there in ***bold italic.*** In most entries, when allowance has been made for the inflection of verbs and nouns (⇨ 1.3), there is a close similarity between the headphrase as it appears at the top of the entry and the forms it takes in examples:

clean forget . . . *I meant to give it to the mail-man and I* ***clean forgot.*** RFW □ . . . *'Of course it is. I'd* ***clean forgotten*** *. . .'*

In some entries there are differences between the *forms* or *endings* of certain types of words given in the headphrase and those appearing lower down in the examples. In some cases it is a matter of the choice of different *words*, or of a change of *pattern*.

7.3.1 The use in headphrases of the reflexive forms *himself* or *oneself* represents the following set of reflexive pronouns: *myself, himself, herself, itself, oneself, yourself, ourselves, yourselves, themselves.* The appropriate choice from this set is given, according to context, in the illustrations, and printed in ***bold italic***:

give oneself airs *'. . . It's only ignorant people that* ***give themselves airs.****'* □ . . . *You never saw such* ***airs*** *as that child* ***gives herself.***

Similarly, the use of the abbreviations *sb's, one's* and *his* in a headphrase represents the full set of possessive adjectives – *my, his, her* etc. Again, the appropriate choice from this list is made, according to context, in the example sentences (⇨ 1.4).

The use of *sb's* in a headphrase can also stand for the possessive form of nouns (e g *John's*) and possessive phrases introduced by *of* (e g *of the minister*). Note how these are treated in examples:

hold sb's hand . . . □ *Come here, love, and* ***hold*** *Granny's* ***hand*** *till we cross the street.*

over sb's head . . . □ *President Nixon was appealing for support . . .* ***over the heads of*** *the leaders . . .*

7.3.2 *Obligatory choice of words.* When one of two or more words shown as alternatives in an entry *must* be chosen to make an acceptable idiom, then whichever word is chosen for illustration is printed in ***bold italic*** (⇨ 1.1):

bear/carry one's cross . . . *And she smiled, and was* ***carrying her cross*** *ever so bravely really.* TT □ . . . *We should help to* ***bear one another's crosses*** *. . .*

the crusading spirit etc . . . **n:** spirit, ⚠ temper, note, mood . . . ***The crusading note*** *is markedly absent.* NS □ . . . *a talent for self-humiliation. It goes with* ***the crusading spirit.*** NS

Even when the list of words given in the entry stands for a much wider choice, the word actually selected for illustration will appear in ***bold italic*** if its place in the headphrase is marked by *etc*:

day-to-day life etc . . . **n:** life; work, duties; expenditure, administration . . .

a Minister to be answerable to Parliament for the ***day-to-day conduct*** *of a service.* DM

In some idioms, alternation between two or more words at one point is paralleled by alternation at another. In such cases, the matching words actually used in example sentences are printed in ***bold italic***:

once a gentleman etc, always a gentleman etc ... ***Once a rifleman always a rifleman,*** *they say* ... □ *'I thought* ***once a student always a student*** *...'*

Sometimes, for special effect, words are substituted for some of those which normally make up the idiom. Any such replacements appear in bold italic in the examples – which are identified as nonce usage:

set a thief to catch a thief (saying) ... (NONCE) ... ***'Set a policeman to catch a policeman'*** *works only when the set policemen have the will to catch.* ...

Where an article, determiner, modal etc forms part of the headphrase and another member of the same class appears in an example, it is printed in bold italic:

can't help oneself ... **modal**: can't, couldn't, not be able to ... *I might**n't be able to help myself.***

7.3.3 *Optional choice of words.* When a part or parts of a headphrase appear in parentheses, the words enclosed are to be regarded as optional elements in the idiom in question (⇨ 1.2). If such optional words are chosen for purposes of illustration in entries, they are printed in ***bold italic***:

sound the (death) knell of sb/sth ... *The safety regulations have* ***sounded*** *the convertible****'s death-knell*** ...

pull (the) strings/wires ... *sufficiently well-connected to* ***pull the wires*** ...

Note that whichever of two optional alternatives is taken up in an example sentence is printed there in ***bold italic***:

a stroke of (good/bad) luck etc ... *Don't you sometimes feel it was* ***a stroke of bad luck*** *for you to be born with a well-to-do father* ... ?

(arise/rise like) a phoenix from the ashes ... *Hunslet* ... *Football Club has* ***arisen like a phoenix from the ashes*** ...

The abbreviations *sb* and *sth* are used in headphrases to indicate points at which a fairly open set of words can be substituted (⇨ 1.4). However, no such word forms part of the idiom itself and none is picked out in boldface print in examples. (See again **sound the (death) knell of sb/sth** at the head of this section.) Note also that adjectives, adverbs, etc, whose position is not indicated in headphrases but which are interpolated in examples appear there in *light italic*:

pound the beat ... *Mr Forbes* (who) *began his career with the Metropolitan Police* ***pounding a beat*** ... *is* ***pounding a*** *different kind of* ***beat*** *these days.*

7.3.4 *Variation in syntax.* It is not unusual for the order of words in idioms to be changed, since many idioms are subject to regular syntactic 'transformations'. Several such transformations – the change from active to passive being one – are fully explained in 3.1. Here we show briefly how certain syntactic variants are illustrated.

(i) In some idioms with an indirect object, we find the alternation exemplified by *Give John the tie* ↔ *Give the tie to John.* Where they occur, these two patterns are illustrated, as follows:

deal sb/sth a blow [V + IO + O pass] ... *fate* ***dealt him another blow*** ... □ ... *the Hire Purchase system* ***dealt a blow to*** *the second-hand furniture trade.* ...

(ii) In many so-called 'possessive' idioms the substitution of one verb for another (say *have (got)* for *give*) is accompanied by a syntactic change (⇨ 3.2). In possessive entries several variant patterns are illustrated, as in the following one, where those appropriate for the verbs *give* and *have* and the preposition *with* are shown:

give sb etc something to complain etc about ... **V**: give sb, ⚠ have (got), there be. **prep**: with, without ... *stop snivelling or I'll* ***give you something to cry about*** . ▫ *If your hair was falling out like mine you'd* ***have something to complain about.*** ▫ *Now here is a man* ***with something to moan about.***

(iii) Note that syntactic variants which are not general but confined to particular entries are specified in a footnote (⇨ 8.1) and illustrated just above:

(play) a cat-and-mouse game ... *Edgar Wallace mystery about a man whose past catches up ... triggering off a deadly* ***game of cat and mouse.*** TVT ▫ common variant **a game of cat and mouse.**

(iv) Nonce variation in idioms can be partly or wholly syntactic (c f of the normal order of words in **a skeleton in the cupboard** and that in *a cupboard for a skeleton*). Several such variants may be illustrated in a given entry, with the words of the headphrase being picked up in examples in ***bold italic***:

a skeleton in the cupboard ... (NONCE) ... *he had to improvise a third compartment, a secret one,* ***a cupboard for a skeleton.*** PW ▫ (NONCE) ... *opening* ***the cupboards*** *and watching* ***the skeletons*** *fall out.* NS

Explanatory notes in illustrations

7.4 Explanatory notes are sometimes provided (within parentheses and in normal roman print) in example sentences. They are of two kinds:

(i) Where it is helpful to indicate the type of text (advertisement, recipe, broadcast interview, etc) from which an example is taken, this is indicated at the beginning of the example:

one's mouth waters ... (advertisement) ***Mouth-watering*** *Tassajara Bread Book* ...

(ii) Where it is necessary to explain an unusual word or meaning, or to comment on a special stylistic effect, a note is provided at the appropriate point:

an odd fish/bird ... *'Is he really worth a piece* (i e a press obituary) *?' I asked. 'I'd say so' 'He was* ***an odd bird,*** *I said....*

Footnotes

8 When attention needs to be drawn to special features of grammar, pronunciation, meaning or use which cannot easily be pointed out elsewhere in the entry, they are explained in a footnote placed after the illustrations (and separated from them by a large box – ▫).

Grammar

8.1 (i) Structural variants of an expression which are not indicated through the grammatical coding are shown in a footnote (and may be illustrated just above):

be oneself again ... ▫ variant **be (like) one's old self again.**

When one alternative form of a headphrase is more frequently used than the other, the preference is shown:

back the right/wrong horse ... ▫ occurs most frequently in the form **back the wrong horse.**

(ii) When an expression can be used attributively (i e as the modifier of a noun) this is shown as follows:

do it yourself ... □ attrib use *a* ***do-it-yourself*** *manual.*

(iii) When an expression is usually or often used with a particular modal verb, or in a certain tense, this is shown as follows:

be cruel to be kind ... □ often with *you have to, must.*
easy in one's mind ... □ ... usu with *will/would be.*

If an expression is usually or often modified by a particular adverb, this is indicated in a footnote:

cakes and ale ... □ often modified by *not all* as in the last example.

Preference for a negative and/or interrogative construction is shown thus:

the end of the world ... □ often neg.
enter sb's/one's head/mind ... □ ... usu neg or interr.

(iv) Restrictions in the positioning of Adjuncts, Disjuncts etc are indicated thus:

either way ... □ usu front or end position.

When an Adjective Phrase always or usually modifies a *preceding* noun, the preferred order is shown:

worthy of the name ... □ almost always modifies a preceding n.

A footnote is also used when a Prep P always or usually modifies a preceding noun or adjective:

in the making ... □ usu modifies a preceding n, ...

(v) When a noun (or nouns) forming part of the headphrase can be made plural, and this possibility is not illustrated, it is indicated in a footnote:

a disaster area ... □ also pl.
a crumb of comfort ... □ also pl *a few* ***crumbs of comfort****;* ...

When a word that can be substituted in a headphrase is both countable and uncountable, where others are only one or the other, this peculiarity is shown:

easy game etc ... □ game and meat are uncountable nouns (no article); prey is uncountable or countable, e g *He was (an)* ***easy prey*** *for,* ...

(vi) Compounds derived from headphrases are shown as follows:

eat one's words ... □ unusu n compound word-eating.

Common derivatives of headphrases are also shown:

a smart alec(k) ... □ ... adj compound smart-alecky and n compound smart aleckry unusu.

Stress and intonation

B.2 (i) In any idiom, one word is always more strongly stressed (i e spoken with more force) than the other(s). In most cases this is the last 'full' word (i e noun, adjective, verb or adverb) in the phrase or clause: make oneself 'useful, cakes and 'ale, make sth 'work. Because such examples follow a general rule no stress markings need be given in the appropriate entries themselves. When, however, there are exceptions to the general pattern these are always indicated, as follows:

a likely story ... □ ... stress pattern a 'likely story.
let 'em all come ... □ ... stress pattern let 'em 'all come
on sb's/one's (own) head be it ... □ ... stress patterns on sb's/one's 'own head be it, on sb's/one's head 'be it.

cross-references

These examples all show *primary* stress; *secondary* stress is indicated as in:

a maid etc of all work ... □ ... stress pattern a ˌmaid of ˈall work.

(ii) Idioms are usually subject to the normal rules of intonation which allow for variety in pitch pattern. In a few cases, however, there are relatively fixed pitch patterns which serve to distinguish between two or more expressions with the same spelling but different meanings. These pitch movements are always shown in entries where the stress pattern is otherwise identical.

do you mind?[1] an enquiry as to whether sb subjects to some action or event; ... □ stress pattern do you ˈmind?; a medium rising tone on mind?

do you mind?[2] an expression of objection, often aggressive, to sth which is occurring; ... □ stress pattern do you ˈmind?; a fall-rise tone on mind?

Functions of idioms

8.3 In this dictionary information is given not only about the meaning and structure of idioms but also about important aspects of their use. In some cases, such information is given in place of the definition (⇨ 5.2), especially when an idiom is used chiefly to perform a particular function (such as making a comment, issuing a warning or uttering a rallying cry). Note, for example:

let them eat cake (catchphrase) unrealistic or flippant suggestion for remedying the lack of a basic necessity ...

However, such indications usually supplement a definition, and are given in a footnote:

my foot etc(!) ... □ scornful rejection of what another person has said ...
just what the doctor ordered ... □ can be used as a welcoming comment, ...
mark/mind you ... □ used to draw attention to a fact, point of view, etc ...
the compliments of the season ... □ (the) compliments of the season (to you)! may be uttered as a greeting.

Some idioms are used in response to, or as a comment on, a statement, command or question within a wider context. Such uses are shown as follows:

one may well ask ... □ often in parentheses, or in reply to a question already put ...

perish the thought (that) ... □ expression is always imperative, sometimes introducing a *that*-cl, sometimes ... in end position as a comment.

Idioms used to make comments etc may also indicate a particular attitude (ironic, mocking, etc) on the part of the speaker. Note, for example:

once seen etc never/not forgotten ... □ often used to remark ironically on the striking qualities of sb or sth.

like/the hell it is etc ... □ expression emphasizes speaker's negative reaction, ...

Cross-references

9 As is explained in 5, *Definitions*, an idiom which has the same meaning as another is cross-referred to it in a special way: the synonymous idiom is placed at the end of the definition and marked (q v), thus:

the bare bones of sth the essential, main facts or outline (of some matter or situation) and nothing more; a bare outline (of sth) (q v) ...

In many entries, however, another kind of cross-reference is provided (⇨ 9.1). This is positioned at the *end* of the entry, as follows:

a stag party ... ⇨ a hen party.

As is the case with synonymous cross-references, there will usually be a reference back from the entry to which the user is directed:

a hen party . . . ➪ a stag party.

Three other conventions should be noted. When the entries which are referred to each other are adjacent, the form of cross-reference is:

be a case in point . . . ➪ ⚠ . . . next entry.
be a case of sth . . . ➪ ⚠ . . . previous entry

When reference needs to be made to an entry in Volume 1 of the dictionary, the convention used is:
make sense[1] . . . ➪ ⚠ make sense of (Vol 1).

In all the above entries the cross-reference is introduced by ➪ (followed where appropriate by ⚠, ➪ 9.1.1, 9.1.2). However, when the idiom to which reference is made is compared with the headphrase in an explanatory footnote, the convention is a follows:

(I'm) glad to meet you . . . □ warmer than 'how do you do' (q v), but still formal unless stressed, . . .

Uses of cross-references

9.1 The purpose of cross-references placed at the end of entries is two-fold: (i) to warn the user against 'false friends' – expressions which are similar in form but not in meaning, and so are apt to give rise to errors; (ii) to point out important relationships of meaning between entries (other, that is, than sameness of meaning).

9.1.1 *False friends*. Errors can arise in the use of idioms whenever one expression is sufficiently close to another – either in the words which make it up or in the arrangement of those words – to be confused with it. When, for example, two idioms are so close in form as to be almost indistinguishable they may be used in place of each other. Thus it is possible for the learner to say *bargaining counter* (= 'something used in the process of negotiations') when what he means is *bargain counter* (= 'a part of the store where bargains can be had'). Though the intended meaning in such cases will often be clear from the wider context, the effect may also be to cause amusement to the hearer and embarrassment to the speaker. To help the foreign learner to be conscious of pitfalls of this kind – which abound in idiomatic usage – we have cross-referred those entries thought likely to lead to errors, and have marked such cross-references with the danger-sign – ⚠:

a bargain basement/counter a serving area in a shop, or large store, where the goods are sold at less than their usual price . . . ➪ ⚠ a bargaining counter.
a bargaining counter . . . a special advantage, a position of strength in negotiations . . . ➪ ⚠ a bargain basement/counter.

Apart from the case just quoted, in which one idiom is almost indistinguishable from another, the following types of false friend should be noted:

(i) One idiom may contain a word or words present in another and yet be quite unrelated in meaning to it:

be damned etc . . . sb or sth mentioned or suggested . . . is to be defied, rejected, refused, ignored . . . ➪ ⚠ (well,) I'll be/I'm damned etc! . . .
(well,) I'll be/I'm damned etc! . . . exclamation of pleased, or displeased, astonishment . . . ➪ ⚠ . . . be damned etc.

(ii) Two semantically unrelated idioms may contain the same words in different arrangements:

the end justifies the means if the result is considered to be important enough, then any method of achieving it . . . should be welcomed and pursued . . . ➪ ⚠ a/the means to an end.

a/the means to an end (simply) the way(s), method(s), or process(es) that need to be adopted in order to achieve a particular result ... ⇨ ⚠ the end justifies the means.

(iii) Two idioms which are closely similar in form may differ to the extent that one idiom has two or more meanings:

hold sb's hand ... clasp or grasp another's hand; (informal) comfort or support sb during a difficult or trying period ... ⇨ ⚠ next entry.
hold hands ... sit, walk etc beside another person with both or nearest hands linked, usu as a sign of affection ... ⇨ ⚠ previous entry.

9.1.2 *Idioms related in meaning*. In the previous section mention was made of idioms whose form is apt to mislead the learner into thinking that they are related in meaning. There are, however, many idioms that *are* semantically related, in various ways, and it is equally important to point these out to the learner. One type of meaning-relationship (synonymy) has already been mentioned; in this dictionary it is treated as part of the definition (⇨ 5.3). The meaning-relations to be discussed here are shown at the end of the entries.

The pairs of idioms involved fall into two groups:

(i) The first group is made up of pairs of expressions which are *opposite* in meaning (the cross-references being introduced by ⇨, *without* ⚠). Some of these contain adjectives, most of which also contrast when used non-idiomatically:

early on ... ⇨ later on.
the big time ... ⇨ (the) small time.
have a closed mind ... ⇨ have an open mind.

Some idioms which are opposite in meaning contain contrastive verbs:

gain ground ... ⇨ give/lose ground (to sb/sth).
open one's (big) mouth ... ⇨ shut one's mouth etc; ...
start the rot ... ⇨ stop the rot.

Note that the verbs, and the expressions of which they are part, denote a 'reversing' process: one loses ground, as it were, only to gain it again – or gains it only to lose it.

A smaller sub-group of contrastive idioms depend for their oppositeness on nouns;

by accident ... ⇨ by design...
in the past ... ⇨ in future; in the future...
a matter of fact ... ⇨ a matter of opinion.

(ii) The second group is made up of pairs of idioms such as *black(en) sb's eye (for him)* and *have etc a black eye*, in which the meaning of one can be said to follow from, or be implied by, that of the other. (If someone blackens my eye, I have a black eye!) Other examples are:

run short (of sth) ... ⇨ ⚠ short of sth².
raise one's/sb's spirits ... ⇨ ⚠ one's spirits rise/sink.
raise the question etc (of sth) ... ⇨ ⚠ the question (of sth) arises; ...

Note that cross-references between expressions of this type are introduced by ⇨ ⚠.

One of the most important functions of cross-references to Volume 1 is to indicate a connection of the above kind between pairs of entries in the two volumes (⇨ also 5.3). Take for example:

give sb a kick/get a kick doing sth ... ⇨ ⚠ get a kick out of (Vol 1).

Since a sentence such as *Water-skiing* **gives** *me* **a** *tremendous* **kick** implies *I get* **a** *tremendous* **kick out of** *water-skiing* the relationship between the cross-referred idioms is similar to that between, say, *raise sb's spirits* and *one's spirits* *rise*. In the *give sb a kick* entry, readers will also note that the alternative expression shown after the oblique (*get a kick doing sth*) has the same meaning as *get a kick out of*. This is borne out by the example *I* ***get a tremendous kick*** *water-skiing*.

Some entries to which reference is made, while related in meaning to the corresponding entries in this volume, nonetheless show fine lexical differences. Consider:

have etc a head of steam . . . ⇨ ⚠ get up steam (Vol 1).

In both entries there are literal and figurative meanings which match neatly. Thus when a train gets up steam it can be said to have a head of steam (and correspondingly for energetic workers and athletes). The *have* idiom (this volume) is implied by the *get* idiom (Volume 1). Comparison of the entries will show, however, that while the phrase *a head of steam* combines with various action verbs (including *get up*) as well as *have*, the noun *steam* on its own collocates only with *get up*: **have steam* and **produce steam* are both unacceptable. Users of the Dictionary would be well advised to note these fine differences carefully as they refer from one volume to the other.

List of sources

This list records the original texts and subsequent additional texts used as a basis for some of the illustrative quotations (⇨ General Introduction, p x and The content and arrangement of entries, 7, *Illustrations*).

It is arranged in alphabetical order according to the reference initials of the title (the first column on the left) that are used in the text of the dictionary to identify the source. The author, if known, and the full title of the work follow in the second and third columns. The last column gives the edition used with the date of the publication or impression and, in parentheses below it, the name of the original publisher and date of first publication in England if they differ from the edition used.

Reference initials	*Author*	*Title*	*Edition used (+ original publisher and date of first publication)*
AH	William Plomer	At Home	Penguin 1961 (Jonathan Cape 1958)
AITC	Monica Dickens	The Angel in the Corner	Penguin 1960 (Michael Joseph 1956)
ARG		Argosy (magazine)	September 1958
ART	N F Simpson	A Resounding Tinkle	Penguin 1960 in New English Dramatists 2
ASA	Angus Wilson	Anglo-Saxon Attitudes	Penguin 1958 (Secker & Warburg 1956)
BB	Gerald Durrell	The Bafut Beagles	Reprint Society 1956 (Rupert Hart-Davies 1954)
BBCR		BBC Radio	programmes 1973-83
BBCTV		BBC Television	programmes 1967-78
BFA	H E Bates	A Breath of French Air	Penguin 1962 (Michael Joseph 1959)
BM		Blackwood's Magazine	July 1960
BN	Alan Moorhead	The Blue Nile	Heron Books 1965 (Hamish Hamilton 1962)
CM		Cornhill Magazine	Summer 1960
CON	John Wain	The Contenders	Penguin 1962 (Macmillan 1958)
CSWB	Arnold Wesker	Chicken Soup with Barley	Penguin 1959
CWR	Laurie Lee	Cider with Rosie	Penguin 1962 (Hogarth Press 1959)

DBM	H E Bates	The Darling Buds of May	Penguin 1961 (Michael Joseph 1958)
DC	Dorothy Eden	Darling Clementine	Penguin 1959 (MacDonald 1955)
DF	Gerald Durrell	The Drunken Forest	Penguin 1961 (Rupert Hart-Davis 1956)
DIL	Richard Gordon	Doctor in Love	Penguin 1961 (Michael Joseph 1957)
DM		Daily Mirror (newspaper)	21 June 1960
DOP	Aldous Huxley	The Doors of Perception	Penguin 1960 (Chatto & Windus 1954)
DPM	Bernard Kops	The Dream of Peter Mann	Penguin 1960
DS	Ian Fleming	The Diamond Smugglers	Pan Books 1960 (Jonathan Cape 1957)
E	Samuel Beckett	Embers	Faber & Faber 1959
EGD	John Osborne & Anthony Creighton	Epitaph for George Dillon	Penguin 1960 (Faber & Faber 1958)
EHOW	Doris Lessing	Each His Own Wilderness	Penguin 1959
EM	Cyril Hare	An English Murder	Penguin 1960 (Faber & Faber 1951)
FFE	Peter Shaffer	Five Finger Exercise	Penguin 1962 (Hamish Hamilton 1958)
G		The Guardian (newspaper)	April-October 1967, 1971-78
H		Honey (magazine)	August 1960
HAA	Angus Wilson	Hemlock and After	Penguin 1957 (Secker & Warburg 1952)
HAH	Aldous Huxley	Heaven and Hell	Penguin 1960
HAHA	Jennifer Dawson	The Ha-Ha	Penguin 1960 (Blond 1961)
HD	John Wain	Hurry On Down	Penguin 1960 (Secker & Warburg 1953)
HHGG	Douglas Adams	The Hitchhiker's Guide to the Galaxy	Pan Books 1979
HOM	Graham Greene	The Heart of the Matter	Penguin 1962 (William Heinemann 1948)
HSG	Bernard Kops	The Hamlet of Stepney Green	Penguin 1959

ILIH	Kingsley Amis	I Like It Here	Four Square 1961 (Gollancz 1958)
ITAJ	Arnold Wesker	I'm Talking About Jerusalem	Penguin 1960
ITV		(various) Independent Television Companies	programmes 1967, 1974-78
JFTR	Stanley Price	Just for the Record	Penguin 1962 (Michael Joseph 1961)
KLT	Samuel Beckett	Krapp's Last Tape	Faber & Faber 1959
L		The Listener (periodical)	14 February & 4 April 1963, 1971-78
LBA	John Osborne	Look Back in Anger	Faber & Faber 1960 (1957)
LF	William Golding	Lord of the Flies	Penguin 1960 (Faber & Faber 1954)
LLDR	Alan Sillitoe	The Loneliness of the Long-distance Runner	Pan 1962 (W H Allen 1959)
LWK	Laurens van der Post	The Lost World of the Kalahari	Penguin 1962 (Hogarth Press 1958)
MFF	Ian M L Hunter	Memory: Facts and Fancies	Pelican 1961 (1957)
MFM	Field-Marshal Montgomery	The Memoirs of Field-Marshal Montgomery	Fontana 1961 (Collins 1958)
MM	Muriel Spark	Memento Mori	Penguin 1961 (Macmillan 1959)
NDN	W R Geddes	Nine Dayak Nights	Oxford University Press 1957
NM	C P Snow	The New Men	Penguin 1961 (Macmillan 1954)
NS		New Statesman (periodical)	1971-78
NSC		The New Scientist (periodical)	17 September 1959, 10 March 1960
OBS		The Observer (newspaper)	1960-78
OI	Marghanita Laski	The Offshore Island	May Fair Books 1961 (Cresset Press 1959)
OMIH	Graham Greene	Our Man in Havana	Penguin 1962 (William Heinemann 1958)
PE	Hugh Clevely	Public Enemy	Penguin 1961 (Cassell 1953)
PL	C Northcote Parkinson	Parkinson's Law	John Murray 1961 (1958)
PM	William Golding	Pincher Martin	Faber & Faber 1960 (1956)

PP	Robert Harling	The Paper Palace	Chatto & Windus 1951
PW	L P Hartley	A Perfect Woman	Penguin 1959 (Hamish Hamilton 1955)
QA	Graham Greene	The Quiet American	Penguin 1962 (William Heinemann 1955)
R	Arnold Wesker	Roots	Penguin 1959
RATT	John Braine	Room at the Top	Penguin 1960 (Eyre & Spottiswoode 1957)
RFW	Nevil Shute	Requiem for a Wren	Reprint Society 1956 (William Heinemann 1955)
RM	Compton Mackenzie	The Rival Monster	Penguin 1959 (Chatto & Windus 1952)
RT		Radio Times (periodical)	Scottish edition 29 December 1960, 1971-78
SC		The Scotsman (newspaper)	6-29 April 1960, 1971-78
SD	Sir Mortimer Wheeler	Still Digging	Pan Books 1958 (Michael Joseph 1955)
SML	William Cooper	Scenes from Married Life	Macmillan 1961
SNP	H J Eysenck	Sense and Nonsense in Psychology	Pelican 1961 (1957)
SPL	William Cooper	Scenes from Provincial Life	Penguin 1961 (Jonathan Cape 1950)
ST		The Sunday Times (newspaper)	1967-83
T		The Times (newspaper)	1960-75
TBC	Fred Hoyle	The Black Cloud	Penguin 1960 (William Heinemann 1957)
TC	Harold Pinter	The Caretaker	Methuen 1960
TCB	Agatha Christie	They Came to Baghdad	Pan Books 1974 (Collins 1951)
TCM		The Cornhill Magazine	Summer 1960
TES		The Times Educational Supplement (periodical)	15 February, 29 March, 9 August 1962
TGLY	Kingsley Amis	Take a Girl Like You	Penguin 1962 (Gollancz 1960)
THH	John Arden	The Happy Haven	Penguin 1962
TK	Arnold Wesker	The Kitchen	Penguin 1960
TO		Today (magazine)	25 June 1960
TOH	Shelagh Delaney	A Taste of Honey	Methuen 1960

TSMP	Margaret Foster	The Seduction of Mrs Pendlebury	Secker & Warburg 1974
TST	John Wyndham	The Seeds of Time	Penguin 1960 (Michael Joseph 1956)
TT	G W Target	The Teachers	Penguin 1962 (Duckworth 1960)
TVT		TV Times (periodical)	1976-78
UL	Richard Hoggart	The Uses of Literacy	Pelican 1959 (Chatto & Windus 1957)
US	Pamela Hansford Johnson	The Unspeakable Skipton	Penguin 1961 (Macmillan 1959)
UTN	Iris Murdoch	Under the Net	Penguin 1960 (Chatto & Windus 1954)
WDM	Angela Thirkell	What Did It Mean?	Hamish Hamilton 1954
WI		Woman's Illustrated (magazine)	16 July 1980
YAA	Michael Hastings	Yes, and After	Penguin 1962
YWT	William Saroyan	The Young Wives Tale	Hogarth Press 1974

The Bible and the plays of Shakespeare

The Authorized version of the Bible and the plays of Shakespeare are the source of many English idioms. In the illustrative quotations, biblical references are given in the form of the name of the book plus chapter and verse numbers (e g ACTS VIII 32) References to Shakespeare's plays take the form of the title of the play plus act and scene numbers (e g AS YOU LIKE IT II 7).

Abbreviations and symbols used in the dictionary

(For the initials used to identify the source of quotations ⇨ *List of sources*, pp lviii-lxii; for the coding system used in the grammatical pattern ⇨ *Grammatical patterns and codes*, pp xxvii-xxxvii.)

Abbreviations

A	Adjunct	modal	modal verb
adj	adjective	n	noun
adv	adv (phrase, clause)	neg	negative
adv mod	adverbial modifier	no, nos	number, numbers
attrib	attributive(ly)	non-rev	non-reversible
aux	auxiliary verb	O	(Direct) Object
c	century	o	object of preposition
c f	compare	occas	occasional(ly)
cl	clause	pass	passive (transform)
Comp	Complement	pl	plural
Conj	Conjunct	possess	possessive
det	determiner	pp	past participle
Disj	Disjunct	prep	preposition
e g	for example	pres p	present participle
emph	emphatic (transform)	pron	pronoun
esp	especially	q v	which may be referred to
etc	and the rest of these	reflex	reflexive
fig	figurative(ly)	rel	relative (transform)
GB	British (usage)	rev	reversible
i e	that is	S	Subject
imper	imperative	sb	somebody
Inf, inf	infinitive	sing	singular
-*ing* form	non-finite verb form in -*ing* (e g *eating*, *drinking*)	sth	something
		to-inf	infinitive preceded by *to* (e g *to eat*, *to drink*)
interr	interrogative	US	American (usage)
intrans	intransitive	unusu	unusual(ly)
IO	Indirect Object	usu	usual(ly)
lit	literal(ly)	V	verb phrase
		v	verb

Symbols

□ separates collocated words (or definitions) and grammatical information from illustrative quotations (⇨ 7, *Illustrations*)

▫ separates individual illustrations from each other (⇨ 7, *Illustrations*)

⚠ marks words in the lists of collocations (after **S, O, o** etc) that are part of a 'restricted' set (⇨ 6.5, *Collocations*); used with ⇨ marks cross-references both between idioms that are 'false friends' and between idioms that, while related in meaning, are neither synonyms nor antonyms (⇨ 9.1.1, 9,1,2(ii), *Uses of cross-references*)

⇨ see (the entry for, etc)

= is equivalent to, means the same thing as

* marks an unacceptable phrase, sentence etc

? marks an unlikely phrase, sentence etc

A

(and) about time (too) [Disj] (informal) and this is sth that ought to have happened some time ago, is long overdue (in the opinion of the speaker); not before time (qv) □ *John has been promoted,* ***and about time*** *considering all the years he has been with the company and all the hard work he has put in.* □ *'The book you ordered is now in stock.'* ***'About time, too****, if I may say so. Do you realize I've been waiting six months for it?'* □ end position.

above all (else) [Disj/A (PrepP)] especially; most importantly (in addition to all the matters already mentioned or implied) □ ***Above all****, he is blessed with a gift rare in any company and rarest of all in a British one — a naturally romantic stage presence.* OBS □ *He longed* ***above all else*** *to see his wife and family again.* □ *In choosing the curtains for a room you should consider the material from the point of view of texture, its weight, its pattern — but its colour* ***above all****.* □ Disj in ***Above all****, I know, believe, him to be fair*, cf first example; front, middle or end position.

above etc par (value) [A (PrepP)] (commerce) at a price which is higher than etc the original, or face, value **V:** purchase, sell, dispose of. **O:** stock, share; equities, gilts. **prep:** above, ⚠ at, below □ *On the first day of trading in the new issue, interest was keen and at one point the price moved up to 30p* ***above par value****.* □ *This year it has been possible to purchase the stock at a price* ***below par*** *on the market and as a consequence the company will be cancelling £23,514 3 per cent debenture stock on January 1 next.* T

above one's station [Comp/A (PrepP)] (behaving, acting etc in the opinion of other people) in a superior way that one's social level does not entitle one to **V:** get, go; have, get, ideas; educate sb □ *...a lad in the village, a deceitful smooth-tongued boy who'd got* ***above his station****.* ASA □ (letter) *This has curious echoes of something we have not heard for many years, viz. that the workers should not be educated* ***above their station****.* L □ *In a close-knit community such as a village there is an established hierarchy: a farm labourer's wife is seldom allowed to get ideas* ***above her station****.* □ formerly used by some members of the upper classes of those thought to be inferior to them —see second example. ⇨ ⚠ get above oneself (Vol 1).

accidents can happen (saying) (however careful one is) it is possible that sth unforeseen, and possibly damaging, may occur in the future over which one has no control □ *The story was not yet complete. Just as in real life* ***accidents could happen****; a character* (ie a person in a story) *might take control.* OMIH □ *Don't commit yourself to completing the book this year —* ***accidents can happen****, you know.* □ stress pattern 'accidents 'can 'happen. ⇨ ⚠ next entry.

accidents will happen (saying) when some mishap has occurred (eg sth has been broken, sth has been spilt) show forbearance to the person who caused it, or excuse oneself if one has caused it, by saying these words □ *Stop going on so about that broken jug.* ***Accidents will happen****, you know.* □ *The young waiter was obviously unnerved by such distinguished guests and slopped the first bowl of soup over the pop star's dress.* ***'Accidents will happen****,' I murmured to my companion, 'even in three-star restaurants.'* □ stress pattern ˌaccidents ˌwill 'happen. ⇨ ⚠ previous entry.

accidents etc will happen in the best-regulated families etc (saying) mishaps will unfortunately happen whatever precautions are taken to prevent them **S:** accidents, ⚠ it, these things. **modal:** will, can, seem to. **o:** families; schools, hospitals, offices □ (source) ***Accidents will occur in the best-regulated families****, and in families not regulated they may be expected with confidence, and must be borne with philosophy.* DAVID COPPERFIELD (C DICKENS 1812-70) □ *'How does a kid like him get into the drug scene?' 'Don't ask me.* ***It*** *seems to* ***happen in the best-regulated families****, nowadays.'* □ *They called it a computer error and* ***accidents****, we know,* ***can happen in the best-regulated systems****.*

according to sb [A (PrepP)] as has been said, written etc by sb □ *Today's text is taken from the Gospel* ***according to*** *St Matthew.* □ ***According to*** *his uncle the boy is a good-for-nothing layabout.*

according to sth [A (PrepP)] in relation to, corresponding to, sth (some criterion, sth already existing, etc); in accordance with sth (qv) **o:** size, shape; cost, value; specifications, instructions □ *Please arrange the books* ***according to*** *size.* □ (advertisement) *Salary scale £5500 — £8500* ***according to*** *qualifications and experience.* □ *The client complained that the builder had not carried out the work* ***according to*** *the architect's instructions.* □ *We must be prepared to modify our investment plans* ***according to*** *any new circumstances that may arise.*

according to/by one's lights [A (PrepP)] applying, observing, one's own (perhaps limited and narrow) standards of morality, religion, behaviour etc **V:** live, act; behave, manage things □ *Her parents had,* ***according to their lights****, maintained their respective standards of value. She had let hers down.* PW □ *They were open-hearted, and, though austere, their lives were lived justly* ***according to their*** *exacting* ***lights****.* LWK □ *Look here, Parkinson. I'm going to do some plain speaking.* ***By our*** *own* ***lights****, we've played this game pretty clean so far.* TBC

according to plan [A (PrepP)] exactly, precisely, as has previously been planned, arranged, expected etc **S/O:** operation, task; transfer of power; take-over; it, everything, nothing. **V:** go, happen; accomplish, carry out, perform, sth □ *If all goes* ***according to plan*** *he will graduate next year.* □ *What a morning I've* *had! Nothing, but absolutely nothing, has gone* ***according to plan****.* □ *A part of me felt a great tenderness for her—she was as trustful as a baby—but the most important part of me was continuing the operation* ***according to plan****.* RATT

aches and pains [n + n non-rev] considerable fatigue esp in the muscles, or joints, all over one's body **V:** be all, be full of; suffer, feel □ *My body was present to me in a variety of* ***aches and pains*** *which made the external world almost invisible.* UTN □ *He had become like an old man, continually complaining and full of imaginary* ***aches and pains****.*

an/one's Achilles' heel [Comp/O (NP)] a weakness, or fault, in sb or sth which may not be apparent, or known, to anybody but which if discovered can be used to damage, or destroy, him or it (from the legend of the Greek hero with an unprotected place on his heel which eventually caused his death) **V:** be, become; have, expose, find, reveal □ *A social climber can ill afford* ***an Achilles heel****, and this particular weakness on Hutchins' part would probably be disastrous to him sooner or later.* HD □ *Indeed he himself describes 'emotional ambiguity' as a characteristic of his music. And therein, it seems to me, lies at once the source of its attractiveness and* ***its Achilles' heel****.* OBS □ Achilles' with or without apostrophe.

the acid test a thorough, crucial test, or trial, of sb's ability or the truth or viability of sth (from a chemical test using nitric acid to discover the gold content of eg jewellery) **V:** be, become; apply; put sth to, subject sth to, submit (sth) to; stand, withstand □ ***The acid test*** *of an officer who aspires to high command is his ability to grasp quickly the essentials of a military problem.* MFM □ *Its carbon count provides* ***the acid test*** *for the degree of antiquity claimed for an archaeological find.*

an acquired taste [Comp (NP)] a liking for, or appreciation of, sth (eg unusual food, art) which does not come naturally to one, but can only be the result of constant use of, or exposure to, it **S:** snails, squid; beer, rum; abstract painting, jazz. **V:** ⚠ be; become □ *A taste for the work of any original artist is* ***an acquired taste****.* AH □ *For the rest, I can believe that the author would be* ***an acquired taste*** *if you could only put up with his actual writing long enough to acquire it.* SC □ *Most people dislike beer when they first try it, but it soon becomes* ***an acquired taste****.*

across the board [Comp/A (PrepP)] (esp commerce) affecting everybody, or everything, without exception (esp of changes in prices or incomes in a group) **S:** cut, increase, offer. **V:** be, go; operate, be introduced □ *If the Government accepts this argument, it will mean rises in steel prices of 13.4 per cent* ***across the board****, yielding an extra £13.4m in a full year.* T □ *Some efforts have been made of late to bring syllabuses and examinations up to date. Any attempt to cut down on external graded credentials must, however, go right* ***across the board****, or it will fail.* □ *Each insurance agent can tell you about his own company's policies. For* ***across-the-board*** *comparative advice, it is still best to go to an insurance broker.* ST □ attrib use *an* ***across-the-board*** *increase.*

act the fool/the giddy goat act in such a way as to amuse, and perhaps annoy, others; behave irresponsibly □ *Of course, if you will* ***act the giddy goat*** *in front of all your friends you must expect them to treat you accordingly. They may not take you seriously when you want them to.* □ *He doesn't mind* ***acting the fool*** *if it gets him out of doing some work.* □ *Please stop* ***acting the fool*** *with those golf clubs; if you break them your father will be furious.*

(an) act of God (esp law, insurance) a natural catastrophe such as a flood, earthquake, volcanic eruption which causes destruction □ *...insured against all loss or damage including those occasioned by* ***act of God****.* □ ***Some act of God*** *—a typhoon perhaps, or the storm that had accompanied his own arrival—had banked sand inside the lagoon.* LF

act the part/role (of sb) [V + O] pretend, by one's actions, to be a certain (kind of) person; assume a role, or character, for a time; behave in a certain way, that is perhaps untypical of oneself and overdramatic **o:** the stern father, the irate husband; the jilted wife, the cast-off mistress □ HUTCHINS: *If you have taken a job as a chauffeur I shall have to remind you to behave like a chauffeur.* LUMLEY: *Of course, you're a believer in* ***acting the part****, aren't you?* HD □ *He found it hard to* ***act the role of*** *the genial host that night.* □ variant act (the part of) the stern father.

action/panic stations (military) a state of readiness, with everybody in his right position, that is adopted, ordered, before the start of a battle (esp a naval one); a general preparation and readiness for a particular event **V:** take; be at; go to; order sb to □ *When unidentified aircraft are spotted on the radar screens the ship is ordered to* ***action stations*** *as a precautionary measure.* □ *The twins were tumbling and struggling to get upright—to get to* ***action stations****, as it were.* DF □ *When the staff heard that an inspector was in the school it was* ***panic stations*** *all round.* □ often as a command; panic used in non-military contexts, usu facetiously.

active service [O/o (NP)] (military) involvement in actual fighting in a war etc as part of one's duty (as opposed to being in the reserves, having a desk job, etc); (fig) in use **V:** see, request; avoid, escape; be on, go on □ *We regret to inform you that your son has been reported missing while on* ***active service*** *overseas with his regiment.* □ *Granny's old teapot still sees* ***active service****, after all these years.*

after all[1] in the end after everything that has gone before □ *Searched the whole house and garden, he did—and found it in his own pocket* ***after all****.* □ *Though they cut him down by two hundred dollars he got his round figure* ***after all****.* OMIH □ usu end position. ⇨ ⚠ at last.

after all[2] [Disj] contrary to, in spite of, everything that has gone before, what one has said, done etc, what one expected or hoped; nevertheless □ *Perhaps,* ***after all****, I will have a beer.* QA □ *Then Fergus doesn't know* ***after all****!* DC □ *It was only a daughter* ***after all****. When they showed the creature to her, she turned her head away.* WI □ usu end, but occas front, position.

after all[3] [Disj] what is more important, or relevant, considering the circumstances; what should be realized, or remembered; when all is said and done (qv) □ *And what about Jimmy? **After all**, he's your husband.* LBA □ *Who **after all** wants crude sewage and industrial effluent lapping at his door? It is nevertheless an accurate description of 16,000 miles of British rivers.* DPM □ *Of course they're not home from school yet! It's only three o'clock, **after all!*** □ usu front, but occas end, position.

after all one's efforts etc in spite of the trouble (that one has taken) **o:** one's efforts, work; the trouble/fuss (that); the demands (that) □ ***After all my efforts** to prepare the meal nobody wanted to eat it.* □ ***After all the demands** for action not one person could be found to take on the responsibility of organizing the protest.* □ *He surrounds himself with guide books from the library and buys all the touring maps he can find. And **after all that**, he now says perhaps we should go to Cornwall as usual.*

after a fashion [A (PrepP)] (be able to do sth) in a rudimentary, not very skilful, way (esp of skills that are usu acquired through training and practice) **V:** (can) paint (landscapes), skate, dance (a tango), tie knots □ *He's not very clever with his hands. He can mend a puncture on his bike **after a fashion**, but if anything else goes wrong his Dad has to deal with it.* □ *He plays the violin **after a fashion**, but nobody in their right mind would pay to listen to him.* □ usu end position. ➪ ⚠ next entry.

after one's/its fashion in one's/its own particular, different, or perhaps limited, way □ *He wanted to meet our bosses—I may say that **after his fashion** he was quite a big shot* (ie important) *himself.* SML □ *It was an imposing building **after its fashion**, but neither old enough nor beautiful enough to attract the tourists.* □ front or end position. ➪ ⚠ previous entry.

after hours [A (PrepP)] after the normal, or (legally) permitted, period of time for doing sth has finished **V:** open, remain open; serve sb □ *Look, you know as well as I do that I'd lose my licence if I served you drink **after hours**.* □ ***After-hours** drinking is common in some country districts.* □ *Though interest in the new share issue had been high during the day, few **after-hours** dealings were reported.* □ attrib use ***after-hours** drinking, dealings.*

against one's/sb's better judgement [Comp/A (Prep P)] despite one's/sb's opinion of what would be a better course of action or more suitable (esp because of undue pressure or persuasion) **V:** be, go; act; persuade, influence, force, sb □ *I hope you realize that I'm acting **against my better judgement** in allowing you to get engaged before you're eighteen.* □ *If you are going to persuade Mr Skipton, **against his better judgement**, to lead you to the* bas fonds (= the underworld), *I shall really have to accompany you, if only to see that you come to no harm.* US □ *The line of least resistance, backed up by cloudy visions of gain, had brought him here, rather **against** both **his better judgement** and his conscience.* ILIH

against the/one's grain [Comp/A (PrepP)] in a way that is forced, or unnatural and contrary to one's personality or inclinations **V:** be, go; work; force, compel, sb □ *All right for you. I have to work **against the grain**. You know the sort of thing, damned uncomfortable and no special virtue in it.* HAA □ *Her will was forcing her nature **against its grain**.* PW ➪ ⚠ go against the grain (Vol 1).

against the/all (the) odds [A (Prep P)] despite strong opposition, some kind of disadvantage, etc; with little, or nothing, acting in one's favour **V:** win, succeed; fight (on), carry on. **det:** the, all (the). **adj:** heavy, increasing □ *Piggy sought in his mind for words to convey his passionate willingness to carry the conch **against all odds**.* LF □ *They fought on **against** heavy **odds** and finally broke through the encircling forces.* □ ***Against all odds** he succeeded in regaining the camp before his strength gave out.* □ det or adj used, not both.

against/with the tide (of sb/sth) [A (PrepP)] (move, act) in a direction, way, that is opposite to/the same as that of most other people **V:** flow, fight (against); go, swim, flow (with) □ *There was a stampede for the doors; she found herself borne **with the tide of** sweating, struggling humanity out of the hall and on to the pavement.* □ *He knew he would be unlikely to succeed in swimming **against the tide*** (of public opinion) *in this controversial issue.*

against the time etc (when) [A (PrepP)] (formal) in anticipation of, and as a provision for, some event that is expected to occur in the future **V:** save, prepare sth; arm oneself. **n:** time, day ***(when)***; one's/sb's return; a rainy day □ *This I fancy is what I have chiefly to record this evening **against the day when** my work will be done and perhaps no place left in my memory for...* KLT □ *We have now 14 cwt of potatoes in store **against the hard winter** and enough bric-à-brac to stock the entire Portobello Road for a month **against our old age**.* NS □ *The old habit of saving a little something **against a rainy day** has almost entirely disappeared as people see the value of such saving continuously eroded by inflation.*

against one's/sb's will/inclination [A (PrepP)] contrary to one's/sb's desires or wishes **V:** (be forced, force sb to) act, marry; sign sth □ *But then the endless evenings of summer came and I was happy almost **against my will**.* LLDR □ *A Company may be prevented from expanding in a certain area, but it is an entirely different matter to get them to start up in another area **against their will**.* SC

the age of chivalry is (not) dead (saying) the formal, and perhaps exaggerated, courtesies, such as those shown by a man to a woman in former times, have been or are being ignored (or observed) □ *She and I took one quick look at each other and from then on **the age of chivalry was dead**. I knew that she wouldn't hesitate to cheat, lie, bully and blackmail.* LBA □ *Rather grumpily he gave up his seat to her. 'I am glad to see, young man,' she said as she settled herself with all her packages around her, 'that **the age of chivalry is not** quite **dead** among the younger generation.'* □ often used as (facetious) comment on an act, situation etc where one might normally expect some courtesy to be required.

the age of miracles is not past (saying) sth good can happen, or has happened, that seems inexplicable, or is of a kind that might once have been considered to be the work of God □ *Feeling that* ***the age of miracles was not past****, I staggered into the hut with the heavy, heaving sacks, and then went in search of Jacquie and Ian to tell them the good news and get them to help me unpack the birds.* DF □ *The day that any politician stands up and tells us the real truth about our economic situation — on that day only will I believe that* ***the age of miracles is not past****.* □ usu as (facetious) comment on an unexpected but pleasurable event, a complete reversal of a situation to one's advantage etc.

an agonizing reappraisal (of sth) [Comp/O (NP)] (cliché) (a reconsideration leading to) a change in one's attitude, belief or opinion (about sth) that is difficult, or distressing, to make **V:** there be; make, bring (about), compel, force. **o:** the scheme, project, campaign □ *They* (the space feats) *have been so successful that they have been taken for granted, and the death of the Russians is a grim reminder of the hazards of space travel. Their fate will certainly bring* ***an agonizing reappraisal*** *of manned space flights.* SC □ *This means that I'm going to be able to put this Elixir straight into full production, straight on the world market! We must tell the Ministry. It alters our whole timetable.* ***An agonizing—a*** *wonderfully* ***agonizing reappraisal of*** *the entire Copperthwaite Project!* THH

agree to differ allow each other to have differing opinions about sth or things in general, esp in order to avoid (further) argument □ *'The sincere pursuit of truth can never be a Press stunt, Mr Wagget,' the topographer insisted. 'That is where I'm afraid you and I must* ***agree to differ****,' said Wagget loftily.* RM □ *'You don't actually like me overmuch, do you, Moriarty?' He laughed, 'Let's say we* ***agree to differ****.'* TT □ S usu pl *(we, they, you and I)* and referring to the two people etc whose opinions differ. ⇨ ⚠ beg to differ.

ahead of/in advance of one's time [Comp/A (Prep)] further advanced in knowledge, outlook etc than one's contemporaries, to the extent that one is unlikely to be accepted, or recognized, except by following generations; be ahead/ahead of (Vol 1) (qv) **V:** be, come; be born □ *Leonardo da Vinci's notebooks and drawings show him to have had a scientific imagination and technological ingenuity well* ***ahead of his time****.* □ *I always say your grandfather was born* ***ahead of his time****. He would have been a far happier man in today's more liberal-minded society.* ⇨ ⚠ next entry.

ahead of time/schedule [Comp/A (PrepP)] in advance of an arranged, or particular, time **V:** be, come; arrive, depart, be produced □ *'I have an appointment for 10.30,' he told the receptionist. 'I'm a little* ***ahead of time****, I know, but I thought it would be better to wait here rather than walk about in the rain.'* □ *The new section of the motorway was completed in just over eighteen months, nearly two months* ***ahead of schedule****.* ⇨ ⚠ previous entry.

aid and abet [v + v non-rev] (legal) act as an accomplice in some criminal activity; help, encourage sb to do sth undesirable, antisocial, foolish etc **O:** him, her, us, them; the prisoner to escape, the accused in concealing the crime □ *...and her devious husband,* ***aiding and abetting*** *her, thought out new variations on the theme of burglary and blackmailing.* DC □ *He was brought to trial on a trumped-up charge of* ***aiding and abetting****.* □ *You seem to assume that I'm going to* ***aid and abet*** *you in fooling about with this contraption and going against your father's wishes.* HD □ *I have consulted him and he confesses he cannot explain it* (the error in dating) *to himself. It was 'a clerical error of the mind' —which I must perforce plead guilty to* ***aiding and abetting****!* RT □ aiding and abetting often used without O, as in second example; aiding and abetting often preceded by *charge sb with, accuse sb of, arrest sb for*—these verbs often in passive eg *be charged with, be arrested for*.

the aim etc of the exercise the real reason for, the underlying purpose behind, some act or series of acts that may appear pointless or unclear (from the military practice of holding training exercises with a particular purpose) **n:** aim, ⚠ object, point, purpose □ *'I wish I knew* ***the aim of this*** *particular* ***exercise****,' and he launched into an account of some incident that had happened in the ward that day.* THH □ *She has fun and she makes us enjoy it too. And that, I take it, is* ***the point of the*** *whole* ***exercise****.* OBS □ *'I can't see why you waste your time going to those evening classes on art appreciation.' '****The object of the exercise****, I'd have you know, is to improve my mind — and precious little help I get from you!'*

air/parade one's knowledge [V + O pass] show, demonstrate, the (great) amount of knowledge that one has on a subject or subjects, often in a boastful and superior way □ *Why don't you go in for one of those TV quizzes? It'll give you a chance to* ***air*** *all* ***that*** *useless* ***knowledge*** *you've been cluttering your brain up with over the years!* □ *The author seldom misses an opportunity to* ***parade his knowledge****; we are meant to be impressed, but for every fact he gets right there are half a dozen he gets wrong.*

air one's views etc [V + O pass] make one's opinions known, in either speech or writing (the implication sometimes being that the recipients may not like, or want, such opinions) **O:** views, ⚠ opinions; prejudices, ideas □ *He finished by saying that the purpose of the meeting was to* ***air our views****, and to give him ideas which he could think over.* MFM □ *Is our particular personality inherited or shaped by our environment? A distinguished but often controversial author* ***airs his views*** *on the subject of personality.* ST □ *And who asked you to* ***air your opinions****? The nearest you've been to France is the end of Brighton Pier, so I doubt if anyone will be interested in your opinion of the French character.*

airs and graces [n + n non-rev] affected manners intended to give an impression of fastidious refinement (but producing an opposite effect on the observer) **V:** give oneself; be full of □ *She's kind-hearted enough once you get behind all her* ***airs and graces****.* □ *I don't think much of her son—he's so conceited, and as full of* ***airs and graces*** *as a young lord.* □ (NONCE) *The Contessa, the Renata who had billions of lire, a castle here, a villa there, a grand apartment in Milan, was a pal,* ***no airs, only graces****.* YWT □ always pl.

an Aladdin's cave [Comp/O (NP)] a place, a

source, of riches and wealth of a material kind or (fig) of purely aesthetic value, which has to be, or has been, discovered and made used of (from the treasure cave in the story 'Aladdin and the Wonderful Lamp') **V:** be, find sth; discover, reveal □ *It is hard to believe it can be so difficult to make a home among the terraces of Glasgow's beautiful West End housing — **a** veritable **Aladdin's cave** of architectural treasure when you look below the grime.* SC □ *I was taking Susan not as Susan, but as a Grade A lovely, as the daughter of a factory-owner, as the means of obtaining the key to **the Aladdin's cave** of my ambitions.* RATT

alarm and despondency [n + n non-rev] acute fear and hopelessness felt in the face of sth that is happening, or is expected to happen **V:** cause, create, spread (among) □ *So I shall drive into Inverness tomorrow and try to get rid of what we used to call **alarm and despondency** in the war.* RM □ *My purpose in trying to spread as much **alarm and despondency** as I can is twofold. In the first place, it is a service to the cause of historical truth.* NS □ *Wonderful impromptu songs Dylan* (Thomas) *used to make up. I can remember one which described the impact of a vampire on Swansea Town Council, to the **alarm and despondency** of all concerned.* L

alarms and excursions [n + n non-rev] bustle and disorganized activity of a noisy kind (from a stage direction alarums and excursions used in former times to indicate the noise of battle etc off-stage) □ *Having anticipated all sorts of **alarums and excursions** in the auditorium of the Coliseum...* L □ *He wouldn't like staying with us. He's not used to **alarms and excursions**, and you know the chaotic way we live.* □ almost always used facetiously, esp with archaic form alarums.

alive and kicking/well [adj + adj non-rev] (informal) (still) living, in good health, and active **V:** be (very much); find sb □ *In the next kennel was Spot with her newly born puppies, a fine litter of six, all of them **alive and kicking**.* □ *'Is your grandfather still alive?' '**Alive and kicking**, I'm glad to say.'* □ *Korky the Cat is **alive and well** and still digging in dustbins on the front page of 'The Dandy'* (a children's comic).

alive to sth [Comp (AdjP)] completely aware of (the bad effect of sth, the implication of sth) **V:** ⚠be; appear; make sb. **o:** the danger, risk; the seriousness of the situation; the opportunity, the possibility □ *The view of some owners* (of trawlers) *was that the blockade had served its purpose in making the Government **alive to** the difficulties caused by low-cost imported fish.* T □ *'But you may lose all your money if the venture fails!' 'I'm fully **alive to** that possibility, thank you, but I've decided to take the risk.'*

all agog [Comp (AdjP)] eager and full of excited anticipation **S:** he, they, we, I; the crowd, the children. **V:** ⚠ be, seem; leave sb. **A:** for him (to appear), for the results (to come through); to see him □ *I was **all agog** to see again the three-mile long beach of Traigh Swish on whose glittering white sands...* RM □ *The children were **all agog** for the show to begin and for Santa Claus to appear.* □ *They hung about, looking down the street, returned into the bookshop, and then came out again and waited **all agog**.* UTN

all along [A] (informal) continuously during the whole of a period of time (and esp in contexts of deception, secrecy, or simple forgetfulness); all the time[2] (qv) **V:** doubt, suspect, mistrust, sb; know, be sure of, sth □ *'But, darling, the whole thing's been my own silly stupid fault.' 'Yours? Nonsense, Nikki! I'm to blame **all along**.'* DIL □ *There has been slightly too much criticism of this project to be comfortable, **all along**.* NM □ *Her employer said he had suspected the girl of pilfering **all along**.* □ usu end, but occas front, position; ambiguity in last example — either she was pilfering all the time or (more probably) he had suspected all the time.

all along the line etc [A (PrepP)] in every way; at every point; in every aspect (of a matter, situation etc) **o:** line, ⚠ road, way □ *These newer family magazines are making the older ones fight for existence **all along the line** because they are their direct competitors and successors.* UL □ *Alexander let me run this private war in my own way. We gave him success **all along the road** and he was content to leave well alone.* MFM □ *Probably the average child is not very much affected* (ie by educational 'streaming'), *but clearly the child marked 'C' loses **all along the way**.* OBS

all anyhow [A (AdvP)] (informal) carelessly; untidily; any old how (qv) **V:** do, leave, arrange, fix, sth □ *She rushes off to college and leaves her room **all anyhow**.* □ *Give me a minute or two— I can't go into the drawing-room with my hair **all anyhow**.* □ *He stuffed the papers **all anyhow** into his folder.* □ usu end position.

all at once[1] [A (PrepP)] everybody or everything together, at the same time, quickly □ *It would be easier for the waiters if you didn't come in **all at once** for your lunch.* □ *If you gave me a bigger basket I could bring the apples **all at once**.* □ *She couldn't tell them much about the accident. 'Everything just seemed to happen **all at once**,' she said.* □ front, middle or end position.

all at once[2] [A (PrepP)] suddenly and unexpectedly; all of a sudden (qv) □ ***All at once** she found herself telling them everything about the evening.* WI □ *I found myself **all at once** on the brink of panic.* DOP □ ***All at once**, with the diminishing of the pain in his eye, the cold and exhaustion came back.* PM □ front, middle or end position. ⇨ ⚠ at one (fell) swoop.

all being well [Disj] if everything happens as expected; if nothing goes wrong □ *I eventually temporized, and agreed, **all being well**, to return to Pakistan for three or four months annually for the next three years.* SD □ *'See you next Wednesday, my dear,' he said, taking his hat and looking round the ward, sharply, at each of the grannies in turn. '**All being well**,' she said.* MM □ variant if all is/was well.

all the best (informal) may everything go well □ ***All the best** to you, my dear, and to the lucky man.* □ *He lifted his whisky. '**All the best**, boys.'* RATT □ *Goodbye then, and **all the best** till next Christmas.* □ *I'd like to conclude my remarks by wishing Mr Wilkinson **all the** very **best** on his retirement and by saying that all our thoughts go with him.* □ often used as conclusion of letter; often polite, friendly remark with little meaning; also used with *with sb*.

all boys etc together [Comp (NP)] (informal)

members of a closely-knit group, sharing common interests together, perhaps secretively and to the exclusion of other people eg of the opposite sex, of different ages, etc **V:** ⚠ be; remain. **n:** boys, girls; friends, pals □ *The men sat up late exchanging memories of the happy days when they had been* ***all boys together***. □ *There's no need to get all steamed up over a few harmless jokes. I thought we were* ***all boys together*** *here.* □ *'Well Mr Miller,' she said in her* ***all-boys-and-girls-together*** *voice. 'You remember what you said this morning?'* TT □ *I didn't know, until I asked Robert later, that it was the caretaker (Robert called him the 'concierge', to show that we were* ***all cosmopolitans together****).* CON □ boys and girls may be literal in meaning or, more commonly, refer humorously or deprecatingly to adults; attrib use *an* ***all-boys-and-girls-together*** *voice.*

all but[1] [A (PrepP)] all those persons or things referred to, with the exception of (one or more of them); all except **o:** one, two (of the people); one flower, one of the flowers; the slowest, the least able (students) □ ***All but*** *three of the girls passed their first-year examinations.* □ *Although its trunk had been stiffened with cement to stop its splitting and falling,* ***all but*** *one of its branches had withered and died.* DC □ *The maximum of cooperation should be achieved to avoid* ***all but*** *the minimum of disturbance in international payments.* DC

all but[2] [A] almost; very nearly, but not quite □ *The lower wing-tip dipped and* ***all but*** *touched the water as the engines idled and finally spluttered out.* BM □ *...a swathe of convolvulus, the flowers growing so thickly they* ***all but*** *obscured the leaves.* DF □ *He turns and passes the table which has given Pacho, a rich man,* ***all but*** *apoplexy.* BM □ *He himself was* ***all but*** *bankrupt and couldn't help us.* □ *'Was the patient dead when the doctor arrived?' '****All but****.'* □ modifies v, adj or n.

all cats are grey in the dark (saying) differences between persons, animals, or things of a certain kind, are indistinguishable in the dark, or in other obscuring circumstances; any differences which exist no longer matter □ *Having lost my sense of smell, if I didn't see what I was eating I could only guess at it by the texture. It was not unlike* ***all cats being grey in the dark****.* □ *A libertine of the most cynical kind, he even affected not to remember whether a certain woman had been his mistress or not, saying that* ***all cats were grey in the dark*** *anyway.* □ *His persecution mania is such that he suspects everybody. In his state of mind,* ***all cats are grey*** *and pose an equal threat.*

all clear (military signal) (the place is) free of danger now that enemy aircraft have gone, an attack has ended, etc; (fig) (the place is) clear of people, free of obstacles □ ***All clear****, now. They've just left in their car so there shouldn't be anybody in the house.* □ *One of his few memories of the war was sitting in dark and dank air-raid shelters waiting for the wail of sirens to sound the* ***All-clear****.* □ *With both the unions and management actively in support, the Government may now feel it has the* ***all-clear*** *to tackle the problems facing British industry.* □ when not used as signal, may occur with *give, get, sound.* ⇨ ⚠ the coast is clear.

all day and every day [n + n non-rev] continuously; without ceasing; during the whole of one day and for a number of days afterwards □ *I worked* ***all day and every day*** *in my office caravan.* MFM □ *We had glorious weather for our cruise, sunshine* ***all day and every day****.* □ *I wondered what he did,* ***all day and every day****. 'I spend a lot of time writing at the moment. And,' he added, grinning quite sweetly, 'I follow a gentleman's pursuits.'* ST

all the days of one's life [A (NP)] (formal) for as long as one will live, or has lived □ (source) *Surely goodness and mercy shall follow me* ***all the days of my life****: and I shall dwell in the house of the Lord for ever.* PSALMS XXIII 6 □ *They had known only oppression and bitter poverty* ***all the days of their lives****.* □ *Looking at the cheering audience in front of him, he knew that, old as he was, he would treasure this moment of triumph* ***all the days of his*** *remaining* ***life****.*

all dressed up and/with nowhere to go (catchphrase) wearing one's best clothes for a special occasion, but not actually having such a destination (eg because of a change in plans); (fig) obviously prepared for an event which has not taken place □ *'This is little Coral, Mr Redfern,' she said. 'Poor little dear, she doesn't seem to have anyone to love her.* ***All dressed up and nowhere to go****, eh dear?'* HAA □ *We went to the opera last night, but only because Helen's party had to be cancelled at the last minute and we couldn't bear to be* ***all dressed up with nowhere to go****.* □ usu facetious.

all ears/eyes [Comp (NP)] attentive (by listening or looking closely) **V:** ⚠ be; seem, become □ *'So nothing happened?' 'No we just mooched about all Sunday, killing time. There was just one thing though.' Isabel suddenly became* ***all ears****.* PW □ *Mrs Crawley,* ***all ears*** *as a good hostess should be, was pleased that her party had such good results.* WDM □ *Now children, I want you to be* ***all eyes and ears*** *for the first part of the lesson and then we'll have questions afterwards.*

all important [Comp (NP)] (be a matter) of the greatest importance, urgency, necessity etc **V:** ⚠ be, become; make sb/sth □ *If the baby swallows a large object which obstructs breathing, speed of action is* ***all important****. Do not hesitate to lift him by the heels and thump him soundly on the back.* □ *There was at the centre of every 'new' religion that I examined a very solid chunk of Shintoism or Buddhism or both — an* ***all-important*** *continuity.* L □ attrib use *an* ***all-important*** *meeting.*

all in all[1] [Disj] (after) assessing everything (that has happened); after summing up the whole situation (and mentally comparing the good with the bad); all things considered (qv) **V:** taking it, considering it; taken, considered □ ***All in all*** *the battle had achieved what I had wanted.* MFM □ ***All in all****, he had probably been a soft-hearted old thing, despite his brittle bones and acid pen.* PP □ ***All in all*** *and all added up, this would lead you to believe that food is being taken very seriously indeed.* L □ usu front position.

all in all[2] [Comp (NP)] the main object of sb's love and devotion, to the exclusion of everything and everybody **V:** ⚠ be; become, make sb/sth □ *The daughter who had been her* ***all in all*** *had* *left home; all she could look forward to were her fleeting visits, the occasional letter and telephone conversation.* □ *...the urge to make the beloved happy, to do him good, to be* ***all in all*** *to him.* PW

all is fair in love and war (saying) everything wrong, unethical etc that is done can be excused, because the normal rules of society do not apply in situations of personal conflict or of emotional involvement □ *I'm sorry for poor Bill, Elsie, but I love you, and* ***all's fair in love and war****.* RM □ *Alas! I accepted that* ***all was fair in love and war*** *as far as primary things went, but if I could show a bit of decency in secondary ones, so much the better, I thought.* SPL

all is gas and gaiters (saying) everything is fine; the situation, or state of affairs, is ideal □ (source—spoken by a mad old man, a comic character in the novel) *I see her now! My love, my live, my pride, my peerless beauty. She is come at last — at last — and* ***all is gas and gaiters****!* NICHOLAS NICKLEBY (C DICKENS 1872-70) □ *The sun was shining. All sorts of trees were showing signs of life. The birds, in classic phrase, were a-hollering and a-bellering.* ***All was gas and gaiters****.* WDM □ *Do what Uncle Charles advises, and* ***all will be gas and gaiters****.* RATT

all is (not) lost there is no/still some chance of recovery, success etc □ *Despite the defeat suffered by his army, the President could not be persuaded that* ***all was lost*** *and that his only hope was to negotiate with the rebels.* □ *But* ***all was not*** *necessarily* ***lost****. As I said, Desmond was a tough chap and he was determined to get as many of the gang as he could.* DS □ ***All isn't lost*** *yet. Though the judgement went against you here, you can still take your case on appeal to a higher court.*

all is not gold that glitters (saying) (a warning that) sth/sb may not be so good, valuable, admirable etc as it/he appears to be on the surface; beauty is but/only skin deep (qv) □ (source) ***All that glisters is not gold*** *;/Often have you heard that told.* MERCHANT OF VENICE II 7 □ *We should not deter our younger scientists from going overseas to the United States or elsewhere. They will gain valuable experience, and perhaps learn that* ***all is not gold that glitters****.* T □ *Don't be taken in by his stories about all the famous people he knows. Remember that* ***all is not gold that glitters****.* □ glisters is archaic.

all is (not) well (with sb) the general position, or situation, is (un)satisfactory □ *It has taken a little time to recover from the accident but I'm glad to say that* ***all is*** *now* ***well*** *and I'll be back at work next week.* □ *I was beginning to suspect that* ***all was not well with*** *them, as I hadn't had a reply to my last two letters.* □ *There is a widespread feeling that* ***all is not well with*** *the disarmament talks.*

all kinds/sorts of sb/sth many different varieties of people, things etc; all manner of sb/sth (qv) □ *Everybody's been most sympathetic.* ***All kinds of*** *people have come up to me in the street and congratulated me on my stand against the Council.* □ *The new delicatessen caters for* ***all kinds of*** *tastes, provided, that is, you have enough money to indulge them.* □ (football) *His speed and his beautifully placed crosses to the goal-mouth are creating* ***all sorts of*** *problems for the defence.* □ *'And what will you be doing during the school holidays?' 'Oh,* ***all sorts of*** *things—swimming, playing football, watching telly—who knows!'*

all the King's horses and all the King's men can't/couldn't do sth (saying) nobody, no group, however clever, powerful, influential etc, is/was able to do sth □ (source) ***All the King's horses and all the King's men/ Couldn't*** *put Humpty together again.* HUMPTY-DUMPTY (nursery rhyme) □ *If you haven't got a degree or diploma in engineering I doubt whether* ***all the King's horses and all the King's men could*** *get you a job with that particular firm.* □ *The Black Cloud is on its way and neither you nor* ***all the King's horses nor all the King's men****, nor the King himself can stop it.* TBC

all manner of sb/sth (formal) many different varieties of people/things etc; all kinds/sorts of sb/sth (qv) □ ***All manner of*** *people went to the protest meeting, from housewives to old age pensioners, from stockbrokers to bricklayers.* □ *And the foundations of the wall of the city were garnished with* ***all manner of*** *precious stones.* HAH □ *She turns the radio through* ***all manner of*** *stations and back again until she finds some very loud dance music.* R

all men are created equal all people have equal rights and are entitled to equal opportunity (the implication is *not* that all people are of equal merit and ability) □ (source) *We hold these truths to be self-evident, that* ***all men are created equal****, that they are endowed by their Creator with certain inalienable rights...* AMERICAN DECLARATION OF INDEPENDENCE (1776) □ *Much of this argument* (against selective education based on intelligence tests) *arises from a very praiseworthy desire to give all children an equal chance, and to act on the principle that* ***all men are created equal****. Unfortunately the facts make it quite certain that* ***all men are*** *not* ***created equal****, and that heredity clearly discriminates between the bright and the dull.* SNP □ second example departs from original meaning of expression.

all the more reason [Comp/O (NP)] a reason, justification or incentive stronger than others **V:** it/there be, appear, seem; have (got). **A:** for expecting a favourable outcome, for remaining firm, for telling the truth; (for sb) to act now, to insist on one's rights □ *But if anything bad is going to happen, that's* ***all the more reason*** *for being as happy as I can, while I can.* PE □ *'I haven't seen her for some time.' 'So I gather. I hoped that would be* ***all the more reason*** *for your being glad to see her on this occasion.'* EM □ *'It's taken you a long time to make up your mind,' commented Louie, laughing. '****All the more reason*** *to act quickly now,' said Isobel.* HAA □ *Seeing the lack of common purpose among the Opposition Parties, the Government has* ***all the more reason*** *for being confident that it will be able to carry out its major reforms in the next two years.*

all one needs (ironic) what one does not want or need is is the thing or person specified; what will make one's difficulties, disappointments, inconvenience, discomfort worse, or complete, is that thing or person **Comp:** this, that; a visit from Aunt Edith, a power cut □ *Someone has offered Ken a greyhound pup. '****That's all I need****,' his wife objects. 'Nine up* (in a high-rise block) *with three kids under my feet, and now a bloody* *great dog.'* SC □ *Well, nobody could have had more trouble in getting from A to B.* ***All we needed*** *now was to find that the hotel had no record of a booking and couldn't put us up.* □ variant that/this is all I need used as exasperated comment on events.

all of a dither etc [Comp (PrepP)] (informal) very confused and undecided (esp mentally) **V:** ⚠ be, become, feel, get. **n:** dither, ⚠ flutter, tremble □ *I don't think he'll last long in that job. He gets* ***all of a dither*** *the moment there is the slightest suggestion of pressure.* □ *She was trying to walk haughty like, but she was still* ***all of a tremble***. EM □ *I don't mind telling you, nurse, that I felt* ***all of a flutter*** *when they told me that that nice young doctor was going to examine me today.*

all of one hour etc [Comp/A (NP)] fully one hour, or such other precise period of time stated, during which sth happens **V:** be; last, take, live (somewhere). **o:** one hour, ⚠ five days, three weeks, a month, ten years □ *It took the factory* ***all of four months*** *to clear the back-log of orders that had accumulated during the strike.* □ *'Hi!' she said. 'Long time no see.' 'Must be* ***all of eight hours****.' 'Seems like a long time,' she said.* TT □ *'He seems to know a lot about Brazil. I suppose he must have lived there some time?' 'Yes,* ***all of a year****—which of course makes him an expert on the country.'* □ usu indicates that the time spent on sth is long or too long or, ironically, not long enough.

all of one metre etc [Comp/O (NP)] fully one metre tall or long, or such other precise measurement (of size, area, quantity, weight etc) given **V:** be, look, seem; measure, contain, total. **o:** five feet; ⚠ four kilos, ten stone; five kilometres, ten miles; one hectare, five acres; £5000; a thousand people □ *'Why didn't you complain?' 'I wasn't going to start an argument with* him. *He was* ***all of six foot*** *and must have been a couple of stone heavier than me.'* □ *The paddock was* ***all of three acres*** *and it was sometimes difficult to catch the pony.* □ *Some of these seamstresses who work at home put in a forty-five hour week and for that they are paid* ***all of ten pounds****.* □ usu indicates that measurement is (unexpectedly) large or, ironically, not large enough.

all of a piece (with sth) [Comp (PrepP)] consistent (with sth); typical (of sth) **V:** ⚠ be, appear, seem; make sth □ MRS PARADOCK: *You should have led him on by pretending to think it was 1868.* MR PARADOCK: *It was* ***all of a piece with*** *his asking me to form a government.* ART □ *'Goodness isn't* ***all of a piece****,' he said, 'any more than badness.'* ASA □ *Everything I have written is related to everything else and its originator. Such as it is, it is* ***all of a piece****.* AH □ *His bit of success had been good for him; he carried the weight of one who is, for the first time,* ***all of a piece****.* NM

all of a sudden [A (AdvP)] suddenly and unexpectedly (and perhaps in circumstances that appear suspicious to the observer); all at once[2] (qv) □ ***All of a sudden*** *a November meteorite scorched its way across the sky.* NM □ *Why are you so interested in Philip* ***all of a sudden****?* EHOW □ *And what do you know about this* ***all of a sudden****?* R □ front or end position. ⇨ ⚠ at one (fell) swoop.

all or nothing [n + n non-rev] everything or nothing, with no half measures (esp of a total commitment to sth, a course of action, etc) □ *The Museum wasn't interested in acquiring single items of the collection; it would buy* ***all or nothing****.* □ *I'm not going to share you with anybody, you've got to give me* ***all or nothing****.* □ *He is working sixteen hours a day just now, but it has always been* ***all or nothing*** *with him, as you know.* ⇨ ⚠ go the whole hog.

all over (sb/sth) [A (AdvP/PrepP)] on/in every part (of sb/sth); everywhere (on/in sb/sth) **o:** oneself, one's body; the chair, floor; the town, area, place □ *Sand had been blown* ***all over*** *everything in the tent.* □ *I make her wash herself every day* ***all over*** *and if she won't I do it for her.* PW □ *She was covered* ***all over*** *with a strange rash.* □ *Posters plugging the new cigarette scream from hoardings* ***all over*** *the Midlands.* □ cf with third example *She had a strange rash* ***all over*** *her body.*

all right[1] [Disj (AdjP)] (informal) certainly; without a doubt □ *He's a bright child* ***all right****, you must be very proud of him.* □ *Yes, the consignment has arrived* ***all right****, but several of the crates have been damaged in transit.* □ *She pretended to be very busy looking at the shop-windows, but she saw me* ***all right****.* □ *It's him* ***all right****, but if you hadn't pointed him out I would never have recognized him without his beard.* □ follows n, v, adj or adv; often used to prepare for some reservation, as in last example.

all right[2] [Disj (AdjP)] (informal) I note what you say; I acknowledge what you say; I accept what you say □ *'I'll be home rather late tonight.' '****All right****. Have you got your key with you, as I'll probably be in bed?'* □ *'Don't you think we'd better have another meeting this time next week?' 'Oh,* ***all right****, though I'm not sure everybody'll be able to get to it.'* □ *'But you were wrong, weren't you?' '****All right, all right****, so I was wrong! Can't you change the subject?'* □ attitude and tone of speaker can vary from simple politeness, to a certain amount of unwillingness, to a high degree of exasperation and anger.

all right[3] [Comp (AdjP)] (informal) physically, or mentally, well; safe, content, happy etc **V:** ⚠ be, seem, appear, look □ *He held her closely and reiterated, 'You'll be* ***all right*** *while I'm away?'* DC □ *The doctor said I'd be* ***all right*** *again in a couple of weeks.* □ *She looked* ***all right*** *when I saw her in hospital two days ago.*

all right[4] [Comp (AdjP)] (informal) in good order; working properly; safe; undamaged; satisfactory and acceptable **S:** car, cleaner, drill; room, garden. **V:** ⚠ be, seem, appear, look, feel, sound □ *We've given your car a full service, sir, and put in new brake linings. I think every thing should be* ***all right*** *now.* □ *The safe appeared* to be ***all right****, but the thieves had ransacked the rest of the room.* □ *It's all* ***all right****. I've managed to get a seat on the afternoon flight so I should be able to get to the meeting.* □ *I can't hear anything wrong with that record. It sounds* ***all right*** *to me.*

all right[5] [Comp (AdjP)] (informal) tolerable; acceptable; without conspicuous faults; adequate; without obvious drawbacks (sometimes in an implied contrast to other better or worse people or things) **S:** food, bed, accommodation, surroundings. **V:** ⚠ be; seem, appear □ *'It will be one more obligation I have to this horrible family of mine.' 'I think your Aunt is rather a pet,' Nurse Ellen said mildly. 'Oh, yes, she's **all right**.'* DC □ *Oh, how dare she! I clothe my own children. Sarah's dresses are perfectly **all right**.* DC □ *Yes, that's **all right** so far as it goes. But remember that we can only read about a hundred words a minute, whereas we're hoping to translate at least a hundred times faster than that.* TBC □ *'Did you enjoy the concert?' 'Oh, it was **all right** in its way; but it wouldn't have done for the Royal Festival Hall.'*

all right[6] [Comp (AdjP)] (informal) convenient; suitable; reasonable; not forbidden or wrong **S:** it. . .do that, it. . .if he does that. **V:** ⚠ be, appear; make sth. □ *'Will it be **all right**,' asked his secretary, 'if I have a little longer for lunch and make it up later?'* □ *The cathedral doors were open so they thought it would be **all right** to go in.*

all right by/with sb [Comp (AdjP)] (informal) acceptable, not objected to (so far as it concerns sb, but not necessarily sb else) **S:** it; this, that; doing sth; whatever you do. **V:** ⚠ be, seem; make sth □ *'I'll be a little late this evening, John.' 'That's **all right by** me, as I've got some work to do.'* □ *They're not her lips,/But they're such tempting lips/That I'm so glad you're free./And it's **all right**, it's **all right with** me.* C PORTER

all right for sb [Comp (AdjP)] (informal) suitable for, acceptable to, sb **V:** ⚠ be, seem, appear □ *That sort of bike may be **all right for** little kids, but now I'm twelve I want a proper racing model.* □ *All these petrol price-rises are **all right for** you salesmen with your company cars and mileage allowances, but what about me? I soon won't be able to afford to run a car at all.* □ *Working in a nine-to-five office job is **all right for** some, but it wouldn't suit me at all.*

all right on the night/day (informal) satisfactory, well done, when the time comes (esp of a dramatic performance or public event which is being rehearsed, planned etc and which is not going well) **V:** ⚠ be; go, turn out □ *I'm sorry, I don't quite know my lines yet, but I'll be **all right on the night**, don't you worry.* □ *'Far too quickly' was the opinion of all the organizers of Coronation celebrations, for it is but human to take up the attitude that it will be **all right on the day**.* WDM □ esp with *it will*, and used as confident prediction.

all roads lead to Rome (saying) whatever ways, means or methods one chooses, any one or all of them will achieve eventually the same objective (as in ancient and medieval times Rome was considered the political, cultural and religious centre of the European world) □ *In other words, the starting point is quite irrelevant; as **all roads lead to Rome**, so a person's thoughts and associations tend to lead towards his personal troubles, desires and wishes of the present moment.* SNP □ *The religious ferment set in motion by the Oxford Movement and epitomized by the conversion of Newman and others to the Catholic Church might be said to reinforce the saying that **all roads**, sooner or later, **lead to Rome**.* □ Rome, as in second example, is now often used to signify Roman Catholic Church.

all the same [Comp (AdjP)] (have) the same, usu undesirable, characteristics **S:** men, women; students, shopkeepers. **V:** ⚠ be, seem; find sb to be □ *'Men!' she said. 'They're **all the same**! Lazy, useless, faithless good-for-nothings!'* □ *Don't talk to me about shopkeepers! They're **all the same**—cheat you as soon as look at you!*

all/just the same [Conj] (informal) nevertheless; at the same time[2] (qv); mark/mind you (qv) □ *Nicky was impossible to manage unless he trusted one. **All the same**, Prissie must be told not to pamper him.* DC □ *'Well, she has a young man, you know.' '**All the same**, I think she might like to join our Women's Institute.'* PW □ *Pissarro, though he disliked the way Whistler puffed himself up, called him 'an artist **just the same**', and he always kept an eye open for his work.* NS □ front, middle or end position.

all the same (to sb) a matter of indifference, of little importance, or interest, (to sb) **A:** whether you go or stay; if you decide to leave. **V:** ⚠ be; make sth □ *I dragged you out of the gutter once. If you want to go back there it's **all the same to** me.* TOH □ *As long as there's a golf course nearby, it's **all the same to** Henry where we go for our holiday.* □ *Complain to the boss if you like, but it'll be **all the same** in the end.* □ *If it's **all the same to** you, I'd prefer to go shopping by myself.*

all set [Comp (AdjP)] positioned, ready and prepared (to do sth, for some activity, etc) **S:** he, she, they; everything. **V:** ⚠ be, feel, get, look, seem. **A:** to go, to leave, to sign (a document), to buy a house; for a fine old time, for a big argument □ *'**All set**, Mr Carter?' The Navigating Officer switched on a fuel line, and poised his right hand above a key. '**All set**, sir.'* TST □ *I had thought I was **all set** to get married.* SML □ *I thought your invitation said it was an all-fish evening. My goodness, I was **all set** for oysters, clam chowder, lobsters, the lot.* BM □ may be used to check, or confirm, readiness to start, as in first example.

all square (with sb) [Comp (AdjP)] an equal amount of eg points etc in a game or competition; (by repayment etc) clear of any debt or obligation. **S:** he, they, I, we; the team(s). **V:** ⚠ be; remain; make sth. □ *At half-time the teams were **all square** with two goals each.* □ *If I give you back the £5 you lent me, less a couple of pounds for the cigarettes and wine you borrowed on Saturday, will that make us **all square**?* □ *I've just returned his loan, so I'm **all square with** him at last.*

all and sundry [n + n non-rev] all the people indiscriminately, whoever they may be (eg who are present on a particular occasion, who may or may not have a proper interest in the matter) □ *This made Isabel nervous, whereas Harold had declared to **all and sundry** that it was exactly what he had expected.* PW □ *Finally I must mention the constant advice I was given by **all and sundry** about how I should fight the battle.* MFM *I scrubbed and swabbed the last yard of the hallway and opened wide the heavy oak street door, now visible to **all and sundry**.* L

all talk (and no action) [Comp (NP)] (informal) full of ideas, schemes, proposals etc for doing sth but never getting any further than talking about them; a matter of conversation, discussion etc for future action but not ever accomplished; exaggerated, attention-seeking claims, opinions etc **S:** he, they, we, it; this, that. **V:** ⚠ be, seem; find sb □ *'That man Brown said to me he would be coming back with a camera team to make a film about our village.' 'Don't take any notice of him, that fellow's* ***all talk and no action****.'* □ *'James surprised me last night when he spoke of giving up his job to do volunteer relief work overseas.' 'Oh, that was* ***all talk****. He indulges in these flights of fancy from time to time.'*

all things considered [Disj] (after) considering, thinking over, every aspect of a problem, situation etc; if everything (that has happened, etc) is taken into account; all in all[1] (qv) □ *I would,* ***all things considered****, have preferred to retrieve the book and been without the information.* UTN □ *Weren't you a bit harsh with the boy,* ***all things considered****?* □ ***All things considered*** *the quarterly trading figures can be interpreted as indicating an improvement in the balance of payments.* □ front, middle or end position.

all things to all men [Comp (NP)] (saying) (adopt, modify, one's behaviour, one's actions etc) in a way one thinks will be acceptable to the person, or persons, one is with (either in a genuine attempt to please or just to be ingratiating) **V:** ⚠ be, become; attempt, seek, try, to be □ (source) *To the weak became I as weak, that I might gain the weak; I am made* ***all things to all men****, that I might by all means save some.* 1 COR IX 22 □ *Mirroring the confusion of the nation they now lead, there are some loyal to the past; some devotees of Marx, Mao or even Marcuse; still more who seek to be* ***all things to all men****.* NS □ *She was* ***all things to all men*** *and spent most of her life being so, because the men outnumbered the girls at Ford by four to one.* RFW □ ambiguous play on expression in last example, suggesting sexual availability.

all this and heaven too (saying) not only does the Christian believer have a blessed and happy life on earth but he will also gain the final reward of heaven after his death; (fig) not only are the previously mentioned advantages available but also sth else that is even more valuable or important □ *A beautiful, devoted wife; two intelligent, healthy children; a well-paid, interesting job:* ***all this and heaven too****—he's just inherited a villa on the French Riviera.* □ (NONCE) *One is genuinely in touch with things deep in the working of the mind, with the primitive, with sacred mythical time.* ***All this, and science too****! The intellectual bases of social anthropology were laid by Herbert Spencer.* NS

all thumbs [Comp (NP)] clumsy, or awkward, in handling things (either as a permanent characteristic or on a particular occasion); (fig) tactless and insensitive in handling other people **V:** ⚠ be, become; seem □ *When I was a kid, I was* ***all thumbs****; while the others followed those intricate instructions for modelling aeroplanes with absolute precision, my struts were always askew, my dihedrals drooped.* L □ *I'm sorry, I seem* ***all thumbs*** *this morning. I don't seem able to type one short letter correctly. I think I've got a bout of 'flu coming on.* □ *'I have a mind and feelings that are all fingertips...' 'And Josie's feelings — what about them?'* ***'All thumbs.'*** EGD

all the time[1] [A (NP)] continuously and regularly, without ceasing **V:** appear, emerge, develop; vanish, decay □ *New stars are forming* ***all the time****; they emerge in clusters from turbulent clouds of gas.* NS □ *But she was not in that state verging on hysteria* ***all the time****.* DC

all the time[2] [A (NP)] continuously during one whole period of time (esp in contexts of deception, or forgetfulness); all along (qv) **V:** mislead, deceive, humbug, sb; pilfer, remove, sth □ *It wasn't stolen by the burglar, you know. Saunders had it* ***all the time****. The night the burglar came, he saw his opportunity and hid it.* DC □ *I think they're just stringing us along. They obviously have no intention of accepting our proposals, as* ***all the time*** *they've been negotiating secretly with our rivals.* □ usu end, but occas front position; esp with perfect tenses.

all the time (that) [Conj] throughout a period of time (during which sth else is happening); while; for as long as **cl:** (that) I was speaking, I spoke; (that) he was ill; (that) these events were taking place □ *Our neighbour watered the garden for us* ***all the time that*** *we were away.* □ *A crowd of anti-nuclear protesters kept up a continual barrage of heckling* ***all the time*** *the Minister was speaking.* □ *Why must you fidget* ***all the time*** *I'm talking to you?* □ v in subordinate clause (which is usu placed at end) often past continuous; that usu omitted.

all to the good [Comp (AdjP)] of a kind that can bring nothing but advantage or improvement **S:** change, development; it...that he's agreed to talk **V:** ⚠ be; seem, appear □ *It is* ***all to the good*** *that the* (Conservative) *party is to pay greater heed to the voice of youth.* SC □ *Harry had married slightly above him, both socially, which may or may not be* ***all to the good****, and financially, which is beyond all doubt beneficent.* SML □ *I agree there may be a few more visitors than usual, but that's* ***all to the good*** *from the point of view of people here.* RM ⇨ ⚠ be to the bad/good.

all together/told [A] when all the items mentioned are, or have been, counted and totalled; in all (qv) □ *All the real work of the property was done with horses;* ***all together*** *we had about eighty on the place.* RFW □ *I had fourpence a day for my food (I suppose I cost my hard-pressed father less than five shillings a week,* ***all told****).* SD

all too brief etc [Comp [AdjP)] much briefer etc than one considers desirable or suitable **V:** ⚠ be, seem, appear. **adj:** brief, short; familiar, natural, obvious; dreadful, grim; ready, willing, eager, anxious; likely □ *Finally, an* ***all-too-brief*** *mention of the untiring efforts of the Committee to make the evening a success.* □ *Readers who are* ***all too familiar*** *with popular articles on anthropology may be interested to learn that some recent investigations have involved a completely novel approach.* PL □ *She was* ***all too prone*** *to see herself as a case, a moral instance, neatly divided into pros and cons.* PW □ attrib use, *an* ***all-too-brief*** *mention*, usu hyphenated.

all too briefly etc [A (AdvP)] much more briefly etc than one would have liked, than one considers desirable or suitable **V:** disappear, move on; end, wind up. **adv:** briefly, quickly; soon, late; clearly, obviously; eagerly, reluctantly; often □ *He then dealt with the problems facing the firm in the coming months—**all too briefly** in my opinion — before going on to discuss the quarterly sales figures.* □ *I shall be leaving you **all too soon**.* □ ***All too often**, girls leave school and shut themselves into a tiny office prison, with stale air and staler ideas, because they just do not know what they want out of a job.* L □ *I congratulate myself on my good fortune; **all too easily** she might have been the usual sort of landlady, smelling of washing-soda and baking-powder.* RATT

all very fine/well (for sb) [Comp (AdjP)] (informal) reasonable, or understandable, in theory (as it concerns sb) but not reasonable, or understandable, in other circumstances or to another individual **S:** it, that; attitude, behaviour; course of action. **V:** ⚠ be; seem; sound. **o:** him, her, us, them (to do sth); others, the majority. □ *'And when I've done that, I'll compare my results with your observations of those other planets.' 'That's **all very fine**,' said the Astronomer Royal, 'but how do you propose to do all this in a couple of days?'* TBC □ *The doctor told her to avoid worry and get a lot more rest. '**All very fine for** some,' she thought, 'but look at me—a widow with four young children.'* □ *It was **all very well for** Flaubert to complain in 1870 of the incorrigible barbarism of the human race. But in 1939 it was as difficult to feel superior to the mass of mankind as it was impossible to remain aloof from it.* AH □ *Dieting is **all very well**, but it has to be done with a good knowledge of food values.* □ ***All very well for** you to laugh! It's not you that has to clear up the mess.* □ *but*-cl or its equivalent usu present, introducing the 'reality'.

all well and good [Comp (AdjP)] (informal) satisfactory (the implication usu being that other things are not satisfactory) **V:** ⚠ be, seem □ (Fiorella gives up her job and stays at home) ***All well and good**! In spite of a few well-meaning jokes from the family, this seems a thoroughly sensible solution to the problem.* ARG □ *I know my sons are in steady jobs and happily married. That's **all well and good**, but I had hoped they'd be more ambitious for themselves.*

all work and no play (makes Jack a dull boy) (saying) if there is too much concentration on working and not enough time for relaxation or other interests, the worker will become bored and the quality of his work will deteriorate □ *The boy is too wrapped up in his books. **All work and no play** isn't good for anyone.* □ *Try to see the last of the current World Cinema series, 'L'Atalante' (Friday, BBC 2). It should be a way to relax and stop **Jack being a dull boy**.* RT □ (NONCE) *'American society no longer has any viable concept of work': but the trouble is that the youth revolution hasn't such a concept either. **All play and no work makes Jack a dumb jerk**.* L □ often adapted, as shown.

all the year round [A (NP)] continuously throughout a complete year (esp irrespective of seasons or other natural or man-made divisions in the year) □ (advertisement) *Buy a deep-freeze and enjoy fresh strawberries and other garden produce **all the year round**, in season and out of season.* □ (advertisement) *All you need is 'Leg Make-up' which gives legs that golden glamour in a moment—and **all the year round**.* H □ *He had never settled down into a rut like so many people of his age, and he believed that he owed much of his liveliness to the train journeys which he made **all the year round**.* TCM

all's well that ends well (saying) the whole matter, affair etc has had a satisfactory outcome despite earlier difficulties □ (source — title of a play by Shakespeare) ***All's well that ends well**.* □ *I'm sorry you had such difficulty in finding us, but **all's well that ends well** and now we can enjoy ourselves.*

one's/the allotted span (formal) seventy years, as the normal or likely length of a person's life □ *She is a Londoner born and bred and, for a woman some years past **the allotted span**, of a truly remarkable vigour and alertness.* RM □ *If three score and ten years is **my allotted span**, then I have to look at any time that's left to me as being in the nature of a bonus.*

an all-time high/low [O/o (NP)] the highest/lowest point in a scale of measurement, better/worse than any observed or recorded before **S:** (rate, quantity of) production; (share price) index; (one's) morale; (the figures for) crime; moral/educational standards. **V:** hit, reach; be at; ***(high)*** rise to; ***(low)*** fall to, plunge to □ *The year ended with the news that UK automobile production reached **an all-time high** in November.* US □ (reader's letter) *The BBC usually excels in its holiday programmes, but this Christmas I really think it has hit **a new high**.* RT □ *As far as the CID is concerned, morale is at **an all-time low**.* □ *English poetry has reached **an all-time low** in the past decade or two, but it's not as bad as this anthology paints it.* L □ *I hate the in-fighting within the party. My heart was in its boots at the time of the Common Market row; it was **an all-time low** for me.* OBS □ variant a new high/low.

along/on familiar etc lines [A (PrepP)] in a way that is familiar etc **S:** debate, discussion, argument; group, party. **V:** run, proceed, be conducted; work, divide. **adj:** familiar, expected, the same, similar; different; unusual; democratic □ *Luckily the Diamond Research Lab in Jo'burg had been working **along the same lines,** and they'd invented ways of 'labelling' diamonds.* DS □ *So far his argument had run **on familiar lines** but then he turned his attention to the Party Leader and started to attack his policies.* □ *The members of the committee were sharply divided — the divisions being **along ideological lines** rather than being based on any objective consideration of the facts before them.* □ *Pavlov considered these differences to be due to innate properties of the central nervous system. His explanation ran **along the following lines** ...* SNP □ *There are many methods of producing hypnosis; perhaps the most common is something **along these lines**: ...* ⇨ ⚠ next entry.

along/on the lines (of sth) [A (PrepP)] in the style of sth; in the way that **V:** make, construct, fashion, sth □ *I've been thinking of making a dress something **along the lines of** what you are wearing now. Would you mind?* □ *Dave was to type the letter when he had drafted it **along the lines** we had agreed upon.* UTN □ *This world, too, cares much for recognizable success, but does not distribute it **along the lines** on* *which he has been trained to win.* UL □ may modify a preceding n. ⇨ ⚠ previous entry.

(the) alpha and omega [n + n non-rev] the first or beginning and the last or end of sth, thus incorporating the most important features and often the whole aspect of it (from the names of the first and last letters of the Greek alphabet) **V:** ⚠ be, remain; make sth □ (source) *I am **Alpha and Omega**, the beginning and the ending, saith the Lord, which is, and which was, and which is to come, the Almighty.* REVELATION I 8 □ *Adherence to the objectives of the Fourth Plan remains **the alpha and omega** of French economic and financial policy.* T □ *There is nothing like one's first, or one's last, camp. Others may be more beautiful, but those at the beginning and end have a unique quality all their own. They are **Alpha and Omega** and they give, rather than take from one.* LWK □ (television) *This has been an **alpha-and-omega** week's viewing; every programme seemed to be either the first of a new series or the last of an old one.* L □ unusual attrib use, *an **alpha-and-omega** week's viewing*, in last example.

always supposing (that) [Conj] if a possible, or likely, specified condition is met □ *The cloud may have an appreciable heat of its own, and this might compensate us for the loss of sunlight, **always supposing**—as I keep saying—**that** we do find ourselves in the cloud!* TBC □ *Then I will do a teacher training course—**always supposing** I get my degree, of course.*

ancient/past history [Comp (NP)] sth, esp in a person's past, that is no longer the case, or is without significance or relevance to the present matter (and best forgotten) **S:** one's (misspent) youth; first marriage, early love affairs; it, that. **V:** ⚠ be, become; make sth □ *It was all over, Oxford, the students, the Principal, the animals and Mother's friends. It was all the past. It was all **ancient history**.* H □ *'And Tom is engaged to Stella.' 'To Stella! I thought it was her cousin he was keen on!.' 'Oh, that's **ancient history**—he's been going out with Stella for more than a year now.'* □ *I know my name's not Larsen, because I changed it after I quarrelled with my old man. But that's **past history**; never mind that now.* PE □ ancient used facetiously here.

ancient and honourable [adj + adj non-rev] (formal) having been in existence a long time and therefore respectable because of its age **n:** custom, practice, tradition □ *'Mr President, gentlemen,' began the speaker, 'in rising to address this **ancient and honourable** society I must confess to a certain nervousness.'* □ *It was an **ancient and honourable** tradition of his office that each new Mayor should receive his insignia from his predecessor at a ceremony held in the town square.* □ *The meal proceeded according to the **ancient and honourable** custom of grabbing what one could for oneself.* □ usu in attrib position with following n; facetious use in last example.

ancient and modern [adj + adj non-rev] both old and new **n:** songs; styles; attitudes □ (book title) *Hymns **Ancient and Modern** for use in the services of the Church.* □ *For music, we used to borrow songs, mostly from musical comedies, **ancient and modern**, but I fancy I could write as good or better songs myself.* T □ *Because of the various extensions built on from time to time the so-called castle is a jumble of **ancient and modern** (styles) and totally without architectural distinction.* □ often placed after n, as in second example.

and all also; too; included; in addition □ *Duncan had stepped backwards over the gunwale of his boat and fallen, camera **and all**, into the Indian Ocean.* LWK □ (advertisement) *Corns come away cleanly, roots **and all**, after only a few simple applications of Freezone.* WI □ *'Please, Miss, I've finished that one,' said Doreen. 'So have I,' said Sylvia. 'And copied from one another as usual, I suppose, mistakes **and all**.' 'No, Miss,' they said.* TT □ *'The Browns,' she said, looking up from her letter, 'have invited themselves here next weekend.' 'What! Children **and all**?'* □ modifies a preceding n.

and all that (informal) and other similar things (esp when a full list could be tedious, when the speaker assumes that the listener knows what is implied, or when being diffident, dismissive or belittling); next entry (qv) □ *It is commonly thought that some magazines—for example, those predominantly read by working-class women and usually spoken of as 'Peg's Paper **and all that**'—provide little other than undiluted fantasy and sensation.* UL □ *Ah, but he's known her all his life. Childhood sweethearts **and all that**.* EHOW □ TONY: *Why am I on to old Mike? I like him. I always have. He's the salt of the earth **and all that**.* EHOW □ *They know I'm nearly always there and they can come and talk to me if they've got any problems **and that** and I like to be able to do their jobs.* ST □ often derogatory; variant and that as in last example usu associated with working-class speakers.

and all that jazz etc (informal) and other similar things (esp when a full list would be tedious, when its speaker assumes that the listener knows what is implied, or when being diffident, dismissive or belittling); previous entry (qv) **n:** jazz; ⚠ rubbish, nonsense, tripe; stuff, kind, sort of thing; (taboo), crap □ *'In a way, what is dramatic is the same as what is news. ('Man bites dog' **and all that jazz**).* SC □ *The headmaster delivered his usual Speech-Day tripe—honour of the school, devotion to hard work, a healthy mind in a healthy body **and all that crap**.* □ *If you came to work here, you would be expected to show some initiative—dealing with routine correspondence on your own, answering the telephone, making bookings and reservations **and all that sort of thing**.*

and a half [A (AdjP)] (informal) of more than usual size, importance, worth etc □ *Nini was indeed a predicament—in Robert's idiom, a predicament **and a half**.* SML □ *You've got to admire her. She's a woman **and a half** to be able to cope with that awful husband* and *bring up four children.* □ *My goodness, that's a cabbage **and a half**! How do you get them to grow that size?* □ modifies a preceding n.

and how! (informal) yes, indeed; I agree strongly; you can say that again (qv) □ *'He's the fastest of the racing drivers we get on this circuit—good-looking bloke too.' '**And how!**' agreed his daughter fervently.* □ *'Want a lift, mate?' asked the lorry driver. '**And how!** This rucksack's killing me.'* □ *'He's a rich man all right.'*

'***And how!*** *Do you know, he gets more for one of those TV shows than you or I earn in a year.'* □ stress pattern ˌand 'how!.

and I don't know what (all) (informal) and also any number of different things of a type already mentioned (that I cannot remember, describe or be bothered to mention) □ *...chaps with beards and silk scarves marching to and fro with their banners and petitions* ***and I don't know what all*** *and showing off.* TGLY □ *There are boxes of old letters and rags and tins of paint* ***and I don't know what all*** *in the cupboard under the stairs.* □ *We used to go from Delhi to Kalka in our own private* (railway) *coach, which was absolutely slap-up. It had a private bathroom, a great double bedroom,* ***and I don't know what.*** *Father always used to change for dinner in it.* L

and one knows it (informal) one is very much aware of a fact, or truth, just previously stated □ *I wish you'd stop trying to cheer me up with that kind of talk. Alan's not coming back,* ***and you know it.*** □ *Oh yes, Rathbone's completely in our hands—we can expose him at any time* ***and he knows it.*** TCB □ *The upshot was that the police wouldn't have him at any price* ***and Shaw knew it.*** NS

and no mistake/error (informal) there can be no doubt about it □ *If you're in the London telephone book, you're in town, and if not, you live in the provinces. Well, we were in the provinces,* ***and no error.*** CON □ *Well, precious, that's a pretty stirring outfit you're wearing,* ***and no mistake.*** *Never realized how much I adore polo sweaters until this instant.* TGLY □ *I was properly scared* ***and no mistake*** *when the bull began to move towards me.* □ stress pattern and 'no mistake; usu end position.

and so on/forth and other things of the same kind as have been already mentioned (without wishing to go into further detail) □ *'What were you talking about so long with Mrs Green?' 'Oh, just about the children, and the school, and their hobbies* ***and so forth.'*** □ *'You still call me Mrs Gaye. You don't call my husband Mr Gaye or Squadron Leader.' 'I suppose it's because I've known him longer, working with him* ***and so on.'*** DC □ *He went on about the need to work harder, moderate wage demands, invest more* ***and so on and so forth.*** □ on and forth used together (non-rev) to reinforce impression of redundant detail, as in last example.

and that's a fact (informal) what has been previously stated is true (however extraordinary or unbelievable it may appear) □ *However many gallons you say you put in this morning, the tank is empty now,* ***and that's a fact.*** □ *I don't know who he is or where he came from* ***and that's a fact.*** □ *It was just that when I came to the point — well, I hadn't the courage* ***and that's the fact.*** EM □ the instead of a as in the last example is unusual; usu end position.

and that's fact! and that is the truth (as an emphatic addition to some statement regarding one's determination to do or not to do sth) □ *I wouldn't trust him further than I saw him—* ***and that's fact!*** □ *I have no intention of trying to smuggle your camera through the customs,* ***and that's fact!*** □ *I'm not buying tomatoes at 75p a pound,* ***and that's fact!***

and then some (informal) to an even greater degree (than sth else stated or implied) □ *'The Battle for Moscow' (BBC 1), third in the series on the Second World War, had all the faults of the first two programmes* ***and then some.*** L □ *She's as attractive as Marilyn Monroe—* ***and then some!*** □ end position; stress pattern and 'then some.

the angel of death (the forewarning or heralding of) approaching death, personified □ *Some of the patients kept looking expectantly and fearfully at the entrance to the ward whenever anyone was heard approaching, as if watching for* ***the Angel of Death.*** MM □ GEORGE: *Well, did you go to the doctor's?* RUTH: *Yes.* GEORGE: *Well*—(laughing)—*don't stand there with* ***the angel of death*** *on your shoulder—what did he say?* EGD

an angel of light [Comp (NP)] sb who is cheerful, good and kind to others **V:** ⚠ be, appear, find sb □ *Such a self-centred old man! If his wife wasn't* ***the angel of light*** *she is, she'd have left him long ago.* □ *Send Mary to us for as long as you like; we're both so fond of her, and she's* ***an angel of light*** *in the house.*

an angel of mercy [Comp (NP)] sb who helps people who are in need, or who are suffering in some way **V:** ⚠ be, appear, find sb □ *She exempted the nurses. They had been lovely, everything they always said nurses were, regular* ***angels of mercy,*** *so kind and gentle with Stanley and so sympathetic with her.* TSMP

an angry young man (cliché) a young man, esp an intellectual, who objects to the moral, social, political etc attitudes of his time (and tries to change them by means of public protest or action, through his writings, etc) □ *The Prime Minister said that in his youth, if the term had been invented then, he would have been classed as* ***an angry young man.*** OBS □ *Between these assignments he was on the personal Foreign Office staff of Edward Heath during our first frustrated negotiations to join the EEC. Heath called him* ***his angry young man.*** OBS □ first used in late 1950s of a group of young British writers (esp of John Osborne and his play 'Look Back in Anger', though the expression does not appear in it).

another cup of tea (informal) sb/sth quite different from the person(s)/things(s) previously mentioned; a (very) different kettle of fish (qv) **V:** ⚠ be; find sth, regard sth as □ *I don't object to giving you a helping hand now and then, as I've said before; but being made use of like this is* ***another cup of tea.*** □ *He had met several of his room-mate's relatives and not much liked them, but this girl was* ***another cup of tea*** *altogether.* □ *Even if you read French easily, you'll find it's* ***another cup of tea*** *to make conversation in French.*

answer/obey the call (of duty) respond as a matter of conscience, patriotic feeling, religious belief, etc to a demand made of one (either by people in authority or as a result of one's own convictions) □ *I would like to speak to you today about the soldier — about the fighting men who came from all parts of the Empire to* ***answer the call of duty.*** MFM □ *While still a student he felt he had been called to the Mission Field. The time had now come to*

answer that call. □ now thought rather solemn or pompous; sometimes used allusively, as in second example.

the answer is in the affirmative/negative (catchphrase) the answer is 'yes'/'no' □ *We've applied to the Regional District Council for planning permission. If* ***the answer is in the affirmative*** *we can start work within the month.* SC □ *Her instructions had been to go to the hotel and ask if she had left a cardigan behind.* ***The answer*** *having* ***been in the negative****, Marcus appeared and immediately swept her out on to the river bank for a drink.* TCB □ esp facetious.

the answer is a lemon (catchphrase) the reply, or response, to sth is rejection; the result of sth is barren, futile □ *'What did the boss say when you asked him for a rise?'* ***'The answer****, my dear,* ***was a lemon****—not unexpected, but it was worth a try.'* □ *It's pretty depressing to produce a quality article like this, spend thousands of dollars on sales promotion, only to find that* ***the*** *public's* ***answer is a lemon****.* □ wry comment on rejection, failure etc; now rather dated.

answer pat answer immediately (though not necessarily correctly or truthfully) □ *So I answered up like a felon fighting for his freedom, and I* ***answered pat****, because I was telling the truth, which is sometimes a help.* PP □ *'How,' I asked myself, 'can Myrtle love me and not want to read my books? How can a woman separate the artist from the man?'* ***The answer came pat****. Women not only can: they do.* SPL □ variant the answer came pat.

the answer to a maiden's prayer [Comp (NP)] a man who is a particularly suitable partner because of his good looks, wealth, social standing, etc; (fig) sb or sth that is particularly desirable and right (for a purpose) **V:** ⚠ be, seem; find, think, sb □ *Georgina pointedly and formally introduced her nephew. 'If you're anything like your uncle, you're* ***the answer to a maiden's prayer****,' said Mariana.* ARG □ *An unexpected legacy, a win on the pools, or some such* ***answer to a maiden's prayer****, was the only thing that could save him from bankruptcy now.* □ (NONCE) *The more permissive we become as a nation, the less permissive we expect our rulers to be. Fortunately, the first of the Windsors* (ie Queen Victoria) *was* ***the answer to a nun's prayer****.* L

any day [A (NP)] (informal) whenever possible; whenever a choice can be made or stated; every time (qv) □ *You can keep your expense accounts, company cars, overseas travel — give me my country cottage and my books* ***any day****.* □ *'Fish?' 'No, thanks; I'd rather have sausages* ***any day****.'* □ used esp when one wishes to indicate one's strong preference for sth; usu end position; often with *would rather/sooner (do sth)*; stress pattern 'any day.

any day (of the week) [A (NP)] (informal) whenever one wants and without any difficulty □ *Don't think they wouldn't fire you on my say so. We can get a dozen better than you* ***any day of the week****.* AITC □ *Belfounder hasn't anything on us legally. As for young Donoghue, we can buy him* ***any day of the week****.* UTN □ *He thinks he's a good golfer, but my kid brother could beat him* ***any day****.* □ stress pattern 'any day (of the week); usu end position; usu with *can/could (do sth)*.

any and every [det + det non-rev] all different kinds of (people, things etc), taken together and without discrimination (esp in a dismissive or derogatory way) □ *He is a bit stand-offish, I admit, but do you blame him for refusing to meet* ***any and every*** *reporter who wants to interview him?* □ *Should a child be allowed to watch* ***any and every*** *programme that comes his way, or should his parents control his viewing?* □ *The brother is a modern Churchman, which means, as I can see, an attachment to* ***any and every*** *belief save the dogmas of his own life religion.* ASA □ cf the prons *anyone and everyone, anything and everything, anywhere and everywhere.*

any man's money [Comp (NP)] available, eager, to do anything provided there is (financial etc) gain in it **V:** ⚠ be; seem □ *Thus (to a man of Harold's type) barmaids were brassy, blatant, hard-voiced, impudent, vulgar, venal and above all, loose; they were* ***any man's money****.* PW □ *He showed no allegiance to the Party and made no secret of being* ***any man's money****.*

(at) any moment [A (PrepP/NP)] very soon; any time etc now (qv) □ *The U-boat may be hanging round to pick up a survivor or two. She may surface* ***at any moment****.* PM □ *Everything was nightmarish, even Prissie's charming, concerned face that seemed strangely as if it might be distorted into something entirely different* ***any moment****.* DC □ *But she was at home, with the children likely to come in* ***at any moment****, and everyone being so kind, she felt that the least she could do was to keep bright and cheerful.* DC □ usu used with at.

any old how [A] (informal) carelessly; untidily; all anyhow (qv) **V:** do, leave, arrange, fix, set, sth □ *I spend hours checking my piston rings to get the gaps right, and then I have to mess them up just because I haven't got a proper ring expander. Just have to slide the bastards on over the pistons* ***any old how****.* HD □ *'Look,' I said to the carpenter, 'if I was content to have my shelves put up* ***any old how****, I'd have done the job myself instead of paying you to do it.'*

any old place/where [A (NP)] (informal) anywhere **V:** find, call in □ *I don't mind where we go for our holidays. You choose —* ***any old place*** *will do for me as long as there's plenty of sun and food and wine.* □ *Put it down* ***any old where*** *for the time being. I'll put it away later.*

any old time [A (NP)] (informal) at any time **V:** come, call in □ *Just drop in to see us* ***any old time****.* □ *He seems to think he can come to work* ***any old time*** *and sit and drink coffee and read the newspaper while we're slaving away.* □ *'When shall I bring your lawn-mower back?' 'Oh,* ***any old time*** *will do.'*

any time etc now [A (NP)] very soon; (at) any moment (qv) **n:** time, ⚠ moment; second, minute, hour, day, week, month □ *He's approaching sixty-three, so it's very likely he'll be asked to retire* ***any time now****.* □ *They'll be starting* ***any minute now****.* □ ***Any hour now****, the flood should begin to abate.* □ *I shall be rescued* ***any day now****. I must not worry. I have water and food and intelligence and shelter.* PM

anybody's guess [Comp (NP)] (informal) not certain; not known **V:** ⚠ be; remain; seem □ *The stranger will ask where it is all going to lead and* *the answer is* ***anybody's guess****.* OBS □ *What goes on in the mind of a year-old child is* ***anybody's guess****.*

anything but [A (AdvP)] the very opposite of, entirely different from (sth previously or subsequently mentioned); certainly not □ *Going about without a hat in Japan may have given my naturally* ***anything but*** *sallow skin a tinge of the local complexion.* AH □ *Huxley is* ***anything but*** *optimistic for the future of either man or plant on this planet.* SC □ *I expected a rather smooth starchy affair at yesterday's Royal wedding. It was* ***anything but****.* DM □ *I tried to get Johnny to take an afternoon nap like his baby sister. No such luck! He did* ***anything but*** *sleep.* □ front position. ⇨ ⚠ have etc everything but (sth); nothing but sth/do sth.

anything for a quiet life (informal) be prepared to do sth, to adapt one's behaviour, to make concessions, etc in order to preserve calm, to avoid argument or other unpleasantness etc, but without necessarily being persuaded that it is the right thing to do □ *'I'm quite willing to do as I say—just bring them* (a class of schoolchildren) *down into the Hall with mine, and you can hover about among the back row.'* *'****Anything for a quiet life****,' she said.* TT □ *'Be a pal. Come on, now, don't leave me in the lurch.' 'All right, all right. Get behind the wheel and I'll push.* ***Anything for a quiet life****.'* HD □ usu no v present, but cf *He'll/He'd do* ***anything for a quiet life****.*

anything goes no (strict) standards of conduct, or morals, apply or are forced; (almost) anything can be done or attempted □ *The attempted kidnapping broke through a psychological and emotional barrier.* ***Anything goes*** *after that. I can never remember a time when the powerful and the high-born have been subjected to so many humiliations.* OBS □ *It's a situation which makes conventional fictional realism bizarrely unreal—all creation is creation from a void, so* ***anything goes****, everything can be fitted in, helter-skelter.* NS

anything up to [A (AdvP)] (in a scale of measurement of time, quantity, weight etc) from any (low) point to another (higher point specified) without wishing to be precise but establishing nevertheless the top limit □ *It will take us* ***anything up to*** *four months to complete the job.* □ *Estimates varied but there must have been* ***anything up to*** *five thousand people at the rally.*

an apology for sth an inferior kind of sth; a less satisfactory substitute for sth □ *Perhaps it was the grey morning, with the daylight no more than* ***an apology for*** *the departing night.* DC □ *He lost half of his savings when he backed* ***that*** *miserable* ***apology for*** *a horse.* □ *In my opinion, it's* ***the*** *feeblest* ***apology for*** *a marriage I ever saw. How long do you think that girl is going to stick to you?* AITC

an apple for the teacher an attempt at ingratiating oneself with, or bribing, sb in higher authority □ *'Here's an offer from Mr Stephens to arrange cost price transport for all our away matches.' 'That's probably* ***an apple for the teacher****, and best not accepted. If we do decide to put his son in the team we don't want anybody to say it was favouritism.'*

an/the apple of discord (sb or sth that is) a cause of dispute, argument or rivalry; a bone of contention (qv) (from the Greek myth of a golden apple which was to be given to the most beautiful of three goddesses) □ *The girls had got on well together until* ***the apple of discord*** *in the person of a handsome young apprentice arrived in their midst.* □ *His lawyer tried to persuade him to make a more equitable disposal of his property. 'What you have here,' he said, 'is not so much a will as* ***an apple of discord****.'*

the apple of sb's eye [Comp (NP)] sb who is the main object of sb's love, devotion, attention etc **V:** ⚠ be, become; regard sb as □ *I sacrificed everything to make you happy and safe. I won't talk about your father, but you, you were* ***the apple of my eye****.* DPM □ *Far less gregarious, and without political ambition, as a salesman Slater was* ***the apple of*** *Donald Stokes****'s eye****.* NS

are we down-hearted? (No!) (dated catchphrase) we refuse to allow matters (eg the present unfavourable situation, esp in wartime) to make us depressed, dispirited etc □ ***Are we down-hearted? No!****/Then let your voices sing/ and let the music ring...* OLD MUSIC HALL SONG □ *They'll be there in the darkness somewhere where she* (a ship) *sank, asking each other if they****'re down-hearted****.* PM □ *The defeated candidate sprang to the front of the platform, 'Comrades,* ***are we downhearted****?' A thousand throats roared back the answer: '****No!****'* □ rhetorical question, always expecting answer No.

aren't etc we all everyone is etc; who isn't etc? **V:** aren't, ⚠ don't, haven't □ CHILDREN (singing)*: All she wants is gold and silver, all she wants is a fine young man.* HAVA: ***Don't we all****.* HSG □ *'Blood pressure's looking healthier now,' Benkin reported. 'All he needs now is a good night's sleep.' '****Don't we all****,' muttered Sister Wallis, who had been on duty in the theatre since the first operation 14 hours earlier.* TVT □ *'She has had, and is having, many difficulties to contend with, of a personal nature.' '****Haven't we all****?'* TT □ semi-exclamatory comment on condition, activity, desire etc previously mentioned, followed by a question-mark, exclamation-mark, or full stop.

argue the toss [V + O pass] disagree about sth; discuss a matter of dispute □ *A letter was sent to the then Minister for Industry. It did not* ***argue the toss*** *over his ruling. It simply asked for a meeting with him to discuss the matter.* NS □ *Time is pressing. If we delay while* ***the toss*** *is being* ***argued*** *in London and Washington, the operation will never be launched in July.* MFM □ *He thought we might have shown less of his face. Maybe he was right. Anyway, I* ***argued the toss*** *a bit and finally he said keep it in.* PP

arm in arm [A (NP)] with one arm of one person bent at the elbow and linked with the similarly bent arm of the person who walks beside her/him **V:** go, march, stroll, walk; (be) linked □ *'John and Mary had quite a quarrel this evening.' 'Well they must have made it up, because I've just seen them going down the road* ***arm in arm****.'* □ *The police claimed the students had been proceeding along the pavement singing and shouting,* ***arm in arm*** *and six abreast.*

armed to the teeth [Comp (AdjP)] fully equipped with things to fight with (eg guns, knives etc); (fig) fully provided with what is (thought to be) necessary for some task, purpose etc **V:** ⚠ be, look; find sb □ *The Palestine Police Force was* ***armed to the teeth*** *and a large part of it organised in the form of mobile columns with armoured cars.* MFM □ *He was waiting for us with a rope and an axe in one hand, a bulging knapsack on his back. 'For goodness sake!' I said, 'How do you think you're going to do a three-mile climb,* ***armed to the teeth*** *like that?'* □ *The negotiators were in a belligerent mood. They came to the conference table* ***armed to the teeth*** *with statistics on cash-flow analyses and directors' emoluments.*

around/round the clock [A (PrepP)] continuously; throughout the whole of a twenty-four hour period **V:** work, play, perform. **adv mod:** all, right □ *They worked* ***around the clock*** *and over the entire weekend to get the export order ready for dispatch on the Monday.* □ *I have never seen such feasting, feeding, drinking and toasting—at dances, weddings, receptions. It went on* ***round the clock*** *on every day of the five I was there.* L □ *They will succeed; and the bombing will go on, every day and all* ***around the clock.*** MFM □ attrib use ***round-the-clock*** *bombing raids.*

arse over tip [A (NP)] (taboo) with one's feet going up and over one's head and one's behind following in a somersault; head over heels (qv); (fig) (be made) mentally confused or upset (by some event, personal attack etc) **V:** fall, go, go flying, land; send, turn, sb □ *If you happen to trip/And go* ***arse over tip****/Like Horatius, into the Tiber...* MFM □ *But the word solicitor fairly turned her, as Granny Barnacle recounted next day,* ***arse over tip.*** MM □ *...got his punt-pole stuck in the mud, he did, and went* ***arse over tip*** *into the river.*

art etc for art's etc sake art etc with no other motive and no other result than the practice and enjoyment of it **n:** art, knowledge, destruction, change, power □ *Ironically, the man* (Tolstoy) *who was one day to turn his back on art, rejecting it, stood up now as the champion of* ***art for art's sake****—to the dismay of all those who believed that the first duty of a writer was commitment to social reform.* OBS □ *Thus the myth that politicians are honest servants of the public good is accompanied by its counterpart — that they are cynical seekers after* ***power for power's sake.*** L □ ***Violence for the sake of violence*** *has also been increasing much more quickly than other types of crime.* L □ *Oh you, you're just a natural glutton. You* ***eat for the sake of eating.*** □ (stage direction) *He is* ***talking for the sake of it****, only half listening to what he is saying.* LBA □ variants art etc for the sake of art etc, argue etc for argument's etc sake, talk etc for the sake of it.

arts and crafts [n + n non-rev] artistic and semi-artistic activities such as painting pictures, making pottery, carving wood, spinning and sewing etc (with emphasis on individual and traditional skills and non-machine-made creativity) □ *The villagers no longer carry on the* ***arts and crafts*** *practised by their grandfathers.* □ *There is one really good* ***Arts and Crafts*** *shop in the town, where everything is authentic and beautifully designed; all the others are full of factory-made junk to catch the eye of the tourists.* □ (NONCE) *In England she had gone all* ***arty and crafty*** *and picked up with a chap called Laurence Hilton who worked for the BBC and put on plays for the Third Programme.* RFW □ (NONCE) *He never allowed a note of home madeness or* ***arty-craftiness*** *to get into the flat.* HAA □ nonce adj + adj and n compound forms as in last two examples are derogatory (cf arty-crafty); arts and crafts also the name of a British movement dedicated to ideals of traditional skills etc.

as artful etc as a wagon-load etc of monkeys very artful etc, but not malicious or really wicked **V:** ⚠ be, seem; find, think, sb. **adj:** artful, ⚠ clever, crafty, cunning, mischievous. **n:** wagon-load, ⚠ cart-load, barrel □ *I can't leave my youngest son alone in the house for a moment. He's* ***as crafty as a barrel of monkeys*** *and gets up to any number of tricks and then appears all innocence when you return.* □ *Clever as sin, though he could be all wide-eyed and naive when he chose: not that you can tell with a man,* ***artful as a wagon-load of monkeys.***

as bad etc as ever [Comp (AdjP)] bad etc to the same degree as before (even though some change for the better, or the worse, may have been expected); every bit as bad etc (as) (qv) **V:** ⚠ be, look, seem. **adj:** bad, corrupt, weak, devious; lively, cheerful □ *No, doctor, in spite of the treatment, the pain is* ***as bad as ever.*** □ *Although he had become frailer and a little deaf, the old man's mind was* ***as lively as ever.***

as badly etc as ever [A (AdvP)] badly etc to the same degree as before (even though some change for the better, or the worse, may have been expected); every bit as badly etc (as) (qv) **V:** behave, walk, react. **adv:** badly, painfully, weakly, crookedly, well, smoothly □ *It's a fine little car. I know it looks old and rusty but the engine runs* ***as well as ever****, even with seventy-five thousand miles on the clock.* □ *He was limping* ***as badly as ever*** *when I last saw him.*

as bald as a coot [Comp (AdjP)] completely bald (from the water-bird which has a white patch on its head above the beak) **V:** ⚠ be, look, appear □ *All the men in our family have been* ***as bald as coots*** *by the time they reached forty.*

as best one can [A (AdjP)] not perfectly but as well as possible in view of disability, inability or adverse circumstances **V:** struggle, protest; resolve, settle, sth. **modal:** can, could, may, might □ *They could even hear her sobbing. A little pride came back. She hushed herself and looked at her watch* ***as best she could.*** ARG □ *If his last arrow was spent he still struggled* ***as best he could.*** LWK □ *I think we'd better have a full meeting, and I'll explain the situation* ***as best I can*** *to everybody.*

(as) big/round as saucers [Comp/A (AdjP)] (with one's eyes) wide open and staring fixedly at sb or sth, eg in surprise, curiosity etc **V:** be, become; grow □ *He was facing me and walking backwards, and I could see his eyes growing* ***as round as saucers.*** UTN □ *Gradually mothers and children started coming into the famine relief centre, the mothers thin and emaciated, the children with swollen bellies and eyes* ***as big as saucers.*** □ variant with/having eyes as big as saucers.

as big etc as they come [Comp (AdjP)] of a size etc that is not likely to be exceeded; (as) clever etc as they make 'em/them (qv) **V:** ⚠ be; reckon, consider, sb to be □ *If he did really catch a 20 lb salmon, he was lucky; that's about* ***as big as they come*** *in this river.* □ *He's a very shrewd and able man, and if you want a competent administrator I expect he's* ***as good as they come.*** NM

as birds etc go [Disj] according to, or in comparison with, the average quality, size, characteristics etc of birds etc **n:** birds, cats; houses, schools □ *Certainly,* ***as birds go,*** *the oven-bird appears to have more than his fair share of personality and charm.* DF □ *The nearby reconstructed Roman village where, our driver assured us, Hercules had lived, was not much* ***as tourist attractions go.*** DS □ *We are really quite an old family* ***as families go.*** *There was a castle more or less where this house is now, in the thirteen hundreds.* WDM □ *My Hairy Frog was,* ***as frogs go,*** *quite large.* BB □ n in headphrase may be countable or uncountable; front, middle or end position.

(as) black as coal etc [Comp (AdjP)] very dark, black or dirty **S:** face, hands. **V:** ⚠ be, look, turn. **n:** coal, ⚠ soot, the ace of spades □ *Look at your hands, boy, they're* ***as black as coal****—you can't come to the table like that.* □ *What have you been doing down in that cave? Your face and clothes are* ***black as the ace of spades!*** □ adj compound coal-black.

as black as ink etc [Comp (AdjP)] very dark, so that one cannot see clearly **S:** sky, tunnel, room. **V:** ⚠ be, become; grow. **n:** ink, ⚠ night, pitch, the Pit □ *The sky had grown* ***black as ink*** *—we would have to find shelter before the storm broke.* □ *He rushed out of the shelter into the open. It was* ***pitch black,*** *unrelieved even by starlight.* TBC □ *They moved cautiously from the entrance to the tunnel, already having to feel their way with their hands. Ahead it was* ***as black as the Pit.*** □ adj compounds ink black, pitch black, pit black.

(not) as black as it is painted [Comp (AdjP)] better than it, he etc is reputed to be; better than sb else says or judges it, him etc to be **V:** ⚠ be; find sth □ *Conditions in our geriatric wards may leave a lot to be desired but they are* ***not as black as they are painted.*** □ *'I don't envy you your new boss, he's pretty tough, I'm told.' 'Oh, I don't know. Is he really* ***as black as he's painted****?'* □ *'It wasn't an ideal holiday,' said her husband, 'but not quite* ***as black as*** *you seem intent on* ***painting it.****'* □ neg, interr, conditional; active form of paint in last example.

(as) blind as a bat [Comp (AdjP)] unable to see, or read, very easily (but usu not completely blind); (fig) unable to see, or perceive, sth that is obvious to other people **V:** ⚠ be, become; find sb □ *I'm sorry, I can't read it. I'm* ***as blind as a bat*** *without my glasses.* □ *'I can't find the newspaper anywhere.'* ***'Blind as a bat*** *as usual! There it is, by the telephone.'* □ *All I can say is, if you don't see that she comes here just to meet Johnny, then you must be* ***blinder than a bat.***

(as) bold as brass [Comp/A (AdjP)] impudent; aggressive; defiant; in a shameless, insolent, manner **V:** be; come in, return, deny sth, accuse sb □ *There she stood, denying everything* ***as bold as brass,*** *in spite of all the evidence against her.* □ *'Fancy him insulting you in your own house like that! Never mind, you've seen the last of him.' 'I doubt it. He'll be back again,* ***bold as brass,*** *if it suits him.'*

(as) bold/brave as a lion [Comp (AdjP)] courageous, without fear, esp uncharacteristically so in times of danger etc **V:** ⚠ be, become; find, make, sb □ *Puny though he looked, he was* ***as brave as a lion,*** *as all the playground bullies came to learn.* □ *He might have behaved timidly in life; in the book he would be* ***bold as a lion.*** PW ⇨ (as) timid as a mouse etc.

(as) bright as a button [Comp (AdjP)] very clever and quick-witted **V:** ⚠ be, seem; find sb □ *Be careful what you say in front of the boy. He's* ***as bright as a button*** *and can ask the most awkward questions.*

(as) broad as it's long [Comp (AdjP)] (informal) offer little or no clear advantage between two or more things whichever one is chosen, both being equally satisfactory or unsatisfactory; be six of one and/to half a dozen of the other (qv) **S:** it; whether we go or stay. **V:** ⚠ be, seem □ *The plane fare is much dearer of course, but then you save on overnight accommodation and meals. Financially it's* ***as broad as it's long;*** *it really comes down to which way you prefer to travel.* □ *Well, on the figures alone, whether we invest in Germany or France is about* ***as broad as it's long.***

(as) brown as a berry [Comp (AdjP)] very brown (skin), esp from the sun or constant exposure to the weather **V:** ⚠ be, become, look □ *How quickly suntan disappears! You wouldn't think the twins were* ***brown as berries*** *only a month ago.* □ *A little old woman with a wrinkled face* ***as brown as a berry*** *told us our fortunes for ten pence.*

(as) busy as a bee [Comp (AdjP)] very busy and occupied, doing many things, esp in a pleasurable or satisfying way **V:** ⚠ be, keep □ *My wife never has time to get bored. She's* ***as busy as a bee*** *from morning to night.* □ *'Isn't this the programme the children like watching?' 'Yes, but they're upstairs,* ***busy as bees*** *making puppets, so I'm not going to draw their attention to it!'*

as the case may be [A] as facts or circumstances direct, or are applicable □ *Third stage: the assignation is made—at the water-side or elsewhere,* ***as the case may be.*** EM □ *I'll be at work until five, in the pub till seven, and at home after that—so contact me later at one of those places* ***as the case may be.*** □ does not occur in front position.

as chance will/would have it [Disj] by coincidence (the implication not necessarily being that the occurrence, coincidence etc referred to is specially lucky, unlucky or significant); as it happens/happened (qv); as (good/ill) luck would have it (qv); by chance (qv); by accident (qv) □ *I'm going to London myself tomorrow night* ***as chance will have it,*** *so maybe we can travel together.* □ *I was there when the blind went down, throwing a ball for a little white dog* ***as chance would have it.*** KLT ⇨ by design; on purpose.

(as) changeable as a weathercock [Comp (AdjP)] having moods that alter rapidly, opinions that vary from one moment to another, etc **V:** ⚠ be, become; find sb ▫ *If you're going to London, go—and if you're not, stay at home. I can't make any plans with you* ***as changeable as a weathercock.*** ▫ *One moment he's accusing the Party of pandering to the Right, the next he's talking about some sinister communist conspiracy, and a day later he wants a tougher policy towards the Unions. He's* ***more changeable than a weathercock!*** ▫ variant more changeable than a weathercock. ⇨ as steady as a rock.

(as) cheap as dirt [Comp/A (AdjP)] very cheap; surprisingly cheap; very vulgar **V:** be; buy, sell, get, be going (ie be on sale) ▫ *It's odd how people will pay exorbitant prices for forced rhubarb in February and turn up their noses at it in July when it's* ***as cheap as dirt.*** ▫ *They got an old lawn-mower* ***dirt-cheap*** *at a local auction.* ▫ *A friend of mine bought one for £350.* ***Dirt-cheap*** *at the price, he said, but I thought he was a sucker.* ▫ adj compound dirt-cheap.

(as) clean as a new pin [Comp/A (AdjP)] very clean indeed, with no trace of dirt or dust. **S:** house, room, clothes; he, it, they. **V:** be, make, keep sth; end up ▫ *Jim's mam* (= mother) *was a big woman, a Tartar, a real six-footer who kept her house* ***as clean as a new pin.*** LLDR ▫ *You're such a scruffy little beast—I'll bet some respectable little Madam from Pinner or Guildford gobbles you up in six months. She'll marry you, send you out to work, and you'll end up* ***as clean as a new pin.*** LBA

(as) clean as a whistle [Comp (AdjP)] very clean or bare; empty, without anything left **S:** house, room; bone(s). **V:** ⚠ be; leave, pick, sth ▫ *Vultures had been at the carcase and had left the skeleton* ***clean as a whistle.*** ▫ *The feed-pipe's* ***as clean as a whistle****, so I'm afraid, if the oil is not getting through to the burner, the valve must be faulty.*

(as) clear as a bell [Comp/A (AdjP)] clearly and easily heard; having a very pure sound, like a bell **S:** sound, voice; words, song. **V:** be; hear sth, carry, ring out ▫ *She has the voice of a natural singer, effortless and* ***clear as a bell.*** ▫ *She has what you might call a carrying voice. It rings out across the room* ***as clear as a bell.*** *Conversation stops and heads turn towards her.*

(as) clear as crystal [Comp (AdjP)] very clear, that can be seen through or to the bottom; (fig) obvious; that can be understood easily without further explanation; next entry (qv) **S:** water, stream; explanation, argument; it. **V:** ⚠ be, become; make sth ▫ *The river ran* ***as clear as crystal*** *and if you watched closely you could now and then catch a glimpse of a trout hovering over the pebbles on the bottom.* ▫ *We Conservatives have never made too much of these issues* (unemployment and prices). *Let me make it* ***crystal clear****: all things being equal, I would prefer a lower level of unemployment.* NS ▫ adj compound crystal-clear.

(as) clear as day/daylight [Comp (AdjP)] very clear and light, as though day; (fig) obvious; that can be understood easily without further explanation; previous entry (qv) **S:** night, moonlight; statement, argument; it...why he's there. **V:** ⚠ be, become; make sth ▫ *He switched on the floodlights and what had been impenetrable darkness became suddenly* ***as clear as day.*** ▫ *It had been, when I read it, only a vaguely pregnant piece of nonsense. Now it was all* ***as clear as day****, as evident as Euclid.* DOP ▫ *You know, really, it's* ***as clear as daylight*** (why he hasn't come). *Pyle knows I smoke a few pipes before bed, and he doesn't want to disturb me.* QA

(as) clear as mud [Comp (AdjP)] (informal) not apparent, understood, or clearly explained **S:** explanation, instructions. **V:** ⚠ be, seem, become ▫ ALEX: *No matter how high you jump you always return to earth. Never lose sight of it, or you might come down with a bump. Is that quite clear?* PETER: ***Clear as mud.*** DPM ▫ *Yes, he gave me directions how to get there. They were about* ***as clear as mud*** *though. I wish I'd asked him to draw a rough sketch-map.* ▫ (NONCE) *But could I? It was all* ***as clear as a mud-spattered windscreen.*** ▫ facetious comment made when sth is not clear.

(as) clever/smart as paint [Comp (AdjP)] (informal) quick-witted; able at one's work, studies etc; cunning **V:** ⚠ be; think, find, sb ▫ *Mary,* ***as clever as paint*** *and much admired in academic circles, was clearly destined for a brilliant career.* ▫ *He's* ***as smart as paint****, that boy, and the best apprentice I ever had—I never had to show or tell him anything more than once.* ⇨ as thick as two short planks.

(as) clever as sin [Comp (AdjP)] (informal, derogatory) sharp-witted; cunning **V:** ⚠ be, seem; find sb ▫ *Don't trust him an inch—he's* ***as clever as sin*** *and has never yet shown the slightest sign of having a conscience.*

(as) clever etc as they make 'em/them [Comp (AdjP)] (informal) very clever etc; as big etc as they come (qv) **V:** ⚠ be, look. **adj:** clever, wise; miserable, awkward ▫ *The whole family is like that.* ***Clever as they make them****, but can't help boasting of it.* TCB ▫ *He's a cautious old bird, but* ***as wise as they make 'em.*** ASA ▫ *'Good morning, Moriarty,' said Hopalong, and he looked about* ***as miserable as they make 'em****, and he hadn't even started work.* TT

as close as an oyster [Comp (AdjP)] uncommunicative; secretive **V:** ⚠ be, become, remain; find sb ▫ *But we must be* ***as close as oysters*** *over Popsy. We don't want that fellow Prew starting non-stop patrols there.* RM ▫ *You can never get to know George well; he's* ***as close as an oyster*** *about everything, even matters of no particular concern.*

(as) cold as charity [Comp (AdjP)] (sth is) very cold; (sb is) very unresponsive; next entry (qv) **S:** the weather; it, he, they, you. **V:** ⚠ be, remain; find sth/sb ▫ *They say it's too early for snow to lie, but outside it's* ***as cold as charity.*** RFW ▫ *I like our new doctor; the last one was very efficient, but* ***as cold as charity.***

(as) cold as ice etc [Comp (AdjP)] (sth is) very cold; (sb is) very unresponsive; previous entry (qv) **S:** the weather, it; soup, tea, coffee; he, they, you. **V:** ⚠ be, turn, feel. **n:** ice, ⚠ an iceberg; a stone ▫ *The central heating had been switched off and the room was* ***as cold as ice.*** ▫ *You won't melt Sally's heart—it's* ***as cold as an iceberg.*** ▫ *Your soup will soon be* ***stone-cold*** *if you don't hurry up and drink it.* ▫ adj compound ice-/stone-cold.

(as) common as dirt/muck [Comp (AdjP)] so numerous, or plentiful, as to be little prized; vulgar; plebeian; coarse **V:** ⚠ be; find, think, sb □ *I wouldn't say white heather was* ***as common as dirt*** *round here: there's quite a lot if you know where to look for it.* □ *Flashy and vulgar.* ***Common as dirt.*** *But she's got money. I expect that's what he's after.* PE □ *They think they're Mr and Mrs Big since they got that big win on the pools, but they're* ***as common as muck*** *and always will be.*

(as) cool as a cucumber [Comp (AdjP)] controlled; not disconcerted or upset (esp in circumstances where the opposite might be expected) **V:** ⚠ be, stay; find sb □ *I thought there would have been protestations and tears when I told her I wanted to move out of the flat, but no, she stayed* ***as cool as a cucumber.*** □ *I know now it would have been better to have shut the doors and windows and gone to ring the Fire Brigade instead of running about with pails of water, but it's not everybody who can keep* ***as cool as a cucumber*** *in an emergency.* □ (NONCE) *'Yes, you must take everything.' said Magdalen. 'I'll pay for the taxi if you like.' Now she was* ***as cool as a lettuce.*** UTN

as coolly etc as you like/as anything [A (AdvP)] very coolly etc **adv:** coolly, sharply, boldly, savagely □ *When I scolded the child for tormenting the kitten, he answered me back* ***as coolly as you like****, 'Go away, it's not your cat and you're not my mummy.'* □ *He's a really classy darts player. I've seen him score three bull's-eyes one after another* ***as effortlessly as anything.*** □ *The barman was very affable, but he can be* ***as rude as you like*** *at times.* □ also, though less frequently, with adj as in last example.

(as) cross etc as a bear with a sore head [Comp (AdjP)] very bad-tempered; next entry (qv) **V:** ⚠ be, sound; find sb. **adj:** cross, ⚠ surly, grumpy, irritable □ *We'd better hurry — George will be* ***as cross as a bear with a sore head*** *if we keep him waiting.*

(as) cross as two sticks [Comp (AdjP)] very bad-tempered; previous entry (qv) **V:** ⚠ be, sound; find sb □ *Uncle Colin was to take the three children out in the punt so long as they got back in time for Jessica to have a rest before lunch, or she'd be* ***as cross as two sticks*** *by tea time.* WDM □ *Wait till later in the day to ask your father about this; he's always* ***as cross as two sticks*** *till he's had his breakfast and read his newspaper.*

as the crow flies [A] (distance) calculated in a straight line from one point to another, without allowing for detours, ascents and descents, windings of roads or rivers □ *When we stopped, we were not far away from Chesterfield Mews, Robert's old slum. Not far from it* ***as the crow flies****, that is, but...* CON □ *'Just how far are you from your nearest neighbour out there?' 'About a mile* ***as the crow flies****, but three miles up-river by boat and seven miles round by road.'* □ (NONCE) *He could see the jeep snaking round the hairpin bends that multiplied the* ***crow-flight*** *distance tenfold.* ARG □ used after expression of distance, as shown.

(as) cunning as a fox [Comp (AdjP)] sly and scheming, esp in plotting for one's own advantage or in escaping the consequences of wrongdoing **V:** ⚠ be, seem; find sb □ *There is a good deal of crooked dealing in the property business but the people involved in it are* ***as cunning as foxes*** *and know how to keep just on the right side of the law.*

(as) dead as the dodo [Comp (AdjP)] no longer in existence; very much out of date **S:** time, age, world; custom; idea, belief. **V:** ⚠ be, seem □ *Even the briefest glance at Bruce's life reveals the great gulf that divides us from the privileged classes of eighteenth century England. He belongs to a world that seems to us now* ***as dead as the dodo.*** BN □ *The days when the only opportunity for a 'nice girl' to meet a young man was in her parents' drawing-room, or that of a family friend, are* ***as dead as the dodo.***

(as) dead as a doornail [Comp (AdjP)] dead without hope of resuscitation; (fig) without vitality or importance **V:** ⚠ be, seem □ *I know when he talks to me and I look into his army mug* (= face) *that I'm alive and he's dead. He's* ***as dead as a doornail.*** LLDR □ *Her father was a puritanical old tyrant, but though he has been* ***dead as a doornail*** *for two years, she still acts as if any simple pleasure she allows herself is a kind of sin.* □ *The biblical view of the creation of the world has been* ***as dead as a doornail*** *for over a century.*

(as) dead as mutton [Comp (AdjP)] dull; uninteresting; difficult to arouse or stimulate **S:** he, they, you; place; idea. **V:** ⚠ be, seem; find sb/sth □ *Look, Dufton's awful. It stinks. Literally. It's* ***dead as mutton.*** *Warley's alive. I felt that from the first moment I set foot in the place.* RATT □ occas used literally of a dead person, but only by someone deliberately intending to be coarse or callous.

(as) deaf as a post [Comp (AdjP)] completely, or extremely, deaf **V:** ⚠ be, turn, go □ *A man going on eighty marrying a girl of twenty-four. Absolutely digusting. And he's* ***as deaf as a post.*** MM □ *'Fine old gentleman he is. Can be* ***as deaf as a post*** *when it suits him,' which Mr Adams appeared to find a praiseworthy and enviable characteristic.* WDM

(as) deep as a well [Comp (AdjP)] difficult to assess or understand, because he/she keeps his/her thoughts, plans etc to himself/herself **V:** ⚠ be, find sb □ *'I never knew Harold could handle a boat!' 'There's a lot we don't know about Harold. He's* ***as deep as a well.'*** □ rare.

(as) different as chalk from/and cheese [Comp (AdjP)] totally unalike **V:** ⚠ be, find sb/sth □ *The two brothers resembled each other physically, but were* ***as different*** *in their natures* ***as chalk from cheese.*** □ *Attending a cookery class once a week, and running your own house are* ***as different as chalk and cheese****, my girl, as you'll very soon find out.* ⇨ (as) like as two peas/peas in a pod.

(as) drunk as a lord/newt [Comp (AdjP)] very drunk; (as) pissed as a newt (qv); (as) tight as a tick (qv) **V:** ⚠ be, seem; find sb □ *No doubt about it, Pop thought, Charley was* ***as drunk as a newt.*** *It reminded him of the time they had first met and how Mariette had had to lend him pyjamas and put him to bed.* BFA □ *They went off down the road together half an hour ago, singing and swaying,* ***drunk as lords.*** ⇨ (as) sober as a judge.

(as) dry as a bone [Comp (AdjP)] with no moisture (left) **S:** wall, floor; earth, ground; wood; clothes; he, you, they. **V:** ⚠ be, feel, stay □ *No, I don't need to change, this cape keeps me* ***as dry as a bone*** *in all weathers.* □ *There's no damp in this cellar. Feel the walls, they're* ***dry as a bone.*** □ often used when dryness is a desirable condition; adj compound bone-dry.

(as) dry as dust [Comp (AdjP)] very dry, liable to crumble; (fig) very tedious and uninteresting **S:** cake; earth, soil, powder; book, lecture, programme, subject. **V:** ⚠ be, taste; find sth □ *How long have you had this cake in the cupboard? It's* ***as dry as dust****, and tastes stale too.* □ *I can't plant those seedlings till we get some rain: the soil is* ***as dry as dust.*** □ *How different children's schoolbooks are now from the* ***dry-as-dust*** *grammars and manuals of fifty years ago!* □ usu used when dryness is an undesirable condition; adj compound dry-as-dust.

(as) dry as paper [Comp (AdjP)] uncomfortably, or unhealthily, dry **S:** skin, mouth. **V:** ⚠ be, look; find sth □ *His skin looked* ***as dry as paper****, and there were harsh lines ruled from his nostrils to the corners of his mouth.* RATT □ *Because I couldn't breathe properly through my nose at that time, I used to wake up at night with my mouth and throat* ***as dry as paper.*** □ rare.

(as) dull as ditch-water [Comp (AdjP)] very uninteresting, dreary, boring **S:** he, she, it, they; evening, party, holiday; book, film. **V:** ⚠ be, sound; find sth □ *The Andersons are very hospitable and mean to be kind, but, really, an evening spent with them is* ***as dull as ditch-water.*** □ *Bestseller or not, the book sounds* ***as dull as ditch-water*** *to me.*

(as) easy/simple as ABC etc [Comp (AdjP)] very easy to do or understand **V:** ⚠ be, seem; find sth. **o:** ABC, ⚠ (eating) pie, kiss your hand, falling off a log/horse □ *'I hardly think,' Dorothy said, 'that we need quite such an elementary approach.' 'But you do! You let me do it my way, and it will be lovely and all* ***as easy as pie.****'* US □ *First lessons in any subject are usually designed to make you think the whole course is going to be* ***as easy as ABC.*** □ *Why not assemble the kit yourself? It's* ***as easy as falling off a log.***

as far as one can see [Disj] in one's judgement; to the extent that one can judge □ ***As far as I can see****, a war within the next ten years is inevitable.* □ *We don't know of course what the cost of living may be in five years' time, but* ***as far as I can see****, we'll be able to live comfortably enough on our pensions.* □ usu front position.

as far as sb/sth is concerned [Disj] in the way, or to the degree, that sb/sth matters, is involved or is affected □ ***As far as I'm concerned*** *there isn't a shadow of a doubt but that this cloud is travelling towards us.* TBC □ *Don't bring me into the argument.* ***As far as I'm concerned****, the boy can go to London if he likes.* □ *'If your book has sold out why don't they reprint it?' 'I'm afraid that* ***as far as*** *that* ***is concerned*** *the decision is the publishers'.'* □ ***As far as*** *money* ***is concerned*** *I'm in the hands of my bank manager.* □ usu front position.

as far as sb/sth goes [Disj] used to denote, or to imply, a degree of limitation, incompleteness or inadequacy in sb/sth □ *It is an excellent textbook* ***as far as*** *it* ***goes****, but it doesn't include anything to interest the advanced student.* □ *You're too hard on her; she's quite a nice girl* ***as far as*** *she* ***goes*** *and you can't expect everybody to be both an intellectual giant and a tremendous wit.* □ often in phrase *be all right* ***as far as*** *it* ***goes.***

as fast as one's legs can carry one [A (AdvP)] as fast as possible **V:** run, get away, dash off. **modal:** can, could, will, would □ *People may believe, for instance, that they could fight demons. In truth they would not try if they met one. They would certainly run* ***as fast as their legs would carry them.*** NDN □ *Stop nagging at the child to hurry up! He's going* ***as fast as his legs can carry him*** *already.* □ *He had said he was too tired to cut the grass that evening, but when he heard there were free drinks going in the village pub he rushed off* ***as fast as his legs could carry him.*** □ frequently used, as in last example, to indicate willingness or eagerness to go somewhere.

(as) fat as butter/a young thrush [Comp (AdjP)] plump, usu in a pleasant, healthy-looking way **V:** ⚠ be, get □ *There is one poor little runt in the litter as usual, but the other four puppies are* ***as fat as butter*** *and obviously thriving.* □ *'Your little boy is a bit wasted from his long fever,' the doctor said, 'but we'll soon have him* ***as fat as a young thrush*** *again.'* □ first form much more usual. ⇨ (as) thin as a rake/lath; ⚠ next entry.

(as) fat as a pig [Comp (AdjP)] (derogatory) grossly overweight **V:** ⚠ be, get □ *I'll have to stop all these between-meals snacks. I'm getting* ***as fat as a pig.*** □ *You can't miss him—he's red in the face,* ***fat as a pig****, and will be wearing a yellow panama hat.* ⇨ (as) thin as a rake/lath; ⚠ previous entry.

(as) fit as a fiddle/flea [Comp (AdjP)] healthy; active; in good physical condition **V:** ⚠ be, become □ *I'll tell your parents that you're* ***as fit as a flea*** *and having the time of your life.* RFW □ *What with all the walking, climbing, swimming, etc, it was a much more strenuous holiday than I'm accustomed to. But I must admit I've come back* ***fit as a fiddle.***

(as) flat as a board [Comp (AdjP)] absolutely flat (the implication usu being that some roundness or unevenness would be desirable) **S:** face, chest; landscape. **V:** ⚠ be, become □ *The top of the new small-car range is* ***as flat as a board*** *—quite a contrast with what we have become used to.* G □ *Her breasts were not merely small: her whole chest was* ***as flat as a board.***

(as) flat as a fluke/flounder [Comp (AdjP)] very flat, like the fish referred to **V:** ⚠ be, go, fall □ *The soufflé was a bitter disappointment. No sooner had I taken it out of the oven than it collapsed and in three seconds was* ***as flat as a fluke.*** □ rarer than previous or next entries.

(as) flat as a pancake [Comp (AdjP)] very flat; completely flattened; (fig) without interest, being a disappointment or anti-climax **S:** cake, tyre; landscape; voice; surprise, celebration; joke. **V:** ⚠ be, come out, turn out; fall □ *Why didn't you look where you were sitting? You've squashed my hat* ***as flat as a pancake.*** □ *The whole terrain was* ***flat as a pancake****, not a rise or hollow, or even a tree, to relieve its monotonous aspect.* □ *It was supposed to have been a gathering of celebrities, but as most of* *them sent notes of regret for their absence, the whole affair fell* ***flat as a pancake****.*

as for sb/sth [A (PrepP)] with reference to sb/sth; coming to the subject of sb/sth □ *The men there all looked as though they distrusted him, and* ***as for*** *the women, they were all intent on showing their contempt for this rather odd creature.* LBA □ *I enjoy reading Dickens, and some of Thackeray, but* ***as for*** *Sir Walter Scott —you could make a bonfire of all his novels as far as I'm concerned.* □ *You will certainly qualify for a grant to cover the three-year course at a British University. But* ***as for*** *your chances of obtaining a further grant to study abroad, I'm afraid they're rather slim.* □ *Take your elbows off the table, you two boys, and* ***as for*** *you, Anna, stop sucking your fork and get on with your dinner.* □ introduces a second, or subsequent, item of description or discussion, comparing, contrasting or simply adding; often used, as in second example, as a signal that sth dismissive is going to follow; stress pattern ˌas for ˈyou etc.

(as) free as (the) air/a bird [Comp (AdjP)] without ties, duties, obligations etc **V:** ⚠ be, feel, remain □ *It's all very well for a bachelor like Jim to travel the world over, picking up interesting jobs, but a family man can't be* ***as free as air*** *to follow his fancy.* □ *Bring the child down to me for a fortnight. I have a huge old garden where he can be* ***as free as a bird*** *and perfectly safe.* □ *'As far as I'm concerned,' she said to her fiancé, 'you're* ***as free as the air****. If you've decided you don't want to marry me, just say so.'*

(as) fresh as a daisy [Comp (AdjP)] vigorous, lively **V:** ⚠ be, look, feel □ *It was six in the morning, dawn was breaking, but Nick still felt* ***as fresh as a daisy****, ready to dance, drink and talk for hours longer.*

(as) fresh as a rose [Comp (AdjP)] very attractive in a fresh, clean way **V:** ⚠ be, look; find sb □ *She's beautiful, yes, really beautiful,* ***fresh as a rose*** *on the day of the battle or whatever that poem is, and a truly sweet-natured child.* RATT

(as) gay as a lark [Comp (AdjP)] merry, carefree and untroubled (the implication sometimes being that to be so is unexpected or unsuitable in view of the circumstances) **V:** ⚠ be, seem, feel □ *I was sure he would have a hang-over after last night's party, but not Jim—up early and away to work* ***gay as a lark****.* □ *You can hardly expect Louise to be* ***as gay as a lark*** *with her boyfriend away in India and her thinking she's going to fail her exams as well.*

(as) gentle as a lamb [Comp (AdjP)] very gentle, careful not to hurt or harm **V:** ⚠ be, seem □ *He was a big rough-looking fellow but* ***gentle as a lamb****, even when he'd had a few drinks.*

as God is my witness [Disj] I swear, I vow, solemnly; truthfully; honestly; before God (qv) □ *'I gave the baby the medicine, your Honour,' sobbed the girl, 'I've never denied it. But* ***as God is my witness****, I meant no harm.'* □ *'You're pulling my leg!' 'I'm not.* ***As God is my witness****, that's exactly what she said.'*

(as) good as gold [Comp (AdjP)] very well-behaved **V:** ⚠ be, seem, remain □ *I tell you, my children are* ***as good as gold****. Hava even came back to look after me when her mother died; she's just like a little mother.* HSG □ *'Can I come round tonight? I'll be* ***as good as gold****. Can I?' Yeah, Mr Big Heart-Throb, she thought to herself,* ***as good as gold*** *as long as it suits you and not a second longer.* TGLY

(as) good as new [Comp (AdjP)] in as good a condition as when it was new; showing little sign of wear or use **S:** (second-hand) television, table, carpet; watch, radio, typewriter. **V:** ⚠ be, look; make sth □ *If you care to spend £20 on replacement parts for your washing-machine I can make it* ***as good as new****.* □ *He had been lucky enough to pick up a sofa at the auction which was* ***as good as new*** *and cost him under £50.* ⇨ ⚠ make sth look/seem like new.

as good etc as the next (one) [Comp (AdjP)] just as satisfactory as another thing of the same kind **S:** car, washing-machine; government, (political) party. **V:** ⚠ be, look; find sth. **adj:** good, bad; useful, useless; interesting, boring □ *If you have always thought one electric cooker was* ***as good as the next one*** *then it is time you visited our showroom.* □ *I don't know why you're bothering with all those brochures.* ***No*** *package holiday's* ***any better than the next****.* □ variant no/not any better etc than the next (one).

as good etc as the next man [Comp (AdjP)] equally as good, virtuous, able to do sth, as most people are (the implication often being that one is better etc than most people) **V:** ⚠ be, seem, find sb. **adj:** able, good, clever, honest, intelligent □ *The British forces would show, and did show, that when it came to mobile battle they were just* ***as good as the next man****.* MFM □ *I'm* ***as honest as the next man****, I hope, but I see no reason why I should give my hard-earned cash away to the tax man.* □ *He does****n't*** *keep his promises* ***any better the than next man****.* □ variant no/not any better etc than the next man.

(as) good as a play [Comp (AdjP)] amusing; interesting; lively **S:** scene, episode; quarrel, argument. **V:** ⚠ be, find sth □ *I wish you had been in the shop this morning when the boss was trying to give Liz the sack and she wouldn't take it. It was* ***as good as a play****.*

as good as one's word [Comp (AdjP)] completely reliable, trustworthy **V:** ⚠ be, find sb □ *Mrs Turner had been* ***as good as her word*** *in response to Mrs Paxon's appeal and had taken up her temporary abode at the Mitre.* WDM □ *If he said he would lend you the deposit for a house, he will. Uncle Fred has always been* ***as good as his word****.* ⇨ ⚠ sb's word is (as good as) his/her bond.

(as) green as grass [Comp (AdjP)] naive; inexperienced; immature; easily deceived **S:** girl, boy, young man/woman, youth. **V:** ⚠ be; find sb □ *She was* ***as green as grass*** *when she was sixteen but the other girls in the typing pool taught her the ways of their world.* □ *Of course I'll find my way about town all right! I'm not* ***as green as grass****, just because I come from the country.* □ less common variant as green as a cabbage/a leek.

(as) happy etc as the day is long [Comp (AdjP)] very happy etc (esp as a continuous state) **V:** ⚠ be, seem, stay. **adj:** happy, ⚠ cheerful, contented, merry □ *If I didn't have you to worry about, I could be* ***as happy as the day is***

long. ▫ *There was I standing on a chair, singing away,* ***merry as the day is long.*** TOH

(as) happy as a king etc [Comp (AdjP)] completely, or extremely, happy **V:** ⚠ be, become, seem. **o:** a king, ⚠ a sandboy, Larry ▫ *He wasn't a man who enjoyed social occasions, and did not even get on very well with his own family; but in his laboratory he was* ***as happy as a king.*** ▫ *I gave him fifty pence for himself, and a basket of strawberries for his mother, and he ran off home,* ***happy as Larry.*** ▫ *'Where is Grandpa, do you know?' 'Up in the meadow with the children. He's* ***as happy as a sandboy*** *helping them to fly their kites.'* ▫ (NONCE) *Leave the poor sweetie alone. She's* ***as happy as a sandgirl****, dear. It's years since she's been able to wash the nappies out like this.* HAA

(as) hard as flint [Comp (AdjP)] unforgiving, unsympathetic in temperament, character **S:** boss, teacher; look, face. **V:** ⚠ be, look; find sb ▫ *He said he was frightfully sorry, but he had forgotten the number of baskets. She gave him a look* ***as hard as flint*** *and her mouth opened and shut like a spring trap.* DBM

(as) hard as iron/rock [Comp (AdjP)] very firm, strong, unyielding; (as) hard as (a) stone (qv) **S:** muscles; ground, earth; cake, scone; glue. **V:** ⚠ be, feel; find sth ▫ *Mike was a nipper compared to me, but underneath the scruffy draughtboard jersey he wore were muscles* ***as hard as iron.*** LLDR ▫ *The great timbers of La Belle Helene, darkened now by smoke, wormed in places, looking rotten on the surface, but hard in the core,* ***hard as iron.*** ARG ▫ *Some of these modern contact adhesives set* ***as hard as rock****, so you must get the pieces that you are joining in position at the first try.*

(as) hard as nails [Comp (AdjP)] tough; with great physical stamina; (fig) selfish, ruthless in one's dealings with others **V:** ⚠ be, look; find sb ▫ *Although he seemed thin and undersized compared with his cousins, he was really* ***as hard as nails*** *and didn't fall ill half as often as they did.* ▫ *She's ignorant, but she's* ***as hard as nails*** *and pretty sly. Don't you let her in on your private life!* ASA

(as) hard as steel [Comp (AdjP)] physically strong and with mental or moral firmness (esp in circumstances where such qualities are desirable) **S:** soldier, leader; army. **V:** ⚠ be, become; make sb ▫ *An army must be* ***as hard as steel*** *in battle and can be made so; but, like steel, it reaches its finest quality only after much preparation.* MFM ▫ *General discipline and academic achievement improved greatly under the headmastership of Mr Gray, a man* ***as hard as steel****, but very just.*

(as) hard as (a) stone [Comp (AdjP)] very firm; (as) hard as iron/rock (qv); (fig) heartless; unfeeling **S:** ground, earth; heart; he, you, they. **V:** ⚠ be, become; find sth ▫ *I can't do any digging today, the ground's* ***as hard as stone*** *after last night's frost.* ▫ *One would need to have a heart* ***as hard as a stone*** *not to be moved by his pitiable plight.*

(as) heavy as lead [Comp (AdjP)] very heavy; oppressive in weight or colour **S:** suitcase, box; arms, legs; heart; sky. **V:** ⚠ be, feel, look; find sth ▫ *When he woke the following morning his throat felt sore and swollen and his limbs* ***heavy as lead.*** ▫ *It was with a heart* ***heavier than lead*** *that she saw him depart.* ▫ *The sea was sullen and the sky* ***heavy as lead.*** *The storm would break any time now.* ⇨ (as) light as a feather.

(as) helpless as a (new-born) babe etc [Comp (AdjP)] not able to defend, or fend for, oneself **V:** ⚠ be, feel; find sb. **n:** babe, ⚠ baby, child ▫ *There I was, locked in his grasp,* ***as helpless as a new-born babe.*** ▫ *You're lucky to have a husband who can look after himself. Mine is* ***as helpless as a child*** *in the house—I don't think he could make himself a cup of tea.* ⇨ ⚠ a babe in arms.

(as) hoarse as an (old) crow [Comp (AdjP)] very hoarse **S:** voice, throat; speaker, singer. **V:** ⚠ be, sound ▫ *My voice is getting* ***as hoarse as an old crow*** *with this constant reading.* TBC ▫ *You know your throat is not quite better yet. If you go out in this fog, you'll make yourself* ***as hoarse as a crow*** *again.*

(as) honest as the day is long [Comp (AdjP)] very honest **V:** ⚠ be, find sb ▫ *It's easy to say I should have doubted her story, but you ask anyone you like; they'd all say that she's* ***as honest as the day is long.***

(as) hungry as a hunter [Comp (AdjP)] with one's appetite well sharpened, eg by exercise or postponement of a customary meal-time, but not seriously hungry or semi-starved from lack of food **V:** ⚠ be, feel; make sb ▫ *We'd better have supper a little earlier tonight. The boys will be* ***as hungry as hunters*** *after their bike ride.* ▫ *In the sitting-room Pop had poured out a Dragon's Blood for himself and one for Mr Charlton, who felt he really needed it. He was* ***as hungry as a hunter*** *too.* DBM

as if/though to do sth [A] in way that indicates an intention to do sth, esp when the action mentioned is not actually carried out ▫ *He was so annoyed at not getting his own way, that in answer to any alternative proposal he just shrugged his shoulders* ***as though to*** *disclaim any further interest or responsibility in the matter.* ▫ *I lifted the beer glass* ***as if to*** *strike it against the table.* RATT ▫ *He made* (ie a movement) ***as if to*** *leave the room but, thinking better of it, returned to comfort the weeping girl.* ▫ *She went* ***as if to*** *snatch the letter from him, and probably would have succeeded had he not been prepared for just such a move on her part.* ▫ often *made* ***as if to...****, went* ***as if to....***

as if/though it mattered etc! it certainly doesn't matter; I certainly don't care; he certainly does know; etc **cl:** it mattered/matters; I cared; he didn't know; you could ▫ *I asked him where that was, and he named a pretty ritzy part of Hampstead, near the Heath.* ***As if I couldn't have guessed!*** CON ▫ *If Ronnie were here I'd get him to fill it in for me.* ***As if they didn't know*** *how many times I was at work this year. Forms!* CSWB ▫ *'That was Mr Davis on the telephone to say he couldn't attend the meeting tonight.'* ***'As if anybody cared!'*** ▫ used to deny or assert emphatically that sth is the case, a positive expression being used to deny and a negative one to assert (***As if they didn't know!*** = 'Certainly they knew!')

as if/though one's life depended on/upon it [A] in such a way as to indicate that one is doing it with the utmost energy, concentration, devotion **V:** play; hammer, work (away); search; eat □ *The market people stop cheering and laughing and go back to work* ***as if their lives depended on it.*** DPM □ *She has been on her hands and knees all morning, weeding the flower-beds* ***as if her life depended on it.*** □ end position.

as if/though one owned the place [A] in a presumptuous, or domineering, way **V:** come in, go about; talk □ *'How dare you come in here* ***as if you owned the place!****' she called out in her high, grating voice. 'What do you want? I can't see anyone now.'* AITC □ *He's only a summer visitor, but he goes about telling the locals what they should and shouldn't do,* ***as if he owned the place.*** □ end position.

as if/though sth were/was not enough [Conj] in addition to sth, or doing sth, which in itself would appear to be sufficient in the circumstances □ *...and a heavy fragrance of gardenias that overwhelmed in a cloud of intoxication as she came and sat at his side.* ***As if*** *this* ***were not enough****, she had brought with her the bluebells and the rose campion, arranged in an orange and crimson jar.* DSM □ ***As if*** *scalding her arm* ***wasn't enough****, she went and broke her ankle the very next day.* □ *His father gave him £200 to make a fresh start elsewhere,* ***as if*** *it* ***were not enough*** *to have paid off all his debts for him.* □ front, middle or end position.

as if/like there were/was no tomorrow [A (AdvP)] (informal) very energetically; fast; freely (with the implication of slight desperation) □ (headline) *Why people are spending* ***as if there were no tomorrow.*** □ *The last time I saw her was in this Chinese restaurant where she was downing vast quantities of food* ***like there was no tomorrow.***

(as) innocent as a (new-born) babe etc [Comp (AdjP)] completely innocent, either of having done sth, or in one's nature **V:** ⚠ be, look, sound. **n:** babe, ⚠ baby, child □ *There were a lot of unpleasant innuendos in the comedian's patter, but Alice, being* ***as innocent as a new-born babe****, didn't understand half of it.* □ *You just won't see him around for two or three days sometimes, but he'll come out of it looking* ***as innocent as a baby.*** AITC □ variant as innocent as a babe unborn.

as it happens/happened [Disj] by coincidence; by chance (qv); as chance will/would have it (qv); as (good/ill) luck would have it (qv); by accident (qv) □ *Don't worry about having to ask for a loan.* ***As it happens****, I've just been left a legacy by an old cousin of mine.* □ *The janitor had gone back to the school that evening,* ***as it happened****, in order to check the stores.* □ *'You can't park here. Didn't you see the notice saying 'Employees Only'?' 'Thank you, but I am the District Manager,* ***as it happens.****'* □ often used in rather pompous, petulant or aggressive manner, to contradict another person's (impudent etc) assumptions. ⇨ by design; on purpose.

as it is/was [A] already; as the situation is/was at the time of speaking (the implication often that any additional action or change in the situation would probably make things worse rather than better) □ *'Look, Parkinson,' he said. 'There's no need to go on gabbling about this until we know more about it. The Prime Minister suspects I'm off my head* ***as it is.****'* TBC □ *And don't throw your things about—this place is untidy enough* ***as it is.*** TOH □ *The pilot must have done a good job, and they were lucky not to have been killed.* ***As it was****, one of the wings, and the undercarriage and the propeller, had been smashed.* DS □ front or end position.

as it were [Disj] to speak figuratively; so to speak (qv) □ *The twins were tumbling and struggling to get upright—to get to action stations* ***as it were.*** DF □ *He felt himself shivering as if in the midst of all this horror, his body was,* ***as it were****, jogging at his elbow, asserting its claim to a little consideration, trying to get him to put on an overcoat.* HD □ middle or end position. ⇨ ⚠ as one/you might say.

(as) keen as mustard [Comp (AdjP)] very enthusiastic and active **V:** ⚠ be, become; find, make, sb □ *This clansman James Donaldson is* ***keen as mustard*** *on the Monster. He understands absolutely why I object to the notion that the Monster has left Loch Ness.* RM □ *He's just the boy to be our next Troop Leader—****as keen as mustard*** *and very popular with the others.*

(as) large/big as a cabbage [Comp (AdjP)] very large **S:** lettuce, weed; blossom, flower, rose. **V:** ⚠ be, grow □ *Here were hats with pink roses* ***as large as cabbages.*** DC □ *This must be a good year for hydrangeas. All the bushes have heads on them* ***as big as cabbages.***

(as) large as life [Comp (AdjP)] seen, pictured in the imagination, or exhibiting oneself, as one undoubtedly is **V:** ⚠ be, seem, look □ *'You must be crazy. Your uncle doesn't go to nightclubs.' 'But I saw him myself in a disco* ***as large as life****, dancing with a girl half his age.'* □ *I can't believe, sometimes, that granny is dead. If I close my eyes I can just see her knitting away in that old armchair* ***as large as life****, with her specs half-way down her nose.* □ usu in apposition to a n rather than as a Comp; variant (facetious) as large as life and twice as natural. ⇨ ⚠ larger than life.

(as) a/one's last resort (as) a resource, expedient, means of help, etc; (only to be used) when all else fails; in the last resort[1] (qv) **V:** be; keep, use, leave, appeal to, fall back on sth □ *If justice, then, must be seen to waddle at its measured pace in the formal investigations, what about a little informal mud-slinging? How about publicity? 'Publicity is* ***a last resort****,' I was told.* OBS *The place seemed to be impregnable. There might have been a way of entering from the railway side. But I left this* ***as a last resort****; for although I am not frightened of motor cars I am rather nervous of trains.* UTN □ *I discovered that all grassland squirrels made straight for the trees when pursued, and only chose holes in the ground, or hollow logs,* ***as a last resort.*** BB □ *The operation is occasionally successful but so expensive as well as uncertain that it should be restricted to* ***last resort*** *attempts at reconciliation.* OBS □ attrib use *a* ***last resort*** *attempt.* ⇨ ⚠ in the last resort[2]; the last ditch.

(as) lean as an alley cat [Comp (AdjP)] with very little flesh on one's bones (the implication usu being that the person is hardy) **V:** ⚠ be, become, grow □ *Most of the tourist party spent the afternoon lying on their beds with the shades drawn, but Jim, who was* ***as lean as an alley cat,***

suffered much less than the others from the heat and humidity.

(as) light as air [Comp (AdjP)] carefree; untroubled; possibly superficial **S:** tone, mood; he, you, they, we. **V:** ⚠ be, feel □ *For the first week or two after sitting my final examinations I felt* ***light as air****, but of course I soon had to face the problem of finding a job.* □ *'I doubt if my husband and I will still be living together by next summer,' she remarked in a tone* ***as light as air****. I stared at her, not knowing whether to take her seriously or not.*

(as) light as a feather [Comp (AdjP)] very light in weight **V:** ⚠ be, feel, weigh □ *'Can you manage to carry her?' 'Oh, she's* ***as light as a feather****.'* TGLY □ *I don't know why you persist in wearing those old oilskins for fishing, when you can get nylon jackets that are waterproof, windproof, and* ***light as a feather****.* □ always sing, even when talking of objects in pl, as in second example. ⇨ (as) heavy as lead.

(as) light as thistledown [Comp (AdjP)] very light in weight and gentle in movement **S:** movement; fingers; breeze. **V:** ⚠ be, feel □ *To his delight and relief the dentist's touch was, if not quite* ***as light as thistledown****, at least sensitive, and certainly far from the brutal assault he had feared.*

(as) like/likely as not [Disj (AdjP)] in all probability; with an even chance of occurring or not occurring □ *She had left the breech out of the port Oerlikon* (gun)*, and,* ***as like as not****, without her help the rating wouldn't be able to put it together again.* RFW □ *Come now to the average wife's impression.* ***Likely as not****, 'picnic' for her means three hours of cutting, buttering, boiling, packing, and getting the family equipped.* □ *The headmaster could make no promises, of course, but he did say the boy was* ***as likely as not*** *to win a scholarship.* □ as likely as not also used as Comp after *be*.

(as) like as two peas/peas in a pod [Comp (AdjP)] very similar in appearance, but not necessarily indistinguishable; very alike **V:** ⚠ be, seem □ *We haven't met before, but I'm sure you must be Alec Brown's brother from New Zealand; you're* ***as like as two peas****.* □ *An expert could probably tell which was the original and which the copy, but to the layman's eye the three vases were* ***as like as peas in a pod****.* ⇨ (as) different as chalk from/and cheese.

(as) lively as a cricket [Comp (AdjP)] bright, cheerful and active **V:** ⚠ be, remain; find sb □ *My darling daughter awoke,* ***lively as a cricket,*** *just three hours after we'd gone to bed.* WI □ *Some men are old at sixty-five, others are still* ***as lively as crickets*** *in their nineties.*

as/so long as [Conj] provided that □ *I don't mind where we go* ***so long as*** *there's sun, sand and sea.* □ *'Can I take the dog for a run?' 'Yes,* ***as long as*** *you're back before dark.'* □ *The farmers' answer is that* ***as long as*** *we take something like 90 per cent of our butter and cheese from abroad we cannot hope to produce our own butter and cheese economically.* SC

as long as one's arm [Comp (AdjP)] very long **S:** list, schedule, itinerary, column of figures. **V:** ⚠ be, seem □ *. . . and wrote out a shopping list* ***as long as her arm****.* AITC □ *Since they'll only be here for half a day, there's no point in planning an itinerary* ***as long as your arm****.* □ often modifies a preceding n, as shown.

as (good/ill) luck would have it [Disj] fortunately, or unfortunately; as chance will/would have it (qv): as it happens/happened (qv); by chance (qv); by accident (qv) □ ***As ill luck would have it*** *he was on holiday at that time, and it came as a blow to Sir Percy to read in one of the newspapers that Brigadier Rademeyer was very critical of his activities.* DS □ *Soon after three o'clock one of the occasional mortar bombs came over.* ***As luck would have it*** *a steward was bringing him a cup of tea, and this man was killed instantaneously.* RFW □ *He had just the qualifications we wanted, and* ***as luck would have it*** *we happened to have a vacancy.* □ when no adj is used, then context gives meaning. ⇨ by design; on purpose.

(as) mad as a hatter/a March hare [Comp (AdjP)] abnormal in behaviour (ranging from mere eccentricity, recklessness, folly, irresponsibility etc to near-madness and insanity itself); (as) nutty as a fruit-cake (qv) **V:** ⚠ be, seem; think sb □ *Strangely, although Mr Benberg was only an ineffectual dreamer, and Mrs Benberg seemed at times* ***as mad as a hatter****, they had managed to give her the help she had looked for in vain from her mother.* AITC □ *I think you're* ***as mad as a March hare****, and I don't want to see you any more, so please don't ring up, or write and thank me for this.* RFW □ the Mad Hatter is a character in the book 'Alice in Wonderland'; mad as a March hare is derived from the strange behaviour of hares occas observed in March, and usu describes unorthodox and unpredictable behaviour of a flamboyant kind.

as one makes one's bed, so one must lie on it (saying) one must suffer the consequences of one's own actions, of the arrangements one has made for one's life or work □ *'Well,' his mother explained to ours about a month after they'd got married, '****he's made his bed and he can lie on it****, even though it turns out to be a bed of nettles.'* LLDR □ *But I did hear from Robin that she had a sort of stroke after Christmas. Of course,* ***she's made her bed and she's got to lie on it****.* ASA □ (NONCE) *We are not sent on this earth for pleasure alone.* ***You*** *have* ***lain on your bed and now you'll have to make it****.* SC □ often adapted, as shown; stress pattern as one ˌmakes one's bed, so one must ˈlie on it.

as a matter of fact [Disj] the fact is that; and that is a fact; to tell you the truth (qv) □ ***As a matter of fact****, if you stop eating altogether for a day or two and drink only plain water, you will be surprised at how well you feel.* TO □ ***As a matter of fact*** *I doubt if a Tory government could act any differently as things stand, whatever they might wish.* HAA □ *'What would you like for dinner?' 'Just a boiled egg will do, thanks. I'm almost too tired to eat,* ***as a matter of fact****.'* □ used to reinforce a statement, often either implying that listener or reader might not believe it, might be surprised to hear it, etc, or to strengthen contradiction of sth already said or suggested; front or end position.

as a matter of form [A (PrepP)] in a way that is not essential but is either correct procedure or the courteous thing to do □ *It was time new arrangements were drawn up, and Bevill and*

Rose undertook, ***as a matter of form****, to get Martin's views.* NM □ *Although her retirement does not entitle her to attend the dinner, I feel strongly that,* ***as a matter of form****, she should receive an invitation.* □ front or end position.

(as) meek as a lamb [Comp (AdjP)] humble; not resisting or answering back; like a lamb (qv) **V:** ⚠ be, look, sound □ *If he'd thought I would sit there* ***meek as a lamb*** *while he abused my family, he must have got a real surprise.* □ *It was thought he might have resisted arrest, but in the event he accompanied the officers to the Police Station,* ***as meek as a lamb.***

as one/you might say [Disj] a comment attached, often semi-apologetically, to a statement when the speaker himself does not wish to identify himself fully with its content, its implications or its form, or when he thinks his listener may not wish to do so □ *Johnny isn't much of a fighter in the boardroom — a bit afraid,* ***as one might say****.* □ *'You don't see much of your brother, eh? Haven't quarrelled or anything, have you?' 'Nothing like that, it's just that, well, nowadays we move in different circles* ***as you might say****.'* □ front, middle or end position. ⇨ ⚠ as it were; so to speak.

(as) miserable as sin [Comp (AdjP)] very unhappy **V:** ⚠ be, look, sound □ *We saw him walking down the yard, carrying a suitcase and two paper bundles, looking* ***as miserable as sin*** *and wearing the good suit he'd got married in to save it getting creased in the case.* LLDR □ *I'm not letting Peter go to his grandparents unless his cousins are going too. He would be* ***as miserable as sin*** *without company of his own age.*

as much as one's life is worth [Comp (AdjP)] involving danger to one's life; very dangerous; involving oneself in trouble or unpleasantness **S:** it...not to go, it...to arrive late. **V:** ⚠ be; think sth □ *I'm glad your father was persuaded not to go fishing. It would have been* ***as much as his life was worth*** *to have taken the boat out on a night like this.* □ *Some poor fellows are so dominated by their wives that it's* ***as much as their lives are worth*** *to get home half an hour late.* □ *I promised I'd get this done by five o'clock, and it'll be* ***as much as my life is worth*** *if I don't.*

as much as to say [A] as if to say; in a way that is equivalent to saying □ *Wormold made a little gesture* ***as much as to say****, 'I haven't the nerve. Help me.'* OMIH □ *All the time he was boasting about his adventures, Celia was gazing at him with her big round eyes* ***as much as to say*** *'What a wonderful, man you are!'*

as near as dammit/kiss your hand [A (AdjP)] (informal) very nearly; almost but not quite □ *Kirkcaldy, they say, was the birthplace (or* ***as near as dammit****) of the gentleman who founded 'The Scotsman', one John Ritchie.* SC □ *I only hope the Germans are capable of making bloody fools of themselves like this. Or anyone else who gets as far. I tell you we've got* ***as near as kiss your hand****.* NM □ *I* ***as near as dammit*** *missed my train again this morning. I shall really have to get up earlier.*

as near ((to) sth/(to) doing sth) as makes no difference etc [Comp (AdjP)] so close (to sth/to doing sth) that any differences are unimportant **V:** ⚠ be, come. **n:** difference, ⚠ matter, odds □ *'Now Cobb, Stevenson here tells me that you know about this already.' And Stevenson was* ***as near*** *crying* ***as makes no difference.*** TT □ *...Harry, whose shape came* ***as near as makes no matter to*** *a globe.* SML □ *She was* ***as near*** *thirty* ***as makes no odds*** *the year war broke out.* WOM

(as) nervous as a cat/kitten [Comp (AdjP)] apprehensive; easily startled; ready to take fright **V:** ⚠ be, become, feel; find sb □ *'Some of the patients can be pretty difficult at first, especially in the New Town. They think it's asserting the rights of citizenship to be rude to the doctor.' 'Well, I might tell you I was* ***as nervous as a kitten*** *when I started.'* DIL □ *I don't mind being in the house alone in the daytime, but after dark I'm* ***as nervous as a cat****.* ⇨ ⚠ like a cat on hot bricks.

(as) nutty as a fruit-cake [Comp (AdjP)] (informal) abnormal in behaviour (ranging from mere eccentricity, recklessness, folly, irresponsibility etc to near-madness and insanity); (as) mad as a hatter/a March hare (qv) **V:** ⚠ be, seem □ *I'm staying in the house of my Aunt Grizelda, who is 87 years old, has 3 pet monkeys, eats only fish and oats, is* ***nutty as a fruit-cake*** *—but she's a most delightful companion.* □ *The characters in Don Sleeve's new comedy series 'Filthy Showers' are all* ***nuttier than fruit-cakes.*** □ *Ben's* ***a*** *real* ***fruit-cake*** *turning down that offer for his bike.* □ variant a fruit-cake.

(as) obstinate/stubborn as a mule [Comp (AdjP)] difficult to persuade, or force, into doing or thinking anything different from what he does or thinks now **V:** ⚠ be, become; find sb □ *But this is the odd thing, though he's impulsive he's* ***as obstinate as a mule****.* PW □ *But he wouldn't see it.* ***Obstinate as a mule*** *over that, he was.* TST □ *When interested, his powers of concentration were those of a burning-glass, but his trains of thought,* ***as obstinate*** *and as surefooted* ***as mules****, seemed often to lead him far from the place where he was.* AH

as of now [A] starting now (from this moment, day etc) and from now on □ *There was the world, and somewhere in it was Pepina without anyone to turn to. Well, she had,* ***as of now****. She had me.* CON □ *'I heard on the radio this evening that National Insurance Contributions are going up by 13p.'* ***'As of now****?' 'No, from July 14th.'* □ esp in official or semi-official contexts, or humorously in imitation of this; front, middle or end position.

as of old [A] in the old, familiar way; as used to be, and still is, the case □ *Otherwise all was peace, and on the quay the blue-clad hotel porter fussed forward* ***as of old*** *for our packs and coats.* SD □ *I could see that* ***as of old*** *their house was a port of call for all the lonely and the lost of the district.* □ *Your Uncle James was at the wedding, flirting with all the good-looking girls,* ***as of old****.* □ front, middle or end position.

as of right [A] by (legal) entitlement; as sb who is (legally) entitled to sth □ *One third of the total estate comes to you* ***as of right****, you know, whether your husband has left a will or not.* □ *'Come along, Elspeth, let's have some tea,' said Alec. She sat down* ***as of right*** *behind the teapot. Harold sat down too, but Alec remained standing.* PW □ front, middle or end position.

as often as not [A (AdvP)] about as many times as not □ *The baboon 'overlords' have been described as highly aggressive within their groups. In fact,* ***as often as not****, the animals that were attacked evaded the aggressor by feats of rock-climbing which he did not emulate.* NS □ *'You're always up until after midnight, and it's not good for you.' 'That's not true, really it isn't!* ***As often as not****, I'm in bed by eleven.'*

(as) old as the hills [Comp (AdjP)] ancient; very old; not new; not young; dating from far back in history **S:** custom, practice; joke, story; suit, coat. **V:** ⚠ be, look □ *Many of the customs and rituals of this tribe were* ***as old as the hills*** *they dwelt among.* □ *'And anyway,' Rose added, 'I look* ***as old as the hills****.'* ASA □ *'Is that a new dress you're wearing?' 'Good heavens, no. It's* ***as old as the hills****—you must have seen me in it dozens of times.'*

(as) old as Methuselah [Comp (AdjP)] very old (from GENESIS V 27); (derogatory) of an older age group than the speaker **V:** ⚠ be, look □ *'Mr Phillips is still alive, but living with his daughter's family now.' 'Well, you do surprise me! He must be* ***as old as Methuselah*** *— he was a grey-bearded old man when I was a boy.* □ *He said he didn't want to go on a coach-tour with a lot of fuddy-duddies all* ***as old as Methuselah****.*

(as) old as time [Comp (AdjP)] ancient; very old; dating from far back in history; not new or young **S:** area, locality; village, settlement; rite, custom. **V:** ⚠ be, look □ *Geologically speaking, most of the earth's surface is comparatively new, but here and there, rock formations* ***old as time*** *have been exposed by the action of long vanished glaciers or by natural erosion.* □ *There are very few sins that aren't* ***as old as time****.* HAA

as one enchanted etc [A (AdvP)] (formal) in the manner of sb who is under a magic spell which has deprived him of his normal faculties and functions **V:** ⚠ be, appear, stand. **adj:** enchanted, ⚠ bewitched, possessed, deprived of her/his senses □ *I heard no sound after the door closed, and for some time I stood* ***as one bewitched*** *in the middle of the room.* UTN □ ***As one enchanted*** *she wandered aimlessly through the house, picking things up, laying them down again, gazing vacantly about her.*

as one man [Comp/A (PrepP)] acting unanimously; in unison; precisely alike **S:** group, members, workers; company, club, team; children; they (= men or women). **V:** be; stand, rise, drop, stop, walk out, advance, run, think, feel □ ***As one man****, the Bafut Beagles dropped their spears and fled.* BB □ *There were some differences of opinion about hours of work, but on the need for a rise in pay they were* ***as one man****.* □ (NONCE) *The Company,* ***as one woman****, were stunned by this speech.* WDM □ facetious nonce use in last example; occas variant as one.

as one man etc to another [A] in a way that acknowledges or assumes equality with, or similarity between, oneself and another **n:** man, woman; teenager, parent, old age pensioner; worker, teacher □ *'Evening classes,' he would say, 'are the foundation of social democracy.' She smiled* ***as one intellectual to another****.* ASA □ *The boy was pleased that his uncle had spoken to him* ***as one man to another****, instead of adopting the patronising or authoritative tone he resented in so many of his elders.*

(as) pale as death [Comp (AdjP)] very pale on account of illness, shock, fright etc; (as) white as chalk/a sheet (qv) **V:** ⚠ be, go, turn □ *She suddenly went* ***as pale as death*** *and I thought she was going to faint.* □ *His face* ***pale as death****, and his lips trembling, he stammered out the dreadful news.*

(as) patient as Job [Comp (AdjP)] very patient, tolerant, either in the performance of laborious tasks or in the endurance of pain, provocation, opposition etc **V:** ⚠ be, remain; find sb □ *He's so impossibly long-winded. You need to be* ***as patient as Job*** *to listen to him without making some excuse to leave.*

as per usual [A (AdvP)] (informal) as sb usually or habitually does; as sth usually is or happens; as usual etc (qv) □ *He went back in at the door, and Kathie had finished and poured theirs, and Dusty and Chadwick were hardly able to wait. And they sat down,* ***as per usual****, and Hopalong smiled over.* TT □ *That lazy little monkey has gone to school and left her bed unmade again,* ***as per usual****.* □ facetious, and rather dated.

(as) pissed as a newt [Comp (AdjP)] (taboo) very drunk; (as) drunk as a lord/newt (qv); (as) tight as a tick (qv) **V:** ⚠ be, look, find sb □ *After six whiskies Harry was finding it difficult to stay on his feet. 'You're* ***as pissed as a newt****,' Ted muttered. 'I'd better get you to a taxi.'* ⇨ (as) sober as a judge.

(as) plain as the nose on your face [Comp (AdjP)] obvious (though with the implication that the person addressed may not know it) **S:** it...that he's got measles, it...that she's after your job. **V:** ⚠ be, look □ *'What's the matter with Dave recently? He hardly ever answers when he's spoken to.' 'Good lord—it's* ***as plain as the nose on your face****: he's in love!'*

(as) plain as a pikestaff[1] [Comp (AdjP)] clearly visible; obvious; easy to discern or understand **S:** it; reason, significance, implication(s). **V:** ⚠ be; make sth □ *But there's a big 'Private Road—No Entry' notice* ***as plain as a pikestaff****. You couldn't possibly avoid seeing it.* □ *Ma said of course she got it* (= understood). *It was* ***as plain as a pikestaff****.* BFA

(as) plain as a pikestaff[2] [Comp (AdjP)] plain in appearance; not beautiful or handsome **S:** sister, boyfriend. **V:** ⚠ be, look; find sb □ *Looks are something given to us at birth. I'm not any more to blame for my looks than if I were* ***as plain as a pikestaff****.* WI □ *He's* ***as plain as a pikestaff****, poor boy, and keenly aware of it.* ⇨ (as) pretty as a picture; ⚠ (as) ugly as sin.

(as) pleased etc as anything [Comp (AdjP)] (informal) as pleased etc as it is possible to be **V:** ⚠ be, look, sound. **adj:** happy, pleased; sad, worried; annoyed, surprised; good, bad (ie in behaviour); careful □ *She would be* ***as pleased as anything*** *if you wrote to her.* □ *Keep out of the boss's way if you can—he's* ***as cross as anything*** *this morning.* □ *I knew that Mary was going to give me cigars for Christmas, but I pretended to be* ***as surprised as anything****.* □ *I promise to carry them* ***as carefully as anything****.* □ [A (AdvP)] in last example.

(as) pleased as Punch [Comp (AdjP)] elated or delighted on account of sth; like a dog with two tails (qv) **V:** ⚠ be, look, sound □ *He claims not to care what the critics say, but actually he's* ***as pleased as Punch*** *when one of his books is well received.* □ *'We shall look such fools,' the Commander said. 'They are going to be* ***as pleased as Punch*** *in the Naval Intelligence.'* OMIH □ *You're looking* ***as pleased as Punch*** *this morning. Is there any special reason for it?*

(as) poor as a church mouse [Comp (AdjP)] having, or earning, barely enough money for one's needs **V:** ⚠ be, look; leave sb □ *Miss Pilchester was* ***as poor as a church mouse;*** (her brother) *the Brigadier hadn't had a new suit for twenty years and generally wore socks that didn't match.* BFA □ *Being* ***poor as church mice*** *is all very well when you're young, but Sam is nearly thirty now and ought to be looking for a better job.* □ also pl, as in last example. ⇨ (as) rich as Croesus.

(as) pretty as a picture [Comp (AdjP)] very pretty, pleasing to the eye (but not strikingly beautiful or impressive) **S:** girl, woman; cottage, village. **V:** ⚠ be, look; think sb □ ***Pretty as a picture****, she was. And such a happy child.* PE □ *The tiny cottage with its leaded windows and thatched roof was* ***as pretty as a picture.*** □ *You're looking* ***as pretty as a picture****, Granny, in your nice new blouse—and you've had your hair done too!* ⇨ (as) plain as a pikestaff[2]; (as) ugly as sin.

(as) proud as Lucifer [Comp (AdjP)] very proud, arrogant, independent; never willing to accept advice or help **V:** ⚠ be, become; find sb □ *You can't help people who won't admit they need help. He's* ***as proud as Lucifer*** *and would rather starve than take a penny from anyone.* □ *Even if he knows now that he was wrong to quarrel with his son, he's* ***proud as Lucifer*** *and could never unbend enough to try to patch things up again.* □ rather rare.

(as) proud as a peacock [Comp (AdjP)] self-important; openly pleased and proud (of, or on account of, sth); (as) vain as a peacock (qv) **V:** ⚠ be, become; find sb □ *Just look at him strutting about in his Mayoral robes,* ***proud as a peacock!*** □ *When I finally secured a small part in a television play my mother was* ***as proud as a peacock*** *and told all the neighbours about it.*

(as) pure as the driven snow [Comp (AdjP)] innocent; chaste **S:** girl; motives, thoughts. **V:** ⚠ be, look; think sb □ *My relations with Mrs Aisgill are* ***pure as the driven snow.*** RATT □ *I've tried to tell him what kind of a girl she is, but he's convinced that she's* ***purer than the driven snow.***

(as) quick as lightning etc [Comp/A (AdjP)] very swift, sudden or deft **V:** be; answer. **o:** lightning, ⚠ thought, a flash □ *I didn't mean to let the dog out, but he shot past me,* ***as quick as lightning****, when I opened the door to the postman.* □ *He's the best left wing we've ever had in the team,* ***quick as lightning*** *and with excellent anticipation.* □ *'What other moral problem is there in this age?' 'Being loyal to one's friends and behaving properly to women,' I answered* ***quick as a flash.*** UTN □ ***Quick as thought****, she pulled the child out of harm's way, and the lorry crashed into the very spot where he had been standing.* □ used to describe movement, action etc; [A (AdvP)] in last two examples.

(as) quiet/silent as the grave/tomb [Comp (AdjP)] (sth is) very still, noiseless; (sb is) (esp with silent) not speaking, or not disclosing some particular information **V:** ⚠ be, seem; find sth/sb □ *It's only on the surface, you know. Underneath all is* ***quiet as the grave****. Not a sound.* E □ *I do miss the children. The house seems* ***as silent as the tomb*** *without them.*

(as) quiet as a mouse [Comp (AdjP)] quiet and self-effacing by nature; specially quiet for a purpose **V:** ⚠ be, keep □ *'I didn't hear you drive up. How long have you been in?' 'Got him to drop me at the corner.* ***Quiet as a mouse*** *coming in.'* TGLY □ *Bob's sister seems rather shy,* ***as quiet as a mouse****. I only saw her when she was serving drinks.* □ used to describe people.

(as) red as a turkey-cock [Comp (AdjP)] flushed with anger or embarrassment (from a turkey-cock's comb and wattles, which become more conspicuously red when it is excited or angered) **V:** ⚠ be, grow, turn, go; flush □ *The Sergeant-Major, his face* ***as red as a turkey-cock****, was abusing the squad at the top of his voice.* □ *I felt myself turning* ***as red as a turkey-cock*** *when the teacher praised my essay and read it to the class.* □ cf one's face is as red as fire, one's cheeks are on fire, which usu refer only to feelings of shame or embarrassment.

(as) regular as clockwork [Comp (AdjP)] occurring at set times in a way that can be depended upon **V:** ⚠ be; find sb □ *The landlady was sent out for a two-hour walk with the dog, no matter what the weather; whereupon the niece and the respectable-looking middle-aged man promptly went upstairs. 'He's* ***as regular as clockwork****,' Myrtle whispered.* SPL □ *She told the doctor that she always woke up feeling fine; but just around eleven,* ***as regular as clockwork****, this dreadful headache started.* □ *Every single tea-break she says, 'For this relief, much thanks.' Ten times a week,* ***as regular as clockwork****! It gets on your nerves.* □ [A (AdvP)] in last two examples; variant with clockwork regularity.

(as) rich as Croesus [Comp (AdjP)] very wealthy (from the name of a king of Lydia in ancient times) **V:** ⚠ be, become, grow □ *'From what he says,' Cosmo observed, 'our friend Querini is* ***as rich as Croesus****, but dependent upon his father.'* US □ *Royde wants to charter a yacht to hunt this monster and I thought it was a deal right up your street. You don't want to soak* (= grossly overcharge) *him, because although he's* ***as rich as Croesus*** *he hates being soaked. Charge him the top price you'd charge anybody else.* RM ⇨ (as) poor as a church mouse.

(as) right as rain [Comp (AdjP)] in good health, or in one's normal state of health; quite satisfactory; as it should be **S:** he, she, they, we; everything. **V:** ⚠ be, look, feel □ *All you want is rest and fresh air and good food and you'll be* ***as right as rain.*** DBM □ *'Her headaches are not as bad as that,' said Harold. 'Tomorrow she'll be* ***as right as rain****.' '****As right as rain****?' said Irma doubtfully. 'It's a thing we say in England,' said Harold in a rather lofty manner.* PW □ *Cheer up, your wife will be back in a week or two and everything will be* ***right as rain*** *again.*

(as) right as a trivet [Comp (AdjP)] in good health; properly adjusted or repaired; in good working order **V:** ⚠ be, look, feel □ *A month or* *so in plaster and then a little massage and therapy, and we'll have your ankle and you* ***as right as a trivet****.* ▫ *'****Right as a trivet*** *now,' said the mechanic as he crawled out from under the car. 'I've replaced your silencer.'*

as a rule [A (PreP)] almost always, but not invariably; the general rule (qv) ▫ *He frequently changed his address and had all his mail sent to a post-office box;* ***as a rule****, it was picked up and brought to him by a messenger.* TO ▫ *It's lucky for you I'm still up. I'm in bed by eleven o'clock* ***as a rule****.* ▫ *We don't* ***as a rule*** *give credit to customers, but are willing to make an exception in your case.* ▫ front, middle or end position; expression refers to custom, habit, or likelihood; compulsory or rigid rules of behaviour or action are better described as carried out *according to rule*.

(as) safe as houses [Comp (AdjP)] secure; not dangerous; not likely to be a cause of mishap or loss **S:** bridge, path; investment; it. **V:** ⚠ be, feel, look, seem ▫ *With Susan here we feel* ***as safe as houses****. The children dote on her.* PW ▫ *'Do you think that wooden bridge will take our weight?' 'Of course—it's* ***safe as houses****; the farmer takes his cows over it every morning.'* ▫ *He wasn't the type to take risks in hope of a quick profit; anything his money was invested in was sure to be* ***as safe as houses****.*

(as) sharp as a needle [Comp (AdjP)] quick-witted; having plenty of perception **V:** ⚠ be, become; find sb ▫ *One doesn't need to be* ***as sharp as a needle*** *to see that* that *story doesn't fit the facts.* ▫ *Young though he was, the child was* ***as sharp as a needle*** *and sensed the disharmony between his parents in spite of the fact that they never quarrelled in front of him.*

(as) sick as a dog [Comp (AdjP)] vomiting a great deal; (fig) deeply concerned or depressed (often because of a lost opportunity) **V:** ⚠ be, feel ▫ *I had felt some nausea all day and went to bed early, but I was up three times in the night,* ***as sick as a dog****.* ▫ *I saw an ad in the paper for just the car I'm looking for. I was* ***sick as a dog*** *when they told me it had just been sold.*

(as) smooth as a baby's bottom [Comp (AdjP)] (informal) soft and smooth to the touch, or in appearance **S:** skin, hands; fabric; wood. **V:** ⚠ be, feel ▫ *'I'm getting flabby lying here in bed,' he grumbled, 'and look at my hands —* ***smooth as a baby's bottom****. What kind of hands are these for a working man to have?'*

(as) smooth as a billiard-ball/pebble [Comp (AdjP)] very smooth **S:** head; porcelain; surface. **V:** ⚠ be, feel ▫ *I walked slowly round the tree, searching the trunk for any foot- or handholds on the bark which would enable Peter to climb to the top, but the bark was* ***as smooth as a billiard ball****.* BB ▫ *'Perhaps one side comes away,' I said. But there was no sign of any special fastening. The whole thing was* ***as smooth as a pebble****.* UTN ▫ *There are bald heads in plenty to be seen, but his was uncommon in that it was* ***as smooth*** *and round* ***as a billiard-ball****, all over.* ▫ used esp of curved or rounded surfaces. ⇨ ⚠ next entry.

(as) smooth as a billiard-table/glass [Comp (AdjP)] very smooth **S:** lawn, field, road, floor. **V:** ⚠ be, look, feel ▫ *It can take years of careful cutting and rolling to get a lawn* ***as smooth as a billiard-table****.* ▫ *The road was* ***smooth as glass*** *and the tyres didn't grip at all once I started to skid.* ▫ used esp of flat surfaces. ⇨ ⚠ previous entry.

(as) smooth as a mill-pond [Comp (AdjP)] very smooth and calm **S:** sea, water, lake. **V:** ⚠ be, look ▫ *When we set out from the harbour, the sea was* ***as smooth as a mill-pond****, but within half an hour the waves were a metre high.*

(as) smooth as velvet [Comp (AdjP)] soft to the touch, ear or taste, or in appearance **S:** cloth, material; skin; tone, voice; brandy. **V:** ⚠ be, feel, sound, taste ▫ *I don't like that woman. She's always making sarcastic remarks in a tone* ***as smooth as velvet****.* ▫ *You'd better be careful with that malt whisky. It goes down* ***as smooth as velvet****, but it's very potent.* ▫ *Try our* ***velvet-smooth*** *plum brandy!* ▫ [A (AdjP)] in second example; adj compound velvet-smooth.

(as) snug as a bug in a rug [Comp (AdjP)] very comfortable **V:** ⚠ be, feel, look ▫ *I must dry some seaweed and line this crevice. I could be* ***as snug as a bug in a rug****.* PM ▫ *Warmth, to be '****as snug as a bug in a rug****', is of the first importance.* UL ▫ *There's a nice little pension and a cottage on the estate coming to him when he retires. He'll be* ***snugger than a bug in a rug*** *there.*

(as) sober as a judge [Comp (AdjP)] not at all drunk; serious; solemn; not in high spirits **V:** ⚠ be, look, sound ▫ HELEN: *You're drunk.* PETER: *I'm* ***sober as a judge****.* TOH ▫ *It's ironic, when you think of how often he could have been picked up by the police for drunken driving, that he should have met with his first accident when he was* ***as sober as a judge****.* ▫ *They're an odd pair of friends, Sylvia always bubbling over with nonsense and Polly* ***as sober as a judge****.* ⇨ (as) drunk as a lord/newt; (as) pissed as a newt; (as) tight as a tick.

(as) solemn as an owl [Comp (AdjP)] very serious, solemn, earnest etc **S:** expression, face; he, she, you. **V:** ⚠ be, look, appear; find sb ▫ *He felt more like laughing at the child's escapade than scolding him, but,* ***solemn as an owl****, he got through the necessary reprimand.* ▫ *'But I'm serious underneath it all, you see.' 'Yes, you look it.* ***Solemn as an owl****, that's you.' 'I didn't say that, I said serious. I mean every word I say.'* TGLY ▫ often used jokingly or teasingly. ⇨ ⚠ (as) wise as an owl.

as soon as look at sb [A (AdvP)] very readily ▫ *If he starts any of his nonsense with my daughters, boss's son or no boss's son, I'll kick him out of the house* ***as soon as look at*** *him.* ▫ *'I'll not deceive you, Mrs Brown,' the officer said. 'The girl is a good worker but if you were to leave money or valuables lying about she'd steal them* ***as soon as look at*** *you.'* ▫ used to express readiness to take action about, or in defiance of, sb/sth; often preceded by a clause containing future or conditional v.

(as) sound as a bell [Comp (AdjP)] in good condition physically **S:** heart, lungs; engine, motor; he, you, it. **V:** ⚠ be, feel, remain ▫ *Thirty-nine today,* ***sound as a bell****, apart from my old weakness.* KLT ▫ *'Well, you have nothing to worry about,' said the doctor after concluding his examination. 'Heart and lungs* ***as sound as a bell****.'* ▫ used in sing, even with pl.

(as) sour as vinegar/a crab [Comp (AdjP)] very sour in taste; (fig) very bad-tempered, sharp-tongued, unfriendly **S:** wine; fruit; he, she, you, they. **V:** ⚠ be, sound; find sth/sb □ *Don't eat those oranges yet—they're not ripe and* ***as sour as vinegar***. □ *What's the matter with old Mrs Botley? She used to be so cheerful and friendly. Now whenever I pass her in the street all I get is a look* ***as sour as a crab***. □ expression with vinegar used only in literal sense. ➪ (as) sweet as honey.

as the spirit takes/moves one [A] according to one's inclination or eagerness (to do sth) and at a time or times of one's choice **V:** work, speak, write. **conj:** as, when, if □ *They* (= beings from outer space) *ambled* ***as the spirit took them****, through shops and banks and offices and homes, without a care for the raging occupants.* TST □ *'Doesn't your husband work in the garden at all?' 'Oh yes, he does sometimes, but only* ***when the spirit moves him****.'* □ *Asked if he set himself daily periods of work, Ian said that he knew many novelists who did, but he himself preferred to write* ***as the spirit took him***.

(as) steady as a rock [Comp (AdjP)] firm; reliable; (fig) loyal **S:** stepping-stone, ladder; he, she, they. **V:** ⚠ be, feel, look □ *'Is that stile safe?'* ***'Steady as a rock****. You couldn't make it wobble if you tried.'* □ *He would be a good chap to have around one in an emergency, I thought —* ***as steady as a rock****. He'd never get into a flap.* □ *Some of the tribes had changed loyalties several times, but the Warani had remained* ***steady as a rock*** *in their allegiance to their old allies.* ➪ as changeable as a weathercock.

(as) stiff as a poker [Comp (AdjP)] rigid in posture, carriage, or manner **V:** ⚠ be, keep, stand □ *The old lady was sitting upright in her chair,* ***stiff as a poker****, unlike the younger members of her family.* □ *I think he feels quite friendly towards people, but he's* ***as stiff as a poker*** *in company—can't relax at all.* □ adj compound poker-stiff.

(as) stiff/straight as a ramrod [Comp (AdjP)] rigid in posture or carriage **S:** back; he, she, they. **V:** ⚠ be, keep, stand □ *She sat there on the edge of her chair, her back* ***as stiff as a ramrod*** *the whole evening.* □ *The captured general maintained his dignity to the end, walking* ***ramrod-straight*** *to his execution.* □ adj compound ramrod-stiff/-straight.

(as) still as death [Comp (AdjP)] without sound or movement **S:** everything; place; night; he, she, they. **V:** ⚠ be, keep, go, stand □ *Just before the thunder broke, everything suddenly went* ***as still as death****; not a leaf rustled, not a bird sang.* □ *I never knew such a sound sleeper! Once his head touches the pillow, he just lies there* ***as still as death*** *till he's wakened.*

(as) still as the grave [Comp (AdjP)] without sound or movement **S:** everything; place. **V:** ⚠ be, remain, lie □ *There's no use peering through the letter-box. The place is* ***as still as the grave****. They must have forgotten we were coming.*

(as) still as a statue [Comp (AdjP)] not moving, or speaking, esp for a particular reason or purpose **V:** ⚠ be, keep, stand □ *When I was at school, if the headmaster came into the room, we all had to rise and stand* ***as still as statues*** *until he left.* □ *If you both creep down to the reeds and then keep* ***still as statues****, maybe the moorhen will come back with her chicks and you can see them close up.*

(as) straight as an arrow [Comp/A (Adv/AdjP)] in a straight line, path, or direction **S:** line, path, road, route. **V:** be; go, run, drive, fly, throw □ *You won't get lost if you keep to the track. It's* ***as straight as an arrow*** *and goes right through the middle of the wood to the other side.* □ *She has a mind that flies* ***straight as an arrow*** *to the crux of any problem.* □ *He drove the car* ***as straight as an arrow*** *along the line that had been made in the sand.*

(as) straight as a die [Comp/A (Adv/AdjP)] in a straight line, path, or direction; (fig) honest; not ambiguous **S:** line, path, road, route; he, she, you, they. **V:** be; go, run, drive, fly, throw □ *A flagged path has to be laid* ***straight as a die*** *to look well; a stretch of crazy paving is easier for an amateur to manage.* □ *'Well Barrett,' said Mr Collins, 'what do you know about this?' The boy looked round at their faces, and then at Mr Collins. 'Nothing, Sir,' he said,* ***straight as a die****. 'Would you tell me if you did?' said Mr Collins. 'No, Sir,' he said.* TT □ *If there's any fiddling of the books going on in this office, it must be one of the new people. Jenkins has been with me eighteen years and I know he's* ***as straight as a die*** *in everything.*

(as) strong as a horse/an ox [Comp (AdjP)] having great muscular strength; able to do heavy physical work **V:** ⚠ be, become; make sb □ *Physically she had always been broad-shouldered and athletic, and lugging loaded drums and belts and canisters of ammunition about all day made her* ***as strong as a horse***. RFW □ *'She's* ***as strong as a horse****. Got my constitution!' He never would admit that Jenny was in anything but the rudest of health.* AITC □ HARRY: *I can't move my left hand very well. Lost its grip or something....* RONNIE (gripping Harry's hand in a shake): ***Strong as an ox****. You're a sham, Harry boy.* CSWB □ strong as an ox generally used of men only. ➪ (as) weak as water[1].

as such[1] considered alone; not including anything that is, or may be, associated with sb/sth □ *Another condition which exerts a profound influence on learning* ***as such*** *is that of being motivated. Without an intention to learn, little worthwhile learning occurs.* MFF □ *She had nothing against public houses* ***as such***. PW □ *Such intellectual work as I have ever accomplished has always left me with a sense of having achieved nothing; but whether this is because of the nature of intellectual work* ***as such****, or whether it is because I am no good, I have never been able to decide.* UTN □ modifies a preceding n.

as such[2] [A (PrepP)] in that particular capacity, manner, form, or function □ *Headquarters 21 Army Group had been formed out of G.H.Q. Home Forces and* ***as such*** *had been in existence for nearly four years.* MFM □ *It was odd how Harold proved himself a past-master of intrigue. Yet intrigue was only his instrument: he didn't think of it* ***as such****, he thought of it as the means whereby he could...* PW □ *The word 'artist', up there, has a special meaning. It means someone who works in one of the pottery factories putting the designs on crocks.* ***As such****, they get sacked* *just as easily as anybody else when times are bad.* CON

(as) sure as death etc [Comp/A (AdjP)] certain to happen; inevitable; absolutely predictable **V:** be; happen, fall apart. **n:** death, ⚠ fate, (informal) hell □ *With all these clouds gathering it's* ***as sure as death*** *to rain before morning.* RM □ *You'll be found out,* ***sure as fate****, if you try a silly piece of trickery like that.* □ *A retribution* ***sure as fate*** *will overtake him for his evil deeds.*

(as) sure as eggs is eggs [Disj (AdjP)] (informal) quite certainly □ *If there's another gale like the one we had last week, we'll lose a lot more trees,* ***sure as eggs is eggs****.* □ *If he goes on driving like that,* ***as sure as eggs is eggs*** *he'll end up in hospital.* □ front or end position; strictly ungrammatical but used jocularly by educated speakers.

(as) sure/true as I'm sitting/standing here [Disj (AdjP)] without any doubt (said esp of the certainty, or truth, of sth which has already occurred or is predicted) □ *You might think she could never have been so unkind, but these were her exact words to me,* ***as true as I'm sitting here****.* □ *If you don't clean your room this morning, you're not going to the youth club,* ***as sure as I'm standing here****.* □ variant as sure/true as you're sitting/standing there.

(as) sure as (God made) little apples [Disj (AdjP)] (informal) quite certainly □ *'I seem to remember reading somewhere recently about the influx of new blood into the Profession.' '"The Schoolmaster",' said Charles, '****sure as little apples****.'* TT □ *If they appoint Smithson manager there'll be trouble with the staff* ***as sure as God made little apples****.* □ front or end position.

(as) sweet as honey [Comp (AdjP)] very sweet in taste; (fig) very pleasant in speech, behaviour etc (often with the implication of insincerity) **S:** peach; coffee; he, she, they; words. **V:** ⚠ be, sound, become □ *I can't drink this tea. It's* ***as sweet as honey****.* □ *Grow these* ***honey-sweet*** *melons in your own garden!* □ *She's the kind of woman who'll be* ***sweet as honey*** *to your face and as malicious as hell behind your back.* □ *If you don't like the Browns then don't visit them. If you go on being* ***sweeter than honey*** *every time they telephone, of course they'll keep inviting you.* □ adj compound honey-sweet. ⇨ (as) sour as vinegar/a crab.

(as) thick as thieves [Comp (AdjP)] spending much time in each other's company and having common interests **V:** ⚠ be, become, remain □ JO: *What were you talking about to that old mare downstairs?* GEOFF: *I was giving her the rent. I got my grant yesterday.* JO: *You're* ***as thick as thieves****, you two.* TOH □ *I never came across such a closely-knit family before. They're* ***as thick as thieves****, down to the last second cousin.*

(as) thick as two short planks [Comp (AdjP)] (informal) very stupid **V:** ⚠ be, seem □ *It's hopeless trying to explain anything to him —he'll never understand it, he's* ***as thick as two short planks****.* ⇨ as clever/smart as paint.

(as) thin as a rake/lath [Comp (AdjP)] very thin **S:** he, she, you, they; body, frame. **V:** ⚠ be, look, become □ *He was* ***as thin as a rake*** *in spite of his enormous appetite.* □ *I was shocked at his appearance—so grey-faced, and* ***thin as a lath****. He used to be such a powerful-looking fellow.* □ ⇨ as fat as butter/a young thrush; as fat as a pig.

as things stand/stood [Disj] in view of, or taking into consideration, a certain set of circumstances or some particular situation □ *I doubt if a Tory government could act any differently* ***as things stand****, whatever they might wish.* HAA □ *It would have been nice to have visited all these interesting places when we were younger. But* ***as things stood*** *then, there was no chance of it.* □ ***As things stand*** *with me at the moment, I simply can't find time for voluntary work.* □ front, middle or end position.

(as) tight as a tick [Comp (AdjP)] (informal) very drunk; (as) drunk as a lord/newt (qv); (as) pissed as a newt (qv) **V:** ⚠ be, become, sound □ *You'd better keep an eye on Barbara—she's fast becoming* ***as tight as a tick****, and when she gets like that* anything *can happen.* ⇨ (as) sober as a judge.

(as) timid as a mouse etc [Comp (AdjP)] timid to the point of fear of other people; very shy; lacking in courage **S:** he, she, they. **V:** ⚠ be, look; find sb. **n:** mouse, ⚠ rabbit, hare □ *It's no use expecting Arthur to stand up for himself: he's* ***as timid as a mouse****. Somebody else will have to protect his interests.* ⇨ (as) bold/brave as a lion.

(as) touchy etc as hell [Comp (AdjP)] (informal) very over-sensitive etc **V:** ⚠ be, seem; find sb. **adj:** touchy, bad-tempered, angry, grumpy; mean, stingy; tight, uncomfortable □ *In the water they* (= floating mines) *seem to be safe unless they are borne down by a ship. But out of water, on a solid foundation, they are* ***as touchy as hell****.* ARG □ *These new shoes of mine are* ***as tight as hell****. I wonder if I could have them stretched?* □ adj usu conveys strong neg feelings on part of speaker.

(as) tough as leather/an old boot [Comp (AdjP)] very difficult to chew and swallow; physically hardy; able to withstand abuse, criticism etc **S:** meat; he, she, you, they. **V:** ⚠ be, seem; find sth/sb □ *I wish I'd asked for chicken salad. This steak is* ***as tough as leather****.* □ *Dave is not a nervous wreck, but* ***as tough as an old boot****.* UTN □ *'The professor's plans for reorganizing the department didn't meet with much approval, poor man.' 'Don't waste your sympathy. He's* ***tough as old boots****; he won't let their remarks hurt him.'* □ also pl as tough as old boots.

(as) true as steel [Comp (AdjP)] very loyal, dependable **V:** ⚠ be; find sb □ *The captain said he would rather attempt the relief of the fort with twenty men he knew to be* ***as true as steel*** *than with a hundred of their ally's mercenaries.* □ *I have asked a great deal of my wife in the way of hardships and sacrifice in order to further my ambitions, but she has been* ***as true as steel*** *to me throughout and has never complained.*

(as) ugly as sin [Comp (AdjP)] exceptionally ugly **V:** ⚠ be; find sb/sth □ *The house stands by a river in a very beautiful place, though the house itself is* ***as ugly as sin****—rather like a Scotch castle gone wrong.* RFW □ ***Ugly as sin*** *themselves, the two stepsisters hated Cinderella for her beauty.* ⇨ (as) pretty as a picture; ⚠ (as) plain as a pikestaff[2].

as usual etc [A (AdvP)] as sb usually, or

habitually, acts; as sth usually is, or happens; in a way that is expected, because it has happened often before; as per usual (qv) **adv:** usual, ⚠ ever, always ◻ ***As always***, *John is only interested in how to turn the situation to his own advantage.* ◻ ***As ever***, *the train got in just too late for me to catch the early bus.* ◻ *Complete accord,* ***as usual***, *is reported by the Western Foreign Ministers, whose meeting in Washington was part of the extensive preparations for next month's summit conference.* SC ◻ *It was difficult for him to appreciate, in his pain and distress, that not only in other homes, but in his own also, life must go on* ***as usual***.

(as) vain as a peacock [Comp (AdjP)] very vain; (as) proud as a peacock (qv) **V:** ⚠ be, seem; find sb ◻ *His wife was a much less pleasant person than he was, over-dressed and* ***as vain as a peacock***. ◻ *peahen* not used with reference to women.

(as) warm as toast [Comp (AdjP)] comfortably warm **S:** room, house; it; he, she, they. **V:** ⚠ be, feel; find sth ◻ *'Yes, let's all sit down,' said Isabel, 'if Daddy's thoroughly thawed out.' 'Oh, I'm* ***as warm as toast***,*' said Harold.* PW ◻ *'You should be wearing gloves in this weather.' 'I never need them. Feel my fingers—they're* ***warm as toast***.*'* ◻ *The central heating is off, I'm afraid, but come into the kitchen. It's* ***as warm as toast*** *in here with the oven on.*

as we have seen [Disj] as has already been shown, demonstrated or proved ◻ ***As we have seen***, *the earthquakes in the world are confined to fairly definite zones, and it is only in these regions that severe damage will be done.* NS ◻ *If,* ***as we have seen***, *conducted water will not naturally rise above the level of its own source, what methods do we use to enable the occupant of a dwelling above that level to turn on his bath water?* ◻ pron we is essential part of expression.

(as) weak as water[1] [Comp (AdjP)] very weak **S:** beer; arms, legs; he, she, they. **V:** ⚠ be, feel, taste ◻ *The doctor told me the infection had completely cleared up, but not to feel surprised if I felt* ***as weak as water*** *for the next month or so.* ◻ *Well if you can't drink whisky, have a glass of this beer. It's* ***as weak as water***: *even a child could drink it.* ◻ also, esp of tea, as weak as/like dish-water; also, with reference to people, as weak as a kitten. ⇨ (as) strong as a horse/an ox.

(as) weak as water[2] [Comp (AdjP)] (fig) very weak; inadequate; deficient **S:** character, personality; he, she, they; argument, case. **V:** ⚠ be, prove ◻ *He would have worked for his exams all May and June if his friends had left him alone. Unfortunately they didn't, and he's* ***as weak as water*** *when it comes to saying no to a friend.* ◻ *The staff didn't want the proposed changes in office routine, but the arguments they tried to put forward against them were* ***as weak as water***.

(as) welcome as (the) flowers in May/spring [Comp (AdjP)] very welcome **S:** friend, guest, visitor; he, you, she, they; money, cheque, wage-rise. **V:** ⚠ be; find sb/sth ◻ *The small legacy was* ***as welcome as flowers in spring***, *coming just when they were faced with an enormous bill for dry-rot repairs.*

as well (as sb/sth) [Conj] too; also; in conjunction with sb/sth specified; in addition (to sth) (qv); over and above (qv) ◻ *'I thought you said you wanted fruit-juice?' 'So I do, but I want soup* ***as well***.*'* ◻ *When we asked them to stay for the weekend we didn't realise they would be bringing a couple of dogs* ***as well***. ◻ *He had to carry a light sleeping-bag and ground sheet* ***as well as*** *a blanket.* ARG ◻ *The attitudes of the US and Russia seem to have been determined by their desire to avoid conflict* ***as well as*** *by their reluctance to offend France.* SC ◻ *The modernisation of the transport system could prove a rich investment in Highland recovery, lowering freight costs for the inhabitants,* ***as well as*** *providing easier access for visitors.* SC ◻ ***As well as*** *being a terrible gossip, I think she actually tells lies too.* ◻ as well occurs almost always in end position, as well as occurs almost always in middle position, though it can occur in front position.

(just) as well (that) [Comp (AdjP)] fortunate, more convenient, etc (that) **S:** it. . .that I'd come prepared; that; your arrival. **V:** ⚠ be; prove; turn out ◻ *Perhaps, on thinking back, it is* ***as well*** *I had no idea that ahead of me lay the most dramatic and frightening years of my life.* TO ◻ *It was* ***just as well*** *I had taken my umbrella with me, though the weather had looked settled enough when I set out.* ◻ *Actually, I have very little food in the house, so it's* ***just as well that*** *you're not hungry.* ◻ *He hadn't come in his car, which was* ***just as well***, *Jane thought, since he'd be forced to catch the last bus home instead of keeping them all up half the night.* ◻ *'Poor old granny, she has no idea how ill she is.'* ***'Just as well***, *surely,' the nurse said gently.* ◻ can be used (always with just) without following *that*-clause as end comment to sth already specified or described.

as well etc as the next man/person [A (AdvP)] in a way that is equally as good as the way other people do it (often with the implication that it is even better) **V:** speak, write, do (a job); play (music, cricket etc). **adj:** well, clearly, carefully, honestly; (no/not any) better/worse (than) ◻ *I can drive a car* ***as well as the next man***, *let me tell you!* ◻ *She said that normally she could bear pain* ***as patiently as the next person***, *but that this particular attack was as much as she could endure.*

as well sb may/might (do) as may, or might, be expected of sb in the circumstances mentioned ◻ *Our passenger gave no signs of nerves or apprehensiveness,* ***as well*** *she* ***might have done***. BM ◻ *'Peter is feeling very miserable and ashamed of himself.'* ***'As well*** *he* ***may***, *after all the trouble he has caused!'* ◻ stress pattern as ˌwell sb ˈmay/ˈmight (do); usu functions as emphatic comment on some previous statement.

as well do sth (as do sth else) (ironic) it is just as unreasonable, unprofitable to do sth (as it is to do sth else) ◻ ***As well*** *get Maureen to help you* ***as*** *get a cat to help a rat—she's as lazy and as selfish as a pig.* ◻ *'Do you think there'll ever be an International agreement to ban nuclear arms?'* ***'As well*** *expect the two great powers to set up a joint World Peace Fund!'* ⇨ ⚠ it/that is just as well; may/might (just) as well do sth.

as and when [conj + conj non-rev] used to indicate both the manner and time of doing sth (esp in semi-official jargon, when either as or when would be enough and preferable) ◻ *Until* *he recovers, Mrs Jones, just let your little boy eat* ***as and when*** *he likes.* □ *A small committee will be constituted whose sole duty will be to deal with applications for relief* ***as and when*** *they arise.*

(as) white as chalk/a sheet [Comp (AdjP)] very pale in appearance as a result of illness, fear, shock etc; (as) pale as death (qv) **S:** he, she, you, they; face, hands, complexion. **V:** ⚠ be, go, turn □ *I've never seen anyone looking as ill as Geoffrey. His face was* ***as white as chalk*** *when he arrived home from work this evening.* □ *No wonder some bridegrooms looked* ***as white as a sheet*** *on their wedding-day.* SML □ *It was dreadful to see him lying there* ***white as a sheet*** *and in such pain.* □ *Mary has just come in with a face* ***as white as a sheet*** *to say there's been an accident at the corner of the lane.*

(as) white as snow [Comp (AdjP)] very white **S:** cloud; blossom, petal; hair, beard; dress, sheet. **V:** ⚠ be, go, turn □ *The sheets were rough but* ***as white as snow.*** □ *I scarcely knew him when we met again. His hair had gone* ***as white as snow.*** □ *The ground was* ***as white as snow*** *with petals that had drifted down from the apple trees.* □ adj compound snow-white.

as a whole considered with reference to all its parts; at large (qv) □ *For the populace* ***as a whole*** *the sound advice would appear to be the old, old one—moderation in all things, including animal fats.* T □ *It is, however, in the interests of Scotland* ***as a whole*** *that our economy should be better balanced and that the volume of employment should be increased.* SC □ *These molecules begin to appear when the local gas density is 100 times greater than that of the cloud* ***as a whole.*** NS □ modifies a preceding n. ⇨ ⚠ on the whole.

(as) wise as an owl [Comp (AdjP)] (ironic) very wise **V:** ⚠ be, look, seem □ *The child picked up the spectacles and put them on. 'Now you look* ***as wise as an owl,*** *' said his father affectionately.* □ *Although the technical details of the drainage scheme were far beyond their grasp, the City Councillors sat looking* ***as wise as owls,*** *every now and then nodding their heads as if in acknowledgement of a point taken.* ⇨ ⚠ (as) solemn as an owl.

(as) wise as Solomon [Comp (AdjP)] very wise (in the sense of having good judgement rather than much learning or knowledge) **V:** ⚠ be, become, prove □ *In some of the divorce cases you read about nowadays, one would need to be* ***as wise as Solomon*** *to know which party was the more at fault.* □ *He made the wrong choice of career, we now know; but he couldn't have known it then, not if he had been* ***wiser than Solomon.*** □ variant need/display the wisdom of Solomon.

(as) yellow as a guinea [Comp (AdjP)] clearly yellow in colour (because affected by illness or climatic conditions) **S:** skin; he, she, they. **V:** ⚠ be, turn, go □ *I say, it's high time you got a tonic, you're* ***as yellow as a guinea.*** US □ *He used to be a fine fresh-looking fellow, but after fifteen years of West Africa he came home* ***yellow as a guinea*** *and thin as a match-stick.*

as yet [A] up to the present time, or time of speaking, or point reached in a narrative; so far (qv) □ *From this sketchy outline it will be apparent that,* ***as yet,*** *we know very little indeed about the fundamental mechanisms of virus infection.* NS □ ***As yet*** *he had consumed but a pint and a half and was still rational.* BM □ *The only conclusion the unbiased observer can come to must be that there does exist a small number of people who obtain knowledge by means* ***as yet*** *unknown to science.* SNP □ always used negatively or depreciatingly; cf ***As yet*** *we have had no/very few applications* with *Already/to date/up to now, we have had over a hundred applications,* and *He had shown no/little interest in music* ***as yet*** with *Already/by this time he was keenly interested in music*; esp before past participles used as adj eg ***as yet*** *unknown/untried/unprepared etc.*

as you were (catchphrase) return to your former position (from a command used originally in drilling soldiers); (fig) cancel any instruction, whether given by mistake or not □ *Robin mumbled now. He would have given anything to be a small boy once more who, by saying 'I take back what I said' or '****As you were****', could erase a whole conversation.* ASA □ *'I used to look forward to the time when my children would marry and leave home. Now I have three grandchildren to look after nine months of the year.' '****As you were****, in fact!' 'That's right!'* □ also used in everyday situations where speaker wishes to correct something he has said, or to suggest that a present situation is very similar to an earlier one.

ask me another (catchphrase) in quiz games signifies that the contestant has answered successfully so far and is asking for a harder question in order to increase his score; means in ordinary conversation 'I don't know,' 'Who can tell?' □ *'Isn't Tom thinking of getting married?' '****Ask me another.*** *He's had two or three different girl friends recently.'* □ *'Well, David has got his orders from the doctor, but will he keep to them?' 'You can* ***ask me another****, but it's a poor look-out for him if he doesn't.'* □ always used as response to direct question.

assault and battery [n + n non-rev] (legal) wilful physical damage to a person, whether this is slight or serious □ *We retreated into the streets of Rome* (ie a filmset mock-up)*, which were already invaded by a small number of combatants who were, however, more concerned with mutual* ***assault and battery*** *than with the possibility of escape.* UTN □ *That's ridiculous! He can't bring a charge of* ***assault and battery*** *for one slight poke in the ribs!*

at all [A (AdvP)] in any way; to some degree □ *Were you* ***at all*** *surprised to hear that Sarah had decided to become a nun?* □ *If you're* ***at all*** *worried, get in touch with me immediately.* □ *Will you be visiting Venice* ***at all*** *when you go abroad next summer?*

at all costs [A (PrepP)] regardless of effort, trouble, expense, concessions etc; whatever else one/sb does □ *The Germans will fight hard to keep us from the Ruhr, and to keep the war static.* ***At all costs*** *they must stop the war from becoming mobile.* MFM □ *But in so far as we are animals, our business is* ***at all costs*** *to survive.* DOP □ *The Right and Left Wings of the Labour Party are now united by little more than the leaders' desire to avoid a split* ***at all costs.*** □ front, middle or end position; frequently used with *must* and expressions of obligation; stress pattern at 'all costs.

at all events [Conj (PrepP)] however that may be; in any case; whatever (else) happens □ *Neither Parsons nor old Watley could—perhaps I should say* would*—give anything like a precise account of what Robert had said.* ***At all events****, it must have been quite an oration.* CON □ *Certainly—or should the affirmative reply to that question be certainly not?* ***At all events****, I will come with you immediately.* EM □ front, middle or end position; stress pattern at 'all events.

at all hours (of the day/night) [A (PrepP)] at any time during the day/night (esp with the implication that this is an unsuitable time) □ *It's bad enough having her come back from the club* ***at all hours*** *without sitting up after she gets home.* PE □ *The main entrance was open all night, but very brightly lit, as I knew from having passed it by* ***at all hours*** *when going to Dave's flat.* UTN □ *Why, my sister, she couldn't bear to hear a door creak. Her husband had to go round with an oil-can* ***at all hours of the night****.* AITC □ *I used to go dancing* ***till all hours****, but I really need a good night's sleep now—I must be getting old!* □ stress pattern at 'all hours (of the day/night); variant till all hours (of the night).

at all times [A (PrepP)] always; on all occasions **adj:** polite, obliging, friendly; impartial, neutral; vigilant, ready, prepared □ *Don't strike back or curse back if abused; show yourself friendly and courteous* ***at all times****; sit straight and always face the counter.* OBS □ *He was the best kind of teacher, firm yet relaxed, exacting yet ready with encouragement and* ***at all times*** *strictly impartial with his favours.* □ front, middle or end position; stress pattern at 'all times.

at any moment [A (PrepP)] at any (chosen) point or points within a whole range or scale of time **adj:** one, given, particular, single □ *. . .as a result of developments in modern aids to navigation — which enable an aircraft's position* ***at any moment*** *to be known accurately.* NSC □ *I'll see if I can find him for you, but he's out a lot and it's very difficult to know where he is* ***at any*** *given* ***moment****.*

at any price [A (PrepP)] at whatever cost in money, honour, happiness etc □ *My despair began to give way to exasperation and I felt coming upon me that nervous impulse to act* ***at any price*** *which so soon overtakes me in periods of frustration.* UTN □ *I'm enjoying myself here, but we'll go home now if that's what you want. Peace* ***at any price****, I always say.* □ stress pattern at 'any price; phrase *peace* ***at any price*** is used either seriously or jokingly.

at any rate [Disj (PrepP)] whether for this, or another, reason; this much, if no more, being true; at least[2] (qv) □ *I suspected Sadie of having been a little sweet on me at one time;* ***at any rate*** *she was always rather unpleasant in the old days about my being fond of Anna.* □ *There was a silence as the implication of these remarks dawned on the meeting, or* ***at any rate*** *on some of the scientists.* TBC □ *On one theory, they* (the craters) *are due to meteoric impact; on another, they are due to volcanic action of some type.* ***At any rate****, activity on the Moon now is negligible.* NS □ front, middle or end position; stress pattern at 'any rate. ⇨ ⚠ at that/this rate.

at sb's behest [A (PrepP)] (formal) in obedience to sb's command, or in compliance with sb's request (often with the implication of unwillingness); at sb's bidding (qv) □ *Guy, no doubt* ***at*** *Prissie****'s behest****, came in after dinner that evening.* DC □ *'I'm here as the headteacher's secretary,' she said, 'not to run errands* ***at*** *anybody****'s behest****.'*

at best/worst [Disj (PrepP)] taking the most/least favourable view; choosing the most/least hopeful possibility □ *The British people also wanted real success; for too long they had seen disaster or* ***at best*** *only partial success.* MFM □ *When she wanted to talk about her work, he would change the subject, or* ***at best*** *listen condescendingly, as if she were a child telling of school excitements.* AITC □ *I don't think this cake will be as good as the last one I baked for you, but it'll be eatable* ***at worst****.* □ ***At best*** *the army is regrouping, and* ***at worst*** *the advance continues by stealth behind a smooth front of official statements.* □ *I tried to be open-minded about the rock concert, but the music was* ***at best*** *loud and* ***at worst*** *tuneless.* □ front, middle or end position.

at the best of times [A (PrepP)] even when conditions are most favourable; (informal) at any time, and especially now/then □ *Life on a Chinese river barge was,* ***at the best of times****, uncomfortable and monotonous.* BM □ *He was* ***at the best of times*** *a temperamental man and sometimes, after drink, ran about with carving knives.* BFA □ *I can never resist owls* ***at the best of times****, but these two babies were quite adorable.* BB □ *'Good afternoon,' said Florrie. 'What can I do for you?'—which was a silly enough question* ***at the best of times****, and he shoved through the doors on account* (= because) *tea was on the go* (= was being made). TT □ front, middle or end position.

at sb's bidding [A (PrepP)] (formal) in obedience to sb's command, or in compliance with sb's request (often with the implication of unwillingness); at sb's behest (qv) □ *'I don't think your parents like me,' I said. 'Bob's obeying their orders.' She withdrew her hand from mine. 'That's a beastly thing to say. As if they were all-powerful tyrants and Bob danced* ***at their bidding****.'* RATT □ *Remember, I only invited the boy on holiday* ***at your bidding****. I expect you to devote some of* your *time to entertaining him, not leave it all to me.* □ *With an air of authority, as if every jug and bottle in the place existed to do* ***his bidding****, the landlord gave Harold his drink.* PW □ variant (in a more continuous sense of being obedient or subservient to another) do sb's bidding.

at a/one (single) blow [A (PrepP)] by means of one action or effort; at one (fell) swoop (qv) □ *Flies were crawling all over the windows, but with a tightly folded wad of newspaper he was soon disposing of them, six or seven* ***at a blow****.* □ *She could have managed each of her misfortunes separately, but coming as they did* ***at a single blow****, they caused a severe nervous collapse from which she never fully recovered.* □ *'I'm afraid your teeth will all have to come out,' the dentist said. 'I might as well take them all out now and get it over* ***at one blow****, don't you think?'*

at bottom [Disj (PrepP)] fundamentally, essentially, whether this is apparent or not; at heart (qv) □ *The working-classes are **at bottom** in excellent health — so the pastoral descriptions run — in better health than other classes; rough and unpolished perhaps, but diamonds nevertheless.* UL □ *She never seemed to resent her sister's popularity, but I daresay that she was sometimes a little jealous **at bottom**.* □ *What look like generous hire-purchase terms are **at bottom** encouragement to the customer to spend to his last penny.* □ front, middle or end position.

at close quarters [A (PrepP)] very near; with no or very little distance intervening **V:** see, observe, sb/sth; meet, encounter, sb □ *I, for my part, was astonished to see a popular writer **at close quarters**.* AH □ *Now that it was **at close quarters**, but in the shadow, I could see that the offending object was smaller than a football, but much the same shape.* DF □ *Seen **at close quarters** she looked even more formidable.* RATT ⇨ from afar.

at close range [A (PrepP)] at, or from, a point near to where sb/sth is, esp to the extent that this influences how sb may observe, aim at, reach, etc sb/sth else □ ***At close range** a candle can create the most magical lights and contrasting shadows.* HAH □ *His camera was a cheap one and didn't take good photographs **at close range**.* □ *People who watch programmes about murder and violence wouldn't find such things entertaining **at close range**.*

at cross purposes [Comp/A (PrepP)] having different or opposing aims, desires etc, esp to the extent that this interferes with plans or situations where cooperation is important; misleading and/or misunderstanding each other **V:** be, appear, find sb; talk □ *A meeting between the City Council and the Local Residents isn't likely to settle anything. They're **at cross purposes** before they start.* □ *Some young people don't ask their parents for advice. However, John did, and was dismayed to find them **at cross purposes** concerning his future career.* □ *Let's see if we are not arguing **at cross purposes**. Is it the system of voting itself you condemn, or merely the ways in which it can be abused or misused?*

at one's (own) discretion [A (PrepP)] not according to some rule, but as one personally judges to be right, necessary, or suitable □ *...which is not the same thing as manufacturing our own nuclear weapons and, in theory at least, being able to use them **at our own discretion**.* SC □ *I have made out a programme of events for Sports Day, Mr Simpson, but do feel free to make any alterations **at your own discretion**.* □ *As the police officers prepared to surround the house, the Superintendent told them to act **at their discretion** but to avoid the use of fire-arms if possible.* □ middle or end position.

at the double [A (PrepP)] very quickly (originally military) **V:** walk, run, march □ *'I'll go,' said the CSM (=* Company Sergeant-Major*), and was up and away **at the double**.* TT □ *Almost **at the double**, the little party dashed from stone to stone, missing none in the circuit.* SD □ *I called for a member of the staff, who came running **at the double** carrying a hurricane lantern.* BB

at the drop of a hat [A (PrepP)] for little or no reason; with the least encouragement □ *What's done can't be undone, no use crying over spilt milk, two wrongs don't make a right, and all the other old saws that spring to my mind **at the drop of a hat**.* AITC □ *They faced each other, one gaunt, unkempt, trousered, ready to scratch or bite **at the drop of a hat**, the other sleek, feminine.* HD □ (NONCE) *There are other advantages to Fibre-glass Crown — a whole list of them. **At the drop of a hint**, we will tell you all about them.* NS □ (NONCE) *Personally, I would much rather not be treated to the spectacle of a gallstone popping out of some unfortunate's bile duct **at the drop of a surgeon's knife**.* SC

at one's ease [Comp/A (PrepP)] comfortable/comfortably; at a leisured rate of action etc **V:** be, look; do, take, sth □ *'Why should I have to do all the fetching and carrying, while you sit there **at your ease**?' she complained.* □ *The dinner had been a particularly good one and they were both much **at their ease** as they drew up to the blazing fire.* TBC □ *I'm quite fond of travelling, as long as I can do it **at my ease**.* □ *Instead of attending the meeting, he was **taking his ease**, lying in the sun in the park.* □ variant take one's ease.

at one's elbow [Comp/A (PrepP)] very near one; within arm's reach **V:** be; need, have, sth □ *'Can you read Gaelic?' 'Yes, with a dictionary **at my elbow**!'* □ *I've put up bookshelves before, you know — I don't need somebody **at my elbow** telling me what to do.* □ often fig use and with reference to unwanted advice, assistance etc.

at the eleventh hour [A (PrepP)] almost, but not quite, too late to do sth, to take part in sth, for sth to be averted, etc; at the last minute (qv) (for source see MATTHEW XX 1-12) □ *We were in despair of finding an accompanist to replace Jack Stevens who had fallen ill; but **at the eleventh hour**, just as we were thinking of cancelling the performance, we remembered Alice Lyall* □ *His teeth were in a dreadful state, but it is wonderful what, even **at the eleventh hour**, modern dentistry can do.* □ *What happened at the last reorganisation in 1929, when the concept of district councils unexpectedly triumphed, suggests that it would be unwise to rule out completely the prospect of **eleventh-hour** changes.* SC □ attrib use *an **eleventh-hour** decision*; variant leave sth till/until the eleventh hour.

at every turn [A (PrepP)] whatever one does; wherever one goes; constantly **V:** find, meet, encounter, sb/sth □ *He had been trying to get his book finished all that year, but had been thwarted **at every turn**.* □ *'I haven't seen you for months,' she laughed, 'and now I seem to be meeting you **at every turn**!'*

at one's (own)/sb's expense [A (PrepP)] paying for sth oneself/allowing sb else to pay; with sb else paying **V:** live, feed, travel; be brought up □ *I did, however, dislike the dim light, and on the second day provided, **at my own expense**, a more powerful electric bulb.* UTN □ *He ate **at** other people**'s expense** as much as possible.* HAA □ *Harold had been to Bath on business and was travelling first-class **at the** firm**'s expense**.* PW □ *From childhood he had been fed, clothed and educated **at the expense of** various relatives.* ⇨ ⚠ next entry.

at the expense of sb/sth [A (Prep)] involving the ridicule of sb else; involving a cut, loss or reduction made somewhere else □ *Can you keep your good humour if others laugh at you in a friendly way and make witty remarks* ***at your expense****?* WI □ *Now the Chancellor wants to encourage fixed capital investment* ***at the expense of*** *consumer spending.* SC □ *We might say that Hamlet was a highly introverted person, probably with strong neurotic tendencies—a person liable to lose himself in abstract trains of thought* ***at the expense of*** *contact with reality.* SNP ⇨ ⚠ previous entry.

at (its/one's) face value [Disj/A (PrepP)] at (its/one's) nominal, supposed or apparent value (often with the implication that this may not be the real worth) **V:** accept, take, sth □ *Certain phenomena having been reported consistently for thousands of years, certain obvious problems are being raised.* ***At face value*** *they seem to contradict certain widely held beliefs; yet it seems difficult to dismiss these phemonena as being simply due to chance, to misconception, or to fraudulence.* SNP □ *He always accepted* ***at face value*** *any friendly gesture that was offered to him.* HAA □ *His contemporaries had soon formed the habit of accepting him* ***at his face value****, listening almost respectfully when he read papers to literary societies.* HD □ *'I want to sell my car. What do you suppose it's worth?' '****At face value****, about £200, and you aren't likely to get much more, however good its condition.'* □ *accept sth/sb* ***at its/one's face value*** occurs frequently, implying trusting attitude or, in neg, the opposite.

at first [A (PrepP)] at, or in, the beginning; to begin with; at the time of sth starting, or of starting sth □ *Diabetes is symptomless* ***at first****.* NS □ *The earth was formed about two thousand million years ago, along with the rest of the solar system.* ***At first*** *the surface was frozen.* TO □ *I didn't like the work* ***at first****, but after I got to understand it and made friends with the other girls, I came to love it.* □ front, middle or end position; often followed by another statement which may begin with *then, later, afterwards, etc.*

at the first attempt [A (PrepP)] the first time one tries **det:** first, second, third; last, final □ *He struggled to speak.* ***At the third attempt*** *his vocal chords vibrated slightly, and a hoarse whisper came out.* HD □ *Not many people can solve this puzzle* ***at the first attempt****.* □ front, middle or end position.

at first blush [A (PrepP)] after a superficial inspection; when first encountered; when first brought to one's notice; next entry (qv); at first sight (qv) □ *It might appear* ***at first blush*** *that the provision of free secondary education for all has failed to justify the hopes and efforts which have been expended upon it.* SC □ ***At first blush*** *the cliff seemed unscalable, though we had heard the islanders used to climb it in search of seabirds' eggs.* □ somewhat dated — next entry and at first sight more common.

at first glance [A (PrepP)] when first looked at; when not yet scrutinised or carefully considered; previous entry (qv); at first sight (qv) □ ***At first glance*** *one would be pardoned for mistaking a hyrax for an ordinary member of the great group of rodents.* BB □ *It does not seem, therefore, that the content of the suggestion is as important as one might have thought* ***at first glance****.* SNP □ front, middle or end position; *at first look* never used.

at first light [A (PrepP)] at dawn □ *One must remember to wake* ***at first light*** *in order to diddle the savages—and he did not know how quickly sleep came and hurled him down a dark interior slope.* LF □ *Let's pack our gear into the car tonight, and then we can start off* ***at first light*** *and have clear roads—for the first half of our journey at any rate.*

at first sight [A (PrepP)] when first seen: when first considered; at first blush (qv); at first glance (qv) □ *He produced a huge silver case containing what looked* ***at first sight*** *like small cheap cigars.* HD □ *So far we have been considering what would appear* ***at first sight*** *to be a simple case of dynastic assassination. But the matter is a little more complicated than that.* EM □ front, middle or end position. ⇨ ⚠ on sight.

at the foot of one's/the bed [A (PrepP)] in, on or near the bed at the end farthest away from the occupant's head □ *Shall I put your hot-water bottle* ***at the foot of your bed****, or in the middle?* □ *On Christmas Eve the children hang their stockings* ***at the foot of the bed****.* □ *'Ghosts?' 'Actually, I believe there's only one. A little man in a brown coat who stands* ***at the foot of her bed*** *and says nothing.'* DC □ never used to mean *under* the bed.

at full speed [A (PrepP)] at the maximum rate of movement, or progress, appropriate to sb/sth **S:** car, bus, tank, plane; electric saw, drill; engine. **V:** go, run, drive, work, revolve □ *They were away* ***at full speed*** *down the river in a couple of minutes.* RFW □ *My car can just touch 100 mph* ***at full speed****.* □ *Though I was running* ***at full speed****, I could not overtake him.* □ with v of motion at full speed preferred to at top speed (qv).

at a glance [A (PrepP)] with one quick look **V:** know, see, tell, realize, sth □ *You could see* ***at a glance*** *that something had happened to upset her.* □ *I've been in this business so long I can tell* ***at a glance*** *whether an objet d'art is genuine or a clever imitation.* □ usu preceded by *can* or *could*.

at a (rough/wild) guess [Disj (PrepP)] (by) making a guess □ *'****At a wild guess****,' said Mr R Horsfall Turner, town clerk of Scarborough, 'it could cost £500,000,000 to clean up all Britain's rivers.'* DM □ *'How old do you think he is?' 'Forty to forty-five* ***at a guess****, but certainly under fifty.'* □ *He thought that* ***at a rough guess*** *there would still be about a hundred gallons of oil in the tank.* □ *I may be lucky enough to pass the test;* ***at a guess****, I got more than half the answers right.* □ used esp when estimating approximate numbers, costs, amounts; cf last example and *I was lucky to have passed the test, as I got more than half the answers right* ***by guessing****.*

at sb's hands [A (PrepP)] from sb; through the action or agency of sb (almost always with the implication that sb has been unjust, cruel etc) **V:** endure, undergo, suffer, sth □ *I have been subjected to too many insults* ***at his hands*** *to accept favours from him now.* □ *Imagine a child suffering such cruelties* ***at the hands of*** *his own parents!*

at heart [A (PrepP)] in one's real nature, whether this is apparent or not; at bottom (qv) ▫ *I am sick and tired of the silly theory that all men are really just little boys* ***at heart.*** TO ▫ *If Raul had taken off at midnight, he would refuel just before dawn in Santiago, where the ground-staff were friendly, everyone within the Oriente province being rebels* ***at heart.*** OMIH ▫ ***At heart*** *she still preferred her former way of life.* ▫ *I'm not,* ***at heart,*** *as indifferent to criticism as I often pretend to be.* ▫ front, middle or end position.

at sb's heels [A (PrepP)] following close behind sb ▫ *I threaded my way through the crowd with the dog* ***at my heels.*** UTN ▫ *Ready for anything, and especially anything unwelcome, Charles entered Mr Frush's conference room* ***at the heels of*** *Froulish.* HD

at home [Comp/A (PrepP)] in one's own present, or former, dwelling place; in one's own country, not abroad **V:** be, stay, find sb; develop, increase ▫ ***At home*** *there had been a pear tree outside her bedroom window.* DC ▫ SARAH: *Hymie's all right. He's got a business. His children are married and he stays* ***at home*** *all the time.* CSWB ▫ *If boom conditions are allowed to develop* ***at home,*** *price stability will be endangered.* SC ▫ *Sales since October, both* ***at home*** *and abroad, show a marked increase.* T

at large generally; as a unit; as a whole (qv) ▫ *That humanity* ***at large*** *will ever be able to dispense with artificial Paradises seems very unlikely.* DOP ▫ *Too wrapped up in his indignation to notice that Ned was there, he simply addressed the company* ***at large.*** TC ▫ *'Opportunity to do just what?' 'Why, to dig in and find some facts and reveal them to the country* ***at large,'*** *cried Dogson.* HD ▫ usu modifies a preceding n.

at last [A (PrepP)] at the end of a period of time; after a long time of waiting, wishing or striving for sb/sth; at length[1] (qv) ▫ *I leaned for a long time, looking into the mirror of the Pont Neuf.* ***At last*** *I began to want my breakfast.* UTN ▫ *And through all that time she had clung to one fantasy —that, aged and broken,* ***at last*** *in need, he might one day return to her.* CWR ▫ *You've got here* ***at last,*** *thank goodness! I was beginning to be afraid you might have had an accident.* ▫ *She looked for her purse in her handbag, then in her basket and all her pockets, and finally in the car, where* ***at last*** *she found it.* ▫ front, middle, or end position; cannot be replaced by next entry (qv), in the end (qv); cf *lastly* or *finally* used to introduce final item of a sequence or to introduce a further and last statement about sth with last example.

at the last [A (PrepP)] in, during, the final period of sth ▫ *Ah, but you never saw him* ***at the last.*** *He was so patient and grateful—not at all what he used to be.* ▫ *At first, he was enraged at her neglect of Kay, her utter selfishness; and then he was overcome with pity for her disintegration, her utter panic.* ***At the last,*** *however, it was physical nausea that gripped him.* ASA ▫ often used of last period of sb's life.

at the last minute [A (PrepP)] almost, but not quite, too late to do sth, to take part in sth, for sth to be averted etc; at the eleventh hour (qv) ▫ *I'll not expect you then, but if you find* ***at the last minute*** *that you're free after all, just turn up.* ▫ *The dinner's ready except for a few* ***last-minute*** *things like the parsley sauce, so I'll just run upstairs and change.* ▫ *She's known for three weeks that her essay had to be handed in tomorrow, but she will* ***leave*** *things* ***till the last minute,*** *and then do them in a mad rush.* ▫ attrib use *some* ***last-minute*** *shopping*; variant leave sth till/until the last minute.

at least[1] [A (PrepP)] to the (full) amount of, if not more; to the extent of, if not more ▫ *During my holiday I'll spend* ***at least*** *a week in Dorset* ▫ *I shouted after him. 'It's not all that dangerous It won't be high and dry for another fifteen minutes* ***at least.'*** ARG ▫ *British farmers, proud of their efficiency, feel strongly that they should be treated* ***at least*** *as liberally as farmers on the Continent.* ▫ *I must* ***at least*** *go and say goodbye to the rajah before events sweep me out of his life for ever.* TO ▫ *There is little doubt that some* ***at least*** *of the professional military would be pleased if war broke out.* SC ▫ placed before or after the word or phrase modified. ⇨ at (the most.

at least[2] [Disj (PrepP)] whether for this, or another, reason; this much, if no more, being true; at any rate (qv) ▫ JIMMY: *Oh, I'm not saying that it mustn't be hell for them a lot of the time. But,* ***at least,*** *they do seem to have a cause* LBA ▫ *This addition to the range of inducements offered by the Ministry of Commerce* ***at least*** *illustrates the ingenuity of the Government's efforts to widen the province's industrial base.* SC *The soup wasn't very good but* ***at least*** *it was hot and we were too cold and hungry to complain. John is going to give up smoking.* ***At least*** *so he said last night.* ▫ *The boy is not very clever at his lessons; but he tries,* ***at least.*** ▫ front, middle or end position.

at one's leisure [A (PrepP)] without hurrying with no time limit imposed on getting sth finished **V:** visit, survey, observe, sth; finish complete, sth ▫ *She would have preferred the children to go ahead and leave her to follow on at* ***her leisure.*** ▫ *Plastering is not a job you can do* ***at your leisure;*** *you can't allow your trowel to rest for a minute.*

at length[1] [A (PrepP)] after a long time of waiting, wishing or striving for sb/sth; eventually; at last (qv) ▫ *When* ***at length*** *the day broke found the travellers still weary and dispirited.* ▫ *tried for years to find a sponsor for my invention but* ***at length*** *I became discouraged and abandoned the thing.* ▫ front position.

at length[2] fully; in great detail **V:** speak, talk write; explain, deal with, go into, sth. **adj:** some great, considerable, inordinate ▫ *When I se her 'The Case is Altered' she wrote to me at* ***length*** *with an appreciation of character and incident that seemed as genuine as it was detailed.* AH ▫ *Robin talked* ***at great length*** *John's misconduct in the Pelican affair.* ASA *The fourteenth chapter of the Handbook deals at some* ***length*** *with the special conditions and problems of motorway driving.*

at long last [A (PrepP)] after a particular long time of waiting, wishing or striving for s sth ▫ *It was part of her artistic development th she was getting away from naval subjects now;* ***long last,*** *perhaps, the preoccupation with h service life was beginning to fade.* RFW ▫ ... *would merely bring in a rival for promotion*

*W's vacancy when W (**at long last**) retires.* PL □ front, middle or end position.

at long/short range [A (PrepP)] at, or from, a point distant from/near to sb/sth else **V:** shoot, kill; hit, strike; view, observe. **O:** prey, quarry; target; scene, prospect □ *He could kill a stag **at a longer range** than anyone else I knew.* □ *Cuba can't afford to start making H-bombs, but have they found something equally effective **at short range** and cheap?* OMIH □ *'Who is this York Harding?' 'He's the man you are looking for, Vigot. He killed Pyle—**at long range**.'* QA □ *In a family crisis it's often a good idea to seek outside advice. It can be difficult to judge the situation correctly **at short range**; you may need an objective view.*

at the moment [A (PrepP)] now; at the present time; at present (qv); just now² (qv) □ ***At the moment** the Council for Nature is considering the idea of sending around tutors who will, if asked, keep a professional eye on the best field work of the best amateur societies.* NS □ *It is in fact only by importing foreign capital into this country that we are managing to balance our accounts **at the moment**.* OBS □ *'Hullo, Mary, this is David speaking. Is your father in?' 'Not **at the moment**, I'm afraid, but if you ring again in an hour or so, he should be home by then.'* □ front, middle or end position; applies to the present conceived as either a short or long span of time; variant (considered by some to be clumsy and pompous) at this moment in time. ⇨ ⚠ in future; in the future; in the past.

at the moment/time of speaking etc [A (PrepP)] now; then **o:** speaking, writing, reporting, posting □ *What is two thousand pesos? **At the moment of writing**, about eight pounds fourteen shillings.* BM □ *He regretted that **at the moment of speaking** it was not known whether Government support for the scheme would be forthcoming.* □ *We have still not received any payment **at the time of posting**, but if you have sent us your cheque within the last two days, please disregard this reminder.* □ used when giving information, stating a fact, etc, esp to safeguard oneself from having seemed to make a false statement should something occur very soon afterwards which invalidates it.

at a moment's notice [A (PrepP)] immediately on being asked to do sth, or immediately it seems necessary or important to do it; at short notice (qv) **V:** report, return, depart; prepare, produce, sth □ *It was uncertain how long the engine-room repairs would take, so the passengers were advised either to stay on board or be ready to rejoin the ship **at a moment's notice**.* □ *You might have phoned to say you were bringing friends with you. I can't produce dinner for six people **at a moment's notice**.* □ *I want you to keep these tablets in your pocket, because you may need to take one **at a moment's notice**, any time you feel a pain coming on.*

at (the) most [A (PrepP)] in an amount not greater than, or to a degree or extent not more than, sth specified (the implication usu being the likelihood of being less than this); at the outside (qv) □ *Your brother is not taller than I am; he's about one metre seventy, or seventy-two **at the most**.* □ *I'll only be away for a week **at the most**—probably only four or five days.* □ ***At most** the drug may be effective as a palliative; it cannot cure.* □ placed before or after word or pl modified; the two forms are fairly interchangeable, but at the most tends to be used of numbered totals, quantities, and at most tends to modify a v or adj. ⇨ at least¹.

at once¹ [A (PrepP)] immediately; without delay □ *I did not look for a bell, but tried the handle **at once**.* UTN □ *Brigit, her mind free from care, fell asleep **at once**.* DC □ *You had better leave **at once** if you want to catch your train.* □ usu in end position.

at once² [A (PrepP)] simultaneously; at one and the same time (qv); at the same time¹ (qv); both at the same time; at any one time □ *But it wasn't so much a cry as an order; an order delivered in a voice that was **at once** indulgent but firm, bored but implacable.* PW □ *The boys had him summed up pretty quickly as being **at once** a bully and a coward.* □ *The countryside is not quite all dense with the tangle of secondary growth, for only a little of it is cultivated **at once**, and that little changes in place from year to year.* NDN □ occurs before or after adj + adj, n + n etc (where its use is rather formal), and in end position in the sense 'at any one time'.

at one remove (from sb/sth) [A PrepP)] in not too close a connection (with sb/sth) □ *He had no wish for a home of his own, and yet always sought lodgings as a paying guest with some family. It was as if he preferred to enjoy domesticity **at one remove**.* □ *He shows an interest in his staff, but it is a well-rehearsed management technique. The pleasant façade lets him stay **at one remove from** the people round him.* □ usu follows n or v it modifies.

at one and the same time [A (PrepP)] simultaneously; at the same time¹ (qv); at once² (qv) □ *You have to learn to watch the traffic ahead and keep your eye on the driving mirror **at one and the same time**.* □ *She had a compulsive urge to overeat, though **at one and the same time** she despised herself for giving way to it.* □ *He said he was heartbroken when Sheila broke off her engagement to him. **At one and the same time**, however, he had been seeing another woman.* □ used for joining phrases, clauses, or forming link with an immediately preceding sentence.

at one (o'clock) sharp [A (PrepP)] at exactly the specified time □ *The room behind him is heavily garrisoned by tea-chests, cases, valises, packages—all in full marching order. The old man should have been at the flat **at seven sharp** with his lorry.* EM □ *'If you come **at 10.20 sharp**,' answered the receptionist, 'Mr Wood may be able to fit you in between appointments.'* □ *The train came in **sharp at noon**, for once.* □ *If you're not here **sharp at five o'clock**, you'll have to get your own tea ready.* □ sharp usu takes end position, but cf last two examples.

at one/a sitting [A (PrepP)] during the course of one meeting; in one period of activity **V:** finish, complete, deal with, sth; read, eat, sth □ *All members of the Committee agreed that they would prefer to stay on a little longer and finish their business **at one sitting**.* □ *It's quite a short book; you could easily read it **at a sitting**.* □ *She asked me to knit her a sweater, quite casually, as if it was something I could do **at one sitting**.*

at one (fell) swoop [A (PrepP)] by means of

one action or effort; at a/one (single) blow (qv) □ (source) ROSS: *Your castle is surprised; your wife and babes/Savagely slaughtered.* MACDUFF: *What! all my pretty chickens and their dam,/**At one fell swoop**?* MACBETH IV 3 □ ***At one fell swoop**, the earthquake had left him without family, home, or means of livelihood.* □ *I'm going to try to weed the whole garden **at one fell swoop**, because I don't really want to spend another weekend at it.* □ *You have to be a fool to turn down the chance of earning ten thousand pounds in prize money, or even twenty thousand, **at one swoop**.* ⇨ ⚠ all at once², all of a sudden.

at one time or another [A (PrepP)] on an occasion or on different occasions in the past, the precise time or date of which is not recalled, not given or not known □ *The irrational guilt which they felt for her distress could in some degree be expiated by the panic that, **at one time or another**, they all experienced from her erratic driving.* HAA □ *He has indeed **at one or another time** argued both for and against most of the big changes in Turkey over the past thirty years.* OBS □ variant at one or another time. ⇨ ⚠ (at) some time or other.

at the outset (of sth) [A (PrepP)] in the beginning period (of sth); when sb/sth is about to start, or has just started □ *That pleasant glow would fade when the time came to work, but he was always bad at believing this **at the outset**.* TGLY □ *He was fond of the girl after his own fashion, but told her frankly that he did not want to be burdened with a wife and family **at the** very **outset of his career**.* ⇨ ⚠ (right) from the start etc.

at the outside [A (PrepP)] at the highest estimation, or reckoning, of a possible number or amount of time, money, materials etc; at (the) most (qv) **V:** earn, own; yield, produce, sth □ *You know you'd enjoy it. That's what'll be your undoing, not just the offers. I give you two years **at the outside**.* TGLY □ *I don't suppose he earns more than £5000 a year **at the outside**.*

at one's own risk [A (PrepP)] with the consequences of any possible misfortune to be borne by oneself **V:** go climbing, flying, swimming; enter, leave □ *'I daresay I shall find it an ordeal. But I am going through with it, Mr Skipton, because I must.' 'Then, Miss Merlin,' he said quietly, 'it shall be **at your own risk**.'* US □ *Inexperienced climbers who attempt these mountains should remember that they are not doing so **at their own risk** only, but at the risk of those who may be called out to rescue them.*

at one's peril [A (PrepP)] at the risk of serious danger or of incurring severe penalties **V:** go out, venture out; fly, go sailing □ *'You'll go on smoking **at your peril**,' the doctor told my husband, but he was wasting his time.* □ *I told them they would be taking that old boat out **at their peril**.* □ *They can attack us if they like. But if they do so it will be **at their peril**.* □ cf *in peril (of sth)* where people are already in a state of danger.

at a pinch [A (PrepP)] if necessary, but with some difficulty **V:** (can) do, manage, sth; afford sth; sleep; put up, feed, sb □ *I don't claim to be more intelligent than anyone else, and I can understand most things **at a pinch**, but this problem is really beyond me.* □ *I daresay that **at a pinch** we could afford to run a car, but I'd rather have a little extra spending money.* □ *The tent sleeps four comfortably and five **at a pinch**.* □ modified v often preceded by *can/could*.

at present [A (PrepP)] now; just now; at the present time; at the moment (qv); just now² (qv) □ ***At present** the nineteen children—ten boys and nine girls, aged from eleven to fifteen years old—live in a Victorian stone mansion.* TO □ *This summer about a quarter of a million boys and girls will be looking for jobs. Finding one at all will become harder in the next few years, but **at present** the main problem is to find the right one.* OBS □ *'I would like to employ you if I could,' the manager said, 'but we have no vacancies **at present**.'* ⇨ ⚠ in the past; in future; in the future.

at a price [A (PrepP)] by paying a (relatively) large amount of money; by expending, or sacrificing, (relatively) much effort, time, comfort, peace of mind, etc □ *The policy in many countries is to encourage consumption of the local spirits, so Scottish whisky is only obtainable **at a price**.* □ *It was a decision to be taken only **at a price**: if he left his wife, it would mean leaving his children too.* □ *His uncle would let him have £5, he supposed, **at a price**—a ten-minute lecture on how to manage his affairs better.* □ stress pattern ˌat a ˈprice.

at the prospect (of sth) [A (PrepP)] in expectation (of sth), whether welcome or not □ *She brightened visibly, doubtless **at the prospect of** banter with the greengrocer at the corner store, to say nothing of his neighbour.* BM □ *'How will you like having your in-laws to stay?' 'I'm not delighted **at the prospect**, I must say!'* □ *He set off home, smiling to himself **at the prospect of** astonishing his family with his good news.*

at random [A (PrepP)] without aim or purpose, or without making a deliberate choice from a number of possible items or actions **V:** choose, select, pick out, draw, sth; walk, move; shoot, fire, bomb, sth; distribute sth □ *He sees each star formed from many blobs of relatively high density travelling **at random** and at supersonic speed.* NS □ *Then I set off running **at random** down one of the avenues, looking to left and right. Anna could not be far away.* UTN □ *She turned and smiled **at random** to the company behind her.* ASA □ *He translates numbers drawn **at random** from an urn into symbols which he then tries to transmit to the receiver.* SNP

at the risk of doing sth [A (PrepP)] (do sth) though aware sth unpleasant, undesirable, or dangerous may happen as well, or instead **o:** hurting his feelings, offending you, losing their friendship/one's life □ ***At the risk of** strengthening opposition to his one-man rule, General de Gaulle has tried to prevent any attempt at political sniping through what remains of Parliament.* OBS □ *The men may grumble about their conditions of work, but are they prepared to make an open protest **at the risk of** losing their jobs altogether?* □ not usu followed by a n but at the risk of one's life is very common.

at a run etc [A (PrepP)] moving at the speed of running etc **adj:** fast, brisk; slow, gentle. **n:** run; ⚠ walk, stroll, waddle, crawl; gallop, canter, trot □ *But it was a different Alfred, pale, sweating, trembling, coming **at a run** toward him.* PM □ *'Right, Jim,' he said, 'we'll take it **at a waddle** through the village and avoid drawing attention* *to ourselves. Once past the beech hedge we can make a run for it.'* □ *The riders crossed the side of the hill* ***at a slow trot***. □ *'If you must drive* ***at a crawl*** *like this, you should be in the nearside lane. Can't you see you're holding up the traffic?*

at the same time[1] [A (PrepP)] not at a different time; simultaneously; at once[2] (qv); at one and the same time (qv) □ *He gets up* ***at the same time*** *every morning.* □ *It would be easier for me if my family could all have lunch* ***at the same time***. □ *You can't watch television and do your homework* ***at the same time***!

at the same time[2] [Conj (PrepP)] in spite of sth already known or mentioned; nevertheless; however; all/just the same (qv); mark/mind you (qv) □ *I know that before we married you warned me there could never be a divorce. I accepted the risk and I've nothing to complain of.* ***At the same time*** *I'm asking for one now.* QA □ *I was deeply moved. Yet* ***at the same time*** *I took the thing with a grain of salt. I had often known myself to be moved in the past, and little had come of it.* UTN □ *That evening the two girls wandered round with mixed feelings, bemoaning the fate that had landed them into a place which was ten miles from the nearest movie.* ***At the same time***, *they were forced to realise that the Navy had sent them to one of the most lovely country houses in England.* RFW

at second hand [A (PrepP)] not directly; not based on personal knowledge or observation **V:** hear, learn, pick up, obtain, sth □ *Sensations, feelings, insights, fancies—all these are private and, except through symbols and* ***at second hand***, *incommunicable.* DOP □ *I am surprised his book about Ireland was ever accepted for publication; it consists mostly of material taken up* ***at second hand*** *from other travel books.* □ *Tell your wife you got into a fight last night. She'll probably get it* ***at second hand*** *from somebody else anyway, and she'll be all the more angry.*

at short notice [A (PrepP)] without much warning; without much time to get sth done; at a moment's notice (qv) **V:** appear, arise, come up □ *When such questions are placed on the order paper* ***at short notice*** *the extra cost to the Colonial Office and the overseas government arising from telegraphic communication is from £10 to £100.* T □ *I've already said that I'm quite prepared to go somewhere else if it's inconvenient for you to have me* ***at*** *such* ***short notice***. EHOW □ *He had his pipe at the ready in case it should be necessary to put on his don's act* ***at short notice***. HD

at sight [A (PrepP)] as soon as sb/sth is seen; on sight (qv) **V:** read, translate, comprehend, decipher, sth; shoot sb □ *If one of those renegades came prowling round my house, I'd shoot him* ***at sight*** *and ask questions afterwards.* □ *We don't need a concert musician for this job, but we do need somebody who can play accompaniments* ***at sight***. □ at sight and on sight are sometimes interchangeable, but not in expression *be able to read music, make a quick translation, calculation etc* ***at sight***.

at (the) sight of sb/sth [A (PrepP)] when, or because, sb/sth is seen □ *Nobody said anything. Norreys opened his mouth and then closed it* ***at the sight of*** *Henry's face.* WI □ *Keep Susan out of the room just now; she's apt to faint* ***at the sight of*** *blood.* □ *When we drove up to the 'charming cottage' of the advertisement, my heart sank* ***at the sight of*** *it.* □ *It was not the mother of her girlhood, whose full-rigged majesty had towered above her; even physically Mrs Knighton had shrunk.* ***At sight of*** *her Isabel felt a rash of pity.* PW

at a snail's pace [A (PrepP)] very slowly indeed □ *Granny prefers to drive by herself. She knows it irritates young people to have to go* ***at a snail's pace***. □ *'I hear you're writing a novel. How is it coming along?'* ***'At a snail's pace***; *it's a much harder business than I would have believed.'*

at sb's suggestion [A (PrepP)] because sb has suggested, or proposed, sth □ *Early in 1845 Lady Blackford bought the property* ***at the suggestion of*** *Sir Robert Peel.* WI □ *'Edward is compiling an anthology of prose and verse extracts about the dance and dancing.'* ***'At*** *somebody****'s suggestion****? Or is it just an idea of his own?'*

at a tender age [A (PrepP)] when one is still quite young □ *He had been deserted by his mother* ***at a tender age*** *and brought to this country by his grandparents.* □ *Bonnie Langford,* ***at the tender age of 12*** *has already formulated her views on possible stardom.* TVT □ *His interest in medieval music started while he was still* ***of tender age*** *and has since developed until he is now a recognized international authority on the subject.* □ variants at the tender age of 12 etc , of tender age; occas facetious.

at that[1] [A (PrepP)] whereupon; immediately subsequent to that □ *'I wanted you to have a talk with her.'* ***At that*** *his own smile faded.* PW □ usu front postition.

at that[2] [A (PrepP)] moreover; too; also; as a surprising, noteworthy, or preposterous addition □ *'Pay five pounds for a secondhand trunk!' she exclaimed. 'And with a handle missing* ***at that***, *' she added, taking a closer look.* □ *This seems to be to be full of fallacies, and dangerous fallacies* ***at that***. OBS □ *This, he found, was not half so delicious an experience as pinching Ma, who wore nylons and very tight ones* ***at that***. DBM □ follows word or phrase it modifies.

at that[3] [A (PrepP)] possibly; now one comes to think about it (esp with statements indicating doubt, conjecture) □ CLIFF: *He's just an old Puritan at heart.* JIMMY: *Perhaps I am,* ***at that***. LBA □ *'You're enlisting for life as a mannequin,' I said. 'You'll have to spend all your time being a symbol of conspicuous wealth.' And it occurred to me as I said it that it mightn't be such a bad life* ***at that***. UTN □ usu follows word or phrase it modifies.

at that/this rate [A (PrepP)] if that/this is so; according to that/this way of thinking, reckoning, behaving etc; in that case (qv) □ *'I did say to the baby-sitter that we'd be home in time to put the children to bed.' 'We should have left half an hour ago* ***at that rate***. *Why didn't you say so earlier?'* □ *We discussed the matter a bit further, and then I told him, 'But* ***at this rate*** *almost everything one says turns out to be a sort of lie.'* UTN □ ***'At this rate***, *' his father told him, 'you're going to turn out an even greater disaster than your brother.'* □ stress pattern at 'that/'this rate. ⇨ ⚠ at any rate.

at this stage (of sth) [A (PrepP)] at this point in the development of sth, or in the course of a series of events □ *The first milk teeth may appear at anything from five to eight months from birth, and* ***at this stage*** *the child should be provided with something clean and hard to bite on.* □ *'But I understood a great deal could be done to relieve arthritis?' 'Not* ***at this stage****, I'm afraid, apart from analgesics to lessen pain.'* □ ***At this stage of*** *the proceedings I was handed a large coloured reproduction of the well-known self-portrait by Cézanne.* DOP □ stress pattern at 'this stage.

at the (very) thought of (doing) sth/that [A (PrepP)] when, or because, one thinks of sth, or of the possibility of sth occurring □ *He had felt a flush of discomfort* ***at the thought of*** *revisiting the scene of so much folly and embarrassment.* HD □ *'A proper millionaire, they say he is!' She glowed with suppressed excitement* ***at the thought that*** *a man who makes chocolate on a big scale can become rich, and can then fall ill, and that he should have come to 'their' hospital.* HD □ *Imagine walking along a girder a hundred metres up in the air! I shudder* ***at the very thought of*** *it.* □ very tends to be added when what one is thinking of is fanciful, extreme, desirable, alarming or improbable as far as speaker is concerned.

at a time [A (PrepP)] in sequence; separately **S:** grain, bean; shred, fragment □ *I took out my good news of yesterday, and unfolded it slowly, admiring its glittering colour and intricate pattern an item* ***at a time****.* RATT □ *They would eat their meagre ration of rice a few grains* ***at a time*** *to make it seem more and last longer.* □ *Support the patient's head, nurse, and let him have a little brandy and water, just a sip* ***at a time****, though.* □ *They approached the President five* ***at a time*** *to receive their awards.* □ cf *shifting a stone* ***at a time****, shifting one stone* ***at a time****, shifting the stones one* ***at a time****.*

at the time [A (PrepP)] then; when sth specified was/will be happening □ *Although nobody realized it* ***at the time****, the occasion of the Prime Minister's visit was very nearly the worst moment in the whole episode of the Black Cloud.* TBC □ *I'll admit to you now, Jinny, though I held my peace* ***at the time****, that it used to quite embarrass me that in anything you happened to try, you came out top.* AITC □ *You can't rely on seeing the same doctor at each visit. It all depends on which of them is on duty* ***at the time****.* □ *He would read volume after volume of whoever happened to be his favourite author* ***at the time****.* □ only used when accompanied by another statement, usu in different clause of same sentence, which indicates time referred to.

at a time like this/that [A (PrepP)] at such a time, esp an important time, or a time unsuitable for sth specified to take place or be done □ *I don't think she has any friends. She's talked them all away, except for that sanctimonious sister of hers, and she wouldn't want her* ***at a time like this*** (ie when her husband was in state of alcoholic delirium). AITC □ *OK, so you're angry because Frank swindled you over the car deal, but you were wrong to bring it up again* ***at a time like that****. After all, you were both supposed to be celebrating Sue's engagement.*

at times [A (PrepP)] at various times, esp unpredictable or unspecified times □ *Robert and I got on each other's nerves* ***at times****.* AITC □ *He gets a bit depressed* ***at times****—who wouldn't?—but on the whole he's adapting very well to the loss of his leg.* □ *The van gave a lot of trouble on the way home;* ***at times****, it stopped altogether, and James had to get out and tinker with the engine; then it would cough and splutter for a few more miles.* □ front, middle or end position.

at the top of one's voice [A (PrepP)] very loudly indeed **V:** talk, call, shout, scream, yell, shriek, bawl □ *I'd half expected the theatre to be full of people like Bob and Eva, being determinedly witty and theatrical* ***at the top of their voices****.* RATT □ *It was left to Jacob and me to go to the rescue of the Beagle who was lashing about in the undergrowth, screaming* ***at the top of his voice****.* BB □ *All that day I was on the telephone, to the news agencies, to the gallery, to people like Justin Cartridge (who, of course, was bragging* ***at the top of his voice*** *about having recognized Robert from the start).* CON □ pl either at the top of their voices or at the tops of their voices.

at top speed [A (PrepP)] very fast; as fast as possible **V:** pack, remove, study, sth □ *She knew something was up the night when I gave her her bottle and cereal* ***at top speed****.* WI □ *There is a more than adequate supply of material designed to be read* ***at top speed****, and that speed is useless for most worthwhile reading.* UL □ *Get your materials tidied away, boys, and* ***at top speed****. There's another class waiting to come in.* □ also, used literally of vehicles, machines etc, but whereas one would say *What is its* ***top speed****? The* ***top speed*** *recorded is... etc,* one would tend to prefer at full speed (qv) with a v of motion.

at (a) walking pace [A (PrepP)] at the rate of a person walking at normal speed **V:** go, move, progress; ride, drive □ *For some miles now the road was well-nigh impassable, deep-rutted and riven, and we crawled* ***at walking pace*** *past dull, harsh fields.* BM □ *It's very difficult to ride a bike steadily* ***at walking pace****.* □ *Please don't try to hurry me. I can only climb* ***at a walking pace****, or I get quite breathless.*

at what (a) cost/price [A (PrepP)] (fig) at a very great cost in effort, suffering, sacrifice etc □ ***At what cost*** *through long days and sleepless nights she had nursed the old man, she alone knew.* □ *They had achieved independence indeed, but* ***at what a price****!* □ *These young people wouldn't take their privileges so lightly if they realised* ***at what cost*** *my generation had fought for them.* □ frequently used in direct or indirect questions or rhetorical exclamations.

at will [A (PrepP)] as one wishes; by willing sth; by exercising the power of the mind over matter □ *The master plan must never be so rigid that the Commander-in-Chief cannot vary it to suit the changing tactical situation; but nobody else may be allowed to change it* ***at will****.* MFM □ *Discipline was non-existent. Students roamed about the campus* ***at will****, as if there had never been such a thing as a timetable.* □ *A known characteristic of demons is that they can make themselves minute* ***at will****.* NDN □ *In the course of his practice the doctor had come across several cases where children could faint or be sick* ***at will****.* □ usu end position.

attack is the best form of defence (saying) a paradoxical statement based on military tactics, used also to describe methods of argument, or competitive manoeuvres between people or groups in any sphere of activity □ *There is no exact division between defence and attack, and* ***attack*** *may* ***be the best form of defence****.* AH □ *Harold knew that* ***attack was the best form of defence****, and made quite a good show of seeming the injured party.* PW □ ***The best form of defence being attack*** *he rose from his bed next day and rode down to the beach, where the Customs flag was flying over the hulk, and the Preventive Officers were patrolling.* ARG □ variant the best form of defence being attack.

attempt the impossible [V + O pass] try to do sth that cannot be done; try to do sth without any expectation of succeeding □ *Furthermore, he was asked to* ***attempt the impossible****; his Headquarters had to act as a General Headquarters, and at the same time he had to exercise direct command over the fighting and administrative forces allotted to him.* MFM □ *'You're* ***attempting the impossible*** *if you think you're going to reform a hardened character like him.' 'I can't be sure of that unless I've tried, can I?'*

an Aunt Sally sb singled out as a target for abuse, criticism, or ridicule (from the name given to an effigy used as a target for aiming at in fun fairs, etc); an object, or idea, deliberately invented in order to attract destructive criticism, with the object of leading to constructive thought □ *The Party were not sorry to have* ***an Aunt Sally*** *in the person of the Hon Member for Lupton. The more the public concentrated on his faults, the less conspicuous theirs would appear.* □ *More often the enemies are either men of straw, bogus* ***Aunt Sallies*** *such as 'conventional people'; or if the attacks are on real people they usually prove on examination to be a few safe feints.* UL

avoid sb/sth like the plague [V + O + A pass] have such a strong fear, or dislike, of sb/sth that one habitually avoids contact with him/it as much as possible □ *They built these things on top of practically every hill in Upper Burma, put a statue of the Buddha inside, dug a well for his refreshment, and thereafter* ***avoided*** *the place* ***like the plague****.* ARG □ *I don't know whether I've unintentionally offended her or whether somebody has turned her against me, but she has certainly been* ***avoiding*** *me* ***like the plague*** *for the last six months.* □ *Self-important idiots such as Elliot should be* ***avoided like the plague****.*

an awful lot [A (NP)] (informal) very much; very often; to a great extent □ *He's playing the piano* ***an awful lot*** *these days. I wonder what's made him take it up again?* □ *I never liked him* ***an awful lot****, although I couldn't tell you why.*

an awful lot (of sb/sth) (informal) a great number or amount (of sb/sth) □ *Now that the fighting has stopped* ***an awful lot of*** *girls will be getting married and leaving the service, and I don't suppose they will be training any more.* RFW □ *There's going to be* ***an awful lot of*** *lethal stuff coming downward from the top of the atmosphere though — X-rays and ultra-violet light.* TBC

the awkward age [o (NP)] the period of early adolescence when young people have great difficulty in preparing themselves for adult life, and show it **V:** be at, be past/over, get to/near, go through □ *Susan would like to come with us, I'm sure, but don't press her too much. She's at* ***the awkward age****, and rather self-conscious.* □ *He's a tall, shambling sort of fellow who looks as if he'd never got past* ***the awkward age****.* □ *Johnnie, unlike his brothers, was very easy to bring up. He never seemed to have* ***an awkward age*** *at all.* □ used of mental, emotional, or physical characteristics.

an awkward customer [Comp (NP)] a person or animal (rarely a thing) that is difficult and/or dangerous to deal with or manage **V:** ⚠ be, appear; think, find, sb □ *I'll take the matter to the police before I let you do it.' 'I believe you would.' He seemed pleased about it. 'I really believe you would. You're* ***an awkward customer****, aren't you?'* RATT □ *'There's only* ***one awkward customer*** *on the staff,' he told his successor. 'I won't name her, but you'll find out for yourself soon enough.'* □ *A wild cat doesn't seek to attack people but it can be* ***an awkward customer*** *if surprised or cornered.* □ not used of physical clumsiness.

an awkward silence an embarrassed, or embarrassing, silence between people □ *'You can argue with me but not with my staff. In any case it is too late to change anything—If you think it is wrong, that can only mean that you have lost confidence in me.'* ***A*** *somewhat* ***awkward silence*** *followed these remarks.* MFM □ *I never knew what to say to him, and he never knew what to say to anybody at all, so that conversation between us was full of* ***awkward silences****.*

a/the awkward squad (originally military) a group of new recruits; (fig) any inept, clumsy, or otherwise intractable group □ *'Mind you, I don't agree with you about the Barrett boy—good material there. But I mustn't keep you—I see you have* ***a*** *little* ***awkward squad****?' Mrs Southcott turned, and walked back to the boys.* ***Awkward squad****? They'd get* ***awkward squad****!* TT □ *'We want the tents put up quickly before these clouds break,' the Scoutmaster said. 'Get your best boys on the job—and let* ***the awkward squad*** *go off and collect firewood.'* □ usu of new recruits, pupils, trainees.

the ayes/noes have it those who are in favour of/against a proposal are more numerous than those against/in favour of it □ *'Will those in favour of the motion raise their right hands,' continued the Chairman. '****The ayes have it*** *then.' he said, as a forest of hands shot up.* □ *Other raptures might go deeper, but for pure bliss the eyes had it. '****The Ayes have it****.' Yes, indeed they have! It was odd how since she had been with Alec words and even puns had come to mean a great deal to her.* PW □ used esp of voting aye (= yes) or no by a raising of the hand.

B

a babe in arms an infant too young to support itself without being held; (fig) an adult who is, or is thought to be, innocent, helpless or lacking in worldly wisdom (often because he/she is too young) □ *In the same spirit of refusal to condescend to fellow beings by softening reality for them, Mme Dolto makes it a principle to address not just fourteen-year-olds but very* ***babes in arms*** *in adult and intellectual terms.* NS □ *I am not* ***a babe in arms****. I am entitled to go out for a walk by myself if I want to.* EM □ not baby in arms; ⇨ ⚠ (as) helpless as a (new-born) babe etc.

babes in the wood innocent and inexperienced children or adults, who are victims of circumstances or of unscrupulous people (from the old ballad *The Children in the Wood* about a boy and a girl left to die in a wood by a wicked uncle) □ *They looked like a couple of* ***babes in the wood****, Brigit thought, with curious wryness. There were even tears in Prissie's cheeks to keep company with Nicky's.* DC □ *They were just two* ***babes in the wood*** *when they got married. They had terribly earnest discussions about love, compatibility, shared interests. Now look at them!* □ usu pl; often preceded by *(just) a couple of/two.*

back and forth [adv + adv non-rev] (moving) from one place to another and back again, repeatedly and usu in a regular way; backward(s) and forward(s) (qv); to and fro (qv) **V:** move, swing, wander; convey sth, pass, send sth □ *Allergic to seafaring ever since those childhood voyages* ***back and forth*** *between Southampton and the Cape, I detested the confinement, the motion, and the very smell of all ships.* AH □ *The wiper was clicking* ***back and forth*** *with the persistence of a metronome.* EM □ *Her mind flashed messages to itself* ***back and forth.*** MM □ ***Back and forth*** *swung the pendulum* (cf ***Back and forth*** *it swung* or: *The pendulum swung* ***back and forth****) gradually hypnotizing him with its movement.* □ usu end position after v of motion, but can have emphatic front position, as in last example.

a back number an issue of a periodical, or newspaper, earlier than the current one; (informal) sb who is thought to be no longer important, influential, modern in his outlook, etc **V:** be, become; consider, regard sb as; check, consult, look up □ *I spent the morning in the offices of the 'Cork Examiner' in Patrick Street. For four long hours I was deep in* ***back numbers*** *of that cosy old journal.* PP □ *One can't be cut off* (the phone) *perpetually. I still have my Homes to consider. I am not entirely* ***a back number****, Taylor. One must be on the phone.* MM □ *If I'd been marrying a girl like that and I'd had to introduce her to* ***a back-number*** *like me, I'd have pretended I'd dropped myself years ago, if you see what I mean.* CON □ not usu hyphenated.

the back of beyond [o (NP)] a distant isolated place, far from centres of civilization and social activity; a (similar kind of) place that is thought to be backward, dull and unattractive because of its poor social amenities, etc **prep:** at, from, in, to □ *The excitement and interest aroused by the fortnightly visit of the little mail-boat could hardly be appreciated by anyone who had not himself lived at some time in* ***the back of beyond****.* □ *I just can't understand this craze for buying up derelict cottages at* ***the back of beyond****, and cutting oneself off from everything and everyone.* □ *'I'll get all the publicity I want my own way,' Miss Miller retorted, 'and that won't be from some twopenny-halfpenny scandal sheet* (ie gossipy newspaper) *in* ***the back end of nowhere****.'* AITC □ usu preceded by a prep; variant the back end of nowhere found less frequently than headphrase.

back the right/wrong horse support at the beginning (as though betting money on a horse in a race) the person, team, candidate etc that eventually wins/loses; choose, adopt a scheme, idea, course of action, etc, that in the end succeeds/fails □ *He asked cold questions about who had done the work; with the methodicalness of a recording angel, he put down to Drawbell's credit the occasions when he had* ***backed the right horse****—and then turned to the other side of the sheet.* NM □ *The Russians make their mistakes, cause their antagonisms,* ***back their wrong horses****, just as we do.* OBS □ *Publishers, like other people, have their blind spots and little manias; like other people they reject chances of* ***backing a right horse****, and obstinately* ***back wrong ones****.* AH □ occurs most frequently in the form back the wrong horse.

a back seat [O/o (NP)] a position of little importance, power, or responsibility in the management of affairs; a low position in the order of priority **V:** (force/oblige sb to, have to) take, occupy; assign sb/sth to □ *I hope nobody minds if I take* ***a back seat*** *during the discussions, as I'm really only here as an observer.* □ *After so many years in control he found it difficult to accept that he now had to move to* ***a back seat*** *and let others take charge.* □ *Cutbacks in local government expenditure have meant nursery school and playgroup expansion plans taking* (or: *being assigned*) ***a back seat*** *in relation to the maintenance of essential public services.* □ usu sing. ⇨ ⚠ a back-seat driver.

back to front [A (n + n non-rev)] with the back where the front should be, and vice-versa □ *That boy's got his pullover on* ***back to front****.* □ *The windows on the ground floor had rude words written in the grime outside, which Mrs Roper could read* ***back to front*** *as she sat and rocked the baby.* AITC □ *In the* ***back-to-front*** *world that Alice found behind the looking-glass* (in Lewis Carroll's 'Alice Through the Looking Glass'), *the White Queen actually lived in reverse.* L □ attrib use *a* ***back-to-front*** *world.*

a back-seat driver a passenger in a car etc who persists in offering the driver unnecessary or annoying advice or criticism; sb who criticizes, or tries to influence, the decisions, actions etc of others which do not concern him or which (perhaps because of his inferior position) he is unable, or unwilling, to take himself □ *Jack's been travelling over this route for the last ten years so do stop telling him what to do. Not everyone can put up with **a back-seat driver**, you know.* □ *I've no use for all these **back-seat drivers** telling me how to run things without doing a stroke of real work themselves.* □ variant back-seat driving. ⇨ ⚠ a back seat.

(the) backroom boys a group of people, engaged in scientific research, etc, who do not become prominent leaders or managers but who provide a vital service for those who do □ *A firm like this, Professor Carter suggested, would make no use of specialized management techniques, regarded scientists as '**back-room boys**' instead of allowing them a say in policy, and had difficulty in recruiting talented people.* L □ *In the last analysis it's **the back-room boys** who put a nation in front.* T □ almost always pl; sing form normally *be one of **the backroom boys***, rarely *be **a backroom boy***.

backward in coming forward [Comp (AdjP)] (informal) hesitant, or reluctant, to assert oneself, one's opinions or wishes; shy or retiring **V:** ⚠ be, seem; find sb. **A:** rather; (not) usually, (not) often, seldom □ *He was continually being passed over when promotions were made. At the beginning he accepted that it was because he was rather too **backward in coming forward**, but gradually he developed a feeling of injustice as he saw less able, but more aggressive, people overtaking him.* □ *I expect he was too bashful. Poor old Alec! It's the first time I've ever known him to be. He's not usually **backward in coming forward**.* PW □ (NONCE) *Parliamentary pronouncement reflects the views of infuriated constituents, who are never **backward in forwarding*** (= in coming forward with) *their views about the latest outrage on BBC or ITV to their Member.* L □ often neg.

backward(s) and forward(s) [adv + adv non-rev] (moving) from one place to another and back again, rcpeatedly and usu in a regular way; back and forth (qv), to and fro (qv) **V:** move, travel; pass, transfer, switch, sth □ *He began to pace **backward and forward** on the bridge.* PM □ *Then they work the tractor **backwards and forwards** to stamp the earth in.* RFW □ *He began to sway **backwards and forwards** in his chair, feverishly flicking his short fingers.* HD □ ***Backwards and forwards** they swam* (cf ***Backwards and forwards** swam the boys* or: *They swam **backwards and forwards**)—three lengths of the baths in a race.* HAA □ usu end position after v of motion, but may occupy emphatic front position, as in last example.

bad blood (between A and B) [Comp/O (NP)] ill-feeling, enmity (between sb and sb else) **V:** there be; cause, create, make (for) □ *'So I'm to be an efficiency expert?' 'Not quite. Don't like those chaps anyway; there's **bad blood** wherever they are.'* RATT □ *There had been **bad blood between** them for so long that neither was willing to make the first friendly approaches.* □ *The unfair distribution of their father's wealth made for **bad blood between** the brothers.*

a bad etc business [Comp (NP)] (informal) an unfortunate, unpleasant, or deplorable event, state of affairs, etc **S:** it, this, that; death, disappearance. **V:** ⚠ be; consider sth, think sth. **adj:** bad, ⚠ shocking, terrible, sad, unfortunate □ *This pilfering from the offices is **a bad business**; we'll all be suspecting one another if it goes on much longer.* □ *It'll be **a bad business** for everybody here, not just the fishermen, if the river pollution gets any worse.* □ *That was **a terrible business** down at the chemical works last night.*

a bad egg/lot (dated informal) sb who is untrustworthy, wicked (possibly criminally so) etc □ *Their nephew, who was **a** real **bad egg**, got his hands on nearly all the old couple's savings on the pretext that he would buy them a little place in the country.* □ *If I were you, I wouldn't be seen too much with Ken. He's **a** thoroughly **bad lot**.* □ a bad lot (always sing) may refer to a group of people, as in *Don't have anything to do with the Johnsons—they're **a bad lot**!*

bad/good form [Comp (NP)] incorrect/correct social behaviour, esp according to British middle- or upper-class standards **V:** ⚠ be; consider sth, think sth (to be) □ *'I remember,' said Dave, 'you once before told me that it was **bad form** to drink in a pub you didn't know the name of, or to enter a pub without drinking.'* UTN □ *You could go to the reception in your sports jacket but it would be rather **bad form**.* □ *No self-respecting bookie likes to admit to doing well. It is considered very **bad form** in the trade, like driving around in a Rolls Royce, since it tends to discourage punters.* ST □ *In some parts of the world it is considered quite **good form** to belch after food—it shows proper appreciation.* □ becoming dated.

bad etc luck (on sb) [Comp (NP)] (informal) an unfortunate happening (for sb) **V:** ⚠ be, seem; think sth. **adj:** bad, ⚠ hard, rotten, rough, tough □ *'I didn't get that job after all.' '**Bad luck**!* (or: *What **bad luck**!) But I suppose you'll be looking around again?'* □ *'And you, Harold, you are happy, you are not disappointed because Mrs Eastwood cannot come?' 'Well, it was **bad luck on** her, of course,' said Harold.* PW □ *If her husband couldn't get away at that time of year, she thought, well, **bad luck on** him, but she wasn't going to lose the opportunity of a trip abroad.* □ *'I've lost my wallet!' '**Hard luck**!'* □ often exclamation, as in last example, otherwise a comment—either can be said sympathetically or unsympathetically; attrib use a ***hard-luck** story*.

bad news travels fast (saying) unpleasant facts rapidly become known widely (whereas pleasant facts do not attract so much notice) □ ***Bad news**, it is said, **travels fast**. In this country, at the moment, bad news seems to be the only kind of news that travels at all.* G □ *The accident happened at five o'clock. By half past five everyone in the village knew about it. **Bad news travels fast**!*

a bad etc patch a particularly difficult, or awkward, period of one's life (eg in work, money, personal relationships, etc) **V:** have; hit, strike; go through, run into. **adj:** bad, ⚠ black, difficult, hard □ *He went through **a** very **bad patch** last year: he lost his job and his wife left him for another man.* □ *He dreaded the repetition of the writer's **bad patch** when, for three weeks, he had shivered in his bitter attic.* US □ *Don't be* *too discouraged if the words suddenly dry up. I struck* **a** *couple of* **difficult patches** *recently when I thought I was never going to write again.*

bag and baggage [A (n + n non-rev)] with all one's/sb's belongings, often suddenly or secretly **V:** go away, leave; throw sb out, turn sb out □ *His landlady couldn't tell the police where he might be. All she knew was that he'd left,* **bag and baggage**, *without paying his rent.* □ *I can't understand why Ted puts up with a drunken brother-in-law in his house. Most people would have turned him out,* **bag and baggage**, *long ago.* ⇨ ⚠ lock, stock and barrel; hook, line and sinker.

a bag of bones [Comp/O (NP)] (informal) a very thin person or animal, esp one made so by starvation or illness **V:** be (just), be nothing but; look like □ *I'm glad to see you putting on weight again. You were just* **a bag of bones** *when you came home from hospital.* □ *You'll get nothing for your horse. Who's going to buy* **an** *old* **bag of bones** *like that?*

a bag/bundle of nerves [Comp/o (NP)] (informal) overwrought, nervous, easily frightened, etc (often temporarily because of some pressure, threat etc); a nervous wreck (qv) **V:** be, become; reduce sb to □ *'It's all so calm with you. Do you know what it's doing to me?—I'm being strangled!' 'You can't act quicker than the police. If you're* **a bag of nerves**, *it's your fault.'* YAA □ *She's not fit to be a mother; she'll reduce that child to* **a bag of nerves** *with all the scoldings and slappings he gets.* □ *Ever since the break-in she had become* **a bundle of nerves**, *starting at the slightest sound in the house.* □ sing use with reference to several people, as in *The two of them were* **a bag of nerves**!

a baker's dozen thirteen (from a former practice of giving an extra bun, roll etc free to a customer buying a dozen of any one article sold in a bakery) □ *There were twelve occupants of the Maud Long Medical Ward (aged people, female). The ward sister called them* **Baker's Dozen**, *not knowing that this is thirteen, but having only heard the phrase.* MM □ *'I've got witnesses,' I said to him. 'I can get you a dozen more, or thirteen altogether, if it was a baker's that got robbed.' 'I don't want no lies,' he said, not catching on about* **the baker's dozen**. LLDR □ *Let us start, then, with* **a baker's dozen** *of introverts, followed by a similar number of extraverts.* SNP

a banana republic (derogatory) a state that is (considered to be) dependent on primary, agricultural products and that is, therefore, backward economically and politically, and subject to internal disorder □ *Until recently there was a tendency to dismiss whatever happened, good or bad, in South America as just the sort of thing one would expect of* **banana republics**; *but now such simple and derogatory attitudes no longer hold good.* □ (NONCE) *These projects* (in technology) *may properly be described as a lunge into the future, undertaken because of psychological pressures, to prove that we* (the UK) *are not yet* **a banana kingdom**. L □ formerly used of some Central and South American states.

the bane of sb's existence/life [Comp (NP)] sb, or sth, that causes continual trouble or worry to sb, either badly affecting everything he does or occupying his attention more than he wishes **V:** ⚠ be, become; find sth □ *Anne suffers a lot from migraine; it's* **the bane of her existence**, *in fact.* □ *Wet or fine, weeds are* **the bane of** *a gardener***'s life**. OBS □ *I had purchased in Asunción a gigantic mincing machine — this ponderous piece of mechanism was* **the bane of our lives**. *Even when working properly, it shuddered and groaned, emitting at intervals a piercing shriek.* DF □ *I'm getting really fed up with her. She's becoming* **the bane of my life**, *always on the doorstep, asking favours, borrowing things and complaining about all her neighbours.* □ bane sing, even when referring to pl people or things.

bang etc in the middle (of sth) [A (PrepP)] (informal) exactly in the centre (of a space or area, a line of things, etc); suddenly, and perhaps inconveniently, while sth else is happening, while sb else is doing sth, etc **V:** be, stand, fall; happen, explode, yell. **adv:** bang, ⚠ right, slap. **o:** target; road, town; room, carpet; conversation, work; what I was saying/doing □ *I wish you wouldn't interrupt people* **bang in the middle of** *what they're saying.* □ *You would arrange to have your party* **right in the middle of** *my exams!* □ (of a proposal to convert an ocean liner, Queen Elizabeth II, into an offshore casino) *Since the continental shelf falls away steeply from the coastline the QE2 would not be able to anchor itself. Not only that, it would be* **slap in the middle of** *a general shipping line.* ST □ bang and slap more informal and emphatic than right; variant slap bang in the middle (of sth) more informal and emphatic than headphrase.

the bare bones (of sth) the essential, main facts or outline (of some matter or situation) and nothing more; a bare outline (of sth) (qv) **V:** be; give sb, reveal; get, come, to. **o:** story, play, plot; matter, situation, the (whole) business □ *Such are* **the bare bones of** *the plot.* □ *Leaving aside the ethics of it, and stripping the matter to* **its bare bones**, *the plain fact is that no one dares to use the nuclear weapon for fear of mutual suicide.* BM □ *I don't know any more than you about it. My husband just gave me* **the bare bones**—*that Rogers had attacked his wife and the police had to be called in.* □ variant a skeleton outline (of sth).

bare of sth [Comp (AdjP)] without, not having, sth that is normally, or at other times, present **V:** ⚠ be, become; strip sth/sb. **o:** (any) covering, protection; flowers, leaves; decoration □ *With the road to ourselves,* **bare of** *other traffic, we sped on fast.* BM □ *In the winter when the trees were* **bare of** *leaves* (cf *when the trees were* **bare**), *it was possible to see the lake on the far side of the park.* □ *In striking contrast with the rest of the house, his study was austerely furnished and* **bare of** *any ornament.*

a bare outline (of sth) [Comp/O (NP)] a brief statement of the main facts (of some matter or situation) and nothing more; the bare bones (of sth) (qv) **V:** be; give sb, state, quote. **o:** story, play, plot; matter, situation; plan □ *This is* **the bare outline of** *only some of the reactions encountered in the course of this work.* SNP □ *I don't need all the details now, just give me* **a bare outline of** *your plans.* □ *These,* **in bare outline**, *are* *only some of the reactions.* □ variant in bare outline.

a bargain basement/counter a serving area in a shop, or large store, where the goods are sold at less than their usual price or where particularly cheap goods are sold □ *You need to be fairly careful not to be taken in by* ***the bargain counters*** *in some stores. Very often they're full of shoddy goods that they wouldn't dream of selling normally.* □ *Britain is not* ***the*** *only* ***bargain basement*** *of Europe after all. Some of the countries these tourists come from are not as expensive for holiday makers as Brighton or Scarborough.* G ⇨ ⚠ a bargaining counter.

a bargain's a bargain/a promise is a promise (saying) an agreement, or promise, is binding □ *'You're a fool to miss this chance of a higher salary.' 'Maybe, but* ***a bargain's a bargain****. When I took this job I promised to stay for at least three years.'* □ *'Oh come on, Liz, sit down and relax!' 'I will* not*;* ***a promise is a promise****, remember. You said "a couple of drinks and then straight home".'*

a bargaining counter [Comp/O (NP)] a special advantage, a position of strength in negotiations, disputes etc, which one can use to offset, or outweigh, some advantage possessed by the other side. **adj:** strong, valuable; weak □ *The* de facto *occupation by British and American armies of large parts of the Russian Zone was* ***an*** *important* ***bargaining counter*** *for obtaining satisfaction from the Soviet Government on a number of outstanding questions.* MFM □ *Comparatively unproductive groups — pensioners, the chronic sick, students in training—have no* ***bargaining counters****. All they can do to push their claims for more money is to make a big enough nuisance of themselves.* ⇨ ⚠ a bargain basement/counter.

sb's bark is worse than his bite (saying) sb is not so dangerous, bad-tempered, aggressive etc as he gives the appearance of being (esp when one compares what he says with what he does not do) □ *All my friends were terrified by my landlady, but I knew* ***her bark was worse than her bite****.* □ *I don't care whether* ***his bark is worse than his bite*** *or not. I'm not working for somebody who deliberately sets out to be rude to everybody.* □ *There are a number of 'spicy', 'off the shoulder' periodicals, or sex-and-bittiness weeklies and monthlies,* ***whose bark is*** *in an illuminating way much* ***worse than their bite****.* UL □ in last example (sing expression referring to pl things) implication is that the periodicals are not as sexy as they appear to be or would like to be thought.

a batting average (cricket) the average number of runs scored by a batsman in a season or in a series of matches; (fig) sb's record of attainment over a series of tests or experiments; sb's successes, compared with his failures, over a period of time, in his work, etc □ *Turner finished the season as he had started, with a splendid score of 110 which put him at the top of* ***the batting averages*** (ie the printed tables showing the position of various batsmen). □ *Where a number of judges made predictions as to the 'officer' quality and future career of young officer candidates, some people had* ***a batting average*** *of correct predictions very much in excess of that of their colleagues, while others were quite unusually incompetent.* SNP □ stress pattern a 'batting average.

the battle of the bulge (facetious) the struggle to keep one's weight down and esp to reduce the size of one's waistline and stomach in middle age (from the unofficial name given to the Ardennes campaign (Dec-Jan 1944-5) in the Second World War, when German forces attempted a breakthrough and almost succeeded) □ *At a rotund five feet six inches and sixteen stone, Jim is now winning* ***the battle of the bulge*** *as a weight-watcher.* RT

a battle of wits [Comp/o (NP)] a contest in which the intelligence, ingenuity etc of one person, or party, is pitted against that of another, either verbally or tactically; the cut and thrust (of sth) (qv); the thrust and parry (qv) **V:** be... (between); engage in, join in □ *The Russian war of nerves, or* ***battle of wits****, was looked on not as a bluff but as an indication that hostilities would break out at any moment.* MFM □ *It's* ***the*** *usual* ***battle of wits*** *between the cops and the robbers.* DS □ *Unless he was careful to whom he spoke, the professor often found himself engaged in* ***this battle of wits*** *over the question of who took the shortest holiday in the year.* TCM □ also pl battles of wits.

a battle royal a strongly contested fight, or dispute, between two or more persons or parties (from, originally, a fight in which several combatants were engaged (esp in cockfighting)) □ *You'd better attend the Council meeting to-night; we're expecting* ***a battle royal*** *over the new parking proposals for the town centre.* □ *The ladies of the staff affiliated themselves to either the Upper or Lower staffrooms by natural inclination, and throughout my whole term as headmaster* ***a battle royal*** *was waged between them on every conceivable issue.* □ *If his father really thought Paul was intending to enlist in the Army, it wouldn't be an argument they'd be having, it would be* ***a battle royal****.* □ adj always in end position.

a bawling/slanging match a noisy, angry dispute between two or more people with accusations and counter-accusations **V:** be... (between); start; engage in □ *Instead of attacking one another, Robert and the Bloater began arguing in more or less normal voices. For a moment I thought they were going to start* ***another bawling match****.* CON □ (reader's letter) *After sitting through the Dimbleby Talk-in on meat prices (12 Jan, BBC1) which gradually degenerated into* ***an*** *ignorant and ill-mannered* ***slanging match****, I wondered whether...* RT □ *I've never had* ***a*** *real* ***slanging match*** *with a woman before. I told her what I thought of her, and she told me what she thought of me.* □ also pl; stress pattern a 'bawling/'slanging match.

bay the moon [V + O] want sth that one cannot have; engage in a futile pursuit of sth (as dogs are said to bark (ie bay) at night when they see the (unattainable) moon); cry for the moon (Vol 1) (qv) □ (source) *I had rather be a dog, and* ***bay the moon****,/Than such a Roman.* JULIUS CAESAR IV 3 □ *I wouldn't try to shake anyone's belief in an afterlife if it was a comfort to them, but, to me, it is just* ***baying the moon****.* □ *You lost Sue entirely through your own fault and now* *she's gone off with someone else. You're just* ***baying the moon*** *if you expect to get her back now.*

be afraid (that) be sorry to have to say (sth, which may be a polite objection, refusal, expression of an unwelcome fact, etc) □ ***I'm afraid*** *you're wrong. The quotation is from Milton, not Shakespeare.* □ *If you want to catch that train, you'll have to leave now,* ***I'm afraid.*** □ usu first person, present tense; that usu not present; often end position.

be afraid to do sth be reluctant to perform some action through fear of the consequences **Inf:** to speak, say (a word), open (one's mouth in public), move (a step), go (out), act □ *She* ***was afraid to*** *open the gate in case the dog attacked her.* □ *Don't* ***be afraid to*** *tell me if anything goes wrong.* ⇨ ⚠ be afraid etc of doing sth.

be afraid for sb/sth worry, be concerned, feel anxious, about sb and the danger he may be in, or about the way things may develop **o:** him, you, them; his safety, the future □ *Parents,* ***afraid for*** *the safety of their children, have started a campaign for a supervised pedestrian crossing at the road junction near the school.* □ *Growing right-wing unrest together with new waves of extreme left-wing terrorism lead many observers to* ***be afraid for*** *the future of parliamentary democracy in the country.* ⇨ ⚠ next entry.

be afraid etc of sb/sth be in a state of fear about sb/sth **adj:** afraid, ⚠ frightened, terrified. **o:** him, her, them; the authorities; burglars; heights, the dark; flying; horses, wasps; the consequences; what may happen; nothing □ *She was bitter and arrogant and made life impossible for daddy. We* ***were*** *all* ***afraid of*** *her.* DC □ *I was eleven or twelve years old before I stopped* ***being frightened of*** *the dark.* □ *He****'s afraid of*** *nothing and nobody; I've seen him take on boys twice his size in the playground.* ⇨ ⚠ previous entry.

be afraid etc of doing sth be in a state of fear or worry about sth **adj:** afraid, ⚠ frightened, terrified. **o:** getting old, looking silly, making a mistake, losing one's job, hurting oneself/sb, upsetting sb □ *She* ***was afraid of*** *falling ill and having to go to hospital again.* □ *It's no use asking* him *to support you. He****'s*** *absolutely* ***terrified of*** *offending the bosses.* ⇨ ⚠ be afraid to do sth.

be afraid of one's (own) shadow be very timid and easily alarmed, usu without proper cause □ MR GREEN: *I'm afraid of my mother—and she's scared to death of me.* MRS GREEN: *Who could blame her?* ***I'm afraid of my shadow.*** DPM □ *The Government may have only a slim majority of votes, but that does not explain why it* ***is*** *so ineffectual and so* ***afraid of its own shadow.*** □ pl be afraid of their own shadow(s).

(not) be all beer and skittles (not) be always pleasant and free of trouble, hardship etc **S:** life, job, marriage; it; everything □ *Do you think that a life that* ***is all beer and skittles*** *can prove very satisfying in the long run?* □ *Naturally there were gaieties of sorts, public or private, open or secret; but* ***all was not beer and skittles.*** AH □ *Just because it's not on a nine-to-five basis doesn't mean that an actor's job* ***is all beer and skittles.*** □ beer and skittles non-rev.

(not) be/take all day etc (not) take a long time, or too long a time, (to do sth) **n:** day, ⚠ night, evening, afternoon □ *Robert strode angrily towards the door, calling to me over his shoulder, 'Oh, come on—do****n't be all night****!'* CON □ *Tell me what you want me to get in town then, but do****n't take all day*** *over it. I have to catch the 9 o'clock train.* □ *'Can I tell you something, Estelle?' '****Not*** *if you're going to* ***be all night*** *about it.'* □ *'Are you going to* ***take all day*** *shaving?' she shouted to him through the bathroom door.* □ often neg imper. ⇨ ⚠ (not) have all day.

be (only) as old as one feels [V + Comp] (saying) even if one is not old one can 'feel old' (eg tired and weak), and even if one is old one can 'feel young' (eg lively and enthusiastic) □ *Remember what my grandmother, well into her eighties, used to say every morning as she set off for her plunge into the icy Atlantic: 'You****'re only as old as you feel*** *and I feel forty today!'* ⇨ ⚠ feel one's age.

be the bee's knees [V + Comp] be, in sb's estimation, just what is wanted; be the best person, thing, idea etc; be the cat's pyjamas/whiskers (qv) □ *When it comes to tennis, I don't take Jim's reputation too seriously. He may* ***be the bee's knees*** *at his college, but I don't think there's much competition there.* □ *I'm not flattered by Charles's attentions. He clearly thinks he****'s the bee's knees*** *around here, but I don't share his opinion.* □ usu restricted to a fairly trivial context, and/or used ironically; often in construction *sb thinks he* ***is the bee's knees.***

(not) be etc a blind bit of use etc [V + O] (informal) (not) have any, the slightest effect **V . . . o:** be. . .use; ⚠ make. . .difference; take. . .notice, pay. . .attention □ *And something inside me altered as well—though I tried to tell myself that all was just the same and that Kathy's leaving me would****n't make a blind bit of difference.*** LLDR □ *Now it****'s not a blind bit of use*** *your protesting to the committee.* □ *You'd think when that sort of thing* (= a physical assault) *happened in the middle of the West End a hundred people would be around in a jiffy but no one* ***took a blind bit of notice.*** JFTR □ *But even if she* (an officer in the Women's Section of the Labour Party) *follows this advice, and goes to the Labour Women's Conference with a resolution and gets it passed, is the Labour Party at the real conference or in Parliament going to* ***pay a blind bit of attention****?* NS □ usu neg, or interr with neg implication.

be built/made that way (informal) have it in one's nature or constitution to be or do sth □ *I always like to have things tidy about me. I suppose* ***I'm just built that way.*** □ *My sister can make herself agreeable and pleasant to people she doesn't like in the least, but* ***I'm*** *not* ***built that way.*** □ *Jim was never one for loving speeches and flowers on your birthday and so on. He* ***is****n't* ***made that way,*** *but you couldn't get a better husband, all the same.* □ *You mustn't blame her for being nervous if that's* ***the way*** *she****'s made.*** □ often neg.

(not) be born yesterday be sb who is (not) likely to be deceived or taken advantage of; (not) be so foolish or stupid □ ***Born yesterday****? Joe? You're joking — he's the craftiest devil around!* □ *The spiv is a more positive figure, a sort of inverted 'go-getter', a 'casher-in' on disorder.*

For those who occur among working-class people (some of) the favourite phrases are: 'I'm in the know.' 'I ***wasn't born yesterday****.' I know my way around.'* UL □ *Of course I didn't let on to the copper that I'd helped the bloke to hang himself. I* ***wasn't born yesterday****, nor the day before yesterday either.* LLDR □ ***Were*** *you* ***born yesterday****? Fancy giving a knife-grinder a pound note for a 20p job and expecting him to come back later with the change!* □ *He told you that? He must have thought you* ***were born yesterday****.* □ neg, interr, or neg by implication; past tenses only.

be by way of being sth (informal) be considered to be, or have pretensions to being, the thing stated; be a sort of, a kind of, sth □ (A certain book) *had to do with early smoking habits and materials, on which Old Archie* ***was*** *evidently* ***by way of being*** *an expert.* TGLY □ *She's very fond of visiting art galleries and* ***is by way of being*** *an artist herself.* □ *'What's that curious object?' 'It****'s by way of being*** *a parsley chopper, but either it's badly designed, or else I don't know how to work it properly.'*

be the case (that) (formal) be a fact (that); be true (that) **S:** this, ⚠ such; it □ *It is claimed that this is your handwriting. If this* ***is the case****, there will be serious consequences.* □ ***Is*** *it* ***the case that*** *all our actions are determined by our sexual drives?* □ *It might have been thought that the Western Christian influence would have been very great in this troubled scene. But such* ***was*** *not* ***the case****.* BN

be a case in point be a particular example, or instance, of sth already stated in general terms □ *People over the years have changed their minds about the Common Market, and Mr John Stonehouse* ***is a case in point****.* NS □ *Those who go only to the festival concerts with big names attached sometimes miss a deal of excitement.* ***A case in point was*** *last night's appearance of a young piano trio from America.* G ⇨ ⚠ next entry.

be a case of sth be what is required, or unavoidable, given the circumstances **o:** helping oneself, making do; do or die; all hands on deck □ *The implications of my defeat had never really struck me before. It* ***was****n't just* ***a case of*** *muddling through and losing every battle but the last in true British fashion.* BM □ *'Three of our friends are helping to coach Brian with his maths, but he's not making much progress.' 'Maybe it****'s a case of*** *too many cooks spoiling the broth.'* □ BEATIE: *I can't bear sick men. They smell.* JIMMY: *Ole* (= old) *Stan's alright—do anythin'* (= anything) *for you.* BEATIE: *I couldn't look after one you know.* JIMMY: ***Case of*** *heven'* (= having) *to sometimes.* R □ often used to introduce all, or part, of saying that sums up the situation or shows course to be followed; ***be a case of*** *having to* often used of situation where one has no choice but to act in given way. ⇨ ⚠ previous entry.

be the cat's pyjamas/whiskers [V + Comp] (dated informal) be, in sb's estimation, just what is wanted; be the best person, thing, idea etc; be the bee's knees (qv) □ *I was very lazy when I was a young actor. I really thought I* ***was the cat's pyjamas****.* TVT □ *There were thousands of buses in England; let them* (ie the government) *give me some and release me from this static role so that I could practise a mobile counter-attack. The Prime Minister thought that this* ***was the cat's whiskers****.* MFM □ usu restricted to a fairly trivial context, and/or used ironically; often in the construction *sb thinks he* ***is the cat's pyjamas/whiskers.***

be caught/taken short [V + Comp] suddenly need to empty one's bowels or bladder □ *'Now people seem to use anywhere* (as a WC). *Even near the shelters and the platform. You Littluns, when you're getting fruit, if you****'re taken short****—' the assembly roared. 'I said if you****'re taken short*** *you keep away from the fruit. That's dirty.'* LF

be caviar(e) to the general be sth suited to specialized tastes or responses; be sth not appreciated, liked, understood or known to the majority of people (general here = 'people in general') □ *The play, I remember, pleased not the million; 't****was caviare to the general****.* HAMLET II 2 □ *I learned to play the sitar, after a fashion, at a time when, over here, Indian classical music* ***was*** *still* ***caviare to the general****.* □ (NONCE) *Mr MacIntyre has written a sharp, racy book packed—overpacked?—with Irish wit and style about the Dublin arms trial of last year. The result is perceptive entertainment, but, I suspect,* ***Irish coffee*** (black coffee with Irish whisky and topped with cream) ***to the general****.* L

be cruel to be kind (saying) do or say sth painful but necessary to sb, so that greater good may come from it □ *Only you can help.* ***Be cruel to be kind****. Break his idol completely. Tell him now that he is not ready for a life and a friendship so far outside his achievements.* HAA □ *'I'm only* ***being cruel to be kind****,' the physiotherapist said, 'If I don't keep you at these exercises now, you'll lose the use of your shoulder muscles entirely.'* □ often with *you have to/must.*

be/mean curtains (for sb) [V + Comp] (informal) be/lead to the end of (esp) sb's life □ *If you met one (*ie a German Messerschmitt aeroplane*) in a Typhoon or a Spitfire it was likely to* ***be curtains*** *unless you had a great numerical advantage.* RFW □ *And be careful how you drive. If you run into anything big in that cockleshell of a car, it'll* ***mean curtains for*** *you, my lad.*

be a dab etc hand at sth [V + Comp] (informal) be skilful at, experienced in, sth/doing sth **det:** quite a, not much of a, no. **adj:** dab, great; old (= experienced); poor (= bad). **o:** finding excuses, making pancakes; photography, insinuation □ *'The door key was in it* (a lost handbag).*' 'That's distinctly awkward. Unfortunately I****'m*** *not* ***a great hand at*** *picking locks.'* TBS □ *One course in Early Classical Greek Vase Paintings attracted enormous support one year, but only because word got around that the Spartans had* ***been dab hands at*** *pornography.* OBS □ *The kids won't get to make a monkey out of me.* ***I'm an old hand at*** *baby-sitting.* □ *He was obviously annoyed and* ***was no hand at*** *concealing it.* CON □ *'Peter* ***was never much of a hand at*** *letter-writing,' his mother said, looking at the three lines scribbled on half a sheet of paper, 'and he's getting worse as he grows older.'*

be damned etc (informal) sb, or sth, mentioned or suggested (in an immediately previous statement) is to be defied, rejected, refused, ignored etc, in the opinion of the speaker **adj:** damned, ⚠ blowed, darned, hanged, (taboo) buggered □ *'Won't your boss expect you to turn up at the meeting?' 'The boss* ***be buggered****! My time's my own outside office hours.'* □ *'If I were you, I'd clear out of here before you start any more trouble with your Red notions.' 'Red notions* ***be damned****!' he shouted. 'I've nothing against you men, in the main—'* HD ⇨ ⚠ (well) I'll be/I'm damned etc!; I'll be/I'm damned etc if.

be dead against sth [V + Comp] be firmly opposed to (doing) sth **o:** it, the proposal, drink, selling □ *And Reith was against all forms of drinking at that time. He used to try and put the pubs here out of bounds. He* ***was dead against*** *it.* L □ *She would have liked to adopt a baby but her husband* ***was dead against*** *it.* □ *Any responsible lawyer would* ***be dead against*** *an elderly person risking his capital in a private loan. It's my duty to dissuade you if I can.*

be etc dead right/wrong [V + Comp] be absolutely correct **V:** be; ⚠ get sth; have (got) sth □ *'I suppose Kenny Macroon is right in advising me not to camp out on Pillay?' 'He****'s dead right****, Mr Brownsworth.'* RM □ *'I suppose you're angry with me?' 'You****'re dead right*** *I am.'* □ *He's a good judge of character as a rule, but he* ***was dead wrong*** *about Harry* □ *Your measurements must* ***be dead right*** *because a deviation of even 0.5mm in some part of the blueprint will be so magnified in the working model that it constitutes a serious or dangerous defect.* □ *Well done—you****'ve got*** *that design* ***dead right*** *now.* □ *Your parents have made an excellent job of renovating that old cottage they bought last year. They* ***have*** *the whole thing* ***dead right****.* □ be dead wrong not often used.

be the death of sb [V + Comp] (informal, facetious) cause sb a great deal of harm, anxiety or worry; be exceptionally funny or ridiculous **S:** road, steps; job, project; husband □ *Do me a favour, shave that beard off. Oh, you drive me mad—you'll* ***be the death of*** *me—what a son I've got!* DPM □ *Oh, stop grumbling—filling in a few forms won't* ***be the death of*** *you.* □ *This sent her off again* (ie started her laughing again). *'Oh you! You're a holy terror, yes, you are. You'll* ***be the death of*** *me some day.'* US □ with *will/would.*

be a different etc ball-game [V + Comp] (informal, esp US) be a different matter, a separate issue, a new subject **adj:** different, another, whole new □ *'But if Washington learnt the correct lessons from Vietnam, why have they begun interfering in the same way with El Salvador?' 'El Salvador? Central America? Don't you see — that's* ***a*** *completely* ***different ball-game****.'*

be dog tired [V + Comp] be very tired, (esp after work or physical exertion and as a temporary condition) □ *Let him do a little housework if he offers, don't insist that he washes up if he****'s dog tired****.* WI □ *'You're always so brave, but I can tell you're very disturbed.' 'I'm not in the least disturbed. I****'m*** *just* ***dog-tired****.* TGLY □ (NONCE) *'God. I'm tired. I haven't done a thing all day, and I****'m*** *as* ***tired*** *as a* ***dog****.' He put a cushion under his head, punched it and settled down.* AITC □ dog-tired frequently hyphenated.

(not) be sb's doing [V + Comp] (not) be sth that sb has done, instigated, been responsible for □ *'You want to be Queen of England, you let Catherine lie shut up in Kimbolton Castle where it's said you're having her poisoned.' 'You lie about Catherine,' she said harshly. 'Kimbolton Castle* ***isn't my doing****.'* WI □ *'It* ***won't be*** *the head-cashier****'s doing*** *if I get this promotion. He's never liked me.* □ *The difficult situation in which he found himself* ***was none of my doing*** *and I resented having to listen to his complaints.* □ *You can be damn sure the anonymous donors didn't include our local land-owner, anyway. If the new ambulance had* ***been any of his doing****, he'd have wanted to claim credit for it.* □ variant be none/not any of sb's doing.

be doing very nicely, thank you (very much) [V + Comp] (catchphrase) (as though in answer to a question) functioning, continuing or progressing successfully □ (rugby) *A group of worthy sporting gentlemen in Leeds have reformed the club, renamed it New Hunslet, found a new ground, and it****'s doing very nicely*** *so far this season,* ***thank you very much****, albeit in the Second Division of the Rugby League.* RT □ *Neil Lyall* ***is*** *currently* ***doing very nicely thank you*** *out of flogging a product called Pollen-B to an eager public.* NS □ *By the middle of the 18th century Gillow and his three sons had taken a lease on premises in Oxford Street where Selfridges now stands, and for 137 years everything went* ***very nicely, thank you****.* OBS □ *. . . a quite unjustified insult to the Royal Family who do not resemble the Mafia, and comprise an aristocracy far from decayed. Our Royal Family* ***are*** *still* ***doing very well, thank you very much****.* ST □ *At eleven o'clock he was still sitting there with his pipe lit and drawing* ***very nicely thank you****. We seemed to be stuck with him.* □ usu be doing, but sometimes adapted, as in last three examples.

be the done thing [V + Comp] be conventional or approved behaviour, etiquette, procedure □ *For most of us it* ***is*** *still* ***the done thing*** *to get married; and this, perhaps surprisingly, influences not only the girl who cannot wait to leave her boring office job, it also influences the intellectuals, the rebels who feel it is their right to question society's traditions.* ST □ *'When I was young,' their grandmother said, 'it* ***wasn't the done thing*** *for girls to go to dance halls without a partner.* □ *And marriage? Everyone got married in those days, it seemed* ***the thing to do*** *as soon as you got into uniform. Everyone thought they might be killed the next day.* TVT □ *Sartre, I suppose, was the only active European intellectual that one had heard of, and even his philosophy (to those of us eagerly listening to Russell on the wireless) didn't* ***seem the thing****. I say all this not merely to show how insular some of us were, but. . .* L □ variant be/seem the thing (to do).

be downhill all the way[1] [V + Comp] be easy and/or quick progress towards an objective (esp after difficulties are passed) **S:** it, the rest □ *Many politicians on both sides of the border* (ie between England and Scotland) *are already convinced that today's devolution White Paper marks a watershed. From now on they believe it will* ***be downhill all the way*** *for the separatists.* G □ *The police had felt sure all along that Georgie Taylor was their man. Once they had broken his alibi the rest* ***was downhill all the way****.* ⇨ an uphill task etc.

be downhill all the way[2] [V + Comp] be an inevitable process of decline or deterioration **S:** it □ *Between 1900 and 1959 the Conservative Party had, more often than not, a majority both of seats and votes in Scotland. In the 1955 election they polled over 50 per cent and won 36 out of 71 seats; since then it has* ***been downhill*** *almost* ***all the way****. Last October they polled less than 25 per cent and returned only 16 MPs.* NS □ *As good as ever I was? No treatment's going to do that for me. Once you get to my age it****'s downhill all the way****.*

be (just) the drink talking [V + Comp] be a confidence, boast, threat, promise etc made by sb who is drunk, and therefore not necessarily to be believed or relied upon **S:** it, that □ *'How on earth are we to live if Johnny gives up his job in the market?' 'He never will. That****'s just the drink talking****, Mary. I've heard him threaten that most Saturday nights for nearly twenty years.'* □ *He had been in a fight in a Liverpool pub, he told his wife, and had pushed a man against some railings. The man had struck his head on a spike and died, and he'd served time for manslaughter. 'I didn't know whether to believe him,' she said. 'I thought it* ***was the drink talking****.'* ST

be drunk in charge [V + Comp] (legal) be drunk when driving or in charge of a vehicle □ *At first he drove rather fast and then, suddenly subdued by the immensely incredible notion that he might one day become Master of Fox Hounds, slowed down to a silent crawl. He didn't want anybody to think he* ***was drunk in charge****.* DBM □ *'A man who thinks he is too drunk to drive and pulls into a layby to sleep it off can still be booked for* ***being drunk in charge****.' 'That seems a little hard, don't you think?'* □ *'Let me carry the whisky, before you drop it.' 'Yes, you take it—can't have a man* ***drunk in charge*** *of a bottle of whisky.'* □ extended uses humorous.

be dying for sth/to do sth [V + Comp] (informal) be longing for sth to occur, or to possess or experience sth, or for the opportunity to do sth □ *'James,' said Sonia. 'I'm sure everyone****'s dying for*** *a cocktail.* HAA □ *Only Tuesday morning, and* ***I'm dying for*** *the weekend already!* □ *Here you are at last. I've* ***been dying for*** *you to come back and hear the wonderful news.* □ *The remark was lost on Pop who* ***was dying to*** *demonstrate the horn's orchestral variations.* DBM *'Have you read this book?' asked Harold. 'No, but* ***I'm dying to****.'* PW

be the end [V + Comp] (informal) be very bad, annoying, exasperating; be no longer tolerable; be the worst that one can think of; be the (absolute) limit (qv) **S:** friend, wife; behaviour; remark, language. **adj:** absolute, very, bitter □ *Philip asked me if I had another bed I would put into their room. That he should bring her here. God, men* ***are the end****.* EHOW □ *'I asked him what the repairs would cost but I've forgotten what he said.' 'Oh, you really* ***are the end****!'* □ *I'd seen a dirty house before, but his* ***was the end****.* □ *'Then she said, "Of course, we have a higher standard of living to keep up than you."' 'If that****'s*** *not* ***the end****! What a cheek!'*

to be exact etc [Disj] more exactly; if you want it (ie sth previously mentioned) defined absolutely exactly **adj:** exact, ⚠ precise, (strictly) accurate □ *Short of exterminating the illegal diggers, the only solution was to legalize them. This was done, and early last year—on February 6th* ***to be exact****—all prosecutions against diamond diggers and dealers were suspended.* DS □ *'Not bad,' he said. 'Sixty-two minutes from town. From Highgate* ***to be precise****.'* HD □ front or end position.

be (strictly) for the birds [V + Comp] (slang) be worthless; be fit only for people who are easily deceived or misled □ *There was talk of departmental funds being reallocated to the Research section. That****'s strictly for the birds****—not a chance it'll happen.* □ *'You'll get your reward in heaven.' 'I don't believe that rubbish. It****'s for the birds****.'* □ (advertisement) *Does your choice of soap embarrass him (*ie a man*)? As far as he's concerned, the fancy stuff* ***is strictly for the birds****. Give him the clean, fresh smell of Wright's Coal Tar soap every time!* WOMAN AND HOME □ bird ((slang) = 'young girl') in last example gives a double meaning.

be sb's (own) funeral [V + Comp] (informal) be sb's (own) concern, fault, bad luck, etc; (be) sb's look-out (Vol 1) (qv) **S:** it, that. **A:** if he's late, if she doesn't come, if he gets into debt □ *There were always too many passengers for the boat, so that if someone got left behind, it would* ***be****, as far as I was concerned,* ***his funeral****.* NDN □ *If he can't join me on the 19th, that****'s his funeral****—he can't expect me to change all my arrangements now, just for him.* □ *If they've got into debt by splashing out on a house that's far too large for them anyway, it****'s their own funeral****.* □ stress pattern it's 'his funeral or it's his 'own funeral.

be glad etc to see the back of sb/sth (informal) be glad etc to get rid of sb/sth, to see him/it for the last time **cl:** be glad to see, ⚠ be anxious to see, not be sorry to see; hope to see, long to see; hope that one has seen, trust that one has seen, pray that one has seen □ *Then the rows began. Mrs Collins would rake over her husband's first marriage—'She must have* ***been glad to see the back of*** *you.'* □ *All right. That's your message. Now let's* ***see the back of*** *you.* ST □ *All right. That's your message. Now let's* ***see the back of*** *you and your boy-friend as well.* HD □ *'You'll* ***be glad to see the back of*** *the TT (motor-cycle race)?' a reporter asked Gould, as he crouched by the bike. 'Yep ((slang) = yes),' said Gould.* ST □ *I have made it more than clear that by now there* ***were*** *plenty of people* ***anxious to see the back of*** *me.* MFM □ *I shall* ***not be sorry to see the back of*** *1979.* NS

be a good chap etc (and do sth) [V + Comp] (informal) would you please be kind and helpful by agreeing to do sth that I would like you to do **Comp:** a good chap, ⚠ a good boy, a good girl, an angel, a darling, a dear, a sport □ *Would you* ***be a good chap and*** *take one end of the chest of drawers? I can't manage it by myself.* □ ***Be an angel****, Mary,* ***and*** *run downstairs and get the scissors. You'll find them on the kitchen table.* □ *Go on,* ***be a sport****. There's hardly any damage done to your car so there's no need to report the accident to the police.* □ friendly, encouraging introduction to request; be a good boy/girl used by adults to children; certain terms of endearment, like an angel, a dear, a darling used mainly by women.

be good/kind enough to do sth [V + Comp] (formal) be obliging and do what I suggest, what I would like you to do, as a favour or service to me; be so good/kind (as to do sth) (qv) □ *When you have finished your drink, would you* ***be good enough to*** *accompany me to the top of the hill again?* ARG □ *'Thank you, we have enough coffee,' he said in reply to the waiter's query, 'but if you would* ***be good enough to*** *empty the ashtrays?'* □ *As it was a very cold night, the landlady* ***was kind enough to*** *let me have two extra blankets and a hot-water bottle.* □ introduction to polite request, usu with *will/would you.*

be good for sb/sth [V + Comp] be beneficial to sb/sth; be effective in relieving or curing an illness or other unpleasant condition **S:** rest, holiday; drink, meal. **A:** it...to travel widely, it...not...to be on your own too much □ *Ah, there you are my dear boy,—all alone? Come and talk to me, it****'s*** *not* ***good for*** *you to be on your own too much.* FFE □ *Alice spends too much time playing with the big boys next door. A friend of her own age would* ***be better for*** *her, I'm sure.* □ *I'm tired of hearing people say 'It****'s good for*** *the carpet,' when they drop cigarette ash and then proceed to grind it in with the soles of their shoes.* □ *Drink this up hot. It'll* ***be good for*** *your cough.*

be good with one's hands [V + Comp] be skilful at practical work; be able to make/mend articles neatly and/or artistically □ *This man is known to be something of a 'scholar', another is a good 'penman', another* ***is*** *particularly '****good with his hands****', in wood or metal or as a general repairer.* UL □ *There was a lot of banging and clanking and something broke. 'Rudy* ***is****n't very* ***good with his hands****,' Beatrice said.* OMIH

be (all) Greek to sb be sth that sb cannot understand, esp talk or writing that is obscure, allusive or of a very technical nature □ *'But since they deepened the drain at Pomfret Madrigal in '37 everything has been at sixes and sevens and the Monday country absolutely ruined,' which* ***was Greek to*** *the Mertons, but Lady Pomfret evidently understood.* WDM □ *The cleaning women and other manual workers were chosen for their illiteracy, so that if they came on an engineering tool or a formula on a scrap of paper, it would* ***be all Greek to*** *them.* L

be half the battle be an important, or the decisive, contribution towards achieving sth □ *Believing you can make a good recovery* ***is half the battle*** *when you're ill.* □ *I've been adopted as candidate for the constituency, Mabel, and that****'s*** *already* ***half the battle****. Lowdon West is a pretty safe Labour seat.* □ *Having brains* ***is*** *only* ***half the battle****. If the boy's not going to use them he might as well have none.* □ ***be*** *only* ***half the battle*** = 'be important or necessary but not enough in itself'; S often *it, that* or *doing/having sth.*

(not) be happy about sth (not) be satisfied, contented, with sth □ *He can****not be*** *very* ***happy about*** *this measure, which owes its existence solely to the Government's desire to placate their Right wing supporters.* SC □ ***I'm not*** *too* ***happy about*** *leaving David with a baby-sitter. He's sure to panic if he wakes up and sees a strange face.* □ ***Are*** *you quite* ***happy about*** *all these suggestions? Anything you'd like to add?* □ affirmative statements are less frequent than neg statements and tend to be making assertions, or contradicting doubts or questions.

be here to stay [V + Comp] become permanent, successful, established, accepted **S:** fashion, commodity; way of thinking; industrial method, administrative procedure □ *If you're going to do bed and breakfasts in the holiday season you'll get plenty of unmarried couples, especially young people. That sort of thing* ***has come to stay*** *whether you approve or not.* □ *The trouser-suit that so effectively combines elegance and utility* ***is*** *surely, like the 'little black dress',* ***here to stay****.* □ *My wife May learned to drive, then my two farm workers. After 12 months I also learned to drive, and we* ***were*** *on the market* ***to stay****.* L □ *Even if the leaders were to come together to persuade Mrs Gandhi that the time had come for her to retire to Geneva, the old openness of the Nehru period seems likely to have gone for good. The draught excluders (=* enemies of 'open' government) ***have come to stay****.* G □ variant have come to stay.

be/get high on sth (informal) be/become exhilarated, intoxicated, stimulated etc under the influence of sth **o:** LSD, two whiskies; fresh air, good news □ *There are three separate strands to the story—a group of linguistics experts doing research with children, a tribe of South American Indians* ***getting high on*** *a drug of their own making, and...* SC □ *'I'm sure you could* ***get high on*** *this stuff,' Dad said as he put his bottle of cough medicine back on the shelf.* □ *The kids'll settle down. They****'re high on*** *fresh air and each other's company—it's always the same the first day of the holidays.*

to be honest etc [Disj] speaking honestly; saying what I really think **adv mod:** quite, perfectly, brutally, absolutely, totally. **adj:** honest, ⚠ frank, blunt □ *We had a pretty difficult relationship, which we both struggled to overcome. It was give and take and I don't know who gave more. I should think,* ***to be*** *quite* ***honest****, I gave more than she did.* ST □ *Why didn't the drivers have the confidence or,* ***to be blunt****, the courage to call a strike, like the miners?* NS □ *'Would you not like to come and stay with for a while?' '****To be frank****, Alice. I wouldn't. I'm too set in my ways now to fit in with other people's.'* □ front, middle or end position.

(not) be one's/sb's idea of sb/sth (not) be what one/sb thinks of as a normal characteristic of, a proper or representative type of, a person/thing **o:** a good person, a hero; a Prime Minister; bliss, fun, comfort, beauty; a holiday □ *She makes a lot of money by being a photographer's model—she****'s*** *everyone****'s idea of*** *a pretty girl.* UTN □ *Sitting for hours in a crowded pub full of cigarette smoke may* ***be your idea of*** *a pleasant night out, but it* ***isn't my idea of*** *comfort—these low doorways where you're always cracking your head, and stairs like corkscrews.* DC □ MIKE: *Perhaps you could persuade your mother to go away with you for a holiday somewhere. There's that cottage of mine in Essex. It's empty.* TONY: *I shouldn't imagine that a cottage in Essex with me* ***is*** *mother****'s idea of*** *fun at all.* EHOW

be in/out of one's element [V + Comp] feel relaxed and interested/ill at ease and bored □ *Look at Sophie over there—laughing, smoking, drinking, telling jokes, flirting. Totally* ***in her element****!* □ *You should never have taken me along with you. Surely you knew that I'd* ***be*** *right* ***out of my element*** *with all those physchiatrists, psychologists and psychotherapists?* ⇨ a fish out of water.

be like that (informal) be in a particular mood, take up a certain attitude, often an awkward or unco-operative one; be/get that way (qv) □ *'Kate's not coming because, she says, she didn't get a proper invitation.' 'Well if she wants to* ***be like that****, let her stay at home.'* □ *Oh, don't* ***be like that****, Julie! I was only teasing you!* □ always used in inf or imper; often neg.

be the (absolute etc) limit [V + Comp] be sb/sth that disconcerts, exasperates or offends to a marked or exceptional degree; be the end (qv) **adj:** absolute, ⚠ bloody, (dated) giddy □ LOUISE: *Where's Clive?* PAMELA: *Not down yet.* LOUISE: *Really, you children* ***are the limit****. I don't see why you can't all have breakfast together.* FFE □ *'I think it****'s the limit****,' the girl laughed. 'Here I've been in the Wrens three years but no one ever asked if I'd like to go to the party. Daddy comes along at the last minute and walks right in.'* RFW □ *Isn't it Gaelic at all? Well,* ***aren't*** *you* ***the giddy limit****, Father James. And telling everyone in Nottingham that 'Jingalorie' is how you say 'cheerio' in Gaelic.* RM

be loud in one's praise (of/for sb/sth) [V + Comp] praise, commend sb/sth very highly, enthusiastically □ *The minister* ***was loud in his praise for*** *Dan McGarvey, and rightly so, but to most workers in Britain it will be seen as a victory for the rank and file and for the shop stewards.* NS □ *I think you would like to know that he and his friends* ***were loud in their praise of*** *the arrangements on his journey.* MFM

be a man [V + Comp] behave in a firm, courageous way; have, or show, manly qualities □ *Oh, get upstairs to that child!* ***Be a man*** *for once in your life, can't you?* EHOW. □ *'And if ever I do get married,' she continued, 'It'll be to a man who* ***is a man****, not a mother's boy like you.'* □ usu exhortation to sb who is behaving in cowardly fashion, who needs encouragement, etc.

be/take a matter of seconds etc require, occupy a period of time to be measured in seconds etc **o:** seconds, ⚠ minutes, hours, days, weeks, months, years □ *I could place an order for a similar carpet, madam, but it would* ***be a matter of weeks*** *or even* ***months*** *before you got it.* □ *Perhaps I was too old, but it* ***took a matter of minutes*** *to wriggle in or out of the cramped little single seater cockpit.* RFW

be a moment etc [V + Comp] take very little time (to do sth) **Comp:** moment, ⚠ second, minute; (informal) jiffy, tick □ *'Where's Andrew gone now? We should be leaving straight away.' 'He'll not* ***be*** *two* ***seconds****, he's just run upstairs to comb his hair.'* □ *Now, just sit down, like a good chap. My wife'll just* ***be a minute*** *making you a cup of tea and then you'll feel better.* □ with *will* + *just/only/not*.

be neither here nor there [V + Comp] be of no importance or relevance □ *We did all we could to make this parish feel that it was part of a larger whole, in fact of the world—the world to which I myself belonged, though that* ***is neither here nor there****.* PW □ *I maintained my view that our dealing should be with Sadie. That Sadie might still fancy me* ***was neither here nor there****.* UTN □ *It is unfortunate that we should use* welsh *as meaning 'go back on one's obligations'. The fact that the dictionary says the origin of this meaning of the word is unknown* ***is neither here nor there****: the thing that matters is that there are many who believe it to have a 'race' connotation.* NS

be new to the game [V + Comp] be inexperienced in a game, trade or activity □ *It was agreed that, since Bernard* ***was new to the game****, we would not play poker for money that night.* □ *While we* (a forest-fire fighting squad) *waited for the helicopter to arrive and take us to the fire, I drowsed off and woke to hear Bob telling one fellow who* ***was new to the game****, '—nothing to it. Don't volunteer for anything, be last in line, and you'll be all right.'* BM □ *It's easy to see that you****'re new to the game****, Constable Jones. If someone can tell you immediately where he was on Tuesday before last between 7 and 9 o'clock, he's your number one suspect.*

be no/not any better than one should/ought to be [V + Comp] be less than averagely honest, good, trustworthy etc □ *Ledderford is a place where to talk about holidays abroad is one of the almost infallible marks of the stuck-up, the high-and-mighty, who* ***are no better than they should be****.* RATT □ *She was wrong about her son's marriage, of course, but to an old chapel-going countrywoman of the 1930s the word* actress *was synonymous with '****no better than she should be****'.* □ (of 'Western' films in the 1920s) *Girls were either ranchers' daughters, whiter than white, or one of an assortment of types,* ***none*** *of whom* ***was any better than she should be****.* TVT □ euphemism often used of prostitute or woman who accepts more or less casual sexual relationships.

be no great shakes [V + Comp] only averagely or less than averagely good, efficient, suitable, adequate etc □ *The Metropolitan Opera* ***is no great shakes*** *in general, but it has a resource never yet secured for Covent Garden: the service of Karl Böhm in the orchestra pit.* ST □ *She* ***is no great shakes*** *as a field naturalist. She constantly sees birds and plants whose names she does not know.* NS □ *Angputa* ***was no great shakes*** *as a high altitude Sherpa, but he was a very nice person indeed and I got very, very fond of him.* OBS □ *The first episode of 'Kojak'* ***was no great shakes*** *as a plot, but American addicts tell me that the characters grow on you.* NS □ *I daresay the school* ***was no great shakes*** *educationally, but in its relaxed, almost domestic, atmosphere I gained confidence in myself and the trust of others for the first time.* □ often followed by *as* + phrase.

be no oil painting [V + Comp] be a plain or ugly person □ *If Rosa were like this in twenty-five years, well, it would suit him. He would* ***be no oil painting*** *himself by that time.* HD □ *What's the matter with me? I may not* ***be an oil-painting****, but I'm all right in my way.* PW

be no picnic [V + Comp] not be a pleasant, easy task or experience □ *Running a house this size* ***is***

no picnic *these days, believe me.* TGLY □ *Marine archaeology* ***is****, after all,* ***no picnic****. The diver does not, like the digger on land, spend lazy afternoons excavating with camelhair brushes and toothpicks.* OBS □ *'Was it very uncomfortable—painful?' 'Not so bad as I had feared, but* ***no picnic*** *all the same.'*

be no (kind of) place etc for sb [V + Comp] be a place etc by its nature not suited to sb (for reasons of age, youth, sex, temperament, rank, ability etc) **n:** place, enviroment, house, job, work, life, sight, company, philosophy □ *The geriatric wards of most general hospitals* ***are no place for*** *patients that are crippled but not senile.* SC □ *If, however, you don't enjoy organized activities and the almost constant company of your fellow-beings, a holiday camp* ***is no place for*** *you.* □ *'After all, everybody knows that Mars* ***is no place for***— *' She hesitated. 'Absolutely primitive.* ***No kind of life for*** *any woman.'* TST □ *I can't understand young people nowadays. Look at your own Harry—washing-up in a kitchen. That* ***'s no kind of job for*** *a boy with his education.* □ *No wonder he's had nightmares. You're used to it, but a pig-killing* ***is no sight for*** *a child.*

be no/not any respecter of persons [V + Comp] be sb who does not show more regard for one person than for another, and esp is not influenced by considerations of class, wealth, fame, authority etc □ (source) *Of a truth I perceive that God* ***is no respecter of persons****: But in every nation he that feareth him, and worketh righteousness, is accepted with him.* ACTS X 34-5 □ *If anything, the Forfar people err on the side of* ***not being respecters of persons*** *and very quickly puncture any pomposity.* SC □ (NONCE) *Rugby* ***is not any respecter of personalities*** *and there was more ragging of O'Reilly at the banquet after the game.* RT □ *Miss Hellman is indeed a notable teller-off and throughout her life she* ***shows scant respect for persons****.* ST □ variant show scant respect for persons.

be no room at/in the inn [V + Comp] there is a lack or refusal of suitable accommodation, shelter or acceptance □ (source) *And she* (Mary) *brought forth her firstborn son* (Jesus) *and laid him in a manger; because there* ***was no room*** *for them* ***in the inn****.* LUKE II 7 □ *One camera-man who had to sleep outside (* ***no room at the inn****) played a little prank next morning.* OBS □ *Edna's father was a sadist, her harassed mother left her alone one night, and she got sent to a remand home because there* ***was no room at the inn****.* L

be no skin off one's nose [V + Comp] (slang) be a matter, action etc that does not affect one adversely, does not cause one any upset or loss, does not matter to one □ *If he's too proud to accept help, let him get on with it. It* ***'s no skin off my nose****.* □ *Well, even 6p on the rates for a really good Sports' Centre would* ***be no skin off your nose*** *since you don't pay rates anyway.* □ stress pattern ˌno skin off ˈone's nose.

be nobody's business [V + Comp] (informal facetious) be sth, esp excessive or outrageous, best not inquired about, not discussed □ *That was his style all right, no mistaking it. The way he used to treat that wife of his* ***was nobody's business****.* L □ *The house was built to specification and what the furnishings must have cost* ***is nobody's business****.* □ stress pattern be ˈnobody's business ⇨ ⚠ like nobody's business.

be nobody's/no man's fool [V + Comp] be a wise and/or astute person; not be easily deceived or exploited by anyone □ *When it became clear that the prosecution's case ran on the lines that Angela Davis had been tricked into becoming a pawn of the men around her, the defence emphasised that, whatever Angela Davis might be, she* ***was nobody's fool****.* ST □ *Don Moffat* ***is*** *a former soldier and teacher, patient, reasonable, approachable,* ***nobody's fool****.* L □ *'I didn't expect this,' said Martin. 'Didn't you? You must have been working things out,' said Bevill. I thought once more, that in such matters he* ***was no man's fool****.* NM

be not as other men are [V + Comp] be better than many or most people are □ (source) *The Pharisee stood and prayed thus with himself, God, I thank thee, that I* ***am not as other men are****, extortioners, unjust, adulterers.* LUKE XVIII II □ *Some wives are so certain that their husbands* ***are not as other men are*** *that they do not suspect even what may be going on under their own noses.* □ *Amid all the problems that beset him, Charles found time to rejoice that he* ***was not as Hutchins was****, that his soul, stretched as it was on the rack of his ludicrous predicament, was alive.* HD

be nothing to it [V + Comp] be easy; be simple to do □ *How were we going to get launched? 'We just run it down the shingle,' said young George nonchalantly, 'and tip it into the surf.* ***Nothing to it****, old lad.'* ST □ *One of the remarkable things about expert water skiers is the sincerity with which they insist how easy it is. 'There* ***'s*** *really* ***nothing to it****, James said. 'A sense of balance, a love of speed.'* OBS □ stress pattern be ˌnothing ˈto it.

be/go off one's food/oats [V + Comp] (informal) be without/lose one's appetite □ *I'm worried about Keith. He's* ***been off his oats*** *for a week now, feels tired after a long night's sleep and looks as pale as the full moon.* □ *What do you mean,* ***gone off your food****? I cook a three-course meal, and half-way through the soup you suddenly tell me you've* ***gone off your food****!*

be on sale [V + Comp] (esp of specific articles) be available for purchase; be 'for sale' (qv) □ *There* ***are*** *very few hand-made shoes* ***on sale*** *these days.* □ *As long as horror comics* ***are on sale*** *for a few pence in every other stationer's shop, children will buy them.*

be oneself act, behave in a way that is natural, or normal, for oneself (esp in contrast to the affected manner etc that one may occas adopt to impress others) □ *I wish you wouldn't act the sophisticated lady when I bring my friends here, Sheila. You're far nicer when you're just* ***being yourself****.* □ *Actors often complain that they can never* ***be themselves****. They play so many different parts that these can submerge their original personalities entirely.*

be oneself again return to one's normal state (after a temporary illness, shock, emotional upset, etc) □ *Just when I* ***was myself again*** *and victorious, there came a sort of something. A Terror.* PM □ *'He'll pull through now,' the doctor said, 'but he'll never* ***be*** *quite* ***himself again*** *in many respects.'* □ *Charles seems to be recovering from the loss of his wife at long last—quite*

like his old self again *and only occasionally a bit silent.* □ variant be (like) one's old self again.

be an open secret [V + Comp] be a fact, state of affairs, etc which is not publicly acknowledged or officially made known, but which many people are aware of **S:** his whereabouts, her origins, his hide-out; it. **cl:** it. . .that he's resigning, it. . .that she's remarried □ *His hide-out, in the same gimcrack modern apartment where the baby has been staying recently,* ***was an open secret*** *in this small tight township.* NS □ *British cars are rarely advertised on television; it* ***is an open secret*** *that the makers agreed long ago to stay away, for fear of an expensive war of words.* OBS □ *It* ***is an open secret*** *that guns are being imported via Kilkeel, a stronghold of right-wing Unionism, and Ballynahinch. They are brought into Belfast in sand lorries.* NS

be par for the course (informal) be what one would expect to happen/expect sb to do **A:** about; more or less; pretty well □ *'There's been another military coup in Fantasia.' 'The third this year. Well, I suppose that****'s*** *about* ***par for the course****.'* □ *'Sid's already ten minutes late.' 'Give him ten more — twenty****'s par for the course*** *for Sid.'* □ par (golf) = 'the number of shots that has been set as a standard for a good player for each individual hole or for all eighteen holes on a particular golf-course'. ⇨ ⚠ under par.

be a (dead/real) ringer for sb/sth [V + Comp] (slang) be extremely like, be virtually indistinguishable from, sb/sth specified **o:** the Queen; my old headmaster; the one I lost □ *Some of those interviewed, notably the 'false' Eric Morecambe, were not so very like the notabilities they claimed to be being constantly mistaken for, but there was one woman who* ***was a real ringer for*** *the Queen.* □ *Without* ***being ringers for*** *their originals, the actors resembled them sufficiently to help the suspension of disbelief.* OBS □ *It turned out to be her own ofter all. But when a girl comes in to pawn a diamond bracelet that****'s a dead ringer for*** *one on the stolen property lists from the police, you have to be suspicious.* □ ringer = 'a horse illegally substituted in a sale, race etc for one of similar appearance'.

be/make sb ripe for sth [V + Comp] be fully ready for sth **S:** people, masses; school, department. **o:** revolution, love, take-over, development, mischief □ *The hunger, cold and misery then pervading Germany had reached the point of exasperating the masses and* ***making*** *them* ***ripe for*** *revolution.* OBS □ *The girls* ***are ripe for*** *romance, and when a handsome young musical composer moves into the house as a boarder, they all see him as a target for matrimony.* TVT

be a sight for sore eyes [V + Comp] be sb/sth one is very glad to see; a feast for the eyes (qv) □ *'Look who I've brought with me.' 'Jane! What* ***a sight for sore eyes****! I hope you're to be back among us for a while.'* □ *And Kathie and Mac and Miss Flynn came in, and the kettle was well away* (ie was boiling). *'This* ***is a sight for sore eyes****.'* TT

be sitting pretty [V + Comp] (informal) be in a pleasant, comfortable, enviable situation □ *Olivia Newton-John* ***was sitting pretty*** *last month with her version of the Bob Dylan song, 'If Not For You' in the Top 20.* RT □ *I whiled away the minutes watching three strong men plying their charms around a young bright blonde and she* ***was sitting pretty****, proud to be queening it in that masculine stronghold.* PP

be six of one and/to half a dozen of the other [V + Comp] be equal merit or weakness in two persons, things, courses of action that one has to choose between; (as) broad as it's long (qv) □ (source) *I never knows the children. It****'s*** *just* ***six of one and half-a-dozen of the other****.* THE PIRATE (F MARRYAT 1792-1848) □ *I've tried both routes and it****'s six of one and half a dozen of the other****.* □ *As far as qualifications and references are concerned it****'s*** *a case of* ***six of one to a half dozen of the other****. I wish we had jobs for both of them.* □ a half dozen occas used instead of the more common half a dozen.

be so good/kind (as to do sth) [V + Comp] (formal) be obliging and do what I suggest, what I would like you to do as a favour or service to me; be good/kind enough to do sth (qv) □ *Would you* ***be so kind as to*** *help me open this window?* □ *'What will you take?' 'Scotch, if you will* ***be so good****.'* ARG □ introduces polite request, usu with *will/would you.*

to be sure [Disj] it is true; certainly □ *But I remain optimistic that the Seychelles, 'the islands that time forgot', will never become a Costa Brava or a Miami Beach. They will get more visitors,* ***to be sure****, but this will be discerning visitors who will appreciate their particular charms.* OBS □ ***To be sure****, it is always possible for* (a witness) *to say: 'I don't know.' But often he is not prepared to confess his ignorance.* MFF □ front, middle or end position.

be sure to do sth[1] [V + Comp] shall certainly do sth □ *The children* ***are sure to*** *miss their father while he's away.* □ *Prices* ***are****n't* ***sure to*** *rise, but it's very probable that they will.*

be sure to do sth[2] [V + Comp] do not fail to do sth □ *You must* ***be sure to*** *come and see us when you get back to New York.* AITC □ ***Be sure to*** *lock the door when you leave.* □ usu imper, or with *you must/are to.*

be tantamount to sth [V + Comp] be equal to sth in effect or result; be virtually the same as sth **o:** genius, disobedience, a declaration of war, condoning the crime, taking a bribe □ *Coburn hopes that when you watch his death-dealing kung fu* (= Chinese form of karate) *exploits, you might take it as a tribute to Lee's skill in training him. 'That man's talent for the martial arts,' says James Coburn, '****was tantamount to*** *genius. He was the fastest thing I ever saw.'* TVT □ *The discussion failed to point out the insidious influence of team games. Setting one team against another* ***is tantamount to*** *playing at warfare.* RT □ *But then the Prime Minister likes to deceive even when it is not in his interest to do so (another trait he shares with Nixon). It seems, for him,* ***tantamount to*** *a duty.* NS □ *They all suffered from neglect, in some cases a neglect* ***tantamount to*** *cruelty.*

be ten/two a penny [V + Comp] be cheap; be numerous and easily obtainable; be not very valuable, important or interesting □ *It is a sordid fact that equal pay* (for men and women doing the same job) *is bitterly opposed by many of Britain's craft unions, not at the top—where* *declarations of principle* ***are ten a penny****—but where it really matters, on the shop floor.* ST □ *One of the exceedingly dreary things about life these days is that one can never get any cooks — you'd think with all this unemployment around cooks would* ***be two a penny****, but no.* ST □ *'Tabby cats* ***are ten a penny****. What I'd like is an* unusual *cat, like a Manx.' 'What! A cat without a tail?'*

be thankful/grateful for small mercies be thankful for minor benefits, consolations, or for what, though not good, could be worse **modal:** must, should, ought to □ *One ought to* ***be thankful for small mercies****. Muted approval of a modest space research programme is at least an advance on the Astronomer Royal's 'space travel is bunk', uttered* ex cathedra *so very few years ago.* NSC □ *Among the professionals Miss Chisholm found very few takers for global solutions* (of ecological problems)*, although many were optimistic about the possibility of individual answers to individual problems. We must, it seems,* ***be thankful for small mercies****, at least for the time being.* NS □ (NONCE) *At this time of year columists tend to* ***snatch*** *greedily and* ***gratefully at small mercies*** *like the weather.* L

be that as it may [Disj] that may, or may not, be true, but is, in any case, irrelevant □ *'None of the previous applicants* (knows about Burma)*, apparently,' answered the Professor with more than a touch of sourness. 'Still,* ***be that as it may*** *—I want a man who knows upper Burma.'* ARG □ *I rack my memory in vain for its counterpart* (ie of your house) *in literature. But* ***be that as it may****, you will never know what being with you and, indeed, all the Eastwoods has meant to me.* PW □ CLIVE: *I think education is simply the process of being taken by surprise, do you see?* STANLEY: ***Be that as it may****.* CLIVE: *You don't see.* FFE ⇨ ⚠ that is as (it) may be.

be/get that way [V + Comp] (informal) take that attitude, esp become angry, sulky, standoffish, touchy, uncooperative etc; be like that (qv) □ *What's he think this place is—a soup kitchen? I don't want your friend and I don't want his cheques.' 'Ah, now, don't* ***be that way****, Mr Mazzolini,' Trillie said coaxingly.* PE □ *'She won't* let *people help her. We've all tried.' 'Oh well, if she wants to* ***be that way****, you'll just have to leave her to it.'* □ *She was very even-tempered, but she never talked about herself. We got on fine, because maybe* ***I'm*** *a bit* ***that way****. I never sought to pry into her business, nor she into mine.* RFW □ stress pattern 'be/'get that way.

be/feel that way etc inclined [V + Comp] have the tastes, habits or desire to be, do, enjoy sth specified **adv mod:** that way, ⚠ so, thus □ *You see, in a town this size the number of people who take any interest in intellectual pursuits, they're pretty far and few between. So if you****'re that way inclined*** *you tend to keep running across the same crowd.* TGLY □ *Don't encourage his laziness. He****'s*** *too much* ***that way inclined*** *already.* □ *. . . an Opus 1 of astonishing distinction and individuality, suggesting that Webern could well have rivalled Mahler or Strauss in handling the full orchestra had he* ***felt so inclined****.* G □ often in a clause beginning *if/when/unless.*

be thick/thin on the ground [V + Comp] be numerous/few; be dense/sparse □ *As things are, Londoners* ***are*** *too* ***thick on the ground*** *to live satisfactorily with such space-hungry devices as private cars.* NS □ *Speculators* ***are thick on the ground****—literally speaking. They buy up land, sit on it* (ie don't use it) *for a month or two and resell for twice what they paid.* ST □ (TV programmes) *Everyone is always swearing that they are on the look-out for new talent: you can't blame them if it****'s thin on the ground****. After all, statistically there can be only so much of it.* L

be thick with sth [V + Comp] be densely made up of, be full of, sth **S:** the air, the atmosphere, the room. **o:** fog, starch, dust; people; errors; weeds; rumours/reports of □ *Some things are better. The London smog—air so* ***thick with*** *fog and smoke that chest-sufferers could die breathing it, is to all intents and purposes a thing of the past.* G □ *Following the Government's announcement of economies, the air* ***was thick with*** *rumours of redundancies.* □ (a museum) *The visitors' book is accordingly opened, and found to* ***be thick with*** *entries, mostly collective, and monothematic: '20th Sept—23 pupils of—courteous attention—unforgettable morning—' Idly we add our own names, but without comment.* TCM

be the thin end of the wedge [V + Comp] be the apparently insignificant event, action etc that is in fact the beginning of sth widespread, serious or disastrous, often intentionally so □ *For many years, anything more than a mere suggestion of rape was rare in the cinema. Over the years it has become less prohibited and probably it was the famous Jame Wyman film of 1948, 'Johnny Belinda', which was* ***the thin end of the wedge****.* TVT □ *He returned to this country to be greeted by a characteristic attack from Mr Enoch Powell, who claimed that the Ugandan Asians were just '****the thin end of a*** *very thick* ***wedge****' and that as many as a million and a half people from other parts of the world would eventually descend on us.* NS □ stress pattern be the ˌthin end of the 'wedge.

be three sheets in the wind [V + Comp] be very drunk (a sailing boat with sheets (= ropes) fully loosened on all 3 sails cannot be kept on course) □ *Go if you like, but if he****'s three sheets in the wind****, as is very likely by now, it won't be any use trying to talk business with him.* □ stress pattern be ˌthree sheets in the 'wind.

be to the bad/good [V + Comp] be disadvantageous/advantageous for sb/sth □ *I was not to take up my appointment till two months ahead, on Sept 1st, which might* ***be to the good*** *as giving me a chance to rub up on my rusty German but* ***was*** *altogether* ***to the bad*** *financially.* SC □ *In one way and another the public for the first time became conscious of the Early Iron Age and the meaning of prehistory. All this* ***was****, in our view,* ***to the good****.* SD ⇨ ⚠ all to the good.

be too bad (that)[1] [V + Comp] be regrettable, unfortunate (that) **S:** it, that. **adv mod:** just. **cl:** (that) it should rain today, you can't be with us, there's such talented competition □ *Whatever dangers threatened him, he could cope with them, and if he couldn't that would* ***be*** *just* ***too bad****.* PE □ (a telephone call from a blackmailer) *I've been waiting for that parcel* (of banknotes) *since yes-*

*terday. It's **too bad** it hasn't come, because now my price has gone up.* DC □ *My father was over seventy and my mother not much less, and neither of them in the best of health. **Too bad that** they should have a nuisance of this nature thrust on them.* RFW □ *Tuesday's documentary promises to show me 'The Real Che Guevara'. **Too bad that** it clashes with 'Casanova' — another inviting new series on BBC 2.* RT □ sometimes ironic.

be too bad (that)[2] [V + Comp] be inconsiderate, unjust (that) **S:** it, that. **adv mod:** really. **cl:** (that) he didn't let them know, they've left the place so untidy □ *His mother was terribly disappointed. It **was too bad that** he didn't turn up after having promised to.* □ *If only two or three boys were responsible for the damage I think it's really **too bad** they should all be penalized.* □ *'**Too bad of** me **to** keep bothering like this,' said Miss Simpson, darting into the room again, 'but where did you say I'd find the carbon paper?'* □ sometimes ironic; variant be too bad of sb to do sth.

be too clever by half [V + Comp] (informal) be more clever than wise (the implication being that the person referred to is overreaching himself, creating difficulties, rousing antagonism, etc) □ *Under this former backroom boy* (Iain Macleod) *at Tory headquaters—described, was he not, by Lord Salisbury as **too clever by half**?—the Conservatives have done very badly at by-elections.* T □ *...the sources of religious feeling, and all the elements which rat-racing Western man had cast out in becoming 'single-minded', and **too clever by half**.* OBS □ *Mark was hardly spoken to for some time by his superiors and, it is said, the iron entered his soul. This ostracisation was put down to snobbery, and the suspicion that Mark **was 'too clever by half'**.* ST

be too funny etc for words [V + Comp] (informal) be very funny etc **adj:** funny; silly, awful; handsome; exciting; disgusting □ *And the scene in the air-raid shelter with pans on their heads **was** just **too funny for words**.* RT □ *'The Squaw', a ghost story about a black cat's revenge, trapping an American in the Iron Eye maiden at Nuremberg, was thought '**too ghastly for words**' by Edwardian schoolboys, but now seems merely absurd.* OBS □ *Mrs Hamilton Clipp was now happily engaged in making a running commentary on their fellow travellers. '**Are**n't those two little children just **too cute for words**?'* TCB

be etc too good etc to be true [V + Comp] be so good etc that one suspects that there are hidden faults, deficiencies, drawbacks etc **V:** be; ⚠ seem; sound, look. **adj:** good, lucky; (facetious) bad, stupid; English, professional, upright □ *'Z Cars' was doing something, good or bad, for the 'image' of the police force, trying to be more realistic than 'Dixon of Dock Green' who sometimes **seemed too good to be true**.* RT □ *'You can have one of the firm's cars; there's depots at Leeds and Wakefield you'll be visiting a great deal.' 'It's **too good to be true**,' I said, trying to look keen and modest and boyish.* RATT □ *Horham Hall, raspberry pink Tudor in the setting sun, **looks** almost **too English to be true**.* ST □ *Once upon a time, the central figures of fiction tended to **be too good to be true**. With Mr Leslie A Fiedler's book of short stories we have come full circle and the chief characters **are** simply **too nasty to be true**.* T

be too good to last [V + Comp] be very good but not permanent □ *I* (Harold Macmillan) *happened to make a speech at Bedford* (in the late 1950s) *and in the course of it I said, 'Most of our people have never had it so good.' Then I went on to say, 'What is beginning to worry some of us is, is it too good to be true? Or perhaps I should say, **is** it **too good to last**?'* L □ *Kate had been consistently friendly all that week — a state of affairs **too good to last** but at least a welcome change from her usual criticisms and complaints.*

be too good to miss/turn down [V + Comp] be too attractive or profitable to reject □ *Don't want to start making tracks yet awhile, though, do we? This **is too good to miss**. Look at it all.* TGLY □ *Many* (Iranians) *who have opted for the US are starting to come back, bringing their Thunderbirds with them. 'The money **was too good to turn down**.' Sons and daughters, however, think otherwise and can't wait to get back to Los Angeles, New York, and Washington.* SC

be/prove too hot to handle [V + Comp] (informal) be too dangerous to deal with or become involved with □ *'I don't defend people in cases that might **prove too hot to handle**,' he told Barton. 'I'm not an expert in international law.'* □ *The pieces stolen included three early German and Italian iron clocks—four of the best-known brass lantern clocks in the world. 'These were top clocks,' says Illyett, 'the equivalent of Gainsboroughs or Rembrandts in the world of art. Many of them you would think **were too hot to handle**.'* RT

be too little (and) too late [V + Comp] be not enough and too long delayed □ *Mr Barber announced that he was pumping some £185 million more of investment money into the economy. '**Too little and too late**,' was Mr Vic Feather's reply to this gesture, and he proceeded to lead a mass demonstration of workers against unemployment through the streets of London.* L □ *The Government of India Act was 'never fully implemented', because the federal scheme incorporated in it remained a dead letter. In fact, this measure as a whole **was too little and too late**.* L

be too much like hard work [V + Comp] (informal) be too energetic or troublesome an activity, sport, pastime etc for sb to want to do □ CRAPE: *Now answer me this one — Suppose you were born again* — PHINEUS: *I don't know* — CRAPE: *I do. You wouldn't dare to face it. Oh Lord, it would **be** far **too much like hard work**.* THH □ *They could have had as many strawberries as they wanted if they'd come over and picked them, but I suppose that **was too much like hard work**.* □ often facetious.

be/have too much of a good thing [V + Comp] be/experience an unsuitable or unwelcome excess of a commodity, activity or form of behaviour (the implication usu being that less would be right or acceptable) □ *If my strong will and indiscipline had gone unchecked, the result might have been even more intolerable than some people have found me. But I have often wondered whether my mother's treatment for me*

was *not a bit* ***too much of a good thing****: whether in fact it was a good thing at all.* MFM □ *We'd love to have you and Marian and all the children to stay, but you* ***are*** *literally* ***too much of a good thing****, alas.* □ *Pete and Mike decide that if they can't get work, they will start their own business. After a certain amount of bother, they decide that you can* ***have too much of a good thing****.* TVT

be too true [V + Comp] be unfortunately true; be regrettably as described □ *The Glasgow Branch hummed and hawed over a small mortgage on a fine old terrace property. 'Well, you know what building societies are.'* ***Too true****. A former London architect said there was little problem about mortgages on old houses down south where it was accepted that faults could be rectified.* SC □ *If you think I'm just being cantankerous, listen to 'The Times' critic: 'Saturday sport apart, the repeats of "Die Fledermaus" (BBC 2) and "Man Alive" (BBC 2) not to mention "Pets and Vets" (BBC 2) offer the brightest hope in an otherwise dismal day.'* ***Too true****.* NS □ *'Tom said you were an old fool, not to invest in the scheme.' 'Well, I'm old, that****'s*** *only* ***too true****, but he'll maybe find it's himself that's the fool.'* □ generally without be, except when used with *only* as in last example.

be top secret [V + Comp] be highly confidential, privileged (information etc), esp on an international, governmental or military level □ *A colossal amount of paper was in circulation and everything* ***was*** *Secret or* ***Top Secret****.* MFM □ *'May we ask about it?—Unless, of course, it****'s*** *"****top secret****",' she added musingly, with her head on one side, her eyes glinting mischievously.* HAHA

be touch and go [V + Comp] be a situation in which death, or disaster, failure etc will only be, or has only been, narrowly avoided; nip and tuck (qv) □ *My lungs were lacerated. Nine of my ribs were broken. They phoned my wife, Barbara, and warned her that it* ***was touch and go****.* ST □ *It had* ***been touch and go****, in those days, whether she* (a valued servant-companion) *would leave the Colstons and settle down with her brother in Conventry while she had the chance.* MM □ *Minister Macao provides some nifty inspiration for director Michael Moore and his camera team in this* ***touch-and-go*** *yarn about a deadly cargo of 'Nitro 2' and the efforts to keep it afloat as far as Hong Kong.* RT □ often followed by a clause introduced by *whether*; attrib use *a* ***touch-and-go*** *yarn*; touch and go non-rev.

be well etc advised to do sth be wise etc to do sth **adv:** well, ⚠ better; ill □ *When Bill Shankly does decide to go, the board of the day would* ***be well advised to*** *ask him to find his own successor.* OBS □ *Lloyd would probably* ***be better advised*** *not* ***to*** *play Holding in what would be his first Test match.* G □ *Industry would* ***be ill-advised to*** *sit back now and wait for government guidance or help.* NSC

be your age (informal) behave as sb of your age and maturity should, and not as though you were much younger (and less experienced, more irresponsible, etc) □ *For God's sake* ***be your age****, Alan, and stop behaving like a teenager.* RFW □ *'Tra-la-la' sang George, turning up the radio and seizing his wife by the waist. 'There's nothing like a waltz before breakfast.' 'Oh,* ***be your age****,' she said pulling away from him crossly.* □ usu direct or indirect command.

the be-all and end-all (of sth) [n + n non-rev] the main purpose (of sth); all that matters (in sth); the sum total (of sth) (qv) □ (source) *...that but this blow/Might be* ***the be-all and*** *the* ***end-all*** *here,/But here, upon this bank and shoal of time,/We'd jump the life to come.* MACBETH I 7. □ *Not that sexual desire is* ***the be-all and end-all of*** *Dayak love. It has a part in the history of each romance, but...* NDN □ *The book is flagrantly uninformative and is really only useful in preventing one from thinking that the current state of Darwinism is* ***the be-all and end-all of*** *man's knowledge of the origin of the species.* SC

the beam in one's own eye [O (NP)] a major fault in one's own character, outlook etc, which one disregards while observing or criticizing minor faults in others **V:** (not) see, notice; ignore; remove □ (source) *And why beholdest thou the mote that is in thy brother's eye, but perceivest not* ***the beam*** *that is* ***in thine own eye****?* LUKE VI 41 □ *'Do you make this a habit?' she said, 'this going round always seeing the good things in people?' 'I try to—then they are less likely to see* ***the beam in my own eye****.'* TT □ *Mr Charteris has written an appealing and honest sermon on the text that we should attend to* ***the beam in our own eyes*** *before trying to remove the motes from other people's.* T □ often associated with *the mote in sb's eye* (= 'sb's minor fault') as in source quotation and last example.

bear the burden and heat of the day [V + O pass] (formal) have the longest and most difficult part of a task to perform (in contrast with others whose share is (considered to be) easier or shorter) **S:** country, class; section, department; officer, writer □ (source) *These last have wrought but one hour, and thou has made them equal unto us, which have* ***borne the burden and the heat of the day****.* MATTHEW XX 12 □ *The assumption by some Americans that the Allied victory in World War One was solely due to their eventual last-minute intervention was bitterly resented by those who felt they had* ***borne the burden and heat of the day****.* □ *His comments on the present Director-General, however intended, are not likely to enhance the reputation of one who has still to* ***bear the heat and burden of the day****.* L □ burden and heat rev.

bear etc a charmed life [V + O] have a personal history of lucky escape from, or avoidance of, accident, injury or death, although exposed to such risks **V:** bear, ⚠ lead, live, have □ (source) *I* ***bear a charmed life****, which must not yield/To one of woman born.* MACBETH V 7 □ *To his friends it has long been apparent that Creswell* ***bears a charmed life****. Even Creswell, however, has had his moments of adversity.* SC □ *Errol Flynn swung on ropes and leapt from balconies and rode bareback into Technicolour dawns. He rescued a girl and killed his enemy and* ***led a charmed life****.* QA □ *Some girls say that men like a secretary with mothering instincts. But if this is what is called for, you would think that secretaries of 40-plus would* ***lead a charmed life*** *in the job market.* L □ also pl bear etc charmed lives.

(not) bear/stand close examination/ inspection [V + O] (not) be satisfactory, genuine, as good as appearances might suggest, etc, when carefully examined; stand up (to)² (Vol 1) (qv) **S:** he, it, they; character, attitude, motive; proposal, plan □ *'I think he only does you these favours to make himself liked.' 'And does that really matter? Would all our motives* ***stand close inspection****?'* □ *The point made by Stephen Hearst—that 'in matters of politics we are democrats, in matters of culture we are élitist authoritarians'—is an interesting statement of his personal viewpoint, but does* ***not bear close examination.*** RT

bear/carry one's cross [V + O] suffer, or cope with, a disability, grief, irksome responsibility, either as a condition of life or for a period **A:** bravely, lightly, with courage □ (a deferred wedding) *'Still, this isn't the time really, is it?' And she smiled, and was* ***carrying her cross*** *ever so bravely really.* TT □ *Poor soul, she* ***has a heavy cross to carry*** *with those young children and her husband out of work.* □ *We should help to* ***bear one another's crosses*** *instead of shutting ourselves off from other people's troubles.* □ variant have a heavy cross to bear/carry.

bear fruit [V + O] show (usu good) results; come to fruition (Vol 1) (qv) **S:** effort, planning, thought □ *The Gas Council's hitherto rather unrewarding search for natural gas in Britain is soon to* ***bear*** *its first* ***fruit.*** NS □ *I've tried dozens of ways to make him change his mind, but none of them have* ***borne fruit*** *so far.* □ *Our improved methods and modern machines are already* ***bearing fruit*** *in the shape of increased output and better staff relations.*

a bear garden [Comp (NP)] a place or gathering where there is noise and unruly or coarse behaviour (from 16th-17th c places of public amusement where bear-baiting took place) **V:** ⚠ be, become, appear □ *I'm glad you didn't come round to see us last night. Dave had both teams up to the house after the Rugby match and the place was* ***an*** *utter* ***bear garden.*** □ *Get on with your work. Remember this is a classroom, not* ***a bear garden.*** □ not usu pl.

bear sb no ill-will [V + IO + O pass] not be hostile to, resent, sb for sth he is, or sth he has done **det:** no, ⚠ (not) any, little □ *'Enemy' is rather a strong word to use. I* ***bear no ill-will to*** *Julius.* EM □ *I* ***bore*** *Bolshaw very* ***little ill-will.*** *I was always interested in his devices for avoiding work.* SPL □ *The customers vote with little reference to the persuasions of the papers, but* ***bear*** *them* ***no ill-will*** *and continue to buy them. They assume that a great deal they read in the papers is phoney.* UL □ *They do****n't bear*** *their cousins* ***any ill-will,*** *you must understand.*

bear (sb) no/not bear (sb) (any) malice [V + IO + O pass] not feel vindictive or spiteful (towards sb) □ *Mrs Jones called after Dorothy good-naturedly as she angrily withdrew; she* (Mrs Jones) *did* ***not*** *appear to* ***bear malice.*** US □ *My parents were hard on me as a child, but I* ***bear*** *them* ***no malice.*** *That was the way they had been brought up themselves.* □ *Considering that my carelessness was partly responsible for her accident, it is surprising that she* ***bears no malice towards*** *me.* □ variant bear no malice (towards sb).

(not) bear repeating/repetition [V + O] (not) be worth repeating, because it is (not) valid, interesting, important etc **S:** sb's opinion, argument; the joke, matter; it, the whole thing □ *It's their timing and the expression on their faces that makes their act so hilarious—the jokes themselves do****n't bear repetition.*** □ *Look, does the argument really* ***bear repeating****? You've had your say and I've had mine, and neither of us is going to convince the other.* □ *There is so much common sense in his advice that it will* ***bear*** *any amount of* ***repeating.***

beard the lion/sb in his den [V + O + A pass] visit sb of power, importance etc at his home or place of work in order to attack or challenge him, to obtain a favour, etc (the implication being that one is rather afraid but has summoned up enough courage to do so) **o:** den, room, office □ *And I would be late this morning of all mornings. I suppose the Old Man has been waffling around? I'll go and* ***beard the lion.*** TT □ *One of these days somebody will have the courage to* ***beard*** *the manager* ***in his den*** *and tell him what we all think of him.* □ (NONCE) *Each time the principal boy left the stage, Virginia wondered whether she should get up and go through the pass-door at the side of the stage, and* ***beard*** *her* ***in her dressing room*** *for the promised interview.* AITC □ beard the lion may be used alone, but a more specific n/pron usu requires in his den.

beat the band [V + O] (informal) surpass everybody or everything □ *My millionaire grandfather left all his money to research into proving that the pyramids in Egypt were built by visitors from outer space. That really* ***beats the band****!* □ *Gillian* ***beats the band****—she's now claiming that she's a direct descendant of the Queen of Sheba!* ⇨ ⚠ next entry.

to beat the band [A] to a high degree; in a way that surpasses everything □ *What with the noise of the television and the baby howling* ***to beat the band****, I gave up the idea of reading the newspaper and went out into the garden.* □ *Don't worry about waking my wife. She can sleep* ***to beat the band****, that one.* ⇨ ⚠ previous entry.

beat etc one's brains [V + O] puzzle, think very hard, esp in order to solve a problem, find a way of doing sth **V:** beat, ⚠ cudgel, rack □ *I've been* ***beating my brains*** *all evening, trying to thing of an excuse for not going to Martin's wedding.* □ *He greatly despised crossword puzzles. 'People should* ***cudgel their brains*** *to some better purpose,' he often said.* □ ***Rack her brains*** *as she would she could think of no way to raise the money.* □ *After several hours of* ***brain-racking*** *they were still no nearer to a solution.* □ n compound brain-racking.

beat one's breast [V + O pass] hit one's breast with one's fist(s) as a sign of grief, remorse, despair etc; (fig) (pretend to) express remorse for what one has done; acknowledge one's mistakes etc, esp as a form of public apology □ *She wanted to* ***beat her breast*** *and scream but fought down the rising wave of hysteria.* □ *Once again a dismal ritual has been enacted: public figures have searched their grimy little consciences in public,* ***breasts*** *have been* ***beaten.*** NS □ *For my part I was relieved to find that she never indulges* *in any* ***breast-beating*** *about her wartime attitudes.* OBS □ n compound breast-beating.

beat sb/sth hollow [V + O + A pass] (informal) defeat sb decisively in a game, contest or struggle; be greatly superior to sb/sth else **S:** team, side; product, scheme; course □ *I played Max at chess last night and* ***beat*** *him* ***hollow.*** □ *It's a fine whisky, but I know a blend that* ***beats*** *even this* ***hollow.*** □ *'I think the bed is the most uncomfortable in England—in Barsetshire at any rate.' 'It certainly couldn't be more hideous. It* ***beats*** *the state bed at Gatherum Castle* ***hollow.'*** WDM □ *Our boys were* ***beaten hollow*** *by the visiting team.*

beat it (informal) go away, esp swiftly (because either one's presence is not wanted or one does not want to stay) □ *'****Beat it****, you kids,' shouted the shop-keeper. 'You're keeping the proper customers away.'* □ *I wasn't going to stay and have her talk to me like that. I got to my feet. 'About time I* ***beat it****, after that,' I said.* RFW □ *'How do we get out then?' 'I've got a plane—only a small one, a four seater. As soon as there's a suitable break I'll send her over, and then you can* ***beat it****.'* DF □ often imper.

beauty and the beast [n + n non-rev] the union of sb who is beautiful with sb who is ugly or in some way repellent (from the title of a fairy tale) □ (of the film about the giant gorilla King Kong, who kidnaps a beautiful woman) *...a cunning reworking of the* ***Beauty and the Beast*** *fairy tale.* L □ *When Marjorie married a man old enough to be her grandfather, everyone behaved as if it were* ***beauty and the beast*** *all over again.*

beauty is but/only skin deep (saying) the beautiful appearance of sb or sth is not as important, or as durable, as the hidden, or inner, qualities; what looks beautiful on the outside may be ugly beneath; all is not gold that glitters (qv) □ ***Beauty*** *may* ***be only skin deep*** *as they say, but in my opinion a girl's good qualities are all the more easily appreciated if she is beautiful as well.* □ *Women, more than men, the article continued, were inclined to buy a car for its appearance; but all buyers, it concluded, should remember that, as with women, so with cars:* ***beauty was but skin deep.*** ⇨ fine feathers make fine birds.

beauty etc is/lies in the eye of the beholder (saying) there is no absolute standard for beauty etc, and what one person finds beautiful etc may not to be so to sb else **S:** beauty; goodness; political/religious bias; obscenity; value for money □ ***Beauty is in the eye of the beholder****, but what makes the beholders themselves so unattractive?* OBS □ *There is no thought of telling the fable of Joseph. Any* ***religious connotations****, one suspects,* ***remain*** *firmly* ***in the eye*** *and the ear* ***of the beholder.*** OBS □ *But the play is rather more complex than a simple example of 16th Century Christian wish fulfilment.* ***Anti-semitism*** *may well* ***be in the eye of the beholder.*** L

the beauty of it/sth the specially good point about sth; the aspect of sth which gives sb a special satisfaction □ *'Do you know what I'd do with them* (100 miniature whisky bottles) *if I were you?' Hasselbacher said. 'Play checkers. When you take a piece you drink it.' 'That's quite an idea.' 'A natural handicap,' Hasselbacher said. 'That's* ***the beauty of it****. The better player has to drink more.'* OMIH □ *'They're all good shears,' the salesman explained, 'but* ***the beauty of*** *this pair is that the blades have a self-sharpening action.'* □ *'That's* ***the beauty of*** *having only a small car,' he said as he manoeuvred it into a minute parking space.* □ usu occurs as Comp of *that is* or as S followed by *is that.*

one's beauty sleep [O (NP)] sleep that is begun in the hours before midnight and presumed to be esp restful and beneficial **V:** get, have, take; lose. **det:** one's; some, a little □ *Come now, don't get into a tantrum. You must get* ***your beauty sleep*** *for the photographer tomorrow.* MM □ *'He'd just like a cup of coffee, and I'll make it,' said Julie. 'You go to bed, Auntie. Can't have you losing* ***your beauty sleep.'*** PE □ *'Now who says one more glass of port? And then we go to bed?' 'Yes, time to get* ***a little beauty sleep,'*** *Ma said.* DBM □ stress pattern one's 'beauty sleep.

a beauty spot[1] a place much admired and visited for the sake of the beauty of its natural scenery □ *The Guide Book lists all* ***the*** *famous* ***beauty spots****, but if you look you will find other equally delightful places off the beaten track.* □ *You must take a walk to Wakely Cove some afternoon. It's* ***our*** *local* ***beauty spot.*** □ stress pattern a 'beauty spot.

a beauty spot[2] a small, dark, natural mark or mole on the face, arm etc which is thought to add charm to a woman's beauty □ *I used to spend hours trying to scrub off what my mother liked to call* ***my beauty spot****. I thought it disfigured me. Now, I think it's rather an asset.* □ also pl; stress pattern a 'beauty spot; cf *a beauty patch* = 'an artificial black patch placed on the face in former times to simulate a beauty spot'.

a/the bed etc to end all beds etc/to end them all (often facetious) an outstanding, extraordinary example of a bed etc **n:** bed, sports-car, horror-film; lover, bore, gourmet; soprano aria, tragic performance □ *The room Jacquie and I occupied, though large, was dwarfed by an immense feather bed. It was* ***a bed to end all beds****, almost as big as a tennis-court and as thick as a bale of hay.* DF □ *But tonight he was sentimental. Tonight he was* ***the husband and father to end all husbands and fathers.*** AITC □ *Edwards has tried his hand at a variety of genres, sometimes with considerable success. 'Wild Rovers'* (a film) *seems to find him trying a hand at* ***the Western to end them all.*** NS □ stress pattern a ˌbed to end 'all beds/to end them 'all.

a/one's bedside manner the pleasant, reassuring calmness shown by a doctor to a patient who is usu, but not always, in bed (the implication sometimes being that the attitude adopted is overdone and artificial) **V:** have (got); put on; use □ *The new doctor has* ***a*** *good* ***bedside manner****; at least all the old ladies adore him, I hear.* □ *'There, my dear, in your anxiety to walk, these dreams become very real.' He was now exerting all* ***his bedside manner*** *to take the look of white dismay from her face.* DC □ *'Research is your strong point. Isn't it?' 'I'm very flattered,' was all I mumbled. 'No, you're not,' Wensley said. He had* ***his*** *best* ***bedside manner***

fitted on tight, and he might have been telling the patient it wasn't galloping consumption after all. PP

a beef etc baron a wealthy and influential owner, manufacturer or controller of the product or service mentioned; sb of influence in a particular profession **n:** beef, wool, cotton, tobacco, oil; newspaper, press □ *Those who dislike us and call us* ***the wool barons*** *say that we all sink to the mental level of the sheep.* RFW □ *The spirit of John Pierpoint Morgan, American banker,* ***railway baron*** *and book and art fancier, haunts the house and treasures.* OBS

been and gone and done it/sth (informal) really, or finally, have done sth that is unexpected, shocking, likely to cause trouble, etc □ *Suppose he had* ***been and gone and*** *fallen into the water all of a sudden?* ILIH □ *Guess what Tommy's* ***been and gone and done****, sir!'* □ *Did you really tell her that you can't stand women's magazines? I'm afraid you've* ***been and gone and done it*** *then — she's editor of 'Women Today'!*

before God (formal) I swear, vow, solemnly; as God is my witness (qv) □ *'I will bring up your son as if he were my own,' he told the dying woman. 'I promise you that,* ***before God****.'* □ *I know what you must have thought at the time, but I went off to find food, water, for all of us. I couldn't return, Findlay —* ***before God****, I couldn't—I got lost, and then I fell ill myself.* ARG

before one knows where one is very quickly or suddenly; very soon; next entry (qv) □ *I lost no time, took my coat from between my teeth, chucked it up to the wall and was sitting astraddle* ***before I knew where I was****.* LLDR □ *She asked how old Ludovic was. Rising sixteen, said his father, and it would be military service* ***before they knew where they were****.* WDM

before you can say Jack Robinson/knife (informal) very quickly or suddenly; very soon; previous entry (qv) □ *Let me fetch your newspaper for you. It's no trouble to run down to the shop—I'll be there and back again* ***before you can say Jack Robinson****.* □ *I said he could have the marble egg since he admired it so much, and* ***before you could say knife*** *it was off the shelf and in his pocket—as if he was afraid I might change my mind.* □ you occas replaced by I, he etc.

beg, borrow or steal [v + v + v non-rev] obtain sth by any means possible, except by paying money for it □ *'I haven't got a pen, sir.' 'Well,* ***beg, borrow or steal*** *one, but don't bother me.'* □ *The book is rather highly priced for the average pocket, but so well worth reading that is should be* ***begged, borrowed or stolen*** *rather than missed.* □ (NONCE) *Walter Gabriel is a shockingly bad farmer, but somehow he manages to stay cheerful and* ***begs, borrows and*** *generally* ***scrounges*** *his way through life.* RT □ used with or without O.

beg sb's pardon [V + O] apologize for sth one has done or said, or intends to do or say, that inconveniences others, or that is considered rude in polite society □ *'Would you mind taking your hat off, madam, I can't see the stage.' 'Oh, I* ***beg your pardon****, I didn't realize.'* □ *'One of those damn cats,' Nurse Ellen said cheerfully. '****Begging your pardon*** (ie for using the word damn)*, Mrs Gaye.'* DC □ *'But George here agrees with me.' 'Then George,* ***begging his pardon****, is a bloody fool too.'* ⇨ ⚠ I beg your pardon.

beg the question [V + O pass] not deal properly with the matter under discussion, leave it unresolved; not give a full and satisfactory explanation, either deliberately or unwittingly **S:** he, you, they; answer, proposition, statement, theory □ *'Do you think it's your own fault, or the composer's, that you don't understand this music?' 'I'm sure if the composer were here to explain it to me, I might enjoy it more.' 'That may well be so, but you are* ***begging my question****, aren't you?'* □ *Weirdest of all is a theory which states essentially 'that the phenomena of hypnosis result from the subject's motive to behave like a hypnotised person, as defined by a hypnotist, and as understood by the subject.' This is perhaps the most* ***question-begging*** *of all, because it leaves unanswered the two crucial questions as to why the subject should want to behave in this fashion and how he manages to do it.* SNP □ *Is any subject barred from poetry? This is a foolish question, but is so often posed that one might as well ask it and get it over. The answer is no, nothing is barred, providing it can be made into a poem. This is the correct way to* ***beg that*** *particular* ***question****.* NS □ adj compound question-begging.

beggar (all) description [V + O] (formal) be difficult to describe, because of extraordinary beauty, ugliness, oddness etc □ (source) *For* (= as for) *her own person, it* ***beggar'd all description****.* ANTHONY AND CLEOPATRA II 2 □ *The sunset that evening was of a beauty to* ***beggar all description****.* □ *I was accustomed to scenes of misery and squalor but the conditions in which the refugees were forced to live* ***beggared all description****.* □ *Her affected accent and eccentricity of dress combine to produce a comic effect that* ***beggars description****.*

beggars can't be choosers (saying) a person who has insufficient money to do exactly what he likes, or who depends on sb else, must be satisfied with what he can get □ JO: *You won't sleep very well on this couch, Geof.* GEOF: *It's all right.* ***Beggars can't be choosers****.* TOH □ *Joseph himself was not so pleased at Waggett's getting a free ride. 'I'll be turning off some time before Tràigh Swish,' he warned him. '****Beggars can't be choosers****,' said Waggett with a gracious smile.* RM □ *'Small fortune guaranteed within one month, no risk involved. Write Box 27.' Small fortune! Fantastic! I would have preferred a large one, but* ***beggars can't be choosers****, so I took pen in hand.* L □ always pl.

beginner's luck unusual success at the start of learning to do sth, when one first does sth (the implication often being that the success is purely accidental and temporary) **V:** have, enjoy; it be. **A:** just, only, purely, simply □ *Carter gave a sharp yelp. 'You nearly shot me!' He pulled out a hand clasped round a shattered pipe. '****Beginner's luck****,' Wormold said.* OMIH □ *You don't know what you're looking for. But you heard Carmichael's last words and they may suggest something to you when you get there. Who knows—you may have* ***beginner's luck****.* TCB □ pl form beginners' luck occas found.

behind sb's back[1] [A (PrepP)] while sb's back is turned, so he does not see what one is doing (usu because one does not want him to see) **V:** signal, make signs, wink; send messages (to each other) □ *'I shall go and make an omelette,' said Mrs Pettigrew, and casting her eyes to heaven* ***behind*** *Mrs Anthony****'s back*** *for Godfrey to see, disappeared into the kitchen.* MM □ *She was making frantic signs to me* ***behind*** *her husband****'s back*** *to say no more.*

behind sb's back[2] [A (PrepP)] while sb is absent and therefore unable to answer, or defend himself; without sb's knowledge or consent **V:** criticize, carp, gossip; organize sth, fix sth, sell sth □ *They enjoyed talking about him* ***behind his back****, telling stories about his prowess with women, stories that even they might have known were exaggerated.* CON □ STANLEY: *I'll write tonight. I'll say—let's see—'Much as I dislike complaining about people* ***behind their backs****, I feel it is my duty to warn you!'* FFE □ *It will be a bit of a job arranging it all* ***behind her back****, but we should manage.* ⇨ to sb's face; ⚠ go behind sb's back (Vol 1).

behind closed doors [A (PrepP)] in secret; without the public knowing or being admitted **S:** committee, council, society; meeting, reunion, discussion. **V:** meet, gather; hold a meeting, take a decision, decide sth; take place, be held □ *But while the rows over oil are headline news, the fights over coffee tend to take place* ***behind closed doors****, sometimes in a distant Latin American or African capital.* OBS □ *While Parliament talks about the future of our economy, the vital decisions have already been made* ***behind closed doors****.*

behind the scenes [A (PrepP)] (theatre) behind the main stage, or behind the scenery, where the audience cannot see what is happening; (fig) in private; out of the public's eye; in a concealed and perhaps secretive manner □ *On the first night there was a great deal of frantic activity and improvisation* ***behind the scenes*** *when it was realised that the costumes had been mislaid.* □ *Of course, there are lots of those great men who've got timid mousy little wives* ***behind the scenes****.* CON

(not) believe/credit (the evidence of) one's ears/eyes [V + O] be so astonished by what one has heard or seen that one's first reaction is one of disbelief □ *The problem would have been to get them to* ***believe their ears****. Robert to go and have an expensive training as an artist?* CON □ JO: *I saw him again one day, on the street.* HELEN: *Did you?* JO: *I could****n't believe my eyes****. He was thin, weak-chinned, with a funny turned-up nose.* TOH □ *For a moment they stood staring, unable to* ***believe the evidence of their eyes****. It was many months since the Germans had done anything like that.* RFW □ *If we were to* ***credit the evidence of our*** *own* ***ears*** *our darling child had just emitted a string of oaths worthy of a sergeant-major.* □ usu with *couldn't/can't, could hardly/scarcely, not be able/be unable to.*

believe it or not [Disj] it may sound odd to you but (I think) it is true □ MICK: *You know,* ***believe it or not*** *you've got a funny kind of resemblance to a bloke I once knew in Shoreditch.* TC □ *When I married I was a very young girl.* ***Believe it or not****, I'd hardly met anyone outside Bournemouth.* □ *Carlyle wholly resented Jeffrey's refusal to support his application to be a Professor of—****believe it or not****—Astronomy at Edinburgh University.* SC

believe (that) water can/will flow uphill (saying) be able to persist in a belief, despite evidence to the contrary □ *But I had no faith in its lasting. I could no more believe that it would last than I could* ***believe water would flow uphill****.* SPL □ *You might as well try to make me* ***believe that water will flow uphill*** *as convince me that the President was the victim of his crooked assistants.*

(not) believe a word (of sth)/(that) [V + O] (not) believe, even partly, what sb has said, written, or reported **o:** it; his speech, statement, excuse, apology; what he says. **cl:** (that) he says □ *I can get up from my sick-bed, dress, go out, do the shopping, and nearly kill myself, but you do****n't believe a word of*** *it!* DC □ *I've had no trouble myself from any phone calls. Between ourselves, I think it's all made up. I do****n't believe a word of*** *what they say.* MM □ *Well, I hope you're telling the truth this time, but you've made it difficult for me to* ***believe a word*** *you say.*

believe you me [Disj] (informal) you must accept what I say as definite, true; I mean what I say □ *'It's your affair,' I said. 'It is.* ***Believe you me****,' said Sammy, and we left it at that.* UTN □ *You gave him £20 to get rid of him? You don't get rid of spongers that way,* ***believe you me****! He'll be back for more.* □ *You think too little of that boy, you know.* ***Believe you me****, he won't do too badly.*

bell the cat [V + O] do sth which is dangerous to oneself to help or protect others; expose, or make less harmful, the designs or actions of sb thought dangerous to others (from a fable about mice who thought it would be a good idea to hang a bell round a cat's neck but could not find a single mouse willing to do this) □ *One can imagine the possible repercussions of a full judicial enquiry, but the need for such an enquiry is now unmistakable. Who will* ***bell the cat****?* L

below/under one's/sb's breath [A (PrepP)] in a whisper; in a very low tone, (often so as not to be heard by others) **V:** complain, grumble, mumble, mutter; repeat sth, say sth □ *What are you muttering there* ***below your breath****, Simpson? If you don't agree with what I've been suggesting, kindly speak up and give us all the benefit of your opinion.* □ *I called her the worst names I could think of, repeating them again and again* ***under my breath****, but it didn't relieve my feelings very much.* RATT *Decidedly Mrs Carstairs was in good humour. She was humming a tune* ***under her breath*** *as she tripped to the door.* EM.

a/one's besetting sin a typical fault, failing, lack of control, etc; a temptation that one gives in to too easily □ *He's a fine fellow, apart from* ***his besetting sin*** *— he drinks too much.* □ *Interfering in other people's business was* ***her besetting sin****. A self-appointed healer, she seemed to imagine that a few wise words from her could set anybody's life in order.* □ *'The Bingo Age' aptly describes* ***one besetting sin*** *of both major parties in the post-war era; offering quick and easy prizes as vote-catching incentives.* □ also pl.

one's best bib and tucker [n + n non-rev] one's best, or finest, clothes, esp as worn for a special occasion **V:** be in; don, put on, wear □ *'What sort of a function is it? Do I have to put on* ***my best bib and tucker****?' 'Oh no, it's a very informal affair, people will be coming just as they are.'* □ *So we all set off in* ***our best bibs and tuckers****, as instructed, to visit our prospective 'in-laws' and make a good impression of ourselves as a family.*

one's best friend sb whom one can rely on above all others for help or support; sth (esp a valuable object) that gives one security and independence and is therefore worth possessing **det:** our, their □ *'They always did say a boy****'s best friend*** *was his mother, didn't they?' I said nastily. Even while I was sarcastically fending off my mother's instructions, I was automatically obeying them.* CON □ *Mink-hunting is on the increase. Not of the cultivated mink — after diamonds, a girl****'s best friend*** *— but of the financially valueless wild mink.* OBS □ *If you have £5 in one pocket and £5 in the other, you are between two of* ***the best friends*** *you will ever have.* SC □ *'Ah, you can't go far without money,' she said. '****Your best friend****'s your pocket.'* MM □ allusion in second example to catchphrase diamonds are a girl's best friend (qv).

the best man wins (accept philosophically that) sb has defeated one in some competition, has succeeded better than oneself, etc; (declare that) the person who proves himself better than everybody else in some competition will gain the prize, reward etc □ *'Will you marry me?' he repeated. 'No,' Phuong said. 'No?' He took the glass wistfully. '****The best man wins****. Only please don't leave her, Thomas.'* QA □ *She threw down her racket but then went up to the net to congratulate the new champion. '****Best man wins****,' she said, generously enough.* □ *In choosing the man to fill the job, he said he would play no favourites: it would be strictly a matter of merit and experience with* ***the best man winning****.* □ not usu pl.

(in) the best of all possible worlds [A (PrepP)] (in) a state in which all that one could desire could happen; (under) perfect circumstances (the strong implication being that this is not the way things actually are, or are likely to be) □ (source) *All is for the best* ***in the best of all possible worlds****.* VOLTAIRE (1694-1778) □ *It may be true that, if this were* ***the best of all possible worlds****, the food surplus in the developed countries would be sufficient to answer the needs of the starving millions elsewhere.*

the best of British (luck) (to sb) (I wish you) good luck (in some activity) (the implication being that the person addressed will not succeed, or does not deserve to succeed) □ *'Will you get your blessed van out of the way! I've got a train to catch in ten minutes!' 'And* ***the best of British to*** *you,' muttered the milkman under his breath.* □ *I don't for a moment think you'll succeed in raising that much money, but* ***the best of British luck to*** *you, all the same.'* □ often introduced by *I/we wish you* or *And*; usu ironic.

the best of it the most amusing, or suprising, part of an incident or situation □ *We all had a good laugh when Grandpa couldn't find his spectacles.* ***The best of it*** *was that they were up on his forehead all the time he was looking for them.* □ *The show's had rave reviews—and* ***the best of it*** *is that the entire cast thought the opening night was a complete mess.* □ usu followed by *is/was that*.

the best/worst of it/sth is (that) the most/least advantageous aspect of sth is (that) **o:** it; teaching, sailing; being a teacher, being overweight, living here □ ***The best of*** *being a teacher* ***is*** *the long holidays you get.* □ ***The worst of it is that*** *I can't even be sure that they got my cheque.* □ ***The best of*** *patterned carpets* ***is that*** *it doesn't matter if your guests spill their drinks over them.* □ ***That's the worst of*** *being a novelist—we never answer letters.* PW □ variant that's the best/worst of sth.

the best/better part of sth [O (NP)] most of sth, leaving very little over **V:** consume, devour, swallow; contain, hold □ *He ate* ***the best part of*** *a chicken, and gave the rest to the dog.* □ *The gourd must have held* ***the best part of*** *a gallon.* □ *He brought us a bottle of wine and then proceeded to drink* ***the better part of*** *it himself.*

(for) the best/better part of an hour etc [A (NP)] (during) most of an hour or any other period of time specified **V:** take; work (for), be away (for). **n:** hour, ⚠ day, evening, week, year □ *Kingsley studied the papers silently* ***for the best part of an hour****.* TBC □ *Aged between 12 and 18, the entrants have been put through their paces* ***for the best part of a week*** *and judged by a jury of celebrated musicians.* RT □ *He's been away in China* ***for the best part of a year****.*

the best (education etc) that money can buy [Comp/O (NP)] only the very best (object, article etc) that can be bought **V:** be; get, give, have, offer. **n:** education, training; jewellery, furniture □ *They have a beautiful house, full of* ***the best that money can buy****.* □ *If you had given me* ***the best piece of jewellery money could buy****, it wouldn't have pleased me more than this little keepsake.* □ *I'm in a position to give my son* ***the best education that money can buy****, and that's what he's going to get.* □ (NONCE) *Mr Adams, who lived in the Old Bank House at Edgewood, said Kate, had got* ***the best television that money could hire*** *and they were all going to look at the Coronation on it.* WDM

the best things in life are free (saying) activities etc which cost nothing, or very little, give more pleasure, have more true value, than anything for which one might pay a great deal □ *She thought we were mad, getting married when neither of us had two halfpennies to rub together. 'Still,' I said, '****the best things in life are free****.'* □ (NONCE) *Why cook at all when* ***the best things in life*** *according to the telly* (ie television commercials) ***come*** *conveniently* ***processed****, so clean and easy to handle, no more dirty pans.* L

the best-laid schemes of mice and men (gang aft agley) (saying) despite careful planning, or plotting, things often can, or do, go wrong in their actual execution □ (source) ***The best laid schemes o'*** (= of) ***mice an'*** (= and) ***men/Gang aft agley*** ((Scot) = often go wrong). TO A MOUSE (R BURNS 1759-96) □ (NONCE) *All of which shows that I should have held my tongue.* ***The 'best-laid' Press conferences of 'mice and men gang aft agley****.'* MFM □ *'It was* *maddening to have to cancel the children's outing at the last minute like that.' 'It couldn't be helped, so don't let it bother you too much—* ***the best-laid schemes of mice and men****, you know!'* □ often adapted, as in second example.

bet sb anything/what he likes (that) (informal) be prepared to assert, confidently predict (that); I('ll)/you bet (that) (qv) **cl:** (that) it won't happen, (that) he won't turn up, (that) she'll get drunk □ *I* ***bet*** *you* ***anything you like*** *we won't get an invitation to the wedding.* □ LOUISE: *You'd better be off on your ride before you get into any more trouble.* PAMELA: *Oh, it's one of those days. I* ***bet*** *you* ***anything*** *the horse breaks its legs.* FFE □ *I beat Daddy at chess, and he* ***bet*** *me* ***anything that*** *I couldn't.* □ *We* ***bet*** *them* ***what they liked that*** *they'd find themselves no better off than before.* □ first person S is often dropped as in ***Bet*** *you* ***what you like*** *he won't come.* ⇨ I('ll) bet.

bet one's bottom dollar (on sth/that) (gambling) stake all the money one has (on sth/ that); be very certain (about sth, that sth will happen, etc) □ *'I bet you that the day after tomorrow by this time Mommy will be back.' 'What will you bet?' 'I'll* ***bet my bottom dollar****.'* PW □ *He had* ***bet his bottom dollar on*** *an outsider thinking that he'd been given a sure tip by someone 'in the know'.* □ *'I don't think the shopkeeper meant to cheat us.' 'I'll* ***bet my bottom dollar*** *he did—probably thought we were in too much of a hurry to count our change.'* □ *You're not going out again tonight, my boy. You can* ***bet your bottom dollar on*** *that!*

better etc all round (for sb) (if) [Comp (AdjP)] preferable in every way (for sb) (if) **V:** ⚠ be; get, prove. **V:** better, ⚠ easier, pleasanter. **o:** everyone, all concerned, the children. **cl:** if it works, if they leave □ *Last Autumn I thought I should have to give up my business, but things have been* ***better all round*** *since the New Year.* □ *'I don't really enjoy picnics any more,' said grandmother. 'It would be* ***easier all round for*** *you* ***if*** *I stayed at home, because then I could look after the baby and you could do something really interesting with the older ones.'* □ *It'd be* ***better all round if*** *you'd take that thing off your eyes, Mr Lamb, and get on with your work.* CON

better bad now than worse later (saying) it is better to endure, or deal with, sth painful or unpleasant immediately, if by not doing so the situation will only get worse and even more difficult to handle □ *'I ought to have chucked you out before you said a word.' 'You couldn't have, any more than you can now. Too painful.' She said in a muffled voice: '****Better bad now than worse later****.'* TGLY □ *'****Better bad now than worse later****,' the surveyor told him. 'If we hadn't discovered this patch of dry rot now, you'd have had a bill for hundreds of pounds in a year or two.'*

the better the day the better the deed (saying) it is sometimes right to do sth, to work, on a Sunday (which is traditionally regarded, in Christian belief, as a day of rest) □ (partial source) *If it* (a sheep) *fall into a pit on the Sabbath day, will he not lay hold on it, and lift it out? Wherefore it is lawful to do well on the Sabbath day.* MATTHEW XII 11-12 □ *'I may be old-fashioned, dear, but I don't like to see the washing hung out on a Sunday.' 'But, Granny, this is the only day I'm free to come over and help you and, anyway, as people say,* ***the better the day the better the deed****.'* □ usu offered as an excuse, justification etc.

better (off) dead [Comp (AdjP)] being dead would be preferable to being alive (because one's life is miserable, painful, useless, or occas, antisocial, destructive etc) **V:** ⚠ be, think sb □ *They* (the gulls) *told him, with their close approach and flapping hover, that he was far* ***better dead****, floating in the sea like a burst hammock.* PM □ *Why should our good taxpayers' money be spent supporting brutes who would be* ***better dead****?'* □ *He sat alone, thinking. His wife had left him, he'd lost his job—he'd be* ***better off dead****.*

one's/the better half (informal, facetious) one's wife/husband □ *'All alone?' she asked, looking surprised. 'Where's* ***the better half****?' 'Working late,' Jane replied. 'he'll come along later.'* □ *So we meet this fellow in the pub and he invites us, me and* ***my better half****, that is, round to his place.*

better late than never (saying) (offer, be offered, sometimes ironically) an excuse or apology for one's lateness; (accept, point out to sb, that) success in some matter, however long it has taken to come or however small it is, is better than none at all □ *Come along in. I'm sorry you had such a bad journey, but* ***better late than never****.* □ *In fact, I had been given very nearly all that I had been asking for since August.* ***Better late than never****.* MFM □ *'I expect you think I'm too old for a holiday on my own?' 'Not at all,* ***better late than never****, I always say.'*

better luck next time (saying) may you succeed on some future occasion **V:** wish sb; have; hope for □ *'So the party was dismal. Never mind!* ***Better luck next time****!' 'It wasn't the party that was wrong. It was me.'* HAHA □ *I just wrote and said I was sorry he had not passed his exam and wished him* ***better luck next time****.* □ *Never mind! Perhaps you'll have* ***better luck next time****.* □ often verbless clause; used esp to console or encourage sb who has just failed to do sth, win sth, etc.

one's/sb's better nature the more honourable, self-denying, or virtuous aspect of one's/ sb's character **V:** appeal to; make, try, respond to, an appeal to □ *I may have to punish Sam for bullying, but I'll try to appeal to* ***his better nature*** *first.* □ *A cruel and slighting answer hovered on my tongue, but then* ***my better nature*** *re-asserted itself and I made some noncommittal remark.* □ also pl their better natures.

better (to be) safe than sorry (saying) (it is) wiser to be over-cautious and take proper care than to be rash and unthinking (and so do sth foolish that harms one, that one regrets later; etc) □ *Patrick said 'Christ, someone's shooting at us,' and threw himself down full length on the muddy verge. Jenny laughed. He gave her a glare, then smiled reluctantly. '****Better to be safe than sorry****,' he said.* TGLY □ *'You could easily have overtaken the lorry just now.' '****Better safe than sorry****,' the driver replied. 'Just let me use my own judgement, will you?'* □ often introduced by *It is*; used to excuse or justify one's actions or decisions.

the better to see etc in order to see etc better **V:** see, hear, supervise, explain, appreciate □ *I remember being perched on my father's shoulders* ***the better to*** *see over the heads of the crowd.* □ *At this point David took off his shoes* ***the better to*** *avoid being overheard and, carrying them in his hand, tip-toed past the half-open kitchen door into the darkness of the garden.* □ *I had learned a little Russian* ***the better to*** *pursue my scientific researches, and this knowledge was now to stand me in good stead.* □ usu end position.

better/worse still [Conj (AdvP)] (there is) sth better that one can do than what has been previously suggested/(it is, would be) much worse if one decided to do sth other than what has been suggested □ *Why don't we all go out to the pub?* ***Better still****, why doesn't Jimmy pop round to the off-licence and bring something back here?* □ *I think you ought to go cautiously with him, it's no use storming in and demanding a rise.* ***Worse still*** *would be to criticize his handling of your staff.*

better that way [Comp (AdjP)] more suitable, desirable than any other **S:** arrangement, system; it; things. **V:** ⚠ be, seem; go; work □ *He thought: She* (Beatrice) *will go back by the next plane, life will be the same as before, and, of course, it was* ***better that way****; his life belonged to Milly.* OMIH □ *'He is ridiculously generous with both his money and his time.' '****Better that way*** *than the other extreme.'* □ *Fifty years ago ordinary people didn't know so much about medical matters and about what might be wrong with them, and I often wonder whether it wasn't* ***better that way****.*

between the devil and the deep blue sea [Comp/A (PrepP)] (saying) (be faced) with a choice of alternative situations or courses of action, neither of which is welcome or desirable **V:** be, find oneself; be caught □ *His enemy was close behind him, and the bridge over the ravine was rotten and swaying. Caught* ***between the devil and the deep blue sea****, he hesitated.* □ *We'll have to put our hands in our pockets to pay his passage home or else have him sponging on us here indefinitely. Talk of being* ***between the devil and the deep blue sea****!* □ (NONCE) *Mrs Thatcher now stands* ***between the devil and the deep wet*** ((UK slang) here = liberal Conservative) ***sea****.* L ⇨ ⚠ next entry.

between Scylla and Charybdis [Comp/A (PrepP)] (formal) (be) threatened by two dangers, the avoidance of one increasing the likelihood of harm from the other (from a Greek myth about a narrow sea passage between a rock and a whirlpool, each inhabited by a monster) **V:** be; be caught, (try to) steer □ *He would have preferred to be on good terms with both his wife and his mother, but the effort of pleasing one without offending the other was like steering* ***between Scylla and Charybdis****.* □ *Somewhere* ***between the Scylla*** *of too formal a courtesy* ***and the Charybdis*** *of over-familiarity lies the technique of putting people at their ease.* □ rather rare. ⇨ ⚠ previous entry.

between one's teeth [A (Prep P)] with one's teeth tightly closed, clenched (as a sign of anger, pain, or other strong emotion) **V:** say, speak; mutter; force out, spit out □ *'Look, Baxter,' he said* ***between his teeth****. 'You and your honest work. You're the sort of person who'll keep this factory down in the mud, turning out cheap trash.'* CON □ MYRA (has an impulse to make a maternal protective gesture, suppresses it at the last moment. Says quietly, but **between her teeth**): *All the same get out of those clothes.* EHOW □ *He managed an apology of sorts, muttering a few perfunctory excuses* ***between his teeth****.*

(in) between times/whiles [A (PrepP)] in the intervals between events (which are stated or implied) □ (The central heating boiler) *gets made up in the morning, and last thing at night, and* ***in between times*** *nobody goes there.* RFW □ *Films, theatres, concerts, everything she had once dreamed of doing she now did. And* ***between whiles****, for Alec was writing hard, she visited old friends.* PW □ usu front position; stress pattern (in) be'tween times/whiles.

betwixt and between [prep + prep non-rev] neither one nor the other of two things mentioned but having some characteristics of each □ *'Are you glad or sorry your husband hasn't been posted abroad?' 'Sort of* ***betwixt and between****, really.'* □ *I could enjoy life in either the town or the country, but there are no advantages that I can see in living in a* ***betwixt and between*** *district like this.* □ *She had served the family for years in a capacity something* ***betwixt and between*** *housekeeper and benevolent tyrant.*

beyond belief (to a degree) too difficult or impossible to believe, or too wonderful or too dreadful for the mind to grasp. **V:** be, seem □ *The huts they lived in were sordid and filthy* ***beyond belief****.* □ *Imagine these Pyramids being built by physical labour alone! It's almost* ***beyond belief****.* □ *The sunset last night was of a beauty* ***beyond belief****.* □ often modifies a preceding adj or n.

beyond a certain point [A (PrepP)] as soon as, once, a particular stage, or moment in time, has been reached and passed □ *Publicity may help to break down the barrier, but* ***beyond a certain point*** *it is impossible to dramatise administration.* SC □ *He allowed his staff a fair amount of latitude but* ***beyond a certain point*** *he would put his foot down as firmly as the next man.* □ *There are drugs which slow the progress of the disease in its earlier stages but* ***beyond a certain point*** (cf ***once a certain point is reached***) *they become ineffective.* □ variant once a certain point is reached.

beyond (all) measure [A (PrepP)] (formal) to an unusual degree (often excessively, immoderately) **V:** esteem sth, prize sth, value sth; covet sth □ *Since our arrival in Africa I had talked about it incessantly, until even the staff knew that Idiurus kivuensis was the name of a beef* ((pidgin English) = animal) *that I prized* ***beyond all measure****.* BB □ *It's natural for parents to love their children, and Richard's nice enough, but his father dotes on him* ***beyond all measure****.* □ *'Your husband tells me you're a devotee of Henry James?' 'He exaggerates — I do admire his writing but not* ***beyond measure****. He can be very tedious.'*

beyond one's wildest dreams/hopes [Comp/A (Prep P)] (in a way that is) very much greater than one expected, than one could possibly expect, etc **V:** be, lie; succeed □ *And so ended a remarkably successful visit — successful* ***beyond my wildest dreams.*** MFM □ *The Prime Minister said, 'Today, I am amazed at the changes that have come about. They are* ***beyond my wildest hopes.'*** OBS

bid fair to do sth (formal) seem likely to happen, to do sth good or bad □ *It* ***bids fair to*** *be a nice day.* □ *Our scheme for building a new community centre* ***bids fair to*** *succeed.* □ *For a while he* ***bade fair to*** *become a drunkard like his father, but his marriage seems to have steadied him.* □ irregular past tense bade and pp bidden; when phrase is in past tense there is usu a following clause showing that the thing expected did not finally happen, as in last example.

bid sb goodbye [V + IO + O] say goodbye (to sb); take formal leave of sb □ *We have just called in to* ***bid*** *you* ***goodbye*** *and to thank you for all you have done to make our holiday so pleasant.* □ *I tipped him £10 for his trouble and* ***bid*** *him* ***goodbye.*** □ *Have you* ***bidden*** *the children* ***goodbye*** *yet?* □ irregular past tense bade or bid, and pp bidden.

bide one's time [V + O] patiently, wisely await a suitable time or opportunity (for sth one intends to do or say) □ *Harold had something on his mind; he looked slightly portentous. Harold did not always spill the beans at once; he would* ***bide his time*** *and adopt a sphinx-like air.* PW □ *'A bit of hoeing today,' he said. She made no immediate objection, for she must* ***bide her time.*** *Not that Henry was touchy or difficult about his angina.* MM □ *'I don't think you should let the house go for £75,000,' the agent said. 'If you're prepared to* ***bide your time*** *I'm sure I could get you a higher offer.'*

the big battalions the powerful, influential, wealthy etc groups of a community, among nations, etc, who are able to dominate less powerful groups, minorities etc **V:** side with; bring up; face □ *Working-class people mistrust the leaders of* ***the big battalions,*** *but usually with a humorous scepticism towards them and their pretensions.* UL □ *Between* ***the big battalions*** *of organised labour and organised capital, there are 56 million people, all of whom are consumers, who feel they are being squeezed and who have no real voice at all.* OBS □ *In the competition for customers, time and money is on the side of* ***the big battalions*** *of chain stores and supermarkets.* □ often preceded by *on the side of*, as in last example.

Big Brother (a personification of) the forces of a bureaucratic and totalitarian state (which direct, control, interfere with, every aspect of one's, or society's, life) □ (source) *The poster with the enormous face gazed from the wall. '****Big Brother*** *is watching you', the caption beneath it ran.* 1984 (G ORWELL 1903-50) □ *The way things are,* ***Big Brother*** *won't be keeping an eye on us via television. He'll more likely be organizing us to pedal the bicycles to power the machines to get the television going.* NS □ (NONCE) *'Terribly strict country still,' Angela Snow said. '****Big mother*** *is watching you and all that.'* BFA

a big bug (slang, derogatory) sb of importance □ *I daresay the Mayor and a few other* ***big bugs*** *from London will be present at the opening ceremony.* □ *There's the station-master in his frock-coat and top-hat. There must be* ***a big bug*** *getting off the train here.* □ stress pattern a 'big bug.

a big cheese (slang, derogatory) sb who is, or believes he is, a very important person, the most important person in a group, company etc □ *Here comes* ***the big cheese*** *himself. Have we got the red carpet out?* □ *He thinks he's* ***the big cheese,*** *but in fact he's only one of the maggots!* □ not usu pl.

big deal(!) (slang) ironic exclamation suggesting that sth is not very impressive or interesting (though it may be represented as such) □ *'When you've washed the dishes, made the beds, and prepared the vegetables for dinner, I'll give you 50p.' 'Oh thank you!* ***Big deal!****'* □ *There was I with a whole free weekend in front of me, no wife, no children — in a boarding house that described itself as a hotel but had no bar.* ***Big deal.***

a big fish in a little pond [Comp (NP)] sb whose importance and influence are great only in a restricted situation or small community **V:** ⚠ be; prefer to be, would rather be □ *'She'd be more usefully employed in a proper hospital.' 'She couldn't be "Matron" in one of them, and she's the kind that would rather be* ***a big fish in a little pond*** *than* ***a little fish in a big one.****'* □ (Bob) *had lived in London and hadn't enjoyed it. 'Got damned tired of it,' he said. 'Don't like being* ***a little fish in a big pond.****'* RATT □ variants a big fish in a big pond, a little/small fish in a big pond.

a big hit [Comp/O (NP)] (informal) a popular success **S:** player, performer; fashion, play, song, film. **V:** be; make, score □ JIMMY: *Thought of the title for a new song today. Thought you'd like it. If I can slip in a religious angle, it should be* ***a big hit.*** LBA □ *Come along and do some of those conjuring tricks at our next social. You'd be* ***a big hit.*** □ *It seems a very silly play to read now, yet it was quite* ***a big hit*** *in the West End forty years ago.* □ also pl.

a big name (informal) sb who has gained the approval of the public (eg as a commentator, entertainer, sportsman, writer etc) and is well known for his work □ *'Startime' and 'Showtime'* (the seaside theatre entertainments) *do not go in for* ***big names.*** *Their purpose, rather, is to appeal to people's fondness, on holiday as everywhere, for regularity and routine.* ST □ *The pre-war and post-war eras in jazz development were dominated by a small group of* ***big-name*** *bands such as Armstrong's, Ellington's, and Basie's.* □ attrib use *a* ***big-name*** *band, artist, singer.*

a big shot (informal) sb who is, or claims to be, a person of importance and influence (eg in some organization etc, and often in criminal circles) □ ***The*** *one really* ***big shot*** *among us was* ***the*** *one* ***big shot*** *no longer.* CON □ *Nicky, pale-faced and tense, was relishing his power. He was the tough,* ***the big shot,*** *who gave orders with the crack of a whip.* PE □ also pl; stress pattern a 'big shot.

the big stick [O/o (NP)] superior force or power (eg of authority, military strength, economic sanctions, etc) **V:** carry; use, wield (against sb/sth); favour (the use of), threaten sb with □ (source) *Speak softly and carry* ***a big stick.*** SPEECH 1901 (T ROOSEVELT 1858-1919) □ *The*

United States Government's recent action in cutting off aid to Ceylon smelt of the use of ***the big stick*** *against a smaller country.* T □ *Thus, during the Nixon era, interventions such as the terror bombing of Cambodia had to be conducted by stealth and deception. Now Gerald Ford waves* ***his big stick*** *openly.* NS

big talk/words boastful claims, promises, intentions etc which sb makes in order to impress others but which are not likely to be true, to be carried out, etc □ *You may have yer 'ead* (= your head) *full of fine ideas, you may be able to live on air and* ***big talk****—but the rest of us 'ave* (= have) *to pay our way—and pay it with money!* HD □ *I've heard a lot of* ***big talk*** *from her about other members of her family that never came to anything.* □ *They are cheerfully cagey towards both the leaders of the big battalions and their* ***big words****: 'Ah'm* (= I'm) *not buying that,' they say.* UL □ big words rare.

the big time (informal) the top level of some sphere of activity, esp one that gives one a lot of publicity, eg the world of entertainment, or the wealth, success and fame that go with it **V:** be in; make; get (sb) into □ *This isn't an occasion for bread and cheese. We're in* ***the big time*** *now. We're all going for lunch.* CON □ *He was a fairly versatile actor who always gave a sound performance, but he knew he would never make* ***the big time****.* □ *Before trying for* ***the Big Time****, I started out doing the rounds of the sticks* (= provincial) *shows.* L □ *When it comes to keeping all the excitement of* ***big time*** *sport in close-up you need something more than pictures. You need sportswriters you can rely on.* TO □ attrib use *a* ***big-time*** *writer, politician*; stress pattern the 'big time. ⇨ (the) small time.

the Big Top the large tent for the (main) performance of a circus □ *The monkeys are in a side-show. They don't bring them into* ***the Big Top****.* □ *My mind had become a trapeze, swinging emptily under* ***the Big Top****, for any passing acrobat to seize and twirl on for a few seconds.* CON □ usu capital letters but occas lower case.

bigger and better [Comp (adj + adj non-rev)] (sth) larger and more useful etc (than sth else that it replaces etc); (sb) more important, cleverer (than sb else) □ *St Valentine's Day started the card game* (ie the sending of lovers' greeting cards)*—back in the 15th century. Now Valentines are* ***bigger and better*** *each year.* WI □ *When I was a child we never had very much of anything. So I always tried to do everything* ***bigger and better*** *than everyone else.* SC □ (letter) *We have carried major reports which have given reporters opportunities to write at a length and with a depth and individuality which they are often denied on newspapers with more restricted space. Here, at last,* ***bigger*** *does mean* ***better****.* L □ in second example expression is used, rather unusually, as an A.

the bigger etc the better the degree by, or to which, sth is big etc, by that much it is better (more desirable, tolerable etc) **adj:** big, tall, great, small, more, less, young, old, rich, hard, soft, sweet, powerful, long, short □ *'I think we're in for a lot of rain.' '****The more the better****,' said the farmer looking at his parched crops.* □ *'After all, inflation is itself another product of growth economics.' '****The bigger the better****' may well have been a 19th-century truth, but now it has become a 20th-century myth, in my opinion.'* L □ *'How old do you have to be* (to train as a fashion model)*?' 'The general rule is* ***the younger the better****.'* H □ *Stores say cheques are more trouble, but it is largely their own cumbersome procedures that are to blame. I'd have thought* ***the less cash handled the better*** *from a security point of view.* OBS □ *Tony Benn says: 'I expect questions and answer them as they come up.* ***The harder the interviewers press, the more I like it****.'* TVT

bill and coo [v + v non-rev] show mutual affection by words and gesture, often in an overdone and obvious manner (from the behaviour of amorous doves which rub their beaks together and coo gently) □ *The following Saturday night Clough got together with Parkinson* (on a TV programme)*: the two professional Yorkshire lads* ***billed and cooed*** *at each other and Clough was as cute as a canary.* ST □ *I don't mean romance in the way you mean, Dinah. Not romance in the silly Peg's Paper, moon-June,* ***billing and cooing*** *sense—or nonsense.* L □ *We don't wish to indulge in the sort of domestic* ***billing and cooing*** *that fellows like Roberts go in for, with their wives playing University politics.* ASA □ *-ing* form of v is commonly used.

bind/tie sb hand and foot [V + O + A pass] tie sb's hands together and feet together; (fig) take away or restrict sb's freedom of action □ *They* ***bound*** *him* ***hand and foot*** *and placed a gag in his mouth.* □ *A trader who becomes an authorized distributor of a product may soon find that he has agreed to conditions of sale that* ***bind*** *him* ***hand and foot*** *to the manufacturer.* □ *Having your mother to stay here will be worse than having an infant in the house. I'll be* ***tied hand and foot****! I'll go mad!* ⇨ ⚠ tie sb's hands.

the birds and the bees [n + n non-rev] (a euphemistic reference to) matters relating to procreation or sex in general **V:** tell sb about; know about; find out about □ *Whatever its disadvantages, sex education in the schools is an advance upon the process by which children used to find out about* ***the birds and the bees*** *from their embarrassed parents.* □ *Joan's getting to be a big girl now. I suppose it's time you had a talk with her about* ***the birds and the bees****.*

the bird has flown sb who is being sought, or pursued, has gone away, has escaped □ *'All right,' said the old man, 'but forty per cent is all you get, and if there's going to be any arguing you'll find* ***the bird has flown*** *when you get here.'* US □ *Police hurried to the address supplied by their informant, only to learn that* ***their bird had flown*** *less than an hour before.* □ *Harry was so drunk after last night's Rally, we had to put him to bed in our spare room. But when we got up this morning,* ***the bird had flown****.* □ perfect tenses only; used esp of sb who may be a criminal.

a bird in the hand is worth two in the bush (saying) it is better to be content with sth one has, or can be sure of, than risk having nothing at all by trying to get sth more or sth else □ *He had one quite reasonable offer for the manuscript, but turned it down. Then he could find no takers at all. He learnt with a vengeance that* ***a bird in the hand is worth two in the***

bush. □ *'Are you going to take the job at the High School or wait and see if the University will offer you one?' 'I'll settle for* **the bird in the hand**, *I think.'*

a bird of passage a migratory bird which spends different seasons in different parts of the world; (fig) sb who travels from place to place without staying long in any one of them, without settling down, etc □ *The island had been used by many generations of* **birds of passage**, *as they made the long journey south each year in search of warmer weather.* □ *Three months' stay had proved me not to be* **a bird of passage**, *like every past pallid-skinned visitor.* NDN □ *'Who is this Professor Wylie you've been talking about?' 'An archaeologist,* **an** *odd* **bird of passage** *who turns up here every three or four years or so.'*

birds of a feather (flock together) (saying) people of the same sort (will be found together; like attracts/calls to like (qv) □ *'I can't understand why Liz wants to spend most of her evenings in that disco.' 'Well,* **birds of a feather flock together**, *as you know—I've always said your picture of her as basically a home-loving cocoa-drinking wife and mother is wildly wrong.'* □ *'Have you noticed that Bill's starting to behave like Reg did, just before he cracked up?' 'Yes I have. And I wouldn't be at all surprised if they didn't turn out to be* **birds of a feather**.*'* □ often derogatory.

a bird's-eye view (of sth) [O (NP)] a view seen from a higher position looking down as though one were a bird; (fig) an overall summary; a quick examination **V:** get, have, obtain; give; show. **o:** landscape, town; matter, situation, subject □ *I had not realized how very indented the coastline was until I had* **a bird's-eye view of** *it in my first trip in a glider.* □ *In my opening lecture I propose to give you* **a bird's-eye view of** *18th Century French literature. In subsequent lectures we will explore various aspects of it in greater depth.* □ (NONCE) (Fellini's film, 'His Woman') *is by no means* **a Fellini-eye view of** *felony—not, to coin a phrase, on your dolce vita.* T □ in last example *not on your dolce vita* (a travesty of Italian usage) = 'not on your sweet life' (qv).

one's birthday suit [O (NP)] (facetious) (having) no clothing on at all; naked (ie as in one's unclothed state at birth) **V:** be in, wear; find sb in □ *Here's a snapshot of me at six months old, wearing* **my birthday suit**. □ *I thought I had been given a private bathroom, so I was more than disconcerted when somebody walked in and found me in* **my birthday suit**. □ also pl.

bit by bit[1] [A (n + n)] each piece (of a whole thing) at a time; one bit, or piece, after another □ *The only way to tackle one of these plastic model kits is to assemble it* **bit by bit**, *following the instructions carefully.* □ **Bit by bit** *a complete picture was built up of the murderer's movements up to the moment of the crime.* □ usu in front or end position.

bit by bit[2] [A (n + n)] a little at a time; slowly, or gradually; little by little (qv) □ *If I had nothing else to do I could get this garden in order in a couple of weeks. As it is, doing it* **bit by bit**, *it may take me the whole summer.* □ *Your boy is not stupid, Mrs Brown. He does not learn easily but he gets there* **bit by bit**. □ **Bit by bit**, *feeling cautiously for holds and trying not to panic, he hauled himself out of the crevasse.* □ usu in front or end position.

a bit much [Comp (AdjP)] (informal) unwelcome, excessive, unreasonable etc (in the opinion of the speaker); a bit thick (qv) **S:** it, that; everything; situation, sb's behaviour. **V:** ⚠ be, become, seem; be getting □ *Myrtle's voice came to me with reproach. 'You don't sound very enthusiastic!' There is only one phrase for expressing what I felt. It was* **a bit much**. SPL □ *I said, 'Ssh!' and added, 'It's Jake Donaghue.' 'This is* **a bit much**!*' said Hugo. 'I was asleep.'* UTN □ *'I'm not one to interfere with people enjoying themselves,' she said to her neighbours, 'but really the noise is getting* **a bit much**.*'*

a bit of all right [Comp (NP)] (dated slang) sth that is very pleasant to do, watch, eat, have done, etc; very attractive □ *'Well, that was* **a bit of all right**,*' he said, crumpling up his napkin and throwing it on the empty plate.* □ *First prize: a fortnight's holiday for two in one of Paris's luxury hotels—now that should be* **a bit of all right**, *shouldn't it, Kate?* □ *'What's she like?' 'The daughter?* **Bit of all right**, *from her pictures.'* AITC □ when expression describes person, as in last example, it is used to refer to women only.

a bit of a coward etc [Comp (NP)] rather cowardly etc **V:** ⚠ be, seem, appear. **o:** coward; ass, fool, idiot, nuisance; weakling; (taboo) bastard, sod ((taboo) = nasty, unreasonable person) □ *'I'm* **a bit of a coward** *about pain,' he told the dentist. 'Could I have an injection before you start?'* □ (of the Wombles, a children's TV programme) *Then there is young Bungo who is* **a bit of a know-all** *and his friend Orinoco—who is lazy and greedy but perhaps the most lovable Womble.* RT □ used to refer to some personal quality or type of behaviour that is not very positive or good, but not to any marked degree.

a bit of a nuisance etc [Comp (NP)] sth that irritates one mildly **S:** it; working on Saturdays, missing the train; to have to work; delay, inefficiency. **V:** ⚠ be, become; get. **o:** nuisance, ⚠ problem; mess, shambles; (slang) bind (ie sth that hampers or bothers one) □ *It'll be* **a bit of a nuisance** *carrying our bags around with us, but if we put them in the Left Luggage Office we may have to queue up for ages to get them out again.* □ *'How did the school concert go?'* '**A bit of a shambles**, *actually; but we got through the programme without any major disaster.'* □ *I must admit, I wouldn't want to be ugly. The physical thing can be* **a bit of a bind** (ie being beautiful has its problems) *but it is good because it gets you work* (in the theatre). TVT

a bit thick [Comp (AdjP)] (informal) unfair; unreasonable; more than one can, or wishes to, tolerate etc; a bit much (qv) **S:** it, that, this; his behaviour. **V:** ⚠ be, seem; come (it); find sth □ *I moaned about it being* **a bit thick** *sending me out so early to run five miles on an empty stomach.* LLDR □ *This is* **a bit thick**. *I can't have you trailing me all over London.* AITC □ *I cannot say I was pleased. I felt like saying: 'That's* **a bit thick**,*' or 'Come off it, Tom.'* SPL □ *Fifty pounds a week for this house is coming it* **a bit thick**, *isn't* *it?* □ cf *(a bit) thick* = (people who are) stupid, not very clever, as in *He never seems to understand what you're saying—sometimes I wonder if he's not really* ***a bit thick****.*

bite the dust [V + O] (informal) fall from one's horse to the ground; (fig) die; cease to function; suffer a defeat; come to an end □ *Some of these Old Westerns seem to be composed of nothing more than a succession of redskins* (= American Indians) ***biting the dust*** *as they circle round the covered wagons and their heroic defenders.* □ (film review) *From now on he relishes revenge, inviting muggers to come at him. Again audiences in America and elsewhere have been breaking into applause as another mugger* ***bites the dust****.* NS □ CLIFF: *A Fellow of All Souls seems to have* ***bitten the dust****, so the Editor declares that this correspondence is now closed.* LBA □ *Since 1955, no less than nine national newspapers have* ***bitten the dust****.* NS

a bite to eat [O (NP)] some food, often just in small quantity and eaten hurriedly **V:** get, have; grab, snatch; give sb, spare sb. **prep:** without □ *There was hardly time to do more than snatch* ***a quick bite to eat*** *before going out to the airport.* □ *There was no buffet car on the train, and I hadn't had* ***a bite to eat*** *all day.* □ *It would therefore be very disturbing to do work for others without recompense. If the idea that one did so were to spread, one would soon find oneself without* ***a bite to eat****, or without a roof over one's head.* NDN □ often neg, implying that one cannot afford food, one had (had) no time to eat, etc.

bite the hand that feeds one (saying) insult, injure, be unfriendly towards, sb to whom one ought to feel grateful and loyal □ *And we are astonished that Mr Mackay, who in the past enjoyed our hospitality, should turn around and* ***bite the hands that fed him*** *by lending himself to the exploitation of a chimera.* RM □ (NONCE) *But patronage and encouragement of writers and artists do not necessarily make those who exert them liked or respected.* ***Their hands*** *are liable to become deeply indented with scars caused by* ***bites*** *from* ***those they have fed****.* AH □ *He was a neutral figure in all the quarrels between the students and the authorities. This ambivalent attitude to* ***the hand that*** *was* ***feeding him*** *was extended to his colleagues (on the college staff).* L □ (NONCE) *Ministers and officials in Saigon are more restrained about* ***biting the hand that passes the ammunition****. They have not entirely given up hope of persuading Congress to restore at least 300 million dollars to this year's military aid budget of 700 million.* L

bite one's lip [V + O] draw in or grip one's lip or lips between the teeth, to restrain oneself from saying sth, uttering a cry of pain, sobbing etc □ *'You watch your language, or I'll have you in the office.' Joe* ***bit his lip*** *and said no more for a while.* AITC □ *At the thought of Fergus hurrying home to an invalid wife, Brigit* ***bit her lip*** *and turned her head on the pillow.* DC □ *Robert's cheek glowed red in the firelight. He* ***bit his lip*** *and there was a distinct pause before he turned to look at his father.* EM □ also pl bite their lips.

the biter bit sb who seeks to cheat, or take advantage of, another finds that his intended victim has got the better of him □ *The secretary of an Anglo-Irish literary society thought the most practical way for me to get the information I wanted would be for me to lecture to her Society and could she book me for the evening of Saturday, the 30th? '****The biter*** *seems to have been* ***bitten****,' Miss Arnold said in pleasure.* PP □ *He thinks he is fooling the buyer's lawyers in his negotiations for the sale of his land; but I told him he had better take care it didn't turn out to be a case of* ***the biter bit****.* □ bit an old form of pp bitten; often preceded by *it is/was a case of.*

bits and bobs [n + n non-rev] (informal) a collection of miscellaneous objects, of various unrelated pieces of information, etc; next entry (qv); odds and bobs/sods (qv); odds and ends (qv) □ *And he felt in his pockets and pulled out all that was inside, throwing the handful of* ***bits and bobs*** *on the table; fag* ((slang) = cigarette) *packet and peppermints, a pawn ticket, an old comb, and a few coppers.* LLDR □ *In the body of its text a magazine in the newer style is superficially like the old; it is made up of* ***bits-and-bobs*** *of information; short articles on figures in history, Teddy Boys, curiosities from many lands.* UL □ usu not hyphenated.

bits and pieces [n + n non-rev] a collection of small articles, objects, abstract ideas, etc (that may be all different or separate or form part of a larger whole); previous entry (qv); odds and bobs/sods (qv); odds and ends (qv) □ ASTON: *I started to collect wood, for my shed and all those* ***bits and pieces*** *that I thought might come in handy for the flat.* TC □ *'The rations—' She laughed. 'Don't worry about that, honey. It won't be a banquet anyway, just* ***bits and pieces****.'* RATT □ *But picking* ***bits and pieces*** *out of this programme does not help to give an idea of its richness, too rich perhaps to digest at one sitting.* L □ *In everyday life, we often, as it were, fit together recalled* ***bits and pieces*** (ie from the memory) *in a patchy mosaic and fill out the gaps by inference.* MFM □ RONNIE: *We carry* ***bits and pieces*** *of each other, like shrapnel from a war. Ada's strong like you, Sarah, strong! I'm charming, like my father, and weak.* ITAJ

a bitter pill (for sb) to swallow [Comp (NP)] sth that is difficult to accept and distressing to bear **S:** defeat, rebuff, disappointment; closure, shut-down. **V:** ⚠ be; find sth; make sth □ *This is* ***a bitter pill*** *that we* (Scottish railwaymen) *are* ***swallowing****.* T □ *Mr Edmunds had served his constituency well for upwards of twenty years, and his unexpected defeat at the last election must have been* ***a bitter pill for him to swallow****.* □ *If Dennis had fallen in love with a beautiful talented girl I could at least have understood it. It was his deserting me for a common empty-headed little thing like Evelyn that has made it such* ***a bitter pill to swallow****.*

black and blue [Comp (adj + adj non-rev)] marked with a large number of bruises on the body, (either because of an accident or a beating) **V:** ⚠ be; beat sb □ *I don't think I'll go to the reception. My arm is still* ***black and blue*** *and I haven't got a suitable long-sleeved dress.* □ *'Oh God,' I said miserably, 'what did you do it for? Damn you to hell, I'd like to beat you* ***black and blue****.'* RATT □ (an Austrian girl with an imperfect command of English is speaking) *And I have one or two bruises, what you say in English—* ***blue***

and black. PW

(a) black comedy (theatre) (the style of) play in which comic elements are combined with more tragic, macabre, or absurdly evil ones, with the latter on the whole predominating; a situation, an event, with a mixture of farcical and tragic elements □ *I'm told it was the French who first introduced **black comedies** into the theatre, what with Genet and the rest. They've got a lot to answer for.* □ *It was all **a black comedy** on an international scale, with the nations' spokesman outwardly expressing grave concern for the welfare of the Sioux while inwardly praying that they would vanish from the face of the earth.* OBS

a black day (for sb) [Comp (NP)] a day, or some less specific point of time, when sth sad or disastrous happens (to sb) **V:** ⚠ be, become, turn into. **o:** him, her, me, them; workers; nation, stock exchange □ *If your superiors take the same hopeless attitude as you do, Eliot, it will be **a black day for** this country.* NM □ ***The blackest day** I can remember was in the great storm of '52 when three of our boats went down together.* □ *'I wish you would leave me alone,' Fred protested querulously. 'It would be **a black day for** you if I did,' the nurse answered without resentment.*

black(en) sb's eye (for him) [V + O pass] (threaten to) hit sb in the eye and so make it black and bruised; punish or assault sb □ *This job on the drill was a dead loss, and he was going to **black** Frank**'s eye for him** some day, but he would stick to it until he found something better.* AITC □ *The young fool got both **eyes blackened** when he picked a quarrel with a man in the pub.* ⇨ ⚠ have etc a black eye.

the black hole of Calcutta a dark, unpleasantly hot and stuffy building or place, with few amenities etc (from an incident in India in 1756 when a large number of English prisoners were crowded into a small room overnight where many of them died) □ PETER: *Upset? I'm not upset. I just want to get the hell out of **this black hole of Calcutta**.* TOH □ *'What is it like down there?' shouted Pete from the upper cave. 'Like **the black hole of Calcutta**, but a lot wetter,' came the reply.* □ (NONCE) PAMELA: *Stay with us, Clive's telling me a story.* CLIVE: *Yes, it's going to be brilliant! All Gothic darkness and calamities. It's called **the 'Black Hole of East Suffolk'**.* FFE

black etc is beautiful (catchphrase) one's blackness etc is something to be proud of; black etc is a good thing to be **adj:** black, big, small, fat □ (The slogan) *'**Black is Beautiful**' was comprehensive as an ego-booster, a defiant counterblast to the sort of social pressures that filled 'Ebony' with ads for hair-straighteners and skin-lighteners: it remains as demonstrably silly and divisive a generalization as, say, '**white is beautiful**.'* NS □ *South Africa's Supreme Court has lifted a ban on T-shirts bearing the words '**black is beautiful**'. The Court ruled yesterday that there was no substance in the* (Publication Control) *Board's charge that the words '**black is beautiful**' could be prejudicial to good order and the safety of the state.* SC □ *There's no doubt that for the American owner-driver **big is beautiful**.* ST □ *Fran Fullenwider (the name is genuine) is the one and only 60-hipped 17½-stone model girl in London. Positively the fattest, and you can say as much as you like, because Fran says **fat is beautiful**.* RT

a black look [O (NP)] a look of strong dislike, disapproval, resentment etc **V:** give sb, cast. . .at sb; get, attract, draw □ *She cast **a black look** at the box in the corner of the room and observed that she would not spend the night in a house with a yarara* (a poisonous snake), *even if she were paid to do so.* DF □ *I saw his wife giving him **a black look** when he brought out the second bottle of whisky.* □ also pl as in *get several **black looks***.

a black mood [O/o (NP)] a fit of depression, bad temper, etc, usu temporary, though perhaps recurring **V:** have; be in, suffer from □ *This isn't the time to ask the boss a favour. He's been in **a black mood** ever since the Board Meeting this morning.* □ *Yes, the psychoanalyst has helped her a lot, but she still has those **black moods** from time to time when she doesn't care about anybody or anything.* □ often used with *be in/have one of one's, have/suffer from* when expression used in pl.

the black sheep (of the family) that member (of a family or other group) who is thought to be a disgrace to other members of it (because he is a criminal, a wastrel or because he does not measure up to their imposed standards) □ *We know where she has come from (a selfish, cunning and often ruthless New Orleans family, with its **black sheep** and its white wolves) and what she has become: a New York lady intellectual, one of those tough babes.* ST □ *Now every profession has of course got its **black sheep**. If the evidence is available against them, you can be absolutely certain that the professional tribunals will be down on them like a ton of bricks.* L

a black spot a place or area where unpleasant and unwanted things occur regularly and without much chance of improvement eg epidemics, crime, traffic accidents, unemployment etc □ *Northern Ireland's competitive position has been weakened by the Local Unemployment Bill, which is the Government's chosen instrument for steering industries to **black spots** in Scotland and England.* SC □ *Overcrowding in some of our mental hospitals together with unsuitable grouping of patients still make conditions in the wards **the** one **black spot** in an otherwise good record.* □ *Drive with Care! Accident **Black Spot**!* □ stress pattern a 'black spot.

(in) black and white[1] [n + n non-rev] not coloured; having no other colours than black and white □ *Professor Calvin Hall, who has collected records of many thousands of dreams, tells us that about two-thirds of all dreams are **in black and white**.* HAH □ *The older ones* (magazines) *still use **black-and-white** drawings in an unsophisticated style.* UL □ *Most of the councillors were there, and practically all the Town Hall staff, unfamiliar **in the black-and-white** of evening suits.* RATT □ attrib use *a **black-and-white** drawing, photograph, film.*

(in) black and white[2] [n + n non-rev] (consider moral etc matters only in terms of) absolute wrong or right, without recognizing any more subtle variations **V:** see, view, think. **O:** everything, things, events; people □ MONTY: *But she has one fault. For her the world is **black and white**. If you're not white, you must be black.*

She can't see shades in a character. She can't see people in the round. CSWB □ *As children we were taught always to tell the truth and never to tell lies. But now we do not see these things **in** quite such **black and white** terms.*

blacken sb's character/name [V + O pass] make sb's character (through idle gossip etc) seem worse than it really is □ *Some of the press reports amount to an attempt to **blacken the character of** someone who is still a highly respected public figure.* □ *Then **their names** were **blackened** in sensational media coverage.* ⇨ ⚠ next entry.

blacken the picture [V + O pass] describe sb or sth as being worse than he or it is □ *Sometimes Wormold felt a tinge of jealousy towards Paul and he tried to **blacken the picture**. 'He gets through a bottle of whisky a day,' he said.* OMIH □ *Trust your father to **blacken the picture**! You mustn't worry about me, Penny. The doctor says I shall be all right again in a month or two.* ⇨ ⚠ previous entry.

blame the other fellow [V + O pass] evade responsibility for a fault, neglect of duty, etc, by shifting it on to another person □ *Unfortunately it is a common human failing to **blame the other fellow** when something is not done that everyone agrees ought to be done.* SC □ *Face up to the fact that you simply aren't capable of handling the business, will you, and stop **blaming the other fellow**.* □ the other fellow (always sing) does not refer to a particular, identifiable, person.

blaze a trail [V + O pass] be a pioneer, lead the way, in a field of research, or study, or in doing sth new and untried (from the original (US) practice of indicating a way through a forest etc by cutting marks on trees) □ *Antiseptic treatments have been greatly refined and improved since Lister's day, but it was he who **blazed the trail** with his use of the carbolic acid spray during surgical operations.* □ *By its enlightened prison system Sweden had **blazed a trail** which a number of other European countries gradually began to follow.* □ *He's a sound enough physicist and I'm glad to have him in my laboratories but I can't see **any trails** being **blazed** by him. He's more likely to follow than to lead.* □ n compound a trail-blazer; adj compound trail-blazing.

bleed sb white [V + O + Comp pass] take away (almost) everything sb possesses, often by drastic, unfair, or deceptive means (esp of money, but also of physical or emotional resources) **O:** him, her, you, them; taxpayer, customer; nation, company □ *He thought, 'I bet he's regretting the termination of his income. They've all **bled** poor Lisa **white**.'—The poet was, in fact, in a state of excitement. Lisa's death had filled him with thrilling awe.* MM □ *He **bled** them **white** with his demands for more and still more money.* □ *For the whole movement to have come to the aid of a union which was being **bled white** by the practice of the Lump (contract labour outside a Union-controlled wage-paying system, esp in the building trade) would have hindered growth in a key sector of the economy.* NS

bless sb's heart an expression of admiration, affection, close attachment, etc □ *'I can't get the children off to sleep at all tonight,' their mother complained. '**Bless their** little **hearts**,' said their grandfather, 'they'll be too excited about going to the seaside tomorrow.'* □ (early 20th C actor-manager) *Martin Harvey might depend year after year on his bread-and-butter jobs, his 'Only Way' and his 'Treshams', but the little man—**bless his heart**! — did at least* try. OBS □ *'Terence,' he said, 'is battling at the bar. It suits him to the ground. **Bless his** little Kensington **heart**.'* HAA □ bless sometimes used to make an ironic comment, as in last example.

(God) bless my soul(!) (formal) an interjection expressing astonishment or surprise (about sth that has happened, been said, etc) □ *'**God bless my soul!** Fancy finding you here, of all places!'* □ *'I don't understand what keeps you ticking, Charles,' said the Admiral. '**God bless my soul**, even as a mad young lieutenant I wouldn't have done it.'* ARG □ *I had told the boys they could give their friends some beer, but **bless my soul** if they hadn't drunk every drop in the house.*

(God) bless you! an interjection made when sb else sneezes □ *'I think I'm getting a cold,' he complained. And as if to prove his point he started sneezing violently. '**God bless you!**' she said automatically.*

(God) bless you may God reward you for your kindness; thank you □ *'Well, I can spare fifty pence.' '**God bless you**, sir,' the old man said, 'at least I can get something to eat with that.'* □ ***Bless you**, my dear; it's most kind of you to offer to help.*

a blessing in disguise [Comp (NP)] sth that seems unwelcome or unfortunate when it happens but which eventually proves to be fortunate, advantageous **V:** ⚠ be, seem □ *We have heard of **blessings in disguise**, but surely a novel one is the revelation that the injury sustained by D.J. Whyte when playing in last Saturday's 'extra rugby trial' at Murrayfield may have started his complete recovery.* SC □ *Mary nearly broke her heart when Chris lost interest in her, but now she sees the way he treats the girl he went with, she realises it was **a blessing in disguise**.* ⇨ ⚠ a mixed blessing.

a blind alley [Comp/o (NP)] a street, usu short, closed at one end; a cul-de-sac; (fig) sth which one embarks on that may look promising but which (eventually) has no satisfactory result or outcome; a dead end (qv) **V:** be, turn out to be; find oneself in, turn into □ *He took the next turning to the left as he had been told, but found himself in **a blind alley**.* □ *This expensive bucolic setting had offered nothing more than an escape down **a blind alley** and it had taken a crack-brained mechanic, a nymphomaniac, and a deranged careerist to show him that.* HD □ *But remember, when you're fully qualified you'll earn three times as much as him and have a fair amount of job satisfaction while he'll be going from one **blind-alley** job to another.* □ also pl; attrib use *a **blind-alley** job.*

blind drunk [Comp (AdjP)] (informal) extremely drunk; blind to the world (qv) **V:** ⚠ be, get, become □ *His one idea of a good night out is to get **blind drunk**.*

(a) blind fury/rage a state of fury or rage so violent that it prevents consideration of other matters, obscures one's judgement, makes one lose one's self-control, etc □ *Then he swore at her outside* (the house). *He swore so hard that all the village heard, and heard with relish, for such* *performances enliven the evening air but seldom. It was more than* ***blind rage*** *which led the husband to swear outside as well as in.* NDN ◻ *The kitten spat and scratched in* ***blind fury*** *as I worked to free her from the rabbit trap.*

the blind leading the blind (saying) (the situation in which) people without adequate knowledge or experience attempt to direct or guide others like themselves, with the consequence that neither group can help the other or be helped ◻ (source) *Let them alone: they be* ***blind leaders*** *of* ***the blind****. And if* ***the blind lead the blind****, both shall fall into the ditch.* MATTHEW XV 14 ◻ *The staff of the Archaeological Department are insufficiently trained by precept and experience—indeed as regards the students and junior members it is a case of* ***the blind leading the blind****, and the quality of the department is likely to deteriorate progressively.* SD ◻ usu functions as comment or assessment (often preceded by *be a case of*).

a blind spot[1] [Comp/O (NP)] a small area of the retina of the eye which is insensitive to light and which may prevent sb from seeing sth for a short period of time; an area of vision which is obscured because sth blocks it **V:** (there) be; have, cross ◻ *Someone threw a paper pellet at me, but, just as I put up my hand to catch it, it must have crossed* ***my blind spot*** *and it hit me right on the nose.* ◻ *The car's pretty old and the back window's rather small and there are two* ***blind spots*** *because of that. I find I have to use the wing-mirrors rather a lot.*

a blind spot[2] [Comp/O (NP)] a failure in oneself or sb to understand or accept sth, to exercise one's judgement normally (because of a lack of knowledge, a particular prejudice, etc) **V:** be; have, discover ◻ *And it is always interesting to notice that publishers, like other people, have* ***their blind spots*** *and little manias.* AH ◻ *If everybody admires Chagall's paintings so much then I suppose it must be* ***a blind spot*** *of my own that makes me find them so unattractive.* ◻ *The truth about Louise is that she uses people and when she's finished with them throws them away like old clothes. But you'll never convince Peter of that—he has* ***a blind spot*** *as far as she's concerned.*

blind to sth [Comp (AdjP)] unaware of, fail to see or consider (sth that is clear, evident etc) **V:** ⚠ be, appear, seem; become. **o:** (one's/sb's) faults; what is going on; everything around one. ◻ *The little dark man hailed a taxi that was conveniently cruising past and which had been singularly* ***blind to*** *the hails of an agitated woman with parcels a moment or two previously.* TCB ◻ *The General's refusal to convene Parliament is a clear warning that his contempt for 'politicians' who are* ***blind to*** *the higher interests of France is as strong now as it was in 1945.* OBS ◻ *The Cardinal enables us to see the Roman Catholic Church through the eyes of one who knows her well and loves her dearly but is not* ***blind to*** *her faults.* SC ⇨ ⚠ deaf to sth.

blind to the world [Comp (AdjP)] (informal) extremely drunk; blind drunk (qv) **V:** ⚠ be, become, appear ◻ *He may be a nice enough fellow when he's sober. But on the two occasions I have met him he was* ***blind to the world*** *and a perfect nuisance.* ◻ *'Now, hold on a minute, Mrs Brown,' he said into the telephone, 'we're not responsible for your husband's condition. He was* ***blind to the world*** *when he got here.'* ◻ cf *go on a blinder* = '(intend to) get very drunk', as in *I'll bet the team will* ***go on a blinder*** *tonight, with it being the end of the season and them winning the cup and all.*

blink the fact (that) [V + O pass] ignore the truth of sth; decide or pretend not to notice sth ◻ *There is no* ***blinking the fact that*** *junior secondary education has so far failed to develop as a going concern.* SC ◻ *The awkwardness about finishing a novel lies in* ***blinking the fact that*** *though the story is ended the characters are still alive.* SPL ◻ *Our business is on the decline and we can't* ***blink the fact*** *any longer. There just isn't the demand for quality goods there used to be.* ◻ *In the docks dispute,* ***the fact*** *can't be* ***blinked that*** *here are two lots of workers trying to do each other out of a job.* ◻ usu neg.

a blood bath [Comp/o (NP)] a scene, an occasion, of much slaughter and bloodshed **V:** be, end up as; develop into ◻ *It was generally considered that the invasion would be* ***a blood bath****, with fearful casualties; I assured them that the invasion would not be so.* MFM ◻ (of a prison riot) *Then come the army of rifle-bearing troopers,* ***a blood-bath*** *during which some 40 men were killed.* NS ◻ occas pl.

one's blood boils one feels extremely angry, resentful (about sth that has happened, that sb has done) ◻ *At the very thought of Robert Warbeck and all that he stood for, the Chancellor****'s blood boiled*** *in his veins, so that it was an unreasonably flushed and angry man that alighted from his car at the end of the journey.* EM ◻ *'It never cools me down when I drive through Glencoe,' the Macdonald Chieftain declared. 'You know* ***my blood*** *always* ***boils*** *when I drive through Glencoe.'* RM ◻ *Out of range, he looked back at her, bewildered, angry,* ***his blood boiling*** *with resentment.* LLDR

blood is thicker than water (saying) family or kinship ties are very strong and, despite disagreements or differences, (should) unite individual members of a family ◻ *'Are you sure he's your boy? Why didn't you recognize him before?' 'I wasn't too proud of him—wanted to forget him—but* ***blood is thicker than water****.'* DBM ◻ STONE: *And why didn't Lottie come?* BESSIE: *What can you expect? Lottie's husband is a school-teacher and, apart from being Communists, I think they are also vegetarian.* STONE: *That explains it;* ***blood is thicker than water****.* HSG

one's blood runs cold be filled with horror and/or fear (because of an extraordinary, perhaps supernatural, event, a terrible crime, an accident that has happened, etc) ◻ *The way Alice talks of that old man makes* ***my blood run cold****. And Mr Barker, too, when he could still speak. Brutal he was.* ASA ◻ *Was he ashamed of his mother? Didn't he think she was respectable enough to be seen by his young woman? Didn't he like to bring her back to his own home—you should have heard the way she said 'home': it made* ***my blood run cold****.* LLDR ◻ often preceded by *(be enough to) make*.

blood and thunder [n + n non-rev] (facetious) violent and melodramatic action, incidents etc in a story, play, film etc □ *I suppose, for most people, German cinema really means the cinema of the Twenties and the early Thirties — wild chiaroscuro, full of devils, full of mystery, full of* ***blood and thunder****.* L □ *Yet to read this, his eighteenth novel, alongside a handful of others, is to wonder at Mr MacLean's eminence among the scribes of* ***blood and thunder****.* SC □ *Just forget that* ***blood and thunder*** *stuff, will you? I'm sorry to be so lacking in melodrama but honestly your ancestors were probably painted larger than life.* DC □ attrib use *that* ***blood and thunder*** *stuff.*

a bloodless revolution a change of government that takes place without civil war or other bloodshed; any social change in values, customs, morals etc which comes about gradually and without serious disturbance □ *It is often said that there are no working-classes in England now, that* ***a 'bloodless revolution'*** *has taken place which has so reduced social differences that already most of us inhabit an almost flat plain, the plain of the lower middle- to middle-classes.* UL □ ***A bloodless revolution*** *in the distribution of wealth is taking place in Britain.* □ also pl.

a bloodless victory [Comp/O (NP)] a victory gained without warfare, or without injury or other harm to either winner or loser in a fight, dispute etc **V:** be; win, secure, achieve □ (two men are playing draughts using miniature whisky bottles as the 'pieces') *It was obvious that he was torn in two between the desire to win and the desire to keep his head. Now that his opponent had a king, he would no longer play for* ***a bloodless victory****, for the king had freedom of movement.* OMIH □ *The mayor got his own way in the end and the rents of the Council houses were raised. It wouldn't be* ***an entirely bloodless victory*** *though; he had stirred up a good deal of bad feeling.* □ also pl.

a bloody fool (informal) sb who is stupid, or ignorant, has acted foolishly etc (in the opinion of the speaker) □ *What can you expect of a Council consisting half of scoundrels and half of* ***bloody fools****—all just asking to be led by the nose?* □ SAM: *I tell you, Mr Segal, that's what I've missed.* MR SEGAL: *What? Fruit?* SAM: *Oh, don't be such* ***a bloody fool****, of course not. I mean going places, seeing people.* HSG □ *I was just getting the policeman nicely talked round into letting us drive off when* ***that BF*** *Higgins started to wave a five-pound note at him.* □ often used as a direct term of abuse, as in *You* ***bloody fool****! What made you switch the electricity on while I was still fixing the bulb?*; abbreviated form BF.

a bloody shovel (facetious) the calling of sth by its proper (or perhaps coarse) name (by analogy with 'call a spade a spade' (qv)) □ *The writer said that he didn't believe in calling a spade a spade when it was really* ***a bloody shovel*** (ie since most labourers probably refer to it in this way). □ GEORGE: *Farther left you go, the worse the manners seem to get.* RUTH: *Well! The house is still fairly ringing with* ***the bloody shovels*** *of your opinions.* EGD □ in last example the suggestion is that Ruth is tired of George's bluntly expressed opinions.

blot one's copybook [V + O pass] do sth that spoils one's (previous) good record or reputation □ *One of the security branches had some evidence that there might have been a leakage* (of information). *'We don't want to* ***blot our copybook****,' said Captain Smith. 'Nothing very serious has got out, has it?'* NM □ *Though it has* ***blotted its copybook*** *a little of late, the weather so far this year has been quite extraordinarily docile.* SC □ *I've always been interested in racing. When I was eight I* ***blotted my copybook*** *irrevocably with the Geography mistress when she asked what was the Gulf Stream. Up shot my hand: 'Bay Colt by Hyperion, out of Tideway,' I rattled off, 'second in the Derby.'* ST □ also pl blot our copybooks.

a blot on sb's/the escutcheon [Comp/O (NP)] (formal) sb who, or sth which, brings dishonour or discredit upon a family or other group **V:** be; leave, acknowledge □ *Her family were less concerned about the human problem of Leila's illegitimate baby than about having to acknowledge* ***a blot on their escutcheon****.* □ *'You have not only disgraced yourselves and your families,' the headmaster said in his usual pompous style, 'but your conduct is* ***a blot on the escutcheon of*** *this ancient and honourable school.'* □ escutcheon = 'a shield, plaque, or badge bearing a coat of arms'.

a blot on the landscape[1] a construction, an ugly building, a rubbish dump, etc that spoils natural or urban scenery; an eyesore □ *It's a wonderful view, but those electric pylons are rather* ***a blot on the landscape****, aren't they?* □ *To most people the vast development taking place around St Paul's Cathedral and further east in the City are a succession of* ***blots on a*** *hitherto small-scale and charming* ***landscape****.*

a blot on the landscape[2] sb who, or sth which, spoils an otherwise satisfactory situation, is an unwelcome addition or contrast (that one would like to remove); the fly in the ointment (qv) □ *We're a very happy crowd in our office. The boss himself is a bit of* ***a blot on the landscape*** *but, luckily, we don't see much of him.* □ *Life has been just about perfect since we moved here. In fact* ***the*** *only* ***blot on the landscape*** *is this little bit of local jealousy we've just been talking about.* □ also pl *a couple of* ***blots on the landscape****.*

blow by blow [A] (describe an event) as it occurred in every detail (as in a boxing match or game, but esp when reporting a discussion, an argument etc that has taken place elsewhere, at another time) **V:** describe, give, tell, relate, sth □ *I tend to prefer cricket commentators who report a match* ***blow by blow*** *to those who spend their time philosophizing about what happened on the same ground five years ago.* □ *In the hundred days before Hitler's rise to power, of which Messrs Manvell and Fraenkel give a* ***blow-by-blow*** *account, Goering played a leading role.* SC □ *'Who told you about that?' 'Oh, Anne gave us a* ***blow-by-blow*** *account. In front of Jenny.' 'Christ, what a bitch that woman is.'* TGLY □ common attrib use *a* ***blow-by-blow*** *account, description, etc.*

the blow falls sth catastrophic, disastrous or unwelcome happens, either quite unexpectedly or in the way one has feared □ *You really must take some financial precautions now. Then when* ***the blow falls*** *you'll have something in reserve.* □ *When this was completed, we would travel down the river to Asunción. That was our plan,* *but then **the blow fell**. 'Paula says that there's a revolution in Asunción.'* DF □ *Now that **the blow** has **fallen** and her husband has started divorce proceedings she is actually much less miserable than she was.*

blow the gaff [V + O pass] (informal) let out a secret; inform against sb; expose a scheme or plot; spill the beans (qv); let the cat out of the bag (Vol I) (qv) □ *'Well,' said Martin, turning to the grandparents, 'since young Tommy has **blown the gaff** I might as well admit we'll be emigrating to Australia in February or March.'* □ *'I'll do that girl over* ((slang) = assault her) *when I get out,' he swore to his cell-mate. 'They could never have got a conviction if she hadn't **blown the gaff**.'* □ *It is high time **the gaff** was **blown** on all this mind-enhancing rubbish that is attributed to the use of marihuana.*

blow hot and cold vacillate in one's opinions, loyalties etc according to mood or circumstance; refuse, or seem unable, to commit oneself to a positive course of action □ *You're a fool, Dick. While you **blow hot and cold** about whether you want to get married or not, the girl will be off with somebody else.* □ *I am never quite sure what the word 'volatile' means but it means I change, and I **blow hot and cold**—surely.* L □ *He **blows hot** one minute **and cold** the next; I never know where I am with him.*

blow sb a kiss [V + IO + O] press one's fingers to one's lips and then either extend the hand or pretend to blow the kiss toward sb □ *'If you'd seen that much of me once, you wouldn't have stayed in that chair for very long.' 'I'm sure I wouldn't.' She **blew me a kiss**.* RATT □ *People on the platform were waving handkerchiefs and **blowing kisses to** their friends as the train steamed out.* □ *You'd better just **blow** Daddy **a kiss** tonight, in case he gives you his cold.*

blow one's/sb's mind [V + O pass] (informal) give sb, receive, an extreme sensation of pleasure, excitement or shock (eg from taking hallucinatory drugs, or from some extraordinary experience) □ *In the 1960s in America it was almost part of conventional behaviour to take a trip* (ie use LSD etc) *and **blow your mind**.* □ *The first time I got into it* (an Aston Martin DB6 sports car) *I couldn't see above the steering wheel, but all those gauges really **blew my mind**.* OBS □ *You're going to the Blackpool* (George Formby) *Appreciation Society Conference? It's an amazing event, you'll never forget it. It'll **blow your mind**.* RT □ also pl; adj compound mind-blowing.

blow one's own trumpet [V + O] praise oneself; boast about oneself, one's achievements □ *One of the Town Councillors usually attended our prize-givings and had to be asked to say a few words. Most of them took this as an opportunity to **blow their own trumpets** for anything up to ten minutes.* □ *I don't like to **blow my own trumpet**, but I must say the sales conference would have been utter chaos if I hadn't been there to organize it.* □ *Actors are good at **trumpet-blowing** and the temptation increases as their popularity grows and their reputations are made.* L □ (NONCE) *Say good-morning. Remember the interviewer is a human being, not a god. Speak about yourself. Here's one place where you must **toot your own horn**.* H □ n compound trumpet-blowing.

blow sb/sth sky-high [V + O + A pass] make sth explode violently upwards; (fig) destroy, shatter, sth; completely disprove sth; completely disrupt or expose hopes, illusions; explode a myth (qv) **O:** him, her, me, us, them; ammunition dump, troop-carrier; theory; prospect, plan □ *Good God! That boy's left a full can of petrol in the kitchen again! We'll all be **blown sky-high** one of these days.* □ *It helps also to chat, reason, present compromises, explain the cause of a problem, especially if the explanation **blows** a commonly held myth **sky-high**.* RT □ *A publican giving evidence at the trial of a Glasgow councillor and former magistrate who is charged with corruption said that the police wired up his public house* (to record a conversation) *but that the former magistrate called earlier than expected, and all the arrangements were **blown sky-high**.* T

blow one's top [V + O] (informal) express one's anger against, one's dislike of, one's alarm about, sb or sth in a forceful, unrestrained way; do one's nut (qv) □ *I ran to my father, waving the magazine and shouting, 'This is my home, look.' Dad fairly **blew his top**. He told me not to be so silly; that it was a building called a temple, in a country called Egypt and that I had never been there.* OBS □ *She is particularly good at contrasting the Anglo-Saxon and Latin ways of life; usually it is her Anglo-Saxons who **blow their tops**, while hot-blooded Latins slyly keep their cool.* L.

a blue film etc a film etc which contains obscene material, has explicit reference to, or portrayal of, sexual acts **n:** film, ⚠ movie; joke, humour □ *In an odd sort of way, the wheel has come full circle in the film industry. The cinemas were sold as bingo halls, and now the bingo halls are becoming cinema clubs, which normally means they show **blue films**.* □ *Charlie's fine as a stand-up comedian in a working man's club—but frankly his **jokes** are a bit too **blue** for the BBC.*

a blue fit [O/o (NP)] (informal) (show) extreme annoyance, alarm or irritation (about sth) **V:** have, take; throw, fall into □ *It's a good job the boy was safely back before his mother heard of his escapades. She'd have taken **a blue fit** if she'd known he was out in the boat alone.* □ *I can remember the time when a judge would have been horrified almost into **a blue fit** if he had been asked to exercise discretion in favour of a petitioner whose conduct had been that of the person in this case.* ST □ *I'll have to write out my exercise again. The teacher will have **a blue fit** if I hand it in like this.* □ usu with *will/would have* .

sb's/the blue-eyed boy [Comp/O (NP)] a favourite; sb whom another presumes to be incapable of doing wrong, to be the embodiment of perfection **V:** be, become; have □ *She was a good mother to us all but there was no blinking the fact that George was **her blue-eyed boy**.* □ *'I know you're **the blue-eyed boy** round here' grumbled the works foreman, 'but you don't take* me *in.'* □ *Big organizations have **their blue-eyed boys** too, destined for the top jobs and carefully groomed to fill them.* □ usu confined to male sex.

blunt the edge of sth [V + O pass] cause sth to be felt less keenly (by taking appropriate action); take the edge off (Vol 1) (qv) **O:** sb's appetite, hunger; anger, disappointment; pleasure □ *I'll just have a cup of tea and nothing else. If we're going out to dinner I don't want to* ***blunt the edge of*** *my appetite.* □ *It might* ***blunt the edge of*** *his disappointment at not winning the scholarship, if you were to let him know that the examiners all commented very favourably on his papers.* □ *Time would no doubt* ***blunt the edge of*** *her grief, but not make it any less real.*

board and lodging [n + n non-rev] food and accommodation, usu paid for, provided by boarding houses, private houses, etc □ *The Probation Officer got Andrew a job in the paper-mills and arranged* ***board and lodging*** *for him in a Working Boys' Hostel.* □ *I discovered an incredibly charitable arrangement whereby I could get free* ***board and lodging*** *in exchange for being a guinea pig in a cold-cure experiment.* UTN □ cf the simple v *board: I* ***boarded*** *in a small hotel/She makes money from* ***boarding*** *summer visitors.*

Bob's your uncle (informal) (once sth is done, arranged satisfactorily) everything is or will be all right, nothing more will need to be done □ SAM: *This is how we get them married* (he whispers to David, who laughs). DAVID: *And once they're married,* ***Bob's your uncle.*** HSG □ *It's quite simple, really. Turn this knob to the right, then this other knob to the right, press the red button, switch on—and* ***Bob's your uncle.*** □ usu second of two clauses, often introduced by *and*; stress pattern ˌBob's your 'uncle.

a body blow [Comp/O (NP)] sth which affects one or one's plans badly, severely etc; a stroke of bad luck; bad news; adverse criticism **V:** be; deal... to sb/sth, deliver... to sb/sth; inflict... on sb/sth □ *He has had a good many ups and downs in his life but his wife's leaving him was* ***a body blow.*** □ *Withdrawal of the Government cattle subsidy would deal* ***a body blow*** *to the islands' economy.* □ *'I mean do you* intend *to marry her?' 'Oh, you're asking about my* intentions,*' said Sammy. 'That's* ***a body blow***! *You ought to have brought your shotgun!'* (ie for 'a shotgun wedding' (qv)) UTN □ also pl; originally a hard punch to the body in boxing; stress pattern a 'body blow.

body and soul [A (n + n non-rev)] completely; with all one's energies, devotion etc **V:** be sb's, belong to sb, own sb; devote oneself to sb/sth; throw oneself into sth □ *He had flung himself into the project* ***body and soul*** *and if the town did not have the beginnings of a Community Centre by next Spring it would not be his fault.* □ *Don't take a job in that firm: they think they own their employees* ***body and soul.*** □ usu in end position. ⇨ ⚠ keep body and soul together (Vol 1).

a bogey man sb who, because of his apparently mysterious or unknown abilities, is capable of striking fear into one (and esp, in former times, an imaginary person used by parents etc to frighten children into behaving well) □ *She had cowered under the blankets hiding from* ***the bogey man*** *who, her elder brothers assured her, would come and get her if she so much as poked her nose out.* □ *The head-hunters are* ***the bogey men*** *of the Land Dayaks. Little children who wander far from their mother's backs are warned that they lie in wait for them.* NDN □ *The villain* (in magazine stories) *inviting an adulterous relationship seems to be found interesting because he makes a shocking attack on what is felt to count greatly. He is* ***a*** *kind of* ***bogey-man*** *rather than a disguised hero.* UL □ stress pattern a 'bogey man; cf *make a bogey of sth* = 'allow oneself to be more frightened by sth than is necessary or rational'.

a bold/brave front [O/o (NP)] courage, cheerfulness (perhaps exaggerated) in what one says or does in order to hide one's true feelings; a brave show (of sth)[2] (qv); put a bold/brave/good face on (Vol 1) (qv) **V:** show, display, put on □ *Don't be too humble.* Demand *a rise in salary—you're much more likely to get it if you put on* ***a bold front.*** □ *Myrtle did not flinch. When we met at the railway station on Saturday afternoon she was showing* ***a brave front.*** SPL □ *She had talked gaily about adventure, but she hadn't liked it very much when it really came. And now she'd got to go back to it all. Because she was employed by Mr Dakin and she had to earn her pay and show* ***a brave front***! TCB

a bolt from the blue [Comp/o (NP)] a sudden and unexpected event, esp one of an unpleasant or catastrophic nature (as a thunderbolt from a blue sky would be) **V:** be, seem (like); come like/as □ *Jesse can still hardly believe David is in business with him. 'It was* ***a bolt from the blue*** *when he came down from Cambridge and said he'd like to come in the firm with me.'* RT □ *Well, your resignation has certainly come as* ***a bolt from the blue****, Watkins. I was counting on you staying with the firm for at least another three years.* □ also pl *a couple of* ***bolts from the blue.*** ⇨ ⚠ be out of the blue (Vol 1); come out of the blue (Vol 1).

bone idle [Comp (AdjP)] idle, lazy, as an incurable fault **V:** ⚠ be, become, seem □ *...forty-year-old clockwatchers, who were more* ***bone idle*** *than I could have imagined.* SML □ *The boy has a good enough brain but he's* ***bone idle*** *and won't study.* □ *If you weren't so* ***bone idle*** *you could save over £100 a year by looking after the garden yourself.*

a bone of contention a cause of dispute or disagreement between persons or parties (ie like a bone over which two dogs may fight); an/the apple of discord (qv) □ ***A*** *third* ***bone of contention*** *is the U.S. refusal to supply arms and the pressure put on other countries to refuse likewise.* SC □ *I don't think it's a good idea at all to give the boys a motor-bike between them. If they've got to share it'll just be* ***a bone of contention.*** □ also pl *two such* ***bones of contention.***

a boon and a blessing [n + n non-rev] (formal) sth very welcome and much appreciated □ *I let myself in, switched on the light, took up the vacuum flask and out gurgled the bitter coffee Mrs Burton had left those hours before,* ***a boon and a blessing*** *to midnight men.* PP □ (early 19th c advertisement for pen nibs) *The Pickwick, the Owl, and the Waverley pen/They come as* ***a boon and a blessing*** *to men!*

a boon companion a congenial acquaintance, esp sb who regularly joins in one's leisure activities, pleasurable pursuits, hobbies etc □ *Such satisfaction as he got from his relationship with Alec was not personal; like many married men Harold did not have men friends; he had* *acquaintances and* ***boon companions****.* PW □ *A common interest in angling and the amenities of the hotel bar had made* ***boon companions*** *of the two men for the period of their holiday.* □ often pl and usu referring to men rather than women. ⇨ ⚠ a bosom friend/pal.

born and bred (in/to sth) [v + v non-rev] born, reared and educated (in a specified place, in a specified manner, for a specified purpose, etc) **o: *(in)*** the country, Yorkshire; ***(to)*** the life of a farmer, the life of a fisherman □ *A word about Mrs Lucy Odd. She is a Londoner* ***born and bred****, and for a woman some years past the allotted span, of a truly remarkable vigour and alertness.* RM □ BEATTIE: *Think of it! An English girl* ***born and bred*** *and I couldn't talk the language—except for to buy food and clothes.* R □ *I might have wished that I had been* ***born and bred in*** *such a place, where everybody knew or knew about one another and felt their roots entwined.* AH □ *'It's necessary, and so is emptying bloody dustbins,' cried the educated man, 'but there are some classes of society that are* ***born and bred to*** *it and ours isn't.'* HD □ placed after n it modifies.

born to command/rule [Comp (AdjP)] destined to command/rule; of such a nature that one inevitably tends to command/rule **V:** ⚠ be, seem, regard oneself as □ *The English milord was obviously a most masterful person. A man clearly* ***born to command****.* BFA □ *The Conservative Party is about power. It regards itself as the party* ***born to rule*** *and will swallow almost endless reversals of policy or pragmatic decisions to remain in power.* NS

born in the gutter born in poverty, of beggarly or obscure parentage □ ***Born in the gutter*** *and surviving first by good luck and then by his own cunning, Emilio at sixteen was a ripe recruit for any of the gangster mob then prevalent in the city.* □ *'I've hardly had to teach you anything.' 'My mother did that,' the girl replied somewhat shortly. 'I wasn't* ***born in the gutter*** *you know.'* □ cf *rise from the gutter, die in the gutter.*

born in/to the purple born of royal, or very aristocratic, parents (and thus be a privileged member of society) □ *From a very early age the Prince was aware that he was* ***born in the purple*** *and was very conscious of his elevated state.* □ *From the way he talks and behaves you'd think he was* ***born to the purple*** *or something. Whereas the truth is his parents are ordinary middle class, living in the stockbroker belt in Surrey.*

born under a lucky star [Comp (AdjP)] successful and happy, either for the whole of one's life or on one occasion when one has a stroke of luck **V:** ⚠ be, appear, seem; must have been □ *That's how it goes, son; if you haven't been* ***born under a lucky star*** *you just have to work all the harder to get what you want.* □ *'Did the driver survive?' 'Survive! He was hardly scratched. He must have been* ***born under a lucky star*** *when you see what happened to the lorry cab.'*

born with a silver spoon in one's mouth born of wealthy parents; born the heir to a fortune, or comfortable living, etc □ *The son of a Texas oil millionaire, young Elmer was certainly* ***born with a silver spoon in his mouth****.* □ *The son of a Scottish minister,* ***born*** *in Zululand* ***with*** *not* ***a silver spoon*** *but a Box-Brownie* (a type of camera) ***in his mouth****, as I once teased him, he had been obsessed by cameras all his life.* LWK □ also pl born with silver spoons in their mouths.

born within the sound of Bow bells born in the district of London round Bow Church, Cheapside, and hence a true Cockney □ *But I'm a true Cockney myself. Yes,* ***born within the sound of Bow Bells****. Where do you come from?* RM

borrowed time a period of time which one would not normally expect to have at one's disposal, which one gains and continues to have only by chance or good fortune **V:** live on; be a case of; have □ *Johnson had been self-employed for eight years, and never paid a penny in income tax. But he was living on* ***borrowed time****; sooner or later the day of reckoning would come.* □ *He was 30 when the doctors gave him two years to live. Since then he has had eight years of* ***borrowed time*** *and made the most of every one of them.*

a bosom friend/pal a close and dear friend with whom one spends as much time as circumstances allow □ *Jenny and Tina were* ***bosom friends*** *as girls and are still very fond of each other.* □ *On the face of it, they seemed an ill-assorted pair to be such* ***bosom friends****.* □ *He's not the sort I would choose for* ***a bosom pal****, but he's so witty you can't help enjoying his company.* □ often pl referring to two friends; applied equally to men and women. ⇨ ⚠ a boon companion.

a bottle party a party where the host provides the accommodation and perhaps music and some food, and the guests provide the drink, each bringing a bottle of wine, spirits, or beer □ *Julie explained her occasional absences from the flat by saying she was staying with an aunt, and Isabel accepted this just as she accepted* ***the bottle parties*** *that from time to time assembled in Julie's bed-sitting room.* PW □ stress pattern a 'bottle party.

one's bottom drawer a girl or young woman's collection of clothes, linen etc, towards her marriage (though she may start collecting these things without an actual marriage in view) □ *'Six pounds,' I said. 'That's very good money, Mavis. You'll be able to save for* ***your bottom drawer****.' 'You've got to find the chap first,' she said.* RATT □ *I got some lovely towels at the sale, mum. I can't make up my mind whether to start using them or put them in* ***my bottom drawer****.*

one's bounden duty (formal) an absolute, pressing, compelling duty; (in) duty bound to do sth (qv) □ *It's not a case of whether you want to give evidence or not. If you overheard a criminal conversation it's* ***your bounden duty*** *to report it to the police.* □ *You will hear men boast of being good fathers to their children as if that were some special merit and not* ***their bounden duty****.* □ bounden not used in any other current phrase.

bow and scrape [v + v non-rev] (facetious) behave in a servile manner; be over-polite or obsequious □ *A waiter approached us and, with much* ***bowing and scraping****, led us to a table in the dining-room.* RATT □ *Promotion never meant* *so much to me that I was willing to* ***bow and scrape*** *for it.* □ *The reception was all very pleasant, everybody chatting and laughing and enjoying themselves until the Lord-Lieutenant appeared—and then you never saw such* ***bowing and scraping*** *as went on!* □ often the *-ing* forms function as nouns; scrape refers to a backward movement of one foot when bowing.

(play) Box and Cox [n + n non-rev] (two people who) keep failing to meet, to be in one place at the same time; alternate in one's use of a house, room etc or in providing a service etc (from a story—also the theme of a short Gilbert and Sullivan opera — of two lodgers named Box and Cox who shared the same room unknown to each other, one occupying it by day, the other by night) □ *I keep hoping that Michael and Ian will get their home leaves at the same time but it has been a case of* ***Box and Cox*** *with them ever since they were posted abroad.* □ *Spring has been* ***playing Box and Cox*** *with winter for months past. The winter aconites have got mixed up with the snowdrops and the crocuses and look like being overtaken by the daffodils.* SC □ cf use as compound v, as in *We have only one spare bed, but James and George have been* ***Boxing and Coxing*** *for years, so there's been no problem.*

box sb's ear(s) [V + O pass] hit sb about the ear(s), or side(s) of the head, with one's hands or fists, esp as a punishment or expression of anger □ *I was rescued at last by a gracious lady — the sixteen-year-old junior-teacher — who* ***boxed*** *a few* ***ears*** *and dried my face and led me off to The Infants* (classroom). CWR □ *'He'll be waiting round the back to give you a kiss in the dark.' 'I'll* ***box his ears*** *for him if he tries.'* □ variant give sb a box on the ear. ⇨ ⚠ give sb etc a thick ear.

(the) box office (theatre, cinema) the office, with a serving counter, from which tickets for a performance are sold; (fig) the popular attraction, success or failure of a particular show, performance, performer etc judged in commercial terms (ie the number of tickets sold, the number of people who come etc) □ *By the time* ***the box office*** *opened at 10 am there was a queue right around the block. The morning reviews had turned the play into an overnight success.* □ *Phantasi films evidently decided that human beings were bad* ***box office*** *and started on their series of animal pictures.* UTN □ *He is not the figure in the theatre world that he used to be, but he is still pretty good* ***box office.*** □ *For thirty years we looked at 'Spectacular, Stunning, Stupendous!' blazing across a cinema front and wondered if the film was worth seeing. Nowadays* ***the box office*** *adjectives are more likely to be 'Decadent, Daring, Disturbing!'* □ cf modifiers *good/bad* ***box office*** = 'successful, unsuccessful'; attrib use ***box-office*** *appeal, contributions, sales, (a)* ***box-office*** *success*; stress pattern good/bad 'box office.

the boys in blue (facetious) the civil police force □ (of legal advice centres) *How do you manage, as a human being, between clients who call the police 'pigs' and your professional peers who regard them as upright* ***boys in blue?*** ST □ *And she does not hide her admiration for the professors and for the level of intelligence of the pupils any more than she does her loathing for Philadelphia's police chief and for Chicago's* ***boys in blue.*** ST

boys will be boys (saying) (offer as an excuse for the fact that) young boys, and also sometimes grown men, will occas act in a childish, non-adult way □ *I know it's annoying to have our orchards robbed like this, but* ***boys will be boys*** *and apple-stealing is really just part of their life at this time of year.* □ *'Just look at them swilling all that beer, and telling dirty jokes! It's enough to make you sick.' 'Oh, I don't know, you must let them off the leash a bit now and then and remember that* ***boys will be boys****, poor things.'* □ other nouns may occasionally replace boys eg girls will be girls, students will be students.

sb's brain child an idea, project, plan etc that is sb's original conception and for which, as a rule, he expects to be given credit □ *No! This programme is* ***my brain child*** *and I strongly object to somebody taking over the production of it.* □ *The irrigation scheme for which the Development Board take a great deal of credit was, in fact,* ***the brain child of*** *an American consulting engineer holidaying in the district seven years previously.*

brain(s) versus brawn [n + n rev] (the opposition of or possession of) mental intelligence and physical strength □ *In wartime sacrifices are called for from everyone—from the* ***brains*** (= the people with high intelligence) *as well as the* ***brawn*** (= those who are physically strong). □ (cricket) *Thomson, formidable* ***brawn****, not much* ***brain****, pulls a shoulder muscle. Alan Knott softens the blow of defeat.* L □ (boxing) *For once the contest of* ***brain versus brawn*** *didn't produce the right result. For all his too obvious lack of skill, Scanlon had the strength to break through Lloyd's defences.*

a brand plucked etc from the burning [Comp (NP)] (formal) sth saved at the very last moment; sb rescued from, or persuaded to give up, a wrong or misguided course of life **V:** plucked, ⚠ saved, snatched □ *'How do your boys get on after they leave Approved School* (= a kind of reformatory)*?' 'Many of them go back to their old ways, I'm afraid, but even a few* ***brands plucked from the burning*** *would justify our work here.'* □ *He was a tireless organiser of musical evenings, amateur dramatics and poetry readings and was inclined to view anybody not much interested in the Arts as* ***a brand*** *to be* ***plucked from the burning.*** NS

the (top) brass the highest-ranking officers, ie generals, admirals etc, in the armed forces □ *Perhaps* ***the top brass*** *didn't confide in the journalists quite enough: at any rate, the United States government has, on the whole, had the worst press over the Indo-China war that any government has ever had anywhere.* L □ *With* ***their*** *attendant* ***brass*** *they drove down in style from the Admiralty and had lunch with the Captain of HMS Excellent.* RFW □ cf associated word *a brass-hat*, as in *...the appalling rows and intrigues which went on between the 'Frocks'* (ie Cabinet-ministers wearing frock-coats) *and the '****Brass-hats****' in those days.* MFM

a brass farthing [O (NP)] a very small amount of money; our resources; almost nothing; (consider) sth, eg an object, sb's feelings etc, as being of very little worth **V:** (not) have; (not) be worth; (not) care, (not) give □ *And here's me having to put* ***every brass farthing*** *of my allowance into getting a few worn-out old parts off the junk heaps.* HD □ *'Haven't you any money at all?' 'Not* ***a brass farthing.****'* □ *She had already pawned the few articles of any value that she possessed. Nothing she had left was worth* ***a brass farthing.*** □ *He doesn't care* ***a brass farthing*** *what anybody thinks—if he thinks it's worth doing he just goes ahead and does it.* □ often neg or with neg implication.

(a) brave new world (catchphrase) a new era brought about by revolutionary changes, reforms etc in society □ (source) *How many goodly creatures are there here!/How beauteous mankind is!* ***O brave new world,****/That has such people in't.* THE TEMPEST V 1 □ *In his most famous novel, '****Brave New World****', Aldous Huxley warns of the dangers of moral anarchy by depicting a repulsive Utopia, in which Platonic harmony is achieved by scientifically breeding and conditioning a society of human robots.* □ *. . .manifesting the aspirations and optimisms of Soviet Socialism and pointing to* ***the brave new world*** *that a classless society, armed with man's new understanding of the universe and his new tools of commanding it, would enjoy.* T □ almost always derogatory in current usage, following the novel by Huxley.

a brave show (of sth)[1] a beautiful, splendid, exhilarating etc spectacle (to watch) **o:** flowers, bluebells; flags, streamers □ *You should have* ***a brave show*** *of daffodils next spring after planting all those hundreds of bulbs.* □ *A march-past of Highland pipes, with kilts swinging and ribbons flying, always makes* ***a brave show.***

a brave show (of sth)[2] a courageous pretence (of being unafraid, unworried etc, when usu the opposite is the case); a bold/brave front (qv); put a bold/brave/good face on (Vol 1) (qv) **V:** make, put on. **o:** confidence, indifference; not worrying, not caring (what happens) □ *For a while, the child made* ***a brave show of*** *being unaffected by his schoolmate's taunts, but in the end he could not hold back his tears.* □ *With* ***a brave show of*** *confidence which he was far from feeling, he led his party along the narrow ledge of rock.*

the bravest etc of the brave etc one/some of the bravest etc possible of people **adj:** brave, poor, pure, rich, mean, mighty, humble, smart, chic, drab, ugly □ *He's waiting till the boss calms down, and I don't blame him.* ***The bravest of the brave*** *would hesitate to confront the Old Man in his present mood.* □ *I've seen him on the telly. Poor chap. Answering a lot of silly questions from* ***the poorest of the poor.*** *They won't thank him for it.* ASA □ *Who is she to criticize others? She's got in and out of a few beds in her time, though to hear her talk you'd think she was* ***the purest of the pure.*** □ only with adjs that form their superlative in *-(i)est.*

bread and butter[1] [n + n non-rev] slices of bread spread with butter (esp as part of an ordinary English meal eg breakfast or tea) □ *Finally, stuffed with ham, cake,* ***bread and butter****, and pints of dark tea, they moved from the table.* HD □ *After that I cut* ***bread and butter*** *and then washed up the mugs and saucepans and cleaned the kitchen.* UTN

bread and butter[2] [n + n non-rev] one's ordinary means of livelihood, esp at a very basic level and without any extras **V:** be (one's); earn one's □ TERRY: *Do you back horses?* JACK: *Do we? Do we!* JERRY: *They're our* ***bread and butter****, kid.* YAA □ *The 'different matters' which concern students* (in Sweden) *today are* ***bread-and-butter*** *ones—jobs and the Government loans they live on.* OBS □ *'Dear Pyle', I wrote and was tempted for the only time to write 'Dear Alden'* (his Christian name)*, for after all this was a* ***bread-and-butter*** *letter of some importance and it differed little from other* ***bread-and-butter*** *letters in containing a falsehood.* QA □ attrib use ***bread and butter*** *matters*, and esp *a* ***bread and butter*** *letter* = 'a letter written as a conventional way of thanking sb for hospitality or some other kindness'.

bread and butter[3] [n + n non-rev] simple and wholesome; without extraordinary features or frills □ *I wish often that I could have fixed my life at that moment—the car rolling smoothly down the narrow street, that wonderful* ***bread-and-butter*** *smell coming from the open spaces nearby—and inside the car the masculinity of steel and oil and warm leather.* RATT □ *'She always seemed a bit insipid to me,' Bob said, 'strictly the* ***bread and butter*** *Miss.'* RATT □ in this sense, only used attrib.

bread and circuses [n + n non-rev] the necessities of life and the provision of amusements, esp as a recipe for keeping the mass of the people contented with their government □ (source — translated from Latin) *Only two things limit their* (the Roman people's) *anxious longing—* ***bread and*** *the games of* ***the circus.*** JUVENAL 60-130 AD □ *'The Bingo age' and 'playing politics with the economy'. The former aptly describes one besetting sin of both major parties in the post-war era, the offering of bigger and better* ***bread and circuses*** *as vote-catching incentives.* T □ (NONCE) *In a society of Mr Crosland's choosing, the significance of education is that it serves in part as a job-qualification, in part as a distraction—part* ***bread****, part* ***circus.*** L

bread and water [n + n non-rev] the minimum diet, ration, on which life can be sustained, esp considered as a form of punishment (for a child, prisoner) **V:** put sb on; be, live, on □ *The prisoner claimed that the kitchen orderly had tripped over his foot by accident, but the Governor gave him ten days on* ***bread and water*** *all the same.* □ *I've a good mind to spank your b- h'mm—well, come downstairs you little minx, and make up your mind to* ***bread and water*** *this week.* DC □ *We couldn't possibly afford a holiday like that! Why, we'd have to live on* ***bread and water*** *the rest of the year.*

break the bank [V + O] (gambling) win so much money that one's winnings cannot be paid; (fig) be more than one can afford **S:** gambler, punters; spending; week-end, party □ (partial source) *You can see them sigh and wish to die,/You can see them wink the other eye/At the man who* ***broke the Bank*** *at Monte Carlo.* SONG (F GILBERT 1850-1903) □ *I'm afraid we'll be staying in Britain this year. A European holiday would just about* ***break the bank.***

break a case [V + O pass] find out who committed a crime etc; collect enough evidence to get sb convicted of a crime etc on which the police, military intelligence etc have been working **S:** policeman, detective, investigator □ *After the war he was tempted into M15 and had been one of the team which eventually* ***broke the*** *Fuchs* ***case****.* DS □ *It was rather vainglorious of me to think that a private investigator could* ***break a case*** *that the police had seemingly had to give up, but I was determined to try.* □ *'****The case*** *is about to* ***break****,' pleaded the inspector. 'Just give me another week on it, sir.'* □ cf the structures *We are about to* ***break the case****/****The case*** *is about to* ***break****.*

break cover [V + O] come out of, or be forced to flee from, a place of concealment **S:** animal; rabbit, fox; enemy □ *Once the fire has been lit and piled with green leaves, it generally takes about three minutes before the smoke percolates to every part and the animals start to* ***break cover****.* BB □ *The others, waiting on the grass, saw Jack and Ralph unharmed and* ***broke cover*** *into the sunlight. They forgot the beast in the excitement of exploration.* LF □ *And suddenly the dog began to whimper. It* ***broke cover*** *and made for the service-door.* OMIH

break one's duck [V + O] (cricket) score one's first run or runs; open one's score; (fig) have a first success in some matter, in relation to sb, etc, esp after trying for some time □ *After ten minutes' play Gower* ***broke his duck*** *with a splendidly-hit four to the boundary.* □ *He could hardly believe he had* ***broken his duck*** *at last, that he was to have a short story published in a reputable magazine.* □ *At such times Patrick would decide that there was still hope of Graham* ***breaking his duck*** *with the women if he could contrive to use the smile on them with reasonable frequency.* TGLY

break and enter [v + v non-rev] force one's way into a house, premises etc by illegal means such as breaking a window, lock, door etc (in order to steal something) □ *It's a treat being a long-distance runner, out in the world by yourself with not a soul to make you bad-tempered or tell you what to do or that there's a shop to* ***break and enter*** *a bit back from the next street.* LLDR □ *The courts call what he does '****breaking and entering****'; in reality it usually means pushing in a poorly-bolted back door and taking a few pounds set aside for the milkman.* OBS □ usu in *-ing* form without O, as in *he was held by the police on a charge of* ***breaking and entering****.*

break even (commerce) have, show, neither a profit nor a loss in some business transaction or sale □ *Some of the older coalfields like Durham, South Wales and Scotland are losing money. If they were told they must at least* ***break even****, how could this be achieved?* DM □ *Whatever its performance, the state factory is bound to stay in business because its main job will be to provide employment, not to* ***break even****.* T □ *The product is starting to sell well but the initial launching costs are high and we are unlikely to reach* ***break-even*** *point until the end of the year.* □ attrib use *(the)* ***break-even*** *point* = 'the point beyond which further sales or income will result in a profit'.

break one's/sb's fall [V + O pass] soften the impact of one's/sb's fall □ *Grandpa lost his footing on the stairs today. I was in front of him so I managed to* ***break his fall****.* □ *Then I found myself falling. There was a kind of exhilaration about it; I imagined a mattress below me to* ***break my fall****, to bounce away from, higher and higher into the sky. There was only the pavement, the cold stone.* RATT □ *Mary came off her horse yesterday, but* ***her fall*** *was* ***broken*** *by a pile of hay nearby.*

break one's fast[1] [V + O] (formal) have breakfast □ *We* ***broke our fast*** (ie we breakfasted) *in an early morning café on crunchy bread rings and butter, goats'-milk cheese and excellent coffee.* BM

break one's fast[2] [V + O] eat after a considerable period of time without food (because one has deliberately not eaten or has been prevented from eating) □ *Does the prisoner understand that if he cannot be persuaded to* ***break his fast****, he will be forcibly fed?*

break fresh/new ground [V + O pass] be a pioneer in some branch of knowledge; work at, try, sth new and different either in itself, or in relation to what one has done before □ *Ponderous and abstruse, his book* ***breaks*** *no* ***new ground****, but nevertheless merits attention for the way it traverses familiar terrain.* NS □ *In the recording field he has just* ***broken new ground****, too, with the issue of his first stereophonic LP.* RT □ *No* ***fresh ground*** *has been* ***broken*** *by this most recent study.*

break one's/sb's heart [V + O pass] (cause to) feel considerable grief, mental anguish, disappointment etc (esp in matters of love and personal relationships, business affairs, etc); weep inconsolably □ MONTY: *She'll* ***break her*** *little* ***heart*** *when she hears he's going to Spain.* CSWB □ *I don't know what's wrong with Mary and she won't tell me. But she's been upstairs crying fit to* ***break her heart*** *all afternoon.* □ *The fellow's a pest. I wouldn't* ***break my heart*** (cf *It wouldn't* ***break my heart****)* *if I never saw him again.* □ *She was so young and innocent that it nearly* ***broke my heart****; in a queer but pleasurable way it actually hurt me to look at her.* RATT □ *'I've been kept pretty hard at work this morning, I can tell you.' 'You're* ***breaking my heart****! Isn't that what they pay you for?'* □ can be ironic, as in third and fifth examples; also pl *it would* ***break their hearts****;* adj compounds broken-hearted, heart-breaking.

break the ice [V + O pass] do or say sth to remove or reduce social awkwardness or tension, esp at a first meeting, or at the start of a party etc □ *Virginia felt that if he did not come now, and meet Spencer, and have dinner as one of the family,* ***the ice*** *might never be* ***broken****.* AITC □ *Such generators were often used to* ***break the ice*** *at parties by making all the molecules in the hostess's undergarments leap simultaneously one foot to the left.* HHGG □ *'Nice to see you, boys,' he said quite quietly. Ned and I murmured the usual formula, and* ***the ice*** *was just* ***breaking*** *up nicely when Ned, the fool, couldn't resist adding, 'Haven't seen much of you lately.'* CON □ unusual intransitive construction with particle *up* in last example.

break one's journey [V + O pass] in the course of a journey, make a stop sufficiently long to enable one to shop, pay a visit, have a rest, etc □ *He would have caught an express, but had discovered that if he travelled by a slower train he could change trains at Stotwell, and* ***break his journey*** *for long enough to visit the Oak Lounge.* HD □ *We* could *drive from Glasgow to Portsmouth on the Thursday, but I'd rather we left the day before and* ***break our journey*** *somewhere just north of London.*

break one's neck (doing sth/to do sth) [V + O pass] try one's utmost, act recklessly (to do sth); take a great deal of trouble (to do or get sth) □ *If so many women think they are the biggest bargain a man can ever get and think they are hard done-by, then why do they practically* ***break their necks to*** *get married?* DM □ *Now that the American party has produced this bomb, you're thinking it's obviously unreasonable for our people to* ***break their necks trying*** *to save a couple of months.* NM □ *You're not exactly* ***breaking your neck to*** *get me that book from the library, are you?* ⇨ ⚠ (at) break-neck speed.

break the news (to sb/about sth) [V + O pass] (be the first to) inform sb of sth (generally sth unwelcome or exciting) □ *I had a letter this morning telling me I've failed my exam. That's bad enough, but I don't know how I'll* ***break the news*** *to Dad.* □ *I had a wonderful surprise this morning. Ann and David rang up from New Zealand to* ***break the news*** *that they're having a baby.*

break no bones [V + O pass] not injure oneself or sb else in spite of a (possibly) serious fall, accident etc (the implication is not necessarily that actual bones could have been broken) □ *No, I don't expect to enjoy myself on the school outing. If I can get the children there and back again without any of them* ***breaking any bones*** *I shall be thankful.* □ *And he bundled out into the corridor and nearly knocked over a man just passing. 'Oh, I'm having quite a little chapter of accidents.' 'In the words of the classics,' said the man, '****no bones broken****.'* TT □ *'****No bones broken****, I hope?' said Tommy's father, as the small boy came in, glowing from his first riding lesson.* □ often non-finite, as in last two examples.

break the peace [V + O] (legal) cause a disturbance, as an offence for which one can be arrested and punished □ *He was very noisy and abusive, and alarmed the other customers. The proprietor was very forbearing in not sending for the police and having him charged with* ***breaking the peace****.* □ *'If you* ***break the peace*** *in this way again, you'll go to prison,' said the magistrate.* □ *That argument in the pub last night got badly out of hand. Max has been charged with causing* ***a breach of the peace*** *and has to appear in court tomorrow.* □ variant a breach of the peace used only in legal context. ⇨ keep the peace.

break the rules [V + O pass] infringe, not keep to, the rules or regulations by which a game is played, a school or club is run, etc; do sth that runs counter to accepted behaviour □ *'I don't want to play snakes and ladders with Billy any more,' the child replied. 'He keeps* ***breaking the rules****, and making up new ones.'* □ *Your boy knows the school rules as well as I do myself—he's just one of those who think that* ***rules*** *are made to be* ***broken****.* □ *As a diplomat he* ***breaks every rule*** *in the book but is immensely popular everywhere he goes.* □ variant, rules are made to be broken, is sometimes used as an excuse, or as an encouragement to others, not to observe them.

break the silence[1] [V + O pass] interrupt a natural or normally continuous period of silence **S:** cry (of a bird), (the sound of) running feet, (an odd) noise; nothing □ *We were comfortably dozing off in our deck-chairs when a piercing shriek* ***broke the*** *afternoon* ***silence****.* □ *Nothing* ***broke the silence*** *of the night but an occasional seabird's call.* □ *Suddenly* ***the silence*** *was* ***broken*** *by a single shot.*

break the silence[2] [V + O pass] (try to) end an awkward or embarrassed silence between two or more people, by starting a conversation etc **S:** he, she, I, you, we, they; host, hostess □ *I left him to* ***break the silence****. Our steps remained the only noise, until he remarked, as though casually: 'Walter Luke didn't say much tonight, did he?'* NM □ *This knowledge was the trouble. We all knew too much. It was Randall who* ***broke the silence****.* CON □ *After what seemed an eternity,* ***the silence*** *was* ***broken*** *by our host's son facetiously remarking 'Well! Lots of weather we've been having lately!'*

break the sound etc barrier [V + O pass] go faster than the speed of sound; similarly, cross any other specified point or obstacle **n:** sound, heat, space, speed; pain, (social) class □ *When Concorde was tested over the west coast, the sonic boom created as it* ***broke the sound barrier*** *affected a swathe of country fifty miles wide.* □ *What was Dr Roger Bannister's exact time when he* ***broke the four-minute-mile barrier*** *at Oxford in 1954?* TO □ *In the stratified society of a Jane Austen novel* ***the class barriers*** *are never* ***broken*** *with impunity. Wealth is not a prerequisite, but to be of good family is.*

break the speed-limit [V + O pass] exceed the maximum speed allowed by law □ *Policemen nowadays seem more interested in where you're parking than in whether you're* ***breaking the speed-limit****.* □ *You must realize that* ***the speed-limit*** *is there for a reason. It is not there to be* ***broken****!*

break the spell [V + O pass] destroy an infatuation, fascination, illusory experience, etc by a return to reality □ *I had seen photographs of women that streamlined their shapes and made them look so alluring that you knew it was all a trick, that once* ***the spell*** *was* ***broken****, and they moved, you would see that they were just ordinary, if pretty, women.* CON □ *Then it was over, and she turned and vanished leaving* ***the spell*** *un-****broken****, and an incredulous murmur rising after her.* WI □ *I wish something could* ***break the spell*** *that binds her to that worthless fellow.*

break sb's spirit [V + O pass] destroy, suppress, sb's desire for independence, his right to decide for himself, his sense of pride, delight in life, etc □ *The life of convicts in nineteenth-century Australia was one of hard labour, heat, disease, and poor food, with the threat of the lash or the gallows if they showed rebellion — enough to* ***break*** *even the proudest man****'s spirit****.* □ *I'm not surprised Featherstone's a widower: any woman****'s spirit*** *would be* ***broken*** *by life with that old miser!*

(a) breaking point the place or time at which

sth, which is subject to considerable pressure, strain, or stretching, breaks or is likely to break; (fig) a similar moment when sb loses, or is about to lose, his courage, patience, control of his temper, etc **V:** be at, be near to, reach □ *Some of these special nylon mountaineering ropes have* ***a breaking point*** *considerably higher than those of the old type.* □ *The reaction to this news was too much for a nervous system which must have been already strung to* ***breaking point***. EM □ *I warn you that my patience is at* ***breaking point***. *I won't stand for much more of this behaviour.* □ (stage directions) *(Alison carries on with her ironing. This is routine, but she is getting close to* ***breaking point***, *all the same.)* LBA

(at) break-neck speed [A (PrepP)] with the greatest speed that one can manage, often dangerously fast **S:** drive, move, dash along □ *He flung himself into the car and drove off* ***at break-neck speed*** *to fetch the doctor.* □ (the announcement of the Prix Goncourt) *All bookshops which have any intellectual pretensions clear their best windows and stand ready to welcome in the winner as it arrives with the* ***break-neck speed*** *of a stop-press edition.* UTN ⇨ ⚠ break one's neck (doing sth/to do sth).

a breath of fresh air [Comp/O (NP)] an opportunity for breathing in or from the open air, (eg by leaving a stuffy enclosed house or room, by opening a window, etc); (fig) (sb or sth that makes) a refreshing and welcome change **V:** be, seem like; want, get □ *Nonsense! One can't stay shut up in here for ever. I want* ***a breath of fresh air***. EM □ *Graham had stopped the car, saying that it was a fine night and what about* ***a breath of fresh air***? TGLY □ *Amid the clamour of the oil lobby and other interested parties, this* (the refusal by 60 per cent of Detroit constituents to accept a tax cut for themselves) *came like* ***a breath of fresh air***. T □ note that the title of the novel *'A Breath of French Air'* (one of the sources used in the compilation of this dictionary) is a play on this expression.

the breath of life signs of breathing in a person's body as an indication that he is still alive, surviving etc; (fig) sth that invigorates one, gives (new) meaning to one's life or actions □ *Actually Nora would have stayed chained to her husband's bedside, had it kept* ***the breath of life*** *in him a second longer.* NM □ *'Doesn't your husband get tired of being so much in the public eye?' 'Oh no, on the contrary; it's* ***the breath of life*** *to him.'* □ *In this fiery demagogue, opposition to all established order had become* ***the*** *very* ***breath of life***.

a breath of wind (any indication or sign of) a light amount of wind, a little breeze □ *Not* ***a breath of wind*** *rose to stir the dense fog which had settled over the snow-bound countryside.* EM □ *'Lovely day, isn't it?' 'Yes, too hot, almost. We could do with* ***a breath of wind***.*'* □ *It was a likely-looking lake, but wet-fly fishing is hopeless in a dead calm. Had there been even* ***a breath of wind*** *to ruffle the surface, we might have had some luck.* □ ***A breath of wind*** *stirred the sails — a welcome change after being stuck two miles offshore all afternoon in a dead calm.* □ often neg or implied neg, as in examples.

breathe fire and slaughter etc [V + O] threaten to destroy and kill sb, to punish, to take reprisals etc; (facetious) become angry, make a great deal of fuss, and perhaps intend to take some positive action **O:** fire and slaughter, ⚠ fire and brimstone, fire and venom □ (source) *And Saul, yet* ***breathing*** *out* ***threatenings and slaughter*** *against the disciples of the Lord, went unto the high priest.* ACTS IX 1 □ *This was the mouth of the cannon, which seldom* ***breathes*** *forth anything but* ***threatening and slaughter***, *made to speak the language of affection and sorrow of parting friends.* L □ *Some kids had got in and mucked up the Labs. The Head's* ***breathing fire and slaughter***, *but he hasn't found the culprits yet.* □ (fishermen's rights) *Rampant Scottish peers have emerged from their glens* ***breathing fire and brimstone***. *The 20-odd Tory MPs with fishing constituencies are looking distinctly unhappy.* SC □ *His fortunes were closely linked with a legendary figure called Moses Idwal Valentine, now dead, who dominated the Manchester police force and* ***breathed fire and venom***. ST

breathe one's last [V + O] die, or be about to die □ *Her condition worsened during the night and towards midday the following day she* ***breathed her last***. □ *When you come to* ***breathe your last***, *you may be sorry to have this cruelty on your conscience.* □ euphemism.

breathe etc a sigh of relief [V + O pass] inhale or exhale a breath of air, perhaps audibly, as an indication of one's relief after a moment, or situation, of some danger etc **V:** breathe, ⚠ give, heave. **prep:** with □ *Brigit* ***breathed a sigh of*** *deep* ***relief*** *as she heard Nicky shrilly making some explanation, and then the rapid patter of feet approaching the door.* DC □ ***A sigh of relief arose*** *from the crowd as the fireman reappeared with the child in his arms and prepared to descend.* □ *The leaves of the gallant thorn trees looked as if they were about to crumble to ashes, and greeted the sunset* ***with a sigh of relief*** *that was echoed in our own exhausted senses.* LWK □ *Windbags and bigots who* ***heaved a sigh of relief*** *when Tom Driberg left the House of Commons had better get back under cover again.* NS □ variant a sigh of relief arose.

bricks and mortar [n + n non-rev] a house or houses, buildings in general, esp as a physical, concrete reality or as objects with a value suitable for the investment of money □ *This place has a mellowness about it, although the new town is only about forty years old, proving that* ***bricks and mortar*** *alone do not make a city.* BM □ *On the left, half-hidden by pines, there was the biggest house I'd seen in Warley. It was a physical extension of Jack, at least fifty thousand pounds' worth of* ***bricks and mortar*** *stating his superiority over me as a suitor.* RATT □ *People always used to tell me: put your money in* ***bricks and mortar***, *there's nothing safer. So I bought my house.* TVT

bridle one's tongue [V + O pass] restrain oneself from speaking too frankly, too rudely, etc; watch/mind one's tongue (qv) □ *'It is a relief to be able to talk plainly. My wife tells me that its lack is, well, one of my faults.' She smiled. 'And I am told that, given a year or so, I am to be cured of it—taught to* ***bridle my tongue***.*'* TT □ *His language is appallingly coarse sometimes. He might at least try to* ***bridle his tongue*** *in front of the children.* □ also pl; often as *to*-inf after another v as in *try, learn, seem unable, be asked, to* **bridle one's tongue**.

bright and early [A (adj + adj non-rev)] early in the morning; before most people have got up from bed **V:** be up, get up; emerge, start work □ *'Yes, it's true. I heard it on the 7 o'clock news.' 'Goodness, you must have been up* **bright and early** *this morning!'* □ *There's no sense in my getting up* **bright and early** *if you're going to sleep half the morning.*

the bright lights (the glamour of) city life; big cities thought of as centres of gaiety, entertainment, and opportunities for enjoyment □ *'Well, a week tonight and it'll be back to* **the bright lights**.' *'Don't talk of it,' he groaned. 'I wish I could stay here for ever.'* □ *I've never really been lured by* **the** *proverbial* **bright lights**. *Acting never really struck me as all that glamorous.* OBS

a bright spark [Comp (NP)] (informal) a lively and intelligent person, esp one who is young and expected to do well, eg a child, pupil, junior member of a profession, etc **V:** ⚠ be, regard sb as, think sb to be □ *'She's* **a bright spark**, *that littlest one of George's, isn't she?' 'Yes, she's a lively child.'* □ *I heard a Conservative Member — and one who would undoubtedly consider himself among* **the brighter sparks** *of the back benches — give it as his settled opinion that Heath's chances of gaining the necessary majority first time round were three to one on.* NS □ *Tell them they've got to do the sum themselves, as an initiative test, and* **some bright spark***'ll usually save your face by coming up with the answer.* □ frequently used ironically, esp with some, as in last example.

bring sb (bad/good) luck [V + IO + O] be the cause of sb having a special, almost supernatural or superstitious, advantage/disadvantage □ *I wish we had never left our old home. This house has* **brought** *us nothing but* **bad luck** *ever since we moved into it.* □ *Aunt Annabel had found a black kitten, plump and playful, and if no owner turned up perhaps Bridget would like it. It would* **bring** *her* **luck**. DC □ *The stalls were full of charms and bracelets that, if you listened to the salesman, would* **bring good luck to** *everybody who bought them.* □ *They say that breaking a mirror* **brings** *one seven years'* **bad luck**, *and I started mine in two seconds flat by cutting my finger on one of the pieces.* □ bring sb luck = 'bring sb *good* luck'.

broach the subject etc [V + O pass] introduce a topic, suggestion, request etc for the first time **O:** subject, matter; idea, topic; the question (of an increase in salary, our marriage) □ *Now, he knew, was the time to* **broach the matter**. *The only question was, should he give her the present before or afterwards?* □ *It was no use making for the door because I still had to* **broach the subject** *of her taking a job in America.* SPL □ *'Are your parents quite willing that you should study in London?' 'I haven't* **broached the subject** *with them yet.'* □ often followed by *(of sth) to/with sb*; often used when one is not confident of a favourable response.

(in) broad daylight [A (PrepP)] (in) the full light of day; (fig) (do sth in) daylight or public conditions which make it unexpected, outrageous or unsafe □ *The Eshobi path is bad enough* **in broad daylight**, *but by night it is a death-trap.* BB □ *I thought with bitter regret of the time she had been a stranger to me and I wouldn't have cared if she'd walked the streets naked* **in broad daylight**. RATT □ *Nobody on the site had questioned their authority to move the caravan and they drove off with it* **in broad daylight**. □ *I had intended to be up before the dawn, but when I awoke it was* **broad daylight**.

broaden etc one's horizons [V + O pass] enlarge the range of one's interests, knowledge, attitudes, activities etc **V:** broaden, ⚠ enlarge, extend, widen □ *They must spread their wings a little. They must make friends in many places. Nothing* **widens one's horizons** *like having friends.* PW □ *There are too many specialists urging the concert-goer to* **extend his horizons** *and widen his perspectives when all they mean is, 'you must like what I like.'* T □ *Children in stories tend to have drama in their lives which real children are, in general, denied. To this extent, all storybooks, whether 'education-oriented' or not, serve to* **broaden the horizons of** *young readers.* □ **One's horizons** *are inevitably* **enlarged** *through contacts with people from other countries.*

broken/fractured English imperfect English, as spoken by sb to whom it is a foreign language not yet mastered □ (source) KING HENRY: *'Therefore, queen of all, Katharine, break thy mind to me in* **broken English**, *wilt thou have me?'* KATH: *'Dat is as it shall please de roi mon père.'* HENRY V, V 2 □ *'Who are you?' they asked in French. 'Ah, English,' they murmured and changed gear into* **broken English**. BM □ *The Brazilian Alberto Cavalcanti, despite his* **fractured English**, *made a number of films at Ealing.* ST

a broken home a home, or family background, in which the parents are divorced or separated □ *Many of the boys who come before the Juvenile Courts are from* **broken homes**, *but by no means all of them.* □ *After all the bitterness of the divorce, Lesley had to pull herself together and ensure that her children survived the handicap of* **a broken home**.

a broken marriage a marriage which has ended in the divorce or separation of the partners □ *He is a man who has always learnt to count the pennies and to risk the pounds. That's why he's not a member of the Country Club— nothing to do with* **his broken marriage**. OMIH □ *He had thirty years to look back on, he thought bitterly, with nothing to show for them but a ruined career and* **a broken marriage**. □ also pl.

a broken reed [Comp/o (NP)] sb or sth likely to fail when his or its strength is tested, usu because of some prior stress or experience **V:** be; lean on, trust in, be let down by □ (source) *Lo, thou trustest in the staff of* **this broken reed**, *on Egypt; whereon if a man lean, it will go into his hand, and pierce it.* ISAIAH XXXVI 6 □ *After the scandal he continued to hold high office, but even the most naturally sycophantic of his colleagues avoided close involvement, regarding him as* **a broken reed**. □ also pl.

a Bronx cheer [O/o (NP)] (esp US) a vulgar sound produced by the air being forced through tight lips; ironic applause, generally in disapproval and intended to be offensive (from the Bronx, a district of New York) **V:** give, get; greet sb with, respond with □ *The Chancellor's* *plea that additional measures to pump extra money into state investment would keep the increase in the dole queues lower got the Westminster equivalent of* ***a Bronx cheer*** *from the Labour benches.* G □ *When the referee awarded the title to the winner, the crowd, who disagreed with him to a man, gave him* ***the Bronx cheer****.*

brook no delay etc [V + O] be such as not to allow for any delay etc **S:** situation, crisis; plan, scheme. **O:** delay, ⚠ hesitation, inefficiency, interference, vagueness □ *I thought this over for a week and then decided that I wouldn't wait; Janet Prentice might well be in trouble that would* ***brook no delay****.* RFW □ *With satisfaction he noticed himself becoming accepted and integrated into the community of the hospital, finding his place in a society that* ***brooked no vagueness*** *as to questions of society.* HD

one's brother's/sb's keeper [Comp (NP)] acknowledge responsibility for sb's conduct or welfare **V:** ⚠ be, become □ (source) *And the Lord said unto Cain, Where is Abel thy brother? And he said, I know not: Am I* ***my brother's keeper****?* GENESIS IV 9 □ *But I'd stopped thinking about Alice and I was walking steadily. I* ***wasn****'t Alice* ***'s keeper****; let George take care of whatever guilt there was to bear.* RATT □ *'Charity begins at home, let me remind you,' she stormed. 'You're so busy* ***being*** *every Tom, Dick and Harry* ***'s keeper****, you've no time for your own family.'* □ often neg.

(a) brute fact/necessity (a) fact/necessity which is harsh and inescapable □ *'****Brute necessities****', the more pressing hardships of working life, have been greatly lessened.* UL □ (Mescalin visions) *are the stuff of which the mind's antipodes are made. It is* ***a brute fact*** *of experience which, whether we like it or not, we have to accept.* HAH □ *That's nothing to shudder at.* ***Brute necessity*** *has driven men to stranger diets than raw fish, I can tell you.*

brute force/strength physical power which is unallied to skill, judgement, intelligence etc □ *On the whole, then, strong emotions may prepare us for the primitive type of battle in which* ***brute strength*** *and endurance and speed of flight determine survival.* SNP □ *He couldn't break the rock for all his* ***brute strength****, but Jake, who had been a quarryman, picked up his mallet and broke it neatly into four pieces.* □ *The bout was a classic example of* ***brute force*** *meeting more than its match in boxing skill and experience.*

the buck stops here responsibility, or blame, is accepted here, and will not be passed on to sb else □ *Harry Truman* (US President 1945-53) *had a sign on his desk reading '****The buck stops here.****'* NS □ *The Armed Forces may curse them* (politicians) *and try to overawe them and blind them with science and appeal to emotive considerations of prestige and morale, but they know very well* ***where the buck stops****, and they don't (on the whole) try to cheat.* ST □ *Glib talk of the need to summon a five-power conference 'to reach a sensible and humane solution'* (to the war in Vietnam) *is simply evasive nonsense. The harsh truth is that* ***the buck*** *started here and that it* ***stops here*** *as well.* NS ⇨ pass the buck.

a bucket shop (derogatory) premises where unauthorised betting or gambling takes place; (fig) an organization dealing in the sale of stocks and shares without the legal sanction of membership of a Stock Exchange; a travel agency which sells very cheaply esp air tickets obtained by the agency by semi-legal means □ That *company! Well, Brian may call them stockbrokers but I say the firm's* ***a bucket shop****.* □ *...the doubtful facts and figures of the claim-jumper turned administrator—a more bloody cooked-up set of figures I've never seen even in a* ***bucket-shop*** *circular.* HAA □ *The fortunes won and lost in the Australian mineral share market in the late sixties suggest that the gap between the respectable stock-broker and the* ***bucket shop*** *operator may not be as wide as one may like to suppose.* □ also pl; attrib use *a* ***bucket(-)shop*** *circular, operator etc.*

a buffer state/zone [Comp (NP)] a country, or area, situated between two powerful forces which are likely otherwise to be in conflict **V:** ⚠ be, act as; constitute, represent □ *It was on the tip of my tongue to say that I didn't want to act as* ***a buffer state*** *between him and Ned, but I didn't say it.* CON □ ***A buffer state****, should it cease to function as such, may well find itself the battleground of opposing forces.* □ *Recent research in Brazil has highlighted the importance of the mangrove swamps as* ***a buffer zone*** *between the sea or the Amazon and the dense forest.* □ also pl.

Buggins' turn (informal) the procedure whereby posts are given not to those most capable of filling them but to relatively mediocre candidates as a reward for long and undistinguished service □ *Nowhere is the principle of* ***Buggins' turn*** *more firmly established than in the Labour movement — and the great psychological strength of X's position is that, having run for the office six times, he's regarded as having earned it.* NS □ *When the results of the election were known, James, who had been narrowly defeated, made no secret of his annoyance at being the victim of* ***Buggins' turn****.* □ Buggins is an invented name which to English ears is both undistinguished and slightly comic; often preceded by *the principle of.*

bulk large [V + Comp] be a prominent, or the main, item in some context or perspective; (fig) dominate sb's thinking on some subject **A:** on the horizon; in sb's mind, in sb's thoughts, in the public eye □ *Coming back on deck, he was surprised to find that the island so dimly discerned an hour ago now* ***bulked larged*** *on the horizon.* □ *I think I can guess what* ***bulks largest*** *in your mind at the moment. A comfortable chair and a long cool drink.* ILIH □ *If retirement were not* ***bulking*** *so* ***large*** *on the horizon he might have risked the investment.* □ *The population explosion is another threat which* ***bulks large*** *in the public eye at the moment.*

bully for sb (informal) a mocking expression of approval or praise; well done! bravo! good for sb(!) (qv) □ *'Out of a Hole' gives every intimation that it is the work of the most exciting novelist to come along in years.' Well,* ***bully for*** *Peabody, even though he must have been dead out* (ie drunk) *to write that.* JFTR □ *'I told him I had better things to do with my money than help people who can't help themselves.' '****Bully for*** *you, I hope you're pleased with yourself. I daresay you are.'* □ stress pattern bully for 'sb..

the burden/onus of proof the obligation to prove sth claimed **V:** be upon, fall upon, lie on; rest with □ *The rule under which, in criminal prosecutions,* ***the burden of proof*** *lay throughout on the prosecution was approved by the Supreme Soviet and written into the code.* OBS □ ***The onus of proof*** *rests with him. If he cannot make good his claim that you were present, there is no need for you to prove you were not.* □ usu functions as S of clause.

burn one's boats/bridges (behind one) take some irrevocable step and thereby commit oneself to a course of action; leave oneself with no means of escape □ ALISON: *I was cut off from the kind of people I'd always known, my family, my friends, everybody. And I'd* ***burnt my boats****. After all those weeks of brawling with Mummy and Daddy about Jimmy, I knew I couldn't appeal to them without looking foolish and cheap.* LBA □ *'Perhaps it's a pity you* ***burned your boats****.' 'That's possible,' said Martin. 'Perhaps it wasn't sensible to invest your future in one man.'* NM □ (NONCE) *So he was really doing it.* ***Putting a match to his boats and bridges*** *right in front of my eyes.* CON □ *'You've sold your house before you've got your emigration clearance to go to Australia?' 'Yes, It's the only way I'll have the courage actually to go—I just* had *to* ***burn my boats behind me****.'*

burn the candle at both ends exhaust, or make too great a demand on, one's physical or mental resources by overwork or over-indulgence in some activity □ *It's a bit silly going away on a day-trip after you've been on night duty. In this kind of job you can't* ***burn the candle at both ends****.* □ *At the end of each term I'd go home to my parents with all the symptoms of someone who has well and truly* ***burnt the candle at both ends****: a permanent hangover, not a penny in my pocket, and a desperate need to catch up on lost sleep.*

burn one's fingers [V + O pass] cause oneself trouble or harm through miscalculation, foolishness etc □ *I don't like artists in public life, and when the artist is as good at his art and as old a friend as you, I hate it. Not only because you inevitably mess things about, but because I don't like to see you* ***burn your fingers****.* HAA □ *I'm not going to interfere with people's private lives any more, even in the most well-meaning way.* ***My fingers*** *have been* ***burnt*** *once too often.* □ *If you've never played the stockmarket this is not the time to start. You're liable to* ***get your fingers burnt****.* □ variant get one's fingers burnt.

burn the midnight oil [V + O] stay awake late into the night, esp to work or study □ *I expect you'll be* ***burning the midnight oil*** *for the next week or two, getting ready for your exams.* □ *I doubted whether, even with much* ***burning of the midnight oil****, I could assemble the anthology by the deadline suggested.*

the burning question a question whose answer is hotly debated or on which a great deal depends □ *Entry or non-entry into the European Common Market was one of* ***the burning questions*** *in British politics in the early 1970s.* □ *It's not whether we can get a good meal at The Apéritif or not, but whether we could pay for it if we did—that's* ***the burning question****.*

the burnt child dreads/fears the fire (saying) one is unwilling to repeat an experience which one has found to be unpleasant; once bitten, twice shy (qv) □ *He would be better off getting married again, but I suppose it's a case of* ***the burnt child fearing the fire****. His first marriage was a disaster.* □ *The boy's had a fright, but it'll do him no harm.* ***The burnt child dreads the fire****, so he's not likely to make the same mistake again.*

bury sb alive [V + O + Comp pass] cover sb totally with earth, rubble etc, though without killing them (after an explosion, cave-in etc); (fig) live in obscure, or confined, circumstances □ TONY: *It is the night Mother refers to in her inimitable way as The Night The Bomb Fell.* MIKE: *Yes. And your father and your mother were* ***buried alive*** *for hours.* EHOW □ *I couldn't understand why a man who had always been so fond of the social scene should suddenly want to* ***bury*** *himself* ***alive*** *in a one-horse village at the back of nowhere.* □ *We don't have the feeling of being* ***buried alive*** *here because so many of our friends come to visit us.* □ often pass.

bury the hatchet [V + O pass] come to friendly or peaceful terms with sb else; make some gesture to signify the end of hostility between two people, groups, sides in an argument □ (headline) ***Bury The Hatchet*** *Serious efforts are now being made by both Bulgaria and Yugoslavia to put their relations on a better footing.* SC □ *I had acquainted Hugo with something which he needed to know, and we had exchanged not unfriendly words. But it is possible to break the ice* (qv) *without* ***burying the hatchet****.* □ *Those two are the best of friends now.* ***The hatchet*** *was* ***buried*** *years ago.*

bury the past [V + O pass] deliberately forget about, cover or break one's connections with, sth or everything that has happened in the past; let bygones be bygones (qv) □ *But I thought the past was the past. I was too optimistic. You and I are not like the people here—we have no confessional box where we can* ***bury the*** *bad* ***past****.* OMIH □ *Well, let's admit there were mistakes on both sides; we'll* ***bury the past*** *and try to make a fresh start.* □ *With the marriage of their children, the two families could finally look on* ***the past*** *as being* ***buried****, and their reconciliation was complete.*

(the) bush telegraph a mysterious, unofficial way of conveying information or rumour □ *By the way, I have it by* ***bush telegraph*** *that Davy, Brian and their pals are proposing to descend upon us for Whitsun.* □ *The company's collapse came as a shock to none of its employees. Even at our obscure provincial depot* ***the bush telegraph*** *had brought the news that all was not well at head office.*

the business end (of sth) (informal) the part of a tool, instrument, weapon etc with which one performs its particular function **o:** tin-opener, spade; gun, rifle □ *We used to have a way of testing whether there was any guts left in a battery. What we did was to lay our tongues on the little brass strip at* ***the business end****. If there was any juice remaining, then we used to get a tingling feeling in our tongues.* TGLY □ *And she avoided answering — this time by fussing about with the window opener, getting it behind the cupboard without breaking any of the bulbs* *and shades with* ***the business end****.* TT ▫ *Emerging cautiously, but not cautiously enough, from cover, I found myself looking down* ***the business end of*** *a double-barrelled gun.*

the business in hand [O/o (NP)] the matter or topic being dealt with or discussed at the time of speaking **V:** state, summarize; complete; attend to, get down to, get on with, return to ▫ *The proceedings were then opened by Lydia, who briefly stated* ***the business in hand****, namely to choose a secretary and treasurer for the Committee.* WDM ▫ *This is neither the time nor the place to exercise your wit, my boy. Kindly settle down, and attend to* ***the business in hand****.* ▫ *Instead of getting on with* ***the business in hand****, he worked out a hundred and one futile schemes intended to save time in the end.*

business is business (saying) (justify oneself in) refusing to be diverted from some business arrangement, or opportunity, on such grounds as friendship, family ties, sentiment, pity etc ▫ *The real victim of this crisis should be the neo-colonial myth and its rhetoric.* ***Business is business****.* NS ▫ *Certainly, I'll be sorry to see them put out on the street. But* ***business is business****, and they haven't paid any rent for two months now.*

a busman's holiday a holiday, or leisure time, spent in doing the same kind of thing as one does at work ▫ (a journalist in Ireland) *I thought I would make it* ***a busman's holiday*** *and write up my visit to the 'Cork Examiner'* (= a paper), *so I sat down and in half an hour I had done my piece.* PP ▫ *I'm not going to let you help with the washing-up. You get enough of that at home without making* ***a busman's holiday*** *of your evening out.*

but good [A] (informal) very well, efficiently, thoroughly etc ▫ *And out of the door, out of it, out of the stale sweet stink, away from the words on the wall which showed the staff were known* ***but good****, 'taped' as the kitchen* (ie kitchen staff) *said.* TT ▫ *'Shall I get rid of him, boss?' 'Yes, you get rid of him* ***but good****!'* ▫ when used after an imper, as in last example, it carries the threat of punishment in case of failure.

but me no buts (saying) do not offer any objections or modifications to what I have said, ordered etc ▫ *'I've already seen it, son,' he said. 'Doesn't apply to me.' 'But Mr Collins—' '****But me no buts****,' he said. 'You just take it round to the others.'* TT ▫ *These are my orders, and I want you to* ***but me no buts****; just get along and do as I say.*

buy it/that [V + O] (informal) believe, accept a proposal, explanation, suggestion (the implication often being that such a belief or acceptance is likely to prove misguided) ▫ (Working class people) *are cheerfully cagey* ((informal) = distrustful) *towards both the leaders of the big battalions and their big words: 'Ah'm* (= I'm) *not* ***buying that****,' they say.* UL ▫ *'And I'm very grateful to you, Ron. I want to give you a nice present.' Ron relented a little. 'All right,' he said, 'I'll* ***buy it****.'* HAA ▫ *'I'll tell him a pigeon flew in at the window and knocked his precious vase over.' 'And do you really think he'll* ***buy that****?'*

buy a pig in a poke [V + O] (saying) purchase sth or agree to sth without first having an opportunity to judge its value or all the relevant facts ▫ *'Well I'll take it now.' 'You mustn't* ***buy a pig in a poke****,' he said. 'You mightn't like it.'* PW ▫ *'This is an entirely new type of appointment and we don't know exactly how it will work.' 'So if I accept it,' I replied, 'I am* ***buying a pig in a poke****?'* ▫ (NONCE) *Until the wells are sunk nobody will know for sure whether or not this is bonanza time for the oil industry, but it would be surprising if every* ***poke*** *were opened without their being a fairly plump* ***pig*** *at the bottom of several of them.* NS

by accident [A (PrepP)] as a result of a chance or a mishap, rather than through a plan or arrangement; by chance (qv); as chance will/would have it (qv); as it happens/happened (qv); as (good/ill) luck would have it (qv) ▫ *You might cut yourself* ***by accident****; you wouldn't cut yourself on purpose.* ▫ *Completely* ***by accident*** *my uncle happened to be booked into the same hotel as I was.* ⇨ by design; on purpose.

by/from all accounts [Disj (PrepP)] according to all available information; according to what has been said or reported ▫ *My mother's family had been in Africa since the European beginning.* ***By all accounts*** *more restless, bold and adventurous than most, they had always been in the forefront of what we called 'progress'.* LWK ▫ *I had never met him; he was clearly a fine soldier. But* ***from all accounts*** *he was completely worn out and needed a rest.* MFM ▫ *The hotel was,* ***from all accounts****, very well run as far as the comfort of the guests was concerned.* ▫ front, middle or end position.

by all means [Disj/A (PrepP)] of course; certainly; please do ▫ *'That leaves us just enough time for our little chat before lunch,' returned Rogers equably. '****By all means****, Sergeant. I repeat, I am at your service.'* EM ▫ *He sat down again. 'Look, Norah,' he said, 'I'll come straight to the point if I may.' '****By all means****.'* TT ▫ *Conscious now of the pitfalls spread around him, Harold said warily, 'If you think there is anything to be gained by telling me,* ***by all means*** *do.'* PW ▫ used as way of agreeing to, or strengthening, an invitation, suggestion, instruction etc; not to be confused with *by every means*, where *means* = 'methods of achieving an object'. ⇨ by no means.

by any chance [Disj (PrepP)] perhaps; conceivably; possibly ▫ *You know Ernie Ollershaw? Not in the game yourself* ***by any chance****? Don't get me wrong, I mean the straight* ((informal) = legal) *side of it.* HD ▫ *I was wondering if* ***by any chance*** *you could lend me five pounds until the end of next week?* ▫ used in wording of a question when the speaker wishes, either from politeness or caution, not to appear to know what answer he will get. ⇨ ⚠ by chance.

by anybody's/sb's standards [A (PrepP)] according to anybody's/some particular person's scale of values; according to views or tastes which are generally held or held by a particular individual or group ▫ *'Thirty years ago,' he said, handing the paper back to me. 'That's a lot of years judged* ***by anybody's standards****.'* PP ▫ *Internationally famous teams such as Real Madrid are expensive to run* ***by our standards****, but because of the prestige they have won and the crowds they have shown that heavy* *expenditure can be financially rewarding.* SC.

by and by [A] in the near future; after a little time □ *You'll be getting married and having a family* ***by and by****, and then you'll understand why parents want to protect their children.* □ *Young Smith on his first day was sent to the galley to try his apprentice hand at peeling the potatoes.* ***By and by*** *the captain came down.* SD □ *'Things are bound to get better* ***by and by****.' 'Oh yes, I've heard that before—everything will be all right in the sweet* ***by and by****'* □ sometimes used as n, esp the sweet by-and-by, from (source) *In* ***the sweet by-and-by****/We shall meet on that beautiful shore.* HYMNS (S R BENNETT 1836-1898)—expression now normally has ironic overtones.

by chance [A (PrepP)] accidentally, fortuitously, unpredictably etc rather than through some plan or arrangement; by accident (qv); as chance will/would have it (qv); as it happens/happened (qv); as (good/ill) luck would have it (qv) **V:** find, discover, notice, sb; come on, come across, meet; happen, come about □ *He sees each star formed from many blobs of relatively high density travelling at random and at supersonic speed through the turbulent cloud, converging* ***by chance****, coalescing and compressing one another.* NS □ *Karma is a theosophical belief that nothing happens* ***by chance*** *but forms part of a continuous chain of cause and effect.* □ *'I didn't try to get off with your girl-friend,' he protested. 'I just ran into her* ***by chance*** *on the way home from the library.'* ⇨ by design; on purpose; ⚠ by any chance.

by common consent [A (PrepP)] as agreed by all concerned; as a result of an unspoken agreement, perhaps following custom □ *Anyone stands a chance of becoming a headman. Appointment is* ***by common consent****, and except by mistake will not be given to a man who seeks government by his own will.* NDN □ ***By common consent*** *the ladies remained in the room after dessert.* EM

by/in comparison (with sb/sth) [Conj (PrepP)] when, if, sb/sth is compared with sb/sth else □ *It seems quite a lot of money to me but* ***in comparison with*** *the sums you handle every day it's nothing.* □ *Hughes was a totally unscrupulous villain.* ***By comparison****, his brother, for all his faults, seemed a positive angel.* □ by comparison often used without with to express contrast, as in last example.

by courtesy of sb [A(PrepP)] (formal) by the kind permission, or favour, of sb or of some group; (fig) by the agency of sb or sth (the implication often being that sth has been given or lent free of charge) □ *No less than eighteen of the pictures currently exhibited at the Gallery are there* ***by courtesy of*** *Lady Mercer.* □ *Liquor was paid for at the bar but coffee and soft drinks were served* ***by courtesy of*** *the management.*

by definition [A (PrepP)] (establish that sb or sth has some characteristic) because it is an essential aspect of sb's or sth's identity, function, name or description □ *For the intellectual is* ***by definition*** *the man for whom, in Goethe's phrase, 'the word is essentially fruitful.'* DOP □ *'I don't look upon myself as an intellectual. I just teach five hours a day and enjoy myself in the evenings like everyone else.' 'But you're a graduate, so you're an intellectual* ***by definition****!'*

by design [A (PrepP)] intentionally; as planned; on purpose (qv) **V:** do sth, happen, meet □ *By some fatality, certainly not* ***by design****, this doctrinaire apron* (ie a poster pinned to her person) *collapsed twice more at the very moment when I happened to be the person nearest to her.* AH □ *Three times Wilson had been on the spot to thwart his plans. Whether or not this was* ***by design****, further interference could not be tolerated.* ⇨ by accident; by chance.

by dint of sth [A (PrepP)] through, as a result of, (doing) sth **o:** expenditure; application, patience, (hard) work □ *Many men and women of mediocre capacity used to manufacture an annual novel.* ***By dint of*** *repetition and with luck, many of them made some kind of name for themselves.* AH □ *The police had now,* ***by dint of*** *persistent enquiry over several weeks, obtained enough evidence to convict.* □ o normally refers to some action which is laborious or tedious.

by fair means or foul [A (adj + adj non-rev)] by any available method, regardless of whether the chosen method is honest or not; by hook or by crook (qv) **V:** get, win, sth; beat, catch, trap, sb □ *A foreign agent forgets about codes of honour;* ***by fair means or foul****, he is expected to bring home the information.* □ *And if you want a salmon, or a couple of rabbits to take home with you, just say so, and I'll get them —* ***by fair means or foul****.* □ (NONCE) *I want that site and I've offered him a reasonable price for it. I've tried* ***fair means****, but I won't hesitate to use* ***foul****.*

by far the best etc/(the) best etc by far [Comp (AdjP)] (the) best etc to, or by, a great degree **V:** ⚠ be, become, seem. **adj:** (the) best, ⚠ better; (the) worst, worse; (the) greatest, greater; (the) smallest, smaller □ *It seemed to me to be* ***by far the best*** *hiding place for a suitcase on the top floor of Coombergana.* RFW □ *Overspending in the fashion shops is* ***by far their biggest*** *temptation.* TO □ *Shanghai's population is* ***greater by far*** *than that of any other Chinese city, outstripping that of Peking by three million.* □ *Of the two poems the young man submitted for the competition, the shorter was* ***by far the better****.*

by the fire(side)/round the fire [A (PrepP)] beside, or near, the fire used for heating a room; (fig) at home; in domestic comfort **V:** fall asleep, relax, sit, stay □ *This was Rosa's father's Sunday afternoon, and he had been spending it as he always did, in his armchair* ***by the fire*** *with the 'News of the World'* (a Sunday newspaper) *on his knee, fast asleep.* HD □ *He was as completely relaxed as the grey tomcat asleep* ***by the fire*** *with its head on my feet.* RATT □ *Let's not go out tonight. What we need is an evening* ***by our*** *own* ***fireside****, just the two of us together.* □ *It was a really nice, relaxing evening — the four of us just sat* ***round the fire*** *and chatted.* □ round the fire used only when a number of people involved as in last example.

by/in fits and starts [A (n + n non-rev)] spasmodically, irregularly, over a period of time, without any discernible pattern of action **V:** do sth; function, progress; study, talk, work □ *The other unsolved problem which I had upon my hands was the problem of Mars* (a dog)*, and about this I worried* ***in fits and starts****.* UTN □

He's been trying to learn Spanish for three years, but I tell him it's no use studying ***by fits and starts***. □ *A few seconds later the monkey's eyes would droop once more, her head would start to nod, until eventually, after many* ***fits and starts*** *and sudden awakenings, her head would sink downwards and rest peacefully on her paws.* DF □ use without by/in, as in last example, unusual.

by guess and by God [A (n + n non-rev)] through no ability, knowledge, planning of one's own **V:** achieve, build, do, sth; find one's way; succeed in doing sth □ *We had no map, and Jamieson had damaged the compass in a fall, but* ***by guess and by God*** *we succeeded in making our way through the mist to a spot not far from our destination.* □ *I think this house was built more* ***by guess and by God*** *than anything else. There's hardly a step on the staircase that's the same height as another.*

by hand [A (PrepP)] by personal messenger, rather than through the official postal service; using one's hands rather than some form of machinery **V:** send, deliver, despatch; make, do, sth □ *If you're sending that account to old Johnson, you'd better get it delivered* ***by hand***. *He's too fond of claiming that our bills get lost in the post!* □ *Jenny's ballroom dress had over a thousand sequins on it, each of them sewn on* ***by hand***. □ *We're trying to preserve the old ways on this farm. We use horses to pull the plough, and milk our cows* ***by hand***. □ letters, packages etc to be delivered personally are marked 'by hand'.

by hook or by crook [A (n + n non-rev)] in whatever way one can; by any available means; by fair means or foul (qv) **V:** get (hold of); seize, grab; succeed, truimph □ *And do not worry, my dear Skip, because I will 'ave* (= have) *that picture* ***by 'ook*** (= hook) ***or by crook***. US □ *As soon as he heard there was to be an evening party for the impresario, he determined that* ***by hook or by crook*** *he would be present too and get himself introduced.*

by the hour [A (PrepP)] for hour after hour; for considerable periods at a time □ *I found myself lying* ***by the hour*** *close to the water, ready to pounce on the new-hooked prizes.* BM □ *Bobby kept all his old comics and sat reading them* ***by the hour***. □ end position.

by intent [A (PrepP)] (informal) quite deliberately, so that one bears full legal or moral blame whether or not one actually succeeds in carrying out one's plan □ *Yes, you stole the rubies—but I decided to steal them from my employers in the first place. I had already broken faith* ***by intent***. ARG □ *I should say that a man who passed secret documents to the enemy, even though they were false papers planted in the hope that he would pass them on, was still guilty of treason* ***by intent***.

by itself/oneself[1] [A (PrepP)] alone; without company; on one's/its own[1] (qv) **V:** be, go; be situated, stand. **adv mod:** all, absolutely, completely □ *'Why have you followed me? I thought I said I wanted to be* ***by myself***,' *she said.* PE □ *'My wife hasn't come back with the car yet, I'm beginning to get worried.' 'Did she go* ***by herself***?' □ *'Which bottle of wine did you ask me to bring?' he shouted from the foot of the stairs. 'The hock—it's standing all* ***by itself*** *at the far end of the shelf.'*

by itself/oneself[2] [A (PrepP)] without help or without anything/anyone else giving support or power; on one's/its own[1] (qv) **V:** work, move; do, lift, make, sth. **adv mod:** all, absolutely, completely □ *My room is in the old part of the house. The door opens* ***by itself*** *if you don't latch it.* PW □ *Baby walked* ***by himself*** *this morning—all the way from that mat to the bookcase.* □ *You're going to do yourself an injury some morning, turning that heavy mattress all* ***by yourself***! *Why can't you ask one of us to give you a hand?* □ *The trouble with these automatic washing machines is that they work happily* ***by themselves*** *for some time but then suddenly break down.*

by and large [Disj] taking everything into account; speaking generally; on the whole (qv): □ *This is quite a full programme, and* ***by and large*** *surely a sensible one; there is no black magic in all this, but simply the application of the usual scientific methods.* SNP □ *He loved me as much as he could love anyone and he was a loving man* ***by and large***. ASA □ *He may have a cousin who teaches, married a girl in Nottingham and settled there. But* ***by and large*** *the family live near and have always lived near; each Christmas Day they all go to tea at Grandma's.* UL □ non-rev; front, middle or end position.

by/in leaps and bounds [A (n + n non-rev)] at a rapid pace towards higher, larger, faster, better levels or standards **S:** inflation, population, prices, scientific knowledge. **V:** advance, get on, improve, increase, progress □ *Publishers are well aware that rumours of possible prosecution of a book on the grounds of obscenity are likely to send the sales up* ***by leaps and bounds***. □ *I thought Johnny was never going to learn to read, but since he got this new teacher he's getting on* ***by leaps and bounds***. □ TONY: *God knows there is material progress. Hundreds of millions of people progressing* ***in leaps and bounds*** *towards a materially-progressive heaven.* EHOW

by the light of sth [A (PrepP)] in, or with the help of, the light shed by sth **V:** dress; read, see; study, work. **o:** the moon, the sun; a candle, a reading lamp □ *Fuseli got the inspiration for some of his best and wildest pictorial ideas by studying the statues on Monte Cavallo* ***by the light of*** *the setting sun.* HAH □ *At night, alone,* ***by the light of*** *his candle, the old man would lovingly count and recount his miser's hoard.* □ *Rolling ho-o-ome, rolling ho-o-ome/* ***By the light of*** *the silvery moon.* STUDENT SONG □ variants by daylight, by moonlight.

by/from the look of sb/sth [A(PrepP)] judging by the appearance of sb/sth, or from the apparent circumstances, surrounding facts, etc **o:** it, things; the weather; his wife □ *'You are a very mystifying young man.' 'Not young. It's you, Professor, who are young* ***by the look of*** *things.'* OMIH □ JO: *Is this the wedding group?* PETER: *My brother's wedding.* JO: *They only just made it,* ***from the look of*** *his wife. You can tell she's going to have a baby.* TOH □ ***By the look of*** *the sky, it's going to rain before the day is over.* □ *David can't be arriving tonight,* ***by the look of*** *it. We'll wait another half hour, and then go to bed.*

by means of sth [A (PrepP)] by using sth or

some method; with the help of sth □ *The general idea is to link up the islands as far as possible with the national road system* ***by means of*** *a short sea crossing.* SC □ *Two similar sets are used simultaneously, and communications between the operators are maintained* ***by means of*** *a built-in telephone.* NS □ *Jackson set out to deceive me and only got my agreement* ***by that means.*** □ variant by this/that means

by mistake [A (PrepP)] unintentionally; as the result of misjudgement, carelessness, mishap etc □ *You can't go on taking tablet after tablet till you've taken twenty,* ***by mistake.*** RFW □ *Who's going to feed you? Certainly not Aunt Annabel. She would be giving you the cat's meat* ***by mistake.*** DC.

by no means [A (PrepP)] (formal) certainly not; in no way; of course not (qv) □ *'Am I right in assuming that you too were at Miss Catterick's flat on the night in question?' '****By no means.****'* □ *It has* ***by no means*** *been proved that 'nuclear deterrence' is anything but a basically aggressive and finally disastrous policy.* □ emphatic; front or middle position; stress pattern by 'no means. ⇨ by all means.

by reason of sth [A(PrepP)] (formal) because of sth; as a result of sth; on the grounds of sth □ *He therefore went up to his study, a room that deserved the name of 'den' more than most,* ***by reason of*** *its hole-like aspect and the remarkable gamey smell coming from the wallpaper.* ILIH □ *Judge Lorne Stewart said that* ***by reason of*** *their refusal to authorise a transfusion the parents were in the legal sense neglecting their child.* OBS

by return (of post) [A (PrepP)] by the first possible postal delivery after the receipt of a letter, mail-order etc **V:** fill (an order); get, receive, send, (an answer); reply, respond, write □ *For a stamped, addressed envelope you could get* ***by return*** *a free sample of custard powder, face powder or flea powder.* PP □ *What cheek! She takes three weeks to acknowledge our invitation and now she wants an answer* ***by return*** *of post!*

by right of sth [A (PrepP)] on the basis of a right or legal entitlement **o:** birth, conquest, inheritance; possession, tenure □ *Warbeck's claims to the English crown* ***by right of*** *birth led to his execution for high treason.* □ *If you and your father before you have pastured cows on this strip of land for fifty years, then I think these two acres are yours* ***by right of*** *tenure.* □ *'It's all right, Bill,' he said jokingly, 'I fancied your wife myself, once upon a time, but she's yours* ***by right of*** *conquest now.'* ⇨ ⚠ next entry.

by rights [A (PrepP)] according to what should be happening (and, by implication, is not); as would be expected by sb who knew all the facts in the case **V:** ought to be, should be (doing sth) □ *Yes, I know I should be in bed* ***by rights.*** *But being in the trade* (ie being a doctor) *myself, I thought I could take a few liberties with ward routine.* DIL □ *...an aged character who should* ***by rights*** *have been dozing out his days in an olde-worlde almshouse.* PP □ *He took all the credit for making a success of the hotel when,* ***by rights****, it should have gone to his wife.* ⇨ ⚠ previous entry.

by the same token [Conj (PrepP)] following logically from the same circumstances, or the same argument □ *No one can deny that France has as much right to have nuclear weapons as Britain. But,* ***by the same token****, every other country can claim the same right.* SC

by the scruff of one's/the neck [A (PrepP)] by the loose skin of an animal's neck; (seize or hold sb) by gripping the back of his neck, coat collar etc **V:** carry, hold, pick up, sb/sth; eject, grab hold, seize □ *The mother bear has to teach him that blueberries are good to eat. She has little difficulty in doing this; she simply picks him up* ***by the scruff of the neck****, carries him to the nearest blueberry bush and dumps him into it.* SNP □ *And, observing substantial slices of potato adhering to the peel in the bucket, he seized Smith* ***by the scruff of the neck*** *and kicked him vaguely into the rigging.* SD □ *A second policeman, approaching from the rear, was able to grasp him* ***by the scruff of the neck*** *and the seat of the trousers.* □ in second sense, always in context of violent or aggressive behaviour.

by the skin of one's teeth [A (PrepP)] narrowly; by a small margin **V:** avoid sth, escape; catch a train; pass an examination □ (source) *And I am escaped* ***with the skin of my teeth.*** JOB XIX 20 □ MYRA: *There.* (laughing) *I've done it. Only* ***by the skin of our teeth.*** EHOW □ *We had a breakdown on the way and expected to miss the last ferry service; but we caught it* ***by the skin of our teeth.*** □ *I made an awful mess of my Maths paper. If I pass, it will only be by the skin of my teeth.* □ with, as in source example, not normally used.

by some fortunate etc chance/coincidence/by what fortunate etc chance/coincidence(?) [A (PrepP)] for some reason which one cannot fully explain **adj:** fortunate, lucky; extraordinary, odd, strange; unfortunate, unhappy □ *It was a man who had been at college with him, a medical student, but* ***by some odd chance*** *Charles had never learnt his name.* HD □ *I should have missed my connection, but* ***by some fortunate chance*** *the train from Crewe was twelve minutes late.* □ *I thought I was locked out, but* ***by some lucky coincidence*** *I'd forgotten to lock the back door that morning.* □ *Why, it's Williams!* ***By what fortunate chance*** *do we have the doubtful honour of your company****?*** □ ***By what unfortunate chance*** *he had contracted typhoid fever, he was never to discover.* □ formal use of relative what in last example; interr use of what in fourth example.

by then [A (PrepP)] at a time in the past or the future (when sth else has happened or will have happened); next entry (qv); by the time[1] (qv) □ *We didn't manage to get to the shops until the second day of the sales.* ***By then****, of course, all the best bargains had been sold.* □ *Phone the family a bit later on. Your father will be home* ***by then*** *and I know he'll want to have a few words with you.*

by this/that time [A (PrepP)] when sth is completed or sb has finished doing sth; next entry (qv); previous entry (qv) □ *I got out my knitting and Jimmy smoked several cigarettes.* ***By this time*** *Sally had stopped crying.* WI □ *I'll run the car down to the garage and fill her up.* ***By that time*** *you'll have read your mail and we can start off.* □ this used with reference to past time, that to past future time.

by the time[1] [A (PrepP)] when some process has been completed, or an event has taken place; previous entry (qv); by then (qv) □ *Her breakfast tray was obviously prepared by Nurse Ellen with great care.* ***By the time*** *it came in Brigit was ready for the comfort of food and hot coffee.* SC □ ***By the time*** *we got to Goldhawk Road it was nearly dark.* UTN □ *Not so long ago it used to be thought that if a person was not a Socialist* ***by the time*** *he was 21, he had no heart.* □ followed by finite clause usu without *that*.

by the time[2] [A (PrepP) as a result of some action or series of events □ ***By the time*** *she'd paid her rent, and her electricity bills she had little left from her pension for food.* □ *Be quiet, you fool!* ***By the time*** *you've finished banging about on the bottom of the boat there won't be a fish left on this side of the bay.* □ followed by finite clause usu without *that*.

by trial and error [A (PrepP)] using a process of adjusting methods, eliminating errors, until the correct answer, method, solution is found **V:** discover, demonstrate, prove □ *Teachers in every field of psycho-physical skill, from seeing to tennis, from tightrope walking to prayer, have discovered,* ***by trial and error****, the conditions of optimum functioning within their special fields.* DOP □ (trying to please a lover) *Then,* ***by trial and error****, she had discovered the personality he liked—or so she thought; but was she really his creation?* PW □ ***Trial and error*** *calculations of this kind are particulary suited to an electronic computer, which can work out the amount of earth-shifting necessary for three miles of road in an hour—a tremendous saving in time and effort.* NSC □ attrib use *a* ***trial and error*** *calculation;* trial and error non-rev.

by turns [A (PrepP)] alternately; turn and turn about □ *It was a grey drizzling September morning, muggy and cold* ***by turns****.* RATT □ *She was laughing and crying* ***by turns*** *for the best part of half an hour.*

by virtue of sth [A (PrepP)] (formal) because of sth; by reason of sth; by the authority or influence conferred by sth □ *Nor does it mean that this very uniqueness of the individual cannot be studied. He is unique* ***by virtue of*** *his social upbringing, his schooling, his sex, his age, his genetic inheritance and so on.* MFF □ *She selected four* (keys) *and putting them in the black suede handbag which, perhaps* ***by virtue of*** *her office, she always carried about the house, descended to Charmian's bedroom.* MM

by the way/by [Disj (PrepP)] incidentally; in passing (qv) □ *'He's absolutely demented about me,' said Susie. '****By the way****,' she said, 'how did you know I wanted a caretaker?'* UTN □ *'****By the way****, I nearly forgot, Lumley,' she said as he held the door open for me to get out of the car, 'my husband wants you to meet the 2.45 at the station.'* HD □ *'I won't be in next Tuesday evening,* ***by the by****,' she added, 'in case you were thinking of calling then.'* □ by the by used less frequently than by the way; introduces a topic not immediately connected with the preceding topic of discussion.

by/from the way (that) [A (PrepP)] judging by, from, the behaviour of sb/sth or some other evidence **V:** conclude, judge; know, realize; see, tell □ *She had a bad conscience, though, I could see* ***from the way*** *she avoided my eye.* UTN □ *The petrol gauge didn't work properly but I thought* ***by the way*** *the indicator was jumping about that the tank was nearly empty.*

by way of sth[1] [A (PrepP)] by a route which includes a specifically named place; (fig) by following some development or process which involves sth named **V:** come, get (there), go, travel □ *But there is good news yet to hear and fine things to be seen,/Before we go to Paradise* ***by way of*** *Kensal Green* (a London suburb). THE ROLLING ENGLISH ROAD (G K CHESTERTON 1874-1936) □ *I can easily come home* ***by way of*** *the Post Office and get your stamps.* □ *Of the writers who matter today, all must go to Wyndham's* ***by way of*** *Wigan Pier* (ie achieve success in the theatre through works of social realism like George Orwell's 'The Road to Wigan Pier'). DPM □ *The opponents of comprehensive education point with some justification to the fact that the high road to success in the sixties was via Oxford and Cambridge* ***by way of*** *a first-rate grammar school.*

by way of sth[2] [A (PrepP)] as a kind of sth; as a particular version of sth; in the way of sb/sth (qv) **o:** apology, greeting, payment; justification, holiday; payment; supporting evidence □ *It looked quite a cosy little domestic picture, but,* ***by way of*** *greeting, he started straight away to grumble about having to have a fire at all.* CON □ *Noel and Colin,* ***by way of*** *a complete change, criticised Mr Justice Stareleigh's ruling in Regina v Stickleback.* WDM □ *But you must have a rest. What are you thinking of doing* ***by way of*** *a holiday this year?*

by word of mouth [A (PrepP)] as a spoken message, esp as contrasted with other means of communication **V:** hear (about sth), learn (about sth), get to know (about sth); pass (from one person to another) □ *The rapid growth of group therapy slimming clubs stems not from massive advertising campaigns, but basically* ***by word of mouth****, from women who have lost weight through attending the classes.* SC □ *I'm so pleased you've been able to come this evening, and I hope you didn't mind getting your invitation* ***by word of mouth****, but I didn't know how to contact you.* □ *Do you mean that it's only a* ***word-of-mouth*** *transaction so far? That there's no written contract?* □ in attrib use, *a* ***word-of-mouth*** *transaction,* by not included.

(in) bygone days/days gone by [A (PrepP)] (in) the past (the reference being to ancient or recent times ot to an earlier period in one's life) □ *A girl could be worked like a slave in these hotels for £15 a year. But these are* ***bygone days*** *and thank God for it.* OBS □ (The Islanders) *regard law and order as their natural enemies. Of course, they used to be pirates* ***in days gone by****.* RM □ ***In days gone by*** *it was usual for the other directors to talk inaudibly at board meetings, thus convincing the chairman that he was going deaf.* PL □ *I would not wish to survive all my friends, and become a recluse living on memories of* ***days gone by****.* RT □ front, middle or end position; stress pattern (in) 'bygone days, (in) ˌdays gone 'by.

C

cakes and ale [n + n non-rev] material comforts, merry-making etc in contrast to a severe or ascetic style of life. □ *Dost thou think, because thou art virtuous, there shall be no more* ***cakes and ale****?* TWELFTH NIGHT II 3 □ *There's no point in arranging a home-coming party for Aunt Elizabeth. She'd be more likely to appreciate a prayer-meeting than* ***cakes and ale****.* □ *Going in for beauty contests at this level is not all* ***cakes and ale****. We've got a lot to think about.* □ often modified by *not all* as in last example.

a calamity Jane (informal) a pessimistic person who is always expecting the worst to happen, exaggerates fears, enjoys telling tales of woe, etc □ *I've not been nearly as ill as my aunt made out. She's* ***a real calamity Jane****; you've only got to catch a bad cold for her to start thinking of coffins.* □ *During a very minor outbreak of typhoid fever in Aberdeen a few years ago, there were quite a few* ***Calamity Janes*** *in other parts of the country who wouldn't accept mail postmarked from there, for fear of infection.* □ usu, but not necessarily, said of a woman.

call sb's bluff [V + O pass] challenge or defy an opponent's supposed power, knowledge etc and thus expose the fact that his claims are a pretence (from the game of poker, where when sb is 'called' he has to show his hand) □ *The colonel's temper was beginning to fray. If only, I thought, he had* ***called our bluff*** *from the start and told us firmly that he knew the figures but wouldn't say.* QA □ *They thought of me as having definitely chosen a life of cosy provincial mediocrity and, outwardly, I had. I should have gone mad if* ***my bluff*** *had been* ***called*** *and I'd been asked to settle into that position for good.* CON □ *Cheek is one of his professions, and here he was exercising it even before opening his mouth. When* ***his bluff*** *was finally* ***called****, he carried off his resignation with dashing style.* ST □ call their bluff when referring to several people.

call it a day (informal) decide or agree to stop (doing sth), either temporarily or for good □ *We'll have one more* (drink) *and* ***call it a day****. Then I'll wander back and see how they've balled up that new front page.* PP □ *'I'm engaged to Susan,' I said. 'I'm going to work for her father. But that isn't the reason we've got to* ***call it a day****. It's impossible for us to love each other in Warley.'* RATT □ *'Tell them we've* ***called it a day****,' said Luke with fatigue. 'They can see the fireworks about tea time tomorrow.'* NM

call it etc what/which you will etc [V + O + Comp] (you can) accept a name or description already given, or choose another of your own **O:** it, her, him, them. **V:** will, ⚠ like, choose □ *Objectivity, impartiality, neutrality,* ***call it what you will****, may have been justified when you thought you were dealing with rival religious factional trouble.* RT □ *'A hurricane, a typhoon—a storm' (he was describing a violent wind), '****call it what you will****,' he barked.* L □ *He'd known a fellow who had got half a dozen of the lads together ('****call 'em what you like****—thieves?') and sent them out to strip tiles from houses that had just been bombed.* L □ *That was obviously the bit of cant or idealism in Rhodes,* ***call it which you will****, that we all need to make us tick.* HAA □ in parenthesis to main construction, usu middle or end position.

call sb names [V + O + Comp pass] taunt and jeer at sb □ *'Is it true, what Billy says, that you punched his nose so hard that it bled?' 'Yes, sir. But he was* ***calling*** *me* ***names****.'* □ *We had the most ridiculous school uniform you ever saw. No wonder the kids in the street used to* ***call names at*** *us* (or: ***call*** *us* ***names***). □ *Let the record show that Archbishop Salvidge, Unionist boss in Liverpool, implored Conservative Central Office: 'It is not sufficient to* ***call*** *socialists* ***names****; send us arguments.'* NS □ *To the other village girls Mother (as a girl) was something of a case, yet they were curiously drawn towards her. One gathered that there were also quarrels at times, jealousies,* ***name-calling****, and tears.* CWR □ usu said by children quarrelling with each other or being impudent to their elders, and not likely to be used by adults except in deliberate imitation of childish usage; n compound name-calling; variant call names at sb.

the call of nature[1] the urge to go and live in undeveloped, sparsely inhabited regions; the call of the wild etc (qv) □ *There was no time of year I didn't hate having to live and work in Birmingham, but it was in the spring that I felt* ***the call of nature*** *most strongly and began, like the citizens in Hardy's poem, to 'dream of the south and west'.*

the call of nature[2] the natural desires, instincts etc, of the human race or of animals □ *You must expect George to start being interested in girls at his age. It's* ***the call of nature****.* □ *We don't know how the mature salmon, after years spent in the ocean, find their way to the river spawning-beds where they were hatched, but* ***some call of nature*** *brings them back there.*

the call of nature[3] the need to pass water or empty the bowels □ *'What's the bus sitting here all this time for?' 'Don't ask me. I thought when the driver left, it was just to answer* ***the call of nature****, but he's been gone a very long time.'* □ euphemism.

the call of the wild etc the compulsion to go and live in, work in, explore, regions that are undeveloped, sparsely inhabited, unspoilt etc; the call of nature[1] (qv) **o:** the wild, ⚠ the hills, the West, the prairie □ *Several times my father made an attempt to settle down, but* ***the call of the wild*** *would prove too strong and off he would go again.* □ *Who were these noble pioneers who opened up the first overland routes from the east to California? An adventurer who heard* ***the call of the west*** *in 1846 wrote: 'Among them are some of the vilest outcasts in the country.'* SC □ cf *the wilds* (= a wild or secluded place) as in *a lonely hut in* ***the wilds*** *of Alaska*, or *come back from* ***the wilds*** *to civilization.*

call the shots [V + O pass] (informal) have

control of a situation; decide, determine, what others do □ *The British Prime Minister said the British Government had full confidence in the Canadian Government's decisions. Which surprised* me, *Marc thought. I was the one who said the British would never stand by and let Trudeau* ***call the shots***. ST

call a spade a spade [V + O + Comp] call sth by its own name and not by a euphemism; describe sth straightforwardly as being what it is, even if this should give offence □ *There is, of course, a '****calling a spade a spade****' arrogance which makes a few working-class people overdo the rougher elements in their speech when with others from a different class.* UL □ *He believes in* ***calling a spade a spade*** *and if he wants to empty his bladder he doesn't ask where he can wash his hands.* □ *I wouldn't live anywhere except London. But I like the Scots. They* ***call a spade a spade****, they say what they mean and they have a sense of humour.* SC

(a/one's) callow youth a young person/ young people in general, with inexperience, immaturity; this stage in life □ *'These are not the opinions you used to express twenty years ago.' 'I should hope not. I believed a lot of things in* ***my callow youth*** *that I don't believe now.'* □ *I was sorry for Henry,* ***a callow youth*** *from the provinces. I found him rather boring, but there was more to him than my colleagues would allow.* □ youth an uncountable n in first example.

the calm before the storm a period of unnatural or false calm immediately preceding a storm; an expected outburst of violent activity, passion, disorder etc □ *There is less activity in the kitchen now,* ***the calm before the storm****. A few waitresses wander around, a porter sweeps the floor.* TK □ *The ominous stillness which my father preserved throughout the whole of my halting explanation was only too clearly* ***the calm before the storm***. □ (NONCE) *Every time the pain receded he hoped it was going for good, but each recession proved to be no more than* ***a calm before another storm***.

the camera cannot lie (saying) a photograph gives a true record of events □ ***The camera cannot lie*** *perhaps, but photographic experts can do almost anything now by fading out some parts and superimposing others.* □ *Who says* ***the camera can't lie****? You look as if you could be your own grandmother in this photo.*

can/could always do sth[1] be able to do sth whenever one wishes, or as soon as required □ *Fortunately, I* ***can always*** *fall asleep as soon as I go to bed.* □ *His French was not perfect but he* ***could always*** *make himself understood.* □ sometimes said sceptically or humorously.

can/could always do sth[2] have the chance or possibility of doing sth, usu as an alternative to sth else or as a last resort □ *Short of going down to the village for a quick one at the wine-shop, there was nothing to do until lunch-time. Of course, he* ***could always*** *have a nice read.* ILIH □ *Debbie's friend has backed out of their holiday arrangements. She* ***could always*** *go by herself I daresay, but I don't think she'll want to do that.* □ *This looks like the kind of shop that might sell camping gas. I* ***can always*** *ask, anyway.*

can breathe (easily/freely) again (informal) feel one's usual self again, relax, when a period of crisis, tension, or special effort, has ended □ *'Good news,' she said. 'Dad'll be out of hospital in a couple of days. And now that we* ***can*** *all* ***breathe again****, what about a cup of tea?'* □ *We're right in the middle of the Bed and Breakfast Season, she wrote, but once August is past and we****'re able to breathe easily again****, we'll drive over some Sunday to see you.* □ *He heard the security guard's footsteps receding and* ***breathed freely again***. □ positive use only; usu with *can/could/be able to*, but occas in simple past tense.

can(not) call one's soul etc one's own (not) be free from, have to suffer, continual interference with one's privacy or independence **modal:** can(not), could (not), (not) be able to. **O:** soul; ⚠ house, time □ *'And how Cousin Emily would have begun arranging everything and not let Mr Adams* ***call his soul his own****,' said Lady Pomfret.* WDM □ *'No mother ever gets on with her son after he is twenty,' she said. 'Not if he has an ounce of spirit and* ***calls his soul his own****.'* □ *I might have more success out of doors than in, and now that I have* ***a*** *small* ***patch*** *of earth I* ***can call my own****, I'm ready for instruction.* RT □ *'Living right on the campus,' explained the professor, 'I* ***could never call my time my own****. That's why I've moved out here.'* □ pl *They* ***couldn't call their souls their own****;* usu neg with modal.

(no) can do (dated slang) one can('t) do it; it will be (im)possible for one to arrange □ *'I'd like to book a table for six this evening, about 7.30.' '****Can do****. What name, please?'* □ *'Will you dine with me?' 'Sorry,' answered Terence, 'as your dear Elizabeth would say, "****No can do****".'* HAA

can/could do no wrong be in such a privileged position, be so much favoured by sb, that anything one does is thought to be right **A:** in his wife's eyes; as far as his followers are concerned □ (source) That the King ***can do no wrong****, is a necessary and fundamental principle of the English constitution.* SIR W BLACKSTONE 1723-80 □ *The hero's progress as a concert pianist is dizzy, impeded only by a penchant for causing grievous bodily harm to policeman; for Ruth, he* ***can do no wrong***. OBS □ *'That's news to me. I thought Chris* ***could do no wrong*** *in your eyes?' 'I've been having second thoughts about him.'* □ *My mother's so pleased I'm back home again, and bringing wages into the house and all that, believe me, I* ***can do nothing wrong***. □ variant can do nothing wrong.

can do worse than be quite correct or sensible in acting in a particular way; can't/ couldn't do better than (qv) **modal:** can, could; might. **adv mod:** a lot, a great deal, much. **cl:** settle here, marry my niece, model yourself on him □ *During that long grieving week-end* (after the assassination of President Kennedy) *many of them expressed their anguish in ways they would try to forget. But politicians* ***can do worse than*** *display their emotions in public.* ST □ *But an English tourist* ***could do worse than*** *plan his tour among Shakespeare's Italian towns. He won't regret it.* OBS □ *'It's not a bad buy, is it?' 'Well, you've got the cash to spare and you* ***might do*** *a lot* ***worse****.'*

can a duck swim? (informal) yes (said in answer to a question which the speaker thinks is foolish or unnecessary because, from his point of view, it allows only the answer 'yes') □ *'Can I fill your glass again?' '**Can a duck swim?**'* □ *'I didn't know one could do that with flats,' said Lydia, rather impressed. 'Didn't the landlord object?' '**Can a duck swim?**' said Aubrey. 'Gold, my girl, gold did it.'* WDM □ *I had already trudged five miles of dreary moorland road when a lorry-driver pulled up and asked if I wanted a lift. '**Can a duck swim?**' I thought to myself.* □ emphatic.

can/could hardly be described as cannot/could not be said to be or do sth □ *Since it* (the Commonwealth) *is not an organisation with any set and specific purpose, and **can** indeed **hardly be described as** an organisation at all, there is a temptation to conclude that it does not amount to much.* SC □ *The job **could hardly be described as** offering much opportunity for promotion.* □ *He **could hardly be described as** young. He's forty if he's a day.* □ a form of understatement; active construction in *You **could hardly** have **described** our home **as** a haven of peace*; one can hardly call sb beautiful etc/a child etc used actively or passively, as in *You **could hardly call** Peggy **beautiful** and yet she seems to be the centre of attraction everywhere she goes.*

can have sth for the asking [V + O pass] can have sth/be available free on request, or if wished for, or very easily **O:** it, money, help, admittance, fame, love □ *Why was Pepys never knighted? At any time between 1684 and 1688, at least, Pepys **could** surely have **had** it **for the asking**.* NS □ *Squares of material from old sample books, which **can be had for the asking** from most large drapery stores, can be joined together to make attractive cushion-covers or even bed-spreads.* □ *Virginia was full of a limitless ambition, which arose from her vitality and her youthful belief that the world **was hers for the asking**.* AITC □ variant be sb's for the asking. ⇨ ⚠ next entry.

can have sth for the catching etc [V + O pass] can catch etc sth/be available to be caught etc **O:** fish, berries, profits, opportunities. **O** catching, picking, grabbing, having, taking (away) □ *As long as there **is** fish **for the catching** there will be fishermen's families in these islands.* □ *I'm getting rid of this old table. If any of you want it you **can have** it **for the taking away**.* □ *So now I'll go call the Answering Service and get reassurance that I'm not forgotten by the rich and famous, that there **are** still contracts in the offing, royalties **for the gathering**, people **for the snubbing**, invitations **for the turning down**.* JFTR □ variant be (sb's) for the catching etc. ⇨ ⚠ previous entry.

can/could ill etc afford to do sth not be justified, because of one's own behaviour or shortcomings, in doing sth; be in no position to do sth **adv mod:** ill, ⚠ hardly, scarcely. **Inf:** to criticize, to complain, to say anything □ *He had been guilty of some pretty shady transactions himself and **could ill afford to** criticize others for doing the same sort of thing.* □ *'Janet should have let you know if she was going to be late for lunch.' 'Maybe so, but you **can hardly afford to** speak. You wander in for meals any old time you like.'*

can etc take a joke [V + O] accept with good humour being the object of teasing, facetious remarks, playful or disconcerting tricks, etc **V:** can('t) could(n't), (not) be able to; (must/should/ought to/will) learn to □ *He danced and rode well, and was courteous to ladies; he **could take a joke** and make one.* NS □ *Young Womersley in the costing department has written a humorous ditty about the sales director to the tune of 'I Who Have Nothing', and believes—quite erroneously—that the sales director **can take a joke**.* TVT.

can/could well believe it think sth is very likely to be true; be prepared to believe sth even without actual proof □ *They had always gone through a street where, so it was said (and she **could well believe it**), a famous mass murderer had done his stuff.* TGLY □ *'Do you know that Margaret hasn't once driven over to see her father since he's been ill?' 'I **can well believe it**. She always was a heartless girl.'* □ stress pattern can ˌwell beˈlieve it; pron it usu refers to sth already mentioned.

can you beat it! (informal) exclamation of consternation, or shocked amusement, about sth that has occurred, or that sb has done □ *Well, **can you beat it**! Here's George Wrangle writing to say he's coming up for Easter with his wife, all five of their kids, his Aunt Dorothy, and their Alsatian dog Rasputin.* □ *When I answered the advertisement I found they wanted me to do all the housework and pay for my keep as well. **Beat that if you can!*** □ stress pattern ˌcan you ˈbeat it!; variant beat ˈthat if you can!

can you imagine! (informal) an exclamation expressing one's own, or inviting another's, astonishment; would you believe it? (qv) □ *Then I went to Portugal. My sister was living there and she wanted me to come. I was able to fix up some lectures down there. Portugal! **Can you imagine!** I was delighted.* OBS □ *My uncle says he is going to put a bathroom into the cottage himself. **Can you imagine!** He doesn't know the first thing about plumbing.* □ may express either shocked or pleasurable surprise; stress pattern ˌcan you ˈimagine!

can't/couldn't do better than be entirely correct, sensible, well-advised in acting in a particular way **cl:** read it yourself, consult your teacher, invest your money in property □ *For this part of the story I **can't do better than** read from my notes of the case.* DS □ *If you are really interested in finding out more about our local antiquities you **couldn't do better than** have a chat with the Vicar.*

can't/couldn't do sth for the life of one etc (informal) be wholly, totally, unable or unwilling to do sth **V:** imagine, think, understand, comprehend sth. **A:** for the life of one, ⚠ for one's life, to save one's life □ *'There are certain aspects other than material that have to be borne in mind.' Pop said that he **couldn't** think **for the life of him** what they were.* DBM □ *She lived by the easy laws of the hedgerow, loved the world, and made no plans, had a quick holy eye for natural wonders and **couldn't** have kept a neat house **for her life**.* CWR □ *Mozart really* did *compose masterpieces at a sitting. When the fit was on him he quite literally **could not** have refrained from composing even **to save his life**.* ST □ *The Italians have provided most of the cinematic humour to* *leak out of the Second World War, though* ***for the life of me*** *I* ***can't*** *recall that they or we had much to laugh at.* RT □ for the life of one used in front, middle or end position.

can't do sth for love (n)or money (informal) be completely without the ability or means to do sth; be quite unwilling to do sth **modal:** can't, couldn't; won't, wouldn't □ *The speech therapy has helped Anne a lot. A few weeks ago she* ***couldn't*** *have sounded an 's'* ***for love nor money.*** □ *There is such a glut of strawberries this week that growers* ***can't*** *get rid of them* ***for love or money.*** □ *I* ***couldn't*** *spend a night in that house alone,* ***not for love or money.*** □ *There was a time when* ***no*** *American* ***would*** *have chosen London as a place to live.* ***Not for love or money****, or free hamburgers.* TVT.

can't/couldn't do sth for toffee (informal) lack the natural or practical ability needed to do sth □ *Carlo's my brother, the little one, he* ***can't*** *sing* ***for toffee****, though he's the dead spit of me, only not so gay.* US □ *You think I despise these young fellows because I'm jealous. But it isn't that at all. I* ***can't*** *write* ***for toffee.*** HAA

can't/couldn't do sth often etc enough do sth eagerly, lavishly or insatiably **V:** thank sb, apologize; go there, get away; spend, try, sth. **A:** often, ⚠ fast, soon, hard □ *He used to make excuses not to visit there but now he* ***can't*** *go* ***often enough****. I wonder what the attraction is?* □ *The children had never seen anything like the bluebell wood before. They* ***couldn't*** *pick the flowers* ***fast enough.***

can't/couldn't go wrong (informal) be sure to make a success of sth, or not make any mistakes, not become confused, etc in doing sth □ MRS ELLIOTT: *Well, he didn't really have much chance to get on. But you will, George, I'm sure. With all your talent, you just* ***can't go wrong.*** EGD □ (advertisement) *You* ***cannot go wrong*** *with COLOR-GLO, because your own hair colouring controls and safeguards the final effect.* H □ *You* ***can't go wrong*** *if you're advised by me. Auntie Alice is always right.* RATT □ *I took the files away and I settled down to work. It was good solid reading and I* ***couldn't go wrong.*** *The first two articles wrote themselves.* PP □ in first example you can't go wrong is addressed to a particular person, in second it is a general statement.

can't hear oneself think (informal) one is subjected to, irritated or distracted by, too much surrounding noise, esp loud talk, music, or general uproar **modal:** can't, couldn't; can hardly; not be able to □ MRS ELLIOTT (she crosses to lounge and opens door) : *Do put that telly down a bit, there's good children. We* ***can't hear ourselves think*** *in here.* EGD □ *Everybody kept talking louder and louder till you* ***couldn't hear yourself think.*** □ *He was singing 'Onward Christian Soldiers'. 'Are you having a prayer meeting?' Brown asked. 'I* ***can hardly hear myself speak.'*** □ RATT □ variant can't hear oneself speak.

can't help oneself be unable to control, or avoid, behaving in an undesirable or unsuitable way **modal:** can't, couldn't; not be able to □ CISSIE: *Has your father still got that job?* RONNIE: *No, he's a store-keeper in a sweet factory now. Look.* (Shows her a biscuit tin full of sweets.) *Jelly babies.* ***Can't help himself.*** *Doesn't do it on a large scale, mind, just a handful each night.* CSWB □ *It is natural, but mistaken, for an alcoholic's relatives to feel that he* ***could help himself*** *if he tried.* □ *It's no use my promising not to cry when you go. I might* ***n't be able to help myself.*** ⇨ ⚠ help oneself[1].

can't help doing sth find it natural to do sth; find it unavoidable to do sth **modal:** can't, couldn't, not be able to □ *I put my arm round her waist—when anyone looks woebegone I* ***cannot help*** *trying to cheer them up.* SPL □ *Yet she* ***could not help*** *sometimes asking herself: How with all this deceit can I possibly be happy?* PW □ *Given all the changes that are going to come, and the fraying away of exclusively Commonwealth trade links, I* ***can't help*** *wondering where that will leave the Commonwealth.* L

can't/couldn't help it/that[1] be unable to avoid (doing) sth; be unable to control or change events etc □ *I'm sorry to be sniffling like this, but I've got such a cold I* ***can't help it.*** □ *It's a sordid dump of a place. I'm sure nobody would live there if they* ***could help it.*** □ *Yes, she is a stupid girl—she* ***can't help that****, I suppose, but what infuriates me is the way she's always so damned pleased with herself.* □ cf stress patterns she can't 'help it, she can't help 'that.

can't/couldn't help it/that[2] one is not to be blamed, or held responsible, for sth □ *They can't sue me for damages. There's a warning notice about electric fences at the farm gate.* ***Can*** *I* ***help it*** *if trespassers won't look where they're going?* □ *'You can't go out now, Kate! We've come all the way from Leeds, just to see you!' 'I* ***can't help that****, I'm still going to the theatre.'* □ often said in unfriendly or aggressive way.

can't/couldn't say be unsure about, or not know, either the answer to a question or about sth specified or understood **A:** for sure, for certain, at present □ *'Do you think that a European Security Conference would be a waste of time at the moment?' 'That one* ***can't say.'*** L □ *'When did you go to this cupboard last?' he asked. 'I really* ***couldn't say*** *for sure, Mr Rogers.'* EM □ *'Did you ask how long the repairs would take?' 'Yes, but the foreman wasn't there, and the mechanic* ***couldn't say.'***

can't/couldn't stand/bear the sight of sb/sth[1] not like, or be seriously upset (physically or emotionally) by, the actual sight of sb/sth **o:** blood, tears; him being made a fool of, dirt all over the place □ *She had always wanted to be a doctor. 'Ever since I was eight. I went to school here and did my O-levels and A-levels. But I* ***can't stand the sight of*** *blood.'* ST □ *Dad often works from the top ladder himself but he* ***can't bear the sight of*** *other people doing it.* □ *I* ***can stand the sight*** *of blood all right. What gives me the horrors is having to de-louse a patient.* □ usu neg or neg implication; front position if contradicting an assumption, as in last example.

can't/couldn't stand/bear the sight of sb/sth[2] find objectionable or intolerable, dislike very much; hate/loathe the sight of sb/sth (qv) □ PETER: *And don't bring that little fruitcake parcel* (description of an acquaintance) *either! I* ***can't stand the sight of*** *him.* TOH □ *Oysters? I* ***can't bear the sight of*** *them.*

the candid camera a concealed camera to take an unposed photograph or make an undirected film, esp of people who do not know their actions are being recorded □ *Most practical jokes are, for everyone except their perpetrator, tedious and boring and often, like '**Candid Camera**' (a TV series) embarrassing to the onlooker.* SC □ *At the Gate* (cinema) *incidentally, there is a terribly **candid-camera** record of an 81-year-old American writer. It is called 'Henry Miller Asleep and Awake'.* NS □ *My real objection to flag days is a disapproval of licensed begging, of extortion by **candid camera** methods, everyone watching to see whether you buy a flag or try to escape.* OBS □ attrib use *a **candid-camera** shot, picture.*

canvass the idea etc (that) [V + O pass] introduce or suggest an idea etc for discussion and/or acceptance **O:** idea, ⚠ theory, notion, possibility □ ***The idea that** the Blue Nile might be blocked or poisoned at its source in Ethiopia as a means of destroying Egypt had been **canvassed** in every age.* BN □ *It may be thought unlikely that he has been dead for years though **this theory** on his absence has been actively **canvassed**.* OBS □ ***The idea**, **canvassed** in a famous 'Times' leader in 1968, **that** a large part of the observed inequality of wealth is due to the age structure of the population is a long way off the mark.* NS □ *But **the possibility that** these children might have suffered quite the same fate, regardless of their upbringing, is never even **canvassed**.* SNP □ often pass; idea etc usu sing, esp when followed by that.

cap in hand [A (NP)] (formerly) holding one's cap instead of wearing it, as a sign of respect from sb in the lower classes when speaking to, or being addressed by, a social superior, employer etc; (fig) subserviently, with humility, as sb begging for favours, etc **V:** go, present oneself; ask, beg, for sth □ *The taxi-driver, **cap in hand**, withdrew, and Alec who, as usual, was bareheaded, asked if he might take off his overcoat.* PW □ *All pensions should be at or above subsistence level. Retired workers should not have to go **cap in hand** to ask for supplementary allowances.*

a capital offence etc an offence etc legally punishable by death **n:** offence; ⚠ murder, treason; charge, punishment □ *Nine out of the 13 executed came within the category of **capital murder** because their crime was committed 'in the course or furtherance of theft.'* OBS □ *Sheep-stealing was still **a capital offence** in early 18th century England, although the penalty began to be less often enforced.*

a captain of industry a prominent leader of an industrial or commercial firm □ *He was Ned Roper, **captain of industry**, off to London to grace with his presence a party given by his old friend, Mr Robert Lamb, the well-known artist.* CON □ also pl; often used facetiously.

a captive audience an audience with little or no freedom to stay or go away; people or groups who cannot choose whom or what they listen to or watch □ *'Isn't the publication of a book a way of trying to manipulate your readers?' 'They don't have to buy or read my books. But students are to some extent **a captive audience**.'* OBS □ (NONCE) *He went to a show featuring Blackstone, a famous magician. This, decided Bradbury, was the life for him, and with the aid of a paper moustache he performed shaky tricks in front of **an audience** of **captive** relatives.* OBS □ occas pl.

a captive market a group of consumers with little or no choice where or from whom they buy goods □ *Nearly all the newly emerged countries are starting their own industrialisation programmes. So we have to start again, and make our goods dominant, and we won't get them out there any more on the basis of any form of **captive market**.* L □ occas pl.

a card-carrying member etc a fully affiliated and accredited member of an organization (esp of the Communist Party, to which the term was originally confined); a committed supporter of, or believer in, a particular principle or practice **n:** member, ⚠ communist; membership □ *Green had just become **a card-carrying Communist** when I first met him in '48, must have been attached to the Party for some years previously.* □ *Or take that daft Children's Charter of the National Council of Civil Liberties (and I speak with sadness as **a card-carrying member**). Children have a right to be free of religious or political indoctrination, it says. Meaning what?* OBS □ *The Communist Party, the second largest in Italy after the Christian Democrats, picks up nearly nine million votes, despite the fact that **card-carrying membership** is only a million and a half, and declining.* L □ also pl. ⇨ ⚠ a fellow traveller.

a cardinal error etc a fundamental or basic error, sin etc, which is likely to be accompanied, or followed, by other errors, sins etc **n:** error, ⚠ sin; virtue, grace □ *'My late husband,' said Miss Hopgood's Aunt, 'always said committees were **a cardinal error**. Why* cardinal, *I do not know, but those were his words.'* WDM □ *It's **the cardinal sin**, I think, to let life bore you.* HAA □ *Austria for their part, made **the cardinal mistake** of dropping Schmied and restoring the famous Walter Zemnan—a goal-keeper previously omitted precisely because he had lost form.* ST □ *Mediaeval philisophers named justice, prudence, temperance, and fortitude as the Four **Cardinal Virtues** of natural man, as distinguished from faith, hope, and charity, the theological virtues.*

(not) care/give a damn etc (informal) not care at all about, be completely unaffected by (sb/sth) (often with the implication that one might or should care); couldn't care less (qv) **O:** a damn; ⚠ a tinker's curse/cuss; two hoots; twopence/tuppence; a fig, a rap. **A:** for anyone; about anything; what they think, who gets it, whether they do or not □ *You don't care, that's all. You do**n't care a damn** how it hurts James and Nicholas.* HAA □ *The government we had in those days, when we were the world's richest country, did**n't give a damn** whether the kids grew up with rickets or not.* CON □ *I do**n't give a tinker's curse** who rules any one of these places so long as every man there is given parity of social, economic and cultural opportunity to be himself.* L □ *The truth of the matter is that I could **never** really have **cared twopence** about who won the Tory Party leadership.* NS □ *Why should playwrights **give a fig** for what 'the public' or Mr Monahan or anyone else, including myself, wants?*

RT □ *Vanity made you set out after the King, when you did**n't care a fig** for him.* WI

care killed the cat (saying) used in exhortations to people to cheer up, take a lighter view of life, etc □ (source) *What though **care killed a cat**, thou hast mettle enough in thee to kill care.* MUCH ADO ABOUT NOTHING V 1 □ *Never mind what you ought to be doing—the work will get done sometime. Relax, enjoy yourself! It was **care killed the cat**, remember?* □ MRS STONE (suddenly sings): *You die if you worry, you die if you don't, so why worry at all? It's only **worry that killed the cat**, anybody can tell you that.* HSG

care of used in postal directions to a person not permanently living at, or working at, the address given □ *I completed the letter to Sadie's solicitor, and asked him to send the typescript to me **care of** Mrs Tinckham.* UTN □ *You should try writing to him **care of** the BBC. They'll probably send the letter on to him.* □ written abbreviation is c/o.

a caretaker government etc a government or administration which has actually been replaced but which continues to function until its successor is properly organized; an interim administration asked to function temporarily during a change-over **n:** government ⚠ administration; arrangement; president □ *The sudden resignation of Signor Tromboni's Government confirms the profound crisis in Italian politics — even granting that Signor Tromboni was selected for the purpose of forming **a Government** of the **caretaker** sort.*

the carrot and the stick [n + n rev] (offer) as the hope of reward and the threat of punishment a means of making sb try harder □ *Elaine* (a young swimmer) *has to be coaxed. She benefits from **the carrot-and-stick** approach — I say, right, give me a couple of top swims and you can go home early. So she thinks she's getting out of work when she's actually putting more into it.* RT □ *'We emphasise to the men that their conduct might secure a place at a government training centre.' He laughed, a trifle nervous. 'That's **our** only **carrot**.'* NS □ either part of expression may be used alone, as in last example.

carry the can [V + O] (informal) (be manoeuvred or forced to) accept the blame or responsibility (for sth specified or understood); have all the work and worry of sth fall upon oneself (instead of upon another person or group) □ *Mr Waller (replying to the Attorney-General in the Vassall inquiry) said, 'I know there was a feeling in the Foreign Office that the Foreign Office were **carrying the can** in this particular case.'* SC □ *Samantha Ryder-Rose is on the* (contraceptive) *pill, and scatty about a gorgeous man at the office who's had three wives. Needless to say, mummy and daddy hover in the background to **carry the can** should the pill go down the wrong way.* L

carry conviction [V + O] be convincing; seem true or authentic **S:** speaker; account, argument, lie. **det:** some, more, less. **adj:** total, absolute □ *Mr Jack Jones is fond of fulminating against the supposed iniquities of the Industrial Relations Act, but he would **carry** more **conviction** if he showed that he was capable of looking after his own cabbage patch.* OBS □ *The grace, humanity and plausibility which he manages to inject into a dubious argument make his essays an unfailing delight to read even when, on occasion, they fail to **carry** complete **conviction**.* L □ *Don't get so fiery. Truths don't have to be shouted at people in order to **carry conviction**.* □ often neg or neg implication; det and adj not used together.

carry/win the day [V + O] be victorious (on the day of battle); (fig) win; overcome the opposition of others □ *...left me free to give my personal views on a wide range of subjects, often to the extreme annoyance of my two colleagues in London, especially when they found that my personal views, with which they mostly disagreed, often **carried the day** in the end.* MFM □ (on nuclear disarmament) *...with some hope that it will command a majority, and perhaps do something to reconcile the multilateralists with the unilateralists who **won the day** this year.* T □ *I must be one of the people that the proposed new compulsory seat-belt law is meant to bring into line. Although I do occasionally 'belt up'—say on a motorway — sloth has usually until now **won the day**.* NS

carry/hold one's liquor [V + O] (informal) be able to drink alcohol without becoming drunk, or much affected, physically or mentally □ *He's the most delightful old rogue, and the quickest and surest way to his heart is to prove to him that you can **carry your liquor**.* BB □ *Now that grandpa's getting older he can't **hold his liquor** as he used to, so tell the boys not to keep filling his glass.* □ *She took drink for drink with the rest of them and **carried her liquor** like a sailor.* □ often with *can/can't*.

carry one's point [V + O pass] succeed in persuading others involved to agree with what one says about sth, or suggests should be done, etc □ *Having **carried his point** about not overloading the boat, he got them to settle among themselves what should be left behind.* □ *Look, Margaret, we've all agreed now that it's hopeless to think of going away next week-end. You've **carried your point**, and there's no need to be thinking up fresh arguments every half hour.*

carry sb shoulder high [V + O + A pass] carry sb supported on one's arms and shoulders as a sign of acclaim, enthusiastic approval **S:** admirers, followers, team-mates. **A:** through the crowd; from the field □ *In Leningrad, the scene of his previous triumph and defeat, Lerica was met by an enthusiastic crowd flying red banners which **carried** him **shoulder high**.* ST □ *Such a view was clearly not shared by the dockers, who greeted the release of their colleagues from Pentonville as a triumphant victory, and **carried** them through the streets **shoulder high**.* L

carry sth too far [V + O + A pass] preach and/or act beyond a reasonable or suitable limit; go too etc far (qv) **adv mod:** too, ⚠ rather; a bit, a shade, a trifle □ *One of the attractions of the school is a '6.45 a.m. dip in the Irish Sea every morning'—a prospect which many serving officers may think is **carrying** image-making a shade **too far**.* T □ *It's very rude to reject well-meant offers of help. You can **carry** independence **too far**.* □ *Come on, Bob, give me a serious* answer. You've ***carried** this teasing **far enough**.* □ *I don't believe in repressing children myself but* *it's **carrying** things **a bit far** to let them rule their parents.* ▫ *Change was all very well but it could be **carried too far**.* TSMP

carry weight [V + O] be important, influential, convincing, effective etc **S:** director, secretary; statement, argument; factor, influence. **adj:** no, a lot of, some; more, less; a good deal of ▫ *If such representations are to **carry weight** they will have to avoid bias and be of a high intellectual standard.* SC ▫ *She disapproved — disapproved violently — of what the reviewer had said: it was pernicious rubbish, she knew, and could **carry** no **weight** with any thinking person.* PW ▫ *But what you do won't **carry** anything like the same **weight**. On the Peace Committee, for example, an ex-professor's not much, but a Professor's just what we need.* HAA ▫ *Legal penalties and moral obligations will inevitably **carry** less **weight** than fear of reprisals by violent criminals and their associates among whom they must live when the case is over.* ST ▫ *The old girl didn't seem very worn out by the climb; she was like a tough, stringy old chicken. I was blowing a bit, but of course even in those days I was **carrying** too much **weight**.* CON ▫ in horse-racing, the better horses are handicapped by the addition of weights to their saddle, so that all begin with a more or less equal chance of winning—last example reflects this.

case the joint [V + O pass] (slang) inspect premises as carefully as possible, esp with a view to burglary; take a good look at a restaurant, hotel etc, on some pretext or other before deciding to eat or stay ▫ *...care, of the sort with which a burglar studies a house. I think it is called '**casing the joint**'.* ▫ *There was a disco going on in the village hall and Gus went in to **case the joint** for us. He came out shaking his head. 'No bar, and the music's lousy.'* ▫ (a shop-lifter) *...inspecting the store layout, the alertness of the assistants, the absorption of the other customers. I was '**casing the joint**' in cold blood, relating to people not as human beings but as obstacles to be surmounted, problems to be solved.* SC

cash and carry [n + n non-rev] a trading concern (esp a wholesale business supplying retailers) supplying for 'cash down' (qv) goods which must be taken away by the purchasers (because of the saving on accounting and delivery costs, such a concern offers goods at cheaper rates) ▫ *Robbs' have been supplying animal feeding-stuff to the whole county for three generations, but since even the small farmers have their own transport now they run their business on a **cash-and-carry** basis.* ▫ *'You'd find it much cheaper to buy a small van and stock your shop from the **Cash and Carry**.' 'But then I'd have to employ somebody to mind the shop while I was away, and to help me with the loading and unloading.'* ▫ attrib use *a **cash-and-carry** store, business.*

cash down [A] payment of money for goods or services, at time of purchase; (less often) of a gift or loan given ▫ *You won't get a better used car for the price anywhere, the salesman assured him, 'and don't forget you get 5 per cent discount for **cash down**.'* ▫ *Our hypocrisy had gained us nothing—not even a reliable ally, while theirs had procured arms, supplies, even **cash down**.* QA

cast one's net wide etc [V + O + A pass] cover a wide field of supply, activity, inquiry etc; make sure that no source of obtaining what one wants is overlooked **A:** wide, ⚠ widely, farther ▫ *It's about time you started **casting your net** out a bit **wider** isn't it? Most people are thinking seriously about husbands at your age.* HH ▫ *'This is a tentative list of contributors for the "History",' he said. 'I wrote to them last night when I got back to London.' 'You've **cast your net wide**,' she said.* ASA ▫ *The antique dealers are **casting their nets farther and farther**. The shepherd's wife up the glen was telling me she was offered £50 for a pair of china figures she had on her mantelpiece.* ▫ *'Bishop's Move' is the sort of middle-brow story that used to be the staple of magazines like 'The Strand'. It's an example too of how **widely** the editors have **cast their net**.* SC ⇨ ⚠ spread one's net.

a casual remark sth said by way of conversation; a passing comment not meant to be the basis of an argument, discussion, or inquiry ▫ *He was as deliberate in his speech as he was in his work, weighing his words momentously, even if they were only going to add up to **a casual remark**.* AITC ▫ *Your uncle is a touchy* (= ready to take offence) *old devil, isn't he? He has just interpreted **a casual remark** of mine, that it was nice walking weather, to mean I was wanting him out of my way.* ▫ also pl.

a cat may look at a king (saying) there is no reason why a superior should be protected from certain kinds of behaviour from, or contact with, inferiors ▫ *As the personalizing technique* (eg in the popular press) *becomes yearly more machine-tooled, we sink further into a dream of an intimate world in which not only **may a cat look at a king** but a king is really a cat underneath, and all the great power-figures are Honest Joes at heart.* UL ▫ *'Take your drinks into the public bar, if you don't mind, gents,' the landlord said. 'I'm sure these ladies could do with a little privacy.' 'So what? **A cat may look at a king**, you know.'* ▫ sometimes said to justify rather insolent behaviour.'

the cat's got sb's tongue (informal) said to or about sb, esp a shy child, who does not answer when spoken to, or is silent when he should say something ▫ *'What is your dolly's name?' the visitor asked, trying another question. '**The cat's got her tongue**, I think,' the mother replied for her.* ▫ *'I wanted a ride on the pony too.' 'Well, **had the cat got your tongue**? Why didn't you say so when it was being offered?'* ▫ also interr as in second example. ⇨ ⚠ lose/find one's tongue.

(have/lead) a cat-and-dog life (lead) a life of frequent or constant quarrelling **S:** man and wife, brother and sister; partners, colleagues ▫ *You miss a woman when she's been living with you in the same house for six years, no matter what sort of **cat-and-dog life** you **led** together* LLDR ▫ *You're lucky to have children that play so nicely together. My two **fight like cat and dog** all the time.* ▫ *Mike and Pete got on well enough with the rest of the crew but **fought like cat and dog** with each other on every issue of the day.* ▫ variant fight like cat and dog.

(play) a cat-and-mouse game (keep

another person in) a state of suspense and uncertainty, treating him cruelly and kindly by turns □ *'Look!' he said suddenly as if he'd decided to cut short* ***the cat-and-mouse game****. 'From tomorrow morning — in fact from an hour ago—I'm Managing Director and Editor-in-Chief of this outfit.'* PP □ *Why didn't the train drivers have the confidence or, to be blunt, the courage to call a strike, like the miners? Instead they* ***play a*** *tiresome and irresponsible* ***cat-and-mouse game*** *which both harasses their travelling fellow-workers and drives more and more commuters on to the already chaotic roads.* NS □ *'Accidental Death' — an Edgar Wallace mystery about a man whose past catches up with him, triggering off* ***a*** *deadly* ***game of cat and mouse****.* TVT □ variant a game of cat and mouse.

catch sb's attention [V + O pass] make sb take notice of sb/sth (often, but not necessarily, with the further implication of arousing sb's interest) □ *He was idly turning over the pages of a magazine when an article by a former colleague* ***caught his attention****.* □ *The first requisite for an advertisement is that it should* ***catch*** *people****'s attention****.*

catch one's breath [V + O] break the rhythm of one's breathing by an involuntary gasp or sharp intake of breath, expressing shock, surprise, pain etc; cause one to gasp, cough, choke etc □ *He* ***caught his breath*** *for a second and felt a slight pain round the heart as he heard Eric's voice.* HAA □ *He had seen her dance before, and been exhilarated by her skill, but he had never seen her dance like this. Behind him, Norreys* ***caught his breath****, but the King heard nothing.* WI □ (NONCE) (a child playing with water) *You could put your head in it, and open your eyes, and see the sides of the bucket buckle, and hear* ***your caught breath*** *roar.* CWR □ *Helen was so beautiful that it quite made you* ***catch your breath****.* TVT □ *The cold* ***catches your breath*** *as soon as you put your nose out of the door.* □ *The neat whisky* ***caught his breath*** *and some seconds went by before he was able to reply.*

catch (a) cold [V + O] become ill with a cold in the head, usu brought on by exposure to cold, wet, or infection □ *'Go back to bed, Prissie,' said Fergus with a note of protectiveness in his voice. 'You'll* ***catch cold****.'* DC □ *But she wore flimsy shoes in all that snow! No wonder she wrote to us once that she had* ***caught an*** *awful* ***cold*** *and been under the care of two doctors.* WI □ *In fact, several other controlled trials that were just as thorough and that have greater statistical significance and greater relevance to the problem of* ***catching cold*** *have been carried out.* L □ catch a cold usu used of specific instance of such an illness, and catch cold of the exposure, infection etc which leads to it, but countable and uncountable uses of n often interchanged.

catch one's death (of cold) [V+O] become seriously ill, starting with a cold in the head; catch a severe cold □ CLIVE: *He's sitting down under the apple tree.* LOUISE: *Sitting? In this weather! Without an overcoat? He'll* ***catch his death****. Tell him to come in at once.* FFE □ DAVIES: *I could* ***catch my death of cold****, with that draught. Just shut that window and no one's going to catch any colds.* TC □ SEGAL: *What on earth are you doing? Sam, get back into bed at once, do you want to* ***catch your death of cold****?* HSG □ *She* (blew) *her nose extremely hard. This stentorian call startled Pop into saying: 'You sound as if you've* ***caught your death****.'* BFA □ often used, with *will, shall,* to predict that sb will catch a cold or to warn him against catching one.

catch sb's eye[1] [V + O pass] look at sb with the special intention of making him look at, or take notice of, one in return; exchange a glance of amusement, sympathy, shared knowledge, etc with sb □ *Have a double* (whisky). *Then you don't have to* ***catch*** *the waiter****'s eye*** *twice.* RATT □ *He said, 'This is my first and it looked at one time as though it was going to be my last public appearance.' He* ***caught*** *Carter****'s eye****. Carter was frowning.* OMIH □ *'I think perhaps one oughtn't to,' said Hugo, and he was deadly serious. Then I* ***caught his eye*** *and we both laughed enormously.* UTN.

catch sb's eye[2] [V + O pass] happen to be observed by sb; be noticeable by one's/its very nature □ *As I turned, something* ***caught my eye*** *in the wall behind the bookcase.* UTN □ *To the villages around, it was a patch of bare skyline, a baldness among the woods, a wind-scarred platform which* ***caught*** *everybody****'s eye****, and was therefore just the place for a gibbet.* CWR □ *'There's only one thing that can put you at the top,' he* (a newspaper reporter) *said, 'and that's a real out-and-out scoop. Something that really* ***catches*** *the public****'s eye****.'* HD □ *Lilian turned out to be a pretty blonde, a little past her prime but, in her* ***eye-catching*** *silk dress, still very attractive.* □ adj compound eye-catching.

catch etc sb's fancy [V + O pass] (informal) strike sb as pleasing, desirable (to observe, do, know more of, have, use etc) **V:** catch, ⚠ take, tickle □ *'I can always tell the married men.' Pause, while he looked round. 'They have that* tamed *look!' I can only repeat that the remark had* ***caught my fancy****. It did not* ***catch*** *Myrtle****'s****.* SPL □ *The only thing in the auction sale that* ***caught my fancy*** *was a little French clock.* □ *Victoria took a bath and attended to her face and hair with the meticulous care of a young women who is shortly to be reunited to a young man who has* ***taken her fancy****.* TCB □ (video tape recorders) *For £1,000 anyone can own the equipment, take it where they want to and say with it whatever* ***takes their fancy****.* L □ *The* (marriage) *alliance of the 'Democrat' Roosevelts with their far grander 'Republican' collaterals was bound to* ***tickle*** *the public****'s fancy****.* NS

catch fire ignite; start to burn; (fig) (suddenly) become interested or interesting, lively, enthusiastic **S:** wood, paper; idea, project; broadcast, discussion □ *We collected sticks to boil our kettle, but they were damp and would not* ***catch fire****.* □ *She was standing far too near the open hearth and her nightdress* ***caught fire****.* □ *If the Liberals want the country to* ***catch fire*** *for them they must take up its hopes and grievances and dress them in the force and conviction they deserve.* G □ *After a polite parade of statistics and points of view the programme '****caught fire****' when it developed into an impassioned debate between personalities.* RT

catch etc sb's imagination [V + O pass] rouse the interest, engage the thoughts and feelings of esp of a specified group or kind **V:** catch, ⚠ capture, seize, grip, fire □ *As a design for the world of tomorrow socialism has* ***caught the imagination of*** *the young, although it is, in my view, the wrong answer to the right problem.* L □ *The period 1919-21 saw a phenomenal rise in trade union membership; the Bolshevik Revolution in Russia had* ***seized the imagination of*** *millions of working people, and fierce industrial battles flared as post-war boom lurched back into slump.* OBS □ (Gordon Banks) *And no goalie in modern times has* ***captured the imagination of*** *kids more.* TVT □ *Helen Cresswell wrote 'Lizzie Dripping', the children's series about a day-dreaming girl that* ***caught the imagination of*** *many a young viewer.* RT □ *Europeanism has failed to* ***catch*** *the Conservative* ***imagination*** *because Mr Heath is not, despite all that has been written about him, a particularly imaginative European.* NS

catch it (informal) get a scolding; be punished; get it (in the neck/where the chicken gets the chopper) (qv) □ *She spied, she pried, she crouched, she crept, she pounced—she was a terror. Each morning was a war without declaration; no one knew who would* ***catch it*** *next.* CWR □ *Look at your shirt—all torn! You'll* ***catch it*** *from your mum, when she sees it!* □ used mainly with reference to minor misdemeanours at school or home, and in forms with *catch* rather than *caught* as in *I didn't half* ***catch it*** *from my wife last night for being so late.*

catch sb napping [V + O + Comp pass] (informal) find sb out in error; gain an advantage over sb, because he has not been alert to the possibility of this happening □ *Stevenson would have loved to find any excuse to get me fired, but I was wise to him and wasn't going to be* ***caught napping.*** □ *'You* ***caught*** *me* ***napping*** *that time,' he said, surveying the chessboard. 'You've got me into a hopeless position now. The game's as good as over.'*

catch a packet [V + O] (informal) get into real trouble; suffer severe injury or misfortune; receive a severe reprimand □ *'Somebody's* ***catching a packet,'*** *Poll said and Mr Charlton caught a glimpse of two bare-shouldered girls fighting each other like wild white cats.* DBM □ *'Some fools have taken their boat out,' he said, lowering his binoculars. 'They'll* ***catch a packet*** *if they try to go round the point.'* □ *He* ***caught a packet*** *from me when he* did *turn up. He'll think twice about staying out all night again, without a word of warning.* □ (demolition) *It's a dirty old job, I've had my share of nails through my feet from old beams, and a few smashed fingers. But I've never* ***caught a packet,*** *touch wood.* ST

catch sb red-handed [V + O + Comp pass] discover, capture sb, while he is doing something wrong or committing a crime (originally, from a murderer caught with blood still on his hands); catch in the act (Vol 1) (qv) □ *Virginia* ***caught*** *Helen* ***red-handed,*** *shut the door and leaned against it. 'Reading my letters again, Helen?'* AITC □ *An atmospheric pressure cabinet may cause some burglars to be* ***caught red-handed,*** *for it is connected with the police through a central station, and the burglar unwittingly 'contacts police' when he tampers with the safe.* SC □ *Over there* (the USA) *it is vital not to be* ***caught red-handed*** *lying to the people or their representatives, because Establishment excuses about the public interest do not get a sympathetic hearing.* NS

catch/take sb unawares [V + O + Comp pass] surprise and disconcert sb **S:** question, cry, shot; appearance, arrival; decision □ *I wanted to wait until I could present my story in a more dramatic way; when* ***caught unawares*** *I usually tell the truth, and what's duller than that?* UTN □ *'Good-bye, Jim.' 'Good-bye, Doctor.' The use of his first name* ***took*** *Wormold* ***unawares.*** OMIH □ *For once, Martin was* ***taken unawares.*** *He was disconcerted to see me. 'Are you all right?' he asked.* NM □ *Top soloists can be capricious and eccentric in the extreme. A conductor has to be very much on his toes if he is not to be* ***caught unawares*** *by an unscheduled speed change.* RT

catch/get a whiff of sth [V + O] feel, briefly, a smell of sth; (fig) sense sth in a social or emotional atmosphere **o:** smoke, scent; intrigue, hostility, unpleasantness □ *At seven, I made the mistake of picking her up out of her cot. She* ***caught a whiff of*** *my special party perfume, felt a strange silken-clad body against her.* WI □ *The interview went better than I thought it would. Sometimes I thought I* ***caught a whiff of*** *hostility in his answers but he behaved very reasonably on the whole.*

(play) catch-as-catch-can [V + O] (get) what one can how and when one can (the implication often being a disregard for moral or ethical rules of behaviour; originally a form of wrestling in which 'no holds are barred') □ *He found he had no need to* ***play catch-as-catch-can*** *for air. He blew deeply and regularly into the tube until the lifebelt rose and strained at his clothing.* PM □ *I whiled away the minutes watching three strong men plying their charms around a young bright blonde, her arms fully occupied with drink and defence. I sat engrossed by this* ***catch-as-catch-can*** *until the peace of my evening was suddenly shattered.* PP □ *He complained that I was taking away his customers. It's time he woke up to the fact that it's a case of* ***catch-as-catch-can*** *in this trade.* □ stress pattern ˌcatch-as-ˌcatch-ˈcan.

cause and effect [n + n non-rev] the action or circumstance producing change, and the change itself which results necessarily from it □ *Events moving from another direction also instituted a chain of* ***causes and effects.*** PE □ (The Metropolitan Police Commissioner said) *'During my service, I have seen penal sanctions become less and less punitive, and at the same time have witnessed the gradual growth of violent crime in London.' But this simple* ***cause-and-effect*** *sequence is not a sufficient answer to the problem of rising crime.* SC □ attrib use *a* ***cause-and-effect*** *sequence.*

cause a ripple (on the surface) [V + O pass] have a noticeable effect; alter; disturb **S:** event, change, crisis; remark, insult. **A:** hardly, scarcely; not □ *The cut* ***caused*** *hardly* ***a ripple*** *in the foreign exchange market, where it had long been discounted.* T □ *Not one of his insulting remarks* ***caused*** *even* ***a ripple on the surface*** *of her composure.* □ *The lead character combines second-rateness with an abrasive wit and candour that*

causes *a few* ***ripples*** *of outrage amongst the theatre's more staid patrons.* G □ *...an affair which normally might scarcely* ***cause a ripple*** *but which is a further potential embarrassment to an Australian Government facing an imminent General Election.* L □ usu neg or neg implication.

cause etc a stir [V + O pass] (informal) cause lively interest, discussion, controversy among a group, profession, or the general public **S:** (sudden) entry, appearance; action, decision. **V:** cause, ⚠ create, make. **adj:** considerable, tremendous; something of a; no end of a □ *The hypothesis that recent ancestors of* Homo sapiens *were forced to live as amphibious animals has* ***created a stir*** *among scientists and laymen.* NS □ *One evening she was able to announce, 'I am going to be married.' The news, understandably,* ***caused*** *no small* ***stir****.* □ *Researching the circumstances of the crime for an article, he found that people remembered 'it* ***made*** *quite* ***a stir*** *at the time' and little else that he had not got from old newspaper files.* RT □ *Such revelations of corruption in high places were bound to* ***cause a*** *considerable* ***stir****.*

the centre of attraction [Comp (NP)] a place where, or a person to whom, people are drawn (to the comparative neglect of other places available, or of other people in a company) **S:** ⚠ be, become; make sth □ *Joe was in his element,* ***the centre of attraction****, congratulations, and crude masculine jokes.* AITC □ *Celia pleaded a headache and left the party early. The truth was that she is so used to being* ***the centre of attraction*** *wherever she goes that she could not bear to be outshone.*

the centre of things [o (NP)] the place where interesting and important activities are going on **V:** be, live, work, operate. **prep:** at, in, near □ *My half-conscious thought had been, 'It's fat white grubs like him that crawl about at* ***the*** *so-called "****centre of things****" — and you're no more real than he is.'* CON □ *We've put a day-bed for father in the lounge. He likes to be in* ***the centre of things*** *and the doctor says it will be better for him, too.* □ *It is one of those books written by a journalists which gives a first impression of the author being present at all the world's trouble-spots at just the right moment. It conveys, possibly a little misleadingly, the sense of being close to* ***the centre of things****.* SC

a chain is (only) as strong as its weakest link (saying) each person or feature in an enterprise or process must be equally reliable and efficient; a project or process may fail because of a single weakness or fault □ ***A chain is only as strong as its weakest link****, and so we're putting the whole point of the trip at risk if we bring the children along.* □ *On his showing at Wembley last Saturday Smithson would seem to be* ***the weak link in the chain****, and may well lose the British relay-team the Gold Medal they covet.* □ (NONCE) *Written journalism is a fundamentally lonely profession followed by gregarious people. Television is done in a crowd* ***whose strength is its weakest member****.* L □ variant the weak(est) link in the chain.

a chance acquaintance/companion a person met quite by chance □ *The boy had been climbing on the rocks with a couple of* ***chance companions****, young holiday-makers like himself, when the accident occurred.* □ *I don't know what made me start confiding in him. He was* ***a chance acquaintance****, after all, someone I'd met on a train journey.*

chance one's arm/luck [V + O] take the risk of receiving a rebuff, being found out to be wrong, suffering a loss or defeat, etc in the hope of gaining sth □ *'I don't know the answer,' he said to the quiz master, 'but I'll* ***chance my arm*** *and make a guess.'* □ *He considered the pros and cons of making the investment for a full week and then decided to* ***chance his arm*** *and hope to get a return for his capital.* □ *He risked saying, when this* (singing) *had gone on some time, 'You're a little ray of sunshine these days,' but that made her huffy so he didn't* ***chance his luck****.* TSMP □ pl in *would they* ***chance their arm****?*

a chance encounter/meeting a meeting that has not been arranged or foreseen □ *A film began, quite wildly at first. It showed a bicyclist, some woodland scenery, a punctured tyre,* ***a chance encounter****, a gentleman raising a straw hat.* OMIH □ *It was during* ***a chance meeting*** *with Jeffries at a concert that I first heard of his interest in the research project.* □ also pl; chance (='happening by chance') occurs in other, less common, collocations, such as *They usually cost upwards of £20, this was* ***a chance bargain****.*

chance would be a fine thing (informal) it would be very pleasant, gratifying to get an opportunity to do, experience sth specified, but one is very unlikely to be so lucky (the implication occasionally being that what one wants may be foolish or unsuitable, although enjoyable) □ *'Why don't you apply for that management job—you'd be very good at it.' '****Chance would be a fine thing****. Everyone knows that it's been promised to Maxwell in the Finance Department.'* □ *'Enjoy yourself, Anne, but no unsuitable holiday romances with a passionate, dark-haired stranger!' '****Chance would be a fine thing****! My mother and aunt are coming with me. I won't even manage a quick visit to a disco.'*

(the) chances are (that) it is as likely to happen, or to have happened, as not (that) □ *I'm not going to let you go off on that long drive as you are, with all that drink in you.* ***The chances are*** *you'd fall asleep at the wheel.* PE □ *I think we may assume that he has good reason for revenge.* ***The chances are that*** *he was engaged in some sort of underground during the war.* ARG □ *Virginia sighed. 'I wish I knew what he looked like.' '****Chances are*** *you never will,' the nurse said, going to the door.* AITC □ stress pattern (the) ˌchances ˈare.

one's/the chances are slim there is a possibility that sth could happen or be done, but it is not very likely **V:** be, look, appear, seem □ *Senator Humphrey collected enough votes in Wisconsin to indicate that he need not yet retire from the race, even if* ***his chances are*** *very* ***slim****.* SC □ ***The chances*** *of my marrying again* ***look*** *rather* ***slim****.* TVT □ *Even if President Ford had chosen Senator Baker to run with him,* ***the chances*** *of the Republicans capturing the South would have* ***been slim****. With Mr Dole* ***the chances are*** *much* ***slimmer****.* G

change/turn one's coat [V + O] transfer one's loyalty, services etc from one country, political party, religious sect, etc to another (always said with the implication (sometimes untrue) that the person concerned has done this, not because his beliefs or principles have altered, but because he finds it expedient or profitable to do so) □ *Accusation and counteraccusation have been laid on pretty thick. So-and-so used to be a communist, so-and-so wants to abolish religious teaching altogether, X has* ***turned his coat*** *and Y is suborning his employees.* NS □ *'The Vicar of Bray' is a well-known English song about an 18th century Anglican clergyman who managed to stay the priest in the same parish for many years by* ***changing his coat*** *with every swing of political or religious opinion.* □ n compound a turncoat.

change colour [V + O] blush, flush, or grow pale; (esp neg) show (no) emotion in one's face whether accompanied by growing red/pale or not □ *If this young man means nothing to her, as she claims, why did she* ***change colour*** *at the mention of his name?* □ *I saw him suddenly* ***change colour****, but before I could reach him he had slipped off his chair on to the floor in a faint.* □ *There was a great scene in the movie where the kid goes to a bar and gets drunk with Mary Maxwell, and as he gets drunker she starts* ***changing colour****.* RT

change course [V + O] take a different direction from that in which one has been moving till now **S:** dog, fox; ship; industry, management □ *The fox suddenly* ***changed course*** *through the culvert and up into the spinney, and left the panting hounds snuffling about the banks of the lane.* □ *It's a a winding river that* ***changes course*** *twenty times in as many miles.* □ *The Belgians are* ***changing course*** *smartly leftwards under the banner of workers' control.* NS □ *The view that criticism of South African racial policies should be soft-pedalled could only be justified if there were the slightest chance of* ***a*** *spontaneous* ***change of course****.* SC □ *The river had* ***changed its course*** (ie made a new bed for itself). □ *This information made me* ***change my course*** (ie adopt a different plan of action altogether). □ sometimes interchangeable with change one's/its course as in fifth and sixth examples; variant a change of course.

change and decay [n + n non-rev] the action of natural or historical processes on oneself, one's surroundings □ (source) *Swift to its close ebbs out life's little day;/Earth's joys grow dim, its glories pass away;/* ***Change and decay*** *in all around I see;/O Thou, who changest not, abide with me.* ENGLISH HYMNAL 363 □ *Autumn, the season of* ***change and decay****...* □ *All around were* ***change, decay****, and new life. It was the fictionist rather than the poet in me who took a keen interest in the social revolution going on all round me.* AH □ *'The Vanishing Hedgerows' (BBC 2) was a different kind of country matter:* ***change and decay*** *in all around he sees—he being Henry Williamson who for many years has farmed as well as written.* OBS

change the face of sth [V + O pass] make sth very, or unrecognizably, different **o:** the world, Britain; child education, surgical practice □ *The distinct hope of direct talks between President Nixon and Chou En-Lai before the end of 1971 represented one of the most momentous diplomatic coups of this and many a year. The Pope thought that it might '****change the face of*** *the world'.* L □ *They worked under good leadership, and they* ***changed the face of*** *Britain's cattle—a review of the foreign blood now being introduced to improve our beef herds, by Graham Rose.* ST □ variant the changing/changed face of sth.

a change for the better/worse [Comp/O (NP)] an improvement (or the reverse) of sth already existing or that has gone before **V:** be, seem; show, indicate □ *Each innovation is assumed to be better than its predecessors, simply because it comes after them: any change is* ***a change for the better*** *so long as it is in chronological succession.* UL □ *Within an hour of receiving the injection the patient's condition had* ***changed for the better****.* □ *The provision of an hourly bus service to and from our village has been* ***a change for the worse*** *as far as I am concerned. People now go into town to shop, and I have lost a lot of trade.* □ variant change (v) for the better/worse.

change gear [V + O] (informal) alter, adjust, one's approach to sb/sth, or one's way of dealing with sb/sth, as appears suitable or necessary (from the operation of a geared vehicle) □ *'Who are you?' they asked in French. 'Ah, English,' they murmured, and* ***changed gear*** *into broken English.* BM □ *Teaching so many different age-groups in the course of a day, it often took me quite a few minutes to* ***change gear*** *when a fresh lot came in.* □ *The new patient was a noisy sleeper with a wide repertoire. Any pause in his reverberating snores only indicated that he was* ***changing gear*** *into whines, grunts, or even whistles.*

change hands [V + O] pass from one owner to another **S:** money, jewels; collection, property □ *The hotel has* ***changed hands****, I believe, since I stayed there. It may be better managed now.* □ *The book had long been out of print but I managed to obtain a somewhat tattered copy that looked as if it had* ***changed hands*** *many times.* □ *'How did he get past the gate-keeper without credentials?' 'I expect it would be a matter of money* ***changing hands****.'* □ *All over the world a great demand for diamonds and other precious stones has arisen. They* ***change hands*** *a dozen or more times until finally they disappear and cannot be traced.* TCB

change/swap horses (in mid-stream) [V + O pass] transfer (unexpectedly or awkwardly) one's preference for, or trust in, one person or thing to another; change the policy etc through which sth is to be achieved before the task is completed □ (source) *I am reminded in this connection* (his renomination for the Presidency of the US) *of a story of an old Dutch farmer, who remarked to a companion once that it was not best to* ***swap horses when crossing a stream****.* ABRAHAM LINCOLN 1809-65 □ *When the 'New Mathematics' syllabus was adopted most schools introduced it at the lower end of the curriculum only, and pupils who had completed two or more years' instruction under the old system were not required to* ***change horses in mid-stream****.* □ *As an ex-Communist seeking affiliation with the Scottish National Party, the election caught him just as he was* ***swapping horses****.* SC □ *Your style* *skids from cliché to cliché. Apron strings are outgrown, age-old rivals contend, and* ***horses*** *are* ***changed in midstream****.* NS

a change is as good as a rest (saying) a change of work or occupation can be just as restorative, refreshing etc as resting □ *So we'll all forget work for a few hours and enjoy ourselves. What about it?* ***A change is as good as a rest****. A few drinks?* DPM □ *'I'm sure you didn't come here for the week-end just to work in my garden.' 'Oh, but I enjoy it! And* ***a change is as good as a rest****, you know.'* □ *She insisted that she was feeling well enough to go to the party, though I don't think her doctor would have agreed that* ***a change was as good as a rest*** *in her case.*

a change of face/front [O (NP)] a change in one's attitude or behaviour towards sb/sth; a genuine change to a different viewpoint or objective; a change of tactics without a change of objective **V:** make, execute; order. **det:** a, the; this; one's □ *The fact of the matter was that the Government, to meet a crisis in its own ranks, made* ***a*** *sudden* ***change of face****.* MFM □ *'I'm very much concerned about Mother's being left alone here.' 'Oh! Alan, really!' cried Mrs Craddock. Alan looked bewildered at* ***her change of front****.* HAA □ *He* (Mr Wilson) *was right to realize that, whatever the Prime Minister's aims were in 1967 the Leader of the Opposition in 1971 cannot support entry* (to the European Common Market) *on Mr Heath's terms. The ways, however, in which he has chosen to make* ***this change of front*** *and then to justify it have been devious and divisive.* NS □ a change of front originally a military term.

a change of heart [O (NP)] a real change in the feelings of a person, group, or nation, esp one which leads to understanding, co-operation and friendliness where there has formerly been indifference or enmity **V:** notice; signal; cause, produce □ *There is danger of being so pre-occupied with defence that we would miss or discourage* ***a*** *Soviet* ***change of heart*** *that would possibly lead to a settlement.* OBS □ *At the moment, he's pretending to be blissfully unaware of* ***any*** *approaching* ***change of*** *mind or* ***heart****. 'Rumours,' he says, and smiles his angelic smile.* L □ *Industry's part has been to act more responsibly. The changing economic climate as well as public concern have influenced* ***this change of heart****.* G

the change of life that period in a woman's life when menstruation (gradually) ceases and she becomes no longer capable of childbearing □ TONY: *What's the matter?* MYRA: *Giddy. No, leave me alone.* TONY: *You're not still having* ***the change of life*** *are you?* EHOW □ *The somewhat vague symptoms of her disease were erroneously attributed to '****the change****', a mistake which many doctors of that time were all too apt to make.* □ *Men too go through* ***a*** *less definable* ***change of life****, characterized physically by a redistribution of body weight or hormone imbalance, and psychologically by feelings of inadequacy and lost youth.* □ sometimes called simply the change; popularly, and sometimes in fact, asssociated with varying degrees of physical or emotional upset.

change the record [V + O] (informal) used in protests against hearing the same request, remark, complaint etc too often (record = disc for a record-player) □ *'When I was a boy I didn't do this, I didn't have that!'—I wish Grandpa would* ***change the record*** *occasionally.* □ *'****Change the record****, will you?' shouted Anne from the kitchen. 'Do you realize you've been whistling the same tune over and over, all the time you've been fixing that window?'*

change one's spots [V + O] (try to) be or do sth that is against one's nature □ (source) *Can the Ethiopian* ***change*** *his skin, or the leopard* ***his spots****? Then may ye also do good, that are accustomed to do evil.* JEREMIAH XIII 23 □ *Nothing has been said or done since last June to convince the voter that Labour in opposition has* ***changed its spots****.* NS □ *I had classed Jean Pierre once and for all. That he should secretly have been* ***changing his spots****, secretly improving his style, ennobling his thought, purifying his emotions: all this was really too bad.* UTN □ *The leopard has not really* ***changed its spots****. For all the populist rhetoric, National Front propaganda prefers the real red meat of racialism.* NS

change the subject [V + O pass] start a different topic in the course of a conversation or discussion (perhaps because it is embarrassing, distressing, boring etc) □ *When she wanted to talk about her work, he would* ***change the subject****, or at best listen condescendingly, as if she were a child telling of school excitements.* AITC □ *I* ***changed the subject*** *and leading on from our previous talk I asked him what sort of people the smugglers had been.* DS □ JO: *What day was I born on?* HELEN: *I don't know.* JO: *How old was I when your husband threw you out?* HELEN: ***Change the subject****.* TOH

change one's tune [V + O] (informal) (be influenced by events or circumstances to) alter one's opinion or attitude; think or speak about sb/sth in a way pretty much the opposite of how one formerly did; sing a different song/tune (qv) **S:** politician, businessman, union leader; rival, competitor □ *When I was in Germany I saw what the Russians were really like. I was a bit of a Communist before the war, but I soon* ***changed my tune****.* RATT □ *In June, Ismail said to Cailliand that Bruce was a liar: the climate of Senner was very bearable. In July when the rains came, he* ***changed his tune****.* BN □ *These evening lectures at the works have been a great success, despite all the jeremiads I was treated to when I started them. Even some of my dear brother directors have* ***changed their tune****, and the union bosses are quite enthusiastic now.* ASA

change one's ways [V + O] lead one's life differently; form habits suited to a new pattern of life or work □ *I'm not against modern methods of teaching at all. It's just that I'm too old to* ***change my ways****.* □ *She has her own idea of how a house should be run and you'd never get her to* ***change her ways****.* □ *I think we'll manage to live comfortably enough on my pension. We'll have to* ***change our ways*** *a bit though, and live more simply.* □ often neg or with the suggestion that change is difficult.

a chapter of accidents a number of successive accidents, mishaps, occurring to one person or group or connected with a particular place or activity □ *Andy bundled out into the* *corridor and nearly knocked over a man just passing. 'Oh, I'm sorry, I'm having quite* ***a*** *little* ***chapter of accidents****.'* TT □ *'What* ***a chapter of accidents****,' said Anne's mother when the girl had finished explaining how she had come to arrive six hours late.* □ *We've had a proper* ***chapter of accidents*** *this morning,' the school Matron told the headmistress. 'I've just about emptied the First Aid box.'* □ not used of really serious accidents or misfortunes, or ones involving serious injury.

chapter and verse [O (NP)] (give) the exact source of a text from the Bible, or of any other quotation; (provide) substantiating or authoritative detail **V:** quote, give; want, expect □ *I haven't got one of those memories that can quote* ***chapter and verse****, but I think I can give you the gist of the passage that you're asking about.* □ *'You weren't the first young man she's slept with. She's notorious for it—' And, he, pressing his advantage home, went on to give* ***chapter and verse****.* RATT □ (of a man hanged for a murder of which he may have been innocent) *The answer in Hanratty's case is a sadly familiar one to lawyers who practise in the criminal courts. He could not give* ***chapter and verse*** *for his truthful Rhyl alibi, so he tried to concoct himself one in Liverpool.* L □ non-rev.

charity begins at home (saying) one's first care must be for one's family; one cannot care for others and neglect one's family □ ***Charity*** *and beating* ***begins at home****.* WIT WITHOUT MONEY (J FLETCHER 1579-1625) □ *To say, in politics, that* ***charity begins at home*** *is often a polite way of saying that the voter is a selfish brute who doesn't give twopence for the under-developed nations.* NS □ *Before you busy yourself with telling us how to put the rest of the world right, just remember that* ***charity begins at home*** *and get on with the job of putting Britain right.* RT

chatter like a magpie talk rapidly and excitedly, esp about nothing very important □ *And as they* (school children) *started to get everything ready,* ***chattering like*** *a lot of* ***magpies****, she turned back to Miss Elliot.* TT □ *I was looking forward to exchanging news with Morton after all these years, but I could hardly get a word in, because of* ***his chattering magpie*** *of a wife.* □ *The crowd* ***chattered like monkeys*** *the whole time, especially when they recognised personages whose faces they knew from newspapers and news films.* AH □ often said of individuals who do this habitually; when attention is directed to the behaviour of a group of people, chatter like monkeys/sparrows also used; variant a chattering magpie.

cheap at the price [Comp (AdjP)] so well worth having, or so much desired, that the price (not necessarily in money), however high, does not seem too much **S:** place; settlement, agreement; house, business. **V** ⚠ be, seem, find sth □ *He was buying time. He needed time. He wanted to stay in this country. Maybe he thought he'd be the Big White Chief within ten years. Maybe he thought it was* ***cheap at the price****.* PP □ *'And I had to lend Colin £5. I don't suppose I'll ever see it again.' 'Well, if he keeps out of your way for a while because he can't pay you back, it'll be* ***cheap at the price****.'* □ *In the end he was driven to confess and face a prison sentence, feeling that to clear his conscience would be* ***cheap at any price****.* □ almost always after *be* and with reference to sth already stated or understood.

cheek by jowl (with sb/sth) [A] close together, esp side by side **V:** stand, sit, lie, live □ *The other two took no notice of him at all, though they were standing* ***cheek-by-jowl****.* RATT □ *'The Womenfolk' was a programme from Scotland about a group of trawlermen's women in Aberdeen. Once they would have all lived* ***cheek by jowl*** *in the villages of Fittee or Torry.* L □ *Her locker was always untidy. A hair-comb would be lying* ***cheek by jowl with*** *a half-eaten apple.* □ *Caracas has nowhere to grow but upwards, and surprising extremes of wealth and poverty are crowded* ***cheek by jowl****.* OBS

a chequered career/history [O (NP)] the life, record, of a person, nation, institution etc characterized by many changes of function and fortune **V:** have, enjoy, experience □ *Behind this is a lesson for those who buy cheap Italian shares like La Centrale's. La Centrale has had* ***a chequered history*** *from the time when its electricity undertaking was nationalised in 1963.* ST □ *'When I was working as a zoo-keeper—' 'A* what, *did you say?' 'Oh, I've had* ***a chequered career****. I could tell you a few things more surprising than that.'* □ *The National Health Service after 25 years—nearly its entire life—has its ailments. Tony Osman looks at the service's* ***chequered history****.* ST □ sometimes, but not necessarily, slightly derogatory, implying instability or inefficiency.

chew the cud (of sth) [V + O] chew food regurgitated from the first stomach (of ruminant animals); (fig) recall and consider, reflect upon, sth already said or done □ *The small sturdy Kerry cattle were* ***chewing the cud*** *within the shelter of the white ring fence.* PP □ *During the evening, moodily* ***chewing the cud of*** *these reflections, he gradually convinced himself of Alec's bona-fides.* PW □ *Whenever you two get together you do nothing but* ***chew the cud of*** *schoolboy memories. I've heard these stories so often I'm bored stiff.*

chew the fat/rag [V + O] (informal) discuss sth often but not essentially in a grumbling or argumentative way; have an argument or (near) quarrel with sb over sth; talk casually □ *After all, I argued, if you take over someone else's wife, the chances are that he won't lose much time in coming round to* ***chew the fat*** *a bit.* CON □ *And then the bloody door had to open and there was Dusty and Chadwick* ***chewing the fat*** *and smoking very nicely thank you.* TT □ *'The other typists won't like you appointing the new girl to be your private secretary.' 'Oh, it'll give them something to* ***chew the rag*** *about in their coffee breaks.'* □ *You heard that Victor* (held awaiting trial) *got moved to Lewisberg? They gave him a television and he lives on steaks and eggs. They tell me the convicts there sit around* ***chewing the fat*** *in a rose garden most of the day.* ST

a child in such/these matters [Comp (NP)] knowing little about, or still preserving one's childish innocence about, sth already referred to or understood **V:** ⚠ be, seem, appear □ (reader's letter) *I am* ***a child in these matters*** (the money market)*, but I cannot but observe that since the collapse of the negotiations*

(Brussels) *my modest portfolio of ordinary shares has increased in value by 14 per cent.* T □ *Since we all know James is* ***a child in such matters*** *we should have insisted on his taking legal advice about what should be due to him in copyright fees.* □ *It wasn't the sort of show I should have taken my mother to at all. Fortunately, she is rather* ***a child in these matters****, and most of the comedians' innuendoes were lost on her.*

the child is (the) father of the man (saying) the influences and experiences of childhood determine one's character as an adult □ (source) *So was it when my life began;/So is it now I am a man;/So be it when I shall grow old.../* ***The child is father of the Man.*** MY HEART LEAPS UP (W WORDSWORTH 1770-1850) □ *All educationists agree that* ***the child is the father of the man****—and yet there is a shameful lack of provision, by almost all local Authorities, of Nursery Schools for underprivileged children.*

child's play [Comp (NP)] sth that is quite easy to do; kid(s') stuff (qv) (sometimes said to forestall or deny any assertion to the contrary) **V:** ⚠ be, seem; make...of sth □ *I've had audiences of the Pope, I've been received by the Queen, I've met Elsa Maxwell, but that's* ***child's play*** *to getting hold of you, Professor Middleton.* ASA □ *The appeal of Transcendental Meditation is that it is* ***child's play****. It doesn't demand exercise, discipline or restraint; you needn't give up drink, or meat or sex; you don't have to retreat from the world or believe in God.* ST □ *He has electric shears that make cutting a hedge* ***child's play.*** (or: *that make* ***child's play*** *of cutting a hedge).* □ *'Isn't it awfully difficult to work those machines?'* ***'Child's play****, my dear girl. Let me show you.'* □ stress pattern 'child's play.

children should be seen and/but not heard (saying) children should be quiet and respectful in the presence of their elders, speak only when spoken to, etc □ *'My grandfather brought up his children in ways that astonished people. Their whole social life was spent with their parents.' 'I thought the rule was that* ***children were seen and not heard****.' 'They were constantly seen and very, very much heard.'* L □ *Whilst our forebears may have thought that* ***children should be seen but not heard*** *in the home, nowadays it is more likely that they are neither seen nor heard there; increasingly, it appears that the young seek to avoid the company of their parents.* RT □ (referring to the average size of a Victorian family) *No wonder they said* ***children should be seen and not heard****. With so many of them it would have been absolute chaos if they'd all been speaking at once.* TVT □ extreme and dated view of family and school discipline; expression may still be used to rebuke a child whose behaviour is annoying.

chill sb's/the spine etc [V + O pass] cause feelings of fear and horror; freeze sb's/the marrow/blood (qv) **O:** spine, ⚠ marrow, blood □ *'A collection of horror stories,' the blurb went on, 'guaranteed to* ***chill the spines of*** *the most sceptical readers.'* □ *Sensuous, witty, wise—her qualities need no inventory from me, and she can also* ***chill the marrow*** *with an item like 'The Intruder'.* G □ *The chemical industry, which is supposed to have bent the Minister's ear with* ***spine-chilling*** *stories about what would happen if...* NS □ *Wendy—who appears in 'Shadows', the series* (TV) *of children's* ***spine-chillers****—is far too down-to-earth to take ghosts seriously.* TVT □ adj compound spine-chilling; n compound spine-chiller.

a chink/crack in one's armour a vulnerable point in one's protection from attack, or in one's position in an argument etc; an imperfection or flaw of which others may take advantage □ *As Harold was shutting the door, something on the wash-stand flashed a lipless grin at him—it was Alec's false teeth in a tumbler. Far from being disgusted, Harold was touched by this evidence of imperfection,* ***this chink in Alec's armour****.* PW □ *'You were saying how you'd told her she was too much of a do-gooder to do much good.' 'I'll save it till later. One thing though—I think I've detected* ***the crack in her*** *shining* ***armour****.'* TT □ *His* (advertising) *copy seemed to me to be based on a very nice estimate of* ***the chink in the*** *intellectual* ***armour*** *which most 'New Statesman' readers and writers wear in order to protect themselves from vulgar, commercial appeals.* NS

a chinless wonder (informal) a type of (young) upper-class Englishman thought of as being both effete and pretentious □ *I'm tired of watching films that show forelock-tugging Cockney privates, dim Scottish stokers, and clueless Welsh batmen being tally-ho'd by the insidious, condescending, upper-class tones of a* ***chinless wonder*** *officer.* RT □ occas pl; attrib use *a* ***chinless wonder*** *type.*

a chip of/off the old block [Comp (NP)] a child very like its father in appearance and/or character (the reference being to a chip struck off a block of wood) **V:** ⚠ be; think, find, sb □ *Edmund Burke said of the Younger Pitt that he was 'not merely* ***a chip of the old block****, but the old block itself'.* □ *He was privately not at all displeased that one of his hefty daughters should be* ***a chip of the old block****.* RM □ (Congratulations and thanks) *also to David Dimbleby for his splendid commentary.* ***A real chip off the old block*** (Richard Dimbleby, his father, was a well-known radio and TV commentator). RT □ most often said of a son.

chips with everything (catchphrase) symbol of lower-class and unimaginative taste in food or anything else (popularized from the title of a play (1962) by ARNOLD WESKER) □ *There used to be a restaurant in Chancery Lane called '****Chips with Everything****'. This was a nice irony, since Arnold Wesker's play of that name was intended to point up the low expectations of 'the working class'—that is to say, most people, the other ranks. Nevertheless '****Chips with Everything****' eventually came to be a name for a smart restaurant.* L □ *The village restaurant is cheaper than most (about £5 a head, with wine) and offers a brave selection of local dishes, as well as the more conventional* ***chips-with-everything*** *fare.* ST

chock-a-block (full) (with sb/sth) [Comp (AdjP)] (informal) filled to capacity (with a number of persons or things) **S:** cupboard, drawer; room, theatre. **V:** ⚠ be; fill, pack, sth. **o:** rubbish, remnants; guests □ *This started off as my cupboard, and now it's* ***chock-a-block***

full with *your books and papers.* ▫ *If anybody else comes, don't let them in. The place is* ***chock-a-block*** *already.* ▫ *'He is an historian.' 'Well, you've certainly come to the right place.' Yves was in no way abashed. 'Italy's* ***chock full of*** *history.'* ASA ▫ *My aunt sent me a hamper* ***chock-full of*** *all kinds of goodies.* ▫ *Don't fill a pressure lamp* ***chock full*** *or the oil will flood the burner.* ▫ variant chock(-)full (of/with sb/sth).

chocolate box pleasing in a stereotyped or conventional way (ie pretty rather than beautiful, original, or artistic, and likely to make a suitable cover for a box of chocolates) ▫ *The Hall of the average Oxbridge College usually displays the portraits of its worthies. There they are, straight from the* ***chocolate box****, the ministers, judges, cardinals and archbishops, beneficent tycoons.* NS ▫ *She paints flower pictures that are quite pleasant in a* ***chocolate-box*** *sort of way.* ▫ *The mother had a faded* ***chocolate-box*** *prettiness that left me quite unprepared for the outstanding beauty of her daughter.* ▫ attrib use *a* ***chocolate-box*** *prettiness.*

chop and change [v + v non-rev] (informal) fluctuate, vary constantly, from one thing to another; keep changing one's opinions, plans, jobs etc ▫ *You never know what sort of clothes to put on in the morning, when the weather keeps* ***chopping and changing*** *like this.* ▫ *You've got your room all different again! You're a great one for* ***chopping and changing****, aren't you?* ▫ *He was never content with anything he had written until he had* ***chopped and changed*** *it about twenty times.* ▫ *You'll never make any headway at anything, if you keep* ***chopping and changing*** *jobs like this.*

the/God's chosen (people) the Jews, esp in Old Testament history, but also as a general term for Jewish people anywhere; those who are 'saved' (with reference to the Christian doctrine of salvation by election or redemption) ▫ (source) *But you are* ***a chosen*** *generation, a royal priesthood, a holy nation, a peculiar* ***people****.* 1 PETER II 9 ▫ *The problem then was to establish whether Antichrist had come and who he was. And the tradition could be, as Hill brings out, highly political; Antichrist is a holder of political power who persecutes* ***God's chosen people****.* NS ▫ *His death-bed was racked with doubts as to whether he was numbered among* ***the chosen****.*

the chosen few a relatively small number of persons selected for, or finding themselves in, a position of favour or privilege ▫ (source) *For many are called, but* ***few are chosen****.* MATTHEW XXII 14 ▫ *If all went well* ***the chosen few*** *would be masters of the world and mowing down the many, the snob-ridden aristos, the mighty tycoons and their bourgeois friends.* PP ▫ *The Professor is giving a dinner-party tonight, but that's just for* ***the chosen few****. The rest of us are invited to a wine-and-cheese party next Wednesday.* ▫ *Fears have been expressed that as higher education comes to be less and less a privilege of* ***the chosen few****, we shall be faced with a glut of unemployable graduates.*

a chosen instrument/vessel (formal) sb/sth to whom/which the mission or duty of working out a divine purpose has been entrusted; sb/sth chosen to carry out a special mission ▫ (source) *But the Lord said unto him, Go thy way: for he is* ***a chosen vessel*** *unto me, to bear my name before the Gentiles, and Kings, and the children of Israel.* ACTS IX 15 ▫ *Whether Smith was a religious maniac genuinely believing himself* ***a chosen instrument****, or just a shrewd charlatan, is debatable.* ▫ *Northern Ireland's competitive position has been weakened by the Local Employment Bill, which is the Government****'s chosen instrument*** *for steering industries to black spots in Scotland and England.* SC ▫ *Like many others who have the arrogance to see themselves as* ***chosen vessels*** *for the regeneration of the world, he was narrow-minded and bigoted in the extreme.*

chuck it (slang) abandon, give up (a job, a task); stop doing sth more or less immediately; pack it in (Vol 1) (qv) ▫ *'It's why I took this job —to get out of this country. But it's pretty foul really, having to go off just when I've met you,' said Edward. 'I've half a mind to* ***chuck it****.'* TCB ▫ *Oh,* ***chuck it****, will you! I've had enough of your grumbling.* ▫ *I'm feeling a bit tired. I think I'll* ***chuck it*** *for tonight and go to bed.* ▫ *You're not going to persuade me however much you say, so you might as well* ***chuck it****.* ▫ in second meaning, often used in imper to stop sb whose behaviour is irritating.

circumstances alter cases (saying) one's opinion, judgment, or treatment of sb/sth may vary according to the circumstances ▫ *Recognition of the fact that* ***circumstances alter cases*** *required more flexibility of mind than he possessed.* PW ▫ *'I understood your father had always set his face against having a TV set in the house?'* ***'Circumstances alter cases****; he can't get about now as he used to, and he's glad of it to pass the time.'*

circumstances beyond one's control [o (NP)] conditions or events one is not responsible for, is powerless to affect, and hence should not be blamed for **prep:** due to, owing to; as a result of, because of; through ▫ *All the aspects of the plan that were within reach of my own hand were worked out and determined. What took longer, of course, was the part which depended on the decisions of others and on* ***circumstances beyond my control****.* LWK ▫ *The contractors pointed out that failure to complete the work by the agreed date had been entirely due to* ***circumstances beyond their control****—the exceptionally severe winter, and strikes in the supply industries.* ▫ *No reason for postponing the programme was given except the usual unspecified 'owing to* ***circumstances beyond our control****'.* ▫ *When rain came to ruin the schedule of location filming Roy Boyd took over the Bradshaw part.* ***'Circumstances beyond our control****,' explained Avengers executive Brian Clemens. 'Sometimes you can't beat the English weather.'* TVT ▫ cf not be within one's control, as in *We're hoping the new baby will be a girl, but that****'s not within our control****, of course.*

circumstantial evidence a number of facts or details that point strongly to a certain conclusion ▫ *No jury likes to convict on* ***circumstantial evidence*** *alone.* ▫ *His experience was that eagles only took interest in the dead lambs. Away back in the fifties he was new to sheep farming but refused to be stampeded into taking* *action against the eagles on the* ***circumstantial evidence*** *of the time. The event proved the wisdom of his caution.* SC □ *'Jack said he wasn't going to be home between the match and the dance.' 'Well, there's* ***circumstantial evidence*** *in the bathroom that he was. No stopper on the toothpaste as usual, and two dirty towels flung in the bath.'* □ used esp of contributory evidence of this kind which may or may not add up to a presumption of guilt in a court of Law.

a city slicker (slang) a smart, fast-dealing, fast-talking person from a city—possibly not entirely honest (esp in implied or stated contrast to an ordinary town or country person) □ *...talking away until the Commander bustled back. 'Now fire off your questions,' he barked, genially enough. 'One at a time, mark you. I'm not one of those* ***city-slickers*** *you're probably used to.'* PP □ *It would disturb them no end to set about going to a thing like that* (a strip show) *in the full knowledge of what they were going to get. I'm talking about the solid citizen, naturally, not* ***city slickers*** *like you and me.* TGLY □ *Would he, however, be prepared to say: 'We intend to prevent people — speculators, property developers,* ***city slickers****—from borrowing large sums of money and then repaying them in depreciated currency.'* NS

civil disobedience organized non-aggressive refusal to obey the law (often as part of a campaign for political reform) □ (in Northern Ireland) *More seriously, the minority as a whole has now renounced parliamentary politics and opted for direct action, ranging from* ***civil disobedience*** *and demonstration to bullets and gelignite.* NS

Civvy Street (military slang) civilian life in contrast to life in one of the armed forces, whether on active war service or not □ *Spike Mays, ex-trooper of the Royals and then a signalman, was repatriated from India in 1934 and sent on a telegraphist's course as a preparation for '****Civvy Street****'.* NS □ *You can call it War Service if you like but as a training instructor at Catterick he was in a lot less danger of copping it than plenty of the people in* ***Civvy Street****.* □ *Remember when the Groupie* (Group Captain) *drove his Mercedes into the camp swimming-pool? Remember Coronation night in the Naafi? Remember how dull* ***Civvy Street*** *seemed—and how lonely?* TVT □ sometimes written without capitals; stress pattern 'Civvy Street.

a clarion call a loud rousing call or sound (as of a trumpet); any inspiring summons to, or appeal for, action □ *I'll wring that cock's neck, one of these mornings. I can do without* ***a clarion call*** *right under my window at the break of dawn.* □ *At present NATO is in the doldrums. It needs a roll of drums and* ***a clarion call****—to put its house in order while the going is good.* MFM □ *Revolution was in the air when Mary Wollstonecroft sounded* ***a*** *new* ***clarion call*** *to battle in 1792 with her vigorous work 'A Vindication of the Rights of Woman'. She urged women to improve their minds and their status.* L □ stress pattern a 'clarion call.

a clash of wills etc a situation in which the views, aims etc of two persons or groups are in conflict with each other **o:** wills, ⚠ interests; personalities, temperaments; ideologies □ *Secondly, nothing has changed as regards* ***the clash of interests*** *between Britain and France on the agricultural question, and nothing is likely to change for at least a generation.* L □ *It seems as if, for some people,* ***a clash of wills*** *is inseparable from sexual excitement.* SML □ *It may be argued that it is not* ***the clash of*** *Protestant and Catholic* ***ideologies*** *as such that have caused the present troubles in Ulster.* □ *Keith and Brian are both men who tend to dominate whatever scene they find themselves in and there's always* ***a clash of personalities*** *when they meet.*

class distinction(s) (placing people in) different ranks in the social scale, according to birth, economic status and/or occupation □ *To isolate the working-classes in this rough way is not to forget the great number of differences, the subtle shades, the* ***class distinctions****, within the working-classes themselves.* UL □ *The new meritocracy will have* ***class distinctions*** *of its own.* □ *Our pupils come from families in all walks of life: no boy who has been refused admittance here has been the victim of* ***class distinction****.*

the/a classic example (of sth) a long established and widely known instance or illustration (often ***the***); a typical or striking instance or illustration (often ***a***) □ *The capacity to retain one's faith and fortitude throughout affliction and adversity, of which Job's is* ***a classic example****, is given to few men.* □ *Great truths may seem to have been stumbled on by accident, witness* ***the classic examples of*** *Archimedes' bathwater and Newton's apple, but...* □ *To many of its inhabitants Birmingham is* ***a classic example of*** *a city disfigured by planners' blight.* RT □ *Some people can bore you even when they're talking about a subject that interests you. Margaret Thatcher on 'law and order' is* ***a classic example****.* DM

clean forget forget completely, esp sth one should have done or kept in mind that has present relevance □ *There's a letter came the other day for her from England. I meant to give it to the mail-man and I* ***clean forgot****.* RFW □ *'It's nearly nine o'clock.' 'Of course it is, I'd* ***clean forgotten****. It was talking to you about that fellow Goodrich.'* PW □ occurs most frequently in first person uses.

a clean sheet[1] [O/o (NP)] a record free of anything to one's dishonour or discredit **V:** have, give sb; start with, begin with □ *'I don't know anything about the man's past history,' he told the Inspector, 'but I can give him* ***a clean sheet*** *for the five years he's been working here.'* □ *'If this lark goes on much longer,' he said, 'you and me'll have to get married as well.' Ma said she thought it wouldn't be a bad idea perhaps—just as well to start with* ***a clean sheet*** *about these things.* DBM

a clean sheet[2] [o (NP)] an opportunity either to do sth for the first time or to start afresh as if for the first time **V:** start (again) with, begin with, turn to □ *It's a new appointment in the Department so he starts with* ***a clean sheet****.* □ *All the wallpaper—layer and layer of it—and all the paint must go, so that we could start with* ***a clean sheet****.* SC □ *The tradition of making lists on the arbitrary basis of the calendar stems from the common human impulse to wrap up the muddle of the old year, label it, and turn to 1 January as* *if to* ***a clean sheet****.*

cleanliness is next to godliness (saying) to be clean is good religious practice □ (source) *Slovenliness is no part of religion.* ***Cleanliness is****, indeed,* ***next to godliness****.* J WESLEY 1703-91 □ *Our grandmother kept both the house and us children in a constant state of spit and polish, quelling our complaints with frequent reminders that* ***cleanliness was next to godliness****.* □ *'I thought Sunday was supposed to be a day of rest?' 'Oh well, it's a good chance to wash the kitchen floor while the children are all out, and* ***cleanliness is next to godliness*** *after all.'* □ expression perhaps linked with the purification rituals laid down in Leviticus and the Pauline doctrine of the body as the temple of the Holy Ghost and not to be defiled, but not now said very seriously.

cleanse the (Augean) stables [V + O pass] thoroughly reform some section of public life, big business, etc where there has been an accumulation of corrupt practice (from one of the twelve labours of Hercules in Greek myth) □ *The one problem which the government must now tackle is urban decay. And this is first dependent on clearing up bureaucratic communications at local level: a* ***cleansing of the Augean stables*** *of lethargy, buck-passing and stalling.* L □ *It had really been an eye-opener to him, he said, to see what went on, when he thought of the distinguished men who apparently were either too cynical or too flabby to protest. Such a* ***cleansing of the stables*** *as he could see was needed, no wonder the nation was so slack.* HAA

clear the air [V + O pass] freshen the air or atmosphere; (fig) deal with openly, and possibly dispel, doubt, suspicion, jealousy, grudges between persons or groups □ *Do you mind if I open the windows, just for five minutes, to* ***clear the air****?* □ *In the sultry thundery weather of that week I longed for a real storm to break and* ***clear the air****.* □ (astrologist's forecast) *You may have to write a difficult letter to an acquaintance but it should* ***clear the air*** *quite a bit.* WI □ *This talk did a great deal to* ***clear the air****. It was the beginning of a friendship between Grigg and myself.* MFM

a clear case of sth [Comp (NP)] an unmistakable, easily identifiable, case or instance of (sth, doing sth, or sth having happened) **V:** ⚠ be, seem; look like. **o:** murder, arson; discrimination; being victimized □ *There must have been some doubt as to the manner of his death because the widow was able to draw his Life Insurance money. In* ***a clear case of*** *suicide they usually withhold payment:* □ *Giving Jamieson a place in the school team was* ***a clear case of*** *favouritism —and didn't the boys know it!* □ *His lawyer thought that Johnson's was* ***a clear*** *enough* ***case of*** *discrimination on grounds of colour to warrant taking legal action against the landlord.*

clear one's/sb's character [V + O pass] prove or show that one/sb is innocent, honest, respectable etc, after having been accused of something to the contrary □ *When the police-sergeant had finished, Julius reiterated his plea to be allowed to go to bed. 'Now that all* ***our characters*** *have been* ***cleared****,' he said with a poor attempt at irony, 'I presume that there is no point in keeping us up any longer.'* EM □ *My son did not do this horrible thing, and I want you to find out who did. I'm willing to spend every penny I have to* ***clear his character****.* □ *You don't need to try to* ***clear your character*** *with me, my dear. I know you too well to believe malicious gossip of this sort.*

clear etc one's conscience [V + O] (try to) atone for some real or imagined failure, etc **V:** clear, ⚠ salve, square, ease □ *Ned was making him a bit of a sermon, to* ***clear his*** *own* ***conscience*** *for being a business man and making money.* CON □ *But he was being kind to himself not to me. It was the sort of kindness which, when there is a gash in a close relationship, one performs to* ***ease one's conscience****, to push any intimate responsibility away.* NM □ *At present he has a cause, although it would be cheap and unfair to imply that he pursues it simply to* ***salve his*** *own over-demanding* ***conscience****.* OBS □ *I would not have been able to* ***square my conscience*** *if so large a sum had been given to me, simply for doing my duty.* MFM □ esp in *to*-inf constructions after *try, manage, be able etc.*

clear cut [Comp (AdjP)] clearly outlined, distinct, definite and unambiguous **V:** ⚠ be, seem, appear; consider sth as □ *I consider the problem viewed as above is very simple and* ***clear cut****.* MFM □ *Nearly 500 college students acted as subjects in this experiment and the results were* ***clear cut****.* MFF □ *It would be better to make a* ***clear-cut*** *decision to retire all employees at 65 than to continue the present rather invidious system of considering each case on its own merits.* □ *But there is no* ***clear-cut*** *division, in my opinion, between what constitutes art and what doesn't, though the opposite extremes are easily enough recognized.* □ *We cannot allow any of you to leave the building. Our instructions on that point are* ***clear cut****.* □ attrib use *a* ***clear-cut*** *decision, separation.*

clear the decks (for action) [V + O pass] get ready for any sort of activity, business, by removing anything not essential to it or by performing any tasks that are a necessary preparation for it □ *The morning's session was described as mainly to present facts and* ***clear the decks****.* T □ *...ordering that all British women and children, and all non-essential British male civilians, were to be evacuated from Palestine at once.* ***The decks*** *were now* ***cleared for action****.* MFM □ *If we're going to dance, some of you can give me a hand to* ***clear the decks****. Carry the small stuff into the hall, and shove the rest out of the centre of the room.* □ clear the decks can also be used of eating every bit of the food laid out on a table for a meal.

clear one's/sb's head restore one's mental faculties; reduce confusion, fatigue, or congestion from a cold, etc □ *I'm not making much progress with this essay. I think I'll take a little walk to* ***clear my head****.* □ *It's your own fault if you've got a hang-over. Still, I'll make you some coffee. It might* ***clear your head*** *a bit before you go to work.*

clear of sth [Comp (AdjP)] free or freed from sth; past, beyond, a place, time, stage of progress, life, or work **V:** ⚠ be, get; rise, soar. **o:** town, traffic; work, commitments; encumbrances □ *We had a slow journey north. It took us an hour and a half to get* ***clear of*** *London in* *the first place.* □ *He made for the Western Highway by a short cut through suburban roads I did not know. I did not talk to him till we were* ***clear of*** *the houses.* RFW □ *I have a study group to take this afternoon. I should be* ***clear of*** *that, though, by half-past three or four.* □ *I hope I've passed in all my subjects. It would be nice to be* ***clear of*** *exams for a while.*

clear one's throat [V + O pass] cough, or make a slight coughing noise, either to relieve a feeling of congestion, or as a warning or nervous preliminary to saying something □ *He* ***cleared his throat*** *and took a swift but profound sniff at the inhalant to do the same for his nasal passages.* TO □ *Pyle* ***cleared his throat*** *and it was the signal for an approaching intimacy.* QA □ *They scratched their heads, shuffled their feet, glanced helplessly at each other, and then one of them eventually plucked up the courage to speak. 'Masa,' he said, having* ***cleared his throat*** *several times.* BB □ also pl *They* ***cleared their throats.***

clench one's hands etc [V + O pass] hold both one's hands tightly closed, hold the jaws or teeth rigidly closed, esp indicating aggression, concentration, endurance under strain, nervous tension, etc **O:** hands, ⚠ fists; jaws, teeth □ *'Don't* ***clench your hands*** *like that. Just relax,' the doctor said. 'I'm not going to hurt you.'* □ *I can't get anything out of the child about who he is or where he came from. He just stands there with his* ***teeth clenched*** *and refuses to answer.* □ *From the tone of his voice you would have thought him calm enough, but I observed he had his* ***fists clenched*** *till the knuckles shone white.*

a clever dick (informal) sb who is clever, smart, in a superficial or insolent way, who is always ready to correct others or score over them in some way, esp verbally; a smart aleck (qv) □ DAVID: *What's love? How can I recognize it? I never saw any in this house.* BESSIE: *There he goes again —* ***clever dick.*** *Didn't I give you enough food?* HSG □ *'I used to work stripped to the waist in Germany,' I said. 'I nearly went mad with sunburn and I caught cold every time the wind changed.' '****Clever Dick,****' she said. 'Think yer knows everything doncha* (= you think you know everything, don't you)*?'* RATT □ clever dick often used to reproach sb sarcastically.

click one's heels [V + O] bring the heels of one's boots/shoes sharply together as part of a military salute or other formal greeting □ *The chief of police rose to his feet, bowed to us, and then* ***clicked his heels*** *together with such vigour that one of the constables dropped his rifle.* DF □ *Introductions were accompanied by a considerable amount of* ***clicking of heels*** (or: ***heel-clicking****) and kissing of hands, formalities she was unused to in an English drawing-room.*

click one's tongue [V + O] make a short sharp sound (by drawing the tip of one's tongue sharply away from the teeth-ridge) to indicate disapproval, annoyance with sb/sth or oneself, impatience etc □ *'How do you do?' said Susan. There was an undertone of defiance in her voice, and Briggs* ***clicked his tongue*** *in disapproval as he noted that no 'my lady' followed the form of words.* EM □ *Gerald sketched to him his doubts over Melpham. Mr Cresset* ***clicked his tongue*** *in a shocked way. 'It would be a terrible thing if that were true,' he said.* ASA □ *'What have I said wrong now?' she wondered, as she heard the examiner* ***click his tongue.***

the climate of opinion what, in any given period or place, the majority of people think, believe and feel □ *We tend to forget how much courage, in view of* ***the climate of opinion*** *in his time, Darwin showed in propounding his theory of the Evolution of Species.* □ *Artists and writers, no less than political reformers, have their part to play and often indeed subtly create that change in* ***the climate of opinion*** *which makes reform possible.* □ *There is a sound tape of this hair-raising affair buried deep in a drawer* (in Broadcasting House)*, never, given* ***the*** *present* ***climate of opinion*** *about language, to be heard.* L □ *Pornography, abortion, contraception, illegitimacy — and indignation. The frequency with which these factors cropped up and coincided in the week's news testified to the continuing unease felt in Britain about* ***the moral climate*** *of the Seventies.* L □ variants the moral, financial, economic etc climate = 'the general attitude towards, or the general conditions existing in, some section of public life'.

climb the wall(s) [V + O] (informal) be distraught, be harassed or exasperated almost beyond endurance or reasonable behaviour; go up the wall (Vol 1) (qv) □ *'I don't work there,' she answered. 'At least, only this afternoon, because Lucy Hall wanted to go to a wedding; and she's going to start* ***climbing the walls*** *on Monday when she finds how I've left things.'* PE □ *He really is an awful child. He had my wife* ***climbing the wall*** *the last time he stayed here, and you know how good* she *is with children.* □ *I'd better get along home, or Dad'll be* ***climbing the wall,*** *wondering what's happened to me.* □ esp inf and continuous tenses.

clinch a deal [V + O pass] (informal) make a business, or other, agreement final and binding □ *Many British firms are prepared to undercut one another and other western countries to the extent that may be necessary to* ***clinch a deal.*** T □ *You'll be happy to know I've sold her a stone;* ***clinched the deal*** *just before she got married.* HSG □ *I'm not saying that Robert didn't find Jenny attractive, but he didn't marry her for love. I'm sure it was her having the capital to set him up in business that* ***clinched the deal.*** □ pl *He* ***clinched*** *a couple of* ***deals;*** variant that clinches it, is said of sth that confirms a decision already made or nearly made, or of sth that finally settles or proves an argument.

clip sb's wings [V + O pass] restrict (the scope of) sb's activities; make it difficult or impossible for sb to realize his ambitions □ *She'll find that having a baby to look after will* ***clip her wings*** *more than she thinks.* □ ***Clipping the wings of*** *the Church was a main objective in 16th century England under the Tudors.* □ *'He thought he'd presented a good thesis, but he didn't get his PhD in the end.' 'That'll* ***clip his wings,*** *poor Charles. He was hoping it would get him an appointment to a university teaching job.'*

cloak and dagger [n + n non-rev] (stories etc that are) full of intrigue, fighting and adventure; (similar situations or behaviour in real life that are) full of—possibly contrived—mystery and intrigue □ *He writes historical romances of the* ***cloak and dagger*** *sort. I don't care for that kind of stuff myself, but I believe they are very popular.* □ *What's more, Ellsberg almost seems to enjoy his notoriety. At the Boston restaurant he insisted, in true* ***cloak and dagger*** *style, that his table should be a corner one.* RT □ *If the rifles had really been intended for use by the Defence Forces of the Republic (a very different thing, of course, from the Irish Republican Army), then there would have been no need for all the Le Carré-type* ***cloak-and-dagger*** *play in which the business was enwrapped.* L □ usu attrib use, as shown.

a close call [Comp (NP)] (informal) escape from, avoidance of, mishap, danger, embarrassment etc by a narrow margin; a close/narrow shave/squeak (qv); a narrow escape (qv); a near miss [2] (qv) **V:** ⚠ be, seem □ *In those cold valley cottages, a child could sicken and die in a year, and it was usually the strongest who went. I was not strong; I was simply tough, self-inoculated by all the plagues. But sometimes, when I stop to think about it, I feel it must have been* ***a*** *very* ***close call.*** CWR □ *I'll never ride in a car with Stephen again. We may have got here in one piece, but there were too many* ***close calls*** *for my liking.*

a close friend etc an intimate friend with whom one has a relationship of trust and affection, with whom—as opportunity offers—one is happy to spend one's time **n:** friend; ⚠ friendship, relationship □ *Cornelius (1824-1874) was* ***a close friend*** *of Wagner and Liszt.* RT □ *But their friendship was safely founded on distance —it was always* ***the closest friendships*** *that were most liable to break.* OMIH □ *Of our four children, Johnny and Peter could never agree and have drifted further apart, but the two youngest were, and still are,* ***close friends.***

close on [adv mod] nearly; almost; pushing forty (qv); rising twenty etc (qv) **det** (numeral) + **n:** fifty men, a dozen chairs, ten years, five miles, twelve pounds, midday □ *I expected them for lunch but they didn't arrive till* ***close on*** *two o'clock.* □ *Furniture and fittings, I'll take four hundred or the nearest offer. Rateable value ninety quid. You can reckon water, heating and lighting at* ***close on*** *fifty.* CON □ *Well, I don't know his age exactly, but he must be* ***close on*** *seventy.* □ *Not far to walk to the post-office, you say! It must be* ***close on*** *a mile.*

close (the/one's) ranks [V + O pass] (military) adopt a close formation; (fig) combine strongly, whatever one's individual differences, in a group in order to achieve or defend a common purpose **S:** workers, bosses; Civil Service, Cabinet □ *The nations of the free world would be well advised to* ***close their ranks*** *and co-operate whole-heartedly and unreservedly.* MFM □ *In the past we have not shirked competition, and if employers and workers* ***close their ranks*** *to meet the challenge the Scottish economy ought to benefit from membership of the Common Market.* SC □ *'I wonder would you mind accepting my most sincere apologies for all that I might have ever said?' 'You mean we should* ***close the ranks****?' 'Something like that,' she said.* TT □ *The Marquis* (a character in a play) *regards life as a gigantic spree whose real reward is outwitting fools and outdaring knaves. But inevitably, the Munich establishment* ***closes ranks****, depriving its tormentor of money, mistress and mystique.* NS

a close etc relation/relative sb with whom one has a strong etc tie of blood or kinship **adj:** close, ⚠ near; distant □ ***Close relatives*** *are not always close friends.* □ *Unless you were* ***a near relation*** *of the patient, the Sister wouldn't consider you were entitled to such information.* □ *I have heard that the hedgehog is* ***a distant relation*** *of the domestic pig.* □ not to be confused with a close/distant relation(ship) = 'closeness of feeling, interchange, connection between persons, facts, conditions', as in *There is* ***a close relation(ship)*** *between mental and physical abilities in the child under two.*

a close season a period of the year, varying from place to place and from species to species, during which it is illegal to kill or catch certain animals, birds, fish, esp the time during which they are breeding or rearing their young □ *He recognized the necessity of* ***a close season*** *during the time of breeding, but he could not help wishing that birds would stagger the business,* (ie not all breed at the same time). RM □ *There seems to be* ***no close season*** *for football nowadays. In the old days only schoolboys and village lads played it in the height of summer.* □ *This* (German) *chap said: 'It is for us, we are sure, the end of the war.' So I said: 'Well, my dear fellow, the thing to do is to keep as far from the Eastern Zone as possible, because, though we might possibly have* ***a*** *sort of* ***close season****, being sportsmen, for Germans, it's very doubtful if the Russians will.'* L □ also used of other sports or activities which are temporarily suspended.

a close second [Comp (NP)] almost as successful, satisfactory etc as the winner or leading item in a competition or contest **V:** ⚠ be, come; run sb/sth □ *The river's probably contaminated in some way. Human sewage is the main offender, with industrial waste* ***a close second.*** DM □ *It seems likely at this stage that Benson will win the Cup for the best all-round competitor, with Tait running him* ***a close second.*** □ *In a recent survey it was found that though Britons still drank more tea than any other beverage, coffee now came* ***a close second.***

a close/narrow shave/squeak [Comp (NP)] (informal) escape from, avoidance of, mishap, danger, embarrassment etc, by a narrow margin; a close call (qv); a narrow escape (qv); a near miss[2] (qv) □ *When there were mishaps or setbacks or* ***close shaves*** *like the Cresset affair of last night, he saw himself as the artist caught up in a web of other people's trickery.* ASA □ *He appears to belong to that generation of 'playboys' who made a habit of getting themselves killed in motor-cars, a fate Max has happily managed to avoid, though there was at least* ***one narrow shave.*** NS □ *A very tall thin man with a squint rose from a table near-by. 'You said he had a paunch.' 'Not a paunch—ponch. It's the local dialect for squint.' It was* ***a*** *very* ***narrow squeak.*** OMIH □ *'Would it not be an additional safeguard,' suggested Dr Bottwink, 'if the British constitution were rationalized to some degree? You have had* ***a close squeak****, like William Pitt before you. The next man may not* *be so lucky.'* EM □ a close shave and a narrow squeak are the usual collocations.

a close etc thing [Comp (NP)] a fine balance between life and death, success or failure, doing or not doing sth, one person and another in competition (though finally determined one way or another, usu fortunately) **V:** ⚠ be, seem. **adj:** close, ⚠ close-run, near □ *John and I managed to throw ourselves to one side as Barry and the bike crashed past. It was* ***a near thing.*** TVT □ *It was going to be* ***a near thing*** *whether Luke got his headship; wasn't that true? So if one could do anything to bring it about, one had to.* NM □ *To think I might have been married to that woman! It was* ***a close thing*** *once, believe it or not.* □ *The favourite that year* (in the Leeds Piano Competition) *was a brilliant Russian named Vladimir Krainov, but Sebastien Risler of France was there too, as was Armenta Adams of the United States. Clearly it was going to be* ***a*** *very* ***close thing.*** RT

close/near to sb's heart [Comp (AdjP)] of deep interest and concern to sb; dear to sb's heart (qv) **S/O:** subject, project; your welfare, the future of the service. **V:** ⚠ be, seem, remain; have, keep, sth □ *After lunch Joker found an opportunity to talk to Ian Carmichael on a subject* ***near to*** *his* ***heart.*** RM □ *They had discussed during the morning a neat plan for flooding a small competitor with orders beyond the power of his commission. It had been a scheme* ***close to*** *everyone****'s heart****, and they had adjourned to the Metropole for drinks in a haze of bonhomie.* HAA □ *The history of the Scottish regiments is* ***close to the hearts of*** *the Scottish people; almost every family in the land has had a relative serving in the Black Watch, the Gordons, the Argylls, or some other regiment perhaps now disbanded.* TVT □ *'It's the first time I've been in charge of anything on this scale, and I realise that if you don't organise it yourself, it doesn't get done.' A sentiment* ***close to the hearts of*** *captains everywhere.* TVT □ *'The welfare of the firm,' he concluded, 'is something I will always have* ***near to*** *my* ***heart.'***

a closed/sealed book (to sb) [Comp (NP)] a matter about which there is no body of knowledge, or which sb specified knows nothing about or cannot understand **V:** ⚠ be; find sth □ *In a huge area which until now had been* ***a closed book*** *Baker had compiled a mass of original information.* BN □ SECOND COMEDIAN (continues to stare into the goldfish bowl): *The open sea is* ***a closed book to*** *this goldfish.* ART ⇨ an open book.

a closed shop (industrial relations) the practice, ruling, or agreement under which only people belonging to a recognized trade union are employed in a factory, workshop, trade or profession □ *The scheme was therefore the antithesis of restriction, for it prevented the operation of a* ***closed shop*** *policy in the motor industry.* T □ *Lord Fulton himself, the outgoing chairman, replying to a member who challenged the Henniker appointment (*to the chairmanship of the British Council*) with the words 'You seem to be involved in some sort of* ***closed shop****', said, changing the metaphor, that there had been a 'very broad trawl'. But the question 'Who made the trawl?' remained unanswered.* NS

closing/opening time the end/start of the two statuory periods (GB) when public houses or bars may legally sell or serve alcoholic drinks □ *It was nearly* ***closing time****, and she began to make sandwiches for lunch. She heard Joe lock and close the front door. She heard him stop in the bar to pour himself another drink, which he brought into the kitchen.* AITC □ *By now it was about* ***opening time.*** *It seemed useless to start ringing up the night clubs at this hour* (for information)*, so there was nothing to be done but to work Soho* (ie go round the Soho pubs). UTN □ *I don't know how long the zoo stays open at this time of year, but there'll be a notice at the gates telling you about* ***closing times.*** □ applicable also to shops, banks, libraries, museums etc but out of context the meaning above may be assumed.

clothed and in one's right mind have oneself organized mentally and physically to start the day's work, to meet others, go about one's business, etc □ (source) *Then they went out to see what was done; and came to Jesus, and found the man, out of whom the devils were departed, sitting at the feet of Jesus,* ***clothed, and in his right mind****: and they were afraid.* LUKE VIII 35 □ *I'm a slow starter in the mornings. Come round about 10 o'clock. I should be* ***clothed and in my right mind*** *by then.* □ *'How was Steve to-day?' '****Clothed and*** *very much* ***in his right mind****; I think he'll be out of hospital very soon now.'*

cloud one's brain etc [V + O pass] interfere with, obscure, one's understanding and judgement **O:** brain; ⚠ vision, judgement □ *In general, I consider that excessive smoking and drinking tend to* ***cloud the brain.*** MFM □ *It was your innate modesty, no doubt, that* ***clouded your vision****, and prevented you from seeing that you were the person aimed at by the criminal all the time.* EM □ *It is not easy sometimes to prevent* ***one's*** *moral* ***judgement*** *from being* ***clouded*** *by self-interest.* □ pl cloud their brains etc.

a cloud no bigger than/the size of a man's hand a small indication, perhaps not recognized as such, of coming disturbance, trouble, or of widespread change not necessarily disastrous □ (source) *Behold, there ariseth* ***a little cloud*** *out of the sea,* ***like a man's hand.*** *And he said, Go up, say unto Ahab, Prepare thy chariot and get thee down, that the rain stop thee not.* 1 KINGS XVIII 44 □ *It was an unpleasant little incident, soon forgotten but recalled afterwards as being* ***the cloud no bigger than a man's hand*** *that might have warned us of the course events would take.* □ *Reactionary and repressive regimes are never very prone to take note of* ***clouds the size of a man's hand.*** *They ignore the signs until disaffection becomes too widespread to control.* □ *The reporter reminded me that only three years before I had been listed as an 'undesirable radical campus speaker'. The following day* ***a cloud no bigger than a man's hand*** *appeared on my otherwise serene horizon.* OBS

a cloud on the horizon/in the sky a threat or indication of trouble to come □ *But no industrial picture, however bright, is likely to be without one or two small* ***clouds on the horizon.*** SC □ *The Home Office is a particularly* *treacherous ministry. Everything seems to be going smoothly, there is not **a cloud in the sky**, when suddenly there is a case, an issue, a human story in which the newspapers take an interest.* NS □ not/without a cloud on the horizon/in the sky is used of a trouble-free prospect.

the coast is clear no danger or interference threatens; there is nobody about who might be an obstruction or a nuisance (originally a smuggler's term) □ ***The coast's clear**. I've just heard you can go ahead. Have your novel printed. It's OK by the Home Office.* SML □ *I noticed them peering up and down the far main-passage in the manner of people making sure that **the coast was clear**.* TST □ *There's such a scramble for the bathroom in the mornings, I think you should stay in bed till I give you a knock. Then you can get up and have your bath when **the coast's clear**.* ⇨ ⚠ all clear.

the cobbler should stick to his last (saying) people should confine themselves to doing the things they know how to do, are supposed to do, and should not make pronouncements on matters they are ignorant of □ *Diversification may be all the rage in the nation's boardrooms but I can't help thinking that there was a good deal to be said for the old saying about **the cobbler and his last**.* NS □ *That's what comes of **the cobbler not sticking to his last**—see what a mess you've got your affairs into by setting yourself up as your own lawyer.* □ (NONCE) *As the husbandry of resources comes back into the picture, and **the cobbler returns to his last**, and the need to build your own windmill becomes ever more obvious, more and more folk in smocks and aprons will doubtless be wanted to dispense know-how from the studios.* L □ less common variant let the cobbler stick to his last.

a cock and bull story [O (NP)] a long-winded and complicated story, but especially an extravagant and untrue account of events given as an explanation or excuse for sth **V:** tell; invent, make up □ *He's been telling **some cock-and-bull story** to the 'Daily Tale' about seeing the footprints of this imaginary monster on Pillay and hearing it roar.* RM □ *'This address book business, Kingsley,' said McNeil, 'doesn't seem to apply at all in my case. As far as I'm aware we never met until a few days ago. **Cock and bull story** evidently.'* TBC □ *There are many variations on the theme of what really took place, many fabrications and much lying by Oppenheimer before he admitted in 1954 to the Personnel Security Board that he had invented **a cock and bull story** because 'I was an idiot'.* NS □ also hyphenated; stress pattern a cock and 'bull story.

cock an/one's ear(s) [V + O pass] erect one's ears; (start to) listen attentively; have one's interest aroused by sth heard □ *The loudspeaker gave a few snappy barks. Jasmine* (a donkey) ***cocked her ears** and broke through with frenzy leaving Pop on the ground and everybody scattered.* DBM □ *A Minister of the Crown is expected to lift his eyes from the written evidence and **cock his ear** to catch the sounds from the outside world.* L □ *There's some bird in that tree that I've never heard before. When you go for the milk, **cock an ear** in that direction and see if you recognize what it is.*

(the) cock of/o' the walk (the) person in a group who exercises most authority in it, whom the others obey, defer to, are careful to keep on good terms with □ *He wouldn't want to take a job in Manchester, where he'd be nobody in particular. He's **cock of the walk** here and that's what he likes.* □ *She was a bit slower than when I'd seen her last, as if she'd bumped into a wall during the last ten years through walking in the **cock o' the walk** way she always had.* LLDR □ attrib use, *a **cock o' the walk** way, manner*, not usu pl, or preceded by *a*.

a coffee-table book a handsomely produced and illustrated book that is easy to admire, suitable for casual study or entertainment, but an unimportant contribution to literature or scholarship □ *Masses of radiant, somewhat chocolate-boxy, photographs interspersed by an excellent simple text saves this from being just **another coffee-table book**.* SC □ *'Edward Heath: Prime Minister' contains some good illustrations, appears in large print on very good paper and looks as expensive as it is. But except for the purpose of lying unopened on **the coffee table**, 'Heath and the Heathmen'—which is cheap and looks nasty—is much the better buy.* L □ *Mino Milani's slightly rhetorical account of the world's main civilisations for **this** junior **coffee-table** (Coke table?) **book** drops in a few quotations from original sources.* L

a cog in the machine [Comp (NP)] sb who plays a necessary but subsidiary or insignificant part in an undertaking, business, administration etc **S:** ⚠ be, become; regard sb as □ *It was becoming abundantly clear that, unless I made some determined move, I should become **a** permanent **cog in the machine**.* SD □ *'We may be only **cogs in the machine**, but where would the big shots be without us?' 'Rubbish, people like us are easily replaced.'*

coin money [V + O] (informal) earn or gain a lot of money (rather easily); make large profits from very little outlay □ *With a big house like that full of bed-and-breakfasters every night, the woman must be absolutely **coining money**.* □ *Thomson's Garage gone bankrupt? They're always so busy I could have sworn they were **coining money**.* □ *I wouldn't say we were **coining money**, but business is steady enough and we can afford what we need.* □ usu inf or continuous tenses.

coin a phrase/word [V + O] invent a new expression, word; put a new twist to a familiar phrase □ *Sweep these* (quotas) *away, give the Irish farmer unlimited access to the markets both of Britain and the Six at the prices set in Brussels, and the Irish, to **coin a phrase**, will make a bomb.* L □ *His affairs are in a very bad way: overdraft at the bank, HP payments fallen behind, local tradesmen refusing any more credit. You name it, he owes it—if I may **coin a phrase**.* □ forms to coin a phrase, if I may coin a phrase often used as an aside by a speaker or writer introducing a novelty of this kind, and also, in a self-deprecating way, to apologise for using a cliché rather than an original phrase.

cold comfort little, or no, comfort or consolation □ *'Hasselbacher, you've never felt the need of money, have you? But then, you have no child.' 'Before long you will have no child either.' 'I* *suppose not.'* ***The comfort*** *was as* ***cold*** *as the daiquiri* (a drink). OMIH □ *Scottish ratepayers can expect only 'rough justice' if they appeal against their new assessments. This* ***cold comfort*** *message, at a time when rateable values are soaring by more than 100 per cent in many cases, was spelled out by several delegates.* SC □ *'I just told Sheila that if Jim's the philandering type it's as well to find out now and not after they're married.' 'That may be true, but it's* ***cold comfort*** *to offer the girl at the moment.'*

a cold fish [Comp (NP)] a person who is never much moved by emotions of any kind, and is considered to be unattractive for this reason **V:** ⚠ be, seem; be regarded as □ *She leads young men on and then she turns prim and proper on them. She's a born teaser, she'll never change. It wouldn't surprise me if she told Bob* (her husband) *about her young men's antics. They're* ***cold fishes****, both of them.* RATT □ *'The only point about dropping the second atomic bomb,' said Martin, his tone neutral, the last edge of feeling dried right out, 'must have been for purposes of comparison.' As soon as we went inside the canteen at Barford he made a similar remark, and was immediately denounced by Luke as* ***a cold fish****.* NM

(a) cold fury (a) fury no less strongly felt and no less chilling in effect for its being held in some sort of control □ *But it was the eyes I noticed more than anything else: large, and set at a slight slant in the golden face, they stared up at me with a look of such* ***cold fury*** *that I was thankful the animal's feet were tied.* BB □ *I could see from the set of his face and the way he gripped the arm of the chair that he was in* ***a cold fury****.*

cold hands and a warm heart (saying) a conventional comment sometimes made with reference to sb's hands being cold □ *'Goodness, how* ***cold your hands*** *are,' the nurse said, 'but never mind — that means you have* ***a warm heart****.'* □ *'****Cold hands and a warm heart****, eh?' he said as they shook hands, trying to strike a light-hearted note with his prospective daughter-in-law.*

a cold snap a sudden, short period of cold weather, either out of season or unusually cold even for the season □ *The lilac buds were all frosted during* ***that cold snap*** *we had last week. We shan't have any blooms this year.*

(stone-)cold sober [Comp (AdjP)] (informal) completely sober, in the sense that one has either been drinking no alcohol or too little to be affected by it **V:** ⚠ be, become; make sb □ *He was smoking a cigar, emblem of the celebration of that night, but he had drunk little and was* ***cold sober****.* NM □ *Will you promise me something — now,* ***stone-cold sober*** *in broad daylight?* RATT □ (NONCE) *I'd like a drink first. I can't go to a show like that* ***stone sober****.* OMIH

the cold war a state of affairs where countries or groups struggle for supremacy by means of propaganda, economic pressures, etc but without declaration of hostility or actual fighting □ *It would distress Yugoslavia if the United States withdrew her interest in Europe. A rapprochement between America and Russia would weaken Yugoslavia's position.* ***The cold war*** *has not been altogether to Yugoslavia's disadvantage.* SC □ *Holding a Summit meeting, in fact, is a continuation of* ***the cold war*** *by other means; and so is sabotaging it.* BM □ *We hear a lot nowadays about* ***the cold war****, but any trader will tell you that the war between two manufacturers of the same goods can be quite a hot war.* OMIH □ *Khruschev did more than any American politician to propagate the belief that war was obsolete in the nuclear age. Our people were much more bound by the* ***cold-war*** *party line.* NS □ attrib use *a* ***cold-war*** *attitude.*

collapse of stout party (catchphrase) a solid, pompous person is dumbfounded, powerless to say or do anything further after he has been (suddenly) outwitted, proved wrong in an assumption, etc □ *To many people Victorian wit and humour is summed up by* (the magazine) *'Punch', when every* (cartoon) *joke is supposed to end with '****Collapse of Stout party****', though this phrase tends to be as elusive as...* R PEARSALL 1975 □ *'An Inspector Calls' is not nowadays a disturbing play. Perhaps we relish too much the way in which all the Birling* (family name) ***stout parties collapse****.* L □ (NONCE) *When I pressed the prosecution's main witness to confirm my client's story of blamelessness, he said, what he had charitably omitted previously under examination, that after the incident the defendant had been swaying about and reeked of drink.* ***Collapse of slim solicitor****.* L

collar and tie [n + n non-rev] a respectable appearance, or a proper sense of occasion (esp so in the case of men whose jobs would make the wearing of a collar and tie unsuitable or inappropriate during working hours) □ *When my father came home from the pits and had his bath, he would always put on* ***collar and tie*** *whether he was going out anywhere or not.* □ *A few of the farm-workers, looking rather uncomfortable in their* ***collars and ties****, attended the funeral service.* □ *'You can't go visiting your Aunt Doris in hospital without a* ***collar and tie****,' his wife nagged at him.* □ used esp formerly when casual clothes for men were less common, and used esp of men whose jobs would make the wearing of a collar and tie unsuitable or inappropriate during working hours; attrib use *a* ***collar-and-tie*** *job, function etc.*

collect/gather one's wits [V + O] make a (fairly rapid) mental adjustment to a change in circumstances, to an unexpected occurrence, shock, surprise etc □ *I was tempted to set off again then and there for Holborn Viaduct. But on second thoughts I decided that I had better* ***collect my wits*** *a little before attempting to face Hugo.* UTN □ *I like an early morning cup of tea in bed. It gives me time to* ***gather my wits*** *again.*

Colonel Blimp the embodiment of most of the undesirable qualities of an elderly reactionary as regards politics, the social scene, military affairs, etc (from a character created by David Low, the cartoonist, during the 1930s) □ *The fact that the Duke of Kent, a major in command of an armoured-car squadron, accompanied the regiment, did not amuse one Dublin paper, which described the decision to let a member of the Royal Family go as one worthy of* ***Colonel Blimp*** *at his worst.* L □ *Bertrand Russell was frothing because the bookstall staff wasn't there at 7.30 on a Sunday morning. I didn't dare to ask him why he had turned suddenly into a spindly,* *hopping **Colonel Blimp**.* L □ *Mr Greene's trouble is that he is behind the times. He imagines **Colonel Blimp** is still alive, when in fact Mr Blimp Jr is angling for a fat, tax-free job in Brussels.* NS □ occas pl.

the colour bar the exclusion of people from certain social amenities or legal rights because they are coloured or of coloured descent □ *Already* (in the Thirties) *with her courage and independence Nancy Cunard made no bones, whether in the United States or in Europe, about her complete indifference to **the colour bar** and her partisanship on behalf of those who were suffering most by it.* AH □ *The unimportance of **colour bars** in Brazil requires no mystic explanation. The Portuguese were too few to populate their vast empire.* NS □ *In 'Basketball Game', a 14-year old black boy meets a white girl neighbour of his own age and class, but this is in Nashville, Tennessee, and their calf-love breaks against **the colour bar**.* L

come (now) used as a mild expression of reproach, urging sb to be sensible, to talk or behave reasonably □ *Ah, **come now**, darling, don't upset yourself.* DC □ *'And the place was disgustingly filthy.' 'Oh, **come**, Linda, that's not quite true—a bit untidy perhaps.'* □ ***Come now**, be a good girl and eat up your pudding. Daddy's waiting for you.* □ milder expression than come, come (qv).

come alive [V + Comp] become interested or interesting; show animation, purpose; take life[2] (qv); come to life (Vol 1) (qv) **S:** girl, audience; book, performance □ *For Stein was the older: she **came alive** in the 1890's when, at Radcliffe, she studied psychology under William James.* G □ *To anyone hoping to see this important event **come alive** through Mr Griffith's dramatic insight, the evening* (ie TV) *was a profound disappointment, for all we were given were talking heads.* L ⇨ ⚠ bring to life (Vol 1).

(not) come amiss [V + Comp] (not) be unwelcome, unsuitable (ie be very welcome, most suitable) **S:** wage-increase, better allowance; loyalty, support, courtesy, help □ *'Wouldn't you like to have a few extra pounds in your pocket every week?' 'It would**n't come amiss**.'* □ (reader's letter) *May one ask why HRH Princess Anne could not have graced the cover? In her impeccable outfit she would adorn this issue, and a little patriotism would **not come amiss**.* RT □ *I was glad to be seated in front of a good fire, and the glass of brandy pressed upon me did**n't come amiss** either.*

come/go as one is (informal) pay a visit, attend a function or performance without dressing formally, without taking any special pains about one's appearance □ *'But I'm not dressed to go out and meet people. Give me half an hour.' 'Now, don't fuss but just **come as you are**.'* □ *Where are you thinking of going to dinner? I hope it's some place where we can **go as we are**. If not, I'd rather stay at home and scramble some eggs or something.* □ esp in direct invitation come as you are.

come clean [V + Comp] state or confess sth fully and frankly **A:** with you, with his constituents; about the facts; on this point □ *Let's **come clean** with you, Lewis. That's a very good reason but it isn't the real reason, and you both know that as well as I do.* NM □ *Now **come clean**, Myra. What's really eating you up? You've been talking around and around it.* EHOW □ *But if MPs do demand, as they should, a little trust from those of their party workers who toil to put them in office at each election, then the least they can do is to **come** a little **cleaner** about themselves.* NS

come, come expression used to urge sb to be sensible, to talk or behave reasonably, with a stronger suggestion of reproach or rebuke than 'come (now)' (qv) □ *'**Come, come**, Miss Jenkins, be careful what you are saying,' the detective sergeant interposed. 'You were seen at Edgbaston that morning, you know.'*

come a cropper (informal) have a severe fall (though not from any great height); (fig) suffer a reversal of fortune; make a mistake with disastrous results □ *He was performing 'stunts' on his bike as boys will, caught his foot in the chain and **came a** real **cropper**.* □ HELEN: *Now you're going to listen to a few home truths, my girl.* JO: *We've had enough home truths.* HELEN: *All right, you thought you knew it all before, didn't you? But you **came a cropper**.* TOH □ *You try too hard, which makes you an insufferable do-gooder, and one of these days you'll **come** such **a** lovely **cropper**—And do you know what everybody will stand round and do? Cheer.* TT

come and go[1] [v + v non-rev] be transitory; come and then go, to be replaced by sb/sth else, or others of the same kind □ *For men **may come** and men **may go**,/But I go on for ever.* THE BROOK (A TENNYSON 1809-92) □ *But there are sadnesses of growth, moods that **come and go** with the awakening consciousness of passing time.* HAA □ *Institutions **come and go** and the Board, like its predecessors, is to go. We venture to believe it will not be the last in the line.* NS

come and go[2] [v + v non-rev] arrive and depart, go in and out, etc as part of a pattern of (free) activity; occur intermittently **S:** visitor, employee; the public; breeze; pain □ *She was chained to her place. But other people were not; other people could **come and go** as they pleased; people without home ties could take the longest journeys.* PW □ *Oh, I think we should take the car now Mummy's offered it, and it'll be so useful with the children. We can just **come and go** as we please.* ILIH □ *It shares many of the common devices of classical comedy — the adjoining houses in a street, with creaking doors through which all characters **come and go*** NS □ often part of the longer expression *be/feel free to **come and go** as one pleases.*

come hell or high water [Disj] whatever the opposition or difficulties may be □ *She was right of course. I was fuddled. On the third day I just had to sleep, **come hell or high water**.* TST □ *If he says he'll have the 3rd edition on the streets by five o'clock then, **come hell or high water**, he will.* □ *He's an extremely brave little man who would gladly **go through hell and high water** for Walmington-on-Sea's safety. He is also a very good bank manager there.* RT □ expression means 'even if hell or high water comes'; variant go through hell and/or high water.

come it strong (informal) emphasize, exaggerate, one's speech or behaviour for effect; speak very, or unduly, forcefully about sth **adv**

mod: a bit, too, rather, very □ *'Religion! Religion, in one form or another, has been the cause of most of the trouble in this world.' 'Well, that's* ***coming it*** *a bit* ***strong****, isn't it?'* □ *You can hardly* ***come it*** *too* ***strong*** *when warning children of traffic dangers nowadays.* □ (a young golfer) *He dressed in a flamboyant manner and affected white golf shoes in an age when that was considered to be* ***coming it*** *a bit* ***strong*** *if you were anything above scratch.* SC ⇨ draw it mild.

come one, come all (informal) anybody that cares to do so can come, take part, etc; it makes no difference how many people come; if one comes, everybody comes □ *'A lot of people are going to take objection to your speech, as you've outlined it to me.' 'It's intended to be provocative —****come one, come all****, I'm ready to take them on.'* □ *'I wish we could invite just Jack by himself.' 'Well, it's impossible. You know how the Andersons gang together in everything they do. It has to be a case of* ***come one, come all****.'*

come to pass (biblical) happen; occur; (formal) happen according to, or contrary to, expectation □ *Many in the country hope that the famous 'amnesty' for journalists in prison, which has been talked about for the last few years, may really* ***come to pass****.* OBS □ *Because this isn't a fairy story but the true story of a man and the company that he made his life's work, not* quite *everything has yet* ***come to pass****.* ST

come rain, come shine whatever the weather is like; whatever happens; in any case/event (qv); wet or fine (qv); (in) fair (weather) and/or foul (qv) □ *OK then.* ***Come rain, come shine*** *we all meet here about 9 o'clock tomorrow morning.* □ *Almost every Saturday evening,* ***come rain or shine****, snowstorm, blizzard or hail, this intrepid young lady attended open-air political meetings.* SNP □ (NONCE) *Every Thursday,* ***come winter storm and summer sun****, he cycled fifteen miles to Cork and fifteen back.* PP □ *He had a cheerful philosophy of life—not so far too severely tested—that enabled him,* ***come storm or shine****, to make the best of things as they were.* □ *'Now be sure to meet me at the station.' 'Don't worry —* ***come rain or shine****, I'll be there!'* □ variants come rain or shine, come sun or shower, come storm or shine/sun.

come etc thick and fast [adv + adv non-rev] come etc in large numbers or great quantity **V:** come, grow, fall; lay on, pile on, bombard □ *By midnight on Christmas Eve the snow was* ***falling thick and fast****.* □ *The first guests were announced.* ***Thick and fast*** *they* ***came****, filling the Hampstead double drawing-room.* ASA □ *There are also many new sorts of paint on the market. Over the last few years, technological advances have* ***come thick and fast****.* OBS □ *It is in this first part of the book that the clichés of both style and situation* ***fall thick and fast****.* L □ *At one stage, as the objections from Mr Stable and Judge Gillis* ***grew thick and fast****, even Hain admitted to doubts about dismissing his counsel.* NS □ *Los Angeles, during the 20s and 30s, was arid for sensations, dreams and miracles — and Mrs McPherson* ***laid*** *them* ***on thick and fast****.* RT

(now I) come to think of it now that the person, event etc just mentioned or just about to be mentioned has been thought of or recalled □ *Did he say anything special?' I asked. '****Now I come to think of it****,' said Dave, 'he did.'* UTN □ *They don't like undertakers in Russia.* ***Come to think of it*** *they don't like them anywhere.* DPM □ *He could never,* ***now he came to think of it****, remember having seen a professional window-cleaner at work in a college.* HD □ MILLY (giggling): *I walked out.* MYRA: *What for this time?* MILLY: *But it's always the same reason. Yes,* ***come to think of it****, it is.* EHOW □ almost always first person sing, though sometimes in forms if/when he/you come(s) to think of it; front, middle or end position.

come true [V + Comp] actually happen as foretold, dreamed, hoped for, etc **S:** dreams, longings, hopes □ *Granny Valvona remembered everyone's horoscope all the day, checking up to see the points where it* ***came true****.* MM □ *And now it had all* ***come true****, Anne's childhood longings. The offer of four years in Russia, studying at the Moscow Choreographic School.* WI □ *'You've got to make it* ***come true****,' he says gently. 'You've just got to work and be so determined that it's got to* ***come true****, because you believe in it.'* ST

come unstuck [V + Comp] (informal) meet with a mishap, misfortune, a reverse **S:** plan, plot; arrangement, project □ *He had not felt like somebody for a long time, not since the publisher had written so encouragingly about the book, which had somehow* ***come unstuck*** *since then, and had lain untouched in its drawer for weeks.* AITC □ *Poor chap. He'd* ***come unstuck****. Unfortunately for Patterson's story the engine was intact, and when they tested it a few days later with a new propeller, there was nothing wrong with it.* DS □ *The two front benches at Westminster have been parties to a conspiracy to put off the difficult and dangerous day of choice. What has happened in the last few weeks is that the conspiracy has* ***come unstuck****.* NS

come up roses (informal) happen in the best, most desired, way possible **S:** everything; plan, experiment; it; life □ *For ten years everything in my life seemed to be* ***coming up roses****. Then, suddenly, disaster — job, marriage, health, religious faith, all four began to fail.* □ often in continuous tenses.

come one's way be found, met with, without deliberate intention or effort **S:** money, fortune; chance, offer, proposal; prospect, possibility □ *Of all the impudent suggestions that ever had* ***come his way****, none had astounded him more.* TST □ *At this point, however, a more novel fortune* ***came our way****. A squalid hut-floor, dated by coins to about AD 300, was found to cover the adit* (= entrance) *of a mineshaft, which must therefore have been of earlier date.* SD □ *You seem to be afraid that life might pass you by without giving you time to enjoy it to the full and so you are always ready to take advantage of any chances that* ***come your way****.* WI □ *His father was a share cropper, tilling other people's land, though he worked at any job that* ***came his way****, including a stint at building roads.* ST

come what may/might [Conj] in spite of, disregarding, whatever (else) may happen (while doing sth or as the result of doing sth) □ ***Come what might****, he would never leave John.* ASA □ *My mother taught us to speak the truth,* ***come what may****, and so far as my knowledge goes none of her children have ever done anything* *which would have caused her shame.* MFM □ *This glorious sense of having won,* ***come what may****, was entirely new to him.* HD □ *The army must be withdrawn; and the best way of achieving this while bringing the contending parties to their senses is to tell them now that in 12 months' time the withdrawal will take place,* ***come what may****.* NS □ front, middle or end position.

comic opera (theatre) farce or comedy set in operatic form; (fig) a farcical situation, or the farcical behaviour or appearance of people □ *Who would have the power to fire this hybrid armament? Those who sat through the* ***comic opera*** *of the Multilateral Force will realise at once that this is where we came in.* NS □ *The assembly consisted largely of sashed and bemedalled men with here and there a* ***comic opera*** *dowager—broad of bosom and resplendent in diamonds and nodding feathers.* □ *A race can be won or lost simply on the speed with which a rider mounts and dismounts his cycle during a race. And this is the sort of skill riders like Atkins work hard at during practice, though it's an exercise which adds a touch of the* ***comic opera*** *to his rigid training routines.* TVT □ attrib use *a* ***comic opera*** *figure, scene.*

comic relief [O (NP)] the temporary relief from tension, distress, tedium etc afforded by a comic scene or character in a tragedy or serious play, or film; an amusing incident in real life **V:** afford, supply, provide □ *Shakespeare, in his tragedies, often includes a few short scenes where the antics and conversation of jesters, simpletons, or homespun wits provide* ***comic relief****.* □ *This theme of the passing of great days is useful to film men, and was well exploited in 'Big Jake' recently in order to pass off the same boring Western material and provide* ***comic relief****.* NS □ *It gives a touch of* ***comic relief*** *to the working day, after all, when you get a really crack-pot customer. Believe it or not, I was once asked for a tin of tartan paint.*

coming events cast their shadow(s) before (saying) there are often early indications, perhaps unrecognized, of future events or changes □ (source) *'Tis the sunset of life gives me mystical lore,/And* ***coming events cast their shadows before****.* LOCHIEL'S WARNING (T CAMPBELL 1777-1844) □ *But it is a truism that poetry can reflect* ***coming events****—and the most momentous* ***coming events*** *were acts of violence.* AH □ *Last year Britain exported an English-bred Arab* (horse) *to Kuwait—and in October a Kuwait businessman bought Crabbet Park Equitation, the riding school and stables, thus importing a real Arab patronage — a case, perhaps, of* ***coming events casting their shadow before****?* OBS □ can refer to gloom or depression felt about a known but unwanted event which is soon to happen.

coming(s) and going(s) [n + n rev] arrival(s) and departure(s); movement(s) in and out □ *There's been a tremendous amount of* ***coming and going*** *in the flat upstairs all morning. I'm dying to know what's going on up there.* □ *As the doors opened and shut to the* ***comings and goings*** *of men and women, most of whom smiled at Virginia, she could see the desks and typewriters and filing-cabinets and drawing-boards.* AITC □ *The window looked down only on the side entrance to a club. He noted the* ***comings and goings*** *of the club porter.* MM □ *'As long as he pays his rent and keeps his room decent, his* ***comings and goings*** *are no business of mine,' said his landlady firmly, and no more was to be got out of her.* □ *Paragraphs about his* ***goings and comings*** *had leaked into the papers from time to time over the last few years.* DS □ rev, but usu in order given in headphrase; in a possess construction form is always pl.

commit oneself declare or reveal one's opinions, attitudes, feelings, likely courses of action, etc **A:** to the press; in front of me; about anything; very far □ *When asked by a press representative whether he thought intervention was justified he managed to talk for a full ten minutes without* ***committing himself*** *one way or the other.* □ *Some of the people did not answer, some of them answered grudgingly and hurried away, unwilling to* ***commit themselves*** *too far with this stranger.* AITC □ often neg or with neg implications.

common decency the helpful, considerate, or courteous behaviour that would be expected of any reasonable person □ *Ask any half-dozen working-class people what they understand by religion, and very easily, but not meaninglessly, they will be likely to answer with one of these phrases: 'doing good', '****common decency****'.* UL □ *I think you might have had the* ***common decency*** *to tell me you wanted to get married.* LLDR □ *Since Mrs Robson does so much baby-sitting for us out of the goodness of her heart, it would be only* ***common decency*** *to ask her to dinner some evening.* □ often used to reproach sb for not behaving well, as in constructions *it's only* ***common decency*** *to do sth, you might have the* ***common decency*** *to do sth.*

the common good the general welfare; what is best and most advantageous for a country, community, or group as a whole □ *They are assailed by a mass of abstractions; they are asked to respond to 'the needs of the state', and 'the needs of society', to study 'good citizenship', to have in mind* ***the*** *'****common good****'.* UL □ *It was the more difficult as there was no true unity, and no nation was willing to make any sacrifice of sovereignty for* ***the common good****.* MFM □ (penal reform) *Yet the hard-liners must be heard, their suggestions must be received as born of a genuine anxiety and a desire for* ***the common good****. They still think that brutality pays in dealing with brutal offenders.* NS □ often in construction *do sth for* ***the common good****.*

common ground [O (NP)] a basis for shared interests, understanding, objectives etc **V:** find, discover, establish, have □ *Although we think differently and serve different masters, we do have sufficient* ***common ground*** *to be able to talk together.* TBC □ (Italy, 1960) *For all the differences of doctrine which divide the parties of the Right and Left respectively, on practical issues each wing of the Christian Democrats tends to find more* ***common ground*** *with other parties than with the opposite wing.* SC □ *'All right,' I said, relenting. I smiled, 'I'll do something about it.' 'What will you do, darling?' she said looking at me. Reflection was over for her, if not for me. We were on* ***common ground*** *again.* SPL

the common herd (derogatory) the mass of

people in general, esp the working or lower classes; the majority of people in a group □ (source) *...when he (*Caesar*) perceived* ***the common herd*** *was glad he refused the crown, he...offered them his throat to cut.* JULIUS CAESAR I 2 □ *I knew Felicity wouldn't come with us. Catch her consenting to mix with* ***the common herd*** *at anything so vulgar as a fairground show.* □ *'Why on earth study Sanskrit, when there are so many modern languages that could be useful to him?' 'Oh, that's Steve all over—anything to be different from* ***the common herd****.'*

common knowledge [Comp (NP)] what everybody (in a community or group) knows or is aware of **V:** ⚠ be, become □ *It is, of course,* ***common knowledge*** *that a substantial proportion of electors are opposed to entry into the European Common Market.* SC □ *Micky's prison record was doubtless a matter of* ***common knowledge*** *in the district.* PE □ *It seems to be fairly* ***common knowledge*** *that you and your particular pals have got some racket that brings you in pretty big money.* HD □ *How do you reconcile people's undoubted nervousness about air-travel with the* ***common knowledge*** *that statistically it's the safest way to go from A to B?*

the common man the average man, esp one typifying that section of a community not politically, academically or artistically ambitious, but hard-working and sensible and entitled to their rights as contributing members of their society; the man in the street (qv) □ *From then on has developed, with increasing elaboration, all the well-known cant of '****the common man****'; a grotesque and dangerous flattery, since he is conceived as the most common or commonplace man.* UL □ *The popularity of Burns is due to the fact that he wrote to, for, and about* ***the common man*** *in verses and terms that he could understand.* □ *One general criticism made about the Festival programmes was that they appealed too exclusively to cultivated tastes. There was nothing in them for* ***the common man*** *to share and enjoy.* □ *While the candidate's wife was explaining how he would get 'fascinated by other people's trains and ring roads', his agent was worrying about his image ('We had quite a problem trying to relate him with* ***the common man****').* NS

common or garden [adj + adj non-rev] ordinary, not unusual or remarkable (from horticultural classifications distinguishing a common flower or plant from rarer members of its species) □ *If this monster isn't entirely imaginary, it is nothing more extraordinary than a* ***common or garden*** *seal.* RM □ *He leant forward across the table towards that* ***common-or-garden*** *Nottwich face on which he felt he could rely for incredulity, reassurance, the easy humour based in experience.* OMIH □ *Psychiatry doesn't consist of listening to beautiful blondes lying on couches telling you all about their sex life. Before you get to that you have to sweat it out for years with ordinary* ***common-or-garden*** *lunatics.* DIL □ sometimes hyphenated; usu attrib.

the common/general reader sb who reads for entertainment, interest, or to increase his general knowledge, but who is not qualified to understand writing of a highly technical or specialised nature □ *Modern science is centrally mathematical. Having no mathematics, or very little,* ***the 'common reader'*** *is excluded.* L □ *The detailed results are comprised in the Meddleton-Snooperage Report (1956) but there is no reason why they should not be presented in a simplified form for* ***the general reader****.* PL

the common etc run (of sb/sth) the usual, typical, kinds (of person or thing) **adj:** common, ⚠ general, normal, ordinary. **o:** people, folk; members, trade unionists, soldiers □ *I am writing particularly of the majority who take their lives much as they find them; of what some trade union leaders, when they are regretting a lack of interest in their movement, call 'the vast apathetic mass'; of what song-writers call, by way of compliment, 'just plain folk'; of what the working-classes themselves describe, more soberly, as '****the general run of*** *people'.* UL □ *He may be brilliant at his job, but as far as making a success of his personal life is concerned, he's not so different from* ***the ordinary run of*** *mankind.* □ *I enjoyed that book you lent me. I like reading something out of* ***the normal run****.* □ *His teachers say he is an intelligent enough boy but nothing out of* ***the common run****.* □ construction *different from/out(side) of* ***the common run***, means 'not conforming to the general pattern'.

common sense natural good sense and intelligent understanding, as distinct from learning, acquired information, etc □ *I stood there silenced. Of course there were lots of* ***common-sense*** *arguments I could have brought up, but* ***common sense*** *itself told me that it would be a waste of time.* CON □ *'Please,' he said, 'wonder more than half-consciously about this question and tell me your answer.' 'Oh,' she said, 'I think in that case, other people do exist. That's my answer. It's only* ***common sense****.'* MM □ *What Gielgud gives us is this* ***common sense*** *and easy goodwill, plus something deeper, larger.* NS □ *His manner had certainly changed, ever so slightly, at the idea of paying her a salary. He clearly preferred people to work for nothing. But that, thought Victoria, was a sign of* ***common sense****.* TCB □ attrib use *a* ***common-sense*** *argument.*

the common touch [O (NP)] a natural ability to adapt oneself to all types and classes of men, to accept, and be accepted by, them on good terms **V:** have, keep; lack, lose □ (source) *If you can talk with crowds and keep your virtue,/Or walk with Kings—nor lose* ***the common touch*** *...* IF (R KIPLING 1865-1936) □ *Celia, of course, prided herself on* ***her 'common touch'****, particularly with 'characters' like Mrs Wrigley; in Esher her 'friends', she was always most emphatic in stating, were the dustman, the milkman, and the old woman who dealt in second-hand clothes.* HAA □ *David Frost is the single most important phenomenon of the television age, and the first who has grown up with the Box. He walks with Kings, and keeps* ***the common touch****.* L □ *Giscard maintains that the idea that he lacks* ***the common touch*** *was something invented by the Press and politicians because of his background.* ST □ *The fans are ordinary working folk who want to enjoy a night out and get value for money. That's why wrestling will always be around—it has* ***the common touch****.* TVT

the company one keeps the kind of people one mixes with (the suggestion often is that the company is superior) ▫ *He rails at his inadequacy in such 'complex and sophisticated society'. It is as though the boy from the down-town grocery store never quite felt up to* ***the company he kept.*** NS ▫ *What made the experience bearable was* ***the company I kept,*** *working for the Long Island daily paper, 'Newsday'.* NS ▫ *The British girls* (gymnasts), *visibly awed by* ***the company they were keeping,*** *watched Nadia's astonishing gravity-defying routines with small murmurs of disbelief, and, at the end, they stood and applauded her.* RT ⇨ ⚠ keep bad etc company.

comparisons are odious (saying) people or things should be judged on their own merits and not measured against sb/sth else; it is not always tactful or in good taste to make comparisons ▫ *You will remind me that* ***comparisons are odious,*** *I dare say, but I am convinced that a poorly educated countryman is superior in every way to his city counterpart.* ▫ *One has a certain scale of values, of course, but when it comes to weighing Dante and Shakespeare against each other I find that* ***comparisons are*** *both* ***odious*** *and inapplicable.* ▫ *Since in this field* ***comparisons,*** *far from* ***being odious,*** *are much in order, I must confess that I find Hester Chapman's account ('Mary II, Queen of England') a subtler and more thoughtful study.* ST

the compliments of the season greetings of goodwill at Christmas and the New Year **V:** wish, give, sb; send sth with ▫ (Christmas morning and the host is dangerously ill) *'He did in fact instruct me to ask all the party to see him as soon as they had breakfasted in order to wish them'—his voice faltered—'****the compliments of the season,*** *sir.'* EM ▫ *'I want to give her a present for being so kind, but I don't think she'd like me to.' 'Wait another month and send it with* ***the compliments of the season.*** *She couldn't take offence at that.'* ▫ (the) compliments of the season (to you)! may be uttered as a greeting.

compound a felony [V + O pass] in return for a money payment or other consideration, agree not to prosecute sb, bring a charge or inform against him, for a crime he has committed ▫ *I had in a sense* ***compounded a felony,*** *and if he were to steal anything again it would go hard with me. But I couldn't have done otherwise: I could remember the time when I was desperately in need of fifteen shillings myself.* RATT ▫ *The police officer explained that he couldn't strike a bargain with Smith not to prosecute: this would be* ***compounding a felony.*** *But if Smith gave him information about his associates, this might be used in mitigation of his sentence.*

a con(fidence) trick a manoeuvre whereby sb's confidence and trust is obtained in order to deceive, swindle, or otherwise take advantage of him ▫ *But we are not so surprised that the Chancellor said so little about where the main burden of paying for this increase is to fall. For that represents* ***the*** *first* ***confidence trick.*** AH ▫ *The TUC wants to set up a special working party — to hammer out the details. Most of the cabinet still regard this sort of offer as little better than* ***a con trick.*** NS ▫ also pl; a person who behaves this may be called a confidence trickster, a confidence man, (informal) a conman.

(hanging) concentrates the mind wonderfully (saying) (knowledge that one is to be hanged) keeps one thinking of, makes one focus sharply on, that only ▫ (source) *Depend upon it, Sir, when a man knows he is to be hanged in a fortnight, it* ***concentrates his mind wonderfully.*** S JOHNSON 1709-84 ▫ *There is something that* ***concentrates the mind*** *even more* ***wonderfully*** *than the propect of being hanged in a fortnight; it is the prospect of taking part in 'Any Questions?'* (a radio programme) *in a week's time. What desperate reading of the newspapers! What solemn analysis of the more sober periodicals!* L ▫ *As during general election transmissions, ITN's frontmen will be Peter Snow and Robert Kee. 'If we were to ignore the Common Market completely, people would ask why. The referendum* ***concentrates the mind wonderfully,*** *like* ***hanging.'*** TVT ▫ *The one certainty is that most parents worry too much and too soon. The O-level may be a very bad exam, but it* ***concentrates the mind wonderfully,*** *and in most subjects a determined spurt in the fifth year will see you through.* OBS

concert pitch the tuning of musical instruments (eg a piano) so that the note A in the treble staff has 440 vibrations to the second; (fig) a high degree of fitness, preparedness, concentration etc ▫ *Some of their periods were spent in thinking how late it was; and others in watching car-headlamps moving along the main road. It is hard to keep one's concentration up to* ***concert pitch*** *in this sort of scene.* SPL ▫ *He had screwed himself up to* ***concert pitch*** *for this encounter and the longer it was delayed the more he feared his confidence would ebb away.*

confirm one's worst fears [V + O pass] prove/show that one's fears (that sth undesired would happen) were justified; cause sb's fear to be felt even more strongly ▫ *The goose he was now eating might well be part of the same living bird that had wrapped its neck about his legs the previous day. Pop, a moment later,* ***confirmed*** *Mr Charlton****'s worst fears*** *by laughing uproariously: 'This must be the joker that was under the table yesterday and heard us talking.'* DBM ▫ *I thought my patient might be too old and weak to survive the operation.* ***My fears,*** *however, were not* ***confirmed*** *and he made an excellent recovery.* ▫ *The news of a proposed Welsh Assembly fell on the old market town of Mold, in Clwyd, but lightly. It seemed to be like* ***the confirmation of a worst fear,*** *and to that extent best dismissed with a shrug.* G ▫ variant the confirmation of one's worst fears.

a confirmed bachelor [Comp (NP)] a man who from principle and/or long-established habits is not likely to marry **V:** ⚠ be, become; make sb ▫ *I was then thirty-eight years old and* ***a confirmed bachelor.*** *Women had never interested me and I knew very few; I disliked social life and dinner parties.* MFM ▫ confirmed may also be used to describe persons with other strongly entrenched habits, beliefs, as in, a confirmed drunkard, invalid, atheist.

confound the prophets/critics [V + O pass] be successful, turn out well, in spite of the predictions or warnings of others to the contrary □ *Some thought I was to be ticked off for my behaviour at the meeting on the 10th September. But* **all prophets** *were* **confounded**. *Mr Alexander offered me the appointment of Chairman of the Western Union Commanders-in-Chief Committee.* MFM □ *In the event, this small local Festival,* **confounding the critics**, *drew many visitors and cleared its expenses without a subsidy from the Arts Council.*

confusion reigns a situation is characterized by confusion, muddle, disarray, uncertainty etc □ (a 'character-reading' following a person's answer to a questionnaire) *Money has no importance in your eyes, but one sometimes wonders what you do consider important.* **Confusion reigns** *in your behaviour as well as in your accounts.* WI □ *At the reception centre,* **confusion reigned** *and no one knew how many more victims of the flood were still to arrive.*

(make) confusion worse confounded (saying) (be the cause of) worsening of an already existing state of confusion □ (source) *I saw and heard, for such a numerous host/Fled not in silence through the frighted deep/With ruin upon ruin, rout on rout,/* **Confusion worse confounded**. PARADISE LOST II 995 (J MILTON 1608-74) □ **Confusion** *even* **worse confounded** *was the prevailing theme of the Congo saga last week.* OBS □ *I agree—the committee's got itself into a bad mess, but we'll have to give them more time to present their report. To bring in somebody new at this stage would just* **make confusion worse confounded**.

one's conscience pricks one one feels guilt or remorse to a greater or lesser degree □ *He was a quite impossible person to have in the same house as children. All the same,* **my conscience** *is* **pricking me** *a bit about turning him out.* □ *As far as all the killing goes, it happened when he was living within his own primitive culture and he's certain he was right. I'm sure* **his conscience** *isn't* **pricking him** *at all.* RT □ **The pricks of conscience** *must have been bothering her for she came round two days later with a peace-offering of vegetables from her garden.* □ variant the pricks/prickings of conscience.

consider the lilies saying do not worry and do not strive to provide oneself with material benefits, but trust to providence for what is needed □ (source) **Consider the lilies** *of the field, how they grow; they toil not, neither do they spin...even Solomon in all his glory was not arrayed like one of these.* MATTHEW VI 28-9. □ *Instead of men and women playing their fantastic tricks before high heaven, we are asked to* **consider the lilies**, *to meditate on the unearthly beauty of 'mere things' when isolated from their utilitarian context.* HAH □ *I think Marjorie had made it her philosophy of life to* **consider the lilies**. *At any rate, she toiled not, neither did she spin.*

a consolation prize [O (NP)] an additional prize given to sb who, though not the winner of a set award or prize is considered to have done well enough to merit some recognition of his efforts **V:** win, get; offer, give, sb □ *The brewery combine that ran the slogan competition offered £1000, £500 and £200 as first, second, and third prizes and one hundred* **consolation prizes** *of a cask of beer delivered free to the door.* □ *I thought that after coming second in so many of his class subjects, Nick ought to have been given* **a consolation prize** *at least.*

conspicuous/distinguished by one's/its absence [Comp (AdjP)] more the focus of interest for not being present as expected, than if one/it were actually there **V:** ⚠ be, become, seem □ *I turned on Jacob* (who had run away when poisonous snakes escaped), *'I noticed that you were* **conspicuous by your absence**, *my noble and heroic creature.' 'Yes, sir,' said Jacob, beaming.* BB □ (Jo is pregnant) HELEN: *Where's the loving father?* **Distinguished by his absence**, *I suppose.* JO: *That's right.* TOH □ *The usefulness of a history source book of this sort would be much enhanced by the cross-references which are so* **conspicuously absent**. □ sometimes used to comment on the absence of sb/sth as an observable fact without special significance; distinguished less usu than conspicuous; variant conspicuously absent.

contain oneself restrain oneself, hold back, from expressing strong feelings **modal:** can(not), could (not), (not) be able to; have to, must □ *But at that point Nicky could* **contain himself** *no longer. Oblivious of the fact of how he frightened Sarah he began banging on the door and screaming.* DC □ *'You're always trying to sort out people's ideas for them. It's not a very endearing characteristic.' 'I know, but hearing such utter drivel I find it hard to* **contain myself**.*'* □ *And then you had to be careful how you held him,* (a young fox) *for he would be so overcome with joy at seeing you again that he could no longer* **contain himself**, *and the resulting stream could drench you if you were not careful.* DF □ in last example, there is a play upon the figurative meaning and the purely physical meaning (= 'urinate').

contemplate/gaze at one's (own) navel [V + O] engage in a typical Yoga discipline in which concentration is said to lead to union of the soul with the 'universal spirit' (also used, in a more general way, when describing people whose thoughts and interests are too much turned in on themselves) □ *He's been reading up about Yoga and now he's trying to practise it. He'll be up in his room this very minute sitting in the fourth position or* **contemplating his navel**. □ *I do like poetry, and modern poetry as well, but not the introspective stuff. Some of these young chaps are so busy* **contemplating their own navels** *they don't realise there's a world going on about them.* □ esp in continuous tenses.

a contradiction in terms [Comp (NP)] the use of two terms in a statement, definition or description that (seem to) contradict each other's meaning **V:** ⚠ be, appear, seem □ *In plain clothes among uniforms, a harmless drudge among men of action, I was politely designated, as* **a contradiction in terms**, *a 'civilian officer' on the Naval Staff.* AH □ *Touchy CID men said that all this was* **a contradiction in terms**, *that detectives couldn't do their job if drinking with an informer could be called associating with known criminals.* ST

conventional warfare/weapons weapons or the means of waging war that exclude atomic or hydrogen bombs, lethally poisonous gases or disease-carrying bacteria □ *'Hawthorne, I* *believe we may be on to something so big that the H-bomb will become* ***a conventional weapon****.' 'Is that desirable sir?' 'Of course it's desirable. Nobody worries about* ***conventional weapons****.'* OMIH

a conversation piece[1] a painting or drawing showing a pair, or small group, of human figures in a natural scene from daily life—perhaps a little formalized; a scene in real life that strikes one as being like a picture of this kind ▫ *Above the mantelpiece hung* ***a*** *charming little 18th century* ***conversation piece*** *by an unknown artist.* ▫ *Only one rule, none the less rigid for being unspoken: 'no member of the College may ever bid against another.' If at the preview two students find that they want the same article,* ***a conversation piece*** *on the following lines takes place.* BM

a conversation piece[2] any object of an interesting or unusual kind (eg a picture, table-ornament) which often provides a subject of, or stimulus to, conversation ▫ *Personally, I think it's the most hideous and complicated ornament I ever saw, but we always put it at the centre of the table when we're giving a dinner-party. It makes* ***a*** *useful* ***conversation piece****.*

cook the books [V + O pass] (informal) falsify facts or figures in order to make one's financial, or other, affairs seem better than they are ▫ *Like a great many people who are very bright in other directions, he lost all his wits when confronted with a column of figures. 'Come and testify to my character, darling,' he said. 'Joe's practically accused me of* ***cooking the books****.'* RATT ▫ *No sensible observer blames the Minister who on the floor of the Commons suppresses essential facts or even 'improves' the record where he feels that national or even Party interests require it. But it is a different thing when in his retirement he continues to* ***cook the books*** *to his own greater glory.* NS

cook one's/sb's goose [V + O pass] (informal) spoil or ruin one's own or another's chances of success either in general or in a particular way ▫ *His alibi would hold, he thought, unless somebody actually identified him as having been a passenger on the later train. In that case, of course,* ***his goose*** *was* ***cooked****.* ▫ *That fellow Carter thinks he's just going to walk in and take over this whole department, but I'll find some way of* ***cooking his goose*** *for him, mark my words.* ▫ *I warned her to check the date her application form should be in, but she always knows best. Well, she's* ***cooked her goose*** *now, because by this time next year she'll be too old to qualify for a grant.* ▫ also pl *I've* ***cooked their goose****.*

cool(/)calm and collected [adj + adj non-rev] not flustered, upset, or in a panic ▫ *Thank God there was somebody there* ***cool and collected*** *enough to give first aid. The boy might easily have bled to death.* ▫ *If you think Steve's being unfair to you, try to reason with him in a* ***calm and collected*** *way instead of flying into a temper.* ▫ (advertisement) *Always* ***cool and collected****—always crisp and neat, and she's buying her Lambretta with the fares she saves by riding to work.* TO ▫ *And one woman on the board successfully played the game of sailing against the prevailing wind by simply being* ***cool, calm and collected****.* OBS.

a cool customer[1] [Comp (NP)] (informal) sb who is impudent or presumptuous in a calm self-assured way **V:** ⚠ be, seem; find sb ▫ *'By the way, I took a packet of cigarettes out of your handbag. I didn't realise I had run short.' 'Well, you're* ***a cool customer****, I must say.'* ▫ *She's* ***a cool customer****, Sue. Just rings up and says 'Sorry I can't make it to the office to-day. Tell the boss, will you?'*

a cool customer[2] [Comp (NP)] (informal) a person who is not nervous or excitable, but will keep his head under the stress of circumstances or his own emotions **V:** ⚠ be, seem; find sb ▫ *There are many more wide-famed names, worn by* ***cool customers*** *with straight eyes and straight lefts* (a boxing term) *whose delight is the tough assignment and whose only raison d'être is to ferret out murky truth wherever it lies.* RT ▫ *At 43, Mr Marsh is the youngest chairman British Rail has ever had and without doubt* ***a cool customer****.* RT

a cool hand on a fevered brow [O (NP)] (facetious) the soothing effect of tender attendance and sympathy, esp upon the sick **V:** lay, place ▫ *I had often heard the expression about laying* ***cool hands on fevered brows*** *but I had never until then experienced it. It was most satisfying.* DIL ▫ *Florence Nightingale was a very determined and business-like woman, not just a ministering angel flitting about the wards with her famous lamp in order to lay* ***a cool hand on fevered brows****—though she did that, too.* ▫ *'Is that really and truly the impression I give?' she said. 'It is—the portable angel of mercy,* ***the cool hand on the fevered brow****, the lot.'* TT

cool one's heels [V + O] (informal) be kept standing and/or waiting (usu with some loss of dignity); be prevented from doing sth one wants to do until some time has elapsed ▫ *The threat comes from the experienced Pakistani politicians who have been* ***cooling their heels*** *for the last four and a half years.* SC ▫ *So you may imagine how unhappy it makes me to have to* ***cool my heels*** *at Newhaven, waiting for the trains to run again.* UTN ▫ often in constructions *leave sb to/let sb* ***cool his heels****.* ⇨ ⚠ kick one's heels.

cop it (informal) get into trouble; receive a punishment or scolding; catch an illness, be involved in an accident, be wounded or killed, etc ▫ *'You'll* ***cop it*** *from old Miss Devenish for not doing your homework,' his sister said.* ▫ *With three of our party down with malaria, we couldn't help wondering who would be the next to* ***cop it****.* ▫ *Maybe you don't care whether you kill yourself or not, but remember that if you hit something it may be the other fellow that* ***cops it****.*

cops and robbers [n + n non-rev] (informal) the law versus criminals, esp as the theme of a film, story, TV series, etc ▫ *These things frighten the small man, but they don't frighten the big ones. It's the usual battle of wits between the* ***cops and the robbers****.* DS ▫ *I used to love the 'chase' sequences in the* ***cops-and-robbers*** *silent films of my youth, everybody dashing in and out of doors and windows, up and down stairs and over roof tops at top speed.* ▫ *One chapter —called 'The Battle of Two Civilisations'— puts Irish and English civilisation at each other's throats in a* ***cops-and-robbers*** *situation. The* *truth is infinitely more subtle.* L □ attrib use, *a **cops-and-robbers** film*, hyphenated.

corner the market (in sth) [V + O pass] (commerce) buy up, or secure control of the supply of, a commodity in order to obtain a monopoly and (often) push up prices **o:** corn, oil, tobacco, cocoa □ *The town was already quite well provided with window-cleaners, who had **cornered the** really profitable **markets**.* HD □ *Is it not curious that we should have given an American-owned firm such a handsome subsidy, allowed it to **corner a** small but vital **market in** our aircraft and atomic energy industries, and then sat by while it ran trade unionists into the ground?* NS □ (quack religions in the USA) *Every third street corner in those days had some cosmic huckster buying and selling futures in humanity, **cornering the market in** optimism, because nothing, we thought, could be worse than the present.* NS □ *'The Prodigal Son' is not great art, but it is good show-biz, and certainly more successful than 'The Seven Deadly Sins', Covent Garden's bid to **corner the** same **market**.* L

the corridors of power the higher levels of government, administration etc where men (either for reasons of personal ambition, or to further a cause or their convictions) compete and intrigue for power and position (a phrase coined by C P Snow in the 1950s and later used by him as the title of one of his novels) □ *Among others close to the Duke of Edinburgh, one might mention the photographer Baron, the naturalist Peter Scott, the artist Edward Seago, and two scientists who are also potent in **the corridors of power**—Sir Harold Hartley and Lord Zuckerman.* OBS □ *But in the rare atmosphere of **the corridors of** medical **power** which lead to the council rooms of the Royal Colleges, psychiatrists are regarded as long-haired drop-outs who lack the mental discipline and capacity to understand real ailments and problems.* NS

cost sb dear affect sb's health, happiness, prestige etc adversely and seriously **S:** foolishness, rashness, intemperance, cruelty; it...to admit his error □ *'In fact he* (R A Butler) *is a very considerate man and usually observant,' says a friend. 'But when he's preoccupied, he simply doesn't notice things.' Politically, this absent-mindedness was to **cost** him **dear**.* ST □ *Mr Gamble's first fight on behalf of his students and their parents has **cost** him **dear**. 'But I hope,' he told me, 'that our experience has a lesson to teach.'* RT

cost (sb) a fortune etc (informal) cost a large sum of money; (esp) be much more costly than other things of its kind, or cost more than one is willing or able to pay **O:** a fortune, ⚠ a packet, a pretty penny, the earth, a bomb □ *See, Janet, this huge yellow rose wreath here from Mrs Pettigrew. It must have **cost** her **a fortune**.* MM □ *The party was very good and we didn't leave until very late, so it was a jolly good thing we did take Sally with us or the baby-sitter would have **cost a fortune**.* WI □ *'All going to France. For a holiday. Place in Brittany.' '**Cost** you **a pretty penny**, won't it?'* BFA □ *'That's a queer house of yours, Pomfret Towers,' said Mr Adams. 'It must have **cost a pretty penny** to build.'* WDM □ *It looks as though it must have **cost a bomb** and intends to sell for one—that is if £200 for a velvet jacket and jersey trousers is considered explosive.* SC.

cost sb his life be the cause of sb losing his life, of his death □ *But remember that one false move could **cost** Sally **her life**. If you try to get in touch with anybody while I'm out, you'll be murdering her yourself.* TO □ *He made his way apprehensively along the ledge, well aware that one false step would **cost** him **his life**.* □ *Smoking, he said, was a filthy habit that had **cost** many people **their lives**.* □ also cost sb his sight, reputation etc used of anything one would not willingly be without.

cost money have to be paid for; not be obtainable for nothing **S:** good housing, proper food, decent transport; it...to travel □ *Even to sleep on the pavement there* (in the slums of Calcutta) *can **cost money**: protection money to the goondas, the thugs who'll kick a man's brains in while he sleeps if he won't pay up.* L □ *All I'm saying is that you can't just come up to me and say 'I'm pregnant. Now it's your move' as coolly as that. These things **cost money**, and I just haven't enough.* HD □ JO: *Why do you wear black shirts? They make you look like a spiv.* GEOFF: *They do, Jo, but I can't be too particular. Good clothes **cost money**.* TOH

the cost of living what it costs a person to maintain life and health at a reasonable standard having regard to food, clothing, housing and all necessary requirements □ *And anybody who sees the Common Market coming to our rescue is a wild optimist. **The cost of living** will go up and up.* NS □ *The trade figures for August showed a bountiful surplus of £87 million, and for once even the **cost-of-living** index* (ie the official statistical measurement) *contained some encouragement: last month it rose by less than 0.1 per cent, which was its lowest increase for 12 months.* L □ attrib use *the **cost-of-living** index.*

could go sth (informal) could enjoy sth: would like to have sth (esp to eat or drink) □ *The kettle's nearly boiling—**could** you **go** a cup of tea?'* □ *My companion, badly shaken, nodded dumbly and began to shamble off. As I started after him, I remember thinking that I **could**n't half **go** a beetroot roll.* SC □ *'I hope I won't snore so much tonight.' 'I hope so too. I **could go** a night's peace.'*

could/would (cheerfully) murder etc sb (informal) an expression of intense anger or exasperation with sb where the possibility of actually killing him is seldom seriously thought of **V:** murder, ⚠ kill, strangle, throttle, break sb's neck. **A:** cheerfully, with pleasure; with one's bare hands □ *By this time the audience was perfectly quiet and every mother **would cheerfully** have **murdered** a child that raised its voice.* WDM □ *I **could murder** you, you know, when you do this teasing act while I'm trying to be serious.* □ *I **could** have **killed** him at times for being so practical when what I wanted from him was a little imagination.* AITC □ *He swore that if ever he caught the fellow that had poisoned his dog he **would strangle** him with his bare hands.* □ *Heartfelt thanks for a beautiful serial. At times I **could** have **throttled** Emma for her neglect of Charles (played so lovingly by Tom Conti).* RT

could swear (that) feel perfectly sure (that) □ SARAH: *I thought Prince dealt the cards.*

CISSIE: *What's the matter with you, Sarah? Hymie dealt them.* PRINCE: *I* ***could have sworn*** *Sarah dealt them.* CSWB □ *There was the slow movement of the last quartet in date, again music one* ***could*** *have* ***sworn*** *one knew in every detail.* T □ *I can't find my nail scissors anywhere and yet I* ***could swear that*** *I put them back in the drawer myself not half an hour ago.* □ *I* ***could swear*** *the man at the next table was sitting opposite me in the train.* □ in past tense, the meaning is that one's certainty has now been proved wrong.

couldn't agree more (catchphrase) agree completely with, approve of, an opinion expressed by sb else □ *'Liberty's the most sickening claptrap of all,' she was saying. 'Liberty to conscript, Liberty to sit back on solid dividends and pour out woolly-minded platitudes.' 'I* ***couldn't agree more*** *about the woollymindedness,' said Terence.* HAA □ *'I'm afraid I've been boring you,' he said 'with all this talk about the office.' And his two listeners, though too polite to say so,* ***couldn't*** *have* ***agreed more.*** □ PEPPER: *After all, what happens when a boxer gets knocked out in the ring? He's lost the fight.* MRS VINEGAR: *I* ***couldn't agree more.*** ART

couldn't care less (catchphrase) be utterly indifferent to, unmoved by, a fact or situation, esp one which might be expected to hold one's interest, or affect one's feelings or conduct; (not) care/give a damn etc (qv) □ *But even if Chou En Lai cared about Asian reactions, it is possible that his colleagues* ***could not care less*** *and are bent simply on the increase of Chinese might.* SC □ *Muriel would have liked to stand up for this handsome stranger's chance, but the cunning which Cupid injects in female hearts warned her to be cautious. 'I* ***couldn't care less,*** *' she said severely.* RM □ (mental nursing) *Perhaps the hardest and most discouraging* (burden) *is a largely justifiable feeling that the outside world, and even the bosses of their own small hospital world, just* ***couldn't care less.*** NS

a counsel of perfection a piece of advice that is difficult, or impossible, to follow because it does not take into account the shortcomings or frailties of human nature □ *'When you have done all that, you will have solved the problem* (of reasonably priced accommodation for visitors, students etc in London). *I reckon that it will take ten years.' The unfortunate thing is that these fierce and indeed rather radical* ***counsels of perfection*** *are unlikely to be followed.* NS □ *For a fellow who's made such a mix-up of his own life, he's uncommonly full of* ***counsels of perfection*** *for other people.* □ ('Woman's Hour' programme note) *How to be a Good Mum or Dad:* ***counsels of perfection*** *from those who'd like to be, or have, one!* RT

count one's blessings [V + O] realize how much one has to be thankful for, and not grumble □ SONIA: *As you get older, days don't last so long. Tuesdays and Thursdays become one and soon they all roll in together. Still, I mustn't grumble, I must* ***count my blessings.*** DPM □ *My upbringing as a child had taught me to have resource within myself. I was also taught to* ***count my blessings*** *and this I certainly did.* MFM □ *To Luke it seemed that he had wasted years of his life, and perhaps his health for good, just to have all snatched away within sight of the end. On the other hand, Martin found considerable comfort for himself and he began to* ***count his blessings.*** NM □ commonly uttered to urge oneself or others to be grateful for what one has, or they have (in the forms *one must/you should* ***count one's/your blessings***).

count one's chickens (before they are hatched) [V + O] be too confident too early of one's success in realizing an ambition, obtaining a result, acquiring possessions, etc □ *She's been boasting all over the village about her son going to Oxford and now he hasn't been given a place. It shows you that you shouldn't* ***count your chickens before they're hatched.*** □ *He had been* ***counting his chickens*** *and borrowing money on the strength of his expectations as his uncle's sole heir. When the old man married his housekeeper, that put him in a proper fix.* □ (NONCE) *I should have known better than to start* ***counting my criminals before they were behind bars.*** RT □ *don't* ***count your chickens*** often uttered as warning not to be prematurely confident.

count the cost [V + O] assess what advantages and/or disadvantages there are, were, or may be, in doing sth; decide whether sth is, was, or will be, worth doing □ *Day trippers* (to France) *plunge at their target with all the urgency of commandos in a raid. Their time abroad is precious. They don't stop to* ***count the cost.*** TO □ *Dr Doug Smith, the Lions' manager, did his rounds and* ***counted the cost*** *of a victory on the previous afternoon in a bad-tempered, ill-mannered slog against the province of Canterbury.* L □ *Riding out, they didn't* ***count the cost;*** *they had one end in view—to serve their king.* PW

count the days/hours [V + O] know how many days/hours must go by before some desired event, and count them off one by one until then; look forward to sth with eagerness □ MRS ELLIOTT: *And while he's been in hospital all these weeks, he's known he's got somewhere to come back to. He's known that somebody wants him, anyway, and that's a great deal. To know that someone is* ***counting the days*** *until you come home.* EGD □ *I hope Judy is enjoying the School Party as much as she was looking forward to it. She's been* ***counting the hours*** *since she got up this morning.* □ mainly continuous tenses.

count etc oneself fortunate/lucky [V + O + Comp] recognize that one is lucky, concerning sth specified or understood **V:** count, ⚠ consider, think, reckon □ *'Still, I think Isabel can* ***count herself lucky,*** *' she said quietly, 'to have an opportunity to get away, when so many young mothers are more or less house-bound.'* PW □ (unemployment in Scotland) *Yet thousands of Glaswegians will* ***count themselves lucky*** *if they can afford a day trip to Largs and a plate of ice cream this summer.* NS □ *David* (due to be discharged from prison) ***counts himself*** *particularly* ***fortunate*** *that his family have not abandoned him.* RT □ *Every reporter who has worked any length of time in the courts has been, at one time or another, identified by an eager witness as the accused.* ***Consider yourself lucky*** *if you are identified as a pickpocket—there are worse crimes.* SC □ often followed by *that*-clause, *if*-clause or *to*-inf.

count heads [V + O] reckon how many persons are present, doing sth, etc; use the calculation, whether precise or not, as a basis for deciding which of two or more opinions, policies etc to favour □ *Even with a supervisor about, there were so many children in the pool that one could have gone under and never be noticed. I did try to* ***count heads****, but the amount of activity going on made it impossible.* □ *If that is good which meets the wishes of the greatest number, then quantity becomes quality. This kind of undifferentiation can lead to a world in which every kind of activity is finally made meaningless by being reduced to* ***counting of heads****.* UL □ *If you were simply to* ***count heads*** *I dare say there would be more people in favour of capital punishment being restored than against it.* □ *Gormley and Daly* (miners' leaders) *both wanted to avoid a row in the wages debate and* ***a*** *quick* ***head-count*** *showed that Scargill's £20 resolution had only the barest chance of winning.* OBS □ variant (a) counting of heads; n compounds a head-count, head-counting.

count (the) pennies [V + O] (informal) calculate costs carefully and minutely; be economical, or, possibly, mean □ *I'll marry her if I have to put her in the family way to do it. I'll make her daddy give me a damned good job. I'll never* ***count pennies*** *again.* RATT □ *'It's all part of the man's character,' the Chief explained. 'A man who has always learnt to* ***count the pennies*** *and to risk the pounds.'* OMIH □ *Then, we went to a restaurant off Piccadilly and had dinner. That was very expensive too. I wasn't in the mood to* ***count the pennies****.*

count sheep [V + O] try to induce sleep by counting (with one's eyes closed) imaginary sheep jumping one after another over a stile □ *But these were surface thoughts—hardly more real to her than* ***counting sheep*** *and sometimes deliberately induced to encourage sleep—with which she beguiled the weary hours.* PW □ *'I often wonder if anybody ever does* ***count sheep*** *jumping over a stile to send themselves to sleep.' 'Well, I do, for one. I find it very effective, too.'* □ *'Was I looking cynical and superior?' he asked. 'I was thinking about sheep.' 'What,* ***counting 'em****? Trying to put yourself to sleep?'* PE

a country cousin a person who lives in the country □ *Londoners themselves are infrequent visitors to the city's showpieces. If it were not for the tourists and* ***the country cousins****, most of these establishments could close their doors.* □ *Some of your smart friends make me feel like* ***a*** *real* ***country cousin****.* □ *At this time of year* ***country cousins*** *often ask townees to advise them on shows to see in London.* NS □ often pl; a somewhat patronising term implying that such a person is, or would be, at a loss in (superior) urban society and/or surroundings.

a course of action (a planned programme of) activity to achieve some desired end; the procedure adopted to get sth done, effect some change, etc □ *One's friends find nothing easier than advising* ***a course of action*** *which involves ceasing to go to bed with one's young woman.* SPL □ *The Chancellor of the Exchequer seems apprehensive that pressure will be brought to bear on the Government to agree to a modest revaluation of sterling as part of the general realignment. He obviously is opposed to such* ***a course of action****.* SC □ (on the Nazi concentration camp, Auschwitz) *Each one of us carries in himself the seeds of all possible actions. If sometimes there may be an abyss between two* ***courses of action****, at other times it is only a question of degree.* L

(change) the course of history [V + O pass] (change) the sequence of events in time that make up the world's history □ *Throughout* ***the*** *whole* ***course of history*** *empires have flourished only to decay.* □ *'This is one of those moments,' Wormold said, 'which might* ***change the course of history****.'* OMIH □ *He tells us repeatedly that the birth of Christ, and the creation of the Church, was 'an event which* ***changed the course of*** *human* ***history****,' but denies that it has in any way improved, or was intended to improve, the world.* NS

the course of justice the procedures and just application of the laws of the land, esp as administered in courts of law □ (source) *Though justice be thy plea, consider this,/That in* ***the course of justice****, none of us/Should see salvation: we do pray for mercy...* MERCHANT OF VENICE IV 1 □ (criminal intimidation of witnesses) *There have recently been a number of disturbing cases in our courts in which witnesses have been so terrified of the possible consequences of telling the truth that* ***the course of justice*** *has been made extremely difficult.* SC □ *You can't interfere with* ***the course of justice*** *at this stage. Even if you persuaded the plaintiff Watson to drop the charge, the police have obtained sufficient independent evidence to bring charges themselves.*

the course of true love never did run smooth (saying) any love affair will have its troubles, problems, difficulties □ (source) *Ah me! for aught that ever I could read,/Could ever hear by tale or history,/* ***The course of true love never did run smooth*** MIDSUMMER NIGHT'S DREAM I 1 □ *Muriel told herself that somehow she must see Bill and warn him how much* ***the course of true love would be smoothed*** *if he could give her father an assurance that nobody should ever persuade him to come to the microphone and talk about the monster.* RM □ *If* ***the course of love runs smoothly*** *and Princess Anne can tell the Queen that absence* does *make the heart grow fonder, friends are saying there will be a betrothal announcement.* L □ (NONCE) *It's odd that Mr Taylor seems to believe that a labyrinthine maze of argument, speculation and intellectual kleptomania is necessary to establish such homely conclusions. But then* ***the course of true analysis never does run smooth****, even for bestsellers.* NS

court death etc [V + O] behave in a way that invites death, danger etc, or in a way that gives the impression that these are being sought **O:** death, ⚠ disaster, trouble, danger □ *In a sense, of course, all battles are fantastic, since they are an abrogation of reason, a deliberate* ***courting of death****.* T □ *He drove faster and more wildly.* ***Courting death****, their own and anyone else's, was the one possible chance of escape.* HD □ *His kindly serious face looked rather anxiously round the harbour, weighing up, it seemed, whether to risk overwhelming Brown with in-*

formation or to ***court the danger*** *of leaving him in perplexity on some point.* ILIH □ *I warned her she was* ***courting trouble****, staying away from her classes whenever the fancy took her to do something else instead.* □ variant a courting of death etc.

a cover address an address, eg of an agency, one's employers, etc, through which mail will reach the addressee, though not addressed to him at any place of residence □ *His routes are, first by Russian and Polish ships from the port of Antwerp, secondly, to* ***cover addresses*** *in Switzerland, and thirdly to West Berlin for passage through to the East.* DS □ *It might take some time for the news to reach my brother. All I had was* ***a cover address****, care of a bank in Sao Paulo.*

cover the ground[1] [V + O pass] travel, or range about, over territory **det:** the; a lot of, a good deal of; more, less □ *We* ***covered a lot of ground*** *on our tour of Spain.* □ *What with continually slicing or pulling his ball into the rough, my uncle* ***covered*** *about* ***twice as much ground*** *as the average golfer in going round a course.*

cover the ground[2] [V + O pass] deal with a subject, proposed arrangements, etc, completely, less fully, etc **det:** the; a lot of; more, less, the same □ *Asked if the course could be shortened to two years, the professor replied that the majority of students would not be able to* ***cover the ground*** *in less than three years.* □ *Mr Macmillan was fresh from his week-end at Rambouillet with President de Gaulle. Their talks, although less formal than the others,* ***covered*** *largely* ***the same ground****.* OBS □ *'We haven't succeeded in* ***covering as much ground*** *as we hoped, today,' the chairman said.* □ *When I started to study Economics I didn't realise there was such* ***a lot of ground*** *to be* ***covered****.*

cover a multitude of sins [V + O] compensate for, or serve as a mask for, sins, faults, shortcomings □ (source) *And above all things have fervent charity among yourselves: for charity shall* ***cover the multitude of sins****.* I PETER IV 8 □ *'What job does he do?' 'Economic Mission, but that* ***covers a multitude of sins****.'* QA □ *The girl isn't worth her salary—she could leave tomorrow and I wouldn't shed a tear. But as far as my partner is concerned, a pretty face* ***covers a multitude of sins****.* □ *That shame-faced phrase 'I'm just a housewife'* ***covers a*** *greater* ***multitude of sins*** *than we care to admit. It enables us to forget, for example, that despite the advent of labour-saving technology, housewifery is still for most women a sentence to 'hard labour' for life.* NS □ can be facetious, as in second example.

cover one's tracks [V + O] continue to leave no evidence of where one has been or what one has been doing □ *Finn suggested that we should heave* (the cage) *into the river, but I was against this. We decided eventually to leave it where it was. It wasn't as if we really cared about* ***covering our tracks****, or as if this were possible anyway.* UTN □ *Nobody ever knew what Johnson might be up to. It was second nature to him to* ***cover his tracks*** *even when negotiating business that was perfectly legitimate and above board.* □ (a jockey) *He is a grave, dedicated man, like a monk in a grimly penitential order, who* ***covers his tracks*** *with charm and polite jokes.* RT □ *Competitors were invited to produce punning 'Guardian' headlines. I was told the 'Guardian' men themselves went in for this, though they seem to have* ***covered their tracks*** *remarkably well.* NS

crack a bottle [V + O] open a bottle of wine etc to have a drink; take part in social drinking with another or others □ *That's wonderful news! I can't think of any better reason for* ***cracking a bottle****. Bring your wife round to our place and we'll have a little celebration together.* □ *Drink brings out the worst in some people but he was as cheery an old sinner as ever* ***cracked a bottle****.* □ *I know an amusing little place, licensed of course, impeccable service, marvellous cabaret. Why don't we nip along there, you and I, and* ***crack a bottle****?* L

crack a joke [V + O pass] tell a funny story; make a humorous remark that causes laughter □ *In spite of the growing army of hopeless alcoholics, in spite of the hundreds of thousands of persons annually maimed and killed by drunken drivers, popular comedians still* ***crack jokes*** *about alcohol and its addicts.* DOP □ HENRY (irritably): *Could a horse be trained to stand still and mark time with its four legs?* ADA: *Oh.* (Pause) *The ones I used to fancy* (= bet on, in races) *all did.* (She laughs. Pause) *Laugh, Henry, it's not every day I* ***crack a joke****.* E □ *I was not very good at lessons, so some teachers were always getting at me and showing me up in front of everyone. I defended myself by* ***cracking jokes*** *at their expense.* TVT

cramp sb's style [V + O] (informal) prevent sb from doing sth as freely, or as well, as he might otherwise do □ *It* ***cramped her style*** *to talk to Alec in this local public place, where they couldn't even use their natural voices, much less endearments.* PW □ *We search them occasionally, both physically search them and also search their cars, and we watch them. And I think this tends to* ***cramp their style****.* L □ *Do you find that having a student-teacher 'observing' in the classroom* ***cramps your style****?* □ *Here also there are potential problems with spare parts, fuel nozzles, and so forth. Diversification, the programme seemed to say, is fine in peacetime, but it* ***cramps one's style*** *in war.* L

a crash course/programme [O (NP)] an organized course or plan for sth to be learnt/done at top speed or much more quickly than is usual **V:** offer, provide, lay on; attend □ *The University offers* ***a crash course*** *in Russian—from beginners' to Entrance Examination level in one year.* □ *Parliament will be summoned at the earliest possible moment so that* ***a crash programme*** *of financial recovery can be undertaken.* T □ also pl.

a crashing bore [Comp (NP)] sb who irritates his listeners with an excess of dull, uninteresting talk; an excessively tedious task, situation etc **V:** ⚠ be, become, turn into; find sb/sth □ *'All she's concerned with is pushing that dirty politician up the dirty political ladder. Also, she's* ***a crashing bore****,' he added.* EM □ *'It* (our relationship) *doesn't work any more.' 'Is it Larrie?' asked John abruptly. 'Oh! God, of course not,' said Elvira. 'He's* ***a crashing bore*** *and I wish he wouldn't come to the office.'* ASA □ *'I'm awfully sorry, old man,' he said, 'but Eva invited some friends up. Personally, I'd rather go out.*

They're ***crashing bores****, but there it is. Some other time, eh?'* RATT

create/make a bad etc impression [V + O pass] cause people to have a bad etc opinion of sb/sth, whether this is a true judgment or not **adj:** bad, ⚠ poor, unfavourable; good, splendid, favourable □ *The fears about tying ourselves to the common agricultural policy seem justified. The zeal the Six have displayed in trying to complete all their arrangements, including those for fishing, before other countries are admitted, has also* ***created a bad impression****.* SC □ *It remains to be seen how much the pupils learn by Miss Hamilton's methods, but it certainly* ***creates a good impression*** *to see a class busily engaged and looking happy.* □ *Your protégé may be all you say, Andrew, but* ***a*** *rather* ***poor impression*** *was* ***created*** *at his interview and I don't think he'll get the job.*

create (bloody) hell/murder [V + O] (informal) make an uproar; cause trouble; be aggressively angry □ *My, what a temper! I wish you'd have seen her just now.* ***Created bloody murder*** *when she heard there was a chap from the 'Courier' at the stage-door.* AITC □ *The boy's father came up to the school prepared to* ***create bloody murder****, but he gradually calmed down as the facts of the case were explained to him.* □ *'Some children are extraordinarily plucky,' the dental surgeon was saying, 'while others start* ***creating murder*** *at the first sight of the drill.'* □ *If the odd 10 per cent of the population doesn't swear, that's OK with me, but when they start* ***creating hell*** *because the majority of people do swear they are nut cases.* RT □ *'There's a chap* ***creating****,' said the senior and dirtier of the waiters. 'Says he doesn't like the tipple.'* CON □ *My wife won't half* ***create*** *when I tell her I'm giving up this job and going back to sea again.* □ create by itself, as shown in last two examples, has much the same meaning.

creature comforts [O (NP)] those things which man physically needs and enjoys, such as warmth, food, clothing, household amenities **V:** enjoy, love; miss, need □ *The bath is prepared with much child-like glee. Beatie loves her* ***creature comforts*** *and does with unabashed, almost animal, enthusiasm that which she enjoys.* R □ *No, thank you. I'm far too fond of my* ***creature comforts*** *to go camping.* □ *The Home couldn't have been better run as far as* ***creature comforts*** *were concerned, but too little was done to interest and occupy the minds of the residents.*

a credibility gap the degree to which one finds it difficult to believe what one is asked to believe □ *Nell Dunn sets up* ***an*** *unbridgeable* ***credibility gap*** *between herself and her audience with the dire consequence that Maro's further adventures are devoid of all interest and significance.* NS □ *...a talk on Radio 3 about the natural and supernatural interpretations of Biblical events—and in particular the Resurrection. '****The credibility gap*** *seems to me to rule out deliberate deceit by the disciples or that the women had gone to the wrong tomb.'* L □ (the merits of the English system of criminal justice) *There seems to be a terrifying communications gap, and consequently* ***a*** *rapidly widening* ***credibility gap****. On one side are ranged the Establishment, authority, the middle class; on the other side, the young, the black, students and the working class.* L

a credit to sb [Comp (NP)] sb/sth of which one can be justly proud, esp sb/sth whose good qualities, excellence etc are, to a greater or lesser degree, the result of one's own efforts; do sb credit (qv) **V:** ⚠ be, appear; become, turn out □ SAM: *What a lovely daughter you have! She's* ***a credit to*** *you.* HSG □ *The boy is still very young, you must remember. He may mend his ways and turn out* ***a credit to*** *his family yet.* □ *'It's not a case of accepting the cheapest tender,' the councillor pointed out. 'We want to build a community centre that'll be* ***a credit to*** *the place.'* □ *'It's my wife, really, that looks after the garden.' 'Well, it's* ***a credit to*** *her.'*

creep and crawl [v + v non-rev] behave in a timid, subservient way □ *There was Bates, doing every odd job that was flung at him, just to keep in the bosses' good books. And what good did all his* ***creeping and crawling*** *do him in the end?* □ *I don't mind accepting a favour if it's freely granted, but I'm damned if I'm going to* ***creep and crawl*** *for one.* □ *You should either stand up to his fits of temper or ignore them. The more you* ***creep and crawl*** *trying to placate him, the more pleasure he gets in taking it out on you.*

a creeping Jesus (informal, derogatory) a term for the kind of person, esp a professing Christian, to whom non-sympathisers attribute (often with good reason) hypocritical humility, tiresome piety, intrusive evangelism, etc □ *He had in his service a pious, soft-spoken, tip-toeing unmarried middle-aged Irishman for whom Guy felt much affection, and whom he called Tony to his face and* ***Creeping Jesus*** *behind his back.* MM □ *'If your despair does not lend you compassion, then I can only limit its field of devastation.' 'My God!' cried Hubert, 'you talk about compassion, you* ***creeping-Jesus*** *Karamazov. I attempted to speak to you directly out of our despairs and desires, and you throw it back in my face.'* HAA □ attrib use *a* ***creeping-Jesus*** *Karamazov*; in last example, reference is to a character in Dostoyevsky's novel 'The Brothers Karamazov'.

a creeping paralysis (informal) physical or moral paralysis from a disease that manifests itself slowly and gradually □ *Eventually, nothing in this big world can move the 'common man' as a 'common man'. He is infinitely cagey; he puts up so powerful a silent resistance that it can threaten to become a spiritual death,* ***a creeping paralysis*** *of the moral will.* UL □ *In the early years of the following century the movement finally succumbed to* ***the creeping paralysis*** *that had set in with the death of its founder.*

crime doesn't pay (saying) criminal behaviour is not only wrong, but foolish from a practical point of view (ie as one is likely to be found out and punished) □ *He* (the chief of police) *was a lank and scowling man, whose polished boots and belt proclaimed his importance; he had only recently taken over this post, and it was obvious that he intended to prove to the inhabitants that* ***crime did not pay****.* DF □ *Whatever may be the case in real life, 98 per cent of the thousands of crime novels published put across the unmistakable message that* ***crime doesn't pay****.* □ *Last month Mr Feather* (a union leader) *urged employers to adopt a firm line in resisting unofficial pressure—if they do not, he warned, they would be demonstrating that '**crime pays**'.* SC ⇨ it pays to do sth.

(shed/weep) crocodile tears [V + O pass] (shed) false tears; (express) feigned sorrow (from the moaning, sighing noises attributed to a crocodile that is luring a person towards it to be devoured) □ *Molly has her father twisted round her little finger. No matter how badly she's behaved she's only got to **shed** a few **crocodile tears** and he forgives her.* □ *This country above all has an obligation to Cyprus not to follow the easy path of greeting President Makarios with a deaf ear and **a crocodile tear**.* NS □ *Too many vested interests—which include men who are now **weeping crocodile tears** over the damage Lonrho has done to the capitalist image—have too much to lose and too little to gain from radical reform.* L

crook one's finger[1] [V + O pass] bend one's finger into the shape of a crook or hook □ *She perched on the edge of the chair drinking tea with **her** little **finger crooked** above the handle of the cup.* □ *The doctor told her to spend a few minutes **crooking** and uncrooking **her fingers**, several times a day, in order to keep the arthritic joints as supple as possible.*

crook one's finger[2] [V + O pass] with the palm upwards crook one's forefinger in sb's direction as a summons or invitation to approach □ *He caught sight of Mary Pearson's husband, and beckoned also to him. As Bevill **crooked his finger**, Pearson gave a relaxed smile and came unconcernedly into the ring.* NM □ *Across the heads of the other guests I saw Anne **crook her finger** at me and point to the empty place at her side on the divan.*

crook one's finger[3] [V + O] make the slightest beckoning sign and expect others to react immediately □ *I love the cool way you assume that I've just been sitting here waiting for you to **crook your** little **finger**. You take too much for granted.* RATT □ *He's got delusions of grandeur, that fellow. Thinks he's only got to **crook his finger** and we'll all run about to do his bidding.* □ *You know that, too, don't you? **Crook your finger**, and they'd come running. Whatever tidying up there was to be done, they'd be glad to do it for you.* ST

a cross between sth and sth sb/sth that is neither of two things mentioned, but resembles or contains elements of both (from cross-breeding in animal husbandry, horticulture etc) □ *And the strange noises she* (a monkey) *was making sounded like **a cross between** a bird cry **and** the friendly greeting of a cat.* BB □ *All this understanding then, this going about like **a cross between** St Francis **and** Thomas More comes to nothing then, when it doesn't happen to be your particular little fad.* HAA □ *A harassed French waitress came to operate a large patent wooden-handled bread-slicer about the size of an old-fashioned sewing-machine: **a cross** somewhere **between** a guillotine **and** a chaff-cutter.* BFA □ *On the first Sunday of each September, Venice stages The Historical Regatta. Imagine **a cross between** a Coronation **and** the Boat Race, and you'll get some idea of the pageantry and excitement.* TVT

cross one's bridges when one comes to them (saying) one should not worry about a problem that may never arise; a future problem, even if inevitable, will be better dealt with later when its nature is more precisely known □ *I decided to report that conversation about the use of the bomb to Hector Ruse. To him it seemed almost unbelievably academic. 'I fancy our masters will **cross that bridge when they come to it**,' he said.* NM □ *If only one did not have to face a stranger who might regard her as a usurper! She shook herself mentally. Don't **cross your bridges** prematurely, Sarah Isbister.* WI □ *'How could you keep up those enormous mortgage payments, though, if you fell ill or lost your job?' 'How, indeed. But I don't believe in **crossing my bridges before I come to them**.'* □ variants one will cross that bridge when one comes to it, don't cross your bridges before/until you come to them.

cross the Great Divide [V + O] (cliché) die □ *Then I remembered something that Charles had said: 'Zombies* (here = conventional suburban types) *always "pass away" or "**cross the Great Divide**" or "go into the sunset". And they "lose" people like they lose a parcel or a glove.'* RATT □ divide = 'high mountain range separating two valleys or territories'.

cross my heart (and hope to die) (informal) an expression used to emphasize the sincerity of a promise or the truth of a statement (cross my heart refers to the sign of the Cross and hope to die = 'may I die if this is not true') □ *'Now, don't you go telling your parents where we've been today, or I'll knock your head off.' 'I won't,' replied the younger boy, '**cross my heart and hope to die**.'* □ *'But—oh, never mind.' She stroked my hair gently. 'But what?' 'You'll think I'm silly.' 'I promise I won't. **Cross my heart**.'* RATT □ *You'll maybe not believe me but, **cross my heart**, she buys chicken livers and fresh cream every day for those two cats of hers.*

cross one's mind [V + O] occur to one without being deliberately reasoned out or striven for **S:** thought, idea; suspicion; it...that he might know; □ *The thought of murder **crossed my mind**, of course, and I put it out of my head.* RFW □ *The thought **crossed his mind**, among other thoughts, that Jean's brain might be undergoing a softening process.* MM □ *The speculative possibilities are endless and every columnist, Congressman, and armchair diplomat is teeming with theories that never **crossed his mind** a year or a week ago.* L □ *It never **crossed his mind** that, if she were to deceive Froulish, her unfaithfulness would take the form of simple quid pro quo prostitution.* HD □ *'Does it never occur to her that she's taking up too much of your time?' 'She's so self-centred, it would never **cross her mind**.'* □ *One of the things I liked most about Shaw was the way he always said and did what would only **cross the minds of** others.* NS □ common use in past simple tense with *never*.

cross sb's path [V + O pass] come into contact with sb, in the course of his travels, business, mode of life, etc □ *'I'll report him to Mr Hogg down at Divisional Office,' he said. 'He'll wish he never **crossed my path**.'* TT □ *I know you can't get on with Clark, but you shouldn't let that worry you. You'll be working in such very dif-*

ferent departments, there'll be no need for you to ***cross his path*** *unless you want to.* □ *I had heard a lot about Barker, and he of me, but up till then* ***our paths*** *had never* ***crossed.*** □ variant our/ your/their paths cross.

cross one's/the Rubicon [V + O pass] take an action, start a process, which is important, and which cannot be reversed; the die is cast (qv) (when, in 49 BC, Julius Caesar crossed the river Rubicon, a natural boundary between the province he commanded and Italy governed by Pompey, he started a civil war) □ *Persons using the bridge do so at their own risk, the notice said. Superstitiously she had always avoided* ***crossing*** *it, as if it was a sort of* ***Rubicon.*** PW □ *Of four models in the £900-£1,000 class two are French, one Japanese, and only one British. Such previous bargain buys as the VW Beetle and the Mini have* ***crossed their Rubicon*** *into four figures.* NS

(to) crown it all[1] [V + O] (to) complete or embellish sth □ *They gave us a delicious meal and,* ***to crown it all,*** *a very rare old brandy which must have cost a fortune.* □ *It was a very happy anniversary for mum and dad; all their old friends rallied round, the grandchildren behaved like angels, and* ***to crown it all*** *my brother George, whom they hadn't seen for eight years, flew over from Canada specially for the occasion.*

(to) crown it all[2] [V + O] (to) surpass, be more important or much worse than (though connected with), what has gone before or has been previously mentioned □ *Agriculture and industry were largely at a standstill. Food was scarce and* ***to crown it all*** *there was no central government in being.* MFM □ *'I've a good mind to throw you out of the house,' his father said. 'You're lazy, dirty, and impudent and now,* ***to crown it all,*** *I find you're dishonest as well.'* □ *We had a perfect week-end with nothing to do but eat and sleep and enjoy the scenery — and* ***crowning it all,*** *glorious sunshine.*

one's crowning glory that which, above all else, gives beauty, distinction or fame to sb/sth □ *He considered that Edinburgh was the most beautiful city in Britain and that the New Town was* ***its crowning glory.*** □ *His impersonation of Charlie Chaplin conveyed little of that art which was* ***the crowning glory of*** *the silent cinema.* □ *Father had all us girls wear our hair long. When we complained, as we frequently did, he would remind us that a woman****'s crowning glory*** *was her hair.* □ (saying) *a woman****'s crowning glory*** *is her hair.*

the crowning success the performance, achievement etc, which, although others are good enough, is the most successful, popular or praiseworthy □ *Miss Hopgood and Miss Crowder gave a talk on the Riviera. But* ***the crowning success*** *was a talk by Miss Pemberton on Home Cooking for the Coronation, with a practical demonstration.* WDM □ *In a lifetime of outstanding services to education, Sir Geoffrey has told me that he considers the establishment of this Institution to be* ***his crowning success.***

a crumb of comfort some small amount of consolation, or alleviation, in an unpleasant or undesired situation □ *I'm sure that* ***the*** *only* ***crumb of comfort*** *for many readers over the budget is the assumption, 'Oh well, when we're* (the Labour Party) *back we'll repeal it.'* NS □ *'Three hours to wait in this God-forsaken hole!' 'Let's see if there's a waiting-room open. I've got a flask of coffee and a few sandwiches with me.' 'Well, that's* ***a crumb of comfort,*** *anyway.'* □ also pl *a few* ***crumbs of comfort;*** often in construction *the only/sole* ***crumb of comfort.***

crumbs (that fall) from the (rich man's) table things that remain after a rich man has finished, and which a poor person can have (does not refer to charity freely given out of goodwill and at some sacrifice) □ (sources) *There was a certain beggar named Lazarus desiring to be fed with* ***crumbs from the rich man's table.*** LUKE XVI 20-1 □ *Yet the dogs eat of the* ***crumbs which fall from their master's table.*** MATTHEW XV 27 □ *...the announcement of grants for the improvement of older property in development areas. In reality, of course, these particular* ***crumbs from the rich man's table*** *will amount to no more than the tarting-up of some of the meanest and most miserably laid-out areas of the 19th century housing in the country.* NS □ *In Scotland it is illegal to remove articles from garbage containers put out by householders, but many policemen turn a blind eye on the poor 'bucket-pickers' rummaging for the* ***crumbs that have fallen from the table.*** □ *At least these programmes prove one thing: that the working man is not prepared to be pushed around and to be content with the* ***crumbs from the rich man's table.*** RT

(when) the crunch comes (informal) (when) it is a time of crisis or confrontation or necessary decision; if/when it comes to the crunch/push (Vol 1) (qv) □ *'We stayed as long as we could,' he said. '****When the crunch came*** *we were ever so reluctant to pull out, we really were, but there was no alternative.'* OBS □ *The white knitters insisted that they would not start training Indians as full-fashioned knitters until a 'compromise' was accepted: eight Indian jobs would have to be given back to whites.* ***The crunch came*** *at the beginning of the night shift at 10 p.m. on Tuesday.* NS □ *The Housing Finance Bill is the most dogmatic piece of legislation in years. Mr Walker is going to find it more difficult than his colleagues did,* ***when the crunch comes,*** *to effect an about-turn.* NS

the crusading spirit etc the committed enthusiasm with which one tries to advance a project, idea, movement etc **n:** spirit, ⚠ temper, note, mood □ *At that time there was* ***a crusading spirit*** *in the atmosphere at the Headquarters, which took much of its inspiration from Eisenhower.* MFM □ *There is no limit to the capacity of men to believe what they want to believe, especially if they are leader-writers. Talk to politicians, however, and the tone is different.* ***The crusading note*** *is markedly absent.* NS □ *For Ackerley, like Lawrence, possessed a talent for self-humiliation. It goes with* ***the crusading spirit.*** NS

the crux of the matter etc [Comp (NP)] that part of a situation, problem, argument etc that presents the most difficulty, the solution to which makes other aspects of the situation (etc) easier to deal with **V:** ⚠ be, become; make sth. **o:** matter, ⚠ problem; dispute, argument □ *'So the cloud will be hitting the atmosphere during* *what would generally be the daytime?' 'That's right. And it will not be hitting the atmosphere during the night.' 'And that's* ***the crux of the matter****,' continued Weichart.* TBC ▫ *That, in fact, is* ***the crux of the matter****. If we believe in ourselves and our ability, we need not be afraid of economic competition or political integration.* L ▫ *But neither Mr Carr nor Mrs Rossi quite comes to grips with* ***the crux of the argument****.* L

cry/laugh all the way to the bank (catchphrase) (cry =) apologize for or pretend to deplore/(laugh =) openly rejoice in the fact that one has, or is making, a lot of money ▫ (referring to source) *Some years ago Liberace successfully sued for libel the 'Daily Mirror' columnist, Cassandra. During the trial, the defendant's counsel was cross-examining Liberace about various alleged excesses. Liberace, angry, replied that if he was as absurd as counsel was suggesting, then he wished the court to know that he was* ***crying all the way to the bank****. The jury laughed, and effectively the case was won.* OBS ▫ *However carefully they* (suppliers of glamorous underwear by mail order) *do it they often offend somebody, like the religious objectors who write furious letters—'They say I'll suffer for it in the hereafter,' says Lewis Cligman. 'It makes me* ***cry all the way to the bank****.'* ST ▫ (a TV chat-show) *Parkinson took a pummelling from both his guests—not that that should stop him* ***laughing all the way to the bank****.* L

cry havoc (and let slip the dogs of war) threaten, incite oneself and others, to wage war mercilessly on sb/sth; cause disruption and destruction, literally or figuratively (Havock! was an old military command — forbidden since the time of Richard II—to slaughter indiscriminately and without mercy) ▫ (source) *Caesar's spirit, ranging for revenge,... shall in these confines, with a monarch's voice* ***cry 'Havoc!' and let slip the dogs of war****.* JULIUS CAESAR III 1 ▫ *We are back to the days of robber-baron government. Next year, instead of sending a complaint to the Board of Inland Revenue, I shall lock my gates, take my shotgun down from the wall,* ***cry 'havoc' and let loose the dogs****.* NS ▫ *Those who hate bureaucracy must learn to work with bureaucracy to save it from itself, rather than* ***cry havoc*** *in the wilderness.* L ▫ (NONCE) *'In the event of an emergency'! What had given rise to such a phrase? The Emergency of 1914-18, the Boer Emergency, the Hundred Years Emergency?* ***Cry havoc, and let loose the dogs of emergency****!* ▫ often adapted, as shown.

cry wolf [V + O pass] give or spread a false alarm; be an alarmist by nature though with no intent to deceive (from the fable of the shepherd boy who called 'Wolf' so often, in order to tease, that his neighbours in the end ignored his genuine call for help) ▫ *When the voices, especially those of the Press, really have something important to speak to him* (the common man) *about, he gives them the old smile and continues to read the funny bits. They have* ***cried 'wolf'*** *too often.* UL ▫ *The people are told that they are in a more perilous condition than ever in the past. Why on earth should they believe it? '****Wolf****' has been* ***cried*** *time after time. No one is now going to pay any attention until the wolf gobbles him up.* NS

a crying evil etc [Comp (NP)] sth wrong that demands to be put right, be redressed, abolished etc as **V:** ⚠ be, become; turn into. **n:** evil, ⚠ scandal, shame; need, necessity ▫ ***The*** *great and* ***crying need*** *everywhere was going to be coal. We had 148 mines working, producing 40,000 tons a day; not nearly enough.* MFM ▫ *Wilberforce awakened the world's conscience to the iniquity of the slave trade, but it was not until 1807 that the Act was passed which put an end to* ***this crying evil****.* ▫ (from a letter) *P.S. It is* ***a crying shame*** *to say I have ever hidden anything from the Income Tax; Mr Pellew would not let me.* US ▫ *It's* ***a crying scandal*** *the prices they charge in that hotel, considering the poor service they give.* ▫ *I said I needed a new coat,* last *winter, and did without, but it's* ***a crying necessity*** *now.* ▫ pl crying evils etc.

(a voice) crying in the wilderness (sb) preaching a cause, uttering a warning, advising reform, etc in vain and ignored by the public ▫ (source) *For this is he that was spoken of by the prophet Esaias, saying,* ***The voice*** *of one* ***crying in the wilderness****, Prepare ye the way of the Lord, make his paths straight.* MATTHEW III 3 ▫ *Nevertheless Smith* (of the Criminal Investigation Department) *is adamant that if he had another kidnapping case tomorrow he would allow no publicity whatsoever. So long as people believe that crime stories sell newspapers, he may well be* ***crying in the wilderness****.* L ▫ *Mr Herron proposed a bold, but hardly revolutionary, redesigning of the Church's structure. As he recognised, there is an inbuilt resistance to change in the Kirk. But he is not* ***a voice crying in the wilderness****.* SC ▫ *Ever since he published his 'Conditions of Happiness' Mr Rattray Taylor's has been* ***a voice crying in the wilderness****. He has continually warned me about the spiritual, intellectual and ecological doom which lies ahead unless we mend our ways of living, thinking and feeling.* OBS ▫ also pl voices crying in the wilderness.

crystal clear [Comp (AdjP)] plain to understand; definite and unambiguous **n:** situation, position; views, attitude; orders, instructions. **V:** ⚠ be, become; make sth ▫ *The direct result of the meeting in Berlin on the 5th June was to make the Russian position* ***crystal clear****.* MFM ▫ *All this was happening within days of the announced date—28 July—when Mr Wilson was committed to making his own views on the Common Market* ***crystal clear*** *once and for all.* L ▫ *Mr Heath and Miss de Haviland, we were solemnly assured, were 'very old friends'. How ungallant, therefore, of Miss de Haviland to have made it* ***crystal clear****, on a radio interview last Monday morning, that the only time she had previously met the Prime Minister was on a transatlantic voyage 10 years ago.* NS ▫ often used in constructions *it was* ***crystal clear*** *that..., he made it* ***crystal clear*** *that...*

a cuckoo in the nest [Comp (NP)] an interloper; sb who shares in or takes over privileges, tasks that belong to others **V:** ⚠ be, appear, become ▫ *Paul Hogarth, himself a notable graphic journalist, describes Houghton as '****an*** *uneasy* ***cuckoo in the*** *Victorian middle-class* ***nest****' and represents him as an observer who* *became all too aware of the ugliness and corruption around him.* OBS □ *The signs are that soon it* (the Open University) *will be turning out as many graduates per year as four or five of the new universities put together. In other words it will soon cease to be a portent and become an inescapable influence, a fat* ***cuckoo in the nest***. NS

a cultural desert [Comp (NP)] a place or community where there is little or no artistic or academic activity or any interest taken in such pursuits **V:** ⚠ be, become, make sth □ *However, she seemed happy with him and had adopted most of his views, including the one that Australia was* ***a cultural desert*** *that no decent person would dream of living in.* RFW □ *This place is* ***a cultural desert****, in the Institute and out of it. The men talk of nothing but football, promotion, or their cars.* □ *He makes a point of returning each year to live theatre, but in Glasgow —* ***a cultural desert****, he calls it — the halls are gone, so he must work in Edinburgh.* RT □ *Basingstoke is well-known as* ***the*** *all-time* ***entertainment desert*** *with absolutely no recent theatrical tradition.* TVT □ desert occas has other attrib adjs or nouns, as in last example.

a culture vulture (informal, derogatory) a 'hanger-on' of the arts; a person who attends lectures and concerts, visits art galleries, reads the 'best' books, etc as a matter of duty rather than pleasure, and partly or mostly to increase his own prestige □ (review of a play) *Richard Benjamin's husband, wine snob,* ***culture vulture*** *and compulsive talker, is a true monster. His whole life is spent in creating a fashionable image to applaud.* OBS □ *Many works of art have been given 'to the nation' by private benefactors, or have been bought by public subscription through organisations like the National Art Collection Fund to save them from the clutches of* ***the*** *American '****culture vulture****'.* SC □ pl culture vultures.

one's cup is full etc one's joy, sorrow, satisfaction etc is complete; one has more joys, sorrows etc than should rightly be the lot of any one person **V:** is full, ⚠ runs over, overflows □ (sources, PSALM 23) ...***my cup shall be full***. BOOK OF COMMON PRAYER □ ...***my cup overflows***. SCOTTISH METRICAL PSALMS □ ... ***my cup runneth over***. (BIBLE: AUTHORIZED VERSION) □ *Even my school-teacher (whose heart was of stone) brought me a bagful of sweets and nuts. Finally Jack told me I'd been prayed for in church twice, on successive Sundays.* ***My cup was full****, I felt immortal.* CWR □ *Edinburgh's cultural life does tend to be rather stop-go. For three brief weeks* ***the cup is filled*** *to overflowing; at other times — particularly in the early summer — it can run perilously dry.* SC □ *Life is just as sweet for swans as it is for us,' he said. 'Now that they have been on telly,* ***their cup*** *of happiness must* ***be*** *truly* ***overflowing***.*'* L

sb's cup of tea [Comp (NP)] (informal) what one likes, is interested in, can do well, etc **V:** ⚠ be, seem, look like □ *Coombargana is my home and I would not willingly live anywhere else, but architecturally I will admit that the house isn't everybody****'s cup of tea***. RFW □ *This pain can be increased until the experimenter's research is completed, or until the subject decides that psychological research is not* ***his cup of tea***. SNP □ *Certainly Frank was doing very well for himself. Import-export was booming, but it wasn't* ***his cup of tea***. TO □ *'You may find this sort of job rather difficult.' 'But it's just* ***my cup of tea****! It's absolutely made for an unfrocked nurse.'* DIL □ *Undemanding creatures that they are, ants will eat just about anything. Left-overs, meat, bread, sugar, any dead insect, are* ***their cup of tea*** *and ants need no coaxing.* TVT □ usu neg; positive uses are usu emphatic and indicated by the advs *just, exactly, absolutely*.

the cup that cheers (but not inebriates) tea □ (source) *And while the bubbling and loud-hissing urn/Throws up a streamy column, and* ***the cups/ That cheer but not inebriate*** *wait on each,/So let us welcome peaceful evening in.* THE WINTER EVENING (W COWPER 1731-1800) □ *Good, you've put the kettle on.* ***The cup that cheers****, that's what I like. None of your coffees and cocoas for me.* □ *'Thank you,' he said. '****The cup that cheers but not inebriates****.' But his thoughts strayed longingly to the cosy pub he had just left.*

cupboard love (informal) (a show of) affection sustained by the thought of what one can get out of a situation for oneself □ *'It's only* ***cupboard love*** *that brings the boy round here so often,' the old man said sadly 'He knows I'll always give him a bit of money when he leaves.'* □ *'But I thought that couple old Mrs Smith rented her basement flat to were absolutely devoted to her.' 'Just* ***cupboard love****; they were always coming up to cadge from her — money, food, furniture, anything and everything.'*

the cure/remedy is worse than the disease (saying) the cure is more painful, or does more harm, than what it is supposed to put right □ *I tell him that if he'd smoke less he'd cough less but he says* ***the cure*** *would* ***be worse than the disease***. □ *But the execution of convicted terrorists to prevent rescue attempts by their colleagues which may involve the murder of yet more innocent people would have to be carried out immediately to be effective: and this would make nonsense of our judicial processes. Thus* ***the remedy*** *would* ***be worse than the disease***. NS □ (NONCE) *The importance of Sam Brittan is that he is making a sustained attempt to explore the causes of our present discontents, and to suggest* ***some remedial*** *which, unlike most of those currently on offer, does not threaten to* ***be worse than the disease***. ST

curiosity killed the cat (saying) an obstructive or teasing answer to a question; a warning to mind one's own business, not interfere, in case harm is done to sb; a reproof for something of this kind already done □ *'Didn't you ask him why he'd stayed out so late?' 'Yes, but all he said was "****Curiosity killed the cat****"!'* □ *Now boys, remember that* ***curiosity killed the cat****; don't go picking up any strange objects on the beach, especially if they're metal.*

curl one's/the lip(s) [V + O pass] make a sneering grimace with one's lip(s) □ *The later adolescent who first arrives in this egocentric community will find he still goes 'up' to Oxford and 'down' again. His college servant will address him as 'sir', the last place on earth where this can be done without the merest* ***curling*** *of*

the lips. OBS □ *He was a very narrow-minded pedant, academic rather than scholarly, and far too ready to* ***curl the lip*** *when such subjects as 'modern studies' or 'student rights' came up for discussion.* □ *Nine hoods* ((US) = gangsters) *run onto the stage. They look as if they had just stolen a mound of hub-caps. Their flat-top hair styles are smothered in grease and their T-shirts are blackened. Some of them flex their muscles at the audience and* ***curl their lips***. L □ more often in sing form, esp when expression is used to describe an attitude of mind rather than the actual facial gesture.

the curse of Cain the lot or fate of sb who has to live a vagabond life, who wanders or is forced to move from place to place in a profitless way □ (source) *And now* ***art thou*** (ie Cain) ***cursed***. . .*a fugitive and a vagabond shalt thou be in the earth.* GENESIS IV 11-12 □ *He had fled in panic and now returned to England hoping to clear his name. Whatever happened could be no worse than living under* ***the curse of Cain***, *in terror and concealment, as he had been.* □ *'And why has he never married? Because he was so madly in love with that absurd mother of his, who clung to him like an octopus. Talk about* ***the curse of Cain***,*' she went on, though nobody had, 'the curse of Oedipus is ninety thousand times worse.'* US

a curtain lecture a cautionary or scolding talk given in private by a relative, teacher, close friend, etc (originally a nagging talk from a wife to her husband, in a four-poster bed with the curtains drawn) □ *On the following morning my landlady invited me into her sitting-room where she delivered* ***a curtain lecture*** *on the subject of late hours and noisy company.*

a cushy number etc (informal) a job or situation in life that is pleasant, easy, undemanding and, often, financially comfortable as well **n:** number, ⚠ job, life, billet □ MR STONE: *The taxi game never changes; too many new boys taking it up; they all think it's* ***a cushy life***; *they'll learn soon enough.* HSG □ *I'd like to get out of General Practice. You don't know of any* ***cushy jobs*** *in the Public Health department, do you?* □ *The impression I came away with was the familiar one of people with* ***a cushy job***, *who dimly realise that any change must be for the worse.* NS □ *But it had been the Foreign Office which subsidised his writing. 'I thought it would be* ***a cushy number***. *When I went to Belgrade as press attaché to the British Embassy, my predecessor, a charming fellow, said I couldn't have picked a nicer spot. He'd written three books in a year.'* RT

a custard pie a stage property in simple slapstick comedy (thrown at people, clapped down on their heads, etc) □ *Ronald Barker is actually, by training and instinct, a traditional actor shipwrecked on the wilder shores of farce, Tamburlaine let loose among* ***the custard pies*** *of Light Entertainment.* RT □ use attrib *a* ***custard-pie*** *comedy,* ***custard pie*** *entertainment.*

the customer is always right (saying) it is good policy in trade never to contradict or argue with a customer □ *It's mostly older people we deal with—little old ladies. It's nice to try to please them. Of course you get the other sort and then you just have to put up with it.* ***The customer is always right***, *isn't she?* ST □ (in Marks and Spencer stores) ***The customer*** *might not* ***always be right*** *but she always comes first — whatever her demands.* TVT □ *The Democratic Party openly proclaim that the American people are looking for something to take their minds off their troubles. And since* ***the customer is always right*** *in the land of consumer sovereignty, palliatives and exhortations are what they ordered and what they will get.* NS

cut both/two ways be capable of having opposite or contradictory interpretations, results, effects, etc **S:** argument; policy, procedure □ *What you've just defined as liberty can* ***cut both ways*** *you know. If A is to be at liberty to do whatever he likes short of harming others, B is equally at liberty to think A is harming himself and to try to stop him.* □ *The speaker argued that the imposing of sanctions could* ***cut more ways than one***, *weakening our own economy from loss of trade and possibly stiffening resistance in a country that felt it was being ganged up on.* □ variants cut several ways, cut more ways than one.

cut one's cables [V + O] (do sth to) sever one's connections with one's family, profession, country etc in an final way; burn one's boats (qv) □ *There was still time to draw back, he reflected, before he* ***cut his cables***, *became a 'defector' — that ugly word which bore so little relation to the strength of his political convictions.* □ *'I've got to make a success of this job I've taken on,' he said, 'because I've* ***cut my cables*** *as far as getting back into the Civil Service is concerned.'*

cut the cackle (and come to the hosses) (informal) start business instead of talking about it; say sth frankly instead of going round the subject □ *I had the feeling, quite new, that I had this time* ***cut the cackle and come*** *straight* ***to one*** *single, stark, wonderful* ***hoss***. SML □ *The old man dug out his relics of idealist speculation, and talked proudly on, while all they wanted, that night of all nights, was to* ***cut the cackle*** *and hear his intentions about Barford and Luke's scheme.* NM □ *News items will only win an important place if they can be personalised or there is an increasingly popular 'no-nonsense', '****cut the cackle****' and 'let's face it' approach.* UL □ hosses = 'horses'.

cut a caper [V + O] perform a few springing dancing steps more or less on the spot where one stands, either in the course of a dance, or to express sudden pleasure, exuberance of spirits, etc; (esp pl) behave in an unusual or fantastic manner in order to attract attention □ (source) SIR TOBY: *What is thy excellence in a galliard* (a lively dance), *knight?* SIR ANDREW: *Faith, I can* ***cut a caper***. TWELFTH NIGHT I 3 □ *'How are you feeling, Harold?' 'I feel pretty good,' said Harold repressively. 'Not more than that?' 'Oh, I could dance!' Alec* ***cut a caper*** *on the pavement.* PW □ *'What's got into Robert?' the old lady said sourly. 'Bowing people into their seats, kissing the women's hands and* ***cutting capers*** *like a stage Frenchman in a farce.' 'I think he's had a bit too much to drink,' said her daughter.*

cut one's coat according to one's cloth (saying) adapt one's way of life to one's means or other (restricting) circumstances □ *After World War Two, the Americans felt they had no* *choice other than to accept the active leadership of the West. Their reasoning was that if they did not fill the power vacuum, then the USSR would. In those palmy days the US did not have to* **cut her** *political* **coat to suit her** *economic* **cloth**. NS □ (the buying of rare books and manuscripts) *The British are scholarly and timid,* **cutting their coat to the measure of their** *threadbare* **cloth**, *devoid not only of money but often of imagination.* NS □ (NONCE) *Don Revie knows he must* **cut his cloth according to the way he expects the opposition to play**. *If he knows they are going to string a line of beefy blokes across the penalty area then Macdonald, for all his ability, is going to be running into a brick wall.* TVT □ often used with *one must*, to give advice, warning etc.

cut and come again help oneself from, take some of, a large joint of meat, etc, as often as one pleases or as long as it lasts □ *'Perhaps I haven't given some of you enough,' said their host, 'but there's plenty of turkey here for you all to* **cut and come again** *as often as you like.'* □ *This travel book is the ideal present for me. I like a book where I can* **cut and come again** *without losing the thread of a story.* □ (rehearsing an opera) *In any case, the soloists share with trained sportsmen and experienced statesmen a variety of* **cut-and-come again** *stamina which is dumbfounding for the watching layman.* RT □ attrib use *a big* **cut-and-come-again** *cake*.

cut corners [V + O pass] (informal) go straight across the bend of a road instead of following its curve, or, sometimes, proceed in a straight line over territory served by a winding road, etc; (fig) take a short or quick way of doing sth, or of achieving one's object (often with the implication that this is unwise or dangerous, that sth essential is missed out or not properly done) □ *There'll be no* **cutting corners**, *you understand, just because you are the boss's son. You'll have to learn the business and get your engineering qualifications like anyone else.* □ *With really cheap clothes, manufacturers can keep prices down only by* **cutting corners** *on both materials and workmanship.* OBS □ *Each hour-long show can take up to six months to prepare. Were we to scale our ideas down,* **cut corners** *and play safe, we would risk coming up with that depressing thing — the 'special' that looks like an 'ordinary'.* TVT □ *He drives himself to a lot of race meetings, a fast,* **corner-cutting** *driver in his big Mercedes.* TVT □ n compound (here used attrib) corner-cutting.

cut a dash [V + O] present a dashing appearance; impress others by one's bearing and dress □ *She was merry and well-fed and confident, serene in the knowledge that she was doing a worth-while job; she could put on her Number Ones* (officer's dress uniform) *and doll herself up smartly to go home and* **cut a dash**. RFW □ *Fashion is great fun this Autumn — you'll be* **cutting a** *military* **dash** *in braids, brass buttons and swaggering Guards-type greatcoats.* H □ *From this spirited sketch of my great-great-grandfather seated on his phaeton behind a pair of fine horses, I could well imagine him* **cutting a** *tremendous* **dash** *in Hyde Park's Rotten Row of a summer morning.*

cut sb dead refuse to greet or recognize sb that one, in fact, has met or knows □ *We women play such nonsensical games with men,* **cutting** *them* **dead** *as a ploy and doing awful things like that.* RT □ *Oh yes, he did take offence, and very much so. I've run into him several times since then and he has simply* **cut** *me* **dead**.

cut and dried[1] [adj + adj non-rev] completed in every detail and either already in force, or ready to be put into execution **S:** plan, agreement, contract, schedule of work □ *It seems clear at this stage that Britain made a mistake in not getting in at the start when she would have had the opportunity with her partners to shape the treaty in accordance with her interests. It is now* **cut and dried**. SC □ *'Well worth it,' said the Agent. 'A thousand's not high if it helps you to avoid a crack-up.' Duncan argued it a bit, on principle, but the Agent had the thing* **cut and dried**. TST □ *'You chaps have got to deliver the goods.' 'That's bound to happen. It's* **cut and dried**, *and nothing can stop it now,' said Martin.* NM

cut and dried[2] [adj + adj non-rev] formal; inflexible; predictable; not likely to adapt to change, emotional pressure, etc **S:** person; attitude, response; mode of thinking, method of work □ *Unwillingly he had to consider Alec as a person, not as someone coming under a business heading, not even as a client, for his relations with his clients were also* **cut and dried**: *very little personal feeling could, in the nature of things, come into them.* PW □ *She was a very* **cut-and-dried** *little person with a very* **cut-and-dried** *way of speaking in short sentences that sounded as if they had been culled from 'How to Speak English in 100 Easy Lessons'.* □ attrib use *a* **cut-and-dried** *person, way of speaking*.

cut each other's/one another's throats [V + O] engage in mutally destructive rivalry, esp in commerce □ *The essence of business is to combine. Suppose I had started on my own? There'd just been two of us* **cutting each other's throats**, *and neither of us able to expand at all.* HD □ *For so long as they can rely on us* (the British) *to stay for ever, so long will all parties* (in Northern Ireland) *postpone any kind of negotiation — and so long will the situation grow hopelessly worse. It may at first seem an irresponsible plan to announce that we are 'leaving and letting them* **cut each other's throats**'. NS ⇨ cut one's own throat; cut off one's nose to spite one's face (Vol 1).

cut one's eye-teeth [V + O] reach the stage where one is experienced, has one's wits about one, knows the ways of the world □ *She's not such an innocent little piece as you think. Believe me, that girl* **cut her eye-teeth** *a long time ago.* □ *He was happy to have some mature company for a change. Having to spend so much of his time with a gang of inarticulate youths who hadn't* **cut their eye-teeth** *yet had been getting him down.* □ *You've no idea what you're talking about. Wait till you've* **cut your eye-teeth** *before you start advising the boss.* □ often neg.

cut a fine etc figure [V + O] present a fine etc appearance; give a good etc impression of oneself **adj:** fine, ⚠ handsome, neat; sorry, ridiculous, an abject □ *No doubt he'd been looking forward to the wedding, ever since it was announced, as an invaluable chance to* **cut a**

figure *and do some good public relations work.* CON □ *Why don't you take my place? You'd* ***cut a*** *far* ***finer figure*** *at the head of a procession than me, anyway.* □ *They'd been ducking him in the water. Poor fellow, he* ***cut a sorry figure.*** □ *It was a shame to laugh, but she* ***cut*** *such* ***a ridiculous figure*** *flopping back on to the ice every time she tried to get up that I couldn't help it.* □ when used without an adj = 'make oneself conspicuous in the hope of being admired'.

cut it/things fine [V + O + A] allow only a minimum quantity, esp of time; have barely the required amount of sth or time to do sth **adv mod:** a bit, rather, too □ *'Will it be OK if we get to the station ten minutes before the train leaves?' 'I think that would be* ***cutting things*** *rather* ***fine****. We have to buy our tickets and look for the right platform, you know.'* □ *Oh, here you are at last! You've* ***cut it*** *a bit* ***fine****, haven't you? We were just about to leave without you.* □ *She's a very economical caterer, but inclined to* ***cut things fine*** *at times. I suppose she underestimates students' appetites.*

cut the (Gordian) knot [V + O pass] by a single decisive action, stroke of inspiration, etc, find the solution to a difficult and complicated situation or problem (from a story of Alexander the Great who, faced with the challenge of a knot so cunningly tied that no one had been able to unloose it, simply slashed through it with his sword) □ *At one stroke he had* ***cut the knot****, by-passing all the preliminaries — the manoeuvring for position, the attacking at one point and giving way at another.* PW □ (NONCE) (a football commentator) *His good temper, crisp approach and fairness make him the perfect disentangler of a disputed Notts* (= Nottinghamshire) *County penalty decision (* ***Gordian Notts****, as it were), illustrating his points with flashbacks.* NS

to cut a long story short [Disj] briefly; in brief □ ***To cut a long story short****, by the time Desmond came out* (of prison) *in October '53, they were firm friends, and Desmond had agreed to look out for a safe market in Europe for Sammy's stones.* DS □ *Well,* ***to cut a long story short****, just after this flying spout passed close to where I was standing, out of the loch came something I can only describe as a huge horse's head on top of a snaky neck.* RM □ ***To cut short a long story****, the matter was finally settled in accordance with the Australian view—as of course it had to be.* MFM □ *If only she really would* ***cut a long story short*** *instead of assuring everybody that that's what she was about to do.* □ accompanies an account of sth done or proposed when the speaker feels that the full details are not necessary, would be boring, would take longer than there is time for, etc; minor variations occur, as in last two examples.

cut loose (from sb/sth) become, make oneself, independent (of sb/sth); disassociate oneself (from sb/sth) **o:** family, background, associates; tradition, convention, the past □ *Those boyhos* (= fellows, here critics) *don't want to chuck away their rule books and* ***cut loose****. They like the feeling of power — the weekly make-or-break piece with their names big under it.* JFTR □ *'Do you remember Dollie at all?' he asked. 'Dollie Stokesay?' Robin blushed involuntarily 'Yes, of course,' he remarked with what he hoped was a casual air. 'I was fourteen or fifteen when you* ***cut loose from*** *her.'* ASA □ It could be frightfully interesting, but one's kept so infernally busy, and, then again, once you're in on what's happening, it's difficult to ***cut loose***. HAA

cut one's losses [V + O] close a business, shop etc that is not making money before losses mount any higher; bring any unsatisfactory or unprofitable situation to an end before matters get worse □ *I said that there seemed to me two possible courses: one, to* ***cut your losses****, break up Barford, and distribute the scientists among the American projects: two, to reinvest in Luke.* NM □ *This party is degenerating rapidly into a rabble. I think the best thing you and I can do is to* ***cut our losses*** *and depart.* □ *It's tempting to hang on to shares you once paid a lot of money for, in the hope that they'll appreciate. But if I were you, I'd sell out now and* ***cut my losses****.*

cut one's own throat [V + O] (informal) adopt, or persist in, a course of action (through pride, folly etc) which can only bring harm to oneself; cut off one's nose to spite one's face (Vol 1) (qv) □ *37 per cent of those covering up to 10,000 miles a year were prepared, they said, to abandon car. 'The manufacturers have* ***cut their own throats*** *with unreliable rust-heaps.'* OBS □ *Dr Banda had to choose between doing business with the white-ruled states of Southern Africa or boycotting them, as African ideology demanded. By adopting the latter course, he would have* ***cut*** *his country'****s throat****.* L □ *We'll take over your business and put you in as manager at a fair salary. We can't stop you from trying to go it alone, but if you do you'll be* ***cutting your own throat****.* ⇨ cut each other's/one another's throats.

(at) cut rates/prices (commerce) (at) reduced rates, prices, esp at certain seasons, or for a particular class of customer or consumer □ *They did the laundry for everyone who stayed there, rather than let it be sent out into the village; they did it* ***at cut rates*** *and of course there were always rows about it.* CON □ *Old-age pensioners can travel on the town buses and get into the cinema* ***at cut prices*** *in off-peak hours.* □ *It would be very expensive to stay in this hotel for a summer holiday, but they do offer* ***cut rates*** *in the winter months, and for long-term residents too.* □ attrib use *a* ***cut-price*** *holiday, excursion.*

cut and run [v + v non-rev] make a quick or sudden escape (from a sailing ship cutting its anchor rope and running before the wind, when hoisting the anchor would be too slow for evasive action) □ *To* ***cut and run****, to walk out, as Elspeth had, was quite unthinkable to Isabel: it was not in the pattern of civilized behaviour.* PW □ *I've not met the man. I've tried to, but he wouldn't see me. But if you decide to* ***cut and run****, you'd best do it early before he and his mother have got into the way of you.* ASA □ *Kersey invokes 'the old American custom of self-defence when his son-in-law talks of* ***cutting and running*** *as the best answer to the threats.* NS

cut sb/sth short [V + O + Comp pass] interrupt sb when he is speaking; not allow sb to finish speaking; interrupt a conversation, lesson etc □ *I introduced myself again, but he* *cut* me *short* with a kindly 'of course'. PP □ 'When I consider my behaviour to you just now, believe me, I—' 'That's what I came to see you about,' said Camilla, ***cutting*** him ***short*** without ceremony. 'I rather think you owe me an explanation.' EM □ We were ***cut short*** at this point by a thunderous knocking at the door. UTN □ 'Not at all,' he said. 'Delighted. Well, I'm afraid we must ***cut*** our conversation ***short***. The discussion's four minutes overdue.' ASA

cut-throat competition/rivalry (commerce) intense trade rivalry, in the course of which competitors are prepared to accept short-term sacrifices to secure a longer-term advantage □ *One doesn't have to look far for instances of* ***cut-throat rivalry*** *among the Common Market countries. To give just one example, when the firm of Pechiney was hestitating between Hamburg and Dunkirk as the site for a new aluminium plant, Dunkirk clinched the deal by advancing 30 per cent of the capital investment cost.* L

a cut-throat price (commerce) a low price charged by a shop etc which suggests some sacrifice of profit; a high price bid for materials in short supply □ *The poster on the window read: '5% reduction on all refrigerators, washing-machines and vacuum cleaners. Many other household appliances at* ***cut-throat prices****'.* □ *It is no use buying raw commodities at* ***cut-throat prices*** *if the result is to impoverish prospective customers.*

the cut and thrust (of sth) [n + n non-rev] the techniques characteristic of political factions, rival business interests, etc; methods of argument or sustained repartee; a battle of wits (qv); thrust and parry (qv) (from sword-play, fencing) **o:** debate, argument, controversy □ *Harrison, however, is perhaps too high-minded for* ***the cut and thrust of*** *University politics.* OBS □ (Meetings of The British Medical Council) *Anyone who expects much of* ***the cut and thrust of*** *debate at these affairs is likely to be disappointed.* NS □ *There is far too much emphasis on factual information and too little on* ***the cut-and-thrust of*** *disagreement.* L □ (football) *I think the attacker of 35-plus is also less inclined to throw his entire being into a* ***cut-and-thrust*** *penalty area confrontation.* TVT □ occas hyphenated; attrib use *a* ***cut-and-thrust approach***.

D

the daddy of them all [Comp (NP)] (informal) the founder, originator, and often the most successful exponent, of a popular movement, school of thought etc; sb who has been successful and engaged in some sphere of activity longer than his associates **V:** ⚠ be; be regarded as; look like □ *Running the 'Meet my next guest' shows of which Americans are so fond, are in the afternoon Mike Douglas, in mid-evening David Frost, or in the hours around midnight when there are three on view, all, of course, at the same time: Johnny Carson —* ***the daddy of them all****— Dick Cavett and Merv Griffin.* L □ *Meantime a newly-formed, science-based company in California (interestingly, an off-shoot of 'Syntex',* ***the daddy of them all****) is now conducting trials with a uterine contraceptive system.* L □ *'Picasso has just celebrated his 90th birthday, hasn't he?' 'Yes, and in so many other respects, he's* ***the daddy of them all****.'*

one's daily bread [O (NP)] the food one needs and/or gets each day; one's means of subsistence generally **V:** get, give, (not) want, (not) lack; earn, work for □ (source) *Give us this day* ***our daily bread***. MATTHEW VI 9 □ *British business is not, as certain people appear to believe, a jungle in which the weakest go to the wall, but simply a civilised and harmonious way of earning* ***one's daily bread***. RATT □ *All the world knows what a soft and merry life the film reviewer leads, lounging back in the morning dark while outside others dig ditches or rob banks for* ***their daily bread***. NS

the/one's daily dozen [O (NP)] a few routine exercises practised daily in order to keep oneself fit **V:** do, perform □ *Third in our series of basic health requirements:* ***The daily dozen***. SC □ *My husband does* ***his daily dozen*** *every morning as soon as he rises. He says it does him far more good than an extra five minutes in bed.*

the daily round the common tasks or duties of one's working day □ *The nurses came on* ***their daily round*** *of washing, changing, combing and prettifying the patients before the matron's inspection.* MM □ *'And what have you been doing while I was away?' 'I? Oh nothing.* ***The daily round****, you know. Looking after the children, missing you.'* PW □ *I was as keen to get away as he was. After two summers the Gulf becomes a jail and* ***the daily round*** *something of a drag.* BM

the damage is done (saying) it is too late to prevent the occurrence of sth undesirable □ *I wish you wouldn't make promises on my behalf. Oh, well,* ***the damage is done*** *now, I suppose, and I shall have to send him a cheque.* □ *If we join the EEC* (European Economic Community) *we shall burn our bridges behind us. The Labour Party Conference should set the scene for one last great effort to prevent* ***the damage being done***. NS □ *When it comes to preventing other people from interfering with their work, legal action can only be taken after* ***the damage*** *has* ***been done***. OBS

damn all [Comp/O (NP)] nothing at all; none or so little as to be not worth mentioning or considering **V:** be; get, receive, give □ *If that's what they do with the money they collect, they'll get* ***damn all*** *from me the next time they come round for subscriptions.* □ *On the morning of the great day he will be riding down the route of the procession to make sure everything is all right. 'Although by that time,' he added needlessly, 'there's* ***damn all*** *one can do.'* RT □ (concerning wage increases) *The percentage game played absolutely straight would still have a built-in bias in favour of the better off. That was what Vic*

*Feather meant when he snapped: 'What's 40 per cent of **damn all**?' at a reporter who challenged him about the iniquity of some groups of low-paid workers who had dared to ask for 40 per cent rise.* NS □ variants (taboo) bugger all, fuck all.

damn and blast (sb/sth) [v + v non-rev] can be used to curse sb/sth violently; or, esp if the speaker often uses strong language with unnecessary or inappropriate freedom, merely to comment adversely on a situation or occurrence that annoys or inconveniences him □ *The engine spluttered and stopped. '**Damn and blast**!' my father exclaimed. 'The bloody petrol's run out.'* □ *Oh, **damn and blast** Bennie Hyman. What's it got to do with him?* ILIH □ *I'll have to swallow about a handful of pills to get to sleep, and then I won't wake up if the phone rings, which won't be any good either, **damn and blast** it.* JFTR

damn etc it (all) an expletive accompanying a plea, protest, argument, accusation etc **V:** damn, ⚠ dash, hang □ *'But **damn it all**,' said Weichart, 'the Cloud must speed up as it falls through the sun's gravitational field.'* TBC □ *But **dash it**, I am not a babe in arms. I am entitled to go out for a walk by myself if I want to.* EM □ *'You might let me finish what I'm saying, **damn it**.' 'But you told me yourself, **hang it all**, that you wanted that holly bush dug out!'* □ front, middle or end position.

damn with faint praise not condemn, but mention for praise only qualities of such slight merit as to imply that more valuable or important qualities are lacking □ (source) ***Damn with faint praise**, assent with civil leer,/And, without sneering, teach the rest to sneer.* EPISTLE TO DR ARBUTHNOT (A POPE 1688-1744) □ *'But your book wasn't so unkindly reviewed as you say.' '**Damned with faint praise**—I would rather it had been violently attacked, which arouses people's interest at least.'* □ used esp in literary or other forms of professional criticism.

a damp squib an event, statement, publication etc intended to be interesting, exciting, startling etc that fails in its effect □ *After these fireworks, the final communiqué on the visit was **a damp squib**.* L □ *I forget the year, but I know the date was Guy Fawkes' Day, so I was able to make something of the '**damp squib**' theme when the speaker duly called 'Captain Longhurst' and I extracted the evidence from my pocket and read it out.* ST □ *'Here's your girl,' he said to Bill. 'Handle her carefully; she's liable to explode.' 'Like **a damp squib**,' Cindy said. She spoke to Bill, 'I tried to flirt with him, but it all fell flat.'* PE □ also pl; often used with *a bit of, something of*; attrib use *the '**damp squib**' theme*; a squib = 'firework that explodes loudly'.

a damsel in distress [O (NP)] (facetious) a (young) woman who needs help with a practical difficulty, in an unpleasant situation, etc (from a stock character in old tales of romantic chivalry) **V:** rescue, save □ *The students come to him with personal problems too; he seems to have a way with tormented youths and **damsels in distress**.* □ *'What were you doing in Barfield at that time of night, anyway?' 'Rescuing **a damsel in distress**. She'd missed her last bus and was walking home.'* □ (NONCE) *The team have set their tale in that storybook time when knights were bold and brave in shining armour, minstrels sang of love and battle, **damsels** were **distressed** and all the castles looked like something out of Disneyland.* TVT

one's dancing etc days are done etc one can no longer dance etc because of age, disability, changed feelings or views **pres p:** dancing, fighting, mountaineering, flirting. **Comp:** done, ⚠ over, past □ *Former bar-room brawler and hell-raiser Robert Conrad stars in a new series here—but he says **his fighting days are over** now because: 'I carry the Bible with me everywhere. I get a lot of strength from it.'* TVT □ *'Does Isabel try to keep you guessing?' 'No,' said Harold, stiffening. 'But wives sometimes do, you know; it's a habit women have. And I don't like it. **My guessing days are over**.'* PW □ *People don't have much more to offer once **their dancing days are over**.* □ headphrase may be used figuratively to complain about or emphasize old age, restriction of activity or pleasure etc, as in last example.

danger/dirty money extra payment above usual wages for doing particularly dangerous or dirty work □ *No amount of **danger money** would tempt me to work on these oil rigs they're constructing in the North Sea.* □ *Two constantly recurring themes among all who were writers were economic duress and violent fluctuations of readership. **Danger money**, they felt, was no better deserved at the coal face.* NS □ *Big stores have had difficulty finding men to play Santa Claus in their Christmas bazaars. Possibly they want **danger money**, or **dirty money** for all the chimney work they have to do.* SC

a Daniel come to judg(e)ment (saying) sb who makes a wise decision or ruling about sth that has perplexed others (see DANIEL V 14-16); or may be said in approval of sb whose opinion, decision etc agrees with that of the speaker □ (source) SHYLOCK: ***A Daniel come to judgment**! yea, a Daniel!/O wise young judge, how I do honour thee!* THE MERCHANT OF VENICE IV 1 □ *'I shall have to toss for it.' He tossed a penny in the air, 'Muriel will call,' said her father in the tone of **a Daniel come to judgement**.* RM □ ***A Daniel come to judgement** could hardly have disentangled the truth from falsehood in this case, much less an inexperienced young District Magistrate like me.* □ *My friend had plied me with official transcripts of the hearings in the hope of converting me to his passionate view that Senator McCarthy was either John the Baptist resurrected or **Daniel come to judgement**.* L

(a) Darby and Joan [n + n non-rev] a faithful loving married couple (a couple thus named are referred to or described in a number of 18-19th c ballads) □ *My parents won't mind the isolation of the cottage one bit. They're **a** real old **Darby and Joan**—there's no company they enjoy better than each other's.* □ *Newbury had a bumper attendance for the Hennessy Cognac Gold Cup and it was good to see many young race-goers there. Too often race-course crowds look like a reunion of the local **Darby and Joan** club.* ST □ used for middle-aged or elderly people; attrib use *the **Darby and Joan** club.*

a dark horse [Comp (NP)] somebody who is secretive, or unusually reserved, about his feelings, activities, plans, skills or abilities **V:** ⚠ be;

find, think, sb □ JERRY: *Did Jim ever tell you about my old man's money, Mrs Mount?* JEAN: *I don't know—I suppose so.* JERRY: *He's* **a dark horse** *is old Jim. I bet he never told you nothing.* YAA □ *'Well, Mr Highmore, you are* **a dark horse**,*' said Mrs Paxon who had joined them, 'I've not heard an amateur* (actor) *like that for a long time.'* WDM □ MRS ELLIOT: *It seemed a funny thing to say, and especially after all these years. Of course, she always was* **a dark horse**. EGD □ *Whatever the outcome of the election, Mr Michael Foot —* **the dark horse** *— emerges more and more as a figure of moderation and sound sense.* NS □ occas pl *a couple of* **dark horses**.

(not) darken sb's door(s) (again) (not) enter a building, sb's home etc, (the implication being that the person has become either a reluctant or an unwelcome visitor); (not/no longer) want or be allowed membership of or association with a society, group, business concern, etc □ *If anybody had spoken to me like that when I was a guest in their house, it would be a long time before I would* **darken their door again**. □ *'Go! Now!' shouted his indignant, but slightly inebriated father, adding, with a touch of melodrama, 'And* **never darken my doors again**!*'* □ *Dylan Thomas wrote to Pamela Hansford Johnson: You'll be interested to know the BBC has banned my poetry. After my poem in the 'Listener', the editor received a host of letters complaining of the disgusting obscenity of two of the verses. I shall* **never darken** *Sir John Reith***'s door again**. L

darkest Africa the most remote, inaccessible parts of Africa (from the fact that the regions referred to were the last areas of the continent to be explored by Europeans; also linked with 19th c missionary zeal to bring the light of Christianity to those that 'walk in darkness') □ *Like the earth of a hundred years ago, our mind still has its* **darkest Africas**, *its unmapped Borneos and Amazonian basins.* HAH □ *I'm not going to have you beetling around on your own. Next thing I know you'd be heading for Burma or* **darkest Africa**. TCB □ *I do most of my listening* (to radio) *on Fridays when I go to my country cottage at Chiddingfold in* **darkest Surrey**. RT □ *Africa seems to cast a spell over many of the Europeans who go there to work. A remarkable number of them are irresistibly drawn back by the magic of* **the dark continent**. □ frequently adapted as shown in examples; variant the dark continent.

the darkest hour is that/comes before the dawn (saying) it is often when things seem to be at their worst that they improve □ *Don't give up. Try to believe that* **the darkest hour is that before the dawn**. *Tomorrow, or the next day, something may happen that will make you feel life is worth living after all.* □ *Your share certificates aren't worth the paper they're printed on at present—but hang on to them. Even in the stock market the oddest things can happen that prove* **the darkest hour comes before the dawn**. □ *That was* **my darkest hour**, *but the rescuers turned up and everything was suddenly much brighter.* □ may be said to console or cheer oneself or another in difficulty, despair, danger etc; variant one's darkest hour.

dash/shatter sb's hopes [V + O pass] cause sb to abandon altogether, or to lose confidence in, their hope(s) of doing or getting sth □ **All hopes** *that the European proletariat would rise and come to the rescue of Russia, utterly ruined by years of war, civil war, and intervention, were* **dashed**. ST □ *Shares soared and the nation joyfully awaited the glad news that the Chancellor would announce to the House of Commons on his return from the International Monetary Conference. But* **hope** *was soon* **dashed** *by a torrent of cold water from official quarters.* L □ *Well, I'm sorry to* **shatter your hopes**, *but I don't believe your furniture will fetch anything like the price you mention.*

Davy Jones'(s) locker the sea as a grave (from Davy Jones, a personification of something like an evil spirit or devil of the sea who delights in drowned men, foundered ships etc) □ *Ah, well, well, I believe when the Excisemen blew up the 'Cabinet Minister' and put all that good whisky in* **Davy Jones's locker**, *Davy Jones himself was warning you to keep off the grass.* RM □ *He was a fine seaman, poor fellow, but ended up in* **Davy Jones' locker**.

dawn/day breaks the first morning light comes; (fig) a period of time begins that brings or promises to bring change, a new outlook—often, but not necessarily, for the better □ **Dawn** *was* **breaking** *when we came in sight of the walls of Pekin.* BM □ *Suddenly, everyone is a lot more optimistic about the economy, but the Chancellor's new* **dawn** *won't* **break** *overnight.* OBS □ *I suppose we must accept this not unwelcome period of passivity* (on the part of insurgents), *and hope that we will not really be strung from the lamp-posts* **when the great day dawns**. NS □ n compound daybreak; variants if that day should ever dawn, when the great day dawns, begin to see the break of day, break of day.

the dawn chorus burst of bird-song at dawn, particularly prolonged and audible in spring and early summer □ *I crawled into the tent at 3a.m. promising myself four hours sleep at least but I'd forgotten about* **the dawn chorus**, *and didn't drop off till 4.30.* □ *Angus McDermid's picture of radio in Africa, beginning with the pleasing comparison of stations coming on the air in the morning with the starting-up of* **the dawn chorus**, *was illustrated with extracts from a play.* L

a day dream used of letting one's imagination wander pleasantly, esp about things one would like to do or have happen to one □ *I sat thinking of New York, wondering whether I'd like it as a place to work in, one of those damned, stifling, dreadful summers, but those were* **day dreams** *all right.* PP □ *Muriel would say that if he was capable of mixing her up with her twin sister he could hardly be as much in love with her as he pretended to be. Then he fell back upon* **a day dream**. *Dick had arrived and made an immediate impression on Elsie.* RM □ *I would have spent an hour* **day-dreaming** *an imagined place, to no particular end.* L □ also used as v as in last example.

day etc in (and) day etc out [A (NP)] every day; continuously or repeatedly over a long period of time **n:** day, ⚠ week month, year □ *The same thing happened to Sartre when he ar-*

*rived in America after the war. He had been wearing the same old suit, **day in day out**, for five years, and he was swept straight off to the tailor's.* OBS □ *And ever since I grew up I've weighed ten and half to eleven stone **year in year out**.* □ *You get more variety in your work, Betty. You're not slaving **week in week out** in a hot kitchen, like me.* □ *Life on the tennis roundabout has its drawbacks. 'You see the same faces **day in, day out**.'* TVT □ front, middle or end position; stress pattern day ˌin day ˈout.

the day/time is not (so) far off/distant when it will soon be the time when (sth happens, is said, etc) □ *My aunt is still just able to care for herself, but **the day is not far off when** she'll need to employ a daily help or go into a nursing-home.* □ ***The day** may **not be far distant when** the small-scale techniques can be used in large-scale mapping.* NSC □ ***The time isn't so far off** as you think **when** minute computers will take over most jobs.* □ often used to introduce predictions about the near future; variant the day/time is approaching when.

a day etc or two a short period etc of days etc **n:** day, minute, week; inch; glass; word □ *As a matter of fact, if you stop eating altogether for **a day or two** and drink only plain water, you will be surprised—after the hunger pangs of the first twelve hours are over—at how well you feel.* TO □ *For **a moment or two** after a wave had passed he could see right into it, but the waves were nothing but water—there was no weed in them, no speck of solid, nothing drifting.* PM □ *I think your skirt should be **a centimetre or two** longer.* □ *He may take **a glass or two** of wine with his evening meal, but otherwise he doesn't drink.* □ stress pattern a ˈday or two.

day and night [A (n + n rev)] continuously throughout all 24 hours of each day; continually, most of the time, whether it be day or night, **V:** work, study, slave; guard, watch over, sb/sth □ *There was a ten feet high electrified double wire fence all round, and dogs and guards patrolling between the fences **day and night**.* DS □ *For one like Stanfield a thousand typists toil **day and night**. Not for one minute would he let an important document exist in one copy.* UTN □ *He had worked **night and day** for it; few scientists had been more devoted and whole-hearted in their science.* NM □ JIMMY: *Nearly four years of being in the same room with you, **night and day**, and I still can't stop my sweat breaking out when I see you doing something as ordinary as leaning over an ironing board.* LBA □ front, middle or end position.

the day of days a very special day because sth important or pleasant takes place then; a noteworthy day, in general or to sb in particular; a red letter day (qv) □ GEORGE: *Now let the wine flow on **this day of days**. Bring out the golden goblets.* EGD □ *In all parts of the country open-air entertainments had been planned to celebrate the Coronation, and when **the day of days** dawned cold and wet, many hasty revisions had to be made.*

the day of sb/sth is over/finished sb/sth has outlived/outlasted his/its usefulness and importance, or has already been rejected or superseded; have had one's day/time (qv) □ *I can't say that I liked the new machine with its thick wings and its enormous Sabre engine, but **the day of** the Spitfire **was** practically **over** in Europe.* RFW □ *He needn't think he's going to be first just because he's the son of a peer. It's time he realized that **the days of** his sort **are over**.* □ *It should not be assumed from this that **the day of** the family trust **is over**. In particular it will still be possible to arrange trusts to keep capital out of the hands of the irresponsible young.* G □ also pl the days of sb/sth are over/finished. ⇨ ⚠ the days of sb/sth are numbered.

the day of reckoning the day or time when debts, or (fig) misdeeds, shortcomings will have to be paid for; a testing time when the degree of one's success or failure will be exposed □ *As late as the end of July they* (the Chinese, 1900) *allowed food to reach the garrison. They wanted to exterminate the 'foreign devils' and foreign influence, including if possible the Pekin Legations, but at the same time they wanted to leave themselves room to manoeuvre on **the** inevitable **day of reckoning**.* BM □ *Whatever his majority, Mr Heath has Mr Wilson's unqualified assurance that **the 'day of reckoning'** has merely been postponed.* L □ *'All that drinking, and the late nights he keeps, don't seem to have affected his health, anyway.' 'Not so far, but there'll be **a day of reckoning** yet.'*

a/one's day etc off a/one's regular and recurring time off duty **n:** day(s), ⚠ week; morning, night; period □ *'How nice of you all to come,' she told the nurses, 'especially on **your day off**.'* DM □ *You thought you were being a comfort to him, and all the while he was deceiving you with his Italian servant, lying in her arms (I don't know where) on **her days off**.* PW □ *I've a good mind to take **a day off** and go down to Brighton with you. The office could get on without me, for once.* ⇨ ⚠ one's off etc days.

daylight robbery [Comp (NP)] flagrant overcharging for goods or services **V:** ⚠ be; find sth □ *Even allowing for wages and other overheads it's **daylight robbery** to charge 60 pence for a cup of tea.* □ *Father is quite out of touch with prices nowadays. If ever he does a few errands for me he always comes back muttering about **daylight robbery**.* □ often an expression of opinion rather than a fact.

the days of sb/sth are numbered sb/sth will live, last, only a short time longer; the death or end of sb/sth is inevitable and will come sooner or later □ *Lord let me know mine end, and **the number of my days** that I may be certified how long I have to live.* BOOK OF COMMON PRAYER: PSALMS XXXIX 5 □ *Tommy feels that **his days are numbered** and that a grandchild, once a possibility, is fast becoming a daydream.* TVT □ *The Conservative Party has been much more successful than Labour in attracting middle-class support but now there are signs—that **the days of** an automatic bonus to the Conservative Party may **be numbered**.* NS □ *Like harem slaves they* (cars) *are bought for their bodily beauty and changed before it begins to fade. Some, it is true, survive tattily to become dowdy wives rather than flashy mistresses, but even **their days are numbered** for all cars now it seems are born with the fatal disease of obsolescence.* SC ⇨ ⚠ the day of sb/sth is over/finished.

a day-to-day arrangement etc an arrangement etc that is valid, renewable, only on or for each day as it comes **n:** arrangement, ⚠ allowance, commitment; basis, footing ◻ *Myrtle was continuing our relationship on* ***a day-to-day basis****.* SPL ◻ *Your accounts are in confusion but you don't care. Organising the future is* ***a day to day affair*** *for you.* WI ◻ a day-to-day basis/footing usu follows prep *on.*

day-to-day life etc a daily routine or continuous pattern **n:** life; work, duties; expenditure, administration ◻ *The local quality of the* ***day-to-day life*** *of a working-class man is still illustrated by the way he will still* (1950s) *trudge half-way across town with a handcart or old pram, transporting a sixth-hand kitchen table he has picked up cheap from someone who knew someone.* UL ◻ *The railways are starved of first-class technical men, and the small and enthusiastic band who keep the wheels turning are so engrossed in* ***day-to-day duties*** *that there is little opportunity to think out what the long-term solution may be.* NSC ◻ *He said that an independent corporation for the medical profession on the lines of the BBC and the Arts Council would be one without the need for a Minister to be answerable to Parliament for the* ***day-to-day conduct*** *of a service.* DM

dead and alive [adj + adj non-rev] lacking animation; lacking interest in oneself, others, or one's surroundings; boring; without a lively atmosphere of active interested engagement **S:** performer, speaker, lecturer; reception, occasion, affair ◻ *In the play he is the complete petit-bourgeois,* ***dead-and-alive*** *from the moment he was old enough to think, killed by the formalism handed down through the ages.* L ◻ *These civic receptions are pretty* ***dead-and-alive*** *affairs as a rule. You won't miss much by not going.* ◻ *'Sue,' the director protested, 'you can't come on to the stage and say "Folks, I have wonderful news for you" in that* ***dead-and-alive*** *tone of voice. You're supposed to be bursting with excitement.'* ◻ often hyphenated esp in attrib use *that* ***dead-and-alive*** *tone of voice.* ⇨ ⚠ more dead than alive.

dead beat [Comp (AdjP)] exhausted, esp temporarily after too much work or other demands on one's physical or mental energy **V:** ⚠ be; feel, look ◻ *You look* ***dead beat****, and no wonder. There was no need to dig the whole potato patch in one go.* ◻ *The present specimen,* ***dead beat****, robbed of his loose cash in the pursuit of disgusting pleasures, loitered with an empty stomach in a ghastly dawn.* HD ◻ *In Sandford's play, Edna is a tramp and a drunk, the dramatist's message is that something should be done for* ***deadbeats*** *like Edna.* ◻ n compound a deadbeat = 'sb who does not have, or has lost, the will to work, to contribute anything to the society of which he or she is a member'; stress patterns (adj) ˌdead ˈbeat, (n) a ˈdeadbeat.

dead and buried/gone [adj + adj non-rev] long dead, separated from the living; (fig) forgotten or otherwise relegated to the past **S:** wife, father, friend; love, quarrel, hope, memory ◻ *Ten years ago I was gamekeeper to the old squire—Squire Lawson-Hope and his dear wife Letty. She's been* ***dead and gone*** *this many a year.* RT ◻ JO: *You're forty years old. I hope to be* ***dead and buried*** *before I reach that age.* TOH ◻ *Consciously, he is able to experience a past which is, in actuality,* ***dead and gone****.* MFF ◻ *Whether the Scottish Nationalist Party really have a case or not, it should be argued in terms of present issues and not in terms of old grievances better* ***dead and buried****.* ◻ SAM: *I am* ***dead and buried*** *and live only in the imagination of a neurotic young man; you are fickle, and you'll forget all about this, then I'll be really dead.* HSG

a dead cert/certainty [Comp (NP)] (racing) a horse, dog, that will certainly win; sth that will certainly happen; sb/sth that is sure to do what is expected or forecast **V:** ⚠ be, seem; regard sth as ◻ *'Do you ever put any money on a horse yourself?' 'I'm not such a mug. Unless of course it's* ***a dead cert****.'* AITC ◻ *I hoped that the governor and all the rest of his pop-eyed gang were busy placing big bets on me, and the more they placed the happier I'd be. Because here was* ***a dead cert*** *going to die on the big name they'd built for him.* LLDR ◻ *What had seemed in the opening stages to be* ***a dead certainty*** (i.e. a girl) *had lured Patrick, earlier in the year, to a rugger club dance. As it turned out,* ***the dead certainty*** *was just a naughty little tease after all.* TGLY ◻ *'Do you think your brother would lend me his car for the weekend?' 'I'd say it's* ***a dead certainty*** *that he won't, but ask him if you like.'* ◻ also pl.

dead certain/sure (of/about sth) [Comp (AdjP)] completely, absolutely sure (about sth) **V:** ⚠ be, seem, regard sth as ◻ *I'm* ***dead certain*** *he has a lot of money stashed away that he never lets on about.* ◻ *We locked all the doors when we left. I'm* ***dead sure of*** *that.* ◻ *I'm not saying that if you put on a clean shirt and brush your hair you'll get the job, but it's a* ***dead-sure*** *thing you won't if you go for an interview looking the way you do now.* ◻ attrib use *a* ***dead-sure*** *thing*; adj compounds dead-certain/sure; stress patterns a ˌdead-sure ˈthing, ˌdead-ˈcertain/-ˈsure.

dead drunk [Comp (AdjP)] so drunk that one is incapable physically and/or mentally **V:** ⚠ be, get (sb) ◻ *It was the night I went and got* ***dead drunk*** *because the world didn't have any bottom any more.* TST ◻ *There was a bloke lying on the road* ***dead drunk****, so we pulled him over on to the verge and left him propped up against the hedge.*

a dead duck [Comp (NP)] sth which is either abandoned, or doomed to fail **S:** plan, project, scheme, undertaking; idea. **V:** ⚠ be, become ◻ *A statement of future plans issued recently by the IBA significantly predicts no change in the present structure of commercial television. For the next few years at least, the fourth channel is* ***a dead duck****.* NS ◻ *After the evictions and the demolition all we have is a stretch of ugly waste ground as a memorial to another of the Council's* ***dead ducks****.* ⇨ ⚠ a lame duck.

the dead and the dying [n + n non-rev] newly dead and dying persons as in the aftermath of battle, natural disasters, large-scale epidemics ◻ *Being over seventy is like being engaged in a war. All our friends are going or gone and we survive amongst* ***the dead and the dying*** *as on a battlefield.* MM

dead easy/simple [Comp (AdjP)] extremely easy to understand and do **V:** ⚠ be, look; make sth ◻ *It'd 'ave* (= It would have) *been* ***dead easy*** *to burgle the Scarfedales' house, except* *that there worn't* (= wasn't) *anything much worth pinching.* LLDR □ *'It's* ***dead easy,*** *the 'bishop' assured him; 'they'll all be ready and waiting for you at the church, and the bus drops you a few yards away.'* BM □ *'The strategy's* ***dead simple,*** *he said, setting his mug down after a long swig.* CON □ *He won't even tackle a* ***dead simple*** *job like changing the battery though you couldn't fit the leads into the wrong connections if you tried.* □ attrib use, *a* ***dead simple*** *job*, not common.

a dead end [O/o (NP)] a path, road, which has no exit in the direction in which one is travelling; (fig) that stage in one's work, art, research, enquiries etc where one can make no further progress; a blind alley (qv) **V:** reach, come to □ *They still talked of Alexander Goodrich, not with the reverence of old days, for they too felt as the reviewers did (and some of them were reviewers) that Alec's art had reached* ***a dead end.*** PW □ *I shall pass over the details of my quest shortly, because it ended in* ***a*** *complete* ***dead-end.*** RFW □ *His school hadn't worried about what work he would ever do, and now he was in what he called a* ***dead-end*** *job.* L □ attrib use *a* ***dead-end*** *job*; sometimes hyphenated even when not used attrib.

dead from the neck up [Comp (AdjP)] stupid, or uninterested in any kind of mental, artistic, political etc activity **S:** boy, pupil, blonde, boxer, chorus-girl; boss. **V:** ⚠ be; find, think, sb □ *And there they were, two old ladies,* ***dead from the neck up.*** TT □ *Goodness, Patrick's cousin is hard work! He's very correct, very courteous—and* ***dead from the neck up.*** □ (NONCE) *But even so, by Christ, I'd rather be like I am—always on the run and breaking into shops for a packet of fags and a jar of jam—than have the whip-hand over somebody else and be* ***dead from the toe-nails up.*** LLDR

the dead hand of the past etc the influence of any firmly established tradition, code of conduct or procedure, which prevents or hinders reform, improvement, enlightened action **n:** the past, bureaucracy, legal precedent, dogma, authority, the Church □ *England has progressed in many ways towards egalitarianism. None the less, to an outsider like myself, it would appear that in some respects you are still under the power of* ***the dead hand of the past.*** EM □ *There's nothing in the White Paper* (on devolution) *which will bring jobs to Scotland, eradicate poverty in Scotland.* ***The dead hand of the Treasury*** *remains on our country.* G □ *Lord James hopes that, freed from* ***the dead hand of*** *university curricular* ***control,*** *they* (Colleges of Education) *will be transformed from geese into swans.* NS □ *No action, however urgent, can be taken without being duly 'authorized'.* ***The dead hand of bureaucracy*** *exerts its paralysing influence everywhere.*

a dead heat an instance of two or more persons, horses, cars etc finishing a race so close together that it is impossible to say that one has beaten the other; an instance of sb/sth being indistinguishable from another, in merit, rate of work, time of occurrence, etc □ *They can't both get the Chair* (= Professorship) *of course, but it looks like* ***a dead heat*** *between Ross and Clarke at the moment.* □ *In the new Riksdag* (= Swedish Parliament) *the Social Democrats have retained power only in* ***a dead heat****—175 seats to the Social Democrats and the 19 Communists who support them, and 175 to the three 'bourgeois' opposition parties.* OBS □ *Come along with us, Joe. Let's have three* ***dead-heating*** *for last place.* CON □ *-ing* form in last example unusual.

a dead letter[1] a letter, package etc undeliverable by the Post Office because it is incorrectly addressed or because the addressee cannot be found □ *The label may have come off that parcel you're expecting. You should enquire at the* ***Dead Letter*** *Office—or rather the 'Returned Letter' Office, as it's called nowadays.* □ also pl.

a dead letter[2] a law, agreement etc no longer in force or that has been allowed to lapse □ *Some of the obligations imposed on employees would be unworkable or unenforceable or would quickly become* ***dead letters.*** T □ *After discussions the councillors agreed that the '10-day rule' would be reviewed each time it was to be enforced. In fact, the rule has become* ***a dead letter.*** OBS

a dead loss [Comp (NP)] (informal) sb/sth from whom no profit, advantage, use, or interest can be got **V:** ⚠ be; think, find, sb □ *I'm an individualist, which is* ***a dead loss*** *these days when everyone gets pushed steadily up the N.H.S.* (= National Health Service) *ladder, unless you fall off with a coronary on the way.* DIL □ *This job on the drill was* ***a dead loss,*** *and he was going to black Frank's eye for him some day, but he would stick to it until he found something better.* AITC □ *Madge didn't tear* (a manuscript) *up for that, but out of pique, because I broke a lunch date with her to meet a woman novelist. The latter was* ***a dead loss,*** *but I came back to find 'Mr Oppenheim' in pieces.* UTN □ *Larry, who lives in the attic, must be the world's champion cadger and is* ***a dead loss*** *about the house.* TVT □ occas pl *a couple of* ***dead losses.***

dead men (informal) empty bottles, esp beer or spirits bottles whose contents have been (recently) drunk □ *Here, take this carton and go round collecting the* ***dead men,*** *will you? Then we'll see exactly what we've got left.* □ *I was longing for a pint of beer, but could find nothing in the larder but* ***dead men.*** □ *'There's still a bottle behind the typewriter.' 'That's* ***a dead man*** *too.'* □ usu pl.

dead men tell no tales (saying) men who have been killed do not give away incriminating evidence. □ *'You won't get away with this, you know.' 'Why not?* ***Dead men tell no tales.'*** □ may be used as a threat to kill, or be given as a reason for killing.

(in the/at) dead of (the) night [A (PrepP)] (in the) middle hours of the night when it is darkest and most quiet □ *One thing I can't stand* ***in the dead of the night*** *is a cat miauling.* DC □ *Coca-Cola, though it can taste like nectar on the appropriate occasion, is some way short of the ideal winter drink for* ***dead of night*** *in the Alps.* SC □ *The joints and timbers of the old house kept up an uneasy sighing and creaking which, easily enough ignored in the daytime, took on an eerie significance* ***at dead of night.*** □ usu occurs as prep p.

dead on time [Comp/A (AdjP)] at exactly the expected or appointed time **S:** he; train;

procession; customer, comet. **V:** be; arrive, pass by, walk in, appear, occur □ *The towing aircraft appeared* **dead on time**, *and far behind it a small winged object streaked across the sky.* RFW □ *Always when she arrived so* **dead on time** *it seemed like a coincidence. But it wasn't; so what could have kept her now?* PW □ *The Safety First slogan competition was won by a fourteen-year-old schoolboy, with his punning entry 'Better five minutes late than* **dead on time**.*'* □ *We want to make a good impression on your parents, so we'd better take care to be* **on time** *when we go for lunch on Sunday.* □ *'***Dead on three o'clock***!' he exulted. 'Just when I told you I'd get here!'* □ variants (be) on time and dead on two o'clock etc.

dead or alive [adj + adj rev] whether dead (possibly killed) or alive □ *Citizens are no longer encouraged to become casual agents of the law by posters announcing rewards for the capture of 'So-and-so,* **Dead or Alive**.*'* □ (reader's letter) *I have one criticism of the series, which concerns the irritating non-character, Peter Grant. The search for him detracted from some of the episodes in the middle of the run. I hope Peter will be found—* **dead or alive** *—in the first of the new series.* RT □ *No one knows where Harry is, nor if he is* **alive or dead**. TVT □ usu in order of headphrase, but note the last example; often preceded by *I want him, He's wanted, Bring him back.*

dead pan [Comp/A (NP)] an expressionless face; an expressionless way of saying or doing sth; an attitude which is deliberately assumed in order that others may be uncertain whether one is joking, means what one says, etc **V:** be, appear; speak, behave □ *He may have been pulling my leg, of course. With that* **dead pan** *of his, you never know how to take what he's saying.* □ *'Just to tide me over till I can get a decent, steady job,' said Robert, all* **dead-pan**. CON □ *Perhaps it was inevitable that the surviving papers should have reported the news* **dead-pan**. NS □ *When Rosemary tells stories in that* **dead-pan** *way of hers, it's difficult to know if they're supposed to be funny or not.* □ attrib use, *that* **dead-pan** *way of hers*, usu hyphenated; occas hyphenated when used as Comp or A.

dead silence complete, unbroken silence □ *There was almost* **dead silence** *for the next quarter of an hour, as the star fields on the edge of the cloud were carefully compared by the assembled astronomers.* TBC □ *'Listen, Hugo, it's Jake Donaghue here. I want to see you as soon as possible about something very important.' There was* **dead silence**. UTN □ *He heard me through in* **dead silence**, *giving no sign of approval or disapproval until I had finished.* □ *The darkness and* **dead silence** *of the cave began to oppress him.* □ usu with *there is/was* or prep *in*; variant be/keep dead silent.

dead still [Comp (AdjP)] not changing one's position, stance, perhaps even one's facial expressions, at all; absolutely still **V:** ⚠ be; stand; keep, stay, remain □ *I stood* **dead still** *on the floor of the store room. There was a silence into which it seemed to me I had just let loose a vast quantity of sound.* UTN □ *'Try to keep your whole arm* **dead still**,*' the doctor said. 'I won't hurt you too much.'* □ *It's not much use trying to fly a kite on a* **dead still** *day like this.* □ *On the* **dead still** *surface of the lake the further bank was reflected as if in a mirror.* □ adj compound dead still, n compound dead stillness (of the night, the forest etc); attrib use *a* **dead still** *day.*

dead to sth [Comp (AdjP)] (formal) impervious to and unaffected by sth **V:** ⚠ be, become. **o:** shame, pleasure, feeling □ *Are you* **dead to** *shame, that you could behave so disgracefully in front of everyone?* □ *I do not know of any spur to increasing my capacity for response* (other) *than the realisation that I am* **dead to** *something in which better-equipped people find delight.* L ⇨ ⚠ deaf to sth.

dead to the wide [Comp (AdjP)] physically exhausted or actually deep in sleep; either just managing to keep going or having given up the effort altogether **V:** ⚠ be, appear; find sb □ *Day in and day out she'd worked her fingers to the bone at that fag-packing machine, coming home at night* **dead to the wide** *yet cooking his dinners and mending his britches* (= breeches, type of trousers). LLDR □ *'Where's Jimmy, then?' '***Dead to the wide** *on the divan in the back room. That last whisky was too much for him.'* □ possibly variant of *dead to the world* (*the wide world* being a familiar collocation). ⇨ ⚠ next entry.

dead to the world [Comp (AdjP)] deeply asleep, unconscious as a result of physical exhaustion, sedation etc **V:** ⚠ be, appear; find sb □ *Jane's* **dead to the world** *at the moment. She's been travelling for 48 hours with no chance to rest.* □ *He's under heavy sedation. He'll be* **dead to the world** *for the next 24 hours or so.* □ has similar meaning to *dead to the wide* but tends to denote greater degree of withdrawal and is not confined to physical exhaustion. ⇨ ⚠ previous entry.

a dead weight [Comp (NP)] a heavy burden; sb/sth difficult to move, carry or manipulate because bulky and inert **V:** ⚠ be; find sth □ *Perfecto does not fight, but, giving a curious musical groan, drops,* **a dead weight**, *to the pavement, where he hangs from the policeman's grip.* BM □ *A curling-stone moves smoothly enough over the ice but it's* **a dead weight** *to carry.* □ *Gaitskell found* **the dead weight** *of conventionalism at Winchester very oppressive.* T □ *John may be a good teacher but he's* **a dead weight** *socially.*

the dead wood sb/sth out-of-date, or not relevant or useful, esp in a government, administration, educational system, etc (from horticulture) **V:** cut out, get rid of; leave; contain. **det:** the; much, a lot of □ *Opportunity was taken to get rid of a great deal of inefficient material in the lower ranks, but in the higher ranks* **much dead wood** *was left untouched.* MFM □ *Clichés apart, it was sad to see how* **much dead wood**, *how much muckage, we left in, but we thought at the time we were doing a good job of streamlining on the English language.* L □ *Harvey would like to see more practising jumpers both on the British Showjumping Association's Council and on the board of selectors. 'There's too* **much dead wood**: *people who scarcely ever go to a show so don't have a clue what's going on and who's in form.'* RT □ *Nor was it merely a matter of reshaping, refinancing, revitalising.* **The dead wood** *of obsolete and erroneous ideas had to be uprooted.* SD □ often used with v *cut* *out*. ⇨ ⚠ cut out (the) dead wood (Vol 1).

(the) deaf and dumb [n + n non-rev] (these) unable to hear and (hence) to speak, as a congenital defect ▫ *He knew the system of signs, the 'finger alphabet', whereby* ***the deaf and dumb*** *communicate.* ▫ *'Perhaps he's* ***deaf and dumb****', said the woman with the pinafore. 'Can't you say anything?' called the man on the fire escape.* UTN ▫ also [adj + adj non-rev] as in second example.

deaf to sth unable to hear accurately or perceptively from want of skill or training; (fig) determined not to listen to or be affected by sth **V:** be, become. **o:** niceties of tone, indications; appeal, instructions, reason ▫ *Large lorries covered with Arabs tore along in the middle of the track and were* ***deaf to*** *all intimations of the horn.* TCB ▫ *The poor woman pleaded with the manager not to press charges against her son but,* ***deaf to*** *her entreaties, he put the whole affair in the hands of the police.* ▫ *There is often a switch to politics of violence when authorities are* ***deaf to*** *the politics of argument.* ⇨ ⚠ dead to sth, blind to sth.

deal sb/sth a blow [V + IO + O pass] strike sb/sth a blow; (fig) cause a severe disappointment, setback, reversal of fortune, etc ▫ *He was just beginning to take heart again after the death of his wife when fate* ***dealt him another blow****. His younger son was drowned in a yachting accident.* ▫ *There's no doubt that the Hire Purchase system* ***dealt a blow to*** *the second-hand furniture trade —except in the case of genuine antiques which could always find a market.* ▫ *'Did you hear that Helen's husband has lost his job?' 'Oh, poor things. They've had enough trouble lately without being* ***dealt a blow*** *like that.'* ▫ *When I went to Hollywood, TV had* ***dealt the*** *heavy* ***blow*** *and it was like living in a factory town.* RT ▫ *The arrival of Michel from France looks like* ***dealing a*** *severe* ***blow to*** *Anglo-French relations.* TVT ▫ also pl ***deal sb/sth*** *several heavy* ***blows****.*

(the) dear (only) knows (saying) nobody knows; I don't know; there's no means of knowing ▫ ***Dear knows*** *when I'll get home tonight so don't wait up for me.* ▫ *The research costs of a safe cigarette are estimated at £50 million and* ***dear knows*** *what the final figure may be.* ▫ *'How are you going to get all that luggage into the van?'* ***'Dear only knows****. We'll try anyway.'* ▫ *I was going to meet all that gang again and what we were all going to say to each other,* ***the dear only knows****.* CON ▫ often followed by *what-*, *when-*, *how-* etc clauses; possibly contraction of *the dear Lord* or a corruption from the French or Italian (*Dieu, Dio*).

dear me/oh dear a mild exclamation of anxiety, sympathy, consternation etc ▫ ***Dear me****! Just look at the time! I had no idea it was so late.* ▫ *Her eyes reddened and the damp streaks of tears lay on her cheeks. '****Oh dear****!' she said. 'I'm sorry to be like this.'* DC ▫ *Shaw got through to him* (on the telephone) *and said: 'Hallo old man, I hear you're dying.' A bewildered and startled Le Mesurier replied: '****Oh dear****. Am I?'* NS ▫ *I know you don't have a big salary, but* ***dear me****, Alice, there are plenty of people with much less who manage to make both ends meet.* ▫ often interchangeable, but oh dear more likely in cases of sudden and/or genuine alarm or distress; dear me accompanies remonstrance, objection, claim; stress patterns ˌdear 'me, ˌoh 'dear.

dear to sb's heart dear to sb; much loved or liked by sb; close/near to sb's heart (qv) ▫ *The concept of individual freedom is* ***dear to*** *Tory* ***hearts****.* NS ▫ *No place on earth, however beautiful, could be* ***dearer to my heart*** *than these few acres of wood and stream.* ▫ *Her hair had been tinted with one of those blue rinses so* ***dear****, at that time,* ***to the heart of*** *the older American matron.* ▫ *This satirical sketch material is* ***dear to the*** *German* ***soul*** *but out of place here.* NS ▫ sometimes said lightly or sarcastically, as in last example; variant dear to the soul of sb.

one's death agony/throes the last moments before a person or animal dies, whether in conscious pain or not; (fig) the final stage in the break-up of an empire, institution, industry etc ▫ (mock headline) *Loch Ness Monster Hit By a Flying Saucer? Groan Heard By Drumstikit Man May have Been* ***Death Agony****.* RM ▫ *The break-up of* (the Cloud's) *neurological activity is bound to lead to the most terrifying outbursts —what we might call* ***death throes****.* TBC ▫ *Ten miles short of our destination, after* ***a death agony*** *of rattles, shudders and minor explosions, the engine finally gave out.* ▫ *Even in* ***the throes of death****, his chief concern was that no one should be too much troubled on his account.* ▫ variants a death agony, the death throes, the throes of death; often used with *in*.

(on) one's death bed (on the) bed or other place where one is dying; (at or about) the time/place where sb/sth dies or ends ▫ *Bernard's always spoiling for a fight. He'll rise from* ***his death-bed*** *if there's an injustice to attack.* HAA ▫ *All Prissie had was a letter written by her old nurse* ***on her deathbed****, confessing to a mix-up of babies.* DC ▫ *By the end of the Wars of the Roses, English feudalism was already* ***on its death-bed****.* ▫ *Some of these verses are new to print, not least the 'Epitaphs', said by Florence Hardy to have been dictated* ***on*** *the author****'s deathbed****.* NS ▫ *A* ***death-bed*** *repentance is all very well but what good will it do for his victims?* ▫ attrib use *a* ***death-bed*** *conversion*; written as one word, or two, or hyphenated esp if used attrib.

a death blow [O (NP)] a blow, or other injury that kills; (fig) sth that destroys, puts an end to, sth **V:** deal, give, deliver, inflict ▫ *The police surgeon stated that the victim had been struck several times about the head and shoulders.* ***The death blow*** *had been the one which was inflicted just above the right temple.* ▫ *Pop stared blankly at Charley giving* ***the death blow*** *to a pink and purple ball that went up with a crack like a Roman Candle.* BFA ▫ *The Company might have weathered the slump if that had been all. But the withdrawal of a government subsidy was* ***a death blow****.*

death/old age comes to us all (saying) a remark often passed on the subject of (sb's) death, old age emphasizing that everyone will ultimately die/experience the problems of old age ▫ HELEN: *No, he's dead.* JO: *Why?* HELEN: *Why? Well, I mean,* ***death****'s something that* ***comes to us all****.* TOH ▫ *She gets impatient with the old chap being so slow and confused. She ought to remember that* ***old age comes to us all****.*

□ *I little thought when I was speaking to Tom last Thursday that I'd be at his funeral today. But there you are,* ***it comes to us all****.* □ variant it comes to us all, an example of popular sententious language—it = 'death'.

death or glory [n + n non-rev] death/utter failure or glorious victory/success are the only outcomes to a hazardous enterprise (from the regimental badge of the 17th/21st Lancers (a regiment of the British Army), showing a Deathshead and the words 'Or Glory') □ *While on military service, I was chiefly concerned with keeping my head down. I was never one of your* ***death or glory*** *boys.* □ *Jack treats all his business deals as* ***death or glory*** *contests—he doesn't know how to compromise.*

a death rattle [Comp/O (NP)] a rattling sound sometimes occurring in the throat of a person very near to death **V:** be, sound like; hear □ *'I'd just like my little biography finished before the Baron dies, that's all.' 'I didn't hear* ***any death rattle*** *this afternoon,' I said.* PP

(sign sb's) death warrant (complete by signing) an official document authorizing either the execution of a legal sentence of death or a procedure that hastens and ensures the death/end of sb/sth; (fig) finally thwart sb/sth □ *...the Welfare moves in 'the blood is bled away' and that 'the gift of the council house is* ***the death-warrant of*** *the Gypsy people.'* L □ *By revealing his knowledge of their plans the foolish fellow was* ***signing his*** *own* ***death warrant****.* □ *The Minister of Transport is shaping the future of soccer. And, without meaning to,* ***signing the death warrant of*** *many little clubs.* TVT □ also pl (sign their) death warrants.

a decent/good sort [Comp (NP)] (informal) a likeable person who behaves fairly, kindly, is good company, etc **S:** he, she; cousin, neighbour, boss. **V:** ⚠ be; find, think, sb □ *If the husband were* ***a decent sort*** *and let his wife have an extra shilling or two, then she could be relieved of a deal of fine calculation.* UL □ *But she still smiled, wasn't touchy like some. She was* ***a good sort****—would likely make somebody a good wife one day.* TT □ also pl; expression a decent/good chap used without implication that *decent* is opposite to *indecent* or *not correct*, whereas to describe sb as *a decent man, woman, girl etc* would imply that they were respectable persons unlikely to conduct themselves improperly.

declare an/one's interest [V + O pass] make known to others any facts which (whether they do so or not) might influence one's opinions, decisions or actions in a particular set of circumstances □ *Films in the 'can'* (= ready to be shown) *have had to be held over until next spring. Here I must* ***declare an interest****, for my own film on Vietnam, made this summer, is one of those that will have to wait till March at the earliest.* NS □ *Asked about the Suez action of 1956, Sir Frank said: Here I must* ***declare my interest****. My wife is an Egyptian of Lebanese origin, and I am therefore prejudiced.* L □ *Lord Redcliffe-Maud's committee is already looking at the desirability of tightening up on public* ***declarations of interest*** *by councillors: this is obviously most important where planning and building contracts are concerned.* OBS □ variant a declaration of interest.

decline and fall [n + n non-rev] the process or sequence of events leading to a final and complete loss of power, prestige, popularity etc (cf esp the title of Edward Gibbon's famous history (18th c) 'Decline and Fall of the Roman Empire') □ *A myth was growing up about the Nile in the early 18th century. This was a new kind of* ***decline and fall****, where the sophisticated past was overwhelmed by the primitive present, and the great river, flowing out of nowhere, carried one back and back towards the mysterious origin of things.* BN □ *The Pop world is a milieu where reputations* ***decline and fall*** *with more than usual rapidity.* □ *There have been few sadder tales in the last decade than the* ***decline and fall*** *of the British Post Office.* NS □ also [v + v non-rev], as in second example.

one's declining years [o (NP)] one's old age, when physical and mental powers are becoming weaker **V:** be in; save for, put sth aside for □ (from a letter) *There has been bitterness between your parents and yourself, I know. But the time is come, surely in* ***their declining years****, for you to make what amends you can.* MM □ *He does a pretty hard day's work for a man that's supposed to be in* ***his declining years****.* □ *Our pensioners deserve a better deal than they get; it is not always possible for a working-man with a large family to put something aside for* ***his declining years****.* □ esp following prep *in*.

deep in thought etc [Comp (AdjP)] temporarily wholly engaged in thinking, either because one is in a pensive mood, or because one is thinking carefully about sth, considering a problem, etc **V:** ⚠ be, appear; sit, stand. **n:** thought; discussion, argument; a book, his homework □ *Some students scribbled away furiously, others sat* ***deep in thought****, and others glanced in all directions as if seeking inspiration from any source.* □ *'He's far away,' she said, indicating her uncle who, oblivious of the chatter around him, was* ***deep in a book****.*

defeat one's/its (own) purpose etc [V + O] interfere with, spoil, or undo an intended effect or purpose **O:** purpose, ⚠ end(s), aim □ *In fact the middle course is so uncommitted and colourless that by following it he risks losing his audience and* ***defeating his purpose****.* L □ *Those who are out to line their own pockets can do little harm—mere greed* ***defeats its own ends****.* TCB □ *'Tell John you can't go, and then you can make that long-promised visit to Kate and Andrew.' 'That doesn't sound a bad idea but it would* ***defeat my aim****, which is to have a long quiet weekend clearing up arrears of work.'*

deliver the goods [V + O] (informal) do what is expected of one, make good one's promise, achieve desired results □ *I should commend especially Mr Hyde's consideration of Stalin as a commander. There's little doubt that in this sphere Stalin emphatically* ***delivered the goods****.* NS □ *'I don't see the difficulty,' said Berill. 'You've been doing splendidly, why, you've been* ***delivering the goods****.'* NM □ *The film business does not need creative geniuses. We need people who can* ***deliver the goods****. That's what I'm doing now.* ST

delusions of grandeur/power [O (NP)] exaggerated, false or insane assumptions that one is far more highly placed, powerful, influential, than is in fact true **V:** ⚠ have, develop, suffer from ▫ *I think he has developed* ***delusions of grandeur*** *after playing police officers for so long—he needs a change of role.* RT▫ (reader's letter) *What splendid arrogance. What superb independence. And yet it was also a symptom of a complaint common to Press Lords —* ***delusions of power****.* ST ▫ *These* ***delusions of grandeur*** *can be dangerous; commentators, in a word, are expendable; if one's face is not staring from the* (TV) *screen, it might just as well be another.* L

(not) demean oneself (not) lower oneself, esp in one's own esteem, by behaviour that falls short of one's usual standards or by doing something (eg a menial task) that is beneath one's dignity ▫ *'I'll help with the washing-up first.' 'No, don't do that. I would****n't*** *like you to* ***demean yourself****.* PE ▫ *Listen at key-holes? I would****n't demean myself*** *to do such a thing!'* ▫ *He's the sort that would****n't demean himself*** *to sit down and have a cup of tea with the workers in the canteen.* ▫ neg, interr and conditional; sometimes said sarcastically to, or about, sb whose standards are thought to be pretentious or false, as in first and last examples.

the demon drink (facetious) alcoholic drink, particularly as the cause of poverty, violence, deterioration of character, etc ▫ *It was easy to see how even a family which had had as good food as it wished and a few extras could be down to bread-and-scrape off an orange-box inside a month if* ***the 'demon drink'*** *took hold.* UL ▫ *At first, anyway, the Budget is certain to be thought 'fair'. What could be more virtuous than old-age pensioners and milk? And what could be worthier of stern discouragement than tobacco and* ***the demon drink****?* NS ▫ *Nobody who lived among the tenements of Glasgow when Benny Lynch was in his prime will ever forget Scotland's first World boxing champion, who punched his way into folklore until being counted out by* ***the demon drink*** *in 1946.* TVT ▫ drink is in apposition to demon.

a den of iniquity [Comp (NP)] a place associated with criminal or immoral activities **V:** ⚠ be, become; find, make, sth ▫ *People think Soho is* ***a den of iniquity****. It isn't. We get more churchgoers round here than any other part.* RT ▫ *His daughter Maureen, 17, would like to be a cryptologist but probably won't because it would mean studying in London, a city her father tends to regard as* ***a den of iniquity****.* ST ▫ also pl dens of iniquity.

a den of thieves [Comp (NP)] a meeting-place of thieves and rogues; a shady or disreputable organization, place of business, entertainment etc **V:** ⚠ be, become, turn into; make sth ▫ (source) *And* (Jesus) *...said unto them, It is written, My house shall be called the house of prayer; but ye have made it* ***a den of thieves****.* MATTHEW XXI 12-13 ▫ *She shouldn't be chasing after that character. He's no good for her, and if she appears in* ***that den of thieves*** (Sporting Club) *looking like that, the wrestling won't all be in the ring.* AITC

dereliction of duty (formal) neglecting or failing to do one's duty esp in an official or appointed role ▫ *Two minutes away from the accident or ten, Constable, it's* ***dereliction of duty*** *in either case, as you'll find out when I get you back to the station.* ▫ *Marie Helene had no compassion for her mother-in-law's role as a wronged wife, when it sprang from such* ***dereliction of*** *wifely* ***duty****.* ASA ▫ word *dereliction* now mainly confined to this expression and legal uses connected with the abandonment or neglect of property or rights. ⇨ devotion to duty.

desperate diseases etc call for/require desperate measures/remedies (saying) extreme, violent or repressive actions, procedures involving great risk are justified as being the only effective response to dangerous situations **n:** diseases, difficulties, situations ▫ ***Diseases desperate*** *grown/By* ***desperate appliances*** *are reliev'd,/Or not at all.* HAMLET III 9 ▫ *Amputation of the whole limb may seem* ***a desperate remedy****, but gangrene is* ***a desperate disease****.* ▫ ***Desperate times call forth*** *desperate men applying* ***desperate measures****.* SC ▫ *Of course, I knew nothing whatsoever about graphology, but* ***a desperate situation calls for desperate remedies****.* SNP ▫ *Locked in a telephone booth, Miss Murphy resolved that she must take* ***the desperate measure*** *of breaking the glass.* ARG ▫ often modified lexically and/or grammatically.

the devil/Satan finds/makes work for idle hands (saying) when people don't have enough work to do they get into, or make, trouble ▫ (source) *In works of labour, or of skill,/I would be busy too;/For* ***Satan finds*** *some* ***mischief*** *still/* ***For idle hands*** *to do.* DIVINE SONGS FOR CHILDREN (I WATTS 1674-1748) ▫ *I hope you won't mind, Mr Chadwick, but I have just had occasion to, well, reprimand your class. Perhaps if you had left them some work to do before leaving them?* ***The Devil*** *always* ***makes work for idle hands****.* TT ▫ ***The Devil finds work for idle hands****—A light-hearted look at a serious subject in today's new series, 'Four* ***Idle Hands****'.* TVT

(why should) the devil have all the best/good tunes (why must) what is wicked or worldly have a claim on what is attractive and interesting, while what is virtuous or worthy is dull and dreary ▫ (source—referring to Wesley's defence of setting hymns and sacred songs to the music of popular songs) *He did not see any reason* ***why the devil should have all the good tunes****.* (R HILL 1744-1833) ▫ *What makes Kingsley Amis's change of heart all the more bitter is because he is so* funny, *dammit: that he should join the enemy has come as a cruel blow to the Lefties who believed that for once* ***the devil*** *didn't* ***have all the best tunes****, or rather jokes.* NS ▫ ***The devil has all the best tunes****, and his advocates the best arguments, which might explain in some measure why Robert Robinson is an unparalleled performer on radio and television.* L ▫ *Every age, however, has seen attempts at a* (religious) *come-back, marked by the reluctant abandonment of dogmas which have become indefensible and the adoption of popular new ideas on the principle of taking* ***the devil's best tunes****.* NS

the devil one knows is better than the devil one doesn't (saying) it is better, easier, to tolerate, cope with, sb/sth evil, unpleasant or undesirable who/which is familiar and understood, than to risk having to cope with sb/sth unknown, who/which may prove worse □ *Unless a population is brought by desperation to the verge of revolution, there will always be more people who prefer* ***the devil they know to the devil they don't.*** L □ *The Mamelukes, in moments of violence, behaved infinitely more cruelly to the Egyptians than the French did. But this was not the point. The Mamelukes were* ***the devil they knew*** *and Bonaparte was not.* BN □ *And like everyone else, we scientists are just a teeny* (=little) *bit resistant to change, particularly if we are not 100 per cent certain that the change will be for the better.* ***Better the devil you know****, etc.* NS □ *Some women stick to men who are very far from being ideal, either because they think* ***the devil they know is*** *likely to be no worse than any other* ***devil they*** *might encounter—or because they can't be bothered to start all over again.* TVT □ variants better/rather the devil one knows than the devil one doesn't, prefer the devil one knows to the devil one doesn't.

the devil looks after his own (saying) success, good fortune, comes to those who least deserve it □ JO: *You'll end up an old down-and-out boozer knocking back the meths.* HELEN: *It'll never come to that.* ***The devil looks after his own****, they say.* TOH □ *He's the greatest swindler there is in the whole building business and a living proof that* ***the devil looks after his own****.* □ often used jokingly about a stroke of good fortune, lucky escape etc, without any real suggestion that the person concerned is undeserving.

a/the devil of a fellow etc [Comp/O (NP)] an extreme example of some aspect of sth or some type of person **V:** be; have, take. **n:** fellow, fine looking woman; job, situation; time; way □ *I was* ***the devil of a fellow****. I was the lover of a married woman, I was taking out the daughter of one of the richest men in Warley, there wasn't a damn thing I wouldn't do.* RATT *'****Devil of a fine-looking woman****, that,' commented the colonel as Estelle passed through the lounge.* □ *It'll be* ***the devil of a nuisance*** *if the car isn't ready to pick us up tomorrow.* □ *Poor soul, she deserves a holiday and I hope she enjoys it. She's had* ***a devil of a time*** *these last two years.* □ *That line of seaweed's going to take* ***a devil of a time*** *to build.* PM □ frequently, but not necessarily, with a strong disparaging implication; in last two examples a devil of a time means respectively 1, 'a harassing, difficult experience', 2, 'a very, or unusually, long time'.

(the) devil take sb/sth (saying) an exclamation of annoyance with, or about, sb/sth □ *'No, the damned Customs took it.' I said, and as I had a gulp at the whisky I added, '****Devil take them****!'* UTN □ *I'm going out. If people don't chose to come when they've said they would, then* ***the devil take them****.'* □ *'****The Devil take it****!' he exclaimed, slamming down his book. 'I should have been at the dentist's an hour ago!'* □ devil spelt with or without a capital.

a devil with the men/women [Comp (NP)] a philanderer, flirt etc; attractive to the opposite sex, esp to flatter one's own vanity and extend one's conquests regardless of broken hearts etc **V:** ⚠ be, turn into; make sb □ JO: *You're not really going to marry her, are you? She's* ***a devil with the men****.* TOH □ *It's an extraordinary thing that when a man gets a reputation of being* ***a devil with the women*** *they absolutely line up to be the next victim.*

the devil's advocate [Comp/O (NP)] a censorious critic of sth who deals only with points in its disfavour, eg in formal debate with another, or before going on himself to give the other side of the question (from an official of papal courts whose duty it is to advance all possible arguments against a proposed canonization) **V:** be; act, play □ *The Witbowers' ultimate view of the artist is anti-romantic, but before they reach it they give* ***the devil's advocate*** *full scope.* T □ *He was secretly pleased about his son's decision but, in order to test the firmness of his resolve rather than to dissuade him, decided to play* ***the devil's advocate*** *for a while.* □ *Adamson loved a battle of wits and was willing to be* ***a devil's advocate*** *on any subject just to keep a good argument going as long as possible.* □ with capitals or small letters.

devoid of sth [Comp (AdjP)] without, not having, sth desirable (as an undesirable condition) **V:** ⚠ be; seem, appear. **o:** quality, merit; intelligence, beauty; goodwill, generosity □ *The child seems to be quite* ***devoid of*** *any sense of right or wrong. Not surprising really, when you think what his parents are like.* ⇨ ⚠ free from sth; free of sth.

devotion to duty [O (NP)] exceptional conscientiousness in carrying out one's duty (often used in formal citations accompanying the award of medals, prizes, for courageous or faithful service (military or civilian)) □ *The brave and brilliant work of your gallant pilots and crews and the* ***devotion to duty*** *of the ground staffs have aroused our profound admiration.* MFM □ (The English) *left the church almost roofless, demolished the two transepts and severely vandalised the choir. But their thorough* ***devotion to duty*** *423 years ago has led to an astonishingly ambitious project today — a medieval abbey is being painstakingly rebuilt, stone by hand-fashioned stone.* □ (review of a novel) *Post-mortem shows his plot skin and bone, his character skeletal, his imagination exclusively visual—even perhaps after so long, his* ***devotion to duty*** *is somewhat casual.* ST ⇨ dereliction of duty.

diamond cut diamond (saying) (a situation in which) two persons or parties are equally matched in cunning or power □ (Wormold 'phoned) *'Bring a gun.' 'Can't you bring one?' Carter asked. 'I don't happen to own one.' he replied. 'Nor do I' and he* (Wormold) *believed he caught in the receiver the metallic sound of a chamber being checked.* ***Diamond cut diamond*** *he thought, and smiled.* OMIH □ *It's a case of* ***diamond cut diamond*** *with those two and both of them are afraid of going too far in their demands of each other.*

a diamond etc of the first water a diamond of the finest quality (water here refers to clarity and lustre); (fig) sb/sth of superlative quality or that is outstanding within a given field **n:** diamond, gem; artist, soprano, prevaricator; performance, writing □ *'Oh, thank you!' she enthused gratefully. 'You're a real gem,* ***a diamond of the first water****.'* □ *The great Lord Salisbury was a sickly baby and grew* *up into a frail introverted schoolboy. At Oxford he was still 'a **neurotic of the first water**'.* NS □ *Sir Charles Cochran, who dazzled the town with many **an entertainment of the first water** in the twenties and thirties, was a man of great taste.* OBS □ (piano competition) *As well as being **a** musical **experience of the first water**, and of vital importance to those taking part, it actually was a sporting occasion—the bookies in Leeds truly were offering odds on the finalists, and why not?* RT

diamonds are a girl's best friend (catchphrase) diamonds, or gifts with a lasting cash value, esp from a lover or succession of lovers, are an insurance for one's future □ (source) *Men grow cold as girls grow old, and we all lose our charms in the end./But square cut or pear-shaped these rocks don't lose their shape—**diamonds are a girl's best friend**.* (from a song in the musical comedy GENTLEMEN PREFER BLONDES, 1949) □ *Quote from Zsa Zsa Gabor: '**Diamonds are a girl's best friend**, and a dog is a man's best friend. Now you know which sex is smarter.'* TVT □ *Isadora slept around a good bit, acquiring children by Gordon Craig and Mr Singer, of those sewing machines. The latter also provided yachts, houses, a holiday in balmy Paignton, and **a girl's best friend (diamonds)**.* NS

did he fall or was he pushed? (catchphrase) a humorous or ironic enquiry into the cause of some apparent injury or accident (originally a music-hall joke) □ *I was lying half under the car trying to spot an oil leak when my cousin arrived. '**Did you fall or were you pushed**?' he asked jocularly.* PE □ *'I hear Tom has moved in with Emma at last.' 'Poor girl, **did she fall or was she pushed**, I wonder?'* □ *And what about Rudolf Diesel, who disappeared from a channel steamer in 1913—**was he pushed, did he fall**, did he drop out? Nobody knows.* NS

die the death [V + O] (be condemned to) die, be killed; (fig) come to a sudden or irreversible end; cease to function **S:** career, performance; show, play; actor, singer □ (source) *For God commanded, saying, Honour thy father and mother: and, He that curseth father or mother, let him **die the death**.* MATTHEW XV4 □ *He went into the Editor's office prepared to **die the death** but was let off with a warning.* □ *With rather more distinction she played Judy Garland's kid sister in 'Presenting Lily Mars', after which her film career **died the death**.* ST □ *It's awful to '**die the death**' in front of an audience and in my 'down' period it happened to me. You couldn't win.* TVT □ always absolute.

die hard take a long time to die; (fig) persist despite opposition, reason, or the advance of knowledge **S:** customs, (old) habits; ideas □ *Customs **die hard**; and I'm glad of it for there are many Gaelic customs which I would hate to see die, and with them our individuality as people.* RT □ *The notion is that one is free to make any kind of postulation in psychology seems to **die hard**.* SNP □ *I had been given a chapter to write, and here were the facts for writing of the chapter. I almost wondered why I took the trouble. But force of habit **dies hard**.* PP □ *He presumably thinks that Scotland is 'too poor' to mount its own defence system (I should have thought that even the most **die-hard** critics had given this argument up).* L □ *As 'peace-maker' the Prime Minister would gain popularity with the public and with **diehards** in his own party.* NS □ n compound diehard, as in last example used to describe sb who retains long-held and possibly outdated principles, ideas etc; attrib use *as **die-hard** attitude.*

die in a ditch die alone in some forsaken corner, esp as a penniless vagrant □ *A year ago, when Miss Taylor had been admitted to the ward, she had suffered misery when addressed as Granny Taylor and she thought she would rather **die in a ditch** than be kept alive under such conditions.* MM □ *'Let me sleep in your barn, ma'am,' he pleaded. 'You couldn't drive an old man out to **die in a ditch**, on a night like this, would you, ma'am?'* □ often in unconsidered assertions that one would rather die in a ditch than do sth. ⇨ ⚠ wouldn't be seen dead (in a ditch) with sb/in sth.

die in harness/one's boots die while still going about one's daily business or duties □ *I'm as fit as a fiddle. Mixing with the 'Coronation Street' youngsters keeps me youthful. No, I'll never retire. Actors **die in harness**.* TVT □ *Please God, he thought, don't let me **die in harness**. When he did die he would find St Peter at the Pearly Gates looking at his watch and saying: 'Oh, Standish, you're just in time to ref* (= referee) *that Colts match with Lucifer's.'* TGLY □ *I don't want to think up things to do when I retire. I'd rather **die in my boots**.* □ variant die with one's boots on.

the die is cast (saying) a decision, gamble etc has been made and cannot be revoked; cross one's/the Rubicon (qv) (a translation of the Latin, *iacta alea est*, ascribed to Julius Caesar when he crossed the Rubicon) □ *Now it was done; **the die was cast**: she hadn't realized that a doubt still lingered, but there must have been one, to judge by her relief.* PW □ *The country really does not yet know where it's going. **The die** has not yet **been cast**.* L □ *The lot of the Scottish Labour MPs in all this has not been a happy one. The devolutionary **die was cast** without their Government even consulting them.* NS □ *Eighteen months after the 'preliminary canter' the Corporation finally gets down to committing itself to building an opera house. On Dec 14, 1969, **the die is cast** and the Corporation takes the plunge.* SC □ die a rarely used sing form of dice.

die laughing (informal) be quite overcome by mirth, or laugh to the point of exhaustion □ *'You can be sure we'll do right by you and send you back into the world an honest man.' Well, I could have **died laughing**, especially when straight after this I hear the barking sergeant-major's voice calling me and two others to attention and marching us off like we was* (= as though we were) *Grenadier Guards.* LLDR □ *Yes, he told us the whole story. **Laugh**? I nearly **died**!* □ *A beleaguered Britain, which was the greatest fortress in history, has somehow been scaled down to the size of a location for an early Ealing comedy. At times it becomes increasingly hard to believe that nobody **died laughing**.* NS □ esp in constructions, *nearly **died laughing**, could have **died laughing**.*

die like flies die in very large numbers, esp

during a famine, epidemic etc □ *For instance, in places like Kimberley, where most of the European miners go back to their homes every day, if you X-rayed them* (to detect diamonds) *every time they left the mine they'd* ***die like flies***. DS □ *A Government Official said: 'We have given up cremating them because the refugees are* ***dying like flies****, and we do not have enough fuel, so we bury them.'* SC □ *Nepalese soldiers sitting by the stage looked baffled by it all. Elderly colonels began dropping off* ***like flies*** *in the back row.* ST □ in last example, writer has combined expression with drop off (= 'fall asleep') (Vol 1) (qv).

die a natural etc death [V + O] die from disease or old age; die from natural causes or otherwise; cease to exist; be superseded or forgotten **adj:** natural, violent, slow, painful; a hero's, well-deserved □ *There was no reason to suppose that he had not* ***died a natural death****. The other three* ***died violent deaths****, Von Freidburg poisoned himself, Kerizel shot himself, and Friedel was killed in a motor accident shortly afterwards.* MFM □ *As a boy, he says, his ambitions were to ride in the Grand National and to go big game hunting. But since the war, such objectives have* ***died a natural death****.* OBS □ *Has the cycle of booms and slumps been throttled or has it* ***died a natural death****, or is it just lying dormant?* NS □ *When he was told he would have to pay his own expenses, his enthusiasm for the trip* ***died a sudden death****.*

a difference/different in kind [Comp (NP/AdjP)] a difference/different in a way that places sth in another class or category from what it is compared with **V:** ⚠ be, seem □ *There is* ***a difference in kind*** *between what many people call 'the flu', ie a feverish cold, and the true epidemic influenzas.* □ *'People quite cheerfully dodge paying their fares on buses who wouldn't dream of stealing 50p from their neighbour to buy a ticket with.' There seems to be* ***a difference in kind*** *between the two actions, though I don't know if this feeling is justified.'* □ *London occupies a special position only in being the largest and therefore the most congested city. Its traffic problems are not* ***different in kind*** *from those of any other big city.* SC

(a) difference of opinion [O (NP)] (instance of) two or more persons, or parties, thinking differently on the same subject, coming to different conclusions from the same set of facts, etc; disagreements of a more quarrelsome kind **V:** have; settle, resolve □ *One can be right or wrong about matters of fact like the latitude of Paris or the number of square yards in an acre, but in matters of aesthetic judgement you have to allow for* ***difference of opinion****.* □ *The point is that honest* ***differences of opinion*** *are almost inevitable among experienced commanders, especially if they are also men with very definite views of their own.* MFM □ *'You and your husband are happy together, I take it?' 'Certainly, we are. We have* ***our differences of opinion*** *from time to time of course. What married couple doesn't?'* □ *'I sell cars—till the end of this week, that is. After that I'm out of a job.' 'You mean you've got the sack?' 'I had* ***a*** *small* ***difference of opinion*** *with the owner.'* PE

a (very) different kettle of fish [Comp (NP)] (informal) sb/sth quite different from sb/sth else previously mentioned; another matter, subject, altogether; another cup of tea (qv) **V:** ⚠ be; find sb □ SAM: *Hamlet wasn't an important man. Where would he have been if Shakespeare didn't rescue him from obscurity? Now Shakespeare was* ***a different kettle of fish****.* HSG □ *Peter Terson has specialised in studies of the way society tramples on instinctive adolescent energy. But his latest play is* ***a very different kettle of fish****: an amiable farcical romp.* G □ *I'm not the stuff that martyrs are made of: I don't have any sort of built-in sanctity. I'm glad to have been able to stand as a sort of witness to the Church, yes, but that's* ***a very different kettle of fish****.* L ⇨ ⚠ a fine etc kettle of fish.

a different matter etc [Comp (NP)] a state of affairs or consideration that is different from one previously mentioned **V:** ⚠ be, seem; make sth. **n:** matter, ⚠ thing; story, proposition. **adv:** very, quite a; entirely, altogether (front or end position) □ *The barrage does not, of course, prevent infiltration, but makes it difficult and serves as a warning system. A concerted attack would be* ***a*** *very* ***different matter****.* SC □ *Yet he still retains the capacity to make an important contribution towards the sanity of this Government. Whether he will ever summon up the energy to make it is* ***a different matter****.* NS □ *The task of influencing an Army which dwells among an alien population is easy. But an Army which dwells among its own folk is* ***a*** *wholly* ***different proposition****.* MFM

dig a pit (for sb) [V + O pass] contrive to trap, or trick, sb or (through miscarriage or mismanagement of one's plans) oneself **o:** oneself; his enemy, the unwary □ (source) *He that* ***diggeth a pit*** *shall fall into it; and whoso breaketh an hedge, a serpent shall bite him.* ECCLESIASTES X 8 □ *The sort of middle-aged or elderly trendies who try to get with it are* ***digging a pit for*** *themselves of no mean depth.* L □ *I strongly object to the type of paper where examinees, instead of being given a straightforward chance to show what they* do *know, have* ***a pit dug for*** *them in every question.*

dim and distant [adj + adj non-rev] imperfectly recollected/imagined because it is far back/ahead in time **n:** past, future; time(s), days; memory □ *At school we were led to believe that physical torture belonged to the* ***dim and distant*** *past and that times were better now.* □ *One day, in* ***dim and distant*** *times many travellers assembled at a traditional English inn to go on an outing to the Cathedral of Canterbury.* L □ *I would like to believe in the ultimate perfectibility of the human race in some* ***dim and distant*** *millennium but the pointers are notably lacking.* G □ *I hear of people recalling incidents from their early childhood—and even their infancy—but my* ***dim and distant*** *past is very dim indeed to me.* □ often part of a prepositional phrase.

(the law of) diminishing returns [O (NP)] (a theory which states that one receives) less and less profit in proportion to the increase in outlay, expenditure of money, work, effort etc **V:** show reveal; lead to □ *The increase in remembering which results from an increasing number of repetitions shows* ***a diminishing return****.* MFF □ *There is* ***a law of diminishing returns*** *that* *becomes operative in old age, I find. One takes longer and longer to do less and less as the years go by.* ▫ *'Inadmissible Evidence'* (a play) *appeared to proclaim that the protagonist already knew in his guts that increased doses of sex, selfishness, and booze provided* ***diminishing returns***. NS ▫

a ding-dong (battle etc) (informal) a fight, argument or dispute in which there is an extreme display of actual violence or angry disagreement **n:** battle; ⚠ argument, confrontation, fight, contest, match ▫ *Two of the children were engaged in* ***a ding-dong battle*** *in the bicycle shed, surrounded by a circle of gaping class mates.* ▫ *In the Common Market discussion quite a few times we had the pleasure of hearing the questioner say he'd just received the information he sought and was grateful; the BBC is wrong in supposing the greater* ***the ding-dong***, *the greater the fun.* L ▫ *Nobody had got upset, nobody had shouted or been unpleasant, they'd all abided by the rules of the debate, but no punches had been pulled.* ***Ding-dong*** *all the time.* TSMP ▫ *'Let's have* ***a ding-dong,*** *' a drunken voice called out from the back of the bus, but no one joined in his feeble efforts to start one.* ▫ in last example ding-dong = 'sing-song' (from Cockney rhyming slang).

a dirty dog (informal) sb who has behaved badly, meanly, selfishly ▫ *Was he equally defeatist in his heart? Maybe he sympathised with the ambassador of whom he writes, '****Dirty*** *little* ***dog*** *has got the wind up and wants to get out of the country.'* OBS ▫ *'****The dirty dog****! He might have slowed down a bit!' I said, wiping mud off my jeans.* ▫ *I see you've finished all the whisky, you* ***dirty dogs***. *You might have saved me a little.* ▫ *The tone of the book* (by a French writer) *is naive. 'Le fair-play' is British. Why then were the British* ***dirty dogs*** *enough to hound the poor innocent Irish Nationalists 'rightly struggling to be free'?* SC ▫ not always said very seriously; not used of a person for his physical appearance or habits—such a person might be called a dirty pig (qv).

the dirty/thick end of the stick [O/o (NP)] the most unpleasant, heaviest share in an arrangement, division of labour or responsibility etc **V:** get, have; be left with ▫ *It* (neighbourly helpfulness in the working classes) *starts from the feeling that life is hard, and that 'our sort' will usually get '****the dirty end of the stick****'.* UL ▫ *In most divorce cases the woman, even if she has been very little or not at all at fault, is left with* ***the dirty end of the stick*** *both financially and socially.* ▫ *It's the care staff who have* ***the thick end of the stick*** *in the running of the hostel, and I think their salaries should be increased to match the teachers.*

a dirty great bill etc (informal) a very, or unexpectedly, large bill etc; sth possibly large and/or dirty, disliked, resented or scorned by the speaker **n:** bill; hole, stain; boots, bag ▫ *It's bad enough to get your car half wrecked in the process of being serviced, without having to pay* ***a dirty great bill*** *for the privilege.* ▫ *Saw her coming round the stairs rattling* ***her dirty great bunch*** *of keys. And Mrs Southcott gave a last little toss and jangle and sorted out the Yale she wanted.* TT ▫ *No thanks. The last time I borrowed your boots I came home with two* ***dirty great blisters*** *on my heels.*

a dirty old man [Comp (NP)] (informal) a (type of) lewd or lascivious older man; sb considered to be interested in sex, or in young girls as 'sex objects' in a way not at all suitable for his years **V:** be; find sb; turn into, regard sb as ▫ *They thought I was* ***a dirty old man***, *of course. They thought I must be hard up if I was reduced to trying it on with a girl who'd be too tired to do anything but sleep all night.* CON ▫ *I'm going to stay a bachelor. Changing imperceptibly from gay young to* ***dirty old***. DIL ▫ *'I'd love to go to France before I get too old to enjoy it.' 'You're not old, silly.' 'I'm very old. I'm twenty-five. A genuine* ***DOM***.*'* RATT ▫ also pl; occas abbreviated to DOM, as in last example.

a dirty pig (informal) sb who is (offensively) dirty in his or her personal or domestic habits, or who is offensively coarse or obscene ▫ *To tell someone that he stinks like a polecat is to insult him. The same goes for the expression '****dirty pig****'. This is an insult to the pig which is a clean animal until some person makes it dirty.* SC ▫ also pl. ⇨ ⚠ a dirty dog.

a dirty etc trick [Comp/O (NP)] a mean or dishonest action, esp one from which another person suffers **adj:** dirty, ⚠ rotten, mean, filthy. **V:** be; play (on sb), do (on sb) ▫ *'You don't think they'll try and pay us out by doing nothing about the Garryboo pier?' asked Murdo MacCodrum. 'Ach, they would not do* ***a dirty trick*** *on me, like that,' the councillor protested.* RM ▫ *'Well if I let you play,' said the child, 'you've got to play fair, and none of* ***your dirty tricks***, *like moving pieces when you think I'm not looking.'* ▫ *There has been some suspicion over the last two years that the periodic explosions have been organized by a '****dirty tricks****' department to discredit the SNP.* G ▫ in last example *a department of* ***dirty tricks*** is used to describe part of a business or political organization with the specific task of disrupting the work of rivals or opponents by questionable means.

a dirty word [Comp/O (NP)] an oath or obscenity **V:** be, sound like; say, use ▫ *At first he looked down his nose as though I'd said* ***a dirty word*** *in church.* HAA ▫ *To the new generation, science sounds like* ***a dirty word*** *(when all the old* ***dirty words*** *are everywhere in print) while the new mysticism seems to many to hold the secret of the universe.* NS ▫ JIMMY: *She gets letters. Letters from her mother, letters in which I'm not mentioned at all because my name is* ***a dirty word***. LBA ▫ *In Red China 'bonus' is* ***a dirty*** *capitalist* ***word***. OBS ▫ often used now in conjunction with the name of sth that is deplored or scorned by some specified person or group.

dirty work[1] [O (NP)] necessary work of a dirty, unpleasant, or laborious kind **V:** get, do; be left with ▫ *Which of us is to do the hard and* ***dirty work*** *for the rest—and for what pay?* SESAME AND LILIES (J RUSKIN 1819-1900) ▫ PETER: *A private* (soldier) *is far more important than you think. After all, who does all the* ***dirty work****?* JO: *Yes, a general without any army wouldn't be much use, would he?* TOH ⇨ ⚠ dirty work at the crossroads.

dirty work[2] [Comp/O (NP)] criminal, dishonest, or discreditable activities or behaviour **V:** there be; go on; do (for sb) ▫ *It's a cad's trick, isn't it, to put it mildly? I mean, whom does he take me for wanting me do his* ***dirty work****?* PW ▫ *The St Ermin's Hotel where Labour's National Executive is staying this week has something of a political history of its own. In the Fifties all sorts of dark plots and* ***dirty deeds*** *were reported as being hatched there.* NS ▫ variant dirty deeds occas used for facetious effect as in last example. ⇨ ⚠ next entry.

dirty work at the crossroads dishonest, shady, or simply unpleasant, activity ▫ *There must have been* ***dirty work at the crossroads*** *for all that amount of tainted meat to have found its way into the market.* ▫ *We can expect some* ***dirty work at the crossroads*** *tonight, with all that drunken football crowd in town.* ⇨ ⚠ dirty work[1,2].

(do) a/one's disappearing act [V + O] absent onself so that one cannot be found as expected or when wanted; do a bunk (qv); sth cannot be found where one might expect it to be ▫ *Now that I have time to sit down and read the paper, it's* ***done a disappearing act****.* ▫ *You've only got to suggest a collection for 'poor old so-and-so' or maybe for Oxfam or the Salvation Army, for Jack to* ***do his disappearing act****.* ▫ ***The disappearing act*** *by the man who's come to the end of his tether, says goodbye to his wife in the morning, never turns up at the office, is never seen again, has reached the point where they have a special phrase for it—'human evaporation.'* L ▫ also used seriously or lightly when it is not unusual for sb to absent himself or for sth to get lost.

a disaster area a district which has been badly damaged or devastated by natural forces or war; (facetious) a room, or other defined area, which has suffered some minor disruption or calamity **V:** be; declare sth (to be) ▫ *The President declared the west coast of Florida* ***a disaster area****.* ▫ *Over the past eighteen months the reserves of the voluntary aid organisations have been drained by appeals from* ***one disaster area*** *after another.* ▫ *The tension of the cup-tie finally exploded in violence which left the visitor's goalmouth looking like* ***a*** *minor* ***disaster area****.* ▫ *The children's bedroom was* ***an*** *absolute* ***disaster area****—toys, books and clothes were strewn across the floor.* ▫ also pl. ⇨ ⚠ a distressed area.

discretion is the better part of valour (saying) it is sometimes better, wiser, more sensible to exercise discretion or caution than to be courageous, determined, or foolhardy ▫ (source) FALSTAFF: ***The better part of valour is discretion****; in the which better part, I have saved my life.* I HENRY IV V 4 ▫ *When Desmond and his 'valuer'* (of diamonds) *came into the garage Charlie recognized among the guests a certain Johnny, who had been a fellow prisoner of Desmond's in jail. Desmond and his 'valuer' withdrew and conferred. They decided that* ***discretion was the better part of valour****. Johnny would certainly beat up the 'valuer', and probably both of them.* DS ▫ *Collins ignored the tribunal's findings until one day a policeman arrived with a rail warrant and his marching orders. Reluctantly he decided that* ***discretion was the better part of valour****, although during the first year of the Bevin Boy scheme* (compulsory work in coal mines — Second World War) *500 young men like him decided to risk prosecution and 147 were sent to prison.* OBS ▫ (NONCE) *It was 1878. The staff of Rules Restaurant had even built a special door for Bertie* (the Crown Prince)*, opening directly into his curtained-off corner, saving a walk past less distinguished diners.* ***Discretion****, then,* ***was the better part of adultery****.* TVT

dish etc the dirt [V + O pass] (informal) reveal information about somebody or something scandalous, underhand, improperly conducted, etc **V:** dish, ⚠ spill, make with ▫ *'Really, my dear,' he was saying, 'fun's fun, and I like mine feelthy* (= filthy) *but you can't really suppose I would have* ***dished the dirt*** *about you if I'd guessed I was speaking to your daughter.' 'You would and did,' said Bernard.* HAA ▫ *I think it's just as well for Robert to have found out that his wife is not the paragon of virtue he supposed. I'd never have had the courage to* ***spill the dirt*** *myself though.* ▫ *'But what do you know about Brother Golding? Give,* ***make with the dirt****.' 'Why are you so interested in him?' Chadwick said.* TT

a dismal etc failure [Comp (NP)] a complete disappointment **V:** ⚠ be, become; turn into. **adj:** hopeless, miserable; total, unmitigated ▫ *The question of whether or not Britain requires a national incomes policy is by no means closed. The Government are against such a policy because attempts to apply it hitherto have been* ***dismal failures****.* SC *He cast his first spell when he was twelve. 'It was to help me through an examination, and it was* ***a dismal failure****. I'd have been much better occupied learning my French verbs.'* ST ▫ *I didn't know John was a vegetarian until I served the roast lamb, and then I dropped the bottle of wine—the evening was* ***a total failure****.*

a disorderly house [O (NP)] premises doing business that is in violation of public law and morals, eg an unlicensed drinking-house, brothel, gambling den **V:** run, keep ▫ *Police raided the premises known as the Dean Club on the night of March 14th and found ample evidence that the proprietor had been running* ***a disorderly house*** *under the cover of this name.* ▫ *When Queen Elizabeth visited the ruins of Pompeii in 1980, the Italian authorities ordered policemen to position themselves in such a way that the royal visitor should not be embarrassed by over-explicit drawings on the walls of the Romans'* ***disorderly houses****.*

a displaced person a person forced to leave his native country, or ejected from it, as a result of military action, political pressure, etc and not yet accepted as a national by any other country (the expression originated in World War II) ▫ *In addition there were about one million civilian refugees who had fled into our area from the advancing Russians; these and '****Displaced Persons****' were roaming about the country, often looting as they went.* MFM ▫ for a time, such people were referred to as DPs.

the distaff side women, as contrasted with men (the distaff is a stick to hold wool or flax for spinning by hand) ▫ *I could tell you a thing or three. He was alwdys a great one for* ***the dis-***

taff side, *could never resist a bit* (= young woman). TT ▫ *If there is any blue blood in the family it must have been introduced somewhere on* ***the distaff side***. ▫ *Of the women, successful British singers like Shirley Bassey and Petula Clark could have been doing what they're doing now if rock 'n' roll had never happened and Cilla Black,* ***the distaff side*** *of the Mersey invasion of the 60s look, is set fair to become the Gracie Fields of 1984.* RT ▫ expression *on* ***the distaff side***, as in second example, indicates the female (or mother's) branch of a family.

distance lends enchantment to the view (saying) flaws and faults are not so apparent at a distance; (fig) one's ideas of far-off times or places may be idealized and unreal ▫ (source) *'Tis* ***distance lends enchantment to the view***,/ *And robes the mountain in its azure hue.* PLEASURES OF HOPE (T CAMPBELL 1777-1844) ▫ ***Distance lends enchantment to the view***, *but so does propinquity. A Sung painting of far away mountains, clouds, and torrents is transporting, but so are the close-ups of tropical leaves in the Douanier Rousseau's jungles.* HAH ▫ *I look back on my childhood as a time of almost unsullied happiness and I don't think that this is merely a case of* ***distance lending enchantment to the view***. ▫ *They're talking of California as if they were going to live in a paradise on earth.* ***Distance lends enchantment to the view***, *I suppose.*

a distressed area part of a country in which there is serious long-term unemployment with consequent hardship ▫ *You can still believe it's January 1933, when 4,000 in the town are unemployed. The number didn't decrease much until the war was well under way, and today West Cumberland, to the local workers, is still* ***a distressed area***. *Officially, it's a development area.* ▫ occas pl. ⇨ ⚠ a disaster area.

disturb the peace [V + O pass] disregard the state's requirements to behave in a peaceful, orderly way; cause or take part in a quarrel ▫ *'You're* ***disturbing the peace***, *that's what you're doing,' replied their long-suffering neighbour. 'Turn that music down, or I'll phone the police.'* ▫ *I'm not sure whether having a transistor going full blast* (= playing very loudly) *in a public vehicle constitutes* ***a disturbance of the peace*** *or not, but it certainly ought to.* ▫ variant a disturbance of the peace.

divide and rule [v + v non-rev] (saying) it is easier to obtain and maintain control and mastery of an empire, a nation, or other large group, if it is divided into parties, or factions, that either rival each other or are not motivated by a common interest ▫ *We are still struggling to overcome the vestiges of the feudal order and of the communalism which was encouraged by the policy of '****divide and rule****'.* MRS I GANDHI ▫ *The three men, who had exclusively and unsuccessfully directed the government's policy for three years, played out their trio to the last. It had been an unequal trio which had allowed the Minister to* ***divide and rule*** *with personal power.* NS ▫ (NONCE) *I was surprised to read as shrewd a judge as Brian Winston suggesting that the single-handed interview had had its day, and that the job might be better done by a panel of journalists. Doesn't Brian know that this is the set-up most favoured by the politicians themselves? And why not? They know how to* ***divide and win*** *the debate.* L

(the) divine right the right, or entitlement to do sth, believed to be directly ordained by God ▫ *That there is* ***no divine right*** *whereby Britain will without exertion automatically stay a leading second-class power has not yet sunk in.* T ▫ *...the royalty of that middle-class womanhood, which is so eminently secure in* ***its divine rights***, *that it can afford to tolerate the parliament, and reasonably free assembly of its menfolk.* LBA ▫ *The Department of Health can advise and influence, but it is careful not to be caught 'interfering' with* ***the divine right*** *of doctors to be the arbiters of medicine.* ▫ expression ***the divine right*** *of Kings* refers to the belief that royal authority was divinely conferred and not dependent on the will of the people.

a/the division of labour the allocation of the various duties necessary to a main body of work, undertaking or project, amongst those who are employed on, or take part in, it ▫ *I do the cleaning and maintenance work around the kennels. George does the actual handling of the dogs, rearing the pups and so on. It makes* ***a*** *pretty fair* ***division of labour*** *on the whole.* ▫ *In a recent survey of married couples both of whom were in full employment it was found that* ***the division of labour*** *was heavily weighted against the wife, who, in all but a few cases, continued to be responsible for 70 to 80 per cent of all domestic commitments.* ▫ *I want to argue that the central theme of the improving society will be the attempt to break down the rigidities of* ***the division of labour***. L

the dizzy heights (of sth) [O/o (NP)] (cliché) an extremely high and exalted level of (sth) **V:** ⚠ rise to, reach; fall from. **o:** fame, popularity; office, wealth ▫ *For three and a half years he* (James Prior) *sat in the Cabinet, eventually rising to* ***the dizzy heights of*** *Lord President of the Council and Leader of the House of Commons.* NS ▫ *In 1956 my BBC salary had risen to* ***the dizzy heights of*** *£20 14s a week. I was offered a job of weekend commentating by ABC at £5000 a year. Naturally I took it.* ST ▫ *'Have you ever thought of going in for one of the international competitions?' 'Good heavens, no. I'm just a working musician, I don't operate at* ***these dizzy heights***.*'* ▫ sometimes ironic, as in second example.

do a sb [V + O] do, behave, as a named person did or would do ▫ *And of course, there is no question of the society under its present control* ***doing a*** *Clore* (the name of a well-known developer) *on its valuable property sites.* OBS ▫ *He had contemplated '****doing a*** *Charles March' (a friend of mine who, years before, had given up society and career in order to become a doctor).* NM ▫ *'Kids have never given him half a chance,' said Steve. 'He might go and* ***do a*** *Richie on us* (be an excellent and popular teacher like Miss Richie). TT

do as I say, not as I do (catchphrase) follow my advice, not my example ▫ (source) *Preachers say,* ***Do as I say, not as I do.*** PREACHING (J SELDEN 1584-1654) ▫ *But despite his mother's well-meaning efforts, Simon comes to the inevitable conclusion that parental guidance* *is really a case of 'Don't do **as I do—Do as I say**.'* TVT

do as/what one is told obey orders; be obedient to one's parents, teachers, superiors at work, etc **A/O:** as/what one is told, as/what sb tells one, as sb says □ HELEN: *Come on, Jo, shift those books.* JO: *I'm sorting them.* HELEN: *Jo, **do as you're told**.* TOH □ *For once he was prepared to admit that I was in charge in the battle area and he must **do what he was told**!* MFM □ *'Pickup' is graced by several superlative performers, all of whom spent a decade or more **doing what they were told**, and usually coming out on top as a result.* RT □ *Catherine was arrested with her husband, but freed after a week. 'They take the view in Spain that a wife **does what** her husband **tells her**.'* OBS □ *Although he dreamed of being 'one of the three As'—author, artist or actor—he was apprenticed at 15 as an accountant because 'you **did what** your father **said** in those days.'* RT □ variants do as/what sb says/tells one.

do as you would be done by (saying) one should treat others in the way that one would hope to be treated by them □ (source) ***Do as you would be done by** is the surest method I know of pleasing.* LETTER TO HIS SON (EARL OF CHESTERFIELD 1694-1733) □ *She is the loveliest fairy in the world — and her name is Mrs **Doasyouwouldbedoneby**.* C KINGSLEY □ popularized as a saying by Kingsley's use in 'The Water Babies' and sometimes accompanied by the warning *or you'll be done by as you did* (Mrs Bedonebyasyoudid—also a character in 'The Water Babies'—found life deservedly difficult).

do/try one's best [V + O] have good intentions (in all things) which one carries out as well as one can; be conscientious, hard-working, anxious to please etc; do/try one's damnedest (to do sth/for sb) (qv) **adj:** very, level, honest. **A:** for the children, for his patients; in that respect; always □ *Henry's school reports were something of a disappointment to his parents and they didn't know whether to find the 'General Remarks' item, 'always **does his best**', a consolation or not.* □ *Aunt Maud brought me up. She **did her best** for me, but she only had the money she earned as a nurse.* DC □ *I have **done my** muddled, unhappy, but none the less honest **best**. I ask no privilege, except the right of every Englishman for a fair trial.* G □ *Some months later, he said: 'We're looking for a new commentator for the Boat Race. Will you take it on?' I said: 'Oh yes, I'll **do the best I can**.'* L □ SAM: *Listen, Davy; don't settle for second best like your mother and I did. Do you understand what I mean?* DAVID: *Of course.* SAM: *Then promise me you'll **try your best**.* HSG □ variant do the best one can.

do/try one's (level/very) best (to do sth) make a determined effort, use every means available, to do sth whether the aim is praiseworthy or not **Inf:** to provide (a good home); to stop sb; to please, spoil, sth □ COLONEL: *I **did my best to** stop her, but she was in such a state of mind, there was simply nothing I could do.* LBA □ *Edmund Gosse's father was a minister of the Plymouth Brethren and also a scientist who **did his best to** resolve what the nineteenth century saw as a conflict between religion and science.* SC □ *The girl is lucky to be alive. Somebody **did his best to** strangle her and probably would have succeeded if she hadn't had her dog with her.* □ *And, until the birth, Henry VIII **tried his best to** please Anne and keep her happy for the sake of the son and heir he so confidently expected.* WI.

do better to do sth gain advantage by doing sth specified instead of doing sth else already, or about to be, mentioned **Inf:** to wait; to save (one's money); to forget (the matter) □ *If it's clothes you want, Jimmy, Spenser will let you buy anything you want, although you would **do** much **better to** wait until we get to the States.* AITC □ *'I am revolted by men who don't work,' continued Fiorella. 'You'd **do better to** work instead of nattering.'* ARG □ *It'd have **been better** selling the car than having it locked in the garage never used.* □ with *will/would*; variant it would be better doing/to do sth.

do one's bit [V + O] do one's (share of) duty, esp as a voluntarily accepted responsibility (an expression popularized in Britain during World War I when anybody furthering the war effort either as a soldier or a civilian could be spoken of as doing their bit) □ *I thought I ought to **do my bit**. I wasn't much use for anything, but they were glad to have anyone then.* ASA □ *Unambitious but out to **do his bit** Gunner Goodman had become a quarter-master sergeant when I parted from him two years later, and I wish him well.* SD □ (a hostel providing temporary accommodation) *Almost 5,000 kids come through our doors in any one year and it's unusual to hear anything more from them again when they walk out after three days. We have **done our bit**, but who knows where they go then?* RT

do oneself a bit/piece of no good [V + IO + O] incur loss or harm through misjudgement, folly, carelessness etc □ *'You believe it might work?' I said. 'When he started talking about it, I thought he'd **do himself a bit of no good**.'* NM □ *'Look at you,' she sneered. 'Loafing around from morning till night. I **did myself a** real piece **of no good** the day I married you.'* □ *It is tempting to try to get a higher return for your money, but take your broker's advice or you may **do yourself a bit of no good**.* □ *bit* used more frequently than *piece*.

do a bunk [V + O] (informal) go away without warning; disappear from one's usual haunts, place of residence, a place of danger, etc, esp to avoid trouble or sb/sth one doesn't want to have to cope with but sometimes for no very serious reason and not for long; (do) a/one's disappearing act (qv) □ *We talked about the dough* (= money) *we'd crammed up the drainpipe. Mike thought we should take it out and both of us **do a bunk** to Skegness or Cleethorpes for a good time.* LLDR □ *When the enforcing officers arrived at the farm, the bankrupt had already **done a bunk**, leaving his wife and family to cope as best they could.* □ *These boys have more cheek than courage. If a policeman appeared they'd soon **do a bunk**.* □ also used in the meaning of 'a dash and bid for escape', in the expression make a bunk for it; *make* cannot be substituted for do in do a bunk.

do sb credit [V + IO + O] a person's achievements, actions etc are in his or sb's else's favour;

his achievements etc show, or add to, his or sb else's good qualities, ability, worth; a credit to sb (qv); reflect credit on/upon (Vol 1) (qv) **adj:** (not) any; (not) much; (not) sufficient □ *But his wide-ranging sympathy, though it no doubt* ***did*** *me* ***credit****, didn't do anything to make me less uncomfortable.* CON □ *'If this is your own work, as I presume it is,' said his tutor, 'it* ***does*** *you* ***credit****.'* □ *This exhibition, from which many of his best paintings are absent, doesn't* ***do*** *the artist* ***credit****.* □ *If you help a neglected, deprived child, he or she may well grow up to* ***do*** *you* ***credit****.* OBS □ *Wilkinson, it's not that this pitiful attempt at an office budget doesn't* ***do*** *you sufficient* ***credit****. It doesn't* ***do*** *you any* ***credit*** *at all.* □ often in neg constructions, as in third and last examples.

do/try one's damnedest (to do sth/for sb) [V + O] (informal) do everything in one's power (to do sth/for sb); do one's utmost(to do sth/for sb); do/try one's best (qv) **Inf:** to win; to prevent it; to prove the truth of sth. **o:** the boy; his constituency □ (Her trainer) *has no fears for her once she is in the water and racing. 'She's a natural competitor and she'll* ***do her damnedest to*** *win everything she's in.'* RT □ *You must realise that, at the end of a career of 40 years,* ***doing one's damnedest for*** *an Army that one loved, one was in a certain state of, not mutiny, but almost despair.* L □ *In the same bill is a worthy documentary from Switzerland, 'Katutura', about the plight of the black South African. The title means 'total insecurity': the 37-minute film* ***does its damnedest to*** *show why.* NS □ *They* ***tried their damnedest to*** *stop the pop festival in the village but failed.*

do the donkey work [V + O pass] do the drudgery, esp the hard and/or uninteresting part of the work as contrasted with the parts that require skill and reflect credit on the doer □ *Valcareggi points the moral: 'There are people who can invent things, fantasists, makers of the final pass. You can't make them* ***do a lot of donkey work****.'* L □ *But at the last moment the Labour reformers who had* ***done the donkey work*** *were excluded from the committee and it was packed with rather more elderly, uncommitted folk.* NS □ *I don't know anything about gardening, but I could* ***do the donkey work*** *for you if you want to make a rockery.* □ donkey-work can be hyphenated.

do/get a double take [V+O] react with full understanding to a situation following a first reaction that was incomplete because, at the beginning, one did not fully understand that situation □ *Even today, though, Dr Stoppard finds herself up against male prejudice. 'I can almost hear them thinking, "What does she know?" When I tell them I'm a member of the Royal College of Physicians, they* ***do a double-take****.'* TVT □ *'Wouldn't you think that people might be less bigoted in this day and age?' English people keep on asking me about Ulster. 'You would certainly think so,' I answer. And immediately I find myself* ***doing a double-take****. 'Why would you think they might be?' I wonder.* L □ *I always* ***get a double take*** *when I tell that joke. People smile politely, then a second or two later there's a loud laugh from them when the point has sunk in.*

do one's duty [V + O] perform an allotted task faithfully and well; act in accordance with what one feels to be one's moral or social obligations □ *...and to* ***do my duty*** *in that state of life, unto which it shall please God to call me.* BOOK OF COMMON PRAYER □ *England expects every man will* ***do his duty****.* LORD NELSON (before the Battle of Trafalgar) □ *Oh help, help! I am dying of exposure. I am starving, dying of thirst. I have* ***done my duty*** *for you and this is my reward.* PM □ MILLY: *Do come and* ***do your duty****, Myra—I can't cope with all these people any longer by myself.* EHOW □ *Our Dad wasn't a particularly loving father but he* ***did his duty*** *by us.*

do sb a favour [V + IO + O pass] do sth to oblige or help sb out of courtesy or goodwill, and sometimes as a result of being asked to do so □ *I thought I was* ***doing you a favour*** *by coming to warn you, but it looks as if death for you might be the best solution.* OMIH □ *Anybody'd think I was asking you to risk your neck for me, instead of just suggesting that you* ***do me a*** *little* ***favour****.* HD □ *'****Do me a favour****, Baxter,' said Robert, jigging the cup up and down in his hand. 'Scrub off. Take a powder* (= go away)*.'* CON □ *'****Do me a favour****, will you?' said Ralph Reader. 'Don't write about me only in connection with the Boy Scout Gang Show. I've done other things, you know.'* SC □ imper **do me/us a favour** introduces a rude or aggressive suggestion as in last two examples; person A *asks/begs a favour (of sb)* but person B almost always does sb a favour. ⇨ ⚠ do (sb) a good/bad turn.

do good [V + O] act with virtuous helpfulness towards others, esp in promoting social reforms, organizing or supporting charities etc **det:** much, a lot of, no end of, a great deal of □ *Ask any half-dozen working-class people what they understand by religion, and they will be likely to answer with one of these phrases: '****doing good****', 'common decency', 'helping lame dogs'.* UL □ *I think my husband would've been very shocked and rather grieved to have seen the Empire breaking up. We had a great position in the world and* ***did*** *a great deal of* ***good****.* RT □ *No-one on a hospital management committee would dream of telling a surgeon what operation his patient needs; but any* ***do-gooder*** *knows what is right for a deprived child.* OBS □ *The National Federation of the Blind say* (that the charities) *are out of touch with the real problems of the blind, and representative of Victorian philanthropy and* ***do-gooding****.* OBS □ n compounds a do-gooder, do-gooding are usu derogatory, suggesting blundering amateurism or over-righteousness. ⇨ ⚠ next entry.

do sb/sth good [V + IO + O] be beneficial to sb/sth; improve sb's health, or happiness, or the condition of sth; serve to correct a fault in sb/sth □ JO: *Will you get me a drink of water, Helen?* HELEN: *No, have a dose of this. It'll* ***do*** *you more* ***good****.* □ *'Guy needs cheering up,' Prissie was continuing. 'He works too hard and he looks awfully thin. A night out will* ***do*** *him* ***good****.'* DC □ *You're welcome to use our cottage any weekend we're not going to be there ourselves. It* ***does*** *the place* ***good*** *to be aired, anyway.* □ *Harry's been getting much too cocky lately, and it'll* ***do*** *him* ***good*** *to be taken down a peg or two.* □ if special emphasis needed, use expression do sb a power/world of good (qv). ⇨ ⚠ previous entry.

do good by stealth (and blush to find it fame/known) (saying) do good quietly and inconspicuously, either because one wishes to avoid praise or thanks, or because one thinks this is the most effective way to help sb, or improve sth □ (source) *Let humble Allen, with an awkward shame,/* ***Do good by stealth, and blush to find it fame***. IMITATIONS OF HORACE (A POPE 1688-1744) □ *At some stage the moderate members of the government must cease trying to* ***do good by stealth*** *and instead make a virtue of attempting to rationalise the pay of notoriously touchy groups.* NS □ *'What if they realize that it's not that a free house at all, but that you are paying the rent?' 'I shall tell them of course. I like to* ***do good by stealth*** *but I wouldn't* ***blush to find it known****.'* □ *We must take into account their innate conservatism and not try to bring about changes overnight. Social reform is often best* ***done by stealth****.*

do (sb) a good/bad turn [V + IO +O pass] perform some kindly action, esp of one's own free will and when not asked for, that helps, benefits or pleases sb; do sth that displeases sb, that is to sb's disadvantage, usually without intending to □ *He'll go a long way out of his way, a long way to* ***do you a good turn****. And there's another thing he is, and that's emotional.* PW □ *He liked* ***doing good turns*** *and letting one know it; but that had always seemed to me more amiable than not liking to* ***do good turns*** *at all.* NM □ *I'm afraid I* ***did you*** *all* ***a bad turn*** *when I introduced you to the Barkers.* □ do sb a bad turn less common than do sb a good turn and implies conscious constrast with a good turn. ⇨ ⚠ do sb a favour.

do one's homework [V + O] (informal) make suitable preparations, find out the necessary facts or possibilities, before answering questions, starting up an enterprise of one's own, or making an appraisal or criticism of another's work or of a general situation □ *Carwyn James had* ***done his homework*** *before the tour started, and his basic ideas were sound.* L □ *I can't sit quiet while my company—and others—are subjected to the uninformed criticism of hospital plans expressed by Mr Piachaud. He should* ***do some homework*** *and make sure he has a fair view of the enemy before swinging his crusader's sword.* NS □ *From 11.0 p.m. until 2.0 a.m. he puts in three hours' solid work. He makes sure he* ***does his homework****. How well, listeners will be able to decide for themselves when 56-year-old Mr Davies answers questions live on Radio 4's 'It's Your Line' on Tuesday.* RT

do sb an/the honour [V + IO + O] pay deserved tribute to sb □ *'I don't want to open their bloody Sale of Work!' 'I know, George, but how can you refuse? I'm sure they think they're* ***doing*** *you* ***an honour****, poor things.'* □ *He is a very great man and his compatriots don't* ***do*** *him enough* ***honour*** *in my opinion.* □ *They* ***did*** *me* ***the honour of*** *asking me to chair the Commission.* □ when used with definite article, as in last example, particular form of tribute is specified. ⇨ ⚠ next entry.

do the honours [V + O pass] act as host; perform the main social duties appropriate to a public function or private occasion □ *'If I am called away this evening before our dinner party,' he told his eldest son, 'I shall rely on you to* ***do the honours*** *of the table for me.'* □ *How very kind of you to bring me a bottle of my favourite brandy. But, first, let me* ***do the honours*** *of the house and offer* you *a drink.* ⇨ ⚠ previous entry.

do I/am I to understand etc? is it true that? is it the case that? **V:** understand, ⚠ gather, take it □ *'****Do I understand*** *that you're suggesting I should change my employment?' Charles asked him with dignity.* HD □ *'****Do I gather*** *that I am no longer welcome here?' he asked. Their averted faces were answer enough.* □ *'****Do I understand*** *you to say you* cannot *pay your bill, sir?'* □ *At first she seemed not to understand him at all and then she asked him if* ***she was to take it*** *that he was never coming back.* □ indicates uncertainty, dismay, incredulity or protest about what is stated in the following clause; am I to understand etc more usual in reported speech.

do sb/oneself an injury [V +IO +O] cause or inflict bodily harm, or do say sth that damages one's own or another's reputation, chances of success, etc □ *When he thought of this man Reilly, who had worn a monocle, he wanted to seek him out and* ***do*** *him* ***some*** *physical* ***injury****.* HD □ *He laughed so hard and so long I began to fear he would* ***do himself an injury****.* □ *There are people who may try to* ***do*** *you* ***an injury****. Please stay at home for a few days. Don't come to the theatre.* OMIH □ *He chose to think Patterson had* ***done*** *him* ***an injury*** *by getting the post he thought he was entitled to.* ⇨ ⚠ do sb/oneself a mischief.

do it yourself do practical jobs like house-painting, carpentry, interior decorating, etc, with the help of a manual and/or one's own commonsense instead of employing a tradesman; handle a subject or project untrained or unaided □ *No point in getting a builder in to do such a simple job. Why not* ***do it yourself****?* □ *As long as the specification is correct you can fit any make of brake lining. Extraordinarily, some people make their own, which is taking* ***do-it-yourself*** *a bit far.* ST □ *The superstitious half of his* ***do-it-yourself*** *creed involved the fate of his immortal soul, a factor which affected him to the end of his days.* L □ *Cape have just published his first book, 'An Occult Primer', which they claim is the first* ***do-it-yourself*** *manual on the subject.* ST □ *The* ***DIY*** *department in the basement supplies just about everything in the way of tools or material that the home-handyman requires.* □ n compound do-it-yourself; attrib use *a* ***do-it-yourself*** *manual*; often abbreviated to DIY.

do sb/sth justice [V + IO + O pass] give sb/sth the treatment, acknowledgment, praise that is deserved; do (ample/full) justice to (Vol 1) (qv) **adj:** ample, scant; no (= not any) □ *To* ***do*** *it* ***justice****, the Africa Korps behaved itself commendably well amidst the current temptation to destroy.* SD □ *I saw your picture in the 'Courier'. It doesn't* ***do*** *you* ***justice*** *though.* RATT □ *Last year's revival* (of the opera, 'Eugene Onegin') *in the company's international season* ***did*** *it scant* ***justice****.* SC □ *The accusation that there is little interest in Gaelic literature throughout the Hebrides* ***does*** *the people of these islands* ***a*** *grave* ***injustice****.* □ neg variant do sb/sth an injustice, often with such adjs as *grave*, *serious*; neg expression more formal than headphrase.

do sb/oneself a mischief [V + IO + O] (informal) do some physical harm to sb or oneself □ *'My orders are to bring him in,' went on the corporal. 'Take his sword, Fred, he might* ***do himself a mischief****.'* TVT □ *She lets the baby play with anything he can lay hands on. He'll* ***do himself a mischief*** *one of these days.* ⇨ ⚠ do sb/oneself an injury.

do more harm than good [V + O pass] achieve an effect which is more damaging than beneficial □ *What is needed is a new drug which will relieve and console our suffering species without* ***doing more harm*** *in the long run* ***than*** *it does* ***good*** *in the short.* DOP □ *In general I was convinced that 'speaking'* (giving unasked-for advice) *to people was liable to* ***do more harm than good****.* SML □ ***More harm than good*** *would be* ***done*** *by pumping in public money* □ *Enjoying entertainment and loving talent, I ought to understand and appreciate Showbiz. But in fact I detest it. Increasingly it* ***does*** *far* ***more harm than good****.* NS □ *I always said that* ***more harm than good*** *would* ***come of it****, and now I'm proved right.* □ used esp as warning against, or criticism of, actions, institutions etc which are motivated by good intentions but not, in effect, helpful; variant more harm than good comes of (doing) sth.

do the necessary/needful [V + O pass] (informal) perform some action, or task, that is expected or required □ *She's our mother after all and if she's no longer able to look after herself it's up to Diane or me to* ***do the necessary*** *and have her to stay.* □ *When the kick came in, centre-half Dempsey jostled aside Osgood to reach the ball first and head just wide. The forward might have* ***done the necessary*** *a shade better.* ST □ *'Here, Peter,' she said, handing him the rubbish bin, 'go and* ***do the needful****.'*

do no good [V + O pass] not be useful or effective in achieving any purpose **det:** no; (not) any, (not) much; little; what □ *Archie is always being punished by his teacher, but it* ***does no good*** (or: ***never does any good***). □ *It may be assumed that the inquiry now being conducted by the TUC* (= Trades Union Congress) *into unofficial strikes will distinguish between impatient gestures, which may* ***do little good*** *but are not altogether blameworthy, and the stoppages which are part of a campaign to cause trouble in industry.* SC □ *You could complain* (about delays) *to the Department of Trade and Industry, who oversee civil aviation. But that is unlikely to* ***do much good*** *either.* ST □ *'We're getting a very poor picture on BBC2 tonight.' 'Try switching it off, and then on again.' 'I don't see* ***what good*** *that'll* ***do****.'* ⇨ ⚠ much good may it do sb; no good.

do no/not do any harm [V + O pass] have no bad effect, or result, and possibly have a good or useful one **S:** it; a walk in the fresh air, a word of advice. **A:** to take a walk, to eat less; for Jane to take the children out □ *Maybe he can't help you but it* ***does no harm*** *to ask.* □ *I do believe you are willing, Prissie, but it wo****n't do any harm*** *for Nurse Ellen to take the children out.* DC □ *It would****n't do*** *you* ***any harm*** *to walk to work for a change.* □ *'These tablets should help your indigestion,' the doctor said, 'and remember that, at our age, a little less to eat and drink never* ***does any harm.****'* □ *Perhaps he can't help you but* ***there's no harm in*** *asking.* □ variant there's no harm in (doing) sth, where's the harm in it?

do no more than do sth be sufficient, or adequate, only to meet a particular need or purpose **V:** cover, pay for, provide, sth; amuse, soothe, sb. **adv mod:** no; little; (not) any, (not) much □ *The £15 fee* ***did no more than*** *cover my expenses.* □ *Even if they* ***do little more than*** *help her to forget her troubles for a few hours, I think a couple of sleeping pills would be a good idea.* □ *Such half-hearted reforms can't* ***do much more than*** *serve as palliatives for the time being.* □ *The business is washed up; a loan will* ***do no more than*** *delay the day of reckoning.*

do nothing/not do anything by halves do anything one is engaged in completely and thoroughly; extend oneself to one's limits in one's activities, emotions etc □ *No doubt a rapid volley of telegrams would shower upon them from all parts of the country, and possibly even from abroad, for Walter* ***did nothing by halves****.* HD □ *George was* ***not*** *the man to* ***do things by halves****. He would either refuse to support the venture at all or send us a very handsome cheque.* □ (a golf enthusiast) *He made models of the greens and worked out every angle, putting his theories into successful practice and even playing with a red ball in the snow. Pop* ***never did anything by halves****.* TVT □ *So ends a weekend which began with sheets of tropical rain, typical of a city which does* ***not do anything by halves****.* T

do one's nut [V + O] (informal) get into a state of alarm or consternation; lose one's temper, self-control; blow one's top (qv) □ *I'm* ***doing my nut*** *because the doc says I may be impotent by Christmas.* JFTR □ *Oh, Lesley, be careful what you're doing! The boss'll* ***do his nut*** *if anybody jams up that copying machine again.* □ nut = head.

do or die [v + v non-rev] (catchphrase) (resolve to) make a determined, or desperate, attempt to do sth (the price of failure not necessarily being death) □ *I had to get down that rock face,* ***do or die****, before nightfall.* □ *I was only riding as an individual* (ie not one of a team) *so there didn't seem to be a great deal of honour at stake—though that of course has since been disproved; apparently it should always be* ***do or die****.* OBS □ *Only four contestants were left in the slow-bicycle race, all of them wobbling along the track with identical* ***do-or-die*** *looks on their faces.* □ attrib use *a* ***do-or-die*** *look.* ⇨ ⚠ never say die.

(sb can/could) do the other thing (informal) do what you like, let him do what he likes etc, I don't care □ *You're twenty-one, and you're married to me. So what? If she doesn't like it, she* ***can do the other thing****.* AITC □ *I'm telling you this, and if you don't like it,* ***you can do the other thing****: I think you killed Christine.* PE □ *'****Do the other thing****, then!' she flared at him. 'There's no pleasing you.'* □ *'You pamper those children ridiculously,' said their father. 'If they won't eat the food you set before them, let them* ***do the other thing****.'* □ often follows *if*-cl.

do one's own thing (catchphrase) allow one's natural abilities, tastes, interests, feelings etc to guide one's way of life, work, pastimes, or behaviour (the implication often being that self-expression is a desirable end in itself); follow one's (own) bent (qv) □ *The popular* *catch-phrase of the moment — '**doing one's own thing**'—is symptomatic of a widespread revulsion of thought and feeling against the kind of regulations which the education system has imposed.* SC □ *It's very much a characteristic of today, this **doing your own thing**, the idea that in the last resort our liberation is only possible through what we see and feel and taste.* RT □ *I feel pleased that I can involve other women and perhaps help them by providing pin-money. So **do your own thing** and who knows where it might lead: no matter if the home gets a little dusty.* ST ⇨ ⚠ do one's thing.

do sb a power/world of good [V + IO + O pass] (informal) be very beneficial to sb (esp to their health, good spirits, morale) **S:** holiday, breaks; exercise, diet; getting away □ *Astonishing what a man can do with a bit of training. Oh, it'll **do** us **a power of good**.* THH □ *'If you don't mind me saying so,' Ma said, 'a few days in the country'd **do** you **a world of good**.'* DBM □ *That was why he had saved his cigarettes—an intact packet of ten. A smoke now would **do** him **the world of good**.* HD □ *Aubrey was really extraordinary with that boy. It will **do** him **all the good in the world** to feel he is someone and get a bit of importance.* WDM □ variant do sb all the good in the world; less emphatic form do sb/sth good (qv).

do sb/sth proud [V + O + A] entertain, reward, honour, sb lavishly or generously; praise or otherwise testify to the merits of sb/sth in a full and fitting way **S:** restaurant, hotel; press, radio; performer □ *There had been quite a correspondence in 'The Times' and 'The Telegraph'. 'The papers have **done** you **proud** certainly,' said the stockbroker's wife.* HAA □ *Finally he had a brainwave and remembered the name of some extra-special superb restaurant, where we could **do** ourselves really **proud**, and re-directed the driver again.* CON □ *You may think that he was not **doing** me as **proud** as all that* (= was not paying me a very special compliment). SML □ *How such a cantata could go unrecorded so long is a mystery. Nikolaus Hamoncourt and his Vienna forces **do** it **proud**.* NS

do the rest [V + O] complete a job or process, esp one begun by sb/sth else □ (an attempted murder) *There must be only a slight mark, as if she had fallen against the lamp as it hung from the hook. The real fall would **do the rest**.* □ *'Once you have signed up with us,' the Travel Agent assured him, 'you have to pack your own suitcase and turn up at the airport at the time we tell you, but we'll **do the rest**.'* □ often *will/would* **do the rest**.

do the right etc thing[1] [V + O] behave, act, in a way that is morally or ethically proper, that seems just and fair **adj:** right, ⚠ decent, proper, honourable □ (World War 1 volunteer) *I never regretted joining up. I'm no churchman, I can tell you. But I felt I **did the right thing**.* SC □ *Clearly they were of the opinion that Jack had **done the decent thing**, had put himself in the right by his generous apology.* LF □ ***do the right thing** by the girl, woman, Jane etc* can be understood to mean 'marry sb who has the right to expect it'.

do the right etc thing[2] [V + O] act wisely, prudently etc **adj:** right, ⚠ sensible, wise; wrong □ *If she took sides in their disputes, as she sometimes did, she never knew if she was **doing the right thing**—it was like interfering between husband and wife, they both resented it.* PW □ *'Should we have waited till morning to phone you, doctor?' 'No, you **did the right thing**. I've given the boy a sedative and we'll get him into hospital right away.'* □ *Anyway the whole atmosphere of the place was stuffy and institutional. No spark. Everyone seemed to be afraid to expand. People were too afraid of **doing the wrong thing**.* ST □ *Joseph Lambton was **doing the sensible thing**, keeping out of harm's way until the rum and the beer and the brandy settled down.* RATT

do/drive a roaring trade/line (in sth) [V + O pass] be very successful in selling particular goods or providing a particular service □ *Temporary cafeterias set up at one end of the hall are **doing a roaring trade** refreshing the hungry multitudes before and after the show.* TO □ JIMMY: (reading a Sunday newspaper) *Grotesque and evil practices going on the Midlands. Startling Revelations this week! Pictures too. Well—I'll bet Fortnums must be **doing a roaring line in** sacrificial cocks!* LBA □ *The electricians' strike lasted so long that anybody with the foresight to stock up could have **done a roaring trade in** candles and oil-lamps.* □ *As the only blacksmith in twenty square miles of this countryside, my great-grandfather **drove a roaring trade**.* □ drive rarer in use than do, line rarer in use than trade.

do/go the rounds [V + O] make a number of visits, calls, inspections etc covering a certain area, often including certain groups of people □ *Every Christmas* (they) ***did the rounds** of their own people and then of ours on a visit of goodwill.* SML □ *Several high level party delegations from Moscow have **done the rounds** to inspect the party organisation all over Italy, and they seem to have departed satisfied.* L □ *I'm afraid that the doctor can't come to see you immediately—he's out **doing his rounds*** (= seeing his patients). □ variant do one's rounds often indicates a procedure carried out regularly.

do sb/oneself a service/disservice [V + IO + O pass] do something that will or should benefit sb/oneself (or the reverse) □ *The Cuilleband Report may be **doing a service to** more than the railwaymen directly affected* (by the proposed improvements). NS □ *Since he doesn't realize that his arrogance is antagonizing people I think you would be **doing** him **a service** if you told him so.* □ *Constables' pay has kept broadly in step with the average industrial earnings. If the police were too far ahead of the general body of industrial workers it would be **doing a** great **disservice to** the workers.* DM □ *It is surely worth trying to put matters into some kind of perspective. Neither our politicians nor our newspapers **do** us **any service** by trying to frighten us out of our wits.* NS □ *I decided not to bother contacting Duvivier in Paris and thereby **did myself a disservice**, as subsequent events were to show.* □ *I think I **do** the army and **myself a disservice** in always concentrating on military subjects.* G

do the spadework [V + O pass] perform the (hard) tasks that are a necessary preliminary to the success of a project □ *Some of the prime movers to the third* (aid to undeveloped countries) *conference* **did a lot of spadework** *beforehand, urging delegates to play everything very cool in the belief that the rich would be more impressed by rational debate than by emotive polemic.* NS □ *Theory and exercises are very boring, I know, but you can't be a real musician without* **doing the spade-work**. □ *The Impressionists certainly brought in new attitudes in art, but where feeling for Nature and skill in capturing its moods were concerned,* **much** *humble* **spade work** *had already been* **done**. G □ spadework written as one word, two words or with a hyphen.

do one's stuff [V + O] (informal) do what one is expected to do; show how well one can do sth; carry out the duties, activities usually assigned to or associated with one □ *Training in the 5th Corps was ordered to be hard and tough; in rain, snow, ice, mud, fair weather or foul, at any hour of the day or night—we must be able to* **do our stuff** *better than the Germans.* MFM □ *Some day a war might come again and I would have to leave my peace and go and* **do my stuff** *as my father had before me.* RFW □ *Jennings remembers his manager, Bill McGarry, telling him bluntly that he didn't know a thing about goalkeepers and wasn't fussy whether Jennings trained every day or not, so long as he* **did his stuff** *on the day.* TVT

do one's thing [V + O] (informal) perform in a way commonly associated with one; go into one's act/routine (Vol 1) (qv) □ *Dad usually stumps up for anything we want badly. But first, you've got to let him* **do his thing** *about not being able to afford it.* □ *It's quite amusing to listen to him* **doing his thing** *with tourists in the lounge bar. I don't suppose he buys a single half pint for himself, the whole of the summer season.* □ (fashion shows) *Few can mould crêpe so skilfully and his white pants suits are a tour de force of supple tailoring. Revers and huge collars* **are his thing**, *overlapping each other on widely cuffed coats.* ST □ variant be one's thing. ⇨ ⚠ do one's own thing.

do time etc [V + O] (criminal slang) serve a prison sentence **O:** time; ⚠ (slang) bird, porridge □ *Sammy's a well-known Jew from Jo'burg. He was* **doing time** *for illegal possession.* DS □ *The regime in children's prisons is not unnecessarily harsh or punitive but it is a prison regime and the children themselves are well aware of it. They get a certain amount of pride at having* **done 'bird'** *before their 17th birthday.* ST □ *The two dozen or so members of gangs '***doing porridge***' are a drop in the ocean of potential villains, says Mr Payne.* SC □ *He's* **doing** *fifteen* **years** *for armed robbery.* □ variant do x months/years, with actual period of imprisonment specified.

do the trick etc [V + O] (informal) accomplish what is desired; be sth that (finally) solves a problem, achieves an object, has a required effect, etc **O:** the trick, ⚠ the job; it □ MICK: *You'll be tarring over the cracks on the roof.* ASTON: *Yes* (pause). MICK: *Think that'll* **do it**? ASTON: *It'll* **do it**, *for the time being.* TC □ *Bevin and Citrine and the TUC* (Trades Union Congress) *generally, refused in 1931 to accept the analysis of the crisis with which Macdonald and Snowden presented them. Bevin refused to believe that cuts in wages would* **do the job** *(and he was proved right).* OBS □ *I said that if I was not taken to see the Marshal I would leave Berlin and return to the British Zone—which, of course, I would hardly have done! However, this* **did the trick** *and I was taken to Marshal Zhukov's residence.* MFM □ *'The next three or four hours will probably decide the business. If oxygen doesn't* **do the trick***'—Dr Bennet shrugged his shoulders as if to say, 'There's your answer.'* PE

do the/one's usual [V + O] (informal) do what is customary; do sth that one is in the habit of doing whether this is a mode of behaviour or just a customary task □ *'Have you planned your summer holiday?' 'Not really; I expect we'll be* **doing the usual** *and taking the caravan up the West Coast somewhere.'* □ *'Coffee will be served in a few minutes — Miss Wotherspoon, would you be frightfully kind and* **do your usual**? *Thank you so much.' Miss Wotherspoon's usual was to trudge down to the school kitchen, make the coffee, and carry it up.* HD □ *It was a very pleasant gathering on the whole. Our chairman, of course,* **did his usual** *and spoke far too long.*

do well to do sth etc be well advised, find it in one's own interests, to remember or do sth specified **Inf:** to remember, to bear in mind; to call off, postpone; to think again □ *Those who criticise India will* **do well to** *remember the depths of her start, and the height of her hopes.* ST □ *At this time the Scottish and New Zealand rugby teams would* **do well to** *call off their forthcoming visits.* SC □ *I can only commend Mankiewicz's literate, witty, caustic and penetrating script of an order of writing many modern film directors would* **do well to** *study.* RT □ *You* **do well to** *ask if you can help me to mow the lawn now that it's finished!* □ usu with *will/would*; often used ironically in the simple present and past tenses as in last example.

do etc wonders/miracles (for/with sb/sth) [V + O] be extraordinarily successful in achieving something, producing some result; work a miracle/wonders (qv) **V:** do, ⚠ work, perform, achieve □ *'I think,' he said, 'Murley was one of the movers of the economy. Bernard had* **done wonders** *but the cost of living, you know, does rise so.'* HAA □ JERRY: *Old Jack here has been* **doing wonders with** *her.* JEAN: *How is she?* JACK: (putting his arm round Cairy's shoulders): *She's fine.* YAA □ *Mr Goodrich tells me that you can* **work wonders with** *the miserable pittance that a robber Government still allows us to call our own.* PW □ *The bath and the drink had* **worked wonders** *and Sir Julius was by now sufficiently recovered.* EM □ *Some patients expect their doctors to* **do miracles** *in the way of instant relief.* □ *This annual 'Book of Records' has* **done wonders for** *the name of Guinness and has made the McWhirters wealthy men.* ST □ *It is hard to believe that children who are so physically handicapped have produced woodwork and pottery of such a high standard. Miss Murphy has* **wrought wonders with** *her pupils.* □ wrought occurs much less frequently than worked in this phrase.

do one's worst [V + O] be as difficult, unpleasant, harmful etc as possible □ *Grieve drives towards Charing Cross* (in Glasgow) *where he says the planners have* ***done their worst****. High on a flyover above the old cross he points to the sandstone relics of the Victorian days.* RT □ *She's with me at the house. I decided to have her up here, for a time at least, and let the gossips* ***do their worst****.* CON □ *The weather could* ***do its worst*** *for all he cared. He had enough provisions and fuel was laid in.* □ the expressions *let sb/sth* ***do his/its worst****, he etc can* ***do his worst*** indicate defiance.

do you know (informal) a comment, or exclamation, introducing a statement, esp one which may cause some surprise □ ***Do you know****, that's the first time I've heard of burglars having children. Makes them quite human doesn't it?* DC □ *'You switched off the hot plate before we left, I suppose?'* ***'You know something****, I don't believe I did!'* □ *I had the old Chesterfield suite recovered while he was away and* ***do you know****, he hasn't noticed yet.* □ almost always front position; stress pattern do you 'know; variant (less formal) you know something(?).

do you mind?[1] an enquiry as to whether sb objects to some action or event; if you don't mind [1] (qv) □ *I think I'll go along to the club this evening for a game of snooker.* ***Do you mind****?* □ stress pattern do you 'mind?; a medium rising tone on mind?

do you mind?[2] an expression of objection, often aggressive, to sth which is occurring; if you don't mind [2] (qv) (according to the context, could be the equivalent of 'get out of my way', 'stop interrupting', 'you're sitting in my seat' etc) □ JO: *Hold my hand, Geof.* GEOF: ***Do you mind****? Halfway through this?* (he is brushing the floor) TOH □ (TV stars about weight-watching) DIANA DORS: *Actually, I'm just getting the weeniest* (= slightest) *bit bored of reading about me in the round.* ***D'you mind****?* TVT □ stress pattern do you 'mind?; a fall-rise tone on mind?

do's and don'ts [n + n non-rev] (informal) instructions; detailed guidance □ *My* ***do's and don'ts*** *for employing any kids are: first, to see the job is done properly. And I pay on the dot.* OBS □ *Many people dream of retiring to a cottage by the sea or in the country. But, when the time comes, can they be sure the dream matches up the reality? Today's programme looks at the* ***do's and don'ts*** *of making a move.* TVT □ *'You Can Take It' is a useful manual of* ***Do's and Don'ts*** *for the ambitious amateur photographer.*

dodge/duck the issue [V + O pass] avoid dealing with a situation, answering a question or argument, directly □ *'Would you let your daughter marry a bear? Come on now, yes or no?' You then appear to be the one to be hovering and qualifying and* ***dodging the issue*** *while he stands there quivering with certainty and righteousness.* NS □ *This led to an attack on the delegates by Keith Jackson of Liverpool accusing them of* ***ducking*** *all* ***the issues*** *at stake.* NS

doesn't one know it! (informal) an added comment to the effect that sb is very well aware, or too much aware, of sth previously mentioned □ SARAH: *He knows he can go to her—she'll feed him.* CISSIE: *He's her son, for God's sake.* SARAH: ***Don't I know it****.* CSWB □ *'The Browns made a big mistake in not buying that house when they first came here.'* ***'Don't they know it!*** *It'll cost them twice as much now.'* □ *He's handsome all right—and he* ***doesn't half know it!*** □ variant sb doesn't half know it (!) = 'sb is very well aware of sth'.

the dog days high summer; (fig) a time of tedium, apathy etc (in the Roman calender, the 6 or 8 weeks of greatest summer heat when the influence of Sirius, the Dog-star, rising with the sun was thought to increase its heat thus causing difficult conditions, pestilence etc) □ *My first full week of retirement from the daily production of '24 Hours' coincided with the very end of* ***the dog days*** *of repeats and try-out series which disfigure the schedules of late summer.* L □ *If the French did accept the rather presumptuous identification of Gaullism and France, their acceptance had the colour of acquiescence, passivity; precisely the qualities which, as Ophuls shows, made possible* ***the*** *shameful* ***dog days*** *of the Pétainist regime.* NS

dog ears/-eared turned-down corners on the pages of a book, or in bundles of papers (usually the result of much, or careless, handling but sometimes done deliberately to mark a place). □ *'Don't do that,' she snapped. 'I hate a book full of* ***dog ears****. Use an old envelope or something to keep your place.'* □ *He asked me to read his novel, a* ***dog-eared*** *manuscript that told its own story of having gone the rounds of probably a score of publishers.*

dog eat dog ruthless competition that takes no account of loyalties or fellow-feeling □ *Bluff Court was far too large to live in. You needed to keep twenty servants to wait on you and another twenty to wait on them. It was very* ***dog eat dog****.* DBM □ (NONCE) *The world of books has always suffered from its petty promotional aspect, in that its* ***dogs****—not to mention its bitches—****eat each other*** *till their teeth fall out, but Melvyn Bragg has the proper open-minded respect for artistic achievement.* RT □ (an Englishman criticizes his compatriots' theatrical production in New York) ***Dog does not eat dog****; but I can no longer repress a cry of anguish.* OBS □ neg variant dog does not eat dog = 'one doesn't harm or destroy one's own kind'.

a dog in the manger [Comp (NP)] a person who selfishly prevents others from using or enjoying sth which he keeps for himself, though he cannot use or enjoy it (from Aesop's fable of a dog sitting in a manger and preventing the ox from eating the hay) **V:** ⚠ be, become □ *Who would get the commission? No one.* ***That*** *filthy* ***dog in the manger*** *would not have accepted any—that was certain; and had taken care to see that no one else profited.* US □ *To these major attitudes towards 'Them' may be added one or two minor but recurrent ones, the 'I ain't a gentleman, you see' attitude: a dull* ***dog-in-the-manger*** *refusal to accept anything higher than one's own level of response.* UL □ *It is not merely that it* (the BBC) *finds itself in a* ***dog-in-the-manger*** *role—not wanting the fourth channel for itself but still firmly determined to do everything in its power to deny it to ITV* (= Independent Television). NS □ attrib use *a* ***dog-in-the-manger*** *attitude, role etc.*

the dog it was that died (saying) sb has become the victim of his own attempt to harm another □ (source) *The man recover'd of the bite,/* ***The dog it was that died.*** ELEGY ON THE DEATH OF A MAD DOG (O GOLDSMITH 1730-74) □ *'I have come back,' he said to Beatrice, 'I am not under the table* (= poisoned). *I have come back victorious.* ***The dog it was that died.****'* OMIH □ *Be sure you have your facts right. If you make an attempt to discredit a man in his position and fail, it may be a case of '****the dog it was that died****'.*

dog one's/sb's (foot)steps [V + O pass] be sth that one/sb never seems able to escape from **S:** ⚠ bad luck, misfortune; unhappiness; sickness □ *Bad luck still seems to be* ***dogging*** *the European Movement****'s footsteps****.* □ *He worked hard enough on his farm, God knows, but drought and pestilence* ***dogged his footsteps*** *season after season.* □ *That tiresome old bore, Perkins, seems to be* ***dogging my footsteps*** *these days. I swear I can't go anywhere but he turns up too.* □ (NONCE) *But we were winning. At all points success* ***dogged our steps****. The great walls of the citadel emerged as our picks cut through the encumbering debris.* SD □ use in last example depends on paradox in that the meaning must be deduced from an apparent contradiction in terms.

a dog's breakfast/dinner [Comp (NP)] (informal) a mess; a situation, undertaking, piece of work, room etc that is mismanaged, untidy etc **V:** ⚠ be; make sth; feel like □ *You've made* ***a*** *right* ***dog's dinner*** *of your attendance register, Mr. Smith. I'll issue you a new one and you can get it copied out so that other people can make sense of it.* □ *As for the party I don't remember much of it. I felt like* ***a*** *second-class* ***dog's dinner****.* JFTR □ *The battle was really almost lost before it began. The whole business was* ***a*** *complete '****dog's breakfast****'.* MFM □ *He was prepared readily to accept assignments which most officers would have regarded as the kiss of death, and to the horror of Mountbatten, who knew* ***a dog's breakfast*** *when he saw one, he agreed in 1942 to assume command of the Army of Burma.* NS

a dog's life [O (NP)] a pattern of life in which there is not much pleasure or freedom, in which one has to take orders from others, etc **V:** have; lead (sb) □ *He is leading* ***a dog's life*** *in that store, fetching and carrying from morning till night.* □ *My old man* (= father) *would never hang himself, worse luck. Maybe mam* (= mother) *would have to leave him first, and then he might do it, but no—I shook my head—there wasn't much chance of that even though he did lead her* ***a dog's life****.* LLDR □ *It's* ***a dog's life*** is often an expression of temporary or not serious dissatisfaction.

a Don Juan a womanizer, breaker of hearts, sexual libertine, etc (from a 14th century Spanish aristocrat who figured as the 'hero' of many poems and plays and of Mozart's opera 'Don Giovanni') □ *The occasional bachelor in a* (English working-class) *neighbourhood is likely to be living at home with a widowed mother. He is not thought of as a man-on-the-loose and therefore as* ***a*** *potential* ***Don Juan****.* UL □ *'And there's another thing, Mister* ***Don Juan****,' she said, her arm round Rosa's shoulders. 'Get out and do some work, even if it is your last night. And next time you meet a decent girl, leave her alone, will you?'* HD □ *Pete's virility has to be established. 'He's a pistol,' explains an office girl-friend. Tillie amiably assents, side-tracking the girl's attention by a chummy discussion of* ***Don Juanism****.* NS □ also pl; variant Don Juanism.

don't be too sure said by a second speaker to a first who has just made an unwarranted assumption, over-confident remark, etc □ *'Thank God. I never need to wonder where my wife is or what she is doing.' '****Don't be too sure****,' she answered teasingly, 'maybe I'm leading a double life.'* □ *'Henry will be away at the university by next winter, so we'll have a spare bedroom.' '****Don't be too sure****,' her husband said. 'He hasn't been doing so well at school this year.'*

don't call us, we'll call you (catchphrase) a statement intended to hint that it may not be possible to keep a promise, or to keep people at a distance (from the statement traditionally made by theatrical directors to aspiring actors, actresses, chorus girls, etc after an audition) □ *'The parts shouldn't be too difficult to obtain.' 'I'll ring up in a day or two, then, and call to collect them if you've got them.' 'No,* ***don't call us, we'll call you****.'* □ *What good is a cosy Utopia that raises students' expectations and then dashes them in a world that has no use for more than 10 per cent of them? The rest, waving their special aptitudes, could be channelled relentlessly towards the car factories or the collective farms.* ***Don't call us, we'll call you****.* G □ now normally used ironically; call in headphrase = 'make a telephone call to'.

don't do anything I wouldn't do (catchphrase) used as ironic advice in leave-taking □ *Well, got to run along now, Charleyboy. Got to see a man about some scrap iron.* ***Don't do anything I wouldn't do****. See you all about five.* DBM □ *Off on your holidays tomorrow, are you? Be sure to enjoy yourselves then, but* ***don't do anything I wouldn't do****.*

don't give me that (catchphrase) what nonsense! do you expect me to believe that? what you've just said is not true and you know it, etc □ *'Didn't know where you lived,' he muttered. '****Don't give me that****.' Robert grated. 'An administrative wizard like you couldn't be baffled by a simple problem like finding my address.'* CON □ RUTH: *You've a lot to learn yet, George. If there weren't people like the Elliots, people like you wouldn't exist.* GEORGE: ***Don't give me that****, Ruth. They drive you mad, and you know it.* EGD □ (writing dialogue for a play) *He put a fresh sheet in and typed: Gregory: But this is really quite farcical. Breathing heavily, Bowen now x-ed out his original line of dialogue and typed: Gregory: You're just pulling my leg. Then he got up and stumped around the room for a bit, made another line of x's and typed:* ***Don't give me that****.* ILIH

don't just stand there (do something) (catchphrase) act effectively, esp in a time of crisis or trouble □ ***Don't just stand there, do something****! Your great brute of a dog is going to attack my little cat! Look, he's got him by the throat!* □ *He remembered one of their quarrels. 'Why don't you* ***do something****, act some way, any way at all? You* ***just stand there****—'* OMIH □ *'The investigation of an affair of this nature is* *entirely outside my sphere.' 'Do you mean that you're going to* ***stand there*** *and* ***do nothing,*** *you ridiculous person?' said Mrs Carstairs.* EM □ often an appeal or demand though the speaker himself may not know what should be done; stress pattern don't just ˌstand there, ˈdo something; reference to standing need not be taken literally.

don't look now, but a request that another should look at sb/sth without drawing attention to himself, without being seen to be looking □ (of a television series) ***Don't look now, but*** *the Daleks are coming back. Dr Who zooms off on a new series of adventures soon.* OBS □ '***Don't look now but*** *I think your father's among that party that just came in.' 'Good Lord, let's finish our drinks and get out of here. I'm supposed to be at my French class tonight.'* □ *It was Sir Thomas Beecham (who else?) who once became aware that a soloist had slowed up and was now several bars behind the orchestra.* '***Don't look now***,' *he hissed to his players,* '***but*** *I think we're being followed.'* RT □ used as a sort of 'joke' phrase when the speaker thinks another will be interested, surprised or dismayed by what he is about to see.

don't make me laugh (catchphrase) a bitter, scornful, resentful etc response to a statement or suggestion □ *Mind you, in a way it's the poor bloody wives I'm sorry for. Legalized bloody prostitution, that's what it is. Look at their faces, that'll tell you all right. Ever-loving wives?* ***Don't make me laugh***. TGLY □ DAVID: *Anyway, what can you do with two hundred pounds?* SAM: *You can build up the business into a really posh layout; or you can take a world trip before you begin.* DAVID: ***Don't make me laugh***, *a world trip? You're living in the past. All I could do is buy a motor-scooter or eight new suits.* HSG

don't mention it a courteous reply to sb's expressions of thanks or gratitude, to sb's apology for a mistake, trouble caused, etc; you're welcome (qv) □ PHILIP: *Well, Myra, I'm sorry all this has been foisted on you.* MYRA: *Oh,* ***don't mention it***. EHOW □ *'Thank you, constable, for your help.'* '***Don't mention it***, *ma'am—that's what we're here for.'* □ *I paid your milkman for you—£3.20 for the week, he said—and you can give me that. As for taking care of Billy,* ***don't mention it***. *He was no trouble at all.*

don't mind me[1] (informal) don't bother about me; don't let concern for me interfere with your plans etc **O:** me, him/her, us/them □ HENRY: *Have you been there* (beside me) *long?* ADA: *Some little time.* (Pause). *Why do you stop?* ***Don't mind me***. (Pause). *Do you want me to go away?* E □ *'You will see my bicycle now.' He threw his leg across the saddle and settled himself comfortably in riding position. The seconds went on ticking by while he went on sitting there and Bowen watched him.* ***Don't mind me***, *Bowen wanted to say to him; go brrmmm, brrmmm if you want to.* ILIH □ *Father says go to the cinema and* ***don't mind him***, *he'll be perfectly happy with his book.* □ said more or less sincerely, but without criticism of person to whom it is addressed; stress pattern ˌdon't mind ˈme; fall-rise tone on me.

don't mind me[2] (informal) don't bother about me; don't let concern for me interfere with your plans etc □ PETER: *Oh, go to hell! Go on, have your blasted family reunion,* ***don't mind me***! TOH □ '***Don't mind me***, *I just love getting my feet wet.' she said stepping into a puddle in order to pass him.* □ *His wife leant over and switched the TV to another programme. 'That's right,* ***don't mind me***!' *he said.* □ said sarcastically, resentfully, or agressively, to draw attention to a grievance; stress pattern ˌdon't mind ˈme; rise-fall-rise tone on me.

don't 'Now Norah' etc me (informal) do not speak to me in the terms, or call me by the name, that you have used **Comp:** 'Now Norah', 'Granny'; 'ever so sorry' □ *'Now Norah—' he said, and put his pen down carefully.* '***Don't 'Now Norah' me*** *please, I've had just about enough* (= as much) *as I can stand.'* TT □ '***Don't you 'Granny' me***, *my girl,' she said to the nurse. 'My name is Mrs Adams, and that's what you'll call me.'* □ *'I forgot to collect your transistor, Dad—ever so sorry.'* '***Don't 'ever so sorry' me*** *in that don't-care tone of voice! The shop'll be closed by now or I'd send you straight back for it.'* □ expression is aggressive, conveying resentment or defiance; Comp is always repetition of all or part of the statement which causes resentment or defiance.

don't shoot the pianist etc (he's doing his best) (catchphrase) be tolerant towards a well-intentioned person who only means to please, entertain or try to do something worthwhile, whether he is making a success of it or not (from the first example, said by the author to have been a notice in a 19th c American saloon bar) **O:** pianist; artist; translator; policeman; secretary □ (source) ***Please do not shoot the pianist. He is doing his best***. IMPRESSIONS OF AMERICA (O WILDE 1854-1900) □ (NONCE) *I must declare my interest in the piano interlude, 'Peter Grimes Fantasy', which was commissioned by 'Music Now' (a TV series). This piano was fine, expertly tuned.* ***The pianist was 'shot'*** *(****doing his best****) in the music room of Tyvie Castle.* L □ *I happen to have read one of M. Orieux's earlier biographies in his own language — and can assure the reader that this tone is entirely his own. So* ***don't shoot the translator, she is doing*** *more than* ***her best***. NS □ ('audience participation') *It is as well to recall that: (a) participation need not necessarily be a virtue (I should not add much to a pas-de-deux in 'Swan Lake'), (b) participation can take many forms, from mental communion to* ***shooting the artist***. OBS □ used as a whole, in part, or allusively; in second example shot means 'filmed', making the whole sentence a complicated play on headphrase.

don't tell me surely it can't be possible (that sth is true or has occurred) □ *'Really, dear, I couldn't say when they went to the park.* ***Don't tell me*** *they're not home yet.' Brigit shook her head.* DC □ *'What did you mean, he's a business friend? What business?* ***Don't tell me*** *he's anything to do with that publisher.' 'He's in a much better racket than that. He's a bookie.'* AITC □ '***Don't tell me*** *you're Millie's grandchild, the one that had the yellow hair down to her waist!' 'Yes, that was me.'*

done etc to a turn [Comp (AdjP)] cooked for just the right amount of time and ready to eat (from roasting meat on a spit) **V:** ⚠ be; seem. **pp:** done, ⚠ cooked, roasted □ *'Is your egg right for you?' '**Done to a turn**—white solid and yolk soft, just how I like it.'* □ (NONCE) *Like some wine with this? I've got some 'Entre Deux Mers' **chilled to a turn**.* BM

(for) donkey's years (informal) a long, or very long, time (perhaps arising from an old tradition that one never sees a dead donkey) □ *Mrs Scarfedale had set to working at the tobacco factory to earn enough for herself and Jim. She stayed hard at it **for donkey's years** and she had a struggle to make ends meet.* LLDR □ *It would take **donkey's years** to collect all the necessary information for their survey unless they could enlist a research team.* □ *It's **donkey's years** since I've eaten semolina pudding. I didn't think people made it any more.* □ often *not have done sth **for donkey's years**.*

dot and carry (one) [v + v non-rev] (informal) move with a limping, or unsteady, gait □ *If she rested in the daytime, Lennie went **dot and carry** up the stairs with cups of tea and vivid sugar cakes from the bakery on the corner.* AITC □ *In waters so hazardous with reef and shoal our explorations were dependent on the availability of some local navigator, but in this **dot and carry** way we did manage to visit most of the islands in the group.* □ *'I got a punishment exercise from old **Dot-and-Carry-One**.' 'James, I have forbidden you to use that nickname for Mr Simpson. An artificial leg is nothing to make fun of.'* □ attrib use, *this **dot and carry** way* as in second example, indicates uncertain or irregular progress of any kind.

dot the i's (and cross the t's) be meticulously correct in what one does or says; make clear in every detail something which may be obvious or well enough understood already □ *There are many **i's** to **dot and t's** to **cross** before we can feel certain about the exact relationships described here in broad detail.* SNP □ *The shares may not break through the chart barrier at around their current 42p until full-year figures are produced, **dotting the i's**, but then they should move smartly ahead.* ST □ *The novelist's own belief had been that the scandal lay, not in the political field, but in an indefinable, though very definite, impression of sexual indiscretion, of the unnecessary **crossing and dotting** of **the t's and i's**, which were perfectly well known, but not to be advertised.* HAA □ *'I see you've got my point,' the lawyer continued. 'There's no need for me to **dot the i's and cross the t's** then.'* □ usu in order of headphrase.

a double agent a person who is employed as a spy, agent-provocateur etc by the Secret Services of two countries, one of whom he is deceiving on behalf of that other to whom he owes allegiance □ *'Will he* (our man) *be able to start again if he's blown* (ie his disguise is penetrated)*?' 'He has a trick worth two of that. Struck right home into the enemy camp. Recruited **a double-agent** in the police-headquarters itself.' 'Aren't **double agents** always a bit tricky?'* OMIH □ *Like numerous other academics he enjoyed the battle of wits carried on in the Intelligence world behind the military battles. 'Running a team of **double agents** is very like running a club cricket side.'* NS

a double bind (informal) a situation in which one has to choose between two things, two courses of action, etc, both unfavourable or undesirable; a dilemma **V:** be; be in, put sb in, find oneself in □ ***The double bind** I found myself in was very simple: if I left the country now I would not be allowed back, but if I stayed, I would be forbidden employment, and probably imprisoned.*

a double chin a heavy fold, or folds, of flesh or fat visible between the jaw line and the neck □ ***The double chin** he had had when he was twenty-five was a rather larger double today, his complexion was pastier, and his pugnose was now approximating to a bulldog's nose.* RM □ *The fat man's eyes glared and all his **double chins** shook with rage, as he thumped the table.* □ one can have several, three etc double chins.

a double cross the betrayal or exploitation of two different persons or parties by sb who pretends allegiance to each but is in fact using them against each other □ *The Italians had said they were fed up with the war. It seemed that at any given moment they were prepared, if we would land on the mainland of Italy, to come in with us. I remarked that this looked like **the** biggest **double-cross** in history.* MFM □ *Madge is being **double-crossed** by Sammy, who ditches her for Sadie.* UTN □ *Some agents made errors, which were surely detected and exploited in Germany; and the Germans themselves were also operating a **double-cross** system to feed us misinformation.* NS □ (NONCE) *And the lovers of power, the councillor, the footballer, the **treble-crossing** womaniser, and a thousand others are all there.* PP □ attrib use *a **double-cross** system*; used as n, v or attrib n or adj; variant, treble crossing, in last example unusual, but easily understood.

double Dutch something, esp sth spoken or written, that cannot be understood or that seems to be gibberish; meaningless sounds or words □ *How can anybody understand this Constitution? It's difficult enough for educated Africans and Europeans to understand it, but for the masses it must be absolute **double Dutch**.* L □ *'I expect the name Paul Temple is as well known in Europe as it is here. Except in Holland, where they've never heard of him.' 'But you said just now—' 'Yes, I did—but in Holland, for some **double-Dutch** reason, he's called Paul Vlaanderin.'* RT □ *Sometimes an older brother or sister seems to have an intuitive knowledge of what a toddler is trying to say in a **double-Dutch** that defeats even his own parents.* □ often hyphenated; attrib use *some **double-Dutch** reason etc.*

double or quits [n + n non-rev] a bid in a gambling game, when the winner alone stakes his stake for the second game, throw of the dice, etc, and it is agreed that if the loser loses a second time he will pay double this stake, but if he wins, his debt is cancelled and no money passes □ *'I should be against any compromise. You've either got to show some faith now—or give the whole thing up in this country.' '**Double or quits**,' said Rose, 'if I haven't misunderstood you, my dear chap.'* NM □ *So with Consols it's a **double or quits** situation. If interest rates rise, then the income is inadequate and the capital* *value drops.* G □ may be spoken as an actual offer or challenge as in first example.

double quick [A] very fast; as quick(ly) as possible (the implication usually being that speed is, or will be, expedient or necessary) □ *'And if it starts to spit, then turn it off* ***double-quick****. It's quite a reliable old contraption.' He gave the geyser a familiar and affectionate slap on its smooth white flank.* TGLY □ *Now then, Freddie, —off to bed and in* ***double-quick*** *time, too. It's me that'll get into trouble if your mother comes back and finds you still up.* □ *'I feel badly* (= ill),*' I fibbed. 'Well, get outside and get some fresh air then,' he shouted. I did as I was told,* ***double quick*** *because if ever Dad goes as far as to tell me to get some fresh air I know it's time to get away from him.* LLDR □ often hyphenated.

(do) a double shuffle [V + O] (take) corrective action to get back into step when marching; (fig) (take) some hurried action to correct a situation, or alter the direction of an argument □ *The three of them fell into step. This meant that every now and then Simon had to* ***do a double shuffle*** *to catch up with the others.* LF □ *We had about twenty minutes' notice that Arthur and family were coming to see us, so we all had to* ***do a double shuffle*** *to clean the place up before they arrived.* □ *'Now who would like to see my slides?' said their hostess brightly. 'I wouldn't,' he started to say abstractedly, but being a master of* ***the double shuffle****, coughed as if he had caught his breath unexpectedly, and added 'miss that for the world.'*

double talk talk, sth said, that is capable of more than one interpretation or that is intended to mean something opposite to, or different from, what the words actually used might indicate □ *I'm sure I don't know whether all this sophisticated* ***double talk*** *your friends indulge in is just a pretentious habit or whether they've found a way of being able to insult each other with impunity.* □ *The managing director's speech was a masterpiece of* ***double talk****. The workers thought they were being promised the earth, but the shareholders knew there weren't going to be any changes that were going to come out of their pockets.*

(a) double think (informal) believing two contradictory things at the same time □ *At the heart of Christanity there seems to me to be* ***a*** *stark* ***double-think****: 'the world' is worthless, corrupt and doomed, at the same time as being precious, sanctified and glorified.* □ *Mr Jackson's guilty of a bit of* ***double think*** *about Mary. He values her work, but won't promote her because he believes women are inferior to men.*

(not) doubt sb's word [V + O pass] (not) disbelieve what sb has stated, reported, promised etc □ *'You might be Harold Martin's daughter.' 'I am. I've just told you.' 'No need to take me up. I'm* ***not doubting your word****.'* AITC □ *Yes, I would like to see your references. It's* ***not*** *that I* ***doubt your word****, but it's always better to do business matters in a businesslike way, isn't it?* □ *'Have you found the murderer of Hasselbacher? Was it Carter?' 'After what you said, naturally I checked. He was with Dr Braun at the time. And we cannot* ***doubt the word of*** *the President of the European Traders' Association, can we?'* OMIH □ *I've already said I would tell nobody about this. Do you* ***doubt my word****?* □ *I believe you're* ***doubting my word****. Ask Jack, if you don't believe me.* □ almost always neg, interr or conditional; positive uses tend to imply that doubt should not be present, as in last example.

a doubtful proposition [Comp (NP)] a proposed undertaking which will be difficult to carry out and could easily fail; a statement, assertion etc that is arguable and perhaps false **V:** ⚠ be; find, think, sth □ *To take on the job of hand-rearing a week-old baby* (ant-eater), *therefore, was* ***a*** *very* ***doubtful proposition****, to say the least.* DF □ *After the taking of Alexandria and Cairo, Napoleon's campaign to annex Egypt from the Ottoman Empire began to seem less of* ***a doubtful proposition****.* □ *'If you show people that you trust them, they will not let you down.' 'Well, if that has been your invariable experience you are a lucky man. It seems to me to be rather* ***a doubtful proposition****.'* □ also pl.

a doubting Thomas a sceptic; sb who will not believe anything unless he has satisfied himself as to its truth, seen the evidence with his own eyes, etc (from the name of one of the 12 disciples of Christ, see JOHN XX 25-29) □ *'And I didn't believe in those flying saucers till I saw one with my own eyes.' 'You're a bit of* ***a Doubting Thomas****, what?'* RM □ *The experiment has worked. It didn't really need doing, since Einstein's theory had already been tested under far more extreme conditions. But such a test had to be performed, if only to lay the* ***doubting Thomases*** *to rest.* L □ *The workers have all been paid a month's wages, which will make Christmas a good deal brighter for them, and confound* ***doubting Thomases*** *like me.* L

(a trip) down memory lane (cliché) nostalgic recollections of the past; an event, experience that recalls the past, esp one's own **V:** take (a trip); go, travel, wander □ *'I'm not a nostalgic person at all,' says Elspet Gray, referring to* ***her trip down Memory Lane*** *in 'With Great Pleasure' (Sunday 10.10 Radio 4). 'I'm very forward-looking.'* RT □ *The Queen Mother took* ***a trip down memory lane*** *yesterday during an informal visit to the Angus village of Glamis where she spent her childhood.* SUNDAY EXPRESS □ *Remember square-bashing and the days of the short back and sides? Whether you do or not, take* ***a trip down memory lane*** *to the time of National Service.* TVT □ *I do not want to travel too far* ***down memory lane*** *in this piece, but I remember the time when Mr George Brown arrived panting in Brighton to persuade an alarmed General Council to accept a voluntary wages policy.* NS

a down payment [O (NP)] part of the total price of goods or property, paid at the time of agreeing to purchase; a deposit **V:** make; request, ask for □ *The Building Society have agreed to give us an 85 per cent loan which means we shall have to make* ***a down payment*** *of nearly £500.* □ *We usually ask for* ***a down payment*** *on made-to-measure suits for new customers, sir. Will that be all right?* □ *It was the sort of wedding where the cost of the ceremony and reception go as* ***a down payment****, and you then continue dishing out your wages every week for life.* LLDR □ also pl.

down to sb/sth [A (PrepP)] even including the

final item of a comprehensive list of persons or things **o:** the last woman, the youngest man; the last detail; the final stages; the present day □ *In the course of a séance dance, the witch doctor was able to describe correctly, in minute detail, the hidden article,* ***down to*** *the colour of the wrappings and the nature of the locality where it was buried.* SNP □ *From Thomas More, through Rousseau, and a dozen others* ***down to*** *Lenin, many thinking, feeling men, disgusted by the ugly squalor of existing social systems which maintained and propagated the poverty and misery of mankind, have sought a solution.* NS □ *We had everything packed,* ***down to*** *the very last teaspoon, when the removal contractor phoned to say he couldn't come till the next day.* □ *The patients were of the middle sort from well-to-do workmen* ***down to*** *impoverished pensioners.* L

down tools [V + O] stop work at the end of the day, for any official break, or as part of a strike or other protest; (fig) pause in, or discontinue, any activity □ *Conditions from the point of view of the professional astronomer were poor, the 'seeing' was bad—there was too much wind at high levels. So nobody was sorry to* ***down tools*** *for the midnight snack.* TBC □ *He had realised that he could not carry on without taking some decisive step to help himself. It was then that he had '****downed tools****' and retreated here, he explained.* HAHA

down under [A] in the antipodes, and esp Australia or New Zealand □ *Actor Warren Mitchell who plays Alf Garnett, the outrageous cockney character from the series 'Till Death Us Do Part', talks to Alan Whicker about his approach to comedy* ***down under****.* TVT □ *Edward Heath became the first British yachtsman since the war to win the Sydney-Hobart race. Oh Lord, yes, he said, it was very much his object to show them* ***down under*** *that we're not as effete as they thought.* G

down with sb/sth (catchphrase) an exclamation, or exhortation, that expresses hatred of sb/sth or a desire to destroy sb/sth □ TONY: *God knows there is material progress. Hundreds of millions of people progressing in leaps and bounds towards a materially-progressive heaven.* MYRA: *Are you pleased about it or are you not?* TONY: *Of course I'm pleased.* ***Down with*** *poverty.* EHOW □ *'****Down with*** *the Rich': Berger's writing is at its stirring best when predicting the overthrow of authority.* NS ⇨ up (with) sb/sth.

drag one's feet [V + O] proceed unwillingly, or with delaying tactics, in a course that one must or should take □ (The convoy system) *was a tremendous success. And the people at the Admiralty were amazed. They still* ***dragged their feet*** *for some time to come. But by August it was perfectly clear that this was the answer and they must simply go ahead full speed, and they did.* L □ (advertisement) ***Drag your feet*** *much longer and you'll end up kicking yourself. Save As You Earn is the most profitable guaranteed National Savings plan ever.* OBS □ *The site could temporarily be used as a sewage pumping station, if only to remind our* ***foot-dragging*** *friends that we are still aware of the problem, and hope that they are.* SC □ attrib use ***foot-dragging*** *friends, bureaucracy etc.*

draw (a) blank [V + O] fail to obtain, learn, find sth one is searching for, or hopes to get (from drawing a blank ticket in a lottery, but draw blank is a hunting term for failure to start game in a covert etc where one hoped to find it) □ *So we wanted it known for certain if there really were any diamond mines in Liberia. We had nothing to go on, and the British and American Embassies in Monrovia, who were equally worried about the problem, had also* ***drawn a*** *complete* ***blank****.* DS □ *I came upon various interesting objects, but not the typescript. There was no sign of the thing. Finn had* ***drawn a blank*** *too. We searched the other rooms, but without much hope.* UTN □ *Well, he might be at his club, but if you* ***draw blank*** *there, I don't know where to suggest.*

draw blood [V + O pass] injure sb sufficiently seriously to make him bleed; (fig) hurt sb's feelings; arouse injured resentment; score a victory over sb □ *And although the future Prime Minister* (Disraeli) *was smaller and not so strong he was like lightning on his feet. Besides, he had been taking boxing lessons for three years. Soon he succeeded in* ***drawing blood*** *from his opponent, and at last the boy collapsed.* OBS □ *'Oh, Clun feels doubts about Pforzheim's proficiency in Arabic,' Gerald said. 'I hope he raises that in the discussion,' said Theo. 'Pforzheim'll make rings round our Arthur.' 'Well, you must let me know if he* ***draws blood****.'* □ *Dawson doesn't care about the critics. Anyhow, critical disclaim can hardly* ***draw blood*** *from a man who went through the swamp fever of the provincial clubs in the Fifties.* TVT □ *First* ***blood*** *was* ***drawn*** *by the home team, with a goal scored within five minutes of the start of play.* □ ***draw*** *the first* ***blood*** = 'be the first to draw blood, or to score in some contest'.

draw breath [V + O] live; (begin/continue to) exist □ *She was as kind a woman as ever* ***drew breath****.* □ *The warning signs were clear before the new government* ***drew breath****.* OBS □ (late 17th c) *Verse drama would have to be overtly formal, and probably composed in strict couplets, if it were to stand a chance in* ***drawing breath****—the language had lost its innocence beyond hope of recovery and only discipline could restore it to delight.* ST □ *She won't want for a friend as long as I* ***draw breath****.* ⇨ ⚠ next entry.

draw/take (a/one's) breath [V + O] breathe; breathe in; pause to breathe **adj:** deep, long, another, one's last. **A:** lightly, painfully □ *I suppose Sir Mortimer had to seem to be talking to somebody but in fact, he was entirely self-sufficient. He hardly* ***drew breath****.* L □ *Sarah* ***drew a*** *deep* ***breath*** *before replying.* WI □ *Charles Lamb said he wished to* ***draw his*** *last* ***breath*** *through a pipe and exhale it in a pun.* □ *A useful trick, if ever you want to avoid being interrupted, is not to* ***draw breath*** *at the end of a sentence but to carry straight on, breathing when you can in mid-flow.* □ *As he slid the third slide under the microscope he* ***drew his breath*** *sharply, causing his colleague to look up from his work.* □ *'****Take*** *two or three deep* ***breaths*** *before you jump in,' said the swimming instructor. 'You can hold your nose if you like.'* □ draw never followed by pl breaths. ⇨ ⚠ previous entry.

draw/make comparisons [V + O pass] compare sb/sth with sb/sth else □ *No one is so much* *disliked as he who persists in '**drawing comparisons**', he spoils the party spirit.* UL □ *'She runs her house in quite a different style from Mrs Rose,' the home help replied, 'but they're both very nice ladies to work for, and I see no call to **make comparisons**.'* □ *Punish or reward a child as he deserves, but don't **draw comparisons** with his brothers or sisters.* □ often used to suggest that the comparison is unjust, or tactless, instead of being based on merits or demerits objectively considered.

draw sb's/the enemy('s) fire [V + O pass] cause the enemy to concentrate gunfire etc; (fig) cause sb to concentrate attack, criticism, unwelcome attentions, etc in a particular direction, against particular groups, objects etc in order to divert such attack from sb/sth else □ *There was no shortage of police volunteers to **draw the** killer**'s fire** by attacking the front of the building while an attempt was made to rescue his hostages from the rear.* □ *Elsie feared that tempers were rising and, brave girl, she **drew** her father**'s fire** upon herself.* RM □ *'I can't imagine being afraid of a woman,' Harold said, trying not to sound unsympathetic. 'Oh, can't you? Well, you don't know Elspeth. We shall get through it somehow. You must **draw her fire**, Harold. Play up to her, won't you?'* PW

draw it mild [V + O + A] moderate one's speech or behaviour; not exaggerate a description, overstate a case (from a request for mild, or light, beer in public houses etc where different kinds of beer are sold on draught) □ *Oh, come on, Bill. **Draw it mild**. That's no sort of language to be using in front of kids.* □ *Conditions were, in fact, even worse than I had described but I **drew it** a bit **mild** for fear of not being believed at all.* □ often imper. ⇨ come it strong.

draw/point a moral [V + O pass] perceive and/or point out that there is a moral lesson to be learnt from sth that has happened, a story etc □ (source) *He left the name, at which the world grew pale,/To **point a moral**, or adorn a tale.* THE VANITY OF HUMAN WISHES (S JOHNSON 1709-84) □ *Tales deliberately concocted so that we may **draw a moral** from them don't appeal greatly to children and no class I ever taught were much interested in 'Aesop's Fables'.* □ *A riffle through the daily papers turned up little to lighten the general gloom except an item that told how when a wolf escaped in a zoo, people were put behind bars. There is obviously **a moral** here somewhere waiting to be **drawn**.* SC □ *Our mother was **a** great **drawer of morals** and the various fortunes of our neighbours provided her with numerous examples of what we should emulate or avoid.* □ *We also believe that, given the facts, people nowadays are anxious to make up their own minds—and that we shall not always need to draw obvious conclusions or **point** familiar **morals**.* NS □ *A grave defect of the English oratorio was the inadequacy of the libretti so enthusiastically produced by the Anglican poetasters* ((derogatory) = versifiers) *who found in the most murky episodes of the Old Testament fit material not merely to adorn a tale but to **point a moral**.* L □ variant a drawer of morals.

draw sb's/sth's teeth/fangs [V + O pass] render sb/sth harmless, take away from sb/sth the means to cause fear or harm □ *Scottish independence, the speaker said, was more a matter of personal characteristics than of national ambition. In any case, **the teeth of** the Scottish Lion had been **drawn** over three centuries ago.* □ *He was an elderly homosexual, who had corrupted a few boys in his time, but was comparatively harmless now. **His fangs** were **drawn**, he declared sadly.* AITC □ *The British family, possible loss of earnings apart, does not have to budget for possible illness. The National Health Service has **drawn the teeth of** that bogey.*

dread the moment (when) [V + O] be worried about, or merely not be looking forward to, sth that will, or may, happen □ *Pauline spent three wretched hours at the cinema **dreading the moment when** she must go home and face her husband again.* BM □ *'The Principal wants to see you in his room,' Jane said. 'Oh dear,' Mary whispered hastily to her neighbour, 'this is **the moment** I've been **dreading**.'* □ *The thought of having to take my turn at climbing down the rope-ladder scared me stiff, but when **the dreaded moment** came I found it much less of an ordeal than I expected.* □ variant the dreaded moment.

dress the part [V + O] clothe oneself suitably for what one has to do, for the role or function one has to perform—perhaps merely in order to conform with convention or the expectation of others □ *Charles seemed not to realize the sacred duty of **dressing the part**. Even as an undergraduate he had not worn corduroys or coloured shirts.* HD □ *You can't possibly open the Highland Games without **dressing the part**. You'll have to hire a kilt and all the trimmings.* □ *'I thought of phoning to warn you it would be a dirty job, but'—he added, glancing at Jim's grubby jeans—'I see you**'re dressed for the part**, so that's all right.'* □ *'I expect that'll be the old lady's solicitor that came in just now.' 'He**'s dressed for the part**, anyway. You don't see many people wearing a morning coat and striped trousers, even at a funeral, nowadays.'* □ variant be dressed for the part.

the dress rehearsal [Comp/O (NP)] the final practice performance of a play, with full costume, scenery etc in the same form as it will be presented to the public; (fig) an episode which precedes a similar but more significant event **V:** be; hold, stage □ *'**The dress rehearsal** didn't go too well.' 'Oh well, they know now what can go wrong. It'll be all right on the night, you'll see.'* □ *He was going to stage Myra's wedding all over again, as if to rub in the fact that the first one had been nothing but **a dress rehearsal**, and this time she was* really *getting married.* CON

dressed to kill (informal) dressed in very fine and striking-looking clothes (the implication usually being that there is a lack of taste, a gaudiness, too many adornments, etc) □ *Brenda Rawnsley, **dressed to kill** in the New Look, chartered a four-seater aeroplane, with money borrowed from the bank, and flew across the Channel one summer Sunday in 1948.* OBS □ *She had done her utmost to remind him of the conditions agreed on when he asked her out, insisting on paying her share and backing this up by having **dressed** as hard not **to kill** as she could, short of frumpishness.* TGLY

(in) dribs and drabs [n + n non-rev] (informal) (in) small irregular amounts; by irregular action **V:** get, impart, reveal, sth; approach, deal with, tackle, sth □ *She had concocted the whole story from* **dribs and drabs** *of gossip picked up at back doors and in the shops.* □ *Wales have given British soccer many great players. But always* **in dribs and drabs**. *If only they had all arrived in the same generation, then Wales would certainly have been potential world champions.* TVT □ *Certainly there is an illiteracy problem in Britain by the old measure—a reading age of the average nine-year-old. It is tackled at the moment* **in dribs and drabs**, *a volunteer teacher scheme here, a local authority class there.* NS □ also used as [A (PrepP)] as shown in second and third examples.

drink/drain the cup of sorrow etc [V + O pass] (formal) experience great sorrow etc **o:** sorrow, ⚠ sadness; humilation, shame □ *I was mistaken in supposing that I had* **drained the cup of humilation** *to the dregs. My ex-wife was now to inform me that 'our' child was not my own.* □ *After all their high hopes for their sons, they've had* **a bitter cup** *to* **drink**: *one a drug addict, one in jail, and now the youngest diagnosed a dangerous psychopath.* □ variant drink a bitter cup = 'experience humiliation'.

drink like a fish (informal) drink too much alcohol too often, as a regular habit □ *He claims that it was the loss of his wife that drove him to drink, but believe me, he was* **drinking like a fish** *long before that.* □ *'Who's Alphonse?' Pop said. 'He is the chef. He is not an easy man.' Drinks, Ma thought. She knew. Nearly all cooks* **drank. Like fishes**, *too, though perhaps you couldn't blame them.* BFA □ *It stands to reason, doesn't it, that you can't have money for clothes, or anything else, if you* **drink like a fish**.

drive a hard bargain [V + O] (have the means, power, or cunning to) force a bargain; contrive an exchange of goods and services that is either unfair or to one's own advantage □ *'Whether we buy the furnishings along with the house depends on what you're asking for them.' 'Look, I'm not trying to* **drive a hard bargain**. *If you care to get any reputable valuer in to look at the stuff, I'll let you have them at his valuation.'* □ *Goran chief executive, 40-year-old Archie Gilchrist, has been hunting a purchaser. It was a pretty tense period, he admits, and Pao coming along in the nick of time, has managed to* **drive a hard bargain**. ST □ *Now that the supplying countries have* **driven a hard bargain** *and cashed in again at the expense of the UK consumers, we can begin to reckon up the cost of not having this sugar business thought out and properly agreed.* SC

drive sb mad etc [V + O + Comp pass] cause sb to lose his/her sanity; (fig) make sb angry, exasperated, distraught etc; send sb crazy (qv) **Comp:** mad; (informal) ⚠ daft, crazy; (slang) crackers, bonkers □ *It* **drove** *one man* **mad**: *another to his grave. It caused bitter controversy and cost a fortune. Now it merely exasperates. It is the new Palace of Westminster, more famous as the Houses of Parliament.* SC □ *It's always me who's the louse, and honestly, Jim, you're so God damn forbearing and unselfish that sometimes it's enough to* **drive** *a man* **mad**. AITC □ JO: *There's a gas stove in here. How do I light it?* HELEN: *How do I—with a match. Wouldn't she* **drive** *you* **mad**? JO: *I know that, but which knob do I turn?* TOH □ *'Gosh!' she said. 'Who'd work in a dry-cleaning shop. This afternoon nearly* **drove** *me* **crackers**.' PE □ *I offered to look after the two boys for her while she was in hospital but I'm just about* **driven daft** *with the pair of them, although I'm used enough to children.*

drop one's aitches [V + O pass] omit the initial 'h' sound in a word where it is present in received pronunciation, as is done in some dialects, eg in some London speech □ *'And when she has to make a public appearance, it's embarrassing for both of them.' 'Why should it be?' Randall asked. 'You mean she* **drops her aitches** *or something?'* CON □ *'It was the 'eadmaster kept us back, miss—'e told 'er and me to wait be'ind and 'elp with the milk bottles.' 'Now Harry, say all that again without* **dropping your aitches**.' □ often used to suggest, or indicate, origins that might be found socially unacceptable; *aitch* is name of letter 'h'.

drop a brick/clanger [V + O pass] (informal) say, or do, sth that causes embarrassment, or that should not have been said or done in the company present □ *Still careless of how many* **bricks** *I* **dropped**, *as long as I could be of some use, I asked him why he didn't come back home: at least he had friends there who could keep an eye on him.* CON □ *My series is honest—it really is, I may have made a few technical blunders, politics are so complicated even the most seasoned MPs* **drop bricks**. TVT □ *'I wouldn't know how to behave at a grand function like that,' the old man said. 'I'd be* **dropping bricks** *the whole time and upsetting you by doing everything wrong.'* □ *Mary did not realise what* **a clanger** *she had* **dropped** *when she asked her hostess if the soup came out of a tin.* □ drop a clanger is the more informal expression.

drop dead[1] [V + Comp] (informal) die suddenly (in the middle of some normal activity) □ *I said that, of the things one has to expect from old age, I put blindness, being totally bedridden, and* **dropping dead** *as the worst, in that order.* □ *'***Dropping dead**,' *he boomed 'has no terrors for me.'* ST □ *I've got enough money in my pocket to last me the rest of my life—provided I* **drop dead** *this afternoon.* OBS

drop dead[2] [V + Comp] (slang) a coarse and/or violent recommendation to sb to stop bothering one, interfering etc; get knotted (qv); get lost (qv); get stuffed (qv) up yours etc (qv) □ PAMELA: *Mummy says she's common, but that's just because she wears shocking pink socks and says '***drop dead***' all the time.* FFE □ *She could see the point of sex being frank, free and open as Patrick had unwisely put it. What was meant by the expression in practice was a frank, free and open (and immediate) scuttle into bed with some man; to tell them all to* **drop dead**, *however frankly, freely and openly did not count as that.* TGLY

drop a hint [V + O pass] refer indirectly to something; make a suggestion indirectly, or tactfully, in order to give the listener an opportunity to do something that the speaker wants him to do □ *Fiorella couldn't help* **dropping** *a few* **hints**. *Gianpaolo, like a true working man, was utterly impervious to hints. He didn't even* *answer.* ARG □ *I knew that in this matter his temperament would work like mine; we said yes, but we did not like to be managed. Nevertheless I could* ***drop a hint****.* NM □ *'Is it true that me and him are—sort of cousins, in a way?' 'Your mother's great-auntie used to* ***drop hints*** *about goings-on in the sixth viscount's days, but I never paid any attention to them, and my advice to you is to do the same.'* EM □ *His visit to France, which was to have started last Tuesday, was postponed on his plea of influenza. Dark* ***hints*** *were* ***dropped*** *about a 'diplomatic illness'.* OBS ⇨ take a hint.

a drop in the bucket/ocean sth of inconsiderable value, importance, esp as compared with something larger in total or in kind **adv mod:** only, just, no more than a. **adj:** mere, single, tiny □ (source) *Behold, the nations are as* ***a drop of a bucket****, and are counted as the small dust of the balance.* ISAIAH XL 15 □ *According to Karl, the diamond which Kutze had lost on Beit Bridge was* ***a*** *mere* ***drop in the ocean****. The Copperbelt was lousy with IDB smuggled stones.* DS □ *In fact, the total resources of the hospital services would furnish no more than* ***a drop in the bucket*** *by comparison with the needs of the community.* L

drop sb a line etc [V + IO + O] (informal) write sb a brief note etc **O:** line, ⚠ note, letter □ BARNEY: *Here, I'll have to be going. As I say, maybe we can do business together and make some money for both of us. I'll read it through again, and* ***drop*** *you* ***a line****.* EGD □ *Relax with an ice-cool drink. Day dream about Marlon Brando or some celebrity you admire, then* ***drop*** *him* ***a note*** *to say so.* WI □ *'I think,' his solicitor advised, 'that before threatening your tenant with the law, you should* ***drop*** *him* ***a letter*** *yourself.'* □ esp of casual, or friendly correspondence, or of an attempt to keep communications on this footing.

drop names [V + O] (informal) over-use the names of celebrated or influential persons in order to impress others with one's acquaintance with, or knowledge of, them; over-use scientific, technical, specialist words and terms in order to impress a lay audience □ *By* ***dropping*** *a sprinkling of the right* ***names*** *and enough technical jargon I was able to pick up secret files left lying on desks.* OBS □ *The book is strictly for members and sympathisers but as there are thousands of them, it is sure to give a lot of pleasure. It is unpretentious, it can present* ***names*** *without* ***dropping*** *them, and the tone is contagiously warm.* L □ *A brief broadcast talk, already crowded with information, is not the place to give references; had I done so, the accusations of* ***name-dropping****, now gratuitous, might have had some point.* L □ *Most secret agents are snobbish about their calling. They enjoy '****name-dropping****' about cut-outs, postboxes, burnt contacts, double agents, conscious and unconscious agents, de-briefing and the rest.* DS □ second sense less usu than first; n compound name-dropping.

drown one's sorrows [V + O] (informal) drink wine etc to comfort oneself, to forget one's troubles □ *'You're in trouble, aren't you?' she said. He shrugged his shoulders slightly. 'Who isn't?' 'Well, there's something in that. Better have another drink and* ***drown our sorrows****. I'll buy you one this time.'* PE □ *They talk about drinking to* ***drown your sorrows****, but the more Andrew drinks the more melancholy he gets.* □ *We arrived in Edinburgh on the evening after an International rugby match and found the pubs packed out with Welshmen celebrating and Scotsmen* ***drowning their sorrows****.* □ often used lightly.

a drug on the market [Comp (NP)] an article, or commodity, not in much demand and difficult to sell **V:** ⚠ be, become; make sth □ *Second-hand cars were* ***a drug on the market*** *in Kuwait, where every other semi-skilled inhabitant tore* (= drove very fast) *sumptuously around in a Chevrolet or Mercedes, imported at cut-throat prices, duty free.* BM □ *The publisher has been accused of using the word 'novel' in connection with these three related stories and two pieces of reportage, to conceal the fact that the book is* ***that*** *supposed* ***drug on the market****, a collection of stories.* NS

a dry/dummy run an experimental, or trial, performance of a mission, project, the working of a machine, etc □ ***A dummy run*** *of the rescue apparatus, with weighted sacks instead of people, had been organized for the following week.* □ (headline) ***Dummy Run*** *With Metric System, Advantage Of Trial.* T □ *It is too early to assess the success of the scheme but if the rest of the '****dry run****' trips* (to continental hotels) *are as successful as last weekend's I don't think that many clients will forfeit their deposits on summer bookings.* OBS □ *It was as tricky a piece of advertising copy as I'd ever had to handle, and the crumpled papers in my waste-basket testified to the number of* ***dummy runs*** *that had preceded the final layout.* □ attrib use *a* ***dry/dummy run*** *trip.*

a/the dumb blonde (cliché) stereotyped figure of femininity, esp as a sex-object or booster of male morale □ (reader's letter) *I write in praise of Charles Marowitz's fascinating talk on* ***the dumb blonde****. And, of course, he is right:* ***the dumb blonde****, beautiful and desirable, does not need brains, providing that she is loving and sympathetic.* L □ *She is alone by choice as much as circumstance, she says.* ***No dumb blonde****, with clockwork eyelashes this one, but a woman as shrewd as she is beautiful.* TVT □ *I used to resent being type-cast as* ***a dumb blonde*** *all the time, but now that I've proved I can do serious parts I'm quite content to cash in on my physical appearance for some years to come.* RT □ also pl.

dust and ashes[1] [n + n non-rev] the decomposed state of sb long dead □ (source) *...earth to earth,* ***ashes*** *to* ***ashes****,* ***dust*** *to* ***dust****; in sure and certain hope of the Resurrection to eternal life,...* BOOK OF COMMON PRAYER □ *Edward Fitzgerald could not visit a museum or read history without thinking: 'The men who did this are dead.' He saw the dead writers and those they had written about as what they exactly were at the present moment;* ***dust and ashes****.* NS

dust and ashes[2] [n + n non-rev] sth previously pleasant which has become unpleasant, bitter □ *...in his frenzied search to regain those wondrous secret childhood games beside which all the pleasures of the adult world were* ***dust and ashes*** *in his mouth.* HAA □ *Chanel* (in her autobiography) *has produced a gripping success story, which at the same time most morally ex-*

poses the ***dust and ashes*** *of that success.* L

the dust of ages [o (NP)] dust that has lain undisturbed for a long time; (fig) the obliterating effects of the passage of time **prep:** under; in, from; with □ *By courtesy of the local commandant, the labour problem had been solved and Ugarit* (an archaeological site) *was fast emerging from* ***the dust of ages****.* SD □ *The books on the upper shelves were thick with* ***the dust of ages****.* □ *Under the psychoanalyst's skilful questioning, memories long buried in* ***the dust of ages*** *began to reform themselves.*

the dust settles (saying) the upset, consternation, confusion, resentment etc aroused by sth slowly lessens, subsides □ *As* ***the dust*** *began to* ***settle*** *yesterday, one or two facts about Thursday's controversial programme became established.* OBS □ *Has there been a leak? Downing Street* (home of the British Prime Minister) *flatly denied it. Had the journalists been afflicted by some collective delusion? They remained silent. Once* ***the dust*** *had* ***settled****, the one certain thing was that for the time being unemployment was being left to respond to the medicine already prescribed.* L □ often in subordinate clauses beginning *when, till, after etc.* ⇨ raise a dust.

Dutch courage (informal) courage lent by strong drink, either in the form of assertions as to what one can or will do, or carried over into action □ *We've finished the whisky. Fancy that now. Just when you need your* ***Dutch courage*** *most!* OMIH □ *I woke up thinking: 'I've got to change my hair, I've got to get it cut.' I drank a whole bottle of wine for* ***dutch courage*** *and took myself to 'Scissors' in King's Road, London, before I could have any second thoughts about it.* TVT □ *After my fourth drink it began to seem possible that I could tell my wife what had happened, so I left the pub hoping that my* ***Dutch courage*** *would last till I got home.*

a Dutch treat (informal) an outing, entertainment, social gathering, etc where each person pays his own share of the expenses □ *'I thought Gerald had invited you all for this game of golf and dinner at his club-house.' 'Oh no, he has organized it because he's a member, but it's to be* ***a Dutch treat****.'* □ *'You're spending too much money,' Jenny said. 'I'd much prefer to* ***go dutch*** *on our evenings out.'* □ variant go Dutch = 'share the cost of an outing etc'; both headphrase and variant sometimes written with small *d.*

(in) duty bound to do sth [Comp (AdvP)] required to do sth because it is one's professional duty to do so, or out of a sense of moral obligation; feel obliged to do sth because it is 'one's bounden duty' (qv) **V:** ⚠ be, feel □ *'Since you are turning me out,' I said, 'you are* ***in duty bound to*** *make a constructive suggestion.' 'You were never in, Jake,' said Dave, 'but I will try to think.'* UTN □ *'I cannot sell you these tablets unless you have a doctor's prescription,' the chemist replied, and added stiffly, 'as* ***in duty bound****.'* □ *It's nice for an old woman to have somebody drop in for a chat, but I wouldn't like you to feel* ***duty bound to*** *come every other day.*

a duty call [O/o (NP)] a visit made to sb as part of one's routine of work (eg as a doctor, diplomat etc), or of one's social obligations **V:** make, pay, receive; go on □ *I'm afraid I can't give you an appointment at 4.30. That's the time Dr Simpson keeps free to make* ***his duty calls****.* □ *Any diplomat will tell you that most of the first couple of months of a new posting are taken up with tedious but necessary* ***duty calls*** *on the Foreign Ministry and on other diplomatic missions.*

duty calls (cliché) there is work that one must do now; there are obligations that one cannot escape (esp as a reminder to oneself or others that a pleasurable interlude must come to an end) □ *'Stay and have another drink, won't you?' 'There's nothing I'd like better, but* ***duty calls****, I'm afraid'* □ *He had once wanted to become a monk, but with a widowed mother and two younger sisters to support, he had realized that* ***duty called*** *and that he was obliged to train for a professional career.*

a dyed-in-the-wool reactionary etc [Comp/O (NP)] a thoroughly imbued and committed person of a specified type (the reference is to wool that is dyed before being spun or woven) **n:** reactionary, conservative, socialist; rogue, villain □ *Some people see you as* ***a dyed-in-the-wool reactionary****. Others think of you as an out-of-date 19th century classical liberal. Your son suggests calling you a libertarian anarchist.* L □ *'Are you making reflections on my morals, old man?' 'Yes, I am. You're nothing but* ***a dyed-in-the-wool*** *inconsiderate* ***rogue****.'* DIL □ *The programme's title is, in this case, slightly misleading. Both the featured guests are to be found more often on the rock-orientated 'Sounds of the 70s'—but they could open the ears of a few* ***dyed-in-the-wool traditionalists****.* RT □ *His real name wouldn't mean anything to you and the last thing I want to do is to throw a man's past in his face, unless he's* ***a double-dyed villain****.* DS □ *If anyone tells you he sat there wholly at ease, looking forward to the moment when the Speaker would call upon him to make his maiden speech, he is* ***a liar of the deepest dye****.* ST □ often, but not necessarily, used of old-fashioned or reactionary qualities; variants, using the same metaphor, a double-dyed reactionary etc, a reactionary etc of the deepest dye, almost always derogatory (or jestingly so).

E

each and every [det + det non-rev] each single individual (person or thing) in a group of people or things, without exception; every last/single one etc (qv) **n:** one (of you, them etc); person, householder; item, object; situation, recommendation, objection; time □ *There is not one of you men and women who is not a volunteer. In the hands of* ***each and every*** *one of you lies a civilization.* TST □ *The astonishing thing was that* ***each and every*** *one of the patients thus treated* *made a better and quicker recovery than any patient in the control group.* □ ***Each and every*** *discovery can only be examined against historical evidence, and historical evidence means here the story as we receive it from Bede.* ASA □ tautological expression used for emphasis (cf each one, every one).

each/every man for himself (and the devil take the hindmost) (saying) everybody does what he can to further his own interests, to protect himself, to save his own life etc without considering the interests etc of anybody else; (the) devil take the hindmost (qv) □ *This is a case of* ***each man for himself****, Briggs, and if you don't make a clean breast of it to the police I shall have to give them the information in my own interests.* EM □ *For years he had tried to justify to himself that final act of treachery. He no longer bothered now. In Sefton's world it was* ***every man for himself****.* ARG □ *He had no regrets about leaving the crowded existence of a big impersonal city with its attitude of* ***every man for himself and the devil take the hindmost****.* □ each/every man for himself can be used alone with the rest understood; used as warning remark, or reflection on people's behaviour, or as recommendation that one should act in this way.

each (one)/everyone (according) to his taste(s) (saying) (one must accept the fact that) what one (or sb) likes or dislikes is not, or may not be, liked or disliked by sb else □ *'I like working for the magazine.' '****Everyone to his taste****,' Helen said, with the air of one who has long outgrown such childish things.* AITC □ *'Company'* (a musical play) *is as far removed from 'Hair' as it is from 'Mahagonny'.* ***Everyone to his taste****, however, and plenty of people will love it.* L □ used to affirm that tastes differ (but to suggest, perhaps, that one's own taste may be superior).

each way/both ways [A (NP)] (horse-racing) (bet money on a horse in the hope of it) either winning or gaining second or third place (as opposed to a bet 'to win' only or 'for a place') **V:** back a horse, the favourite; put £5 on a horse □ *'Queen's Rook won't lose,' said Sammy, 'but we're covered anyway by the four-thirty. Twenty-five quid* ***each way*** *on the two of them just to please you.'* UTN □ *The favourite came in third which must have pleased the bookies as few people had been cautious enough to back it* ***both ways****.*

an eager beaver (informal) sb who is, or who makes himself, particularly enthusiastic and busy about sth, often in minor matters and, without any particular need □ *We were a mixed bunch of 24 students of several nationalities and from all walks of life. We were all* ***eager beavers*** *and wanted to learn, a fortunate minority.* SC □ *The House of Lords is now inhabited by a fascinating mixture of aged celebrities, public-spirited experts and political* ***eager beavers*** *who would like to do something useful if they knew what their function was.* NS □ formerly US army slang for a particularly zealous recruit who is anxious to please; repeated vowel pattern.

an early bird (informal) sb who gets out of bed early in the morning or does something earlier than most other people (either as a habit or on a particular occasion) □ *You're a bit of* ***an early bird****, aren't you? I didn't expect to see you down for breakfast after that party last night.* □ *'Shall I leave the door open?' 'If you don't mind,' she said. 'I expect several little* ***early birds*** *will be in soon.'* TT ⇨ ⚠ next entry.

the early bird catches the worm (saying) the person who seizes the earliest opportunity of doing sth (eg getting up before others, reacting faster than others to a situation, etc) will get what he wants, be successful at the expense of others etc □ (music hall song) *She was one of* ***the early birds****/And I was one of* ***the worms****.* □ (NONCE) *At eleven o'clock in the morning I was certainly no* ***early bird****—but the plan still looked fair enough to* ***catch some*** *sort of* ***worm****.* PP □ *'****The early bird gathers the worm****,' Mother was saying, and it would be best, if I was to cut new ground, to set out rather early.* MM □ usu comment or recommendation to act; sometimes in the construction *it's* ***the early bird*** *(who/that)* ***catches the worm****.* ⇨ ⚠ previous entry.

the early days the early period of one's life, career etc; the beginning of a historical process, the development of sth, etc **det:** the, those, one's □ *He has no equal—proving that he was not wasting his time in* ***those early days*** *as a third-rate stand-up comic in second-rate clubs.* T □ *Most old people are fond of recounting the experiences of* ***their early days****.* □ ***The early days*** *of the nuclear power programme were marked by some very expensive technical mistakes and considerable bureaucratic bungling.* □ *Since* ***the early days*** *of the Valois régime English* corps de ballet *have been notoriously well drilled.* ST ⇨ ⚠ next entry.

early days yet (saying) (it is) rather too soon to come to conclusions about, or to pass judgement on, a situation that has still to develop □ *'I'm beginning to think I shall never be a grandmother.' 'For goodness' sake it's* ***early days*** *to be talking like that!'* □ *I hadn't managed to bring the committee round to my way of thinking, but it was* ***early days yet*** *and I still had a few cards up my sleeve.* □ usu with *it's/it was* as reminder or recommendation to be patient, not to be anxious. ⇨ ⚠ previous entry.

early on [A (AdvP)] soon after the start of an event, proceeding, discussion etc (that has taken place in the past) □ ***Early on*** *these new discoveries put a strain on the Rhodes selling machinery, and the Diamond Syndicate more or less collapsed.* DS □ *Moreover I agree with what Alexis said* ***earlier on*** *that the only way to test a hypothesis is by predictions.* TBC □ *'Isn't it a lovely morning?' 'It was ever so cold* ***early on****,' said Bobby Reynolds.* TT □ usu with past tenses of the v that is modified. ⇨ later on.

early to bed and early to rise, (makes a man healthy, wealthy and wise) (saying) if one lives sensibly and without excesses one will benefit physically, materially and mentally □ *We knew how to breed 'em* (= them) *good. We were resourceful, imaginative, tough, reliable. We were* ***early to bed and early to rise, healthy, wealthy and wise****.* CON □ (NONCE) *It has had to be* ***early to bed and early to rise*** *with me most of my life but though I'm certainly* ***healthy*** *and I may be* ***wise****, I'm still waiting for the* ***wealth****.* □ (parody) ***Early to rise and***

early to bed,/Makes a man healthy, wealthy and dead! O NASH 1902-71 □ usu comment, or recommendation to act.

earn/turn an honest penny etc [V + O] earn some amount of money as a result of one's (honest) work **O:** penny, ⚠ copper; cent, dollar; coin □ RONNIE: *This notion of* ***earning an honest penny*** *is all my eye. A man can work a whole lifetime and when he is 65 he considers himself rich if he has saved a thousand pounds. Rich!* CSWB □ *Soon Elliott was* ***turning*** *further* ***honest coppers*** *by giving poetry recitals as well as lectures.* L □ BLACK: *Look, give us a break—help me* ***earn an honest coin****—I'm not really a traveller in tombstones.* HSG □ often used euphemistically or self-mockingly to hide one's interest in money.

earn one's/its keep [V + O] be sufficiently useful, helpful and profitable to balance any expense incurred (eg in housing, feeding or maintaining oneself or itself) **S:** assistant; cow, pig; tractor, van; duplicator □ *Jill more than* ***earns her keep*** *with the help she gives me about the house and looking after the children and so on.* □ *I don't keep hens any more. What with the high price of feeding-stuff and the little I got for eggs, they weren't* ***earning their keep****.* □ *Though it's quite expensive to hire and maintain, the new copying machine is* ***earning its keep*** *as we've been able to reduce the number of office staff.* ⇨ ⚠ next entry; make a/one's living.

earn a/one's living [V + O] (have to) work, for a wage or salary, in order to obtain the food, services etc necessary to maintain oneself **adj:** (a) good, decent, respectable; (one's) own □ *He had always gathered that manual workers belonged to Unions and that anyone who tried to* ***earn a living*** *with his hands without the blessing of the Unions was in a very dangerous position.* HD □ *It's high time you were* ***earning your*** *own* ***living****, my boy. You can't expect me to support you for ever.* □ pl *They* ***earn their living(s)*** *on the land.* ⇨ ⚠ previous entry; make a/one's living.

one's/sb's ears burn be aware that, think that, other people are or have been discussing one, one's (good or bad) character, etc (from the physiological fact, or belief, that one's ears become hot or flushed with blood in embarrassing situations) □ *Well, some folk****'s ears*** *must have been* ***burning*** *tonight. I never heard such a lot of gossip as went on in that back kitchen.* □ *'Did he have anything to say about me and my new ventures?' 'Not really, your name was mentioned in some connection or other, but it was nothing to make* ***your ears burn****.'* □ often with *must have* or *make*.

one's ears/eyes deceive/do not deceive one what one thinks one has heard or seen is not actually/is actually true or a fact; one's senses mislead/do not mislead one into thinking something has happened □ *Do* ***my eyes deceive me****, or are those real orchids you have growing in that pot?* □ *That's the train coming now if* ***my ears don't deceive me****.* □ usu interr (expecting a confirmation of what one hears or sees) or conditional (with neg *if...not, unless*).

ease sb's conscience/mind [V + O pass] give sb some relief from worry, guilt or fear; set sb's mind at ease/rest (Vol 1) (qv) **S:** news, report; verdict, decision; it...to know everyone was safe □ *'It would* ***ease my mind****,' said Martin, 'if I could explain a little what I mean.'* NM □ *Doctors must use their own judgement of course, but in many cases the patient****'s mind*** *is greatly* ***eased*** *if his treatment is explained to him.* □ *I'm sure my husband wasn't offended by anything you said last night. Still, if it'll* ***ease your mind****, I can ask and make sure.* □ also pl ease their consciences/minds; usu with *will/would*.

easier said than done [Comp (AdjP)] (saying) suggesting some course of action is very much easier than actually carrying it out (esp if the person proposing it expects others to do it) **S:** it; writing the letter, moving house, putting up the new shelves; to write the letter, to move house, to get agreement to the plan. **V:** ⚠ be, look, seem □ *The essence of all reducing diets is to eat less—often* ***easier said than done****—and keep eating less than before.* RT □ *Wormold thought, I have no arsenic or cyanide. Besides I will have no opportunity to drink with him. I should have forced that whisky down his throat.* ***Easier said than done****, off the Elizabethan stage.* OMIH □ *Forcing a child to eat is* ***easier said than done****.* □ often rueful comment on the difficulty of doing sth.

East is East and West is West and never the twain shall meet (saying) there are, there may be thought to be, great differences in people or things (eg races, cultures, beliefs, attitudes) which are fundamental and not likely to be brought together □ (source) *Oh,* ***East is East, and West is West, and never the twain shall meet****,/Till Earth and Sky stand presently at God's great Judgement Seat.* THE BALLAD OF EAST AND WEST (R KIPLING 1865-1936) □ *The courses available for students have been arranged on the usual assumption that* ***the Arts are the Arts and the Sciences the Sciences, and never the twain shall meet****.* □ *The professional film critics have separated the 'commercial' films from the 'artistic' pieces of cinema, determining that* ***never the twain shall meet****.* NS □ twain = archaic form of *two*; often adapted, as in second example; either first or second part can be used alone, as in last example; originally comment on the difference between Asian *(Eastern)* and European *(Western)* cultures and occas still used in this way.

East, (or) West, home's best (saying) one's home (ie one's house, home town, native land, etc) is where one is likely to be happiest, esp in comparison with other places one may be at the time, may have visited, may have returned from etc; there's no place like home (qv) □ *'I was born there. Yes. It is a very small town, some old walls, a castle in ruins—'* ***'East or West,'*** *Beatrice said,* ***'home's best****.'* OMIH □ sentimental jingle often written on calendars, door-knockers, pottery etc.

easy come, easy go (saying) what has been acquired too easily or quickly, without effort or trouble (eg money, friends, knowledge) is (likely to be) spent, lost □ *What you chiefly notice* (about American society), *after the shock of seeing so much stuff lying around, is precisely that it does lie around and is easily lent or given away. We might produce a sour British phrase to explain that—'****easy come, easy go****'—but we would be wrong.* L □ *There is a popular notion that* *speed of learning is related negatively to the amount remembered. The learning of the bright student who acquires knowledge with ease and speed is felt to be unstable:* ***easy come, easy go****.* MFF □

easy/gently does it (saying) handle, move, lift, lower, an object with great care so as not to damage it; handle a situation, deal with a person, with great delicacy, patience etc so as not to ruin it, upset him, etc; softly, softly (catchee monkey) (qv) □ *We'll slip the edge of the blanket under you and use it to slide you on to the stretcher. There you are, you see,* ***easy does it****!* □ *I won't ask her yet what's the matter, he decided.* ***Easy does it****. He plied her with drinks and little attentions, and was rewarded by seeing colour return to her cheeks and naturalness to her manner.* PW □ *'No call to get worked up,' Mr Fiske said. '****Gently does it****.'* AITC. □ advice to sb, or caution to oneself, to act patiently etc.

easy game etc [Comp (NP)] sb or sth that is or can be easily attacked, victimized or taken advantage of **V:** ⚠ be, appear, become; make sb. **n:** game, ⚠ meat, prey □ *She was* ***easy game****, or rich material, for satirists. She is said to have been a mainstay for certain satirical novelists of the twenties.* AH □ *Down on the coastal plain lay the great Roman cities which must now or shortly be battlefields in the main advance and therefore* ***easy meat*** *for any dog that came along.* SD □ *He was rich, he was young, he was foolish. He was* ***easy prey*** *for any scheming woman who came along.* □ game and meat are uncountable nouns (no article); prey is uncountable or countable, eg *He was (an)* ***easy prey*** *for...*

easy in one's mind [Comp (AdjP)] more relaxed and reasonably content about sb, sth, some situation, etc **V:** ⚠ be, feel, seem; make sb □ *Phone us in the morning, Lilian. Your mother won't be* ***easy in her mind*** *till she knows you got back safely.* □ *I know he's said he doesn't need the money just now, but I'd be* ***easier in my mind*** *if we got out of debt now while we have the chance.* □ *He feels* ***easier in his mind*** *now that the whole story is out.* □ also pl; usu with *will/would be*.

easy money [Comp/O (NP)] money in return for very little work, trouble, or initial outlay (the implication often being that some dishonesty is involved) **S:** selling cars, teaching, flower-arranging, giving pop concerts. **V:** be, appear, seem; make □ *Here we have the case of a hitherto conscientious official tempted by what seemed to be* ***easy money*** *into not thinking too closely about the possible consequences of what he was asked to do.* SC □ *One treated them with tact, with finesse, and after a time, perhaps, one got an occasional good racing tip from them and made a little* ***easy money****.* PE □ *Taking parties of six to eight people round the bay for an hour at £5 a head seems pretty* ***easy money*** *to me.* ⇨ ⚠ a fast etc buck.

easy on the eye [Comp (AdjP)] (informal) quite pretty, good-looking (in the opinion of the observer or speaker) **S:** girl, woman; nurse, secretary. **V:** ⚠ be, find sb. **adv:** very, rather □ *Peggy is not quite so good-looking as her sister but very* ***easy on the eye****, all the same.* □ used to describe a woman. ⇨ ⚠ next entry.

easy/hard on the eyes etc [Comp (AdjP)] (be sth) causing little strain (considerable strain) to one's eyes etc **V:** ⚠ be; become, get, grow. **o:** the eyes, the hands, the legs, the feet; the skin; the nerves, the digestive system □ *This close italic print is very* ***hard on the eyes****.* □ *A museum attendant's job doesn't sound arduous but actually, for an older man, it's likely to be* ***hard on the legs****.* □ *You have to be careful about soap powders. For all their claims some of them are rather* ***hard on a*** *delicate* ***skin****.* □ *Johnnie's driving this time, so let's hope our return journey will be* ***easier on the nerves****.* ⇨ ⚠ previous entry.

easy/hard on sb's/the pocket [Comp (AdjP)] easy/difficult to afford **V:** ⚠ be, become, get; make sth □ *Package tours have made foreign travel, within a limited range, surprisingly* ***easy on the pocket****.* □ *These price increases are always* ***hardest on the pocket of*** *the lowest-paid worker.*

an easy rider (esp US) sb who wanders from place to place (esp on a motor-bike) without settling, and trying to lead an uninvolved life; sb who takes advantage of what society, a situation etc offers but without contributing himself □ *Knievel* (a stuntman) *has no truck with those slovenly* ***Easy Riders****: his superstars are Elvis and John Wayne.* NS □ *He* (a militant striker) *approves of the Labour Alliance — 'there's no* ***easy riders****, no opportunists' — but has not joined their ranks.* NS □ originally a black American term for (i) sb good at sexual love, (ii) a guitar, the present meaning has developed from the theme of the film 'Easy Rider' (1969).

easy terms [O/o (NP)] (finance) low interest rates on, or a long period in which to repay, a loan to buy goods, services etc, esp in hire-purchase arrangements **V:** get, offer, let sb have. **prep:** (buy) on; (offer sth) on □ *'****Easy terms*** *available' ran the poster across the shop window. 'Why not refurnish your home now?'* □ *I'm sure that, as a salaried woman, you'd get a loan on* ***easier terms*** *from your bank than from any finance company.* □ *Most* ***easy terms*** *cost the customer a great deal more than if he had been able to buy the goods outright.*

eat sb alive/for breakfast [V + O + Comp pass] (informal) be able to dominate, make maximum use of sb and then discard him, esp in a sexual relationship **O:** him, us, you, them; that type of man, a married man □ *You want to steer clear of Gloria. She'd* ***eat*** *someone as green as you* ***for breakfast****.* □ *'But watch out for Jack Wales. Bags of money, about seven foot tall and a beautiful R.A.F. moustache.' I laughed. 'I* ***eat*** *those types* ***for breakfast****,' I said.* RATT □ *He'll get* ***eaten alive*** *if he tries anything on with Barbara.* □ esp used of a woman's domination etc of a man in a sexual relationship.

(let us) eat, drink and be merry (for tomorrow we die) (saying) we should enjoy ourselves while we can because life is uncertain; we should not concern ourselves about the future □ (source variously ascribed but see) *A man hath no better thing under the sun, than to* ***eat****, and to* ***drink****, and to* ***be merry****.* ECCLESIASTES VIII 15 □ ***Let us eat*** *and* ***drink: for tomorrow we*** *shall* ***die****.* ISAIAH XXII 13 □ *Let's leave the rest of this work for another day. I'm in the mood to* ***eat, drink and be merry*** *and the rest of you had better be too.* □ (NONCE) *He holds the* *broad view that taking one year with another, as all good Chancellors of the Exchequer do, it is not only pleasant but prudent to* ***eat, drink and be merry for tomorrow is another day****.* NS □ usu said in support of a selfish, pleasure-loving attitude, or in a disapproving spirit.

eat humble pie (have to) be more respectful or apologetic than one has been before, usu because one has been proved wrong in one's opinions or statements (from, in former times, 'umbles'—the entrails of a deer—served in a pie to huntsmen etc while the nobility etc had better meat) □ *If John's wife did take him back, would she have the sense not to make him* ***eat humble pie*** *for the rest of his life?* □ *Both sides claimed afterwards that there had been straight and frank talking, but it seemed obvious that the Government were cock-a-hoop and the TUC* (Trades Union Congress) ***eating humble pie****.* SC.

eat like a horse (informal) eat well, consume large quantities of food, either on one specific occasion or as a habit □ *It doesn't seem fair that I should have a constant struggle to keep my weight down while you can* ***eat like a horse*** *and always stay the same.* □ *Cosmo was eating little, Matthew was pretending to eat sparingly, but putting a surprising amount away, and Dorothy Merlin was* ***eating like a horse****, stuffing food into her small frame.* US □ often used disapprovingly of greedy people.

eat a peck of dirt/dust before one dies (saying) one is bound to take in with one's food a certain amount of dirt from the air, in the course of one's life □ *'I wonder if these strawberries have been washed properly? They taste a bit gritty to me.' 'What of it? You've got to* ***eat a peck of dirt before you die****, anyway.'* □ (of a married couple in an illustrated advertisement) *They need more sleep in their eyes, they need at least a little rumpling and staleness, just as the room needs at least a small crack in the plaster, and the sunbeams a suggestion of that* ***dust*** *which, whether we come from it or not, we all* ***eat a peck of before we die****.* RATT □ *The truth is, that all alcohol is filth. But we are compelled to swallow* ***our peck of it****, as it were,* ***before we die****, in order to conform to the conventions of an idiot society.* US □ peck = 'a dry weight measure, equal to 2 gallons'; usu preceded by *one/ everybody has to/is bound to, we/you (all) have to.*

eat oneself sick (on sth) (informal) eat too much (of sth, esp at one meal) so that one either feels sick or (occas) is actually sick and vomits **o:** sweets, chocolate, ice-cream □ *Come to London and have a slap-up lunch with me on expenses. We'll* ***eat ourselves sick on*** *lobster at Premier's.* HAA □ *She'd* ***eat herself sick on*** *ice-cream if I let her.*

eat/drink (sth) till/until it comes out of one's ears (informal) eat/drink excessively □ *Her cooking is disappointingly received by her two children, Kate, 12, and Matthew, 10. 'I think they'd* ***eat*** *beefburgers and chips and sausage and mash* ***until it came out of their ears****.'* RT □ *We've got* ***butter coming out of our ears*** *in the canteen at work, ever since the 'more dairy products' petition was handed in.* □ variant (have sth) coming out of one's ears.

eat one's words [V + O] (be forced to) take back what one has previously said was true, certain etc (because of changed circumstances, new evidence, etc) □ *They can't* ***eat their words*** *fast enough about Donald. I must say he seems to have been very tactful all round.* ASA □ *If the Government agree to '****eat their words****' and pump in more public money what is going to happen?* T □ *No Prime Minister is committed to the expulsion of South Africa at the moment, although some are having to do a certain amount of* ***word-eating****.* SC □ unusual n compound word-eating.

ebb and flow [v + v non-rev] move backwards and forwards regularly and continuously as the tides of the sea do, sometimes decreasing and sometimes increasing in quantity; fluctuate, alter, in intensity □ *Pigeons wandered unconcernedly about the station concourse seeking the odd crumb here and there while round them the tide of commuters* ***ebbed and flowed****.* □ *He lay in a comfortable half-doze, just aware of the noise of the traffic as it* ***ebbed and flowed*** *in the street.* □ *After such a heavy lunch he found it difficult to follow the course of the arguments as they* ***ebbed and flowed*** *around him.* □ first sense used of people or things, second sense used of conversation, noise, abstract ideas, etc. ⇨ ⚠ next entry.

the ebb and flow (of sth) [n + n non-rev] the constant movement (of sb or sth) changing in quantity throughout a period of time; the decrease and increase in intensity (of conversation, noise, abstract ideas, etc) **det:** the, an; this, that □ *The cameraman and his sound-recordist had to catch* ***the ebb and flow*** *of conversation and the peaking of tension between one member of the family and another.* L □ *I knew by experience that she suffered* ***this*** *mysterious* ***ebb and flow of*** *mood, but I felt slightly reassured if I could link it with some external event.* SPL □ *Thus there was a continual interchange at Cairo,* ***a*** *constant* ***ebb and flow*** *of strange faces and of strange goods displayed for sale.* BN ⇨ ⚠ previous entry.

eff and blind [v + v non-rev] (slang) curse and swear □ *They wouldn't let him mess around with the radio so he started* ***effing and blinding*** *and threw their books on the floor.* CSWB □ *I'm a Londoner and have played Cockney characters all my life. My image is that of a drunken old cow. When I'm not working, I don't swear all the time. If I go out I don't go* ***effing and blinding*** *everywhere.* RT □ usu occurs in *-ing* form or (eg with *start*) as *to*-inf; eff = 'fuck', blind = 'blind me' or 'blimey'; euphemism.

either way [Disj (NP)] whichever of the two is considered or chosen; whether sth is true or not; however things turn out; one way or the other (qv) **V:** (not) matter, (not) be important, (not) care; win, lose □ *'I'm not a Templar after all. Nicky and Sarah aren't Templars. We're nice people!' 'It didn't matter,' said Fergus. 'I loved you* ***either way****.'* □ *In the days of good Hollywood comedies, such a marital quarrel used to end with a reconciliation in which the career-woman gave up her career. Today the husband changes his job.* ***Either way*** *it is a fairy-tale.* T □ usu front or end position.

an elder statesman sb who has held (high)

office in government, business management, etc, for a long period and who, though he may have retired, is still likely to be asked for opinions and advice ▫ *It was to be expected that the chairman of the Parliamentary Party might also be given a free run* (ie be returned unopposed by any other candidate) *in view of the widespread affection felt by everybody for* ***this elder statesman***. T ▫ *Cicero distinguished his year in office by undoing the lethal conspiracies of Catiline; after which he grew yet further, from statesman to* ***elder statesman****, from doyen to oracle.* OBS ▫ also pl elder statesmen.

an embarrassment of riches (the state of) having more things to choose from, to use, etc than one can really cope with or than one actually needs (from the French phrase *embarras de richesses* which is also used in English) ▫ *But* ***an embarrassment of riches*** *is perennial on radio. One of the problems for anyone with catholic tastes is that last Saturday, for example, he'd have to choose between the 'Arts Commentary' on Radio 3 and 'The Entertainers' on Radio 4.* L

the emperor has no clothes (saying) (some sensible person at last points out that) what the majority of people blindly accept as existing or true (because other more influential people have said so), does not in fact exist, is completely false etc ▫ (source) In a fairy story an emperor is persuaded by two swindlers that they have fitted him with a suit of fine clothes that are 'invisible', but do not in fact exist; he pretends to admire them until—*'But* ***the Emperor has nothing on*** *at all!' cried a little child.* THE EMPEROR'S NEW CLOTHES (H C ANDERSEN 1805-75) ▫ *The last story concerns a European couple and the way in which the wife, seeking to immerse herself in India, still retains her ability to see that* ***the emperor*** *(in the guise of mysticism or eastern eroticism) very likely* ***wears no clothes*** *at all.* SC ▫ expression, esp when based on the title of the story, often adapted and modified.

end one's/its days [V + O] spend the last part of one's/its life in a particular way or place (esp after having done sth else in the main period of one's/its existence, or having served some other purpose) **S:** he, she, we, you, they; retired bank manager, statesman; racing-horse, pit-pony; paddle-steamer, steam engine. **A:** in peace; in the country, on the farm; in a junkyard, in a museum, as a tourist attraction ▫ *I am reminded of this by a letter from an old friend who writes to me that he has decided to* ***end his days*** *in Hollywood.* L ▫ *A much-loved pre-war Riley Kestrel* (car) ***ended its days*** *stuffed in the Michelmores' kitchen doorway.* RT ▫ usu modified by an adv phrase of manner or place in end position.

an end in itself [Comp (NP)] looked at as sth in its own right, even though it was originally undertaken for another purpose **S:** ritual, ceremony; meeting, reunion. **V:** ⚠ be, become; regard sth as ▫ *We almost came to look upon a meeting at the summit as* ***an end in itself****, as though what we were seeking to achieve was a meeting for its own sake.* BM ▫ *She goes to see all his films half a dozen times each, she can repeat scraps of gossip about him, but this is* ***an end in itself****. She doesn't even consider the idea of getting any closer to the man.* CON ▫ *To be progressive, 'forward-looking', 'as modern as tomorrow', is still one of the desirable* ***ends-in-themselves***. UL

the end is not yet (formal) there are more (or worse) things going to happen, to be said, to be endured (before one can have better things, before a situation improves etc) ▫ (source) *For all these things must come to pass, but* ***the end is not yet****. For nation shall rise against nation, and kingdom against kingdom.* MATTHEW XXIV 6-7 ▫ *Meanwhile, the Sahara desert grows, increasing its acreage year by year and within itself growing ever more desert-like as oases, unconserved, degenerate. And* ***the end is not yet***. SC ▫ *Cheer up,* ***the end is not yet****. We've still got another couple of weeks to raise the money.*

the end justifies the means if the result is considered to be important enough, then any method of achieving it, whether right or wrong, should be welcomed and pursued ▫ *The hazard to which revolutionaries are particularly prone is not that they will think that* ***the end justifies the means****. It is that they will allow the means to dictate the end.* L ▫ *Whatever the director's intentions, 'Straw Dogs' is a 'wartime'* ***ends-justify-the-means*** *movie.* NS ▫ (NONCE) ***The means becomes the end****. Law courts are intended to do justice; then the law courts become more important than justice.* RT ▫ unusual attrib use in second example. ⇨ ⚠ a/the means to an end.

(at) the end of the rainbow (fig) the place where all one's hopes are fulfilled (from folklore, in which anyone who could locate where a rainbow's end touched ground would find gold buried there) ▫ *Since World War Two, more than one and a quarter million Britons have emigrated to Australia, and for millions more it's still* ***the end of the rainbow***. TVT ▫ *In 1918 the City of the Angels* (Los Angeles) *was the brimming pot of fool's gold* ***at the end of the*** *American* ***rainbow****, and the roads into LA were packed with hopefuls and dreamers of every kind.* RT

the end of the road[1] the final place, goal, at which one is aiming, where one can find peace, satisfaction etc; (a) journey's end (qv) **V:** it be... (for sb/sth); reach, come to, arrive at ▫ (source) *Though your heart be weary, still journey on/Till you come to your happy abode,/Where all you love and are dreaming of/Will be there at* ***the end of the road***. (popular song sung by) SIR HARRY LAUDER 1870-1950 ▫ *The shop stewards have welcomed the news of a government subsidy with all the calmness and generosity of men who feel they have won a just battle. But it is by no means* ***the end of the road*** *for the Upper Clyde.* NS

the end of the road[2] the point at which no further progress is possible, where one is forced to stop, beyond which there is no more hope, where life finishes, etc **V:** it be...(for sb/sth); reach; be at, come to, arrive at ▫ *Father Paul Byrne is Director of the Shelter Housing Aid Centre to help families in London. 'When a family comes to SHAC you know you're at* ***the end of the road*** *for that family, that even the local authority social workers have given up hope of being able to do anything for them.'* OBS ▫ *For* *him, irrational literary movements like Dada and Surrealism mark* ***the end of the road*** *for bourgeois literature.* L □ *We have, in fact, got to* ***the end of the road****, where the man who determines that objective* (of scientific research) *has got to justify it to a form of shareholder, whether it be the electorate and their representatives in Parliament, or the shareholder in a company.* NS

the end of the world [Comp (NP)] (informal) completely disastrous for sb; (mean that) sb's comfortable way of life etc will have to stop or change **S:** defeat, failure; refusal, reluctance, unwillingness (to act); it. **V:** ⚠ be; seem (like), look like □ *Once a lad had served his time (as an apprentice) he could always try some other job, knowing that failure wouldn't be* ***the end of the world****.* L □ *Refusal* (by the Transport and General Workers' Union) *to pay would not be* ***the end of the world****. The court could then order the seizure and sale of enough union property to pay the fine.* NS □ often neg.

the end product what is finally manufactured after a number of processes have been gone through; (fig) the final result (eg a kind of person, an idea, a conclusion) that is achieved after some kind of process or effort (eg a type of education, a series of discussions, etc) is completed □ *Most of the assembly workers spread through this vast plant never get a sight of* ***the end product****.* □ *But a group of pictures organised into a sequence is enormously more powerful than the same slides shown individually.* ***The end product*** *can express much more than most of us can express with words.* RT

end to end [A (n + n)] with the (short) side of one touching the (short) side of the next, and the longer sides forming a continuous line **V:** lie; put, place, lay, sth □ *Put your two card-tables* ***end to end*** *over by the window and the kids can have their meals there for the time being.* □ *At the foot of each page were snippets of useless information such as that if all the cockroaches in London were laid* ***end to end*** *they would stretch right across the Atlantic and back again.* □ often occurs in *if*-cl.

the enemy at the gate(s) the threatening presence of enemy forces very close to one's homeland, one's cities etc; (fig) any imminent threat to, or attack on, oneself, a particular form of society, one's beliefs □ *For centuries Britain had had to wage no foreign wars within her own confines. Things were rather different in the last war as the civilian population had the reality of* ***the enemy*** *overhead as well as* ***at the gate****.* □ *There is today* ***a*** *new* ***enemy at the gate****. Inflation may have become a capitalist bogey word—but in fact it is a far more terrifying spectre for socialists than for anyone else.* NS ⇨ ⚠ next entry.

the enemy/traitor within (the gate(s)) a traitor; sb who acts, or is thought to act, against the interests of the family, group, society etc of which he is a member □ *Wherever Jenny had got to, there was not much left of that elaborate structure of love and obligation which the two of them had been struggling to assemble.* ***The enemy*** *had been* ***within the gates****, he intoned.* TGLY □ *Books are felt to be alien, and* ***the traitors*** *are* ***within the gates****. Mr Wain has met people 'employed in university literary studies' who actually concur in their pupils' self-important supposition that the present is different from anything preceding it and so renders the past irrelevant.* L ⇨ ⚠ previous entry.

the English etc dearly love a lord (saying) the English etc have a high regard for titled nobility, are flattered to have dealings with or be noticed by any of its members **S:** the English shareholders; they, we □ *Mr Worsthorne holds that the common people defer to birth but not to mere position:* ***they dearly love a lord*** *but they can't stand a bureaucrat.* L □ *Their contribution towards management is often negligible but their names lend weight to a directors' list, for* ***shareholders*** *too, it seems,* ***dearly love a lord****.* □ *It is rather remarkable that almost two centuries after the fall of the monarchy, and after not one but half a dozen French revolutions, the President of the Republic should claim descent from the Bourbons and the Minister of the Interior from a niece of Charlemagne.* ***The English*** *are not the only people who* ***love a lord****.* ST

an Englishman's home is his castle (saying) (in England a citizen is, or thinks he is, entitled under Common Law to consider that) his home is a place in which he may do as he wishes, where he may remain private, and from which he may exclude anybody □ (source) *For* ***a man's house is his castle****, et domus sua cuique tutissimum refugium (and his own home is to each person the safest place of refuge).* INSTITUTES (SIR EDWARD COKE 1552-1634) □ *'He is a milord?' 'Down to the ankles,' Angela Shaw said. 'And like every* ***Englishman*** *he's sure* ***his home is his castle****.'* BFA □ *Jack clearly enjoys his home and his privacy. 'The old bit about* ***an Englishman's home being his castle*** *fits me to a T.'* TVT □ used of a man/men alone, and, by implication, of men and women together but not used of a woman/women alone.

enough/plenty to be getting/going on with [Comp/O (AdjP)] (be, have) as much as one needs or can use, temporarily; (have done) an adequate amount of work (so as to be able to rest); (have obtained) a reasonable amount of information (so as to know how to act etc) **V:** be; have (got), have completed □ *Jacob, however, had better luck at the top of the tree, and soon lowered down a bag of twenty specimens, which I thought was quite* ***enough to be getting on with****.* BB □ *Ned was now going to bed with Myra, and Stocker knew all about it or* ***enough to be going on with****.* CON □ *'Have you got all the paper you need?' 'I've got* ***plenty to be going on with****, thanks.'*

enough is as good as a feast (saying) what one has got, done etc should be quite sufficient and anything more is not needed, will bring no additional pleasure or benefit etc; next entry (qv) □ *'Why can't we have more blackberries, Mummy?' 'Because* ***enough is as good as a feast****. You'll have blackberries coming out of your ears if you eat any more.'* □ *Then she decided to go and say good-bye to the Larkins and then, a moment later, impulsively decided not to after all.* ***Enough****, after all,* ***was as good as a feast****.* BFA □ warning to oneself or others that enough has been said or done.

enough is enough (saying) what one has said, done etc, is quite or more than sufficient, so that nothing else needs to be said etc; previous entry (qv) □ *But on the last day, since I had been a diligent bottle-washer, the chief chemist took me by the arm and said '**Enough is enough**. But before you go you shall do something that really matters.'* NS □ *And for nearly four years the trio barn-stormed the world, earning both cash and credit, until Miss Ross decided **enough was enough**.* T □ *'She said she wanted to commit suicide.' 'Now that's enough!' Stanley was sharp. He glared at Alice. '**Enough's enough**.'* TSMP □ usu said as indication or warning that what is going on must be stopped.

enough to make one weep etc [Comp (AdjP)] (informal) be so distressing or disgusting that one needs to weep etc **S:** destruction, slaughter; smell, sight; neglect. **V:** ⚠ be, become, find sth. **Inf:** to make one weep, ⚠ to make one cry, to make one throw up; to make a cat laugh; to drive one to drink □ *This absurd posturing is **enough to make you throw up**.* □ *It's **enough to make you weep**, seeing all that food go to waste.*

enough of a fool etc (to do sth) [Comp (NP)] sufficiently foolish etc to perform some action **V:** ⚠ be; appear, seem. **n:** fool, ⚠ coward, idiot; man, lady □ *'He wouldn't take the cliff path in the dark, would he?' 'He might, the fellow's **enough of a fool** to do anything.'* □ *I had no doubt that Sadie thought it quite possible that I would be **fool enough** to buy Mars* (a dog). UTN □ *You aren't **man enough** to scrape up a miserable seventy-five pounds without all this whining.* HD □ *Married, you call yourselves. Well, I'm **lady enough** never to have asked any questions about that.* AITC □ variant fool enough etc (to do sth); enough (of) indicates the degree of foolishness etc; usu followed by *to*-inf.

enough/'nough said (informal) one doesn't need to say any more, because one's meaning or intentions have been made clear. □ *'But, my dear Roderick,' Waggett protested,* 'verb. sap. *means—well, it's short for something. I don't remember what, but it's the same as "Amen" or "**Enough said**".'* RM □ ***Enough said**. If you feel like doing your training here, you only have to say so.*

enter/join the fray [V + O] take part in a fight, quarrel, dispute etc (that has already started); (fig) put oneself forward as a contender in some competition (eg for election, for a position of power, etc) □ *'Now don't you **join the fray**,' she pleaded with her husband. 'There's enough people shouting their heads off in here already.'* □ *Earlier in New Hampshire, where none of his serious rivals **entered the fray**, Senator Kennedy also polled well.* SC

enter sb's/one's head/mind [V + O] occur to sb/one; arise, be considered, in sb's/one's mind **S:** thought, idea; matter, question; it...to speak to her, it...that she might need help. **A:** not, never, hardly, seldom, rarely □ *Any other thought regarding her had never **entered his mind**.* DC □ *Economy was important to him but on this occasion the matter of money never **entered his head**.* TBC □ *I wonder, did it ever **enter your head** to collect your shoes from the repairers' when you were in the village?* □ *It* did ***enter my head** to ask her why.* □ also pl enter their heads/minds; usu neg or interrog, but see last example.

(not) entertain the idea etc [V + O pass] (refuse to) accept, consider, an idea, suggestion etc made by sb else **O:** idea, notion; suggestion, proposal; doubt, suspicion □ *I assure you our firm simply would **not entertain the idea** of advancing a loan without security.* □ *This was a case of suicide. **Any** other **suggestion** is simply **not** to be **entertained**.* EM □ *That any child of his might be mentally handicapped was **a notion** he could **not** bring himself to **entertain**.* □ *He did **entertain the idea** of an overseas post at one time, but decided the risks were too great.* □ usu neg or with neg implication.

(one's/sb's) entrances and exits [n + n rev] (the acts of, the places for, the times of) coming onto or leaving a stage in a play etc, or coming into and going out of a room etc (often in a rather dramatic way) □ (source) *All the world's a stage,/And all the men and women merely players:/They have **their exits and their entrances**...* AS YOU LIKE IT II 7 □ *She moved towards the door, as if **her entrances and exits** depended on her own volition and concerned no one but herself.* PW □ *Lunch was very good and there was some claret which pleased Mr Downing, but owing to Doris**'s exits and entrances** they could only speak of matters of outside interest.* WDM

to err is human (to forgive divine) (saying) it is in the nature of mankind to sin and to make mistakes (and therefore one should be as forgiving as possible) □ (source) *Good-nature and good-sense must ever join;/**To err is human, to forgive divine**.* ESSAY ON CRITICISM A POPE 1688-1744 □ *To abandon him* (your brother) *now would almost certainly lead to further terms of imprisonment. Your parents illustrate the old saying '**to err is human, to forgive divine**'.* TVT □ *'I shouldn't have lost my temper, though.' 'It probably didn't improve matters, but **to err is human**. We can't be perfect all the time.'*

an error of judgement [Comp/O (NP)] a mistake in one's assessment of a situation, in some aspect of a course of action that one has undertaken (the mistake may affect only part or the whole of what one does) **V:** there be; make, commit. **adj:** serious, gross; minor, small; regrettable □ *Though he has made serious **errors of judgement** he has always been a staunch supporter of the principles on which Ataturk founded the Turkish Republic.* OBS □ *He showed me the report of the court of enquiry: the master and second mate were criticised for **errors of judgement** but not blamed for the deaths among their crew.* RT □ *I notice that in this Diary I described the Jenkins plan as '**the** one gross **error of judgement** he made as Home Secretary'. Let me make amends and admit that this was **one** gross **error of judgement** I have made as a diarist.* NS

the error of one's/sb's ways [O/o (NP)] the mistakes, sins, omissions etc that arise from the way one/sb lives, that are present in one's/sb's thoughts, beliefs etc **V:** (force sb to, be made to) see, learn, recognize; teach sb; point out to sb □ *He admits to having expected the deed to be done then and there. But he soon learnt **the error of his ways**.* NS □ *Having seen **the error of his ways**, St Laurent's* (fashion) *shows are now as* *organised and civilised as limited space allows.* SC ▫ *True, he dislikes their racial system, but he is more concerned to propound the advantages of dialogue than lecture the whites on* ***the errors of their ways***. SC

escape (sb's) attention/notice [V + O] be missed, not be observed or noticed (by sb) **S:** point, fact; comment, observation; it...that costs have risen ▫ *It surely cannot have* ***escaped*** *the professor****'s attention*** *that there has been a big swing in economic opinion on the EEC since the 'Observer' poll of a decade ago.* L ▫ *But the guilt-ridden anxiety and deep depression felt by these patients may often* ***escape notice***. SNP ▫ *It will no doubt have* ***escaped the notice of*** *those living south of Alderley Edge, but last Thursday people in the greater Manchester area had 3.4p slapped on their rates.* T ▫ often neg, with the implication by the speaker that a fact needs to be emphasized or brought out (because sb has overlooked or suppressed it).

the eternal triangle the sexual relationships (with their accompanying tensions, jealousies etc) between one man and two women, or one woman and two men ▫ *It was so fascinating; she knew Dollie and her 'Don Juan', and now this wife. For some it would just be* ***the eternal triangle***. ASA ▫ *Long Island has developed its own tawdry suburban version of the* crime passionel, *in which murder supplants divorce as a solution to* ***the eternal triangle***. NS

even as [Conj] (do sth, happen) at the very same time as, just when (sb does sth else, sth else happens) ▫ *'We're going to have a storm, I think,' Andrew said, and* ***even as*** *he spoke the first flash of lightning shot across the sky.* ▫ ***Even as*** *she remembered his reassuring words Brigit imagined she heard a faint stirring in the direction of the fireplace.* DC ▫ *But* ***even as*** *they sat there congratulating themselves on their success, the forces of the law were gradually closing in.* ▫ functions as subordinating conj.

even if/though [Conj] in spite of the fact or belief that sth is the case, did happen, or might have happened, etc ▫ *I don't regret lending her the money,* ***even if*** *I never see it again.* ▫ *The plea of diminished responsibility in his case failed,* ***even though*** *there was some evidence to show abnormality of personality.* OBS ▫ *That was a nice bit of steak —* ***even if*** *a little overcooked.* ▫ functions as subordinating conj with both conditional and concessive meaning; occas in non-finite constructions with participle as in last example.

even now/then[1] [A (AdvP)] not at this or that moment (any more than previously) **V:** (not) manage, succeed; understand, believe ▫ *I could never do sums at school — in fact I have difficulty in adding up a column of figures correctly,* ***even now***. ▫ *They put another two men on the job but* ***even then*** *they couldn't move it.* ▫ *He consulted two other doctors who both confirmed the original diagnosis but he didn't believe it* ***even then***. ▫ usu in neg constructions.

even now/then[2] [A (AdvP)] (formal) at this or that precise moment (while sb is or was doing sth else) **V:** plan, plot; arrange, prepare; invade, attack ▫ *While we are talking and debating, the opposition is* ***even now*** *forming an alliance with the dissidents in order to overthrow the established government.* ▫ *The news was that the mob had broken down the barricades and were* ***even then*** *preparing to storm the palace.* ▫ with continuous tenses and A often in middle position between aux and main v.

even odds [Comp (NP)] (horse-racing) an equal chance, in the opinion of the backers, bookmakers etc of a horse winning or losing; (fig) equally likely to have happened, to happen **V:** ⚠ be, become; make sth ▫ *Heavy betting in the morning had the favourite in the Derby being quoted at* ***even odds*** *an hour before the race began.* ▫ *Well, father's bound to be at the bowling-green or in the pub, but it's* ***even odds*** *which.* ▫ *'They're very keen that this first baby should be a boy.' 'Well, the* ***odds*** *are* ***even*** *that it will be, aren't they?'* ▫ either *The* ***odds*** *are* ***even*** *that he'll be late* or *It's* ***even odds*** *that he'll be late.*

even so [Conj] nevertheless; in spite of sth (that has happened, may or may not be true etc) ▫ *In the end the Executive struck out the word 'proper', but* ***even so*** *the phrase was more than Mr Nicholas, Mr Cousins' representative, would stomach.* OBS ▫ *Across the road one of the finest collections of art-nouveau and imperial postcards in the world is, as always, never open. But,* ***even so***, *there are more things worth seeing in this city than you can assimilate in one visit.* OBS ▫ *The scientific profession does still tend to operate as though the new Baconian revolution had not yet taken place.* ***Even so***, *today's scientists can now follow a dozen pathways to distinction.* OBS

ever and anon [adv + adv non-rev] (formal) a number of times, at fairly frequent intervals ▫ *At dawn I had walked into the city, a little gingerly, preceded by a sapper who thrust a bayonet* ***ever and anon*** *into the suspect soil* (ie because of land-mines). SD ▫ *The dog was restless too,* ***ever and anon*** *rising to lay his head on his master's knee.*

ever more[1] [A (AdvP)] (formal) increasingly (anxious, keen etc) as time passes; more and more (qv) **S:** he, she, you, they, we; child, woman, man; administrator, teacher, politician. **V:** be, become, grow, seem. **adj:** anxious; beautiful, dear (to sb); keen, trustworthy; stupid, frightening ▫ *The plane was now two hours overdue; relatives and friends waiting at the airport were becoming* ***ever more*** *anxious and beseiging the staff with almost hysterical demands for news.* ▫ *Despite the scepticism of friends, they had grown* ***ever more*** *attached to the life of the quiet little village they had retired to.* ▫ modifies an adj.

ever more[2] [A (AdvP)] (formal) to an increasing degree (anxiously etc) as time passes, as a situation develops, etc **V:** wait, act, work, speak. **adv:** anxiously; amazingly; carefully, clearly ▫ *The crowds outside in the square waited* ***ever more*** *anxiously for news of the President's health.* ▫ *Encouraged by each small, but positive, piece of new evidence, he pursued his enquiries* ***ever more*** *persistently.* ▫ *It must be apparent to all concerned, that the country is living* ***ever more*** *dangerously on borrowed money.* ▫ modifies an adv.

ever so[1] [A (AdvP)] (informal) very, extremely (bad, good etc) **V:** be, become, seem. **adj:** bad, good; happy, sad; hard, easy □ *Jenny went back to her perch on the stool. 'Can I have another of these chocolates? They're **ever so** good.'* TGLY □ *Six-year-old Guy and his classmates constructed a morality play for modern times on the subject of cheating. 'The lady who was God was **ever so** angry.'* RT □ *We were **ever so** reluctant to pull out, we really were, but there was no alternative.* OBS □ considered substandard by some educated speakers and thought of as being used mainly by women and children; modifies an adj.

ever so² [A (AdvP)] (informal) very, extremely (badly, well etc) **V:** behave; speak, talk; play, act. **adv:** badly, well; happily, sadly; hard, easily □ *I thought your little Johnny spoke his part in the school play **ever so** well. Perhaps he's going to be an actor.* □ CLIFF: *Let's have your arm. I'll do it **ever so** gently.* (Very carefully, he rubs the soap over the burn.) LBA □ *Ever so hard he worked for the firm and what thanks does he get? A TV set and a little thank-you letter!* □ considered substandard (as with ever so¹ (qv)); modifies an adv.

ever so³ [adv mod] (informal) a very great etc number or quantity (of people, things etc) **det:** many, much; few, little. **n:** people; problems, questions; places, countries □ TONY: *And you become certain that there are **ever so** many sides to every question.* EHOW □ *How many people play bridge nowadays, anyway? **Ever so** few as compared with our young days.* □ *There must have been **ever so** little difference between the three of them, but you know what judges are!* □ considered substandard (as with ever so¹ (qv)); modifies a det.

every bit as bad etc (as) [Comp (AdjP)] in all respects or to the fullest extent as bad etc (as); as bad etc as ever (qv) **V:** ⚠ be, look, sound. **adj:** bad, good; important, relevant, effective, useless □ *We went there for a meal and the food was **every bit as bad as** you said it would be.* □ *The holiday was superb. It was **every bit as good as** we had been led to expect.* □ *Teachers are **every bit as responsible as** we* (doctors) *are. And if a child is epileptic, for instance, shouldn't his teacher be told?* L

every bit as badly etc (as) [A (AdvP)] in every way, or to the fullest extent; as badly etc as ever (qv) **V:** act, behave; play; see, speak, talk. **adv:** badly, well; importantly, effectively, clearly □ *When it came to his own turn to perform, he played the guitar **every bit as badly as** those he had been criticizing.* □ *I really don't know why he bothers to wear glasses. He can see **every bit as clearly** without them.* □ *'The parents are as much to blame as the children, don't you think?' '**Every bit**.'* □ in last example ***Every bit*** implies *The parents are **every bit as much to blame as** the children.*

every cloud has a silver lining (saying) there is always some comforting or brighter side to a sad or gloomy situation, sth pleasant that can happen now or in the future, even though it may not be immediately clear □ *Oh well, **every cloud has a silver lining**. I may not be so well off now, but I'll have more time to enjoy my family.* □ *Patrick decided things were far from bad just now. Even **an** alcoholic **cloud** may turn out to **have a silver lining** if taken in time.* TGLY □ (NONCE) *He turns out to be considerably less pessimistic than most writers whom we think of as 'serious', for whom **every silver lining was a cloud**.* L □ often adapted; often said to encourage oneself or sb else.

every day (and) in every way (one is getting better and better) (catchphrase) one can improve, is improving, one's life gradually over a period of time by means of constant self-examination □ (French source) ***Tous les jours, à tous points de vue, je vais de mieux en mieux***. (EMILE COUE 1857-1926) □ ***Every day, in every way, we're getting better and better****. Malcolm Muggeridge doubts that familiar proposition. In an earlier edition of 'The Question Why' (BBC 1) he invited his guests to discuss the question of progress and perfectibility.* L □ (NONCE) *Lorenz devotes a brief chapter to each of his 'sins' in turn, drawing on a variety of sources for his argument that **every day, in every way, things are getting worse** for mankind.* L

every dog has his/its day (saying) everybody will, at some time or other in his life, get his turn at being successful, at being in a position of power □ (source) *Let Hercules himself do what he may,/The cat will mew, and **dog will have his day**.* HAMLET V 1 □ *He has the best financial brain in Parliament—even if—' 'Even if a certain person is Chancellor of the Exchequer and your husband is not? Never mind, his time will come. **Every dog has its day**, and we are all mortal.'* EM □ *Was he hopeful? 'Yes, because if I believe that there is a God, and if I believe that we blacks were created by God, then certainly I can't dismiss the idea that **every dog has its day**.'* L □ often said in encouragement to oneself or others, esp when one or sb else is at the moment unsuccessful etc.

every inch a gentleman etc [Comp (NP)] in all respects a well-dressed, well brought-up person (either because one is in fact or because one is pretending to be) **V:** ⚠ be, appear, look. **n:** gentleman, lady; king, queen; soldier, officer; politician, administrator, businessman □ *He was dressed in a quiet grey suit and looked very well bred and **every inch a gentleman**.* CON □ *Irma in her soft red dress looked **every inch a lady**.* PW □ *George Shipway is very upright, very, very well dressed, **every inch a military man** (which he once was).* SC □ usu said of obvious, superficial distinctions of class, rank etc.

every last/single one etc every person or every item (in a group) included, with no one person or item omitted; each and every (qv) **n:** one (of you, them, us); man, woman, child; bit, crumb, piece; time □ *The other four shook their heads as though butter wouldn't melt in their mouths, **every last one of them** lying in actual sin.* TT □ *And she turned round, and **every last child** got on with its work as though that was the thing.* TT □ *'People don't realise — you are scared every morning when you go down, **every single morning**,' said one miner.* NS

every little helps (saying) even though sth that sb has done for, or given to, one may be small, it is not too small to be of some use; each gift, however small, will eventually add up to a large total □ *'I'm sorry we could only let you have one* (sten gun), *sir.' '**Every little helps**,' he said.*

RFW □ *'I've nothing on me except this 5p, I'm afraid.' 'Never mind,' said the collector, sticking the charity flag on her lapel, '**every little helps**.'* □ said in appreciation of, admittedly limited, help.

every man has his price (saying) nobody is so honest or incorruptible that some particular weakness or (secret) desire cannot be used to bribe or corrupt him □ *The statement that **all men have their price** was true of the men involved in the Watergate break-in. The prospect of continued political influence at the heart of the United States Government outweighed any scruples about their actions being illegal.* □ *But for how long can he escape it* (joining the ruling élite)? *His answer: '**Every man has his price**—I've got a price.' For if he wins his seat at the next election he will automatically join the Establishment.* NS □ expresses a commonly held, cynical belief.

every man jack (of sb) (informal) every one of a large group or of a considerable number of people, with no exceptions. **o:** (of) them, you, us; committee, police force, platoon, government ministers □ *'Come on, Dad, they're only a bit to the left of the Labour Party.' 'Say what you like, they're Trotskyites, **every man jack of** them.'* □ *There's only one way to describe the people who run this country—incompetent. I'd sack the ruddy lot—**every man jack of** them.* □ *To have Robert standing there — the **only man Jack of** us who had got sufficiently away from himself to create anything—it was Hell.* CON □ usu derogatory; unusual sing form in last example; Jack may be spelt with a small or capital J.

one's/sb's every move [O/o (NP)] everything that one/sb does; everywhere that one/sb goes **V:** watch, note; check, follow, control; be aware of □ *I had a feeling that from amidst the leafy cover unseen eyes were watching **our every move**.* □ *From that moment Glatt**'s every move** was recorded.* DS □ *In his heyday of supreme power at Elstree film studios, he had all the clocks removed because he resented time dictating **his every move**.* SC □ used esp if one is suspected/one suspects sb of wrongdoing, crime, an intention to attack sb, etc.

every now and again/then [A (NP)] on a number of occasions, at irregular intervals; every so often (qv); now and again/then (qv); from time to time (qv) **V:** snore, interrupt, look up; buy, sell, sth □ *I wouldn't read the newspapers if it wasn't for this ridiculous idea about being well informed. Conscience stirs me **every now and again**.* ASA □ *Ella soon felt that she could decently abstract herself from the discourse. **Every now and again** Bill's phrases came to her as through pads of cotton wool.* HAA □ *It was a warm squally day; the windows on the garden side were shut against the blast. **Every now and then** the pennons of the pampas clump bowed almost to the ground.* PW

every other/second man etc missing the first, taking the second, and so on alternately; half or approximately half, without actually numbering the particular group or class; (fig) quite a large number of people or things **n:** man, girl; car, office block; song, plan □ *Continue knitting the pattern, increasing once at the end of **every other row** till there are 78 stitches on the needle.* □ *Second-hand cars were a drug on the market in Kuwait: **every other** semi-skilled **inhabitant** tears sumptuously around in a Chevrolet or Mercedes.* BM □ *Kristofferson, an ex-Rhodes Scholar who works out of the country-music tradition, is a gifted lyricist who does something good in **every second song**.* L

every picture tells a story (catchphrase) a picture, photograph etc is able to convey a situation, or express a message, just as easily as (and sometimes better than) a written account; the way sb or sth looks is likely to reveal what has happened, the true story etc (from a caption to an illustration of a person in pain, in an advertisement for a patent medicine (1920-40)) □ *'Well, well,' said Frank's father, eyeing the lipstick mark on his son's cheek, '**every picture tells a story**.'* □ (advertisement) ***Every mirror tells a story**—when you look into the mirror you know the real truth about your complexion.* H □ HELEN (she peers and primps into the mirror): *Oh look at that, **every line tells a** dirty **story**, hey?* TOH □ often adapted, as shown.

every schoolboy knows (the stated fact, the information, is so elementary that) even sb who is still at school has learnt it already, and it therefore hardly needs repeating □ (source) *How haughtily he cocks his nose,/To tell what **every schoolboy knows**.* THE COUNTRY LIFE (J SWIFT 1667-1745) □ ***Every schoolboy knows** where to find Teeside.* OBS □ *The Lord Chancellor, as all first-year law students and **most schoolboys know**, is a very curious animal indeed* (the office combines political, legislative, and judicial functions). NS □ often occurs in *as*-cl or *what*-cl.

every so often at irregular intervals that may be frequent or not; every now and again/then (qv); now and again/then (qv); from time to time (qv) □ *I began throwing them* (the stones) *straight into the cart and **every so often**, when I had cleared a few square feet of ground, I used to pull it after me on to a nice, fresh, stone-filled part.* OBS □ *This make of starter-motor has a good reputation but **every so often** you get one that just won't function properly however much you tinker with it.*

every time [A (NP)] (informal) whenever possible; whenever a choice can be made **V:** give me (= I would choose); opt for, prefer; settle for, take. **O:** classical music, jazz, pop; a Mediterranean climate; plain cooking, home-made bread □ *You never know where you are with ultra-polite people like George. Give me the outspoken type **every time**.* □ *'I'd rather have too much to do than too little, wouldn't you?' 'Oh yes, **every time**.'* □ *People have different notions of how they like to spend a holiday but I'd settle for a quiet seaside place **every time**.*

everything but the kitchen sink [O (NP)] every possible (moveable) object; every abstract thought, argument etc that might be thought useful or relevant **V:** include; produce, carry, bring □ *She was only coming to stay for a few days but she brought **everything but the kitchen sink** with her.* □ *His central theme has to be disinterred from a heap of accompanying debris that includes **everything but the kitchen sink**. But the theme itself is clear and* *important.* L

everything/all (that) the heart (of a man) could desire [Comp/O (NP)] (formal) (sth is) all that one wants (eg health, wealth, success etc); (sb/somewhere has) all the desirable qualities that one wants or expects **V:** be; possess, attain, achieve □ *She said, 'Aye, they're getting for him* ***everything the heart of a man could desire****, saving one thing.' I asked, 'What's that?' she said, 'A wife.'* RFW □ *He tried to reason himself out of his depression, telling himself that he had* ***everything the heart could desire****.* □ *As a place to stay, the island seemed to him to offer* ***all that the heart could desire*** *except the means of earning a living.* □ *My teenage son's just achieved* ***his heart's desire****—a drum set, and he plays it all the time.* □ variant one's heart's desire.

everything in the garden is lovely/rosy (saying) everything is satisfactory, is going well, could not be better □ *'Welcome back, Mistress Odd. How are they all in Nottingham?' 'Oh,* ***everything in the garden's lovely*** *in Nottingham.'* RM □ JACK (consults book): *Bristol, Birmingham and Manchester are taking on extra staff — simply cannot cope with the orders pouring in.* JASON: *In fact,* ***everything in the garden is lovely****.* DPM

everything is going/coming one's way all that is happening is exactly as one had wished; all the things that one had planned are in one's favour □ *When I kissed her on Sunday it had seemed that* ***everything was going my way****.* RATT □ *The public took a fancy to him in that television series last year and now* ***everything*** *seems to* ***be coming his way*** *with offers of work from all over the place.* □ *As usual when* ***things were****n't* ***going his way****, Peter turned quite sulky.* □ in neg constructions S is usu things as in last example.

everything etc under the sun everything etc in the world, anywhere, of any kind, that one can think of **pron/adj** + **n:** everything, anything; nothing; all things, every nation, all places; no subject; the kindest woman; not a rottener trick □ (source) *The thing that hath been, it is that which shall be; and that which is done is that which shall be done: and there is* ***no*** *new* ***thing under the sun****.* ECCLESIASTES I 9 □ *...attitudes which show themselves in the all-pervading gossip about* ***everything under the sun****, but most often about sexual peccadilloes.* L □ *Julius found himself under the cruel necessity of holding his peace about the subject which, of all* ***subjects under the sun****, he most liked to discuss.* EM □ *There's* ***no nation under the sun*** *that doesn't try to protect its military secrets, however meagre, from foreign powers.* NS

the evil eye the (alleged) ability to cast an evil spell, to do sb harm, by means of a malevolent look or glance □ *The priest dropped his eyes to the ground and covered his shaven head with a fold in his robe. 'The camera is a form of* ***evil eye****,' Sefton explained. 'They don't like 'em* (= them)*.'* ARG □ *'There you go,' said Lefty. 'It's like* ***the evil eye****. You don't really believe in it, yet it paralyses you.* □ *Modern science produces the H-bomb which reproduces the heat of the sun; modern magic counters with voodoo, black mass,* ***evil eyes****, the Tarot pack.* T

the evil that men do lives after them (saying) people will remember the bad, wrong things that sb has done long after they have forgotten the good things; the bad things that one does in one's lifetime continue to have an effect long after one's death □ (source) ***The evil that men do lives after them****,/The good is oft interred with their bones.* JULIUS CAESAR III 2 □ (NONCE) *A bald and squat old Babbit* (= ordinary business man) *at the next table with a young woman certainly not his wife, looked around, quickly and guiltily.* ***The evil that men do lives*** *sometimes* ***with them****.* PP □ ***The evil that*** *such* ***men do lives after them****. The dangers from which Dulles saved what he liked to call the Free World no longer frightened us.* OBS □ first meaning derives from original source, second meaning is more usu in current usage.

the exception proves the rule (saying) some single thing that exists or occurs contradicts or diverges from an established theory or belief (eg in behaviour, philosophy, science etc) and therefore serves to confirm or emphasize (the truth of) the theory □ *In spite of her upbringing she emerges from her own pages as exceptionally serene and strong and it looks as if the best the child psychologists will be able to do is regard it as* ***the exception*** *that* ***proves their rule****.* L □ *'Englishmen are supposed to be very reserved, but Ralph will start a conversation with anyone anywhere.'* ***'He's the exception that proves the rule.'*** □ variant it's/he's the exception that proves the rule. ⇨ ⚠ next entry.

an exception to the rule [Comp (NP)] be sb who, or sth which, appears contrary to what is normally accepted, believed etc (eg in matters of behaviour, science etc) **V:** ⚠ be; prove; make sth □ *This small boy was something of* ***an exception to the rule*** *in so far as he appeared to seek knowledge rather than profit.* BM □ *Press tycoons have never been notably successful in turning themselves into writing journalists and this book, far from being the exception that proves the rule, proves that the author is* ***no exception to the rule****.* NS ⇨ ⚠ previous entry.

exercise due/proper care (and attention) [V + O pass] (formal) take all the ordinary and normal precautions (esp those required by custom or law) in a situation with some possibility of danger □ *Residents claimed that the City Engineer's Department had failed to* ***exercise due care and attention****, by leaving a manhole uncovered during the hours of darkness.* □ *Sniping may be a problem and senior officers must* ***exercise due care*** *when travelling about their areas.* MFM □ *Provided you* ***exercise proper care*** *there is no reason why you shouldn't live to a great age.* □ occurs in formal written (and esp (legal) use eg *He was charged with driving without* ***due care and attention****.*

exercise one's right(s)/prerogative [V + O] do sth with the awareness that one is entitled to do it, either legally or as part of a special privilege attached to one's rank, office etc □ *Henry VIII could have* ***exercised his prerogative*** *and prevented Sir Thomas More's execution, but there was to be no Royal Pardon for the gentle scholar.* □ *I decided to take my books across London each day for a change of scenery by* ***exercising my rights*** *as a member and working in the British Medical Association* *building.* DIL

the expectation of life the number of years, based on a general statistical average, that a person may expect to live; the number of years that sb (who is middle-aged or elderly) may, with care or appropriate medical attention, expect to continue to live **det:** the, a(n); one's ▫ *The duration of marriage is related most obviously to* ***the expectation of life****. Since the turn of the century, the impact of medicine has increased the span of life by some 20 years.* OBS ▫ *We none of us have* ***a** great* ***expectation of life*** *nowadays, so why worry? We live in an atomic age, Mr Wormold.* OMIH ▫ *The older one is on joining an insurance scheme, the greater the annual premium, because* ***one's life expectancy*** *is less.* ▫ variant one's life expectancy.

expense/money (is) no object (saying) it does not matter how much money is needed to do sth, to buy sth, etc (either because there is plenty of money available or because there are other, more important, factors involved) ▫ (of a journalist) *'He'll do anything to get his story,' says Veitch. '**Expense is no object**. He can charter a jet or whistle up a helicopter any time.'* RT ▫ *Cooking, when* ***money is no object****, soon becomes ornate, over-elaborate, amazing.* NS ▫ sometimes used as invitation or encouragement to spend, in form ***Expense is no object!***

explode a myth etc [V + O pass] destroy the basis of what is believed or accepted by many people; show sth to be false or no longer true; blow sb/sth sky-high (qv) **O:** myth, ⚠ belief, idea, notion, theory ▫ *The popular picture of the craftworker is a grey-haired tatty figure, wrapped in hessian, producing lengths of knobbly tweed. In recent years a number of individuals have* ***exploded this myth****.* OBS ▫ *Two* ***myths*** *about comedians: they all want to play Hamlet and they're all melancholic. Both are* ***exploded*** *by Richard Briers.* RT ▫ *The author sets out to explore and, let it be said,* ***explode*** *the present fashionable* ***theories*** *about the structure of language.*

explore every avenue [V + O pass] (cliché) examine all the means, opportunities or possibilities that may be available in order to achieve some aim; make all possible inquiries to find out what is happening etc; leave no/(not) any stone unturned (qv) **det:** (sing) every, any, a/this particular; (pl) all (possible), many, several, a number of ▫ *'You don't suspect a man in my position, surely? Why it's preposterous!' 'It is my business to* ***explore every avenue****,' the Inspector answered.* ▫ *I've* ***explored a lot of avenues*** *as they were always saying in the House* (of Commons) *when I was a member, but this time I think I'm barking up the right tree.* WDM ▫ *'Let the public be assured,' the speaker continued, 'that we will* ***leave no avenue unexplored*** *in our efforts to keep down the cost of living.'* ▫ usu associated with official or political figures; (double neg) variant leave no avenue unexplored.

extremes meet two or more people or things of very opposite natures, qualities etc meet, come into contact or conflict with each other, etc ▫ *Alec and his wife are not a bit like each other. I suppose it is a case of* ***extremes meeting*** *and actually finding they could live together.* ▫ ***Extremes*** *of poverty and affluence* ***meet*** *in this mushrooming city.* ▫ often spoken as comment or judgement; variant a/the meeting of extremes.

an eye for an eye (and a tooth for a tooth) (saying) (a warning that) an act of aggression will be met with retaliation of the same kind (esp in personal or national conflicts) ▫ (sources) *If men. . .hurt a woman with child. . .and if any mischief follow, then thou shalt give life for life,* ***eye for eye, tooth for tooth****, hand for hand, foot for foot.* EXODUS XXI 22-4 ▫ *Ye have heard that it hath been said,* ***An eye for an eye, and a tooth for a tooth****: But I say unto you, That ye resist not evil: but whosoever shall smite thee on thy right cheek, turn to him the other also.* MATTHEW V 38-9 ▫ *And in the Protestant areas of Belfast, the talk will be of* ***an eye for an eye and a tooth for a tooth****.* SC ▫ *The minister might preach about God loving his flock and protecting it from harm, but we believed far more in* ***that tooth for a tooth*** *and in an Angry God who would punish us our sins.* SC

the eye of the storm etc the central and strongest point of a storm (often indicated by a small break in the clouds); (fig) the main, central point of a dangerous situation, crisis etc **n:** storm, ⚠ hurricane, whirlwind ▫ *Not having proper navigational aids the pilot had been unaware of the changing conditions and had flown the plane right into* ***the eye of the*** *tropical* ***storm****.* ▫ *But his* (Harold Macmillan's) *warning that the 'wind of change' should not become a 'howling tempest' was a little late; the storm has already broken across Central Africa. Mr Macleod is sailing into* ***the eye of the storm****.* OBS ▫ *While warring factions battled all around him for Spain, a journalist working for a British newspaper paced carefully up and down a solitary cell in* ***the eye of the storm****.* L ▫ *Suddenly all is quiet; daylight begins to filter in; but it is only* ***the eye of the whirlwind*** *and before one can reach the escape hatch the storm is on one again from the rear.* SC ▫ last example is a humorous account of steering one's car through an automatic carwash.

one's/sb's eyes are bigger than one's/his belly/stomach (saying) one/sb is too greedy in asking for, or taking, more food than one/sb can eat; (fig) think that one/sb can do more, enjoy a larger amount of sth, than actually is the case ▫ *'What was the sense in buying two packets of chips when you can't even finish one, Mike?' '**His eyes are bigger than his belly**, that's what's the matter with him,' said his father.* ▫ *The Law Society's Legal Aid budget, including an allowance to publicise the scheme, comes from the State. Given the relatively small numbers of solicitors choosing to practise in the poorer urban areas, the profession**'s eyes** could* ***prove larger than its belly****.* NS ▫ often spoken as criticism or reproach.

F

face down/up [A] with the informative, functional, or otherwise important side hidden/exposed **S:** book, photograph, paper. **V** ⚠ lie; lay, place, deal, sth □ *The fortune-teller asked me to select 16 cards from the pack and these she dealt* ***face up*** *on the table, in the shape of a square.* □ *I don't know what's wrong with this alarm clock but it only goes if it's lying* ***face down***. □ *She laid the book down* ***face upwards***. *It was one of Alec's novels. 'Oh,' said Isabel, when they had shaken hands, 'I see you are reading that!'* PW □ *When she had read through a page of examinee's answers she placed it carefully* ***face downwards*** *on a separate pile.* HAA □variant face downward(s)/upward(s).

face (the) facts [V + O pass] see (and deal with) things as they are, not as one would wish them to be; not avoid acknowledging that sth is difficult or unpleasant □ *I might as well* ***face facts****: good-bye Susan, good-bye a big car, good-bye power, good-bye the silly handsome dreams.* RATT □ HARRY: *But it is an industrial age, you silly girl. Let's* ***face facts***. CSWB □ *It was my homecoming that had precipitated this thing, and I must* ***face the facts*** *and take what might be coming to me.* RFW □ *I began to be aware of the identity of some of the heavily muffled figures, who, like me, were pacing the platform. I supposed they had already seen me, and one another, but didn't feel like* ***facing the*** *stern* ***fact that*** *we were all travelling together.* CON □ *. . .the bid to convince the citizenry that it faces disaster unless prodigal ways are mended,* ***facts faced****, belts tightened, teeth gritted, and wallets opened.* NS □ variant face the fact that.

one's face falls one shows one's disappointment, dismay etc by one's expression □ *Then* ***her face fell***. *I was still sitting there shivering and clutching for something else and she was suddenly sorry that she had failed.* HAHA □ *Macfarlane always takes a supply of soft drink with him to the commentary-box—usually in a gin bottle. 'The first year I did it, the producer****'s face fell***.*'* RT □ usu in simple past tense; also pl their faces fell.

face the music [V + O] (informal) accept the difficulties, criticism, repercussions that follow a decision or action of one's own; meet a crisis, emergency with boldness and confidence **modal:** have to, must, ought to, should □ *Dr Verwoerd will have to* ***face the music*** *of his opponents' criticisms of apartheid.* SC □ (We agreed) *that we should ask the Prime Minister for a new Minister of Defence. But that agreement came to nothing, since my two colleagues declined to* ***face the music*** *on the day of battle.* MFM

the face of the earth [O/o (NP)] the surface of the whole world; anywhere and everywhere **V:** change, cover, disfigure, transform; disappear from; wipe sb/sth off/from □ *The conservationists claim that modern technology and commercial exploitation will change* ***the face of the earth*** *as surely as any Ice Age.* □ *If highway authorities reorganised road networks in such a way that there was no traffic congestion, there'd be so much road space covering* ***the face of the earth*** *that there'd hardly be room for anything else.* □ *Is there a more beautiful county on* ***the face of the earth*** *than Perthshire?* □ *'How will this company of yours relate to Bounty Belfounder* (another film company)*?' I asked. 'Relate to it?' said Madge. 'It'll wipe it off* ***the face of the earth***.*'* UTN □ *How many people go abroad to live, change their names or addresses, die intestate, have heirs who live in Australia or Chile, or just disappear from* ***the face of the earth****?* OBS

face to face (with sb/sth) [Comp/A (NP)] in a directly opposite position (to sb/sth); in the physical presence (of sb/sth); in direct confrontation or competition (with sb/sth) **V:** be, come, find oneself; bring, place, sb; meet, argue; tell, accuse, sb □ *Two people arguing* ***face to face*** *enjoy a greater sense of intimacy and privacy than when made to dispute at a distance with the help of closed-circuit television.* NS □ (stage direction) *Davies turns, shambles across the room, comes* ***face to face with*** *a statue of Buddha standing on the gas stove, looks at it and turns.* TC □ *Securely placed in the middle-class world of a successful businessman, he is suddenly brought* ***face to face with*** *the realization that there are more things to life than making money.* OBS □ *We were* ***face to face with*** *Rommel's forces between the sea and the Qattara Depression.* MFM □ *I'll finish the affair once and for all. And* ***face to face***. *Not by letter. That's cowardly.* RATT

fact/truth and/or fiction/fantasy [n + n non-rev] verifiable information, or an account of sth, that has really happened, as contrasted with imagined or invented incidents □ *She lives, perhaps, in a world of other people's dramas, where* ***fact and fiction*** *are no longer clearly distinguished.* UTN □ *This feature, which provides a contrast with many modern European tales of* ***fact and fiction****, is the small concern shown for 'character', either psychologically or morally.* NDN □ *'Now it's your turn, Emily,' said the quizmaster. 'A swan sings once only, just before it dies.* ***Fact or fiction*** (= true or false)*?'* □ *This shows one of the important factors of myth and folklore—they survive because* ***fact and fantasy*** *are totally dissociated.* RT □ *Of course the difficulty is that in the Indian context, now as before, the dividing line between* ***truth and fiction*** *is elusive.* G □ usual collocations fact and/or fiction/fantasy and truth and fiction.

the fact of the matter is (that) sth is the real truth or the most important aspect of sth being discussed □ *You keep on saying that a camping holiday will be no real rest for me but* ***the fact of the matter is****, you don't want to go yourself.* □ *He said he couldn't afford to run his car any longer, now that he was having to live on a pension—****the fact of the matter being that*** *he'd had several near accidents and had lost his nerve.*

the fact remains (that) sth is true, is undeniable, is still the case (whether regrettable or not, whether likely or not, whatever else may or may not be true) □ *Each* (defence) *Service has developed within itself a system which provides for specialisation where it is wanted, and yet ensures overall unity in direction. But* ***the fact remains that*** *we have not achieved for the three Services in combination a system which is comparable to that which each Service has evolved for itself.* MFM □ *Annabel, either the children or those cats of yours have been at my clippings. No, I don't know either what cats or children would want with Stock Exchange clippings, but* ***the fact remains****, they've disappeared.* DC

facts and figures [n + n non-rev] (items of) precise information, esp in spoken or unspoken contrast with ideas, theories, rough estimates, generalized statements or arguments **V:** ⚠ give, provide, quote □ *We torchbearers of culture* (librarians) *are paid starvation wages, and the hard materialists, the men of* ***facts and figures****, are the lords of creation.* RATT □ *So I told my tale with* ***the facts and figures*** *I knew, the dates, and the changes in the history of the firm.* PP □ *And this time the argument succeeded. The Cheddar teenagers talked* (= gave) ***facts and figures****. They guaranteed to pay the rent.* H

(let) the facts speak for themselves (let) the actual facts noted about a situation or occurrence, or revealed by an inquiry, indicate the conclusion to be drawn from them without further interpretation or explanation □ *'I am suggesting nothing. But do not* ***the facts speak for themselves****?' 'You seem to have jumped to the conclusion that because of what has happened to this unfortunate young man there must have been foul play.'* EM □ *I reserved my complaints about being understaffed and underequipped. It would be better, first, to escort the Visiting Committee round the buildings and* ***let the facts speak for themselves****.*

faint heart ne'er/never won fair lady (saying) a timid or easily discouraged person won't get the best of anything in life □ *Don't give up.* ***Faint heart never won fair lady****—or anything else worth having either.* □ *Mr Whitelaw condemned such critics as '****faint-hearts****': the worst thing to do when the going got tough was to about-turn and march in the opposite direction.* L □ n compound a faint-heart.

a fair cop (informal) the act of catching sb, the occasion of being caught, in crime, misdemeanour, error, evasion etc (esp when this has been brought about by fair or legitimate means) □ *The attitude of the professional thief is quite different. If he's nabbed it's* ***a fair cop****, he pleads guilty, and hopes to be smarter next time.* □ *'My goodness, we treat animals like slaves!' 'I expect you're a vegetarian,' I suggested. 'I ought to be,' Mr Adams replied. 'All right, I admit it,' he added eventually. 'That's* ***a fair cop****.'* OBS □ *I found him at a flat near Fisherman's Wharf. He had dismantled the telephone because he wanted a rest from the Press but he bowed gracefully to* ***a fair cop****.* OBS □ often follows *it's/that's* .

fair do's (informal) just and equitable treatment or appraisal **V:** be; give sb □ *On weekdays, papers come right to the door, with the milk; sometimes for breakfast, but sometimes after lunch, depending on which way the milk lady decides to tackle her journey.* ***Fair do's****.* ST □ *'It's six months and more since he promised to look into that claim for me. It's just not good enough.' 'Come on, John, that's not* ***fair do's****! The man's been ill.'* □ often used as comment on fairness of sth.

fair enough [Comp (AdjP)] (informal) sth which is proposed, or which has taken place, is acceptable **V:** ⚠ be; seem; think sth □ *'Look, I can't lower the price any further because of an agreement with the wholesalers. But we'll forget about any extra charges for delivery.' '****Fair enough****. I'll write you a cheque.'* □ *'I don't see what more you can expect—you were dismissed from the job and offered two weeks pay in lieu of notice. Generous, I'd call it.' 'Well, that's* ***fair enough****. But what about the holiday pay I'm owed?'* □ used to acknowledge fairness of sth; often introduces a qualification.

fair, fat and forty [adj + adj + adj] (catchphrase) a teasing, or derogatory, description of a woman in early middle-age □ (source) *'Who can that comely dame be, on whom our excellent and learned Doctor looks with such uncommon regard?' '****Fat, fair, and forty****,' said Mr Winterblossom; 'that is all I know of her—a mercantile person.'* ST RONAN'S WELL, VII (SIR W SCOTT 1771-1832 □ *It fell to Mr Andrews to propose the toast to the ladies, which, in view of the fact that the representatives present were indisputably* ***fair, fat and forty****, he managed very graciously.* □ expression now usu begins with fair and always ends with forty.

(in) fair (weather) and/or foul whatever the weather is, or will be, like; (in) favourable and adverse circumstances alike; come rain, come shine (qv); in any case/event (qv); wet or fine (qv) □ *Training in the 5th Corps must be carried out in all conditions of weather and climate;* ***in*** *rain, snow, ice, mud,* ***fair weather and foul****.* MFM □ *We've put off this fishing trip long enough. I'm going to set off to-morrow morning,* ***fair or foul****.* □ *It's not everybody that would stick by a man through* ***fair and foul*** *as you have.* □ adj compound fairweather as in *a* ***fairweather*** *friend* = 'one who will desert you should trouble or difficulties arise'.

fair game [Comp (NP)] a legitimate, or suitable, object for exploitation, abuse, ridicule, teasing etc (from animals thought proper to hunt and kill) **V:** ⚠ be; make, think, sb □ *Irma was not an ordinary barmaid, he recognized that. Still, she belonged to the category of barmaids. Barmaids were* ***fair game****, so Irma was* ***fair game****.* PW □ *Not for nothing was the admirably flamboyant Highland Division ('HD') known to its envious friends as the Highway Decorators. The colonnades of Lepcis and its underclad statuary were* ***fair game****.* SD □ *Anyone who takes part in a prohibited demonstration somehow puts himself outside the law and is* ***fair game*** *for any soldier to take a pot shot at.* NS

(with) one's/sb's (own) fair hand(s) [A (Prep P)] (facetious) (by) oneself/sb personally (the reference usu being to a task, service or favour performed by oneself/sb) □ *My suggestion is that we go upstairs to the sitting-room, where we drink coffee and where we listen to music played by Ann****'s fair hand****.* TBC □ *'Did you* *bake those cakes yourself?' 'Yes, **with my own fair hands**.'* □ *The landlord of the inn seemed flattered to have a titled guest, and his wife made up a bed for me **with her own fair hands**.*

fair play behaviour, in a game or contest, that conforms to the rules; personal behaviour, governmental or legal procedure, that conforms to generally accepted principles of impartiality and justice □ *Traditional standards of **fair play** on the football field are so far eroded that terms of suspension for fouling are regarded as a hazard rather than as a stigma.* G □ *The leader-writer explains: 'Democracy assumes **fair play**.'* OBS □ *It is perhaps a tribute to your British instinct for **fair play** that what came immediately to my mind did not also occur to yours.* EM □ (radio panel-game) *Peter Haigh will be in the chair for this series to see **fair play**, and for tonight's session the members of the panel are...* RT □ *Suddenly I felt tired and old, sick of trying to explain, sick of eternally trying to mediate and see **fair play**.* CON □ *see, ensure **fair play*** = 'referee, supervise (and, if necessary, interfere) in order to ensure proper behaviour'.

a fair question [Comp (NP)] a reasonable, or permissible, question; a question that sb is entitled to ask and receive an answer to **V:** ⚠ be; find, think, sth □ *'Before agreeing to purchase, can you assure me that the house isn't in an industrial development area.' 'It's **a fair question** and my honest answer must be "I don't know".'* □ (science fiction story) *'What I mean is,' she said, 'things like that oughtn't to be allowed. If a man is going to be able to walk through a girl's bathroom wall, where is he going to stop?' Which seemed **a** pretty **fair question**.* TST □ *'You'd do better using a spanner.' 'How can I use a spanner if I haven't got one?' 'It's **a fair question**, I must admit.'*

the fair sex (facetious) women □ *I've already told Sir Edgar to appoint one of you younger chaps. If they don't like either of your two faces, there's Prescott or Drake, not to forget **the fair sex**.* ASA □ *His personality, so unlike that of the traditional 'Herr Professor', his attraction for what used to be called **the fair sex**, and the fact that in his spare time he composed songs...* ST □ stress pattern the 'fair sex.

fair (and) square [adj + adj non-rev] just; honest; without deceit, bias or concealment □ *'May I ask where you got that from?' 'Yes, you may. And what's more, I'll even tell you. I told Mr Purnell I'd taken it — everything **fair, square** and above board.'* TT □ *We won't have a local referee for the re-play, and then if we beat them again everybody will know its been **fairly and squarely** done.* □ variant fairly and squarely [adv + adv non-rev].

fair and square[1] [adj + adj non-rev] without deviation in position or direction □ *She had it* (a moving target) ***fair and square** between the rings* (of the sighting device) *at about four-o-clock* (dial position), *exactly as she wanted it.* RFW □ *At length the awaited sign flashed to us from the beach; the commander signalled 'full speed ahead' and we struck the beach **fairly and squarely**.* SD □ variant fairly and squarely [adv + adv non-rev].

fair and square[2] [adj + adj non-rev] unequivocal; without ambiguity, or possibility of mistake or misunderstanding **S:** blame, responsibility, guilt. **V:** rest, lie, fall, stand □ *The Labour Party stands **fair and square** behind the proposition that Britain should leave the EEC.* □ *There hasn't yet been an accident between two roads or two stationary cars. No, the blame rests **fairly and squarely** on the shoulders of the motorist and no amount of verbal smokescreen can obscure this.* ST □ variant fairly and squarely [adv + adv non-rev].

fair to middling [adj + adj non-rev] (informal) less than satisfactory but not really bad; moderate in number, force, or quality □ *'Had* (= have you had) *a good day?' '**Fair to middling**, you know.'* ILIH □ *'So you're going to Paris? How's your French?' 'Oh, **fair to middling**. I can order myself a cup of coffee.'* □ *He was never more than a **fair to middling** student and he was lucky to get as good a degree as he did.* □ *The Cocktail Lounge was almost empty but there was a **fair-to-middling** number of drinkers in the Public Bar.* □ attrib use, *a **fair-to-middling** golfer*, often hyphenated.

fair's fair (saying) an appeal, or a reminder, to act justly and equitably, share a benefit or burden equally, avoid prejudice □ *The letters just lie on the page like lumps of dead cod on a slab. But **fair's fair**. While Cicero's letters may be (to me, at least) vain, fussy, tedious and irresolute, they are also honest and, in their mannered way, affectionate.* OBS □ (NONCE) (advertising sticker on a travel-agent's shop window) ***Fare's Fair**!* □ headphrase = 'fair is fair'.

a fairy godmother a good fairy who bestows some gift, talent, magic protection, etc on a child at birth or on its naming day, and who may continue her help throughout its life (from a character found in many folk tales and children's stories); a person who is a source of protection, help or deliverance □ *She's the family drudge, poor little soul — a Cinderella without **a fairy godmother*** (in the children's story, Cinderella's fairy godmother saves her from the neglect and abuse of her two step-sisters). □ *Completely benumbed, still doped with morphia, I must have fallen asleep, because the next thing I knew a Highlander was talking to me, a stretcher-bearer. This Jock was like **a fairy godmother**. He'd looted some champagne from a burning shop and brought me a bottle.* ST □ (NONCE) *But the report did have one positive result: the Official Solicitor — **the 'fairy godfather'**, as Mr Wilson called him — materialised once again and announced that he was going to apply for the men's release.* L □ also pl.

a fairy story/tale[1] a folk tale or children's story which, if not specifically about fairies, will involve supernatural events and beings, eg ogres, goblins, giants, witches, magic spells, and fanciful incidents □ *Their age divided them from the adult world and their credulity was of a different quality. He was glad that Milly could still accept **fairy stories**: pictures that wept or spoke words of love in the dark.* OMIH □ stress pattern a 'fairy story.

a fairy story/tale[2] an inaccurate account or interpretation of sth, motivated by romanticism, wishful thinking, gullibility or a reluctance to face facts □ *I'm not going to hide things* *from her, or feed her with* ***fairy stories*** *that will make it easier for her and more difficult for me.* AITC □ *Coinneach Mór is not the kind of man to spread* ***a fairy tale****. I am satisfied that the eyes of a man whose professional powers of observation have never been at fault would not have been deceived.* RM □ stress pattern a 'fairy story.

a fairy story/tale[3] a lie □ *'She said you were an old boyfriend of hers, thirty years ago.' 'Damn that for* ***a fairy tale****!'* □ *'I think you're telling me* ***a fairy story****, Peter,' his mother said. 'Your face would be dirty if you'd fallen. You've been fighting again, haven't you?'* □ also pl; stress pattern a 'fairy story.

one's faithful hound (cliché) one's dog, or other close companion (from the frequent occurrence of faithful together with the name of a dog in poems and stories) □ *'Where's* ***the faithful hound*** *today?' 'Oh, I had to leave him at home. He has a sore paw.'* □ *'You don't* eat *them, do you?' he said, with all the disgust of a man asked to make a meal of* ***his faithful hound****. 'If we didn't breed rabbits and poultry for the table,' I replied, 'we couldn't afford to eat meat at all.'* □ *Carter patted his tobacco-pouch as though it were a dog's head, '****My faithful hound*** *shall bear me company.'* OMIH □ last example misquotes the following (which deals with various conceptions of an after-life): (an Indian) *thinks, admitted to that equal sky,/****His faithful dog*** *shall bear him company.* ESSAY ON MAN (A POPE 1688-1744)

fall flat [V + Comp] fail completely in its intended or expected effect **S:** joke, story; performance, play, concert □ *I once made the mistake of taking a sceptical girlfriend to see a Marx Brothers' picture on a sunny afternoon in a huge, almost deserted, Thirties palace of a cinema. For once, Groucho flopped. For much the same reason, I think, he* ***falls*** *a bit* ***flat*** *on television.* L □ *Tonight's Commons' vote on entry into the EEC will be, as has often been said, a decision of historic importance. Yet the great debate in the country and Parliament has* ***fallen flat****.* SC □ *Tastes and habits of humour vary not only from country to country but from region to region within them. A story that makes a West Highlander laugh may* ***fall*** *very* ***flat*** *in Edinburgh.*

fall foul of sb/sth meet, have a confrontation or disagreement with, sb/sth to one's disadvantage or in a way that exposes one's weaknesses, ignorance, misdeeds etc **o:** authorities, police; official, taxman □ *He had been publicly nasty to Churchill in the recent war, he had* ***fallen foul of*** *MI5, and inquisitive Members had asked a lot of questions about him in the House* (of Commons). PP □ *Simkins had got away with a lot of shady dealings for years, but eventually overreached himself and* ***fell foul of*** *the law.*

a fall guy (informal) a comedian's stooge; anybody who is set up in a role only to be dislodged from it, discomfited, ridiculed, blamed etc with the purpose of showing another person to better advantage □ (film review) *Randy Quaid is* ***a*** *well-observed* ***fall-guy*** *again, a simpleton whose trusting affection for Daddy is endlessly betrayed.* L □ *It was a marvellous piece of organisation. A political crank was used as* ***a fall guy****. They shot him and planted a diary on him that explained his motives and proved he was crazy. Everyone fell for it.* ST □ also pl; stress pattern a 'fall guy.

fall/be taken ill/sick [V + Comp] become ill □ *I must expect to* ***fall sick****. I cannot expose the body to this hardship and expect the poor beast to behave as if it were in clover.* PM □ *In '42nd Street', the script had Ruby Keeler taking over from Bebe Daniels, the leading lady who had* ***fallen sick****, going on and dancing her feet off to roars of applause.* ST □ *First there was trouble finding politicians or soldiers willing to serve on the commission, then its leader, Brigadier-General Alfred H Terry, was* ***taken ill****.* OBS ⇨ ⚠ go/report sick.

fall quiet etc [V + Comp] become silent after having been speaking, shouting, laughing etc **adj:** quiet, ⚠ silent, speechless □ *The strangeness of these words struck the two young people. And they* ***fell quiet****.* ARG □ *'Listen, Masa!' he said excitedly. We all* ***fell silent****, and then from the valley ahead a strange cry drifted down to us.* BB □ *The two of them kept shouting more and more loudly. The noise was just at its peak when Ned appeared. They* ***fell silent*** *and he turned his head to look into their faces one after another.* CON □ *The conversation consisted mainly of embarrassed silence on Strindberg's part, floods of French and German from Shaw, who* ***fell speechless*** *when Strindberg took out his watch and said: 'At two o'clock I am going to be sick.'* SC ⇨ ⚠ strike sb dumb/speechless.

fall short (of sth) [V + Comp] be less than a required, satisfactory or desired standard **o:** the average; perfection; one's expectations, specifications □ *There is no point at which we can say anybody beyond this point is tall, or intelligent, or fat, and anybody who* ***falls short of*** *it is the opposite.* SNP □ *The largest absenteeism is in the most tedious, frustrating and dehumanising jobs. The national sickness rate provides a measure of the distance by which we still* ***fall short of*** *having built the good society.* NS □ *If, however, its middle and ending* ***fall*** *a bit* ***short****, 'Mirror, Mirror' can at least claim a startlingly arresting beginning.* L □ *He's full of ideas.* ***His short-fall*** *is in carrying them out.* □ n compound a short-fall = 'deficit; lack'.

a false alarm [Comp/O (NP)] a call for emergency action that is not in fact needed; an occasion of being unnecessarily alerted to do sth or caused to feel panic or alarm **V:** ⚠ be; sound, give □ (a voice from the streets is heard frantically shouting: *Man your posts! Come out! Come out!*) MONTY: *Christ! They've started before time.* DAVE: *It might be* ***a false alarm****.* CSWB □ (earthquakes) *Even though a warning system may give* ***some false alarms****, it is probably worthwhile since quite minor precautions should be able to reduce the number of casualties.* NSC □ *Pop said it was very nice about Mr Charlton and Mariette and had Mr Charlton found out about the baby? 'She's not going to have a baby now.' Ma said. '****False alarm****!'* DBM

a false dawn [Comp (NP)] an indication of success, improvement etc that proves to be an illusion (from the lightness of the horizon before the real dawn) **V:** ⚠ be, prove, turn out to be □ *The following year he was appointed conductor of the reconstituted Royal Opera House at Covent Garden. Alas, it proved* ***a false***

dawn *and for over 20 years he suffered almost total neglect.* OBS □ (a former German officer speaks of 1940) *And we felt that the war would soon be over, that the British could not fight on — and at that time there was no war with Russia. It was like* ***a false dawn****. We had few casualties, although I was wounded twice.* RT □ (of the actress, Marilyn Monroe) *She had long years as a cheesecake 'sweater girl' before breaking into movies, slowly and with* ***many false dawns*** *before the sunburst of her seven years at the top from 'Gentlemen Prefer Blondes' to 'The Misfits'.* L

false modesty affected modesty, esp in denying or minimizing one's good looks, abilities or achievements when these entitle one to feel pride and satisfaction □ *I don't like people who have this* ***false modesty****. I know that I am beautiful.* ST □ *'Any one of 40 actors,' he says, 'could have played that part and been just as successful as I was.' But then, in a profession not normally noted for its* ***false modesty****, Gilmore is a strikingly reluctant interviewee.* RT □ *The book contains 19 references to his own writings, and no more that seven to those of any other individual scholar. No* ***false modesty*** *here; but no false pride either.* NS

(make) a false move (do) sth foolish, rash or mistaken which results in one's discomfiture, defeat, capture, death etc (from chess, as in the first example) □ *Wormold was clinging to the edge of the board with what was left of his foiled pincer-movement, but he had lost his base. He* ***made a false move*** *which enabled Segura to thrust a protected piece into square 22.* OMIH □ *I always had the fear of doing the wrong thing, of making a fool of myself in front of the higher grades. The rich were my enemies, I felt: they were watching me for* ***the*** *first* ***false move****.* RATT □ *He said harshly: 'But remember also that* ***one false move*** *could cost Sally her life. If you try to get in touch with anybody while I'm out, you'll be murdering her yourself.'* TO □ also pl.

(on/under) false pretences [A (Prep P)] (by using) lies about one's identity, qualifications, financial or social position, etc □ *I wouldn't have cared whether his father was an earl or a fishmonger. It's people making* ***false pretences*** *that I don't like.* □ *Could he be arrested now that he was on British territory? What would the charge be? Obtaining money* ***on false pretences*** *perhaps or some obscurer charge heard* in camera *under the Official Secrets Act.* OMIH □ *...the parlourmaid had been deceiving his mother and living here* ***under false pretences*** *for the last year.* RFW □ *do sth* ***on/under false pretences*** is a legal term to describe a criminal action.

fame and fortune [n + n non-rev] fame and wealth, as the twin goals of ambition **V:** ⚠ seek, be off to; find, be at the height of one's; court □ *I told Sheila I was off to* ***fame and fortune*** *in the big city and would invite her to join me in Park Lane as soon as the penthouse was ready.* JFTR □ *Other musicians court* ***fame and fortune*** *for a lifetime and count themselves lucky to possess these unreliable goddesses for a few weeks.* ST □ *Scott started the journal in the winter of 1825 when he was at the height of his* ***fame and fortune****.* NS

familiarity breeds contempt (saying) continued experience of, or association with, sb/sth leads to loss of appreciation, respect, attention etc formerly shown □ *A combination of self-interest and fear usually made Yves obedient to Mrs Portway's orders. The situation unfortunately had gone on too long;* ***familiarity breeds contempt****.* ASA □ *Queen Victoria grew alarmed as rail accidents increased and there appeared to be evidence of railway slackness,* ***familiarity*** *perhaps* ***breeding contempt****.* G □ *There must be familiarity in marriage, that was certain. But too much* ***familiarity*** *was a danger too, it* ***bred*** *if not* ***contempt*** *an apathy of the feelings.* PW □ (NONCE) *Thomas Hardy saw its tumultuous outline daily from his windows, but* ***familiarity*** *only* ***bred*** *fresh* ***wonder*** *at it.* SD □ (NONCE) ***Familiarity breeds attempt*** *and, when kissing the same girl over a long period of time gets too tame—or too stimulating—a fellow is apt to shift into the next gear.* H

a family favourite (cliché) sth likely to be appreciated by all members of an average family; sth (or occasionally sb) that all members of a particular family like, or like best □ *Summer Pudding is* ***an*** *old* ***family favourite*** *made with any mixture of summer fruits you happen to have available.* WI □ *She used to like the record-request radio programmes like 'Housewives' Choice' and '****Family Favourites****' which gave brief glimpses into other people's lives as well as music.* □ *My mother had five brothers, of whom Uncle Harry, a regular visitor and interested in us children, was* ***the family favourite****.*

a family feud bad feeling between two families or family groups, or between two branches of the same family (cf family tree) (this may vary from a distant unfriendliness to a serious intention to harm or even kill) □ *I wouldn't kill for capitalism or Communism or social democracy — I would kill Carter because he had killed Hasselbacher.* ***A family feud*** *is a better reason for murder than patriotism.* OMIH □ *A dispute over an inheritance fifty or sixty years ago led to* ***a family feud*** *which exists to this day.* □ *Romeo and Juliet's love-match was doomed from the start because of* ***the family feud*** *that existed between the Montagus and the Capulets.* □ also pl.

the family fortune(s) [O (NP)] the wealth, perhaps hereditary, that belongs to a family; the assets, or income, however small, that a family may have **V:** make; restore, retrieve; spend, squander, waste □ *'Cleopatra's People' begins in Alexandria, ten years after the Queen's death, with survivors of her family plotting to rescue her heirs from Rome and restore* ***the family fortunes****.* □ *Mummy hoped that I'd acquire a sort of polish and a little glamour—and then hook a rich young man and retrieve* ***the family fortunes****.* RATT □ *I don't have a son or daughter, only a nephew who's dead scared I may run through* ***the family fortune*** *before he can get his hands on it.*

a family joke [Comp (NP)] sth amusing that is frequently said or done in a particular family (often a remark or allusion which would be meaningless to outsiders because they do not know the origin of it); sth/sb found ridiculous by a family **V:** ⚠ be, become; make sth □ *'I hope* *the chicks* (the two daughters of the house) *will bring back some eggs.' This was* ***a family joke*** *at which Mrs Waggett tittered dutifully.* RM □ *I'm tired of having my appetite made* ***a family joke****. I don't eat any more, for my size, than the rest of you.* □ also pl.

a family likeness a greater or lesser degree of physical resemblance between the members and/or generations of a family; (fig) shared characteristics **V:** notice, find, detect. **adj:** strong, distinct, clear, obvious; faint □ *...her similarity to her father, whose image was still fresh in Patrick's mind.* ***This family likeness****, so extreme in general physical outline, extended under better optical conditions to points of detail.* TGLY □ *Now that you tell me who you are, I can see* ***the family likeness****.* □ *I notice* ***a family likeness*** *in the modern German novels that I read.* L

a family man [Comp (NP)] a man with wife and children, esp one who identifies himself fairly strongly with them, likes to spend a good deal of his free time in their company, etc **V:** ⚠ be, become, turn into □ *Some youngsters have found, like* ***family men****, that they are better off on Social Security than working.* ST □ *Then he goes home and takes his children out for walks. You can believe him when he says work is his hobby, and he is, despite all,* ***a family man****.* RT □ *Oh, George's quite different from when you knew him. He's settled down and is quite* ***the family man*** *now.*

family planning methods by which parents may decide the number and timing of the births of their children; birth control □ (of women who work after marriage) *The social benefits of* ***family planning*** *in poor and overpopulated countries must be weighed against people's rights as individuals, their feelings, and religious and cultural values.* □ *Despite the strenuous opposition of some of the less enlightened local church groups, we now have a* ***family planning*** *clinic right next to the supermarket—and they don't ask to see a marriage certificate as you go through the door.* □ attrib use *a* ***family planning*** *clinic.*

family pride high regard for the prestige and good name of one's own family and ancestry **V:** ⚠ show, display, have □ *The Goodwins had always acted as if they were a cut above their neighbours and it was a great blow to their* ***family pride*** *to have to acknowledge this dirty drunken old fellow as a relative.* □ *Whatever your sister has done, there's no need to tell the whole world about it. Have you no* ***family pride****?*

a family tree a diagram giving the line of descent of a family, or related families, as far back as it can be traced (eg families descended from the elder and younger sons of a common ancestor will belong to different *branches* of a family tree) □ (book review) *To follow this approach needs a good grasp of genealogy; fortunately we are provided with a set of* ***family trees****.* SC □ *My great grandpa, despite any impression to the contrary, did not actually grant humble petitions from his bedside — merely industrial patents from a run-down little office near the Louvre. Let us therefore not gasp too excitedly at the loftiness of Mother****'s family tree****.* FFE □ *It is not that Dayaks fear to look down* ***their family tree****, as many of us might, for they do not believe that children are stained by the sins of their forebears.* NDN

a famous victory (catchphrase) an instance of an overwhelming, or unexpected, victory or success □ (source) *'And everybody praised the Duke,/Who this great fight did win.'/'But what good came of it at last?'/Quoth little Peterkin./ 'Why that I cannot tell,' said he,/'But 'twas* ***a famous victory****.'* THE BATTLE OF BLENHEIM (R SOUTHEY 1774-1843) □ *'Well Harry,' said Sir* (Harry's teacher), *'and how did you get on?' 'I never got the stick, Sir, he just told us off.' '****A famous victory****,' said Sir. 'Now go and find a place. Sit next to Charlie there.'* TT □ *...a lady who boasted that she could teach a lamp-post to sing and had indeed gained some* ***famous victories*** *with actors for whom music was a great mystery.* TVT □ often ironic.

fan the flames (of sth) [V + O pass] incite to further activity, a more determined attitude, intenser emotion, etc **o:** rebellion, love, jealousy, ambition, curiosity □ (reader's letter) *No part or class of the community should be made a laughing stock, least of all on television. Such jokes do not promote 'integration'—they merely* ***fan the flames of*** *strife and discontent.* RT □ *You can't put into a student what's not there, but where ability or enthusiasm is already present a good teacher can* ***fan the flames****.* □ *He put more work into the business and got less out of it than either of his two brothers. All the same, I don't think he would have broken with them completely if his wife hadn't been there to* ***fan the flames****.*

fancy oneself [V + O] (informed) be vain, conceited; have a high opinion of one's attractions or abilities □ *'She's ever such a good teacher. Makes me despair.' 'Never comes down from the mountain to visit the Staffroom with her favours,' said Dusty. '****Fancies herself****, and it's easy enough to impress kids.'* TT □ *'Oh, he's good-looking all right,' Tracy agreed, 'but he* ***fancies himself*** *a bit too much for my taste.'*

a fancy man etc (informal) sb who has a relationship with another, not as a suitor or serious lover, but as an escort, spare-time companion, or (casual) sexual partner **n:** man, ⚠ woman; bit □ *Night after night we sat in front of the telly with a ham sandwich in one hand, a bar of chocolate in the other, and a bottle of lemonade between our boots, while mam was with* ***some fancy man*** *upstairs on the new bed she'd ordered.* LLDR □ *Then the rows began. Mrs Collins would rake over his first marriage. Or he'd get it stuck into his head that she had* ***a fancy man****.* ST □ *He never uses the caravan for a real holiday, just for the odd week-end with one of* ***his fancy women****.* □ *'I'm not deceived about your carryings-on,' his wife told him, 'but there's a limit. Just don't bring any of* ***your fancy bits*** *here again as a friend of the family, that's all.'*

far afield [A (AdvP)] far away **V:** travel, move, go, wander □ *Singing coachloads of block-bookings from as* ***far afield*** *as Bristol and Nottingham converge nightly on Birmingham's Bingley Hall.* TO □ *There are outings with jam-jars to a dirty stream a mile or so away, for sticklebacks and red-throats; blackberrying, also with jam-jars, even* ***farther afield****, past the church with the whalebone arches.* UL □ *School* *journeys are few, and have to be within walking distance because there is no money for fares to go **further afield**.* NS □ (NONCE) *Hughie, who thinks nothing of sailing off on his own to Boulogne or even as **far afloat** as Oslo, ran aground in the Thames Estuary.* TVT

far/miles away [Comp (AdvP)] oblivious of one's surroundings or company **S:** I, you, she, they; one's thoughts. **V:** ⚠ be, seem □ *'I've often wondered where you hide yourself,' he said, 'and now I know—gazing out of the landing window at the sights of South London. You were **miles away**.'* TT □ *Mr Wormold, Mr Wormold, your thoughts are **far away**. Come back to earth. We have to find a lottery-ticket at once, before the draw.* OMIH

far/out and away [adv + adv non-rev] to a very great degree □ *Axel Springer owns **far and away** the most influential newspaper empire in Central Europe.* ST □ *'Thompson's Progress' was not the most notorious of Hyne's works but it was **far and away** the best.* SD □ *They were both conscientious scholars, but Davis was **out and away** the abler of the two.* □ more emphatic than *much* or *by far*; comparative or superlative adj which follows far/out and away always preceded by det; stress pattern 'far/'out and away.

far be it from me to interfere etc (but/yet) I would never interfere etc (because I recognize it would not be right or appropriate) **V:** interfere, disagree, pass judgment □ *'You must be the judge,' she said. '**Far be it from me to interfere**.'* TT □ *'**Far be it from me to suggest** any change in your admirable programme, Mrs Paxon,' said Mrs Pemberton, '**but** don't you think it would be better...?'* WDM □ *I did not add the sick kids, with the drains and more personal plumbing, in the dispatches of the last two weeks; **far be it from me to** indulge in self pity.* G □ often followed, or preceded, by a statement which proposes sth very like what has been disclaimed; stress pattern far ˌbe it from 'me to interfere (but/yet).

a far cry from sth [Comp (NP)] very different from sth **V:** ⚠ be, make sth □ *The room is chilly, but full of light—**a far cry from** his Oxford digs, described by Stephen Spender as 'a darkened room with the curtains drawn, and a lamp on a table at his elbow.'* OBS □ *Tea came in on a wheeled table and Gobi began to hand us tea and scones. It was **a far cry from** the Baron's canteen with its bentwood chairs, glass-topped tables and slops of char* (= tea). PP □ *It might be objected by some that it is a study of Paris in the absence of the Parisians: and it is true that Anthony Sutcliffe is **a** very **far cry from** Professor Louis Chevalier, especially as the latter is seen in his recent work.* L

far from sth certainly not; by no means; not at all □ *Life in the outback was **far from** a bed of roses.* □ *It is generally recognized that our present legal methods and procedures for ascertaining the truth and administering justice are **far from** perfect.* SNP □ *Yet the idea of manned space-stations is **far from** new: they were discussed by Konstantin Tsiolkovski, the 'father of space research', almost seventy years ago.* L □ *Mere hints of trouble they may have been, but I took them **far from** lightly.* □ *He answered me in a manner not **far from** insolent.* □ premodifies n or adj; *not **far from*** = 'very nearly'.

far from doing sth[1] [Comp (AdjP)] certainly not doing sth **V:** ⚠ be, find sb/oneself □ *'Who would look after them, if I die?' 'You're **far from** dying, by the look of you.'* □ *She went up to Alec with a winning smile, at the same time hunching one shoulder to give an effect of shyness that she was **far from** feeling.* PW

far from doing sth[2] [Disj (AdjP)] not doing sth (as expected), but, on the contrary, doing sth else □ *I stuck it in a pot and forgot about it, but the plant, **far from** dying, seemed to thrive on neglect.* □ *Everyone was shy at first, but that soon passed and the chairman, **far from** having to prod the discussion, was having to call for order!* H □ *Dr Elton does seem, then, to have proved that Cromwell did not operate a reign of terror. **Far from** deploying an army of spies and officials, he was dependent on the traditional authority of the country gentry.* ST □ *Many Labour MPs were inclined to agree that the party, **far from** simmering down, faced a critical year of argument and discussion.* OBS

far from it [Disj (AdjP)] certainly not; just the opposite □ *Eight years old, Jeremy was much taller than Janice who was six. Janice did not seem to be afraid of him, **far from it**; she used him remorselessly as a mirror to show off in.* PW □ *'Is he generous with his money?' '**Far from it**. He doesn't even like to spend it on himself.'* □ *'I mean, you haven't come into a fortune or anything?' '**Far from it**! Yes,' said Victoria slowly, 'I shall want a job.'* TCB □ follows (as reply or comment) a previous statement in neg, interr or conditional form; stress pattern ˌfar 'from it.

far gone (in sth) [Comp (AdvP)] in an advanced stage (of sth) **S:** he, she, you, they; roof, house, farm; business; country. **V:** ⚠ be, seem. **adv mod:** very, too, so. **o:** debt; love, madness, ignorance; neglect, decay, corruption; decadence, misery □ *The victim of the attack was already **far gone** when the ambulance brought him in.* □ *Nobody will lend us money now. They know we're too **far gone in** debt ever to pay them back.* □ *The roof is pretty **far gone** but the rest of the house is in fair condition.* □ *The city was so **far gone in** decadence that the country's legal system had ceased to operate there.*

far and near [adv + adv rev] (from) everywhere; from all, or many, places or directions **V:** come, arrive, make one's way from; take, get, sth from □ *One used to be able to pick up good furniture quite cheaply at rural auctions, but now dealers come from **far and near** and force the prices up.* □ *When a priceless masterpiece was stolen recently from a famous gallery, people flocked from **far and near** to see the empty space where it had hung.* □ *Experience has taught me that, home or abroad, **near and far**, mankind comes in the same mixture of good, bad and indifferent.* ⇨ ⚠ far and wide.

(not) far removed from sth [Comp (AdvP)] (not) very different from sth **V:** ⚠ be, seem □ *The doleful, taciturn image he represents to the public is **far removed from** the jovial father his family knows.* OBS □ *The 3½ litre Rover V8 engine is **not** so very **far removed from** a now obsolete Buick engine, manufactured in America by General Motors.* ST □ *I know that among journalists can be found people who started their work-*

ing life in jobs **far removed from** *newspapers.* NS □ *The Highland games at Kirkintilloch—with small girls dancing reels and cabers thumping the ground—are* **a far remove from** *the ordered magnificence of the Olympic Games.* RT □ variant a far remove from sth.

far and wide [adv + adv non-rev] (to) everywhere; (to) all, or many, places or directions **V:** look, search, (for sb/sth); reach, spread, scatter □ *'It appears she's come down to infant-teach at Albert Road, the renown of which must have spread* **far and wide**, *because her home is located as far away as—' 'I knew that,' Patrick Standish managed to interrupt.* TGLY □ *Fest's view of Hitler as 'the point of convergence' for the 'intersecting moods of the age' exonerates the Germans, or at least spreads the blame* **far and wide**. OBS □ *By the 8th century the Church at Rome was already a power whose influence reached* **far and wide** *in secular as well as spiritual affairs.* ⇨ ⚠ far and near.

fast/sound asleep [Comp (AdjP)] comfortably and deeply asleep **V:** ⚠ be, fall □ *There's nothing to worry about. I looked into the children's bedroom while I was upstairs and they were both* **fast asleep**. □ *The thieves would have happily resorted to violence—so it was fortunate for the night-watchman that he was* **sound asleep** *in his office for the whole time they were in the warehouse.*

fast bind, fast find/safe bind, safe find (saying) if you safeguard your property it will be there for your use when you want it and/or as you left it □ (police poster) *Going On Holiday? Then remember,* **fast bind, fast find**. *Leave your doors and windows secured with adequate locks and inform a neighbour or your local police officer.* □ *Although the housekeeper did not actually distrust any of her staff, she preferred, on the principle of* **safe bind, safe find**, *to keep the store cupboards locked and have the servants come and ask her for anything they required.* □ *My wife's a stickler for putting things back in their places. '***Safe bind, safe find**,*' she's alway saying.* □ fast here = 'safely; firmly'.

a fast etc buck (informal) money quickly and easily made or earned, esp with disregard for higher values or other people's interests **adj:** fast, ⚠ quick; easy □ *That was when most property was in the hands of Blackpool people—now it's owned by vast companies who don't care about the town and its people, just* **the fast buck**. RT □ *'But we aren't going to chase after every situation that promises to make* **a quick buck**,*' Lee says. 'We want to move cautiously and firmly, building up a reputation here of a bank that offers a good deal more than just lending facilities.'* ST □ *Bess Myerson sometimes gets into trouble, but because she is always and irrefutably on the side of 'the little guy who gets stomped on in New York,' she bids fair to make the Mecca of* **the fast buck** *a marginally more honest city.* ST □ buck (US informal) = 'dollar'. ⇨ ⚠ easy money.

fast and furious [adj + adj non-rev] exciting, frenzied or hilarious □ *Father swore he was right and mother swore he was wrong and, various members of the family siding with one or the other of them, the argument raged* **fast and furious** *for an hour and more.* □ *The shelter had to be completed before darkness fell and as the sun slid down to the horizon the pace of work grew ever more* **fast and furious**. □ *'Life is what yer* (= you) *make it' is a vulgarly unfunny programme where the audience response seems to have been filled in by the sound engineer, with the jokes coming* **fast, furious** *and feeble.* L □ may function as A, as in first example.

a fast worker [Comp (NP)] (informal) sb clever at establishing relations quickly with sb of the opposite sex, either in some particular instance or as a characteristic ability **V:** ⚠ be; think, find, sb □ *'Is it true you got married, Jenny?' she asked at once. 'Why didn't you tell us about it?' 'I didn't know myself until just before it happened.' 'I wouldn't have thought you were such* **a fast worker**.*'* AITC □ *'I don't like the idea of Pat going out with a fellow twelve years older than herself,' said her father. 'Particularly when he's already got the reputation of being* **a** *pretty* **fast worker**.*'* □ also pl.

a fat etc lot of good etc [Comp (NP)] (informal) little or no good etc **V:** ⚠ be, do sb. **adj:** fat, ⚠ damned, great. **o:** good, ⚠ help, use. **cl:** that is, he'll be, you were; they talk □ *Major Penrose said gloomily, '***A damned lot of good** *they'll be in action. As likely as not shoot our fellows in the back.'* BM □ *All the points were first made more than 10 years ago—not least in a Young Fabian pamphlet, some of which we printed in this journal. And* **a fat lot of good** *it did us or them.* NS □ usu ironic and exclamatory; usu front position in an inverted construction.

a fat price etc a high price etc **n:** price, ⚠ sum, profit, return; salary □ *His latest novel has an exotic Italian contessa rudely forcing a young composer away from his wife for* **fat sums** *to satisfy her need for possession.* NS □ *He would hide his diamond hoard near one of the beaches and come back to the coast by plane or boat. It would mean paying* **a fat price** *to a pilot but probably a few hundred pounds would be enough.* DS □ *Willy could pay the excess* (postage)*;* **the fat profits** *of his swindling firm could cope with that.* US □ *Now it happened that Karl had once been a police informer in Kimberley, and he had not forgotten* **the fat rewards** *you could get for successful informing.* SD

the fat years and the lean years contrasting periods of prosperity and hardship in sb's life, a business, a country's history, etc (from GENESIS XLI 1-36) □ *He talks about the debt he owes his wife, Rena, who has helped him through the 27 years of their marriage which, like so many, has faced the problems of coping with* **the fat years and the lean**. TVT □ *We* (Israel) *had* **the fat years**. *Now we'll have* **the lean years**, *divided into several structural units.* NS □ *Like all highly successful writers, he has to pay a huge percentage of his earnings to the Inland Revenue, regardless of the fact that* **the lean years** *for the self-employed outnumber* **the fat years** *by seven to one.* SC □ **The fat years** *are over now for the British doctors of Calgary. A British doctor wouldn't get a licence so easily now, in fact he might not get one at all.* OBS □ either part of headphrase may be used alone; stress pattern the ˌfat years and the ˈlean years.

a fate worse than death [O/o (NP)] (facetious) to be seduced or raped **V:** suffer, meet (with), face, endure; escape □ (article heading) *The lady who escaped **a fate worse than death**.* TVT □ *In 'Callisto' we see the innocent virgin who takes up a cause with such passion that she blindly slides into her seduction without really being aware that it is happening, and she goes willingly to **her fate worse than death**.* L □ (NONCE) (the 'Tantra' carvings) *The smiles of the women suffering **a fate better than death** are charming.* NS

a father figure sb seen, or accepted, as the psychological equivalent of a father (in any relevant role, eg authoritarian, benevolent, protective, repressive, disciplining) □ *Perhaps the authority of **the father figure** was less established in fact. More and more the Victorian family seems to belong to the class of powerful myths.* L □ *Syria, on my count, has had 22 régimes in the past 28 years. But now* (1971) *it seems to have discovered **a father figure**.* L □ *But let us now look back as cricket came out from under the shadow of **that** great **father-figure**, W G Grace.* L □ (a driving instructor) *They were terrified of me as well as the car. Well, I was **a** sort of **father figure** to them, and perhaps they were frightened of their fathers.* OBS □ also pl.

the father and mother of a row etc [Comp/O (NP)] (informal) an outstanding example of a row etc (esp sth noisy, violent or unpleasant) **V:** be, turn into; start, stir up. **n:** row, quarrel, fuss, uproar; crash, thunderclap, storm; lie; mess □ *My views on how to tackle the problem were not considered right and proper and there was **the father-and-mother of a row**.* MFM □ *After a long walk through dark, lonely lanes in what promised to be **the father and mother of all thunderstorms**, I at last chanced upon the church.* BM □ (television programme) *If they were stopped, as 'World in Action' has been stopped from showing 'South of the Border', at least we'd know — and there would be **the mother and father of a** public **fuss** about it.* OBS

the fault is in ourselves, not in our stars (saying) we are not what fate makes us, but what we make ourselves; our own mistakes, lack of ability, misuse of opportunity, etc are the cause of our misfortunes or sufferings □ (source) *Men at some times are masters of their fates:/**The fault**, dear Brutus, **is not in our stars**,/But **in ourselves**, that we are underlings.* JULIUS CAESAR I 2 □ *It is very annoying that we do not always enjoy doing what is right, but **the fault is** probably **in ourselves, not in our stars**.* WDM

fear the Greeks, bearing gifts (saying) be (rightly) suspicious about gifts, or benefits, offered by certain people □ (source) (translated from the Latin, the reference being to the wooden horse given to the Trojans by the Greeks who had first concealed their own soldiers inside it) *Do not trust the horse, Trojans. Whatever it is, I **fear the Greeks, even when they bring gifts**.* AENEID II 48 (VIRGIL 70-19 BC) □ *With colleagues on other newspapers, I have pleaded that the twenty local BBC stations should have access to medium waves as well as VHF. Now Sir John Eden, Minister of Posts and Communications, has answered our prayer. Yet still I **fear the Greeks, gift-bearing**.* ST □ *'A very handsome present, Colin,' the old lady said. 'It must have cost quite a bit. But I was taught a long time ago to **beware of the Greeks who bring gifts**. What is it that you want?'* ARG □ *Any piece of good fortune that came his way he tended to think of as **a Greek gift**, to be paid for later by some counter-balancing misfortune or mishap.* □ often used allusively and with variations in wording; variant a Greek gift.

a feast for the eyes etc [Comp (NP)] sth satisfying and delightful to see etc; be a sight for sore eyes (qv) **V:** ⚠ be; find, make, sth. **o:** the eyes, ⚠ the ears, the senses; the mind, the soul □ *Bales of cheap printed cottons in gay colours made **a feast for the eyes**.* TCB □ *Probably, though, what will most turn on Barbara's admirers is the prospect of a film compilation of the* best 'Carry On's', ***a feast for eyes and senses**, out next March.* TVT □ *Perhaps the audiences of ancient Greeks rose from their seats purified and enlarged, as Aristotle suggests. I haven't seen much from contemporary dramatists that would qualify as **a feast for the soul**.*

a feast of talent etc an abundance and/or great display of talent etc **n:** talent, wit; colour, delights □ *'All About Eve' is another film much requested by viewers. I can only commend Mankiewicz's literate, witty, caustic and penetrating script as chief delight among such **a feast of talent** that one wonders if we will ever see its like again.* RT

a feather in one's cap [Comp/O (NP)] sth achieved that constitutes a victory, triumph, credit for oneself (from a former custom of various peoples, among them the American Indians, of adding a feather to their headgear for every enemy killed) **V:** be, make sth; get □ *Debs'* (debutantes') *mums think it's **a** definite **feather in their caps** if their daughters get asked to Trinity* (College, Cambridge) *Ball. Trinity is very royal and aristo* (= aristocratic), *it has glamour.* ST □ *Desmond had got the names of a number of the men at the mines who were stealing, and these people were sacked and blacklisted. So the Diamond Detectives got quite a lot of **feathers in their cap**.* DS □ *Obviously it would be **a feather in their cap** if they could get this scheme off the ground without a public inquiry.* SC □ also pl a feather in their cap(s).

feather one's (own) nest [V + O pass] look after one's own interests, esp by accumulating money or property (the implication almost always being that greed, selfishness or dishonesty is involved) □ *It is generally assumed that politicians are: 'All twisters/crooks.' 'Only out for their own ends.' 'Feathering their own nests.' 'Looking after number one.'* UL □ *The myth that employers of labour are all unscrupulously exploiting humanity for the sake of profit is balanced by that which presents trade-unionists as all purblind opportunists **feathering their own nest** at the economy's expense.* L □ (NONCE) *The film industry's **own nest-featherers**, and local politicians looking for a vote-catching cause, all have an interest in shouting for stricter controls.* L □ *I'm sure she **feathered her nest** well after they got too old and confused to be bothered with housekeeping accounts.*

feed a cold and starve a fever (saying) eat well if you have a cold, eat little if you have a fever □ *Helen Mirren believes you* ***feed a cold and starve a fever****. Snuffling into a restaurant's paper napkin, she looks at the food arranged in a stainless steel goblet and slaps it on to a large plate.* OBS

feel one's age [V + O] realize from one's failing powers, altered outlook, etc that one is growing old □ *Men of that age and type can't bear the sight of old people. It reminds them that they're getting on. Ha, and he's* ***feeling his age****, I hear.* MM □ *I know I'm not exactly young any more but, really, I never* ***felt my age*** *till this last winter.* □ *Yes, thank you, grandfather is pretty well—****feeling his age*** *of course, but that's only to be expected.* ⇨ ⚠ be (only) as old as one feels.

feel (all) (the) better for (having done) sth [V + Comp] feel that one's physical, or mental, well-being has been improved by (having done) sth □ *The letter could not be posted for another twenty-four hours, but I* ***felt*** *much* ***better for having*** *written it.* SPL □ *I had begun to feel a bit paunchy, but now I'm down to my fighting weight of 12½ stone, and I'm* ***feeling*** *all* ***the better for*** *it.* RT □ *Leave her alone. She's very likely to* ***feel better for having*** *had a good cry.* □ *Of course, sun is welcome, but so are clouds. I* ***feel better for*** *rain on the face, and I revel in snow. For me all weather is good.* OBS

feel the draught [V + O pass] feel unpleasantly cold air blowing gently round one inside a house, room etc; (fig) be made aware of some adverse change, or the threat of such change, affecting one, esp financially □ *Scotland has the unenviable distinction of being top of the unemployment league. Even the prosperous Midlands are* ***feeling the draught****.* SC □ *It* (America) *is on the way out. Finished. Doomed. And then will you fellows in Europe* ***feel the draught****!* ILIH

feel good [V + Comp] feel happy, confident, pleased with oneself, virtuous □ DAVID: *I want to be a crooner. I want to switch on the radio—any time and any day—and hear my voice on records.* SAM: *Why, Davey? Why have you got these crazy ideas?* DAVID: *I* ***feel good*** *when I'm singing.* HSG □ *I might not have let her off with that remark on another occasion, but I had just downed a couple of whiskies and was* ***feeling good****.* □ *People donate money to charities not so much because they are concerned to* do *good, but because it makes them* ***feel good****.* □ *No wonder Mark Twain said of the perils of fame, 'It's a rough business. Shakespeare's dead, Dickens is dead, and I do****n't feel so good*** *myself.'* OBS □ neg variant not feel (so) good = 'not feel well'.

feel like (doing) sth think that one would enjoy, be willing to accept, or take part in, (doing) sth □ *...having to be gay and lively for Joe and always ready to listen when he wanted to talk, and being sometimes kept up half the night if he* ***felt like*** *a party.* AITC □ *Stick the beauty page for another two weeks, and you can come back to editorial. I* ***feel like*** *economizing. You can do two people's work.* AITC □ *They clustered round Mr Roderick eagerly, and some of the other guests, those who* ***felt like*** *hearing the story again, came over and added themselves to the audience.* HD □ *He was cold and chilled. 'Flu coming on,' he thought. He didn't* ***feel like*** *anything to eat.* TO □ *'Does anybody* ***feel like*** *a game of poker?' he asked hopefully, but nobody did.*

feel/look like a million dollars (informal) feel/look extremely well, happy, proud, handsome, beautiful etc □ *I'm on holiday, it's a beautiful morning, and I* ***feel like a million dollars****.* □ *It's good to see you both again. Jake, you* ***look like a million dollars****!*

feel like a new man/woman feel restored to health, completely refreshed or revitalized □ *Take one of these tablets every morning and you'll soon* ***feel like a new man****.* □ *As soon as I started in my new job I* ***felt like a new woman****.*

feel/look like nothing on earth (informal) feel/look extremely ill, miserable, strange, ridiculous etc □ *That dreadful period when you're just coming out of an anaesthetic and* ***feeling like nothing on earth*** *is not the time when you want a visitor, however well-intentioned.* □ *It could have been quite a pleasant room if she hadn't cluttered it up with a hundred and one so-called* objets d'art *that* ***looked like nothing on earth****.*

feel one's oats [V + O] (informal) be in an energetic, lively, perhaps obstreperous, mood and act accordingly (from a horse well fed on oats) □ (Father Christmases, in the big London stores went on strike) *One wonders just what induced them to take such a step. Something obviously has got their back up. Perhaps their reindeer have been* ***feeling their oats****, perhaps...* SC □ *They're a bit rough and noisy but no real trouble—just a bunch of healthy lively kids* ***feeling their oats****.* □ *'I thought I'd be too tired to do anything more than lie about, but I'm beginning to* ***feel my oats*** *already.' 'It's all this fine fresh air and home-cooking that does it.'* □ usu in continuous tenses.

feel the pinch [V + O] (informal) suffer from a lack of sth (usu money) □ *Lisa's money* (a legacy) *will make a great difference to a man of Guy's tastes. He has been* ***feeling the pinch*** *lately.* MM □ (headline) *Press* ***Feeling the Pinch****. The newspaper publishers are claiming that they are being hurt by rapidly rising costs at the same time as circulations remain stagnant.* SC □ *The big fat cat entertainment industry of the past decade is* ***feeling the pinch****; in hard times the record industry cannot take a chance on something new, different and possibly good—they must go for tried and true trash.* G

feel etc small [V + Comp] feel, appear etc inadequate, despised, humiliated **V:** feel, ⚠ look; make sb □ *Harold had been left at the end of the interview* ***feeling*** *very* ***small****. Not* ***looking small****; Alec had saved his face, had managed to give the Inspector the impression that Harold backed him up.* PW □ *One doesn't meet so many men of stature in this puking little world and his greatest thing was that he never made one* ***feel small****.* HAA □ *A good teacher does not indulge in sarcasm. Children can be guided or reproved or, for that matter, punished, without being* ***made to feel*** *or* ***look small****.*

feel one's way [V + O] determine (eg in darkness) where one is going by touching walls, (natural) objects, putting one foot in front of the other cautiously to avoid obstacles etc; (fig) proceed cautiously in an undertaking, adjusting one's plans and ideas according to circumstances **A:** along the passage; through the hazards; towards a solution □ *Is Mrs Gandhi* ***feeling her way*** *towards some kind of 'guided democracy' in which opposition is tolerated provided it is tame?* G □ *'I can't see anything wrong with your idea. When are you going to start on it?' But Miss Heath said it was no good rushing one's fences and she must* ***feel her way****.* WDM □ *It was the first training scheme of its kind and we would have to* ***feel our way*** *carefully to avoid unforeseen difficulties.*

feelings etc run high feelings etc are intensifying **n:** feelings, ⚠ loyalties, resentment, tempers □ *National* ***feelings*** *on the subject* (the military campaign in North-West Europe, 1944) *have tended to* ***run high*** *and in particular American writers have launched heavy attacks on the British conduct of operations.* MFM □ *In committee heads were shaken, not much was said, yet* ***feelings ran high****. Luke was one of those figures who have the knack, often surprising to themselves, of stirring up controversy.* NM □ *And although* ***militancy*** *among workers is* ***running higher*** *now than for decades, it may well die out if it is not nourished and informed with a strategy for social change.* NS

one's feet etc are killing one one's feet etc are sore, causing one pain **n:** feet; shoes, collar, tie, girdle, belt, trousers; suitcase, rucksack □ HELEN: *Oh my God,* ***my feet are killing me****. How I got* (= carried) *that lot from the bus stop I'll never know.* TOH □ *The Northampton Museum of Boots and Shoes has records from ancient times containing complaints from Egyptians that* ***their feet were killing them****—and blaming the shoemakers for their discomfort.* TVT □ *...women, lost in girlish romantic memories, who have forgotten momentarily that* ***their girdles are killing them****.* TVT □ usu first person; not used in this way of other named parts of the body, though the pain in my back was killing me is possible.

(a) fellow feeling [O/o (NP)] sympathy with, and a desire to help or support, other people □ ***A fellow-feeling*** *makes one wond'rous kind.* ON QUITTING THE THEATRE (D GARRICK 1717-1779) **V:** show, demonstrate, display, express □ *The mind is its own place, and the places inhabited by the insane and the exceptionally gifted are so different from the places where ordinary men and women live, that there is little or no common ground of memory to serve as a basis for understanding or* ***fellow feeling****.* DOP □ *The doctor has* ***a fellow feeling*** *for his migraine patients, since he suffers from it himself.*

a fellow traveller [Comp (NP)] sb who, without being a full member, associates himself with, sympathizes with, and supports an organization or principle (esp Communism) **V:** ⚠ be, become; regard sb as □ *Dozens of talented writers in Western countries declared their sympathy with the Stalinist 'experiment' while it was in progress. The more eminent of them were taken on tours of the Soviet Union and, if their enthusiasm survived the experience, they returned to serve on committees dedicated to pro-Soviet causes and to the justification of Stalinism. They were called* ***fellow-travellers****.* NS □ *I've never joined the Labour Party—perhaps because I find it too much of an uneasy mixture of policies and factions. I suppose you could call me a* ***fellow-travelling*** *Socialist Liberal in search of a cause.* □ adj and n compound fellow-travelling. ⇨ ⚠ a card-carrying member etc.

the female of the species is more deadly than the male (saying) a derogatory, or joking, expression used of women, comparing them unfavourably with men □ (source) *But the she-bear thus accosted rends the peasant tooth and nail/For* ***the female of the species is more deadly than the male****.* THE FEMALE OF THE SPECIES (R KIPLING 1865-1936) □ ***The females of the species are most dangerous*** *when they appear to retreat.* ARCHY DOES HIS PART (D MARQUIS 1878-1931) □ *'Both the Richardsons are amusing but Jack's wit is never cruel.' 'Well, you know what they say about* ***the female of the species being deadlier than the male****.'* □ *And what about Margaret (****the female of the species is more deadly than the male****, 'Daily Express') McKearney, billed as the IRA's Number One Single-Handed-Mistress-of-Disguises 21-year-old Long-Legged Blonde Super-Bomber?* G □ an imitation of a possible zoological comment on a species eg a poisonous spider.

the festive season (cliché) the few days around and including Christmas □ *He expressed the desire that if it met with your convenience you should remain as his guest over* ***the festive season****.* EM □ *During December all the counters on the ground floor of the store were given over to the display of gifts, decorations and cards for* ***the festive season****.*

few and far between [Comp (AdjP)] small in number and widely dispersed; scarce; seldom occurring or found **V:** ⚠ be, become, seem □ *Since signal communications were so inadequate, the Command Post could be set up only at places —* ***few and far between****—where the international buried cable system came to the surface.* MFM □ *You see, in a town this size the number of people who take any interest in intellectual pursuits, politics and the arts and that, they're pretty* ***few and far between****.* TGLY □ *Although the Royal Ballet is full of good dancers, it is short of star personalities. Nureyev has not been engaged at all for next season. Fonteyn's appearances have become* ***few and far between****.* NS

a few home truths [O (NP)] outspoken assessment, or criticism, of sb or his behaviour usu in order to point out his faults or shortcomings to him personally **V:** tell, give, sb; hear, learn, listen to. **det:** a few, some, one or two □ *'You heard,' she called back. '****A few home truths*** *might do you a bit of good.'* LLDR □ HELEN: *Now you're going to listen to* ***a few home truths****, my girl.* JO: *We've had enough* ***home truths****!* TOH □ *'Teaching's had me, I can tell you that, and I've been waiting to tell you bloody lot* ***a few home truths*** *for—' 'Try not to swear,' said Richie. 'It only weakens your case.'* TT □ *Having once led a strike, I know* ***one or two*** *uncomfortable, improbable* ***home truths*** *about the business which seem to elude the TV interviewers.* ST □ *I admire 'Man Alive' and I like those programmes in which humble citizens are able to deliver* ***a few home truths*** *to Authority.* L

(in) a few well-chosen words [A (PrepP)] (cliché) (using) a brief, but comprehensive and appropriate, statement or description **V:** ⚠ tell, sb; say, express, sth □ *...all failing to clarify some point that could have been made* ***in a few well-chosen words****, if anybody involved had been capable of doing the choosing.* OBS □ *...and* ***the few, well-chosen words*** *of criticism with which he could quietly splinter someone's too-lengthy conclusion.* TCM □ *He suggested, since I was out of a job, I might like to give him a hand in the shop 'for experience' — meaning he wouldn't pay me. I told him* ***in a few, well-chosen words*** *what I thought of that idea.* □ often facetious, as here.

fiddle while Rome burns (saying) behave frivolously in a situation that calls for concern or corrective action (from a legend that the Roman emperor, Nero, played a violin while his capital was being devastated by fire) □ *Meanwhile, plans are going forward for a new Opera House and an enormous sports stadium and swimming pool in a city where over half the population are inadequately or insanitarily housed. This is* ***fiddling while Rome burns****.* □ (NONCE) (the world's population 'explosion'). *They say that things are so bad nothing can be done. This is awful. The situation must be shown to have some hope, or we might as well* ***dish out violins and start fiddling****.* OBS □ (NONCE) *The novel is rich in evidence of the trivial snobberies and hypocrisies which obsess our upper and upper-middle classes as they* ***fiddle while London smoulders****.* L □ often adapted, as shown.

a field day [Comp/O) (NP)] a day, or other period, full of special excitement, important events, profitable or pleasing activity (from a military term meaning 'a day when troops carry out manoeuvres, have field-practice in mock warfare') **V:** be, make...for sb; have, enjoy □ *Mrs Craddock was delighted by Bernard's speech, delighted by all the speeches; it was* ***a field day*** *for her, of course. She told Eric and Alan so a hundred times and rather loudly.* HAA □ *New York was then abominably plagued by racketeers who made* ***a field-day*** *out of the awkward fact that Manhattan is an island.* L □ *Two people were discussing someone they knew, and having* ***a field day*** *with his reputation. Then it dawned on me that I knew the person they were tearing to shreds.* RT

fight the good fight [V + O] act with strong commitment to sth □ (source) ***Fight the good fight*** *of faith, lay hold on eternal life...* I TIMOTHY VI, 12 □ ***Fight the good fight*** *with all thy might,/Christ is thy strength and Christ thy right.* ENGLISH HYMNAL 389 □ *...missionaries who* ***fought the good fight*** *at the sacrifice of their health (and pockets) and did a great deal of good.* RT □ *The Society chairman had* ***fought the good fight*** *for the conservation society by going round personally to see planning offenders, to argue with them with calm and polite good sense.* NS

fight like Kilkenny cats fight so violently and/or persistently that both, or all, parties are defeated or destroyed (from an Irish story of two cats who fought each other till there was nothing left but their tails) □ *They* ***fought like Kilkenny cats*** *—and the only result of their quarrel was that they both lost the respect of those who had supported them.* □ (NONCE) *The two men fought for the girl, over a period of months, but it was* ***a Kilkenny cat fight****—she was so sickened by their behaviour that she dropped them both.*

fight like a tiger attack sb/defend oneself with ruthless energy/savagery □ *Except as regards its natural prey the weasel is a timid animal but will* ***fight like a tiger*** *in defence of its young.* □ *But he* (Frank Sinatra) ***fought like a tiger*** *for the part of the little Italian Maggio in the film, 'From Here to Eternity'—a gamble which paid off with an Oscar and a new world fame.* H □ also pl fight like tigers.

fight a losing battle [V + O pass] struggle without success to achieve, or prevent, sth □ (obtaining a mortgage on old property) *We too will be joining the rush into suburbia as our hopes and energies rapidly diminish in* ***the losing battle*** *we've been* ***fighting****.* SC □ (reader's letter) *I am trying desperately hard to bring up children in a decent way, and sick and tired of* ***fighting a losing battle****. What assurances have I and mothers like me that scenes of this nature will not be included in children's programmes again?* RT

fight etc tooth and nail fight etc with energy and determination, using every means one has **V:** fight, ⚠ struggle; oppose sb/sth; defend oneself □ *Industry has been pressing hard for the abolition of the fuel-oil duty, which adds to industrial costs; and the local Board has been* ***fighting tooth-and-nail*** *on the other side.* OBS □ CISSIE: *You ought to be ashamed of yourselves, I told them, after the Union* ***struggled*** *hard* ***tooth and nail*** *for every penny you get, and at the first sign of intimidation you want to give in.* CSWB □ *Were I a British subject (a status which under suitable conditions I would deem a great privilege), I would* ***fight*** *British entry into the EEC* ***tooth and nail****.* NS □ *When I ventured to criticize her husband's behaviour she* ***fell upon*** *me* ***tooth and nail****.* □ more often used of struggles to achieve some end than of physical combat.

fighting fit [Comp (AdjP)] in exceptionally good physical condition; fit for energetic action and/or endurance of hardship; in good general health **V:** ⚠ be, become, get □ *This little flyweight* (boxer) *weighs 8 stones, every ounce of him* ***fighting fit****.* SC □ *'And how are you feeling today?' 'Not exactly what you'd call* ***fighting fit****, but improving.'* □ *Mailer scarcely yields to his 50 years. His middle-aged spread has all but vanished. If less disposed to fight, he is* ***fighting fit*** *again.* ST

fighting talk/words a defiant statement or challenge; a declaration which will involve one in having to defend, or substantiate, it □ *'To deride the hope of progress is the ultimate fatuity, the last word in poverty of spirit and meanness of mind.'* ***Fighting words*** *indeed.* NS □ *'I want to race where it comes down to who's toughest, who can push himself the farthest into that kind of exhaustion.'* ***Fighting talk*** *at 21, especially when the event has never been won by anyone under 25.* RT □ often used as a comment when quoting, or reporting, such a statement.

a figment of the/one's imagination [Comp (NP)] sth imagined; sth supposed to be real but which is in fact not so **V:** ⚠ be, seem; regard sth as □ *Among these* ***figments of the imagination*** *appear such varied objects as the* *philosopher's stone, the Oedipus complex, and the houris.* SNP □ *Had I really seen a face peering out from among the reeds or had it been merely* ***a figment of my imagination****?* □ *Long before marriage I suspected that a spoilt child was not just* ***a figment of a*** *stern Victorian* ***imagination*** *but something real and nasty.* OBS

a figure of fun [Comp (NP)] a person who looks, or is made to look, foolish or ridiculous in appearance and/or behaviour **V:** ⚠ be, become, turn into, look □ *To him the novelist was, if not exactly* ***a figure of fun****, then at any rate someone who was playing at life and therefore not to be taken quite seriously as a man.* PW □ *The holiday-maker* (at the seaside) *is portrayed as* ***a*** *bingo-crazed* ***figure of fun****, getting locked out of his hotel, losing the bus station, getting sick on shellfish, chips and beer.* SC □ *No, I'm not going to change my clothes to please you. I intend to be warm and comfortable in the boat whether I look like* ***a figure of fun*** *or not.* □ also pl figures of fun.

fill/fit the bill [V + O] be satisfactory, or adequate, for a defined or understood purpose; satisfy all the requirements of a function or role (bill here refers to a theatre or advertising poster) □ *I would stand there in my sensible shoes that would '****fill the bill*** *on most occasions'.* HH □ *But sometimes solid food doesn't* ***fill the bill****. During illness, for example, or simply between meals.* □ *...a calculating, ingenious book, which is described as a thriller but doesn't quite* ***fit the bill****.* NS □ *For a man who regularly provides* (a radio programme) *with a guide to shopping, John Leese admirably* ***fits the bill****. At 6ft 3ins, and a number of pounds over 300, he admits: 'I'm no gastronome but I do enjoy my food.'* RT *...do whatever heads of state have to do with efficiency and grace. Better still if it is done within the context of a happy family life. Edward VII, an unattractive, self-indulgent roué, would not* ***fit the*** *royal* ***bill*** *today.* L

fill sb's shoes [V + O pass] adequately take over sb's function, role □ *We face, moreover, impending changes in the political leadership of the world's most influential states. The men who* ***fill their shoes****, at whose identity we can only guess, may make an unexpected imprint upon world politics.* L □ *The old doctor was worshipped round here. The son's a nice enough young man, but he'll never* ***fill*** *his father****'s shoes****.*

filthy lucre money, or financial gain, as something to be despised □ (source) *A bishop must be blameless, as the steward of God; not selfwilled, not soon angry, not given to wine, no striker, not given to* ***filthy lucre****.* TITUS I 7 □ PETER: *Inside that safe — packets and packets of lovely,* ***filthy lucre****.* DPM □ (a golf tournament) *No advertisements are allowed to disfigure the scene either inside or outside the grounds—nor is any mention of* ***filthy lucre*** *permitted. All the television directors and commentators have to submit to a solemn lecture forbidding mention of money in any form.* ST □ usu facetious, as here.

the final solution a way of dealing with a problem that will be completely and permanently effective □ *...Treblinka, the notorious concentration camp, where a single-line railway track ended a stone's throw away from the gas chambers, and where the Nazis were putting into practice* ***their final solution*** *of the Jewish problem, by which they meant the Jewish people.* OBS □ *Mescalin can never solve that problem: it can only pose it.* ***The*** *full and* ***final solution*** *can be found only by those who....* DOP □ (BBC investigatory programme about gypsies in Britain) *But what was achieved? There was no verdict, so what action does 'Time for Action' think it is time for? Armed confrontation? Government intervention?* ***A final solution****?* L □ expression now widely recognized as a grim euphemism for the Nazi policy (under Hitler) of mass extermination of Jewish people living in Germany or in countries under German control.

find etc one's bearings [V + O] get to know etc where one is, what to do, in a new location, social situation, employment etc **V:** find, ⚠ get, take; give sb; lose □ *Though I had lived in Birmingham as a child, the city had altered so much it took me some time to* ***find my bearings*** *again.* □ *John's experience had been with a legal practice that didn't do much court work, so the retiring partner agreed to stay on till he'd* ***got his bearings****.* □ *But other fantasies seem to belong to the world of the paranoid. I do not doubt that these are the kinds of fabrications with which those who have* ***lost their bearings*** *in life attempt to re-inject meaning into things.* NS

find etc a better hole [V + O] (catchphrase) find etc a situation, a place, a home, a job etc, which is an improvement on the one that one has now, that one was in previously **V:** find, ⚠ look for, have, get □ (source) (a cartoon picture of the First World War showing a soldier—Old Bill—in a battered, muddy trench saying to another soldier) *Well, if you* ***knows of a better hole****, go to it.* C B BAIRNSFATHER 1888-1959 □ *And will you now please give a thought to our Todday Monster, to Old Bill who has gone off to* ***find*** *himself* ***a better hole****. Let us wish him a safe return to his icy home.* RM □ (work in the BBC) *You learned to examine your craft because you had to tell other writers what needed changing and what wouldn't work. I couldn't have* ***found a better hole****.* SC

find one's feet [V + O] gain experience and the knowledge of what best to do in new surroundings, a new job, etc; achieve a settled outlook and purpose in life □ *The 1st Canadian division had not been in action before and officers and men were just beginning to* ***find their feet****.* MFM □ *It was good experience for her, for it enabled her to* ***find her feet*** *in the new country and to learn a little of its ways.* RFW □ *It may be that our playwrights would have broken out of this* (rigid set of rules and conventions) *in any event. There were signs of it happening as early as 1956, when television drama was still* ***finding its feet****.* RT □ MR SEGAL: *Excuse me, Sam, but you must agree; he's good for nothing.* SAM: *There I disagree with you, Mr Segal. he'll* ***find his feet****.* HSG

find one's vocation [V + O] find, esp after trying other work or activities, the work or function that best suits one's abilities and inclinations **adj:** real, true □ *With two films under his belt Jeffries was directing his third with all the éclat and exhaustion of a man who'd* ***found his vocation*** *late in life.* RT □ (from a diary) *25 September: My first lecture — at last I've* ***found my*** *true* ***vocation****. There were more than 200* *students, ranging from fresh-faced late teens to grizzled heads; I loved them on sight.* OBS ⇨ miss one's vocation.

find sb/sth wanting [V + O + Comp pass] judge that sb/sth does not meet a required, or expected, standard of behaviour, efficiency, suitability □ (source) *Thou art weighed in the balance, and art* ***found wanting****. Thy kingdom is divided, and given to the Medes and Persians.* DANIEL V 27-8 □ *Shaw applauded Nietzsche for laying low false ideals, but* ***found*** *him* ***wanting*** *politically.* NS □ *Our British leaders receive power with modesty; they lose it with resignation, if not with exhilaration. But when weighed in the balance they are not* ***found wanting****.* MFM □ *Fashions in education are constantly changing as various methods are tried and all, in some degree,* ***found wanting****.*

find one's way (to sth) [V + O] reach a destination, or objective, by search, inquiry, or experiment; (facetious) arrive, be found, somewhere by fortuituous or unexplained means **S:** traveller; researcher; coat, key, wallet □ *Don't bother to meet me at the station. I'm sure I'll be able to* ***find my way to*** *your house by myself.* □ *Reluctantly defensive of his family, he is drawn to the liberals, until he sees how they insensitively try to turn individual desperation to immediate political ends. Yet at least he determines, patiently and painfully, to* ***find his*** *own* ***way*** *in****to*** *reality, without selling out his consciousness to any factions.* NS □ *'Here are your cigarettes in the refrigerator.' 'Good God! How on earth did they* ***find their way*** *there?'* □ *The new* (Italian) *Government's first act has been to impose exchange controls on all those suitcases of bank-notes that traditionally* ***find their way to*** *Switzerland the moment there's a money crisis.* L

finding is keeping (saying) if you find something, then it is rightfully your property □ (Colin has picked up a packet with two cigarettes in it, from the gutter.) *'Come on,' Bert said, cajoling, threatening, 'let's 'ave* (= have) *one.' Colin stood firm.* ***Finding was keeping****. 'I'm saving 'em for our dad.'* LLDR □ *'That's my ball! I lost it in the park yesterday!' 'I don't believe you. Anyway,* ***finders keepers****.'* □ said, esp by children, as a claim to ownership, of sth found; variants finders keepers, findings keepings.

a fine body of men etc [Comp (NP)] (cliché) an admirable group of men etc **V:** ⚠ be, seem, appear. **n:** men, women; soldiers, amateurs, sportsmen; criminals, incompetents □ *I have nothing against Air Force pilots. I am sure they are* ***a fine body of men****. I just don't see that having been one qualifies Potter to run this firm.* □ *Philosophers, lawyers, scientists, diplomats, sociologists —* ***a fine body of men****, as Cyril Ray used to say, whenever he had occasion to refer to a provincial police force.* L □ *Do you know who trained our secret police, that* ***fine body of men****?* ILIH □ a conventional compliment, used esp of soldiers or policemen; stress pattern a 'fine body of men. ⇨ ⚠ a fine figure of a man etc.

fine and dandy [adj + adj non-rev] splendid, most satisfactory for one person or group only, or depending on an (as yet) unfulfilled condition □ *John wants to spend the whole vacation up at the log-cabin. As I said, '****Fine and dandy*** *for you, since you like fishing and climbing, but what am I supposed to do with* my *time?'* □ *What do they need another loan for now? I understood that everything was to be* ***fine and dandy*** *once Peter started his new job.* □ *'You can drive here in twenty minutes in your car,' she said. Which would have been* ***fine and dandy****, if I'd happened to have one.* □ often used as ironic comment on arrangements that suit another person.

fine feathers make fine birds (saying) an eye-catching outward appearance is necessary if one wants to attract attention, make a good impression, etc; (ironic) an impressive or showy appearance is no indication of merit or ability □ (source) *It is not only* ***fine feathers*** *that* ***make fine birds****.* FABLE: THE PEACOCK AND THE JAY (AESOP 620-560 BC) □ *As for the Elizabethan episode* (in a pageant), *Miss Crowder in her farthingale had never enjoyed herself so much, so much so indeed that her friend Miss Hopgood felt constrained when they got home to remind her that* ***fine feathers*** *did not* ***make fine birds****.* WDM □ *'****Fine feathers make fine birds****,' I tell him. 'If Susan had as much time and money to spend on her appearance as those Quigley girls have, she'd soon put them in the shade.'* □ *For the Trinity* (College, Cambridge) *May Ball, the fledglings had put on their* ***finest feathers****.* RT □ *But it's all window-dressing really. Our* ***fine-feathered*** *friend must keep well in with Britain and America now, since they weren't defeated by Hitler as he'd hoped.* ILIH □ use of expression with neg often indicates sarcasm; adj compound (attrib) fine-feathered; *a* ***fine-feathered*** *friend* used as term of scorn. ⇨ beauty is but/only skin deep.

a fine figure of a man etc [Comp (NP)] a man etc who is well-developed physically and of handsome, or impressive, appearance **V:** ⚠ be; find, think, sb. **n:** man, woman; sailor, Yorkshireman □ *I caught a glimpse of myself in a mirror and thought that I looked* ***a fine figure of a man****.* UTN □ MYRA: *Do put something on, Tony. You'll catch cold.* TONY: *I know, and then you'll have to nurse me* (drags on his black sweater). MILLY: *Eh, but he's* ***a fine figure of a boy****, that Tony.* EHOW □ *Mr MacLennan,* ***a fine figure of a Highlander*** *of the old school, gave our representative a vivid account of the amazing occurrence.* RM □ *I don't like your skinny pieces. I prefer what our grandfathers would have called '****a fine figure of a woman****'.* □ stress pattern a 'fine figure of a man. ⇨ ⚠ a fine body of men etc.

a fine etc kettle of fish a disagreeable, muddled, perplexing state of affairs **det:** a, what a, such a. **adj:** fine, ⚠ nice, pretty □ *'Here's* ***a fine kettle of fish****,' John said, returning to the car. 'The petrol pump's empty and there isn't another for 40 miles.'* □ *'Well, if they're going to sack me, Eliot,' he said, 'I've left them* ***a nice kettle of fish****.'* NM ⇨ ⚠ a (very) different kettle of fish.

a fine thing [Comp (NP)] an excellent procedure or state of affairs; a deplorable procedure etc **V:** ⚠ be; seem □ *It would be* ***a fine thing*** *if we could present to the electorate next time not only proposals for national superannuation, but a complete all-in plan for modernising social security.* OBS □ *What* ***a fine thing*** *it is that our city has been chosen as the site for the new* *university.* ▫ *Sit somewhere else, indeed! It's* ***a fine thing*** *when a man can't sit down on his own chair for fear of disturbing a cat!* ▫ *Through some slip-up in organization there was no one to meet our distinguished visitors on arrival.* ***A fine thing*** *to have happened when we'd been told first impressions would be important.* ▫ when used alone, as in last example, functions as ironic comment; stress pattern a 'fine thing.

a fine time (to do sth) [Comp (NP)] (ironic) an unsuitable time or too late a time (to do sth) **V:** ⚠ be, seem ▫ *'Jenny, someone on the phone for you.' 'Some joker, no doubt.' '****Fine*** *bloody* ***time to*** *be ringing a girl up, what?' 'Tell them the morning'll do.'* TGLY ▫ *'I don't feel like eating breakfast this morning.' 'Well, this is* ***a fine time to*** *tell me that. I could have saved myself the trouble of making it.'* ▫ *No, I'm not going to let you drive home with all that whisky inside you.* ***A fine time to*** *lose your licence this would be, just when you've got a job that depends on your having a car.* ▫ used as ironic comment; stress pattern a 'fine time to do sth.

fine words butter no parsnips (saying) flattery, expressions of sympathy, vague promises, etc do not help others, do not improve a situation; mere words are not enough ▫ *'****Fine words butter no parsnips****,' went on Bevill gravely, waving a finger at Martin, who in fact had not spoken. 'You chaps have got to deliver the goods.'* NM ▫ *Mr Carter reminded everybody at the so-called 'summit-meeting' in London that* ***fine words butter no parsnips*** *or whatever is the equivalent idiom of Georgia.* L ▫ (NONCE) *But I readily admit that by the end of the chat my unhealthy prejudice, as one born in the Forest of Dean, against Welshmen* ***buttering parsnips*** *with* ***fine words*** *and moist adjectives almost ebbed back within the proper confines of the Race Relations Act.* NS

one's finer feelings the better, or nobler, side of one's nature as contrasted with less worthy sentiments, urges, desires **V:** suppress, show; be governed by; (let)... get the better of one ▫ *I should not have repined because a brother had stamped down* ***his finer feelings*** *and done himself well out of it. Success did not come so often enough to those one was fond of that one's responses could be so delicate.* NM ▫ *I feel sorry for the people I have to evict, too. But if I were to be governed by* ***my finer feelings*** *I'd soon be out of a job and then where would I be?*

the finer points (of sth) the details, or aspects, of an art, skill, game, system etc which can be recognized or assessed only by those who have a full understanding or knowledge of it **V:** grasp, understand, appreciate; be well up in, be (well) versed in; escape, elude ▫ (cricket) *The last ball of that over Skinner hit nearly to the boundary, but took only one run off it. The idea of this—Jenny was pleased with herself for getting one of* ***the finer points****—was to arrange that he, and not his partner, should be up against Lawrence* (the bowler). TGLY ▫ *I don't think your landlord could prosecute, but I'm not well enough versed in* ***the finer points of*** *the law to be certain.* ▫ *Jamieson, who always thought nobody could appreciate* ***the finer points of*** *a picture as he could himself, proceeded to explain just how the artist had achieved his effect.* ▫ *I think Jack's a fool to try and undermine his boss's authority —and he thinks I'm a fool and that* ***the finer points of*** *his subtle plan escape me.* ▫ stress pattern the 'finer points.

one's finest hour the period during which sb, an institution, country etc achieves greatest success, receives credit or renown to a degree greater than at any other time ▫ (source) *Let us therefore brace ourselves to our duties and so bear ourselves that if the British Empire and its Commonwealth last for a thousand years men will still say, 'This was* ***their finest hour****.'* W CHURCHILL (in a speech after the British withdrawal from Dunkirk June 1940) ▫ *It seemed fitting somehow—a definition of national temperament—that he* (a German) *should speak of 1940 as* ***a*** *military '****finest hour****' with the same nostalgia that we do. But when we use the phrase we mean the time of our defeat.* RT ▫ *The Sixties had seen public service broadcasting in* ***its finest hour*** *of liberation, and only a few were aware that distant signals were faintly ominous.* NS

the finished product sb/sth finally completed or evolved (contrasted with the same person/thing at an intermediate stage) ▫ *Education is a life-long process. No young person emerges from school, college, or university as* ***a finished product****.* SC ▫ (Max Wall, comedian) *I'll do whatever comes into my mind on any given night. The trouble is that none of it is written down, and that makes it hard to sell; bookers say they don't know what to expect. They simply can't see it, but I tell them not to worry: I can always visualise* ***the finished product****.* ST ▫ *It is wrong to make a fetish of professionalism, of* ***the Finished Product****. There should be courses in, for example, creative writing, if only to get people to read, to feel that books are theirs.* L

a finishing school a school where rich parents send their children (usu girls) to be 'finished', ie to acquire cultured tastes, social assurance, good manners, etc ▫ *I was sent for a year to* ***a finishing school*** *in Switzerland, but all I learned was to swear in Swiss German and to drink litres of lager fast.*

(add/put) the finishing touches (to sth) [V + O pass] (add) the final details completing or embellishing sth ▫ *Twenty rushed minutes later, she was getting the melon from the fridge and* ***putting the finishing touches to*** *the salmon salad.* WI ▫ *The hut was now completed except for* ***a*** *few* ***finishing touches****.* BM ▫ *'I'm leaving my husband. Shocking, isn't it?' 'But when he's like this, laid up—' Martha laughed loudly. 'Oh yes, isn't that wonderful? That was* ***the finishing touch****. On top of everything else he has to go and get himself shot.'* TGLY ▫ *Rosa brought Glad downstairs,* ***the finishing touches*** *were* ***put to*** *the tea, and they sat down.* HD ▫ sing form, (add/put) the finishing touch (to sth), often derogatory.

fire and brimstone [n + n non-rev] symbols of punishment and destruction, esp as inflicted by God's wrath and associated with Old Testament concepts of God, Hell, and the Devil (brimstone = sulphur) **V:** call down...(on), rain (down)...(on); breathe ▫ (source) *Then the Lord rained upon Sodom and Gomorrah* ***brimstone and fire*** *from heaven.* GENESIS XIX 24 ▫ *Far from being propaganda for the established* *churches, only the fourth* (TV programme) *approaches traditional* ***fire-and-brimstone*** *Christianity.* OBS □ (Britain's in-shore fishermen resist entry to the European Common Market) *Rampant Scottish peers have emerged from their glens breathing* ***fire and brimstone****. The 20-odd Tory MPs with fishing constituencies are looking distinctly unhappy.* OBS □ *Joanna is Joanna. I love her. She just radiates—whether with* ***fire and brimstone*** *when confronted with yet another irritating inadequacy, or conversely, with deep compassion and understanding of other people's problems.* TVT

fire the first/opening shot [V + O pass] make the first move in a contest, quarrel, fight or confrontation □ (headline) *Carter* ***Fires First Shot*** *in Election Campaign. Jimmy Carter formally opened his campaign today with a strong attack on...* □ ***The opening shot*** *in an intensified pro-monetarism campaign was* ***fired*** *by the Chancellor of the Exchequer.* □ *A letter from the owner's lawyer to the tenant, demanding the vacation of the property within 6 weeks, was* ***the first shot fired*** *in a long and tiresome legal battle.*

(need) a firm hand [V + O Pass] (need) strong discipline, control □ *Charmian needs to be bullied. What she* ***needs*** *is* ***a firm hand****. She will simply go to pieces if you don't keep at her.* MM □ *It was obvious to Symes within two days of taking up his appointment that* ***a*** *very* ***firm hand*** *would be* ***needed****.*

a firm offer [O (NP)] an offer to buy or do sth, and one which can be accepted as genuinely meant and almost certain to be adhered to **V:** ⚠ make (sb); reject; obtain (from sb) □ *First, we tried to obtain from them* ***a firm offer****, with satisfactory guarantees, but it was not forthcoming and negotiations were terminated by them.* T □ *I think you're just the man for the job. Go home and think it over; but remember that though it's* ***a firm offer*** *I can't keep it open indefinitely.* □ *No, we haven't sold the boat yet. Several people seemed very interested but nobody has made us* ***a firm offer****.*

first among equals [Comp (NP)] the one of a group who leads or takes special responsibility but who neither feels himself, nor is held by others to be, their superior **V:** ⚠ be; stand □ *On the Parliamentary Committee we are equal, the leader being* ***first among equals****, and the responsibility for party discipline is shared by all equally.* OBS □ *In Dyak society the rich are respected but the poor are not despised. Success is admired because it represents something everyone would like to achieve. The rich man can therefore hope to stand* ***first among equals*** *in the minds of other men.* NDN

a first charge on/upon sth/sb [Comp (NP)] a demand on sth/sb that takes priority over all others **V:** ⚠ be, become; make sth □ *A certain minimum of defence expenditure ought to be* ***a first charge on*** *a nation's resources.* MFM □ *I confess that it was I who sent the bomb which killed the postman and I desire that the welfare of the man's family shall be* ***a first charge upon*** *my estate.* ARG □ *We fully realize that the care of your husband's health must be* ***a first charge on*** *your time during the next few weeks.*

first come, first served (saying) people will be dealt with in strict order of arrival, application etc; there will be no discrimination or favouritism about the order in which people are entitled to buy or receive goods or services □ *Joining up was like anything else—it was a matter of* ***first come, first served****. Quite soon, when the war actually started, everyone would be conscripted; but by that time they, Robert and Ned, would be well ahead with their training, and in a position to get a better share of what was going.* CON □ ***First come, first served*** *should be the rule for hospital waiting lists, but there seems to be little doubt that some National Health patients with a bit of influence can jump the queue in a way not entirely related to the severity of their condition.*

first cousin to sth [Comp (NP)] closely resembling, if not actually the same as, sth else **V:** ⚠ be, look □ *I could never tell whether his eyes were blue-grey or grey-blue, but what I did know was that as a colour it was* ***first cousin to*** *stainless Sheffield steel.* PP □ *Did that teak chest come from Burma? We have one at home that's* ***first cousin to*** *it.* □ *'I wouldn't call it a quarrel, really.' 'Wouldn't you? It was* ***first cousin to*** *one, anyway.'*

the first fine (careless) rapture (saying) any initial period of enthusiastic activity or pleasure which is not, or is not likely to be, maintained at the same high pitch □ (source) *That's the wise thrush; he sings each song twice over,/Lest you should think he never could recapture/* ***The first fine careless rapture****!* HOME-THOUGHTS FROM ABROAD (R BROWNING 1812-89) □ *In an exclusively male party,* (men) *feel a special kind of happy-go-lucky contentment, yet they cannot do without women entirely. Gianpaolo himself, when* ***the first fine rapture*** *had worn off, seemed none too pleased.* ARG □ *Young love,* ***that first fine careless rapture****, comes for most girls not with a crush on a pop star or the gym mistress, but in a passion for ponies.* G □ (NONCE) (football) *By and large, Inter have not had a good season and the team manager has been under fire.* ***The first fine frenzy*** *of his promotion from youth coach last season is no more than a memory.* ST □ (NONCE) *My mood was a text-book case for manics, the classic anti-climax,* ***the first fine careless flatness*** *after the job is done.* PP

(in) the first/full flush of youth etc [A (Prep P)] (in) the freshness, or vigour, of youth etc at its outset/prime; (in) the period when a stimulating activity, state of affairs, emotion begins or is at its height **n:** youth, (early) manhood, (young) womanhood; romance, reform, victory, success; enthusiasm, passion, anger, generosity □ *Most West African lorries are not* ***in*** *what one would call* ***the first flush of youth****.* BB □ *The great likelihood of this relatively early falling off of learning efficiency is something which may be unpleasant for those of us who are past* ***the first flush of youth****.* MFF □ *We should hate to think that Edinburgh, particularly* ***in the full flush of Festival****, was not going to be given the chance of responding to some of the novel invitations to public participation in art experience planned by artists.* SC □ *It is mainly because,* ***in the first flush of romance****, we like to pretend that 'marriage means independence of* *other people' that it so often turns sour.* NS □ *It was a statement he would regret when* ***the first full flush of his anger*** *had abated.* □ *The bottom had fallen out of romanticism with the death of Byron, and Clare's* ***first flush of fame*** *as 'the peasant poet', the literary ploughboy to be patronised and gawped at, was fading.* SC

first and foremost [adv + adv non-rev] firstly and most importantly; taking precedence as a consideration, procedure, function or role □ *Will we now let cars eat men and our cities?* ***First and foremost*** *people want space to live in at a price they can afford.* ST □ *If your problem is dry, cracked nails,* ***first and foremost*** *have a health check. Your doctor may suggest some 'diet-extra' tonic.* H □ *What I've been saying has been based on the assumption that the museum is there for the benefit of the community. On another view the museum is* ***first and foremost*** *a tourist asset.* L □ *When you talk about the National* (Theatre) *most people think* ***first and foremost*** *of Lord Olivier.* ST □ *Now who is going to teach British management to do the job?* ***First and foremost*** *the companies themselves.* L □ usu front or middle position.

the first one has heard of it/sth the first time one learns about it/sth □ *He seemed flabbergasted when told we were going to Sui and it was obviously* ***the first he had heard of it*** *although he was a partner in the Company operating there.* DS □ *Like everybody else in the village, including the wives of the men involved, it was* ***the first she'd heard of it****. And 30 years later, there's still a degree of confusion among the men themselves.* RT □ *I can't stand all this fuss over weddings. I'm telling you now that if I ever do get married,* ***the first you'll hear of it*** *is after it's an accomplished fact.* □ *How do you know about Tony's appointment?* ***The first he heard of it*** *himself was last night.* □ *Really? I've known George for years and it's* ***the first I've heard of*** *him nursing a secret ambition to go into politics.* □ usu Comp of *be*; usu pres or past perfect tense of hear.

one's first impression one's immediate reaction to a new experience of any kind □ *He* (the Prime Minister) *said he wanted my opinion on the proposed operation. I replied that I was not his military adviser. He agreed but said he would like me to study the plan nevertheless, and give him* ***my 'first impression'****.* MFM □ *'I could easily be wrong in my estimation of his character, of course.' 'Not necessarily,* ***first impressions*** *are often correct.'* □ *It's a beautiful place, but I'm not going to launch into a description of it or show you my slides or otherwise interfere with* ***your first impression*** *of it.*

first and last [adv + adv non-rev] altogether; when everything is taken into account; in all respects and/or circumstances □ *It took four years to build the Towers and cost about four hundred thousand pounds* ***first and last****.* WDM □ *I'd go back to Canada if I got the chance.* ***First and last****, the ten years I spent there were the happiest of my life.* □ *'His father wouldn't have done business that way.' 'No, he was a gentleman,* ***first and last****.'* □ *What his dismissal from the cabinet and his translation to the boardroom of a great nationalized industry taught him about himself is that he is* ***first and last*** *an administrator, and that political labels simply got in the way.* NS □ front, middle or end position.

first of all[1] [A (Adv P)] before (doing) anything else; in the first place[1] (qv); in the first instance (qv); to begin with[1] (Vol 1) (qv); to start with[1] (Vol 1) (qv) □ *Brigit was aware,* ***first of all****, of the resentment in Prissie's face. Then it passed, and Prissie turned a hurt but acquiescent look towards Brigit.* DC □ *Well, I tried this and I tried that and still the car wouldn't start, so I went and phoned the AA* ((GB) = Automobile Association)*, which is what I should have done* ***first of all****.* □ an emphatic version of first.

first of all[2] [Conj (Adv P)] (used to introduce what the speaker considers to be) the first or most important item in an argument or process; for a start (qv); in the first place[2] (qv); to begin with[2] (Vol 1) (qv); to start with[2] (Vol 1) (qv) □ ***First of all****, he's not the dear kind old man he'd like you to think he is.* □ *'I don't see why we can't just go ahead and buy the house.' 'Well,* ***first of all****, we simply couldn't afford to pay off a mortgage of £30,000 — which is what we'd need. Secondly, no building society would lend us that much, anyway.'* □ an emphatic version of first.

first principles [O/o (NP)] truths, laws or assumptions which form the basis for subsequent reasoning or illustration; the basis of a whole religious, philosophical, educational etc system **V:** go back to, return to; derive sth from; establish □ *This elegant method is derived here from* ***first principles****, including the background of complex functions.* NSC □ *At least the old authoritarian teaching was reasonably clear on its objectives. But of course Bruner does not suggest a return to* ***first principles*** *in this respect, although in the past he may rather have over-stated the case against all learning by exposition rather than by discovery.* NS □ *Realising that his students were out of their depth, the lecturer decided that he had better go back to* ***first principles****.*

the first step (in/towards sth) [Comp/O (NP)] the first stage in a process or progress **V:** be, regard sth as; take □ *...recommended that the school-leaving age should be raised from fifteen to sixteen as* ***the first step in*** *a long-term plan for improving the education of all boys and girls between the ages of fifteen and eighteen.* OBS □ *You know what'd happen if he did marry you, don't you? Load you down with about five kids in the first four years, that's* ***the first step****.* TGLY □ *'What are you doing, father?' 'I'm taking* ***the first step*** *in a new career.' She looked over his shoulder. 'Are you becoming a writer?'* OMIH □ *Sadat should be supported because he has taken some brave* ***first steps*** *along the road to peace with Israel.* G

first thing (in the morning) [A (NP)] early in the morning; soon after one wakes or rises □ *So I went up* (to London) *alone, with Ned's assurance that he'd follow, either late on the same night or* ***first thing in the morning****.* CON □ HELENA: *Listen, Alison—I've sent your father a wire. Look, dear — he'll get it* ***first thing in the morning****.* LBA □ *Don't suppose you could lend me a pound? Pay you back* ***first thing*** *tomorrow.* □ *'Fancy going off to work on nothing but a cup of tea!' 'I know, but that's all he ever takes,* ***first thing****.'* □ front or end position. ⇨ last thing (at night).

(the) first/next thing one knows [Conj (NP)] (informal) then; next; after that □ *You'd better keep off cigarettes altogether, or,* ***first thing you know****, you'll be back to smoking 40 a day again.* □ *If they let that woman in there* ***the first thing they know*** *she'll have the whole place reorganised.* □ DAVIES: *We used to have a bit of a chat, not any more. I never see him, he goes out, he comes in late,* ***next thing I know*** *he's shoving me about in the middle of the night.* TC □ *One kid came up and asked for an autograph, which I gave. Then there were about 15 kids who also came up to me and I thought, 'Very nice.'* ***Next thing I knew*** *I got a knee in the groin.* RT □ stress pattern (the) 'first/'next thing one knows.

the first thing etc that comes into/enters one's head/mind [O (NP)] a hasty or unconsidered opinion, remark, reply etc **V:** say, blurt out; write, use, give. **n:** thing, words, name, thought, excuse □ *That was just an excuse. I wanted to get back early, and I said* ***the first thing that came into my head.*** □ *We at home can see people caught off balance, saying* ***the first*** *and not the fourth* ***thing which comes into their heads****, which is television's greatest achievement.* ST □ *I tried to draw him aside, muttering by way of explanation* ***the first words that came into my head****. 'Robert's just a bit irritable.'* CON □ *I hope it will not seem patronising if I blurt out* ***the first thought that comes to my mind****, and say that working with the young — as I'm doing these days — is a stimulating thing and full of strange surprises.* L □ *'I wasn't sure about giving my right name to the janitor,' she said, 'so I just gave him* ***the first name that entered my head****, Moll Flanders. I've just been reading about her.'* HD

(put) first things first (catchphrase) (realize that) the most important or necessary considerations, duties must be attended to before any others that arise; get etc one's/its priorities right etc (qv) □ *To represent the many good things in a society massively at odds with itself is difficult for the mass media to do. But* ***first things first****. Is the case for it even recognised?* L □ *'Those four days I spent with you — they started me along the right track, you know, Joe. I began to* ***put first things first****, as I used to do before I got —' 'Before you got successful,' I finished for him.* CON □ *'For heaven's sake, Jinny! Do you have to start being domestic now? Spenser is waiting for us.'* ***'First things first,'*** *Joe said. 'She has to sew my button on first.'* AITC ⇨ ⚠ put sb/sth first.

a fish out of water [Comp (NP)] sb who is uncomfortable, who is at a disadvantage, because in unfamiliar company or unnatural surroundings **V:** ⚠ be, seem, feel (like) □ *I fear that at the best I shall be somewhat of* ***a fish out of water****. There is so little in common between me and my fellow guests.* EM □ (In this novel) *a Classics don is offered a huge sum to write the life of a Hollywood Star of the Fifties now living in seclusion on a South Pacific island. The story reveals the man and his failings, and the* ***fish-out-of-water*** *hero is honestly and nicely observed.* L □ *In my patched jeans and torn leather jacket I felt like* ***a fish out of water*** *amongst all those elegantly-dressed people.* □ attrib use *the* ***fish-out-of-water*** *hero.* ⇨ be in/out of one's element.

a fisherman's story etc an exaggerated story (from one relating to the size of a fish which has been caught or has got away) **n:** story, ⚠ tale, yarn □ *And there, after dinner, while the rest of the guests were spinning* ***fishermen's yarns*** *round the bar, we perched in dark uncomfortable vantage points overlooking badger terrain.* RT □ *Have you heard the one about the pike that tried to eat a mule? Unlike some* ***fishermen's tales*** *this one could be true, because it's been around for 300 years. Izaak Walton told it first.* TVT □ stress pattern a 'fisherman's story.

fit for human consumption [Comp (AdjP)] (official description for foodstuffs) tested and passed as being fit for people to eat **V:** ⚠ be; think, consider, sth □ *Now I think there's a lot to be said for us all having lunch here, don't you? I think there might be one or two scraps still just about* ***fit for human consumption*** *if I can contrive to locate them.* TGLY □ *Meanwhile, Gian-Carlo Menotti's politically supercharged opera, 'The Consul', is performed at Warsaw's Grand Theatre, and James Bond has been passed* ***fit for human consumption.*** L □ *In Britain there is no agreed system for monitoring the alkaloid level in potatoes. Potatoes are only subject, like any other foodstuff, to '****fitness for human consumption****' regulations.* ST □ often facetious and/or fig; variant fitness for human consumption.

fit sb like a glove [V + O + A] fit the wearer perfectly in size and shape; seem as if it were specially made for sb; (fig) be apt and accurate **S:** coat, dress; job; description, adjective □ *Aren't I lucky? The only dress in the shop that I fancied and it* ***fitted*** *me* ***like a glove****!* □ *'Mother', he said to me, 'you make the place like a palace and it* ***fits*** *you* ***like a glove****.'* ASA □ *'Prudent' and 'calculating' are two adjectives which* ***fit*** *President Pompidou* ***like a glove****.* □ (NONCE) *Welsh actor Clifford Evans has virtually cornered a market in Top People parts: he has played a Lord Chancellor, the Head of a British secret Service agency and* ***fits glove-like*** *into the role of a retired politician in the Sunday play.* TVT

a fit of laughter [o (NP)] (a state of) unrestrained or helpless laughter **V:** be in, dissolve in, collapse in; have sb in, keep sb in □ *The attacks of asthma grew more frequent — losing his temper or* ***a fit of laughter*** *could bring one on.* □ *By this time the audience were rolling about in* ***fits of laughter****.* □ *His attempts to manage the bicycle had us all in* ***fits****.* □ *be etc in* ***fits*** implies fits of laughter.

fit and proper [adj + adj non-rev] suitable and correct, esp conforming to accepted standards of social behaviour, religious observance, etc □ *'No,' he said, 'this morning I do not, to be quite honest with you all, I do not really feel that this School is, well—a* ***fit and proper*** *place to have the Word of God read aloud in it.'* TT □ *It's all very well for them saying that marriage is just a ceremony, but now that there's a child coming you'd think they'd want to have things* ***fit and proper****.* □ *As George introduced Peter to Sarah it is only* ***fit and proper*** *that he should be best man at their wedding.*

a fixed idea an idea, or opinion, not only firmly, but often obsessively, held and unlikely to be affected by the arguments of others or even by one's own experience □ *John had* **a fixed idea** *that it was only the lack of a typewriter that prevented him from plunging straight into a novel that would win him immediate fame.* □ *The moratorium should be recorded in some form in the general nuclear tests ban treaty, said Mr Tsarapkin, but he had no* **fixed ideas** *about how this should be done.* OBS

flags fly/fly flags at half-mast flags are hung/hang flags half-way up the flag-pole, instead of the top, as a token of mourning or distress □ ('Black September' Munich Olympic Games 1972) *The air where the doves of peace flew so recently is filled with the strains of Beethoven's 'Eroica'.* **Flags fly at half-mast**. *West Germany's Chancellor Willy Brandt sits among the mourners.* OBS □ JASON: *Wake up, make it lively. This is a wedding.* MRS FISH: *The day I got married was the worst day of my life.* MRS GREEN: *The day I got married all the* **flags flew at half-mast**. DPM

a flash Harry (derogatory) a man whose dress, talk, manner and conduct is more showy, extravagant than is good taste □ *...politics is meant to be boring, and boring people carry it out more competently than* **Flash Harrys**. NS □ *What's the Reid recipe? 'It's Mike Reid being himself. I'm a bit of* **a** *pushing* **flash Harry***—aggressive type, I suppose.'* TVT

a flash in the pan [Comp (NP)] an effort to do sth, that attracts notice but does not succeed; a brief (partial) success which is not followed up; the person who makes such an effort, achieves only such a success (from an explosion of gunpowder in the pan of an old flint-lock gun, which fails to fire the charge) **V:** ⚠ be; think sth, regard sth as □ *Brilliance that has not been tempered by the discipline of long years of apprenticeship to research will not give the 'History' what it requires. We shall get flashy stuff, Middleton, brilliant, unsustained* **flashes in the pan**, *unsupported guesses.* ASA □ *It soon became clear that he would have to follow his success with a new play, but when 'Badger's Green' was shredded by the critics, Sherriff decided that 'Journey's End' was* **a flash in the pan** *and that he should carry out another ambition—to go to Oxford, read history and become a schoolmaster.* ST □ *You've written that McCarthy was a kind of* **a** *ghastly* **flash in the pan** *and that that kind of thing could never happen again.* L □ *Only Winnie the Pooh who has his own adult cult following and who was translated into celluloid* (= made the subject of a film) *can rival Rupert's bid for Top Bear. Beside them both Yogi is just a* **flash-in-the-pan** *colonial upstart.* SC □ attrib use *a* **flash-in-the-pan** *success, upstart etc.*

flat out [A (AdvP)] with all the speed, energy, determination etc one can (from pressing the accelerator pedal of a car right down till it is flat/level with the floor) **V:** ⚠ be, go, ride, work □ *Dennis had allowed Nur Johan a few healthy gallops, but never before had he ridden him* **flat out**. ARG □ *I suppose they* (the police-car) *were just patrolling and saw us immediately after getting the wireless message. Blast their guts. We'll cook them yet: we've got five miles an hour more than they have,* **flat out**, *and in any case they're not taking me alive.* HD □ *My father tended to be influenced by the opinion he'd heard or read most recently. If he had just been down a coal-mine —he was a vicar in a coal-mining village in Northamptonshire—he tended to be* **flat out** *on the side of the miners.* L □ *If we worked* **flat out** *on the circuits all night there was a chance we might have the automatic cut-out working again by morning.*

a flat voice a (deliberately) expressionless tone of voice □ *'I could do some interesting designs blindfold. Here, Joe, tie this behind my head.' He poised his brush. Then* **a flat voice** *spoke from the doorway. 'Mr Lamb,' it said. 'Don't you think you ought to be getting on with some work?'* CON □ *'Shall I make some tea, or shall we have a little drink of something stronger to cheer ourselves up?' 'Whichever you like,' she answered in* **a flat** *little* **voice** *and didn't even raise her eyes.* □ also pl.

flay/skin sb alive [V + O + A pass] punish, penalize, abuse, criticize sb with the utmost severity □ *Harold Wilson is still stuck in one of his bad patches. The pro-Marketeers who dominate Fleet Street have seized the chance of* **flaying** *him* **alive**. NS □ *'If it's one of my boys that did this,' said the woman, surveying the damage, 'I'll* **skin** *him* **alive**.*'*

a flea pit (derogatory) a cheap theatre or cinema □ *'Just keeping my eye on a touring show that's here at* **the** *local* **flea pit**.*' 'One of your shows?' Charles asked.* HD □ JO: *Oh shut up, Helen. Have a look in that paper and see what's on at the pictures tomorrow night.* HELEN: *Where is it? Oh yes. 'I was a teenage—'—what? You can't go there anyway. It's* **a** *proper little* **flea pit**. TOH

fleet of foot [Comp (AdjP)] able to move rapidly **V:** ⚠ be, seem □ *Haydn is not a composer to whom Boulez brings special insights; his account of the Oxford Symphony was buoyant and clean-limbed, no more; and though the finale was* **fleet of foot**, *the phrasing of the slow movement could well have been more pointed.* OBS □ *'I couldn't do it now,' said Uncle Fred, pausing in the tale of his escape, 'but I was* **fleeter of foot** *in those days.'* □ *It's the chamois' leaping powers, more than its* **fleetness of foot**, *that are astounding.* □ variant fleetness of foot.

flesh and blood [n + n non-rev] the human body; the human being; the frailties, fears and passions that all mankind share as physical beings □ *Sometimes she wished that the symptom* (of pregnancy) *hadn't turned out to be a false alarm, for an incarnation of her experience with Alec, its expression in* **flesh and blood**, *with the prime necessity to love it would have banished the warring abstractions that beset her mind.* PW □ *The fortifications were too strong and solid concrete pill-boxes lined the whole top of the hill, and we were only* **flesh and blood**. OBS □ *Something snapped inside Monsieur Bonneval.* **Flesh and blood** *could endure no more.* ARG □ also found in *more than/as much as* **flesh and blood** *can/could endure/stand/take.* ⇨ ⚠ one's own flesh and blood.

flex one's muscles [V + O pass] exercise, test, or show off one's muscles (before doing sth); display one's power, either as a warning or for self-gratification **S:** fighter; army; industry, union, department □ *The first sign that Russia was* ***flexing its muscles*** *as a Sea Power came in 1961 when Soviet warships carried out exercises in the Norwegian Sea.* OBS □ *Feeling in Government circles is that the TUC have had a severe shaking in the last two weeks as the industrial relations court* ***flexed its muscles****.* SC □ *I'd read somewhere that most people can't even understand the* reviews *of his books. 'Sure they can't, said Dee. 'The guy doing the review is always some goddamned expert* ***flexing his muscles****.'* ST □ *It may be difficult to persuade the intellectuals and the artists that they can emerge from the darkness* (of political repression) *without fear. I gained the impression from writers, film-makers and actors that they would have to wait for quite a while before they could* ***flex any*** *imaginative* ***muscles****.* L □ *The tough talkers at the top of the Union tree could find themselves at any moment confronted with the logical implications of their* ***muscle flexing****.* NS □ n compound muscle flexing.

a flight of fancy sth extravagantly imagined, or out of touch with reality or probability □ *How could a voice speak from the chimney? No, when Fergus came home this evening she could not tell him* ***this*** *latest* ***flight of fancy****. He would be as impatient with her as he was with Nicky.* DC □ *In my opinion this poem—so homely and spontaneous and apt and accurate—is worth a hundred* ***flights of fancy****.* SC □ *After I had read Jay's report, I remarked to my boss that Jay would either become Director-General of the BBC or make a fortune in industry. This was received with the modicum of reserve which greeted my* ***flights of fancy*** *at that time.*L

flog a dead horse [V + O] (informal) spend one's time and energy in promoting some activity, or belief, that is already accepted, or widely rejected or outdated □ *You may have amazed people by your advanced views on education forty years ago but now you're just* ***flogging a dead horse****.* □ (NONCE) *I nodded, and muttered maybe I should, but the Baron wasn't letting me leave the subject, he was* ***flogging*** *it until he made it* ***a*** *good* ***dead horse****.* PP □ (NONCE) *One looked in vain for the professional touch, some hint of the craftsman's skill. Detection, it seems, is very largely a question of* ***flogging a horse*** *until its* ***death*** *is beyond question.* L

flood the market [V + O pass] offer/be for sale through every possible trade outlet; produce/be for sale in greater quantity than demand justifies or than can find buyers at a profitable price **S:** farmer, dealer, importer; cars, fruit, wine □ *Last week, as speculative farmers* ***flooded markets*** *with hoarded beef to cash in while prices reached unprecedented levels, an optimistic industry claimed that the peak had been reached.* ST □ *In Western economies if* ***the market*** *shows signs of being* ***flooded*** *by a commodity, be it wheat, coffee or butter, production will be cut back.*

flora and fauna [n + n non-rev] the plants, trees etc that grow in, and the animals that inhabit, a specified region □ *Relics of the* ***flora and fauna*** *of the Pleistocene age have been preserved in fossil form.* □ (mental illness) *Ella had retreated into an underground cave whose pale, albinoid* ***flora and fauna*** *were less real than the vast shadows they cast on the high rocky walls around her.* HAA □ *I wish we could have* ***the flora*** *without* ***the fauna****. These roses are covered with green-fly again.*

a Florence Nightingale a devoted nurse (from the British nurse, also known as *the Lady with the Lamp*, who served in the military hospital at Scutari, during the Crimean War, 1854-56) □ *'I only hope you're feeling better,' he said. 'But I'm sure you are, with so charming* ***a Florence Nightingale*** *to attend to you.'* ASA □ *Should hairy Superbikers become part-time* ***Florence Nightingales****? Glamour-boy Sheene, winner of the World Championships in the 500cc category, on a Suzuki, stopped to save the life of team-mate John Williams in Sweden.* TVT

flotsam and jetsam [n + n non-rev] wreckage, or goods, found floating on the sea or washed ashore; (fig) miscellaneous people, or things, moving/moved about or abandoned □ *It was the duty of Chrissie and Lizzie, their younger sisters, to carry up any* ***flotsam or jetsam*** *marked down by their father in the course of beach-combing operations.* RM □ *It was the poorest and foulest quarter of the city and here the* ***flotsam and jetsam*** *of three continents struggled precariously to survive.* □ *Unfortunately over the last few years the* ***flotsam and jetsam*** *of tower-block living have been dropping out of the balconies, and bottles, cans, toys, flower pots and, horribly, three cats have become lethal weapons, reaching a speed of 100mph from the top storey by the time they hit the ground.* OBS □ often used of the homeless, refugees etc, as in second example.

flourish like the green bay tree (saying) prosper; be conspicuously successful (the implication often being that the flourishing is temporary or undeserved) □ (source) *I myself have seen the ungodly in great power, and* ***flourishing like a green bay-tree****. I went by, and lo, he was gone. I sought him, but his place could nowhere be found.* BOOK OF COMMON PRAYER (PSALMS XXXVII 36) □ *The wicked, he thought, did in fact* ***flourish like the green bay tree****, and it was untrue to suggest that in the morning they were not, yea, they could not be found. They were, and they could.* US □ *The four of them* (delinquent school children) *are so strong. The wide world, she thought, might use them, just as they were — out there where the wicked sometimes* ***flourish like the green bay tree****.* ARG

flower children/people the name given in the 1960s to the young people who rebelled against conventional social pressures, ambitions, obligations, conventional cultural and moral values, in favour of private values, non-aggression, affection for each other, communal living, and oriental religion (their philosophy often being called 'flower power' (next entry) (qv)) □ *Colin Smith reports from San Francisco and finds the city that was once a haven of peace for the* ***flower children*** *has become a battleground for exponents of savage ideologies.* OBS □ *The stalls selling underground magazines, Jamaican patties, loon pants* (brightly-coloured trousers) *and brown-paper sleeping-bags are packed. But not with customers. Just clumps of* ***flower people****, sheltering from the rain.* ST □

*Since his death 10 years ago the German novelist Hermann Hesse has been adopted by the post-hippies, neo-**flower-people**, as one of their major culture-heroes, avatars and prophets.* OBS □ stress pattern 'flower children/people; flower children/people also called 'hippies'.

flower power the name given to the philosophy of the 'flower children/people' (qv) □ *The slogan 'make love not war' sounds all very fine, but dissidence has got to be constructive, and you won't put an end to war with **flower power**.* □ *The Rolling Stones feature in a rock-style Pilgrim's Progress that sees them start off as true believers, become progressively side-tracked into the Slough of Despond during their flirtation with **flower power**, and return to the straight and narrow as the best live rock group in the world.* RT □ stress pattern 'flower power.

flutter the dovecotes [V + O pass] astonish, upset or alarm people who are accustomed to a calm or conventional way of life or thinking □ (source) *...like an eagle in **a dove-cote**, I/ **Flutter'd** your Volscians in Corioli.* CORIOLANUS V 5 □ *Our evidence is not complete but the revelations we expect to make should **cause the** biggest **flutter in the dovecotes** since Eisenberg's release of the Pentagon Papers to the American press.* □ *This proposal is bound to **flutter the** legal **dovecotes**. There's nothing these fellows cling to like established practice.* □ (NONCE) *It was not only a great book. It would **cause a rustle in the dovecotes**, for in it he had pilloried everyone who had ever insulted or injured him.* US □ variant (cause) a flutter/rustle in the dovecote(s).

fly the coop [V + O] (informal) escape, leave (without warning) esp a domestic or work situation, one's responsibilities or obligations □ *The plot was about this doctor who is on the verge of leaving his wife for someone else's. After a highly-charged emotional exchange between them on the matter of why he's **flying the coop**, he's just packing his light-weight suits when suddenly the phone rings.* TVT □ *She could see no way, short of **flying the coop**, out of this oppressive life-style.*

fly high be ambitious □ *One only hoped that in SW1* (a fashionable London district) *they weren't going to find themselves socially too far out of their depth. We must all, even nations, learn not to **fly** too **high**; or, come to that, too fast.* NS □ *He'd have to tell Ma, he thought, about the Master of Foxhounds lark. No, he wouldn't though. He'd keep that after all; she'd say he was **flying** too **high**.* DBM □ *Two more factories,* and *handle your own distribution! That's **flying high**, isn't it?* □ *When the implications of the new* (examination) *system become clear, it is just possible that one or two education boards (which are technically independent of the government) may go it alone and preserve O-level as an élite examination for **high-flyers**.* NS □ n compound high-flyer; adj compound high-flying.

the fly in the ointment [Comp (NP)] sb/sth that spoils, to a greater or lesser degree, an otherwise perfect or very satisfactory situation, state of affairs; a blot on the landscape[2] (qv) **V:** ⚠ be, become; regard sb as □ (source) *Dead **flies** cause **the ointment** of the apothecary to send forth a stinking savour: so doth a little folly him that is in reputation for wisdom and honour.* ECCLESIASTES X 1 □ *'Apparently they don't like poor Lennie.' 'Well, neither do I.' He's **the** only **fly in the ointment** around here, as far as I'm concerned.'* AITC □ JEAN: *I'd swear even before Saturday morning, he had all his clothes packed. I suppose he had his ticket and money ready. I must have been **the fly in the ointment**.* YAA □ *The airlines recognize that the engine will be the quietest of its kind in the world, and therefore acceptable to a market ever more conscious of noise pollution. Even at this stage, however, there is **a** sizeable **fly in the** proverbial **ointment**. Can British Airways be persuaded to give a letter of intent for a substantial order?* NS □ also pl flies in the ointment.

a flying start [O/o (NP)] an initial advantage, or a good beginning, which in itself takes one some way towards the completion of a race, journey, or any other enterprise **V:** give, have, present; get off to □ *The day I put on my demob suit was the happiest day of my life. Granted, I came home to discover that the bloody Library Association had made their exams ten times as difficult, thus giving **a flying start** to the women and the conchies* (= conscientious objectors). RATT □ *Present him with the star and the script and your contracts, and we have **a flying start**. Belfounder hasn't anything on us legally.* UTN □ (a golf tournament) *Jacklin was somewhat bemused by his 78. How it happened he didn't really know. Instead of getting off to **a flying start**, he began in the most depressing fashion with five fives.* SC

a flying tackle [O/o (NP)] an attempt to stop, or capture, sb/sth by hurling oneself through the air at him/it (as is sometimes done to intercept a player carrying the ball in a game of rugby) **V:** make, try; bring sb/sth down in/with □ (an experiment in hypnotic suggestion) *The subject opened his eyes, began to creep forward very slowly, and finally in **a flying tackle** brought the Lieutenant-Colonel down on the floor.* SNP □ *I thought my precious box of specimens was going to slide into the river but Jack retrieved it with **a flying tackle**.* □ also pl.

a flying/lightning visit [O/o (NP)] a very brief visit, often one fitted in between doing other things **V:** pay sb/sth, pay...to sb/sth; beg come, on □ (caption under a press photograph) *Sheikh Mujib during last week's **flying visit** to London.* L □ *A few weeks later, as Robin was leaving the Works after **a flying visit** from the London Office, he met Donald.* ASA □ *We're only passing through, but we'd like to pay you **a flying visit**, if we may.* □ *Another 900 security policemen have been brought in, and the Prosecutor-General has paid **a lightning visit** to Paris.* T □ also pl; a lightning visit is the less common expression and is used for a visit that is sudden or unexpected as well as very brief.

follow one's (own) bent [V + O] do as one's own tastes, inclinations, talents suggest; do one's (own) thing (qv) □ ***Following your** particular **bent** on holiday doesn't necessarily mean being energetic.* H □ *'There ought to be room for all styles of theatre,' says Fry mildly. 'The more differences the better. It's the same with people. The more individuals there are **following their own bent** the healthier we are as a society.'* SC

▫ *Several of the boys who had seemed stubbornly stupid under the former system showed plenty of common-sense when allowed to* ***follow their own bents****.*

follow sb's example [V + O pass] do as sb else has done; act in imitation of sb else (whether or not this is wise); next entry (qv); follow suit (qv) ▫ *We learn from the book that he has* ***followed*** *his mother****'s example*** *in diary-keeping: when it is eventually published, that may be his best book of all.* L ▫ *I'm only talking to you like this because I don't want you to* ***follow my example*** *and rush into marriage with the wrong kind of man.* ▫ *Perhaps every fashion house should* ***follow the example of*** *Nina Ricci who has solved the problem by showing clothes for individual customers and ready-to-wear together.* SC ▫ also pl follow their example(s). ⇨ ⚠ set (sb) a (good etc) example.

follow sb's lead [V + O] accept sb's decision, guidance, or example and do as he does; previous entry (qv); follow suit (qv) ▫ *I had never taken a first-class ticket in my life before but Ned slammed his money down with such a brusque 'Euston, first return' that I had to* ***follow his lead*** *and make the best of it.* CON ▫ *Devlin* (a golfer) *hit a slump which had him walking off a course in disgust, saying he didn't care to inflict his game on other people any longer, which is as laudable a reason for walking off a course as any. Mind you, if we all* ***followed his lead****, the courses would be practically deserted.* SC ▫ *Most of the people didn't know a thing about the scheme; but somebody made an objection and from then on it was a case of* ***follow-my-leader****.* ▫ *He wouldn't leave us here and go on to Jim's place by himself. What he wants is for us all to play* ***follow-my-leader*** *and troop after him like a flock of sheep.* ▫ also pl follow their lead; variant follow-my-leader with the meaning 'a child's game where a number of children run about in single file imitating the actions of the person in front of them as passed down the line by the leader'—fig references to this occur in adverse criticisms of people's behaviour.

follow one's (own) nose [V + O] go straight ahead; act instinctively or pragmatically; act without thought or imagination ▫ *'How do I get to the Post Office?' 'Turn right when you leave the house and then* ***follow your nose*** *till you come to it.'* ▫ *The leaders of men, the best and the worst, live from hand to mouth, from hour to hour,* ***following*** *nothing but* ***their own noses****, and the people follow after, usually with much too much obedience.* RT

follow suit [V + O] do as another has (just previously) done; act, or behave, in the same way as another who sets a precedent or example (from playing a card of the same suit (hearts, spades etc) as that led by the first player in a card game); follow sb's example (qv); follow sb's lead (qv) ▫ (laboratories and workshops in schools and colleges) *The Ministry of Labour is already engaged on a campaign to make factories even safer; the Ministry of Education would be well advised to* ***follow suit****.* NSC ▫ *The popular Press has long found it profitable not merely to report but even to promote archaeological excavation. And now radio* ***follows suit*** *and is, I understand, sponsoring a highly technical archaeological enterprise in the Mediterranean.* SD

(bid sb) a fond farewell [V + IO + O] (say good-bye on) an occasion of leave-taking or parting (the implication now only occasionally being a loving or sorrowful feeling, now usu being ironic or facetious) ▫ *And still ringing in our ears is* ***the fond farewell*** *of the Russian girl employed by the tour operator, who urges us to come again.* L ▫ *On the final day of the book exhibition we left,* ***bidding*** *our neighbour* ***a fond farewell****.* ST ▫ *Our plan was to pick an up-and-coming* (pop) *group to front a series of 13 programmes and then to* ***bid*** *them* ***a fond farewell****. But the reaction to the band and the fan mail was so spectacular that we decided to ask them back for another run.* TVT ▫ (astrological prediction) *Any* ***farewell*** *at the moment will be* ***a fond*** *one, so there's no need to feel anxiety.* TVT

(in) the fond hope etc (with) a hope which, though perhaps foolish or not likely to be realized, is optimistically clung to **n:** hope, ⚠ belief, expectation ▫ ***The fond hope*** *of every gardener is that in high summer the garden will be a riot of colour.* SC ▫ *I had been on my chapter a whole week, and the week looked pretty thin; but it was* ***my fond hope*** *that Mrs Macadam might unlock a door in Whitehall Mansions and thereby unlock more of Waterman than a housekeeper's memories.* PP ▫ *He spent his life in the struggle, sustained only by* ***a fond belief*** *in the ultimate triumph of justice.* ▫ *Indeed there is a rough parallel to the spectacular motorway pile-ups to be found in the early days of railroading, when trains would be dispatched on a line-interval basis* ***in the fond hope*** *that Driver B would be able to stop in time if Driver A got stuck.* ST ▫ *She's not the first that's married a crook* ***in the fond expectation*** *of reforming him.*

food/meat and drink to sb [Comp (NP)] sth that gives sb exceptional satisfaction or pleasure **V:** ⚠ be, come as ▫ *The Burtons' romance was* ***food and drink to*** *a thousand gossip columnists.* RT ▫ *'And they got better and better, real photos, and he was going on great guns about how disgusting it all was that kids should be open to such corrupting influences—' 'I know those words,' said Dusty, and this was* ***meat and drink to*** *him.* TT

food/a dish for the gods [Comp (NP)] particularly fine, tasty or welcome food **V:** ⚠ be, become; regard sth as ▫ *This is an easily prepared summer sweet — which laced with brandy and served with cream becomes* ***a dish for the gods****.* OBS ▫ *I was tired, bored, depressed and very hungry, and a Chinese take-away was* ***food for the gods*** *to me.* RT

food for thought [Comp/O (NP)] a situation, subject, remark, event etc that provides material for, or stimulates, thought, that requires to be carefully considered **V:** there be. . .in sth; find. . .in sth; give (sb), provide (sb with) ▫ *I do not want the Signora to talk of art any more. She gives one such* ***food for thought*** *that one doesn't need more food, don't you agree?* US ▫ *The meetings had, they said uneasily, been interesting. They had provided much* ***food for thought****.* NS ▫ (reader's letter) *If it is necessary* *to reply to some of your readers' comments, keep the replies honest. Or, better still, don't comment at all, and leave the letters page as* ***food for thought*** *to those few who read it.* RT

(you can't) fool etc all (of) the people all the time (saying) (nobody can) fool etc everybody at all times **V:** fool, cheat, deceive; please, satisfy, interest. **det:** all (of), some of; most of; any of; none of □ (source) *You can fool all the people some of the time, and some of the people all the time, but* ***you cannot fool all the people all the time.*** (attributed to ABRAHAM LINCOLN 1809-1865) □ *Mussolini practised the fine art of being all things to all men, changing his principles whenever it was expedient and doing his best to* ***fool all the people all the time.*** OBS □ *Attempts were made in those days to brainwash us into believing we could actually deceive* ***some of the people some of the time.*** *I did not believe it then. Nor do I believe it now.* L □ (Isadora Duncan, a dancer) *She at first simply lay on the stage, then she slowly rose to her full height and with outstretched arms she remained motionless to the end of the composition. Well* ***you can fool some of the people...*** NS □ *Sadly, the lesson we in 'Nationwide' carried back from Scotland is that not only* ***can you not please all the Scots some of the time****, it is very difficult to please any of them even for a moment!* RT □ *There'll be an appreciation by art critic, William Feaver. There's also a possibility of a display at Madame Tussaud's. A case, perhaps, of* ***pleasing most of the people*** *for at least* ***some of the time.*** ST □ stress pattern fool ˌall the people ˈall the time; expression often adapted, as shown.

a fool's errand [o (NP)] an unnecessary, or profitless, errand or journey, esp one that only proves to be so after completion; a wild goose chase (qv) **V:** ⚠ be on; go on; send sb on; find oneself on □ *Every call and investigation goes down on the records — even the false alarms and the various* ***fool's errands*** *that are part of the fireman's lot.* SC □ *No harm in trying, I suppose, but you're going on* ***a fool's errand*** *in my opinion.'* □ *'The man sounded really ill.' 'He'd better be. I'll strangle him if I've been called out in the middle of the night on* ***a fool's errand.'***

a fool's paradise [Comp/o (NP)] a state of contentment that is based on an illusion of one's own, or the deceptions of others **V:** be; live in □ *Sheila's still got that beautiful childish handwriting that looks sort of plaintive when you know it comes from a girl of twenty-six who's living in* ***a fool's paradise.*** JFTR □ *'Is that what they call schizophrenia then? Is that what's wrong with me?' I was still staring abstractedly at yesterday and the two months of* ***fool's paradise*** *that preceded this revelation.* HAHA □ ***The 'fool's paradise'*** *in which Maxwell lived is one in which many managers have basked. Getting accurate figures is tough; so they accept inaccuracy, which is much easier.* OBS

foot the bill (for sth) [V + O] pay directly or indirectly (for sth) (from signing a bill or account at the bottom as a token of agreeing to pay it) □ *No one who cares for architecture can have much doubt that the state should intervene to save this neo-classical masterpiece and should* ***foot the bill for*** *its preservation.* NS □ *Science has created the physical environment in which we conduct our lives. The effects are felt by everyone — and everyone* ***foots the bill for*** *the scientist's electron microscope, test-tube, jar of fruit flies and micro-analyser.* L □ *How is it, in a capitalist country, with the Press entirely owned by rich men, that so much that is printed in some papers, and so little in others, is guaranteed to be damaging to the values of the class which* ***foots the bill?*** ST

footloose and fancy-free [adj + adj non-rev] not bound to any particular place or routine; not in love with sb, and not occupied by thoughts of being in love; without ties or responsibilities □ (source) *And the imperial votaress passed on,/In maiden meditation,* ***fancy-free.*** MIDSUMMER NIGHT'S DREAM II 1 □ *In his heart, George Hill knows that the good times are over, but he says: 'We still feel* ***footloose and fancy-free.*** *We may move on to Portland, Oregon, somewhere near the sea. Who knows?'* OBS □ *Auntie Betty arrives from her home in the Midlands; hoping for a chance of being '****fancy-free****'. Unfortunately, husband Frank has the same idea.* TVT □ *I don't feel that I'm too dedicated, or that I miss out on anything. I did all the socialising bit when I was younger and* ***footloose and fancy-free.'*** TVT □ first adj occas omitted, as in source text and third example.

for and/or against [prep + prep non-rev] supporting and/or opposing **V:** argue, debate, struggle. **n:** case, opinion, argument □ *He has at one time or another argued both* ***for and against*** *most of the big changes in Turkey over the past thirty years.* OBS □ *The cases* ***for and against*** *opera in English at Covent Garden have long been familiar.* T □ *Anything really worth saying could, in her opinion, be said in two minutes. And the same for any arguments* ***for or against.*** WDM □ may follow v or n, as shown.

for ages (and ages) [A (PrepP)] for a long, or comparatively long, time, referring either to the past or to the future □ *'Life is no bed of roses,' they assume; but 'tomorrow will take care of itself'; thus the working classes have been cheerful existentialists* ***for ages.*** UL □ *'You were with him last night, weren't you?' 'Yes, but Mother, he's going in less than three weeks. I shan't see him* ***for ages and ages*** *then.'* PE □ (George is waiting for Josie to get dressed before they go out together for the evening) *I think I'll give Josie a yell.* RUTH: *It won't do any good—not* ***for ages*** *yet.* EGD

for all one cares [Disj (PrepP)] considering how little one cares □ *If you haven't found anyone before that who's fool enough to take you in, you can go and sleep on the Embankment* ***for all I care.*** AITC □ *'Children are that (= so) ungrateful,' grumbled Mrs Wrigley. 'I've got eleven of them but much good it's done me. I might be dead* ***for all they care.'*** HAA □ *'The painter was asking if you want your study done over again in the same colours?' 'Yes; but he can paint it purple and green* ***for all I care****—as long as he hurries up.'*

for all the difference it makes etc [Disj (PrepP)] considering how little difference it makes etc **cl:** it makes; ⚠ there is; I can see □ *I'd been keeping the dope* (pain-killer) *down because I still sometimes got an idea I'd be acquiring virtue by holding off when I wanted it — I wasn't of course.* ***For all the difference it made***

to anyone else I might as well be doped up to the eyes all the time. TST □ ***For all the difference there is*** *between this 'leather-type' material and the genuine article, you'd be a fool to waste your money having your chairs covered in real hide.* □ *Whisky is a fantastic price anyway, so* ***for all the difference a pound*** *or two* ***makes*** *on the price of a bottle I prefer to buy the best.*

for all one's efforts etc [A (PrepP)] despite one's efforts etc **n:** his effort, her education, the frustration □ ***For all*** *Mr Foot****'s*** *courageous* ***efforts****, the 'image' of the Labour Party is slightly less secure.* OBS □ *But he had,* ***for all his dishonesty****, made strong the love of Jill for the lieutenant called Tony.* ARG □ *I must keep this body going. I must give it drink and food and shelter. So long as the thread of life is unbroken it will connect a future with the past* ***for all this*** *ghastly* ***interlude****.* PM □ main clause states that, nonetheless, sth is true, has happened, etc.

for all one/it is worth [A (PrepP)] to the full extent of one's/its powers, resources, energy; as hard as one can **V:** play, run; fight, struggle □ COLONEL: *I think the last day the sun shone was when that dirty little train steamed out of that crowded, suffocating Indian station, with the battalion band playing* ***for all it was worth****.* LBA □ *I'm with another travel firm now, and we're pushing holidays in Britain on to the Americans* ***for all we're worth****.* AITC □ *Mr Salinger plays the ingredients* (of his novel*)* ***for all he is worth****: public opinion polls, left-wing revolutions, hotline exchanges, economic crises.* NS □ *The next thing I saw of him he had climbed over the fence and was running down the road* ***for all he was worth****.* □ *With the wind blowing* ***for all it was worth*** *against them they had a hard time of it at the oars.* ⇨ ⚠ for what sth is worth.

for all one knows etc [Disj (PrepP)] considering how little one knows etc **V:** know, can tell, notice □ *How was I to know you would come back tonight?* ***For all I knew*** *you were never coming back.* AITC □ *He sent me some business without knowing me from Adam; I might have been a complete crook* ***for all he knew****.* PW □ *It might be printed in Greek or Russian* ***for all I can tell****, without my spectacles.*

for all (the world) to see [A (PrepP)] with the purpose, or result, of being freely observed, judged etc by others, by the general public □ *So they painted a nice new board and stuck it up in the playground* ***for all the world to see****.* TT □ *You stay where you are. I'm not having you wandering down the street drunk* ***for all the world to see****.* □ *Once the facts were there* ***for all to see****, the decision—whether taken by the Minister or delegated to the Inspectorate—should be straightforward enough.* G □ *New York is the only place in the US where acute alcoholics, men drinking themselves to death in the street* ***for all to see****, are given this chance* (of rehabilitation). *It's completely voluntary.* OBS

for all that [A (PrepP)] despite sth previously mentioned; nevertheless □ *I'm not going to pretend that I spent* all *my time at Aunt Emily's in a state of outraged sensibility.* ***For all that****, I* was *beginning to find certain details of living in Dufton a bit too sordid to be funny.* RATT □ *The shop is State-owned but* ***for all that*** *the acknowledged personal enterprise of Clara Rothschild (no relation to the others) who has been running dress salons in Budapest since the thirties.* G □ *I turned to go indoors when I saw a girl waiting in the next doorway. I couldn't see her face, only the white silk trousers and long flowered robe, but I knew her* ***for all that****.* QA □ front or end position; stress pattern for 'all that.

for all time [A (PrepP)] for a very long time; until the end of time; for ever[1] (qv); through succeeding ages □ (the British and American Zones of occupation in Germany, 1945) *Some 400,000 of these* (displaced persons) *were Russians and we could reasonably hope that Zhukov would take these off our hands. But the remaining 600,000 would probably remain with us* ***for all time****.* MFM □ *Just when it seemed that the silence was to remain unbroken* ***for all time*** *he paused in the act of buttering a piece of toast, looked very hard across the table, cleared his throat and said in an accusing tone: 'Dr Bottwink, you are a foreigner.'* EM

for all the world like/as if very much, or altogether, like/as if (the implication being that a perceived similarity is surprising) □ *'That sounds* ***for all the world like*** *a lark,' she said in amazement. 'So it should. It is a lark.'* WI □ *Prominent among them was the figure of Anthony Buckridge, creator of 'Jennings', who with his duffle coat and pipe looked* ***for all the world like*** *a prep school master taking games.* NS □ *The only talk-show not to be thrown out of its stride by politics was 'Kaleidoscope', which kept up its nightly commentary* ***for all the world as if*** *people had nothing better to do at such a time than go to the theatre or read a book.* L □ first part of expression functions like adv of degree.

for appearances' etc sake [A (Prep P)] in order to obtain the benefit of seeming to behave in a socially acceptable way etc **n:** appearances', convenience's, safety's □ *'He has a mistress,' I said. 'They* (ie he and his wife) *only live together* ***for the sake of appearances****.'* RATT □ *In Yalta, the Big Three decided to cut up Germany into three parts for occupation purposes. Berlin was supposed to be the vantage-point from which this would be done, and so* ***for convenience's sake*** *Berlin too was cut into three pieces.* L

(just) for argument's sake [A (PrepP)] as a starting point for discussion **V:** ⚠ suppose, say, agree □ *I don't know how much his lordship owes the Exchequer for the privilege of inheriting his father's estate along with his title, but let's suppose,* ***for argument's sake****, that it's a round million in cash.* NS □ *Let's agree* ***for the sake of argument*** *that we each have a 16-year old son who comes to us with this problem. Now what do we do about it?* □ stress pattern for 'argument's sake; variant for the sake of argument.

for sb's benefit[1] [A (PrepP)] in order to help or guide sb, or to suit his interests and wishes □ *Visitors are warned to keep away from the constructional operations. If members of the public choose to disregard the notices put up* ***for their benefit****...* HAA □ *I don't see why you should give up part of your holiday* ***for his benefit****. He wouldn't do the same for you.* □ *It is often necessary to be strict with children* ***for their*** *own* ***benefit****.*

for sb's benefit[2] [A (PrepP)] in order to produce a reaction, often of annoyance, fear, jealousy etc, from a specific person or group □ *I hope Charlie didn't think that remark of mine about picking a very convenient time to be ill was* **for his benefit**: *I quite forgot how often he has to be off work with asthma.* □ *I don't know* **whose benefit** *you think you're crying* **for**. *There's nobody here who's going to let you have your way.*

for the best [A (PrepP)] with good intentions, though the result may not be as desired **V:** ⚠ do, mean, intend, sth □ *In the end the two* (golf) *captains decided upon a complicated set of local rules for the bunkers on this particular course. All this was done* **for the best** ST □ *Your sister shouldn't have interfered, I agree. But she meant it* **for the best** *so don't be too cross with her.*

(all) for the best [Comp/A (PrepP)] (catchphrase) happy or satisfactory in its results, or at least better than was possible or originally foreseen **V:** be; turn out, happen □ ***All is for the best*** *in the best of possible worlds.* CANDIDE (VOLTAIRE 1694-1778) □ *So here she was with the children en route to New Zealand. It had been* **for the best**, *Sarah knew.* WI □ *However, it turned out* **all for the best** *that the sale fell through, as he got a much higher offer shortly afterwards.*

for better or (for) worse [A (PrepP)] whether the result, known or unknown, proves to be good or bad □ (source) *I take thee to my wedded husband, to have and to hold from this day forward,* **for better for worse**, *for richer for poorer, in sickness and in health.* BOOK OF COMMON PRAYER □ MRS ELLIOT: *So things didn't work out then?* RUTH: *No—I've just walked out on him,* **for better or for worse**. EGD □ *Careless talk, which might have drifted away over the moors, has been trapped by the media. A lot of hot air has been translated,* **for better or worse**, *into cold print.* L □ *Some prime ministers, perhaps most great ones, have been interesting in themselves. They were eccentrics either in character or behaviour. Gladstone appeared extraordinary,* **for good or ill**, *to everyone who met him.* NS □ front, middle or end position; variant for good or ill.

for a bit/while [A (PrepP)] (informal) for a short period of time □ *I told him about you and he said that if you were in trouble he would be glad to look after you* **for a bit**. OBS □ *'I'd never go back to school now. What about you?' 'I wouldn't mind going back* **for a bit** *to finish off what I started.'* RFW □ *In 1939 Morris Myerson returned to America and stayed* **for a while** *with his sister in Philadelphia.* ST □ *Prissie unexpectedly hailed a taxi, and pushed the two of them into it, following herself with her suitcase. At least they were safe* **for a while** *in a taxi.* DC

for a change [A (PrepP)] in a way that does not match previous habits, procedures (the implication often, but not necessarily, being that these are, or are becoming, unsatisfactory); for once (qv); for once in a way (qv) □ *Perhaps if it* (a house) *were pulled down they might have a little money in the bank instead of living on overdrafts. Perhaps they could really live in comfort* **for a change**. DBM □ *I suppose you'll be spending your holiday in Devon as usual. Don't you ever think of going somewhere else* **for a change**? □ *'What do you want me to do? Throw the furniture about, or go for you with a kitchen knife?' 'At least that would put you in the wrong* **for a change**. *It's always me who's the louse.'* AITC □ usu end position.

for a consideration [A (PrepP)] in exchange for payment, usu in money but perhaps in the form of some other service □ *One knows practically everybody with an intimacy of detail. One knows, for example, that that old woman is always ready to sit up with an invalid* **for 'a consideration'**. UL □ *'What I did hear I couldn't make out. Something to do with some estate that Ormerod could arrange to have put into Thompson's hands for disposal.'* '**For a consideration**, *no doubt.'* TGLY

for crying out loud! (informal) an exclamation of astonishment, dismay, or annoyance □ ESTHER: *Have you been crying, Ada?* CISSIE: *Leave off, Esther, I tell you.* ESTHER: **For crying out loud** *what's been happening to you two?* ITAJ □ *He's* too *available. I can just hear myself saying:* '**For crying out loud**, *Duke, could you be a little more elusive for a change?'* RT □ *This is the most sinister story I have heard about any politician. If he would do that to his wife, what would he do to us,* **for crying out loud**? NS □ (NONCE) *A wind as cold as winter ran ceaselessly round the harbour with unbroken shriekings and occasional whistles.* '**For crying out gently**, *Charley,' Pop said. 'Where's this? Where have we come to? Lappland?'* BFA □ front, middle or end position.

for days etc at a time etc [A (PrepP)] for several days etc in succession **V:** sit, stand; wait, watch. **n:** days, ⚠ seconds, minutes, hours, weeks, months. **A:** at a time, ⚠ at a stretch; on end; together □ *I was jerked into that zone of unreality one would inhabit* **for seconds at a time** *in the RAF watching a Wimpey* (aeroplane) *scarcely a wing-tip away disintegrate into rather gaudy green orange flames.* RATT □ *Joe never seemed to be in the same job* **for** *more than* **two months at a time**. AITC □ *Along with lethargy often goes television addiction. I'm not talking about the child who has regular favourites—but about the boy who sits mesmerised before the screen* **for hours on end**. OBS □ *Temperatures rose to the lethal limit throughout the whole country and people were obliged to remain indoors* **for weeks on end**. TBC *He realized with a shock that he had not succeeded* **for five minutes together** *in banishing the image of that small dark head.* HD

for dear life [A (PrepP)] vigorously and tenaciously (as one would if trying to defend or preserve one's life) **V:** run, swim; hang on; pull, push; shout; argue □ *'Did you enjoy your pillion-ride?' 'I did not. I was hanging on* **for dear life** *all the way.'* □ *When I left the restaurant the fat man in the corner was still gobbling food* **for dear life**.

for ever[1] [A (PrepP)] until the end of time, or of a person's life; for all time (qv) □ *I just roamed the streets, hoping I suppose to get my hands on another five hundred nicker* (= pounds) *so's the nice life we'd got used to could go on and on* **for ever**. LLDR □ *The colour TV boom is still strong though it will not keep up the pace of the last year* **for ever**. ST □ *In a period of cricket-watching and playing covering the past 25 years, there have been half a dozen Test Matches that will live* **for**

ever in the memory. L □ *'Hey, you!' he shouted, thumping on the door. 'Are you going to be in that bathroom **for ever**?'* □ also used exaggeratedly = 'for a very long time', or ironically; end position.

for ever[2] [A (PrepP)] very frequently, or habitually (but not necessarily continuously) **pres p:** grumbling, helping others, nibbling, having headaches □ *For a man who's **for ever** grumbling about his electricity bills, you're pretty careless about switching off the lights when you leave a room.* □ *...the coolly tender Anna who was **for ever** balancing the claims of her admirers one against the other with the gentle impartiality of a mother.* UTN □ *He's like the rest of you, **for ever** taking umbrage about something. You're making it a perfectly beastly holiday for me, I'm fed up with the lot of you.* US □ usu precedes pres p, as shown, but cf *He's **for ever** up in arms about something or other.*

for example [Conj (PrepP)] by way of illustration; for instance (qv); let us say[2] (qv) □ *But there's speculation in other areas too. **For example**: what is it about a TV spin-off which attracts cash customers to the cinema when the chances are they've shunned it for years?* ST □ *While the trumpet, the horn and the piano were being improved, and the clarinet invented, some instruments—varieties of key-board, **for example**—were falling out of use.* L □ *'But what is the use of an intellectual renaissance that doesn't move the people? Theory and practice only unite under very special circumstances.' '**E.g.** when?' said Lefty. 'Well,' I said, '**e.g.** when the Bolshevik party fought for power in Russia.'* UTN □ introduces or follows specific illustration of general statement; abbreviation e.g. (Latin *exempli gratia* = 'for example') occas used in speech; front, middle or end position; e.g. used in front position only.

for fear of sth/that [A (PrepP)] because of fear of sth happening/that sth might happen **o:** victimization, accidents; hurting her; what neighbours may think. **cl:** (that) he might fall, the boat would sink, nobody would believe him □ *Not all the students have been active in the campaign, but few have dared to stand out against their classmates **for fear of** victimisation, or at least ostracism.* OBS □ *Virginia could understand that Mollie dared not leave the house **for fear of** what Paul might do.* AITC □ *He* (the scientist) *must at all costs keep out of the actual political fray, **for fear of** raising doubts about his integrity and objectivity as a scientist.* OBS □ *The driver said: 'I have no time for Hugh MacDiarmid's opinions. Or his poetry. The man's an atheist.' I smiled politely, **for fear** I might be taken past my stop again.* RT

for the first etc time [A (PrepP)] marks the place (first etc) in a number of occurrences **adj:** first, second, last; hundredth; umpteenth, nth (= any large number, equivalent to umpteenth) □ *'The children aren't home yet?' 'Are you sure?' Prissie seemed surprised and Brigit noticed **for the first time** that it was growing dusk.* DC □ (Beatles' records) *We can appreciate **for the nth time** the dramatic rightness of 'Sergeant Pepper', the richness of the double album and the finesse of 'Abbey Road'.* L □ *Tom, 15 years old and brought up in a village not twenty miles from the sea, was now seeing it **for** only **the second time** in his life.* □ *'Please call me Virginia,' Virginia said **for the tenth time**. Mrs Allen bowed stiffly and continued to call her Miss Martin.* AITC □ *Lennox's wife took the children and left him **for the last time**.* LLDR ⇨ not for the first time.

for free [A (PrepP)] (informal) without payment being required; for nothing[1] (qv) □ *Bowen tried to buy some drinks, conscious of having been fed and made drunk **for free**.* ILIH □ *Many fishmongers still give you an assortment of fishy bits and pieces **for free**.* ST □ *And what did the jolly porter tell him? He said he had the best job in the world. 'Travel anywhere in England, cross-Channel steamers, the Continent—for me, the missus and five kids, all* **for free**.*'* SC

for full/good measure [A (PrepP)] as an extra amount to sth or as an additional item (from shopkeeper adding a little more to weighed goods, lengths of cloth, etc thus making sure he does not give the customer less than what was asked for) **V:** throw in, add, include, sth; display, produce, sth; take, bring, give, sth □ *The argument is that the whole of the military hierarchy should be convicted; some even suggest that President Nixon and his Defence Secretary should be thrown in **for good measure**.* NS *Sometimes Hingley throws in **for good measure** the legends* (about Stalin) *that were manufactured by Trotsky and other political opponents.* OBS □ *I stood waiting and smoking and looking up at the square of night boxed in by the courtyard's roofs, and it could have been a beautiful moment, with the stars thrown in **for full measure**.* PP □ *If Mr Aisgall wanted a divorce, he could afford detectives to trace you here. That would be enough in itself, but **for good measure** they'd ferret out the old boy too.* RATT □ *Hope and Crosby made 'The Road to Singapore' (1939) and thus established one of the most successful and longest running wisecracking duo teams in the movies. **For full measure** they persuaded an up-and-coming sex goddess to join them on their travels.* RT

(just) for fun [A (PrepP)] for amusement, enjoyment or interest, and not for any serious purpose; (just) for a giggle (qv) □ *I'd like to go back again some day **for fun**, say in about ten years' time, and see how it's all getting on.* RFW □ *But the majority bet **for the fun of it**. Their stake is only a small portion of their salary. It's a thrill if they win and it isn't a disaster if they lose.* OBS □ *People don't work on the factory shop floor, or down a mine, **just for the fun of it**.* □ often neg; variant (just) for the fun of it. ⇨ ⚠ in fun.

(just) for a giggle etc [A (PrepP)] (informal) for amusement or enjoyment, not for any serious purpose; (just) for fun (qv) **n:** a giggle, ⚠ a laugh, a joke; (the) laughs □ *'Fancy a round of golf tomorrow, Jim?' Tarbuck knew nothing about the game. Golf, to him, was a game restricted to middle-class followers with old school ties. 'Anything **for a laugh**,' he said.* TVT □ *After leaving school he somehow failed to see eye-to-eye with a succession of exasperated bosses. Then came the night when, at 18, he entered a Butlins talent contest **for a giggle**.* RT □ *I'm more interested in birds* (= girls) *now than fighting. It's these* *mad buggers of 14 who go for the fights. I want to see the football, see the lads win, have a few drinks, and a few laughs. That's what we come* ***for, the laughs***. ST

for good (and all) [A (PrepP)] permanently; for keeps (qv) □ *Alan's been away five years, but from what they say he's definitely coming home* ***for good*** *now.* RFW □ *If he accepted it* (a peerage), *he was accepting the fact that he was out of politics* ***for good***. NM □ *'Wish me luck.' 'Doing what?' 'Going to London.' 'How long for?' I asked him. '****For good****, you ass. I'm leaving Ned's.'* CON □ *If he were to take the responsibility, he needed sanction to join Captain Smith and try to settle 'the Sawbridge question'* ***for good and all***. NM □ *If you borrow money* once, *you're on the slippery slope* ***for good and all***. US □ for good and all emphatic.

for sb's/sth's (own) good [A (PrepP)] so that sb/sth will benefit □ *Our rules try to persuade us that a lot of damned bad food is all* ***for our own good***. HAA □ *Don't think I enjoy finding fault with people. I'm only talking to you like this* ***for your own good***. □ *Piecemeal attacks on the worst excesses of property developers are no substitutes for a policy to ensure that land is used* ***for the good of*** *the community.* ST □ *The Elizabethan Sir Henry Wotton used to call an ambassador a man 'sent abroad to lie* ***for the good of*** *his country.'* NS

for goodness etc sake(!) [Disj (PrepP)] an exclamation of astonishment or protest; in the name of God etc (qv) **n:** goodness, ⚠ God's, Christ's, heaven's, pity's, Pete's □ *The Department of Employment ascribed the rise in Mrs Britain's shopping bill to 'increases in the price of potatoes, and many other goods and services'. Why single out potatoes,* ***for goodness sake****? Few of us eat enough potatoes to knock our budgets more askew than they already are.* SC □ *Battalion headquarters, on our left, had surrendered and I saw the Germans coming across to us. I remember saying to the men; '****For Christ's sake*** *don't shoot now.' That effectively was the end of the battle.* RT □ *'Can you guess why?' Tom smiled at him. There was a silence in which I thought of saying: 'Tom,* ***for Pete's sake*** *stop it!' and rejected the idea.* □ often accompanies appeal, or order, to do or not to do sth.

(not) (just) for (the good of) one's health [A (PrepP)] (ironic) (not) for a trivial reason or purpose □ *There are many conjectures about Mr Nixon's forthcoming visit to Peking but nobody imagines he is going* ***for the good of his health***. □ *'We're safe enough, I tell you.' 'You think those two coppers are hanging around* ***for the good of their health****, then?'* □ *'How many new potatoes have you sold?' 'Oh, I don't know, but several pounds.' 'Several pounds! You ought to have sold several hundredweight, at least, or several tons if you want to persuade the Inspector that you're* ***not*** *in business* ***for your health***.*'* PW □ used to emphasize that the reason is not self-indulgent or capricious; always neg or with neg implication.

(just) for the hell of it [A (PrepP) (informal) because of the brief experience or sensation it offers, esp when this is against the law, conventional practice or one's usual habits □ *In my village, boys have wrecked a beautifully-tended allotment, and smashed all the windows at the railway station, apparently* ***just for the hell of it***. NS □ *There's a difference between speaking necessary truths and embarrassing people* ***for the hell of it***. □ *He is decent, admirable, and has to continue to be so, though it would be very tempting to take him off the rails occasionally,* ***just for the hell of it***. TVT

for instance [Conj (PrepP)] by way of illustration; for example (qv); let us say² (qv) □ *A warning system for earthquakes is probably worthwhile, since quite minor precautions should be able to reduce the number of casualties.* ***For instance*** *many of the 30,000 killed in the great Lisbon disaster of 1755, were buried by the collapse of the roofs of churches where they had gone for shelter.* NSC □ *Too much time* (when travelling) *must not be sacrificed to safety. No one today,* ***for instance****, would think it reasonable to impose speed limits severe enough to prevent* all *road deaths.* OBS □ *Much of the anti-trade-union propaganda is directed at women in the hope they will get at their menfolk: those stories of neglected old people dying of cold during the* (electric) *power work-to-rule,* ***for instance***. NS □ introduces or follows a specific illustration of a general statement; front, middle or end position.

for keeps [A (PrepP)] (informal) permanently; for good (and all) (qv) □ *Supposing he wants to keep her here, in what I believe is called a love-nest, for occasional visits? It isn't likely he would want her* ***for keeps***. PW □ *I asked where Luke was, and who was nursing him. She went on: 'As a matter of fact, if I've got him lying on his back* ***for keeps****, I shall be grateful, as long as I've got him at all.'* NM

(just) for kicks [A (PrepP)] (informal) in order to get excitement or pleasure (perhaps, but not necessarily, of a dangerous or perverse kind) □ *Sheila Cronin is the dominant partner in the relationship with Frank Price. Did she urge him on to beat up Thomas Dolan* ***just for kicks****? Or are they both victims of our society?* TVT □ *'There must be an easier way of doing that!' 'You tell me then. I'm not doing it* ***for kicks***.*'*

for lack/want of sth [A (PrepP)] because there is little, or none, of sth □ *The ships were needed urgently back in England for the build-up of the army, and if they had been damaged on the beaches the whole venture might have met disaster a week later* ***for lack of*** *supplies.* RFW □ *And experience proves that such an institution will die. It is choked by its own perfection. It cannot take root* ***for lack of*** *soil.* PL □ *The dog* ***for want of*** *any better provender was lapping at the whiskey on the floor.* OMIH

for life [A (PrepP)] for the rest of one's/sb's life; permanently □ *Scars of battle from Belfast have marked this soldier* ***for life***. ST □ *The* (wholesale) *firm sells its goods to 'the High Street trader' and the public gets nowhere near its warehouses; any retailer who helps even his brother to buy there is likely to find himself banned from the premises* ***for life***. ST □ *When the British public gives its interest and affection, it gives it, like a dog,* ***for life***. NS □ *If the Battalion got posted to Singapore or Hong Kong I'd probably sign on for another three years. I'd sign on* ***for life*** *if they'd let me drive.* RT □ in the last example for life refers to a maximum period of service in one of the Armed Forces; a similar use occurs where one's working or professional life is referred to.

(just) for love/the love of sth/sb [A (PrepP)] without payment, or material reward, because one likes either the work itself or the person one works for **o:** it, the thing; one's family, friend; firm, party, country □ *As a matter of fact he's one of my best informers. The beggar's name is Miguel. He really does all this* ***for love****. You see, I saved his life once.* OMIH □ MILLY: *Well, I'd cleaned the cottage up all Friday,* ***just for the love of*** *the thing. Cleaned it up some more on Saturday.* EHOW

for the love of God etc exclamation of astonishment, dismay etc **o:** God, ⚠ Christ, heaven, Mike □ *'Look, Robert,' I said. '****For the love of God*** *give it a few minutes' thought. It's a three-hour trip. That means you'll hit London at half past two, having had no sleep.'* CON □ *'****For the love of Mike****!' Jean exclaimed as the glass of whisky was set in front of her. 'You don't expect me to drink all this, do you?'* □ ***For the love of heaven****, child, can't you sit still for one minute?* □ can be used to introduce an appeal, as in first and last examples.

(just) for luck [A (PrepP)] in order to bring good luck □ *When a couple leave for their honeymoon it's the custom to throw an old boot or shoe after them* ***for luck****, or to tie it to the back of their car.* □ *There's your posy, dear, I've put in a little bit of white heather* ***just for luck****.* □ *'That was a nice goodbye kiss,' he said to his little grand-daughter. 'Let's have another one,* ***for luck*** *this time.'* □ sometimes said without much real meaning as in last example.

for a moment [A (PrepP)] very briefly **V:** think...that, believe...that; pause; sit down; glance □ *'What's the matter, darling?' 'Nothing,' she said. For how could she tell him that it seemed,* ***for a moment****, as if Prissie had stood at the foot of the bed watching them.* DC □ *Stand still* ***a moment****, while I straighten your collar.* □ *He might have popped in* ***for a moment****, since he was passing this way.* □ often used without for with verbs of action. ⇨ ⚠ next entry.

for the moment etc [A (PrepP)] temporarily **n:** moment, ⚠ present, time being □ *Carry on* ***for the moment*** *with your own ideas and don't take any notice of your friends' criticism or advice.* WI □ *Evidence will be brought forward later on to show that this suggested usage agrees quite well with common usage in many ways;* ***for the time being*** *let us just note this new way of defining the concept.* SNP □ *With a click sounding in her ears like doom, the receiver at the other end was replaced. This was the worst of all. That,* ***for the present****, was all that Brigit could think.* DC □ used only with present tenses. ⇨ ⚠ previous entry.

for the most part[1] [A (PrepP)] in most cases; mostly (the reference being to the great majority of people or things); in the main (qv) □ *Of the many different animals and birds that were brought to us while we were at base camp, about a fifth were babies, and, although they were charming little things* ***for the most part****, they caused a great deal of extra work for us.* BB □ *Ford's first important film dates from the mid-Twenties, but for ten years before that he'd turned out innumerable two-reelers: Westerns and other frontier films* ***for the most part****.* L □ modifies a preceding n.

for the most part[2] [A (PrepP)] mostly; largely (the reference being to frequency of occurrence, or to preponderance in degree or amount); in the main (qv) □ *...the heroism, the holiness, the sublimity to which mankind perpetually aspires,* ***for the most part*** *in vain.* DOP □ *This August there is a deeper sense of futility in the feverish air. In the Republic, politicians stand aghast and* ***for the most part*** *helpless.* L □ *Then it had carried four lines of heavy military traffic day and night. Now this tarmac miracle of engineering had,* ***for the most part****, disintegrated.* ARG □ modifies v, adj or adv.

for my money [Disj (PrepP)] (informal) in my opinion □ *They* (newspapers) *are there for the record, down in 'Back Numbers'.* ***For my money*** *they can stay in the big bound volumes that stand on the shelves.* PP □ *This performance has a distinguished company headed by the marvellous Ben Luxon and Janet Baker who,* ***for my money****, is just about the top singer we've got.* RT □ *There are two things people get really excited about. One is food; the other is the weekly, or rather daily, wash.* ***For my money*** *it's the washing machine that takes pride of place over the deep-freeze and the double-bed in most people's value scales.* SC □ stress pattern for 'my money.

(just) for the nonce [A (PrepP)] (facetious) temporarily; on this/that (one) occasion (from an Old English form equivalent to 'for the once') □ *Since reading that note the foundations of the scientific approach to life had been so severely shaken that* ***for the nonce*** *he was willing to truckle even to superstition.* RM □ *He let it be assumed* ***for the nonce*** *that he was one of the touring party.* □ *This year he thought he would let a swan get on with motherhood, but that meant getting dad* (here = male swan) *out of the way* ***for the nonce****.* L

for nothing[1] [A (PrepP)] without payment being required; for free (qv) □ *He went to Joan Littlewood's theatre workshop in London and subsisted on scraps once more. 'Except that Bert's Café in Angel Lane used to give you bubble and squeak* (fried potato-and-cabbage leftovers) ***for nothing****.'* SC □ *There is very little art in hitch-hiking as Germaine Greer describes it. It seems rather to be one of the crudest ways of getting something* ***for nothing****.* ST

for nothing[2] [A (PrepP)] without good reason □ *I didn't tell you until I got the doctor's report: I didn't want to have you worrying* ***for nothing****.* □ *In the English version of the tale, Rumpelstiltskin went on his way, while everybody laughed at him for having had all that trouble* ***for nothing****.* L

for old times' sake [A (PrepP)] because of tender, or sentimental, memories of one's past □ *I'd never been to Inverness before, so I decided to drop in on Gordon* ***for old times' sake****.* □ *She had never cared for jazz music, though she occasionally permitted herself a little ragtime* ***for old times' sake****.* HAA □ stress pattern for old 'times' sake.

for once [A (PrepP)] on this/that occasion (if not, or hardly ever, at any other time); for a change (qv) (the implication often being that sth should be done more often than it is) □ *You're early* **for once**, *thank God.* PW □ JO: *Why did you tell me that story? Couldn't you have made something up?* HELEN: *You asked for the truth and you got it* **for once**. TOH □ *But why on earth could it* (the Government) *not have gone one step further and have arranged to have a really scientific election* **for once**? NSC □ *On most occasions, and from most people, Isabel was pleased to hear Harold praised; but* **for this once** *she wasn't.* PW □ (for) this/that once is used when one wishes to indicate the first, or only, occasion of doing sth that is not contrasted with usual habits or procedures in an ironic or critical way.

for once in a way [A (PrepP)] on this/that occasion (if not usually); for a change (qv); for once (qv) □ *'What on earth is the idea, Chris?' 'Oh, just a hunch, a crazy idea, I suppose. But perhaps you'll indulge me* **for once in a way**.*'* TBC □ *'Weren't you at Out-Patients this morning?' 'Yes—and* **for once in a way** *I was seen promptly at 10.30.'*

for one reason or another [A (PrepP)] for a reason not known, not remembered, or not specified; for some reason (or other) (qv) □ *Having* **for one reason or another** *missed the previous broadcasts from Edinburgh, I eventually caught up with the Festival in Anne Howell's Saturday-morning recital from the Freemasons' Hall.* L □ *Even motorists may feel some guilt about leaving a car the whole day in a city street, but* **for one reason or another** *many of them really depend on their cars.* SC □ *Now, what was I doing that day? Anyway,* **for one reason or another**, *I had left the children with a neighbour.*

for one thing (...(and) for another thing) [Conj (PrepP)] as one factor (...(and) as another factor) in support of an opinion, argument, objection, accusation etc □ *Anyway, Robert lived with his mother's parents, whom I seldom saw,* **for one thing**, *I dislike them.* CON □ *There's a pretty widespread dissatisfaction with the way you're going on.* **For one thing** *the way you just disappeared after taking your finals. Your father told me you hadn't even given them your address.* HD □ (someone asks Roman Polanski about his film version of 'Macbeth') *'Are you going to give Shakespeare equal billing?' 'Why should I?' he buoyantly replies. '***For one thing**, *it's already fairly well-known that he is the author.* **For another thing**, *he hasn't got an agent!'* ST □ stress pattern for 'one thing (...(and) for a'nother thing).

for one's/its own sake [A (PrepP)] because one/it is what one/it is; because of one's/its own qualities regardless of social class, importance, usefulness etc **V:** like, love, value, sb/sth; marry sb □ *One of the things that makes Ludovic Kennedy a superb television journalist is his real interest in what makes people think or act the way they do, and his liking for people* **for their own sake**. RT □ *I love materials* **for their own sake** *and I love the feel of them.* OBS □ *She was so outshone publicly by her husband that, as his widow, she could scarcely credit that people might want to come and visit her* **for her own sake**. □ stress pattern for one's/its 'own sake.

for one's pains [A (PrepP)] as a disappointing, or unsatisfactory, return for one's trouble, efforts **V:** be snubbed, repulsed; be wounded, shot □ *He had been unable to get permission to go through to Upper Burma. He tried it without permission and had narrowly missed being shot* **for his pains**. ARG □ *They had grown to look more like sheep; but every now and then one of them reverted to earlier lambhood, tried to take a pull of mother's milk, and got buffeted in the ribs* **for its pains**. SPL □ usu end position after pass V.

for one's (own) part [Disj (PrepP)] as far as one is concerned; in one's (own) opinion; as one's contribution to the proceedings **det:** my, our, their; John's; the committee's □ *'I imagine they'll* (properties) *be ours one day,' Brigit said wearily. '***For my part** *you're welcome to the lot.'* DC □ **For their part**, *the middle-class Indians completely fail to understand why people should give up (even temporarily) the comforts of Western living and roam barefoot around India in the sun.* ST □ *The women sit on sofas by the fireplace and the men stand around the President.* **For my own part**, *I drain two large scotches too rapidly and can't get enough caviar, bad as that combination is, to help absorb them.* OBS □ use of own is commonest with my; stress patterns for 'one's part, for one's 'own part.

for (all) practical purposes [Disj (PrepP)] practically considered, as far as usefully matters; to all intents (and purposes) (qv) □ *There were, after all, four Zulu Kings—more if you are fussy about titles, but four* **for all practical purposes**—*yet this book deals only with the first two.* SC □ (touring in France, 1973) **For practical purposes** *there are two classes of hotel and very little in between.* OBS □ *But* **for all practical purposes**, *the centre has been in power ever since I can remember.* NS

for the price of sth [A (PrepP)] in exchange for what sth costs □ *They* (homosexuals) *only use pubs for picking up boyfriends. They don't booze, themselves, any more than you or I would if surrounded by bedworthy women who might be had* **for the price of** *a few drinks.* RATT □ *Do your realize you could buy a loaf of bread and half a pound of cheese* **for the price of** *that packet of cigarettes?*

for real [Comp/A (PrepP)] (informal) real, not sham or pretended; in a real way, not in a sham or pretended way **V:** be; see, hit, sail, fly □ (recruiting advertisement) *To fly a powerful, high-performance aircraft at great speed and with complete precision, in any manoeuvre, on a mission: this is flying* **for real**. ST □ *As Mr MacIntyre said, with only a touch of Celtic extravagance, 'It* (modern Ireland) *is a dream in which only the knives are* **for real**.*'* L □ *'Everything on this programme,' Peter told us, 'had to be* **for real**. *I did all the stunt work myself.'* RT □ *There are a few magnificent chapel scenes, during one of which the bible gets thumped* **for real** *as the whole congregation goes into a praise-the-Lord jam session.* NS □ *Actually he had got the wrong idea because people who have been cast away* **for real** *say that you don't just lie under a palm tree for most of the time: you have to work about 16 hours a day just to survive.* ST

for reasons/some reason best/only known to oneself [A (PrepP)] for private reasons; for reasons that others cannot guess or cannot understand (the implication sometimes that the person responsible does not himself fully understand why he has done sth) □ *He was getting on well in the business and was in line for a directorship when* ***for some reason only known to himself*** *he gave the whole thing up and bought a small farm in Wales.* □ *The rules say that any application for an extension must be made before the original period has expired, and* ***for reasons best known to himself*** *the Minister let that day pass.* ST □ ***For some reason best known to themselves*** *the vast majority of 15-year olds nowadays leave school under the impression that the first of the Ten Commandments is 'Thou shalt not steal'.* SC

(just) for the record [Disj/A (PrepP)] so that it should be recorded □ *'****For the record****,' he said 'these are the companies that have selling contracts with the Diamond Corporation.'* DS □ *In fact, commentating, like criticism or teaching, has little to do with one's own ability as a performer. But,* ***just for the record****, this is what half a dozen of the BBC's top commentators are like when they emerge from behind the microphone and into the sporting arena.* RT □ *He has apparently no intention of giving evidence before the Commission. It might have been good tactics to put his case forcibly* ***for the record****.* SC □ (reader's letter) *I don't know if James Fenton sees himself as a horny-handed champion of the oppressed but in his article on the political crisis in Lincoln he is,* ***for the record****, wrong on the following points:...* NS □ introduces, or refers to, a statement, fact, item of information, etc that is made deliberately, officially or publicly; as A, middle or end position; as Disj, front or middle position. ⇨ ⚠ off the record.

for the rest [Conj (PrepP)] as far as other things are concerned; apart from that □ *Not much seemed to have changed; there were a couple of new stores and electricity had reached the place while I had been away.* ***For the rest*** *it was unaltered.* RFW □ *That was the only thing she had asked.* ***For the rest****, she had submitted without protest to everything that was arranged for her.* AITC □ *But as far as serious dancing is concerned, Gene Kelly has retired. 'There are certain types of dancing you could do until you're 102, but* ***for the rest*** *I find it too difficult.'* RT □ front or middle position.

for sb's/sth's sake [A (PrepP)] in order to benefit, please, protect or defend the interests of sb/sth □ *Maybe later he would realise that all she had done was* ***for*** *the children****'s sake****, not her own.* WI □ *'Please accept, Father,' she said, 'I'd be so proud of you.' 'I'd make a fool of myself.' 'You wouldn't.* ***For my sake****.'* OMIH □ *Most heads* (of schools) *like things as they are. The excuse is that it is all* ***for the sake of*** *the pupils. The aim is to decorate them with as many certificates and credentials as they can muster.* OBS □ *The convention has been filmed through the eyes of this group that had to switch to Reagan,* ***for the sake of*** *party unity.* ST □ stress pattern for 'sb's/'sth's sake.

for sale [Comp/A (PrepP)] available for purchase; be on sale (qv) **V:** be; offer, put up, display □ *These articles are displayed* ***for sale*** *in chaotic piles, though I have never seen anyone buy anything in Mrs Rinckham's shop except ice-cream, which is also* ***for sale****, and the 'Evening News'.* UTN □ *There were a few empty shops with '****For Sale*** *or To Let' notices on them, but we could find no accommodation except furnished lodgings.* ⇨ ⚠ to let.

for shame(!) exclamation of reproach, usually addressed directly to the person who has behaved badly, or said or done sth shameful □ CISSIE: *You ought to be ashamed of yourselves, I told them—at the first sign of intimidation you want to give in.* ***For shame!*** *I yelled at them—* ***for shame!*** CSWB □ *He picked up a handful of gravel and drew back his arm to throw* (at the hens). *'Stop it Patrick,' Jenny called. 'What do you think you're doing?* ***For shame****. Leave them alone.'* TGLY □ *Get out of here. You say I'm a fool.* ***Shame on you****.* □ variant shame on you(!).

for the simple reason that [A (PrepP)] because and only because (the implication being that, in the speaker's opinion, that one reason is so obvious or incontrovertible that no others are necessary) □ *John Counsell, for example, whose company at the Theatre Royal, Windsor, receives no Arts Council grant* ***for the simple reason that*** *Counsell has never asked for one...* OBS □ *They would not be expecting her to escape* ***for the simple reason that*** *she was a prisoner and could not.* TCB □ *'Why does he take on so many public engagements, if he's always feeling tired?'* ***'For the simple reason that*** *he can't say No.'*

for some reason (or other) [A (PrepP)] for a reason not known, not remembered or not specified; for one reason or another (qv) □ *The other day I found an old doll in the toy cupboard upstairs and I called it Clementine, just to give it a name.* ***For some reason*** *it seems to have frightened Nicky.* DC □ *Here we have an example of an involuntary emotional response giving away a secret which,* ***for some reason or other****, the subject of the experiment wants to keep to himself.* SNP □ *No, I won't have an egg, thank you. I seem to have gone off eggs lately* ***for some reason****.* □ stress pattern for 'some reason (or other).

for some time [A (PrepP)] for a long time □ *I heard no sound after the door closed, and* ***for some time*** *I stood as one enchanted in the middle of the room.* UTN □ *Experiments with tools given their power by an explosive have been in progress* ***for some time*** *here and in the United States.* NSC □ (of a book) *In fact, 'The Case of the Helmeted Airman' has clearly been sitting around* ***for some time*** *gathering dust.* NS

for a start [Conj (PrepP)] (informal) first of all² (qv); in the first place² (qv); to begin with² (qv); to start with² (Vol 1) (qv) □ *Conditions at Mountain Colliery contrasted sadly with the training centre.* ***For a start****, there were no pithead baths.* OBS □ *Jacky Stoller has a most unusual hold over Anthony Valentine.* ***For a start****, she's his girlfriend, and, as producer of 'Raffles' she is, in effect, his boss as well.* TVT □ *'Why don't you take your wife with you on this trip?' 'We couldn't afford it,* ***for a start****, and, anyway, I don't think she'd like to leave the children with somebody else for so long.'* □ HELEN (points to wicker basket): *Hey, you can throw that bloody thing out* ***for a start****.* GEOFF: *What thing?* HELEN: *That thing there. You're not put-*

ting my grandchild in a thing like that. TOH □ accompanies first item in argument, statement of opinion, recommendation or order; often used for emphasis without speaker detailing any further items and perhaps without his having any clear idea of what these might be.

for that matter [Conj (PrepP)] as is additionally, but equally, relevant □ *You oughtn't to have spoken like that to Bernard's friends, or to anybody* ***for that matter****.* HAA □ *He stressed the need to recognize that universities (and polytechnics,* ***for that matter****) are not setting out solely to train people for jobs.* L □ *A man — or a woman,* ***for that matter****—can now encircle the globe with little more luggage than once he used to take to a destination not 60 miles from his own front door.* T □ front or end position.

for this relief etc, much thanks (catchphrase) I am/we are very grateful for this relief etc **det:** this, that, the, which. **n:** relief; consolation, help, service, advice □ (source) BERNARDO: *'Tis now struck twelve; get thee to bed, Francisco.* FRANCISCO: ***For this relief, much thanks****: 'tis bitter cold, and I am sick at heart.* HAMLET I I □ *'It must have fallen from heaven straight into the mind of the artist,' said Berlioz of the second movement of Beethoven's Eighth Symphony, but Beethoven's sketch books show that it was tortured out bar by bar. So Beethoven was a human being, and I am another;* ***for this relief, much thanks****.* ST □ (a film) . . .*a car chase with an airborne sequence of extraordinary dream-like appeal.* ***For this flight of fancy*** *alone,* ***much thanks****.* NS □ *Mr Bibby, who produced a lengthy tome on* (Thomas) *Huxley in 1959, has distilled it well into a compact and elegant little book.* ***For which service, much thanks****.* NS □ often ironic or facetious.

for two pins [A (PrepP)] (informal) with very little persuasion or provocation □ *'I don't usually go round fainting.' 'See how you feel at playtime.* ***For two pins*** *I'd throw a faint myself and come and join you.'* TT □ ***For two pins****, Granny Taylor, I'd be out of that door and down them* (= those) *stairs if it was the last thing I did.* MM □ *'It is a Tableau,' said Miss Pemberton, with awful clarity. 'The whole point is that the scene should be static,' at which point Lydia felt she would resign the whole thing* ***for sixpence****.* WDM □ small sums of money may be substituted for two pins, as in last example.

for want of a better name etc [A (PrepP)] because there is no better name etc that the speaker can think of **n:** name, ⚠ word, term □ *The story regarding these beings, whom we are calling 'demons'* ***for want of a better name****, states that once upon a time there were two kinds of people.* NDN □ *One forgets so quickly one's own youth: once I was interested myself in what* ***for want of a better term*** *they call news.* QA □ *The ballet, 'Unfamiliar Games', is,* ***for want of a better word****, abstract; at any rate, it has no narrative theme.* L □ said to excuse or justify the use of a name etc with which the speaker is not fully satisfied.

for what sth is worth [Disj/A (PrepP)] however much or little value, importance, or significance may be given to sth (the implication being that the speaker is not certain and invites others to be the judge) **n:** it, that; opinion, evidence, report; popularity, position □ *But I'm only giving you the evidence* ***for what*** *it****'s worth****. I'm not giving any interpretation.* TBC □ *He is,* ***for what*** *it* ***is worth*** *(which in terms of public impact does not seem to be much), the 'shadow' Minister of Employment — or Mr Foot's opposite number as the Conservatives' emissary to the trade unions.* NS □ *As a criticism of what is undoubtedly a very remarkable work, it was unfair and inadequate — but not, I think irrelevant. I cite it* ***for what*** *it* ***is worth****.* DOP ⇨ ⚠ for all one/it is worth.

for years etc to come [A (PrepP)] for many years etc, dating from the time of speaking **n:** (many) years, ⚠ a long time, months, weeks □ (illustrated advertisement) *Take a good look! It's the Ronson C.F.L., the new shaver that sets the pace* ***for years to come****.* DM □ *Much has been written about the campaign in North-West Europe and it will be a happy hunting ground for historians* ***for*** *many* ***years to come****.* MFM □ *The drought has been so severe that, even if we do get rain, water supplies will still have to be rationed* ***for weeks to come****.*

forbidden fruit (is sweetest) (saying) sth that is desired because it is forbidden or disapproved of (is the most attractive) (from Eve's eating the fruit of the Tree of the Knowledge of Good and Evil in GENESIS II 1-14) □ *Pity the weight-reducers who work in restaurants, sweetshops and pubs! How awful to have one's will power tested every minute of the day by working with* ***forbidden fruit*** *not allowed on the diet-sheet.* TVT □ *There's bound to be a time when the unquestioning acceptance of home gives way to a critical inquiry of it. Disobeying, contradicting, sampling* ***forbidden fruit****—it's growing up.* OBS □ ***Forbidden fruit is*** *always* ***sweetest*** *and there are some people who enjoy sex more if they feel guilty.* TVT

forbidden ground/territory an area into which entry is forbidden; (fig) a subject, activity etc which is forbidden or disapproved of □ *The second draft was still to be rejected by the New Zealanders, but it laid the foundations for a British counter-proposal. This British document trespassed on* ***forbidden ground*** *in the opposite direction.*L □ *Whatever his motive I'm surprised he lent his presence. Surely the occult is* ***forbidden territory*** *for clergymen.*

a force to be reckoned with [Comp (NP)] sb/sth that cannot be lightly treated, opposed or defied **V:** ⚠ be, become; make sb □ *It's this combination of simplicity and righteousness, verging at times on fanaticism but backed up by hard cash, that has made Gaddafi* ***a force to be reckoned with****.* L □ *Despite the protests about truckling to terrorists, the Provisionals are* ***a*** *political* ***force to be reckoned with****.* NS □ *Some 20 years ago Bayure Nakulema was already* ***a force to be reckoned with*** *in his village of Wayen, in the West African State of Upper Volta.* OBS □ *Regionalism is certainly* ***a force to be reckoned with*** *in Spain, but it has not proved so strong in this election as was thought.*L

force sb's hand [V + O pass] compel sb to do sth other than, or sooner than, he intended (from the tactics of card games) □ *But it had been free science, without secrets, without much national feeling.* That *used to be science; in the* *future,* that *must be science again. Meanwhile, the war had* ***forced their hands****.* NM □ *Wilson has been thinking for some time of a merger with Boots in 12 or 18 months, when the Glaxo profits turned stronger. It was the Beecham bid that* ***forced his hand*** *now.* ST □ *The Labour Party Chairman, Mr Wedgwood Benn, said on 'The World This Weekend' that his proposal for a referendum on entry to Europe might* ***force the hand of*** *the Prime Minister.* L

(by) force of arms [A (PrepP)] (by) warfare; (by) the threat or use of weapons □ *Get what supplies you can from the villagers, but do so without resorting to* ***force of arms****.* □ *But for the presence of British troops, the Communist minority, might have succeeded in seizing power* ***by*** *terrorism and* ***force of arms****.* MFM

force of circumstance [o (NP)] a combination of events and conditions that leaves one little or no choice of action **prep:** ⚠ by, through, owing to □ *It was* ***force of circumstance*** *that led to their getting married. There was nobody else of marriageable age on the island—neither wanted to leave and both were lonely.* □ *The camp contained men from many backgrounds brought together through* ***force of circumstance*** □ *He* (a painter) *hopes that a degree will give him access to 'at least some policy-making role' in graphic education, a subject in which he has grown interested first* ***by force of circumstance*** *but later by choice.* G

(from) force of habit (owing to) the strong inclination to do certain things in a certain way from having always done so in the past □ *Then I did the thing the research man always does. I wondered why I took the trouble. But* ***force of habit*** *dies hard.* PP □ *Three new murders, two new air crashes, one old fashioned strike; I don't know why I buy it* (a newspaper) *really —* ***force of habit*** *I suppose.* TT □ *I'm enjoying a couple of weeks away from work, but* ***from force of habit*** *Monday starts early with 'The News' at 7.0 and 'Today' (Radio 4).* RT

a foregone conclusion [Comp (NP)] an end, consequence, or result that is completely predictable **V:** ⚠ be; think, make, sth □ *Although opinion in metropolitan France still seems solidly behind General de Gaulle's plans for Algeria, the success of the referendum is not* ***a foregone conclusion****. A massive affirmative is demanded.* T □ *How can a students' union, or a nation, hold a great debate if the result is* ***a foregone conclusion****?* SC □ *Many people think it's* ***a foregone conclusion*** *that England will beat Finland comfortably in their World Cup qualifying match at Wembley on Wednesday. I'm one of them.* TVT □ occas pl.

a foreign body [O (NP)] a piece, or particle, of matter introduced from the outside and which should not be present in sth, esp the parts, or tissues, of the body **V:** remove, dislodge, get rid of □ *Removal of* ***a foreign body*** *from the eye, other than by use of a saline eyewash, should be left to the doctor.* □ *We decided that if we first strained the water to get rid of such obvious* ***foreign bodies*** *as grit and insects, and then boiled it well, it would be safe to drink.*

foreign parts [o (NP)] regions, or countries, not one's own (used collectively in a rather imprecise way that covers all or any of them) **prep:** ⚠ in, from □ *After twenty-three years in* ***foreign parts*** *I had smugly assumed that I had long since spanned the whole gamut of bureaucratic ingenuity.* BM □ *'We had a cockatoo,' the old lady recalled, 'that my brother—who was a sailor, you know — had brought home from* ***foreign parts****.'* □ *On his travels Hunt drinks only orange juice and milk, never touching the water in* ***foreign parts****.* TVT

forewarned is forearmed (catchphrase) a warning of danger, or sth unpleasant, to come serves as a preparation to meet it, gives one the opportunity to protect or defend oneself as well as one can □ *'I understand Sir Julius is spending Christmas at Warbeck Hall, chief.' 'Well, thanks for telling me, Sikes.* ***Forewarned is forearmed****. I shan't be sorry to have the chance of giving that windbag a piece of my mind.'* EM □ ***Forewarned is forearmed****. Many of the thousands of holidaymakers travelling abroad would be spared the risk of injury or death if more publicity were devoted to the problems of foreign motoring.* ST

forget more about sth than sb ever knew (saying) one/sb knows much more about a subject/skill than another or others mentioned **o:** camping, cooking; music, football □ *'And Mr Prew has* ***forgotten more about*** *camping out* ***than*** *most people* ***ever knew****,' Miss Wriggleston interposed.* RM □ *To put it kindly, the author is racking his brains. Carlyle, who* ***forgot more about*** *revolution* ***than*** *Reich will* ***ever know****, urged that 'Know thyself' was an impossible maxim till it can be translated into this partially possible one, 'Know what thou canst work at.'* L □ (NONCE) *I would have sold my soul for Uncle Walt* (Disney). *Just him, not the studio. He was a man who'd* ***forgotten more about*** *family entertainment* ***than*** *most people* ***ever learn****.* TVT □ tenses usu as in headphrase.

forgive and forget [v + v non-rev] (catchphrase) dismiss ill feeling, the desire to blame and punish, etc entirely from one's mind □ *Then Holleb gets beaten up, and his apartment smashed to pieces. He must either* ***forgive and forget****, or remember and pursue—see the case through the court.* L □ *Cissie, unknown to Flora, has entered a competition and has made the mistake of winning. Flora is fully prepared to* ***forgive and forget****—as long as Cissie hands over the prize.* TVT □ *You were quite right in what you said to me, that I'd have told you the same. All right, sport, all right.* ***Forgiven and forgotten****.* THH □ *'They* (Irishmen) *bother you?' I said. 'They're all right,' he said magnanimously,* ***forgiving and forgetting****.* PP

forgive sb his trespasses forgive sb for what he has done wrong □ (source) ***Forgive*** *us* ***our trespasses*** *as we* ***forgive*** *them* ***that trespass against us****.* BOOK OF COMMON PRAYER (LORD'S PRAYER) □ RONNIE: *Everyone thinks what I say doesn't count. Like they used to think of Dad. Poor old Harry—poor old Ronnie. But you* ***forgive*** *me* ***my trespasses*** *don't you, Addie?* ITAJ □ *During the First World War it was a shock to many simple people, who had been taught that Christ was the Prince of Peace, and that we were to* ***forgive*** *those* ***that trespass against us****, and that peacemakers were blessed, to see, for example, priests publicly blessing in-*

struments of destruction. AH □ variant forgive sb who trespasses against one.

a forlorn hope (dated military) a small band of soldiers sent out in advance of the main force; a hope that is almost certain not to be realized □ *So the lieutenant with* ***his forlorn hope*** *of followers led the advance attack that was to draw the enemy's fire.* □ *It is to this theatre that Mr Turnell wishes to attach Racine—**a forlorn hope** indeed. He wants us to engage with Racine as we do with Shakespeare.* L □ *I can understand why wages and prices chase each other, but not why they are allowed to: the explanation that it's never possible to stop it without being unfair to somebody is unconvincing when I remember the much worse injustices of* ***forlorn hopes*** *and strategic sacrifices of lives during the war.* L

fortune favours the brave (saying) a person who is willing to take risks is often lucky, and more so than one who is timid or over-cautious □ (cricket commentary) *Well, that was a bit of a swipe—not exactly a text-book stroke—but Botham connected and hit the ball into the stand.* ***Fortune favours the brave!*** □ *Miller made a daring, and dangerous, manoeuvre to overtake, and once again proved that* ***Fortune*** *often* ***favours the brave.*** □ fortune with capital or small F.

(have/take) forty winks (informal) (have) a short sleep, esp a daytime nap □ *'You must make him rest, dear,' he said to Eric; 'you know, feet up and* ***forty winks.'*** HAA □ *I drew my chair up to the fire and thought 'I'll just* ***have forty winks*** *now, before the children come home from school.'* □ *His father, Nick, says that when the TV production team joined him and Annie in their smallish sitting-room in Oxford and the lights began to warm up, Benjamin reacted by* ***taking 40 winks.*** TVT

foul one's (own) nest [V + O] dirty, polute, or bring disgrace to, one's home, family, profession, country etc □ *1972 will be remembered as a vintage year for doom merchants, the year when mankind finally realised that it cannot go on* ***fouling its nest*** *indefinitely, the year of the first United Nations conference on the environment.* NS □ *He upsets every orthodox applecart in sight and* ***fouls his own*** *academic* ***nest*** *with aquiline droppings.* RT □ also pl foul their own nests.

foul play[1] (sport) play that is contrary to the rules of a game; (fig) unfair or unscrupulous dealings □ *It seemed to the spectators that the referee was letting a fair amount of* ***foul play*** *go unchecked.* □ *Manufacturers continue to offer 2p off various goods, but since the abolition of resale price maintenance no one can be sure what figure the 2p is coming off. Many shoppers suspect* ***foul play*** *and this type of* (sales) *promotion has lost much of its appeal in consequence.* ST

foul play[2] (legal) violent crime, esp criminal assault and murder □ *'A sudden death has occurred here,' he said. 'It is inevitable—is it not?—that it must be followed by police inquiries.' 'You seem to have jumped to the conclusion that because of what has happened to this unfortunate young man there must have been* ***foul play.'*** EM □ *The body of an elderly man was found early this morning in the darkened doorway of a High Street shop. According to a police statement,* ***foul play*** *is not suspected.* □ *The commission of inquiry failed to establish any satisfactory reason for the crash. It left open the question whether Hammarskjöld had died as a result of a pilot's error or of* ***foul play.*** RT □ *(not) suspect* ***foul play*** collocation used in police reports.

a founding father [Comp (NP)] an originator and/or patron of an institution, popular movement, school of art or thought, etc **V:** ⚠ be; regard, consider, sb as □ *For some time Australia has been having pious second thoughts about certain* ***founding fathers*** *of its culture.* SC □ *Michael Carreras is the son of Colonel James Carreras,* ***founding father*** *of Hammer horror* (films). ST □ *Mary Tudor was subjected to heavy pressure by her father and his Ministers to acknowledge the Reformation Settlement. But she would not submit. Clearly neither Henry VIII nor the Duke of Norfolk may be counted among* ***the founding fathers*** *of Women's Lib.* L

the four etc corners of the earth/world [o (NP)] the regions of the world distant from the centre (from primitive conceptions of a flat or table-shaped world) **prep:** from, at, in, to. **adj:** four, ⚠ far, distant □ (source) (And God) *shall assemble the outcasts of Israel, and gather together the dispersed of Judah from* ***the four corners of the earth.*** ISAIAH XI 12 □ *There is only one industry here now, and that is tourism. Tourism has grown tremendously, and this place has become known in* ***the four corners of the earth.*** TVT □ *You can almost hear the gasp of steam as the great, gleaming monster pulls out along the shining rails, carrying a boy's imagination and a father's fancy to* ***the far corners of the earth.*** DM □ *Throughout his career, he has exerted a considerable influence, rolling out great editorials like rivers day after day on the most diverse subjects and (since he has been a mighty traveller) often from* ***the corners of the earth.*** OBS □ adj occas omitted, as in last example.

a four-leaved clover a clover with four leaves, instead of three, to a stem (which is believed to bring the finder good luck) □ *The woman gathering rattan may be gladdened by finding a length with the sections five hand-spans apart, the Dayak equivalent of* ***a four-leaved clover,*** *but more useful.* NDN

four-letter(ed) words 'taboo' verbs or nouns, mainly of Anglo-Saxon origin, that denote esp sexual or excretory organs and functions, and used with that meaning, or as forceful swearwords □ *The anonymous author of 'Her' sets himself a task that others have failed at: to rescue from debasement those* ***four-lettered words,*** *'to new-mint these words by writing them in the context in which they are most often spoken.'* NS □ (of 'live' radio phone-in programmes) *Risks have to be taken—even if it does mean the occasional person with an opinion actually getting on the air, let alone the occasional nut-case or* ***four-letter word.*** ST □ (NONCE) *Cognac and cigarettes are passed round, and with them the President's talk grows more manifestly masculine and even includes a peppering of* ***Anglo-Saxon tetragrams.*** OBS □ most of these words are, in fact, spelt with four letters, eg *fuck (n, v)* of sexual intercourse, *shit (n, v)* of excretion, *cock* (penis) and *cunt* (vagina), but the term refers to the class of word and not the actual number of letters in individual words.

the fourth estate the Press (the reference being to the power and influence of newspapers) ▫ *The gallery in which the reporters sit has become* ***a fourth estate*** *of the realm.* HISTORICAL ESSAYS (T B MACAULAY 1800-59) ▫ *'You're a news-hound, Joe,' he said. 'A newspaper reporter,' I substituted, not caring to stand any insolence about* ***the Fourth Estate****.* CON ▫ the Three Estates of the Realm are, in the House of Lords, *the lords temporal* (peers) and *the lords spiritual* (bishops) and, in the House of Commons, *members of Parliament*.

a freak of nature a physical or biological accident; sb/sth that is the result of such an accident ▫ *Still harder was it to realise that this utter isolation was only momentary; the transient creation of* ***a freak of nature****, and that within a matter of days, perhaps of hours only, it must vanish.* EM ▫ *At the far end of the fairground stood the booths where dwarfs, a giant, a bearded women, and other* ***freaks of nature*** *could be viewed for 20p a visit.*

free association the spontaneous and personal association one makes between a given word, object, concept and another word etc ▫ *According to Freud's theory, the 'manifest' dream leads back to the 'latent' dream in terms of symbolization and in terms of* ***free association****.* SNP ▫ *'Did you know there was a group* (of code symbols) *for "eunuch"? Do you think it crops up often in cables? I wish we could use it.' 'Are you every going to marry again?' 'Your* ***free associations****,' Beatrice said, 'are rather obvious sometimes.'* OMIH

free and easy [adj + adj non-rev] relaxed; informal; morally lax **n:** manner, style, way ▫ *'I wouldn't like to call on your parents without an invitation.' 'Don't worry. They're very* ***free and easy****, and as long as you're willing to take them as you find them you'd be welcome any time.'* ▫ *'It's my one chance to get out,' says a South London grandmother. 'Bingo is the only place I can come to on my own,* ***free and easy****, and enjoy myself.'* OBS ▫ *Most of the boys called me* (a schoolmaster) *by my Christian name, outside the lessons if not inside. I had wanted to get on* ***free-and-easy*** *terms with the boys—how else could I find out all about them?* SPL ▫ *I don't believe in this—whatever* you *call it—* ***free-and-easy*** *way of going on. 'Anticipation of marriage' is probably how they put it in your—the advice columns.* TGLY ▫ attrib use, as in *a* ***free-and-easy*** *way*, often hyphenated.

a free fight [o (NP)] group fighting, or struggling or quarrelling, of a disorganized and rowdy kind **V:** turn into, develop into, degenerate into ▫ *By the time the bus came so many people were waiting that it was* ***a free fight*** *to get on it.* ▫ *'Is anybody with that class?' 'Mr Simpson, I think.' 'Well, it sounds more like* ***a free fight*** *than a geography lesson.'* ▫ *I thought this was to be a reasoned discussion about next year's plans. If it's going to degenerate into* ***a free fight****, I'm not going to stay.* ▫ also pl.

free from sth [Comp (AdjP)] without, not having, sth (as a desirable condition) **V:** ⚠ be; find, consider, sb. **n:** blame, care, interference, pain, guilt, anxiety ▫ *It's a little late to admit it, I know, but your mother and I weren't entirely* ***free from*** *blame.* LBA ▫ *The virtues of the Unicorn Opera Group's Handel—so natural and straightforward, yet so stylish and commendably* ***free from*** *tiresome tamperings with the original—have been celebrated before in this column.* ST ▫ *Over the last few years there has been increased legislation to ensure that canned, bottled and preserved foods shall be* ***free from*** *harmful additives.* ⇨ ⚠ devoid of sth; free of sth.

a free loader (informal) sb who makes no contribution to an event of which he is taking advantage; sb who takes every opportunity of being present on an occasion where he can get sth for nothing ▫ *There we were, the usual* ***free-loaders****, already armed with our free hold-alls and drinks, staring beadily around for something else to* ***free-load****, and not what you'd call a celebrity to be seen.* NS ▫ *...the pop music business, where slit throats smile at each other across rooms crowded with boozed* ***free loaders*** *at 'new star' junkets* (= parties*) run by record companies.* L ▫ *There is something about the sight of this hardy ancient* (Mao Tse Tung*) in his flowered straw hat, which makes it difficult, for me at any rate, to have much patience with the pseudo-philosophers and the* ***free-loading*** *'Maoists' who have somehow and elsewhere got aboard the wagon.* ST ▫ adj compound free-loading; variant (v) free-load.

free love (dated) freedom to love and live with a man or woman of one's choice without being bound by marriage ties ▫ (statistics) *...the percentage who said that they believe in God, or who thought that* ***free-love*** *was 'all right in its way'.* UL ▫ *It was a setback that did not daunt Victoria Claffin Woodhull, a pioneer fighter for women's rights,* ***free love*** *and socialism.* OBS

free of sth [Comp (AdjP)] exempt or released from sth usu compulsory or normally present **V:** ⚠ be, become; feel. **n:** tax, charge; domestic duties, religious sanctions; filling in forms ▫ *...a company which he used in Liechtenstein had served only to get export permits and to allow him to take profits out of Germany* ***free of*** *tax.* T ▫ *It says here that Sheik Ahmed—an Arabian mystic—will,* ***free of*** *all charge, draw up for you a complete analysis of your character and destiny.* TOH ▫ *The post-war Southern prosperity* (in the US) *has affected the blacks too. Most of the* (political) *activists come from urban, middle-class homes and they and their parents are at least partly* ***free of*** *the traditional fears.* OBS ⇨ ⚠ devoid of sth; free from sth.

free speech the right to express one's opinions publicly on any subject, esp in so far as this is allowed or disallowed by censorship ▫ *'What's on telly now?' 'Something about* ***free speech****.' Mariette said. 'Freedom of the press or something.'* DBM ▫ *The well-being of mankind depends more directly on the rational production of such necessities as food and medicines than it does on a comparative luxury like* ***free speech****.* NS ▫ *My headmaster was a member of the* (Nazi) *party, but, under the circumstances, allowed an extraordinary degree of* ***freedom of speech*** *to our teachers.* RT ▫ variant freedom of speech.

free with one's hands [Comp (AdjP)] prone to fight, or strike, others with whom one is in disagreement or whom one wishes to control or subdue; prone to touch, or fondle, others in a way likely to be resented **V:** ⚠ be, become; find sb □ *He took his responsibilities as a father seriously but in matters of discipline was rather too* ***free with his hands***. □ *'You can't say Uncle Saunders is a pet.' 'He likes to make himself heard certainly. And he's a bit* ***free with***—' *'Yes?' said Brigit, as Nurse Ellen hesitated. 'Well, I guess I can cope with silly old men who like to pinch.'* DC

free with one's money etc [Comp (AdjP)] generous with one's money etc; over-ready to offer sth not welcome to sb **V:** ⚠ be; find sb. **o:** money, help, sympathy; advice, compliments, criticism □ *Johnson earns more, in my opinion, than any man has a right to, but I've always found him very* ***free with his money***—*which is more than you can say of many in his position.* □ *If you were as* ***free with your help*** *as you are with your advice we could have had the job finished by now.*

a French letter a contraceptive sheath □ *...and sent me after a job in a hot-water bottle factory in Islington. When I got there I discovered it was really a* ***French-letter*** *factory and it wasn't the sort of job you can discuss over cocktails.* NS □ *By this time the shaving process was over and the fat barber said, 'You don't want any of our boss's specials?' 'What are they?' I asked. '****French letters****,' he said, and laughed until he coughed chestily.* CON □ *Laurie John produced and presented his own plan for the restoration of the Alexandra Palace organ. Any programme in which a gentleman is permitted to say that he saw two* ***French letters*** *underneath the organ cannot be all bad.* L

French etc without tears (catchphrase) an easy, pleasant way to learn French etc (from the title of a play (by T RATTIGAN 1911-77), which is a parody of the kind of text-book/manual that promises quick and easy instruction) **n:** French, home decoration, fitness, slimming, cooking, rose-growing □ ***Slimming without tears*** *is Lyn's theme. Too good to be true? Give it a go.* TVT □ ***Spinach Without Tears****: it has been ruined for many of us, who remember it being shovelled into our mouths in childhood as if it were a life-saver.* OBS □ often adapted.

(make) a fresh start [V + O pass] (make) a second, or subsequent, attempt to do sth in which former materials, methods or arrangements are discarded or adapted □ *The death in a Paris park brings two people together. Both are unhappy in marriage—but is it too late for* ***a fresh start****?* TVT □ *This sketch is getting less and less like you the more I work on it. I think I'll tear it up and* ***make a fresh start***. □ *Because of the Law Lords' judgment, a new legal situation had developed and it was time for* ***a fresh start*** *to be* ***made*** *by everyone.* ST

fret and fume [v + v non-rev] show impatience, anxiety, irritation in one's speech and/or behaviour □ *He spent ten minutes at the phone while the others* ***fretted and fumed***. *At length he put the receiver down.* TBC □ *I found the door open and Sadie* ***fretting and fuming*** *about the hall. 'My dear creature,' she said, 'thank heavens you've come.'* UTN

Friday the thirteenth a conjunction of day and date thought to be unlucky and likely to be avoided by superstitious people when arranging a journey, an important function, etc □ *Monsieur Bonneval stolidly attempted to fight his way through the morass of calamities that was engulfing him. It was a losing battle.* ***Friday the thirteenth*** *had not finished with him yet.* ARG □ *'You could fly to Paris on Friday evening and add a day to your holiday.' 'I thought of that, but my husband flatly refused to fly anywhere on a* ***Friday the 13th****.'*

friend and/or foe [n + n non-rev] allies and/or enemies □ *There was not a trace of bitterness at the Labour Executive meeting last week. On the contrary,* ***friend and foe*** *treated each other with a respect that has been absent these many years.* OBS □ *Every now and then a man would leap from the scaffolding or from one of the camera cranes, scattering* ***friend and foe*** *alike.* UTN □ *Women would fight as well as men, and no one would know who was* ***friend or foe***. MFM

a friend in need (is a friend indeed) (saying) a friend who helps one when one needs help (is a true friend) □ *No, we don't see a lot of each other, but I know she would always be* ***a friend in need***. □ (NONCE) *Buskers* (= street entertainers) *have a 'society' of their own, a virtual unofficial union which moves unwelcome newcomers along.* ***A busker in need is a friend in need****, and must, they believe, be helped.* OBS

(your) friendly neighbourhood policeman etc (catchphrase) (your) friendly, familiar, local policeman etc (from the slogan your friendly neighbourhood policeman used in a Police public-relations campaign in the late 1960s) **n:** policeman, postman, milkman; bank; grocer; traffic warden; burglar; vandals; mad dog □ *'Anybody with the slightest admiration for the Queen should wear a buttonhole next Saturday to mark the official royal birthday.' She says it's entirely a non-commercial idea, although we don't suppose* ***your friendly neighbourhood florist*** *will actually be giving buttonholes away next Saturday.* ST □ *I have seen television advertisements which base their main message on misleading implications that a mass-produced brand of butter is made carefully by hand, in* ***friendly neighbourhood dairies***. L □ *Richard Marsh, new chairman of British Rail, says with a smile, 'I know more about the problems of British Rail than anybody else because I created more than anybody else. I'm* ***the friendly neighbourhood expert*** *on British Rail's problems.'* RT □ *Within three weeks my student friend received a welcoming letter from* ***his friendly neighbourhood bank manager****, together with an application form to open an account.* □ usu ironic or facetious.

friends and relations [n + n non-rev] one's immediate circle of acquaintances and family members □ (after a funeral) *That's what shivas* (formal gatherings of family and friends) *are for. For* ***friends and relations*** *to come and try to make the family forget.* HSG □ *He gave a grand party for* ***friends and relations****/And all who'd stuck by him when close to the wall,/And if you just listen I'll make your eyes glisten/With the rows and the ructions of Lannigan's Ball.* IRISH SONG

frills and furbelows [n + n non-rev] frills and flounces as ornamental trimmings on dress; (usu derogatory) any eye-catching finery or anything not essential to the main purpose or value of sth □ *'What did you think of Mrs Reynolds's dress?' 'I thought she looked absurd. But then I always did prefer a good tailor-made suit to* ***frills and furbelows****.'* □ (a newspaper office) *Friday's 'Objects and Subjects' was already shaping with six bright paragraphs on national* ***frills and furbelows****, freaks and frolics.* PP □ *Finger-bowls and napkin rings and flowers! If she would cut out the* ***frills and furbelows*** *and learn to cook a decent meal she would make a better job of running a guest-house.*

from afar [A (PrepP)] (formal) from a distance; from far off; from a long way off **V:** see, view, sth; admire sb □ *But already he was calling out loudly the ancient Bushman greeting: 'Good day, I saw you* ***from afar*** *and I am dying of hunger.'* LWK □ (San Francisco) *I know no other city so splendid* ***from afar*** *and so cosy from close quarters.* L □ *Both those attending the festival and those following it* ***from afar*** *will be delighted to learn that several pubs have had their licences extended to the heady hour of 11 p.m.* TVT ⇨ at close quarters.

from beginning etc to end etc [A (PrepP)] throughout **nn:** beginning. . .end, ⚠ first. . .last, start. . .finish □ *. . .a sober, clear, moving and singularly unbitter book which makes fascinating reading* ***from beginning to end****.* ST □ *The Bach ballet was brimming with brilliance — and I thought it was wrong* ***from start to finish*** *and should never have been attempted.* ST

from the bottom of one's heart [A (PrepP)] with sincerity; with genuinely felt emotion **V:** speak, tell sb, wish sth □ *'I love you. I shall always love you. You're my wife. I wouldn't have it any different.' I was speaking* ***from the bottom of my heart****.* SML □ *In the office Luke and Martin were both sitting down. As Nora saw her husband she said, awkwardly, wishing* ***from the bottom of her heart*** *that she could let herself go: 'Bad luck.'* NM

from a child etc [A (PrepP)] from the time one was a child etc; since childhood etc **n:** a child, a boy, a girl; boyhood, girlhood, (earliest) youth □ *Most people, she was aware, acted from impulse or inclination but* ***from a child*** *she had been acted upon by successive idealisms stronger than any personal desire of her own.* PW □ *'He's been wilful and headstrong* ***from a baby****,' the mother complained, 'and now even his father can hardly control him.'* □ *'And this is Miss King, better known as Annie,' he continued, introducing the new manager to a smiling woman in a flowered overall. 'An old and trusted employee. She's been with us* ***from a girl****.'*

from China to Peru [A (PrepP)] in, throughout, many or all parts of the world □ (source) *Let observations with extensive view/ Survey mankind* ***from China to Peru****;/Remark each anxious toil, each eager strife,/And watch the busy scenes of crowded life.* THE VANITY OF HUMAN WISHES (S JOHNSON 1709-84) □ *Isherwood was a letter writer of exceptional brilliance, and when he moved on from Berlin, original observations made in Copenhagen, in Lisbon, or later* ***from China*** *(literally, as they say)* ***to Peru****, arrived in a very small, regular, and evidently imperturbable handwriting.* AH □ ***From China to Peru*** *the transistor radio has become as necessary a part of the furniture of human life as the cooking-pot.* □ China and Peru non-rev.

from the cradle to the grave [A (PrepP)] at/ in every stage of life; from birth to death □ *I am also local agent for the never-never furniture company, a qualified midwife, a marriage broker, and an undertaker. Jason is at your service* ***from the cradle to the grave****.* DPM □ *Certainly there's no racist like a new racist. 'These labourers,' one manager told me, 'are just bloody parasites on the national economy. And they're looked after* ***from the cradle to the grave****.'* NS □ *In olden times there was a saying that the Co-op took care of you* ***from the cradle to the grave****, provided a pharmacy to delay the event, and then buried you.* OBS

from dawn/morning to/till dusk/night [A (PrepP)] all day; all the time (esp with reference to a repeated pattern of work, mode of living, etc) □ *When the month of Ramadan comes round each year and Moslems have to fast* ***from dawn to dusk****, any display of energy borders upon the miraculous.* L □ *'Oh, it's too utterly boring,' said Sadie. 'I'm simply worn out with the work. On the* (film) *set* ***from dawn to dusk****.'* UTN □ *Later, when her husband was Bolivian Minister in London and Paris, she lived in Compayne Gardens, where the servants were treated as friends and an almost unreal state of happiness seems to have reigned* ***from morning to night****.* L □ dawn/morning and dusk/night non-rev.

from head etc to foot etc [A (PrepP)] over the whole length of one's body; in every part of one's being, nature, character **nn:** head. . .foot, ⚠ head. . .toe, crown. . .toe, top. . .toe, the top/ crown of one's head. . .the soles of one's feet/ shoes/boots □ *And with another explosion the water hit him* ***from head to foot****. He shook it from his face.* PM □ *Every time the phone used to ring I used to shake* ***from head to toe*** *and felt sick in my stomach.* L □ *So the St Michael* (trademark for goods sold in Marks and Spencer's stores) *label is synonymous with good sense, and the housewife clothing her child in St Michael* ***from top to toe*** *feels the warm glow of the prudent.* TVT □ *Britton, a Tory* ***from the top of his head to the soles of his boots****, is taking an unaccustomed look at life from a Socialist viewpoint in playing Labour MP Collinson.* TVT □ *Observable progress is being made in the novel social experiment of educating a democracy* ***from top to toe****.* T □ head etc and foot etc non-rev. ⇨ ⚠ from top to bottom.

from here to eternity [A (PrepP)] forever □ (source) *Gentlemen-rankers out on a spree,/ Damned* ***from here to Eternity****,/God ha'* (= have) *mercy on such as we. . .* GENTLEMEN-RANKERS (R KIPLING 1865-1936) □ *But screw all that* ***from here to eternity****. Trying not to be a bad man took up far more energy than he could, or was prepared to, spare from trying not to be a nasty man.* TGLY □ use often facetious.

from job etc to job etc [A (PrepP)] from one to another of a succession of items, activities, events, plans, persons of the same kind **V:** go, drift, hurry; take, send sb/sth. **n:** job, meeting, agency, shop; disappointment, fad; specialist □ SAM: *You have no trade — no profession — you're not interested in politics and you drift* ***from job to job****.* HSG □ *Meanwhile* *he flits* ***from function to function****, automatically accosted, perpetually propositioned by those who seek his patronage.* ST ▫ *I asked him round, mainly to save the paper and string necessary to send back his script. Ned and I have bumped along* ***from crisis to crisis*** *ever since.* RT ▫ *Pre-school years are to me a confused memory of being taken* ***from one relative to another*** *to be looked after.* ▫ variant from one job etc to another/the next.

from log cabin to White House [A (PrepP)] (catchphrase) from humble, or obscure, beginnings to a position of power, wealth or influence (from the title of a biography of the US president, James Garfield, by W M THAYER) ▫ *It was Bernie who so constantly urged him to control and limit his fantasies by achievement. '****From log cabin to White House****, my dear,' Bernie had said, 'isn't done on a broomstick* (= by witchcraft, magic) *any more.'* HAA ▫ *In the American* ***log cabin*** *story the point is soon reached at which the future millionaire must wear a tie. He explains that he cannot otherwise inspire confidence.* PL ▫ can be used in part and allusively, as in second example.

from the money etc point of view [Disj (PrepP)] looked at, considered, with the importance or function of money etc uppermost in one's mind **n/adj:** money, health, schooling, family; educational, religious, aesthetic, moral ▫ *It's fairly clear that you've found some way of improving on the job* ***from the money point of view****, and I'm here to ask you whether you can trust me enough to let me in on it.* HD ▫ ***From the stock market point of view****, however, Willson means only one thing—the tiny house furnisher and textile wholesaling group he took under his wing last October.* OBS ▫ *She claims that,* ***from an educational point of view****, mixed-sex classes at school have a negative effect.*

from now etc on [A (PrepP)] from now etc into the future **o:** now, ⚠ then; this/that day/year/time; childhood; retiring age ▫ *'Say Hullo to Prissie, Nick,' said Fergus. 'She may be looking after you* ***from now on****.'* DC ▫ *And I began, almost automatically, to pack up my papers. I knew that* ***from now on*** *I should do no more work.* UTN ▫ *'They say he's very rich. A proper millionaire they say he is!' Even Charles took,* ***from then on****, a fresh interest in the frail, scared figure in that bed.* HD ▫ ***From childhood on*** *Tennyson was fascinated by the sound of words.* L ▫ *When Marilyn Frounson was 13 she saw the Royal Ballet perform in her own city. '****From that day on****,' she says, 'all I wanted to do was to come to England and join the Royal Ballet.'* OBS ▫ stress pattern from ˌnow etc ˈon.

from one week's etc end to another continuously over a long period of time **n:** week's, ⚠ month's, year's. **det:** another, the other, the next ▫ *He sits plugged in front of the telly, or reads a cowboy book, or just sleeps, and I suppose the only reason I was pals with him was because I didn't say much* ***from one month's end to another*** *either.* LLDR ▫ *I'll tell you what farming is, my boy. It's work, work, work* ***from one year's end to the next****.* ▫ *I get quite a bit of company at this time of year, but in the winter I often don't have a visitor* ***from one week's end to the other****.* ▫ often follows neg construction

saying what one does not do/have.

from pillar to post [A (PrepP)] in many directions (esp in contexts implying harassment or worried activity) **V:** rush, move; drive, push, chase, sb ▫ *And having crossed the Rhine, we will crack about the plains of Northern Germany, chasing the enemy* ***from pillar to post****.* MFM ▫ *Mr Geoffrey Rippon, our chief Common Market negotiator, continued to proceed* ***from pillar to post*** *and make optimistic noises.* L ▫ *Men with a prison record discover that work and accommodation are hard to find and harder to keep. Too many of them, after having been driven* ***from pillar to post*** *in this way, take to crime again.* ▫ pillar and post non-rev.

from the President etc down/downward(s) including everybody in a group, ie the most important or highest ranking person (whose name or title is given first) together with all those of lesser importance or rank **o:** the President, Mrs Thatcher, the matron, the managing director ▫ *The Commissioner of Police, Bill Syer, and the head of the CID, Bernard Nealon, could not have been more co-operative, and,* ***from Sir Percy down****, we were deeply grateful for their attitude.* DS ▫ *The American party were picked up by 'Christian Action' and joyfully accepted bunk beds in marquees at 35p.* ***From Professor Steinberg downwards*** *they were rigged in anorak and ruck-sack, but they were not doss-house bums.* OBS ▫ *It was, I believed, the perfect answer to criticism that the standard 1.8 litre model lacked power. Apparently, at the time, all the company's top brass,* ***from Lord Stokes downwards****, agreed.* T

from rags to riches [A (PrepP)] from extreme poverty to wealth **V:** ⚠ go, move, pass ▫ *To go* ***from rags to riches*** *in one step could be a severe test of character, but most big pools' winners have ordered their fortunes with great good sense and some generosity.* ▫ *Even if he despised the 'mobsters' over whom he towered in his prime, Hoover understood them. In their own devious way, they were part of the American '****rags-to-riches****' dream.* OBS ▫ *His astonishing success, a political version of the* ***rags-to-riches*** *story, may have gone some way to silence the boring chorus of political pundits.* NS ▫ *The production ignored the truths of the opera, the underlying humanity and tenderness that make it more than a superficial tale of* ***rags to riches****.* L ▫ attrib use *a* ***rags-to-riches*** *story.*

(right) from the start etc [A (PrepP)] at the time when sth started, or was started, and ever since; from the word go (qv) **o:** the start, ⚠ the beginning, the first, the outset ▫ ***From the outset*** *and for most of the time that Mrs Mackay was alive, the police refused finally to accept that she had been kidnapped.* NS ▫ ***From the first****, the Reformation had been quarrelling with the symbolism of Christianity, with all that connected it with the ancient, vanished, pagan world of Europe.* L ▫ *The pundits and columnists have been wrong about Strauss* ***from the beginning****. Their assessment of his chances of nomination was wrong.* ▫ ***Right from the start*** *it was a lovely friendship. We went everywhere together.* TVT ▫ emphasizes the immediate establishment of an attitude or procedure and/or its continuity and consistency thereafter. ⇨ ⚠ at the outset (of sth).

from the sublime to the ridiculous [A (PrepP)] from what is serious, important, dramatic, to what is trivial, foolish, laughable **V:** go, move; switch, change; turn, jump, descend; range; be a short step □ *If she had been rushed to hospital and her life been saved, she would have plunged straight* ***from the sublime to the ridiculous*** *and have got into a lot of bureaucratic difficulties.* RFW □ (headline of an article about fashion shows) ***From*** *Britain's* ***sublime to*** *its frankly* ***ridiculous***. SC □ (NONCE) *When Peter Hall formed his own company and opened at the Aldwych he gave me a part in 'Ondine' and other classics. Then, in 1965, I started in 'The Avengers'* (TV series). ***From the sublime****, you might say,* ***to the****—well, rather* ***different****!* OBS □ sublime and ridiculous non-rev.

from that day to this [A (PrepP)] from then to now **V:** (not) see, speak to, hear of, sb □ *I haven't really got the heart to describe Robert's wedding. I hated it all so much that* ***from that day to this*** *I've never gone down Park Lane except in a taxi with my eyes shut.* CON □ *But Orwell's whole effect was to tell the world that totalitarianism existed on the Left as well as on the Right and that you couldn't be anti-fascist without being anti-totalitarian—the informing political insight governing the interpretation of cultural history* ***from that day to this***. NS □ pres perfect tense.

from/since time immemorial [A (PrepP)] (cliché) from/since longer ago than anyone can remember; from an undated time of origin □ *All the vegetable sedatives and narcotics, all the euphorics that grow on trees have been known and systematically used by human beings* ***from time immemorial***. DOP □ (the Crown Jewellers) *...the workshop benches, the equipment, and, indeed, the craftsmen, look as if they have been there* ***since time immemorial***. RT

from time to time [A (PrepP)] occasionally; at irregular intervals; every now and again/then (qv); every so often (qv); now and again/then (qv) **V:** see, visit, talk to, sb; read, listen to, sth □ *In the main the art of the potter has been a secular art.* ***From time to time****, however, this secular art has been placed at the service of religion.* HAH □ *Most of the literature lies there* (in the shop-window) *year after year, fading in the sun, and is only disturbed when Mrs Tinckham herself has a fit of reading, which she does* ***from time to time****, and picks out some Western, yellow with age.* UTN □ *He read through the letter carefully,* ***from time to time*** *raising his eyebrows or emitting a long slow whistle.*

from top to bottom [A (PrepP)] in/throughout every part of sth **V:** search, study, scrutinize, examine, sth □ *The War Office,* ***from top to bottom****, has been splendid, and every section, both military and civil, has spared no effort to help us get ready for the battle.* MFM □ *She searched the house* ***from top to bottom****, behind sofas, in cupboards, under beds.* MM □ (The architects) *studied the system* ***from top to bottom***. OBS □ top and bottom non-rev. ⇨ ⚠ from head etc to foot etc.

from where one is standing [Disj (PrepP)] (as seen or judged) from one's physical, intellectual or emotional position or situation □ *'All I wanted to do was to fill in the sort of thing I can probably see more clearly* ***from where I'm standing***.*' 'Yes, spectators see more of the game than players, don't they?' he sneered.* CON □ *Your parents aren't interfering just for the sake of it. Try to look at things* ***from where they're standing*** *and be more tolerant.*

from the word go [A (PrepP)] (informal) as soon as is possible, or has been made possible; (right) from the start etc (qv) (from the verbal signal *ready, steady, go!* used to start a race, game etc) □ *'We felt that unless it* (a new system of roads for buses) *was a basis for the New Town, and unless it worked* ***from the word go****, it wouldn't have got off the ground,' says Mr Ken Wright, leader of the busway project team.* OBS □ *It's important to realise* ***from the word go*** *that broadcasters should get out and about among the people. They must take guidance from local people.* RT □ *There's nowhere in the country where there's a properly integrated accident service, where a seriously injured person can get absolutely first-class treatment* ***from the word go***. L

frozen music architecture, statuary etc □ (source) *Architecture is music in space, as it were* ***frozen music***. (F VON SCHELLING 1775-1854) □ *It wasn't large as mansions go, absolutely severe with a flat parapet line and no projections. But I caught my breath as I looked at it, remembering suddenly the Dufton art master's favourite phrase: here was* ***frozen music***. RATT

frozen stiff [Comp (AdjP)] rigid because liquid content has turned to ice; extremely cold or numb with cold **S:** cloth; fingers, toes. **V:** ⚠ be, look □ *I had to leave the clothes on the washing-line. They were* ***frozen stiff*** *and I couldn't fold them into the basket.* □ *But there I am,* ***frozen stiff****, with nothing to get me warm except a couple of hours' long-distance running before breakfast.* LLDR □ *They had another free daiquiri each,* ***frozen*** *so* ***stiffly*** *that it had to be drunk in tiny drops to avoid a sinus-pain.* OMIH

the fruit(s) of one's labour(s) [O (NP)] the result(s) of one's work, seen as giving profit or satisfaction **V:** enjoy, see, savour □ (source) *For to me to live is Christ, and to die is gain. But if I live in the flesh this is* ***the fruit of my labour****: yet what I shall choose I wot (*= know*) not.* PHILIPPIANS I 21-22□ *This compilation seems a never-ending task; I sometimes wonder if I'll live to see* ***the fruits of my labours***. □ *Tom Parker enjoys* ***the fruits of his labours****. His pleasures encompass hunting, shooting, coaching and seeing the stable buckets are painted.* TVT

(at/in) full blast [A (PrepP/NP)] in a state of full or maximum operation, activity etc (from the steel-making blast furnace working at full power) **V:** work (away); go; talk, argue □ *We must marshal our strength up along the Western borders of Germany, to the Rhine if possible, ensure adequate maintenance by getting Antwerp working* ***at full blast*** *at the earliest possible moment;...* MFM □ *We were able to display to him an orderly British excavation* ***in full blast****, the first of its kind, I suppose, in the annals of Breton archaeology.* SD □ *I could visualise the production line, so to speak, when this place was going* ***full blast*** *and sheep were passing through at the rate of three hundred an hour.* RFW □ *It's not so peace-*

*ful in the early morning, when the birds are going **full blast** outside your window.*

full face [A(NP)] with the whole face visible to a viewer (describes a portrait, photograph etc; contrasted with *in profile*) □ *Most of the masks were made **full face**, but two of them, which were worn by the only two women on the scene, were made in profile.* UTN □ *The weakness of his chin is not so apparent in a **full-face** study, which, I suppose, is the reason he chose this photograph for publication.* □ attrib use *a **full-face** study, photograph.*

full frontal (nudity etc) the front of nude human body freely exposed, esp in photography, films, and on the stage; (fig) uncompromising and unequivocal exposure, assertion, display etc **n:** nudity, nude; postures, self-advertising; impudence, intransigence; description, terms □ *A group of girlie magazines, which for 23 years had 'gone its own sweet way' had given a pointer to the times by setting its face against **full frontal nudity**—and going out of business.* G □ *'Die Zeit' is published in Hamburg, and this week carries a double-page spread of four male **full-frontal nudes**, the like of which I've never seen in 'Cosmopolitan'.* NS □ *'Here Comes Everybody' (Certificate X) shows his methods which include screaming physical contact and verbal insults. Language is free and so are **full frontals**.* OBS □ ***Full frontal anarchy** is his cry, and that means flaunting an indiscriminate contempt for all institutions and authority.* NS □ (NONCE) *'Little Blue Room' is bright and breezy, written mostly in the present tense for maximum immediacy, direct, not to say **fully frontal**, easy to read and enjoyable at its best, shallow and quickly forgettable in its more facile passages.* L □ full frontal nudity is the original, and is still the most commonly found, collocation.

full in sb's/the face [A] directly or forcefully towards, into or against sb's face **V:** strike, hit, sb; look sb □ *The sun struck over the wall at the corner. It shone **full in her face**.* AITC □ *The jet of water hit him **full in the face**, blinding and choking him for long enough to enable his assailant to drop the hose and make his escape.*

full of oneself [Comp (AdjP)] self-confident (often selfishly so) **V:** ⚠ be, get, seem □ *Her father said Patrick seemed a bit **full of himself**, but that at any rate he was a sight better than the fancy-necktie brigade* (= young men wearing colourful ties) *who sat in his chair and read his evening paper when they called.* TGLY □ *When he came home from hospital he was too **full of himself** to notice how ill his wife was looking.* □ stress pattern 'full of oneself.

full of beans [Comp (AdjP)] (informal) full of health, good spirits and energy **V:** ⚠ be, look, feel □ *After the first pint Grimsdyke remarked, 'You're looking **full of beans**, Richard. Hard work must agree with you, or something.'* DIL □ *I had a good night's sleep in a hotel and was feeling very **full of beans**.* MFM □ *She was a girl everyone liked. 'A pretty girl—**full of beans**,' remembers Mr Bird.* OBS

full of the joys of spring [Comp (AdjP)] lively; light-hearted; merry **V:** ⚠ be, look, feel □ *She's tiresome, really—down in the dumps one day and **full of the joys of spring** the next.* □ *You can see this in the behaviour of flies if they are subjected to DDT. Their first effort is to fly about, as though they were **full of the joys of spring**, and then they gradually die off.* L □ often facetious.

full of life [Comp (AdjP)] lively; animated; active; interested **V:** ⚠ be, look, feel □ *Why should Prissie be so **full of life** today? Her cheeks were glowing, her large eyes more brilliant than ever.* DC □ *No, they weren't naughty, but you know what children are—so **full of life** they tire you out.* □ *The old fellow's still **full of life**, isn't he? He'd shame people half his age.*

full of one's own importance [Comp (AdjP)] (derogatory) thinking oneself important, influential, indispensable etc **V:** ⚠ be, look; find sb □ *She described the chief of police in terms no lady should use, and told us that he was far too **full of his own importance**.* DF □ *In the last episode of the present series, Fletcher has been out to lunch with the Chairman and comes back more than usually **full of his own importance**—and drink.* TVT

(at) full pelt [A (PrepP)] (informal) with great speed and/or force; at full tilt (qv) **V:** run, race, dash, charge; drive, ride □ *'Wake up! Live dog!' I said to Mars; as I knelt down he sprang from my shoulders; and together we set off down the road **at full pelt**.* UTN □ *Looking backwards as he turned the corner, he charged **full pelt** into the policeman.*

full steam ahead [Comp/A] with as much speed and vigour as possible (from an order given on steam-powered ships) **V:** it be; go, come, proceed; make one's/its way; do, perform, sth; get on (with sth); □ *Turning away from the punch-bowl she was run into by someone who was coming towards it **full steam ahead**.* TGLY □ *Miss Jenkins has been banging away at her typewriter **full steam ahead** for two days to get those documents finished for you. I'm sure she'd appreciate a word of thanks.* □ (advertisement) *Hoover helps you give all your ironing the master touch—just set to the one point on the dial and it's **full steam ahead**.* DM □ (NONCE) *You misunderstand me, Professor Kingsley. I explicitly referred to the immediate present just now. Once our policy is formulated we intend to go **ahead full steam**.* TBC

full stop [Disj] without further qualification; and that is all; and I have no more to add □ *'I find Jerry very tiresome when he's had a bit too much to drink.' 'Well, I find Jerry very tiresome, **full stop**.'* □ *There is no gospel in this theatrical performance* (Jesus Christ Superstar). *The gospel of Jesus Christ is the gospel of the Resurrection, not of the sacrifice of the Cross, **full stop**.* NS □ *I don't have to give you any reasons. You're not going to get a motor-bike till you're twenty-one, **period**.* □ end position; US equivalent, period.

(at) full throttle [A (PrepP/NP)] with the throttle-valve of an engine fully open to allow the maximum flow of petrol vapour or steam; (fig) very energetically □ *She glanced at her wrist watch; they were still about two miles off, though behind her the engine was roaring **at full throttle** and they were doing about fifteen knots.* RFW □ *I know you must have some practice on that motorbike before you take it on to the main* *roads, but is there any need to drive it up and down the drive* ***full throttle****, deafening us all?* □ *No wonder she's worn out! If only she'd do things a little more calmly and quietly instead of steaming through her day's work* ***at full throttle****.*

(at) full tilt [A (PrepP/NP)] with great speed and/or force; with reckless abandon; (at) full pelt (qv) **V:** run, race, dash, charge; drive, ride □ *The animal had somehow managed to get out after all and was pursuing him* ***full tilt*** *down the pathway.* SNP

fully stretched [Comp (AdjP)] extended to the limits of one's capacities or talents **V:** ⚠ be, feel □ *Reith complained to me after John Freeman's 'Face to Face' television encounter with him that Freeman had not asked him what he still wanted to do in order (at what was then an advanced age) to be '****fully stretched****'. What he had in mind—and would have discussed frankly—was Beeching's job of reorganising British Railways.* L □ *He was ambitious for his sons and felt that they were not being* ***fully stretched*** *in the local secondary school.* □ *Brown equalled his own record time in the half-mile yesterday, against weak competition. It seems likely he could have knocked a few seconds off it, if he had been* ***fully stretched****.*

fun and games [n + n non-rev] frivolity, amusement for oneself, esp contrasted with sth more serious, hard work, etc; (euphemism) flirtation or sexual play □ *Meanwhile in Scotland refreshing winds of change are beginning to blow, sweeping away before them the old idea that* ***fun and games*** *are incompatible with the worship of God.* SC □ *Fred Mundy is general manager of the Albert Hall. 'I think it's all worthwhile when you see how dedicated the Prommers* (= people who attend the Proms or Promenade concerts) *are. They may have their* ***fun and games*** *before a concert begins, but once it starts they're as good as gold.'* RT □ *You don't want to get married, I assure you, old man. Not till you're too old to go out in the evenings, anyway. Think of the* ***fun and games*** *you can have yet.* DIL □ MILLY: *Well, love, I'm back.* MYRA: *Oh, Milly, I've never been so pleased to see anyone.* MILLY: *Me, too. A delegation of twenty women for two weeks—not my idea of* ***fun and games****. I changed to an earlier plane and here I am.* EHOW □ *Wensley was in his office and he had a copy of the first edition on his desk and copies of all the other morning papers on the floor and he was sitting there like a man in a trance. 'Not much* ***fun and games*** *tonight,' he said as I came in.* PP

(all) the fun of the fair [O (NP)] all that is arranged or happens to entertain and amuse at a fair, entertainment, social occasion, etc **V:** provide, enjoy, miss □ *Mrs Allen was having a few moments with her weary feet up while the rest of her family enjoyed* ***the fun of the fair****.* NS □ (Edinburgh International Festival) *In Wednesday's programme Mahoney hopes to kaleidoscope* ***the*** *enormous diversity and* ***fun of the fair****, with glimpses of artists at work and play.* TVT □ *It was a great party — not that Johnny here would know. He drank so much before we got there he fell asleep and missed* ***all the fun of the fair****.*

the funeral baked meats (cliché) a meal or refreshment served to mourners after a funeral □ (source) (referring to Hamlet's widowed mother's haste in re-marrying) *Thrift, thrift, Horatio!* ***the funeral baked meats****/Did coldly furnish forth the marriage table.* HAMLET I II □ *Sonia found it difficult to believe that such vulgarity could accompany advancing years. 'Something's gone sadly awry with the gay whirl,' he said. '****The funeral baked meats*** *taste a bit ashy in the mouth, don't you think?'* HAA □ *'Got your* ***funeral baked meats*** *all right?' said Guy. 'What?' said Godfrey. Guy nodded his head towards Godfrey's pocket which bulged with the cakes.* MM

funny business (informal) sth illegal or not quite straightforward; sth prohibited or disapproved of; (euphemism) improper sexual advances or conduct **V:** try (on), start (on). **det:** any, some; this, that □ *In spite of being unable to discover any evidence that the firm was anything other than it purported to be—manufacturers of small electrical components for the export trade—the police and the Home Office felt sure there was some* ***funny business*** *going on.* □ *As a rival he had counted Alec out. Had he been premature? Alec posed, he postured, he talked a lot of hot air. Besides, if he did try any* ***funny business****, had not Irma said she did not love him?* PW □ *She hardly noticed it when, still talking, Anna slipped an arm round her shoulders and nuzzled her slightly, but she noticed it very clearly when Anna's other hand started on some* ***funny business*** *with the shoulderstrap of her nightdress and elsewhere in that area.* TGLY □ *it's a* ***funny business*** = 'it's an odd affair'.

funny peculiar or funny ha-ha funny = 'odd, inexplicable' contrasted with funny = 'comic, amusing' □ (source) *What do you mean, funny?* ***Funny-peculiar, or funny-ha-ha?*** THE HOUSEMASTER (I HAY 1876-1952) □ *'La Bonne Année' opens with an utterly equivocal joke—* ***funny ha-ha or funny peculiar?****—in greyish black and white: after a second or two it dawns that we are watching the closing scenes, culminating in an amorous reunion on a railway platform, of his eight-year-old prize-winning film.* NS □ (Teachers are writing books) *'...and they're trying hard to do a 'Doctor in the House' on teaching,* ***funny ha-ha****!' 'They're not all like that,' said Kathie. 'There was "Spare the Rod".' 'You're right,' he said. 'Some of them are* ***funny peculiar****.'* TT

the funny thing is (that) a/the peculiar, unexpected, or seemingly contradictory thing about sth described is that □ *I'm sorry I showed it* (a witch-doll) *to him, but I thought it was so cute.* ***The funny thing is*** *he seemed to mind it more shut in the cupboard than when he could see it.* DC □ ***The funny thing was that****, as it turned out, Robert wasn't lying. He really did just go out and walk about.* CON □ *Y'know,* ***it's a funny thing, but*** *even the best of us can fall by the wayside and yours truly is no exception.* OBS □ *'He wasn't a bit worried,* ***that was the funny thing****.' 'Oh, he's probably got plenty of money tucked away somewhere that the bankruptcy liquidators can't touch.'* □ variants it is a funny thing (but), that/this is the funny thing.

the fur (begins to) fly a real and bitter argument starts (from animals tearing at each other in a fight) ▫ *I replied that the £1500 had been spent. I produced all the receipts.* ***The fur*** *then* ***began to fly****. The Major-General i/c Administration Southern Command, Salisbury, came to see me and said that this incident had ruined my chances of promotion in the Army.* MFM ▫ *The moment this fact had sunk in,* ***the fur began to fly****. Holloway, accompanied by one of the firm's lawyers took the next plane to Vienna, deliberately telling no one at Lessner and Kamper that they were on their way.* ST ▫ *He's a trouble-maker, I tell you. He spreads stories about people and then sits back to watch* ***the fur fly****.* ▫ *What too of the practical considerations? The 'liberated' lady may not mind wife number two sharing her husband's bed, but two women in one kitchen will almost certainly set* ***the fur flying****!* G ▫ cf *watch/make* ***the fur fly****, get/set* ***the fur flying****.*

(our) furred, four-footed and feathered friends (cliché, facetious) the animal world ▫ *I would hazard that misconstruction of this paltry event spoiled several people's enjoyment of the evening, and not just because of an English weakness for* ***our furred and feathered friends****.* NS ▫ *Editions of 'Nationwide', the teatime circus, which don't give me pussycats or crocodiles, warblers or wombats, just are not good enough: this is Britain, you know, squatters or no, and we like* ***our four-footed and feathered friends****.* L ▫ (a naturalist tries to get released birds and animals to leave his camp) *Those knowledgeable sentimentalists who are forever telling me that it's cruel to lock up the poor wild creatures in little wooden boxes — I'd just like them to see how eagerly* ***our furred and feathered brothers*** *rush back to the wilds as soon as they're given the opportunity.* DF ▫ (homing/carrier pigeons) *Last century, war correspondents from 'The Times' and Reuters were chosen sometimes not so much for their lively use of deathless prose, as for their abilities to clean out birdcages under fire and be kind to* ***the feathered friends*** *at all times. Else the news might not get through.* G ▫ our fourfooted friends and our feathered friends also used.

fuss and bother [n + n non-rev] worried, energetic activity which is (usu) superfluous to the demands of a situation **det:** (not) any, no; lots of ▫ *'Suppose we have a drink,' came Fergus's voice from the doorway. 'I'm sure you need one after all this* ***fuss and bother****.'* DC ▫ *'Why don't we just get married without any* ***fuss and bother****,' Dick said suddenly, as they were discussing what form the wedding reception should take.* ▫ *Oh, my wife is always* ***fussing and bothering*** *about the children's health, when it's perfectly obvious that they're as fit as fleas.* ▫ rare variant fussing and bothering [v + v non-rev].

G

(add to) the gaiety of nations (catchphrase) provide general, or widespread, amusement, pleasure, entertainment etc ▫ (source—referring to the death of the actor, David Garrick) *I am disappointed by that stroke of death, which has eclipsed* ***the gaiety of nations*** *and impoverished the public stock of harmless pleasure.* LIVES OF THE ENGLISH POETS (S JOHNSON 1709-84) ▫ *'Say something amusing,' an unwise lady once demanded of Noël Coward at a Melbourne reception. 'Australia,' he unkindly replied. I don't much care whether these stories are true or not. They* ***add*** *incomparably* ***to the gaiety of nations****.* NS ▫ (NONCE) *And with his talent for coming vividly alive in any human company, he will no doubt go on being popular. Whatever else he does he will surely* ***add to the gaiety of NATO****.* OBS ▫ *They see petrol prices doubling within 18 months, a prospect not calculated to* ***add to the gaiety of nations****.* SC

gain ground [V + O] make a territorial advance in warfare, combat or pursuit; make progress; increase in strength, influence, popular acceptance, etc **S:** army, force; idea, notion; change, development; revolution. **A:** against the enemy; on all fronts, on the fugitives ▫ *At last our men began to* ***gain ground****, forcing the enemy back towards the river.* ▫ *A glance behind confirmed his fears. His pursuer was* ***gaining ground*** *on him rapidly.* ▫ *The writing of the first three words of 'in so far as' as one, is a practice which seems to be* ***gaining ground****.* ▫ *Cottage industries are a growing business. It is a movement very much in tune with the general social changes which have* ***gained*** *enormous* ***ground*** *during the seventies.* G ⇨ give/lose ground (to sb/sth).

gales of laughter/mirth loud sustained laughter ▫ *But it's by no means unusual to see him wandering through the house in* ***gales of laughter****.* OBS ▫ *Whatever answer the stooge gave to his question was lost amidst the* ***gales of laughter****.* ▫ *It's very discouraging to a learner to have his mistakes greeted with* ***gales of mirth****.*

gall and wormwood (to/for sb) [Comp (NP)] sth felt or remembered (by sb) as a painful, or humiliating, experience **V:** ⚠ be, become; make sth ▫ (source) *Remembering mine affliction and my misery, the* ***wormwood and the gall****.* LAMENTATIONS III 19 ▫ GILLESPIE: *The whole world knew that it was* ***gall and wormwood for*** *him to darken any church door.* BOLES: *He'd explain that without trouble — 'You have to pretend to observe appearances, simply for your own safety, Mr Boles.'* L ▫ *The mere mention of another artist's success was* ***gall and wormwood to*** *Petersen, starving for recognition.* ▫ now usu in form and order of headphrase; to used more often than for.

the game is (not) worth the candle (saying) the profits, results, or pleasures gained from doing sth are (not) worth the trouble, or expense, involved ▫ *In business, I ruminated, I'd have to soft-soap (*= flatter*) people whom I despised. But* ***the game was worth the candle****; if I sold my independence, at least I'd get a decent price for it.* RATT ▫ *Is the ban arbitrary and unfair? Chapple thinks he might still be able to defend it even under the Race Relations Act. But*

***the** legal **game isn't worth the candle**.* NS □ *'I've got a bint* (= girl I can go to bed with). *Getting a bit old,' he said. 'What I mean is that **it isn't worth the candle**, as you get older,' he said.* CON

a game that two can play unpleasant, or hurtful, behaviour or action which can lead to retaliation of the same kind □ *Sulking until you get your own way is **a game that two can play**, you know.* □ *You know Jack. He can't help chatting up any pretty girl he meets. It doesn't mean a thing, but if you don't like it why not show him it's **a game that two can play**?* □ *The canal was full of bodies: they must have been caught in a cross-fire, trying to get back, and I suppose every man of us along the bank was thinking, '**Two can play at that game**.'* QA □ variant two can play at that game.

gamekeeper turned poacher/poacher turned gamekeeper sb who uses the knowledge and skills acquired in one trade or role to operate in another which is directly opposite in purpose □ *A police officer who takes to crime is likely to be more successful at it than most. The **gamekeeper turned poacher** has everything going for him.* □ *A clever negotiator for the Union of Distributive and Allied Workers as a young man, now **turned gamekeeper**, Robens (as Chairman) had the inside knowledge to run rings round troublesome union men when necessary.* L □ *Last month I finished a six-week stint working as a barman. Today makes it 24 weeks since I touched a drop and **turned gamekeeper**, and the more I see of **poachers** the tighter I cling to my wagon* (ie cling to my decision to stop drinking). NS □ part of expression may be used, with rest understood from context, as in second example.

a gammy leg a game leg; an injured, or deformed, leg that makes one limp □ *Hopalong* (was) *still looking for a stick to bring and walking about with **his gammy leg** as though he was trying to shake a toffee-paper off the sole of his shoe.* TT

a garden/plaster gnome a coloured figurine used for garden decoration, satirically associated with lower-to-middle-class suburbia and uninformed taste □ *Mrs Brown is a native of South London, the heartland of English fantasy, a society of do-it-yourself and **the** ever-watchful **garden gnome**.* L □ *Despite the knocking* (= adverse criticism) *they've had you can still see **plaster gnomes**, a rabbit and a toad or two, in some gardens.*

gather dust[1] [V + O] be difficult, or tiresome, to keep free from dust or dirt **S:** statue, ornament; china, furniture □ *Why bother keeping all these ornaments? They just **gather dust**.*

gather dust[2] [V + O] remain unused, undealt with, neglected etc □ *And then she played us an unfunny snatch from an old Victor Borge record that has been **gathering dust** on my shelves for the past 20 years.* NS □ *'The Case of the Helmeted Airman' is either the work of a lazy man or the victim of a procrastinating publisher, since it has clearly been sitting around for some time **gathering dust**.* NS □ *Along the spectator fence are the legendary machines of a vanished but not so distant past ready for action. 'I really don't believe folks would rather see these old planes sitting in my museum building **gathering dust**.'* OBS □ esp in *to*-inf and *-ing* constructions, such as *(be) left to **gather dust**, lie/sit/stand **gathering dust**.*

gather etc momentum [V + O] increase etc in speed or force, esp that self-generated from a movement already begun; increase etc in rate, or range, of activity **S:** train, lorry; process, movement, course of events. **V:** gather, ⚠ gain, pick up; lose, run out of □ *It was clear to me that as the American attack **gathered momentum** there would be severe repercussions all along the enemy front.* MFM □ *The boulder seemed to slide almost reluctantly down the first few yards of the incline then, **gaining momentum**, it crashed through the sparse scrub and bounded off the rocky surfaces.* □ *In a few sentences one cannot do justice to a story which depends for its effect upon a sense of **gathering momentum**.* NS □ *Michael Tippett (who was 70 on Thursday) has seemed in recent years to have **gained** rather than **lost momentum**, so that one impressive work has arisen out of another in majestic succession.* OBS

gather ye rosebuds while ye may (saying) seize what pleasures you can before the passage of time removes them or you □ (source) ***Gather ye rosebuds while ye may**,/Old Time is still a-flying.* TO THE VIRGINS, TO MAKE MUCH OF TIME (R HERRICK 1591-1674) □ *Young people like to be together, don't they? At least in the stage you two are in at the moment. **Gather ye rosebuds while ye may**, remember?* TGLY □ (NONCE) *Am I saying that the world is incurable anyway, and that we should **gather roses while we may**? I'm not saying any such thing. I am saying that, when the nations rage furiously together, we should not be misled by their hullabaloo.* L

a gay dog a pleasure-loving, perhaps irresponsible or licentious, fellow; sb who is fond of social life □ *To those who knew them both Goronwy Rees was himself a character of grand proportions; the gayest of **gay dogs**; a bright cork which always bobbed to the surface again after each submersion.* OBS □ *The aforementioned editors have all insisted on promoting Allais as a humorous writer. It is all right to be a satirist, even a wit, but give **a gay dog** a humorous label, and you might as well forget him.* L

gee whizz(!) (dated US informal) exclamation of astonishment, or an indication that one is greatly, and perhaps naively, impressed by sth seen or heard □ *When Phil and I first hit New York, we were still wearing baggy pants. It was the first time we ever saw shoes without laces or socks that came up your legs. We met Buddy and the Crickets up in Montreal; they saw what we were wearing and said '**Gee Whizz!**'* ST □ (NONCE) *The editor of the BBC's 'Election Special', Michael Townson, claims that he's trying to simplify and tidy up the clutter of messages on the screen, not add to them with '**gee whizzery**'.* RT □ *This film's strength is not scientific data but the boyish **gee-whizz** enthusiasm of the Canadian explorers.* ST □ (a television programme) *'Tomorrow's World' has sometimes been described as the '**gee-whizz**' look at science and industry.* RT □ can now be used humorously, with awareness that it is dated; attrib use *the **gee-whizz** enthusiasm, a*

gee-whizz *look at sth.*

(all) sb's geese are swans sb, usu already mentioned, has an exaggerated idea of the merits of his own family, friends, belongings, accomplishments etc □ *'According to Jones, his class-room is full of budding geniuses.' 'Oh,* ***all his geese are swans****. It's the same story year after year.'* □ *It's a common maternal failing to think* ***one's geese are swans*** *but some mothers have the sense to keep that belief to themselves.* □ *Lord James hopes that, freed from the dead hand of university curricular control, the Colleges of Education will be* ***transformed*** *from* ***geese into swans****.* NS □ variant transform/turn geese into swans.

the general rule [Comp (NP)] the customary way of doing things that is understood and usu followed; the way things are usually arranged or are likely to happen; as a rule (qv) **V:** ⚠ be, become; make sth □ *It's* ***a*** *good* ***general rule*** *in First Aid not to give food or drink to anybody in a state of collapse until you know what is the matter with them.* □ *I never understand why patients are woken up between 5 and 6 a.m. to be washed but it seems to be* ***the general rule*** *in hospitals everywhere.* □ *It may be that, in industrial districts, the high wages that can be obtained at an early age have reduced the attractions of postponing wage-earning in favour of a university education. But there seems to be* ***no general rule****.* SC □ does not imply anything legally binding or strictly enforced.

generate/contribute more heat than light [V + O pass] cause argument, disagreement, resentment etc instead of, as might be supposed, giving enlightenment or information **S:** topic, debate; conference; correspondence □ *Maybe the most cogent comment on a topic which so far has* ***generated more heat than light*** *came from Mr Mark Bonham Carter.* L □ *Small islands dependent on one crop can fall into serious difficulties of foreign exchange, and whoever picks up the bill can pick up the political influence with it. To mention Cuba probably* ***generates more heat than light****.* NS □ *The Shockley affair has* ***contributed more heat than light****, and on both sides of the controversy irrational racialism has furnished its inescapable quota of confusion.* L □ (NONCE) (reader's letter) *If these fundamental questions are to be discussed in your pages, may we please have* ***more light and less heat*** *with our physics and metaphysics?* L □ *We have* ***generated a lot of heat****, a lot of screaming, but over 24 years our roles have evolved.* ST □ variants generate a lot of heat, generate less light than heat.

the generation gap a lack of understanding and/or sympathy between people of different age groups, and esp between young people and middle-aged, or old, people □ *Although Bazarov's theme is certainly a serious one with contemporary implications—****the 'generation gap'*** *being topical these days—'this novel is most un-Russian,' says the serial producer, Martin Lisemore.* RT □ *Now, however, Hoover is a victim of* ***the generation gap****. Today, the young revolutionaries preach hate and want to destroy the society Hoover serves and loves.* OBS □ *The Major's friends and comrades, like his widow, had crisp standard-English accents: his daughter to me sounded quite extraordinary in their company: a blurred, hummy youth-voice with strangely down-at-heel vowels. It doesn't much matter: but it underlined* ***the generation gap****.* L

the genie of the lamp/in the bottle a spirit imprisoned in a jar, casket etc, that, if released, has magical or malevolent powers but will do its master's bidding if it can be controlled (from Middle Eastern folklore) □ *The sudden appearance of small boys at crucial moments is an accepted phenomenon in the Middle East. They may well have suggested ancient tales of* ***the genie of the lamp****.* BM □ *The gases writhed in the bell-jar like* ***a genie in a bottle****.* □ *Mrs Mavis Mayo, writing from Germany, had gone the other way, from minor tycoon to housewife and never regretted it. 'An unliberated woman and enjoying every minute of my serfdom. Take warning, sisters, do you really know* ***the genie*** *you are letting* ***out of the bottle****?'* ST □ may be adapted, as shown.

genius is an infinite capacity for taking pains (saying) exceptional creative or inventive capacity is the product of an inexhaustible willingness to take great trouble □ *'****Genius****' (which means* ***transcendent capacity of taking trouble****, first of all).* FREDERICK THE GREAT (T CARLYLE 1759-1881) □ *Success in haute cuisine lies like* ***genius****, in the* ***infinite capacity to take pains****.* OBS □ *There are three types of commanders in the higher grades: 1, those who have faith and inspiration, but lack* ***the infinite capacity for taking pains*** *and preparing for every foreseeable contingency. These fail.* MFM □ *With only limited* ***capacity for taking pains****, he used water-colour as the most ready, serviceable means of expression to hand, and constantly dodged his issues.* L □ often adapted, as shown.

a gentleman's agreement an agreement between people to do sth, when the agreement is not a formal contract or legally binding but depends on the mutual trust and good faith of both, or all, parties □ *The English system of house-buying depends initially upon* ***a gentleman's agreement*** *between the buyer and the seller without any backing from the law.* ST □ *Large sections of the middle class were still on the way up, and thus could feel some confidence that, as a result of* ***an*** *unspoken* ***gentleman's agreement****, God was on their side.* OBS

gentlemen prefer blondes (catchphrase) men of wealth and/or elevated social position find women with fair hair more attractive than women with red or dark hair (from a novel of that title by ANITA LOOS b1893) □ *'Don't bother to turn on your charms for me,' he said coldly. 'I'm not one of* ***the gentlemen*** *who* ***prefer blondes****.'* WI □ *Team spirit abounds among 'Six of the Best', those appropriately named* ***blondes*** *that* ***gentlemen prefer*** *every Monday in 'Billy Dainty Esq'.* TVT □ *If Sharon is a little unsure about dyeing her hair for a role in a TV series, it can only be because part of her, at least, has enjoyed being a* ***blonde****. After all, aren't* ***gentlemen*** *supposed to* ***prefer*** *them?* TVT

the genuine article [Comp (NP)] sb/sth authentic of his/its kind, that conforms exactly to his/its title or description; the real Mackay/McCoy (qv); the real thing (qv) **V:** ⚠ be, look like □ *Anybody that strums a guitar and mugs up* *a few old songs can call himself a folk singer nowadays. But Jeannie Robertson's different—she's* ***the genuine article****.* □ *'Photoplay' declared that every single word* (of his autobiography) *had been written by Valentino himself: it was* ***the genuine article****.* L □ *'It was probably one of those champagne-type sparkling wines they gave you.' 'No, it wasn't. It was* ***the genuine article****.'*

get etc an airing [possess] be stated, or discussed, freely and openly **S:** subject, views, opinions; grudge, fears; differences. **V:** get, ⚠ have (got); give sth. **adj:** good, proper, thorough □ *World War Two has a new lease of life when Mr Roper meets Franz Wasserman, and his old grudge against Hitler* ***gets an airing****.* TVT □ *I mention this, because it illustrates the real tragedy of Slater Walker which has not yet been* ***given the airing*** *it deserves.* G □ *Producer Barrie Sales and presenter Robert Kee feel they will have* ***given*** *the pros and cons* (of Common Market membership) ***a*** *pretty good* ***airing*** *by the finish.* TVT

get away (as) clean as a whistle get away, leave a place, without leaving traces, without being detected or caught (and, often, after having stolen sth) **S:** he, she, you, we; burglar, gang □ *I heard a door click, and then he was coming along the garden path, carrying one quite small suitcase. '****Got away clean as a whistle****,' he said chuckling.* CON □ *Despite the tip-off the police arrived too late. The bank-raiders* ***got away as clean as a whistle****, leaving nothing behind but an empty safe.*

get etc a bad name [possess] gain an unfavourable, harmful reputation (eg because of sth wrong one has done or sth right one has failed to do) **S:** behaviour, attitude; standards, levels (of achievement). **V:** get, ⚠ have; give sb/sth. **prep:** with □ *I don't want to* ***get a bad name*** *among boys for being easy-going in the clinches* (= too ready to respond to their love-making), *but neither do I want to be looked on as an iceberg.* H □ *I don't know if that club really is a den of vice, but it certainly* ***has a bad name*** *in the district.* □ *Rumours of poor educational standards together with intimidation of smaller boys in the playground have* ***given*** *the school* ***a bad name****.* □ often followed by *for* + n or *for* + *-ing* form.

get/give sb the bird [possess] (informal) be hissed off the stage by an audience/give a stage performer an unfavourable reception; be rudely rejected or dismissed/rudely reject or dismiss sb; have one's requests or suggestions rudely or sharply refused/rudely or sharply refuse sb's requests or suggestions □ GEORGE: *Don't panic. I'll not get maudlin. I could probably start howling any minute, only I'm afraid of* ***getting the bird*** *from my audience.* EGD □ *One's known applause and one's known being* ***given the bird****, and I don't think either is of any importance, really.* RT

get busy [V + Comp] (informal) start to work seriously and energetically on sth specified or understood; get cracking etc (qv) □ *As soon as the war is over, I'll* ***get busy*** *and push Blue Seal Ware till it's the rage of the post-war fashion world.* CON □ *I thought I told you to clear up these papers. Come on now,* ***get busy****.* ⇨ ⚠ get going.

get etc a chill on the liver etc [possess] (informal) have etc a mild illness which affects the function of the liver etc (as a result of exposure to cold, wet, draughts etc) **V:** get, ⚠ have (got); give sb. **prep:** with. **o:** liver, kidneys, stomach, bladder □ *Apparently, he* ***got*** *what Dr. MacGregor calls* ***a chill on the liver*** *during that infernal east wind, so I suppose the old boy was feeling low.* RM □ *'They'll* ***get a chill on their stomachs****,' remonstrated Granny, 'eating all that ice-cream.'* □ *Well, if he's* ***got a chill on the bladder*** *I'm very sorry for him. It's a painful complaint, as I well know!*

get/give sb the chop/chopper [possess] (informal) be dismissed, sacked/sack, dismiss sb; be reduced, or dispensed with/reduce, or dispense with sb/sth because of an economy drive, change of policy; die, be killed/kill **S:** worker, staff; department, section; plant, works; airman, sailor □ *A lot of families living here will have to leave if the fish-processing station* ***gets the chopper****.* □ *'A very great friend of mine was with that squadron. Thoroughly decent chap. Went for a Burton over the Ruhr.' We noncoms* (= non-commissioned officers) *used to say* ***got the chopper****. Going for a Burton was journalist's talk.* RATT □ *Owing to lack of space, last week's crop of football platitudes* ***got the chop****, so double helpings* (= twice as much) *this time.* OBS ⇨ ⚠ go for a Burton (Vol 1).

get etc cold feet [possess] (informal) feel etc, esp as time for action approaches, timidity or fear about doing sth **V:** get, ⚠ (begin to) have, give sb. **prep:** with, without □ *He also fails to point out that if Mr Superman signs the policy and suddenly* ***gets cold feet*** *the next day, it is not too late to extricate himself.* ST □ *To this day I don't know how genuine that sudden bit of urgent business was; perhaps he just* ***got cold feet*** *and wanted me to go ahead and soften things up.* CON □ *Make up your mind—now I decide to stay, you start* ***getting cold feet****.* HSG □ *All seemed set, and each day passed* ***without*** *any signs of* ***cold feet*** *on the part of my colleagues.* MFM

get cracking etc (informal) start to move and/or work quickly and energetically (the reference usu being to sth that needs urgent attention); get busy (qv) **V:** cracking, ⚠ moving, weaving □ *'You thievin'* (= thieving) *Radford lot,' the man responded angrily. '****Get cracking*** *from here, or I'll call a copper* ((slang) = a policeman)*.'* LLDR □ *'You and Bill are going to have to* ***get cracking****. You go and see your company tomorrow, Bill,' he urged. 'Make them find Cindy a passage* (to Australia)*.'* PE □ *If you hope to hire a caravan during August, you'd better* ***get moving*** *now. Most of them are booked well in advance.* □ *'Come on, let's* ***get weaving****,' said Hutchin's pupil, settling himself in the cockpit.* HD ⇨ ⚠ get going.

get etc a dose/taste of one's own/the same medicine [possess] receive etc treatment of the same kind as one has given sb else, or of a kind previously referred to **V:** get, ⚠ receive, take; give sb □ *In the rapid changes of fear and favour during those years not a few of the French Revolutionary leaders found themselves having to* ***take a dose of their own medicine*** *on the steps of the guillotine.* □ *There* *is still a large body of opinion that the only effective way to deal with violent criminals is to* ***give*** *them* ***a taste of their own medicine****, although there is no evidence that such methods produce any good results.* ▫ *The most courageous step Einstein took lay in abandoning the theoretical absolutes, which amounts to saying that things are as observed, and not as some conceptual scheme prescribes. Yet his own theory is such a conceptual scheme, and so calls for* ***the same medicine****.* L ▫ *Repressive measures have already fomented opposition and discontent. How can* ***another dose of the same medicine*** *help?* SC ▫ often used in part, or allusively, as shown in third and fourth examples.

get etc a dusty answer [possess] get etc a disappointing, noncommittal, dismissive, or virtually negative answer to a question or request **V:** get, ⚠ receive; give sb; there be ▫ (source) *Ah!, what* ***a dusty answer gets*** *the soul/When hot for certainties in this our life.* MODERN LOVE (G MEREDITH 1882-1909) ▫ *You can try suggesting that you two girls go with him to the boxing match but you'll* ***get a dusty answer****. He thinks that sort of thing's unfeminine.* ▫ *Noël Coward rang up to find out when the ship would be available, but since the whereabouts of HM ships was deadly secret, he always* ***received a dusty answer****.* I FLEMING ▫ *The one was secure; an agnostic having no doubts, never* ***receiving dusty answers****; the other a doubter, with her mind fixed to the God of whom she could not be sure.* ST ▫ *Trenchard, blunt to a fault, informed Reith that the height of the transmitter masts constituted a risk to the lives of his pilots and to their machines. Reith's* ***answer was*** *fairly* ***dusty*** *too, but the two men met and swiftly settled the matter.* L.

get an earful/eyeful of this (informal) listen to/look at this ▫ *'Before you tangle yourself up in any more lies,* ***get an earful of this****,' and he played back the incriminating tape.* ▫ *'I'd never have believed it!' exclaimed his wife, beckoning him to the window. 'Come and* ***get an eyeful of this****!'* ▫ usu imper.

get even (with sb) [V + Comp] get one's revenge (on sb) for sth done to one's own disadvantage; (facetious) retaliate in not very important circumstances ▫ *During all my childhood I listened to her hating him and planning to* ***get even with*** *him. I was frightened of my mother. She was so bitter and unforgiving.* DC ▫ *They were trying to rob him. He would* ***get even with*** *them somehow, he would creep up when they least expected it.* US

get etc a fair/square deal [possess] receive etc just and equitable treatment, exchange of goods or services, value for money, etc **V:** get, ⚠ have; give sb; ask for, want ▫ *How can postmen be convinced that they are* ***getting a fair deal****, when others in the public service receive an increase that is inflationary, though it may be justified on other grounds?* SC ▫ (reader's letter) *Indeed, women do not everywhere* ***get a fair deal****. If they did, there would be no imbalance for 'Radio Times' to help level, in its special issue.* RT ▫ *We're in business for profit of course, but we* ***give*** *our customers* ***a square deal****.* ⇨ get etc a raw deal.

get etc a/one's fair share [possess] get etc a justly divided share **V:** get, ⚠ have (got), receive; give sb; take; pay, contribute. **A:** of the food, of the expenses; in the labour, in bringing up the children ▫ *I'd like to come, but you must let me* ***pay my fair share****.* ▫ (reader's letter) *I have nothing against teenagers. But if they are earning good money they should be prepared to* ***contribute a fair share*** *to the rest of the community.* DM ▫ *It comes as a shock to some of the starry-eyed young people, chafing from the bonds of capitalism and family, to realise that* ***fair shares*** *for all* (in a kibbutz) *means everyone having their prescribed tasks.* OBS ▫ variant fair shares (for all), sometimes used as a slogan. ⇨ ⚠ have etc (more than) a/one's fair share of sth.

get etc a free hand [possess] get etc permission and/or opportunity to make one's own decisions and arrangements in respect of one's work, an undertaking, etc **V:** get, ⚠ have, need; give sb, allow sb; ask for ▫ (UK entry into the Common Market) *The Marketeers claim a victory, the anti-Marketeers are prepared to concede a defeat. Mr Wilson* ***had a free hand****, which is what he wanted all along.* NS ▫ *I had served under some good and sympathetic generals who had encouraged the development of my ideas and* ***given me a free hand*** *in carrying them out.* MFM ▫ *The salon reopened with 120 workers in 1945 and although, when the Communists took power, Mrs Rothchild was nationalised, she has been* ***left an*** *entirely* ***free hand****.* G

get sb's goat [V + O] (informal) make one feel irritated, impatient, or resentful **S:** neighbour, colleague; noise, interruption; impertinence ▫ CHARLES: *It's funny how he* ***gets my goat****. I suppose it's because I've been under authority for so long. I envy him his independence.* OI ▫ *I rather like a good argument. What* ***gets*** *people****'s goat*** *about Andrew is that he doesn't bother to listen to what they have to say.*

get going start to move, work, or function **S:** convoy, procession; factory, store; project, research ▫ *'Do you feel fit for another long walk today?' 'Sure—a little stiff maybe, but I'll be all right once I* ***get going****.'* ▫ *'What brings you down here, Lewis?' 'Oh, just an ordinary visit from headquarters.' 'I didn't know we had much to visit, till you and Walter had* ***got going*** *again,' she said.* NM ▫ *The new hotel is open but it hasn't really* ***got going*** *yet, and won't until the summer season.* ⇨ ⚠ get busy; get cracking etc; next entry.

get sth going start, organize sth and make it work **O:** club, hotel; travel; French class, discussion groups ▫ *I'm sure with all these newcomers to the district we should be able to* ***get*** *the Badminton Club* ***going*** *again in the village this winter.* ▫ *Customers would want a drink as well as food, however good that was. A bar, that's what was needed, to* ***get*** *the place really* ***going****.* RT ▫ *I take no credit for the Charities Drive. The students* ***got*** *it* ***going*** *themselves.* ⇨ ⚠ previous entry.

get etc a good/bad press [possess] receive etc favourable/unfavourable, or inadequate, attention in newspapers and journals **S:** actor; footballer, athlete; book, play. **V:** get, ⚠ have, enjoy, suffer ▫ *Business men and financiers have never* ***enjoyed a*** *particularly* ***good press****. In terms of glamour they have never really been able to compete with lords and ladies, film stars and* *even politicians.* NS □ *I think the book has* ***had an*** *over-****bad press*** *but I'd agree it isn't up to the standard of his previous work.*

get etc a grandstand view (of sth) [possess] obtain etc a clear and complete view (of a relevant area) from a position of advantage **V:** get, ⚠ obtain, have; give sb, there be □ *My father had a very big office and on special occasions, like the State Opening of Parliament, there were some very nice parties. And you* ***got a grandstand view of*** *everything and the spread was marvellous.* OBS

get/have (got) the idea [possess] perceive, understand, esp what another has described, proposed, or demonstrated to one □ (training an agent for espionage) *'He may have recognized my legs under the door* (of the men's lavatory). *Do you think we ought to change trousers?' 'Wouldn't look natural,' Hawthorne said, 'but you are* ***getting the idea****.'* OMIH □ *'Well, do you think you could change a tyre yourself now?' 'Yes, I think I'****ve got the idea****.'*

get in etc one's twopence/fourpence worth (informal) make one's contribution to a discussion, argument, conversation **V:** get in, (want to) have, shove in (with), chime, weigh, in with □ *If the consumer is going to have any influence on the recommendations of a future committee he had better* ***get in his tuppence worth*** *early, often and loud and clear.* ST □ *We did invite some Health Visitors along, and a couple of them did turn up and* ***weigh in with their four penn'orth****.* RT □ *We'd nearly reached agreement when Andrew, of course, had to* ***have his twopence worth*** *on the rights of the tenants, which immediately put the landlord's back up again.* □ stress pattern ˌget in one's ˈtwopence/ˈfourpence worth.

get it (in the neck/where the chicken gets the chopper) (informal) receive a severe reprimand, punishment, unwelcome or disastrous experience; catch it (qv) □ (rugby coaching) *'The coach is bound to* ***get it in the neck****,' he says, 'but you know that when you take it on.'* RT □ *'Just you wait,' the taxi-driver finally exploded. 'You wait till Mrs Gandhi gets in, and then you are going to* ***get it****.'* NS □ *That's another lesson of my life—the day anybody gets the whole story, you* ***get it where the chicken got the chopper****.* HD □ expression get it where the chicken gets the chopper rare.

get knotted (taboo) be quiet; go away; drop dead[2] (qv); get lost (qv); (taboo) get stuffed (qv); (taboo) up yours etc (qv) □ *A nurse called me out to meet one of her superiors, who coldly informed me that I was not running the hospital, and that I would in future adhere strictly to the rules about visiting hours. 'You,' I said 'can* ***get knotted****.'* OBS □ exclamation expressing violent contempt.

get etc one's lines crossed [possess] fail to make proper contact by telephone because of a technical fault; (fig) think one is making genuine contact with people or groups achieving certain aims, when one is, in fact, doing otherwise **V:** get, ⚠ have (got); be. **prep:** with □ (a technical accident when making a phone call) *I keep getting the same wrong number. The* ***lines*** *must* ***be crossed****.* □ *Sometimes an advertising copy-writer will* ***get his lines crossed*** *and produce copy designed to reach the body of the working-classes though appealing to assumptions more characteristic of other classes.* UL □ *Somewhere Parliament and the people have* ***got their lines crossed*** *and it is probably too late to unravel them.* NS □ *He claims to be in constant touch with Albert Einstein but I think he's* ***got his lines crossed****.* NS

get a load of this (informal) listen to, look at, read, become familiar with, fully understand, etc this □ *'You said they'd never sue, didn't you?' he said, thrusting the letter under his lawyer's nose. 'Well,* ***get a load of this****!'* □ *'Prescott was threatening to give in his notice this morning.' 'He can please himself about that, but tell him to* ***get a load of this****—if he does, he needn't think we'll take him back later.'* □ usu imper.

get lost (informal) go away; shut up; don't interfere; drop dead[2] (qv); (taboo) get knotted (qv); (taboo) get stuffed; (taboo) up yours etc (qv) □ *'I think you two should go away and have your argument somewhere else,' said the neighbour, who had come down to his garden gate to complain. '****Get lost****, dad, unless you want a punch up the throat,' one of them told him.* □ (coal-mining) *There is a considerable incentive, for both management and men in the area, to tell the rest of the country to* ***get lost****.* NS □ *As a kid Rosie Casals was always pestering her father for a game of tennis. 'They'd get really fed up with me. They didn't take me seriously and they'd usually end up giving me a nickel to* ***get lost****.'* RT □ often with *tell sb to*.

get/have (got) the message [possess] (informal) have no doubts about what is best, or what sb intends one to do or think **S:** government, council; press, public; leader □ *'They'****ve got the message*** *all right and they're taking action. But how effective it will be and how long it will last remains to be seen,' said an official.* SC □ (conclusion of a review of a fashion show) *In case you didn't* ***get the message****, I thought it was a great collection.* ST □ *Homelessness, said Des Wilson, was living in cold, damp, overcrowded, filthy, verminous rooms: and on that basis, probably at least a million people qualified. The public* ***got the message****, and Shelter's funds topped the magic figure of £1m.* NS

get etc one's money's worth [possess] receive etc full value in goods, or services, for the money one spends; receive more than adequate reward, satisfaction, response etc for the effort one expends **V:** get, ⚠ have (got); want, demand; give sb □ *Only those manufacturers selling cheap, mass-produced goods consumed in such quantities that the products are household words can* ***get their money's worth*** *out of television advertising.* L □ *'I thought you only took a cup of tea in the mornings.' 'That's true, but since I've paid for bed and breakfast this time I* ***want my money's worth****.'* □ *I like to keep up with the practical achievements and future possibilities of technology. After a brisk half hour on information storage and retrieval, I felt I had really* ***had my money's worth****.* NS □ *If it's a fight he wants he'll* ***get his money's worth*** *from me.* □ stress pattern get one's ˈmoney's worth.

get etc moral support [possess] get etc help from sb's presence, sympathy, public approval, etc, as distinct from financial or practical assistance **V:** get, ⚠ have (got); (there) be; give sb, offer, lend. **prep:** with □ *'Here Joe, you try and get him to see reason,' Ned called to me quite angrily. Perhaps it* ***was*** *the lack of* ***moral support*** *from me that made Ned give in. At any rate, the next thing was that we were in a taxi again.* CON □ *'Oh Sir Julius, I am so glad you are still here!' she said. 'You have finished breakfast, I see, but you will stay and* ***give*** *a little* ***moral support*** *while I drink a cup of coffee, won't you?'* EM

get etc more kicks than ha'pence/halfpence [possess] receive etc more pain than profit, more blame or abuse than praise or thanks (said first of performing or organ-grinders' monkeys) **V:** get, ⚠ (there) be. **prep:** with □ *He started work at 14 on his uncle's farm where he* ***got more kicks than ha'pence.*** □ ***There's more kicks than halfpence*** *in editing a collection of contemporary verse. I'll never do it again.*

get nowhere etc achieve little, nothing etc; see no, few, some results for one's efforts **A:** nowhere, ⚠ (not) anywhere, somewhere □ *In four days I travelled six hundred and seventy miles, saw twenty-four residents of Ireland and* ***got nowhere.*** PP □ *Philip's doing fine but George, the other son — well, he's* ***getting nowhere,*** *fast.* □ *Thanks to you, I have grasped that a certain fundamental decency to others is necessary if one's to* ***get anywhere.*** HAA □ *I think we may be* ***getting somewhere*** *now, since those last figures came in. A pattern is beginning to emerge.* □ *Although the committee had decided on its recommendation the previous day, all the sniffing by the best pedigree newshounds of Fleet Street could* ***get nowhere.*** NS ⇨ ⚠ next entry.

get sb nowhere etc [V + O + A] not help sb to become successful, happy, to get what they want **S:** flattery; protests, tears; being honest. **A:** nowhere, ⚠ (not) anywhere, where □ *'I believe you implicitly—and I believe I've said before, you are my best teacher and a good Christian woman—' 'Flattery will* ***get*** *you* ***nowhere*** *—I am, as you know, already spoken for.'* TT □ *In what particularly are we interested in the museum? The simplest way, of course, is to take the catalogue and tick the items. Unfortunately this idea does not* ***get*** *us* ***anywhere;*** *there is no catalogue.* TCM □ *You can turn off the waterworks. Tears will* ***get*** *you* ***nowhere*** *with me.* □ *In those days, films divided sharply between broad comedy and stark tragedy. The halfway house* ***got*** *you* ***nowhere.*** NS □ *Renny's cheerfully optimistic belief that energy will* ***get*** *you* ***anywhere*** *helped.* TVT □ *Dammit,* ***where*** *does being honest* ***get*** *you? If old Philip had been honest where would the Templar family have been today?* DC □ in last example ***where*** *does sth* ***get*** *one?* implies *it* ***gets*** *one* ***nowhere.*** ⇨ ⚠ previous entry.

get etc one's/the priorities right etc [possess] have a true/false scale of values; judge/misjudge what the first claims should be on one's time, money etc and act accordingly; (put) first things first (qv) **V:** get, ⚠ have (got). **prep:** with. **adj:** right, ⚠ straight, clear; wrong □ *Any politician who wishes to be taken seriously in politics must* ***get his priorities right;*** *and this means, in the end, preferring his political career to his business career.* ST □ (reader's letter) *The less you do, the more help you get from Welfare and Voluntary Organisations. So let's* ***get our priorities right,*** *let's help those who, like my parents and many others,* really *tried and got nothing.* RT □ *The Railway Conversion Association League consider the benefits of their scheme self-evident, but they* ***have got the priorities wrong.*** ST □ *A senior member asked me to remind you that we are 20 years more ancient than the first Continental Congress, and maybe you should* ***get your priorities straight.*** L □ the much less common than one's.

get etc a raw deal [possess] get etc unjust or harsh treatment; receive etc insufficient payment or reward **V:** get, ⚠ have; give sb □ *Devereall* ***had a*** *very* ***raw deal*** *from the Secretary of State for War, Hore-Belisha, and was turned out after 18 months in office.* MFM □ *The polytechnics believe that though the Government talks of 'parity of esteem' between the two sectors of higher eductation, they are still* ***given a raw deal*** *in comparison with the universities.* OBS □ *'A Scandalous Woman' is a collection worth reading. But it will reinforce the iron in the soul* (= sense of injury caused by adverse circumstances) *of any lady who feels she is* ***getting a raw deal*** *from life.* NS ⇨ get a fair/square deal.

get rich quick [V + O + Comp] acquire wealth without having to work much, or wait long, for it □ *'Save and Prosper' itself recommends that no investor should put in more than 5 per cent of his savings anyway. Subject to these qualifications, these trusts could be an agreeable way of* ***getting*** *slightly* ***rich quick.*** G □ *'Do you know what you want to do when you leave school, Jimmy?' '****Get rich quick****. Any ideas?'* □ *I'm doubtful if a man ever* ***gets rich quick*** *quite honestly.* □ attrib use *a* ***get-rich-quick*** *property developer.*

get sth right/wrong[1] [V + O + Comp] carry out a task, answer a question, solve a problem, etc, or fail to do so **O:** sum, calculation; it, the thing □ *I* ***got*** *all my sums* ***right*** *in school today, Mummy.* □ *She wasn't satisfied with the sketch she had made of her friend. 'I can't* ***get*** *the mouth* ***right,****' she complained.* □ *We are constantly* ***getting*** *it* ***wrong*** *when we use figures like 80 per cent, 20 per cent—or even vague ones like two to one.* L □ (a television programme) *On 'Nationwide', we use* (the weather) *as a standby topic, to fill in spare seconds between the joins. And we often* ***get*** *it* ***wrong,*** *which is to say that Bob Wellings does.* L

get sth right/wrong[2] [V + O + Comp] understand, or remember, sth correctly, or fail to do so **O:** it, things; song, story □ *It was Seattle she was going to, when she left Oxford, not Settle. The charwoman* ***got*** *it* ***wrong.*** RFW □ *As commonly happens when politicians land their country in a mess by their own folly, they hold that the world's Press has* ***got*** *things all* ***wrong.*** SC □ *Your old man's* ***got*** *the story* ***wrong.*** *That's not what happened at all.* □ O often it, referring to sth previously mentioned.

get sb the sack (informal) be the cause of sb being dismissed from his employment **S:** boss's wife, customers' complaints; laziness, smoking □ *'Breeziness' is, I think, the quality that I most associate with him: certainly it is what* ***got*** *him*

the sack *from the Wilson Government.* NS ▫ *You'll* ***get*** *me* ***the sack*** *if you keep dropping in* (= paying casual visits) *here when I'm supposed to be working.* ▫ *Workers got special rations which many of them flogged* ((slang) = sold) *on the black market, but to be found doing so could* ***get*** *you* ***the sack***. RT ⇨ ⚠ next entry.

get/give sb the sack [possess] (informal) be dismissed from one's employment/dismiss sb from his employment ▫ *I suppose I have really* ***got the sack***. *L.W. says I can't be trusted to do anything but wrap up parcels and that I am the most frightful idiot he has ever had the privilege of meeting in a long career of suffering fools.* ST ▫ (proposal to dismiss old and sick dockers in 1947) *'What other alternative was left to us, much as our hearts went out to them?' a TGWU official asked a strike meeting. He got his reply at once from the back of the hall: '****Give them*** *nine doctors each like the King has got, not* ***the*** *bleeding* ***sack***!' NS ⇨ ⚠ previous entry.

get one's second wind [possess] begin to breathe smoothly again after a period when one's breathing has been irregular or heavy; (fig) become active again after a period of little activity **S:** runner, swimmer, cyclist; lecturer ▫ *I was hoping my aunt had come to the end of her tirade, but no, she had just paused to* ***get her second wind***. ▫ *Jim expressed a desire to go swimming. Lefty had been talking to Dave, and I was just* ***getting my second wind***. UTN ▫ *The play dragged a bit in the middle but* ***got its second wind*** *in time for a rousing finish in the third act.*

get etc a shot in the arm [possess] (informal) get etc an injection from a hypodermic syringe; get etc sth that has a stimulating or restorative effect **S:** patient; institution, industry, economy; project, campaign. **V:** get, ⚠ have (got), give sb; be...(for), provide...(for); bring...(to) ▫ *...and for the first time* ***got*** *the full benefit of* ***that shot in the*** *moral* ***arm*** *derived from his virtual turning-down of Sheila's invitation.* TGLY ▫ *They claim it will* ***provide a*** *much-needed* ***shot in the arm*** *for the half-empty churches and chapels in the area.* TO ▫ *Two momentous legal decisions last week* ***brought*** *joy to the Government,* ***a shot in the arm*** *to the Industrial Relations Act, and gloom to the militants on the picket lines.* ST ▫ *His wit and intelligence would* ***be a*** *welcome* ***shot in the arm*** *for many a chat show.* TVT ▫ *The Chancellor's immediate problem is to* ***give*** *the economy* ***a*** *quick* ***shot in the arm*** OBS

get a slap in the face get a rebuff, a snub; one in the eye for sb (qv) **V:** get; ⚠ give sb; be (for sb/sth) ▫ *Bill assumed he was next in line for the editorship. He* ***got a*** *real* ***slap in the face*** *when they appointed an outsider.* ▫ ***A*** *resounding* ***slap in the face*** *from the people of Norway and Denmark might help the 'Europeans' everywhere to wake up to this.* NS

get etc a/one's slice/share of the cake [possess] (informal) get etc a/one's share of whatever financial or social benefits one is, or feels, entitled to within an industry, business, profession, city, nation etc in which one is a worker, member, citizen etc **V:** get ⚠ have (got); take, grab; give sb; want, need; ask for, demand. **prep:** with. **adj:** a bigger, larger, better; a fair, one's rightful ▫ *'One of my worries is that the lads I knew and loved might be being exploited,' he says of the present situation in the industry. 'I'm all for everybody* ***having a*** *fair* ***share of*** *whatever* ***cake*** *there is. I only hope the results for them will be happiness.'* OBS ▫ *The prosperity of the rich is slowly percolating down to a rising middle class of professional people, traders and officials, but maybe too slowly. The poor, who can see this boom with their own eyes, are starting to* ***want their share of the cake***. L ▫ *Our problem cities desperately* ***need a*** *bigger* ***slice of the*** *national* ***cake***. *A Commission should be empowered to direct resources to the urban black spots within our cities.* G ▫ (medical facilities) *An influential consultant has always* ***demanded*** *and obtained* ***an*** *above-average* ***share of the cake*** *for 'his' patients, not because their needs are necessarily greater but because his voice is louder.* OBS

get etc a standing ovation [possess] get etc enthusiastic applause or welcome with the whole audience or company standing up to cheer or clap **S:** speaker, leader. **V:** get, ⚠ have, receive; give sb. **prep:** with ▫ *He* ***gets a standing ovation*** *and as he moves off stage people are pleading, chanting and stomping for more.* TVT ▫ *The chairman thought that, from where he was sitting at the top table,* (the speech) ***received a standing ovation***. *It certainly evoked prolonged applause.* SC

get sth straight [V + O + Comp pass] understand sth said to one, the nature of a situation, etc clearly and correctly **O:** this; things, the position ▫ *I want you to explain properly why Myra should have done a thing like that. I must* ***get*** *it* ***straight***, *Joe, I must. I feel I could stand it if I could* ***get*** *it* ***straight***. CON ▫ *The item that he had often placed at the head of his undergraduate list of topics to be thought over and* ***got straight*** *— 'Sex' — was still capable of being coolly thought over.* HD ▫ *'****Get*** *this* ***straight***,' *I said. 'I love Alice. She loves me.'* RATT ▫ *Let's* ***get*** *it* ***straight***: *it is the times that have changed, not the men. Old-style centre forwards, so much a part of British soccer for so long, haven't died out. They have simply become obsolete.* TVT

get stuffed (taboo) be quiet; go away; drop dead[2] (qv); (taboo) get knotted (qv); get lost (qv); (taboo) up yours etc (qv) ▫ *When a newspaper calls on Lord Hill to be 'less aloof, less coldly impartial, less rampantly irresponsible', it should be told to* ***get stuffed***. *Everyone has his own solution to Ulster's agony.* L ▫ *'I think you'd better go down and see her. It wouldn't take much to apologize for whatever bloody tip you gave her.' 'She can* ***get stuffed***,' *said Dusty.* TT ▫ direct or indirect imper; exclamation expressing violent contempt.

get there (in the end etc) achieve one's aim, complete a task, etc esp by patience and perseverance **A:** in the end; ⚠ eventually, somehow ▫ *'That's all right, dear,' she said, 'you'll* ***get there in the end***.' *She always answered Bill's unintelligible flights with general reassurance.* HAA ▫ *Jenkins isn't a fast learner but give him time and he* ***gets there in the end*** *—which is more than you can say of some more brilliant intellects.* ▫ *I thought we would have the house ship-shape by now but we're still living in* *the same muddle. I suppose we'll* ***get there eventually****.*

get there first reach, obtain, or achieve sth before another, or others, who would have liked to do so □ *I can usually fill a big basket of raspberries down by the railway bridge but this year somebody had* ***got there first****.* □ *In China, or in the Soviet Union, there is at least some demand for things which Britain can make better than the local competition. Not surprisingly, the Americans* ***got there first****.* NS □ (drugs in the treatment of schizophrenia) *So many people are working in this field—and the drug companies in particular have such an enormous investment in it, because not only would this bring the Nobel Prize to half a dozen chemists, but it would bring untold profits to whichever drug firm happened to* ***get there first****.* L

get/be too big for one's boots [V + Comp] (informal) become/be too self-important, assuming functions and/or authority beyond one's rights, or ambitions beyond one's powers **S:** child; pop-star, footballer □ *Don't try and take that line with me, my lad. You're* ***getting too big for your boots****, talking to me in that tone, and I'm not having it.* TGLY □ MRS BUTCHER: *You're a snotty-nosed big mouth.* MRS FISH: ***Too big for your boots****, that's your trouble.* DPM □ *Archaeology stands at the point of collision between art and science, and there are archaeologists who feel that in invading their art, science has* ***got too big for its boots****.* OBS □ *In the early days of Watergate, the press was the hero uncovering the true facts. But now a body, which was never really respected, is widely regarded as being extremely irresponsible,* ***getting*** *far* ***too big for its boots****, due to be brought down a peg or two.* L

get tough (with sb) [V + Comp] (informal) become violent or stubborn (with sb); take up an aggressive, or sternly disciplinarian, attitude and line of action (towards sb) □ *Sammy's position over the typescript was just dubious enough to restrain him from* ***getting tough****.* UTN □ *The suggestion that it is time for the army to '****get tough****'* ***with*** *the opposition betrays an almost total ignorance not only of the present situation in Ulster but of the whole concept of operations in support of the civil power.* L

get etc the upper hand (of sb) [possess] have mastery over, be more powerful than, sb **S:** enemy; employer, union; passion, temper. **V:** get, ⚠ have, gain □ *I try to be cool and sensible but sometimes my feelings* ***get the upper hand of*** *me.* □ *They were harassed by the Malays, and attacked by the Sea Dayaks who, having* ***gained the upper hand****, were not restrained by a balance of power.* NDN □ *By June 1799, however, Desaix could fairly claim that he* ***had the upper hand****. For nearly five hundred miles he was keeping the enemy off the river, and many of the local sheikhs had submitted.* BN

get etc uptight (about sth) [V + Comp] (informal) become etc tense, over-concerned, guarded or touchy in one's attitude and reactions (to sth) **V:** get, ⚠ be; make sb. **o:** noise, interruptions; relationship; appearance, disability; opposition, criticism □ *I've treated everybody like a gentleman so there's no cause to* ***get uptight****.* RT □ *Please reassure the owners and managers not to* ***get*** *so '****uptight****'* ***about*** *something that makes the day a little pleasant.* T □ *Bentine says he's a man who* ***gets up-tight about*** *situations, not about the individuals that cause them: 'I hate armies, but not soldiers. I suppose that just about sums it up.'* TVT □ *A hero who is illiterate without being uncommunicative, and impotent without* ***being uptight****, is a refreshing conception.* L □ *Where the English usually* ***get uptight about*** *Burns is the title 'National Bard', especially if celebrating Scots indulge in comparisons between the Bard of Alloway and the Bard of Stratford.* SC

get etc one's (own) way [possess] succeed in doing what one wants, or in doing sth in the way one prefers, despite opposition or disapproval **V:** get, ⚠ have; give sb, let sb (have) □ *If he still hesitated it was because he didn't want to yield to the other man's pressure, to Alec's gift for* ***getting his own way****.* PW □ MYRA (laughing): *And what about the roof gardens—did you* ***get your way*** *about those too?* PHILIP: *Yes, everything.* EHOW □ *There was a considerable measure of opposition both locally and in the newspapers throughout Gloucestershire. But the Government* ***had its way****, as it does in such matters.* TBC ⇨ ⚠ go one's own way.

get well etc [V + Comp] recover one's health, or suffer a deterioration in one's health **adj:** well, ⚠ better; worse □ *I'm sorry to hear about Alice. I must send her a* ***Get Well*** *card.* □ *'How is your tooth-ache now?' '****Getting better.*** *Of course, I've told the dentist I simply must have an appointment this afternoon.'* □ attrib use *a* ***get-well*** *card, message.*

get/take what's coming to one [possess] (informal) suffer the results of one's misdeeds or follies; suffer an inevitable fate □ *'What happens to them in the end?' asked Isabel. 'Oh, they* ***get what's coming to them****. Rather a mistake, I think: it doesn't happen in real life.'* PW □ *I don't believe in health fads and all those ways of avoiding this disease or that. You* ***take what's coming to you****, whatever you do.*

get sb where he lives hurt, threaten, criticize, ridicule etc sb in ways that he is specially sensitive to, that will particularly hurt or displease him □ *This, as they say,* ***gets*** *George Meany* ***where he lives****. He now finds himself in direct contact with men who want to dump him.* NS □ *Rugby is a Welshman's second religion. Make a mock of the game itself or a Welsh XV and you really* ***get*** *him* ***where he lives****.*

get/have (got) sb where one wants him [possess] (informal) have sb in a position where he does as one wants him to, or where his actions can be controlled to one's own advantage **adv:** just, exactly □ *He's got you, see?* ***Got*** *you* ***where he wants*** *you. You're the beautiful wife and lovely family that* he *can't leave whenever one of his girl-friends starts turning serious on him.* TGLY □ *'That's all right,' he said boastfully. 'I've* ***got*** *that feller* (= fellow) *just* ***where I want*** *'im* (= him). *'E'll* (= he will) *pay.'* PE

get wise (to sb/sth) [V + Comp] (informal) become aware of sth, or of qualities or behaviour in sb (the reference often being to sth that should have been noticed previously or that sb is trying to hide); make sb aware of sth, or of qualities or behaviour in sb **o:** it, him; their tricks; what's happening □ (advertisement) *I noticed it* (her greasy hair) *spoils her looks. You'd think she'd* ***get wise to*** *it—it's so obvious.* H □ *There aren't many shop-lifters who escape my eye. I've* ***got wise to*** *their little tricks.* □ *'I thought it would give me a chance to* ***put*** *you* ***wise*** *about the practice,' I continued. 'Difficult to think of everything in the rush-and-tumble of the surgery.'* DIL □ *It was that one careless remark of Paterson's that* ***put*** *me* ***wise to*** *where he had really spent the evening.* □ variant put sb wise (to sb/sth).

get sb wrong (informal) misunderstand sb, his motives or actions, or what he says □ *'Not in the game yourself by any chance?' the young man went on in a light casual tone. 'Game?' 'Don't* ***get*** *me* ***wrong****. I don't mean what he was pinched* (= arrested) *for.'* HD □ *'Clever, aren't you?' he said in a very unfriendly way, 'but we won't rest until we clear all this up.' 'Look,' I pleaded, as if about to sob my socks off because he'd* ***got*** *me* ***wrong****.* LLDR □ expression *don't* ***get*** *me* ***wrong*** is used as appeal.

a gift from the gods [Comp (NP)] an unearned, or unexpected, benefit that is greatly appreciated **V:** ⚠ be; come as □ *When we went to buy our tickets back we found that the boat didn't call again till the next day. We were gloriously stranded in Skopelos. The two days there were* ***a gift from the gods****.* SC □ *'I wish the Income Tax would pay me a refund.' 'They would if they owed you one. It's not* ***a gift from the gods****, you know.'*

gild the lily [V + O] try to make perfection more perfect; mask, spoil natural beauty or a good quality by over-decorating it, praising excessively, etc **S:** writer; report, account □ (source) *To* ***gild*** *refined gold, to paint* ***the lily****,/ ...Is wasteful and ridiculous excess.* KING JOHN IV 2 □ (Scotland) *The country that does not depend for one moment on* ***gilding the lily****, but glories rather in craggy individualism.* SC □ *But there are some who feel he overwrites—and even that he had gone slightly over the top* (= exaggerated) *in both the words and the pictures he painted of wartime evacuation. '****Gilding the lily****,' Benny Green accused him of.* RT □ (reader's letter) *But surely '****gilding the lily****' is now the quotation, for if I and the world's thoughtless masses have never known the particular quotation which Tom Driberg knows then we cannot be quoting it—and when Richard Baker uses the cliché '****gilding the lily****' he is using a valid quotation.* NS

gild/sugar the pill [V + O pass] (try to) make sth that is unpleasant, or unwelcome, seem less so □ *We'll have to* ***gild the pill*** *by telling Jones that he's doing such valuable work here that he can't be spared.* □ (Harold wants his wife to leave him for a while) *'You might want to run up to London sometimes, or go to see your mother—' 'We might try it,' Isabel said. 'It's very good of you, Harold,' she added humbly, swallowing* ***the gilded pill****.* PW □ (NONCE) *The danger here is of the personality more familiar in the world of showbiz used as* ***sugar on the pill*** *of a solid programme. Such false casting will only disappoint the viewers.* L □ variants the gilded pill, (the) sugar on the pill.

(a bird in) a gilded cage (sb) confined, or restricted, in his or her mode of life, though with every comfort and amenity □ (source—title of a song) *She's* ***a bird in a gilded cage****.* A J LAMB 1870-1928 □ *'The Government is just finishing the conversion of an extremely pleasant eighteenth-century manor house at Nortonstowe.' 'You want me to allow myself to be fastened up in a cage, albeit* ***a gilded cage****.'* TBC □ *Ingham the untiring money-spinner and Tina* ***the*** *wise* ***bird in a gilded cage*** *are the twin poles of this intricate and bizarre study.* NS

gilded youth young people, esp of the rich upper classes, with the means and leisure to enjoy themselves (translation of French *jeunesse dorée*) □ *Exams* (at Cambridge) *were over, their results as yet unknown, and the students were filling this uneasy vacuum with a glorious display of their own* ***gilded youth****.* RT □ *Sporting a boater, a striped blazer and the aggressive look of a visitor come to hate, Gosling watched disdainfully as* ***gilded youth*** *did its bright young thing.* NS

a gin palace (dated) a garish public house, esp one serving cheap spirits to the poorer classes □ *This looked a more cheerful pub. He went in and got a drink and carried it to a seat. He had been wrong. It was* ***a gin-palace*** *when you got inside.* HD □ *...the inadequacies of that time for the 'lesser society' who had to find their colour and excitement in the music-halls—or in* ***the gin palaces****.* RT □ second example refers directly to the kind of public house defined above; stress pattern a 'gin palace.

a ginger group a group within, or connected with, a political party, popular movement, sectarian campaign, etc which devises schemes, and keeps pressing, for action □ *He joined none of* ***the*** *new* ***ginger groups*** *because he believes in working through his existing organisations—the Chamber of Commerce and the National Pharmaceutical Union.* G □ *Tyndall also said that approaches had been made, 'by innuendo, but with no specific offer', for the National Front to withdraw from elections and become* ***a ginger group*** *for the Tories, outside the party.* OBS

give oneself airs behave, talk, in an affected, pretentious way; think oneself better than one is and try to impress others with one's superiority **adj:** such, terrific, (the) most frightful □ *'He's not a bit conceited—fits in here just like one of ourselves.' 'That's what I'd expect. It's only ignorant people that* ***give themselves airs****.'* □ *They're all snobs, even Julie who's only ten years old. You never saw such* ***airs*** *as that child* ***gives herself****.*

give etc the alarm/alert [V + O pass] alert others to an imminent, or already existing, danger, natural disaster, military or criminal attack—by sounding bells or sirens, or by flashing lights etc **S:** bystander, neighbour, passer-by. **V:** give, ⚠ raise, sound □ *When a baboon group is raiding crops, crossing roads, or even simply moving across country, it is said to have one or more animals 'posted' to* ***give the alarm*** *to the others of any approaching danger.* NSC □ *The daylight raid at the sub-post office in Midland Road, Bedford, was seen by salesmen at a nearby car show-room. As they* ***raised the alarm*** *three men escaped by car.* DM □ (Observer Magazine's 'Whistleblower' campaign on 'threats to the quality of our lives') *If there is something you wish to* ***sound the alarm*** *about, fill in this coupon.* OBS □ *This* (control of internal eye pressure) *is done by regular supervision with sophisticated apparatus that* ***gives the alert*** *as soon as things start going wrong.* OBS

give sb/sth etc the all-clear [possess] give the signal after an air attack that enemy raiders have left; (fig) let sb know that he is now safe, or has permission, to do sth he wants or plans to do; approve, authorize initial, or additional, work on a scheme, product etc **V:** give sb; ⚠ get, have (got), receive. **IO:** garrison, guncrew; applicant; maker, inventor; product, scheme □ (an attempted hold-up) *But this damn fool girl* (an accomplice) *at the cinema got panicky and* ***gave*** *him* ***the all-clear*** *too soon. The cashier only had to let out one peep and the whole place was swarming with people.* AITC □ *Once the Council have* ***given*** *us* ***the all-clear*** *the builders will start at once.* □ *The controversial drug, which causes nausea, has* ***received the all-clear,*** BBCR □ *'****All clear****,' whispered Johnny, tapping gently on the tool-shed window, 'Mum's gone. I won't tell her you've been here.'* □ the words All clear may be spoken to indicate that danger has passed, as in last example.

give sth all one's got [possess] (informal) do sth with all one's strength, energy, devotion etc **IO:** it; her job, the role; their marriage □ *If he does take on the editorship he'll* ***give*** *it* ***all he's got.*** □ (film review) *Burt Lancaster...being grateful for his early circus training which enables him to stunt like Fairbanks. It might not be 'Robin Hood' but Burt* ***gives*** *it* ***all he's got.*** RT □ *I don't suppose she cries any more than most babies, but when she does she* ***gives*** *it* ***all she's got.*** □ esp with present simple tense, *will, be going to.*

give (sb) (back) as good as one gets [possess] (informal) not be outdone by an opponent; retaliate in a fight, argument, abusive exchange of words, etc with as much force, or skill, as has been used against one **IO:** heckler, critic; intruder □ *Old Bunce does beat the girls, but the few times he has beaten Mrs Bunce she has* ***given*** *him* ***as good as she got.*** WDM □ *Bobby Howe says he's noticed a big difference in Clyde. 'He's come out of his shell a lot this season,* ***giving as good as he gets*** *when the lads have a go at him.'* ST □ *'Hullo, lousy,' Pierre said. 'Why bloody hell you turn up?' Angela with her slow drawling voice and luscious smile* ***gave back as good as she got.*** *'This is my friend, Mr Larkin. Mr Larkin—Pierre. Mr Larkin keeps pigs—he'll understand you.'* BFA

give sb etc the benefit of one's advice etc [possess] advise sb (the implication often being that the giver's kindness is not necessarily appreciated by the recipient) **V:** give sb; ⚠ get, have. **o:** advice, experience, superior knowledge; presence □ *Since you're so fond of* ***giving*** *people* ***the benefit of your advice,*** *now that you've got me into this mess perhaps you'll tell me how to get out of it.* □ *Mrs Carstairs gave up her attempts at fraternization with the cook. She paused at the pantry door to* ***give*** *him* (the butler) ***the benefit of her presence.*** RM □ *I daresay you believe you know best, but allow me to* ***give*** *you* ***the benefit of my experience.*** □ usu ironic.

give sb etc the benefit of the doubt [possess] believe the best about sb, unless or until there is clear proof that one is mistaken in doing so **V:** give sb, ⚠ allow sb, let sb have; get □ *There was clearly a conflict of understanding between Mr Wilson and the programme's producers, and the Governors* (of the BBC) *therefore decided to* ***give*** *Mr Wilson* ***the benefit of the doubt.*** L □ *I won't make up my mind about people, I'm always trying to* ***give*** *them* ***the benefit of the doubt.*** RT □ *I would think that, after all the evidence is in, if it is anywhere near balanced, the President would* ***get the*** *very heavy* ***benefit of the doubt.*** L □ *Routes to the top are still difficult because in competition with men, women must be prepared to demonstrate the same level of commitment to their careers. Unlike men, they will not be* ***given the benefit of the doubt.*** G

give sb/get a big hand [possess] (informal) applaud an actor, speaker, instrumentalist etc generously and vigorously/be applauded generously and vigorously; show one's welcome for, or appreciation of, sb warmly and unmistakably/be welcomed, appreciated, warmly and unmistakably **IO:** singer, speaker, artiste □ *'Now,' said the compère, 'this little girl has travelled all the way from Liverpool to sing to us tonight. So let's all* ***give*** *her* ***a big hand.'*** □ ***A big hand,*** *by the way,* ***for*** *Mr Crosland, for managing no effective criticism of the Walker proposal.* NS □ *The founder of the settlement was a Welshman and anybody from Wales* ***gets a big hand*** *up here.*

give sb etc a blank cheque [possess] give sb etc complete freedom, or permission, to do sth (esp to spend money) without reference to anybody else (from the banking practice of signing a cheque and (perhaps) naming the payee but not specifying the amount to be paid) **V:** give sb, ⚠ present sb with; get, have; sign; ask for □ (Conservatives said that) *Mr Wilson intended to* ***ask*** *the nation* ***for a blank cheque*** *to nationalise what he liked.* T □ *He looked expectantly at Marie Hélène, but she said 'I do not* ***give blank cheques.'*** *It was one of her favourite English phrases; the very enormity of so prodigal a behaviour fascinated her.* ASA

give sb/get a blank look [possess] have, show no expression on one's face, esp because one has not understood sth said by sb else, or because one does not wish to give away one's feelings/receive expressionless, or uncomprehending, looks from people either because they do not wish to show their feelings or because they have not understood what one has said or done □ *When I asked Celia if she wasn't excited about tomorrow she* ***gave*** *me such* ***a blank look*** *that I realized that Robert must have intended his return to be a pleasant surprise for her.* □ *I don't think the second-year Russian group have had any conversation practice at all. All I* ***get*** *is* ***blank looks*** *when I make the simplest remark in the language.* □ *He tried to make his face* ***look*** *as* ***blank*** *as possible while he listened to her. It was vital that he did not reveal that he already knew the whole story.* □ variant look blank.

give sb/sth etc one's blessing [possess] ask God to protect sb/sth in his daily life or in his conduct of an enterprise/during the time of its existence; approve, or encourage, sb's action/a particular scheme whether proposed or accomplished **V:** give sb/sth; ⚠ get, receive, have. **prep:** with; without. **IO:** partnership, marriage; scheme, policy; change, amendment ◻ (Fergus's wife who is convalescing in bed) *'Oh Fergus! My lipstick, please.' 'I shall only kiss it off.' 'Not with Sister watching.' 'Sister will* ***give*** *me* ***her blessing****.'* DC ◻ *'I spilled the whole plate of soup into her lap.' 'You wouldn't* ***get*** *her* ***blessing*** *for that.'* ◻ *I asked one or two questions. Would these revelations be made* ***with the blessing of*** *De Beers?* DS ◻ *He had always gathered that anyone who tried to earn a living* ***without the blessing of*** *the Union was in a very dangerous position.* HD ◻ *The great petrol price war enters a new stage today as oil companies begin to* ***receive*** *the Price Commission****'s blessing*** *to raise their prices by as much as 5p a gallon.* G ◻ *Industrial retraining has become a bipartisan policy in the past 10 years, with Labour and Conservative governments* ***giving*** *it* ***their blessing****.* G

give sb the boot [possess] (informal) kick sb, esp sb who he has already been knocked down, is lying on the ground, etc ◻ *I wanted to knock over the table and hit him until my arm had no more strength in it, then* ***give*** *him* ***the boot****,* ***give*** *him* ***the boot****,* ***give*** *him* ***the boot****.* RATT ⇨ ⚠ next entry.

give sb/get the boot [possess] (informal) dismiss, or reject, sb from one's employment, company, favour etc/be dismissed, rejected etc ◻ MILLY: *I wish you'd* ***give*** *him* ***the boot*** *before he drops you. I wish you would.* EHOW ◻ *If the old boy's son hasn't got a job to go to when he comes out of the army, I'll be* ***getting*** *the order of* ***the boot****.* ◻ ***get*** *the order of* ***the boot*** (facetious) is a play on the word order (i) = 'command to leave, go away, etc' and (ii) = 'an honorary distinction, eg the Order of the Garter'. ⇨ ⚠ previous entry.

give sb etc a break[1] [possess] give sb etc a rest, respite, or change from work or activity **V:** give sb; ⚠ get, have, take. **adj:** short; occasional; periodic ◻ *'Do you want me to* ***give*** *you* ***a break****?' 'Not just now. We'll be stopping for petrol around Doncaster and we can change over then.'* ◻ *'But with the children on top of you all day, and then the housework — ' 'Yes?' said Isabel. 'Well, you don't* ***get a break****.'* PW ◻ *We'll* ***take a break*** *now, and you can ask questions when we resume.* ◻ *Children need excitement and activity on holiday as much as adults need to take it easy. This year there are more opportunities than ever to* ***give*** *them (and their parents)* ***a break****.* ST

give sb etc a break[2] [possess] (informal) give sb etc an opening for his talents or abilities, an opportunity to establish himself in an art or profession; give sb etc a piece of good luck that leads to further success etc **V:** give sb; ⚠ get, have; hope for. **IO:** actor, singer; writer; small businessman, farmer. **adj:** lucky; even; bad, lousy ◻ *Mr Daubeny is reticent about the mechanics of his trade. In April 1945, he says, 'I* ***got*** *my first* ***break*** *and managed to put on my first production.'* L ◻ *'You're an optimist.' 'Why not? People have* ***had*** *lucky* ***breaks*** *before now.'* ◻ *In applications for jobs that they're perfectly capable of doing, disabled people should be* ***given an*** *even* ***break****.* ◻ *He's* ***had*** *a lot of bad* ***breaks*** *lately, from what I hear. Particularly with that son of his, Victor.* ST ◻ ***an*** *even* ***break*** = 'a fair chance, compared with others, of opportunity, success, selection etc'.

give (sb)/get a broad grin/smile [possess] give (sb)/get a smile which is a clear indication of great delight, amusement, complacency etc **prep:** with ◻ *The hunters had been grouped around me in a silent and sorrowful circle; now that they saw the creature regain its faculties, they* ***gave broad grins*** *of delight.* BB ◻ *His pursuer pulled up short to greet us* ***with*** *an affable bow and* ***a broad smile****.* BM ◻ *'I've half a mind to ring the fire-alarm while the boys are in the showers,' said Frank, and* ***grinned broadly*** *at the notion.* ◻ variant grin/smile broadly.

give sb/get the bum's rush [possess] (slang) forcibly remove sb/be removed; throw sb/be thrown out (of a room, a meeting, a hotel etc); give sb/get too little time to consider a decision, choice, agreement or refusal **IO:** intruder, heckler, drunk ◻ *One of the Prime Minister's assistants, who had once before been* ***given the bum's rush*** *out of Downing Street when the Heath Government moved in in 1970, found himself bundled out of the Wilson entourage as well.* G ◻ *His heavy drinking reached the point where he was liable to be* ***given the bum's rush*** *the moment he showed his face in any of the local pubs.* ◻ *'I have to answer by return of post* (= immediately)*.' 'Who says you have to? Don't let them* ***give*** *you* ***the bum's rush*** *over this.'*

give sb etc carte blanche [possess] (military) offer etc unconditional surrender on a blank sheet of paper for the victor to dictate his own terms; (fig) allow, or authorize, sb to do, or say, as he likes, make his own arrangements, use his own initiative, etc **V:** give sb, ⚠ get, have (got). **prep:** with ◻ *Fire any questions you like at Pforzheim. He's told me to* ***give*** *you all* ***carte blanche****.* ASA ◻ *You can imagine that IDSO* (= International Diamond Security Organization) *wasn't very popular. We were a private army and we were from London. On the other hand we'd* ***got*** *absolute* ***carte blanche*** *from Sir Ernest Oppenheimer himself, and it would be wise to cooperate with us.* NS ◻ *They employed an interior decorator and* ***gave*** *him* ***carte blanche*** *to do up the place as if it were his own.*

give (sb) etc a civil answer to a civil question [possess] show (sb) etc ordinary and reasonable courtesy in answering an ordinary and reasonable question **V:** give, ⚠ have (got), get; expect ◻ MRS ELLIOT: *Percy! Was that you, Percy?* (She returns to sitting room.) *I suppose it was him, Norah?* NORAH: *Of course it was. I'd know that cat-like tread anywhere. Trust him not to* ***give a civil answer to a civil question****.* EGD ◻ *Since it's called an Enquiry Office you'd expect to* ***get a civil answer to a civil question****, wouldn't you?* ◻ *There's no need to bite my head off. I was only asking* ***a civil question****.* ◻ may be used in part with whole understood, as in last example.

give sb etc a cold etc reception [possess] give sb etc a barely civil or friendly welcome;

give sb etc an uncooperative or hostile response **V:** give sb; ⚠ get, meet with; there be. **IO:** delegate, guest, speaker; remark, suggestion. **adj:** cold, ⚠ cool, icy, lukewarm □ *The Johnsons called again last night, but I* ***gave*** *them* ***a cold reception****. I'm getting rather fed up with them coming here so often and staying so late.* □ *Any proposal that I should part with £50 would* ***get a*** *pretty* ***cool reception*** *from me.* □ *Despite his healthy arrogance he was not best pleased by* ***the lukewarm reception*** *his programme initially* ***got****.* ⇨ give sb etc a warm welcome/reception.

give sb/get the cold shoulder [possess] (informal) reject sb/be rejected by sb **IO:** visitor, stranger; salesman, inventor; relative, colleague □ *As soon as it became clear that his business was likely to fail, his so-called friends started* ***giving*** *him* ***the cold shoulder****.* □ *Perhaps she really didn't know me again, perhaps I was* ***getting the cold shoulder****.* □ *'There's nothing, mark you, that you could do, Bill,' he said. 'Time is what we have to rely on.' It was his stock* ***cold shoulder*** *to kind strangers.* HAA

give credit where credit is due praise, or recognize achievement justly, ie praising the person who deserves it and not another; not fail to recognize an action, or quality, for which a person deserves some praise or recognition; give sb his due (qv) □ *This statement appeared in the Press as having come from me, and, though I have always* ***given credit where credit is due****, this particular credit has always stuck to me.* ST □ (reader's letter) *Let us* ***give credit where credit is due****. From the conversation quoted I should say that the suggestion for reducing the population explosion came from Mrs Williams, not from Bertrand Russell.* L □ *I don't like the man but* ***credit*** *should be* ***given where it is due*** *—he is very good at his job.* □ pass, as in last example, not very common.

give sb etc the creeps etc [possess] (informal) cause one to feel fear, loathing, aversion, nervous anxiety; make one's flesh creep/crawl (qv); make one's hair stand on end (qv) **S:** noise, silence; snake, spiders; sb's face, voice. **V:** give sb; ⚠ get, have. **O:** the creeps, ⚠ the horrors, the willies □ *All this time Finn had been leaning against the door. 'Send him away,' said Magdalen. 'He* ***gives*** *me* ***the creeps****.'* UTN □ *Wasps and moths and things don't* ***give*** *me* ***the horrors*** *the way creeping creatures like cockroaches and woodlice do.* □ DAVID: *Those same cars will be fluttering with white ribbons on Sunday, carrying brides instead of corpses.* SAM: *Shut up, you* ***give*** *me* ***the willies****.* HSG □ *I can put up with him, if I have to, but the fact is he* ***gives*** *me* ***the creeps****.* ST

(sweet airs/noises that) give delight and hurt not (music of a kind to) give nothing but pleasure and enjoyment □ (source) *Be not afeared: the isle is full of noises,/Sounds, and* ***sweet airs, that give delight and hurt not****.* TEMPEST III 2 □ *Don't believe the critic who said that the BBC is backward in innovation. David Cain's music and Adrian Revill's audiospatial illusion filled my room with noises,* ***sweet airs that gave delight and hurt not****.* L □ *It is with an authentic reverence that the nurslings pad on bare feet in the 'Dream House' which La Monte Young and Marian Zazeela fill with* ***sweet sounds that give delight and hurt not****.* ST □ *Alcohol's bad for you, tobacco's bad for you. Now butter, sugar, coca-cola and maybe even milk are bad for you too. What's left that* ***gives delight and hurts not****?* □ (radio review) *The isle was particularly full of* ***noises*** *this week* ***that gave delight and hurt not****.* L

give the devil his due [possess] (saying) if there's anything good to be said about a person or credit to be given, let it be said or given; be just in one's assessment, or treatment, of even an unworthy person □ *You're all talking about George's meanness but,* ***give the devil his due****, he's not a sponger like some I could name.* □ *To* ***give the devil his due*** *whatever racket Frank is engaged in, he's likely to make a success of it.* □ often in parenthesis.

give a dog a bad/ill name (and hang him) [possess] (saying) it is difficult to regain a lost reputation; people continue to condemn, or suspect, sb who has once done, or been accused of doing, sth criminal or very wrong □ *Beginning with the stories of eight selected citizens who have learned the bitter truth of '****give a dog an ill name and hang him****',* (the report) *acknowledges the research objections to destroying or even sealing up criminal records.* NS □ *What gets you into prison in the first place is as little as being on the street and being black. I don't expect improvements because it all holds together on the principle of* ***give a dog a bad name****.* NS □ *Jim Kent's known as a persistent offender, but he's never been accused of violence. Now he's accused of assaulting two police officers. Is it a case of '****give a dog a bad name****'?* TVT

give sb his due [possess] admit that sb does have merits or abilities, even if they are few; admit that there is a valid reason, or excuse, for sb's (apparent) faults; give credit where credit is due (qv) □ *'You're just frightened to take on the job of living, that's all.' 'I hardly think,' said Alan, 'that an enterprise like the new Vardon Hall backs up your diagnosis.' 'No, no, Louie,* ***give*** *Bernard* ***his due****,' cried Isobel.* HAA □ *Pushkin so obviously modelled himself on Byron that it becomes imperative to show that he surpassed him. John Bayley does better than most in* ***giving*** *Byron* ***his due****.* L □ *It was seldom that Kay came to see Gerald. It was seldom, to* ***give*** *her* ***her due****, that the housekeeping and baby care allowed her to come up from Reigate.* ASA

give sb/get the (rough) edge of one's/sb's tongue [possess] speak to sb/be spoken to by sb sharply, rudely, critically etc □ *His voice was unpleasantly dry and sarcastic, except that when he was really* ***giving*** *someone* ***the rough edge of his tongue****, which happened about a dozen times a day, he raised the pitch and barked like a St Bernard.* CON □ *If a child had behaved in my house like that, he'd have* ***got the edge of my tongue*** *whether his mother liked it or not.* □ *The hotel manager is very 'smarmy' with the guests but I can well imagine him* ***giving*** *some poor devil of a waiter* ***the rough edge of his tongue****.* ⇨ ⚠ have etc an edge to one's voice.

give etc free play to sth [possess] allow etc freedom of movement or expression to sth **V:** give sth ⚠ allow, (there) be □ ***There's*** *a little* ***free play*** *on most steering-wheels but there's something wrong if you can turn it as much as* *three inches without getting engagement with the wheels.* ▫ *He had distrusted the cooing, pink-shirted aesthetes because he perceived inside himself the germs of the same disease, and had been afraid of* ***allowing*** *the tendency any* ***free play****.* HD ▫ *She was a woman who* ***gave free play to*** *her emotions, one who both laughed and cried a lot more than most people.* ⇨ ⚠ give sb/sth etc full play.

give sb etc his freedom [possess] consent to a divorce; allow one's husband/wife to leave one for another person or way of life, without putting legal obstacles in the way **V:** give sb, ⚠ let sb have; get, have (got). **IO:** ⚠ husband, wife ▫ *'What are you going to do if he falls in love with another woman?' '****Give*** *him* ***his freedom****, I expect,' Brigit answered light-heartedly.* DC ▫ *They're separated, not divorced. Mark says it is not vindictiveness that prevents him* ***giving*** *Jane* ***her freedom****, but that as a believing Catholic he cannot reconcile such a step with the teachings of his Church.*

give sb etc the freedom of the city [possess] bestow etc a civic honour on sb for public services, entitling him to various benefits **V:** give sb, ⚠ bestow on sb; receive, get ▫ *On the 7th June I flew to Antwerp to* ***receive the freedom of the city****.* MFM ▫ *'Is there any advantage arising from being* ***given the freedom of the city****?' 'Well it's chiefly the honour, but I believe you get a few perks thrown in.'*

give sb/get the fright etc of his/one's life cause sb to have/receive a severe fright; cause sb to be/be suddenly startled **O:** fright, ⚠ shock, surprise ▫ *'We've got the kids, haven't we? They'll pay for them.' 'What with?' asked Prissie wearily. 'I tell you I brought them here to satisfy you, and to* ***give*** *her* (ie their mother) ***the fright of her life****.'* DC ▫ *I knew Billy was waiting to pounce on me but I pretended to* ***get the fright of my life****.* ▫ *And one other veteran, the 76-year-old racket-buster, Senator John McClellan,* ***got the shock of his life*** *when he failed to get an absolute majority in the Primary.* L

give sb etc full marks (for sth) [possess] give sb etc the greatest possible praise and credit (for sth they have done well or perfectly) **V:** give sb, ⚠ award sb; get ▫ *Professor Lehmann received financial support from the American Philosophical Society and the North American Foundation, plus leave of absence from De Paul University, to write his book.* ***Full marks to*** *all three institutions.* NS ▫ (reader's letter) ***Full marks to*** *you* ***for*** *showing such an enjoyable play, which was made all the more exciting by the superb acting of Simon Ward.* RT ▫ *Gort saw clearly that he must, at the least, get the soldiers back to England with their personal weapons.* ***For*** *this I* ***give*** *him* ***full marks*** *and I hope history will do the same.* MFM ▫ ***Full marks for*** *agility were* ***awarded*** *by one distinguished leader-writer* ***to*** *Mr Christopher Chataway,* ***for*** *edging home ahead of other aspirants for Parliamentary time with his new commercial radio Bill.* L ▫ variant, full marks to sb (for sth), used to offer direct praise to sb.

give sb/sth etc full play [possess] give sb/sth etc complete freedom of action or expression **V:** give, ⚠ allow, grant, sb/sth; let sb/sth have. **IO:** him, her, them; sb's imagination, genius, ideas, style, taste ▫ *At St Pancras* (railway station) *Scott* ***gave*** *the style* ***full play****—skyline and windows, ascending chandeliers, cast-iron tracery.* OBS ▫ *In 'Clocks and Clouds' Ligeti* ***gives*** *his taste for ambiguity* ***full play****; a profusion of detail is in a state of constant metamorphosis.* OBS ⇨ ⚠ give etc free play to sth.

give sb furiously to think puzzle sb; make sb think hard, examine his opinions, etc (translation of the French idiom, *donner furieusement à penser*) **O:** the inspector, a child, the neighbours ▫ *I refuse to believe in supernatural phenomena, yet an incident like this* ***gives*** *one* ***furiously to think****.* ▫ *This witness's deliberate provocation of the Court* ***gave*** *the Inspector* ***furiously to think****.*

give sb/get the glad eye [possess] (dated slang) give sb (man or woman) inviting, or amorous, looks to encourage him or her to approach, make a date, etc; give sb the old one two (qv) ▫ *From the old photograph I could easily imagine him as my mother described him —an old peacock, twirling his moustache and* ***giving the glad eye*** *to pretty housemaids.* ▫ *Like a lot of old birds* ***giving the glad*** *in the Circus, or the York Road, Waterloo, more likely.* ASA

give a good etc account of oneself [possess] work, behave, perform in a way that is creditable etc, or that will be approved of, admired etc **S:** player, performers; team, unit; industry; army. **adj:** good, ⚠ splendid, excellent; poor, disappointing ▫ *Since reaching adult life he had not actually been involved in a fight, but he had always imagined that if it ever came he would* ***give a good account of himself****.* HD ▫ *'Ah, here's young Levy now. I think he can be trusted to* ***give a good account of himself****.' There was more clapping while a boy with a violin came round the edge of the cellos and got ready.* TGLY ▫ *They can't always win, I know, but I've never seen the team* ***give*** *such* ***a poor account of themselves****.*

give sb etc a good hiding etc [possess] (informal) give sb etc a severe thrashing, beating; defeat sb overwhelmingly in a game or contest **V:** give sb, ⚠ get; deserve, ask for. **O:** hiding, ⚠ beating, thrashing, trouncing ▫ *I saw my Mum and she told me it was done and she said if I went anywhere near it she'd* ***give*** *me* ***a good hiding****.* TT ▫ JO: *You mean you're running away from somebody.* HELEN: *You're* ***asking for a*** *bloody* ***good hiding****, lady. Just be careful.* TOH ▫ *The outcome of the staff v pupils hockey match was never in any doubt. The staff always* ***get a good trouncing****.*

give sb etc the green/red light [possess] (informal) let sb know etc that it is safe/dangerous to go ahead with his plans, that he is allowed/forbidden to do as he wants in some particular case (from traffic lights) **V:** give sb; ⚠ get, have (got). **IO:** developer, industrialist; plant, company; council ▫ *The Ministry of Agriculture, like the Department of Trade and Industry, refuses to say which companies have been* ***given the green light*** (to increase their prices) *or to discuss the basis of their decisions.* ST ▫ *'Master Drawbell mightn't have* ***seen the red light*** *in time. Never mind,' he said. 'We saved the situation.'* NM ▫ *Enfield Grammar School* *must continue to recruit its pupils on a selective basis despite Patrick Gordon Walker's* ***green light*** *to the local council to go ahead with a comprehensive scheme.* NS □ green/red light can be used alone, as in last example.

give/lose ground (to sb/sth) [possess] retreat (to sb/sth else's advantage); fail to hold one's position or advantage (against sb/sth) □ *If we cancel this autumn's big publicity drive, it'll* ***give ground to*** *our main competitors, but, with the market as depressed as it is, we'll just have to take that risk.* □ *Uncle John's very ill — he's* ***losing ground*** *every day. The doctors reckon he'll be dead in a week.* ⇨ gain ground.

give sb etc ground(s) for complaint etc [possess] give sb valid reason(s) or justification for making a complaint (whether or not the complaint is actually made) **V:** give sb; ⚠ have (got), there be. **prep:** with, without. **adj:** no, little; some; considerable, good. **o:** complaint, complaining; anxiety, fears; supposing sth □ *In his press conference Kissinger reiterated that this demand would not be met. Thieu* ***had*** *good* ***grounds for complaint***. NS □ *But* ***there is ground for anxiety*** *about the growth of crime among young people.* SC □ *The apologists for the modern kind of magazine are usually pert and even morally self-congratulatory about the old-fashioned stuff they have displaced; they* ***have*** *no* ***grounds*** *to be.* UL □ *Whether you dislike Smith or not, you appear to have* ***given*** *him some* ***grounds for*** *believing that you do.*

give sb/sth etc half a chance [possess] give sb/sth etc some opportunity of being, or doing, sth **V:** give sb/sth; ⚠ get, have; there be. **prep:** with □ *...the same hostels full of thieves all out to snatch your last bob if you* ***gave*** *them* ***half the chance***. LLDR □ *He thought he knew how other people ought to live and* ***given half a chance*** *he was determined to make them live that way.* PP □ *'That medicine's doing me no good.' 'You're not* ***giving*** *it* ***half a chance*** *to.'* □ *The more you pray for me, Tony, the more I'm a hardened sinner. Or would be if I* ***had half a chance***. MM □ neg, or in an *if*-cl.

give (sb) etc a (helping) hand [possess] assist (sb) in a task or undertaking **V:** give (sb), ⚠ lend (sb); get, receive □ *'Shall I* ***give*** *you* ***a hand*** *with the washing up?' said Harold.* PW □ *Among the people who had been flying back and forth* (between Britain and America) *throughout the war* ***giving a hand*** *on both sides,...* NM □ DAVIES: *You took me on here as caretaker. I was going to* ***give*** *you* ***a helping hand***. TC □ *'Looking on the bright side', '****lending a helping hand****', 'not being stuck-up or a getter-on', all these are a good deal more healthy than the commercial values which working-class people are constantly invited to adopt nowadays.* UL

give sb/let sb have his head [possess] allow sb, esp in his work or in carrying out a project, to make his own decisions and arrangements, use his own methods (from riding, not curb or guide one's mount) □ *Sir Nicholas made it clear yesterday that they proposed to '****give*** *the shipbuilder* ***his head****' in the construction of these ships.* T □ *The conflict is created by scientists who don't wish to make commercial products and by managers who don't want to* ***give*** *good researchers* ***their*** *expensive* ***heads***. OBS □ *I told the Board that unless I got to run the department in my own way I wanted to leave. Surprisingly, they* ***let*** *me* ***have my head***.

give sb/get hell [possess] (informal) scold or punish sb; make sb suffer; seriously harass, torment, or persecute sb **S:** father, boss; migraine, fever; heat; mosquitoes; enemy bombers □ *I'll* ***get hell*** *if I interrupt him in the middle of making a recording.* □ *'How's the toothache this morning, Jeff?' 'Bearable at the moment, but it* ***gave*** *me* ***hell*** *all night.'* □ *For two years, while she was making up her mind, she had* ***given*** *Charmian* ***hell****, threatening to leave every month.* MM

give (sb) etc the impression (that/of being) [possess] intentionally, or unintentionally, make people think/come to think that sth is so, without precisely defining it or giving an example **V:** give (sb); ⚠ get, gather, form, be left with □ *He certainly* ***gave the impression that*** *he was rather bored by his company.* □ *They can't very well poison a bottle of wine. You could* ***give the impression of*** *being an alcoholic, somebody who doesn't eat but only drinks.* OMIH □ *'I always thought you were a nurse.' 'I wonder how you* ***got that impression****?'*

give sb an inch (and he'll take a mile etc) [possess] (saying) if a particular person is shown any generosity or tolerance at all, he will then increase his demands, be excessive in his claims or behaviour **O:** a mile, ⚠ a yard, (old use) an ell □ *With this government we had to make our stand now because if we* ***gave*** *them* ***an inch they would*** *be quite content to ride roughshod over all our principles in* ***taking the*** *proverbial* ***mile***. NS □ (NONCE) *All that later pessimists have in common with Guy Thorne is the belief that human nature is essentially bestial, and that therefore, if you* ***give*** *'the masses' of humanity* ***an inch they*** *are liable to* ***give you hell***. OBS □ *I like that class a lot. Can't* ***give*** *'em* (= them) ***an inch****, mind, but none the worse for all that.* TT □ often used in part, as shown.

give it a try [possess] (informal) make an effort to do, or obtain, sth **IO:** medicine, treatment; suggestion, proposal; course □ *How silly of him to decide he wouldn't qualify for a grant without ever* ***giving it a try***. □ *'Here, let me* ***give it a try****,' Laurence said. But* he *couldn't unscrew the lid either.* ⇨ ⚠ next entry.

give it/sb a try [possess] (informal) use sth, employ sb, experimentally, to see if it/he works well; give sb/sth etc a trial (qv); give sth a whirl (qv); worth a try (qv) □ *Even if you don't think you'll enjoy listening,* ***give it a try***. *You'll probably be surprised.* RT □ *'Bread sauce? Horrible stuff!' 'Not as I make it. Go on,* ***give it a try***.*'* ⇨ ⚠ previous entry.

give sb a kick/get a kick doing sth [possess] give sb/get a thrill; give sb/get a sharp sensation of enjoyment, power etc **S:** experience, change; trip, flight; crime. **det:** quite a, one hell of a, no end of a □ *'Look,' I said, pointing to the west, 'a good sunset always* ***gives*** *me the hell of* ***a kick****,' I said.* RATT □ *'Half the kids,' one boy told me, 'don't like smoking fags all that much. It's doing it in the lavs* (= lavatories) *and that, because it's not allowed, that* ***gives*** *them* ***a kick***.*'* □ *I* ***get a*** *tremendous* ***kick*** *water-skiing — there's such a sense of* *movement and freedom.* ⇨ ⚠ get a kick out of (Vol 1).

give (sb) a lead [possess] take the initiative in some matter; make oneself responsible, by instruction or example, for events **S:** father; officer, manager; government. **adj:** clear, firm, clear □ *He was emphatic that when the war was over, I must speak out and say these things, and* ***give a lead*** *in the matter.* MFM □ *The General Council rightly seek to* ***give a lead to*** *the Conference by putting forward a motion on the Scottish economy.* SC □ *These people are ignorant, not lazy, and,* ***given a lead****, could quickly improve the quality of their crops and livestock.*

give sb/get a leg up [possess] (informal) help sb to mount a horse, climb a wall, etc by placing a hand under one of his feet to give him an upward heave/be helped in this way; (fig) help sb with money, influence used on his behalf to get, or do, sth he wants or needs/be helped in this way. **IO:** neighbour, colleague; industry, agriculture □ *Hugo began to put his money into films. He started to do this in a vaguely philanthropic way, in order to* ***give*** *the British film industry* ***a leg up****.* UTN □ *Why not just keep on your regular patients and* ***give*** *that new young dentist across the square* ***a leg up*** *by recommending any newcomers to him?* □ *He is determined to achieve whatever he does achieve in life on his own terms. He doesn't want to be* ***given a leg up*** *by his family.* NS

give sb etc a lift [possess] take sb somewhere in one's car, esp on a journey that one is already making **V:** give sb; ⚠ get, have (got); thumb ((informal) = 'signal to passing cars with arm outstretched and thumb cocked') □ *'You won't get back unless you start now,' I added unwillingly, 'I'll* ***give*** *you* ***a lift*** *if you like.'* QA □ *You might have asked that woman with the baskets if she* ***wanted a lift****.* □ *Hikers used to be people who took a walking holiday with rucksacks on their backs. Nowadays, they sit on them by the roadside* ***thumbing lifts****.*

give sth/have a local habitation and a name [possess] give/have a precise identification □ (source) *And as imagination bodies forth/ The forms of things unknown, the poet's pen/ Turns them to shapes, and* ***gives*** *to airy nothing/* ***A local habitation and a name****.* MIDSUMMER NIGHT'S DREAM V 1 □ *Quinton's book cannot, indeed, be taken as totally representative even of Oxford philosophy as a whole. If it must be* ***given a local habitation****,* ***no name*** *would be more appropriate than 'New College Philosophy'.* L □ *If Bergman is hinting at the aboriginal calamity, should he not* ***give*** *it more of* ***a local habitation and a name****?* L

give a man etc enough rope (and he'll hang himself) [possess] (saying) sb allowed sufficient freedom of action will eventually overreach himself, cause his own downfall, come to harm, etc **IO:** a man, these chaps; a thief, a suspect. **det:** enough; ⚠ more, plenty (of) □ *Napier had decided to* ***give*** *Theodore a little further time to surrender—a little* ***more rope*** *with which to* ***hang himself****.* BN □ *Donald's success* (was) *due to factors of which he had no comprehension—desire by some to curry favour with Robin, determination by others to* ***let him have a rope and hang himself****.* ASA □ *Wilson did, from time to time, toy with sacking George. But I suspect that he knew that he had* ***given him enough rope and*** *that George Brown* ***would hang himself****, as he duly did.* L □ variant let a man etc have enough rope (and he'll hang himself).

give sb etc his marching orders [possess] (military) give troops the command to carry out a training march, proceed from A to B, advance to a fighting front, etc; (fig) direct, instruct, dismiss etc sb **V:** give sb his; ⚠ get one's; have (got) one's □ *The answer to the question, 'Who, in a democratic society, is to* ***give*** *the scientists* ***their marching orders****?' is quite simple: democratic society itself and its elected representatives.* NS □ *Mr Heath has been* ***given his marching orders*** *simply because he has been found guilty of the one crime in the Tory charge-book for which there can be no forgiveness. He 'failed' and therefore he had to go.* NS

give sb/sth a miss [possess] (informal) not do sth, not go somewhere, as one might be expected to do, or as one has been in the habit of doing/ avoid meeting sb, or omit him, on a particular occasion, from an arrangment, invitation etc **IO:** film, show; lecture, party; club, restaurant/ boyfriend □ *I asked him why he didn't come back home. 'It is impossible,' he said. He seemed to be psychologically committed to the policy of* ***giving*** *the place* ***a miss****.* CON □ *Hence our profound attachment to and love for the Jesus Bar. We did however* ***give*** *Jesus* ***a miss*** *one night for a sort of token meal in the town.* ST □ *'You know I always see Jake on Friday nights.' 'Well, you'll have to* ***give*** *him* ***a miss*** *for once.'*

give sb/sth etc a new etc lease of life [possess] provide an improvement in, or renewal of, sb's health, vigour, happiness etc; give sb/sth further opportunity of success, popularity **V:** give, ⚠ offer sb; get, have; take on. **adj:** new, ⚠ second, another □ *Far from being too much for her to cope with, the care of her grandchildren seems to have* ***given*** *the old lady* ***a new lease of life****.* □ ***Give*** *your poor old restricted brain* ***a new lease of life*** *with what Dr Edward de Bono calls 'lateral thinking'.* RT □ *'How come that clock's working again?' 'I knocked it off the shelf last night, since when it seems to have* ***taken on another lease of life****.'* □ *He volunteered for the same colliery, which was* ***enjoying****, if that is the word,* ***a second lease of life****, having been condemned in the inter-war years.* OBS □ *In the Benelux countries fears are being expessed that unless the Community is* ***given a new lease of life*** *by enlargement, Germany may reject her present role as its chief financial mainstay* L

give (sb)/get notice[1] [possess] give (sb)/get advance information about sth one/sb intends to do **det:** much, a lot (of), (very) little □ *I sat at the window trying to see who was there to meet me. It was likely to be my father. I hadn't* ***given*** *them much* ***notice****.* RFW ⇨ ⚠ give sb etc warning.

give (sb)/get notice[2] [possess] give/get formal notification that employment is to end **S:** employer, boss; employee, staff; servant. **det:** one's, a week's, a fortnight's □ *My chauffeur's* ***given notice****. He's going to get married.* HD □ *The factory is cutting down all the time. I'm always expecting my husband to come home and say he's* ***got*** *his* ***notice****.* □ *If he wants to get rid of you, he'll have to* ***give you*** *a fortnight's* ***notice****.* □ cf give *(sb) notice to quit*, said of a landlord in relation to a tenant.

give sb/get an old-fashioned look [possess] (informal) give sb/get a reproving, or disapproving, glance **prep:** with □ *When Bob said we'd go out for a pint and come back later, his wife didn't say anything but she* ***gave*** *him* ***a*** *right* ***old-fashioned look*** *and then picked up the tray with the tea things and marched off to the kitchen.* □ *'I don't think it's so damned funny myself.' 'I do,' I said, and grinned a bit more. He* ***looked at*** *me* ***old-fashioned*** *as we say up there.* CON □ *'And then there are all the arrangements, catering— it's enough to put anybody off* (getting married).*' Pat* ***looked at*** *her* ***in an old-fashioned way****, and then obviously decided it was none of her business really.* TT □ variant look at sb (in an) old-fashioned (way).

give sb/get the old one two [possess] (dated slang) give sb/get an ogling look that declares a sexual interest or invitation; give sb/ get the glad eye (qv) □ *'You're a wicked boy to be so late,' she said. Ron* ***gave*** *her what he called his '****old one two****' look.* HAA □ *An atmosphere of heavy hot-eyed sex prevailed, everyone* ***giving*** *everyone else* ***the old one two****, because at the end of the week they'd all be safely home again.* ST

give sb/sth/get the once-over [possess] (informal) assess sb/sth/be assessed rapidly with a travelling glance; calculate sb/sth's suitability for a purpose, role etc/have one's suitability for a purpose, role etc calculated by sb **IO:** patient, applicant; shop, plant; car, boat □ *A thick-set woman peeled the coats off our backs and* ***gave*** *us* ***the once-over****.* CON □ *A man pushed open the swing door, stood uncertainly for a few seconds and went out again. 'Probably* ***giving*** *the place* ***the once-over*** *and deciding he wasn't hungry,' I said.* □ *He wasn't quite sure what his feelings for Lucy were but he wasn't going down to Exeter for the weekend to* ***get the once-over*** *from her parents.*

give or take ten years etc allowing, in an estimate, for a margin of variation or error of ten years etc up or down **O:** ten years; a mile; a pound or two; a few herrings; several inches □ *'What was the size of the traffic when you took over the job?' Blaize shrugged his shoulders. 'About ten million pounds a year,* ***give or take a million****,' he said.* DS □ ***Give or take a handful*** *the herrings are packed two hundred to the barrel.* □ *We got our loo in for Easter,* ***give or take a day or two****, but it doesn't flush yet and we have to use buckets.* OBS □ front, middle or end position.

give sb etc a piece of one's mind [possess] (informal) let sb know, bluntly or angrily, exactly what one thinks of him or of his behaviour **V:** give sb, ⚠ let sb have; get □ *I shan't be sorry to have the chance of* ***giving*** *the old windbag* ***a piece of my mind****. Perhaps he won't have such an enjoyable Christmas.* EM □ *If any child of mine spoke to me like that, I'd* ***let*** *him* ***have a piece of my mind****.* □ *My wife got fed up with his self-pity and* ***gave*** *him* ***a piece of her mind*** *one night.* □ often in first person statements or threats.

give sb the pip [possess] (slang) irritate, or depress, sb □ *He overdoes the name dropping, 'Well, we were having dinner with the Oliviers, when—' It* ***gives*** *some people* ***the pip****. But it shouldn't because it's endearing really.* OBS □ *Can't we change the subject? All this talk about wills and dying is* ***giving*** *me* ***the pip****.*

give sb/get the push etc [possess] (informal) (try to) dismiss sb/be dismissed from one's company, home, employment, public office, a committee etc **IO** husband, colleague, employee, official, member. **O:** the push, ⚠ shove, (old) heave-ho □ (to a hospital patient) *Soon, I suppose, they'll be wanting to* ***give*** *you* ***the push*** *from here. You must rehabilitate yourself, as they would say.* HAH □ *Then if your daughter has to come here with her kids, I'll be* ***getting the push****, I suppose?* □ *If he doesn't resign after this term—which he won't—we'll just have to* ***give*** *him* ***the shove****.*

give sb etc the raspberry [possess] (informal) make a rasping explosive sound with the tongue and lips, as a sign of derision or rejection; treat sb with similar rudeness and contempt **V:** give sb; ⚠ get; draw, earn □ *Snooper Riley and Tugs Campbell* ***gave*** *him* ***the raspberry*** *on the Green today.* OBS □ *Now I am aware that this sort of statement is liable to* ***draw*** *loud* ***raspberries*** *from all sides of the house, not to mention cries of 'No!' and 'Get Away.'* SD □ *Telling them that they are interesting examples of contemporary sociology might* ***earn*** *you a clump round the earhole* (= a blow on the ear) *from Terry or* ***a*** *verbal* ***raspberry*** *from Bob, marginally the more civilised of the two.* RT

give sb a ring/tinkle [possess] (informal) speak to, get in touch with, sb by telephone □ *Viola's in the telephone book. If you like I'll* ***give*** *her* ***a ring*** *tonight.* RFW □ *You'll be all right now, said the kindly neighbour from the flat upstairs. But if you want anything or don't feel well just* ***give*** *me* ***a tinkle*** *and I'll be right down.*

give sb/sth etc a rough etc passage [possess] cause a ship, and/or those sailing on it, to have a rough, dangerous etc voyage; give sb/sth etc a trying, painful, difficult etc time (in the course of accomplishing sth) **V:** give sb/sth; ⚠ get, have, be in for. **IO:** speaker, teacher; legislation, proposal. **adj:** rough, ⚠ stormy; smooth □ *There's a tide rip out there that can* ***give*** *small boats* ***a rough passage****.* □ *You could see, if you cared to, that his leg must have* ***given*** *him* ***a rough passage*** *in its time.* TT □ *The Bill was* ***given a smooth passage*** *through the Commons.* □ *A certain amount of rowdyism had been traditional at Rectorial addresses in Scottish universities and speakers knew they* ***were in for a rough passage****.*

give sb etc a rough ride [possess] subject sb to hard or painful experience(s), abuse or ridicule **V:** give sb, ⚠ get, have; be in for □ *His own GP felt that Geoff had been* ***given a rough ride*** *in hospital.* □ *There was at least an equal chance that Mr Jenkins, if not actually torn limb from limb, would have* ***had an*** *extremely* ***rough ride****.* NS □ *I knew the coloured lads might* ***get a rough ride*** *from spectators and opponents, so I made a point of warning them that players are bound to try any trick to get them rattled.* TVT □ *He went to Joan Littlewood's theatre workshop in London and subsisted on scraps once more. That kind of* ***rough ride*** *has obviously shaped some things in his personality.* SC

give sb/sth etc a (good) run for his/its money [possess] (informal) cause etc another race-horse to strive to the utmost in order to win or run well enough to satisfy or encourage its backers; (fig) provide sb/sth with challenging competition or opposition; provide sb with reward, interest, enjoyment etc in return for outlay or effort **V:** give sb/sth; ⚠ get, have □ *'They all fall for Joe,' Hoylake said. He sighed. 'Mind you, when I was younger I'd have* ***given*** *him* ***a run for his money****.'* RATT □ *I think he's got a bone to pick with you. Something to do with your interpretation of the seals. So we'll* ***give*** *you a bit of* ***a run for your money****.* ASA □ *Le Vieux Puant de Lille is the smelliest cheese in the world — though a really powerful Limburger would probably* ***give*** *it* ***a good run for its money****.* G

give sb etc the run of the house [possess] give sb etc freedom, permission to use one's house as if it were his own **V:** give sb; ⚠ get, have. **o:** the house, the library, the place, his uncle's workshops □ *Jenny* (a lodger) *was sorry she had never bought herself a kitten as she had planned at the start. But she could not* ***give*** *it* ***the run of the house****, and to keep it shut up in her room would have been cruel.* TGLY □ JEAN: *We had absolute trust in the man. They* ***had*** *complete* ***run of the house****.* YAA □ *In the end he landed up with an enlightened clergyman in Truro who* ***gave*** *him* ***the run of his library*** *and taught him all he knew.* SC

give sb/sth etc short shrift [possess] give sb a brief, perfunctory form of confession and absolution before a public execution; (fig) deal with sb/sth summarily, impatiently, in a dismissive way **V:** give sb/sth; ⚠ get, have. **IO:** heckler, critic, intruder; programme, broadcast □ *The Minister* ***gave*** *the deputation* ***short shrift****, telling its leaders he had no sympathy for a campaign that appealed for public support by means of false statements and exaggerated accusations.* □ *Even the man with a roving eye* ***gets short shrift*** *if he goes in for marriage-breaking.* UL □ (reader's letter) *Despite the* ***short shrift*** *which Magnus Magnusson has* ***given to*** *the critics of 'BC: The Archaeology of the Bible Lands', we should like to make further comments on behalf of our 800 or so members.* RT

give sb/sth the slip [possess] (informal) avoid meeting sb; escape sb's notice, supervision or control; avoid carrying out some duty etc esp when this is done without attracting notice or reproof **IO:** a boring colleague, a tiresome neighbour; guard, supervisor; enemy, pursuer □ *Godfrey decided to* ***give*** *Mrs Pettigrew* ***the slip*** *again this afternoon and go and see Olive.* MM □ *Sir Julius has not been here. Funny. He must have* ***given*** *me* ***the slip****. I could have sworn I saw him making off in this direction.* EM □ *I'd given up hopes of getting you here. But you haven't told me how you managed to* ***give*** *the desert* (= a work assignment) ***the slip****, and why you decided to leave.* TBC

give sb etc some rope [possess] (informal) not force sb to follow too strict a discipline or control (from allowing a captive, or domestic, animal a long tether) **V:** give sb, ⚠ allow sb, let sb have. **IO:** child, pupil, student, employee. **det:** some, more, less, a bit of, too much □ *We're an old-fashioned firm, Mr Smith, but not hide-bound. We're not averse to* ***giving*** *a man with ideas of his own* ***some rope****.* □ *You're absolutely hopeless about people you like or who you think like you. You —* ***give*** *them* ***too much rope****. You let them kick you around too much.* ILIH □ *Tony's nearly sixteen. You've got to* ***give*** *kids* ***a bit of rope*** *as they grow older.*

give sb etc something to complain etc about [possess] give sb who is (in the habit of) complaining etc some reason to do so/have some reason to complain etc **V:** give sb, ⚠ have (got), there be. **prep:** with, without. **Inf:** to grouse, to cry, to sulk, to worry □ *I said you weren't to have any more sweets. So just stop snivelling or I'll* ***give*** *you* ***something to cry about****.* □ *'Don't go,' he said. 'Come and live with me. That would* ***give*** *her* ***something to gripe about****.'* AITC □ *If your hair was falling out like mine you'd* ***have something to complain about****.* □ *Now here is a man* ***with something to moan about****. He bought a new car three months ago and it's been back to the garage five times because of poor workmanship or faulty parts.* □ often used as threat or following conditional constructions.

give sb/have something to think/talk about [possess] present sb with/have a problem, difficult decision, etc to make; startle or upset sb/be startled or upset by a threat, defeat etc, or through unexpected or unconventional speech or behaviour □ *The doctor's remark that the wife of any alcoholic should take a close look at herself has certainly* ***given*** *me* ***something to think about****.* □ *'We* ***gave*** *them* ***something to think about****,' said Sam. 'He won't want to come and fight us again in a hurry.'* LF □ *If he went on a cruise and came home with a wife and four ready-made kids the neighbours would* ***have something to talk about****.* □ *To* ***give*** *them* ***something to think about****, Davies has set up an office right in the back garden of his American competitors on the outskirts of Boston.* ST

give and take [v + v non-rev] (be able to) arrange matters sensibly and tactfully with others so that each gains advantage or suffers disadvantage to the same extent; show mutual toleration between people or groups □ *We had to learn how to* ***give and take****, otherwise I think it might have been a very disastrous situation after four years.* ST □ *We often require, in the* ***give and take*** *of social life, to recount our experiences to friends and satisfy their curiosities about us.* MFF □ *What Miss Murphy had long tried to do was to project towards them the sound, friendly,* ***give-and-take*** *attitude she held towards other students.* ARG □ *Don't let Jack overwork you. He never thinks of anybody but himself—it's* ***all take and no give*** *with him.* □ also [n + n]—usu non-rev but see last example; attrib use *a* ***give-and-take*** *attitude.*

give sb etc a thick ear [possess] (informal) give sb etc a blow on the ear or the side of the head **V:** give sb; ⚠ get, need, want □ *Everybody's kids are the same. The only way to impress them is to* ***give*** *them* ***a thick ear****.* RT □ *'Did he* ***get a thick ear*** *for allowing me to leave the country?' 'I gather so, but he didn't say much about it.'* TBC □ *There's a couple of waiters, but they're paid to do waiting, and you can't blame* *them if they look the other way when anyone starts acting rowdy. A man doesn't* ***want a thick ear*** *as well as having to carry things on a tray.* HD □ more often threatened than actually carried out. ⇨ ⚠ box sb's ear(s).

(not) give sb/sth a thought [possess] not think of, or about, sb/sth at all; forget, dismiss from one's mind, or not concern oneself further with, sb/sth **A:** scarcely, hardly. **IO:** her friend, his wife; it, the matter; such remarks, his absence. **det:** a; another, a second; enough □ *'After your wife's death, didn't you miss this bag?' 'I did****n't*** *even* ***give*** *it* ***a thought****. Too many other things to think of, I suppose.'* PE □ *'I wish there was some way I could repay you for your kindness.' 'Please do****n't give*** *it* ***a thought****.'* □ *There will be plenty of young men in America. You wo****n't give*** *this Joe creature* ***another thought****.* AITC □ *The popular Press has long found it profitable not merely to report but even to promote archaeological excavation; so that the other day in Cincinnati I scarcely* ***gave*** *the matter* ***a second thought*** *when I found the eminent excavator of Troy at work in a comfortable study amidst the machinery of the newspaper which is his generous patron.* SD □ *James is going for a week's holiday tomorrow, but he hasn't* ***given a thought to*** *packing his things yet.*

give sb etc three guesses [possess] give sb etc three chances to answer a riddle, to guess who, what or where sb/sth is, etc before being rewarded or punished; delay giving a piece of news to tease sb or to stimulate his interest by speculation (from a formula commonly used in folklore, fairy tales) **V:** give sb, ⚠ let sb have; get, have, take □ (the door bell rings) TONY: *Perhaps it's Philip.* MYRA: *Who is it? I'm not in.* TONY: *I'll* ***give*** *you* ***three guesses****.* EHOW □ *'On the other hand, he mustn't let me slip out of his hands, otherwise someone else might corner me. So what does he do? What does he do?' 'We'll* ***take three guesses****,' I said.* CON

give sb/sth etc the thumbs down [possess] give a gesture, make a statement, expressing rejection or disaproval of sb/sth **V:** give sb/sth, ⚠ get; be. **prep:** with □ *'Love Story' came to be made only after six major studios had* ***given*** *it* ***the thumbs down****.* RT □ *If ever an aspirant presidential candidate* ***got a thumbs-down*** *from the pundits, John Lindasay did this week.* NS □ *Then I heard words in the hall and a split-second later the two plain-clothes men were standing at the kitchen door and I knew it* ***was thumbs down*** *for me.* PP ⇨ next entry.

give sb/sth etc the thumbs up [possess] give a gesture, make a statement, expressing acceptance, approval for, success achieved etc or wishing courage and good luck in a situation where he is likely to need these **V:** give sb/sth, ⚠ get; be. **prep:** with □ *He's absolutely delighted to have scored that goal! See him running round* ***with his thumbs up****!* □ *'The surgeon told me exactly what was he going to do tomorrow, and I'm sure everything's going to be all right.' 'That's the spirit,' Jean said, kissing him. '****Thumbs up****, eh?' '****Thumbs up*** *it is,' he said.* ⇨ previous entry.

give sb the tip [possess] (informal) let sb know that sth is the case, is about to happen or likely to happen, esp so that he may take advantage of such information; tip off (Vol 1) (qv) □ *'How did you know to put your money on that horse?' 'Somebody I won't name* ***gave*** *me* ***the tip****.'* □ *'I hope,' said the Editor, 'that if you do decide to lead another expedition to the Islands you'll* ***give*** *us* ***the tip*** *beforehand.'* RM □ *Well, thanks for* ***giving*** *Jim* ***the tip****. He found it very useful to know what his examiner's foibles were.*

give sb/sth etc a trial [possess] employ sb, use sth, experimentally to see if he/it works satisfactorily, suits one's purposes; give it/sb a try (qv); worth a try (qv) **V:** give sb/sth; ⚠ get, have. **IO:** product; medicine, paint; policy, approach □ (advertisement) *Have found Valpeda of great benefit for tired and aching feet, and sincerely recommend sufferers to* ***give*** *it* ***a trial****.* DM □ *'I don't know what to do about Bobby's fits of temper.' 'You could* ***give*** *ignoring them* ***a trial****, in my opinion.'* □ *'I'm stronger than I look,' the boy pleaded. 'Won't you at least* ***give*** *me* ***a trial****?'*

give sth/sb etc a trial run [possess] test a machine's performance, speed etc under simulated conditions or as a preliminary to final production, sale or use; try out any new project, test the competence of a new employee or assistant experimentally for a period **V:** give sth; ⚠ get, have; do. **IO:** boat, car; programme, method, procedure; assistant, employee, team □ *'The first race isn't till 2 o'clock anyway.' 'I know, but there are drivers on the circuit all morning* ***having trial runs*** *and I find that very interesting to watch.* □ *Besides the recovery in morale, the Eighth Army had been* ***given a trial run*** *under its new commander.* MFM □ *It was decided to* ***give*** *the tinned puddings* ***a trial run*** *of six months in the chain stores of a subsidiary company.*

give sb to understand (that) make sb think sth is true; lead sb to believe (that) (qv) □ *He* ***gave*** *the Prime Minister* ***to understand that*** *in his view the British forces on the eastern flank could and should be more offensive.* MFM □ *The British public had been* ***given to understand that****, before the final decision on Common Market entry was taken there would be a referendum.* SC □ *When I ordered these carpets I was* ***given to understand that*** *fitting was free of charge, and now you have put it on my account as an extra.* □ often used to suggest that one was misled in being made to believe sth; often pass.

give sb etc a warm welcome/reception [possess] give sb etc a kind, positive reception or recognition of his presence, performance etc **V:** give sb, ⚠ accord sb; have (got), get, receive; there be; deserve. **IO:** visitor; team, theatre company; idea, proposal □ *...****a warm welcome to*** *LCDT* (London Contemporary Dance Theatre) *on the opening of their four-week season at Sadler's Wells.* G □ *Emperor Haile Selassie of Ethiopia, flying back to his country after Wednesday's coup, was* ***given a warm welcome*** *when he landed at Khartoum today.* T □ *This shop is one of the most exciting design outlets to be offered to us recently and* ***deserves a warm welcome*** *from architects and designers as well as domestic consumers.* OBS □ *The invitation to come on board* ***got a warm****, not to say rapturous* ***reception*** *from the children.* ⇨ give sb etc a cold etc reception.

give sb etc warning [possess] let sb know one's intentions, that sth is to happen, etc a reasonable time in advance; not upset, or inconvenience, sb with a sudden decision, penalty, task etc **V:** give sb; ⚠ get, receive, have. **det:** some, any; no, not much. **adj:** fair, ample, adequate; insufficient ▫ *The least he could do was to **give** fair **warning** of a change of attitude.* CON ▫ *You might **give me** some **warning** when you're bringing people home to dinner!* ▫ *On April 17th his client had **received** 7 days' **warning** to vacate the premises.* ➪ ⚠ give (sb)/get notice[1].

give way collapse; break; yield to pressure; become loosened; (fig) yield to the pressure of grief, temptation, despair, opposition, argument **S:** leg, support, prop; bridge, trestle; floorboard; prisoner ▫ *The joists were so eaten through by dry rot it was a wonder the whole floor hadn't **given way**.* ▫ *As I put my hand to the door of Sylvia's Café I had a mild attack of pins-and-needles and one leg **gave way** under me.* RATT ▫ *'I didn't mean to **give way** like this,' Mary sobbed.* ▫ *When I refused to allow him to question Phuong without me he **gave way** at once.* QA

give sb/get what for [possess] (informal) punish or scold sb for what he has done/be punished or scolded for what one has done ▫ *'I **gave** one of 'em* (= them) ***what for**,' said Ralph, 'I smashed him up all right. He won't want to come and fight us again in a hurry.'* LF ▫ *You thieving hooligan! I'll tell your father, and he'll **give** you **what for**.* ▫ *For when the governor told me to be honest it was meant to be in his way, not mine. But in my own way, well, it's not allowed, and if I find a way of doing it then I'll **get what-for** in every mean trick he can set his mind to.* LLDR

give sth a whirl [possess] (informal) try sth experimentally in order to find out whether it is suitable, effective, pleasant etc; give it/sb a try (qv) **IO:** it, this; the treatment, your proposal ▫ *A chat show with musical interludes has worked. And the reason it works is that, at this hour of the night, it is what most people who are still awake want to see and hear. Why not **give** it **a whirl**?* L ▫ *I'm prepared to **give** this **a whirl**, Senora, if things are done my way.* ST ▫ *'How can you say it's a rubbishy series if you never watch it?' 'Oh I **gave** it **a whirl** when it started—three or four episodes at least.'*

give sb/sth a wide berth [possess] (nautical) allow a ship room to swing at anchor; steer past a ship at anchor, or past some other hazard, at a safe distance; (fig) avoid coming into contact with sb/sth in the interests of one's safety, convenience, or happiness; steer etc clear (of sb/sth) (qv) **IO:** colleague, father; restaurant, shop ▫ *I think what excited them was the fact that he should be wandering about among us, unheralded, after having **given** the place such **a wide berth** for so long.* CON ▫ *Victoria resolved to **give** this lady as **wide a berth** as possible. Something told her that inventing stories to satisfy that kind of woman was no easy job.* TCB ▫ *A reporter from Lynn actually joined the beaters while we were shooting! He very soon **gave** me **a wide berth** as I very nearly shot him in the legs.* NS

give (sb) one's word (of honour) (that) [possess] accompanies or introduces a claim, or promise, in order to make it more credible (the implication being that the speaker would be a person without honour if the claim or promise were not true) ▫ *I **give** you **my word of honour**, Segura, **that** I didn't even know he existed until tonight.* OMIH ▫ *I will **give** you **my word of honour that** you may safely ride by my side, and I will accept yours.* ARG ▫ *'If I show you my secret den will you not tell my sister or anybody where it is? **On your word of honour**?' '**Word of honour**, I won't, Bill.'* ▫ variants have sb's word (of honour) (that), (on sb's) word of honour, latter used by children.

give sb/sth etc the (full) works [possess] (informal) do, say, provide etc everything one possibly can or undertake to meet some particular need **V:** give sb/sth, ⚠ (formal) accord sb/sth; get. **IO:** audience; visitor, guest; house, car ▫ *I'll **give** them **the works** about London, the Octopus and the need for provincial culture.* ASA ▫ *They are what's known as Category One guests of the British Government, **accorded**, in terms of comfort and deference, **the full works**.* L ▫ *The boat wasn't 'patched up' as you put it. It's **got** a new engine, new sails, fresh trim,— **the works**.*

(I'm) glad to meet you a greeting on the first occasion of being introduced to, or meeting, sb **adv mod:** so, very ▫ *'You're Joe Lampton,' she said. 'I hope you had a pleasant journey.' I suddenly remembered that I should offer my hand. '**I'm glad to meet you**,' I said, meaning the words.* RATT ▫ *'May I introduce myself since our host is so busy? I'm Anne Cairns, and I think you are Bob's mother.' '**Glad to meet you**, Miss Cairns. Do you live in Deepham too?'* ▫ warmer than 'how do you do?' (qv), but still formal unless stressed, eg ***I am glad to meet you*, So *glad to meet you*** *at last*.

glad rags (dated informal) evening dress, or clothes kept for special occasions, parties etc ▫ *'I'm afraid I've only this old tweed doublet and I don't expect Mr Mackay will have **glad rags**.' '**Glad rags**?' 'Evening dress.'* RM ▫ HELEN: *Help yourself to a drink, Peter, and I'll go and put my **glad rags** on.* TOH ▫ *An uninterrupted camera sweep prepares us for something more shattering than the sight of Theo's wife, Hélène, prettily waiting in her Twenties **glad rags** by a Rolls.* NS

(the) glad tidings (formal) very good news ▫ ***Glad tidings** of great joy I bring/To you and all mankind.* ENGLISH HYMNAL 30 ▫ *Staff representatives were given **the glad tidings** that, since the unions were engaged in a wage restructuring exercise with British Rail, the staff too should benefit from a parallel exercise.* NS ▫ *The children raced each other up the stairs, each determined to be the first with **the glad tidings**.*

gladden sb's heart [V + O pass] cheer and please sb ▫ *I took out a tight wad of dividend warrants ringed with a rubber band, and the records in the wad would have **gladdened the heart of** a broker.* PP ▫ *There was one incident which must have **gladdened the heart of** every schoolboy who has ever tried to penetrate his father's sanctimoniousness.* ST ▫ *To **gladden our hearts** in January* Iris histrioides *is the most outstanding of the small early-flowering irises.* SC

a gleam in sb's eye [Comp (NP)] (informal)

sb or sth which is anticipated, for a time, with pleasure and desire, but which has not yet come about **V:** ⚠ be, think of sth as ▫ *This was when we were living in our seedy flat in central London, at a time when you were still* ***a gleam in*** *your father***'s eye** (= before you were born). ▫ *Your car for the twenty-first century may already be* ***a gleam in the eye of*** *a designer—even on the drawing-board.* OBS ▫ facetious.

a glutton for work/punishment [Comp (NP)] sb always willing, or wanting, to work, or to tolerate hardship, physical or mental stress **V:**⚠ be, become; find sb ▫ *He's* ***a glutton for work****—the sort that would rather make a garden seat than sit on it afterwards.* ▫ *You can't afford to be self-conscious if you take part in 'It's a Knock-Out' and it helps if you're* ***a glutton for punishment*** *too.* ▫ *She's an impossible woman! Jack must be* ***a glutton for punishment*** *if he's stayed with her for all these years* ▫ also pl gluttons for work/punishment.

gnashing of teeth grinding the upper and lower teeth against each other, as an accompaniment or reaction to pain, stress, frustration; grind one's teeth (qv) ▫ (source) *But the children of the kingdom shall be cast out into outer darkness: there shall be weeping, and* ***gnashing of teeth****.* MATTHEW VIII 12 ▫ *And so, in a brief blaze of glory and to much weeping and* ***gnashing of teeth*** *in Monrovia and among Monsieur Diamant's friends in Europe, IDSO* (= International Diamond Security Organization) *wound up its activities and prepared to disband.* DS ▫ *Martha Graham has had more influence on an art form than any other woman in history. Passing over much* ***gnashing of teeth*** *and beating of feminine breasts, let's take a quick look at her track record.* RT ▫ *She didn't know what to do. Bill's incompetence had made most of her work over the last three months quite pointless—she could have* ***gnashed her teeth*** *with sheer frustration.* ▫ use often non-literal and facetious, as shown; variant gnash one's teeth.

(not) go any/go no farther/further be stopped, or dispelled; be treated confidentially; be kept secret **S:** illness, epidemic; rebellion, disturbance; story, confidence, rumour ▫ *'We can't cure baldness,' the specialist admitted, 'but sometimes we can keep it from* ***going any further****.'* ▫ *Two people moved forward and began to speak in an attempt to stop this* (quarrel) *before it* ***went any farther****.* HD ▫ *She told me of his discretion: 'You could tell him everything and you knew it would****n't go any further****.'* AH ▫ *He paused before going on with the letter he was dictating. 'I am particularly anxious, Miss Baines, that this should* ***go no further*** *at present —inside this office as well as out.'*

go as/so far as to do sth/that go to particular — often extreme — limits in talking about sth, in dealing with a situation, etc ▫ *The younger Nicholls, indeed, hated his father so much that he* ***went as far as to*** *make two attempts at killing him off.* ST ▫ *The delegates spent a day discussing the prospect of advanced life on other planets. Many* ***went so far****, in their enthusiasm,* ***as to*** *treat the possibility as an accomplished fact.* TO ▫ *Then Beatrice said, 'I wish you hadn't given your word of honour. You needn't have* ***gone as far as that****.'* OMIH

go begging be unwanted; be available for anybody who might want them **S:** job, vacancy; house, site; seat, berth ▫ *'That flat over the stables,' Mrs Middleton said, 'it seems such a pity that it should* ***go begging****. I thought perhaps you would like it.'* ASA ▫ *'Won't you have this last sandwich?' 'Well, if it's really* ***going begging****, I'll eat it.'* ▫ *Why should I work when I could steal? Why settle down to some humdrum uncongenial billet when excitement, romance, danger, and a decent living were all* ***going begging*** *together?* TVT

go etc berserk [V + Comp] become etc filled with a maniacal fury which drives one to attack people or property (from Scandinavian folklore of warriors in battle) **V:** go; ⚠ be; drive sb, send sb ▫ *A young man shot a girl he did not know and then himself. He is believed to have* ***gone berserk****.* T ▫ *Police searched the track* (railway) *for a man who* ***went berserk*** *at two stations. At London Bridge station he attacked the collector, then assaulted three other men.* OBS ▫ *Mr Massey, the master, had to go down and see about the register or something; as soon as he left the room we all* ***went berserk****.* ST ▫ *In the past 18 months the housing situation—in fact, the whole property world—has* ***gone*** *completely* ***berserk****.* ST ▫ may be used seriously or not, as can be judged from context.

go etc blue (in the face) [V + Comp] (informal) appear bluish because of sluggish circulation brought on by cold etc **V:** go, ⚠ turn (sb), be. **A:** with cold, with fear, with fright, with terror ▫ *I could see the way things were going, right enough. His mam* (= mother) *suddenly* ***went blue in the face****.* LLDR ▫ *It was icy cold —enough to* ***turn you blue in the face****.* ▫ *The prisoners* ***went blue*** *with terror.* ⇨ ⚠ go etc purple (in the face); go etc red (in the face).

go/be broke [V + Comp] (informal) go, be, bankrupt ▫ *In the depression of the 'thirties', when everyone was* ***going broke*** *and all the properties were coming under the hammer at a knockdown price, the McConchies were prudently buying land.* RFW ▫ *I told him there was no point in undercutting competitors to get business and then* ***going broke*** *because there were no profits.* ▫ *If we spend money at this rate, we'll* ***be broke*** *in six months.*

go (and) chew bricks etc (slang) go away; be quiet **V:** chew bricks, ⚠ eat coke, fry your face, climb a tree, fly a kite, jump in the canal, jump in the lake ▫ *He thought there was a conspiracy to keep him out of the big* (football) *teams. I said to him: '****Go and chew bricks****, man. The manager's never heard of you, or your club either.'* RT ▫ *'I'm going to get that fellow turned out of here.' '****Go and fly a kite****. Do you think everybody's going to gang up on him, just because he gets your back up* (= annoys you)*?'* ▫ *The fish traps would horrify the Izaak Walton League. (The Izaak Walton League can just* ***go climb a tree*** *because the traps have brought us an average of a dozen fish a day for supper or lunch.)* OBS ▫ *The law might require me to* (open the case), *but I had the power to tell the Law* ***go jump in the lake****, for nobody but I knew the case existed.* RFW ▫ exclamation expressing derision and contempt; esp in direct or indirect imper constructions.

go cold on the deal [V + Comp] (informal) lose interest in, or not carry through at all, a proposed business transaction or other agreement—either because of delays, or as a result of thinking about it more carefully **S:** partner; client, customer □ *I strongly advise you to lend* (money) *to our Italian friend for the down-payment. Otherwise, I shrewdly suspect that he will* ***go cold on the deal****.* US □ *You were keen enough to go fishing when we spoke about it last night. You're surely not going to* ***go cold on the deal*** *now, after I've bought the tackle and hired a boat?*

go etc crackers etc [V + Comp] (informal) become mentally unbalanced or disturbed; start to behave eccentrically or foolishly **V:** go, ⚠ be; drive sb, send sb. **adj:** crackers, ⚠ bananas, bonkers, crazy, mad □ *If I have to share a room with Jimmy for another month, I'll* ***go crackers****.* □ *Why did your aunt give that child a toy drum for his birthday? He'll* ***drive*** *everyone* ***bananas*** *with the noise!* ⇨ ⚠ next entry.

go etc crackers etc (about/over sb/sth) [V + Comp] (informal) become etc obsessively, or extravagantly, interested in, or occupied with, sb/sth **V:** go, ⚠ be; drive sb, send sb. **adj:** crackers, ⚠ bananas, bonkers, crazy, mad □ *'Janet* ***went crackers over*** *that dog,' she told me. 'She spent every minute that she had with him.'* RFW □ *'Jack's looking miserable—what's wrong?' 'He* ***was crazy about*** *this last girlfriend of his—I've never seen him so keen on anyone —and she's just gone off with another man.'* ⇨ ⚠ previous entry.

go dead on sb [V + Comp] (informal) cease to function; cease to respond, or be interested; be, or seem, incapable of development, or completion **S:** machine; radio, computer; class; project, painting, novel, song □ *Charles and I set up our Ferrograph and microphones to record some of the strange night sounds. The machine, which before had worked so well, now* ***went dead on*** *us.* LWK □ *There's a two-way flow between actor and audience, and there's nothing more paralysing than the feeling that your audience has* ***gone dead on*** *you.* □ *'This is one that* ***went dead on*** *me,' he said, moving aside a canvas that stood with its face to the wall.*

go their different etc ways continue their own journeys, disperse in different directions, to their homes etc; having had a common origin or bond, branch or drift apart **S:** travellers, guests; vehicles; members, devotees, disciples, followers, lovers. **pron:** their, our, your. **adj:** different, ⚠ separate; several, various □ *The 'broad front' strategy was to be adopted. And so we all got ready to cross the Seine and* ***go our different ways****.* MFM □ *Why had we suddenly become polite, almost distant? We were like the vicar and the doctor* ***going our separate ways*** *after the squire's tea-party.* CON □ *All the other jazz musicians of his generation have* ***gone their different ways*** *but Steve Lane is a purist— one hundred per cent devoted to the music of the Golden Age.* RT □ *They are all proud to call themselves Americans. Yet, equally proudly, they call themselves Irish and Italian, Polish and Norwegian and German, and* ***go their separate ways*** *together.* TVT

go and do sth[1] (informal) move and do sth □ *Then he straightened and said briskly, 'What about getting Prissie a little brandy, Aunt Annabel? I must* ***go and*** *see about trains.'* DC □ *Will you* ***go and*** *fetch me another four glasses from the cupboard in the hall, Peggy?* □ *'And I've got my violin practice, as well, tonight.' 'Why don't you* ***go and*** *do it now, before tea?'* □ go often superfluous here but reflects fact that one moves somewhere before, or while, acting.

go and do sth[2] (informal) go and functions as a kind of auxiliary to the main verb—itself often do (the implication always being that the main action is wrong, stupid, or regrettable) □ *Day in and day out she'd work her fingers to the bone. And now what had he* ***gone and done*** *by way of thanks?* LLDR □ *'If she was happy in the place whatever made her* ***go and do*** *a thing like that?' 'I dunno* (= don't know)*, Mr. Alan,' he replied. 'I dunno what makes girls* ***go and do*** *the things they do.'* RFW □ *Captain Segura said poor Dr Cifuentes was so scared* ***he went and*** *wet his trousers.* OMIH □ *Oh, yes, isn't that wonderful? On top of everything else he has to* ***go and*** *get himself shot up the bum.* TGLY

go down etc like ninepins be easily overcome, brought down, scattered etc (from a game in which a ball is rolled along the floor at nine bottle-shaped pieces of wood with the object of toppling as many of the pieces as possible) □ *I was a jack of all subjects and a master of none, but General Papers* (ie examination papers on 'general' subjects) *went down before me* ***like ninepins****.* NS □ *This was the batsmen's first taste of body-line bowling and they went down* ***like ninepins****.* SC

go easy on sth (informal) use sth moderately, sparingly, in not too large quantities **o:** butter, bread; beer, whisky; petrol, paint □ *You can have yourself another slice of bread but* ***go easy on*** *the marge* (= margarine) *mind, it's all we've got till I can bring some in from work.* TT □ *And they said '****Go easy on*** *the dope!' I should laugh. If they'd given me anything else to keep the pain away, maybe I would.* TST □ *Try* ***going easier on*** *the brakes, will you, or you'll have me through the windscreen.* □ ***Easy on*** *the paraffin! There's not much left and I can't get any more till next week.* □ usu direct or indir imper, go sometimes omitted, as in last example.

go far last long; meet the needs of users adequately **S:** money, food, supplies; cement, plaster. **adv mod:** very, quite, surprisingly □ *£45 a week doesn't* ***go*** *very* ***far*** *these days.* □ *You only bought half a dozen bottles of wine! That won't* ***go far*** *among thirty people.* □ *A piece of meat will always* ***go further*** *if sliced cold.* □ *You know I'm not extravagant, Jim. I make the money you give me* ***go*** *as* ***far*** *as I can.* □ *'Just take the 2-litre can in the meantime,' the paint salesman suggested. 'You'll be surprised how* ***far*** *it'll* ***go****.'* □ often neg; positive constructions usu comparative, or contradict neg assumption, as in last example. ⇨ ⚠ next entry.

go/get far rise greatly in social position, a profession, or the arts; become very successful, or effective; go/come a long way (qv) **S:** beginner, novice, pupil; movement, crusade. **adv mod:** very, so, that, as □ *His teachers used to say that the boy would* ***go far*** *but I don't suppose that even* they *thought a small village* *school would produce a future Cabinet minister.* □ *She has a good ear and a fine natural voice but she won't* ***get far*** *as a singer, without training.* □ *But political integration seems unlikely to* ***go*** *very* ***far*** *so long as General de Gaulle is in command in France.* SC □ often in predictions; often neg. ⇨ ⚠ previous entry.

go far to do sth/towards (doing) sth help greatly to achieve a desired purpose; go a long way to do sth/towards (doing) sth (qv) □ *The very activity required for rebuilding confidence in his direction of Vardon Hall would have* ***gone far to*** *dispel his depression and distrust of himself.* HAA □ *A promise of accommodation in nine to fifteen months' time doesn't* ***go far towards*** *the solution of our present problem.*

go farther/further and fare worse (saying) (one might easily) go on in the hope of finding sth better, but in fact end up with sth worse □ *The hotel is all right. It doesn't look much from the outside but they make you very comfortable. You could* ***go further and fare worse****.* □ *He's not a bad old stick. One could* ***go farther and fare worse*** *than have Jenkins for a boss.* □ often with *can/could/may/might*, and used to make fairly favourable comment on sb or sth.

go great guns (informal) do sth vigorously, or successfully; be very fashionable or popular □ *Most of the young ones had drifted off to the other room where Terry was* ***going great guns*** *at the piano.* □ *'The old fellow's* ***going great guns****, isn't he?' whispered Anna to me in the middle of his speech. 'I didn't think he still had it in him.'* □ *I myself remember buying a khaki green overcoat in 1969, when the military look was* ***going great guns****.* TVT □ usu continuous tenses.

go green (about the gills/in the face) [V + Comp] (informal) start to look pale, sickly-coloured, from nausea etc **V:** go, ⚠ be; turn sb. **A:** with nausea, with sickness □ *You've* ***gone a bit green about the gills****—are you feeling all right?* □ *The younger ambulance man* ***went green in the face****, and I thought he was going to faint or be sick.*

go/be haywire [V + Comp] (informal) go/be wrong; become/be confused; behave or function in an uncontrolled or crazy way **S:** look; office, switchboard; programme, schedule; things □ *I want the right time. My watch seems to have* ***gone haywire****.* PE □ *Instead, partly due to Mark Cox and Brian Fairlie unexpectedly coming through to the singles final, the original schedule* ***went haywire****.* PE □ *Cooks are traditionally liable to fly off the handle anyway and working conditions in that kitchen were enough to make anybody* ***go*** *completely* ***haywire****.* □ *The phones* ***are*** *completely* ***haywire*** *this afternoon—I keep getting the same number no matter what I dial.*

go it alone (informal) do sth, esp an undertaking of some difficulty, or that takes a considerable time, without the co-operation, assistance, or backing of others □ *Merseyside has been under Government scrutiny since 1949. Liverpool Corporation having till then '****gone it alone****' since the 1930s.* T □ *He put forward all sorts of schemes on how to capitalise on the unused assets of various companies, but his employers wouldn't listen. So he* ***went it alone****.* NS □ *In an age of motor manufacturing giants, it is not easy for the smaller company to* ***go it alone****.* SC

go like a bomb (informal) be an instant and thorough success **S:** party, comedy act, jumble sale; new product, latest book □ *I hope to produce two super courses, and a slight failure with the pudding makes the other women happy and the evening* ***goes like a bomb****.* ST □ *They have been on sale in some London stores—where Treasureware says they have been '****going like a bomb****'—and they are now becoming available in stores around the country.* ST

go/run like clockwork function or proceed smoothly, regularly, according to a plan or a pattern **S:** organization; trip, tour; party; office, laboratory, kitchen □ *We're used to emergency catering, we all know our jobs and everything* ***went like clockwork****.* □ *When Mr Mays had the organizing of the school plays they used to* ***run like clockwork****.*

go etc like the wind move very fast; pass very quickly **S:** sprinter; horse; car; week, month. **V:** go, ⚠ run, speed, be off □ *Harry was on his bike and* ***going like the wind*** *in the direction of the beach.* □ *Your uncle's left this parcel behind, Tommy.* ***Be off like the wind****, now, and catch him before he gets to the bus stop.* □ *Pop only knew that the month at St Pierre le Port seemed to have* ***gone like the wind****.* BFA

go/come a long way make/have made great progress—esp improve one's social or financial status, standard or performance—over a period of time; go/get far (qv) **S:** politician, academic; company, department; movement, theory □ HAVA: *I think David is a lovely boy, he's got such a wonderful* (singing) *voice, he'll* ***go a long way****.* HSG □ *They are very able people and will* ***go a long way****. What they mustn't mind is if somebody pips them to the post for the topmost job.* L □ *Ideas about the educability of the masses have* ***come a long way*** *during the past 100 years.* SC □ go a long way usu in predictions with *will*, come a long way in retrospective statements with *have*.

go a long way to do sth/towards (doing) sth help greatly to bring sth about; go far to do sth/towards (doing) sth (qv) **det:** a; some, a considerable, (not) the whole □ *If you can get some really good stories from Lewis any suspicion of bias will vanish, and it will* ***go a long way to*** *offset the effect of that letter.* RM □ *Dr Buchan* ***goes a long way towards*** *explaining what one commentator has called 'the ballad enigma'.* SC □ *The report's defect can only be dealt with by tightening up and widening legal requirements. This will* ***go some way towards*** *stopping shareholders from backing the wrong jockey instead of the right horse.* OBS □ *'Money doesn't bring you peace of mind.' 'No, but it would* ***go a long way towards*** *it in my case.'*

go native [V + Comp] (informal) adopt the customs of a foreign country or region that one lives in, and abandon those of one's own □ *There were even rumours that Scotland's greatest traveller had long since* ***gone native*** *and married what was quaintly called an 'African princess'.* OBS □ (time-shifts in science fiction story) *I am well aware of your sentimental penchant for the Twentieth Century and its ways my* *dear, but surely it wasn't quite necessary for you to* ***go native****?* TST

go one better (than sb/sth) outbid, or outdo, sb; be rather better than sth similar which was previously offered **S:** rival, competitor; remark, suggestion; joke, ploy □ *I saw the other dealer was determined to have the picture: however high I bid he would* ***go one better****. So I gave up.* □ *The urge to* ***go one better than*** *the next man which seems to dominate most people's lives in one way or another, is something I just didn't have built into me.* CON □ *. . . a powerful pressure, notably from advertising copywriters to sell to all classes the ramified forms of individualism by which their kind of commerce must live, in the stress on the virtue of '****going one better****', 'getting on', 'being wideawake'.* UL

go one's own way follow one's own inclinations; have values, interests, pursuits, work methods, etc not the same as another's, or a group's, with whom one might be expected to conform □ *As far as others are concerned, whatever they tell me to do, I usually* ***go my own way****.* RT □ *After my encounter with Schoenberg had produced what Hans Keller calls productive tension, Nielsen gave me the kind of intellectual and spiritual support I needed to help me* ***go my own way****.* L □ *'The English didn't want us,' so the local saying goes, 'and the Scots didn't want us.' Which left the land on either side of the Tyne to* ***go its own way****, to mature over the hundreds of years its own tough and vital lifestyle.* RT ⇨ ⚠ get etc one's (own) way.

go the pace lead a life of continuous, or excessive, social activity; lead a loose, or dissipated, life □ *'Of course I only got to know her in bed.' 'Good gracious! I know you young people* ***go the pace*** *a lot, but I didn't think you'd be as brazen about it as that.'* DIL □ *What, another dinner in Downhaven? You are* ***going the pace****, my dear.* PW

go phut (informal) collapse; break (down); fail to function **S:** marriage, plans; ankle, electric iron □ *It was an experience she recalls with determined optimism. The marriage had* ***gone phut****. She was unknown in America.* TVT □ *'I shouldn't have to treat it gently.' I told him. 'Other people can bang their car doors shut without the rooflight* ***going phut****.'*

go places (informal) (seem likely to) become very successful, improve one's position **S:** actor, businessman; company. department □ *Raymond, of course, is no run-of-the-mill executive. Firstly he is still only 36, and the City loves nothing better than a young man who's* ***going places****.* OBS □ *Ron, too, was in a dreamy mood, '****going places****' on his looks and personality.* HAA ⇨ ⚠ next entry.

go places (and see people) (informal) be active socially; travel, frequent, places of entertainment, etc for interest or stimulation □ SAM: *I tell you, Mr Segal, that's what I've missed—I mean* ***going places and seeing people****.* HSG □ *Larrie was* ***going places*** *that Mr Vin Salad would only see at the pictures* (= in cinemas). ASA □ *I was tired out and Jenny was in a want-to-****go-places-and-see-people*** *mood, and we had our first quarrel.* □ attrib use *a* ***go-places-and-see-people*** *mood.* ⇨ ⚠ previous entry.

go etc purple (in the face) [V + Comp] (informal) start to look dark red (in the face) through being flushed with blood **V:** go, ⚠ be; turn sb. **A:** with anger, with fury, with rage, with frustration □ *He held the kinds of left-wing views that can* ***turn the face*** *of a retired colonel* ***purple*** *with fury.* □ *The delay was enough to make a patient man* ***go purple in the face****.* ⇨ ⚠ go etc blue (in the face); next entry.

go etc red (in the face) [V + Comp] (informal) start to look red (in the face) through being filled with blood **V:** go, ⚠ be; turn sb. **A:** with anger; with shame, with embarrassment □ *We can behold an outraged member of Women's Lib* ***going red in the face*** *and choking with anger so that she cannot find words to express her contempt.* SC ⇨ ⚠ go etc blue (in the face); previous entry.

go right/wrong (for sb) [V + Comp] turn out well/badly (for sb); happen or be done according/contrary to (sb's) plans or hopes **S:** things, everything, nothing, something; marriage, pregnancy; evening, talks □ *It was a tight schedule but everything* ***went right for*** *us.* □ *Ford did everything he could to dissipate his marvellous talent, but on at least two occasions things defeated him by* ***going right****.* L □ *Nothing* ***goes right for*** *Noddy today.* TVT □ *His main aim in the* (TV) *series is to make the vet less necessary. 'How to prevent things* ***going wrong*** *by treating animals properly in the first place.'* RT ⇨ ⚠ go wrong (with sth).

go the right/wrong way have a favcurable/unfavourable result **S:** contest, dispute; trial, hearing; war □ *He had opened the bag* (of uncut rubies) *meaning to cache the rest where, if the war* ***went the right way****, he could come back and collect them.* ARG □ *His lawyer advised him not to sue; the case could so easily* ***go the wrong way*** *and leave him worse off than before.*

go etc scot-free [V + Comp] go etc without paying the due penalty or suffering punishment (from scot, an old form of tax) **V:** go, ⚠ get away, escape; let sb off □ *Men like the Kray brothers or the Richardson gang are often too canny to get personally involved in the crimes they are planning. It would surely be wrong to let them* ***go scot-free*** *just for lack of fingerprints.* SC □ *It appears that, as the Act stands, if the TGWU* (= Transport and General Workers' Union) *had registered, it could have* ***got away scot-free****.* SC

go to show serve as a proof, or demonstration, of sth previously, or shortly to be, mentioned **S:** it (all), this, which □ *Anna le Page never used any French words mixed in with her conversation in the way that French people were meant to* (ie usually did)*: it must just* ***go to show*** *how long Anna had been living over here.* TGLY □ *He's never looked back since. He's got a boutique and a used car business. It all* ***goes to show****, don't* (= doesn't) *it?* ST □ often followed by *that*-cl, *how*-cl.

go/report sick (esp military) report, in person or through sb else, that one is unfit for duty, one's work, because of illness or injury □ *Belchem was an excellent man to have handy in case de Guignand* ***went sick*** *as he sometimes did after too much hard work and strain.* MFM □ *They agreed, and Desmond was briefed to tell X that his principal had* ***gone sick*** *and was sending a* *junior valuer in his place.* DS □ report sick formal. ⇨ ⚠ fall/be taken ill/sick.

go slow reduce work, or activity, considerably; (industrial relations) reduce work, or activity, considerably as a form of industrial action in place of stopping work altogether **S:** railwaymen, air traffic controllers; railways, ferries □ *There's something wrong with his lungs. Nothing immediately serious but he does have to* ***go slow.*** □ *A* ***go-slow*** *by pilots of British European Airways demanding more pay had little appreciable effect on Easter holiday traffic.* L □ *Between 17 April 1902 and the holding of a special conference on 15 May, Lord Kitchener, the Commander-in-Chief, agreed to what he himself called a '****go-slow****' in the war.* OBS □ n compound a go-slow.

go slumming (derogatory) visit the house of poor people on fact-finding or charitable missions; (condescend to) visit a family, restaurant, pub, place of entertainment, etc of a lower class than one usually visits—perhaps from curiosity □ *She had chosen to go and live in Stepney and share the exposure of its people to the hazards of poverty and war. Her concern with the lives around her seemed so different from that of those who used to* ***go slumming.*** AH □ *'I didn't expect to see you in the Public Bar.' 'Oh, the Cocktail Lounge was frightfully crowded so we thought we'd* ***go slumming.****'* □ often facetious.

go/turn sour [V + Comp] become sour, ie no longer fresh, sweet, wholesome; (fig) become unfriendly, unsatisfactory, unproductive etc **S:** milk, beer; things; life, friendship, attitude, feelings; economic conditions, the market □ *After 25 years as an MP does he wish when things* ***go sour*** *that a career in music might have been possible?* G □ *I was certain in my mind that the whole operation was* ***going sour.*** DS □ *The story centres on an attractive fashion model whose romance* ***turns sour*** *and leads her into a situation of terror.* TVT □ *Commodity shares are fine for the more knowledgeable investor but even he has to be nimble-footed and prepared to switch quickly if the sector shows signs of* ***turning sour.*** OBS □ *Even his humour has* ***gone sour.*** *I think he just doesn't like people any more.*

go steady (with sb) (informal) have a stable relationship with sb of the opposite sex, of the kind that usu leads to marriage □ *I have been* ***going steady with*** *a girl for nearly two years, and we were shortly to be engaged.* WI □ *Half a dozen visits to the Cinema, and then they would be* ***going steady****; and afterwards—well, why not?* HD □ (reader's letter) *I have not got* ***a steady*** (boy friend) *because the boys I like best just aren't the steady kind.* H □ usu continuous tenses; variants be sb's steady/a steady (boy-friend, girl-friend). ⇨ ⚠ next entry.

go steady (with sth) be (more) careful or controlled in one's actions or speech; be (more) careful or controlled (in the use of sth) □ *Here, you two, just* ***go steady with*** *that bottle! I want a couple of drams left for Dad and Harry.* □ *I'd* ***go*** *a bit* ***steady*** *about calling in the police if I were you. They might uncover more than you want found out.* □ ***Go steady****, James. That's no kind of language to be using in front of the children.* □ usu imper. ⇨ ⚠ previous entry.

go straight (informal) give up dishonesty, or crime, as a way of life **S:** prisoner, criminal □ *He'll never* ***go straight****, and if he wanted to, the lot he goes around with wouldn't let him.* ASA □ *By the time Desmond came out of prison in October (19)53, he had no intention of doing what Sammy wanted. He had decided to* ***go straight.*** DS

go too etc far exceed what is right, true, reasonable or just; carry sth too far (qv) **S:** critic, opponent; remark, comment; claim, proposal, policy. **adv mod:** too, rather (too), a bit (too), much too, a great deal too □ JIMMY: *She is a cow. I wouldn't mind that so much, but she seems to have become a sacred cow as well.* CLIFF: *You've* ***gone too far****, Jimmy. Now dry up* ((slang) = be quiet)*!* LBA □ (reader's letter) *After having quite a few drinks, she* ***went too far*** *with another boy and is now expecting a baby.* WI □ *Possibly I* ***went a bit far*** *in urging on him my own plan.* MFM □ *This nonsense about feeling better by tomorrow has* ***gone far enough****. I'm going to phone for the doctor, whether you like it or not.* □ variant have gone (quite) far enough usu implies *have already* ***gone too far****,* too can be premodified by *rather, a bit, a little.*

go trumps (on sth/sb) play a trump card which beats any card of another suit; (fig) outdo, score a success over, sth/sb □ *In the third round of hearts I fully expected to see somebody* ***go trumps on*** *my Queen.* □ (advertisement) ***Go trumps*** *at your next party by wearing this wool and metal weave. It's the newest fashion deal.*

go underground live and work in hiding, under a false identity, etc, esp as a member of a secret, or proscribed, military or political movement **S:** movement, party; dissident, opponent □ *'What about Rudy?' 'I'd have told him to radio London that we were breaking off and then* ***go underground****!'* OMIH □ *Some say 'the General' was secretly executed, others that he escaped and* ***went underground.*** □ *The native healers probably* ***went underground*** *during the 350 years of Spanish rule.* OBS

go the way of sb/sth end in the same way, suffer the same fate, as sb/sth specified (the implication almost always being that this is regrettable) **o:** his father, too many careerists, other small firms; the old ideals □ *He'd better watch himself or he'll be* ***going the way of*** *his father and ending up an alcoholic.* □ *The young pharmacist who has bought the business has already made plans to re-vamp the exterior. So Mr Ewan's shop is destined to* ***go the way of*** *so many small shops in London today.* ST □ *If it* (Gaelic) *loses another generation of children it is lost as a spoken language. It will* ***go the same way as*** *the Cornish and Manx languages have gone.* RT □ *Religious sanctions for human behaviour have long been in decline and it now looks as if moral ones are* ***going the same way.*** □ variant go the same way (as sb/sth).

go the way of all flesh (saying) (live and) die as other men do; suffer any of the changes, hazards, or temptations which men are faced with □ (about Picasso) *Now that the greatest artist of the first half of this century has at long last* ***gone the way of all flesh****, the small talents are doing their best to discredit his phenomenal achievement.* SC □ *'Craze' embroils Jack Palance as a broke antique dealer who kills ladies to satisfy an idol called Chukee. Poor Julie Ege,*

Kathleen Byron, Dame Edith Evans and Suzy Kendall ***go the way of all flesh*** *as he makes his rounds.* NS

go west die; perish; be lost, or got rid of (from the sun sinking in the west) □ *'There always used to be a white horse in that field.' 'Fancy you remembering that, it's a long time since he* ***went west****.'* □ *Even now, when what used to be called compensating moral values have* ***gone west****, the end of 'The Getaway' comes as a surprise.* ST □ *The food mixer must have* ***gone west*** *along with my baking tins, when we moved house.*

go west, (young man) go and develop new opportunities (while you are young and vigorous) (from a 19th c US catchphrase to promote the opening up and development of the Western States) □ *Jacklin will do all right from British golf. In the long run, there could be an end to the fallacy that the only way to make good in this game is to* ***go west, young man*** (= play in US tournaments). OBS □ *The old rebel* ***went West*** *— we've seen it on a hundred Hollywood films. The freed black men* ***went West*** *as well.* RT □ *They wanted 'the right kind' of* ***young man*** *to* ***go West*** *in 1927, and they were misguided enough to accept Pyke.* TVT □ now used in allusion to original catchphrase, or facetiously.

go etc while the going is good leave, escape etc while there is an opportunity to do so easily; do sth while conditions are still favourable or do not involve too much danger or inconvenience **V:** go, ⚠ get away, get out, leave, escape □ MR BUTCHER: *Good luck, son—but* ***go while the going is good****.* DPM □ *Many European planters have already left Ceylon, retiring early to their bungalows in Surrey and Sussex,* ***getting out while the going is good****.* SC □ *I could see that the alcohol would involve us in a rallentando and I wanted to* ***go*** *as far away as possible* ***while the going was good****.* UTN

go the whole hog (informal) go to the full limit of a possible course of action; commit, or involve, oneself to the fullest extent □ *He was rich, but he had refrained from* ***going the whole hog*** *and becoming a millionaire, and he showed the same spirit of restraint in his style of living.* HD □ *'I'm a vegetarian, do you know with what intention? I want to live for 250 years.' 'Lad!* ***Go the whole hog****! Live for ever!'* ST ⇨ ⚠ all or nothing.

go wrong[1] take to crime, vice; start to behave in some socially unacceptable way □ *This chap came from a very good South African family, but he* ***went wrong****, and in 1951 he got a two-year sentence for conspiracy to defraud.* SD □ *'We've been foster parents to eight kids in all,' she said, 'and some of them from terrible backgrounds. They all keep in touch and not one of them has* ***gone wrong****.'*

go wrong[2] err in calculation, judgement, or management □ *Perhaps all you need to do to see where you* ***went wrong*** *is to read the instructions more carefully.* □ *With a skilled instructor to correct you each time you* ***go wrong****, bad driving habits don't get built in.* ST □ *They ask why the young take to drugs, they ask where they, as parents, might have* ***gone wrong****.* SC

go wrong (with sth) fail; prove deficient, or unreliable **S:** something, nothing, anything, what. **o:** experiment; air-conditioning system, lock; metabolism, sense of time, eyesight, left knee □ *My class were watching the demonstration very attentively, no doubt in the hope that something would* ***go wrong*** *and I'd be showered with broken glass and raw egg.* □ *If only I'd made the thing fifty per cent bigger. Then whatever's* ***gone wrong****, it would still have worked.* NM □ *As long as nothing* ***goes wrong with*** *my other ear I won't be too deaf.* □ cf *the experiment* ***went wrong****,* and *something* ***went wrong with*** *the experiment.* ⇨ ⚠ go right/wrong (for sb).

God damn (it) (taboo) damn (it); blast (it) □ MILLY: *What's the matter with you all anyway? — Well,* ***God damn*** *the lot of you. I'm going home.* EHOW □ *For the next ten minutes I want to talk to somebody else, so just take your* ***God-damned*** *dirty hand off my wrist if you want to keep your front teeth.* HD □ *Through prayers and psalms and rackety hymns, the Squire slept like a beaming child, save when a visiting preacher took some rhetorical flight, when he'd wake with a loud '****God damn****!'* CWR □ *I don't know whether these guys are communist or not. But if anybody asks me am I Democrat or Republican I'd say it's none of his* ***goddam*** *business.* NS □ *The other player simply put down his cards and, shaking his head in disbelief, said, 'Pug, you're the* ***goddamnedest*** *lucky player.'* ST □ exclamation of strong irritation, displeasure, or anger; attrib use (GB) *your* ***God-damned*** *dirty hand,* (US) *none of his* ***goddam*** *business.*

God damn sb's eyes (taboo) damn sb; blast sb □ *My name it is Sam Hall, and I hates* (= hate) *you one and all./Yes, I hates you one and all,* ***God damn your eyes****.* GALLOWS' SONG (US) □ CRAPE: *Mrs Letouzel, you cantankerous old bag, what do you mean by complaining about your money? All* you *are asked to provide,* ***God damn your eyes****, are those few small comforts.* THH □ *The lucky sods* (ie vulgar term of abuse) *got there before us,* ***God damn their eyes****.* □ almost always spoken in anger, in hate, or with offensive intention.

God etc forbid let us hope that what is mentioned is not so, cannot be, will never happen **S:** God, ⚠ heaven, the Lord □ *'Look, I must go. I'm late already. I didn't think you would want breakfast.' '****God forbid****.' He made a face.* AITC □ *The housewife might ultimately have some sort of television link with her neighbourhood store.* ***God forbid****, there might even be, with computers becoming smaller and smaller, a computer link to the home.* L □ *You may be right, but I know if I were going to take a wife to Mars, which* ***heaven forbid****, I'd feel a tough, gun-toting Mamma was less of a liability.* TST □ fervent wish which negates another statement.

(may) God etc forgive me possibly a pious appeal for forgiveness, but usu added to an account of sth said or done to note, or point out, that it was wrong, mistaken, mischievous etc **S:** God, ⚠ the Lord; heaven. **O:** me, you, him, them; the poor soul, those responsible □ *I killed and imprisoned and exiled those I loved because the Devil whispered in my ear through your mouth.* ***May God forgive me****!* WI □ *Oh, I hate you with your filthy mind! But how can I expect you to have anything else? You're a Templar! And now,* ***heaven forgive me****, I'm bringing* *another Templar into the world.* DC □ *'Boys,' said the Biffer one evening in the Snorvig bar, 'I never came so near to hitting a man as I came to hitting Waggett this afternoon.' '***The Lord forgive you***, Mr Waggett,' I was saying.* RM □ *That was the night Henry,* ***may he be forgiven****, got us to believe his wife was due to have triplets.* □ pass form may I be forgiven (ie by God).

God etc help sb sometimes a pious appeal, but usu a comment that sb's circumstances are unfortunate, that he is, or is likely to be, in need of sympathy and help though perhaps not likely to get it **S:** God, ⚠ heaven, the Lord □ *Isn't it time that husband of yours was demobbed? The war's been over a year already. We've been living here five years—he hasn't even seen the place,* ***God help*** *him!* CSWB □ *If that's the way he treats his friends then* ***God help*** *his enemies.* □ *Nevertheless,* ***heaven help*** *opponents if they ever play on dry grounds—if, in fact, we ever have dry grounds again.* T □ *Ivy's mother and father think of her as a perfectly ordinary girl, not doing too well in her studies, but 'popular'.* ***Lord help*** *us!* ARG

God helps those who help themselves (saying) one has to make efforts on one's own behalf before God can assist in making those efforts successful □ *Things will come out all right for you.* ***God helps those who help themselves****, if you want another old saw* (= proverbial saying). AITC □ *Fischer emerges not only as the victim of an exclusive dedication to chess, but also as a product of a society where* ***God*** *does indeed only* ***help those who help themselves****. By crushing others.* L □ either advice to lazy, indifferent, or despondent persons or, more cynically, a comment that it is wiser to look after one's own interests than to trust God to do so.

(dear) God in heaven(!) exclamation of surprise or shock □ (Jo is pregnant by a coloured man) HELEN: *And what about the nurse. She's going to get a bit of a shock, isn't she?* JO: *Well, she's black too.* HELEN: *Good, perhaps she'll adopt it.* ***Dear God in heaven!*** TOH □ ***Dear God in Heaven****, I thought to myself, get me out of this mess and I'll never tell a lie again.* □ *'***God in heaven***, Mary, what's happened to you?' 'I fell off my bike.'* □ ADA: ***God in heaven*** *save me from the claptrap of a threepenny pamphlet.* CSWB □ sometimes worked into structure of exclamatory appeal or statement.

God etc knows I don't know; nobody knows; one can only guess **S:** God, ⚠ the Lord, goodness, heaven. **O:** what there is; who arranged it; when to buy; where it landed; how to end it; which ideas □ *'What does he hope to achieve by carrying on like that?' '***God knows***, you'd think he was trying to get himself disliked.'* □ *'I had a most glamourous evening dress,' Eva said. 'Yes,' said Bob, 'and* ***God*** *only* ***knows*** *how it kept up.'* RATT □ *And is this one of the bargains that will be kept when Gerneral Franco dies and is replaced by* ***goodness knows*** *whom?* L □ *'Does it matter now?' she asked. 'He's dead and we're old.* ***Heaven*** *alone* ***knows*** *who lives at Melphan now.'* ASA □ *Here I'm living, my posse of Ghurka Guards, who protect me very amiably from* ***God-knows****-what wherever my headquarters may be.* SD □ *. . .meditating on* ***goodness knows*** *what subtleties of mind and convolution of temperament in his loved one.* SML □ can be modified God or (the) Lord above/only/alone, and goodness or heaven only/alone; attrib use ***God-knows****-what,* ***goodness knows*** *what.*

God etc knows (that) certainly; emphatically **S:** God, ⚠ goodness, heaven, the Lord □ ***God knows****, English rule in Ireland has not been distinguished for wisdom or even common sense.* NS □ *'We can't really afford it,' Brigit answered cheerfully. 'Then you must ask Saunders for money.* ***Goodness knows*** *he has plenty.'* DC □ *He never did become a top-class athlete though* ***heaven knows*** *he tried hard enough.* □ affirms the truth of a statement.

(serve) God and Mammon satisfying spiritual (God) and worldly (Mammon) interests, esp the love of money □ (source) *Ye cannot* ***serve God and mammon****.* MATTHEW VI 24 □ *He* (David Frost) *has built up a financial empire. He is still only 32. He may find other causes beside* ***God and Mammon****.* L □ *Paxton was one of those 'Christian' businessmen who find it a very satisfactory arrangement to* ***serve God*** *on Sundays* ***and Mammon*** *for the rest of the week.*

God moves in a mysterious way, his wonders to perform (saying) God often achieves his purposes in ways which cannot be clearly seen or understood (the first two lines of OLNEY HYMNS 35 (W COWPER 1731-1800)) □ *Her motives would then be buried beneath the issue of a son saved from moral danger.* ***God****—if one could believe in Him, she thought with a little laugh—would once more have* ***moved in mysterious ways His wonders to perform****.* HAA □ (NONCE) *Fowler, of course, knew that language, like* ***God****,* ***works in mysterious ways its wonders to perform****.* L □ (NONCE) *One particular extract from Barrington-Ward's own diary is all too revealing of* ***the way the Establishment*** *(of which 'The Times' was then, of course, an integral part)* ***moves its wonders to perform****.* NS □ (NONCE) *Attention has to be paid to lunch-time nourishment. But* ***the law moves in mysterious ways its functions to perform****, and the only people who can be sure of a square meal are the judge, jury and prisoner.* SC □ often freely adapted, as shown, usu for ironic effect.

God rest him/his soul (dated formal) pious, or affectionate, parenthesis used when referring to sb who is dead □ *As far as I know, my father,* ***God rest his soul****, only met my mother's people at his wedding.* TVT

God speed (sb/sth) (dated formal) may God prosper sb/sth □ *Together we have carried through one of the most successful campaigns in history, and it has been our good fortune to be members of this great team. God bless you and* ***God speed****.* MFM □ *The old man then came upon a group of women mending nets by the shore. '***God speed*** *the work,' he said courteously. 'Is there any kin to James Sangster, once of this place, amongst you?'* □ *All the same, isn't there something, anything, to be said for these* (suburban) *people and their chosen life-styles? As it is, little is allowed to impede the swelling flood of bile. Ayckbourn,* ***God speed*** *him, would have been more balanced and forgiving.* NS □ *Harry's done so much for this school, I think we should* *organize a dinner or something else special, just to wish him and his good wife* ***God speed*** *before they go to Jamaica.* □ now more usu in expression *bid/wish sb* ***God speed***, old-fashioned form of well-wishing, esp for sb starting on a journey, task, enterprise, new way of life.

God willing if God so wills; unless prevented by '(an) act of God' (qv) or by some circumstance over which one has no control □ ***God willing****, this was Richard Nixon's last campaign and he won it going away, for the first time in his life a landslide winner on his own.* NS □ *We've had a lovely holiday and will be back again next summer,* ***God willing****.* □ *I could come and stay for a weekend at the end of April provided you let me know the date pretty soon—and always, of course,* ***D.V.***' *'Cautious blighter, aren't you?'* □ front, middle or end position; variant DV = (Latin) deo volente = 'God willing'. ⇨ ⚠ please God.

God's gift to sb/sth [Comp (NP)] sb/sth that seems specially created to be of use or pleasure, esp to persons of a kind, group or race, or to a place, industry etc **V:** ⚠ be; regard, see, oneself as. **o:** women, lazy cooks; Scotland; the legal profession □ *Anyway, I'm sick of him and his soppy ways, and it may do him a bit of good to find out he isn't* ***God's gift to*** *women.* PE □ *Mr Wilson today contemptuously dismissed the Heath Government as* ***God's gift to*** *militants and troublemakers.* SC □ *'Won't you grow any fruit?' 'No. Only rhubarb,* ***God's gift to*** *Scotland and lazy gardeners.'* □ *Syphilis was* ***God's gift to*** *puritanism since it combined the horrors of a sexually transmitted disease (therefore shameful) with those of a slow and secret killer (therefore fearful).* NS □ often ironic.

a going concern [Comp (NP)] a shop, business, institution etc that is well established, active and sucessful **V:** ⚠ be, become; make sth □ *Labour leaders yesterday started anew the search for a defence policy that would, with luck, keep together the party as* ***a going concern*** *during the next 10 months.* T □ *Junior secondary education has so far failed to develop as* ***a going concern****.* SC □ *This time I accepted* (a new appointment). *I felt that now I could depart with a clear conscience. Behind me I should leave* ***a going concern****.* SD □ *You know the properties will never be* ***going concerns*** *commercially; most of them are terraced farmland which is no longer economical.* L □ *And as Sir Edmund was only eighty-six we hope that he will continue in his ways, for apart from a slight and often deliberate deafness he was* ***an*** *extremely* ***going concern****.* WDM □ last example a parody of normal use.

going, going, gone an auctioneer's warning that an article is to be sold unless there is a higher bid before his hammer goes down at the word *gone* □ *What's happened to Manchester? says the man behind the desk in the planning office. What's happened? Why it's going —* ***going, going, gone****.* OBS □ also in extended use, esp facetious, as shown.

the going rate (for sth) the usual sum paid for goods, or for a service, at any particular time; the general percentage increase being awarded to groups of workers in any one cycle of wage negotiations □ *Chung Ling Soo caught the bullets between his teeth, till one caught him between the eyes and he was killed.* ***The going rate for*** *the secret of the bullet-catching trick is just £2 at Brighton, and there are not many takers.* TVT □ *If certain powerful groups of workers settle their wage claims at 17%, we can expect other groups to look on that figure as* ***the going rate****.*

(still) going strong (still) active and successful; (still) maintaining its/their popular appeal **S:** father, president; business, institution; periodical, orchestra, ballet □ *Kathleen is the only one of the original 'Children's Hour' broadcasters* ***still going strong****.* RT □ (tourism in Britain, 1912) *The Corris Railway is* ***going strong****—five bob* ((informal GB) = five shillings) *for the combined rail-and-coach tour.* ST □ (reader's letter) *May we inform, or reassure, readers that the 'British Journal of Photography' has reached Volume 122 and is* ***still going strong****.* G □ *'I suppose Rockets are* ***still going strong****,' I said. 'I notice that the municipality of Paris is a customer of yours.'* UTN □ after *be*, or may modify a preceding n.

a gold mine any source of wealth, esp a product or idea which brings massive returns to its originator, or to those marketing it □ *That was all right as long as Ballantynes* (publishers) *kept on repeating the success of 'The Lady of the Lake'. Scott himself was* ***a gold mine****.* SC □ *With the North Sea oil speculators' need for coastal development sites some crofters who had scratched a living for generations found themselves sitting on* ***a gold mine****.* □ *Gerald Priestland began with Harmsworth's verdict immediately after the launching of the first 'Daily Mail' in 1896: 'We have struck* ***a gold mine****!'* L

the golden age (of sth) the period when sth is at its best, happiest, most prosperous, most interesting, etc (from the Golden Age in Greek mythology — first and happiest of the successive ages of mankind) □ *For most English radicals, Paine's 'The Rights of Man' provided a bridge between their native traditions and the cosmopolitan revolution; the world of humanity and* ***the golden age*** *which many saw as opening up in the wake of revolution in America and France.* L □ *From about 1880 to 1903 was truly* ***the golden age of*** *mountaineering, when the Lakeland pioneers developed their craft to such a peak that the best of their routes still provide a severe challenge today.* SC □ *In the further corners a few dilapidated carriages still remained from* ***the golden age of*** *horses and prosperity.* EM

a golden handshake [O (NP)] a gift, or gratuity, given to sb on his retirement, or honourable dismissal, from office, a job, service in the armed forces, etc □ ***A golden handshake*** *for workers, financed by a variable payroll tax on employers can no longer be classified as an overfed director's bad dreams.* T □ *We'd both just come out of the forces, blown* (= spent recklessly) ***the golden handshake*** *and were jobless.* SC □ (reader's letter) *I was aware of* ***the 'golden handshake'*** *presented to Sir John when the BBC board, not unaided by leading members of the political Establishment, dislodged the giant in June, 1938.* L

the golden mean the ideal (point of) balance

between too much and too little of sth; moderation in principle and in conduct □ *Trollope's hero and anti-hero personify the excess of virtue and the excess of vice which in his philosophy threatens* **the** *British* **golden mean**. NS □ *Walter Kempowski is an author whose own life approximates to* **a** *sort of* **golden mean** *of contemporary German existence; old enough to remember the Nazis but too young to have fought in the war, hailing from the East, resident in the West.* ST

a golden opportunity a very favourable opportunity to do or obtain sth, esp one that rarely occurs or that, if taken, will provide exceptional rewards **V:** offer, present, afford; take, seize; lose □ *Polytechnics present* **golden opportunities** *to a bright young lecturer. Starting salaries are higher than in universities, and there are unparalleled chances to experiment with new syllabuses.* OBS □ (review of 'This Week's Composer', Radio 3) *Surely* **a golden opportunity** *was lost for demonstrating that Walton's range is wider and deeper and more varied than is usually acknowledged.* L

the golden rule the best, most useful, course to adopt in a particular field or activity **A:** in politics; of advertising; for all young nurses □ *In any relationship—personal, business or social—when in doubt, follow* **the golden rule**. □ *Tell him not to be impatient. That's* **the golden rule** *in politics.* EM □ *'Important business,' I shouted from the floor below. 'Fleet Street. Hustle. Get there first, newspaper man's* **golden rule**.' CON □ *But Tudor knew that* **the golden rule** *of merchandising is to create an appetite for something that you didn't even know you wanted.* L □ when unmodified, as in first example, expression means 'treat others as you would like them to treat you'.

a good address a place of residence which lends social prestige, esp in a city district that tends to have well-to-do, fashionable, or important people living or doing business there □ *'They could have got a far larger house in North London for half the price.' 'Ah, but they wouldn't have had such* **a good address**.' □ *Why the militarily impractical castellations on top of a great house on the Welsh border? Because, then, as now, a castle is* **a good address**. RT

the good book the Bible □ *She even took out* **the 'Good Book'** *from a dusty cupboard and sat it on the table as a testimony to the godliness of her home.* HAA □ **The good book**, *if we are to believe it, says we are entitled to three score years and ten* (= 70 years). *Who am I to argue?* OBS

good clean fun harmless and wholesome enjoyment or entertainment □ *Why not come and have a cup of tea with me and my old mum? Why not make a jolly day of it, with lots of* **good clean fun** *and memories of old times?* CON □ *'Well, what do you think? Very jolly, what?' 'Oh yes,* **good clean fun**.' TGLY □ (film review) *A lot of very funny people are doing their best to see that you get a good 90 minutes' enjoyment. This is* **good clean** *British* **fun**. RT □ *Hamish MacInnes wouldn't, I imagine, class himself all that high as a writer.* **Good clean fun** *in the Alastair MacLean style but somewhat livelier.* SC □ often ironic or derogatory.

a good/great deal [A (NP)] much; often □ *'He seems to think you care* **a good deal** *about Guy,' Brigit said deliberately.* DC □ *The father has to be away from home* **a good deal** *and the boys are getting a bit too headstrong for their mother to handle.* □ *He worries* **a great deal** *about his future.* □ great, not good, in all neg uses. ⇨ ⚠ next entry.

a good/great deal (of sth) a large, or considerable, quantity (of sth) **o:** noise, disturbance; unpleasantness, dissent; charm, enthusiasm □ *There's been* **a good deal of** *discontent, locally, with the new traffic regulations.* □ *'Did he have much trouble getting through the customs?'* '**A good deal**, *I'm afraid.'* □ *According to the campaign committee, revival supporters are generous people and* **a good deal of** *the money is being contributed in small amounts by hard-up enthusiasts who can ill afford it.* TO □ *The young animals spend* **a great deal of** *time and energy exploring, and therefore, learning, their environment.* NSC □ *The all-party approach to the Government sponsored by the STUC* (= Scottish Trades Unions Congress) *may also not achieve* **a great deal**. SC □ great, not good, in all neg uses. ⇨ ⚠ previous entry.

a good/great deal healthier etc [Comp/A (NP)] much healthier etc **adj:** healthier; better, worse; longer, heavier; louder. **adv mod:** too (long, heavy; loud; often) □ *Russian foods seem to be* **a good deal healthier**, *anyway, than ours.* NSC □ *It'll be* **a good deal more expensive** *to have the floor sanded and polished than to lay a fitted carpet.* □ *'I don't often interrupt you, do I?' 'A* **great deal too often**. *I can only suppose you're unaware of it.'* □ *'Can you manage that case?' 'Why not? It's not* **a great deal heavier** *than the one you're carrying yourself.'* □ great, not good, in all neg uses.

one's good deed for the day an action, appropriate to the situation and designed to help another person or other people, that one tries to carry out each day (the reference being to the recommendation to Scouts and Guides, that they should try to do at least one good deed every day, ie sth helpful to others) □ *Half-way through, the door swung open and a Boy Scout came in with Parson's camera.* **His good deed for the day**, *I suppose.* CON □ *Tell them if they want to borrow the lawn-mower they can come and fetch it themselves. Tell them I've done* **my good deed for the day** *already.* □ often facetious.

good egg! (dated informal) good! excellent! □ *'I managed to find a shop that sells all those things you wanted for that Chinese recipe you're going to cook tomorrow.' 'Oh,* **good egg!** *I was beginning to think it would have to be roast chicken again.'*

good and evil [n + n non-rev] what is right and what is wrong, esp as forces or principles influencing, or exemplified by, human conduct □ *But men do not seem to be reliable judges of* **good and evil**: *the help of the same God is invoked by opposed nations, each believing that it has right on its side against a wicked enemy.* AH □ HELENA: *I believe in* **good and evil** *and I don't have to apologize for that. And by everything I have ever believed in or wanted, what I have been doing is wrong and evil.* LBA □ *On the whole, it had been a successful evening. An excess of emotion* *had crept into an argument on* ***good and evil****.* TCM ▫ non-rev when unexpanded, but cf *a power for* ***evil*** *as well as for* ***good****, there is more* ***good*** *than* ***evil*** *in him.*

a good few ((of) sb/sth) (informal) a large, or considerable, number (of sb/sth); a good many ((of) sb/sth) (qv) ▫ *'By the way,' concluded the chairman, 'our treasurer tells me that* ***a good few of*** *you haven't paid your annual subscriptions yet.'* ▫ *'Are there many of the original members about?' 'Oh,* ***a good few****.'*

good for sth [Comp (AdjP)] (informal) able, or likely to, provide sth; fit, or equipped, to do sth **S:** father, punter, backer; oar, boat. **V:** ⚠ be, seem, look. **o:** £10,000, loan, raise; another twenty years, a lifetime, 20,000 kilometres ▫ *He was a rich man in our estimation—***good for** *at least £10,000.* ▫ *If you're thinking of raising money to help with the expenses, you should ask the Club members. They'll be* ***good for*** *a pound apiece.* ▫ *'I'm eighty you know. I can't expect to live much longer.' 'By the look of you, you're* ***good for*** *another twenty years.'* ▫ *The Civic Ball was the event of the year in Warley,* ***good for*** *two full pages in the 'Courier'.* RATT

good for sb(!) exclamatory comment of congratulation or approval; bully for sb (qv) **o:** him, the boss, the kids ▫ *'Yes, sir! The Astronomer Royal is Chief British Liaison Officer to the whole U.S. project.'* ***'Good for*** *him.'* TBC ▫ *'Well, I've persuaded your father to see a doctor.' 'Oh,* ***good for*** *you! You must have been very tactful.'* ▫ (reader's letter) *'But then we never got around to thinking of emotional dependence as a moral virtue,' he writes. Well,* ***good for*** *Mr Cutforth, but I happen to be mystical and sanctimonious enough to believe that emotional dependence* is *important. Had Mr Cutforth ever been lucky enough to fall in love he would probably think so too.* L ▫ usu sincere, sometimes ironic; stress patterns ˌgood for ˈyou(!), ˌgood for Mr ˈCutforth(!).

good for a laugh [Comp (AdjP)] (informal) likely to cause amusement **V:** ⚠ be; find sb ▫ *Some of those interviewed were friendly and communicative; others, voicing distrust of the mass media and the way it has usually handled Women's Lib — always* ***good for a laugh*** *— refused any information.* ST ▫ *You could get Mike to tell a few of his stories. That's always* ***good for a laugh****.*

good for nothing [Comp (AdjP)] idle and useless (the implication sometimes being that the person referred to is a scoundrel or wastrel as well); (sth that is) useless for any purpose **S:** brother, daughter, partner, ally; information; guidebook **V:** ⚠ be; find sth ▫ MR SEGAL: *A lot of good that boy will be to you, anywhere in the world. Excuse me, Sam, but you must agree; he's* ***good for nothing****.* HSG ▫ *I once knew a military man who professed to believe that the French were* ***good for nothing****.* AH ▫ *'Their son's old enough to help his father with the outdoor work.' 'What! That* ***good-for-nothing****?'* ▫ *'Did you have any of your dress material left over?' 'Just a heap of* ***good for nothing*** *clippings.'* ▫ n compound a good-for-nothing; attrib use *a load of* ***good for nothing*** *layabouts*, can also be hyphenated.

good going [Comp (NP)] rapid and/or successful travel, performance, progress **V:** ⚠ be; find sth ▫ *Our Australian roads are straight and good, and relatively empty, but even so an average of over fifty* (miles per hour) *was* ***good going****.* RFW ▫ (reader's letter) *Can anyone beat this? After cracking four eggs, I got ten yolks — two trebles and two doubles.* ***Good going****, eh?* DM ▫ *Nine of our sixth-formers gained entry to Oxford or Cambridge that year, which was pretty* ***good going*** *for a provincial Grammar School.* ▫ *Her work is hand-written. For 'Barbed Wire' she finished an episode a month, which is pretty* ***good going****.* TVT

good grief(!) (informal) exclamation of dismay or displeasure ▫ *'And how old's your boyfriend?' 'Twelve. He says I can go and live with him.' 'Eh?' Pop said. He spoke faintly.* ***Good grief****, bit early wasn't it?* BFA ▫ (reader's letter) *'Tapu' was an insult to New Zealand and the Maori people, the Maori being portrayed as a 'cave-dweller who can reach the heights through education' as the so-called Maori King said in the meeting house.* ***Good grief****, who wrote the script?* RT ▫ often accompanies criticisms or objections.

good heavens etc(!) exclamation of alarm, dismay, surprise; or accompanies an assertion, denial, question, to emphasize it **n:** heavens, ⚠ God, Lord ▫ (a nightmare) *His scream came to an end only for want of breath, and as its sound died from his ears he heard his father saying,* ***'Good heavens****, Nicky, are you being murdered?'* DC ▫ *'Margot, are you thinking of marrying Jim?'* ***'Good heavens****, no,' replied Margot, and from that moment on she began to think of it.* H ▫ *'Am I seeing things, or is that Tony getting out of that car?'* ***'Good God****, so it is! Fancy him turning up here.'*

(it's a) good job/thing (that) (informal) (it is) lucky or convenient (that sth is true, does/did happen, etc) ▫ ***It's a good job*** *I can only think of these things as fast as I can write with this stub of pencil.* LLDR ▫ *Forster himself provided his own explanations.* ***It is a good thing*** *he did, because it must be said that words like 'beauty', 'liberty' and 'democracy' are elastic.* AH ▫ *Someone else shouted 'Cops' and these two chaps that had been smoking scooted. Nobody knew who they were. I said,* ***'Good job****, too.'* ST ▫ *'Perhaps you haven't been in love, Mrs Batey?'* ***'Good thing*** *I wasn't, or I'd have shot myself from disappointment long ago.'* AITC ⇨ ⚠ a good/(not) a bad thing.

a good job well done a necessary, or worthwhile, task or undertaking ably carried out or successfully completed ▫ *The ideal of fine quality, of* ***a good job well done*** *(always a bourgeois rather than working class ideal) had accompanied him into the new world.* HD ▫ *The rescue team came home tired and dirty but glowing with the satisfaction of* ***a good job well done****.*

one's/sb's good lady one's/sb's wife ▫ *Photographers are desperately searching for famous faces. There's a senator — and there's Kenneth Galbraith and there's Jo Levine with* ***his good lady****, and there, there is Bobby Fischer.* NS ▫ *As I was just saying to* ***your good lady****, sir, you don't see many of these old water-driven machines nowadays.* ▫ often used to refer pleasantly (and perhaps obsequiously) to wife of man addressed.

the good life the privileged life, real or imagined, of those who can afford to have whatever comforts, luxuries, pleasures they choose □ ***The good life*** *is not simply a matter of 'putting up with things', of 'making the best of it', but one with scope for having the 'bit extra' that really makes 'Life'.* UL □ *It is not easy to admit that there are limitations on the delights of being rich, handsome and successful. But George Lazenby looks at* ***the good life*** *from an unexpectedly critical angle.* RT

a good/bad listener [Comp (NP)] sb who says little but whose sympathetic attention allows, or encourages, others to talk/sb who pays little attention to what others tell them, perhaps because they prefer to do the talking **V:** ⚠ be, become; find sb □ *Fortunately* ***a good listener*** *is always appreciated. Victoria was an excellent listener to the two men and she began to pick up the jargon fairly easily.* TCB □ *I have too active a mind of my own to make* ***a good listener*** *and, if I cannot say my piece, I direct my thoughts elsewhere.* □ also pl; a bad listener found only occas.

a good/bad loser [Comp (NP)] sb who is good-/bad-tempered when beaten in a game, competition etc, or when surpassed by sb else in any activity **V:** ⚠ be; find sb □ *This was the first British Lions team that had been mentally and physically prepared for the demands of a long tour. This team was not content with our traditional acceptance of being jolly* ***good losers.*** L □ *I am* ***a good loser*** *except at games. Show me a contest with little round balls and oblong pieces of coloured paper and I tremble with anxiety.* NS □ *In the old days I was always trying to beat other fellers* (= fellows)*—and if I lost, I was* ***a bad loser.*** TVT

good etc luck to sb may sb be fortunate and successful in general or in sth he is trying to do or obtain **adj:** good, ⚠ better, the best of □ *However, for the time being I was the boss and I decided to get on with the job in my own way. If later someone else was appointed,* ***good luck to*** *him.* MFM □ (reader's letter) ***Good Luck to*** *Radio 1—but keep it for Radio 1 listeners, leave Radio 2 alone, and let us have our decent programmes back.* RT □ *Some of the modern food experts seem to be eating everything raw now.* ***Good luck to*** *them, let them get on with it.* L □ often used with the meaning 'I wish sb no harm'.

a good many ((of) sb/sth) a large, considerable number (of sb/sth); a good few (of sb/sth) (qv) □ *'Get a nice atom bomb dropping down upon Earls Court tonight,' I said. 'That'ld get rid of* ***a good many of*** *us.'* RFW □ *It seems the place hasn't been used as a builder's yard for* ***a good many*** *years.* HD

(all) good men and true honest, worthy, loyal people, esp as a body of responsible citizens, policemen, jurors etc □ *To live one's life in the close companionship of the Force is to adopt a way of life bound by rules and regulations, discouraging to originality and designed to turn out* ***good men and true,*** *formed to a pattern.* NS □ (reader's letter) *And why should one of the few programmes that one finds a complete delight be shown at an hour when* ***all good men and true*** *are fast asleep?* RT □ always in order of headphrase; modern use often facetious.

a good mixer [Comp (NP)] a sociable person; one who can adjust himself to, and be liked by, various kinds, or classes, of people **V:** ⚠ be; find, think, sb □ *Harold was well pleased with the evening; he told Isabel he hadn't thought Goodrich would be such* ***a good mixer.*** PW □ *An expression heard frequently was that so-and-so was* ***a 'good mixer'.*** *A good mixer of drinks, I came to believe, for it soon appeared to me that* ***a good mixer*** *was a man who had never been known to refuse a drink.* MFM □ also pl.

good money [O (NP)] a lot of money, ie money that is hard-earned, not to be wasted, etc **V:** make, earn, get; pay, spend; cost □ PETER: *Oh, you get* ***good money*** *here—but you work!* TK □ JIMMY: *You spend* ***good money*** *on a new pair of trousers, and then sprawl about in them like a savage.* LBA □ *A great sound of wrath came from Ian. It was, I could see, his first encounter with an irate Scot being pressed to pay* ***good money*** *for nothing.* BM

sb's good name [O (NP)] the present, or possible future, good reputation of sb **V:** destroy, damage, injure. **o:** ***(of)*** the school, your country; the family, anyone □ *'Remember,' he said, 'that at all matches, at home or away,* ***the good name*** *not only* ***of*** *your team but* ***of*** *your city is in your hands.'* □ *He has never quite done that* (written a ruthless book)*, perhaps, because he is too kind to debunk, too civilised to destroy,* ***someone's good name.*** SC

(through etc) sb's good offices [A (PrepP)] (because of) services, efforts, influence exerted on behalf of another or others **prep:** through, ⚠ due to, owing to, as a result of □ *Instead, Parkinson went to London and claimed that the retreat of the Cloud was in a large measure* ***due to our good offices.*** TBC □ *In the following year he obtained,* ***through the good offices of*** *a family friend, a post with a publishing firm which, though not highly paid, he found more congenial.* □ *Two or three years ago the Association of Municipal Corporations undertook to take up with various local authorities the question of swimming baths being made available at morning and night* (ie outside working hours) *for top level training. I have not yet heard of* ***their good offices*** *being called upon. Everywhere, athletic facilities are standing idle for much of the week.* OBS □ *'One of the best purchases I've ever made,' said Richard. 'And entirely* ***owing to your good offices.'*** TCB

good old sb/sth(!) a greeting, or reference, to sb/sth for whom/which one feels affection or appreciation □ *They pressed forward, smiling and laughing, shouting* ***Good old*** *George!* L □ *Only another week, Fay, and we'll be back in* ***good old*** *Bristol, meeting all our friends again.* □ *Cotton or polyester-cotton slacks in a galaxy of colours and three sizes are £1-99, while* ***good old*** *blue denims are only 89p.* SC

the good/bad old days periods in history, or in one's personal past, when conditions of life and work were (in the speaker's opinion) better/worse than they are at present □ *In the 1930s maids' wages were around £25 a year all found. These were certainly not* ***'the good old***

***days**,' and it took another war to end it all.* RT □ HENRY: *That's what hell will be like, small chat about **the good old days**.* E □ *To the miners, decentralisation signals a return to **the bad old days** of cut throat competition, with area boards instead of private owners.* DM □ *It is always to somebody's advantage to persuade you that **the Bad Old Days** ended when you were born.* NS

good and proper [adj + adj non-rev] (informal) proper(ly); valid(ly); thorough(ly) □ *Nobody will be excused their turn of duty except for a **good and proper** reason, such as illness.* □ *He could see just exactly what George was worth and put the screws on* (= blackmailed) *him **good and proper**.* PE □ (I) *caught him with a razor blade at my Renoir book. Clipped his ear **good and proper**.* TT □ *It is right that we should have this scabrous aspect of Genet revealed to us and we get it **good and proper** (or bad and improper) at the Aldwych Theatre.* ST □ usu functions as adv phrase of degree, though adj in form.

good and ready etc (informal) completely, thoroughly, very, ready etc **adj/adv:** ready, large, deep, hot, early □ STANLEY: *I think you'd better go to bed.* CLIVE: *I'll go to my bed when I'm **good and ready**.* FE □ *I meant to get up **good and early** and take a walk before breakfast.* □ good and functions as adv of degree.

good riddance (to bad rubbish) (saying) exclamation or comment of relief at having got rid of, or no longer having to endure, sb/sth unwanted or disliked □ *As Professor Talbot had been nothing but a very selfish, cross, complaining old gentleman and bedridden and senile for the last five years of his life, everyone had felt: And a **Good Riddance**.* WDM □ *These are the sucker students on whom commercial correspondence colleges (many budget for an 80 to 90 per cent drop-out, collect a fat fee and quietly say '**good riddance**') positively thrive.* NS □ *There's nothing worth stealing in the house except your Uncle Michael's silver cups and trophies; and **good riddance to bad rubbish** if they were stolen!*

a good Samaritan a person who helps another in distress or difficulty—perhaps with loss or inconvenience, and certainly with no profit, to himself (in allusion to LUKE X 30-37) □ *Claud Cockburn has taken the story of **the Good Samaritan** and has immersed himself in it imaginatively. Mr Cockburn's key theme is the danger of disinterestedness.* ST □ *I was really in a hurry to get home to watch a football match on telly but I decided to be **a good Samaritan** and turn back with her without saying so.* SC □ also pl.

(a) good etc show(!) a creditable, praiseworthy etc mode of conduct or action, esp in difficult circumstances **adj:** good, ⚠ first-class; bad, poor □ *She felt that his effort for the drowned man had been **a good show** and she told him so.* RFW □ *In the words of Osborne, who leads the raid, the important thing is to put up **a 'good show'**.* NS □ *Once she had put that scarf into Mr Dakin's hands, perhaps her task would be done. He would say to her, perhaps, like on the pictures: 'Oh! **Good show**, Victoria.'* TCB □ *He does admit to once turning down a book about a horrible dog. 'It was full of things like "**Jolly good show**" and "I say, chaps".'* OBS □ *Marcuse argues that such social repression of genuine feeling has gone too far—though it may be **a 'bad show'** for officers to cry it does not mean that 'emotion' need become a term of abuse in everyday life.* ST □ good show! without article an expression of approval or praise; dated upper-class public-school or military slang but still used mockingly as supposedly representative of usage of those groups.

a good/(not) a bad thing [Comp (NP)] desirable, beneficial/(not) undesirable, harmful in nature or result **S:** competition, indirect taxation; democracy, having to fend for onself. **V:** ⚠ be, seem, look like, prove □ *There are some places for which it's not easy to find a properly cogent reason for a national identity—except that independence is **a Good Thing**, in the abstract.* L □ *My caddie suggested that it would be **a good thing** if he accompanied me to Rye for the University match.* ST □ *Fifty years ago, of course, nobody had the least idea that competition in the classroom was **a Bad Thing**.* NS □ *In this remarkable first novel different forms of romance, the real and the spurious, jostle against each other. In case anyone is wondering whether this is **a good thing**, I will tell you that it is **a** very **good thing**.* NS □ esp with capitals, deliberately parodied from Sellar and Yeatman's comic history, '1066, And All That' (1930). ⇨ ⚠ (it's a) good job/thing (that).

the good things in/of life [O (NP)] material comforts, luxuries, pleasures **V:** provide, supply; desire, crave □ *He drove off past the lighted shop windows, full of television sets and bottles of intoxicating liquors and other selections from **the good things in life**.* TGLY □ *His talent has brought him **the good things in life** but not happiness.* NS □ *Brezhnev had made a very fundamental change of policy back in about 1971, when they decided that the Soviet citizenry would be treated with better consumer goods—more food, more of **the good things of life**.* L

(a) good wine needs no bush (saying) anything of good quality will become known and appreciated on its own merits and should not need to be advertised or boasted about (formerly, a bundle of ivy hung outside a building was a sign that liquor could be bought within) □ *If it be true that **good wine needs no bush**, 'tis true that a good play needs no epilogue.* AS YOU LIKE IT: EPILOGUE □ *The revised edition of Janouch's remarkable memoir **needs no bush** from me, but let me commend 'American Violence' available as a sizeable Vintage paperback.* NS □ ***A good wine needs no bush**. If the piece is a good as you say it is, stop talking about it and let me hear it for myself.* □ can be used in part and allusively, as shown.

good works charitable or welfare work □ (source) *Now there was at Joppa a certain disciple named Tabitha: this woman was full of **good works** and almsdeeds which she did.* ACTS IX 36 □ *She put an envelope* (containing a donation) *in Mrs Paxton's hand which that lady, who was very practical and in the cause of **good works** had no shyness or reticence, at once opened.* WDM □ *...produced by the Further Education Department of the BBC at those advanced and sleepy hours usually reserved for minority interests like gods, poetry and **good***

works. RT

the goodies and (the) baddies [n + n non-rev] (informal) the (groups of) people representing good and evil in stories, films etc of adventure, crime, espionage □ *Mr Hurd has very simple ideas of right and wrong. His novel, 'Truth Game', lines up* ***the goodies and baddies*** *as clearly as any two-bit* (= cheap) *Western.* NS □ *It doesn't often happen in world politics that* ***the goodies*** *defeat* ***the baddies****. It happens even more rarely outside strip cartoons that* ***the*** *little* ***goodies*** *beat* ***the*** *big* ***baddies*** *not once but several times.* L

(my) goodness (me)(!) exclamation of (mild) astonishment, pleasure or dismay □ *He looked at me, then put out his hand to feel the texture of my suit. 'High grade worsted,' he said. 'And look at that shirt and tie!* ***My goodness****, Mr Lampton, however do you manage on your* (clothes rationing) *coupons?' 'He has connections,' Reggie said.* RATT □ *'Oh,* ***goodness me****, child,' his grandmother fussed, 'wherever did you learn such a horrid word as that?'* □ *So here you are at last, James.* ***My goodness me****, it has been a long time!* □ stress patterns ˌmy ˈgoodness, ˌgoodness ˈme, my ˌgoodness ˈme.

goods and chattels [n + n non-rev] (sb's) belongings or part of them □ *She piled various* ***goods and chattels*** *into Wayne's pram till you couldn't see the baby for the articles surrounding him.* NS □ *It's amazing, the amount of* ***goods and chattels*** *my husbands finds it necessary to take with him on a fortnight's holiday.* □ *The old boss knew the workers by name—but not this chap. We're just* ***goods and chattels****, nothing more.* □ chattel (legal term for an article of moveable property) not common usage except in this expression.

one's gorge rises one feels nausea or disgust **A:** at the thought (of sth), at the sight (of sth), at the sound (of sth) □ *She knew instinctively of what he was going to talk, and she tried in vain to stop* ***her gorge rising****.* HAA □ *He knew, though* ***his gorge rose*** *at the sight of it, that he'd have to drink the greasy soup or give deep offence to his hosts.* □ variant make one's gorge rise.

grace and favour [n + n non-rev] (formal) goodwill (from a superior) as distinct from duty or obligation □ *Princess Margaret and Mr Armstrong-Jones spent about two hours looking over their new home — the* ***grace-and-favour*** *residence in Kensington Palace, London—yesterday.* DM □ *The police are responsible for the* (mountain) *rescue equipment itself although this responsibility is on what one might describe as '****grace and favour****' terms.* OBS □ attrib use *a* ***grace-and-favour*** *residence.*

gracious living (catchphrase) a luxurious, or refined, standard of domestic furnishings, arrangements and daily management □ *Until now there have not been the same rich pickings for senior members of the Bar as there are in England but most top Scottish Silk can amass somewhere between £10,000 and £20,000 a year. However, they do enjoy* ***gracious living*** *in delightful surroundings.* OBS □ *Myra had become a symbol of possession, achievement, of ease, of having it good: what the ad man, in his sickening dialect, calls '****gracious living****.'* CON □ *All* (transatlantic liners) *had the same idea of* ***gracious living****: that is, you wandered through unaccustomed opulence in a dinner-jacket, then retired to a crowded box to remove your trousers before strangers* (ie returned to a shared cabin). L

(in) the grand manner (with) a confident display of wealth, superiority, authority, ability, style etc □ *There is a touch of* ***the grand manner*** *about her — the overtones of her strong, flexible voice, her elegant frankness.* TVT □ *It is not only the piano that is grand. Here is a hint of* ***the grand manner*** *as well—and that is something that is rare in contemporary life.* T □ *Dickens was a traditional Victorian father* ***in the grand manner****, as the Tuesday series 'Dickens of London' shows.* TVT

a Grand Old Man (of sth) an old, or elderly, person of outstanding ability and a long history of achievement in his own field (first said in 1882 of William Gladstone, British Prime Minister) □ *He looked back over his long years of struggle and victory. For* ***a Grand Old Man of*** *Letters it had become fairly plain sailing.* HAA □ (Fred Streeter) ***The grand*** *but gentle* ***old man of*** *English gardens, who is now an amazing 94, started work when he was 12 for 2s 6d a week.* RT □ *Britain today has two* ***Grand Old Men*** *in her two great ex-Prime Ministers.* OBS □ sometimes abbreviated to GOM; occas pl.

grasp/seize the nettle [V + O pass] deal with a difficult matter firmly; use bold measures to rid oneself of an obstacle, solve a problem □ *Our object must now be to bring the Western Germans into the community of Western nations. But if we were to do this, we would have to* ***grasp the nettle*** *firmly with both hands.* MFM □ *If the extra road space is denied, it can be argued that the effect in time will be to deny car ownership to the lower income groups. Who, may I ask, is going to* ***grasp this nettle****?* L □ *Lord Gladwyn said it was arguable that, if* ***the*** *political* ***nettle*** *had been* ***seized*** *earlier, success would have resulted.* SC □ *'Time for Action', one of the more costly new ventures,* ***grasping*** *daunting* ***nettles*** *by the handful, deserved to go out on the air more often.* L

the grass is (always) greener on the other side (of the fence)/in the other man's field (saying) people are inclined to think that in another country, job etc they would be better off, happier, than they are in their present circumstances □ *He thinks* ***the grass is always greener in the other man's field****. He has a constant feeling that the party was last night and he missed it.* OBS □ *'They do things differently in France. The independent artist is respected over there.' 'Oh, sure.* ***The grass is always greener on the other side of the fence.****'* □ (NONCE) *It is horribly expensive to play golf in America. And when you consider the relatively improved rewards in other parts of the world, then* ***the grass on the other side of the Atlantic*** *does not* ***look*** *all that much* ***greener****.* OBS

the grass roots the basic level; the natural, or popular, sources from which a society, art, political system, etc must draw its strength □ (histories of working-class movements) *Their authors overrate the place of political activity in working-class life, they do not always have an adequate sense of* ***the grass roots*** *of that life.*

UL ▫ *Politically, there was the fact of colonial rule and, initially at least, a lack of contacts at* ***grass roots*** *level between rulers and ruled.* NS ▫ *They were men who admitted no loyalty other than to the international Communist cause, who spoke for no native* ***grass-root*** *aspirations.* OBS ▫ *The Arts Council, sensing* ***a grass-roots*** *movement, show the colour if not the weight of their money.* OBS ▫ *The word 'community', like '****grass-roots****', has come to suggest a lot of well-educated people shouting and swearing in the American manner.* L ▫ attrib use *a* ***grass-roots*** *movement, the* ***grass roots*** *level.*

a grass widow a married women whose husband is temporarily absent on holiday, because of his work, etc ▫ *Look, what about coming round on Tuesday and cheering me up when I'm* ***a grass widow****?* TGLY ▫ also pl.

the gravy train (informal) an easy means of getting much money and other benefits (from gravy (US slang) = 'easily acquired money or financial success') ▫ *North Sea oil has transformed a faintly cranky brotherhood into a serious political force. The aim of most Scottish National supporters is to book their seats on* ***the*** *new high-speed* ***gravy train****.* TIMES LITERARY SUPPLEMENT ▫ ***The Gravy Train*** *Rolls On. Two whole mornings were spent wrangling in parliamentary committee on the correct name for the new Independent Broadcasting Authority.* NS

grease sb's palm [V + O pass] (informal) give sb money either as a tip or as a bribe ▫ *'The waiter says all the corner tables are booked.' 'You should have tried* ***greasing his palm****.'* ▫ also pl grease their palms.

great and small [n + n non-rev] people of all ranks, grades of office, importance ▫ *Cromwell, efficient policeman that he was, filed away all the reports he was sent concerning the treasonable utterances of* ***great and small****, up and down the country.* ST ▫ *Another feature of the last five years has been the introduction at BBC board meetings of the counting of heads of every conceivable subject* ***great or small****.* NS ▫ also [adj + adj non-rev], and always end position when used thus.

the great wen London ▫ (source) *But what is to be the fate of* ***the great wen*** *of all? The monster, called 'the metropolis of the empire'?* RURAL RIDES (W COBBETT 1762-1835) ▫ *The Metropolitan Railway Company wooed commuters with cheap season tickets and the promise of pastoral pleasure at the end of each day's labour in* ***the great wen****.* RT ▫ originally derogatory, but now often used merely to name the city.

(I'm) the greatest (catchphrase) (I am) the best; (I am) better than anyone else—either in a specific group or field or absolutely (from a remark made by the boxer, Muhammad Ali, about himself) **S:** I, you, he, she, we, they ▫ *80% of young people who send me their manuscripts don't want advice. They just want to be told they're the best.* ***The greatest.*** ▫ *O'Connor? No, not Des.* Tom. *Tom O'Connor from Bootle. Never heard of him? In Liverpool,* ***he's the greatest****.* TVT

the greatest thing since sliced bread (catchphrase) sb/sth new, or of recent introduction, that is much admired or appreciated ▫ *I went with the sting of ambition—this was going to be* ***the greatest thing since sliced bread****. I walked out on that stage and I was going to show them Mr Showbusiness.* L ▫ ▫ *My husband uses this stuff now for all repair jobs about the house. He thinks it's* ***the greatest thing since sliced bread****.*

the Greeks had a name/word for it (catchphrase) reminder that a human condition or activity, an idea, scientific theory, physical fact or object, etc has existed and been known about for a very long time ▫ *'I thought I heard a sort of rumbling noise. Yes, there it is again.' 'Rumbling in the guts. My guts were rumbling.' 'Of course, of course—Yes, yes,* ***the Greeks had a name for it****, eh?'* RM ▫ ***The Greeks had a word for*** *the contemptuous disregard North and South showed for their opponents. It is hubristic.* T

green with envy [Comp (AdjP)] extremely, or resentfully, envious of what another has or does **V:** ⚠ be, go, turn; make sb ▫ *I do wish I could handle mine* (ie my pupils) *the way you do yours, it makes me* ***green with envy****.* TT ▫ *However, clothing manufacturers in Leeds are, without doubt,* ***green with envy*** *at the prices Savile Row can charge and get away with.* ST

a grey eminence a background figure in government, administration etc who has considerable power in an influential, or advisory, capacity (anglicization of *éminence grise* (French), often left untranslated in English writing) ▫ *Both are truly* ***grey eminences*** *who have become accustomed to the delectable pursuit, the exercise of influence.* ST ▫ *By then the Six* (a European economic coalition in the 1950s) *had formed the Coal and Steel Community, invented and headed by that French* ***grey eminence*** *of genius, Jean Monnet.* L ⇨ ⚠ the power behind the throne.

grey matter brain tissue; mental powers; intelligence; common sense ▫ MARTIN: *He's all right, really, Joe Turner, not much* ***grey matter****, but a good worker.* OI ▫ *It's not for want of* ***grey matter*** *he does so badly at school. He's just lazy.* ▫ *Encourage the older patients to play card games or do simple jig-saw puzzles—anything that keeps the* ***grey matter*** *in use.*

grievous bodily harm [O (NP)] (legal) the infliction of severe physical injury **V:** cause, inflict; suffer ▫ *In the legal sense the intention to cause* ***grievous bodily harm*** *constitutes murder if the victim dies.* OBS ▫ *Now the neuro-surgeon is charged, jointly with the psychiatrist who recommended the operation, with causing* ***grievous bodily harm*** *to Mrs Williams.* TVT ▫ informally abbreviated to GBH.

grin and bear it [v + v non-rev] (informal) endure sth unpleasant cheerfully or, at least, without complaint ▫ *He would* ***grin and bear it****, pretend he was pleased to act as a model to so great an artist.* US ▫ with *must, have to, will, would; etc*; for reference to past time *I had to* ***grin and bear it****, there was nothing for it but to* ***grin and bear it****,* (occas) *I* ***grinned and bore it****.*

grin like a Cheshire cat (continue to) grin or smile, esp in a senseless or inappropriate way (from an old simile of obscure origin, that was further developed in ALICE'S ADVENTURES IN WONDERLAND (L CARROLL 1832-98) in which there is a Cheshire Cat who could disappear except for his grin which remained visible) ▫ *Gone are* *the days when the photographer's, 'Smile, please', kept us transfixed,* ***grinning like Cheshire cats*** *while he fiddled with his camera.* □ *The population may have vanished, but the hospital remains on its site, like* ***the grin on*** *the face of* ***the Cheshire cat.*** L □ *A face stuck out of the shop door. It made a short speech then, suddenly giving it up, it leered. When the face had gone the leer seemed to hang there, 6ft above the ground,* ***like the Cheshire Cat's grin.*** TVT □ (hallucinations of fever) *They were* ***Cheshire-cat smiles,*** *with no face or outlines, and I could see the room clearly through them.* CWR □ variants have/with a grin (on one's face) like a Cheshire cat, (like) a Cheshire cat's grin/smile, a Cheshire-cat grin/smile.

grind the faces of the poor etc (in the dust) [V + O] oppress poor people, any underprivileged group, by exploiting their labour, or by denying them any chance to improve their conditions **o:** the poor, their subjects, the captives; honest workers □ *What mean ye that ye beat my people to pieces, and* ***grind the faces of the poor****? saith the Lord God of hosts.* ISAIAH III 15 □ *Contemplatives* (= contemplative men) *do not as a rule preach intolerance, or make war; do not find it necessary to rob, swindle, or* ***grind the faces of the poor.*** DOP □ *The trouble at Chobham Farm container depot is not a case of a tyrannical employer* ***grinding the faces of honest men in the dust.***

grind one's teeth [V + O] grind the upper and lower teeth against each other as an accompaniment, or reaction, to pain, stress, frustration etc; gnashing of teeth (qv) □ *Daniel came home slowly, on his fiery feet,* ***grinding his teeth*** *as each rod of pain probed upwards from his toes into his forehead.* US □ *He* ***ground his teeth*** *and forced himself down and the rock was so sharp against his knees that he reopened the wounds of the first day.* PM □ *A hundred yards ahead he saw the gates of the level-crossing start to close and he* ***ground his teeth*** *with frustration.* □ (NONCE) *On hillsides and in deep rough, trolleys are inclined to get on one wheel and turn over. It's one of the most* ***teeth-grinding*** *experiences in golf.* SC □ attrib use *a* ***teeth-grinding*** *experience.*

grist to/for sb's mill [Comp (NP)] sth that one can seize, make use of, turn to one's own purposes **V:** ⚠ be; regard sth as □ (the hairy armadillo) *Nearly everything is* ***grist to his mill.*** *He will eat fruit and vegetables or even a snake, should he happen to meet one.* DF □ *Questionnaires became very popular indeed in the years between the wars. They provided so much* ***grist for the*** *statistical* ***mill of*** *the psychologists' calculating machines.* SNP

grit one's teeth [V + O pass] clench one's jaw so that the teeth close hard against each other; (fig) decide definitely (clenching one's jaw or not) to do sth difficult, to resist pressure, etc □ *The swimming baths terrified me as a child. But rather than be made a fool of by the other boys I would* ***grit my teeth*** *and jump in.* □ *'People are a trial and a trouble, aren't they?' she added, in that voice which must have greased the way to many a confession. But I* ***gritted my teeth*** *against speech.* UTN □ ***Grit your teeth*** *while watching ITV's 'Opportunity Knocks'. But spare a thought for the production team. Every year they audition 10,000 acts, most of them awful, to bring you the 175.* L □ *...convince the citizenry that it faces disaster unless prodigal ways are mended, facts faced, belts tightened,* ***teeth gritted*** *and wallets opened.* NS □ often in construction ***grit one's teeth*** *and do sth.*

grow grey in the service of sth have a long and creditable record of service to sth **o:** country; firm, family; art □ *Who can doubt that such a man,* ***grown grey in the service of*** *a nation, would have acquired an extraordinary prestige?* OBS □ *You would think a well-to-do family would have had more consideration for an old dependent* ***grown grey in their service.*** □ often facetious.

grow old gracefully accept one's advancing years and adjust one's habits and outlook suitably, not trying to appear younger than one is nor becoming resentful, depressed, careless of one's appearance, etc □ *I have a distinct sense of the passing of time, and I do want to* ***grow old gracefully.*** *I don't want to be some kind of ageing pop singer.* RT □ *I don't think he's the type to* ***grow old gracefully****—more likely to write complaining letters to the press and the BBC.*

growing pains vague aches and pains felt by children; (fig) mistakes and troubles that occur when a new enterprise, popular movement, business concern, etc is being set up □ *The result* (of paying high wages) *was splendid service for the first month followed, after pay-day, by 75 per cent absenteeism. This is called '****growing pains****'.* NS □ *The disaffections that threaten to disrupt the three-year-old republic are more than just* ***growing pains.***

a grown man/woman an adult; sb who has, or should have, common sense; sb who will behave reasonably □ *The assumption that the world is divided into good and evil, with each side immediately recognisable on sight, is scarcely creditable in* ***any grown man.*** NS □ *We know and respect each other, and we're both* ***grown men.*** *I think I ought to tell you what this is all about without mincing words. You're in bad trouble.* ST □ *He was too much masked behind his mocking, paternal attitude for any proper relationship with* ***a grown woman.*** MM

a/one's guardian angel a heavenly spirit that watches over, protects and helps one; a person in real life who seems to fit such a role □ *You thought you had* ***a guardian angel.*** *Well, you did, only you were looking for him in the wrong place.* AITC □ *Tony has crashed fast cars, jumped from burning buildings, been swept down rapids, more times than you and I have had hot dinners. 'A stunt man,' he says, 'needs to have* ***a*** *good* ***guardian angel.*** □ also pl.

a guiding light/star [Comp (NP)] sb who gives a lead, or sets an example, that is followed by another or others **V:** ⚠ be, become; see sb as □ (a television programme) *Ian Hendry was in 'The Avengers' for the first nine months of its life. He was* ***the guiding light,*** *the inventive genius.* TVT □ *What I dislike about her is that she is so self-satisfied. She tries to set herself up as* ***a guiding star*** *to everyone she knows.* □ *They said I was a menace to honest lads like Mike and that I was the brains behind the job,* ***the guiding light*** *when it came to making up anybody's mind.* LLDR

a guinea pig [Comp (NP)] sb/sth made use of,

willingly or not, for testing medical, scientific, administrative etc experiments (the reference originally being to laboratory experiments on animals) **V:** ⚠ be; act, serve, as □ *The psychological material at his disposal was still absurdly inadequate, and he was anxious to add to it. I was on the spot and willing, indeed eager, to be* ***a guinea pig****.* DOP □ *I could get free board and lodging in exchange for being* ***a guinea pig*** *in a cold-cure experiment.* UTN □ also pl.

guns or butter [n + n non-rev] symbols of alternatives between which a country must choose, ie national power and prestige, contrasted with the personal welfare and prosperity of its citizens □ (source—translation of a broadcast speech by Hermann Goering, 1936) ***Guns*** *will make us powerful;* ***butter*** *will only make us fat.* □ (NONCE) *In the current Soviet Five-Year Plan, great emphasis is laid on improving the living conditions of the Soviet people. In short, it comes down to: fewer* ***missiles****, more* ***butter****.* L

the gutter press newspapers, weekly papers, etc filled with the kind of material which appeals to uninformed or vulgar tastes □ *'Something that really catches the public's eye. Say an important series of articles on some scandal.' There was something almost fine in the selfless zeal with which he worshipped the glory of* ***the gutter press****.* HD □ (reader's letter) *Report the news by radio as you deem best, but do not drop to the sensational level of* ***the gutter press****.* RT

H

hail and farewell (formal) a greeting, or comment, on seeing sb and saying goodbye to him simultaneously or within a very short space of time (a translation of *ave atque vale*—the Latin poet Catullus's last salutation made at the grave of a brother who had died during his absence) □ *We are here this evening to bid* ***hail and farewell*** *to George Oxford, who has captained our match team for the last few years.* PE □ *Professor Colman and I had been in correspondence with each other at various times but our sole meeting was a '****hail and farewell****' affair of a few minutes' duration in the departure lounge at Orly Airport.* □ often facetious; attrib use *a* ***hail and farewell*** *affair.*

hail fellow well met (with sb) [Comp (AdjP)] friendly in a confident or (too) familiar way, esp when greeting, meeting, approaching or receiving, sb **V:** ⚠ be, become; get. **o:** everyone, me □ *It doesn't do to be too* ***hail-fellow-well-met with*** *employees over whom you may have to exercise your authority later.* □ *The Agriculture Minister has a bluff and cheerful manner. No such* ***hail fellow*** *tactics were involved in the Environment and Transport Councils.* NS □ attrib use *a rather* ***hail-fellow-well-met*** *approach*; shortened form in last example is unusual.

a/the hair of the dog (that bit one) (informal) a glass of beer, spirits etc taken (esp on the morning after heavy drinking) to offset or help to remove the effects of drunkenness □ *Poor old Gitty, looking as though she needed something on the stronger side of tea to do her much good,* ***a hair of the dog that bit her****.* TT □ *I was a dissipated traveller—dissipated in a gentlemanly sort of way, looking forward to the hot bath,* ***the hair-of-the-dog****, the black coffee, and the snooze in the silk dressing gown.* RATT

hale and hearty [adj + adj non-rev] in vigorous good health □ *Being still* ***hale and hearty*** *in spite of his seventy years, my father was able to add to his pension by selling vegetables from his garden.* □ DOBSON: *These places* (youth hostels) *really do cater for the* ***hale and hearty****, don't they?* ITAJ □ esp said of elderly people; [n + n] in last example.

half cut [Comp (AdjP)] (informal) somewhat, but not completely, drunk; half seas over (qv) **V:** ⚠ be, seem, look □ *How many executives can work reasonably effectively unless they are* ***half-cut****?* RT □ *Go and sleep it off, and we'll take the morning tide. These are no waters to be negotiating with a navigator that's* ***half cut****.*

half the fun etc (of (doing) sth) much of the enjoyment (got from sth/doing sth) **n:** fun, ⚠ pleasure, thrill □ ***Half the fun of*** *coming home was to come back to all the things you knew and remembered.* □ *I didn't enjoy all that bobbing around on moorings, brewing up and having bacon and eggs, which yachtsmen say is* ***half the fun****.* TVT

half and half [A] (in) two equal portions; or (in) an equal mixture of two ingredients, qualities, feelings □ *'How do you like your coffee?' Mary asked. '****Half and half*** *please, and no sugar.'* □ *'Are you looking forward to your trip?' '****Half and half****, really. In some ways I'd rather just stay at home and have a good rest.'* □ esp as a response; as a v qualifier, always in end position, eg *Let's share it* ***half and half****,* not * *Let's* ***half and half*** *share it.*

half a loaf is better than no bread/none (saying) having to accept less than one expects, or feels entitled to, is better than having nothing; it is better to compromise in one's demands than risk losing all □ *'You do understand, don't you, that the operation will only partially restore your eyesight?' 'Well, even* ***half a loaf is better than no bread****.'* □ *Realising that they couldn't prevent raw materials coming in through the docks, the strikers decided that* ***half a loaf was better than none*** *and accepted a 10% wage increase instead of the 15% originally demanded.*

half a mo etc [Disj (NP)] (informal) wait for a short time; just a minute (qv) (the implication being, until the speaker does, remembers, thinks of, sth). **n:** mo(ment), ⚠ sec(ond), minute; jiffy, tick □ *'****Half a mo****. Stay a few minutes.' But I was already on my feet.* HAA □ *'There's no bus after 10pm,' he said, studying the time table. '****Half a sec****. There's a later one on Saturdays and Sundays.'*

(in) half a mo etc [O/A (NP)] (informal) (in) a very short time **V:** take, wait, be; be there (***in***); do sth (***in***). **n:** mo(ment), ⚠ sec(ond), minute;

jiffy, tick □ *'Don't go without me,' Jill called. 'I'll be downstairs* ***in half a mo****.'* □ *'I'll ask him when I next see him.' 'Don't be lazy. It'll only take* ***half a tick*** *to ring him up now.'*

half seas over [Comp (AdjP)] drunk, but not helplessly or violently so; half cut (qv) **V:** ⚠ be, seem, look □ *Look at Frank—**half seas over** already, and the party's hardly begun.* □ *He spoke with the careful enunciation of a man who knows he is **half seas over** but does not wish to be thought so.*

half the time [A (NP)] very, or too, often □ HELEN: *I never used to be sure when he was being serious, or when he wasn't.* CLIFF: *I don't think he knows himself **half the time**.* LBA □ *Don't ask Ted! **Half the time**, he's too drunk to know whether he's coming or going.* □ front, middle or end position.

(in) half the time [O/o (NP)] (in) a much shorter time than expected; a considerable, or too long a, time **V:** take; do sth ***(in)*** □ *'Some painter he is!' her husband grumbled. 'I could have done the job myself, in **half the time**, and far better too.'* □ *If I have company on the way, the walk to the village seems to take only **half the time**.* □ *'Johnson didn't finish his literature paper.' 'I'm not surprised. He spent **half the time** staring out of the window.'*

half the trouble (with sb/sth) (informal) a considerable part of what is wrong or unsatisfactory (about sb/sth); a significant contributory cause (of sbs/sth's faults or shortcomings) □ *'The department should be running more smoothly, now that it's fully staffed.' 'That's **half the trouble**. Everybody leaves things for somebody else to do.'* □ ***Half the trouble with*** *kids like Tony is that they've been spoiled. Give children everything and they're satisfied with nothing.* □ often functions as S or Comp of *be*.

a halfway house a resting-place that marks half of a journey completed; the middle stage in a process or undertaking likely to be completed; a compromise between opposite attitudes, procedures etc □ *All this assumes President Nixon's complicity in the original crime or in the subsequent cover-up. Should this complicity be proven Congress will have to bite the bullet and move toward impeachment. There is **no halfway house**.* NS

the hall of fame the number of great and famous persons; those remembered as being outstanding in a particular profession or skill **det:** mountaineering's, the mountaineering, vaudeville's, his country's, the medical □ *One can qualify for **the hall of fame** by murdering sufficient people in a sufficiently interesting fashion.* □ *Men like Walter Parry Haskett-Smith, and the remarkable O.G. Jones have earned their place in mountaineering**'s hall of fame**.* SC

hand in glove (with sb) [Comp/A (NP)] in close, often conspiratorial, association and/or co-operation (with each other) **V:** be, seem; work, operate □ *'You must speak to the doctor, Granny Barnacle,' said Miss Taylor, 'if you really feel you aren't getting the right treatment from the Ward Sister.' 'The doctor, my backside. They're **hand in glove**. What's an old woman to them I ask you?'* MM □ (BBC television) *Our aim is to run two channels **hand in glove**, and in such a way as to provide choice programme by programme.* L □ *Unprogressive managements like this are much too common. They cause half the trouble and work **hand in glove with** communism for the downfall of the system.* SC

hand in hand [A] side by side with hands linked **V:** sit, walk; come in, go off □ *One of the genial moments of the film finds them gazing raptly at an exploding helicopter before wandering off into the desert **hand in hand**.* NS

hand over fist [A] with rapid alternative movements of the hands, as when climbing a rope; pulling, or gathering, sth towards oneself; (fig) continuously and rapidly, esp said of making big profits from business **V:** haul (it) in; make, coin, money □ *I was lucky to land the fish. My reel jammed and I had to lay the rod down and haul the line in **hand over fist**.* □ *They're making money **hand over fist**, but anyone capable of counting up to ten can do that nowadays.* RATT □ hand and fist non-rev; usu end position after inf or continuous tenses.

hand over heart [A] sincerely; honestly **V:** declare, state, affirm, sth □ *I ask you, in a society which repeatedly declares, **hand over heart**, that the child's interests are always paramount in these disputes, how damned hypocritical can we be?* RT □ variant with one's hand on one's heart.

the hand that rocks the cradle (rules the world) (saying) the example and influence of a mother are powerful and far-reaching in their effects □ *And **the hand that rocks the cradle**/Is the hand that **rules the World**.* W R WALLACE 1819-1881 □ *In recent years **the hand that rocked the cradle** has reached out to grasp the stethoscope, the barrister's brief, and the ministerial portfolio.* □ (reader's letter) *What a pity that your Special Report on the Modern Woman was written from the standpoint of the young, educated, English townswoman. This not very lovable of species does not yet **rule the world**, though **her hand** may have ceased to **rock the cradle**.* G

hand-to-hand fighting etc warfare or struggle 'at close quarters' (qv) involving bodily attack and defence **n:** fighting, ⚠ combat; contest, encounter □ *One scene taken from high ground of an attack over open ground, including **hand-to-hand fighting**, showed the horror, the courage, and the bravery of war.* RT □ *Wars become depersonalized, and **hand-to-hand combat** is replaced by machine warfare.* SNP □ *One did not connect the ships with their future; only with their immediate present, their **hand-to-hand encounter** with the grey, monotonous sea.* PW □ variant fight, contend, grapple etc hand to hand.

hands off (sb/sth) (informal) not take, touch, interfere (with sb/sth); not criticize, judge or find fault (with sb/sth) □ *I think it may have been on that very day that the newsbill carried the slogan, **Hands Off** China!* AH □ ***Hands off*** *free English! Up with warmth and spontaneity, down with scholastic rules!* NS □ usu imper; often (part of) a printed or shouted slogan. ⇨ keep one's hands off (Vol 1).

handsome is as handsome does (saying) good looks alone are not enough; character and behaviour are more important than good looks □ *I'm quite pleased with my old Morris, thank* *you.* ***Handsome is as handsome does*** *is my motto for cars as well as people.*

hang fire fail to fire, or delay in firing; (fig) fail to be carried out and completed as expected, or suffer delay in being carried out **S:** pistol, gun; scheme, project; play, show, concert, performance □ *He was checking its action this morning. 'Not much use being quick on the draw if your pistol* ***hangs fire****,' he said.* □ *The completed play had* ***hung fire*** *for five years, with no-one willing to chance his arm on a fairly spectacular production.* SC ⇨ ⚠ hold one's fire.

hanged/hung, drawn and quartered [Comp (AdjP)] suffer a savage process of criminal execution; (facetious) be severely chastized or reprimanded **V:** ⚠ be, have sb, order sb to be □ *He glared at me the message that he would have preferred to transport me to Australia or have me* ***hanged, drawn and quartered.*** G □ *I'll sue the council for every penny it's got! I'll have you* ***hung, drawn and quartered****. And whipped!* HHGG

hanging is too good for sb (catchphrase) sb deserves a much worse fate even than to be hanged **o:** him, the likes of you, traitors □ (source) ***Hanging is too good for him****, said Mr Cruelty.* THE PILGRIM'S PROGRESS (J BUNYAN 1628-88) □ *It's the child molesters that sicken me.* ***Hanging's too good for them.*** □ *She had an unfortunate experience, we know, but now she talks about all doctors as if* ***hanging was too good for them.*** □ used to express disgust or exasperation.

a hanging judge a judge who (esp in former times when the death penalty was allowed for many types of crime) sentenced persons to death much more frequently than was the general practice; still used of judges apt to pass harsh sentences □ *The effect was that of* ***a hanging judge****, a jolly old* bon viveur *sentencing some poor devil of a labourer or clerk to death by dislocation of the neck.* RATT □ *'What's happening here? It looks like a court martial.' 'It is a court martial.' At 11.35 the Colonel came out; he looked hot and angry as he strode towards the lift. There goes* ***a hanging judge****, thought Wormold.* OMIH □ stress pattern a 'hanging judge.

the happiest days of one's life (cliché) one's childhood and school days (often used to remind children how fortunate they are in not being working adults) □ *Schooldays, the saying goes, are* ***the happiest days of your life.*** *If you'd told that to Nicholas Nickleby, hero of Dickens's novel, you'd have got a bitter reply.* RT □ *All this talk of* ***the happiest days of your life*** *is bunkum to me. I have no happy memories of my childhood.* OBS

happy the bride the sun shines on (saying) sunshine is a good omen on a wedding day □ *It was an appropriate day for an artist's wedding;* ***happy the bride the sun shines on****, and happy the painter for whose wedding Nature gives a really convincing imitation of art.* CON □ JO: *A quarter past eleven, and the sun's coming out.* HELEN: *Oh! Well,* ***happy the bride the sun shines on.*** TOH □ not taken seriously, but even a blink of sunshine at a suitable moment could provoke this remark from a guest or onlooker at a wedding.

a happy choice [Comp (NP)] a name, word, gift, location etc that is, or turns out to be, suitably or fortunately chosen **V:** ⚠ be; find, think, sth □ *Whether by chance or foresight her parents had named her Grace. The years had proved it* ***a happy choice.*** □ *'There were so many beautiful caftans I didn't know which to get you.' 'Well it was* ***a happy choice****. Yellow's my favourite colour.'*

(by) a happy/an unhappy coincidence (because) — fortunately/unfortunately — certain events happen together □ *Looking for a second-hand Land Rover, are you? That sounds like* ***a happy coincidence.*** *I have one to sell and I'm sure we can agree on a price.* □ *If* ***by an unhappy coincidence*** *both celebrations were to be held on the same date I should have to forego one of them.*

the happy couple/pair (cliché) a bride and groom or a very recently married couple □ *After the church ceremony relatives and friends went to the bride's parents' house to drink the health of* ***the happy couple*** *in champagne.* □ *There were photos of* ***the happy pair*** *alone, with attendant children, with family. In no picture did they touch and in none did they look happy.* NS

happy days(!) an expression wishing sb well, eg in a toast; □ *'Well, it's nice to be here,' exclaimed Mr Porter, beaming affably around him. He raised his glass. '****Happy days!****'*

a happy ending a successful conclusion to a series of events; a satisfactory settlement of earlier troubles and trials, esp happening at the end of a story, film, play □ (discussing R.L. Stevenson's unfinished novel, 'Weir of Hermiston') *The plot outlined in them* (Stevenson's notes) *was not present when the novel was conceived, but developed later from Stevenson's anxiety to provide* ***a happy ending.*** RT □ *In this instance the kidnappers were arrested and Nicole was returned to her parents, but few such cases have* ***a happy ending.*** □ also pl.

a happy etc hunting ground (for/of sb) a happy after-life, paradise (from American Indian folklore); (fig) a favourable place, source, etc where sb may do, observe, acquire what he wants **adj:** happy, ⚠ good, favourite. **o:** botanists, folklore enthusiasts; pickpockets, gossipmongers □ *The crowded sales floors are* ***a happy hunting ground for*** *pickpockets.* □ *Much has been written about the campaign in North West Europe and it will be* ***a happy hunting ground for*** *historians for many years to come.* MFM □ *Health authorities are also looking at the possibility of a 10 per cent cut in costs. Capital spending —* ***a favourite hunting ground for*** *cutters — is already largely confined to urgent work, or buildings already started.* G

happy landings(!) good wishes for a journey, esp by air (occas used to express good wishes for other types of undertaking—perhaps implying a 'crash' of sb hopes) □ *'I've got a plane. Soon as there's a suitable break I'll send her over.' 'Thanks — thanks a lot,' I said. 'That's O.K.* ***Happy landings****,' said the voice.* DF

a/the happy medium [O (NP)] a proper balance between too much and too little of sth, between two qualities either of which would be undesirable in excess **V:** strike, hit; attain, achieve □ *I don't want to get a bad name among boys for being easy-going in the clinches* (=

close embraces), *but neither do I want to be looked on as a iceberg. Is it possible to strike* ***a happy medium****?* H □ *You tend to laugh at people above you to cut them down to size and at those below you to express your superiority. He'll be looking for* ***the happy medium*** *in 'Frank Muir Goes into Europe'.* RT

hard by [A (AdvP)] (formal) situated very near (to) □ *Not a stone's throw from Whitehall, and* ***hard by*** *the River Thames, there stands an old, decaying building.* NS □ *Never assume a young animal has been deserted. The mother is probably concealed* ***hard by****, waiting for you to go.* □ functions as prep or adv (front, middle or end position).

a hard case[1] (sb in) specially sad or difficult circumstances □ *Everybody that comes to this Bureau is in trouble of some sort but I've seldom heard of* ***a harder case*** *than that poor woman's.* □ *'He'll lose his job as well as his licence.' 'The court can't make exceptions for* ***hard cases****.'* ⇨ ⚠ hard cases make bad law(s).

a hard case[2] sb with a hard or unsympathetic character; sb who has followed a life of crime or evil ways for so long that he is not likely to change □ *'She looks* ***a*** *right* ***hard case****, that one,' said old Mrs Jennings.* □ *School became unbearable when the kind Miss Dear was supplanted by* ***a hard case*** *called Miss Turnbull.* OBS □ *'You can't jump to conclusions from their age,' the Probationer Officer objected. 'Some of these boys are just in need of care and training and some are* ***hard cases*** *at fourteen.'* ⇨ ⚠ next entry.

hard cases make bad law(s) (saying) being lenient in applying a law (because of the hardship it will cause) leads to that law becoming less effective □ *Legislation restricting the freedom of the great majority cannot be justified merely because it ensures the protection of a tiny minority.* ***Hard cases make bad laws.*** OBS ⇨ ⚠ a hard case[1,2].

hard cash [O/o (NP)] coins or notes contrasted with cheques, banker's cards, etc **V:** want, prefer. **prep:** in (terms of), in the form of □ *I don't have that much money on me — not in* ***hard cash*** *anyway. Will you take a cheque?* □ *What it will cost in terms of* ***hard cash*** *the ratepayers of Oxford may shudder to think.* T □ *Victoria toyed hopefully with the idea that Mrs Chipp might press upon her a parting present in the form of* ***hard cash****.* TCB

hard cheese(!) (dated slang) interjection or comment expressing sympathy, sincere or ironic; hard lines (on sb) (qv); hard etc luck (on sb) (qv) □ (tossing a coin) *'Heads', Muriel quavered. But when the paternal hand was lifted it was tails. '****Hard cheese****,' said Elsie, accepting her victory like the good sportsgirl she was.* RM

the hard core (of sth) the solid or permanent part of sth □ *It was the 'regular content' of the Services which was* ***the hard core of*** *our fighting efficiency.* MFM □ ***The hard core of*** *racial antagonism used to be in the mines where the white miners fought a long and bitter battle to retain the privileges of the European worker.* NS □ *At once, the* ***hard-core*** *Tories of the old Government, headed by Wellington and Peel, resigned.* ST □ often used of the strongly committed members of a political or religious group; attrib use *a* ***hard-core*** *Tory.*

a hard day at the office (catchphrase) facetious reference to a busy and tiring day, sometimes used as a plea for relaxation or amusement or as an excuse for laziness, bad temper, etc □ *At opening time, glasses polished and lager at the cool and ready, I'd greet the first few customers and we'd talk in clichés for half an hour. '****Hard day at the office****?' I'd ask and they would say something on the lines of 'Yes. Mustn't grumble.'* NS

a hard day's night staying up late or all night, possibly on special duties, but esp to drink, dance etc □ *It's been* ***a hard day's night****, And I've been working like a dog./It's been* ***a hard day's night****,/I should be sleeping like a log.* (P MCCARTNEY b1942) □ (New Year's Eve) *It's* ***a hard day's night****—and from 11.0 pm on Radio 4 Scotland Tom Fleming will be launching the jollifications with a look back at 1975 through records and sound archives.* RT □ expression is a facetious variant of next entry (qv).

a hard day's work etc a day spent working hard **n:** work, graft; ploughing, teaching, climbing **A:** on the farm; in the kitchen; at the coalface □ *He doesn't know what it is to do* ***a hard day's work****.* □ *We are sitting in the bar and the Goodies are resting from* ***a hard day's filming*** *for the first of their new series.* RT □ *Often, after* ***a hard day's work*** *in the ward, I was too tired to change my clothes and go out.* □ similarly ***a hard day*** *in the fields, etc.*

hard fact(s) facts which can be examined and checked; information as opposed to general statements, expressions of opinion, etc □ *The way to fight emotionalism is with a cool head;* ***hard facts*** *versus fake evidence.* NS □ *The ideas generated seem to stem from bouts of reverie entangling with* ***hard facts****.* L

hard and fast[1] [adj + adj non-rev] fixed; inflexible; precisely defined **n:** rule, regulation; category, class distinction □ *These stages may now be discussed in more detail but first it must be emphasized that they do not present* ***hard and fast*** *categories.* MFF □ *We must make it a* ***hard and fast*** *rule not to allow any parent to enter a classroom without first speaking to the headmaster.* □ often in neg constructions.

hard and fast[2] [adv + adv non-rev] firmly; immovably **V:** stick, fasten, jam, weld (sth) □ *The thawed surface had frozen again and now the runners of the sled were stuck* ***hard and fast*** *to the ice.* SC □ *The boulder was wedged* ***hard and fast*** *in the crevice and nothing short of an explosive charge could have moved it.*

hard and fast[3] [adv + adv non-rev] with energy, speed, all one's attention **V:** play; run, row, swim □ *He played the Do You Know So-and-So game* ***hard and fast*** *from all angles, social, political, and even religious. It's a well-known game, its object being the humiliation of those with less money than yourself.* RATT □ *If there'd been any danger, you'd have seen me running* ***hard and fast*** *in the opposite direction.*

a hard life [O (NP)] a life made difficult by hard work, poor natural conditions, poverty, ill health, persecution etc **V:** lead, live, have □ *Shepherds in those hills lead* ***a hard life*** *compared with those who work the lowland pastures.* □ *But those white South Africans who espouse the* *cause of black emancipation to some purpose have **a hard life**, even if their professional and family lives are not ruined by a series of treason trials.* SC ▫ ***Life is hard**, George. Anyone who thinks it isn't is either very young or a fool.* EGD ▫ *'They had every size in the shop except the one I wanted.' 'Oh, it's **a hard life**, all right.'* ▫ variant life is hard; *it's **a hard life*** and life is hard are popular remarks about the quality of life in general, or as expressions of casual, perhaps mock sympathy for oneself or sb else, usu in not very serious circumstances.

hard lines (on sb) exclamation or (sympathetic) comment on an event, or state of affairs, which is unfortunate, undeserved or unjust (for sb); next entry (qv); hard cheese(!) (qv) ▫ *'**Hard lines**!' said a bystander sympathetically. 'Now you'll have to wait half an hour for the next bus.'* ▫ *It would be **hard lines on** a serious student to be turned down in favour of a lay-about like Charles.*

hard etc luck (on sb) exclamation or (sympathetic) comment on sb's misfortune in general or some particular case of it; previous entry (qv); hard cheese(!) (qv) **adj:** hard, ⚠ bad, tough, rotten, foul, lousy ▫ *So he didn't inherit a penny? That was **hard luck**, after all the years he worked for the old devil.* ▫ *'You are not disappointed because Mrs Eastwood cannot come?' 'Well, it was **bad luck on** her, of course,' said Harold.* PW ▫ *Like it's a man's life in today's professional army, but if you don't want to be in the infantry, **tough luck**.* NS ▫ *Oh, **was**n't that just **my bad luck**?* ▫ variant be sb's/one's hard etc luck.

a hard luck story a story, or version of events, told by sb who is trying to win sympathy, help, financial assistance, etc for himself ▫ *'He says it's not his fault.' 'Nothing ever is. He's always got **a hard-luck story** to excuse his failures with.'* ▫ *At first glance he was one of nature's second fiddles. **A** walking bloody **hard-luck story**.* JFTR

a hard/tough nut to crack [Comp (NP)] (informal) a problem difficult to find an answer to, a situation difficult to deal with effectively; sb likely to resist efforts to conciliate, influence or intimidate him **V:** ⚠ be, seem; make sth/sb ▫ (building a motorway) *But the difficult terrain of the Pennines, and the congested urban development along the remainder of the route will both be **hard nuts to crack**.* T ▫ *I didn't think any of them* (= girls you fancy) *were too **tough nuts** for you **to crack**. I should hate to think you were losing your grip.* TGLY ▫ a hard/tough nut is 'sb who resists physical or mental strain, or has no sympathetic or tender feelings'.

hard of hearing [Comp (AdjP)] rather, or very, deaf **V:** ⚠ be, become; make sb. **adv mod:** a little, a bit, somewhat, quite, so ▫ *Since your father's getting so **hard of hearing** you must all learn to speak up instead of losing patience with him.* ▫ *Certainly he enunciates beautifully — a fact borne out by an award as 'Television's Clearest Speaker of the Year', chosen by the deaf and **hard of hearing**.* L

hard on sb [Comp (AdjP)] dealing with, punishing or criticizing sb/sth (too) harshly; being unfair by either blaming too much or praising too little **V:** ⚠ be; find, think, sb. **adv mod:** a bit, rather, very. **o:** son; partner, colleague ▫ *I don't like to be **hard on** an old man but I'm going to have to tell him, one of these days, what a lying old fraud he is.* ▫ *Roy Hudd was actually heard to say that King Edward VII would be remembered for reforms—which seems a bit **hard on** Lloyd George (who was really responsible for them).* L

hard on sb/sth [Comp (AdjP)] having a damaging or destructive effect on sb/sth **V:** ⚠ be, seem; make sth. **o:** tyres, brakes; shoes, jumpers ▫ *The washing-machine is a great time saver, but my one anyway, is **hard on** clothes.* ▫ *'Mumps now,' she continued. 'That's another illness that's far **harder on** grown-ups than on children.'* ▫ *The trad* (= traditional) *British cooked breakfast is **hard** both **on** wives/mothers and **on** the digestion.* OBS

hard/close on/upon sb's/sth's heels [Comp/A (AdjP)] immediately or soon after sb/sth in time, order of procedure, merit etc **V:** be; arrive, appear, come, follow ▫ *The appearance of Briggs with the tea-things brought the conversation to an end. **Hard on his heels** came Sir Julius, rubbing his hands and oozing geniality.* EM ▫ *A cold and agitated wind came hurrying ahead, and **close on its heels** came the rain.* BB ▫ *Personally, I find Henry James the most boring writer there is, but your precious Nabokov, 'Lolita' apart, is **hard on his heels**.* ▫ may precede or follow *come* or *be*.

hard put (to it)/pressed to do sth [Comp (AdjP)] able to do sth only with great difficulty **V:** ⚠ be; appear, seem ▫ *Even with the three of us working, we were still **hard put to it to** cope with all the work.* DF ▫ *The ground beneath us shook so violently to a series of shocks that we were **hard put to** keep our feet.* TST ▫ *Young women were burdened with large families that they were **hard pressed to** feed and clothe.* SC ▫ *Robin Day has been unable to get together the balanced panel he had wanted and was **hard pressed to** keep things moving.* NS

hard to say/tell [Comp (AdjP)] difficult to make a firm statement about, esp because too little is, or can be, known about it **S:** that; it...why they did it, when to operate, how to do better. **V:** ⚠ be, become; make sth ▫ *'How old a man is he?' 'About my age, probably, though it's **hard to say**.'* ▫ *All this time Finn had been leaning against the door, looking abstractedly into the middle distance. Whether he was listening or not was **hard to tell**.* UTN

the hard/soft sell (informal) sales technique by which the customer is pressed into buying by facts, figures, argument or the seller's force of persuasion/sales technique by which the customer is persuaded to buy by attractive presentation, indirect suggestion, etc ▫ *In fact a cooling-off period for insurance deals of this kind is going to be made law — yet another reason for the decline of **the hard sell**. It's no use wasting all the time and effort if the man can change his mind as soon as he's had time to think about it.* ST ▫ *'It depends on what you want from a machine, sir,' replied the assistant who was clearly a master of **the soft sell**. 'If you're happy with the quality of reproduction from this, there's no need to pay more for the best.'*

hard to take [Comp (AdjP)] difficult to accept

without bitterness or grief; difficult to believe, to accept as being true **S:** disappointment, rebuff, misfortune. **V:** ⚠ be, become; make sth □ *Be patient and kind with her, John. The loss of a young child is very* ***hard to take****.* □ *I joined the Army when I was 17. The discipline was dreadful, and the loss of freedom* ***hard to take****.* TVT □ *What is* ***harder to take*** *is Hawkridge's account of his own moral indignation.* NS

a hard taskmaster/taskmistress sb who makes others work, and does so strictly or harshly □ *But Glyn is* ***a hard taskmaster****. The winter is spent doing tough practical work on the mountain to get the dogs fit.* RT □ *Mark was promoted swiftly through the ranks by Valentine, who perhaps recognised himself in* ***this hard taskmaster*** *and man of scrupulous honesty.* ST □ also pl.

the hard way [A (NP)] the most difficult, least convenient, method (of doing sth, of achieving one's object) **V:** do, learn, sth; find out sth □ *Such things as electric starters and windscreen wipers were not so long ago regarded as rather sissy accessories not really required by the virile and competent motorist who much preferred to do things* ***the hard way****.* SC □ *'Ludovic has acted in school plays.' 'The best beginning for anyone,' said Aubrey, 'now that people aren't allowed to be born in a barn and learn it all* ***the hard way****.'* WDM □ *As for the strike committee, they have found out* ***the hard way*** *who their real friends are. The stopping of strike pay by one of the two unions involved and the comparative lack of interest shown by the union leadership in their cause, give the phrase 'official strike' a hollow ring.* NS □ *'I rose to my present position* ***the hard way****,' he answered, 'but it doesn't follow that I should expect my sons to do the same.'*

hard words reproaches, criticisms, accusations, made or exchanged □ *There were some* ***hard words*** *between us, that I will admit. But if it came to threats, what could I do?* EM □ *Those who have nothing but* ***hard words*** *for the present generation of university students have little idea of how hard most of them work.*

hard work never hurt etc anybody (yet) (saying) popular pompous remark justifying one's own or another's efforts or criticizing idleness **V:** hurt, ⚠ killed, harmed; did (any) harm to anyone, did anyone (any) harm □ *'Me a breakdown?' said Harold, as if a breakdown was a thing that only happened to writers with too much time on their hands, and too much money. '****Hard work never did anyone any harm****.'* PW □ ***Hard work never killed anybody****. It's too much rich living that gives people coronaries.*

a hard/harsh world [Comp (NP)] life seen as a struggle against natural conditions, misfortune, and esp competition from one's fellow men, etc **V:** ⚠ be, seem; find it □ (a teacher defends his classroom methods) *This is* ***a hard world****— they've got to learn to give and take some hard knocks before they're very much older.'* TT □ *Emily's protected upbringing had not equipped her for the realities of* ***a harsh world****.* □ often *it's* ***a hard world*** as comment on an instance of hardship, etc.

harden one's heart [V + O] not allow oneself to be misled by the love, sympathy, pity etc one does in fact feel □ *The impulse to feed* (the released animals) *was almost irresistible, but we had to* ***harden our hearts*** *and ignore them.* DF □ *If he could have cried, he would have cried now at the unfairness of it all. He* ***hardened his heart****. This was no time for thoughts of anything but the immediate problem.* US

a hardened criminal etc sb so accustomed to a life of crime, wrong-doing, that he is unlikely to repent or change his ways **n:** criminal, ⚠ sinner, reprobate □ *Guy had told him, 'The more you pray for me, Tony, the more I'm* ***a hardened sinner****.'* MM □ *'And was that all you did in Paris? No wine, woman and song?' 'Certainly not. I'm a family man, not* ***a hardened*** *old* ***reprobate*** *like you.'* □ also pl; sometimes used facetiously of other faults.

(not) harm etc a hair of sb's head (not) injure sb, even in the slightest way **V:** harm, ⚠ hurt, touch □ *'Come, dear,' the nurse soothed her, 'you know I wouldn't* ***harm a hair of your head*** *if I could help it, but I've got to give you this little injection, just to make you better.'* □ *That's a lie. I swore at him and told him to get out of my way, but I* ***never touched a hair of his head****.* □ usu in neg or conditional constructions.

a hat trick [O (NP)] three related achievements, successes, awards etc in sport or some other activity (from, formerly, a cricket club presenting a new cap to any member who took three wickets with three successive balls) **V:** do, score, achieve, bring off □ *George Seaton wrote and directed, he was already a double Oscar winner by this time, but his script was too proud or too profane to make it* ***a hat trick****.* RT □ stress pattern a 'hat trick.

hatch a plot etc [V + O pass] devise a plan, arrange (by oneself or with others, and usu secretly) to do sth, which will be revealed only when completed or carried into action **O:** plot, ⚠ conspiracy, plan, scheme □ *So the next time I ran into Ned we* ***hatched a scheme*** *for going to see Robert together.* CON □ *The St Ermin's Hotel has something of a political history of its own. In the Fifties, all sorts of dark* ***plots*** *and dirty deeds were reported as being* ***hatched*** *there.* NS □ *When Caryl Brahms was writing ballet reviews for the 'Daily Telegraph' she and S J Simon* ***hatched a plot*** *to write a novel about a murder in the ballet, with Arnold Haskell as the corpse.* G

a hatchet man/job sb/sth employed to reduce staff and cut down expenditure in a business or public service; sb/sth used to attack, discredit or get rid of opponents (eg within a political party, government system); a destructive critic/criticism of anything □ *Brown is regarded by the Left as* ***a hatchet man****; they haven't forgotten the way he treated Bertrand Russell.* OBS □ *We used to do our homework in the train to and from school— but that was in the days before Lord Beeching did* ***his hatchet job*** *for British Rail.* □ *The 'Times Literary Supplement' suggested that the programme 'tends to select only those books about which it can say something commendatory.' Well, in the age of* ***Hatchetman*** *that makes a nice change.* L □ stress pattern a 'hatchet man/job; also pl.

hate sb's guts [V + O] (informal) hate or dislike sb intensely □ *I just had to tell someone.*

*Funny it happened to be you, and you **hate my guts**.* QA □ *...and I wishing to God she'd asked him* (a police detective) *in, though on second thoughts realizing that that would seem more suspicious than keeping him outside, because they know we **hate their guts**, and smell a rat if they think we're trying to be nice to them.* LLDR

hate sb/sth like poison (informal) dislike sb/sth intensely □ *The Earl and Gillies's father **hated** each other **like poison** I believe.* WDM □ *'Look,' I'd say, 'Why don't you get a book, duck?' But she never would, **hated** them **like poison**. She sneered: 'I've got more sense, and too much to do.'* LLDR

hate/loathe the sight of sb/sth [V + O] dislike sb/sth very much; find sb/sth objectionable or intolerable; can't/couldn't stand/bear the sight of sb/sth (qv) □ *He **hated the sight of** army officers, whom he regarded as idle and effeminate.* OBS □ *'You don't love me any more, do you, Charles?' 'To be frank, Amanda, I **hate the** bloody **sight of** you!'*

have etc an/the air of sb/sth [possess] look like sb/sth; function or behave as sb/sth does or would be likely to do **V:** have (got); ⚠ give sb, lend sb/sth. **prep:** with □ *Her house is the marvel of the film colony. Its mock stonework, narrow interstices and naked fuseboxes **have** somewhat **the air of** a ruined keep.* ST □ *He picked up his tankard with a rather weary gesture, and drank from it. He **had the air of** a man who is turning over a number of things in his mind.* CON □ *The portrait utterly fails to convey the sitter's character. It **gives** him, in fact, **the air of** a languid aristocrat.* □ *This technique—for it is often no more than a technique, **lends an air of** profundity to the discussion.* NS

have etc all day [possess] (informal) have etc (at the time of speaking) much or any time to spend or waste **V:** have (got); ⚠ there be. **prep:** with. **A:** for that, for reading; to hang around, to read books □ *Stop mucking about and tell me what you want brought back from town. I **haven't got all day**.* □ *'No, we can't,' the girl at the Enquiry Desk answered brusquely. 'We're busy people in this office. We **haven't got all day** to fill in forms for people.'* □ *'We must go. We're keeping your wife up and she should be getting plenty of rest just now.' 'Oh, don't go! She **has all day** for that. A bit of company will liven her up.'* □ esp neg in first person; positive statements usu assertive and often suggest that others have ample time or opportunity compared with oneself. ⇨ ⚠ (not) be/take all day etc.

have (got)/with all one's marbles [possess] (slang) be in full possession of one's senses or wits □ *The uncle claims he was butted at a séance by a goat which had died the previous October. John thinks his uncle may not have **had all his marbles**.* NS ⇨ lose one's marbles.

have (got)/with all the marks of sb/sth [possess] be likely to be sb/sth, because he/it shows the signs of being so **o:** a schoolma'am; a hasty departure, having been done on the cheap □ *Williams **has all the marks of** a successful and rather ruthless man.* TO □ *'An amateur job, would you say, Sergeant?' the Inspector asked. 'It's **got all the marks of** it, sir.'* □ *I think he knew he was dying. At any rate, his last novel **had all the marks of** having been written in haste.*

have etc all the money etc in the world [possess] (informal) have etc a very great amount of money etc **V:** have (got); possess; get; there be. **prep:** with. **n:** money, wealth; advantages; influence; leisure, time; patience □ *They **have all the money in the world**, with wool up at its present price, but they've got to do their own housework just like everybody else.* RFW □ *He **has all the advantages in the world** of birth and education, so why does he want to go and be a nurse in a leper hospital?* □ *Nobody could put up with such behaviour, even if they **had all the patience in the world**.* □ ***Having all the time in the world** is hard for a writer, who can always say 'I'll start tomorrow.'* SC □ *Though we were late in starting, he strolled along as if **there was all the time in the world** to get there.* □ *His voice was quiet, calm, and unhurried. He seemed to **have all the time in the world**.* RT

have (got) another think/guess coming [possess] (informal) be forced to think again, to revise or alter one's opinions or plans □ DAVIES: *If you think you're better than me you'**ve got another think coming**.* TC □ HELEN: *In any case, bearing a child doesn't place one under an obligation to it.* GEOFF: *I should have thought it did.* HELEN: *Well, you've **got another think coming**.* TOH □ (NONCE) *If you think I'm going to sit still and play noughts and crosses after listening to all that dreary crap, you've bloody well **got another guess coming**.* HAA □ almost always in aggressive statements made to or about another person.

have etc ants in one's pants [possess] (informal) be very restless, excited or excitable **V:** have (got), ⚠ get. **prep:** with □ *She's **had ants in her pants** all week—waiting for the exam results.* □ *Emergency. Action stations. I said I should be ill. I can feel the old scar in my leg tingling. Salt in my trousers. **Ants in my pants**.* PM

have/give sb a bad etc time (of it) [possess] suffer (a period of) ill-health, poverty, persecution etc **adj:** bad, ⚠ hard, rough, thin □ *Dad's beginning to get his strength back now, but he's **had a bad time of it**.* □ *But in each class there are born a certain number of natures with a curiosity about their best self—for the pursuit, in a word, of perfection. They **have**, in general, **a rough time of it** in their lives.* MATTHEW ARNOLD 1822-88 (quoted in UL) □ *By now we were weak and thirsty and the flies and stinging insects were **giving us a bad time**.* □ *The small independent dealers have **had a thin time** in the past two or three years.* T

have etc bags under one's eyes [possess] have a puffiness or swelling in the loose skin below one's eyes, as a sign of lack of sleep, ill-health, or as a general indication of old age. **V:** have (got), ⚠ get; there be. **prep:** with □ *Observe **the bags under his eyes**, the look of lascivious satisfaction.* RATT □ *You could point to **the bags under his eyes**, the bags under his chins and the bag that was his belly.* PP □ *He's only twenty-three, but he'**s got bags under his eyes** already!*

have (oneself) a ball (informal) enjoy oneself greatly, perhaps doing sth one shouldn't **A:** in the Mediterranean, with his prize money, criticizing the neighbours □ *Is he sorry for himself? Not on your life. He's* ***having a ball*** *while it lasts.* H □ *We were subjected to Colin Davies* ***having a ball*** *teaching the Promenaders how to sing.* RT □ *In the airline's advertising the girls are referred to as 'Love Birds'. You get the feeling that one of these days Women's Lib is going to* ***have a ball*** *with Air Jamaica.* OBS

have (got)/with bats in the belfry [possess] (informal) be mad, eccentric, odd (esp in regard to some subject that obsesses one) □ *He's not the first in the family to* ***have bats in the belfry****. His grandfather used to sit up half the night composing letters of warning to all his acquaintances about the end of the world, or whatever his current obsession happened to be.* □ *'What was that old man at the bus-stop trying to tell us?' 'Some rigmarole about sheep and poppies—****bats in the belfry****, if you ask me.'*

have (got) to/must be seen to be believed be almost impossible to describe convincingly because it is so beautiful, ugly, unusual, untidy, ridiculous etc **S:** view; squalor, filth; conditions, sufferings □ *The sun went down in an explosion of colour that would* ***have to be seen to be believed****.* □ *The squalor of those crumbling red sandstone tenements* ***has to be seen****, not just to bring the housing figures alive, but* ***to be believed****.* NS ⇨ ⚠ seeing is believing.

have etc a bee in one's bonnet [possess] be obsessed with sth (usu with the implication that it is unimportant, irrelevant or foolish) **V:** have (got), ⚠ get. **prep:** with □ *For years Ford****'s had a bee in his bonnet*** *about the Irish and the English. Thinks he's got a God-given mission to bring the two races together under the Established Church.* PP □ *Scientists and doctors are no more immune to* ***bees in their bonnets*** *than other members of the community.* T □ *She was always a crank.* ***Got a bee in her bonnet*** *about Mussolini later on—the Shavian 'great man', you know.* ASA

have etc a/one's bellyful/a basinful (of sb/sth) [possess] (informal) have etc as much as one can tolerate of sth, or of sb's actions or company **V:** have; ⚠ give sb; get □ *If Robert's coming round tonight, I'm going out. I've* ***had a bellyful of*** *his company this week.* □ *Can't you think of anything exciting for us to do? I've certainly* ***had a basinful of*** *slumping in front of the television.* □ often perfect tenses, as shown; basinful more polite than bellyful.

have/give sb best [possess] (informal) know more than, be stronger than, intimidate or outwit, sb □ *If it ever comes to a fight there's no doubt which dog will* ***have best****.* □ *David hates to* ***give*** *anyone* ***best*** *in an argument so he never learns anything from what other people have to say.*

have etc a black eye [possess] show etc severe bruising and swelling of the area round the eye caused by an accident or by a deliberate blow **V:** have (got), ⚠ get; give sb. **prep:** with □ *I walked into a door in the dark and* ***gave*** *myself* ***this black eye****.* □ *When the women of our street could think of no more bad names to call Frankie Butler for leading their children into fights that resulted in* ***black eyes****, torn clothes and split heads...* LLDR □ often pl. ⇨ ⚠ black(en) sb's eye (for him).

have etc a black mark (against one) [possess] have etc a note, in an official record, that one has done sth wrong, incorrect etc, eg of a schoolchild's conduct, an employee's performance; receive a sign of disapproval of one's actions **V:** have (got), ⚠ get; give (sb); there be. **prep:** with, without □ *In our school if you* ***got*** *three* ***black marks****, your name was read out at prayers, and if you got six, your parents were sent for.* □ *I don't know if the firm will actually sack me for having lost the contract, but it'll certainly* ***be a black mark against*** *me.* □ *He left the bank after 40 years' service* ***without a*** *single* ***black mark against*** *him.* □ *The Nicholsons will be* ***giving*** *me* ***a black mark****, I suppose, for not turning up at their party.*

have etc blue blood (in one's veins) [possess] be a member of, be related to, the upper classes (from the greater visibility of the veins in persons with fair skins) **V:** have (got); ⚠ there be. **prep:** with □ *A young upstanding Tory's the romantic thing to be now, especially* ***with*** *any* ***blue blood in your veins****.* PP □ *The* ***blue-blooded*** *sons of noble families were not averse to mending their fallen fortunes by marrying the daughters of wealthy manufacturers and industrialists.* □ adj compound blue-blooded.

have etc a brain(-)wave [possess] have etc a sudden inspiration, a good idea **V:** have (got), ⚠ get; give sb □ *Pop confessed he wasn't all that gone on David either, and urged Ma to put her thinking-cap on. Ma was always the one who* ***had the brainwaves****.* HSG □ brain wave, brain-wave, brainwave are all possible.

have etc the brains etc (to do sth) [possess] have sufficient intelligence etc to enable one to do sth **V:** have (got). **prep:** ⚠ with, without. **O:** brains, ⚠ intelligence, nous, (common) sense, wit, vision □ *I would like to see the school-leaving age lowered, instead of raised, for children who don't* ***have the brains to*** *profit from class-room teaching.* RT □ *It was a good thing somebody* ***had the intelligence to*** *switch off all the power when the first explosion occurred.* □ *'Don't give him another thought,' said Stephen. 'If the fellow just* ***hasn't the sense to*** *see what he's losing.'* WI □ *Times had changed and my father had* ***had the wit to*** *change with them.* RFW □ *Macmillan* ***had the vision****, but not the guts* ***to*** *face his own destiny.* RT □ *He* ***had the*** *political* ***nous to*** *know what to say if, for example, a live film of an IRA chief being interviewed was suddenly slotted into the programme.* L □ often neg.

have etc a bun in the oven [possess] (dated slang) be etc pregnant **V:** have (got); give sb; there be. **prep:** with □ *Ah! The erring daughter. Who's* ***got a bun in the oven****? Who's got a cake in the stove?* TOH □ *Mr Otway is bisexual and only married Gillian because* ***there was a bun in the oven****.* L

have one's cake and eat it (too) have, or enjoy, two things simultaneously even though one normally excludes the possibility of the other; have etc it/things both ways (qv) □ *Cambridge has been shouting for a by-pass for the past 20 years. Now that plans have been drawn up, people do not like them. Cambridge cannot* ***have its cake and eat it****.* T □ *'If Bernie likes to give me the money, I shall be glad to have it. But*

I certainly shan't feel under any obligation.' 'Bravo! Eric, bravo!' she cried. 'You want to ***have your cake and eat it****.'* HAA □ often neg; often with *can*.

(not) have etc a cat in hell's chance (of doing sth) [possess] (informal) (not) have etc a slight chance (of achieving sth); next entry (qv); (not) have etc a dog's chance (of doing sth) (qv); (not) have etc a ghost of a chance (of doing sth) (qv) **V:** have (got), ⚠ get; stand, give sb; there be. **prep:** with, without □ *'Their daddies will have arranged it* (a future marriage) *all,' Charles said. 'You* ***haven't a cat in hell's chance****, frankly. Unless you thoroughly misbehave, if you see what I mean.'* RATT □ *It wasn't cowardice. It was common-sense. If I'd thought I* ***had a cat in hell's chance of*** *holding him against the current, I'd have dived in.* □ usu neg.

(not) have etc a chance in hell (of doing sth) [possess] (informal) (not) have etc a slight chance (of achieving sth); previous entry (qv); (not) have etc a dog's chance (of doing sth) (qv); (not) have etc a ghost of a chance (of doing sth) (qv) **V:** have (got), ⚠ stand, get; give sb; there be. **prep:** with, without □ *I just thought* ***there was*** *half* ***a chance in hell*** *that the old man was the vain fool he turned out to be.* ASA □ *Had I been the man whose case was heard before me, I should have* ***stood a*** *snowball's* ***chance in hell of*** *getting off* (ie an exceedingly remote chance). NS □ *Under half of the men found work, and even this represented an achievement. 'To be quite frank,' said one genial manager, 'we jump the queue. Otherwise our chaps would****n't stand a chance in hell****.'* NS □ usu neg.

have etc a chip on one's shoulder [possess] have etc a grudge or grievance, either about one's circumstances in general or about sb/sth more specific, which makes one quarrelsome, discontented, ready to take offence, etc **V:** have (got), ⚠ get; wear; there be. **prep:** with, without □ *You'll get on all right with Carson if you take him the right way. He* ***has a chip on his shoulder*** *of course — feels he knows more about the business than the people he sees being promoted above him.* □ *Where would Mr Goodrich be* ***without his chip on the shoulder****, his grievance against women? It was that that made him tick, to use a vulgarism.* PW □ *If* tourists *are an insensitive lot, the* toured *are terribly touchy. First, in new countries one really must be aware of* ***the Chip****. It's hopeless to admire the old colonial buildings: one must admire the skyscrapers.* L □ (NONCE) *For God's sake* ***take that chip off your shoulder****. I didn't like telling you when the others were around — but you were bloody offensive to me.* RATT

have etc clean hands [possess] have committed no crime, done no wrong or harm, either in general or in a particular case **V:** have (got). **prep:** ⚠ with, without □ (source) *He that* ***hath clean hands*** *and a pure heart; who hath not lifted up his soul unto vanity, nor sworn deceitfully.* PSALMS XXIV 4 □ *No state throughout history has* ***had*** *completely* ***clean hands****. A civilised society is one which sees the evil in itself and provides means to eliminate it.* NS □ *He was talking about the old colonial powers, England and France, and how they couldn't expect to win the confidence of Asiatics. That was where America came in now* ***with clean hands****.* QA □ *Let no mud be thrown; few people's* ***hands are clean****. Just let us think again.* CSWB □ *If the stock market is actually aiming to protect investors rather than just* ***keep its hands clean*** *it must be more selective in allowing these dealings.* ST □ *The global inflation now engulfing us all might be termed the masterpiece of 25 years of centre misrule. Nor can the men of the centre be described as exactly* ***clean-handed****: they have spilt much blood in their time.* NS □ variants keep one's hands clean, sb's hands are clean; adj compound clean-handed.

have etc a clear conscience [possess] have etc no reasons for, or feelings of, guilt **V:** have (got), ⚠ keep. **prep:** with, without □ *'It must be a great burden nursing your old mother at home for so long.' 'Oh, I prefer to do that and* ***have a clear conscience****, than let her go into one of those "homes".'* □ *Paul Foot's documents present their evidence persuasively enough to show that no jury faced with it could have convicted Hanratty* ***with*** *anything like* ***a clear conscience****.* L □ *Here are the recipes, and I guarantee that the family will find them as delicious as an ordinary dessert — and slimmers can enjoy them* ***with a clear conscience****.* WI □ variant keep one's conscience clear.

have (got)/with a clear head[1] [possess] have the ability (as a permanent characteristic) to think clearly, make accurate appraisals, sensible decisions, etc □ *All the examiners commented that he* ***had an*** *impressively* ***clear head*** *and considerable powers of independent criticism.* □ *I can't understand how Monica got herself into such a predicament; she's usually so* ***clear-headed****.* □ adj compound clear-headed.

have (got)/with a clear head[2] [possess] have one's state of mental alertness unaffected by alcohol, fatigue or illness □ *I'm not going to touch a drop of anything till we've had a definite 'yes' or 'no'. I've a feeling that we're going to surprise the world in the next three or four days, and I want to* ***have a clear head****.* RM □ *He does have pain-killing tablets for his arthritis, but he wouldn't take them today — said he wanted to* ***keep his head clear*** *for the TV interview this evening.* □ variant keep one's head clear; adj compound clear-headed.

have etc a clear idea (of sth) [possess] have etc precise knowledge or understanding of the nature, cause, possible outcome, etc (of sth) **V:** have (got), ⚠ get; keep; give sb. **prep:** with, without. **A:** of the outcome, of the progress; (of) what to do; (of) how to proceed □ *Though Ernest Bevin foresaw the General Strike and to some extent prepared for it, he did not* ***have a clear idea of*** *what the strike was meant to achieve and certainly did not consider the implications of victory.* OBS □ *And they* ***have no clear idea*** *what she* (a merchant ship) *is, where she came from or when she sank. External sources provide few clues.* OBS □ *He confessed to distrusting this particular employee without* ***having any clear idea*** *why.* □ *Peter is a dreamy, drifting sort of fellow, but his sister is a young lady* ***with a*** *very* ***clear idea of*** *where she is going and what she wants from life.*

have etc a closed mind [possess] have etc a mind unable or unwilling to accept new ideas, consider other opinions, either in general or about sth in particular **V:** have (got). **prep:** ⚠ with, without □ *A final word: this is not a play for* ***closed minds****, established beliefs, or misplaced Puritanism.* ST □ *He believes in the literal truth of the whole Bible and* ***has a closed mind*** *on the subject. So we don't bother trying to argue with him.* □ *'They have no interest in anything that happens beyond the parish boundary.' 'People* ***with closed minds****?' 'That's right.'* ⇨ have etc an open mind.

have etc a/the constitution like/of a horse/an ox [possess] be strong and vigorous; be able to do hard work; be able to withstand the effects of illness, accident, or old age to a surprising degree. **V:** have (got), ⚠ possess; need; develop. **prep:** with □ *'Mrs Pettigrew* ***has a constitution like a horse****,' said Dame Lettie, casting a horse-dealer's glance over Mrs Pettigrew's upright form.* MM □ *He's been getting through three bottles of whisky a week for as long as I can remember. He must* ***have the constitution of an ox*** *or he would have killed himself long ago.* □ *He****'s got*** *courage, ingenuity and* ***a constitution like a horse****—just the man you need to lead an arduous expedition of this sort.* □ *A week on tour with Ray in Scotland makes you realise that a snooker professional* ***needs the constitution of an ox****, a certain talent as a comedian and raconteur and a fairly formidable drinking capacity.* RT □ indefinite article used with like, definite article used with of, as shown.

have etc sb/sth covered [possess] have sb, or a place, in the direct line of fire from a pistol, gun etc **V:** have (got), ⚠ get, keep □ *You will observe that I also* ***have*** *you* ***covered****. From under the table you can only give me a painful wound. If I see the slightest sign of you raising that pistol above it, I will kill you.* ARG □ ***Keep*** *them* ***covered*** *while I try to fetch help.* □ *A voice on the loud-hailer said 'OK, Beeblebrox, hold it right there. We****'ve got*** *you* ***covered****.'* HHGG

have one's day[1] [V + O] be important, useful, fashionable etc only for a period (but be (likely to be) superseded by sb/sth) □ *Our little systems* ***have their day****;/They* ***have their day*** *and cease to be.* IN MEMORIAM (A TENNYSON 1809-92) □ *It was rather like during the War, when private armies sprang up and* ***had their day*** *until they made a mistake and were disbanded or swallowed up.* DS □ *He's just another of these public idols that will* ***have his*** *little* ***day*** *and be forgotten, like many another before him.* ⇨ ⚠ have had one's day/time.

have one's day[2] [V + O] be successful, be influential, be happy, enjoy life, etc only for a period, (but with the emphasis on these good things rather than on their impermanence) □ *Time drag heavy. She do that. Time drag so slow, I get to thinkin' it's Monday when it's still Sunday. Still, I* ***had my day****. I had that alright.* R □ *I don't believe in loading youngsters with responsibilities. Let them* ***have their day*** *is what I say. The world will close in on them soon enough.* ⇨ ⚠ have had one's day/time.

have (got)/with the devil's own luck [possess] be unusually, or exceptionally, fortunate □ *When there was company he had supper in the nursery and played card games with Nannie, in which pursuit he* ***had*** *all old Lord Pomfret's skill and also what his uncle Roddy called* ***the devil's own luck****.* WDM □ *He raised his rifle and fired. By a stroke of* ***the devil's own luck****, the bullet sped straight to its mark.* □ *Fancy him not being hurt at all! But then, he* ***has the luck of the devil****, that boy — always has had.* □ variant have etc the luck of the devil.

have (got)/be (sth) to do with sb/sth[1] be related to, or connected with, sb/sth; have as its subject **S:** book, chapter; argument, process. **O:** something, nothing, little, (not) a great deal □ *Some years ago I published an autobiographical book 'Double Lives'. It* ***had to do with*** *my progenitors and my own early life.* AH □ *A touring fringe company from Paris are offering their version of 'Robinson Crusoe', an anarchic pageant which* ***has little to do with*** *the story as we know it.* L □ *It seems that the first step in germination by abrasion* ***has to do with*** *weakening and cracking in the outer spore layer, which keeps out water.* NSC

have (got)/be (sth) to do with sb/sth[2] work with, concern or interest oneself in, sb/sth **O:** something, nothing, (not) much, little, a lot □ *A man like Angus that's* ***had to do with*** *boats and these waters all his life doesn't need advice from you.* □ *I had never* ***had much to do with*** *children and felt awkward with them.*

(not) have etc a dog's chance (of doing sth) [possess] (informal) (not) have etc a slight chance (of achieving sth); (not) have etc a chance in hell (of doing sth) (qv); (not) have etc a cat in hell's chance (of doing sth) (qv); (not) have etc a ghost of a chance (of doing sth) (qv) **V:** have (got), ⚠ stand, get; give sb; there be. **prep:** with, without □ *I've entered my name for the 1000 metres, but I* ***haven't a dog's chance of*** *winning. The competition is very strong this year.* □ *'Now, get out! And I want your resignation by the morning, Wensley.' Then Wensley said, 'I don't think so, and I'll tell you why. A: I'm not the resigning sort. B: You do****n't stand a dog's chance*** *and I'll tell you why.'* PP □ *'Will he catch his train, do you think?'* ***'Not a dog's chance****! But he's determined to try.'* □ usu neg.

have done it this time etc [V + O + A] (informal) have done sth serious that cannot be undone; have made a foolish, or serious, blunder in speech, conduct or work **S:** he, you, I, they; our team, the Government; the stupid fool. **A:** this time, ⚠ now, again □ *It was dramatic and touching with the baby inside Virginia, but what about after it was born? What would life be like then? A baby! Well, he* ***had done it this time****, all right.* AITC □ *Oh God! I****'ve done it again****. When will I learn to hold my tongue?* □ *There was an iron-shaped hole with charred edges where she had started to iron her dress. 'You****'ve done it now****, haven't you?' her mother said.*

have etc sb's ear [possess] have access to sb esp on a higher social or administrative level than oneself, be able to influence him, obtain his help, etc **V:** have (got), ⚠ get, win. **prep:** with □ *So 'Maori' (a nickname)* ***had*** *Tedder****'s ear****—they were both good airmen.* MFM □ *Luckily Zamyatin had the support of Gorki who, in turn,* ***had*** *Stalin****'s ear*** *and he was allowed to go on living in Paris until his death.* SC □ *But it turned out that the eccentric Browne* ***had the ear of*** *Leonard Elmhurst, millionaire owner of Dar-*

tington Hall. ST ▫ *If sent through the regular channels, the information was sure to be suppressed. Somehow, he must* ***win the ear of*** *the President himself.* ▫ sing form used when referring to two or more people, as in *He must* ***win the ear of*** *both men.*

have etc an edge to one's voice [possess] have, show, a certain degree of anger, nervousness, exasperation etc in the way in which one speaks **V:** have (got); ⚠ there be. **prep:** with ▫ *'The facts, Robert, the facts!' Ned cut in.* ***There was an edge to his voice****, this time, that revealed how sick of it all he was getting.* CON ▫ *The child repeated his lesson again, more correctly but* ***with an edge to his voice*** *that showed that tears were not far off.* ▫ *'You have a ten-minute tea-break, don't you?' was all the manageress said, pausing at the canteen table. But* ***her voice had an edge to it*** *that sent the girls scurrying back to their work.* ▫ variant one's voice has an edge to it. ⇨ ⚠ give sb/get the (rough) edge of one's/sb's tongue.

have etc elbow room [possess] have etc sufficient space beside, or all around, one to move one's elbows sideways (so as to eat, play an instrument, sit comfortably etc); (fig) have freedom, within certain limits, to experiment, negotiate, manoeuvre **V:** have (got), ⚠ get, gain; give sb; there be. **prep:** with. **det:** some, more; no, (not) any, enough, a little, too little ▫ *The gallery was fitted with tiers of narrow wooden seats which* ***afforded*** *their occupants very little* ***elbow room****.* ▫ *As an independent school we* ***have*** *enough* ***elbow room*** *to try out new theories and methods of education.* ▫ *This* ***gaining*** *of more air to breathe, more* ***elbow room*** *for thought, so to speak, looks like being a very cautious probing of the possible.* L

have etc enough luggage etc to sink a battleship [possess] (facetious) have a considerable, or excessive, amount of luggage etc **V:** have (got); etc there be. **prep:** with. **O:** luggage, money; food, drink; confidence, conceit ▫ *I thought you said your mother was only coming for a week. She****'s got enough luggage*** *there* ***to sink a battleship****.* ▫ *We've had hundreds of applications since we advertised. People* ***with enough degrees to sink a battleship*** *have written in.* ST

have etc enough and to spare [possess] have more than a sufficient amount (of sth mentioned previously) for oneself so that there is some for others if they want it **V:** have, get; there be. **prep:** with. **O:** food, drink; money, riches; jobs; room, ▫ (source) *How many hired servants of my father's* ***have*** *bread* ***enough and to spare****, and I perish with hunger!* LUKE XV 17 ▫ *Yet whenever I went out, even into areas just vacated by other disappointed hunters, I would* ***find*** *game* ***enough and to spare****.* LWK ▫ *'Listen, Findlay,' he babbled, 'there's money down here —millions of it. Be sensible,* ***there's enough*** *here* ***and to spare*** *for both of us.'* ARG ▫ enough used either after the n or as Comp to *be* (as in last example).

have etc an enquiring etc turn of mind [possess] have etc an enquiring etc mental outlook or aptitude **V:** have, ⚠ possess; be of; lack. **prep:** with, without. **adj:** enquiring, academic, mathematical; religious; gloomy, optimistic ▫ *He's a child* ***with a more enquiring turn of mind*** *than his brother.* ▫ *The affair much irritated the French, and not least General de Gaulle, while those* ***of a democratic turn of mind*** *were concerned that a man could be kidnapped in broad daylight on the Boulevard St Germain by French 'parallel police' acting under orders from the head of a foreign security organisation.* NS

have etc an even/a fifty-fifty chance (of doing sth) [possess] have etc an equally balanced possibility, opportunity (of sth happening, of succeeding in sth, or not) **V:** have (got), ⚠ get; give sb, offer sb; it be, there be. **prep:** with ▫ *I think it was his enthusiasm as much as anything else that decided me to go ahead.* ***It was*** *after all* ***an even chance****, and this has always seemed generous odds to me.* OBS ▫ ***It was a fifty-fifty chance*** *which staircase he would use so I tossed a penny and waited hopefully at the Baker Street exit.* ▫ *Right now you got something to sell. You got assets. I'm gonna be fair with you, Tagliaferri; I like to* ***give*** *everybody* ***an even chance****.* ST ▫ *There are only two of us being considered for the job and I happen to know that we're about equal as regards qualifications and experience. So, I suppose I'****ve a fifty-fifty chance of*** *getting it.* ▫ *I still wouldn't* ***give*** *the whole operation* ***better than an even chance****, but, at the time, I didn't even think there was that.* L ▫ variants have etc a better than even/fifty-fifty chance, have etc better than an even/a fifty-fifty chance.

have etc everything but (sth) [possess] have etc almost all the things that one needs for a task etc except for (one, often vital, thing) **V:** have (got), ⚠ get; give sb; there be; find. **prep:** with ▫ *He had the feeling that he now had almost all the information he needed, that he* ***had everything but*** *that one last piece of the jigsaw that would make the whole situation clear.* ▫ *'What about the attic?' 'I went right through it —* ***found*** *the most amazing things —* ***everything but*** *what I was looking for.'* ▫ *I particularly asked Margaret to write and let me know if she would be home for Christmas and here's a great long letter that* ***tells*** *me* ***everything but****.* ⇨ ⚠ anything but; nothing but sth/do sth.

have (got)/with an eye for etc the main chance [possess] do sth concentrating on one's own interests, on what one considers will be profitable, and ignoring the interests of others **prep:** for, on, to ▫ *But to talk of 'sincerity' helps no more than to talk of 'utter cynicism'. Clearly a man may not be altogether a conscious manipulator but still* ***have an eye on the main chance****.* UL ▫ *This is how Alec had seen it, in his book: not as an act of self-abnegation on her part, but as something done* ***with an eye to the main chance****.* PW ▫ *If, as his critics allege, Mr Wilson* ***had*** *too much of* ***an eye for the main chance****, that certainly doesn't emerge from his account of his relationship with Ministerial colleagues.* L

have (got)/with an eye to (doing) sth [possess] do sth for the sake of sth else, with the main or further purpose of sth else happening, or in the hope of achieving sth **o:** the future, further developments, possible closure, quick profits; cornering the market, impressing the general manager □ *Schweppes' first big acquisition was the right to distribute Pepsi-Cola, which they bought in 1953, clearly* ***having an eye to*** *the battles to come.* OBS □ *'Gunpoint' is a conventional Audie Murphy Western, made very much* ***with an eye to*** *television, about a small town sheriff pursuing a nefarious gang.* RT □ *There is something about the tone of these letters that makes me feel sure they were written* ***with an eye to*** *getting them published at a later date.*

have etc eyes in/at the back of one's head/neck [possess] (informal) (seem to, need to) have the ability to see in all directions at once (because a lot is happening around one, because there is sth suspicious going on, etc) **V:** have (got); ⚠ there be. **prep:** with □ *You need to* ***have eyes at the back of your head*** *to keep that kid out of mischief.* □ *Jack came out quickly, and closed the door. 'Collins* ***has got eyes in the back of his neck****,' he said, 'and he's only waiting for a chance like this.'* TT □ also pl *They've* ***got eyes in the back(s) of their head(s)****.*

have etc eyes in one's head [possess] (informal) be observant; be able to notice one's surroundings, what sb is doing etc **V:** have (got); ⚠ there be. **prep:** with □ *Well, it's getting pretty obvious about you and Katie, and I'****ve got eyes in my head*** *as well as anyone else.* TT □ *There's a notice outside that says 'Please knock before entering'.* ***Have****n't you* ***got eyes in your*** *idiot* ***head****?* □ *Her purse wasn't lost at all. It was lying on the hall table where anybody* ***with eyes in his head*** *would have seen it.* □ also pl *They've* ***got eyes in their heads****!*

have etc a face-lift [possess] receive etc cosmetic surgery to reduce sags and wrinkles caused by ageing; be re-decorated, reconstructed, modernized or otherwise improved **V:** have, ⚠ get; give sb. **prep:** with □ *Concrete has* ***had a face-lift*** *in recent years and is no longer its old forbidding grey self.* OBS □ *Even* ***getting one's face lifted*** *can't do much for nose-to-mouth lines.* TVT □ *Mrs Lauder* (of Estée Lauder Cosmetics)*, in her sixties, is a very good ad for the products—peach skin and so on —'and no* ***face lift****', she said, insisting that I check for scars round her hairline.* ST □ *The Lincoln Centre has now had a time to settle down, not only as a group of buildings devoted to the arts but as a factor in the* ***face-lifting*** *of New York's slummy West Side.* L □ also pl; variant have/get one's face lifted; n compound face-lifting.

have etc a fair crack of the whip [possess] (informal) have etc an equal opportunity with others to say sth, to show what one can do, or to play one's part in an undertaking **V:** have, ⚠ get; give, allow sb □ *Mr Botha believes that Africans should now be* ***given a fair crack of the whip*** *in the Zimbabwean Government.* T □ *'The press never* ***gives*** *doctors* ***a fair crack of the whip****.' There is some truth in this. Often we are not fair to doctors, expecting them to be not only dogmatic, but also omniscient.* NS □ *For the newspapers, and for the broadcast political discussions, gladiatorial engagements between the front benches are the main theme. In 'Yesterday in Parliament', on the other hand, the ordinary Member does* ***get a fair crack of the whip****.* L □ *Nowadays Sylvester very rarely appears with the orchestra at public preformances in London. This is so that Victor Jr, who has laboured for years behind the scenes, should* ***have a fair crack of the whip****.* ST

have etc (more than) a/one's fair share of sth [possess] have etc (more than) a usual, or expected, amount of sth (without the implication that others are either entitled or deprived) **V:** have (got); ⚠ enjoy; be blessed, favoured, gifted, with. **prep:** with. **o:** (good/bad) luck; adventures; good looks, talent, intelligence; disappointments □ *Up to the time he got into films he had made steady progress in the business of acting. Clearly he* ***had*** *a more than respectable talent and* ***a fair share of*** *the necessary luck.* TVT □ *Certainly, as birds go, the oven-bird appears to* ***have more than his fair share of*** *personality and charm.* DF □ *Business, so the saying goes, is people. Even more so is local government, a service-oriented industry* ***with more than its fair share of*** *loyal, and perhaps sometimes excessively dedicated, staff.* OBS ⇨ ⚠ get etc a/one's fair share.

have etc a familiar etc ring (about/to it) [possess] sound familiar; seem already known to one **S:** message, request, plan; name; music. **V:** have (got), ⚠ there be. **prep:** with. **adj:** familiar, old-fashioned, convincing, ironical, foreign □ *If this casino confrontation* ***has about it a familiar ring*** *today, it could be because among the representatives of British Intelligence in the casino that night was Ian Fleming, who more than a decade later was to make this moment the central point of 'Casino Royale'.* OBS □ *Unfortunately, Mr Tranter's descriptive excellence is not equalled in his writing of dialogue, which* ***has a stilted ring*** *to say the least.* SC

have etc a/the feeling (that) [possess] think etc that sth is the case, will happen, etc, though there is no reason for thinking so **V:** have (got), ⚠ get; give sb, leave sb with □ *She took the two bottles of whisky, half a bottle of brandy, and all the tins of soup. She* ***had a feeling that*** *she and Joe were going to need them.* AITC □ *He was very pleasant but I* ***got the feeling that*** *he didn't much like me, all the same.*

have etc feet of clay [possess] have etc some fundamental weakness or fault that injury, challenge or attack will reveal (from DANIEL II 31-35, describing a statue with a head of gold, and other parts progressively less durable and valuable, down to feet made partly of clay which, when struck by a stone, caused the whole to collapse) **V:** have, ⚠ possess. **prep:** with □ *Why don't you directly refute Lenin's thesis that imperialism is a colossus* ***with feet of clay****, and 'a bugbear'?* T □ *Every twisted corporate saga of recent years has had the same effect—showing that an erstwhile management hero* ***had****, among other things, administrative* ***feet of clay****.* OBS □ (NONCE) *The phrase 'high ideals' is commonly used derisively. If anyone else seems to be trying to 'live by principle' he may be a fool or prig; look for* ***the clay feet****.* UL

have etc one's/both feet on the ground [possess] have plenty of commonsense; know what one is doing and why; not be likely to be led into foolish undertakings; be realistic **V:** have (got), ⚠ keep. **prep:** with □ *'If my brother hadn't been with me I daresay I would have been* *talked into lending them the money.' 'Yes, It's a good job John* ***has both feet on the ground****, since you haven't.'* □ SYLVIA: *I want a home, Peter.* PETER: *I'll build one for you.* SYLVIA: *What, with dreams? I want a boy* ***with his feet on the ground****.* DPM □ *The working classes are at bottom in excellent health: rough and unpolished perhaps, but diamonds nevertheless; not refined, not intellectual but* ***with both feet on the ground****.* UL

have etc (the) first refusal [possess] be given etc the option to buy sth before it goes on the open market, or to accept a gift etc before it is offered to sb else **V:** have: ⚠ give, promise, sb □ *Mr Cadbury* ***gave*** *Lord Rothermere a firm option,* ***first refusal*** *on the papers should they ever come into the market.* T □ *No one has the* dedicace (= has my new book dedicated to them) *so far, but you can* ***have the first refusal****, if you like.* PW □ *'Look,' I said, 'I have a private customer waiting for an early oak bureau and I have* ***promised*** *him* ***first refusal****. I'll ring you if it does not suit him.'*

have etc a fit of (the) giggles [possess] succumb to etc irrepressible giggling for a short time **V:** have (got), ⚠ get; give sb □ (reading a script) *It's no wonder that in the middle of one steamy love scene Jenny* ***had a fit of the giggles*** *as her imaginary romp continued on another page.* TVT □ *I laughed a lot, particularly at Milligan's sport with cigarette commercials, but that doesn't persuade me to excuse his tendency to laugh at himself.* ***A fit of giggles*** *in the middle of a sketch is no substitute for a good script.* RT

have etc a fit [possess] suffer a physical seizure with convulsions; (fig) become wildly or excessively alarmed, dismayed, angered **V:** have; ⚠ take, throw □ *The car started up. 'Look the other way please,' Helena laughed, 'as I take this corner. The instructor would* ***have a fit*** *if he saw me.'* HAHA □ *I went along to interrogate him and he practically* ***threw a fit****, ending up by shouting at me: 'You English swine, what right have you got to be in this country anyway!'* DS □ often with *would* in (exaggerated) predictions of how sb might react.

have etc a flea in one's ear [possess] be reprimanded, rejected or humiliated **V:** have, ⚠ get. **prep:** with □ *If he tried to take over my little operation, he'd soon* ***get a flea in his ear****.* □ *...Duncan, who sank even lower in his chair like a discouraged Cupid* ***with a flea in his ear*** *from Venus.* US *He thought all he had to do was come and ask for his job back, but he soon* ***had a flea in his ear*** *from me, and* he *won't be back.* □ often *send sb away/off, go away, leave* ***with a flea in one's ear****.*

have a/one's fling [V + O] enjoy a short or long period of unlimited pleasure; allow oneself some special extravagance of behaviour, expenditure etc □ *He's only young once. Let him* ***have his fling****. He'll settle down, you'll see.* □ *It's nice for a bride to be able to dress up and be the centre of attraction, without having to feel guilty about it. And you never forget it, it's probably the last chance you get to* ***have*** *a bit of* ***a fling****.* TT

have (got) sb fooled [V + O + Comp] deceive or mislead sb; puzzle sb **S:** problem, task, puzzle; player, opponent □ *'I thought he was really ill.' 'He* ***had*** *me* ***fooled*** *too.'* □ *...the phoniest account of wage-slavery and incestuous relations ever. That really read as if it had been written by an American butterfly collector, but it* ***had*** *everybody* ***fooled*** *from Fleet Street to Pinewood.* JFTR

have (got)/with form [possess] (police slang) have a criminal record of some kind, esp one including a prison sentence, which can be consulted by the police □ *Mimi has a child whom she adores and a husband who* ***has*** *what English criminal lawyers call '****form****'.* NS

have etc the fortune/misfortune to do sth [possess] be lucky/unlucky to do, have, or be sth specified **V:** have (got), ⚠ be sb's. **prep:** with. **adj:** great, good ***(fortune);*** great ***(misfortune)*** □ *Israel has* ***had the fortune to*** *attract a nucleus of Jewish scientists from the Western countries.* NS □ *In his late forties he* ***had the misfortune to*** *lose the sight of one eye.* □ *It* ***was my good fortune to*** *have parents who were both understanding and tolerant.*

have etc a friend at court [possess] have access to sb who will help one by using his influence in an important place **V:** have (got), ⚠ get. **prep:** with □ *He had just mentioned Hector Rose* (a Permanent Secretary of State)*, for whom perversely he had taken a liking—and I teased him about his* ***friends at court****.* NM □ *'My brother has spoken so often and so well of you.' 'Well, it's good to know you* ***have a friend at court****,' said Robert, 'I was nervous about meeting you all.'*

have etc a frog in one's throat [possess] have a (temporary) loss or roughening of the voice, eg as might be caused by catarrh in the throat **V:** have (got), ⚠ get. **prep:** with □ *He started to speak, but coughed instead. 'Excuse me, I* ***had a frog in my throat****.'* □ *'What's the matter with you—have you got a sore throat?' 'I'm all right,' he answered hoarsely. 'It's just that I often* ***get a frog in my throat*** *first thing in the morning.'* □ *Against all odds (and, apparently, doctor's advice) he soldiered on for four long acts, without a top or a bottom to his voice and* ***a frog*** *in the middle. Our sympathies went out to him. But what, in opera's name, are understudies for?* NS ⇨ ⚠ have etc a lump in one's throat.

have (one's) fun enjoy oneself (doing sth) □ *Even Nicky had pink in his cheeks. In response to Brigit's question he admitted that they had* ***had fun*** *catching the kitten.* DC □ *All I know is you've* ***had your fun*** *and now I'm going to have a baby.* HD □ *All right, then, we've* ***had our fun****. Settle down now and get out your Geography work-books.* □ with possess usu indicates selfish enjoyment or a pleasure that is, or should be, temporary.

have etc a (great) future [possess] have etc good prospects; be likely etc to succeed; be likely etc to lead to success **S:** actor, minister; discos, supermarkets; plastics, detergents. **V:** have (got). **prep:** ⚠ with, without. **A:** ahead (of one/sb); before one □ *And Twiggy? Time alone will tell whether she* ***has a future*** *at this game. Her present is exquisite.* NS □ *Apprentices are, or should be, people* ***with a future****.* SC □ *Indeed, just about the only clear message to emerge from this book is that violence* ***has a great future*** *ahead of it.* L □ *I suppose any mother would like to see* *her son in a nice respectable job* ***with a future.***

(not) have etc a ghost of a chance (of doing sth) [possess] (informal) (not) have etc a slight chance (of achieving sth); (not) have etc a cat in hell's chance (of doing sth) (qv); (not) have etc a chance in hell (of doing sth) (qv); (not) have etc a dog's chance (of doing sth) (qv) **V:** have (got), ⚠ stand, get; give sb; there be. **prep:** with, without □ *'Perhaps you'll make it up again with Angie.'* ***'Not the ghost of a chance.*** *She's avoiding me like the plague.'* □ *Believe me, if I thought I* ***had the ghost of a chance*** *I'd apply for the job myself.* □ *'If Harry were to pay us back the £200 he borrowed, things wouldn't be so bad.' 'Yes, but* ***there isn't the ghost of a chance of*** *that.'* □ *Anyone* ***with the ghost of a chance of*** *getting a visa was queuing outside the consular offices.* □ usu neg.

have etc the gift of the gab [possess] (informal) have the ability to talk fluently and at length **V:** have (got), ⚠ possess. **prep:** with □ *Harry's a good person to invite to dinner parties. He's* ***got the gift of the gab*** *so conversation never flags when he's around.* □ *He's an ex-insurance man* ***with the gift of the gab*** *and a shrewd brain for business.* TO □ *Very remarkable chap, you know. Unusual to find a sense of responsibility* ***with*** *such* ***a gift of the gab.*** ASA □ *And it is true that one of Shaw's problems as a playwright is that he cannot resist* ***his*** *own* ***gift of the gab,*** *his desire to charm through whichever character currently has his or her mouth open.* RT

have etc the gift of tongues [possess] have knowledge of, and skill in, the use of a language or languages; have the ability to interest, delight, or inspire others in conversation or speeches **V:** have (got), ⚠ possess; be blessed, favoured, with; speak with. **prep:** with □ *Pope John Paul II makes a point of giving at least some of his speeches in the language of the country he's visiting. He* ***has the gift of tongues*** *in a way shared by none of the world's secular leaders.* □ *A man* ***with the gift of tongues,*** *he could speak fluently in four languages, and could get by in as many more.* □ *The chapels made wide use of lay preachers. They were 'one of us'* ***with*** *what admirers called '****the gift of tongues****', but doubters knew as 'the gift of the gab'.* UL □ *'You know,' Matthew said, 'this is most illuminating, and admirably put.' And Daniel himself was genuinely moved; he had been* ***speaking with the gift of tongues.*** US

have etc the gift/power(s) of total recall [possess] have etc the ability to recollect, as one chooses, events, one's past, what one has studied, read or listened to, wholly and in correct detail **V:** have (got), ⚠ possess; be blessed, born, with; lack. **prep:** with □ *...those people* ***with powers of total recall*** *who can identify any quotation and remember the names of all the horses who won the Derby.* SC □ *What special quality made E Nesbit so good at distilling the atmosphere of childhood, the small details that assume enormous importance? It was, for a start,* ***the gift of total recall*** *which, perhaps precociously, she had cultivated.* RT □ *Kempowski combines* ***the gift of*** *near-****total recall*** *with a chilling knack of letting his characters condemn themselves out of their own mouths.* ST

have (got)/with a good etc head of hair [possess] have hair that grows thickly to cover the scalp **adj:** good, ⚠ fine, magnificent, lovely □ *I don't think you'll grow bald, Bill. Your father lived to be 76 and still* ***had a good head of hair*** *on him.* □ *At thirty-five she still* ***had a head of hair*** *like black silk cotton, curly and thick as it fell to her fat olive shoulders.* DBM □ *Granny Green would never fail to tell the nurses after her hair was done, 'I* ***had a lovely head of hair*** *till you cut it off.'* MM □ ***With that head of hair*** *you don't need a hat.* □ usu said of hair that can be admired or envied.

have etc a good etc/one's innings [possess] (be allowed to) enjoy a long life or have a period of popularity, power etc; have a satisfactorily long turn at officiating, performing, speaking etc (from cricket) **V:** have, ⚠ get; give sb. **adj:** good, ⚠ fair, long □ *Being dead I don't think about. I have* ***had a good innings,*** *and it would be quite nice to have a rest.* L □ *None of these sirens would have* ***had an innings*** (a chance to marry him) *if Mrs Arbuthnot had been alive.* ST □ *I don't think he'll be re-elected president. People are feeling he's* ***had a long*** *enough* ***innings*** *and that the honours should go round.*

have etc (no) good reason (for (doing) sth) [possess] have etc (no) valid motive, explanation or justification (for doing sth) **V:** have; ⚠ there be; see; know. **prep:** for, with, (not) without □ *Last week's annual get-together of Wintrust shareholders was a jolly affair and* ***for good reason.*** *There was plenty to celebrate, what with thumping good increases in profits, assets and dividends last year.* OBS □ *I think he is very genuinely sorry to leave and probably* ***with good reason,*** *for he belongs to the soil here.* NS □ ***Without*** *any* ***good reason for*** *doing so, Mr Bludgeon was inclined to abandon a class halfway through a lesson, to the astonishment and delight of the pupils.* □ *...the woods at evening, the two figures* ***for no good reason*** *locked together, the shadows in the background...* RATT □ *He hit her again two weeks later,* ***for no better reason*** *than that he was half drunk and discouraged.* AITC □ *Her apprehension had* ***not been without reason.*** *Now it had flowered into this very real problem.* DC

have etc a good time [possess] (informal) enjoy oneself generally or on a particular occasion, eg as at a party, on a holiday, etc **V:** have, ⚠ give sb, treat sb to □ *Apparently he had taken an overdose of sleeping tablets. 'But why do it in Brighton? That's where one goes to* ***have a good time.'*** DC □ *He finds life largely acceptable so long as the big worries (debt, drink, sickness) keep away, and so long as there is adequate scope for '****having a good time****'.* UL □ *If the weather's fine we can* ***give*** *the kids* ***a good time,*** *with pony rides and picnics on the beach.* □ *I know Angie's just a* ***good-time*** *girl. But she's fun to take out and it doesn't bother me who else she goes out with.* □ *Most of the canoes were swamped but the water was warm* ***and a good time was had by all.*** ST □ often derogatory, as in *She's only interested in* ***having a good time;*** attrib use *a* ***good-time*** *girl;* variant, (and) a good time was had by all (often facetious or ironic), may end a description of a pleasant or social occasion. ⇨ ⚠ have/give sb a high old time.

have got it badly (informal) esp be very much in love with sb, but used also of other enthusiasms, infatuations or crazes □ *'I like her.' He paused and chose a little colloquialism which he remembered hearing somewhere. 'She**'s got it** very **badly** over you, Robin.'* ASA □ *'Steve's always had plenty of girl-friends, but it's different this time.' '**Got it bad**, has he?'* □ *Most of the twelve-year-olds had dreams of being ballet-dancers or show-jumpers. I'**d got it badly** too, but it was skin-diving in my case.* □ variant (informal) have got it bad.

have etc the grace etc to do sth [possess] have etc a sense of what is suitable, polite or considerate, behaviour and thus do sth specified **V:** have (got). **prep:** ⚠ with, without. **O:** grace, ⚠ courtesy, (good) manners, (common) decency, □ *Why could she not **have the grace to** accept the polite lie he had told her?* HD □ *I did **have the grace to** feel a bit ashamed when I got a picture postcard from a Chelsea address.* CON □ *Announcing at the last minute that he couldn't attend the meeting after all, he might have **had the courtesy to** explain why.* □ *He was unnecessarily rude but at least he **had the decency to** apologise afterwards.*

have etc green fingers [possess] have greater than usual ability to grow plants, flowers, crops, successfully **V:** have (got), ⚠ possess. **prep:** with □ *Williamson's farm rated as an A during the war, and in the ensuing decades flourished under his **green fingers**.* OBS □ *Potted plants always die with me. I'm afraid I **have**n't **got green fingers**.* □ *'Nasty frost though, very nasty. It's a wretched nuisance.' 'I'm sure you are **green-fingered** enough to manage, Mr Purnell,' she said.* TT □ adj compound green-fingered.

have etc guts [possess] (informal) be a tough, persistent, courageous type of person **V:** have (got); ⚠ show. **prep:** with. **det:** no; plenty of, some □ *'She **has got guts**; no one can deny that,' said a colleague.* OBS □ *Don't give up like that, Harry. **Show** some **guts**, man, and refuse to be beaten.* □ *The bloody fool's **got guts**, I'll say that for him.* PE ⇨ ⚠ next entry.

have etc the guts to do sth [possess] (informal) have etc sufficient courage, determination, or defiance of opposition, to be able to do sth specified **V:** have (got). **prep:** ⚠ with, without □ *He also saw in Lansbury the good-natured but woolly-minded pacifist who would not **have the guts to** use force.* OBS □ ALISON: *I used to hope that one day, somebody would **have the guts to** slam the door in our faces, but they didn't.* LBA □ *Would you have **had the guts to** join Xerox in 1959? Volkswagen in 1950? IBM in 1946?* L □ *At last! A writer **with the guts to** present us with a sincere, true-to-life situation.* RT ⇨ ⚠ previous entry.

have had one's chips (dated slang) be dead or dying; suffer a serious loss of prestige, favour, position; have had it (qv) **S:** he, she, they, you; firm, company; project □ *'Here's another case of somebody drinking weed-killer from a lemonade bottle.' 'Well, if it was that Paraquat stuff, he**'s had his chips**.'* □ *'I think Goldilocks* (a nickname) ***has had his chips**.' 'The push?' he said. 'From here, anyway.'* TT □ JO: *It doesn't really matter if you do fancy her, anyway, beause she's gone. You're too late. You**'ve had your chips**.* TOH

have had one's day/time [V + O] be too old, worn out, to be of much or any further use; not be able to function as one used to; the day of sb/sth is over/finished (qv) □ *'I'm afraid these shoes **have had their day**.' 'They certainly have. Throw them out.'* □ (alleged experiments on patients that are in hospital with terminal diseases) *It seems the attitude has been that these patients **have had their day** anyway, so that even if things go wrong there's not much harm done* □ HAVA: *Going to die? Please, Mr Levy, don't speak that way; you scare me.* SAM: *Listen, be a good, sensible girl—I**'ve had my time** and I'm going to die—what's more natural than that?* HSG ⇨ ⚠ have one's day[1,2].

have had enough be unable or unwilling to stand any more of sth, eg pain, worry, interference, disappointment, hard work, etc **adv mod:** (just) about, more than. **A:** of sb, from sb □ TONY: *I'm waiting for that moment when you put your foot down about something and say you**'ve had enough**. But you never do.* EHOW □ *The work was hard but the pay was good. I had no complaint against the company, but I suddenly felt I **had had enough**.* □ *The Marquis stood in the middle of the haymarket offering gin to all comers. They came all right. But the police **had had enough**. They managed to arrest him on a charge of furious driving.* L

have had it (informal) have come to the end of one's life or career; not be able any longer to continue an activity or a relationship, or to command the respect or interest of others; have had one's chips (qv) □ *I was thinking: 'Well, that's that. I**'ve had it**,' and deciding that I was now in some kind of outer-room to heaven.* TST □ *Sometimes I think I**'ve had it**, I really do. I get phases of desperation and my husband and I agree we'll manage to live somehow on his salary.* SC □ PHILIP: *Why don't you recognize the fact that we**'ve had it**? We've served a purpose.* MYRA: *You mean we should leave it all to the youth?* EHOW □ *I hope nobody wants a last drink because if they do they**'ve had it**.*

have (got)/with one's hands full [possess] have plenty of work to do, or so much that one cannot take on anything else **A:** at home; with all these papers to correct; coping with the rush of orders □ *I won't stay for coffee. I can see you **have your hands full** this morning.* □ *Its task was also to arouse amongst the educated public a new sense of values in matters relating to the material heritage of India. It **had its hands full**.* SD □ *Somebody else will have to see to the curtains and lighting. I'll **have my hands full** helping with all the changes of costume.* □ *Joe Sugden**'s hands are full** with the Emmerdale Farm Annual General Meeting coming up.* TVT □ variant one's hands are full.

have etc (no) hard feelings [possess] have or retain (no) feelings of resentment, or bitterness, about sth said or done to one by another person **V:** have; ⚠ bear sb; there be. **prep:** with (no), without (any) □ *He thought I was wrong and said so. I **bear** him **no hard feelings** for that.* □ *They had both agreed that the engagement had been a mistake. They broke it off, apparently **without hard feelings** on either side.*

have etc a hard row to hoe [possess] have a long and wearisome task or a difficult and arduous style of life (from the hand-hoeing of weeds among rows of field plants) **V:** have (got); ⚠ give sb; it be. **prep:** with □ *It's a curious thing about the English race: they hate brains. People who have a little flash of poetry or genius in their make-up* ***have a hard row to hoe***. ST □ *'He's very young to be appointed Headmaster, isn't he?' 'Yes, some of the older staff don't like the idea at all. And* ***it'll be a hard row*** *for him* ***to hoe*** *in other respects as well. The school is going comprehensive next year.'*

have/give sb a hard time [possess] have/ give sb difficult work; be in a situation in which people harass, obstruct, or demand too much of one/harass etc sb else □ *The eldest of four sons, he was always the rebel. His father had died and his mother had problems. He recalls: 'I suppose it was my individuality coming out, but she certainly* ***had a hard time*** *from me.'* TVT □ *I would kill any fox that I found doing specific damage to stock, and I'd do it with the local pair if I knew they were* ***giving*** *somebody* ***a hard time***. *But I don't know that they are.* SC □ *West Yorkshire sent a man to cut down all the bunting from the lamp-posts. It was 'a traffic hazard'. The man they sent was not only on the gala committee, he was the man who traditionally put the bunting up. He was* ***given a hard time***. G

have (got)/with a (good) head for figures [possess] be good at arithmetic, at calculating □ *I* ***have no head for figures****—drawing and making things with my hands is what I can do best; whereas my sister Maureen, blessed* ***with a*** *superb* ***head*** *not only* ***for figures*** *but also for words, draws cows and ants to look much the same.* □ often neg, esp in have no head for figures.

have (got)/with a (good) head for heights [possess] be able to stand on, move along, or look down from, a high place without feeling giddy or afraid □ *I judged the distance, looked at the drop, and decided I was not a daring fellow. I* ***had no head for heights***. UTN □ *Any fit person* ***with a head for heights*** *could learn to do rock-climbing.* □ often neg, esp in have no head for heights.

have etc a head of steam [possess] have etc steam pressure, to drive an engine, etc; (fig) show an increase in enthusiasm, energy, rate of work, feeling etc **V:** have; ⚠ develop, get up, produce; there be. **prep:** with. **adj:** good, powerful □ *After reading or listening to nearly 100 speeches, I cannot honestly report that anyone here has* ***got up*** *much of* ***a head of steam*** *about what the Tanzanian delegate described as the 'increasingly iniquitous status quo'.* NS □ (rugby) *But in the loose, especially in the concluding 20 minutes, it was the Irish forwards who were able to* ***produce a*** *more powerful* ***head of steam***. ST □ *It could happen that Fitzwilliam will beat Crowe to the London stockmarket scene. Whatever finally emerges, Crowe shares still seem to* ***have a*** *good* ***head of steam***. OBS □ *He offers her £100 to get an abortion, but she sweeps out on* ***a*** *proud* ***head of steam****, hating and loving him at the same time.* SC ⇨ ⚠ get up steam (Vol 1).

have etc a head start [possess] have etc a certain advantage over others, or above what is usual at the start of a race, competition, course of study, etc **V:** have (got), ⚠ get; give sb. **prep:** with □ *In her time (she* ***had a head start*** *as RADA's youngest student at 16) she has played Rosalind, Lady Macbeth, Cleopatra, Beatrice, Desdemona and Titania, and Ophelia last year in the West End.* OBS □ *In 'Winner Takes All', Tarbuck takes bets from contestants gambling on their ability to choose the right answer from six possibilities. And 'being a bookie's son* ***gives me a head start***.*'* TVT □ *Whether chairing a panel game, quizzing a politician, or talking of books, Robinson gives a display of language which may or may not help to communicate. Readers of 'Brewer's Dictionary of Phrase and Fable'* ***have a head start*** *in keeping up with him.* L

have etc a healthy respect for sb/sth [possess] have etc a respect for, fear of, caution about, sb/sth which it is wise to have for one's own good **V:** have, ⚠ feel, show; give sb. **prep:** with □ *The confrontation over Cuba must have* ***given*** *the Russians* ***a healthy respect for*** *the United States Administration.* OBS □ *Don't worry. I have a healthy respect for the Law.* □ *A man* ***with a*** *more* ***healthy respect*** *than myself* ***for*** *firearms, especially for one pointed in my direction, would be hard to find.* □ healthy (= 'preserving one's safety or comfort') also occurs in the expressions *have a healthy dislike of sb/sth, at a healthy distance.*

have a heart(!) be more tolerant, considerate, merciful, helpful etc □ *'****Have a heart****, Jake,' he said. 'If you don't help me to get away now I may not be let out for days.'* UTN □ *He dropped the window with a crash, and was staring angrily up the line when a rich husky voice from inside the compartment summoned him back. '****Have a heart****, partner! I'm refrigerated to the marrow as it is!'* HD □ exclamatory appeal to sb.

(not) have (got) the heart to do sth [possess] (not) be willing, or able, to do sth which could, or does, cause distress either to oneself or another **det:** (not) much, little, no. **Inf:** to refund the money, to turn them out □ *We disposed of the car when Maurice died. It was his really; we* ***hadn't the heart to*** *use it somehow.* RATT □ *She* ***had not the heart to*** *spoil his pleasure with her own troubles.* RFW □ *The child was in obvious need. Who could* ***have the heart to*** *refuse him?*

have (got)/with a heart of gold [possess] have a noble, kind, helpful, loyal etc nature (which may be contrasted with a rough and unpleasing exterior) □ *Everyone behaved as if they were under contract to live up to the tradition of the outspoken Yorkshireman* ***with a heart of gold*** *underneath a rough exterior.* RATT □ *The hero, a Tory MP, has as his loyal ally a rugged Labour MP, who, though he makes foolish radical speeches in the House,* ***has a heart of gold***. OBS □ *You* ***'ave 'earts*** (= have hearts) ***of gold*** *like my friend, Cavaliere Skipton. I cannot love you enough!* US □ *We are anything but strangers to the small town in Montana with its store and sheriff's office, the bullying deputy, crooked gambler, and even a whore* ***with a heart of gold***. *We have seen it before in scores of Western movies.* NS

have (got)/with a heart of stone [possess] have an unfeeling, callous, pitiless nature □ *It* *could not be said that she* ***had a heart of stone****, for this usually implies some conscious rejection of pity.* ASA □ *Elspeth was extremely photogenic. The pictures of her leaving the court would have moved* ***a heart of stone****.* PW □ also pl have hearts of stone.

have etc a heavy/light heart [possess] be filled with feelings of despondency, grief, sorrow/joy happiness, relief (the reference always being to a condition caused by sth, not a general characteristic of the person specified) **V:** have; ⚠ there be. **prep:** with □ ***There were*** *many* ***heavy hearts*** *in the little fishing village that night.* □ *He recalled* ***with a heavy heart*** *the tone of her voice when she had murmured 'a double wedding' with all too evident pleasure at the prospect.* RM □ *We finally found my kitten locked up in the cupboard under the stairs. It was* ***a light-hearted*** *little boy that went to bed that evening, I can tell you.* □ adj compound heavy-/light-hearted; variant (informal) be heavy/light of heart.

have etc a hide/skin like a rhinoceros [possess] show etc insensitivity to attack, criticism, slights or insults **V:** have (got); ⚠ need. **prep:** with □ *Angrily the men returned 10 minutes later to tell their mates, 'We had no impact. These men* ***have hides like a rhinoceros****.'* OBS □ *To stand up and oppose Churchill in person* ***needed the skin of a rhinoceros****.* ST □ *But how do you identify your dedicated social climber? She will certainly have Cardin or Yves St Laurent labels sewn into her chain-store coat.* ***Her hide is as thick as a rhinoceros*** *in a bullet-proof body-stocking.* ST □ frequently adapted, as shown.

have (got)/with high hopes [possess] be optimistic and ambitious in one's hopes **A:** of winning the cup; for her clever son; that he will succeed □ *Our* (medical) *team* ***has the highest hopes*** *I assure you. We'll have you out of here in no time!* HAHA □ *Local owner Albert Burnett* ***has high hopes*** *of winning Newcastle's Gosforth Park Cup with Shamrock Star.* DM □ ***Hopes are high*** *that the National Exhibition Centre, soon to be built just outside the city will restore Birmingham's rate of industrial expansion.* NS □ *'The Long March of Everyman', Radio 4's 26-episode history of the British underdog, set off last November* ***with high hopes****.* L □ *Everyone's* ***hopes ran high*** *for Plessey had recently taken over the computer-based numerical control system for making machine tools.* RT □ variants hopes are high; hopes run high.

have/give sb a high old time [possess] (informal) enjoy oneself immensely, esp in an exuberant or jolly way/entertain sb in such a way that he enjoys himself immensely □ *I'm a bit of an old fogy, but I still flatter myself I can rise to the occasion. We should* ***have a high old time*** *tonight and no mistake, heh?* DIL □ *'Oh, yes,' said Dollie, 'we* ***had a high old time*** *all right. I enjoyed myself.'* ASA ⇨ ⚠ have etc a good time.

have etc Hobson's choice [possess] have etc the option of taking either what is offered or nothing (from the 17th c carrier who would not offer a free choice of horses, but hire out one only in its proper turn) **V:** have (got), ⚠ get, take; give sb; there be. **prep:** with □ *In America it is still possible to choose from a fairly large selection of architect-built homes, rather than simply* ***taking Hobson's choice*** *and thanking your lucky stars that you've found anything that's remotely habitable.* ST

have (got)/with hollow legs [possess] (facetious) have a large appetite □ *Lydia told Minor not to eat too much cake as they would be having tea in half and hour. 'That's all right, Miss Lydia,' said Nanny. '****Hollow legs*** *they* ***have*** *at their age.'* WDM

have etc a home (of one's own) to go to [possess] used esp in reproachful or aggressive comments or questions suggesting that sb's own home is where he should be, rather than where he is **V:** have (got). **prep:** ⚠ with (no), without □ JO: ***Have****n't you* ***got a home to go to****, Geof?* TOH □ *I'm tired of entertaining Tony at all hours of the day and night. It's not as if he* ***had****n't* ***a home of his own to go to****.* □ *There's no need for us to stay here if we're not welcome. After all, we do* ***have a home of our own to go to****.* □ esp in neg and interrog constructions; also pl have homes (of their own) to go to.

have (got)/get a hunch (that) [possess] (informal) have/get a premonition or strong feeling (that sth is the case, or is about to happen) (the implication often implying being a shrewd or inspired guess that is later proved correct) **cl:** (that) he will come, (that) you were going to ask me □ *Purvis's description of him is right. Nationality, on the face of it, British. But I* ***have a hunch that*** *he might not be.* ARG □ *I had a couple of chits about Waterman from the Baron during the war. So today I just* ***had a hunch*** *he might want a note on Waterman. Instinct.* PP □ *I had worked on this job for ten years and* ***my hunch is that*** *the peers were getting poorer.* L □ variant sb's hunch is (that).

have etc an idea (that) [possess] have etc reason to think that sth is the case or is likely to happen **V:** have (got), ⚠ get; give sb. **prep:** with. **det:** no, (not) any, (not) the least. **adj:** good, shrewd, vague □ *He said he* ***had an idea that*** *Miss Prentice had gone abroad.* RFW □ *No, I don't know where he spends the night when he doesn't come home, but* ***I've a*** *good* ***idea*** *who he'll be with.* □ MILLY: *Myra, what are you going to do?* MYRA: *I* ***have no idea****.* EHOW □ ***Have*** *you* ***any idea*** *what it costs to put a man into space?* □ *'Of course he speaks Welsh. It was his first language.' 'Really? I* ***had no idea****.'* □ *I didn't press him but I* ***got the idea*** *he'd be willing to cooperate.* □ *Me a teacher! What* ***gave*** *you* ***that idea****?* □ dets listed not used before an adj; often neg implying lack of information or inability to make up one's mind about sth, esp have no idea.

have etc an idea of sth [possess] have etc an impression, understanding, of sth studied or explained to one; know sth from experience or instruction **V:** have (got), get; give sb. **prep:** with. **det:** some, (not) much, no. **adj:** good, fair rough, poor; □ *I see you've done social research work before so you should* ***have a*** *good* ***idea of*** *the kind of information we want.* □ *The annual careers guide is a valuable introduction,* ***giving some idea of*** *the range of opportunities open to school-leavers.* OBS □ *'You mean you keep them lying about on your desk?' 'Oh, I lock them away at night.' 'You haven't* ***got much idea of*** *security, have you?'* OMIH □ dets listed not used before an adj.

have etc sth in one's blood [possess] have etc sth as part of one's nature, character, through heredity or custom **V:** have (got), ⚠ get; there be. **prep:** with □ *The desert**'s in my blood**; and when I go home after the war I'll take a sackful of sand with me!* SC □ *Shirley Anne can reasonably claim to **have** betting **in her blood**. Her father, Tom Baines, is a well-known London bookie with several shops.* ST □ *When local people of Welsh descent come together they can start up a choir straight away. 'The harmonies are there, aren't they? It**'s in the blood**, isn't it?'* OBS

have etc sth in one's favour [possess] have etc sth as an advantage or asset, helping one towards a desired result **V:** have (got); ⚠ be. **prep:** with, without. **S/O:** youth, a sound constitution; years of experience; the wind, climatic conditions □ (a fishing competition) *Everything **was in** the postman**'s favour**—years of practice, expert knowledge of the river, the support of the crowd.* TO □ *'Our side haven't much chance with the ball in this wind.' 'Oh well, if it doesn't drop, it'll **be in our favour** in the second half.'* □ *Though Frank **had** youth and good looks **in his favour**, a shrewd girl was more likely to settle for Alan's £10,000 a year.*

have it (that) suggest, state, declare, that sth is the case, is true **S:** tradition, the story; rumour, local gossip; some, others; the police, his wife □ *Tradition **has it that** Bridge of Allan copper was used in the first coinage of halfpennies, struck for the Coronation of Queen Mary in 1543.* SC □ *The legend **has it that**, during a recruiting drive in 1795, the Duchess of Gordon put a golden guinea between her lips and said she would kiss any man who enlisted.* TVT □ *Disappeared. Rumour **had it** he was killed in a reprisal raid up in the Fermoy area.* PP

have etc it/things both ways [possess] (try to) combine two ways of thinking or behaving, satisfy two demands, obtain two results, etc that are, or might be thought to be, exclusive of each other; have one's cake and eat it (too) (qv) **V:** have (got), ⚠ get; want □ *Victorian critics of the monarchy were able to **have it both ways**, denouncing the Queen for her avarice, the Prince of Wales for his extravagance.* L □ *To be admired for one's talents or to be loved for oneself? Men **want it both ways** and I am surprised that women do not make a little more pretence of giving it—especially when they want to marry the men in question.* SPL

have (got) it good [possess] (informal) enjoy prosperity, comfortable conditions of life, etc □ *Myra Chetwynd, the fashion model, had become an important symbol. A symbol of possession, of achievement, of ease, **having it good**, what the ad man, in his sickening dialect, calls 'gracious living'.* CON □ BESSIE: *You'll cry—you'll see—when I'm gone—you don't know when you**'ve got it good**. Didn't I give you everything you wanted?* HSG □ *All the complaints about food, accommodation and facilities come from people who I know for a fact have never **had it better**.* □ *Mr Macmillan was still riding the wave that had taken him to landslide victory in the '**never had it so good**' election of 1959.* L □ *Greig **has never had it so good**. Late in his career he is enjoying well-earned luxuries.* OBS □ variant you've never had it so good (a catchphrase since its use in 1959 by the Conservative Party as a campaigning slogan for re-election to office).

have (got) it made [possess] (informal) be sure of (continued) success **S:** firm, hotel, store; businessman, actor □ *Why go to the Outer Hebrides to open a hotel? If you stay here in the middle of Birmingham, you'll **have it made**.* □ *To hear the Group talk you'd think they**'d got it made**—just because they got a two-minute spot on a Regional TV show.*

have etc it/things one's (own) way [possess] (informal) be allowed to have the last word in an argument; succeed in doing what one wants, or doing sth in the way one wants, despite some opposition; dominate a situation, eg a sporting contest **V:** have (got), ⚠ get; want □ *All right then, **have it your way**. I'm tired of arguing.* □ *That's James all over, he's got to **have things his own way**.* □ *In the second half, the heavier Welsh pack **had things** pretty much **their own way**.* □ stress patterns have it 'one's way, have it one's 'own way.

have etc the jitters etc [possess] (informal) be in an unsettled, fearful, nervous state, esp when awaiting or undergoing some serious trial or ordeal **V:** have (got), ⚠ get; give sb. **prep:** with. **O:** the jitters, ⚠ the shakes, the willies □ *When her hand trembled as she handed Brigit her cup of hot chocolate, she laughed shakily and apologized. 'I'm sorry. I've **got the jitters**.'* DC □ *Meet me for coffee before my exam. If I've someone to talk to it will keep me from **getting the shakes**.* □ *You're **giving me the willies** the way you keep jumping up and running to the window.*

have (got) a (hard/tough) job to do sth/doing sth do sth only with great difficulty □ *It now seems that earlier estimates of a business boom were over-optimistic and that the Administration will **have a job to** prevent a recession.* SC □ *Malta doesn't make anything much or grow anything—in fact, it **has a job** supporting itself.* L □ *'John's not fit to drive.' 'I know, but you'll **have a hard job** stopping him.'*

have (got)/with a kick like a mule [possess] (informal) have an unmistakeably definite effect on the recipient, spectator etc resulting in his being stimulated, galvanized, stunned or stupefied **S:** drink, drug; play, film, piece of music; her presence; his conversation □ *You be careful. Some of these home-brews **have a kick like a mule**.* □ *He gave me a small glass of some raw spirit **with a kick like a mule**.* □ *For amateurs of exotic dancing there was the Ballet de Rio de Janeiro in a voodoo piece, Zuinaaluti, **with a kick like a mule** but curiously little flavour of its own.* T

have/give sb kittens [possess] (informal) react to a situation, or piece of information, with surprise and alarm, or with fussy and excited behaviour/act in such a way as to cause sb else to be alarmed □ *My mum thinks money is for saving. She'd **have kittens** if she knew how much I paid for this coat.* □ *She'd been giving the baby a half aspirin and a teaspoonful of whisky every night to make him sleep. The doctor **had kittens** when he found out what was going on.*

have etc the knack (of it) [possess] have or learn a practical skill **V:** have (got), ⚠ get; learn

□ *I know you're used to painting with a brush, but a roller's far quicker once you* ***get the knack of it****.*

have (got)/with a/the knack of doing sth [possess] have an aptitude for, or a tendency towards, acting or behaving in a certain way **adj:** (un)happy, (un)fortunate □ *He always* ***had a knack of*** *falling out with anyone in time.* PP □ *The Bank of England* ***has a*** *happy* ***knack of*** *not doing these things at the expected moment and then doing them when expectations have been temporarily postponed.* T □ *Dr Jackson* ***has the knack of*** *putting nervous patients at their ease.*

have (got)/get the last laugh [possess] be the rival, competitor, opponent etc who after alternations of fortune, is finally successful, outdoes another or others □ *President Pompidou could* ***have the last laugh*** *over his old chief, General de Gaulle, who, many believed, cherished hopes of becoming the first President of Europe.* OBS □ *One can only wish the former civic dignitary luck in his labours between now and Friday morning and hope that he* ***has the last laugh*** *after all.* G □ variant he who laughs last laughs longest/loudest.

have etc the last word [possess] (be allowed to) speak etc last in an argument, discussion etc —this being regarded as decisive, or closing off further debate; be the final authority or judge in an office, the home etc **V:** have (got), ⚠ get; let sb have, give sb □ *If the negotiations fail and the Government says that the outcome is unsatisfactory, the people must* ***have the last word*** *in a referendum.* ST □ *There wasn't any point in arguing, so I got up and put on my tie and shoes. Here the police* ***had the last word****.* QA ⇨ ⚠ the last word (in sth).

have etc a long face [possess] have etc a dismal, disappointed or disapproving expression on one's face **V:** have (got), wear, pull. **prep:** with. **det:** a, such a, what a □ *I suppose they lost at the match, because I can't think of any other reason why you should* ***have such a long face****.* LLDR □ *How shocked she was, because in a novel —I forget its name—somebody, some naughty, naughty women broke up a happy home. Oh,* ***what a long face*** *she* ***pulled****!* PW □ *'She says "No"?' I said with hardly any hesitation, 'She hasn't made up her mind. There's still hope.' Phuong laughed. 'You say "hope"* ***with such a long face****.'* QA □ ***The longest faces*** *in Llandudno last week belonged to the Communists in the National Union of Mineworkers.* OBS □ *Is anything wrong with Paul? He says he's all right but I can't remember seeing* ***a longer face****—helooks ready to burst into tears.*

have etc a long way etc to go [possess] have etc much still to do, learn, change, improve; have a long time to wait (until sth happens) **V:** have (got), ⚠ there be. **prep:** with. **O:** long way, ⚠ fair way, some distance, far, a lot further, a bit. **A:** still, yet □ *Housing and sanitary conditions have improved under the new administration but* ***there's a long way to go*** *yet.* □ (popular breeds of dogs) *But the King Charles Spaniel* ***has far to go*** *before it dethrones the Miniature Poodle.* OBS □ *'Will I ever be as good a player as Geoff?' 'Perhaps, but you****'ve a fair way to go*** *before that day comes.'*

have etc a lot to be grateful/thankful for [possess] (cliché) be, in some or many respects, fortunate or more fortunate than others **V:** have (got); ⚠ find. **prep:** with. **O:** a lot, much, a great deal, a good deal □ *Of course I would like to be able to get about as I used to, but I realize I* ***have a lot to be thankful for****.* □ *When they look back, and especially when they look abroad (for example, at Northern Ireland), the Greeks* ***find much to be thankful for****.* OBS □ *He's not complaining, he's a man* ***with a lot to be grateful for****.*

have(got)/with a lot to learn [possess] not be well enough informed, or experienced in general or about sth in particular **A:** from us, from your example, from animals; about life, about the theatre, about running a newspaper □ *Far from this country learning about road safety from America, the Americans* ***have a lot to learn*** *from us.* L □ *He****'s got a lot to learn*** *and ten more years to learn it in. Or rather, he****'s got a lot to*** *un****learn****.* L □ *The youngster* ***has a lot to learn*** *about his world, and the simple acts of play help him to explore.* TVT

have (got)/with a lot to put up with [possess] (informal) have much to endure as a pattern of life or work **O:** much, enough, a good deal □ *'Tell me it all, my lad,' she said. 'Get it off your chest. I can see you****'ve had a lot to put up with****.'* LLDR □ *My mother* ***had much to put up with****, poor soul, but survived her trouble with an increasing sweetness to the age of eighty-four.* SD

have etc a lump in one's throat [possess] feel etc a constriction in one's throat as a result of strong emotion caused by beauty, love, sadness, grief, relief, gratefulness **V:** have (got), ⚠ get; give sb; there be. **prep:** with □ *Seeing him step out of the plane and down the gangway* ***gave*** *me such* ***a lump in my throat*** *that when we finally met I was quite unable to speak.* □ also pl *Several* ***had a lump in their throat(s)****.* ⇨ ⚠ have etc a frog in one's throat.

have (got)/with a memory like a sponge/sieve [possess] have/lack the ability to absorb and retain information, to keep in mind the details and practical arrangements of daily life and work □ *I* ***have*** *normally* ***a memory like a sponge****: I used often to fill in spare moments by presenting pages of print before my mind's eye.* RATT □ *I wouldn't depend on John. He****'s got a memory like a sieve****.* □ *Of course I forgot. What do you expect of someone* ***with a memory like a sieve****?*

have etc (a) method in one's/sb's madness [possess] there is a pattern and/or purpose in one's/sb's irrational or unusual behaviour **V:** have (got), ⚠ (there) be. **prep:** with □ (source) *Though this be* ***madness****, yet* ***there's method in'****t.* HAMLET II 2 □ *Yet Theodore's appalling reputation does not fit this absolutely. He was far too emotional to be a calculating villain, and* ***there was no*** *real* ***method in his madness****.* RM □ *By the time they do realize* ***there is a*** *crafty* ***method in their*** *opponent's apparent* ***madness*** *he has won the match.* BM

have (got)/with the Midas touch [possess] have the ability to make a financial success of all one's projects or undertakings (from the Greek myth of King Midas to whom the gods granted that everything he touched turned into gold) □ *Candidates for your financial wizard-work, **your Midas touch**, are queueing up and falling over each other.* PW □ (marine salvage) *'Not until we have shifted every grain of sand out there will we leave the "Atocha's" grave,' says the man **with the** real **Midas Touch**.* OBS □ *'Your father knows how to reward talent — but your father plans to give talent leisure, and of that we have a very shrinking supply.' 'My father,' James said grimly, '**has King Midas's touch**.'* HAA □ King not usu used; stress pattern have the 'Midas touch.

have etc a mind to do sth [possess] have the intention, or feel a strong desire, to do sth **V:** have (got), ⚠ be in, find oneself in. **prep:** with. **det:** (half) a, no □ *When they heard I **had a mind to** walk the whole length of the Downs from west to east they recommended keeping to the ridge the whole way.* L □ *Miss Pilchester remembered some stock exchange figures and **found herself in half a mind to** ask Pop what he thought she ought to do with her 3% War Stock.* DBM □ *I **had no mind to** let such moments of contemplation be ruined by miserable yearnings for a woman I could not find.* UTN

have etc a mind of one's own [possess] be (habitually and characteristically) capable of forming opinions, making decisions, etc independently; be determined to act as one thinks right or suitable for oneself **V:** have (got). **prep:** ⚠ with; without □ *'I'd like to know who's been putting such ideas into your head.' 'What do you mean? I **have a mind of my own**.'* □ *I'd discover something unimportant to disagree with her about so that she'd think me an intelligent type **with a mind of my own**.* RATT □ *By the time he was fifty Eric began to display what looked like **a mind of his own**.* MM ⇨ ⚠ know one's own mind.

have etc mixed feelings [possess] react to a person, situation, event, piece of news, etc with confused or conflicting feelings, such as love and hate, joy and sorrow, contempt and pity **V:** have, ⚠ there be, show. **prep:** with. **A:** about him; on this subject □ *Christopher Seaman **has mixed feelings** about musical competitions. 'These have often been the means of discovering great talent. But there's always the danger that some youngsters will be beaten and simply pack it in.'* RT □ *Miss Quentin's admirers, who have been regretting her recent retirement from the limelight, will hear **with mixed feelings** the report that she is bound for Hollywood.* UTN □ *When I read somewhere this week that a Peterborough citizen had raised only £5 after three weeks of fasting in aid of the Ethiopian victims of famine **my feelings were**—well, let's play it safe and say **mixed.*** NS □ *Victoria went to bed that night in a turmoil of **mixed feelings**.* TCB □ variant one's feelings are mixed.

have etc mixed motives [possess] do sth for more than one reason (the implication sometimes being that the motive(s) may be discreditable) **V:** have (got): ⚠ there be. **prep:** with □ *I don't believe that most people are more concerned to feel good than to do good when they support charities or send donations to relief funds — and even if they do **have mixed motives** that doesn't prevent their money from doing good.* □ *His **motives** in taking on the job were '**mixed**', he says, and he denies getting the same personal kick out of multiplying business assets, so clearly and sucessfully shown by his chairman.* SC □ *Like Frick and Mellon and other transatlantic billionaires, Morgan collected fine and rare things for **a mixture of motives**, partly to satisfy his sense of power and because there was little outlet for his vast wealth.* SC □ variants one's motives are mixed, a mixture of motives.

have (got) one's/its moments [possess] (informal) have short periods that are happier, more interesting, more successful, etc than are usual in the course of one's life or work; have sth of interest or amusement here and there; have unpleasant short periods contrasted with pleasant ones **S:** life, partnership; play, speech. **adj:** happier, lighter, livelier; gloomier, off □ *You miss a woman no matter what sort of cat and dog life you led together—though we **had our moments** that I will say.* LLDR □ *Like any other of Chaplin's films, even the poorest of them, 'Limelight', **has its moments**.* □ *And somebody who was so lively so much of the time was bound to **have his** off **moments**.* TGLY □ *Life as a funeral director **has its** lighter **moments**.*

have etc more goodness etc in one's little finger than sb [posses] be a very much better, kinder, more virtuous person than (another) **V:** have (got); ⚠ (there) be. **prep:** with. **n:** goodness, imagination, understanding, guts. **cl:** than sb has in his whole body, than the rest of them put together, than the whole lot of you □ *She **has more goodness in her little finger than** he has in his whole body.* POLITE CONVERSATION (J SWIFT 1667-1745) □ *Your father knew what would happen. He's a man **with more sense in his little finger than** these committee members have in their whole bodies.* □ *She **had more animation in her little finger than** you two put together.* LBA □ *If you **had as much courage in your whole body as** she **has in her little finger**, you'd have followed her.* □ variant have etc as much goodness etc in one's whole body as sb has etc in his little finger.

have (got)/with more money than sense [possess] spend one's money foolishly (the reference being either to general extravagance or to a particular item of expenditure) □ *You **had more money that sense** when you bought that white overcoat. It's never out of the cleaners.* □ *When we heard of a student, **with more money than sense**, who bought a portable television for his room, we felt much the same mixture of pity and contempt that we felt for each other when, in our last year, we saw ourselves embarking on 'careers'.* L

have etc a mouth to feed [possess] have sb requiring food and/or general support as a personal responsibility or expense **V:** have (got); ⚠ (there) be. **prep:** with. **det:** another; one less; a lot of, so many □ *'He'll have to stay with us for a while.' 'Poor you—another mouth to feed.'* □ *We were hoping to **have** children: more and more **mouths to feed**.* □ *My grocery bills are just about the same as they were ten years ago when I **had** twice as many **mouths to feed**.* □ *Some refugees were turned away. **There were** too many hungry **mouths to feed** already.*

have etc a mouth like the bottom of a

parrot's cage [possess] (informal) have a mouth that tastes unpleasant, eg after drinking or smoking too much, or during illness **V:** have (got), ⚠ get; give sb. **prep:** with □ *For heaven's sake go and fetch me a cup of tea. **I've got a mouth like the bottom of a parrot's cage**!* TBC

have etc a natural bent (for sth/doing sth) [possess] have etc an in-born talent for sth, ability to do sth well **V:** have (got); ⚠ show; it be, there be. **prep:** with. **o:** singing, painting, teaching; running other people's lives; mathematics, music, athletics, card-games □ *Rawlins **had a natural bent for** mathematics and was a theoretical rather than an experimental scientist by aptitude.* NM

have etc neither rhyme (n)or reason [possess] make no sense **V:** have (got), ⚠ show; give sb...(for sth); there be...(in/to sth). **prep:** with, without. **det;** neither, no, little □ (source — referring to More's having advised an author to turn some prose into verse) *Yea, marry, now it is somewhat, for now it is rhyme; before, it **was neither rhyme nor reason**.* T MORE 1478-1535 □ *This formidable way of dealing with correspondents extended to virtually all the things they wrote about. People who sent in poems might be told **there was neither rhyme nor reason** in them.* L □ *Her officials can **give no rhyme nor reason** for her decisions; she certainly takes not the slightest notice of the local education authority's views.* NS □ *My first action on being appointed headmaster was to do away with a mass of petty rules and regulations that **had neither rhyme nor reason** to them.* □ *English spelling and pronunciation must seem to the foreigner to be totally **without rhyme or reason**.* □ *The country, already burdened with Cambodian refugees, cannot quite look after its own; there are better reasons here for inter-country adoption that in Korea, but **there is little rhyme or reason** to the manner in which it is conducted.* L

have (got)/with a nerve [possess] (informal) be bold, insolent, presumptuous etc **adj:** bloody, colossal, terrific □ *'What's he (an aircraft) up to?' 'Making a survey, I suppose. Photocopying everything he can. He's **got a bloody nerve**.'* RFW □ *God, you **have a nerve**. Whenever I think about it, I could break your neck.* RATT ⇨ ⚠ next entry; have (got)/with the nerve etc to do sth; of all the nerve etc(!); what a nerve etc(!).

have (got)/with the nerve etc (to do sth) [possess] have the boldness, courage, confidence in oneself, necessary to do sth **O:** nerve, ⚠ courage, confidence □ *I worked with about five different guys before I **had the nerve to** tell Capitol that I wanted to leave unless they let me do it the way I wanted.* RT □ *A young woman gave Wormold a grave encouraging nod. Wormold made a little gesture as much as to say, 'I **haven't the nerve**. Help me.'* OMIH ⇨ ⚠ previous entry; next entry; of all the nerve(!).

have (got)/with the nerve etc to do sth [possess] (informal) show impudence, presumption, impropriety in doing sth **O:** nerve, ⚠ cheek, face, gall, (brass) neck; impudence, impertinence □ *Macmillan **has the nerve to** suggest that the American intervention in Lebanon in July 1958 was a vindication of what the British and French did in 1956.* L □ *Ten shillings (a fine) and I spend six months inside and the judge **has the cheek to** ask me if I had the ten bob on me now.* ST □ *I don't think I'd **have the face to** ask for a holiday just at that time.* RFW □ *I was a leader writer on everything. I can't imagine how I **had the gall to** hand out all that instant advice.* L ⇨ ⚠ previous entry; have (got)/with a nerve; of all the nerve etc(!).

have (got) no business (to do sth/doing sth) [possess] do what is not one's duty or responsibility; be wrong, foolish or interfering (in doing sth) **det:** no, (not) any, what. **A:** to give you orders, to change the programme; giving you orders, reading other people's letters □ *Actually he **had no business to** give you any orders at all. You're not part of his command.* RFW □ *I warn you that the regular club members think nobody else **has any business** making proposals.* □ *He bathes every morning in the Thames. He's lately had three months away with a bad leg. 'I hope he stays that way,' interjected his landlady. '**He's no business** being in the water at his age.'* ST

have (got)/there be no call to do sth [possess] (informal) have no need, reason or excuse for doing sth **det:** no, (not) any; more, less. **Inf:** to come here, to be rude, to let sb do sth, to take offence □ *You **had no call to** come down here. You'll catch your death of cold.* EM □ *If we lose the match, I'm in the dumps. But **there's no call to** go around kicking some poor devil's windows in.* ST □ *'Don't you dare put those cases in the van before I get back.' '**No call to** get worked up,' Mr Fiske said.* AITC

have etc no/an inkling (of sth) [possess] have no/some knowledge, awareness (of sth) **V:** have (got), ⚠ get; give sb. **prep:** with (no), without (any). **det:** a; no, some, (not) any. **o:** it, any of this, what was going on □ *I do now **have an inkling of** what the immigrants face from the authorities.* NS □ *At the turn of the century a large majority of people were only two generations removed from country life — they **had some inkling of** what it was about.* TVT □ *The middle-aged lovers were so quiet and normal that he **had no inkling of** what had happened since he last saw them.* WDM □ *The report is frightening enough but **gives** only **an inkling of** the sufferings of ordinary people.*

have etc a no (more) nonsense [possess] tolerate no false, pretentious, unnecessary, unsuitable, foolish, extravagant etc quality in the appearance or function of things, in the character, conduct or any particular action(s) of people **V:** have; ⚠ there be; stand. **prep:** with, without. **A:** about it, about paying □ *The enjoyment of fireworks, according to Hugo, ought to be an education in the enjoyment of all worldly splendour. 'You pay your money,' said Hugo, 'and you get an absolutely momentary pleasure **with no nonsense** about it.'* UTN □ *Granny will look after you while we're out, and when she tells you it's time to go to bed **there's** to **be no nonsense**.* □ *'He thinks he's only got to shout and lose his temper and then everyone will scurry around and do what he wants.' 'Does he? Well, I'm **not** going to **stand any nonsense** of that sort from him.'* □ (a performance of 'Twelfth

Night') *Maria alone is allowed to be real. Patricia Hayes plays her an elderly **no-nonsense** nanny.* L □ attrib use, *a **no-nonsense** approach, attitude,* always hyphenated.

have etc no remedy but to do sth [possess] have etc only one thing one can do to improve a situation, help oneself, get rid of a danger or nuisance **V:** have (got); ⚠ there be. **prep:** with □ *Mr Henderson has driven his critics and opponents into a position where they **have no remedy but to** break the law.* SC □ *A fine place to have a breakdown! Well, if **there's no remedy but to** get out and walk, we'd better start.*

have etc no time to lose [possess] need to hurry, act swiftly, in order to do sth, prevent an accident or disaster, make use of an opportunity while it is available, etc **V:** have (got); ⚠ there be. **prep:** with (no), without (any). **det:** not much, not any □ *The Tories have a unique opportunity to steal a march on their political opponents. They **have no time to lose**.* SC □ *You'd better get your things together. **There's no time to lose**.* □ *'Could I still catch the 6.50?' 'Yes, you **haven't any time to lose**, though.'* ⇨ ⚠ lose/waste no time (in doing sth).

have etc a nodding/bowing acquaintance (with sb/sth) [possess] know sb slightly; have occasional casual contacts (with sb/sth); have a superficial, or patchy, knowledge (of sth) **V:** have (got), ⚠ obtain; give sb □ *'Who was that?' 'A Mrs Parker, just **a nodding acquaintance**. We say "Good morning" when we meet or pass a remark about the weather.'* □ *The plane back to Cuba had few passengers; a Spanish woman with a pack of children, a Cuban cigar exporter **with** whom Wormold **had a nodding acquaintance**...* OMIH □ *I have made sporadic raids into these 150-year old documents* (a naval captain's log books), *and have **established a nodding acquaintance with** one of history's bystanders.* L □ *Working there would be a means of **obtaining** at least **a bowing acquaintance with** Greek, and after a few weeks he found he could often pick up the drift of a simple conversation.*

have etc none/nothing to speak of [possess] have etc very little; have etc not enough (of sth) to merit mention or notice **V:** have (got), ⚠ get; there be. **prep:** with, without. **det:** no, (not) any, (hardly) any. **n:** crime, harm, pain; work; snow, money □ ***There is no** work **to speak of** in a small modern house like this.* □ *'Do you have much work to do?' 'No indeed, **none to speak of**.'* □ *'Does your husband help you with the house work?' 'Not really, **not to speak of**.'* □ *And look how successful marriages are in India. **There is hardly any** divorce **to speak of**.* OBS □ *Normally, **there** should **be no** carbon monoxide **to speak of** in the air of a house using gas for heating or water-heating.* L □ (TV play) *It **had no** plot, **no** action **to speak of**; nothing but this tremendous spate of words.* SC □ *And **with no** money to spare, or **none to speak of**, we'll find the going tough.*

have etc nothing better to do (than) [possess] not be able to fill one's time in a more profitable way; not have anything more worthwhile to do (than the activity mentioned) **V:** have (got); ⚠ can think of; there be. **prep:** with, without □ *I went—for I **had nothing better to do**—to the Press Conference.* QA □ *Do you think people **have got nothing better to do than** look at you?* TOH □ *One man told me he and some of his friends were sitting around one evening and **for want of anything better to do** (= because they **had nothing better to do**) went up the road and broke the man's arm.* ST □ *The other day, stepping out of Broadcasting House and consulting my wristwatch with the usual gesture, I was pounced upon by a military-looking lady in a trilby. '**Haven't** you **anything better to do than** flap your hand at me like that?' she demanded.* L □ variants for want of anything better to do (than), have better things/something better to do (than).

have etc nothing/something between one's ears [possess] (informal) be/not be stupid; have/not have a frivolous or superficial mental outlook **V:** have (got); ⚠ there be. **prep:** with, without □ *He's a handsome, sensible enough looking boy, but you don't need to be talking to him very long before you realise he **has nothing between his ears**.* □ *How did you get into such a mess, you great idiot? **Nothing between your ears**, that's your trouble.* □ *Chorus-girls don't become stars on looks alone; they've got to **have something between their ears** as well.*

have (got)/with nothing/something to hide [possess] have done nothing/something wrong; have been/have not been frank or honest in a particular action, relationship etc □ *The MP concluded by saying that he had asked for reporting restrictions to be lifted because he **had nothing to hide**.* G □ *I can leave the constable here while I go back for a search warrant. But if you **have nothing to hide**, why put us to all that trouble?* □ *That's another cause for suspicion. Nobody goes about under an assumed name unless he **has something to hide**.*

have etc nothing (much) to shout/write home about [possess] (informal) have etc nothing that is specially fine, valuable, important or interesting **V:** have (got), ⚠ there be. **prep:** with, without. **O:** nothing, (not) anything, not much; something □ *Irwin Russell is in the 'Dictionary of American Biography' for being one of the first Southerners to see the literary possibilities of the Negro, and to exploit a form of Negro dialect in his own verse. **Nothing to shout about** today.* L □ *The acting was marvellous, and I can only suppose that it was on the actors' fees that the vaunted £100,000 spent on the programme was used up: **there was nothing** else **to write home about**.* NS □ *I've seen his work. He **has nothing to shout about**.* □ *You should be used to John's changing his mind by this time. Now, if he were to make a plan and stick to it we'd **have something to write home about**.* □ have etc something to shout/write home about = 'sth that is worthy of special mention, is particularly fine, interesting'.

have etc (a) nuisance value [possess] have etc an annoying, or disruptive, quality that can be put to some use **V:** have (got), ⚠ possess; give sth; there be...in sth. **prep:** with □ (a boy's pets) *And, not least, grass snakes which **had a***

*tremendous **nuisance value** in my constant guerrilla warfare with my countless maiden aunts. A snake in any aunt's bath was worth any petty punishment that might ensue.* SD □ *Other members come to be admitted* (to a Cabinet), *some with a claim to special knowledge but more because of **their nuisance value** when excluded.* PL

have etc sb's number [possess] (informal) know or discover what sb's character, social position, motives etc really are **V:** have (got), ⚠ get, take □ *I didn't believe my wife when she said you were just a fairweather friend but she **had your number** all right.* □ *All swank and no cash —it didn't take me long to **get his number**.* □ *She told him she didn't intend to go on modelling. 'Pity,' he said, brushing her body upwards and downwards with his eyes. 'I always—' Before he had got half-way through his sentence she had **taken his number**.* CON

have etc occasion to do sth [possess] (formal) need, or find it suitable or convenient, to do sth **V:** have (got), ⚠ find; give sb; there be. **det:** no, (not) any, little, frequent □ *President Mitterand's speech expressed admirably the sentiments which inform French relations. But he himself has **had occasion to** note the changes of sentiments.* SC □ *She seldom wore them* (evening dresses), *indeed she seldom **had occasion to** do so.* HAA □ *If you do **find occasion to** come to London be sure to visit us.* □ *I'm not going to buy expensive kitchen gadgets that **there**'ll **be** little **occasion to** use.* □ *'I never hear you criticizing your husband.' 'Maybe I **have no occasion to**.'* ⇨ ⚠ take occasion to do sth.

have etc an old head on young shoulders [possess] have, as a young person, wisdom, caution, tastes etc that are usu associated with mature or older people **V:** have, ⚠ (can't) put. **prep:** with □ *The demand was for the Young Conservatives to **have old heads on young shoulders**.* T □ *'In a few years' time he'll be wishing he'd listened to my advice.' 'Very likely, but in the meantime you **can't put an old head on young shoulders**.'* □ you **can't put an old head on young shoulders** (saying) = 'you can't expect wise, mature behaviour from the young'.

have etc sth on the go [possess] have etc sth currently happening, being done, being offered, made available **V:** have (got); ⚠ (there) be. **prep:** with. **O:** too many things, a business deal, preparations for dinner, a new painting, a closing-down sale, a Christmas pantomime □ *Sometimes he doesn't feel like writing his quota of 600 words a day. But he always **has** a book **on the go**.* TVT □ *That's the trouble. **With** so many things **on the go** at the one time, how can he give any of them his proper attention?*

have got/with one foot in the grave [possess] be so old or ill that one is not likely to live much longer □ *Some of us stay nymphs and satyrs till we **have one foot in the grave**.* SML □ *...known and respected for his kindness to unfortunate born-losers, who have lost their way in life, who find themselves alone, crazy, forgotten and **with one foot in the grave**.* ST □ *If you knew how many pensioners bother me with the most trivial complaints. They're the only type that really need me. I think they're lonely. They live in small rooms, **one foot in the grave** and one half out.* YAA

have etc one law for the rich, and another for the poor [possess] have etc a social system in which rich and successful people can avoid legal restrictions and penalties that poor or working-class people have to submit to **V:** have (got); ⚠ there be. **prep:** with □ *'**There's one law for the rich—**,' 'There's nowt* (= nothing) to choose between them (political parties).*' These, and a hundred similar apophthegms are repeated unquestioningly every day, as they have been for decades.* UL □ (NONCE) *The feeling that **there was one law for the workers and another for the gentry** did much to undermine faith in the justice of the previous incomes policy.* NS

have/be one of one's good etc days live through/be a day when one feels well etc, when one acts more/less efficiently, when one is in a good etc mood **adj:** good, ⚠ on (= good); bad, off (= bad); better, best; worse, worst □ *I shouldn't go in and see him now if I were you. He's **having one of his bad days**, swearing at everything and everyone.* □ *By 11 o'clock I knew it was going to **be one of my better days**; the thoughts were all assembled and the words flowed freely on to the paper.* □ variants have one's good etc days, have/be a good etc day.

have etc one over the eight [possess] (informal) have etc too much to drink **V:** have, ⚠ take; be □ *The Irish playwright roundly declared himself completely unembarrassed by his previous screen appearance, when he **had one over the eight**.* SC □ *The most widely accepted story was that he had met several of his former shipmates and they had persuaded him to **take several over the eight**.* RT □ *I'm not surprised you're feeling sick this morning—you **were** definitely **one over the eight** at the party last night.* □ be one over the eight = 'be drunk'.

have (got)/with a one-track mind [possess] (informal) have a mind preoccupied, or dominated, by a particular subject, interest or purpose □ *Carpenters, as a breed, I have discovered, **have one-track minds**: engage a carpenter and tell him he must make a variety of cages for animals, and he immediately goes all to pieces.* DF □ *The caption reads: 'Freddie Laker was in the right—OK?' Also in this room: a brightly coloured painting of Laker surrounded by flags of the world, a framed photograph of a Laker DC 10, a map of the world, and 14 model aeroplanes. 'This man,' I thought to myself, '**has a one-track mind**.'* OBS □ also pl have one-track minds.

have (got)/with only oneself to blame/thank (for sth) [possess] because of one's own faults of character, actions or failings, be solely responsible for sth unpleasant which happens to one **O:** only oneself, no-one, nobody but oneself □ *We sent our soldiers into war with weapons and equipment that were inadequate; we **have only ourselves to blame for** the disasters that early overtook us in the field.* MFM □ *'If women don't join unions,' said Barbara Castle, 'they **have nobody but themselves to blame**.'* ST □ *'I don't think you need feel very sorry for him,' Harold said. 'He **had only himself to***

***thank**. He didn't take care of himself.'* PW

have etc an open mind [possess] have etc a mind that can accept more than one point of view, that is ready to absorb new ideas, to abandon or change former opinions **V:** have (got); ⚠ keep, preserve. **prep:** with □ ***I've an open mind**. I've nothing against angels, for those who want to put their trust in them.* AITC *As Mr Morley can only have heard old recordings of some of the famous artists past their best, I feel he should at least have **kept an open mind** on the quality of their voices.* RT □ *My two colleagues considered it was preferable to let the planners tackle the problems **with an open mind**.* MFM □ *At 14 he was strong, cheerful, open-hearted and—what was equally important—unusually **open-minded**.* ST □ *His experiences there were not unusual, but less than usual was his **open-minded** and appreciative attitude to some of the things he found there.* OBS □ *Mr Koestler is an asset to our culture; a cogent and persuasive reasoner, his **mind is open**.* ST □ also pl have open minds; adj compound open-minded; variant sb's mind is open. ⇨ have etc a closed mind.

have (got)/with other/bigger fish to fry [possess] (informal) have sth more important, interesting, profitable to do □ *What? You're walking out on me? You've **got other fish to fry**? Is that it?* EHOW □ *We can't expect the Cloud to give endless time to talking to us, it's **got bigger fish to fry**.* TBC □ *At 80 he* (a composer) *still **has other fish to fry**. 'What I really want to do is turn John Van Druten's play "The Voice of the Turtle" into a musical.'* ST

have etc outside interests [possess] have etc concerns, (eg sports, the arts, social or political activities, not connected with one's work or home-life **V:** have (got); ⚠ develop. **prep:** with, without. **det:** (not) any, some, no, (too) many, a few □ *'**Have** you any **outside interests**?' 'I don't know what you mean.' 'Did you belong to any societies at the university?'* NM □ *Chief among his **outside interests** are playing croquet and attending concerts of pre-baroque music.* RT

have etc the patience of Job/a saint have etc unlimited patience, either in the performance of laborious tasks or in the endurance of pain, provocation, opposition etc **V:** have (got); ⚠ need, require; try, test. **prep:** with □ (source) *Behold, we count them happy which endure. Ye have heard of **the patience of Job**, and have seen...that the Lord is very pitiful and of tender mercy.* JAMES V 11 □ *Patience is a very necessary qualification for coastguard skippers: Commander Sigurdur Arnason of the 'Odinn' appears to **have the patience of Job**.* L □ *Perry realised at once that here was a major new talent, a man who could film animals as they are, using the skills of the stalker and **the patience of a saint**.* RT □ *In the end her father gave her a good smacking and I wasn't surprised. That child would have **tried the patience of a saint**.*

have etc pins and needles [possess] have a (more or less painful) prickling sensation, esp in a limb, when blood starts to circulate freely again after pressure or a cramped position **V:** have (got), ⚠ get; give sb □ *As I put my hand to the door of Sylvia's Café I **had** a mild attack of **pins-and-needles** and one leg gave way under me.* RATT □ *Terror made him catch his breath; **pins and needles** surged in his fingers.* TGLY

have etc a place in the sun enjoy etc a position of equal, or shared privilege with other nations, groups, professions, institutions etc **V:** have (got) ⚠ get, want, fight for, keep; buy oneself. **prep:** with, without □ *There are things we can do to help if we summon up the will. It is not impossible to enable the poor of the world to improve their lot, to feed themselves and to **have a place in the sun**.* L □ *I never resent it when people in the behavioural sciences overstate their case somewhat, because they have had to **fight for a place in the sun**; they've had to fight to be recognised by universities and to get their departments, so naturally they can't be too diffident in appraising their own worth.* L □ *If Robert wanted to go on indulging his belief that business men were robots whose only justification was to minister to the needs of artists, Ned equally wanted to make a dent in this egoism, and at the same time **buy himself a place in the** creative **sun**.* CON

have (got) a point [possess] say sth sound, difficult to deny, etc esp in an argument, expression of opinion, justification of behaviour, etc; have (got) something (there) (qv) □ *A German once said that 'in Britain they think that soap is civilisation.' When you reflect that we spend more money on advertising and marketing detergents than we do on our whole educational system, you must admit he might just **have a point**.* SC □ *'If some people have mopeds, everyone will want mopeds. Then they'll want cars and before we know where we are we'll have a capitalist system.' He **has a point**.* OBS

have (got)/with one's/its points [possess] have valuable or useful elements, characteristics, capabilities **adj:** good, strong; weak, bad □ *The argument **had its points** of course.* SML □ *Counsel will speak as if he had a strong case though he may know very well it **has its** weak **points**.* □ *As a wife for Peter, I was prepared to concede that Daphne might **have her points**.* □ when not modified by an adj, the expression has a favourable meaning.

have etc one's pound of flesh [possess] receive etc the full amount of anything due to one legally or by previous agreement, though hardship, suffering and even death (of the other person) may result from obtaining it (from Shakespeare's THE MERCHANT OF VENICE, in which the usurer Shylock obtains the promise of a pound of the merchant Antonio's flesh as security for a loan and then tries to enforce it in a court of law) **V:** have (got), ⚠ get; take; want, demand; pay □ *It would have cost Brown less to have forgotten the debt than to try to trace the couple through a detective agency, but he hated being diddled and swore to **have his pound of flesh**.* □ *I should also mention that, Britain having now agreed to **pay** France **her pound of flesh** through the Common Agriculture Policy, the French have sanctioned the creation of a free trade area in industrial goods covering the whole of Western Europe.* L □ *'It sounds like a fair rise in salary but you're left with pickings once the Income Tax send out their new assessment.' 'Yes; trust them to **take their pound of flesh**.'*

have etc (the) presence of mind (to do

sth) [possess] have etc the ability to decide and do quickly what is needed in a situation or crisis **V:** have (got), ⚠ show, take. **prep:** with ◻ *The child would have pulled the steaming soup plate over on top of her if George hadn't* ***had the presence of mind to*** *grip the other side of the tablecloth.* ◻ *Disaster was averted. I grabbed a cigarette with sweating hands and lit it. Justin Cartridge leaned across and said to me, 'I thought you* ***showed presence of mind*** *there.'* CON ◻ ***A*** *curious cold* ***presence of mind*** *seemed to descend on him. Everything became very clear to him; he know exactly what he must do.* PE ◻ *His mates ran to help the struggling man while the foreman,* ***with*** *greater* ***presence of mind,*** *jumped into the pit and switched off the current.*

have etc reason to believe/for believing etc [possess] have etc adequate evidence or justification for believing **V:** have; ⚠ there be; see; give sb. **prep:** with, without. **adj/det:** good, little; any, no, some, every. **Inf:** to believe, to know, to object, to fear, to change. **A:** for believing, for supposing; for his belief, for their attitude, for my action ◻ ***There is*** *good* ***reason to believe*** *that recurrence is not due to fresh infection from outside the body.* NSC ◻ ***There was reason to suppose*** *that the impending 'total' war would be catastrophic.* AH ◻ *We* ***have reason to believe*** *that in every country there are agents of this group, some established there many years ago.* TCB ◻ *'These escape lines are very dangerous,' he grunted. I* ***had*** *every* ***reason to know*** *they were dangerous.* OBS ◻ *The Chancellor, no doubt,* ***had*** *good* ***reason for*** *his anti-inflationary warning.* SC ◻ *The people of Rumbur Valley have yielded less to outside influences. Nature provides for their basic requirements and they can* ***see*** *little* ***reason to change.*** RT ◻ *The mescalin taker* ***sees*** *no* ***reason for doing*** *anything in particular and finds most of the causes for which, at ordinary times, he was prepared to act and suffer, profoundly uninteresting.* DOP ◻ *With the threat of being instantly forced out of business should it prove not to be the case, the government* ***has given*** *the company good* ***reason to*** *make sure its statements are true.* NS

have etc a red face [possess] feel or look embarrassed ashamed, conscious of error/make sb feel embarrassed etc **V:** have (got); ⚠ give sb. **prep:** with ◻ *I'm sure he feels embarrassed. Anyone who virtually accuses a colleague of stealing his money and then finds it in his own coat pocket* deserves *to* ***have a red face.*** ◻ *Eventually he did the job himself, and then casually pointed out that I must have mixed the samples up. I went home* ***with a red face.*** NSC ◻ *He's so damned cocksure about winning the race I'd like to see somebody* ***giving him a red face.*** ◻ *I was doing one of my imitations of the boss when I turned to find him standing in the doorway watching. He just shook his head and went off, but* ***was my face red!*** ◻ *The burglar-alarm people had failed to sensitise the bank flooring and* ***their faces*** *must have* ***been*** *as* ***red*** *as anybody's on the morning after.* NS ◻ variant one's face is red, esp in exclamatory form was my face red!

have etc a right to sth/to do sth [possess] be etc (legally) entitled to have or do sth; be etc fully justified in doing, expecting, demanding, receiving sth **V:** have (got); ⚠ give sb. **prep:** with, without. **det:** a, the; no every, some, (not) much, (not) any. **o:** the property, consideration. **Inf:** to know, to be told, to be present ◻ *What has been going on here? I am a magistrate. I* ***have a right to*** *be told.* ARG ◻ *'You had so many beautiful things, and Clementine — '* ***'Had a right to*** *some?' said Fergus softly.* DC ◻ *You may like him* (a boy) *well enough to just push him away and tell him firmly that you're not the type. If he persists, you* ***have a*** *perfect* ***right to*** *slap his face.* H ◻ *And* ***what right*** *have you* ***got to interfere,*** *I'd like to know?*

have (got)/with the ring of truth etc seem likely, either by what is said or by the way it is presented, to be true etc; ring true etc (qv) **S:** story, report, account; testimony. **o:** truth, ⚠ sincerity, authenticity; folly, madness ◻ *His account conflicted with that of the other witnessess and yet his story* ***had,*** *for me,* ***the ring of truth.*** ◻ *'We should feel wonder at nothing at all in nature except only the Incarnation of Christ.' In the seventeenth century, the phrase seemed to make sense. To-day it* ***has the ring of madness.*** DOP ◻ distinct from with a ring of merriment, scorn, incredulity etc in his voice indicating a quality of sound.

have etc a roof over one's head [possess] have etc a place to live in, a house of one's own (and often, by implication, the security and amenities that go with it) **V:** have, ⚠ get, give sb; be; need, want. **prep:** with, without ◻ *And if you add on rates, insurance, heating etc, he is paying something approaching half his income just to* ***have a roof over his head.*** ST ◻ *All she craved for the children* ***was a roof over their heads*** *and a school nearby.* WI ◻ *If Bernard hadn't paid all Bill's debts, we shouldn't* ***have a roof over our heads.*** HAA ◻ *Blood-hounds and grand pianos do not normally figure among the possessions of those who publish pathetic appeals for* ***a roof over their heads.*** T ◻ *You can have the cottage, such as it is. It would* ***be a roof over your heads*** *and much cheaper than a hotel, while you look around for something better.*

have (got)/with a roving eye [possess] have a watchful, inquisitive, acquisitive disposition; look for chances to flirt, or have love affairs ◻ *Hubert took Bill's arm. 'Come and have a long talk.' Unfortunately Mrs Curry's* ***roving eye*** *had seen the undesirable confluence and her large mauve form bore down upon them.* HAA ◻ *They know he has also been out with Mrs Cooper, and with that Mrs Winter who was here a term or so ago, and with at least three of the students we have had here recently — in fact that he* ***has*** *what he himself calls* ***a 'roving eye'.*** TT ◻ *Even the man* ***with a roving eye*** *gets short shrift if he goes in for marriage-breaking; before that, he comes under dispensations more indulgent than those accorded to women on the loose.* UL

have etc a rude awakening [possess] have an experience that causes one, suddenly and forcibly, to realize sth unpleasant or unwelcome **V:** have, ⚠ get; give sb; there be, it be; be due for, deserve. **prep:** with ◻ (the effect of the Spanish Civil War, 1936-39) *The older generation* ***had a rude awakening.*** *The younger* *generation grew up taking it all for granted.* NS □ *The Rolls-Royce men* ***had a rude awakening****. Those who felt that, having become technical engineering assistants with considerable responsibility, they should therefore be able to find comparable jobs, experienced difficulty because their expertise was specific to Rolls-Royce.* L □ *I* ***had*** *many* ***rude awakenings*** *and frustrations before I was finally given a part in 'Seagulls Over Sorrento', the comedy with Ronald Shiner.* TVT □ *If Brown thinks he's just going to walk into Jim's job when he retires he****'s due for a rude awakening****.*

have etc one's say [possess] be allowed to express one's opinion, have one's comments, advice etc listened to in full whether these are accepted or not/allow sb to express his opinion etc **V:** have, ⚠ get; give sb □ *At Hyde Park Corner pacifist speakers were usually allowed to* ***have their say*** *along with everyone else.* NS □ *The work gets done in the best possible way, because everyone feels he has* ***had his say****.* NDN □ *He began to talk like a man who has an unwilling audience but who will* ***have his say*** *whether anyone listens to him or not.* PM □ *It was a natural development to attempt to* ***give*** *people who rarely have an opportunity to express their views on television* ***their say****.* L

have (got)/with a screw loose [possess] (informal) be a little mad or eccentric □ *If you employ a message boy* ***with a screw loose*** *because you can get him for peanuts, you must expect him to do stupid things.* □ *It wouldn't have been such a bad idea for your son and my daughter if he had a nice job with prospects, but a crooner? Hava, you've* ***got a screw loose****.* HSG □ occas pl *He****'s got a few screws loose****.*

have etc second sight [possess] have etc the (supposed) ability to see, or know about, events taking place in the future or in another place **V:** have (got); ⚠ be blessed, favoured, gifted, with. **prep:** with □ *The Hottentot groom who believed that horses* ***have second sight****, cried out...* LWK □ *Every village has its tale of some old inhabitant* ***with second sight*** *who...* □ *'I don't know what made me ring you just then.' 'It's lucky you did. You must* ***be gifted with second sight****.'*

have etc a second string (to one's bow) [possess] have etc a second person, commodity, skill etc, available for a purpose or as a means of livelihood, either as a replacement for, or an alternative to, a first (from archery) **V:** have (got), ⚠ get; (there) be, it be. **prep:** with. **det:** a second, another, more than one; two, several □ *I'll just jot down that telephone number. We have a baby-sitter that can usually come but it does no harm to* ***have a second string****.* □ *When I doubt my literary competence, I can tell myself that I am primarily an actor and that writing* ***is*** *just* ***another string to my bow****.* RT □ (the acceptance of modern medicine in a primitive society) *Gradually more and more people began to regard medicine as the first rather than* ***the second string to their bow****.* NDN □ *I've discovered now that it's important to* ***have a second string*** *and not to be totally reliant on acting. That's how the restaurant came about.* TVT □ *Now he's working hard at his school exams, determined to be an actor, but sensible enough to realise that the profession is loaded with disappointments.* ***Two strings to your bow*** *is a minimum requirement.* OBS □ often adapted, as shown.

have second thoughts [possess] arrive at an opinion, decision which further thought has changed from one previously held **A:** about it, about resigning; on the matter; as to how we should proceed □ *I took some pictures of the gunpit in which he had died. I was going to send them to his family. Thank God I* ***had second thoughts****.* SC □ *Then one morning I woke up thinking: 'I've got to change my hair, I've got to get it cut.' I drank a whole bottle of wine for dutch courage and took myself to Scissors in the Kings's Road, Chelsea, before I could* ***have*** *any* ***second thoughts*** *about it.* TVT □ *English property law bends over backwards to allow both parties time for* ***second thoughts*** *or to withdraw if their circumstances alter.* ST □ *I was tempted to set off again then and there for Holborn Viaduct. But* ***on second thoughts*** *I decided that I had better collect my wits a little before attempting to face Hugo.* UTN □ *He did not give the Executive quite the statement that appeared in 'Tribune'.* ***On second thoughts*** *he had made one or two additions, the most important being a reference to a mixed economy.* OBS □ variant on second thoughts = 'having thought further (about the matter)'.

have to (go and) see a man about a horse/dog (catchphrase) absent oneself on unspecified business; go to urinate □ *'Do you want to hear me practise my new piano piece, Dad?' 'Can't,' said his father, rising. 'I* ***have to go and see a man about a horse****. Ask your mother to listen to you.'* □ second meaning euphemistic.

have seen etc it all (informal) have a long and rich experience of life in general or of sth specific **V:** seen, heard, done, been through □ *They sat and looked at each other, the wise old man who* ***had seen it all*** *and the blasé young sophisticate who thought he had.* □ *As careers go, Moira Redmond* ***has done it all****. Well not quite, she says.* TVT □ *You may distress your analyst but hardly shock him. After a few years in practice they've* ***heard it all****.*

have etc a sense of guilt etc [possess] have etc feelings of guilt etc **V:** have; ⚠ feel, experience, suffer. **prep:** with, without. **det:** a, some, (not) any, no, a slight, a faint, a heavy, a great, much, little. **n:** guilt, ⚠ loss, shame □ *She would rather that she had not had to fire the Oerlikon* (an anti-aircraft gun), *but she* ***felt no*** *particular* ***sense of guilt****.* RFW □ *I drove on, musing about how impossible it was for anyone to divine the precise nature of Robert's suffering. Wounded pride;* ***sense of loss****; all that, yes.* CON □ *'But you forget,' said a colleague, 'the man* ***has*** *no* ***sense of shame****.'* NS ⇨ ⚠ next entry.

have etc a sense of humour etc [possess] have etc a quality of, sensitivity to, understanding of, humour etc (as a permanent quality of character) **V:** have, ⚠ possess, be blessed, favoured, gifted, with; lose one's; acquire. **prep:** with, without. **det:** a, some, (not) any, no, a great, much, little. **n:** humour, ⚠ fun, mischief; occasion, duty, proportion, values, the ridiculous □ *His family could boast of little* *but their integrity, their* ***sense of humour****, and their appreciation of pleasant things.* DC □ *I know he can be a stern man when necessary, but he's not like that at home. He* ***has a*** *great* ***sense of humour****.* OBS □ *...a country which is, on the whole, tolerant, inhabited by decent people* ***with a sense of duty****.* L □ *Tom Fleming comes closer than any to filling part of the gap left by Richard Dimbleby's death. It is his voice and* ***sense of occasion*** (= feeling for what is right on a particular occasion) *that now provides the commentary to national and state ceremonies.* RT □ (the merits of individual football players) *These questions are discussed with a scholarship and passion which occasionally make me think the community has* ***lost its sense of proportion****.* NS □ *Working in television news as a reporter is to live in a slightly unreal world,* ***with a*** *somewhat false* ***sense of values*** (= an understanding of what is important in life). L ⇨ ⚠ previous entry.

have etc a sense of one's own importance [possess] feel that one is important (the implication sometimes being that one is not as important as one thinks one is) **V:** have; suffer from, be afflicted with. **prep:** with. **adj:** tremendous, overwhelming, enormous □ *The Chancellor of the Exchequer's* ***sense of his own importance*** *had had time to re-establish itself.* EM □ *Of course, John always* ***had an*** *immense* ***sense of his own importance****.*

have etc a shot (left) in the/one's locker [possess] have etc a reserve of ammunition; (fig) have a remaining source of money, influence, information, argument etc that one can use **V:** have (got). **prep:** ⚠ with, without. **O:** a shot, another shot, a shot or two. **A:** still, yet □ *But counsel* ***had another shot in his locker****. 'Is it not true,' he asked, 'that you did, as someone has said, persecute this long-suffering man with your malignant fidelity?'* PW □ *He'd been staving off bankruptcy for some years but now he'd exhausted his credit. He* ***had****n't* ***a shot left in the locker****, and soon everyone knew it.* □ also pl *He* ***has several shots in his locker****.*

have etc a/that sinking feeling [possess] (informal) have etc a sensation of panic, helplessness or fear **V:** have (got), ⚠ get; there be. **prep:** with □ *As soon as I saw Chris I* ***had a*** *terrible* ***sinking feeling****. I knew she'd only have come if something was wrong.* □ *Julian's house was so large and had so much land surrounding it that* ***a sinking feeling*** *to do with butlers came over Jenny, but none appeared.* TGLY □ *'Son, you'll just have to leave your animals behind.' 'Well, supposing we did that?' I asked,* ***a sinking feeling*** *in the pit of my stomach. 'How do we get out then?'* DF

have etc a sixth sense [possess] have etc a special sensitivity beyond those of the five senses (sight, hearing, smell, taste and touch), believed to warn one of danger, help one understand others, etc **V:** have (got); ⚠ develop; show; give sb. **prep:** with □ *It seemed to Harold, whose training and experience* ***had given*** *him* ***a sixth sense*** *in such matters, that with every word an agreement was being reached.* PW □ *He would have abandoned the task altogether, had not* ***some sixth sense*** *told him that it was worth while to persist.* EM □ *Pop drew a deep breath and told her, in a swift flick of description, almost ecstatic, how he* ***had a*** *kind of* ***sixth sense*** *about flowers and their perfumes.* BFA

have etc a sneaking suspicion etc [possess] feel etc a secret, rather furtive, suspicion etc **V:** have (got); ⚠ there be; feel; retain. **prep:** with. **n:** suspicion, ⚠ belief, hope, pride, sympathy, admiration, envy, weakness. **A:** that he stole it, that I can do it; with their cause; for John's ruthlessness; of such people □ *I even* ***had an*** *occasional* ***sneaking suspicion*** *that the director had taken a certain pride in these defects as proof of honesty.* NS □ ***There was a sneaking belief*** *that the Conservatives would still beat Labour at the next election.* T □ *If a man eludes police pursuit for long enough people begin to* ***feel****, though few would confess to it,* ***a sneaking sympathy*** *with him.* □ ***I've a sneaking weakness*** *for old-fashioned thrillers.* NS □ *We* (as boys) *accepted Hitler and Mussolini as bogeymen, while* ***retaining a sneaking admiration*** *for the country that could produce the Auto-Union and Mercedes racing cars.* TVT

have (got)/with a soft centre [possess] have a weak, or sentimental, tendency to yield to pressure, which is not apparent at first □ *People might think I'm a hard nut* ***with a soft centre****, but I have a genuine feeling for music.* TVT □ *She marries a man apparently as unemotional and self-possessed as herself, but Peter turns out to* ***have a soft centre****, and, when he breaks down, Emily can offer him no more than 'ordered coldness'.* L

have (got) something (there) [possess] (informal) show good sense, shrewdness, understanding of a situation, in a comment, piece of advice, criticism, argument etc; have (got) a point (qv) □ *In her diary Janet had written that this house and this view had made Bill what he was. Perhaps she* ***had got something there****.* RFW □ *'The faults in others that people are most aware of are those they have themselves.' 'You know, I think you* ***have something there****.'* □ *The chap that first said there was no fool like an old fool certainly* ***had something****.*

have (got)/with something etc to lose (by sth) [possess] risk losing money, health, prestige etc by doing sth **O:** something, ⚠ anything; everything, much, plenty a lot, a great deal; nothing, (a) little □ *But the United States may* ***have much to lose by*** *precipitate action and much to gain from patience.* SC □ *Miss Littlewood said would I be good enough to read one of the parts since an actor hadn't turned up for the session? I* ***had nothing to lose*** *so wasn't embarrassed.* OBS □ *After all, a depressed area* ***has little to lose by*** *believing in luck and may even, through such irrational hopes, come to believe in itself.* NS

have (got)/with something etc to offer [possess] be able to provide opportunities, facilities, help, inducements etc **O:** something, ⚠ anything; everything, much, plenty, a lot, a great deal; nothing, (a) little. **A:** to students, to tourists, to investors; by way of accommodation; in return for their money □ *If we expect to attract tourists we've got to* ***have something to offer*** *them.* □ *John could usually be relied upon for helpful advice but for once he* ***had nothing to offer****.*

have (got)/with something etc to say for oneself [possess] be talkative, communicative, in general; be able to explain, excuse or justify one's conduct on a particular occasion **O:** something, ⚠ anything; much, plenty, a lot, a great deal; nothing, (a) little ▫ *The girl kept away, not turning up very often for the communal evening meal and not* ***having much to say for herself*** *when she did.* TGLY ▫ *Sir Thomas turned to Dennis. 'What* ***have*** *you* ***got to say for yourself****?'* ***'Nothing****,' Dennis answered.* ARG ▫ *I don't think he's the chap for the job. We'll see if he* ***has anything*** *more* ***to say for himself*** *at his interview.*

have etc something etc to show for it [possess] have etc some tangible, or demonstrable, evidence of gain; get a proper return for money, time, energy etc expended **V:** have (got), ⚠ get; there be. **prep:** with, without. **O:** something, ⚠ anything; much, plenty, a lot, a great deal; nothing, (a) little ▫ *'I seem to remember you spending twenty pounds on a handbag last week.' 'Well, at least, I've* ***got something to show for it****.'* ▫ *I didn't make much money out of the series—in fact I* ***had nothing to show for it*** *at the end.* ST ▫ *These Americans have been sustained only by pride in their companies, and when the war is over they will* ***have nothing to show for it*** *but their wounds.* L

have etc a sporting chance (of doing sth) [possess] have etc the possibility but not the certainty (of achieving sth) **V:** have (got), ⚠ get; stand; there be; give sb. **prep:** with, without ▫ *Labour leaders yesterday started anew the search for a* modus vivendi *on defence policy that would, with luck,* ***stand a sporting chance of*** *acceptance by the next annual party conference in Blackpool in October.* T ▫ *Wouldn't it be terrible to start work if you didn't feel* ***there was a sporting chance of*** *being interestingly interrupted?* DIL

have etc a spot of bother/trouble [possess] (informal) experience etc some danger, difficulty, disturbance or inconvenience **V:** have, ⚠ meet (with); there be; give sb. **prep:** with ▫ *We* (twins) *were a bit of a handful at school, and naturally made merry blaming each other for* ***any spot of bother****.* TVT ▫ *If 'Delos' sails into Ancona she may be impounded owing to* ***a spot of bother*** *with the Italians.* ST ▫ ***'Had a spot of trouble****,' he said. 'In fact, had a load of trouble with the bird.' He jerked his head towards the helicopter.* BM ▫ ***There*** *seems to have* ***been a spot of trouble*** *in the outer office. Somebody let off a revolver, I understand.* TCB ▫ often an understatement.

have etc a sting in the tail [possess] have etc an unsuspected and unpleasant feature or result **V:** have (got); ⚠ there be; hide. **prep:** with ▫ (source) *And they had tails like unto Scorpions, and* ***there were stings in their tails****: and their power was to hurt men five months.* REVELATION IX 10 ▫ *Our first colony; now our last. It should come as no surprise if Ireland proves* ***the*** *deadly* ***sting in the tail*** *of British decolonisation.* NS ▫ *The Act ended 150 years of religious bigotry, but his triumph* ***had a sting in its tail****. It gave the country an appetite for reform.* ST ▫ *The Sugden family turns out to see Joe get his meal. But* ***there's a sting in the tail*** *sprung upon them all.* TVT

have etc a streak of cowardice etc (in one) [possess] be cowardly to some degree or in relation to some things; have cowardice etc as one of one's character traits **V:** have (got); ⚠ there be. **prep:** with. **o:** cowardice, cruelty, madness, vanity ▫ *Like many another bully he* ***had a streak of cowardice*** *in him.* ▫ *Talman* ***has a streak of self-criticism*** *which makes it difficult for him to be certain he is right on any particular issue.* OBS ▫ *Indeed, my father, a school-master not* ***without a puritanical streak in him****, thought there was too* much *entertainment in Bradford.* OBS ▫ usu derogatory; variant have a cowardly etc streak (in one).

have (got)/with a sweet tooth [possess] be fond of, greedy for, sweet foods and drinks ▫ *Does a cauli* ***have a sweet tooth****? Is it true that a teaspoonful of sugar sprinkled around a cauliflower plant will produce a whiter head?* OBS ▫ *Harry is the only one of us* ***with a sweet tooth****. If it weren't for him, I wouldn't bother making puddings at all.* ▫ *But caring for her looks doesn't stop her* ***having a sweet tooth****. 'I still can't resist fudge, candy and chocolate cookies,' says Marge.* TVT

have etc one's tail between one's legs [possess] (informal) have, etc feelings of dejection, apprehension, humiliation or surrender (from the behaviour of dogs) **V:** have (got); ⚠ carry; go off, slink away, come back, with; ask, apologize, with. **prep:** with ▫ *'I've always known Mr Golding was that sort of man,' said Miss Flynn, 'and she sent him packing* ***with his tail between his legs****, and he won't forget that in too much of a hurry.'* TT ▫ *I think he hopes that I'll crawl back,* ***carrying my tail between my legs****, and ask for my job again.* ▫ also pl have their tails between their legs.

have (got) sb/sth taped [possess] (informal) know all about sb/sth; be able to manage, influence, control sb/sth (from, originally, having taken sb's/sth's measurements with a measuring tape) ▫ *Now that he knew how much Goodrich was worth, now that he* ***had him taped****, Goodrich had become much more manageable to his imagination.* PW ▫ *All right, I* ***had them taped****; I was free to go ahead and feel sorry for them. If we* ***have****, as you say,* ***got*** *everything* ***taped*** *and our plans are known, then it's easy for the other side to* ***have got*** *us* ***taped****, too.* TCB ▫ *When it comes to playing Continental beauties, Madeleine Hinde* ***has*** *the market* ***taped****.* TVT

have etc teething troubles [possess] have etc pain, feverishness, minor ailments when cutting one's first teeth; (fig) have etc difficulties and setbacks when new **S:** baby; machine, business, industry, administration. **V:** have, ⚠ experience, suffer from. **prep:** with ▫ *On the credit side, the best of the manufacturers' guarantees offer servicing at appointed dealers. If a new car is* ***having teething troubles****, nine times out of ten free servicing is available locally.* ST ▫ *We were hopeful last week that the progressive elimination of the* ***teething troubles*** *(which were anticipated) would result in a steady and sustained improvement of the services.* T ▫ *The first supertankers* ***had teething troubles****. During sea tests the huge metal plates of the hulls buckled.* TVT

have etc a temperature [possess] have a body temperature higher than normal **V:** have (got), ⚠ run. **prep:** with. **det:** a, a bit of a, quite a ▫ JO: *I've got a cold.* BOY: *I think you have too. Yes, you've* ***got a bit of a temperature.*** TOH ▫ *It was found, when her turn came, that she was* ***running a temperature.*** MM

have (got)/with sb/sth to thank (for sth) [possess] attribute to sb/sth the responsibility for sth which has happened to one **O:** one's family, one's wife; sloth, callousness. **o:** success, recovery; failure, accident ▫ *Again, she* ***had*** *Fergus* ***to thank for*** *seeing that she had a pleasant nurse.* DC ▫ ***For*** *his defeat and downfall he really* ***has*** *two men* ***to thank.*** NS ▫ *'We had to wash in cold water except for a Saturday bath —no warmed bedrooms or vitamin foods.' 'Perhaps that's* ***what*** *you****'ve got to thank for*** *the rheumatism that's crippling you today.'* ▫ used equally to praise sb/sth, to express gratitude or to blame.

have etc a thick head[1] [possess] (informal) have etc a dull or stupid mind **V:** have, ⚠ possess. **prep:** with ▫ *When will you get it into* ***your thick head*** *that you can't license a car without an Insurance Certificate?* ▫ *You're a fence-post short. You need 21, not 20. You could have worked that out for yourselves if you* ***had****n't such* ***thick heads.*** ▫ *You won't enjoy teaching this class as much as your last one. They're a pretty* ***thick-headed*** *lot.* ▫ n compound a thick-head = 'sb who is stupid'; adj compound thick-headed; variant be thick in the head.

have etc a thick head[2] [possess] (informal) have etc an aching head; one's/sb's brain is temporarily dulled, or confused, by alcohol, drugs, a blow etc **V:** have, ⚠ give sb: there be. **prep:** with ▫ *It's the morning after the old soldiers' reunion and* ***there are thick heads*** *all round.* TVT ▫ *No more brandy, thanks. I'll* ***have a thick*** *enough* ***head*** *as it is.*

have etc a thick/thin skin [possess] have etc a low/high degree of sensitivity to criticism, reproach, insult ⚠ etc **V:** have (got); develop, grow. **prep:** with ▫ *Hinchcliffe is not afraid of or dependent upon the large landowners of the region who still sit on top of the social pyramid as did their great-grandfathers. 'It's feudal here,' says Hinchcliffe, 'but I* ***have a thick skin.'*** OBS ▫ *The Service manager has had to* ***develop a thick skin,*** *for few owners ever expect a Rolls-Royce to go wrong, and when it does they are liable to be incensed.* ST ▫ *One of 'Razor' Reynolds's tutorial groups was not the milieu for students* ***with thin skins.*** ▫ *This is the cheapest holiday-flight time for families, and probably the most embarrassing for all but the* ***thickest-skinned*** *parents; watch fellow holidaymakers pale as you enter the aircraft with that potential dynamo of noise.* G ▫ *Furthermore, your own profession* (journalism), *I think, is a very* ***thin-skinned*** *one: they can dish it out but they can't take it. When people start criticising the press, the press scream, 'It's a foul blow, you can't do that to me. I am engaged in great public service.'* L ▫ adj compound thick-/thin-skinned.

have etc the time[1] [possess] know etc the correct time of day; have a watch or clock with which to verify the time of day **V:** have (got); ⚠ tell sb, give sb. **adj:** right, correct ▫ *'Good evening,' she said. '****Have*** *you* ***the time*** *please?'* RATT ▫ *Ask inside, they're bound to* ***have the time.*** ▫ esp interr.

have etc the time[2] [possess] have etc sufficient time to do sth (sometimes with the implication that one has ample time, or more time than energy or inclination) **V:** have (got), ⚠ get; there be. **prep:** with ▫ *Because of the depression and the film mania, thousands of girls, many of them hanging around Hollywood, learned to tap. They* ***had the time.*** ST ▫ *If you want a rock garden, OK—but don't expect me to do anything about it. You're the one that's* ***got the time,*** *anyway.*

have/give sb the time of one's/his life [possess] (informal) enjoy oneself greatly doing sth, either on a particular occasion or during a certain period, eg a party, a holiday/enable sb else to enjoy himself greatly ▫ *I'll write to her tomorrow and tell her that you're as fit as a flea and* ***having the time of your life.*** RFW ▫ (travel agent's advertisement) *Whether you choose to go by King-Flight, King-Train, or King-Coach, you'll* ***have the time of your life*** *with Lunn's.* RT ▫ *And there they were now* ***having the time of their lives*** *letting themselves go in cheering me.* LLDR

(not) have etc time to turn round [possess] (informal) (not) have etc some time to spare from work, engagements etc **V:** have (got), ⚠ get; find. **prep:** with (no) ▫ *I wrote as soon as I* ***had time to turn round*** *after the mass of work that came upon me at the invasion.* RFW ▫ *I simply can't go rushing off to visit distant relatives.* ***I've scarcely time to turn round*** *these days.* ▫ often neg or with neg implication.

have etc sth to hand [possess] have etc sth present, nearby, in one's possession, etc and readily available **V:** have (got); ⚠ (there) be; come. **prep** with, without ▫ (broadcast opera) *For me, at least, it is virtually impossible to follow an extended work of this kind without some guide to take the place of the visual aspects which would make all plain.* ***Having*** *a score* ***to hand*** *induced me to pursue Gluck's 'Alceste' to the end.* L ▫ *The Conservatives therefore require a doctrine which permits them to live alongside organised trade unions. That doctrine* ***is,*** *fortunately, already* ***to hand*** *and is called free collective bargaining.* NS ▫ *I* ***have*** *a few comments on items in the 25 June issue, just* ***to hand,*** *some of which may be positive contributions.* NS

have etc too much money etc for one's own good [possess] have etc money etc, ie sth normally desirable in itself, to such a degree or in such a quantity that it becomes a disadvantage **V:** have (got), ⚠ possess, own; give sb; there be. **prep:** with. **O:** ***(much)*** money, time; ***(many)*** interests, graduates ▫ *They* ***have too much*** *pocket* ***money for their own good,*** *these youngsters.* ▫ *This is hardly a socialist rallying call with which to face Mrs Thatcher when she decides that* ***there are too many graduates for*** *society****'s own good.*** NS ▫ *'I'm All Right, Jack' was probably the Boulting Brothers' greatest hit —a scathing comedy aimed both at the trade unions and the employers. A bit* ***too serious*** *and direct* ***for its own good*** *at times.* TVT ▫ *'I wash my hair every day.' 'Then you're* ***washing*** *it* ***too often for its own good.*** *You'll be drying out all* *the natural oils.'* □ variants be too serious etc for one's own good, do sth too often etc for one's/its own good.

have etc a touch of class [possess] have etc a superior quality **V:** have (got), possess; give sth; there be; get. . .from. **prep:** with □ *Even before Best's arrival Fulham already* ***had*** *more than* ***a touch of class*** *in former England captain Moore.* OBS □ *The Kingston Bridge* (in Glasgow) *and its concrete pillars dominate the skyline. It was not until they built this that I realised how much I missed Victoriana. Next to these monstrosities, the old buildings* ***have a touch of class****.* L □ *Manchester is a working-class city and remains so. The last has not been heard nor the final chapter written on Manchester, a town* ***with a*** *real* ***touch of class****.* NS

have etc a touch of the sun [possess] suffer from too much exposure to the heat of the sun; (facetious) suffer from lesser degree of sunstroke as the only possible explanation for foolish or (slightly) mad-sounding behaviour or talk **V:** have (got); ⚠ be; get. **prep:** with □ *I've* ***got*** *rather a headache.* ***A touch of the sun****, I expect.* PE □ *'I'm still hoping,' he articulated distinctly, 'that this will turn out to be some foolish joke on your part.' 'Perhaps* ***a touch of the sun****. It has been hot lately.'* HD □ *Edward looked at her doubtfully and said, 'You do feel all right, Victoria, don't you? I mean you haven't* ***had a touch of the sun*** *or—a dream, or anything?'* TCB

have/get two bites at the cherry [possess] have a second opportunity to do sth; make a second attempt at doing sth □ (source) *I believe he would* ***make three bites of a cherry****.* (F RABELAIS ?1495-1555) □ *Any national museum or library can bid at the auction, but if their valuation is below the price it sells for, they should not then* ***have a second bite at the cherry****.* ST □ *Not content with getting an order in the National Industrial Relations Court, the Company immediately rushed to the Chancery Court for* ***another bite at the*** *same* ***cherry****, this time relying on Common law remedies.* ST □ often adapted, as shown.

have etc a (nasty etc) turn¹ [possess] (informal) feel ill, faint or sick, esp suddenly and temporarily **V:** have, ⚠ take, get. **adj:** nasty, ⚠ queer, funny, little □ *'Jenny, what is it? You're trembling, darling. Was it so bad?' 'It was all right. I just* ***had a little turn****. It'll go off. I'm all right.'* TGLY □ *Don't lock the door, grandfather, when you're having a bath. What if you* ***took one of your turns*** *in there?* □ *'I* ***had another funny turn*** *this morning.' 'Well, don't you think it's time you saw the doctor?'*

have etc a (nasty etc) turn² [possess] (informal) have etc an upset, shock **V:** have; give sb. **adj/det:** a nasty; ⚠ quite a, such a, what a, something of a □ *Hearing his voice in the hall* ***gave*** *me* ***quite a turn****. It was so exactly like his father's.* □ *It was only a nightmare but the poor child is frightened to fall asleep again, she's* ***had such a turn****.*

have etc a vested interest (in sth) [possess] enjoy a right or a privilege allowed in law to a person or group; enjoy a privilege long established in favour of a person or group **V:** have (got); ⚠ (there) be. **prep:** with. **A:** in the armaments trade, in the research station, in maintaining private medicine, in delaying the change-over □ *Only our habit of national self-deception permits us to ignore the fact that British politics are class politics; and those who would deny it almost invariably* ***have a vested interest*** *of their own for doing so.* NS □ *Both those opinions come from* ***vested interests in*** *expanding road space.* L □ *Management of the news is part of a perpetual battle between the press and Government and* ***vested interests****.* SC □ a vested interest = 'a person or group having the privileges defined above'.

have etc the vices/defects of one's/its virtues/qualities [possess] have etc the bad qualities which are inseparable from (and perhaps the result of) one's/its good qualities **V:** have; ⚠ show, reveal; allow sb; suffer from; be. **prep:** with, without □ *She* ***had the vices of her virtues*** *and her constant generosity and unselfishness were felt by some of those nearest to her to be a sort of tyranny.* □ *Perhaps Matron does cause minor resentments among the staff, but we must* ***allow*** *her* ***the defects of her qualities****. Everybody loved her predecessor but the hospital wasn't half so well run then.* □ *I recommend enamel paint for the woodwork. It wears and washes well and* ***its*** *only* ***defect is that of its qualities****—it chips more easily than other paints if it gets a direct knock.* □ ***Every virtue has its*** *attendant* ***vice****, and the reverse side of the steely restraint, which contributes to Boulez's special distinction as an interpreter* (of others' musical compositions), *has been a recurrent primness.* OBS □ variants every virtue/quality has its vice/defect, its vices/defects are those of its virtues/qualities.

have (got)/with a way of doing sth [possess] be apt, likely, to do sth or behave in a particular way □ *Mice can be found in the communal middens, and ladybirds* ***have a way of*** *appearing in the mucky bits of back-gardens.* UL □ *Johnny's* ***got a way of disappearing*** *if he thinks there might be work for him to do.* □ *At least officially he was thinking of Barbara, but thoughts of Buckmaster* ***had a way of*** *keeping on breaking in.* ILIH

have/give sb a/the whale of a (good) time [possess] (informal) enjoy oneself greatly/enable sb else to enjoy himself greatly □ *We talked about moving to a quieter spot, but the children were* ***having*** *such* ***a whale of a time*** *and had made so many friends of various nationalities that we decided to stay.* SC □ *They* (amateur actors), *of course, are* ***having the whale of a time*** *and it is sad but true that if an actor, or orator, or preacher, or after-dinner speaker is enjoying himself, nobody else is.* NS □ *I always thought the servants in big country houses must* ***have the whale of a good time*** *and now I know it.* RFW

have (got) what it takes (to do sth) [possess] (informal) have the necessary qualities of character, intelligence, or the special abilities, to do sth **Inf:** to reach the top, to be a star □ ***Have*** *you* ***got what it takes****? Elizabeth Jones chose car ferrying as a career because 'I love engines, and a gipsy existence.'* H □ *I still enjoy trying to paint pictures but I realised some time ago that I didn't* ***have what***

it takes to *reach the top.* □ *As a commentator on the American scene you don't have to* ***have what it takes to*** *come up with beginners' stuff like, 'It must be so terribly bad for them, always eating on stools at counters instead of sitting down for their meals.'* NS

have (got)/with a wicked etc tongue [possess] have the habit of speaking unkindly, unjustly; be a scandalmonger or troublemaker **adj:** wicked, ⚠ spiteful, malicious, sharp □ *I'm sorry for, well you know what. I've* ***got a wicked tongue*** *and I've probably been unfair.* TT □ *People won't believe her. They know she* ***has a malicious tongue.*** □ *Don't be frightened of her. She's a woman* ***with a sharp tongue*** *and a kind heart, you'll find.* □ also pl *They* ***have wicked tongues.***

have etc a will of iron [possess] have etc the firm determination to achieve what one wants or thinks right **V:** have (got); ⚠ need, require. **prep:** with □ *She looked and behaved just like a first-class cook,* ***with*** *a high complexion shadowed by the faintest of moustaches, a tiny appetite, and* ***a will or iron.*** ARG □ *You don't* ***need a will of iron,*** *either—just a few minutes a day, or whenever you feel like doing the exercises.* TVT □ (NONCE) *But though her warm Mid-Western accent might lull certain innocents into believing in the motherly image, opponents know that she also* ***has a whim of iron.*** ST

have (got)/with a will of one's own [possess] have sufficient independence of opinion and determination to do what one wants (the implication usu being that one has determination at least equal to that of sb else) □ *He is clever, Gerald, you know, and his little heart is so big. But he* ***has a*** *little* ***will of his own,*** *too, like me, Gerald.* ASA □ (Brigit's legs are, temporarily, paralysed) *I always knew they* ***had a will of their own*** *and one day they would say they were having a rest.* DC

have etc sb's (bare) word (for sth) [possess] have etc only what sb says or promises without also having any (esp written) proof or supporting evidence **V:** have; ⚠ there be; take, accept □ ***His bare word*** *isn't enough. He must prove that he wasn't anywhere near the scene at the time.* □ *Well, we only* ***have his word for*** *it, of course, but I suppose we must believe him.* □ *I'm not saying the story is true or untrue. All I'm saying is that I'll not* ***take*** *Jenny****'s bare word for*** *it. She's a little troublemaker, anyway.*

have etc a year etc to go [possess] there is still a year etc that must pass, be travelled, be obtained or be accomplished **V:** have (got); ⚠ there be. **prep:** with. **O:** a year, 3 days, 5 miles, a few more yards, 20 pages □ *Most of the African leaders have refrained from public commitment on their attendance, although* ***there are ten days*** *only to go before the conference opens.* T □ *He was well ahead of the other runners when* ***with*** *only* ***a couple of yards to go*** *he tripped and fell.* □ *'How's the Restoration Fund progressing?' 'We'****ve*** *still* ***got a hundred pounds to go*** *before we reach our target.'*

haven't (got)/without a clue [possess] (informal) not know (anything about) sth; not know how to do sth; lack understanding in general □ *'Is the Exhibition open on Sundays?' 'Sorry, I* ***haven't a clue.'*** □ *My boyfriend is mad keen on motor racing and he wants to drag me along with him. But I* ***haven't got a clue*** *what to wear.* H □ *I wish you wouldn't talk about me as if I'm an impotent, shrivelled old woman* ***without a clue*** *in her head.* TOH □ *'Fred must have felt a bit unwanted last night.' 'Oh, he's so* ***clueless*** *he probably didn't notice.'* □ adj clueless indicates general foolishness, inadequacy etc.

haven't etc an earthly (chance) (of achieving sth) [possess] (informal) have no likelihood of achieving sth **V:** haven't (got); ⚠ not stand; there not be. **prep:** without □ *By the way, Bernard, another little victory for you. All the dear locals at your feet. I did my best to say you were the biggest Bolshie since Aneurin Bevan, but I* ***hadn't an earthly.*** HAA □ *Any candidates* ***without an earthly chance of*** *passing would be tutored by me.* □ *'Any hope of getting a ticket for the match?'* ***'There's not an earthly,*** *I'm afraid. You've left it much too late.'* □ *Once the weather broke, the climbers* ***had no earthly chance of*** *reaching the summit.* □ form have no earthly chance (of achieving sth) less usu and more formal.

the haves and the have-nots [n + n nonrev] the wealthy contrasted with the poor; privileged contrasted with under-privileged people (the reference usu being to income but also to health, intelligence, talent etc) □ *The gulf between* ***the haves and the have-nots*** *appeared to have changed little from the days of British rule.* NS □ *The result is an unshakable conviction among* ***the have-nots*** *that American society is based on two quite distinct sets of laws: one for the affluent, the other for the black and the poor.* L

hawks and doves [n + n rev] militarists and pacifists contrasted; those who are aggressive in military or political affairs, contrasted with those who favour negotiation, compromise, moral persuasion, etc □ *Meanwhile, Mrs Gandhi's Cabinet is still divided roughly 50-50 between* ***hawks and doves.*** L □ *Abba Eban always tried to defuse the situation. When he was in America they asked him 'Are you* ***a Hawk or a Dove****?' He replied, 'Israel isn't an aviary.'* ST □ *Not that he was an anti-Vietnam* ***dove,*** *or anything like it; his feud with McNamara was basically personal.* NS □ *The fire Bob Hope has been drawing, particularly over his '****hawkishness****' over Vietnam puzzles him.* RT □ can be used in part and allusively; adj hawkish(ness) is acceptable, but not doveish(ness).

he who hesitates is lost (saying) unless you grasp an opportunity quickly, either someone else will, or it will be lost; □ *Well, you know what they say—****he who hesitates****. . . If I were you, I'd write now.* □ *Dusty* ***hesitated*** *and* ***was lost,*** *because the Old Man got stuck into him.* TT □ (NONCE) *'And to think I very nearly married that woman!'* ***'He who hesitates is sometimes saved*** *as James Thurber remarked in another connection.'* □ may be a comment on delay or vacillation of any sort.

the head of the table the end of a table usu occupied by the host or hostess, the father of a family, etc □ *Sir Julius took his place at* ***the head of the table*** *with a malevolent look at Dr Bottwink who sat on his right.* EM □ *We drifted into the dining-room where there was some argu-*

ment as to who should take ***the head of the table.*** □ at formal dinners, guests one especially wishes to honour will sit to the right and left of that position.

head over heels/ears [A] with one's body circling, or turned upside down; (fig) helplessly, completely **V:** fall, roll, turn; be, go. **A:** into the river; across the stage; in love, in debt □ *You must all be aware from the peculiar behaviour of space as seen from our ports that we are now tumbling along* ***head over heels.*** TST □ *Extraordinarily, he demonstrates a* ***head over heels*** *roll which lands him up against the marble steps of the hotel foyer.* RT □ *'But you would be absolutely right as Romeo,' said Jessica. 'Can you still say your lines?' 'I could to you,' said Ludovic, who was by now* ***head over ears*** *in love.* WDM □ *I'm* ***head over ears*** *in debt and that's why I'm selling the house.* □ head and heels/ears non-rev; attrib use *a* ***head over heels*** *roll.*

sb's head rolls sb is executed or assassinated, esp by beheading; (fig) sb is punished, made to suffer loss, position, rank, credit etc □ *The throne was auctioned to the higher bidder,* ***whose head*** *duly* ***rolled*** *a few weeks later.* SC □ *'Would you mind if I did needlework while we talk?' she asks. A vision passes before my eyes of those ladies who knitted while* ***heads rolled.*** ST □ *Mr Crossman insisted that* ***heads*** *must* ***roll.*** *Lord Hillman's inquiry must produce the replacement of the present system.* L □ *The talk, though, is that only second rank* ***heads*** *will* ***roll,*** *most likely that of the deputy police chief.* L □ *Later, he modified his attitude, saying that there would be a departmental inquiry and that '****heads*** *may* ***roll****'.* G □ ***heads*** *must/will* ***roll*** used to express a demand or prediction.

one's head rules/governs one's heart wisdom, commonsense, caution or self-interest, determines one's conduct — not one's passions, sentiments or sympathies □ *It was typical of Stephen that, even in the matter of choosing a wife,* ***his head*** *should* ***rule his heart.*** □ *I know* ***my head*** *always* ***rules my heart.*** *If I did a film with some man and fell madly in love with him, I'd never leave the children or anything like that.* TVT □ variant one's heart gets the better of/runs away with one's head.

one's head swells one thinks very highly of oneself □ *This film is about a boy jockey (Jeremy Spencer)* ***whose head swells*** *along with his list of winners.* TVT □ *They didn't stint their praises. I expected to see* ***your head swell*** *visibly.* □ *Cartridge thinks it's no good letting me get recognition too fast. It might give me* ***a swollen head.*** CON □ *If you go off for a year on one of those courses, all your mates are dead sure you're going to come back* ***swollen-headed.*** □ variants have/suffer from/give sb a swelled/swollen head; adj compound swollen-headed.

head to tail [Comp/A (n + n non-rev)] placed, or following each other, in a continuous line and all facing in one direction; placed in rows or stacks with the head of one alongside, or on top of, the tail of the next **S:** tanks, trucks; barges, elephants; bottles, sheaves (of corn). **V:** be; lie, stand, move □ *A convoy of army lorries was proceeding along the road* ***head to tail.*** □ *In their sleeping compartment they would lie on their bunks,* ***head to tail,*** *their great pink and wrinkled tummies bulging and deflating as they breathed.* DF □ *You'd have got another two rows of roses in that box if you'd arranged them* ***head to tail.***

heads I win, tails you lose (catchphrase) one person, group, gets all the advantages of a so-called bargain, exchange of services, etc; whatever the arrangements, rules, choices available, one person or group will always win, do better than the other □ (source) *A game which a sharper once played with a dupe, entitled, '****Heads I win, tails you lose****'.* J W CROKER 1780-1857 □ *However, when it comes to renting theatres out for profit,* ***heads we win, tails you lose*** *is the rule. The average rent demanded is in the region of a thousand pounds a week against 20 per cent of the box office takings, whichever is larger.* OBS □ *When a child does well at school it's because he's clever, when he does badly it's because we can't teach him. You'll have to get used to the* ***heads I win, tails you lose*** *attitude of parents.* □ occas heads we win, as shown; attrib use *a* ***heads I win, tails you lose*** *attitude.*

heads or tails(?) [n + n non-rev] the obverse or reverse side of a coin tossed or spun to decide an issue, heads often being the positive or winning side, unless sb is to get his choice, obtain an advantage, etc by first guessing correctly the side which will face upwards □ *Since neither of us can make up our minds, we'll toss for it.* ***Heads*** *we go to the cinema,* ***tails*** *we stay at home.* □ (tennis) *'****Heads or tails****?' their father asked, looking at Tony. 'Heads.' 'Heads it is, so you get the first service.'* □ can be used as an invitation to settle an issue in this way.

hear/see the last of sb/sth [V + O pass] be finished with sb/sth as a subject of discussion or argument; be finished with, having to cope with or being affected by, sb/sth □ *The murders continue to be the subject of books, magazine articles, newspaper stories: 'I don't think we've* ***heard the last of*** *Jack the Ripper.'* RT □ *'You haven't* ***heard the last of*** *this, Chadwick,' said Mr Purnell, 'not by a long chalk you haven't.'* TT □ *Well, he's gone to Australia right enough. Let's hope we've* ***seen the last of*** *him.* □ *Leaked or not, 'copyright' or not, the 'Sunday Times' gave it wonderful publicity and* ***the last*** *has not been* ***heard of it.*** NS □ usu neg; positive uses often expressions of hopes or wishes.

one's heart bleeds for sb (informal) one feels sorry for, pity for, sb □ ***My heart bleeds for*** *poor old Mike. First he loses his job, and now his wife has gone off with his best friend, Pete.* □ *'I'm just off to Mexico and Latin America—I get so bored with these business trips!' '****My heart bleeds for*** *you! I wish I had problems like yours instead of being stuck at my desk all day.'* □ sometimes facetious.

one's heart misses etc a beat a sudden surge of fear, hope or other emotion causes a break or catch, real or imagined, in one's heartbeat or breathing **V:** miss, ⚠ lose, skip □ *For a moment she thought she saw a face looking at her through the window and* ***her heart missed a beat.*** □ *'Now I know something about you,' said Cosmo Hines. Daniel****'s heart lost a beat.*** *Someone was going to recognize him at last, and for what he was.* US □ also pl Their hearts miss etc a beat.

the heart/root of the matter the essential nature, or the most important aspect of, a situation, a means of doing sth, or a subject being discussed **V:** seem to be; contain, reach; get to □ *Then she had to investigate what seemed* ***the heart of the matter****. The mystery of Clementine.* DC □ *And then one thinks of Hill's books which, whatever their shortcomings, have—in the phrase of Oliver Cromwell that Hill likes to quote—'****the root of the matter****' in them.* NS

one's heart sinks one feels despondent, disappointed, fearful etc □ *When this reviewer is sent a work dealing with the aesthetics, the theology, the politics or the science of Ruskin* ***his heart sinks****.* NS □ *I showed them a drawing of the animal, and everyone shook their heads over it and said sorrowfully that they had never seen it.* ***My heart sank****.* BB □ *There was still a multitude of tasks to be performed before dinner was ready to be served and* ***his heart sank*** *to see yet another visitor in the pantry.* EM □ *Here at last was Challowsford and with* ***a sinking heart*** *Sarah wondered what kind of reception awaited them.* WI □ also pl their hearts sink; variants feel one's heart sink(ing), with a sinking heart, make sb's heart sink.

heart and soul [A (n + n non-rev)] energetically; enthusiastically; devotedly **V:** devote, dedicate, oneself to; fling, throw, oneself into □ *They made the governor think they were* ***heart and soul*** *on his side when he wouldn't have thought any such thing if he'd had a grain of sense.* LLDR □ *This Greek composer has flung himself* ***heart and soul*** *into the life of his country.* ST □ *Josephine Barstow throws herself* ***heart and soul*** *into the part of Natasha, singing the lyrical music beautifully.* OBS □ *Miss Bates has dedicated herself to her profession* ***heart and soul****.* □ middle or end position. ⇨ ⚠ next entry.

one's heart and soul [n + n non-rev] all, or a great deal of, one's energy, enthusiasm, devotion, sincerity of feeling **det:** one's, all one's, one's whole □ *He's a man* ***whose heart and soul*** *were clearly in the venture from the start.* □ *Peter must make a success of this project and I hope with* ***all my heart and soul*** *that he will.* □ *'Isn't Jill bothered about her husband, then?' 'Not enough—* ***her heart and soul*** *are bound up in that boy of theirs.'* ⇨ ⚠ previous entry.

heart to heart [A (NP)] (informal) confidentially, sincerely, as between friends **V:** talk sth over, discuss sth □ *Did you ever think of discussing these problems* ***heart to heart*** *with your husband?* □ *Then I had one of those big* ***heart to hearts*** *with the doctor who said if you go back you could lose your foot.* RT □ *She takes up problems the day they're presented, replies by return post. She finds the time by cutting out what she calls '****heart to hearts****'—lunches with non-working girl friends.* ST □ end position; attrib use *a* ***heart-to-heart*** *(talk).*

hearth and home [n + n non-rev] (informal) home, esp a family house (the implication being home comforts and surroundings) □ *The farther her children were from* ***hearth and home*** *in adult life, the more highly did my mother tend to think of them.* □ *Aerial warfare apart, it's a long time since any Englishman has had to fight in defence of* ***hearth and home*** *on his own territory.*

(a) heaven on earth [Comp (NP)] a physical location, a place where one lives or works, a set of personal circumstances or relationships, where conditions are ideal and lead to great happiness—or the extreme opposite **V:** ⚠ be, become; make sth. **n:** heaven, ⚠ paradise, hell □ *The 175 acres of field and woodland at the Children's International Village at Sedlescombe, Sussex, is* ***a heaven on earth****.* □ *Why did he make Saturday afternoon such* ***hell on earth****? Anger throbbed violently in her temples.* LLDR

the heavens open rain falls in torrents □ *Thunder rumbled around and it grew dark. We had just made it to the house when* ***the heavens opened****.* □ *What we didn't need was for* ***the heavens to open****—and would you believe, come straight through the roof.* TVT

the heavy father the idea, or practical example, of a father as a stern disciplinarian, who controls the activities of his family as he thinks good for them **V:** come (over sb); play, act □ *But how about a man who preaches liberation and yet when his daughters are seeking marriage partners, can show himself the very caricature of* ***the heavy*** *Victorian* ***father****?* NS □ *He takes very little notice of the children as a rule. It's only in public that he likes to come* ***the heavy father****; and the heavy husband too, for that matter.*

heavy etc going [Comp (NP)] difficult movement or work, eg over rough or steep ground, against currents, when carrying weights, etc; (fig) laborious or boring work or activity; sth, eg a lesson, piece of writing or music, that is difficult to understand or enjoy **V:** ⚠ be; make, find, sth. **adj:** heavy, ⚠ hard, rough, tough □ BEATIE: *Still got your allotment, Jimmy?* JIMMY: *Yerp* (= yes). BEATIE: *Bit* ***heavy going*** *this weather.* R □ *Some days he had dictated like a man possessed for five or six hours. It had been pretty* ***heavy going****, but she had stood up to it.* PP □ *I must admit that I found Mr Grigg's Welsh chapters* ***heavy going****.* L □ (astrological prediction) *It could be fairly* ***tough going*** *this week, and you could get depressed.* WI □ *But we'll never know how well the greats of years ago would have fared in the football of today. I suspect they would have* ***found the going*** *much* ***harder****.* TVT □ *For teenagers* ***the going is*** *pretty* ***tough****; they are coping with themselves and at the same time with the transformed relationships with others.* OBS □ variants the going is heavy etc, find the going heavy etc.

heavy necking/petting (informal) caresses and fondling that are more intimate than kissing or cuddling but that stop short of sexual intercourse □ *Prolonged kissing is more frustrating than having sea-sickness and lockjaw at the same time. Then the* ***heavy necking*** *and* ***petting*** *begins, and the next step is going too far.* H □ *I didn't know this was a debate on marriage, I thought we were just on about, well,* ***heavy necking****.* TGLY

hedge one's bets [V + O] make a number of smaller bets to protect oneself from possible loss on a main stake (from gambling); (fig) not commit oneself to a single course of action, a definite opinion, etc □ *Diversification? You could call it industry's way of* ***hedging its bets****.* □ *In fact, the committee* ***hedge their bets*** *at* *every turn, and the final impression is rather confusing.* SC □ *'Scotland's people are looking forward — but they are looking back, too,' said Fyfe Robertson,* ***hedging his bets*** *on his new show, 'Robbie' (BBC 1).* L □ *One can find oneself using a range of stylistic tricks or ties—which are insurances, water-wings, crutches, face-savers,* ***hedging of bets****, playing safe.* L

the height of folly etc [Comp (NP)] (an instance of) extreme foolishness etc **V:** ⚠ be; think, find, make, sth. **o:** folly, silliness, foolishness, madness; bad manners, cheek, arrogance, perversity □ *It would be* ***the height of folly*** *not to finish his course now, whether he wants to practise as a dentist or not.* □ *The claim of the Conservatives to be the national party is valid, and it is* ***the height of silliness*** *for those on the Left to deny it.* NS □ *I call it* ***the height of bad manners*** *for a guest to tell one how to cook.* □ often in the construction *be* ***the height of folly*** *(for sb) to do sth.*

hell-bent on doing sth [Comp (AdjP)] recklessly or blindly determined on doing sth **V:** ⚠ be; seem, appear. **o:** getting his revenge, making the trip, causing a sensation, climbing to the top □ ***Hell-bent on*** *getting his revenge he embarked on hard training for a return fight.* □ *She is* ***hell-bent on*** *winning Tsuda's total love and admiration because it would be intolerable to her to make do with less.* L □ (NONCE) *It would be refreshing if the social scene was graced and littered by a few more people who weren't* ***heaven bent on*** *being so utterly ordinary.* NS

(all) hell breaks/is let loose fierce rioting, or a great amount of uproar and disorder, breaks out □ *If they should somehow find out that the rescue* (space)*ship had not, in fact, even yet been able to take off from Earth—that was when* ***hell*** *would start* ***breaking loose****.* TST □ *Then I wrote right across the* (examination) *paper: If the next three hours are going to determine my future then I'm not bothered. Afterwards, I folded my arms and waited for* ***hell to break loose****.* TVT □ *I realised that if they* (two IRA hunger strikers) *died* ***all hell*** *would* ***be let loose*** *among the Catholics in Northern Ireland.* L

hell for leather [A (NP)] (informal) with the greatest possible energy and speed **V:** run, ride, drive, work, go (at sb/sth) □ *We've started them all right. A whole lot of mad March hares streaking* ***hell for leather*** *across the open country.* ARG □ *'Do nightingales sing all day?' 'All day, all night,' Pop said. 'Like everything else in the mating season, they go* ***hell for leather****.'* DBM □ *For some reason, absence of information often goes hand in hand with* ***hell for leather*** *expansion.* OBS □ *She wrote the first draft in one* ***hell for leather*** *month.* OBS □ end position; attrib use ***hell-for-leather*** *expansion, a* ***hell-for-leather*** *hurry.*

hell has/knows no fury like a woman scorned (saying) there is no one more vindictive than a woman who has been slighted (esp one whose favours or advances have been rejected) □ *Heav'n has no rage, like love to hatred turn'd,/* ***Nor Hell a fury, like a woman scorn'd****.* THE MOURNING BRIDE (W CONGREVE 1670-1729) □ *So I said to myself,* ***hell knows no fury like a woman scorned*** *and it's no use my telling Muriel at this moment that I thought she was Elsie. That'll only make her vicious.* RM □ (NONCE) *Elated, George prepares. But* ***hell hath no fury like a woman's scorn****, the woman being his wife, Lil.* TVT

a/the hell of a sth (informal) a considerable, remarkable, impressive etc sb/sth **o:** guy, fellow, girl; lot, (long) time, speed, row, nuisance □ *Unfortunately we don't believe in eternity now, although they tell me the moment you're atomized lasts* ***a hell of a long time****.* HAA □ *'She must have been going at* ***the hell of a pace****,' Teddy said.* RATT □ *It must be something very important because there certainly seems to be* ***a hell of a lot of it****.* HHGG □ *'She said you were* ***the hell of a chap****,' Viola remarked. 'Fighter Command, three rings, and a chest full of ribbons.'* RFW □ JO: *Old Nick'll get you in the end.* HELEN: *Thank God for that! Heaven must be* ***the hell of a place****.* TOH □ occas spelt helluva. ⇨ ⚠ one hell of a row etc.

the/to hell with sb/sth (informal) sb/sth doesn't matter, is not going to be considered or bothered about **o:** him, all such pessimists; work, the future; waiting any longer □ *But I was sick and tired of being a tenant at the mercy of absentee landlords. So I threw my hands up and said:* ***the hell with*** *it, I'll explore Brooklyn.* L □ *And too many self-styled lovers of our countryside are concerned only with what they can see and do in their own lifetime—and* ***to hell with*** *posterity.* NS □ ***To hell with*** *what passes for local democracy if the consequence will be bad housing and bad environmental planning for so many of our citizens.* NS □ used to express irritation, weariness etc.

Hell's Angels (gangs of) young motor-cyclists who project a tough image of themselves by driving at reckless speeds on the roads and wearing black, decorated, leather clothes □ *Items range from the copper studs used in leather work which sell at 5p a dozen. 'We get rid of thousands to* ***Hell's Angels*** *for decorating their jackets.'* ST □ *Despite the leatherware on the cover, the four angels of the title aren't* ***Hell's Angels*** *but a bunch of Texan teenagers who act and talk tough, but aren't really.* NS □ *The wind comes straight from Alaska and the Japanese equivalent of* ***Hell's Angels*** *can be heard at night weaving their way through the dunes.* L □ occas sing a Hell's Angel.

help oneself[1] do what one can for oneself (rather than expecting or demanding help from others) □ *Oxfam, Christian Aid and similar organisations devote as much of their funds as can be spared to supplying communities with the means to* ***help themselves****.* □ *The surgeons have done a wonderful job on your knee but you've got to* ***help yourself*** *now.* ⇨ ⚠ can't help oneself.

help oneself[2] serve oneself with food, or anything else offered to be used or taken away; take sth that is not offered, without payment, permission etc □ *The waitress only clears the table between courses. The food is all laid out on side tables and you* ***help yourself****.* □ *Did you see him* ***helping himself*** *out of my box of cigarettes all evening? Cheek!* □ *He's been* ***helping himself*** *to paint out of the store-room.*

help a lame dog over a stile give help to sb who is in difficulty or trouble □ *The charitable* *precept always to **help lame dogs over stiles** is shared by the world's major religions.* □ *My Aunt Gloria surprised us all by becoming a nun at the age of sixty and founding the **Lame Dog** Society to care for the poverty-stricken, sick and homeless.*

a hen party a social occasion restricted to, or attended only by, women □ *The first time I was asked to do an act for **a hen party** I nearly didn't accept.* ITV □ (astrological prediction) ***A hen party** will be extremely successful.* TVT ⇨ a stag party.

the herd instinct the desire or compulsion to be like, behave like, seek the company of, other people, esp those of one's own age or social group □ *'Why don't some of this crowd go out by the side door?' '**Herd instinct** I suppose.'* □ *The other factor behind these huge receptions is **the herd instinct**. People rarely do things in ones or twos but in groups of five, ten or a dozen.* L

here below [A (AdvP)] in this life (contrasted with heaven 'above') □ (source) *Man wants but little **here below**,/Nor wants that little long.* THE HERMIT (O GOLDSMITH 1728-74) □ *If his* (the American plantation slave's) *lot **here below** was miserable, he was encouraged to hope for pie in the sky. And he was freely allowed the consolation of religion.* L □ *I do not know the name of the lady who announces the trains at Victoria Station, nor do I expect to meet her **here below**.* NS □ often facetious.

here goes (informal) a signal or announcement that sth will start, that one is about to do sth, immediately □ *'**Here goes** then.' Davidson went to the lean-to, taking a torch from his trouser pocket. He ducked through the broken door and disappeared.* PM □ *'**Here goes**,' murmured the headmaster to his companion as the curtain started to rise on the yearly School Play. 'I warn you that you're going to be extremely bored.'* □ *Jack really tells this story far better than I do because I'm no good at imitating accents, but since he won't oblige, **here goes**.* □ fixed form, pres tense only.

here and now [adv + adv non-rev] immediately; in this place and at this moment; in present circumstances □ *If our funds had been in better shape nothing would have given us more pleasure than to present him, **here and now**, with a brand new bicycle.* TCM □ *I'm telling you **here and now** to let this rubbishy idea drop.* HD □ JO: *The time to have taken care of me was years ago, when I couldn't take care of myself.* HELEN: *All right, but we're talking about **here and now**.* TOH □ *Those who work in news are, by the very nature of the business, ensnared by **the here and now** and they have little time for the more graceful enduring things of life.* L □ n form the here and now.

here and there [adv + adv non-rev] in, to and from, various places; scattered about in a random way □ ***Here and there** under china animals or French paper-weights, were neat piles of letters or press cuttings or thousand-franc notes.* UTN □ *We still have the Lord knows how many hydrogen bombs stored **here and there**, waiting for some madman to set them off.* EHOW □ *The words themselves became an obsession with him and he spent a longer and longer time each day staring at them and shifting them **here and there**.* TCM □ *It's dreadful. **A pound here and a pound there** and before you know where you are your whole week's wages are gone.* □ variant a pound etc here and a pound etc there. ⇨ ⚠ next entry.

here, there and everywhere in many different places; all over the place; moving about; to or from many different places □ *Rumours fly from ear to ear of apparitions **here, there and everywhere**.* NDN □ *I think you should get yourself a big filing cabinet, instead of having your papers lying around **here, there and everywhere**.* □ *'Don't you have a regular run then?' 'No, just **here, there and everywhere**, wherever there's a load to be picked up.'* ⇨ ⚠ previous entry.

here today and gone tomorrow (saying) a philosophical comment on the transitory nature of man, his works, or any forms of life; also said of sb who is always on the move or with whom one has only a brief contact □ *That's the trouble with you office fellows. You all worry too much by half. After all, **here today and gone tomorrow**.* DBM □ *Nick does come home to see us quite often, but you could easily have missed him. **Here today and gone tomorrow** is his style.* □ *You should be looking after your regular customers, Joe, not a whole lot of tourists who'll be **here today and gone tomorrow**.*

here/there we go (again) sth said or done before is, or is about to be, repeated □ *'I was engaged once but it didn't work out.' 'Why not?' Virginia asked with a slight sigh. **Here we go again**. He wants to talk about his love troubles.* AITC □ VAIZEY: *Geoffrey Howe, do you believe that faster and more successful economic growth necessarily means greater fairness and equality?* HOWE: ***There you go again**! Greater fairness and equality; they don't necessarily tie up.* L □ in everyday use expresses exasperation, tedium or resignation that sth is about to happen.

here's to sb/sth a common form of toast **o:** you, her, us all; the bride; the success of our new venture □ *You'll need a stiff whisky before your interview. Well, **here's to** you, and I hope you get the job.* □ *He raised his glass. 'Your mother,' he said. '**Here's to** her.'* AITC

hewers of wood and drawers of water [NP + NP non-rev] people or classes whose lot it is to labour at necessary, if often menial or unskilled, tasks for others □ (source) *And the princes said unto them, Let them live; but let them be **hewers of wood and drawers of water** unto all the congregation.* JOSHUA IX 21 □ *There will always be 'factory hands and the like' — **hewers of wood and drawers of water**. There is no such thing as the classless society, even in the Soviet Union.* RT □ (NONCE) *In other words, the majority of children had no need of an academic qualification since they would be spending their lives **hewing wood and drawing water** for their grammar-school-educated masters.* NS

hey presto magician's or conjuror's phrase accompanying the successful completion of a trick; announcement of, or comment on, anything done with surprising ease and swiftness □ *Now you unlock it the same way—19-6-14—and **hey presto**, it opens.* OMIH □ *They adopt the* *ultra-conservative remedy of Professor Friedman and Mr Enoch Powell. Stop the rise in the volume of money and* ***hey presto****, all will be well.* NS □ *There was a brief pause for Ed to muster his army. Then* ***hey presto*** *the furniture van arrived.* OBS

the hidden persuaders advertising and its techniques as they indirectly influence people to think, believe, or desire to have, things they might not otherwise have done (from the title of a book by V PACKARD 1957) □ *But despite his long experience in films, on TV and on the stage, George Baker is finding it hard to break into the field of* ***the hidden persuaders*** (TV commercials). OBS

hide and seek [n + n non-rev] children's game with varying rules, but basically one seeker finds a number of hiders and brings them to a 'den' within a stated time; (fig) elusive or teasing tactics with another person, group etc □ *Go on now, kiddies,* ***hide and seek****; now we are playing* ***hide and seek****; run away and hide.* HSG □ *He would say in answer to pestering that he was to hold a ceremony at a particular time and place. While this game of* ***hide and seek*** *was still going on, a young man named Laduh fell ill.* NDN

high days and holidays [n + n non-rev] days when festivals, celebrations are held; special occasions generally □ *Fish, potatoes, bread and milk were our regular articles of diet, with a chicken or a piece of pork and a bottle of cheap wine on* ***high days and holidays.*** □ (NONCE) *He goes back to sleep when the alarm goes off, forgets even agreeable appointments and gets* ***high dates and holidays*** *wrong by just one day.* OBS □ high days, high-days or highdays.

high and dry [Comp (adj + adj non-rev)] above a water or tide line; (fig) abandoned, ignored, left in isolation, by changes of circumstances **S:** boat, dinghy; trader, merchant; firm, industry. **V:** ⚠ be (left); lie □ *I saw, in the sharp silver light of the full moon, that the mine was left* ***high and dry*** *by the ebbing tide.* ARG □ *After lunch they strolled down again to the beach. The landing craft lay* ***high and dry*** *far from the sea.* RFW □ *Had the laughter receded only to leave me* ***high and dry****, staring through these windows, never wanting to go inside?* HAHA

high jinks (informal) fun and frivolity □ *...croquet on the lawn, theatricals in the great hall, the younger boys knocking up at cricket with the footmen behind the stables,* ***high jinks*** *in the servants' halls when the upper servants had retired.* L □ ***High jinks*** *at a camera club outing games didn't tell us anything about photography as a visual art and powerful modern mode of expression.* RT

high and low[1] [adj + adj non-rev] of all classes, ranks □ *Listen, children of the world, both* ***high and low****, rich and poor. I shall speak the truth.* HSG □ *London life,* ***high and low****, is drawn upon extensively, though the story about an old working-class woman seems to me the least successful.* NS □ *Troubles, like death, come to* ***high and low.*** □ usu follows n which it modifies; may function as [n + n], as in last example.

high and low[2] [adv + adv non-rev] everywhere; in every possible place **V:** search, hunt, look, scour □ *My Hairy Frogs settled down very nicely in their large tin. For many weeks I searched* ***high and low*** *to try to find some females to go with them, but without success.* BB □ *Anyway, we've hunted* ***high and low****, boy, believe me. Not a bloody twitter.* ILIH

high and mighty [adj + adj non-rev] self-important and arrogant with a presumption of being superior to others □ *'Music is for people,' he says. Consequently he harbours no* ***high and mighty*** *ideas against music that is intended frankly for entertainment.* RT □ *If Jenny had not had the fear of being thought* ***high and mighty****, she would not have hoisted and edged her way on to Patrick's lap.* TGLY □ *And to talk about holidays abroad is one of the almost infallible marks of the stuck-up, the* ***high and mighty****, who are no better than they should be.* RATT □ attrib use *a* ***high and mighty attitude****;* may function as [n + n], as in last example.

a high profile [O (NP)] a visible, active, presence in a situation **V:** adopt; keep, maintain □ *They specifically queried the* ***high profile*** *tactics which were adopted by the army over the weekend.* G □ *The Chairman of Lambeth Council's community affairs committee criticised* ***this high profile*** *adopted by the police.* G □ ***The high*** *and impressive* ***profile*** *maintained by the Chancellor of the Exchequer throughout the year has enhanced his chances of succeeding to the Prime Ministership.* □ attrib use ***the high profile*** *tactics.* ⇨ a low profile.

high spirits exuberant happiness, vitality, confidence etc □ *She had been a gay young girl, I believe, but by this time had lost most of her* ***high spirits.*** UL □ *What had really gone were the jokes, the* ***high spirits.*** OBS □ *Bunder, who seemed in* ***high spirits****, was telling a story which he punctuated, as Charles approached, with bursts of laughter.* HD □ *You are quick to spot bright ideas, so there should be plenty of enthusiasm and* ***high spirits.*** TVT

high summer the middle of the summer season, constrasted with early or late summer □ *Mr Charlton stood there staring too, thinking of how spring had passed, how quickly the buds of May had gone, and how everything now had blossomed with full,* ***high summer.*** DBM □ *It was heavy and thundery outside; early August and beginning to get that washed-out feeling of* ***high summer*** *when the freshness has gone from the leaves.* HD

(it is) high/about time (that) the time is (long) overdue when sth should happen or be done □ *'I've put those shelves up in the kitchen.'* ***'High time****—I've waited long enough.'* □ *So I think* ***it is about high time that*** *some organization applied some careful thought to deciding what kind of relationship between the House of Commons majority and the proportion of votes cast for the different parties would be desirable.* NSC □ *I said* ***it was high time*** *you fell in love with somebody.* PW □ *'Well, I'm waiting.' 'What for?' 'Don't you think* ***it's about time*** *you kissed me?'* DBM □ *that*-cl contains a v in the past tense; high/about time, (too)! used as a comment.

high, wide and handsome striking; impressive □ *The day was riding* ***high, wide and handsome*** *into the deeps of the incredible blue sky.* LWK □ (film review) ***High, wide and*** *meticulously* ***handsome*** *re-creation of Cromwell, his life and strife.* RT

the higher you climb etc the harder you fall (catchphrase) the risk of disappointment, disgrace or failure increases in proportion to the height of one's ambition, position in life or profession **V:** climb, get, go, rise □ *Parents and careers masters tend to advocate the safe jobs and professions.* ***The higher you climb the harder you fall*** *of course but the rewards for a youngster with guts and talent in striking a line of his own can be enormous.* SC □ *It is easier for an employee in a business that has failed to get another job than the man who ran it.* ***The higher you get the harder you fall.*** □ (NONCE) ***The bigger you are, the harder you fall.*** *Malcolm Allison has attracted more than the usual band of knockers—people who consider him too big for his boots and gloat when he doesn't find success.* TVT

the highways and byways (of sth) [n + n non-rev] all the roads or routes, large and small; (fig) the main forms or trends of sth, as well as its less well-known aspects **V:** explore; go (out) into. **o:** Wales; physics, comic verse, life, the printing trade □ *By lectures, excavations and other contacts, I took the museum into* ***the highways and byways of*** *Wales.* SD □ *Is the Labour opposition so involved in the parliamentary processes that it does not think it important enough to go out into* ***the highways and byways****?* NS

hire and fire [v + v non-rev] employing staff, esp on a temporary and insecure basis, and then dismissing them □ *...an industry accustomed to on-site* ***hiring and firing*** *and much casual labour.* OBS □ *Certainly in the first half of this century, one remembers the proprietors better than the editors. The tycoons naturally tend to survive the men they* ***hire and fire.*** L □ (NONCE) *Local government appeals to certain people partly because, unlike industry, it has no record of being a* ***hiring-firing*** *kind of place to work.* OBS

history repeats itself (saying) sth that has occurred in the past, happens, or is likely to happen, again □ ***History*** *may* ***repeat itself*** *in a general way, as in the rise and fall of empires, but not exactly enough to enable us to learn from the mistakes of the past.* □ *I, personally, do not subscribe to the theory of* ***history repeating itself*** *and I think that a new march on Rome is out of the question.* L □ *But the tendency of* ***history*** *is to* ***repeat itself*** *in every way but one; and the new element is unfortunately and usually the only one that matters.* L

hit the bottle [V + O pass] (informal) drink too much habitually or over a period of time □ *I suppose every school has at least one master who begins fairly early to* ***hit the bottle****, ending up as a quiet soak.* CON □ *She seemed all right for a while after her marriage but I'm afraid she's* ***hitting the bottle*** *again.* □ usu infin after *begin, start,* or in continuous tenses.

hit the/score a bull's eye [V + O pass] hit the small innermost circle of a shooting target, dartboard etc; hit, strike, any physical object with an accurate aim; (fig) make a successful diagnosis, judgement, choice, prediction **S:** darts player, marksman, archer; inventor, writer, critic □ *'There's no chance of the Cloud missing the solar system, of it being a near miss?' 'That Cloud is going to* ***score a bull's eye*** *plumb in the middle of the target.'* TBC □ *Patricia Highsmith is a brilliantly talented novelist and she has* ***hit the bull's eye*** *often in the past.* ST

hit the ceiling/roof [V + O] (informal) lose one's temper suddenly and violently; be violently startled or frightened □ *Phelan found out that the source of the leak in the Hughes organisation had been Gregson Bautzer. He gave Dietrich this titbit of information, and Dietrich* ***hit the roof.*** ST □ *Don't creep around so quietly! I nearly* ***hit the ceiling*** *when you spoke.* □ *The mere mention of James Bond to Sean Connery at that time was enough to make him* ***hit the roof*** *without the aid of ejector seat or any other item of sophisticated Bond gadgetry.* TVT

hit sb/sth hard [V + O + A pass] affect sb/sth adversely **S:** misfortunes, losses; administration, disease, climate. **O:** nation, family; farmers, workers; livestock; economy, industry □ *The advent of commercially viable television* ***hit*** *the cinema very* ***hard.*** □ *The recent rise in National Insurance contributions for the self-employed will* ***hit*** *small shopkeepers* ***hard.*** ST □ *Higher prices for food will increase pressure for further wage increases and better pensions for those* ***hardest hit*** *by the rising cost of living.* SC □ *The Institute of Pacific Relations,* ***hard hit*** *financially by the withdrawal of tax exemption, is leaving New York for a cheaper base in Vancouver, British Columbia.* T

hit the hay [V + O] (informal) go to bed □ *I just said, 'Sure, let's* ***hit the hay****, James.' I set the clock to arouse us in ample time.* BM □ *Don't wait up for me. The Greens have invited me to supper after the concert and by the time I walk back from there I'll be ready to* ***hit the hay*** *anyway.*

hit etc the headlines [V + O] (informal) become important or prominent news; attract press notice and public attention **S:** story, report, news; actress, boxer. **V:** hit, ⚠ make, reach □ *Although much of Malcolm MacDonald's work was done behind the scenes, he says he didn't mind. 'I've never wanted to* ***hit the headlines*** *anyway,' he says.* RT □ (the Sudan's civil war) *There's been plenty of killing, hunger and suffering, yet it never* ***hit the headlines*** *like the conflicts in Biafra and the Congo.* L □ *Meanwhile Diana Ross does attempt to show that far from being just a junkie who* ***made the headlines****, Billie Holiday was a very considerable artist, the greatest of all jazz singers.* NS

hit the jackpot [V + O] win a lot of money at poker from the jackpot ie the pool of money staked in bets; (unexpectedly) make, inherit etc a lot of money; do, or produce, sth that is a spectacular financial success **S:** gambler, punter; scheme, project; play, production □ *Writers of dream-like fantasies take a big gamble. It is all or nothing. John Hawkes* ***hit the jackpot****, George Macbeth loses his shirt.* L □ *They* (dress designers) ***hit the jackpot****, fall from grace and just when you think they have sunk without trace, pop up again.* SC □ *The subjects he chose were always interesting and the writing distinguished, but only one, 'Invasion 1940',* ***hit the jackpot.*** L

hit and miss [n + n non-rev] guesswork; random procedures which have some successes and some failures □ FIRST COMEDIAN: *Go for spontaneity. Just give the dialogue its head.*

SECOND COMEDIAN: *This seems a damned* ***hit and miss*** *way of doing things.* ART □ *The problem is that authenticating old violins has always been something of a* ***hit and miss*** *business.* ST □ *Like so many youngsters of the time his early education was* ***hit and miss****. 'I didn't really get stuck into any proper schooling until I was eight.'* TVT □ functions as a Comp, or attrib, as shown in third, and first and second, examples respectively.

hit and run [n + n non-rev] the behaviour of motorists who do not stop after causing an accident; (when the 'hitting' as well as the running is deliberate) methods in guerilla warfare, gang wars, attacks by hooligans, etc **n:** driver, victim; accident, cases; tactics, action, attack □ (newspaper report) ***Hit and Run****. Charles Lumley (23) was admitted to hospital last night. This is believed to be another case of a motorist failing to stop after knocking down a pedestrian.* HD □ *Oh, we'll manage this little old blackmailer. After all there have been much worse things in the Templar family than* ***hit and run*** *drivers and blackmail.* DC □ *The guerillas have clearly decided that there is no need to face the Pakistan Army directly, or even to disrupt their activities by ambushes and* ***hit and run*** *actions.* L □ always attrib, as shown.

hither and thither [adv + adv non-rev] from one place to another in a varying, or aimless, pattern of movement **V:** move; dart, dash; scurry, run □ *The water was clear to the bottom and bright with tropical weed and coral. A school of tiny, glittering fish flicked* ***hither and thither****.* LF □ *He gave himself up to the surging sea of memory, washed* ***hither and thither*** *by the chance currents of the conversation that flowed around him.* ASA

hold (oneself) aloof (from sb/sth) separate oneself in a superior way, keep apart (from sb/sth) □ *The people who really had a genuine interest in art couldn't scoff and* ***hold aloof*** *because his pictures really were the freshest and strongest thing we had to boast of.* CON □ *That region near The Boltons which is not quite of Kensington, turns its back to Earl's Court,* ***holds aloof from*** *Chelsea, and a hundred years ago was called New Brompton.* AH

hold one's breath [V + O] not breathe, for some practical reason, eg during a medical examination, under water, etc; not breathe because one's attention is concentrated on sth temporarily, one is gripped by wonder, fear etc □ *He* ***held his breath*** *and waited, tightening his grip on the chain.* ARG □ *A miraculous evening. The sky broke like an egg into full sunset and the water caught fire. He* ***held his breath****.* US □ *These little slapstick performances occurred quite frequently, during which everyone* ***held their breath****, for if they did not serve their purpose in promoting smiles, there were usually tears instead.* L □ cf *Everyone* ***held his breath*** and *They all* ***held their breath****.*

hold court [V + O] (formerly, a monarch would) preside at functions in his own court, receive guests, hear appeals, etc; (fig) be the admired, or respected, central figure in a gathering of people □ *Now at Calcutta the hospitable Caseys* ***held court****—old friends with time for everything and everybody in years of unparelled stress.* SD □ *In the kitchen, Jimmy and Kay helped their father to make sandwiches while in the front room the new baby* ***held court*** *amid a circle of admiring relatives.* □ *The professor could often be found* ***holding court*** *at a coffee table in the students' common room around eleven o'clock.* □ often humorous or derogatory.

hold sth dear [V + O + Comp pass] value, cherish, sth **O:** customs, beliefs, institutions, traditions □ *This loose plot provides the excuse for short cartoon scenes which cheerfully fragment the myths we are supposed to* ***hold dear****.* L □ (cricket commentaries) *Long may we enjoy the happy summer days, never for a moment missing one word of these fascinating and expert exchanges on the game we* ***hold*** *so* ***dear****.* RT □ *The reviewer was scared stiff at the thought of the seething, inattentive masses of young Americans who were listening to, looking at, and reading the wrong things and paying no heed to all we* ***hold dear****.* NS □ usu as part of a relative clause *(that/which) we* ***hold dear****.* ⇨ hold (one's) life etc cheap.

hold fast to sth (informal) adhere, cling, to sth with determination or stubbornness **o:** principle, theory, belief, code □ *'Just because she's a lady born,' repeated Briggs firmly,* ***holding fast to*** *his antiquated creed, 'she's your superior, Susan—whatever she may have done.'* EM □ *When they* (institutions) *are constituted for the service of God, it is even more important to* ***hold fast to*** *what is best in them.* AH

hold the field [V + O] not (yet) be superseded or supplanted **S:** artist, scientist; theory, idea; belief, fashion □ *For some years I* ***held the field****, always with an appreciation of the hard fact that my position was the outcome of circumstance, not merit.* SD □ *The years following World War II saw a great change. Until then the political and economic assumptions of the 19th Century had, by and large,* ***held the field****.*

hold one's fire [V + O] not fire a gun etc immediately, because one does not know where one's enemy is, to save ammunition, etc; (fig) refrain from saying or doing sth, esp of a critical or aggressive nature, until one learns more or until the right moment comes □ *Once he seemed to rush, but there was no shot. Evidently he had lost patience, but was* ***holding his fire*** *till he was certain.* ARG □ *The IRA extremists seemed to be* ***holding their fire****, while the Vanguard forces of Unionist activism were regrouping.* L □ *'He should have telephoned if he couldn't be here.' 'Well,* ***hold your fire****—he may have met with an accident.'* ⇨ ⚠ hang fire.

hold the floor [V + O] speak, or address an audience, at great length or with determination to finish what one has to say; monopolize a conversation or discussion (the floor = where members of an assembly sit and from where they speak) □ *Politicians and farmers expressed the pros and cons of entry. But it was Geoffrey Rippon fresh from the Luxembourg negotiations, who* ***held the floor****.* L □ *There was no interrupting her tirade. She had* ***the floor*** *and meant to* ***hold*** *it.* ⇨ ⚠ take the floor.

hold the fort [V+ O pass] take charge of defending, controlling, looking after, sth/sb in the absence of others □ *She wanted me, for* *reasons of her own, to* ***hold the fort*** *all day, and her method of making sure that I did was to keep me a prisoner.* UTN □ *Mrs Carstairs was speaking to Washington on the transatlantic telephone. 'You know, I ought really to be there to look after you— Yes, dear, I know, and after all I am doing my little bit to* ***hold the fort*** *while you are away.'* EM □ *Your old man's sitting here* ***holding the fort****—talking his head off—and you don't back him up.* YAA

hold good be or remain true, valid, or applicable; hold true (qv) **S:** statement, declaration; conditions; promise, undertaking □ *Years ago there used to be a doctrine called 'Ministerial Responsibility'. As a 'convention' of our constitution that may no longer* ***hold good****.* NS □ *As for the company's shares, they may well show some improvement. But we said last year that they were not for widows and orphans and that still* ***holds good****.* ST □ *'I've always managed to pick up a job when I needed one.' 'I know, but you can't depend on that kind of luck* ***holding good****.'* ⇨ ⚠ hold water.

hold/stand one's ground [V + O] defend and/or maintain one's position in a battle, contest or argument □ (a herd of buffalos stampede) *I* ***stood my ground*** *because, in some strange way, now that my uneasiness was explained I was not afraid.* LWK □ *On the industrial relations legislation the Government seem resolved to* ***stand their ground*** *and make no concessions of substance.* SC □ *The witness stoutly* ***held his ground*** *despite Defending Counsel's skilled efforts to confuse him and discredit his testimony.* OBS

hold/stay one's hand [V+ O] refrain, at least temporarily, from taking action □ *The Diamond Detectives* ***held their hand****. All went well, and de Graaf was on his way to the bus with a fortune in his pockets when the detectives pounced.* DS □ *The landlord was persuaded to* ***stay his hand*** *till other accommodation was found for the occupying tenants.* □ *What did surprise me was the way the newspapers interpreted Wilson's temporary* ***staying of his hand****. They seemed to see it as the product of his desire to help the Liberals.* NS □ stay one's hand is more formal.

hold sb's hand [V + O pass] clasp or grasp another's hand; (informal) comfort or support sb during a difficult or trying period □ *Come here, love, and* ***hold*** *Granny* ***'s hand*** *till we cross the street.* □ *Jack has to go to the Infirmary to have that sore eye examined and I know he'll want me to go and* ***hold his hand****.* □ *The industry can't expect the Minister to come and* ***hold its hand*** *every time it runs into trouble.* ⇨ ⚠ next entry.

hold hands [V + O] sit, walk etc beside another person with both or nearest hands linked, usu as a sign of affection □ *We sat in silence then,* ***holding hands*** *until the taxi pulled up at the cottage.* RATT □ *It was a difficult courtship and there was relief all round when finally it was official and the pair could stop pretending. At least for the first time they could* ***hold hands*** *in public.* RT ⇨ ⚠ previous entry.

hold one's head high [V + O + A pass] have, show, confidence (or pride) in one's worth, good character, ability etc □ *Now he and Lindsay 'feel we can* ***hold our heads high*** *again.' But it will be difficult to forget they felt like 'lepers and social pariahs'.* RT □ *India is now undeniably one of the world's leading industrial nations, so it has good reason to* ***hold its head high*** *in the world.* □ also pl *Now they can go about with* ***their heads held high.***

hold one's horses [V + O] (informal) go, or work, more slowly; wait a moment, to consider one's action or until sb else is ready; curb one's impatience, impetuosity, enthusiasm etc □ JASON: *Back to work everyone.* TOM: ***Hold your horses****. Where is Peter?* DPM □ *Then all the people involved in the Commonwealth Architects' competition were told to* ***hold their horses****—because time would be needed to organise an exhibition in which the entries could be put on show.* NS □ often used as check or warning.

hold it (informal) stop doing sth, or wait a while before continuing with it □ *'All right,* ***hold it****, Bill,' said Jane, looking at him sternly. 'We haven't started on the food yet.'* □ *We may as well start. No,* ***hold it****—I think that's John coming down the lane now.* □ an instruction or warning.

hold (one's) life etc cheap [V + O + Comp] consider sth, esp a condition or quality usu valued, to be of little value or importance **O:** (one's) life, ⚠ (one's) honour, one's good name, (one's) humanity □ *There's those that* ***hold life cheap****, but they're not our kind. We've got to show we're different from people like that.* OI □ *Even miserable wretches like these do not* ***hold life*** *so* ***cheap*** *that they will give it up without a struggle.* □ may reflect one's attitude towards others or oneself. ⇨ hold sth dear.

hold one's/its own [V + O] keep what position or popularity one has; not be outdone or made to look smaller in competition or contest with another or others **S:** industry, nation; cult, fashion; rider, runner □ *It was a decent background for the girl to have; she would be able to* ***hold her own*** *in feminine society in the Western District.* RFW □ *How much of a start he had had he could not tell, but Nur Jehan* (a horse) *seemed to be still* ***holding his own****.* ARG □ *In spite of the advances in recording technology some of the 'hit' records of the Big Band Era can* ***hold their own*** *with anything produced today.* NS □ *'When you consider the strong challenge from the hamburger,' said Lock, 'the sausage is* ***holding its own*** *extraordinarily well.'* OBS

hold one's peace [V + O] (decide to) remain silent; not say anything, or pass an opinion, about sth esp when this would be unwelcome or cause trouble □ *Julius found himself under the cruel necessity of* ***holding his peace*** *about the subject which he most liked to discuss.* EM □ *I'll admit to you now, Jimmy, though I* ***held my peace*** *at the time, that it used to quite embarrass me.* AITC

hold the purse strings [V + O pass] be the person who controls the supply of money, who decides how money is to be spent, etc □ *I* ***hold the purse strings*** *and they must come to me for money.* ST □ *The hero of Moravia's new novel is an Italian filmwriter with pretensions to direction, hampered by the need to keep in with a mogul who* ***holds*** *court and* ***purse strings****.* L □ *Many a small child has been dressed up to the nines in the hope that, by tugging at the heart-*

strings of an elderly relative, he will ***loosen the purse strings****.* ST ▫ unusual form in last example = 'be the person who, with control over the supply of money, decides that more money will be made available'.

hold sb/sth responsible (for sth) [V + O + Comp pass] think that sb/sth is the cause (of sth); treat sb as the one responsible (for sth/ doing sth to sb) (the implication being a duty or obligation that should be fulfilled) **o:** failure, accident; loss, theft, disappearance; abuse, misuse ▫ *The first question is whether the scientist can be* ***held responsible for*** *the eventual misuse of his discoveries by others.* NS ▫ *If you take the car don't* ***hold me responsible*** *if you have a breakdown on the way.*

hold/keep the ring [V + O pass] be in charge of a fight, contest or dispute; conduct and control a fight or dispute **S:** police, army; UN observers; peace-keeping force ▫ *A diplomat's duty is not to the disinterested search for 'truth'. It is for others to* ***hold that ring****.* L ▫ *The federal government is doing its best to make the election fair and legal. A new Police Commissioner and a strong team from the Federal Elections Commission are* ***holding the ring*** *in a firm and much needed way.* L

hold sway be supreme in power, control, influence or popularity **S:** monarch, government; creed, culture; idea, emotion. **A:** over half a continent; in men's hearts; among the rank and file ▫ *It is doubtful if Alexander the Great could have* ***held sway*** *over the vast territories he overran and subjugated even if he had lived to try.* ▫ *James, our janitor, was the real boss of our school and* ***held sway*** *for thirty years while headmasters came and went.* ▫ *To experts income tax figures have their elasticity; there is a considerable No-man's Land where the precision of mathematics does not* ***hold sway****.* PW

hold one's tongue [V + O] say nothing; remain silent ▫ *Jo's little girl* ***holds her tongue*** *and glowers at the grown-ups.* L ▫ *If I hear anything about it* (my engagement) *I shall know where it comes from, so* ***hold your tongue*** *like a good girl for a few days.* WDM ▫ *Well let me tell you here and now, my lad, that you had better brighten your ideas up. Now* ***hold your tongue****.* TT ▫ when imper, expression is either advice to say nothing, or sharp order to stop talking; also pl *Tell them to* ***hold their tongues****.*

hold true remain true, or be consistent with all known facts **S:** statement, description, account; theory, model; hold good (qv) ▫ *Yet the French police made no effort to prevent his leaving with the child, saying they could do nothing until an offence had been committed. The same apparently* ***holds true*** *in this country.* RT ▫ *This theory of language teaching is supposed to* ***hold true*** *whatever the mother tongue of the children.* ⇨ ⚠ next entry.

hold water [V + O] (informal) be sound, valid, capable of standing up to examination or testing **S:** theory, argument; explanation, reason, excuse; belief, need. **det:** much, a lot of ▫ *The tempting theory that he was a double agent does not* ***hold water****. Gehlen was, and is, a Nazi.* NS ▫ *The belief, say, that French garage men are ghastly doesn't* ***hold water****.* RT ▫ *'I could arrange an alibi, half a dozen of them for that matter, should that prove necessary.' 'Yes, but would they* ***hold water****?'* ⇨ ⚠ hold good, previous entry.

hold etc the whip hand (over/of sb) [V + O pass] have control, power (over sb); be in a position of special advantage or power (over sb) (the implication usu being that this is callously or unscrupulously used to benefit oneself) **V:** hold, ⚠ have, keep ▫ *He's doing it to take it out of me. Just to show that things have changed since he married me, and that he* ***holds the whip hand*** *now.* NM ▫ *The other team,* ***holding the whip hand****, seemed to relax midway through the first half.* ST ▫ *By Christ, I'd rather be like I am than* ***have the whip hand over*** *somebody else and be dead from the toe-nails up.* LLDR ▫ *Newspapers are now for the first time entirely subordinate to advertisers. I see no way out of this impasse, other than by maintaining a great daily net sale and thus* ***keeping the whip hand of*** *the advertiser.* ST

(a) hole and corner business etc sth carried out secretively, furtively because those involved are doing sth dishonest or disapproved of; sth which for no very sensible reason the people involved feel guilty or ashamed about **n:** business, ⚠ stuff, dealing; affair, method, proceeding ▫ *The selection conferences smacked of a piece of* ***hole-in-corner business****.* NS ▫ *Whoever her companion was, he wasn't her husband but I couldn't imagine her having* ***the*** *kind of* ***hole and corner affair*** *that had to be conducted in a dusty workroom.* TST ▫ *You have an absolute faith in democracy. You dislike* ***hole-and-corner government****, the stench of privilege and patronage which clings around Westminster and Whitehall.* NS ▫ *Unfortunately, I can't indulge in* ***this hole-in-corner stuff****. I have to come out in the open and print my information.* PP ▫ *In some respects their attitude towards sex activity does come from a long way back. But for them it is all rather scrabbily* ***hole-and-corner****.* UL ▫ functions as Comp in last example; variant a hole in (the) corner business etc.

a hole in the wall a very small shop, pub etc, esp in a row of buildings ▫ *The Comrie Bookshop is as inviting* ***a hole in the wall*** *as you could hope to retreat into anywhere in wintry Perthshire.* SC

holier than thou [Comp (AdjP)] self-righteous; self-admiring and slighting towards others **S:** attitude, manner; preacher, moralist. **V:** ⚠ be, seem; make sb ▫ (source) *I have spread out my hands all the day unto a rebellious people...which say, Stand by thyself, come not near to me; for I am* ***holier than thou****.* ISAIAH LXV 2,5 ▫ *I have decided to resign myself to being surrounded by prolific parents. The* ***holier than thou*** *attitude which they adopt towards anyone who doesn't have children is too deeply ingrained.* OBS ▫ *When those who earn their livings by* (writing for popular newspapers) *find themselves under attack they counter-accuse their accusers of being '****holier than thou****', of smugness, of hypocrisy.* UL ▫ (NONCE) *Something odd happens to Englishmen who go to California. Gerald Heard, Aldous Huxley and Christopher Isherwood went madly native, often more* ***mystical than thou****.* ST ▫ attrib use *a* ***holier than thou*** *attitude*; sometimes adapted, as in last example.

a hollow laugh an insincere, forced or sceptical laugh **V:** give, produce □ *'You're looking fit,' I said, after we had shaken hands. He gave **a hollow laugh**, said 'That's something to the good, anyway,' and quickly changed the subject.* □ *They held little sherry parties full of frenzied chat and **hollow laughter**.* □ *I heard a Conservative Member give it as his opinion that Heath's chances of gaining the necessary majority first time round were three to one on. I gave **a hollow** knowing **laugh**.* NS □ variant hollow laughter.

a holy terror [Comp (NP)] a formidable, dominating person; sb who makes himself a nuisance to others, eg an over-lively, naughty or impudent child **V:** ⚠ be, turn into, become □ *Pity anyone who tried to take advantage of my grandmother who was known as '**the holy terror**' among the local shopkeepers and tradesmen.* □ *His first Commanding Officer 'was a non-drinker and non-smoker, but **a holy terror** if it came to a rough and tumble.'* L □ *Oh you! You're **a holy terror**, yes, you are. You're supposed to be a gentleman, and that's how you carry on!* US □ also pl holy terrors.

a holy war (formerly) a war fought to defend one's religion, or to force conversion to it; (fig) a campaign, struggle or contest which has, or claims to have, idealistic motives and morally or socially worthy aims □ *The banner of the newly-founded Dockers' Union depicted a docker wrestling with the serpent of capitalism, and carried the legend: 'This is **a holy war**, and we shall not cease until all destitution, prostitution and exploitation are swept way.'* OBS

a home bird someone who chooses to spend most of his time at home because he is happiest there □ *But other than dining out, which I like, I'm **a home bird**. I'm not one for a big social whirl.* ST □ also pl home birds.

home and dry [Comp (AdjP)] safe and successful after a struggle or negotiation to achieve sth **V:** ⚠ be; get (sb) □ *Once McGovern acquired a credibility problem of his own, Nixon was **home and dry**.* NS □ *Overall, Raynaud now has 23 per cent of the company in his pocket, and with the backing of Bolding directors he is as good as **home and dry**.* OBS □ *The essentials* (of a musical play) *are technical expertise and unflagging vitality, and in these respects the production is **home and dry**.* L □ sometimes said in anticipation of a success felt to be assured.

a home from home [Comp (NP)] a place where one feels as comfortable, happy, welcome etc as in one's home **V:** ⚠ be; make sth, feel like □ *We don't run this hotel on a purely commercial basis. We try to make it **a home from home** for our guests.* □ *A caravan, bought by sixth formers in the area, has been set up in the school's adventure playground as **a home from home** for these children — and their parents.* OBS

home in one [Comp (AdjP)] successful in a first attempt to reach, strike, find, guess, identify, sb/sth **V:** ⚠ be; get (sb) □ *My drive had taken me to the edge of the green. 'Now let's see you get **home in one** for a birdie* (ie one stroke below par for a hole in golf)*,' said Mike.* ST □ *'You can munch this stuff at any hour of the day. It's a logical extension of TVP.' 'Textured Vegetable Protein?' 'That's right. **Home in one**.'* L

Homer sometimes nods (saying) even the best, or cleverest, of people have lapses, make mistakes (nod = fall momentarily asleep) □ (sources) *I am aggrieved when good **Homer sleeps**.* (HORACE 65-8 BC) □ *We learn from Horace, '**Homer sometimes sleeps**';/We feel without him, Wordsworth sometimes wakes.* DON JUAN (BYRON 1788-1824) □ *D J Hall's enormous 'Journey into Morning' appears to be the final working out of a too-intense classical education: **Homer nods** and so do I.* OBS □ *Occasionally **Homer nods**. It isn't enough to account for the expatriate Highlanders' support of George III during the American Revolution with the statement that it is puzzling. It isn't.* RT

honest to God/goodness(!) [Disj] honestly; truthfully □ *She was a silly cat if ever there was one. I can assure you. **Honest to God!** She was a sight for sore eyes.* TOH □ *'We want to trust you while you are in this establishment,' he said. 'If you play ball with us, we'll play ball with you.' (**Honest to God**, you'd have thought it was going to be one long tennis match.)* LLDR □ *I'm an **honest to God** real, live human being.* RT □ *Naturally the dissidents are furious, and none more so than the Medical Practitioners' Union which has been an **honest to goodness** union for 57 years.* NS □ *I must have looked like Charlie Chaplin imitating a penguin. The whole house rocked with **honest to God** belly laughs.* TVT □ in Disj use, uttered as a cry of disgust or exasperation; in attrib use = 'real, genuine'.

honesty is the best policy (saying) honesty is not only a moral virtue but has practical advantages; it is safer, and often more profitable, for a man to be honest than dishonest □ *'I could knock 5p or 10p off their change and they'd be none the wiser.' 'It's not worth the risk — **honesty's the best policy**.'* □ *Would it not have been kinder in the end to tell the woman that her baby had no chance at all of being born? That would have been honest; but he doubted whether the coiner of the phrase about **honesty being the best policy** had known a great deal about expectant mothers.* TST

(there is) honour among thieves (saying) law-breakers, cheats etc may have certain standards of conduct of their own which they will adhere to □ *'Somebody must have helped him carry the stuff away but he's sticking to it that he did the whole job himself.' '**Honour among thieves**, eh?'* □ *The contractors are all trying to do each other out of business and will use any mean trick they can turn their minds to. **There's** more **honour among thieves**.*

hook, line and sinker [A (NP)] (believe sth) completely either because of one's own credulity or because of the skill with which has been deceived (from angling, a fish swallowing not only the baited hook but part of the tackle as well) **V:** swallow, take, accept, believe, fall for, sth. **O:** the bait; his story, this old trick; the new product □ *Their attitudes and my father's eventually made me critical too at about 15. Up to then I had swallowed Nazi teaching, **hook, line and sinker**.* RT □ *It was a poor excuse but Mary swallowed it **hook, line and sinker**.* □ *The island* (Isle of Man) *is rather poorly policed against fraud. 'Our trouble is we're very suspicious of honest people but we fall **hook line***

***and sinker** for con-men.'* L □ always in order of headphrase. ⇨ ⚠ bag and baggage; lock, stock and barrel.

hop it (informal) go away, esp to avoid sth unpleasant or on the orders of sb who wishes to get rid of one. □ *I can't have you kids playing here when I'm working. Go on, **hop it**.* □ *I'm warning you, Kevin, take a tip from a friend, **hop it**! Get out!* TK □ often imper.

hope against hope (that) continue to hope (that sth is the case, will happen, etc) though one's reason tells one this is useless, foolish □ *It was then I heard Phuong's step. I had **hoped against hope that** he would have gone before she returned.* QA □ *There is another kind of truth, which counts blessings and **hopes against hope** and which has quite often been proved right in the long run.* L

hope deferred (maketh the heart sick) (saying) the experience of not having one's hopes fulfilled or realized (makes one depressed or discontented) □ (source) ***Hope deferred maketh the heart sick**: but when the desire cometh, it is a tree of life.* PROVERBS XIII □ ***Hope deferred maketh the heart sick**, as the Book of Proverbs tell us, but so do other feelings or emotions and there would appear to be no way of shortcircuiting the horrid connection.* WDM □ (a castaway) *There was illness of the body, effect of exposure. There was food-poisoning that made the world a mad place. There was solitude and **hope deferred**.* PM

hope springs eternal (in the human breast) (saying) feelings of hope are natural to mankind; one rarely accepts that the worst is inevitable □ ***Hope springs eternal in the human breast**;/Man never is, but always to be blest.* AN ESSAY ON MAN (A POPE 1688-1744) □ *I remember with the batteries, we'd try the old ones time after time. Even when we were quite sure they were as dead as a doornail. **Hope springs eternal**, that's what it is. When nothing else does.* TGLY □ (imprisonment) *All the time you think you're not going to be there as long as you're supposed to be. **Hope springs eternal**, you know.* ST

hope and trust (that) [v + v non-rev] hope (that sth is the case, will happen, etc), one's hope being strengthened by belief or an optimistic conviction □ *We have observed the changes all over Africa as a result of the policies of your Governments. We **hope and trust that** these changes will affect our own deplorable state.* OBS □ *We have arranged for you to take up your appointment on 30th Sept in the **hope and trust that** you will have fully recovered from your illness by that date.* □ occas used as a n, as in second example.

hopping mad (about/over sth) [Comp (AdjP)] (informal) really annoyed and angry (about sth) **V:** ⚠ be, go; make sb □ *We have a rough and tumble tradition of politics in this country that perhaps offends the sensibilities of more civilized nations. A lot of people in Washington are **hopping mad about** this.* L □ *I'll be **hopping mad** if I've gone to all this trouble to make lunch, and they phone to say they're not coming.* □ *Cruelty to animals is a subject upon which Mr Adams holds passionate views. 'I feel bitterly angry,' he explained, looking bitterly angry. 'Makes me **hopping mad**!'* OBS

a horn of plenty an unlimited, or copious, source of supplies (from the Latin *cornucopia*, a ram's horn overflowing with fruit and flowers, an emblem of plenty) □ *The morsels offered by '1001 Jokes and Anecdotes for Every Occasion' make singularly cheerless reading but doubtless the book will be **a horn of plenty** for after-dinner speakers up and down the country.* □ *I need help and am not going to be assisted by TV pictures of cheery credit managers showering £5 notes out of **a horn of plenty**.* ST □ occas pl horns of plenty.

a hornets' nest [O/o (NP)] (provoke) attacks, criticism, abuse from or quarrelling among several people **V:** rouse, stir up; bring about one's ears □ *I have never regretted stirring up **hornets' nests**. The first time I did so was shortly after the Second World War, by defending Wilhelm Furtwängler against accusations of Nazism.* OBS □ *I wonder if the reporter knew, when he quoted the learned judge's remarks, that he was going to rouse such **a hornets' nest**.* □ *A merger of the departments would certainly save money but you'll bring **a hornets' nest** about your ears.*

a horse of another colour [Comp (NP)] a person, matter or affair of a quite different kind **det:** another, a different, the same. **V:** ⚠ be; find sb □ (source) SIR TOBY: *He shall think, by the letters that thou wilt drop, that they come from my niece, and that she is in love with him.* MARIA: *My purpose is indeed, **a horse of that colour**.* TWELFTH NIGHT II □ *You can't have friends sharing the room for the same rent, but if you want your brother to stay for a week or so, that's **a horse of another colour**.* □ *After eight years I knew what was thought of Charles Hill by the BBC. 'I hope,' I said, 'that he will recognise that we are **a horse of a different colour**.'* NS

hot air fake rumours, empty boasts, threats or promises not likely to be carried out □ *If the merger rumours are just so much **hot air**, then the shares have been artificially inflated, and we can expect a scramble for the exit in due course.* OBS □ *He posed, he postured, he talked a lot of **hot air**.* PW □ *He's just a **hot-air** merchant who wouldn't say boo to a goose if it came to a fight.* □ *Political prophets and creative drama departments have in common the ability to generate considerable quantities of **hot air**.* G □ attrib use *a **hot-air** merchant*.

hot at sth (informal) (quite) accomplished or able in a particular activity, skill, branch of knowledge, etc **V:** be, get, become. **adv mod:** pretty, (not) so, quite, rather, very □ *Ask Jimmy about it. He's pretty **hot at** diagnosing engine troubles.* □ *Here Julia—since you're so **hot at** crosswords, try this one.* □ *He's good at English and languages but not so **hot at** Maths.* □ not so hot a (self-)deprecating reply to such questions as *How are you feeling? What was the film like? How's your French?* ⇨ ⚠ hot on sb/sth.

(all) hot and bothered [adj + adj non-rev] (informal) harassed by the need to hurry, pressure of work, anxiety, apprehension etc **V:** be, get (sb), make sb □ *And Pat was coming up from the bottom, **all hot and bothered**, unbuttoning her coat.* TT □ (official secrets) *'Nothing very serious has got out, has it?' 'If one thing gets* *out, another can. That's why we get **all hot and bothered**.'* DM

a hot line a secret and special telephone link, eg between a head of state and a supreme military commander □ *'People seem to think that I have **some hot line** between here and Jerusalem,' said Mrs Golda Meir's sister.* ST □ *There are double- and triple-safe precautions against any maniac getting on to **a hot line** and blowing up half the world.*

hot on sb/sth (informal) an enthusiastic admirer of sb, devotee of sth; well-informed on a subject **V:** be, be considered, think oneself. **adv mod:** (not) so, not too, pretty, quite, extremely □ *I was also **hot on** cross-country running. I boxed in the RAF, too, and I'm a bit of a tennis nut.* RT □ *I always thought he was pretty **hot on** Kenny Brown's sister.* □ *I'll help you if I can but I'm not too **hot on** Income Tax law.* ⇨ ⚠ hot at sth.

the hot seat [O/o (NP)] (informal) the electric chair as a means of executing criminals; (fig) a position in which one is esp open and vulnerable to criticism, attack, questions etc, as in TV or public press interviews, radio phone-in programmes **V:** occupy; sit in, be in □ *Not here. If he's for **the hot seat** he'll be transferred to another prison.* □ *Somehow WOSU* (= a radio station) *manages to get spokesmen of authority to occupy **the hot seats** and deal with questions thrown at them.* L □ *If you put yourself in **this hot seat**, you are asking to be shot down. So we got thrashed at the outset by the critics.* ST

a hot spot [Comp/o NP] (informal) a difficult or dangerous situation **V:** be (in), find oneself in, get sb into □ *I remember seeing the Commander of the Guards Division in **a** very **hot spot** in a place called Happy Valley, not far from where the tank battle took place.* L □ *I would be in **a hot spot** if the payment didn't come through before he tried to cash my cheque, but I had to risk that.* □ also pl hot spots.

hot under the collar [Comp (AdjP)] (informal) embarrassed, indignant, or annoyed; in a worked-up excited state, esp in an aggressive way **V:** ⚠ be, become, get, grow; make sb □ *The Vicar, despite years of practice, still got **hot under the collar** when she addressed him like this.* ASA □ *If you do get stopped, remember that most policemen enforce the law on the basis of common sense and just about the worst thing you can do is to get **hot under the collar**.* ST □ *If a client enlarged on the iniquities of the income tax, and grew **hot under the collar**, Harold's eyes would stray towards the door.* PW

a house etc divided against itself (cannot stand) (saying) a family, nation, political party, etc that is weakened by internal dissension, quarrelling or fighting (cannot survive, will be easily overcome by others, etc) **n:** house, family, nation □ *Every **kingdom divided against itself** is brought to desolation; and every **city** or **house divided against itself shall not stand**.* MATTHEW XII 25 □ ***A band of rebels** thus **divided against themselves could not stand** against a secure government.*

a house of cards a house, tower etc built by balancing playing-cards; (fig) an imaginative, over-ambitious project that cannot be realized; a state of affairs that exists mainly in sb's imagination or wishful thinking □ *But the Federation is like **a house of cards**: disturb one and the whole structure wobbles.* OBS □ *The trouble with any such elaborate pretence is that if you expose one detail **the** whole **house of cards** comes tumbling down.* □ *Soberly considered, Fest's psychological reconstruction* (of Hitler's character and career) *falls to pieces like **a house of cards**.* OBS □ often follows *like*.

a household name/word [Comp (NP)] a name, eg that of a prominent public figure or a widely-used product, which is so well known that it is part of the currency of ordinary conversation **V:** ⚠ be, become; make sb/sth □ *He talks about the big companies which are **household words** and of the smaller ones too.* ST □ *Becoming **a household name**, however, brought its problems for Slater with his every move being headline news.* OBS

how/what about (doing) sth?[1] (informal) invitation or suggestion to do or have sth **o:** (having) a cup of tea? (painting it) pink? (calling him) John? □ *'**How about** having a cup of coffee with me?' 'All right,' she said.* H □ ***What about** a drink? It's nearly opening time.* UTN □ ***What about** asking a busload of these orphans to see the horse run, Banks said to Piggott.* SC □ *'**How about** bringing your own father round to a Marxist way of thinking?' I asked. Ajit laughed —nervously. 'You can't teach an old monkey new tricks.'* OBS

how/what about (doing) sth?[2] (informal) request for information, assistance, explanation; reminder that sb/sth should be remembered, done, or taken into account **o:** the return journey, money to pay for it; carrying my bag, letting them know; the daft things you do yourself □ *'Thank you,' jotting down the flight times to Dublin. '**How about** getting back, Saturday or Sunday?'* □ *When he told me we were aground I said, 'Splendid. Now, **what about** a boat to put me on shore?'* MFM □ *You're the last one to talk about wasting electricity! **How about** all the times you fall asleep with your bedside lamp on all night?*

how about it/that(?) (informal) exclamatory question asked about sth just done, discussed or discovered; challenging remark, often made to sb with whom one disagrees, or whose behaviour one wishes to change □ *'They're going to publish my novel,' he said, '**how about that?**'* □ *If you start working in earnest, you might just pass. So now, **how about it?*** □ *'I can park here if I like.' 'And your car can be towed away if you do, so **how about that**!'*

how come (that)? (informal) how does/did it happen (that)? what is the explanation (of sth)? □ *'**How come** he was a Red* (= communist), *then?' 'It's been the romantic thing to be for a century now.'* PP □ *He was told that the whole edition had been sold out. He asked the bookseller: '**How come?**' And the man replied: 'These days people want to forget, so they read books.'* L

how crazy etc can you get? (informal) you are being completely crazy; is there any limit to how crazily you behave? **adj:** crazy, stupid, selfish, pompous, hypocritical □ *'Here's a man had his dog's teeth crowned with gold.' 'Really, **how crazy can you get?**'* □ ***How pompous can***

you get**? You had me under your spell for a moment. Now you've broken it.* EGD □ *'Good God!' Bob broke out at last. 'What a conversation!* ***How vicious can *some of* ***you*** *women* ***get?****'*

how dare you (do sth) shocked and reproachful reaction to wrong, presumptuous or impudent behaviour **V + O:** say such things, speak to your mother like that, use this room □ *'I don't know what you've pinned on those two boys, but you cane either of them, and I'll drag you down to the Divisional Office myself.' '**How dare you**, Mr Golding! I will not be talked—'* TT □ *At the heart of all her disillusion and anguish there was a nerve that throbbed with hatred.* ***How dare he*** *treat her so,* ***how dare he****?* PW □ also with other pronouns, as shown.

how do you do? form of greeting when being introduced on first meeting □ *'Veronica, this is Mr Lockwood whom you remember my having mentioned so often. This is Miss Roderick.' '**How do you do?**' said Lockwood bemusedly.* HD □ *Run out to the garden, Gillian, and tell your brother I want him to come and say* ***how d'you do*** *to Mrs Smith.* □ more formal and distant than '(I'm) glad to meet you'.

how the hell etc? (informal) how? in what way? **n:** (flaming/merry) hell, ⚠ devil, blazes, heck, dickens □ MYRA (furious): ***How the hell*** *did I come to have such a tenth-rate little snob for a son?* EHOW □ usu indicates the speaker's bad temper, hostility, scorn etc. ⇨ ⚠ what the hell etc? where the hell etc? who the hell etc? why the hell etc?

how many times/how often do I have to do sth? complaint that one's opinions, statements, requests or orders have not been heeded or remembered; complaint that one has heard sth more often that is necessary or desirable **cl:** do I have to say it, must I tell you, do you have to be reminded; must I listen to that story, do we hear the same excuse □ *'But I don't know the man,' he shouted, losing his temper at last. '**How many times do I have to** say it?'* □ *Turn round, Gladys, this minute. Yes, my girl,* ***how many times do you have to*** *be told?* HD □ *I know I was wrong and I've said so.* ***How often do we have to*** *go over it?*

how on earth/in the world? (informal) how? in what way? □ *But* ***how on earth*** *do you propose to equip yourself with this information-carrying capacity?* TBC □ emphasizes questioner's bewilderment, indecision etc.

how right/wrong you are(!) you are absolutely correct/incorrect in an opinion or assessment □ *'No after-dinner speech should last longer than ten minutes.' '**How right you are!**'* □ *I hesitated as to whether to listen to it at all and wondered if radio could really add anything to Olivia Manning's subtle and exciting masterpiece.* ***How wrong I was!*** L □ also with other pronouns as shown. ⇨ ⚠ what on earth/in the world? where on earth/in the world? who on earth/in the world? why on earth/in the world?

how's the world been treating you? (informal) a polite inquiry on meeting a friend or acquaintance after not too short a space of time □ MRS ELLIOTT: *Oh come in, Mr Stuart. You know everyone don't you?* GEOFFREY: *Yes. Good evening everyone. And* ***how's the world treating you****, Mr Elliott?* EGD □ *Hullo, Jane. I wondered if you'd be here.* ***How's the world been treating you*** *since I saw you last?*

a howl/storm of protest etc [O/o (NP)] strong and usu widespread protest against, or objection to, sth ordered or suggested **V:** raise, set off, start up. **o:** protest, ⚠ rage, anguish □ *German officials and newspapers had treated the killings with discretion. Now, however, the lid was off. The Puchert 'execution' set off* ***a howl of protest*** *from Hamburg to Munich.* TO □ *It must be clearly understood that those bland words amount in many cases to a sentence of death. The Labour Movement should raise* ***a storm of protest****.* NS □ *This view will doubtless be greeted with* ***howls of*** *enraged* ***anguish*** *at Essex.* NS

a howling success [Comp (NP)] (informal) a very great success; sth that receives much praise and (loud) acclamation **V:** ⚠ be; turn into, make sth □ *His first lecture was* ***a howling success*** *with the shop stewards and with my dear co-director Simpson.* ASA □ *His second play was not* ***the howling success*** *he was confident of but attracted quite large houses in the provinces.* □ *I've done a bit of amateur operatics myself, though I've always described my singing as* ***a*** *'**howling success**'.* RT □ sometimes with facetious double meaning, as in last example.

a howling wilderness a desolate tract of country without amenities or beauty; a place, period or sphere of life without attraction or interest □ *He found him in a desert land, and in* ***the*** *waste* ***howling wilderness****.* DEUTERONOMY XXXII 10 □ *The hospital was an enormous building,* ***a howling*** *honeycomb* ***wilderness*** *of white tiles and dark green paint.* □ *Culturally Bradford was not* ***the howling wilderness*** *I had been led to expect.*

a hue and cry [n + n non-rev] general outcry and alarm, often with shouting, searching, chasing □ *They couldn't find you. I tell you there's been a big flap on, not to speak of* ***the hue and cry*** *going on in camp.* BM □ *There were no threats, no checks,* ***no hue and cry****. I was a stranger with no passes or credentials, yet no one even noticed my coming or my going.* OBS □ hue (old use) refers to the sound of a horn.

huff and puff [v + v non-rev] speak or act in an important or threatening way but, finally, be indecisive or ineffective (from 'I'll huff and I'll puff and I'll blow your house down' spoken by the big bad wolf in a children's story, THE THREE LITTLE PIGS); puff and blow (qv) □ *In short we badly need the finest élite that we can get to cope with all the changes in the way that we live and work. The masses can* ***huff and puff*** *but they are powerless to alter the way things are.* NS □ *So there's a fair amount of* ***huffing and puffing*** *in Mr Mintoff's attitudes. But his performance is matched in London.* L

hum and ha(w) [v + v non-rev] make inarticulate noises, indicating nervousness, indecision etc, before or while speaking; (fig) take a long time to make a decision or to say what one really means or wants to; waver in one's intentions □ (film review) *John Fraser and James Fox flounder miserably and Derek Nimmo* ***hums and ha's*** *with quiet desperation.* RT □ *When Richard Buckle organised the gala performance for the 'Save the Titian' fund, Richards and Piper were* *quick to act, while others **hummed and hawed**.* ST □ variant um and ah.

the human predicament (cliché) the complexity of man's life in general, esp as a quasi-philosophical study □ *Secondly, if we are to be convinced that the rigid Victorian marriage was a better frame for dealing with **the human predicament** than current licence...* L □ *Christians are those who actually celebrate a death and see it as a fertile extinction, a seed sown, not a lamp quenched. In the next week (*Holy Week of Easter*) Christians are preoccupied with **the human predicament** at its point of high intensity.* G

humanly possible [Comp (AdjP)] at all possible for humans to do; possible according to any natural law **V:** ⚠ be, appear; think, regard sth as □ *Even twenty years ago, many of the sports records recently achieved (and doubtless soon to be broken) would have been thought not **humanly possible**.* □ *'Perhaps they'll make up their quarrel and things will be as they were before.' 'It's **humanly possible** I suppose, but — knowing them both — most unlikely.'* □ (reader's letter) *And it is to be hoped that his programme will stimulate greater interest. Would it be **humanly possible** to obtain a copy of the script?* RT □ often neg or with neg implication.

hunger is the best sauce (saying) nothing stimulates the appetite better than hunger □ *But if we listen to working-class people at work and at home we are likely to be struck first by the degree to which they still draw on oral and local tradition. In three minutes two women used these phrases: 'If it's not there y'can't put it there,' 'Well, **'unger's t'best sauce**.'* UL

the Hungry Forties the period in 19th c Britain (before the repeal of the Corn Laws) when poor people often went hungry owing to the high price of flour and bread □ *I have not forgotten the experiences of **the 'Hungry Forties'** of the last century; but I think also of the Russian serfs and of the Italian attitude towards civil servants even today* (early 1950s). UL □ *Industry is a vital prop to the whole domestic economic structure, says 'The Review', which adds that possibly as a legacy of **the hungry thirties**, there is an extreme element among the precocious intelligensia which almost believes that industry is the enemy of the people.* T □ can be adapted, as in second example.

huntin', shootin', fishin' (facetious) prestigious pastimes of the moneyed, leisured or aristocratic classes □ *Kennedy has been on holiday up in North Scotland. 'We took a fortnight and I've been having a real **huntin', shootin', fishin'** kind of holiday.'* RT □ *'What do they talk about then?' 'Oh, a bit about local affairs, but mostly **huntin', shootin', and fishin'**, as you'd expect.'* □ the omission of 'g' from the participle imitates the clipped enunciation ascribed to these classes.

hurt sb's feelings [V + O pass] injure sb's self-esteem by criticism, neglect, misunderstanding, by insults either intended or taken as such □ *He sometimes writes letters like that when he's working hard to get rid of people without **hurting their feelings**.* ST □ *Mr Blake has always been a good friend to you. It'll **hurt his feelings** very much if you go off to Canada without paying him a farewell visit.* □ JO: *Don't go, Geof! I'm sorry. Please stay.* GEOF: *Don't touch me.* JO: *I didn't mean to **hurt your feelings**.* TOH

hurt/injure sb's pride [V + O pass] lessen or take away sb's estimation of himself, his worth or abilities □ (astrological prediction) *You could easily say the wrong thing or reveal a secret. Your partner will be touchy, and **pride** can be easily **hurt**.* H □ *He gets furious on these occasions, not because he's lost money but because it **injures his pride** that he's been conned.* ST

husband and wife [n + n non-rev] man and wife; a married couple (the implication usu being the stability, closeness etc associated with marriage) □ *We stopped being lovers; we became **husband and wife**.* RATT □ *I'm sure they can settle this difference themselves. It's not for you to come between **husband and wife**.* □ *This is a book of jaunty travellers' tales by a **husband and wife** team who covered 12,000 miles from London to Australia by scooter.* □ *Their cartoons and jokes (which are often very funny, when they forgot the narrow run of **husband and wife** bickerings) are in the new sophisticated style.* UL □ attrib use *a **husband and wife** team.*

hustle and bustle [n + n non-rev] (situation when one has to) do a number of things in a hurry, with some fuss □ *'And he's never on time. God, the times I've waited for him.' 'Well,' said Clyde, smiling. 'It's all this **hustle and bustle**. I don't like that.'* ST □ *'You can easily finish your report while I pack, and we can post it when we go.' 'I can't work with people **hustling and bustling** round me.'* □ also functions as [v + v], as shown.

I

I ask you (informal) have you ever heard anything so ridiculous? □ *The most ridiculous looking women go up to her and tell her their old men* (=husbands) *think they look just like her. They're covered with paint, they have navy blue hair roots. **I ask you**.* TVT □ *Throwing money about, that's all she's doing. Twelve pounds eighteen on flowers! **I ask you**!* TCB □ addition to statement or question, inviting the listener to recognize how difficult, surprising or ridiculous it is, rather than expecting an answer; front, middle or end position; stress pattern ˌI ˈask you.

I beg to differ (formal) I am afraid I must disagree □ *Sir Julius has characterized the events which we have recently witnessed as un-English. Respectfully, **I beg to differ**. This could only have happened in England. It is, indeed, an essentially English crime.* EM □ *'England has one of the worst climates in the world!' '**I beg to differ**!'*

□ polite but firm expression of disagreement; first person, unless in reported speech.

I beg your pardon I must object, disagree; I must have misheard, misunderstood, you (because if I did hear you properly, then I am offended) □ *'Of course, I've always thought that Mahler's best work was his Fifth Symphony.'* '***I beg your pardon****, most people would hold that the Ninth was incomparably greater.'* □ *'How that dangerous idiot ever got on the committee, I shall never know.'* '***I beg your pardon****, he happens to be a friend of mine.'* □ in this meaning of the expression there is a fall-rise tone on pardon; I beg your pardon? (formal) with a high rising tone on beg, or Pardon? (informal) with a high rising tone, is used in conversation to mean 'Please repeat what you have just said'; I beg your pardon! (formal) with a low falling tone on pardon or Pardon! (informal) with a low falling tone is used in conversation as an equivalent to *Excuse me!* or *Sorry!* to mean 'I apologize for what I have just done/said'. ⇨ ⚠ beg sb's pardon.

I('ll) bet (informal) I don't believe you, what you say; I very much doubt it (esp in commenting on what sb says he will do or has done) □ *'I'll be home early tonight, darling.' 'That'll be nice,' she answered mechanically, and, as the door closed, added,* '***I'll bet****!'* □ *'He says Chelsea will win the Cup next year with their new team.'* '***I bet****! They'll be lucky to stay in the First Division!'* □ stress pattern 'I'll bet. ⇨ next entry; ⚠ bet sb anything/what he likes (that); you (can) bet your (sweet) life (that).

I('ll)/you bet (that) (informal) I am convinced, certain (of sth); I emphatically agree (that sth is the case); bet sb anything/what he likes (that) (qv); you (can) bet your (sweet) life (that) (qv) **cl:** (that) not many people earn £50,000 a year; (that) you didn't know that □ *When manufacturers make up mothproof material into suits and coats, why don't they add mothproof lining?* ***I bet*** *there are many others, like myself, who have perfectly good tweed suits with motheaten interiors.* TO □ *You ask anyone in this house what their secret is.* ***I'll bet*** *you find they've all got one.* DC □ ALISON: *I'm sorry. I wasn't listening properly.* JIMMY: ***You bet*** *you weren't listening.* LBA □ *'Veronica,' he said aloud. 'You didn't know, you didn't know.'* '***You*** *bloody well* ***bet*** *I didn't know,' replied Bunder, who had not caught the first word.* HD □ stress pattern I('ll)/you 'bet; when present, O clause usu without that. ⇨ previous entry.

I can tell etc you an addition to a statement, expression of opinion, etc which underlines or reinforces it **V:** can tell, ⚠ (can) assure, (can) promise □ *'Are you sure you want to stay here? It's very quiet. After your interesting life—' 'Interesting!' 'When I could never get over being scared.* ***I can tell you****, this will be heaven.'* DC □ *It'll be a damned long time,* ***I assure you****, before he gets another offer of help from me.* □ front, middle or end position.

I can't/couldn't say (that) a more polite, less blunt, way of making a statement neg, eg 'I can't say I agree' = 'I don't agree' **S:** I, you, one □ *Well, you are entitled to your opinion but* ***I can't say*** *I agree with you.* □ ***I can't say that*** *I liked the new machine with its thick wings and its enormous Sabre engine.* RFW □ *He had plenty of faults but* ***you couldn't say*** *he was mean.*

I can't tell you I cannot adequately say, indicate, express **O:** how glad I am, how upset I was; what pleasure it gives me □ *I just* ***can't tell you*** *how glad I am to see you. I just* ***can't tell you****. You're the first human face I've seen for ages.* UTN □ *Dear James, she wrote, I have just heard of your wife's death.* ***I can't tell you*** *how sorry I am.*

I dare say [Conj] I suppose; it seems to me safe to say; I think it likely, probable etc □ *He doesn't like me—* ***I dare say*** *he suspects me because I refuse to treat him either as a clown or as a tragic hero.* LBA□ *'I hope it hasn't put your housekeeper out, Mr Alexander, having three extra suddenly thrust upon her.' 'Oh,* ***I dare say*** *I shan't lose her because of you, Miss Isbister. She is devoted to me.'* WI □ *I can be with him in thought, of course, prompting him, encouraging him.* ***I daresay*** *your wife's thoughts are with you now.* PW □ front, middle or end position; dare say usu two words.

(well) I (do) declare(!) (dated informal) an exclamation of surprise, dismay, or disbelief □ *'****Well, I declare****,' said Mrs Hatchett. 'You should have had your tea long ago. I thought the nurse was looking after you.'* DC □ *And this young lady is Brenda?* ***Well I declare!*** *How time passes, to be sure.* □ *Ooh, now* ***I do declare****, we've got him rattled.* TGLY □ usu with either well or do.

I don't know (that) I am not sure, am doubtful, would be inclined to disagree (that sth is the case, would be correct, suitable or possible etc); not know about (Vol 1) (qv) **O:** that I agree, that he's right □ ***I don't know that*** *being called to the Bar is going to help me much.* RFW □ *'I had not thought you cared.' 'I didn't,' said Ella.* '***I don't know that*** *I do even now, for James.'* HAA □ *'He's ruined his chances of promotion.' 'Oh,* ***I don't know****,' said Miss Ferguson.*

I don't know what the world's coming to a complaint, serious or humorous, about (changes in) present-day conditions, morals etc □ *What with strikes and rising prices everywhere* ***I don't know what the world is coming to****.* □ MR GREEN: (after a customer tries to get goods without paying for them) *Clever bloke—aren't you—get away from my stall.* MRS GREEN: ***What's the world coming to****—it's full of lousy good-for-nothings.* DPM □ variant what's the world coming to?

I don't mind if I do (catchphrase) used when accepting sth, esp an alcoholic drink (popularized by 'ITMA', a radio programme of the early 1940s which featured a Colonel Chinstrap who was very fond of a drink and used this phrase) □ *'This is the best Highland malt* (ie malt whisky)*.' Carter said across the table,* '***I don't mind if I do****.'* OMIH □ *And he took out his case and offered them* (ie cigarettes) *round. 'Senior Service?' Chadwick said,* '***I don't mind if I do****.'* TT □ *Jury foremen were usually chosen by someone saying: 'Here Bill, you have a go,' and Bill saying* ***he didn't mind if he did****.* NS □ usu first person, but occas used in second and third, as shown.

I don't think (informal) contradicts an immediately preceding statement by oneself or sb else, in order to emphasize either that it was ironically intended or that one does not really believe it □ *'I believe our hostess has planned guessing games for after supper.' 'That'll be great fun,* ***I don't think****.'* □ *Of course, I'll have made my fortune by then,* ***I don't think****.* □ (of geriatric day care) *They must like my pretty face,* ***I don't think****, to bring me so often.* G

I, for one I definitely, certainly **pron/n:** I, you, he, she; Mrs Jones; my uncle □ *Being a naturalist and ornithologist I am always hooked by 'The Living World' (Wednesday, Radio 4). This time the listeners have their go in 'Talking Point', and* ***I, for one****, won't miss that!* RT □ *When Bill got killed it was the end of everything for me. I never thought about it being the end of everything for other people—for* ***his mother, for one****.* RFW □ *Patrick made up his mind to be as nice as possible to Lord Edgerstoune. It was up to him to show the old boy that* ***he for one*** *was not given over to any unworthy prejudice.* TGLY □ stress pattern ˌI for 'one.

I like that! an exclamation of astonished protest, esp about sth said or done which is felt to be untrue or unfair □ *'I mean we're quite all right in our way, but nobody's going to mind what happens to us.'* ***'I like that!'*** *Harold exclaimed. 'Jeremy and Janice* (the children of the two speakers) *would mind, I hope, if anything happens to us.'* PW □ BOY: *I'm trapped in a barbaric cult—matrimony.* JO: *Trapped!* ***I like that!*** *You almost begged me to marry you.* TOH □ stress pattern I like 'that!

I may/might say/add it is perhaps appropriate, helpful, informative etc that I should tell you this (ie what is said in a preceding, or following, statement) □ *'Veronica will never communicate with you any more.* ***I may say****, in case you're puzzled, that this little gift of mine,' he waved his hand to indicate the room and its furnishings, 'was made at her request.'* HD □ *Come, children, show your mother your new things. Sarah,* ***I might say****, would have given her eyes for a ballet dress.* DC □ *Fireworks, for example, were once no more than bonfires (and to this day,* ***I may add****, a good bonfire on a dark night remains one of the most magical of spectacles).* HAH □ may/might interchangeable.

I mean (to say)(!) (informal) accompanies (and usu precedes) an explanation, or justification, of sth one has said or done □ *Of course you should type it out again!* ***I mean to say****, just look at it!* □ □ *We walked straight out again and found another hotel.* ***I mean to say****, if you're going to pay £30 for bed and breakfast you expect the place to be at least clean, don't you?* □ *It's a hell of a tough game,* (rugby) *League.* ***I mean*** *they don't care, you know?* OBS □ first person only.

I must/have to fly (informal) I must leave immediately and hurry off to where I ought to be, am expected, etc □ *'And by the way, I must be off.' He glanced at his watch, 'Yes* ***I must fly****.'* PW □ *I wish we could have finished this discussion, but* ***I must fly****.* □ have had to always substituted in future and past time constructions; usu first person subject.

I must say it is appropriate, or sensible, for me to agree with sth, comment on sth, or point sth out; the preceding, or following, statement is forced from me by surprise, anger, sudden pleasure, etc □ *'That depends on how much energy is required to heat the Cloud,' remarked Weichart. 'And on its opacity and a hundred and one other factors,' added Kingsley. '****I must say*** *it seems very unlikely to me that much heat will get through the gas.'* TBC □ *They can't eat their words fast enough about Donald.* ***I must say*** *he seems to have been very tactful all round.* ASA □ *'I just thought Mr Templar might have cheated.' 'Well, that's a nerve,* ***I must say****,' Uncle Saunders declared.* DC □ *'****I must say*** *I'm surprised at you, Michael—isn't your mother one of the school cleaners?' 'Yes, Miss,' he said. 'And what do you think she and your father would say if they knew they had a liar for a son?'* TT □ first meaning of expression (first and second examples) stress pattern I must 'say; second meaning of expression (third and fourth examples) stress pattern I 'must say.

I say(!) mild exclamation; or as an introduction to a question, suggestion, reproach etc (associated with upper-middle class speech habits, and often used by writers as a caricature of them) □ *'****I say****, Jane,' she said, crossing to the window. 'What a wonderful outlook you have here.'* □ *'****I say****, mother,' said Lavinia. 'Well, darling?' said Lydia. 'I really can't help not liking arithmetic, mother. Do you and father mind?'* WDM □ *Simon Stern, a freelance illustrator of children's books, does admit to once turning down a book about a horrible dog. 'It was full of things like "Jolly good show" and "****I say****, chaps".'* OBS

I should say/think so etc(!) I absolutely agree/approve; I think that the situation, or action, described is appropriate or desirable **A:** jolly well, certainly. **O:** so, not; it is, they can't, I won't, you ought to □ *'I'm sorry I was so rude to your friend.' '****I should think so!*** *What a way to behave!'* □ *'You're not going to accept this offer, are you?' '****I should say not!*** *The farm buildings alone are worth £50,000.'* □ *Might have helped?* ***I should*** *jolly well* ***think so*** *but he wasn't there to ask.* □ stress pattern I should 'think so; not, I won't etc echo a neg statement or question expecting answer 'No'.

I should worry! (ironic) why should I worry? I won't worry □ SAM: *All my life I worked in the open air and you bet your life, I'm going to die there.* BESSIE (off): *All right,* ***I should worry!*** *It's your funeral!* HSG □ *One or two of the sheets were rather greasy.* ***He should worry****. The cold had affected the membranes of his nostrils so that he couldn't smell anything.* HD.

I shouldn't wonder (informal) I would not be surprised; I think it possible or likely □ *How you come out with all this, a detective, a man that has to mix with criminals—and bringing them to my house before long,* ***I shouldn't wonder****.* HD □ ***I shouldn't wonder*** *if Alan was over at your father's house now, getting in his own version of the story.* □ used in end position as a comment on sth one has supposed or predicted might happen, or in front position to introduce *if*-cl.

I('ll) tell you what (informal) introduces a proposal, suggestion or piece of advice □ DAVIES: *No, no, I never smoke a cigarette.* ***I'll tell you what****, though, I'll have a bit of that tobacco for my pipe, if you like.* TC □ ***Tell you what!****' he cried excitedly, 'Come to my place in *town next Sunday night.'* HD □ ***I tell you what****, my darling girl. If you nag at him this time when he does come back, next time he may not come back at all.* AITC

I won't say no (to sth) (informal) a formula for accepting sth offered **o:** that; a drink, a lift □ *I don't mind walking home, as a rule, but if anybody offers me a lift tonight* ***I won't say no****.* □ DAVIES: *Well, it don't fit too bad. How do you think it looks?* ASTON: *Looks all right.* DAVIES: *Well,* ***I won't say no to*** *this then.* TC □ *I daresay he* ***wouldn't say no to*** *a brandy. I want one too.* BFA □ *He's never* ***said no to*** *cake yet, and I don't suppose he'll start tonight.* AITC □ usu first person, but also in reported statements as shown.

I would if I could but I can't (catchphrase) I would like to do sth worthwhile, but I am unable to □ JASON: *Sonia, marry me while there's still time.* SONIA: ***I would if I could but I can't****, because you'll be burying me tomorrow.* DPM □ *'Have some sense, and stop scoffing. The cakes'll still be there tomorrow.' 'I know.* ***I would if I could but I can't****.'* □ used as a confession.

I'll be bound I am perfectly sure that sth mentioned is the case, will happen, etc □ *'He's got some other reason,* ***I'll be bound****.' 'You mean it's part of his plan for marrying Myrtle?'* SPL □ *Bob won't spend the whole evening collecting subscriptions. He'll be in the pub by now,* ***I'll be bound****.* □ usu end position.

(well,) I'll be/I'm damned etc! (informal) exclamation of pleased, or displeased, astonishment **Comp:** damned, ⚠ darned, hanged, blowed □ *'****Well, I'll be damned!****' he exclaimed when he had unwrapped Susan's gift. 'I've been trying to get a copy of this book for years.'* □ *'****I'll be blowed****,' said Jill. 'That's the Browns' car now and I distinctly told them not to come before 6 o'clock.'* ⇨ ⚠ next entry; be damned etc.

I'll be/I'm damned etc if (informal) I'm unable, or determined not, to do sth; it certainly is not the case that **Comp:** damned, ⚠ darned, hanged, blowed. **cl:** if I do, if I understand you, if it is, if they will □ *'You must agree that their terms are very reasonable.' '****I'm damned if*** *I do.'* □ *I know I have that receipt somewhere but* ***I'll be blowed if*** *I can find it.* □ *They wanted to leave their caravan sitting in her garden all winter and* ***she was hanged if*** *she was going to let them.* □ usu first person. ⇨ ⚠ previous entry; be damned etc.

I'll be seeing you (informal) a form of leave-taking or of signing off a letter to sb one meets fairly frequently or is likely to meet again soon □ *'Don't you need your key?' 'Got a pass key.* ***I'll be seeing you****.'* OMIH □ *I've got to ring off now, Betty. The baby's woken up.* ***Be seeing you****.* □ often with I'll omitted.

I'll believe it/that when I see it (saying) until I have proper evidence (eg by actually seeing it), I remain very sceptical □ *If there is any temptation to make a practical demonstration of this weapon — on the whole* ***I shall believe that when I see it****—then the scientists are likely to have their own views.* NM □ *In the meantime they transferred Sister Burstead, on the first of January, to another ward. '****I'll believe it when I see it****,' said Granny Barnacle. She saw it before that weekend.* MM □ *'Did you tell your mother I'd be around with the car to pick her up at seven sharp?' 'Yes, she said* ***she'd believe it when she saw it****, but would be ready just in case.'* □ usu first person and sing but third person in reported speech as in last example.

I'll eat my hat (informal) (the situation is so ridiculous, sth is so unlikely to happen etc that) I can promise to do something equally ridiculous such as eating my hat without really expecting that I will have to do so □ *They're always late—if they get here a minute before eight o'clock,* ***I'll eat my hat****.* □ (critic's comment after quoting an excerpt from a book) *If that isn't long-winded bosh,* ***I'll*** *go* ***eat my hat****.* NS □ *Jenny keep a secret! She'll have told a dozen people by now, or* ***I'll eat my hat****.*

I'll live/survive (informal) sth which has happened isn't going to bother or affect, me much □ *'And you thought John was your friend! He doesn't behave much like one.' 'Oh, don't go on about it.* ***I'll live****.'* □ *'We're so late this morning that you'll have to go off without your sandwiches now. I'm terribly sorry.' '****I'll survive****,' he answered drily.* □ also he'll, you'll etc, where effect is more dismissive of sb's interests, and sometimes callous.

I'll say it is an emphatic form of agreement with an immediately preceding statement **O:** it is, I am, you are; she does; they won't □ *'It's a pretty dull programme, don't you think?' '****I'll say it is****. Shall I switch off or try another channel?'* SML □ *'Estelle isn't going to the disco unless she gets a proper lift home.' '****I'll say she isn't****,' her father agreed.*

I'll see you in hell first (informal) I defy you; I will never agree to what you are ordering or proposing I should do **O:** you, him, them; the lot of them, you bastards □ *I won't keep my mouth shut, and you won't buy me off.* ***I'll see you in hell first****.* □ *'Perhaps, for the sake of peace, you should go and apologise.' '****I'll see her in hell first****.'* □ always first person, or third in reported speech.

I'm afraid a tag expressing regret, or apology, and added to a piece of news or information which is expected to be unwelcome or unpleasant □ *I can put you up for the night but you'll have to sleep on the sofa,* ***I'm afraid****.* □ *I'm sorry, Mrs Gaye—* ***I'm afraid*** *Nicky is being difficult this morning.* DC □ *'She hasn't broken her leg, has she?' '****I'm afraid*** *so.'* □ *'Have you got two tickets for tomorrow night's performance?' '****I'm afraid*** *not, madam.'* □ *so* and *not*, in last two examples, refer to a preceding clause.

I'm all right, Jack (catchphrase) I have been lucky, clever, or careful enough to make sure that I am safe, comfortable etc, and I don't care what happens to you or anyone else (orig *Fuck you* ***Jack, I'm all right*** but usu as shown below) □ (reader's letter) *If the '****I'm all right, Jack****' philosophy is to disappear then those who propose the remedies will have to show how they would be called upon to endure the same hardships that they prescribe for others.* T □ *'He's no need to worry about redundancies. Most weekends he gives the boss a hand in the garden.' 'Looks like a case of* ***I'm all right Jack****.'* □ not usu used by person who has this attitude but by sb else who assumes it in him.

I'm sorry (but) usu expresses no real apology or regret but emphasizes that one will stick to an opinion, policy etc whether others can accept it or not □ *'Only a fool could think there was any advantage for Scotland in devolution.'* ***'I'm sorry but*** *I don't agree.'* □ *Humphrey Burton replies* (to a reader's letter)*:* ***I am sorry but*** *I am absolutely unrepentant about the way I introduced the Leeds Piano Competition.* RT

the (very) idea! what a preposterous, insulting, unsuitable, ridiculous etc idea, way of behaving, etc □ *He might find himself in the same* (regiment) *as Ned; and this might mean having to obey him as an officer.* ***The idea!*** CON □ *What! Me go off to a party and leave you here on your own?* ***The very idea!*** □ *She'd been furious. All day she kept exclaiming, '****The very idea****,* ***the very idea****,' over and over.* TSMP

if any if, indeed, there is any/you have any □ *What happens to the surplus,* ***if any****? It belongs to the local committee who can dispose of it as it sees fit.* TO □ *In many small private schools teachers were recruited from the genteel poor and their qualifications,* ***if any****, were of the lowest.* □ *I'm afraid you'll just have to appeal to his generosity,* ***if any****.* □ follows n to which it refers.

if anything if anything, or something, definite can be said, this is it □ *The painting she was working on was a good, vigorous action picture;* ***if anything*** *I think she was a better draughtsman than a painter.* RFW □ *'We used to look very nice then, didn't we, Charles?' said Evelyn Ramage, as she showed the old snapshots. 'My dear Evelyn, you look* ***if anything*** *more beautiful now,' answered Charles Murley.* HAA □ *He had not, it is true, displayed any overt hostility. His behaviour had been,* ***if anything****, rather casual.* UTN □ front, middle or end position; accompanies description or assessment of sb/sth, often contradicting or correcting a previous suggestion or assumption.

if anything happens to sb if sb should die, be killed, suffer a (fatal) accident □ *Always at the back of the wife's mind, though probably not consciously, is the knowledge that* ***if 'anything happens' to*** *the husband she will have to manage on her own.* UL □ *I ought to tell you, Mr Wormold, that I have saved enough money to leave Milly in comfort* ***if anything*** *were ever to* ***happen to*** *me.* OMIH □ *I felt it in my bones that* ***something*** *had* ***happened to*** *him.* □ *He should have been here hours ago; I hope* ***nothing****'s* ***happened to*** *him.* □ variants something happens to sb, nothing happens to sb used similarly but without *if*-cl.

if at all if, indeed, sth is to happen, or sb can do sth, at all □ *In Harold's plans for the evening, this stage was to have come later in the conversation* ***if at all****.* PW □ *As soon as he* (the witness) *is interrogated, he may have to deal with features of the original* (story) *which he can recall but vaguely* ***if at all****.* MFF

if at first you don't succeed, (try, try again) a moral maxim, of the kind that used to appear in old-fashioned copy-books for schoolchildren □ (source) 'Tis a lesson you should heed,/Try, try again. ***If at first you don't succeed,/Try, try again****.* TRY AND TRY AGAIN (W E HICKSON 1803-70) □ (reader's letter) *About seven years ago he applied to become Labour candidate, got an interview but was turned down. His aim has always been to become an MP.* ***If at first you don't succeed****—but spare us the forced grin.* NS □ *Armed with the maxim he had once sung everyday for his schoolteacher mother—'****If at first you don't succeed, try, try, try, again****'—he achieved his three goals one by one.* RT

if one believes that, one will believe anything (catchphrase) if one accepts the truth of sth extremely unlikely (that has been referred to), one is easily deceived, has no critical judgement □ *There is a story about the Duke of Wellington, who having been approached by a stranger with the words 'Mr Jones, I believe?' replied, '****If you believe that, you will believe anything****.'* □ *It was put out that the first statement was entirely true because at that time there hadn't been anything going on and I say,* ***if you believe that, you'll believe anything****.* ST

if the cap fits, (wear it) (saying) if anyone thinks a description, or piece of advice or criticism, applies to himself, he should accept it, and be warned by it □ *I have noticed that there are some classrooms where the pupils have been in at least five minutes before their teacher appears. I will name no names but,* ***if the cap fits, wear it****.* □ *'You shouldn't have ranted on so much. Jenkins might have thought you were getting at him.' 'Well* ***if the cap fits,*** *let him* ***wear it****; if not, he doesn't need to bother, does he?'*

if one dies in the attempt (do sth) however much trouble, pain, danger etc is involved □ *She could still look attractive in the right clothes, and she made up her mind that one day,* ***if she died in the attempt****, she would have them again.* AITC □ *He could have followed at his own pace but he was determined to keep up with the rest* ***if it killed him****.* □ TONY: *What's wrong with mother?* MILLY: *She's tired. Come on, we've got to be gay* ***if it kills us****.* EHOW □ *That settles it. I'll get you sacked* ***if it's the last thing I do****.* HD □ sometimes implies the risk of one's life but usu just an expression of determined intention; variants if it kills one, if it's the last thing one does; usu first person or reported speech in second variant.

if ever[1] if at any (other) time; if on any (other) occasion □ ***If ever*** *I offended you, it was entirely unintentional.* □ *'I won't be using the oil stove.' 'Well,* ***if ever*** *you do, be sure to keep the children well away from it.'* □ order of S and ever may be reversed eg ***If ever*** *I offended you...*/***If I ever*** *offended you....*

if ever[2] if anything ever happened, was ever seen (etc) at all, then it/he is a prime example □ *'Then he's ill.' 'Ill? Ha!* ***If ever*** *I saw a gentleman in the pink—* (= excellent health)*.'* US □ *The effort to prove that the deceased was a superman often took the form of saying that '****if ever*** *there was a born soldier'—or 'saint on earth', or 'leader of men'—it was he.* AH □ *Really, Nick!* ***If ever*** *there was a stubborn idiot, you're a prime example.* □ *They seemed destined to follow utterly different paths* ***if ever*** *two youths did.* CON □ usu front position. ⇨ ⚠ next entry.

if ever there was one of that there is no doubt; that is certainly true □ JO: *And then he ran off with that landlady's daughter.* HELEN: *She was a silly cat* ***if ever there was one****.* TOH □ *Then I had a meeting with the miners' agent, Mr Trevor James—there's a good man* ***if there***

ever was one. ST ▫ *Dunkirk, a complete military defeat* ***if ever there was one****, became — in Priestley's terms—the saga of the little ships.* L ▫ *She hadn't spent hours slaving over a hot stove! That was a shop-bought cake* ***if ever I saw one***. ▫ order of ever and there may be reversed; usu end position; variant if ever I/I ever saw one. ⇨ ⚠ previous entry.

if God did not exist, it would be necessary to invent him from the French EPITRES (VOLTAIRE 1694-1778) ▫ (reader's letter) *Don't let the 'NS'* (= New Statesman) *become a destructive killjoy.* ***If the Jubilee had not existed we should have had to invent something*** *to celebrate.* NS ▫ ***If colour film had not existed*** *when Paul Newman hit the screen* ***it would have been necessary to invent it****. The blaze of those blue eyes made him an overnight heart-throb.* TVT ▫ often adapted or parodied, as shown.

if one has done sth once one has done it a hundred etc times one has warned people, given advice, etc very many times **cl:** (if) I've said it, I've told you, he's warned them; (if) it's happened, I've had it explained to me. **det:** a hundred, ⚠ fifty, a thousand, a dozen ▫ *I knew we'd have an epidemic sooner or later.* ***If I've said it once I've said it a hundred times***. ▫ *Give him a warning, did you say?* ***If he's been warned once he's been warned twenty times***. *Tomorrow morning he gets the sack.* ▫ (reader's letter) *Why do we have so many previews?* ***If they are shown once they are shown a dozen times***. TVT ▫ often serves as reproach to, or complaint about, sb who repeatedly forgets or ignores such warning of advice; occas complaint about having heard something more often than is necessary or desirable.

if he/it is a day used to make confident claims about sb's age, or about time that has elapsed ▫ *Why do you keep referring to him as 'young Dr Morton', mother? He's forty* ***if he's a day***. ▫ *'I can't remember when I last played a game of golf. It's a long time anyway.' 'Fifteen years* ***if it's a day****,' his wife said.* ▫ immediately follows n denoting age, time etc.

if I'm any judge (of sb/sth) if I am competent, or qualifed, to know about, or give an opinion, on such matters ▫ *Why do you feel this personal interest in me?* ***If I'm any judge*** *at all, you're not a man with a big streak of inquisitiveness.* HD ▫ ***If I'm any judge of*** *children, that boy is going to grow up to be a real headache to his parents. I thought the violinist was the best of the lot—* ***not that I'm any judge***. ▫ accompanies assessment of sb's/sth's nature, worth etc and usu implies speaker's confidence in his own judgement; front, middle or end position; variant, indicating greater uncertainty, not that I'm any judge.

if/when in doubt, do sth if you are in doubt (ie not sure what to do in circumstances), then do as indicated ▫ *Don't ask others whether they think you are fit to drive.* ***When in doubt, don't***. ▫ (espionage) *You will find us in different makes and colours of car.* ***If in doubt,*** *look at the number. It will add up to twenty-three.* ARG ▫ *According to Paul Gallico, the two main maxims a cat gives to her kittens are 'never stay where you are put', and '****when in doubt,*** *wash'.* ▫ brief, pithy way of giving general or personal advice; main cl usu short imper construction.

if it wasn't for sb/sth (doing sth) if sb/sth did not exist, had not stepped in to help or hinder **V:** wasn't, were not, had not been ▫ ***If it wasn't for*** *her, you wouldn't be alive today.* ▫ ***If it hadn't been for*** *the storm, they could have rowed over to the mainland to collect their mail.* ▫ *They said he would never have done it* ***if it hadn't been for me*** *talking him into it.* LLDR ▫ *My two youngest aren't on their own feet yet.* ***Were it not for them****, I'd retire tomorrow and make do on my pension.* ▫ variants were it not for sb/sth, had it not been for sb/sth; main clause states what might have happened.

if one knows what is good for one a threat accompanying advice, or an order, to do or not to do sth ▫ *'I'm going up to see her,' she said. 'Stay away,* ***if you know what's good for you****.'* AITC ▫ *Nah* (= now)*, listen. You better,* ***if you know what's good for you***. PE

if (my) memory serves me right if I remember correctly ▫ *I think he had been married before—a short and unhappy affair in his early twenties,* ***if my memory serves me right***. RT ▫ *I was paid,* ***if my memory serves me right****, six shillings for the mid-week meeting and seven shillings for Saturday nights.* RT ▫ front, middle or end position.

if need be if it was/were to be necessary or advisable ▫ *'How many men were employed to erect it?' 'We would use a thousand, ten thousand* ***if need be****.'* TBC ▫ *She wanted someone to look up to, he wanted someone to look down on, protectively and* ***if need be*** *patronizingly.* PW ▫ *Commerce is another field of critically important activity which has always shown an ability to develop outside the law,* ***if need be***. L ▫ front, middle or end position.

if only[1] if for no other reason or purpose, or in no other respect or manner, than the one specified **A:** because I prefer peace to getting my own way; to please my wife; for its sentimental value, for a change; temporarily ▫ *'Do you think he is telling the truth?' 'Yes, I do;* ***if only*** *because it's too strange a story for a simple fellow like him to invent.'* ▫ CONNIE: *They expected Russia to attack the United Nations plan* ***if only*** *to upset the West. Power politics!* CSWB ▫ *It was months since he had burst out of the strait-jacket of his upbringing — here was a chance to benefit by that escape* ***if only*** *in a small matter.* HD ▫ reason, manner etc indicated by following A.

if only[2] if it were possible that; provided that **cl:** he would help; they hadn't left; we'd answered in time ▫ ***If only*** *I could get away for a bit from all this work and muddle!* ▫ ***If only*** *he suffered them* (illnesses) *in her care, then she was spared the intolerable deprivation of losing him.* NM ▫ ***If*** *he had* ***only*** (or: ***If only*** *he had*) *taken my advice, he might have been a rich man today.* ▫ expresses desire for particular event which is unlikely to happen, or which has not happened yet; expresses vain regret about sth in the past which one wishes one had, or had not, done.

if there is one thing sb hates etc, it is there is one thing sb dislikes very much, or finds distasteful, offensive, intolerable etc **V:** hate, ⚠ detest; can't bear, can't stand; won't allow; like, enjoy ▫ ***If there was one thing*** *Myrtle* ***hated it was*** *to be told she ought to go to bed earlier.* SPL

□ ***If there's one thing I can't stand, it's*** *kids jumping down from their chairs when they're supposed to be having a meal.* □ ***If there's one thing I enjoy it's*** *a cup of tea in bed before I get up.* □ usu derogatory and often expression of temporary annoyance.

if one values one's life if one wishes to remain alive; (fig) if one wishes to avoid serious unpleasantness, a quarrel, etc □ *Never speak a word of this to a living soul.* ***If you value your life****, never say one word.* WI □ *'I don't know that I've anything smart enough to wear,' she said pursing her lips; this was to make me contradict her, which* ***if I valued my life*** *I had to do, but fast.* CON □ may be said seriously, but often (esp in second person) merely exaggerated threat accompanying order, or advice, to do sth.

if and/or when at such time as sth may happen, esp sth which is expected to take place but which one does not wish to be too definite about □ *And* ***if and when*** *you and I do get married, we've somehow to keep old Waggett safely parked in the Outer Hebrides.* RM □ *'Of course he'll get a higher salary eventually.' '****If or when*** *he qualifies.'* □ if and when non-rev.

if wishes were horses, (then) beggars would ride (saying) everybody would be rich, talented, successful, popular etc if wishing was all that was required □ *'His parents think he should go to university and do computer science.' '****If wishes were horses, beggars would ride****. That boy had the greatest difficulty in passing O level Maths.'* □ *'Some unknown relative might die and leave us a lot of money.' 'And* ***if wishes were horses, then beggars would ride****. Now think of something practical.'*

if the worst/it comes to the worst if circumstances become too difficult, troublesome or dangerous; if a project, plan etc fails □ *Surely it's more important for Tony to be free than to fuss about some bricks and a roof —* ***if it comes to the worst*** *you'll always take me in.* EHOW □ *I adopted Paula's attitude, saying that* ***if the worst came to the worst*** *we could make our way across the river into Brazil.* DF □ *Things look very black.* ***Should the worst come to the worst*** *there will be civil war within a month or two.* □ main clause states what could, or should, happen; variant should the worst come to the worst.

if you ask me (informal) as I understand it; if you care to know what I think □ *And what would they want all those towers and wires for?* ***If you ask me****, it's a death-ray that they're building.* TBC □ *'****If you ask me****, I think he's an escaped loonie* (= lunatic)*,' said the second woman.* UTN □ *'My dad used to say that only fools read books.' 'He only said that because he didn't know how to read. He was jealous,* ***if you ask me****.'* LLDR □ front, middle or end position.

if you can't beat them, join them (catchphrase) if a rival faction, political party, business firm, foreign power, etc continues to be more successful than one's own, it is better to go over to their side and get what advantages one can from the alliance □ *All too often, the attitude of the workers' representatives, heavily outnumbered, has been '****if you can't beat them, join them****.' They've had to dance to the bosses' tune.* L □ *The Celts were early exponents of the principle, '****If you can't beat 'em*** (= them)***, join 'em****.' By the second century AD, nearly three-quarters of the Roman army of occupation of Britain consisted of Celts.* RT

if you can't stand the heat, get out of the kitchen (catchphrase) if the pace of life, difficulties or tensions produced by important work etc, prove too much for you, don't complain but get out and leave it to others (orig said by President Truman c1950) □ *The idea seems to have gone around that he is responding to Harry Truman's famous dictum: '****If you can't stand the heat, get out of the kitchen****.' Since he is not winning, he is returning to the easier pickings of British golf.* OBS □ *A cool and rational approach was essential, but an academic with no experience of '****the heat of the kitchen****' would be written off as a mere word-spinner.* RT □ often used allusively, as in second example.

if you don't mind[1] (informal) if sth doesn't inconvenience, or displease, you; do you mind[1] (qv) **S:** you, he, they; your father, the neighbours □ *Oh—that's something Prissie is going to post for me. Prissie,* ***if you don't mind****.* DC □ *I'll have to leave a little of this,* ***if you don't mind****. You gave me an enormous helping.* □ polite addition to request or proposal, often when objection not really expected. □ stress pattern if you don't 'mind.

if you don't mind[2] (informal) an angry, or sarcastic, request or rebuke; do you mind[2] (qv) □ *'****If you don't mind****!' said Jack, swiftly retrieving his glass before it reached Patrick's lips.* □ *'You're making an awful fuss about a few pence.' '£3.75* ***if you don't mind****, and I want it now.'* □ stress pattern if you 'don't mind.

if you know etc what I mean (informal) added to a statement, sometimes when the speaker feels he has been rather obscure or imprecise, but often as a verbal habit **V:** know, ⚠ see, get □ *Over there I've been offered a television chat show, which could be very interesting and a lot of fun. But I'm sorry it had to be American,* ***if you know what I mean****!* RT □ *He's emotional, and it doesn't do to be emotional if you're not married,* ***if you see what I mean****.* PW □ *And when George Devine was around he would always at least find out if one was still alive,* ***if you know what I mean****.* ST □ *Oh no, I wouldn't say Jack's attractive. He's handsome, but he knows it,* ***if you get my meaning****.* □ *I won't say my last secretary wasn't good at her job, but with the new girl all the work's done faster and everything seems more under control.* ***You know what I mean?*** □ middle or end position; person who uses expression probably does so frequently; variants if you get my meaning, you know what I mean? (latter as separate sentence).

if you like (informal) if you want an example; you must agree; that's certain etc □ JIMMY: *And there's Hugh's mum, of course. I'd almost forgotten her. She's been a good friend to us,* ***if you like****.* LBA □ *Eighteen years faithful to an unfaithful man; there was a proof of staunchness,* ***if you like****!* PW □ *I was a Red myself once. I even sat at the feet of Waterman and he was a phoney old prophet* ***if you like****.* PP □ stress patterns ˌthere was proof of staunchness, if you 'like, ˌhe was a phoney old prophet if you 'like.

if one likes that kind/sort of thing (usu

derogatory) implying the speaker's indifference to, distaste or disapproval of sth which may interest or attract others, eg a (type of) book, entertainment, social function □ HELEN: *Have you seen a picture of the house? Do you like it?* JO: *It's all right* ***if you like that sort of thing*** *and I don't.* TOH □ *There were fields and orchards as far as the eye could see. No doubt,* ***if you like that sort of thing****, it was all very beautiful and peaceful.* □ *'Jack thought the show was very funny.' 'I daresay* ***if he likes that kind of thing****, he would find it funny.'* □ *'Oh, it was a very good performance* ***for those who like that sort of thing****—I'm just not very keen on ballet.'* □ usu second person; usu middle or end position; variant for those who like that sort of thing.

if you must know (informal) added to a piece of information given to sb who has been asking for it inquisitively, tiresomely etc □ *This,* ***if you must know****, is a child I knew in the hospital.* DC □ (a telephone call) *'Is anyone with you, Hasselbacher?' 'Yes, friends.' 'What friends?' '****If you must know****, Mr Wormold is here.'* OMIH □ *'Where did you meet him?' '****If you must know****, I met him on a number eleven bus.'* UTN □ front, middle or end position; stress pattern if you 'must know.

if you please[1] formal, or anxiously, polite request □ *Now where shall we all sit? Mrs Johnston, over here* ***if you please****, and Andrew next to Mrs Johnston!* □ *'Shall I sit you up a little?' '****If you please****, nurse.'* □ *And Jenkins—knock at the door* ***if you please*** *the next time you interrupt one of my classes.* □ usu abbreviated please; sometimes, spoken in a peremptory tone, more an order than a request.

if you please[2] (ironic) what do you, what would anyone, think of that? (the reference being to a situation or proposal that seems to the speaker to be unjust, unreasonable, ludicrous etc) □ (Walter's father has forbidden motor cycle racing) *And we've had one or two almighty scenes already. Nothing of that sort till I'm twenty one,* ***if you please****.* HD □ *Then there are the parents, who want some say in the fate of their children, and these days even the children themselves demand to be heard,* ***if you please****.* NS

if you will[1] (formal) if you are willing, able or free to do sth □ *Mrs Allen sat down again. 'You may bring me a small glass too,* ***if you will****.'* AITC □ *'Oh, I nearly forgot, sir. Mr Wickham said he had the Tranter documents ready for you to sign.' 'Good. Go and ask him to bring them in now* ***if he will****.'* □ usu just polite addition to request or suggestion; also used in third person, as shown.

if you will[2] (formal) if you wish to go that far in describing, or criticizing, sb □ *No, you are wrong there. The old Prof was a snob and a bore, a pretentious ass,* ***if you will****, but as far as his work was concerned not a charlatan.* □ *A number of distant relatives were always present—camp-followers or hangers-on,* ***if you will****.*

if you'll pardon/excuse the liberty (dated or ironic) added when sb feels that what he is doing—or esp saying—may be thought presumptuous, interfering or over-familiar □ *'I don't know. Angels are funny people—****if you'll pardon the liberty****.' She bobbed her head towards the corner of the room, where she had taught Virginia to believe that her angel stood to guard her.* AITC □ *'****If you'll excuse the liberty****, Miss,' the housekeeper said. 'I think you should change for dinner. Mr Robert's parents would expect it.'*

ifs and buts [n + n non-rev] conditions, objections and exceptions sometimes contrasted with a firm policy, a clear statement of opinion, etc □ ***Ifs and buts*** *are the stuff of politics, Mr Parkinson. As a scientist I am concerned with the facts.* TBC □ *It is the resentment that gives rise to the nagging* ***ifs and buts*** (in the 36th National Democratic Convention). NS

ill at ease [Comp (AdjP)] nervous, worried, embarrassed, dissatisfied, awkwardly shy, etc **S:** visitor, stranger, guest. **V:** ⚠ be, feel, appear; make sb □ *With men of his own sort* (ie business men) *he was sometimes* ***ill at ease****, especially with the bigwigs. They made him deferential.* PW □ *A young man stood in a curious attitude, half arrogant and half obsequious, by the girl's side. He was obviously rather* ***ill at ease****.* HD □ *But by and large* (domestic) *employers have become timid,* ***ill-at-ease****, and guilt-ridden. They no longer feel that they have a right to have their work done for them.* NS □ as Comp only, even when hyphenated.

the ills etc that flesh is heir to the numerous diseases, pains, griefs, disappointments, accidents that mankind is liable to suffer **n:** ills, ⚠ shocks, pains, afflictions □ (source) *To die: to sleep;/No more; and, by a sleep to say we end/The heart-ache and* ***the*** *thousand natural* ***shocks/That flesh is heir to****. . .* HAMLET III 1 □ *The longer Christmas holiday brought the mildest weather for a decade, and a blessed apparent break from* ***the*** *daily national* ***ills that*** *British* ***flesh has been heir to*** *since the end of the Second World War.* L □ *Jesus did not live a cloistered existence nor was he spared* ***the shocks that flesh is heir to****.* G

imagine things [V + O] have illusions; suppose on a particular occasion that sth is so when, in fact, it is not □ *Mummy's sick, darling. She* ***imagines things****.* DC □ *'Look at that policeman. What shall we do?' 'That dick's* ((slang) = policeman) *not after you. Don't start* ***imagining things****.'* AITC □ *Was it a face he had seen peering between the reeds or was he starting to* ***imagine things****?* □ usu continuous tenses or as *to*-inf after *start, be inclined etc*.

improve the occasion [V + O pass] (formal) use an existing situation to obtain some advantage, or point out a lesson to be learned from it □ *Dad was in a spending mood, so I thought I might as well* ***improve the occasion*** *by buying something useful.* □ *When a child has had a bad shock it's no time to* ***improve the occasion*** *with a moral lecture on road safety.* □ sometimes facetious, as in first example.

in the absence of sb/sth [A (Prep P)] when, or where, sb/sth is absent or lacking □ *The formulas of politeness tend to become meaningless* ***in the absence of*** *good will.* SC □ ***In the absence of*** *more solid evidence most of his admirers will prefer to think her mistaken—if not, indeed, malicious.* □ *The difficulties of bringing up a pair of spirited boys* ***in the absence of*** *a father were beginning to weigh her down.* □ *Julia was always* *more relaxed and communicative* ***in*** *her father* ***'s absence***. □ *Our typewriter was frequently in pawn and* ***in its absence*** *we had to make do with pen and paper.* □ variant in sb's/sth's absence refers to sb/sth that does exist but is temporarily absent cf ***in the absence of*** *a father* and ***in*** *her father* ***'s absence***.

in the abstract [A (PrepP)] as an idea, theory etc, and not related to specific persons, objects, facts, figures or examples **V:** consider, examine, contemplate, study, sth □ *Harold paused in his unexpectedly sympathetic analysis of Alec's character to consider emotion* ***in the abstract***. PW □ *I don't care for moral problems, posed* ***in the abstract***, *or for fictitious examples either.* □ *We acknowledge that 20 thousand light years away is a greater distance than 12 thousand light years, but only* ***in the abstract***. *Neither figure has any real meaning for us as a concept.* □ occas also modifies a preceding n.

in accordance with sth [A (Prep P)] conforming with and/or acting upon sth; according to sth (qv) **o:** the law, the rules of the Society; established procedure, an old custom; your expressed wish □ *Trespassers may be prosecuted* ***in accordance with*** *the law.* □ *When asked why Her Majesty's Ambassador in Paris was described as Ambassadeur de l'Angleterre, the reply was that he was only so described on his personal invitation cards* ***in accordance with*** *long-established tradition.* SC □ (a business letter) *Dear Mr Brown,/* ***In accordance with*** *your instructions of May 27th, a transfer of credit has now been arranged whereby you may operate your account from the Mill Street, Richborough, branch of this bank.*

in addition (to sth) [A(PrepP)] also; as well (as sb/sth) (qv); over and above (qv) □ *Two main kinds of waves travel outward from the centre of an earthquake.* ***In addition***, *there are surface waves.* NSC □ ***In addition to*** *the general plot which I have just outlined, I had also made it clear to the Eighth Army that 'bellyaching' would not be tolerated.* MFM □ front, middle or end position.

in advance [A (PrepP)] before, or for a future period or occasion **V** pay, book, prepare; warn, know, sth □ *The rent will be £20 a week, paid* ***in advance***. □ *There's always a Morro crab to start with at the Nacional* (a restaurant). *That's prepared* ***in advance***. OMIH □ *There's always a great demand for tickets. You'd better book your seats well* ***in advance***. □ *No one can possibly know* ***in advance*** *how he would react in circumstances like these.* L □ attrib use *(an)* ***advance*** *payment, booking, notice.*

in an advisory etc capacity [A (PrepP)] being present, or acting, only in an advisory etc function or manner **V:** act, write, speak. **adj:** advisory; official, unofficial; general, menial, professional □ *Though he was no longer strong enough for the heavy handling work in the Yards they retained his services* ***in an advisory capacity***. □ *He avoided all social contact with women and tolerated their existence only* ***in a menial capacity***. □ *Roy Fuller is a Governor of the BBC: he writes here* ***in a private capacity*** (ie not as a spokesman for the BBC). L □ *I have flexes running under carpets at home myself though,* ***in my capacity as*** *a fire prevention officer, I frequently warn people not to.* □ variant in one's capacity as sth.

in agreement (with sb/sth) [Comp/A (PrepP)] (be) of the same opinion (as sb about sth); (do sth) as a result,or indication,of agreeing (with sb about sth) **V:** be, find oneself; act. **O:** colleague, committee; proposal, recommendation, suggestion □ *I take it we are* ***in agreement***? □ *I find myself so completely* ***in agreement with*** *your letter of 18 September that I cannot believe there is any great difference in our concepts.* MFM □ ***In agreement with*** *this suggestion we all set off for Bournemouth the following morning.* □ *Peter nodded* ***in agreement***, *drew the curtains and switched off the ceiling light.*

in (the) aggregate [A (PrepP)] (formal) when added up; when considered together instead of separately □ *Those pension increases will* ***in aggregate*** *cost the country an additional £5m a year.* □ *No one of his faults was very serious but* ***in the aggregate*** *they made him an unbearably irritating person to live with.* □ *Domestic consumption of coal has certainly decreased.* ***In the aggregate***, *however, demand is still high.* □ usu front or middle position.

in all/total [A (PrepP)] altogether; all together/told (qv) **n:** fifty-six, a hundred, a dozen; twenty persons, forty items □ *I did quite a lot of flying at the London Aeroplane Club, I did about a hundred hours* ***in all***. RFW □ *It seemed we were to be a cosy round-table party, fourteen* ***in all***. PP □ ***In total*** *there must have been twenty vehicles in the pile-up.* □ often modifies a preceding n, as shown.

in all/everything but name having all the qualities and functions of sb/sth specified, although not (formally or legally) called so **n:** president, monarch; husband, wife; prison; the same product □ *Within his own fiefdom a feudal overlord was a monarch* ***in all but name***. □ *They've been living together a good while. You would say they're man and wife* ***in everything but name***. □ usu modifies a preceding n.

in all conscience [Disj (PrepP)] certainly; surely; it cannot be denied □ *This moment* (in the play) *is not as hilarious as,* ***in all conscience***, *it should be; it is awkwardly staged.* OBS □ *And we discovered shortly that the gallant Eighth Army though destructive enough* ***in all conscience***, *was not our only foe.* SC □ *She began as a straight novelist in her early twenties and hit a blank spot. 'I'd read enough thrillers* ***in all conscience***, *so my husband suggested I tackle one.'* SC □ often gives special emphasis to statement containing *enough, (not) much, (too) many, plenty (of)*; middle or end position in clause or phrase.

in all one's/its glory/majesty [A (PrepP)] in a beautiful, magnificent, finely dressed, etc state; displaying power, importance, fame etc **V:** appear, arise, emerge; parade □ (source) *And yet I say unto you, That even Solomon* ***in all his glory*** *was not arrayed like one of these.* MATTHEW VI 29 □ *Was it really on Hampstead Heath that Linnaeus fell on his knees at the sight of gorse blooming* ***in all its glory***? T □ *Alcatraz* (once a big American prison) *can now be inspected just like any other stately home or palace anywhere else in the world, totally untarted up,* ***in all its*** *crumbling* ***glory***. OBS □ *But the husband* *in all his majesty is singularly backward in a number of intellectual situations.* TO □ occas modifies a preceding n, as shown.

in all honesty/sincerity [A (PrepP)] completely truthfully, sincerely **V:** say, declare, answer, promise; act, do sth □ *A few students answered this correctly, and a few abstained from answering, but the majority declared unhesitatingly and* ***in all sincerity*** *that the man returned the book to the shelf.* MFF □ *Can you* ***in all honesty*** *claim that none of this has been your own fault?*

in all probability/likelihood [Disj (PrepP)] very probably; more likely to happen, or be the case, than not □ *Any day Jenny half expected a bowl of soup, garnished* ***in all probability*** *with a bit of chalky underdone rice and a piece of string or two, to turn up as evidence of the cock's death.* TGLY □ *Why should we go so far out of our way to visit somebody who* ***in all likelihood*** *moved out of the district years ago?*

in all shapes and sizes [A (PrepP)] (occur) variously formed or produced **V:** come, grow; find sth □ *Feet come* ***in all shapes and sizes*** *which the average manufacturer tends to overlook.* SC □ *Tropical orchids, on the other hand, are found* ***in all shapes and sizes*** *and have a wide colour range.*

in all weathers [A (PrepP)] in all kinds of weather (reference being to esp outdoor life and work in variable climates) **V:** be out; work, fly, sail; deliver sth □ *He was a van boy on a dray working* ***in all weathers*** *for twelve hours a day.* OBS □ *Her father was a powerful fifty-year-old, with the grainy red brown complexion of a man accustomed to being out* ***in all weathers.*** □ an ***all-weather*** *aircraft* is one that can fly in all weathers.

in answer/reply (to sth) [A (PrepP)] as a verbal answer, or other response (to sth) **V:** say, declare □ *'Fergus hasn't given me anything yet,' she said lightly,* ***in answer to*** *Guy's question.* DC □ *I threatened to set the dogs on them and after flinging a few ill-aimed stones* ***in reply,*** *they scrambled back over the fence.* □ ***In answer to*** *this summons I presented myself at the Magistrates' Court at 10 a.m. the following morning.*

in any case/event [Conj (PrepP)] whatever happens or is done, regardless of any (other) fact or circumstance; anyway; anyhow; come rain, come shine (qv); (in) fair (weather) and/or foul (qv); wet or fine (qv) □ *Such murders, moreover, are often committed by the palpably insane who are,* ***in any case,*** *automatically immune from the death penalty.* OBS □ *Admittedly his microphone was not working, but* ***in any event*** *most of the 1,000 delegates did not seem in the mood to listen to the vice-chancellors.* NS □ *The owners should be compensated, especially as the state will be taxing them* ***in any event.*** NS □ case is more informal than event; front, middle or end position.

in any shape or form [A (PrepP)] (informal) in whatever way, form, sth appears, is presented □ *Never again did he sample tobacco* ***in any shape or form.*** DF □ *She behaved as if she couldn't welcome sex from me* ***in any shape or form;*** *and I took her at her face value.* RATT □ *You can give me eggs as often as you like. I'm very partial to them* ***in any shape or form.*** □ often modifies a preceding n.

in as/so much as [Conj] to the extent that; in so far as (qv) □ *I never claimed perfection for my father.* ***In as much as*** *we are all fallible, I suppose he was too.* □ *One can actually take infant mortality as a crude index of social well-being generally (at least* ***in as much as*** *good feeding, healthy surroundings, good medical care and freedom from violent stresses are important to social well-being generally).* L □ *The captain's 'little blow up',* ***in so much as*** *the waves were from 6 to 18 feet high, was what I'd have called a storm.* □ introduces subordinate clause.

in bed [Comp/A (PrepP)] resting or sleeping; confined because of illness; as a sexual partner **V;** be; rest, lie; snore □ *I hope I haven't rung too early. Were you* ***in bed?*** □ *You should be* ***in bed*** *from the look of you, Miss Smith. Don't come in tomorrow unless you're feeling better.* □ *Brigit had one fierce unhappy qualm that perhaps being ill* ***in bed*** *gave Nicky an aversion to her.* DC □ *I love Alice. She loves me. I'm happy with her. Not just* ***in bed*** *either.* RATT

in the best/worst of taste [Comp/A (PrepP)] polite/impolite; conforming/not conforming to the rules of polite society; according to what is most/least acceptable and admirable in current conventions of furnishing, decoration, dress etc □ *I thought his remarks about her were* ***in the worst of taste.*** □ *His behaviour was not* ***in the best of taste.*** *He swore, slurped his soup, didn't attend properly to what people were saying to him, and kept breaking in on other people's conversations.* □ *Wilson's flat was small, but decorated and furnished* ***in the best of taste.*** □ in the best of taste often neg.

in a big/small way [A (PrepP)] extensively; importantly; seriously/modestly; on a large etc scale (qv) **V:** invest, do business; become involved, fall for sb □ *They're receivers of stolen goods* ***in a big way,*** *but the countries where they operate don't care, so long as they take a cut in taxes and import licences and so on.* DC □ *Her father was a poultry breeder* ***in a small way.*** *I don't think there was ever much money to spare* □ *The Army has gone into business* ***in a big way,*** *investing in construction firms, agriculture, and tanks.* OBS □ *It was now fairly clear that we were heading for trouble* ***in a big way.*** MFM □ *I fell for Irma* ***in a big way,*** *Harold.* PW □ *Always assuming that spring is the right description of this chilly season, Nature dictates* ***in a big way*** *at this time of the year* T □ also modifies a preceding n as shown.

in black and white [A (PrepP)] in writing or in print; as black letters on white paper (esp as clarification or confirmation of sth said verbally, as more legally binding) **V** get, have, sth; put sth down, state sth □ *This letter's from your mother saying she agrees to your coming with me. Now we have it* ***in black and white.*** SPL □ *This view, indeed, has become so much a commonplace that one feels almost ashamed of putting it down* ***in black and white*** *again.* SNP □ *'Perhaps I could have it all* ***in*** *what's called* ***black and white*** *from the family solicitor,' he said.* HAA

in a body [A (PrepP)] all together at the same time, as if many or a number of persons were one **S:** audience, crowd, assembly; department, faculty. **V:** rise, leave; resign □ *I asked them if they were all prepared to resign* ***in a body****, led by me, if anything less than eighteen months' National Service with the Colours was decided upon by the Government.* MFM □ *The audience rose* ***in a body*** *and cheered him to the echo.*

in sb's book [Disj (PrepP] (informal) as sb thinks; as information, experience and tastes lead him to believe; in sb's/one's opinion (qv), in sb's view (qv); to my mind (qv); to sb's way of thinking (qv) □ *Donald Burton insists on altering his appearance for each role he undertakes. In my view, quite fatal. They must know who you are and what you are going to do as soon as you step on the stage,* ***in my book****.* OBS □ *Here* (ie in a film) *she was teamed with Dana Andrews and Henry Fonda. 'Which should she marry?' asked the posters rhetorically. Neither,* ***in my book****, because both were miscast.* RT

(never) in (all) one's born days [A (PrepP)] (never) at any time during one's life, before a particular occasion (the reference often being to sth seen, heard or done that is unpleasant or regrettable) □ *A man who came level with them on the same side called out derisively: 'Did you ever see such a game?' '****Never in all my born days****,' Fred replied.* LLDR □ *They get on my tit-ends, they do straight. You've* ***never*** *met such a bloody shower* ***in all your born days****.* TT □ *She's a fine one to preach self-denial!* ***Never in all her life*** *has she had to do without anything she really wanted.* □ variant (never) in (all) one's life.

in brief/short [Conj (PrepP)] briefly; in as few words as possible; as a summing-up; in a word (qv) □ ***In brief****, the evidence purported to show that animal (or saturated) fats increase the amount of cholesterol in the blood and increase the likelihood of coronary thrombosis.* T □ *It would need a book to tell properly but,* ***in brief****, she started an extra-mural diploma course and got a place at Bedford College, London, four years later.* ST □ front or middle position.

in broad daylight [A (PrepP)] in the full light of day (esp thought of as providing (un)suitable or (un)likely conditions for sth to happen) **V:** happen, take place; shoot, rob, sb □ *We were walking along Holland Park Avenue. It was* ***broad daylight*** *and the mist had cleared.* UTN □ *'Nothing happens to a woman* ***in broad daylight****,' he said. 'She'll turn up.'* DC

in sb's case [A (PrepP] in the particular instance or example provided by sb etc (the implication often being of a contrast with other people of a roughly similar group) **det:** sb's, sth's; that, this; some, (a) few, (not) many □ *Briefly,* ***in*** *my own* ***case****, two matters cannot have been right.* MFM □ *I never forget a face, but* ***in*** *your* ***case*** *I'll make an exception.* G MARX □ *But* ***in the case of*** *Scotland they* (these facts) *are tragic because we cannot afford such wastage.* SC □ ***In some cases*** *only swirls of patterned colour are seen. In others there may be vivid recalls of past experiences.* HAH ⇨ ⚠ in that case.

in the cause of sth [A (PrepP] (formal) in order to support, defend, or promote sth **o:** liberty, one's country, justice for all □ *Mr Herter could find no better reasons for going to Paris than the desirability of living up to President Eisenhower's offer to go anywhere* ***in the cause of*** *peace.* SC □ *The idea of a hero's death* ***in*** *England****'s cause*** *rated pretty low with any of us.* □ (printed beneath an advertisement reading: Don't let the extremists wreck our freedom and our economy.) *Issued by Aims of Industry* ***in the cause of*** *free enterprise.* NS

in Christendom [A (PrepP)] anywhere; everywhere □ *He said, 'I think I am the happiest man* ***in Christendom****,' and I think he really felt that way.* L □ *Rich American visitors, served by Arab waiters, pay Israeli pounds to eat international breakfasts while looking through huge picture windows at what must be the finest view* ***in Christendom****.* L □ *'You're exactly what the American's call a "sad sack", isn't he Geoff?' 'I should just say he is, ma'am, the biggest god-almighty sad sack* ***in Christendom****.'* TBC □ usu modifies a preceding n, as shown.

in/under the circumstances [A (PrepP)] in the special situation (determined by one's relationship to other persons, things, events that have occurred or are likely to etc) **det:** the, no, (not) any; such, certain, these □ *Could firms be forced to move against their wishes?* ***In such circumstances*** *they might decide not to expand at all.* SC □ *To tell a white lie, he thought, was excusable* ***in the circumstances****.* □ *Old People's homes vary considerably in the standard of care they offer, but I would not* ***under any circumstances*** *send a relative of mine to* that *one.* □ front, middle or end position.

in cold blood [A (PrepP)] calmly; deliberately; callously; without (the excuse of) passion, enthusiasm etc **V:** shoot, kill; plan, consider □ *The ambushes and pitched battles were fought in fury. And afterwards, prisoners were shot* ***in cold blood****.* PP □ *Secondly, thank you for all you say about my new adventure in the East.* ***In cold blood*** *I'm sometimes a little terrified when I think of the immensity of the task.* SD □ often used in collocation *a murder* ***in cold blood****/a* ***cold-blooded*** *murder.*

in common etc parlance [Disj/A (PrepP)] (formal) (using) part of the vocabulary of ordinary people, or of a more specialized group **adj:** common, vulgar (= common); medical, schoolboy, 16th century □ *If an expression is* ***in common parlance*** *one tends to use it regardless of strict accuracy, as a woman will talk of 'hoovering' her carpets though her vacuum cleaner may be of a different name and manufacture altogether.* □ *'What is the cause of these black-outs* (fainting fits)*?' 'Cardiac arrest—****in common parlance****, temporary heart failure.'* □ *'****In vulgar parlance****,' said McNeil amiably, 'what Chris is saying is that individuals in the Cloud, if there are any, must be highly telepathic.'* TBC □ *And Mr Rawstorne's yacht has the reputation of being what* ***in nautical parlance*** *is called a lively craft.* □ *I don't think I understand more than about half of the contract we had to sign when we bought our house. It's all written* ***in the parlance of*** *lawyers trying to sound high skilled and mysterious.* □ variant in the parlance of sb.

in common with sb/sth together with, like, sb/sth □ *Tony,* ***in common with*** *many of his generation, had no very clear idea of what he wanted to do in life.* □ *The main issue is that of compensation for United States interests expropriated —* ***in common with*** *Cuban* *interests—in the agricultural reform.* SC

in confidence [A (PrepP)] confidentially; as a private message, confession etc **V:** say (sth), tell (sb), be given sth. **adj:** strict, absolute, total □ *'Naturally,' she added, 'all that I say to you now is **in confidence**.'* UTN □ *Olive had promised to write and tell Eric **in** strictest **confidence** about his difficulties with Mrs Pettigrew.* MM □ *'That would make a good story for your paper.' 'Too true, it would. But I cannot use information given me **in confidence** in that way.'*

in confusion[1] [A (PrepP)] in a disorderly, or muddled, state or manner **V:** flee; break up, collapse; begin, end □ *The room had been thoroughly ransacked and the contents of drawers and cupboards lay **in confusion** on the floor.* □ *The once orderly ranks now fled **in confusion**.* □ *Unhappily there is more than one interpretation of the Labour party's drama. The week opened **in confusion**.* OBS

in confusion[2] [A (PrepP)] muddled in one's ideas; perplexed or embarrassed **V:** look on, listen □ *'They've altered this part of the town completely since I was here last,' he complained, peering through the windscreen **in confusion**.* □ *'Oh dear,' he gabbled to the naked figure, 'wrong room, I'm so sorry,' and scuttled out again **in** considerable **confusion**.*

in conjunction (with sb/sth) [A (PrepP)] acting, working or planning together (with sb/sth) □ *The Ninth American Army attacked northwards on the 23rd February, **in conjunction with** the Canadian Army attack.* MFM □ *At least two other pre-school centres built and financed by private trusts and administered **in** close **conjunction with** the Inner London Education Authority are in the pipeline.* □ *Planning teams were set up under the nominal leadership of Brown but were told to work **in conjunction**.*

in connection with sth [Conj, (PrepP)] arising from sth; about, concerning, relevant to sth **det:** this, that, the same, another, a different. **o:** that; the alleged theft, the catering arrangements; what you've just said □ *Preventive detention orders have been made against 12 more people, '**in connection with** an alleged conspiracy in the Volta region'.* OBS □ *'I want to see the manager,' she said, laying an envelope on the counter, '**in connection with** this letter I received from him yesterday.'* □ *'Your tenants are not giving you any more trouble, I hope?' 'No, I've come to ask your advice **in another connection**.'* □ *Some people need their illnesses. Cure them and you deprive them of an excuse for inadequacy. **In that connection** (or: **In connection with** that), consider my father-in-law.* □ if with is omitted, *this, that etc* must be used.

in contrast (to/with sb/sth) [Conj (PrepP)] contrasted with (sb/sth); being opposite or different (from sb/sth) **adj:** marked, sharp, striking, great □ ***In contrast to** the subterranean life which Granny Walton lived, Granny Trill's cottage door was always open and her living-room welcomed us daily.* CWR □ *In marked **contrast to** the normal response to a cut in Bank rate, prices on the Stock Exchange drifted lower after the news.* T □ *In desert lands a puncture is rare. (This **in great contrast to** the thorn bush of the Somalilands where thirty punctures in a day, three or four at a time, are common enough).* BM

in the course of sth [A (PrepP)] during a specified period of time or activity; while engaged in (doing) sth **o:** his life, the month; their researches, their inquiries; listing the contents □ *These tidal waves have hardly any effect on ships in the open sea, since there is only a very gradual rise of perhaps a few feet on the sea's surface **in the course of** several minutes.* NSC □ ***In the course of** preparing a half-hour film report for '24 Hours' on the Army in Northern Ireland I had a long interview with him at his headquarters.* L

in the (normal/ordinary) course of nature etc [A (PrepP)] as part, or as a result of a natural or inevitable process or progression **o:** nature, ⚠ events, things □ *People will dose themselves for minor ailments which **in the course of nature** would clear themselves up in a few days.* □ *It was no special treat for John. He gets more than enough of dining out **in the ordinary course of events**.* □ *Sinden, in fact, could well be next occupant of one of the great theatrical thrones, that eminence where Sir John Gielgud and Sir Ralph Richardson now stand but cannot, **in the course of nature** remain for many more years.* TVT

in one's cups [Comp/A (PrepP)] (when) drunk, under the influence of alcohol; in drink (qv) □ *I've come to know him pretty well these last ten or twelve years. And odd facts drop out when a man's **in his cups**.* PP □ *My mother was merely a horrified looker-on, my father **in his cups** already predicted the gallows for me.* ST □ *Mr Hughes employs as guards four or five Mormons, a group he admires for their integrity (you can't pay them to talk) and their sobriety (they don't spill anything **in their cups**).* OBS

in sb's day/time[1] [A (PrepP)] at the time when sb was alive, or young, or in the prime of working life, or in a position of authority □ *The kind of light entertainment put out now is not nearly as good as it was **in my day**.* RT □ *The place is not kept as it was **in** your grandfather**'s time**. It would break his heart to see the garden now.* □ *Lung cancer, traffic accidents and the millions of miserable alcoholics are facts even more certain than was **in** Dante**'s day** the fact of the Inferno.* DOP □ stress pattern in 'my day, in your 'grandfather's time.

in sb's day/time[2] [A (PrepP)] at a period, or periods, in one's past life (esp used in claims to have done, or experienced, sth specified) □ *The Auberge did not satisfy the artistic and creative soul of Monsieur Bonneval. **In his day** he had been a great cook.* ARG □ *Dorothy was more boring than even Daniel, who had met some bores **in his time**, could have believed possible.* US □ *I also have been deeply moved into bad poetry **in my day** and no critical response could match one's own embarrassment when one is left with some poor words on the printed page.* NS □ stress pattern in my 'day/'time.

in days of old/yore [A (PrepP)] (formal) in ancient times; in times long past □ *It's a pastiche historical romance of the '**in days of old** when knights were bold' genre.* □ *I believe, sir,* (palaeontologist) *is the word for one who studies the fossilized remains of the prehistoric monsters that used **in days of yore** to roam the earth.* RM

in (the) dead of winter in the severest part

of a winter season (esp in a cold climate where growth of vegetation ceases and people's outdoor activities diminish or are difficult) □ *'It's a wonderful house, Frank,' he said, 'with great gardens ablaze with all the colours in the rainbow.' 'That's not likely* ***in dead of winter****,' said Frank, and his little mouth pursed tightly.* ASA □ *If you had to live here* ***in the dead of winter****, you wouldn't think it so delightful. We were snowed up for weeks on end last year—that's why we store up fuel and provisions every autumn.*

in depth [A (PrepP)] thoroughly and exhaustively (esp contrasted with generally, broadly or superficially) **V:** study, treat; deal with, go into. **O/o:** field, topic, subject □ *In this fourth Stockton Lecture I have decided to interpret 'education for corporate responsibility' broadly rather than* ***in depth****.* ST □ *Mr Linklater, whose more recent works have taken him into studies* ***in depth*** *of Scottish history, breaks new ground with his excellent analysis.* SC □ *I think that everybody who has helped other people with personal problems, and who has pursued the study* ***in*** *any* ***depth*** *comes to the conclusion that there are interactions going on within the mind itself.* L □ attrib use ***in-depth*** *treatment, analysis, scrutiny.*

in detail [A (PrepP)] with every detail, item etc of sth included, mentioned etc **V:** recount, examine, enter, render, sth □ *In future, a claim for expenses must be rendered* ***in detail*** *and accompanied by receipts.* □ *The Princess was taken to see the cardboard vessel which had carried off the lovers during the final chorus. She inspected the rigging* ***in detail****.* ST □ *Just give me the gist of what he said. I haven't time to listen to the whole thing* ***in detail****.*

in dribs and drabs (informal) in small irregular amounts; piecemeal **V:** get, impart, reveal, sth; approach, deal with, tackle, sth □ *Wales have given British soccer many great players. But always* ***in dribs and drabs****. If only they had all arrived in the same generation, then Wales would certainly have been potential world champions.* TVT □ *Certainly there is an illiteracy problem in Britain by the old measure—a reading age of the average nine-years-old. It is tackled at the mement* ***in drabs and drabs****, a volunteer teacher scheme here, a local authority class there.* NS □ *She had concocted the whole story from* ***dribs and drabs*** *of gossip picked up at back doors and in the shops.* □ dribs and drabs non-rev.

in drink [Comp/A (PrepP)] (when) drunk (the implication often being only slightly, or partially, so); in one's cups (qv) □ *It was spoken* ***in drink****, but it happened to be true. Half drunk myself, I loved him for it.* NM □ *'Was he drunk at the time of this accident?' 'Not what you'd call drunk. I would say he was* ***in drink****—a bit happy, maybe had a glass or two.'*

in droves [A (PrepP)] in large numbers **n:** fans, suppporters, shoppers. **V:** come, arrive, go (by) □ *When he collects the rates all the women come* ***in droves****. They pay twice over to have five minutes longer with him.* RATT □ *There'll be a big crowd at the match. They've been going down the road* ***in droves****.* □ *I had to shut the windows. The flies where coming in* ***in droves****.*

in due course [A (PrepP)] at a proper and suitable time in the future; eventually in a natural, or inevitable, sequence of events □ *Naturally, I have that possibility* (poisoning) *in mind. I shall search the deceased* ***in due course****.* EM □ ***In due course*** *the Bill became law; the first election under the new Act took place in August 1872, at Pontefract.* SC □ *True pyrotechny began with the use of combustibles in sieges and naval battles. From war it passed* ***in due course*** *to entertainment.* HAH □ front, middle or end position.

in earnest [A (PrepP)] serious(ly) and not light(-ly) or joking(ly); heavily; fiercely **V:** speak, argue, fight; sleet, snow, blow. **adj:** dead(ly), sober, grim □ *It is not surprising that Jeffrey besought Carlyle not to be 'so dreadfully* ***in earnest****'. The rugged Carlyle did not attempt to hide his contempt for Jeffrey's social charm.* SC □ *I once knew a military man who was heard to say, not humorously, not in a moment of exasperation, but* ***in*** *deadly* ***earnest****, 'I must say I can't stand civilians!'* AH □ *The snow did not start to fall* ***in earnest*** *until after darkness had set in.* EM □ *I just wanted to give the boy a fright, but I'll be angry* ***in earnest*** *if he does it again.* □ *No more playing at soldiers, it's war* ***in earnest****.* □ may modify a preceding n or adj, as in last two examples.

in effect [A (PrepP)] really; actually; as proves to be the case in practice; virtually □ *I stood on the tarmac at Rabat Airport to see Colonel Gaddafi greeted by King Hassan of Morocco and to observe what was* ***in effect*** *his baptism in international affairs.* L □ *The procedure could* ***in effect*** *deprive parents of their right to be represented legally before a court.* OBS □ *This ingenious arrangement safeguards against overturning and* ***in effect*** *allows the machine to float on its two driving wheels so that it behaves like a front wheel drive tractor.* NSC □ *Let the unions, the editorial said* ***in effect****, work out their own destiny—and let socialists and politicians leave them to it.* NS □ usu middle position.

in the end [A (PrepP)] at the end of a period of time; finally; after other possibilities, choices, lines of action, have been tried □ JO: *Which knob do I turn?* HELEN: *Turn 'em* (= them) *all, you're bound to find the right one* ***in the end****.* TOH □ *They tried very patiently to teach me to glide, to use every muscle sinuously.* ***In the end*** *they confessed to failure.* TO □ *The more he dithered* (about accepting the offer of a job) *the more desirable to the others the appointment seemed, but* ***in the end*** *he said No.* NM □ front, middle, or end position; used to introduce or refer to a further and last statement about sth.

in essence [Disj (PrepP)] essentially; if one confines oneself to the essentials or gist of a matter □ *The two stories* (in the 'Washington Post') *were* ***in essence*** *what the 'New York Times' would have published on Wednesday and Thursday if it had not been prevented.* OBS □ ***In essence*** *therefore both BBC 1 and ITV had to adopt competitive policies if they were to remain in a 50-50* (audience) *position.* L □ front, middle or end position.

in the event [Conj (PrepP)] as actually happened at the time, contrasted with what was expected to happen □ *Someone was bound to go too far, to overstep the mark, to let everyone down.* ***In the event*** *no one did.* NS □ *I'd been* *warned by an anxious press lady* (= woman journalist) *not to bring up politics, which Mr Bennett apparently considered a very private matter.* ***In the event****, he seemed anxious to set the record straight.* RT □ usu front position.

in the event of sth [A (PrepP)] if sth specified happens or is done **o:** war, his death; his resignation, his refusing; a successful outcome □ *He gathered that* ***in the event of*** *war with the US, Pearl Harbor was to be the first target.* OBS □ (a 'Miss World' rehearsal) *They tried on the crown for size over their rollers and practised kissing each other* ***in the event of*** *victory.* RT □ *There seemed to be no more certainty of St Peter's Hall getting the land* ***in the event of*** *the council's scheme being accepted than otherwise.* T □ *'I'll try to get a joint of lamb for Sunday, but the butcher may not have any left by now.'* ***'In that event****, I'd like chicken—I haven't had any for ages.'* □ *'What will be done if the report says the roof of the school hall is in a dangerous condition?'* ***'In such an event****, the hall will be closed and it won't be used again until the necessary repairs have been carried out.'* □ if of is omitted, *that, such an* must be used.

in excess (of sth) larger, greater, heavier, longer etc than a specified amount **adv mod:** far, much; greatly, slightly, little. **O:** figure, total; speed, rate □ *Trains now travel at speeds far* ***in excess of*** *those which a motorist can attain on the M1.* NSC □ *This is slightly* ***in excess of*** *the comparable total for the preceding year at £54,860.* T □ *You may eat less than me but if you're fat you're still eating* ***in excess of*** *your body's requirements.* □ may function as Comp, or modify a preceding n.

in the extreme extremely; to a degree (qv) □ *Christopher Seaman has been conducting for many of the world's top soloists. It's no easy task either. They can be capricious and eccentric* ***in the extreme****.* RT □ (sports match) *Time and again movements broke down through passes going astray, and much of the play was scrambling* ***in the extreme****.* ST □ always modifies a preceding adj.

in (the) face of sth (although) faced with sth; in defiance of sth; despite sth **o:** danger, obstacles, opposition; all the evidence □ *He had resolved to be patient* ***in face of*** *the many difficult situations that he knew must arise during the Christmas visit.* ASA □ *Now he intends,* ***in face of*** *all the obstacles, to take 'a quiet look at France' for his next travel film.* RT □ *We have a long sea journey, and at the end of it we will have to land on an enemy coast* ***in the face of*** *determined opposition.* MFM □ *No such view can be maintained for one moment* ***in the face*** *of the evidence.* SNP

in fact [Disj (PrepP)] really; truly; to be strictly accurate; in point of fact (qv) □ *You believe that you are careful and efficient, but* ***in fact*** *you are not good at organisation.* WI □ *'You look tired, Jilly.' 'I am tired,* ***in fact****.'* □ *I want your frank opinion. Is he* ***in fact*** *likely to recover?* □ often accompanies correction of sth believed by sb else to be true; front, middle or end position.

in sb's/sth's favour [A (PrepP)] so as to recommend, support or defend sb or sth **V:** speak, testify; say a word, allow this much; be one point □ *I am sure, headmaster, it would help if you would speak* ***in his favour*** *when Tom's case comes up.* □ *The old couple haven't a word to say* ***in*** *their daughter-in-law****'s favour****. She can't be as bad as all that!* □ *...as fairly and persuasively as a scientist will present the case* ***in favour of*** *a particular belief he holds.* L ⇨ ⚠ next entry.

in favour of sb/sth [A (PrepP)] so as to favour, or give preference to, sb/sth other than the person or thing previously mentioned **V:** decide, vote, opt; work, operate. **o:** expansion in other directions; making useful social connections; younger men; bigger boats □ *William Wells's miffed* (= offended) *feelings at being passed over* ***in favour of*** *John Stonehouse have now brought the whole issue out into the open.* NS □ *It may be that in industrial districts the high wages that can be obtained at an early age have reduced the attractions of postponing wage-earning* ***in favour of*** *a university education.* SC □ *The modern Army looks, not for 'cannon fodder', but for intelligent and motivated young men. Any selectivity there is in recruiting operates* ***in their favour****.* □ variant in their favour. ⇨ ⚠ previous entry.

in fear of one's life [A (PrepP)] fearing that one may be killed; (fig) feeling alarm at (the possibility of) being scolded, punished, bullied etc **V:** go; live, work □ *At the far end of the open space a stream of people came running in as though* ***in fear of their lives****.* NS □ *A surly old bear, that's what he is! Why should we all be creeping about* ***in fear of our lives*** *because he mustn't be disturbed?* □ *I don't know how you can live here. I'd be* ***in fear of my life*** *every time I stepped outside the door.* □ often used with *go*, as in go in fear of one's life (Vol 1) (qv).

in fear and trembling [A (PrepP)] in a frightened, or cowed manner, **V:** be, go; approach, wait □ (source) *...but now much more in my absence, work out your own salvation* ***with fear and trembling****.* PHILIPPIANS II 12 □ *But when he got to Belgrade, he found that Tito had just broken with Stalin. 'I arrived* ***in fear and trembling****. I was also followed everywhere by the sound of breathing, the heavy breathing of the Jugoslav Secret Service.'* RT □ *Tim, though not* ***without fear and trembling****, had defied his father and no great harm had come to him.* □ preps *with, (not) without* occas used.

in the final/last analysis [Disj (PrepP)] ultimately; undeniably and most importantly; as the end of an examination, or line of reasoning, shows; in the last resort[2] (qv) □ *Plants get it from sunlight, and animals get it from plants, or from other animals of course. So* ***in the last analysis*** *the energy always comes from the sun.* TBC □ ***In the last analysis****, you do want the thing to work and what works for other people ought to work for you too.* OBS □ ***In the final analysis*** *the West Indies lost the series because their batting failed at two crucial moments.* □ usu front or middle position.

in the first instance [A (PrepP)] at the beginning; as a first step; first of all[1] (qv); to begin with[1] (Vol 1) (qv); in the first place[1] (qv); to start with[1] (Vol 1) (qv) □ *It's very good of you to come to the rescue like this. Why I didn't ask you to take charge of the arrangements* ***in the first instance*** *I can't imagine.* □ *The problem* *was solved by heating alone, and refrigeration was used only to dry out the buildings* ***in the first instance***. NSC □ usu end position.

in the first etc person [A (PrepP)] using the first, second or third personal pronouns in speech or writing **adj:** first, ⚠ second, third □ *Formal invitations are usually issued and accepted* ***in the third person***. □ *The afternoon brought a note from the hotel,* ***in the third person***, *'Miss Merlin has been invited to give a lecture this evening and thinks it might interest Mr Skipton to attend.'* US

in the first place[1] [A (PrepP)] as a first step; before anything else or further is done; anyway; first of all[1] (qv); in the first instance (qv); to begin with[1] (Vol 1) (qv); to start with[1] (Vol 1) (qv) □ *'What Chris is saying is that individuals in the Cloud must be highly telepathic.' 'Then why didn't he say so* ***in the first place****?'* TBC □ *With better site supervision many of the things that lead to complaints could not happen* ***in the first place***. OBS □ *They were punished by being ignored and excluded. Of course, they needn't have gone there* ***in the first place***. OBS □ middle or end position.

in the first place[2] [Conj (PrepP)] first and foremost; first of all[2] (qv); for a start (qv); to begin with[2] (Vol 1) (qv); to start with[2] (Vol 1) (qv) □ ***In the first place***, *as Boswell urged, Christ's death was intended to appease God's wrath and thus to reconcile Him to admitting sinners to Heaven; while in the second place, such a God would be so evidently morally contemptable that to worship Him would itself be an act of gross moral cowardice.* L □ ***In the first place*** *he feared another act of treachery on the part of the Leadership of the Movement. He also saw in Lansbury the good-natured but woolly-minded pacifist. Thirdly he saw the hand of the 'intellectuals' in this.* OBS □ accompanies the first of a number of statements, reasons or arguments; usu front position; often followed by *in the second place/second(ly), etc.*

in a flash [A (PrepP)] quite or very suddenly, quickly; in a space of time too short to be measured; in a trice (qv) **V:** disappear, vanish; cure sb □ *Flynn sliced through the defence of the two England centres.* ***In a flash*** *he was past them and clean over the England line.* ST □ *It is advisable to keep greyhounds leashed in parks because small dogs could prove too much of a temptation, and they can kill* ***in a flash***. TVT □ ***In a flash*** *she realized how superficial, and in a sense how vulgar, her reaction to the book had been.* PW □ front, middle or end position.

in the flesh [A (PrepP)] in one's/sb's bodily presence; in person[1] (qv) □ *John Ogdon is playing Tchaikovsky 1, which is a bit predictable, but as he plays it better than anybody else I've heard* ***in the flesh***, *I suppose the choice is justified.* RT □ *Their idol is appearing for only 10 or 12 minutes, but their appreciation of him* ***in the flesh*** *is such that they have converged on Belle Vue tonight from Newcastle, Peterborough, London, Bristol, Birmingham.* TVT

in for a penny, in for a pound (saying) having spent some money, gone to time and trouble, decided on some action, one may as well etc go much further (than one originally intended) □ *The new carpet made everything else in the room look so shabby that it was a case of* ***in for a penny, in for a pound*** *and we ended up with fresh wallpaper and new curtains, too.* □ *'Look here, Lydia,' said Colin, 'don't tell me that Effie and Ruby are going to London,' adding rather coarsely that if they did they would be bound to get into double trouble;* ***in for a penny, in for a pound***. WDM □ may be uttered (following *oh well*) before taking action.

in full [A (PrepP)] to a complete amount; with nothing omitted; verbatim **V:** pay, report, recount, sth; publish sth □ *Anything he has ever borrowed from me he has always repaid* ***in full***. □ *Crossman* (a Government Minister) *boldly decided to publish the report* (which was highly critical of the Government) ***in full***. NS □ (reader's letter) *One must of course withhold judgement on Bergamini's book until it has been published and read* ***in full*** *but on the face of it, its allegations must seem utter nonsense.* SC

in full etc measure [A (PrepP)] abundantly; in ample quantities (the implication sometimes being that there is more of whatever is referred to than is desirable) **adj:** full, ⚠ good, ample □ *There were possibilities of trouble and they descended on the North-Eastern front* ***in full measure***. MFM □ *For two years they knew happiness* ***in full measure*** *and then Jane fell ill.* □ *If you like folk singing you'll get it* ***in good measure*** *tonight*. ⇨ ⚠ in a measure.

in full view of sb/sth [A (PrepP)] wholly and clearly visible by sb/from somewhere □ *The owners were protesting against the proposed erection of storage tanks* ***in full view of*** *the hotel.* □ *It was bad enough to have his mother come to see him off at all, and to be hugged and kissed* ***in full view of*** *his grinning classmates was the last word in humiliation.*

in the fullness of time [A (PrepP)] (as is likely or bound to happen) when sufficient time has passed **V:** re-emerge, take over; grasp, realize, sth □ ***In the fullness of time***, *when the album was stuffed to overflowing, new pictures were placed between pages in strict chronological order.* L □ *I knew you'd be back for them, Sefton,* ***in the fullness of time***. ARG □ front, middle or end position.

in fun [A (PrepP)] not seriously; as a joke **V:** speak; say, do, sth □ *'I know Celia will never see forty again.' 'Oh come,' I said. 'She was exaggerating when she told you that. She was* ***in fun***.*'* CON □ *Grandpa didn't mean he was going to eat your ice cream, you silly girl. He only said it* ***in fun***. □ often preceded by *only* or *just*, as shown. ⇨ ⚠ (just) for fun.

in future [A (PrepP)] from now/then onwards (as the occasion arises) □ *'You could have insured your luggage, you know, for quite a small sum.' 'I know, and that's what we'll do* ***in future***.*'* □ *Oh, Peter—* ***in future***, *when I have a client in the office with me, please knock before you come in.* □ *That was when he decided that* ***in future*** *he'd better carry an extra gallon of petrol in the boot.* □ front, middle or end position. ⇨ in the past; ⚠ next entry; at the moment; at present.

in the future [A (PrepP)] at a time or times, or during a period, still to come **adj:** near, (not too/so) distant, immediate, foreseeable □ *He foresaw that he was going to have some anxious times, some very awkward moments* ***in the*** *near*

future. PE ◻ *The sun's heat will eventually destroy the earth, but that's* ***in the*** *distant* ***future***, *by some millions of years.* ◻ *It is fear of the unknown which frightens the businessman who has to rely upon a number of constants when making his plan for expansion* ***in the*** *immediate* ***future***. SC ◻ *A little work at French and German plus a little influence and charm will make you manager* ***in the*** *not-so-distant* ***future***. HAA ⇨ in the past; ⚠ previous entry; at present; at the moment.

in general...in particular broadly speaking or considered, without specifying or taking into account individual cases or exceptions, contrasted with singling out a special instance or example of its kind ◻ *The authors, who are Danish, clearly intend it as a kind of manual to guide the under-17s in their dealings with adults* ***in general***, *and with teachers and parents* ***in particular***. SC ◻ *About midnight I came to and realized we'd been talking about the world* ***in general*** *and nothing* ***in particular***. PP ◻ ***In general*** *the demonstrators have learnt from one another.* OBS ◻ HELENA: *It's almost as if he wanted to kill someone with it. And me* ***in particular***. *I've never seen such hatred in someone's eyes before.* LBA ◻ used one after the other, usu in order of headphrase, or separately with implied contrast; end position as a n modifier, usu front or middle position as a clause modifier.

in a good cause [Comp/A (PrepP)] for a good purpose; in order to achieve sth worthwhile or valuable **V:** be; fight; suffer, be wounded ◻ *Medical research volunteers can console themselves that not only are they suffering* ***in a good cause*** *but they are actually being paid to be ill.* ◻ *Noel said his evening and his wife's digestion were going to be ruined, but he supposed it was* ***in a good cause***. WDM ◻ *And when his Mum went away for a few days it was all* ***in a good cause*** *—she was probably making an attempt on the John O'Groats to Lands End cycling record.* TVT ◻ sometimes facetious or ironic.

in good/bad faith [A (PrepP)] sincerely; genuinely/with insincere purposes or aims **V:** act, intervene, negotiate, do business ◻ *The police would have found it difficult to inspire confidence unless they were negotiating* ***in good faith***. ◻ *There was a record of broken promises, of deals handled* ***in bad faith***.

(all) in good part [A (PrepP)] without becoming angry or offended; not annoyed or provoked (by what sb says etc) **V:** take, accept. **O:** criticism, banter, his remarks; it, everything ◻ *I thought her uncle's teasing remarks might have upset her, but no, she took it* ***in good part***. ◻ *'And some damn heated to-and-fros* (= arguments) *we have too, I can tell you. You ought to hear us at it—well, you already have, haven't you?' 'Yes, I—'* ***'All in good part***, *naturally.'* TGLY

in good time [A (PrepP)] a little, or well, before an appointed time or date, esp so that one can be ready for unforeseen difficulties or use the time to do sth else **V:** arrive, return; examine, consider, plan, sth ◻ *D-day was to be on the 5th June and I had to be back* ***in good time***. MFM ◻ *The train doesn't leave till 10.20 a.m. but you'll need to be there* ***in good time*** *if you want a corner seat.* ◻ *The matter should be quickly settled so that it can be considered* ***in good time*** *by the constituency parties and the trade unions in readiness for next year's conference.* T ⇨ ⚠ in time[1,2].

(all) in good time [A (PrepP)] after a reasonable or appropriate space of time, long or short, but not immediately ◻ *'Oh Harold,' she exclaimed, 'why all this mystification?' 'You'll find out* ***in good time***,*' he said grinning at her as he might have grinned at Irma.* PW ◻ *'Tell me all about yourself and Spencer and your house and everything.' 'I will* ***in good time***. *Right now, I'm only interested in getting you out of this pigsty.'* AITC ◻ *'It's not a bed I want,' Brigit cried out in anguish. 'It's* (the use of) *my own two feet!' 'I know, darling, I know.* ***All in good time***.*'* DC ◻ always said in response to sb's wish, or demand, for sth *now*. ⇨ ⚠ in time [1,2].

in one's heart (of hearts) [A (PrepP)] as one would, or should, admit to oneself if not to others; actually, if secretly **V:** know, believe; regret, hope. **adj:** inmost, secret ◻ ***In his heart*** *he wept for his own guilt and failure and for the echo of her words which he would spend the rest of his life trying to refute.* WI ◻ *Was he* ***in his heart of hearts*** *beneath that assuming English exterior, beginning to worry?* NS ◻ *I think officers and men knew* ***in their hearts*** *that if we lost at Alam Halfa we would probably have lost Egypt.* MFM ◻ *'Oh, I knew you'd take it like this,' Milly said, 'I knew it* ***in my heart of hearts***.*'* OMIH ◻ front, middle or end positions; adj used only with in one's heart.

in the heat of the moment [A (PrepP)] when extremely, though temporarily, angered, excited, enthusiastic, upset etc ◻ *He was sure that my anger, roused* ***in the heat of the moment*** *by an unfortunate remark, would be forgotten just as soon as the remark itself.* MFM ◻ *They were all shouting at me to hurry up and* ***in the heat of the moment*** *I forgot to pick up the envelope with the tickets.* ◻ *What the students were demanding* ***in the heat of*** *regional* ***debate*** *is probably less important in the long run than the spirit which informs their outlook.* L ◻ similarly in the heat of the argument, chase, struggle, excitement, etc as in last example; front, middle or end position.

in the heyday of sth [A (PrepP)] in/during the time when sb/sth was most popular, successful, or highly thought of ◻ *Munich, which* ***in the heyday of*** *the Nazi period was to be honoured as the 'Capital of the Movement', was then the focal point of all the forces of nationalism, right-wing radicalism and Nazism.* OBS ◻ ***In the heyday of*** *banner art no trade union branch had 'arrived' until it possessed its own Tutill* (manufacturer's name) *banner.* OBS ◻ (greyhound racing) ***The dogs' heyday*** *was when they were the only place a working man could regularly legally bet.* L

in high places at the top levels of government or administration; among people of power and influence **n:** corruption; friends, allies ◻ *I had sacked a peculiarly incompetent and indolent officer who had friends* ***in high places***. SD ◻ *The idea that she was murdered seems a little less extraordinary now. We know more about the CIA, the right wing of the FBI, blackmail and counter blackmail* ***in high places*** *today, don't we?* ST ◻ *I tried to develop radio as an art form in its own right, and nothing could be more cal-*

culated to induce apoplexy ***in High Places*** *than this.* NS ▫ *Insurance agent Kirby has stumbled on corruption* ***in high places****—information he can sell to the British Civil Service.* TVT ▫ usu modifies a preceding n, as shown.

in sb's honour [A (PrepP)] out of respect or admiration for sb or for his achievements, services; as a compliment to sb **V:** write, compose, paint, build, sth; name, call, sth ▫ *The new municipal building is to be called the Sir John Bolt Hall* ***in honour of*** *Sir John's many services to the community.* ▫ *There were three small pictures hanging on the far wall: 'Especially chosen* ***in your honour****,' Mrs Thompson said.* RATT ▫ *The feline hero of this memoir already enjoys the distinction of having a poem* ***in his honour*** *included in the 'Oxford Book of Modern Verse'.* OBS ▫ may modify a preceding n, as in last example.

in the hope of sth/that [A (PrepP)] (do sth) because one hopes that a favourable result will follow **o:** better luck next time, a good feed; finding a partner, attracting a larger audience. **cl:** that you'll agree, that nobody would notice, that their sins will be forgiven ▫ *The American company have been drilling in the Western Desert* ***in the hope of*** *striking large reserves similar to those in neighbouring Libya.* SC ▫ *Writers will write what they want, in answer to the need within them and* ***in the hope that*** *there is an audience who wants to see their plays.* RT

in a hurry[1] [Comp/A (PrepP)] (be) hurrying; (do sth) hurriedly (the implication being that there is insufficient, or barely sufficient, time for the activity etc suggested) **V:** pack, dress, revise. **det:** a, no, (not) any, rather a. **adj:** great, terrific, tremendous. **Inf:** to catch the bus, to get there first, to finish by 5 o'clock ▫ *'Did you speak to Jack about getting a job for me?' 'He was* ***in a hurry*** *to catch a train, but he'll see me on Monday morning.'* ▫ *I'm not* ***in any*** *special* ***hurry****, except that I've to collect Julia from nersery school at 12.15.* ▫ *I'm sure to have forgotten something. I always do when I have to pack* ***in a hurry****.* ▫ *Art restoration is finicky work. You simply can't do it* ***in a hurry.*** ▫ *to*-inf often, but not always, used after *be*.

in a hurry[2] [A (PrepP)] (informal) quickly; easily; willingly; perhaps ever (again) **V:** forget, come back, cross me again, re-marry ▫ *'It seems to have made a profound impression on you.' 'It's not the kind of experience you forget* ***in a hurry****.'* ILIH ▫ *He spoke about her as if he was going to murder her. 'I'll give her something she won't forget* ***in a hurry****.' he said.* CON ▫ *His remarks didn't bother me but I doubt if my wife will forgive him* ***in a hurry****.* ▫ *I smashed him up all right. He won't want to come and fight us again* ***in a hurry****.* LF ▫ *And she said, 'Their Mummy has found someone she likes better than the master, and she won't come back* ***in a hurry****.'* PW ▫ usu in constructions with *won't/wouldn't*.

in one's imagination/fancy [A (PrepP)] not in actual fact but in contemplation, daydream or illusion **V:** contemplate, picture, envisage, see ▫ *I have to admit that the Venice I saw was not quite up to the standard of the Venice I had visited so often* ***in my imagination****.* ▫ ***In fancy*** *he was on the mat in the yellow drawing room trying to explain to his wife why he had not immediately asserted himself as a father.* RM

in itself/oneself considered, or judged, in isolation — ignoring causes, results etc **n:** honour, courage; an evening's entertainment, the meal ▫ *Not only is the success an honour* ***in itself****, but it means that the team will be Scotland's representative in next season's European Cup competition.* SC ▫ *Jullien's conducting was an exciting performance* ***in itself****.* OBS ▫ *'They show,' said Miss Murphy, 'a certain courage. Courage* ***in itself*** *should be worth something.'* ARG ▫ placed immediately before or after n referred to.

in a jiffy etc [A (PrepP)] (informal) very soon; quickly; almost immediately; in a moment etc (qv); in two twos/ticks (qv) **o:** jiffy, ⚠ tick ▫ *'Where's Irma?' one of them asked. 'Just gone out to powder her nose, I think. She'll be back* ***in a jiffy****.'* PW ▫ *I asked him that conundrum you told me and he had the answer* ***in a tick****.*

in kind[1] [A (PrepP)] (pay sb) with goods, or services, instead of money ▫ *He's paid £70 a week beside what he receives* ***in kind****—a rent-free cottage, firewood, milk and potatoes, and so on.* ▫ *At various other times French television teams were allegedly given payola* (= bribes) ***in kind*** *to put Hava's clients in a favourable light.* L

in kind[2] [A (PrepP)] with the same kind of treatment, language etc as one has received or been subjected to **V:** pay back, answer, retaliate ▫ *Abba Eban is probably just the right kind of figure to stand up to the extreme provocation of some of the hotter challenges. He never replies* ***in kind*** *and always tries to defuse the situation.* ST ▫ *A fat lot of good informing the police will do, if there were no witnesses. I'd have paid him back* ***in kind*** *with my two fists.*

in the land of the blind the one-eyed man is king (saying) even a limited, or partial, ability gives one an advantage over those who have none ▫ *In effect, he* (a racing commentator) *makes the* (TV) *picture second best, and, in so doing, continues in a quite remarkable way the work of those who used to broadcast on sporting events via Daventry, and when* ***in the realm of the*** *listening* ***blind, a one-eyed commentator*** *could* ***be king.*** L ▫ often adapted, as shown.

in the last resort[1] [A (PrepP)] as the only thing left to try, do or accept in difficult circumstances; if nothing else succeeds; (as) a/one's last resort (qv) ▫ *Until now direct rule* (for Ulster) *from Westminster has been assumed to be the ultimate deterrent, the policy to be imposed* ***in the last resort****.* NS ▫ *I can, if I really want to get nasty, run the court meetings on strictly procedural lines.* ***In the last resort*** *I can adjourn meetings.* SC ▫ front, middle or end position. ⇨ ⚠ the last ditch.

in the last resort[2] [Disj (PrepP)] as an examination of the facts, or a line of reasoning, finally makes clear; in the final/last analysis (qv) ▫ ***In the last resort*** *the battle is won by the initiative and skill of regimental officers and men.* MFM ▫ *We all need to remember that* ***in the last resort*** *there is no such person as 'the common man'.* UL ▫ *Tavener's ideas are usually strong ones and are carried through with conviction but* ***in the last resort*** *it is difficult to avoid a feeling of thinness of invention.* L ▫ usu front or middle position. ⇨ ⚠ (as) a/one's last resort.

in lieu (of sth) [A (PrepP] (formal) instead (of sth); replacing sth **o:** rent; quarters, accommodation □ *The statement in Parliament that married personnel received quarters, or an allowance* ***in lieu*** *had caused intense irritation in the Army because it was untrue—the allowance* ***in lieu*** *being inadequate to get any reasonable accommodation.* MFM □ *'Don't bother about any pay tonight,' he said. 'Keep it* ***in lieu of*** *notice.'* HD

in the light of sth [A (PrepP)] according to the way of seeing, or understanding, sth which is suggested **V:** consider, think of, analyse, sth. **o:** reason, common sense; subsequent events, your remarks, the evidence; a parent's concern for his children □ *When people are going through difficult times they don't always see things* ***in the light of*** *reason.* □ ***In the light of*** *our own general expectations about events, we construct, out of a few elements, an account of what was likely to have occurred.* MFF □ *'In murdering anyone you have to avoid scandal!' 'I hadn't thought of it* ***in that light*** *before.'* OMIH □ variants, with reference to sth said earlier, or in contrast to it, in this, that, another, a different light.

in the long/short run [A (PrepP)] eventually; ultimately; (considered) over a long period and reaching an eventual solution or result (considered) over a short period **V:** agree, cooperate; help, benefit, sb □ *'Mrs Pettigrew keeps the whisky locked up.' Alec made a note. 'Do him good* ***in the long run,*** *' he commented. 'He drank too much for his age.'* MM □ *Dublin, London and Belfast are all concerned in Northern Ireland's future and* ***in the long run*** *tripartite agreement must be sought.* SC □ *We were always beginning jobs and then being forced to break them off, which* ***in the long run*** *wastes more time than the odd ten minutes spent smoking.* RATT □ ***In the short run****, he'll get very sick;* ***in the long run****, he'll get fit and strong again.* □ front, middle or end position. ⇨ ⚠ next entry.

in the long etc term [A (PrepP)] looking, or planning, ahead for a long etc period, esp when considering what policy, action is possible, most suitable or effective **adj:** long, ⚠ short, medium □ *The conditions in which some of the travellers* (gypsies, people in show business, etc) *have been forced to live have long caused concern.* ***In the long term*** *permanent accommodation is the best solution.* SC □ *Such a reorganisation* (of alliances) *could only come about as the result of changes in our society so radical that they are unimaginable* ***in the short term.*** □ *More seriously, the dockers would perhaps have hazarded the* ***long-term*** *future of their own port and their jobs in it.* ST □ *Forms of saving or paying in advance for* ***short-term*** *if recurrent purposes, as with the payings-in for Christmas or holidays...* UL □ *Britain's North Sea oil reserves will ease her financial problems* ***in the short*** *and* ***medium terms.*** □ *The* ***long-term*** *effects cannot be predicted—too much depends on the international political and financial situation.* □ front, middle or end position; attrib use *a* ***long-term*** *investment, a* ***short-term*** *advantage,* ***medium-term*** *growth.* ⇨ ⚠ previous entry.

in a loud etc voice [A (PrepP)] loudly, hoarsely etc **V:** proclaim, declare, announce sth. **adj:** loud, low, hoarse, piercing; cold, angry, cheerful □ (stage direction) *Takes letter and reads contents* ***in a*** *dead flat but* ***loud voice****—as though it were a proclamation.* R □ *Ever since Christine's death, he had been reserved and silent, only speaking to George when it was necessary and then* ***in a cold voice.*** PE □ *'Of course not, Dolly,' he said* ***in a voice*** *that tried to express an infinite sufference of human stupidity.* RM □ describes either physical quality of sound, or mood, attitude conveyed by speaker; sometimes followed by clause as in last example, in which case adj usu omitted.

in the main [Disj (PrepP)] mainly; generally; usually; almost always; for the most part[1,2] (qv) □ ***In the main****, the art of the potter has been a secular art—but a secular art which its innumerable devotees have treated with an almost idolatrous reverence.* HAH □ *Though General de Gaulle's visit to Canada and the United States will be* ***in the main*** *a State occasion, like his visit to this country, there are a number of important questions which he is likely to raise with President Eisenhower.* SC □ *Some days of course, she's still very unwell. But* ***in the main*** *she's hideously bored, I'm afraid.* HAA □ front, middle or end position.

in the making evolving or being made **n:** history, nation; writer, artist; neurotic misfits; a new deal, a TV series □ *Dickens' depiction of the American scene in 'Martin Chuzzlewit' was deeply resented over there, and indeed he did not allow for the fact that he was observing a nation* ***in the making.*** □ *I could have taken a different literary example—namely, what a critic does when he looks at a first novel and says: 'Here is a great writer* ***in the making.****'* L □ *Hopefully, a new philosophy of medicine, less heroic and individualistic, more logical and democratic, is* ***in the making.*** OBS □ usu modifies a preceding n, but see last example.

in a manner of speaking [Disj (PrepP)] (informal) as could be said; as one way of putting it would be □ *'What are you doing hanging about there?' 'Well, sir, hanging about is my job,* ***in a manner of speaking.*** *My card, sir.' And Robert found himself reading: 'Metropolitan Police, Special Branch'.* EM □ *Rose thought he had gone for his paper—which he had* ***in a manner of speaking.*** *He had it under his arm and grapes in his other hand.* TSMP □ accompanies statement, esp description or definition of sth.

in the manner to which one is accustomed [A (PrepP)] (catchphrase) matching a standard (of living) no less comfortable, refined or luxurious than one is used to **V:** maintain, keep, support, entertain, sb □ *A Victorian suitor would be expected to satisfy a girl's father that he could support her* ***in the manner to which she was accustomed.*** □ *She had to find herself a job. She did—as a telephone operator. It was hardly calculated to keep her* ***in the manner to which she*** *had* ***become accustomed.*** OBS □ *That most prestigious of dog shows, Crufts, takes place next week and Tim Heald finds out what it costs to keep a champion dog* ***in the manner to which he is accustomed.*** RT

in a matter of minutes etc [A (Prep)] in a relatively short time **o:** minutes, ⚠ seconds, moments; (a few) hours, two weeks □ *It could have been captured* ***in a matter of minutes*** *and its defence soundly organised with time to spare.*

MFM □ ***In a matter of hours****, the assailant's car was identified.* TO

in the meantime [A (PrepP)] meanwhile; meantime; during a previously defined, or understood, period □ *Prissie in her clear self-possessed voice* (was) *saying that she could take over very well, at least* ***in the meantime****.* DC □ *Only the blindest optimism would lead anyone to believe that Ulster will find peace for many years.* ***In the meantime*** *the continuation of any kind of coherently ordered existence depends almost entirely on the army.* NS □ front, middle or end position.

in a measure [A (PrepP)] (formal) partly, or largely, but not wholly **det:** a, some; great, no small □ *There is a theory that there are 'murderees', people themselves* ***in a measure*** *responsible for the crimes committed against them.* □ *The success of Mr Kruschev's farm programmes depends* ***in great measure*** *on the production of these lands.* OBS □ *Large charitable organizations, that get no funds from national governments, finance their international aid programmes from money given by private citizens. This work* ***in no small measure*** *helps raise living standards in the world's poorest countries.* ⇨ ⚠ in full etc measure.

in the middle/midst of sth [A (PrepP)] while sb is engaged in (doing) sth (the implication often being that he is busy or harassed); while some activity, or action, is in progress **o:** (all) this noise, hubbub, disturbance; activity, movement; breakfast, lunch □ ***In the midst of*** *all this, Jimmy had to go and get his finger jammed in a keyhole.* □ *He hadn't taken two spoonfuls when the Emergency bell rang. 'Damn it,' he said, 'Why do I always have to be interrupted* ***in the middle of*** *a meal?'* □ *He found it almost impossible to concentrate on business details.* ***In the middle of*** *reading something, his attention would wander.* PE

in one's mind [A (PrepP)] mentally; in one's thoughts **V:** see, picture, sth □ *Prissie would make a wonderful wife for Guy. No doubt already* ***in her mind*** *she was admiring this house as its mistress.* DC ⇨ ⚠ next entry.

in one's mind's eye [A (PrepP)] as pictured mentally **V:** see, picture, behold, sth □ *The summers I look back on myself all,* ***in my mind's eye****, turn into 1959 which was so hot for so long that reservoirs turned into patches of cracked mud.* L □ *Frowning, he saw the chart now* ***in his mind's eye*** *but not clearly.* PM □ *Edward Burne-Jones, then a very young undergraduate, wrote describing what he had seen* ***in his mind's eye*** *—the abbey and long procession of the faithful.* OBS ⇨ ⚠ previous entry.

in a moment etc [A (PrepP)] very soon; quickly; almost immediately; in a jiffy etc (qv); in two twos/ticks (qv) **o:** moment, ⚠ minute, second □ *Just rest, dear. The doctor will be here* ***in a moment****.* DC □ *Oh, please come in and wait for Jack. He'll be back* ***in a minute****.*

in one's more sober etc moments [A (PrepP)] when one does, or can, think more calmly, realistically etc **V:** realize, admit, acknowledge, recognize, sth. **adj:** more sober, more lucid, gayer, less optimistic □ *Thus the driver who has his new car scratched by an incompetent lady may be moved to call out some deprecatory remark concerning women drivers, without,* ***in his more sober moments****, necessarily endorsing the anti-feminist position implied.* SNP □ *She did sometimes* ***in her gloomier moments*** *despair of ever completing the task she had taken on.* □ *I couldn't remember how I knew he was an adopted child. Perhaps in one of* ***his more communicative moments*** *he had told me so himself.*

in name (only) entitled to bear a name, or dignity, but not functioning or behaving as such □ *Finally a compromise was arrived at. Nura would marry Rati, but be a husband* ***in name only****.* TO □ *Well, he may be a minister, but he's a Christian* ***in name only*** *if that's how he treats people.* □ usu modifies a preceding n, as shown.

in the name of sth/sb [A (PrepP)] naming or using sb/sth as an authority, precedent, example, justification etc **o:** freedom, religion; the Company, his master □ *There have been more wars, persecutions and massacres perpetrated* ***in the name of*** *religion than from any other single cause.* □ *...the encouraging precedent of the Clyde Steamer services, which at one time British Railways wanted to contract* ***in the name of*** *the company.* SC □ *These duties will require your direct contact* ***in my name*** *with the several governments, military staffs and agencies of NATO nations.* MFM □ *If what has happened to Dr Verwoerd awakens disgust, how much more disgust is awakened by the things now being done* ***in his name****.* SC □ in the name of sb/sth common when n refers to a group or organization; in sb's/sth's name common when n is a pron or denotes an individual (specified by name or function). ⇨ ⚠ next entry.

in the name of God etc used as an oath, expletive or exclamation; for goodness etc sake(!) (qv) **o:** God, ⚠ heaven, all that's holy □ *Now, why does he want to come busting in here,* ***in God's name****?* □ *'It's almost time to go and try again. Does anyone want to?'* ***'In heaven's name****, no!' said Leicester.* TBC □ *Johnny!* ***In the name of all that's holy****! How did you get here?* ⇨ ⚠ previous entry.

in the nature of sb/sth [Comp/A (PrepP)] like sb/sth; similar (to sb/sth); as having the character of sb/sth □ *Of course, underground explosions are more* ***in the nature of*** *simple outward pushes on to the surrounding rock.* NSC □ *The ease with which he found the stones came* ***in the nature of*** *an anticlimax.* ARG □ *I hoped they would look upon me* ***in the nature of*** *an adviser and helper rather than as an overseer or critic.* ⇨ ⚠ next entry.

in the nature of things [Disj (PrepP)] things, circumstances being what they are; as is likely or inevitable, either generally or in particular circumstances □ *Some productions were,* ***in the nature of things*** *less good than others and occasionally a kindly critic would give a timely warning.* NS □ *Although* ***in the nature of things*** *it was unlikely that any other baby could have been as sweet as little Stephen, any baby at all would have been better than none.* TGLY □ *His relations with his clients were also cut and dried, very little personal feeling could* ***in the nature of things*** *come into them.* PW □ front, middle or end position. ⇨ ⚠ previous entry.

in the nick of time [A (PrepP)] (informal) at precisely the right, or most opportune, moment; just in time not to be too late (to achieve or avoid sth) **V:** arrive; save, rescue, sb □ *Hess* (Hitler's deputy) *was convinced that there must be statesmen in Britain who could be brought to see reason* ***in the nick of time.*** NS □ *On the other side are those who* (think) *that we should continue as we are going now and that technology will come to the rescue* ***in the nick of time****, as always.* L □ *I nearly cooked a chicken for supper last night but I remembered* ***in the nick of time*** *that Jack's a vegetarian, so we had a cheese soufflé instead.*

in no time (at all) [A (PrepP)] extremely quickly; very soon □ GEORGE: *I'm all right, I'd like a cup of tea though.* MRS ELLIOT: *It's all ready. And I'll get you something to eat* ***in no time.*** EGD □ ***In no time at all*** *they were buckling on their safety belts and coming down to Woodbourne Aerodrome.* WI □ ***In*** *less than* ***no time*** *I would be standing, clammy and paralysed, in front of a group of earnest students.* BM □ DAVIES: *I'll give you a hand! We'll put up that shed together! See? Get it done* ***in*** *next to* ***no time!*** TC □ no may be modified by *less than* or *next to*, as shown; front, middle or end position.

in no uncertain terms etc [A (PrepP)] (speaking) plainly and emphatically so that no one can be mistaken about one's meaning etc **V:** say so, explain; protest, resist. **n:** terms, ⚠ fashion, manner □ *I broadcast a printed manifesto forbidding the practice* ***in no uncertain terms****—and even that did not completely stop it.* SD □ *You see he went on to do what Granny would have called 'coupling your name' with Terence Lambert's and* ***in no uncertain terms.*** HAA □ *This island monster clearly has no connexion at all with the Loch Ness Monster and I have said as much in the columns of the 'Daily Tale'* ***in no uncertain fashion.*** RM □ *The word 'no' didn't exist for her in English: but she had shaken her head* ***in no uncertain fashion.*** PW

in a nutshell [Disj (PrepP)] (informal) in a brief and concisely worded form □ *Incredibly (when you think about it), the President was running on his record. He was governing and seen to be governing, and that* ***in a nutshell*** *was the campaign.* NS □ *. . .this problem which,* ***in a nutshell****, is a problem of the relation between body and mind generally.* SNP □ often used with v *put*, as in put in a nutshell (Vol 1) (qv).

in one piece [A (PrepP)] (informal) safe and unharmed **V:** return; escape; be retrieved □ *We never mixed it with German fighters if we could avoid it, for our main duty was to get home* ***in one piece.*** RFW □ *Usually, depressed adolescents endure a few grey years and emerge, more or less* ***in one piece****, into adult life.* ST □ *I was so glad to see the car back* ***in one piece*** *that I forgot to ask him if he had filled up the tank again.*

in sb's/one's opinion [Disj (PrepP)] as sb thinks; as information, experience etc lead him to believe; in sb's book (qv); in sb's view (qv); to my mind (qv); to sb's way of thinking (qv) □ *But a surgeon specialist at the same hospital said later that he disagreed. He said: '****In my opinion****, the vertebra is compressed not fractured.'* DM □ *I have now much pleasure in announcing the winner of the entry which was,* ***in the*** *unanimous* ***opinion of*** *all the judges, the best.*

in opposition (to sb/sth) [Comp/A (PrepP)] fighting, contending, arguing against, sb/sth; contrary to, or defying, sb/sth **V:** be, stand: leave, resign; marry, write □ *The two wings* (of a political party) *would not do so well separately and* ***in opposition to*** *each other in an election as they have done together.* SC □ *If Jenny chooses to marry you* ***in opposition to*** *my wishes, I cannot of course prevent her.*

in order to do sth so as to do sth; with the aim of doing sth; so that sth will happen, be done, become possible □ ***In order to*** *make these calculations it is essential to have as much information as possible about the terrain through which the road is to go.* NSC □ *Three ministers in the South African Government yesterday gave a Press Conference* ***in order to*** *put their side of the case.* SC □ *'Why did we leave so early?' '****In order that*** *the old man might go to bed.'* □ variant, in order that sb may do sth, less often used.

in the ordinary way [A (PrepP)] normally; usually; according to (one's) usual habits □ *You were lucky to find me in.* ***In the ordinary way*** *I'd have been off to work by now.* □ (advertisement) *And although* ***in the ordinary way*** *these books would cost £4, £5 or more, members of the Club are privileged to buy them for only £1!* □ usu front or middle position.

in other words [Conj (PrepP)] put a different way; differently expressed; that is (to say)[1] (qv) □ *Without compassion people become self-centred and greedy—****in other words*** *subject to all the Seven Deadly Sins.* TO □ *Pressure on the surface of an object varies with the depth of the object below the surface of the water.* ***In other words****, the farther down you go, the greater the pressure.* □ front or middle position.

in one's/its own right because of what one is in oneself (by nature, character, achievements, interest, usefulness etc) and not because of a relationship, or connection, with sb/sth else □ *There were some prominent Masons in the National Assembly, but they were influential* ***in their own right*** *rather than as Masons.* L □ *Among Reich's fellow students was Annie Park, whom he married in 1921 and who later became a well known analyst* ***in her own right.*** OBS □ *If Fife is to become a regional authority* ***in its own right****, Kirkcaldy is likely to become the administrative centre for the county.* SC □ *The packaging of goods for sale has become a large industry* ***in its own right.*** NSC □ usu modifies a preceding n or adj, as shown.

in passing [Disj (PrepP)] incidentally; in addition; by the way (qv) **V:** note, observe (sth); state, remark □ ***In passing*** *I would claim that such programmes might well prove what I have always suspected— that nothing would make more compulsive viewing than the 'unpacking' of the human mind.* L □ *I note* ***in passing*** *that it was the judges, who now condemn it, who invented the ritual in the first place.* L

in the past [A (PrepP)] at a time or times, or during a period of time, before the time of speaking or that has long ago elapsed **adj:** recent; dim and distant □ *If any of these things were true Guy would not have given up so easily.* ***In the past*** *he had had more tenacity than that.* DC □ *The fact that rock layers exist which have* *been folded into mountain ranges demonstrates the action of these forces* ***in the past***. NSC □ *The seal-woman bore seven sons to that exiled son of Clan Donald and thus populated the island with Macroons* ***in the*** *dim* ***past***. RM □ ***In the*** *recent* ***past*** *there have been unmistakable signs of strain in certain parts of our economy.* ⇨ in future; in the future; at present; ⚠ at the moment.

in peace [A (PrepP)] undisturbed; unharassed; quiet(ly) and free(ly), esp to do as one likes **V:** live, die; sleep, work □ *The main object of the couple's lives, the one thing they still had to do before they could die* ***in peace***, *was to guide Robert into a job where he'd be safe from the sack.* CON □ *'Oh, there's a man sweeping leaves.' 'That's all, dear, Just a man with a barrow. So you can sleep* ***in peace***.*'* DC

in person[1] [A (PrepP)] physically present, as distinct from being simply known; in the flesh (qv) **V:** be acquainted with; meet; see, sb □ *And when he appeared* ***in person***, *his conversation continued in exactly the same tone as his letters.* AH □ *She has a charm that more beautiful women often lack. But until you actually meet her* ***in person*** *you can't know what I mean.*

in person[2] [A (PrepP)] oneself personally, in contrast with sb else, esp sb acting as an agent or substitute **V:** attend to, sth; see, interview, consult, sb □ *You must go yourself. Dr Kingsley will be flattered if you go to see him* ***in person***. TBC □ *Sorry not to look after this* ***in person***; *I'm madly busy getting ready to go to the States.* UTN

in a pig's ear [Disj (PrepP)] (slang) never; not likely □ *'I will drive of course. You may sit behind me.'* ***In a pig's ear*** *I may sit behind you, Bowen thought to himself.* ILIH □ *'I'm sure he's an honest fellow.' 'Honest?* ***In a pig's ear***! *You're a poor judge of character.'* □ *'As a local resident you'll be expected to give a donation.'* ***'In a pig's ear*** *I will! Let the church-goers see to their own church roof.'* □ precedes or follows repetition of an immediately previous request, proposal, expression of opinion.

in place of sth/sb [A (PrepP)] instead of, to replace, replacing, sth/sb □ (recipe) *Make it up in exactly the same way but substitute 1 level tablespoonful of flour and used vanilla essence* ***in place of*** *the lemon essence.* WI □ *Even grafting new blood vessels* ***in place of*** *the diseased coronary arteries has been tried.* NSC □ *The agency have rung up. Do you want another girl sent along* ***in place of*** *Miss Lewis?* □ *Jill has gone to another job. Whoever comes* ***in her place*** *will find it hard to match her efficiency and flair.*

in plain English [A (PrepP)] bluntly, or straightforwardly, expressed **V:** express oneself, make one's point □ *What I meant* ***in plain English*** *was that it would be easier to stand him a meal if he was on the spot: but I didn't put it that way.* CON □ *If you want the flat to yourself for some reason this afternoon, why don't you say so* ***in plain English***? ⇨ ⚠ plain speaking.

in point of fact [Disj (PrepP)] as is actually the case, the truth, a fact; in fact (qv) □ *There had been rumours of a Turkish invasion. Now* ***in point of fact*** *the rumour of the arrival of the Turks was entirely true.* BN □ ***'In point of fact***,*' he told me, 'it's not strictly true that I still have to pick up the checks. Quite often I get a free lunch.'* ST □ *He looks more like a great musician, a famous surgeon even, than anyone's idea of a painter who is also a genius.* ***In point of fact*** *Kandinsky began by studying law at Moscow University.* G □ front, middle or end position.

in principle [Disj (PrepP)] (considered) as a general idea, belief, theory, plan (omitting details, special circumstances etc) **V:** admit, accept, agree (to sth) □ *Though he* (the Minister of Agriculture) *had agreed* ***in principle*** *that Charollais bulls should be imported at a convenient opportunity, this would not be done for the time being.* T □ *A programme of positive eugenics is unthinkable in a society which respects the rights of individuals. But it is* ***in principle*** *possible.* L □ *At home she had always been in rebellion against her mother.* ***In principle*** *she accepted and even applauded her.* PW ⇨ ⚠ (as) a matter of principle; on principle; on the principle of sth/that.

in private [A (PrepP)] privately; when or where alone, or with one other person **V:** argue, fight; discuss, arrange, sth □ *It's when a man—or woman—starts to drink a lot* ***in private*** *that he's in danger of becoming an alcoholic.* □ *I could feel that he was waiting for Luke to leave. He had something to say to me* ***in private***. NM ⇨ next entry.

in public [A (PrepP)] publicly; able to be seen, or heard, by anyone **V:** argue, brawl; debate, discuss, sth □ *She could have thrashed both James and Bernard for losing their tempers* ***in public***. HAA □ *He had made his views known* ***in public*** *on many occasions, so his decision not to vote along party lines should have come as no surprise.* ⇨ previous entry.

in question involved, or already being discussed **n:** person, gentleman, young lady; affair, publication, travel agency □ *He asked, 'How's Timothy?' 'Beginning to fall in love at last,' she said. Gerald asked, 'Do I know the girl* ***in question***?*'* ASA □ *The gentleman* ***in question*** *has had a few brushes with the law in connection with property deals.* □ *At last the object* ***in question*** *is usually knocked down* (= sold at an auction) *to some outsider for ten times the price either student could pay.* BM □ always modifies a preceding n, which is always common (rather than proper), though the person etc may already have been specifically named.

in the raw unrefined; not made to seem more pleasant, acceptable etc than it is **n:** life, nature, warfare □ *I admire Ibsen's stagecraft but I find it more and more difficult to sit through hours of life* ***in the raw***. HAA □ *Just in case you leap to the conclusion that the title* ('Savage') *indicates a film about primitive life* ***in the raw***, *perhaps it should be said that it's no such thing.* TVT □ usu modifies a preceding n; esp in the collocation *life* ***in the raw***.

in reality [Disj (PrepP)] really; actually; factually, or (more) accurately, considered or defined □ *The Prime Minister* (of France) *is responsible to Parliament, but is not* ***in reality*** *head of the Executive.* OBS □ *The courts call what he does 'breaking and entering';* ***in reality*** *it usually means pushing in a poorly bolted back door and taking a few pounds set aside for the milkman.* OBS □ front, middle or end position.

in/with regard to sth (formal) concerning,

referring to, sth; as far as sth is concerned; with respect (to sth) (qv) **o:** request, application; report, notice, statement □ *Marshal Tito delivered a report on the tasks before the alliance* ***in regard to*** *the further development of Socialism in Yugoslavia.* SC □ ***With regard to*** *your request for an additional assistant, I can only say at this stage that this is being considered.* □ *I foresee no difficulties* ***in that regard.*** □ variant in this, that regard. ⇨ ⚠ in terms of sth.

in respect of sth (formal) with special reference to (a particular cost, item, time etc) **o:** rates, water charges; equipment; lighting; the current quarter, financial year □ (They) *announced that the amount to be expended* ***in respect of*** *the current year under the trust deed is £19,157.* T □ *. . .and on the other hand a tendency for like to marry like* ***in respect of*** *intelligence.* L □ *Substantial increases can be now expected* ***in respect of*** *gas and water costs.* ⇨ ⚠ with respect to sth.

in response (to sth) [A (PrepP)] as a verbal answer, or physical/emotional reaction (to sth) **o:** question, inquiry, appeal; encouragement, provocation □ ***In response to*** *Brigit's question he admitted that they had had fun catching the kitten.* DC □ *If you treat a child with consistent care and kindness you are bound to get some trust and affection* ***in response.*** □ *Money sent* ***in response to*** *the broadcast appeal will be used to buy blankets and medical supplies.*

in return (for sth) [A (PrepP)] as payment, recompense or retaliation (for sth received, or done to or for one) **o:** your kindness, his insolence, benefits received □ *'She likes to feel one is doing something for her.' 'And what does she do* ***in return****?'* PW □ *Let me buy the gin* ***in return for*** *all your kindness while I have been staying here.* □ *Sarah, plump and placid, gave her a wide friendly smile* ***in return.*** DC

in the right etc spirit [A (PrepP)] with the correct, or a suitable, mental or emotional attitude or response **V:** approach, accept, view, interpret, sth. **adj:** right, ⚠ proper; wrong □ *Men of first-rate ability described transcendental experiences which come to those who, in good health, under proper conditions and* ***in the right spirit****, take the drug.* DOP □ *You're approaching marriage* ***in the wrong spirit*** *if you're already making arrangements in case it doesn't work out.* □ *I would rather have done the job myself but nevertheless accepted his offer of help* ***in the proper spirit.*** □ *Ghost stories are perhaps the only kind of folk tale which we can still take* ***in the spirit in which*** *they* ***are offered.*** □ variant in the spirit in which sth is intended/meant/offered.

in the round [A (PrepP)] in entirety, including all aspects and qualities; solidly; in three dimensions **V:** see, view; describe, capture, sb/sth □ *We do need literary popularisers like Rowse whose enthusiasm for, and love of, Shakespeare communicate themselves to the reader, firing his imagination and making him see the plays, the lines, the characters vividly and* ***in the round.*** OBS □ *One does not expect from anyone's diary history* ***in-the-round.*** *What, however, one is entitled to ask for is some kind of easily recognisable impression of the author.* NS □ *In a country place characters emerged '****in the round****' and in variety.* AH □ MONTY: *For her the world is black and white. She can't see shades in character—know what I mean? She can't see people* ***in the round.*** CSWB

in a row successively, one after the other over a long or short period of time □ *Which jockey rode 11 winners* ***in a row*** *in the 1959-60 National Hunt Season?* TO □ (of a rugby match between Scotland and England) *It's the fact that we are going for a fourth win* ***in a row*** *over England that makes it important for us not to take them lightly.* RT □ usu follows n referring to a number of incidents etc.

in the same way [Conj (PrepP)] similarly; likewise **adv mod:** much, exactly □ *She swears she didn't mean to leave Nurse Ellen down there to die.* ***In the same way*** *she says she only pretended to kidnap the children.* DC □ *Young athletes need encouragement.* ***In*** *much* ***the same way****, young artists need the guidance of established performers.*

in the same etc way (as sb/sth) [A (PrepP)] using the same etc methods, displaying the same etc features, conforming with the same etc rules or laws, (as sb/sth) **adv mod:** quite, just, much, exactly. **adj:** the same, a different; other, various □ *One of the hallmarks of ideological fanatics is that they do not use words* ***in the same way as*** *other people.* SC □ *Two children born of the same parents and brought up* ***in*** *exactly* ***the same way*** *may grow up to be very different in character.* □ *Fred was handsome too, though* ***in a different way****, having fair hair and blue eyes.* □ *'How does this coffee grinder work?' '****In*** *much* ***the same way as*** *the old one, only it's electric so you don't have to turn the handle all the time.'*

in search of sb/sth looking for and hoping to find sb/sth **V:** come, go; travel the world □ *Because baboons roam widely during the day* ***in search of*** *food we do not use hides.* NSC □ *Mr Blearney and several of the guests came* ***in search of*** *him.* HD □ *The more people who visit the island* ***in search of*** *peace and quiet, of course, the less likely they are to find it.*

in secret [A (PrepP)] secretly; without the knowledge of others, or of anyone outside a small group of people who have the same information □ *First* ***in secret*** *she had to practise walking until she was reasonably strong.* DC □ *They pretended that they had broken off their relationship but continued to meet* ***in secret.*** □ *I daresay that they turned to older religions in times of stress — and not entirely* ***in secret*** *either.*

in self-defence [A (PrepP)] in order to protect one's life, reputation, rights etc □ *Any disaster in their view must be the work of terrorists, gangsters and intimidators. Africans shot in the back must have been shot by the police* ***in self-defence.*** SC □ *I felt I had to leave home* ***in self defence.*** *I simply wasn't being allowed to grow up.* □ legally admissible excuse for killing, wounding, striking sb — if there is sufficient provocation; legal formula *to plead* ***self defence.***

in a sense [Disj (PrepP)] if interpreted, understood, considered, in one way rather than in any of several other possible ways **det:** one, a certain, another; this, that; not any; some, every □ ***In a sense****, Beaverbrook was not a character* *of the first importance. He wasn't a serious character, he wasn't an Archbishop of Canterbury or a Home Secretary.* L □ *Thus the conclusions to be drawn from the list of executions are* ***in no sense*** *scientific. Much more detailed evidence is needed about the background to the murderers and their crimes.* OBS *Although the father earns a high salary the family would be better off* ***in many senses*** *if he had a lower-paid job in Britain.* □ *He is a small, mean little man. Small* ***in every sense*** *of the word, with a small man's aggression.* EGD □ can be used to emphasize preceding adj, as in last example.

in the shape/form of sth/sb specifically; in particular (introduces a word or words which provide a particular instance of a general idea introduced earlier) □ *No provision whatever for advanced level work* ***in the shape of*** *a laboratory or practical room* (had been made). NSC □ *This walking stomach* (a young racoon) *had a quarter of a pound of minced steak or heart, and fruit* ***in the shape of*** *bananas, guavas, or pawpaws.* DF □ *The following morning the boss announced a pleasant surprise* ***in the form of*** *a two-day holiday with pay.* □ *After facing these dangers, he was trapped for us by what he considers a worse hazard—an interviewer,* ***in the shape of*** *Jim Crace.* RT

in silence [A (PrepP)] without saying anything □ *She handed him back the manuscript* ***in silence****, with her remarks written between the lines and on several attached loose sheets.* TCM □ *They sat there a moment* ***in silence****. 'I suppose —' he began. 'We'd better go—' she said at the same moment.* WI

in a similar etc vein [A (PrepP)] a similar etc mood, manner, style; dealing with similar etc subject matter **V:** go on, continue, ramble on; work, paint, compose, write. **adj:** (a) similar, (the) same, (a) different; (a) lighter, popular, melancholy □ *Many other stories* ***in a similar vein*** *could be quoted from historical writings of many countries.* SNP □ *There were many more tributes* ***in the same vein****. We tend to overpraise the dead.* NS □ *'Those big pop eyes of yours are glinting with lust,' Charles would have said. 'Is it the girl or the car?' We would have continued* ***in this vein*** *for some time, becoming more and more outrageous.* RATT □ *The poem opened with the description of a night out* ***in the vein of*** *'Sweeney Agonistes'* (a poem by T S Eliot), *designed to show the mastery of vernacular which Eliot felt a modern poem required.* ST □ often modifies a preceding n as shown; variant in the vein of sb/sth.

in/into the (wee) small hours [A (PrepP)] in the first few hours after midnight, often as prolongation of the day before **V:** continue, go on, sit up □ *Dick Thompson was shot last night, or rather* ***in the small hours****.* TGLY □ *So far I had not mentioned to anyone the signal I had received* ***in the small hours*** *of that morning.* MFM □ *It is not surprising that the discussions that went on* ***into the wee small hours*** *in the Craigcrook became increasingly unprofitable.* SC

in so far as [Conj] to the extent that; in the sense that; in as/so much as (qv) □ *But* ***in so far as*** *we are animals, our business is at all costs to survive.* DOP □ *This small boy was something of an exception to the rule* ***in so far as*** *he appeared to seek knowledge rather than profit.* BM □ ***Insofar****, then,* ***as*** *I was concerned, the 'ground force command' problem was closed by the end of 1944.* MFM □ occas written insofar as.

in so/as many words [A (PrepP)] clearly; explicitly; in exactly the same words as are claimed, or reported, to have been used □ *'Have you told her definitely that you're going?' 'Not* ***in so many words****.'* SPL □ *No one's said anything,* ***in so many words****, but it's fairly clear that you have found some way of improving on the job from the money point of view.* HD □ *I thought he was being a selfish, little pig and I told him so* ***in as many words****.* □ often neg or neg implications.

in the space of sth [A (Prep)] within, during, a period not exceeding a specified period of time **o:** five minutes, two years, a few hours □ (about a series of television films) *This week it's Norway. Then Germany, Denmark and Iceland, all* ***in the space of*** *the next five weeks.* RT □ *There she was sitting talking to me, just her usual self, and then* ***in the space of*** *a few minutes she was dead.* □ *One can't expect a newly independent state to have solved its economic difficulties* ***in the space of*** *only two years.*

in spite of oneself (do sth) compulsively or only half willingly, esp contrary to one's formed opinions, real wishes, etc **V:** laugh, cry, shudder; go back; watch, listen (to), forgive, envy, sb □ *'You see,' (and* ***in spite of herself*** *she couldn't help half smiling), 'there is a woman, a harpy, who has got her claws into him.'* PW □ *I've seen him settle down in front of TV and be so tired that he falls asleep* ***in spite of himself****.* □ *It takes a certain kind of courage to be so ruthless.* ***In spite of myself*** *I almost admire him.*

in spite of sth [Conj] despite, notwithstanding, sth; succeed although opposed or hindered by sth; (fail) although supported or aided by sth **o:** one's inclinations; poverty, wealth; many warnings, the dangers involved, all the doctor's efforts □ *The waiting list for Chelmsley* (a hospital) *is 150 and* ***in spite of*** *the over-crowding,* ***in spite of*** *the 40-bedded children's wards, they're going to try to accept them.* NS □ *Britain,* ***in spite of*** *her wealth and power, was beginning to sense the danger of standing alone in a more hostile world.* OBS □ *'The Government can make enormous mistakes and we can still survive.' 'As long as we have our Civil Service?' 'No, no. Even* ***in spite of*** *it.'* L

in (full) strength [A (PrepP)] with force and vigour; with all the resources and/or personnel available; in large numbers **V:** attack; be present, turn up □ *If Rommel attacked* ***in strength****, as was expected soon, the Eighth Army would fall back on the Delta.* MFM □ (reader's letter) *The civilian population used to turn out* ***in strength*** *every evening to watch our guard mounting parade in the town square.* RT □ *The Robinsons from Westhill Farm were there* ***in full strength*** *down to the latest grandchild.*

in (the grand/great) style [A (PrepP)] on a very lavish scale, or in accordance with high (or perhaps false) standards of social behaviour **V:** live, entertain, travel, get married □ *Phrases like 'very fancy' and 'doing it* ***in style****'—that is, in the style in which posh folk are hazily assumed to pass their every day—strike the same note.* UL

□ *He was born in a seedy area of Manchester and can remember moving* (house) *with the family belongings piled on a handcart. Now he's doing it* ***in style***. TVT □ *He and his wife live* ***in style***. *He is very proud of his children.* SPL □ *Wilders Fergus, then a rising man of business, married Elvira Summerfield and set up house* ***in the grand style***. L □ *If this is provincial Rep* (= repertory theatre), *it is being conducted* ***in the grand style***. NS □ often used in expression *do it/things* ***in style***.

in succession [A (PrepP)] one after another in an unbroken sequence **adj:** quick, rapid, swift; unending; monotonous □ *The tray* (of drinks) *came past again, and this time I took a couple.* ***In*** *rapid* ***succession*** *I tossed them back.* CON □ *He lost three more* (fish) ***in*** *quick* ***succession*** *then handed the rod to Koji without a word.* BM □ *This'll be the fourth year* ***in succession*** *that we've not had a proper holiday.* □ may modify a preceding n.

in sympathy (with sb) [A (Prep P)] because, or in order to demonstrate that, one shares the feelings, or approves the attitude or actions etc of others □ *If she could shed tears* ***in sympathy with*** *a child she would not be able to lie in her own bed and listen to him cry.* DC □ *During the Glasgow bus strike, transport employees in various other towns declared 24 hour strikes* ***in sympathy***.

in the teeth of sth battling against, resisting or overcoming sth **o:** the gale, the wind; the opposition, the evidence; his parents' disapproval □ *We'd be quicker trying a zig-zag course than rowing* ***in the teeth of*** *this wind.* □ *The whole idea of these lectures was a pet one of mine carried through* ***in the teeth of*** *a good deal of opposition.* ASA □ *She won a travelling fellowship to Turkey* ***in the teeth of*** *stiff competition from fifteen men.* SC

in ten etc seconds etc flat [A (PrepP)] (informal) in a period lasting a few seconds, or as otherwise indicated, but always implying a surprisingly short time **adj:** ten, ⚠ five, eight. **n:** seconds, ⚠ minutes, days, weeks □ *It was worse than Deadly Nightshade. It would kill us* ***in five seconds flat*** *if we were to eat it.* LLDR □ *She spent 9 months on the first half of her novel, and then she came back early from holiday and finished the rest of it* ***in three weeks flat***.

in terms of sth as far as sth is concerned □ *The new plague is a tic called '****in terms of****', which is a bureaucratic substitute for any preposition of real meaning, or simply a way of padding out intellectually thin copy. '****In terms of*** *public opinion,' one paper announced recently, 'the government's anti-inflation policies are proving popular.' In other words, the government's anti-inflation policies are proving popular.* NS □ *There seems to be no real attempt to ascertain what industries cost the nation* ***in terms of*** (= in) *foreign exchange for imports of raw materials.* SC □ *The Social Democratic and Labour Party action, while it can perhaps be explained* ***in terms of*** (= by) *the pressure exercised by the Party's supporters, in fact marks a significant shift by the Party back towards Nationalist politics.* L □ *In recent weeks, in spite of losing 2-0 to Australia, West Indies cricket has begun to rebuild itself* ***in terms of*** *strength* (= rebuild its strength). OBS □ *It's a better job* ***in terms of money*** (or: ***in money terms***) (= a better paid job), *but doesn't carry the same prestige.* □ *These figures expressed* ***in terms of a percentage*** (or: ***in percentage terms***) (= expressed as a percentage) *minimise the situation emotionally.* ⇨ ⚠ in/with regard to sth; with respect (to sth).

in that case [Conj (PrepP)] since, or if, that is so (the reference being to a state of affairs, incident, line of argument, etc previously mentioned); at that/this rate (qv) □ *When I say that I have no references, his face falls. '****In that case*** *I fear we cannot take you on,' he says.* ST □ *'I'm very fussy about tea.' 'You had better make it yourself* ***in that case***.*'* □ front, middle or end position ⇨ ⚠ in sb's case.

in their hundreds etc [A (PrepP)] in large numbers; abundantly **V:** come, arrive; die, emigrate; be published. **n:** hundreds, ⚠ thousands, dozens □ (advertisement) *This is one reason why so many women find a regular glass of Lucozade a comfort in the business of coping with life. And write to say so* ***in their hundreds***. T □ *Instruction books on how to sail come* ***in their dozens***, *most of them routine, dull, dreary.* SC □ *I'm covered in midge bites! They were out* ***in their thousands*** *tonight.*

in theory...in practice [A (PrepP)] as sb/sth should behave, perform, function (according to general principles or laws) contrasted with what sb/sth actually does, or is only able to do □ *'That's all very well* ***in theory***,*' Gerald answered, 'but it won't be so easy* ***in practice***.*'* ASA □ *'And you finish work for the day at 5.30 p.m?' 'Yes,* ***in theory***, *but seldom* ***in practice***.*'* □ ***In theory*** *anyway, the missile might be fitted to quite different types of aircraft — perhaps slower-moving machines with great endurance.* NSC □ ***In practice***, *mind you, Dawson clearly loves a Lord although he's such an egalitarian* ***in theory***. □ two parts of expression used together, or separately with the other implied.

in this day and age [A (PrepP)] (cliché) nowadays (esp when there is a reference to conditions, beliefs or behaviour felt to be suitable or unsuitable in modern times) □ *There are too many at very low levels of pay and it is not right* ***in this day and age*** *that a significant number will still be earning less than £20 a week.* L □ *'Anyway,' Stanley said, squirming, 'it's nothing to worry about. Cataracts don't make you blind, not* ***in this day and age***.*'* TSMP

in this respect [A (PrepP)] with reference to a particular factor or feature (or particular factors or features) **det:** this, that; no, (not) any; every, some, all, certain, other □ *He was a 'majorities' man, and was impatient of minorities.* ***In this respect***, *of course, he ran counter to one of the most important traditions in the Labour Party.* OBS □ *But forces adequate in strength for the job in hand could be supplied and maintained provided these forces had complete priority* ***in all respects*** *as regards maintenance.* MFM □ *She's rather too severe with the children but an excellent teacher* ***in other respects***.

in time[1] [A (PrepP)] at, or before, the right or proper time; not too late **V:** come, arrive, leave; diagnose, find, stop, sth. **adv mod:** just, precisely. **A:** for dinner; to catch the bus □ *'Your* *parents must be very glad to see you home again.' I nodded. 'I'm glad I came* ***in time*** *to help them out with this.'* RFW ▫ *The realisation came—somewhat belatedly but still* ***in time****—that it was fundamentally a political war.* NS ▫ *One has completely lost a crippling backache, another had visited the healer just* ***in time*** *to avoid a gall-bladder operation.* NS ⇨ ⚠ in good time; (all) in good time.

in time² [A (PrepP)] eventually; gradually throughout a period of time **V:** disappear; be solved, resolved, healed ▫ *Could one garrulous old lady reduce her niece to desperation? Perhaps,* ***in time****, she could.* DC ▫ *This is a sad and rather comic misunderstanding, but one which will no doubt be cleared up* ***in time****.* NS ▫ front, middle or end position. ⇨ ⚠ in good time; (all) in good time.

in time (to/with sth/sb) [A (PrepP)] maintaining the same rate and rhythm (as sth/sb) **V:** sing, dance, sway, pull, stamp ⚠**:** ***(to/with)*** the music, each chorus, the chiming of the clock; ***(with)*** the conductor, the soloist, each other ▫ *Since Miss Brown takes the trouble to play for you, we want you to march out smartly* ***in time to*** *the music.* ▫ *He looked on, quietly humming to himself* ***in time with*** *the chug-chug of the engine.* ▫ *The old sea shanties served a useful purpose in that they helped men hauling on ropes, winches and stays to pull* ***in time with*** *each other.*

in time of war etc [A (PrepP)] (formal) in/during a period characterized by war etc (esp with reference to conditions which affect nations or large groups of people **o:** war, peace, trouble; famine, hardship, prosperity ▫ *My mother could not come twelve thousand miles from Australia* ***in time of war*** *to meet Bill's girl.* RFW ▫ *That's right. It's* ***in time of trouble*** *you find out who your friends are.* ▫ *There's a good deal of unselfishness shown* ***in time of adversity****.* ▫ *London was supposed not to be safe for children* ***in war time*** *so I was sent to live with a family in the south-west of England.* ▫ more informal variants in war time, in peace time; their attrib use ***peace-time*** *conditions,* ***war-time*** *conditions.*

in/into a towering passion/rage in/into an uncontrolled, or frenzied, state of anger **V:** be ***(in)***; get, go, fall, fly, ***(into)***; push, put, send sb, ***(into)*** ▫ ***In a towering passion*** *at having his new car damaged he dragged the other driver from his seat and punched him several times about the head.* ▫ *Just being contradicted can put him* ***into a towering rage****, but I've never know him to sulk or to bear grudges.*

in a trice [A (PrepP)] very quickly; often in one short swift movement, action, decision etc; in a flash (qv) **V:** disappear, vanish; be healed ▫ ***In a trice*** *Weston had picked up his own special piece of equipment, and nipped swiftly up the steps in time to bring up the rear of the party.* TO ▫ *The yardsticks by which we can measure these events and judge them cannot be conveyed* ***in a trice****.* L

in true naval etc fashion/style [A PrepP)] in typically naval etc style or manner **adj:** naval, military; rustic, man of the world, schoolgirl ▫ *They got off the bus and headed towards Grant Alexander's car. Terry,* ***in true boy fashion****, whistled when he saw it. 'Gee! What a beauty!'* WI ▫ *We should have set off an hour before, but Angus* ***in true West Highland style*** *said there was no hurry and would we not be the better for a dram in our stomachs first.* ▫ *Birmingham-born but London-based, Carol got her television break* ***in true story-book fashion****.*

in turn [A (PrepP)] in succession; one after another; in an orderly sequence **S/O:** participants, shoppers, suspects; questions, answers ▫ *The younger children came forward* ***in turn*** *to be given a present from the Christmas tree.* ▫ *Bottwink and Briggs were then searched* ***in turn****, without protest and without result.* EM ▫ *He put his left foot on one end of the twisted cloth and screwed the other with both hands. He did this* ***in turn*** *to each piece of clothing and spread the lot in the sun to dry.* PM ▫ usu end position. ⇨ ⚠ next entry.

in (one's/its) turn [A (PrepP)] as must happen, or can happen, in the course of events, in a natural pattern of life or work; (act) backwards and forwards, one person or thing opposing another ▫ *Here, when Spring* ***in its turn*** *does come, there are no false starts.* OBS ▫ *Mrs Maugham was her godmother and she* ***in turn*** *became godmother to the poet and critic John Lehmann.* L ▫ *He never lost his concern for the paper, and we* ***in our turn*** *were totally delighted when he agreed to start writing regularly for the paper again.* NS ▫ *He struggled to free himself from the twisting weeds which* ***in turn*** *wrapped themselves more and more closely round his legs.* ▫ front, middle or end position. ⇨ ⚠ previous entry.

in the twinkling of an eye [A (PrepP)] instantaneously, or very quickly **V:** change; vanish, disappear ▫ *(source) . . .but we shall all be changed, In a moment,* ***in the twinkling of an eye****, at the last trump.* I CORINTHIANS XV 51-2 ▫ *Her moods could change from sweet to sour,* ***in the twinkling of an eye****.* ▫ *I want to win* (a bet on a horse race) *but I don't want the savings of a lifetime wiped out* ***in the twinkling of an eye****.* G MARX ▫ front, middle or end position.

in two shakes (of a lamb's tail) [A (PrepP)] (informal) quickly and easily; almost at once ▫ *As I thought, it's just a loose connection. I'll have it fixed up for you* ***in two shakes of a lamb's tail****.* ▫ *Don't worry about the money.* ***In two shakes*** *I can be on to Fred about a loan.* ▫ front, middle or end position; sometimes first part can be used alone.

in two twos/ticks [A (PrepP)] (informal) quickly; within seconds or minutes; willingly, or eagerly, and without delay; in a jiffy etc (qv); in a moment etc (qv) ▫ (reader's letter) *I don't like to hear people sneering at positions and titles they'd have accepted* ***in two twos*** *if they'd got the offer.* SC ▫ *Would I bother the doctor about a little thing like that? Yes I would.* ***In two twos*** G ▫ *Jim didn't expect the water to be so cold. He was in and out again* ***in two ticks****.*

in unison (with sb) [A (PrepP)] together (with sb) and at the same time (as sb); in close association (with sb) **V:** act; speak, shout; condemn ▫ *Once in a while they would act* ***in unison*** *and move a spanner on a particularly difficult nut and bolt.* ART ▫ *The Church of England, through its leaders and* ***in unison with*** *the Church of South Africa, has constantly denounced the evil of the policy of apartheid.* SC ▫ middle or end position.

in vain [A (PrepP)] vainly; without achieving a desired result **V:** die, sacrifice oneself, suffer □ *The turnover of tyrants has been frequent and quick enough to ensure that very few freedom fighters can be seen to have died* ***in vain***. NS □ ***In vain*** *Sarah had striven to reassure him.* WI □ *It's an enchanted place — I rack my memory* ***in vain*** *for its counterpart in literature; perhaps you can think of one.* PW □ front, middle or end position.

in sb's view [Disj (PrepP)] as sb sees, understands or estimates; in sb's/one's opinion (qv); in sb's book (qv); to my mind (qv); to sb's way of thinking (qv) □ ***In*** *the editor* ***'s view*** *there was nothing in the article that went beyond legitimate comment and so he printed it.* □ *The films seem to draw on a force somewhere in one's psyche— that's why they really are demoniac* ***in my view***. L □ ***In*** *the Russian* ***view*** *diets rich in animal protein are bad for three reasons—* NSC □ *Bruce McFarlane,* ***in the view of*** *many fine judges, was the greatest English historian of his generation.* NS □ front, middle or end position; used in form in sb's view with prons, attrib adjs, and individuals specified by name or function (as in first three examples); form in the view of sb used with nouns denoting a functional or professional group, as in last example.

in view of sth because of sth; considering sth; bearing in mind the fact or possibility that □ *I had told Alexander privately that* ***in view of*** *my promise to the soldiers, I refused to attack before October.* MFM □ ***In view of*** *the success you were having, why didn't you stay there?* L □ ***In view of*** *the numbers expected to attend, special parking facilities have been arranged.*

in sb's/sth's wake [A (PrepP)] fairly closely behind sb/sth; following sb's/sth's path or progress; after sb/sth in time, usu though not necessarily as a result **V:** come, follow, leave □ ***In the wake of*** *the Events of May 1968 the French Government found itself obliged to offer something in the way of concessions to its rebellious students.* L □ *They are artists pure and simple.* ***In their wake*** *come younger artists still in the chrysalis stage, profiting by their inspiration.* OBS □ *The article was illustrated by photographs of the damage and destruction the hurricane had left* ***in its wake***. □ *'Come and talk to her,' said Lucy, and she clove a way through the crowd, Lord Mellings following* ***in her wake***. WDM

in a way [Disj (PrepP)] not exactly or wholly; if one considers some aspect(s) or detail(s) of a situation etc **det:** a, no, (not) any; some, several, many □ *'I suppose you are going,' said Lydia. 'Yes, we are,' said Lady Pomfret. 'I wish* ***in a way*** *we weren't.'* WDM □ *The absent-minded professor — is that the role you cast me for, Sergeant? Well, it is true enough* ***in a way*** *I suppose.* EM □ *It has always been accepted that the Emperor Theodore was a mad dog let lose, and so he was* ***in many ways***. BN □ *Except for the lighting and the normal technical requirements of a filming session the programme was* ***in no way*** *'staged'.* OBS □ front, middle or end position.

in its/one's (own) way [A (PrepP)] if one accepts that it/he has a special character; in a perhaps unusual way which is characteristic of itself/oneself **V:** shine, excel, be admirable; love, value, appreciate sb/sth □ JIMMY: *I'm not talking about Webster, stupid. He's all right though,* ***in his way***. LBA □ ***In their own way*** *they are as heavenly as are the great masterpieces of landscape painting.* HAH □ *She must have loved him* ***in her way***: *hadn't she been fond of me and hadn't she left me for Pyle?* QA □ *'I still have faith in God* ***in my own way***,*' he says.* OBS □ front, middle or end position.

in the way of sb/sth such as sb/sth; as regards sb/sth; by way of sth² (qv) **n:** nothing, not much; something, anything; little, a great deal. **O:** new staff; change; fresh vegetables, drink; organized planning, nursing invalids □ *It won't be very easy for him to absorb many* ***in the way of*** *new staff.* OMIH □ *There appears to be an absence of strenuous or routine activities in dreams—there is little* ***in the way of*** *working, buying or selling, typing and so forth.* SNP □ *Most of my life is spent in hot climates so I don't need much* ***in the way of*** *clothes.* TVT □ *We have nothing very remarkable* ***in the way of*** *scenery round here, I'm afraid.* □ *In the wake of the Events of May 1968 the French Government found itself obliged to offer something* ***in the way of*** *concessions to its rebellious students.* L □ usu modifies a preceding n.

in a whisper [A (PrepP)] whispering instead of using one's normal voice **V:** say, confide, announce. **adj:** low, loud, hoarse □ *'Don't you find it awfully irritating?' 'Actually I do,' Aunt Annabel confided* ***in a whisper***, *giving a quick nervous glance towards her husband.* DC □ *'I'll tell you, mate; only keep it under your hat,' he said* ***in a*** *hoarse* ***whisper***. BB □ *It is a stage convention that other actors do not hear remarks made* ***in a*** *loud* ***whisper*** *for the benefit of the audience.* □ almost always end position after v.

in a word [Disj (PrepP)] briefly; in as few words as possible; in brief/short (qv) □ *From the day our schooldays began, we were taught, implicitly, that every other boy was a potential rival. We had,* ***in a word***, *the perfect training for careerists.* CON □ *You certainly picked the right person for that job, James.* ***In a word***, *she's the best engineer this firm's ever employed.* □ usu introduces summing-up or different wording of sth already described or explained; not to be understood literally.

in word and (in) deed [A (PrepP)] not only as one claims, or promises, but also as one does □ (source) *...let us not love* ***in word***, *neither in tongue; but* ***in deed*** *and truth.* I JOHN III 18 □ *The Victorians viewed all this with that odd blend of humbug and charity that marks them* ***in word and deed***. L □ *He's just another of these hypocrites who are pacifists* ***in word*** *but not* ***in deed***. □ commonly varied in structure, as indicated.

in a year's etc time [A (PrepP)] after a year etc (precisely or approximately) has elapsed **n:** years's, ⚠ a year or two's, a couple of months', a week's, two hours' □ *There may be some action for you, Rose, not now, perhaps* ***in a year*** *or so* ***'s time***. NM □ *The bomb, set to go off* ***in two hours' time***, *was placed behind a large waste container.* □ *I'll see you again* ***in a couple of weeks' time***, *Mrs. Smith. Ask the receptionist to make an appointment for you, on your way out.*

industrial action [A (NP)] strike, go slow,

work-in, esp one backed by a union. **V:** take, threaten; plan, propose □ *If the **industrial action** takes place, it is right that the public should know that the Government stand ready to take whatever action is necessary.* ST □ *Perhaps the progressive Swedes regard it as 'reactionary' not to allow army officers to belong to a trade union, with the right to take **industrial action** and the risk of being locked out if fellow members of their union are ordered out on strike.* SC

injured innocence [O (NP)] attitude of sb wrongfully attacked or blamed □ *'Did I see you throw a half-smoked cigarette over the wall just now, Jones?' 'What me, sir?' he replied, the very picture of **injured innocence**.* □ (cricket) *There was prolonged applause once when he stopped 20 paces from the wicket and put down a marker. Proctor revolved with the astonishment of the **injured innocent**, and took another 12 paces to his usual mark.* OBS □ usu ironic; variant the injured innocent.

innocent of sth[1] [Comp (AdjP)] not guilty (of sth); completely without an unpleasant quality **S:** suspect; loiterer, layabout. **V:** ⚠ be, seem, appear. **O:** action; offence, crime; malice □ *Whatever else Fisher had done he was **innocent of** that particular crime.* □ *Even a three year old child may not be **innocent of** deceit.*

innocent of sth[2] [Comp (AdjP)] without, lacking, sth; devoid of sth (qv) **V:** ⚠ be, seem, look □ *She glanced at the plain wooden door, **innocent of** knocker or bell, but made no move to knock or open it.* HD □ *The untarred road wound away up the valley, **innocent** as yet **of** motor cars.* CWR

the ins and outs (of sth) [n+n non-rev] the details, intricacies, complications of sth **O:** affair, procedure, profession □ *At the back of the announcement that 'Ah* (= I) *keep myself to myself' there can be a hurt pride. It is difficult to believe that a visitor from another class could ever realize all **the ins and outs** of one's difficulties.* UL □ *Since **the ins and outs of** racing—cunning, subtlety, villainy and sheer commonsense—are so complex they merit a programme to themselves.* NS □ *I knew there had been a tremendous row between them but I never did hear **the ins and outs**—not that I want to.*

inside every fat man there's a thin man trying to get out (catchphrase) a fat man feels he presents a distorted image of his true self to the world □ (source) *Imprisoned **in every fat man a thin one is** wildly **signalling to be let out**.* THE UNQUIET GRAVE (C CONNOLLY 1903-70) □ *They say that **inside every fat man there's a thin one trying to get out**—and I feel much happier since I lost a couple of stones.* □ (NONCE) *William's barbs are in fact an expression of affection and concern for his **fat friend**, part of a campaign to bounce a **thin friend out** of her.* NS □ (NONCE) *I would, however, be the first to admit the validity of the comment 'that **inside each** hardened **sceptic there is a superstitious old wife crying to be let out**.'* SC □ *But Lord Lambton thinks that playwriting was a second choice not to farming but to politics: 'Like Cyril Connolly's **fat man, there's a politician struggling to get out** of William* (Douglas Home).*'* ST □ adaptation common, as shown here.

an interested party a person, or group, who will profit or lose (financially or otherwise) by a business deal etc and is therefore not likely to make an impartial judgement or decision about it □ *Perhaps he held no shares in that particular Company, but if his wife did that makes him **an interested party**.* □ (reader's letter) *Of course I know that **the interested parties**—builders, speculators or whatever — can always turn round and tell me that someone deposited a plan somewhere that would have told me all.* SC

into the bargain [A (PrepP)] as well; as sth added to what has already been done, received, given etc □ *We do the thinking for a bunch of nitwits and allow ourselves to be pushed around by 'em* (= them) ***into the bargain**.* TBC □ *We got away all right, and had a good feed **into the bargain**.* LLDR □ *I know it's a bit thick to rob you of a cheroot and then grill you with personal questions **into the bargain**.* HD □ usu end position.

inverted snobbery the practice of identifying oneself with the lower classes, less educated people, vulgar tastes, etc for no sensible reason, or from affectation, or from fear of being thought a snob □ *Hence the aggressive 'plain man', the embattled low-brow tone of many columnists and leader-writers; the **inverted snobbery** of those film critics who insist that they are 'simple and ordinary men in the street'.* UL □ *She seemed to think every man in a suit was bourgeois, which was just **inverted snobbery** of the worst kind.*

the Iron Curtain the Westernmost boundary of the group of Eastern European states politically and economically dominated by the Soviet Union □ *The phrase '**Iron Curtain**' was first used just about a quarter of a century ago* (ie 1945) *but behind **that Iron Curtain** there are millions of other small ones that have been an accepted part of the Russian social scene for a great deal longer than that.* L □ *I just wanted to record my personal conviction that one should meet writers and scholars from behind **the iron curtain** whenever possible.* T □ attrib use ***iron curtain** policy, countries, secrecy.*

the iron enters (into) one's/sb's soul sb becomes emotionally affected (esp hardened and embittered) by (his own or another's) suffering □ (source) *. . .Joseph, who was sold to be a bond-servant; whose feet they hurt in the stocks: **the iron entered into his soul.*** PSALMS CV 17-18 □ *He seemed to have recovered from the death of his wife, but **the iron entered his soul** and he never wrote a note of music again.* □ *'A Scandalous Woman' is a collection worth reading. But it will reinforce **the iron in the soul of** any lady who feels she is getting a raw deal from life.* NS

an iron fist/hand in a velvet glove firm control or severe treatment, either applied with such skill that it is not resented, or hidden under apparent courtesy and goodwill □ *'Bernard,' says Lady Dartmouth, 'this kind lady and I are just discussing whether I have **an iron hand in a velvet glove**. What do you think?'* ST □ (NONCE) *Does that **velvet voice** (I wonder) conceal **a tongue of iron**? Has he threatened his cast with dismissal if it does not constantly increase productivity?* NS □ may be used in part, or allusively.

iron rations small pack of food in a fairly concentrated form carried by soldiers, explorers, climbers etc for use in emergencies □ *It was rather like waiting to go out on a raid into enemy territory; we had our* ***iron rations****, our rope-soled shoes, pocket compasses, our faces were blacked and we had been given full instructions.* CON

sb/sth is dead, but he/it won't lie down (catchphrase) a person, institution, feeling, belief, topic etc continues to exist, exert some influence, or demand some attention, even when he/it has outlived any real function, or is thought to be destroyed or forgotten □ *The supermarket killed off his trade but his shop's still there. They****'re dead but they won't lie down****, both him and the business.* □ *Twice he dismisses with scorn Professor Wollheim's query: do you or don't you want for ordinary people a higher standard of living? But the query* ***won't lie down****.* L □ (NONCE) *Penda* ***died*** *in AD 655 and it was not many years after that before England was fully Christianised. Yet the old dark demon of Penda's England* ***refuses to lie down****.* RT

it/sb beats me (informal) I cannot understand, cope with, sth/sb **cl:** why they keep it up; how they do it; what she sees in him □ *'Now, what d'ye* (= do you) *think of the idea?' '****It beats me****, that's what I think about it.'* HD □ *Haven't you got these dishes done yet?* ***It beats me*** *what you people do with your time.* HD □ *'I can't get rhubarb to grow in my garden.' 'Well, why that should be so certainly* ***beats me****.'* □ *His teacher at school seems to be able to handle him but he* ***beats me****.* □ weary or baffled comment on events; inversion possible, eg ***it beats me*** *why he does it* = *why he does it* ***beats me****.*

it can't be helped there is nothing one can do to improve a situation, undo a wrong or foolish action □ (advertisement) *Sufferers from indigestion have surprised me by suggesting that* ***it can't be helped****.* DM □ *They* (new nations) *may well be more conformist and allow less scope for individual liberty.* ***It can't be helped****. Each nation must make its own history.* RT □ *You need reassurance from another person. But if it's not there* ***it can't be helped*** *and you must manage on your own.* TVT □ usu advice to oneself or others that one should resign onself, forget about sth, go on to sth new, etc.

it can't happen here etc (catchphrase) we are safe from sth unpleasant, unjust, dangerous, terrifying **A:** here, ⚠ there; to me, to us □ *Years ago when we read of the terrifying range of drug-addiction in the US we thought* ***it can't happen here****. Well it hasn't yet (quite).* SC □ *The word cancer was never mentioned in these early tests and though I did wonder I always thought 'Oh no,* ***it can't happen to me****.'* OBS □ *Nobody is immune against misfortune. To declare '****It cannot happen to us****,' is to ask for and to get trouble.* G □ *The invasion of the Falkland Islands has left red faces on those who insisted that* ***it could never happen there****.* □ *People who smuggle pets into Britain ignore the very real danger that those animals may carry rabies back to this island. They need to remember that* ***it can happen here****.* □ esp an expression of blind or smug optimism; variant it can happen here occas used as corrective or warning.

it/that (all/rather) depends [Disj] perhaps; possibly □ *'Would you marry him if he asked you?' 'Well, I wouldn't like to say.* ***It depends****.'* □ *'Can we watch the football on TV?' the children asked their father. '****That depends****,' he replied. 'Have you finished your homework?'* □ *'Well, are you coming to dinner on Thursday?' Bill asked anxiously. '****It all depends****,' Alison replied teasingly.* □ occas used, without further explanation or elaboration, as vague, or deliberately teasing, answer to question or suggestion, as in last example.

it does not do to do sth it is not advisable, socially acceptable, to do sth, to take some course of action **Inf:** to refuse; to be too modest, friendly, talkative; to dress shabbily □ *'Mind you,' he said confidentially to Gerald, '****it doesn't do to*** *be too modest. You can pass a lot of business up that way.'* ASA □ *In the old days* ***it would never have done*** *for a professor* ***to*** *be on such familiar terms with his students.* □ *'How old did you say?' 'Seventy-five. Seventy-nine to the Council.' 'Of course,' said Alec. '****Doesn't do to*** *let on too much.'* □ used as warning or advice.

it/that figures (informal) it/that seems right, reasonable or likely □ *'Somebody told me he'd won money on the pools.' 'I never heard that, but* ***it figures****. They certainly have more money to throw around than they used to.'* □ *She finds it difficult to adjust her style of expression to the various narrators. Such phrases as '****That figures****,' from King Henry are at odds with the carefully studied period background.* SC □ *'He hasn't taken long to forget Carrie.' 'Who says he has? I think* ***it figures*** *that a man who has been happily married is more likely than another to want to fill the gap.'* □ also ***it figures*** *that* as shown.

it ill becomes sb to do sth (formal) sb's own character, status, record, makes it unsuitable, or even wrong, for him/her to do sth **adv mod:** ill, well; little, hardly, scarcely. **Inf:** to complain, object, criticize, condemn □ *He had elected so many years ago* (for a life of) *scholarship on solid dividends,* ***it*** *would* ***ill become*** *him now* ***to*** *criticize the source of his misspent independence.* ASA □ ***It ill becomes*** *a Scottish newspaper, valuing Scottish identity,* ***to*** *decry the right of the Ukraine, a nation of some 47 million people, to a seat at the UN.* SC □ expression of somewhat smug disapproval.

it/that is all according (informal) dependent on, related to, a previously stated or implied circumstance, or a likely outcome □ *Fair enough; but was it worth coming something over a thousand miles to look at this harbour and think these thoughts? Ah, well now,* ***that was all according****, wasn't it?* ILIH □ *I don't know what time he'll get back.* ***It's all according****.* □ considered substandard.

it is all/as much as one can do (to do sth) one can do sth only with difficulty; to do sth is as much as one is capable of doing in a given line of activity □ *'Will you be wanting more pie, Jan?' 'Thanks, but* ***it'll be all I can do to*** *finish what I have.'* □ *No crops were planted. Except in north-west Europe and the far northland* ***it was all Man could do to*** *exist.* TBC □ *'This time last year,' he said, '****it was as much as you could do***

to *get a word out of that girl.'* TT

it is all in the day's work it is a task or job that one expects, or is accustomed, to do in the course of one's work or duties that is therefore not burdensome or demanding (though perhaps considered so by others) □ *'But that's hardly fair on Carmichael,' Brownsworth objected. 'Forget it,' Carmichael said.* ***It's all in the day's work****, for me.'* RM □ *Despite the problems they insist that* ***it's all in the day's work****. The Abbey puts on about a dozen weddings a year for Royalty or 'near' Royalty.* □ *The warden has proved himself able to bring the best out of the most difficult people.* ***It was all part of the day's work****.*

it is (not) for sb to do sth (not) sb's function or responsibility to do sth □ *'When will I be allowed to go home, nurse?' 'Towards the end of the week, I should think, but* ***it's for the*** *doctor* ***to*** *decide.'* □ ***It is not for*** *Hanoi* ***to*** *criticise Saigon democracy but it is a pity all the same that manipulation has robbed the election of credibility.* SC □ ***It's not for*** *me* ***to*** *say whether you can borrow the car or not, tonight. You'd better ask Eric.* □ *What people might be driven to do in such terrible circumstances* ***is not for*** *us* ***to*** *judge.* □ often neg.

it is/has (just) gone midnight etc it is just after, or within a short time after, midnight or any other named time of day **n:** midnight, ⚠ ten o'clock, 5 p.m., noon □ ***It's gone midnight*** *and we've all got work to do in the morning.* □ *We tried going to a party last Saturday night. I say tried, because* ***it was gone ten*** *before we finally got there.* WI □ ***It had just gone nine o'clock*** *when I got into the office but Rankin chose to consider that I was late again.* □ pres or past simple tenses.

it is idle to deny etc (that) it is mistaken, foolish, or serves no useful purpose, to deny etc sth **V:** deny, protest; hope, expect, suppose. **O:** that I'm flattered; his ability; anything better, otherwise □ ***It*** *would be* ***idle to deny that*** *when Lydia had a letter from Lady Pomfret asking if they would dine at Pomfret Towers on Saturday week, she felt slightly uplifted.* WDM □ ***It is idle to*** *suggest* ***that*** *Cymediethas yr Iaith* (a Welsh Nationalist Movement) *has won more sympathy from 'magistrates' benches' than it has from the public generally.* NS

it/that is just as well it/that is fortunate or desirable (that a situation is, that sth has been done or has happened, as described) **cl:** that I stayed at home, that I didn't say anything, that you can't understand Spanish □ ALISON: *Mummy made me sign everything else over to her, when she knew I was really going to marry Jimmy.* HELENA: ***Just as well****, I imagine.* LBA □ *'Helen says we're sailing on the eleventh of May. I shan't be seeing you much longer.'* ***'Just as well*** *for you,' he said. 'Ending this is probably the most sensible thing you've done.'* AITC □ *As a revolutionary, Buchner was a failure. Perhaps* ***that is just as well****, or we shouldn't have had the plays.* L □ HELEN: *I've come to look after you.* ***It's just as well*** *by the look of things.* TOH □ ***It is just as well that*** *the schoolteachers themselves are not expected to participate in this refreshing ordeal, because some of them would not fare too well.* SC □ often used alone as an elliptical reply, or comment on sth already mentioned; variant it is just as well that. ⇨ ⚠ as well do sth (as do sth else); may/might (just) as well do sth.

it is (just/quite) like sb to be/do sth (informal) sb acts as his character or usual habits would lead one to expect □ *Then he offered me his cigarette case.* ***It was like*** *him* ***to*** *carry cigarettes for his visitors, though he did no smoke himself.* NM □ *Ned smiled as if* ***it*** *were* ***just like*** *Robert* ***to*** *forget who his real friends were.* CON □ ***It isn't like*** *me* ***to*** *come empty handed, but I've been down in the cow sheds with the men.* WDM □ *We got into Ned's car without another word.* ***It wasn't like*** *Ned* ***to be*** *so taciturn.* CON

it is more than one's job is worth (to do sth) to do sth would mean being dismissed from one's employment **Inf:** to let you in without a pass, to tell anybody that, to falsify my report □ *Strict regulations, sir.* ***It's more than my job's worth to*** *let you in without a pass* □ *. . .stuck in freezing dressing-rooms, pacifying the 'jobsworths' — theatre hands who always tell you* ***it's more than their job's worth to*** *do anything at all—and ending up exhausted.* TVT

it is no wonder (that) it is/is not surprising (that) **det:** no, (not) any; a; small, little □ *He was lucky to get off with shock and a few bruises.* ***It's a wonder*** *he wasn't killed.* □ ***It's no wonder*** *you can never find anything when you want it. What the good of having filing cabinets if you won't use them?* □ *How cold and gloomy it is in here.* ***No wonder*** *you had a nightmare.* DC □ *The Austin wasn't up to much — and* ***no wonder*** *after seventeen years' misuse.* RATT □ ***It is small wonder that*** *attempts have been made to use post hypnotic suggestion as a curative agent.* SNP □ *Most of the audience left before the performance ended, and* ***little wonder****.* □ variant no/small little wonder (can be used as comments on some earlier statement).

it is not/has to be it (usu an unwelcome event or situation) is unavoidable, must be accepted, is ordained by fate, etc □ *Although I don't look forward to the children growing up and leaving home I know* ***it has to be****.* □ *It was a big change to go over to basing our defence organisation on nuclear weapons; but* ***it had to be****.* MFM □ *He might well have been defended by a far worthier pen than mine.* ***It was not to be****, however, for worn out with his valiant struggle for peace Lionel Stokesay died in 1940.* ASA □ pres or past simple tenses.

it is only a little one (facetious) an illogical reason given to excuse or mitigate sth (illogical because size is irrelevant to its (un)suitability) (source—referring to having given birth to an illegitimate baby) *If you please, ma'am,* ***it was a very little one****.* MR MIDSHIPMAN EASY (F. MARRYAT 1792-1848) □ *Perhaps it is not for the reviewer to talk, since he produced a book on Johnson himself, but as the girl said,* ***it was only a little one****, a wicked publisher seduced me, and I have promised never, never to do it again.* NS □ *It is not only the piano that is grand (and its owner would clearly scorn to plead that* ***it is only a little one****); here is a hint of the grand manner as well—and that is something that is rare in contemporary life.* T □ stress pattern it is ˌonly 'little one.

it is a question of what is really involved is; the essence of the matter is; a matter of (qv) **adv:** only, all, chiefly, simply, just. **o:** atmosphere, compromise; what I want; getting him to accept, restoring his self-confidence ▫ *'You see,' explained Simenon, '**it's** all **a question of** atmosphere. The story counts but people count more. I watch people, I read, I think. Bit by bit the characters build up.'* RT ▫ *And in this case the interests hadn't even been conflicting; **it was** just **a question of** acquainting each party with what the other wanted for full agreement to be reached.* PW ▫ *'I didn't see that the man was vulgar in any way.' '**It's** not **a question of** that. You don't understand. Americans, if you'll forgive me, Spenser, don't understand the difference between being a gentleman, and just not being one.'* AITC ▫ *'Where would you like me to book you a room?' 'I'm afraid **it's** not **a question of** where I'd like you to book me one, but whether you can book me one that I can afford.'* ▫ *I can't tell you if James will be free to help you this summer. **It's a question of** whether he's accepted for this training course or not.*

it is a woman's/lady's privilege to change her mind (saying) reversing, or changing, a decision previously made is tolerated when done by a woman more readily than when done by a man ▫ NORAH: *I thought you were going to the club.* JOSIE: ***It's a woman's privilege to change her mind.*** EGD ▫ *'I don't like this wallpaper after all. Is it too late **to change my mind**?' '**It's a lady's privilege**, isn't it?'* ▫ first part can be used alone alluding to second part, as shown.

it never rains but it pours (saying) incidents, troubles, visitors, business orders, etc tend to come together in large numbers or in rapid succession ▫ '(Your) *classroom's been mucked up.' 'I would be late this morning of all mornings.' 'And it's all over the School,' she said, 'You were supposed to be on playground duty.' 'Christ Almighty! **It never** bloody **rains but it pours**! I quite forgot.'* TT

it pays to do sth it is profitable, or advantageous, to do sth; one is wise; or sensible, when one does sth **adv:** always, never, sometimes ▫ *And so the chain went on, and because **it pays to** advertise, and all good goods are advertised goods, the advertisers were happy, the readers were happy, and the editors may be.* PP ▫ *'They certainly cause some damage.' But the French find **it pays** not **to** complain. English day-trippers have brought the unfashionable Channel ports a taste of big business.* TO ▫ *There probably wouldn't be a mike in a place like this, but it's the drill, you know, that counts. You'll find **it** always **pays** in the end **to** follow the drill.* OMIH ▫ ***It** never **pays to** believe you must be cleverer than your opponent.* ⇨ crime doesn't pay.

it/that remains to be seen sth is not yet known or decided **cl:** whether it will succeed; how it is to be managed; what the reaction will be ▫ *What Mr Laird is trying to do—and **it remains to be seen** whether he will succeed—is to reduce the risk of waiting for trouble.* SC ▫ ***It remains to be seen** whether I would ever again be able to hold a conversation with Hugo.* UTN ▫ *'They're taking action. But how effective it will be and how long it will last **remains to be seen**,' said an official.* SC ▫ *'I think I'm your man, Professor Neave.' '**That remains to be seen**,' Neave answered.* ART ▫ usu followed by clause beginning *that, what, how, when*, or esp *whether*, or with such a clause replacing it as S, cf ***it remains to be seen** how long* and *how long **remains to be seen***.

it shouldn't happen to a dog nobody should have to suffer such misfortune, punishment, pain, abuse etc **S:** it, that (kind/sort of thing) ▫ *'Echoes of a Summer': glutinous slop about a kid dying of a bad heart and her divided parents; **shouldn't happen to a dog**, certainly not to Jodie Foster.* NS

it so happens (that) by chance it is true, it is the case, that ▫ *Something gleamed palely on the fist. **It so happened that** Charles had never seen a knuckle duster before, but he recognized it.* HD ▫ *He would have been travelling on the train that crashed if **it** hadn't **so happened** he'd been working late that night.* ▫ *if **it** hadn't **(so) happened** he'd been working late = if he hadn't **happened** to be working late.*

it takes all sorts etc (to make a world) (saying) people vary very much in character and abilities and this is necessary and desirable **n:** sorts, ⚠ kinds, types ▫ *People have their own ideas. Some like danger. Some like security. **It takes all sorts to make a world**.* PP ▫ *Palmer said icily that fire-irons weren't iron, they were brass. 'Seems funny to me calling them iron then,' said Ruby. 'But **it takes all sorts to make a world**.'* WDM ▫ *'I don't understand Bill. How can anyone spend so much time fiddling with a car?' '**It takes all kinds**—he probably thinks you're silly spending every Saturday afternoon at a football match.'* ▫ sometimes a (tolerant) comment on sb's peculiar habits or nature; first part can be used alone alluding to second part, as shown.

it takes one all one's time (to do sth) one can just manage, and no more, to do sth; one does, achieves, sth with some difficulty **Inf:** to do the housework, to keep the weeds down, to manage the accounts ▫ *Our collection had reached such proportions that **it took us all our time to** cope with it.* DF ▫ HELEN: *Anyway, it's your life, ruin it your own way. **It takes me all my time to** look after myself, I know that.* TOH ▫ emphasis may be on time it takes (to do sth) or on effort expended.

it takes two to do sth some actions or situations are such that one person alone cannot be entirely responsible—another must share the blame or credit **Inf:** to make a quarrel, to build up a happy marriage, to call a truce ▫ *Remembering that **it takes two to** make a quarrel I held my tongue.* ▫ *Had we parted or not? It seemed like it, yet somehow I felt sure that Myrtle had not. **It takes two to** make even a parting.* SPL ▫ *It appears that she found him uninteresting in bed. Well **it takes two to** make a marital failure.* NS

it/that will never/won't do a comment on an occurrence, situation or state of affairs that is unsatisfactory and should be remedied—indicating either sympathy or an intention to ensure that matters are improved ▫ *Mr Charlton confessed that he had no car. Pop was stunned.*

*'No car, no car?' he said. '**That'll never do**.'* DBM □ *It has not escaped my notice, Miss Ross, that you've been coming in late every second or third morning. What you may not realize, and what I am now pointing out to you, is that **it** just **won't do**.* □ *In 1864 Theodore had clapped in chains one of Her Majesty's consuls. **This** clearly **would not do** and a British rescue mission was mounted with a field-marshal at its head.* OBS

it's all in the mind (catchphrase) mental attitudes, not physical conditions, influence one's state of health, behaviour, reactions etc **S:** it; travel-sickness; whether you're too old at 40 □ *You could get high on water if you believed it was whisky. **It's all in the mind**.* □ (professional footballers over 30) ***Whether you carry on or not is all in the mind**, not the body, and some of the blokes around today prove that.* TVT □ *Is there an organic difference that explains why some people get seasick and others don't or **is it all in the mind**?*

it's as simple etc as that (informal) no other explanation, or reason, is necessary **adj:** simple, ⚠ easy, straightforward □ *I've an open mind. If you believe in them* (angels), *that makes them believable. If you don't, not. **It's as simple as that**.* AITC □ *The advertisement said 'Satisfaction guaranteed or your money back' but, in the event, **it was**n't **as straighforward as that**.* □ PEPPER: *After all, what happens when a boxer gets knocked out in the ring? He's lost the fight. **It's as simple as that**.* ART □ often neg.

it's the gipsy etc in one it is that gipsy-like part of one's character, (developed by background, upbringing etc), which makes one behave in a certain way **n:** gipsy, Puritan, idealist; Frenchman; jounalist, artist □ JO: *I'm never at one school long enough to show them something.* HELEN: *That's my fault, I suppose.* JO: *You* will *wander about the country.* HELEN: ***It's the gipsy in me**.* TOH □ *'He's married now but he's still got a roving eye.' '**It must be the Latin in him**.'* □ *I'm in love with you, and that's as plain as can be. You and you alone bring out **the gipsy in me**.* POPULAR SONG

it's an ill wind (that blows nobody (any) good) (saying) few situations, or events, are so unwelcome or disastrous that nobody at all gets any benefit or profit from them; one person's misfortunes may be another's good fortune □ (Already redundant) *scientists and engineers from the factories in the West of Scotland are looking to the teaching profession which may find that **it is an ill wind which blows nobody good**.* SC □ *But for whom is any weather 'worse'? Sunbathers? Skiers? Tomatoes? Ducks? Obviously any weather is good for some people and purposes, so why label it? **It's an ill wind**.* OBS □ sometimes first part can be used alone with the rest implied.

it's later than you think (catchphrase) there is less time, or opportunity, left to achieve sth, or avert disaster etc, than one deceives oneself into believing □ (source) *Ah! the clock is always slow;/**It is later than you think**.* SPRING (R W SERVICE 1874-1958) □ *Enjoy yourself! **It's later than you think**.* POPULAR SONG □ *There's still a hard campaign ahead for those who see the need for persuading the rest of us that **it is later than we think**.* NS

it's a long road/lane that has/knows no turning (saying) nothing goes on for ever; there is sure to be a change some time that will give relief, or improvement □ *We didn't reach it after. But we will. Very shortly. **It's a long road that has no turning**, as they say.* THH □ (reader's letter) *I hope that these children may grow up into a different community in Denby (as an Educational Priority Area). The process may be slow, but **it's a long, long lane that has no turning**.* L

it's love that makes the world go round (saying) usu a comment on love between people as both desirable and necessary (translated from an anonymous French song) □ *And the moral of that is—Oh **it's love, 'tis love, that makes the world go round**!* ALICE IN WONDERLAND (L CARROLL 1832-98) □ *As the squat mauve figure walked off with her chin pressed close to Eric's shoulder, they reminded Bernard of Alice and the Duchess. **It's love**, he thought, **that makes the world go round**.* HAA □ ***It's** not **love**, but money **that makes the world go round** for the villains in 'The Sweeney'* (TV series) *on Monday.* TVT

it's never too late to mend (saying) it is always possible to (try to) improve one's character, habits, attitude to others, however long one has been wrong or at fault □ *'Do you think I should go back and live with Rob again?' 'You can try. **It's never too late to mend** and the breakup may have made him see sense.'*

it's not what you do etc, it's the way that you do etc it (catchphrase) the effect, impact, of an action depends on the style, manner, in which it is performed **V:** do, say, use, wear, play □ *'Listen to him trying to convince himself,' said Goldy. 'Ever hear that Fats Waller song, "**It's not what you do, it's the way that you do it**"? Well them's* (= those are) *my sentiments—some can, some can't.'* TT □ ***It's not what I say** to people. **It's the way that I say it**. People believe me when I say something's going to be great.* OBS □ ***It's not what you wear, it's the way that you wear it**—meaning that you don't necessarily have to spend a fortune to look good.* TVT □ *'What do you suggest I write about, then, to stand a chance next year?' '**It isn't** so much **what you write as the way that you write it**.'* ST

it's a small world (saying) one is likely to meet, or hear about, someone one knows or has some connection with, however distant, anywhere one goes □ *'That's all right, Mrs Southcott,' he said. 'You know my name?' '**It's a small world**,' he said.* TT □ *When I boarded the train at Milan the only other occupant of the compartment was a neighbour of ours in Leeds. 'Well, well **it's a small world**,' I said as we shook hands.* □ *I remember suddenly looking up over Robert's shoulder and seeing two familiar faces. 'It's a small show,' I said. I think I meant to say 'It shows what **a small world it is**.'* CON

it's (quite/really) something (informal) it's an important, valuable achievement, possession etc □ ***It's something** to have a family after all, nuisances though they can be at times.* PW □ *Her last novel he calls 'one of the very few significant modern works of fiction'. D S Savage is a hard man and coming from him **that***

is really something. L □ *Being independent* ***is quite something.*** □ in second example, *that* refers back to earlier statement; last example = ***It's quite something*** *being independent*; variant it's no small thing.

it's the thought that counts (saying) the goodwill, or affection, that lies behind an action, gift etc is more important than the action etc itself □ (Boy gives Jo a ring) JO: *Did it cost very much?* BOY: *I got it from Woolworths!* JO: *I'm not proud.* ***It's the thought that counts.*** TOH □ *'I came down to help you cut the sandwiches, but I see you've done it already.' 'Never mind,* ***it's the thought that counts.****'*

an ivory tower studies, interests (esp academic or artistic) that cut one off from the realities, struggles of life; observation and imagination in place of direct experience (first used by the French critic, SAINTE-BEUVE (1804-69), about the poet, de Vigny, *en sa tour d'ivoire*) □ *There were indications that the chief constable lived somewhat in* ***an ivory tower****, barely able to accept that men under his command could be guilty of truly infamous conduct.* T □ SARAH (posing the real question): *What's wrong with socialism that you have to run to* ***an ivory tower****? The city is human beings. What's socialism without human beings, tell me?* ITAJ □ ***The ivory tower*** *it would seem is close to being a sweat-shop, and the academic tots up nearly as many hours as the average senior business executive for very much less pay.* SC □ *She is not interested in* ***ivory-tower*** *couture but designs clothes that the ordinary woman can wear and look good in.* RT □ attrib use ***an ivory-tower*** *mentality, detachment etc.*

the Ivy League the group of older US universities (including Harvard, Yale, Princeton, Columbia) conferring academic and social prestige on those who have taught or studied there □ *Even if McGovern had been underplayed by the British press, why should that be a matter for* ***Ivy League*** *professorial rebuke?* NS □ *You would be a party surrounded by fellows with their* ***Ivy League*** *suits and dreams of safe havens in IBM or some other secure corporate body.* RT □ attrib use *an* ***Ivy League*** *campus, professor etc.*

J

a jack in office (derogatory) an official, esp in a public or administrative post, who feels his position makes him very important and often behaves in a way that causes him to be resented by subordinates or clients □ *But he really must repair the damage. If he doesn't use the authority that becomes him, all* ***the*** *little* ***jacks-in-office*** *and the ignorant* arrivistes (= upstarts) *will win.* HAA □ *Busy Mr Creevey, the Whig diarist, testified with equal fervour to the Duke's amazing naturalness and absence of pride: 'considering the impostors that most men in power are—the insufferable pretensions one meets in every* ***Jack in Office****—the uniform frankness and simplicity of Wellington makes him to me the most interesting object I have ever seen in my life.'* ST □ capital or small J.

Jack is as good as his master (saying) an employee is not, or need not necessarily be, inferior to his employer; an employee's worth is equal to that of his employer □ *At least these programmes prove one thing: the touching of the forelock days are over, and* ***Jack is as good as his master****—and more power to his lungs on this type of show.* RT □ *The Member* (of Parliament) *is no longer to be regarded as the superior person whom the constituency should be jolly grateful to have. This almost egalitarian,* ***Jack's-as-good-as-his-master*** *spirit informs the whole report.* NS □ attrib use *a* ***Jack's-as-good-as-his-master*** *spirit, attitude*; always capital J; may be used ironically to deplore trends in modern industrial relations; the expression more power to his lungs is a play on more power to his elbow (qv).

a jack of all trades (and (a) master of none) (saying) sb who can do varied types of work; sb who has knowledge and ability in varied skills and crafts □ *Wolfenden described the background of a typical rural policeman. 'He has to be* ***a Jack of all trades.*** *For minor crimes like petty theft, he sometimes has to change into civilian clothes and act as his own CID* (= Criminal Investigation Department) *officer.'* TVT □ (NONCE) *This is a malpractice, I have noticed, to which historians talking about literature are particularly prone, sometimes even Christopher Hill, that highly distinguished* ***jack of all trades and Master of Balliol.*** L □ *Her father, Reuben 'Buck' Clafin, was* ***a*** *feckless, loutish* ***jack-of-all-trades*** *who wandered the Middle West, in and out of jobs.* OBS □ (NONCE) *I was* ***a jack of all subjects and a master of none****, but General Papers* (in exams) *went down before me like ninepins.* NS □ *Natural prostaglandins are such* ***jacks of all trades*** *that unwanted side effects tend to be numerous and severe.* NS □ (NONCE) *Maybe it's because of her parentage that Stacey Gregg who plays Lynn Baxter in 'Crossroads' is such* ***a Jill of all talents.*** □ capital or small J; sometimes hyphenated; sometimes derogatory implying no real ability in any of the trades; occas a Jill of all trades (and (a) mistress of none) used to describe a woman and derived from the traditional pairing of Jack and Jill, as in the nursery rhyme of that name.

jam tomorrow (catchphrase) the promise of, or confidence in, better conditions of life, work, pay in the (near) future; pie in the sky (qv) □ (source) *The rule is,* ***jam tomorrow*** *and jam yesterday—but never jam today.* THROUGH THE LOOKING-GLASS (L CARROLL 1832-98) □ *With the most promising movies one or two months hence, it's a case of* ***jam tomorrow.*** *But make a note of 'Theatre of Blood' opening in London on May 31.* ST □ *There remained just one major uncertainty. It was the state of the domestic economy and the extent to which its difficulties might overshadow the* ***jam-tomorrow*** *prospect of the Common Market.* L □ *There are other sharply* *observed characters, notably Peter's rich Belgravia parents, father a fascist-minded brigadier, mother a White Queen with thoughts of **jam yesterday**.* L □ attrib use *a **jam-tomorrow** attitude, prospect*; last example contains allusion to source.

a jaundiced eye etc [O (NP)] a way of considering sb/sth characterized by (prejudiced) disfavour, disgust or disillusion **V:** have, cast... on; take; look upon with. **n:** eye; ⚠ view, outlook □ *Perhaps I was still looking at the world through **jaundiced eyes**, but I soon become unable to concentrate, to feel enthusiastic about the exam, or to see any future in the medical profession at all.* DIL □ *In the past most schemes have failed to reach their target profits because the prices kept falling below forecast. So **a** more **jaundiced view** is now being taken of forecasts.* ST □ *'You're back!' said Lily and cast **a jaundiced eye** on him. 'What do you want this time?'*

one's jaw drops one's face shows astonishment or disappointment, perhaps by gaping a little □ *People**'s jaws drop** when Don Ferguson* (composer of sentimental verses for Greetings Cards) *tells them what he does for a living. 'I often hear a muffled 'Oh my God,' and some people even walk away from me.'* TVT □ *Dennis had insisted on paying for the meal but **his jaw dropped** when he saw the bill.*

(a/Dr) Jekyll and (Mr) Hyde [n + n non-rev] sb who has, or seems to have, a dual personality, who shows two apparently contradictory aspects of his character (from DR JEKYLL AND MR HYDE (R L STEVENSON 1850-94), a story of physical and mental transformation by a mysterious drug) □ *'Alec, are you the man who is making the anonymous telephone calls, or not?' 'I don't know,' he said. 'If so, I am unaware of it. But I may be **a Jekyll and Hyde**, may I not?'* MM □ *There is the haunting fear that behind the urbane face of the Turkish Government's **Dr Jekyll** lurks a **Mr Hyde**. That a duality exists in Turkey's psyche, creating complex internal tensions, is undeniable.* OBS □ *So who (or what) is John Smith* (= any average person)*? This ancient question can be as perplexing for the individual himself as for the sages who try to understand the **Jekyll and Hyde** character of human life.* RT □ attrib use *the **Jekyll and Hyde** character of life.*

the jet set (informal) people who on business and/or for pleasure can afford to travel frequently and far (ie by jet aircraft) and live expensively and luxuriously in other respects also □ *Building luxury hotels at £100 a night for **the jet set** is not what I call industrial development for the benefit of the islanders.* □ *'What's his line?' 'Earth-moving machinery — General Manager in Singapore and points east for a world-wide company.' 'Oh, one of **the jet set**.'* □ (opera) *I suspect, but have no proof, that this is not laziness but due to the fact that the power of visiting **jet-set** singers is such that nobody dares to direct them, even if there is time.* NS □ WANDA: *You think I look like **a jet-setter**? But I'm not! I'm a part-time housewife, part-time mother and part-time actress.* RT □ attrib use *a **jet-set** life-style*; n compound a jet-setter.

the jig is up (saying) all hope of success in a scheme, plan or deception must be abandoned □ (of the film industry) *To hear some people talk, you might think that **the jig was up**; annual admissions halved since 1963, the number of cinemas reduced by a quarter.* OBS □ *A week or so later, whan the spokesman finally had to admit that **the jig was up** in the East, one local newsman conceded to me that perhaps the BBC hadn't been lying after all.* L ⇨ ⚠ the game be up (Vol 1).

the job etc in hand [O/o (NP)] the task or occupation one is already engaged upon, that is one's immediate concern **V:** tackle; get on with, get down to, cope with. **n:** work, ⚠ task, business, matter □ *He could do far more for his chosen profession in getting on with **the job in hand** than by interfering in the detailed scholarship of a period that was not his own.* ASA □ *'Engineers,' Douglas Birkinshaw explained, 'have a habit of concentrating on **the job in hand**. What one thought of most was getting the best out of the equipment at that time.'* OBS □ *...sweltering and freezing alternately, grumbling, throwing up hands in despair, and somehow getting through **the job in hand**.* L □ *The proceedings were then opened by Lydia who briefly stated **the business in hand**, namely to choose a secretary and treasurer for the Committee.* WDM □ *Justin's mind, as so often, is occupied by thoughts other than those appertaining to **the** practical **matter in hand**.* BM

a job lot [Comp (NP)] a miscellaneous collection of persons or articles, usu approximately all of a kind but not differentiated or sorted out according to their value or usefulness **V:** ⚠ be, seem; find sb/sth □ *While this conversation was going on the rest of the company had been looking through the properties* (= costumes etc for amateur theatricals). *They were rather **a job lot**, lent with an enthusiasm that hardly made up for their deficiencies.* WDM □ *'What a beautiful old plate!' 'Yes, it was the only thing worth having in **a job lot** of crockery I picked up at an auction for £12.50, but a bargain at that.'* □ *The extra student helpers were **the** usual **job lot** you'd expect after scraping around at the last minute.*

a job of work [Comp (NP)] a difficult, important task or commitment; sth worth doing or that has proved to have been well done **V:** ⚠ be, become; look like. **adj:** real, hard; good, satisfactory, splendid □ *An assignment is **a job of work** that overrides any personal feelings a reporter may have.* DM □ (He) *shuffled in and out of the Ministry under Mr Healey's awful eye, and hoping to God that they would move on soon to a post where there was **a** real **job of work** to be done.* ST □ *To vary the pace and tone of your reading to suit a wide range of stories over almost half an hour is **a** hard **job of work**.* L □ *The surgeons did **a** good **job of work** on my smashed knee-cap and I was able to get about fairly easily after a couple of months.*

a Job's comforter sb who perhaps means to sympathize with a depressed or unhappy person but who depresses him/her further by pointing out the hopelessness of his/her case, that worse may still be to come etc; one who offers 'cold comfort' (qv) □ (source) *Then **Job** answered and said, I have heard many such things: miserable **comforters** are ye all.* JOB XVI

1-2 ▫ *When the marathon talk-in at No 10 Downing Street* (residence of the British Prime Minister) *finally broke up without agreement, it then became open season for the chorus of* ***Job's Comforters*** *and the massed prophets of gloom (if not doom).* L ▫ *'Well, do exactly what the doctor says. A cousin of mine ended up losing the sight of an eye over an infection like that.' 'Thanks very much! You're* **a** *proper* ***Job's comforter****, aren't you?'*

jobs for the boys the provision of paid employment for favoured groups within a hierarchy, profession, administration etc (the implication being that the work of these groups is not really necessary) ▫ (job advertisement) *At the same time they've turned the old feudal, paternalistic structure upside down so that it's no longer soft* ***jobs for the boys*** *but work for those who are able and ambitious.* ST ▫ *And he would not run it like a museum curator. No more* ***jobs for the boys*** *in the BBC Scottish Symphony Orchestra, allowing them to bow 'n blow us their repertoire of TV programme theme music.* L ▫ *Look, Dad, I'm really keen on the engineering course. The days of teacher, librarian or other* ***jobs for the girls*** *and then with luck a quick marriage are over.* ▫ last example ironic play on headphrase. ⇨ ⚠ a soft job.

jog/nudge sb's arm/elbow (to do sth) [V + O pass] touch or push against sb's arm with one's own as a signal that he/she should notice sth, do/say or not do/say sth; (fig) remind, persuade, pester sb to do sth ▫ *I've told your husband he'll have to book in good time, so you* ***jog his arm*** *when he seems to be forgetting.* ▫ *Jane* ***nudged my arm*** *when they asked if anybody spoke French but I didn't want to be involved in the argument.* ▫ *The Department have been* ***jogging my elbow to*** *get all the reports in before the new Director takes over.* ▫ *He* ***jogged*** *the waitress****'s arm*** *and she dropped the heavy tray she was carrying. Bits of china were scattered everywhere.* ▫ last example shows literal meaning of expression ie 'give a slight knock to sb's arm/elbow'.

jog one's/sb's memory [V + O pass] remind sb of/about something; help or stimulate sb to recall sth ▫ *Never heard of anybody called Mary Woodson, eh? Well, here's a snapshot of her and you together at Newmarket that might* ***jog your memory****.* ▫ *He emptied his pocket of the notes and scraps of paper he had used to* ***jog his memory*** *and document his story over the previous days.* DS ▫ *'I think Alan's forgotten all about that fiver I lent him.' 'Then I think it's time you* ***gave his memory a jog****.'* ▫ variant give sb's memory a jog; also pl give their memories a jog.

John Bull the English nation; a nickname for, and a burly symbolic figure representing (in political cartoons etc), the typical average Englishman ▫ ***John Bull*** *at any rate went about his empire-building without troubling his head over universal ideas.* L ▫ *'It'd be better all round if you'd take that thing off your eyes, Mr Lamb, and get on with your work,' he said, the honest, bluff* ***John Bull****.* CON ▫ *This is Shaw the Irishman speaking: and, if we wish to be reminded why his other island* (= Ireland) *continues to hold* ***John Bull*** *in such loathing, we should listen.* ▫ last example refers to the play JOHN BULL'S OTHER ISLAND (G B SHAW 1856-1950).

a Johnny-come-lately a person who has recently joined a social, administrative or working group (which does not like him to presume equality with or superiority to existing members) ▫ *'Long-distance driving used to be a specialised job,' John explains. 'But now the roads are crowded with new, young "Cowboys" out for a quick buck.' What angers the old hands most is that these* ***Johnny-come-latelys****, with their heavy drinking and brawling ways, give lorry drivers a bad name.* RT ▫ *We simply stand dumbfounded before these natural cathedrals* (canyons in Utah, US). *Here man himself is* ***a Johnny-come-lately****.* L ▫ *It is a sad, but safe, bet that when the first Nobel award is given for research into extra-sensory perception it will not go to any long-serving member of the Society for Psychical Research but to some* ***Johnny-come-lately*** *convert.* NS ▫ attrib use *a* ***Johnny-come-lately*** *convert.*

join the fray [V + O] become a participant in a fight, contest, argument (or simply some fairly lively activity) that is already taking place ▫ *We passed a dog fight. Buster was only too eager to* ***join the fray*** *but I had him on the lead and hurried on as fast as I could.* ▫ (an electoral contest) *Mr Kudal had a lot of influence in certain low quarters. 'That is why people get worried when they hear Kudal has* ***joined the fray****.'* ST ▫ *'What's happening?' 'Billy's birthday party. Come in and* ***join the fray****.' But Mr Bolton excused himself, saying he would call again another day.*

jolly good(!) (dated informal) exclamation, or emph comment, of approval or admiration ▫ *'I think he's gone and extended his sick leave. Since he saw the doctor. Going to stay another week or two.' 'Perfick* (= perfect)*,' Pop said. '****Jolly good****.'* BFA ▫ *'We've planned a picnic, if you want to come.' 'Oh,* ***jolly good!*** *When do we start?'*

a jolly good dinner etc (informal) a very, thoroughly good dinner etc; thorough, complete, punishment etc **n:** dinner, meal; discussion; dressing-down, hiding (= beating) ▫ *You know from the way he talks about the kids and his work that he must be* ***a jolly good teacher****.* ▫ *I know several restaurants where you can get* ***a jolly good meal*** *for less than £5 a head.* ▫ *'You do that once more' his father said, looking up from his paper, 'and I'll give you* ***a jolly good hiding****.'* ▫ *And we can control a whole area from this height. We have* ***a jolly good search*** *every night before the guard goes on duty.* ST ▫ in last two examples, good means 'thorough, complete'; in all examples jolly intensifies adj good.

jolly hockey sticks (catchphrase) a manner or language suggestive of schoolgirl life and interests, esp the breezy, athletic style once associated with English public schools for girls ▫ *The first impression is a manner which would do well opening the choicest of country fêtes, and a vocabulary rich with 'chum', 'crumbs' and bags of* ***jolly hockey-sticks*** *advice.* G ▫ *Fiona Monro-Crighton brings a touch of* ***jolly hockey sticks****, St Trinian's style, to the opening of an exhibition of lithographs by Ronald Searle.* SC ▫ (headline) *Not so* ***Jolly Hockey Sticks****: Glas-*

gow Sherriff Court was told that Mr Purba, who plays for one of the Indian hockey sides in the city, grabbed his hockey stick from under the counter and chased the masked youths from his shop. SC □ hockey sticks may be hyphenated.

jolly well[1] [A (AdvP)] (informal) (do sth) very well, ably, satisfactorily □ *My grandfather's not one of the helpless kind in a house. He can cook a meal and iron his shirts, and do it* ***jolly well****, too.* □ end position after v.

jolly well[2] [A (AdvP)] (informal) certainly, most emphatically (do sth) □ *'Will you come back for me?' 'No. If you don't want to come now you can* ***jolly well*** *walk home.'* □ *He is both grateful for his good fortune, and convinced that he has* ***jolly well*** *earned it.* NS □ *Don't keep saying that Tom couldn't have been there, I'm telling you he* ***jolly well*** *was.* □ middle position only between S and v.

a jot or tittle [n + n non-rev] the least item or detail **det:** (not) a; (by) one; every □ (source) *Till heaven and earth pass,* ***one jot or*** *one* ***tittle*** *shall in no wise pass from the law, till all be fulfilled.* MATTHEW V 18 □ *And* ***no jot or tittle*** *of this morning ritual was ever omitted.* RT □ *I don't suppose all the preachers and philosophers that ever lived have changed human nature by* ***one jot or tittle****.* □ *'The Darkness of the Body' is sexy enough — indeed it's one of the sexiest novels I've read for ages—and, in its long and detailed couplings, few* ***jots*** *miss being jotted,* ***or tittles*** *escape being touched in.* L □ jot = the smallest Greek letter, *iota* (ι); tittle = the dot over the letter *i.* ⇨ ⚠ not one whit etc.

(is your) journey really necessary? (catchphrase) an expression questioning whether a journey or some other activity, occupation, must be undertaken or is worthwhile (from a caption on British Government posters and advertisements, during World War 2, discouraging citizens from internal travel in the interests of fuel economy, priority of troop movements, etc) □ *But the energy consideration might well be part of the argument when it comes to a national policy for industrial relocation. Whether one considers goods or passengers there is an argument for a campaign on the lines of: '****Is your journey really necessary?****'* G □ *But from time to time we all sit back, whatever our occupation, and ask ourselves the question: 'Is what I am doing worth while? Whither am I going?* ***Is my journey really necessary?****'* SD □ *These are only a few of the reasons why Kissinger****'s journeys are really necessary****.* NS

(a) journey's end goal or conclusion of a period in, or process of, life or work — and often death itself; the end of the road[1] (qv) □ *At 3 a.m. one day we drew up on the quay-side at Dunkirk,* ***journey's end*** *for me; for we were to part at Dover.* BM □ *We were too old to start all over again. All we had was this place and each other till we died. This was* ***journey's end****.* □ *It was Rameau himself who first codified what was to become the classical system of key-relations. It remains a mystery why he so completely lacked the feeling for a long-range tonic as a point of departure and* ***a journey's end****.* L □ modern use frequently without article or possess, perhaps influenced by title of successful and well-known play JOURNEY'S END (R C SHERRIFF b1896) about World War 1.

(you can) judge/tell a man by the company he keeps (saying) (it is reasonable or legitimate to) estimate sb's character from the kind of people he associates with, or from the activities, pastimes etc he chooses to spend time on □ STANLEY: *People still* ***judge a man by the company he keeps****. You go around with a lot of drifters and arty boys, and you'll be judged as one of them.* FFE □ ***You can tell a man by the car he keeps****. The car, in our contemporary society, is the chief determinant of social class or moral worth.* SC

a judg(e)ment of Solomon a just and shrewd passing of judgment on a case, esp an unconventional one that is also effective in opposing a wrong-doer or in fitting the punishment to the crime (first example is ironic, an allusion to the circumstances only of the story in I KINGS III 16-27) □ *A French judge at the conciliation hearing divided custody of the child—then only a year old—between the two parents, giving three months' custody to each alternately.* ***This judgment of Solomon*** *was greeted by most French lawyers with incredulity.* ST □ *'The reversing of the directions of motion means that the rockets will go back along their paths—' 'So it means that those who sent the rockets will get 'em* (= them) *back again. Ye gods, it's* ***the judgment of Solomon****.'* TBC □ (NONCE) *The* ***judge*** *offered a* ***Solomon****-like compromise. I should place a set of my fingerprints in a sealed envelope and submit them, not to the university but to the court, there to repose until the litigation was finally resolved.* OBS

jump the gun [V + O] start a race before the starting-gun or other signal; (fig) do sth too soon, before the usual or proper time □ *I had to open veins and things, which worried me a bit, because the last doctor I knew who did the same thing* ***jumped the gun*** *and ten minutes later the blood was running down the stairs.* DIL □ *Is it necessary now to give the plot of 'A Clockwork Orange?' It's been serialised, discussed on all the media, defended and attacked for the last month. Sociologists and others have* ***jumped the*** *film critics'* ***guns****.* OBS □ *The Department of Health and Safety at Work which gains new powers in two weeks' time, on April 1,* ***jumped the gun*** *yesterday and sent a mobile Laboratory, with three inspectors, to Pitsea* (refuse dump) *to see what caused the death of the lorry driver three days ago.* G

jump the queue [V + O] get on to a bus, be served with goods in a shop, etc before other people who have waited in a line to do so; (fig) obtain promotion, a council house to rent, publication of one's book, etc before one's proper turn is due □ *This sailor looked, and was, very strong. If someone* ***jumped the queue*** *he would give them a sharp crack on the head with his enormous wooden spoon.* OBS □ (training centres for the unemployed) *Under half found work, and even this represented an achievement. How was it done? 'To be quite frank,' said one genial manager, 'we* ***jump the queue****. Otherwise our chaps wouldn't stand a chance in hell.'* NS □ *One reason why Harold was not at ease with Alec was because he distrusted the quality of imagination; it was a rogue quality that* ***jumped***

the queue. PW □ (NONCE) *They were put in the flats that families on the housing list wouldn't touch. But to the locals it looked as if they were* ***jumping the*** *housing* ***list***. OBS □ n compounds queue-jumping, a queue-jumper.

just about (informal) almost; very nearly; pretty well etc (qv) □ *With the acquisition of Johnson, who must be* ***just about*** *the fastest winger in the business, the team should do better next season.* □ *I've taken* ***just about*** *all I can stand from dear, simple, kind Derek.* AITC □ JIMMY: *Now Nigel is* ***just about*** *as vague as you can get without being actually invisible.* LBA □ *'She's* ***just about*** *the nastiest creature I have ever played,' says actress Eileen Peel.* DM □ qualifies n, v, adj, adv, prep p.

just another game etc [Comp (NP)] merely another item or person without characteristics or merits to distinguish it or him/her from others of the same kind **V:** ⚠ be, turn into; make sth. **n:** game; book, lecture; toyshop □ *Even experienced professionals are prone to World Cup nerves: no-one can play in front of millions of TV viewers and pretend it's* ***just another game***. □ *It was pitiful to see her mother ageing and be unable to help her, to see her father turning into* ***just another*** *poor old* ***man***. RFW □ *Unless you can prove that this is going to be something more than* ***just another*** *women's* ***magazine*** *we are not prepared to back it.*

just anybody etc absolutely anybody etc, regardless of suitability **pron/adv:** anybody, ⚠ anything; anywhere, any time, anyhow □ *A charming man, I thought, and clever too. Did you know he was on the staff at Westminster? They don't give those posts to* ***just anybody***. AITC □ *She must have been fond of him. It's not the sort of sacrifice you make for* ***just anybody***. □ *Well, if you will put things down* ***just anywhere***, *you're bound to mislay them.* □ *You're supposed to be here by 8 o'clock, not* ***just any time*** *you feel like showing up.* □ often neg or with neg implication.

(it is) just as one feared etc (an event, situation, already described or about to be described, is) exactly as one was afraid etc it would be **V:** feared; ⚠ thought; expected, hoped, foretold □ *'There you are,' James said, tossing the letter over to her. '****It is just as I feared***. *"Your case has been carefully considered and we regret to inform you—" but read it for yourself.'* □ ***Just as I thought***! *Now get back into bed and don't have me coming upstairs again. You're very naughty children.* □ *His greed overcame his caution and he fell,* ***just as we had hoped***, *straight into the trap we had prepared for him.* □ often Disj; often without S or v; past def and past perf tenses only.

just as one/it is unaltered in any aspect; not improved, adorned, or adjusted to any standard □ *'Don't you ever wish I was blonde and beautiful?' 'No, I love you* ***just as you are***.*'* □ *I'm content to be* ***just as I am***. *I'm not interested in making a lot of money, or a name for myself either.* □ *I think your garden is very nice* ***just as it is***. *The kids couldn't play in it if you filled it with flower-beds and rockeries.* □ Comp of S or O (first two examples); or modifies preceding adj (last example).

just as you like etc do as you want to, have your own way, give sb/sth anything you choose to, etc (often, though not necessarily, implies the speaker's disapproval, disagreement or indifference) **V:** like, ⚠ please, wish □ CLIFF: *The sweet-stall's alright, but I think I'd like to try something else.* JIMMY: ***Just as you like***, *my dear boy. It's your business, not mine.* LBA □ *Well, I'm sure it would do you less harm to take a sleeping pill than to lie tossing and turning all night, but* ***just as you wish***. □ *'I'd like to give your secretary something for all the trouble she's taken.' '****Just as you please***, *she certainly won't expect it.'*

(go to the funeral) just for the ride (saying) (attend a function, take part in a project or undertaking not for its apparent purpose or in common with others but) for any pleasure or profit one may get (from 'I went to the funeral just for the ride', a line in an anonymous campfire community song) □ *The banal truth is that I was staying with some friends in the neighbourhood and* ***went to the funeral just for the ride***, *hoping to glimpse some members of the Académie Française.* NS □ *Things were to get tougher from then on and if anybody had thought he was coming on this expedition* ***just for the ride*** *he was soon disabused.* SC

'just growed' (like Topsy) (saying) a person, institution, custom etc has come into existence nobody knows when and how (from quotation given first but expression now usu found in form of headphrase) □ *'Where were you born?' 'Never was born!' persisted Topsy. 'Do you know who made you* (ie God)*?' 'Nobody, as I knows on,' said the child. 'I 'spect* ***I grow'd***.*'* UNCLE TOM'S CABIN (H B STOWE 1811-96) □ *Topsy did not have an illegitimate baby. Miss Ophelia kept far too firm a hand on her for that to happen. To account for her own origin she said she '****just grow'd****'.* NS □ *There is no real logic to Grangemouth, the 'boom town' of Stirlingshire —and indeed, of Scotland. No king or abbot fostered her into being.* ***Like Topsy*** *she '****just growed****'.* SC □ (NONCE) *If the* ***Topsy-like growth*** *of the consumer movement is allowed to continue much longer they won't be able to see the consumer for consumer protection laws.* OBS

just the job/ticket [Comp (NP)] (informal) exactly the person, thing, situation, that is needed or wanted, that would be appreciated **V:** ⚠ be; think, find, sth □ *It is easy, of course, to see how he was a success with patients. For a certain type of mentally ill person Cannon was* ***just the job***. NS □ *Anyway Jane and I knew we were in for a smashing time the moment we set eyes on the place—three dance halls, two sunbathing parades—****just the job****!* UL □ *Thanks for lending me your big lawn mower—it was* ***just the ticket****! I even managed all that long grass behind the house.* ⇨ ⚠ just the thing.

just like that [Prep (AdvP)] (do/say sth) in such a sudden, summary, unexplained, irresponsible etc way that others are surprised, aggrieved or resentful □ *'Look here, Madge,' I said, 'you can't turn me out* ***just like that***.*' 'You arrived* ***just like that***,*' said Madge. It was true. I sighed.* UTN □ RONNIE (goes to a drawer and takes out a notebook): *Did you know he once started to write his autobiography? There, a whole notebook full, and then one day he stopped!*

Just like that! CSWB ▫ *Oh yes, he has dreadful moods, and then he'll come out of them,* ***just like that****, and be as happy as Larry.* ▫ sometimes, esp when recounting an incident, accompanied by a snap of the fingers on that indicating that the event occurs quickly, easily or casually.

(it/that is) just one's luck (saying) (an event or coincidence is) of the annoying or inconvenient kind that is likely to happen, or that happens too often ▫ *'There's no need to take food. We can stock up when we get there.' 'It's a Wednesday, remember.* ***It*** *would* ***be just our luck*** *if we arrived to find all the shops shut for the afternoon.'* ▫ *'The plumber called while you were out.' 'Oh,* ***is****n't* ***that just my luck****! I've waited in all day for him and he comes just when I slip out to the shops for a few minutes!'* ▫ *'Bob's broken arm had only just mended and he fell off a ladder and concussed himself badly.' '****Just his luck****,' Jack replied. 'He's the most accident-prone person I know.'*

just a minute [Disj (NP)] wait for a short time, ie until the speaker does sth/remembers, thinks of sth, etc ▫ *When one's wife, just as one is in a hurry to leave for the office, exclaims: '****Just a minute****, dear — let me fix your tie for you,' what she is really doing as she straightens it is to express her love. This conclusion has been reached by a consulting psychologist called in by the Tie Manufacturers' Association.* SC ▫ *'I'll phone and find out if there is a late train on weekdays.' 'Good idea. Oh,* ***just a minute****. I believe I have a timetable in my briefcase.'* ▫ *Hey,* ***just a minute****! Where do you think you're going with my handbag?* ▫ *'My ticket entitles me to a seat!' 'Now then,* ***just a minute****, sir. I'm afraid it only entitles you to travel to the destination named.'* ▫ sometimes a remonstrance or objection, halting sb in what he or she is saying or doing; in the expressions *wait/hold on/hang on* ***a minute***, just may replace the v to give the headphrase, but it may also be added to give ***just*** *wait/hold on/hang on* ***a minute***.

just now[1] [A] at or around the time of speaking ▫ *I'll take a note of that* ***just now*** *if you can give me a slip of paper. I don't trust my memory.* ▫ *'Want one?' he asked, holding up the bottle. 'Not* ***just now****. Tell me something, darling. Where did you get the typewriter?'* AITC ▫ *I didn't want a drink* ***just then*** *and nobody offered me one later.* ▫ variant just then used esp with neg and in reported accounts as in last example.

just now[2] [A] during a longer or shorter period including the recent past and near future; at the moment (qv); at present (qv) ▫ *You'll have no difficulty finding accommodation* ***just now****. It's not like the summer season, when I've known people have to sleep in their cars.* ▫ *'And what's your son doing* ***just now****?' 'Oh, he's still in the same job.'*

just on midnight etc [A (PrepP)] (informal) very nearly, or exactly a particular point or period of time, weight, quantity, distance etc **o:** midnight, two years ago, opening time; 32 miles to the gallon; ninety, fifty years old; 10 miles from here ▫ *To say that the train was late was an understatement: in fact, it was* ***just on*** *midnight when it finally reached London.* ▫ *I've kept a record these last few weeks and the car seems to be doing* ***just on*** *32 miles to the gallon, which is not bad for an old banger.* ▫ *He was* ***just on*** *ninety when he died.* ▫ *Even before he won the Presidential election* ***just on*** *two years ago, M. Pompidou was already saying in private that he saw no future for Europe without Britain.* L ▫ *Now I'll betake myself to the pub. There I'll wait, it's* ***just on*** *opening time.* PW

(it is) just one of those things (catchphrase) (it is) the kind of thing that can and does happen although one cannot explain or understand why ▫ ***It*** (a love affair) ***was just one of those things,/Just one of those*** *fabulous* ***things****/—A trip to the moon on gossamer wings...* POPULAR SONG ▫ *'Why did McIntyre leave?' he asked, his hand round the glass. 'Oh,* ***just one of those things****,' Mr MacDougall said, 'you know the way it is.'* OMIH ▫ *Bournemouth, for instance, sells a lot of town maps, so does Blackpool. Yet Southend doesn't. 'I don't know why,' admits Dennis Stevenson. '****It's just one of those*** *curious* ***things****.'* ST

(not) just etc a pretty face [Comp (NP)] (not) just sb that has good looks without other qualities, abilities to recommend him/her **V:** be; be seen as. **adv mod:** (not) just, (no/little) more than ▫ *Proving irrevocably that she is****n't just a pretty face****, zany Lena has seven 'O' levels.* TVT ▫ *They should watch, in particular, Dr David Owen who now faces his greatest test as a domestic politician. Failure could mean that he is seen as* ***little more than a pretty face****.* NS ▫ *You think I'm* ***just a pretty face*** *but you're wrong. There are lots of things I want to do and you can't stop me.* ▫ (NONCE) *Miss Collins has progressed and proved she is* ***not just a pretty voice****. She has written many fine songs as well as hitting the charts with her moving interpretations of songs by other top writers.* TVT

just right (for sb/sth) [Comp (AdjP)] exactly and completely suitable (for sb/sth, or for a function or purpose) **V:** ⚠ be, seem; make sb ▫ *Guy will be all right when he marries a nice girl. Perhaps he'll marry Prissie. She would be* ***just right for*** *him, plenty of sense and shrewdness in that little head of hers.* DC ▫ *'All the same, he wasn't a bad chap,' Wormold said. 'But* ***not right for*** *a husband,' the grown-up Milly replied.* OMIH ▫ *I saw a duvet cover that would be* ***just right for*** *Peggy's room.* ▫ *'You didn't think I was too facetious?' 'No, no. The tone was* ***just right for*** *the occasion.'* ▫ neg variant not (just/quite) right (for sb/sth).

just so[1] [Conj (AdvP)] quite, exactly, so; that is true ▫ *'I ordered this carpet four months ago, you know.' '****Just so****, madam, but I'm afraid we've been having delivery problems because of the transport strike.'* ▫ *'You're not showing a very Socialist attitude.' 'Socialists have to be realistic too.' 'Oh yes,* ***just so****— "What's yours is mine and what's mine is my own".'* ▫ used to give assent or agreement, sometimes of a provisional or even sceptical kind.

just so[2] [Comp (AdjP)] (sth) done or arranged with great precision, correctness, tidiness, cleanliness etc ▫ *I told her that her friends were coming to see her, not to inspect the house. But you know mother, she always has to have everything* ***just so****.* ▫ *We had to keep every instrument and bit of equipment* ***just so*** *or the old boy* *would blow his top* (= be very angry). ◻ *I expect you're used to having everything* ***just so****, Mr Jenkins, but I warn you we are pretty slapdash here. No time to be anything else.* ◻ end position.

just the thing [Comp (NP)] (informal) a most suitable and/or satisfactory object, arrangement, job, event, pastime etc **V:** ⚠ be; think, find, sth. **A:** for you, for keeping my papers in; to do him good; (that) we need ◻ *The billiard table, covered over by trestle table boards and with a big white cloth, was* ***just the thing*** *for the eats* (= food), *the champagne and the glasses.* DBM ◻ *Also I had a curious faith in Finn's intuition. It often happened that Finn made some unexpected suggestion which when I followed it up turned out to have been* ***just the thing****.* UTN ◻ *I've got some homemade soup in the pan.* ***Just the thing*** *to warm you up.* ◻ *'Tom is a maniac behind the wheel.' 'Well, his accident—thank God it wasn't any worse—might be* ***the very thing*** *to bring him to his senses.'* ◻ (espionage) *'Sometimes I send postage stamps to a small nephew.'* ***'The very thing****. We could put a microphotograph on the back of one of the stamps.'* OMIH ◻ variant the very thing. ➪ ⚠ just the job/ticket.

just what the doctor ordered [Comp (NP)] (catchphrase) sth that is exactly right and/or desirable for sb to do, have or obtain **V:** ⚠ be, seem ◻ *'Oh, isn't it lovely,' Rose said, the minute they were in the park. 'Yes,' said Stanley, accepting the compliment, 'very refreshing.* ***Just what the doctor ordered****.'* TSMP ◻ *With their* (ie the publishing company) *slipping, and a clutch of aggressive new editors on the general book side being encouraged to search for hot new properties to restore the firm's fortunes, the Irving-Hughes book looked* ***just what the doctor ordered****.* L ◻ *In the northern corridor, 1st Armoured Division was out in the open and was being furiously attacked by the enemy armour; which was exactly* ***what the doctor ordered****, so long as I was the doctor in question.* MFM ◻ can be used as a welcoming comment, as in first example.

justice must not only be done, it must be seen to be done (saying) there is no proof that justice is obtainable and effective unless its procedures and results can be observed by everybody ◻ *Bank of England backing might clothe a CSI with some authority. But the premise that* ***justice ought not only be done but be seen to be done****, is much more important than the invisible, guiding hand.* G ◻ ***Justice*** *to W. Longstaff* ***had been done****. Murray-Hamilton would accept that without much trouble.* ***Justice*** *to W.L.* ***must*** *now* ***be seen to be done****.* SML ◻ (NONCE) *If* ***justice*** *, then,* ***must be seen to waddle*** *at its immemorial pace in the formal investigations, what about a little informal mud-slinging?* OBS ◻ *Life was more orderly (then). Events moved more slowly.* ***Justice was seen to be done****. There was little violence.* TVT ◻ (NONCE) *Some deep lemming instinct requires us to push informality to the limit. It is* ***not enough to be relaxed****—we* ***have to be seen to be relaxed****.* TVT

K

keen on sb/sth [Comp (AdjP)] (informal) in love, or infatuated, with sb; enthusiastically interested in (doing) sth **V:** ⚠ be, get, become; make sb. **o:** Alice, the riding master; music, gardening, sport; studying wild life, keeping up family traditions ◻ *Thomas Brown, author of an unpublished novel, is* ***keen on*** *Alice, a flapper* ((1920s slang) = teenage girl) *with a rich aunt and a studio.* L ◻ *Being* ***keen on*** *an older girl or a member of staff was quite common among second and third form girls, thought merely silly, and quickly outgrown.* ◻ *He rarely switches on to hear any of the classical music he professes to be so* ***keen on****.*

keen on (doing) sth/to do sth [Comp (AdjP)] (strongly) in favour of (doing) sth or of sth being done; eager to do sth or see sth done **V:** ⚠ be, become; make sb. **o:** the idea, what you suggest; Jones for this particular post; prescribing tranquillizers. **Inf:** to go abroad, to have Jones as a colleague, to learn to play the flute ◻ (reader's letter) *My girlfriend and I would like to go on holiday together abroad next summer but our parents are not* ***keen on*** *the idea.* TVT ◻ *Terence was expected to follow* (his father) *into the Diplomatic Service. 'I wasn't* ***keen to do*** *that and said so.'* RT ◻ *Applications from young men* ***keen to*** *join the expedition came from far and near.* ◻ *Local people are* ***keen*** *enough* ***on*** *having the ferry service if it's laid on for them. What they don't want is to have to pay for it.* ◻ neg use common.

keep bad etc company [V + O] associate with undesirable etc people **adj:** bad; better, distinguished; all kinds of ◻ *Counsel said that the youth was of weak character and had been* ***keeping bad company****.* ◻ *At one stroke, Mr Rees had succeeded in infuriating both the Welsh and English establishments. To the former, he was revealed as* ***keeping*** *very* ***bad company****. To the latter, he was a traitor.* ST ◻ *One may* ***keep all kinds of company*** *for all kinds of causes.* NS ◻ *'Lord This and Lady That,' Emily said, scanning the Conference guest list. 'You'll be* ***keeping distinguished company*** *next week.'* ➪ ⚠ the company one keeps.

keep the ball rolling keep an activity, organization etc going, functioning etc ◻ *Corinne and Andrew have left school now and so can no longer be members* (of a Youth Orchestra). *They regret it, but see the necessity for new players coming up. You've got to* ***keep the ball rolling****.* OBS ➪ ⚠ set/start the ball rolling.

keep/bear sb company be a companion for sb either for a short period, or more permanently ◻ *Virginia came in alone and stopped just inside the door when she saw Mollie. 'Oh—hullo,' she said vaguely. 'Been* ***keeping*** *Joe* ***company****?'* AITC ◻ *I'm really glad my father has married again. He needs someone to* ***keep*** *him*

company *in that lonely old house.* □ *Carter patted his tobacco-pouch as though it were a dog's head—'my faithful hound shall* ***bear*** *me* ***company****.'* OMIH □ bear sb company now dated.

keep/lose one's cool [V + O] (informal) retain/fail to retain one's presence of mind, temper, impartial attitude, composed manner, etc □ *I don't know if anyone remembers my colleague who joined the hippy community out there 'to* ***keep his cool*** *and bring up his wind'.* ST □ *There followed three MPs and Robin Day, all of them* ***keeping their cool*** *as if nothing had happened.* NS □ *...the face of an intelligent man in a wide-open, mass-persuasive society, who is not to be taken in, who has* ***kept his cool*** *and his irony.* L □ *The 2,700 visitors from 32 countries waited several hours to register* ***with no*** *noticeable* ***loss of cool****.* OBS □ (a 19th c publisher) *He even moved Lamb to* ***an*** *uncharacteristic* ***loss of cool****: 'The more I think of him, the less I think of him. The lesser flea that bites little fleas!'* NS □ variant (with) no, some etc loss of cool. ⇨ ⚠ next entry; keep/lose one's head; play it etc cool.

keep etc a cool head [possess] not become flustered, angry or excited in a crisis or difficult situation **V:** keep, ⚠ have (got). **prep:** with □ *It's not so hard to get out of a skid if you* ***keep a cool head****.* □ *What the advocates of repression desire is the atmosphere of heightened emotion. The way to fight their emotionalism is* ***with a cool head****; hard facts versus fake evidence.* NS □ (press photograph caption) *This woman turned her programme into a hat to help her* ***keep a cool head*** *during the heated tennis battles in the sun of Wimbledon yesterday.* DM □ also pl *They had to* ***keep a cool head****;* use in last example is facetious. ⇨ ⚠ previous entry; keep/lose one's head; play it etc cool.

keep sth/it dark (from sb) [V + O + Comp pass] hide sth, keep sth secret (from others), sometimes merely in a negative, ungenerous way; keep in the dark (Vol 1) (qv) □ *'Annette's going on with the idea of taking Elspeth's job when she gives it up.' I stared at him. Elspeth had been* ***keeping it dark from*** *me.* SML □ *Anyway, Strether wanted his identity* ***kept dark*** *and for Hiscock that meant* ***keeping it dark from*** *everybody, including the other directors and his own wife.* ILIH □ often keep it dark, referring to sth already mentioned.

keep a dog and bark oneself (saying) employ, or have the services of, sb to do sth and yet choose to do it oneself □ *'I'm busy. What about* you *sewing your button on, if it can't wait?' 'What?* ***Keep a dog and bark myself****!'* □ *I don't believe in* ***keeping a dog and barking myself****, so I'm perfectly happy to let my husband go out and start my car on cold mornings.* RT □ *The agent Hugo Read said: It's the old adage, isn't it, that if you* ***have a dog****, you don't* ***bark yourself****. From the point of view of management here, the Duke interferes very little with the detail.* L □ occas modified, as shown.

keep early etc hours [V + O] go to bed early etc **adj:** early; ⚠ late; regular; odd, peculiar, strange □ *His friends do not* ***keep late hours****: he left their house soon after ten.* PE □ *'I wish we could persuade you to stay with us, but I expect you are more comfortable at the hotel.' 'Not more comfortable, certainly,' he said, 'but you see I* ***keep*** *rather* ***odd hours****—I'm not properly house-trained yet.'* PW □ *We have to* ***keep regular hours*** *here or else my wife would never be out of the kitchen.* □ *All I say is, he* ***keeps*** *very* ***strange hours*** *for a man who says he's a wages clerk.* □ regular, odd etc refer to working routines, mealtimes etc.

keep one's ears/eyes open [V + O + Comp pass] (informal) live, go about one's business, as an alert, receptive, wide-awake person in general; be quick to notice, obtain information about, sb/sth in particular or of a particular kind **A:** for misprints, for the bread van; in case the baby cries; to catch the rumours, to find out what you can □ *I want you to* ***keep your eyes*** *and* ***ears open*** *and report to me.* OMIH □ *I've been* ***keeping my ears open*** *to see if anyone said anything about Coombargana, but I haven't heard anything.* RFW □ *A democracy has to be a continual to-and-fro tug of interests. So the successful running of a democracy means* ***keeping your eyes open*** *as much as you can.* L □ *When Dodd set off for Madrid last Friday he drove one of his ordinary Rolls. 'I think they will be* ***keeping an eye open*** *for the other one,' he says.* ST □ *The important thing is to* ***keep a weather eye open*** *for Susie opening the gate and running out into the road.* □ variant keep an ear/an eye/a weather eye open. ⇨ ⚠ next entry; keep an/one's eye on (Vol 1).

keep one's eyes peeled/skinned (for sth) [V + O] (informal) watch carefully (for sth) □ *Don't move,* ***keep your eyes peeled****, and be prepared to wait for several hours— then you might catch a glimpse of Rumpelayer's Blue-backed Sea-thrush.* □ ***Keep your eyes skinned for*** *any movement in the house opposite. The police think it's a terrorist cell and they want our help.* □ ***Keep your eyes peeled****, Lil, and tell me if you see a blink of sun on those hills ahead.* ARG □ often imper. ⇨ ⚠ previous entry; keep an/one's eye on (Vol 1).

keep oneself/sb fit [V + O + Comp] exercise one's body to keep it in good physical condition □ *Apart from squash, Rae* ***keeps fit*** *with early morning runs around Clapham Common, London, which borders his home.* TVT □ *George claims he can 'still shake a leg with all the youngsters at the discos. I enjoy a bit of a rave-up.* ***Keeps me fit****.'* TVT □ *A* ***keep-fit*** *class, specially adapted for the elderly, is an ideal way to get exercise without overdoing it.* ST □ *Fear of being thought a* ***keep-fit*** *crank made her give up the exercises while staying at the hostel.* □ also intrans, as in first example; attrib use *a* ***keep-fit*** *class, enthusiast etc.*

keep the flag flying behave in a way, do sth, which shows that oneself, one's cause, an institution or activity, is not defeated yet and can still survive (hauling down one's flag is a signal or token of military surrender) □ *British golf fans tend to see Jacklin as something of a standard-bearer, playing for Queen and country and* ***keeping the Union Jack flying*** *in a foreign land.* OBS □ *It's true that newer crime writers like Julian Symons and Edmund Crispin have* ***kept the flag flying****.* RT

keep (oneself etc) going (cause sb/sth to) continue moving or striving, or keep up a pattern of life, work etc in spite of tiredness, obstacles, difficult circumstances **O:** himself, them; one's system, body; company, plant □ *I'm shagged* ((slang) = exhausted)—*had to have a nip* (= drink) *to* ***keep going***. OBS □ *He writes non-stop day and night when he's in the mood and* ***keeps himself going*** *with cigarettes and black coffee.* DM □ *It took 400 tons of rail and timber for every mile of track. It was said that whereas the Union Pacific* (Railroad) *was sustained by whisky, the Central Pacific was* ***kept going*** *on tea.* L □ *The end to be desired is rescue. I must* ***keep*** *this body* ***going***. PM □ passive as in *we were* ***kept going*** *on coffee.*

keep sb guessing allow sb, usu deliberately, to remain uncertain of one's intentions, or about the actual facts of a case □ *If Winterhalter* (a portrait painter) *might seem to have been something of a snob he was never a lackey. Queen Victoria complained of his not answering letters and he sometimes* ***kept*** *her* ***guessing*** *about a commission.* ST □ *The Government were, of course, entitled to* ***keep*** *everyone* ***guessing*** *for security reasons.* SC □ *Of course, we were* ***kept guessing*** *as to their real intentions.* □ passive as in last example.

keep/lose one's head [V + O] think, act, calmly and sensibly/excitedly and foolishly in an emergency, difficulty; retain/lose one's powers of judgement when being subjected to persuasion, flattery, criticism etc □ *If your father hadn't* ***kept his head*** *and switched off at the mains they'd have both been electrocuted.* □ *He was torn in two between the desire to win and the desire to* ***keep his head***, *but his head was clouded by anger as well as whisky.* OMIH □ *She sounded apologetic and he hastened to reassure her. 'I think you did pretty well,' he told her. 'Didn't* ***lose your head***.' PE □ *As always she has* ***kept her head*** *while others around her have been* ***losing theirs***. ST □ also pl keep/lose their heads. ⇨ ⚠ keep etc a cool head, keep/lose one's cool; play it etc cool.

keep the home fires burning (dated catchphrase) maintain in good order one's family home, or a domestic or civil front, while awaiting the return of those serving in the army etc (from a popular song of World War I) □ *'Oh, yes,' she said. 'I'm a young war widow. Haven't you heard the pater* (= father) *talking about it? It's quite moving. Only he forgets that there are two million others. Most of them at least* ***kept the home fires burning***.' ASA □ (NONCE) *Our holiday pleasure rests on* ***keeping the fires of hospitality burning***. *Freedom for British tourists depends directly on maintaining and improving Britain as a good place for foreign tourists to come to.* OBS

keep one's mouth/trap shut [V + O + Comp pass] (informal) not reveal information, express an opinion, advice or a promise, etc; shut one's mouth etc (qv) □ *Spies are trained to* ***keep their mouths shut*** *and they don't often lose the habit.* DS □ *Your brother knocked down a man and killed him. I have proof of this but I will* ***keep my mouth shut*** *if you pay me a hundred pounds by midday tomorrow.* DC □ *Philistine and the Furies pursued Whistler. He was the artist who did not simply—perhaps wisely—***keep his trap shut** *and get on with painting.* NS □ ***Your mouths*** *should be* ***kept shut***, *and your eyes open.* ⇨ open one's (big) mouth.

keep mum (informal) stay silent, say little or nothing (for a period); say nothing about sth in particular as a matter of policy or by request; mum's the word (qv) □ ***Keep mum*** *during all his favourite TV programmes—don't chatter when he's playing his best-loved disc.* WI □ *Oh, one snub's enough for me. I'm* ***keeping mum*** *now, thank you.* □ *Even that theatrical old fool Portway wasn't prepared to disagree with the great Stokesay. He smelt a rat, but he* ***kept mum***. ASA

keep one's nose clean [V + O + Comp] (informal) keep out of trouble (eg not break the law, flout regulations, get into debt) □ *I'll tell him to* ***keep his nose clean*** *when he goes out* (of prison), *but I know he'll be back.* OBS □ RUTH: *Give me that letter.* JOSIE: *Oh, that. Oh, yes.* RUTH: *Thank you very much. Kindly learn to* ***keep your nose clean*** *in future, will you.* EGD □ also pl *They should* ***keep their noses clean***.

keep open house [V + O] be willing to receive guests or visitors, invited or uninvited, at any time or at specified times □ *Well, it's very nice to be able to* ***keep open house***, *I suppose. But it's not everybody that can afford to be so hospitable.* □ *In the evenings, he'd* ***keep open house*** *for his cronies with endless champagne and caviar and half a dozen girls that some agent used to procure for him.* DS

keep one's own company not mix with others in a friendly or social way (either as a permanent habit or temporarily because of one's circumstances or mood) □ *Some of us tried at first to be neighbourly but they seemed to want to* ***keep their own company***. □ *He* ***kept his own company***, *thinking gloomily that somehow he ought to have foreseen the tragedy and taken steps to prevent it.* TBC

keep one's own counsel form one's own ideas, opinions, plans and not talk about them, so that others are never sure of one's attitude or intentions □ *He listened to all the suggestions put forward, took notes from time to time, and* ***kept his own counsel***. □ *As for what I'm going to do with the money—if I get it—I'll* ***keep my own counsel***. □ *They were advised to* ***keep their own counsel***.

keep the peace [V + O] enforce or observe the state's requirements to behave in a peaceful, orderly way; prevent or avoid a quarrel □ *The Canadian government had made plans for a mounted force to* ***keep the peace*** *on the prairies.* OBS □ *On the following day he was fined $25 and bound over to* ***keep the peace***. ST □ *I wasn't keen* (on a career in the Diplomatic Service) *and said so. But to* ***keep the peace*** *and in the hope of learning some French I went off to a crammer near Boulogne.* RT □ n compound peace(-)keeping; attrib use *a* ***peace-keeping*** *force.* ⇨ break the peace.

keep the pot boiling[1] earn enough to maintain an adequate standard of living (the implication often being that this is barely sufficient) □ *Even with the bits of gardening and house-jobbing I do in the evenings it's not easy to* ***keep the pot boiling***. □ *Sometimes he's lucky and sells a picture for a good price and we think, 'Oh well, that'll* ***keep the pot boiling*** *for a bit.'* □ *Contemporary critics saw nothing more than a producer of* ***pot-boilers***, *but recently literary* *historians have begun to take him more seriously.* □ n compound a pot-boiler = (derogatory) 'a novel, article, painting, song etc written etc by a person of talent merely to add to his/her income, with the implication that the work is of poor quality'.

keep the pot boiling[2] keep a situation active, interesting, amusing or disturbing, upsetting □ *It was not for nearly half an hour that Churchill did arrive and in the meantime someone had to* ***keep the pot boiling****. This was brilliantly done by my hero, A. P. Herbert.* ST □ *There was continuing concern about America's 'energy crisis'. To* ***keep the pot boiling*** *the Oil Producing and Exporting Countries decided to demand a 10 per cent increase in revenues.* L □ *It seems to have been in about 1962 that the Ministry of Health decided that fluoridation was to be crashed through* (= introduced speedily). *A number of circulars since then have* ***kept the pot on the boil****.* L □ variant keep the pot on the boil.

keep one's powder dry [V + O + Comp] (military) have one's equipment and resources ready; (fig) be in a state of readiness to cope with a possible emergency (the original reference being to gunpowder) □ *It doesn't sound like business for a long time. Still it won't do any harm to watch out and* ***keep our powder dry****.* NM □ *No man was ever more fit than the Afrikaner to hold the motto: Have faith in God but* ***keep your powder dry****.* OBS

keep a safe etc/one's distance [V + O] stand, move etc some distance away from sb/sth; not associate, or have only a formal relationship, with sb; not let oneself become involved in a situation, project etc **adj:** safe; ⚠ discreet, judicious, suitable □ *You'd better* ***keep your distance****. There's going to be an awful smell when I lift the lid.* □ *I* ***kept a discreet distance*** *until the hunters joined me; then we went forward and removed the rat from the net.* BB □ *She reflected that, when she had first arrived, she should have* ***kept her distance*** *with the woman and refrained from confidences.* MM □ no adj used with keep one's distance.

keep sb's seat etc warm for him [V + O + Comp pass] (informal) occupy a chair, house, business, professional or official position until a second person is ready to do so (esp in order to prevent a third person establishing a claim to it) **O:** seat, place; constituency; post □ *'Don't get up.' 'That's all right, I was only* ***keeping*** *it* ***warm for you****.'* □ *His constituency at South Leeds was being* ***kept warm for him*** *although he was only able to visit once or twice a year.* OBS

keep a secret [V + O pass] not pass on to any third person sth which has been told to one confidentially by another □ *'I wonder if you can* ***keep a secret****?' 'Me,* ***keep a secret****? What, I'm the grave's only rival with a good secret, I am.'* RM □ *One can't expect children to* ***keep secrets****.* □ *I must say,* ***their secret****'s been well* ***kept****.*

keep one's side of a/the bargain [V + O pass] carry out what one has undertaken to do in an exchange of services or favours □ *I don't think we need put anything down in writing. If I can't trust you to* ***keep your side of a bargain****, I don't know who could.* □ *He said that if I'd play cards with him, he'd take me out for a drink. Now the wretched man's not* ***keeping his side of the bargain****.* □ ***His side of the bargain's*** *not been* ***kept****.*

keep smiling show courage and cheerfulness; refuse to appear discouraged □ *But with so many problems besetting the world, from war to pollution and injustice, I find it difficult to* ***keep smiling****.* RT □ *If you're a nurse this sort of* ***keep smiling*** *thing is what you've got to do, give your patients a charge of confidence.* SC □ (astrological prediction) *Tuesday looks difficult; it'll be hard to* ***keep smiling****, though people around you are happy.* TVT

keep a straight face [possess] not smile or laugh when one really wishes to; not display amazement, doubt, disbelief etc though these are felt **V:** keep, ⚠ have (got). **prep:** with □ *The doleful taciturn image Clement Freud represents to the public is far removed from the jovial father his family knows. 'That's not to say he can't* ***keep a straight face*** *for as long as he likes,' says his 15-year-old son, Dominic.* OBS □ *He learned to* ***keep a straight face*** *playing cards during his National Service.* TVT □ *I knew he couldn't be feeling as funny as he looked, all covered with mud and dripping weeds, so I managed to* ***keep my face straight****.* □ (TV news programmes, US) *And there are John Chancellor and Walter Cronkite reporting horrendous things* ***with a straight face*** *and, saving the Administration's presence, with admirable objectivity.* L □ variant keep one's face straight.

keep etc oneself unspotted from the world keep oneself morally and spiritually uncorrupted by worldly practices and pleasures **V:** keep oneself; be, remain □ (source) *Pure religion and undefiled before God and the Father is this, To visit the fatherless and widows in their affliction, and to* ***keep himself unspotted from the world****.* JAMES I 27 □ *Purity in lesser degree is required of those who have to earn their livelihood in the world at large, and are presumably less likely therefore to* ***keep themselves unspotted from it****.* T □ *She is not very bright, but the only completely good person I know. Maybe you have to have a fairly low I.Q. to* ***remain unspotted from the world****.*

keep watch [V + O pass] be on guard duty (against intruders or enemies); keep sb, a building, an area, etc under observation **A:** for marauders; at the airport; over their stores □ *They took it in turns to* ***keep watch*** *after that, in case Simmons should come back to continue his search.* □ *She came so quickly after him that she might have been* ***keeping watch****—and almost at once there was another constraint in the room.* NM □ *'I don't think the patrol van's gone by yet.' 'You don't* think*! You're supposed to be* ***keeping watch****, you oaf.'* ⇨ ⚠ keep a close watch on (Vol 1).

keep/break one's word [V + O] (not) do as one has promised to do □ *I promised not to go out of this territory and I* ***kept my word****.* □ *What was Querini up to? Was Wouwermans* ***keeping his word*** *to hang on to the picture?* US □ *You've* ***broken your word*** *already by not being there at nine.* □ cf *he never* ***broke a promise****, she* ***kept*** *all but one of* ***her vows****.*

kick oneself (informal) reproach oneself; be angry or vexed with oneself (for sth one has done or failed to do) □ *I* ***kicked myself*** *all the* *way back to the hotel for having behaved like a carefree man in a quite embattled town.* NS □ *When Elsie had departed, Bill Brownsworth could have* ***kicked himself*** *for not having given a bold affirmative to that question.* RM □ *Bolshaw then looked at me suddenly. 'Would you like to join me in this work?' I could have* ***kicked myself*** *for having politely professed interest.* SPL □ often with *could (have)*.

kick the bucket [V + O] (informal) die □ *Mr Wickham, their agent for many years past, said that if he* ***kicked the bucket*** *Mrs Merton could run the place standing on her head.* WDM □ *They sleep so well I think that every scruffy head's* ***kicked the bucket*** *in the night and I'm the only one left.* LLDR

kick the habit etc [V + O pass] (informal) completely abandon, give up the habit etc (the reference usu being to sth harmful or foolish) **O:** habit, addiction; smoking, drink; this stupid fear □ *Formerly a 20-a-day smoker, Dr John Dunwoody* ***kicked the habit*** *when he was a GP.* RT □ *He had been on hard drugs too and one of the very few who have managed to* ***kick it*** *sweating it out on their own.* OBS □ *Gilmore is tall and wiry with fair hair. He has* ***kicked his Yorkshire accent***. RT

kick one's heels [V + O] find oneself with nothing particular to do; be forced to wait about idly, esp because of delays caused by others □ *Bob Gurney, the oldest player, was* ***kicking his heels*** *and pulling on his pipe in the corridors a couple of days later.* ST □ *Sent to* ***kick his*** *gilded* ***heels*** *around the Mediterranean, Maximilian's liberal deportment in Italy roused resentful suspicions—never quite quenched—in his elder brother the Emperor Franz Joseph.* NS ⇨ ⚠ cool one's heels.

kicking and screaming [A] (informal) offering (strong) physical protest or resistance **V:** lie, roll about, wake, come to; drag, push, carry off, bundle in, sb □ *I used to have the most dreadful nightmares. I'd wake up* ***kicking and screaming***. □ *We aim to drag the Co-operative Movement,* ***kicking and screaming*** *if need be, from the 1930's into the 1960's.* OBS □ *I can't stand much more of this noise. When I'm carried off* ***kicking and screaming*** *to the nut-house you'll know who to blame.* □ usu in order of headphrase.

kid(s') stuff (informal) an easy task or procedure; child's play (qv) □ *'What about the General Knowledge test?'* ***'Kids' stuff,'*** *Leslie said loftily, 'I've seen last year's paper.'* □ *Western Europe could then face a period of nationalist rivalries which would make the Gaullist extravagances of the 1960s look like* ***kid stuff***. NS

kill oneself doing/to do sth (informal) spend a great deal of effort to do or achieve sth (the implication frequently being that more effort is used than the situation or results calls for) □ *I've since noticed there's a kind of racial difference between the boys with the BBC and those with the other outfits. The BBC wallahs are* ***killing themselves to*** *be British, and the other mobs are getting ulcers trying to be all slick and American.* JFTR □ *We plan to leave about 6.45 a.m. but don't* ***kill yourself to*** *get here in time.* □ *They're not children now, Penny. Why should you* ***kill yourself*** *running around after them?*

kill the fatted calf (saying) give a hospitable welcome with the best of food and treatment, esp to a returning or visiting member of one's own family but also to any favoured guest □ (source) *And bring hither* ***the fatted calf***, *and* ***kill*** *it; and let us eat and be merry: For this my son was dead, and is alive again; he was lost, and is found.* LUKE XV 23-24 □ *Her mother, who never stinted them of feasts for ceremonial occasions,* ***killed the fatted calf***. PW □ *They are rich cultural snobs who are prepared to* ***kill*** *any number of* ***fatted calves*** *in return for finding their marshy and unprofitable estates to be one of England's 'historic treasure-grounds'.* ASA □ *I shouldn't worry over her reception of you. After all, you could hardly expect* ***a fatted calf***, *could you?* WI

kill the goose that lays the golden eggs (saying) destroy (out of greed or thoughtlessness) a source of continuous future profit □ *'The Times' contained the predictable well-turned warnings about the folly of* ***killing geese that lay golden eggs***, *through excessive wage demands.* L □ □ *Tea production falters.* ***The goose that lays*** *Ceylon****'s golden eggs*** *is being tormented to death.* SC □ *It is always hard to see whether the North Sea* (oil) *is profitable and whether the Government action is* ***killing*** *off* ***the*** *golden* ***goose*** *before it* ***lays*** *any* ***golden eggs***. G □ structural variation possible, as in last example.

kill or cure [v + v non-rev] either kill the patient or cure him; if not by chance successful, be likely to prove not merely ineffective but disastrous **S:** medicine, drug; treatment; doctor; handling, journey □ *'I've such a stiff shoulder I can hardly get my clothes on and off.' 'Well, I've got some horse liniment in the shed that'll* ***kill or cure*** *you.'* □ *'The outboard motor won't fire.' 'Hit it with that hammer under the stern seat.' 'Sounds a pretty* ***kill-or-cure*** *technique to me.'* □ attrib use, *a* ***kill-or-cure*** *technique etc,* common.

kill sth stone dead [V + O + Comp pass] (informal) completely end or destroy sth, make it unable to continue **O:** the notion, any such proposal; conversation; his ambitions as a politician, their budding romance □ *A face-to-face encounter with Miss MacLaine* ***kills stone dead*** *any notion that her motives might be frivolous, her principles half-baked.* RT □ *...plenty of real people in 'The Family'* (a television programme) *which for sheer entertainment value alone* ***killed*** *all its fictional counterparts* ***stone dead***. L

kill time etc [V + O] try to make (a period of) time, in which one has nothing to do, pass as pleasantly as possible **O:** time, ⚠ an hour or two, a wet afternoon □ *Even a horizontal raid* (flight above the range of ground-fire) *would be a way of* ***killing time*** *and* ***killing thought***. QA □ *If I had to* ***kill the evening*** *until Hugo's return I might as well kill it searching for Hugo as any other way.* UTN □ *Breaking my flight in Madrid, I found I had a couple of* ***hours*** *to* ***kill***.

kind/sort of (informal) rather; somewhat; partially; to some extent □ *But I'm* ***kind of*** *plump, sergeant, as you see. So the postman here couldn't haul me out.* TO □ *It tastes rather like Russian salad — only* ***sort of*** *drier.* OMIH □

*'Were you relieved when they said they couldn't come?' '**Kind of**, but only because I was so tired.'* □ *No, it's not your husband on the phone, madam. It's a strange voice, sinister **sort of**.* DC □ *You'll have to put the question **kind of** indirectly, so that she needn't answer unless she wants to.* □ may qualify an adv, adj or v. ⇨ ⚠ of a kind/sort.

a kindred spirit sb who shares one's interests, tastes and with whom one feels at ease □ *She made George her confidant, professing to find in him **a kindred spirit**.* PE □ *Shaw saluted Nietzsche as **a kindred spirit** (though it is unlikely that Nietzsche would have returned the compliment).* NS □ *The outspoken ambition of our class was to become one's own boss. He knew he wasn't the leader of **kindred spirits** any more.* LLDR

a King Charles's head [Comp (NP)] an obsession (of sb's); a fact or topic constantly referred to whether really relevant or not (the head of this executed monarch kept intruding into the thoughts, conversation and writing of Mr Dick, an amiable eccentric in DAVID COPPERFIELD (C DICKENS 1812-70)) **V:** ⚠ be, become □ *He wasn't prepared to listen endlessly to complaints of how little her children appreciated her. It was fast becoming **a King Charles's head**.* □ *And here too, Martin has had a raw deal. The question of his candidacy at Ludlow gradually became **a King Charles's head**.* NS

King Log...King Stork a ruler, overseer, boss etc (King Log) who does neither harm nor good, is not feared but is ineffective, contrasted with one (King Stork) who makes his power felt in a destructive or tyrannical way (from Aesop's fable of the frogs who asked Jupiter for a King; dissatisfied with the log he threw down for them, they were sent a stork instead) □ *'You promised to be as great a tyrant as Clun in your editorial supervision,' he said laughing. 'I suspect we've avoided **King Log** to be landed with **King Stork**.'* ASA □ *'Wax' was about an old fellow, once awe-inspring to his family. When they take him up to the hospital to have him certified and put away as a loony, the family find that their old **log** is changed to the **stork** he used to be by the breezy doctor who syringes out his ears.* L

the king of the castle the one who is in the highest position (used literally in children's games) □ (source) *I'm **the king of the castle**/ Get down you* (or: *And you're the*) *dirty rascal.* NURSERY RHYME □ *The beautiful rich have an infuriating ease about them. **Kings of the castle** indeed.* YWT

the King's/Queen's English standard English as contrasted with regional dialects, slang, substandard or foreign forms; English as opposed to any other language □ *Bayswater after the War became steadily more cosmopolitan so that now, if any survivors of this earlier population happened to hear **the King's English** spoken in the street, they looked up in amazement.* AH □ *He has one of the most flexible voices in radio, although he says that coming from Somerset meant he had a hard time at first convincing producers that he could speak **the Queen's English**.* RT

a king's ransom [O/o (NP)] a very great, perhaps incalculable, sum of money **V:** cost, be worth, pay sb; not exchange sth (for) □ *An emerald of that size, unflawed, would be worth **a king's ransom**.* □ *I wouldn't even stay in the same district as Dr Grimsdyke, sane or insane, if you paid me **a king's ransom**.* DIL

Kingdom come heaven; the next world; Christ's second Kingdom after the Day of Judgement □ PETER: *Let me die with my eyes full of flowers! I am old—I go to **kingdom come**.* DPM □ *You left the gas jet on again. One of these days we'll all be blown to **kingdom come**.* □ *'Retire?' The bright-eyed widow gathers lace gloves, 'I hope to work here until **Kingdom come**.'* OBS □ uses often irreverent.

kiss the Blarney Stone [V + O] have the ability or intention to flatter, persuade or deceive people with one's talk (from an inscribed stone in the castle wall of Blarney, near Cork in Ireland, kissing which is supposed to give one such powers of persuasion) □ *It's not necessary to have **kissed the Blarney Stone** to be a successful salesman. That's another outdated notion of yours.*

kiss it better kiss a young child as a 'cure' for a minor bump or injury □ *Did you bump your knee when you fell? Come here and I'll **kiss it better**.* □ *Who* wouldn't *have a sore head after a night like that! What does he expect me to do about it — **kiss it better**?* □ ironic use in second example where person referred to is adult.

the kiss of death [O (NP)] a blighting or destructive effect on sth/sb **V:** give, administer □ *Films about art have got to be about life, and to be sacred and solemn about it is the surest way of administering **the kiss of death**.* RT □ *He was prepared readily to accept assignments which most officers with an eye on promotion would have regarded as **the kiss of death**.* NS □ *The production team really* care *(professionally, of course) about viewers' reactions, and this could soon put **the kiss of death** on the programme.* L □ parodies next entry (qv).

the kiss of life [O (NP)] mouth to mouth resuscitation by expanding the lungs of sb who has stopped breathing; (fig) action, influence or change of circumstance that (re)vitalizes an art, science, industry, political or religious system etc; a shot in the arm (qv) **V:** give, administer □ *Only 81 days to Christmas, and already love is all around, **a kiss of life** breathed by tired tycoons into a moribund industry.* L □ *The stagnant condition of the British economy cried out for a shot in the arm. Whether the Chancellor of the Exchequer**'s kiss of life** can make much difference may be regarded as doubtful* L □ expression parodied in previous entry (qv).

kissing cousins cousins, esp a pair of opposite sex, who have a close personal or emotional relationship as well as a family one □ *She measures everybody against Frank who was **a kissing cousin** of hers in her teens.* □ *When we saw each other we just embraced. What else? They called those of us who were left 'the dangerous **kissing cousins**'.* ST

(a) kitchen-sink drama/play a play about family life in the working and lower middle classes which is intended to be realistic and is often socially and politically didactic (a trend esp of the late 1950s and early 1960s) □ *Morris's magic, of course, is out of date, caught as we are* *between* ***kitchen-sink drama*** *and women's magazines.* NS □ *He is not a man to be rattled easily, not even when* ***kitchen sink plays*** *drove out verse from the theatre, just when every critic was convinced it had come to stay.* SC □ *The* ***plays*** *I put on weren't* ***kitchen sink****, if you follow me, they were the bucket below the drip in the kitchen sink.* SC

(one's) kith and kin [n + n non-rev] members of one's family or racial group □ *The French troops were given orders no longer to pamper their '****kith and kin****' and the whole movement collapsed at once.* NS □ (reader's letter) *By signing the Treaty of Rome we shall forgo the right to elect those who make our laws, the right to keep such links as we think fit with* ***kith and kin*** *in the Commonwealth, the right to decide what is best for our country.* SC □ kith now used only in this expression.

knee-high to a grasshopper [Comp (AdjP)] (informal) still just a small child (usu with reference to one's own or another's past) **V:** ⚠ be, stand □ *I wouldn't miss 'The Rolling Stones' Story' (Sat Radios 1 and 2) because I've been a good old Stones' groupie since I was* ***knee-high to a grasshopper****.* RT □ *I've seen him leading in these huge horses, when his father came off the field, when he was no more than* ***knee-high to a grasshopper*** *as the Americans say.* SC

a knight in shining armour (cliché) sb who is gentlemanly, gallant and brave, esp one seen in the role of lover, rescuer or defender □ *Kay says Cassidy, 27, is 'very romantic'. 'He's also a gentleman. My mother always hoped I'd meet* ***a knight in shining armour****. Somehow I think I've found one.'* TVT □ *Cress is a young woman whose marriage is going wrong. Along comes* ***a knight in shining armour****—tender, understanding, romantic.* TVT □ (NONCE) *Lord Brockway is a professional nonconformist,* ***a knight in*** *rather dusty white intellectual* ***armour****. British politics over the last half-century would have been less honourable without his presence.* SC □ also pl knights in shining armour.

knock sb cold [V + O + Comp pass] (informal) render sb unconscious or severely stun him; severely shock or stupefy sb **S:** blow, impact; shock; incident; report, news □ *He was just in time to dodge the full force of the boom as it swung round. Even so, it* ***knocked*** *him* ***cold*** *and he'd have slipped off the deck if I hadn't grabbed him.* □ *She was pale but she was taking it all right. You could say that for Jin; she would never let you* ***knock*** *her* ***cold****.* AITC

a knocking shop (slang) a brothel □ *He knew exactly the sort of second-rate, profiteering road-house Mrs Curry would have made of Vardon Hall. 'Pretty easy to imagine, I should think,' a retired admiral mumbled, '****a*** *high-class* ***knocking shop****.'* HAA □ *. . . a spate of detail about how and where she'd had it off with her long string of lovers. Curiously, though, even if every page reads like a* ***knocking shop*** *gazette, the effect is cheering and resiliently human.* L □ also pl; stress pattern a 'knocking shop; attrib use *a* ***knocking-shop*** *gazette.*

know all the answers [possess] (informal) believe that one's information, opinions, judgments are correct and not hesitate to express them freely, or ignore other people's views **V:** know, ⚠ have (got). **prep:** with □ *The researchers say: 'The broadcaster often seems to give the impression of* ***knowing all the answers****.'* ST □ (reader's letter) *We saw how a lecturer in a college of education* ***had all the answers****.* RT □ *I am an ordinary person with everyday problems myself. I'm not a specialist* ***with all the answers****.* ST □ usu derogatory.

(not) know any better (not) be able to act appropriately, to behave well (through (lack of) experience, (bad) upbringing, etc) □ *Let's face it, you and I would never dream of paying so much. We poor men in the street simply do****n't know any better****.* OBS □ *Their patience with teenage hooligans is remarkable. 'After all,' one teacher said, 'most of them do****n't know any better****, do they?'* □ *What do you think you're doing, you two? — fingers filthy, eating with your hands, talking with your mouths full. It'd be hard for a stranger to believe that you* ***knew any better****.* □ usu neg or interrog. ⇨ ⚠ know better (than to do sth).

know (sth) as well as I do understand perfectly well, in spite of one's claim or pretence that one does not; know sth very etc well (qv) **O:** implications, consequences; that he will, why he doesn't, when it'll go. **pron:** I, you; anyone, anybody (does) □ *'Come to London and have a slap-up lunch with me on expenses.' How she does fuss, thought Ella. She must* ***know as well as I do*** *that I shan't really go.* HAA □ *'Why can't you make yourself look a bit more attractive?' 'You* ***know*** *why* ***as well as I do****. Where's the money for nice clothes and hair-dos, I'd like to know?'* □ *Mr Stanton* ***knows as well as anybody*** *that the average pupil does* not *have more sense than his teachers.* □ may be followed by clause introduced by *that, why, when, etc.*

know best know what should be done, thought etc, better than anyone else □ *This is not a government which believes in consultation. It is a government which is sure it* ***knows best****.* NS □ *'I want to get up.' 'But the doctor said you were to stay in bed, and surely he* ***knows best****?'* □ *I warned him the bridge wouldn't bear his weight but some people always* ***know best****.*

know better (than to do sth) be wiser, better informed, or more sensible (than to do or believe sth) □ *There was hardly any light but he* ***knew better than to*** *waste time because of what was coming.* PM □ *All kinds of irritating conditions exist through the disregard of the needs of the school by responsible persons who should* ***know better****.* NSC □ *In 1971 he was 26 — old enough to* ***know better than to*** *go to India with some friends and post home some toy elephants containing cannabis.* NS □ in constructions with *should, ought to, be old/big enough to*, the suggestion is that one *doesn't* ***know better****.* ⇨ ⚠ (not) know any better.

know different (informal) have evidence, information or an opinion contrary to sth stated or suggested □ *The newcomers think that if old Fred didn't get the nomination this time he would loyally stand down and make way for a younger man. The party bosses* ***know different****.* G □ *You can't tell some people anything. They always* ***know different****.* □ judged non-standard by some careful speakers; often suggests a superior, self-satisfied attitude in the people concerned.

know (all) the dodges/tricks [V + O] (informal) know the clever procedures, manoeuvres etc needed to achieve or obtain sth; be up to² (Vol 1) (qv) □ *'I can fix it. I know what to do.' He laughed. 'I **know the dodges**,' he said.* AITC □ *Thames and Hudson* (a publishing company) *specialise in books on the history of art and when it comes to opening windows from their texts in the form of pictures they **know all the** better **tricks**.* SC

know etc for certain/sure know etc with absolute certainty and accuracy (that sth is as described, that a given fact is correct) **V:** know; ⚠ (can) say, (can) tell □ *It might have been another man speaking. Just then, I **knew for certain** the effort he was making.* NM □ *He asked his friends how many murders there had been in Belfast during the week. Nobody **knew for certain**.* NS □ *'He says that it was the speed that killed Dave. Is that true?' 'It might be. I don't **know for sure**, but it's quite possible.'* TBC □ *I think Jack means to call this evening for his books, but if you ring again at lunch-time he'll be in himself and can **tell you for sure**.* □ *'Did this witness remain in the room the whole time?' Paul hesitated, 'I can't **say for certain**.'* □ may be followed by, or refer back to, clause introduced by *that, what, where etc.*

know a good thing etc when one sees etc it have the knowledge or shrewdness to recognize the usefulness or value of sb/sth, or the opportunity to do or obtain sth profitable; recognize sb/sth as being one of a particular class or kind **O:** a good thing, bargain; gentleman, scoundrel; Irish accent; string of lies; explosive situation. **V:** sees, ⚠ hears, meets, comes across. **O:** it, him, her; one □ *In spite of his contempt for naturalistic art, the old visionary **knew a good thing when he saw it**.* DOP □ *There are at least two things that people have come to agree about Terson: **he knows a good** piece of **dialogue when he hears it**.* RT □ *I **know** bloody **obstinacy when I meet it** so I quit arguing with him.*

know/tell a hawk from a handsaw [V + O + A] be well-informed, intelligent, discerning □ (source) *I am but mad north-north-west; when the wind is southerly, I **know a hawk from a handsaw**.* HAMLET II 2 □ *The absent-minded professor, that favourite figure of British humour —is that the role you cast me for, Sergeant? But in matters of ordinary life, I flatter myself that I **know a hawk from a handsaw**.* EM □ *Mr Foot cannot **tell a hawk from a handsaw** if he supposes that the wastage of unemployment, and the idiocy of the Industrial Relations Act, spell revolution.* NS

know sb and his kind be familiar with and informed about the type of person sb is □ JIMMY: *You see, I **know** Helena **and her kind** so very well. They're a romantic lot. They spend their time mostly looking forward to the past.* LBA □ *He's had several letters he's never bothered to answer. We **know** him **and his kind** in this office—can't be bothered with what they call 'red tape'.* □ often derogatory.

know how many beans make five (informal) be astute, clear-headed, sensible in practical matters □ *'There'll be some reason that suits her for taking a lower-paid job.' 'I wouldn't worry about Deborah if I were you — she **knows how many beans make five**.'* □ *'The poor old sausage,' Laker said of her affectionately. 'She was a bit of a wheeler-dealer. Bright! She **knows how many beans make five**.'* OBS

know sth inside out [V + O + A pass] know, be skilled in, every aspect of sth **O:** job, trade; subject; book, play □ *I don't know how good he is as a general solicitor but he certainly **knows** Income Tax Law **inside out**.* □ *You've read that book so often, Tony, you must **know** it **inside out**.* □ *It was strange going back to 'Time and Time Again'; it was a play we **knew inside out** but, with a new director, it was like doing a new play.* TVT

know sth like the back/palm of one's hand [V + O + A] be thoroughly familiar with the features and details of sth **O:** road, route; area, town; place □ DAVIES: *All I got to do is to go down to Sidcup tomorrow. I got all the references I want down there. I **know** that place **like the back of my hand**.* TC □ *Mr Sutcliffe obviously **knows** the Pennine Way **like the back of his hand**.* RT □ *I **know** Warley **like the palm of my hand**. In fact, much better, because I don't know the palm of my hand.* RATT

know one's man/opponent [V + O] have assessed accurately sb one has to deal with □ *She had in her life before met men prepared to sacrifice the prospect of money in order to gain a social ambition. To that extent she felt she **knew her man**.* MM □ *I've gone to every fight of his I could, and watched him on TV too, studying his style. It's a great help to **know your opponent** when you step into a Championship ring.*

know no bounds [V + O] be excessive or unlimited in scope or intensity **S:** grief, exultation; licence, revelry; ambition. **det:** no; ⚠ hardly any, scarcely any □ *Her glory, happiness and pride therefore **knew no bounds** when one evening she was about to announce, 'I am going to be married.'* ARG □ *His admiration for Britain **knows scarcely any bounds**, and of course all his plans for the 'second Europe' are largely dependent on our joining it.* L □ *Excitement in 'Highland Estate' **knew no bounds** on the day 'they' arrived.* TBC

know one's onions/stuff [V + O] (informal) understand the nature of one's work, activities or studies and be competent in the performance of them □ (laying bets on horses) *'Let's put something on Little Grange alone.' 'Nonsense,' said Sammy. 'What's the use of caution when you **know your onions**?'* UTN □ *The first prerequisite at all levels were commanders who **knew their stuff** and were determined in spite of all difficulties to get their own way.* MFM

know one's own mind [V + O] know what one wants to do; be able to make a firm choice or decision □ *Ralph turned to him quickly. This was the voice of one who **knew his own mind**.* LF □ *After the war audiences had changed and I was trying to get through to people who didn't seem to **know their own minds** any more.* RT □ *'Well,' her mother replied calmly, 'you are twenty-five and old enough to **know your own mind**.'* ⇨ ⚠ have etc a mind of one's own.

know/keep one's place [V + O] know, and behave in a way suitable to, one's position in society or employment (usu an inferior or subordinate position) □ *In the Victorian suburb everyone '**knew his place**'. Whereas it is part of the American tradition that everyone's place is at the top.* L □ DAVIES: *I've seen better days than you have, man, I'll be all right as long as you **keep your place**. Just you **keep your place**, that's all.* TC □ *When I was a kid, we had never heard the word teenager. You **kept your place** in those days. You were a nobody.* TVT □ also pl know/keep their place(s); now thought, esp by young people, to be dated concept and expression.

know etc the ropes [V + O] be familiar with the customs and procedures of an institution, administration, community, business etc, esp so that one knows what to do, what advantages to obtain for oneself, etc **V:** know; ⚠ learn; show sb □ *He was en route with his lady for leave in Italy. They had done it the previous year and **knew the ropes**.* BM □ *'How did you manage to get hold of a boat at all?' She grinned. 'I've been here long enough to **know the ropes**.'* RFW □ *Philip agreed to stay on in the job another week to **show** the new man **the ropes**.*

know etc the score [V + O] know etc the true state of affairs, how matters really stand **V:** know, ⚠ see, find out; give sb, let sb know, explain □ *Miss Stevenson **knows the score** and still has the courage to live with it.* NS □ *Many stock market men think they **know** what **the score** is. They are telling their friends to fill up with First National shares, for a grand merger with Sears Holdings is on the way.* OBS □ *But it would be very interesting if someone could go and sort of **see** what **the score** is, kind of thing.* ILIH □ JIMMY: *Shouldn't think you'll last five minutes without me to **explain the score** to you.* LBA □ *Number One, who gives her name as Miss Tina Tietjen, management and training adviser for the Industrial Society, **gives** them **the score**.* SC

know etc a thing or two (about sth) [V + O] (informal) know etc much; know etc sth useful, interesting, important **V:** know; learn; tell sb, show sb □ *The gist was this: Myra, who **knew a thing or two about** eligible men, had married two men from our town. And why? Because we knew how to breed 'em* (= them) *good.* CON □ *This arises mainly from the conviction that in most things the Americans can '**show** us **a thing or two**' **about** being up to date.* UL □ (NONCE) *'But what do you know about Brother Golding?' 'I could **tell** you **a thing or three**,' he said. 'We were on the same Emergency Training what-have-you just after the War.'* TT □ tell, show etc often preceded by *can/could*; stress pattern ˌknow a ˈthing or two.

know sth very etc well [V + O + A] know, be aware of sth, in spite of one's claim or pretence that one does not; know (sth) as well as I do (qv) **O:** implications, consequences; what he means, that he's serious. **adv mod:** very, ⚠ perfectly; (dated) full, jolly □ CLIVE: *I don't know what 'cultured' means. I always thought it had something to do with pearls.* LOUISE: *Nonsense, you **know perfectly well** what your father means.* FFE □ *Although Prissie kept saying, 'But there's nothing to be frightened of, you silly boy,' he **knew very well** that there was.* DC □ *There was no excuse for making such a scene. If you have a complaint you **know** the procedure **perfectly well**.* □ *'He can't understand why you avoid him.' 'Can't he? He **knows jolly well** why.'*

know etc one's way about/around [V + O] be familiar with a locality, subject, procedure; be capable and well-informed in general **V:** know ⚠ find, learn □ *Any Tom, Dick or Harry can work as a guide and give not only wrong information, but cause further chaos by not **knowing his way about**.* NS □ *To **know one's way around** the intellectual history of the 19th century is to be familiar with instances of generosity and friendship.* NS □ *The author has at least four previous books to his credit and **knows his** Irish **way around**.* OBS □ *He is very modest, attributing a lot of his business success to luck, but it does emerge in the course of an interview that Martin has **learnt his way about**.*

know what sb/sth is know what the character of a person or thing is like, understand how he/it is likely to behave or function (the implication often being that he/it is unreliable, difficult to handle, etc) **S:** you, we (all), everybody; Anne, Jack □ JIMMY: *Is your friend Webster coming tonight?* ALISON: *He might drop in. You **know what** he **is**.* LBA □ *I can't be bothered with carbons* (= copies of a typewritten document). *I have no manual skill and you **know what** carbons **are**—so there was only one copy.* UTN

know what one is doing (informal) understand the nature and purpose of one's action(s); do sth deliberately, whether wisely or foolishly □ *They're very intelligent people. They **know what they're doing**. They're not fools.* ST □ *Musicians are a cynical lot, and they take it out on any conductor who doesn't **know what he's doing**.* L □ (cattle auctions) *Most of the big spenders have their own private stools round the edge of the ring and a confidence all their own. 'Those blokes really **know what they are doing**,' Cox said.* RT

know what it is to be/do sth have personal experience of being/doing sth **Inf:** to be ill, to be hungry; to lose a husband, to do a hard day's work □ *He **knows what it is to be** ill, to be in pain, to be disappointed. But he has no inclination to compile a hard-luck story.* AH □ *Till he was ten years old he never **knew what it was to** play with another child.* □ neg variant have no/not have any idea of what it is to be/do sth.

know etc what love etc is have personal experience and understanding of the true nature of love etc **V:** know; ⚠ find (out), learn, discover. **n:** love; gratitude; security; poverty; work □ *Emotionally he was quite unawakened and didn't **know what love was**.* PW □ *Believe me, I **know what poverty is**, and it's not selling a few stocks or shares to keep your car on the road.* □ *If they put him in the loading gang he'll soon **find out what work is**.* □ know often neg; find out, learn, discover usu positive.

know etc what's what (informal) know what should be known of the facts, arrangements, rules of behaviour, etc in a given situation **V:** know, ⚠ learn, find out; tell, show, sb, let sb know □ *Anyone who **knows** who's who and **what's what** in broadcasting knows that the people in it who matter, at whatever level, are no more morbid than members of the CBI* (= Confederation of British Industry). L □ *Stevie Smith* *is also proud of the way a certain kind of innocence has clung to her all her life: 'Angels aren't the only ones who do not* ***know what's what****.'* L □ *Not that I was Anybody, you understand: just a piano-player in some of those Amusing Little Places. Darling Steve, buttering up his betters, professionally* ***aware of who was who****, but discreetly overlooking who was rightfully whose.* L □ cf variant know/be aware of who's who = 'be able to identify the people who are important, and possible useful to oneself'.

know where one is going (saying) know clearly what one's motivations and objectives are in life or in a particular line of activity □ *I felt there must be something wrong with me: everybody else seemed so definite and knowledgeable. They* ***knew where they were going****.* L □ *I* ***know*** *on the whole* ***where I'm going*** *and I know, thank God, who is going with me.* WDM □ SAGAN: *But you hold on anyway, you go on.* BARDOT: *Yes I go on, I don't really* ***know where I am going*** *but I get there.* OBS

know which/what side one's bread is buttered (on) (saying) know where one's interests lie; know who to please, what work to choose or continue, in order to ensure one's livelihood, comfort or success □ *Professor Clun said, 'They're all the same, these old soldiers. On the scrounge. They* ***know*** *very well* ***which side their bread's buttered****.'* ASA □ ***Knowing on which side their bread is buttered****, they* (the people of Eire) *now like the English, who allow them to enter the UK freely and make money.* NS □ *'He didn't come near* us*,' said Godfrey, 'so why should he come to see you?' 'At least,' she said, 'I should have thought he* ***knew what side his bread's buttered****.'* MM □ *Her mouth twisted. 'You're a timid soul, aren't you?' 'I* ***know which side my bread is buttered on****,' I said.* RATT □ (NONCE) *You must expect literary and academic people to lose some respect for you if you're going to go on churning out twaddle for the popular press.* ***You can't have your bread buttered on both sides****.* □ can be used as (part of) a cynical comment on sb's motives; variant you can't have your bread buttered on both sides in last example possibly influenced by have one's cake and eat it (too) (qv).

L

a labour of love [Comp (NP)] a task, or commitment, not undertaken from necessity or for profit, but for the satisfaction of a devoted interest **V:** ⚠ be, become; make sth □ *And she took me round the stables and there was her long life's* ***labour of love****; eight chestnut hunters (=* horses) *and each a king.* PP □ *It was* ***a labour of love*** *to clean the plugs and top up the battery.* TGLY □ *I complain only on the unfashionable ground that writing a history book ought to be* ***a labour of love****.* NS

labour the point [V + O pass] continue to repeat, or explain, sth said and understood already □ *'Do I know best?' she bullied him. 'Now, now,' Matthew said, 'that is so obvious that none of us needs* ***labour the point****.'* US □ *'Mr Golding did tell me.' He seemed relieved. 'So there's no need for me to, well,* ***labour the point*** *then, is there?' he said.* TT □ *'It has always seemed to me, and I fear that I have* ***laboured the point*** *more than once in print'—she smiled in childish glee round the room—'that the Roman missionaries made so many compromises.'* ASA.

the labourer is worthy of his hire (saying) anyone who works for another is entitled to a proper wage, or due return, for his labour □ (source) *And into whatsoever house ye enter, in the same house remain, eating and drinking such things as they give: for* ***the labourer is worthy of his hire****.* LUKE X 5, 7 □ *Nurses have too long been made the victims of their sense of vocation.* ***The labourer is worthy of his hire****.* □ *'I say,' Mr Mackay exclaimed, 'friend Joseph doesn't mind asking favours from his friends. I hope he'll decide that* ***the labourer is worthy of his hire****.'* RM

(all) labourers etc in the vineyard fellow-workers in a profession, undertaking, public cause, etc, esp irrespective of their status, work contribution or remuneration (see MATTHEW XX 1-14) **n:** labourers, ⚠ workers, toilers. **adj:** same; hospital, industrial □ *He is there to help the* ***labourers in the*** *hospital* ***vineyards****, from consultants to kitchen-hands, first to recognise and then to solve, their problems.* NS □ *I said 'Ah well, Father Macalister, we* ***all work in the*** *same* ***vineyard****.' And then he gave one of those affected sighs of his and said 'Very true, Colonel, but we planted it.'* RM □ *...which, in the jargon of the Act, apparently means the British Medical Association, and the BMA alone, would be able to speak for the* ***workers in the*** *medical* ***vineyard*** *in any negotiations with authority.* NS □ *It* (ie being a TV commentator) *seemed, and still seems to me, a cheaply gained celebrity, if celebrity is what you want; the more so if you have* ***toiled*** *so many years* ***in the*** *increasingly barren* ***vineyard*** *of fiction.* L □ variant (all) labour/work/toil in the vineyard.

ladies first (saying) a reminder of, or allusion to, polite procedure in serving food or drink, entering a room or vehicle, etc □ *And then Mr Collins pulled open the doors from inside the Hall — and the noise seemed to be switched off. 'Now,' he said, '****Ladies first****—let yours come on in please, Miss Elliot.'* TT □ *'Look, Mummy's tasting your medicine and it's quite nice. Here, Bobby, you can take yours and Janice will see there's nothing to make a fuss about.' 'No,' said Bobby. 'It's always* ***ladies first****.'* □ often ironic or jocular.

ladies and gentlemen [n + n non-rev] a form of address (often as an introduction to a speech) or a descriptive reference (cf 'men and women', 'husbands and wives') □ *I don't think I quite understand what is being said here—if you could repeat your argument again, very slowly this time,* ***ladies and gentlemen****, and define the terms you are using.* TCM □ *...where some* ***ladies and gentlemen*** *of the Press were hoping* *to waylay him.* SC

(my) Lady Bountiful [Comp/O (NP)] a woman (or source of supply personified as such) who dispenses charity, gifts, favours etc (the implication often being, in the case of individuals, a condescending patronage (from a character in a 17th c play)) **V:** be, see oneself as; play, act. **det:** my; the, a; no □ *I resent her coming round to play* ***Lady Bountiful****. Tell her we're not so poor that we can't feed and clothe ourselves.* □ *And several of Goldy's lot* (= schoolchildren) *were making a great to-do of taking her case off the seat and opening the johanna* (= piano) *for her—might have been* ***the Lady Bountiful*** *lobbing out tanners.* TT □ *Their living is hard wrung from the soil. Dame Nature is* ***no lady bountiful*** *in these regions.*

a lame duck [O (NP)] a disabled or disadvantaged person, ship, vehicle etc; an organization, or business firm, not able to function effectively, esp because of financial difficulties **V:** aid, assist, bail out □ *You're always getting yourself involved with* ***lame ducks*** *who have enough gumption to know a soft mark when they see one.* □ *Rolls-Royce has gone bankrupt but the cost of picking up the pieces and avoiding massive redundancy is as yet incalculable. Now* ***another lame duck****, the Harland and Wolff shipyard in Belfast, is to have further help from the Government.* SC □ *UCS had been labelled by the Government as a prime species of* ***lame duck*** *which unless it took steps to get up and walk, would be cut down as an example to the rest of industry.* L □ attrib use *a* ***lame duck*** *industry.* ⇨ ⚠ a dead duck.

a land fit for heroes to live in (catchphrase) a country, nation that can reward those who have fought in its defence with good conditions of life and work as civilians (based on the first quotation but used now in the form of the headphrase) □ (source) *What is our task? To make Britain* ***a fit country for heroes to live in.*** LLOYD GEORGE (Prime Minister) NOV 1918 □ *In 1914 Great Britain went to war, and the men who came back from the war found quite quickly exactly the opposite of* ***a land fit for heroes.*** L □ *But if the United States is hardly today, as North Vietnam or even perhaps China are,* ***a land fit for heroes to live in****, it is a least now once again a plainly more secure ground than these for itinerant academics and scriptwriters.* L

a land flowing with milk and honey a place of abundant resources, easy living; a/the promised land (qv) □ (source) *And I am come down to deliver them unto a good land and a large, unto* ***a land flowing with milk and honey.*** EXODUS III 8 □ *Around the time that Huckleberry Finn decided that he should light out for the territories, California became, once and for all,* ***the land of milk and honey*** *for gold-diggers, waitresses wanting to be discovered and East Coast academics.* NS □ *California is* ***the land of milk and honey****—milk by the gallon and honey by the quart. Everything comes in extra-super-giant-economy packs.* TVT □ variant the land of milk and honey.

(in) the land of Nod (have gone to) sleep (perhaps originally a pun on *'dwelt* ***in the land of Nod****, on the east of Eden.'* GENESIS IV 16) □ *'Father's* ***in the land of nod****, I think.' 'Well, leave him be; he's had a tiring day. And don't turn off the TV or he'll wake up.'* □ *Let's get you bedded down and off to* ***the land of Nod.*** TGLY □ usu facetious; with or without capital N.

larger than life [Comp (AdjP)] larger in size than the person/object represented; dramatically exaggerated, so as to seem more impressive than he/it is **S:** model, portrait, figure; actor, statesman; incident, event. **V:** ⚠ be; appear, make sth □ *These masks were a little* ***larger than life*** *and this fact accounted for the extraordinary impression of closeness which I received when I first opened the door.* UTN □ *'Fergus—I have the Templar blood, the blood of robbers and murderers and...' 'Just forget that blood and thunder stuff, will you? I'm sorry to be so lacking in melodrama, but honestly your ancestors were probably painted* ***larger than life.****'* DC □ *Trivial incidents of his childhood began to flood his memory with a significance* ***larger than life.*** ⇨ ⚠ (as) large as life.

(and) last, but not/by no means least [Conj (AdjP)] (cliché) precedes the final item in a cited list of people, or things, in order to emphasize that sb/sth is no less important than the others previously mentioned □ *Large numbers of medical personnel had to be employed, special hospitals had to be set up, psychiatrists had to be employed to determine the degree of incapacity,* ***and last, but not least****, a considerable financial sacrifice was involved in boarding out men under this category.* SNP □ *They thanked every member of the Committee by name, and similarly everyone who had sent a donation,* ***and last, but not least****, the caretaker of the Hall whom the catering and cleaning arrangements had kept early and late at work, for over a week.* □ *I have ventured to bring with me a selection of his books: 'Happy Days Among the Heather', 'Wandering in Wester Ross',* ***and last but by no means least*** *one of his earliest books, 'Land of Heart's Desire'—a gem, Mr Carmichael.* RM

the last ditch [Comp/o (NP)] the last resource, the last remaining position one can use in order to resist or counter-attack military, political or social pressure; the last effort one can make to ensure one's safety, or to avoid/defeat in a contest, argument etc **V:** be; fight to/in, resist to/in, make one's stand in/at; □ *It is all very well for politicians who are spared the sufferings of those they claim to lead and represent to talk of resisting oppression to* ***the last ditch.*** □ *All this has no doubt bred a reasonableness, a remarkably quiet assumption that violence is* ***the last ditch.*** UL □ *An Army spokesman said: 'Whether it's a* ***last ditch*** *effort or not we cannot be sure. But they are certainly pulling out all the stops.'* ST □ *The attitude 'I won't have a television in the house' is dying; but there are still a few* ***last-ditchers*** *holding out against what they are content to dismiss as the goggle-box or idiot's lantern.* NS □ attrib use, *a* ***last ditch*** *effort*, may or may not be hyphenated; n compound, a last ditcher, may or may not be hyphenated ⇨ ⚠ (as) a/one's last resort; in the last resort[1].

the/one's last gasp [o (NP)] one's last few breaths before death; (fig) (when people, machines, sources of energy or supply show, give) a last spurt of action, or effort, before exhaustion (the implication being that it is either too late, or only just in time, to be effective) **prep:** at, to, until □ *Society clings to its irrational attitude that you must on no account die until you have exhausted all and every artificial means medicine has invented to keep you ticking over to* ***the last gasp****.* RT □ *I hope you brought another torch or a spare battery. This one's at* ***its last gasp****.* □ *The story of what has happened to 'Collier's', 'Saturday Evening Post' and, more recently, 'Look' is familiar. They all had huge readerships right up to* ***the last gasp*** *but they got their sums horribly wrong.* L □ *'I wish you had consulted me a year ago when this trouble started,' the doctor scolded her gently. 'Some of you women* will *wait until* ***the last gasp****.'*

the last lap [O/o (NP)] the final circuit in a race; (fig) the final stage of a journey, contest, course of study, long-term undertaking, etc **V:** enter, reach. **prep:** in, on, at □ *As they entered* ***the last lap*** *Johnson was still running third.* □ *It has become something of a favourite pastime to gather at the quayside and watch tipsy trippers cover* ***the last lap*** *back to the ship.* TO □ *'He has had good grades until this year.' 'Agreed, but it's* ***the last lap*** *that counts and he is not working as a final-year student must.'* □ *It has been a hell of a business completing this contract. Thank God, we're on* ***the last lap*** *now.* □ *Here in Basrah, in sight of safety, he felt instinctively sure that the danger would be greater than during the wild hazards of his journey. And to fail at* ***the last lap*** *—that would hardly bear thinking about.* TCB

one's last penny etc each detail of one's income or expenditure, esp (down) to the last remaining (small) unit of currency; all, or all that remains, of one's money **n:** penny, ⚠ halfpenny; bob, dollar, dime □ *I want justice for my son, if it costs me* ***my last penny****.* □ *When Fergus arrived and said, 'Everything all right?' she would answer, 'Well, Nurse Ellen did fall down that awful hole, and Nicky was chased by someone called Clementine who doesn't exist, and a blackmailer has taken* ***our last penny****, but otherwise, yes, everything is all right.'* DC □ *Virginia felt sure that she knew exactly the price of everything on the list and would count the change to* ***the last halfpenny*** *when she returned.* AITC □ *Before the invitation came to review novels for the 'Listener' (which he carried on for no less than 11 consecutive years) he was down to* ***his last 30 bob*** ((slang) bob = shilling, formerly unit of British currency). □ literal uses of expression usu specify a precise amount in an appropriate unit of currency while fig uses usu take form of headphrase.

the last rites/sacrament(s) a religious ceremony performed at a time of impending death, a burial etc; anything which is seen as acknowledging, or symbolizing, the end of sth □ *'What is your feeling about the service?' said Tempest. Godfrey looked round at the waitresses. 'Very satisfactory,' he said. Tempest closed her eyes as one who prays for grace. 'I mean,' she said, 'poor Lisa****'s last rites*** *at the crematorium.'* MM □ *He blamed everybody in turn for the high mortality rate in the ward, often ingeniously, as in his idea that the sight of the priest constantly arriving with* ***the Last Sacrament*** *might frighten people into their coffins.* L □ (reader's letter) *Humphrey Littleton read* ***the last rites*** *over half an hour of Wednesday night's jazz programme. Another nail in the coffin!* RT

the last shall be first (and the first, last) (saying) those that are despised, or underestimated, may prove superior to their supposed betters □ (source) *But many that are* ***first shall be last****; and* ***the last shall be first****.* MATTHEW XIX 30 □ *It is not equality, as they claim, that most revolutionaries seek but that* ***the last should be first****.* □ *He seemed the least promising of my pupils—but there you are,* ***the last shall be first*** *and the teacher's darlings pass into oblivion.* □ now used in order, and with emphasis, of headphrase.

one's/its last etc state is worse than the first (saying) an attempt at change, or improvement, may leave sb/sth in a worse condition than before **adj:** last, ⚠ latter, second □ (source) *When the unclean spirit hath gone out of a man, then goeth he, and taketh with himself seven other spirits more wicked than himself, and they enter in and dwell there: and* ***the last state of*** *that man* ***is worse than the first****.* MATTHEW XII 43-5 □ *So do we not do better to proceed gradually, to persuade rather than to bully, to avoid a violent reaction that will leave* ***our last state worse than our first****?* OBS □ *Many an employee who has thought it would be more profitable to go into business for himself has found* ***his latter state worse than his first****.* □ *By the time Stanley had finished tinkering with the clock* ***its second state was worse than the first*** *for it struck twelve at every hour of the day.*

the last/final straw [Comp (NP)] an additional burden beyond endurance **V:** ⚠ be; find sth; prove to be □ *I suppose my resistance to illness had become weakened during five years of war, and the aeroplane crash was* ***the last straw****.* MFM □ (NONCE) *This easy assumption that a cook's day off could as well be one day as another may have been* ***the last straw that broke the back of her patience****, but Mrs Robbins declared that she had been going to give in her notice anyway.* □ *His Christmas at Warbeck, he felt, was becoming a whole series of disagreeable surprises. The presence of yet another unexpected guest was* ***the last straw****.* EM □ *'Don't even have ketchup,' he said, as if this serious gastronomic omission were* ***the final straw****.* BFA □ headphrase is reduced form of the less commonly used saying *it's* ***the last straw*** *that breaks the camel's back.*

last thing (at night) [A (NP)] immediately before retiring to bed or falling asleep; at the latest possible or reasonable time (the implication being that other matters have been attended to) □ (advertisement) *Just one spray when you get up and that glorious morning-fresh feeling and heavenly perfume are still there* ***last thing at night****.* H □ *The next thing they decided* (about chocolate), *however, was that it was good for loving. This idea, is of course, pretty well exploded by now even among those who like a cup of* ***cocoa last thing****.* TVT ⇨ first thing (in the morning).

the last thing one wants etc (to do) a most unlikely, unsuitable, or personally disagreeable object, person, state of affairs, action to take, etc **V:** wants, ⚠ wishes, expects;

needs. **Inf:** to do; to happen; to see; to discuss □ *Reform, in a sense, is* ***the last thing*** *that the IRA* (= Irish Republican Army) *in either its Provisional or its Official manifestations, actually* ***wants.*** □ *His real name wouldn't mean anything to you and* ***the last thing I want to do*** *is to throw a man's past in his face unless he's a double-dyed villain.* SD □ *Even when I felt that the galley stove was* ***the last thing I wanted to*** *see again, there were few days when I didn't have at least one proper meal.* SC □ *In fact, a complete rest is often* ***the last thing one needs.*** *To continue to be active but with a change of occupation may be far more beneficial.* ST □ ***The last thing he expected*** *of the stranger was that he would be travelling first-class with a third-class ticket.* PW □ *The subject of his wife's illness was* ***the last thing that*** *Bernard* ***wished to*** *discuss at that moment, his brother-in-law the last man with whom he would discuss it any time.* HAA

last one's time [V + O] continue to exist, or be sufficient, during one's own lifetime, although perhaps not much longer **S:** it; the present régime, the reservoir, the carpets we have □ *The roof will* ***last our time,*** *Mary. I'd rather spend the money on making things a bit easier for us.* □ *As long as they see it* ***lasting their time*** *and probably that of their grandchildren, not too many people are going to spend sleepless nights worrying about the run-down of natural resources.* □ may imply selfish outlook which disregards prospects of others or of future generations, but may simply indicate practical outlook; stress pattern ˌlast ˈour time.

one's last will and testament [n + n non-rev] a legal document—superseding any other previously made—which gives instructions for the disposition of one's property after death, sometimes including general remarks, recommendations etc which are not legally binding □ *The doctor's 'Well, how's Granny Taylor this morning? Have you been making* ***your last will and test—*** *' would falter when he saw her eyes, the intelligence.* MM □ *...featured the fighter pilot, Richard Hillary, whose book 'The Last Enemy' was* ***a*** *kind of* ***Last Will and Testament*** *for the British who fought in the Second World War — for those, at any rate, who thought about it at all deeply.* L

the last word (in sth) [Comp (NP)] sb/sth that, of its kind, cannot be surpassed (ie is as good, or as bad, as it is possible to find), or that sets a new standard as yet unchallenged **V:** ⚠ be; become, seem; make sth. **o:** women; competence, luxury, laziness □ *She's always going on about women's feelings and intuitions as though she was* ***the last word in*** *women.* ASA □ *Don't talk to me about untidy kids. I've got two at home that are* ***the last word.*** □ (advertisement) *The luxurious interior sprung mattress is guaranteed by the manufacturers for 5 years against fair wear and tear and is* ***the last word in*** *night-time relaxation.* OBS □ *'Yield to the Night': A sombre condemned cell drama focussed on convicted murderess and understanding prison official. Until 'Room at the Top', this was* ***the last word in*** *British cinema realism.* RT ⇨ ⚠ have etc the last word.

(famous) last words a (recorded) utterance that was the last sb made before dying; a foolish, misjudged or boastful remark, or opinion, passed before an accident, reversal of fortune, etc □ *There is also a fatalistic note; the victim of the crime, in her* ***last words,*** *declares, quite unprotestingly, that it is what she expected.* AH □ *'Poor bird,' said Sir Alex sounding genuinely concerned. When I asked what his parrot's* ***last words*** *were he looked rather shocked.* OBS □ (Another publisher) *asked me to write a book for children about the stage on the strength of the 'Whicharts'. My own editor said I could certainly do so, but warned me that there was no money in children's books. These were* ***famous last words,*** *weren't they?* RT □ *'Of course, they're edible,' he answered cramming another handful of berries into his mouth. I hoped it wasn't going to be a case of* ***famous last words.*** □ when expression is used to refer to a foolish remark it is given in full, and use in such a context is frequently facetious.

late in the day [A (AdjP)] later in time, after more delay, than is appropriate, desirable, or likely to produce good results **adv mod:** rather, much too; a little, somewhat, not too □ *I am sure we all appreciate Mr Isaacson's anxiety to complete this work in the best possible way. I feel, however, that it is rather* ***late in the day*** *to call in new technical advisers.* PL □ *I'm an old man. Your offer has come too* ***late in the day*** *for me.* □ *Without Hitler's approval he was nobody. Hess does not seem to have thought of that till remarkably* ***late in the day.*** L □ *This is the second book in which he has unwisely, and too* ***late in the day*** *for comfort, remembered things better now forgotten.* NS □ almost always modified.

the/one's late lamented sb/sth (formal) sb fairly recently dead and still mourned; sb/sth that no longer lives, or exists, for whom/which the speaker may not necessarily feel regret **n:** mother, chairman; Himmler □ *I hope you will do so. It was* ***your late lamented*** *mother's strongest wish for you.* □ *In the presence of his widow, of course, any criticism of* ***the late lamented*** *was studiously avoided.* □ *I'm not talking about actual complaints against the Government: you go to prison for that. Do you know who trained our secret police, that fine body of men?* ***The late lamented*** *Himmler, with personal supervision.* ILIH □ *I don't really like my new car. It's very economical on fuel but it isn't nearly as comfortable as* ***my late lamented*** *Morris Minor.* □ n may be omitted, as in second example, when expression is used literally.

later on [A (AdvP)] later (the implication usu being later within an understood period or process) □ *It was uncertainty on this issue which was to lead to trouble* ***later on.*** MFM □ *James had to visit a patient but he hopes to join us* ***later on.*** □ *'He doesn't mention a price.' 'Oh yes he does, but* ***later on,*** *near the end of his letter.'* □ front, middle or end position. ⇨ early/earlier on.

laugh like a drain (informal) laugh noisily, raucously □ (of a television programme) *Take 'Faulty Towers', for example: I hated it first time round, but when it was repeated this year on BBC 1, I* ***laughed like a drain.*** L □ *Mademoiselle Dupont was horrified. Ma, on the other hand, started* ***laughing like a drain.*** BFA

laugh till/until one cries etc laugh so long, or so hard, that one's eyes water, one becomes almost hysterical **A:** till one cries, ⚠ until the tears ran down one's face; so much one is almost crying ▫ *The Riley Kestrel* (a car) *ended its days stuffed in the Michelmores' kitchen doorway. 'I was trying to teach Jean to drive in it. We* ***laughed till we cried****.'* RT ▫ *Sometimes when I'm writing something for the script I phone Warren to tell him and we're both* ***laughing so much we're almost crying****.* RT ▫ *I regret to admit that I could do nothing more sensible than sit down on a rock and* ***laugh until the tears ran down my face****.* BB

laugh and the world laughs with you, (weep and you weep alone) (saying) other people are more willing to share your joys and successes than to help, or sympathize, in your sorrows or failures; people want cheerful, not melancholy, company ▫ (source) ***Laugh and the world laughs with you;/Weep and you weep alone****;/For the sad old earth must borrow its mirth,/But has trouble enough of its own.* SOLITUDE (E W WILCOX 1855-1919) ▫ *The banner-motto for the whole paper is 'Smile Dammit Smile!' '****Laugh and the world laughs with you****', Ella Wheeler Wilcox's lines have hung on the walls of unnumbered working class living rooms.* UL ▫ (NONCE) ***Smile and the world smiles with you*** *may work in London or Leeds. Smile in Cambridge and see where it gets you.* ST

the laughing academy (informal) a lunatic asylum and institution for the care, education etc of mentally handicapped, or mentally ill, people ▫ *Well, if I worried about that sort of thing I'd end up in* ***the Laughing Academy*** *in one of those waiter's jackets with the arms sewn together.* JFTR ▫ (a film review) *Any questions about the dubious taste of mocking the insane is dispelled by the unreality of* ***this*** *particular celluloid* ***laughing academy****.* OBS

laughter and tears [n + n rev] (a display of) amusement and sorrow/pity contrasted or mingled ▫ (a radio programme) *The next half-hour or so will be full of* ***laughter and tears****.* T ▫ *The sudden relief from strain had left her in a tremulous state between* ***tears and laughter****.*

the law is an ass (saying) a legal procedure, judgment or enactment is stupid or unjust ▫ (source) *'You indeed are the more guilty of the two, in the eye of the law; for the law supposes that your wife acts under your direction.' 'If the law supposes that,' said Mr Bumble, squeezing his hat emphatically in both hands, '****the law is a ass****—a idiot.'* OLIVER TWIST (C DICKENS 1812-70) ▫ (advertisement) ***The law is an ass****. Minimum office temperatures are clearly laid down by law. Maximum office temperatures are not. It can top 100°F in the office (as it did in many last summer) and the law offers employees no word of comfort.* ST ▫ *You may be stopped from doing something innocent, which will make you think* ***the law's an ass****.* TVT ▫ *On camera, they make you believe* ***the law is an ass****, and worse, when it comes to dealing with people of the incorrect pigmentation.* NS

the law of the jungle self-preservation; the survival of the strongest, or most uncrupulous ▫ *The Robens Committee of 1972 had been told, in written evidence, by W H Thompson, a leading union solicitor: 'The only law that rules in factories is* ***the law of the jungle****, and it is a jungle where innocent persons are maimed and mutilated and their lives laid waste.'* G ▫ *The chief French grumble about Dr Kissinger's speech is that he is applying '****the law of the jungle****' or 'the doctrine that might is right'.* OBS

the law(s) of the land the law as enforced in a particular country at a particular period ▫ *The success was because in those days, and up to 1961, there were no betting-shops.* ***The law of the land*** *said you could only bet at a racecourse.* L ▫ *Same with judges — you stick them in a uniform to make it clear that it's* ***the laws of the land*** *you're up against, and not just a prejudiced old man.* OBS

the law of the Medes and Persians any established and rigidly followed code or practice ▫ (source) *Now, O king, establish the decree and sign the writing, that it be not changed, according to* ***the law of the Medes and Persians****, which altereth not.* DANIEL VI 8 ▫ *She could be flexible. After all, it's not* ***a law of the Medes and Persians*** *that afternoon tea must be drunk at four precisely.* ▫ (NONCE) *Nurse, who after* ***the Mede and Persian code of*** *the nursery quite rightly held all education to be superflous, having got on very well without it herself. . .* WDM

law and order [n + n non-rev] maintenance of, uniformity with, the laws under which the members of a society, community, nation are governed and protected **V:** establish, maintain, uphold ▫ *'One outstanding advantage left behind by the old colonial regime in Sierra Leone,' says Siaka Stevens, 'is the establishment of* ***law and order****, without which no progress would have been possible.'* RT ▫ *In this situation it is common to say that nothing can be done until* ***law and order*** *is restored. But intransigence in Northern Ireland on both sides makes it necessary to take the long view.* SC ▫ *And yet, if abused, '****law and order****' become the strongest (because the official) forces for oppression.* NS

a law unto oneself [Comp (NP)] sb who does as he wishes, sets his own standards, etc regardless of the rules or conventions of a community, social group, profession etc **V:** ⚠ be; become, remain ▫ *Abd-el-Rahman, the ruler of Darfur, had died, and the tribes who inhabited that vast province were now largely* ***a law unto themselves****.* BN ▫ *If Sam Silkin has any self-respect, he will demand the demotion of police officers who decided to act as* ***a law unto themselves****.* NS ▫ *I've been in this business for thirty years; I know everything about showgirls; but I don't know Tillie. She's a mystery; she's* ***a law unto herself****.* PE ⇨ ⚠ take the law into one's own hands (Vol 1).

lay sth bare [V + O + Comp pass] expose sth fully to the eye, or to the light of day; reveal, or communicate, sth fully so that it can be known and understood **O:** his chest, the original surface; one's soul; the facts, their motives ▫ *Professor Eric Birley, Robin's father,* ***laid bare*** *the headquarters of the fourth-century fort in the 1930s.* ST ▫ *There is little that any further inquiry could discover that was not* ***laid bare*** *by the Royal Commission on the Press.* T ▫ *He* ***laid bare*** *his soul to her in a way he would not willingly have done had he been entirely sober.* ▫ *Here we have all the elements of the prophetic dream—the strong emotion indicating the importance of* *the dream, the symbolic way in which the information is wrapped up, and the special skill of the interpreter who can* ***lay bare*** *its innermost meaning.* SNP □ in active constructions O almost always in end position.

a lay figure [Comp (NP)] a jointed wooden frame used by artists instead of a living model for arranging garments, draperies, on; (fig) a person given, or performing, only a nominal function **V:** ⚠ be; see, regard, sb as □ *The realisation had come to her slowly; the Queen was* ***a lay figure****, lacking even the power to dismiss a maid-of-honour without the King's approval.* WI □ *'Sometimes I think you treat your agents like* ***lay figures****, people in a book. It's a real man up there—isn't it?' 'That's not a very nice thing to say about me.'* OMIH

lay a/one's ghost etc [V + O pass] exorcize a supernatural spirit; rid oneself, or another/others, of a threat, obsessive or irrational fear, doubt, suspicion **n:** ghost, ⚠ spirit, bogey, demon □ *Included are ancient recipes for everything from curing warts to* ***laying ghosts****.* □ *But a series of tests carried out by multiple screening at a single visit* ***lays the ghost*** *of a number of diseases and furnishes a healthy profile.* L □ ***The*** *Agheila* ***bogey*** *had been* ***laid*** *and we were leaguering as an Army beyond that once-dreaded position, where hitherto only our advanced patrols had penetrated.* MFM □ *I discovered a tendency in myself to be unwarrantedly sharp towards those features in working-class life of which I disapprove. Related to this is the urge to* ***lay one's ghosts****; at the worst, it can be a temptation to 'do down' one's class, out of a pressing ambiguity in one's attitude to it.* UL

lay sb/sth low [V + O + Comp pass] knock, bring down sb/sth into a horizontal, flattened position; reduce, or lower sb/sth in esteem, importance; weaken or destroy sb/sth □ *Crops had been destroyed and many buildings* ***laid low****.* □ *We had a bad time last winter. The whole family was* ***laid low by the flu*** (= influenza) *epidemic. The house looked like a hospital for weeks.* □ *A current advertisement tells us of an author who 'takes on the greatest evolutionists of all time, Charles Darwin, Desmond Morris, Robert Ardrey, Konrad Lorenz — and* ***lays*** *them all* ***low****.'* L

lay oneself/sb (wide) open (to sth) [V + O + Comp] invite, expose oneself to criticism etc **o:** attack, criticism, exploitation, ridicule □ *Not to defend oneself would be to* ***lay oneself****, and one's children,* ***open to*** *oppression, slavery or extermination.* AH □ *One can, however, admire a researcher who* ***lays himself open to****, and suffers, attack from his subjects.* SC □ *I was pleased to see how the ineptitude of the drawing* ***laid*** *Davies* ***wide open****; a good thing about drawing is that it's difficult to fake things with it.* OBS □ *Of course, you're* (ie comedians) *always* ***laying yourself wide open****, and that's half the fun—though it still frightens me. We're always walking the knife-edge between being very funny and very silly.* RT

lay sth waste [V + O + Comp pass] destroy sth; render sth useless **O:** crops, fertile country, houses □ *The emperor vanished with his army into the wilderness of the Ethiopian plateau, murdering, torturing, and* ***laying waste*** *the country as he went along.* BN □ *. . .factories where innocent persons are maimed and mutilated and their lives* ***laid waste****.* G □ *There was a time, after all, not that long ago, when children seemed quite capable of walking past a golf course without being seized with an overwhelming desire to* ***lay waste to*** *it.* SC □ variant lay waste to sth.

lead sb to believe (that) cause sb to believe (with or without intention to deceive) that sth is true, is a fact, when this is false or, at least, uncertain; give sb to understand (that) (qv) □ *Bolshaw had* ***led*** *me* ***to believe*** *he was at death's door.* SPL □ *This will take time; only the blindest optimism would* ***lead*** *anyone* ***to believe*** *that Ulster will find peace for many years.* L □ *The report reveals that even this relatively informative company last year did not tell shareholders that profits were much less than their record dividend* ***led*** *them* ***to believe****.* ST □ *But my father was already dead these ten years or more, or so I had been* ***led to believe****.* □ pass as in last example.

lead a busy etc life [V + O] be continuously, or characteristically, or for a particular period, a busy etc person **adj:** busy, active; idle; dangerous; lonely; sober; downtrodden □ *To say you* ***lead a busy life*** *is not an answer to whether you take enough exercise.* □ *Little boys* ***lead a*** *lazy* ***life****. Little girls work, feeding the fowls.* NDN □ *'Who's the Red Vulture?' 'Captain Segura of course,' Dr Hasselbacher said. 'What* ***a sheltered life*** *you* ***lead****.'* OMIH □ (of oil-rig workers) *Insurance premiums are extremely high in view of the dangerous* ***lives*** *they* ***lead****.* SC ⇨ ⚠ bear etc a charmed life; lead/live a double life/two lives.

lead sb a dance [V + IO + pass] make sb follow one in bewilderment from place to place; subject sb to the vagaries of one's way of life; cause sb a lot of unrewarding exertion or worry **det:** lively, fine, pretty, awful; a hell of a, no end of a □ *Also an acute tactician, he* ***led*** *the Royal Navy* ***a*** *lively* ***dance*** *before they finally pinpointed and sank Atlantis.* OBS □ *Nosey is the nickname of a young Arab stallion who has just featured in a film shot on Dartmoor,* ***leading*** *a BBC crew* ***the dance*** *of its life in the course of it.* RT □ *They marvelled that a man so brilliant could be so difficult. He* ***led*** *them a hell of* ***a dance****.* ST □ *Helen, the youngest,* ***led*** *her family* ***a*** *dreadful* ***dance*** *in which drink, opium and conversion to the Church of Rome all figured.* NS

lead/live a double life/two lives [V + O] alternate, or combine, two roles in life each with its own activities, colleagues or acquaintances; esp, but not exclusively, do this illegally or secretly (under an assumed name, with intent to deceive, etc) □ *It was hard to imagine the respectable Mr Archibald* ***leading a double life****, but the evidence of the photograph of M. Jean Dupont (which could possibly have been a freak likeness had the French passport not been found in the said Archibald's possession) was incontestable.* □ *She was free to go to London when she liked. She was no longer pricked by guilt,* ***her double life*** *had become second nature to her.* PW □ *Mother spent several odd years in that village pub,* ***living her double life****, switching from barroom rages to terrace meditations, and waiting while her twenties passed.* CWR □ *Sonia is leaving to get married. She's not going to try and* ***live two lives****. It isn't easy, I know. I've seen plenty* *of girls before you wear themselves out trying to run a house and a job.* AITC ➪ ⚠ lead a busy etc life.

a leading/lesser light/luminary sb whose position in a community, profession etc is pre-eminent/respected (but less so than sb else referred to) □ *...to solve a murder which relates to the activities of a gang of brutal London crooks and, eventually, some of* ***the leading lights*** *of the small town where the action takes place.* NS □ *Entries would be accepted only from writers 'sponsored' by others already recognised in dramatic circles. 'Well, of course, anyone would do, really. Say* ***a leading light*** *in the local amateur dramatic society.'* NS □ *J F Peabody, that lovable old drunken critic praised my novel. A lot of* ***the lesser lights*** *followed his lead, and because it was written in the first person they snuffed at autobiography.* JFTR □ (reader's letter) *The prisoner in the dock was not Wal Hannington at all but* ***a lesser luminary*** *of the National Unemployed Workers' Movement.* NS

a leading question/remark [O (NP)] a question asked, or worded, so that one can hardly avoid giving the answer or showing a reaction that the questioner hopes for **V:** ⚠ ask, put □ *Secondly, Decca argues that* (during trials of a navigating aid) *the Agency asked pilots* ***leading questions*** *which invited critical answers.* □ *Pier Angeli, when asked* ***a*** *rather* ***leading question****, slapped her interviewer on his left cheek and flounced out of the studio.* L □ *'Of course, I wouldn't ask your mother out alone. I mean, not unless it was sort of—well, in a family way—I mean, if she was my mother-in-law.' He looked so scared when he had said this. 'It sounded like* ***a leading remark****. It wasn't meant to. My God, I've only met you a few times.'* AITC

a leap/shot in the dark [Comp/O (NP)] an action, diagnosis, answer etc which is risked in the hope that it is correct **V:** be, seem ***(leap/shot)***; make, take ***(leap)*** □ *We are calling for a halt to progress, for prevention and preservation, for safety first and no* ***leaps in the dark****, because it's all that we are capable of.* NS □ *It has always been usual for a new kind of work to be considered in an unacademic manner, realising that a just estimate requires a certain generosity, a readiness to take* ***a leap in the dark****, or risk a rash generalisation.* L □ *Give your poor old restricted brain a new lease of life with what Dr Edward de Bono calls 'lateral thinking'. For what we all need, he maintains, is a little less logic, and a bit more creative, imaginative,* ***leap-in-the-dark*** *headwork.* RT □ *'Irma?' 'Yes, Irma; you've seen her, haven't you?' Harold had no means of telling whether this was* ***a shot in the dark****. Having hesitated, he saw that he was lost. 'Well, I have seen her,' he admitted in a low voice.* PW □ attrib use ***leap-in-the-dark*** *headwork.* ➪ ⚠ look before one leaps.

learn a/one's lesson [V + O pass] learn from sth that one has done, or that has happened to one, what (not) to do again in similar circumstances □ *He also* ***learned an*** *important* ***lesson****. Having warred for his first four years with the 'Leicester Mercury and Evening Mail', he gradually took on board the idea that good press relations were essential.* ST □ *The trouble was that he expected everybody to be as honest as himself, but I think he's* ***learned his lesson now.*** □ *For every £1 saved on helping them to live at home, £5 is spent to help them live in hospital. This is* ***the lesson*** *that is now to be* ***learned*** *by national, as well as local, government.* NS □ *'I am doing this,' he had told her, 'for moral reasons. I believe —I firmly believe, it will do the old man good.* ***Teach*** *him* ***a lesson****.'* MM □ variant teach sb a lesson = 'make plain to sb that sth he has done, has said, or believes to be true, is wrong or misguided (the realization usu coming as a result of unpleasant experience)'.

the (very) least one can do [Comp (NP)] an action that is the minimum that duty, gratitude, courtesy etc requires of one **V:** ⚠ be, seem; feel, consider sth □ *But now that she was at home, with the children likely to come in at any moment and everyone being so kind, she felt that* ***the least she could do*** *was to keep bright and cheerful.* DC □ *But if MPs do demand, as they should, a little trust from those of their party workers who toil to put them in office at each election, then* ***the least they can do*** *is to come a little cleaner about themselves.* NS □ CLIVE: *If we can't afford a chateau in Brittany, if we can't install scholars in our library, because we haven't got a library, then* ***the least we can do*** *is get in a young charming tutor for the girl, someone with tone, of course.* FFE □ *I insist. Giving you a lift home is* ***the very least I can do*** *after your staying so late to help me.*

least said, soonest mended/forgotten (saying) lengthy recriminations, explanations, excuses, are often a mistake as they tend to exaggerate the importance of a (perhaps trivial) mistake, misunderstanding, quarrel etc □ *In most* (phrases) *the note is one of cheerful patience: 'you've got to take life as it comes', 'grin and bear it', 'ah well,* ***least said, soonest mended****'.* UL □ *What has happened is an illustration of my belief that '****least said, soonest mended****'. Because I made some off-the-cuff remarks on prices, which were misinterpreted as a pledge or something of the kind, I have had to bear up under a good deal of abuse.* NS □ *'Oh dear, I must apologise the next time we meet.' 'Oh, I don't think she took what you said at all seriously, and perhaps* ***least said, soonest forgotten****.'*

leave/let sb/sth alone [V + O + Comp pass] not take, touch, interfere with sb/sth; not try to influence, or alter, sb/sth; next entry (qv) □ *Among the botanical jewels of those forest rides are profusions of orchids. As some species take up to fifteen years to flower it is, to say the least, good manners to* ***leave*** *them* ***alone****.* L □ *Mrs Thatcher, who seems unable to* ***leave alone*** *anything that is going along well, must be longing to get her interfering hands onto this educational success story created under Labour.* NS □ *Some of the spectators went out to meet the cricketers, Horace's mother in the lead. He told her, several times and loudly, to* ***leave*** *him* ***alone****.* TGLY □ *All this turmoil of emotion makes me fearfully sick — I can neither eat nor sleep. If he doesn't soon* ***let*** *me* ***alone*** *he'll be the death of me.* TCM □ O usu middle position but end position if O is clause or long phrase, as in second example ➪ ⚠ leave/let well alone; let alone.

leave/let sb/sth be not interfere, or tamper, with sb/sth; previous entry (qv) □ JERRY: *Good* *morning*. (Cairy ignores him.) JEAN: *Say good — CAIRY: No! JEAN:* ***Leave*** *her* ***be*** *then —* ***let*** *her* ***be***. YAA □ *Some treatments are administered without any certainty that they will prove helpful and some, I believe, are actually riskier than* ***letting*** *the patient* ***be***. ⇨ ⚠ leave/let well alone; let alone.

leave sb cold [V + O + Comp pass] not interest, amuse or excite sb **adv mod:** rather, quite; completely □ *Instrumental music, oddly enough,* ***left*** *me rather* ***cold***. DOP □ *He was then the guest of Lord Rothschild, who's invited him over to view several fine gardens, which* ***left*** *Mr Streeter* ***cold***. OBS □ (book review) *If Mr Chips makes you melt, this misspelt, irreverent account of japes and whizzes will* ***leave*** *you* ***cold***. OBS □ *Red scare-mongering may even persuade a few small colleges of education to disaffiliate, but this banging of the anti-communist drum will* ***leave*** *most students quite* ***cold***. NS

leave sb holding/to hold the baby etc [V + O + Comp pass] (informal) cause, or allow, sb to be burdened, or inconvenienced, by an unwelcome duty or responsibility; cause, or allow, sb to take the blame for sth **n:** baby; ⚠ bag, parcel □ *'Is it a character reference the Finance Company want?' 'No. Alan's asking you to be his guarantor. In other words, if he can't complete his payments you're* ***left holding the baby***.' □ *'And you would* ***leave*** *us* ***to hold the baby****?' Dave was incoherent with indignation. 'You go off to Paris and leave here your stolen property to be found by the police, no?'* UTN □ *This was what Kissinger and Nixon, their various minions and dimly remembered predecessors, laboured so fervently to stave off. Nobody wanted to be the one caught* ***holding the bag***. NS □ *It reflects a subconscious reluctance to be* ***left holding the parcel***. *They don't want to be in government at this particular moment, thank you very much, and reckon that so long as Heath is their leader, they stand no danger of it.* NS

leave one's/its mark [V + O] have had an influence on, caused a change in, sb/sth that can be seen and recognized **A:** on the school; wherever he goes; here □ *The gentry took over the house in turn; a painter, a mad poet, then someone retired from the City. Each* ***left his mark***, *brick floors were covered with boards, doorways blocked up or altered to make way for unheard of luxuries such as bathrooms.* ARG □ *In Philip's life, however, there has been no exact equivalent of the philosopher-courtier, Baron Stockmar, who largely formed Albert's views on monarchy. The most comparable figure is Dr Kurt Hahn, Philip's headmaster at Salem and Gordonstoun, whose ideas have manifestly* ***left their mark***. OBS ⇨ ⚠ make one's mark.

leave much to be desired [V + O] (formal) be unsatisfactory, inadequate; be less than, fall short of, a required standard **det:** much, a lot, a good deal, a great deal, something □ (reader's letter) *The way in which the evidence was handled may* ***leave much to be desired*** *but this does not necessarily mean that the evidence is unconvincing or that the 'allegation' is fake.* NS □ *Her entrance with bare feet was silent, and so the armadillo (whose sight apparently* ***left much to be desired****) was unaware of her presence.* DF □ *'We'd best get ourselves seated,' Graham said. 'I should suggest near the back. The acoustics of this place* ***leave a great deal to be desired***.' TGLY

leave no/(not) any stone unturned [V + O pass] (cliché) search for and examine every possible solution to a problem, any means of accomplishing sth; explore every avenue (qv) □ *Once faced with a loss of initative the Government* ***left no stone unturned*** *in collecting data for 'The Times' solicitors to use in defending its conduct before the Commissioners.* SC □ *It was suggested that further leaks* (of privileged information) *might subsequently have taken place. Mr William Whitelaw promised that* ***no stone*** *would be* ***left unturned***, *but again this did not soothe all doubts.* L □ *So obvious is their sympathy and good faith, and so convincing their depiction of this obsessive recluse that the inquisitive reader must ultimately applaud them for their refusal to* ***leave any*** *available* ***stone unturned***. L

leave the room [V + O] go to the lavatory to relieve oneself □ *'All right, I must just nip down to the toilet first — didn't get a chance what with the meeting and everything.' 'Yes,' he said, 'you can* ***leave the room***—*I'll mix the necessary.'* TT □ *Before sleep, the subject* ***leaves the room***, *gets into bed, and may remain mentally active for as long as ten minutes.* MFF □ euphemism used esp by children in a classroom asking permission to go to the lavatory.

leave sb speechless [V + O + Comp pass] so astonish, delight or outrage sb that he is incapable of responding, objecting etc, or cannot do so adequately □ *'Yes, it's for sale if you can afford it,' the dealer replied, mentioning a sum that* ***left*** *him* ***speechless***. □ *15-year-old Adrian Dannatt has amazingly adult views on everything from girls to money. Since he* ***left*** *me* ***speechless***, *I'll leave him to explain in his own words.* TVT □ *'I suggested to Mr Collins,' she said, 'that you ought to marry Miss Elliot.' 'And this decision on my part would improve the moral climate of the School?' 'I think so,' she said, and she really did, 'don't you?' 'Richie, you* ***leave*** *me bloody* ***speechless***.' TT

leave sb/sth standing [V + O + Comp pass] (informal) exceed sb/sth in speed, ability, worth, popularity etc so greatly that his/its own progress, achievement, seems negligible (from racing) □ *He started swinging his way uphill at a pace that* ***left*** *the others* ***standing***. □ *Mike Mansfield doesn't attempt to compete with the wilder dressers in his world. He doesn't need to. Wearing today's classics with confidence and colour, his own special supersonic style* ***leaves*** *most men* ***standing***. TVT □ *Field mushrooms are difficult to obtain but for flavour* ***leave*** *the cultivated commercial product* ***standing***. ST

leave undone those things which/that one ought to have done sin, or act foolishly, by omitting to do what is right, necessary or advisable, esp in stated or implied contrast to, or in conjunction with, doing things which one ought not to do **det:** those; many, a host of; several; a single □ (source) *We have* ***left undone those things which we ought to have done****; And we have done those things which we ought not to have done; And there is no health in us.* BOOK OF COMMON PRAYER □ *This is the time* *of year when his sins both of omission and commission begin to catch up with the average back-green gardener. Not only has he* ***not done those things which he ought to have done****, but the mistakes as well as the triumphs of former seasons are emerging relentlessly from the decent obscurity of their winter retreat.* SC □ *The one-sided contemplative* ***leaves undone many things he ought to do****; but to make up for it he refrains from doing a host of things he ought not to do.* DOP □ *'I think it is quite dreadful about Pomfret Towers,' and so seriously did she speak that Lord Pomfret wondered if he had* ***left undone one*** *single* ***thing that he ought to have done*** *and came to the conclusion, that, humanly speaking, he hadn't.* WDM □ often facetious; usu adapted.

leave/let well alone [V + O + Comp] not interfere with, or try to improve, an already satisfactory or adequate arrangement, state of affairs, standard of working or production, etc □ *Alexander let me run this private war in my own way and supported me to the hilt; we gave him success all along the road and he was content to* ***leave well alone****.* MFM □ *In almost every sentence the translators could not* ***leave well alone****.* T □ *The living room is well furnished, and almost aggressively expresses Mrs Harrington's personality. We are let know by it that she is a Person of Taste; but also that she does not often* ***let well alone****.* FFE ⇨ ⚠ let alone; leave/let sb/sth alone; leave/let sb/sth be.

leaven the (whole) lump [V + O] enliven, transform, a company, community, state of affairs of which one/sth is only a part □ (source) *Know ye that a little leaven* ***leaveneth the whole lump****?* I CORINTHIANS V 6 □ *Communes are not for every man. They are not Gardens of Eden. They will not revolutionise society. But they help to* ***leaven the lump****. They reproach. They stimulate. They cry aloud that man need not be a slave.* OBS □ *It is good for slow learners to be in a class of mixed ability. A few bright and interested minds can* ***leaven the whole lump****.*

one's left hand does not know what one's right hand is doing (saying) one acts secretly, or for reasons not known to oneself, or in a way that seems haphazard or contrary to one's interests or principles □ (source) *Take heed that ye do not your alms before men, to be seen of them: But when thou doest alms,* ***let not thy left hand know what thy right hand doeth****.* MATTHEW VI 1, 3 □ *You could be leading a double life at the moment,* ***not letting your left hand know what the right hand is doing****.* TVT □ *'New Scientist's' editorial* ***left hand*** *obviously* ***didn't know what its*** *publicity-conscious* ***right hand was doing****.* NM □ *Certainly the Dorset business is an illuminating instance of* ***a*** *governmental* ***right hand not knowing what the left hand is doing****.* ST □ *We both knew the temptations of action, and how even clear-sighted men did not enquire* ***what their left hand was doing****.* NM □ adjs may be reversed, as in one's right hand does not know what one's left hand is doing; variant not let one's left hand know what one's right hand is doing, in which adjs are similarly reversible.

left and/or right [A/o] both sides or all directions (the implication being 'alternately', 'simultaneously' or 'indiscriminately' according to context) **V:** look, turn; lie; converge, disperse. **prep:** to; in; on; at; from □ *But she soon saw it was all just fun, and really she felt quite proud of Ron's adaptability—he was giving the old one-two look* ***left and right****.* HAA □ *Then I set off running at random down one of the avenues, looking to* ***left and right****.* UTN □ *A sudden breeze blew in, scattering the papers* ***right and left****.* □ *He was at that time being attacked* ***left and right*** *for his views.* □ *I've tried to make this rag into a decent newspaper and I can't have the people who represent it going about insulting everybody* ***right and left****.* AITC □ *I've been up and down the High Street twice and neither* ***left nor right*** *is there any such shop as you mention.* □ may be preceded by verbs *look, turn, lie* with or without prep *to*; rev. ⇨ ⚠ next entry.

left, right and centre [A] everywhere; at, to, or from all, or many, points; in all respects □ *In the Council Offices they were tearing what was left of their hair and putting up notices,* ***left, right and centre*** *about what was not allowed to the 'tourists'.* TST □ *The poor were sacrificed* ***left, right and centre*** *to make money for a privileged few.* RT □ *'No sign of yours* (= your class) *yet, Dusty?' 'They're a right lot — let you down* ***right, left and centre****.'* □ usu in order of headphrase; *centre* always end position. ⇨ ⚠ previous entry.

a left-handed/back-handed compliment an ambiguous compliment; a compliment that the recipient might not think flattering, or that is qualified by an additional comment that displeases or amuses □ *'I was quite nervous about meeting you — but here you are, just a nice ordinary person I feel quite at home with.' Esther smiled to herself at* ***the left-handed compliment****, but understood well enough what her mother-in-law meant.* □ *I felt quite flattered when Jane said that she knew her father would like me. Then I found out that he likes plump women who believe men are superior beings—a bit of* ***a back-handed compliment****, I felt.* □ also pl.

lend one's/an ear [V + O] hear, listen to sb/sth, esp in response to an appeal or request to do so □ *Most people are only too keen to talk about their disabilities to anybody willing to* ***lend an ear****.* NS □ *'I'm afraid I've been running on* (= talking continuously) *about myself again.' 'Well, I should think so.' 'It's you* ***lending your*** *pretty little* ***ear*** *in sympathy that does it — '* TGLY

the length and breadth of sth [O/o (NP)] the whole area of the land, or in most or many places within it **V:** travel, journey, walk **prep:** throughout, through; across; over **n:** land; island; Britain; airfield; sb's estates □ *Throughout* ***the length and breadth of*** *the land, people were shivering in ill-heated houses as they read the morning papers, ate their breakfasts, and grumbled about the weather.* TBC □ *Just before the 'off' the race-reader takes over, and his stride for stride account of the event goes to Manchester where other voices disseminate it, with only a few seconds' time-lag,* ***the length and breadth of*** *the country.* OBS □ *In an age of sport, with playing fields so much in demand over* ***the length and breadth of*** *Britain,...* SC □ *But now, still eagerly talking, Illich has led me through* ***the length and***

breadth of *the gardens, and finally up to the roof, where he is to conduct his Tuesday seminar.* OBS □ *She let the words stay, and we walked* ***the length and breadth of*** *the station. Then we began to talk again but the words were stilted.* PP □ prep may be omitted after a v, as in last example.

the less/least said (about sb/sth) the better (saying) sb/sth is an unpleasant subject; little, or nothing, can be said in sb's/sth's favour □ *I think* ***the less said about*** *this battle* ***the better****, for I fancy that whatever I do say will almost certainly be resented.* MFM □ ***The less said about*** *Arnold Wesker's 'The Old Ones' at the Royal Court,* ***the better****. In the past, Wesker has done good things with the Jewish comic tradition but this time he falls sadly short.* L □ (of a football match) *Tommy Docherty and Jack Charlton, who had so much to say before this game, ran out of words after it. Docherty was almost laconic. '****The least said the better****,' he rapped.* G

the lesser of two evils [Comp/O (NP)] sth little better, or more welcome, than the alternative offered or available **V:** be, seem; choose, prefer □ (astrological prediction) *In business you may have to choose between* ***the lesser of two evils****—pick the one which does least harm.* TVT □ *It was considered that this alternative would be* ***the lesser of two evils****.* MFM □ (reader's letter) *I now see the truth of Mr Harold Wilson's dictum at the last general election that the choice before the electorate is* ***the lesser of two evils****.* L □ *A loss of land would be compensated by a greater measure of political support. For Israel it is* ***a choice of evils****, but there is no point in pretending that the preservation of the status quo is likely to be a happy solution.* SC □ variant a choice of (two) evils; in last example a choice of evils suggests choices available are equally unattractive.

to let available for hiring, for renting □ ***To let****: rooms, flats, houses, caravans. Contact Swindle and Crook Co. Ltd.* □ used of accommodation. ⇨ ⚠ for sale.

let alone [Conj] how much less likely, less probable (is it that one would find, do etc this thing that the one just mentioned); much less (qv) □ *No hot drinks,* ***let alone*** *sandwiches, were available.* SC □ *You would not hurt an earthworm,* ***let alone*** *a big dog.* UTN □ *At the time, however, I could not begin to read the words,* ***let alone*** *trust myself to sing.* ST □ *...the Ministry, whose experts seem never to have entered a chemistry laboratory,* ***let alone*** *worked in one.* NSC □ *All in all, it is difficult to imagine a biography of Richardson more definitive than this one,* ***let alone*** *more readable.* L □ *The professor must be confusing me with some one of the same name. I've not missed a lecture once,* ***let alone*** *often.* □ usu in neg construction; precedes n, v, adj or adv. ⇨ ⚠ leave/let sb/sth alone; leave/let sb/sth be; leave/let well alone.

let bygones be bygones (saying) allow old or former mistakes, offences, causes of contention to be forgotten; bury the past (qv) □ *Don't you go worrying your little head about that. That's all over—finished and done with, as they say. Let's* ***let bygones be****—what's that word? Oh yes!* ***bygones****.* TGLY □ *Well ahead of the tourist deluge, Chopin chose Majorca for a winter holiday. It was a calamity. The islanders today are happy to* ***let*** *such* ***bygones be bygones****—they treasure the composer as an immortal asset.* OBS □ *Sender hasn't* ***let bygones be bygones*** *without a murmur. He has laid down stringent conditions for the end of his self-imposed exile.* L

let the dead bury their dead (saying) it is better to concern oneself with the living, with present and future life and work, than with the remembering of rituals connected with people, institutions, events, customs that are dead or finished □ (source) *And another of his disciples said unto him, Lord, suffer me first to go and bury my father. But Jesus said unto him, Follow me; and* ***let the dead bury their dead****.* MATTHEW VIII 21-2 □ *'Stop picking on the poor man.' Virginia continued to bang the broom against the skirting-board as she swept. 'It's done with.* ***Let the past bury its dead****, Helen.'* AITC □ *One does a great writer no service by raking out and publishing his juvenilia unless they have some intrinsic merit.* ***Let the dead bury their dead****, and let ghouls not disinter them.* □ *Sunday night's 'Brother, Can You Spare a Dime?' (BBC 2) was a prize American example of how to* ***let the dead bury the dead*** *with a bit ot toe-tapping on the edge of the grave.* NS □ often adapted or allusive, as in second example.

let the dog see the rabbit (catchphrase) do not get in the way of another who wishes, or whose job it is, to see or do sth □ *Pop went up to the steps of the hotel and gave Mademoiselle Dupont a prolonged parting sample of amorous affection that even had the children cheering from the car. 'Here, stand back and* ***let the dog see the rabbit****!' Ma called.* BFA □ *'There's a whole lot of connections going in under here. I don't know which is the speedometer cable.' 'Well, get your head out of the way and* ***let the dog see the rabbit****.'* □ facetious.

let 'em all come (catchphrase) a response to the intrusion, competition or opposition of others that may express open welcome, resigned acceptance, or determination to defy them □ *'I never thought we asked this lot,' Ma said, 'Hardly enough stuff to go round.' '****Let 'em all come****.' Pop said.* DBM □ *'Don't worry, Mollie,' said Joe, trying to laugh off his resentment. 'Why didn't you bring, Paul?* ***Let 'em all come****. We're having open house.'* AITC □ *He was a mean-gutted rat, and if he's a measure of the coming revolutionary I'd say* ***let 'em all come****.* PP □ 'em = 'them'; stress pattern let ˊem ˈall come.

let fly (at sb) (with sth) aim, throw sth (at sb/sth) vigorously or recklessly; express one's resentment, criticism (of sb/sth) without restraint **o: *(at)*** opponent, critic, pupil; ***(with)*** one's fists, a stone, a faster ball □ *One of these gas-bullets that hit the Moon three months ago would finish us. Sooner or later the Cloud will probably* ***let fly with*** *some more of 'em* (= them). TBC □ (of a tennis match) *When Newcombe held a game point for it Smith* ***let fly with*** *an ace so fast and accurate that the Australian had no chance to return it.* OBS □ *His voice was louder as he* ***let fly at*** *Francis Getliffe, Luke, me, all liberal-minded men.* NM □ *'I'm sorry,' she said, 'Sometimes your cold-blooded look does some-*

'Sometimes your cold-blooded look does something to me and I have to ***let fly****.'* PP

let (oneself) go allow full expression to one's mood, inclinations, feelings, esp temporarily □ *Victoria had been entertaining the three other typists and the office boy with a vivid performance of Mrs Greenholtz paying a visit to her husband's office. Secure in the knowledge that Mr Greenholtz had gone round to his solicitors, Victoria* ***let herself go****.* TCB □ *I cried for about ten minutes when I got back to the Wrennery but I suppose it does one good to* ***let go****.* RFW □ *Myrtle was a little vulgar, and I must say that I like it. People who cannot* ***let themselves go*** *on occasion will not do for me.* SPL ⇨ ⚠ next entry; let sb go; let/leave go(of sb/sth).

let oneself/sth go [V + O + A] allow oneself, one's appearance, business, house, garden etc to deteriorate; run to seed (Vol 1) (qv) □ *She would be a good enough looking woman yet if she hadn't* ***let herself go****.* □ *'You're* ***letting yourself go****, my girl!' her father told her, eyeing the dowdy skirt and jumper, her lustreless hair. 'Your mother would always keep herself a picture though she had four to look after.'* □ *'I was vexed,' said Alice, 'they've fairly* ***let*** *the place* ***go*** *since Dad was gardener there.'* ⇨ ⚠ next entry; previous entry; let/leave go (of sb/sth).

let sb go realease one's grip on sb; release sb, an animal, from captivity; allow sb to proceed on his way □ *I took the wrist with the watch upon it, and twisted it. 'Jake, you're hurting me,' said Anna. I* ***let*** *her* ***go*** *and lay heavily upon her breasts, completely limp.* UTN □ *Sometimes the web caught a wasp by mistake. Then the spider had to dismantle the web. The wasp had to be* ***let go****, because it was dangerous.* HD □ *The police had taken Bates in for questioning but, after having established his identity and made a few routine inquiries, they* ***let*** *him* ***go****.* □ *Well, if you've a train to catch we'd better* ***let*** *you* ***go****. I'll get the rest of your news another time.* ⇨ ⚠ next entry; previous entry; let (oneself) go.

let/leave go (of sb/sth) release one's grip (on sb/sth) □ *You're mad, Robert! For heaven's sake* ***leave go of*** *me!* EM □ *His fingers were so numb and quivering. In a few minutes he would have to* ***let go*** *and risk breaking his back or limbs on the rocks below.* □ *You cross the road with Granny, Sue—and don't* ***let go of*** *her hand till you're on the other pavement.* ⇨ ⚠ previous

let sb/sth go hang not bother oneself about sb/sth either through carelessness or through defiance **V:** family, friend; job, project □ *From now on he was going to please himself and* ***let*** *the world* ***go hang****.* □ *Your average modern playwright feels obliged to don his philosopher's cloak and shout out moral conclusions when he tackles such a subject; Sherriff prefers to give all his attention to particular characters and places, and philosophy* ***may go hang****.* NS □ *'But Billy said he might want to go, and if so there won't be room for me in the car.' 'You come if you want and* ***let*** *Billy* ***go hang****. He's had plenty of time to make up his mind.'* □ variant sb/sth may/can go hang.

(not) let/allow the grass (to) grow under one's feet (not) be inactive, or waste time, when one should be doing sth necessary or helpful to oneself □ *He says his publisher tells him there's a lot of advance interest in this book —he's working on the publicity side himself, making the right contacts and so on. Oh, he's cute, Alec is. He does****n't let the grass grow under his feet****.* PW □ *Court Line, who are Britain's biggest package-tour airline as well as the stock market's hottest take-over tip at the moment, are* ***not letting the grass grow under their feet****. They are currently boosting their jet fleet from 10 to 12.* SC □ *The directors themselves* ***allowed the grass to grow under their feet*** *after international defenders Paddy Mulligan and Johnny Fulham were transferred for almost £30,000 a couple of seasons ago.* ST

let it be said as one may as well admit, or make known □ (a job) *It suited him because in an era of form-filling and letter-writing there was no paper work to be done, for,* ***let it be said****, Joe had difficulty in reading and writing.* TBC □ *Here am I turning out to be right again, which causes me no surprise,* ***let it be said****.* TGLY □ *Inside each of Edna O'Brien's stories is a full-length novel: quiescent,* ***let it be said****.* L □ usu middle or end position; almost always within commas or parentheses.

let it go (at that) not choose, or bother, to say or do anything more about sth which might be thought to require further examination, attention, action □ *Either the slight gloss of irony which I put on the words had escaped him altogether, or he preferred to* ***let it go****; I could not tell which, at the moment.* CON □ *I went carefully through the dead man's personal records yet Waterman was still a man in a mist as far as I was concerned. But something attempted, something done, I told myself and thought I would* ***let it go at that****.* PP

let it etc ride (informal) let a process, developing situation, take its own course, continue as it has begun; ignore or take no action about sth said or done **O:** it; ⚠ things; the matter □ *Sometime that night we should have to* (discuss tactics)*; but just for this brief space we put the tactics out of our minds, we gave ourselves the satisfaction of* ***letting it ride****.* NM □ *Could the doctor after all be depended on to understand Rose? Might he not take it too seriously and have her taken away? It might be better just to* ***let things ride*** *for the moment.* TSMP

let me see I am thinking, trying to remember □ *If the insurance company pays up I might invest in—* ***let me see****—Guy, what do you think of these Bolivian oil rigs?* DC □ *'I'm the professora from England.' 'Oh, the professora from England! Forgive me—it's so very hot—now* ***let me see****: Senorita Elena Lawrence?'* BM □ *I think it was in August, '64 we were there. No,* ***let me see****, that was the summer Julia was expecting our eldest and we didn't go abroad at all. It must have been '63.* □ used to allow speaker, in course of main statement, to slow down for consideration, more exact definition or identification; front, middle or end position.

let me tell you let me assure you; you can be quite sure of this □ ***Let me tell you****, when you've caught your food for four flaming days with a filed-down can opener, two bootlaces and a flaming hat for a fishing-net, it kind of gets you after a while.* BM □ *She isn't as feeble as she makes out,* ***let me tell you****. I've watched her when she didn't know I was watching. She can move about quite* *easily when she likes.* MM □ *Your mother's quite right—you do always look a mess. And that old mac,* ***let me tell you****, is going into the furnace before the week's out.* □ used to emphasize a preceding or following statement, threat, promise etc; front, middle or end position.

let (her) rip (informal) allow, or arrange for, a vehicle, machine to proceed at full speed; let a plan of action be carried out with speed and vigour; do/say sth without restraint or moderation **O:** her, it, them. **A:** with the machine-guns, with a volley of abuse; in private □ *For the next two days the radio astronomers were hard at work on the aerials. It was late in the afternoon of 9 December that a crowd assembled in the lab to watch results. 'OK.* ***Let her rip****,' said someone.* TBC □ (reader's letter) *He was particularly concerned about what was actually said by General Eisenhower when he triggered off the D-Day invasion. 'OK!* ***Let 'er*** *(= her)* ***rip****' was agreed as probable but needed confirmation.* L □ *Jackie Charlton's singing voice is so awful that he daren't even* ***let rip*** *in the bath.* RT □ O and A never used together.

let sleeping dogs lie (saying) do not provoke, disturb or interfere with sb/sth that is giving no trouble though he/it might, or could, do so □ *For the time being there was no fear of public alarm, and for this reason the Prime Minister resolved to* ***let sleeping dogs lie****.* TBC □ *For although we all go on so much about oppression we give little thought to its varieties; and there are clear similarities between the '****let sleeping dogs lie****' tolerance of Horthy's and of Kadar's Hungary, both autocratic rather than totalitarian.* L □ (NONCE) *I started talking about the Golden Section. This was silly as it roused* ***the sleeping dog*** *in L.W.* ST □ (NONCE) *'Who'd like to go for a walk round the yard?' I could not have said anything sillier in the circumstances. Any schoolmaster will tell you, even I can tell you, that you should always* ***let sleeping boys lie****.* SPL

let sth slide allow sth to remain unattended to and esp to decline or deteriorate **O:** things, everything; matters; work, research □ *We are trying to get more people in the UK to eat herring in some form or other. The home market used to be a big one. I think the British market has been* ***let slide*** *and we must get back into it.* SC □ *As an author he* (G B Shaw) *controls everything from the renting out of his own electrotypes to the width of his margins and the fonts of his title-pages. Nothing, but nothing, is* ***let slide****.* L □ *'It is kind of you to offer,' she wrote, 'and there will be plenty for you to do in house and garden if you come. I've had so much to do looking after my two invalids I've had to* ***let*** *everything else* ***slide****.'* □ pass as in first two examples.

let sth slip[1] fail, esp through delay, negligence or misunderstanding, to obtain, enjoy, make use of, sth **O:** opportunity, chance; occasion. **A:** between/through one's fingers; from one's grasp □ *He's a born cadger—never* ***lets slip*** *an opportunity of getting something for nothing.* □ *But you've always wanted to see Venice! It would be crazy to* ***let*** *a chance like this* ***slip****.* □ *When in 'Habit' Jeannine says, 'I want last year,' her impossible request is poignant: but in sorrow she is able to value at last the love she has so casually* ***let slip****.* L □ *Tell me more about this profitable transaction I'm supposed to have* ***let slip*** *through my fingers.* □ pass as in *The chance was* ***let slip****.*

let sth slip[2] reveal, stupidly or carelessly, information, an opinion etc that one does not wish to be known; say sth casually, or indirectly, though hoping it will be noted **O:** ...it... (that you were leaving); anything; remark □ *Now remember you told the Carsons you'd be out of town last Friday, and don't* ***let*** *it* ***slip*** *that you weren't.* □ *You should have brought Jack's present when the children were in bed. One of them is bound to* ***let*** *something* ***slip*** *before tomorrow.* □ *'What makes you think Mrs Fraser lent them the down-payment?' 'Oh, a remark she* ***let slip*** *herself about it paying them to keep in with her.'* ⇨ ⚠ a slip of the tongue/pen.

let them eat cake (catchphrase) unrealistic or flippant suggestion for remedying the lack of a basic necessity, eg by suggesting sth still harder to get (often attributed to Queen Marie-Antoinette, 18th c, when told that her subjects had not enough bread, but actually an older saying) □ *One of the exceptions, wife of a former Ambassador at Moscow, thought the miners should show a little 'Russian' patriotism. I don't think she said '****Let 'em*** (= them) ***eat cake****'—neither did Marie-Antoinette for that matter—but it didn't seem far from her thoughts.* L □ *'****Let them eat cake****.' It is, naturally, in Harrods that Marie-Antoinette is taken seriously. There, £1.50 buys admission to a schoolboy's paradise: the buffet tea, eat as much as you like, on the fourth floor: 75p if the schoolboy is under 11.* G □ (NONCE) *Until the war, no self-respecting Cambodian ate dogs. Dogs were for the Chinese, and paddy rats for the Vietnamese. Cambodians enjoyed snake-meat ('****Let them eat snake****!' said the queen, or as the great Khmer poet put it,...)* NS □ (NONCE) *Let us assume that on the first ballot the candidates are Mr Heath, Mr du Cann and Mrs Margaret ('****Let 'em eat Spam****') Thatcher.* NS

let us say[1] let us agree that; do you agree that? □ *We both seem rather uncertain about our movements.* ***Let us say*** *that we will meet here for lunch on Sunday, and if either of us can't manage we'll let the other know.* □ *'What fee would you want for your contribution?' 'I prefer people to offer me a fee, and then I'll tell them if it's not enough.' '£50 then,* ***let us say****, and your expenses?'* □ introduces, or invites confirmation of, a proposal or suggestion; front or end position.

let us say[2] [Conj] introduces, or refers back to, an example; for example (qv); for instance (qv) □ *Don't you sometimes feel it was a stroke of bad luck for you to be born with a well-to-do father who's got ideas about educating you—when if you were son of,* ***let's say****, a chimney sweep you could have been happily employed as a garage hand?* HD □ *If the wave-length was too short the radio waves would stream out of the atmosphere away into space instead of being bent round the Earth, as they must be to travel from London to Australia,* ***let us say****.* TBC □ front, middle or end position.

let's face it [Disj] (cliché) let us speak frankly, boldly; let us admit that what I say is a fact □ (reader's letter) ***Let's face it****, 90 per cent of the* *world swears. If the odd 10 per cent doesn't, that's OK with me, but when they start creating hell because the majority do swear they are nut cases.* RT □ *I can't help noticing how little space in this vast compilation my friends and I occupy.* ***Let's face it****—we aren't Whitaker's Almanac people.* L □ *We've both had affairs which have seemed important at the time—well,* ***let's face it****, any relationship is important isn't it, whether it's a physical one or a mental one?* ST □ *Why did he come to bingo? '****Let's face it****,' he said, 'I come here for the money I might win.'* OBS □ *Any wedding list* (of guests), ***let's face it****, is going to have omissions.* L □ usu front or middle position; almost always in parenthesis to a main statement which is often not very revealing or challenging.

the letter of the law etc [O/o (NP)] the law literally and rigidly defined or enforced (esp in stated or implied contrast to *the spirit of the law*, ie its general purpose or desired effect) **V:** observe, uphold; stick to, abide by. **adj:** strict, exact. **o:** law; constitution; agreement; one's promise □ *A policeman, if he is to do his job well, cannot abide by* ***the*** *strict* ***letter of the*** *law. He has to be familiar with his neighbourhood and abide by its ethics to some extent.* SC □ *In claiming that an unbaptised child could not be counted Christian, the rector of Akenham stuck callously close to* ***the letter of the law*** *on theological grounds.* NS □ *But to More and others its rejection heralded the divorce of politics from morality. It was no comfort to More that Cromwell observed* ***the letter of*** *parliamentary* ***legislation****.* L □ (price freezes) *A manufacturer who wants to honour* ***the letter*** *but not the spirit* ***of his pledge*** *simply has to bring out a whole range of slightly improved products—and he can jack his price up.* OBS □ *Codes of ethics in advertising, for instance, should be adhered to* ***in spirit as well as in letter****.* NS □ *'The new edition,' say Kestrel, '****maintains the spirit as much as the letter of the*** *original* ***work****.' I find it hard not to take this remark as ironical.* G □ variants in letter observe/maintain the spirit as much/as well as the letter of the law etc, in spirit and/as well as in letter .

Liberty Hall a home, institution etc where people can do as they please □ *'But I'll tell you this,' he says, waving a hand in the direction of the main prison, 'I'd rather be here than there.' Not that the hostel is* ***Liberty Hall****. The prisoners function under a system of rules.* RT □ *Bert is always carping or nagging at his wife or kids about something though he honestly believes his home is* ***Liberty Hall****.*

lick sb's boots/arse [V + O] (informal/taboo) behave in a servile, toadying way to sb one hopes to please or conciliate, esp sb ranking as one's superior or sb whom one fears □ *He caved in straightaway. If you just spoke roughly to that chap, he was* ***licking your boots*** *the next moment.* RATT □ *. . .a new series about an up-and-coming executive who suffers all kinds of humiliations, tests, frustrations and tediums in his route up the ladder,* ***licking the boots*** *above, stamping on the fingers below.* ST □ MONTY: *I bet we have a revolution soon. Hitler won't stop at Spain, you know. You watch him go and you watch the British Government* ***lick his arse****, until he spits in their eye. Then we'll move in.* CSWB □ *Daniel felt fury that snobbery like this should exist, that the duke's descendant should be prized above the great artist. He thought of Shakespeare's* ***boot-licking*** *to Southampton, and was ashamed both for Shakespeare and himself.* US □ n compounds a boot-/an arse-licker, boot-/arse-licking; attrib use *a/an* ***boot-/arse-licking*** *attitude.*

lick/smack one's lips/chops [V + O] (informal) show (greedy) enjoyment, or anticipation, of sth, perhaps by the action described □ *The children,* ***licking their lips****, watched while the cake was carefully cut into equal portions.* □ *Maybe the old man has left all his money to charity. It's too soon to be* ***licking your lips****.* □ *'Honest, mam, I can't tell you one half of what went on, because you wouldn't want to hear it.' (Not much, I thought, I could see her as large as life* ***licking her chops****.) 'Tell me it all, my lad,' she said. 'Get it off your chest.'* LLDR □ *Don't apologise to Max because we had that argument when he was there. He loved every minute—I couldn't almost hear him* ***smacking his lips****.* □ *The whole thing is an odd mixture of insistent* ***lip-smacking*** *hedonism and pert comedy, pleasant enough to read in an English mid-winter but not really adding up to anything.* OBS □ lick one's chops suggests crude or vindictive enjoyment; attrib use ***lip-smacking*** *enjoyment*; often continuous tenses.

a lick of paint [O/o (NP)] a coat of fresh paint (the implication usu being a skimpy job of renovation instead of thorough repair or treatment) **V:** need, want; apply, put on □ *Most amateur sailors are familiar enough with the business of making do with what they have got. Our boats are lucky to get as much as* ***a*** *seasonal* ***lick of paint****.* G □ *It's wonderful what half a pound of putty and* ***a lick of paint*** *will do.*

lick one's wounds [V + O] brood, console oneself, or try to restore oneself, after any form of defeat, injury or loss □ *'Where's George?' 'Gone off home to* ***lick his wounds****, I expect. You were pretty severe with him.'* □ *Essex University this week resembles a battlefield from which the chief protagonists have temporarily departed, bloody and battle weary. The senior administrators remain,* ***licking their wounds*** *and sharpening their claws for the inevitable ferocious battles to come after the Easter vacation.* NS □ *We have got to have peace—peace to* ***lick our wounds*** *and make a new world—and to do that we must try to understand each other.* TCB

lie awake [V + Comp] be unable to sleep though having gone to bed for that purpose □ *I've not much sympathy with him. He spends half the day snoozing and then complains because he* ***lies awake*** *at night.* □ *In reality, it was Lisa Brooks who had black-mailed Charmian so that she had been forced to* ***lie awake*** *worrying throughout long night hours.* MM

lie doggo (informal) remain in hiding or inactive, esp temporarily; next entry (qv); play possum (qv) □ *We are cheered by the discovery of a chemical dip for stopping the needles coming off Christmas trees. They can* ***lie doggo*** *in a cushion for months before popping out to pierce their chosen victim in his tenderest spot.* SC □ *. . .a snake clambering along a length of twig, blissfully unconscious the twig is another kind of in-*

sect ***lying doggo.*** L □ *As for his* (President Carter's) *money policies, Wall Street was* ***lying doggo*** *for a while, and the stock-market trod water, until it saw what kind of a wild Liberal we had in there.* L

lie low remain in hiding or inactive, esp as a temporary policy; previous entry (qv); play possum (qv) □ *He could get out of London,* ***lie low*** *for a bit, living on the fat of the land in George's house.* PE □ *But nobody up here believes that our dear old monster was killed by this flying saucer. We think it's* ***lying low.*** RM □ *As for the theatre, he says, 'The period of serious theatre is past. It's back in the hands of the frivolous people. We have to* ***lie low*** *and wait.'* RT

life begins at forty etc (saying) people of 40 are mature but still fit, will generally have established their values, be freer from emotional, financial and career problems, responsibilities of child-rearing, etc **adj:** forty, ⚠ thirty-five, sixty □ *'Any Questions' came from Brussels, with Marghanita Laski, Richard Crossman and others bandying about answers to questions on English sex-life and hot-water bottles, does* ***life begin at 40****, and how is public opinion to be converted to preserving the environment.* RT □ *Nordin stressed that women themselves, instead of just thinking 'Isn't there more to life than this, what about being well and happy?' need to be more assertive and go along to their doctors and say so. The adage that* ***life begins at forty*** *could be less of a bad joke and more of a reality to many women.* RT □ *At 35 we need to settle down to our lives and shed fantasies. To the despondent I whisper, as one who knows, that real* ***life begins at 60.*** ST □ chiefly humorous or consolatory, but sometimes serious; other ages may be substituted according to speaker's wishes.

(a matter etc of) life and/or death [n + n non-rev] that which determines whether one lives or dies; that which is crucial to the success, or survival, of sb/sth in a function or field of activity **n:** matter, ⚠ question, issue □ *What might be a reasonable measure of precision in a small matter might be quite unreasonably lacking in precision when it is* ***a matter of life and death.*** SNP □ *Mr Wilson also spoke about the Government's handling of Ulster: this has been sacrificed a little to keeping votes for the Common Market—* ***an issue of*** *literally* ***life and death*** *to hundreds of thousands and to British soldiers there.* L □ (consultant speaking) *Considering what we are expected to put into society, considering that we have to be available night and day, and ready to accept responsibility for* ***life and death*** *decisions, society is just not giving us a good enough return.* L □ *There was a time when people would go to the cinema to see almost anything. Now you either make a good film that's commercially viable or you don't make anything at all. As simple as that—* ***life or death.*** RT □ ASTON: *You've got to have a good pair of shoes.* DAVIES: *Shoes? It's* ***life and death*** *to me. I had to go all the way to Luton in these.* TC □ attrib use *a* ***life and death*** *decision.*

life is (not) a bed of roses (saying) life (for certain people, in certain circumstances, etc) is (not) easy or pleasant □ *I felt that I should explain to them that* ***life*** *here* ***is not a bed of roses.*** NS □ *'****Life is no bed of roses****', they assume, but 'tomorrow will take care of itself': on this scale the working-classes have been cheerful existentialists for ages.* UL □ *No, I can hardly call our relationship* ***a bed of roses****, even at the end.* DS □ *With all due respect to Mr Hamer, if he imagines that the one broadcast a year which is the most that many jazz musicians get enables them to wallow in* ***a bed of roses*** *then he is ignorant of some rather crucial realities himself.* L □ *She sees mouths, she says,* everywhere. *Her husband, for whom* ***life is not*** *all* ***roses****, has grown used to his bedroom slippers saying goodnight and the newspaper singing.* OBS □ used in whole or in part but always including roses.

life is hell (cliché) usu an assessment of, or grumble about, specific circumstances rather than expressing a pessimistic view of life in general **A:** for them; when she is here; on wet Sundays □ *'If you automatically fell in love with the most attractive woman you saw, in the first place your* ***life*** *would* ***be hell.****' 'I see what you're getting at,' I said. 'A man who's on the way up is continually raising the standard of the women he can fall for.'* CON □ *All right, he can come.* ***Life is hell*** *anyway just now—one more or less to cater for isn't going to make much difference.* □ *Having failed to get Turner the sack, the overseer determined to* ***make life hell for*** *him instead.* □ *For the young commercial artist* ***life*** *in the Bentley Colliery near Doncaster* ***was hell.*** OBS □ variant make life hell for sb.

life/it is one (damn(ed)) thing after another (catchphrase) life is a succession of tiresome incidents, duties etc □ (source) ***Life is*** *just* ***one damned thing after another.*** F W O'MALLEY 1875-1932 □ *I'm sincerely sorry for that poor guy. He loses all his money in Cuba, and then this happens to his son.* ***It's*** *been* ***one thing after another.*** ST □ *Most* ***life*** *in retrospect* ***is one damn thing after another****, and we are more geared to accepting this in art as well than we used to be.* NS □ That, *the theory says, is why* ***life is 'one damn thing after another'*** *because known brain mechanisms prevent any particular sensory mode from activating the pleasure areas for very long.* ST

life is too short (for sth/to do sth) (saying) no part of one's life should be wasted on sth (in the speaker's opinion) so unnecessary, tedious, frivolous, profitless etc **o:** that, vain regrets; doing what a machine will do for you **Inf:** to study everybody's foibles, to be fussing about a few specks of dust □ (advertisement for dishwashers) *This is insane—every day I wash up dozens of dishes. Not to mention knives and forks and pots and pans. In a year, it must run into thousands.* ***Life's too short.*** OBS □ *The game has a great fascination for some people but as far as I'm concerned* ***life's too short*** *for playing chess.* □ *Do you think I'm going to worry about what somebody said somebody else had said about me?* ***Life's too short for*** *that.*

life is (not) worth living one gets (no/little) satisfaction or pleasure, perhaps temporarily, from the way one has to live □ *If people wasted nothing and lived with carefully calculated economy, they might be able to save a modest amount. It would mean a bare, oatmealy sort of life, for very little at the end;* ***life*** *'would****n't be worth***

living'. UL □ *It was my only one-and-three* (1s 3d, former British currency) *and I was saving it for a packet of tips* (= cigarettes) *this morning—I was reckoning on it for getting me through today because I don't think* ***life's worth living*** *without a fag, do you?* LLDR □ *It was one of those beautiful spring mornings that made you feel* ***life was*** *really* ***worth living***. □ *It exaggerates the issues of survival to the point of obliterating the overwhelming significance of justice and of liberty. After all, survival is not enough; what matters is a* ***life worth living***. □ *I love the autumn. Those clear days when the air is crisp and the trees are such lovely colours — it* ***makes life worth living***. □ often, but not exclusively, neg or neg implications; variant make life worth living.

life and/or limb [n + n non-rev] one's survival and/or preservation from accident or injury **V:** threaten, endanger; risk □ (in New York) *Meanwhile, the burnings go on. Teenagers throw bottles at firemen as they risk* ***life and limb*** *to put out a blaze that nobody cares about.* OBS □ *As many of these cavers were perched high on the friable rock-face, the fact that the search was conducted without loss of* ***life or limb*** *is remarkable.* OBS □ *The railway train, that threat to* ***life and limb*** *of the Victorian age, is now almost 200 times safer than the motor car.* RT □ variant a risk/threat/danger to life and limb.

the life and soul (of the party) [n + n non-rev] sb who by his high spirits, wit, social assurance, etc animates a party, or gathering, and thus tends to keep everybody interested and lively **V:** ⚠ be, seem; make, think, sb □ *Last week we had an office get-together and, as Joan was ill, she wasn't able to come. Tom was there, though, and was* ***the life and soul of the party***. H □ *With a grin that dares you to keep glum when he's around, Bruce Forsyth is, every affable inch of him, the* ***life and soul of the party***, *the host who keeps pouring even if you're not thirsty.* RT □ *The two children are cousins, William and Janet, observing huge adults, loathing a* ***life-and-soul*** *uncle, admiring a riding-instructress.* L □ *There was all this agonizing over going and then once there, she was* ***the life and soul***. TSMP □ sometimes ironic or derogatory; unusual attrib use *a* ***life-and-soul*** *uncle*.

one's life and times [n + n non-rev] (the story of) one's life including, and in relation to, contemporary conditions, events and personalities □ *On her general views of* ***her life and times*** *Miss Hellman can be frail and evasive. One could wish her to have been less elliptic about the larger issues.* OBS □ *Anthony Murphy plays Tom Brown. 'To me it's Anthony Murphy's Schooldays', he says, though in fact* ***his life and times*** *at Westminster in 1971 have little in common with Tom Brown's days at Rugby in 1828.* RT □ *This was the signal for guests to take up viewing positions around my mother, who slowly turned the pages, delivering an informal lecture on* ***the life and times of*** *each portrait.* L

(one/another of) life's little ironies (an instance of) events made sad, vexing, or possibly comical by the circumstances in which they occur □ *'Not that the little fellow won't be loved of course, but they only had a fourth child in the hope of a daughter.' 'There you are, and Jim and Maureen would give everything for a son —****life's little ironies*** *again.'* □ *'It really is* ***one of life's little ironies*** *that the roles I play on television are nothing like the work I do away from it,' he said.* TVT □ can be used alone as sad, mocking etc comment on events.

(not) lift/raise a finger [V + O] be, or feel oneself to be, incapable of the slightest physical effort; not bother to, or be prevented from trying to, help sb **A:** to help himself, to save his friends; on their behalf □ *They would****n't*** *even* ***lift a finger*** *to save their own grandmother from the Ravenous Bugblatter Beast of Traal without orders in triplicate.* HHGG □ *There has been no indication that American Servicemen resent being stationed in Europe. But it is a costly commitment in terms of money rather than blood. Western Europe has* ***not lifted a finger*** *to help the US in Vietnam.* SC □ *He explains: 'I can't call myself a pacifist any more. The Government only* ***lifts a finger*** *when the situation becomes untenable through action.'* L □ *If they* ***raise a finger*** *in protest they make themselves liable to punishment under emergency powers.* SC

the light of day [O/o (NP)] daylight contrasted with darkness or artificial lighting; circumstances of seeing and/or being seen, of being exposed to notice or for use; the stage at which a difficulty, problem, mystery etc becomes clarified or resolved **V:** (not) see; emerge into; be exposed to □ *And now, this spring morning, with* ***the*** *honest* ***light of day*** *on the world, my neighbours and I were watching the young naval lieutenant and the fair-haired rating at work.* ARG □ *A surprising number of colleagues are reluctant to accept Alec Issigonis as a serious engineer. They cite for example his three years at Alvis between the Minor and the Mini, which he spent working on a car which never saw* ***the light of day***. ST □ *The truth of the matter has been the exact opposite—certainly since President Pompidou took office. But the truth has only now begun to emerge into* ***the light of day***. L □ *Now the job was done, the main leaks plugged, the final arrests made, and Blaize was on his way out of the shadows and back into* ***the light of day***. DS ⇨ ⚠ see (day)light; see the light.

light relief [Comp/O (NP)] a short respite in the midst of serious work, instruction, discussion **V:** be, prove; provide, afford, offer □ *If they were not to be regarded as serious programmes, why waste the excellent speakers who made up the panels each evening (even if on at least one occasion there was introduced—for* ***light relief****?—a woman really unfitted to speak on the subject)?* RT □ *I daresay he thought that passing round his holiday snapshots would prove some* ***light relief*** *for those mourners not seriously upset by the recent ceremony.*

lightning never strikes in the same place twice (saying) an unusual event, or sth that happens by chance, is not likely to be repeated in exactly the same circumstances or to the same people □ *She says 'What's the use of buying another car to have it stolen again?' 'Tell her* ***lightning*** *does****n't strike in the same place twice***. *She's had hers.'* □ *Fifty years ago my housemaster at Wellington College summoned me to his study and sent me packing. 'You're not looking well, boy. You need a holiday,' he told me. I am a great believer that* ***lightning*** *can, and* *often does,* ***strike twice in the same place****, but, alas, no one has ever again speeded me on my way in such a totally unexpected fashion.* OBS

the lights are going out all over Europe (catchphrase) (Europe's) civilization, culture etc is in decline, is about to perish or be destroyed □ *Folk-memory, let alone contemporary history, has attributed to Edward Grey one memorable phrase. On the morning war broke out in 1914, the Foreign Secretary looked out of his office window and noticed the gas-lights of London being extinguished. He observed, with a touch of that melancholy which marked him increasingly as he approached old age, that* ***the lights were going out all over Europe*** *and would not be lit again in his lifetime.* L □ (NONCE) (reader's letter) *Listen to our lady of the green ink* (obscure reference), *Clivo, alivo, and remember her* ***when the lights go out all over*** *your* ***European*** *culture circus. You could do worse, artistically, than the 'Sydney Bulletin'.* L □ (NONCE) *These were the years when the big circuses disappeared. Chipperfields decamped for South Africa, Bertram Mills, the greatest circus of all, dissolved itself.* ***The coloured bulbs had gone out all over Britain.*** RT □ *Marcel Boulesten was the first TV chef in the world. In the early pre-war days of television he was a great success.* ***When the lights went on*** *again, Boulesten was dead: but the BBC were still not convinced that an Englishman could do the job.* L □ variant (when) the lights go on used to refer to the end of the Second World War and itself alludes to the words of a popular song *We're going to get lit up* ***when the lights go on*** *in London.*

and one's like and people like him, her etc □ *It's all very well for you to sneer at her for a do-gooder. There's many would be a lot worse off without your Aunt Agnes* ***and her like****.* □ *'You* ***and your like*** *are trying to make a war with the help of people who just aren't interested.' 'They don't want Communism.' 'They want enough rice,' I said. 'They don't want to be shot at.'* QA □ often used in either praise or blame. ⇨ ⚠ next entry.

and the like and so on; together with things, or people, of approximately the same kind □ *They use the money to buy food—rice, millet,* ***and the like****—but it is so hard to get protein that the children are seriously malnourished.* NSC □ *'At supper parties* ***and the like****,' says Colonel Allen, 'the Princess is often placed not necessarily with the most senior but instead with the younger officers and their wives.'* RT □ (reader's letter) *Perhaps my children will one day be 'factory hands* ***and the like****', but in common with any mother who cares I want the very best for my children, which includes education.* RT ⇨ ⚠ previous entry.

like anything [A (Prep P)] (informal) very much; very quickly, loudly, ably, successfully etc □ *I wanted this pair of white Oxford Bags* (trousers of a particular style) ***like anything****, which I would never have thought of a year ago, and this skinny top too.* OBS □ *Joy is a warlike chatelaine: 'I shoot a starting pistol at them* (trespassers) *and they run* ***like anything****.'* L □ *Give it to Robert to do. He can add up figures* ***like anything****.* □ *He'd laugh* ***like anything*** *when you told him, I expect?* □ end position after v.

like attracts/calls to like (saying) one tends to choose the company of, or feel a preference for, sb of the same class, upbringing or character as oneself; birds of a feather (flock together) (qv) □ *I thought, moving away from the district, and sending him to a good school, he'd have a chance of making a new and better set of friends. But* ***like attracts like*** *wherever you go.* □ *The facts he reports imply that* ***like calls to like*** *and that a member of a middle-class healing profession is instinctively, if unconsciously, encouraged to make his greatest efforts on behalf of the kind of people whose daily practical, intellectual and emotional problems and experiences are most recognisably similar to his own.* NS

like a bad penny [Comp/A (Prep P)] again and again, when not wanted or liked, but usu difficult to avoid etc (like the damaged, or counterfeit, coin one may continue to find in one's change) **V:** be; turn up, keep turning up □ *I purposely didn't introduce you to my sister-in-law at the party, because once she gets an entry into anybody's home she keeps turning up* ***like a bad penny.*** □ *The conditioned response, once it is firmly established, can be extinguished dozens of times, but it will always return,* ***like the proverbial bad penny****.* □ variant like the proverbial bad penny.

like a bat out of hell [A (Prep)] (informal) quickly; at top speed (qv); like a bullet out of/from a gun (qv); like a shot (qv) **V:** go, rush out be off □ *Then I put four hundred crisp smackers* (= £400) *in my wallet, and heaved myself out and on to the 3.20 train that went* ***like a bat out of hell*** *towards Euston.* JFTR □ *When I saw him tearing out of his front door* ***like a bat out of hell*** *and into the phone-box I thought his wife or one of the kids must have taken ill or something.* □ also pl like bats out of hell

like a bear with a sore head [Comp/A (PrepP)] in a surly, irritable way **V:** be; go around, act □ *'My friends were telling me how much they enjoyed Bill's company at the club dinner.' 'They should come and see him now. He's* ***like a bear with a sore head*** *in the mornings.'* □ *'Do hurry up. You know your grandfather gets* ***as cross as a bear with a sore head*** *if lunch is kept waiting.*

like billy-o(h) [A (Prep P)] (informal) vigorously; successfully **V:** go, run; burn; sell □ *I play a mass murderer whom nobody would suspect, and I've been going around killing people* ***like billy-o****.* TVT □ *Maxwell Reed and Dinah Sheridan act up John Gilling's script* ***like billy-o****. Co-writer/director Robert S. Baker pulls out all three stops as the storm mounts to a teacup frenzy.* RT □ *The home-made jam and cakes and sweets sell* ***like billy-o*** *and the garden produce too, but there is always a fair amount left on the soft goods stalls at the end of the Sale.*

like blazes etc [A (Prep P)] (dated informal) vigorously; as fast, hard, loud, violently etc as possible **V:** run, row; try; blow. **n:** blazes, ⚠ the devil, hell □ *When I rose at 7 the next morning the wind was still blowing* ***like blazes****.* □ *A skiff went by with a burden of charming girls rowing* ***like blazes*** *in tight white shirts and tight white shorts.* US □ *Don't blame me. I tried* ***like hell*** *to dissuade him.* □ *When I first shot him he jumped* *out of the gig and ran* ***like the devil****, singing out that he would deliver all he had if I'd only spare his life.* OBS

like a bull at a gate [A (PrepP)] in a headlong, vigorous or aggressive way; without care, finesse or tact **V:** go, charge, at sth; barge into sth □ *Try to approach her the right way. She's dead scared of policemen and you'll get nothing out of her if you go at it* ***like a bull at a gate****.* □ *'Maybe there's some more,' I said, pulling out half a dozen drawers. 'No,' he said, 'this is the lot.' 'How do you know, you lousy sod?' He barged past me* ***like a bull at a gate****. 'Because I do.'* LLDR □ also pl like bulls at a gate.

(like) a bull in a china shop [Comp/A (PrepP)] in a way that is too clumsy, rough, coarse, vigorous etc to suit one's company or surroundings, or to handle a delicate situation **V:** be, feel; behave, barge about □ JEAN: *I wish I could mark everything fragile, that's how I feel, tucked in here. Listening to her, I feel* ***like a bull in a china shop****.* YAA □ JO: *Start barging around just* ***like a bull in a china shop****. You don't have to let her push you around.* TOH □ *His method is the time-honoured one of* ***the bull in the china shop****; rushing at everything, pillaging anthropology, psychology, the natural sciences, and any other source conveniently to hand in a mad quest for evidence, 'insight', or anecdotes.* NS □ (NONCE) *I broke a thermometer and he told Sister he did it. He's really awfully sweet, you know. But he does make me feel* ***like a piece of china in a bull shop*** *sometimes.* DIL

like a bullet out of/from a gun [A (AdvP)] (informal) at once; swiftly; at top speed; like a bat out of hell (qv); like a shot (qv); **V:** be off; come, speed (ahead); answer □ *Well, as soon as I read that bit in the 'Daily Tale' about the Loch Ness Monster being seen in Little Todday and Great Todday I was off* ***like a bullet out of a gun****. I mean to say, I don't want to miss seeing this monster.* RM □ *'Would you care to take on the job yourself?' His 'No!' came* ***like a bullet from a gun****.*

like a cat on hot bricks [Comp/A (PrepP)] (informal) restless(ly); nervous(ly); unable to sit/lie still, settle one's attention **V:** be; fidget, bob up and down □ *Jenny, you're* ***like a cat on hot bricks****. I wish you'd either sit down with a book or some sewing, or go out for a walk.* □ *I don't know when he'll get the results of his exam, but he'll be* ***like a cat on hot bricks*** *until he does.* □ *I knew nothing would make eleven o'clock come any sooner but I was* ***as restless as a cat on hot bricks*** *and couldn't sit the concert out.* □ variant as restless/nervy as a cat on hot bricks. ⇨ ⚠ (as) nervous as a cat/kitten.

like the cat that stole the cream [Comp/A (PrepP)] (informal) smug; (self) satisfied; gloating **V:** be, look; smile, have an expression □ *'This is one of Esther's old school photos. Can you spot her?' 'I think that must be her holding the Cup and looking* ***like the cat that stole the cream****.'* □ (NONCE) *From that moment the debate was lost. Churchill sat up, gloating at his critics with a discreet twinkle,* ***like a cat*** *presented* ***with*** *an unexpectedly large bowl of* ***cream****.* L □ frequently adapted.

like a cat with nine lives [Comp/O (PrepP)] hardy; with unusual powers of survival; fortunate in one's escape(s) from accident or death **V:** be; act, behave □ *Jamieson has had several severe illnesses in the last number of years, each of which could easily have finished him off. But he's* ***like a cat with nine lives*** *and will probably live to see ninety.* □ *The daring things that boy gets up to would make your hair curl. Fortunately he seems to* ***have nine lives, like a cat****.* □ *It's not just a case of* ***having nine lives*** *with* ***that*** *old* ***cat****—it's more like ninety-nine!* □ variant have nine lives (like a cat).

(like) Caesar's wife (like) sb who is pure, chaste, honest etc □ *I know that as a class they* (barmaids) *have a name for being chaste. That's why I said it would be the first thing people said about them—if they weren't, I mean. Everybody would be on the look-out. They have to be* ***like Caesar's wife****.* PW □ (paid leave of absence for maternity) *Cumbria Education Committee has recommended that a distinction* (between married and unmarried teachers) *should be preserved. As one of its advocates explains: '****Like Caesar's wife****, the village schoolteacher has to be above suspicion.'* ST □ *Nowadays Her Majesty's judges are treated as though they were* ***Caesar's wives*** *and we should be unsuspicious. This is nonsense.* NS □ can be used of either sex.

like the clappers [A (PrepP)] (informal) noisily; busily; quickly; with gusto and vigour **V:** go, be off, move, run □ (photo caption) *'Star-studded entertainment' at the Three Tuns with Clive at the organ and one of the regulars, Frank, going* ***like the clappers*** *on the bones* (bones, as sometimes spoons, used for percussion). RT □ *'I wouldn't surrender to anyone else but you, you big strong man,' I could feel her thinking, 'but seeing it's you, I'm going to surrender* ***like the clappers****.'* CON □ *The doctor's run off with the minister's wife, eh? The village tongues will be going* ***like the clappers*** *this morning.* □ *I didn't wake till 8.30. It was no breakfast and off down the road* ***like the clappers*** *for me this morning.* □ *'She* (the car) *really feels hungry for speed and goes* ***like the clappers*** *of hell,' he says.* TVT

(like) the curate's egg sth that is good and bad in parts, is of mixed quality (from an illustrated joke in 'Punch' in 1895, showing a nervous curate breakfasting on a boiled egg at his bishop's table: 'I'm afraid your egg is bad, Mr Jones.'—'Oh no, my lord, I assure you! Parts of it are excellent!') □ *Religious broadcasting,* ***like the curate's egg****, is good in parts; but much of it seems to swing uneasily between intellectual trendiness and drearily undevotional bathos.* □ *This is a British film of no mean significance; it has more than its moments; it has frankly terrible lines like 'We're contemporaries in a common grief', or words to that effect; it is* ***your curate's egg****, but home-laid.* NS □ *RCA has a new album due out next week. It's likely to be* ***the*** *usual* ***curate's egg****, but no one with a serious interest in popular song will be able to ignore it.* OBS

like a dog with two tails [Comp/A (PrepP)] delighted(ly); proud(ly), esp because one now owns, or has achieved, sth; (as) pleased as Punch (qv) **V:** be; run around, hop about □ *The old chap's been* ***like a dog with two tails*** *since he got the news—wants everyone to know his grandson is being called after him, too.* □ *Some* *men feel or feign indifference about their successes, but Paul is* ***as pleased as a dog with two tails*** *that he's been chosen for the award.* □ variant as pleased as a dog with two tails.

like father etc, like son etc (saying) a child turns out to be like its parents in character, tastes, opinions, habits etc **n:** father...son, ⚠ mother...daughter; master/man...maid □ *It was intellectual dishonesty again.* ***Like father, like son****, I bet you he knew all about it.* ASA □ *Jean-Claude is acquiring the respectability that quite rightly eluded his father. But if there is any real threat to the power of the Duvaliers, no one doubts that it will be a case of* ***like father, like son****.* L □ (advertisement) ***Like Father, Like Son****. The standard set by 'The Times' Correspondents of the past is the standard we set ourselves today.* ST □ *It's a good, old-fashioned craftsman's business. The old man's spent his life making beautiful furniture with meticulous care and all his workers are the same—* ***like master, like man****.* □ ***Like mother, like daughter****. Two year old Joanna Hayes—as you can see here—looks like growing up to be a little girl just like her mum, eternal teenager Wendy Padbury.* TVT □ almost always comment on particular pair and on particular aspect of similarity.

like a fishwife [Comp/A (PrepP)] loud(ly) and vulgar(ly), abusive(ly) (from, formerly, street-sellers of fish crying their wares) **V:** scream, shout (at sb); behave, act, carry on □ *And goodbye to Alice. I could see her now screaming at me* ***like a fishwife****, naked, with her figure beginning to submit to middle age.* RATT □ *I used to act* ***like a fishwife*** *and scream and shout and I got it out of my system.* TVT

like a fly in amber [Comp/A (PrepP)] forever fixed, preserved (the implication being perhaps a lack of function or development) □ *The little scene so briefly glimpsed may have had some significance for me that I cannot guess at now. All I know is that my memory retains it,* ***like a fly in amber****, to this day.* □ *At times, he had been envious of those who found stardom. But then those were actors who mainly had to go on repeating themselves. He might have been stuck* ***like a fly in amber****. 'Success is not always the same as fulfilment,' he said.* TVT

like greased lightning with great speed (the reference esp being to a single act or direction of movement or motion) **V:** run off, go past, ride away; draw one's gun; throw the switch □ *There was a phone call. Then he ran down the stairs* ***like greased lightning****, jumped on his bike and rode off.* □ *Dave Rio practises daily to maintain his position as the fastest draw* (= drawer of a gun) *in the British Fast Draw Association. 'I like people to think, don't tangle with Dave Rio, he's* ***greased lightning****.'* OBS

like/the hell it is etc (informal) it isn't, you aren't, they can't, etc **V:** it is; you are; I will; they can □ HELEN: *The house is half mine.* PETER: ***Like hell it is****. I could throw you out tomorrow.* TOH □ *'She'll be nice to you.' '****Like hell she will****.' He leaned over and ground out his cigarette on the egg-smeard plate. 'The old girl hates my guts.'* AITC □ *'The window cleaner's asking if he can come tomorrow afternoon.' '****The hell he can****. I'm giving a bridge party.'* □ *'I've decided to come in on this deal with you after all.' '****The hell you have****. Now, isn't that great. I must ring and tell Simpson at once.'* □ expression emphasizes speaker's negative reaction, with rising tone on will, can, etc; the hell it is etc may also be used to express relief, surprise, disbelief, disappointment etc of the other speaker's remark as in last example, with falling tone starting on hell.

like it or lump it (saying) whether willingly or resentfully; next entry (qv) □ *I've explained already. While you're staying with your grandmother you go to church on Sunday mornings,* ***like it or lump it****.* □ *'John won't enjoy that daily journey by public transport.' 'He'll have to* ***like it or lump it****, I'm afraid. We can't afford to run a car any more.'* □ *'****I don't like*** *you smoking so much, Beryl.' 'Then* ***you must lump it****. I don't see myself giving it up.'* □ like and lump non-rev; variant (if sb doesn't like it,) sb must lump it.

like it or not/no [Disj] whether one likes sth or not (the implication usu being the latter); obviously; inevitably; previous entry (qv) □ *Mr Stewart should be made to realise,* ***like it or not****, that he is about fifty years behind the times.* SC □ (reader's letter) *World governments were more vitally interested in Nixon's economic policies and what the devil he was doing to the international money markets.* ***Like it or not****—and many palpably did not — other industrial countries had to make sacrifices to bail out the dollar because there didn't seem to be any alternative.* L □ *All wars end eventually but* ***like it or no*** *some of us are not going to survive this one.* □ HELEN: *There'll be money in the post for you every week from now on.* JO: *Until you forget.* HELEN: *I don't forget things. I'm going to see you through this* ***whether you like it or not****.* TOH □ *For the days of private patronage are over, and most field archeology now comes directly out of our rates and taxes,* ***whether we like it or no****.* SD □ front, middle or end position; variant whether one likes it or not.

like a (hot) knife through butter/margarine [A (PrepP)] easily; without meeting resistance or difficulty **V:** slice into; cut into; go in □ *'There you are—* ***like a knife through butter****,' said the demonstrator as the powered shovel swung back with its load.* □ *I never wanted to notice much while running in case it put me off my stroke so I wasn't far now from going into that last mile and a half* ***like a knife through margarine****.* LLDR □ *To watch him you'd think splitting the slates was* ***as easy as cutting butter with a hot knife****.* □ *The 'trio of baptism' is as fine a trio as Verdi wrote until the last act of 'La Forza'. It goes through you* ***like a hot knife through butter*** *and was gorgeously sung on this exciting occasion.* G □ variants like/as easy as cutting butter with a hot knife; margarine rarely used.

like a lamb [PrepP)] obediently; submissively; without protest or complaint; (as) meek as a lamb (qv) **V:** come, go; follow, take sth □ *He went up to his solicitor's office* ***like a lamb****, while Mrs Pettigrew waited in the car below. He did not even attempt to circumvent her wishes, as he had half-hoped to do.* MM □ *Billy's been such a good boy, Mrs Smith—never once got out of bed and took his medicine* ***like a lamb****.* □ also pl like lambs.

like the look/sound of sb/sth [V + O] be

favourably impressed by what one has seen of/heard about sb/sth □ *Sillitoe* ***liked the look of*** *Desmond and believed him.* DS □ *We can stroll past anyway and if you* ***like the look of*** *the boat I can arrange for you to inspect it and have a trial run tomorrow.* □ *...just because you don't want to leave this man you're running to all the time, John, Jack, whatever his name is. I don't* ***like the sound of*** *him.* AITC □ *'I hope they'll find at the hospital that there's nothing seriously wrong.' 'I hope so too, but I don't* ***like the look of*** *him.'* □ *You'd better take your mac with you—I don't* ***like the look of*** *that sky.'* □ neg constructions may express opposite meaning, or indicate worry about sb's health, the running of a machine, weather conditions, etc.

like mad/crazy [A (PrepP)] (informal) with much, or the maximum of, effort, energy, enthusiasm, concentration etc **V:** try, swot, struggle; dance □ *Most of us have experienced that excruciating pain when our calf muscles double up into a knot. We rub the calf* ***like mad*** *and the pain gradually eases.* DM □ *I have been gardening long enough never to decry any unusual tip: that pot plants flourish best on the TV set;* (and) *that tea leaves make hydrangeas grow and flower* ***like mad.*** OBS □ *Apart from poor old Mabel's spotty face, there's her owlishness—always got her head in a book and peering* ***like mad.*** UL □ (tennis) *Holmberg said later: 'Whenever I got him in trouble he served* ***like crazy.*** *There was nothing I could do. He played too well.'* DM □ *The trouble is that a self-absorbed masochist, over-compensating* ***like crazy,*** *would almost certainly bore you stony-eyed in real life.* L ⇨ ⚠ next entry.

like a mad thing [Comp/A (PrepP)] like a madman; acting as a madman would; not trying to behave sensibly, or with suitable restraint **V:** be; rush around, carry on, shout and scream □ *The champion was in real trouble as he got up glassy-eyed and bleeding from the mouth, and Patterson chased him* ***like a mad thing*** *round the ring.* DM □ *We both struggled with the bottle, broke a glass, and sat on the floor laughing* ***like mad things*** *and toasting each other.* UTN □ *As soon as Tom put his nose in at the door his wife started raging at him* ***like a mad thing.*** ⇨ ⚠ previous entry.

(like) a new man/woman (like) sb who has gained, or regained, happiness, good health, etc **V:** be, become; feel; look □ *There's nothing to be frightened of, Mrs Smith. Let me arrange for you to have these infected tonsils removed and, I assure you, you'll be* ***like a new woman*** *in no time.* □ *'Retirement didn't suit John,' his wife went on. 'He was getting so depressed, you'd hardly believe it. It's not much of a job he's got, but keeping busy for three hours a day and feeling he's useful has* ***made a new man of*** *him.'* □ variant make a new man/woman of sb.

like nobody's business [A (PrepP)] (informal) with unusual intensity, excess, frequency etc □ *Naturally, if you've been oppressed for 300 years by a bunch of white slobs you are going to hate whites* ***like nobody's business.*** L □ *God knows where he's got it from but he's been spending money* ***like nobody's business*** *for the last three months or more.* □ *The boat's probably going* ***like nobody's business.*** *So you get on top of it and sort of haul, haul all the canvas up into a great packet.* L ⇨ ⚠ be nobody's business.

like/as one of the family [Comp (PrepP)] accepted into a family group though not closely related **V:** ⚠ be like; count as, look upon sb as. **adv mod:** just; more □ MRS ELLIOT: *You've met George, haven't you?* GEOFFREY: *Oh, yes, we've met several times, haven't we?* MRS ELLIOT: *Yes. He's been here a long time now.* GEOFFREY: ***Like one of the family,*** *in fact.* EGD □ *I'm glad you got the job but I'm sorry you're leaving. You've been more* ***like one of the family*** *than a lodger.* □ *'I thought you said you'd had enough of entertaining guests this summer.' 'Oh, but I don't mind Peter! He counts* ***as one of the family.*** *We don't have to put on any style for him.'*

(like) a red rag to a bull [Comp/A (PrepP)] sure, or extremely likely, to provoke resentment, attack, violent action **V:** be; act □ *The word 'family' was* ***like a red rag to a bull*** *for a section of the audience. 'Family, Family?' shouted a man. 'What is this thing called "family"? It is the root of all our trouble.'* NS □ *Our Mike seems to feel that the very notion of profits is* ***a red rag to the bull*** *in the machine shop, and suggests that this information ought to be imparted more delicately.* G □ *When their kisses reached one of its climaxes she felt, as she often did, like making some little satisfied, appreciative noises, and was only held back by the thought, based on experience, that such noises were liable to act* ***like a red rag,*** *or rather a green light,* ***to a bull.*** TGLY □ (NONCE) *While discussing the current promiscuous scene, George is accused by his former shipmates of being 'past it'. Saying that to George is like* ***waving a pair of red panties at a bull.*** TVT □ *You should know by now that Geoffrey always loses his temper if you let the conversation get on to politics. You might as well* ***wave a red rag at a bull.*** □ variant wave a red rag at a bull.

like Rip van Winkle like sb unaware, or only recently concious, of changes in himself, others, general circumstances, world affairs (from the story of the same name by W IRVING in which the main character, Rip Van Winkle, slept for 20 years) □ *I came back then to find the association which had sustained me in war and prison irrevocably dissolved and I wandered,* ***like*** *a kind of* ***Rip Van Winkle,*** *into a strange new world with nine years of unshared and uncommunicable experience separating me from it.* LWK □ *But few share Prendergast's faith in the ability of his union.* ***'Like Rip Van Winkle,*** *it is still fast asleep,' says a broadsheet issued on Monday.* NS □ *I had taken my degree in law at Oxford, but I hadn't enjoyed it much. 'It was a bit* ***like Rip Van Winkle,*** *Dad,' I said. 'I was so much older than the others, and things had changed so.'* RFW

like a sack of potatoes [Comp/A (PrepP)] (sb's physical appearance is) shapeless and unwieldly; in an ungraceful manner **V:** be, look; walk, waddle along □ *The poor thing has a figure* ***like a sack of potatoes,*** *anyway, and a tubular dress is the last thing she ought to wear.* □ *There must also be realism. A man doing a fall from a building and who is supposed to be unconscious or dead has to fall* ***like a sack of potatoes.*** TVT

like a scalded cat [A (AdvP)] reacting to a sudden pain, panic or fear by flight **V:** run, tear off; fly out, jump □ *At the sound of the shot one little boy ran* **like a scalded cat** *for the horizon but the other jumped up and down eagerly shouting, 'Where's the dead rabbit? Where's the dead rabbit?'* □ *That girl's a bag of nerves. I just gave the back of her hair a flick in passing and she was out of her chair* **like a scalded cat**.

(like/as) sheep etc to the slaughter [Comp/A (PrepP)] (as) unwitting and helpless victims **n:** sheep, ⚠ lambs; a sheep, a lamb. **V:** lead, drive, sb; flock □ (source) *He was led* **as a sheep to the slaughter**. ACTS VIII 32 □ *Many* (of my fellow-students) *perished in the 1914-18 war, to which my generation flocked* **like sheep to the slaughter**. SD □ *John Reid, whose team was full of green young things led* **the** *Canterbury* **lambs to the slaughter** *by Laker and Lock*. ST □ *The Jeremiahs are already on our backs, warning us against intervention and shepherding us,* **lambs to the slaughter**, *towards the indefensible stupidity of another statutory incomes policy*. NS

like a ship without a rudder [Comp/A (PrepP)] (in an) unmotivated or unguided (way) **V:** be: drift (about), be borne along □ *His appointment was in my judgement a great mistake and under him the Army drifted about* **like a ship without a rudder**. MFM □ *He lapsed into a state of fatalism and,* **like a rudderless ship**, *allowed what would to befall him*. □ variant like a rudderless ship.

(like) ships that pass in the night (be, or do sth, like) people or groups who meet briefly and probably for the only time in their lives □ (source) ***Ships that pass in the night**, and speak to each other in passing;/Only a signal shown and a distant voice in the darkness*. TALES OF A WAYSIDE INN (H W LONGFELLOW 1807-82) □ ***Like ships that pass in the night**, Sybil and I, for all the passing and re-passing which practically amounted to a regular service, were still now no more that a couple of ships alone in the night*. SML □ *Not for her the lines about* **ships that pass in the night**. *It was certainly unfortunate that the young man should prove to be just on the verge of departure*.

like a shot [A (AdvP)] immediately; with great speed; like a bat out of hell (qv); at top speed (qv); like a bullet out of/from a gun (qv); willingly; eagerly **V:** be off, go; accept sth; buy sth □ *That dog's getting deaf. He used to be off down the path* **like a shot** *when Charlie tooted his horn*. □ *You'd be glad to be back in the RAF in another war, and you know it. If it happened again, I'd be back in the Wrens* **like a shot**. RFW □ *Young people like to be together, don't they. At least in the stage you two are at at the moment. Anyway—I'd be into that flat* **like a shot** *if I was in your shoes*. TGLY

like etc the sound of one's own voice [V + O] be in the habit of talking a lot or too much (the implication usu being lack of attention to, or impatience with, other people's information or opinions) **V:** like; ⚠ be fond of; like listening to □ HELEN: *Have you got your breath back? Because there's some more I've got to get off my chest first*. JO: *You don't half* **like the sound of your own voice**. TOH □ *The interviewer* **was** *too* **fond of the sound of his own voice**. *His guests could hardly get a chance to speak a word for themselves*. □ *Brian's an interesting talker if you like. In my opinion he* **likes the sound of his own voice** *too much to be called a good conversationalist*.

like a stuck pig [A (PrepP)] in the manner of a pig that is being killed **V:** ⚠ bleed; scream, screech, squeal □ *I was bleeding* **like a stuck pig** *and it would have been all over with me, if Mike hadn't given me first aid until the ambulance men turned up*. □ *The dignified and elegant peacock, when it opens its mouth, screams* **like a stuck pig**.

like/as a thief in the night [A (PrepP)] unforeseen and/or unobserved **V:** come; creep in; steal away □ (source) *For you yourselves know perfectly that the day of the Lord so cometh* **as a thief in the night**. *For when they shall say, Peace and safety; then sudden destruction cometh upon them*. I THESSALONIANS V 2-3 □ *'Oh,' he said to himself, 'these erotic throes that come* **like thieves in the night** *to steal my High Churchmanship.'* MM □ *One day, perhaps, you glimpse a figure in a mirror, and realize, with a shock, that the funny little woman is you. The years,* **like a thief in the night**, *have stolen what you were*. □ use of as now unusual.

like a ton of bricks [A (PrepP)] with physical weight, violence, force or noise; with severity, pressure or criticism; totally; overwhelmingly **V:** descend; burst in; be, come, down on sb □ *The fondest father does not welcome his offspring landing on his bed* **like a ton of bricks** *at 5.30 in the morning*. □ *If I print it, I shall have the Home Office down on me* **like a ton of bricks**. SML □ *If the evidence is available against them, you can be absolutely certain that the professional tribunal will be down on them* **like a ton of bricks**. L □ *She gave Arthur a pleasant smile which settled on him* **like a ton of bricks**. HHGG

like water off a duck's back [Comp/A (PrepP)] making little, or no, impression; having no effect **S:** advice, reprimand, criticism; experience; it. **V:** be, seem; act □ *I keep telling the boys not to bang doors but it's* **like water off a duck's back**. □ *I went as a stagehand at the Winter Garden working on the Folies Bergère. We all used to say that being surrounded by a French company of nude girls was* **like water off a duck's back** *but that was a lie. I can remember every one of them to this day*. NS □ *Had he ever seen Mummy on television? '***Like water off a duck's back***,' said Felicity. 'He never watches anything I'm in.'* TVT

like wildfire [A (PrepP)] rapidly and extensively **V:** spread, travel, go through □ *The weakened refugees had little resistance to infection of any kind and cholera spread through the camps* **like wildfire**. OBS □ *In a community where everybody knew everybody else's business the news that John Thomson's wife had dumped him in the horse trough to sober up travelled* **like wildfire**. □ *The incident started when two police officers went into the club to arrest a man. The Appeal Judge said that as they tried to take him out pandemonium broke out. 'Everyone got excited. Hysteria and aggressiveness travelled* **like wildfire**,*' he said*. G

a likely story (ironic) an improbable version, account, of sth that has happened, of sth that one/sb has done or may do □ MRS PARADOCK:

And what happened about the government? Did you agree to form one or not? MR PARADOCK: *I wasn't approached.* MRS PARADOCK: *That's **a likely story**.* ART □ *Who would have the power to fire this hybrid arrangement? The French President? The British Minister? Both by agreement, perhaps—**a likely story**.* NS □ *'Did you get your typewriter back, then?' 'No. He said he'd jammed the slide and had to put it in for repair.' '**A likely story**! He's probably pawned it till next pay day.'* □ often used alone, or with *that's*, as an exclamatory comment; stress pattern a 'likely story.

(one's) likes and dislikes (of sb) [n + n non-rev] people or things, which one likes contrasted with those one doesn't; fads and foibles in general, esp when these are many or obsessive, or are a nuisance to other people □ *He had been brought up to think that in business matters, and in most other matters, **his likes and dislikes** didn't count—just as he had been taught to eat what food was put before him.* PW □ *If I've had any success I believe it's because I have the taste of the ordinary man. In **my likes and dislikes** I don't feel any different now than when I was struggling for work as a dancer, 50 years ago.* OBS □ *The housekeeper is catering for 250 students on a pretty tight budget: she can't study **the likes and dislikes of** every individual.*

the likes of sb (informal) people like us; anybody of our humble, privileged, criminal, intellectual, handicapped etc class or kind **o:** us, him, them; the Sinclairs □ *It's not for **the likes of** us, who've never had to go without anything we really needed, to condemn them.* □ SYLVIA: *The bloody nerve—how dare you. I'm a respectable girl—I'd never mix with **the likes of** you.* DPM □ *What I say is, council houses were never meant for **the likes of** the Sinclairs. They're being subsidised off the rates working people have to pay.* □ *'The judge gave him six years.' 'Not half enough. People have got to be protected against **the likes of** him.'* ⇨ ⚠ not have seen etc the like (of sth)/sth's like; not see etc sb's/sth's like(s) again.

one's (own) line of country sth one knows a lot about, or can do well □ *Since then I've had a variety of jobs in **my own line of country**—deep drilling in Brazil, and I've been up the Gulf with an oil concern.* ARG □ *Well, infant care is not exactly **my line of country**, but I expect Keith would survive a couple of hours of my looking after him.*

the line etc of least resistance [Comp/O (NP)] the easiest course of direction or action; the procedure that gives one the least trouble though another may be more suitable or effective **V:** be; take, choose, follow. **Comp/O:** line, ⚠ path, way, course □ ***The line of least resistance** backed up by cloudy visions of gain, had brought him here, rather against both his better judgment and his conscience.* ILIH □ *'There has been slightly too much criticism of this project to be comfortable. It may have been a mistake,' said Rose, 'not to take **the course of least resistance**, and pack them all off to America.'* NM □ *If you succeed* (in remembering your dream) *then turn on the light and write it down. Because if you take **the path of least resistance** and say: 'Aha, I have the dream and I'll remember it in the morning,' the chances are you won't.* L

line one's (own)/sb's pocket(s) [V + O] make, or gain, a lot of money, esp by some easy, cunning or dishonest method; cause, or allow, sb to do this □ *They used public appointments to **line their own pockets**. They combined fraudulently during elections to keep the plum jobs in the hands of their families and their friends.* L □ *But what incensed his contemporaries was that he accused Sir Humphry Davy of **lining his pocket** at the Society's expense.* OBS □ *Theoretically, ITV-2 could appease its critics and **line its pockets** at the same time. No one has yet demonstrated that it can be done.* OBS □ *Some provincial man, doing well, with a comfortable wife and children in a suburban house. Just the type who **lines the pockets of** the vice racketeers on his business trips to the metropolis.* HD

one's/a line of thought a way, or system, of thinking; a chain of reasoning or speculation; one's train of thought (qv) **V:** take, follow, pursue □ *Those essentials are: (a) A religion; (b) An education élite, who are not afraid to take **an** independent **line of thought** and who will not merely follow the 'popular cry'.* MFM □ *Now, wait a minute—if I take on the assignment, then I'll need a camera-man, and that could be Philip who you're so keen to give a start to—is that **your line of thought**?* □ also pl *different **lines of thought***.

a lion in the path/way a difficulty or obstacle (real or supposed) given as a reason/excuse for not doing sth □ (source) *The slothful man saith, there is **a lion in the way**; a lion is in the streets.* PROVERBS XXVI 13 □ *Would it be so easy to ask? But if **lions in the path** thought they would have an easy job with Harold they were mistaken. Once his mind accepted its new orientation it would go on boldly.* PW

the lion lies down with the lamb (saying) peace and goodwill prevail; enemies are reconciled; the aggressor ceases to attack and the victim to fear (adapted from ISAIAH XI 6-7) □ *In Martin Luther King's dream, not only was **the lion** going to **lie down with the lamb**, but white was going to be brother to black.* L □ *Fenner, a conchie* (= a conscientious objector) *in the first world war, gave the impression he really believed **the lion** could be made to **lie down with the lamb** under nothing more compelling than the hypnosis of goodwill.* NS □ (NONCE) *The whole of England was now in an orgy of Coronation Committees. Temporary differences were forgotten in the common cause, **Parish Councils lay down with Town Councils**, nor were the Mothers' Unions unheard.* WDM

the lion's share (of sth) [O/o (NP)] very much the largest and best portion of sth; the whole of sth (from AESOP'S FABLES, in one of which the lion claims threequarters of his kill and allows a quarter to any animal brave enough to fight him for it) **V:** claim, get, grab; keep; end up with □ *Polanski subscribes to the view that life is a jungle and so long as society makes sure that none of its members is actually starving, he sees no reason why **the lion's share of** the spoils should not go to the most talented.* ST □ *Scotland must stake a firm claim for **the lion's share of** the oil proceeds because she is* *entitled to benefit from the exploitation and because her need is the greatest.* SC □ *This misuse of the nation's money is partly due to the determination of specialists—the aristocrats of the profession—to keep* ***the lion's share of*** *medical practice under their control and within the hospitals where they reign supreme.* NS

one's lips are sealed (cliché) one will keep silent, give no information away about an understood subject □ *'This salmon was illegally come by, I'm afraid, so don't tell anyone you got a bit.' '****My lips are sealed.****'* □ *Disclosing that sort of information was very wrong of him. On such matters a doctor's lips should* ***be sealed*** *even to members of a patient's family.* □ *Mind over matter, or magic? Watch 'Into the Unknown' and judge for yourself. Hooper's little package which enables me to emulate the feats of Uri Geller cost me £2 and for this price* ***my lips are sealed.*** TVT

a litter lout a person who leaves discarded articles anywhere out of doors instead of disposing of them properly □ *For the litter problem surely results from laziness and selfishness—few* ***litter louts*** *act out of deliberate anti-social spite.* SC □ *'****Litter lout****!' Jane said tartly, as he tossed the empty packet out of the car window.*

a little bird told me (that) (facetious) I know (that) but will not tell you how, or from whom, I know □ *'I do paint a little, but only as a hobby. How did you know, anyway?' 'Oh* ***a little bird told me.****'* □ *That was your boss's wife with a beautiful bunch of roses from her garden. It seems* ***a little bird*** *had* ***told her*** *it was my birthday.* □ *'The bike'll be safe enough for the time being, Miss Gittings,' he said. 'You* are *Miss Gittings?' 'Why, yes, but—well—' '****A little*** *dicky* ***bird*** *must have* ***told me,****' he said, and pushed his cap back on his head.* TT □ in last example, *dicky bird* is a child's word for a bird, used here facetiously by an adult.

a little (sth) goes a long way a particular substance is economical in use; a good quality, attitude, action etc may be effective beyond the degree to which it is shown or given; a short experience of sb/sth is as much as is good for one or as much as one can tolerate **n:** trust, perfume, paint; kindness. **A:** with me; in your case; at our age □ *The price of this exquisitely-shaped little bottle had been ludicrous, but how reassuring the saleswoman's '****A little goes a*** *very* ***long way****, madam.'* WI □ *She gave me back my confidence in myself.* ***A little*** *trust* ***goes a long way*** *sometimes.* □ DOCTOR: *I think we'd better tactfully put an end to the evening now,* ***a little*** *kicking over the traces* ***goes a long way*** *at this age.* THH □ *Because* ***a little of*** *it goes such* ***a long way*** *you actually save money by buying Diamond Floor Polish instead of cheaper brands* □ *I have few old friends, only one from Oxford. I don't need people very much, frankly.* ***A few*** *people* ***go a long way*** *with me.* ST □ used as comment or judgement on sb/sth; variants a few go a long way, a little of sb/sth goes long way.

little green men (facetious) extra-terrestrial beings □ *What possible natural object could be launching signals like this? You begin to ask—is it intelligence from a planet? We really did think of* ***little green men.*** RT □ *Personally I have enough on my mind without worrying about another Ice Age, anti-Christ, or Earth being taken over by rats, ants or* ***little green men.*** □ occas sing.

(just) sb's little joke [Comp (NP)] sth said, or done, that irritates or offends though (perhaps) not intended to do so **V:** ⚠ be, regard sth as. **adv mod:** just, only, merely □ *On Floor Nine, 'we research into the instruments that do the research'—Mr Henderson****'s little joke.*** RT □ *'Jimmy's not a bad boy, just too high-spirited,' his mother claims. 'Well, be sure to remember if ever he slashes your tyres again that it's* ***just his little joke.****'* □ *I was told I wouldn't grow if I gave way. Besides I'd get deaf and have to wear glasses. And, gentle readers, I'll thank you not to draw any untoward conclusions from the fact that I'm five foot six, slightly deaf in one ear and am getting my spectacles strengthened next year. That's merely one of God****'s little jokes.*** G □ used as ironic comment on events or circumstances.

a little learning/knowledge is a dangerous thing (saying) partial or superficial knowledge, information, leads to more serious errors than complete ignorance □ (source) ***A little learning is a dang'rous thing****;/Drink deep, or taste not the Pierian spring.* AN ESSAY ON CRITICISM (A POPE 1688-1744) □ *That's what comes of trying to be your own lawyer.* ***A little learning is a dangerous thing.*** □ *They* (political leaders) *know what they're doing. They're not fools. The public, now—they're not trained to it. Your average man's not educated you see. He's mis-educated.* ***A little knowledge is a dangerous thing.*** *So I think we're in the right hands really.* ST □ *'****A little learning is a dangerous thing,****' as the saying goes. In fact, it's very dangerous when Selwyn is involved.* TVT

the little man the under-dog as a type; sb who does not expect, and is not expected, to achieve a desired and acknowledged status financially, socially or professionally □ *In strip-cartoons, in magazine short stories, in the intimate gossip-columns, the hero is* ***the little man****: 'Just Joe', as a song title has it.* UL □ *So a lot of shopkeepers are self-employed. Value Added Tax is a headache for* ***the little man.*** ST □ *Even Chaplin's earliest film appearances show the actor working at his art. The character of Charlie* ***the little man****, the baggy-trousered bowler-hatted tramp, can be seen evolving behind the surface gagging, the energetic slapstick of the day.* OBS □ *'I'm* ***the little man****'s man. I've always stood up for him,' says Robbie who himself stands six feet two inches in his stockinged feet.* RT

a little of what you fancy does you good (catchphrase) periods of enjoyment resulting from pleasant pastimes of one's own choice are beneficial (from a music hall song sung by Marie Lloyd 1870-1922) □ *There was a coherent economic philospohy in the Macmillan era:* ***a little of what you fancy does you good.*** NS □ *'Come on, drink up.* ***A little of what you fancy does you good.****' 'This will do me nicely, thank you. "Little" is the operative word in my case.'* □ *Learn to walk today, and the energy crisis of 1990 won't hurt so much. Eat less meat, and even Brussels has less power to annoy you. But perhaps after all,* ***a little of what you*** *don't* ***fancy does you good.*** *Some of you, at any rate.* NS □ expression sometimes used with sexual innuendo and often as excuse for drinking, but neither of these should be assumed in uncertain contexts.

little pitchers/pigs have long ears (saying) people, esp children, often listen to, pick up and understand, what they are not meant to hear □ *Now, now, James. We'll leave that till later, if you don't mind.* ***Little pitchers have long ears.*** □ (staff quarrel in a school hall) *'You make me sick,' said Kathie. 'If only you —' 'Keep it down, ladies and gents, only* ***little pigs have long ears.****'* TT □ allusion in headphrase is to handles of a pitcher; esp used as warning, directly addressed to particular person(s); pigs (old usage) = 'earthenware vessel such as jug, pitcher, bed-warmer'.

the little woman (dated or facetious) sb's wife; the married woman, esp viewed in a stereotyped domestic role □ MILLY: *On Sunday afternoon Jack went off to play golf and* ***the little woman*** *hung some new curtains in the living room.* EHOW □ (a vacuum cleaner) *Runs on a motor like a lawn-mower. No effort by* ***the little woman****. No tubes trailing all over the place.* OMIH

live to fight another day have another chance to engage in a fight, contest, confrontation etc, either because one has not been too badly beaten to try again or because (as in the full quotation given first) one has avoided or not finished it for the time being □ (source) *He that fights and runs away/May* ***live to fight another day.*** ANONYMOUS (17TH C MISCELLANY) □ *He saved the men of the BEF* (British Expeditionary Force). *And being saved they were able to* ***fight*** *again* ***another day****: which they did to some purpose, as the Germans found out.* MFM □ (test matches, 1972) *So England got away. Good. I'm delighted for you. The Australians hooked you but they couldn't gaff* ((angling) = land) *you. We* ***live to fight another day****.* ST □ (NONCE) *The Army's entry into the 'no go' areas forced the MPs of the main Opposition party into a particularly difficult position. How could they make the protest expected of them, yet* ***live*** *politically* ***to talk another day****?* L

live happily ever after (cliché) the stock phrase used at the end of a children's/traditional/fairy tale, romantic novel, etc to express the assumption that the hero, heroine etc will in future enjoy a life of unflawed happiness □ *With the average English novel, though, the puppets are paraded before us and then packed away in their places to* ***live happily ever after*** *—or to pay the penalty for what they have done.* NS □ *He told himself that one day he would live in a palace, and drive the biggest, most expensive car in the world, and marry the most beautiful girl in the world, and they would have a family and* ***live happily ever after****.* OBS □ *Well, what with the frock and the wedding and all the fuss, there's only one thing left. The* ***living happily ever after****. That you have to do yourself.* ST □ *In fact, of course, most intelligent adults have enough sense to realize that it takes more than a touch of love fever to set them on the road to* ***happily ever after****.* ST

live and let live [v + v non-rev] (saying) tolerate others, and refrain from ruling on, or trying to direct, the way they run their lives □ *'I like life to be happy and cosy, you know.' 'Do you?' said Ella. 'Well, I'm afraid it isn't.' 'It can be if we make it. It's just a question of* ***live and let live****, really, isn't it?' Mrs Curry reproved.* HAA □ *Thus with 'permissiveness'. Even if it means '****Live and let live****,' which is perhaps more what sensible people, like Tony Crosland, might mean by the term 'permissiveness', it is too general and begs too many questions.* OBS □ MARTIN: *And as for Joe and Betty Turner, well, they're not the neighbours I'd have chosen and never will be, but we* ***live and let live****.* OI □ used alone as recommendation to practise tolerance etc.

live etc the life of Riley (informal) have, or enjoy temporarily, an easy, carefree, pampered or luxurious life **V:** live, ⚠ lead; have; enjoy □ *And I am not going to be assisted* (to cut down expenses) *by ten-page colour spreads persuading my beloved family that they can* ***live the life of Riley*** *(or possibly Nubar Gulbenkian) for 2p down and eternity to pay.* ST □ *This 'mustering' duty, no joke at all, made me abandon the notion that these sheep farmers* ***led the life of Riley****.* OBS □ *Discotheque stuff with jet-setting birds is rubbish. But people seem to think I'm either doing that or suffering and looking for Miss Right. I'm not looking for Miss Right. I* ***have the life of Riley****.* TVT

live to see the day survive until the time when sth happens often (the implication being that one may die first instead) □ *'Things will be easier for you when you retire.' 'If I* ***live to see the day****!'* □ *Even now, the youngest of us may* ***live to see the day*** *when almost all our food will be processed from vegetable and mineral proteins.* □ *The Jacksons are finding life hard now that Mr Jackson's been made redundant.* ***May I never live to see the day*** *when that happens to us.* □ *Christ Church, until recently the only Oxford college that specifically stated women could not be members, has just gone co-educational. I* ***never thought I'd see the day****—but I'm glad I have.* □ variant never think to see/one would see the day; *may I* ***never live to see the day*** expresses wish that sth unpleasant may not happen in one's lifetime.

live etc to tell the tale survive an experience so that one may tell others what actually happened, (the implication being that one might have died in the course of it) **V:** live, ⚠ survive, be alive □ *This enormous study, which occupied him for ten years, was completed by Solzhenitzyn six years ago: it is dedicated to those who did not '****live to tell the tale****'.* ST □ *The small band of kinsmen were soon observed, superbly stalked, and finally massacred by the Matabele at dawn of a very still day and only my mother's mother, her sister, brother, and coloured nurse miraculously* ***survived to tell the tale****.* LWK □ *We can see the funny side of our detention now, having* ***lived to tell the tale****, but it wasn't very amusing at the time.*

a live wire a wire through which an electric current is passing; (fig) a lively, active person □ *...designed so that the power is automatically cut off before* ***the live wires*** *are exposed should the cable be dangerously damaged or cut.* ST □ *'We haven't had any* (written reports) *yet. Perhaps I rather over-emphasized the need of secur-*

*ity.' 'You can't. No use having **a live wire** if it fuses.'* OMIH □ *For two such **live wires** as Roger and Lamb to loaf across the finishing line just behind a small boy—naturally it made the effect all the better.* CON □ word play on lit and fig senses in second example.

one lives and learns [v + v non-rev] (saying) one picks up many useful or surprising pieces of information, has often to adjust one's opinions, in the course of one's life **S:** we, one, you (impersonal) □ *You were in luck, my lad. It must be your bonny blue eyes, though—all she likes as a rule is having a lot of money spent on her and being promised she's going on films on TV. Well, **we live and learn**.* TGLY □ RAMBLER: *There's meant to be a path coming out here.* FARMER: *Are you sure? I never knew that.* RAMBLER: *Quite certain. It's here on the official map.* FARMER: *So there is. **One lives and learns**.* OBS □ ***We live and learn** and it's never too late, I suppose, to add to one's towering storehouse of knowledge, but I never though that, so late in life, the information would reach me that Sir Richard Burton had a morbid fear of honey.* NS □ usu comment on an occcasion of doing this.

lo and behold see! notice! □ *He dramatically presents the five accused with their platefuls of rice. **Lo and behold**, four of them proceed to eat it. The fifth however is moving his jaws desperately in a vain attempt to swallow at least some of the rice, but without success.* SNP □ *The doctrines were put into practice, and, **lo and behold**, the inflation became worse than before, while unemployment rose.* ST □ *...a complete medieval group around the church at Cogges—the kind of thing that survives in only a handful of English towns. And **lo and behold**, it is all to disappear—something unique destroyed for a handful of villas and a bit of road space.* ST □ expresses and/or invites surprise about statement it introduces.

(all) a load/lot of (old) rubbish etc [Comp/O (NP)] (informal) mistaken; nonsensical; not worth serious consideration; worthless nonsense **S:** it, you; sb's opinion, sb's views; book, play, programme. **V:** be find sth; talk. **o:** rubbish, ⚠ nonsense; garbage; (taboo) balls, cobblers, crap □ *The idea of the classless society is **a load of old rubbish**. John Carrier is one of the many sociologists who maintain that the withering away of the class barriers is a contemporary myth.* ST □ *If you think that astrology is nothing more than **a load of old nonsense**, how do you account for the fact that...?* NS □ *Most leading theologians claim that this argument is **a load of dingo's kidneys**.* HHGG □ *Modern psychology, it had explained, was replacing the old Freudian ideas of the unconscious by a simpler, more common-sense control of thought by action. Bernie had said it was **all balls**.* HAA □ *'Jack knows a lot about computers, doesn't he!' 'Garbage! He knows the jargon and he shouts louder than anyone else in an argument, that's all.'* □ variant, all rubbish, garbage etc! used as dismissive exclamation.

(the) local colour [O (NP)] geographical, architectural and social details that give authenticity to the setting of a novel, play, film etc; people, customs, dialects etc typical of any given place, esp as sought by writers, artists, photographers, tourists **V:** use, seek out; supply, provide □ *Like Scott, Macaulay used '**local colour**'. Like him, and like Carlyle, he travelled over all the historic scenes about which he was writing.* L □ (the speaker meets a novelist in a public park) *Why, hello. I didn't expect to see you in this place. Looking for **local colour**, I suppose?* HD □ *We all used to go with our notebooks, writing down dirty street rhymes, skipping games, commercials from Radio Luxembourg, and all the rest of **the local colour** which would prove invaluable in later life.* NS

the local rag (informal) a provincial, or district, newspaper (often a 'weekly') which gives a lot of space to items of purely local interest; (facetious) any newspaper published and printed outside London, New York, Washington □ *The majority of the members of the Council wouldn't have noticed if the entire Town Hall staff had gone to work naked. But there were some who, for the sake of publicity in **the local rag**, appointed themselves as scourgers of the pampered bureaucracy.* RATT □ *When does a man start collecting cuttings on himself? The poet when his first slim volume gets pecked at by the week-end critics? The politician when he gets his first one-inch notice in **the local rag**?* PP

the local talent (informal) the girls/young men in any particular place that are available to 'chat up' (Vol 1) (qv), be danced with, taken about as holiday companions □ *And because most publishers had realised the best way to attract custom to their booth was to have a beautiful girl sitting in it, the whole place teemed with **local** and imported **talent**.* ST □ *'There's a disco in the Town Hall tonight.' 'Then I daresay the boys will take the chance to look over **the local talent**, but I'll settle for an early night.'*

lock etc the stable door after the horse has bolted etc (saying) take precautions too late to be effective; having suffered theft, damage, loss etc, try to avoid a repetition or worsening of these **V¹:** lock; ⚠ shut, bolt, close. **V²:** bolt; run away, gone, disappeared; escaped; been stolen □ *Also, although the family's remaining valuables are now lodged with the bank, he has installed an electronic 999 dialling system. 'It can be expensive, **locking the stable door after the horse has bolted**.'* RT □ *Between 1968 and 1969 the average price of tea at Colombo auctions dropped by 13 per cent. A government takeover of plantations would be one more case of **bolting the door after the** prize-winning **horse has escaped**.* NS □ *How you fare during the demolition of adjoining property will depend largely on the attitude of the firm involved. The police have no power to halt proceedings, though they will **shut the stable door** for you, attending promptly if a fire breaks out, or someone is hurt.* OBS □ bolt = 'fasten with a bolt', and bolt = 'run' are never used together in any variant of the expression.

lock, stock and barrel [n + n + n non-rev] the whole of sth already named, or understood; complete with all parts, items, possessions etc (from the three component parts of a rifle) **V:** sell sth; dispose of, get rid of, sth □ *It was the Saigon pied-à-terre of a rubber planter who was going home. He wanted to sell it **lock, stock and barrel**.* QA □ *'So you're moving out tomorrow?'*

*'**Lock, stock and barrel**. Leave not a trace behind!'* RT ◻ *There is increasing talk in the United States about getting Government support for cultural institutions. The problem is how this may be done without destroying the private citizen's interest and turning them over **lock, stock and barrel** to the state.* T ◻ *The 12,000 acres include two villages owned by the estate, **lock, stock and barrel**, vicarage, pub and school —and two villages partly owned.* L ◻ functions as A. ⇨ ⚠ bag and baggage; hook, line and sinker.

(all) Lombard Street to a China orange (saying) heavy odds in favour of sth; a strong likelihood that sth will happen or be done **V:** be; lay, wager ◻ *It's **Lombard Street to a China orange** that they bring in a verdict of unsound mind.* ◻ (NONCE) (Liberal Party politics) *They didn't vote on it, of course, and it's **all Cyril Smith to a China orange** that someone will try to reopen the issue before long in one of the party's myriad committees.* G

a lone wolf/bird [Comp (NP)] sb who lives, works, as far as is possible, without the social support of others; sb of solitary habits **V:** ⚠ be, seem; find sb ◻ *Here's one little boy that can look after himself. He was at once **the lone wolf** and the boy who got to the top though everyone tried to kick him down.* HAA ◻ *Perhaps a certain kind of shyness had helped to make him a bachelor. He is in some ways **a lone bird** but he cannot be called lonely.* UL ◻ also pl.

(Mr/Miss) Lonely Hearts person(s) in need of love, friendship, sympathy (the implication usu being that one is too shy or inhibited to find it for him/herself) ◻ *WDR-TV in Cologne present a programme in which three or four lonely men or women appeal for a partner in marriage. Newspapers condemned the idea, but for the **lonely hearts** themselves, the programme has drawn an enormous response.* TVT ◻ *Contents seem to have been reminiscent of women's mags today: fashion news and drawings, cooking hints, sentimental stories with happy or moral endings, and even a **lonely-hearts** question-and-answer service.* NS ◻ *Nevertheless it would be a mistake to cast her in the role of **Miss Lonelyhearts**. Her pathological lack of trust in others was amply compensated in herself.* T ◻ attrib use *a **lonely hearts** service, column etc* (ie one which attempts to deal with personal problems of correspondents).

the long arm of the law etc the far-reaching power and influence of the law etc **o:** law; Washington, the Vatican; the Mafia ◻ *He had been living in Switzerland, under a false name, for several months when **the long arm of the law** finally caught up with him.* ◻ *Although I've no doubt that **the long arm of Washington** could extend as far as Nortonstowe, I can't believe that our Government can relish being told what to do on their own territory.* TBC ◻ *The American police have found it difficult to combat the Mafia. Persuading former members to give evidence against the organization is nearly impossible—**the Mafia has a long arm,** and most of those who help the authorities are murdered.* ◻ variants the law etc has a long arm, the law's etc arm is long.

a long haul [Comp (NP)] a long journey, voyage or flight, esp one involving transport of passengers or goods; a continuous, sustained, or protracted process or endeavour **V:** ⚠ be; prove; make sth ◻ *My forces were based on Benghazi and Tobruk, and it was **a long haul** by road from them.* MFM ◻ *While European cruise fares have been rising substantially **the long haul** fly-cruise ones have become more competitive.* SC ◻ *That's something which is only just beginning. It's all going to be **a long haul**, but I know of no more worthwhile and exciting challenge.* OBS ◻ *It's like when I go to the race-track. Sometimes I am up at the end of the day, sometimes I'm down. But over **the long haul**, on balance, I don't win.* OBS ◻ (air transport) *This, coupled with the higher unit cost of flying, meant that once again there was a hiccup on **short-haul**.* G ◻ variant a short haul is usu confined to transport as in last example attrib use ***short-haul** services.*

long in the tooth [Comp (AdjP)] ageing or old (originally said about horses) **V:** ⚠ be, get. **adv mod:** a bit; rather; too; so ◻ *And when's that nice girl, though she's a bit **long in the tooth** for that, Margot Phelps going to get married?* WDM ◻ *'Would you like her yourself, Reggie?' 'My God, would I not! She's terrific. A trifle **long in the tooth**, mark you, but she has style, real style.'* RATT ◻ *'Journalism is great fun when you're young,' he said. 'But I'm getting a bit **long in the tooth** to be jumping in and out of aeroplanes.'* RT ◻ *'I think it's time you went in for something less strenuous than squash.' 'Come, come. I'm **not as long in the tooth as that**, surely?'* ◻ variant (not) as long in the tooth as that/sb.

a long line of teachers etc [O/o (NP)] a succession of people representing a family, type or profession **V:** found; come from; be one/the first/the last of. **n:** teachers, miners, doctors ◻ *He does not see himself as particularly 'progressive'. He comes from **a long line of** vigorous non-conformist **teachers**.* NS ◻ *The MP, Norman Pentland, whose death caused this by-election, was the last of **a long line of miners** to represent the constituency.* NS

long live the King etc may the king etc live a long time; may sb's/sth's presence and influence continue **S:** the King, the President, the Conservancy Board; sentimental feeling; hunting the fox ◻ *So the village school stays open, for the time being at least, and **long live our** present **incumbent**.* SC ◻ (Arts Council maintenance grants to artists, poets etc) *I can think of few things less likely to reap dividends in the shape of an art that is vigorous, self-confident, and authentically uncoopted. So, for the young author, **long live confusion**, emergencies, humiliation, and (brief) periods of penury!* OBS ◻ (NONCE) *An elderly American woman, one of hundreds of thousands of foreigners who visit Canterbury each year, wonders if Becket will grant her an audience. You tell her he was assassinated 800 years ago. **Thomas Becket is dead. Long live Thomas Becket**.* TVT ◻ exclamation of loyalty to superior, or of approval of sb/sth one wishes to remain, enjoy, see effective; variant, the King is dead, long live the King, which is used to proclaim simultaneously the death of a ruler and the succession of his heir, is parodied in last example.

the long and (the) short of it etc (informal) the essential information about a situation, event; the main point, or final result, of a discussion, argument, descriptive account, etc **o:** it; ⚠ the matter, the affair □ *When he returned with the drinks he said,* ***the long and short of it*** *is this. Bunder and them* (= those) *pals of his aren't bad at the job. They could do all right if they were content to stick to it and do one job at a time. But they aren't.* HD □ *Your mother went with him; it was a mad thing to do, but they did it. Anyway,* ***the long and short of it*** *is, they never got to Glasgow. They crashed near Doncaster, and your father was killed.* PE □ *'So we are to expect no help from the Council?' 'That's* ***the long and the short of it****, I'm afraid.'* □ often S or Comp of *be*; long and short non-rev.

a long shot [Comp (NP)] an attempt to hit a very distant target; an attempt to achieve sth that may, but is not likely to, be successful; a guess that has some, but not much, chance of being correct **V:** ⚠ be, seem; think sth. **adv mod:** a very, a pretty; quite a, rather a □ *Cuspatt and Pforzheim are both very keen to start other excavations that might throw up the same thing, though it's* ***a*** *very* ***long shot****.* UTN □ *Their committee had read 'Journey's End' and were lukewarm, but one man urged Sherriff to send it to George Bernard Shaw for an opinion. It was* ***a long shot****, but worth the risk.* RT □ *It was* ***a*** *desperately* ***long shot****, but the Transvaal is closely linked with Holland and when I got back to Oxford I addressed a letter to the Postmaster of Settlers. Too* ***long a shot*** *because I never got an answer.* RFW ⇨ ⚠ not by a long chalk/shot.

long time no see (informal) I haven't seen you, we haven't met, for a long time □ *'Hi, Kathie!' 'Hi there!' she said. '****Long time no see****.'* TT □ *'Hello, Peter.* ***Long time no see****.' 'Well, don't blame it all on me. You know where I live.'*

look as if/though butter would not melt in one's mouth appear demure, incapable of anything other than correct behaviour □ *One of the children ate the bar of chocolate I left in the cupboard, after I'd told them not to touch it. I think it must have been Tom—he* ***looks as if butter wouldn't melt in his mouth****. and that's always a bad sign.* □ *I knew John had left his wife but not that he was living with Anna. You can't mean it! She always* ***looks as though butter wouldn't melt in her mouth****.*

look as if/though one has been dragged through a hedge backwards (informal) look untidy, dishevelled; look as if/though one has slept in that suit etc for a week (qv) □ *And the women in those tight slacks and not bothering with soap and water. And their hair* ***looking as though they'd been dragged through a hedge backwards****.* TGLY □ *Joyce, I just don't know how you manage to get yourself so untidy. You* ***look as if somebody's been dragging you backwards through hedges*** *all the way home from school.* □ variant look as if/though sb has been dragging one backwards through hedges. ⇨ look as if/though one has (just) stepped out of a bandbox.

look as if/though sth has been stirred with a stick (informal) look untidy, in a muddle, in disarray □ *I'd been away one weekend! And he had the kitchen* ***looking as if*** *it* ***had been stirred with a stick****.* □ *We can't invite Jack and Moira for supper tomorrow evening. The house* ***looks as though*** *it****'s been stirred with a stick*** *and there isn't enough time to get it tidied up for them.*

look as if/though one has seen a ghost look pale, shocked, frightened □ *'Is anything the matter, John? You* ***look as if you've seen a ghost****.' 'May I sit down a minute? I've just had some bad news.'* □ *'There must have been a bad accident along the road—there are two badly damaged cars and there's broken glass everywhere.' 'Yes, somebody's been seriously injured. Helen was passing just as it happened and she came in* ***looking like a ghost****.'* □ variant look like a ghost.

look as if/though one has slept in that suit etc for a week have crumpled clothes; look untidy, dishevelled; look as if/though one has been dragged through a hedge backwards (qv) **O:** that suit, ⚠ that dress, those clothes; it, them □ *You can't go for an interview in that suit. It* ***looks as though you've been sleeping in it for a week****.* □ *I'm rather sorry I bought this dress. A three-hour car journey and it's so crumpled it* ***looks as if I've been sleeping in it for a week****.* □ *The 'Sandwiches Picasso' were served to friends by that valiant pair, Gertrude Stein (constantly '****looking as though she had been feeding hens in the rain****') and Alice Toklas.* NS □ variant, look as if/though one has been feeding hens in the rain, has form and meaning similar to headphrase. ⇨ next entry.

look as if/though one has (just) stepped out of a bandbox look neat, fresh, well-groomed □ *I don't know how you manage it, Jean, but whatever you've been doing you always* ***look as if you've just stepped out of a bandbox****.* □ *Mrs Clark's three little girls always* ***look*** *very pretty—fair curls and* ***as though they'd stepped out of a bandbox****—but, at their age, they should be running around and getting into mischief, not behaving quite so beautifully.* □ bandbox = 'light cardboard box for millinery'. ⇨ look as if/though one has been dragged through a hedge backwards; previous entry.

look bad/not look good not be conventionally correct, and likely to make others think badly of one **S:** it...not to attend the funeral; it...to neglect the others; it...if we didn't give a subscription □ *'I wouldn't worry about that, Dad,' I said. 'It's not as if she was a young girl that you were responsible for. She was a grown woman.' 'I know,' he replied. 'But it* ***looks bad*** *all the same. As if we didn't care.'* RFW □ *'Would****n't look good*** *if she sued,' he could say (saying 'it would****n't look good*** *in the Press' is the best way to cloak an altruistic urge in any boardroom).* OBS □ *'What's the hurry? They're not in your way, are they?' 'No, but it* ***looks*** *so* ***bad****, if anyone calls, having the breakfast things still lying on the table at 11 o'clock.'* □ *So the Scottish Labour MPs are looking for ways out. The obvious one is an emergency meeting of the SLP, to reverse the ruling. It would undoubtedly '****look bad****' but it is a necessary exercise.* NS ⇨ ⚠ next entry.

look bad etc (for sb) be ominous; suggest probable failure, trouble or disaster **S:** it; things; the situation; prospects. **adj:** bad, ⚠ black; not (too) good; worse; better. **o:** the men under arrest, the fish trade, Manchester United □ *'Lots of girls run away from home of their own accord.' 'Not this kind of girl, Sergeant, and not from this kind of home. It* ***looks bad****.'* □ *A year ago, when things* ***looked*** *so* ***black****, I might have spoken differently, but I really feel that 1918 has turned the corner for us.* ASA □ *I wouldn't say yet that their marriage won't break up, but things are* ***looking*** *a little* ***better*** *than they did six months ago.* □ *He had been unsure of his welcome as Sandings all along and it certainly did****n't look good*** *that none of the family had bothered to come and meet him at the station.* ⇨ ⚠ previous entry.

look before one leaps (saying) don't act rashly, without considering what the result may be □ *The virtues and faults of both writers are those of their protagonists: Emily watchful, fastidious, ruthless but lacking in life; the vital, vivacious Vivienne, needing to* ***look*** *more carefully* ***before she leaps****.* L □ *The super-activist will always feel annoyed when asked to* ***look before he leaps****—one cannot help that.* NS ⇨ ⚠ a leap/shot in the dark.

look one's/its best [V + Comp] look as specially attractive, beautiful, healthy, tidy etc as possible **S:** complexion, hair; garden, lawn; house □ *Virginia wished that she had brushed her hair and renewed her lipstick before coming up here. Millie never lost an opportunity to tell you when you were not* ***looking your best****.* AITC □ *If you ask me, I think your family worries you. All this running in and out of your room—I don't think the doctor would approve. And he's coming this afternoon, so you must be* ***looking your best****.* DC □ *We don't have much time for bedding flowers. The garden* ***looks its best*** *in spring when the fruit trees and lilacs and so on are blossoming.*

look black [V + Comp] show no sign of hope, or improvement, in the future **S:** things; life; the future □ *'I know things* ***look black*** *at the moment,' said William, seeking to console his son. 'But who knows what's round the corner?'* □ *Not even alcohol could change his gloom; without a doubt everything—his job, his marriage, life—* ***looked*** *extremely* ***black*** *from where he stood.*

(not/never) look a gift horse in the mouth (saying) (not) look for, or point out, faults in sth freely offered (examination of a horse's mouth reveals a lot about its age and condition) □ *'He's settled the proceeds of this new book of his on Jeremy and Janice and on — on any other children we may have.' The pause grew longer. 'What makes him think that this book is going to be a success?' she asked again. 'Darling, I don't think we ought to ask that question. Isn't there something about* ***not looking a gift horse in the mouth****?'* PW □ *'Why did you let Nora stay on after I'd gone?' 'Why* ***look a gift horse in the mouth****? The poor girl didn't have much fun though. My heart wasn't in it.'* AITC □ *I was just trying to decide whether it would be a good thing to make my way to the pub with him or not — it was one of Mother's maxims* ***never*** *to* ***look a gift-horse in the mouth****—when he started making little nibbling noises again with his lips, and I ran away.* HAHA □ *They gave me a sachet of it* (bath lotion) *after, but I looked like a walnut for days. The next time you get* ***a gift horse*** *give it a good* ***look in the mouth****.* NS □ *Being one who always* ***looks gift horses in their mouths****, I will be contrary enough now to argue about the purpose of the huge amounts of money which the Levy Board are dishing out to racecourses in Scotland.* SC □ expression frequently adapted, as shown.

look here pay attention to this; listen to me; let me explain □ ***Look here****, my good fellow, I told you that you'd got to put your nose to the grindstone. That meant this kind of thing has got to stop.* SPL □ *'Just a minute, dear — let me fix your tie for you.' '****Look here****, honey, lay off my tie, and give me a kiss.'* SC □ *'For myself—' He paused. Daniel waited. '****Look here****,' said Cosmo briskly, 'seeing is all very well, but for my own part, I like my amusements a bit more active. Can you direct me to pleasant pastures?'* US □ front position.

look, no hands (informal) see how skilful and daring I am (originally from children showing off that they can ride their bicycles without holding the handlebars) □ (driving test) *Another lady was fond of giving a hand signal and changing gear at the same time—* ***look no hands****. She did it during the test.* OBS □ *What woman (what man) could plod through Juliet Mitchell's latest offering, 'Women's Estate', with any pleasure other than a certain '****look****, ma,* ***no hands****' pride that a woman can write a book every bit as jargon-ridden as a man?* NS □ *'I wouldn't want you to strain yourself,' she said. 'No strain,' he said. '****Look****'—and he spread them, '****no hands****.'* TT □ (NONCE) ***Look, no script****! Oxford historian A.J.P. Taylor gives the first of six impromptu talks (10.50 BBC 1) on 'The War Lords'.* RT □ often now used in mocking reference to assumed cleverness of others.

look the other way turn one's eyes, deliberately or by chance, to look in the opposite or a different direction from sb/sth; (decide to) ignore sb/sth that invites or demands one's attention; turn a blind eye (on/to) (Vol 1) (qv) □ *'Would you mind if I took one of these books—as a keepsake?' 'I'll* ***look the other way****.'* QA □ *'Who started the fight, Jenkins?' 'I don't know, sir. I was* ***looking the other way*** *when it began.'* □ *But so many of the reports* (on pollution) *told the other story. Of factories belching out ugly fluids, in complete indifference. Of everyone* ***looking the other way****.* ST □ *There is no capital punishment there—and no punishment at all, it seems, for officials who* ***look the other way****.* OBS □ *Other men spotted where his weakness lay. The British security system, however, appears to have been* ***looking the other way*** *as 'Vassal — Master Spy' leaped in and out of bed, filmed his documents and pocketed the roubles.* SC

look/feel the part [V + Comp] seem to others or oneself suitable in appearance or face to a real or pretended role, function □ *'The successful business man's well-groomed wife! Do I* ***look the part****?' she asked, parading herself before him.* □ *I don't think the music-making is always as good at the Albert Hall* (as at the Royal Festival Hall)*, but I love the atmosphere and if possible I stand with the rest of the Prommers. The majority of the people in the Proms don't* ***look the part*** *but they're all extremely knowledge-*

able. RT ▫ (yoga exercises) *And I began to feel extraordinarily supple — though whether this was the influence of leotard and tights I don't know. There's nothing quite like a leotard and tights to make you* **feel the part**. *Even if you don't quite* **look** *it.* TVT

look sharp etc [V + Comp] hurry; be brisk, active in doing sth **adj:** sharp, ⚠ alive, lively ▫ *'Finish it later,' he said with a threatening look. 'The fire needs making now, so come,* **look sharp** *and get some coal from the cellar.'* LLDR ▫ JASON: *Back to work, everyone.* JOHN: *Come on, break it up.* JACK: **Look lively**, *get cracking.* DPM ▫ *Get a couple of hands* (= men) *to sling these bags on board, Mr Pearson — and tell them to* **look alive**. *We're due to cast off in 10 minutes.* ▫ *'It was there six months ago and no mistake,' replied his master. 'You'd better* **look sharp** *and find it, else you'll soon know what'll happen to you.'* NS ▫ usu direct or indirect imper forms.

look sb's way look at sb, esp glance in his or her direction ▫ (stage direction) *Segal is offended and sits back and reads a newspaper, and through the next scene he is very interested, though every time Daniel or Sam* **looks his way** *he quickly reverts to the paper.* HSG ▫ *The headmaster speaks to us, and knows our names and that. In my last school if the head passed you in the playground or in the corridors he'd never even* **look your way**. ▫ *Leslie was careful not to* **look** *his father***'s way** *when he suggested this, in case his mother would guess that the two of them had thought it up together.* ▫ neg often implies deliberately ignoring or snubbing sb.

(the) loose ends/threads [O (NP)] minor matters which prevent a project, investigation, story, argument etc from being thoroughly or satisfactorily completed (from finishing off neatly a piece of weaving, sewing, knitting etc) **V:** tie up, tidy up ▫ *Nor was there ever much editing to do after Ford had finished a film—* **no loose ends** *for the front office to start monkeying with.* L ▫ *Nothing will be held up, fortunately. Johnson completed the survey before he had to go in to hospital and his assistant is tying up* **the** *few* **loose threads**. ▫ *And so IDSO wound up its activities and prepared to disband. The next few months were spent in tidying up* **loose ends** *and discussing with De Beers the retention of a skeleton organization to keep a watching brief.* DS ▫ *A nasty husband and in-laws and a suspiciously keen police inspector are sketched in, but too many* **threads** *hang* **loose** *at the end, and it's hard to care about any of it.* NS

loose talk unconsidered statements, gossip, about people or affairs; careless release of privileged information ▫ *Dormitories were considered undesirable, perhaps as encouraging* **loose talk** *at night. The upper servants had their own rooms, the lower servants slept if possible no more than two to a room.* L ▫ *I'm not saying there's a serious leak of information —a bit of* **loose talk** *in the pubs would have been enough.*

the/one's lord and master [n + n non-rev] sb who has control over, and commands the allegiance of, a feudal, political, religious etc group; a husband as the dominant partner in a marriage ▫ *This job on the drill was a dead loss but it was worth it to have Jin so pleased with him, and making so much fuss of him when he came home, treating him like* **the lord and master** *he should be if this marriage was going to amount to anything more than a lot of glorious tumbles in bed.* AITC ▫ *I should be very interested to see whether she sticks to her own 'Trumpet Voluntary' or whether she bows to the wishes of* **her** *future* **lord and master** *and orders 'The Wedding March'.* DIL ▫ second meaning ironic or facetious.

Lord/Lady Muck (facetious) a (type of) person with pretensions to grandeur, importance, gentility, superior habits and tastes ▫ *'Well,' said Madame Houdin* (a procuress) *bleakly, 'I suppose he's got to have a choice. He'll take Louise, they all do, but he'll want to feel he's the Sultan, the great* **Lord Muck**, *he'll want to walk slowly up and down their serried ranks.'* US ▫ *Acting beyond the idea of the group, 'being stuck up* (= conceited)*', 'turning y'* (= your) *nose up at other people,' 'acting like* **Lady Muck**'*—all these are much disliked and not very sensitively discriminated.* UL

the lord(s) of creation mankind (from GENESIS I 27-29); men contrasted with women; races/classes who may think themselves, or be considered, superior to others ▫ *Except in North-west Europe and the far Northlands it was all Man could do to exist. No initiative could be taken.* **The Lord of creation** *was beaten to his knees by his environment, the environment that he had prided himself on being able to control.* TBC ▫ *As well as domestic tasks, women cleared and tended the garden patches, carried water, fed the pigs and fowl, while* **the lords of creation**, *when not hunting or fighting, took their ease.* ▫ expression ironic or facetious.

lose/save face [V + O pass] suffer/avoid a humiliating loss of prestige ▫ *So if the Fascists want to go through the Highway they'll have to fight for it. But we guess they'll want to stick to the main route so as not to* **lose face**—*you follow?* CSWB ▫ *He was content to warn Bullivant to behave himself, seeing that no* **face** *had been* **lost** *by either side in the equal contest.* LLDR ▫ *But now that we can go into what's called a man's world, we have certain advantages over them. We're not so concerned with* **saving face** *as men are. We find it easier to say we're sorry or ask for a favour. Men are afraid to do this lest other men think they're not up to the job.* ST ▫ *Virginia did not argue. If Helen wanted to lie her way out of the situation to* **save** *her* **face** *with Eldredge, that was all right.* AITC ▫ *We shall have to merge some parts of our national sovereignty; but this is progress in international relations — a step taken for mutual benefit, not* **a loss of face**. ▫ *It must make him* (Colonel Gadaffi) *a problem, and even a danger, for President Sadat who is seeking a* **face-saving** *way out of the Middle East deadlock.* L ▫ adj compound face-saving; variant a loss of face.

lose one's grip [V + O] (have to) let go of sth one is grasping; (fig) lose one's ability to understand and deal with either matters in general or a particular situation ▫ *When they were hanging upside-down, the locust gave an extra hefty kick, and the galago's feet* **lost their grip**, *so that they fell through the leaves clasped together.* BB ▫ *There (where the age of retirement has been* *fixed at 60) we are told, people are found to* ***lose their grip****, in some degree, at the age of 57.* PL □ (a football match) *Ahead by 2-1, Barrow show no signs of* ***losing their grip****. It is Newport who lack the effort and are doing all the flustered, careless, bad things.* OBS

lose/take heart [V + O] feel one's courage, hope, enthusiasm weakened/strengthened **A:** ***(take heart)*** from that, from these words, from his example □ *She is doing quite well, I must admit that—but so was Golding, and one day something like this will happen to her, and she'll* ***lose heart*** *like the rest of us.* TT □ *The Supporters Club fell from 7,000 to 2,000 last year. 'Well, the way the team played up till Christmas you couldn't blame anybody for* ***losing heart****. But it'll be back to 10,000 next season.'* ST □ *We all know those people with powers of total recall who can identify any quotation and remember the names of all the horses who won the Derby. So let the Watson's boys who don't shine in general knowledge* ***take heart****. Knowledge assumes many forms and so does ignorance.* SC □ *Yet all over the world whenever I spoke of the Bushman a look of wonder would come into the eyes of ordinary people and I* ***took heart*** *from that.* LWK

lose one's life [V + O pass] die in warfare or a natural disaster, as a result of an accident or criminal attack □ *As a young man he had nearly conquered Kanchenjunga, where he failed to prevent some fellow climbers from* ***losing their lives****.* ST □ *In 1953 large areas of the East Coast were inundated and there were more floods in London's East End. Altogether 300 people* ***lost their lives****.* SC □ *British observance of Armistice Day is not just, or mainly, a celebration of war and death. It is primarily a public promise that a country's Government and private citizens will work to promote peace, to make sure that all* ***those lives*** *were not* ***lost*** *in vain.* □ *Although earthquakes that are large enough to be registered by instruments occur almost daily in some parts of the world, those which are so severe that they cause* ***loss of life*** *are comparatively rare.* NSC □ variant (a) loss of life.

lose/keep one's/its looks [V + O] not be/still be as good looking as when one was younger, when sth was newer □ *I know how it is, old man: Christine's older than you; she's* ***lost her looks****; and you get restless.* PE □ *'I think he's strikingly handsome still.' 'Beginning to* ***lose his looks****, though—too much soft living.'* □ (upholstery) *Hide, almost prohibitively expensive, will* ***keep its*** *good* ***looks*** *through years of hard wear with the minimum of attention.* SC

lose one's marbles [V + O] (slang) no longer possess one's senses or wits □ *Perry told Sherry, 'You and I are acting,' which came as a huge relief for most of us temporarily convinced that the two lads were* ***losing their marbles*** *for real.* OBS □ *'Maybe I am an old woman,' she says, 'but that doesn't mean I've* ***lost*** *all* ***my marbles****.'* NS ⇨ have (got)/with all one's marbles.

lose one's nerve [V + O] lose one's courage or self-control; panic □ *In the 1950's Labour may have lost the battle but only because it first* ***lost its*** *own* ***nerve****.* NS □ *Anthony Butt's death had been doubly horrible, in its cause and in its details. To the very last he never* ***lost his nerve****.* AH □ *Zeman* (the goalkeeper), *once so polished and authoritative, played like a man who had* ***lost his nerve****, running about his area like a chicken with its head cut off, utterly confused by crosses* (= cross kicks). ST □ neg usu not lose rather than keep.

lose/waste no time (in doing sth) [V + O pass] do sth quickly, without delay **det:** no, not any; not much, little □ *Ford was coming, the papers said, and would be recruiting Irish technicians, for this was to be the start of an Irish film industry. I* ***lost no time in*** *seeking out the Irish producer of the film.* L □ *The Government seem resolved to* ***waste no time in*** *getting their proposals for reorganisation of local government finalised.* SC □ *But national prosperity is in the interests of unions as much as it is in those of employers. Once Mr Barber has announced his Budget proposals* ***no time*** *should be* ***lost in*** *having another exchange of views.* SC □ *After all, I argued, if you take over someone else's wife, the chances are that he wo****n't lose much time in*** *coming round to chew the fat* (= argue) *a bit.* CON ⇨ ⚠ have etc no time to lose; waste not, want not.

lose one's rag (informal) express one's anger, irritation, impatience etc in an uncontrolled way □ *His wife says: 'Barry's really very good-tempered. It's very rarely that he* ***loses his rag****. And I pick at him a lot, expecially after a hard day with the hotel and the kids.'* RT □ cf lose/keep one's temper/cool (qv).

lose one's shirt [V + O] (informal) lose everything one has; suffer a severe financial loss, esp in gambling or speculation □ (audience response) *It is all or nothing. John Hawkins hits the jackpot* (= wins everything), *George Macbeth* ***loses his shirt****.* L □ *Not many industries manage to run up a near-record order book and then proceed to* ***lose their shirts****. But British Shipbuilding has.* OBS ⇨ ⚠ put one's shirt on (Vol 1).

lose/keep one's temper/cool [V + O] express/not express one's anger, irritation, impatience etc in an uncontrolled way □ *She frowned. 'I shall* ***lose my temper****. You'll make me* ***lose my temper****. Why do you hide so much from me?'* HD □ *I didn't* ***lose my temper*** *because time can be expensive. I used to, but the leading ladies always cried and it took half an hour to put back their make-up.* SC □ *He was extremely insulting—and very silly too. I don't know how I managed to* ***keep my cool****.* □ cf lose one's rag (qv).

lose the thread (of sth) [V + O pass] fail to maintain, or fail to follow and understand, a consecutive or logical line, pattern, in sth **o:** story, narrative; argument, debate; remarks, conversation □ *He stopped and, for a moment, appeared to have* ***lost the thread of*** *his remarks.* ASA □ (reader's letter) *Surely someone as experienced as Martin Jenkins should know that in a radio play the listener should never be puzzled —while he is working things out the action has gone on, and he* ***loses the thread*** *completely.* L □ *Nevertheless, 'All God's Dangers' is a rare and remarkable narrative. Nate rambles but he does not* ***lose the thread****.* G □ *Conversation is different. It rambles, material overlaps, statements aren't always clear,* ***the thread*** *gets* ***lost****.* OBS ⇨

⚠ pick up the threads (Vol 1).

lose/find one's tongue [V + O] be reticent, or silent, when expected to speak/reply after being reticent or silent ▫ *'Now,' she went on, 'you must call me Aunt Flo and we shall be great friends.' But the boys, faced with this flamboyant and somewhat terrifying figure, had* ***lost their tongues****.* ▫ STANLEY: *I tell you, children are the most selfish things in the world. So he drinks. I drive him to it. So I hear.* (Walter says nothing.) *Well, have you* ***lost your tongue****?* FFE ▫ *At first when I arrived I was a catalyst to a little company bored to death with each other who* ***found their tongues*** *again with a stranger arrived from home.* NS ⇨ ⚠ the cat got sb's tongue.

lose one's touch [V + O] lose some of one's former ability to do sth eg hold an audience, attract the opposite sex, make pastry ▫ *'Pretty little thing, eh? Very jolly,' Ormerod was saying reflectively. 'Knows how to get herself up at inconsiderable outlay. Not very communicative on the other hand, and went off to bed after about twenty minutes. I must be* ***losing my touch****.'* TGLY ▫ *The infant seemed to know it was in competent hands and quietened down surprisingly quickly. 'I see you haven't* ***lost your touch****,' her son-in-law said.* ▫ also pl lose their touch.

a lost cause [Comp/O (NP)] a project, aim or ideal which a group has devoted itself to supporting, and which is not likely to receive, or has not received, sufficient support **V:** be, prove; support, champion, further ▫ *Then leaning towards his brother, he said deliberately, 'She's incurably romantic, of course. The avant-garde's* ***a lost cause*** *and that's enough for her.'* ASA ▫ *'Good evening, all,' she said. 'Guess who I've brought.' There was of course a dead silence. Mrs Villars, used to championing* ***lost causes****, said was it Mr Churchill, which went down very well.* WDM

a lost soul [Comp (NP)] a wandering spirit of the dead which cannot find a home in heaven, earth or hell; a sinner, unbeliever, who has put himself beyond the power of redemption; an unhappy, defeated or bewildered person **V:** ⚠ be, feel, consider oneself ▫ *Outspoken agnosticism was a rarity then and my mother grieved for me as* ***a lost soul*** *and prayed that God in his goodness would lighten my darkness.* ▫ *'But a professor is such a distinguished position,' Marie-Hélène protested. 'Oh,' said Kay, 'to give Daddy his due, he couldn't live on distinction. He's far too much of* ***a lost soul*** *for that.'* ASA ▫ also pl.

a lot to ask (of sb) [Comp (NP)] greater or better than one is justified in expecting or hoping for **V:** ⚠ be, seem; find sth. **pron:** a lot, a great deal; not much, little. **o:** anyone, him; a friend ▫ *'What do you expect me to do, miss—unpack all the boxes?' 'Could you?' She wanted to have her possessions round her. 'Be* ***a lot to ask****.' He shook his head.* AITC ▫ *'Would it be* ***too much to ask*** *what you feel it's worth?' 'Could take a squint at it tomorrow,' Pop said, 'and let you know.'* DBM ▫ *'I only want him to write or phone home occasionally to tell us where he is and if he is well.' 'It's* ***little to ask of*** *a son, certainly.'* ▫ *A chance to earn a fair living and a house for yourself and your family doesn't seem* ***a lot to ask****.*

a lot of/much water has run etc under the bridge (saying) much time has passed, much has happened, many things have changed, since a particular event occurred **V:** run, ⚠ flowed; gone, passed. **A:** since then; in 20 years; during the interval ▫ *I mean, they start handing out their impressions of life, and one thing and another, not realising* ***a lot of water has run under the bridge*** *since they were young.* ▫ *According to those who should know* ***a lot of water has*** *already* ***passed under the bridge*** *and the problems are beginning to recede.* G ▫ *I wonder what he thinks when he looks over at the manor and the estates that once belonged to him?* ***A lot of water*** *can* ***run under*** *a lot of* ***bridges*** *in ten years.* RM ▫ *In 1970 they played the match at St George's again and Pat Marston and I walked round together.* ***Much water****, and a certain amount of other fluids,* ***had passed under the bridge*** *in the intervening 39 years.* ST ▫ (NONCE) *Without ungallantly going into too much detail, Lucille Ball was a leading Goldwyn Girl in 'Roman Scandals' in 1933, and if she could dance and sing in those days, then, as Sam Goldwyn himself used to say, we have* ***passed a lot of water*** *since.* L ▫ last example a pun on usu meaning of *pass water* = 'urinate'.

loud(ly) and clear(ly) [adj + adj/adv + adv non-rev] public(ly); unambigous(ly); for all to hear and notice **V:** ring out, go out; give the message; state sth; get the message ▫ *And if that is indeed what has been happening in Britain, then the drum-beats ring out* ***loud and clear****—militancy pays, brothers, and not just for a few privileged hot-heads, but for the working population at large.* ST ▫ *The Israeli electorate said two things* ***loudly and clearly*** *last Monday.* NS ▫ *Are we getting our money's worth? That is a crude, vulgar question, a question that tends not to be popular with educationists. But an eminent educationist is now asking it* ***loud and clear****.* SC ▫ *A voice,* ***loud and clear*** *but not strident, suddenly rose above the noise of the argument and started to preach sense to the hotheads in the group.* ▫ loud and clear also used adverbially, in third example.

loud and long [adj + adj/adv + adv rev] loud(ly) and continuous(ly) for a few seconds or minutes **V:** be; laugh; cheer, applaud; hold forth ▫ *Asked if he had really said that, he opened his mouth and laughed* ***loud and long****.* NS ▫ *'What's that rope for, mate?' He called back: 'It's to 'ang mesen wi'* (= hang myself with), *missis,' and she cackled at his bloody joke so* ***loud and long*** *you'd think she never heard such a good 'un* (= one). LLDR ▫ *As the audience consisted mainly of the children's parents and relatives, the applause for each item was* ***loud and long****.* ▫ *Carlo, dancing triumphantly on the seat of the cart, whooped* ***long and loud*** *to tell the other peons we had been successful, and when they galloped up we all gathered round our quarry.* DF ▫ usu in order of headphrase.

love at first sight falling in love with sb (or of two people, mutually) on the first occasion of seeing or meeting; an immediate liking for sth ▫ *'Love's Labour Lost' was one of Shakespeare's early plays and it's brimming over with the excitement of* ***love at first sight****.* RT ▫ *The couple first met in 1968. Phillips was still a cadet at*

Sandhurst and the Princess appeared more interested in the older, debonair Richard Meade. It was not, in short, ***love at first sight****.* RT □ (NONCE) *He wasn't by any means brought up on wine. He'd scarcely tasted it until, playing hockey for Oxford in Germany, he had a half-bottle of hock put before him. It was* ***love at first taste****.* ST □ often Comp of *be*.

love is blind (saying) being in love with sb blinds one to shortcomings in the loved one □ ***Love is blind****, and lovers cannot see/The pretty follies that themselves commit.* MERCHANT OF VENICE II 6 □ *'His wife's not just plain. Where were his eyes when he met her?' 'Ah well,* ***love is blind****, you know.'*

love sb and leave sb (catchphrase) have a short-lived romantic attachment to, or relationship with, sb; have a passing affection for sb/sth □ *Her son, the legacy of a GI who'd* ***loved*** *her* ***and left*** *her was now about thirty years old.* □ *'It's a case of* ***love*** *me* ***and leave*** *me with the tourists and summer visitors,' the village postmaster explained. 'They don't put anything into the place.'* □ *Well, Jenny, I'm afraid I shall have to* ***love*** *you* ***and leave*** *you. Something rather urgent's come up at the office.* TGLY □ in last example *I shall have to* ***love*** *you* ***and leave*** *you* used as facetious form of leave-taking.

love me, love my dog (saying) (some people think that) true affection, regard for sb should extend to everybody and everything closely connected with that person □ *'She'd take it as a personal insult if I said those regular Sunday visits to her parents were getting a bit of a bore.' '****Love me, love my dog****, eh?'* □ *The mangy beasts of voters, normally good for no more than a kick up the rump, are treated like royalty.* ***Love me, love my dog****. In the last few days I've patted the heads of numerous unsavoury hounds.* NS □ *I'd like it very much, of course, if Marjorie shared my love of music, just as she'd like me to enjoy gardening and pony-trekking, but we've never taken a '****love me, love my dog****' line with each other.*

love not wisely but too well love with good but misguided intention, or to such an excessive degree that one suffers for it □ (source) *Speak of me as I am. . ./. . .then, must you speak/Of one that* ***lov'd not wisely but too well****.* OTHELLO V 2 □ (It is) *a small, young, and poor organisation of lay volunteers and sympathetic clerics of all creeds, which gives advice and comfort to couples who* ***love*** *each other* ***well, but not wisely****.* G □ (NONCE) *It is easy to* ***water not wisely but too well****. More houseplants die from over-watering than from any other single cause.*

the love of money is the root of all evil (saying) all, or most, of the evil done, or suffered, by mankind arises from greed for gain □ (source) *But they that will be rich fall into temptation and an snare. For* ***the love of money is the root of all evil****.* 1 TIMOTHY VI 9-10 □ *There is a good deal of truth to the injunction that* ***the love of money is the root of all evil****, but when the theme is sung by a chorus of multi-millionaires one begins to wonder if there isn't something phoney about the message.* SC □ ***Money*** *may not* ***be the root of all evil****, but it can produce the sort of problems that will pressure even the most stable of marriages.* □ sometimes shortened form, money is the root of all evil, is used, as in last example. TVT

love's young dream the blissful state of young people in love, esp for the first time □ *No, there's nothing half so sweet in life/As* ***love's young dream****.* LOVE'S YOUNG DREAM (T MOORE 1779-1852) □ MR FISH: *Look at them,* ***love's young dream****.* MR GREEN: *If I had a fiddle I'd play 'Hearts and Flowers'.* MRS FISH: *Real romantic.* DPM □ *'Well, and how's* ***love's young dream****?' Sheila asked Jenny. 'Aren't you the lucky girl? My, but you look radiant.'* TGLY □ may refer, as in second and third examples, to the young lover(s); often facetious.

a loved one sb with whom one has a close, affectionate and usu continuous relationship (esp in context of death or of actual or possible separation) □ *. . .the effect on anyone who has had* ***a*** *close relative or* ***loved one*** *who took their own life.* ST □ *The manner of singing is traditional and has fixed characteristics. It aims to suggest a deeply felt emotion (for the treachery of* ***a loved one****, for example) but the emotion has not the ingrown quality shown by the crooners.* UL □ *The idea was that there was nothing for you out of Bermondsey. The place to be in is Bermondsey, with your* ***loved ones****. Go and work at the factories which are on the doorstep.* L

a low profile [O (NP)] an unaggressive, unassertive, self-effacing attitude, way of behaviour in conducting one's life, work or a particular undertaking **V:** ⚠ keep, preserve, maintain; adopt, cultivate □ *I admire the brisk creativeness of American English. '****Low profile****' is a perfect vivid phrase for 'conciliatory demeanour'.* NS □ *Here you have a genuine Underground Press, of* ***low profile*** *and high seriousness: a placid flow of original research and pottering scholarships.* ST □ *Mr Heath has told friends that he plans to keep* ***a low profile*** *and that he wants to avoid putting himself in the position of stealing the show from Mrs Thatcher.* SC □ *Such ideas excited medieval man and led to such gigantic projects as building Winchester Cathedral. Today's practising Christians tend to adopt* ***a lower profile****. There is a search for the essentials in the faith in greatly changed conditions.* OBS □ *The incident was significant, however, for what it suggested about Army tactics. The '****low profile****' attitude of recent weeks was being abandoned and military rather than political factors were now dominating the situation.* L □ attrib use *a* ***low-profile*** *attitude*; use of comparative or superlative forms of adj, as in fourth example, unusual. ⇨ a high profile.

the lower orders (dated or facetious) people of the lower social classes □ *Working-class people have not only improved their lot, acquired more power and possessions, but no longer feel themselves members of '****the lower orders****', with a sense of other classes, each above them and each superior in the way the world judges.* UL □ *The local swimming pool was an agreeable place, with a high entrance fee imposed to keep out* ***the lower orders****.* SPL

lower/raise one's sights [V + O pass] lower/raise one's standards; be content to achieve less/determined to achieve more than one had originally hoped or expected to (from adjusting the device on a rifle, telescope etc that helps one to aim or observe) ▫ *'What are you trying to prove?' said Chadwick. 'Nothing, wacker, nothing at all—only that we ought to* ***lower our sights*** *a bit and chatter less about "professional status".'* TT ▫ *Unless political leaders can* ***raise their sights*** *to match the situation, there must be acute anxieties for parliamentary government in the next few years.* NS ⇨ ⚠ set one's/sb's sights high.

one's luck holds one continues to have good luck ▫ *'I haven't had to see a doctor for over twenty years.' 'Well, let's hope* ***your luck holds*** *for another twenty.'* ▫ ***My luck*** *continued to* ***hold*** *and at sundown I managed to bring off another extremely difficult shot.* LWK ▫ *I've never seen so little traffic on this route. If* ***our luck holds*** *we shan't be late after all.*

the luck of the draw (the way in which) chance, fortune, decides what some people may be, do, get or suffer, and others not (from drawing lots with straws or marked papers to select who will do, or get, sth) ▫ *The French-speaking Belgians usually get rather short commons in such catalogues, because Maeterlinck is hardly big league, and Hergé (the creator of Tintin) and Simenon are not quite respectable. But that's* ***the luck of the draw.*** NS ▫ *But* ***the luck of the draw*** *ordained that Billy had the auburn curls, and his sisters their father's lank locks.* ⇨ ⚠ next entry.

(just/all) the luck of the game the element of luck, as opposed to skill, that operates in a game, research, scientific activity, etc ▫ *I'm no better than him really. It was* ***just the luck of the game****—if we went on now and played another set, he'd probably beat me.* ▫ DOCTOR (he looks at the retort): *Oh my God: coagulated. The whole damm thing's coagulated. Clear it out, clear it away, it's three weeks' consolidated work, oh no, it's nothing, no—it's* ***all the luck of the game****, isn't it?* THH ▫ often said to make light of one's success or excuse defeat. ⇨ ⚠ previous entry.

lucky at cards, unlucky in love (saying) a superstition about card-players ▫ *'And I couldn't concentrate on beggar-my-neighbour* (a card game). *Merry would have won in any case.* ***Lucky at cards, unlucky in love*** *is her motto, isn't it, Merry?' Miss Merriman, with her usual calm, said she had never had time to consider love.* WDM ▫ *'Never mind, Felicity,' her grandfather said, '****Unlucky at cards, lucky in love****,' but Felicity obviously thought her brother's 15p win was the better bargain.* ▫ comment made during or at end of, a session of card-playing; usu facetious; variant unlucky at cards, lucky in love also usu facetious.

a lucky dip a bag, box etc of wrapped articles from which sb takes sth, either as a gift at a party or for a fixed price at a sale, fair, toy bazaar, etc; a situation where what one gets, takes place or what happens may chance to please one, be useful, etc or not ▫ *Among other film seasons the National Film Theatre's* ***lucky dip*** *of over 100 films from Paramount is to be scrutinised attentively.* NS ▫ *'Why not take your holiday somewhere you'll be sure of some sun?' 'It's* ***a lucky dip****, wherever you go.'* ▫ *But for the last month they have been delving into* ***a lucky dip*** *of political ideas, pulling out a strange array of disconnected decisions. The people wait, hungry for action.* NS ▫ occas pl.

M

mad etc (at/with sb/sth) [Comp (AdjP)] (informal) angry, annoyed, with sb about sth **V:** ⚠ be, get; make sb. **adj:** mad, ⚠ furious, wild ▫ *It's my big brother's ball. He'll be* ***mad at*** *me for losing it.* ▫ *It wasn't the happiest of occasions. They'd forgotten to advertise his lecture in the press and he was pretty* ***wild at*** *that, for a start.* SC ▫ *Well, if he's as stupid as you say there's no use getting* ***mad at*** *him about it, is there?*

mad etc about sb/sth [Comp (AdjP)] (informal) keenly or excessively interested in, enthusiastic about, sb/sth; mad on sb/sth (qv) **V:** ⚠ be, become. **adj:** mad, ⚠ crazy, wild, nuts ▫ *Queen Charlotte was* ***mad about*** *watches and kept 25 of them in a case beside her bed.* L ▫ *They were* ***wild about*** *Marty. Girls? Thousands of them, mobbing him at stage doors.* H ▫ *He wasn't exactly* ***crazy about*** *being visited, because nearly three weeks had gone by before I got a postcard with the scrawled message, 'Come if you like.'* CON ▫ *Dick was then eleven, full of go and football* ***crazy*** (ie ***crazy about*** *football).* ▫ *He said the modern generation was money* ***mad*** *or pleasure* ***mad*** *(ie* ***mad about*** *money etc), or only interested in what they could get out of life.* TGLY ▫ adj compounds football-crazy, money-mad etc.

a mad dog a dangerously or foolishly violent, irresponsible or eccentric person ▫ *It has always been accepted that the Emperor Theodore was* ***a mad dog*** *let loose, a sort of black reincarnation of Ivan the Terrible.* ▫ *It's not* ***mad dogs****, but men who can calculate the risks and bide their time, that we need for a project like this.* ▫ *Kingsley got up and paced the room, talking as he walked, 'Even so, it's a* ***mad-dog*** *scheme. Consider the objections.'* TBC ▫ attrib use *a* ***mad-dog*** *scheme.*

mad on sb/sth [Comp (AdjP)] (informal) keenly or excessively interested in sb/sth; mad etc about sb/sth (qv) **V:** ⚠ be, become ▫ *Between all this, Carole Alden also manages to bring up a 13-year-old daughter and a son of 11 ('both* ***mad on*** *horses, which helps in this home').* ST

a maid etc of all work a servant expected to do, or help with, all domestic duties; a general drudge **n:** maid, girl; man, boy, lad ▫ *Lennie was their assistant. Barman, pot-boy,* ***maid of all work****, he had worked in the Olive Branch since he left school.* AITC ▫ *He charged into the kitchen, bellowing loudly for Celeste, the kitchen maid, and Bragon* ***the man-of-all-work****, her lover.* A ▫ may be used unaltered for both sexes, though boy, lad may be substituted for maid; sometimes hyphenated; stress pattern a ˌmaid of ˈall work.

make answer/reply [V + O] (formal) answer; reply ▫ *'What did you do before?' she asked. 'I* *was a student of history,' I* ***made answer****.* PP □ *He presented an Address from the House of Commons to which Her Majesty was graciously pleased to* ***make reply****.* T

make an/one's appearance [V + O] be visible; come into view; join a company; be present at, take part in, a public or formal occasion **adj:** public; welcome; unexpected □ *'Mrs Hatchett, just what are you talking about?' 'My ghost, madam. In the past he has only* ***made his appearances*** *at night, and silently.'* DC □ *It was a rare event for Jim to* ***make an appearance*** *before noon, any Sunday morning.* □ *Already a very ill man, he* ***made his*** *last public* ***appearance*** *at a CND* (= Campaign for Nuclear Disarmament) *rally in August, '64.* NS

make a beginning/start [V + O pass] begin a task, project etc; achieve a starting point from which to continue a course of action or study, a profession or trade, a relationship; make a start (on) (Vol 1) (qv) **adj:** good, bad; small □ *The only practical way is to* ***make a*** *small* ***beginning*** *and then try to extend it.* □ *You've* ***made a start****, anyway. If your clients are satisfied they're likely to bring you more business.* □ *He hadn't won our confidence yet but* ***a*** *goodish* ***beginning*** *had been* ***made****.*

make bold to do sth risk doing sth; dare, have the courage to do sth **Inf:** to say; to ask, to inquire; to deny □ *I* ***make*** *so* ***bold to*** *say Bobby Jones's feat of the so-called Grand Slam will not happen again because today golf has turned into a money-making industry.* L □ *The only person to whom a Question* (= a question asked in the British Parliament) *could properly be put down was the Prime Minister, so I* ***made so bold as to do*** *so.* ST □ variant be/make so bold as to do sth.

make one's bow/début [V + O pass] appear, be shown, in public or before a particular audience, for the first time **S:** actor, dancer; play □ *'The Dream of Peter Mann'* ***made its bow*** *at the Edinburgh Festival which is about the only affinity between Bernard Kops and T.S. Eliot.* DPM □ *It was not till her father's death that, at the age of eighteen, she* ***made her début*** *in a small part at the Lyceum.* MM

make bricks without straw [V + O + A pass] do sth without proper or sufficient material, information etc □ (source) *Ye shall no more give the people* ***straw*** *to* ***make brick****, as heretofore: let them go and gather straw for themselves.* EXODUS V 7 □ *Sheila has lovely hair anyway. The best hairdresser in the World couldn't do much with mine. You can't* ***make bricks without straw****.* □ *He quotes them extensively nevertheless, together with other equally suspect evidence, because otherwise he would have no* ***straw with*** *which to* ***make his bricks****.* OBS □ *The alleged romance was a triumph for the* ***bricks-without-straw*** *school of British journalism and a harmless enough distraction while Mr Heath made up his mind about the next phase of his fight against inflation.* L □ attrib use *the* ***bricks-without-straw*** *school of journalism.*

make a cat laugh (informal) be especially comic, ludicrous or incongruous □ ('Nairn's Journeys', BBC 1) *To see Nairn waddling through the Zurich woods dropping hints about his amorous past would have* ***made a cat laugh****.* L □ *You should hear the upper-class accent she puts on for the benefit of customers. It's enough to* ***make a cat laugh****.* □ usu with *would*, or preceded by *it's enough to*.

make certain/sure[1] check, verify, that one is fully and correctly informed about a fact, situation or state of affairs □ *Before you sign up for a course,* ***make sure*** *that the school is attached to an established model agency, for agents are often unwilling to take on girls trained elsewhere.* H □ *'I think Mr Brown has gone out,' the landlady said 'but I'll run upstairs and* ***make certain****.'* □ *A 'full' service should included attention to ignition timing, carburettor adjustment and the air filter. If you are in doubt, the short answer is to* ***make sure*** *by asking.* OBS □ *Check that the price of your package tour includes medical insurance.* ***Making certain of*** *that before you go on holiday can save you a lot of money later.* □ expression refers to previous sentence or is followed by *that*-cl; variant make certain/sure about/of sth.

make certain/sure[2] ensure a particular result **S:** government, industry; decision, move; take care (not) to do sth (qv) □ *The original Mr Parker was an 18th century lawyer who* ***made sure*** *that Shirburn remained in the family, which now devotes itself to farming and running the Oxfordshire County Council.* NS □ *Stalin wholeheartedly approved the 'Dragoon' landing. It* ***made certain*** *that his forces would get to Vienna before ours!* MFM □ *'Simpson has withdrawn.' 'Then that* ***makes*** *Edward's election* ***certain****: most of our members distrust Bolton's radical views.'* □ expression has NP in middle position or is followed by *that*-cl; variant make certain/sure of sth.

make a change[1] [V + O pass] bring about an alteration, esp one meant as an improvement to existing conditions, arrangements etc **det:** any; no; some; a lot of. **adj:** slight; sweeping, fundamental, extensive □ *You haven't half* ***made a change*** *here, Mrs Black. You must have worked very hard to get the place cleaned up like this.* □ *Having checked over the leadership problem and* ***made the*** *necessary* ***changes****, I was satisfied that I had a team which would collectively handle the task.* MFM □ *I promise you there'll be some sweeping* ***changes made*** *if I take over this department.*

make a change[2] [V + O] be a contrast to, or relief from, what is usually said, done or used **adj:** welcome, pleasant. **A:** from the usual, from a fish and chip diet, from greasing axles. □ *'Sorry about those,' Patrick said, indicating them with one hand while he found his key with the other. This meant that he had no free hand to touch Jenny with, which* ***made a change****.* TGLY □ *She only twisted her head round as I passed and grinned and said: 'Been gallivanting?' 'That's right.* ***Makes a change****.'* H □ *Harvey Weiss's 'Gadget Book' is perfect for unhandy men, with the sort of instructions that get you there in the end. His gadgets too,* ***make a*** *good* ***change*** *from the usual 'craftsmen only' things.* L □ not pl.

make sth clear/plain (to sb) [V + O + Comp pass] make sth fully and unambiguously understood **O:** attitude, position, view; that he was in no mood to argue, that he was opposed to change. **adv mod:** abundantly, quite, very □ *The title of his last work ('I turned round and* *looked at the injustice which was done under the sun') completed shortly before his death* ***makes*** *his attitude at that time abundantly* ***clear***. L □ *Mr Wilson added: 'What I hope I have* ***made clear*** *is that I have not become a rich man since leaving No.10* (official residence of the British Prime Minister).*'* L □ *We* ***made*** *it quite* ***clear to*** *him that they must include a visit to all or any diamond mines in Liberia.* DS □ *Once the intention to do no such thing* (ie get legal aid) *was* ***made plain*** *they gave all the help they could.* ST □ *He has certainly* ***made plain*** *the principles on which the Budget had been designed.* ST

make sb's day [V + O] be an experience, occurrence, that makes one feel the day has been especially satisfying or significant **S:** you; it, that. **A:** just, certainly, really □ (reader's letter) *It* ***makes my day*** *when somebody actually takes the trouble to pick up a pen and express appreciation.* OBS □ (cricket) *Like Jack Parker I revered Surrey and idolised Jack Hobbs. To hear Jack talking of the great man and of my other childhood heroes* ***made my day***. RT □ *That just* ***makes my day***. *Everybody's talking about me, and the police have been grilling Cindy, and I'm the only person who doesn't know about it.* PE □ often ironic, as in last example.

make etc a decision [V + O pass] decide, esp after previous consideration or doubt **V:** make; reach, arrive at, come to. **adj:** final, firm; hasty □ *Having* ***made a decision*** *Mr Wilkinson would have been wiser to admit frankly that the millions lost on Blue Streak were part of the cost of rearmament.* SC □ *'Sorry,' he would say in answer to questions about his future, 'but I'm not* ***making any*** *major* ***decisions*** *just now.'* HD □ *The girl watched him seriously; it seemed to him that she was considering the whole of the situation and* ***any decision*** *she* ***reached*** *would be final and call for immediate action.* OMIH

make do (with sth) manage with sth, accept sth, although it is not adequate or satisfactory or desirable □ *I didn't have time to buy any food today. You'll have to* ***make do with*** *the left-over cold meat from yesterday.* □ *When we reached the cottage we found that neither beds nor bedding were provided, so we* ***made do with*** *sofas and curtains.* □ *Sorry! Only potatoes left now. You'll just have to* ***make do***. □ often preceded by *have to*.

make do and mend (a policy whereby one continues to) manage with equipment, clothing, furnishings, machinery etc which one already possesses, esp by repairing or adapting them □ *The short term dominates every decision, and in the short term Donovan can always* ***make do and mend***, *always muddle through.* OBS □ *For these are not people who control their lives, except in the immediate sense. That is one thing they share, the other is their need to* ***make do and***, *if possible,* ***mend***. NS □ *I know I could do the decor in a big way—far better than the old* ***make-do-and-mends*** *that are at it now, but the right people don't know it.* HAA □ *In the slump that followed, the Government poured out propaganda of the* ***make-do-and-mend*** *variety, exhorting workers to economise and find new ways of using up waste.* OBS □ n compound a make-do-and-mend; attrib use *the* ***make-do-and-mend*** *variety.*

make an effort (to do sth) [V + O pass] exert oneself physically or mentally; try, or show willingness (to do sth) **det:** some, every; little; no, (not) any. **adj:** determined; (not) the slightest. **Inf:** to appear willing, to co-operate, to smile □ BEATIE: *Oh yes, we turn on the radio or a TV set maybe, or we go to the pictures—but isn't that the easiest way out? Anything so long as we don't have to* ***make an effort***. R □ *Some woe appeared to be weighing her down, though she was clearly* ***making an effort to*** *bear up.* SPL □ *Ned realized that he had been a fool to start provoking Robert by insinuating that he had no time for his old friends, and he* ***made a*** *lame* ***effort to*** *back out.* CON □ (reader's letter) *His property is not fenced and though I* ***make every effort to*** *keep the dog confined, I feel that he should put up some sort of barrier.* TO

make (both) ends meet match expenses to income; live reasonably well without getting into debt □ *I have to keep writing if I'm to* ***make ends meet*** *and when I am homeless I can settle down to nothing.* UTN □ *What was it like to be a Roman legionary? Just how did a medieval peasant* ***make ends meet****?* RT □ *I also took odd jobs—telephonist, clerk, so on. Eventually, I just couldn't* ***make both ends meet*** *and I had to go back home.*

make/pull a face [V + O] grimace in order to show dislike, disgust, impudent defiance, or in order to amuse, anger, or frighten sb □ *Joe took a drink of whisky and* ***made a face***. *He was at the stage when alcohol is repulsive and essential at the same time.* AITC □ *I* ***pull a face*** *and say 'Do you really have to go?' and she* ***pulls a face*** *and says she does.* RT □ *Wormold began to* ***make faces*** *in the glass. 'What on earth are you doing, Father?' 'I wanted to make myself laugh.'* OMIH □ make/pull faces (pl) may imply either a variety, or repetitions, of grimaces.

make one's farewells [V + O pass] say good-bye to sb; see, visit, people to say good-bye before leaving a district, job etc □ *As he was* ***making his farewells***, *a photographer (clearly by pre-arrangement) leaped out of what looked like a cupboard in the Senator's office.* NS □ *By the evening she had* ***made*** *all* ***her farewells***, *including the most difficult of all.* PW

make (sth) fast [V + O + Comp pass] (esp nautical) fasten, tie up, attach etc securely **O:** boat, her; door, gate □ *We went up between the mud flats till we came to a tumbledown jetty. Janet brought the boat alongside this and* ***made her fast***, *and went ashore.* RFW □ ***Make fast*** *to the turret* (of a submerged tank) *if you can.* RFW □ *The butler had gone the rounds of the ground floor as usual about 11 p.m.,* ***making*** *all* ***fast*** *for the night before he, too, retired.* □ in nautical contexts, O often omitted.

make one's flesh creep/crawl [V + O +A] (informal) cause one to feel fear, loathing, aversion, nervous anxiety; give sb etc the creeps etc (qv); make one's hair stand on end (qv) □ *I was woken up in the middle of the night by a weird, high-pitched, monotonous wailing that* ***made my flesh creep***, *sent my heart-beat rocketing and caused me to break out into a cold sweat.* □ *He* ***makes my flesh crawl****: his cat-like walk, his husky voice, his black clothes, his perpetual grin—there's something really sinister about him.*

make a/one's fortune [V + O pass] earn, or gain by other efforts, much wealth **adj:** considerable, immense; small □ *He has* ***made a fortune****, bought his family a fabulous house and 'had a ball'* (= had a wonderful time). H □ *He* ***made a*** *small* ***fortune****, intent on marriage and settling down.* OBS □ ***Fortunes*** *are being* ***made*** *by creating flavours, smells and textures as substitutes for the real thing in processed and synthetic foods.* OBS □ sometimes an exaggeration.

make sb free of sth allow sb full rights in, or free use or enjoyment of, sth **O:** guest, visitor; child; student. **o:** house, pantry; books □ *He kindly* ***made*** *me* ***free of*** *his library to pursue my researches.* CWR □ *Whooping and cheering, they escort me to the city, bring me a beer and a big chop,* ***make*** *me* ***free of*** *their homes.* TCM

make free with sb/sth be over-familiar with sb; treat, use, sb/sth casually or presumptuously as if belonging to oneself **adv mod:** too, very, rather. **o:** wife, secretary; belongings; food, drink □ *His idea was that it didn't do for an officer to* ***make*** *too* ***free with*** *the men under his command.* □ *Mrs Carstairs was breathing heavily in indignation. 'This gentleman seems to have been* ***making free with*** *your pantry in a remarkable way, Briggs.'* EM □ *The second christening, which took place in church, was a somewhat rowdy affair; I was three years old and I cheeked the parson and* ***made free with*** *the holy water.* CWR

make/win friends and influence people (catchphrase) refers to business or political friendship and influence (from the advertising slogan for Pelmanism, a commercial course for memory training, personality development) □ (book title) *How to* ***win friends and influence people****.* (D CARNEGIE 1937) □ *I must confess that I do not believe that cancelling luncheon engagements is a very good way of* ***making friends and influencing people****, or indeed, a substitute for a European policy.* SC □ *For my face is, not innocent exactly, but unused. I mean unused by sex, by money, by* ***making friends and influencing people****, hardly touched by any of the muck one's forced to wade through to get what one wants.* RATT □ *Nobody ever takes me seriously, or pays the least attention to what I say. Sure, I can* ***make friends****—but I can't* ***influence people****.* □ (NONCE) *The magic words are 'Labour Party', guaranteed to* ***lose friends and*** *fail to* ***influence people****—certainly in the cost-accounted 95-percent mortgage four-bedroom detached belt. Why do we bother to canvas here anyway?* NS □ usu humorous or ironic; stress pattern make/win ˌfriends and ˈinfluence people.

make good do well in life and work, contrasted with being unable to rise from the lowest social or economic level, or with being an idler, rogue or criminal; achieve a desired and acknowledged status financially, socially or professionally □ *It is probably due to his protection and advice that I remained at Sandhurst, turned over a new leaf, and survived to* ***make good.*** MFM □ *'I suppose it's a small price for getting rid of him.' 'It's a small price for ruining the lad's chances of* ***making good****. I've no doubt at all he'll get into worse company now.'* ASA □ *He was the white-collar one of the family, the one who was going to* ***make good*** *and redeem all their fortunes.* CON □ *They give an exotic atmosphere to the story of the bullfighter who dreams of the glory, tastes failure, and finally* ***makes good****.* OBS

make good sth[1] carry out, fulfil, sth **O:** one's promise, threat, accusation □ *They'll probably realize that I might be bluffing but while there's just the possbility that I could* ***make good*** *my threat, they'll lay off the strong arm stuff.* TBC □ *With the 1938 Munich agreement, the guarantors of Czechoslovakian independence, led by Great Britain and France, had refused to* ***make good*** *their word.* OBS □ *He made many other fine promises that have still to be* ***made good.*** □ O follows an adj Comp; usu in end position.

make good sth[2] supply a need; repair, restore, or compensate for sth **O:** loss, waste; damage, deterioration □ *Dr MacInnes is much concerned at the underequipment of the Glenelg team, and regards* ***making good*** *the lack of a stretcher as particularly important.* SC □ *The tragedy and waste of the last year—the growth forgone, the thousands unemployed—cannot be* ***made good.*** NS □ *In addition to the fee, any expenses incurred by me really ought to be* ***made good.*** □ O follows an adj Comp.

make good one's escape/flight effect, complete satisfactorily, an action or procedure **O:** escape, flight □ *I had had more than my fill of her boring chatter and when Tom and Louise came up I was thankful to* ***make good*** *my escape.* □ O follows an adj Comp.

make a good death/end [V + O] die with dignity, courage, pious resignation, etc □ (source) *I would give you some violets, but they withered all when my father died. They say he* ***made a good end.*** HAMLET IV 5 □ *You could say he* ***made a good end****. A shell-burst caught him as he was ferrying wounded across the river.* □ *'Did she* ***make a good death****?' 'I don't know. A good death,' she said, 'doesn't reside in the dignity of bearing but in the dispositions of the soul.'* MM

make a good etc showing [V + O pass] behave, perform or function creditably etc; appear to be satisfactory etc in amount or quality **adj:** good, splendid; satisfactory; poor, unsatisfactory □ *Christ can only help you through your will to help yourself. How do you think you have* ***made*** *such* ***a good showing*** *with your life so far?* AITC □ *He* ***made a*** *very* ***poor showing*** *in Parliament during the debate on the National Service Act.* MFM □ *It is an interesting question whether the various parts of the country make a contribution to the university population in proportion to their share of the general population. It seems that this is not so and that some parts of the country which might be expected to* ***make a good showing*** *fail to do so.* SC

make good etc time walk, drive, fly etc or complete a journey quickly etc **adj:** good, satisfactory; disappointing, slow □ *I did not talk to him till we were clear of the houses and* ***making good time*** *on the highway out to Bacchus March.* RFW □ *I* ***made slow time*** *down the steps but once on the flat I was all right, of course, and walked over to the enclosure.* RFW

make the grade [V + O] (informal) reach a desired standard in ability, education, social or popular acceptance, etc **S:** manager, executive;

husband, lover; athlete. **A:** for an administrative post; in show business; with his wife's friends □ *The graduate knows that the first degree has been devalued simply because of the increased number of qualified students applying for a static number of jobs. Only those students who can pass through the finest sieve* ***make the grade****.* ST □ *The other wives looked at him with approval, as at a husband who had* ***made the grade****; with their eyes and sometimes with their tongues they complimented Isabel on him.* PW □ *She wasn't a bit happy when she went off with the boat this morning. She was afraid she wouldn't* ***make the grade*** *with you.* RFW

make great etc strides [V + O pass] progress, develop, improve rapidly **adj:** great, ⚠ tremendous, terrific, enormous □ *Due chiefly to the* ***great strides made*** *in the field of prosthetics* (ie artificial limbs, valves, pacemakers etc) *much can be done to help those children to lead more comfortable or active lives.* ST □ *I specialised in guided projectiles, which were then in their infancy. I had the very great honour to work under Sir William Penney. We* ***made enormous strides****.* L □ *I thought Johnny was just stupid but he's* ***made*** *such* ***tremendous strides*** *since he went to his new school, I'm sure the teaching must have been at fault before.*

make one's hair stand on end cause one to feel extreme fear, dread, horror; give sb etc the creeps etc (qv); make one's flesh creep/crawl (qv) □ *Steve and Jack gave a talk about their trek across the Polar ice cap. It was very interesting but it* ***made my hair stand on end*** *just to hear about the dangers they faced.* □ *Jane's gone rock climbing with her new boyfriend once or twice. She says that it* ***makes her hair stand on end*** *when she looks down at hundreds of feet of empty air.*

make haste hurry; move, act, or carry out a task, quickly □ *I shouted 'Hey!' and Finn came slowly on. He never* ***makes haste****.* UTN. □ *'I'm not ready.' 'Well then you had better* ***make haste*** *and be ready.'* AITC □ *I wish she'd* ***make haste*** *to finish it.* □ sometimes followed by *to*-inf as in last example.

make hay while the sun shines (saying) make the best use one can of opportunities, favourable conditions, etc, as long as these last □ *I've heard about* ***making hay while the sun shines*** *but it's a bit mean to start chatting up your brother's girlfriend while he's in hospital.* □ (NONCE) (Patrick is having affairs with two girls) *I must say Patty-boy does seem to be going in for some pretty dedicated* ***haymaking while the sun shines****. Only snag is there's going to be a spot of rain spreading from the west before very long.* TGLY □ *For years stockbrokers complained they could not make the City function because of the Labour Government; now after three years of Heath's laissez-faire,* ***make-hay-while-the-sun-shines*** *measures they still complain bitterly of the harvest they haven't reaped because others have not sown it properly.* OBS □ attrib use, *a* ***make-hay-while-the-sun-shines*** *attitude*, unusual. ⇨ ⚠ make hay of (Vol 1).

make headway [V + O pass] move forward in an intended course or direction; progress satisfactorily; make progress (qv) **S:** boat, dinghy; project, scheme; student, trainee. **det:** no; little; some. **adj:** rapid; slow; noticeable □ *On some narrow stretches they* ***made*** *such feeble* ***headway*** *against the current that it saved time to carry the canoes and walk.* □ *A course of Thackeray, that's my prescription, soon weed out these little faults. Then you might* ***make*** *some real* ***headway****.* HD □ *He said that the total defence expenditure must be reduced to £600 million. No* ***headway*** *was* ***made*** *on this proposal.* MFM

make sb's heart bleed cause one/sb to feel extreme sorrow and pity □ *But you should have seen poor old Jim. It would have* ***made my heart bleed****, if I hadn't guessed he'd been such a sodding fool, getting wed with a nice tart and then making a mess of it all.* LLDR □ *The quiet pain and loneliness he suffered after his wife's death* ***made*** *his daughter****'s heart bleed****.* □ pl make their hearts bleed; sometimes ironic.

make history [V + O pass] have done, or taken part in, sth important enough to be recorded in the world's or one's country's history; do sth unusual or important, esp sth never done before, in an art, science, profession or sport **adj:** medical, legal; racing, golfing □ *We were deeply stirred. Then Churchill stood up, his eyes full of tears. 'We have* ***made history*** *tonight,' he said.* L □ *'Some people are going to* ***make history*** *and some aren't,' Taffy said. 'I think this'll go down in the history books. It deserves to.'* ST □ *It is, no doubt, an enviable life: travelling the world, staying in first-class hotels, being at the centre of events, watching* ***history*** *being* ***made****.* L □ *Then there was a confused reference to the Beard case, which* ***made*** *legal* ***history*** *back in 1920.* RT □ *Floyd Patterson* ***made*** *boxing* ***history*** *at the Polo Grounds here tonight by sensationally defeating Sweden's Ingemar Johansson and becoming the first man ever to regain the world heavyweight title.* DM

make it [V + O] (informal) achieve what one intends, plans or hopes to do or obtain □ *I should be up at half past seven tomorrow morning. I'll never* ***make it****. I'll just have to be late.* TOH □ *Often, on holiday, the travelling turns out to be the best bit. Arriving has a certain brief triumph—'Well, we* ***made it****'—but made what?* SC □ *He left me in February 1955 to take up an appointment as a scriptwriter with the BBC. I was very sorry to see him go and I told him that he could have a job with me any time he wanted it, because I didn't expect him to* ***make it****.* RT □ *You know that film stars have* ***made it*** *when their Press officers start protecting them from Press exposure rather than courting it.* ST □ *I want to be taken seriously as a short story writer and, by God, I hope I* ***make it****.* L □ objectives achieved range from arriving on time to realizing a life's ambition.

make it one's business to do sth be determined, or be careful, to do sth thought necessary or desirable □ *If Ned had known you were in this kind of state, he'd have* ***made it his business to*** *help you.* CON □ *There is this old aunt in Putney. I shall* ***make it my business to*** *call on her.* DC □ *I* ***made it my business to*** *know all commanders and to insist on a high standard.* MFM

make it snappy (informal) be quick to do or in doing sth required, requested etc □ *Micky slapped a pound note down on the counter. 'Make* *that three* (ie drinks)*,' he ordered. 'And **make it snappy**.'* PE □ *'May I ask a favour of you?' 'Ask away, but **make it snappy**. I should have been out of here five minutes ago.'* □ often imper.

make itself felt cause one/others to be keenly aware of sth **S:** emotion; power, influence; move, action □ *He was having his tonsils out, which is a severe operation for an ageing man; but even his fear did not **make itself felt** in any marked way.* HD □ *In another few weeks the full effects of the shortage will **make themselves felt** both in industry and at home.* □ *Dislike of a person can **make itself felt** even if never expressed.* ⇨ ⚠ make one's presence felt.

make etc (sb/sth) a laughing stock [V + O + Comp pass] make a person, institution or object appear ridiculous **V:** make; be, become □ *Mike said that once the papers had really established my character they weren't going to explode it all later and **make** themselves **a laughing-stock.*** JFTR □ *He and his attempts to revive the old customs **are** just **a** local **laughing stock**.* □ *I couldn't argue with a man like that in public. He'd **make a laughing stock of** me.* □ variant make a laughing stock of sb/sth.

make (sb's) life a misery [V + O + Comp pass] cause sb to be miserable, unhappy or to suffer pain, discomfort in daily life □ HELEN: *Don't worry, you'll soon be an independent working woman and free to go where you please.* JO: *The sooner the better. I'm sick of you. You've **made my life a misery**.* TOH □ ***The lives of** those women, already far advanced, were **made a misery** by the Matron who treated them with unremitting despotism.* UTN □ *Terence Bendicson hates cars. They are a vicious enemy—smelling, roaring, spewing out pollution, and generally **making life a misery**.* NS

make sth (look/seem) like new clean, mend, polish etc sth so well that it looks as it did when new □ *Between them was a card on which was written: 'The Marks' Dry Cleaning Service **Makes** Your Clothes **Like New**.'* PE □ *There are no dents in the body—a re-spray will **make** your car **look like new**.* ⇨ ⚠ (as) good as new.

make a/one's living [V + O] gain sufficient money, esp earned income, to support oneself (and one's family) **adj:** (a) good, comfortable; meagre, bare. **A:** by writing; off the land; in some other way □ SARAH: *Dave is making furniture by hand.* MONTY: *He **makes a living**?* SARAH: *They live! They're not prosperous but they live.* CSWB □ *The outer world is what we wake up to every morning of our lives, is the place where, willy-nilly, we must try to **make our living**.* DOP □ *Company executives travelling by air are notoriously indiscreet—you can overhear enough on air planes to **make a** good **living** if you know how to make use of it.* RT ⇨ ⚠ earn one's/its keep; earn a/one's living.

make oneself/sb look etc a fool etc do or say sth that directs the amusement, criticism or scorn of others upon oneself/sb; make a fool of (Vol 1) (qv); make a fool of oneself (Vol 1) (qv) **V:** look, ⚠ seem, appear. **Comp:** a fool, ⚠ an ass, an idiot □ *Having been **made to look a fool** torments some people far more than consciousness of having done wrong ever could.* □ *The practical question, therefore, is whether the Americans will **make themselves look silly** by wasting their substance* (= money) *on preparations for another manned flight.* NSC □ variant make oneself/sb look etc foolish/silly/ridiculous etc.

make a loss/profit [V + O pass] lose/gain money in a financial transaction □ *Although so far this year Exeter's Theatre Royal has still **made a loss**, its future is much brighter than earlier in the year when there was talk of closing down.* T □ *It is a Working Men's Club, run as a non-**profit making** concern.* □ adj compounds loss-making, profit-making.

make one's mark [V + O pass] become successful and well-known generally or in certain circles; especially contribute to or influence an art, science, sport etc **A:** in his chosen profession; on the stage □ *Bellew quickly **made his mark**. Within a few years of his return from India, he was reckoned the most popular Church of England preacher in London.* L □ *Malcolm, who is a quiet but determined young rider has now **made his mark** on the international show jumping front.* ST □ *Perhaps expectations were too high after **the mark made** by 'Revival' at this year's Dublin Theatre Festival.* OBS □ *Will the international school **make its mark** in education?* ST □ also pl *They both **made their mark**.* ⇨ ⚠ leave one's/its mark.

make a match [V + O] arrange or effect a marriage **adj:** good, excellent; unhappy. **A:** for his daughter; between them; of it □ *In order to **make a** good **match** for his daughter a dowry of a score or so head of cattle was required.* SC □ *Know where he's gone? Off again to see that ex-wife of his in Ostberg. Mark my words they'll **make a match** of it again some day.* US □ *He had only met the dowager once; but that did not diminish his need to improve his finances by **making a match** of convenience.* NS □ *He was still a bachelor despite the efforts of all the village **matchmakers** on his behalf.* □ *Oh, don't take Lucy too seriously. **Matchmaking** is definitely her favourite hobby. Just warn your new boyfriend about her.* □ n compounds a matchmaker, matchmaking.

make matters/things worse [V + O + Comp pass] worsen an already dangerous, undesirable or awkward situation or condition □ *They were born expressly to hate and destroy one another, and the fact that they maintained a crude ceremony in their manners only **made matters worse**.* BN □ *To **make matters worse**, Harvie, in part two, goes on to cast doubts on the very probability theory on which the experiment was based.* SC □ *'That's the best I can do,' she said, her deliberate patience no way to stop his grumbling. And the fact that he detected it **made things worse**.* LLDR □ often *to **make matters/things worse*** in front position, expressing result (not purpose).

make merry be lively, boisterous, in a sociable way—laughing, talking, singing, dancing, eating, drinking etc—when celebrating a festive occasion □ JASON: *Wake up, make it lively. This is a wedding. Bring out the bunting, **make merry**, look alive, if you can.* DPM □ *Henry and I* (twins) *looked alike, dressed alike, thought alike, did everything together as kids. We were a bit of a handful at school, and naturally **made merry** blaming each other for any spot of bother.* TVT □

n compounds a merrymaker, merrymaking.

make etc mischief [V + O pass] play (provoking) pranks; do or say sth calculated to upset or annoy others, to disrupt arrangements or proceedings; provoke misunderstanding or hostility betwen people by malicious gossip or lies **V:** make, ⚠ do, cause □ *He would have been happier if his cargo had consisted of more freight and fewer passengers. Passengers, having nothing to occupy them, were always* ***making mischief*** *one way and another.* TST □ *He had never in the past hesitated to* ***make mischief*** *if it served his curiosity.* MM □ *She had a tactless tongue, but it came from a honest heart, not from a desire to* ***do mischief****.* AITC □ *I advise you to ignore Ada's insinuations about your sister-in-law. She's a known* ***mischief-maker****.* □ n compounds a mischief-maker, mischief-making.

make money [V + O pass] earn money, or acquire it by other means, eg speculation, ingenuity, dishonest practice **det:** some, a bit of; a lot of; (not) much, (not) any. **A:** out of the deal, from sub-letting; by writing novels; for the Club □ *People think so much of* ***money*** *these days that they underrate women — or themselves—if they're not actually* ***making*** *it.* RT □ *The way he saw it, Ned was making him a bit of a sermon, to clear his own conscience for being a business man and* ***making money****.* CON □ *You're a Templar. You must know ways of* ***making money****. They all did, didn't they?* DC □ *I like the way you edit this magazine, but you'll never* ***make*** *any* ***money****.* L □ *Today golf, too, has turned into a* ***money-making*** *industry.* SC □ adj and n compound money-making.

make a move [V + O pass] take some action **det:** a, any, some, no; a single □ *The high sales target is less important than the methods by which the target is supposed to be hit: the canny manager has to be fully satisfied on both counts — the means and the end—before he* ***makes a move****.* OBS □ *I knew that the guys might try to get me. I was trying to find out what was going on in town before I* ***made any move*** *whatsoever.* OBS □ *It seems that we were both anxious to patch up our quarrel but were each waiting for the other to* ***make the*** *first* ***move****.*

make a/one's name [V + O] become famous, or well-known in certain circles; make a name for oneself (Vol 1) (qv) **A:** as a novelist; in the legal profession; with his invention □ *I infallibly know that I shall* ***make a name*** *and that soon. But I should like to be a legend.* L □ *Livingstone had been exploring since 1849, and back in the mid-1850s* ***made his name*** *as the first white man to walk across Africa.* OBS □ *Born in New York, Mr Condon certainly* ***made his name*** *over here with his novel 'The Manchurian Candidate'.* SC □ also pl make their names(s).

make no mistake (about sth) [Disj] do not be misled by appearances into believing sth that subsequent events or further information will show to be untrue or not the case □ *Alison looks very quiet and retiring but,* ***make no mistake about*** *it, she's a very determined career woman.* □ *Most Britons believe that this country could never have the sort of race riots experienced in the United States in recent years.* ***Make no mistake****, it could happen here.* □ imper.

make no odds [V + O] not affect an issue, argument, result or probability (from betting); what's the odds? (qv) **det:** no; ⚠ (very) little, not much. **A:** whether he's there or not; how it's achieved; which way we do it □ *With talented children it* ***makes*** *very* ***little odds*** *which method is used. They will learn to read by, or in spite of, any method.* □ *'You should have tried to dissuade him.' 'It would have* ***made no odds*** *if I had.'*

make old bones [V + O] live to be an old man or woman □ *Slightly underweight people of active habit have a better chance of* ***making old bones*** *than their well-covered brothers and sisters.* □ *I have a feeling I won't* ***make old bones****, you know. I take after my mother's people and they were a short-lived family on the whole.* □ *When not admiring the clothes, I made a mental note of the faces that would* ***make*** *beautiful* ***old bones****.* SC □ often neg.

(one can't) make an omelette without breaking eggs (saying) (one cannot) achieve a desired victory, reform, or other (important) aim without sacrificing sth, causing loss or damage to sb/sth involved □ (reorganizing the Indian Archaeological Department) *It is not difficult to count both the losses and the gains.* ***You can't have omelettes without breaking eggs****, and I have no doubt that the omelette which eventually emerged justified the breaking of a good many eggs.* SD □ (NONCE) *The one thing the experiment demonstrates, if such proof were necessary, is that* ***broken eggs*** *do not in themselves* ***make an omelette****.* L □ (NONCE) *It was all in a good cause — perhaps — as my favourite political slogan has it you* ***can*** *indeed* ***break eggs without making an omelette****.* NS □ reversing the phrases make an omelette and break eggs (as in second and third examples) changes the sense to give meaning 'disruptive change does not always lead to the desired end'.

make or break etc be crucial in making sb/sth either a success or a failure, kindly or unkindly thought of, etc **V:** break, ⚠ mar, destroy. **O:** boy; reputation; firm; enthusiasm □ *The women's tongues ruled the neighbourhood. They could* ***make or break*** *a character.* AITC □ *When Britain comes into Europe, the shock of facing reality will either* ***make or destroy*** *her.* OBS □ *The Itinerant Theatre scheme of the Greater London Arts Association will be* ***made or broken*** *within the next two weeks.* ST □ *Those who really know in the movie business know that Homer K. Pringsheim is the power behind the throne and the* ***maker or breaker*** *of many a film career.* UTN □ *Terence Hodden is an English bachelor and some sort of 'middle manager' who is being given a* ***make-or-break*** *chance with a Roman firm.* T □ n compound a maker-or-breaker; attrib use *a* ***make-or-break*** *chance.*

make a/one's pile [V + O pass] (informal) amass a fortune or a great deal of money, esp in business □ *'Think of all the philanthropists you have ever known!' 'They didn't start being generous till they had* ***made their pile****,' said Mrs Eastwood.* PW □ *Sometimes self-made men would have Grade Ten wives whom they'd been hooked by before they'd* ***made their pile****.* RATT

make one's point [V + O pass] propose, and usu gain acceptance for, a particular opinion, argument etc **det:** one's; a, the; one. **adj:** obvious, additional; important; minor □ *Dr Both-*

wick with the air of a debater who has ***made his point****, sat back in his chair complacently enough.* EM ▫ *A comparison of the layout of a magazine in the older style with one in the newer style* ***makes my*** *general* ***point*** *even more forcefully.* UL ▫ *I'll just* ***make the*** *obvious* ***point*** *that the mere fact of being brought up in a town where everything was shabby, dirty, dwarfish, peeling and generally lousy was another thing that helped to make most of us competitive.* CON ▫ *Hingley also seeks to contrast the real facts of Stalin's life and the legends. This, too, is quite a good idea which becomes rather tedious when* ***the point*** *has been* ***made****.* OBS ⇨ ⚠ take etc sb's point; miss the point (of sth).

make one's presence felt [V + O + Comp] make others keenly aware of one's presence or existence by force of personality, superior ability, aggressive behaviour, etc ▫ *At this point their father, out of a desire to* ***make his presence felt****, told the children to sit up and behave themselves.* ▫ (race-horses) *And even before the halfway stage of the season, the new flow of American-bred youngsters are already* ***making their presence felt*** *in our two-year-old races.* OBS ▫ *Most constructive criticism in any society comes from a minority and, since the democratic way of* ***making your presence felt*** *is to speak, rather than go out in the street and start throwing things, the minority are 'vocal'.* L ⇨ ⚠ make itself felt.

make progress [V + O pass] move forward; advance further towards success or completion; make headway (qv); improve in one's health after injury or illness **S:** convoy, column; survey, project; patient, wounded (man). **det:** no, (not) any; some; little, (not) much. **adj:** good, better; rapid; slow ▫ *The snow here was firm and smooth but not icy and so we* ***made*** *better* ***progress****.* ▫ *But the general disarmament conversations seem to be* ***making*** *no* ***progress*** *and might as well be suspended now.* SC ▫ *Though not a brilliant scholar, James is* ***making*** *steady* ***progress*** *in most subjects.* ▫ *At the hospital, the two survivors were* ***making progress*** *but were not well enough to be questioned.* ▫ *Some* ***progress*** *was* ***made*** *towards agreement.*

make the punishment fit the crime (catchphrase) punish sb as nearly as possible in the way he caused others to suffer ▫ (source) *My object all sublime/I shall achieve in time—/ To* ***let the punishment fit the crime****— /The punishment fit the crime.* THE MIKADO (W S GILBERT 1836-1911) ▫ *It's the old story of* ***making punishments fit crimes*** *rather than individuals, already seen to be wrong in relation to child offenders and anyone still open to reformative influences.* NS ▫ *'Molese over-reacted— but then so did Julius Rudel in firing him. Did* ***the punishment*** *really* ***fit the crime****?' he asked.* L

make the running [V + O pass] in a race, take the lead and/or set the pace which other competitors must maintain if they hope to win; (fig) take the lead in a conversation, argument, course of action, forcing or encouraging others to conform and compete **S:** competitor; firm, industry ▫ *Johnson after having* ***made*** *most of* ***the running*** *previously had left himself with nothing in reserve for the last sprint.* ▫ *At dinner he talked little; but he opened up readily if you* ***made the running****.* MFM ▫ *With the cool relations that exist between the airlines and the BAA* (British Airports Authority), *the danger is that all* ***the running*** *will be* ***made*** *by the unions, goaded by 'subversives'.* OBS ▫ *Excellent results from Sir Jules Thorn last week focused stock market attention on other electronics firms, which as a sector can hardly claim to have* ***made the running*** *this year.* ST ▫ *At the tea party Alec certainly* ***made the running*** *with Irma.* PW

make oneself scarce (informal) go away, esp leave a group or company because it is wise or tactful to do so, either in one's own interests or sb else's ▫ *The only way I could have punished them was by keeping them in after school, and I had every intention of* ***making myself scarce*** *the moment the bell sounded.* SPL ▫ HELEN: *I've come here to talk to my daughter. Can you* ***make yourself scarce*** *for a bit?* TOH ▫ *The assistants know exactly when to appear with a ready-heated piece of glass, when to* ***make themselves scarce****.* OBS

make a scene [V + O pass] display, to another person or publicly, one's anger, disapproval, opposition, grief etc in a noisy, unpleasant or embarrassing way ▫ *I could hardly face the thought of seeing Magdalen at once. She would expect me to* ***make a scene*** *and I didn't feel energetic enough to* ***make a scene****.* UTN ▫ *He longed to escape from Caroline—her whining or scolding importunities, and the dreadful public* ***scenes*** *she* ***made****.* OBS ▫ *She was terrified she would burst into tears and* ***make a scene****. Somehow or other, though, she managed to get up calmly and walk with David towards the lift.* WI

make sense[1] be intelligible; convey a meaning **S:** remark, comments; sentence, text; painting, sculpture. **def:** no, (not) any. **adj:** grammatical, logical, musical ▫ *I wrote out the advertisement on the back of an old envelope and read it aloud to see if it* ***made sense****.* PP ▫ *You have to wait close on three extended movements for one of its* (a musical composition's) *major inspirations, which wouldn't* ***make sense*** *without them.* L ▫ *Often, what a child tries to say at that age* ***makes*** *no* ***sense*** *to anyone but his mother.* ▫ often neg. ⇨ ⚠ make sense of (Vol 1).

make sense[2] be or seem sensible, wise, correct **S:** behaviour, rule of conduct; arrangement, procedure; it... (to do sth). **det:** no; little; a lot of. **adj:** good, sound ▫ *It* ***makes sense*** *to have better advice and selection.* L ▫ *Only the top division of 12 clubs should operate on a national basis; the other three sections should be regional. This* ***makes*** *a lot of* ***sense****.* OBS ▫ *They all have their peculiar notions of reward and punishment which never seem to* ***make sense*** *to the outside world.* NS

make etc a speech [V + O pass] speak formally to an audience on a specific subject and/or on a specific occasion; speak to sb as if one were speaking formally to an audience etc **V:** make, ⚠ deliver, give. **adj:** long, short; after-dinner; boring, amusing ▫ *I* ***made*** *some eighty* ***speeches*** *in four weeks, most of them impromptu and all fully reported.* MFM ▫ *Cindy* ***made a*** *sincere little* ***speech*** *in which she thanked everyone for their kindness, especially George.* PE ▫ *The man with the screwdriver sat down on top of* *the ladder and began to* ***make a speech****.* OMIH □ *speak* may have the same meaning, as in *I've been asked to* ***speak*** *on Founder's Day*; n compounds a speech-maker, speech-making.

make a (big/tremendous) splash [V + O pass] (informal) do sth conspicuous and extravagant, esp spend a lot of money on a social function, a treat for oneself, etc □ *In all these acts one is 'aving* (= having) *a go, a fling,* ***making a splash****. It is a short-lived splash, but a good one, because most of the rest of life is humdrum and regulated.* UL □ *He hadn't much appetite for the feast he had insisted on providing. It wasn't simply self-indulgence, the wish to compensate himself for the lean times he'd been having; nor was it, wholly, the desire to* ***make a splash*** *and assert himself in front of Ned.* CON

make/take a stand [V + O pass] resist and not flee the enemy forces, or a physical attack; (fig) adopt and make known a firm attitude of defence against, or opposition to, sb/sth **adj:** last, firm, determined. **A:** against their pursuers; at that point; on this issue □ *The Americans swung in between us and the Indians, bunched them like sheep into a compact body. How they wailed and cried, for the poor Indian felt he had* ***made his*** *last* ***stand****.* OBS □ *'We'd like to have you on our platform.' Bernard thought that the moment had come to* ***make a stand****. 'I'm afraid that's quite unlikely,' he said.* HAA □ *Which is not at all to say that when* ***a stand*** *has to be* ***made*** *on some clear issue of principle one is without means.* L □ *He shook his head. He had* ***taken his stand****, and he was not going to be persuaded to change his mind.* AITC □ take a stand usu fig.

make sth stick (informal) prove, substantiate, validate, or make effective, esp sth said about or against sb/sth **O:** charge, accusation; agreement; decision □ *I believe that under the British system of government, a Minister can take an unpopular decision which he believes to be right and* ***make*** *it* ***stick****.* L □ *Above all, there was the question: could the Provisionals* ***make*** *a cease-fire* ***stick****, or were there breakaway groups who would carry on the fight?* L □ *The word 'ruthless' also comes up, but is never quite* ***made*** *to* ***stick****. 'I can understand people saying that,' said an acquaintance, 'but to be ruthless one must be aware of doing harm, and I am sure that is beside the point.'* ST □ *The charge is that the producers of the programme either deliberately misrepresented its nature, or foolishly slid into changing its purpose during production — or both. Of course, it is a matter of judgement whether* ***the charge sticks*** (or: *is* ***made*** *to* ***stick***). L

make sb tired [V + O + Comp] (informal) be or appear tiresome, exasperating, difficult to understand or deal with **S:** argument, discussions; manners, ways; he, you □ *'Why did you agree to come here with me, then?' 'I thought you were a gentleman.' 'You* ***make*** *me* ***tired****.' 'Take me home please.'* PM □ *If I thought you believed it I might argue with you but that kind of soppy condescending talk just* ***makes*** *me* ***tired****.* □ O often me, us.

make/cause trouble [V + O pass] show or stir up physical violence, or other kind of disturbance; cause difficulties, friction etc in the lives of others **det:** more; a lot of; (not) any. **A:** for anyone; between husband and wife □ *'You seem to have come here,' the professor said 'with the sole purpose of* ***making trouble****.'* OMIH □ *It wasn't clever to make a pass at the secretary like that. She can* ***make trouble*** *for you with the boss.* □ *I'll go. I don't want to* ***cause*** *any* ***trouble****. God knows I didn't come here for that.* AITC □ *I don't say that she's a* ***trouble-maker*** *by intention, but trouble arises wherever she's around for long.* □ n compound a trouble-maker.

make oneself useful do useful work; do a specific, perhaps small, task to help or oblige sb □ *Tom spent all his summer holiday in the fields,* ***making himself useful*** *in the hope that his father would relent and allow him to leave school.* □ HELEN: *If you're going in there take these flowers with you and put them in water. You might as well* ***make yourself useful****.* TOH □ *Now, if you want to* ***make yourself useful*** *will you grind some coffee and put it in the percolator?* □ often part of a direct request to do sth.

make one's voice heard be audible when one speaks; have others consider or accept one's opinion, decision, protest etc □ *I tried to warn him but couldn't* ***make my voice heard*** *above the roar of wind and water.* □ *'I'm surprised the Professor hasn't opposed these changes.' 'Don't worry, he'll* ***make his voice heard*** *yet.'* □ *People won't do as they should — simply get moving and work through one of our political parties. They should* ***make their voices heard****.* G

make/pass water urinate □ *...Robert standing in the lee of a slag-heap* ***making water*** *while two nuns look the other way.* CON □ *'Do you have any pain when you* ***pass water****?' the doctor asked.*

make sth work cause sth to function effectively **O:** machine, car; scheme, arrangements; system □ *He found no faults in any of the parts but still couldn't* ***make*** *the wretched lamp* ***work****.* □ *If Colombia reverts to more conventional democracy, the rest of Latin America will be waiting to see if she can* ***make*** *it* ***work****.* OBS □ *Simpson resisted the appointment very strongly and he finally told Jenkins that his advice remained against it, but he would accept it and try and* ***make*** *it* ***work****.* ST □ passive as in *It can be* ***made*** *to work.*

a male chauvinist (pig/swine) man whose attitudes and behaviour towards women are governed by the assumption that his is the superior sex (catchphrase of the early 1970s, associated with the women's liberation movement) □ *Under no circumstances will I watch 'Miss United Kingdom' (Friday, BBC1). I have been* ***a male chauvinist pig****, I admit it. But I am at last gaining a sneaking respect for women and I think these contests are degrading.* RT □ *I am writing this review whilst coping with howling children, and therefore am sensitive to being dubbed* ***a male chauvinist pig****.* L □ *Jack's* ***a*** *real* ***male chauvinist swine****. Both he and his wife work full-time, but he refuses to help with the housework.* □ *The Unions, sometimes accused of being strongholds of* ***male chauvinism*** *claim with some truth that women workers themselves are singularly unenthusiastic about membership, support or office-bearing.* ST □ *I envy my wife's unvarying progress through tea, half a* *grapefruit, a boiled egg, coffee, bread and lime marmalade. As I stamp around the kitchen preparing these things (no* ***male chauvinist pigs*** *in our sty) a mad menu of possibilities flits through my mind.* NS □ variant male chauvinism.

a man about town (dated or facetious) a man, esp of the upper classes, who is knowledgeable about and habitually frequents the restaurants, clubs, theatres and other social meeting places of a city □ *Bellew's* (a Church of England clergyman) *name appears in many mid-Victorian memoirs, but rather those of authors, journalists, bohemians,* ***men-about-town****, than of ecclesiastics.* L □ *'Quite the* ***man about town*** *you've become, haven't you?' she said scathingly, 'with your talk of decent little eating-places and sharing jokes with critics at a preview.'*

a man etc after one's own heart [Comp (NP)] sb etc of exactly the kind one likes best, because he etc matches an ideal **V:** ⚠ be, seem; find; reveal oneself/itself to be. **n:** man, woman, companion; house, village; occupation, task □ *John's* ***a man after my own heart****: he likes music, poetry, wine and long-distance walking in the mountains.* □ *To Pop, it now began to seem that he might have met* ***a character after his own heart*** *and kind.* DMB □ *Near Huelgoat, in the middle of Finistère, we found* ***an oppidum*** (= a Roman fortified town) ***after our own heart****.* SD

the man at the top the head of an administration, or of a financial, industrial, or trading concern of some size and complexity—either as an individual or as a type □ *Lewis had created a situation whereby it was possible for* ***the man at the top*** *to fiddle elections, embezzle union funds and do away with potential rivals.* ST □ (aircraft construction) *Inevitably new inventions during the development period would suggest modifications on the whole design. Mid-course decisions have often proved unfortunate for Britain, and more depends on the judgement of* ***the man at the top*** *than on any other single factor.* SC □ *In the case of unusual complaints, it is best to try to go straight to* ***the man at the top****.*

man and beast [n + n non-rev] the human race and all animal kind contrasted either with vegetable and inanimate matter or with each other **conj:** and; or, nor □ *The birds may be drawn to casual death against the wings and into the engines of aircraft. This phenomenon can be fatal to both* ***man and beast****.* OBS □ *In Antarctica the sea is the source of life and food. Lichens spread on stones during the milder season but nothing to support* ***man or beast****.* □ *When the wind is in the east/'Tis neither good for* ***man nor beast****.* POPULAR RHYME (ANONYMOUS)

man bites dog (catchphrase) a definition of what constitutes 'news', sth worthy of being reported, esp in the popular press □ (source) *When a dog bites a man that is not news, but when a* ***man bites*** *a* ***dog*** *that is news.* C A DANA 1819-97 □ *Deviation from the norm is, by definition, interesting and newsworthy. This crude rule of thumb seems to play a considerable role in shaping the output of the mass media, and, in simple cases of the '****Man Bites Dog****' variety, probably works quite well.* NS □ (reader's letter) *That sort of thing, though it undoubtedly descends to the level of '****man bites dog****' journalism, is perhaps unavoidable nowadays.* L □ *The hourly snippets of news had left one with the impression that, war or no war, there wasn't much news; no* ***dog*** *had been* ***bitten****.* L □ pass, as in last example, unusual and facetious.

man and boy [n + n non-rev] for all or most of one's life; from the time of speaking back to when one was a boy □ *Bert Thomas has worked for British Leyland, Longbridge,* ***man and boy*** *for 30 years.* RT □ *If anyone has been with the BBC* ***man and boy*** *it's Charles Chilton. He told how he joined up before Broadcasting House was even opened.* L □ functions as an A (of duration).

the man for the job sb whose qualifications, ability or temperament are suitable for a post or special task □ (advertisement) *Whereas in Spain it has been usual to employ people who are friends of friends, in Rumasa* (wine growers and distillers) *they take on* ***the*** *best* ***man*** *(or rare indeed in Spain, woman)* ***for the job.*** ST □ (cricket) *In three tests Greenidge opened with Fredericks without ever looking quite* ***the man for the job****.* OBS

a man etc in his position a man etc wielding the power, holding the responsible post, earning the large income, etc that he does **n:** man, ⚠ woman; anybody; people. **det:** his, her, your, our, their □ *What's* ***a man in his position*** *doing playing around with a bunch of gamblers and crooks?* □ *I'd have thought* ***a man in your position*** *would be travelling First-Class.* □ pl men in their position; stress pattern a man in 'his position; not the same as in his, your etc position (= 'in his, your etc particular circumstances as an individual') as in ***In his position****, I'd probably have done the same.*

the man in the street the average citizen, esp that category of people who do not have the special knowledge or skills appropriate to sth being discussed; the common man (qv) □ *The miners are talking about the possible necessity of strike action to defend their industry. This puzzles* ***the man in the street****.* DM □ ***The man in the street*** *never learned of the existence of life in the Cloud, for as time went on events took such a turn as to make secrecy quite imperative.* TBC □ *All major brands (of petrol) have comparably high quality: '****The man in the street*** *cannot discern the difference and doesn't want to be able to.'* ST ⇨ ⚠ the common man.

the man etc one most loves to hate [Comp (NP)] sb or sth that one takes a positive pleasure in disliking, despising or criticizing **V:** ⚠ be, become; make sb. **n:** man; actor, politician, announcer; show, programme □ *For every viewer who 'mustn't miss him tonight' there is another for whom he is* ***the man one most loves to hate****.* □ *Enid Blyton, the most materially successful children's writer ever, has become* ***the writer parents, teachers, librarians*** *and even* ***her*** *own* ***ex-readers most love to hate****.* NS □ (TV news bulletins) *Longer versions of the same inserts are interspersed with comments from, on or against one of* ***the Men You Love To Hate****, often Enoch Powell.* L □ *On the other hand, the loud-mouthed, over-confident types can serve a purpose: as* ***those contestants the public loves to hate****.* TVT

a man of action sb with physical or practical prowess, who engages in vigorous exploits; sb who is swift and decisive in doing things or getting things done, in implied contrast to sb who plans, debates or weighs circumstances carefully □ *Success, of course, is infectious, and in every age intellectuals have always been charmed by literate* ***men of action***. BN □ *Alan, eager to prove himself* ***a man of action****, was for breaking down the door without waiting for the police.* □ *The deadly nyloned legs, high-kicking in slow motion, evoke an atmosphere of fetishism which, even in a film that is constantly hopping about between* ***action-man*** *stuff and ragged farce, comes as a rather surprising change of tone.* OBS □ attrib use ***action-man*** *stuff.*

a man etc of few words [Comp (NP)] a man etc who does not talk much at any time, and who, when he has something to say, does so as briefly as possible **V:** ⚠ be: regard sb as. **n:** man, ⚠ boy, woman, girl □ BOY: *I'm* ***a man of few words****. Will you marry me?* JO: *Well, I'm* ***a girl of few words****. I won't marry you but you've talked me into it.* TOH □ *Commander Beasley, who always described himself as* ***a man of few words****, said he remembered hearing about it.* WDM □ (NONCE) *Be a good girl and fetch me a new sheet of paper. Engineer Cifuentes is* ***a man of many words***. OMIH

a man of God an ordained priest, minister, clergyman etc of a Christian Church □ (decay of cathedral buildings) *And yet who's to blame? Surely not the Dean and Chapter. Theologians, mild* ***men of God****, they must rely on technical advisers; conservation is not their job.* NS □ *A Congregationalist minister from Ipswich tried to hold an impromptu ceremony. The rector sallied out to object. There were high words between the two* ***men of God***. NS □ *A rabbi was not considered really* ***a man of God****. He was considered a man who knows the law, ie the teachings of the Talmud. They went to my father to ask all kinds of questions about the law.* L

the man/lady of the house the (co-) householder, esp of a family home □ SARAH: *Look at him!* ***The man of the house****! Why don't you talk to me? I'm your wife, aren't I?* CSWB □ *If it's* ***the lady of the house*** *you want to see, that's my mother-in-law and she's not in.* □ *Sir Walter Scott built himself a mansion, Abbotsford, in the Scottish borders, so that as his literary reputation grew he would have the satisfaction of feeling himself* ***master of a*** *suitably imposing* ***house***. □ variant (formal or facetious) master/mistress of the house (ie a large household with servants). ⇨ ⚠ master/mistress in one's own house.

a man of letters (formal) a writer of essays, poetry, criticism, novels etc intended, or likely, to be of lasting literary worth □ *When one meditates on the material and personal disadvantages with which Samuel Johnson started, and simultaneously reflects on his achievement as* ***a man of letters*** *and a moralist...* L □ *All at once respectable* ***men of*** *science and* ***letters*** *can think of nothing so exciting as to go off on a military expedition to Egypt.* BN

a man etc of (many) parts [Comp (NP)] a man with a (wide) range of gifts and interests **V:** ⚠ be, become; make oneself. **n:** man, ⚠ lad, (young) woman □ *This is Francis Crawford of Lymond,* ***a*** *hard-riding, hard-living* ***man of parts****, and something much more complex than a mere iron-fisted soldier.* SC □ (paperback 'thrillers') *Not an author gets through to print who is not '****a man of many parts****', and if he has not been a pianist in a brothel or a cowboy on the South American pampas, he is at least a Regius Professor of Divinity.* NS □ *It follows that a good psychologist must be* ***a man of*** *several* ***parts****. He must be original and creative, but he must also be critical and destructive.* SNP

a man etc of substance [Comp (NP)] sb who owns a considerable amount of money, property, or land **V:** ⚠ be, become; make sb. **n:** man, ⚠ woman; person, citizen, country squire □ *You have made a fine acquisition and I shall not be the last to envy you deeply. If I were* ***a man of substance****, I am afraid I should not have brought it to your attention* (ie I'd have bought it myself). US □ *Ideally, the candidate we'd like to put forward would be* ***a man of*** *some* ***substance****, already known in the country.* □ man is n usu used; also pl men of substance.

a man/woman of his/her word [Comp (NP)] sb who keeps promises, does as he/she says he/she will **V:** ⚠ be; find sb; regard sb as □ *You're* ***a woman of your word****, I see. Most people would have made this weather an excuse not to come so far to visit a grumpy old man.* □ *There was no point at all in the death of this pretty young woman, except that Buffet presumably wished to demonstrate that he was* ***a man of his word***. NS □ also pl men/women of their word.

a man/woman of the world [Comp (NP)] sb with much experience of different types of society, public affairs, business etc and esp one inclined to take a practical, tolerant, or perhaps cynical, view of most matters **V:** ⚠ be, become; think sb □ MICK: *I mean, you're* ***a man of the world****. Can I ask your advice about something?* DAVIES: *You go right ahead.* TC □ *He belonged to a good club but Harold was* ***man of the world*** *enough to know that obscurity was sometimes a safer passport to a club than fame.* PW □ *Byron had gained the friendship of Lady Caroline's mother-in-law, the Machiavellian Lady Melbourne,* ***a*** *fascinating though elderly* ***woman of the world***. OBS □ *The boatman smiled nervously, shrugging into it a* ***man-of-the-world*** *laugh.* YWT □ attrib use *a* ***man-of-the-world*** *laugh.*

a man or a mouse [n + n non-rev] brave, determined, as a man should be, or timid and evasive like a mouse □ *Are you* ***men or mice*** *that you give up your lands and rights so easily?* □ (report of a trial in court) MR DURAND: *'Did she say anything after you had punched and hit her?' 'She said: "I am glad you did that—I wanted you to show me you are* ***a man****, not* ***a mouse****".'* T □ usu with *be*, and often interr.

man proposes but God disposes (saying) we may declare our intentions, make plans, but it is God, fate etc that decides whether they will be realized or not □ *In life,* ***man proposes, God disposes****. In the plastic arts the proposing is done by the subject matter; that which disposes is ultimately the artist's temperament.* DOP □ *We were told after 1937 that never again would the people of the Mississippi River be at the mercy of heavy rains. Well, Roosevelt and the Army Engineers might* ***propose****, but this spring* ***God disposed*** *of their cunning precautions.* L □ *He* *always lets her have her say, but in the end you'll find that* ***Linda proposes but Peter disposes****.* □ often adapted or parodied, as shown.

(every) man, woman and child [n + n + n non-rev] every living person □ *I fear you will be preparing for a situation in which* ***every man, woman and child*** *will meet their death, in which not an animal, nor any plant will remain alive.* TBC □ *You'd better ask Miss Bates about that. There's not* ***a man, woman or child*** *in the village but she knows their whole history.*

man's inhumanity to man (catchphrase) (the problem of) people's capacity for maltreating or exploiting others □ (source) *And man, whose heaven-erected face/The smiles of love adorn — /****Man's inhumanity to man****/Makes countless thousands mourn!* (R BURNS 1759-96) □ *The basic job of 'The Tonight Show' is to entertain. If our ten million viewers thought we were going to do 90 minutes of* ***man's inhumanity to man*** *every night, they'd rather watch test patterns.* L

a man's life [Comp (NP)] life and work that is suitable (only) for strong and active men **V:** ⚠ be; regard sth as □ *At Coldfield, new recruits are allocated to their regiments—it's* ***a man's life*** *in today's professional army, but if you don't want to be in the infantry, tough luck.* NS □ *A few had wives who'd stuck it out but it was* ***a man's life*** *really in the lumber camps.* □ used as part of a recruiting slogan by the British Army (echoed in first example).

a man's man [Comp (NP)] a man fond of masculine pursuits and masculine company, and less attracted by domesticity or the society of women. **V:** ⚠ be; think of sb as □ *In many ways he was limited. He was* ***a man's man*** *who thought that the roar of male laughter was one of the sweetest sounds on earth.* L

many are called but few are chosen (saying) although many persons may wish to qualify for entry into an élite or private group, only a few will have the ability or good fortune to succeed □ (source) *And when the king came in to see the guests, he saw there a man which had not on a wedding garment...Then said the king to the servants, '...cast him into outer darkness.'...For* ***many are called, but few are chosen****.* MATTHEW XXII 11, 13, 14 □ ***Many are called and few are chosen****, we know, but 38% is too great a second year drop-out for any university.* □ *In the Gipsy kingdom the 'rai', the wholly acceptable non-Gipsy friend, is a phenomenon. As with that kingdom* ***many are called but few are chosen****.* L

many hands make light work (saying) many helpers get a task completed more easily and quickly than one person working alone □ *We'd have to clear the lounge for the painters coming in the morning. The children can help too:* ***many hands make light work****.* ⇨ too many cooks spoil the broth.

many happy returns (of the day) the form of greeting to sb on his or her birthday □ *On 21 December, Dame Rebecca West was interviewed on Radio 3 for her 80th birthday. Dame Rebecca coped with devastatingly destructive tact.* ***Many happy returns*** *to her.* L

(for) many a long day (for) a very long period of time □ *Bowed shoulders and apprehensive glances showed an office working as it had not worked* ***for many a long day****.* SD □ *He made his way sadly downhill, knowing he was not likely to see her again* ***for many a long day****.* □ *'Women,' sighed Grimsdyke reflectively. 'Well, there's one thing,' I told him firmly. 'It's going to be* ***many a long day*** *before I get involved with another one.'* DIL

many a mickle makes a muckle (saying) small amounts of money, property, time, effort which are trifling individually can add up to a lot □ *Prudent and earnest savers, well schooled in the doctrine that* ***many a mickle makes a muckle****, and that if the pence are looked after the pounds will look after themselves, find that...* T □ *On the principle of '****many a mickle makes a muckle****' you could probably improve your fingering technique by devoting even 15 minutes a day to serious practice.*

many moons ago [A] a long time ago, esp referring to an earlier period of one's life **V:** be; happen □ *And I tell myself the tale again as I told it to myself those* ***many moons ago****.* PP □ *I weighed no more than him myself at that age, but that was* ***many moons ago****.*

many a time [A (NP)] many times; frequently; next entry (qv) □ *That post-box has always been there. You must have passed it* ***many a time****.* □ front, middle or end position.

many's the time many times; frequently; previous entry (qv) □ *My wife used to daydream rather a lot at one time you know.* ***Many's the time*** *I've opened a door or come round a corner, just like that, and seen her—miles away.* TT □ *'He says he doesn't drink much.' 'Well,* ***many's the time*** *I've seen him hardly able to stand.'* □ front position.

a mare's nest [Comp (NP)] a reported discovery, event, situation of a wonderful or startling nature which proves to be a hoax or a misinterpretation of true facts **V:** ⚠ be; find, consider, sth □ *Can you imagine what your position would be, Professor Kingsley, if you were responsible for public alarm over what turned out to be* ***a*** *mere* ***mare's nest****?* TBC □ *Visit·of A.S. seems perfectly above board. Showed no uneasiness or consciousness of being followed. And if you ask me I think it's all* ***a mare's nest****!* TCB

mark time [V + O] (military) move one's feet up and down in a marching motion without moving forward; (fig) make no advance, take no action for the time being, possibly until a suitable moment arrives □ *The soft-drinks makers have sociology on their side. The drift from the pubs, the lure of TV, and the new generation of rich teetotal teenagers have all helped them to go up, while beer* ***marks time****.* OBS □ *After all, life is a matter of taking risks, stretching yourself to limits and maybe finding you can go further than you first thought. The rest is* ***marking time****.* RT

(you) mark my words (you) notice and remember what I say, am telling you □ MRS ELLIOT: *But he'll have his own way in the end,* ***you mark my words****. He'll show them all—and you.* EGD □ *Know where he's gone? Off to see that ex-wife of his in Ostberg.* ***Mark my words****, they'll make a match of it again some day.* US □ usu imper form used as a warning or confident forecast; front or end position.

mark/mind you [Conj] let me remind you (and

myself); nevertheless; all/just the same (qv); at the same time² (qv) □ *In fact I do not know anything; so I do not bother to say anything any more. I used to once, **mark you**!* HH □ '***Mark you**, said Blaize, 'occasionally it happened that an entirely innocent trader came under suspicion.'* DS □ *Colossal* (house), *isn't it? **Mind you**, they don't use half of it.* RATT □ *If the insurance company pays up, and **mind you**, I don't expect them to,...* DC □ imper form used to draw attention to a fact, point of view, etc that contrasts with, or modifies, a previous statement; usu front or end position.

a marked man [Comp (NP)] sb whose conduct or reputation makes him liable to be distrusted, avoided, or perhaps hunted, captured or killed **V:** ⚠ be, become; make sb □ *The fact that he'd been convicted was a much more serious blow. It meant that he was now **a marked man** in Rhodesia, which was his field of operations.* DS □ *Smithers had made one financial blunder too many. From then on he was **a marked man** in the organization.* □ also pl.

a marriage of convenience a marriage arranged in order to strengthen the political, social or financial position of one or both parties □ *Friendship, a more lasting commodity than love, is as likely to result from **a marriage of convenience** as from any other.* □ *He might **marry** again **for convenience** (ie make **a marriage of convenience**). Elderly widowers often do.* □ also pl marriages of convenience; variant marry for convenience.

the marriage of true minds (formal) any alliance or relationship based on mutual respect, identity of interests, beliefs held in common □ (source) *Let me not to **the marriage of true minds**/Admit impediments.* SONNET 116 (SHAKESPEARE) □ RUTH: *Yours should look an intriguing couple on the dance floor tonight. I'm tempted to come myself.* GEORGE: *Why don't you?* RUTH: *I should hate to break up **this marriage of true minds**.* EGD

marry in haste, repent at leisure (saying) a marriage hastily entered into is liable to result in one's regretting it over a long period □ (source) *Thus grief still treads upon the heels of pleasure:/**Marry'd in haste**, we may **repent at leisure**.* THE OLD BACHELOR (W CONGREVE 1670-1729) □ '***Marry in haste, repent in leisure**,' she thinks. But how much and how often will she disappoint him?* L □ use of in, as in second quote, is rare.

marry money [V + O] marry a wealthy person (implication is not necessarily that financial gain is the only reason) □ *'She made a fortune,' Godfrey remarked. 'Retired in 1893 and **married money** both times. I wonder what she has left?'* MM □ *'Who is she?' 'Her father owns a factory near Ledderford. He's on the Warley Council.' She looked at me with a curious pity. 'Money **marries money**, lad. Be careful she doesn't break your heart.'* RATT □ money marries money (second example) is a saying = 'sb who is wealthy is likely to choose as a marriage partner sb else who is also wealthy'.

(not) the marrying kind etc [Comp (NP)] (not) a person who would enjoy, or be suitable for, married life **V:** ⚠ be, seem, appear. **n:** kind, ⚠ sort, type □ *'But marriage with Terence—it's so difficult to say.' She gave a high-pitched laugh. 'He's what's called "**not the marrying kind**", I suppose.'* HAA □ *'Why is it so strange?' Virginia asked. Mollie shrugged her shoulders, as if it were obvious, 'Because he's **not the marrying kind**, that's all.'* AITC □ *So far as women are concerned, some are **the marrying type**, some are not.* WI

master/mistress in one's own house [Comp (NP)] in fact as well as in name, the head of one's household, whose decisions etc must be accepted **V:** ⚠ be, remain; make oneself □ *The point of departure for an understanding of the position of the working-class father in his home is that he is the boss there, the '**master in his own house**'.* UL □ *The garden is to be closed: no one may enter, and no one from the house may leave. Please note that I am not joking, and that from now on I intend to be the **master in my own house**.* NS □ *There is one thing that has to be made clear—that while I am her daughter-in-law in* her *house, I am **mistress in my own**.* ⇨ ⚠ the man/lady of the house.

a matter of sth [Comp (NP)] sth as the main factor; dependent mainly on sth (some condition or (factor); it is a question of (qv) **V:** ⚠ be, become; make sth. **adv mod:** just, only; mainly, simply. **o:** patience, will-power, luck; economic viability; finding the right backers, adjusting the intake-valve, knowing when to take a chance □ *But it has never been simply **a matter of** economics either for the promoters of the Common Market or for Britain. The inspiration of the Common Market was largely political.* SC □ *Her physical condition was improving. With that back to normal this curious paralysis would leave her. It was merely **a matter of** shock to the nerve centres.* DC □ *'I've no idea when I'll set up as a director; it's not the sort of thing you can put a time limit on.' And he adds, 'It's very much **a matter of** finance too.'* RT □ *The school teachers felt it was all **a matter of** their being levelled up to university status, and wanted degrees in higher education.* NS □ *I had done it straight on to the typewriter; I've translated so much of Jean Pierre's stuff now, it's just **a matter of** how fast I can type.* UTN

a matter of concern etc [Comp (NP)] a state of affairs, problem, topic about which people feel/do not feel concern **V:** ⚠ be, become; make sth. **adj:** ***(concern, interest)*** national, general; some, considerable, the greatest; ***(indifference)*** complete, utter. **n:** concern, ⚠ interest; indifference □ *Mr Patrick's admirably vivid account of his experiences with the Young Team are of importance as an intelligent discussion of what is, or ought to be, **a matter of** national **concern**.* NS □ *When and if local commercial radio comes in, the amount and quality of its serious programmes will be **a matter of** constant **concern**.* L □ *One object of gerontological studies is the prolongation of useful and enjoyable life: surely **a matter of interest** to most people?* SC □ *'Eric comes of a very good family.' 'Who a man's forbears were is **a matter of** complete **indifference** to me.'* □ also pl matters of concern etc.

(as) a matter of course [Comp/A (NP)] (in accordance with) a natural process or usual procedure □ *We, in these times and climes, take* *a child's survival into adulthood* ***as a matter of course****. By grace of inoculations and antibiotics, many if not all of the killer diseases of childhood have been eliminated or reduced.* OBS □ *He thought it would be* ***a matter of course*** *for the sons of former pupils to receive preferential treatment instead of having to compete on equal terms with other entrants.* □ *It was a country, Shaw maintained, writing of his 1860s boyhood* (in Ireland), *in which Protestant and Catholic despised, insulted and ostracized one another* ***as a matter of course****.* L □ *The pill may have made sex for young women more widespread, more* ***matter-of-course****, but it doesn't invalidate the urge to get married. What it might rule out is the old pressure to marry the first boy that gets them pregnant.* ST □ adj compound matter-of-course.

a matter of fact sth precisely known, probable, measurable; sth felt (by sb) to be true, unarguable □ *It's one thing to debate matters of opinion, but foolish of you to argue about ascertainable* ***matters of fact****.* □ *No man can take it out of himself at your age as he did when he was twenty or thirty, and that's* ***a matter of fact*** *you should accept for your own good.* □ *The security, the calm, the* ***matter-of-fact*** *tenderness which came from her — that is what was important.* RATT □ *Although one was aware in a general sense of the pollution, danger, noise, for which the motor car, and oneself the buyer, are responsible, some details he* ***matter-of-factly*** *delivers are enough to make you put a match to your AA card.* NS □ *With a* ***matter-of-factness*** *that robs the remark of offence, Albert Bressand observes: 'We are considered the cream of our generation.'* OBS □ adj compound (attrib) matter-of-fact means 'flat', 'unemotional', 'unpretentious'; adv compound matter-of-factly; n compound matter-of-factness. ⇨ a matter of opinion.

a matter of moment etc [Comp (NP)] an enterprise, task, state of affairs, problem of considerable importance **V:** ⚠ be, become, seem. **det:** some; great; little; no. **n:** moment, ⚠ importance, consequence □ *My 'standing' whilst on this tour therefore became* ***a matter of*** *some* ***moment*** *in Whitehall.* MFM □ *I was silent, a poor partner for both my partners* (= people seated on each side of me), *but that seemed* ***a matter of*** *no* ***moment****, for the blonde had at last got the financier all to herself.* PP □ *I was dealing with an emergency and had* ***matters of*** *greater* ***consequence*** *on my mind than how to address a superior officer.*

a matter of opinion [Comp (NP)] sth about which opinions are likely to differ, that cannot be evaluated, measured, known, with certainty **V:** ⚠ be; regard, treat, sth as □ *Playing football is best. Watching football is next best. Almost everything outside the act of playing or watching football is, indeed,* ***a matter of opinion****.* L □ *'The sprouts are half-cooked again.' 'I call them perfectly cooked, nice and crisp. It's all* ***a matter of opinion****.'* □ also pl. ⇨ a matter of fact.

(as) a matter of principle [Comp/A (NP)] (in accordance with) a rule of conduct or procedure which is often ethical and may be either generally accepted, or adopted by an individual for his own guidance □ *'I had no intention of shooting anything, Sir.' 'Quite, quite. I appreciate that, but* ***as as matter of principle****, I like people to ask my permission before they land on Pillay.' 'I'm sorry sir. I hadn't realized I was trespassing.'* RM □ *He had made it* ***a matter of principle*** *to rise at six and put in two hours work before breakfast.* □ *'It is sometimes kinder to lie.' 'You mean you don't think that telling the truth at all times is* ***a*** *binding* ***matter of principle****?'* ⇨ ⚠ in principle; on principle; on the principle of sth/that.

a matter of time [Comp (NP)] sth that is inevitable sooner or later **S:** it. . .before he dies, it. . .before they close. **V:** ⚠ be; seem. **adv mod:** only, just, simply, merely □ *He became more and more daring as the path got worse, until I felt it was only* ***a matter of time*** *before he fell.* BB □ *She talks of getting better but I think she knows it's just* ***a matter of time****.* □ *He thought an Australian republic was inevitable: it was only* ***a matter of time****.* L □ *It will only be* ***a matter of time*** *before the company finds itself in the knacker's yard along with Rolls-Royce and Upper Clyde Shipbuilders.* OBS □ *He has yet to prove that he can bowl consistently well anywhere else, although he has so much ability that this should be merely* ***a matter of time****.* OBS □ *it* as S can refer back to a previous sentence etc.

one may/might as well be hanged/hung for a sheep as a lamb (saying) if the penalty for a more serious crime, offence, act of foolishness, etc is no greater than that for a less serious one, then one may as well continue in one's criminal, foolish etc behaviour □ *At least they had big splendid vices, not mean little ones. After all,* ***you might as well be hanged for a sheep as a lamb****.* DC □ *I pushed her back on to the pillows. She made a feeble resistive movement. I was deciding* ***I might as well be hung for a sheep as a lamb.*** SPL □ (Victoria has no money to pay her hotel bill) *Deciding that* ***she might as well be hanged for a sheep as a lamb****, she went down to the restaurant and worked her way solidly through the entire menu.* TCB

may/might (just) as well do sth considering the circumstances, it is reasonable to do sth, no harm will come from doing sth □ *Since no one else has applied for the job, we* ***may just as well*** *give it to Kevin. After all, even though he hasn't got the right qualifications, he's been working in the field for over ten years now.* □ *I* ***might as well*** *go home. I don't see why I should stand around waiting. He's over an hour late already.* □ precedes or follows clause or sentence explaining the action. ⇨ ⚠ as well do sth (as do sth else); it/that is just as well.

may/might I ask what etc? rhetorical question, sometimes merely a formal accompaniment to a query, but often ironic, challenging or dismissive **O:** what, ⚠ who, why, when, where, how? □ *Fergus's arm tightened round Brigit. 'And* ***what, may I ask****, is this song of hate in aid of****?****'* DC □ *'I used one of your library tickets.' 'Did you?* ***May I ask who*** *gave you permission to do that****?****'* □ *But we don't have any real use for a caravan — and* ***where, might I ask****, do you propose to keep it****?*** □ what etc may precede or follow may/might I ask; might used less frequently than may.

may (very) well may possibly, or probably, be or do sth **modal:** may, might, could □ *Her inten-*

tion ***may well*** *be to instil respect by creating apprehension and suspicion.* SC □ *At this point a hypnotist will remind us that if a patient goes into a trance, or if he goes only into a reverie, he* ***may very well*** *see visions within and a transfigured world without.* HAH □ *One of the major civil liberties battlegrounds of the seventies* ***could well*** *be the struggle to publish the secret rulings vouchsafed to some civil servants which affect the rights of many million people.* ST □ *I merely mourn the temporary loss to the Labour Party of a man who* ***might very well*** *have become its next leader.* NS

one may well ask one is reasonably, or entirely, justified in asking, wondering (about sth) □ *What then,* ***you may well ask****, happened to poor Willie Whitelaw, whose expressive, lugubrious face we used to see earlier?* NS □ *Readers of this shabby but disturbing story* ***may well ask*** *how much connivance in high places allowed this remunerative racket to be carried on for so long.* SC □ *'Miss Wildewinde! Where are you going?' '****Well may you ask****!' she said furiously.* DIL □ *Did I think there was any chance of Robert marrying her—* ***well might*** *Annette* ***ask****!* SML □ often in parentheses, or in reply to a question already put; construction beginning with well, as in third example, used to make forceful comments etc.

mean business [V + O] be serious in one's intentions, determined to carry out sth one has planned to do □ *From the moment the African Heads of State stepped off their planes here last week, they showed they* ***meant business.*** OBS □ *Tempest rose, pushing back her chair as if she* ***meant business.*** MM □ *It was reassuring to my ego to be with a woman who was within my reach, who wouldn't egg me on unless she* ***meant business.*** RATT

mean it etc be fully serious when making a promise or threat, announcing an intention or opinion **O:** it; ⚠ every word (of it), what I say □ *If you tell the police about this I'll kill myself. I* ***mean it.*** DC □ *Sometimes I think he's parodying the ordinary kind of political pomposity, and then, God help me, I see he* ***means every word.*** EHOW □ *They must surrender unconditionally all their forces in the areas I have named; if they refused, I would go on with the battle. They saw at once that I* ***meant what I said.*** MFM □ *My old lady gave me bones to chew and I used to get dog biscuits as well. No, I* ***mean it.*** *Dog biscuits are full of calcium.* TVT

mean well have kindly intentions in general or in doing/saying sth in particular □ *I find her terribly interfering. It is not enough that she* ***means well.*** □ JAMES: *But there's just a chance — perhaps they* ***mean well****, perhaps they'll come back with a new saw and a decent plough and a pair of goats.* OI □ *To my mind, programmes like this do more for racial understanding than all the* ***well-meaning*** *speeches in a hundred Hansards.* RT □ often used as a damning or dismissive comment on sb; adj compound well-meaning.

a/the means to an end (simply) the way(s), method(s), or process(es) that need to be adopted in order to achieve a particular result □ *Harold felt that conversation should either be* ***a means to an end****, a business deal, or taking soundings for one.* PW □ *The secretary who had proved so susceptible to his charm was his direct link to a senior executive. For him, she was no more than* ***an*** *attractive* ***means to a*** *more desirable* ***end.*** ⇨ ⚠ the end justifies the means.

meanwhile, back at the ranch (catch-phrase) returning, or turning our attention back, to the main location in a story, field of activity, etc (from the screen captions indicating change of scene in silent 'Western' films) □ *The week has been marked by increased cordiality in Brussels, Dublin and Moscow towards Mr Wilson.* ***Meanwhile, back at the ranch****, Mrs Thatcher has succeeded in replacing Mr Heath, and ousting other likely candidates, as Leader of Her Majesty's Opposition.* NS □ ***Meanwhile****, as the Inspector pursues his special mission in Amsterdam,* ***back at the ranch*** *his pupil and protégé comes under suspicion of bent practice.* RT

measure one's length [V + O] fall, throw oneself, flat on the ground etc **A:** on the floor; at the foot of the stairs; in the pool □ *They dance pretty rough here. You're not the first to have* ***measured his length*** *in the course of an eightsome reel.* □ *The dog's leash got round my ankle somehow and I* ***measured my length*** *in the mud.*

meet one's end [V + O] die or be killed; be destroyed □ *There was a bullet wound in the left shoulder, but death was due to drowning. That is how my brother came to* ***meet his end.*** RFW □ *He died in his sleep — shock to the relatives of course, but there are worse ways of* ***meeting one's end.*** □ *'Where's that Dresden figure that used to stand on the mantelpiece?' 'It* ***met its end*** *at the hands of our cleaning woman.'* □ euphemism.

meet sb half-way [V + O + A] in return for a similar concession, give sb sth that he wishes, or demands, so that both parties may agree, or establish, a working arrangement □ *Unprogressive managements which had made little attempt to* ***meet*** *the workers* ***half way*** *and sort out real grievances would be driven to put their house in order.* SC □ *'I think I'll cut the whole remark out.' 'That would be* ***meeting*** *the Home Office more than* ***half-way.****'* SML

meet etc sth head on [V + O + A pass] meet etc sth directly, head first, in physical contact; (fig) approach and deal with sth directly **V:** meet, tackle, confront, deal with, crash into, collide with. **O:** wall, post; issue, problem, decision □ *It was as if we'd been fused together, melting into each like amoebae, but violently, like cars crashing* ***head on.*** RATT □ *Lord John Russell dodged the decisions that Peel, so the nation felt, would have met* ***head on.*** NS □ *Critics have found them to be somewhat lacking in emotional depth; skirting round problems rather than meeting them* ***head on.*** ST □ *But as a report on women's changing status, 'Working to the End' is unlike anything I have read, and tackles the broadest issues* ***head on.*** SC □ stress pattern meet sth ˌhead ˈon; attrib use *a* ***head-on*** *crash.*

meet one's maker [V + O] die; be destroyed □ *'The Frost Programme' added nothing to our knowledge of the death penalty, despite having a Mr Don Reid, who had seen many a man* ***meet his maker*** *in the electric chair.* L □ (replacement of worn banknotes) *As these tired old notes* ***meet their maker*** *in Essex, a new load is on its* *way into our pockets.* TVT □ euphemism; often facetious, as in second example.

meet one's match [V + O] encounter sb who can equal, or perhaps outdo, one in combat, argument, strength of will, etc □ *The fellow was not as flabby as he looked and I began to fear I had* ***met my match***. □ *In me he'd* ***met his match*** *and I'd never give in to questions no matter how long it was kept up.* LLDR □ *If she hoped to rouse her father by this slight impertinence she had* ***met her match****, as Lord Pomfret paid no attention to her at all.* WDM

sb's memory is green sb has not been forgotten after death; others have not allowed their memories of sb to fade or die □ *America may be withdrawing from the paddy fields of South Vietnam, but the war is still not over, and* ***the memory*** *of those who died* ***is*** *very* ***green***. L □ *She ought to be proud to gather in the facts while Waterman****'s memory's green***. *In a month's time he'll be as dead as cold cod.* PP □ *The tiny churchyard is scarcely able to contain those who gather there, some still to mourn, others out of community feeling and to* ***keep memory green***. RT □ variant keep (sb's) memory green.

men etc may come and men etc may go (but I etc go on for ever) (saying) men etc leave, die, perish, and are replaced by others (but other specified people or objects are not) **S¹:** men, dictators; fashions, philosophies. **S²:** I, he; civil servants, farmers; stone walls □ (source) *For* ***men may come and men may go,/ But I go on for ever***. THE BROOK (A TENNYSON 1809-92) □ ***Styles may come and styles may go but the 'little black dress' goes on for ever***. SC □ ***Detectives may come and detectives may go, but George Dixon*** (a TV policeman) ***outlasts them all***. RT □ often adapted in structure and vocabulary.

(all) men/women of goodwill (cliché) right-minded, progressive, peace-loving people □ TONY: . . .*a record of murder and misery. Yet on you go, all jolly and optimistic that right will prevail.* MIKE (with great sincerity): *It's a question of getting agreement between* ***men of goodwill*** *everywhere.* TONY (laughing incredulously): *Good. Let's drink to that.* EHOW □ *It is obviously hoped that* ***all men of goodwill*** *in the party would be willing to work together to give the Labour movement the unity, stability, and sense of purpose that it has been lacking.* T □ *It now became increasingly apparent to* ***all women of goodwill*** *(for in Northbridge the male element was on the whole not much considered) that Mrs Noel Morton must be the right person* (to become President of the Coronation Committee). WDM □ *It is also a novel of ideas, by turns ironic and challenging, which illuminates the predicament of* ***any man of goodwill*** *who finds himself a prisoner of the political stresses and incurable human obviousness of this or any time.* ST □ expression is associated with political speakers, etc.

mend one's manners [V + O pass] be, become, more civil or refined in speech and behaviour □ *I will implement my promise to send you twenty-five pounds, but not until you write to me in a proper and civil strain. So come off your high horse and* ***mend your manners****, and send me something remotely publishable.* US □ *She's not an attractive child.* ***Her manners*** *need* ***mending*** *for a start, and when she's not noisy and silly she's probably sulking.* ⇨ ⚠ mind one's manners.

(Robin Hood and his) merry men the leader and companions-in-arms, attendants, followers etc of a rebel or guerrilla band or of any fringe or anti-establishment group (from Robin Hood, a legendary outlaw 'hero' in 12th-13th c England) □ *He is not* ***Robin Hood*** *and the Mamelukes were scarcely* ***a merry lot****, but they were men fighting for what they believed to be their rights.* BN □ *I wondered where she might have gone. A Dover postmark might mean anything. Even back to* ***Tito and his merry men***. PP □ expression often adapted, as shown.

might is/makes right (saying) having the power to do sth gives one the right to do it; a plea of justice or fairness is ineffective against a superior force □ *The chief French grumble about Dr Kissinger's speech is that he is applying 'the law of the jungle' or 'the doctrine that* ***might is right***'. OBS □ *There are two lessons to be learned from the miners' strike. The second is that, however justified a union's claim, industrial* ***might*** *alone* ***makes right***. NS □ *Let us have faith that* ***right makes might*** *and dare to do our duty as we understand it.* ABRAHAM LINCOLN (in speech, 1860) □ rev only as a rallying call, affirmation of faith in one's cause, etc as in last example.

a mile off [A] across a considerable separating distance; clearly and unmistakably **V:** hear, see, smell; sense. **O:** ship, target; uncertainty, interest, greed, anxiety □ *'Does baby cry a lot?' 'I couldn't say that, but when he does you can hear him* ***a mile off***.' □ *Of course she's in love with Eric. I should have thought anyone could see that* ***a mile off***. □ *If he tries to be 'pally' with working-class people, to show that he is one of them, they 'smell it* ***a mile off***', *they can immediately detect the uncertainty in his attitudes.* UL □ main v often used with *can/could*.

milk/suck sb/sth dry [V + O + Comp pass] obtain from sb all the money, help, information, (emotional) support etc he has to give **O:** parent, teacher; subject, topic, theme; soil, land □ *If Kipling was interested in a subject or a way of life he could fasten himself on a man and* ***milk*** *him* ***dry*** *of all relevant information in an hour or less.* L □ *They're nomad cultivators, never replenishing the soil. When they've* ***milked*** *the land* ***dry*** *they move on somewhere else.* □ *It's hard work keeping him amused: I feel* ***sucked dry*** *after an hour in his company.*

(full of) the milk of human kindness (full of, characterized by) kindness, affection and goodwill towards others □ (source) LADY MACBETH: *Yet do I fear thy nature;/It is too* ***full o' the milk of human kindness****/To catch the nearest way.* MACBETH I V □ *Only a man* ***full of the milk of human kindness*** *could have continued to befriend the proud and obstinate young man.* SC □ *. . .a man in whom experience had somewhat soured* ***the milk of human kindness***. NS

milk and water [n + n non-rev] sth that is inoffensive but feeble or colourless **n:** person; attitude, doctrine, opinion, manner □ *They* (popular fiction) *claim to be stirring, but are as*

milk and water *compared with what one may find in almost any sex-and-crime novelette.* UL □ *The clergy subscribe to the new pragmatism in religion, their approach is conciliatory and their sermons are* ***milk and water****.* □ *Caute claims to destroy the myth that the fellow traveller was a* ***milk-and-water*** *communist who lacked the courage to join the party.* NS □ *You wouldn't look twice at any of his paintings—****milk-and-water*** *stuff, reproduced by the dozen for suburban parlours.* □ attrib use *a* ***milk-and-water*** *communist,* ***milk-and-water*** *stuff.*

the mills of God grind slowly (but they grind exceeding small) (saying) the processes whereby reforms are brought about, virtue is rewarded, crime is punished, etc are often slow but the end result may be perfectly achieved □ (source) *Though* ***the mills of God grind slowly****, yet* ***they grind exceeding small****.* (H W LONGFELLOW 1807-82) □ *'As a result of the findings of the commission of inquiry a high-up civil servant was severely reprimanded and posted to the Ministry's branch department at Bangor.' 'Well,' said Gerald, '****the mill grinds slowly****.'* ASA □ *The Home Office is naturally chary of haste in these matters. But even if* ***the mills*** *are* ***grinding slowly****, I hope they are grinding in the right direction.* NS

one's/the mind/imagination boggles one cannot accept, imagine, conceive an idea, suggestion, supposed incident or state of affairs **A:** at the idea; to think of it □ *To take one example,* ***the mind boggles*** *at the idea of having to do a sum of multiplication or division by Roman numerals.* OBS □ *Steve looked at me. 'Imagine what it's like to be in my place.' 'For once, Steve,* ***my imagination boggles****.'* SPL □ *One of our most eminent senior knights in a crash helmet doing a ton?* ***Mind-boggling****. 'Of course it's* ***mind-boggling****,' says Sir Ralph indignantly.* RT □ *As usual, the styles (of plot and sub-plot) don't mix. Songs include such* ***mind-bogglers*** *as 'A Message from the Man in the Moon'.* RT □ also occas boggle the mind as in *The quantities of bad amateur verse written and printed* ***boggle the mind****.* BBCR; adj compound mind-boggling; n compound a mind-boggler.

one's/the mind goes blank one's brain does not act; one cannot remember, think, answer etc □ *Each time she tried to imagine what it would be like on Saturday afternoon* ***her mind went blank****.* TGLY □ *As long as I was in the bus I was safe. I tried to* ***make my mind a blank*** *as it speeded up on the main road.* RATT □ *I had such a struggle to keep from thinking about my own worries that I found it best to* ***keep the mind a*** *complete* ***blank****.* CON □ *'Impossible to remember,' she replies candidly. '****My mind's a blank****, 24 hours after I've finished a programme.'* TVT □ variants one's/the mind is a blank, keep/make one's/the mind a blank, make one's/the mind go blank.

mind one's manners [V + O] remember, take care, to be polite, courteous □ *Mrs Robertson isn't really used to children. I hope you told them to* ***mind their manners****.* □ *David Watkins should* ***mind his manners*** *before sneering at magazines that don't go out of their way to cater for his own particular interest in architectural history.* NS ⇨ ⚠ mend one's manners.

mind over matter the mind as opposed to the body, or physical objects or phenomena □ *The power of* ***mind over matter****, and the ability of one mind to communicate with another, are perennial topics of speculation and experiment.* L □ *Phrases which we commonly use like '****mind over matter****' and 'higher nervous activity' imply that there is something going on on top of something else.* RT □ *It's quite common for dice-players to concentrate their will on throwing a six, though they know very well it's a coincidence and not a triumph of* ***mind over matter*** *if they do.* □ often preceded by *the power of, a/the triumph of.*

mind one's own business [V + O] concern oneself with one's own affairs, one's own life and work, without being unduly curious about, or interfering with, what others do; never mind² (qv) □ *He earned his bread at an honest, useful craft that he had taught himself without being helped, and* ***minded his own business****, and looked the world in the eyes.* HD □ *The English love of* ***minding other people's business*** *was being indulged and meetings were held 'in support of the persecuted Armenians'.* AH □ TONY (slowly): He's staying here? MYRA: *Tony,* ***mind your own*** *bloody* ***business****. I've never interfered with anything you did.* EHOW □ *'Will you get your men out of the place before they succeed in killing someone.' 'Perhaps it would be better, sir,' the foreman replied, 'if you were to* ***mind your own business****.'* HAA □ variants mind your own business! (imper) = 'that's my affair', 'keep out of this', mind other people's business.

mind/watch one's p's and q's [V + O] (informal) be very careful and correct in one's procedure, speech or behaviour (p's = pleases, q's = thank-yous) □ *Matron's not very keen on a man for this job, so you'd better* ***mind your p's and q's*** *if you want to keep it.* □ *If we had been* ***minding our p's and q's*** *we would have been referring to Mr Hislop as Professor Hislop, for that is his correct title in Sweden.* SC □ often with *need to, ought to, must, had better.*

a mine of information a person, book etc from whom or which much information on a subject or various subjects can be obtained **adj: *(mine)*** absolute; unexpected; veritable. **adj: *(information)*** useful; valuable; miscellaneous □ *Constance Cruikshank does not deal with this subject in her excellent 'Lenten Fare and Food for Fridays', though it is* ***a mine of information*** *on all other matters to do with food for vigils and for feasts.* OBS □ *We can now disclose, with the indispensable help of the 'Daily Mail's' sports page (what* ***an*** *undetected* ***mine of information*** *!), why Leeds lost such things as, in 1965, the league title.* NS

a ministering angel a benign angel; a woman who serves the needs of others with tenderness and care □ (source) LAERTES (Ophelia's burial): ***A ministering angel*** *shall my sister be.* HAMLET V I □ *She hurriedly recombed her hair so as to make it less exuberant and more in keeping with the role of* ***ministering angel*** *and experienced traveller.* TCB

miss the boat/bus [V + O] lose an opportunity to do or obtain sth □ *'Did she think I would marry Sybil?' I enquired. Henry shook his head. 'I think she's thought for some time that you've* ***missed the boat****!'* SML □ *I have an intense aware-*

ness of the opportunity the Open University offers to chaps who like me have perhaps ***missed the boat****.* RT □ *I think most French perfume houses* ***missed the boat*** *years ago because they become fixated on the belief that if a 1/4 oz bottle did not cost £4 to £5, nobody would buy it.* ST □ often with present or past perfect tenses.

a miss is as good as a mile (saying) narrowly missing success in doing or obtaining sth has the same practical result as failing completely; conversely, a narrow escape from failure, danger, death etc is as successful as an easy escape □ *'You couldn't have failed the exam by much, according to this list.'* ***'A miss is as good as a mile****. I've got to do the whole year over again.'* □ *'Careful! You just missed that rock by inches.' 'What of it?* ***A miss is as good as a mile*** *if you know what you're doing.'*

miss the point (of sth) [V + O pass] not grasp, or misunderstand, the meaning and/or purpose of a remark, joke, lesson etc **o:** the joke, the whole affair, holding such a celebration □ *Her husband was going to make a joke. She waited for it, her whole mind concentrated upon not* ***missing the point*** *when it came.* RM □ *This capacity for* ***missing the point*** *has, of course, always been characteristic of philosophers.* SNP □ *Some suggestions for livening up the* (Edinburgh) *Festival (such as pop concerts on Arthur's Seat) seem less than helpful. They* ***miss the point of*** *the affair.* L ➪ make one's point; take etc sb's point.

miss one's vocation [V + O] not be doing, earning one's living at, the type of work best suited to one's capabilities □ *You have a marvellous way with children, Sue! Don't you think you may have* ***missed your vocation****, working in an office?* □ *I'm not convinced Sam's right, but I can see he's* ***missed his vocation****. He should have been a lawyer.* □ sometimes said, not very seriously, to compliment sb on a talent not connected with his usual occupation; usu with present or past perfect tenses. ➪ find one's vocation.

the missing link popular term for a primate at the evolutionary stage between the apes and the earliest species of man; a connection between the parts or stages of a process, inquiry, argument etc **V:** be; look for; supply, provide □ (Dyak myth) *He* (a man who had run away into the jungle) *stayed there so long that he took the form of an orang-utan, and his children were like him. The wife, on this theory, is* ***the missing link****.* NDN □ *The identity of the forger of the Hughes letters was* ***the*** *only serious* ***missing link*** *in the investigation of the crime.* ST

mix one's drinks [V + O] consume several different kinds of alcoholic drinks in the course of an evening, at a party, etc—with supposedly more harmful effects than drinking the same amount of one kind □ *He had consumed so much vodka, and had* ***mixed his drinks*** *to such an extent that it was considered by experts that it would be two days before he 'surfaced'.* MFM □ *He wanted more than anything in the world to get drunk. Perhaps if he* ***mixed his drinks*** *sufficiently it might be enough. After the whisky, he could have a gin, and then, if he had any money left, a glass of stout ought to finish him off.* HD

a mixed bag etc [Comp (NP)] a group or collection of people, objects, items, stories etc of various kinds **V:** ⚠ be, seem. **n:** bag, ⚠ bunch, lot □ *Now it is there* (ie has been built), *the village clearly offers splendid opportunities to* ***its mixed bag*** *of first arrivals.* ST □ *The houses were* ***a mixed bag****, in every style from mullion and half-timber to what, from its white walls and dark green roof and profusion of ironwork, I took to be Spanish.* RATT □ *These poetry recitals —from the British poets, from Shakespeare, or* ***mixed bags*** *of prose and poetry, humour and pathos—occupied more and more of his time.* L □ *We were* ***a mixed bunch*** *of 24 students of several nationalities and from all walks of life.* NS □ *His characters are* ***a mixed lot****, in background, in class, in reaction to their situations.* NS

a mixed blessing [Comp (NP)] sb or sth which, though giving pleasure or benefits one would not wish to be without, still has some faults or disadvantages **V:** ⚠ be; make sb/sth □ *You know how devoted I am to Jeremy and Janice; the only time I've ever felt they were****n't an unmixed blessing*** *was when they would behead the conversation.* PW □ *Illich is now so influential in the US that he has almost attained the status of guru. This—and his refusal to be specific about solutions—make him something of* ***a mixed blessing****, even to radical reformers of Western society.* NS □ (NONCE) *He realises that evils, like* ***blessings****, are apt to be awkwardly* ***mixed****.* OBS □ occas variant a not unmixed blessing . ➪ ⚠ a blessing in disguise.

mixed company a social gathering that includes women, or women and children, as well as men, hence the need for a certain decency or restraint in speech and behaviour □ CRAPE: *All the things you want to do—why you'll bloody well have to set to and do them!* HARDRADER: *I'll remind you, Crape, that you are in* ***mixed company****.* THH □ *Many of the acts that were put on for the evening's entertainment would have been thought quite unsuitable for* ***mixed company****, even a few years ago.* □ esp with the prep *in*.

a (crazy) mixed-up kid [Comp (NP)] a young person who finds it difficult to adjust socially, doesn't know what he wants, and may be pessimistic, neurotic or rebellious **V:** ⚠ be, become; turn into □ *This is nevertheless a serious and moving book. Which is more than can be said of John Rechy's latest effort, which packs in just about every available cliché about* ***crazy mixed-up kids****.* NS □ *Whatever pessimistic comment Wisemen has to make can be read in the faces of these truly* ***mixed-up kids****.* OBS □ *'You beautiful, uncomplicated brute.' 'No,' I said. 'As they say in the films, I'm just* ***a crazy mixed-up kid****.'* RATT □ *Perhaps I was* ***a crazy mixed-up teenager*** *too. Only no one told me.* TVT

the mixture as before a gathering of people, or an event, entertainment, novel etc, which is a repetition of, or much the same as, a previous one; (from, formerly, chemists labelling bottles in this way when repeating a prescription for a customer) □ *'Who's going to be there?' 'Oh,* ***the mixture as before****, I expect — Hay and Betty's sister, George and his current girl friend. You know, the usual Saturday night crowd.'* □ (a fashion show) *This* (discomfort) *made one less than charitably inclined to see* ***the mixture as***

***before**, only with different athletic accessories —motor-cycles, Olympic hurdles, boxing gloves.* ST □ (NONCE) *The British, at least that influential junior section of the comic-reading public who fork out their weekly 3p and 4p, prefer **the recipe as before**.* OBS

moan and groan [v + v non-rev] complain; grumble □ *He dresses pretty well for a man who's always **moaning and groaning** about how little he earns.* □ *Well, sack him if he's so unsatisfactory. Why keep him on, and **moan and groan** to me?* □ *Anyway, I went through the movements with the minimum of **moans and groans** and can now touch my toes without cheating.* TVT □ also [n + n non-rev], as shown.

the moment of truth a turning-point or moment of crisis when sb has to face the reality of his condition, moral or economic health, etc (from bull-fighting, the moment when the matador must successfully kill the bull with a plunge of his sword) □ (reader's letter) *I was surprised that the English matador referred to by correspondents did not mention that in Spanish abattoirs **the 'moment of truth'** (slaughtering with a sword) is practised on captive cattle.* RT □ *Britain found herself so reduced in status that she had to knock on Europe's door. On the whole, Mr Middleton is, if anything, surprised that **the moment of truth** did not come sooner.* T □ *That a man as much in need of thinking well of himself as Coleridge should be brought to make such a bleakly shameful confession is a measure of the havoc that opium addiction can bring; but Miss Lefebure sees **this moment of truth** as a sign that he had passed the crisis.* NS

money can't buy everything etc (saying) there are certain things in life (health, married contentment, etc) that cannot be bought **O:** everything; happiness, health, peace of mind □ *'I wish I had a pound for every hundred he's got.' 'You're a lot better off than he is, son. I tell you, **money can't buy** you **happiness**.'* □ *Say you don't need no diamond rings/And I'll be satisfied./Tell me that you want the kind of things/That **money** just **can't buy**.* CAN'T BUY ME LOVE (P MCCARTNEY b1942)

money for jam/old rope (informal) money or profit easily earned or obtained; a task or undertaking completed with little or no outlay of money, energy, or time; a piece of cake (qv) □ *If the house could keep itself clean we wouldn't be employing her, would we? What does she expect — **money for jam**?* □ (a bank robbery) *Weston nipped swiftly into the back of a large car that waited outside. It started immediately. 'Gawd, a piece of bleeding cake!' '**Money for old rope**.'* TO

money isn't everything (saying) in many cases, there are more important considerations than how much money sb has or can earn □ *From time to time people have genuinely believed that **money** 'doesn't matter', **isn't everything**, and so forth, but no one has ever failed, on being told 'Mr X is a millionaire' to look at him with keen interest.* UL □ *Freddy? Well, he's not marrying the Greek. Emrys put a stop to that, said **money wasn't everything**.* US

money talks (saying) the possession of wealth enables one to get favoured treatment, exert political pressure, promote one's own interests, etc □ *He* (the working-class man) *sees a gulf between publicly professed morality and the reality. He feels fairly sure that in the end the cash-nexus wins—'**money talks**'.* UL □ *Why did the Attorney General not seek an order against the merchant banks as well? You can choose whatever moral you like: that the pressure of public opinion is still irresistible, or that **money** still **talks**.* NS

money well spent [Comp (NP)] a sensible purchase or outlay of money, not only for its immediate financial value but for the use, pleasure, security etc one derives from it **S:** subscription, membership; £50; new engine. **V:** ⚠ be; think sth, regard sth as □ *Considering the weather, and that you have a cold already, I'd have thought that £2 on a taxi would be **money well spent**.* □ *So you brought the van for £200? I'd regard that as **money well spent**.* □ *'A Private Enterprise'* (film) *is a shade more public than its title suggests, being financed by the British Film Institute Production Board, and thereby proving our **money** can be **well spent** in the cause of art.* NS

monkey business/tricks mischievous, boisterous or fraudulent action or behaviour **det:** some; (not) any; a bit of; too much □ *Robert thundered after the kid and swung him up on his shoulder. He stood there with a benign smile, but I could see, as we hurried up, that he was holding him very tightly to prevent any **monkey business**.* CON □ *If that's all the profit that's shown, there must have been a bit of **monkey business** going on with the account books.* □ *This is dangerous stuff for amateurs to handle. So do exactly as I tell you, boys, and no **monkey tricks**!*

the monstrous regiment of women women as administrators, reformers, agitators, successful managers, etc—and thus as objects of (male) resentment or scorn; women as a class or in unwelcome numbers □ (source) *The First Blast of the Trumpet against **the Monstrous Regiment of Women**.* JOHN KNOX (title of pamphlet, 1558—when Elizabeth I and Mary were Queens of England and Scotland respectively) □ (It) *relates the story of the Empress Maud, daughter of Henry I. England was not ready for **a monstrous regiment of women** at the time of Henry's death, so the throne went to Stephen, Maud's cousin, rather than to the Empress herself.* OBS □ now usu facetious.

a moonlight flit/flitting (informal) move house, decamp (with one's possessions), by night or secretly eg to avoid paying rent due, to escape creditors □ HELEN: *What are all these books doing all over the place? Are you planning **a moonlight flit**, Jo?* TOH □ *The business is plagued by **moonlight flitting**—people moving out of a small business as soon as they've collected enough down-payments on customers' orders.*

a moot point/question [Comp (NP)] a subject on which there are, or may be, different opinions, which can be debated or discussed but not, as yet, settled **V:** be, appear; regard sth as □ *Whether he could have bitten as successfully with his body stretched out was rather **a moot point**, but it was not the sort of experiment that I cared to make.* DF □ *'She'd be less neurotic if she had more to do.' 'That's **a moot question**.'*

more beautiful(ly) etc than ever [Comp/

A] more beautiful(ly) etc than in the past **adj:** more beautiful, lovelier, livelier; more anti-social, noisier. **adv:** more beautifully, more gracefully; more grumpily, more insensitively; worse □ *I can't believe that Anna's 45 now—she's* ***more beautiful than ever****.* □ *John's* ***livelier than ever*** *since he remarried.* □ *The last time I saw him he was drinking* ***worse than ever****.* □ *Alec should have gone into politics. His speech last night managed to say his usual nothing at all* ***more gracefully than ever****.*

more by good luck than (by) good management/judgement [A (PrepP)] mainly because one has been lucky and not because one has used much care, skill or forethought **V:** succeed, win; survive, be rescued □ *'You dirty bastard,' his friend said, and tried to kick me in the groin.* ***More by good luck than good management*** *I turned sideways.* RATT □ *We got the outboard engine working again but* ***more by good luck than good judgement****.* □ *If this reception doesn't end up as a fiasco it'll be* ***more by good luck than by good management****.* □ front, middle or end position.

more dead than alive [Comp (AdjP)] in a poor physical condition owing to illness, shock or injury **V:** ⚠ be; appear, look □ *It wasn't till the early hours of the morning that a policeman found him lying,* ***more dead than alive****, in the side street where he had been beaten up.* ⇨ ⚠ dead and alive.

the more fool you you are foolish **pron:** you, he, she, we, they □ *'I insisted on paying my own share of the bill.'* '***The more fool you****. He just would just have handed it in and claimed the lot as expenses anyway.'* □ *Fred told his parents that the new teacher didn't give homework — and* ***the more fools they*** *to believe him without checking with the school.* □ the O forms him, her, us, them also used; stress pattern the ˌmore fool ˈyou.

more (work etc) in it etc than meets the eye more involved in it than one might at first suppose **V:** (there) be; have, contain, do. **n:** work, skill, poverty, difficulties. **A:** in it, in their friendship; to all this; here □ *'Remember that you have to adjust the washing-machine for me before you go.' 'That'll only take a few minutes unless there's* ***more to it than meets the eye****.'* □ *Your smile may reveal a set of nice white teeth but there is* ***more than meets the eye to real oral hygiene****.* □ *This brings us to the natural and endemic sin of investigative reporting. This is the tendency to write a prose which hints more than it says, which suggests there is* ***more in things than meets the*** *reader's* ***eye****.* NS □ *The required medical examination was so cursory as to be farcical. If there was* ***more wrong with anybody than met the eye*** *it was not likely to be spotted.* □ *A modern primary classroom may look like a free-for-all to the older fashioned of us but there's a lot* ***more work done than meets the eye****.* □ *Disaffection may be* ***more widespread than meets the eye*** *on conducted tours of this sort.* □ *'Janey said he's had a gin or two but was nowhere near drunk.' 'He may have been* ***more so than met the eye****.'* □ variant more than meets the eye in it etc.

more in sorrow than in anger [Comp/A (AdjP)] feeling more sorry than angry; feeling more upset than resentful—though one might justifiably be angry □ HAMLET: *What, looked he frowningly?* HORATIO: *A countenance* ***more in sorrow than in anger****.* HAMLET I 2 □ *I feel it my duty to speak out against the rape of the cinema.* ***More in sorrow than in anger*** *I have long time held my peace, but...* NS □ (NONCE) *Pakistanis, schooled and moulded under the Raj, told me* ***more in anger than in sorrow*** *how disgusted they were that traditional British standards of fair play had been so far eroded.* L □ *When it was all over, Vic Feather having decided that evasions and* ***more-in-sorrow-than-in-anger*** *tones were the best way to keep the temperature down, the vote was taken.* NS □ front, middle or end position; attrib use *a* ***more-in-sorrow-than-in-anger*** *attitude.*

more means worse (catchphrase) allowing more people to have access to public facilities leads to a lowering of standards in education, the arts, commodity distribution, etc □ (referring to source) *Throughout the sixties Kingsley Amis continued to campaign against what he sees as a deliberate erosion of educational standards. He coined the phrase '****More*** *will* ***mean worse****' in 1960, while still following his academic career. It is constantly misquoted — '****More means worse****' — which irritates him, and is taken as further gloomy proof of the decline of literacy.* NS □ *Whether* ***more means worse*** *or not it is certainly going to have to mean different. No government can afford to maintain the staff-student ratio, the residential, social and recreational facilities of our older universities for such numbers.* SC □ *Perhaps an anthology, even of this kind, should be selective rather than representative.* ***More****, as the man said,* ***means worse****.* L □ (NONCE) *It was a bit of cheer for us 40-year olds, the news that the birth-rate is back to its record low level of vintage 1933.* ***Fewer*** *must* ***mean better****, I said to myself, wittily reversing Kingsley Amis's old propaganda.* NS

the more the merrier (catchphrase) enjoyment will grow in proportion to the number of people taking part; anybody/everybody is welcome to come □ *'You'll come, Mr Waggett, and your daughters and your friend there. Where's Mrs Waggett?' 'I'll go across and fetch her if I may,' said Paul Waggett, who was much gratified by the invitation. 'Yes, of course,* ***the more the merrier****, what?'* RM □ *I had previously understood that it was not permissible to send presents to royalty and that they were always politely returned, but I was evidently wrong.* ***The more the merrier*** *seems to have been the motto (there were 2,583 wedding gifts to Princess Elizabeth in all) and if I had sent in half a dozen egg cosies and three boxes of Turkish Delight, they would clearly have been acceptable.* NS

more or less[1] [adv + adv non-rev] approximately; roughly; just about □ *Matters that are down to earth do not interest you. You manage to make your accounts balance* ***more or less*** *and that is enough for you.* WI □ *By halfway through '55 we'd* ***more or less*** *got the whole picture of what amounted collectively to the greatest smuggling operation in the world.* DS □ *The station lies a mile* ***more or less*** *from the village itself, so someone will come to meet you.*

□ *Looking down towards the three Rocks he planned the line to descend across the trenches, parallel* ***more or less*** *to the High Street.* PM □ *In that way the benefits would be distributed* ***more or less*** *evenly.* □ may modify v (first two examples), or a n, adj or adv (other examples).

more or less[2] [adv + adv non-rev] in an amount, or to a degree, that varies slightly according to individual persons, occasions or conditions □ *Citizens will probably steel themselves for a further levy. It is a familiar experience accepted with* ***more or less*** *resignation.* SC □ usu modifies adj or n in this sense.

more or less[3] [adv + adv non-rev] virtually; practically □ ALISON: *Hugh tried to seduce some fresh-faced young girl once, but that was the only time we were* ***more or less*** *turned out.* LBA □ *Eddie, as the son of the eldest brother, was* ***more or less*** *the boss.* OBS □ *I got through* ***more or less*** *unscathed, but Hugo received a blow in the eye.* UTN □ *'About their education?' he said slowly. 'Well, we've* ***more or less*** *decided on that, haven't we?'* PW □ may modify a v (first and last examples) or a n, adj or adv.

more power to his elbow one approves of what sb is trying to achieve and wishes him strength for, and success in, his efforts □ *Gay* (homosexual) *groups objected beforehand* (to a violent TV thriller), *with the support, it is stated, of Mrs Whitehouse who wished them* ***more power to their elbows.*** L □ *Some Members of Parliament of both parties are to ask questions of the Government about the unfortunate mishandling of Mr Cressett's market-garden.* ***More power to their elbow****, I say.* ASA □ (NONCE) (reader's letter) *The working man is not prepared to be pushed around. Jack is as good as his master and* ***more power to his lungs*** *on this type of show.* RT □ usu used without a v, as here, to express a fervent wish or hope; last example includes idiom 'Jack is as good as his master' (qv).

(one must not be) more royalist than the king (one should not strive to) outdo one's model, leader, mentor ie in enthusiasm, loyalty, strictness, in adhering to dying customs, etc (translation of anonymous French saying *Il ne faut pas être plus royaliste que le roi*) □ (reaction to Rugby School, originator of Rugby football, having introduced Association football into their sports curriculum) *What is one to do?* ***One must not be more royalist than the king.*** TES □ *He's a Catholic convert, and, rather oppressively* ***more papist than the Pope.*** □ *She was a Cornish girl but in forty years of marriage she's become* ***more Scottish than the Scots.*** □ *In their passionate attachment to the monarchy, citizens of the Old Commonwealth often tend to be* ***more British than the British.*** □ frequently adapted, as shown, sometimes with facetious intent.

more sinned against than sinning having suffered more or greater wrongs than one has committed □ (source) *I am a man/* ***More sinned against than sinning.*** KING LEAR III 2 □ *Was the root cause of his hopeless plight the epileptic fits he suffered as a child? The betrayal by his parents who helped to commit him to a Remand Home? Either is feasible. But was ever a man* ***more sinned against than sinning****?* ST □ *'However, in view of all you tell me, I am quite willing that she should, well, come back.'* ***'More sinned against than sinning****,' said the CSM. 'Never did like the looks of him.'* TT □ (NONCE) *James Prior must not be seen to plot or to leak* (= let secret information be known) *too openly; and indeed he is doing neither. If anyone is* ***more leaked against than leaking****, it is Prior.* NS

the more so because/(in) that especially because □ *The considerable town of Sverdlovsk, formerly Ekaterinburg, was under snow when we reached it, beneath a dark grey sky. It was a forbidding aspect,* ***the more so because*** *one knew it to be the place where the Czar Nicholas II and his family had been done to death.* AH □ *I'm extremely angry with James for telling you this, and* ***the more so in that*** *he'd promised me that he wouldn't.* □ stress pattern the 'more so because/in that.

more than anything (else) (in the world) [A] very much; above all **V:** want, need; (would) like; dislike, hate; miss □ *'No, a whisky, please,' Charles replied, for he wanted* ***more than anything in the world*** *to get drunk.* HD □ *I accepted the beer but what I wanted* ***more than anything*** *was a cup of tea.* □ *Did you hear Harry put that pompous ass in his place? I enjoyed that* ***more than anything.*** □ ***More than anything else****, I dislike people saying behind my back things they wouldn't say to my face.* □ front, middle or end position.

more than a bit/little [adv mod] quite; considerably **adj:** drunk; nervous, excited, disappointed □ *Like everyone else, I was* ***more than a bit*** *curious to hear what he had to say.* CON □ *I was still* ***more than a little*** *nervous of my colleagues and superiors and very anxious to please.* UTN □ *He gave Harold a nudge and a wink, and Harold realized for the first time that he was* ***more than a little*** *tipsy.* PW

more than one can say/tell [A] very deeply, keenly **V:** miss; love; be sorrier; be more grateful □ *I don't know if you will miss me; but I will miss you* ***more than I can say.*** MFM □ *I'm sorrier* ***than I can*** *possibly* ***say*** *that you should have been brought into all this.* □ *I'm her beau; she's my belle,/And she knows I love her/* ***More than I can tell.*** OLD MUSIC HALL SONG □ usu end position.

more than one can say for/of sb/sth [Comp (AdjP)] certainly not true of or applicable to the person or thing in question **V:** ⚠ be, seem □ *Over-long and sometimes over-written, this is nevertheless a serious and moving book. Which is* ***more than can*** *be* ***said of*** *John Rechy's latest effort.* NS □ *'You have everything. You're even good-looking.' Her dark eyes twinkled. 'Which is* ***more than one can say for*** *your Uncle Saunders.'* DC □ *John's not afraid of work, and that's* ***more than you could claim for*** (or: ***more than could*** *be* ***claimed for***) *some of your brilliant friends.* □ variant more than one can claim/say for sb/sth; both as Comp after *this/that/which is*; pass as shown. ⇨ ⚠ the most (that) one can say/claim (for/of sb/sth).

more than enough [Comp/O (NP)] considerably, or a great deal, too much/many **V:** be; hear, take, suffer. **det:** enough, ⚠ sufficient; plenty □ *I can't do more for Eric. I've done* ***more than enough*** *for Eric. Eric has ruined me.* MM □

*You will hear **more than enough** on this subject in the pages that follow.* UTN □ *Don't pass your problems on to your uncle. He has **more than plenty** of his own just now.*

more than ever (before) [A] to a greater extent, more often, than previously **V:** want, need, love; miss; dislike, resent □ *Prone in bed, plaster from waist to knees, Charles felt **more than ever** at a disadvantage in dealing with this man.* HD □ *He doesn't take proper care of himself, and he's smoking **more than ever** in spite of what they told him at the hospital.* □ *'Does old Tom still come to see you?' '**More than ever**, now that he hasn't got his family within easy reach.'* □ front, middle or end position.

more than glad etc (to do sth) [Comp (AdjP)] extremely glad (about sth); most willing or eager (to do sth); only too glad etc (qv) **V:** ⚠ be; appear; make sb: **adj:** glad, delighted; sorry; keen; ready. **Inf:** to help; to get rid of it □ *When Pop was able to get to his feet again he was **more than glad to** observe that Charles was already in charge of things at the reception desk.* BFA □ *Please call on me if I'm needed, I'm **more than ready to** help.* □ *I never thought your magazine would succeed but I'm **more than delighted** that it has.* □ *My husband's going into town anyway. He'd be **more than glad to** give you a lift.* □ often used when offering help or accepting offers from others.

more sth/more often than sb has had hot dinners (informal) (do sth) in great numbers; very frequently □ *Mrs Duff has organised **more** marches **than most** of the legions of people she feels for **have had hot dinners**.* NS □ *Look, lady, will you stop telling me what to do? I've clipped dogs for shows **more often than** you'**ve had hot dinners**.* □ preceding v always in pres or past perfect tense.

more than likely [Comp/Disj (AdjP)] very probable; probably **Inf:** to arrive late, to give trouble □ *Frost and low lying fog are **more than likely** in South Eastern regions.* □ *Remember that there's a work-to-rule on and your train is **more than likely** to be late.* □ *You'll find your grandpa in the pub, **more than likely**.* □ *I'd have thought Derek was the one to suspect, rather than any of the staff. **More than likely** that thought crossed his father's mind, and that was why he wouldn't call in the police.*

more than once [A] quite frequently □ *Since I took up London cycling again, I have **more than once** found myself pedalling up a new one-way street the wrong way.* L □ *Bottomley rose and fell **more than once**, recovering from bankruptcy and exposure to become a popular idol during the 1914-1918 war.* SC □ *The true expert might even win some respect for his knowledge, however inferior he might be as a teacher: I have seen this happen **more than once**.* L □ variants on more than one occasion, in more than one case/instance.

more than welcome [Comp (AdjP)] warmly and hospitably invited or received in sb's home, a company etc; much needed and appreciated **S:** sister, visitor; advice, help; gift, offer; reform. **V:** ⚠ be, appear; make sb □ *I wish you'd come down to Cornwall. I need hardly say you'd be **more than welcome**.* □ *I am enclosing a copy of the script and any comments you care to make would be **more than welcome**.* □ *The banks have recently had plenty of heavy hints that a greater degree of restraint in lending would be **more than welcome** to the authorities.* OBS □ often used as formula when issuing invitations etc; often with *will/would*.

more to the point [Comp/Disj (PrepP)] more important(ly), more relevant(ly), to the discussion, the situation etc □ *Colin well knew that it was wrong, and dangerous, which was **more to the point**.* LLDR □ *Ernest faced the implications of defeat and **more to the point** faced what would have been the implications if it had taken place.* OBS □ *What is **more to the point**, the London firm can't give us any guarantee on delivery dates.* □ which is **more to the point** in middle and end position, and *what is **more to the point*** in front position.

more trouble than one/it is worth [Comp (NP)] cause more trouble, inconvenience than is offset by the amount of use, pleasure or profit one gets **V:** ⚠ be; find sb □ *I don't know if I could manage one* (a servant) *now—if we could find one. And some are **more trouble than they are worth**.* PW □ *'Why don't they have tables here?' Patrick asked. 'I'm not sure, but I rather fancy they were **more trouble than they were worth**.'* TGLY □ *If you're only cooking for two these electric blenders and mixers and things are probably **more trouble than they're worth**.*

more's the pity [Disj] unfortunately; one is sorry to say; it is all the more to be regretted when one considers sth previously mentioned □ *Girls do not, **more's the pity**, want to sleep with a man because he writes good novels.* SML □ *Apart from a few sentimental attachments like those I've never had a sense of personal identity with possessions, **more's the pity**.* ST □ *The lad from Harringay, 'who had found typography without organised history or principles left it with both.' **More's the pity** then, that this finely produced book should not picture some outstanding examples of his work.* NS □ *Decisions like these showed that the actions of the present Government were not all of a single tough-minded piece. The **more the pity**, then, that the verdict on United Clyde Shipbuilders was delivered with such apparent indifference.* L □ middle or end position, unless introducing *that*-cl; variant the more the pity (usu followed by *that*-cl).

the morning after (the night before) (catchphrase) (one's condition on) the morning after a previous evening's heavy drinking □ *Have you got any aspirins, Mary? I've got a bad case of **the morning after the night before** groaning in bed upstairs.* □ *Most of the cast look as though they were living through **a** perpetual **morning-after**.* L □ *The day dawns in typical Dawson fashion! Birds creaking on foggy rooftops, Les and his wife Meg with that **morning after** feeling from a farewell party.* TVT □ n compound a morning-after; attrib use *that **morning after** feeling*.

morning, noon and night [A] repeatedly throughout either a long (working) day or both day and night **V:** work, study, practise □ *By slaving **morning, noon and night** to turn his own little patch of England from wasteland into proud and self-respecting acres, Williamson was making his own gesture of support for Mosley's* *crusade.* RT □ *They seem to be working night shifts at the factory so we have to put up with the thumpings and vibrations* ***morning, noon and night****.*

the most (that) one can say/claim (for/ of sb/sth) the only praise or recommendation (and that not much) which one can give sb/ sth □ *Probably* ***the most that can be said of*** *this week's debates on the Budget is that they have served to clarify the objectives which the Government have in mind.* SC □ *I've not had a competent lab assistant since Joe left. This one brews a better cup of tea than the last but that's* ***the most you can say****.* □ *After that, Hoskins delivered an appallingly dull lecture.* ***The most you could claim for*** *it was that it only lasted 20 minutes.* □ say may be followed by either for or of, claim may be followed only by for; often used with *be...that*-cl; pass as shown. ⇨ ⚠ more than one can say for/of sb/sth.

one's mother's etc apron-strings one's mother's etc domination and influence **V:** be tied to, be free of, escape from, cut (loose) from, outgrow. **n:** one's mother's, ⚠ one's wife's, a woman's □ *Phil took a dim view of Jim's coming marriage. It'll make no difference,' I told him. 'Jim's not the kind of guy that lets himself get tied to* ***a woman's apron-strings****.' 'Just you wait and see,' Phil replied gloomily.* □ *Big boy now! But he'll have to go a long, long way to escape* ***mother's apron-strings****.* TVT □ *In 1887 the white dominions would still stand by* ***the mother country*** *in the South African and two World Wars, but they were already free of* ***her apron-strings****, and their industrial ambitions would in the next few years wreck Joseph Chamberlain's dream of an imperial common market.* OBS □ *Teenage ideas about entertainment can lead to problems. Obviously you want them home at a reasonable hour, but you don't want them tied to* ***your apron strings****.* TVT

a mother's boy (derogatory) a boy or man whose character and conduct is too much marked by maternal influence (the implication being that he is effeminate or has restricted scope for normal development) □ *And what have you ever done for him that's so wonderful, may I ask? I'll tell you. Turned him into a snivelling little neurotic.* ***A mother's boy****.* FFE □ *...quoting Freud: 'A man who has been the indisputable favourite of his mother keeps for life the feeling of a conqueror!' What does that tell us? Millions of men have been* ***Mummy's boys****. Not all turn into Stalins.* OBS □ variant (rather more contemptuous than headphrase) a mummy's boy, with capital or small M; in contrast, his mother's boy, his father's boy, her granny's girl, etc refer to likeness in physique or character or a specially affectionate or valued relationship.

the mountain labours and brings forth a (ridiculous) mouse (saying) (ridiculously) little is achieved after a great deal of effort, commotion and fuss (translated from a line of the Latin poet, Horace) □ *And to observe* (him) *making a veritably undistinguished little joke is to watch* ***the mountain labouring and bringing forth*** *not* ***a mouse*** *but a sort of jelly-baby* (ie a child's sweet). NS □ *One clause changed! All those meetings and paperwork to* ***bring forth a mouse****!*

(if) the mountain will not come to Mohammed/Mahomet, Mohammed/ Mahomet must go to the mountain (saying) (if) people or circumstances won't change or adjust to suit oneself, one must change or adjust to fit them; an assumption or course of action has been mistaken and one has to do the opposite of what one intended (Mohammed is said to have commanded Mount Safa to come to him as miraculous proof of the power of Islam; when it didn't he thanked God for preventing the destruction that would have been caused and said he would go to the mountain instead) □ *The thirteen counties* (of Wales) *could not for a moment be expected of their own volition to focus on Cardiff; the last thing* ***the mountains*** *were prepared to do was to* ***come to Mahomet****. It was for* ***Mahomet*** *to* ***go to the mountains****.* SD □ *'I'm glad I haven't got to go back there,' said Victoria. 'Only if I don't go back, how can I get hold of Edward?' Dakin smiled. '****If Mohammed won't come to the mountain, the mountain must come to Mohammed****. Write him a note now.'* TCB □ *Freitag has, he says happily: 'reached a stage in my life where I've stopped pushing. From now on, I'm letting* ***the mountain come to Mohammed****.'* TVT □ often modified, grammatically and/or lexically, as shown.

one's mouth waters saliva flows at the thought, smell, prospect of food; one's greed or desire to have sth is aroused □ *The mussels were bigger down there. Hunger contracted under his clothes like a pair of hands. But as he hung there,* ***his mouth watering****, a lump rose in his throat.* PM □ *Gates* (= number of spectators at a match) *for the MCC Tour of India would* ***make*** *an English county Secretary****'s mouth water****.* L □ *I led her round the cages again and pointed out the specimens, some of which were so unusual that they* ***made my mouth water*** *just to look at them.* DF □ (advertisement) ***Mouth-watering*** *Tassajara Bread Book — Recipes from Tassajara, the first Zen Monastery in the western world.* L □ adj compound mouth-watering; variant make sb's mouth water.

move heaven and earth (to do sth) [V+O] make every effort, use all the influence or power of persuasion one has (to achieve or obtain sth) **Inf:** to change things, to win approval □ *Brezhnev made a very fundamental change of policy back in about 1971, when they decided that the Soviet citizenry would be treated with better consumer goods — more food, more of the good things in life. And he is* ***moving heaven and earth to*** *get that accomplished.* L □ *'I have two possible buyers coming this afternoon — one is from a national collection.' 'How much do you want? I'll* ***move*** *all my bit of* ***heaven and earth****.'* L

move house [V+O] change one's place of residence, esp together with one's furniture and goods □ *At the time he was* ***moving house****: he had just been appointed to the BBC Scottish Orchestra.* OBS □ *They felt they simply couldn't face the bother of* ***moving house*** *again so soon.*

the moving spirit [Comp (NP)] the person who activates or leads others in a group, enterprise, reform, revolution etc **V:** ⚠ be, become; make sb. **A:** among them; in the affair; of the enterprise; behind the revival □ *Nxou, who was* *not only **the moving spirit** among the three but the outstanding personality in the little community, was utterly dedicated to his hunter's role.* LWK □ *These two were **the moving spirits** without whom discontent might never have grown into rebellion.*

Mr/Miss Right (informal or facetious) the ideal, or entirely suitable, person for one to marry **V:** meet; wait for □ *I used to think a lot about meeting **Mr Right** and the rest of it, but the way I look at it nowadays, I'm lucky if I can hold on to a Mr Not-too-bad.* TGLY □ *And don't tell us it* (the reason you haven't married) *is because you're still waiting to meet **Miss Right**. A man meets a girl he'd like to marry just as soon as he wants to, and not before.* CON □ *I could get married whenever I wanted but I'm going to make sure it's the right one. When **Mr Right** comes along, I'll know all right.* DPM □ *...that never to be forgotten moment — the one that always cracks my heart in films — the moment when **Miss Right** and Mr Wonderful recognize each other.* NS □ often in expression *when **Mr/Miss Right** comes along.*

Mrs Grundy the personification of a narrow, disapproving and censorious attitude (from a character in SPEED THE PLOUGH (T MORTON 1764-1838)) □ *The dogs provided a bet for the working classes. In your town, in your free time, and not **Mrs Grundy** or the police would stop you from having your bet.* L □ *We admit marital infidelity in theory, but have no way of coping with it in practice, which is quite as hypocritical as anything dreamed up by **Mrs Grundy**.* NS

a Mrs Mop (derogatory or facetious) a female house or office cleaner (from a character in the BBC 'ITMA' radio comedy series of World War 2) □ *Ashton's own wife and mother earned their living as cleaners and he objects that Members of Parliament should worry more about sweat shops in Hong Kong and South Africa than about **Mrs Mops** in the House of Commons.* OBS □ *Today's generation* (of sub-editors) *monotonously describe charwomen as **Mrs Mops**, rag-and-bone men as Steptoes and brash businessmen as whiz-kids.* L

much/little as/though one does sth [Conj] although one feels, desires etc sth very much/very little **V + O:** admires one's parents, dislikes the idea, enjoys driving; wants to see them, should like to stay □ ***Little as he** liked the plan he would have to fall in with it if the others were all agreed.* □ *I felt that Hugo's personality could very easily swallow up mine completely and **much as I** admired him I don't want this to happen.* UTN □ *If he would feel freer at the hotel she musn't press him to stay in their hugger-mugger household, **much as she** would like to* (ie like to press him to stay). PW □ ***Little though I** felt like it, I struggled out of bed and made my way downstairs.* □ conj of concession — main clause states what one nonetheless thinks, feels, proposes to do etc.

much good may it do sb may sb benefit from his actions; may sb's actions do him good □ *Each year is published a volume called 'Book Auction Records'. The dull and industrious may thus trace the ever-rising price history of any famous title. **Much good may it do them** for, to all except those who live by it, prices are a poor pointer to real value.* NS □ *Oh, let him have the old mower if he says it's his — and **much good may it do him**.* □ *'I'll get a lawyer and sue him.' '**Much good it**'ll **do you**. It costs more to collect a small debt than to let it go.'* □ ironic and dismissive remark made about or to sb whose actions are mean and contemptible, or simply unlikely to achieve the desired result; occas used with *it will/will it*, as in last example. ⇨ ⚠ do no good; no good.

much less even less, not so much, as has already been indicated; let alone (qv) □ *The Brigadier, who couldn't remember the last time he had had a holiday at all, **much less** one in France, merely stood bemusedly in the rain.* BFA □ *Dr Schlossberg says Kerwin gave him a pile of health forms and he filled out about 20 of them, without even shaking hands with the applicants, **much less** examining them.* ST □ *She must behave very differently at her work, if that's what they say. At home she doesn't know how to be civil, **much less** obliging.* □ may modify n, adj, adv or v.

much mistaken [Comp (AdjP)] greatly mistaken; having made a greater mistake than one is aware of **V:** ⚠ be, appear; confess oneself □ *Unless I am **much mistaken**, the attitudes described in this first part will be sufficiently shared by many other groups which go to make up 'the common people' to give the analysis a wider relevance.* UL □ *You might think that he was a typical conscientious policeman. But if you thought so, you'd be **much mistaken**.* □ often with *unless one is...*, or *one would be...if.*

much of a muchness [Comp (PrepP)] not greatly different from one another; more or less like one another **S:** doctors, teachers; standard, quality; care, treatment, service. **V:** ⚠ be, appear; find sth □ *And it is a matter of fact that to the well-trained reader, or eater, these judgements become pretty exact, people being **much of a muchness**.* L □ *Quite gross differences exist in the degree of sturdiness enjoyed by the natives of different parts of even so small a territory as Britain, despite the fact that the quality of medical care is **much of a muchness** everywhere.* NS □ *'Which photograph do you like best?' 'They're all **much of a muchness** really.'*

much to one's relief etc giving one much relief etc; making one feel greatly relieved etc **n:** relief, ⚠ sorrow, dismay, horror; surprise, delight □ *The evening hadn't been a success, and Blaize had finally got back to his hotel at five in the morning after the girl, **much to his relief**, had parted with the also traditional 'Pas ce soir. Peut-être demain* (= Not tonight. Perhaps tomorrow)'. SD □ *Noel said* (it was) *a very good idea and in his voice there was no trace of self-consciousness, **much to** his Lydia**'s relief**.* WDM □ *'Geoffrey passed his entrance exam, then?' 'He did, **much to** everyone**'s surprise**.'* □ *She snubbed him good and proper — **much to my delight**, for George thinks he has women eating out of his hand.* □ front, middle or end position.

mud sticks (saying) an accusation against sb/sth, whether proved true, false or slanderous, has a damaging effect on one's/its reputation that is not easily got rid of **det:** some (of the), a little, a bit of the □ *'No school would employ him now.' 'But the court cleared him absolutely.'*

'All the same, ***mud sticks.'*** □ *It would only be the word of a Mart*(ian) *against his own. Very likely they'd put her down as space-crazed. All the same, some of the* ***mud*** *might* ***stick****; it would be better to settle with her here and now.* TST □ (air-navigation aid system) *Both British air corporations use Decca as standard equipment. The system has its faults and it cannot give pilots a clear picture of the ground over which they are passing, but neither can any other navigating aid now in use. Nevertheless, since some* ***mud*** *always* ***sticks****, the FAA's* ((US) = Federal Aviation Agency) *criticisms can be extremely damaging to Decca's foreign sales chances.* NSC

a mug's game [Comp (NP)] (informal) a habit, practice, occupation that is not beneficial to oneself, and is sth only a foolish person would (try to) do **V:** ⚠ be; turn into; find sth □ *If you tried to 'live according to religion', well, you would soon find it was '****a mug's game****'.* UL □ *I'm not so daft as I would look if I tried to make a break for it on my long-distance running, because to abscond and then get caught is nothing but* ***a mug's game****, and I'm not falling for it.* LLDR □ stress pattern a 'mug's game.

mum's the word (informal) keep silent, don't say anything (about sth specified or understood); let's keep this a secret; keep mum (qv) □ *Now, when we get to the gate,* ***mum's the word*** *until I give you the signal.* □ *I'm not supposed to be here, you know, so* ***mum's the word****.* □ used as request or mild warning.

mutton dressed as lamb a middle-aged or elderly person, esp a woman, who dresses, uses hair-styles and make-up etc, in a style suitable only for sb much younger □ *Bohan, of the House of Dior, is pained at the spectacle of* ***mutton dressing as lamb****, though he believes that the line between the older woman and the younger has certainly become less sharp.* RT □ *'There's absolutely nothing worse than* ***mutton dressed as lamb****. The sort of middle-aged or elderly trendies who try to get with it are digging a pit for themselves of no mean depth. A middle-aged don* (= university lecturer) *in a Beatle haircut is one of the most offensive sights known to man.* L □ may be used, alone, as a scornful comment on sb's appearance.

a mutual congratulation(s) society [Comp/O (NP)] (facetious) a pair, group, of people who are engaged in complimenting or congratulating each other **V:** be, become; conduct, form, make □ *There were many speeches and we developed into* ***a*** *sort of* ***mutual congratulation society****.* MFM □ *You'd think kids and parents and teachers had nothing to do with exam successes, the headmaster and the Education Committee chairman made such* ***a mutual congratulations society*** *of it.*

my/one's country right or wrong (saying) (one will support, be loyal to) one's country at all times, even if one finds its policies or actions mistaken or morally wrong □ (source, proposing a toast) *Our country! In her intercourse with foreign nations, may she always be in the right; but* ***our country, right or wrong****.* (S DECATUR 1779-1820) □ (questionnaire) *After each statement, you are requested to record your personal opinion regarding it. . . . 13: '****My country right or wrong****' is a saying which expresses a fundamentally desirable attitude.* SNP □ *The fans have an absolutely single-minded loyalty that has not been common in Britain since its jingoistic days.* ***My team right or wrong****. Anyone who shows tolerance to the enemy is a traitor.* OBS □ occas substitution of another n for country.

(all) my eye (and Betty Martin) (informal) completely untrue or nonsensical, esp of sth said that is intended to deceive or mislead one but does not do so □ *'Maybe there's nothing in it after all. Maybe it's* ***all my eye****.' 'I'll go on for a bit. I'll let you know soon enough if I think the whole thing's a front.'* PP □ *This notion of earning an honest penny is* ***all my eye****. A man can work a whole lifetime and when he is 65 he considers himself rich if he has saved a thousand pounds. Rich!* CSWB □ *That was* ***all my eye and Betty Martin*** *about her having a headache. She just wanted to stay at home in case her boyfriend phoned.* □ usu Comp after *it's/that's*; my always used regardless of S. ⇨ ⚠ next entry.

my foot etc(!) (informal) rubbish! nonsense! **n:** foot, ⚠ eye; aunt Fanny; (taboo) backside, arse □ *The staff nurse was passionately angry and insulted that Charles should have said this was something she could not understand. 'Can't understand,* ***my foot****,' she said. 'That's the line all you dirty cads take.'* HD □ *'Everything that was said this afternoon was plain, sober fact.' 'Sober fact,* ***my eye!****'* TBC □ *'Take for example all these Cockneys coming down* (to work at picking hops). *Strictly, in law they ought to pay tax on that. I mean if the law is to be interpreted in the strict letter.' 'Strict letters,* ***my aunt Fanny****,' Pop said.* DBM □ *'You must speak to the doctor, Granny Barnacle,' said Miss Taylor, 'if you really feel you aren't getting the right treatment.' 'The doctor* ***my backside****. What's an old woman to them, I ask you?'* MM □ scornful rejection of what another person has said (and usu following a repetition of his or her words). ⇨ ⚠ previous entry.

my God(!) exclamation of great astonishment, dismay, despair □ TONY: ***My God****, you aren't Rosemary?* ROSEMARY: *Yes, I am. Who did you think I was?* EHOW □ *Marlowe directed the six-inch finder telescope on the Moon. '****My God****,' he exclaimed, "it's boiling!'* TBC □ *'Had you been afraid to take it* (a car) *into a garage to get* (the bumper) *straightened — in case they should recognize the car?' 'No!* ***My God****, no!'* DC

N

a nail in sb's/sth's coffin [Comp/o (NP)] sth that hastens, or further ensures, the death, end, failure etc of sb/sth **V:** be; knock, hammer, into □ (football) *While Everton retain their narrow lead at the top, they go to the far north with the sad duty of probably knocking in* ***the*** *last* ***nail of*** *Carlisle****'s coffin****, a friendly club without the resources to live among the leviathans of this world.* ST □ (reader's letter) *Other* ***nails in the coffin of*** *science-as-organised-commonsense were knocked in by Planck with the quantum theory (1900), Einstein with...* NSC □ *'Have one?' he said, proffering his cigarette case. 'No thank you, you can keep your* ***coffin-nails*** *for yourself.'* □ n compound a coffin nail.

the naked ape man thought of as no more than an evolutionary refinement, a special kind of animal □ *Jimmy Reid* (a former Communist) *says that he is more at home with Christians than with humanists, or rationalists 'who will see man in terms of* ***the naked ape****—man is not an ape'; and he believes profoundly that 'good Christians are my allies'.* NS □ *Other essays assault reductionist accounts of men as 'nothing but'* ***naked apes****, territorially-minded geese and so on.* L

a name to conjure with [Comp (NP)] an influential name; a name denoting a person, group, business undertaking, etc whose achievements, opinions, wishes etc are respected **V:** ⚠ be, become; make sb/sth □ *Well, the great thing about 'Monsieur Diamant' is that he's completely respectable. He's* ***a name to conjure with*** *in many communities besides the diamond world.* DS □ ***His name****, little known to the public, is one* ***to conjure with*** *in Hollywood. Those who really know in the movie business know that Horner K Pringsheim is the power behind the throne and the maker and breaker of many a film career.* UTN □ *Hawick and Bill McLaren are* ***names to conjure with*** *in rugby.* RT

to name (but/only) a few citing only these □ *Kenneth Harris, who this week reports on a visit to Barbados, is best known to readers for his conversations with celebrities—Callas, Olivier, Piggott, Rigg, Thatcher* ***to name a few****.* OBS □ *At Palacerigg Nature Centre things get more unusual. You walk up a path watched—or more likely ignored—by wolves, foxes, deer, wildcats, badgers,* ***to name but a few****.* RT □ precedes or follows short list of examples or instances which could be greatly extended.

one's name is mud (informal) one is disliked; one has made oneself resented or unpopular, perhaps temporarily □ *In fact only a few of the old regulars use it* (Wheatley's pub in Heathcote)*—most of them have decamped down the road to Northcote, where Wheatley****'s name is mud****.* OBS □ *You know how much your family make of such occasions.* ***Your name****'ll* ***be mud*** *if you don't go down to Plymouth for this wedding.* □ also pl their names are mud.

the name of the game [Comp (NP)] (catchphrase) the real nature of sth; what one has most to do or consider in respect of an activity, procedure etc **V:** ⚠ be, become □ *She relinquished the part after eight months to broaden her scope as an actress. Sex is still basically* ***the name of the game****, but at least the context of drama lends it a more legitimate ring.* TVT □ *The days of the get-rich-quick operators, grab-the-money-and-go boys, are over. Guarantee is* ***the*** *new* ***name of the game*** *and there are a lot of travel agents, tour operators, airlines, hotel and leisure groups whose interests are best served by making sure that the rules are observed.* L □ *If* ***the name of the game*** *is survival, our children's if not our own—and I believe it is—then it must be argued that the media presume to know too much about the issues which concern us and those which do not.* L

name (no) names [V +O] (not) identify by name sb one is describing, praising, criticizing or accusing □ *Now it is easy enough to write about such-and-such a politician's supporters but it is more convincing to* ***name names****.* NS □ *Mrs Meir's* (a former Prime Minister of Israel) *own choice* (of a successor) *could be Sapir, but she's too sharp to* ***name names****.* ST □ *His recipes for solving the problem — better education for young officers, greater integration between the Services, abolition of the Chiefs of Staff—will bring a tired smile to the lips of some battle-scarred warriors,* ***naming no names****.* OBS □ *I'd run a mile if some disc jockey asked me on their shows, I will* ***name no names****, but with Jimmy Young I feel he'd get me out of any difficulty I got into, he'd fill the gaps.* RT

a narrow escape an escape from danger, the unwelcome attentions of others, etc which is only just managed or contrived; a close call (qv); a close/narrow shave/squeak (qv); a near miss[2] (qv) □ *Returning to the mountain hut for the night, the climbing party had* ***a narrow escape*** *from falling rocks.* □ *Tim had* ***a narrow escape*** *from the clutches of Barbara last year. I had* ***an*** *even* ***narrower one*** *this Christmas after she claimed I proposed to her at the office party.*

nasty, brutish and short [adj + adj + adj non-rev] without safety, comfort or refinement and too soon ending in death □ (source) (in a state of nature) *...the life of man, solitary, poor,* ***nasty, brutish, and short****.* LEVIATHAN (T HOBBES 1588-1679) □ *It's easy for a film-maker of Tarkovsky's skill to paint a horrifying picture of life in 15th-century Russia:* ***nasty, brutish and short****, at the mercy of ruthless and quarrelsome nobles, invaded by marauding Tartars...* L □ *Dr Ackroyd wrenches mortality figures out of the realm of tables and statistics and makes them begin to hurt by pointing out that 'People without food do not simply lie down quietly and die. The way to death is* ***nasty*** *and* ***brutish and*** *often not* ***short****.'* NS □ *Far from being* ***nasty, brutish and short****, the life of Gerald Potter is a saga of subtle personal and artistic frustrations.* RT □ (NONCE) *From the days ('****nasty, British and short****,') when Africans were hunted as foxes, to the* *present time, any real progress seems inchlike and precarious.* L

a nasty piece of work [Comp (NP)] (informal) an unpleasant, dishonest, dangerous, cruel etc person **V:** ⚠ be, seem; find sb □ *Sorrowing over the fate of Hector at the hands of Achilles, whom I classed as **a** rather **nasty piece of work**, I had nurtured a mild but lasting prejudice against things Greek.* BM □ *'Indeed I tried to raise objections to the situation, but it was no good. He's Inge's white-haired boy. I agree with you,' he added, 'he's **a nasty piece of work**.'* ASA □ also pl nasty pieces of work.

one's native heath the country, district, town etc in which one was born, grew up, etc □ (source) *Speak out, sir, and do not 'Maister'* (= Master) *or 'Campbell' me—my foot is on **my native heath** and my name is MacGregor!* ROB ROY (W SCOTT 1771-1832) □ INTERVIEWER: *Do you ever consider a return to **the native heath** at all?* P G WODEHOUSE: *It's rather difficult; my legs have gone, you know. I don't know whether I could survive in the city any longer.* L □ *This led our discourse naturally into the realms of entertainment and the arts, our Caledonian* ((facetious) = Scottish) *friend contributing a spirited defence of the traditional songs and dances of **his native heath**.* CON

nature abhors a vacuum (saying) just as, in physics, an unsealed vacuum is impossible to maintain, so, in life, a space, period of time, position, field of inquiry or study, etc will not be left empty for long □ (source) ***Nature abhors a vacuum***. ETHICS (B SPINOZA 1632-77) □ *Roskill hadn't begun his career as a Naval historian; there just wasn't anybody in the Navy or in the academic world concerned with it* (modern Naval history)*, and **nature**, as you well know, **abhors a vacuum**.* L □ *I filled the vacant place, **nature** thus waywardly expressing her **abhorrence of a vacuum**.* SD □ (NONCE) *A considerable part of **nature** regards Saturday afternoon television as **a vacuum**, and accordingly **abhors** it. The amount of time devoted to horse-racing is especially resented.* L □ variant nature's abhorrence of a vacuum.

the nature of the beast [Comp (NP)] (facetious) what is characteristic and to be expected of a (type of) person **V:** ⚠ be; consider, regard, sth as □ *A common attitude is that a girl must not be dirty and noisy but if a boy is, well, that's just **the nature of the beast**.* □ *It is perhaps in **the nature of the beasts** that public attention should light upon the broadcasting authorities, as distinct from programme makers, in moments of confrontation.* L

nature, red in tooth and claw nature thought of as a savage force; (a matter of) fierce competition □ (source) *Man.../Who trusted God was love indeed/And love Creation's final law—/Tho' **Nature, red in tooth and claw**/ With ravine* (= seized prey)*, shrieked against his creed.* IN MEMORIAM A H H (A TENNYSON 1809-92) □ *The spectacle of '**nature red in tooth and claw**' does not make cooperation a less relevant ideal.* NS □ *And possibly a first-night house* (=audience)*, a late-night house a shade tired and hungry, is not the best group to present such a rending, tearing, **nature-red-in-tooth-and-claw** compilation to.* NS □ (views about the business man's secretary) *If she is not raising a laugh for being dumb, she is being attacked for being ambitious and **red in tooth and claw**—or sexy, and black in bra and briefs.* L □ unusual attrib use *a **nature-red-in-tooth-and-claw** compilation.*

the naughty Nineties the last decade of the 19th c, seen as a period of freedom, laxity or decadence in social mores, entertainment and the arts compared with conventional Victorian standards □ ***The Nineties** in which Lady Chalkham had been a young woman, were cheaply referred to as 'gay' or 'naughty'. I doubt if they were, except that wealth and over-confidence allowed some kinds of people in some ways to be frivolous and irresponsible.* AH □ *Until the 1880s paid holidays were virtually unheard of, but by **the Naughty Nineties** the working class was taking regular trips to the seaside, football grounds and music halls.* RT

near and dear (to sb) [adj + adj non-rev] physically or emotionally close (to sb) and valued (by sb) □ *A natural irritability began to verge upon mania, as if the body itself had developed a neurosis. All this was disturbing to me, and must have taxed the forbearance of those who were either **near or dear to** me, or both.* AH □ *'You realise the highway must go* somewhere*?' 'We can't see the matter with an impartial eye, I'm afraid. We're fighting to save the amenities of a place that's **near and dear**.'* □ *There was no need for questions: she talked as any woman talks on that old, old subject **nearest and dearest to** herself* (ie her own experiences, feelings and opinions). PP □ used as Comp, or modifies preceding n. ⇨ ⚠ one's nearest and dearest.

a near miss[1] an attempt to hit, reach or achieve sth that very nearly succeeds □ *In this state he almost derailed a nearby couple, and when the man's hand shot out for revenge he felt the wind of **a near miss** blowing by the side of his face.* LLDR □ (of an attempt to kill a team of foreign agents) *So far they've only scored one out of three, and **a near miss** of course.* OMIH □ *'4000 miles?' 'That's such **a near miss**,' the quiz-master said, 'that I think we'll give you a mark. The correct answer is 3982 miles.'* □ also pl.

a near miss[2] a narrow and fortunate escape from, or avoidance of, death, injury, or other mishap; a close call (qv); a close/narrow shave/ squeak (qv); a close etc thing (qv); a narrow escape (qv) □ *Unfortunately, bottles, cans, toys, flower pots and, horribly, three cats, (reaching a speed of 100 mph, if from the top storey* (of a 30-storey block)*, by the time they hit the ground), have been landing in the playground below. Two **near misses** a fortnight ago were too much for the headmistress who felt she could no longer be responsible for this hazard.* OBS □ *He did survive but whether he lives to be fifty or a hundred he'll never have **a nearer miss**.* TVT □ *'Your Aunt Ada was here till a few minutes ago.' 'Wow! That was **a near miss**. Thank God I walked up from the station.'*

near/close to the bone/knuckle [Comp/A (PrepP)] too frank or inconsiderate in its exposure of a fact or truth; coarse or lewd to a degree that many people would find unacceptable or offensive **S:** remark, criticism, question; joke, story. **V:** be, come, get, go; perform, act, play, sth. **adv mod:** (much) too; rather, a bit, a little (too), very □ DAVE: *Anyone would think it's your experiment that failed, you with your long face.* RONNIE: *O my God, how* ***near the knuckle*** *that is.* ITAJ □ *Another pointed out that, in a recent British book, the therapist was said to have bathed his patient. This, he thought, was a bit* ***near the bone.*** ST □ *To the charge that his jokes are* ***near the knuckle****, he innocently replies: 'Blue is in the eye of the beholder.'* TVT □ *Creasey, who is frankly unable to imagine which way the second programme might swerve, is intrigued. 'It's going out as live. We're playing it very* ***close to the bone.****'* TVT □ in third example, *a blue joke* = 'an improper joke'.

one's nearest and dearest [n + n non-rev] (facetious) one's family, esp those one lives with □ *We found later we shared many tastes, not least that for getting up at around six and then playing Mozart piano concertos very loudly and thus making life a hell for* ***our nearest and dearest.*** OBS □ (space travel) *It is rather perturbing to think of going off on a fast journey and returning considerably younger than* ***one's nearest and dearest*** *who stayed at home.* L ⇨ ⚠ near and dear (to sb).

(or) the nearest offer the highest price offered below one previously stipulated or suggested by sb offering sth for sale □ MICK: *Furniture and fittings, I'll take four hundred* ***or the nearest offer.*** TC □ *I expected to have to come down a bit from £5000 but* ***the nearest offer*** *I got was £3500 and I wasn't willing to let the car go for that.* □ abbreviated o.n.o. eg in newspaper advertisements.

a necessary evil [Comp (NP)] sth undesirable, imperfect or, in some respects, harmful that cannot be done without for practical reasons, or the complete lack of which would be worse than the ill effects that it already produces **V:** ⚠ be, become; make, find, sth □ (source) *Government, even in its best state, is but* ***a necessary evil****; in its worst state, an intolerable one.* COMMON SENSE (T PAINE 1737-1809) □ *Scientists may still regard politics as an evil, but at any rate they no longer shut their eyes to it. They have been forced to recognise that—at the very worst—it is* ***a necessary evil*** *in which their very understanding compels them to play an inescapable part.* OBS □ *Martin was a secretive man: but keeping scientific secrets, which to Smith seemed so natural, was to him a piece of evil, even if* ***necessary evil.*** *In war you had to do it, but you could not pretend to like it.* NM □ *'We asked everyone we could, you know, we didn't discriminate. We had our personal friends, of course, one has to have them.' Mrs Knighton spoke as if personal friends were* ***a necessary evil.*** PW □ also pl.

necessity is the mother of invention (saying) a lack, or need, of sth produces the will to supply it □ (source) *Art imitates Nature, and* ***necessity is the mother of invention.*** R FRANCK 1624-1708 □ ***Necessity*** *may* ***be the mother of invention*** *in evolutionary processes too, but if an animal has to evolve a liquid storage system, a maternal pouch, prehensile tail, or whatever, in order to survive in its enviroment, then how did it survive to evolve it?* □ *He successfully lied his way out of the situation with an* ***invention born of necessity.*** □ (NONCE) ***Necessity****, I suspect, has* ***been the mother of*** *Sadler's Wells's* ***concentration*** *on production and scenic standards. Deprived, by the limitations of their charter and their finances, of great singers' services, they have been able to concentrate on the opera itself.* NS □ (NONCE) ***Gambling was born of necessity.*** ST □ variant invention is born of necessity.

neck and crop [n + n non-rev] bodily; completely □ *She was a Victorian servant girl who had been turned out* ***neck and crop*** *by her employers when they discovered she was going to have a baby.* □ functions as A.

neck and neck (with sb/sth) [Comp/A (AdvP)] in equal position in a race; not able to get ahead of another; equal in ability, popularity, usefulness, cost etc (with sb/sth) **V:** be; run, finish □ *They used to call it a draw, when two horses finished* ***neck and neck.*** *But with the sophisticated cameras and timing devices they have now they can almost always declare a winner.* □ (The Oxford Book of Twentieth Century Verse) *Eliot leads the field with 29 pages, with Hardy (25), Auden (24) and Yeats (21) not far behind. Larkin* (the editor) *himself is limited to a modest six pages (which makes him* ***neck and neck with*** *Day Lewis and two pages behind Graves).* NS □ *Sales analysis shows these two products still vying* ***neck and neck*** *to corner the market.* ⇨ ⚠ win/lose by a (short) neck.

(in our) neck of the woods (informal) (in) the place where we etc live, are etc ((US) originally a forest settlement) **det:** our, your; this, that; another. **adj:** (a) pleasant, (a) remote □ *The audience was disgusted and some left before the end. We don't go in for wife-swapping too much* ***in our neck of the woods.*** □ *I see you are the representative from the Manchester Branch. How's business* ***in your neck of the woods*** *just now?* □ *A vast sign at Spokane's bustling airport says there will be only 'one great International Exposition' in the United States in the 1970s. With all the frustration and feuding which it has brought* ***this*** *usually placid* ***neck of the woods****, it may be just as well.* OBS □ *At the end of Radio 3's Italian Weekend, I felt as if I been at a houseparty whose host had organised a whirlwind of visits for his guests so that we could meet everyone of any consequence* ***in a*** *most richly endowed* ***neck of the woods****, culturally speaking.* L

neck or nothing [n + n non-rev] (saying) risking death or injury in order to do or obtain sth; risking total failure in the hope of complete success □ *'Well, it's* ***neck or nothing****,' he thought to himself as he set his horse at a high windbreak hedge in the hope of outdistancing his pursuers.* □ *A good climber takes only carefully calculated risks. The urge to go at it,* ***neck or nothing****, in a spirit of bravado is not uncommon in beginners, and is the first thing they have to unlearn.* □ *At the next throw he doubled his stakes in a* ***neck-or-nothing*** *bid to recoup his losses.* □ attrib use *a* ***neck-or-nothing*** *bid.*

need etc one's head examined etc [V + O + Comp] (facetious) show oneself (in sb's opinion) to be stupid in one's behaviour, opinions, or tastes **V:** need, ⚠ want; have; get. **Comp:** examined ⚠ tested; examining; testing □ *Any European who doesn't see the period 1945-1973 as one of striking tranquillity* ***needs his head examined.*** *We may live in a violent world,* *but not, at present, in a violent corner of it.* NS □ *I, for example, went back to what everyone accounted a sort of neo-Georgian poetry. Of course, it wasn't. Anyone who thinks my poetry is neo-Georgian* **needs their head examining.** L □ *'I always think of you as being dashing and romantic and good-natured at the same time. Like Charles the Second.' 'What!' George laughed. 'My poor child,' he said kindly, 'I think you ought to* **have your head examined**.' PE □ *Those commentators who have belaboured the point that football can do without George Best* **want their heads testing**. *Of course it can do without him, but the real question is: what will it be like without him?* NS

need sth like (one needs) a hole in the head [V + O + A] (informal) not need sth at all; be better, happier, safer etc without sth □ *The tendency for DDT to accumulate in the fatty tissues of mammals is not denied, but we are invited to console ourselves with the thought that there is no evidence to date that moderate accumulations do us any harm. I still can't help feeling that I* **need** *that DDT* **like I need a hole in the head**. NS □ *They* **need** *four secretaries* **like I need a hole in the head**. *I mean these girls in short skirts look great but think about trading in four of them for a little grey-haired old lady who knows how to type.* SC □ *They've got a billion dollars in it* (supersonic travel*) already. But, I must say, we* **need** *it* **like a hole in the head**. *Why do people need to get somewhere faster than they already can?* L

need etc a long spoon (to sup/eat with the devil) (saying) need to keep at a cautious distance, have some safeguard, or possibility of escape or withdrawal, or sceptical attitude, when associating with sb/sth or involving oneself in an argument, decision **V:** need, must have, have to have, want □ *But how did he know I had any whiskey left in the cave? It would be* **the Devil** *who was* **wanting a long spoon** *if he was* **taking brose** ((Scottish) = oatmeal gruel) *with Father James. What a man!* RM □ *There are no liberals dancing in the streets of America today because they did all that in 1968 when Lyndon Johnson admitted that they had defeated him. It was then—it would almost certainly be now — a premature celebration. Who* **sups with history must have a long spoon**. NS □ *Weekend prime time ought to bring out whatever humility lurks within the religious broadcasting departments in all its full cringe. But it doesn't. Instead we have more than our quota of low cunning, plain deceit and matey evasion. A critic really does* **need a long spoon** *to get most of it down his craw* (= throat). NS □ expression frequently adapted, as shown.

need/require no introduction [V + O] sb's work or achievements is/are well known in general or to a particular audience, company, group etc so no further explanation or information is needed **A:** from me; here; to Celtic scholars □ *Two fairly new faces and one very familiar one make up the trio of presenters. Barrister turned playwright Nemone Lethbridge and Alasdair Clayre, Open University don, poet, songwriter and much else besides, are the new people: Ned Sherrin, however,* **needs no introduction**. RT □ (review of books) *Isaac Bashevis Singer* **needs no introduction** *from me, as they say.* L

(look for) a needle in a haystack etc (look for) sb/sth almost impossible to find, to distinguish or isolate from the crowd or mass which contains him/it **n:** haystack, ⚠ bundle of hay, (old use) bottle of hay □ *Somewhere along that waterfront there might be somebody who knew her. I walked till the straps chafed raw places on my legs, and hardly felt them, but it was like* **looking for a needle in a bundle of hay**, *of course.* RFW □ *There is an excusable feeling that trying to find any practical benefit from SALT* (US-Soviet Strategic Arms Limitation Talks), *or other set-piece conferences, is like peering through the wrong end of telescope in search of* **a needle** *that is not* **in the haystack**. L □ (NONCE) (a novel) *'The Odessa File' looks likely to pull off a very similar coup. The plot concerns* **another needle** *lost* **in another haystack** *and our young hero has to find it before the balloon (or in this case a rocket) goes up.* L □ (NONCE) *All I could do was to go on searching, alone, at random, like a man approaching* **a haystack** *with a piece of cotton in his pocket, ready to thread* **the** *first* **needle** *he finds with it.* CON

needless to say [Disj] of course; as you might expect; obviously □ *The playing of the English Chamber Orchestra is superb.* **Needless to say**, *Peter Pears give a highly perceptive account of the hero himself.* OBS □ *The last Labour government made uneasy and often desperate attempts to curry favour with the City and big business establishments, and even to seek the help of their supposedly 'liberal' fringes—* **needless to say**, *to no avail.* NS □ *The grass on the 'lawn' was a foot high. David offered to remedy this by sprinkling some petrol on it and setting it on fire. He wasn't allowed to,* **needless to say**. □ front, middle or end position.

needs must (when the devil drives) (saying) circumstances make it necessary or unavoidable (for sb to sth) □ *I could no more have climbed that wall, in ordinary circumstances, than flown over it, but* **needs must when the devil drives**. □ *I don't think the walls need re-painting; but* **needs must**, *I suppose, if I'm to get any peace.* □ *'It's all in a good cause,' grinned the photographer when one of the family expressed a mild qualm. '***Needs must when the devil drives***.'* □ elliptical construction with S and main v of must understood; sometimes facetious. ⇨ ⚠ next entry.

needs must/must needs do sth (formal) must necessarily, unavoidably do sth; (ironic) inconveniently choose or happen to do sth □ *'A labourer! Your parents didn't send you to Oxford for that!' 'Honours degrees are ten a penny now, it seems. And even a philosophy graduate* **needs must** *eat.'* □ *It was abundantly evident that, as director of the new Institute of Archaeology which would shortly be opened in London, I* **must needs** *have something more than paper-knowledge of the Near Eastern field.* SD ⇨ ⚠ previous entry.

neither fish, flesh nor good red herring/ fresh meat [Comp (NP)] (saying) vague; ambiguous; difficult to identify or classify **V:** ⚠ be; find sb □ *A man may consider himself an atheist, an agnostic or a believer, and good luck to him.*

But to call yourself a religiously-minded man without professing a religion is to be **neither fish, flesh nor good red herring**. □ *Another bout of leap-frogging next year could be fatal for the 'Mail'* (a newspaper), *whose hybrid formula,* **neither fish nor flesh**, *has so far failed to win it the two million sales it needs to break even.* NS □ *As a business-man, journalist and writer, I was* **neither fish, fowl nor fresh meat**. *So at the age of 45, I packed it all in* (= stopped doing it) *and we came up here.* TVT

neither hide nor hair of sb/sth [O (NP)] no trace of sb's/sth's existence or presence **V:** see; find, discover, reveal □ *As well as about 500 British pilots, more than 280 Americans, Germans, Indians, Canadians, Danes, Swedes, Israelis, French—even two Chinese ('came at the end of the War and* **neither hide nor hair of** *them again')—have passed through the school.* TVT □ *'What do you mean? Hasn't he been in?' 'I've seen* **neither hide nor hair of** *him.'* □ *The place seemed to stink of cats, but I* **never saw hide nor hair of** *one all the time I lived there.* □ hide and hair non-rev; variant never see hide nor hair of sb/sth.

a nervous wreck [Comp (NP)] a person who is suffering psychological damage from, or has broken down under, mental or physical stress; a bag/bundle of nerves (qv) **V:** ⚠ become; turn (sb) into, make...of sb, leave sb □ *His experiences in solitary confinement had left him* **a nervous wreck**, *incapable of concentrating on any task or mixing with strangers.* □ *This fellow is quite madly in love with me. He keeps calling and trying to get in at all hours, and when he doesn't call he rings up, and I'm just* **a nervous wreck**. UTN □ *These constant changes of policy were making* **a nervous wreck** *of me.* RT □ also pl; often facetious or exaggerated.

the net result the end or final result in a process, enquiry etc contrasted with provisional or temporary findings □ *I never lied about my misdeeds; I took my punishment. For myself, although I began to know fear early in life, much too early,* **the net result** *of the treatment was probably beneficial.* MFM □ *I tried to cultivate a small vegetable plot, but as* **the net result** *of my efforts was a row of lettuces without hearts and a few worm-eaten carrots it hardly seemed worth the trouble.* □ *Do you mean that even if I undergo these two operations* **the net result** *may be that I will be no better than I am at the moment?* □ usu S of *be*.

the nettle, danger (...the flower, safety) a dangerous course which is the best or only way to ensure one's safety, freedom, success (from I HENRY IV II 3) □ (a football team, Tottenham Hotspur) *Even at this late stage, Tottenham could take heart from that other Hotspur who, admittedly while talking to himself, observed 'out of* **this nettle, danger**, *we pluck* **this flower, safety**.' G □ *The day after Mr Neville Chamberlain had stung his fingers upon* **that nettle danger** *at Munich in 1938 I stood in the foyer of the Café Royal in Regent Street. Beside me was a minor Secretary of State, and I can still hear his words. 'Today,' he said, 'I am ashamed to be an Englishman.'* SD

never to be forgotten [Comp (AdjP)] (cliché) unforgettable; memorable □ ...*that memorable night in March, at the end of the jetty, in the howling wind,* **never to be forgotten**, *when suddenly I saw the whole thing. The vision at last.* KLT □ *I've only once been more embarrassed, and that was on the* **never to be forgotten** *occasion when the bottom fell out of a seven-pound bag of gooseberries I had with me on the bus.* □ *People as gullible as that are an encouragement to crime. There is such a thing, in the* **never-to-be-forgotten** *words of a legal friend of mine, as culpable innocence.* □ attrib use *the* **never to be forgotten** *occasion, the* **never-to-be-forgotten** *words.*

never cease to wonder etc (at sth/sb) continue to be surprised (by sth/sb) even after long familiarity **V:** wonder (at sb/sth), marvel (at sb/sth), be amazed (at/by sb/sth), be surprised (at/by sb/sth); ask oneself (why/whether/how); regret sth; wonder (that), marvel (that), be amazed (that), be surprised (that) □ *After a few days Madame Lebrun saw to it that I was provided with water or fruit-juice instead of wine at table, though she* **never ceased to wonder at** *this strange preference.* □ *I* **never cease to be amazed by** *people who profess to be so 'furious and disgusted' by fox-hunting. Their compassion is admirable but misplaced.* RT □ *The workmen had a way of setting about their business as if nobody else were in the room,* **at** *which I* **never ceased to marvel**. SML □ *While I do not feel responsible for the accident, I* **never cease to ask** *myself whether it could not have been foreseen and averted.* □ *It isn't right for elderly people to cut themselves off from their friends. My parents retired to the country and have* **never ceased to regret** *it.* □ *It's a racket, of course, but it pays. I* **never cease to be** *amazed that people can be so easily deceived.*

never have etc a dull moment [possess] (catchphrase) have etc no lack of interesting, exciting, amusing etc things to do or see **V:** have; ⚠ (there) be. **prep:** with □ *This can hardly be recommended as a book for sensitive romantics. Mutilations, human sacrifices and the wild excesses of Cartimandua, the voluptuous Queen of Brigantia, ensure that* **there is never a dull moment**. SC □ *We listened to Radio 4 over most of the holiday and* **there was never a dull moment** *and never a false note.* RT □ *It was a very good play* **with never a dull moment** *all evening.* □ *He turned abruptly away and went quickly down to Prospect Cliff. 'Exhausted myself. Mustn't overdo it.' Plenty to do on a rock.* **Never a dull moment**. PM □ often verbless comment as in last example.

never let it be said (that) (informal or facetious) never let the criticism be made (that) □ *Don't measure yourself by others' successes and failures.* **Never let it be said** *you've done less than your best: that is the standard to set yourself.* □ *'Would you mind if we thought it over?' I asked. 'But of course, Doctor. Think it over at your leisure.* **Never let it be said that** *we rushed a client into purchasing a property he didn't want.'* DIL □ *'You mean you want me to get out?' he asked tractably. '***Never let it be said that** *I wouldn't oblige a lady.'* AITC

never mind[1] don't worry; don't consider (sth) important □ *You're a naughty boy to frighten Sarah like that, and to tell lies. But* **never mind**, *it was just a game, wasn't it?* DC □ *'Could any girl be more unfortunately placed?* ***Never mind,****' thought Victoria, 'I'm alive, aren't I?'* TCB □ *You might as well take the clothes away now.* ***Never mind*** *if you can't spare the money at the moment. You can pay me later.* □ *I don't fancy the pub tonight, somehow. But go yourselves, and* ***never mind*** *me. I'll be quite happy reading the paper or watching TV till you come back.* □ imper, often followed by consoling or encouraging remark.

never mind[2] don't inquire (because you won't be told); mind one's own business (qv) □ *'How much was the bill?' '****Never mind****—what you don't know won't hurt you. I'll get most of it off "expenses" anyway.'* □ *We got hold of a copy of the letter—* ***never mind*** *how—before it left the solicitor's office.* □ *'Where are you going?' Sue repeated, running out after him. '****Never mind,****' he answered roughly. 'You get back inside. I'll be no more than a hour.'* □ imper, often curt, replying to, or forestalling, question.

never mind (doing) sth [V + O] forget about; stop, or don't start, doing sth **O:** the excuses, the apologies, the explanations; that, all that; worrying about that □ *'Since you're here at last,' he said, interrupting her explanation, '****never mind*** *the excuses — start serving the customers.'* □ *'You're snoring again, John,' his wife said, shaking him by the shoulder. 'Sorry, dear.' '****Never mind*** *saying you're sorry. Turn over on your side, and stay that way.'* □ *'I could give you a recommendation that would probably get you a job in a school.' 'Listen, George,' Charles said wearily. '****Never mind*** *the missionary zeal. I don't want honest work. I'm like you, I prefer to be a parasite.'* HD □ imper, often curt, and usu followed by order or recommendation to do sth else.

never etc miss a trick/move [V + O] (informal) not fail to notice, or attend to, details (esp ones which, as an expert, professional etc, it is important to observe) **S:** director, conductor, teacher, coach. **adv:** never, not; hardly ever, rarely, seldom □ *You need something more than pictures. You need sports-writers you can rely on. Men who* ***never miss a trick.*** TO □ *Notice the way they disguise the thinness of Twiggy's voice by putting a sax or strings in unison along with her. Conductor-arranger Peter Maxwell Davies does****n't miss a trick.*** ST (Billy Wilder) *He's a perfectionist. He notices a flicker of an eyelid that isn't right. A speck of dust on a prop. I've never known anyone so alert. Billy* ***never misses a trick.*** RT

never put off/leave till tomorrow what you can do today (saying) carry out a task or duty as soon as you can □ (source) ***Never leave that till tomorrow which you can do today.*** MAXIMS (B FRANKLIN 1706-90) □ *The feminist movement which emerged in France in 1970 was inspired with a sort of do-****not-put-off-till-tomorrow-the-revolution-you-can-bring-about-today*** *attitude.* ST □ (NONCE) *Like most of us, Byron's Don Juan believed in* ***putting off till tomorrow what need not be endured today****: 'Let's have wine and women, mirth and laughter,/ Sermons and soda water the day after.'* NS □ *'The form doesn't have to be sent in till the 18th, anyway.' '****Never put off till tomorrow what you can do today****—besides, if you stick it away in a drawer you might forget about it.'* □ sometimes facetious or cynical.

sb/one never said/spoke a truer word (cliché) sb/one was right □ *'Your lawyer should have told you you were making a big mistake.' 'He did, and he never said a truer word. But I thought I knew better.'* □ *'Evening, Mr Lampton, and how are the town's finances?' 'We're solvent,' I said. 'A damned sight more than can be said for the country,' said the woolman heavily. 'By God, but you* ***never spoke a truer word****, Tom.'* RATT □ used to give emphasis to a preceding statement; seldom used in first person.

never say die (catchphrase) don't despair; keep trying; keep your courage up □ (Mrs Salad has to appear in court on a charge of shoplifting) *Gerald patted her shoulder. He could find nothing to say but '****Never say die****, Mrs Salad. It'll be all over soon.'* ASA □ *Now Warhol's distributors have a plan for inviting 100 people from cinema queues to a second Festival showing* (of 'Trash', a film not yet given a censor's certificate) *at lunchtime next Saturday, seats free, everything legal and above-board.* ***Never say die.*** ST □ *Those gutsy* ((slang) = determined, courageous) *little ladies just* ***never say die****. And with a special two-hour TV spectacular bouncing them back into their search for stardom, let's hope they make it there this time.* TVT □ *The newspapers have given away their editorial bias. 'The New York Post', which is the* ***never-say-die*** *liberal evening paper, has had encouraging headlines every night.* L □ attrib use *the* ***never-say-die*** (= determined, courageous) *paper.* ⇨ ⚠ do or die.

never a word etc (formal) no word(s) etc; not a single word etc **n:** word, grumble; look, glance; thought □ *They watched and listened, but spoke* ***never a word.*** □ *Life was hard for my mother, but* ***never a grumble*** *passed her lips.* □ *If you choose to enjoy yourself and spend all your money with* ***never a thought*** *for tomorrow, you must bear the consequences yourself.* □ *I have no sentimental feeling for 'Whiteoaks'. I would leave the place tomorrow with* ***never a*** *backward* ***glance****.* □ sometimes follows prep, esp *with*; sometimes used to give emphasis to a statement.

new/fresh blood [O (NP)] newcomer(s) and/or fresh ideas, skills, methods, likely to improve or invigorate an administrative body, business firm, institution, sport, field of study, etc **V:** have, get; need, want; infuse, inject, put, bring. **A:** in(to) the business; on (to) the staff; here □ *Into this somewhat hidebound 'staff atmosphere' it was vital to inject* ***new blood****.* MFM □ *'Captain Prettyman's retiring as Master next year,' she said. 'You're the sort of chap they ought to have.* ***New blood*** *to pep them up.'* DBM □ *It is some six months since I last watched 'Coronation Street', and what a change for the better are the recent episodes. There's* ***fresh blood*** *in the show, and Ray and Deirdre's marriage has brought into the programme an element of realism.* TVT

a new boy/girl [Comp (NP)] a recently enrolled pupil in a school (esp with the implication of being unfamiliar with procedure and only partially accepted by other pupils); any recent member of a community, society, group of workers, etc **V:** ⚠ be, feel; think oneself □ *I* *was unable to get my two colleagues to agree and, as I was then* ***a 'new boy'*** *in Whitehall, I did not force the issue at that time, being much occupied with other matters.* MFM □ *Seven of the players in this list are regular members of the Test team, while Hayes,* ***the 'new boy'****, Willis, and the five extra players would add spark to the team.* L □ *'I have a comfortable room with a nice outlook,' my aunt wrote, 'and the staff are very kind. But I still feel very much* ***a new girl****.'*

a new broom (sweeps clean) (saying) sb recently appointed to office or a responsible post (starts with an energetic programme of reform and change, sometimes not welcomed by those already there) □ *Some officers from the War Office were present at the conference; they evidently regarded me as* ***a new broom*** *and an unpleasant one at that.* MFM □ *Our books and arts coverage this week has all been organised by him* (John Gross) *in his first week as the new Literary Editor. We welcome him not in any sense as* ***a new broom*** *but rather as a very old friend.* NS □ (NONCE) (The) *new Assistant Commissioner at once embarked on a whirlwind programme of '****new brooming****' which, predictably, ended in an almighty row with the Commissioner.* NS □ *I've complained before about putting jazz under the rule of the same chap who hires comics. When in December Robert Ponsonby succeeds William Glock as head of BBC Music, he should take the opportunity afforded by '****new broom****' licence to inject some logic.* L □ attrib use ***new broom*** *licence, a* ***new broom*** *attitude, approach.*

a new deal [O (NP)] a programme of political, social and economic reform (often New Deal, first used of President's Roosevelt's policy, 1923-35, in the US); any plan or arrangement intended to improve others' life or work **V:** offer, promise, ensure; secure, obtain □ *At the start of 1935, Lloyd George launched* ***his 'New Deal'****, which proposed a National Development Council to revive the British economy and, by slum clearance, road building and restored agriculture, to eliminate unemployment.* OBS □ *The strike lasted four weeks, with no man daring to cross the female picket lines and the bosses cowering in their factories. Eventually the Leeds ladies got* ***a new deal****; 1s 2d on the basic rate (compared with 1s 1d for men).* ST □ *Where are the Scottish Athletes' Club, that group which began in a blaze of publicity promising* ***a new deal*** *for the athlete?* ST

a new look an altered form, style, appearance given to sth whose basic function remains the same (from a fashion in women's clothing made popular by Christian Dior in 1947) □ *It's difficult to say how you have an idea for a* (beauty treatment) *product. It could start as a problem you're trying to overcome, or it might be a fashion idea to go with* ***a new look****.* ST □ *'The blades of the knives and the prongs of the forks seem very short to me.' 'But that's* ***the new look*** *in table cutlery,' the assistant explained.* □ *The reshuffle of ministry portfolios at the weekend gave the Cabinet* ***its*** *long-expected* ***new look****.* L □ (headline referring to the introduction of billiards, table-tennis, afternoon tea, etc as inducements to religious instruction) ***New Look*** *Sunday School Defended.* T □ attrib use *a* ***new look*** *Sunday school.*

news from nowhere sth one/everybody knows already; sth too obvious, or too trivial, to be worth announcing, pointing out □ ((source) book title ***News from Nowhere*** W MORRIS 1834-96) □ *'My colleague was most intrigued by your problem. He says it's a very interesting legal point.' 'Well, that's* ***news from nowhere****! I was hoping to hear you could resolve it.'* □ *The lame conclusion to his embarrassing jaunt* (ie documentary film) *was that Cambridge is a pillar of the Establishment ('I still can't stand it, but that's my problem'), which is* ***news from nowhere****.* NS

the next best thing the most satisfactory substitute available for sb/sth that one does not, or cannot, have □ *The Hutchings Crusade are in Birmingham now because a local committee invited them as* ***the next best thing*** *after an unsuccessful attempt to book Billy Graham.* TO □ *He wasn't the first person to make the wistful discovery that* ***the next best thing*** *to being creative yourself is to become, in one way or another, necessary to someone who is creative.* CON □ *In a cage, however, I could not provide the Pouched Rats with a stream, so they used* ***the next best thing****, which was their water-pot.* BB

next door/thing to sth [Comp (NP)] almost the same as sth; almost as good, or as bad, as sth **V:** ⚠ be; regard, consider, sb/sth as □ *I had given her the manuscript to read, and I strongly suspected that she had not read it. For Myrtle not to have read it seemed to me* ***next door to*** *perfidy.* SPL □ *I've never met your wife but anybody who can put up with you must be* ***next thing to*** *a saint.* □ *'I never said it was a real diamond in the ring.' 'No, but when she assumed it was you let her think so. I call that* ***next door to*** *telling a lie.'* □ *As a medical examination it was* ***next door to*** *farcical, but I was passed A1.*

next to nothing [O/o (NP)] almost nothing; a very small amount **V:** know, understand, read; eat, live on □ *It has also been mentioned that* ***next to nothing*** *is definitely known either about the trace itself or about the way it continues to exist.* MFF □ *He now sleeps for an hour or two in twenty-four and does rigorous exercises for five. He reads voraciously and writes copiously. He eats* ***next to nothing****. At 28 his hair is grey.* L □ *He knew a small printer in the street behind the Fishmarket who, for* ***next to nothing****, had made a die for him with his letter-heading in small script.* US □ *After that* (ie drama school) *there's the road and all the slog of touring with everyone mucking in, living on* ***next to nothing****, and smiling through a mist of tears.* NS □ *Because you are English, you are so proud and stuck up. What does it mean to be English?* ***Next to nothing****. Here we spit upon the English.* TCB

nice one, Cyril (catchphrase) you've done well; you've gained an advantage for yourself (originally part of a football chant) □ *He earns thousands, just welcoming people to the night-club—he got the job because his father knows the club's owner.* ***Nice one, Cyril****.* □ *Charlie Pinney runs heavy horse handling courses for the Agriculture Training Board—which means he gets free and sometimes nubile labour to work his farm, and gets paid for telling them how to do it (****nice one, Charlie****).* ST □ Cyril often used but may be replaced by any name; informal or ironic.

nice and quiet etc/quietly etc (informal) pleasantly and/or suitably quiet(ly) etc **adj:** quiet; gentle; easy. **adv:** quietly; gently; smoothly □ *You'll be the only one sleeping on this floor, which will make it* ***nice and quiet*** *for you.* DC □ *'That's to say a received message would appear as words on a television tube.' 'Well, what's the matter with that? It'll be* ***nice and easy*** *to read.'* TBC □ *Now, move the gear-lever into first position and let the clutch in* ***nice and gently****.* □ nice and functions as adv mod (of degree, extent) of adj/adv it precedes.

nice/lovely weather for ducks (catchphrase) rainy weather, esp as a sarcastic comment with the meaning 'Very wet today, isn't it?', 'What a rainy day!' etc □ *'****Nice weather for ducks****,' said Jim when he arrived at last, soaking wet. 'But since I'm not a duck, do you think you could lend me a change of dry clothes?'*

nice work if you can get it (saying) expression of envy, commenting on what someone has been lucky or clever enough to get or do □ ***Nice work if you can get it****. This week, Peter Barkworth stars in a play about a man, recently made redundant at his work, who makes a success on his own as a snail-farmer.* RT □ ***Nice-Work-If-Can-Get-It*** *Department. Where were my Lords Thomson, Kearton, McFadzean and Ritchie-Calder last weekend? They were the personal guests of the President of the Lebanese Republic, no less, and flew out with wives for what was described as a 'glorious shindig'* (= lively party) *over the Whit weekend.* OBS □ *I think it was Brian Howard who, not over-anxious for a crack at the enemy, protested to his conscription board: 'But I am the civilisation you are fighting to defend.'* ***Nice work, if you can get it****.* NS

the nigger in the woodpile [Comp (NP)] the person responsible for spoiling sth **V:** ⚠ be; regard, consider, sb as □ *He thought the English Revolution was just around the corner. Then suddenly he found you were* ***the nigger in the woodpile****. You could have got him run out of this country. Maybe even got him hanged.* PP □ as a result of changing social attitudes, many speakers find expression offensive.

a (big) night out an evening of social enjoyment outside one's home at a restaurant, drinking-place, theatre, dance-hall, party etc □ *Ambrose, the bandleader, once looked back wryly: 'We used to attract people from the provinces. It was* ***their big night out.*** *But unfortunately they drove the other people — high society — away. We were over-popular.'* NS □ *The hero, after* ***a night on the town*** *and various adventures, has a knife-and-bottle fight with a fellow-worker which ends in court.* NS □ variant a night on the town.

night starvation (dated catchphrase) hypothetical reason for loss of physical or mental vigour (originally suggested by the advertisers of Horlicks Malted Milk, a bed-time drink made from this product being recommended as a remedy) □ GEORGE: *Behind that brooding cloud of mascara, she's got her eye on George, Josie has. Because not only does she suffer from constipation, but* ***night starvation*** (ie no sexual life) *as well.* EGD □ (NONCE) *Drawbell, whose Christian name no one had been known to utter, whose friends called him 'CF', had begun to sign himself 'Cyril Drawbell'. 'A bad case of* ***knight starvation*** (ie he wanted to be made a knight), *said someone.* NM

a nine day(s') wonder [Comp (NP)] a person or event that attracts a lot of notice and is the subject of much talk for a short time but is soon forgotten **V:** ⚠ be, become; regard sb/sth as □ *The eye of the world is upon him. But that must be small consolation as the criminal settles down to a ten-year stretch. A front page splash* (ie in the newspapers) *may have made him* ***a nine-day wonder****, but what is he to do with other nine years and 356 days?* SC □ *But if he were patient, some day he would be listened to in a way that did effective good. Not now. It would be* ***a nine days' wonder****, he would be ruined and powerless.* NM □ *If the General Strike of 1926 had been more than* ***a nine-day wonder****, Chancellor Churchill would simply have wanted to take the BBC over.* L □ also pl nine day wonders.

nine times out of ten [A (NP)] almost always □ (of big winners of football pool prizes) *They've all said, 'no publicity'. But straightaway, before you even knock, by the district, by the look of the house, by the street,* ***nine times out of ten*** *you can predict who's going to play ball.* ST □ *It is very hard to argue from results in history.* ***Nine times out of ten****, the results of what anybody wanted to do in the past turn out to be not what they intended.* L

a nine to five job etc regular work as an employee, esp in an office, shop, factory **n:** job, ⚠ day; mentality; man □ *I think sometimes of the friends who left school at the same time as me, when I made up my mind to go to art school. Some of them went straight to* ***9 to 5 jobs*** *and within three months they looked like old men.* OBS □ *Peter would have hated being cooped up in* ***a nine-to-five job****. He's always loved daring physical pursuits: sailing, motor-racing and flying.* TVT □ *Like good local newspapermen they have to be dedicated to this job:* ***a 9.0 to 5.0 mentality*** *is useless.* RT □ *He is in the office by 7.30 each morning, ready to start a 16-hour day. 'It's the only way,' he says. 'You can't get to the top and stay there with* ***a nine-to-five mentality****.'* RT □ *Yeats's admiration for aristocrats, beggars and terrorists, and his complementary distaste for thrifty* ***nine-to-fivers*** *who 'add the halfpence to the pence', must have persuaded many a young hopeful that it would be not merely tiring but downright uncultured to get a job of work.* L □ emphasis may often be either on the restrictions this pattern imposes or on the freedom from responsibility outside these hours; nine to five may or may not be hyphenated; n compound a nine-to-fiver.

nip and tuck [n + n non-rev] a situation in which failure, an unfavourable outcome, will only be, or has only been, narrowly avoided; be touch and go (qv) □ *Tell him that it'll be* ***nip and tuck*** *if I manage to snatch a few minutes to see him at all on Tuesday, much less give him a couple of hours.* □ *Waugh said he had a whole convent of Poor Clares praying it would be fine for the fête, and throughout the morning it was* ***nip and tuck****. Until the very hour of the fête we were not to know who would gain the day, the*

Poor Clares or the Powers of Darkness. TCM

the nitty gritty (of sth) (informal) the basic, essential, unadorned facts (of sth) **o:** modern living, student life; industrial relations, business management □ *All this of course is* ***the nitty gritty of*** *industrial relations. But what the politicians and the leader-writers want is the glamour stuff — a way of keeping the trains running, the lights burning and the dustbins emptied.* NS □ *After such a rare exposure to* ***the nitty-gritty of*** *modern living, to plunge into the culture-cushioned limbo of J I M Stewart's world is like taking a sauna bath in reverse.* ST □ *And because it's Jimmy Young doing the asking and the locals talking back, the series will be getting down to* ***the*** *real* ***nitty gritty***—*are you conned in the supermarkets, and how? Can you do as well from National Assistance as from Life Insurance?* RT □ *Major Macfarlane will be behind the TV cameras, explaining the ritual of Trooping the Colour. He'll be there to 'add* ***the*** *humble* ***nitty-gritty****' — which means everything from identifying major-generals and regimental marches to explaining why guardsmen have to go into training to wear their bearskins.* RT □ often preceded by *(get) down to.*

no chance (informal) there is no possibility that sth will be done or allowed or will happen □ *A League* (football) *club taking on a lad when he'd been at work for three or four years?* ***No chance***—*if he isn't taken on to the books while he is still at school, he has more or less had it today.* TVT □ *'At all sorts of important meetings up and down the country people listen to what I have to say, but at home,' he shook his head ruefully, '****no chance****.'* □ *Peter and I wanted to persuade the others that there was no need for the stuffed shirt formality of previous years.* ***No chance****. We were both ordered to wear evening dress.* NS □ used as short rueful comment or reply.

no/not any distance [Comp (NP)] not far; a short or relatively short distance **V:** ⚠ be; seem, look □ *Let's walk there—it's such a fine evening and it's really* ***no*** *great* ***distance****.* □ *The church was on the opposite side of the lake, a long way round by road but* ***no distance*** *by water, and most families had or shared a boat.* □ *It does****n't*** *seem* ***any distance*** *to the station now that I've got used to walking it.*

no end of a fuss etc (informal) a very great fuss etc **V:** cause, create, stir up. **n:** a fuss, a flap, a surprise, a disappointment, trouble □ *Dad likes his steak grilled two minutes on each side and he makes* ***no end of a fuss*** *if it's not just right.* □ *How nice to see you again! Jane will get* ***no end of a surprise*** *when she comes in and finds you here!* □ *'You're meeting some kind of a VIP, aren't you?' Young Mr Shrivenham groaned again. '****No end of a flap*** *about this fellow. I don't know why. Even the hush-hush boys are in a flap.'* TCB □ *The police have had* ***no end of trouble*** *trying to track down mail bag thieves.* T □ *The other workers may see it as favouritism and that's something that can cause* ***no end of dissatisfaction*** *among them.* □ stress pattern ˌno ˈend of a fuss etc.

no/(not) any exception [Comp/O (NP)] sb/sth that conforms to a usual kind, rule, pattern **V:** be, prove; allow □ *Helen Cresswell writes books that are impossible to put down, once started. Her last one, 'The Winter of the Birds' is* ***no exception****.* OBS □ *August is usually a wet month here and this year has proved* ***no exception****.* □ *The notice says 'Keep Out: That Means You', so why did you think you were* ***any exception****?*

no fear (informal) no; certainly not □ *'Go up and see,' said Jack contemptuously, '****No fear****!' 'The beast had teeth,' said Ralph, 'and big black eyes.'* LF □ *'Did you see Robert safely off?' 'At half past six in the morning?* ***No fear****! We said goodbye last night.'* □ *'Don't tell me you paid £100 for that old wreck!' '****No fear****. Twenty pounds, I said, take it or leave it.'* □ emph neg answer to an order, request, suggestion etc.

no fewer/less than sth as much as sth (the implication being that this is more than might be expected) □ *No self-respecting campus is without its thesis on some aspect of the social implications, and, as a result of the Surgeon-General's Commission on Violence,* ***no fewer than*** *50 further pieces of research are allegedly awaiting publication.* L □ *Since 1955* ***no less than*** *nine national newspapers have bitten the dust* (= ceased to exist). L □ *Crimes involving robbery rose 3 per cent. This is disappointing as during 1974 there had been a drop of* ***no less than*** *7 per cent.* BBCR □ *Out of 115 candidates* ***no fewer than*** *108 gained their certificates.*

(of) no fixed abode/address (legal) (having) no permanent place of residence, and no home or business address through which one can always be traced or communicated with □ SAM: *I, Samuel Levy,* ***of no fixed abode****, am being charged with loitering and soon I must leave London for ever.* HSG □ *Some of the reality behind that coldly clinical euphemism of the magistrates' courts and social security offices — '****no fixed abode****' — is brought to life in a report published this week by the Notting Hill Social Council.* NS □ address now more usu than abode.

(there are) no flies on sb (saying) sb is astute; sb is well able to look after his own interests and avoid being deceived or taken advantage of **det:** no, not any; not many, few □ *Both men suitably reflect the Co-op's* (= Co-operative Stores) *image: grainy North-country business men, but who could be taken for lay preachers.* ***No flies on*** *either of them — and both with handshakes like a vice.* OBS □ DAVE: *Look, I'm a bright boy.* ***There aren't many flies on*** *me, and when I was younger I was even brighter.* ITAJ □ *I have seen the same professor move in a single two or three-hour faculty meeting from being a pipe-ruminating, academic statesman, in his expression, his gestures, and even his voice, to a Northern,* ***no-flies-on-****Charlie, light-voiced urchin.* L □ attrib use *a* ***no-flies-on-****me businessman.*

(there is) no fool like an old fool (saying) a comment on an instance of foolishness in a person of advanced years, because he is expected to think and act sensibly and, if he does not, probably cannot be corrected □ *'Surely Tom's thinking of making a match of it with the tailor's widow, he goes there so often.' 'Don't you believe it. It's the daughter he's after—****no fool like an old fool****.'* □ (NONCE) ***There's no ghoul*** (= gruesome ghost) ***like an old ghoul*** *and the Devil* *is currently riding high at the box-office.* NS

no go [Comp (AdjP)] (informal) not possible; not allowed; not desirable **V:** ⚠ be, seem, look □ *A child could wriggle through the 20 inch gap, but it was clearly* ***no go*** *for a man of his weight.* □ *I tried very hard to make him take some money for the fish, but it was* ***no go.*** □ *As far as my parents were concerned, for me to hitch-hike across the Sahara was definitely* ***no go.*** □ *'How did you get on with the boss?'* ***'No go,*** *I'm afraid. I can't take more than two weeks' holiday at once, so I can't visit my cousins in Hong Kong.'* □ sometimes used as comment or response, as in last example. ⇨ ⚠ next entry.

a no-go area/district (informal) an area into which, or from which, movement is restricted; an area over which the police have no control etc □ (of a ban on Gypsy encampments) ***'No go' areas*** *should be rarities and temporary ones at that: a solution to some immediate difficulty.* L □ *Under no circumstance, would we be prepared to contemplate* ***no-go areas*** *in the United Kingdom.* BBCR □ *There is going to be no* ***area*** *in London which is* ***no-go.*** G ⇨ ⚠ previous entry.

no good nothing good; no good result; an end condition without value, or positively bad **V:** ⚠ ...come of, ...result from; come to..., result in... □ *It's over. They've never even for one minute suspected me. And the chap's dead and he has no dependants. absolutely* ***no good*** *can come of my going to prison now.* DC □ *...another of these food subsidies that result in* ***no good*** *to anyone. Those who cannot afford to drink milk at 9p a pint can't afford it at 8p either, and those who can won't notice the difference.* SC □ *He was deceitful even as a child. I knew he would come to* ***no good.*** □ usu functions as S or o, as shown. ⇨ ⚠ do no good; much good may it do sb.

no half measures no compromise; no moderation, or medium standard, in behaviour or performance □ *We'll pull the place down and re-build.* ***No half measures.*** T □ *I've seen many a thing like that happen with him. If you do have a disagreement with Ford, it becomes an all-out fight. He does****n't go in for half measures.*** RT □ *There'll be no expense spared. When the Parkers entertain they do****n't believe in half measures.*** □ *There are* ***no half measures*** *with Gary Player. Like one of the Grand Old Duke of York's fabled corps, when he's up he's up and when he's down he's down.* SC □ variant not believe in/go in for half measures.

(with) no holds barred (with) any form of gripping, handling or holding allowed in wrestling contests; (fig) (with) free use, in speech or action, of any methods one can employ in a contest, argument, quarrel etc; (fig) (with) disregard for conventions of honour, decency, fairness, courtesy etc □ *The Japanese wrestler, Antonio Inoki, said in Tokyo yesterday that he might break Muhammad Ali's arm — just to prove his fight* ***with 'no holds barred'*** *against the world heavyweight champion was not fixed* (= fraudulently arranged to give a previously agreed result). G □ *'You're making it just as hard as you know how, aren't you?' 'You bet I am.* ***No holds barred*** *on this one.'* TGLY □ *Thus with 'permissiveness'. If it means* ***'no holds barred'*** *or 'anything goes', then plainly a complete libertarian position is as foolish as the fear that such all-out permissiveness is possible anyway.* OBS □ *Surely a lot of these blokes would like to see a real* ***no-holds-barred*** *nude show?* TGLY □ attrib use *a* ***no-holds-barred*** *fight.*

no idle jest [Comp (NP)] sth, often a threat, said with serious intention which should not be misunderstood as a joke, exaggeration etc **V:** ⚠ be; see, find, sth to be □ *She was doing this not only to save Guy's life (for she knew by the haunted look in his eyes that this threat to take his life was* ***no idle jest****) but for Prissie too.* DC □ *When the garage man said 'This job'll cost you plenty in my time and your money,' I just laughed. But it was* ***no idle jest.*** *It took him three days and cost me £200.* □ gives emphasis, usu to S of preceding v.

no joke [Comp (NP)] an arduous or unpleasant duty, state of affairs, experience etc **V:** ⚠ be; find sth □ *Preparing fourteen pounds of meat when the temperature is over a hundred in the shade is* ***no joke.*** DF □ *This 'mustering' duty,* ***no joke*** *at all, made me abandon my notion that these sheep farmers led a life of ease.* OBS □ *It was often a case of sealing oneself into the tent to cook and sleep while the rain and midges beat their frustration on the roof. Midge-bites were* ***no joke.*** SC.

no lack/want of sth [Comp/O (NP)] plenty of sth **det:** no, never any, not any. **V:** there be; find, meet, encounter; show, display, demonstrate □ *There is* ***no lack of*** *recognition of the apparent danger of pollution to human and animal life.* DM □ *Then I looked about for something to use as a blanket. There was* ***no lack of*** *textiles.* UTN □ *'What cheek to go uninvited.' 'Oh, George has* ***never*** *shown* ***any lack of*** *that!'* □ *A man with money to spend has* ***no lack of*** *friends.* □ *With the house and the garden and three young children to look after, there is****n't any want of*** *things to do, I can tell you!.*

no laughing matter [Comp (NP)] a subject, state of affairs, about which one should not be amused, nor which one should treat lightly **V:** ⚠ be; think sth, regard sth as □ *For actors, the craft of creating comedy is often* ***no laughing matter.*** RT □ *Pat laughed, but you could see it was* ***no laughing matter.*** TT □ *It's not a good joke, I admit, but you must blame Julius for it, not me. In any case, I do not need telling that income-tax is* ***no laughing matter.*** EM

no less (a person/place) (than sb/sth) a person, place, occasion etc so famous, important, unexpected etc as to command respect, notice, surprise etc **n:** the Queen, the President; the Brighton Pavilion; Crufts □ *It will be a very grand occasion.* ***No less a person than*** *the Queen herself will perform the opening ceremony.* TVT □ *'It's a stupid brute of a dog she has.' 'Nevertheless, since it was breed champion last year at* ***no less a place than*** *Crufts it must be worth a lot of money.'* □ *They were the personal guests of the President of the Lebanese Republic,* ***no less,*** *and flew out with their wives—champagne en route.* OBS □ *She reckons it's a great event for her. Ian Hunter has invited the Mayer-Lismann Opera Workship to the Brighton Festival in May. At the Brighton Pavilion,* ***no less.*** OBS □ variant sb/sth, no less.

no/not any longer [A (AdvP)] for no further period of time; no more (qv) □ *But he could* *concentrate **no longer** on Prissie's feelings, for there was something in his pocket he had to show his father.* DC □ *He took off his spectacles. Deprived of them, his eyes seemed paler and larger and colder; his round red face was**n't** jolly **any longer**.* RATT □ *I'm sure you're all hungry. I do**n't** think we should wait **any longer** for Bob. I can keep his meal warm in the oven.* □ *My mother, **no longer** young, had lost the resilience that had helped her to cope with earlier misfortunes.* □ *It had come to the stage where his parents could **no longer** believe a word he said.* □ front, middle or end position.

no man is an island nobody lives in complete independence of others □ (source) ***No man is an Island**, entire of it self.* MEDITATION XVII (J DONNE 1571-1631) □ *It is mainly because in the first flush of romance, we like to pretend that 'marriage means independence of other people' that it so often goes sour. **No man is an island**, nor are a man and a woman.* NS

no man's land the area lying between two opposing army fronts; disputed, unapportioned, or merely desolate territory; (fig) conditions of life, or a mental state, where one feels oneself to be confusedly without place or function □ *He was not clever and he did not bother about administration; his whole soul was in the battle and especially in the actions of fighting patrols in **no-man's-land**.* MFM □ *A beachcomber betimes, I am fascinated by the lure of the shore at low water. That fluctuating margin between the tide marks, neither land nor sea, truly a **no man's land**.* ST □ *Ralph Richardson plays Hirst, a wealthy boozer with a mind so bombed that fantasy and memory, pretence and reality, even night and day, have elided into a '**no man's land**' populated mainly by fading photos and ghosts from the Thirties.* NS □ (reader's letter) *For five years our house has been a battle field between my husband and youngest son, now 19 years old, with me, as the little bit of '**no man's land**' between.* TVT

no/what matter (that/if) it doesn't matter; it's not important □ *'I may not be able to leave the office in time to get your coat from the cleaner's.' '**No matter**. I can pick it up tomorrow.'* □ HENRY: *Never met Ada, did you, or did you, I can't remember, **no matter**, no one'd know her now.* E □ *Indeed, the Inspector would almost certainly think that they were in collusion. But **what matter**, since apparently he didn't care if they were.* PW □ short answer, parenthetical comment, or introducing dependent clause.

no matter what[1] whatever person, thing, event, statement etc **det:** what; who(m); which; when; how (many ways/often/much) □ *I'm going to take next week off work, **no matter what** happens* (ie as a result or as possible cause of prevention). □ (advertisement) ***No matter what** make of electric razor you use, you'll find Lectric Shave gives you a closer, smoother, and much more comfortable shave.* DM □ *But **no matter** how he turned his head he could see nothing but a patch of darkness.* PM □ *Because we know so much about Johnson, and yet find he never lied or cheated, it is possible to feel a deeper affection for him than for any other English writer, **no matter how** great our differences of political or religious views.* NS □ introduces dependent clause.

no matter what[2] despite what (is said, occurs etc) **det:** what, who, how (clever, greatly, often) □ *'There, my darlings!' she crooned* (to her cats). *'There! You shan't starve, **no matter what** your wicked master says.'* DC □ *It's her house as well has her husband's **no matter who** the titular owner is.* □ *But all the same Robert didn't like working for Ned, **no matter how** clever Ned was at not making him feel like an employee.* CON □ *He's such a sap I can't help tormenting him **no matter how** greatly I despise myself for it.* □ introduces dependent clause referring to sb/sth the exact nature of which is known, rather than to various possibilities.

no mean/small feat etc [Comp (NP)] a considerable feat; a quite, or very, important, sizeable, significant feat etc **V:** ⚠ be; find, consider, sth. **n:** feat, achievement; reputation; tribute; poet; batsman □ *Warwickshire have been in the doldrums for a few years now, but last month they drew with Worcestershire 1-1, **no mean feat**, and the result of tomorrow's match will be watched with interest.* T □ *He saved himself by climbing along the parapet, which would have been **no small feat** even for a man half his age.* □ *The voice in question belongs to Jimmy Helms, a singer of **no mean reputation** in his own right.* OBS □ *The adding of fresh entries and some bits of pruning too are, very properly, the work of Janet Adam Smith. **No mean anthologist** herself, she was wife of the late compiler and had a discernible hand in the original.* NS □ *The team will be strengthened by one, if not both, of the all-rounders Julien and Boyce and also Derryck Murray who is **no mean batsman**.* OBS □ *Sir Frederick Ashton, the retired director of the Royal Ballet, was so impressed with her* (Marilyn Trounson's) *dancing last year that he wrote a ballet, 'Lament of the Waves', especially with her in mind. **No small tribute** to someone who was only 22.* OBS

no more [A (AdvP)] for no further period of time; no/not any longer (qv); not ever again **det:** no, (not) any, never (any) □ *I bore the pain till I could bear it **no more** and had to ask for another injection.* □ *Griffith can't bring himself to condemn what he calls Irish 'activism'. He explains: 'I ca**n't** call myself a pacifist **any more**. The Government only lifts a finger when the situation becomes untenable through action.'* L □ *He had no interest in the place except to visit his old parents. After they died he **never** came back **any more**.* □ *It's **no** use* (pretending) ***any more**, I do love Fergus—I've lied to you about it, but now I'm telling you the truth.* DC □ usu end position.

no more do etc I I don't either; I am your equal in that respect **V:** do; ⚠ have; can; would. **S:** I, you, he; Anne □ *My husband doesn't like having lodgers in the house, and **no more do I**, but we need the money and that's that.* □ CRAPE: *I've never heard of no* (= any) *Ministerial Bounty.* LETOUZEL: ***No more had I**, Mr Crape. And the Doctor made it perfectly clear that I was not supposed to have done either.* THH □ *Don't be silly, Mary—you'll just hurt yourself. If I can't shift it, **no more can you**.* □ *'I wouldn't have had the courage to say that.' '**No more would Jack***

if he hadn't had a few drinks beforehand.' □ follows immediately after neg statement.

no names, no pack-drill (catchphrase) when no culprit, defaulter etc can be identified or named, no blame or punishment will follow; when criticism etc is expressed in general terms, both accuser and accused are safeguarded (from the military term, pack-drill = 'disciplinary exercise carrying heavy equipment') □ (corruption in the Home Forces in Britain, World War 2) *There were many more such classic stories, of that we could be sure; but* ***no names, no pack-drill.*** L □ *She was the very one to speak to poor old Miss Gittings, nice decent young woman, not like some,* ***no names, no pack-drill.*** TT □ (reader's letter) *As a teacher I have often wondered how much anything said by any of us is remembered over the years. I would welcome examples. Of course —* ***no names, no pack-drill.*** OBS □ *In a panic, feeling she would be lost to him unless he testified, Harold said; 'You were right, Alec. I am — well, I am interested in Irma.' 'Well, my boy, I congratulate you. I won't ask you any questions —* ***no names, no pack-drill*** *— but go ahead, I wish you luck.'* PW

no news is good news (saying) no communication, information, from or about sb/sth tends to mean that all is going well, that no disaster or trouble has occurred, that no help is needed □ *She was too worried to go across the passage for Mrs Batey's comfort. Mrs Batey would tell her that* ***no news was good news*** *and that if there had been an accident, she would have heard about it all too soon.* AITC □ (a newsprinters' strike during the course of the longer dockers' strike, 1972) *For such apparently self-sufficient men, the dockers' depth of resentment over their public image is remarkable. They were glad there were no newspapers, they said. '****No news is good news****.'* NS

(there's) no peace/rest for the wicked (saying) fear, worry, harassment is the lot of wrong-doers □ (source) ***There is no peace****, saith my God,* ***to the wicked.*** ISAIAH LVII 21 □ HAVA: *Don't cry, because your husband is sleeping now.* (spirit of) SAM: *Yes, but dreaming heavy —* ***no rest for the wicked.*** HSG □ *'Oh dear, I'll have to go,' Mrs Batey said equably. '****No peace for the wicked****, they say.'* AITC □ ***No rest for the wicked****, his mother always said. But I'm not wicked, he told himself.* LLDR □ *But for actors, like* ***for the wicked, there is no rest****. People don't understand that when actors are not working, they are not resting.* TVT □ often merely comment on being harassed, interrupted, required to do sth, with only a teasing, derogatory implication.

no room to swing a cat (saying) restricted, or overcrowded, space to live or work in □ *I'd rather live in this old house with all its inconveniences than in one of those pokey bungalows where you have****n't room to swing a cat****.* □ *It was supposed to be my workshed but there is****n't room to swing a cat*** *now, my wife's filled it so full of household gear.* □ (NONCE) ***Cats*** *do* ***not*** *get* ***swung*** *too much in Japan and by the same token the man who wants to swing a golf club has his problems.* OBS □ (NONCE) *The crucial defect of this government's white paper was that it proposed to draw boundary lines tightly around the built-up areas of the conurbations, leaving them no breathing,* ***no catswinging****, no developable space.* NS □ (NONCE) *For example, sets had rarely been used before in* (Studio) *Pres B and getting them up there was a bit like* ***swinging a cat*** *in a coal cellar.* RT

no/not (any) secret [Comp (NP)] a matter of public or local knowledge **V:** ⚠ be; make of sth... □ *It was* ***no secret*** *that there was some anxiety about the business. The Ministry of Finance had ordered an inquiry at the beginning of last year.* NS □ *My dislike of Jim Paterson is* ***no secret*** *round here but anybody that thinks I'd be capable of deliberately setting fire to his shop must be off his head.* □ *It has been* ***no secret*** *that he carried out abortions in the provincial maternity clinic.* ST □ *I have****n't*** *made* ***any secret*** *of my intention to take business from him. He's had a monopoly, and overcharged, here long enough.*

no/not any slouch [Comp (NP)] (informal) an able and effective worker, performer etc esp in some particular art, skill, activity **V:** ⚠ be; regard, consider, sb as. **A:** as a writer; at playing the market; in the kitchen □ *She shows discrimination and choice in her reading. And of course, as a writer, her father was* ***no slouch****. Eugene O'Neill.* RT □ *He proved himself to be* ***no slouch*** *at playing the market, quadrupling his £50,000 inheritance in less than two years.* □ *Hansen is a fine tender writer and is* ***no slouch*** *at plot-making either.* SC □ *The three houses are all owned by the Church Commissioners who are* ***no slouches*** *when it comes to property.* ST □ JO: *She's a devil with the men.* PETER: *Are you, Helen?* HELEN: *Well, I do****n't*** *consider myself* ***a slouch****.* TOH

(there is) no smoke without fire (saying) signs, indications of sb's presence or involvement (but esp rumours, scandal etc) don't arise from nothing, always have some cause or basis **det:** no, ⚠ (not) any, never (any) □ *Soon after sunrise the first column of smoke stood upright on the eastern horizon. My pulse quickened.* ***No smoke without fire****; no fire without man! Could it, by some miracle, be a sign of River Bushman?* LWK □ *When her name and the Duke's were mischievously linked in the Press, the Duke encouraged her husband to bring a libel action, from which he won £2000. Nevertheless many people shook their heads and muttered, '****No smoke****—'* ST □ *But* ***there is seldom any smoke without fire*** *and it was clear to me that the rumours* (of looting by British troops) *were being spread in London by a colonel that I had removed from my Tac Headquarters.* MFM □ *My man and I had been married for seven years. We all know the myth about the itch* (ie that after seven years of marriage the partners experience (usually temporary) discontent with the relationship) *and we joke about it, but now and again I had my misgivings that* ***there is never smoke without fire****.* YWT

no stranger to sb/sth [Comp (NP)] well-known to sb; familiar to a group, in a locality, etc; familiar with, and having had much experience of, sth **V:** ⚠ be, seem, appear □ *But of course Prissie was* ***no stranger to*** *him. No indeed, he counted on Prissie for everything now.* DC □ *Sergiu Commissiona,* ***no stranger to*** *the Royal Opera House orchestra pit, was conduct-*

ing an opera there for the first time. ST ▫ *Waris Hussein, who directs, is* ***no stranger to*** *the subtler regions of the human spirit.* RT ▫ *Michael Carreras is the son of Colonel James Carreras, founding father of Hammer horror* (films), *and* ***no stranger to*** *the principle of leeching on to an established success and extracting the plasma that remains.* ST ▫ also pl.

no/(not) any such thing[1] [Comp (NP)] not as just previously described **V:** ⚠ be, seem ▫ *'That kid of theirs is a whining brat, anyway.' 'He's* ***no such thing****. He just wasn't well the afternoon you saw him.'* ▫ *Byron's name is there too, and Charles Greville's who gallantly called Holland House 'a house for all Europe'. Of course it was* ***no such thing****.* NS ▫ *'That was a fine show of surprise you put on.' '****No such thing****! I was genuinely taken aback.'*

no/(not) any such thing[2] [O/o (NP)] not that which is ordered, suggested, planned, implied, or accused **V:** ⚠ do; say; agree to ▫ JIM: *I'll take her back to her room.* JEAN: *I'll call Brock.* JIM: *You'll do* ***no such thing****!* JEAN: *I won't have her left on her own.* YAA ▫ *'It's dead easy,' the 'bishop' had assured him, 'the bus drops you a few yards away.' The bus did* ***no such thing****.* BM ▫ *Am I saying that the world is too much with us, and it's incurable anyway, and that we should gather roses while we may? I'm* ***not*** *saying* ***any such thing****. I* am *saying that when the nations rage furiously together we should not be misled by their hullabaloo.* L ▫ *'There's room for the machine at the back of your office.' 'What! And a couple of chattering lads to work it? I'll agree to* ***no such thing****.'*

(there is) no time like the present (saying) now is the best time to do sth ▫ *The senior of the officials merely said: 'Come on,* ***there's no time like the present****.' No platitude has ever sounded to me more profound and original.* LWK ▫ *'It's over in the office, Headmaster. I'd be very happy to go and get it, but it would be easier if you'd —' '****No time like the present****.'* TGLY ▫ *The way I've got it worked out is this.* ***There's no time like the present****. The booze is on the house, and it's good; I'll get her tanked up and then take her out in the car.* CON

no/not any trouble etc (at all) [Comp (NP)] no, or very little, work, worry or inconvenience, or only as much as is willingly accepted **V:** ⚠ be; find sb/sth. **n:** trouble, ⚠ bother, problem ▫ *'You'd like the children out of the way, too,' Brigit said. 'Oh no, dear, they're* ***no trouble****.'* DC ▫ *Twenty years ago it would****n't*** *have been* ***any trouble*** *to me to slate the roof myself. But I'm too shaky to work on ladders now.* ▫ *'Well, thank you for explaining it all so clearly. I've taken up a great deal of your time.' '****No trouble at all****, Mrs Jones. That's what lawyers are for.'* ▫ *Then the assistant kindly filled them* (the suitcases) *with tennis rackets and things so they could get the weight, and back and forwards they went again.* ***No bother****.* TSMP ▫ *How does the ex-world champion adapt himself to the normal traffic conditions we all face every day? '****No problem****,' says Damon.* OBS ▫ part of clause or, in form of headphrase, used as short reply or comment.

(there are) no two ways about it (saying) there is only one correct or suitable way to act, speak or think with reference to sth and that is the way indicated ▫ *What was my decision.* ***There were no two ways about it****. I must try to get back my typescript at once.* UTN ▫ (a tennis champion speaks) *You've got to make your opponent fear you, to take away his confidence. You have to hate your opponent—****there are no two ways about it****.* RT ▫ (the manager of a chain-store bookshop speaks) *A thief's a thief.* ***No two ways about it****. Don't give me any of this psychological nonsense.* SC ▫ *And as for education,* ***there's no two ways about it****. The chances of a working-class child going to University are still minute, compared with a middle-class child.* ST

no way [Disj] (informal) definitely no; definitely not ▫ *There was* ***no way*** *that vast treasures of wealth were going to be stored there.* HHGG ▫ *'It's a small world. They'll find you.' '****No way****. I'll disappear.'* ITV ▫ *I don't like to see people who are neither politicians nor villains discomfited* (in BBC interviews). *That's not my scene.* ***No way****.* RT ▫ *This* (a fatal accident to a driver on a racing circuit) *affected Jody Scheckter very badly and he said straight afterwards that he was going to quit,* ***no way*** *was he going to continue, he was too young for this sort of nonsense.* OBS ▫ S and auxiliary v following this Disj are reversed, as in last example; often used as short emph reply or comment.

no/(not) any way of doing sth no means whereby one can do sth **V:** there be; (can) see; think of. **o:** doing, telling, knowing, getting, stopping ▫ *Is the picture of an old man asleep under the eyes of a young girl merely that? Or is it of St Peter in prison being visited by the delivering angel? There is* ***no way of*** *telling.* HAH ▫ *If there was* ***any way of*** *knowing what the weather would be like, I wouldn't have to pack so many different kinds of clothes.* ▫ *One may alleviate the symptoms or hasten the cure, but once a cold has started there's* ***no way of*** *stopping it.* ▫ *I needed a hundred and twenty pounds by that evening and saw* ***no way of*** *getting it that wouldn't land me in even greater trouble than I was in already.*

the noble savage the type or idea of (primitive) man, unrefined but also uncorrupted by civilization, education etc ▫ (source) *I am as free as Nature first made man,/Ere the base laws of servitude began,/When wild in woods* ***the noble savage*** *ran.* THE CONQUEST OF GRANADA (J DRYDEN 1631-1700) ▫ ***The Noble Savage****: six programmes on the impact of white 'civilisations' on native cultures.* RT ▫ *He was fonder of her than anyone, but her 'bright' simplicity, her self-confident censoriousness, would make her unbearable to live with. She was, he supposed, his unattainable vision of* ***the noble savage****.* ASA ▫ *She was all loving to me at first, but then she got sarcastic and said she couldn't stand the sight of me. 'Here comes* ***the noble savage****,' she called out when I came home.* LLDR

nobody/anybody in his/their right mind could/would do sth no sane or sensible person would do such a thing (the implication often being that sth that has already been done, or that is being contemplated, is an act of a mad person, or, more usu, is stupid, irresponsible etc) ▫ *He must have been insane, temporarily at least.* ***Nobody in his right mind could*** *have* *reason to murder a whole family.* □ *I was in excellent health, and* none *of the cinemas sported a film that* ***anybody in his right mind*** *could want to see.* SPL □ JO: *Would you go and live with her if you were me, Geof?* GEOF: *No, I don't think I would.* JO: *Neither* ***would anybody in their right mind.*** TOH □ with anybody there must be expressed or implied neg.

a nod is as good as a wink (to a blind horse) (saying) a hint, sign or suggestion can be accepted and/or acted upon without further elaboration, public acknowledgement, etc □ *'We shan't forget what you've done for us, and it's time we did something for you.' Bevill went on: 'Now you can forget everything that I've told you. But* ***a nod's as good as a wink to a blind horse.****'* NM □ *But, darling, you don't really think this League of his can be dangerous, do you?—No, no, of course one can't discuss it over the telephone, but* ***a nod's as good as a wink****, and I promise I'll be very careful.* EM □ *Her eyes kept straying to the clock and,* ***a nod being as good as a wink to a blind horse****, I said I had an appointment to meet a friend, and left.*

none the less [Conj] nevertheless; in spite of sth said, done or occurring □ *I felt the lesson to be salutary, but was sorry,* ***none the less****, that it had had to be administered at this moment and in this form.* DOP □ *The Government admitted that many discretionary trusts were set up for quite other reasons than the avoidance of tax.* ***None the less****, it will in future rarely be possible to establish such trusts without incurring heavy tax penalities.* G □ *'It's a bit early to send a child of ten to bed.' 'She'll go when I tell her to,* ***none the less****.'* □ front, middle or end position.

none other than sb [Comp/O (NP)] a named person himself (the implication being that he is sb famous or important, or sb unexpected in the particular circumstances) **V:** be; find, discover, see □ *He had no son. His heir was* ***none other than*** *William Pitt, then Prime Minister and Chancellor of the Exchequer.* EM □ *The whole position* (about lie-detectors) *was put in a nutshell by* ***none other than*** *Daniel Defoe, who in 1730 published a pamphlet,...* SNP □ *Then, one day, I found a guardian for them in whose hands I could safely leave them while I got on with my work. This guardian was* ***none other than*** *Pavlova the Patas monkey.* BB

(there are) none so blind/deaf as those who will not see/hear (saying) people will not see/hear what they are stubbornly determined to avoid seeing/hearing □ ***None so blind as those that will not see. None so deaf as those that will not hear.*** COMMENTARIES (M HENRY 1662-1714) □ (reader's letter) ***There are none so blind as those who will not see.*** *My microfilm of the Cavalli score has been available to any who wished to examine it and, unlike Mr Hicks, a few critics have taken advantage of this and acquired an idea of the many immensely detailed problems that arise when preparing the work for performance.* L □ ***There are none so deaf as those who will not hear*** *the truth. Who has ever said that imperialism can be overthrown by a mere push of the shoulder?* T □ *'Can't he see that Mary can scarcely drag herself around?' '****None so blind as those that won't see****. It would spoil his holiday if he had to admit his wife was a sick woman.'*

none/not any too not very; not sufficiently **adj:** clean; clever; happy; likeable. **adv:** cleanly; easily; quickly; silently; surely □ *The lights in the roof of the compartment were* ***none too*** *bright or could it be that at thirty-five he was beginning to need glasses?* PW □ *His suit of clothes, however, was* ***none too*** *well-fitting* NS □ *Her distressed, well-meaning, but* ***none-too-****bright parents are now convinced that the girl is a dangerous lunatic, so they take her to the doctor.* NS □ *In the end I agreed,* ***none too*** *happily, to say nothing of the affair meantime.* □ *The occasion was the Arab Summit and he was then, at 28, the leader of a three-month-old revolution that seemed* ***none too*** *likely to last.* L □ used for understatement, adj/adv used always contrasting with meaning of whole expression.

none too soon [A (AdvP)] (almost) too late; later than is suitable or desirable **V:** leave, arrive; find, recover, sth □ *They were eventually spotted by a helicopter team, and* ***none too soon****, for when they were picked up one had already died from exposure and the other two could not have survived the night.* □ (a hallucinatory experience) *It was inexpressibly wonderful, wonderful to the point, almost, of being terrifying. And suddenly I had an inkling of what it must feel like to be mad.* ***None too soon****, I was steered away from the disquieting splendours of my garden chair.* DOP □ *'Try to put up with him—he'll only be staying a few more days.' 'All right, then. But, if he was leaving this minute, it would be* ***none too soon*** *for me.'*

nooks and crannies [n + n non-rev] small spaces, sub-divisions, eg alcoves, corners etc, in a location, building etc □ *In every major city there are students on camp beds in* ***nooks and crannies*** *and others 'crashing' on the floors of friends' flats.* OBS □ *Peter Reiss runs the Mathaser Bierstadt, a vast complex of halls,* ***nooks and crannies****, where you can drink for 14 hours a day.* RT □ ***Every nook and cranny*** *of this peaceful 18th-century house held tangible memories of Marceau.* RT □ *I decided that we had better spread out in a line across the stream, and wade up it turning over every movable stone and searching* ***every nook and cranny*** *that might harbour a Hairy Frog.* BB □ variant (in) every nook and cranny.

not all/always (that)/what one/it might be [Comp (NP)] imperfect; less satisfactory, suitable, efficient **modal:** might, ⚠ should, ought to □ *'Well, Amy,' he said as they hurried away, 'I may* ***not*** *be* ***all that I might be*** *as a husband but I've never knocked you about.'* □ *Humphrey's intervewing was* ***not all it might*** *have* ***been****. He already knew too many of the answers, so his probing tended to be a bit oblique.* OBS □ *In a place like this, where people are accustomed to a measure of autonomy in running the affairs of their own community, relations with the new metropolitan district councils are* ***not always what they might be****.* G □ *We're* ***none*** *of us* ***all we should be****. People's faults are tolerated in proportion to the degree of affection we feel towards them.* □ *The Englishman abroad is* ***no*** *longer* ***all that*** *a gentleman* ***ought to be****. Along the once peaceful coast of northern France they're calling our summer tourists 'The Noisy*

Ones'. TO □ all and what never used together; always and that never used together.

not altogether not very; not particularly **adj:** happy; satisfied; indifferent (to sb/sth) □ *Do you think it wise of her to see so much of him? I'm* ***not altogether*** *happy about his influence on her as he's a good deal older and more sophisticated.* □ *It seems to me that she's* ***not altogether*** *indifferent, but is pretending to dislike him because it's expected of her.* □ *The Chief Constable said that he was* ***not altogether*** *satisfied with the proposed security arrangement for the Royal visit.* □ may be used for understatement, eg ***not altogether*** *indifferent* = 'rather interested'.

(we are) not amused (catchphrase) one resents, or regards coldly, sth done or said □ (source—a written comment on the occasion of having been imitated by a Groom-In-Waiting) ***We are not amused.*** QUEEN VICTORIA 1819-1901 □ (lack of academic interest in feminist issues) *Ms Oakley, as a professional sociologist and committed feminist, is, however, not surprised.* ***Nor is she amused.*** NS □ *In place of the scholarly tome that many people expected of him, Mr Maddox has produced a polemic, and not a very good one at that. As the woman said,* ***we are not amused.*** NS

not as/so young as one used to be/(once) was [Comp (AdjP)] old or growing old (the implication being that there is loss of vigour, good health or good looks) **V:** ⚠ be; feel, look □ *The journey up to the West End might be rather trying for Mother who was* ***not so young as she used to be.*** HAHA □ *'She used to change husbands like some people change jobs, but she and Henry have been together for seven or eight years now.' 'Just as well—she mightn't find it so easy to get a fourth. She's* ***not as young as she used to be.****'* □ *'You've turned into a proper stay-at-home, haven't you? You never want to go anywhere or do anything.' 'I think you forget I'm* ***not so young as I was.****'*

not at any price [A (PrepP)] not at all; not for any inducement □ *The grumblers, who do****n't*** *want to go on a picnic* ***at any price,*** ... TO □ *I would****n't*** *want him on my staff* ***at any price.*** □ stress pattern not at 'any price.

not bad [Comp (AdjP)] quite, or even very, good; not half bad/badly (qv) **V:** ⚠ be; find, think, sb/sth. **adv mod:** so; too; at all. **A:** for a beginner, for four hours' work; at all; considering sth □ *'What price do you get for the scampi you land?' '£2 a pound, at the pier-head.' 'That's* ***not bad.****'* □ *'****Not bad*** *for a beginner,' Andrew said as they left the court. 'We'll make a tennis-player of you yet.'* □ *He had the understanding that comes from ten years of early-morning breakfasts to know what is in my range and what is not. That's a great asset in a director.* ***Not bad*** *for a husband, either.* RT □ *Next morning at breakfast Creevey joked about the tea* ***not*** *being too* ***bad,*** *considering it was country tea. No it was not, corrected the Duke with devasting candour, he had brought it specially from Paris.* ST □ *The second mate took one look at me and he said: 'Up the rigging.' I was very frightened. The first part was****n't*** *so* ***bad.*** *Pretty solid really.* L □ *'A very nice wine, my dear.' He took another mouthful, and added '****Not bad*** *at all.'* □ MR STONE: *How are you, Sam?* SAM: ***Not*** *so* ***bad.*** *How are you?* HSG □ *'Nice place you have here, Mr Liversedge,' he said admiringly. '****Not*** *too* ***bad, not*** *too* ***bad,****' Jack said modestly, rather pleased by this tribute from someone with class.* PE □ may be used as comment or answer, as in last three examples.

not/never bat an eyelid V + O] show no surprise, concern, or alarm (about sth unusual that happens) □ *If Cosmia had spread out her arms and flown out of the window I would****n't*** *have* ***batted an eyelid.*** JFTR □ *The sound of the crash brought everyone to their feet—except John who* ***never*** *even* ***batted an eyelid*** *and stolidly went on eating his dinner.*

not to be outdone in order to show oneself as good as, or better than, another **A:** by his sister, by the neighbours; in a matter of generosity; as a marksman □ *The Capri was launched to motoring correspondents in Cyprus in the spring of 1969: everyone who could possibly pen a line about the car was flown to the island. A year later, and* ***not to be outdone,*** *Rootes launched the Avenger. The company took 16 chartered jets, 120 journalists, 400 dealers, and 40 cars to Malta.* ST □ *Peggy showed off her new dancing steps and Walter,* ***not to be outdone*** *in a matter of entertaining visitors, his prowess at handstands, cartwheels and backward somersaults.* □ *Carry and display your subscription list to date* (= until the present time). ***Not to be outdone*** *by their neighbours, people will often contribute more than they originally planned to.* SC □ front or middle position.

not before time [A (PrepP)] at a time when sth is overdue, almost too late; (and) about time (too) (qv) □ *At the moment Australia is negotiating a* (sugar) *deal with Japan, and the present haggle is reported to be between £220 and £260 per ton. It's certainly goodbye to cheap sugar—and perhaps* ***not before time*** *so far as the developing countries are concerned.* NS □ *At about five o'clock she got up and went and found Dev in his kennel and got his supper for him. Then she got her clothes-brush from her quarters and gave him a grooming with it,* ***not before time.*** RFW □ *It all points to a wind of change blowing in the direction of the Ordinary shares, now 39p: and* ***not before time*** *either.* OBS □ often end position, preceded by *and* or *but*.

not a/one (little) bit [A (NP)] not at all; not in any way □ *My ankle's fine since you strapped it up. It does****n't*** *hurt* ***a bit*** *(or: it's* ***not a bit*** *sore) now.* □ *She must be a cold-hearted creature. As far as I could see the news did****n't*** *upset her* ***one bit.*** □ *'You'll be busy at something. I'll take a walk till Jack comes home.' '****Not a bit.*** *Just come right in and we'll have a drink and a chat.'* □ *Don't do that ever again. You brought me up short and, I don't mind telling you, I do****n't*** *like it* ***one bit.*** TSMP □ *'They did****n't*** *like the idea* ***one little bit,****' said Adrian Metcalfe, one of the organisers, 'but we coaxed them.'* TVT □ follows v; often short neg answer, esp in form not a bit.

not a bit of it not at all □ *Sybil looked so like Marlene Dietrich that you might have thought she would never have had a book in her hand, that nobody would ever even have shown her one.* ***Not a bit of it.*** *Once during a lull when we were in bed she recited the whole of one of Hamlet's soliloquies.* SML □ *'Now what would you say was the future of a body like NISP?' 'To get more* *votes than any other party and make you Prime Minister.' '**Not a bit of it**!' said Lefty triumphantly.* UTN □ used as short emph denial of sth previously suggested or supposed.

not by a long chalk/shot not by any small amount, in any small degree (from, formerly, chalking up scores in games etc) □ *And he dug the pot out of the cupboard, found the tea—and the C.S.M. was right, it wouldn't last the week, **not by a long chalk**—and began to organize the cups and beakers and what not.* TT □ (reader's letter) *Not every bank has abandoned the weekday evening session, **not by a long chalk**.* NS □ *Asked if he was short of money, he said: '**Not by a long shot**.' He said that he had about £37 in savings.* T □ *'I don't suppose', she says resignedly, 'you can take me home with the first lot?' 'Well, I don't know, Mrs B,' says the ambulance man with a raised jolly voice. 'It's **not** time yet **by a long chalk**.'* G □ used to emphasize previous neg statement. ⇨ ⚠ a long shot.

not do a hand's turn [V + O pass] not, or hardly, do any work, or make any effort □ *His father had been something big in the City and had left him plenty of money so there was **no need** for him to **do a hand's turn** if he hadn't wished.* □ *Her mother says Kate **never does a hand's turn** in the house and I say, in that case, her mother didn't bring her up properly.* □ *She's **never done a hand's turn** for me in her life.*

not do a stroke (of work) [V + O pass] not do any, or any item of, work □ *Every time she goes away, I **never do a stroke** in the house. Everything gets covered in dust — and Madeleine just accepts that.* ST □ *The 'Olympic Bravery' weighed 250,000 tons and was on her way to be laid up in mothballs in a Norwegian fjord **without** ever having **done a stroke of work**: obsolete the day she was completed.* TVT

not a dry eye in the house [Comp (NP)] (facetious) everybody in the audience or a company is crying or deeply affected **V:** ⚠ be, find □ *A Philippe de Broca film gave us poor Jeanne Moreau as a spinster art-mistress deciding not to put her head in the gas oven.Twenty years ago there might **not** have been **a dry eye in the house**: at Cannes there was hardly an open one.* NS □ *His closing peroration* (= formal speech) *is a funny parody of the worst kinds of sentimentality, fake patriotism, pseudo-religiosity, mock-humility. 'All a man can say is, here I am, and I'm saying it to you tonight.' **Not a dry eye in the house**.* L

not eat you (informal) not actually terrifying, or likely to harm you (esp said as an encouragement to sb who appears frightened) □ *Come on, dear, sit on Father Christmas's lap and get your present. He wo**n't eat you**, it's a man under all those clothes and the beard.* □ *I know he's got a reputation for being fierce, but at least you can try asking for a rise even if he doesn't give you one. He ca**n't eat you** after all.* □ *Come in, come in, don't hang about outside like frightened sheep. I wo**n't eat you** despite what you may have heard about me.* □ usu with *will/can.*

not far to seek [Comp (AdjP)] easily and quickly found, surmised or ascertained **S:** reason, motive, cause, answer. **V:** ⚠ be, seem □ (reader's letter) *Gwynfor Evans drives him to a very unacademic frenzy. The reason is **not far to seek**. Mr Wright is a centralist; for him, Welsh nationalism is parochial, narrow and claustrophobic.* G □ *'How can you put up with the noise?' 'I try to. But if I'm ever carried out of here stark staring mad the reason wo**n't be far to seek**.'* □ *'How come all these sausage rolls were left?' 'Taste one and the answer's **not far to seek**.'*

not fit to wash sb's feet [Comp (AdjP)] incomparably inferior to sb (in allusion to JOHN XIII 5-16) **V:** ⚠ be; think sb, regard sb as □ *I never got over his savage piece of demagogy when he murdered poor old George Lansbury. Neither Bevin nor I nor any of us, Chris, were **fit to wash** George Lansbury**'s feet**.* L

not for all the tea in China [A (Prep P)] refuse to do sth, no matter how great the reward, compensation □ *Old Ron said he would**n't** go up to London again **for all the tea in China**. Rush and bustle it was the whole time.* L □ *It was great to see that officious bastard taken down a peg. I would**n't** have missed it **for all the tea in China**.* □ *'I would**n't** be saddled with this white elephant* (= useless, usu costly, possession) ***for all the tea in China**,' announces Quinn, looking around the boat.* OBS

not for the first time [A (PrepP)] as has happened sometimes, or often, before □ *She was telling herself, **not for the first time**, that there was a time and a place for everything—and that the office was definitely not the place for imitations of the boss's wife.* TCB □ *On Wednesday Mr Jenkins sat, cigar at ready, looking vaguely apprehensive. Mr Anthony Wedgwood Benn promised us a speech from him: but **not for the first time** Mr Benn was misinformed. Mr Jenkins sat tight.* NS □ (an ITV series) *'McMillan and Wife—The Face of Murder.' The police are baffled. **Not for the first time**, Sally McMillan becomes personally involved. Yes, she gets kidnapped.* TVT □ front, middle or end position. ⇨ for the first etc time.

not/never for a/one (single) minute/moment [A (PrepP)] absolutely not/never at all (do sth) **V:** expect; think, consider; believe, suppose □ *I would also like a cold shower, an iced drink, and about four hundred tons of D.D.T., but I do**n't** expect **for a minute** I'll get them.* DF □ DAVID: *Look, Dad, no one thinks **for one moment** that you're going to die.* HSG □ JIMMY: *I hope you wo**n't** make the mistake of thinking **for one moment** that I am a gentleman. I've no public school scruples about hitting girls.* LBA □ *What! James put money into your business? I can tell you now, he would**n't for one moment** consider it.* □ *Not everybody is going to agree with us, and if they don't agree with us they say: 'Well, you are being divisive—dividing the nation.' I do**n't** believe that **for a moment** either.* L □ *Biddy, it's all right now. It's over. They've **never** even **for one minute** suspected me.* DC □ *It says a good deal for the buoyancy of Victoria's temperament that the possibility of failing to obtain her objective did **not for a moment** occur to her.* TCB □ *'You don't suppose he's changed his mind about me, do you?' '**Not for a single moment**. He's overworked and irritable as a result, but he's very much in love with you.'* □ can be used alone as emph denial; neg or neg implication, with v in middle or end position.

not for nothing[1] [Comp/A (PrepP)] not without cause or a reason **V:** be; argue; choose, elect, sb □ *If you ask José Maria Ruiz-Mateos how it is that Rumasa has succeeded in a way that has become the envy of Spain, he replies that there are three main answers: 'Work, work and work.' It is* ***not for nothing*** *that the bee* (ie a symbol of hard work) *has been adopted as their symbol.* ST □ (reader's letter) *The worst evil lies in the training of performing animals. It is* ***not for nothing*** *that this is carried out in strict secrecy, protected by Acts of Parliament.* RT □ *This tale comes near to being a masterpiece.* ***Not for nothing*** *was the author a sometime winner of the Grand Prix de la Nouvelle.* SC □ *The man himself. Standing there immaculate in jet-black silk-and-mohair evening dress. Mentally you note that* ***not for nothing*** *has the kid from the back-streets of San Francisco been voted among America's top 10 best-dressed men.* TVT □ may precede v for emphasis, as in last three examples where S and v are reversed.

not for nothing[2] [Comp/A (NP)] not without result or a definable consequence **V:** be; study, learn, sth; teach, prepare, sb □ *Ian was the best sniper we had. 'You see,' he used to say, 'it's* ***not for nothing*** *I spent half my boyhood poaching deer.'* □ (an unsatisfactory marriage) *For this state of things Isabel was herself a great deal responsible.* ***Not for nothing*** *had she studied the art of marriage and made it for her husband, and almost for herself, a pre-digested meal.* PW □ *He was****n't a schoolmaster for nothing****; he saw corners of a room before he saw the centre.* CON □ may precede v for emphasis, as in second example where S and v are reversed; variant not a schoolmaster etc for nothing = 'the person displays skills or talents particularly appropriate to being a schoolmaster or some other specified profession'.

not for want of trying [Comp/A (NP)] not because one hasn't tried to do or obtain sth **V:** be; fail, lose sth □ *Sir John Donaldson never in fact fought as a Conservative parliamentary candidate (there are those who fancy that this may* ***not*** *have been* ***for want of trying****).* NS □ *He's taken hundreds of exposures. If he doesn't get a few first-class photographs to submit it wo****n't*** *be* ***for want of trying****.* □ *When he has not won, it has* ***not*** *been* ***for want of trying****, or for want of doing anything that would have helped before the race.* G

not for worlds/the world [A (Prep)] not on any account; not for any reason or purpose **V:** hurt, injure, offend, sb; give up, renounce, sth □ *'No, darling,' she said, 'it's all settled. I would****n't*** *have you give it up now* ***for worlds****. You need the opportunity it offers you.'* HAA □ *Now Alistair was the kind of chap who would****n't for the world*** *have said anything deliberately to hurt anyone's feelings.*

not give sb/sth houseroom [possess] not want to have, or not tolerate having, sb/sth in one's house, place of business, or as any part of one's surroundings or belongings □ *£70 for an old sagging settee that I, for one, would****n't give houseroom*** *to!* □ *'Well, you have had an affair with Mr Golding, and then, before that, there have been Mr Moriarty and Mr Miller.' 'Miller!' she said, 'I would****n't give*** *him* ***houseroom****.'* TT □ *Normally, I would* ***not give*** *this sort of luxurious introspection* ***houseroom****, reckoning, as I do, that, for better or worse, the television is part of our lives and the children will make what they can of it.* L

not give etc sb/sth the time of day [possess] ignore sb; treat sb/sth as being of no importance or interest **V:** give; ⚠ get sb/sth; be worth □ *That's part of his holiday—mixing with the natives. If you ran into him in London with his posh friends he would****n't give*** *any of you* ***the time of day****.* □ *Our neighbours on the left weren't over-friendly from the first. Now, since we've lowered the tone of the terrace by offering bed and breakfast we do****n't*** *even* ***get the time of day****.* □ *It does not seem unduly harsh to argue that immigrants to another country should obey its laws, and that their children, if educated by the state, should speak its language. Beyond this, I cannot see why any Act of Uniformity should be* ***given the time of day****.* NS □ (film review) *The fact is the rubbish I have seen this week is* ***not worth your or my time of day****.* NS

not grow/get any younger/thinner [V + Comp] grow or be old(er)/fat(ter) □ *Your father takes on too much. He forgets he's* ***not growing any younger****.* □ *'And how are you keeping, Miss Gittings?' 'Well, I don't suppose there's any real cause for complaint, you know,' she said. '****None of us are growing any younger****, are we?'* TT □ *I'm* ***not getting any younger****, and I can't afford to lend people money I may never get back in my lifetime.* □ *He says to me, Marcus, you villain, I haven't seen you since 46. You have****n't grown any thinner****.* TCB □ *Earlier* (she met) *the Queen's mother, the Duchess of Teck, a jovial lady weighing 240 lbs. 'Ah, Madame Scalia, I see* ***neither of us*** *has* ***grown any thinner*** *since we last met.'* NS □ variant none/neither (of them) grows/gets any younger/thinner.

not half(!) (informal) very much so! yes, indeed! □ *'You'll be glad when you've finished that job, I'm sure.' '****Not half!*** *What a bore it's been!'* □ *'Was the weather bad in the South too, this Easter?' '****Not half*** *it was. It never stopped raining the whole weekend.'* □ *'The garage man wouldn't have been trying to cheat me, would he?' '****Not half*** *he wouldn't! He'd cheat his own grandmother for two pence.'* □ exclamatory affirmative reply to a question or suggestion; a neg construction in the preceding sentence often repeated in verbal tag following not half; in last example, first sentence of reply means 'Yes, of course he would'.

not half bad/badly (informal) (be) quite good, really good; not bad (qv); (do sth) quite well, really well □ *I say, Daphne, this cake is****n't half bad****! You must bake another soon.* □ *Johnny's getting to be quite a little musician. He was playing a Chopin Study just before you came in, and* ***not half badly*** *either.* □ *So here's this 35-year-old man, good on a horse and* ***not half bad*** *with a squash racket.* TVT

not half be sth [V + Comp] (informal) be sth wholly or to an exceptional degree **Comp:** funny; strange, odd; a nuisance, a bother, a trial □ *He may be a nice dog, but he wo****n't half be*** *a nuisance when we go on holiday!* □ *What a racket to be making in the middle of the might. There wo****n't half be*** *complaints from the neighbours* *tomorrow morning.* ▫ *It* ***wasn't half*** *dangerous with them* (= those) *tree trunks falling.* LF ▫ *For such an angelic looking child she ca****n't half be*** *stubborn sometimes.*

not half do sth [V + O] (informal) do sth wholly or to an exceptional degree ▫ JO: *You do****n't half*** *like the sound of your own voice* (= talk excessively). TOH ▫ SARAH: *He did****n't half*** *upset them; they wouldn't let him mess around with the radio so he started effing and blinding* (= swearing and cursing) *and threw their books on the floor.* CSWB

not harm/hurt a fly [V + O] be kind and gentle in character and always unwilling to cause harm or unhappiness to others ▫ *One of the most dismal features of alcoholism is the way the character degenerates. It doesn't always happen; there are those quiet gentlemanly chronics who* ***never hurt a fly****, and even the occasional saintly ones.* OBS ▫ *I want to sell your mother a beautiful memorial stone; one that would be worthy of your dear dead father. Such a fine, kind man, would****n't harm a fly****. I knew him well.* HSG ▫ *While everybody has been moralising about Best, who has****n't hurt a fly*** *though he may have hurt himself, nobody has as much as noticed the utter disgrace of our display in Berlin.* L ▫ often with *would(n't).*

not have etc a bean [possess] (informal) not have any money at all **A:** not; hardly, scarcely. **V:** have (got), ⚠ have left. **prep:** without ▫ *'****Have*** *you money* ***left****, Jack?' '****Not a bean****. I didn't realize it was going to be such an expensive evening.'* ▫ *I* ***hardly*** *ever* ***have a bean*** *on me and have to borrow most of the time.* RT ▫ *So much for making their fortune in Canada! They came home again last month* ***without a bean****.*

not have/without a care in the world [possess] be perfectly happy; have no worries or responsibilities ▫ BOY: *Once, I was a happy young man,* ***not a care in the world****. Now! I'm trapped into a barbaric cult—matrimony.* TOH ▫ *Because the future was uncertain and threatening, he was forced to behave as if he* ***hadn't a care in the world****.* PE ▫ often follows *as if/as though*; can also follow *think*, as in *You'd think he* ***hadn't a care in the world****.*

not/never have etc the foggiest etc idea etc [possess] (informal) have no idea whatsoever of/about sth **V:** have (got), ⚠ get, give sb. **prep:** without. **adj:** foggiest, ⚠ faintest, remotest, slightest; least. **n:** idea, ⚠ notion, conception, clue ▫ *'What's the time, Bill?' 'I haven't the foggiest.'* ▫ (choosing presents) *'What do you think — an Arlesian doll or a quotation from Mistral in poker-work?' and when she did not answer, he said again, 'Which do you think, darling?' 'I* ***haven't the foggiest idea****,' she said violently.* ASA ▫ *My old lady used to say I lacked ambition. Maybe she was right. I wanted to do something but I had****n't the faintest*** *what.* JFTR ▫ *That was something poor old Father never understood. He* ***hadn't the faintest conception*** *of the forces he was up against.* HAA ▫ *I've* ***never had the slightest notion*** *of becoming an actress, though many people seem to assume one will follow in one's parents' footsteps.* SC ▫ *'How would you set about changing a tyre, for instance?' 'I* ***haven't the least idea****.'* ▫ n may be omitted after foggiest, faintest.

not have a hope (in hell) (of sth) [possess] (informal) have no chance at all of success **o:** it, compensation; of catching the train, of finding them ▫ *In the long run Mrs Thatcher's policy* ***hasn't a hope****.* NS ▫ *Our hero aims to coax his recalcitrant stunner into a better attitude: but he* ***hasn't a hope****.* L ▫ *Sounds fine: you decide you're not going to sleep with anyone till you get married and so you don't. But you see, you* ***haven't got a hope in hell****. Not these days.* TGLY ▫ *The British have got the journalism they've been prepared to pay for—and they don't like paying much.* ***What hope has*** *a headline like 'More Pumps Needed in Maharashtra' against 'Second Peer in Call-Girl Scandal'?* L ▫ *'I'm supposed to interview her,' Virginia said, 'for my newspaper!' 'You****'ve got a hope****.'* AITC ▫ variant (ironic) sb's got a hope! with stress pattern 'sb's got a hope!, has neg implication; variants without a hope (in hell), what hope does sth/sb have? ➪ ⚠ what a hope!

not have a leg to stand on [possess] (informal) have no convincing argument to offer in one's defence, or to win others over to one's side **V:** have (got), ⚠ leave sb without ▫ *Shut up and go away, and take your bloody bypass with you. You* ***haven't got a leg to stand on*** *and you know it.* HHGG ▫ *It would sort itself out, he decided, no-one wanted a bypass, the council did****n't have a leg to stand on****.* HHGG

not have/without one penny to rub against another (informal) have no money (left) ▫ *They can gamble until they* ***haven't one penny*** *piece* ***to rub against another****, but that's the end of it. There's no borrowing from the house here.* ▫ *They gave him an advance on his wages—just as well, since he'd arrived* ***with*** *practically* ***not one penny to rub against another****.* ▫ (NONCE) *Even poor old Bernie Cornfield, who was yesteryear's wizard of finance,* ***hasn't got one billion to rub against another*** *and has just got out of jail.* OBS

not have seen etc the like (of sth)/sth's like not have seen etc anything similar previously; not have seen etc anything of its kind that is so good, bad, unusual etc before **adv:** not, never, (not/none) ever. **V:** seen, ⚠ heard; known; tasted. **A:** in one's life; before ▫ *'I guess you****'ve not seen the like of*** *this before,' said Boles, openly enjoying the young man's discomfiture at the prospect of using the dry closet which provided the only toilet facilities.* RT ▫ *Lead shots have been found, linked in pairs with pieces of brass wire. At least, that's what they appear to be—but* ***none*** *of the ordance experts consulted* ***have ever seen their like****.* OBS ▫ *There are many social scientists who wish so to enlarge the consciousness of individuals and of communities that, if it were done, we would be dealing with a regenerate creature* ***the like of*** *which we* ***have not*** *previously* ***seen****.* L ▫ *Ah, boys, you* ***never saw the like of*** *what I was seeing. A great head was staring at me out of the wave, the size of a sack of barley with two eyes as big as pancakes.* RM ▫ *Sixteen pounds that cabbage weighed! In twenty years of gardening and judging shows I****'ve never known the like****.* ▫ *Did you* ***ever hear the like of*** *the cheek that boy gave his father? I'd have given him a damned good hiding.* ➪ ⚠ the likes of sb; not see etc sb's/sth's like(s) again.

not have etc a thing (to do) [possess] have nothing (to do) **V:** have (got), ⚠ there be. **prep:** without. **adj:** single, blessed, blooming, damned □ *They're turning us out at the end of the month and* ***there isn't a thing*** *we can do.* □ *Just leave it to me. You* ***haven't a thing to*** *worry about.* AITC □ *On Tuesday we fished all day and came home* ***without a*** *blooming* ***thing.*** □ *'What is the dress for, Prissie?' 'Guy wants to take me to dinner. And I* ***hadn't a thing to*** *wear.'* DC □ expression not have a thing to wear = 'not have any clothes suitable, new or fine enough for a specified purpose'.

not have etc a word of truth in sth [possess] be completely untrue **V:** have, ⚠ there be. **prep:** with not, without. **o:** it, them □ *I don't know who started this rumour of us going bankrupt but* ***there isn't a word of truth in*** *it. Business has never been better.* □ *He looks so naive that he gets the tourists to swallow whole stories* ***without a word of truth*** *in them.* □ *Judge Clarke said: 'It has been suggested that she is being threatened by other inmates. I don't express any opinion on whether* ***there is a word of truth in*** *this or not.'* G □ *It's my guess that the story did****n't have a word of truth in*** *it* (or: *did****n't contain a word of truth***).

not if/though one lives to be a hundred (informal) never in one's lifetime, however long that proves to be; next entry (qv) □ *'You'll* never *be old, George,' the woman said. '****Not if you live to be a hundred****.'* PE □ *Leave it growing—it's a rare specimen. You may* ***never*** *see one again* ***though you live to be a hundred.*** □ *'You'll come round to a different way of thinking as you get older.' 'No I won't,* ***not if I live to be a hundred****.'* □ *They'll tell you that such and such a thing could only happen once in a lifetime or that you'd* ***never*** *see the same thing again* ***if you lived to be a hundred****. But of course things happen in duplicate, and even triplicate if you're around enough in the right places at the right time.* SC □ emph neg; usu repeats previous neg.

not/never in a hundred etc years (informal) never, however long one tries, goes on, etc; previous entry (qv) **adj:** hundred, ⚠ thousand, million □ *In the end I told her to give up—that she was wasting her money and would* never *learn to drive,* ***not in a hundred years****.* SC □ *People will always find something to grumble about. It's human nature and you wo****n't*** *change that* ***in a million years*** *of progress.* □ *I envied him his talent. I knew I could never paint a picture like that,* ***never in a thousand years****.* □ emph neg; usu repeats previous neg.

not in the least not at all **adj:** stupid; cold; concerned. **adv:** stupidly; apologetically □ *It would be easy to think he was stupid. But that is where you would be wrong, for he is* ***not in the least*** *stupid.* □ *It's* ***not*** *cold* ***in the least****.* □ *I told Sarah the dog seemed to be limping a little but she was****n't in the least*** *concerned.* □ *'Would it be inconvenient to have lunch half an hour earlier today?' '****Not in the least****.'* □ *Half an hour before we were to meet, James rang up to announce,* ***not in the least*** *apologetically, that he couldn't make it.* □ *I would never have guessed you were Harry's brother. You're* ***not*** *like him* ***in the least****.* □ modifies adj, adv, past participle or prep p; these may follow not or least; may be used alone to answer polite enquiry.

not know anything about sth but know what one likes (catchphrase) have little knowledge about sth, not claim to be a judge of sth, esp an art or craft, but have one's own tastes and preferences **o:** music, painting, poetry; fashion □ *'I can't think of anything more ghastly than all that fake Regency.' 'I like the Regency style,' Robin said doggedly. 'Yes, darling, you do****n't know anything about*** *it,* ***but*** *you* ***know what you like****.'* ASA □ *I may* ***not know*** *so* ***much about*** *music as you lot,* ***but I know what I like*** *and I'm not ashamed to enjoy it.* □ *But although many of the people who work for Shelter are—almost by definition—apolitical, they* ***know what they don't like****. And what they are determined not to like is the whole Martin ethos.* NS □ may be used disparagingly of people thought to have poor taste; variant know what one doesn't like.

not know sb from Adam (informal) not know sb at all; have no idea who sb is; have never met sb (and would not, therefore, recognize him) □ *'Isn't that your old girl-friend Linda over there?' 'Do****n't know her from Adam****.'* □ *'But surely you know Jack Simpson?—both of you being in the same line of business?' 'I've heard a lot about him, of course, but we've never met. Would****n't know him from Adam****.'*

not know if/whether one is coming or going (informal) be confused in, and about, what one is doing, esp because one has too many things to attend to; next entry (qv) □ MRS STONE: *How are you, Bessie?* BESSIE: *Don't ask me; what with one thing and another, I do****n't know if I'm coming or going****.* HSG □ *What a morning! I do****n't*** *really* ***know whether I'm coming or going****. This is the first time I've sat down since arriving.* TT □ *But he couldn't find it, and paused in the doorway of the lounge, uncertain how to look or feel. 'Doesn't Daddy look funny?' Janice giggled. 'He does****n't know whether he's coming or going****.'* PW

not know if/whether one is on one's head or one's heels be disorientated, confused, over-busy, over-stimulated etc; previous entry (qv) □ *To tell you the truth the doctors have pumped her so full of drugs she does****n't know whether she is on her head or her heels*** *half the time.* □ *A few years earlier I should have lost my temper and argued furiously. I did have a faint sensation of* ***not knowing whether I was on my head or my heels****. However I pulled myself together.* SPL □ *I don't think you* ***know whether you're on your head or your heels*** *this morning. Sit there and calm down for ten minutes.* □ variant (taboo) not know if/whether one is on one's arse or one's elbow.

not know one is born (informal) take life for granted without worry or inquiry; live in such happy and comfortable circumstances that one does not realize one's good fortune □ *'One dumb Mart's* (= Martian) *costing me plenty. These hick Marts do****n't know they're born****.' 'H'm,' said the Agent. 'They act dumb, and the way their faces are makes them look dumb,' he said, 'but they were a mighty clever people, once.'* TST □ ALISON: *I didn't have much to worry about. I did****n't know I was born****, as Jimmy says.* LBA

▫ *You could evidently threaten* (her with) *the doctor, the matron, or your relations, and she would say no more than, 'You people do**n't know you're born**,' and 'Fire ahead, tell your niece, my dear.'* MM

not know the meaning of the word [V + O] have no understanding, experience, of sth ▫ *'Poetry!' said Percy. 'Dylan Thomas did**n't know the meaning of the word**. It isn't poetry, it's a leg-pull.'* MM ▫ *Moriarty doesn't know what war is, does**n't know the meaning of the word**.* TT ▫ *I object to sitting listening to somebody who does**n't know the meaning of Christian charity** talking about it.* ▫ *Until 20 years ago, the Asmat people of New Guinea, had **never known the meaning of work**, still less the value of money or the sense of trying.* RT ▫ word may refer back to a n (as in first two examples) or refer forward (as in last two examples), in which case word may be omitted; frequently used for deliberate overstatement.

not know what to do with oneself not know how to occupy one's time; be/feel uncomfortable or embarrassed ▫ *Oh, I like having a job. I would**n't know what to do with myself** if I was at home all day.* ▫ *So she'd run out of the flat into the Fiat; but once in Warley she did**n't know what to do with herself**. She turned up St Clair Road with the idea of going home.* RATT ▫ *The poor beasts were so tormented by flies they did**n't know what to do with themselves**.* ▫ *A grown man and woman lisping and babbling at each other like that! I tell you, I do**n't know where to put myself** when they start that baby-talk.* ▫ variant not know where to put oneself, usu meaning 'feel uncomfortable or embarrassed'.

not know what one is missing not realize how good sth one dislikes, or choses not to avail oneself of, really is ▫ *The British sportsman shoots a good many native birds, too, but nothing like as many as he could. If pheasants, why not thrushes? From my own experience, I'd say the inconsistent Englishman does**n't know what he's missing**.* OBS ▫ *This is the India that few people have or make the opportunity to see and appreciate. They **don't know what they are missing**.* ST ▫ *I regret all the years I could have been enjoying classical music. But I was ignorant, you see, I did**n't know what I was missing**.*

not know where/which way to look/turn one's eyes (informal) be embarrassed, awkwardly self-conscious, etc **adv:** not, hardly, scarcely ▫ *It would be historically more correct to picture the embarrassment, in that setting* (Versailles) *of those who came with the news of defeat at Blenheim. In a place resplendent with emblems of victory they can **hardly** have **known which way to look**.* PL ▫ *A baby in the same carriage was bad enough but when the girl calmly opened her blouse and pulled out her breast to feed it, the prim old bachelor did**n't know where to look**.* ▫ *The child was ashamed of the affectionate fuss his mother was making of him in front of his schoolmates and did**n't know where to turn his eyes**.* ▫ *Her parents live in Berkshire where she was brought up. Now, when neighbours say they saw Pam on telly* (= television) *last night, her Mum does**n't know which way to look**.* TVT

not know/be sure where one's next meal/penny is coming from live without security; live on the edge of poverty, want, or starvation ▫ *They would not have expected a man with a full belly to have the same look as one who did **not know where his next meal was coming from**.* SML ▫ *Mr C G Baker, was a classic of the favoured 'ordinary' type of Pools winner—conscientious, hardworking and, up to that Saturday, **never** quite **sure where his next penny was coming from**.* ST ▫ (NONCE) *Palmer's foresight in his business affairs means that when retirement ultimately comes, he wo**n't have any qualms about where his next set of golf balls is coming from**.* ST

not know where/which way to turn not know what to do, how to help oneself, or obtain help ▫ *Every line of investigation had brought me to a dead end and I did**n't know where to turn**.* ▫ *The prospective parents objected to blood transfusions, and the surgeon did **not know which way to turn** in order to save the child.* OBS ▫ *A service to Jura would require Government assistance. The islanders do **not know which way to turn** next, but they still live in hope that ships will again call at Craighouse on a regular basis.* SC ▫ *'We're so pleased to see you,' she said. 'Luckily there's no one much here at the moment—sometimes we just do**n't know where to turn** so as to fit people in.'* TCB

not let the sun go down (up)on one's anger/wrath (saying) limit one's anger or bad temper, not carry it over from one day to another ▫ (source) *Be ye angry, and sin not; **let not the sun go down upon your wrath**.* EPHESIANS IV 26 ▫ *She'll cry herself to sleep if she's not forgiven. Come on, James—do**n't let the sun go down on your wrath**!* ▫ *She's a very irritable old lady, my mother. But she does try **not** to **let the sun go down on her anger**.* ▫ on now more common than upon.

not (bloody) likely no; certainly not; not on your (sweet etc) life(!) (qv); not on your nelly (qv) ▫ *But the idea* (of chasing after them) *never occurred to me. In any case what was I to do? Knock him flat and drag Kathy back by the hair? **Not likely**.* LLDR ▫ *'Perhaps John will do the dishes for a change,' she said, winking at her mother-in-law. '**Not likely**,' John said, 'with two women in the house with nothing better to do.'* ▫ *'Jenny will write my speech for me.' '**Not bloody likely**! or even **not Pygmalion likely**!' said Jenny.* ▫ short emph comment or reply; not bloody likely (taboo) may either give extra emphasis, or be (facetious) conscious imitation of Eliza Doolittle's reply in PYGMALION III by G B SHAW 1856-1950.

not a little quite; very **adj:** weary, jealous, wary, surprised. **adv:** wearily, wildly ▫ *She was **not a little** weary of having to cook Christmas dinner for ten people each year.* ▫ *In fact he was **not a little** surprised by the results of my work, and asked a number of questions which were forceful variants on the theme 'Are you sure?'.* NSC ▫ *So all in all there was quite a bit of work to do before he got through his pile of plates—work that was **not a little** tedious.* TBC ▫ *He was shouting, **not a little** wildly, for someone to let him out.* ▫ used for understatement.

not long for this world [Comp (AdjP)] likely,

or certain, to die soon, or have (had) a very short life **V:** ⚠ be; seem □ *Lord Warbeck was* ***not long for this world****. He had made that clear in his letter of invitation. After him there would be more Warbecks of Warbeck Hall.* EM □ *Of the children thus affected at birth, most are* ***not long for this world*** *anyway and there is a strong argument for not subjecting them to painful and ultimately ineffective operations.* □ *Mrs Bennet sat with them for half an hour, a frail presence* ***not long for this world****.*

not matter a damn etc be of no importance, consequence **S:** result, outcome; it...whether he came, it...how we did it. **O:** a damn, ⚠ (taboo) a bugger, fuck □ *It did****n't matter a bugger*** *to me which of them finished the job, so long as it got finished.* □ (NONCE) *Ford Prefect knew that it did****n't matter a pair of Dingo's Kidneys*** *whether Arthur's house got knocked down or not.* HHGG

not to mention/speak of sth/sb [Conj] and also; and as may be assumed; and, perhaps; more importantly; to say nothing of sth/sb (qv) □ *It was a vast territory, consisting not only of built-up areas, but also of fields, woods and a number of lakes,* ***not to mention*** *three airports.* L □ *A barrel of 500 large herring sold for £1-45, which would have bought a good supply of meal,* ***not to speak of*** *whisky, at that time.* SC □ *They sent a plane with food for you, but they couldn't find you. I tell you there's been one big flap on back in Fairbanks,* ***not to speak of*** *the hue and cry going on in camp.* BM □ *This gallery was to put on a one-man show and give everyone a chance to see my work and talk about it and make me famous,* ***not to mention*** *buy it and make me rich.* CON □ precedes last single item, or group of items, of pair or list.

not mince matters/(one's) words [V + O] speak frankly, bluntly, or coarsely □ *The Home Secretary saw no reason to* ***mince matters****. 'Any revelations you make, Professor Kingsley, will be regarded by the Government as a serious contravention of the Official Secrets Act.'* TBC □ *A letter from Carson, written in his old age (1933) when he no longer needed to* ***mince his words****, tells it all.* NS

not a moment too soon [A (NP)] almost too late, or at a time already overdue **V:** come, arrive; happen; reach, get, sb □ (reforms in the police force) *Anger, dismay, open criticism all add up to a picture of morale so low that it is clear that Mr Mark's radical changes come* ***not a moment too soon****.* NS □ *But if there is a genuine revival, Dr MacIntosh feels that it has come* ***not a moment too soon****. 'The situation is desperate for the preservation of Gaelic, it really is,' he says.* RT □ *'We got him* ***not a moment too soon****,' the surgeon told me, 'the appendix was badly perforated.'*

not much[1] (informal) no; certainly not □ *'Mum was asking in the last letter if you were ever going to get a commission.' '****Not much****,' he said 'I get more fun this way.'* RFW □ *'Shall we see you at the Baby Show?' '****Not much*** *you will. What would I be doing at an affair like that?'* □ *Some people think we're a second-rate team now.* ***Not much*** *we aren't, as they'll very soon find out.* □ often precedes short emph answer to previous question or statement.

not much[2] (informal, ironic) certainly; very much so □ *'Honest, mam, I can't tell you one half of what went on, because you wouldn't want to hear it.' (****Not much****, I thought. I could see her as large as life licking her chops.)* LLDR □ *Chucked 'issen* (= threw himself) *from the hospital window. Dead?* ***Not much*** *'e aint* (= he isn't). *The brainless bastards had put him in a ward six floors up, which finished him off proper.* LLDR □ *'Surely Jenny wouldn't lie over a trifle like that.' '****Not much*** *she wouldn't. Lying's second nature to her.'*

not much cop [Comp (AdjP)] (informal) of slight, or no, value or advantage **V:** ⚠ be; look; think sth □ (Davies tries on a pair of shoes Aston has given him) DAVIES: *They'd cripple me in a week. I mean, these ones I* (= I've) *got on, they're no good but at least they're comfortable.* ***Not much cop****, but I mean they don't hurt.* TC □ *'What fee are they paying you?' '£20.' 'That's* ***not much cop****. Take your Income Tax and your fares* (ie travelling expenses) *off that and you might as well stay at home.'*

not much of a sth[1] [Comp (NP)] lacking skill, ability, value, competence **V:** ⚠ be; prove, find sb. **n:** mechanic, tennis-player, cook; gift, reason, treat □ *'Tell me, do you service these* (vacuum cleaners)*?' 'I send Lopez. I'm* ***not much of a*** *mechanic. When I touch one of these things it somehow seems to give up working.'* OMIH □ *Doctor! He's* ***not much of a*** *doctor if he's been treating you for three months for an illness you haven't got.* □ *Here's a sketch Robin did of his father. It's* ***not much of a*** *likeness, is it?*

not much of a sth[2] [Comp (NP)] sb/sth that is unpleasant only to a minor or insignificant degree (the implication being that the event or state is not as disagreeable as might be expected) **V:** ⚠ be; prove, find sb. **n:** nuisance, burden, mess, disability, lie; complainer □ *'I'm sorry to be such a nuisance, nurse.' 'You're* ***not much of a*** *nuisance, my dear. I wish that most of my patients were as easy to do for.'* □ *Jim's* ***not much of a*** *fusser* (= does not make a fuss) *about his food so what Mrs Hodgkins was giving them must have been pretty awful.* □ *'What have you been doing to yourself now?' 'I nicked my finger with the vegetable knife—****not much of a*** *cut really. The bandage is just to keep it clean.'*

not need to tell sb/say sb is already aware of sth being referred to; the information is already known, or can probably be guessed, by sb **adv:** not, hardly, scarcely □ *Well, the telephone account has come in and I do****n't need to tell*** *you it's a shocker.* □ *I* ***need hardly tell*** *you that if this story of yours becomes public there will be very grave repercussions indeed.* TBC □ *If that's the company you were with you do****n't need to tell*** *me who paid for the lunch.* □ *We both wish you the best of luck and* ***need hardly say*** *how sorry we are not to have seen you before you sailed.* ⇨ ⚠ next entry.

not need any telling be already willing, ready, or eager to do sth which one is told, invited, or urged to do **adv:** not, never, hardly □ *'Eat plenty, there's a lot more if you want it.' But the men did****n't need any telling****, after their long day in the fields.* □ *'Watch carefully now, children,' the conjuror said, but they* ***hardly needed telling****, so keen were they to catch him* *out if they could.* ▫ *'Look on the floor* (= ground),*' Bert called out. Colin* ***needed little telling****: snapped down to the gutter, walked a hundred yards doubled-up like a premature rheumatic, and later shot straight holding a packet with two whole cigarettes protruding.* LLDR ▫ variant need little telling. ⇨ ⚠ previous entry.

not on your (sweet etc) life(!) (informal) certainly not; not (bloody) likely (qv); next entry (qv) **adj:** sweet, ⚠ blooming, bloody ▫ JASON: *Marry me tomorrow and we will merge in every way.* SONIA: ***Not on your life****—business and pleasure don't mix.* DPM ▫ *'It would be very nice if you could come on the Committee,' said Lydia, 'I'm terrified of it.' '****Not on your sweet life****,' said Mr Wickham with sad want of gallantry.* WDM ▫ *In the worlds of commerce and industry, your secretary is your subordinate: in the Civil Service,* ***not on your life****. Rating in the hierarchy goes up thus: Assistant Principal, Principal, Assistant Secretary, Under Secretary, Deputy Secretary, Secretary!* SML ▫ *And so Max Faulkner advises club golfers to think seriously about using women's clubs. But will you?* ***Not on your life****, and neither will I, because for some reason we'd find it an affront to our tatty masculinity.* SC ▫ short emph comment or reply.

not on your nelly (slang) no; certainly not; not (bloody) likely (qv); previous entry (qv) ▫ PETER: *Playing chess? I'll give you a game.* ALEX: ***Not on your Nelly****—I only play against myself.* DPM ▫ *Pop asked with some concern if he shouldn't give him* (the baby) *a piece of fried bread to be going on with? Ma said '****Not on your nelly****,' in a voice very near to severity.* BFA ▫ *They even had a meeting and asked me if I would release them from their obligations. I told them: '****Not on your nelly****. All I want is the chance to prove you wrong.'* RT ▫ short emph comment or reply; capital or small N.

not (the) one etc to do sth [Comp (NP)] not sb who, from character, principles or habit, would be likely to do sth **V:** ⚠ be, seem; consider sb to be. **n:** (the) one, ⚠ a/the man, woman, person ▫ *When her English butler, Robert, asks for an increase in the housekeeping, she refuses. However this British underdog is* ***not one to*** *take defeat lying down.* TVT ▫ *The Home Secretary was* ***not a man to*** *offer a staunch defence to a losing argument. When an argument led him to an awkward impasse he simply changed the subject and never referred to the old topic again.* TBC ▫ *Quiet, genial and studious, Eric Varley, Minister of Energy, is* ***not the man to*** *waste public money.* NS

not one whit etc [A (NP)] not (in) the smallest amount or degree **V:** care, worry; upset, disconcert, disturb, sb. **n:** whit, ⚠ jot, iota ▫ *Mrs Thorpe seemed a bit baffled but it did****n't*** *faze* (= disconcert) *Mr Thorpe* ***one whit****. He took it good-naturedly in his stride, answering everyone, neglecting no-one.* RT ▫ *Forgive me, my dear friend, for writing and accept my sincere gratitude for all you have done—this sad end to it can****not*** *diminish that by* ***one jot****.* HAA ▫ *Some of 'Amarcord' looks remarkably authentic — the village square for example—but tails quickly off into familiar bits of studio, the front offices, the canteen, the dubbing theatres, barely disguised by a few antique film posters. Of course it does* ***not*** *matter* ***one iota****.* ⇨ ⚠ a jot or tittle.

not the only pebble on the beach [Comp (NP)] just one of a number of people or things equally available, suitable, or desirable **V:** ⚠ be; look like ▫ *Peggy's just playing hard to get. Let her see she's* ***not the only pebble on the beach*** *and she'll act very differently.* ▫ (a restaurant) *We go in, come out, say hello, smile. Just one of the hundreds and thousands,* ***just one*** *little* ***pebble on the beach*** *to them, but they always do us well.* ST ▫ *'While you're wondering whether it's worth the price, someone else may snap it up.' 'So what? It's* ***not the only pebble on the beach****. There's a lot more people selling caravans than buying them at this time of year.'* ▫ variant just one pebble on the beach.

not a patch on sb/sth [Comp (NP)] not nearly so good, bad, beautiful, funny etc as sb/sth **V:** ⚠ be; think, reckon, sb. **o:** his father, your garden; what happened here ▫ *He's growing up a very nice boy, but* ***not a patch on*** *his father for looks.* ▫ *Your aunt is eaten up with self-pity. No trouble anyone ever had is* ***a patch on*** *what she's had to suffer.*

not one's place (to do sth) [Comp (NP)] not within one's authority, the terms of one's employment, etc (to do sth); presumptuous, interfering, over-familiar, of one (to do sth) **V:** ⚠ be, seem; think sth ▫ *'I think it's a matter for her to decide, sir,' said Briggs uncertainly. 'I'm sure I don't want to stand in your way but it's not my place to give orders.'* EM ▫ *Don't let yourself be taken advantage of. You're nurse-companion to the old lady, It's* ***not your place to do*** *personal washing for the whole family.* ▫ rather dated; sometimes used by servants etc in talking deferentially of the limits of their authority, as in first example

not a sausage (dated slang) nothing at all ▫ *Can't hear you, old man,* ***not a sausage****. Up a bit. I still can't hear you.* PM ▫ *I thought Stanley would have to pay some of his expenses himself?' 'Well, he didn't.* ***Not a sausage****.'* ▫ *Fred was going to write to us regularly once he got settled over there, but that's six months gone by and* ***not a sausage****.*

not say boo to a goose be very/too timid or gentle ▫ *I don't know why, but everybody in the yard expected to see some scruffy, half-baked, daft sort of piece that would****n't say boo to a goose****.* LLDR ▫ *Rose's heartbeat quickened. Stanley could****n't say boo to a goose*** *but he made her sweat. It was no good flaring at him —his eyes were quite fixed and steady and she was losing.* TSMP ▫ *Oh, she looks as if she ca****n't say boo to a goose*** *but some of these quiet little things can be wonderfully stubborn.* ▫ with *can, could, would.*

not one's scene [Comp (NP)] (informal) surroundings, company, employment, recreation etc not suited to one's temperament or abilities **V:** ⚠ be, seem; think sth ▫ *The camp, we were told, was 'regimented', there was 'strict discipline', children were taken for walks 'crocodile fashion', an atmosphere of 'uncanny quiet' permeated the whole place. Now you and I may feel that is* ***not*** *quite* ***our scene****—but I had supposed that good order and discipline — to say nothing of peace, quiet and calm — were* *just the values it stood for.* NS □ *In 1974 he heard that the producer of the Tattoo was retiring. 'I did**n't** think it was **my scene** but was persuaded to apply. And here I am.'* RT □ (a BBC interviewer speaks) *I don't like to see people who are neither politicians nor villains discomfited. It's all too simple to specialise in making people squirm. That's **not my scene**.* RT □ *'These affairs always end up the same way,' he grumbled, 'everybody looking to me to tell them what to do.' 'Oh? I'd have thought that **was** just **your scene**!'* □ variant be sb's scene, used for emphasis or contradiction.

not see it/that happening not expect that sth suggested, promised or wished for will happen □ *The islanders don't want to leave, and probably wouldn't if there were a subsidy to reduce freight charges. But they do**n't see that happening**.* □ *'Will he really take things easier?' 'He promised the doctor he would, but I ca**n't see it happening**.'* □ esp after *don't/can't*.

not see etc sb's/sth's like(s) again sb/sth has been outstandingly good, able, praiseworthy, impressive etc and is unlikely to be equalled by anyone/anything in the future **adv:** not, never, not ever. **V:** see, ⚠ look upon, meet, come across □ (source) *He was a man, take him for all in all,/I shall **not look upon his like again**.* HAMLET I 2 □ (reader's letter) *I enjoyed the Gene Kelly interview on 'Film 74' (5 Nov, BBC1). Barry Norman can indeed shed a furtive tear that we will **not see** Kelly**'s like again**.* RT □ *The Seychelles are a blissfully forgotten corner of the earth, and if forgotten places appeal to you, they should be seen soon. I know I shall **never see their like again**.* ST □ *In this country we shall **not** easily **see the** remote **likes of** Greaves again—which is the problem: where are the exciting prospects a football season should produce?* L □ *Of Lady Ottoline it may be said, in a phrase much hackneyed by amateur obituarists, that we shall **not look upon her like again**—but then, who had ever looked upon it before?* AH □ with *shall/will* and usu first person. ⇨ ⚠ the likes of sb; not have seen etc the like (of sth)/sth's like.

not see the wood for the trees be unable to understand, deal with, a main subject, issue, problem etc because one is confused by, or too closely involved in, numerous or complex details □ *Whether viewers find this series as fascinating as I do is difficult to judge. I may **not** be able to **see the wood for the trees**, being involved in it.* DM □ *The second part is made up of separate chapters on Peake's individual novels, his shorter prose pieces and his poems. A criticism of his* (ie the author's) *method is that one can**not see the wood for the trees**.* SC □ *A wise historian usually stops twenty or thirty years before his time, because—like the rest of us—he ca**n't see the wood for the trees**.* □ (NONCE) *His own research was devouring him. Even his friends thought he was in danger of **missing the wood in contemplation of the trees**.* OBS □ (NONCE) ***Distinguishing the wood from the trees** is the task facing Scotland's rugby club delegates when they meet in Edinburgh on Friday to debate the formation of a national league competition.* SC □ (NONCE) *He never had time to think because he was always reading papers. He **saw every tree**, but **never the whole wood**.* MFM □ frequently adapted, as shown.

not/hardly sleep a wink not get any sleep/get very little sleep □ *Many said they would **not sleep a wink** but in fact they slept more soundly and exhaustedly that night than on most nights.* MM □ *I **hardly slept a wink** all night because of that howling wind.*

not so/too hot [Comp (AdjP)] (informal) not very good, healthy, satisfactory **V:** ⚠ be, look, feel □ *Beaumont runs in the fourth semi-final and goes out* (ie does not qualify to run in the final race). *'Got away all right,' he says flatly. 'The rest of it was**n't so hot**.'* ST □ *'How are you feeling this morning?' '**Not too hot**, actually. My stomach's been upset these last two days.'* □ *In other words, so long as a programme denouncing the evils of capitalist society is matched by one showing that things under socialism are **not too hot** either, once the heavy mob gets in charge, honour is satisfied.* L

not so much a programme, more a way of life (catchphrase) sth which becomes an obsession or a life's work, rather than the more limited, modest activity it may appear to be (from the title of a BBC TV series shown during the 1960s) □ (NONCE) *Well, we are used to 'Play for Today' being **not so much a drama, more a way of life**, so that the gritty unlit quality* (of the pre-credit sequence) *should have prepared us for a gritty, unilluminated, long, hard look at ourselves.* L □ (NONCE) *'Don't tell me you have a drink problem too?' '**Not so much a problem, more a way of life**. It's my friends that do the worrying.'* □ frequently adapted, as shown.

not so (as) you'd notice (informal) possibly, but, if so, not noticeably (the implication often being 'not really', 'not at all') □ CHARLES: *Some people said that maybe the radiation was clearing.* RACHEL: *Do you think it is?* CHARLES: ***Not so's you'd notice**.* OI □ *Were dire warnings voiced by those omniscient organs, the 'Financial Times' and the 'Economist'? **Not so you'd notice**.* NS

not a (living) soul [Comp/O (NP)] (nobody at all **V:** there be; see, know, tell to sth □ ADA: *Is there anyone about?* HENRY: ***Not a living soul**.* E □ *'I was captivated by the life around here,' he says. 'I love the corner bakeries still making their own bread, the walks across the moors where you do**n't** see **a soul**.'* TVT □ *It's the truth. There's **not a living soul** of my kin left anywhere in the world.* SC □ *'You aren't expecting anyone, are you, Carter?' 'No, why?' 'I thought—the way you watched the door—' 'I do**n't** know **a soul** in this town. I told you.'* OMIH □ *Well, the monster's asleep in the cave and snoring like an earthquake. But **not** a word of this to **a living soul**, Kenny.* RM □ *For close on two months he saw **not a living soul**.* □ *...when you see how many items in any evening are recorded. Sometimes I wonder whether **any living souls** are actually inside TV's Tower of Babel at White City on any given night.* ST □ variant, if/whether any living soul(s), in interr sentences.

not (know sb) to speak to not (know sb) well enough for an exchange of greetings, conversation etc to take place □ *'You know her, of course?' '**Not to speak to**. After all, she's hardly of our square little circle down here.'* YWT □ *I* *know his work and had attended some of his lectures but had never met him* ***to speak to*** *before.* ▫ *Mary Ashley—she's the dark-haired girl in your office isn't she? I've seen her around but I do**n't know** her **to speak to**.*

not speak ill of the dead (saying) not say anything slighting, or critical about sb who has died, esp to those who knew him (a free translation of the Latin proverb mentioned in first quotation) **modal:** ought to, must, should ▫ *The rational explanation for **not speaking ill of the dead** ('De mortuis nil nisi bonum') is obvious. We don't want to distress the bereaved, and the dead can't hit back.* OBS ▫ *'Now, now. Mary. One is **not** supposed to **speak ill of the dead**.' 'Why not, I want to know, if they deserve it?'* ▫ almost always neg.

not/never suffer fools gladly not be tolerant of, or patient with, people who are, or are assumed to be, stupid or foolish ▫ (source) *For ye **suffer fools gladly**, seeing ye yourselves are wise.* II CORINTHIANS XI 19 ▫ *Mark was obsessed with hard work and problems. He did**n't suffer fools gladly** and anybody not prepared to work 100 per cent for Mark was a fool to him and he could be hard on them.* ST ▫ *This strange mixture of aesthete and athlete could scarcely be called stupid. Liddell Hart, who **never suffered fools gladly** or otherwise, commented that he 'had a good intelligence and an exceptionally open mind'.* NS ▫ *'Who cares about grease on your lapel?' 'I do.' 'Well, the waiter'll bring you something.' She sighed, as if it were a tremendous effort to her to **suffer fools** as **gladly** as she did.* US ▫ occas used without neg as in last example.

not tonight, Josephine (catchphrase) facetious way of delining an offer (supposedly said by Napoleon to his first wife, Josephine) ▫ *A small boy touting lottery tickets approached Harry Bannion. '**Not tonight, Josephine**,' he countered.* ILIH ▫ *Silly, but fun all the same—pillowslips for couples who have a communication problem at bedtime; if it's a case of **not-tonight-Josephine** (or Joe) you may put the No-side up.* NS

not trust sb an inch/as far as one could throw him [V + O + A pass] (informal) believe sb to be dishonest, unreliable, likely at any time to do sth criminal, wrong or foolish if not prevented ▫ *'No offence, Steve?' And Steve laughed. 'Not between old comrades in arms,' he said, and backed out and along the top corridor away from a tyke you could**n't trust as far as you could throw him**.* TT ▫ *No, young Victoria, I'm going to have you right under my eyes. I'm not going to take any chances on your running out on me. I do**n't trust you an inch**.* TCB ▫ (NONCE) (racing) *Of course, there are murky sheep in every walk of life, and in view of the money involved it is hardly surprising that there are a few characters engaged in the sport who can **not** be **trusted as far as you can kick a block of concrete**.* ST

not turn a hair [V + O] not show fear, dismay, surprise, excitement etc in circumstances when such a reaction might be expected **adv:** not, never, hardly ▫ *It was a swingeing sentence he got but he did**n't turn a hair** as he sat in the dock. You'd have thought the judge was talking about somebody else.* ▫ *If they had fireworks at the Gymkhana he would put one under Edith's skirts, just to see what happened. Probably **never turn a hair**, he thought.* DBM ▫ *He had tried to convey to her without other people's noticing it how glad he was to see her, and he had much admired the way his love was able to receive the quick signals of affection **without turning a** single fair **hair**.* RM ▫ *With very little visible protest we acquiesced in having a European destiny thrust upon us, we even accepted the bankruptcy of perhaps our proudest national company **without turning a hair**.* NS ▫ variant without turning a hair.

not unduly worried etc [Comp (AdjP)] not very, or excessively, anxious; (ironic) not as anxious as it would be natural to be **V:** ⚠ be, seem, feel. **adj:** worried, ⚠ disturbed, anxious, distressed ▫ *I discovered that he had not eaten anything. I was **not unduly worried** by this, for some creatures when newly caught refuse to eat until they have settled down in captivity.* BB ▫ *It was a bit of a shock to be declared redundant, but since I had a tidy sum of money saved I was **not unduly anxious** about finding another job immediately.* ▫ *It was the Negro who had been sweeping the passage. He said, 'Policia* ((Spanish) = the police)*!' No one seemed **unduly disturbed**. The fat woman drained her wine, the girl who was called Teresa pulled on her second stocking.* OMIH

not want any part of sth [V + O] not agree to take any part in, to be in any way associated with, sth **o:** it; this scheme; what you're suggesting ▫ TONY: *Oh, Christ! Seven years or so of establishing oneself as a* sound *young man—I want to opt out. I do**n't want any part of** it.* EHOW ▫ *I did**n't want any part of** this silly reception. It was all so crass.* CON ▫ usu in first person; variant (formal) want no part of it.

not want to know (informal) deliberately not seek information about, contact with, sb/sth that may involve one in worry, work, trouble etc ▫ *I'm advertising like mad for a housekeeper or a maid, but they do**n't want to know**, do they?* ST ▫ *She must have suspected that some at least of the extras the boy was bringing home from the shop were stolen, not given to him. But if so, she did**n't want to know**.* ▫ *The gap between school training and work training is, indeed, one of the greatest failures of the British system. 'In general schools do**n't want to know** anything to do with the world at work,' says Mr Hayes.* G

not waste words [V + O pass] speak as briefly, or as seldom, as possible, either habitually or on a particular occasion (the implication usu being that what is said is to the point and effective) ▫ *The cheek of them, walking into the ward like that! Sister did**n't waste words** telling them what to do. 'Out!' she said, and they went a lot faster than they came in.* ▫ *Miss Adelaide Small, the editor who had replaced Virginia's mother, was a dry, business-like woman who **wasted no words**, and no sympathy on anyone who made a mistake.* AITC ▫ *Once she starts a story no one can stop her from finishing, but she does **not waste words**.* TVT ▫ usu pass ***not a word** was **wasted***; variant waste no words.

not waving but drowning behaviour, or actions, not indicating (as might be thought) well-being, personal and social assurance, etc but (if rightly interpreted) failure to cope, distress, need for help, etc □ (source) *Oh, no no no, it was too cold always/(Still the dead one lay moaning)/I was much too far out all my life/And* ***not waving but drowning***. NOT WAVING BUT DROWNING (S SMITH 1902-71) □ *This dictum goes with the observation that most funny people are unhappy. But there's more to it. If you look hard at Blake, and Erasmus and Rabelais, what do you see? Not just the sentimentality of men* ***waving while*** *they are really* ***drowning***, *but three fools insisting that Aristotle was on to something when he pointed out that we are the only species with the gift of laughter.* SC □ *Except in the sonnets and poems, Shakespeare's formal sense is disguised and does not threaten. No matter how wrong this idea might be, it does give the poet bobbing in Shakespeare's wake the momentary illusion that he might be* ***waving instead of drowning***. ST □ often adapted, as shown.

not the whole etc story [Comp/O (NP)] not all, only part, of what there is to be known, learned, about sth **V:** be; hear, know. **adj:** the whole, ⚠ half the, the end of the □ *While his faults of character may be partly due to deficiencies in upbringing and education, it's* ***not the whole story***. *Many boys with a worse home and an unhappier school-life have proved that these are not insuperable obstacles.* □ (income tax) *The single person or the married couple without children are even more heavily penalised.* ***Nor*** *is that* (or: *And that is* ***not***) *by any means* ***the whole story***. NS □ *A systematic long-term change of this kind suggests the action of natural selection and indicates that female skeletal characteristics confer greater fitness. But is this* ***the whole story***? L □ *'Producer in one company, drama adviser in another, lecturer and occasional actor,' says the blurb of one of his books, but that is* ***only half the story***. L □ *As nothing whatever is known of Shakespeare's personality such an assertion can neither be proved or disproved. But this is* ***not the end of the story***. *The Oedipus complex can be adduced to explain the actions of any particular person.* SNP □ sometimes interr with neg implication as in third example; variant only half the story.

not with a bang but a whimper (catchphrase) not having a spectacular, magnificent, or terrifying conclusion or downfall but collapsing or fading out in an insignificant way □ (source) *This is the way the world ends/* ***Not with a bang but a whimper***. THE HOLLOW MEN (T S ELIOT 1888-1965) □ (the Nixon administration, US) *This is the way it ends.* ***Not with a*** *big* ***bang***, *as many had feared. And not with with an embarrassed sigh of relief, as others had hoped.* ***But with*** *veiled accusations and self-justifying* ***whimpers*** *from an Administration that finds the buck can no longer be passed on.* NS □ *BBC 2's Sunday night goes out* ***with a whimper*** *rather than* ***a bang***. *Still, it's supposed to be a day of rest.* L □ *As a colleague I respected, he merited better than he got—and better than he dealt himself. Sadly,* ***the bang*** *of his going will dwindle into* ***the whimper*** *of his political suicide.* L □ often adapted, as shown.

not a word no mention (to be) made; no information (to be) given, or received **A:** to your father; about what's happened; of this □ *Well, the monster's asleep in the cave and snoring like an earthquake. But* ***not a word*** *of this to a living soul, Kenny. We must be patient till Thursday comes.* RM □ *I've always been a coward. Saunders is so overpowering. But if Guy is in trouble of course I will help. And* ***not a word*** *to Saunders.* DC □ *'Have you heard when or whether the Canadian team are coming over?' '****Not a word****.'* □ usu imper; often (part of) verbless clause, as in second example where last sentence = 'And don't say anything to Saunders'.

not to worry (informal) I'm not going to worry too much; don't worry; let us not worry □ *'Quite a whirl of events—at least you'll know that you've been married.' 'Won't I just?' she said. 'Still,* ***not to worry***.*'* TT □ (from a yachtsman's diary) *The seas are certainly changing. They are looking much more formidable.* ***Not to worry***. *Can't last for ever (or can it)?* SC □ *What a shame making you listen to all this.* ***Not to worry***, *I'll get it sorted out somehow.* □ used as mild suggestion usu recommending sb else not to worry on one's behalf.

nothing but sth/do sth [Comp/O (NP)] only sth/do sth **V:** be; hear, see, do. **A:** a fake; disaster; grumble, complain □ *We've heard* ***nothing but*** *moans all day.* □ *You've done* ***nothing but*** *grumble ever since we arrived. Shut up or cheer up!* □ *Her life's been* ***nothing but*** *disaster upon disaster but her courage never fails.* □ front position. ⇨ ⚠ anything but; have etc everything but (sth).

(there is) nothing etc to choose between A and B (there is) no, or very little, difference between two, or a number of, people or things **pron/n:** nothing, ⚠ not anything; not, hardly, a pin; not much, very little. **o:** this and that, the old and the new, France and Britain □ *It's only the gold mounting that pushes the price of this model up. For capacity and length of service there's* ***nothing to choose between*** *this and the cheaper pen.* □ *'That treacherous devil. It's the last time I do anything for anyone.' 'Can you stand up?' 'Drew a knife on me. My leg hurts. They're all the same in the end.* ***Nothing to choose between*** *them.'* ILIH □ (Lydia) *thought to herself that as far as conscientiousness went* ***there was hardly a pin to choose between*** *the Earl and his Countess, except that she had perfect health.* WDM □ *As a test of speed or an obstacle course, cyclocross leaves* ***little to choose between*** *the top riders, but champions are made in those brief moments when guts count most.* TVT

(there is) nothing doing (informal) no; one doesn't, and won't, agree to do what is requested, suggested or ordered; one can't get, find, succeed in doing, sth □ JASON: *Just get rid of Peter Mann. Get him away from here—as far as possible.* ALEX: ***Nothing doing***. *I'm in the middle of my game.* DPM □ *'Listen,' Daniel said to Querini, 'It won't hurt you if you let this go. You'll get something better in time. No thanks, Wouvermans,* ***there's nothing doing***.*'* US □ *'Did you get that stain out of your skirt.' 'I tried with everything I could think of, but* ***nothing doing***.*'* □ *She went first to the door and examined it. Certainly* ***nothing doing*** *there. This wasn't the* *kind of lock you picked with a hairpin.* TCB ⇨ ⚠ something/nothing doing.

nothing/(not) anything (else) for it (but to do sth) [Comp/O (NP)] no other action or procedure (is) possible or suitable in the circumstances **V:** there be, seem; (can) see ▫ *Roughly Charles tore the letter open. It is true what Bernard tells you* (ie I am his mistress, not his niece, and will not see you again). *There is* ***nothing for it****. I am sorry. V.* HD ▫ *Do you know he wanted me to write a book about him? I soon crapped on that* ((taboo) = rejected that suggestion), *as you can imagine. But I shall more or less have to get this article out; I ca****n't*** *see* ***anything for it****.* ILIH ▫ *I chafed at the delay, but there seemed to be* ***nothing for it but to*** *wait a year and go to Oxford when I could get into College.* RFW ▫ *We're going to Eve's party, baby-sitter or no baby-sitter. We'll put Sally in the carry-cot and take her with us if there's* ***nothing else for it****.*

nothing if not sth [Comp (NP)] undeniably and/or noticeably having some quality, either as a permanent characteristic or on a particular occasion **V:** ⚠ be; think, consider, sb. **adj:** active; just; professional. **n:** a model of tact, a trouble maker, a professional ▫ *Bruce Forsyth relishes this new television series, his first for BBC — 'because it's a family game, giving teams from different generations something to do. An active show—and I'm* ***nothing if not*** *active.'* RT ▫ *Harold was (so he believed)* ***nothing if not*** *just; and in the light of justice, with the wish to square the account between him and Alec, he was prepared to reconsider the case of Irma.* PW ▫ *'Sister Burstead was cross with Granny Duncan?' said the matron. 'She was* ***nothing****,' said Miss Taylor, '****if not*** *cross.'* MM ▫ *And those are only two examples of the type of reporting that clogs every page. Michner is* ***nothing if not*** *a master of the banal.* SC ▫ *At this time Belton who was* ***noted for nothing if not for*** *persistence was making his third attempt at locating the sunken vessel.* ▫ *Leading scientists are* ***characterised by nothing if not by*** *their extreme taciturnity on every topic save their adopted specialism(s).* L ▫ variants noted, renowned etc for nothing if not for, characterized, typified etc by nothing if not by sth.

nothing in particular [Comp/O (NP)] nothing worth special mention; nothing much at all; no single item of special importance or interest among other things done, thought or said **V:** be; do, notice, buy, enjoy, want ▫ *The most transporting representations of the Cherubim are those which show them as they are in their native habitat—doing* ***nothing in particular****.* HAH ▫ *Professor Matthew's talk on the Fourth Piano Concerto was about* ***nothing in particular****.* NS ▫ *Edward Short had never met me; he had* ***nothing in particular*** *to discuss but he thought it would be useful to have a brief talk before the summer break.* NS ▫ *'Is there anything you want for your birthday?' '****Nothing in particular****. You just give me a nice surprise.'* ▫ cf *not in particular* = 'not specially, not more than anything else' as in *'Are you fond of poetry, too?' 'Not in particular. If somebody finds me some to read I often enjoy it, but I never seek it out, if you know what I mean.'*

nothing is/can be farther from one's mind/thoughts (than sth) sth previously mentioned, or to be defined, is an opinion, wish, intention one definitely does not have ▫ *'I'm not lying about this, you know.' '****Nothing could be farther from my thoughts****, my dear chap. I'm merely amazed.'* ▫ *It seemed a disloyalty to Madge to declare that* ***nothing was farther from my mind than*** *the idea of marrying her—especially as it now occurred to me that Madge might well have been using my alleged aspirations as a lover to make up Sammy's mind.* UTN ▫ *In short this looks like a genuine offer of international inspection made by the United States and applicable to her own territory. Russia should jump at it* (= accept it eagerly). *But* ***nothing*** *seems to* ***be farther from her thoughts****.* SC ▫ (a television series) *When Reginald Iolanthe Perrin set out for work on the Thursday morning, he had no intention of calling his mother-in-law a hippopotamus.* ***Nothing could*** *have* ***been further from his thoughts****.* RT ▫ alternative spellings farther/further.

nothing is sacred (catchphrase) there is no subject or situation, however sublime, important etc, which is not, or cannot be, treated frivolously, with disrespect, etc ▫ *He sets out to amuse by offending as many people as possible, He makes racial jokes, sick-and-sin jokes,* ***nothing is sacred*** *and he is there to tell us.* NS ▫ *With George V, the Edwardian social scene disintegrated pretty sharply. Headstrong girls were mocking their chaperones (****was nothing sacred****?).* NS ▫ frequently facetious.

nothing/not anything like far from; not at all; nowhere near (qv) **adj:** enough, ready; crippled. **n/pron:** 5 miles; the same salary; it ▫ *We would need a circulation of 30,000 for the paper to survive and so far we had* ***nothing like*** *it.* ▫ *The paradox was that, as they worked against time, Luke had* ***nothing like*** *enough to do.* NM ▫ *At the same time, many Forces have been at* ***nothing like*** *full strength.* T ▫ (bad luck in losing a football match) *That time the ball went in, and we won one-nowt* (= 1-0). *And we played* ***nothing like*** *as well as we played tonight.* ***Nothing like*** *it.* OBS ▫ *Nonsense! Eric's* ***nothing like*** *crippled—just got a slight limp.* ▫ HARRIS: *You mentioned your elder brother. How had you got on with him?* RIGG: *Four years between children is a big gap: so as children we weren't so close.* ***Nothing like*** *so close as we are now.* OBS ▫ may also modify an adv ***nothing like*** *as well.*

nothing loath (to do sth) [Comp (AdjP)] (facetious) very willing(ly), eager(ly) **V:** ⚠ be, appear; find sb ▫ *'Do tell me more about your children, Mr Wicklow,' upon which Roddy,* ***nothing loath****, expatiated with the false modesty of a doting parent upon the virtues of his offspring.* WDM ▫ *'Here, take a swig of this.'* ***Nothing loth****, Robin took the flask and raised it to his mouth.* ▫ *I'd no sooner got out the sherry than Brian walked in. Of course, he was* ***nothing loath to*** *take a drink.* ▫ *As you can imagine, I was* ***nothing loath to*** *miss the Sunday morning church parade and readily volunteered to walk the dogs instead.* ▫ alternative spellings loath/loth.

nothing/neither more (n)or less than exactly; unequivocally; merely; just **adj:**

pleasant, agreeable, polite. **n:** tyrant, dictator; businessman. **cl:** we'd imagined, you'd expect □ *But in Ethiopia* (1868) *the British sought no gain of any kind. In other words, the whole vast expensive operation was* ***nothing more or less than*** *a matter of racial pride. Theodore had affronted a great power and now he was to be punished.* BN □ *The reception I got was* ***neither more nor less than*** *polite, and our relationship was maintained on that level for the duration of my visit.* □ *Its performance is good enough but* ***nothing more nor less than*** *you'd expect from any car in the £5000—£6000 range.* □ *You're not fit for such a climb and it's* ***nothing more nor less than*** *folly to attempt it.*

nothing/(not) anything of the kind/sort [Comp/O (NP)] not at all what has been supposed, suggested or claimed **V:** be, prove; do, know, say □ *He had visions of hulking brutes, members of race-gangs with razors at the ready, or at best, sailors on shore full of high spirits and liquor.* ***Nothing of the kind****! The patrons of the Golden Beach Club were as meek and docile a tribe as the inhabitants of any third-class compartment on a suburban electric train.* HD □ PETER: *Give me another chance. You know you love me.* SYLVIA: *I know* ***nothing of the kind****.* DMP □ *For the convenience of the moment it would be pleasant to record that the 'New Statesman' was a formative influence of my career in journalism. Alas,* ***nothing of the sort****. I grew up with 'Chick's Own', the 'Sporting Pink' and the 'Whippet Breeders' Gazette'.* NS □ *Theodore claimed that he was of royal blood and in the direct line of kings descending from Solomon and Alexander the Great. He was* ***nothing of the sort****. He was the son of a small local chieftain.* BN □ *Here* (on a nail in the fencepost) *she was to affix a small piece of the pink handkerchief if she wanted to get into communication with Darin. So far, Victoria reflected bitterly, there had been* ***no*** *need for* ***anything of the sort****.* TCB □ may be used alone as emph denial.

nothing/little short of sth completely/nearly sth **adj:** disastrous, rude, perfect. **n:** a disaster, perfection, cheating □ *Obviously, the most serious question mark hangs over production grants. The NFU* ((GB) = National Farmers' Union) *make no bones about it! 'The loss of these grants in hill and upland argriculture would be* ***nothing short of*** *disastrous.'* SC □ *To have withheld such important information at the stage discussion had now reached was* ***nothing short of*** *wilful deception.* □ *Colin, who was in a state* ***little short of*** *ecstasy at being seated beside a football hero in the flesh, hardly noticed what he ate.* ⇨ ⚠ next entry.

nothing short of sth (can/will do sth) nothing except sth (can/will do sth) **pron:** nothing, (not) anything, nobody; no means, no remedy. **o:** a miracle; an angel, a weight-lifter; a direct request to go; being born again, tying sb hand and foot □ *As the dreaded hour drew near, I thought that* ***nothing short of*** *a miracle* ***could*** *reconcile me to leaving.* BM □ *Then, under the impression that* ***nothing short of*** *a world catastrophe* ***would*** *shake them into consciousness...* DF □ *Or,* ***short of*** *being born again as a visionary, a medium, or a musical genius, how can we ever visit the worlds which, to Blake, to Swedenborg, to Johann Sebastian Bach, were home?* DOP □ *If a woman wanted to commit suicide, there was* ***no means*** *of stopping her* ***short of*** *putting her under actual restraint.* PE □ *So although he might wish to send some message* ***nobody*** *could receive it.* ***Short of*** *having this special receiver.* TBC □ variant short of (nothing sth can/will do sth), often with question. ⇨ ⚠ previous entry.

nothing succeeds like success (saying) success brings one the confidence in oneself and respect from others that lead to opportunities for further and greater success(es) □ ***Nothing succeeds like success****—for a while at least—and publishers can be fairly certain of a good response to that book of an author's which immediately follows his best-seller.* □ *The 50 or more important public engagements throughout the world that await the winner* (of the Leeds Piano Competition) *underline the fact that* ***nothing succeeds like success****.* □ (NONCE) *As Mr Chamberlain observed on another occasion, 'There are no winners.'* ***Nothing succeeds like failure****.* SC □ (NONCE) *If Fellini's motto is* ***nothing succeeds like excess****, it is bad advice to lesser artists.* NS

nothing to touch sth [Comp/O (NP)] nothing so good, so effective, that reaches such a standard of excellence, as sth **V:** (there) be; see, find, meet; taste. **pron:** nothing; (not) anything, another; (never) anything, another; nobody, no-one; (very) little. **O:** it, him; the old pros, a good fresh herring □ *Laddie, the first racing donkey they bought, is now 30—'There's* ***nothing to touch*** *him in a sulky trap* (= small cart)*,' said Mrs Roberts proudly.* OBS □ (advertisement) *When it comes to going, there's* ***very little to touch*** *an Alfa. And it isn't just because of the mph* (= miles per hour). OBS □ *Dad's one of the older generation of football enthusiasts and thinks there's* ***no one*** *playing now* ***to touch*** *the old pros like Stanley Matthews.* □ *'This is very fine port, don't you think?' 'You could call it magnificent. I've* ***never*** *tasted* ***another to touch*** *it.'*

nothing venture/risk, nothing gain etc (saying) if one is too timid to risk failure, loss, a rebuff etc, one finishes by having nothing **V:** gain, ⚠ win; have □ *By midday Tuesday I had the answers, a neat, typed list of names and addresses, and muttering* ***nothing venture, nothing gain****, I dictated a letter to go to all the club secretaries.* PP □ *'I wish now that I had invested some capital in his business as he wanted me to. But who could have guessed then that boating would become so popular?' 'Ah, well,* ***nothing venture, nothing win****.'* □ ***Nothing venture, nothing have*** *in love like everything else. If the girl turns you down, you're no worse off than you were before.* □ *The idea came, and the risk followed, the risk of failure, the risk of being called to account afterwards—****Nothing risked****, said the Duke,* ***nothing won****, and stepped back unnoticed. It was worth trying, anything was worth trying.* WI

now and again/then [adv + adv non-rev] occasionally; at irregular intervals within a short or long period of time; every now and again/then (qv); every so often (qv); from time to time (qv) □ ***Now and again*** *he shook his head,* *as if to clear it, like a boxer recovering from a knock-out.* HD □ BESSIE: *Yes, I am the only mourner. No one ever cared for my poor husband like I did.* SAM: *Why didn't you show it* ***now and again****?* HSG □ *Although the water was up to his elbows, he moved swiftly like an otter along the side, then across to the other bank, disappearing* ***now and then*** *under the surface.* TO □ *I wish we hadn't sold the car now, because she never gets out at all and if I could take her out into the country* ***now and then*** *I think she'd like it.* RFW □ usu front or end position.

now I've seen everything (catchphrase) comment on an occasion of witnessing sth very unusual, unexpected, unsuitable, or ludicrous (the implication being that nothing the speaker might see in the future would be sufficiently extraordinary to surprise him) □ *Not long ago Christine Bell watched about a dozen men trying to persuade a cockerel to crow for a dawn scene. She said nothing but the look in her eyes was enough. '****Now I've seen everything****,' they seemed to say.* TVT □ *'Well, well; John Thomson sitting reading his Bible!* ***Now I've seen everything****.' 'I'm just looking up a reference, you ass.'*

now is the time for all good men to come to the aid of the party (supposed) rallying call to members of a political party □ *Our hospital should be modernised, not closed.* ***Now is the time for all good men to come to the aid of the party****. Lots of lobbying. Lots of letters to the press.* □ (NONCE) *The Department has asked the question: does the social value of particular railway practices justify a subsidy? This is where* ***all good socialists*** *can* ***come to the aid of the railways****.* NS □ *Saturday night* (ie New Year's Eve) *this week is quite obviously* ***the time for all good men to come to the aid of the party****.* RT □ often facetious, as in last example where party = 'social gathering'.

now it can be told (catchphrase) the time for official, tactical, respectful, or deferential secrecy or concealment is over □ *This was but one in a short-lived but snappy series of '****now-it-can-be-told****' movies, all shot* (= filmed) *in the early 50s and all—like 'The Godfather'—to do with Mafia-inspired rackets.* RT □ ***Now it can be told****, the true story of my Desert Campaign. It began last year in Addis Ababa as I was trying to sneak home in time for Christmas, though I wasn't all that anxious to leave.* L □ *Nudging our way into the* ***now-it-can-be-told*** *department, a series about dockers was planned, scripts were written and they lie a-mouldering on a BBC shelf —whether for lack of quality or courage is impossible to say.* NS □ *'The Press were sympathetic but they got things so* wrong,*' she says sadly. And in her defiant* ***now-it-can-be-told*** *autobiography she leaves other biographers standing—embarrassed by her chilling honesty.* TVT □ attrib use, as in *her* ***now-it-can-be-told*** *autobiography*, always hyphenated.

(it is) now or never [adv + adv non-rev] (sth must be done, decided etc) immediately or all hope or opportunity of doing sth later must be given up □ *If it were any time but now! But Lennie had said* ***it was now or never****, and his eyes were on her, ready to light up in hope, or turn away in defeat.* AITC □ (testing a theory about intimidating wild animals) *This bull came thundering up to an absurd knee-high hedge and told me almost in so many words that he could hop over it just when he pleased and would gore me as soon as look at me. I felt* ***it was now or never*** *and went right up to him and stared him out.* ST □ *If it was a case of* ***now or never*** *I'd understand you driving over even in this fog—but you've got six whole months in which to see Martin.* □ *Do you want any of these strawberries? Because* ***now or never*** *is the time. There won't be any left once the children get their hands on them.*

now then[1] replaces, or precedes, a statement or question that checks, warns or reproves sb □ *The police barred my way. They had orders to let no one out. '****Now then****!' said one of them.* UTN □ *'****Now then****, you lads in the corner,' said the landlord, stretching up to look over the heads of the drinkers at the bar, 'we'll have less of that.' 'Less of what?' said one cheekily. 'You know what. Just cut it out.'* □ *'****Now then****!' their father said, flinging open the bedroom door. 'What's the noise about? Do you want your bottoms smacked?'*

now then[2] can replace, but more often precedes, a statement or question that either suggests sth to sb, or requests sth of him □ *You know what your parents want, and I've just told you what your class teachers think of you.* ***Now then****, are you going to be a sensible girl and stay on at school?* □ ***Now then****, Larry, show us what you can do. The stable's looking to you to win this race.* □ *'Well, that's the report and the recommendations—which of course we are not bound to adopt.' He laid down his papers, took off his glasses and leant back. '****Now then****, anybody want to comment?'* □ *At long last a waitress deigned to notice us, if notice is the word for the weary indifference with which she stood, her pencil poised above her pad, and said '****Now then****?'*

now then[3] follows a defiant statement of opinion or intention; so there(!) (qv) □ BEATIE: *Oh, for Christ's sake let's stop gossiping.* PEARL! *I aren't gossiping. I'm making an intelligent observation about the state of television,* ***now then****.* R □ *Rose knew she'd deliberately raised her voice when she told Elsie off and said, 'She's the best friend I've ever had and just you remember that with your outsider talk.* ***Now then****.'* TSMP

now then[4] neutral conversation filler in any position, sometimes indicating a momentary pause for thought, but often just verbal habit □ *Take a look at this letter—* ***now then****, where did I put it? Oh, yes, here it is—and tell me what you make of it.* □ *'You're a little love, aren't you?' she went on, bouncing the baby gently on her knee. '****Now then****, who's a good boy, who's granny's pet?'*

now you see it, now you don't (catchphrase) one is probably being misled; one cannot be sure sth is so but one had better be careful and watchful (from the patter of thimble riggers (ie tricksters at fairs etc) who by sleight of hand made it difficult for customers to identify which of three thimbles has a pea under it) **pron:** it, him, her, them □ *Looking from the viewpoint of the economy as a whole the economist compares the two situations and asks what is produced when the miner is unemployed? The answer is nothing. Hence to employ him 'costs' nothing. (****Now you see it, now you don't****.)*

There is no doubt that Michael Posner sees it. NS □ *Mr Nixon's entitlement to any credit for having 'wound down' the war does not bear any close examination. Much the same motif of '**now you see him, now you don't**' goes for the other Nixon achievement that at first sight seems unassailable — his opening of the door with communist China.* NS

now you're talking (informal) what you say or suggest is something I agree with, approve of □ *'Feel like a sandwich?' 'Not much.' 'A drink, then?' '**Now you're talking**.'* □ *'Couldn't you pick some passage that illustrates a central theme or tendency of the book?' '**Now you're talking**,' replied the novelist, who was quite docile so long as the word 'plot' was not uttered.* HD

nowhere/not anywhere to be seen etc not visible; absent, gone, lost, disappeared etc **Inf:** to be seen; ⚠ to be found; to be heard; to be met with □ *I hurried down to the platform and into the refreshment room. Steve was **nowhere to be seen**.* SPL □ *Children treated their parents with a respect such as is **nowhere to be seen** in these degenerate days.* □ *Then quite suddenly rain-clouds condensed over the whole globe. Within three days **not** a break was **anywhere to be found**. The Earth was as completely cloud-shrouded as normally is the planet Venus.* TBC

nowhere near (informal) far from; not at all; much less than or different from; nothing like (qv) **adj/n:** (being) intoxicated, (being) finished; as/so pleasant as sth; the same (thing), midnight □ *Joe was **nowhere near** being intoxicated but he had drunk enough to feel restless.* AITC □ *I'm afraid the house is **nowhere near** ready for occupation yet.* □ *I bought this card of wool to mend your jersey, but now I've brought it home I see it's **nowhere near** the same colour.* □ *I wouldn't call it a holiday going off to live in a place that's **nowhere near** so comfortable as your own home.* □ *'Is the six-monthly sales report ready yet?' '**Nowhere near**, I'm afraid. Jack's been off work ill for a week.'* □ may be used alone as comment, answer etc. ⇨ ⚠ far from sth.

null and void [adj + adj non-rev] (legal) invalid; not binding or enforceable; cancelled; without value, significance, worth **V:** be, become; declare, consider, sth **O:** a law, the treaty, the marriage; our agreement, the arrangement; his remarks □ *Now, 33 years later, Prague's anger at the* (Munich, 1938) *Agreement has not diminished. The Czechoslovak Government wants it declared **null and void** from the moment it was signed.* L □ *On September 4 the Durham selectors chose Mr David Reed, MP for neighbouring Sedgfield, by 77-75, but this was declared **null and void** by Labour's National Executive after a number of votes were found to be invalid.* ST □ *I have a great respect for your father and if any part of this agreement is made on your part without his knowledge and consent I shall consider it **null and void**.* □ *He spoke in haste and when he was irritated by pain. It would be kind to take the personal remarks he made on that occasion as **null and void**.* □ functions as Comp.

number one [o (NP)] (informal) oneself and one's own interests, well-being etc **V:** ⚠ look after, take care of, (only) care about □ *'Do you mean to say he had a secret store in his tent while the others were going short?' 'That's exactly right. Trust a quartermaster to look after **number one**.'* □ *Jimmy Reid, front-line fighter, has not forgotten the support students gave Upper Clyde Shipbuilders in their struggle. 'A significant number of students care about social problems and not just about "**number one**".'* RT □ *Martial, the Latin poet, appeals salaciously to what George Orwell called 'the unofficial self' which lurks in all of us — that randy, bilking, lie-abed little fellow, foul-mouthed but when needs be sycophantic, who urges us to look to our bellies and take care of **Number One**.* OBS ⇨ ⚠ next entry.

(the/one's) number one/two the person who is the head/immediately subordinate to the head, of an organization, department etc □ *'Are you a holiday-maker too?' 'No, I live here. I work in the Marine Research Station.' 'Indeed! I used to know old Watkins very well. Who's **Number One** there now?'* □ *'You don't usually get the job of meeting the top VIPs off the plane do you?' 'Thankfully, no. However the Ambassador himself is home on leave and **my number one** is laid up with gastric flu.'* □ *Our benefactor rose to rejoin his family, waving aside our offers of refreshment, his good deed done. So we fell back on **his number two**, the café owner, and persuaded him to join us with a round of the dark-foamed beer that was flowing in such abundance all about us.* ARG ⇨ ⚠ previous entry.

nurse a grievance etc [V + O] continue to think about a resentment etc; not allow it, or other painful or undesirable feelings/mental reactions, to fade or be forgotten **O:** grievance, ⚠ grudge, resentment, anger; sorrows, grief; (old) wounds, hurt feelings □ *Amongst the criminals employed by her husband had been one who **nursed a grievance**. The French court had sentenced him to no less than eight years' imprisonment and that was a gross miscarriage of justice.* SD □ *James White, MP, accused the 'Talk-In'* (a television programme) *of turning a serious subject into a 'wrestling match'. Barbara Maxwell who is on the production team of the 'Talk-In' and would, she said, be 'very upset if I felt anyone **nursed a grievance**' spoke to him and passed on his comments to me.* RT □ *Once you have worked for the 'Guardian', you never get it quite out of your blood. Of course not everyone has been happy there. Kingsley Martin was miserable. Malcolm Muggeridge even today seems to **nurse a grudge** against the paper he left all of 40 years ago.* NS □ *If you feel you are misunderstood, don't **nurse hurt feelings** — speak out and clear the matter up.* TVT □ *Educated Scots can be found who see the end of these old grievances in Union. It is sheer hysteria, they say, to **nurse wounds** and curse the cure at the same time.* RT

the nuts and bolts (of sth) [n + n non-rev] the small items, tasks, techniques, procedures etc subordinate, but necessary, to a large undertaking **o:** the political machine; film production; an education system □ *He is a Party Man. The unloved and unthanked amateur politician who keeps **the nuts and bolts of** the political machine well-oiled between elections.* TVT □ *Shaw was involved in the practicalities of theatrical* *business to the uppermost bristle of his eyebrows.* ***The nuts and bolts of*** *performance and production stick out tangibly everywhere in the volume.* L □ *No longer does the Queen speak only to local bigwigs—she is likely to chat to anyone in a crowd who catches her eye. Such tours are* ***the nuts and bolts of*** *the Queen's job and a cancellation is very rare indeed.* OBS

O

an object lesson [Comp (NP)] sth learned or taught by the study and use of actual objects etc; a practical demonstration by sb of an idea or principle, esp as an example or warning to others **V:** ⚠ be, serve (as); receive. **A:** in good manners; on the folly of gambling; for us all; to his children □ *The ladies England-Scotland hockey match was truly* ***an object lesson*** *for our pampered, over-paid footballers. There was no kissing and cuddling when goals were scored.* TVT □ *We had at least been treated to* ***an object lesson*** *in how not to beach a boat.* □ occas pl; stress pattern an 'object lesson.

the object of one's affection(s) (formal) a person with whom one has fallen in love or with whom one has a romantic relationship □ *Pepper once again goes undercover, this time as a parolee. And, as such, she becomes* ***the object of*** *a bank robber****'s affections****.* TVT □ *Monica becomes his mistress, little realizing that the reason for his frequent visits is not to lie in her arms but to be near* ***the object of his*** *real* ***affection****, whom ultimately he seduces.* PW □ sometimes facetious.

an odd fish/bird [Comp (NP)] (informal) an eccentric person; a person whom others find hard to understand or tolerate; a queer fish (qv) **V:** ⚠ be, seem, be thought □ *This is not to say that Mr Hughes is anything but* ***an*** *extremely* ***odd fish****, if we are to believe what we have been told. He has not been seen in public for 16 years.* OBS □ *It would be smug and vain of me to suggest that he was merely* ***an odd fish*** *I took pity on. He, I think, fell in love initially with* ***the*** *much* ***odder fish*** *I was.* ST □ *'Is he really worth a piece* (ie a press obituary)*?' I asked. 'I'd say so.' 'He was* ***an odd bird****' I said, 'I only saw him about a half dozen times.'* PP □ also pl *a couple of* ***odd fish/birds****.*

odd jobs various tasks, esp of a manual kind, needing to be done as they occur but not providing a steady, continuous pattern of work □ *They await him for the first hand of cards, yet sometimes* (instead of playing) *he busies himself with* ***odd jobs*** *about the house.* ARG □ *At the age of 17 he went out to New Zealand. Before long —it was during the slump—he was wandering about the country getting* ***odd jobs****.* OBS □ *You seem a handy sort of bloke. How would you like to stay on here as an* ***odd-job*** *man—bed and board and £40 a week?* □ attrib use *an* ***odd-job*** *man* = 'one employed to do odd jobs in a house, garden, school etc'.

an/the odd man out [Comp (NP)] an extra person when others are arranged or grouped in pairs or sets; a person different from, not at ease with, or not accepted by, others in a group, profession, social setting, etc **V:** ⚠ be, become; make sb □ *Nine was an awkward number for a week-end of bridge games because it meant that one of us had always to take a turn at being* ***the odd man out****.* □ *Helen did most of the talking, occasionally bringing Virginia into the conversation deliberately, as if she were* ***the odd man out*** *at the party.* AITC □ DAVE: *I'm not saying I'm useless, but machinery and modern technique have come about to make me* ***the odd man out****.* ITAJ □ can refer to a person of either sex; also pl.

the odds are (that) it is (very) probable that sth stated is true, did or will happen (from racing, where the odds—ie betting figures—on/against indicate how much/little confidence there is in a horse winning) □ *In the old days a pop star would approach his 30s with some trepidation, because* ***the odds were that*** *he would be abandoned by his public.* TVT □ *How much the premiums* (for medical care insurance) *cost depends on whether people qualify for any kind of discount.* ***The odds are that*** *they do.* G □ *Don't depend on us coming.* ***It's odds on*** *we won't get a baby-sitter—not on Christmas Eve.* □ variant it's odds on (that).

odds and bobs/sods [n + n non-rev] a miscellaneous collection of articles or items, usu remnants or things of little value; next entry (qv); bits and bobs (qv); bits and pieces (qv) □ *The paper-shop window is a litter of* ***odds-and-bobs****; if the light is kept on at nights the children make it a meeting-place.* UL □ *So I was a bread winner when I was nine. I did* ***odds and sods*** *to get things by any means.* ST □ expression odds and sods (taboo), can be used to refer to people.

odds and ends [n + n non-rev] a miscellaneous collection of articles or items, usu remnants or things of little value; previous entry (qv); bits and bobs (qv); bits and pieces (qv) □ (stage direction) *Down R* (= Right) *is heavy chest of drawers, covered with books, neckties and* ***odds and ends****, including a large, tattered toy teddy bear and a soft, woolly squirrel.* LBA □ *It isn't often I go there—it's just got a few* ***odds and ends*** *in it one doesn't often want.* EM □ *It is one of those thoughts which make you realise how long it is since you rearranged the lumber in the attic of your brain, and threw out all the* ***odds and ends*** *you've been saving.* NS □ (Working-class taste in furnishing and decoration is) *nearest of all, though, to the prosperous nineteenth-century middle-class style; the richness showing well and undisguised in an abundance of* ***odds-and-ends****, in squiggles and carvings, in bold patterns.* UL

(a matter etc) of academic interest/concern [Comp (NP)] (sth) that is no longer so important (because circumstances, viewpoints etc have changed) and is therefore not likely to affect a situation but may perhaps interest theorists or historians **V:** ⚠ be, become; make sth. **A:** entirely, just, merely, only, purely; no, then. **n:** matter, ⚠ problem, question. □ *It's* *only **a matter of academic interest** to me now, as you might say, but I thought it would be interesting to know.* EM □ *However, I suspect that Sir Keith's intentions are not **of academic concern**, merely.* NS □ *These **questions*** (about the attempts to prevent the spread of communism) *are **academic**. But they are practical, too, since the real nature of the Cold War and its origins need to be examined.* L □ variants an academic question, the matter etc is (purely etc) academic.

of all the nerve etc(!) (informal) what insolence; what presumption; what a nerve etc(!) (qv) **n:** nerve, ⚠ cheek, impudence □ *Well **of all the nerve**! As though bringing the filthy things* (ie magazines with 'nude' photographs) *into the School wasn't bad enough in the first place, you go leaving them about!* TT □ *'That creature—**of all the nerve**—that vile woman—' She prowled round the room like an angry leopard, too aroused to keep still.* AITC □ expression of strong disapproval and displeasure. ⇨ ⚠ have (got)/with a nerve; have (got)/with the nerve (to do sth); have (got)/with the nerve to do sth.

of all people etc[1] especially; more than any other person etc **n:** people; ⚠ places; things □ *I should have thought that you **of all people** would be able to trust me.* EM □ *'I go out for relaxation.' 'Surely **of all places**, one's home is where one should be able to relax.'* □ may precede or follow n or pron it modifies; stress pattern of 'all people etc.

of all people etc[2] a particularly unsuitable, unlikely, or incongruous, choice or coincidence **n:** people; ⚠ places; things □ *But Tolstoy pushes his argument just a little bit too far. He portrays Napoleon, **of all people**, as a passive instrument in the hands of his army.* L □ COLONEL: *Sweetstall. It does seem an extraordinary thing for an educated young man to be occupying himself with. Why should he want to do that **of all things**?* LBA □ *A questionnaire running to some 196 questions is now being prepared so that an unoffending public can be asked—**of all things**—about privacy.* NS □ may precede or follow n or pron it modifies; main stress usu falls on n or pron modified, as in second example where stress pattern is *Why should he want to do 'that **of all things**?*

of all shapes and sizes having many different shapes and sizes; of many kinds □ *KLM mustered vehicles '**of all shapes and sizes**' to take passengers' luggage to the waiting flights, but no freight could be loaded.* T □ *Have you thought about picking a pup from the Dogs' Home at Battersea? I know there are some lovely ones there **of all shapes and sizes**.* TVT □ *Shells **of all shapes and sizes** strew the long narrow beach.* OBS □ *My young niece was enchanted by her first trip to a toy shop. Soft toys **of every shape and size**—I thought I'd never get her out again.* □ immediately following n which it modifies; shapes and sizes non-rev; variant of every shape and size.

of all time that there ever has been or will ever be **n:** reception, understatement; greatest genius, biggest liar □ *'When we get married,' Ned said to me almost threateningly, 'We're going to have the reception **of all time**.' 'Oh,' I said feebly. '**Of all time**,' he repeated.* CON □ *'Smooth,' said Pete Murray, 'is* the *misnomer **of all time** when applied to me.'* RT □ *A current advertisement tells us of an author who 'takes on the greatest evolutionists **of all time**, Charles Darwin, Desmond Morris, Robert Ardrey, Konrad Lorenz—and lays them low'.* L □ *Mozart was, after all, not a mere purveyor of music but one of* the *supreme dramatic geniuses **of all time**.* OBS □ modifies a preceding n.

of one's choice that one chooses or has chosen **n:** man, woman; profession; route; day, time □ *Meals in Bulgaria, on a tour like ours, could be eaten in any restaurant **of one's choice**.* SC □ *I'll be the happiest man in Her Majesty's Kingdom to see my girl settled down with the fellow **of her choice**.* □ modifies a preceding n.

of course (not) [Disj (PrepP)] naturally (not); as might be expected (not to happen); certainly (not); inevitably (not); by no means (qv) □ *The barrage does not, **of course**, prevent infiltration, but makes it difficult and serves as a warning system.* SC □ ***Of course,** this is just speculation, Hawthorne. He may not be the right man after all.* OMIH □ *'Who's Joe?' 'You know him. The Economic Attaché.' 'Oh, **of course**, Joe.' He was a man one always forgot.* QA □ *'You'll condescend to come in and say good night to me, I suppose?' '**Of course** I will. I shan't be very late.'* PE □ Q: *Are the arts a waste of time, and could we get along just as well without them?* A: ***Of course not**. Life would be dingy and deplorable without the makers of music and of rhymes, the tellers of tales, the painters of pictures.* TO □ front, middle or end position.

of the first magnitude classifiable as among the best, worst, biggest, most important, etc of one's/its kind (from the astronomical classification of stars according to their degree of brilliance) **n:** problem, task; power; industrial complex; controversy, dispute □ (a French theatre company rehearses) *Both Hirsch and Chaton, stars **of the first magnitude**, respond to the delicate guidance they are getting.* ST □ *The Soviet Union which, with colossal efforts over two generations, had converted itself into an industrial and technological power **of the first magnitude**...* L □ *...an enemy whose use of demolition caused us bridging problems **of the first magnitude**.* MFM □ *To effect the arrest of any one of the first three I have enumerated would clearly provoke a scandal **of the first magnitude**.* EM □ modifies a preceding n.

of (good etc) standing having an established (good etc) reputation, acknowledged status **adj:** good; some; no; not much, no special □ *The objections on this occasion came, not from malcontents and rabble-rousers, but from men **of standing** in the locality.* □ (telegram) *No traces* (ie nothing known against) *Professor Sanchez and Engineer Cifuentes stop you may recruit them stop presumably men **of** their **standing** will require no more than out-of-pocket expenses.* OMIH □ *When William Berry bought the 'Sunday Times' it was a paper **of no particular standing**.* L □ modifies a preceding n; absence of adj implies good standing.

of a kind/sort in existence, but not quite adequate or satisfactory □ *'I believe there's food laid on, **of a kind**, at the Coach and Horses,' he said.* CON □ *There's a road **of a kind** from the* *lakeside to the foresters' hut. A jeep could do it but not that car you have there.* ▫ *The Channel Islands and the Isle of Man have independence* ***of a sort****. So why not Cornwall?* OBS ▫ *There is a stable* ***of sorts*** *in the barn. Shall we put your pony there?* ART ▫ modifies a preceding n; variant of sorts. ⇨ ⚠ kind/sort of.

of late [A (PrepP)] recently; continuously, or intermittently, over a recent period ▫ *You've been very irritable* ***of late****. If you feel tired or unwell you should do something about it.* ▫ front, middle or end position

of/to little/no avail [Comp (PrepP)] not effective **V:** ⚠ be, seem; consider sth to be ▫ *I tried to persuade him not to resign but it was* ***of little avail****. Now he's going to have difficulty finding a new job.*

of a morning etc [A (PrepP)] on any morning etc; on some or most mornings etc **n:** morning, ⚠ afternoon, evening; Sunday; day, night. **adj:** fine, stormy; spring, summer('s); busy ▫ *Grandfather likes his nap* ***of an afternoon****. It's best not to visit him until 4 o'clock or so.* ▫ *There is no healthier or more enjoyable activity than leaping over hedges on horseback* ***of a*** *fine* ***morning****.* NS ▫ *Sometimes* ***of an evening*** *when the long shadows fall across the grass...* SC ▫ *When you've had enough of feeling good like the first man on earth* ***of a*** *frosty* ***morning****...* LLDR *We lived on a diet of bread, milk and vegetables with perhaps bacon or sausage* ***of a Sunday****.* ▫ *It could be very eerie sleeping up in the attic when,* ***of a*** *winter's* ***night****, the wind howled round the house.* ▫ middle or end position; day and night always modified.

of necessity [A (PrepP)] necessarily; compulsorily; unavoidably ▫ *At the Royal Court* (Theatre), *the play had* ***of necessity*** *to be played within the proscenium arch.* THH ▫ *Though* ***of necessity*** *accepting the need for new roads through the central area, it puts these on a more modest scale.* SC ▫ *We don't* ***of necessity*** *have to attend all these functions but it doesn't do any good to be thought anti-social.* ▫ usu middle position.

of note (formal) notable; well-known; highly regarded; worthy, or requiring, to be noticed, recorded or remembered ▫ *Nayantara Sahgal is Mrs Pandit's daughter and, it seems, a novelist* ***of note*** *in India.* L ▫ *But although the scientists sat around for a couple of hours or more nothing* ***of*** *further* ***note*** *happened.* TBC ▫ *The next event* ***of note*** *was the kidnapping on the 26th January of an ex-Army officer and a British judge.* MFM ▫ follows n or pron it modifies.

of old/yore[1] (formal) associated with, or that existed in, ancient or long-past times **n:** men, seafarers; hero; superstition ▫ *They* (people eating only meat) *seem to feel continuously hungry, and their thoughts may sharpen but their senses are often subdued. Why then did the Fathers* ***of old*** *speak of meat as passion's stimulant? Perhaps they got their physiology wrong.* OBS ▫ *His characters talk of ration books or public schools or trips to colonies or (God help us) the yellow-brown photos* ***of yore****. Nostalgia is the fashion in the theatre just now.* NS ▫ modifies a preceding n; sometimes facetious.

of old/yore[2] [A (PrepP)] (formal) formerly; in ancient or past times; at, or from, a previous period of one's life ▫ *Here, on the moors where* ***of old*** *the young sprigs of the nobility flew their hawks, the Branston and District Model Aircraft Club try out their skills.* ▫ *I know what you're going to tell me — 'Be more like the girl he married and love him as you did* ***of yore****.'* ▫ *The first question was whereabouts I was going to live. I was not drawn to Chelsea, which I knew* ***of old****.* AH ▫ usu follows v, as in last two examples; sometimes facetious.

of the old school embodying the traditional, perhaps old-fashioned, characteristics of his class, trade, profession etc **n:** butler, actor, lawyer; gentleman; diplomat ▫ *Lucking, an impeccably English butler* ***of the old school*** *(except, perhaps, for his carpet slippers) meets one at the door.* RT ▫ *His father, Gene Mullendore, a tough, crusty cattle baron* ***of the old school****, had started to go blind.* ST ▫ follows n or pron it modifies. ⇨ ⚠ the old/new school.

of the order of sth about, around, the figure of sth; of the same importance, or magnitude, as sth **n:** figure, sum; discount; arrears, debt, loss; saving. **o:** 30 degrees; one part in a thousand; £12,000 annually ▫ *And* (the Cloud) *will move through the angle AEB which must be something* ***of the order of*** *thirty degrees.* TBC ▫ *These small discharges were just audible from the rim of the crater, occurring with a frequency* ***of the order of*** *a hundred a minute.* NSC ▫ *A saving in fuel* ***of the order of*** *15% is expected after the installation of the new machinery.* ▫ *The capture of Brill must rank as a turning-point not only in Netherlands history but in world history: an event* ***of the order of*** *the fall of the Bastille, or the execution of Charles I.* L ▫ modifies a preceding n.

of one's/its own accord [A (PrepP)] voluntarily; spontaneously; without persuasion, interference etc **V:** move, disappear; revive; stop ▫ *Meanwhile in the drawing-room Edith had,* ***of her own accord****, told her cousin Sally that she was sorry.* WDM ▫ *He could not stop his mouth twitching; but it would stop* ***of its own accord****, he believed, once he was in the fresh air.* US ▫ *Brought into the open, such difficulties have a happy knack of going away almost* ***of their own accord****.* TVT ⇨ ⚠ next entry.

of one's own free will [A (PrepP)] voluntarily (the implication being that there has been a deliberate choice from two or more actions open to one) **V:** surrender; follow, accompany, sb ▫ *Do you take part,* ***of your own freewill****, in any social or political organisation outside your ordinary work?* WI ▫ *He walked straight into the prison* ***of his own free will*** *and shut the door behind him.* FFE ▫ *...threaten to torture them until they agreed to come with us* ***of their own free will****.* LLDR ▫ usu middle or end position; freewill occas written as one word, as in first example. ⇨ ⚠ previous entry.

of the same stripe belonging to the same etc kind, class, rank, creed, character-type etc **det:** the same (as); different; his; any; that ▫ *There's one in our school* ***of the same stripe****—slam them down, show them who's boss. They don't make the best teachers.* ▫ *Our deep solemnity about these matters is triggered by the suspicion — which is shared by all serious political commentators* ***of whatever stripe****— that the Chinese,* *like the Russians, know what they're doing.* L □ modifies a preceding n.

of that ilk[1] (Scots, formal) of that same name/place, eg a landowner whose title or surname is the same as the name of his estate □ *At the crossroads about a mile from Monboddo the travellers' carriage was met by His Lordship* ***of that ilk*** *who invited them to dine and rest at his house that night.* □ *The explanation that the Macaulay concerned was not the cricketer but Thomas Babington* ***of that ilk*** *he swept aside as of no consequence.* SC □ modifies a preceding n.

of that ilk[2] (facetious) of the same kind as another **det:** that; her own; the same; his □ (reports published by local naturalist, antiquarian etc societies) *Hundreds* ***of that ilk*** *are produced every year by printers down cobbled alleys.* ST □ *There is every likelihood that he will be able next Easter to hand over the presidency to a successor* ***of his own ilk.*** NS □ *What obligation is there after all for motorists to give lifts to people* ***of her ilk****?* ST □ modifies a preceding n.

off the cuff [A (PrepP)] (informal) without previous preparation or thought (from a supposed habit, formerly, of after-dinner speakers making a few pencilled notes on the starched cuffs of evening-dress shirts which they could glance at casually, instead of reading from a written paper; the first example carries a punning allusion to this) **V:** speak, reply; do sth □ *He was asked to sing for his supper. Realising that this was not the moment for a professional performance he instantly stood up and sang a few lines,* ***off the cuff****, although not without notes.* SC □ *This is a checklist which a builder may use or may put aside, playing his estimate* ***off the cuff*** *instead.* ST □ *Protestant and Catholic children are brought together in a studio for a party to precede an* ***off the cuff*** *discussion with parents.* TVT □ *The discovery of what the majority 'wants' is not a simple matter. On hanging, for instance, it is doubtful whether the* ***off the cuff*** *opinions of almost everybody are worth a tinker's cuss.* L □ attrib use *an* ***off the cuff*** *discussion.*

off and on [adv + adv rev] occasionally, sometimes, or frequently, but not continuously or regularly □ *Of course, I haven't met her but being famous as an author* ***off and on****, she gets all the sympathy.* MM □ FISCHER: *You're kind of out of touch with real life, being a chess-player. I've thought of giving it up* ***off and on****, but I always considered: what else could I do?* L □ *It tells the story of an old comedy double-act Leslie and Lane. '****Off and on****, I used to be part of a double act myself,' says Bass (who played Harry Leslie).* TVT □ *At that time I think I was still living* ***on and off*** *with Bianca in Kedar Street.* KLT □ *He's the man I work for* ***on and off****, taking bets on commission.* AITC □ front, middle or end position.

off one's own bat [A (PrepP)] (informal) entirely by oneself; on one's own initiative; without direction, advice, or approval from anyone □ *I didn't expect him to be a writer. We don't know where he gets the brains from, to be quite honest. He did it all* ***off his own bat*** *though — I'll say that for him.* RT □ *But Joan was enthusiastic.* ***Off her own bat****, at home, she worked out the whole operation — vehicles, staff, finance, building.* OBS □ *Since your builder put the window in* ***off his own bat*** *I don't see that I'm responsible for the extra cost.* □ front, middle or end position.

off the record [Comp/A (PrepP)] unofficial(ly); confidential(ly); not (so as) to be recorded, quoted, used as evidence etc **V:** be; speak tell, inform, let sb know □ (after a drinking session) *Indiscretions now flowed unchecked from their lips, and the only shred of caution remaining to one of them was to preface his disclosures with, 'This is* ***off the record*** *— right?'* SC □ *One of the committee members, whom I won't name, told John* ***off the record*** *the appointment was as good as his.* □ *You could buy yourself a drink at any time of the day, whenever you felt like it, and even fiddle one now and then* ***off the record****, if you were careful.* AITC □ *The camera followed the delegates even when they visited each other's missions for semi-private* ***off-the-record*** *talks.* RT □ attrib use *an* ***off-the-record*** *statement, talk.* ⇨ ⚠ (just) for the record.

an officer and (a) gentleman a combination of roles, or qualities, thought desirable in an officer in the British armed services; (fig) an honourable character which is valued in a man as highly as professional skill □ *Guinness describes his years in the Navy as the best acting performance he's ever given. He played* ***an officer and a gentleman****, very cool, very calm.* OBS □ *The nights spent in marching, the days in hiding, always in terror of being addressed because, as* ***officers and gentlemen****, the fugitives could not speak any other language than their own.* HD □ *You will behave at all times as* ***officers and****—save the mark—as* ***gentlemen****.* BBCTV □ (NONCE) *It is curious to think that a fictional crook helped make the name Albany world famous. But at least he was* ***a cricketer and a gentleman****.* TVT □ expression used now to suggest dated upper-class type.

oil and water (do not mix) (saying) incompatible people (cannot be made to combine, work together, etc) □ *Oh, she means well, but she's not my sort.* ***Oil and water don't mix****, no good trying.* TSMP □ *The team tried hard to mix fresh news and comment only to find they were* ***mixing oil and water****.* L □ usu in order of headphrase.

the old Adam the unredeemed part of (a) man's nature, prone to sin and error □ (film review) *This Jean (Lee Grant) is charming, but something of an irrelevance. Is it mandatory to have an Eve around to raise* ***the old Adam*** *in audiences?* NS □ (reader's letter) *Bless them, they are not, as the Rev Bailey says, 'like boars on heat'; they are merely human, and without* ***this old Adam****, none of us would be here.* L

an old bag (slang) an elderly woman (referring contemptuously or facetiously to her loss of good looks, poor figure etc) □ *When the photographer had done with us ('I'm* ***an*** *ugly* ***old bag****,' lied Helene 'and I hate having my picture taken'), we went to lunch.* RT □ PETER: *His name was Oedipus, he was a Greek I think. Well,* ***the old bag*** *turned out to be his mother.* TOH □ CRAPE: *Mrs Letouzel, you cantankerous* ***old bag****, what do you mean, by complaining about your money!* THH □ also pl.

old before one's time [Comp (AdjP)] older in

looks, physical condition, mental outlook, etc than is right or reasonable for one's age **V:** ⚠ be, seem; get ▫ *She made all the other girls I'd been out with seem dingy and clumsy and* ***old before their time***. RATT ▫ *He was getting* ***old*** *then long* ***before his time***. *He'd come in from his sermons complaining of rheumatism and the cold.* ASA

old etc beyond one's years [Comp (AdjP)] more mature, knowledgeable, blasé etc than most others of one's age **V:** ⚠ be, seem; strike sb as. **adj:** old, ⚠ wise, experienced, shrewd ▫ (reader's letter) *He has been less than diligent in his form work and shows none of the promise of earlier years. He has of course always been '****old beyond his years****' and he has perhaps stayed on too long.* NS ▫ *From Nick's comments on the exhibition I could see that he* ***had an appreciation*** *of what was good in art far* ***beyond his years***. ▫ *Though* ***old beyond her years*** *in some respects, I felt she was emotionally immature and certainly not ready for marriage.* ▫ variants have/show wisdom/understanding/appreciation beyond one's years, with a wisdom/an understanding beyond one's years.

an old boy former pupil of a school or college, esp a public school attended by children of the monied classes, attendance at which is (or was) assumed to confer privileged status for life ▫ *There were, of course, very many* ***old boys*** *of the College and others who hated him and all that he so successfully stood for.* NS ▫ *Non-executive directors grace the boards of many companies for window dressing and little else. Their seats are sinecures secured on* ***the old boy net***. ST ▫ *Mr William Hamilton reminded Mr Godber that 'there was a unanimous decision by the all-party Expenditure Committee that these appointments were made on the principle of '****the old-boy network****'.* NS ▫ *An awful lot of* (County Council) *decisions are taken on the* ***old boy*** *basis and, largely because working people can't spare the time, these bodies were overweighed with lairds, clergy, and retired military gentlemen.* ST ▫ old girl is used literally of a former pupil but does not carry the same socio-political implications; variant the old(-)boy net(work) = 'system whereby, unofficially, appointments to government, administration, armed service etc posts are arranged to favour people of one's own background, education etc'. ⇨ ⚠ next entry; the old boy etc.

old boy etc (informal) familiar or friendly form of address to sb of any age (or to a dog, horse etc) **n:** boy, ⚠ man, chap; girl, thing ▫ *'Your message? What message,* ***old boy****?' 'It's from somebody called Elspeth,' Harold said.* PW ▫ *Gerry, who once flew a Spitfire, has a moustache and still calls people '****old boy****'.* OBS ▫ PAMELA (in a wildly affected, cheerful voice): *Well then, bye-bye, darling. You're sure there's nothing I can get you from the village?* CLIVE (matching her accent): *No, thanks,* ***old girl***. *Just bring back the usual papers.* FFE ▫ *'I thought it was the lady's privilege to be late,' Anne greeted him coldly. 'Awfully sorry,* ***old thing****, but it wasn't my fault, really.'* ▫ associated, though not exclusively, with upper middle-class talk, and sporting or service types. ⇨ ⚠ previous entry; next entry.

the old boy etc (informal) a middle-aged or elderly person, or a person older than the speaker **n:** boy, chap, fellow; girl; bean ▫ ***The old boy*** *was fond of rum, and there is a noble simplicity in his advice about rum today, which is merely hot rum-and-water with sugar.* OBS ▫ *My landlady nearly frightened me off the room with her list of do's and don'ts, but she turned out to be not such* ***a*** *bad* ***old girl*** *after all.* ▫ *'I wonder what* ***the old bean*** *would say if we drank a dram instead of this horrible sherry,' Catriona muttered to her sister.* RM ▫ used with reference to sb already mentioned or known; not *the old man*, unless in meanings covered by 'the old man' (qv), 'the/one's old man etc' (qv). ⇨ ⚠ old boy etc; previous entry.

the old brigade/guard (informal) the senior members of a community, profession etc whose standards, beliefs and practices are being, or are likely to be, challenged or superseded ▫ *This transition period—* ***the old brigade*** *don't like change. They don't like loss of authority.* MM ▫ ***The old guard*** *in the Chief Rabbinate supports re-election of Rabbi Nissim as Sephardi Chief Rabbi and opposes Rabbi Goren as Ashkenazi Chief Rabbi.* T ▫ *Ray Milland presents himself, in a confusing self-portrait, as alternately one of the boys and one of* ***the old guard***. L ▫ *Fewer than a third of GPs are members of the college, which is not always popular with* ***old-guard*** *(and sometimes young-guard) doctors.* OBS ▫ attrib use *an* ***old-guard*** *doctor*.

an old buffer etc (slang) an elderly man **n:** buffer, ⚠ codger, geezer; dear ▫ *'He must be through in the Saloon Bar.' 'No, he isn't. There's nobody there except a couple of* ***old buffers*** *playing dominoes.'* ▫ *What all have in common is reliability of performance. That goes as much for Charles Hill, in his amiable-****old-buffer*** *role as for Dr Saunders, clearly an articulate woman.* L ▫ (a diver brings up a rotting briar pipe) *You can feel a personal connection with a thing like that. You can imagine some* ***old geezer*** *puffing away at it under the rigging.* RT ▫ *I gave the money to* ***an old dear*** *who came to the door collecting for some charity or other.* ▫ buffer, geezer, codger used of men, dear used of women.

old enough to be sb's father/mother [Comp (AdjP)] too much older than sb for a marriage, liaison etc to be suitable or likely ▫ *'It's merely that I am* ***old enough to be your father***. *That's all I remembered.' 'I wish you hadn't. Could you possibly imagine that I am forty-five and you are twenty-five?'* ARG ▫ MRS ELLIOTT: *Of course, she was always a dark horse. But as for her and George — it's ridiculous. Why she's* ***old enough to be his mother***. EGD ▫ said to show disapproval of a relationship or to refuse it.

an old flame (dated slang) sb one was formerly sexually, or emotionally, involved with ▫ (film review) *He is due to be quizzed by a local lady correspondent for the Washington 'Daily News',* ***an old flame*** *whose political convictions are at odds with her sexual ones.* NS ▫ *I felt remorsefully that my behaviour in Sally's ward had ended her nursing career. But can a bridegroom start employing* ***his old flames*** *the night before his wedding, however well they are extinguished.* DIL ▫ *His third wife, Hélène, was* ***an old flame***. *They* *had first met playing tennis at the BBC club 20 years previously; they met again and married in June, 1972.* TVT

an old fogey [Comp (NP)] (informal) a dull or narrow-minded reactionary person, often elderly, who is out of touch with the times he lives in **V:** ⚠ be; turn into, become ▫ *I'm not such* ***an old fogey*** *as to think that parents can order their children's lives nowadays.* EM ▫ *Whenever useful, they mention their opponent's age, 'seventy-two-year-old Mr B' or 'sixty-five-year-old Mr C'; democracy is youthful and forward-looking; clearly these are* ***old fogies***. UL ▫ *Longford rallied a committee of 50 people representing members of the law, the medical and teaching professions, the church and youth leaders. He is anxious to avoid allegations of '****old-fogeyism****' and was pleased to say that nine members of his committee were under 30.* RT ▫ alt spelling fogy (pl fogies); adj form old-fogeyish; n form old-fogeyism.

old hat [Comp (NP)] old-fashioned; out of date; already known, accepted, or practised and not new or original; old stuff (qv) **S:** idea, theory; process, method; style, fashion. **V:** ⚠ be, become; make sth ▫ *It is a mistake to try mixing checks; this is now* ***old hat*** *in the fashion world. A bold check or plaid jacket can find a mate in a plain skirt.* SC ▫ *He has no time for the school of contemporary musicians who, as far as he can see, think that anything done last week is* ***old hat***. RT ▫ *I sent a copy to Geoffrey Elton and he thanked me for it very politely but he said: what* ***old hat*** *ideas these were that all these chaps had in the 17th century.* L ▫ attrib use *an* ***old-hat*** *idea, opinion.*

an old maid an (elderly) woman who is not, and probably never will be, married (the implication often being that remaining unmarried is an indication of personal failure, of lack of emotional warmth, etc); (fig) a person of either sex who is too precise, tidy, conventional, fussy, prudish etc ▫ *'You want to be* ***an old maid****?' she'd ask Goldie. My father used to warn Goldie that it didn't pay to be too clever. Men didn't like smart girls.* ST ▫ *'I've been far too busy all my life to think about love,' Miss Mellings answered in a tone of superior rebuke. And there spoke* ***a*** *real* ***old maid***. ▫ *All accountants, even toughs like me, have a bit of* ***the old maid*** *in them; a neat and tidy desk gives me the same satisfaction as a clean shirt and underwear.* RATT ▫ *His respect for conventional forms of behaviour (illustrated by his shocked repudiation of Violet Hunt) had a fussy,* ***old-maidish*** *quality.* L ▫ also pl; adj form old-maidish, used only in fig senses; n old maidishness, used only in fig senses. ➪ ⚠ an old woman.

the old man (informal) a person in authority over others, eg a leader of a political group, a ship's captain, a headmaster of a school, an office boss, etc ▫ *What can I do? And I would be late this morning of all mornings. I suppose* ***the Old Man*** *has been waffling around?* TT ▫ *We're thirty miles north of the convoy, all on our own, going to send off the signal in an hour's time.* ***The old man****'ll be up for that.* PM ▫ *'No doubt,' he said, 'you'd like to sit in* ***the old man****'s office on your big, fat fanny* (= buttocks) *and run the show.'* AITC ▫ not 'the old boy etc' (qv). ➪ ⚠ next entry.

the/one's old man etc (informal) one's husband/wife or father/mother **n:** man; ⚠ woman, lady, girl ▫ (a school kitchen) *'Mrs Lipscombe's doing a couple of yards of jam-roll.' 'Blackcurrant?' 'You and your stomach,' she said. '****My old man****'s just the same.'* TT ▫ *I was lucky. I went straight into Hornchurch Rep* (= repertory theatre). *Before that* ***my old man*** *was supporting me with £5 a week — but he said he'd never give me anything once I'd left the* (Drama) *school.* RT ▫ *When I was a kid,* ***my old lady*** *gave me bones to chew and I used to get dog biscuits as well. No, I mean it.* TVT ▫ *'It's a bargain,' said my brother Jack. 'Let's buy it between us and keep it for* ***the old girl****'s birthday.'* ▫ not 'the old boy etc' (qv). ➪ ⚠ previous entry.

the old/new school those following a former/current way of thinking, or code of practice, in politics, religion, medicine, the scientific, artistic or academic spheres, etc ▫ (interviewing politicians) *George Brown was always voluble—Some of* ***the older school*** *like Henry Brooke found it extremely difficult at first — Macmillan had the greatest charm of any.* RT ▫ *For Mother belonged to* ***the old school*** *who would not accept grants from local authorities — 'or rather,' she would say, 'money from the taxpayer's pocket'—for her daughter's education.* HAHA ▫ ***The new school*** *of top concert pianists have faultless techniques with, however, that special individual quality missing.* ➪ ⚠ of the old school.

(the) old school tie a man's neck-tie of design and colour exclusive to ex-pupils of (esp) a public school; (fig) such a tie as symbol of the patronage and preference given, esp formerly, in adminstrative, business or social circles to those entitled to wear it ▫ *Spruce young men in pin-stripes come in and out. My heart sinks. Landlord versus tenants? Private money versus legal aid.* ***Old school tie*** *versus no tie at all?* ST ▫ (extract from a pre-election opinion poll) *They know what they're doing. They're not fools. So I think we're in the right hands really. I vote for* ***the old school tie*** *and all that.* ST ▫ *There are a lot of people* (ie pupils) *here who, if asked, say they go to a school near Windsor or Slough, or that they go to grammar school, because if you say you go to Eton, people write you off. Nobody who has left here in the last 10 years would dream of wearing* ***an old school tie***. OBS ▫ occas pl.

old soldiers never die (they only fade away) (catchphrase) comment on the dogged persistence, cheerfulness etc of long-serving, or retired, soldiers etc (from an anonymous soldiers' song of World War 1) ▫ (Bill is helplessly drunk) *Mrs Curry smiled graciously. 'You're quite all right, aren't you, dear?' she said to Bill. '****Old soldiers never die****.'* HAA ▫ (NONCE) ***Old Airmen Never Die*** *— they just fly smaller planes. Denis Lill spent seven years in the New Zealand Air Force. Now he finds that building and flying model aircraft can provide much of the interest for the real thing.* TVT ▫ (NONCE) (headline, with pun on '*fall out*') ***Old Soldiers Never Die — They Just Fall Out****. People and places change — often for the worse. Certainly this is true of the old soldiers who fall in for tonight's reunion at the Village Hall.* TVT ▫ (NONCE) *But at* *the end of the day there is no such thing as 'good landlords' because* ***good landlords die*** *or* ***fade away****, leaving behind Hong Kong merchant bankers or worse.* ST □ (NONCE) *If we did a 'Ministry of Transport car test' on an ageing footballer, we wouldn't find a lot wrong with the bodywork. The fact is that* ***old footballers never die. They only lose a bit of their spark.*** TVT □ often adapted, as shown.

old stuff [Comp (NP)] sth one knows about, or could have informed oneself about, already; old hat (qv) **S:** suggestion, proposal; idea, notion, belief. **V:** ⚠ be, appear, have become □ (images in dreams) *Tunnels and wells and drops of water, all this is* ***old stuff****, just sexual images from the unconscious, the libido.* PM □ *I daresay anything he had to say in the lecture would have been* ***old stuff*** *to you but since I'm not an anthropologist I found it very interesting and informative.*

old Uncle Tom Cobbleigh and all (catch-phrase) everybody □ (source) *For I want for to go to Widdicombe Fair,/With Bill Brewer, Jan Stewer, Peter Gurney, Peter Davey, Daniel Whiddon, Harry Hawk,/****Old Uncle Tom Cobbleigh and all.*** BALLAD □ (NONCE) *Victor Matthews was very much a man of the pushing, abrasive, acquistive Britain advocated by Edward Heath, Peter Walker, Jim Slater, Lord Robens, Lord Sandys, 'Tiny' Rowland, Reginald Maudling and* ***old Uncle John Poulson and all****. They and their creed have fallen into discredit.* NS □ *We have heard a good deal of the demand for 'national unity'. Mr Edward Heath, who roared like a lion last February, now coos like a dove —offering consultation and co-operation with* ***Uncle Tom Cobbleigh and All.*** NS

old, unhappy, far-off things tragedies, or sorrows, of the historical, or one's own, past □ (source) *Perhaps the plaintive numbers flow/For* ***old, unhappy, far-off things****,/And battles long ago.* THE SOLITARY REAPER (W WORDSWORTH 1770-1850) □ *Occasionally I found myself passing the house which had once filled Mrs Ternandez with hope and her husband with suspicion, and I thought of* ***old, unhappy*** *and already* ***far off things.*** AH □ (NONCE) *Well, those* ***unhappy far-off slights*** *are ended and contemporary scholarship is in the process of erecting a massive seven-volume shrine to Henry Lawson.* SC

an old wives' tale a legend, myth, account of historical, or supernatural, events such as old women handed on to rising generations; an unsupported piece of information, recommended practice, etc □ (popular superstitions, esp cases of good and bad luck) *On certain occasions they laugh readily at them as '****old wives' tales****'. But usually they take care to follow their directions.* UL □ *The point is I don't want to hear a lot of* ***old wives' tales*** *about sheep being carried off and chickens and children and all that sort of thing.* RM □ *I've chosen the upright freezer rather than the chest type. You don't get more warm air rushing in when you open the door than when you lift a lid—that's* ***an old wives' tale.*** TVT □ *I completely lost my appetite. This business of a pregnant woman having to eat for two is* ***an old wives' tale.*** TVT

an old woman a woman past middle-age; (fig) sb, male or female, who is fussy and timid □ *Jack, even my grandmother doesn't fuss about things being neat the way you do—and she is* ***an old woman****. You just act like one.* □ *Don't be such* ***an old woman****, Anne. What can possibly happen to you on a package tour when everything's arranged for you? Stop worrying and go away and enjoy your holiday.* □ *You're behaving like a couple of* ***old women****!* ⇨ ⚠ an old maid.

olde worlde (jocular) that seems to belong to, or that imitates, a bygone era in appearance, sentiment or style □ *'I don't like substitutes,' he says. 'If I can't have sheepskin, I don't want simulated. That's why I like this place. It's* ***olde worlde****.'* NS □ *Something else that is mildly feminist, comes naturally to the radio, and has the same* ***olde-worlde*** *flavour is 'Petticoat Line'.* L □ *The very phrase 'spoilt child' has an* ***olde worlde*** *ring.* OBS □ attrib use, *an* ***olde-worlde*** *flavour*, usu hyphenated; pronounced either old world or oldy worldy.

the oldest profession prostitution □ *They felt the police weren't enough to clear the streets in their neighbourhood of the girls on the game* (ie who are prostitutes). ***The oldest profession*** *is alive and well in Birmingham.* OBS □ (NONCE) *I never saw a clearer, and more confused, confession of failure. It made me wonder why Miss Raeburn bothers to keep going in* ***her oldest****-but-one-****profession*** (ie giving advice to others). L

an olive branch [O/o (NP)] a token of peace, peaceful intentions, desire for reconciliation (often in drawings etc depicted as a twig carried in the beak of a dove, see GENESIS VIII 8-11) **V:** hold (out); extend, proffer; carry □ *But apparently the official invitation to become a Commission member was intended as* ***a*** *mutual* ***olive branch*** *extended between him and the Prime Minister.* NS □ *The American tenor, Michele Molese, had interrupted a performance to shout at a music critic. Two weeks later, Tony Scotland described the incident and the subsequent proffering of* ***an olive branch.*** L □ occas pl.

on account of sb/sth [A (PrepP)] because of sb/sth; for reasons connected with sb's/sth's existence, presence, action etc **o:** the children; him; the storm, the recent strike; having misread the instructions □ *The Browns will be higher up the housing priority list* ***on account of*** *their children.* □ ***On account of*** *the high winds the fishing vessels had not put out to sea.* □ *Charmian did not, however, mention the other diplomat whose name I forget, who later committed suicide* ***on her account.*** MM □ MR SEGAL: *Sam, what's come over you? You make me sad talking like this.* SAM: *Don't upset yourself* ***on my account****. It hasn't been a bad life.* HSG □ variant on sb's account.

on all fours [A (PrepP)] with knees, toes and hands on the ground; on (one's) hands and knees (qv) **V:** move, crawl, crouch □ *Harold encouraged them* (ie his children)*; the beach seemed to go to his head as it did to theirs, he crawled about* ***on all fours****, or lay prone or supine while mounds of sand were heaped upon his body.* PW □ *He ran downstairs. Lotte was still* ***on all fours****, reddening the tiles.* US □ CLIVE: *He got one of the girls to crouch* ***on all fours*** *so he could use her back for a table.* FFE

on all sides/every side [A (PrepP)]

everywhere; involving many and various people; on either/every hand (qv) □ ***On all sides*** *the importance of training youth is recognised.* SC □ *His refusal to convene an extraordinary session of Parliament is criticised* ***on all sides***. OBS □ *It is not just by the young and by disaffected groups but* ***on every side*** *that doubts about the old values are being expressed.* □ ***On every side***, *we have the unedifying spectacle of men piling one evasive, unsatisfactory statement upon another.* NS □ front, middle or end position.

on approval [A (PrepP)] to be kept, paid for, etc only if found satisfactory or suitable **V:** be, have sth; send sth □ *Goods sent* ***on approval*** *must be paid for at the time of ordering, but if goods are returned within 7 days customers will get their money back in full.* □ *'Shouldn't Brigit have interviewed her in the usual way? This is so out of order.' 'It was to be a surprise. Prissie understands that she's here* ***on approval***.' DC □ end position.

on (an/the) average [A (PrepP)] taking account of use, production etc over a period **V:** eat, drink; consume; use □ *Each one of us uses,* ***on average***, *180 pounds of paper products every year.* T □ *My husband enjoys an occasional three or four course blow-out but he eats* ***on average*** *much less than I do.* □ *It is quite obvious that if,* ***on the average***, *the patient suffering from a physical disorder stays in bed for two days and is then discharged, whereas the mental patient* ***on the average*** *stays for twenty years, then the number suffering from physical disorders, is 3,650 times as great as those suffering from mental disorders.* SNP □ front, middle or end position.

on balance [Disj (PrepP)] when all aspects of a situation, the points for and against a decision, course of action, etc have been considered **V:** consider, reckon, estimate, judge, sth □ (lie-detecting machines, etc) *Our modern procedures produce much less emotion than the witch doctor was capable of generating and,* ***on balance***, *it is not certain that the advantage lies with our modern technique.* SNP □ *For what my judgment of the war was worth, I thought* ***on balance*** *that Luke should stay where he was.* NM □ ***On balance***, *the Government are right to try to find out on what conditions membership* (of the European Economic Community) *can be obtained.* SC □ front, middle or end position.

on the basis of sth [A (PrepP)] taking account of sth; using sth as a criterion **o:** ability; need; evidence, findings □ *It may be that some countries are sending more students to the universities than they should send* ***on a basis of*** *ability.* SC □ *Nevertheless the FAA* ((US) = Federal Aviation Authority) *reached its conclusions on the efficiency of Decca as a navigation aid solely* ***on the basis of*** *results obtained from this low-powered installation.* NSC □ *You could try to register as a part-time student. They might be prepared to accept you* ***on that basis***. □ variant on that basis, refers to an earlier phrase or clause.

on sb's/sth's behalf[1] [A (PrepP)] as the representative of, spokesman for, sb/sth **o:** wife, client; the Society; all here □ *I will be attending tomorrow's county council meeting and, if necessary, will speak* ***on*** *my wife****'s behalf***. SC □ *It is evident from the observations by Mr Butler and Sir Donald Kaberry* ***on behalf of*** *the Conservatives and by Mr Morgan Phillips* ***on behalf of*** *Labour yesterday that the parties are going to intensify their drive to win youth to their ranks.* SC □ *His wife must be credited with bringing Caruso forward: he sang his first 'Bohème' with her. She could storm at the venal managers and agents* ***on his behalf***. OBS

on sb's/sth's behalf[2] [A (PrepP)] in support of, in order to promote the benefit or interests of, sb/sth **n:** testimony, plea; intervention, efforts, precautions. **o:** prisoner, accused; others □ *Mr Wilson's plea* ***on behalf of*** *old-age pensioners will certainly be popular.* SC □ *It was stated* ***on behalf of*** *the prisoner that he had a record of good behaviour and had been under considerable strain at the time of his outbreak.* □ *Mr Gamble's fight* ***on behalf of*** *his students and their parents—and untimately* ***on behalf of*** *all young people and all parents—has cost him dear.* RT □ *He moved with ease in the highest circles throughout Europe, and English royal personages had been known to bestir themselves* ***on his behalf***. L □ *We reported Professor Alexander Kennedy as implying that these methods* (ie brainwashing) *were used* ***on*** *Britain****'s behalf*** *during the war.* OBS

on both counts [A (PrepP)] (legal) with regard to both etc charges; in both etc respects; for both etc reasons **det:** both; ⚠ two, three; several; all □ *Four years later the Judge in Allahabad High Court pronounced Mrs Gandhi guilty* ***on two counts***. G □ *The canny manager has to be fully satisfied* ***on both counts****—the means and the end—before he makes a move.* OBS □ *Presley's film debut was a brave effort giving, as it did, a chance for him both to act and sing. Presley scored* ***on both counts***. RT □ *I had a bad conscience about Madge. I'd lived there rent-free. Also I knew that Madge wanted us to get married, only I had wanted otherwise. So* ***on both*** *these* ***counts*** *I felt I had no rights at all in Earls Court Road.* UTN □ ***On all counts*** *it would be advisable for the Government to take the risks of expanding the economy.* SC □ *The Parliamentary party has fought, and it is fighting, the European Communities Bill* ***on two*** *main* ***counts***. ST □ front, middle or end position.

on business [A (PrepP)] about matters to do with one's profession or trade **V:** be, come; go, travel, see (sb) □ *'I came here* ***on business***.' *'I never knew you go anywhere for anything else.'* HD □ *Bowes had got to know the place a bit from having been there* ***on business****—he was a salesman for nautical gear of all sorts.* SC □ *'I'd like to* (come),' *George smiled at her. 'But I've got to go out* ***on business***.' PE

on the (off) chance (of sth/that) [A (PrepP)] (informal) because one hopes that, with luck, sth may happen **V:** call, drop in; phone; write. **cl:** ***(of)*** a free meal; a game (being played); its finding me; ***(that)*** you could help us, we wouldn't be seen, the train was running late □ *Thus is avoided the aggravating experience of spectators having to turn up* ***on the off chance of*** *a game being played.* T □ *I'm going to the hairdresser but I'm too early, so I've just dropped in* ***on the chance of*** *a cup of coffee.* □ *It* *was from England; it was from Dave, who knew my partiality to the Brasserie Lipp and evidently sent the wire there* ***on the off chance of*** *its finding me.* UTN □ *I came* ***on the chance that*** *we could go to a cinema and have some supper out.* AITC □ *'I'm going to try another reading, just* ***on the off chance****.' He once more studied the graph.* NM □ *I was staying only a few blocks away from Edward G Robinson's house in Beverly Hills. I phoned* ***on the off-chance****, fully expecting to be stonewalled by the usual imperturbable butler. Instead Mr Robinson himself answered and within minutes had agreed to see me.* RT □ on the off chance often used, as in last two examples, without of/that, when what is hoped for is understood or previously mentioned.

on the cheap [A (PrepP)] cheaply; without paying the usual, or a fair, price **V:** get, buy, make, sth □ *It is perfectly possible to make films of high technical finish* ***on the cheap*** *using first takes and actors working at weekends for a percentage.* NS □ *There was no real difference of principle between those who wanted to make their own nuclear weapons and those who wanted to shelter* ***on the cheap*** *behind the nuclear weapons of others.* OBS □ *The somewhat arthritic rulers of football may well be right when they claim that television is getting football '****on the cheap****'.* L

on (the) condition that provided that sth specified is done, or agreed to, in exchange; on the understanding that (qv) **V:** agree; co-operate; play; lend, borrow □ *Press representatives were allowed to take photographs* ***on the condition that*** *none would be published before he had seen the prints.* □ *Let's go out then. But* ***on condition that*** *I pay for myself for everything.* TGLY □ *I'll make you a rich man—a damned sight better off than you'll ever be in local government—****on one condition****.* RATT □ *We only lent it to you* ***on that condition****.* □ *On balance, the Government are right to try to find out* ***on what conditions*** *membership can be obtained.* SC □ variants on one/this/that condition, on these/those conditions, on what condition(s).

on the contrary [Conj (PrepP)] quite the opposite to what has just been suggested, asserted etc □ *There was none of the bitterness that has so often broken out in the past.* ***On the contrary****, friend and foe treated each other with a respect that has been absent these many years.* OBS □ *I think he was a little ashamed of being so successful. I,* ***on the contrary****, felt proud of him for being so versatile.* UTN □ *Ernest Bevin always favoured the idea of workers being directly represented on the boards that ran nationalised industries. Herbert Morrison,* ***on the contrary****, believed boards should represent the public.* OBS □ front or middle position.

on credit/tick [A (PrepP)] without (full) payment being demanded, or given, at the time of purchase **V:** buy, sell, get, sth □ *They* (= men) *run their businesses, the nation, world commerce* ***on credit****. But your* (= housewives') *charge accounts are not credit, they are frivolous and unnecessary spending calculated to inspire bankruptcy.* TO □ *She's very understanding: if I'm hard up by the middle of the week she'll always let me have a few groceries* ***on tick*** *till Friday.* □ expression on tick informal, and usu used of small transactions with no formal agreement.

on the dot (of noon etc) [A (PrepP)] (informal) promptly; as soon as asked, expected or required **V:** pay; arrive; finish. **o:** noon, 4.30, 9pm, two □ *The Earl was a big spender: and he paid his bills* ***on the dot****.* L □ DOCTOR: *Attend to the X-ray equipment inside and let's have the negatives* ***on the dot****, in my hand, the minute I give the word.* THH □ (the front doorbell rings) MRS ELLIOTT: *That's him now. Right* ***on the dot*** *as usual.* EGD □ *'Are you sure it's me you want?' I asked. 'Of course I'm sure. It's important, too. See you're there* ***on the dot****.'* RATT □ *Work, the vocations apart, is not the centre of life: an easy pace, pack up* ***on the dot of 4.30****, no sackings.* L □ usu end position.

on either/every hand [A (PrepP)] (formal) to left and right; everywhere; on all sides/every side (qv) □ *It was necessary, when driving at night, to keep a sharp look out for the boulders which frequently rolled down the steep slopes* ***on either hand****.* □ ***On every hand****, although the flashes could not be seen through the fog, the leaping guns were pouring a hissing mass of steel across the valley.* SD □ front, middle or end position.

on an empty/a full stomach [A (PrepP)] at a time when one's stomach is empty/full **V:** drink; take medicine; go to bed □ *Oliver Gillie writing on hangovers points out that it is unwise to take aspirin-based products* ***on an empty stomach****, and recommends that breakfast should be eaten first.* ST □ *People with heart conditions shouldn't take hot baths* ***on a full stomach****.* □ *Pop agreed that perhaps it* (coffee) *wasn't a bad idea at that. At least it would save him from going to bed* ***on a*** *completely* ***empty stomach****.* BFA

on an even keel [Comp/A (PrepP)] maintaining steady progress, an undisturbed course of life or action, a well-balanced emotional state **V:** be; keep, stay, be/get back, live □ *'The hour of crisis is past. The ship of state is back* ***on an even keel****, and we must put behind us the fear of capsizing,' he maintained.* NS □ *His life was fascinating but it was also lived* ***on a*** *fairly* ***even keel****.* RT □ *It's been difficult for him to concentrate, with all the stress he's been under lately. When he's* ***on an even keel*** *again I'm sure he'll make a serious effort to finish his book.*

on the face of it [Disj (PrepP)] apparently; seemingly; judging by the (insufficient) amount of evidence available □ ***On the face of it****, Andrew* (deserted by his wife) *was better off than most women in the same situation. The social services department quickly offered a home help and day nursery places for the children.* ST □ *Purvis's description of him as a gentleman is right. Nationality,* ***on the face of it****, British. But I have a hunch that he might not be.* ARG □ *So we wanted to know for certain if there really were any diamond mines in Liberia.* ***On the face of it****, there was no reason why there shouldn't be.* DS □ *Dave was constantly making this suggestion; I can't think why, as there were few pieces of advice which,* ***on the face of it****, I was less likely to follow.* UTN □ front, middle or end position.

on a firm etc footing [Comp/A (PrepP)] in a particular state; having a particular status or relationship (with sb) **V:** be; put, get, start, meet, continue. **adj:** firm, sound, solid; an equal, the same, a different; bad, better, familiar; peace(time), war(time) □ *They fought dilatory governments and a sometimes hostile, usually indifferent, public to put wildlife protection* ***on a sound footing***. SC □ *I feel that is so essential for men and women to approach each other* ***on an equal footing****; this is why I believe women must be given equal pay and equal opportunities.* ST □ *Michael Hurll, who's produced every one of Cilla's series, started* ***on a*** *very* ***bad footing*** *with her.* RT □ *It was precisely because Dr Bottwink was not quite* ***on the footing of*** *a guest that Briggs found it necessary to explain why it was no trouble to climb a flight of stairs.* EM □ *Lord Simonds said that the applicant might proceed* ***on the footing that*** *there was jurisdiction, but should confine himself to the single question before the committee.* T □ *The people of that country are also beginning to show the strains of having to remain indefinitely* ***on a*** *war* ***footing***. L □ variant on the footing of sth/that.

on foot [A (PrepP)] walking, contrasted with any means of transport **V:** go, travel; arrive, leave; see, explore □ (from a game-warden's diary) *Suspicious activity through glasses: two chaps with some sort of contraption ducking down in the rushes. Circle round* ***on foot****, challenge them.* ST □ *I packed up my manuscripts in a brown-paper parcel, and left* ***on foot***. UTN □ *We creep out to see as much as we can of this wonderful city* ***on foot*** *before the 'real' sightseeing of the day begins by coach.* OBS

on the ground/(the) grounds of sth [A (PrepP)] for reasons based on sth indicated **V:** agree, object, to sth; argue against sth. **o:** (ill-) health, hardship; public amenity, economy; religious conviction □ *The Board agreed to Jenkins's retirement* ***on grounds of*** *ill-health without loss of pension rights.* □ *Miss Kazacos obtained the decree in the Divorce Court* ***on the ground of*** *adultery by her husband.* DM □ *The Chancellor was absolutely right in concluding that it would be wrong, both* ***on the grounds of*** *stable prices and the balance of payments, to add in any way to purchasing power by his budget.* SC ⇨ ⚠ next entry; on moral etc grounds.

on the ground(s) that [A (PrepP)] for reasons based on the fact or belief that **V:** agree, object, (to sth); argue (against sth) □ *Signor Segni resigned on February 24, after the Liberals had withdrawn their support* ***on the ground that*** *the Government was drifting to the Left.* SC □ *Shopkeepers in Staveley have been asked to take down advertisement signs put up without permission* ***on the grounds that*** *the signs cause an injury to visual amenities.* T □ *They hoped to contest Lisa's will if possible,* ***on the grounds that*** *Lisa, when she made it, was not in her right mind.* MM □ *His leadership can be criticised* ***on all kinds of grounds****: that he is uninterested in policy making...* NS □ variants, on this/that ground, on those/other/all kinds of grounds, used when reasons are given in a preceding or following clause. ⇨ ⚠ previous entry; on moral etc grounds.

on (one's) hands and knees [Comp/A (PrepP)] with knees, toes and hands on the ground; on all fours (qv) **V:** be; go (down), crawl, proceed, retreat □ (imitating a frog) *Sarah,* ***on hands and knees*** *again, was giving sideways leaps and croaking happily.* G □ *I feared that the Night Sister might see me passing by; so I manoeuvred the first part of the corridor* ***on my hands and knees***. UTN □ hands and knees non-rev.

on sb's/one's (own) head be it (saying) the choice or responsibility is sb's/one's own and if there are unpleasant consequences that person/one oneself must suffer them □ ***On his own head be it****, if people don't like him. What does he expect, the way he carries on?* □ *I'm sure you're wrong to sink all your capital in this scheme. However,* ***on your own head be it***. □ *Viewing for me begins on Sunday with 'Hero's End' (11.00 pm BBC1). This fascinating programme I do know about, as I had a large part in the making of it. So* ***on my head be it***. RT □ often used as a warning; stress patterns on sb's/one's 'own head be it, on sb's/one's head 'be it.

on the home etc front [A (PrepP)] in the sphere, or field, of (a) civilian life, work and defence in time of war; (b) the internal affairs of a country contrasted with foreign policy etc; (c) the affairs of regional, professional, religious etc groups **adj:** home, domestic; Scottish; industrial, educational; Protestant □ *...general City opinion interpreting the reduction* (in the bank rate) *more as an external measure than any relaxation in the credit squeeze* ***on the home front***. T □ *What happens* ***on the wages front*** *during the next few months will be of paramount importance.* T □ *It is not just woe* ***on the City front*** *for Slater Walker Securities.* G □ variant on that front with reference to an earlier clause etc; front, middle or end position.

on the hour/half-hour exactly at an hour/half-hour, eg 12, 3, 6.30, of the day; every hour/half-hour of the day □ *If you told him one o'clock he'll be here* ***on the hour****—just you see if he won't.* □ *At 7 o'clock* ***on the hour*** *the surgery doors are shut.* □ *The Modley bus will take you there — the stop's at the bottom of the road. Going back, it's* ***on the half-hour*** *from the bus-station.* RATT

on (an) impulse [A (PrepP)] without previous thinking or planning □ ***On impulse****, I picked up the phone and dialled my sister in Pretoria.* □ *What he did carelessly* ***on an impulse*** *he will now regret for the rest of his life.*

on a large etc scale [A (PrepP)] in large etc numbers; involving much etc expense, organization etc; in a big/small way (qv) **adj:** large, grand; small, moderate □ *Only on 28 July did the President formally announce his decision to commit American troops* ***on a large scale***. L □ *Ken is the same physical type as his brother though* ***on a smaller scale***. □ *As in all general engagements* ***on a grand scale****, the tactics and objectives of the combatants have become confused.* L □ *I did feel myself inferior to Robert. I was the one with the common sense, but he was the one who was living* ***on the grand scale***. CON □ *The movement matters first because of its extraordinary extent. Negro action* ***on this scale*** *has never been seen in the South.* OBS □ *Action so far has been confined to a few* ***small-scale*** *raids across the border.* □ variant on this/that scale with reference to an earlier clause etc; attrib use *a* ***small-scale*** *raid, a* ***large-scale*** *invasion.*

on sb's merits [A (PrepP)] according to good qualities which sb/sth has and disregarding other considerations **V:** judge, decide; select, appoint. **det:** his, her, its, their □ *I judge goods, like people,* ***on their merits*** *and not by their expensive packaging.* □ *'Oh yes,' he said, 'some of them have a great deal of merit, but music publishers don't buy songs* ***on their merits*** *nowadays.'* T □ *Every case should be decided* ***on its merits.*** L □ *Selection should be made purely* ***on merit.*** NS □ variant on merit.

on moral etc grounds [A (PrepP)] for moral etc reasons **adj:** moral, ethical, religious; educational, economic, political; health, compassionate; several, various. **V:** agree; refuse, object; admit sb; release sb □ *The Home Secretary asked a consultant psychiatrist to determine whether she ought to be released (or transferred to hospital)* ***on health grounds.*** NS □ *The Ministry released her* ***on compassionate grounds.*** PW □ *Parents are more likely to object to operations or blood transfusions* ***on religious grounds*** *than any other.* OBS ⇨ ⚠ on the ground/(the) grounds of sth; on the grounds(s) that.

on no account [A (PrepP)] not for any reason or in any circumstances **adj:** no, not any, never any □ *This patient must* ***on no account*** *be left unattended, even for one minute.* □ ***On no account*** *would she speak to any of them, though afterwards she wanted to discuss what the prospective buyers looked like.* TSMP □ *'Would you consider taking on the editorship yourself?' '****On no account****!'* □ *The 'autovia'* (= train) *would start at four in the morning and could* ***not, on any account,*** *wait for us if we were late.* DF □ *I had told the children they must* ***never on any account*** *go into a friend's house to play without first telling me where I could find them.* □ often with *must, will, would*; front, middle or end position.

on occasion [A (PrepP)] sometimes; occasionally □ *The room was evidence that she could let herself go, and that was what I liked. People who cannot let themselves go* ***on occasion*** *will not do for me.* SPL □ *If* ***on occasion*** *he mistrusted his own powers, it was not a mistrust that he intended others to share.* HAA □ ***On occasion*** *she could express herself on matters of sex in good old English words that would have shocked her father and puzzled her mother.* RFW □ front, middle or end position.

on the one hand...on the other (hand) [Conj (PrepP)] used to indicate contrasting facts, opinions, procedures etc □ (growth of cottage industries) ***On the one hand*** *it is a movement very much in tune with the general social changes which have gained enormous ground during the seventies: and,* ***on the other,*** *it is an antidote to the instant, throw-away fashion styles which dominated the sixties.* G □ ***On the one hand*** *one rule limits the women's colleges to 300 members, excluding graduates and research students, while another* (rule) *allows the total number of women to be one-fifth of the male undergraduate population.* T □ *Should a community allow a child to die because its parents object to a needed operation? Should anyone,* ***on the other hand,*** *ever be given the right to make vital decisions about another person's child?* OBS □ on the one hand occas introduces first statement without being followed by on the other (hand), as in second example; on the other hand very often introduces an addition or correction to a previous statement in which on the one hand has not been used, as in third example; front, middle or end position for each expression in its own clause.

on an optimistic etc note [A (PrepP)] so as to suggest, or cause, sad etc feeling **V:** start, open; end, close; continue. **adj:** optimistic; bitter, angry; despondent; hopeful, cheerful □ *The discussions ended* ***on an optimistic note*** (or: ***on a note of optimism***). □ *The Minister concluded his speech* ***on a*** *more* ***cheerful note*** *with references to a slow-down in the inflation rate.* G □ *I do not want to end this chapter* ***on a bitter note.*** MFM □ variant on a note of optimism etc. ⇨ ⚠ strike etc a false etc note.

on one's/its own[1] alone; without the support of anyone or anything further; by itself/oneself[1] (qv) □ *Lord Hailsham, the Lord Chancellor, describes Lord Masserene and Ferrard as 'almost a House of Lords* ***on his own****'. He has a range of titles.* OBS □ *A bowl of soup, thick with meat and vegetables, was a meal* ***on its own.*** □ *The thought of the voyage was enough* ***on its own*** *to make her feel sick without ever going on board.* □ modifies a preceding n.

on one's/its own[2] [A (PrepP)] without prompting, guidance, assistance etc; by itself/oneself[2] (qv) **V:** function, work; decide, choose; improve □ *Suppose you had to dump that clown you have with you — could you get here* ***on your own****?* ST □ *I'll give my wrist a day or two to see if it gets better* ***on its own*** *before I go to the doctor.* □ *'But nobody comes here who would steal them or borrow them without asking.' 'I wouldn't have thought so either, but books don't walk off shelves* ***on their own.****'* □ usu middle or end position.

on one's own (account) [A (PrepP)] as one's own employer **V:** set up, open shop; start, launch out □ *All the customers want their car jobs done by Brian. It's a pity he can't find the capital to set up* ***on his own account.*** □ *When the war came Madame Schiaparelli closed down and Madam Mirman opened up—****on her own.*** ST □ *He tried to show an intelligent interest in the family. What school did Glad go to? Did Stan* (an assistant hairdresser) *think of starting* ***on his own****?* HD

on one's own account [A (PrepP)] for one's own benefit or pleasure; for, on behalf of, oneself □ *What use has all this love ever been that men forced on me? Love is persecution. All I want is to be left alone to do some loving* ***on my own account.*** UTN □ *But Isabel went through much agony of mind wondering if the secret of her relationship to Alec would come out, and Harold* (her husband, also having an affair) *was no less alarmed* ***on his own account.*** PW

on one's own admission [Disj (PrepP)] as one oneself admits, confesses □ *The authorities concerned have* ***on their own admission*** *been lax in enforcing the anti-litter regulations and in prosecuting those who infringe them.* SC □ *On the left, a man who takes exercise regularly and is careful, but not fanatical, about his diet. On the right a man who,* ***on his own admission,*** *has 'given up'. You have been warned.* ST □ usu front or middle position.

on one's own terms [A (PrepP)] in ways, or on conditions, that one chooses oneself □ *'After the Ball is Over' is a melodramatic song, a commercial song taken over by the people; but they have taken it* ***on their own terms***. UL □ *A young peer of the realm with a famous mother and an even more famous grandmother told me the other day that he is determined to achieve whatever he does achieve in life* ***on his own terms***. *He doesn't want to be given a leg-up by his family.* NS □ *Mr Heath prefers to do things in secret and make his decisions public only* ***on his own terms*** *and when he considers it is to his advantage.* NS

on/under pain of death etc [A (PrepP)] with the risk that, if one disobeys, one incurs the penalty of death etc **o:** death, expulsion, excommunication; his father's disapproval, social ostracism; being forcibly ejected □ *Civilians were forbidden* ***on pain of death*** *to give shelter or food to any enemy fugitive.* □ *Were I cultural commissar for this country I would force everyone,* ***on pain of 40 years hard*** (labour) *in the sociology mines, to buy and read this book.* SC □ *Finally, we both rounded on him and told him to shut up* ***on pain of being dumped*** *by the roadside to finish the journey on foot.* □ *The executive has already succeeded in changing union rules to prevent members,* ***on pain of suspension***, *from taking industrial action without prior permission from headquarters.* NS □ usu middle or end position.

on paper [Disj (PrepP)] as described; when judged entirely on written record or statements, tables of figures, etc **V:** be, look, seem. **Comp:** all right, good, promising □ *I would think that I haven't changed as much as,* ***on paper***, *I would seem to have changed.* L □ ***On paper***, *the certificate of origin system* (ie of wine) *which came into force that October looked foolproof.* ST □ ***On paper*** *the IRA has an elaborate command structure: a GHQ (in Dublin), Brigade Staffs and Brigade Councils, battalions, companies.* OBS □ front, middle or end position.

on present etc form [Disj (PrepP)] judging by sb/sth's previous and/or current actions, behaviour, progress etc (from form = record of horse's performances in previous races) **adj:** present, ⚠ current, recent; past □ *The South Africans clearly hope to get the Ovambo back to work and though it* (their persuasion) *might have the desired effect,* ***on present form*** *it looks highly unlikely.* ST □ ***On recent form*** *I reckon he'll manage university entrance quite comfortably.* □ *If I saw that a horse would win* ***on form***, *I would want to see that horse move in the market* (ie have more people betting on it) *before I would back it.* OBS □ on form (without modifying adj) used esp with reference to horse-racing.

on sb's part shown, or done, by sb **o:** the Government; parents, students, doctors □ *Yugoslavia's international position is difficult. Since the end of last year there have been endeavours* ***on her part*** *to patch up peace with the USSR.* SC □ *I feel sure there will be no objections* ***on*** *anybody****'s part*** *to that.* □ *In the first place, he feared another act of treachery* ***on the part of*** *the leadership of the Movement.* OBS □ *There must be a vast number who would like to see much more personal responsibility* ***on the part of*** *both doctor and patient.* DM

on principle [A (PrepP)] because of a moral, or reasoned, code of conduct that one follows **V:** oppose, resist, sth; object (to sth) □ *Offering extra money was the wrong line to take with my father who* ***on principle*** *would have tried to make a good job of the house anyway.* □ *I object* ***on principle*** *to spending £15 or £20 merely to fill my stomach.* □ front, middle or end position. ⇨ ⚠ next entry; in principle; (as) a matter of principle.

on the principle of sth/that guided by belief in the truth, expediency, or likelihood, of sth **o:** first come first served, looking after number one, fending for yourself. **cl:** ***(of)*** doing nothing for himself, dressing well; ***(that)*** the taking of life is always wrong, what can't be cured must be endured, a child that has been quiet for half an hour is doing something he shouldn't □ *The orderlies, anxious to be off duty, dispensed food* ***on the principle of*** *first come first served and late-comers often had to beg cocoa and a slice of bread in the kitchens.* □ *Some are vegetarians simply because they prefer that type of diet, others* ***on the principle that*** *the taking of life is always wrong.* RT □ *My constable's companion, had,* ***on the principle that*** *if they are young they are probably guilty, arrested the lookout couple.* NS □ *Bob's a lazy devil. He gets through life* ***on the principle of*** *doing nothing for himself that he can get other people to do for him.* □ *She works* ***on the principle of*** *dressing particularly well when she feels depressed—says it always cheers her up.* ⇨ ⚠ previous entry; in principle; (as) a matter of principle.

on purpose [A (PrepP)] deliberately; not by chance; by design (qv) □ JO: *How could you give me a father like that?* HELEN: *I didn't do it* ***on purpose***. *How was I to know you'd materialize out of a little love affair that lasted five minutes?* TOH □ *'I failed my O-levels,' he says, 'more or less* ***on purpose***, *simply because I didn't want to be moulded into the kind of life they had mapped out for me.'* RT □ esp end position. ⇨ by accident; by chance.

on the quiet/QT [A (PrepP)] (informal) privately; secretly **V:** warn, inform, sb; borrow; make money □ *'I've been meaning to have a word with you as a matter of fact.' 'Well, here I am.' 'I'd like it more* ***on the quiet***, *you know.'* OMIH □ (a boy is repairing an old motor-bike his father has forbidden him to have) *'Of course,' he said bitterly, 'I'm handicapped all along the line. No money and having to do the job* ***on the quiet***.*'* HD □ *I warned a few of my regular customers, strictly* ***on the QT***, *that they'd better fill their tanks now because there would be no petrol by the weekend.* □ expression on the QT informal; end position.

on reflection [Disj (PrepP)] after thinking further about a matter □ *I thought of telephoning elsewhere for assistance, but* ***on reflection*** *I decided that there was no one to whom I felt inclined to speak frankly of my predicament.* UTN □ *The suspicion did cross my mind, even as he spoke, that the man was lying and* ***on*** *further* ***reflection*** *I was sure of it.* □ front, middle or end position.

on a shoestring [A (PrepP)] with very little

money or resources, esp capital and stock for starting or running a business **V:** make, produce, operate, work, run, sth □ *So the organisation grew but still lacking the sort of influential and wealthy support so characteristic of that around Stansted and Cublington. We still had to operate* ***on a shoestring***. NS □ *Technically, it is a Presentation show and not Light Entertainment: 'It was made* ***on a shoestring*** *budget,' said Eric.* RT □ attrib use ***a shoestring*** *budget/operation.*

on the side [A (PrepP)] (informal) as a sideline; in addition to one's main job, or source of income; secretly; discreetly □ *While drawing up deeds he wrote poetry, did a little newspaper work* ***on the side****, ran off sometimes to see life on the waterfront down-river at New Orleans.* L □ *He would not wish to kowtow to* (= act obsequiously towards) *the customers, though some of his fellows do that, and get cups of tea and tips* ***on the side***. UL □ *Most of the people at work knew he was having some fancy woman* ***on the side*** (= having an affair). □ usu end position.

on sight [A (PrepP)] as soon as sb/sth is seen; at sight (qv) **V:** love; hate, detest; kill □ ALISON: *Hugh and I disliked each other* ***on sight****, and Jimmy knew it.* LBA □ *A couple of thugs were sent after him with orders to shoot* ***on sight***. □ *There were more than 200 students, ranging from fresh-faced late-teens to grizzled heads; I loved them* ***on sight****. All nerves vanished.* OBS □ on sight and at sight sometimes interchangeable, but for verbs denoting emotions on sight is used. ⇨ ⚠ at first sight.

on the sly [A (PrepP)] (informal) secretly (the implication often being that one intends to deceive) **V:** smoke, drink; meet (sb); bet (on horses) □ *His mam hadn't even seen the girl, and that was what made it worse, she shouted. Courting* ***on the sly*** *like that and suddenly upping and saying he was getting married.* LLDR □ *While there, Chubb testified, Jackson stayed at a different hotel from the main party because he was '****on the sly****'.* ST □ *She says she has given up smoking but I think she goes to her room and has one* ***on the sly*** *sometimes.* □ usu end position.

on spec [A (PrepP)] (dated slang) as a speculation, guess or gamble; in the hope that sth positive may result □ *We heard of the cottage through a friend and took it* ***on spec****—Mary was anxious to get settled somewhere.* □ *Last June, the Government said Govan could go ahead with construction of the ships, worth £6m,* ***on spec***. ST □ *For five years I read on average 30 plays a week, unsolicited plays sent in* ***on spec*** *by hopeful writers.* NS □ usu end position.

on the spot[1] there at the time and place an event happened □ *There I was* ***on the spot*** *and willing, indeed eager, to be a guinea-pig.* DOP □ *ITN had a man* ***on the spot*** *interviewing Turkish paratroopers as they dropped from the sky.* NS □ *The artists (especially the ones* ***on the spot****) learned that the truth is objective after all, and that ensuring it is told is a full-time job*—their *job.* NS □ *Rover* (car manufacturer) *also hopes to send out engineers at some stage to do an* ***on-the-spot*** *check.* ST □ *The news item was followed by an* ***on the spot*** *report from the scene of the fire.* □ usu modifies preceding n; attrib use *an* ***on(-)the(-)spot*** *check, report.*

on the spot[2] [A (PrepP)] immediately; promptly **V:** pay, agree; give (the correct answer), undertake (to do sth) □ (collecting for a charity) *Another of my successes on this occasion was John Lennon, who whipped out his cheque book and gave me the bread* (= money) ***on the spot***. OBS □ *John Williams, to comply with* (Rugby) *Union rules, should have refused that League offer* ***on the spot***. □ *Machiavelli set to work on 'The Prince'. Not that it was much consolation. If the Medici had offered him a job, he would have abandoned the book* ***on the spot***. NS □ *It was no use, however, my trying to think it all out* ***on the spot****, especially with the* (sore) *head that I still had.* UTN □ end position.

on the spur of the moment [A (PrepP)] impulsively; as soon as one thinks of (doing) sth **V:** answer, speak; decide; rush off □ *I've taken a job at Coombargana, as a parlourmaid. I did it* ***on the spur of the moment*** *without really thinking.* RFW □ *The intention to kill or do grievous bodily harm was possibly conceived only* ***on the spur of the moment***. OBS □ *Last year he pushed off to Hong Kong* ***on the spur of the moment***. RT □ *'They nearly all happened in the early morning hours,' said the* (Scotland) *Yard man. 'They were usually* ***spur of the moment*** *attacks.'* TVT □ attrib use *a* ***spur of the moment*** *attack.*

on the strength of sth [A (PrepP)] using sth as one's main supporting reason, excuse, argument etc (for doing sth) □ *They experience a thrill and they call it love. They get married* ***on the strength of*** *this feeling and they still call it love.* HSG □ *Rohauer extracted £250 from the Moroccan Tourist Board* ***on the strength of*** *his dubious rights to this film.* ST □ *It's your birthday, do you say? Well, we can have a drink* ***on the strength of*** *that.*

on the surface [Disj (PrepP)] superficially; as far as can be judged from external appearances □ *The results of the conference appeared* ***on the surface*** *to be gratifying.* MFM □ ***On the surface*** *he doesn't appear to be a miser, but you find out about him, really.* DC □ front, middle or end position.

on that score [A (PrepP)] about that particular (aspect of a) matter; for that particular reason **V:** dislike, resent, sb; object (to sb), quarrel (with sb); please, satisfy, sb. **det:** that; this, another, other; the same; various □ *He would do all that we sought and would see it was done at once; I had no doubt* ***on that score***. MFM □ *You're a good teacher and I've nothing to say against you* ***that score***. TGLY □ *A more serious objection is* ***on another score****— that working in groups is destructive of individual judgement.* NS □ *I have nothing to say against you* ***on the score of*** *your teaching capabilities.* □ less common variant on the score of sth.

on these lines [Comp/A (PrepP)] of a particular kind; in a particular style; in a certain way; by a certain procedure or method **det/adj:** these, the same; different; the usual; the right. **o:** the Arts Council, your own set-up, last winter's series. □ *An independent corporation for the medical profession* ***on the lines of*** *the BBC or the Arts Council would be one way 'lifting medicine out of the realm of party politics'.* DM □ *I didn't get much: one or two things* ***on*** *very*

***simple** classic **lines**, but I had some CLOTHES!* OBS □ *When Johnson was Professor of Mathematics 30 years ago the subject was being taught **on** very **different lines**.* □ *The CBI committee's ideas of bringing the compulsory retirement age for executive directors down to 65 seem to be **on the right lines**.* ST □ *Isabel experienced a curious thrill of pleasure at the idea that her thoughts and those of Alexander Goodrich were running **on the same lines**.* PW □ variant on the lines of sth.

on these terms [A (PrepP)] according to conditions, or arrangements, suggested or laid down **det:** these; his, their; such; the same, different, (not) any other □ *The children promised to sit quietly and to go to bed immediately afterwards, and **on these terms** they were allowed to sit up and watch the film with their parents.* □ *You must allow me to pay my share; I couldn't accept your hospitality **on any other terms**.* □ *I sent for Phillips because it seems necessary to remind him of **the terms on which** he was employed here.* □ *Sure, the vicar likes people to enjoy themselves, but it's got to be **on his terms**, not theirs.* □ variants on the terms proposed, on the terms agreed, the terms on which.

on time [A (PrepP)] punctually **V:** finish sth; detonate sth; deliver sth □ *Do you set great store by punctuality and make a point of being **on time** for work and social appointments?* WI □ (advertisement) *Once settled on a Greece or Elba Halcyon holiday, all we ask is that you get yourselves to the airport **on time**.* ST □ *Blake, British Rail's construction engineer in charge of the Scottish section of the programme, says with quiet confidence that work will be completed **on time**.* SC □ end position.

on one's tod [A (PrepP)] (informal) alone; without others present or helping □ (source) ***On one's Tod** Sloan* (rhyming slang = 'on one's own'). □ (a prisoner) *At night you can listen to your radio till 10 o'clock then it's lights off and you're **on your tod** and you say Christ Almighty, when am I going to get out of here?* ST □ *A third Scottish Labour MP was described to me by one of his comrades as 'an arrogant bugger — the only man I've seen at a conference eating his breakfast **on his tod**.'* NS □ *And then, after being driven round, you go round **on your tod** the next day accompanied by a sizeable hangover.* ST □ end position.

on top of sth besides, as well as, in addition to, sth □ *The situation is in some ways even improving, thanks to our incredible good fortune in finding so much gas and oil on our doorsteps, **on top of** the advantages of already having a big coal industry.* ST □ ***On top of** the set-piece sessions were the policy committees on agricultural production and consumption, on security, and on trade.* NS □ *It was unthinkable that he should be handed over to the attentions of a disciplinarian father **on top of** everything else.* HD

on the understanding that having made an agreement that; on (the) condition that (qv) **cl:** if you are not satisfied with the goods you may return them; I pay for my own keep; it was a permanent post □ *All reputable mail-order firms will send you goods **on the understanding that** you can return them within a stated period, if you're not satisfied, and get your money back.* □ *Ned should take along a youth of his own age **on the** more or less explicit **understanding that** he was going to spiral up to being head of the design department.* CON □ *Of course they want money. They would only agree to take part **on that understanding**.* □ variant on this/that understanding with reference to an earlier clause etc.

on the whole [A (PrepP)] generally speaking; taking everything important into account and not giving much importance to minor details; by and large (qv) □ *To pretend, however, that the struggle to gain his own way had been wholly unpleasant would be untrue. He had, **on the whole**, enjoyed it.* HAA □ ***On the whole**, it had been a successful evening.* TCM □ *'How are they taking the news?' 'Pretty calmly **on the whole**.'* □ *The Services may curse them* (politicians) *and try to overawe them but they know very well where the buck stops, and they don't (**on the whole**) try to cheat.* ST □ front, middle or end position. ⇨ ⚠ as a whole.

once again/more[1] [A] one more time **V:** say, sing, recite, sth □ *'That was better,' said the conductor. 'Let's have it **once again** from bar twenty, and then you can go.'* □ *If you say that **once more**, I shall scream.*

once again/more[2] [A] again as formerly **V:** meet, be reunited, come together □ *He argued that it was best to leave them alone because it seemed somehow probable that after death — whenever it came — he would meet all these things **once again**.* LLDR □ *'Only three weeks to go,' he wrote, 'and we'll be together **once more** and making up for wasted time.'*

once bitten, twice shy (saying) sb who has suffered a particular kind of misfortune is extremely cautious about incurring it again; the burnt child dreads/fears the fire (qv) □ *'He never married again?' 'No, **once bitten, twice shy**, I suppose — though that hasn't deterred some others I know.'* □ *'Do you always check applicants' references?' '**Once bitten, twice shy**. I always do now.'* □ used to explain or justify care or caution.

once and for all [A] now and from this time onwards **V:** understand, settle, establish, confirm, sth □ *Will the cameras prove, **once and for all**, that the dream of finding people on other planets is completely without foundation?* TO □ STANLEY: *Now you listen to me, my boy. You get this through your head **once and for all**; I'm in business to make money.* FFE □ *The only scheme he can get government backing for is the arrangement by which an author would get a **once-and-for-all** payment (a kind of additional 'lending royalty') on each new book of his bought by a library.* NS □ attrib use *a **once-and-for-all** payment.*

once a gentleman etc, always a gentleman etc sb will always be a gentleman etc in spite of changed circumstances **n:** gentleman, lady; Catholic; teacher; thief; whore □ *'Would he allow the other prisoners to feel that he thought himself a cut above them?' 'Of course he wouldn't. **Once a gentleman, always a gentleman**.'* □ ***Once a rifleman, always a rifleman**, they say. I joined up in the Rifle Brigade during the last war, and I never lost that peculiar sense of clannishness, of pride in my silver-plated badge, black buttons and green facing on my battle-dress.* RT □ *She laughed. 'I* *thought* ***once a student always a student****. Aren't you a student of history now?' 'Probably, maybe a different kind of history.'* PP □ stress pattern ˌonce a gentleman, ˈalways a gentleman.

once in a blue moon [A] (informal) very seldom; on rare occasions **V:** happen, occur; appear; perform □ *He* (a film director) *never looked through the view-finder or watched the daily rushes, and he consulted the script* ***once in a blue moon****.* L □ *One official view is that Wednesday's near-riot is one of the hazards of Continental competition — 'the sort of thing that happens* ***once in a blue moon****.'* SC □ *Honegger's huge dramatic oratorio has been performed only twice before in London, once with Ingrid Bergman as Joan. 'It's a* ***once in a blue moon*** *sort of thing,' said one of the violinists.* OBS □ front, middle or end position; attrib use, *a* ***once in a blue moon*** *sort of thing*, unusual.

once in a lifetime [A] likely to occur once only in the life of any one person □ *She was brought up to believe you fell in love and got married* ***once in a lifetime****.* □ *You haven't really achieved anything as a player unless you play in a Cup Final. It is usually a* ***once-in-a-lifetime*** *experience—unless you play for Celtic or Rangers.* TVT □ *W.C. Fields was a* ***once-in-a-lifetime*** *phenomenon who was as much of a surprise to his audiences as to the directors unfortunate enough to be assigned to his pictures.* RT □ attrib use, *a* ***once-in-a-lifetime*** *experience, phenomenon*, often found.

once in a while/way [A] occasionally, or intermittently, over either a long or short period □ *There isn't much upkeep with the hearses except to give them a lick of paint* ***once in a while****.* ST □ *Even the most reputable actresses had to suffer that thankless role of the dutiful wife of the 'great man'* ***once in a while****.* RT □ *The sailors sat with the great red-rusted sphere of the mine between them.* ***Once in a while*** *they would act in unison and move a spanner on a particularly difficult nut and bolt.* ARG □ *'Don't you ever drink tea?' 'Oh,* ***once in a way*** *I might. But I prefer coffee or fruit juice.'*

(only) once removed (from sth) very slightly different (from sth); not much different (from sth) □ *The whole essay was a skilful exercise in plagiarism* ***once removed****.* G □ *Lord Stokes is only one of a whole raft of men, commonly regarded as rich, who, in our presence* ***once removed*** (ie on radio or TV), *have proclaimed that money is, at the best a bore, and at the worst, an unmitigated pest.* SC □ *Reproved for boorishness, he would at once switch over to an exaggerated courtesy* ***only once removed from*** *insolence.* □ usu follows n.

once seen etc never/not forgotten (saying) memorable because of beauty, ugliness, strangeness etc **V:** seen, ⚠ heard, read □ *'Did you ever make the trip to the Falls?' 'Twenty or more years ago, but* ***once seen, never forgotten****.'* □ *It was at Tavistock Square that I first met Lady Ottoline Morrell, who,* ***once seen****, could* ***not*** *be* ***forgotten****.* AH □ *Bellamy has a very strong idiosyncratic personality that excites powerful likes and dislikes. His voice,* ***once heard****, will* ***not*** *quickly be* ***forgotten****.* RT □ often used to remark ironically on the striking quality of sb or sth.

once too often [A] once again, with, this time, unpleasant or disastrous consequences □ *One day at the Principal's little termly tea-party for her third-year students, the laughter happened* ***once too often****.* HAHA □ *You've often dozed off with a lighted cigarette between your fingers. One day when I'm not here to watch you you'll do it* ***once too often****.* □ often, with *will*, used as warning; end position.

once upon a time [A] some time, or a long time, ago □ *This is an older story, as old as Genesis. Maybe it could even start in the old way, and that, as I remember, was '****Once upon a time****'.* PP □ ***Once upon a time*** *there was a wife who ran her house with the organized precision of an electric clock. Everybody hated her and her husband ran away with a girl who couldn't tell the time.* TO □ *Rommel's forces* (would be) *dispirited and defensively minded, looking over their shoulders for the next position to which to withdraw—as had been the case in the Eighth Army* ***once upon a time****.* MFM □ used esp as the opening of a story, fairy tale, etc for young children; usu front position.

one after another/the other first one person or thing, and then another, and then another up to any number or amount □ *I saw him scrutinising us,* ***one after the other****, for long periods at a time.* L □ *We were in* ***one*** *furnished room* ***after another*** *for months and months.* EHOW □ *The sad 1930s gang of social or psychological cripples knock over* ***one*** *hick town bank* ***after another****, until the moment comes when they bite off more than they can chew.* L □ expression may follow or precede n or pron or be interrupted by a n (as in ***one*** *town* ***after another****).*

one and all [n + n non-rev] (informal) everybody relevant, with no individual left out □ *And Woodgate (or Hopalong as he was known to* ***one and all****) shut the door carefully like a man whose doors were always slammed by other people.* TT □ *I didn't kiss her but all women; I know they're stupid and unaccountable, ruled by the moon* ***one and all****, poor bitches.* RATT

one big happy family (catchphrase) a community, work-group, school etc in which all members have a good relationship and common interests □ *There was a lot wrong with the phrase* ***one big happy family****. Her family had been big. She'd had five sisters and three brothers and it had been far from a happy experience.* TSMP □ *But after the clichés like 'We're* ***one happy family****' four dissimilar personalities emerge—the only true common factor a shared ambition for greater success.* RT □ adj big usu present.

one day [A (NP)] at some undefined time, often but not necessarily in the future □ *'I think maybe I'd like to be a TT rider* (ie take part in the Tourist Trophy motorbike races on the Isle of Man) ***one day****,' he said.* OBS □ *And she was really concerned—would likely make somebody a good wife* ***one day****.* TT □ ***One day*** *people wake up to the experience that what was important yesterday no longer matters in the same way.* L □ front, middle or end position. ⇨ ⚠ one of these days.

one for (doing) sth [Comp (NP)] (informal) sb who likes, or is strongly in favour of, (doing) sth, who does sth often or whenever he can **det:** a (great); quite a, not much of a. **o:** freedom, fresh air; interfering; (wearing) bright colours □ TONY: *Of course she didn't reproach me. My mother is a great* ***one for*** *freedom.* EHOW □ *I was never* ***one for*** *rows and trouble, you know that. Peace is more my line.* LLDR □ *Fred was always* ***one for*** *the girls and he doesn't seem to get any less susceptible as he grows older.* □ *We are great* ***ones for*** *sticking labels on animals that have more to do with our own prejudices and attitudes than with ethnology or zoology.* SC □ *Petipa was a great* ***one****, we are told,* ***for*** *latching on to topical themes.* OBS

one for the road (informal) a last drink before setting off for home, on a journey, etc □ *'I think I ought to go.' '****One for the road****.' 'Mustn't drink all your whisky,' he muttered.* QA □ *Don't press a driver to have* ***one for the road****, unless it's in the form of black coffee or hot soup.* □ *'How about* ***one for the road****?' 'No thanks. If I drink any more, I won't be able to drive straight.'* □ often part of suggestion or invitation as in last example.

one good turn deserves another (saying) if A does sth to help or please B, then it is natural, pleasant or fair if B does sth similar for A □ *That* ***one good turn deserves another*** *was an axiom with Harold; he would not have dreamed of doubting it.* PW □ *I'll dig over that patch for you on Saturday. You've just about kept us in fresh vegetables these last two months, and* ***one good turn deserves another****.* □ often used to emphasize that it is normal to repay a favour, and thus to suggest that one has done nothing unusual.

one hell of a row etc (informal) a dreadful, terrible quarrel etc; an exceptional, outstanding person **o:** row, dust-up; mix-up; rat, nice guy □ *You'd better get that job finished or there'll be* ***one hell of a row*** *when the boss comes round.* □ *You knew that wherever you went people would say to themselves, 'This must be* ***one hell of a world-beater*** *to have a wife like that.'* CON □ *I've always found him* ***one hell of a nice guy****.* ⇨ ⚠ a/the hell of a sth.

one in the eye for sb [Comp (NP)] (informal) a setback, serious blow, for sb; get a slap in the face (qv) **V:** ⚠ be, seem; regard sth as □ *And now the jury's decision is being hailed as a triumph for Press freedom and* ***one in the eye for*** *the Whitehouse brigade* (censorship). ST □ *That's* ***one in the eye for*** *Kenneth Little who suggests that the roots of British racial prejudice lie in our 'almost unique' class consciousness.* NS □ *'Hope I'm not interrupting anything?' Which was* ***one in the eye for*** *anyone the cap fitted.* TT

a one-horse town etc (informal) a town or place where there is not much business done or entertainment offered; a poorly equipped business or service **n:** town, ⚠ place; firm, outfit, business □ *'This* (Hollywood in the 1930s) *was* ***a one-horse****, one-tank* ***town****, a beautiful quiet place. It was really dead.* RT □ *He'd started up* ***some one-horse*** *trading* ***concern*** *in a semi-derelict warehouse.* □ also pl.

one etc in a thousand/million [Comp/O (NP)] sb/sth of superlative character or quality, rarely found **n:** one, a man; a feat; a chance, an opportunity □ *'What's your new secretary like?' 'Reasonably competent—not a patch on Jean.' 'Ah, but she was* ***one in a thousand****.'* □ *But I didn't get my rest. Mrs Burton was there pottering about, her sketchy sabbatical dues* (ie church-going) *long done, but this was* ***a chance in a million*** *and she was seizing it and she said, 'Coppers, wasn't they sir?'* PP □ *Having said all that, the garish colour reminds one of the worst excesses of the Ziegfield Follies; but no matter, it's still* ***a musical in a million****.* RT

a one-man band etc a musician or entertainer who plays two or three instruments simultaneously, usu in the street; (fig) a person doing several things by himself which are usu shared with others **n:** band, ⚠ show, circus □ DR BROCK: *A doctor's* ***a one-man band****. Everything—everybody.* YAA □ *But what has grieved Jim Slater more than anything is having his Slater Walker Securities tagged as* ***a one-man band****.* OBS □ *'I'm by no means* ***a one-man-show****,' says Dame Margaret Miles, who* (is) *headmistress of Mayfield Comprehensive School, Putney.* RT □ *A lot of people share Hailsham's view that* ***his one-man****'s* ***circus*** *was more responsible than any other single factor for rousing the Tory rank and file.* ST

one man's loss is another's gain (saying) what sb must, or chooses to, do without is made use of, or enjoyed by, another □ *'She learned to cook at The Three Cocks hotel at Fordington,' Pop said. 'And it's never been the same since she left there.' 'I can only say the Cock****'s loss is your gain****.'* DBM □ *Fancy you not liking smoked salmon—and I got it as a special treat for you! Ah, well,* ***your loss is my gain****, as the fox said to the farmer when he ran off with the chicken.* □ loss and gain rev.

one man's meat etc is another man's poison etc (saying) what seems good or pleasing to one person may be bad or unsuitable for another **n:** meat...poison, religion... superstition, realism...obscenity, chore... relaxation □ *But there is no such agreement with respect to experiences of 'beautiful' and 'ugly';* ***one man's meat is another man's poison****.* SNP □ *That perspicacious proverb about* ***one man's meat being another man's poison*** *could well be stretched to cover the undoubted fact that* ***one man's rubbish is another man's treasure****.* SC □ *The chief difficulty in finding a generally accepted definition of humour is the fact that* ***one man's meat is another man's poison*** *and that many people cannot understand why other people find something funny.* L □ *'****One man's superstition is another man's religion****,' says Stewart Sanderson. 'I prefer to use the word "belief".'* RT □ *The way* ***one man's meat is another man's poison****, so* ***one woman's ideal husband is another woman's pain in the neck****.* TVT □ often adapted, as shown; in such adapted sayings the 'favourable' and unfavourable' nouns may be reversed; a comment on the variability of human judgement or taste.

a one(-)night stand a single performance of a play, concert etc, esp one of a series of performances in different places; a sexual encounter lasting only a single night (or possibly one in a succession of brief encounters) □ *Edo de Waart is not so famous in Britain—a situation he feels is partly his fault. 'I find it difficult to give my* *best when I am guest conducting.* ***One night stands*** *don't really appeal.'* OBS □ *His sex life is in danger of deteriorating into a succession of* ***one-night stands***.

one of the boys [Comp (NP)] (informal) one of a well-established social or work group; sb who has a favoured relationship, which is not granted to many □ *He gave no sign of wanting to please, nor was he patronising. He made efforts to do the job without falling into the trap of trying to be* ***one of the boys***. ST □ *Most of these little literary magazines just take in each other's washing and you don't get published unless you're* ***one of the boys***. □ (a 'pet' greylag goose) *Calling him down when he's up high and travelling fast, is easy if yours happens to be a voice he listens to. But he doesn't listen to just anyone. You have to be* ***one of the boys***. SC

one of nature's gentlemen/ladies [Comp (NP)] sb who is courteous and considerate as a result of character and temperament rather than birth, upbringing or education □ *Donald Sinden who worked with More on the film 'Doctor in the House' describes him as '****one of nature's gentlemen****—and a joy to work with.'* TVT □ (reader's letter) *I was born of a working-class family. My father was a humble dustman,* ***one of Nature's gentlemen.*** L

one of these days [A (NP)] at an undefined time in the future □ *Alec rose and shook hands. 'You'll be seeing me again* ***one of these days.****'* PW □ *'I could go places if I wanted to,' said Ron. 'Yes,' said Bernard. 'But not to prison. That's where Mrs Curry will put you* ***one of these days****.'* HAA ⇨ ⚠ one day; next entry.

one of those/these days [Comp (NP)] a day that is full of mishaps, when one has more to do than one can cope with, etc **V:** ⚠ be; turn into □ *I had the feeling as soon as the Johnsons trooped in for coffee that it was going to be* ***one of these days***. □ *But in 1971, running for Britain's juniors against West Germany, she was fourth in one race and last in another. 'Just* ***one of those days****,' she said.* ST □ PAMELA: *Oh, it's* ***one of those days***. *I bet you anything the horse breaks its legs.* FFE ⇨ ⚠ previous entry.

one and only [det + det non-rev] emphatically; absolutely; the only; the sole □ *Fran Fullenwider (the name is genuine) is the* ***one and only*** *60-hipped, 17½ stone model girl in London.* RT □ *Again the good bread, no meat, fine vegetables and salad and, the* ***one and only*** *time, a glass of beer.* OBS □ *Charles, whose nerves had been sorely tried by inactivity and pain, made his* ***one and only*** *scene with me.* LWK □ usu preceded by *the* or *his, her etc.*

one and the same [det + det non-rev] emphatically, absolutely the same **n:** person; time, moment; thing, entity; process □ *'Do you know who killed Robert?' 'Of course.' He sipped his sherry and added, 'And Lord Warbeck. And Mrs Carstairs. It was all* ***one and the same*** *person.'* EM □ *I can't be in the kitchen and running backwards and forwards at* ***one and the same*** *time.* □ *We have no policemen here and we need none. There is love between us, because we are* ***one and the same***. ST □ may modify, and/or stand in place of, a n (as in last example).

one swallow does not make a summer (saying) one fortunate incident etc should not be taken to mean that the general situation has improved or is about to □ *Could I say yet that everything was all right?* ***One swallow did not make a summer****, though I conceded that most people would think it meant they could reasonably look forward to a warm spell of weather.* SML □ *The revival of Scottish football fortunes —which Tommy Docherty seems to be inspiring—is long overdue. But Docherty himself is cautious: 'We will have setbacks — and* ***one swallow doesn't make a summer****.'* RT □ often used as warning against premature optimism.

the one(s) that got away people who in contrast to others, escape death, danger, matrimony, indoctrination etc (from the big fish that, in anglers' stories, was nearly caught, or broke the line or slipped the hook just before it could be landed) □ *The four Hertfordshire schoolboys who survived four nights out in the Carneddau are, in the words of John Ellis-Roberts, chief warden of the Snowdonia National Park, '****the ones that got away****'.* OBS □ *He took so long to make up his mind about his first really serious girlfriend that she went off and married someone else. He thought of her now, a little ruefully, as* ***the one that got away***.

one thing and another [o (NP)] (informal) various events, items, matters, tasks, topics etc **prep:** (what) with, about, by, from □ *It was an hour before we'd finished with cows and* ***one thing and another****. Then I started to clip. We've about 450 sheep and 250 lambs.* ST □ *What with Cindy's marriage and selling the house, and* ***one thing and another****, I've got an awful lot to see to.* PE □ *'You're like all the rest!' Susan broke out. 'Badgering and bothering me about* ***one thing and another****!'* EM

one too many an additional step etc beyond what is suitable, safe, tolerable, forgiveable etc **n:** step; remark, insult; drink, cigarette □ *She had it in her power to send him to jail for quite a long stretch. He had forged her signature on* ***one too many*** *cheques.* ASA □ *He never behaves like that unless he has had* ***one too many*** *drinks.* □ *'I think,' said Professor Clun, 'that some people have made* ***one*** *imaginative leap* ***too many*** *and show little sign of being able to return to the realm of reason.'* ASA □ *From the way he was lurching about you could see he'd had* ***one too many*** (ie ***one*** *drink* ***too many***). □ pl n in end position, sing n in middle position.

one up for/to sb (informal) sb has acted skilfully, wisely etc **o:** organizer, producer; team; Labour, Conservatives □ *Casals was the first to have this idea* (that there should be two winners if final choice is difficult) *in relation to the cello competition he presided over in Mexico, but the organizers wouldn't allow it.* ***One up to*** *Imperial Tobacco* (the sponsors, who did allow it). G □ *So far then,* ***one up for*** *Mr Russell (and hooray for Glenda Jackson's unheralded appearance).* ST □ exclamation indicating approval.

(in) one way and/or another [A (PrepP/NP)] by some means, methods etc or other □ *The full scandal had not got into the papers, but* ***one way and another*** *his career was at an end.* ASA □ *If you help a neglected, deprived child, he or she may well grow up to do you credit. They may not actually show you gratitude, though quite often they do. but the chances are that you* *will get thanks* ***one way or another****.* OBS □ *Not that everybody in our yard hadn't been a struggler—* ***one way or another****. You had to be.* LLDR □ *The writer may feel on reflection that he has been pressed,* ***in one way or another****, to change what should have been left as it was.* L ⇨ ⚠ next entry.

one way or the other [A (NP)] whichever of two possible events happens; with either of two possible reactions; with one of two possible judgements; either way (qv) **V:** care, have strong feelings; decide; matter; concern sb; (not) make any difference □ GEOF: *Before I met you I didn't care* ***one way or the other****—I didn't care whether I lived or died.* TOH □ *By now I had just sufficient whisky in me not to care much* ***one way or the other****.* UTN □ *I am convinced that there are very many people, non-committed politically, who would just not be interested in this type of play,* ***one way or the other****.* RT □ *About a concept like obscenity they* (a jury) *can only decide whether or not the object in question is acceptable to them—and they decide that,* ***one way or the other****, the first minute they see it.* L □ often neg or with neg implications. ⇨ ⚠ previous entry.

one with sb/sth [Comp (AdjP)] (formal) united with, forming an integral or indistinguishable part of, sb/sth **V:** ⚠ be, seem; become; make sb. **o:** Nature, the universe; all mankind; the dust □ *The reader must feel intimately* ***one with*** *the dream that is being presented to him, and he will not feel this if he has to puzzle over a nuance, or follow even a moderately involved sentence-structure.* UL □ *The artefacts survive when those that made them are* ***one with*** *the dust.*

the only begetter (formal) the sole originator or inspiration (of sth) □ (source) *To* ***the onlie begetter*** *of these insuing sonnets, Mr W.H., all happiness.* DEDICATION prefacing the SONNETS (W SHAKESPEARE 1564-1616) □ *Parts were good—and so was the acting; but it came a long way behind Evelyn Waugh,* ***the onlie begetter*** *of this sort of thing, lacking his incisiveness and genuine hard-heartedness.* L □ (opening ceremony of the Open University) *And Harold Wilson emphasised his role as* ***Onlye Begetter****, by reading into the record great chunks of previous speeches on the subject.* NS □ archaic spelling of only often used; sometimes facetious.

an only child the sole child of one's parents, (the implication often being that such a child is indulged, or deprived of companionship) □ *A friend of mine from a nearby street was* ***an only child*** *and seemed to have no father.* UL □ *It was common knowledge that* ***only children*** *had a difficult time of it and were liable to be immature.* TGLY □ *The fact of being* ***an only child*** *and therefore essentially a loner does not help in the task of jollying other people on.* ST

only connect (catchphrase) link facts, experiences, events etc to form a meaningful pattern; establish a link between oneself and others to improve understanding □ (source) ***Only connect*** *the prose and the passion, and both will be exalted, and human love will be seen at its highest.* HOWARDS END (E M FORSTER 1879-1970) □ *'****Only connect****', could well serve as the motto of Professor Young's study. Starting with a biologist's view of man, his object is to emphasise the inter-connectedness of things.* NS

only fair etc [Comp (Adj)] simply, barely, fair, just etc; no more than fair, just etc **V:** ⚠ be, seem. **adj:** fair, right, proper; natural, polite, human. **A:** to warn you, to point out, to make clear; that he should know □ *It is* ***only fair*** *to warn you that I shall make a very determined effort to evade the police.* HD □ *However it is* ***only fair*** *to say that major results can hardly be expected in a space of only 12 months.* G □ *To show a little bias in favour of one's own kin is* ***only natural****, surely?* □ *'It is nice that he shows such gratitude.' 'Nice, but* ***only proper****, after all.'* □ used to give warning, apology etc.

only to find etc with the sole result being disappointment, inconvenience, discomfort etc **Inf:** to find, ⚠ to discover, to realize, to be informed □ *I can sympathise with the exasperation of tourists—in Paris for a single day—arriving at the Louvre* ***only to find*** *it closed by a strike.* NS □ *...the story of a rising in 1816 in Algiers from which the Consul's family escaped and joined the British fleet,* ***only to find*** *themselves caught up in a sea battle.* NS □ *Throughout the day one or other of us would have an idea and rush with some fresh offering to the cage, to try to tempt the armadillos,* ***only to have*** *them treat it with disgust.* DF □ *Many's the book I've bought home from the library* ***only to discover*** *I've read it before.* □ in end position following a main clause.

the only good Indian etc is a dead Indian slogan expressing hatred for the enemy, racial antagonism, sectarian bigotry, etc (now more usu quoted when exposing or deploring such attitudes in others) **n:** Indian, German; Protestant, Catholic; landowner; fox □ (source) ***The only good Indian is a dead Indian****.* (attributed to the US General P H SHERIDAN 1831-88) □ *Her father had been a prisoner-of-war in the 1914-18 War and though he did not quite subscribe to the idea that* ***the only good Germans were dead ones*** *he certainly jibbed at Elizabeth marrying one of 'them'.* □ *The conscripts would take up one of the constant refrains of the Corporal—'****the only good Kaffir is a dead one****.' They used the word* onmenslik *to describe Africans. It means 'not human'.* NS □ *He was the kind of man who is provoked by some item of news into exclaiming, 'I can't stand the Babylonians!' or '****The only good Visigoth is a dead Visigoth****!'* AH

(but) only just [A] barely; with difficulty; by a narrow margin **V:** manage, get by, survive □ (looking at photographs) JO: *Is this a wedding group?* PETER: *My brother's wedding.* JO: *They* ***only just*** *made it, too, from the look of his wife. You can tell she's going to have a baby.* TOH □ *The air strip was small and I asked the pilot if we could get off. He said he thought we should manage it; and we did,* ***but only just****.* MFM □ *'It's after eight o'clock, now.' '****Only just****. I can still catch the bus if I hurry.'* □ but included only after comments or replies.

only too aware/conscious of sth/that [Comp (AdjP)] fully aware of sth; aware of sth to a degree that facts and circumstances have made unavoidable **V:** ⚠ be, appear; make sb. **o:** shortcomings; danger, risk, hardship, hunger; request; possibility □ *Both mines admitted* *that they were* ***only too aware of*** *the traffic* (ie diamond smuggling). DS ▫ *The boy is* ***only too aware that*** *he is less able than others of his age.* ▫ *Lindsay was* ***only too conscious of*** *the limits of his efforts at educating the unemployed to relieve suffering.* NS

only too glad etc [Comp (AdjP)] very glad etc; esp glad etc; more than glad etc (to do sth) (qv) **V:** ⚠ be, become, seem. **adj:** glad, ⚠ happy, pleased; willing, ready. **Inf:** to come, to get away, to help; to do what I can, to forget. **cl:** the whole thing; if he succeeds; that you've come ▫ *Most English writers have been* ***only too glad*** *to get out of the working class, if they have had the misfortune to be born into it.* NS ▫ *Lord Reith was big enough to discern the flaws which all of us have in our characters, and which most of us are* ***only too happy*** *to hide from ourselves.* L ▫ *I saw at once he was a very decent chap and* ***only too willing*** *to help in any way.* MFM

only too well [A (AdvP)] to a greater degree than is right, pleasant or good for oneself or others **V:** know, understand; like, enjoy; hear, look after ▫ *'Anybody I happen to know?' 'As a matter of fact, yes. Remember Bonachea Leon?'* ***'Only too well.'*** ST *...ignorant dupes of an establishment which has learnt* ***only too well*** *how to divide and rule.* NS ▫ *She would have preferred* (the children) *out of the way; Jeremy didn't like company while Janice liked it* ***only too well.*** PW ▫ *Like a lot of deaf people, father could hear* ***only too well*** *when he wasn't meant to.*

ooh and aah [v + v non-rev] make sounds of astonishment, wonder, horror etc, esp to show enjoyment and relish ▫ *The audience of young children* ***oohed and aahed*** *as the acrobat flung himself into a triple somersault.* ▫ *Their* (the Sunday papers') *interest, whether in news-reporting or in fiction, is often increased by the '****ooh-aah****' element — a very 'ordinary' girl is knocked down by a man who proves to be a film-star.* UL ▫ *In the Christmas edition of 'Tomorrow's World' (a fairground of scientific wonders for children) the famous illusion of Pepper's Ghost, which once drew* ***oohs and aahs*** *of astonishment from an audience in London's Egyptian Hall, will be re-enacted.* RT ▫ oohs and aahs [n + n non-rev]; attrib use *the* ***ooh-aah*** *element.*

open the ball [V + O pass] be the person chosen, or choosing, to start proceedings (from leading off the first dance at a ball) with one's partner ▫ *I was sent for by the Prime Minister. The P.M.* ***opened the ball*** *by asking if I had read the newspaper reports about the fighting in Haifa.* MFM ▫ *Though the incident was unlikely to end in anything other than a shooting-match neither besiegers nor besieged were keen to* ***open the ball.***

an open book [Comp (NP)] sb/sth with nothing secret or mysterious about him/it; sth/sth that is easily understood and interpreted **S:** my life, his face, his mind; the moorland, international law. **V:** ⚠ be, look like. **A:** to me, to a man like him ▫ *He is tough and shrewd when he has to be. But he is* ***an open book****—deviousness does not seem to be part of his personality.* ▫ *I tell you, the mysteries of religion are* ***an open book*** *compared with those of psycho-analysis.* ▫ (television stars) *Their contributions to the taxman are huge and their life is* ***an open book*** *to the public.* TVT ⇨ a closed/sealed book to sb.

open the floodgates (of sth) [V + O pass] release a great force of emotion, destruction, rebellion etc previously held under control (from the opening of gates, eg at a lock or reservoir, that hold back or release a volume of water) **o:** grief, passion; violence, famine and disease ▫ *Five minutes of dead silence is going to* ***open the flood gates of*** *their indignation like the bottom coming out of a bag of cement.* ART ▫ *The bereaved woman is stunned and withdrawn, but presently* ***the floodgates are opened*** *and natural grief has its way.* ▫ *Help has been too little and too late or too far from where it was most needed.* ***The flood-gates of*** *famine and pestilence are already* ***open.*** SC ▫ floodgates or flood-gates.

open one's (big) mouth [V + O] (informal) say something (the implication often being that sb speaks too readily or indiscreetly) ▫ *Everything I say is wrong this morning. I'm frightened to* ***open my mouth.*** ▫ *If you so much as* ***open your mouth*** *about it to her — you can pack your bags and go.* EGD ▫ *Trust you to go and* ***open your big mouth****! Dick was supposed to have been visiting his mother last night.* ▫ *You're afraid it's your fault he's hooked on to us. Because you've* ***opened your mouth*** *too wide.* HD ⇨ shut one's mouth etc; keep one's mouth/trap shut.

open Pandora's box bring about (esp in the hope of obtaining, achieving sth) a host of troubles previously unknown or under control (from Greek mythology, in which Pandora, the first woman, received from Jove the gift of a box — subsequently opened by her husband —in which all the troubles that could afflict mankind had been safely sealed) ▫ *Our quest for North Sea oil is like the* ***opening of Pandora's box****: havoc will prevail as the object of our desire is distributed.* OBS ▫ *Given China's traumatic experiences during her initial contact with Western capitalism in the last two centuries her new leaders will be cautious about* ***opening Pandora's box*** *again.* ST ▫ *Peckinpah is an artist I admire immensely, and I wouldn't want to ban his film* ('Straw Dogs'), *but outside the conventional, allegorical framework of the Western his personal obsessions have exploded like grotesque forces from* ***some Pandora's Box.*** NS ▫ variants the opening of Pandora's box, a Pandora's box.

an open question [Comp (NP)] a question that cannot be, or is not yet, answered; a matter that cannot be, or is not yet, decided **V:** ⚠ be, remain; leave sth ▫ *Whether any adolescent would have benefited from a kind of upbringing he didn't actually have is always* ***an open question****, isn't it?* ▫ *'You seem to have got little thanks for your kindness. Never mind, you'll get your reward in heaven.' 'That's* ***an open question.****'* ▫ *Mr Buckle maintains that, as a choreographer, Nijinsky has influenced all the best of his successors. Stravinsky and Ansermet thought that his choreography suffered from his ignorance of music, which they probably exaggerated.* ***The question*** *therefore remains* ***open*** *and Mr Buckle may be right.* ST ▫ *'La Fauvette' is not merely a long work; it is a big work. Whether it is also a great work is* ***a question*** *I prefer to leave*

open. OBS □ variant the question is/remains open.

open season for sth [Comp (NP)] the months of the year when specified animals, birds, fish may be killed legally; a time or occasion when (doing) sth seems to be specially prevalent **V:** be, become, seem. **o:** salmon (fishing), pheasant (shooting); student-bashing □ *The hard-line Republicans were also extremely active in the war of words. To them it seemed that* ***open season for*** *Republican-bashing had been declared again.* L □ *When the marathon talk-in at No 10 Downing Street finally broke up, it then became* ***open season for*** *the massed prophets of gloom (if not doom).* L

an open sesame (to sth) [Comp (NP)] an easy means of access to a place, to a social, government, academic or business circle, or to a particular commodity (from the magic words Open Sesame! which caused the door of the robbers' cave to open in the 'Arabian Nights' story of 'Ali Baba and the Forty Thieves') **V:** ⚠ be, become; make sth □ *They are precious, almost faery regions, steeped in mystery and rich with treasure, to which the '****Open Sesame****' costs rather more than three shillings and sixpence.* AH □ *His relationship to the Lord Lieutenant, had he let it be known, would have been* ***an open sesame to*** *every drawing-room in the county.* □ *Coke* (= cocaine) *is* ***the*** *latest* ***open sesame to*** *that elusive 'good time' at the heart of the American dream, and at least five million Americans have now tried it.* OBS □ *Although ENA* ((France) Ecole Nationale d'Administration) *is only 30 years old, it is* ***a*** *well-established* ***open-sesame to*** *power, and the first generations of 'Enarques' (ENA graduates) are now prominent administrators, including the four most important men in France.* OBS

an open and shut case [Comp (NP)] a legal case, or other matter, about which there should be no doubt or argument because all the evidence points to only one verdict or conclusion **V:** ⚠ be, appear; make sth; have □ *As soon as the results of the forensic tests came in, the inspector in charge knew he had* ***an open and shut case*** *against Wilson.* □ *Nobody reproduces one and a half pages of critical text word for word from 'unconscious memory'. It's* ***an open and shut case*** *of deliberate plagiarism.* □ occas pl.

open to sb [Comp (AdjP)] available to, obtainable by, possible for, sb **S:** opportunities, choice; post, facilities; it...to write to your M.P., to complain. **V:** ⚠ be, become; make sth. **o:** all; pupils, men and women under 40 □ *Yet the Ombudsman system has certain attractions. It is simple and* ***open to*** *all.* SC □ *The annual careers guide is a valuable introduction, giving some idea of the opportunities* ***open to*** *school-leavers of fifteen, sixteen, seventeen and eighteen.* OBS □ *These concessions are* ***open to*** *cash customers only.* □ *'Why me?' 'Because I think you are the best man for the job. But it's* ***open to*** *you to refuse.'* □ *If it were* ***open to*** *me to say who should or shouldn't receive a grant, you'd get one right away.*

open to sth [Comp (AdjP)] liable, susceptible or vulnerable to sth; of a kind that can be affected or influenced by sth **S:** project, scheme, job; boss, teacher, husband. **V:** ⚠ be, become, seem. **o:** abuse; misinterpretation; suggestion, correction, persuasion; being abused □ *The scheme is, of course,* ***open to*** *abuse. Laws of this type, however liberally conceived, will always be* ***open to*** *being used oppressively.* NS □ *Overweight children are more than averagely* ***open to*** *chest infections.* □ *The wife is often responsible, out of this fixed allowance, for any replacements — of crockery, furnishings, and so on; the more thoughtful of these husbands will be* ***open to*** *suggestions, will promise something out of the next payment of over-time.* UL □ *I believe these figures are the most recent available but I am* ***open to*** *correction.*

open to question etc [Comp (AdjP)] questionable; arguable; uncertain **S:** it...whether he will agree, what they will think, how they will react. **V:** ⚠ be, seem, remain. **o:** question, ⚠ doubt, argument □ *But it must be* ***open to question*** *whether the nation got good value for the money Labour spent.* SC □ *It remained* ***open to question****, no matter what the courts found, whether Mr Ince had been rightly convicted for the offence.* T □ *Whether the field research was necessary or not is certainly* ***open to question****.* L □ *Whether the truth, and nothing but it, is a successful vote-getter remains* ***open to doubt****.* RT □ *The rightness or wrongness of the decision taken is, of course,* ***open to argument****.* MFM

the opium of the people (saying) sth used to give people false satisfaction with, or compensation for, the harsh facts and conditions of their lives □ (source) *Religion is the sigh of the oppressed creature, the feeling of a heartless world, and the soul of soulless circumstances. It is* ***the opium of the people****.* CRITIQUE OF HEGEL'S PHILOSOPHY OF RIGHT (K MARX 1818-83) □ *People sit drugged, all night, before their television sets. It's* ***the*** *new* ***opium of the people****. And what a panic if the hub of the household hiccups, halts, and dies.* SC

one's opposite number a person occupying the same, or a very similar, position as oneself, but in a different country, party, university, business firm, or other group □ *We—or rather* ***our opposite number*** *on the other side—are going to drop a very small tactical bomb.* OI □ *The Greater London Council planners, however, and* ***their*** *Labour* ***opposite numbers*** *came to a less comforting and more realistic conclusion.* ST □ *By being a little extravagant in giving a present to* ***your opposite number*** *you should receive co-operation.* WI

or else otherwise sth unpleasant will happen, be done, as a result □ (from a letter) *It was a hundred and fifty pounds I asked for. You sent only a hundred. The other fifty had better arrive tomorrow* ***or else****.* DC □ *I expect they've found the car and are telling these chaps to have us over* ***or else****.* QA □ *He was the man without mercy, the ruthless one, who must be obeyed* ***or else****.* PE □ *Last year I was told to put on weight* ***or else****. I was down to six stones.* ST □ unfinished threat or warning.

or I'm a Dutchman of that I'm very certain; unless I'm much mistaken □ *'There's a Force 7 wind blowing.' 'Yes — and worse to come* ***or I'm a Dutchman****.'* □ *If it's not a genuine 16th century piece* ***then I'm a Dutchman****.* □ *One thing had the habit of leading to another and this would be so whether he got more amorous or more senti-*

mental, and one of the two he was soon going to get ***or she was a Dutchman***. TGLY □ follows an emphatic assertion; always first person except in reported speech; variant if sth is (not) so, (then) I'm a Dutchman.

or rather put more exactly, more accurately □ *'You're going to say I must go,' I said. 'You must,' said Anna, '****or rather*** *I must.'* UTN □ *The Arabs pointed to the Cloud,* ***or rather*** *to a blackness in the sky, which by now was about seven degrees across, looking like a yawning circular pit.* TBC □ used to correct or modify a preceding statement.

or so approximately □ *The losses so far reported have come from only a half-dozen* ***or so*** *companies.* T □ *This place was about two miles from Mastodon. A mile* ***or so*** *along the coast a country house was occupied by a secret naval party.* RFW □ *I'll keep on for another hour* ***or so***. *Then if there's no improvement I'll turn in.* TBC □ *There is, I am told, a tribe far up the Amazon that makes a great march down to the sea every five years* ***or so***. OBS □ follows, or refers to, a specific number, quantity, time, distance etc.

or something (informal) or some similar thing, person, condition, activity etc □ *There was no need to spend all that money on a present. She would have been just as pleased with a bunch of flowers* ***or something***. □ *'He said: "Is that George's little tart?" She flushed deeply and added, 'I thought he was drunk* ***or something***.*'* PE □ HELENA: *She's going to church.* JIMMY: *You're doing what? Have you gone out of your mind* ***or something****?* LBA □ HELEN: *Turn yourself into a bloody termite and crawl into the wall* ***or something*** *but make yourself scarce.* TOH □ modifies a preceding n, v, adj or clause.

or whatever (informal) or any other/others of the kind indicated (the reference being to things, persons, groups, actions etc) □ *He can be an eminent professor, an eminent lawyer, an eminent surgeon* ***or whatever***. *He's still a stupid man.* □ *'I expect she'll only have to shed a few tears and you'll give in to her.' 'No, not if she weeps, screams, goes down on her knees and prays* ***or whatever***.*'* □ *I always enjoy those sermons in which Christians are likened to birds in their little nests* ***or whatever***. G □ follows n, v, adj or clause; variants or however, or whenever.

ordeal by fire/water any test of courage, endurance etc (from the medieval form of trial being by ordeal, based on the belief that supernatural intervention would prevent the accused, if innocent, from being burned by fire or drowned) □ *I don't have a hope of getting the job after* that *interview—talk about* ***an ordeal by fire****!* □ *The villagers are beginning to calculate the damage caused by last night's floods. They also have the depressing task of cleaning up the mess left after their* ***ordeal by water***. □ (NONCE) *Another cup was rinsed on to the floor, refilled and put like a live coal into my hands—the* ***ordeal by tea***. QA □ (NONCE) *Only perhaps here and there someone, pausing for a moment to recover his strength before further* ***ordeal by chatter****, was aware of some slight strain or disturbance in the atmosphere.* ASA □ often adapted for facetious effect.

the order of the day [Comp (NP)] the procedure or business for a named day, esp debates in the House of Commons; the accepted practice, common routine, usual position **V:** ⚠ be, seem, become □ *Hand-outs were issued to the delegates, giving* ***the order of the day*** *for each session of the conference.* □ *Self-discipline was* ***the order of the day*** *at home and at school.* RT □ (They) *hold parties on Saturday. They get a bit drunk. The lights are off and sex is very much* ***the order of the day***. NS □ (towers for TV cameras) *From that time onwards a form of staircase, complete with handrail, has been* ***the order of the day****, for which I and all my successors may be truly thankful.* ST □ (NONCE) *Until recently paraffin lamps were* ***the order of the night***. T

(only) the other day etc [A (NP)] very recently **n:** day, ⚠ night; evening, morning, afternoon; week □ *Do you remember what we were saying* ***the other day*** *about the Cloud slowing down?* TBC □ *'We have our own job to do in Africa,' Mr Macmillan said* ***the other night***. SC □ *I said: '****Only the other day*** *the Russians put out that they have discovered huge new diamond fields somewhere inside the Arctic Circle.'* DS □ *Your three months can't be up already! It seems* ***only the other week*** *that we went down to the station to meet you.* □ front, middle or end position.

the other side [o (NP)] the after-world, spiritual life after death, now esp associated with the beliefs and practices of Spiritualism, but also with 'crossing the river of Jordan', Christian symbol of passing from earth to heaven **prep:** on; to; from □ *When the day that he must go hence was come, many accompanied him to the Riverside. So he passed over, and the trumpets sounded for him on* ***the other side***. THE PILGRIM'S PROGRESS (J BUNYAN 1628-88) □ *In spite of her glamorous contacts both here and on* ***the Other Side****, Mrs Twigg seems a cosy, kindly, well-intentioned lady.* L □ *You'll be glad to hear the latest from* ***the Other Side***. *Well, George Sand has sent word that she and Chopin have 'made up all their differences, Liszt has more or less given up womanising and Beethoven is more humble.'* NS □ often, but not necessarily, capitals O and S.

the other etc side of the coin the contrasting, or contrary, aspect of a matter **adj:** other; (only) one; two, both; reverse, darker; more pleasing □ *Mr Bell feels so guilty of his own priviliged position in society that he is determined to romanticise* ***the other side of the coin****, and to idealise mores* (= customs) *into positive values.* RT □ *Before deciding to reject or accept the maker's guarantee* (on new cars)*, the buyers should look at* ***both sides of the coin***. *On the credit side the best of them offer unquestioned after-care servicing at appointed dealers. In too many unforgivable cases precisely the opposite happens.* ST □ *During the recent Lord's Test, a happy streaker* (= sb who runs naked through public places) *leapt into millions of homes, and even the magistrate was amused. The Headingley despoilers are* ***the darker side of the*** *same 1970s* ***coin***. G

other than sb/sth except, but, apart from, sb/sth □ *Does anybody* ***other than*** *yourself know this?* □ *Games should normally require no equipment* ***other than*** *a ball or stick; they should* *make use of available materials, of the lamp-posts, the flagstones, and the flat ends of houses.* UL □ *He had never once thought of himself as a man with whom a woman* ***other than*** *his wife could fall in love.* PW □ *It's a nice jersey but I wish you stocked it in a colour* ***other than*** *pink.* □ precedes n or pron, esp in neg, interr or conditional constructions.

other than (do) sth different(ly) from sth □ *Have you ever known her to be* ***other than*** *kind and considerate?* □ *A lot of the social visiting we have to do is a bore but we never come here* ***other than*** *willingly.* □ *With the bottle standing there on the table when he came in I couldn't do* ***other than*** *offer him a drink.* □ precedes adj, adv or v, esp in neg, interr or conditional constructions.

other things being equal [Disj] provided that outside circumstances remain the same, are unaltered □ *Finally, few people are so free of earthly vanity as not to find it pleasant,* ***other things being equal****, to be on matey* ((informal) = friendly) *terms with someone whose face is displayed all over London on posters twelve feet high.* UTN □ *'Wouldn't you like your husband to be earning another £5000 a year?' 'Of course I would,* ***other things being equal****. But not if he has to go to Singapore, which is I guess what you're getting at.'* □ front, middle or end position.

other times etc, other manners etc (saying) in other, or different, times, customs were different also (from the French expression *autres temps, autres moeurs*) **n:** times... manners, ⚠ days...ways, countries...customs □ *When the doctors don't know what's wrong with you they call it a virus infection; in the 16th century they'd have called it a 'humour'.* ***Other days, other ways.*** □ (NONCE) ***Other countries, other customs****: 'Not even a cosy on it!' I heard a Lancashire matron say as she regarded with disfavour the pot of tea served her in the lounge of a London hotel.* □ (NONCE) *'Ah well!' she sighed. '****Other days, other stays****, they say. But you'd not remember the whalebone* (corset), *dear.'* ASA □ often adapted to express other contrasts.

the other way about/(a)round [A] in a direction opposite to the one suggested; the opposite of what is expected or supposed **S:** bed, table; room, house; situation, relationship, result. **V:** be, face, turn; work □ ASTON: *You want to sleep* ***the other way round****.* DAVIES: *What do you mean?* ASTON: *With your feet to the window.* TC □ *Somewhere or other I've heard the comment that capitalism is the exploitation of man by man and that socialism is* ***the other way about****.* □ *To most people acting is glamorous, business isn't. It works* ***the other way around*** *for me.* RT □ end position.

the other woman the woman whom a man loves, or has a regular relationship with, in preference to, or as well as, his wife, □ *One can appreciate the mistrust of '****the other woman****', the Jezebel, the home-breaker, the woman who sets out to wreck an existing marriage or one just about to start.* UL □ SONIA: *I don't believe in marriage; not even for mothers and fathers. I have always wanted to be* ***the other woman****.* DPM

our man in Paris etc (catchphrase) a diplomatic representative, secret service agent, foreign correspondent of a newspaper, etc who works in the place specified; any well placed person from whom one can obtain special services or information **o:** Paris, Washington, Burma; Harley Street, the dispatch department □ *'Dear Mr Ambassador, I knew times had changed in England but never in my wildest dreams — ' So begins one letter among the dozens which have inundated* ***our man in Paris*** *in the aftermath of the Leeds rampage* (disorderly behaviour at an international football match). NS □ *'But I'm not in your Service. Why do you pick on me?' 'Patriotic Englishman. Been here for years. We must have* ***our man in Havana****, you know.'* OMIH □ *Next Sunday in 'The Observer' Walter Schwarz—until recently* ***our man in Jerusalem****—opens a special inquiry into the revolution in the Kibbutzim.* OBS

out-herod Herod [V + O pass] be extremely wicked, cruel, violent etc (the reference being to King Herod, ruler of Palestine when Jesus Christ was born, who 'slew all the children that were in Bethlehem, and in all the coasts thereof, from two years old and under', MATTHEW II 16); (fig) exceed sb named in a quality mentioned or understood □ (source) *I would have such a fellow* (ie an actor who exaggerates his role) *whipped...; it* ***out-herods Herod****: pray you, avoid it.* HAMLET III 2 □ *Reports are reaching us of acts of brutal barbarity by the invading army, who seem to be* ***out-heroding Herod*** *to a scarcely conceivable degree.* □ *In ambition, arrogance, astuteness and effectiveness the new military dictator already* ***out-napoleons Napoleon****.*

out loud [A] clearly and audibly, esp without fear **V:** say, state, speak; declare, testify. **O:** belief; intention; criticism, opposition □ *Children often relieve their feelings by muttering things they would not dare to say* ***out loud****.* □ (marriage ceremonies) *Probably the very fact that we have spoken* ***out loud*** *and let everyone know what we feel makes it more incumbent on us to hold to what we said.* ST

out of the corner of one's eye [A (PrepP)] with an indirect, secretive, casual glance **V:** see, notice, look at, watch, observe, sb/sth □ ***Out of the corner of my eye*** *I saw Reggie take Susan away, and the next ten minutes were a blur of new faces and half-heard names.* RATT □ *I turned my attention to the package. I had already noticed* ***out of the corner of my eye*** *that it came from France.* UTN □ *Even when he was writing on the blackboard he'd be watching you* ***out of the corner of his eye****.* □ front or end position.

out of hand [A (PrepP)] at once; summarily; without investigation or consideration **V:** reject, condemn; refuse, turn down, dismiss, sth □ *No one thought he had any talent; most of what he wrote was rejected* ***out of hand****.* OBS □ *It was the largest wage claim in the history of the land. And when the employers rejected it* ***out of hand*** *in November it was simply dropped.* NS □ *Martin's proposal to get rid of the man* ***out of hand*** *was indefensible.* NM □ *Applied science is more often condemned* ***out of hand*** *than given a genuine trial.* OBS

out of hours [A (PrepP)] during times when public houses are shut or a licence-holder may not sell alcoholic drinks □ *For a long time I have kept a stock of whisky with Mrs Tinckham, in* *case I ever need a medicinal drink, in quiet surroundings, in central London,* ***out of hours***. UTN □ *There is a small back parlour where the landlord will serve drinks* ***out of hours*** *to a privileged few.* □ attrib usu ***out-of-hours*** *drinking.*

out of the mouth(s) of babes and sucklings (wise, shrewd, perceptive remarks or questions can come) from very young, naive or untaught persons □ (source) ***Out of the mouth of babes and sucklings*** *hast thou ordained strength because of thine enemies, that thou mightest still the enemy and the avenger.* PSALMS VIII 2 □ *'What could a boy like that suggest that Bill at the garage hasn't thought of?' 'You never know.* ***Out of the mouths of babes and sucklings****, remember.'* □ (NONCE) *There are occasions, in the City as elsewhere, when ingenuous questions* ***out of the mouths of babes and suckers*** (= people easily deceived) *can confound the experts—or at least defy glib replies.* OBS

out of sight, out of mind (saying) sb who, or sth which, is no longer present, visible etc tends to be soon forgotten □ *Such instances of recall are, however, by no means frequent and it still seems to be largely a question of '****out of sight, out of mind****'.* MFF □ *The end is still unhappy.* ***Out of sight, out of mind****, I say, or would if it weren't for those redeeming bits of humour and madness before brutality sets in.* NS □ *'Good,' said Rose, 'who's talking about good? I don't want to do her good, I just want to keep her* ***out of sight and mind****, thank you very much.'* TSMP □ usu a comment on sb or sth that can easily be forgotten, or on sb of a forgetful nature.

an out and out scoundrel etc a complete, thorough, unmitigated, scoundrel etc **n:** scoundrel, rat, swine; disaster, failure; opposition □ *Yet the Labour leaders managed to steer the conference into throwing out a resolution expressing* ***out-and-out opposition*** *to the EEC* (= European Economic Community). SC □ *We did wring a few concessions from him however —the meeting wasn't* ***an out-and-out failure****.* □ *Maurice Denham gives an awesomely good account of* ***an out-and-out coward****.* TVT □ *As the Conservatives move to the right, they wish the Labour Party to move further to the left. For* ***an out and out socialist*** *this is a defensible position.* L □ n usu refers to an unpleasant person, negative qualities, etc; adj often hyphenated.

the outside world [o (NP)] places, people, activities etc which are not not those of an enclosed community, group, profession **prep:** in, from, for □ *They found me a job in* ***the outside world****. It was they, the Sister, the Doctor, and the social worker who* (arranged it). HAHA □ *This is the first time that I have actually been snowed up. I take it that we are still cut off from* ***the outside world****?* EM □ *There are many signs of such a reversion to tradition, accompanied as in the past by vast claims of empire and contempt for* ***the outside world****.* SC

outstay one's welcome [V + O] tire, or inconvenience, one's host by staying longer than is reasonable or expected □ *It's better not to* ***outstay one's welcome****, especially on a first visit.* □ *'How long will you stay?' 'A month, I should think; mustn't* ***outstay our welcome****.'* TSMP □ often with *must not, ought not, not wish to.*

over and above [prep + prep non-rev] besides; as well (as sb/sth) (qv); in addition (to sth) (qv) **o:** that; his regular wage, our love for her; what was asked □ *In Corelli III* (a hospital ward) *there would probably be nobody,* ***over and above*** *the patients, except the Night Sister.* UTN □ *I denied being too busy, because,* ***over and above*** *any consideration of courtesy, I was genuinely pleased to see him.*

(all) over again[1] [A] (do sth) once more; (do sth) (for) a second time □ *I'll tell you what you have to do and then you'll say it* ***over again*** *after me.* □ *I was adding up this long column of figures when some idiot phoned, so I had to start* ***all over again****.* □ *I'm not sure I could stand seeing the film* ***all over again****.* □ end position after V or V + O.

(all) over again[2] [A] (be sb/sth) repeated; (be sb/sth) in identical or very similar form or character □ *Even if you hadn't written I'd have known who you were. You're your mother* ***all over again****.* □ *What's the point of another meeting? It would just be last night* ***over again****.* □ end position after *be* + Comp.

over sb's head [A (PrepP)] without taking account of people in positions of authority between onself and the person(s) being favoured or appealed to **V:** go, ask; promote, appoint, select □ *President Nixon was appealing for support for his incomes policy,* ***over the heads of*** *the leaders, to the rank and file trade union members.* ST □ *Well you know what my attitude was in the Home Guard. Never listen to any complaints* ***over the head of*** *a man's commanding officer.* RM □ *In September 1937, Lord Gort was promoted* ***over the heads of*** *many senior officers to be the youngest-ever CIGS.*

over here/there [A] the country etc where one is/is not at the moment of speaking (irrespective of one's own nationality), esp one separated by sea, a channel etc from another, eg Britain vis à vis the US, Eire, France; the Americas vis à vis Europe □ *Interest rates on U.S. Treasury bills were sharply declining and with the Budget* ***over here*** *also adding to the strengthened appearance of sterling the £1 rate on New York moved up sharply.* SC □ *Would they be returning to the States? Perhaps, but they hoped for a renewal of contract with ITV for another series, 'the pace of life, even in London, is so much less frenetic* ***over here****.'* TVT

over my dead body [Disj (PrepP)] (informal) (sth will be allowed to happen/be done) only if I am dead, ie I am determined that sth specified will not occur □ *Both he and his wife have seen what can happen to a place as popular as Tintagel. 'Souvenir shops?* ***Over our dead bodies****,' said the farmer's wife.* TVT □ *'My new boyfriend hasn't got any money. But that's all right; he's going to give you a cheque.' '****Over my dead body*** *he's going to give me a cheque.'* PE □ *Les Underwood, the burly leader of the white knitters (who last month said that there would be a multiracial knitting section '****over my dead body****') was a signatory to the agreement.* NS □ almost always first person sing, and even in reported speech, as examples show, often rendered in direct original form.

over and over (again) [A] repeatedly; on many occasions □ *His girlfriend Jean doesn't share his guilt at all, and has to say so* ***over and over again*** *as Gordon tries to make matters right with the dispossessed Miss Partington.* L □ *He's been warned* ***over and over*** *by his doctor to stop smoking, but will he?* □ front, middle or end position.

over to you (informal) it is your turn, responsibility, decision etc (now); (from over (to you), signalling the end of a radio transmission with readiness for a reply) □ *Anne waylaid her husband in the hall as he came in. '**Over to you**,' she hissed quietly, tossing her head in the direction of the lounge. 'I've had enough of them and they're your friends anyway.'* □ *...the shameful practice of the Courts refusing transcripts* (of trials) *to press and public where a man's liberty may be at stake.* ***Over to you****, Lord Hailsham* (the parliamentary head of the judiciary). NS □ *'That's entirely the wrong way to do it.' '**Over to you**, then, smart boy!'*

overshoot the mark [V + O] exceed the permitted limits in a contest; (fig) do sth inaccurately, or with poor judgement or taste □ *The enchanted landscape remains gloriously within the realm of fairy-tale fantasy. Only the final reconciliation scene* ***overshoots the mark****, and the result becomes inflated.* G □ *He wildly* ***overshot the mark*** *with his last statement: he'd clearly made no attempt to check the figures.*

overstep the mark [V + O] exceed, in one's behaviour or language, what is right, morally acceptable, etc □ (Russia) *would watch the situation carefully and ensure that she did not '**overstep the mark**' anywhere by careless diplomacy.* MFM □ MICK: *You could come busting into a private house, laying your hands on anything you can lay your hands on. Don't* ***overstep the mark****, son.* TC □ *She's* ***overstepped the mark*** *in trying to change. Change was all very well but it could be carried too far.* TSMP

owe sb a debt of gratitude [V + IO + O pass] be in a position where one feels, or should feel, a real obligation to sb for sth given, or done, on one's behalf □ *We* ***owe*** *the Allied Forces in general, and the Desert Air Force in particular* ***a*** *very great* ***debt of gratitude****.* MFM □ *Finally, ladies and gentlemen, I am sure you will all agree that we* ***owe a debt of gratitude to*** *the Vintners' Company for the use of their fine Hall.* □ occas pl *several* ***debts of gratitude***; often used in rather formal or stereotyped statements.

one's own flesh and blood those of one's family group with whom one has a genetic or 'blood' relationship □ *Listen, Lottie — you should be ashamed of yourself — your own father —* ***your own flesh and blood*** *and you never came — after all the years he slaved for you.* HSG □ BEATIE: *You can't even help* ***your own flesh and blood****. Your daughter's bin* (= been) *ditched. It's your problem as well, isn't it?* R □ *I get sick to death of hearing about* ***flesh and blood*** *and then reading all those scandalous stories in the newspapers. You can't open a paper these days without reading about old folk being neglected.* TSMP □ rarely without own in above meaning; may be understood to include one's husband or wife. ⇨ ⚠ flesh and blood.

one's own man/woman [Comp (NP)] a person of independent judgement and character **V:** ⚠ be; become; seem; remain; come across as □ *John Reith was, as the phrase has it,* ***his own man****. He was never satisfied, for himself or for the BBC, with less than the first and the best.* L □ *I told him quite quietly, but straight, 'I'm your housekeeper, Mr Snow, but* ***my own woman*** *—and I choose my own friends.'* □ *'Peg will agree with her husband of course.' 'Why "of course"? She's* ***her own woman****.'* □ no neg construction.

one's own master/mistress [Comp (NP)] a person in control of his/her own affairs, not a wage-earner or sb who has to obey the orders of others **V:** ⚠ be; become; seem; remain □ *John Hodgson, farmer, Denbighshire, flexible income (from £0 to £5000) for flexible hours: We're having the hell of a time* (= a very difficult time) *at the moment. But I am* ***my own master****.* ST □ *The university vice-chancellors are no longer* ***their own masters****, but have to be prepared to accept group decisions.* T

one's own worst enemy [Comp (NP)] sb whose own faults or shortcomings are, much more than anything that has happened or been done to him, the cause of his failure or unhappiness **V:** ⚠ be; become; seem □ *And if the Cheineys seemed* ***their own worst enemies****, who is to say with conviction that the perpetual threat of homelessness did not contribute to their despair?* RT □ *If Reith eventually proved to be* ***his own worst enemy****, then one must logically seek the first signs in his unnaturally cloistered upbringing.* L

P

the pace is etc too hot (for sb) the increasing pressure of events, circumstances, competition etc is greater than sb can cope with **V:** is, ⚠ gets, grows, becomes; find sth □ *He left a trail of bad debts and bouncing cheques, and when* ***the pace got too hot for*** *him he came back to Jo'burg and pretended to go sick.* DS □ *I used to think I could drink with the best of them, but* ***the pace is too hot for*** *me here. These fellows must have guts of iron.* □ *In any year about a third of the students on this crash course* ***find the pace too hot for*** *them and drop out before Christmas.* □ *I was last in the race because the other competitors* ***set too hot a pace for me.*** □ variant set too hot a pace (for sb).

pack one's bags [V + O pass] (decide to, prepare to) leave one's home, residence, place of work, etc and live, stay, work elsewhere □ *Believe me, if I'd been married to that woman I'd have* ***packed my bags*** *years ago.* □ *After eight years in Washington (eight years is long enough for a correspondent to be in one place, too long maybe) he is* ***packing his bags*** *and moving to Brussels to spearhead the BBC's European* *coverage.* RT ▫ *Almost every week since she's been here the cook's threatened to* ***pack her bags*** *over some trifling incident or other.* ▫ *The delegation****'s bags*** *were* ***packed*** *and they were all set to leave when they received new instructions from their Government. They unpacked and stayed.*

pack the house [V + O pass] (be able to) attract a full audience, fill a theatre, concert hall, etc **S:** band, singers; show, play ▫ *The fact that 'Peter Pan' still* ***packs houses*** *with delighted kids says a lot for Barrie, or for the staying-power of the Victorian imagination, or both.* ▫ *The band still plays to* ***packed houses.*** ▫ variant a packed house.

pack sb like sardines [V + O + A pass] accommodate, seat etc a number of people in the minimum of space, as with sardines in a tin ▫ *Yes, the good old 'Margate Belle'. Oh dear, what times I've had in her in the sweet long ago.* ***Packed like sardines*** *and all enjoying ourselves.* RM ▫ *Even* ***packing*** *them* ***like sardines*** *into wards planned for half the number of beds, many cases requiring hospital treatment could not be admitted.* ▫ (NONCE) *We were* ***packed*** *together, eager* ***sardines*** *well up in the sky, a loading far above the engineering specifications.* NDN ▫ usu in passive form; pl O only.

a pack of lies an account of something that is totally, or largely, untrue **V:** be (nothing but); tell sb; (have to) listen to; come out with ▫ *'You got my letter?' 'Yes, I wish you hadn't written it.' 'Why?' 'Because it was* ***a pack of lies****. I trusted you, Thomas.'* QA ▫ *Mr Freeman said that if men in business had vacillated and changed their minds as the Ministry had done, they'd have been a laughing stock. Mr Chataway retorted that we'd been listening to* ***a pack of lies*** *for the last ten minutes.* L ▫ *Artistic embellishment gave way to invention and the day's events ended up as* ***a pack of lies.*** NS.

pack a punch [V + O pass] be capable of delivering a powerful blow; (fig) an exceptionally powerful effect **S:** boxer; book, play, rhetoric; alcoholic drink ▫ *He was beside himself with rage and, for so slight a youth, certainly* ***packed a punch.*** ▫ *'The Naked Civil Servant' is a film which looks behind Crisp's life from the age of 18, warts and all. It pulls no* ***punches****, but* ***packs*** *plenty.* TVT ▫ (advertisement) *You're pretty slinky?* ***Pack a punch*** *with Max Factor's Frost on your lips.* H ▫ *A lot of people don't realize, till they've drunk too much of it, what* ***a punch*** *this kind of cider* ***packs.*** ⇨ ⚠ pull one's punches.

paddle one's own canoe [V + O] make one's own decisions, depend on one's own efforts, in life or work ▫ *'Could somebody not have advised him differently?' 'I daresay several probably tried to, but he prefers to* ***paddle his own canoe.'*** ▫ *Birkett made his way up fast, thanks to his father's influential friends. My achievements were less spectacular but at least I could say I had* ***paddled my own canoe.*** ▫ *The boy's been feather-bedded at home long enough—at 19, he should be learning to* ***paddle his own canoe.*** ▫ also pl paddle their own canoe(s).

a (fully) paid-up member etc [Comp (NP)] a member of a club or society who has paid his subscription and any other dues and is therefore entitled to all the privileges and perquisites of membership; anybody who has a secure place for himself in some sphere **n:** member; teacher, supporter; sympathizer, opponent ▫ *It was Edmund Burke, by no means* ***a paid-up member*** *of the Angry Brigade, who reminded George III that the principle of governmental accountability had been settled once and for all when Charles I lost his head.* NS ▫ *I feel quite certain that there is something worrying the teachers apart from salary. If you said that everyone, however they were educated, if once they became* ***fully paid-up teachers*** *would earn the same, and if this same was substantially more than the teachers earn now, I still don't think that the status-seekers would be satisfied.* L ▫ *He was a smooth-tongued old reprobate who could talk to one's grandmother like* ***a paid-up supporter*** *of the Moral Rearmament League.* SC ▫ use is usu humorous though sometimes in sneering way.

a pain in the neck [Comp (NP)] (informal) sb/sth that is disliked, is annoying or tiresome; **V:** ⚠ be, become; find sb/sth ▫ *The way one man's meat is another man's poison, so one woman's ideal husband is another woman's* ***pain in the neck.*** TVT ▫ (reader's letter) *I don't often* see *Philip Jenkinson, as I find his mannerisms* ***a pain in the neck****, but I do read his film notes.* RT ▫ *We talked of everything save the war, and parted with alcoholic poisoning and a restored sense of proportion. They're a grand lot, these Free French, at heart — and stomach. But they're* ***a pain in the neck*** *to the British military mind.* SD ▫ *Moral choices, I thought, are* ***a pain in the neck.*** SML ▫ *Writing letters is* ***a pain in the neck*** *to me, and I arrange everything I possibly can by telephone and think the expense well worth it.* ▫ *Picnics are a treat to some and* ***a pain in the neck*** *to others.* ▫ almost always sing, even after pl S + V.

paint a gloomy etc picture (of sth) [V + O pass] describe events etc emphasizing their gloomy etc nature **adj:** gloomy, pleasant, depressing, frightening, rosy, more/less cheerful. **o:** events, conditions, circumstances; the future, tomorrow; the weather prospects, life in Britain ▫ *The weather forecast* ***paints a gloomy picture*** *for tomorrow. I think we can give up the idea of entertaining our guests in the garden.* ▫ *On the strength of a one-sided report by some academics, they* ***paint a rosy picture****, holding out expectations of local lads in managerial jobs, with rising demands for professional services of all kinds.* L ▫ *People who don't want to make room for them are naturally going to* ***paint the worst*** *possible* ***picture of*** *the habits and activities of any minority group, whether they be gypsies, West Indians, students or down-and-outs.* ▫ *After bad weather during the summer,* ***a gloomy picture*** *is* ***painted*** *for the harvest.*

paint the town red [V + O + Comp] enjoy a lively, boisterous time in public places, often attracting the notice of, or causing some disturbance to, other people ▫ *'I shan't be in for supper, I'm going out.'* ***'Painting the town red,*** *eh? Who's the lucky man? I mean you're not going on your own, are you?'* TGLY ▫ *Two thirds of the crew went on shore leave. They spent too much money,* ***painted the town red****, and one or two of them got themselves locked up and had to be bailed out next morning.* ▫ often preceded by *going to,* or used in past tense.

a paper tiger [Comp (NP)] a person, or group, that is less powerful, or dangerous, than he/it seems or claims to be **V:** ⚠ be; think sb; regard, consider, sb as □ *Goronwy Rees is a commentator rather than an advocate: the dragons are seen but not slain. Though, as he would be the first to admit, not a few of the dragons in these pendulum years have turned out to be only* ***paper tigers*** *in disguise.* L □ *The Chinese Communist Party today defended Mr Mao Tse-Tung's thesis that 'Imperialists are* ***paper tigers****' and that Communists must 'despise the enemy strategically while taking full account of him tactically!'* T □ *Mr Khruschev recently criticized the '****paper tiger****' idea, remarking that western tigers nowadays 'have nuclear teeth'.* T □ attrib use *the* ***paper tiger*** *idea.*

par excellence especially; pre-eminently; more/better than other people/things of his/its kind (from the French) □ *The United Nations, after all, is* ***par excellence*** *an instrument of the gradual readjustment of the status quo. Within it, élites talk to élites. The bureaucracy will carry on much as before.* NS □ *If Cooper has no notable works of scholarship or research to his name that is because he is,* ***par excellence****, a teacher.* □ usu in middle position.

(about) par for the course [Comp (NP)] (approximately) the usual standard of achievement, the normal procedure, time or effort expended, etc (from par = 'the number of strokes a good player should take for any or all holes of a particular golf-course') **V:** ⚠ be; think, find, sth □ *I intuitively sympathise with all those cool-headed sophisticates who argue that a bit of bugging and burglary is* ***par for the*** *American political* ***course****.* NS □ *How many people felt vicarious enjoyment when confronted with headlines which read: 'Headmaster Sacked in School Row'? The column inches written about him were tepidly for and yawningly against. Which is* ***about par for the course****.* G □ (I decided) *when I was prepared to repay it, what securities I could possibly put up as collateral, and prepared for the 20-minute argument with the bank manager which I seemed to recall was* ***about par for the course****.* ST □ *In the 12 minutes after the Queen's arrival, at least 50 people were presented to her before she unveiled the plaque, in the foyer—50 is* ***about par for the course****.* OBS

a paragon of virtue [Comp (NP)] a person without faults or vices **V:** ⚠ be; seem; find sb □ *The police argument* (is that) *an innocent man has nothing to fear from talking freely to a policeman. This reasoning might be acceptable if all policemen were* ***paragons of virtue****, which of course they cannot be.* NS □ *And every camp and unit has a certain amount of 'borrowing' from the establishment. I'm not accusing anyone of being dishonest, but neither would I insult the typical soldier by calling him* ***a paragon of virtue****.* RT

the parish pump a symbol of small-town gossip, purely local politics and interests (from, formerly, communal village pumps where neighbours would meet when drawing water) □ *As far as I could see, life as a revolutionary was much the same as life round* ***any*** *other* ***parish pump****: pretty damn dull to the passer-by.* PP □ *It is particularly necessary that member nations should learn to look outwards at what is going on in the world beyond the NATO area—and not just inwards at* ***their*** *own* ***parish pumps****.* MFM □ *For the Liberals, the survey will confirm that their new strategy of community politics, dismissed by their opponents as issue-dodging* ***parish-pumpery****, pays off and that even people with basically different outlooks respond to direct and repeated contact.* ST □ *Mr Edwards had obviously hoped the discussion would look to the future. As it was, the bulk of the audience took refuge in digging up the past, in* ***parish-pumping****, back-biting and mud-slinging—a not very edifying evening's viewing.* SC □ unusual n forms parish-pumpery and parish-pumping.

parity of esteem [O (NP)] (formal) equality in the degree of official or public regard, respect given to sb/sth, (the implication being that there is inequality in reward, in salary, etc) **V:** enjoy, have; grant, accord, sb □ *Despite their conviction that they are doing a worthwhile job, most polytechnics believe that, though the Government talks of '****parity of esteem****' between the two sectors of higher education, they are still given a raw deal in comparison with the universities.* OBS □ *In the consideration of an applicant's outside interests it is obvious that membership of a County Cricket Club and of a local Literary and Debating Society do not enjoy* ***parity of esteem****.*

part of the furniture/furnishings a person thought of as a permanent fixture in a house, office, institution etc and, as such, accepted, made use of, or ignored □ *The messenger 'boy' had been there so long he seemed to be* ***part of the*** *Bank* ***furnishings****. The thought that he might have a wife to go home to, that he might fall ill, or die, or wish to retire, never entered anybody's head.* □ *Otherwise, the sight of Mrs P complete with black hat and garish make-up might have proved irresistible. As it was, she was accepted as* ***part of the furniture****, at least until the grown-ups came at the end to collect their offspring.* TSMP

part and parcel of sth [Comp (NP)] an integral part of sth (parcel (archaic) = 'component of a whole') □ *Do I fight or flee? Do I conform or rebel? Do I put my foot down or let my children do as they please? These are fairly usual day-to-day decisions that are* ***part and parcel of*** *being human.* ST □ *Visconti's last film, made when he was a sick man, is hardly his best, but still full of his feeling for style as* ***part and parcel of*** *content.* G □ *Assault and robbery, cattle-driving and train-wrecking were* ***part and parcel of*** *his terrorizing tactics.* PP □ *Both girls* (school children—one too fat, one too thin) *suffer at the hands of their friends from jibes and teasing. But nothing is ever going to stop; it is* ***part and parcel of*** *being young.* RT □ part and parcel non-rev; no pl form.

a Parthian/parting shot/shaft an action, gesture, remark etc esp of a hostile or critical kind, made at the moment of departure or in other circumstances which make a reply impossible (the ancient Parthians are said, even when in retreat, to have continued hurling missiles at the enemy) □ (Virginia has married against her mother Helen's wishes, instead of accompanying her to America) *Virginia* *throught that it* (the letter) *was* ***a parting shot*** *from Helen, or, less likely, a gesture of reconciliation; but it was not Helen's writing.* AITC ▫ (house prices) *At the end of the report we are still not much nearer explaining what was special about 1971. As* ***a parting shot****, the Building Societies Association refers to 'low supply' causing a dearth of properties on the market.* ST ▫ *Robert Robinson is an unparalleled performer on radio and television. Nobody thinks as quickly on his feet; nobody steps into a verbal dust-up with more relish; and nobody is his peer when it comes to loosing* ***the Parthian shaft****.* L ▫ also pl; shaft less common than shot.

a/the parting of the ways [O/o (NP)] a place where a road, or route, branches; (fig) a point when one must decide on a course of action that excludes another or others **V:** reach; come to, be at ▫ *It is at this point that the country came to* ***a parting of the ways****. It was the basic error in the manner in which the Government responded to the threat of economic recession which led to the chain of disasters from which we are now suffering.* NS ▫ *I had to find myself a play and a new management. Hugh Beaumont, of H.M. Tennent, with whom I had been closely connected for much of my theatrical life, and I had come to* ***the parting of the ways****.* OBS

a/one's party piece [O (NP)] a particular song, piano piece, recitation etc that one performs well enough to offer, or be asked for, to entertain friends at a party etc; an item of a person's repertoire that is (too) often included in performances **V:** ⚠ do, perform, give ▫ *James hasn't done* ***his party piece*** *yet. Come on, James, we can't let our southern visitors go without hearing my favourite Scots song.* ▫ *Doubtless the '****party piece****' feeling will persist as long as Walton seems willing to be known as the composer of only half a dozen continually available works.* L ▫ attrib use *the* ***party piece*** *feeling.*

pass all understanding [V + O] lie beyond the range of the human mind; (exaggeratedly) exceed what sb finds reasonable or likely; pass (sb's) comprehension (qv) ▫ (source) *And the peace of God, which* ***passeth all understanding****, shall keep your hearts and minds through Christ Jesus.* PHILIPPIANS IV 7 ▫ (transcendental perception) *This given reality is an infinite which* ***passes all understanding*** *and yet admits of being directly and in some sort totally apprehended.* DOP ▫ *How any politician could imagine that, in a world war, Britain could avoid sending her army to fight alongside the French,* ***passes all understanding****.* MFM

pass the buck [V + O pass] (informal) evade responsibility, or blame, by shifting or attributing it to another (from the card game of poker, an object passed to the dealer but no longer used in the game) ▫ *The Minister of the Interior is roused from his bed. Off he goes to* ***pass the buck*** *to his suave Chef de Cabinet, who dumps it in the Police Commissioner's lap.* OBS ▫ *If you lose a race, it's always a question of* ***passing the buck****. The owner blames the trainer, because the trainer told him the horse would win. The trainer can't admit he's wrong, so who's he going to blame? The jockey.* RT ▫ *For most members of the staff it is a complex situation and it can produce a whole range of unpleasant practices, such as making doubly sure that someone above you has initialled all your items of work so that, in case of unpleasant repercussions,* ***the buck*** *has been* ***passed****.* L ▫ *The reaction from some of the other boroughs, however, bodes ill for any rapid improvement. They comprise a mixture of* ***buck-passing****, half truths, petulant lectures about their own impotence in the matter.* NS ▫ n compound buck-passing. ⇨ the buck stops here.

pass (sb's) comprehension etc be too difficult for sb to understand or accept; pass all understanding (qv) **S:** it, that; behaviour, cruelty, kindness. **O:** comprehension, ⚠ understanding; belief ▫ *What comes over people in the January sales* ***passes my comprehension****.* ▫ *He talked in terms of figures that* ***pass the comprehension of*** *most people.* ▫ *I'm not* against *drink, I just don't like the stuff. I expect, to you, that* ***passes understanding****.* ▫ *'They clear £10,000—£12,000 a year in that crummy little café.' 'No!' 'It* ***passes belief****, I know, but I've seen the auditors' statements with my own eyes.'* ▫ S cannot refer to a person.

pass muster be among those of a number of persons or things interviewed, inspected, examined etc that are found to be adequate **S:** argument, case; work, studies; decorating, carpentry ▫ *Faulty arguments, which the statistician would recognize as such immediately, often* ***pass muster*** *in the popular Press because they are disguised in such a way that their statistical nature is not recognized.* SNP ▫ *Though my work at school was never as good as it could have been, it* ***passed muster*** *and I even did well.* ST ▫ *The argument that the Government have made no serious attempt to defend the long-term interests of New Zealand also does not* ***pass muster****.* SC

pass (the) time [V + O] fill, make less tedious, (periods of) time when one needs distraction from boredom, impatience, anxiety etc ▫ *Inevitably, therefore, television is in perpetual danger of being turned into a mere domestic appliance for* ***passing the time****, painless and undemanding.* NS ▫ *I suggested that we should perhaps fish —to* ***pass the time*** *I said, but of course we all realised that it was for our next meal.* BM ▫ *I fell in with anything anybody suggested, chiefly because one way of* ***passing time*** *seemed as good as another till I could get back to London and see Philip again.* ▫ cf *pass one's time (doing sth)* which has positive or purposeful implications.

pass the time of day (with sb) offer, or exchange, a short greeting; make a comment, or a few remarks, about the weather or some other general topic, eg 'Good morning!', 'Cold, isn't it?', 'Baby looks well!', 'Rushing as usual, I see!' **o:** her; my neighbour, the traffic warden; other strollers in the park ▫ *I gave it to one of the priests there. He knows me. I've* ***passed the time of day with*** *him on the street. You know the way they'll talk to anybody.* AITC ▫ *This room was referred to by Robert and me as the big room, and by its racier inhabitants, I gleaned from* ***passing the time of day with*** *them in the lavatory, as the snake-pit.* SML ▫ *I wonder if there really is anything in the wind, or whether this man has just dropped in to* ***pass the time of day****.* NM ▫ (NONCE) *Florentines might have stepped out of a crowd scene in any of the old-master* *frescoes. Expert* ***passers of the time of day****, they charm, they accommodate, they bawl appalling intimacies in public.* RT

patience is a virtue (saying) usu a comment on an occasion when patience is shown or needed □ ***Patience is a virtue****/Possess it if you can./It's seldom found in woman/And never found in man.* ANON □ *Most of us agree that* ***patience is a virtue****, 'and at times,' says Jack, 'I wish I were more slow and patient as an actor. But if I took more time, I'd lose my momentum because I operate best under pressure.'* TVT □ *'When am I going to get my lunch? It's after one already.' 'Now, now. You'll get it as soon as I can manage. Remember that* ***patience is a virtue****.'*

patriotism is the last refuge of a scoundrel (saying) a claim to patriotism may be the only good thing to be said of a scoundrel, or it may be made an excuse for crimes or faults (source, as headphrase, SAMUEL JOHNSON, 1709-84, but often adapted) □ *And Burton's second reason for doing these Jubilee plays: was it a fit of patriotism? 'I suppose I'm as patriotic as the next man. Besides, as Dr Johnson said, "****Patriotism is the last refuge of a scoundrel****" and I'm a bit of a scoundrel.'* RT □ *Bottomley's rise to wealth and fame and his ignominious fall is the kind of fantastic story that needs no embellishment. His patriotic speeches during the 1914-1918 war pulled in the recruits and put money in Bottomley's pocket. In his case Dr Johnson's saying that* ***patriotism is the last refuge of a scoundrel*** *was apt for once.* SC □ (NONCE) *'Why Sandhurst then?' 'My father dropped hints about it and, at the time, it seemed like a good idea.' But he admitted that his real love is diplomacy, which he describes as '****the last refuge of the*** *incurable* ***romantic****'.* RT □ (NONCE) *To brand yourself a puritan is only slightly less damaging than to let it be known that you are, on the whole, in favour of respectability. To approve of respectability is* ***the last refuge of a suburban mind****.* SC □ as explained, headphrase is ambiguous in meaning.

patriotism is not enough (saying) there are values and considerations more important than the defence, or prosperity, of one's country □ (source) *I realize that* ***patriotism is not enough****. I must have no hatred or bitterness towards anyone.* EDITH CAVELL (last words of a British nurse before being executed in 1915 for assisting wounded prisoners-of-war to escape) □ (remembering a friend killed in World War I) *I am no more reconciled to his death, or persuaded that it was necessary, than I am to the death of all those slaughtered contemporaries of many nations. Perhaps after all the greatest thing said in those days was that '****patriotism is not enough****'. It took a woman to say that.* AH □ (NONCE) *Personally I feel a demand for simplicity in my Christmas music which has eluded many great composers. But simplicity, like* ***patriotism, is not enough****.* RT

the patter of little/tiny feet (facetious) (the sound of) young children in the home, around one □ (source) *I hear in the chamber above me/* ***The patter of little feet****,/The sound of a door that is opened,/And voices soft and sweet.* THE CHILDREN'S HOUR (H W LONGFELLOW 1807-82) □ (reader's letter, from a married woman) *There is distinct disapproval of the fact that I enjoy my job when I should be yearning for* ***the patter of tiny feet****.* OBS □ *'You've got my mother's granny-complex going again, inviting us here,' said Anne. 'She can't wait for* ***the patter of little feet****.'* □ often used with reference to the *desire* to have a child.

(a) Paul Pry a meddlesome, inquisitive, but not necessarily malicious, person (from the central character of the comedy, PAUL PRY (JOHN POOLE 1786-1872)); a Nosey Parker (qv) □ *He poked his head forward like* ***a*** *born* ***Paul Pry****, put out his hand and said 'Good afternoon. Won't you sit down?'* PP □ *'I don't intrude, I hope?' he says—* ***Paul Pry****—and all the time he knows he damn well does intrude, but he can't contain his curiosity.*

pay (sb) a compliment [V + IO + O pass] say, or do, sth that expresses admiration of sb or of his actions **IO:** manager, workforce; colleague, wife. **adj:** great, unexpected, doubtful. **A:** on her appearance, on their speeches; about his cooking; in/by coming here tonight; by their presence □ *'I should have been more use to him than any of you.' I said: 'I believe you would.' She flashed out: 'It isn't often you* ***pay me a compliment****.' 'It was meant.' I said.* NM □ *The old chap hardly ever leaves the house now. He's* ***paid you a*** *great* ***compliment*** *in coming to hear you speak tonight.* □ *'What a charming man!' 'He sets out to be a great one for* ***paying compliments to*** *the ladies and all that.'* □ *Being* ***paid*** *fulsome* ***compliments*** *on my ability to manage had become insufficient recompense for being given too much to do.* □ *Of course I don't object. I haven't taken out copyrights on my teaching methods. If a colleague* ***pays*** *me* ***the compliment of*** *adopting any of them, I am only too pleased.* □ variants pay sb the compliment of doing sth, pay (sb) compliments; the second variant usu used to express complimentary remarks (cf pay/give/offer/send one's compliments (to sb) = 'convey greetings, in person, in writing or through sb else (to sb)').

pay a dividend [V + O] provide benefit, reward, good results **S:** the undertaking, his bold policy, a little extra care. **adj:** good, big, handsome, unexpected □ *By the middle of May I had visited every formation in the United Kingdom. It was an immense undertaking but I believe that it* ***paid a*** *good* ***dividend****.* MFM □ *All the scientists they wanted were working elsewhere on work that would* ***pay dividends*** *in one year or two, not in the remote future.* NM □ *Unlike most managers in Irish football, Tuohy was given a free hand and he quit just when his methods looked like* ***paying a*** *handsome* ***dividend****.* ST □ *You know as well as I do that honesty has never* ***paid*** *what one would call* ***a*** *thumping* ((informal) = very large) ***dividend****.* DC □ *Its wires were tapped, and for months Dubois's chief assistant listened to every word exchanged by phone. Dubois passed the recordings to his good friend, Mercier. Before long this arrangement began to* ***pay*** *big* ***dividends****.* TO □ adj usu present when dividend sing.

pay the penalty (of sth/doing sth) [V + O] suffer as a result of wrong-doing, error, misfortune; next entry (qv) **o:** folly, improvidence, self-indulgence; being too generous, honest; selling too early, not having an agent □ *I had drunk not wisely but too well and* ***paid the***

penalty of *my folly with a severe headache next morning.* □ *The keen competition for business that followed the removal of restrictions meant that many companies allowed extremely easy terms, and it is now that they are* ***paying the penalty.*** T □ *I attempted to relieve the enemy pressure on the Fifth Army at Salerno, but* ***paid the penalty of*** *finding my own reserves were exhausted and that supplies to replenish them were not forthcoming.* MFM □ *Young* ***paid the penalty of*** *his craft, which decrees that the manager* (of a football team) *must be blamed for disappointing results irrespective of who is at fault: it is manifestly the directors themselves in this case.* ST

pay a/the price (for sth) [V + O pass] suffer a loss or disadvantage, either in return for something else gained, or as a penalty for wrong-doing or error; previous entry (qv) **adj:** heavy, considerable; small, high. **o:** error, miscalculation; treason, disloyalty □ *Indeed once-demoralised villagers have been considerably fortified by the presence of the Fouj. But they* ***pay a heavy price****. As guerilla action intensifies. . .* NS □ *Everything conspired to convince one that this* (play) *was truth, not fictional contrivance. Of course* ***a price*** *sometimes has to be* ***paid for*** *verisimilitude. The narrative-line was sometimes hard to follow, and so were the Liverpool accents.* NS □ *Cacoyannis says that normally he finds it imperative to live alone. Even to have a maid living in his Montmartre flat 'brings an obligation', he says. 'When you want company, sometimes you don't get it: that's* ***the price*** *one* ***pays.****'* OBS □ *Measures to reduce the use of motor vehicles inside cities would be a superficial inconvenience but it would be* ***a*** *small* ***price to pay*** *if it saved cities from strangulation or destruction by urban motorways.* ST □ *There would no doubt be a lot of vulgarity, a little disorder—but that would not* ***be too high a price to pay for*** *the rediscovery of the election as public festival.* SC □ *He is an accomplished speaker, in a style which is unmistakably his own; and if he makes the occasional silly remark that* ***is a small price to pay for*** *the avoidance of bromides.* OBS □ variants be a heavy/small price to pay (for sth), no price is too high to pay.

pay one's/its way [V +O] maintain oneself/ itself from what is earned income from work, or services, without getting into debt; earn one/it's keep (qv) **S:** he, she, we; country, institution, enterprise; plant, machinery □ *You may have yer 'ead* (= your head) *full of fine ideas, you may be able to live on air and big talk, but the rest of us 'ave* (= have) *to* ***pay our way****—and pay it with money!* HD □ (the Cultural Revolution, China) *The villagers speak well of the Red Guards. 'They* ***paid their way****.' (They were issued with coupons with which their hosts could draw supplies from the country stores.)* L □ *It gradually became obvious that Britain could no longer* ***pay her way*** *alone. We had entered the war as the world's biggest creditor: we had emerged as the world's biggest debtor.* L

peace and good will [n + n non-rev] peaceful conditions (esp contrasted with war or hostility) characterized by friendly and helpful intentions **V:** bring, promote, show; be a/the time/ occasion of □ (source) *Glory to God in the highest, and on earth* ***peace, good will*** *toward men.* LUKE II 14 □ *The first thing the delegation did when it got to San Francisco to help in founding the United Nations and bringing* ***peace and good will*** *to everybody was to switch its entire set of hotel reservations.* L □ *I think we should bury the hatchet and invite them to spend Christmas with us as we used to. It is supposed to be the season of* ***peace and goodwill*** *after all.* □ goodwill, written as one word or two, or hyphenated.

peace in our time freedom, or deliverance, from war during our lifetime; peace as a fact, not something to be hoped and worked for in the future; peace for us now, whatever may happen to others in the future □ (source) *Give* ***peace in our time****, O Lord. Because there is none other that fighteth for us, but only thou, O God.* BOOK OF COMMON PRAYER □ *It is also natural enough to recall the Munich betrayal of 1938 when the British Government — and, lamentably, for a moment the 'New Statesman' — thought selling Czechoslovakia was a bargain for '****peace in our time****'.* NS

one's (own) peace of mind freedom from anxiety, guilt, fear **det:** one's; no, a little □ *I could see that the Earls Court Road phase of my life was over, and that* ***that peace of mind*** *was gone beyond recall. Madge had forced a crisis on me.* UTN □ DOCTOR: *And goodbye, goodbye, goodbye. I'm talking to* ***my peace of mind****, that's all. To my careless existence! Goodbye!* THH □ *It all represents, no doubt, the reaction of an impatient and frustrated man. But for* ***his own peace of mind****—as well as for that of the world—Mr Nixon only needs to come to terms with one simple fact.* NS □ *It was an unkind, stupid thing to say and I shall have* ***no peace of mind*** *until I've apologized and been forgiven.*

peace and plenty [n + n non-rev] freedom from foreign wars or internal disturbance, lawlessness etc together with prosperous, or comfortable, conditions of life **V:** live in, enjoy; be a land of □ *These lush, well-watered islands ought to have been a land of* ***peace and plenty.*** □ *The mellow perfection of house and gardens suggested a home where generations of a family had lived in* ***peace and plenty.*** □ *Two little girls, in long white nightdresses accompanied the Queen of the Festival. One carried a cardboard dove and the other a cornucopia, to represent* ***Peace and Plenty.***

peace and quiet [n + n non-rev] freedom from physical, or mental, disturbance caused by others or by one's surroundings **V:** get, want, enjoy. **prep:** for (= to get); for the sake of. **det:** some, a little, a bit of □ (She was) *so desperate that you eventually drove her away to find a place where she could get some* ***peace and quiet.*** AITC □ *Sussex, with its fabulous beauty, its groomed cottages, its glossy cows and immense trees, was to him a stage-set, a fake, something supported by the prosperous in search of* ***peace and quiet*** *and food in their weekends out of town.* HD □ *The police chief himself, hearing of our assault upon the door of the bank, had relented and sent someone to the bank manager, suggesting something be done for* ***peace and quiet.*** BM □ *'The kids are just going to sit around whining and grumbling all afternoon if they can't go skating with their friends.' 'Oh, all right then' he said crossly, slap-*

ping a fiver down on the table, 'anything for a bit of ***peace and quiet****.'*

peace with honour peace, instead of war, on conditions that do not discredit either side (the reference being either to the avoidance of war or to the terms on which a war has been, or should be, ended) □ *Lord Salisbury and myself have brought you back peace—but a* ***peace*** *I hope* ***with honour****, which may satisfy our Sovereign and tend to the welfare of the country.* LORD BEACONSFIELD (on his return from the Congress of Berlin, 1878) □ *It is two years now since the Paris Agreement was signed in the name of* ***Peace with Honour****, and both sides are insisting so rigidly upon what they conceive to be their honour that there still is no peace.* L □ *The dishonesty of the Nixon Administration was nurtured during the time when the war in Vietnam was described as a moral crusade and the cease-fire as '****peace with honour****'.* NS

a pearl of great price (formal) sb/sth precious and of great worth, that should be valued highly □ (source) *The Kingdom of heaven is like unto a merchant man, seeking goodly pearls: who, when he had found* ***one pearl of great price****, went and sold all that he had, and bought it.* MATTHEW XIII 45-6 □ *But the result has been a mutual confidence between you and me, and mutual confidence between a commander and his troops is* ***a pearl of*** *very* ***great price****.* MFM □ *Her mother was at pains to make clear to him that in marrying Felicia he would be acquiring* ***a pearl of great price****.* □ occas pl pearls of great price.

the pearly gate(s) (usu facetious) the gates of heaven (of which St Peter is, in Christian mythology, the custodian), in allusion to St John's vision of heaven □ (source) *And the twelve* ***gates*** *were twelve* ***pearls****; every several* ***gate*** *was of one* ***pearl****.* REVELATION XXI 21 □ *When he did die he would find St Peter at* ***the Pearly Gate*** *looking at his watch and saying: 'Oh, Standish, you're just in time.'* TGLY □ *To ensure popularity in the hereafter,* (he) *has persuaded a local bishop to bless his earthly habitation, champagne whirlpool bubble tub and all. Given that his main design idea is sticking twinkly bits on himself and his belongings,* ***the pearly gates*** *should make him feel at home.* L

a peck(ing) order (informal) a graded system that determines who dominates, or is dominated by others, in a poultry flock, or in a group of animals or people □ *The whole flock* (of chickens) *could be ranked according to* ***the*** *so-called* ***peck order****. The top bird in the flock displaced all the others, the second bird could only be pecked by the top one, and so on.* NS □ *Within each* (chimpanzee) *community there is a hierarchical system,* ***a peck order****, where males are dominant to females, with an order of dominance within the sexes. At top is the chief male, to whom all others bow.* SC □ *All unsupervised working-class children settle their disputes and* ***pecking orders*** *by fighting.* ST □ *That painful experience was a lesson for medium-sized countries which try to save bigger neighbours from their own folly. There is* ***a pecking order*** *beyond which it is unsafe to venture.* NS

a peeping Tom sb who furtively and secretly looks into house windows etc in order to see people undress, make love, etc (from 'Peeping Tom of Coventry', a tailor who was said to have been the only person to peep through his window at Godiva, wife of an 11th c Lord of Coventry, when she rode naked through the town on horseback) □ (referring to a television programme) *A person under hypnosis is Godiva. Decent people should turn away their eyes. This programme is making us all into* ***Peeping Toms****.* SC □ *This family has every right to live its life its own way, so long as it is lawful. Private lives should remain private and '****peeping Tom****' instincts do no one any credit.* RT □ (resentment towards tourists) *What an insult to treat us as if we were simply picturesque. We're not picturesque: we are living our lives in our own way. What is this stranger but* ***a peeping Tom****?* L □ *But there is another more positive argument for a move towards the open society, whether or not it reduces corruption or discourages '****peeping Tom****' journalists.* NS □ attrib use *a* ***peeping Tom*** *photographer.*

a peg to hang sth (on/upon) a topic, occasion, incident used as an opportunity, or pretext, for expressing one's views etc **O:** his views, (their) dislike of their neighbours; Jack's dismissal □ *Whatever subject the professor lectures on nowadays you can depend on him to make it* ***a peg to hang*** *his own religious views* ***on****.* □ *Peter Sedgwick takes as his starting point a day of demonstrations against German rearmament in 1955 and uses it as* ***a peg to hang*** *an analysis of some of the general characteristics of the British Labour movement in these post-war years.* NS □ *Nemone Lethbridge, for example, claims Gabrielle was persecuted for her left-wing connections and classroom informality. 'Her subsequent affair with a pupil was* ***a*** *convenient* ***peg upon which to hang*** *her martydom.'* L

the pen is mightier than the sword (saying) statesmen, writers, philosophers etc direct and control world and human affairs, changes, progress more effectively and lastingly than conquerors, leaders of armies; legislation, persuasion and instruction can do more than the use of armed force □ (source—itself based on older variants) *Beneath the rule of men entirely great/****The pen is mightier than the sword****.* RICHELIEU (E G BULWER-LYTTON 1803-73) □ (after having been wounded in war) *I had time for reflection in hospital and came to the conclusion that the old adage was probably correct:* ***the pen was mightier than the sword****. I joined the staff.* MFM □ *And just as those whom the press criticises may show great powers of resistance, those whom the press sets out to elevate are not always raised. If Lord Lytton really thought* ***the pen was mightier than the sword****, he must have made a great opponent in a duel.* NS □ (NONCE) (para-military violence compared with law enforcement by the police) *It quickly became apparent that* ***the gun is mightier than the whistle.*** G □ (NONCE) *Doodle expert Michael Bentine gets together with Spike Milligan in 'Quick on the Draw' to show that* ***the pen*** *can* ***be*** *just* ***as mighty as the*** (spoken) ***word*** *when it comes to raising laughs.* TVT

a pen portrait a written description □ *Each week in its heyday the 'Isis' provided* ***a pen portrait*** *of one of the big men on the Oxford* *campus: a printed 'This is Your Life'.* NS ▫ also pl.

pennies from heaven unexpected, or incidental, benefits in money or other form ▫ *The Vicar, like his wife, counts his blessings, loves the house, but knows that the Church cannot bank on* ***pennies from heaven****. 'I think it is totally unjustifiable to keep houses of this kind; considering the sort of expense that's involved in their upkeep and maintenance.'* L ▫ *'Who would expect a day like this at the end of November?'* ***'Pennies from heaven****, you could say. What a pity we can't make better use of it than this.'* ▫ *Every time it rains, it rains* ***pennies from heaven****./Don't you know each cloud contains* ***pennies from heaven****.* POPULAR SONG (T BURKE and A JOHNSTON)

penny dreadful (weekly) paper of a crude, sensational kind aimed at older children ▫ *If Victorian children liked to be amused, and occasionally scared, they were also supposed to be edified. Good parents ensured that their offspring read not just* ***penny dreadful*** *comics, but moral stories like 'The Wide Wide World' and, of course, 'Little Women'.* RT ▫ also pl; attrib use *a* ***penny dreadful*** *comic.*

the penny drops (informal) one now understands sth that was previously unnoticed or puzzling (from machines where a coin must drop down from a slot before it can work the mechanism that delivers a bar of chocolate, ticket etc, or releases a door lock) ▫ *I gradually froze, to such an extent that I eventually found myself huddled over the blurred picture thinking how poor it was and that there wasn't even a commentary. It was quite a time before* ***the penny dropped****. I suppose I can now claim the doubtful distinction of being the only BBC commentator who has actually forgotten to commentate.* ST ▫ ***The penny*** *is finally* ***dropping*** *for investors with matured National Savings Certificates.* (Our) *recent campaign for a better deal on National Savings showed that there is general ignorance of the abysmally low interest rate being paid on these matured certificates.* OBS ▫ *Why he is silly is hard to say at first—until, as Mr Powell might say,* ***the penny drops****.* L

a penny for your thoughts (informal) tell me what you are thinking about ▫ ***'A penny for your thoughts****,' Muriel said suddenly. 'My thoughts?' Bill ejaculated with a startled expression. 'Oh, my thoughts? I really don't know. Not worth a penny anyway.'* RM ▫ ***'Penny for them****, Miss Elliot?' She turned from the window as though she had only just that second stopped to glance out on her way up. 'Hello, Mr Woodgate—'* TT ▫ *Watching Enoch Powell cheerfully swapping compliments with Robin Day on Monday night, I found it hard to fathom his real thoughts.* ***I'd give****, though, a good deal more than* ***a penny for them****.* NS ▫ said to sb who looks abstracted; variants I'll give you a penny for your thoughts, (a) penny for them/'em.

penny plain or twopence/tuppence coloured in cheap or more expensive (attractive or merely showy) form (from, formerly, paper cut-outs of characters and scenery for toy theatres) ▫ *Adapter Ian Cotterell describes the eight-part serialisation of 'Hard Times' as part reading, part dramatisation; a radio way, as he puts it, of presenting Dickens '****penny plain and tuppence coloured****'.* RT ▫ *Frances shows surprisingly good taste when you allow her to choose a garment for herself; not like her sister, who always comes down strongly in favour of* ***the twopence coloured****.* ▫ both parts of headphrase can be used alone and allusively, as shown in second example.

penny wise (and) pound foolish [adj + adj non-rev] (saying) economical in small things but extravagant and reckless in larger and/or unnecessary items of expenditure ▫ *'I never waste food.' 'But you're often* ***penny wise and pound foolish*** *even in that. I've known you buy a tin of fruit and a jar of cream to embellish some stale sponge-cake, when it would have been cheaper to throw it out and make a rice pudding.'* ▫ HELEN: *Oh! My fur! Do you like it? It's a wedding present from that young man of mine. He spends his money like water, you know,* ***penny wise, pound foolish****.* TOH ▫ (NONCE) ***'Penny wise or pound foolish****?' Play this fascinating game and find out what sort of woman you are with money.* WI ▫ (NONCE) *He's only in business in a small way and it seems to be getting smaller. Mind you, he keeps his end up by economizing on paying his round* (ie of drinks, when with friends). ***Penny wise and pound wise*** *as well.* TGLY ▫ (NONCE) *Hughie admits to being* ***pound-wise*** *(boats don't depreciate although it is unlikely they keep pace with inflation) and* ***penny-foolish****. Hughie, who thinks nothing of sailing off on his own to Boulogne or even as far afloat as Oslo, ran aground in the Thames Estuary. 'We'd been too mean to buy new charts,' he says.* TVT

people who live in glass houses shouldn't throw stones (saying) one should not criticize others for faults and mistakes similar to those which one has oneself ▫ *'He got that job through influence, not on merit —what are you looking at me like that for? It's true, isn't it?' 'Of course, it's true, but I was thinking that* ***people who live in glass houses shouldn't throw stones****.'* ▫ (NONCE) (reader's letter) *I fell out of my chair* (= I laughed heartily) *at breakfast when I saw Eric Hobsbawm accuse* anyone *of being a 'remote doctrinaire'; not being at a plate-****glass*** *university* (ie one of the newest universities) *of course, he can afford to* ***throw stones****.* NS ▫ (NONCE) *We would like the rich to acknowledge that all their talk and advice on the economy, and their continual admonishment to the rest of us to pull up our socks, is for them a part-time exercise. What really concerns them and occupies their waking hours is the acquisition of personal wealth. Every time they pretend otherwise they* ***aim a brick*** *straight through their own precious* ***glass house****.* OBS

perfidious Albion the treacherous, untrustworthy English (translated from the French *Albion perfide*) ▫ *One might have expected Community membership to bury phrases like '****perfidious Albion****' for ever. But after not hearing it for years, I've heard it and read it three or four times in the past three months.* L ▫ *The French laughed at the English, did not trust them, and invented such phrases as '****Perfidious Albion****'. I understand Michelin have issued a guide to British hotels and restaurants, not so much to guide the uninitiated as to make it clear that not* *one British restaurant deserved three rosettes.* TVT

a period piece a novel, play, film, that reproduces the activities, life-styles and manners of a previous era; a building, article of furniture, dress etc surviving from, and typical of, a previous era □ *'Follow Me'* (a film) *gave me an eerie sense of having strayed into a projection room where they've not bothered to change the reels since 1955. It's* ***a period piece****, directed at a distance by Carol Reed from a script by Peter Shaffer, reworking his stage play, 'The Public Eye'.* NS □ *'What about the old lady's furniture?' 'Mostly junk, but there are two or three* ***period pieces****, a German wall-clock for instance, that would fetch a bit of money.'*

perish the thought (that) may the thought, idea (that sth may happen) never become fact □ ***Perish the thought that*** *Scotland with so many glorious links with Europe should take fright at the prospect of moving in with the Six.* SC □ *He imagined his young daughter saying 'She's Mr Goodrich's dolly girl, really, but he keeps her here and sometimes he lets Daddy play with her.'* ***Perish the thought!*** PW □ *For someone who says: 'Television is a girl's best friend,' it's a while since Aimi has been seen. 'I'd hate to think that people have forgotten all about me and how clever I can be,' she says.* ***Perish the thought****.* TVT □ expression is always imperative, sometimes introducing a *that*-cl, sometimes in middle position (eg as a disj in parenthesis), or in end position as comment.

the permissive society the kind of society (eg Great Britain since the 1960s) that tolerates freedom of moral choice to its members in everything except criminal activity, and esp freedom in sexual relationships **det:** the, this, a □ *Oxford footnote to* ***the permissive society****: Somerville College* (for women) *has this term allowed men into breakfast on Saturdays and Sundays. Apparently the college authorities, having sensibly decided they cannot possibly stop men staying overnight, are hoping that this tactical concession will limit such activities to the weekends.* NS □ *Tony and Jacky have one of the most unconventional relationships on the theatrical scene. They don't live together and they are both wary of marriage. 'For these* ***permissive society*** *days I suppose we're positively old-fashioned.'* TVT □ attrib use ***permissive society*** *days, morals, standards.*

one's pet aversion/hate [Comp (NP)] (cliché) sb/sth one dislikes more than anything else, or dislikes very much **V:** ⚠ be; become, make sb/sth □ *Having made that trivial criticism, I hasten to say that any list implicitly condemning three of* ***my 'pet aversions'*** *commands my instant and fervent admiration.* ST □ *In the reshuffle she was given a table to share with Judy, who was* ***her pet aversion****.* □ *The old lady produced with some pride a steaming dish of mussels—not knowing they were* ***a pet aversion of*** *my father's.* □ *I expect, like most of us, you have '****pet-hates****'. I can't stand someone who says on meeting: 'How are you?' and before you can answer goes on and on about her own problems.* TVT

a Peter Pan [Comp (NP)] an adult who in some mental, or emotional, respect has not fully grown up (from the title and central character of the play by J M BARRIE 1860-1937) **V:** ⚠ be; remain, find sb □ *In his boyish enthusiasms and lack of respect for conventional values, Frank was a bit of* ***a Peter Pan*** *to his dying day.* □ (reply to reader's letter) *I think your letter should be more tinged with pride than frustration that after all these years your husband is still jealous. When faced with* ***a Peter Pan*** *of your husband's vintage, I'd tell him that you're tickled pink that he feels this way about you. Don't grumble.* TVT □ (NONCE) *Brautigan has never allowed the reality-principles to get him down. Unlike most of his countrymen, nagged at by their psychiatrists to grow up and assume responsibility, he has elected to live in* ***a Peter-Panery*** *of his imagination.* SC

(arise/rise like) a phoenix from the ashes (be) (like) sb/sth reborn after apparent death or destruction (from the Phoenix, a mythical Arabian bird, the only one of its kind, which lived 2,000 years, then set itself on fire, and re-emerged as new) □ *There is an annual political event that we can call* ***Phoenix-from-the-ashes****. It consists of Mr Harold Wilson doing his turn at the Party conference. This performance follows numerous predictions of trouble at the grass roots, and doubts as to whether he is any longer in control of the party. Mr Wilson duly receives a standing ovation. All the papers write 'Wilson triumphs', 'undisputed master'.* NS □ *The story has a happy ending though—as factual stories tend to do. Hunslet RL* (Rugby League) *Football Club has* ***arisen like a phoenix from the ashes****, and under brand new management to boot.* RT □ *Genetic immortality can hardly be equated with* ***a phoenix rising from its ashes****; the strain is pretty diluted by the time a third generation baby sits on his great-grandfather's knee.* SC

physician, heal thyself (saying) doctors, lawyers, ministers of religion, teachers etc sometimes cannot do for themselves what they profess to be able to do for others □ (source) *And he said unto them, Ye will surely say unto me this proverb,* ***Physician, heal thyself****: whatsoever we have heard done in Capernaum, do also here in thy country.* LUKE IV 23 □ *Estée Lauder, grand lady of the beauty* (ie cosmetics) *business says of her male competitors: 'They are all jealous of me because it takes a woman to know what it* feels *like.' On the other hand, there is the* ***doctor-heal-thyself*** *thing—it really would not do for the manufacturer herself to be covered in blackheads and spots.* ST □ *For the moment he felt ashamed at having dropped that girl-finding project* (for a friend who couldn't get girls to 'date' him) *so thoroughly, before recollecting the duty of* ***physicians*** *to* ***heal themselves****. He went to the phone and dialled.* TGLY □ thyself = 'yourself'; expression usu a form of reproach.

pick sb's brain(s) [V + O pass] obtain information from sb (esp sb with greater or more specialized knowledge of a subject) for one's own use □ *If these supplicants realize that they are* ***picking the brain*** *and soliciting the help* ***of*** *a professional man, they do not always show it, either by offering him a fee, making him a present, or even thanking him.* AH □ *You're lucky to have him* (as your estate-agent), *Mrs Merton. There isn't a better man in Barsetshire. We must*

pick *his* ***brains*** *about Starveacres Hatches, Sally. I want to know if there's really a spring in the river bed.* WDM ▫ *'Oh Jack, before you ring off, do you mind if I* ***pick*** *your* ***brains*** *on a minor legal matter?' 'Not at all—if it's anything I can help you with.'*

pick and choose [v + v non-rev] select one, or some, from a number of possible alternatives (the implication usu being an over-fastidious process of rejection and selection) **O:** one's work-mates, who(m) one works with; what job one likes, which subjects one will study ▫ *Persons can make up their own minds with whom they will work because there are plenty of people close at hand from whom to* ***pick and choose.*** NDN ▫ *Unless the law is changed and dentists are no longer allowed to* ***pick and choose*** *whom they will treat and what work they will carry out under the NHS. . .* OBS ▫ *The tragedy is that what is called social violence sometimes attracts genuinely idealistic and otherwise respectable people. But you can't* ***pick and choose*** *which laws you obey.* L ▫ *By the time she had finished* ***picking and choosing*** *there was a queue of customers reaching nearly to the door.*

pick one's nose etc [V + O] remove (often idly or unconsciously) dirt from the nostrils etc with a finger(nail) **O:** nose, ⚠ ears, teeth, nails ▫ *. . .old or down-and-out men in reading-rooms of public libraries. A few resume their endless cult reading; some turn leaves aimlessly or stare blankly for ten minutes at one page; some just sit and look at nothing,* ***picking their noses.*** UL ▫ *They were born in Kentucky, where children* ***pick*** (= pluck the strings of) *guitars instead of* ***their noses.*** ST ▫ (film review) *. . .the slobbish* (slob = 'oafish person') ***nose-picking*** *keeper who releases the maniac Hammersmith.* NS ▫ generally held to be an unacceptable thing to do, and so sometimes used to describe briefly a person who is unaware of the effects of his behavior on other people; n/adj compounds nose-picking, nail-picking.

the pick/best of the bunch [Comp (Adj P)] the best of a number of persons or things **V:** ⚠ be; look, think sb ▫ *The Fosters were all good-looking girls, and Ada was* ***the pick of the bunch.*** ▫ *Such TV programmes therefore do little to bridge the gap between the working scientist and the public. 'Horizon' is perhaps* ***the best of the bunch,*** *though most weeks it should have more time to develop its fabulously rich material properly.* RT

pick sb's pocket [V + O pass] steal money, or small articles, from sb's clothing **det:** his, the man's, the public('s), their customers' ▫ *'He's just asking to get* ***his pocket picked,'*** *said Larry as they watched the big man stuff the notes into a hip pocket and turn to lean his elbows on the bar again.* ▫ *Over the years, he says, he bombarded most of Washington's high officialdom with his information. He was possessed by the idea that only he cared about the systematic* ***picking of*** *the American* ***pocket*** *in Indochina and, when no one replied to his letters, tended to consider that it was all a plot.* NS ▫ also pl; n compound a pickpocket.

pick and shovel [n + n non-rev] tools that are used in, or are symbols of, heavy labouring work ▫ *It would have taken a dozen men with* ***picks and shovels*** *three months to do what we've done today, with this comparatively small earth-moving machine.* ▫ *What a waste of an education! we would say sadly, 10 years ago, of a young man like Tom. Now, the* ***pick and shovel*** *jobs are as scarce as any others.* OBS ▫ (Cambodia) *The period from 1960 to 1966 saw Sihanouk at the height of his popularity and dynamism. His peasants grew used to having him pay them a flying visit. He may not have been an ardent labourer but the public relations of the* ***pick-and-shovel*** *prince were grounded in good sense.* ST ▫ attrib use, as in *a* ***pick-and-shovel*** *job*, with or without hyphen.

the (very) picture of health etc [Comp (NP)] completely, or extremely, healthy etc **V:** ⚠ be, look; find sb. **o:** health, misery, good humour, innocence, contentment ▫ *I was further irritated by the fact that while I was choking and sneezing and using up a sackful of paper handkerchiefs, he remained in complete possession of his human dignity, and looking* ***the picture of health.*** UTN ▫ *Her children were well cared-for and* ***the picture of health.*** ▫ *Johnny stood by the door,* ***the picture of misery,*** *waiting to be taken to school.* ▫ (a monkey) *By her antics she would lure them closer and closer to the cage, looking* ***the picture of*** *cheerful* ***good humour,*** *while her shrewd eyes judged the distance carefully. Suddenly the long and powerful arm would shoot out through the bars.* BB ▫ *He's just as troublesome as most babies though he looks* ***the very picture of contentment*** *at the moment.* ▫ usu unchanged after pl S, as in second example.

(see) pictures in the fire (see) shapes and scenes imagined from the pattern of glowing coals in a hearth fire (esp as a childish, or idle, pastime); idly watch the play of flames and embers ▫ *It just occurred to me that one of these evenings you might feel slightly surfeited with* ***pictures in the fire*** *and relish the notion of a foray into the smoke. Soho and so forth.* TGLY ▫ pun here on *smoke*— which is also a slang name for London.

pie in the sky [Comp/O (NP)] (promise, or hope, of) comfort and bliss in heaven, or wealth, happiness, better conditions of life and work at some indefinite time in the future; jam tomorrow (qv) **V:** be; get, promise sb ▫ (source) *Work and pray (work and pray)/Live on the hay (Live on hay)/You'll get* ***pie in the sky*** *When you die./(That's a lie.)* THE PREACHER AND THE SLAVE (J HILL 1879-1914) ▫ *When the slave arrived in Prostestant North America he would have no hope, as he had in Catholic Brazil, of working out his freedom. If his lot here below was miserable, he was encouraged to hope for* ***pie in the sky.*** L ▫ *We'd say that life was going to be hard, 'dreadful' hard. We reckoned that the public had had enough of silver linings and* ***pie in the sky,*** *and we'd try out something different just for a change.* NS ▫ *'You've so much to live for, you're going to Australia soon and—' 'Oh, that was* ***pie in the sky,*** *I see it all now, clear as crystal.'* TSMP ▫ *If, on the other hand, industry and the unions carry on with the old habits of lackadaisical supply response and* ***pie-in-the-sky*** *wage claims, then inflation will not be cured without major economic collapse.* L ▫ attrib use *a* ***pie-in-***

the-sky wage claim.

a piece of cake [Comp (NP)] (informal) a task, commission, manoeuvre etc that is very easy to carry out successfully; money for jam/old rope (qv) **V:** ⚠ be; seem; find sth ▫ *In the summer of her 18th year, after leaving school, she was a delegate to the Labour League of Youth conference in Bavaria, worked as a housemaid in a Newcastle hotel and made lids for boot-polish tins in a Chiswick factory. After this, Oxford was* ***a piece of cake.*** OBS ▫ (after robbing a bank) *...crowding into the back of a large car that waited outside. It started immediately. 'Gawd* (= God)*,* ***a piece of*** *bleeding* ***cake****!' 'Money for old rope.'* TO ▫ *I met Jim as we clocked out for the day. 'How did it go?' he asked. 'Oh, I replied, '* ***piece of cake*** *really, a real cushy number.'* NS ▫ sometimes without the indef art when used as reply, as in last example.

pig in the middle [Comp (NP)] person, or group in a helpless position between, or made use of by, others (from a children's game where the 'pig' tries to catch a ball tossed from one to another of a pair or ring of people; if he succeeds, the thrower becomes 'pig') **V:** ⚠ be, become, find oneself ▫ *Getting the ball safely back into Dick's* (the bowler's) *hands turned out to be troublesome, with a sort of* ***pig-in-the-middle*** *touch when the fielders on either side of him threw it to and fro in the hope that sooner or later he would catch it.* TGLY ▫ *But we have a more reliable account of Skene House's visitors during the Covenanting wars, when Aberdeen found itself playing the unwelcome role of* ***pig-in-the-middle.*** SC ▫ may be hyphenated, as in second example; attrib use *a* ***pig-in-the-middle*** *situation*; occas pl pigs in the middle.

pigs may/might fly (saying) wonderful, and seemingly impossible, things may happen ▫ *'Perhaps he'll let you have it cheap, since you are a relative.' 'Oh yes, and* ***pigs may fly****.'* ▫ *She had said hopefully to Rose that once Alan was qualified they might move back south, but Rose had replied, rather cruelly, that* ***pigs might fly.*** TSMP ▫ (NONCE) *If each individual were morally regenerated (the general wish of these authors), the world could indeed become a better place. Equally,* ***if pigs had wings they might be taught to fly.*** G ▫ variant if pigs had wings they might be taught to fly; implies speaker does not believe that things referred to will happen.

a pillar of society etc [Comp (NP)] a (type of) person on whom society depends for its security and well-being; a helper and supporter of a creed, party, community or working group, family etc **V:** ⚠ be, become; think sb, regard sb as. **o:** society, the establishment, the community, the Church, Western democracy ▫ *He is unostentatiously successful as an accountant. He and his wife live in style. He is very proud of his children. Steve is now respected by others. I should like to call him* ***a pillar of society.*** SPL ▫ *David Meroro, leader of the South West Africa Peoples' Organisation is a quiet prosperous businessman in his early fifties. Younger fighters for Namibian independence regard him as* ***a*** *rather conservative* ***pillar of the community.*** OBS ▫ *Mr Wilson, once execrated both as dangerous and slippery, is displayed before our admiring eyes as* ***a pillar of the*** *Western* ***alliance*** *and a stout defender of the mixed ecomony.* NS ▫ (NONCE) *Goodbye, Bill, and thank you so much for everything. You were one of* ***the pillars of the tour.*** OBS

a pillar/tower of strength etc [Comp (NP)] sb who shows and/or imparts great moral strength, capability, fortitude etc **V:** ⚠ be; prove, find sb. **o:** strength, common-sense, rectitude, security, comfort. **A:** to me, to his associates, to the weaker members ▫ *I can't begin to tell you what* ***a pillar of strength*** *your husband has been in our troubles here.* ▫ *She was so kind and helpful when my mother was ill last year. She was* ***a*** *real* ***tower of strength*** *to me.* ▫ *But these were not silly hot-blooded youngsters who had blatantly decided to cock a snook at the law. The five defendants were aging* ***pillars of respectability*** *in the small and tightly knit local community.* NS ▫ *I wouldn't embarrass him by telling of some of the things he's done to help people. But there's an awful lot of people who've got good reason to be grateful to him. When I had some emotional trouble years ago he was* ***a pillar of comfort*** *to me.* TVT

pin money (informal) money earned by a woman for her personal use, distinct from a regular income or allowance which she may be receiving ▫ *I bet she doesn't work for a living either, or else does a job for* ***pin money.*** *What good's a girl like that to you? Get one of your own class, lad, go to the people.* RATT ▫ *I haven't got a job; but I do teach a little French when I feel like it—just for* ***pin-money****, you know.*

(see) pink elephants (informal) have visionary hallucinations accompanying delirium tremens (the DTs), an advanced condition of alcoholism ▫ *Terry has a drink problem that's going to lose him his job before long, but he just laughs it off. 'Time to worry when I start* ***seeing pink elephants****,' he says.* ▫ *The first one to bump up against* (the phenomenon) *was one Constable Walsh. It may be that others before him saw things, and just put them down to a new kind of* ***pink elephant.*** TST ▫ *A familiar set-piece of 19th century travels, the banquet which progresses into an epic drinking match, ends for Dufferin with an early morning expedition to an off-shore island where he bemusedly encounters not* ***pink elephants*** *but red-nosed flying rabbits.* L

a pipe dream a hope, belief, plan that will never come true (from allowing one's mind to wander in idle reflections on 'what might be' while smoking tobacco or opium) **V:** be; have, entertain, hold on to ▫ *Mr Peter Rees has* ***a pipe dream*** *that one day the British Royal Family will be emperors of Europe* NS ▫ JASON: *Sonia, at last — now I know you're free. No* longer holding on to ***pipe dreams*** *in the sky.* DPM ▫ *We may wish to provide the blind with artificial eyes that enable them to see—and this is not just* ***a*** *silly, unrealisable* ***pipe dream.*** NS ▫ *Their hope is that in the year and a half between now and the elections there may appear a capable new leader able to command popular support while keeping the military's interests at heart. In the way of Argentine politics, even* ***pipe dreams*** *like this may come true.* L

piping hot [Comp (AdjP)] sizzling, or steaming, hot **S:** dinner, soup, coffee, water; news, publication. **V:** ⚠ be; come, arrive ▫ *'That soup* *looks half cold.' 'No, it's fine. I can't take things **piping hot**, anyway.'* □ *This reporter was found to have had two unauthorised radio monitors installed in his car. It was therefore little wonder that he got his information about police moves while it was still **piping hot**.* □ piping as an intensifier occurs only in this expression.

pitch and toss [v + v non-rev] move, be swung or thrown about unevenly in all directions, esp a boat in rough seas □ *As they **pitched and tossed** along the dusty rutted track Peter could hear, in the back of the van, the canister sliding about and the two men swearing.*

a plague/pox on both your houses may misfortune fall upon both of you (= contending, rival patrons, parties, families, institutions etc) for I do not sympathize with, or approve of, either of you □ (source—the speaker has been hurt in a street brawl between supporters of two rival 'houses', ie family groups) MERCUTIO: *Help me into some house, Benvolio, or I shall faint./**A plague o' both your houses**!/They have made worms' meat of me.* ROMEO AND JULIET III 1 □ *The atmosphere is one of uncertainty. One senses a distinct feeling of '**a plague on both your houses**' and the voter looking towards the fringe parties to fill the political vacuum.* T □ *When I hear the Festival of Light, Lord Longford, Malcolm Muggeridge or Mrs Mary Whitehouse and the so-called underground Press, Kenneth Tynan, George Melly or the National Council for Civil Liberties going hammer and tongs at each other, I can only say, '**A plague on both your houses**.' They positively live off each other's abuse.* OBS □ *So long as the battle between the Provisionals and the Unionists took place a long way off* (ie in Northern Ireland) *the British public were inclined to say: '**A plague on both their houses**.'* NS □ (NONCE) *'A lot of people in Washington are hopping mad about this—' 'All around the country I think there's perhaps a higher tolerance than there would be in the city. There's a sort of **pox-on-both-your-houses** kind of reaction, I suspect.'* L □ (NONCE) *I agree with Kate Millett. I support Women's Lib. But **a plague on both their theses**. All the exhortation and counter-exhortation go back to Mary Wollstonecraft and the cultivation of true independence of spirit.* L □ attrib use *a **plague on both your houses** attitude, reaction.*

plain clothes ordinary civilian wear of soldiers, policemen etc, constrasted with uniform □ *Mrs Reynolds told me afterwards that she knew it was the eve of D-Day—not from anything I said or from the way I behaved, but because I had taken my **plain clothes** there and had put them away in a wardrobe.* MFM □ *Four-year-old Billy took a poor view of my turning up in **plain clothes**—not a whistle or handcuff in sight—and complained bitterly that I was 'just an ordinary man'.* □ *Police at five yard intervals lined the exit from the station and **plain-clothes** men mingled with the crowd.* □ *Some days later a **plainclothes** dick* ((slang) = detective) *knocked at the door. And asked for me.* LLDR □ not the same as *(in) mufti*, which applies mainly to military personnel; attrib use *a **plain-clothes** policeman* .

a plain Jane a girl, or young woman, of less than average good looks □ *The long stories and serials often have startling surprises, as a young man proves to be really wealthy or a girl finds she wins a beauty competition, even though she has always thought of herself as **a plain Jane**.* UL □ *As every reader of the 'Express', 'Mirror', 'Mail', 'Guardian' or 'Sun' is now dramatically aware, two academic psychologists have shown to their own satisfaction that pretty girls enjoy the cruder seaside picture postcards, whereas, in the words of the society's press release, '**plain Janes** prefer cleaner humour'.* NS

plain living and high thinking a simple and moderate way of life (materially), combined with great interest and activity in intellectual and spiritual matters □ (source) *Rapine, avarice, expense,/This is idolatry; and these we adore:/**Plain living and high thinking** are no more.* O FRIEND! KNOW NOT (W WORDSWORTH 1770-1850) □ *Both of them are galloping romantics seeing 'we British' as a race of free-thinking independents eager for a life of **plain living and high thinking**— and 'productivity' expunged with dishonour from the language.* NS □ *...a hard, lonely man brought up in the school of **plain living and high thinking**, and never fully at ease with any colleague.* G □ (NONCE) *This whole series ought to be a wonderful and long overdue reminder that Twenties' and Thirties' literature was not all **high thinking and low living**.* L □ usu in order of headphrase.

(all) plain sailing [Comp (NP)] a matter of simple, straightforward procedure and progress (corruption of *plane sailing* (nautical) = a simplified means of navigation using a plane chart to determine position and course) **V:** ⚠ be, become; find sth □ *Having solved the caging problem, I felt that the three banded armadillos ought to be **plain sailing** for, normally, armadillos are the easiest of creatures to keep in captivity.* DF □ *National advertisers have also been slow to recognise the existence of this new maverick. Neither has it been **all plain sailing** on the editorial side.* ST □ *In my case the ambition was there, and the urge to master my profession. But it required advice and encouragement from the right people to set me on the road, and once that was forthcoming it was **plainer sailing**.* MFM

plain speaking telling the truth, expressing one's opinion, giving orders, rebuking or criticizing sb/sth, without suppressing anything or trying to make what one says pleasant or more acceptable □ *When they had wakened Parkinson and told him of the call, Kingsley said: 'Look here, Parkinson, I'm going to do some **plain speaking**. By our own light we've played this game pretty clean so far.'* TBC □ *There is no doubt that all this **plain speaking** was having some effect; we had definitely worked up considerable alarm in Government circles.* MFM □ *This* (type of) *conversation would take place only when it was understood to be an exchange of opinion with **plain speaking** on both sides.* NDN ⇨ ⚠in plain English.

play all one's cards [V + O pass] use every means, argument, resource in one's power □ *'Is there nothing you can do to avoid bankruptcy?' 'Not any more. I've staved it off for a couple of years but I've **played all my cards** now.'* □ *'The* *prisoner is bound to be convicted, isn't he?' 'Don't be too sure; the defence haven't* ***played all their cards*** *yet.'*

play one's cards well etc [V + O + A pass] use successfully etc the means (at one's disposal) of fulfilling one's wishes, gaining an objective; play it/things right (qv) **A:** well, right, properly, skilfully; badly, stupidly; with skill, cunning, forethought □ *This grouping was good, and if we* ***played our cards properly*** *the successful outcome of the operations in Tunisia was certain.* MFM □ *Then Mother would turn and watch him go. 'You know, I could have married that man', she'd murmur, 'if only I'd* ***played my cards right****.'* CWR □ *Decisions taken across the Channel could not affect Scotland more adversely than the decision currently taken a few miles this side of it. They might even, if we* ***play our cards with skill****, affect Scotland much more favourably.* SC □ *I should have thought you were in a perfect position to become the old lady's heir. You must have* ***played your cards*** *very* ***badly****!* □ often occurs in a conditional clause with *if*. ⇨ ⚠ play a/one's trump/winning card.

play fair (with sb) play a game according to the rules and established procedure; (fig) act justly and honestly; deal with sb, or with a situation involving other people, without deceit or prejudice; play straight (with sb) (qv) **A:** in the distribution of jobs; over the allocation of sites □ (room in a car for only one person to get a lift) *A well-turned out young lady of seventeen was a vast improvement on the heavily-laden gaunt man, but we had to* ***play fair*** *and, taking a coin, we tossed it for the place, and the lady won.* BM □ *Any idea that women ought to* ***play fair*** *by the men's rules in business gets swept away by an overwhelming sense that no one is* ***playing fair*** *at all.* OBS □ (book review) *Mr Fleetwood in his ambivalent swings between realism and surrealism has not* ***played*** *entirely* ***fair with*** *us. But very readable.* ST □ *Another thing. The club never* ***plays fair with*** *tickets. We go to every match yet we don't get a chance of buying them for Wembley. There should be a coupon system the way other clubs do, saving up the programmes.* ST

play sb/sth false [V + O + A] (formal) make a dupe of, betray, sb/sth; deceive, mislead, sb **S:** you, their allies, his wife; memory, life, his judgment. **O:** me, their employers, his country, her husband; (in final position, replacing O in middle position) with me, with both of them, with her affections □ *Why should I trust you? You promised my family safe conduct across the border and you* ***played*** *them* ***false****.* □ (reader's letter) *I think Fritz Spiegl's memory must have* ***played*** *him* ***false*** *when he recounted the story of his discovery and reconstruction of the Donizetti opera.* RT □ *'She was a woman of the world,' he claimed 'and knew the chances of the game. It wasn't as if I'd* ***played false with*** *the affections of a young girl.'* □ facetious use in last example.

play sb's game [V + O] willingly, unwillingly, or unknowingly, conform with sb's policy, methods, aims and thus promote his interests rather than one's own □ *Hitherto Dublin governments have* ***played*** *Britain****'s game****. They have given no assistance, and precious little sympathy, to the Ulster minority.* NS □ *And blackmail? If Guy went to the police there was no doubt that he would have to serve a prison sentence. But was one so weakly to* ***play the game of*** *this horrible blackmailer with his writing like the slimy trail of a garden slug?* DC □ *He's trying to needle you into saying something rash. You'll only be* ***playing his game*** *if you lose your temper.* □ *It does not in fact take long for her to be visibly coarsened. Whereas in 1915 she can still worry about whether or not Lloyd George has 'played the game', by 1919 she is coldly commenting about a political opponent, 'He is* ***playing our game*** *at the moment.'* NS □ last example plays on contrast between this entry and next. ⇨ ⚠ next entry, play the game.

play sb's/the same game [V +)] deliberately (and esp as a means of gaining one's own ends) either (pretend to) co-operate with sb or (try to) match or outdo him by using methods similar to his; play 'a game two can play' (qv) □ BESSIE: *Come on, darling. Davey, come on, Kiss me and shake your uncle Solly by the hand.* DAVID: *Leave me alone.* (Turns his back. Sam goes over to him and reasons with him.) SAM: *Go on Davey.* ***Play their game****. It's nearly over. Wait and see what I've got in store for you.* HSG □ *There is no doubt that when ITV first appeared it quickly took the larger share of the audience and was pushing up to 70 per cent when the BBC decided to* ***play the same game*** *and fought back. Schedules came into their own and the men who control them became extremely important.* SC □ *No. If* ***playing his*** *dirty* ***game*** *is the only way of winning an election I'd rather lose.* ⇨ ⚠ previous entry; next entry.

play the game [V + O] do what is right, fair, honourable; do what is expected of one as a loyal ally, supporter, or as an honourable opponent in fair competition □ *He spoke of a generation of peace, and his other goals — progress, prosperity. He then stated: 'The important thing in our process is to* ***play the game****.'* NS □ *Listen. We've come to say this. First you've got to give back Piggy's specs. If he hasn't got them he can't see. You aren't* ***playing the game****.* LF □ *'You think these heroics* (ie saving my life) *will get her. How wrong you are. If I were dead you could have had her.' 'I didn't mean that,' Pyle said. 'When you are in love you want to* ***play the game****, that's all.'* QA □ expression typifies the qualities and attitudes expected in a 19th c and early 20th c leader of men, empire-builder, man of honour — the ideal product of the public school. ⇨ ⚠ previous entry; play sb's game.

play hard to get (informal) pretend to have less interest than one feels towards sb of the opposite sex; try to set a high value on oneself by not readily accepting a/any proposal, invitation, employment etc □ *'You should have seen her — all maidenly and mysterious.' 'You never know, Steve, you've said yourself that she's a very attractive woman — ' 'Richie?' he said. 'Not on your life — she was just* ***playing hard to get****.'* TT □ (recruitment procedures) *The Army might be rather choosy at the beginning but it's just a case of 'the old maid* ***playing hard to get****'. Once you've done your basic training, you try getting out!* RT □ *You can be sure he has every intention of being present at a prestigious affair like that. When he says he'll try to fit it in if he* *can that's just because he likes* ***playing hard to get****.* □ usu continuous tenses.

play it/do sth by the book [V + O + A pass] (informal) act strictly according to the rules □ *She grew increasingly frustrated in her job as a journalist for although the newspaper's firm rule that she* ***play it*** *—everything she did and wrote —* ***by the book*** *was designed to guard against dishonesty and law-breaking, it also had the effect of stifling all individual initiative.* □ *He pretended that the much-praised main course had been cooked strictly* ***by the book****, but in fact he'd thought it up in a panic-stricken few minutes, half an hour before everybody arrived, having discovered that he'd forgotten to buy the ingredients for the dish he'd planned.*

play it etc cool [V + O + A] (informal) not get angry, excited, enthusiastic, perturbed etc **O:** it, ⚠ the whole thing, things, everything □ *Just cos* (= because) *he comes from the democracy with the lolly he thinks he can say what he likes. I don't know what the hell his game is, but I've got to* ***play it cool****.* JFTR □ *He thought Labour's Patrick Gordon Walker was a real gentleman too. As Indian immigrants poured into Smethwick in the early 1960s, Gordon Walker* ***played it cool****.* OBS □ *Some of the prime movers of UNCTAD III did a lot of spadework beforehand, urging delegates to* ***play everything*** *very* ***cool****, in the belief that the rich would be more impressed by rational debate than by emotive polemic.* NS ⇨ ⚠ keep/lose one's cool; keep etc a cool head; keep/lose one's head.

play it/things right [V + O + A] handle a situation, carry out what one means to do, with the necessary skill or cunning to be successful; play one's cards well etc (qv) □ *'And this time I'll* ***play it right****,' she muttered to herself. This time she wouldn't show so plainly how crazy she was about him.* WI □ *The picture could change hands for about £3000 and if he* ***played it right*** *he could get a commission from both parties.*

play it/things safe [V + O + A] avoid risks, or a particular risk; take the course of action in which there seems to be least chance of danger etc although another course, if successful, could bring greater success **O:** it, things, this one □ *Weston had always* ***played it safe****. But now the time had come to gamble—and a tiny slip could cost him his daughter's life.* TO □ *In that year fighter-bomber tactics had progressed enormously and I was definitely out of touch and for a week I* ***played it*** *very, very* ***safe****.* RFW □ ***Playing things safe*** *has never been his way. 'I've always felt that we must constantly be stretching ourselves, never be content with what we think are our limitations.'* RT □ *One can find oneself using insertions, conjunctions, pauses, exlamations, saving clauses, false loadings—which are face-savers, hedgings of bets,* ***playing safe****. Almost any of them can be used properly as signs that we are aware of other points of view, of qualifications.* L □ O occas omitted, as in last example.

play it straight [V + O + A] deal with a situation in a straightforward and honest way; not magnify, minimize, or distort facts (from an actor's way of playing his role, and from the batsman returning the ball in cricket) □ *The extraordinary and incontrovertible thing about the movement is that it has spread like a contagion, without central organisation. It has been passed on by newspaper stories and the Southern Press has largely* ***played it straight****.* OBS □ *'"Routine inquiries", shall I say, sir?' 'No,* ***play it straight****. Tell him he is under suspicion as a result of our investigations and unless he satisfies you down to the last detail you'll be bringing him in on a charge.'*

play one's last card [V + O pass] use the sole means or argument, the last chance, left to one □ *Madge looked at me through her real tears. She* ***played her last card****. 'If it's Anna,' she said, 'you know that I wouldn't mind. I mean, perhaps I'd mind, but that wouldn't matter. I just want you near me.'* UTN □ *But, alas, when she turned again to the audience, many other people had risen to support the Vicar in his signal for departure. Mrs Middleton* ***played her last card****. 'I know, children,' she said, 'the Vicar is hungry, that is what it is. Now, all of you, off! Then,' she added, 'we will all be ready to sing again.'* ASA

play a lone hand manage one's life, plan and carry out a project or undertaking, often by one's own choice, without the co-operation or support of others (from card games, esp euchre, in which one can play with a partner or against all the other players) □ *When I went to school in London I had learnt to* ***play a lone hand****, and to stand or fall alone.* MFM □ (discussing a draft for a letter) *'I say, would you mind very much leaving out that last bit about me?' Bill Brownsmith asked anxiously. 'But why? I want to impress this fellow Waggett with the fact that I am not* ***playing a lone hand*** *in this matter.'* RM □ *What would Edward do when he found she had vanished? Would he go to Mr Dakin? Would he* ***play a lone hand****?* TCB

play possum [V + O] pretend death, unconsciousness, sleep etc in order either to protect oneself from (further) attack or interference, or to avoid having to do something specific, cope with a difficult situation (source (US) is referred to in the first quote); lie doggo (qv); lie low (qv) □ *The opossum, furthermore, has a facial pose in its repertoire that has provided the base for a common figure of speech—'****playing possum****' or feigned death. This is a trick several other animals can play.* ST □ *'You can peep in and see if Daddy's awake, but you're not to waken him,' I heard her say in an unnecessarily clear voice — and this I took as an invitation to* ***play possum*** *if I wanted to.* □ *'Thomas.' He was hitting at my door, but I* ***lay possum*** *as though I were back in the rice-field and he was an enemy.* QA □ uncommon variant lie possum.

play second fiddle (to sb) [V + O] (informal) be subordinate in position, or function, to another person; be (considered) of secondary importance or interest **o:** another woman, his brother, this outsider □ *I was asked to stay on as housekeeper after he married but I couldn't bear the idea of* ***playing second fiddle to*** *another woman after having been in charge for all those years.* □ *After the birth of a first baby it is very common for a husband to feel he is having to* ***play second fiddle****.* □ *This was a remarkable switch in one so ambitious as Stanley, now quite deliberately trying to undermine his own great scoop. If he did manage to 'bring Livingstone* *back alive' he clearly would have to* **play second fiddle**. OBS □ *The most obvious danger of 'The Sextet' repertory is that the international 'name', in this case Billie Whitelaw, can upstage inadvertently and leave the others to* **play** *nothing but* **second fiddle**. RT □ (NONCE) *At first glance he was one of nature's* **second fiddles**. *A walking bloody hard-luck story*. JFTR

play straight (with sb) use no deception, take no unfair advantage, in one's dealings (with sb); play fair (with sb) (qv) □ *I had been examining Pyle's innocent question: 'Are you* **playing straight**?' *It belonged to a psychological world of great simplicity, where you talked of Democracy and Honor without the* u *as it's spelt on old tombstones, and you meant what your father meant by the same words.* QA □ *However we decide to present your case in court, Mr Simpkins, I expect a client to* **play straight with** *me in this office.* □ *He never* **played straight with** *anyone. That's why he came to a sticky end.*

play truant/hook(e)y [V + O] be absent from school without permission or good reason, and usu without the consent or knowledge of one's parents; (facetious) fail to be present at a place, or time, when one has a duty, or obligation, to fulfil □ *Always* **playing truant**; *wouldn't learn Latin and that. Besides, me* (= my) *mind was always on other things, like football and swimming.* RT □ *They went everywhere together. Elizabeth* **played truant** *from her office and Terence let important contacts go unheeded.* HAA □ *This was* **playing hookey**. *I had to get up north to Yale and there, the next autumn, I discovered the most beautiful of the New England States: Vermont.* L □ (animals as objects of superstitious beliefs) *Why should a party of Welsh gamblers,* **playing hookey** *from chapel, renounce cards for life, merely because of a hare's accidental arrival among them?* NS □ play hook(e)y esp US.

play a/one's trump/winning card [V + O pass] do, or say, sth that achieves the success desired (the implication often being that one has held this most powerful action etc in reserve until a suitable time arrives) □ *'Oh, it doesn't matter if you don't want to go to the dance,' he said, and* **played his winning card**. *'There'll be lots of other pretty girls there.'* □ *'I'd like to think I'm going on this trip,' my sister said, 'but you wait and see—as soon as I'm about ready to go, father will* **play his** *usual* **trump card** *and feel one of his attacks coming on.'* □ *Age, in the case of so sophisticated a woman, was as good* **a card to play** *in the sexual game as youth.* □ comparative construction in last example. ⇨ ⚠ play one's cards well etc.

plead guilty (to sth) (legal) admit guilt formally in a court of law (thus avoiding trial before sentence is passed in relation to a particular charge); (informal) acknowledge, admit an error, fault, failing etc **o:** manslaughter; that; a fondness for gossip; having forgotten to reply to his letter, embezzling the funds □ *Both men cheerfully* **pleaded guilty** *and paid a fine of £300 without turning a hair.* DS □ *'When did you leave Germany, Dr Hasselbacker?' Beatrice asked. 'In 1934. So I can* **plead** *not* **guilty**, *young lady,* **to** *what you are wondering.'* OMIH □ *We residents can all* **plead guilty to** *a certain amount of selfishness in not wanting a ring road routed here.* □ *'I never believed he was half as ill as he made himself out to be.' 'I'm afraid I must* **plead guilty to** *having thought the same myself.'* □ usu first person sing in fig use; in Scotland and US, past tense of plead is pled.

please God [Disj] may God grant sth; may it please God to allow, or forbid, sth □ SARAH: *So he's a cook in Paris.* MONTY: **Please God**, *he'll be a hotel manager one day.* CSWB □ *Well, that's over. We'll never,* **please God**, *have to come here again.* □ *She leapt to the telephone, 'That'll be Margaret ringing now,* **please God**.' □ *Television in this country is (and,* **please God**, *it will remain so) a place where intelligent writers can address a vast audience.* RT □ accompanies statement (positive or neg) of sth hoped or supposed; front, middle or end position. ⇨ ⚠ God willing.

plight one's troth [V + O] agree to marry (from a response in the Anglican marriage service) □ *You pays your money and you* **plights your troth**: *marriage, we are often told, is on its last legs, but it simply isn't true.* ST □ *Although she has received two proposals of marriage from fans of 'Sale of the Century', she has no intention of* **plighting her troth** *at the moment.* TVT □ use outside context of church service usu facetious; first example includes a play on expression 'you pays your money and (you) takes your choice' (qv).

the plot thickens (facetious) the plot of a play or novel, a situation in real life, suddenly becomes complicated, more intriguing □ (source) *Ay, now* **the plot thickens** *very much upon us.* THE REHEARSAL (G VILLIERS, DUKE OF BUCKINGHAM 1628-87) □ *Insurance agent Kirby has stumbled on information which he can sell to the British Civil Service. But first he needs more proof. He goes to the New Forest to meet his contact.* **The plot thickens**. *Kirby re-doubles his efforts.* TVT □ *There are several alternatives which make more sense in terms of even spacing. This, though, is where* **the plot thickens**. *The Department of the Environment prefers services to be at least a mile, and preferably two, from a motorway interchange.* ST

plough a lone/lonely furrow [V + O] (cliché) carry out one's work, or main activities, alone; try to teach, or exemplify, sth with little or no help or sympathy from others □ *The flood-tide of* (religious) *revival is particularly gratifying to men like Arthur Blessitt, a 30-year-old Louisiana-born preacher who for years* **ploughed a lonely furrow** *among the acid-heads* (= drug-users, esp of LSD) *of Hollywood.* L □ *Compared with the galaxy of talent which has been poured out on the elaboration of this thesis* (ie changing inherited structures of government) *in Latin America, Africa has been inadequately served. Thomas Hodgkin, Leonard Barnes, and Basil Davidson have* **ploughed a lone furrow**, *but they are now reaching emeritus status* (= retirement) *and have no successors.* NS □ *He didn't go out much, one didn't meet him at parties—he* **ploughed his own furrow**. *Contemporaries assumed that his cocoon was a chosen protection rather than a prison.* ST □ *'Because you know, darling,' she looked so deep and straight into Eric's eyes, 'it's* *the* ***ploughers of lonely furrows*** *who get there, who matter.'* HAA □ variants plough one's own furrow, a plougher of a lonely furrow.

ply a/one's trade [V + O] carry on a/one's skilled occupation □ *They had pulled down the old smithy where his grandfather had* ***plied his trade*** *and a metal shed with four petrol pumps in front now occupied the site.* □ *She was taught to dismantle, clean, and check a Browning .300 and to load the belts into an aircraft; she mastered that without difficulty and settled down to* ***ply her trade*** *from December 1941 to June 1943.* RFW □ *Though their work was cleaning, and dishing up food, few of them were the ordinary charwoman type; mostly they were obviously welcoming the chance to earn a little extra money by* ***plying the*** *only* ***trade*** *they knew.* HD □ also pl ply their trade(s).

poets etc are born, not made (saying) no amount of instruction can make a poet etc of anyone not naturally gifted to be one (translation of the Latin *poeta nascitur, non fit* = a poet is born, not made) **S:** poets, leaders of men, great singers, mediums □ *Stop worrying if you can't do it, son, and tell your teacher to remember that* ***poets are born, not made.*** □ (Wagnerian opera) *Great* ***Wotans****, it is said,* ***are born, not made****. Each generation of singers seems to produce one supreme exponent of the role.* SC □ *Maybe* ***writers are born rather than made****; but they still need spotting and cultivating, and they can easily be unmade by bad habits.* L

the point of no return [O/o (NP)] the point at which an aircraft must continue its flight because there is insufficient fuel left to turn back; (fig) the stage at which one has so far committed oneself, at which affairs have so far progressed or deteriorated, that stopping or reversing a process is no longer possible **V:** reach, pass, be at/beyond, bring to □ *While talks have been going on in Rome, the withdrawal of British personnel and equipment was slowed down to avoid reaching what is known in Whitehall as '****the point of no return****'.* ST □ *Every year about 150 young men become fully fledged priests in the Roman Catholic Church. Sunday's play in the 'Red Letter Day' series concerns the big moment when a man reaches* ***that point of no return*** *and goes through the ceremony of ordination, a moment comparable in layman's terms to a wedding day.* TVT □ *'You have been granted a reprieve to a life sentence. You are coming out of this condemned cell today.' Strangely enough, I didn't feel in the least happy, because my mind was made up to* ***the point of no return****.* L □ *Unless the Government tackled a crash programme of advanced training for teachers the country's educational system would run down beyond* ***the point of no return****.*

a/one's point of view [O (NP)] an opinion, estimation, assessment that is shaped by one's own character, age, interests, or aims **V:** have, take, press, put forward. **adj:** different, another, the same, the opposite □ *James said nothing. It took him longer to work round to new* ***points of view*** *than his wife: after all, she had not the same personal jealousy to contend with.* HAA □ *Miss Bawden explains about writing for children. 'You need only to have* ***a*** *different* ***point of view****. Children are as emotionally sophisticated as adults, but they just don't know so much.'* RT □ *They also wrote to MPs, and one way and another they pressed* ***their point of view*** *on the BBC from many angles.* L □ *'Don't you agree that the government should economise more?' 'Well, it all depends on* ***your point of view****, doesn't it?'* □ *From* ***another view-point*** *that same hero could be regarded as a villain.* □ n compound a viewpoint.

a poison-pen letter [O (NP)] an anonymous letter that accuses, maligns or slanders sb **V:** write, address; receive □ *But she had decided by now that the Baptists were probably not in the conspiracy. To all the other clergymen she was busy addressing* ***poison-pen letters****.* ASA □ *From where I am, the character Charlie Chaplin plays is a little loud-mouth who gets what's coming to him and then expects us to feel sorry for him. (And while you're writing* ***the poison pen letters*** *you may as well know that I think Busby Berkeley's dance numbers are the bore of the century.)* TVT □ *No explanation should accompany* (the return of the manuscript)*, and the address should be in printed characters—as if a* ***poison-pen*** *had written them.* PW □ usu attrib, as in headphrase.

a poker face a face that expresses nothing of one's intentions, emotions or reactions (as desirable when playing the card game, poker) **V:** have, assume, adopt, wear, put on □ *So at Christie's wine auction last month in London, it came under the hammer as Lot 73. The bidders, all* ***poker faces*** *and dark suits, were described to me by the auctioneer as 'mostly Americans, some Swiss, a few oil-men, almost no English'.* TVT □ adj compound poker-faced.

poles etc apart [Comp (AdjP)] completely dissimilar **S:** brothers, groups, teams; studies, products. **V:** ⚠ be, seem; regard sb/sth as. **n:** poles, ⚠ worlds, oceans □ *A young man once said to me, during a discussion about the impact of television on society, that at least it had made it possible for him to talk to his own father. Before, they had been* ***poles apart****: now they had a shared experience about which they could argue.* L □ *My mother's people had little schooling and were uncorrupted by class. My father's people were from the same county, but* ***oceans apart****.* TVT □ *Though* ***poles apart*** *ideologically, Communism and Anarchism are often confused by the simple die-hard conservative voter.*

a/the policeman's lot is not a happy one (catchphrase) a policeman has many unpleasant duties to perform □ (source) *Ah, take one consideration with another—with another,/* ***A policeman's lot is not a happy one****—happy one.* PIRATES OF PENZANCE (W S GILBERT 1836-1911) □ *Today, when crime is on the increase, and public respect for the force is decreasing,* ***a policeman's lot is not a happy one****.* □ *When there is so much anxiety about violence and disorder, it may be good policy to try to make* ***the policeman's lot a happy one****.* SC □ *With such a small per cent profit margin it is only the huge investment by punters that brings them the profit they have to work so very very hard for. Ah, well —* ***the bookmaker's lot is not a happy one****.* □ often adapted, as in last example.

pomp and circumstance [n + n non-rev]

magnificent and/or ceremonious display and procedure □ (source) *Farewell.../The royal banner, and all quality,/Pride,* ***pomp and circumstance*** *of glorious war!* OTHELLO III 3 □ *On Saturday the Open University dishes out degrees to its first batch of 900 graduates. It's all happening in a welter of academic flummery at Alexandra Palace. Not that the* ***pomp and circumstance*** *is anything unusual; they've been at it ever since the opening ceremony beneath the chandeliers of the Royal Society.* NS □ *When royal princesses are married with great* ***pomp and circumstance****, I wonder how many who grumble at 'needless expenditure' take care not to miss the spectacle on their television screens.* □ (NONCE) (advertisment for 'The Times' newspaper) *No* ***Pomp****, Just The* ***Circumstances****.*

the poor are always with us (saying) there are, and always will be, people who live in poverty (requiring our help and efforts on their behalf) □ (source) *Why was not this ointment sold for three hundred pence and given to the poor?...Then said Jesus, Let her alone: against the day of my burying hath she kept this: For* ***the poor always ye have with you****; but me ye have not always.* JOHN XII 5-8 □ *Bruce Taylor, with his corrugated face, red tie and bandaged thumb represents* ***the poor who are always****—even in 1971—* ***with us****. It does no harm to be reminded of this from time to time.* L □ *This week's '2nd House' (8.40 BBC 2) deals with* ***the poor****—they****'re*** *still* ***always with us****—and with the second helping of gruel that Oliver Twist had the temerity to ask for.* RT □ (NONCE) (reader's letter) *Sir, I must join issue with Mr Bishop. Anyone who works in the life assurance world will know that* ***the rich are*** *very much* ***with us*** *still.* NS

poor little rich girl a young woman of a rich or noble family, or wealthy in her own right, seen as being in many respects deprived (= poor), perhaps having too many social demands to meet and too few opportunities of developing personal interests □ (source) ***Poor little rich girl****,/You're a bewitched girl,/Better beware!* N COWARD 1899-1973 □ *'Apparently George left me some money.' 'So now you're a* ***poor little rich girl*** *to add to all your other troubles.'* PP □ (reader's letter) *Without being too fanciful, I think that Mr Waugh is really trying the '****poor little rich girl****' line. People like him always seem to me to be excessively shocked to find that the difficulties of the rich are regarded with less sympathy than those of the poor.* NS □ (NONCE) *'The life you lead sets all your nerves a-jangle,/Your love affairs are in hopeless tangle', and although Noel Coward's song was directed at a girl, the same conditions often apply to* ***poor little rich guys****.* NS

the poor man's sb/sth sb/sth that is an inferior substitute for another well-known person, institution, expensive food, etc **n:** Bertrand Russell, Bardot; caviare, opera; Hilton □ *If Mike wasn't also a sixpenny philosopher as well as an agent he'd have left me and my fattened head right then, but he can't resist the temptation to be* ***the poor man's*** *Bertrand Russell.* JFTR □ *In his wake he has left imitators —* ***the poor man's*** *Robert Robinson, those jocular iconoclasts who have neither his erudition, mental reflexes, nor command of language.* L □ *At the heart of this empire is Dr Derek Paul Stevenson, tanned and urbane ('****The poor man's*** *Rex Harrison' the girls at HQ are once said to have christened him: though not that poor) who has been BMA secretary since 1958.* □ *'What's on these biscuits?' 'I forget what it's called—something Norwegian out of a tin. I've tasted it before,* ***a*** *sort of* ***poor man's*** *caviare.'* □ *There was an attempt for a few seasons to make a wining, dining and virtuoso music centre of Ledlanet House. But* ***this poor man's*** *Glyndebourne did not* survive.

poor old sb/sth unfortunate (ie expressing some degree of sympathy for sb/sth) **n:** Ma, Peter, chap; milkman, waiters; Birmingham; tree, house, doll □ *I've got a feeling sometimes that if the money lasts five years it may be long enough.* ***Poor old*** *Ma.* RFW □ (a dog) *We've just got Rover back. The* ***poor old*** *chap's been in quarantine.* □ *It's not their fault that the postal services cost us so much but I bet* ***the poor old*** *postmen don't get many tips at Christmas now.* □ *'I hope I'm not given a job there.' 'That's what everyone says, but* ***poor old*** *Manchester wasn't such a bad place to live in once.'* □ old may, or may not, refer to age; may be used, as in first and last examples, as sympathetic comment or exclamation; the, those etc possible when expresion part of a clause.

poor relations poorer, or really poor, member(s) of a family; sb/sth with less power, prestige, respect or approval than another or others **det:** a, the, one's □ *In those pre-Welfare days a man of substance would be expected to do something for his* ***poor relations****, perhaps even accommodate one or two of them in his, usually, spacious home.* □ *Short stories have for too long been the* ***poor relations*** *of literature, no longer cared for in the home.* SC □ *This transmission was something of a rarity in that ITV, which has tended to be* ***the poor relation*** *when it comes to Eurovision transmissions, took the match live.* L □ usu pl.

(the) poor thing (the) poor creature □ *'Your sister was tired and upset,' Prissie said. 'The doctor came and I don't think he gave her much hope of walking,* ***poor thing****. Just imagine that. Never being able to walk again.'* DC □ *I had Meg's children to stay with me for the weekend but the weather was so bad* ***the poor things*** *didn't get out much.* □ *Cathy didn't pass her exam, did you know?* ***Poor thing****, she was terribly disappointed.* □ used to express sympathy and concern esp for women and children; may be used (usu without the) as sympathetic comment or exclamation; the used when expression is S or O of a clause.

a poor thing but my/mine own (catchphrase) sb/sth not very beautiful, notable or valuable but having the merit, or attraction, of being owned, executed etc by oneself □ (source) TOUCHSTONE: ***A poor*** *virgin, sir, an ill-favoured* ***thing****, sir,* ***but mine own****; a poor humour of mine, sir, to take that that no man else will.* AS YOU LIKE IT V 4 □ *To those in whom the faculty of visualization is strong my inner world must seem curiously drab, limited, and uninteresting. This was the world—* ***a poor thing but my own****—which I expected to see transformed* (by mescalin) *into something completely unlike it-*

self. DOP □ *I'll feel safer in the Mini,* ***a poor thing but my own****. I'm not used to powerful cars, nor to a left-hand driving position.*

pop the question [V + O] make a proposal of marriage to a woman □ *What about that young man you've been going out with so long? Hasn't he* ***popped the question*** *yet?* □ *There's an old tradition that in a Leap Year it is acceptable for a woman to* ***pop the question****.* □ dated euphemism.

a port of call a port at which a ship stops temporarily on a voyage; (fig) a place where one (habitually) stops for a short time, eg to pay a visit, have refreshments, make an inspection, buy or sell sth □ *In the old days the island was* ***a*** *regular* ***port of call*** *for sailing-ships on the South Pacific run to take on water and fresh meat and vegetables.* □ *'Anyway, thank God this is* ***the*** *last* ***port of call****. Now we can go and have a drink.' 'But Richard, you just can't go wandering into pubs. We've got to go to* (departments where we can buy) *glass and china, and linen and blankets, yet.'* DIL □ *It would seem natural enough in his role of inquisitive tourist to make the excavations* ***a port of call****.* □ also pl ports of call.

positive thinking an optimistic and determined mental attitude that helps one to achieve success in any kind of undertaking □ (source) *The Power of* ***Positive Thinking*** (title of a book by N V PEALE 1954) □ *'And it's just, I think, a bit of charm, a bit of warmth and a bit of guts that has got me by.' As well as a lot, he might have added, of* ***positive thinking****.* RT □ *Technically the Americans were superior but, as in all the tennis matches, the real difference was not so much one of class but attitude. As Mrs King said: 'We know how to* ***think positively****.'* G □ *If you think you may have discipline problems you probably will.* ***Think positive****, and assume you'll get their attention and co-operation.* □ variant think positive(ly).

possession is nine parts etc of the law (saying) being actually in possession of sth is the greatest possible advantage in establishing one's right, or power, to have it and keep it (nine = nine out of ten parts) **n:** parts, ⚠ points, tenths □ *Whether originally intended as a gift or a loan, the artist allowed the picture to hang in your house for upwards of thirty years.* ***Possession being nine points of the law*** *his widow can't reclaim it now, on hearsay evidence alone.* □ *Rigsby's new furniture attracts admirers — two of whom believe* ***possession is nine-tenths of the law****.* TVT □ (NONCE) *Occupying other people's houses is not a criminal offence in this country. It is usually a matter for the civil courts.* ***Possession is many parts of the law****. Provided a person has not been caught breaking in, then he is afforded a measure of protection by the law.* TVT

postpone/put off the evil hour/day delay sth one would like to avoid but cannot □ *It would be a great relief to me if the pubs would keep these individuals a few hours longer and release them into the atmosphere at intervals instead of all at once. Even if it only* ***postponed the evil hour****, at least it would happen when the streets were quieter.* SC □ *'It wouldn't cost all that much to redecorate the kitchen.' 'It's not the expense, it's the thought of having to move everything out and then back again that makes me keep* ***putting off the evil day****.'* □ *Janice is always the same at bedtime. She's got to tidy out her schoolbag, or get her nails cut, or put the cat out — anything to* ***postpone the evil hour****.* □ usu facetious.

the pot calls the kettle black (saying) sb criticizes another for a fault which he has himself in an equal degree □ JASON: *Marry me now. Sonia, we have witnesses — we could become one here and now.* SONIA: *Don't be a dirty old man, you dirty old man.* JASON: *Huh,* ***the pot calls the kettle black****.* DPM □ DAVID: *But Dad — surely you loved her once.* SAM: *Yes — once. Things happen between husband and wife that no one else can know about.* BESSIE: *Listen to who's talking.* ***The pot calls the kettle black****. I'm going to tell you a few things about Sam.* HSG □ ***The pot*** *is often entitled to* ***call the kettle black*** *when they share the same hob, but I thought Malcolm Muggeridge was pushing it a bit when he called Ronald Searle 'a gargoyle' on Sunday night.* NS

pound the beat [V + O] (informal) patrol an allotted district on foot (often used in implied contrast with higher, or more prestigious, grades of police duty) **S:** police constable; policeman; (slang) cop, copper. **det:** the, a, one's □ *Mr Forbes, who was born of a Scottish farming family, began his career as a policeman with the Metropolitan Police* ***pounding a beat*** *in the East End. When he retired he was national co-ordinator of the Regional Crime Squads in Britain.* SC □ *Television cop Denis Waterman — Det. Sgt. Carter in the 'Sweeny' — is* ***pounding a*** *different kind of* ***beat*** *these days. With a new album capturing both imagination and sales, he's emerging as a Dylanesque, guitar-strumming singer.* TVT □ *For this peccadillo he was demoted and sent back to* ***pound the beat****.* □ often as inf or in continuous tenses.

the power behind the throne [Comp (NP)] the *real* controller of policy and action, as distinct from the titlular head of a state, institution, business firm, household etc **V:** ⚠ be, become, make sb □ (possibly derived from) *A long train of these practices has at length unwillingly convinced me that there is* ***something behind the throne*** *greater than the King himself.* WILLIAM PITT 1708-78 □ *More than one ambitious politician, complacent in the belief that he was* ***the power behind the throne****, has found himself quietly returned to the obscurity from which he had been rash enough to emerge.* NS □ *'He enjoys rushing around telling the "help" to do this and do that and showing he's boss.' Mrs Elton said this with a forgiving smile intended to indicate that she was* ***the power behind the throne****.* □ *So every guru has his chila, every champ his manager, every gangster his mouthpiece — and the perennial aim of* ***the power behind the throne*** *is to outlast the power upon the throne.* ST ⇨ ⚠ a grey eminence.

(all) power corrupts, (and absolute power corrupts absolutely) (saying) the more power one has and exercises, the more one's moral character is corrupted □ (source) ***Power*** *tends to* ***corrupt, and absolute power corrupts absolutely****. Great men are almost always bad men.* LIFE OF M CREIGHTON (LORD AC-

TON 1834-1902) □ *Lord Acton observed the tendency of* ***power to corrupt****. What he did not note is that power physically improves the politicians to whom it is given.* L □ *John Mortimer's play, 'I, Claudius', adapted from two novels by Robert Graves, is a tragically ironic meditation on Lord Acton's epigram that* ***all power corrupts****. The upshot of the play is that rather does it corrupt those upon whom it is exercised, especially—and this is the fine and melancholy heart of the play—when it is exercised for their good.* ST □ (NONCE) *And like Mr Wilson at that time, Mrs Thatcher will now have a honeymoon period with radio, television and the newspapers.* ***All power attracts and newly acquired power attracts absolutely****.* NS □ frequently adapted, and seldom used in full original form.

a power in the land [Comp (NP)] of significant importance and influence in the life of a country (without necessarily holding any official position) **V:** ⚠ be, become, make sb □ *Sanjay Gandhi first became* ***a power in the land*** (of India) *in 1976.* □ *The Church of England, even though it is the 'established' religious authority, is not* ***the power in the land*** *it used to be.*

the powers that be any governmental, legislative, managerial body □ (source) *For there is no power but of God:* ***the powers that be*** *are ordained of God.* ROMANS XIII 1 □ *To cut a long story short,* ***the powers that be*** *agreed to back us with an initial half a million pounds in dollars, and later, when we'd spent this huge sum, they put up another half-million.* DS □ *Yet last autumn's fever in the price index, which should have made* ***the powers-that-be*** *aware of something out of the ordinary, did not apparently alert civil servants to cost increases that companies were no longer going to be able to bear.* ST □ *No doubt a confrontation on this scale would be deplored by* ***the powers that be*** *in the Labour Party, but it might actually turn out to be a godsend.* NS □ often used when the speaker does not know, or feels no need to name, the particular authority responsible for sth; usu written without hyphens; be in headphrase is a (seldom used) subjunctive form.

a practical joke a trick intended to make sb feel ridiculous, or physically uncomfortable □ *The thought that the whole threat to his life might be* ***a*** *nonsensical* ***practical joke*** *came to Wormold.* OMIH □ *...and the Argyll Rooms in the Haymarket, where a* ***practical-joking*** *aristocrat once emptied a sack of rats among the dancing women.* TVT □ often O of *play*; attrib use *a* ***practical joking*** *aristocrat*; variant a practical joker.

practice makes perfect (saying) repeated exercise in a skill, or craft, is the way to become a master of it □ GOLIGHTLY (He throws the darts. They all miss the board): *Oh. Never mind.* ***Practice makes perfect****. I should be.* THH □ *When I take a look at my lads in the Middlesborough Junior side, they're satisfied if a long ball lands a few yards away from the target. Well I tell them, I'm not satisfied:* ***practice*** *really can* ***make perfect****.* TVT

practise what one preaches live and act in a way one believes in, or recommends others to do □ *One does not have to be very old to see that not everybody* ***practises what he preaches****.* AH □ *It is time that they looked at the electoral system, from the viewpoint of fair competition between political parties and equal rights for voters. So far, the Conservative and Labour parties have shown no sign of* ***practising what they preach****.* SC □ *David* (Simon's father) *advises: 'Cut the apron strings and let Simon learn about life the hard way.' But he finds this is easier to* ***preach*** *than to* ***practise****.* TVT □ often introduced by phrases like *Why don't you* ***practise what you preach****? You should/ought to* ***practise what you preach****.*

praise be (to God) let us be thankful (that); I am thankful (that) □ *Nobody went short of food. We were never as hard up as that,* ***praise be****.* □ *What is more effective than clumps of white foxgloves, or palest yellow and cream, in woodland glades or in a shady border? Today these too have disappeared from most catalogues. Thompson & Morgan,* ***praise be****, still list both these foxgloves.* ST □ *'Did you have a hang-over?' 'Awful.* ***Praise be to God*** *I didn't have to go to work that morning.'* □ often in parenthesis and often, even in full, not piously intended.

praise the Lord and pass the ammunition (catchphrase) (let us) be devout, and prepared to fight, defend ourselves against enemies, too (from a comment attributed to a US naval Lieutenant (Howell Forgy) at the attack on Pearl Harbor, 1941, and subsequently incorporated in a World War 2 popular song) □ *He was once good enough to refer to me as a Cromwellian figure, no doubt because I have always tried both to* ***praise the Lord and*** *to* ***pass the ammunition****.* MFM

precious few/little (informal) very few; very little **n:** spectators, students, supporters; sympathy, help, assistance □ *To someone who has never been collecting, it may seem as though we gave ourselves a lot of unnecessary trouble by pampering our animals. The answer is, of course, that unless you pamper them you will get* ***precious few*** *back alive.* DF □ *Even the Nabokovian to-and-fro at the end of the book about his habits and opinions gives* ***precious little*** *away.* NS □ *I took the remaining pieces of gauze off the lamp, but even then it gave* ***precious little*** *light.* UTN □ *'Have you told the boss about your predicament?' 'What's the use?* ***A precious lot of*** *sympathy or help I'd get from him.'* □ variant a precious lot (of sth) = 'very little (of sth)'.

a pregnant silence/pause a silence while one waits for sth expected to be done or said, or in which one is aware of remarks, criticisms etc which might be made but are not □ *I said I was to see Dr Pood. With a slight bow, the beginnings of a Mona Lisa smile, and* ***a pregnant silence****, he ushered me into a waiting room.* AH □ *'I'm a very reasonable man, I'm sure. If anyone can't get on with me, it's not my fault.'* ***The pregnant silence*** *that followed this assertion was broken by Thompson's suddenly recalling that he had a phone call to make and we made the most of this diversion to change the subject.* □ *The jokes are not so devastatingly funny, after all. It's the perfect timing,* ***the pregnant pause*** *in exactly the right place, and so on, that makes their act such a success.* □ also pl.

present company excepted/excepting

present company (the statement that has been made, the matter referred to) does not apply to the person(s) present, but applies to other people not present on the occasion, or to people in general □ *I do find that people in this town,* ***present company excepted*** *of course, are pretty inhospitable.* □ *He was holding forth again, 'There are few literary critics whose opinions one can respect — ' there was a deliberately long pause '—****excepting****, if I may say so,* ***present company****,' but this was delivered in a tone that made it quite clear that he did not mean this at all.* □ a polite formula in parenthesis.

press/push the point [V + O pass] insist on sth (already) defined being understood, accepted, or done □ *Staff seem to have disregarded the request for more economy in the use of paper. Will you please* ***press the point*** *at today's meeting?* □ *I suggested that he should draw up a will but as he clearly felt that such a step threatened him with imminent dissolution I didn't* ***press the point****.* □ *She would have liked literally to stand there until he stripped and climbed in* (to the bath), *but he refused and she did not* ***push the point*** *beyond making a few remarks about trusting him and not being easily fooled and so on.* TSMP □ push rarely used.

pretty well etc [A (AdvP] (informal) almost; very nearly; just about (qv) **adv:** well, ⚠ nearly, much □ ***Pretty well*** *every country in Western Europe has had a motor-car boom.* OBS □ *Though still struggling on they were* ***pretty nearly*** *exhausted.* □ *I gather that the Truman quotation has since been argued over. Nevertheless,* ***pretty well*** *every educated Arab I've spoken to either here or in the Middle East, believes it.* L □ *She* ***pretty well*** *knew what he would say, that he could tell her nothing definite.* PW □ *Numerous studies have shown that Americans consider themselves members of the working-class or the middle class to* ***pretty much*** *the same extent as do people in England, France, or Germany.* SNP □ modifies adj, adv, v, prep p.

prevention is better than cure (saying) it is better, wiser, easier etc to prevent illness, or some other trouble, than to cure it afterwards □ (advertisement) *Many doctors prefer a natural food, rich in dietary fibre, which will help you to avoid constipation, rather than having to resort to purgatives. The reason is obvious—****prevention is*** *always* ***better than cure****.* RT □ *So far, there had been nothing between them* (ie his wife and her tutor) *that he could put a finger on—but Alan's term had still some time to go and Lellie was already hero-worshipping.* ***Prevention being better than cure****, the sensible course was to see that the situation should never develop.* TST □ *The cost of accidents in 1975 will have been in the region of £930 millions. This certainly seems to justify a modest investment in improvements to existing safety systems on the assumption that in the long term* ***an 'ounce' of prevention is worth a 'ton' of cure****.* SC □ variant an ounce of prevention is worth a pound/ton of cure.

prick the bubble (of sth) [V + O pass] reduce to its real size something which has been greatly inflated; destroy an illusion that sb has used for his comfort or protection **o:** indifference, self-esteem, complacency, vanity □ (predicted relations between personality and birth date) *Now, since Professor Eysenck is known among scientists for his tough-minded Behaviourism, one suspects that he went into this question determined to* ***prick this*** *absurd* ***bubble*** *once and for all.* OBS □ *Soldiers shot dead the driver of an IRA gunman's car, which crashed, killing three children and grievously wounding their mother. The casual slaughter finally* ***pricked the bubble of*** *communal callousness.* G □ *Mr Bateson is a great* ***bubble-pricker****, and he is at his happiest when he confronts an imposing, highly organised scholarly structure whose pretensions have been overblown.* NS □ n compound a bubble-pricker.

sb's pride and joy [n + n non-rev] sb/sth that sb is especially proud and pleased to have, to do, or to be associated with □ *I daresay the worst of them was once his mother****'s pride and joy****, but they've all gone a long way downhill since then.* □ *I interviewed a number of prospective daily men. One was too emotional and perhaps hoped to be more than a servant. Another would do anything but cook. A third seemed to have been born in a tiny green baize apron:* ***his pride and joy****, he explained, was to clean silver in all his waking hours.* AH

the primrose path [O (NP)] self-indulgence and the satisfaction of easy pleasures as a way of life that seems pleasant but leads to unhappiness or (spiritual) destruction **V:** tread, take, go down □ (source) *Himself* ***the primrose path*** *of dalliance treads.* HAMLET I 3 □ *...some of all professions that go* ***the primrose way*** *to the everlasting bonfire.* MACBETH II 3 □ *It was odd how Harold who had never since his marriage taken a step along* ***the primrose path****, never gone off the rails in any way or wished to, proved himself a past-master of intrigue.* PW □ *'I think she's far too nice a girl just to be taken to bed whenever you can spare the time. And I also happen to like you too much as a person to see you going the way you're going.' '****The primrose path*** *of dalliance?'* TT ⇨ keep to the straight and narrow (path) (Vol 1).

a private eye (informal) a private detective, a criminal or civil investigator, engaged by sb to work for a fee □ *He even knew how he would feel as he stood at the tall olive-green front door (intrepid, like* ***a private eye*** *still on case after warning from Mr Big).* TGLY □ *Among these* (films) *is 'Shaft' a fast-moving* ***private-eye*** *flick with plenty of action, a strong plot and credible hero.* OBS □ also pl private eyes; attrib use *a* ***private-eye*** *flick.*

one's private life that part of one's life not connected with public affairs, professional duties, employment or means of livelihood □ ***Your****, er,* ***private life*** *is, and ought to be, no concern of mine—I mean, it ought not to be any concern of mine as long as it does not interfere with your work as a teacher.* TT □ *'Friends and relations?' 'I've lost touch in the last ten years.' Her gaze wandered. She said, 'Not a single photograph. Have you* ***no private life****?'* OMIH □ *I don't agree that* ***the private lives of*** *public men should be exempt from reasonable scrutiny. Men without wisdom in managing their own affairs should not be managing ours.* □ *This scathing polemicist of the daily columns is* ***in private life*** *the mildest-mannered of men.* □ cf one's private life (sing or pl) and in private life (sing only).

a prize ass etc [Comp (NP)] sb/sth outstandingly good or bad of its kind **V:** ⚠ be, become, turn into, look. **n:** ass, idiot; pupil; example, instance; pastime ▫ *'My dear Middleton,'—Gilbert affected the use of surnames even for his most intimate friends, — 'don't, for heaven's sake, be* ***the prize ass*** *of all time. Can't you see it's the greatest thing that's ever happened?'* ASA ▫ *It's true that in the natural sciences the same names are applied to precisely defined concepts as are used much more vaguely in ordinary speech. The word 'atom' is* ***a prize example*** *of this.* L ▫ *There are too many people trying to run this affair. We'll end up in* ***a prize muddle*** *with nobody knowing who's supposed to be doing what.* ▫ a prize ass/idiot mildly derogatory.

procrastination is the thief of time (saying) valuable time is wasted, it becomes too late, one grows too old, etc while one puts off doing what one ought to do ▫ (source) ***Procrastination is the thief of time;*** */Year after year it steals, till all are fled.* THE COMPLAINT: NIGHT THOUGHTS (E YOUNG 1683-1765) ▫ *'Remember you have to change that tyre before we leave.' 'I'm remembering — time enough.' 'Time enough, now, but maybe not enough time later.* ***Procrastination is the thief of time.'*** ▫ (NONCE) *You have to consult, and* ***consultation is the thief of time****; but the alternative is any number of family variants on the occasion my husband and I turned up in Paris with two typewriters and only one toothbrush between us.* OBS

the prodigal (son) (returns) a son who leaves his family early, esp for a life of pleasure and extravagance (exhausts his resources, repents etc and returns home); sb who absents himself from a community, profession, religious or political group to follow other interests (returns and resumes his former way of life, loyalties etc) (all this in contrast to the behaviour of other members of a family who unselfishly do their duty, live respectably, economically etc in allusion to LUKE XV 11-32) ▫ *'They've got the painters in next door.' 'That'll be for the* ***return*** *of* ***the prodigal son****. I hear that all is forgiven.'* ▫ *'Well!' she said brightly, 'so* ***the prodigal's returned****. I suppose you spent a huge fortune on some drawing or other.'* ASA ▫ (NONCE) *It wasn't only to please his hearers that he was coming (=* uttering) *all this stuff. It was to claim the status of* ***the*** *non-****prodigal son****. He had stayed in the district and Robert hadn't.* CON ▫ *He had been what is termed a 'lapsed Catholic' but the Church is always ready to receive back* ***her prodigal sons****.* ▫ often adapted, as shown.

prolong the agony [V + O pass] make an unpleasant experience, tense situation, etc last longer than it needs to, either through mismanagement, for dramatic effect, to gain sympathy, etc ▫ *The extra resources created by my self-denial will immediately be seized by whichever sector of the community is least prepared to exercise self-denial in any form. In other words, the effect of individual self-denial is merely to* ***prolong the agony*** *and make the final reckoning even ghastlier.* NS ▫ PETER: *Now you must rest and take it easy.* SONIA: *Now he worries about me —now, when it's too late. All my life he drives me to this point and now he wants to* ***prolong the agony****.* DPM ▫ *Why must adjudicators always* ***prolong the agony*** *like this? They should announce the winners and awards first and make their general comments afterwards.*

(I) promise (you) I assure you ▫ *'Pauline,' I said after a while, 'you made it up.' '****I promise you*** *I didn't; I'm not nearly clever enough.'* BM ▫ *'Did you brush your teeth, Tommy?' 'Yes, mum.' '****Promise****?' '****Promise****.' 'All right, give me a kiss and go to bed.'* ▫ many speakers do not use promise (v) in this meaning; usu first person, pres tense, introducing clause; promise? in second example = 'do you assure me (that sth is true, is the case)?'

promise (sb) the earth/moon [V + IO + O pass] make a promise (to sb), but the promise is too extravagant and cannot, or will not, be kept ▫ *This week Sir John Betjeman makes a nostalgic journey through Metroland — the swathe of suburbs cut through rural Bucks, Herts and Middlesex by the Metropolitan Railway Co in the 20s. Its original brochures* ***promised the earth****; Robert Lacey talks to three residents about the reality of the dream now.* RT ▫ *'And then Lettie,' said Charmian, 'has been so cruel about her wills. Always* ***promising*** *Eric* ***the earth****, and then retracting her promises.'* MM ▫ *In the Heath prospectus both means and end were taken care of. This was not to be yet another government which* ***promised the moon*** *but did not say how it would get there.* ST

a/the promised land Canaan, promised to the Israelites by God, as in GENESIS XII 5-8; heaven, or any earthly place, situation or conditions where people are promised, and hope to get, happiness and security; a land flowing with milk and honey (qv) **V:** reach, come to, cross into, hope for, long for ▫ *Nobody any longer expects that neo-Keynesian fine tuning of the economy can bring us swiftly, painlessly but prosperously into* ***the promised land****.* NS ▫ *In 1913 there was plenty of socialist theory, but virtually no socialist practice. There was a vision of the road ahead, down which all good men would march abreast, but very little knowledge of what* ***the promised land*** *would look like.* NS ▫ (early 19th c migrations of population to the American West) *But whatever their motives, whether an insane hope of a better condition in life, or a desire of shaking off restraints of law and society, or mere restlessness, certain it is that multitudes bitterly resent the journey and after they have reached* ***the land of promise*** *are happy enough to escape from it.* SC ▫ variant the land of promise.

prone to sth[1] [Comp (AdjP)] liable to incur (and suffer from) sth **V:** ⚠ be, become; make sb/sth. **adv mod:** very, less, more, equally. **o:** accidents, infection, hay-fever; misinterpretation, interference, abuse ▫ (cattle-breeding) *There is a world demand for the Brown Salers from south-east France (the white version is* ***prone to*** *skin cancer) and they may well be seen in Britain soon.* ST ▫ (a radio ham) *Early morning reception was less* ***prone to*** *interference from relays on similar wave-lengths.* OBS ▫ *That it may be* ***prone to*** *abuse is no argument for turning down a relief system from which thousands will benefit* ▫ *What awfully bad luck! Poor thing, she* *seems to be* ***accident-prone***. □ adj compound accident-prone

prone to sth[2] [Comp (AdjP)] having a propensity, or liking, for (doing) sth **V:** ⚠ be, become; make sb/sth. **adv mod:** very, less, more, equally. **o:** anger, laughter, tears; fainting, losing/lose his temper, skidding/skid on wet surfaces □ *'Will he be very angry, do you think,' 'Well, he's a man* ***prone to*** *anger and this does seem an occasion for it.'* □ *Outsiders regard them as undisciplined, rather comic and no fighters; resenting this, they are* ***prone to*** *demonstrative acts of heroism.* NS □ *I've found it a difficult cabbage to grow, very* ***prone to*** *shooting up to length instead of forming a compact heart.* □ *Whether the reason for it* (heavy social drinking) *is climatic or temperamental, or both, it is a recurrent theme in Irish history. Irish emigrants, both to America and the UK, have been notoriously* ***prone to*** *take the habit with them.* SC □ adj compound laughter-prone .

the proof of the pudding (is in the eating) (saying) the true value of sb/sth (can be judged only from practical experience and not from appearance, theory etc) □ *Another question remains: does food taste better if a recipe precedes it? I doubt it. Sometimes, of course, the recipe is fascinating and the food deadly, and—on rare occasions—the food excels the recipe: but* ***the proof of the pudding is*** *still* ***in the eating***. L □ *The chance Mr Heath has of rushing the package through Parliament, carrying reluctant Tories along, is partly dependent on its contents and on the concessions he may or may not have made in the mysterious deal over sterling.* ***The proof of the pudding***—NS □ *You'd have thought this message was not one to appeal to today's world but* ***the proof of the pudding is in the eating****, and upwards of 2 million have bought his books and crowds flock to hear him speak.*

a proper/right Charley/Charlie [Comp (NP)] (informal) a stupid, inept, freakish etc person, or one who appears to be so **V:** ⚠ be, seem, look □ *These night-watchmen* (precursors of the police), *introduced in Charles II's reign, were practically useless. The public jeered at these men and called them 'Charlies', after the King. Today many people still use the term '****a proper Charlie****' when they want to describe someone who isn't all that good at doing his job.* OBS □ *'What do you mean "the lights still won't work"?' the foreman said, peering at the dashboard. 'You're* ***a right Charlie****, aren't you? How the hell could the lights work if you don't switch on the ignition?'* □ (headline) *The Don't Do It Yourself Men: Here are some of the adjectives used to describe the men who'll never make* (= become) *Husband of the Year: lazy, untidy, jealous, inconsiderate, unappreciative;* ***a proper Charlie****; the only thing he can do properly is watch television.* TVT

a prophet of doom [Comp (NP)] a person who holds and spreads pessimistic views about present and future conditions in world affairs, etc **V:** ⚠ be; think, make, sb □ *Toynbee has spent his life comparing the ways civilisations rise and fall. He chose a career which made him almost inevitably* ***a prophet of doom***. NS □ *I am* ***no prophet of doom*** *as far as our newspapers are concerned. I am confident that our newspapers are going to be more prosperous, more influential, more worthwhile, ten or twenty years from now.* BBCTV □ *...and Professor Milton Friedman, arch-priest of the money-supply school of economists and* ***prophet of*** *inflationary* ***doom***. L □ *When the marathon talk-in at no 10 Downing Street finally broke up without agreement and with some recrimination on all three sides, it then became open season for the chorus of Job's comforters and the massed* ***prophets of*** *gloom (if not* ***doom****).* L

a prophet (is) without honour in his own country (saying) sb (is) recognized as a great thinker, teacher, writer, artist etc except by his own family, associates, countrymen etc □ (source) *Is not this the carpenter's son? ...And they were offended in him. But Jesus said unto them,* ***A prophet is*** *not* ***without honour,*** *save* ***in his own country*** *and in his own house.* MATTHEW XIII 55-57 □ *Also on the programme are 'If', who seem to be in the position of* ***prophets without honour*** *etc. Highly regarded in America, their musicianship has yet to cut a lot of ice in this country.* RT □ (NONCE) *And a lot of County Sligo where he spent his youth is now known as the Yeats country: there are bars called the Yeats Lounge and The Poet's Rest, though Yeats must have been unique among Irish writers in apparently having been in a bar only once in his life. Nonetheless* ***a prophet was being honoured in his own county****, by his own neighbours, even if they were a bit late, and the reasons were financial as much as literary.* L

(the) pros and cons [n + n non-rev] (the) various points, or arguments, in favour of and against persons, procedures, situations, plans **V:** give, set out, present; argue, discuss □ *She was all too prone to see herself as a case, a moral instance, neatly divided into* ***pros and cons***. PW □ *There are, says Dominic, various advantages and disadvantages in having a father whose name is a household word. But as far as he is concerned* ***the pros and cons*** *cancel each other out.* OBS □ *After setting out* ***the pros and cons****, he simply advised Mr Jenkins to do what he felt he ought to do.* NS □ *ITN'S 'First Report' opened its first Common Market postbag on May 1 and has been running questions and answers ever since. Producer Barrie Sales and presenter Robert Kee feel they will have given* ***the pros and cons*** *a pretty good airing by the finish.* TVT

protest too much affirm, or deny, sth so exaggeratedly that one's sincerity is doubted □ (source) HAMLET: *Madam, how like you this play?* QUEEN: *The lady doth* ***protest too much****, methinks.* HAMLET: *O, but she'll keep her word.* HAMLET VIII 2 □ *'It hardly needs to be said,' is a favourite phrase of Starritt's when protesting the willingness of the* (Special) *Branch to protect vulnerable informers. Starritt* ***protests too much****—it* does *need to be said that the Branch failed to protect Lennon after it was obvious that his cover was blown.* NS □ *There is tremendous fun in this occasionally over-virtuous show which does* ***protest too much*** *at times.* L

proud of sth/sb [Comp (AdjP)] highly pleased and satisfied with, or glorying in, sth one has done or sb/sth one is associated with **V:** ⚠ be, feel; make sb. **o:** our achievement, the school's record; being an Englishman; the regiment, her two handsome sons □ *In education our post-war architectural record is surely second to none. From the pioneering Hertfordshire schools of the 1950s to the architectural adventurousness of the new universities, we have much to be* ***proud of****.* OBS □ *She had stuck to the job because the aunt who had brought her up was so* ***proud of*** *her and liked to boast about her and show her off when she came home in uniform.* DC ⇨ ⚠ next entry.

proud of sth [A (AdvP)] protruding, or extending, above sth **V:** ⚠ stand, be, rise. **o:** the surface, the rim, its surroundings □ *The filler should be worked firmly into the dent or groove and built up until it stands* ***proud of*** *the surrounding surface. When it is quite dry, start rubbing away the surplus filler.* ST □ *As soon as the sediment starts creeping up the shoulder of the bottle, stop pouring. You should now have a glass of star-bright beer with a head* (of foam) *that stands* ***proud of*** *the glass but does not overflow.* G ⇨ ⚠ previous entry.

prove one's/the case/point [V + O pass] demonstrate that one's/the affirmation, argument, criticism etc is true □ *He gave the Prime Minister to understand that in his view the British forces on the western flank could and should be more offensive; they were not fighting as they should, and he quoted the casualty figures to* ***prove his case****.* MFM □ JIMMY: *Anyone who doesn't like real jazz hasn't any feeling either for music or people.* HELEN: *Rubbish.* JIMMY (to Cliff): *That seems to* ***prove my point*** *for you.* LBA □ *'What about the railway station?' he said. 'It's hardly ever used these days.' A quick survey* ***proved the point****.* H

prunes and prism(s) [n + n non-rev] affected gentility and precise enunciation; genteel and narrowly correct behaviour □ (source) *'Father' is rather vulgar, my dear. The word 'Papa', besides, gives a pretty form to the lips. Papa, potatoes, poultry,* ***prunes and prism****, are all very good words for the lips; especially* ***prunes and prism****.* LITTLE DORRIT (C DICKENS 1812-70) □ *'Papa, potatoes,* ***prunes and prisms****,' said over and over again was supposed, at one time, to be the correct formula for producing a pretty mouth.* SC □ *'I like nasty things better than nice things,' said Jessica, with such a* ***Prunes and Prisms*** *of diction that all the grown-ups (except Nurse) had to laugh.* WDM □ *Susan was not at all the* ***prunes-and-prisms*** *miss that I thought a 'private governess' education might have made her.* □ not widely-used; attrib use *a* ***prunes-and-prisms*** *miss.*

Pseuds' Corner (catchphrase) a place to which one relegates people with pretensions to knowledge, taste, interests, artistic ability which they do not have (from the section with this title in the magazine 'Private Eye'; pseud = pretentious, false person) □ *The one article connected with my own studies contained so many errors of fact it was a short step to wondering whether the rest might not be contributions from* ***Pseuds' Corner*** *too.* SC □ *They go to more trouble dressing simply, eating simply, and finding simple pleasures than you and I are ever likely to in our so-called artificial lives. It's all* ***pseuds' corner*** *stuff to me, what they preach about natural life-styles.* □ *Some of the more academic writings on rock music I have found both valuable and enlightening, and I do not share the reactions of those who send off to '****Pseuds' Corner****' all writings about rock which use words longer than 'super' or 'danceable'.* L □ attrib use ***Pseuds' Corner*** *stuff.*

a pub crawl (informal) an evening/a day spent drinking in a succession of public-houses □ *And, since the cold weather had set in, they had allowed their earlier custom of* ***a*** *weekly* ***pub-crawl*** *to lapse.* HD □ *Ronnie, seven years his senior, was big and hearty, a great beer drinker, a jolly companion on* ***a pub-crawl****.* PE □ *But tell me—you see, I have to ask you, Alec hasn't told me anything—didn't he want to take you* ***pub-crawling****?* PW □ with or without hyphen; variants a pub-crawler, pub-crawling.

public property [Comp (NP)] known to everybody or anybody **S:** facts, incidents, situations, relationship; his failure, bankruptcy, dismissal; sb's quarrel with sb **V:** ⚠ be, become; make sth □ *For, ever since the rich Mr Macfadyen's proposal to the Admiral's daughter had become* ***public property****, there had been a growing feeling that unless he married her out of hand she would go on being engaged all her life and probably die an old maid while her parents survived her.* WDM □ *It's* ***public property*** *now that during his last two years of office the man was senile, but his name carried so much weight his colleagues thought it worthwhile to cover up for him.*

publish and be damned make your accusation as publicly as you like and 'be damned to you', ie the speaker does not care, will not pay you money or do anything else in exchange for your keeping quiet; the speaker refuses to be blackmailed (attributed to the DUKE OF WELLINGTON 1769-1852 as referred to in the first quotation) □ *Kenneth Bourne has edited a selection of unpublished letters from the celebrated nineteenth century tart Harriette Wilson, the lady who reputedly was told by Wellington to '****publish and be damned****'.* G □ *It did not seem right that the Count, who must by now be rising ninety, should die without hearing his wife's confession. It was true that when Daniel had last broached the matter she had flown into one of the silly tantrums of the aged and had said, '****Publish and be damned****!'* US □ *The 'Observer', in common with most other London papers, seemed to have taken absolutely no notice of the magistrates' warning, and published the confession in full with a '****publish and be damned****' attitude echoed in the Press many times since.* OBS □ (NONCE) *The story had two morals: not only the obvious 'Now wash your hands' but also '****Publish and be saved****'. Semmelweis* (a 19th c obstetrician) *did not publish soon enough, to the detriment of both human welfare and of his own mental health.* L

puff and blow [v + v non-rev] breathe noisily from physical exertion; threaten, protest and exclaim imprecisely; huff and puff (qv) □ *You're in poor trim. A man of your age shouldn't be* ***puffing and blowing*** *after climbing one flight of stairs.* □ *It is a compromise, and however much Mr Cousins may* ***puff and blow****, it will undoubtedly be accepted by the annual conference.* OBS

a puffing billy (dated informal) a railway-engine of the (old) steam-driven type □ *The* *splendid mechanical beast which now we condescendingly call* ***a puffing billy*** *or an old iron horse: a hundred years ago, it was as magical as a space-ship.* L □ variants (used by children) a puff-puff, a puffer.

pull sb's leg [V + O pass] (informal) say sth, in a joking way, to tease, fluster or deceive sb, esp temporarily □ *'She's probably got some chap at home who's just as steady as she is, waiting to marry her.' 'No, do you think so?' 'Go on, I'm* ***pulling your leg****.'* TGLY □ *'Would you place yourself* (as a writer) *in a direct line of descent from Kafka? 'No' replied Froulish shortly. 'My masters are Dante, Spinoza, Rimbaud, Boehme, and Greig.' Hutchins champed agitatedly on his pipe-stem. His face lost a little of its buoyant expression; he was not sure whether* ***his leg*** *was being* ***pulled****.* HD □ *'Poetry!' said Percy. 'You're making a bloody fool of yourself supporting that charlatan. It isn't poetry, it's* ***a leg-pull****.'* MM □ *The young Norwegian, who was a bit of* ***a leg-puller****, took a bowl of cream of tomato, and proceeded to empty half a dozen sardines into it. The others looked on in astonishment.* TBC □ also pl pull their legs; n compounds a leg-pull, a leg-puller.

pull one's punches [V + O pass] in a boxing match etc, use less force in one's punches than one could do; (fig) describe, criticize or rebuke sb/sth less forcibly, or adversely, than one could do or others would do **S:** writer, critic; programme, play, story. **det:** one's, no, (not) any, few □ *It is interesting to note that 'The Fight Against Slavery', which BBC 2 is waging, has been accused of* ***pulling its punches****.* L □ *Even in comment on the individual poems Mr Stallworthy* ***pulls his punches****. To call the address to Eros 'curious and disturbing' is just mealymouthed. It is, in fact, homo-erotic.* SC □ *I liked the story because it* ***pulled no punches*** *—making clear than an assignment is a job of work that overrides any personal feelings a reporter may have.* DM □ (reader's letter) *In his Richard Dimbleby lecture, Lord Goodman* ***pulled few punches****.* L □ *Nobody had got upset, nobody had shouted or been unpleasant, they'd all abided by the rules of debate, but* ***no punches*** *had been* ***pulled****.* TSMP □ often neg, as shown. ⇨ ⚠ pack a punch.

pull rank (on sb) [V + O] (try to) make use of one's social, or official, rank or position to gain advantages, priority etc that one is not really entitled to; make one's inferiors in rank or position feel aware of that difference **o:** students, the other passengers □ *But in his present position Owen ought to be even a little more than a good European. He ought to be appalled at the way the Cabinet has behaved, he ought to be* ***pulling rank****, creating a stink.* NS □ *He called for a revival of the Dunkirk spirit to attack inflation. At Dunkirk 'we did not* ***pull rank****, we abandoned snobbery and did not really insist on the retention of status symbols.'* SC

pull (the) strings/wires [V + O pass] manipulate others for one's own advantage (as one might control string-puppets); use indirect pressure, influential friends, etc to obtain posts, favours or to avoid duties, penalties □ *They like giving people aid as long as it enables them to* ***pull strings*** *and influence governments.* L □ PHILIP: *Myra dear, I don't know how often I've told you that I don't believe in this—you can do more by quietly* ***pulling strings*** *than you ever can by mass protests and committees and that kind of thing.* EHOW □ *All that was necessary to avoid the statutory period of National Service was a relative or two sufficiently well-connected to* ***pull the wires****.* □ HARRIS: *How does a young actress get her first important role?* RIGG: *Sometimes luck, but basically it's because the producers and directors study you, note your improvement. There's a lot talked about* ***string-pulling*** *and going to bed with directors, but the basic thing is how good your acting is.* OBS □ n compounds a string-/wire-puller, string/wire pulling.

pull one's weight [V + O] work to the full measure of one's capacity; do one's fair share in a joint effort or undertaking (from rowing, esp as one of a boat-crew) □ *If each one of us does his duty, and* ***pulls his*** *full* ***weight****, then nothing can stop the Eighth Army.* MFM □ *Don't let us forget either, that wool prices are dropping. Or that both partners in an estate have to* ***pull their weight****.* WI □ *Producer Gerry Glaister's favourite cartoon shows a TV tycoon bawling out one of his junior executives with the accusation 'You've been with us for 18 months and you haven't got an ulcer—you can't be* ***pulling your weight****'.* RT

pure/plain and simple [adj + adj non-rev] exact(ly); not more, less, nor other than □ *It is madness* ***pure and simple*** *to race wildly on a bicycle down a country road, chasing a motor-car.* HD □ *To the rest of us, it was a joke,* ***pure and simple****, but Ned, though there were undoubtedly times when he saw it as we did, would often get into a very solemn mood about the Book.* CON □ *You're going to exit this world one way or the other, so you might as well choose the manner of your own demise. With me it's gluttony,* ***pure and simple****. I love my food.* TVT □ *Now—a column in the 'Observer' having succeeded one in the 'Guardian'—Des likes to think of himself as a journalist* ***plain and simple****: never again a public man.* NS □ modifies a preceding n.

a purple patch/passage an extremely, or too, ornate portion in a literary work, music, painting, architecture etc □ *If he had confined himself to the dialogue and action and cut out* ***the purple patches*** *where he describes the scenery and moralizes on the folly of mankind and so on he might have found a publisher for his novel.* □ *...the great prima donna singing not only famous* ***purple patches*** *but the entire works to which these patches belong.* T □ *Doesn't a brutally edited version of Mr Callaghan's* ***purple passages*** *make them seem more dramatic and sensational than they really are?* SC

purse one's lips [V + O pass] draw one's lips tightly together, esp indicating disapproval, doubt, concentrated thought □ *The other man gazed at a spot on the wall over Sefton's head, screwed up his eyes and* ***pursed his lips****.* ARG □ *I still thought I had never heard such a silly idea in my life as Tom's proposition. Also, I thought Myrtle would see it in exactly the same light. Tom* ***pursed his lips****, and smiled.* SPL □ *In the also-ran enclosure, Yamaha's mechanics* ***pursed their lips*** *when Gould told them he'd had trouble* *with his brakes.* ST ▫ *Through the dirty fog of feckless slum living faint rays of moral precept would shine from time to time, and she would feebly and grumblingly attempt to reproduce something of the* ***pursed-lipped****, self-righteous matriarchy of her own girlhood home.* HAA ▫ *Mrs Allan disapproved of the free way in which the younger girls gossiped about their friends. She returned to her desk* ***with pursed lips****.* ▫ adj compound pursed-lipped; variant with pursed lips.

push/press one's luck [V + O] rashly, or optimistically, risk sth that depends on one's luck continuing, even though one's luck has already been unusually good; attempt sth that could only succeed if one were extremely lucky **A:** too far, too hard, (any) farther ▫ *'What's wrong with a drop of rain? I've had plenty of wettings all my life and never taken any harm.' 'All right, but remember you're getting older—and don't bother* ***pushing your luck****, that's all. Take your umbrella, as I say.'* ▫ *If any of the pups* ***pushed his luck*** *too far in the mauling and scrapping games they enjoyed, his mother would give him a sharp nip on the nose.* ▫ *But Ashmore was cleverer than that. He came into money and wisely didn't* ***press his luck*** *after that. Directors are like alchemists, their hour is brief.* OBS ▫ press less often used.

push and shove [v + v rev] struggle, esp among others doing likewise, to make one's way through a crowd, eg by pushing, jostling, thrusting with elbows, shoulders or knees ▫ *The tea for the kiddies, originally planned to be on trestle tables in the market place, had to be in the Church Hall where the crowding, the noise, the greed, the* ***pushing and shoving*** *were of an unusually high standard.* WDM ▫ *I don't like having to* ***push and shove*** *in order to get onto a bus.* ▫ rev but usu in order of headphrase.

pushing forty etc (informal) approaching the age of 40 etc; rising twenty etc (qv); close on (qv) (the reference usu being to a decade or other marked point in sb's life, such as a qualifying or retirement age) **n:** forty, ⚠ fifty, sixty, sixty-five ▫ *One thing I think mustn't be long when you're* ***pushing 40*** *is hair; it can look all right from behind, but people can get such a shock when you turn round.* TVT ▫ *Athlete? At* ***pushing 70****—emphatically yes. 'Look at this,' he says, thumping a picture in a glossy motorcycle brochure. 'Isn't she something? I've just bought her, 750 cc.'* RT ▫ *It's not when he's* ***pushing 65****, but long before, that a man should give thought to how he will occupy his time after retirement.* ▫ less likely to be used of anyone *under* 40.

put sb/sth first [V + O + A pass] consider sb/sth to be more important than anything else and act accordingly **n:** one's wife, children; duty, comfort ▫ *I said I sympathized with the French officers in 1940 who looked after their families; they didn't anyway* ***put*** *their careers* ***first****.* OMIH ▫ *I'm as disappointed as you, Julie, that I can't take you out tonight, but a doctor sometimes has to* ***put*** *his patients* ***first****.* ▫ *'And do be careful.' 'Don't worry. No matter how much of a hurry I'm in to get somewhere I always* ***put*** *safety* ***first****.'* ⇨ ⚠ (put) first things first.

put it etc differently etc [V + O + A pass] describe, express or explain sth differently etc **O:** it, ⚠ the matter, the question, things. **adv** differently; this way, another way, more clearly, (very) well, as well ▫ *'Malice' always seems to me too strong a word for what clever, amusing and delightful writers do in conversation. Arthur Marshall* ***puts it differently****: 'On the whole he liked people to behave badly—he was amused, he loved it.'* L ▫ *The travelling population* (ie esp gypsies) *of Britain is between 18,000 and 25,000 — and even most of the 50-year-olds haven't been to school. Let's* ***put it*** *this way: we owe these people 10 years of education.* OBS ▫ *'We don't know what lies ahead. And, anyway, we may as well leave the place looking brighter than we found it.' Or, to* ***put it another way****, they intend to leave their mark. And for that they deserve a king-sized 'A' for Achievement.* H ▫ *'Does that sound silly?' 'No. Not one little bit. I've always felt like that myself, only I can't* ***put it as well*** *as you.'* RATT ▫ *But history is no help to a modern caterer trying to persuade—or as he would* ***put it****, 'educate'—customers to accept a food they never ate at Mother's knee.* N ▫ variants as sb would put it, I don't know how to put it.

(to) put it mildly (to) make an understatement; (to) describe sth in less harsh or realistic terms than it probably merits; to say the least (of it) (qv) ▫ *'Well,' he said, 'whoever did it certainly knows the names of some of the members of the staff.' 'That's* ***putting it mildly****—knows their habits very well too.'* TT ▫ *'I could say the conditions of sale were not clearly explained to me.' 'You would be* ***putting it*** *very* ***mildly*** *indeed if you said that. In my view, you've been the victim of deliberate misrepresentation.'* ▫ *Saying that Victoria was taken aback is* ***to put it mildly****. She was completely flabbergasted.* TC ▫ *Sinister circumstantial evidence was found. Local people spoke of hearing the sounds of a struggle. Suspicion,* ***to put it mildly****, turned towards Thurtell, and although no body had been found he was arrested.* OBS ▫ often Disj; put usu in the continuous tenses or as *to*-inf.

to put it no higher [Disj] without exaggerating, or making any greater claim for or against sth (though perhaps one justifiably could) ▫ *She had thought somehow that love with Patrick would make everyhing stop, but in fact everything seemed to be going on in much the same way as before,* ***to put it no higher****.* TGLY ▫ *A poem of hers appeared in the local paper in a tribute to his memory that was,* ***to put it no higher****, heartfelt.* ▫ front, middle or end position.

put sth right/straight [V + O + Comp pass] correct an error, unsatisfactory situation, etc; redress an injustice; set/put the record straight (qv) **O:** it, this; the matter, things; these misunderstandings, the worst of the defects, the wrong you have done these people ▫ *Is it too late to recognize the mistake and try to* ***put it right****?* SC ▫ *From what I had learnt the troops had their tails down and there was no confidence in the higher command. This would have to be* ***put right*** *at once.* MFM ▫ *'I was of course, relying on Mr Robert to* ***put*** *things* ***right*** *with his lordship.' 'A great mistake to rely on Robert for anything.' said Julius soberly.* EM ▫ *I dare say he'll forget all about it* (ie the money he owes me), *now he's* *gone away; but then Mr Sands will see to it that things are* ***put straight****.* HAA

put sb right/straight (about etc sth) [V + O + Comp] (informal) correct sb in an error; acquaint sb with the true facts, proper procedure, etc (about etc sth) **O:** you, him; his teachers, them all. **prep:** about, on, concerning, over □ (reader's letter) *If your writers had wanted to quote a factually correct case it would have been better to counterpose Marx and Bernstein or Marx and Sidney Webb. Really! Any one of our audiences in Hyde Park could have* ***put*** *you* ***right****.* RT □ *Snap out of it, you dreamer, get down to earth. This is journalism. All you need is a sublime confidence that you can* ***put*** *absolutely anyone* ***right on*** *how to do his job.* ST □ *In his 78th year, J. B. Priestly does very much want to try and* ***put us straight about*** *a state of mind which troubles him in contemporary society.* SC

a Pyrrhic victory [Comp (NP)] an unprofitable victory, success over another force, person etc, where losses are greater than is justified by anything gained (King Pyrrhus of Epirus defeated Roman army in 279 BC, but with so great a slaughter of his men that he said 'One more such victory and Pyrrhus is undone') **V:** ⚠ be, appear; make sth □ *So many windows were broken, dustbins upturned, air let out of bicycle tyres, and heads split as a result of* ***pyrrhic victories*** *in gang raids—for he seemed suddenly to be losing his military genius—that it became dangerous for Frankie to walk down our street.* LLDR □ (reader's letter) *Internment was Mr Faulkner's victory over Westminster, and over wisdom. It was* ***a*** *shameful,* ***Pyrrhic victory****, putting back any settlement by months, perhaps years.* SC □ *So it looks as if the politicians have won. My only point is that it has been* ***a Pyrrhic victory****. In no country in the world are politicians held in greater or more open derision than they are here.* NS

Q

Queen Anne is dead (saying) your news is stale; everybody knows (this) already □ *So we Britons have little or no real influence in world affairs—and* ***Queen Anne is dead*** *too. The distinguished lecturer hardly needed to labour a point which we have stopped bothering to remind each other of.* SC

a queer fish [Comp (NP)] (informal) a strange, odd person; a misfit; an odd fish/bird (qv) **V:** ⚠ be; find, think, sb □ *All sorts of cultists and* ***queer fish*** *teach all kinds of techniques for achieving health, contentment, peace of mind.* DOP □ *One of the last men to join this expedition was Denon,* ***a queer fish*** *in this amphibious operation, since he was a civilian and already aged 51.* BN

the question (of sth) arises sth specified must be considered and discussed **o:** legal liability; his future career, your successor; what to do, how to tackle the problem, when to sell □ *When he was sixteen* ***the question of*** *a career* ***arose****.* PE □ *We've decided to shut down your post, and* ***the question arises****—what are we to do with you?* OMIH □ *In the summer of 1945* ***the question arose*** *whether the nation should make grants of money to the principal commanders in the field.* MFM ⇨ ⚠ raise a question; raise the question etc (of sth).

the question of the hour [Comp (NP)] the question, matter of debate, etc that attracts interest at a particular time **V:** ⚠ be, become; make sth □ *The nation was thrilled, shocked, sympathetic. Whether Edward would abdicate in favour of his brother became* ***the question of the hour****.* □ *The British visitor is possibly better placed than most to arbitrate with some detachment on* ***the question of the hour****. This, in essence, is whether the Merion Golf Course has been made too difficult.* OBS □ also pl questions of the hour.

a quick-change artist an actor who makes rapid changes in costume, appearance, make-up etc to perform a quick succession of roles; (fig) a person able or likely to switch functions, opinions, interests etc rapidly □ *Any teacher whose timetable covers different age groups and different abilities has to be something of* ***a quick-change artist****.* □ *'Yesterday he wanted to hitch-hike all the way. Now he wants to borrow my car.' 'Oh well, he's not* ***the*** *only* ***quick-change artist*** *in the family?'* □ also pl.

the quick and the dead [n + n non-rev] the living and the dead □ (source—see also ACTS X 42) *He ascended into heaven; From thence He shall come to judge* ***the quick and the dead****.* BOOK OF COMMON PRAYER □ (of the funeral of King George V) *There have been times in history when the death of a monarch has seemed to mark the end of an epoch, but on that day I seemed to have been more impressed by* ***the quick*** *than* ***the dead****.* AH

quick/slow in/on the uptake [Comp (AdjP)] mentally alert/sluggish; quick/slow to grasp information, pick up a meaning, suggestion or hint **V:** ⚠ be; find, think, sb □ *Malone was both clever and* ***quick in the uptake****.* SML □ *The interested parties—builders, speculators, or whatever—can always turn around and tell me that I am too* ***slow in the uptake****.* SC □ *'Men are* ***slow on the uptake*** *sometimes,' said Pat, and she said it as though her experience was a wide one and deep as you like.* TT

a quick one [O/o (NP)](informal) a single alcoholic drink, esp taken to refresh one, or to cheer one up, and fitted in before, after or while doing sth **V:** have; go for, have time for □ *We'll go downstairs and have* ***a quick one*** *before we start on the next batch of letters.* □ *After lunch, Bill went for* ***a quick one*** *to the local pub. The meal had been oppressive.* HAA □ STANLEY: *We can stop in at the Red Lion for* ***a quick one****.* FFE

the quickness of the hand deceives the eye (catchphrase) a swift action, skilfully performed, makes a spectator believe that what appears to have happened has actually happened, although this is not so (from the patter of conjurors and players of card tricks) □ *'Rhumb Line' is a chilly little scrap of black comedy in which* ***the quickness of the*** *writer's* ***hand deceives the*** *reader's* ***eye***. NS □ *'I say,' said Lord Mellings when they had finished, 'you do sing well.' 'An illusion,' said Aubrey. 'I can make a noise like a good singer.* ***The quickness of the hand deceives the eye****.'* WDM □ (NONCE) *The closing of music halls put the big illusionists out of business, and the clubs and cabaret shows are much more demanding for the men out to prove that* ***the hand is quicker than the eye****.* TVT

a quid pro quo sth given that is equivalent to a gift or favour received; sth done in retaliation for injury etc (from *quid pro quo* (Latin) = something for something else) □ *'What's this you've brought?'* ***'A quid pro quo****. Last night we drank all your whisky.'* □ *She worries about accepting hospitality she can't return but I tell her people don't conduct their friendships on* ***a quid pro quo*** *basis.* □ (NONCE) *Only Secretary of the Treasury Connally cushioned the jolt to the public—who hadn't known that the dollar was even trembling on its pedestal—by saying that the agreement to devalue was* ***a quid*** *for many a* ***quo****.* L

(a/an life/air of) quiet desperation (catchphrase) (a life characterized by) silent or controlled, but despairing, struggle esp again circumstances □ (source) *The mass of men le* ***lives of quiet desperation****.* WALDEN (H THOREAU 1817-62) □ *Her husband is gentle: 'Ov the years he has perfected small attentions wh his imagination drifts from me.' Is she happy? C leading* ***a life of quiet desperation****?* L □ *He h* ***that air of quiet desperation*** *so often seen the faces of those who are trying to make a j of an alcoholic wife or husband.* BBCR □ (fil review) *John Fraser and James Fox flound miserably and Derek Nimmo hums and ha's* (makes noises indicating hesitation or doub *with* ***quiet desperation****.* RT

quite so perfectly true; I agree with you; I agr (that) □ *'We should have booked our flight befo the prices went up.'* ***'Quite so****, my dear, but it a bit late thinking about it now.'* □ (rain stopp play at the test match) *As Maddock said to Ma tin Jenkins that sodden Monday evening: 'W hope that the music you have heard today h pleased you—or as much as it could have do in the circumstances.'* ***Quite so.*** L □ short rep or comment, often expressing ironic agreeme (second example) or introducing a qualifyi statement beginning with *but, however* (fir example).

R

a race/fight against time [Comp (NP)] an effort to complete sth before, or by, a given time or before sth else happens to prevent its success **V:** ⚠ be, become, turn into □ *'Yes,' she said grudgingly, and I could see she was beginning to stiffen and I knew the rest was* ***a race against time****, and I said, 'These questions may seem somewhat personal and irrelevant, but I must get this financial background straight if I am to get your son straight.'* PP □ *It was now, I realised,* ***a fight against time****: if I could keep this solitary specimen alive until we reached England, I felt sure that I could find something it would eat.* BB

rack one's brains/memory [V + O] make anxious and determined efforts to think of, or recall, sth specific or suitable **A:** to find a solution; for an explanation □ *All night I have been tossing and turning,* ***racking my brains*** *to think what could have possessed that poor young man to kill himself.* EM □ *I* ***racked my brains*** *and tried hard to picture the feelings of anger and indignation.* HAHA □ *I* ***racked my memory*** *in vain for its counterpart in literature: perhaps you could think of one.* PW

a/the rag and bone man etc [n + n non-rev] a street trader who, formerly, bought and sold old clothes, household waste or discarded articles; the place, activity, of such buying and selling **n:** man, ⚠ merchant; shop, trade □ *It was the same with his 'hand cart'. The five pounds would never have run to a good one, and he had found* ***a rag-and-bone man*** *willing to sell him the ruins of an old pram for five shillings.* HD □ *At the same time I* (moved) *away with an awkward shuffling gait, holding the two coats over my arm like* ***a rag-and-bone merchant****.* CON □ *She had enjoyed a Wesleyan childhood and, through t dirty fog of feckless slum living—the long ra* ***and-bone years*** *of Stepney, and the lazy od job existence of the country—faint rays moral precept would shine from time to tim* HAA □ *Yeats, in a fine phrase about a mo emotional, sexual state, wrote about* ***the 'r and bone shop*** *of the heart'. Mr Wilson is t* ***rag and bone man*** *of social democracy.* NS ***rag-and-bone years*** = 'years when one depe ded on the rag-and-bone trade', or more gene ally, 'a makeshift existence'.

the rag-tag and bobtail (of sth) [n + n no rev] (derogatory) the lower classes general the ordinary members of a communit profession etc who are of no individual impo tance **o:** city, parish; clan, army □ *All the peop of whom you and I are* ***the ragtag and bobta*** *all the camp followers of western civilization, w have taken it for granted that, even if we did n live up to those exalted ethical standards, we d a great deal better than anyone else.* NM □ *Th householders in the Square paid for the upkeep the central gardens and didn't want* ***the rag-t and bobtail*** *making use of them.* □ *If he's prominent barrister or a solicitor with a big co nection he'll have plenty of money; but* ***the rag tag and bobtail of*** *the profession don't make a that much, you know.* □ formerly often tag an rag or tag, rag and bobtail, but now almost alwa in order of headphrase.

the rag trade (informal) business concerne with the designing, making, or marketing, c women's clothes □ *Big-timers in the fashio business in Rome and Paris are frenetically ad ing the finishing touches to their autumn colle* *ions while lesser fry* (ie smaller, less important, businesses) *in* ***the rag trade*** *are thinking up their ollections for spring.* SC ▫ *Our daily weather ontinues to dictate the trivial scenarios of our ives — and remains manna to* ***the rag trade****, he tourist industry, and heaven knows what else.* IS

gs and tatters [n + n non-rev] old, torn or worn-out clothes, soft furnishings, papers etc; the poor remains of a former way of life, system, creed etc **V:** be in; dress in; reduce to ▫ *They found several hundred pounds in the house when he died—enough to show that there had been no need for him to half-starve himself and go about in* ***rags and tatters****.* ▫ *They're not like our children. Any picture books they're given are educed to* ***rags and tatters*** *within a week.* ▫ *For even he, illiterate and unimpressive in the* ***rags and tatters*** *of our civilisation, knew that without his gods life would lose its meaning and inevitably ead towards disaster.* LWK ▫ nouns can be used eparately.

in/pour cats and dogs rain very heavily ▫ *We'll meet at the parking place in the village about 9 o'clock, and decide then whether it's a day for the boat, or for walking. If it's* ***raining cats and dogs****, of course, we won't expect you o turn up at all.* ▫ *We went to Ireland but we can hardly say we saw it. It* ***poured cats and dogs*** *every single day.* ▫ only in impersonal constructions with *it*.

e rain falls on the just and the unjust saying) virtue does not ensure all benefits or protect against all hazards ▫ (source) *For he maketh his sun to rise on the evil and on the good, and sendeth* ***rain on the just and*** *on* ***the unjust****.* MATTHEW V 45 ▫ *'What have I done to deserve this?', a common cry of men and women in distress, presupposes a logic of punishment and reward in a world where, unfortunately,* ***the rain falls*** *equally* ***on the just and the unjust****.* G ▫ ***Rain*** *may* ***fall on the just and the unjust****—but not, at least while this Prime Minister is in charge, government largesse* (= generous giving).

aise Cain/(merry) hell[1] [V + O] behave in an extravagantly noisy, unrestrained or riotous way (Cain, from GENESIS IV 5-12) ▫ *They* (railroad builders) *slept in dormitory trains, they* ***raised Cain*** *in mobile track towns with fly-by-night saloon keepers, gamblers, whores.* L ▫ *What did he do in the interim? 'Opted out, got reacquainted with friends I hadn't seen in years, lazed around the Caribbean, Mexico and Hawaii, hooked a 210 lb marlin, and* ***raised*** *a whole lot of* ***hell****,' he said.* TVT ▫ *Former bar-room brawler and* ***hell-raiser*** *Robert Conrad (remember 'Hawaiian Eye' and 'Wild Wild West') stars in a new series here.* TVT ▫ *She seems so quiet usually — I got quite a shock seeing her* ***raising merry hell*** *with the rest of us at the party last night.* ▫ n compound a hell-raiser.

aise Cain/(merry) hell[2] [V + O] complain, protest, exert one's authority, etc angrily or violently ▫ *And keep that puppy off the sofa. Your mother will* ***raise Cain*** *if he piddles on it again.* ▫ *If I were the headmaster of that school, I'd* ***raise hell*** *with the education office till they got those potholes in the playground filled in.* ▫ *We both knew that coppers put bets on horses. Eric St Johnson, who was then the Chief Constable, was on the telephone and* ***raising merry hell*** *about it.* L

raise a dust [V + O pass] cause a considerable amount of trouble, fuss, commotion; kick up[2] (Vol 1) (qv) **det:** a, the; some; a lot (of), such a ▫ *'Bad-tempered bitch! Where's she gone, anyway?' 'Probably to the manager's office to* ***raise a dust*** *about your using her typewriter.'* ▫ *Any day now, your wife's going to find out about your girlfriend and* ***raise the dust*** *accordingly.* ▫ *'There'll be threats of staff resignation, protest meetings by parent groups, and a whole lot more besides.' 'Oh well, you can't re-organize a whole school without* ***raising some dust****. It'll all settle soon.'* ⇨ the dust settles.

raise one's/sb's eyebrows [V + O pass] express, by facial gesture, one's surprise, doubt, scepticism or disapproval/cause others to display similar feelings ▫ *Our more conventional archaeological friends sometimes* ***raised their eyebrows*** *and sniffed a little plaintively at 'all this publicity of Wheeler's'!* SD ▫ ***Eyebrows*** *were* ***raised*** *in the Treasury when the Prime Minister hinted at an imminent devaluation of the pound.* ▫ (reader's letter) *Your claim that 'the biggest drum in the world' was made in the Rhaedr factory has* ***raised certain eyebrows*** *and could be challenged (see the 'Guinness Book of Records').* RT ▫ *As well as their scientific knowledge, they have developed special equipment which would* ***raise an eyebrow*** *or two in Wardour Street.* RT ▫ *Master Sharify* (posing as a doctor) *was unmasked not because of some professional ineptitude but because some of his fellow labourers recognised him as a chap who had been in the place before, employed as a porter. In his performance as a healer Abdul had caused not* ***a*** *single* ***raised eyebrow****.* NS ▫ variants raise eyebrows, raise some/certain eyebrows used of people other than the S.

raise sb's hackles [V + O pass] cause sb to feel and show anger, resentment, antagonism etc (from the hackles, neck feathers, of a bird raised in aggressive display) ▫ *But his justification of this added support might have been calculated to* ***raise the hackles of*** *those members of the theatrical profession who are not already jealous of the money spent on the National.* L ▫ *Scots often say they feel more at home in Copenhagen or Oslo than in London. And even in the most British of Scots* ***the hackles*** *could be* ***raised****.* NS ▫ *If Robin Day,* ***raiser of hackles*** *and freezer of cockles to successive Prime Ministers, can complain that he was in danger of being reduced to a commissionaire whose only job is to open and close the doors of 'Panorama', what power and influence can we credit to his rivals?* ST ▫ *I think I agree with Mr Pettifer's views of the* (Vietnam) *war, and he has reported it with great distinction, but* ***my hackles rise*** *when I am presented with only one veteran in nine who dissents, and he legless.* L ▫ *Mr Lumet has had the guts and flair to take Serpico's story which resulted in a comb-out of the New York constabulary and its high-ups, and make a lot of it stick: you could* ***feel*** *even case-hardened* ***hackles rising*** *at the press show.* NS ▫ n compound a raiser of hackles; variant (feel/make) one's/sb's hackles rise. ⇨ warm the cockles (of sb's heart.)

raise/rear its (ugly) head [V + O] arise;

become apparent and esp threatening **S:** war; envy; sex; political self-interest; religious intolerance □ *Then another question* ***raises its head****. If we call a* (musical) *style 'more advanced', what is it in it that makes it more advanced?* L □ *'I think that anyone who is born a Catholic is bound to find all this rather difficult to understand.' Robin saw that his mother was about to spring at the* ***rearing*** *of Rome****'s ugly head****, so he turned the conversation.* ASA □ *But when he learns that officialdom has again* ***reared its head*** *and is planning the destruction of his last home, his fighting spirit returns.* TVT □ *After their first night together, Terence said, 'Darling Elizabeth, you can't imagine what a relief it is that sex has at last* ***reared its ugly head****,' and Elizabeth agreed.* HAA □ also pl raise/rear their (ugly) heads.

raise hopes [V + O pass] make sb more hopeful that sth will happen **det:** my, his, their. **adj:** false; fond; foolish □ *'You'll be rung if there are any fresh developments. Mustn't* ***raise*** *your* ***hopes****, though,' he added. 'She may never recover consciousness again.'* PE □ *The fall, over the last week, in the number of notified cases has* ***raised hopes*** *that the epidemic is running itself out.* □ *It's true that the experiment hasn't worked according to plan, and Luke was right to tell us so. I'm not going to* ***raise*** *false* ***hopes****, so I shan't say any more about that.* NM □ *His* ***hopes*** *had been* ***raised*** *by what his interviewer said to him, so he was particularly disappointed when he didn't get the job.*

raise a laugh/smile [V + O] amuse sb, one's companions, an audience (either deliberately or not) enough to make them laugh/smile □ MR PARADOCK: *I want to be made up to look like an electronic computer. I want to* ***raise a laugh****.* ART □ *The bird-brained* (= stupid) *secretary has finally pushed the mother-in-law off her perch as the comedian's favourite target. If she is not* ***raising a laugh*** *for being dumb, she is being attacked for being ambitious.* L □ *When a plush circular couch in the centre of the stage alarmingly started to spring to pieces* (the audience) *took it in good humour—perhaps too good—it* ***raised*** *more* ***laughs*** *than any other part of the operetta.* G □ *Baby was usually full of chuckles but that morning I couldn't* ***raise*** *even* ***a smile****.*

raise (the) money etc [V + O pass] obtain (the) money etc, esp for a particular purpose and use, and esp by such means as selling property, borrowing, getting subscriptions or donations from the public **n:** (the) money, ⚠ (the) funds, a loan; (slang) the necessary, the wind □ *I'm sorry, Aunt, I'd much rather you took the cheque back. I'll* ***raise the money*** *somehow to pay off this lot.* ARG □ *The 'Salute the Soldier' campaign brought into being committees not only to* ***raise money****, but also to show the unity of purpose of the country with the Army in the task which lay ahead.* MFM □ *The Townswomen's Guild had already drawn up for the winter a programme of sales of work, coffee mornings and other* ***fund-raising*** *activities.* □ *Was his daughter careless and naive when she unconsciously blackened Sterne's character by publishing some of his letters to* ***raise the wind****?* NS □ n compound fund-raising; attrib use *a* ***fund-raising*** *scheme.*

raise a question [V + O pass] ask a questio[n] esp one not likely to be answered, either at a[ll] or quickly; cause a question to be asked **de[t]:** the, a; some, several. **adj:** awkward, basic, o[b]vious. **A:** what to do; why/how to do sth; abo[ut] its worth, about the future of the schoo[l] ...more... than she answers □ *That explanati[on] should satisfy them, but if anyone* ***raises an*** *awk[]ward* ***question****, refer him to me.* □ *Anoth[er] speaker* ***raised the question*** *why it was, if soci[al] workers were already in contact with th[e] household, that more effective steps had not bee[n] taken to avert the tragedy.* SC □ *Christoph[er] Hitchens* ***raised some*** *basic* ***questions*** *abo[ut] the future of the Socialist International.* NS □ *Th[e] 'marriage' made world headlines and here was [a] chance for the principal character to expla[in] everything. Unfortunately, her account* ***raise[s]*** *more* ***questions*** *than she answers.* SC ⇨ ⚠ ne[xt] entry; the question (of sth) arises.

raise the question etc (of sth) [V + O pas[s]] introduce sth specified for discussion and/[or] settlement **det:** the; this, these. **adj:** delicat[e], important, crucial. **n:** question, ⚠ subjec[t], matter, issue. **o:** improved facilities, immigra[]tion control; his recent dismissal; a suitab[le] marriage □ *Mr Vorster said it was premature [to]* ***raise the question of*** *South Africa joining th[e] Organisation of African Unity.* G □ *I intend [to]* ***raise the subject of*** *improved canteen faciliti[es] for out-patients and visitors at the next gener[al] meeting.* □ *I took the liberty of* ***raising the sub[]ject*** *with his lordship just now and he expresse[d] the desire you should remain as his guest over th[e] festive season* (= Christmas). EM □ *Since Fran[ce] has no hope of providing herself with a usab[le] armoury of nuclear weapons except after som[e] years and at heavy cost, and since General d[e] Gaulle is determined that as a great Power sh[e] must have them, this will probably be* ***the*** *mo[st] important* ***issue raised****.* SC ⇨ ⚠ the question ([of] sth) arises; previous entry.

raise the roof [V + O] (informal) make a lot o[f], or too much, noise, esp by shouting, singin[g], applauding etc □ *Reader, who is now 71, wa[s] born in Somerset the son of a Salvation Arm[y] bandmaster — hence his love of simple bloo[d-]and-fire melodies that* ***raise the roof****.* SC □ *Th[e] wolf's hearing is probably more acute than [a] dog's, because it must be aware of prey or [of] danger. But it doesn't* ***raise the roof*** *if it hear[s] an unexpected sound. It will keep quiet for saf[e]ty.* RT □ *The water boiling behind him, Hollan[d] went on to break the world 1500 metre freesty[le] record as well — by 10.02 seconds. The crow[d]* ***raised the roof****.* RT

raise one's/sb's spirits [V + O pass] cause s[b] to feel more optimistic, cheerful, confident e[tc] □ *I'm so glad you came. Your telling us how we[ll] your friend got on after the very same operati[on] has* ***raised*** *Donald****'s spirits*** *considerably.* □ *I[n] point of fact, the working population wanted [to] have* ***their spirits raised*** *and to be mad[e] enthusiastic for the cause.* MFM □ ***My spirit[s] rose*** *when I heard that I had been selected f[or] interview for the job of assistant manager.* ⇨ ⚠ one's spirits rise/sink.

rake muck [V + O] look for, and make know[n] evidence of scandal, improper or corrupt con[]duct in private or public life (from the episod[e] in THE PILGRIM'S PROGRESS (J BUNYAN 1628-88) referred to in the second example) □ *Since the medicos are well aware of what can and can't be done, one is slow to see the benefits of starting a public scare. Yet experience proves that it rarely hurts to* ***rake muck****, even if, in the short run, you're handing ammunition to the wrong man.* OBS □ *When Theodore Roosevelt reacted against the weekly 'investigative' journalists of his day, he borrowed a character from 'The Pilgrim's Progress' as a jibe with which to label them—the Man with the* ***Muck-Rake*** *who would not look up from the filth on the floor when a celestial crown was offered him. But 'The Washington Post' is not in the same business as the* ***muck-rakers*** *in the decade before World War One.* ST □ (film review) *After the urban* ***muckraking*** *of 'Serpico', Sidney Lumet clearly turned with blissful relief to a rustic idyll of dear old Texas.* G □ *Consumer protectors also go after quack medicines, loan sharks and landlords who gouge the blacks. Such volunteer vigilantes are in the great American tradition of* ***muck-raking*** *journalists.* L □ originally (esp in GB) derogatory, the expression is increasingly used of laudable activities; n compounds a muck-raker, muck-raking; attrib use *a* ***muck-raking*** *journalist*; variant muck rake (v).

(the) rank and file [n + n non-rev] (military) ordinary soldiers; ordinary, undistinguished people; members of a group or organization **A:** of serving men, of the Party, of the profession □ *But this must surely be the same rule for all its members, and to be so no less for officers than for* ***rank and file.*** T □ *Their year of office is past the half-way mark. Before the year is out they will once again take their place among* ***the rank and file*** *of the Church of Scotland's ministers.* RT □ *There are increasing signs that* ***rank-and-file*** *trade unionists recognise the need for greater responsibility.* SC □ attrib use, *a* ***rank-and-file*** *trade unionist*, frequent and usu hyphenated.

rant and rave/roar [v + v non-rev] complain, protest, or enthuse, vehemently and lengthily **A:** about the delay, about the disgrace to the family; on the subject (of sth) □ *He was* ***ranting and raving*** *about something or other, I forget exactly what, but it was clearly a load of rubbish.* ST □ *You'll have to excuse Peter's enthusiasms—he's been* ***ranting and roaring*** *about Norway ever since he got back.* □ *A Liberal MP said yesterday that while people* ***ranted and raved*** *about skivers* ((slang) = absentees), *shirkers and scroungers, he was amazed that a large number of his constituents bothered to work—they would be better off not doing so.* SC □ *The boy in 'Fathers and Families' wants to join the army. This is an enormous shock to his dad, who would have preferred to* ***rant and rave*** *about his wanting to become a painter.* L

a rare bird [Comp (NP)] sb/sth of a kind seldom seen or met with (occasionally rara avis (Latin) from SATIRE VI (JUVENAL 60-130)) **V:** ⚠ be, become □ *They found a South African police officer of English origin—****a*** *very* ***rare bird*** *these days—with only a faint South African accent.* DS □ *Great scientists who are also highly cultured men of letters are not quite such* ***rare birds*** *as is sometimes made out.* L □ *Pat Mulcare is something of* ***a rara avis*** *at championship level—the total amateur.* OBS □ (fashion notes) *The not-matching jacket is still a big deal. Suits are* ***rare birds*** *and suddenly look smashing* (= very attractive). ST

raring/rearing to go etc (informal) eager, physically or mentally poised, to go, or to do, sth; hardly to be restrained from going, or doing, sth **Inf:** to go, to leave; to have a bash ((slang) = to attempt); to fight □ *There is now a new management for the companies in the group, freshly plucked from a profit centre of GEC,* ***raring to go.*** ST □ *The inspector lets students drive round the track a couple of times before commenting on their driving. 'They're always* ***rarin'*** (= raring) ***to have a go****, so I usually get that over first,' he says with a wry grin.* RT □ *Fundamentally these boys are good. My boy was* ***raring to go*** *to work to help the home.* ST □ *They were the oldest* (pupils) *and the most illiterate, a C stream of fourteen-year-old louts* ***rearing to leave*** *and start work at the factories round about.* LLDR □ originally rearing, as of a horse, but now usu raring.

the rat(-)race a continual, and often compulsive and undignified, struggle to get ahead of others in business, a profession, social status, etc □ *Robert and Ned and I first got to know each other at the age of about seventeen, just at the point where* ***the rat-race*** *of adolescence quickens its pace and boys begin to see life in competitive terms.* CON □ *Forecasts of standing room only on earth may be wildly exaggerated, but life should be more comfortable, less of* ***a rat race****, if there are not too many of us.* SC □ *Who ever needed Mr Jay to tell them that business is* ***a rat race****, and that it is 'not logic and reason' but the 'ancient survival imperatives' (our old friends, aggression, status-seeking, hunting comradeship, etc) that 'dominate the corporation'.* NS

rats desert etc a (sinking) ship [V + O] (saying) cowardice, or prudence, makes people desert a friend, employer, cause etc if danger or loss threatens **V:** desert, ⚠ leave, quit, forsake □ *He determined to fly out of this country* (Britain, May 1940) *as soon as he could get a plane. Halifax asked me why he was in such a hurry. I said 'because he's frightened—he's* ***the*** *first* ***rat*** *to* ***leave the ship.****'* L □ *The other union members, Will Paynter and Alf Allen, walked out* (of the Commission on Industrial Relations) *five months ago when the TUC began to mutter about non-cooperation. Moderate academics like Bill Macarthy have for months been refusing appointments. They know* ***a sinking ship*** *when they see one.* NS □ often used in part and allusively, as in second example.

rats etc and snails and puppy-dogs' tails an imaginative description of unpleasant attributes of character **n:** rats, ⚠ frogs, snips □ (source) *What are little boys made of?/****Frogs and snails and puppy-dogs' tails.*** NURSERY RHYME □ *'I love you too much, that's the trouble. Can't you see?' I held out my hand. 'What do you think I'm made of, darling?' '****Rats and snails and puppy dogs' tails,****' she said.* RATT □ rats, frogs and snips in different versions; facetious or gently jocular. ⇨ sugar and spice (and all that's/things nice).

a rattling good etc yarn etc (dated informal) extremely, and esp exhilaratingly or excitingly, good yarn etc **adj:** good, ⚠ fine, fast. **n:** yarn (= story); ⚠ price; pace, tempo; game □ *All in all, then,* ***a rattling good*** *Celtic* ***yarn*** *with a few fragments of wit-and-wisdom thrown in—good value for the price of your paperback copy when it comes out.* NS □ *'Buy your flags,' I used to yell. 'Rattles at* ***rattling good prices****,' I used to try to be funny.* ITAJ □ *Taken as it ought to be, at* ***a rattling fast pace****, it is quite a spirited piece of music.*

a raving beauty [Comp (NP)] a ravishingly beautiful girl or woman **V:** ⚠ be; become, turn into □ *She passed on the news* (about cosmetic preparations) *in phrases of ardent sincerity to her readers, who believed, with each new discovery, that they were going to be transformed into* ***raving beauties*** *overnight.* AITC

a/one ray etc of hope [Comp/O (NP)] a possibility of sth good happening, or being brought about, which will alter, or improve, an unsatisfactory, or depressing, state of affairs **V:** be, remain; discover, discern, allow, admit. **n:** ray, ⚠ glimmer, flicker □ *There is* ***a ray of hope*** *for share-holders tied up in Ralph Hilton Transport, suspended last July.* ST □ *By 1980, The Hudson Report tells us, we will be in an irreversible decline. The film admits* ***rays of hope****. Bellini does not.* RT □ *But* ***one ray of hope*** *emerged in the recent Budget proposals to ease the present difficulties in buying the older house.* SC □ *There must be* ***a glimmer of hope*** *because there always is, but not talking about divorce doesn't make it easier to come together again.* TVT

a ray of sunshine [Comp (NP)] (informal) sb/sth that brightens, cheers, one's life **V:** ⚠ be, become; find sb □ *She sang more than usual. He risked saying, when this had gone on some time, 'You're* ***a*** *little* ***ray of sunshine*** *these days,' but that made her huffy* ((slang) = annoyed). TSMP □ (reader's letter about a television programme) *In these years of economic and social depression, 'Dr Who' has been* ***the*** *only* ***ray of sunshine*** *in our lives.* RT □ also pl rays of sunshine; often, but not necessarily, facetious or ironic.

reach etc rock bottom [V + O] (fall to) the lowest possible level **S:** prices, numbers; television programmes; football team. **V:** reach, ⚠ hit; fall to, be at □ *Congregational attendance had dwindled to handfuls* (ie only a few people). *A few Sundays ago it* ***reached rock bottom*** *when the minister preached to his wife, the organist and the two presiding officers for that date.* SC □ *The effect of deferments will not be physically noticeable for at least several months. By then, unemployment will have* ***fallen to rock-bottom****.* ST □ *During the week Jean trains herself. 'Mentally it's difficult,' she says. 'You* ***hit rock bottom*** *if you're not skating well and you have no trainer to help.'* RT □ *Contractors argue that they are forced to quote* ***rock-bottom*** *prices to get the business, and the Government then refuses to amend the figures to compensate for increased wages.* ST □ attrib use *a* ***rock-bottom*** *price.*

reach the top (of sth) [V + O pass] achieve success at the highest level in business, a profession, sport, politics, branch of entertainment, etc; get to the top (of the ladder/tree) (Vol 1) (qv) □ *Starting as a clerk in a shop which peddles rags, he rips through the garment jungle to* ***reach the top of*** *his outwardly glamorou profession.* TVT □ *It is not surprising that h moved with effortless ease, up the special ladde which the Army keeps for its favourite sons; c that, when he* ***reached the top*** *he should hav become, in the words of Harold Nicolson, 'th darling of the Cabinet'.* NS

read sb like a book [V + O + A] understan clearly what sb's character is, what hi thoughts, reactions, intentions are □ *'I'm nc really very expert at this beating about the bush 'No,' she smiled. 'Any woman can* ***read*** *you* ***lik a book****, James.'* TT □ *Godfrey looked across th fireplace at Mabel Pettigrew and decided to giv* (her) *the slip again this afternoon and go to se Olive. Mabel Pettigrew thought: I can* ***read*** *hir* ***like a book****.* MM □ *It's useless to try to deceiv Mary. One look at my face, and she* ***reads*** *m* ***like a book****.* □ often used with *can.*

read sb's mind/thoughts [V + O] knov what sb thinks, wants, or plans, to do, esp on specific occasion □ *'If you tell me what's wrong I can do something about it,' I said. 'I can't* ***rea your mind****.'* RATT □ *She must, he thought, be a clever as she was pretty to have* ***read hi thoughts*** *so accurately.* OMIH □ *I didn't precisel* feel *guilty, but that's how you do tend to act whe someone* ***reads your thoughts****.* CON □ *'Woul your children like to come out in the boat with m tomorrow or Sunday?' 'You must be a* ***mind reader****. I was just plucking up my courage t ask.'* □ n compound a mind-reader.

read the Riot Act [V + O pass] read the open ing section of the Riot Act (1714) to a riotou assembly (after which they must disperse or b chargeable with felony); (fig) declar authoritatively that a course of action, or con duct, must stop □ *In late 1820, 'riots broke ou repeatedly in Oxford, with the Vice-Chancello* ***reading the Riot Act*** *and the Oxfordshire Yeomanry called in.'* L □ CISSIE: *One* (shop steward *wagged his finger at me and cried: 'We're no taking your advice, we're not taking your advice!' First I* ***read the Riot Act*** *to them and the I lashed out.* CSWB □ *'You've never gone short Joseph.' My mother always called me by my ful name when she wanted to* ***read the Riot Act****.* RATT □ fig use sometimes facetious.

ready for anything [Comp (AdjP)] alert and or willing to do, or cope with, anything, however unusual or unforeseen it may be **V:** ⚠ be, feel, seem □ *The non-fasting starch eaters, bursting with delicious potatoes, French rolls, cakes and ale as well as with their fair share of protein, seem* ***ready for anything*** *except thought.* OBS □ *Gilden is a rather grim mill village north-east of Warley. It has the appearance of being* ***ready fo anything****: the narrow windows of the millstone grit houses might suddenly sprout rifles.* RATT □ *The one thing I miss from the days we wore our hair in crewcuts is that I was so fit, full of boundless energy, enjoying dreamless sleep, always* ***ready for anything****.* TVT

ready, steady, go [v + v + v non-rev] said to start off esp a children's race; said when two or more persons are starting to do sth together □ *'Come on, I'll race you. I'll give you a start* (= let you start before me) *and win* (= beat) *you easy.' 'Come on an'* (= and) *try.' 'Right—* ***ready, steady, GO****!'* TT □ *We're not pushing* *together. I'll give you a* ***ready, steady, go*** *and on 'go' shove as hard as you can.'*

(in) real life [A (PrepP)] (among) living people; (in) life as most people live it, contrasted with life, behaviour, situations etc as depicted in novels, films, plays etc □ *'I like things that are the fashion,' Patrick said almost at random. 'Except for those kind of liquorice allsort women's hats you see in advertisements—good job nobody wears them* ***in real life****.'* TGLY □ *Did people act* ***in real life*** *as they did in detective stories?* PE □ *On Saturday evenings she's Cynthia Wentworth, Birmingham's champion Ballroom dancer.* ***In real life****, she's Doreen Ruddle, waitress in the New Street Golden Egg.* □ *The secret of these films was their skilful use of actual locales and direct sound recording. In other words, they were like* ***real life****.* RT □ *This series was intended to show the ups and downs of a* ***real-life*** *family, prepared to have almost every detail of their lives made public by a television crew who stayed with them.* L □ front, middle or end position; attrib use *a* ***real-life*** *family.*

the real Mackay/McCoy sb/sth that is absolutely genuine, esp people and alcoholic drinks; next entry (qv); the genuine article (qv) □ *Most of them aren't folk-singers at all. They copy the style but they're not* ***the real Mackay****.* □ *'In that case, burgundy,' Angela Snow said. 'A good one, mind,* ***the real McCoy****,' Pop said. 'The best.'* BFA □ *Each, as the French say, to his own crust, and* ***the real McCoy*** *has always had more fascination for me than the mental gymnastics of the fiction writer. For a start, truth is almost always stranger than fiction.* SC

the real thing not a substitute for, or imitation of, an activity, situation, product or object; previous entry (qv); the genuine article (qv) □ *Denis Lill spent seven years in the New Zealand Air Force. Now he finds that building and flying model aircraft can provide much of the interest of* ***the real thing****.* RT □ *Local flavours are being extinguished as giant breweries swallow smaller firms, and keg is replacing draught. However, Ian Nairn (sampling* ***the real thing****) reports that true beer-lovers of Britain are fighting back magnificently.* ST

really and truly [adv + adv non-rev] certainly; positively; sincerely □ *'Perhaps you're too critical.' 'Nobody could enjoy a show like that. It was* ***really and truly*** *awful.'* □ *She turned to him and smiled. 'So you* ***really and truly*** *are not disappointed with our old Elsinore.'* ASA □ *'Please, Miss, can I be excused?' 'Sue, do you* ***really and truly*** *want to go* (ie to the lavatory)*—you can't wait till Assembly, and slip along then?'* TT

reap the benefit(s) (of sth) [V + O pass] benefit from the result of one's own, or another's, forethought, efforts etc **o:** his hard work, a sound education □ *I could not myself attack; Rommel must provide that opportunity for me. But in order to* ***reap the*** *full* ***benefit*** *I must correctly forecast the design of his expected attack and determine in advance how we would defeat it.* MFM □ *You had better slow down a bit. What's the point of all this toiling and saving if you don't live to* ***reap the benefit of*** *it?* □ *The White Paper insists that the economic performance of the Six owes a lot to the creation of the Community, that Britain will* ***reap*** *similar* ***benefits*** *by going in.* L

reap what/where one has (not) sown be rewarded or punished (not) in accordance with what one has done to deserve it □ (source) *Thou art an hard man,* ***reaping where thou hast not sown****, and gathering where thou has not strawed* (= strewed). MATTHEW XXV 24 □ *In future, the Indian will* ***reap where he has sown****, and I, for one, can only hope that, under the new stimulus, he will sow twice as hard and reap threefold.* SD □ *She and her four brothers and sisters were brought up to believe that one* ***reaped what one sowed****. Honesty, diligence and good works were regarded as cardinal virtues.* RT

received opinion(s) etc (formal) widely held and accepted opinion(s) **n:** opinion(s), ⚠ ideas, wisdom □ *Certainly,* ***received opinions*** *have become more sophisticated than they were a few years ago.* NS □ *What he says is often polemical because it is a necessary corrective to* ***received opinion****.* SC □ *As instruments and techniques were improved and refined,* ***received ideas*** *about the nature of the universe took a series of heavy jolts.* OBS □ *At moments, the author's naïveté is all too obvious, and her dependence on the* ***received wisdom*** *of 20th century pundits is no help to her at all.* NS

the recording angel the angel who keeps a record, to be used on the Day of Judgement, of what men have done in their earthly lives (an allusion to REVELATION XX 12-15 though not itself a Biblical term) □ ***The Recording Angel*** *responsible for the world of letters still doubtless raises an eyebrow at the curious company some good writing keeps.* L □ *He* (Pepys, 17th c diarist) *was* ***his*** *own* ***recording angel****—and an angel with tatty wings and an interestingly complicated conscience at that.* SC □ *I've never had much use for tape recorders as a tool of journalism. Still, scribblers today all seem to want to be* ***recording angels****—or at least that was my experience last week.* NS

the red carpet [O/o (NP)] a strip of carpet (traditionally red) for important visitors to walk on from where they get out of a car etc to the entrance of a building; a symbol of respectful or deferential reception and attention **V:** put down/out, lay down/out, roll out □ *At the entrance to the building half a dozen French Republican Guards in full ceremonial dress of brass, plumed helmets and swords, stood on either side of* ***the*** *diplomatic* ***red carpet****.* OBS □ *I wondered what my reception would be in Whitehall. I didn't fancy* ***the red carpet*** *would be out; some form of mat, perhaps.* MFM □ *It would have been quite inconceivable that, as a minister, I would have lived the life of a patient in a 54-bed ward of a massive mental hospital. Every obstacle would have been put in my way by the civil servants, or, alternatively,* ***the red carpet*** *would have been laid out by the hospital authorities.* NS □ *They needn't expect to be given the* ***red carpet*** *treatment. This is a factory, not a country club.* □ attrib use ***the red carpet*** *treatment.*

a red herring (across sb's path/track) [O (NP)] a diversionary topic, incident etc (to deflect attention from the truth, main subject, a purpose etc) (from, formerly, a bundle of pickled herrings used in a drag-hunt or drawn across a fox's trail to destroy the scent and confuse the hounds) **V:** draw, ⚠ pull; raise □ (NONCE) *I never saw a more skilled drawer of* **red herrings**. *Whenever he got in a difficulty, he would start a hare or pull* **a red herring across the track**. L □ *He had made it as plain as he could that he did not intend to become editor. If they chivvied him, he would raise* **the red herring** *of his projected work on England under Edward the Confessor.* ASA □ *'It's hard on Robert, of course,' Ned went on; he was trying to ignore* **the red herrings** *and get on with the story.* CON

a red letter day a day specially looked forward to, or remembered, when sth remarkable and usu pleasurable will happen, or happened; the day of days (qv) (from calendars that have saints' days and holidays printed in red and other dates printed in black) □ *Bevill was looking forward to it* (a laboratory test) *like a child. 'I believe tomorrow is what I should call* **a Red Letter Day**,*' he said earnestly, as though he had invented the phrase.* NM □ *The day I found the husk of an old coconut was* **a red letter** *one for Pooh. It became his favourite toy.* DF □ *My father said the day I was born was* **a red letter day**. *He received final demands* (ie usu printed in red) *for all the household bills.* TVT □ also pl.

the red light district a district within a town or city where there are brothels, frequently indicated by red lights □ *As an officer in the Salvation Army, she has spent the past 30 years helping the prostitutes in* **the red light district** *of Amsterdam — and the elderly.* TVT □ (NONCE) *Carl Meier is the Frankie Howerd of Munich. He entertains nightly in typical Bavarian fashion in a* **district** *where* **lights** *are frequently* **red**. RT

the red meat (of sth) the more powerful, or coarser, stuff (of sth) (from meat, ie beef or mutton contrasted with lighter kinds of meat such as veal or poultry) **o:** practical politics; adventure; pornography; the power game □ *The newly-elected MP, hungry for* **the red meat of** *practical politics, has a long time to cool his ardours on the backbenches.* SC □ *Some journalists argue privately that the wave of support for Enoch Powell indicated that large sections of the public were starved of* **the** *good* **red meat of** *opposition to the liberal consensus.* L

(cut the) red tape (dispense with or simplify) formalities of business, or administrative, procedure (from lawyers, government officials, etc formerly keeping their papers and records in bundles tied with red tape) □ *Englishmen of this type are obviously energetic. They like to be irreverent and are fond of* **cutting red tape**. L □ *An East German* (railway) *guard can send back a whole load of goods if it is a couple of items short of what appears on the invoice. There is a lot of* **red tape** *to be* **cut**. NS □ *Beaverbrook simply wanted to get things done. He hated* **red tape**. L □ *Nothing will ever convince the average Briton otherwise than that the corridors of public services reverberate with snores, broken only by the occasional clatter of teacups and the rustle of* **red tape**. SC □ *Cuspatt was all right but in the last resort these Museum fellows were as much bureaucrats as they were scholars — tied by a lot of* **red tape**. ASA □ can be used allusively, as in third, fourth and fifth examples.

a redeeming feature [Comp/O (NP)] a characteristic in sb/sth that (partly) atones for other faults or shortcomings; a saving grace (qv) **V:** be, prove; have, possess. **det:** a, the one; only; some; no □ JO: *Where's the kitchen?* HELEN: *Through there. It's* **the** *only* **redeeming feature** *in this entire lodging house.* TOH □ *He's not so bad as my mother makes out. When she dislikes anybody she doesn't allow them* **a** *single* **redeeming feature**. □ *I admit I've always had a really nice head of hair —* **my redeeming feature**, *you might say.*

Reds under the bed (facetious) Communists, left-wing activists, seen as threats to Western democracy, the instigators of industrial unrest, etc □ (1974) *A South Wales Labour MP said to me 'If only Roy Jenkins was to come out clearly and publicly on the side of the miners. Because Roy's a moderate, he could stop all this talk about* **Reds under the bed**.*'* NS □ *It surely cannot be seriously maintained that Communists, fellow-travellers and other '***Reds under the beds***' nowadays constitute the main class of person who potentially put the state at risk?* L □ *The hunt for* **reds under the** *Hollywood* **bed**, *led by the US Committee on Un-American Activities in 1947, has become a legend.* RT □ (NONCE) *I should not have thought that fascism was likely to threaten Western Europe at the present time. Brenton must see* **swastikas under the bed**. L □ expression used mainly to satirize point of view defined above.

sb's/the reflected glory fame, notice, credit obtained from association with sb/sth famous, widely respected or admired **V:** bask, bathe, in; enjoy, relish □ *After his apprenticeship he worked for Joe Manton, the greatest gunsmith in England and a legend in his own lifetime. But James was not content to bask in anyone***'s reflected glory**. TVT □ *And, of course, it is a very remarkable achievement of your father's. All sorts of people have congratulated me. I don't think it's* **a glory** *to be sneezed at, you know, even if it is* **reflected**. HAA □ *Time was, when Cilla Black used to guest* (= appear as a guest) *on the Beatles' TV shows and bask in* **the reflected glory**. *Now it's the other way around, and Ringo Starr is on her show.* RT

regardless of sth/sb irrespective of, unrelated to, sth/sb **o:** class, creed, sex; Party; merit, suitability □ *The manifesto promised equal franchise rights to all citizens,* **regardless of** *race, class or creed.* □ *The stagnant condition of the British economy — according to most competent observers,* **regardless of** *political persuasion—cried out for a massive shot in the arm.* L □ *Once, in order to gain a little peace and quiet, he offered a class of 14-year-olds a £1 prize for the longest essay,* **regardless of** *merit, to be written in 30 minutes.* □ *Because, still, at that moment,* **regardless of** *who was managing them, the psychology of playing Leeds was: you would not get past them.* RT

reign supreme (cliché) prevail; be dominant **S:** specialist, head, housekeeper, baby; silence, confusion, self-interest □ *This misuse of the nation's money is partly due to the determination of specialists—the aristocrats of the profession—to keep the lion's share* (= the larger, or largest, part) *of medical practice under their control and within the hospitals where they* **reign supreme**.

NS ▫ *Confusion* ***reigns supreme*** *when a nice Catholic girl brings home her new boyfriend, a nice Jewish boy, in tonight's 'Play for Today' (BBC1).* RT ▫ *During a card game, Lorrie Dellman announces to her friends that she had had more than a passing flirtation with their respective husbands. Paranoia* ***reigns supreme*** *among the women, causing much marital conflict.* TVT

relieve one's/sb's feelings [V + O pass] (cause one/sb to) feel less grief, anger, resentment etc by giving it outward expression ▫ *Again a file drawer was noisily closed. 'Ethel,' Miss Jenkinson said, 'unless you can* ***relieve your feelings*** *more silently, I shall return you to D3.'* OMIH ▫ *I called her the worst names I could think of, repeating them again and again under my breath, but it didn't* ***relieve my feelings*** *very much.* RATT ▫ ***Her feelings*** *were* ***relieved*** *by a good cry.*

relieve the monotony [V + O pass] make a change of any kind in a dull, or boring, pattern of life or work ▫ *'She says she's not in hospital to roll bandages for nurses.' 'You'd think she'd be glad to—* ***relieve the monotony*** *and all that.'* ▫ *'Please do be awfully careful.' 'We'll both be careful, I've dragged you into it.' 'Oh that's all right.* ***Relieves the monotony****.' 'Yes, but take care of yourself.'* TCB

render (sb) a service [V + IO + O pass] (formal) do sth to help, or oblige, sb ▫ *If you're ever in a position that I can be of any help to you, don't hesitate to ask. When a man* ***renders*** *me* ***a service*** *at considerable inconvenience to himself, I don't forget it.* ▫ *What Elsie didn't understand was that any* ***services rendered*** *were reciprocal and that there was no obligation on either side.* TSMP ▫ *I'm sure he gets a good few payments on the side 'for* ***services rendered****' that don't go through the books.* ▫ n often pl; construction often pass, esp following *for*, as in last example.

rest assured be certain; feel completely confident **A:** of that, of a good recovery; that nobody blames you in the least, that I won't do that ▫ *'Do I look the part?' Jenny asked. 'Oh yes,' he said, 'I don't know which part you mean, quite, but you look it,* ***rest assured*** *of that.'* TGLY ▫ *I took the matter up at once with M. Coulet and was informed by him that he had received no complaint and that I could* ***rest assured*** *that the allegations were without foundation.* MFM

revenge is sweet (saying) there is pleasure and satisfaction in avenging a wrong done to one ▫ *Reprehensible behaviour, perhaps, but* ***revenge is sweet*** *even if it takes no more serious form than discomfiture.* SC ▫ ***Revenge is*** *all the* ***sweeter*** *when admiration is its strategy, authenticity its weapon.* L

rich and/or poor [n + n non-rev] rich and/or poor people either implying all classes, or contrasted ▫ ***Rich and poor*** *live side by side but in conditions of extraordinary disparity.* ST ▫ *Nor does he omit the plagues, famines and diseases which made life a lottery for everyone,* ***rich or poor****, until the most recent times.* NS ▫ (3rd United Nations Conference) *The* ***rich-poor*** *confrontation game ended here this week with a victory on points for the rich countries who have successfully resisted all demands for fundamental changes in their trade and aid policies.* ST ▫ attrib use *the* ***rich-poor*** *confrontation.*

ride high have a long or short period of success, confidence in one's/its ability, popularity etc **S:** he, she, they; company, firm; club; product ▫ *Politically, at the age of 42, she is riding high, shadow Home Secretary, top of the poll for the shadow cabinet and a member of the National Executive Committee.* NS ▫ *'Would you say that the Presidency is as strong today as it was?' 'I can say that it is certainly not as strong as it was in February of this year. We were* ***riding*** *very* ***high*** *in terms of our legislative programme.'* L ▫ *When timber is* ***riding high*** (ie is selling for a very good price) *such men make good money, so today they are living off the fat and waiting for the inevitable improvement, predicted to begin early next year.* L ▫ nearly always continuous tenses.

ride etc a/one's high horse [V + O] be haughty, arrogant, proud **V:** ride, ⚠ be on; mount, get (up) on; get (down) off; get down from; come down from; come (down) off ▫ *Mr Jenkins* ***rides a high horse*** *with style and on this occasion rhetoric gave it wings.* NS ▫ *I have stood a great deal from you without complaint, but after your last ridiculous and offensive letter I am going to dig my toes in. So* ***come off your high horse*** *and mend your manners and send me something remotely publishable.* US ▫ *I know you think you should be considered above suspicion but it wouldn't be very clever of you to* ***get up on your high horse*** *and refuse to answer questions.*

ride etc a/one's hobby-horse [V + O] be active in promoting, try to promote, a cause, way of life, method of work, etc (the implication usu being that most people don't think it is of great interest or importance) **V:** ride, ⚠ be/go off on, be/go on about; have a; it be a...of one's/sb's ▫ *Their resolutions are politely acknowledged, appropriately pigeon-holed and usually forgotten—perhaps because there are too many organisations bent on* ***riding*** *too many* ***hobby-horses*** *to the winning post.* SC ▫ *I now have a horrible suspicion that he hasn't much sense of humour, that he's an earnest, even perhaps* ***an*** *inveterate* ***rider of hobby-horses****.* L ▫ *The two young men went on endless walks, Hitler reciting his own poetry, dashing off a quick drawing in his sketchbook, or* ***going on about*** *one of his* ***hobby-horses****.* OBS ▫ *Authority is obsessed with details like school uniform, and line-up of late-comers at a particular point on the hall floor. The staff superior to this sort of thing usually* ***have hobby-horses*** *of their own.* L ▫ *'Probably another case of dietary deficiency. I always maintain—' 'Oh dear,' sighed Jane. 'There****'s*** *Dad* ***off on his hobby-horse*** *again.'* ▫ variant a rider of hobby-horses; hobby-horse = 'a long stick with a horse's head modelled on one end', used in primitive plays, country dances or as a child's toy.

ride a tiger [V + O] take a foolish, or dangerous, course of action that is likely to have disastrous results for oneself ▫ (source) *There was a young lady of Riga,/Who* ***rode*** *with a smile on* ***a tiger****./They returned from the ride/With the lady inside,/And the smile on the face of the tiger.* ANONYMOUS ▫ *'I can take it or leave it.' 'So you say, but anybody who experiments with drugs is* ***riding a tiger****.'* ▫ *'I vote SNP* (= Scottish National Party) *because I think the bigger the vote for the SNP, the better the deal Scotland gets from Westminster* (ie British Parliament).*' 'Well, you're **riding a tiger**.'*

ride (the crest of) the wave [V + O] be at a high, or the highest, point of one's powers, success, popularity □ *There will be a call for the utmost economic realism, a process which may well seem uncomfortable to those who have been accustomed to the exhilarating experience of **riding the crest of the waves**.* T □ *'My role is to do people who are **riding the crest of a wave** of success,' Stanley Baxter says. 'I wouldn't impersonate anyone who was on the slide.'* TVT □ *At the start it seemed that Mr Macmillan was still **riding the wave** that had taken him to landslide victory in the 'never had it so good' election of 1959.* L □ *Michael Tippett, who was 70 on Thursday, has arrived at this crucial moment in his life **on the crest of a** creative **wave**.* OBS □ *I think he* (President L B Johnson) *is something like a Greek tragic figure: a man who **was on the crest of the wave** as an innovator and reformer in terms of domestic legislation, and who made a fatal move in escalating the Vietnam war.* L □ variant (be) on the crest of the wave.

a rift in the lute a first sign of trouble to come, esp a flaw in a relationship that is likely to result in a quarrel or estrangement □ (source) *It is **the** little **rift** with**in the lute**,/That by and by will make the music mute,/And ever widening slowly silence all.* THE IDYLLS OF THE KING (A TENNYSON 1809-92) □ *And the implication is that, since they came together, there has never been **a rift in the lute**, either sentimental or creative. They made theatrical history together, and may do so again.* OBS □ *These happy days in Inverness were, however, marred by the widening of '**a rift in the** matrimonial **lute**' due entirely to disparity of age and incompatibility of temperament.* SC □ *This was **the** first **rift in the lute**. It was clear to me that the Western Powers must now prepare for a continuous struggle with the communist East, which would last for many years.* MFM

right/straight away [A] now; immediately **V:** do sth; start, go; admit, say, sth □ *'Have you remembered to phone your sister?' 'Oh no—I'll do it **right away**.'* □ *'Would you like to see it?' 'You had better show it to me **right away**.'* □ *We are reprinting and anyone who wants it—free, but not free postage—should write **straight away**.* NS □ *He said **straight away** when he fell that it was Clementine* (who had pushed him). DC

right/true enough [Comp/Disj (AdjP)] (informal) expression of agreement that what sb else has said is sufficiently correct or accurate □ *'She's a good-looking girl, **right enough**.' 'I thought you would be impressed.'* □ *'After all, we don't know what other people may be thinking.' 'That's **true enough**. But it's often pretty easy to guess.'* □ ***True enough**, you can't expect sweet reason from that bunch of screwballs.*

sb's/one's right(-)hand (man)/right arm [Comp (NP)] sb's/one's chief assistant, esp a capable and/or indispensable one **V:** ⚠ be, become □ *The Republican Party, led by Kemal Ataturk**'s right-hand man**, Ismet Inou, was defeated.* SC □ *The conversation swung around to progress on his book about his relations with Howard Hughes, **whose** accountant and **right hand man** he had been.* ST □ *You've been **my right hand** here so long, Miss Jenkins, I don't know how I'm to run this little business of mine without you.* □ *Some say that you were Di Stefano**'s right arm**. At this moment it's all that's needed* (to formulate a recommendation for your deportation). ST

(not) right in the head [Comp (AdjP)] (informal or facetious) (not) sane; (not) mentally or psychologically normal **V:** ⚠ be, seem; think sb □ *There was a third daughter, much younger and **not** quite **right in the head**, poor thing.* □ *He's an old friend of mine called Joe Shaw. He's never been in prison. I've often wondered whether he was **right in the head**.* CON □ BEATIE: *But I love him.* JENNY: *You're **not right in the head** then.* R

right now/then [A] (informal) at this/that moment □ *'You should take a packet of sandwiches with you.' 'Common sense tells me so, although, **right now**, I feel I never want to see food again.'* □ ***Right now**, we guesstimate* (= calculate partly on a basis of fact and partly by guesswork) *that there are over 2,000 youth bands in Britain, and that at least one new band is formed every week.* OBS □ ***Right now** I'm not actually writing anything because getting the concerto finished on time has exhausted me. But I have plans.* RT □ *Her mother still does all their washing and ironing, and her father delivers it in the car. But **right then** he was taking time off from the laundry round to finish building them a sauna.* TVT

right off the reel [A (PrepP)] without hesitation; without needing, or taking time, to consider, to recall, to ascertain, or to check facts and figures (from rope, thread etc smoothly unwound from a reel) **V:** tell, answer, recite; give, supply, sth □ *'Can you tell me what these improvements would cost?' 'Not **right off the reel**, but if you care to call or phone back this afternoon I'll have it worked out.'* □ *Why spend hours searching for a Biblical reference when you know somebody that can probably give you the answer **right off the reel**?*

the right/best people people of high social or professional standing, esp seen as desirable or influential acquaintances □ JIMMY: *Reason and Progress, the old firm, is selling out! There's going to be a change-over. A new board of Directors, who are going to see that the dividends are always attractive, and that they go to **the right people**.* LBA □ *You won't get far setting up an advertising agency from scratch unless you know **the right people**.* □ *Oh yes, there are other hotels, but I couldn't tell you much about them: they're not patronised by **the best people**.*

right and/or proper [adj + adj non-rev] correct and/or suitable; conforming with accepted standards □ *My views on how to tackle the problem were not considered **right and proper** and there was the father-and-mother of a row* (= a very heated argument). MFM □ *Charley boy was lucky all right, and Pop could only hope that he would, in the shortest possible time, show his appreciation of the fact in the **right and proper** way.* BFA □ *One can question whether it is **right or proper** to waste such talents on such high-class trash.* SC □ attrib use *the **right and proper***

way, approach.

right royal exceptionally fine, splendid, sensational, immoderate etc **n:** party, celebration, welcome; argument, fight ▫ (actors in a television series) *'Coronation Street's' Albert Tatlock was 80 on August 6, and all his friends at the Rovers Return gave him a* ***right royal*** *party.* TVT ▫ *The boy's just had a* ***right royal*** *dressing-down* ((slang) = severe scolding) *from his father as well as being punished at school.* ▫ attrib use only.

right and wrong [n + n non-rev] what is honest, just, morally admirable, contrasted with what is not ▫ *'So young, Terry. So sure of* ***right and wrong****. It's rather sweet.' 'It's not sweet at all,' I said brusquely. 'There have to be standards—without standards where are you?'* TST ▫ *We need not despair so long as we retain the ability to distinguish between* ***right and wrong****.* NS ▫ *We often say 'Is he a good baby?' of a child too young to* ***know right from wrong*** *when all we mean is 'Is he easy to care for?'* ▫ variant know right from wrong. ⇨ ⚠ next entry.

right and/or wrong [(adj + adj non-rev] morally justified or not; factually correct/incorrect; (do sth) rightly or wrongly ▫ *I don't know yet whether I was* ***right or wrong*** *to conceal the truth from him.* ▫ *If you must lift weights from ground level, remember there is a* ***right and*** *a* ***wrong*** *way to do it.* SC ▫ *Two vital questions stand out in the book. The first is how* ***right or wrong*** *Lenin was in his treatise on imperialism in 1916...* L ▫ *However,* ***rightly or wrongly****, the man in the street, the literary critic and the artist have usually shown much more interest in a rather different kind of analysis.* SNP ▫ functions as Comp or attrib; variant rightly or wrongly [adv + adv non-rev]. ⇨ ⚠ previous entry.

right you are (informal) I will do as you say; I agree to what you ask, propose ▫ JIMMY: *Go out and get me some cigarettes, and stop playing the fool.* ALISON: *The shop on the corner will be open.* CLIFF: ***Right you are.*** LBA ▫ *'Here! Let me carry that for you.' '****Right you are****, then, but I don't think you're much fitter than I am.'*

righteous anger/indignation anger, resentment that is, or that sb feels is, morally justified ▫ *Dr Fisher talks of the Churches doing their divine work of enduring, healing and reconciling. Is there not room for a little* ***righteous anger*** *and even condemnation?* SC ▫ *The man's eyes, formerly nebulous with beer, now become deep and self-centred with* ***righteous anger****. 'You should keep your thievin'* (= thieving) *fingers to yoursen* (= yourself)*.'* LLDR ▫ *Mr John Godson is not alone in deriving satisfaction from a feeling of* ***righteous indignation****. But he is unique in the depth at which he can cultivate this emotion.* G

the rights and wrongs of sth [n + n non-rev] the particular aspects of a situation, procedure, way of behaving, which may be considered right or wrong, esp morally or legally **o:** the case, the situation; corporal punishment; what they did ▫ *'I don't care for John's language, certainly,' Gerald replied, 'but as to* ***the rights and wrongs of*** *the case, I haven't enough knowledge to judge.'* ASA ▫ *Miss Jordan tells the story of unhappy marriage and indiscreet affairs with a clear sense of* ***the rights and wrongs of*** *the matter.* SC ▫ *And quite frankly, I have no intention of discussing* ***the rights and wrongs of*** *corporal punishment with you.* TT

ring a bell [V + O] remind sb of sth; be, or seem (to sb), likely, true or correct (from trials of strength or other amusement machines on which the bell rings if the player is successful) **S:** name, address; play, story. **A:** in my mind; with the majority there ▫ *'Have you ever heard of a man called Armas? Castillo Armas?' 'The name* ***rings a bell****,' Mark said. 'He was in the news a few years ago, wasn't he?'* ST ▫ *Ursula Andress (some called her 'Undress') became a star. It cost her a broken marriage and broken love affairs but Ursula Andress still* ***rings bells*** *in the mind as a sex symbol.* TVT ▫ *As literary editor of the 'Daily Express', 'Wives' was the series that gave me greatest satisfaction — because it* ***rang*** *so many* ***bells*** *with our readers of all classes.* NS

ring the changes [V + O pass] vary one's procedure, choices, action within a possible range of things to be or do (from the style of bell-ringing found in English churches) ▫ *Traditionalists will tell you to drink red wine with meat, dry white with fish, and sweet white with desert. But there's no reason why you shouldn't* ***ring a few changes****.* OBS ▫ *The craze for separates has made a big impact on children's clothes, particularly the pinafore dress under which you can* ***ring the changes*** *from sweaters to blouses.* SC ▫ *She says: 'I like to* ***ring the changes*** *in my acting career. In repertory I played a 60-year-old woman, I was a prisoner in "Within These Walls" and a gangster's moll* (= a criminal's girl-friend) *in "The Sweeney".'* TVT

ring true etc [V + Comp] seem or sound true, sincere, genuine, likely/untrue, insincere, false, unlikely; have (got)/with the ring of truth etc (qv) (from a coin being rung, ie thrown, spun on a counter, etc to hear if it is a counterfeit made of inferior metal) **S:** story, account; analysis, interpretation. **adj:** true, ⚠ false, hollow ▫ *This piece of agonised juvenile self-analysis* ***rings true****.* L ▫ *Spies are trained to keep their mouths shut and they don't often lose the habit. That's why true spy stories are extremely rare, and personally I have never seen one in print that* ***rang*** *completely* ***true****.* DS ▫ *Sometimes I tried to link the disintegration of our private lives with the disintegration of affairs in the world. Yet it* ***rang false****. People can concentrate on their private lives, I thought, in the middle of anything.* SPL ▫ *It organises rallies to promote friendship between men of two sides who, a few months ago, were killing each other. But for many this* ***rings hollow****.* L

a ringside seat [O (NP)] a seat in the front rows round a boxing, circus, auction etc ring; (fig) a position from which one can observe, experience, what is happening very closely and clearly **V:** obtain, get; enjoy ▫ *Yet who now believes that the court surrendered to anything else but a political imperative? Certainly no one with* ***any*** *kind of* ***ringside seat*** *in Whitehall.* NS ▫ *I can't get you into the docks, I can't give you any inside information, I can't wangle you* ***a ringside seat*** *while the country's drug traffic is being arranged, in fact I can't help you with your articles* (for your newspaper) *at all.* HD ▫ also pl.

a ripe old age [O/o (NP)] a full, or more than

averagely prolonged, span of life **V:** reach; enjoy; live, survive, to □ *In spite of all these harmful habits he cheated his heirs by living to* ***a ripe old age****.* □ *So, by* ***the ripe old age*** *of 10 or so, most children will probably feel they are ready to supplement their income* (ie pocket money) *with a bit of freelance work.* OBS

rise and fall[1] [v + v non-rev] vary frequently and sporadically **S:** sound; voice, music; waves; price, demand □ *Nearby the long banner which said 'Socialist Possibility'* ***rose and fell*** *upon the surge.* UTN □ *Our voices* ***rose and fell****; sometimes the bitterest remark was a whisper.* NM □ *He always felt unwell on the small inter-island ferry. The motion of the waves* ***rising and falling*** *upset his stomach.* □ ***The rise and fall of*** *beef and butter prices seem not to affect our consumption per head of these commodities in any significant degree.* □ *The opinion polls that claim to chart* ***the rise and fall*** *in the popularity* ***of*** *the various political parties seem to get less accurate the closer we get to a General Election.* □ variant the rise and fall (of sb/sth) [n + n non-rev].

rise and fall[2] [v + v non-rev] increase and then decline in power, popularity etc **S:** civilization, reign, government □ *Toynbee has spent his life comparing the way civilisations* ***rise and fall****. He chose a career which made him almost inevitably a prophet of doom.* NS □ *The decades passed, administrations* ***rose and fell****, reputations were made and lost, successive Chancellors eased and squeezed the economy.* NS □ *'What's that huge book you're reading?' '"****The Rise and Fall of*** *the Dutch Republic".'* □ (Large oil tankers) *are now lying like dinosaurs in a dole queue in deep water harbours from the Hebrides to the Pacific.* ***Their rise and fall*** *is charted this week in 'Discovery'.* □ variant the rise and fall of sb/sth [n + n non-rev].

rise/arise and shine(!) [v + v non-rev] (informal) wake up; get up; get dressed and ready □ (source) ***Arise, shine****; for thy light is come, and the glory of the Lord is risen upon thee.* ISAIAH LX 1 □ *All right, so it's the first day of their holiday, but it's past eleven o'clock so just you go and tell them to* ***rise and shine*** *double-quick****!*** □ (advertisement) ***Rise and shine!*** *Go to work on an egg!* □ *'****Arise and shine!****' called Grimsdyke heartily. 'For I'm to be married today—today! Yes, I'm to be married today!'* DIL

rising twenty etc [Comp (AdjP)] not much younger than twenty etc; close on (qv); pushing forty etc (qv) **adj:** twenty, ⚠ thirty, forty-five □ *She was a solid, shortish blonde of* ***rising thirty*** *with a skin as hard as marble.* BFA □ *She asked how old Ludovic was.* ***Rising sixteen****, said his father.* WDM □ *It did not seem right that the Count, who must by now be* ***rising ninety****, should die without hearing his wife's confession.* US □ *Arnold is* ***rising 28****. Alec Bedser bowled his best when he was in his early thirties.* T

risk one's neck [V + O] (informal) chance losing one's life as a penalty for crime, or in an accident caused by courage, foolhardiness, or stupidity; be liable to incur any danger, penalty, loss etc **A:** for you, for so little; by trying to pass him □ *The car in front was weaving about the road as if the driver was drunk or ill and I wasn't going to* ***risk my neck*** *by trying to pass him.* □ *Anybody'd think I was asking you to* ***risk your neck*** *for me, instead of just suggesting that you do me a little favour.* HD □ *'Summer of 77' (10.15 pm, BBC2) recalls the official and volunteer rescue teams* ***risking their necks*** *to save the luckless, often the plain stupid, who get themselves capsized, on fire, marooned by the tide or stuck up cliffs.* RT

the road to hell is paved with good intentions (saying) blame, or punishment, is incurred by having good motives which are either not put into practice or which have evil or harmful results □ ***The road to hell*** *may* ***be paved with good intentions*** *but there are many worse pavements; and one need not be ashamed to be a product of a tradition of well-meaning.* AH □ ***The road to hell****, however,* ***is paved with good intentions****: Mr Petrie reminds us how W.T. Stead and Josephine Butler 'procured' a little girl by payment, to show up the white slave traffic* (= trade in prostitution) *and thus, their intentions still laudable, frightened her out of her wits.* OBS □ (NONCE) *'How else do you think a newspaper man works except by personal contacts like this? You're a disappointment to me, Lumley, you really are.' '****The road to Fleet Street****,' said Charles, with mock solemnity, '****is paved with disappointments****. I've taught you a useful lesson.'* HD

rock 'n roll [n + n non-rev] rock and roll, ie 1950s style in popular (dance) music with a steady, insistent rhythm □ *Raving Rupert, billed as Elvis Presley's double, is knocking himself out singing old* ***rock 'n roll*** *numbers in very short black trousers and a very long gold lamé jacket.* ST □ *Most blasts from the past—like the annual* ***R 'n R*** *revival — are a waste of time, but occasionally there's some gold among the dross.* RT □ occas R 'n R; attrib use *a* ***rock 'n roll*** *number*; 'n = 'and'.

a rod/stick to beat sb with a fact, incident, argument etc that is used against sb/sth in order to blame, penalize, or impose a course of action □ *From the author of 'Cathy Come Home', 'Edna the Inebriate Woman' and 'Down and Out in Britain' we now have* ***another*** *published* ***rod with*** *which* ***to beat*** *the insensitive back of our social consciences.* SC □ *Our prisons are going to be dynamite some day. There's plenty of* ***sticks to beat*** *the inmates* ***with*** *if they don't behave but precious few carrots of hope.* ST □ (NONCE) (Why align himself) *with the senseless farrago of Fascism — an extremely unstable Romantic idea? Partly because it was* ***a stick with*** *which* ***to test*** *conventional British wisdom is one answer that emerges.* SC

a rogues' gallery a collection, file, of photographs of known criminals; people/things classified, in sb's opinion, as dishonest, dangerous, undesirable □ *Most of us who care about words at all have* ***a*** *personal* ***rogues' gallery*** *of usages, neologisms and pronunciations we would prohibit if we could.*

a rolling stone (gathers no moss) (saying) a person who moves a lot from place to place, from job to job (does not accumulate property, real friends, or social ties) □ *'I'm a bit of* ***a rolling stone*** *down the avenues of medicine,' he explained.* DIL □ *Originally* ***a*** *'****rolling stone****' by inclination, with a genuine curiosity about unusual places and people, he had, through failure and lazy indulgence, become a purveyor* *of picaresque, sentimental cynicism.* HAA □ *'Marshport must be so limited and limiting,' Mr Eastwood took her up. 'Harold saw a good deal of the world when he was in the Army and was glad to settle there. I'm sure Isabel wouldn't want him to be* ***a rolling stone****, would you, Isabel?'* PW (NONCE) *And, indeed, she could be depended upon to go her own way, gathering any money that came within her path. Perhaps if* ***a stone rolls*** *slowly enough it will* ***gather moss****, and what Alice Cresset gathered, she didn't waste on foolishness.* ASA □ a rolling stone can be used alone alluding to complete expression.

a Roman holiday an occasion of people enjoying the spectacle, or an account, of others suffering, being hurt or even killed (the reference being to the arenas of ancient Rome) □ (source) There *were his young barbarians all at play,/*There *was their Dacian mother—he, their sire,/Butcher'd to make* ***a Roman holiday****.* CHILDE HAROLD'S PILGRIMAGE IV (G GORDON, LORD BYRON 1788-1824) □ *'Don't let us keep the local gentry waiting,' Bernard cried hastily, a little too loudly. 'The least I owe my son is his freedom to show me off to the country-gentleman commuters. They need* ***a Roman holiday****.'* HAA □ *You and your filthy newspapers would have got hold of it and what* ***a Roman Holiday*** *you'd have made of it.* PP

Rome was not built in a day (saying) time, patience and hard work are needed for a difficult, or important, undertaking □ *Only about a month ago Mr Shore's successor answered a question in the House of Commons on this very point by saying he hoped to make an announcement shortly. What could be fairer than that?* ***Rome wasn't built in a day****, old boy.* G □ ***Rome****, the schoolboy knows,* ***was not built in a day****; but the Oklahoma schoolboy knows that Guthrie, the first State capital, went up in an afternoon.* L □ (NONCE) *I suppose there have been worse planning decisions than Maplin Airport. There were several in Augustan Rome who thought that the simple construction of piers into the sea constituted an offence to Neptune which would surely be punished. Yet* ***Rome was not destroyed in a day****.* NS

room (and) to spare (for sb/sth) [Comp/O (NP)] plenty of space or accommodation **V:** ⚠ be; find, have. **o:** another car; them all; both of you □ *'But you use your garage yourself, don't you?' 'That's all right. There's* ***room and to spare for*** *another car.'* □ *Only the parents were invited though I am sure she has* ***room and to spare for*** *all of them—she's probably the kind that can't be bothered having children around.* □ *The gap was not so narrow as it looked and even Tom got his bulk through with* ***room to spare****.*

root and branch [n + n non-rev] wholly; thoroughly; in all particulars **V:** destroy, condemn, oppose, sth; involve sb □ (source) *And the day that cometh shall burn them up, saith the Lord of hosts, that it shall leave them neither* ***root nor branch****.* MALACHI IV 1 □ *What are we to think of statesmen who take the country without arms into unnecessary war? Was it really so reprehensible to oppose their policies* ***root and branch****?* L □ *They were not, he said, under any entitlement to convict of wilful fire-raising because this depended* ***root and branch*** *on the use of inflammable liquid.* SC □ (scientists examine their consciences) *For the only* ***root-and-branch*** *'solutions' which could give a man an absolute reason for not working at Barford on the bomb, were not open to many. But no other faith touched the problem.* NM □ functions adverbially in first examples; attrib use, *a* ***root-and-branch*** *solution, positivist,* always hyphenated.

the root of it/the trouble [O/o (NP)] the primary cause of trouble, a malfunction, illness, scandalous rumour, etc **V:** find, discover; be (at), get to □ ASTON: *I'm mending this plug.* DAVIES: *What's the matter with it?* ASTON: *Doesn't work.* DAVIES: *You getting to* ***the root of the trouble****, are you?* TC □ *'Why can't she get on with her sister?' 'Jealousy—that's what's at* ***the root of it****.'* □ *I don't know how many times he's been into the hospital for tests but they haven't found* ***the root of the trouble*** *yet.* □ ⇨ ⚠ get to the bottom of (Vol 1).

a rose by any other name would smell as sweet what matters is what people or things are, not what they are called □ (source) *What's in a name? that which we call* ***a rose/By any other name would smell as sweet****.* ROMEO AND JULIET II 2 □ *The hope was that the 'Stockholm rose' could be ceremonially unveiled at the opening day next week. Unfortunately, the United Nations has found no roses waiting to be named. And they have rejected the idea that* ***a rose by any other name would smell as sweet****.* NS □ (NONCE) *'One better than that,' said Chadwick, 'is to give the place a nice new fancy name altogether. Bags of swank.'* ***'An Elementary School by any other name still stinks.'*** TT □ often adapted, as in last example.

rose-coloured/rose-tinted spectacles etc life in general, or sb/sth in particular, seen or thought of too optimistically **V:** see sth through, look at sth; wear, put on; take off one's. **n:** spectacles, ⚠ glasses, lenses □ *I don't remember ever being really unhappy as a child, and I don't think I am seeing those years through* ***rose-coloured spectacles****.* □ (reader's letter) *Thank you, ITV, for 'Shades of Greene', an adult series that for once tried hard to look at life as it is, instead of through* ***rose-tinted lenses****.* TVT □ *The real test, though, will come on the field of play, Alec Lewis was quick to remind me. Even he, in his hour of triumph, was not wearing any* ***rose-tinted spectacles****.* ST □ (NONCE) *And I think it is high time he discarded his* ***Marxist spectacles*** *(at least when writing about music).* L □ nonce uses, as in last example, with adjs that suggest national, sectarian or political prejudices.

a rose is a rose is a rose (catchphrase) a rose is what it is, and neither is, nor means, more than what it is □ (source) ***Rose is a rose is a rose is a rose****.* SACRED EMILY (G STEIN 1874-1946) □ (after taking the drug mescalin) ***A rose is a rose is a rose****. But these chair legs were chair legs were St Michael and all angels.* DOP □ (NONCE) *But Hungary did not win the World Cup, and their place in the history of the game must be rather like that of a very great athlete who has failed to win an Olympic medal. As Gertrude Stein might have said,* ***a cup is a cup is a cup****.* ST □ (NONCE) *Elsewhere she ruminates:*

Enough of supposed imaginings. ***A story is a story is a story****, even a good one like 'The Lord of the Rings'.* L □ *A drunk man talked endlessly in the drab bar, as though he were saying in the style of Gertrude Stein '****Cuba is Cuba is Cuba****'.* OMIH □ (NONCE) (advertisement) ***A rose is a rose is a thing of beauty*** *except when something goes wrong. And so many things can—from nitrogen starvation to greenfly to blackspot to mildew and so on.* TVT □ often adapted, as shown.

(not) roses all the way [Comp (NP)] (not) always a pleasant and easy life, experience, task **V:** ⚠ be, seem, become; find sth □ (source) *It was* ***roses, roses all the way****/With myrtle mixed in my path like mad.* THE PATRIOT (R BROWNING 1812-89) □ *Verdi* (received) *endless offers of pensions, titles, professorships, and final assumption into the national consciousness of newly united Italy. Of course it was****n't*** *entirely* ***roses all the way****.* NS □ *Asked what he did, he said he was a plumber. But he only plumbed when he had to and that wasn't often. Plumbing, let it be clearly understood, is* ***not roses all the way****.* ARG □ (NONCE) *Back on board by midnight, I find Henryk Szeryng has joined our company. With flautist Larrieu, harpist Mildonian, cellist Janigro and others, it has been music,* ***music all the way****.* ST

a rough diamond [Comp (NP)] an uncultured, uncouth person who has good and useful qualities **V:** ⚠ be; find sb; regard sb as □ *He plays the chairman of a northern local Labour Party. 'He's a bit of* ***a rough diamond****, but honest. I've met hundreds like him.'* TVT □ ***Rough diamonds*** *we might be, but by God, we were the boys. We were resourceful, imaginative, tough, reliable.* CON □ *It is fairly safe to formulate as an axiom that no English writer who portrays farm-labourers as* ***rough diamonds*** *with hearts of gold actually knows them.* R

a rough house [Comp (NP)] (informal) hard fighting; disorder; (exchange of) physical or verbal abuse **V:** ⚠ be, become, turn into □ *This battle for which we are preparing will be* ***a*** *real* ***rough house*** *and will involve a very great deal of hard fighting.* MFM □ *I'm sure a referee is within his rights to stop a game if he sees it degenerating into* ***a rough house****.* □ *It almost looked to me as if Kingsley expected us to intercept it* (a letter)*, as if he wanted to force our hand. And didn't he* ***rough-house*** *poor old Harry just a bit too much?* TBC □ rare variant rough-house sb (v) = 'subject sb to physical or verbal abuse'.

rough it [V + O] (informal) accept, or endure, an uncomfortable way of life, travel, accommodation etc □ *I want a man who knows Upper Burma, who is prepared to* ***rough it*** (and) *who can drive a jeep.* ARG □ *If Bowen had acquired his Portuguese fleas in the course of* ***roughing it****, being put up by a brigand in a cave, dossing down on straw in a tavern yard, that kind of thing, he considered that he would have felt differently about them.* ILIH □ *Delicate made 'e* (= he) *is, and only a boy. Stands to reason 'e couldn't* ***rough it*** *with the others.* ASA

rough justice harsh, or summary, judgements, punishment, or reward, not based on any exact, or carefully considered, degree of right or wrong, good or bad, etc **V:** be, find sth; deal out; get. . .from □ *He alleged that by late afternoon, when a decision was being made, he could recognise only three committee members who had sat through the whole proceedings. 'That is not justice,' he said. 'It is not even* ***rough justice****.'* SC □ *Most policemen have a natural scepticism about jury trial. They prefer the* ***rough justice*** *of the magistrates' court where there is a 90 per cent conviction rate.* ST □ *Land which has today a valuable development potential may tomorrow have lost its value (and vice versa) and from the country's point of view to deal with development rights in this manner* (ie at a flat rate of £20 an acre at present values) *is a* ***rough*** *but acceptable* ***justice****.* NS

rough and ready [adj + adj non-rev] acceptable, if refinement, precision or expertise are not required **S:** he, she, they; manner, method; calculations, solutions □ *Our Nigerian and Ghanaian fellow-delegates are as* ***rough and ready*** *and pragmatic as we are.* OBS □ *Breath-analysers and blood tests will be more reliable than the old* ***rough and ready*** *ways of judging a driver's sobriety or insobriety.* SC □ *It is helpful to begin with a* ***rough and ready*** *classification.* NS □ predic or attrib use.

a rough and tumble [n + n non-rev] a fight which a number of persons take part in, not necessarily with any serious attempt to injure; rough and competitive conditions of life or work □ *If it had to come to* ***a rough-and-tumble****, our fellows could have thrown the Glamorgans over their heads, for Cornish wrestling was strong in those days.* RT □ GEOFFREY: *Oh, there's nothing I enjoy more than* ***a*** *good old intellectual* ***rough and tumble****, and I only wish I could stay and slog it out with the two of you, but there isn't time, unfortunately.* EGD □ *I began to learn the* (facts of life) *for myself in* ***the rough and tumble*** *of school life.* MFM □ DIMBLEBY: *Do you feel you have been damaged by* ***the rough and tumble*** *of your political career?* GEORGE BROWN: *Not at all.* L

(just) round/around the (next)/(every) corner [Comp/A (PrepP)] likely, or sure, to happen, to be achieved soon (esp as an optimistic, or foolish, conviction) **V:** be; lie, wait □ *We are told to believe in an Eldorado* ***round the corner*** *and in the building of a great new Europe, whereas what we actually face is a sordid little enterprise that will leave everything much the same only more so.* L □ *The summer of 1940—German style: the Wehrmacht is triumphant, there are luxury goods in the shops and peace is* ***just around the corner****.* TVT □ *There was, beyond this, not a positive belief that the important friendship was lying mysteriously* ***round the corner****, but a negative void which only a magical chance meeting could fill.* HAA

a round robin a petition, or protest, with the signatories' names arranged in a circle so that no one is seen to have headed the list, been the instigator, etc □ *The former National Librarian of Wales who organized the payment of the fine, said in* ***a round robin*** *to magistrates that a chasm had opened between the younger and older generations in Wales.* NS □ also pl.

rude health [O/o (NP)] vigorous good health **V:** enjoy; be in; return to □ *'And how are you these days?' 'Not so bad—as well as I'm likely to be. Can't expect to be in* ***rude health*** *at my* *age, you know.'*

rue the day (that) [V + O] regret (the occasion) that (one did sth) **S:** he, you, they; the young woman; John □ *Don't be a foolish boy. Your father left school as soon as he was fourteen and lived to **rue the day**.* □ *There are several amusements to be had from witnessing the birth of an ambitious new television drama-series. Who are we supposed to get hooked on? Who is doomed to **rue the day** he ever took this juicy part?* NS □ *I can't back out now but I **rue the day that** I let myself get involved with this project.*

ruffle one's/sb's feathers [V + O pass] (cause one/sb to) show aggression, loss of composure or self-assurance □ *'I should only be a clog on your activities, a tie when you wanted to lunch or dine with your admirers. Do not argue, Harold.' 'I wasn't going to,' said Mr Downing, **his** gentle **feathers ruffled** for once.* WDM □ *I had concluded that it was no longer any good jollying people along. They had to have **their feathers ruffled** and be jolted out of their apathy.* L

a rule of thumb a means of measuring, assessing sth which is based on precedent, practice, and experience only (and which therefore cannot be depended upon in all cases and in all details) □ *It is impossible to calculate all these factors because they vary widely from one share to another. As **a rule of thumb**, the bigger the company the easier it is to buy and sell.* OBS □ (writers of 'popular' literature) *Thus, one of them says that two of his **rules-of-thumb** are never to put in any 'boring description', and to make sure to get dialogue on the first page.* UL □ *Taboos come and go—**the** old **rule of thumb**, which ordained that words considered unsuitable in a family context were also unfit for the air, no longer applies.* L □ *A **rule-of-thumb** guide is: bottle the beer when it no longer tastes sweet.* OBS □ attrib use, ***a rule-of-thumb** guide*, always hyphenated; hyphens optional in headphrase.

rule the roost [V + O] be the one who directs others in a community, business, household etc; be more important, popular, have more influence, than other persons/things of a similar kind (the allusion probably being to cocks in a poultry yard, though there is an older version rule the roast) □ (early detective stories) *But Holmes, with his ability to deduce 17 facts about a man by examining his hat, and with the indispensable assistance of brave, loyal, bewildered Dr Watson — Holmes **rules the roost**.* RT □ (fashion notes) *We've been wearing the traditional clothes of other countries for a good few years now. Indian prints, Peruvian ponchos, and Chinese Mao jackets have **ruled the** ethnic **roost** in so swift a succession that one wonders what's to be next.* OBS

rules and regulations [n + n non-rev] directions for conduct or procedure, specifying what is required or forbidden □ *There are few more difficult things a man can do than find out precisely what his rights are. This week, for the first time, the random **rules and regulations** which govern the never-ending contest between 'us' and 'them' are brought together in a guide prepared by the National Council for Civil Liberties and published by Penguin Books.* ST □ *Jeremy, with his insistence on **rules and regulations**, his instinct for decorum in all things, seemed to her a spoil-sport and a life-denier.* PW

one's ruling passion [Comp (NP)] one's predominant desire, ambition or interest **V:** ⚠ be, become; make sth □ *Philosophy has withdrawn from what Hume called 'the republic of letters', a republic of which he thought himself to be very much a citizen, admitting that 'love of literary fame' was **his ruling passion**.* L □ *If she could be said to have **a ruling passion**, it was for order and cleanliness and she brought what she could of it to the eccentric household she married into.* SC

a rum go [Comp (NP)] (dated slang) an odd and puzzling occurrence, state of affairs **V:** ⚠ be, seem; find sth □ (source) *'I expect,' he said, 'I was thinking jest* (= just) *what **a Rum Go** everything is.'* KIPPS (H G WELLS 1866-1946) □ *'My first wonder was whether this business was an elaborate camouflage for desertion,' but in case it was not he wanted the colonel to know the details. 'It was', he remarked sagely, '**a** very **rum go**.'* ST

run amok be in a state of pathological frenzy and liable to attack/kill people; be, get, out of control; behave violently or extravagantly □ (headline) *Man **Runs Amok** on Railway. The two-and-a-half hour drama began at London Bridge station when a man was challenged for his ticket. He attacked the collector, then assaulted three other men.* OBS □ *As the mediamen **run amok** in this quiet backwater, literally millions of ordinary hard-working people will be forced to pay 6p every day to subsidise their so-called activities.* G □ *Teddy Roosevelt was the first man of his time who saw clearly that America was no longer a rural nation, but an industrial giant **run amok**.* L ⇨ ⚠ run riot; run wild.

run sb/sth close be very nearly as fast, successful, good, bad etc as sb/sth specified □ *'Thomson in the lead as they come round the bend,' went on the excited voice of the commentator, 'but the lanky Dutchman **running** him **close**!'* □ *I don't know what year my dad's car is but it must **run** yours pretty **close**.* □ *The failure of each attempt, I believe, has invariably been clear in advance, despite the claims of participants (particularly Mr Wilson) that they had fought a damn **close-run** thing.* NS □ adj compound, attrib or predic, close-run; attrib use, *a **close-run** thing*, always hyphenated.

run its course [V + O] start, develop, decline and then end, esp as an inevitable process **S:** the seasons, another year; the illness, his grief □ *He would build it in the summer months, he said, it would dry out better. But summer **ran its course** and the breeze blocks and timber still lay in the corner of the garden.* □ *I don't believe in swallowing all that chemist's muck for a cold. Go to bed, or stay indoors anyway and let it **run its course**.* □ *His grief for Irma had been a natural manifestation of feeling, without guilt or afterthoughts: it had **run its course** and purged itself, leaving no complications.* PW ⇨ ⚠ (let sth) take its course.

run the gamut of sth/from sth [V + O pass] experience, or include, everything within a given span or range (gamut = range of musical notes within a singer's or instrument's capacity) **o:** ***(of)*** emotions, human fears, political affiliations; ***(from)*** palest pink to deepest crimson, A to Z, discomfort to agony □ *Barrault, the greatest master of his art, could* ***run the*** *whole* ***gamut of*** *human emotions in mime.* □ (newspaper publishing) *The empire left by D.C. Thomson, Scotland's small-time Citizen Kane, still churns out a profitable flood of print that* ***runs the gamut from*** *'Beano' to the markedly right-wing 'Courier and Advertiser'.* NS

run the gauntlet (of sb/sth) [V + O] accept, or have to suffer, attack, criticism, annoyance (from sb/sth) (from gauntlet, a corruption of an obsolete word, = 'course, passageway', the reference being to, formerly, military or naval punishment where the culprit ran between two rows of men all striking at him with rope-ends) □ *Between me and the railway line there now stretched a thin but regular cordon of police. To* ***run the gauntlet of*** *both police and trains was more than I could bear.* UTN □ *As soon as I had* ***run the gauntlet of*** *local reporters and photographers and settled in at the Balmoral Beach Hotel...* OBS □ *The consequential legislation will, he promises, force the Government to* ***run a*** *far severer* ***gauntlet*** *than the vote after a six-day debate.* L

run a mile (from sb/sth) be anxious, or careful, to avoid sb/doing sth □ *Mrs Middleton laughed. 'People who are unsociable don't manage great business.' 'My dear mother, I assure you I* ***run a mile from*** *people unless I have to do business with them.'* ASA □ *Five years ago I could have been made into a boring, heartless climber* (ie social climber) *whom everyone* ***ran a mile from.*** HAA □ *I'd* ***run a mile*** *if some disc jockeys asked me on their shows. I will name no names, but with Jimmy Young I feel he'd get me out of any difficulty I got into, he'd fill the gaps.* RT □ *To deal with us during the 1926 strike and to protect the scabs, they drafted 200 people from Devon into our area. The law was very strong and most people would* ***run a mile*** *if they saw a policeman then.* ST □ often conditional *would* ***run a mile*** + *if*-cl/*to*-inf.

(the) run of the mill (that which is) average in kind, class and quality □ *This imaginative historical drama about the preacher who attracted a fanatical personal following is lifted out of* ***the run of the mill*** *by the effective use of Stephen Boxer's music and by David Calder's attractive playing of the hapless Naylor.* G □ *This Sheila was not by any means an irresistibly attractive Sheila, but just a* ***run-of-the-mill*** *everyday Sheila.* TGLY □ *There are the same preoccupations, but what rescues the book from* ***run-of-the-mill*** *New York-Jewish childhood novels is the manner of the telling.* NS □ usu attrib, as shown.

run riot behave, do sth, without discipline or restraint; spread, proliferate to an excessive or uncontrollable extent **S:** children, revellers; roses; famine, one's imagination □ *Many people's idea of a private school that calls itself 'Progressive' is of one where children are allowed to* ***run riot.*** *Nothing could be farther from the truth.* □ *Although she's moved into the income bracket where accountants tell her how much she can allow herself and where the taxman* ***runs riot,*** *the biggest change in her style of life is that she is now completely her own woman.* OBS □ *If by that time the population was not fed, and housed, famine and disease would* ***run riot*** *through Germany.* MFM □ *'It's the thought of Alice,' Teddy said, 'unchaste thoughts are* ***running riot.'*** RATT □ (a television programme) *But everyone working on 'Man from Atlantis' loves the chance it gives them to let their imaginations* ***run riot.*** TVT ⇨ ⚠ run amok; run wild.

run a risk (of sth) [V + O pass] put oneself, or be put/find oneself, in a position where death, injury, punishment, loss or defeat is possible; take risks (qv); take a chance/chances (on sth) (qv) **det:** a, the; some, little; less; more. **o:** imprisonment, infection; feeling ill, losing it all, being jailed □ *Whatever Henry may say,* (your bosses in) *London wouldn't want you to* ***run a*** *silly* ***risk.*** OMIH □ *If working class men celebrate and get drunk they are likely to do so in a public bar, and* ***run more risk of*** *being picked up than the man who keeps his drinks at home.* UL □ *This readiness to* ***run*** *considerable* ***risks*** *to help those whose religious policies Hicks approved must be borne in mind when we are tempted to dismiss the Puritan money-lender as a hypocrite.* NS □ *Their chest movements are paralysed, and unless the patient is artificially ventilated, using a respirator, he* ***runs the risk of*** *asphyxiating himself.* L □ *The same* ***risks*** *would be* ***run*** *if we doubled the guard.*

run short (of sth) have little/few (of sth) left, remaining **o:** time; money; butter; helpers □ *If television* ***runs short of*** *money, at least radio can draw attention to itself as the cut price, dirt cheap medium.* OBS □ *Tell your mummy I'm sorry. I've not a drop of milk I could give her. We've* ***run short*** *ourselves this weekend.* □ *Time is* ***running short*** (or: *We're* ***running short of*** *time*), *ladies and gentlemen, and we won't be able to allow encores for the remaining items on the programme.* ⇨ ⚠ short of sth².

run wild (be allowed to) indulge in unrestrained activity, usu of a fairly harmless nature **S:** children, hooligans, soldiers; gang, mob □ *When they first arrive the children* ***run wild*** *for a week, exploring every corner, climbing every tree.* TO □ *He led the gang of twelve-year-olds in our street against the same age group of another district which had outflanked us and left us a mere pocket of country in which to* ***run wild***—*a few fields and allotment gardens, which was reason enough for holding an eternal grudge against them.* LLDR □ *'A matter for the police he thinks.' 'The police?' Moriarty said, and several of the passing class looked at him. 'Not again, surely?' 'I suppose you'd let them* ***run wild****?' 'They* ***run wild*** *anyway,' Moriarty said.* TT ⇨ ⚠ run amok; run riot.

run with the hare and hunt with the hounds (saying) try to keep on friendly terms with two opposing parties; have an interest in both of two opposing objectives so that one acts a double part oneself □ *A man who through force of circumstances had tried to act as a bridge between the avant-garde and traditional culture was simultaneously rejected by both sides after a long and honourable career. Serve him right, say the heartless in either camp; no good ever comes from trying to* ***run with the hare and hunt with the hounds.*** OBS □ *Others look less indulgently on Shirley Williams's apparent lack of toughness, her dislike of being disliked. They think it* *is due less to sensitivity than to a shrewd instinct for **running with the hare, hunting with the hounds**.* OBS

a running battle/fight (military) continued hostilities by a fleeing army, band of soldiers, against their pursuers; (fig) a quarrel, argument etc sustained between two parties over a period of time □ *Since he announced schemes of house-building and other developments he has been involved in **running battles** of wits and litigation with his crofter tenants.* ST □ *Neutrality: he had found it at last. **The running fight** between himself and society had ended in a draw.* HD

running repairs repairs that are, or can be, made to a machine, vehicle etc without interfering with, or seriously affecting, its use meantime **V:** effect, make, do; carry out □ *Parker's long and varied experience should enable him to cope with any **running repairs** that might be necessary on the voyage.* □ *We'd carried out **running repairs** to the tyre with our emergency kit.*

rush one's fences [V + O pass] be too impetuous and hasty in dealing with a task, or problem, and probably be inefficient, or fail, as a result (from cross-country hunting on horseback) □ *He had great wisdom and his advice on these matters was always sound—as time went on he often restrained me from **rushing my fences**.* MFM □ *As a biographer, I am only too well aware of the pitfalls which lie in wait for the writer whose impatience, over-confidence or lack of sympathy with his subject tempt him to **rush his fences**.* L

S

sackcloth and ashes [n + n non-rev] symbols of self-abasement and penitence (from Old Testament accounts of humbling oneself by wearing sackcloth and scattering ashes over one's head and body, referred to in first example) **V:** clothe in; cover (oneself with). **pp:** clad in □ (source) *If the mighty works, which were done in you, had been done in Tyre and Sidon, they would have repented long ago in **sackcloth and ashes**.* MATTHEW XI 21 □ *School uniform is a symbol of subduing the self to the team: the **Sackcloth and Ashes** tradition. I reckon we can do without it.* OBS □ *We can be sure that by next week he will be scourging himself, fasting, clad in **sackcloth and ashes**.* NS □ clad old pp of clothe.

a sacred cow [Comp/O (NP)] sb/sth that is greatly respected and revered, esp by a particular nation or group, so that attack or criticism is not tolerated (from the Hindu belief that the cow is a sacred animal that must not be killed for food) **V:** be, become; attack, ridicule □ (reader's letter) *It seems from your correspondence column that Harold Wilson is **a sacred cow**. We cannot afford **sacred cows**.* NS □ *Wedlock is best known as a folk satirist, gently jibing at the traditional British **sacred cows**, but he adds: 'I've got a lot of respect for the real folk traditions.'* TVT □ *Psychiatry has become rather **a sacred cow** and appears to have taken over the role once held by the parish priest.* RT

a sad sack [Comp (NP)] (informal) a person usu dispirited and gloomy in behaviour and views **V:** ⚠ be; think sb □ *'Oh, Chris, you're exactly what the Americans call **a sad sack**. Isn't he, Geoff?' 'What, Chris **a sad sack**? I should just say he is, ma'am!'* TBC □ *But the best performances are Stephen Moore's Phil and Ivor Roberts's Arthur, two **sad sacks** kept equally clear of compromise or condescension.* OBS

a sadder and (a) wiser man [Comp (NP)] sb who has learned a lot from a failure, misjudgment or mishap **V:** ⚠ be, become □ (source) ***A sadder and a wiser man**,/He rose the morrow morn.* THE ANCIENT MARINER (S T COLERIDGE 1772-1834) □ (a boxer may have been drugged before a fight) *Alberto is **a sadder and wiser man** now. All he wanted to say about the doping allegations was, 'Basically, someone tried to prejudice me; that's as far as I want to go.'* ST □ *The British trade unions are **a sadder and a wiser bunch** after Friday's Court of Appeal decision in the Railway Ballot case.* T □ occas adapted, as shown.

a safe bet [Comp (NP)] a venture, method etc that is almost sure to be successful; an opinion that is almost sure to be correct **V:** ⚠ be, become; make sth □ *Diet books are notoriously **safe** publishing **bets**, but this one has broken all records.* ST □ *If rest and freedom from responsibility is what you are sure you want, then a one-centre holiday arranged by a reliable travel agent is probably **your safest bet**.* OBS □ *There is no set age, of course, at which children should be released from parental protection but it is **a safe bet** that five is too young.* ST □ in second meaning, usu in the construction *it is **a safe bet** that*-cl.

a safe job work in which one's pay and continued employment are secure **V:** be; have, find, prefer; give up □ *Anybody who wasn't a fully qualified careerist when he left that school must have been abnormally well protected against it, either by having **a safe job** in the family business to go to, or by laziness, or stupidity.* CON □ *With **a safe job** in the Civil Service you should have no difficulty in raising a mortgage.* □ also pl.

safe and sound [adj + adj non-rev] unharmed; secure against (further) harm □ *'I don't think we shall ever see them again. I feel it.' 'Come, come, dear. They'll be back **safe and sound**, you'll see.'* TST □ (In former times) *one could go walking in even quiet areas, leaving one's door unlocked meantime, and return with person and property still **safe and sound**.* RT □ *I carefully wrote these grisly particulars on a label and tied it to his top-coat button. 'We'll soon have you **safe and sound** in bed, sir,' I said confidently.* TVT

safe and sure [adj + adj non-rev] safe to use, reliable and efficacious **n:** drug, medicine; method, procedure; investment □ (advertisement) *Used by doctors, 'Larson's' is **safe and sure**. Contains no drugs.* DM □ *The valuation crisis that has hit Nation Life Property Bond (slogan '**safe and sure**') may well be unique.*

OBS

safety first a slogan aimed at preventing accidents on the roads, in industry and in the home; a policy that makes avoidance of risks more important than chances of gain or improvement □ *There's little point in drilling your children in the rules of* ***safety first*** *if they see you ignoring traffic regulations yourself.* □ *What's happening, therefore, is that we are calling for a halt to progress, for* ***safety first*** *and no leaps in the dark, because it's all we are capable of.* NS □ *Is the price of this* ***safety first*** *policy too high? Is it a price we need and will the rules work?* ST □ attrib use *a* ***safety first*** *policy.*

safety in numbers [Comp/O (NP)] (one has) better protection against ill luck as a member of a group; (finding) a variety of activities, friends and interests makes one less vulnerable **V:** there be, seek; find □ *Realizing that they could not* (escape) *and that there was a certain* ***safety in numbers****, they stood their ground.* TO □ *Stick with the gang on those beach parties. There's* ***safety in numbers****.* H □ *The University of Texas is a refutation too, with its 40,000-odd students on the Austin campus alone, of the old saw that there's* ***safety in numbers****. Just reading the local press makes one continually aware of a massive discontent.* NS □ *there's* ***safety in numbers*** often used to reinforce warning or piece of advice.

one's salad days when one is young, innocent, inexperienced etc; when an institution, adventure, is new □ (source) ***My salad days,****/ When I was green in judgment, cold in blood.* ANTONY AND CLEOPATRA I 5 □ *I'd been very smart, even in* ***those*** *green* ***salad days****, and I'd made a carbon copy of the book.* JFTR □ *It purports to modernise the NHS* ((GB) National Health Service) *and correct the faults discovered during the service****'s salad days****.* NS □ stress pattern one's 'salad days.

the salt of the earth [Comp (NP)] people, esp ordinary ones, whose character and actions are felt to be specially valuable and admirable **V:** ⚠ be; seem; think of sb as □ (source) *Ye are* ***the salt of the earth****: but if the salt have lost his savour, wherewith shall it be salted?* MATTHEW V 13 □ *I like him. I always have. He's* ***the salt of the earth*** *and all that.* EHOW □ *The small businessman likes to think of himself as* ***the salt of*** *the nation's economy, if not of* ***the earth****.* OBS □ *Ten years ago, this kind of* (propaganda) *material would not have persuaded* ***salt of the earth*** *Labour men to quit and throw in their hand with a minority party.* NS □ occas attrib use *a* ***salt of the earth*** *Labour man.*

(the) same again(?) a request for, or invitation to have, a repeat of whatever (alcoholic) drink one has just had □ *We'll have one more and call it a day. Then I'll wander back* (to the office). ***Same again?*** PP □ *Charles was suddenly jerked into attention by the word 'Guinness'. 'No thanks,' he said hastily. 'I'll just have* ***the same again****.'* HD

same here (informal) I agree, share your feelings, etc □ *'I'm nearly falling asleep.' '****Same here****. I think I'll put this work aside and go to bed.'* □ *'Paul distrusts him.' '****Same here****,' put in Sophie unexpectedly, 'though I don't know why.'*

the same(/)old story [Comp/O (NP)] the usual, expected tale of events as heard, or experienced, many times before **V:** be; hear, tell. **A:** always, (over) again □ *The villain of the piece — as is often the case in the theatre — is the box-office: 'It's always* ***the same old story****, money, money, money.'* OBS *When voters complain that election promises have not been implemented they are treated to* ***the old story*** *of unforeseen 'circumstances beyond our control'.* NS □ *The last time I passed, the building was just a hole in the ground: another 'development' was on the way. It is* ***the same story*** *all over the city.* ST

(it's) the same the whole/all the world over (saying) (be) found everywhere and be much alike □ ***It's the same the whole world over****,/It's the poor what gets the blame.* POPULAR SONG (ANONYMOUS) □ *Patients are much* ***the same all the world over****, whether you see 'em* (= them) *being ill at the Government's expense in hospital or being ill at home.* DIL

san fairy ann (dated slang) without doing, or achieving, anything; ineffective; powerless; harmless (comic adaptation of French *ça ne fait rien*) □ *Women in the USA have developed a taste for malt liquors flavoured with lemon, raspberry and so forth, which probably gave conservative brewers a laugh until these '****fairy-ann*** *beers' secured 2% to 3% of the market.* ST

(what is) sauce for the goose is sauce for the gander (saying) what is thought suitable treatment for a woman should be so for a man; behaviour etc expected from one class of person should be expected from another □ *He thought that* ***what is sauce for the goose is sauce for the gander****. 'When I came to your mother I was a virgin. We men have no right to ask of women what we're not prepared—'* ASA □ (reader's letter) *We, the electorate, are forced to vote within a system designed to give unfair advantage to one contestant. Not so the Parties, for when it comes to electing a leader a system of proportional representation is used. Should not* ***the sauce for the goose*** *also* ***be the sauce for the gander****?* SC □ goose and gander rev.

save one's (own)/sb's bacon [V + O pass] (informal) avoid, or save sb from, death, injury, loss, punishment etc □ *With this lie I'd temporarily* ***saved my bacon****, perhaps for long enough to escape.* □ *On a cold and frosty afternoon when horse-racing's abandoned, the dogs can* ***save the*** *bookie****'s*** (= bookmaker's) ***bacon****.* L □ *'I'm surprised you didn't get a bawling out from your wife.' 'I would have, too. It was you being with me that* ***saved my bacon****.'*

save one's breath (to cool one's porridge) [V + O] not bother to speak, advise, object etc (the implication being that one is not heeded or obeyed) □ *His incomprehension was getting me down. 'Make some effort to follow me* (= understand what I am saying) *or I'll* ***save my breath****.'* CON □ *In the end, of course, a civil outfit can't fight a government, and a month later we were thrown out. I might have* ***saved my breath to cool my porridge****.* OBS □ *If it's the job he wants to see me about, tell him he can* ***save his breath****.* □ often with *can, may/might as well, might have.*

save the day [V + O pass] turn possible defeat, or failure, into victory or success □ *In a corps de* *ballet every little wrong movement stands out, whereas when you are doing a solo you can **save the day** by making up some sort of step.* OBS □ *As cavalry the Mamelukes had no equal in the world. Once unhorsed, however, they were heavily encumbered by their arms, and it was left to their Bedouin infantry to **save the day**.* BN

save sb's/one's life etc [V + O pass] rescue sb/oneself from, or avoid, death, punishment, loss of reputation, trouble etc **n:** life, ⚠ neck, skin □ *I might go up there to **save my life** but not for much less.* □ *The Area Museums Service has been a **life-saver** for some of the smaller collections which have no qualified staff.* OBS □ *He'd have gone on all morning with his tale of woe. Your arrival was a **life-saving** interruption.* □ *Having sensibly changed his faith to **save his skin** he found the sloughing of national loyalties equally painless.* NS □ *I blame the owner, not the dog — but that won't **save its neck** if it's caught worrying sheep.* □ also pl save their lives etc; n compounds a life-saver, life-saving; adj compound life-saving.

(God) save the mark (ironic) precedes, or follows, a description that the speaker feels is not likely to be correct or appropriate □ *His eyes would inquire mutely after Phuong, while his lips expressed with even more fervour the strength of his affection and of his admiration — **God save the mark**—for me.* QA □ *You will behave at all times as officers and —**save the mark**—as gentlemen.* BBCTV □ *This evening, the delegation is to attend a civic reception after being entertained, **save the mark**, to a lecture on the City's water supply system.* □ sometimes facetious.

save the situation [V + O pass] solve a political, business, social, domestic etc difficulty **adj:** a dangerous, an awkward, an embarrassing □ *We **saved the situation** and now it's up to those chaps not to let us down.* NM □ *One of his knees touched hers and, after wriggling to and fro for a moment, started trying to push itself between her own two. Luckily, the waiter came up with the bill just then and **the situation** was **saved**.* TGLY □ *He said that not only had I saved his life, but I had **saved a** bad **situation** between the US government and the Dominican Republic.* OBS

save one's/sb's soul [V + O pass] ensure one's/sb's spiritual well-being in this world or the next □ *The genius of Tolstoy subdued the overbearing pretensions of Tolstoy the spiritual path-finder, intent on teaching others how to live and **save their souls** before he had any idea of how to save his own.* OBS □ *For Oeberg there was a question of greater importance to us, to the Americans and the Swedes and the other Europeans, than to the Vietnamese. It was **our souls** that would need **saving**.* OBS

a saving grace [Comp/O (NP)] sth which prevents, saves, one from being altogether bad; a redeeming feature (qv) **V:** be, prove; have, possess. **det:** a, the; one, some; his; only □ (rugby football) *Dickinson is well aware of the danger of Scottish complacency. Perhaps that 12-35 thumping* (= resounding defeat) *the Scottish received in Cardiff on 5 February might prove **a saving grace**.* RT □ *No one is completely evil, darling. They all have **some saving grace**, even the Templars.* DC □ *In that year fighter-bomber tactics had progressed enormously and I was definitely out of touch; **the saving grace** was that I knew that myself.* RFW

say cheese mime the word 'cheese' so as to obtain a natural-looking smile for a photograph □ *Well, smile! **Say cheese**! You can look quite pretty when you smile.* HAHA

say I/I say that is my view, opinion; that's what I (always) say (qv) □ *Why should we get involved? Let them settle their differences themselves, **say I**.* □ *Better dead, **I say**, than suffering like that. I hope somebody would put me out of my misery if I were in her condition.* □ say I more formal, and rare; middle or end position; stress patterns say 'I, 'I say.

say/be one's last word [V + O pass] give/be one's final opinion, decision or command, which will not be changed or repeated **A:** on the subject; about that □ *I do think I was treated unfairly, but I've **said my last word** on the subject so we can forget about it, if you don't mind.* □ *Neither Professor A. K. Cairncross nor the Government spokesman had **said their last words** on this figure.* SC □ *'Bed!' repeated their father. 'Now, that**'s my last word** to both of you.'*

to say the least (of it) [Disj] (and that is) stating sth, describing sb/sth less forcefully, critically, than one easily could; (to) put it mildly (qv) □ *To be stranded in the middle of Buenos Aires with a lorry-load of animals and nowhere to keep them was, **to say the least**, a trifle disconcerting.* DF □ *...a thoughtful and readable novel which is, **to say the least of it**, a pleasant change from some of the squalid muck and pretentious pornography which is flooding the market.* ST □ middle or end position.

say a mouthful [V + O] (informal) say sth very true, very perceptive, or sth that the listener or reader thoroughly agrees with □ *The man who said we'd be frozen up in mid-January **said a mouthful**.* □ usu past tenses.

can't say no (not) have the strength of mind, or the good sense, to refuse an invitation, proposal etc □ *In Dufton, artists' models were thought of as tarts, not quite professionals, but simply the kind who **couldn't** be bothered to **say no**.* RATT □ *You know me — when somebody phones and says 'Come on over' I just **can't say no**.* □ *I'm just a girl who **can't say no**.* OKLAHOMA! (O HAMMERSTEIN) □ *Of course you'll end up doing most of the work if you don't learn to **say no**. Why shouldn't your office colleagues do their fair share?*

to say nothing of sth/sb [Conj] and also; and as may be assumed; and, perhaps, more importantly; not to mention/speak of sth/sb (qv) □ *...failed to justify the hopes and efforts (**to say nothing of** the cost) which have been expended upon it.* SC □ *Coming on top of a 38 per cent pay rise, plushy new offices and meeting rooms for MPs—**to say nothing of** an underground car park in New Palace Yard — the proposals for a new Parliamentary Building in Bridge Street might well have stretched the public patience to breaking point.* NS □ *Glasgow has fine buildings and botanic gardens, and the great river Clyde with its tradition of shipbuilding, **to say nothing of** the glorious scenery as the river unfolds.* RT river unfolds. RT

say one's piece [V + O] make what is virtually a formal statement of one's opinion, thanks, protest etc □ HELEN: *I brought you some money.* JO: *You know what you can do with that.* HELEN: *All right! You've* ***said your piece****. I'll leave it on the table.* TOH □ (the David Frost Programme, BBC TV) *He has encouraged ordinary, not particularly articulate people, to* ***say their pieces****.* L □ *Aware of protocol about queens, but feeling I ought to express the thanks of those 30,000 children, I approached and* ***said my piece****.* OBS

say the right/wrong thing [V + O pass] say sth tactful/tactless, that pleases/displeases the listener, that succeeds/fails in bringing about an intended result □ *Poor Gran* (= Grandmother)*! She tried so hard to like me, poor dear, and she was* so *careful to* ***say the right thing****.* HAA □ *She looked at me rather strangely when I said it must be quite a challenge to have such a handsome and talented husband. Did I* ***say the wrong thing****?*

(just) say the word (just) state one's requests, wishes etc and they will be immediately and/or willingly complied with □ (source) *Lord, I am not worthy that thou shouldest come under my roof, but* ***speak the word*** *only, and my servant shall be healed.* MATTHEW VIII 8 □ *'If you think I could help by being here for a bit,' he said, '****just say the word****, you know.'* ARG □ DAVIES: *I'd look after the place for you. I'll be your man, you* ***say the word****,* ***just say the word****.* TC □ *Jack's the one who thinks it's sensible to wait but he* ***has only to say the word*** *and she'd marry him tomorrow.* □ variant have only (got) to say the word.

says/sez you (informal) that is what you say or may think (the implication being that the speaker doubts whether a previous statement or claim is true, or whether a previous threat will be carried out) □ *'Leave the rubbish bin where it is, Mary. One of the boys will put it out for you in the morning.' '****Says you****. I'll be the one putting it out whether I do it now or in the morning.'* □ *'I'm going to go for* (= fight) *that fellow one of these days and make him wish he had never been born!' '****Sez you****! He could flatten you with one hand.'* □ defiant expression of disbelief.

scare etc (sb) stiff [V + O + Comp pass] frighten sb very much **V:** scare, ⚠ worry, frighten □ *Byron's first nanny entranced his ears with the language of the Bible, and* ***scared*** *him* ***stiff*** *with lurid tales of the Devil.* L □ *'You don't seem worried,' Pyle said. 'I'm* ***scared stiff*** *— but things are better than they might be.'* QA □ *Things at present are not nearly so catastrophic as every newspaper, every television newsflash, suggests, yet we are all* ***worried stiff****.* NS □ often pass.

a scarlet woman (dated or facetious) a whore; a seductress □ *Within this formula, Anouilh provides a preposterously phoney biography about the Man's marriage (above his station* (= of a higher social class than himself)*), his elopement (with '****a Scarlet Woman****', former mistress of the Count).* L □ (NONCE) *Diana was considered far too* ***scarlet a lady*** *for her job as a presenter of the children's programme 'Seeing and Doing'.* TVT □ now usu facetious; occas pl.

a school of thought opinion(s) held about sth which is/are shared by a number of people **det:** a; one, two; another; several; different □ ***One school of thought*** *maintains that mankind's view of nature reflects himself.* G □ *To the question of 'Where do we go from here?' there are broadly* ***two schools of thought****.* OBS

scissors and paste [n + n non-rev] the assembling of existing items of news, entertainment etc for re-presentation without adding anything new, or drawing any new conclusions from them □ *As well as using the* ***scissors and paste****, she has re-interviewed all the people Mr Hutchinson first approached and interviewed a few more besides.* L □ *More relevant than Betty's industrious discovery of forgotten film is the second of the night's* ***scissors-and-paste*** *jobs, 'The Siege of Dien Bien Phu' in ATV's 'Turning Points' series.* ST □ attrib use, *a* ***scissors-and-paste*** *job, collection, survey*, often found.

scoop the pool [V + O pass] win all the money staked in a gambling game; get all the prizes, profits, sales, success, applause etc □ *At a local shooting match, he* ***scooped the pool****, coming home with four cups and over £70 in prize money.* □ (fashion notes) *You'll* ***scoop the pool*** *in a knitted collar like the one on his Sambo tweed dress with the Donegal air.* H

a scorched earth policy [O (NP)] military tactics of retreating from enemy forces, burning and destroying food, fuel and shelter as one goes **V:** adopt, apply, advocate □ *I rebelled against* ***the 'scorched earth' policy*** *which had advocates in Whitehall; their reasoning was that as the Germans advanced inland towards London, so we would burn and destroy the countryside as we retreated.* MFM □ *If I had my way now I would apply* ***the scorched earth policy*** *to all those trippers who are swarming over the island to look for this imaginary monster.* RM

scorn delights and live laborious days put work above pleasure; devote one's life to satisfying an ambition, one's sense of duty, etc □ (source) *Fame is the spur that the clear spirit doth raise/(That last infirmity of noble mind)/ To* ***scorn delights, and live laborious days****.* LYCIDAS (J MILTON 1608-74) □ *It used to be a romantic notion that poverty was good for artists and that others, too, would be none the worse of* ***scorning delights and living laborious days****.* SC □ *One advertisement shows a young man, looking like a budding scholar who* ***scorns delight and lives laborious days****, filling in his 'pools' coupon at home and despatching it.* UL

scrape (the bottom of) the barrel [V + O pass] (informal) use the last part(s) of one's resources; (esp) use the least satisfactory part(s) of one's resources □ *'That was Sue on the phone. She wanted to know whether all seven of them could come round for lunch tomorrow. I said it would be okay.' 'But that's impossible! Even if we* ***scraped the barrel*** *it wouldn't be nearly enough.'* □ *'I notice that the new president of Acirema is a 70-year old, ex-actor, ex-TV-chatshow-compère.' 'Good Lord! They must really have* ***scraped the bottom of the barrel*** *to dig him up.'*

scratch A and (you) find B only a surface veneer, or disguise, hides the fact that A is still to a large extent B □ (saying) ***Scratch*** *a Russian* ***and you'll find*** *a Tartar.* □ *That's what 'The Lord of the Flies' is about.* ***Scratch*** *almost any* *small boy* ***and you find*** *a savage.* ▫ ***Scratch*** *the surface of a civil servant* ***and you****'re likely to* ***find*** *absolutely anything.* OBS ▫ ***Scratch*** *Morris's documentary approach to people and television* ***and you*** *will* ***find*** *another side to him.* TVT ▫ often expresses an assumption about all members of a particular nation, creed, class or profession.

scratch one's head [V + O] (lightly scratch or rub one's head and) wonder, be puzzled, what to do, think or answer ▫ *He glanced at my acquaintance who was* ***scratching his head*** *in a faintly worried fashion.* SC ▫ *When Lord Shawcross described an unknown, corrupt politician as being held in public esteem, the nation* ***scratched its head*** *and could think of only one politician in the last 30 years held in anything approaching public esteem.* NS *'This caused a bit of* ***head-scratching*** *at the BBC, but they are letting it go out as I wrote it,' says Speight.* ST ▫ also pl scratch their heads; n compound head-scratching.

scratch a living [V + O pass] earn, grow, produce, with great difficulty just enough to live on **adj:** bare, meagre, scanty, precarious. **A:** from the soil; (by) selling from door to door ▫ *Others deal in second-hand clothing, scavenge for firewood or take in washing. It allows them to* ***scratch a living*** *while they look for a better-paid job.* SC ▫ *The* (film) *company was kept alive by Aitken's brother Roy, who still* ***scratched a*** *precarious* ***living*** *distributing Griffith's masterpiece on an individual booking basis.* ST

scratch the surface (of sth) [V + O pass] give sth (only) brief or slight study, investigation, or treatment **A:** only, just, hardly, merely. **o:** subject, problem; electoral reform ▫ *They say they are only* ***scratching the surface of*** *the subject, but already they are surprised by the quality and diversity of the material available.* RT ▫ *Despite the numerous attempts to induce industry to move into the development areas and to decentralise offices from Central London, we have only* ***scratched the surface of*** *the problems.* L ▫ *Allport, who has written the classic introduction to this field, discusses some fifty definitions without doing more than* ***scratching the surface.*** SNP

scream etc blue murder shout out loudly, make a great deal of noise and fuss (because one objects to sth that is happening) **V:** scream, ⚠ shout, yell, cry; be ▫ *He'll scream blue murder if you promote Jack Simpson instead of him—but Jack'll do the job better.* ▫ *A few of his utterances are liable to make our Union chaps* ***cry blue murder****, but as long as he's kept in check, it won't do any harm for them to be made to think a little beyond their mental horizon.* ASA ▫ (The photographers) *were the queerest-looking bunch your ever saw, and I use my words advisedly. One of them came over and tried to turn my face round with his hands and before I knew what I was doing I was* ***yelling blue murder.*** JFTR ▫ SARAH: *There'll* ***be blue murder*** *if it carries on like this. All our life is it going to be like this?* CWSB

scrub it/that [V + O pass] (informal) stop (doing) it/that; delete, cancel it/that ▫ MICK: *This bag's very familiar.* DAVIES: *What do you mean?* MICK: *Where'd you get it?* ASTON (rising, to them): ***Scrub it.*** TC ▫ *I couldn't dictate at all that morning. I'd get half-way through a letter and have to* ***scrub it*** *and start again.*

the scum of the earth [Comp (NP)] the class, or kind, of person thought (by sb) to be worthless or despicable **V:** ⚠ be; think, consider, sb ▫ (dockers' strike, 1972) *'****Scum of the earth*** *is what we are,' said a huge man in a club near Smithfield meat market, with heavy sarcasm.* NS ▫ (trial of mercenaries, Angola, 1976) *To the People's Prosecutor, with his customary rhetorical flourish, they* (the accused) *were '****the scum of*** *capitalist* ***society****'.* L ▫ sometimes adapted, as shown in second example.

seal sb's fate [V + O pass] determine (part of) sb's future for better or worse ▫ *I had received a card to say my application was being considered but was still awaiting the letter that would* ***seal my fate.*** ▫ *'That's the man I'm going to marry,' Esther told her friend. 'He may not know it now but* ***his fate*** *is* ***sealed****.'* ▫ also pl seal their fate.

the seamy side (of sth) [Comp/O (NP)] the unpleasant, or immoral, aspects (of sth) **V:** be; see, experience, have. **o:** life, the capital; domestic service, politics ▫ *When a man had seen as much of* ***the seamy side****, you know, as Bill, it could hardly be expected that he was going to be upset.* HAA ▫ *Cyril Pearl writes with indignation and relish about* ***the seamier side of*** *Victorian life.* NS ▫ *Mr Skipton knows a lot about Flemish domestic life.* ***The seamy side****, I believe. I suppose even this delightful city has* ***its seamy side.*** US ▫ *Janet expressed her views about* ***the*** *'****seamy side of*** *motherhood' in the first book published in England which openly advocated abortion reform.* L ▫ stress pattern the 'seamy side (of sth).

search one's heart/soul [V + O pass] closely examine one's feelings, motives, the nature of one's actions ▫ *I'd get tired of listening to mother* ***searching her soul*** *when I knew damn well that she'd always do exactly what suited her best, in the end.* ▫ *The poor, the sick, the aged, the unemployed, had been counted and analysed by a generation of private and official inquirers. There was information. There were theories. There were* ***searchings of heart.*** NS ▫ *There might be some* ***heart-searching*** *by the judiciary on their interpretation of 'reasonable doubt' when there is a conflict of evidence.* L ▫ *Black Mountain seems to have acquired a mystical value for him in the process of writing about it, and becomes the occasion for some dubious* ***soul-searching.*** ST ▫ also pl search their hearts/souls; n compounds heart-searching, soul-searching; variants searching of heart, searching of soul; usu found in n forms.

search me (dated slang) I don't know; I haven't the slightest idea ▫ *'I thought Ailsa Craigs were onions,' said Hopalong. 'Are they?' '****Search me****, mate.'* TT ▫ *'Why doesn't he want to go?' '****Search me.*** *You'd think anybody would jump at the chance of a trip like that, with all expenses paid.'*

(the) second best sb/sth that is less good than the best ▫ SAM: *Don't settle for* ***second best*** *like your mother and I did. Marry a girl who shares your interests.* HSG ▫ *They want the cane completely banned in schools — but as* ***a second best*** *they think they have found a useful piece of case law.* NS

a/one's second childhood etc [O/o (NP)] a period of seeming able to act, feel, think as one did when a child **V:** have; enjoy, revel in. **n:** childhood, ⚠ boyhood, girlhood □ *There's a new 'Paddington Bear' series starting on Monday (5.40 BBC 1) and if these don't lure you into* ***your second childhood****, nothing will.* RT □ *Released from these responsibilities, my mother seems to have enjoyed* ***a second girlhood****—or perhaps the one she'd never really had.*

(in one's) second childhood (at) a stage of life when one's mental powers fail through age or illness □ *He's a dear old chap, but over ninety and* ***in his second childhood****. He couldn't tell you the day of the week.* □ *He's taken to repeating himself quite a lot. It may be the first sign of approaching* ***second childhood.***

second nature [Comp (NP)] a learned ability, or habit, that comes as easily to sb as if he had been born with it **V:** ⚠ be, become, seem. **A:** to him; with her □ *Harold had never confided much in Isabel. It had been a deliberate policy and become* ***second nature****.* PW □ *She's the kind of person who isn't very good at doing nothing, to whom work is* ***second nature****.* RT □ *Professionalism is already* ***second nature*** *to Michael. He has been acting since the age of two.* OBS □ always used without det.

a second etc opinion [O/o (NP)] an assessment, valuation or diagnosis, by another person, who has been consulted because there is doubt or argument **V:** get, have; accept; ask for. **det:** a second, ⚠ a third; another □ *The native miners and dealers insisted on being paid cash, and there was no question of getting* ***a second opinion*** *on a value.* DS □ *Is a National Health patient who has been recommended to have an operation entitled to demand* ***another opinion****?* □ *Neither is convinced by the other but both have agreed to abide by* ***a third opinion.***

the second/third time around/round the second/third occasion of doing, or attempting, sth □ *When you've failed as spectacularly as I did, it destroys for ever all the secret, private fears that can hound and even persecute the wealthy and successful. It's made* ***my Second Time Round*** *a damn sight happier and more contented than the first time.* TVT □ *Have spent every night this week watching re-run of 'Rock Follies'. Even better,* ***second time around****. And* ***third time around.*** TVT

second to none [Comp (AdjP)] equal with any other and better than most **V:** ⚠ be, seem; find sb/sth □ *The British soldier is* ***second to none*** *in the communities of fighting men.* MFM □ *For convenience shopping the supermarket is* ***second to none****, but, compared with the general shop around the corner, it is a most impersonal institution.* SC □ *In education our post-war architectural record is surely* ***second to none****.* OBS

see both sides (of the question etc) [V + pass] understand why one person, or group, thinks or supports sth and why another does not **o:** question; ⚠ argument, conflict; situation □ *Frankenheimer succumbs to the same tactical error — that of* ***seeing both sides of*** *every* ***question****. It's an admirable trait in a democrat, but a disaster in a man of action.* L □ *Roxanne Pitt has been travelling, writing, lecturing, frequently about the Israeli-Arab conflict. As someone with Jewish blood, brought up in Egypt, she can* ***see both sides****.* OBS

see the colour of sb's money ascertain that sb has enough money to pay (for sth) □ *Don't believe a word he says. Don't let him have the car until you* ***see the colour of his money.***

see/think fit (to do sth) consider it correct, convenient or acceptable (to do sth) **Inf:** to go, to stay (away); to refuse; to take (a bath); to ignore sth □ *I was just entering the street when I met her, apparently already on her way to wherever she was* ***seeing fit to*** *go.* SPL □ *'The Times' did not* ***see fit to*** *print the letter, and now I see that the proposal was not needed.* L □ *What happens to the surplus, if any? It belongs to the local committee, who can dispose of it* ***as it sees fit****.* TO □ JIM: *You're full of self-pity.* JEAN: *I talk* ***as I think fit****.* YAA □ variant as one sees/thinks fit.

see the funny side (of sth) [V + O] (be able to) see sth amusing in a situation that some people would find only annoying, regrettable or inconvenient **o:** it, things; life; a situation □ *They really howled for your blood, all except the Chief. There were moments when I thought he* ***saw the funny side****.* OMIH □ *Life is a dance towards death, and Rowlandson* ***saw the funny side of*** *it.* NS □ *This could be a difficult week. Luckily, you can* ***see the funny side of*** *life, especially if you have a good friend to share troubles with.* TVT

see etc how the land lies find out what the shape of a coast-line is, so that one can sail along it, or land on it; observe the shape, arrangement of geographical features, streets and buildings, etc in a town, or furniture in a room; (fig) observe the attitudes of others so that one can decide whether it is possible to do sth one plans to do **V:** see, find out, learn, know, discover, show (sb), reveal □ *I'll consult Joseph Macroon and if he's willing for Kenny to take us there tonight in the 'Morning Star' I think it would be a good thing for you to* ***see the lie of the land****, Carmichael.* RM □ *It was about half past six on a cool summer evening, but the bar was thick with smoke; it took him a moment or two to* ***see how the land lay****.* PW □ *Bunder and Simons had given him addresses that they recommended, but to accept either would have meant the end of his policy of strict neutrality, and he was determined to preserve it until he* ***saw how the land lay****; so he found a place for himself.* HD □ *Their first few questions* ***showed the lie of the land****. The interviewers were much more interested in my family connections than in my competence at the job.* □ variant see etc the lie of the land.

see etc how the other half lives observe, or experience, the life of people different from one's own kind in class, race, occupation, or interests **V:** see, learn, (not) know, get an idea of, have no idea of □ *'Got to get out and see life, General,' Pop said suddenly, in a burst of enthusiastic admonishment. '****See how the other half lives****. See the world. What about it?'* BFA □ *I did have the grace to feel a bit ashamed of myself when I got a picture postcard from a Chelsea address, smudgily inscribed, 'Come and* ***see how the other half do it****.' I really ought to have thought about him more, I told myself.* CON □ stress pattern ˌsee how the ˈother half lives.

see sb hung/in hell first/before doing sth (informal) emphatically reject the idea of doing, or agreeing to, what sb wants □ *Go to work for the man that put me out of business? I'll* ***see*** *him* ***in hell first****!* □ *Your father talks as if he'd* ***see*** *them* ***hung before*** *he lifted a finger to help, but he'll probably end up putting his hand in his pocket for the children's sake.* □ in constructions with *will, would.*

(not) see the joke [V + O] (not) understand why sth said, or done, is amusing □ *The nice thing about Mary is that she can always* ***see the joke****. I couldn't bear working with someone who didn't have a sense of humour.* □ *There is nothing worse than someone who can****not see the joke****.* G □ *Few spectacles give more enjoyment than that of the great and powerful slipping on a banana skin. The satisfaction, however, is neither uniform nor universal. And many do* ***not see the joke*** *at all.* NS ⇨ ⚠ take a joke.

see life [V + O] observe and/or experience various ways of living and behaving, esp those thought to be different from one's own, new, or stimulating □ *We 'av'n't* (= haven't) *much money but we do* ***see life****.* UL □ *Vicky began to like the place and her company less and less. She had to remind herself that at least she was* ***seeing life****.* TCB □ PRINCESS ANNE: *We know all the people on the estates. We try to look after them, and we go and talk to them, and they tell us about their problems. I mean, you do* ***see life****.* L ⇨ ⚠ next entry.

see life (steadily and see it) whole have a balanced and mature reaction to people, events, fashions and opinions □ (source, referring to Sophocles) *Who* ***saw life steadily, and saw it whole****:/The mellow glory of the Attic stage.* TO A FRIEND (M ARNOLD 1822-88) □ *Now, Mr Skipton, like me, you are an artist. You know the duty of the artist is to* ***see life whole****.* US □ *Bogus mystics and half-baked runaway daughters are thick on the ground: prolonging childhood into after years, the legions of those who cannot bear to* ***see life*** *clear and* ***whole****.* L ⇨ ⚠ previous entry.

see (day)light [V + O] see a solution, or end, to a problem or difficulty □ *Obtaining visas for half the Arab states in the Middle East is a formidable business, and expensive too. But at the end of a fortnight I thought I could* ***see daylight****.* BM □ *'I begin to* ***see light****,' broke in McNeil. 'If communication occurs on such a scale then it becomes doubtful whether we should talk any more of separate individuals!'* TBC ⇨ ⚠ next entry; the light of day.

see the light [V + O] realize, after being formerly mistaken, what one should properly do or think □ *One of the most deeply committed Christians I know was a rabid atheist before he* ***saw the light****.* □ (in a Conservative Club) *What brings you here, anyway? Thought you were a red-hot Labour man.* ***Seen the light****, eh?* RATT □ *Paul, 17, 'still says he wants to be slapstick comedian like me, but I have doubts about that. He'll* ***see the light****.'* TVT ⇨ ⚠ previous entry; the light of day.

see ourselves as others see us realize what impression we make on others; (be able to) view ourselves objectively □ (source) *O wad* (= would) *some Pow'r the giftie gie* (= gift give) *us/ To* ***see oursels*** (= ourselves) ***as others see us****!* TO A LOUSE (R BURNS 1759-96) □ *To* ***see ourselves as others see us*** *is a most salutary gift. Hardly less important is the capacity to see others as they see themselves.* DOP □ *Is there a way to* ***see yourself as others see you****—and what would such an ability do to you?* RT

see reason [V + O pass] think, or act, sensibly after studying the facts, being given advice, etc; see sense (qv) □ *He's a thoroughly tiresome fellow, but he will* ***see reason****.* EM □ *From then on, one just had to live from day to day, always hoping that it wouldn't be so long, that* ***reason*** *would be* ***seen*** *by the higher authorities.* ST □ usu with *will* or *would.*

(make sb) see red (make sb) become extremely angry □ *It's just that I* ***see red*** *when I think anyone is trying to muscle in on my property.* AITC □ *What* ***made*** *most of them* ***see red*** *was their assumption that we were somehow downgrading the scientist from the place where he belongs.* NS □ *Charles* ***saw red****. His livelihood was in danger, and after so much fatigue his nerves were raw.* HD

see sb (all) right (informal) look after sb's interests; ensure that sb has all that he needs or wants □ *Old man Barnett said that his son would never get a penny of his money but that he was very fond of his daughter-in-law and the children and would* ***see*** *them* ***all right****.* □ *You do the job properly. If it costs more than you've estimated I'll* ***see*** *you* ***all right****.* □ *I'd like to live here again with you if you'll have me. I'll pay you two quid a week regular* (= regularly) *for my board, and* ***see*** *you* ***right****.* LLDR □ usu with *will* or *would.*

see sense [V + O] think or act sensibly, esp after considering the facts or the opinion of others; see reason (qv) □ SAM: *Maybe you can help him. Help him to* ***see sense****: persuade him to give up his crazy ideas.* HSG □ *'I'm not going to take on more than one public engagement a week this winter.' 'Well, I'm glad you've* ***seen sense*** *at last.'*

see service [V + O] be in employment or in use **S:** troops, police; aircraft, vehicle. **adj:** long, many years', continuous; active. **A:** as a policeman; in the police force; as a mobile coffee-stall; in this kitchen □ *Just remember that Baxter's a man who has* ***seen service*** *in the tropics and will know more about the conditions than you.* □ *The design for a nuclear vessel, currently being put forward by one British firm, may perhaps* ***see service*** *for a reason which is not so much economic as political.* NSC □ *Granny's old tea-pot still* ***sees*** *active* ***service****.*

see the sights [V + O pass] look at, visit, the places typical of, or famous in, a city, district, country □ *The mystery and history of his religion made him* ***see the sights*** *and hear the sounds of the city with eyes and ears that never took anything for granted.* SC □ *'I suppose you've finished* ***seeing the sights*** *for a bit now?' 'Oh no, there's a lot of stuff in and around Lisbon we've still got to see.'* ILIH □ *'You look hot,' she added to Victoria. 'I've been walking around* ***seeing the sights****.'* TCB □ *Lester Piggott's at home wherever he goes, does no* ***sight-seeing****, and treats New York much the same as Newmarket.* TV □ n compounds a sightseer, sight-seeing.

see stars [V + O] (informal) be briefly blinded,

perhaps with flashing sensations, or by a blow (on the head) □ *My God, what a lump! You must have* ***seen stars*** *when you got that.* □ *I didn't feel a thing at the time. There was a bang, I* ***saw stars****, and then I woke up lying on the floor of the hut.*

see them come and see them go outlast a succession of events, persons or things □ *I've* ***seen 'em*** (= them) ***come and*** *I've* ***seen 'em go*** *—six monarchs in all from Edward VII to the Queen — and I still don't rate Royalty.* RT □ *'Well, you watch her* (a baby with a cold)*, that's all.' Mrs Batey said. 'I've* ***seen them come and*** *I've* ***seen them go****, and they sometimes go quicker than they come.'* AITC □ usu perfect tenses.

see one's way (clear) to do sth (formal) find that it is possible, or convenient, to do sth **Inf:** to attend; to oblige sb; to accept □ *If you could* ***see your way to*** *say nothing further on the subject, I should be very much obliged.* EM □ *On the assumption that Mrs Cooper can* ***see her way clear to*** *face up to the situation here, I am quite willing that she could come back.* TT

see etc which way the cat jumps see how sb will act, or react; see what events will happen **V:** see; ⚠ guess, (not) know; be sure □ *It will be interesting to* ***see which way the cat jumps****, now that his profit-making can no longer be reconciled with a clear conscience.* □ *A jury usually takes its cue from the judge's summing up but one can never* ***be sure which way the cat*** *will* ***jump****.*

see etc which way the wind is blowing see etc what is likely to happen; see etc what others think, feel, want, or are planning, esp to check before taking action, or a decision, oneself **V:** see; ⚠ find out, learn; know □ *Shall we still go bumbling* (= wandering aimlessly) *up the middle (in which case today's low-rated shares could be the best bet)? Why not wait and* ***see which way the wind is blowing****, with the flexibility to jump in quickly?* ST □ *Wiser men* ***knew which way the wind was blowing****, cut their losses and got out before the regulations blocking currency were enforced.* OBS

see the world [V + O] travel, live, and/or work in many parts of the world □ *I adore* ***seeing the world*** *and when you read this, I'll be in the middle of a hectic cabaret tour of Teheran, Hongkong and Australia which lasts three months.* TVT □ *You've* ***seen*** *so much more of* ***the world*** *than I have.* QA □ (old slogan) *Join the Navy and* ***see the world!*** □ *We joined the Navy to* ***see the world****,/And what did we see? We saw the sea!* I BERLIN b1888

seeing is believing [v + v non-rev] (saying) one needs to see sth before one can believe it exists, or happens □ *'Ultimately, anyone's experience of the unknown has to be personal.' In other words,* ***seeing is believing*** *and you either believe it or you don't.* TVT □ ***Seeing is believing*** *— 'TV Times' got Anita Harris up a rope on Wimbledon Common, London — thanks to some crafty camera-work.* TVT □ (NONCE) *James Stewart's reading was inspired: the timing, the pauses, the laboured breathing, were masterly. And pure radio:* ***hearing was believing.*** L ⇨ ⚠ have (got) to/must be seen to be believed.

sell like hot cakes be bought readily, or eagerly, by large numbers of people □ *I translate Breteuil because it's easy and because it* ***sells like hot cakes*** *in any language.* UTN □ (a chair) *Made from first-class materials, it retails at more than £250. At the moment it is* ***selling like hot cakes*** *in Switzerland but is slow* (ie few are being bought) *in Britain.* ST

sell the pass [V + O pass] betray one's cause or allies; help those who should be one's enemies or opponents (from an incident in ancient Irish history when a body of soldiers sent to defend a pass let the enemy through in exchange for money) □ *It would seem that the self-appointed leaders of the pupils have* ***sold the pass*** *to the enemy.* SC □ *There is, especially among younger workers, a great thirst for socialism which will never be quenched by the opportunist posturing of men and women who have long since* ***sold the pass****.* NS □ *At some point* ***this*** *vital* ***pass*** *in the battle of communication was* ***sold*** *and it would be fascinating to know just when and where.* L

sell sb a pup [V + IO + O pass] (informal) sell sb sth that is worthless, or not worth the price paid; swindle sb in any bargain or arrangement □ *Supposing I lend you what's necessary to buy a partnership somewhere? I won't* ***sell*** *you* ***a pup****, and I'll even send business your way.* RATT □ *De Beers automatically accepted the custom that* (the post) *should be filled by a retired member of the South African police. On one of these occasions Pretoria* ***sold*** *them* ***a*** *real* ***pup****.* DS □ *That car's caused you nothing but trouble — you were* ***sold a*** *real* ***pup*** *there.* □ often pass.

sell sth/sb short [V + O + A pass] (commerce) agree to sell sth one does not yet have in the hope of obtaining it quickly and cheaply enough to make a profit; cheat sb in value or quantity; belittle oneself or sb/sth else **O:** sterling, dollars; country, economy; oneself, one's friends □ (artistic integrity) *More crap* ((taboo) = rubbish) *has probably been talked about* ***selling*** *oneself* ***short****, usually by disgruntled failures, than about even the popular problem of sex.* NS □ *Any book runs the risk of* ***selling*** *its characters* ***short*** *in some department.* OBS □ *'I like my body. There's nothing wrong with it and other people like it.' Modesty is not one of Beth Porter's strong points and she is certainly not one to* ***sell*** *herself* ***short****.* TVT

send a boy on a man's errand/to do a man's work send, or appoint, sb to do sth that requires more strength, skill, experience etc than he has □ *The appearance of 18 and 19 year-olds in the early casualty lists gave rise to murmurings at home about* ***boys sent to do men's work****.* □ *Floyd Patterson was described as 'game', but* ***a boy on a man's errand*** *when he was knocked out by Sonny Liston in the first round.* BBCR

send sb crazy [V + O + Comp pass] (informal) seriously disturb, or upset, sb; greatly arouse, or excite, sb; drive sb mad etc (qv) □ *But sleep is necessary. Lack of sleep was what* ***sent*** *people* ***crazy****.* PM □ *The Group have many better singles to their credit, yet this is the one that* ***sends*** *the fans* ***crazy*** *wherever they perform.*

send sb packing send sb away, dismiss sb from a job, swiftly and with very little courtesy or consideration, because he is not wanted, has behaved badly, etc □ *Mr Woodgate cleared the*

Hall. ***Sent*** *them* ***packing*** *in double-quick time, saw it myself.* TT □ JEAN: *I thought he's certainly not the type for my Cairy. Too damn rough. I* ***sent*** *him* ***packing*** *last year.* YAA □ *The pay is good but you have no job security. If you don't bring in enough orders you're soon* ***sent packing.***

send etc word [possess] send etc news, a message, request, order by a messenger etc **V:** send; ⚠ hear; get, have, receive; (there) be. **A:** of it, of the meeting; about their movements; that his wife was ill; when he might be expected □ *'The programme has been changed.' 'I know, Sire; the Queen* ***sent word*** *altering it late this evening.'* WI □ *'Fancy Jim not telling us he'd got through* (= passed) *his exam!' 'He only* ***got word*** *this morning.'* □ *On the Friday I had still* ***had*** *no* ***word*** *from America.* NM

(these things are) sent to try us (saying) (adversities, inconveniences are) intended by God to test our worthiness, courage, patience, faith **det:** these; such; one of the □ *The disastrous droughts of the past few years* ***are*** *just biblical plagues* ***sent to try us.*** NS □ *A chap with a machine-gun came and stuck the barrel in my ribs and told me to get back.* ***These*** *are the* ***things*** *that* ***are sent to try you.*** TVT □ final pron occas you, as shown.

serve sb right (informal) be a just, or suitable, penalty for sb **S:** it. . .if you failed, it. . .for being an idiot □ *Helen wanted everything. It would* ***serve*** *her mother* ***right*** *if she ran straight back to Felix and said, 'Forgive me, I will marry you.'* AITC □ *It* ***serves*** *the beggars* ***right*** *for being out marching when they should have obeyed the law and stayed at home.* L □ HYMIE: *Why didn't I go home* (ie to get my head bandaged)? MONTY: *Because you know Lottie would say '****serves you right.****'* CSWB □ serve/serves you, them, the brute(s) right as an exclamation (without S).

serve one's/its turn [V + O] be useful for a purpose or for a particular period **S:** servant, assistant; stove, fridge; drill, razor □ *It* ***served its turn*** *well, did that little car, because John developed into a very fine driver.* RFW □ *Now the cleaning woman has* ***served her turn,*** *they'd be happy to get rid of her.* □ also pl serve their turn. ⇨ ⚠ next entry.

serve sb's turn [V + O] be good, or useful, enough for sb's purpose □ *A reliable lad that'll do what he's told will* ***serve my turn*** *perfectly well.* □ *Anyone who sees something of Servicemen's reading, of the popularity of American and English comics (with the cruder English boy's comics* ***serving their turn*** *when the supply of hotter material runs out) knows something of all this.* UL ⇨ ⚠ previous entry.

set/start the ball rolling be the first person, or item, to start a group programme, activity, discussion etc □ *The cabbies* (= taxi drivers) *are waiting for Lefty, the guy who's going to organise them and* ***set the ball rolling.*** L □ *All that is required is a rough sketch, or joke idea, involving up to four people, with your own caption or 'Laughline' to* ***set the ball rolling.*** RT □ *I was willing to* ***start the ball rolling*** *by submitting at once a paper giving the War Office views.* MFM ⇨ ⚠ keep the ball rolling.

set (sb) a (good etc) example [V + IO + O pass] show, or maintain, a (good) standard of work, behaviour, for others to copy **adj:** good, ⚠ fine; bad, poor □ (the start of a school day) *'Is she in? She usually is by now.' 'She's certain to be, I think.' 'Yes,' said Miss Flynn, 'she certainly* ***sets*** *us all* ***a good example.****'* TT □ *They look to employers to make a firm stand against excessive union demands and under their leadership the public sector has been called upon to* ***set an example.*** SC □ *They're following* ***the good example set*** *by their teachers.* □ *Is that* ***the example*** *you* ***set*** *your younger brothers?* □ omission of adj implies example is good. ⇨ ⚠ follow sb's example.

set fair [Comp (AdjP)] in a stable and favourable condition (for sth to happen or be achieved) (from set fair, a position on a barometer dial) **V:** ⚠ be, seem; turn to. **A:** for success; to succeed □ *When I last spoke to you the economic barometer seemed to be* ***set fair.*** *But in the latter half of the year it began to fall.* T □ *The weather was hot, we had swamps and water close by, and everything was* ***set fair*** *for the winged horrors, but they never appeared in quantity.* BM □ *Cilla Black, the distaff* (= female) *side of the Mersey invasion of the 60s look, is* ***set fair*** *to become the Gracie Fields of 1984.* RT

set the pace [V + O pass] fix a rate of racing, running, walking which others (try to) keep up with, or surpass; take the lead, be foremost, in any activity involving co-operation, or competition, with others □ *With Roddy* ***setting the pace,*** *the boys tore uphill and arrived with bursting lungs.* □ (advertisement) *It's the Ronson C.F.L.—the new shaver that* ***sets the pace*** *for years to come.* DM □ *It was he who* ***set the pace*** *and established the style of a very agile and pert production.* G □ *Italy was from time to time quoted as the success story of the Common Market—its most backward member becoming the* ***pace-setter*** *in economic growth.* NS □ n compound a pace-setter.

a set piece a display, procedure, scene, (public) event that takes place in a set pattern (from, originally, an elaborate fireworks display on fixed frames) □ (rugby football) *There was every indication that it was at* ***the set piece*** *that the Lions could get the sort of ball needed to win the Test matches.* L □ *Except when there is* ***a set piece*** *and a vote at 10 p.m., the House of Commons, these days, is a placid place after dinner.* NS □ *I like a garden to look as if it had just happened even if more care has been expended on the planning than in any* ***set-piece*** *flower-bed or border.* SC □ *Trying to find any practical benefit from Strategic Arms Limitation Talks, or other* ***set-piece*** *conferences, is like peering through the wrong end of a telescope.* L □ attrib use *a* ***set-piece*** *flower-bed, conference.*

set/put the record straight [V + O + Comp pass] provide a correct account, explanation etc of facts, events; put sth right/straight (qv) □ *I'd been warned by an anxious press-lady not to bring up politics. In the event, he seemed anxious to* ***set the record straight.*** RT □ *All in all, this is a profoundly depressing volume. Perhaps, as Dame Rebecca felt, it had to be written to* ***set the record straight,*** *but it is impossible to read it without feeling a frisson* ((French) = shudder) *of true fear.* L □ *But before the discussion proceeded any further* ***the*** *Labour* ***record*** *would have to be* ***put straight.***

set one's/sb's sights high [V + O + Comp pass] be, or make sb, ambitious about one's/his future, or in an aim or project; have, set, a high standard of work, morals or behaviour □ *From the Careers Guide brought out by the National Union of Teachers some parents may be able to see that they, or their children, are being over-ambitious; others that they have not* ***set their sights high*** *enough.* OBS □ *The Italians are upset that, in* ***setting their sights*** *so much* ***higher*** *the Americans are imposing unattainable and unrealistic standards which could put paid to economy cars.* L □ *Of the many reasons I have to hold Persinger in loving remembrance, none is greater than his* ***setting my sights high*** *from the beginning.* OBS ⇨ ⚠ lower/raise one's sights.

set a thief to catch a thief (saying) sb experienced in crime, or cunning, is the most suitable person to catch, or prevent, another person of the same type □ *The effectiveness of the CID* ((GB) = Criminal Investigation Department) *depends on professional skill and training and then on integrity. It really is utter nonsense to say you must* ***set a thief to catch a thief****.* L □ *The President's response was to appoint a presidential task force headed by his chief troubleshooter. Apparently the reason behind this choice was that* ***it takes a thief to catch a thief****.* SC □ (NONCE) (reader's letter) *'****Set a policeman to catch a policeman****' works only when the set policemen have the will to catch* (ie expose corruption). NS □ variant it takes a thief to catch a thief.

set the tone (of/for sth) [V + O pass] establish the atmosphere, mood, social or moral level (of sth) **o:** meeting, discussion; campaign, movement □ *If the policy was to promote high morale throughout the Army, the War Office must itself* ***set the tone****.* MFM □ *His obvious boredom at the entire proceedings* ***set the tone for*** *what promised to be a remarkably cheerless Christmas dinner.* EM □ *The first party political broadcast of the election clearly* ***set the*** *style and* ***tone of*** *the government campaign.* NS

(soon) settle sb's hash [V + O pass] (informal) (quickly) end sb's annoying behaviour, defiance, complaints, interference etc □ *He hasn't any claim on you at all. Don't worry. A good lawyer will soon* ***settle his hash****.* □ *'That's* ***settled their hash****. I think,' their father reported. 'No more squabbling this afternoon.'* □ *Promising herself she would soon* ***settle*** *the janitor****'s hash****, Miss Murphy strode off down the corridor with the requisition sheet in her hand.* □ stress pattern usu settle 'sb's hash.

the seven deadly sins the seven faults of character or behaviour, any one of which could bar one's soul from heaven (from medieval Christianity) □ *Morally, of course, the Americans know as much as any of us about* ***the seven deadly sins****.* L □ *I tend to steer clear of the curious mixture known as the Ten Commandments. I prefer to be guided by* ***the Seven Deadly Sins****—or the reciprocal I should say. The most insidious one for me—I'm too old for lechery now—is sloth.* TVT □ *It is a sad facet of human nature that to be called naive is more wounding than to be accused of all* ***seven Deadly Sins****.* OBS

the seven-year itch boredom, restlessness, desire for sexual variety that is supposed to set in about seven years after marriage □ *My man and I had been married for* ***seven years****. We all know about the myth about* ***the itch****, and we joke about it, but now and again I had my misgivings that there is never smoke without fire.* YWT □ *It was a very happy marriage, but it only lasted four years. In the old days we had* ***the seven-year itch****; these days everything goes at a much faster pace.* TVT

the seventh heaven a state of perfect bliss, extreme happiness and satisfaction □ *She's so smart it's not true. Matthew's in* ***the seventh heaven****. I'm afraid he's a snob, but I do think that's the least of the vices, don't you?* US □ *Laura's unmistakable preference for his company that evening had raised Tom's spirits to* ***the seventh heaven****.* □ usu with *be in the/one's.*

sex appeal the (degree of) attractiveness a man or woman has for sb of the opposite sex □ *Actress Pam Grier smoulders evil and* ***sex appeal*** *as the panther woman.* TVT □ *Whatever* ***sex appeal*** *Jimmy had was greatly enhanced by his resemblance to the star of a popular TV series.*

shake one's head[1] [V + O] move one's head a little from side to side to express refusal □ *'Will you drive, Mr Alan?' I* ***shook my head****; I wanted to be able to see the countryside.* RFW □ *He said 'Anything more?' in a low voice and when she* ***shook her head*** *his thin dark face cleared and brightened.* DC □ *He brushed past the ticket-seller* ***with an*** *impatient* ***shake of his head****.* ST □ variant with a shake of one's head.

shake one's head[2] [V + O] move one's head from side to side to give advice or a warning □ *It's not a fair game of chess if you're going to stand there* ***shaking your head*** *every time Jim looks as if he's going to make a wrong move.* □ *Hugo* ***shook his head*** *at me and put his finger to his lips and gave his attention to Lefty.* UTN

shake one's head[3] [V + O] move one's head slowly from side to side, to express sorrow, concern, perplexity, disapproval **A:** over the news; at such behaviour; in disgust □ *'My poor cousin has passed away. His end was very peaceful.' Dr Bottwink, his hands thrust deep into his pockets,* ***shook his head*** *slowly from side to side.* EM □ *Then she took out Mr Greenholtz's recommendation* (of herself) *and* ***shook her head*** *over it. 'We must do better than that,' said Victoria.* TCB □ *This was clearly a lie. I* ***shook my head*** *over it.* UTN □ *Right from his earliest academic days he gave them history lessons they had never heard before, and his fellow dons* ***shook their heads*** *gravely.* RT □ n compound head-shaking.

shake a leg [V + O] (dated slang) stir oneself; show some physical energy and activity; dance, esp informally or socially □ ***Shake a leg*** *now, Ginger, there's a good sort. There's all that pile to be priced, and you know it's my half day.* AITC □ *Father of two, and now 50, George claims he can 'still* ***shake a leg*** *with all the youngsters at the discos. I enjoy a bit of a rave-up. Keeps me fit.'* TVT

shake etc like a jelly/leaf shake, tremble etc with fear, apprehension, nervousness **V:** shake, ⚠ tremble, quiver, wobble □ *Ma, who had recovered equilibrium, now spoke down the speaking tube,* ***shaking like a jelly****.* DBM □ *He was* ***trembling like a jelly,*** *so that I was hard* *put to it to know what was going on.* LLDR ▫ *Sir Thomas Beecham maintained that he asked Leon Goossens to play the tuning note for the orchestra whereat Leon's oboe* **wobbled like a jelly**. *When he had finished, Sir Thomas turned to the orchestra, saying 'Gentlemen, take your choice.'* RT ▫ *We arrived at the dentist,* **quivering like jellies** *, tormented by the dimly-understood horror of exposed nerves.* SC ▫ *You could hear shrapnel after that, you could count it. Bong, chong, boom.* **Shaking like a leaf** *you'd be.* L ▫ *They even more kindly invited all women passengers into the cockpit; one of them emerged* **shaking like a leaf**. *'They asked* me *to fly the plane.'* NS ▫ esp continuous tenses.

shake one/sb rigid [V + O + Comp pass] (informal) frighten, upset, or astonish, sb ▫ *'It reely* (= really) **shook me rigid**.*' Kevin lurked behind a power-drill to drown his complaint; 'It's crawling with drunks and loonies.'* NS ▫ *'Are you a Christian?' It* **shook me rigid**. *In my whole living life I'd never been asked that one before.* JFTR ▫ *I was never so glad to get out of a car in my life. He had us all* **shaken rigid**. ▫ usu past simple tense.

shall be etc nameless will not be referred to by name **S:** my informant; who, that, which. **V:** shall be, shall remain; must be, had better be; prefers to be ▫ *'How do you know?' 'On good authority. My informant, however,* **shall be nameless**.*'* ▫ *I entitled it 'The Silencer' and added an author's preface to the effect that I owed many of the ideas contained therein to a friend who* **should be nameless**. UTN ▫ *During the Somme battle that summer an infantry brigade, which* **had better remain nameless**, *was to be the leading brigade in a divisional attack.* MFM ▫ *It's perfectly true, and we both know it, that there are certain lady judges, who* **shall remain nameless**, *who have also been known to give* you *some extraordinary marks.* OBS ▫ usu as rel clause following *who, which, that*.

Shanks's pony/mare [O/o (NP)] on foot; walking **V:** ride, use, go on ▫ (high cost of petrol) *Others had bought or now used a moped or motorcycle. Four per cent said that they had already made a reluctant return to* **Shanks's pony**. OBS

the shape/taste of things to come [O (NP)] future events; future conditions of life and work (from a book of that title, published 1933, by H G WELLS) **V:** foretell, indicate, portend ▫ *When Baron de Coubertin reformulated the Olympic ideal in 1908—'The most important thing in the Olympic Games is not winning but taking part,'— he could hardly have foreseen that in the 1970s this would be regarded as a pious, fatuous hope with not an inkling of* **the** *grim* **shape of things to come**. NS ▫ *Looking back over my journal, I see that events of my first week at California State University in San Jose pretty much foreshadowed* **the shape of things to come**. OBS ▫ *A lady constituent has invaded his garden to request an autograph on behalf of her dog. The invasion, David Steel says, is uncharacteristic: 'But I hope that it's not* **a taste of things to come**.*'* RT

share and share alike an equal division, or use, of commodities, facilities etc ▫ *Nothing to do except go over to Mac's there and drink his beer, and he comes over here to drink mine. A* **share and share alike**, *with no one to worry you, and all the time in the world.* TCM ▫ *It was* **share and share alike** *in the early days. We had to borrow boxing boots, for example. Henry would wear them, do three rounds, whip them off, and I would have my fight in them.* TVT ▫ often in construction *it is (a matter of)* **share and share alike**.

sharp practice actions which do not break the law but which are intended to deceive others and profit oneself ▫ *But imagine two apparently identical piles of shirts, the first labelled Hongkong and the second carrying no origin mark, but costing more. All those people who assume that the high-priced pile is British and better may simply be paying extra for a bit of* **sharp practice**. L

sharpen one's/sb's brain/wits [V + O pass] (cause to) become more mentally alert, able, inventive or cunning **S:** you, he, we, they; danger, risk, challenge ▫ *Steve's a nice chap but far too easy-going. He'll need to* **sharpen his wits** *a bit if he hopes to get on in business.* ▫ *The revival of her novels during the past winter had* **sharpened her brain**. *Her memory had improved, and her physical health was better than it had been for years.* MM

shine like a good deed in a naughty world (catchphrase) be pleasing and praiseworthy in sharp contrast to the less pleasant background, circumstances etc ▫ (source) *How far that little candle throws his beams!/So* **shines a good deed in a naughty world**. MERCHANT OF VENICE V I ▫ *I recommended a visit to Franklin Schaffner's 'Planet of the Apes', a science fiction film which in retrospect* **shines like a good deed in a naughty world**. NS ▫ *One house especially has been extensively redecorated and redesigned. The Vaudeville Theatre* **shines** *forth* **like a good deed in this naughty world**. OBS ▫ (US networks) *Still, the attempt now being made is a brave one. In the America of the moment it* **shines like a good deed in a grey world**. L ▫ *Until recently, unpressurized draught beer has been available in only one railway station in the country, namely the BR* (= British Rail) *buffet at Lincoln Central, where the hand-pumped Bass* **shone like a good deed in a naughty world**. G ▫ may be adapted, as shown.

a shining example (of sb/sth) [Comp (NP)] sb who, or sth which, is a perfect instance of a particular type, and sets an excellent model for others to follow **V:** ⚠ be, become; regard sb as. **o:** a happily married couple; efficiency, leadership, integrity ▫ *The final achievement in the Second World War resulted from the bigness of the men who were selected to act in the critical positions — amongst whom Eisenhower was* **a shining example**. MFM ▫ *Friends regard Joan and Phillip as* **a shining example of** *a happily married couple.* ST ▫ *A 'Border Industrialisation Programme' tries to bring together American know-how and cheap Mexican labour in* **a shining example of** *good neighbourliness.* OBS ▫ *John Bentley is* **a shining example of** *an ordinary man who was not content with his corner in the pub.* NS

a shining light [Comp (NP)] (sb/sth) outstandingly good in any field of activity **V:** ⚠ be, become; turn into ▫ (source) *He* (John the Baptist) *was a burning and* ***a shining light**: and ye were willing for a season to rejoice in his light.* JOHN V 35 ▫ *He is also the undisputed expert in the field of medieval and renaissance music, and his Early Music Consort of London is* ***a shining light*** *in the vast field of British music and musicians.* G ▫ also pl.

(steer) the ship of state (cliché) (guide, govern) a nation and its affairs ▫ *The hour of crisis is past.* ***The ship of state*** *is back on an even keel, and we must put behind us the fear of capsizing.* NS ▫ (NONCE) ***The*** *Dayak* ***canoe of state*** *as it sails along, often has as many claimants for the captaincy as there are crew.* NDN

(all) shipshape and Bristol-fashion [Comp (AdjP)] in good order; tidy; well-organized and fully equipped (the reference being to the time when Bristol was an important commercial port for sailing-ships) **V:** ⚠ be; keep sth; find sth ▫ *One of the most curious expressions in common use is '****all ship-shape and Bristol-fashion****'. Bristol City is given over to a convoluted mass of Bristolians in motor-cars, travelling in disorganized chaos.* ***Bristol-fashion****, whatever it may have been in the days of tall ships, is today a bit of a muck.* G ▫ *Jim Larkin arrives at a Devonshire hotel to find everything* ***shipshape and Bristol-fashion****—only there's no owner, no staff and no guests.* SC

shiver my/me timbers (dated nautical slang) exclamation of astonishment or amusement ▫ *And Danny Kaye's comment on the ship as he arrived to play Captain Hook? '****Shiver me timbers****, it's a real treasure.'* TVT ▫ (film review) *You'll* ***shiver your timbers*** *as Wily Wisdom wrecks a rocket, dowses the diver and collides with the Commodore. It may not be clever but it's clean!* RT ▫ now facetious.

(know where) the shoe pinches (know in which way) a situation proves troublesome ▫ *Any working housewife with a family to feed* ***knows where the shoe pinches*** *without studying cost of living indexes.* ▫ *There's no merit in taking on responsibilities and then finding excuses to shed them as soon as* ***the shoe*** *begins to* ***pinch****.*

shoot one's bolt [V + O] find that there is nothing further one can do to attack sb, defend oneself, or achieve one's aim; make one's final effort (from bolt = arrow, hence 'have no weapon left') ▫ *I think I've* ***shot my bolt*** *here. I've done what little I can and I must go and start somewhere else.* L ▫ *With that I had* ***shot my bolt*** *in Seattle, but there remained one faint hope of contact in America.* RFW ▫ *At the fag-end of your life* (ie in one's old age) *you don't care much what you say or what is said to you. One has* ***shot one's bolt****, and it is too late.* NS ▫ also pl shoot their bolt(s); esp perfect tenses.

shoot first and ask questions afterwards/later (catchphrase) kill, or wound, anyone who might be an enemy, and find out afterwards whether one was right or wrong ▫ *Such gunfighters came from various backgrounds, approached their jobs differently, but all shared one characteristic: they were killers. They tended to* ***shoot first and ask questions afterwards*** *and they did their best to take no chances.* TVT ▫ often used as comment on sb's ruthless, or casual, attitude to an enemy.

shoot a line [V + O] (dated Royal Air Force slang) suggest by one's remarks that one's standing, work, achievements etc are better, or more important, than they actually are ▫ *When I was new to England I tried once or twice to explain to people how we lived, and found that they thought I was* ***shooting a line****.* RFW ▫ *I've watched that bastard going and coming about the world,* ***shooting a line*** *about his responsibilities as a British newspaper man.* PP ▫ *I always fall for* ***any line*** *that people* ***shoot****.* HAA ▫ GEORGE: *The one thing I never* ***shoot a line*** *about is the R.A.F.* EGD ▫ *Either he's* ***shooting a*** *phony* (= untrue) ***line*** *or you are.* HD ▫ *I've heard of* ***line-shooting****, but even* she *can't expect us to believe that ridiculous excuse for her behaviour yesterday—she lost her temper and was extremely rude, that's all.* ▫ *Jack must be the world's best* ***line-shooter****. He convinces all his girlfriends that they're the only one for him—and he always has at least three around at a time.* ▫ n compounds line-shooting, a line-shooter.

short back and sides an old-fashioned, or regulation, hair-cut for men and boys where the hair is cut very short ▫ *Remember square-bashing* (= military drill) *and the days of* ***short-back-and-sides****? Whether you do or not, take a trip down memory lane to the time of National Service.* TVT ▫ *The American GIs* ((US) = enlisted soldiers) *had bespoke hair-cuts that suited the head, whereas the British habit was to have the universal* ***short back and sides*** *and grease the hair.* TVT ▫ esp associated with service in ranks of British Army.

(on) short commons (having) barely enough food, esp over a period of time ▫ *The father of this brilliant group, bright and sensitive in his own right, must have chafed under the weight of obscurity and* ***short commons****.* NS ▫ *Tell them they must make the food last. We'll all be* ***on short commons*** *if the supply ship doesn't get through on time.*

a short cut (to sth) [Comp (NP)] a shorter way than the one usually taken to go from one place to another; a quick way, avoiding most of the usual work or trouble to achieve sth **V:** ⚠ be, become; look like; make sth. **A:** to the village; across the fields; through the side-streets; to success, to recovery, to a degree in Medicine ▫ *He made for the Western Highway by* ***a short cut*** *through the suburban roads I did not know.* RFW ▫ *There is* ***no short cut to*** *these qualifications.* ▫ *Persuading foreigners to hold your money, be it as a reserve currency, an investment or a trading medium, is one of the best* ***short cuts to*** *wealth and power.* G ▫ *The most crucial point he makes is that, because the drug is* ***a short cut to*** *religious or quasi-religious ecstasies, the ecstasy it affords is not the real thing.* ST ▫ also pl.

short for sth [Comp (AdjP)] a shortened form of a name **S:** Jo; Ina, NUT. **V:** ⚠ be; regard sth as. **o:** Joseph, Georgina, National Union of Teachers ▫ *Is Ina your baptismal name—or is it* ***short for*** *Georgina or Williamina or something?* ▫ *'Can't we call you Charley?—after all it's* ***short for*** *your other name.' 'Please call me*

Charley if you wish,' Mr Charlton said. DBM □ *She prefers to be called Katharine but everyone* ***calls*** *her* ***Kate for short.*** □ variant call sb/be called Joe etc for short.

a short life and a merry (one) (saying) a life full of pleasure and enjoyment (is best), even if it is shortened thereby **V:** have, live, choose □ *'You should be taking care of yourself.' 'Why? I might prefer* ***a short life and a merry.'*** □ (children's clothes) *Parents are having to decide whether to buy expensive, quality garments made to last, or cheap clothes which have* ***a short life and a merry one.*** SC □ (NONCE) *Some of the stresses can be avoided, and some reduced, although it is, of course, up to the individual to decide if he wants to. Not everyone chooses* ***a long life and a dull one.*** ST

short of sth[1] [Comp (AdjP)] less than sth; below (a particular level) **V:** ⚠ be, lie, stop. **adv mod:** just, only, a little; far, considerably, (not) much □ *At last he struck the wall and followed it, stopping a few feet* ***short of*** *the point where he believed St Sabas to be lying.* ARG □ *'How tall is he?' 'Just* ***short of*** *six feet, I'd guess.'* □ *The car's performance was far* ***short of*** *what I'd been led to expect.* □ *Middle-brow translantic comedy is a school that seems incapable of stopping situation humour* ***short of*** *farce.* NS

short of sth[2] [Comp (AdjP)] without, lacking, enough of sth **V:** ⚠ be, find oneself, go. **o:** money, food, ideas, friends □ *Chaps like you are always* ***short of*** *money. If you don't take the cash you'll regret it tomorrow.* UTN □ (dieting) *If you simply eat less you may go* ***short of*** *some of the nutrients essential for health.* RT □ *It's not ideas he's* ***short of,*** *it's energy to carry them through.* □ *If the family is hard up, then it is usually the mother who goes* ***short,*** *who pinches herself on food and clothes.* UL □ of can be omitted where O is understood from context, as in last example. ⇨ ⚠ run short (of sth).

short and sweet [adj + adj non-rev] lasting too short a time, but, nevertheless, welcome or pleasing; short at least, even though that may be its only merit **V:** be; make sth, keep sth □ *At the moment, our opportunities of meeting are* ***short and sweet,*** *but that will all change soon.* □ *The golden rule for after-dinner speeches is to keep them* ***short and sweet.*** □ (some schoolboys are to be punished) *These boys won't be away long, Mr Chadwick — we aim here to make everything* ***short and sweet.*** TT □ Comp or modifies a preceding n.

short and to the point [Comp (AdjP)] short, or brusque, but incapable of being misunderstood **S:** statement, order, explanation, speech. **V:** ⚠ be; make sth, keep sth □ *I opened Miss X.Y.'s letter first. It was* ***short and to the point,*** *and my spirits rose incredibly. She praised my book.* SPL □ *He paused to say, 'But I don't suppose you want to listen to my troubles?' Jane's reply was* ***short and to the point.*** *'No, Dave, I don't.'*

shoulder a burden (of sth) [V + O pass] perform a duty, accept a responsibility, that involves considerable work and sacrifice **det:** a, the; many, some. **adj:** a heavier, the heaviest, a considerable. **o:** famine relief; running the place, nursing her invalid mother □ *He* ***shouldered a*** *heavy* ***burden of*** *teaching and supervision, now reflected in the growing achievements of a brilliant galaxy of pupils.* NS □ *Who cares whether the doctor wears a frock coat or a boiler suit so long as he is prepared to* ***shoulder the burden of*** *our woes?* SC □ *We have* ***shouldered burden*** *after burden nobody asked us to, and now Lord Rothschild says we shall end up poorer than Portugal.* L □ *The mood of idealistic imperialism has been replaced by an almost bitter determination to see to it that 'undeserving' allies and 'ungrateful' client states should now* ***shoulder*** *some of* ***the burdens*** *which Americans themselves have suddenly discovered to be oppressive.* NS

show (sb) a clean pair of heels [V + IO + O pass] get ahead of, or away from, sb/sth very fast; make much better progress than a competitor **IO:** you; competitors, enemy □ *I wasn't claiming that Bob was a world-class sprinter, but he could* ***show*** you ***a clean pair of heels*** *anyway.* □ *Ian watched him nervously, ready to* ***show a clean pair of heels*** *as soon as the fuse was lighted.* □ *For once, the amateurs of the press* ***showed*** *the professionals of politics* ***a*** *very* ***clean pair of heels.*** NS □ *Only a week ago, British Leyland could still* ***show*** *Slater Walker Securities* ***a clean pair of heels.*** OBS

show/fly the flag [V + O] make known one's support of, loyalty to, alliance with, one's/a country, party, movement etc **A:** for Britain, for his old school; in support of the objectors □ *'****Showing the flag****' as he does at these sporting events is part of his one-man campaign to rehabilitate national pride.* OBS □ *Drake wondered if the company had put a black spot against his name. In fact, it was decided that he had* ***shown the flag*** *for Britain, the Empire, and the systems.* OBS □ *Anne* ***flew the flag*** *by reappearing* (after her fall) *but her score left her in 24th place. It was a disappointing end for her and the rest of the British team.* OBS □ fly the flag usu confined to advertisements for British Airways. ⇨ ⚠ wave the flag.

show etc one's hand [V + O] let others know one's intentions, resources, capabilities (from card games) **V:** show, ⚠ reveal, disclose □ *By 1805 Muhammed Ali felt strong enough to* ***show his hand.*** *He besieged the Turkish governor in the citadel, took him prisoner, and set himself up in his place.* BN □ *He and his daughter know the use and power of money, and they know how to wait and watch and to be silent and not* ***show their hand.*** NS □ *Blessed England, where bureaucrats feel obliged to* ***show*** *at least part of* ***their hand*** *before they place it.* L

show a leg [V + O] (dated slang) rise from bed or sleep □ *'Come on, you lazy so-and-sos,' said Brian, lifting the tent flap, '****show a leg.****'* □ *It's often 11 o'clock before he* ***shows a leg.***

show/prove one's mettle [V + O] give proof of one's courage, worth, determination □ *He is a good cricketer with a tough streak under a very pleasant and diplomatic exterior, and he has* ***shown his*** *captaincy* ***mettle*** *over the past few years with Glamorgan.* L □ *He was confident enough to welcome a bit of heckling at his meeting, judging that it gave him a chance to* ***prove his mettle.***

show one's paces [V + O] show what one can do in a particular activity, skill or study (from horses in a show or sale-ring) □ *She felt that like* *a champion in any field he must be given the chance to* ***show his paces****.* PW □ *The first and second prizewinners appeared with Yehudi Menuhin in his Festival Orchestra in a programme designed, I suppose, to* ***show their paces****.* ST

show promise [V + O pass] show signs of an ability, or talent, that is not yet fully developed or perfected; seem to progress towards a satisfactory, or favourable, outcome **S:** actor, musician; performance, work; season, campaign. **adj:** great, considerable, little; (not) any, not much. **A:** as a footballer; of becoming a violinist □ *It is 69 years since an anonymous critic wrote in 'The Era', 'Master Charles Chaplin as a newsboy known as Sam* ***showed promise****.'* OBS □ *A painting which, if executed by a 16-year-old could be said to* ***show*** *great* ***promise****, would, in the case of a man of 50, be an argument for taking up golf or carpentry instead.* □ *The article remarked on the distinct* ***promise shown*** *by several young players.*

show signs (of sth/that) [V + O] indicate the presence, or approach, of a physical or mental condition; indicate that one/it is likely to be/do sth **det:** many, few; no, (not) any, some; every (sign); little (sign). **o:** age, boredom; wear and tear; complying, being interested. **cl:** that he might break down, that would lead one to believe it □ *Sarah retains much of her energy, but* ***shows signs of*** *her age and her troubles.* CSWB □ *I suspect that Duchêne is not a religious man. (He* ***shows signs of*** *having once been a socialist.)* NS □ *He waited for Froulish to ask what that was, but the novelist was rolling himself a cigarette and* ***showed no sign of*** *hearing, so he went on.* HD □ *The speech of Dr Verwoerd before the attempt on his life* ***showed*** *no* ***signs*** *that the Government might lean to moderation.* SC □ *'The younger one, Toby,' says Miss Smith, '****shows every sign of*** *becoming an actor.'* RT □ *'This suit is* ***showing*** *some* ***signs of*** *wear, I'm afraid.' 'That's putting it mildly.'* □ *Only twice as we talked on did Martin Gray* ***show*** *any* ***signs of*** *anger.* OBS □ *Furthermore, workplace inequality* ***shows little sign of*** *being removed on a major scale.* NS □ signs occas sing, as shown—in those cases, det (any, no, little etc) must be used.

show one's teeth [V + O] use one's authority, or one's power, to intimidate or punish □ *The guarantors determined, one cold Wednesday morning, to* ***show their teeth****. They exercised their contractual right to replace Polanski and Braunsberg as producers.* ST □ *Matron looked a comfortable, motherly soul but she soon* ***showed her teeth*** *if any of the inmates gave signs of having minds of their own.*

show (sb) who's boss [V + IO + O pass] (informal) make it clear (to sb) that one is in charge, that one has authority over him □ *Buddyboy was a beautiful, clever dolphin—but also a rebel who would change the act and wreck the show. Hubbard hated him and had to* ***show*** *him* ***who was boss****.* TVT □ *You must* ***show*** *your plants* ***who's boss****. Snip off the two leaves above the growing 'tips' and this will encourage the lower foliage to sprout sideways.* TVT

show willing let sb understand that one is willing to do sth whether actually required to or not; ensure that one is seen as a co-operative, agreeable person □ *I think she has plenty of helpers as it is, but I'd better go along and* ***show willing****.* □ *I wish now that I hadn't half-heartedly concurred that early August day. But I wanted to* ***show willing*** *to Ike.* MFM □ in opposite meaning, neg constructions more usual than show unwilling.

shrink heads [V + O pass] (informal) give psychiatric treatment or therapy □ *Finally there may appear a statistical appendix tabulating the* ***heads*** *that have been successfully* ***shrunk*** *and comparing this proportion with the failures of some less intensive regime in the NHS.* NS □ *'I want to ask* ***this shrink*** *a few questions. Make an appointment for me—police business.' 'You know, he doesn't have to answer questions concerning a patient?'* ITV □ n compound a head-shrinker = 'psychiatrist' (reduced form a shrink in second example).

a shrinking violet (facetious) a timid, shy, unassertive person □ *In the past we have tended to see Mr Healey, not perhaps as* ***a shrinking violet****, still less as the gentlest and meekest of spirits, but rather as an eclectic politician.* NS □ *In black velvet with chiffon jabots, these ankle-length dresses would make even* ***a shrinking violet*** *look regal.* SC □ *I remember him there, a long, thin, silent shadow behind Chapman's corpulence. One has heard of* ***shrinking violets****: here was a shrinking cactus.* RT

shrug one's shoulders [V + O] raise, then drop, one's shoulders, usu to show indifference, but perhaps helplessness □ *Asked if he wanted to spend a night in the cells, he merely* ***shrugged his shoulders****.* □ *Felix stared at Virginia unhappily. Chris looked at Felix,* ***shrugged his*** *fleshy* ***shoulders*** *and took his sherry over to the fire.* AITC □ (stage direction) *He shrinks, looks at them for a sort of forgiveness, and then,* ***shrugging his shoulders****, turns and goes.* ITAJ □ *There is no excuse, however, for active members of the Labour Party to* ***shrug their shoulders****, blame the Government and leave it at that.* NS □ (He) *tends to worry excessively over the very slightest infringement of the social code which most people would dismiss* ***with a shrug of the shoulders****.* SNP □ also used fig to suggest mental attitude of indifference, helplessness; variants give/with a shrug of one's/the shoulders.

shudder to think (cliché) dislike thinking; hate to think; be afraid to think **O:** what her kitchen must be like, what he'll do to her; how much money has been wasted on it; of it, of how long it'll take □ *Imagine having to live in such conditions and sleep five or six to a room! I* ***shudder to think*** *of it.* T □ *His clothes are nearly dropping off him with age and dirt and when he last took a bath I* ***shudder to think****.* □ often follows O clause, as in second example; S is often *I*.

shut one's mouth etc [V + O] (informal) not start to speak; stop speaking; keep one's mouth/trap shut (qv) **O:** mouth, ⚠ trap, face, gob □ *'Go on.' 'No. You're so convinced you're right that I might as well* ***shut my mouth****.'* □ LETOUZEL: *Use your brains, you silly little fellow, or else* ***shut your mouth*** *while the rest of us use ours.* THH □ *Baader's reply is a rapid spate of German four-letter words, telling the judge to* ***shut***

his trap *as he is only a 'jailer of the capitalist system'.* ST □ *'**Shut your gob**,' he said, but quiet like, 'or I'll kick you out.'* LLDR □ also pl shut their mouths etc; used esp as brusque or rude command. ⇨ open one's (big) mouth.

sick at heart [Comp (AdjP)] unhappy; anxious; harrowed by doubt, disappointment, fear or grief **V:** ⚠ be, become; feel; make sb □ *He himself had come out of it* (the First World War) *so old with killing and so **sick at heart** that he had only one clear instinct and that was to get away from the scene as quickly as possible.* LWK □ *I left the Near East **sick at heart**, ferociously determined to make any new institute in London first and foremost an effective medium for the enlargement of technical understanding.* SD

sick of the sight/sound of sb/sth [Comp (AdjP)] (informal) wearied, disgusted, irritated by sb/sth that one has seen or heard too often; next entry (qv); sick to death of sb/sth (qv) **V:** ⚠ be, get, become □ (a 'Honeymoon Hotel' in America) *And if in time they get **sick of the sight of** each other in all the various permutations of beds and baths and mirrors, the young husband can take himself off to one of the bars.* ST □ *'He sang that well.' 'It's his party piece* (ie what he always sings). *His wife must be **sick of the sound of** it.'*

sick and tired of sb/sth [Comp (AdjP)] (informal) wearied, bored, exasperated, irritated by sb/sth; previous entry (qv); next entry (qv) **V:** ⚠ be, get, become □ *'There are times,' said Luke, 'when I get **sick and tired of** you wise old men.'* NM □ *I get **sick and tired of** you in that baggy cardigan and no collar on.* TSMP □ *'I am **sick and tired of** children coming into this room without knocking,' old Flynn said.* TT □ (reader's letter) *We have become throroughly **sick of** his snide remarks towards our colleagues.* NS □ non-rev though either sick of or tired of can be used with same meaning.

sick to death of sb/sth [Comp (AdjP)] (informal) wearied, bored, annoyed by; previous entry (qv); sick of the sight/sound of sb/sth (qv) **V:** ⚠ be, get, become □ *I read of Paris fashion till I'm **sick to death of** it.* SC □ *Mr Maddox, currently the outstanding editor of 'Nature', now wishes it to be known that he is **Sick To Death of** prophecies of doom.* NS □ *Can't we change the subject? I'm sure that, after a school day, James is **sick to death of** kids and conversations about kids.*

side by side (with sb/sth) [A] one beside the other; closely together; in collaboration (with sb); placed together for comparison **V:** stand, sit, walk; live, work, fight, grow up; study sth, look at, compare, place, sth □ *They stood **side by side** like a bride and a bridegroom at the altar.* □ *...the long houses where animals and humans lived **side by side**.* TVT □ *I had, according to Lord Kilmuir, carried that off with distinction and success and Macmillan had to work **side by side with** me.* L □ *He was forever refining and improving his comedy pieces; it is interesting, for instance, to view **side-by-side** two versions of his famous billiards sketch.* RT □ *The correct way to conduct the trial would have been a **side-by-side** comparison between Decca and the competing system.* NSC □ attrib use rare except as shown in last example, *a **side-by-side** comparison, evaluation, check etc.*

a sight better etc (than) [Comp (AdjP)] very much better etc (than) **V:** ⚠ be; think, find sth. **adj:** better, worse; later, sooner; more interesting; less expensive; more carefully □ *I didn't like being a prisoner but it was **a** damned **sight better than** being dead.* RATT □ HELEN: *If you spent as much time on me as you do on them* (= those) *fiddling bits of greenery I'd be **a** damn **sight better off**.* TOH □ *We thrash matters out like that, which is **a sight more pleasant** in my opinion **than** the atmosphere of an official discussion.* TGLY □ (race-course gambling) *'Done!' he said. 'What a sportsman! But we'll make **a sight more than** fifty pounds.'* UTN

a sign of the times [Comp (NP)] sth that shows the nature of, or changes in, the politics, economics, social etc values of any particular period **V:** ⚠ be; regard sth as □ *They have broken from fundamental Conservative philosophy—that nationalised industries should be allowed to charge what the market will bear and make a profit. Perhaps they were too distracted by other **signs of the times**.* L □ *I would be impressed by many things about the Escort 1300 GL—but it's **a sign of the times** that I'd need nearly £1,800 to get one.* TVT □ *One of the most divisive elements in our society seems to me to be the so-called generation gap. I feel that it is **an** important **sign of the times**, all the same.* OBS □ often follows *it/this is*.

sign/take the pledge [V + O] swear, formally promise, to abstain from alchohol (the reference being to written forms of undertaking to do so introduced by 19th c Temperance Societies) □ *'Don't bring me into it,' I said. 'It's like a drunkard wanting you to witness his **signing the pledge**. You feel personally responsible when they go back on it.'* CON □ *When I went to work among them they were an alcholic community. I made them **take the pledge**. It wasn't easy. It took months.* ST

signed (and) sealed (and delivered) [adj + adj + adj non-rev] properly completed, endorsed (and presented to the relevant person or body); with all legal, or usual, formalities having been completed □ *'I would never dream of going without an invitation.' 'Well, we'll see that you get one, **signed, sealed and delivered**.'* □ *Paris still seems determined to have an agreement on sterling balances **signed and sealed**.* OBS □ (NONCE) *But their manoeuvres in the show do support the comforting notion that a girl is incomplete without a man. And not merely a man — a husband, **signed, sealed and** securely **shackled**.* RT

(speech is silver but) silence is golden (saying) it is desirable, and may be more effective, to remain silent □ (source) *As the Swiss inscription says: 'Sprechen ist silbern, Schweigen ist golden' (**Speech is silvern, Silence is golden**).'* SARTOR RESARTUS III (T CARLYLE 1795-1881) □ *I'm thinking of putting up a '**Silence is golden**' placard in this office. Nobody can hear themselves think.* □ (advertisement appeal, Royal National Institute for the Deaf) *Ask the deaf if **silence is golden**.* RT □ often used as recommendation to remain silent.

silence reigns there is total silence; no one speaks □ *An almost eerie **silence reigned** after* *the noise of the motors had faded away.* BM ▫ ***Silence reigned*** *throughout the rest of the shop except for the whispering voices of a few assistants.* UTN

the silent majority those who lack the ability, or the interest, to make their opinions or reactions known through the media, organized demonstrations, pressure groups, etc ▫ ***The silent majority*** *had always previously meant the dead. Today it has come to mean the great soft mass of the living who put up with things, who get on with their jobs, pay their fines, rates and taxes.* OBS ▫ (the radio series 'Any Questions?') *What I like to think is that our audience really is made up of* ***the*** *so-called '****silent majority****'—which is not so silent on Friday nights.* RT ▫ *Every four years American election commentators invent a new concept to describe the blue-collar protest vote. Four years ago* (ie 1968), *the catchphrase was '****the silent majority****'; earlier, we had 'the forgotten Americans' and 'the white back-lash'.* NS

a silly billy [Comp (NP)] sb who behaves foolishly or childishly **V:** ⚠ be; think, find, sb ▫ *Phil was just teasing you. Now stop crying and don't be such* ***a silly billy****.* ▫ (advertisement) ***Silly Billy*** *had made up his mind. 'I want a hi-fi system,' he thought, 'and a hi-fi system I shall have.'* OBS ▫ PAMELA: *I think it's wonderful of you to take it so well. I'm sure I'd be complaining all the time. I'm* ***a*** *real* ***silly-billy*** *about pain.* FFE ▫ esp said of, or to, a child, or about sth not very serious; also pl; may be either capital or small S and B.

the silly season the late summer when, with Parliament in recess and many people on holiday, there tends to be less activity of national importance, and therefore more space is taken up in the news media by items of trivial entertainment value ▫ ***The silly season*** *is upon us. Journalists at a loss for stories are looking for the tallest hollyhock, a gargantuan marrow and the greatest gooseberry.* SC ▫ *When I read last Saturday's 'Times' leader predicting yet another 'Liberal revival', my first instinct was to believe that* ***the silly season*** *was beginning to take its toll even in Printing House Square.* NS ▫ *At the tail end of* ***the silly season*** *(which, for the BBC, seems to begin about June) nothing is more depressing than to come back to a whole series of repeats of programmes you have already seen or heard.* L ▫ *Thousands of unwanted mediamen have descended on Witchunt. Their aim: to hold a* ***silly season*** *festival in this quiet backwater.* G ▫ attrib use *a* ***silly season*** *festival, story.*

the silver screen the cinema (screen) ▫ *I was shy about girls and in the main transferred my adolescent fantasies to the stars of* ***the silver screen****.* RT ▫ *You became a legend of* ***the silver screen****./And now the thought of meeting you makes me weak at the knees.* P MCCARTNEY b 1942 ⇨ ⚠ the small screen.

Simon Pure [Comp (AdjP)] sb who is genuinely what he says he is; sb whose conduct and character are faultless (from Simon Pure, a character in an early 18th c play) **V:** ⚠ be; appear, stay ▫ *Perhaps in a society that needs to cling to some remnants of faith, the preachers dwindling and political leaders in gaol, the union man must be* ***Simon Pure****.* NS ▫ *The Disciplinary Tribunal suspend usually to a maximum of five years. The whole of that time the struck-off solicitor must be '****Simon Pure****'. His conduct will be examined.* TVT

the simple life [O/o (NP)] a simple, independent way of life, esp in the country, contrasted with the complications, stresses and materialism of modern town life **V:** lead, live; go back to, prefer, choose ▫ *'The Times' carried letters saying that we must change our whole set of aspirations and go back to* ***the simple life*** *(as in most countries of the world where people scrape a meagre existence up to an average age of about 35).* NS ▫ *He finally deserts the barrister's wife, with all her tiresome intellectual pretensions, and flies off with his Angiolina to lead* ***the simple life*** *in Ischia.* PW

sing a different song/tune [V + O pass] (be made to) change one's opinion about, or attitude towards, sb/sth; change one's tune (qv) ▫ *'Anna says she wants to have a large family.' 'Maybe by the time she's had one or two she'll be* ***singing a different tune****.'* ▫ *My father's bankers thought he had gone completely mad. Today they* ***sing a*** *very* ***different song*** *as they watch the sales figures rise month by month.* ST

sing sb's/sth's praises [V + O pass] praise, commend, sb/sth enthusiastically (and, usu, often) ▫ *After enjoying a perfect cross-country ride, Meade was* ***singing*** *Eagle Rock* ***'s praises*** *at Badminton and he would dearly love to ride the horse in Russia.* OBS ▫ *If he adopts the same position he will be accused by those who now* ***sing his praises*** *not only of illogicality but of jettisoning principle for the sake of expediency.* NS ▫ *You won't endear yourself to the doctor by continually* ***singing the praises of*** *his predecessor.*

single blessedness (facetious) the unmarried state ▫ (source) *But earthlier happy is the rose distill'd/Than that which withering on the virgin thorn/Grows, lives, and dies, in* ***single blessedness****.* MIDSUMMER-NIGHT'S DREAM I 1 ▫ *Valerie wouldn't give up matrimony for the illusory freedom of* ***single blessedness****.* RT ▫ *Neil is the only one still enjoying* ***single blessedness****. The rest of the group are all family men now.*

sink one's differences [V + O pass] agree to forget, or suspend, hostility or disagreements, between two or more people ▫ *This is such a peculiarly nasty specimen of Tory Government that it behoves all decent Socialists to* ***sink their differences*** *and unite to bring it down.* ST

sink like a stone sink straight down immediately ▫ *'Do you think that life-belt is any good?' 'It would probably* ***sink like a stone****. It's been hanging there for about twenty years.'* ▫ *My only chance of survival, it seemed to me, lay in releasing my hold on the life-line and deliberately* ***sinking like a stone****.* CON

sink or swim [v + v non-rev] perish or survive; fail or succeed **V:** leave sb to, let sb. **A:** together; on one's own ▫ *It is seldom argued that capsizers of pleasure craft should be left to* ***sink or swim****.* SC ▫ *The attitude finds expression in a great number of formal phrases 'Y've* (= you have) *got to share and share alike'; 'y've got to 'elp* (= help) *lame dogs'; 'we must all pull together'; 'it's* ***sink or swim*** *together'.* UL ▫ MILLY: *Personally I think we should let the younger generation* ***sink***

or swim *without any further comment from us.* EHOW □ *Preferential import agreements with New Zealand must be transitional only, and afterwards that country, 'one of the richest in the world', must be prepared to* ***sink or swim*** *on its own.* L

sinking sand(s) an area of loose, soft, shifting sand into which people or objects may sink and be covered over; quicksand(s); (fig) a shaky moral foundation to one's life □ *I've got rather interested in this Catholic business. The affair with Elvira made me realize what* ***a sinking sand*** *I've lived on.* ASA □ usu pl.

the sins of the fathers (are visited upon the children) (saying) the sins and mistakes of any generation have an effect upon succeeding ones □ (source) *I the Lord thy God am a jealous God, and visit* ***the sins of the fathers upon the children*** *unto the third and fourth generation.* BOOK OF COMMON PRAYER □ *In the British response to imperial collapse, there was also a kind of guilt—people did feel that perhaps they deserved it: both through* ***the sins of their*** *colonial* ***fathers*** *and their wilful incomprehension.* G □ *Screening* (for inherited disease) *offers parents the choice of risking or not risking that a child born to them will suffer from the genes, if not* ***the sins, of his fathers.*** OBS □ often adapted, as shown.

(all) sisters etc under the skin sharing fundamental qualities and only differing superficially **n:** sisters, brothers; Christians, savages □ (source) *For the Colonel's Lady an' Judy O'Grady/Are* ***sisters under their skins!*** THE LADIES (R KIPLING 1865-1936) □ *Who better than Barnard* (a heart surgeon) *to know that we're* ***all brothers under the skin?*** NS □ *The actor and the politician are* ***brothers under the skin*** *linked by a common need for public approval, sharing a constant quest for the bigger role.* TVT □ *We share the same basic tenets whether or not we claim they are supernaturally authorised. We are* ***all Christians*** *nowadays* ***under the skin.*** NS

sit/be bolt upright be sitting, or sit up suddenly, with one's back very straight (as a conventionally formal posture or because one is surprised etc) □ *She had black hair and a fur jacket and* ***sat bolt upright*** *and disdainfully, as if giving the car its orders rather than driving it.* RATT □ *Thick and fast the guests came, filling the Hampstead double drawing-room, covering the gold-and-white couches,* ***sitting bolt upright*** *on the little Empire chairs.* ASA □ PAMELA: *I told him the next time he heard you coming upstairs he was to wait till you came up to the bed, then* ***sit bolt upright*** *and shout 'Go to hell!'* FFE □ sit used much more often than be.

sit tight (and wait) do nothing, either as a safeguard against making a mistake or so as to wait for an opportunity to get what one wants □ *'Then why don't you* ***sit tight*** *when you've got it* (ie position and respect)*?' 'That's not so easy,' said Martin.* NM □ JEAN: *I've been driven crazy, here all night—listening to her. What could I do? We'll have to* ***sit tight and wait.*** YAA □ *He would like to do autocross or grass-track racing: 'They're fairly safe, but with Formula One, if a tyre bursts or something you just have to* ***sit tight*** *and hope for the best.'* OBS

(are you) sitting comfortably(?) (catch-phrase) from a question preceding the telling of a story in the former BBCR programme, 'Listen with Mother', for under-fives □ (title of consumer-interest feature about chairs) ***Are you sitting comfortably?*** SC □ *The star that night of the Tyneside Working Men's Club is* ***sitting comfortably****, so he begins.* NS

a sitting duck/target [Comp (NP)] a bird or animal shot at while resting or nesting; (fig) sb/sth that is easy to attack, criticize, or make use of **V:** ⚠ be, become; make sb □ *The Government draw the conclusion that henceforth deterrents* (ie rockets) *on fixed sites would be* ***sitting targets*** *for the enemy.* SC □ *And would the local council,* ***that sitting target****, itself be allowed to make a programme, or would it be considered too political?* L □ *Caryl Brahms remembers well her first encounter with Ned Sherrin. 'It was in the early 1950s, when I seemed to be* ***a sitting duck*** *for anyone wanting a collaborator.'* RT

six of the best (dated school slang) a punishment by caning or strapping □ *He turned to Gerald with a mock schoolboy expression. 'Let's get the pi-jaw* ((dated slang) = pious moral talk or reproof) *over, Father,' he said, 'or is it to be* ***six of the best****?'* ASA

the sixty-four thousand dollar question the important, crucial question or point, on the answer or solution to which much depends (from the American quiz game in which this was the top prize) □ *Congress simply had no right to ask them what came, nauseatingly, to be known as* ***the $64,000 question****: Are you now or have you ever been a member of the the Communist Party?* NS □ *Anyway, what is culture? That really is* ***the $64,000 dollar question*** *that the more percipient of the sixth formers are beginning to ask.* SC □ when preceded by *that's*, used as comment; cf the earlier form the sixty-four dollar question, from the fact that $64 was the highest award in a CBS quiz show.

a skeleton in the cupboard [Comp/O (NP)] sth criminal, or shameful, in one's own past, in one's family history, or in the conduct of private business or national affairs, which is kept concealed **V:** (there) be; have, hide, find □ *Reticence and taste for privacy seem to have been Thomas Hardy's motives rather than* ***any*** *grisly* ***skeleton in the cupboard.*** SC □ (a novel of nouveau-riche Victorian life) *There are, of course,* ***skeletons in cupboards****, dirt swept under carpets, violent death and other horrors hastily suppressed.* NS □ (NONCE) *But the two main compartments were his business life and his home. Now at a moment's notice he had to improvise a third compartment, a secret one,* ***a cupboard for a skeleton.*** PW □ (NONCE) *Lew Archer moves through the flashy corrupt world of Southern California, opening* ***the cupboards*** *and watching* ***the skeletons*** *fall out.* NS

a skeleton staff the smallest possible number of staff needed to provide essential maintenance and services □ *Originally the office was to be run on* ***a skeleton staff****. Now the immediate target is 75.* NS □ *Within a generation, the laicizing of the church may have become* (inevitable), *if, at the present rate of decrease, the church is left with only* ***a skeleton staff*** *of clergy.* T □ *Practically everybody* (in the town) *is working class — the middle class are just* *represented by* ***a skeleton staff****, as it were, to do the doctoring and the lawyering and so on.* CON

skin and bone [n + n non-rev] very, or too, thin; emaciated **V:** be, become; waste away to, be reduced to. **adv mod:** all, nothing but, just □ *He could see nothing attractive in women that were all* ***skin and bone****.* □ *She's gone to* ***skin and bone*** *now, poor girl. Stomach ulcers.* US □ *I don't know why you carry saccharin to put in your tea and coffee. You're nothing but* ***skin and bone*** *as it is.*

the sky's the limit there is no limit (to what can be achieved, obtained, charged etc) □ (Post Office Savings accounts) *The minimum deposit allowed is 25p, but* ***the sky's the limit****.* TVT □ *For a young man with his qualifications and record —provided he's ambitious enough—* ***the sky's the limit****.* □ *As to barrister's fees, if a case drags on for days, possibly weeks, or if it is followed by an appeal,* ***the sky's the limit****.* ST

a slap-up meal etc (informal) a plentiful, well-served meal of good food (often in a restaurant) **n:** meal, ⚠ lunch, dinner, tea □ *Before I leave, I'm going to take you all out for* ***a*** *really* ***slap-up meal****.* □ *If I'd thought a couple of days ahead to invite Reg Varney for a picnic, it would certainly have been* ***the*** *more* ***slap-up kind****.* TVT

sleep like a log/top sleep soundly and heavily and/or comfortably □ *I've got rather a headache. I* ***slept like a log****, and now I feel lousy.* PE □ *'I was fair jiggered* (= exhausted) *last night,' says Les. '****Slept like a log****—woke up in the fireplace. Terrible joke that.'* TVT □ *Mademoiselle Dupont said she hoped the children had not been frightened by the storm? '****Slept like tops****,' Pa said.* BFA □ *She snuggled into bed and* ***slept like a*** *comfy old* ***top****.* HAA

sleep rough sleep out of doors wherever one can **S:** vagrant, tramp; runaway; traveller □ *But the boy would constantly 'go missing' at nights from his foster home because his mother had taken to* ***sleeping rough*** *in the park.* NS □ *But you never get used to the travel. For months at a stretch, it can be like* ***sleeping rough*** *in luxury hotels.* RT □ the similar *live rough* may refer to a vagrant's life, (temporary) conditions without proper shelter etc.

sleep tight (informal) may you sleep well □ *Good night.* ***Sleep tight****./Don't let the fleas bite.* CHILDREN'S RHYME □ *'Good night, Pat,* ***sleep tight****.' 'Good night, Kath,' she said.* TT □ PAMELA (to Walter in the schoolroom): *Goodnight.* WALTER: ***Sleep tight****.* PAMELA: *Mind the bugs don't bite.* FFE □ usu preceded by 'Good night' and addressed to sb about to go to, or already in, bed.

sleight of hand skill and speed in handling objects, esp in performing tricks for entertainment; (fig) dexterity and cunning in general, esp with intention to deceive □ *The officer hardly looks down as he jabs the key forward, always finding the keyhole first time, a sort of professional* ***sleight of hand****.* ST □ *In yet another strategic* ***sleight of hand****, the British sent a lowly captain, who bore a strong resemblance to Montgomery, on a tour of the Mediterranean theatre of war.* OBS □ (NONCE) *It's ridiculous the things that have been happening in the famous Dome where the* ***sleight-of-tongue*** *talkers of the T.U.C.* ((GB) = Trades Union Congress) *Conference moved out to let the* ***sleight-of-hand*** *merchants in.* TVT □ attrib use *a* ***sleight-of-hand*** *merchant.*

a slice of life a story, play, film that portrays aspects of people's lives realistically □ *'What do theatre-goers want?' 'More than a story of* ***a slice of life****. They want a flavour, an aroma up the nostrils—that's what they'll remember five years on.'* OBS □ *It was one of the most moving pieces of documentary radio I have ever heard broadcast;* ***a*** *remarkable* ***slice of*** *real* ***life****.* L □ *They haven't yet learned the lessons of that French pioneer of* ***slice-of-life*** *naturalism, Antoine.* NS □ occas pl slices of life ; occas attrib use ***slice-of-life*** *naturalism.*

a slice off a cut cake is never missed (saying) taking a little of sth already being used hardly matters, or will not be noticed □ *Round the basic features of life—birth, marriage, copulation, children, death—the old phrases cluster most thickly. On sex: '****A slice off a cut cake is never missed****' (on the easy sexual habits of some married women).* UL □ *I'm your little bit of fun, I'm* ***the slice off the cut cake*** *that'll never* ***be missed*** *— You smug, hypocritical swine!* RATT □ used esp of (casual) sex with a married woman.

sling one's hook [V + O] (dated slang) leave secretly, hastily, or casually, esp a place one is expected to stay in; hook it (qv) □ *I've plenty to feel guilty about, but not her, really. She saw to that. Anyhow she's gone, walked out,* ***slung her hook****.* PW □ (a residential school for young offenders) *And I'll lose that race and I'll let him know it when I'm about to get out—if I don't* ***sling my hook*** *even before the race.* LLDR □ also pl sling their hook.

the slings and arrows (of outrageous fortune) the various injuries, losses, disappointments of life □ (source) *Whether 'tis nobler in the mind to suffer/****The slings and arrows of outrageous fortune****,/Or to take arms against a sea of troubles,/And by opposing end them?* HAMLET III 1 □ (cricket) *Talk about* ***the slings and arrows of outrageous fortune****! On Friday, Arnold had had three slip catches put down in three successive balls — some sort of melancholy record surely?* ST □ (NONCE) *At each stage on the diagram we place an animal who is more complex, better able to withstand* ***the slings and arrows of nature****.* L □ *If only the decision were so simple, then how confidently he could stand up, armoured fore and aft, to face* ***the slings and arrows*** *from Right and from Left.* NS □ now usu facetious.

one's slip is showing a woman's underskirt hangs lower than her dress; (fig) sb is revealing sth about his character, or opinions, that he usually keeps hidden □ *She's the kind of woman that loves to be able to tell you that you need to get your hair done or that* ***your slip is showing****.* □ (reader's letter) *Sir, Patrick Marnham****'s slip is showing****. In an article he reveals that his real aim is to use the problems of immigrant absorption and poverty to besmirch the name of Israel.* NS □ *'I'm afraid you've lost your poster,' I said, much as one might say, 'Excuse me saying so, but* ***your slip is showing****.' And I picked it up for her.* AH □ also pl.

slip sb's/one's memory/mind [V + O] be

forgotten by sb/oneself **S:** fact, piece of information; it. . .that she was away; to warn you □ *It* **slipped** *Wormold's* **memory** *that his nephew was now long past seventeen and had probably given up his* (stamp) *collection long ago.* OMIH □ *He's* my *child, too—a fact which sometimes seems to* **slip your memory**! □ *What Stocker actually did think of Celia, I never found out. Or if I did, it's* **slipped my mind**. CON

a slip of a boy etc [Comp (NP)] just a young boy or girl **V:** ⚠ be; consider sb as, think of sb as. **det:** just a, no more than a. **adj:** mere, tiny, slender. **n:** boy, ⚠ girl, thing, creature □ *True, the Scots-born granny didn't hang about the heather for long. As what my father would have called '***a slip of a girl***' she ventured to Creswick in the goldfields of Victoria.* L □ *In that Club—more of a mausoleum, really—they'd look on a man in his forties as* **a** *mere* **slip of a boy**. □ *Being such* **a** *little* **slip of a thing** *you can pick up a dress to fit you in any chain store!* □ applied to adults denotes slightness of body.

a slip of the tongue/pen sth said/written that it was not one's intention to say/write □ *The nervous strain of addressing a large conference can sometimes cause speakers to make silly* **slips of the tongue**: *like Harold Wilson calling Harold Macmillan 'Harold Wilson' for example.* NS □ *He turned red in the face and went stamping and bumbling away.* **A slip of the tongue**, *you see: but what did it signify?* THH □ *Yet one cannot doubt the depth and power of the love that brought them together — Wells, as* **an** *interesting* **slip of the pen** *reveals, considered their relationship a marriage.* L ➪ ⚠ let sth slip².

a/the slippery slope [o (NP)] a situation that could rapidly lead to danger, error, moral decline, ruin etc; the process of such a decline **V:** be on; go down, slide down □ *These two episodes could mark the start of* **a slippery slope** *leading to the unquestioning acceptance of the use of guns by the Police.* L □ *Mr Short was confident yesterday that the Government was not embarking on* **a slippery slope** *without realizing it.* G □ *'All borrowers get on* **the slippery slope**.' *'I am on it. And I am sliding down it at a rate too great for me to bear.'* US □ *The serious gambler may cut down other expenditure when he loses, but won't go down* **the slippery slope** *into debt and a life of lies, while a compulsive gambler will lose his last penny and then devote all his energies to getting more.* OBS □ occas pl.

the slough of despond (formal) a state, or period, of depression and despair □ (source—referring to a slough in which the pilgrim flounders on his allegorical journey) *The name of* **the slough** *was* **Despond**. PILGRIM'S PROGRESS I (J BUNYAN 1628-88) □ *Though he is now in Washington's Valhalla, this brilliant Russian Jew, who was all for America, was driven by his compatriots through* **the slough of Despond** *before he could get there.* L □ *The Rolling Stones become progressively side-tracked into* **the slough of Despond** *during their flirtation with flower-power, and return to the straight and narrow as the best live rock group in the world.* RT

slow but sure [adj + adj non-rev] (catchphrase) slow but thorough □ *The dullard, on the other hand, may have to toil long and hard at his learning task, but he is thought to have learned it well:* **slow but sure**. MFF □ *'You'll not hurry old Tom with any job, I'm afraid.' 'Ah, well,* **slow but sure** *is a good motto.'* ➪ ⚠ next entry.

slowly but surely [adv + adv non-rev] slowly but inevitably □ **Slowly but surely** *and relentlessly, the lost ground was recovered and we began to pass from the defensive to the offensive.* MFM □ *The first ingredient acts on weeds through the leaf and* **slowly but surely** *kills them.* RT □ *Nottingham is* **slowly but surely** *changing.* NS ➪ ⚠ previous entry.

small beer/potatoes [Comp (NP)] sb/sth of no great importance or value (from small beer = beer with low alcoholic content) **V:** ⚠ be, seem; see sb as □ (source) IAGO: *She was a wight, if ever such a wight were,—* DESDEMONA: *To do what?* IAGO: *To suckle fools and chronicle* **small beer**. OTHELLO II 1 □ *The actual demands set out in the document are* **small beer** *indeed.* L □ *In the end, art is* **small beer**. *The really serious things in life are earning one's living and loving one's neighbour.* OBS □ *This boy was big for his years and thought he was no* **small potatoes**. *He dressed in a flamboyant manner, and affected white golf shoes.* SC □ *But these achievements, impressive enough in themselves, were* **small potatoes** *compared with his real aspirations.* NS

the small change (of sth) coins, or notes, of low value; (fig) the more trivial elements, business, practices (of sth) **o:** conversation, religion, sex □ *Will you leave me some* **small change** *before you go? I've got nothing to pay for my newspapers with.* SML □ *To hear it* (the quality of the language) *was to be reminded how used we have become to hearing lines spoken on television which are* **the** *most worn and shabby* **small change of** *speech.* L □ *My resignation to an existence spent handling* **the small change of** *medicine had already turned into enthusiasm.* DIL

(the) small fry the children of a family, community etc; people in an administration, profession, trade, or art who are thought not to be important; small unimportant institutions, businesses etc (from fry = newly-hatched fish) □ *It was decided to have a staff dinner-and-dance on 18 December and an afternoon party for* **the small fry** *on a date to be decided later.* □ (gift suggestions) **Small fry**, *nephews, nieces would consider super: ball-point pen, visit to a zoo, home-made ice-lolly set.* H □ *An American landing-craft and a British destroyer shared the tiny harbour with a handful of* **smaller fry**. SD □ *Big-timers in the fashion business in Rome and Paris are frenetically adding the finishing touches to their autumn collections while* **lesser fry** *in the rag trade are thinking up their collections for Spring.* SC □ also, in third and fourth examples, smaller, lesser fry; stress patterns 'small fry, 'lesser fry.

the small of one's back that part of the back between hip bones and rib-case □ *'The pain runs from* **the small of my back** *right down my left thigh,' he told the doctor.* □ *I could feel her hands seeking each other in* **the small of my back**. *She locked me to her, then she said, 'It's a little experiment.'* UTN

(the) small print/type those parts of a legal document, contract, hire purchase agreement, etc which have warnings, excluding or saving clauses, in small print which may be difficult to read and, therefore, easy to overlook □ *Make sure you read* ***the small print*** *before signing the lease.* □ *Not being a lawyer's clerk for nothing, he is adept at drawing up unreadable* ***small print*** *in legal contracts.* L □ *It is important to follow their instructions carefully, but you may need a magnifying glass to read* ***the*** *very* ***small type*** *in which they are printed.* TVT □ small type usu used in literal sense.

the small screen (the) television (screen) □ *I moved away from the North not long after, so most of my Rugby League since then has been viewed on* ***the small screen.*** RT ⇨ ⚠ the silver screen.

small talk [O (NP)] light conversation, as at parties, when entertaining visitors at a superficial level, etc **V:** have, make, exchange □ *De Gaulle had humour, but he had no* ***small talk:*** *none of the easy charm of the Frenchman.* L □ *He made some* ***small talk****, staring down Whitehall, so that I could see his knave of diamonds profile. Then he turned full on me.* NM □ *André Previn and Oscar Peterson pulled off another impossible trick, of sitting exchanging riveting* ***small talk*** *while a thousand people in the audience sat there eavesdropping.* L □ stress pattern 'small talk.

(the) small time (informal) entertainment, commerce, crime etc on a small scale that does not bring much profit, public notice, or other reward □ *At that date he was still in* ***the small time****, a North Country comedian doing the circuit of working men's clubs.* □ *In these years occur the first productions at the Royal Court of all Shaw's early plays. Commercially, it was* ***small time.*** L □ *Long gone are the days when Dundee depended on 'jute, jam and journalism', although the empire left by D C Thomson, Scotland's* ***small-time*** *Citizen Kane, still churns out a profitable flood of print.* NS □ *...a helpless prey to a company of* ***small-time*** *criminals, too stupid to defend herself when, innocent, she is brought to trial.* ST □ attrib use, *a* ***small-time*** *criminal*, often found. ⇨ the big time.

a smart alec(k) (informal) sb who thinks he knows more, can do things better, than others and looks for chances to prove it; a cocky impudent person; a clever dick (qv) □ *He's such* ***a smart alec****—he thinks he knows everybody else's jobs better than they do themselves.* □ (F D Roosevelt) *In his 40th year he was paralysed by poliomyelitis. Yet throughout the 12 years of his Presidency, the press, including the most* ***smart-aleck*** *photographers, respected a convention never to photograph him in movement.* L □ *There's a new breed of highbrows talking and writing about film-making. They make Katherine* (Hepburn) *sound bullying and* ***smart-alecky*** *which she most certainly is not.* RT □ *Hamilton seems to be as fair as a critic might reasonably be expected to be in these trying times, and with one glaring exception he avoids the* ***smart-aleckry*** *that disfigures his magazine.* L □ also pl; attrib use *a* ***smart-aleck*** *photographer*; adj compound smart-alecky and n compound smart aleckry unusual.

(a) smash and grab (raid) [n + n non-rev] (a) theft from a shop carried out by smashing a window and grabbing goods □ *He's never been known to carry a gun.* ***Smash and grab*** *is his line.* □ *If all incomes are going to be broadly determined by political means—of which union collective bargaining is one—then it is preferable that the decisions should be made in Parliament rather than in the* ***smash-and-grab*** *of the world outside.* ST □ usu attrib, as in full headphrase.

smell a rat [V + O] (informal) be suspicious that sth is wrong □ *A milkman had several times seen a dark-green Mercedes passing slowly in front of the Tunisian Embassy.* ***Smelling a rat,*** *he had jotted down the licence number: F-AX160.* TO □ *Even that theatrical old fool Portway wasn't prepared to disagree with the great Stokesay. He* ***smelt a rat****, but he kept mum* (= quiet). ASA □ *Everybody* ***smells a rat*** *in a doctored obituary, even the widow.* OBS

smoke like a chimney (informal) smoke (esp) cigarettes frequently, or almost continuously □ *Miss Greece had a cigarette though and the papers said 'Miss Greece—never seen without a cigarette in her hand—* ***smoked like a chimney.****'* RT □ *'How many cigarettes do you smoke, do you think?' '20 a day—unless I'm worried or upset. Then I* ***smoke like a chimney.****'* □ also pl *They* ***smoke like chimneys.***

a smoke screen temporary cover, esp in naval or land warfare, provided by smoke from ships, smoke-bombs etc (to help an escape, redeployment); (fig) behaviour, or talk, that prevents observation or understanding of oneself, what one is really doing, etc □ *The 'Daily Mirror' calls Thorneycroft's plan* ***a smoke screen.*** BBCR □ *...an apparent insensitivity which added as much to* ***the smoke screen*** *of shyness that cut the children off from their parents as did Bernard's inept artificiality.* HAA □ also pl; stress pattern a 'smoke screen.

a smooth operator etc [Comp (NP)] (informal) sb with an agreeable, persuasive manner who usu manages to manipulate people and situations to suit his own purposes, good or bad **V:** ⚠ be, seem; regard sb as. **n:** operator, ⚠ character, customer □ *What Raine has is an iron hand in an iron glove which is beautifully wrought so that people don't realize that the glove is made of iron until it hits them. She's quite* ***the smoothest operator*** *in the place.* ST □ *They're a dour lot up there. They'd suspect anybody as ingenuous and friendly as Brian of being* ***a smooth operator.*** □ *Her stepfather was taking Virginia away to a life of college boys and* ***smooth characters*** *with fast cars.* AITC

smooth sb's/sth's path etc [V + O pass] make things easier for sb, either in general or so that he may do or obtain sth; help a desired situation, or objective, to be accomplished more quickly **n:** path, ⚠ way, passage □ *The only thing to do is to go straight to the President. I'll* ***smooth your path*** *there.* TBC □ *He had a lot of explaining to do and The Board of Inquiry had no intention of* ***smoothing his passage.*** □ *Good behaviour in the international sphere, like good manners in society, may* ***smooth the path of*** *international intercourse.* SC □ *Trade unionists pay only lip service to the need for research. Certainly they could do a lot more than they are doing to* ***smooth the way*** *for its application within the industry.* SC

snakes and ladders [n + n non-rev] a board

game where a counter falling on a snakes's head goes back to the tail and falling on a ladder's foot goes on to the top of it; (fig) an endeavour to do, or obtain, sth where progress alternates with setbacks □ *A social worker in North London describes the process of getting a council house as being like a game of* ***snakes and ladders****. If you are overcrowded or share a lavatory then you get so many points and move up the ladder: if you move to a different borough then you drop down a snake.* ST □ *In common with all other working women they also had no security of employment. The war was a brief, adventurous game of social* ***snakes and ladders****.* RT □ often with *a game of*, as shown.

a snap vote etc [O/o (NP)] a vote etc taken, sth done, quickly without fully considering the consequences **V:** have, call, take; reach, arrive at. **n:** vote, ⚠ election; decision, judgment □ *We could probably talk about it for hours. Suppose we take* ***a snap vote*** *just for the hell of it?* TBC □ *This could result in* ***a snap election****.* OBS □ *In the first place the contradictions are very striking, when seen from outside, and* ***the snap judgment*** *is tempting.* L □ also pl.

a snare and a delusion [n + n non-rev] sth that seems right, safe, suitable or pleasant but is not so □ (source) *Trial by jury itself, instead of being a security to persons who are accused, will be* ***a delusion****, a mockery,* ***and a snare****.* LORD DENMAN (judgement in O'Connell v the Queen, 1844) □ *America, however, insists that negotiation on numbers without a scheme for checking them would be* ***a snare and a delusion****.* SC □ *The rocks had increased considerably in size and were placed like a series of steps. This was* ***a snare and a delusion****, for each rock had been so cunningly placed that it was quite impossible to step from it to the next one.* BB

(the) snares and pitfalls (of sth) [n + n non-rev] (the) temptations and hazards (of sth) **o:** this world, city life; buying a house, living abroad □ *'If John had come straight home none of this would have happened.' 'Ah well, life is full of* ***snares and pitfalls*** *and no one is proof against them all.'* □ *He knew a great deal more than his partners about* ***the snares and pitfalls of*** *playing the stock-market and was determined to proceed warily.*

so far until now (and still); as yet (qv) □ *Brigit liked her at once.* ***So far*** *she was the only thing she liked about the Montpelier Square house.* DC *Goodness knows what size he is, but he's the biggest* (albatross) *I've seen* ***so far****.* SC □ *The stocking trade have* ***so far*** *done singularly little for their large, heavy and problem customers.* OBS □ front, middle or end position.

so far, so good up to now the arrangements are satisfactory though incomplete □ *The pile was going up, the first instalment of heavy water had arrived;* ***so far, so good****.* NM □ *'Let's have it. What happened?' Don Vicente asked. '****So far, so good****,' Mark said.* ST □ (acting on radio or television) *'You've got to be able to put your ideas over with conviction and without hesitation.'* ***So far so good****, but not necessarily enough to achieve a thoroughly professional performance for a thoroughly professional medium.* RT □ never expanded to include S or V; used as comment on effectiveness of sth/sb.

so help me (God) (formal) as God helps me; with the help of God (esp concluding a solemn or legally sworn oath); (informal) I am sure; I assure you; I declare □ *Do you solemnly swear to tell the truth, the whole truth and nothing but the truth,* ***so help you God****?* □ *I'm telling you the truth,* ***so help me God****, whether you believe it or not.* □ HARRY (rising and facing her in a rage): *I'll throw this book at you—****so help me*** *I'll throw this book at you.* CSWB □ *Sunny Italy, eh? Well it doesn't look like it now,* ***so help me*** *it doesn't.* □ (television comedy series about prison life) *Members of the criminal classes will stop him in the street and say, earnestly, 'Good series, that 'Porridge', Mr Barker;* ***so help me****, it's* like *that, inside.'* RT □ headphrase always used in full when formal.

so ignorant etc it isn't true (informal) extremely, unbelievably, ignorant etc **adj:** ignorant, rich, efficient, hideous, comfortable □ *You don't know a thing—you're* ***so ignorant it isn't true****.* TGLY □ *But you must know* (her)*!* The *Mrs Jones! She's* ***so smart it's not true****.* US □ *'Have you read his latest novel?' 'Yes. It's* ***so tedious it isn't true****.'*

(or) so it seems (or) it seems so; it may be true, may be the case (but perhaps not) □ *Irma was her substitute.* ***Or so it*** *had* ***seemed*** *then.* PW □ MILLY (drily): *And he's going to marry her next week?* MYRA: ***So it*** *would* ***seem****.* EHOW □ *It was hours later,* ***or so it seemed*** *to my feet, and we were still walking along the Old Kent Road.* UTN □ middle or end position.

so many words etc [Comp (NP)] just words etc; nothing more than words etc **V:** ⚠ be, become. **adv mod:** just, only. **n:** words, names; bits (of paper), entries (in the index) □ *They are asked to respond to 'the needs of the state' and 'the needs of society', to study 'good citizenship', to have in mind the 'common good'. In most cases, the appeals mean nothing, are* ***so many words****.* UL □ *Hold on, Patrick. All these politicians are just* ***so many names*** *to me.*

so much as do sth only, merely, do sth; (not) even do sth **V:** touch; glance at; hint; move, fidget □ *The skink was so poisonous, that even if you* ***so much as*** *touched its body you immediately fell to the ground writhing in agony.* BB □ *All the time she had been speaking he hadn't* ***so much as*** *glanced at her.* □ *He had never in his life* ***so much as*** *handled a gun, but that was no insuperable objection.* OMIH □ *Hector Rose happened to feel a morbid fear of cancer; he tried to avoid* ***so much as*** *hearing the name of the disease.* NM □ often neg, or as part of *if*-cl.

so much the better/worse (for sb/sth) better/worse by that much (for sb/sth) □ *'I seem to have made my curry hotter than usual.' '****So much the better****.'* □ *If Ned could find some means of integrating his contribution in the general framework, all right; if not,* ***so much the worse for*** *the general framework.* CON □ *In the old days I was always trying to beat other fellers* (= fellows)*. Now, I concentrate simply on improving my own play. If I happen to win,* ***so much the better****.* TVT □ exclamation strongly welcoming/dismissing sb/sth.

so much for sb/sth which indicates how little, in one's opinion, sb's values, views etc can be taken seriously or respected **o:** equality;

good resolutions, your promises; medical opinion; the honest Mr Jones □ *When a King reigns, his wife is Queen. When a Queen reigns her husband is a Prince.* ***So much for*** *equality of the sexes.* OBS □ *'If I were a dictator,' announced Longford on 'Panorama' last week, 'I would start by abolishing striptease.'* ***So much for*** *his priorities.* NS □ ***So much for*** *the pious statements of Bill Davies when he bought control of Aintree Racecourse in 1973, proclaiming himself to be the proud saviour of the Grand National.* G

so much nonsense etc [Comp (NP)] total, complete, nonsense etc **V:** ⚠ be, seem. **adv mod:** just, simply. **n:** nonsense, rubbish, drivel, (taboo) cock talk □ *The idea of us trying to do all that without the authorities finding out is just* ***so much nonsense.*** □ *The men who sit opposite are entirely wrong and all their arguments are* ***so much drivel.*** PL □ *All this talk about being deeply concerned is* ***so much hot air.***

so near and yet so far [Comp (AdjP)] near but not near enough to be effective or have a desired result (the reference being to a place, time, relationship, or an effort to do/obtain sth) **V:** ⚠ be, seem, appear □ (source) *He seems* ***so near and yet so far,****/He looks so cold: she thinks him kind.* IN MEMORIAM A H H (A TENNYSON 1809-92) □ *The cat sat in front of the bird cage in an agony of frustration at being* ***so near and yet so far.*** □ *'I fancy she's interviewing some other young lady, but she may have gone by now.' Cold panic clutched at Victoria's heart. Was it to be* ***so near and yet so far****?* TCB □ sometimes used alone as an unhappy comment on circumstances.

so sharp one'll cut oneself likely to overreach one's capabilities, come to harm, etc by trying to be too clever □ *'Let him take care he's not* ***so sharp he cuts himself****, that's all.' 'Oh, I'm sure Jack'll have everything arranged so as to keep on the right side of the law.'* □ *I cannot help recalling a brutal Northern saying—'Yon* (= that) *lad's* ***so*** *bloody* ***sharp****,' they used to say, ''appen* ***'e'll cut 'isself*** (= perhaps he'll cut himself) *one of these fine days.'* L

(a) so and so (informal) sb/sth who/that does not need to be named; (derogatory) a unpleasant person □ *The American habit of repeating your name in conversation after you've been introduced is rather a good one. If you say, 'What will you have to drink, Mr* ***So and So****?' it sounds friendlier and he's likely to be favourably impressed by you.* □ *Jack's* ***a*** *real* ***so and so****. Don't let yourself be upset by what* he *says about your work — he'd disapprove of the Archangel Gabriel.* ⇨ ⚠ such and such.

so to speak/say [Disj] to speak figuratively; as it were (qv) □ *This fact is reflected in practical problems met with in colour printing. For magenta does not,* ***so to speak****, respond well to being used subtractively.* NSC □ *In the early centuries of Christianity many pagan rites and festivals were baptized,* ***so to say****, and made to serve the purposes of the Church.* DOP □ middle or end position; usu accompanies fig description or fig use of a word. ⇨ ⚠ as one/you might say.

so there(!) (facetious) that's how things are, that's the position, and you needn't bother to argue; now then[3] (qv) □ *I held out my hand. 'What do you think I'm made of, darling?' 'Rats and snails and puppy-dog tails,' she said.* ***'So there!'*** RATT □ *Besides, he has made more money than all of those clever fellows put together.* ***So there*** *again.* NS □ *Mildred's not very nice really, with all her sneers and '****so there****'s'.* RT □ exclamation (usu associated with children) which follows defiant or accusing words which express determination, or refusal, to do sth.

so what? (informal) what follows (from that)? what is important, interesting, relevant (about that)? □ (reader's letter) *The contention of the wholly Christian panel was that if there was no resurrection and no Son of God then human beings are faced with annihilation at death.* ***So what?*** RT □ *You're twenty-one and you're married to me.* ***So what?*** *If your mother doesn't like it, she can do the other thing.* AITC □ rhetorical question prompting answer 'nothing'.

a soap opera a radio or television series about domestic life, the fortunes of a family or community, presented in a contrived, sentimental, or melodramatic way □ *'The Family' must be the best TV for years.* ***A*** *real-life* ***soap opera*** *without the soap—which, for sheer entertainment value alone, killed all its fictional counterparts stone dead.* L □ *If ITV-2 puts on rather* ***less soap opera*** *and rather more 'quality' programmes, it might begin to nibble at the posher kinds of advertising that are the backbone of such* (quality) *papers.* OBS □ *. . .big names now happy to drive into the TV studio along with quiz contestants and* ***soap opera*** *stars.* TVT □ also pl; attrib use *a* ***soap opera*** *star*; stress pattern a 'soap opera.

soap and water [n + n non-rev] these simple means of washing (usu as contrasted with special preparations for skin care) □ *Cleansing cream does not replace* ***soap and water*** *for young skin treatment.* H □ *Charles often used to mimic him—'****Soap and water****'s cheap enough, goodness knows. A person doesn't have to be rich to be clean.'* RATT □ *Farrah is basically a* ***soap and water*** *girl but also uses a special soap wash that she splashes off with cold water.* TVT □ attrib use *a* ***soap and water*** *girl.*

(a) sob story/stuff (informal) a story, film, account of circumstances, etc intended to arouse the listener's sympathy □ *Then we have the various 'Hospitals' series* (on television) *which combine the appeal of* ***the sob story*** *and sensationalism under the guise of 'a slice of life'.* G □ *The boys sometimes get round the piano and sing* ***some*** *real old* ***sob stuff*** *from their days in the Forces.* □ stress pattern (a) 'sob story/stuff; no article used with stuff.

sober fact etc (a) fact contrasted with sth believed, imagined or feared; (a) fact as it is and not exaggerated or twisted **n:** fact, ⚠ truth, reality □ *Philip Landowne gives you the* ***sober facts*** *on a controversial issue too often clouded by emotional and parental prejudice.* H □ *I don't think he has ever told anybody where* ***in sober fact*** *he* did *get his money from.* □ *People often talk in a loose way of 'working day and night', but on this occasion it was* ***the sober truth.*** □ no article used with fact, reality; variant, in sober fact/truth, is a Disj.

a sobering thought [Comp (NP)] sth thought of, or brought to one's attention, that makes one feel serious, unsettled or anxious **V:** ⚠ be, seem, appear □ *We pay a comedian more for a few hours' entertainment than a Cabinet Minister can earn in a year. It's* ***a sobering thought****.* □ *I hadn't even got as far as Mrs Macadam, and that was* ***another sobering thought*** *to add to the morning's total.* PP □ *In another twenty or thirty years Claire might be —* ***a sobering thought****!—very like her mother.*

a soft answer (turneth away wrath) (saying) a mild or peaceful reply, esp to some accusation, slight or criticism (reduces anger or hostility) □ (source) ***A soft answer turneth away wrath****: but grievous words stir up anger.* PROVERBS XV 1 □ *'Now the Baron's joined in. He wants to give up his thoughts on Waterman. "For what they're worth," he said, and I said yessir* (= yes, sir). *D'you* (= do you) *think I said right?' 'It seems* ***the*** *right sort of* ***soft answer*** *to me,' I said.* PP □ *As her father's favourite, Sally did pretty much as she liked and was an adept at* ***the soft answer which turns away wrath****.*

soft/wrong in the head [Comp (AdjP)] (informal) mentally subnormal; weak, sentimental, foolish etc in one's opinions, actions **V:** ⚠ be, go; make sb □ *I wondered if I hadn't gone* ***soft in the head****. I had in a sense compounded a felony, and if he were to steal anything again it would go hard with me.* RATT □ *I knew women made chaps a bit* ***soft in the head****, but I never thought I'd run into a benefit night at Bedlam like this.* DIL □ *The stone had been a light biscuit colour originally — sometimes I wonder if all nineteenth-century architects were a bit* ***wrong in the head****—and a hundred years of smoke had given it an unhealthy mottled appearance.* RATT

a soft job employment in which one does not have to work very hard for one's money □ *We'll check and sign these later. It's* ***a*** *nice* ***soft job*** *here.* TST □ *Anybody who thinks teaching in a nursery school is* ***a soft job*** *should try it.* □ also pl. ⇨ ⚠ jobs for the boys.

a soft option [Comp (NP)] an easier course of action, or study, than others available and possible **V:** ⚠ be; regard, view, sth as □ *Biology teachers are scared stiff that biology should be regarded as '****a soft option****' (which means that pupils should like it).* SC □ *What he has chosen this time is* ***the soft option****. What all his list* (of speakers) *have in common is reliability of performance; you can switch them on and let them go.* L □ also pl.

soft pedal (on) sth [V + O pass] (informal) mention, deal with, a matter in a quiet, unemphatic way, so as to minimize its importance (from the use of the soft pedal in piano-playing) **O:** side, aspect, facet; fault, flaw, imperfection □ *One leading Conservative MP remarked yesterday: 'We would certainly try to get an incomes deal with the Unions and* ***soft pedal*** *on the legislation.'* G □ *The view that criticism of South African racial policies should be* ***soft-pedalled*** *could only be justified if there were the slightest chance of a spontaneous change of course.* SC □ *There may be aspects of a man's character — and some of his actions — which it is natural and perhaps fitting to* ***soft-pedal*** *in an obituary.* □ may be hyphenated; stress pattern soft 'pedal sth.

soft soap (informal) flattery; behaviour designed to ingratiate oneself with sb, or flatter sb; behave in a way designed to ingratiate oneself with sb □ (reader's letter) *I have no doubt there are peaceful and happy deaths, but there are many that are agonising and terrible, and the programme* ('Dying and Bereavement') *gave only the* ***soft soap****.* RT □ *In business, I ruminated, I'd have to* ***soft-soap*** *people whom I despised, I'd have to steer the conversation towards their favourite subjects, I'd have to stand them meals and drinks.* RATT □ *I think it is vital that the Left should take uncompromising attitudes and set uncompromising standards. Whatever may be the case elsewhere, the forces in this country are too unequal for an alliance based on mutual* ***soft-soaping****.* NS □ used as n or v; when v, usu hyphenated; n compound soft-soaping.

a soft/easy touch [Comp (NP)] (informal) sb easy to borrow or steal (money) from, or to overcharge for goods or services **V:** ⚠ be, become; treat, regard, sb as □ *Cash slipped through Lynch's fingers and he became known as* ***a soft touch*** *for anyone who could spin him a sad tale or offer him a good time.* TVT □ *He'd only met us once, but he must have realized you're* ***an easy touch****.*

softly, softly (catchee monkey) (saying) let 'gently, slowly and cautiously' be the maxim; easy/gently does it (qv) □ *'Keep him in a good humour. I don't want him alarmed till we're ready to move.' '****Softly, softly, catchee monkey****?' 'That's the idea.'* □ *Can we not, after all, have socialism on the* ***softly, softly*** *principle? The answer from experience is hardly encouraging.* NS □ *From ten this morning, drive quietly in Darlington, Britain's first 'softly, softly' town which begins a two year project to reduce noise levels.* G □ attrib use a ***softly-softly*** *approach.*

sole and heel [v + v non-rev] renew, or repair, the soles and heels of shoes □ *...in a little shop off the Rue aux Laines, where he had been forced to take his shoes for* ***soling and heeling****.* US □ *The* ***soles and heels*** *are made of real leather.* □ similarly [n + n non-rev], as in second example.

some (men) are born great etc, some achieve greatness etc, and some have greatness etc thrust upon them (saying) some people possess particular qualities, some acquire them, others are made to assume them (from TWELFTH NIGHT II 5) **adj/n:** great/greatness, wealthy/wealth, pessimistic/pessimism □ *A haven of utter silliness in a wilderness of sanity, they were there to amuse, to entertain, to divert.* ***Some*** *of them* ***were born silly****,* ***some achieved silliness****,* ***some had silliness thrust upon them****.* NS □ often adapted.

some men etc are more equal than others (catchphrase) although there may be an external appearance of equality of status and privilege between members of a particular group, society etc, some members in fact receive favoured treatment **n:** men, women; animals; areas, cars □ (source) *All animals are equal but* ***some animals are more equal then others****.* ANIMAL FARM (G ORWELL 1903-50) □ *We're all called senior managers, but the company car may be an ordinary family saloon right up to a Mercedes.* ***Some men are*** *clearly* ***more equal than others****.* □ *In Aberdeen, local authority family houses were reported to be occupied by single* *men while families waited to be rehoused because those single men were necessary to the oil industry.* ***Some citizens*** *seem to* ***be more equal than others.***

some of one's best friends are English etc (catchphrase) an argument used (often unconsciously) to clear oneself of a charge of prejudice against persons of a specified race, creed, class or profession **n:** English; Catholics; Americans; communists; lawyers; layabouts □ *'Engineers are just thick metal-bashers, artists lie around all day doing nothing.' 'Actually,' says Geoffrey,' '**some of my best friends are engineers.**'* RT □ *It is not so long ago that bookmakers were presumed to wear bright check suits and to be the sort of people it didn't do to be seen talking to. Nowadays* ***some of one's best friends*** *can* ***be bookmakers*** *and it's quite all right.* OBS □ *I am far from being anti-American, indeed* ***some of my best friends****, etc. However...* NS □ often facetious.

(at) some time or other [A (PrepP/NP)] (informal) on an occasion in the past or future, the precise time or date of which is not recalled, not given or not known □ *'When did you say he'd be back?' 'Oh,* ***some time or other*** *tomorrow—he was vague about it.'* □ variant (at) some or other time. ⇨ ⚠ at one time or another.

someone or other some person, or thing, not (yet) known, or impossible to identify; any one of a number of possible persons, things, places, times, means or methods **pron:** someone, somebody, something. **adv:** sometime, (at) some time, somewhere, somehow, (in) some way □ *Phone the office.* ***Someone or other*** *will be sure to know his present address.* □ *I had hardly set foot in England before* ***somebody or other*** *exclaimed 'Oh, but you don't look in the least like your books!'* AH □ *He was ranting and raving about* ***something or other****, I forget exactly what.* ST □ *'I know I have some carbon paper* ***somewhere or other****,' she said, rummaging through the drawers.* □ *There wasn't a day gone by during which —* ***at some time or another****—she didn't think of him with a great rush of love.* WI □ *Difficult though it might be, she intended to get to Baghdad* ***somehow or other****.* TCB □ *We'll have to get round that difficulty* ***some way or another****.* □ another frequently used thus *at* ***some time or another****, (in)* ***some way or another****.*

something/nothing doing (informal) activity, work etc (not) taking place □ *Above the trees by the river birds were rising, sure sign of* ***something doing****. Maybe a fox or an angler, but it was worth investigating.* □ *Let's go round to Jack and Mary's. There's always* ***something doing*** *there on New Year's Eve.* □ *It became what reporters call a watching brief:* ***nothing*** *much* ***doing****, but always the possibility of trouble, so newsmen hang around.* L ⇨ (there is) nothing doing[2].

something else again [Comp (NP)] an entirely different matter, situation **V:** ⚠ be, appear; remain □ *Not all his compositions have been received as he would wish; even his playing has not lately been doing full justice to itself. But his teaching remains* ***something else again.*** G □ *The search for 'something pure', in a country racked by self-doubt is at least an understandable commitment. Whether the Jesus freaks have got their bearings right is* ***something else again.*** L

something has (got) to give (catchphrase) the strain, pressure, demand on sb/sth is too great to be kept up or resisted □ *Europe cannot continue to enjoy the security afforded by American defence power* and *become the commercial and perhaps political competitor of the US.* ***Something has to give.*** ST □ *There is no sign that the South Vietnamese* (soldiers) *are all ready to take over. 'If we pull out at this rate,' an officer of the 23rd told me, '**something's** just* ***got to give.**'* NS □ *It was more an ego split than a marriage split. Angie likes stardom, Burt likes stardom.* ***Something had to give.*** TVT

something like (informal) exactly what one wants, likes, expects, hopes for; that etc is more like it (qv) **S:** this, that; £1000, a holiday in Greece □ *'Now, this is* ***something like****!' the tutor said, giving Polly's exercise full marks.* □ *You say he's put the price up to £1,000? Now, that's* ***something like****!* □ stress pattern something 'like; often follows *this/that is*; used as enthusiastic comment about sth.

something like sth[1] approximately; roughly **o:** that number, that quantity; a dozen, a score □ *The outline road programme is on* ***something like*** *the scale required.* SC □ *There must have been* ***something like*** *a dozen pills left in the bottle.* □ adv mod + prep followed by a n indicating amount or scale.

something like sth[2] something (esp an emotion, attitude etc) very similar to sth **o:** panic, terror; exasperation, irritation □ *A wave of* ***something like*** *alarm went through the phalanx. Mr Madden was on the warpath. No one could doubt it.* ARG □ *I detected* ***something*** *very* ***like*** *insolence in the manner, if not the matter, of his replies.* □ *The second proposal was so much less outrageous that the first that it met with* ***something like*** *approval.*

something etc like sth[1] something etc of the same kind or category as sth **pron:** something; (not) anything, nothing. **o:** a snack, sandwich; beer, whisky; magazine, light novel □ *Grandad has so few wants now that I usually end up giving him* ***something like*** *a pair of socks for his birthday* □ *You have such highbrow literature in this house! Isn't there* ***something like*** *a detective or adventure story I could read in bed?* □ *'Can I offer you a sherry — a whisky and soda?' 'Oh, no,* ***nothing like*** *that for me, please.'* □ pron + prep + n.

something etc like sth[2] rather similar etc to sth **adv mod:** something, nothing, (not) anything; somewhat; much, rather. **o:** this, that; yours, mine □ *They're very useful chests. We have one at home* ***something like*** *yours.* □ *I couldn't say the baby was* ***anything like*** *either of them.* □ *This coat that's been left behind is* ***nothing like*** *the one I was wearing. If somebody took mine instead of theirs it must have been deliberately.* □ adv mod something etc modifies prep like.

(see) something nasty in the woodshed (see) something shocking that leaves a deep and lasting impression on one (from COLD COMFORT FARM (S GIBBONS b1902) referred to in the first example) □ *The extraordinary thing is that people who have never read the book will talk* *about Aunt Ada Doom's* (character in the novel) *famous cry, 'I* ***saw something nasty in the woodshed****', almost as if it was a quotation from the Bible or 'Hamlet'.* L □ *Lamont Johnson's 'You'll Like My Mother' is just entertainment of the* ***something-nasty-in-the-woodshed*** *school.* NS □ attrib use *the* ***something-nasty-in-the-woodshed*** *school.*

something/somewhat of a sth quite a, rather a, sth: **o:** authority (on); wit, bore; surprise, understatement, fiddle □ *I found myself again living in Bayswater, a quarter on which I thought myself* ***something of an*** *authority.* AH □ *He was a simple man—and* ***somewhat of a*** *worried one.* TCB □ *It was certainly* ***something of a*** *problem to know where to go next.* UTN □ *French day-trippers to England are still* (ie 1960) ***something of a*** *rarity.* TO

something old, something new, something borrowed, something blue items to be included in a bride's attire in order to bring good luck □ *A bride must not see her groom before the ceremony on her wedding-day, and should wear—and still usually does—'****something old, something new, something borrowed, something blue****'.* UL

something etc out of the ordinary/usual a person, thing, event, opinion, remark etc that is different, unusual (the implication sometimes being that the person etc specified is better, more interesting or valuable); a person etc who/that is not different, unusual or better than other people etc **pron:** something, (not) anything; nothing □ *Well, I do have something special for this evening.* ***Something*** *really rather* ***out of the ordinary.*** BM □ *Florrie came in, and began to back out on the rebound as soon as she saw that* ***something out of the usual*** *tea and natter was up* (= happening). TT □ *He's a healthy, intelligent boy but* ***nothing out of the ordinary****.* □ *Oh, he'll turn up, I daresay. It's* ***nothing out of the usual*** *for David to be late.* □ *I've read his novel and if you're expecting* ***anything out of the ordinary****, forget it.*

somewhere etc along the line at some point etc during the process of growth, development, manufacture or assembly **A:** somewhere; where, at what point; at various points, at some point □ *But* ***somewhere along the line*** *I could have been a different person.* RATT □ *Anthropologists, as far as I know, are still unable to pinpoint just* ***where along the line*** *man and the anthropoid apes branched into two distinct species.* □ *Wild-cat strikes among the many different trades employed in the car industry can hold up production at* ***any point along the line.*** □ *In this programme Hugh Ross will be telling us about people in North Uist who still believe that* ***somewhere along the line*** *they have seals for ancestors.* RT

somewhere, over the rainbow (catch-phrase) at some time, or in some place, one would like to believe in □ ***Somewhere, over the rainbow****, skies are blue,/And the dreams that you dare to dream really do come true.* E Y HARBURG b1898 □ ***Somewhere over the rainbow*** *in the domain of fantasy, a phoenix rises from the ashes, a sea monster defies detection, a mermaid combs her golden tresses.* RT □ *Among the football experts, Jimmy Hill is my favourite. He is not a lyrical reporter like Geoffrey Green of 'The Times' (who nearly always manages to say '****somewhere, over the rainbow****' in his radio talks).* NS

the/one's son and heir [n + n non-rev] an only, or eldest, son □ *'But you know who Mr Robert is?' 'Of course I do, sir. His lordship****'s son and heir****.'* □ *I hear you're now a happy father. How's* ***the son and heir*** *behaving himself?*

a son of a bitch (taboo) a swine; a thoroughly unpleasant person **det:** a, the; you □ *Finally,* ***the son of a bitch*** *walked out of one of the buildings near the runway there.* OBS □ *Toulmin quotes a scientist at the first atomic test as saying, 'We are all* ***sons of bitches*** *now.'* OBS □ *Still the outboard motor wouldn't start. 'Come on,* fire, ***you son of a bitch****!' Tom swore, yanking at the cord.* □ term of abuse to or about sb, and occas of objects; sometimes said warmly rather than in violence or hate.

a son of a gun (dated slang) a chap, fellow (the usu reference being to sb already named or understood) **det:** a, the; that; you. **adj:** lucky, stupid; miserable; impetuous □ *Well, Freddy's won again. He had the rest beaten to a frazzle,* ***the*** *old* ***son of a gun****.* □ *'Nobody would employ him but you.' 'I know. He's* ***a*** *lazy* ***son of a gun*** *but he's so likeable in every other way.'*

a son of the soil a person born and bred in a rural district, and esp one who continues to work on the land □ *Although he's a successful smalltown lawyer, avid for learning and self-improvement, Brill is still* ***a son of the soil****. He cherishes the image of the ploughman as his ideal.* NS □ also pl sons of the soil.

a song-and-dance act etc an item in a variety show, usu involving one or two performers; sb who performs such an item; (fig) sth often, or predictably, done by sb and/or in particular circumstances **n:** act, ⚠ team, duo; man □ *Its authors have become, as an American diplomat put it the other day, '****the*** *favourite* ***song-and-dance act*** *on the television chat shows'.* L □ *The alliance between Mr Callaghan and Mr Wilson is one of the most affecting sights the present government has to offer. Harold and Jim travel the world like* ***some*** *well-loved* ***song-and-dance act****.* NS □ *For 17 years, after a false start in John Colliers, the tailors, he has been* ***a song-and-dance man****, a professional entertainer.* NS □ also pl.

sooner or later [adv + adv non-rev] at some time; inevitably □ ***Sooner or later*** *in British football there will have to be reorientation of thinking.* SC □ *Why not now? She has to know about it* ***sooner or later****.* AITC □ *Meadows and his colleagues found that 'if present trends continue' then we are heading for environmental catastrophe* ***sooner rather than later****.* NS □ front, middle or end position; variants sooner rather than later, probably sooner than later = '(sth referred to will, is likely to, or should, happen) relatively soon rather than after some time has passed'.

sooner you etc than me (informal) I am glad that it is you and not I (who has to do sth) **pron:** you; her, him, them □ *'I spend half my life in cars or trains, I think.' 'Well,* ***sooner you than me****.'* □ HELEN: *Christ! What the hell's she got in here*

—***sooner her than me***—*what's this?* TOH □ expression of relief that one is not affected in the way indicated.

soothe the savage breast calm anger, rebellious feeling, etc □ (source) *Music has charms to* ***soothe a savage breast.*** THE MOURNING BRIDE (W CONGREVE 1670-1729) □ *I discovered also that the appropriate look or word could '****soothe the savage breast****' and bring him to heel.* L □ (NONCE) *Mr Villars as a schoolmaster and a priest had found private theatricals an excellent* ***smoother of the savage breast.*** WDM

a sore point (with sb) [Comp (NP)] a matter which causes feelings of anger or resentment among a group of people or in an individual whose identity is either specified or implied by the context **S:** income tax, rates, price increases; refusal, obstinacy, neglect. **V:** ⚠ be, become; make sth. **o:** hill-farmers, housewives □ *The treatment of Gaelic by Official Scotland is* ***a sore point.*** RT □ *Then there is* ***the sore point*** *of the income tax—not the national personal income tax, which everybody pays, but the additional income tax that has nothing to do with the rates that many states now impose.* L □ *The secrecy with which they got married is still* ***a sore point with*** *Tina's parents.*

sorely tempted (to do sth) [Comp (AdjP)] very much inclined, drawn (to do sth) **V:** ⚠ be; feel; seem □ *Wormold looked at the champagne bottle and at Captain Segura's head. He was* ***sorely tempted to*** *bring them together.* OMIH □ *'Shut the shop for a couple of days, and come with us, Jim.' 'I'm* ***sorely tempted to.****'* □ usu implies that the action is not performed.

sorry for oneself [Comp (AdjP)] pitying oneself (the implication being that this is sth to be avoided) **V:** ⚠ be; feel, appear; make sb □ MYRA: *Oh—do stop being* ***sorry for yourself*** *all the time.* EHOW □ *'Mother is a little difficult sometimes,' Cindy admitted reluctantly. 'In what way?' 'Oh—moody. A bit—a bit* ***sorry for herself.****'* PE

a sorry state etc [Comp/O (NP)] an unsatisfactory, deplorable, pathetic, or tragic state etc **V:** be; reveal, present, tell. **n:** state, ⚠ sight; excuse, tale □ *The facts quoted would reveal* ***a sorry state*** *of affairs in any community.* SC □ *The patients (victims of advanced cancer) were led to believe that the radiation doses they were getting might improve* ***their sorry state.*** NS □ *Kean and Scott, the tiny house furnisher and textile wholesaling group, was in* ***a sorry state*** *when Wilson bought a controlling stake.* OBS □ *All the British Officers of the relief force were invited and* ***a sorry sight*** *most of us were, with our dirty torn uniforms and unshaven chins.* BM □ *Mr Nichols has never written better and* ***his sorry tale*** *has a dreadful fascination.* NS

the soul of courtesy etc [Comp (NP)] sb who regularly displays courtesy or some other good quality **V:** ⚠ be; remain; appear. **n:** courtesy, ⚠ honour, wit, discretion, tact, kindness □ *M. Couve de Murville, the French Foreign Minister, who, whatever business has to be conducted, is always* ***the soul of courtesy,*** *stated shortly before the meeting that he would be able to attend only the morning session.* T □ *Where her husband and family are concerned she is* ***the soul of discretion.*** NS

(the) sound and fury [n + n non-rev] noisy talk, activity, disturbance, excitement etc □ (source) *It* (life) *is a tale/Told by an idiot, full of* ***sound and fury,****/Signifying nothing.* MACBETH V 5 □ *There was an immediate outcry, and a demand for retaliation. There seemed, though, to be* ***more sound and fury*** *than substance in the protest.* L □ *All* ***the sound and fury*** *were over and Tommy and I stood looking at each other in the suddenly empty kitchen. 'She's nuts,' he said sadly.* NS □ *The old people sit talking in groups or play cards or dominoes, or simply watch* ***the sound and fury*** *of the 'activity area', with its jukebox.* OBS

sound in wind and limb [Comp (AdjP)] in good physical condition (used originally of horses) **V:** ⚠ be; seem, appear □ *Shirley Temple was America in microcosm — lovable and loving, vitamin-packed, gold of heart, pure of soul, bright of mind, white of skin, and* ***sound in wind and limb.*** SC □ *The doc reckoned that anyone who could climb all these stairs for his interview was* ***sound*** *enough* ***in wind and limb*** *to be passed fit.* □ (NONCE) *It's a wonder you're back so* ***safe in wind and limb.*** *Cobb's a big chap, as I remember.* PP □ *There were countless expedients for acquiring* ***soundness in wind and limb,*** *such as the Litesome Supporter Belt, which guaranteed 'Commando Fitness' to those it encircled.* NS □ wind and limb non-rev; variant soundness in wind and limb.

sound the (death) knell of sb/sth [V + O pass] be the reason for sb/sth ending, going out of fashion, or being replaced **o:** small shopkeeper; steam engine; private ownership, public transport □ *The safety regulations have* ***sounded*** *the convertible****'s death-knell*** *(which matters little).* NS □ *One tourist had recently been killed by a stray bullet and the death* ***sounded the knell of*** *the all-in-tour.* OMIH

sour grapes deprecation as a form of consolation to oneself, about what one would like to have, but cannot (from a fox, in the Greek fables of Aesop, who, when unable to reach grapes growing on a vine, said he could see they were sour) □ *Several critics of the programme found nothing to talk about except my hair. Another spoke of my being beringed, suggesting, I suppose, that I was homosexual. It's a wedding ring. I think a lot of the criticism was* ***sour grapes.*** ST □ *True, she* (Jane Austen) *couldn't bear to hear about married bliss, but that was possibly* ***sour grapes.*** NS

sow the dragon's/dragons' teeth [V + O pass] do sth, though this may not be one's intention, that causes future trouble, dissension, warfare etc (from the Greek myth of Cadmus who planted a dragon's teeth from which, later, armed warriors sprang up) □ *From the military point of view the expedition had achieved its aims. We had drawn* ***the dragon's teeth*** *but many will say that we had also* ***sown*** *them.* BM □ *For two precious hours more I went patiently through each reproach, and all the others, too, that sprang up like giants from* ***dragons' teeth sown*** *innocently in the wake of each explanation.* LWK □ *The survival of private enterprise now depends on subsidy and patronage: no amount of juggling with tax rates will alter the fact. But the danger is that Mrs Thatcher will try, that she will*

sow dragon's teeth *among the resentful middle class, that she will, in short, sharpen appetites that she cannot satisfy.* NS

sow etc the seeds of sth [V + O pass] be responsible for actions, statements or conditions which are likely to produce future discontent, better understanding, etc **V:** sow, ⚠ plant; carry, have (in it). **o:** discontent, war; dissension, bitterness; hope, wisdom, better understanding □ *Clearly there was much fertile ground in which evil persons could* ***sow the seeds of*** *discontent and trouble.* MFM □ (the Munich Agreement, 1938) *Its main effects at the time were to hand large frontier areas of Czechoslavakia over to the Germans and to* ***sow the seeds of*** *an enduring Czechoslovak bitterness against the Western powers.* L □ *Leadership which is evil, while it may temporarily succeed, always* ***carries*** *within itself* ***the seeds of*** *its own destruction.* MFM

sow (one's) wild oats [V + O pass] go through a youthful period of careless, or reckless, pleasure-seeking □ *If he were really and truly courting her it would be a very good thing, I believe—and the children would respond. But as it is, they are merely getting used to seeing a young man* ***sowing*** *what young men like to call* ***their wild oats.*** TT □ *If they keep on dancing they may not marry so soon. Why shouldn't girls* ***sow their wild oats*** *too?* OBS □ MYRA: *Tony, before you settle down to being an honest electrician, I wish you'd take that money and —* TONY: *What?* ***Sow*** *a few* ***wild oats****?* EHOW □ *But* ***the wildest oats sown*** *by our hero go no further than such mild prep school debaucheries as giving up work, or keeping a pet bat.* OBS

sow the wind and reap the whirlwind (saying) start sth that seems fairly harmless and have to suffer unforeseen consequences that are grave or disastrous □ (source) *But the calf of Samaria shall be broken in pieces. For they have* ***sown the wind, and*** *they shall* ***reap the whirlwind.*** HOSEA VIII 6-7 □ *America revelled at the beginning of the century in the latest ingenuity of the glorious industrial revolution* (motor transport): *today we have* ***reaped that whirlwind.*** L □ *He has been almost a classic example of the self-destructiveness of revolution.* ***The whirlwind*** *that now strikes him was of his own* ***sowing.*** T □ either part may be quoted with assumption that other part will be understood.

spare sb's blushes [V + O pass] not do, or say, sth which would make sb embarrassed □ *Funny, he told me he was going to tell you* (about the gift of money)*, but I expect he was too bashful. He wanted to* ***spare your blushes.*** PW □ *'If I'm not driving myself, I'd rather have my wife at the wheel than anyone else.' 'Spare my blushes, will you, Jack, and give the windscreen a wipe.'*

spare no expense etc [V + O pass] not economize in money or trouble **O:** expense; ⚠ effort, pains. **A:** to make/in making the occasion a success; as far as their education is concerned; towards that end □ *The invitation was very impressive.* ***No expense*** *had been* ***spared*** *as far as size and thickness of paper and gold lettering went.* TSMP □ *In some ways it all seemed too good to be true. All those splendid buildings and equipment, no ostentation but* ***no expense spared.*** OBS □ *He submitted himself to this procedure no fewer than 163 times, and* ***no effort*** *was* ***spared*** *in standardizing the experimental conditions.* MFF □ *You did what you could* ***with no pains spared.*** *There may be much to regret, but you have nothing to blame yourself for.* □ often pass; variant with/and no expense etc spared.

spare the rod and spoil the child (saying) a child has to be (physically) punished when necessary so that he may learn to behave properly, know what is right, etc □ (source) *He that* ***spareth the rod*** *hateth his son: but he that loveth him chasteneth him betimes.* PROVERBS XIII 24 □ *The very phrase 'spoilt child' has an olde worlde* (= old fashioned) *ring. To* ***spare the rod*** *was, traditionally, to* ***spoil the child.*** OBS □ *Advocates of laissez faire and excessive leniency are on the left; those of '****spare the rod, spoil the child****' on the right.* SNP

(in) one's spare time [A (Prep P)] (at) times when one is not carrying on one's regular job □ *'Guy wants to take me to dinner. You don't mind, do you, Mrs. Gaye?' 'What you do* ***in your spare time*** *is your own business, Prissie.'* DC □ *I like John well enough, in moderation, but not to the extent of spending almost all* ***my spare time*** *in his company.* □ *'I didn't know you painted.' 'It's just a* ***spare-time*** *occupation.'* □ attrib use *a* ***spare-time*** *hobby, interest etc.*

(the) sparks fly there is sharp disagreement, argument, or quarrelling □ *We had just started on this plan and* ***the sparks*** *used to* ***fly*** *when I insisted on obedience.* MFM □ *Those who held their breath at the prospect of* ***the sparks*** *that could* ***fly*** *around the studio when three star comediennes were cast in the same show together have been disappointed.* RT □ ***Sparks*** *look like* ***flying*** *in the Systems Control Centre of the University of Manchester Institute of Science and Technology when its chief returns from America in a few weeks.* G

speak one's mind [V + O] say exactly what one thinks □ *He impressed most of the senior officers who had to deal with him as a man who learned quickly, thought hard, and* ***spoke his mind.*** ST □ *There was nowhere I could retreat to, no need to be pleasant to anyone, I could afford the luxury of* ***speaking my mind.*** RATT □ *As hostess and President she felt she ought not to have* ***spoken her mind*** *so freely.* WDM □ also pl speak their minds .

speak now, or forever hold one's peace now is the only time when a claim, objection etc should be made □ (source) (If anyone knows a reason why two people should not marry) *Let him* ***now speak****, or else hereafter* ***for ever hold his peace.*** BOOK OF COMMON PRAYER □ *I hope you haven't any vital evidence to contribute, because if so you'd better* ***speak now or forever hold your peace.*** ASA

speak/talk the same etc language [V + O] (not) share a way of expressing oneself; (not) draw upon common experiences, training, ideas, values etc that make real communication and understanding possible **det:** same, sb's; a different, not. . .the same, not. . .sb's, another □ *He* ***talked a different language****; it was demotic English of the mid twentieth century, rapid, slurred, essentially a city dialect and, in origin, essentially American.* HD □ *Watching him and*

Sawbridge facing each other across the table, I could hear them ***speaking the same language***. NM □ *As a TUC* ((GB) = Trades Union Congress) *official put it, 'it looks as if we and industry and the Treasury are at last beginning to* ***talk the same language***.*'* OBS □ JIMMY: *I don't think I could take Webster tonight.* ALISON: *I thought you said he was the only person who* ***spoke your language***. LBA □ *'Westminster Hotels' has already been told to prune its maintenance budgets again. Sir Charles says that the pruning is absurdly gentle. But the two sides* ***talk different languages***. ST □ *Round about this time Rosburg was a formidable golfer* ***in anybody's language***. SC □ *'£6000 is a comfortable income, I'd think.' '****Not in their language***.*'* □ variant (not) in sb's/anybody's language.

speak the truth [V + O] not tell lies; tell (sb) the truth (qv) □ *She brought her family up in her own way; she taught us to* ***speak the truth***, *come what may* (= whatever the consequences may be). MFM □ *'You know Captain Segura?' 'He is a friend of my daughter.' 'How can I tell that you are* ***speaking the truth***?*'* OMIH □ *Whatever lies her tongue might still be impelled to tell, her face at last* ***spoke the truth***. DC ⇨ tell (sb) a lie (about sth).

special pleading (legal) presentation of a (legal) case by referring to special, or unusual, circumstances; (fig) biased evidence, or argument, in favour of, or against, sb/sth □ *Marilyn Butler nowhere refers to Royles's paper, for if he is right, she is wrong. Marilyn Butler's account requires a little too much* ***special pleading***. NS □ *Still, if much* ***special pleading*** *is required to convince us that 'Titus' is a masterpiece, it is certainly revealed in this splendid revival as a work that every Mozartian should know and love.* ST □ *As spring and Budget-time approaches, the cries grow louder of* ***special pleaders***, *cranks, and high-minded reformers.* T □ n compound a special pleader = 'one who presents evidence of kind defined above'.

the spectator etc sees more/most of the game (saying) sb not actually taking part in an activity is better placed to observe and judge it then those directly involved **n:** spectator, ⚠ onlooker, looker-on □ *'What the hell can you know about it, anyway,' I said angrily. 'You've never been married.' '****The spectator sees more of the game***, *doesn't he?'* DIL □ ***Onlookers see most of the game***, *but not at Hampden Park on Saturday when thickening mist forced the referee to stop play midway through the second half.* □ *'All I wanted to do was to fill in* (details). *I can probably see more clearly, from where I'm standing.' 'Yes,* ***spectators see more of the game*** *than players, don't they?' he sneered.* CON

speed the parting guest [V + O] (formal) bid a civil, or ceremonious, goodbye to sb leaving one's house after a visit, a social function, etc □ (source) *True friendship's laws are by this rule express'd./Welcome the coming,* ***speed the parting guest***. ODYSSEY XV (A POPE 1688-1744) □ *Noel and Mr Wickham went out with them to help with coats and* ***speed the parting guests***. WDM

spend one's/its force [V + O pass] exhaust one's/its power esp to affect, or harm, sb **S:** raider, attacker; storm; disease, epidemic; anger □ *The Speyside fire, thanks to heavy rain during the night, seems to have* ***spent its force*** *though many acres are still smouldering.* SC □ *The deflationary aspect of the episode had pretty well* ***spent its force*** *by now.* TGLY □ *Though* ***a spent force***, *Sir Roy will make one last effort to save what he can of this old* (province). OBS □ esp past tenses; variant a spent force.

spend money as if it's going out of fashion (informal) spend money freely; next entry (qv) (the implication often being that one is spending more than one can really afford) □ *In spite of the world recession, there are still some people in the early 1980s who are cheerfully* ***spending money as if it's going out of fashion***. □ *I'm getting worried about Jack—he's* ***spending money as if it's going out of fashion***. *He doesn't earn all that much, so I only hope he came by it honestly.*

spend money like water/spend (money) like a sailor [V + O pass] spend money as freely as if it were in endless supply, or like a sailor on shore leave; previous entry (qv) □ HELEN: *It's a wedding present from that young man of mine. He* ***spends*** *his* ***money like water***, *you know.* TOH □ *Ford* ***money*** *is being* ***spent like water***—*nearly £10 millions so far this year. The television screens are stiff with Ford advertising.* G □ *In the years to come, when the oil is ashore and the Scots are* ***spending like sailors*** *and even the Government is lavishing undreamed of largesse...* SC

spick and span [adj + adj non-rev] fresh, clean, and tidy in every detail, way (originally referring to obsolete terms of manufacture) **V:** be, appear; be left; make sth □ *The bed had been made, fresh towels were in the bathroom and everything was* ***spick and span***. TCB □ *One's almost ashamed of its* (Freetown, 1954) *being an English possession—particularly after visiting Leopoldville or Elizabethville in the Belgian Congo, which are as* ***spick and span*** *as Brussels or Antwerp.* DS □ *These* ***spick-and-span*** *children of hers put my lot to shame.* □ attrib use *a* ***spick-and-span*** *child.*

spike sb's guns [V + O pass] frustrate the aims, intentions, or ambitions of sb (from making an old fashioned firearm useless by driving a spike into the touch-hole through which the charge was ignited) □ *The Second World War is getting very generous treatment on both BBC channels perhaps to* ***spike the guns of*** *a certain series in production at Thames TV.* L □ *Listen, we'll get married tomorrow. That will* ***spike*** *the old lady****'s guns***. *God, I would like to see her face!* AITC □ *They'll do anything to* ***spike the guns of*** *the opposition, even at the risk of underpricing themselves out of business.* □ *He smiled with satisfaction—he had made a confession of an action that troubled his conscience and* ***spiked*** *John****'s guns*** *at the same time.* ASA

spill the beans etc [V + O pass] (informal) give away information, deliberately or unintentionally; blow the gaff (qv); let the cat out of the bag (Vol 1) (qv) **O:** the beans; ⚠ it; the lot, everything. **A:** about her husband's plan, to the police, at the Council meeting, wherever she went □ *Harold did not always* ***spill the beans*** *at once; he would bide his time and adopt a sphinx-like air.* PW □ *Many diplomatic wives find it easier* *not even to know* ***the beans*** *they must not* ***spill*** *—but there are other ways of being indiscreet.* OBS □ *You can't keep a secret — you see no reason why you shouldn't* ***spill the beans.*** TVT □ *He didn't know what he was going to do with her, not now she'd* ***spilled the beans*** *all over the place.* TSMP □ *But after a bit I just wanted to tell him all about it and I think it did me good to* ***spill it.*** RFW

spin sb a yarn [V + IO + O pass] tell sb a fanciful story, esp one designed to mislead , impress, or get rid of, sb □ JASON: *Just get rid of that young man.* ALEX: *How?* JASON: ***Spin*** *him* ***a yarn,*** *a tall story.* DPM □ GEOF: *Do people ever tell the truth about themselves?* JO: *Why should she want to* ***spin*** *me* ***a yarn*** *like that?* GEOF: *She likes to make an effect.* TOH

the spirit is willing (but the flesh is weak) (saying) one's intentions and desires are good but laziness, love of pleasure, etc may prevent them from being put into action □ (source) *Watch and pray, that ye enter not into temptation:* ***the spirit*** *indeed* ***is willing, but the flesh is weak.*** MATTHEW XXVI 41 □ *I won't promise to be up to see you off. You know how it is —* ***the spirit is willing but the flesh is weak.*** □ *Miss Shepherd and Miss Kahn may be said to enter into the spirit of things,* ***but the flesh****—notably in dimly sketched dance routines —****proves*** *all too* ***weak.*** NS □ either part may be used alone with assumption that other part will be understood.

one's spirits rise/sink one feels more/less cheerful, optimistic **A:** a bit, a little, somewhat; higher/lower □ *I hastily fed the Idiurus* (= flying mice) *with the ripe fruit he had procured, and they enjoyed them thoroughly.* ***My spirits rose,*** *and I began to have hopes once more of landing them in England.* BB □ *Tom began to outline his plans.* ***My spirits rose*** *a little.* SPL □ *When nothing happened* ***her spirits*** *would begin to* ***sink*** *lower and lower. In hospital at this time the sister had frequently found her in tears.* DC ⇨ ⚠ raise one's/sb's spirits.

one's spiritual home [Comp (NP)] the place where one is, or thinks one could be, happiest; the country and its inhabitants to which (for reasons of ancestry, temperament, sentimental feeling, etc) one feels a stronger attachment than to one's own country **V:** ⚠ be, become; make sth □ *I have met third and fourth generation Scots-Canadians who still feel that some township or island of the Scottish Highlands is* ***their spiritual home.*** □ *Yet he was obviously a first-rate leader. He should have been a German or a Russian. Either place was* ***his spiritual home*** *if spiritual is the word.* PP

the spit and image/spitting image of sb/sth [Comp (NP)] sb/sth exactly, or extremely, like another; next entry (qv) **V:** ⚠ be, look; find sb □ *She was trying to make* (Alice) *feel thoroughly uncomfortable by references to the good looks of her lover—'****the spit-and-image of*** *Jean Marais, darling.'* RATT □ *He were* (= was) *a grand man. He died in his 70s lifting weights. A great way to go. And Leon is* ***the spitting image of*** *him.* TVT □ *I've seen any number of seals bobbing up out of the water all round us and all of 'em* (= them) *looking* ***the spitting image of*** *my butcher in Nottingham.* RM □ spitting is a corruption of spit and.

the (dead/very) spit of sb/sth [Comp (NP)] sb/sth exactly, or extremely, like another; previous entry (qv) **V:** ⚠ be, look; think sb □ MICK: *Yes, it was a curious affair.* ***Dead spit of*** *you he was. Bit bigger round the nose but there was nothing in it.* TC □ *If ever a boy was* ***the spit of*** *his father it's Michael.* □ *He lived in one of a row of council houses each* ***the very spit of*** *the other.*

spit and polish [n + n non-rev] meticulous, or excessive, cleaning and polishing (esp care of personal or working/fighting equipment in the armed forces) □ *The Israeli forces are refreshingly free of the* ***spit and polish*** *tradition of the British Army.* SC □ *Councillor John Kidd told the meeting that some of the fire engines were so old they were only held together by* ***spit and polish.*** SC □ *To a man their husbands will be* ***spit-and-polished,*** *and dressed in their best, all hat-tipping civility.* ST □ *Field Marshal Lord Napier may seem to the present generation a slightly comic figure, the apotheosis of the* ***spit-and-polish*** *school of Victorian generals.* BN □ attrib use *the* ***spit-and-polish*** *school*; variant (be) spit-and-polished.

splice the mainbrace [V + O pass] (nautical slang) serve out grog (ie spirits mixed with water) to sailors; have a drink, or drinks, of spirits □ *I think we can congratulate ourselves on a fine run. Let's go below and* ***splice the mainbrace.*** □ *Too frequent* ***splicing of the mainbrace*** *had given Marsden's face a permanent flush.*

split hairs [V + O pass] quibble, or argue, on minor points □ (reader's letter) *A kidnapping is a kidnapping whether the child be hidden by a vindictive parent or by a stranger. To* ***split hairs*** *over these cases being civil or criminal offences is unworthy of us all.* RT □ *These days it's no good just doing surgery, y'know. The* ***hairs*** *of specialization are* ***split*** *finer than that. In America, so they tell me, they have a man for the right kidney and another man for the left kidney.* DIL □ *And both the Zenda stories are good bad books rather than bad good books—a Christmas game of* ***hair-splitting*** *which doesn't seem so witty by the New Year.* NS □ n compound hair-splitting.

a split second a measure of time seen either as precisely calculated or as being too short to calculate □ *Then suddenly there he was. Cool, calm, timed to* ***the split second,*** *with the minimum of hand luggage to save waiting for baggage at the other end.* TVT □ *In* ***a split second*** *she saw it coming, and raised her hands too late. She felt no pain as it struck her.* AITC □ *For* ***a split second*** *the squirrels watched us without movement; then they fled.* BB □ *...that built-in stop-watch possessed by Royals* (the Royal family), *who are used to having to dispense small change of gracious conversation to a* ***split-second*** *schedule.* ST □ attrib use ***split-second*** *timing,* ***a split-second*** *schedule*; often follows preps such as *in, to, for.*

spoil the ship for a ha'porth/ha'penny worth of tar (saying) make a whole undertaking useless by trying to economize on a small but necessary item (ship, orig sheep referring to tar as an insecticide or disinfectant for sores;

ha'porth/ha'penny = halfpenny's worth/ halfpenny) ▫ *If you're willing to pay £90 for a coat why* ***spoil the ship for a ha'porth of tar****? Get yourself a smart hat, too.* ▫ *It would only have needed a kilo or two of weed-killer every spring to keep the garden right.* ***Spoiling the ship for a ha'penny worth of tar*** *I call it.*

the sport of kings formerly hunting as a sport, esp on horseback, now (horse-)racing ▫ ***The*** *so-called* ***Sport of Kings*** *has always had social respectability. The racecourse, especially on a big occasion, does exude wealth and success.* OBS ▫ *Piggott is not a particularly attractive man physically, but he has power, a charisma and a rare talent: the king of* ***the sport of kings****.* TVT ▫ *In the beginning the promoters* (of dog-racing) *tried to get people like colonels onto the board, aping horse-racing, but they failed; it was never to be* ***a sport of kings****.* L

a spot check [O/o (NP)] a test, or investigation, of persons, products etc made usu without warning and usu at random **V:** have; make, carry out ▫ *You can't go on X-raying men* (ie possible diamond thieves) *again and again. All you can do is have* ***an*** *occasional* ***spot check****, and make the men think you're X-raying them when sometimes you're not.* DS ▫ *The Federal Health Ministry in Bonn denied reports that West Germany had halted imports of Israeli oranges after poisoned fruit had been found but a spokesman said* ***spot checks*** *were being made on imports.* SC

a sprat to catch a mackerel/whale [Comp/O (NP)] (saying) sth of relatively small importance etc that is sacrificed, risked, or offered in the hope of securing a much greater gain **V:** be, set up sb as; throw ▫ *He was deliberately being set up, as he put it, as '****a sprat to catch a mackerel****'—the IRA assassin who he was convinced would come after him.* G ▫ *What the Law Society has launched on the Tyne and Tees is* ***a sprat to catch a mackerel****. Solicitors might have just cause to thank their professional body for the business it stands to attract.* NS ▫ *Dickie asked me to be in 'A Bridge Too Far' and be* ***a sprat to catch a mackerel*** *because I have, strangely, some distinction to my name, though no great box-office worth, and other actors are sort of tempted, if I've said OK to a role.* RT ▫ also pl sprats to catch mackerels.

spread like a rash extend thickly, esp in visible form ▫ *Every rainy spell added to the damp rings that* ***spread like a rash*** *across the thinly plastered walls.* ▫ (popular newspapers) *The* (picture) *'strips'* ***spread like a rash****, from the bottom corner of the back page through all the inner pages, take over a page of their own, and still crop up here and there elsewhere.* UL

spread like wildfire travel with great speed and/or force **S:** news, rumours; rebellion; disease, plague, infection ▫ *This business would* ***spread like wildfire*** *if it once got out, even without the help of newspapers or radio.* TBC ▫ *A genuine response is only possible if the document is immediately released, otherwise misunderstandings about it could* ***spread like wildfire****.* G

spread one's net [V + O pass] prepare to catch sb or to get sb in one's power or influence **det:** one's; a, the. **A:** for him; to catch the unwary ▫ (source) *A man that flattereth his neighbour* ***spreadeth a net*** *for his feet.* PROVERBS XXIX 5 ▫ *In fact contacting Rohauer is not easy: having* ***spread his net****, he waits quietly for someone to stumble in.* ST ▫ *When the police had gathered fresh men and* ***spread the net*** *systematically over the area, a suspect would be picked up even if it were pitch dark.* HD ⇨ ⚠ cast one's net wide etc.

spread etc one's (own) wings [V + O] (have the confidence to) extend one's activities and interests **V:** spread, ⚠ stretch, try ▫ *Oh, but they must* ***spread their wings*** *a little. They must make friends in many places.* PW ▫ *Malvern* (Festival) *was the creation of a burgeoning 19th-century middle class, who by the turn of the century and after, were anxious to* ***spread their*** *cultural* ***wings*** *a bit.* L ▫ *Farrah Fawcett-Majors wants to* ***try her own wings*** *in a TV movie with husband Lee Majors.* TVT

spring clean thoroughly clean and tidy; freshen, put into good order or condition **O:** house, room; body, mind; procedure, drills ▫ *Modern governments are like slovenly housekeepers who sweep the dust under the carpet and slap some new paint on the rotting wood. They never* ***spring clean****.* TVT ▫ MICK: *I was just doing some* ***spring cleaning****. How do you think the place is looking?* TC ▫ *When* (the raccoon) *discovered that the padlock would not yield he devoted half an hour a day to it, and the rest of the time he devoted to other good works. Among these were his* ***spring-cleaning*** *activities.* DF ▫ *There's nothing like a whole day's walking on the hills, I find, for giving both lungs and a cluttered brain* ***a*** *good* ***spring clean****.* ▫ n compounds a spring clean, spring cleaning; attrib use ***spring-cleaning*** *activities.*

spring a leak [V + O pass] crack, or perforate, so that water etc enters or escapes; (fig) cause, or allow, (privileged) information to get out **S:** boat; floor, ceiling; pipe, radiator ▫ *Don't tickle him till I get his nappy* (= baby's napkin) *on or he's sure to* ***spring a leak****.* ▫ *'Would it be possible for Kingsley to* ***spring a leak*** *if we put him under sudden arrest?' 'I fear Kingsley may have deposited some document in any of a thousand possible places.'* TBC

one's/the springs of action the instincts, motives, urges etc that underlie the behaviour of individuals or groups ▫ *I believed that* ***the springs of action****, as Lowes Dickinson once said, lie deep in ignorance and madness. I wished to cultivate my understanding and to be sane.* AH ▫ (In the novel) *a cult of 'Lord Shardik' springs up around the enormous animal. People respond to the bear in different ways, their reactions serving to define their type just as it discloses* ***their springs of action****.* SC

square the circle [V + O pass] attempt to do what is impossible; (try to) solve a seemingly insoluble problem ▫ *There are always new ways of* ***squaring the circle*** *just around the next technological corner.* L ▫ *Tolstoy knew very well from past experience that the gulf between master and peasant could not be bridged. The way to* ***square the circle*** *was to get hold of the peasant children when they were young, and educate them.* OBS

a (good) square meal a satisfying meal of nourishing food ▫ *Not once in those years did Ned visit London without looking up Robert and* *taking him out for **a good square meal**.* CON □ *These tapes should be a great source for students of the nuances of political cliché. I am still mulling over Mr James Prior's observation that, after all, one can eat only so many **square meals** a day.* L

a square peg (in a round hole) sb whose character and abilities are not suited to his position or employment □ *I was **the** proverbial **square peg in the round hole**—I should be out there* (ie on the battle front) *snatching real pictures. But no one seemed to have time to listen.* SC □ *Generically speaking, he is a misfit, **a round peg in the squarest of holes**.* OBS □ *There is a witty script by Garry Michael White which opposes two different types of social **square pegs**.* L □ (NONCE) *...education which is more concerned with developing individuals than with moulding them into **pegs suitably rounded to fit** an array of **round holes**.* L □ usu in form of headphrase, but square and round rev; frequently adapted as shown.

the staff of life bread, or any other staple food which supports life in a particular society □ *The dough was kneaded in long rolls, each **a** literal '**staff of life**', and left to rise before being divided into sections for baking.* RT

a stag party (informal) a party, gathering, attended by men only □ *The Western has always been the venue for the Warley NALGO Men's Evening, **the** Town Hall's annual **stag-party**.* RATT □ *If his friends were going to give him **a stag-party** it must be* two *nights before their wedding; she wasn't going up the aisle to be met by a hung-over bridegroom* (ie who was suffering the unpleasant effects of too much alcohol). □ also pl. ⇨ a hen party.

stage and screen [n + n non-rev] the theatre and the cinema □ *They had paid a lot of money presumably to be near us, and Princess Anne, and the stars of **stage and screen**.* NS □ attrib use *a **stage and screen** actress*; variant (stars of) stage, screen and television.

stage a strike etc [V + O pass] arrange a strike etc, often for special effect, or in a dramatic manner **n:** strike, ⚠ sit-in, demonstration, rebellion; entry □ *The Fort Jameson secondary and trades school was closed after students had **staged a** sit-down **strike** in protest at the proposed visit to the school of the Monckton Commission.* OBS □ *'Marie is a little late.' 'She always is. She likes to know the other guests are all here before she **stages her entry**.'* □ also pl.

stamp one's foot [V + O] bang one's foot on the ground in a gesture of anger, annoyance, impatience etc □ *'Don't keep saying that!' Helen **stamped her feet** lightly. 'I've never asked you to pay me back.'* AITC □ *The audience signified their disapproval with that slow **stamping of feet** that's apt to put the wind up performers of any kind.* □ n compound foot-stamping.

one's/sb's stamping(-)ground the place where one/sb lives, is active, or is often to be found (originally referring to the habitats of wild animals) **adj:** main, favourite, preferred; former, latest. **o:** street vendors; prostitutes; lawyers, bankers □ *As a youngster he was a big lad, mixing it with the other tough kids in Islington, London, and **his** favourite **stamping ground** was the brightly-lit streets of Soho.* TVT □ *Master Sharify was unmasked because some of his fellow labourers at **his** latest **stamping ground** recognised him as a chap who had been in the place before.* NS □ *London is **the** main **stamping-ground** for private landlords.* L □ stress pattern one's/sb's 'stamping(-)ground; sometimes hyphenated.

stand a chance (of sth/doing sth) [V + O pass] have the possibility of achieving sth **det:** a; any, some; no; little, not much. **adj:** good, better; worse, poor □ *We **stand an** extremely good **chance of** getting through the Russian defences.* L □ *I'm afraid Lisa's family do not **stand a chance**. I doubt if their advisers will let them take it to court.* MM □ *Great numbers of people were smuggled into the country and hidden in remote and distant settlements where they **stood less chance of** being detected.* ST □ HETTIE: *What a man! I simply melt—oh, one night, just one night with him and then I wash dishes all my life.* RAYMOND (to Paul): *So **what chance** do we **stand**?* TK □ *If I had wanted to be an actor then I don't think I would have **stood much chance**.* TVT □ *The first thing to be said about the latest scheme for Piccadilly Circus is that it **stands a** far better **chance of** being built than any of the projects published since 1959.* NS

stand and deliver [v + v non-rev] formerly, a highwayman's command when stopping travellers to rob them of money or valuables; now facetious □ *It can't cost any more to provide a tourist with bed and breakfast in August than in March or November. A prices system adjustable to what you can squeeze out of somebody seems very like the modern equivalent of '**stand and deliver**'.* □ *One young Dutchman asked a sensible question about aid to the developing countries but without success. As he said after: 'You can never get these people to **stand and deliver** on anything.'* NS

stand easy [V + O] (military) stand in a relaxed posture with the feet apart and the hands clasped behind the back □ *The men '**stood easy**' throughout so that they could lean and twist, and look at me all the time if they wished to.* MFM □ *He paused, and then he said, 'You can **stand easy**, Prentice. Sit down.'* RFW ⇨ stand to attention (Vol 1).

stand firm [V + O] not yield to, or be destroyed by, enemy attack, stress or pressure, violent weather, etc; not be persuaded, or bullied, to change a decision or opinion **S:** fortress, outpost; sea-wall, barricade; employer, government. **A:** against the onslaught, against temptation; in the face of pressure; on this issue □ *In spite of repeated attempts to storm or fire the gates, the citadel itself still **stood firm**.* □ *If I had not **stood firm** and insisted that my plan would be carried through, we would not have won.* MFM □ *'Come on,' Best said, cajoling, threatening, 'don't be mingy* (= ungenerous), *our Colin. Let's 'ave* (= have) *one.' Colin **stood firm**. Finding was keeping.* LLDR

stand four-square [V + O] be positioned in the exact, or approximate, shape of a square; (fig) stand solidly, firmly, uncomprisingly **S:** house, table; citizen; policy. **A:** in the middle (of sth); in his complacency; to the winds; against change of any kind □ *It was a late 17th century stone-built farmhouse that **stood foursquare** in* *the middle of a scatter of later outbuildings.* □ *She flung a hand and a smile in the direction of Judy, who* ***stood four-square*** *in the front row, with her feet planted and her arms folded.* AITC □ . . .*the ideal of the whole man who can be serious without solemnity and cheerful without cheapness, and* ***stands four-square*** *in integrity and sound sense.* UL □ four-square or foursquare.

stand to gain etc be in a position where one is likely to gain etc **V:** gain, ⚠ win, profit; lose, forfeit. **O:** £3000, considerable prestige, your licence; ***(lose, forfeit)*** more than you gain □ *I've nothing to offer you—no money, next to no equipment, not much trade. What do you* ***stand to gain?*** HD □ *On BIG's* (a building-contracting company) *latest hush-hush budget, the architects* ***stand to collect*** *fees of £1,818,000.* ST □ *These income bonds have guaranteed cash-in values, so the life company* ***stood to lose*** *a packet.* OBS □ (reader's letter) *That is only one rule; there are hundreds that* ***stand to be altered*** *if we sign the Treaty of Rome.* SC

stand still [V + O] not progress, develop, or take positive action **S:** time, conditions, education; we, the police, his rival □ *Seeing time apparently* ***stand still*** *for three years while the rest of the world surges ahead in the race of life, the* (Oxford) *student cannot help wondering what are these intangible values he is suppposed to be acquiring.* OBS □ *Police departments have not* ***stood still****. More men have been sent to cities in the north, and over 85 arrests were made last year.* OBS

stand the strain (of sth) [V + O] cope physically or mentally (with sth) **o:** work, demands; excitement, worry, distress □ *Commanders and staff officers at any level who couldn't* ***stand the strain****, or who got tired, were to be weeded out and replaced—ruthlessly.* MFM □ *It's a very lucrative job if you can* ***stand the strain of*** *almost constant travel.* □ *It's doubtful if his heart would* ***stand the strain of*** *another major operation.* □ often neg with *can/could.*

stand etc tall [V + Comp] bear oneself bravely, or self-confidently, with consciousness of one's merit, status, rights etc **V:** stand, ⚠ ride, walk □ *He* (a badger) *didn't waste any time pottering around. After* ***standing tall*** *for a moment, he shambled up the well-worn trail into the wood and disappeared.* SC □ *Doesn't matter if you eat corn mash and saddle your own horse; you can still* ***ride tall****. Folks'll respect you if you respect yourself.* BBC TV □ (NONCE) *Groups came together for the common purpose of seeing films unavailable elsewhere. So if you don't feel like dropping in at your local* (cinema)*, the remedy is often to hand:* ***sit tall*** *at a Film Soc* (= society). NS

stand the test of time etc [V + O] prove to be of more than temporary, or immediate, interest, use or value **o:** time, ⚠ exposure, familiarity; re-reading, re-examination □ *Perhaps there is the germ of a novel there based on a theme that has already* ***stood the test of time.*** SC □ *His pictures sell for quite large sums now but who is to say whether they will* ***stand the test of time.*** □ *But although he assumed the difficult dual role of experimenter and subject, his methods were so thorough that his conclusions have* ***stood the test of*** *repeated* ***re-examination.*** MFF

the star turn [Comp (NP)] the main performer, or item in a programme of entertainment; a notable, interesting, or amusing person or event **V:** ⚠ be, become; make sb □ *Then he set the waste-paper basket on fire with a cigarette-end which made me pretty angry but which, for the children, was* ***the star turn*** *of the evening.* also pl.

stark raving/staring mad/bonkers [Comp (AdjP)] (informal) insane; demented; wildly angry, reckless, enthusiastic; **V:** ⚠ be, go; drive sb □ *Griffith refers to him* (George III) *as having 'gone potty—* ***stark staring mad****'.* RT □ *Pop gave the* (TV) *screen a cursory, whipping glance and wondered if everybody on it had gone* ***stark, staring mad.*** DBM □ HARRY: *She's mad, your mother, she's* ***stark raving mad****!* CSWB □ *And I've found Gittings—she's the one that went* ***stark raving bonkers****, isn't she?* TT □ always in order of headphrase.

start etc a hare [V + O pass] introduce a subject for discussion, perhaps just to stimulate conversation but usu with the aim of turning people's minds from the main subject **V:** start, ⚠ raise, put up. **det:** a; many, several □ *The conscious decision was made to give an overall picture of the Festival. Almost* ***every hare*** *that was* ***started*** *could have been profitably pursued.* L □ *Lord Citrine said* (about Ernest Bevin)*: 'Whenever he got in a difficulty he would* ***start a hare*** *or pull a red-herring across the track.'* L □ *There will be many* ***hares put up*** *for us to chase—that the money is more urgently needed for slum clearance—that. . .* NS □ *We mustn't* ***raise hares*** *we cannot, at this time, chase.* TT

start the rot [V + O pass] begin a process of deterioration in personal life, society, industry, administration etc □ *Miming to records on TV* ***started the rot****, and discotheques pretty well killed immediacy stone dead.* L □ ***The rot*** *had* ***started*** *last Christmas and the cameras were already there. They photographed the unity of the board gradually deteriorating.* RT □ *It has become fashionable for teenagers of the 60's, now securely employed bank clerks, to pinpoint the day the Beatles disbanded in 1970 as the day* ***the rot set in.*** RT □ variant the rot starts/sets in. ⇨ stop the rot.

a state of affairs (all) the circumstances and events relevant at one time to a person, group, country, undertaking, profession or world situation **det:** a, the, this. **adj:** desperate, deplorable; existing, present □ *Under the emergency regulations almost any adverse comment on* ***the state of affairs*** *in South Africa may be treated as an offence.* SC □ *Indian democracy* (1971) *might have been damaged if the Lower House had again comprised a group of warring parties. That was* ***the state of affairs*** *before the election.* SC □ *There are two principal reasons for* ***this state of affairs****—a philosophical reason and a chemical reason.* HAH

a state of grace [O/o (NP)] the condition of a Christian believer whose sins have been forgiven and who has hope of eternal salvation; (fig) a favourable condition, or status, according to some social, ethical or aesthetic viewpoint **V:** attain, achieve; aspire to, be received into □ *I watch London Airport dwindle merci-*

fully among the gravel-pits, and am received into ***the state of grace*** *that, beyond the lowering English cloud-banks, awaits us all in the sunshine and cumuli above.* OBS □ *Faith and works,* ***state of grace****, day of judgement — the book is soaked in these phrases of the Christian discipline.* NS □ *The Greater London Council has applied, this summer, for permission to restore Albury Street to* ***its*** *former* ***state of grace****— cobbles and all.* ST ⇨ fall from grace (Vol 1).

the state of play the score so far, esp in a game of cricket; (fig) the stage reached, so far, in a dispute, negotiation, or activity involving several persons or groups □ *The next TV visit to Lord's* (cricket ground) *isn't until 3.40, but there'll be flashes giving* ***the state of play****.* □ *It is a most agreeable intellectual exercise, or a painless education in* ***the state of play*** *of the human scientists.* OBS □ *This highly readable summary of* ***the*** *present* ***state of play*** *will be as illuminating to the professional as to the cultivated amateur.* L

a stately home a house formerly, or still, lived in by the British nobility and gentry, esp those houses built on a lavish scale in extensive grounds which in recent years have been opened to the public □ (source) *The* ***stately homes*** *of England,/ How beautiful they stand!/ Amidst their tall ancestral trees,/O'er all the pleasant land.* THE HOMES OF ENGLAND (F HEMANS 1793-1835) □ (parody) *The* ***stately homes*** *of England/How beautiful they stand,/To prove the upper classes/Have still the upper hand.* THE STATELY HOMES OF ENGLAND (N COWARD 1899-1973) □ *Mr Lees-Milne has worked much with the National Trust and written upon the* ***stately homes*** *of England.* SC □ *Alcatraz* (a former American prison) *can now be inspected just like* ***any*** *other* ***stately home*** *or palace anywhere else in the world, totally untarted up, in all its crumbling glory.* OBS □ *In those early days they catered mainly to the crowned heads of Europe and the* ***stately home*** *trade.* TVT □ attrib use *the* ***stately home*** *trade, business, circuit.*

stay etc the course [V + O] continue running till one completes a race, whether one wins or not; (fig) carry on and endure till the end in any struggle or activity **V:** stay, ⚠ last, survive □ *Knowing observers are unimpressed by Senator Kennedy's successes and point out that 'front runners' are unlikely to* ***stay the course****.* SC □ *I see this new work needs seven harpsichordists, 52 tape recorders and 16 film projectors. My curiosity is aroused but I may not* ***stay the*** *90 minute* ***course.*** RT □ *His father was a violent animal who reckoned to be drunk every evening and who again and again gambled away his money but somehow* ***lasted the course****.* NS □ *To his credit, Mr Millar has* ***survived the course****, bloody but only slightly bowed.* OBS

(a) stay of execution [O (NP)] a delay in, or postponement of, enforcing a court order; a delay in, or postponement of, some process or activity (the implication usu being that the process or activity, is/will be unpleasant) **V:** win, secure, obtain; ask for □ *The eviction order goes through, but counsel asked for* ***a stay of execution*** *until accommodation could be found for the defendant's children.* □ *'Do you want to go home and think about it?' 'No, if you really think the tooth should come out I'll have it done without* ***stay of execution****.'*

stay put [V + Comp] remain where one/it is or has been put; remain where one is in a general way, ie not travel, escape, seek promotion, etc **S:** family, shopkeeper, teacher; furniture, decorations □ *'Ronald, sit down here and* ***stay put****,' Tempest said to her husband.* MM □ *...the ideal conditioning cream for hair that won't* ***stay put****.* □ *By* ***staying put****, by digging our caves or cellars and staying in them, we shall be able to hang on.* TBC □ *Pious people that they are, they hope that the answer to their prayers will be, above all, that Britain will* ***stay put*** *exactly where she is, both in Northern Ireland and in the Common Market.* L

staying power [O (NP)] the capacity to continue running, working, fighting, living etc, esp under stress **V:** possess, have; lack; display □ *Given enough time and distance, a man will always catch up on a horse because he has more* ***staying power****.* □ *The fact that 'Peter Pan' still packs houses with delighted kids says a lot for Barrie, or for the* ***staying-power*** *of the Victorian imagination.* L □ *People learning because tap dancing is 'quaint and fashionable' lack the* ***staying power*** *and will soon be moving on to something else.* OBS □ stress pattern †staying power.

steady on be more careful; stop going, talking, so fast □ ***Steady on****, you two, you'll be hurting each other in a minute.* □ *He began to trot round the room, dusting the ornaments, as he spoke. Gerald was forced to turn round in his chair to speak to him. '****Steady on****,' he cried.* ASA □ ***Steady on****; if it is indescribable, don't describe it.* NS □ reproachful reminder or warning.

steal the show/scene [V + O pass] in a play, film etc, receive more applause and notice than the leading actor or actors; get more attention and admiration in a company, on a social or business occasion, than the person or thing which is expected to receive most attention □ (He) *stars as the bemused professor trying to prove that we all come from tree houses. The Chimp,* (chimpanzee) *of course, completely* ***steals the show****.* RT □ *Babies are notorious* ***scene-stealers****.* NS □ n compound a scene-stealer. ⇨ ⚠ stop the show.

steal sb's thunder [V + O pass] detract from what sb is saying, or doing, by accompanying it with dramatic remarks or actions of one's own, or with material stolen from him □ (source —referring to stage-thunder effects designed for a play of his own being used in a performance of 'Macbeth') *Damn them! They will not let my play run, but they* ***steal my thunder****!* J DENNIS 1657-1734 □ *Helen was the one who was getting married. She would not have the* ***thunder of*** *her wedding* ***stolen*** *by a presumptuous daughter coming up with a wedding of her own.* AITC □ *By then Mr Powell had* ***stolen*** *everyone****'s thunder*** *with his extraordinary speech at Stockport.* L

steam radio (informal) sound broadcasting contrasted with television □ *I'd forgotten what good value* ***steam radio*** *was till I had to spend those weeks in bed.* □ *My father maintains that you got better tone quality from the old plug-in type of* ***steam radio*** *than from any but the most* *expensive of transistor sets.*

steer etc clear (of sb/sth) be careful to avoid meeting, using, becoming involved with, sb/sth; give sb/sth a wide berth (qv) **V:** steer, ⚠ keep, stay □ *'What the hell's going on here?' said Robert. People were beginning to* ***steer clear of*** *me and Cartridge, and he must have wanted to investigate.* CON □ *Her eight trips to England had generally some practical purpose but these letters* ***steer clear of*** *such dry stuff.* L □ *Opium has been a cash crop for centuries, and it's hard to see why a peasant farmer should jeopardise his livelihood to safeguard overprivileged youngsters in the States who can perfectly well* ***keep clear of*** *his produce if they wish.* L

steer etc a middle etc course [V + O pass] adopt a policy and line of action that avoids extremes etc **V:** steer, ⚠ hold (to), keep (to). **adj:** a middle; ⚠ one's own, an independent, a cautious □ *The reporter, whose business is to present relevant facts in an acceptable form, could and should* ***steer a middle course.*** L □ *But 95 per cent of ordinary practising psychiatrists like myself, who run an area service, use both methods, and we* ***hold a middle course.*** L □ *Working hard at school had a very definite negative rating. But my mother had taught me to love books and feel the fascination of learning. So I* ***steered a middle course.*** ST

stem the flow (of sth) [V + O pass] check, or stop, sth **o:** words, tears; diamonds (into illicit channels); our best brains (to the States) □ *I took out a packet of cigarettes and offered* (him) *one, hoping to* ***stem the flow*** *a bit, but he accepted it and lit it without breaking his conversational rhythm.* CON □ *There is a need for a great many local industries to be set up to* ***stem the flow of*** *young people to the cities.*

stem the tide (of sth) [V + O pass] check, stop, or make some progress against, sth thought of as continuously growing or threatening **o:** enemy assault; barbarism, drunkenness, thefts; squatters □ *It is Britain that stood alone in 1940/41 and then, with American aid,* ***stemmed the tide.*** MFM □ *The second argument looks to the home rather than the school for methods of breaking the cycle of deprivation and* ***stemming the*** *rising* ***tide of*** *illiteracy.* NS □ *So how can* ***this tide of*** *distress be* ***stemmed?*** OBS

a step forward etc [Comp (NP)] sth done to bring a desired objective nearer, to improve a situation **V:** ⚠ be, represent. **adj:** big, definite; small; another. **A:** forward, ⚠ in the right direction, on the road towards sth □ *The high cost of defence is not being seriously tackled, except in the United Kingdom — where the Defence White Papers are* ***steps in the right direction.*** MFM □ *Nobody can pretend that this is* ***a step in the right direction.*** OBS □ *Anyone who has heard good stereo reproduction knows that* (this) *represents* ***a*** *big* ***step forward*** *towards that ideal.* RT □ *If one could divert some of the resources, now underemployed in the overproduction of tea, into agriculture for domestic consumption, it would be* ***a*** *small* ***step forward.*** NS □ *I did think that this was* ***a*** *very big* ***step on the road towards*** *getting a revolutionary situation where the capitalist system would be divided.* ST

a stepping stone (from sth) (to sth) [Comp (NP)] a means of reaching a higher professional or social level, or a more advanced stage in building, learning etc (from a stone, or line of stones, laid in a stream to enable persons to cross without getting their feet wet) **V:** ⚠ be, represent; regard sth as □ *He deplores what he suggests is 'a new feeling among some young BBC reporters that a correspondent's job is only* ***a stepping stone to*** *something else.'* RT □ *We had liberated a large part of Holland; we had* ***the stepping stone*** *we needed for the successful battles of the Rhineland.* MFM □ *There, blocks of buildings form a vast triangle of sooty architectural* ***stepping-stones from*** *1844* ***to*** *the present.* OBS □ stress pattern a 'stepping stone.

sterling stuff [Comp (NP)] (dated informal) a person, endeavour or achievement of high quality and solid worth **V:** ⚠ be; find sth □ ***Sterling stuff****, these old merchant-kings, but sometimes they can't see far enough beyond the counting-house to be of use to people like ourselves.* OMIH □ (golf) *The British were four up with seven to play but the Americans set about them with level fours for the last seven holes. This really was* ***sterling stuff*** *and all credit to them.* ST □ can be used without v as an approving comment.

the sticking point the limit, beyond which one cannot or will not go, or be persuaded to go □ *When it came to* ***the sticking point****, this shy, introverted man was capable of rare courage and resolve, however infuriatingly pale and insipid he appeared at less critical moments.* L □ ***The*** *other* ***sticking point*** *was over the length of Norway's coast which should have the special protection of the interim period.* SC □ *He's not going to keep lending you money. There'll be* ***a sticking point.*** □ stress pattern the 'sticking point.

a stickler for sth [Comp (NP)] sb who is fussy about, and insists on, particular behaviour in himself or others **V:** ⚠ be, become; make sb. **o:** punctuality, (the) truth, etiquette, hygiene □ *As a man he was* ***a stickler for*** *pudency* (= decency, propriety) *in word and deed.* NS □ *Darwin may be a frontier city 1,000 miles from anywhere worthwhile, but it is still* ***a stickler for*** *its own conventions.* L □ also pl.

sticks and stones will break my bones but names will never hurt me (saying) jeers and verbal abuse (should) cause one no real damage □ *I don't know what the hell his game is, but I've got to play it cool.* ***Sticks and stones will break my bones, but words*** *etc, etc.* JFTR □ *Miller's production shows us that 'The School for Scandal' is a very moral piece, a demonstration that* ***sticks and stones*** *aren't all that may injure the unwary. Words, too, are infinitely dangerous.* NS □ often adapted.

a stiff drink etc a drink with a high alcohol content **n:** drink, ⚠ one; whisky, gin □ *I left and had myself* ***a*** *real* ***stiff drink.*** *I have been shocked only twice in my life and this was the second time.* OBS □ *'I feel I need a little—' 'I'll bring one in to you. Sit down.' '****A stiff one.****'* MM □ also pl; with *need, could do with,* used by, or about, sb who needs to be restored or livened up.

a stiff letter [O (NP)] a letter that requests, demands, or complains about, sth in straightforward terms **V:** write, send □ *They* (working-class people) *suspect that public services are not so readily and effectively given to them as to the people who can telephone or send* ***a stiff letter***. UL □ occas pl; used by, or with reference to, educated people who can complain in an articulate way.

a stiff upper lip [O (NP)] courage and self-control in the face of danger, difficulties, grief etc **V:** keep, have, wear, maintain □ *'How's he taking it?' 'Badly, I think, but he tries to keep* ***a stiff upper lip****.'* □ *And men are brought up with this awful burden of having to have* ***a stiff upper lip*** *and not crying at all.* RT □ ***The stiff upper lip*** *that Tory ministers have so far worn in public in the face of every attack is now under a good deal of strain.* NS □ *It says much for* ***the stiff upper lips*** *of my parents that none of their anxiety was transmitted to their children.* ST □ *And who would have found the South Pole if wives had not agreed on* ***a stiff*** *and homebound* ***upper lip****?* YWT

the still small voice (of conscience) one's sense of right and wrong (still = 'quiet'); the voice of conscience (qv) □ (source) *And after the earthquake a fire; and after the fire* ***a still small voice***. I KINGS XIX 12 □ *'But burglars don't stay the night,' I protested to myself, but again* ***the still small voice*** *piped up.* PP □ *It is easier to fight down* ***the still small voice*** *that tells you you are wrong than the one that tells you you may be found out.*

still waters run deep (saying) a quiet person can have much knowledge, cunning, strong emotions, etc □ *'She's never shown any sign of having a mind of her own before.' 'Perhaps she's never needed to.* ***Still waters run deep****.'*

stink like a polecat/to high heaven (informal) have an offensive smell because contaminated by dirt, disease, or contact with sth unpleasant □ *And to tell someone that he* ***stinks like a polecat*** *is to insult him. But it also insults the polecat, which stinks by glandular reaction to stress, but which smells rather attractively at other times.* SC □ *We'd been sleeping in our clothes for nearly a week and must have been* ***stinking to high heaven***.

stinking drunk/rich [Comp (Adj P)] (informal) extremely, perhaps offensively, drunk/rich **V:** ⚠ be, become, get □ PETER: *I want to be* ***stinking rich****, open the most super-colossal Superstore you ever saw.* DPM □ *Oh, no, I've got to stay sober. I don't want to think afterwards I was* ***stinking drunk*** *the night my boy died.* QA

stir the/one's blood [V + O pass] arouse enthusiasm, courage, excitement (in one) □ *The Rhodesian agreement was the best of a bad job. There was just nothing around to* ***stir the blood***. L □ *Speak for yourself. The sound of bagpipes doesn't* ***stir my blood***.

a stitch in time (saves nine) (saying) immediate action taken as soon as sth goes wrong saves a lot of work later □ *'Must you stop to mend that now?' 'I prefer to—* ***a stitch in time saves nine****.'* □ *'He'll wait till the water's coming in on him before he mends that roof.' 'He doesn't believe in* ***the stitch in time****, then?'*

one's stock in trade the qualities and methods one characteristically uses, or offers, in dealing with a situation or other people **S:** treachery, false promises; conciliation, flattery □ *Dickinson, for example, spreads a useful awareness that treachery is* ***your stock-in-trade***. US □ *False alibis are put forward. Extraneous issues damaging to police credibility are introduced. All these are part of* ***the stock-in-trade*** *of a small minority of criminal lawyers.* L □ *'Welcome, Professor Middleton!' she cried. 'We meet as shades on the other side of the Styx.' Such allusions were, perhaps,* ***her stock in trade*** *for academical visitors.* ASA □ *People want, or say they want, consensus in politics, and yet reject or have doubts about those very politicians who have made consensus* ***their stock-in-trade***. NS

one's/sb's stock is high/low one/sb is thought well/badly of (from the varying prices at which stocks/shares are sold) **A:** with the public, with the Browns; in college; at home; everywhere □ *If a September attack was ordered by Whitehall they would have to get someone else to do it.* ***My stock was*** *rather* ***high*** *after Alam Halfa! We heard no more about a September attack.* MFM □ *I don't suppose a Labour Government****'s stock*** *has ever* ***been*** *so* ***low*** *in this country.* ST

stolen sweets etc are sweeter/the sweetest (saying) stolen, secret, unearned, or undeserved pleasures are often the most enjoyable **n:** sweets, ⚠ pleasures, fruits, kisses □ *Mick's Field was thereafter forbidden to us but, for no better reason than that* ***stolen sweets are*** *always* ***sweeter****, we did sometimes play there.* RT □ *'The cat's only choosy about what's put on her plate. Otherwise, she's an incorrigible thief.' 'Ah well,* ***stolen fruits are sweetest****, you know.'* □ *That so good, so homely, and so secret an eating place should be almost within arm's length of Piccadilly Circus, and as good as invisible, gave meals there almost the* ***sweet taste of stolen fruit***. AH □ variant the sweet taste of stolen fruit.

a stone's throw ((away) from sth) a very short distance (from sth) **adv mod:** not, just, scarcely □ *Not* ***a stone's throw from*** *Whitehall, there stands, amidst all the hum and bustle of the great metropolis, an old decaying pile.* NS □ *A seagull was drifting over the water* ***a stone's throw from*** *the rock.* PM □ *Police and demonstrators have fought viciously in Red Lion Square, only* ***a stone's throw from*** *this office.* NS □ *In the dark night at Le Tirage,* ***within a stone's throw of*** *the Germans, Bill had gone forward to attach the gadget to the German mines.* RFW □ ***Within a stone's throw*** *there must be four hundred places run by Italians, with an average of six girls called Pepina working in each.* CON □ variant within a stone's throw (of sth).

stoop (so low as) to do sth [V + Comp] lower, demean, oneself by doing sth; stoop to (Vol 1) (qv) **Inf:** to do sth; to eavesdrop; to ask sb □ *That a paper of such stature should* ***stoop so low as to*** *have a colour supplement. Why, it was nothing more than a cheap, nasty comic* (= children's magazine). ST □ *'Everyone has to make sacrifices: no one more than I who have to part company with valued and faithful colleagues,' said Asquith, and Churchill never* ***stooped to*** *point out how near that came to the old lie about 'this will hurt me more than it hurts you.'* L

stop a bullet/one [V + O] (slang) be shot, and wounded or killed □ (There was) *one shambling, ill-shaven slob. It was gratifying to learn that he*

stopped a bullet *shortly before the end.* L □ *Finally, he saves his first master, Charlie's, life by* ***stopping a bullet*** *during the Indian Mutiny.* OBS □ *You know they're armed but you concentrate on your driving to keep your mind off whether this is going to be the time you* ***stop one***.

stop (sb/sth) (stone) dead [V + O + Comp pass] (cause sb/sth to) stop immediately and completely □ *As I did so, a figure appeared round the corner of the corridor. All three of us* ***stopped dead***. UTN □ *'Perhaps you need a new battery?' 'I'd have had some warning if it was that. The transmission just* ***stopped dead***.*'* □ *With a cunning twist of his foot he* ***stopped*** *the ball* ***dead*** *before kicking it into the goal mouth.* □ *'Why do you let that lousy little mongrel follow you round everywhere?' I said it good and loud, and even the blokes with mouthfuls of crisps were* ***stopped stone dead*** *in mid-mastication.* JFTR.

stop the rot [V + O pass] halt, or put right, a process of deterioration, esp in social or industrial conditions, practices, or standards □ *Depending on the age and condition of the houses concerned,* ***stopping the rot*** *meant either improving the existing buildings with the help of council grants, or simply bringing the bulldozers and eventually replacing them with more modern accommodation.* RT □ *It* (the discovery of many new diamond fields) *nearly bust* (= destroyed) *the diamond trade. But then De Beers, who must have had terrific guts, stepped in again and* ***stopped the rot***. DS □ *'No, no,' he said, 'I didn't so much mean likely culprits, but what you think we can do to* ***stop the rot***. *We must take a firmer line.'* TT ⇨ start the rot.

stop short (at sth) not complete a distance, action, statement, study etc □ *He ran down towards the main road,* ***stopped short*** *when he saw the police car and doubled back up the alley.* □ *'Right. Down to the beach with you.' Pauline made to obey and then* ***stopped short***. WI □ (Ella has not yet fully recovered from mental illness) *Remembering de Morgan's theme of a wife in Bedlam, however, he* ***stopped short***, *and made a mental note not to mention Jane Eyre either.* HAA □ *This view recurred so often (particularly among churchmen whose acquaintance with France* ***stopped short at*** *Joan of Arc) that a common origin seemed likely.* NS □ variant stop sb short = 'prevent sb from completing sth'.

stop the show [V + O] attract so much attention, applause etc from an audience, or company, that proceedings are halted □ *This is Brenda Arnau of 'Oh! Calcutta!' fame where, statuesque and starkers* ((slang) = completely naked), *she* ***stopped the show*** *wearing nothing but her talent.* TVT □ *'I don't know that I've anything smart enough to wear,' she said, pursing her lips. 'Smart?' I choked 'You'll* ***stop the show***.*'* CON □ *By the time the Rainers came to Britain in 1827—the first time 'Silent Night' had been sung here—the carol had become their* ***showstopper*** *everywhere they went.* TVT □ *Len Deighton was born in a workhouse. The maternity hospital needed to set up an annexe in what had once been the local workhouse, though you can see the possibilities as* ***a*** *conversational* ***show-stopper***. G □ n compound a show-stopper/showstopper. ⇨ ⚠ steal the show/scene.

stop and start [v + v non-rev] proceed with pauses, halts, or interruptions □ *The bus* ***stopped and started***, *picked people up, let them down, and pursued its interminable course again unhurriedly.* AITC □ *But a totalitarian, one-party state is committed to the belief that it's always and everywhere totally right. Give me our mixed, blundering,* ***stop-and-start*** *system any day.* L □ *Harrison was then called in and, with many* ***stops and starts***, *gave his version of what had occurred.* □ attrib use *a* ***stop-and-start*** *system*; variant stops and starts [n + n non-rev] as in last example.

a storm in a tea-cup [Comp (NP)] a lot of fuss, disturbance, fear about sth that is, or eventually proves to be, of very little importance **V:** ⚠ be; regard sth as □ *And really it was all such* ***a storm in a teacup***, *to make this fuss about somebody coming back unexpectedly to spend a Sunday!* PW □ *Let us suppose that the whole matter comes to nothing, that it turns out to be* ***a storm in a tea-cup***, *a chimera.* TBC □ (NONCE) *The key element in* ***the*** *whole* ***tea-cup storm*** *seemed to be the government's devotion to 'competition'.* L

(so) the story goes so people say; so it is said □ ***The story goes*** *that, totally ignorant of navigation, he ranged alongside ships in the Channel, cupped his hands and shouted up 'Where am I? Which way to Stavanger?'* OBS □ *Jim has never been happier. His relations with Mr,* ***the story goes***, *are a model of serenity, quite different from those that existed in 1964-70.* NS □ *His son trained as a doctor at Trinity. Turned to religion, evangelical Low Church and all that, and decided to take Holy Orders.* ***So the story goes***, *anyway.* PP □ without so when introducing *that*-cl; with or without so when in parenthesis; always with so in main clause as end comment.

a stout fellow/feller (informal) a good, dependable, helpful etc person □ *He coughed, drank again, poked at the hole in his knee, and called Pop* ***a stout feller***. *He knew the committee would be eternally grateful.* DBM □ *The fiesta is in honour of St John the Baptist, it seems, local patron saint: Mr Graves was at St John's College, Oxford; there have been several St Johns,* ***stout fellows*** *all.* RT □ feller = fellow; use often facetious; expression can also be applied to a girl or woman.

a straight answer [O (NP)] an honest and/or unambiguous answer **V:** give, get; want, expect □ *Would you rather I didn't come?—and, please, I want* ***a straight answer***. □ *Subtle people, like myself, can see too much ever to give* ***a straight answer***. *Aspects have always been my trouble.* UTN □ occas pl.

straight from the shoulder [A] directly; frankly; forcefully (from boxing) **V:** speak, tell; give, deliver, get, sth □ *Johnson always says what he thinks you'd like to hear. I prefer a man who speaks* ***straight from the shoulder***. □ *This was a rebuff* ***straight from the shoulder*** *and there was no way to conceal his embarrassment.* □ *What's really the matter with me, doctor? I'm not a child, you know—you needn't be afraid to give it to me* ***straight from the shoulder***. □ *The editor of a down-to-earth,* ***straight-from-the-shoulder***, *fearless magazine in Berkeley, California, announced to a breathless world that* *the United States has been busy breaking the codes of the Soviet Union.* L ▫ attrib use *a* ***straight-from-the-shoulder*** *magazine, answer etc.*

(a) straight man a comedian's partner in a subordinate role assisting with situations and dialogue to highlight the main actor's performance; sb who supplies a stimulus for another's wit ▫ *The whole* (Morecambe and Wise) *show can absorb a tremendous amount of damage from flat scripts simply because of the sheer pleasure provided through watching the two men work. Neither is* ***the straight man****. Each leads to the other.* L ▫ (a television series) *'Basil Brush' is back for teatime (5.05 BBC1). The puppet whose outrageous jokes are a delight to connoisseurs of all ages also has Roy North back in the role of* ***straight man*** *to a fox.* RT ▫ stress pattern (a) 'straight man.

the straight and narrow (path/way) [O/o (NP)] righteousness and virtue; strict conformity to a religious, moral, political, or professional code of conduct **V:** tread, follow, forsake; keep to, stick to, hold to, depart from, stray from, tire of, keep on, encourage on, bring up in, guide along ▫ (source) ***Strait*** *is the gate,* ***and narrow*** *is* ***the way****, which leadeth unto life, and few there be that find it.* MATTHEW VII 14 ▫ *Certainly Australian wool producers got such an economic fright as would keep them in* ***the straight and narrow path*** *for the rest of their lives.* RFW ▫ *The exquisitely proportioned classical building of Inigo Jones evoked a closed world in which there was no room and patience for anyone who deviated from* ***the straight and narrow path****.* RT ▫ (Everyman's 'English Pronouncing Dictionary') *Deep in the English character, there is an instinct for a U and non-U* (= social acceptability and social non-acceptability) *of pronunciation as strong as it ever was. Meanwhile, for anyone needing help along* ***the straight and narrow****, Jones and Gimson will go with thee and be thy invaluable guide.* L ▫ *The Rolling Stones become progressively sidetracked and return to* ***the straight and narrow*** *as the best live rock group in the world.* RT

strain at a gnat (and swallow a camel) (saying) have scruples, make difficulties, about doing or allowing sth only slightly wrong or unsuitable, but remain unconcerned about doing or allowing sth really wrong, outrageous, or dangerous ▫ (source) *Woe unto you, scribes and Pharisees, hyprocrites! Ye blind guides, which* ***strain at a gnat, and swallow a camel****.* MATTHEW XXIII 23-4 ▫ *The Manifesto Group grumbled about the closed shop in journalism. But it also accepted the most extreme and anti-libertarian proposal in Mr Foot's new industrial relations legislation, which deprives workers of legal protection against unfair exclusion from a trade union. Having* ***swallowed this camel****, it was somewhat superfluous to* ***strain at a gnat****.* NS ▫ *But there are bigger issues at stake today than the merits of individual performances. Socially, artistically and economically the symphony orchestra is a beleaguered beast. In others words, we may be present at one of those crucial moments when it is not sufficient to* ***strain at gnats****.* OBS

strained relations hostile, or suspicious, feelings between persons, groups, or nations which could lead to open enmity or warfare ▫ *Professional jealousy had led to* ***strained relations*** *between the two men.* ▫ *...no Turkish or Olympic airlines from Athens on account of the present* ***strained relations****, and an Air France strike.* L ▫ *When* ***relations*** *became even more* ***strained*** *as a result of having now to live, as well as work, in close proximity, the research work began to suffer.* SC ▫ strained may follow *be, become*, as shown.

(in) straitened/reduced circumstances [A (Prep P)] (in) poverty or (living on) an income which is less than average, or a good deal less than formerly ▫ *She was well aware that* ***in*** *their* ***straitened circumstances*** *she was unable to provide for the child as she would like.* T ▫ *Though living* ***in reduced circumstances*** *themselves my parents still felt an obligation to help those even less fortunate.* ▫ *Loyal friends responded to heavy hints about* ***reduced circumstances*** *with cash and dainties.* NS

strange etc bedfellows [Comp (NP)] people, or things, one would not expect to find close together, or to be closely associated with each other, because of their very different nature, uses, habits etc **V:** ⚠ be, seem, prove, make. **adj:** strange, ⚠ odd, uncomfortable, incompatible ▫ (source) *Misery acquaints a man with* ***strange bedfellows****.* TEMPEST II 2 ▫ (reader's letter) *But it is hardly the first time in history that* ***strange bedfellows*** *have worked together for the same cause.* NS ▫ *Hollywood's bread and butter is now television. In some ways, feature films and television make* ***uneasy bedfellows****.* RT ▫ *Pathos, humour and terror, in this book, prove rather* ***incompatible bedfellows****.* SC

a stranger in a strange land [Comp (NP)] (facetious) sb unfamiliar with his surroundings and company **V:** ⚠ be, become; remain ▫ (source) *And* (Zipporah) *bare* (Moses) *a son, and he called his name Gershom: for he said, I have been* ***a stranger in a strange land****.* EXODUS II 22 ▫ *For the first time in 22 years I now know what people are talking about. I can watch the telly! Before, except when I was among actors, it was like being* ***a stranger in a strange land****.* TVT

a straw in the wind [Comp (NP)] an incident, rumour, expression of opinion, etc that indicates how a situation may be developing, what changes are planned or happening **V:** ⚠ (there) be, represent; see sth as ▫ *I had to set myself to wait, picking up any rumour from Barford,* ***any straw in the wind****.* NM ▫ *Maybe it is* ***a straw in the wind*** *that Peking broadcasts to the USSR have stopped saying, 'Hello, dear comrades and friends.'* L ▫ *It's something more than mere hooliganism. There have been one or two other* ***straws in the wind*** *recently.* TT ▫ ***The straws in the*** *fashion* ***wind*** *indicate a shrinking attachment for jersey and knitting.* SC ▫ *There are* ***straws in the wind*** *that this type of political campaign may take over sometime in the future from the industrial militancy of the present executive.* NS

a straw man [Comp (NP)] a man who takes on business commitments with limited means; an imaginary person set up as an opponent (and then demolished) **V:** ⚠ be; regard sb as ▫ *A second ideological feature of Mr Wilson's memoirs is his inability to recognise or to portray his various opponents and critics as anything but **straw men**.* L ▫ ▫ variant a man of straw.

the stream of consciousness the events and circumstances (including one's own reaction to them) of one's life as continuously experienced and interpreted by oneself; the imitation of this in books, films etc as a means of telling a story, portraying a character ▫ *Above all, he* (Tyrone Guthrie) *showed how important the use of **the stream of consciousness** could be for radio drama.* L ▫ *This is all contained in **the stream of consciousness** snippets, usually unpunctuated, that are a feature of M. Simon's other fine novels.* ST

streets ahead (of sb/sth) [Comp (NP)] (informal) far better, more efficient, cleverer etc (than sb/sth) **V:** ⚠ be, keep remain ▫ *The Focke-Wulf was a better fighter than anything we had till the Tempest became operational, and in the Messerschmitt 262 jet fighter they were **streets ahead of** us.* RFW ▫ (reader's letter) *The star's talented mimicry is **streets ahead of** that of any other impersonator.* RT ▫ (advertisement) *We're **Streets Ahead Of** The Rest! In linen hire and garments it's the care we take that makes us great.* OBS

the streets (are) paved with gold (saying) it is a place, esp a city, where one can get rich quickly ▫ *Some feel that, by merely coming to New Zealand, fortune is about to smile on them, that **the streets are paved with gold**.* WI ▫ (why young people run away to London) *It used to be the bright lights and the promise of excitement, of **the streets paved with gold**, drawing, by and large, the more motivated and adventurous.* RT

strengthen sb's hand [V + O pass] increase sb's power to do sth in the face of opposition or competition ▫ *This gave the Prime Minister the realisation that although Britain may have been satisfied with what the Government was doing, Scotland was not. That **strengthened the hand** of the Secretary of State* (for Scotland) *in dealing with his cabinet colleagues.* OBS ▫ *The power stations, which have so far coped remarkably well with the problems thrown up by the miners' strike, will be disturbed by an overtime ban and work-to-rule. This will both **strengthen** the miners' **hand** and produce a drastic worsening of the problems of keeping the country adequately supplied with fuel.* SC

stress(es) and strain(s) [n + n rev] demands made, or pressures put, upon materials, persons, or social, economic or political systems ▫ *He was a fine driver and mechanic, but when it came to working out complicated problems of **stresses and strains**, he was all at sea.* PE ▫ *Curtis confesses that sometimes he isn't up to coping with the **stresses and strains** of a large family.* TVT ▫ *It turns out to be a straightforward, chronological account of a very normal life punctuated here and there with the usual **strains and stresses**—jobs and people.* L ▫ usu in order of headphrase.

stretch the (long) arm of coincidence the strange chance that causes events to happen at the same time, people to meet, when one would not expect it, etc is used as an (almost) implausible explanation for sth ▫ *The author has managed to trace many incidents in which **the long arm of coincidence** brought Katharine in fleeting touch with members of the family into which she was later to marry.* SC ▫ *But I hesitate to believe that an animal which has existed since the days of St Columba at least would at this date fall a victim to a 'flying saucer'. This is to **stretch the long arm of coincidence** too far for even the most credulous historian.* RM ▫ *Either incident, I suppose, might have been an accident, but taken together they rather **stretch the arm of coincidence**.* NS

stretch a point [V + O] extend a regulation, or definition, to cover sb/sth not usu included in it; not keep strictly to required, or normal, procedure ▫ *'What is the boy's date of birth?' '23rd October — next week.' 'In that case I think we could **stretch a point** and call him 16 now.'* ▫ *And after I'd talked big and waved my wartime status at them a bit, they consented to **stretch a point** and take me along too.* TST ▫ stress pattern 'stretch a point.

strictly etc speaking [Disj] speaking with strict accuracy etc **A:** strictly; broadly, generally, roughly ▫ *Social psychology, **strictly speaking** deals with the behaviour of people in groups.* SNP ▫ *A 50-50 position* (between BBC1 and ITV audience numbers) *was achieved during the Sixties and, **broadly speaking**, has prevailed ever since.* L ▫ ***Roughly speaking**, I think no such contact is to be expected, but only **roughly speaking*** L ▫ ***Generally speaking**, scholars writing on the Scottish Enlightenment tend to ignore the development of law and legal thought.* SC ▫ front, middle or end position.

strike an attitude/pose [V + O pass] make deliberate use of physical posture, or gestures, to emphasize what one says or feels; speak or write about one's opinions, intentions or feelings in a dramatic or artificial way ▫ *Hylda Baker came out from behind the bar, **struck an attitude** and began to declaim.* ST ▫ *What merit is added to a perfectly good radio* (news) *story, when, having written it, you then memorise it, **strike a pose** under a palm tree, and tell it to a camera?* L ▫ *If you want brass band music, you get amateurs; bandsmen don't **strike attitudes** about it, nor consider money somehow dirty, but it's an amateur movement.* G ▫ *Amsterdam is one of the least hung-up communities in the world and that's reflected in their police force. Nothing astonishes them—they try to understand and not **strike** moral **attitudes**.* TVT

strike etc a bad patch [V + O pass] (informal) start, or have, a period of personal, business or professional difficulties etc **V:** strike, ⚠ hit, suffer ▫ *'**Struck a bad patch**?' asked Mrs Jones. He bit his lip. 'I am destitute.'* US ▫ *I admire my colleagues' persistence and ingenuity. Still, occasionally, every one **strikes a bad patch**.* NS ▫ *We've both **hit a bad patch**, Mark. You're in a terrible spot, and I've just been faced with the knowledge that my life's work has crumpled.* ST ▫ *He was reminded of **a** particularly **bad patch struck** at the beginning of his career.* ▫ also pl *He **struck** several **bad patches**;* pass use unusual.

strike a chord [V + O pass] produce a mental,

or emotional, response in sb (of recognition, sympathy, joy, fear etc); ring a bell (qv) **adj:** familiar, sympathetic, happy; ominous. **A:** in my mind, in human hearts; among those present □ *If I chance on a poem that* ***strikes a*** *familiar* ***chord****, matches up with something in my own experience, then I'm inclined to think it's a good one.* □ *The anti-census agitation* ***strikes a*** *responsive* ***chord*** *among those who are anxious about the invasion of privacy in the age of the computer.* SC □ *It suddenly occurred to Pop that he had heard these ominous words somewhere before. They* ***struck a*** *faint and unpleasant* ***chord*** *in his mind.* BFA

strike sb dumb/speechless [V + O + Comp pass] silence sb by astonishing, bewildering or terrifying him □ *In the face of such astute reasoning, Rafael was* ***struck dumb****.* DF □ MRS BRYANT: *Well, do you know what? I was* ***struck dumb****. I was* ***struck dumb*** *wi'* (= with) *shock.* R □ *An earlier, and a greater writer* (ie Dr Samuel Johnson), *had been uncharacteristically* ***struck dumb*** *by the dark, brooding malevolence of the place.* SC □ usu pass. ⇨ ⚠ fall quiet etc.

strike etc a false etc note act, speak or write with a lack of accuracy, appropriateness, or sensitivity **V:** strike, ⚠ hit, sound. **adj:** a false, a jarring, a discordant, a sour; the right, the proper, a more pleasing; a worldly; a spiritual, an austere; a cheerful □ *It would be rare for even an accomplished pianist to get through such a difficult piece without* ***striking a*** *single* ***false note****.* □ *First the vivacity of his mind became apparent, his openness to new impressions, then some comment, softly yet sharply* ***striking*** *exactly* ***the right note****.* AH □ *To* ***strike a sour note*** *about what is actually a most pleasurable occasion, the booklet leaves much to be desired.* OBS □ *The Armada emerged as a disaster, not a triumph. The grief at Philip's court* ***struck a*** *more* ***human note*** *than any of the English scenes.* L ⇨ ⚠ on an optimistic etc note.

strike gold [V + O pass] discover a rich source of information, wealth, happiness, enlightenment etc □ *'I expect you'll be off* (= will not like any longer) *this girl too in a few months' time.' 'No, this time I've* ***struck gold****.'* □ *With one van he opened up a small delivery business, somewhat tentatively, but soon found that he'd* ***struck gold****.* ⇨ ⚠ strike lucky.

strike it rich (informal) become rich, esp suddenly **A:** in business, as the result of speculation; by becoming sb's heir, by making a wealthy marriage □ SONIA: *Everyone who made a terrible fortune has been out of their mind. There was a man with motor cars in America and that man who* ***struck it rich*** *with frying oil.* DPM □ *He now felt less like an anthropologist who has* ***struck it rich*** *than a shagged-out* ((slang) = tired out) *school-master* (who) *must be in position at nine-fifteen the following morning.* TGLY

strike a light (dated slang) an exclamation of astonishment or protest □ PETER: *Jason, it's me.* JASON: ***Strike a light****, look who it ain't* (= isn't). DPM □ *'Have you got those sandwiches ready?' '****Strike a light****, Jim! It's only two minutes since you asked me to make them.'*

strike lucky be lucky, esp find sb/sth one is looking for, or of a kind that one hopes for □ *It was the Americans who first drilled for oil here and* ***struck lucky****.* L □ *Presently I* ***struck lucky****: on inserting the net handle into a clump of grass and wiggling it gently, I disturbed a Que-fong-goo* (a kind of lizard). BB □ *The only thing to do was to keep on photographing the whole sky, night after night. Some day he would* ***strike lucky****.* TBC □ (architectural styles) *The Queen Anne answer,* ***the*** *great* ***lucky strike****, the hitting of the jackpot was as simple as it proved irresistible.* L □ n compound a lucky strike; variant make/get a lucky strike. ⇨ ⚠ strike gold.

strike while the iron is hot (saying) make immediate use of an opportunity; do sth while conditions are favourable □ *His aunt was in a good mood and, thinking to* ***strike while the iron was hot****, he put Tina's proposal to her then.* □ ***Striking the iron while it was hot****, Daniel said they might as well stroll along to look at it now. He would first telephone the dealer to say they were coming.* US □ can be used as recommendation to act quickly; variant strike the iron while it is hot.

a stroke of (good/bad) luck etc [Comp/O (NP)] an instance of (good/bad) luck; a chance event, or circumstance, that works for/against one **V:** be; seem; have, experience. **n:** luck, ⚠ fortune, fate □ *I thought I had had* ***a stroke of luck****. Myrtle rang to tell me that she had been promoted to a better job in the firm.* SPL □ *By* ***a stroke of*** *sheer* ***good luck*** *the 'Nautilus', of which he was skipper, was called upon to accompany Captain William Perry.* L □ *Don't you sometimes feel it was* ***a stroke of bad luck*** *for you to be born with a well-to-do father who's got ideas about educating you?* HD □ *Alan Webb has the central role as a publican who decides to celebrate what he believes to be* ***a stroke of good fortune****.* ST □ a stroke of luck/fortune (ie no adj) suggests *good* luck.

strong language/words free or excessive use of swear-words, esp in abuse; forceful expression of one's views, intentions □ *We could hear a few yelps of pain and a good deal of* ***strong language*** *as Jim groped his way through the darkness of the cellars.* □ *Genius?* ***Strong language****, laddie.* ST □ *If we do not accept the rules of the Western system, the only option is to join Comecon. These are* ***strong words****, but there is no prospect of recovery for this nation by continuing to steer a path between these two clear alternatives.* G □ may be used as comment or judgement.

a strong man a professional performer of feats of strength as an entertainment □ *Bertram Batell's Sideshow: launched two years ago, now with nine ballets in the repertoire, as well as acrobatic acts and* ***a*** *memorable* ***Strong Man****.* OBS □ *Johnny Carter, our neighbour and* ***a*** *local* ***strong man*** *in his youth, could shatter a handful of hazelnuts in his fist.* □ stress pattern a 'strong man.

strong meat [Comp (NP)] a set of beliefs, or the language or theme of a book, play, film etc, thought unsuitable for people who are easily upset or shocked **V:** ⚠ be; find sth □ (source) *Ye are become such as have need of milk, and not of* ***strong meat****.* HEBREWS V 12 □ *Morris's magic would be too* ***strong meat*** *for most of us these days, caught as we are between kitchen-sink* *drama and women's magazines.* NS □ *A darker imagination is at work in this story of betrayed love and revenge.* ***Strong meat*** *and very good.* NS

a strong point [Comp (NP)] an ability, quality, asset that sb/sth has to a marked degree **V:** ⚠ be, become; make sth. **det:** a; my, his, your. **A:** of mine, of the system; of/in our family, of/at this particular university, of/with most small boys □ *Sometimes Wormold forgot he had altered a figure. Addition and subtraction were never* ***his strong points.*** OMIH □ ***A strong point*** *of his system is that the fast learner forges ahead very fast and the slow learner can take as long as he needs.* T □ *Modesty is not one of Beth Porter****'s strong points****, and she is certainly not one to sell herself short.* TVT □ *Herbs, too, are* ***a strong point*** *at White Moss House, by Rydal Water in the Lake District.* T □ may be followed by prep phrase, as shown; often neg.

(the) strong silent man/type [Comp (NP)] (cliché) a powerful or dependable man who does things and doesn't talk much, esp as a type in romantic fiction **V:** ⚠ be; find sb □ *Bill's* ***the strong silent type****, says Mabel. He's shy, adores the children.* TVT □ *No synopsis can do justice to its extraordinary sense of heroism without heroics of* ***strong silent men*** *who are not dumb but just as intelligent as the slick traders they scorn.* NS □ article usu used with type; stress pattern (the) ˌstrong ˈsilent man/type.

one's/sb's strong suit [Comp (NP)] what one/sb knows most about or does best; the power or influence which one/sb can exert most effectively (from the suit of playing cards in which one holds most winning cards in bridge, whist etc) **V:** ⚠ be, become; make sth □ *He was only an adequate batsman. Bowling was* ***his strong suit*** *and had got him his place in the team.* □ *But humour had never been Harold****'s strong suit****, and he did not feel like laughing.* PW □ *Unfortunately lyricism is not Robbins****'s strongest suit****, and the Mozartian quality of the music was not really translated into dance.* G □ often neg.

stuff and nonsense [n + n non-rev] foolish or false beliefs, ideas, talk □ *And how could anything be after her? What sort of thing? Oh,* ***stuff and nonsense****, it was time she got over her childish fears.* TGLY □ *The books are written off as a morass of* ***stuff and nonsense****. But what all the critics overlook is the pace at which a Blyton production moves.* L □ often used to express strong disagreement.

the stuff that dreams etc are made of [Comp (NP)] the very essence of dreams etc; have it in one's nature, character, to be, or do, sth **n:** dreams, legend; heroes, revolutions; good cooks, headlines □ (source) *We are such* ***stuff****/ As* ***dreams are made on****, and our little life/Is rounded with a sleep.* TEMPEST IV 1 □ *For most little girls pony books are* ***the stuff that dreams are made of****, and their little lives are bounded by the stable.* G □ *I'm not* ***the stuff that martyrs are made of****: I don't have any sort of built-in sanctity.* L □ *I'm not* ***the stuff dictators are made of****. I'm only really comfortable as an underdog.* TBC □ *This is* ***the*** *very* ***stuff of which archaeology is made*** *— small, insignificant finds, which add to our knowledge of the past.* OBS □ variant the stuff of which dreams etc are made.

a stuffed shirt [Comp (NP)] (informal) a self-important but empty person **V:** ⚠ be, become; find sb □ *But these aren't big people at all, Yves. These are frightfully, frightfully, unimportant people. They're what are called* ***stuffed shirts****, Yves.* ASA □ *Pete and I volunteered for the Press Ball committee because we wanted to persuade the others that there was no need for the* ***stuffed shirt*** *formality of previous years.* NS □ *The '****stuffed-shirt****' diet put out by the BBC didn't appeal to him at all: he liked the dance music from Fécamp, a Continental station.* L □ attrib use *a* ***stuffed-shirt*** *manner,* ***stuffed shirt*** *formality.*

a stumbling block [Comp (NP)] sth that hinders or prevents progress **V:** ⚠ be, become; find sth □ *At the centre is a resolution in a world which puts so many* ***stumbling blocks*** *in the way, to hold on at least to 'self-respect'.* UL □ (live radio commentary — golf) *We soon came up against* ***the*** *elementary* ***stumbling block*** *that in order to describe the play you had to see it, and in order to see it you had to be within range of the players.* ST □ stress pattern a ˈstumbling block.

subject to sth[1] [Comp (AdjP)] liable to sth; bound, or likely, to incur sth **V:** ⚠ be, become; make sth. **o:** tax, duty; atmospheric interference, distortions; colds, depression □ *What is one to make of his barefaced pretence that the Immigration Board is not* ***subject to*** *Government influence?* OBS □ *This habit of blushing stuck to her, she was* ***subject to*** *it even in private.* PW □ *It emerged not only that such a job existed, but that it was particularly* ***subject to*** *bribery.* HD

subject to sth[2] [A (AdjP)] conditional upon sth; provided that sth specified happens, or is the case **o:** his parents' consent, the Board's approval; supplies being available □ *In the end they agreed,* ***subject to*** *his parents' consent, to take Mark on as a trainee.* □ *One precaution that must be observed is to prevent the sheet from coming into contact with the steam pipes.* ***Subject to*** *that, it remains easy to handle.* NSC □ *An air corridor to Berlin twenty miles wide was to be established, and the free use of this corridor was permitted,* ***subject to*** *one hour's notice being given to the Russians of an aircraft entering their zone.* MFM

such as it is/they are poor, inadequate, though it is/they are □ *You're welcome to borrow the lawn-mower,* ***such as it is****, any time you want it.* □ *The text,* ***such as it is****, is predominantly smug ('there is no longer an acute overall shortage of housing in most parts of England and Wales').* NS □ *Sustained panic about our place in the world isn't really a reasonable frame of mind in which to face up to the realities of the modern world,* ***such as they are****.* L □ in parenthesis after n phrase it modifies.

such is life (catchphrase) that's what life is like; that's life (qv) □ *Dear me, and here we were expecting a quiet weekend; but* ***such is life****, I'm afraid.* □ *No, he didn't get the degree he was hoping for. But* ***such is life****, I suppose.* □ usu expressing, or recommending, acceptance of life's disappointments.

such and such a particular event, object etc that has been specified previously but which is not directly named in a later report ▫ *People would say: 'Are you going to do* ***such and such****?' and I'd say: 'Oh no, I'd* never *do that.' And it was very definite.* ST ▫ *A stereotyped letter arrives from the factory pointing out that* ***such and such*** *is not covered by the warranty.* ST ▫ stress pattern 'such and such. ⇨ ⚠ (a) so and so; next entry.

such and such a man etc a particular, a given, man etc **n:** man, politician, artist; thing, occasion; sum of money; place, seaside resort ▫ *He seldom asked himself whether he liked* ***such and such a man****: he esteemed him according as he fitted into the categories Harold knew.* PW ▫ *Now it is easy enough to write about* ***such-and-such a politician****'s supporters but it is more convincing to name names.* NS ▫ *Did one show one's hand? Did one betray one's anxiety that* ***such and such a thing*** *should happen? One did not.* PW ▫ BARDOT: *Journalists and photographers are on my heels everywhere I go. My trips are not trips—they're feature stories people are doing on me in* ***such and such a country****.* OBS ⇨ ⚠ previous entry.

a sucker for sb/sth [Comp (NP)] (informal) one who is easily duped by sb/sth; sb who cannot resist the attraction or temptation of sb/sth; sb who likes, is greatly impressed or interested, by sth **V:** ⚠ be, become; make sb. **o:** a hardluck story; kids, sweet things, antique knick-knacks; televised athletics, sentimental films, science fiction ▫ *Anybody that knew* ***a sucker for*** *a hardluck story when he saw one could get a fiver out of George.* ▫ *Dickie Davies is* ***a sucker for*** *boat shows and blames himself to the tune of £5,000 for his brand-new cabin cruiser.* TVT ▫ CHARLTON: *But I know what you mean: if you're* ***a sucker for*** *a ball game, you're* ***a sucker for*** *life. You never forget your heroes.* TVT ▫ *She kept this radiant smile even when singing the Magnificat. I'm* ***a sucker for*** *this kind of thing and the tears rolled.* G ▫ also pl.

a sudden death finish/play-off (sport) an additional contest to decide between people or teams who have achieved equal results, eg after a given period of extra time ▫ *In these tournaments, instead of requiring the winner to be two up, we have* ***a sudden death finish*** *in the 7th game.* ▫ *If two teams are level at the final whistle, they compete in* ***a sudden death play-off****.*

suffice (it) to say etc (that) (formal) it is enough to say etc (that); I will say etc no more than (that) **V:** say, ⚠ point out, state, stress ▫ *It would be idle to attempt to describe the prevailing excitement.* ***Suffice it to say that*** *frenzied attempts were made to decode the incoming message.* TCB ▫ *I have discussed such relationships and will not do so again here.* ***Suffice it to stress that*** *the concept of status is not purely defined in terms of position.* NSP ▫ *He was wounded and spent a year in hospital, but won't talk about it: 'I don't like heroes—****suffice to say*** *I was a soldier.'* RT

sufficient unto oneself [Comp (AdjP)] not dependent on others, esp for companionship, moral support, sympathy etc **V:** ⚠ be, become; remain ▫ *Because they meant so much to each other emotionally, they were* ***sufficient unto themselves****.* PW

sufficient unto the day (is the evil thereof) (saying) anything unpleasant will be quite difficult enough to bear when it happens without worrying about it beforehand ▫ (source) *Take therefore no thought for the morrow.* ***Sufficient unto the day is the evil thereof****.* MATTHEW VI 34 ▫ *Governments have a great capacity for ignoring the problems of the future.* ***Sufficient unto the day is the evil thereof*** *is their motto.* SC

a sugar daddy (informal) an elderly man who supports a girl, or young woman, in return for sexual favours ▫ *'La Paloma': deliriously mock fantasy about a cabaret singer and* ***her*** *sickly sweet* ***sugar daddy****.* NS ▫ stress pattern a 'sugar daddy.

sugar and spice (and all that's/things nice) imaginative description of pleasant attributes of character ▫ (source) *What are little girls made of?/****Sugar and spice****/****And all that's nice****./That's what little girls are made of.* NURSERY RHYME ▫ *Come, Mr Skipton, y're* (= you are) *not made of* ***sugar and spice****. The easy way is not for you.* US ▫ (Jessie Matthews's) *stage success was followed by a string of buoyant films—cobweb thin, some of them, but enchanting in their own* ***sugar-and-spice*** *way.* TVT ▫ attrib use *a* ***sugar-and-spice*** *way.* ⇨ rats etc and snails and puppy-dogs' tails.

suit/fit one's/sb's book [V + O] be convenient for one's/sb's purposes; agree with what one/sb wishes or intends to do ▫ *I believe even the most civilized of Englishmen still think that Catholic historians falsify or deny whatever doesn't* ***suit their book****.* ASA ▫ *Dawson wouldn't have taken Mark into partnership if it hadn't* ***suited his book****.* ▫ *They were not truths about America; but they showed truths about the British, selecting and distorting American evidence to* ***fit their book****.* L

the sum total (of sth) [Comp (NP)] all (of sth); the whole (of sth) **V:** ⚠ be, represent ▫ *Two grocery shops and the general store are* ***the sum total of*** *local industry.* T ▫ *She'd rather not have to live alone, and I think that's* ***the sum total of*** *her feeling for him.*

one's Sunday best etc [O/o (NP)] one's newest, smartest, clothes **V:** wear, dress in, put on. **n:** best, ⚠ suit, dress, hat ▫ *My clothes were* ***my Sunday best****.* RATT ▫ *In addition, as part of their public strategy, the demonstrators invariably wear* ***their Sunday best*** *and carry their most impressive school-books.* OBS ▫ *And there were the clothing workers themselves, dignified but a little prim in* ***their Sunday best****.* RT ▫ *Recall for a moment some of the routines of working-class life: as to clothes, the persistence of* ***the Sunday suit****.* UL ▫ such clothes formerly, esp among middle class or working people, kept for Sundays (when one went to church, visited relatives or friends but did not work, or play games, etc).

sure enough [Disj (AdjP)] (informal) exactly as one had expected, or as had been said, forecast etc ▫ *'Well, you can see for yourself what a mess it's made of the beach.' And* ***sure enough*** *when Mr Mackay looked at the sand it was scored and striated in every direction.* RM ▫ *First of all she went to the bombed buildings of the King's Road. There,* ***sure enough****, was Godfrey's car.* MM ▫ *'Am I being a nuisance?' he asked, and* **sure**

enough *he was but I could hardly say so.*

a sure-fire method etc [Comp (NP)] a certain, reliable method, etc **V;** ⚠ be; think, find, sth. **n:** method, ⚠ way, solution; success □ *A small item in the newspaper can easily be missed, but a short announcement on the radio, put out several times during the course of the day, is* ***a*** *more* ***sure-fire method****.* L □ (answer to reader's letter) *No, it's not the thing to do. Yours is* ***a sure-fire method*** *to block the drains.* TVT □ *'Play for Today' on BBC1 kicks off with what looks like* ***a sure-fire success****, 'Bar Mitzvah Boy'.* RT □ also pl.

sure of oneself [Comp (AdjP)] extremely, or excessively, self-confident; sure that one is competent, correct **V:** ⚠ be, feel, seem; look, sound □ *I hated Joe Lampton, but he looked and sounded very* ***sure of himself****; he'd come to stay, this was no flying visit.* RATT □ *He refused to tell me by what methods he was going to bring about this miracle, but he was so* ***sure of himself*** *that I began to wonder if he really would be able to get me one of these creatures.* BB

sure thing [Disj] (informal) of course; naturally; it is certain; I admit; we all know □ *'They wouldn't be so cruel!' '****Sure thing****, they would. Don't underestimate their ruthlessness.'* □ *I've been luckier than a lot of people,* ***sure thing****, but that doesn't mean I'm satisfied with things as they are.* □ ***Sure thing*** *it rains if I plan to wash blankets.* □ front or end position; esp Scots or US.

a surprise packet (informal) any person, thing, or event that surprises one through some quality or content □ *'All he said in the letter was that he'll be bringing* ***a surprise packet*** *with him.' 'Could be a new girlfriend, I suppose.'* □ *'Let me mix you one of Julian's specials. It's a sort of long cocktail—' 'I've been caught with Julian's drinks before, I want to know what's in* ***this surprise packet****.'* TGLY □ also pl.

surprise, surprise (ironic) just as one would expect; it's really no surprise □ *A new steel works has just been constructed. So there's not much lack of work. There is however,* ***surprise, surprise****—an acute lack of housing.* NS □ *Somebody announces that we are here for an investiture,* ***surprise, surprise****, and we ran off. Today's list is exceptionally long, with 176 people.* ST □ comment, or rejoinder, often in parenthesis.

the survival of the fittest (the theory of) survival by natural selection, ie only those forms of plant and animal life best adapted to their surroundings are able to survive □ *Reduce men to animals, and still a little dogged altruism remains. It isn't all self-interest and* ***the survival of the fittest****.* NS

the suspension of disbelief the readiness to accept as real what one knows to be impossible or unlikely □ (source) ***That*** *willing* ***suspension of disbelief*** *for the moment, which consititutes poetic faith.* BIOGRAPHIA LITERARIA (S T COLERIDGE 1772-1834) □ *Was he so unnatural a child as to be unable to make* ***a*** *positively eager* ***suspension of disbelief****?* L □ *There isn't a moment when* ***disbelief*** *is* totally ***suspended****. It may, however, prove a socially useful film.* OBS □ *If the team goes on next season to put itself back in the first division, the dream could just possibly come true. I for one think it worth while to* ***suspend my disbelief*** *for a time.* NS □ variant suspend (one's) disbelief.

swallow the dictionary [Y + O] use uncommon and, esp, long words □ *'I'm a palaeontologist.' 'A what? You'll sprain your jore* (= jaw), *if you start in trying to* ***swallow the dictionary*** *all at one go.'* RM □ *He may be an expert but can he talk to school-children? They'll not sit still for half an hour listening to some chap that's* ***swallowed the dictionary****.* □ infin or perfect tenses.

swallow/pocket one's pride [V + O] humble oneself, esp in order to do or obtain sth, or to admit error or guilt □ *Where money was concerned she had little* ***pride****. What little she had she* ***swallowed*** *and wrote to Elvira.* ASA □ *He had more practical matters to deal with. Having* ***swallowed his pride****, he did not intend to prostrate himself for nothing.* NM □ *The Americans have* ***swallowed their pride*** *in order to make a deal which could have been made years ago.* NS □ *But he needed the aid and companionship of his wife.* ***Pocketing his*** *badly-damaged* ***pride****, he hurried to the door of Madame's locked room.* ARG

swear black is white say emphatically or stubbornly that sth is the true, is the case, when it is not true, not so □ *Don't believe a word that child tells you. He'd* ***swear black was white*** *if he thought it was to his advantage.*

swear blind (that) (informal) say emphatically or stubbornly (that sth is the case although it may not be so) (the implication sometimes being that the actual truth is disregarded) □ *They aren't going to get me on this racing lark, this running and trying to win, because it's not the way to go on at all, though they* ***swear blind*** *it is.* LLDR □ *It would be just like Peter to slide a few notes into my handbag if he thought I was hard up, but he* ***swears blind that*** *it wasn't him.*

sweat blood [V + O] be in an agony of effort or fear □ *You're too used to* ***sweating blood*** *for your money. But that's not the way to get it. Just lie on your back and whistle and it'll come.* UTN □ *He must have* ***sweated blood*** *dragging himself out of there with a broken leg.* □ *'You look frightfully composed and superior.' 'If I may say so, sir, that's just what struck me about you.' 'Good God! I've been* ***sweating blood*** *at the thought of this afternoon for a week.'* DIL

sweated labour work by underpaid employees, usu working in cramped and unsafe conditions □ *It is now argued that imports from countries which exploit cheap labour should be controlled. Complaints of* ***sweated labour*** *will give place to complaints of sweated environments.* ST □ (NONCE) *What did he want out of you this time? More* ***sweated manuscript-reading****?* ILIH □ *To compete in the labour market the fashion industry has had to take its workers out of* ***the sweat shops*** *and pay them more.* SC □ cf a sweat shop = 'a cramped, unhealthy factory or workshop where employees are underpaid'.

sweep the board (clean) [V + O + Comp pass] win all the cards, stakes, at a card or gaming table; win all the prizes, awards, honours connected with an event or activity; have an exceptional run of success, popularity □ *Starbrook had his first taste of success when his* *club put in for an area event and '**swept the board clean**, scooping up all the prizes'.* RT ▫ *The colt's trainer, Alec Head, **swept the board** in the three-year-old races in France this season.* OBS ▫ (fashion notes) *The odd jacket is the runner-up to yesteryear's blazer and we know how that **swept the boards**.* SC

a sweeping statement [O (NP)] a statement expressed in terms that are far too general and that do not allow for exceptions **V:** make; favour, be given to ▫ (It) *is as ridiculous as it would be to suggest that all journalists are ignorant charlatans who make **sweeping statements** in the mistaken belief that their readers know as little as they.* NS ▫ *He's much given to **sweeping statements** about trades unions, foreigners and working wives.*

sweet Fanny Adams/f.a. nothing at all; nothing of much value or importance (from (i) a girl so named murdered in the 19th c and chopped to pieces, then (ii) sailor's slang for tinned mutton, then (iii) sth of little value or appeal, or (iv) nothing at all) ▫ *We're going to get it* (school sports) *over at the double. I'm not going to 'ave* (= have) *you all standing there doing **sweet fanny adams**.* SPL ▫ (reader's letter) *What other subject would the BBC be prepared to have discussed in front of millions of viewers by someone who, on his own admission, knows **sweet Fanny Adams** about it?* RT ▫ *I have always been keen to discover what it is that puts editors apart from mortal men and the answer in Johnson's case was the usual and resounding **sweet f.a.*** PP ▫ *I went to a junior secondary school, which carried a stigma. Then I was thrown out at 15 as though I was **sweet Fanny Adams**.* SC

sweet sixteen (and never been kissed) (catchphrase) past childhood but still young enough to be innocent, unworldly, inexperienced etc ▫ *A woman trapped in the rubble of her wash-house said she was about to have a baby. I was **sweet 16**, wide-eyed, and had no idea what to expect next.* OBS ▫ *I was just **sweet sixteen** when I went through the portals of the District and National with my first ham sandwich.* JFTR

the sweet smell of success (catchphrase) what draws people to seek success and/or to admire it ▫ *One might expect that Gilmore would be savouring **the sweet smell of success** now, having spent more than 20 years as he says, 'in and out of character parts, and flop musicals'.* RT ▫ *This brings us back to the book which also gives off **the sweet smell of success**. As a Pan Books paperback, costing 60p, it has sold nearly two million copies.* SC

sweetness and light [n + n non-rev] harmony and reason (popularized as terms in artistic, cultural, moral and political doctrines and criticism by M ARNOLD 1822-88) ▫ (source) *Instead of dirt and poison we have rather chosen to fill our hives with honey and wax; thus furnishing mankind with the two noblest of things, which are **sweetness and light**.* THE BATTLE OF THE BOOKS (J SWIFT 1667-1745) ▫ *'**Sweetness and light**' is simply reason active in society. We must find a use for intelligence in our society.* L ▫ *It would clearly be foolish to suppose that a warm welcome for table-tennis tourists means the end of Chinese isolationism and the immediate inauguration of a new policy of **sweetness and light**.* NS ▫ *Reith's sojourn* (as Lord Commissioner, representing the monarchy) *at Holyroodhouse, we gather, was not all **sweetness and light**. At times he could be unbearable.* SC ▫ *Diana is a bit baffled as to why she's constantly cast in parts that tend to lack **sweetness and light**.* RT

swing the lead [V + O] (dated slang) (try to) deceive with a false or exaggerated account of sth; esp feign illness in order to avoid work, a duty etc (from casting a sounding-lead at sea) ▫ *'Poor Mrs Spencer,' said Kathie, 'she does have a lot of trouble.' 'Trouble?' said Dusty, 'she's **swinging the lead**—sick headache!'* TT ▫ a n compound a lead-swinger.

the swing of the pendulum (the pattern of) alternation in public opinion and taste ▫ ***The swing of the pendulum** since 1968, observable last year, is expected to enable Labour to regain Glasgow, to hold Aberdeen, perhaps to capture Dundee.* SC ▫ (in East Germany) *Stalin, about whom nobody had a bad word to say while he was alive, suffered from **the swing of the pendulum** and became the wrong person to name things after.* SC ▫ *A great many people thought that **the pendulum** of permissiveness had gone too far, and that it was about time it began to **swing** back again.* ST ▫ *You never know **how the pendulum** will **swing**: our middle-class grandparents sold their pianos and now the grandchildren are buying them back again.* ▫ variant (how/which way) the pendulum swings.

swings and roundabouts [n + n non-rev] a matter of balancing profits against losses (from fairgrounds—if customers favour the swings, money is lost on the roundabouts) ▫ *As to whether it's better to be 20 now than then—it's a matter of **swings and roundabouts**.* TVT ▫ *'It's just **swings and roundabouts** in politics,' said Mr Foulkes lightly. 'You're never rejected for long.'* ST ▫ *A study of the fairly momentous changes in Italian family life indicated that there, as elsewhere, they were **gaining on the swings what they** were likely to **lose on the roundabouts**, but that is progress, I suppose.* L ▫ (producers are also consumers) ***What** people **gain on the roundabouts** at work obviously matters more to them than **what they lose on the swings**.* G ▫ variants what one gains on the swings one loses on the roundabouts, gain on the swings what one loses on the roundabouts — swings and roundabouts rev in both variants.

T

a tail-end Charlie sb (habitually) late, slow or ineffective: (dated RAF slang) the rear-gunner in a bomber aircraft ◻ *The bad teacher will always be showing how good he is, will let the weaker skiers be the* ***tail-end Charlies****—learning little and feeling worse and worse.* ST ◻ *Over the barriers jumped the team to effect a rescue, when another bull, something of* ***a tail-end Charlie****, mopped up* (= defeated) *the lot of them.* L

the tail wags the dog [V + O pass] a part controls the whole; a subsidiary associate, group, element, factor etc dictates the course of action for a more important associate etc ◻ *The Scots should appreciate that within the British economy they occupy a subordinate position. They ought not to expect* ***the tail to wag the dog****.* SC ◻ (NONCE) *Can* ***the*** *Libyan* ***tail wag the*** *Egyptian* ***dog****? Can Gaddafi influence or effectively contradict Cairo?* L ◻ (NONCE) *For one thing, craft chapels* (union branches) *have established a tradition of near autonomy which sometimes makes the more militant* ***tails*** *appear to* ***wag the*** *union* ***dog****.* NS ◻ *Because of ideology, because of distrust and hostility between the great powers, no one feels able to bring any pressure to bear on Iraq. The same goes for Iran. Small* ***tails wag*** *big* ***dogs*** *on both sides.* L ◻ *The specific danger he visualises is that in bowing to pressure to widen the operation beyond the scope of his company's own feasibility study, 'One could end up being* ***the dog*** *that is* ***wagged*** *by its own* ***tail****.'* SC

take the air [V + O] be out of doors; go for a walk ◻ *Cuckoos were still calling across the fields in their late bubbling voices and a few people were wandering among Ma's flower-beds,* ***taking the air****.* DBM ◻ *'Where are you going now, for goodness' sake?' 'Nowhere—just to* ***take the air*** *on the lawn before I go to bed.'*

take sth/it amiss [V + O + A pass] be offended by sth said or done that was not intended to have this effect **O:** it; the criticism, advice, review of his book; my remarks, his interest ◻ *'When are you two going to get married? I'm glad you didn't* ***take it amiss*** *when I said that.' He wagged his globe-shaped head with satisfaction.* SML ◻ *She's so touchy about being able to look after herself that your offers of help may easily be* ***taken amiss****.* ◻ *Please don't* ***take it amiss*** *if I say I'd rather you didn't come to the station to see me off.*

take etc another course [V + O pass] change; change one's plan, pattern or line of procedure **S:** events, matters; illness, epidemic; government, management. **V:** take, ⚠ follow, pursue. **det + adj:** another, a different, the same; the right; a predictable ◻ *That, then, was what they expected. Events, however, were to* ***take another course****.* TBC ◻ *The disease does not necessarily* ***follow the same course*** *in every person who contracts it.* ◻ *Rarely has a Budget left more uncertainty in the public mind as to* ***the course*** *business may be expected to* ***take*** *in the immediate future.* SC ◻ *I think you are* ***taking the wrong course*** *with that boy in constantly criticizing him.* ◻ also pl *There are* ***several courses*** *open to us to* ***take****.*

take sb/sth as one finds him/it [V + O + A] accept, be willing to tolerate or welcome, sb/sth without wishing him/it to be different; take sb/sth as he/it is/comes (qv) **O:** her, the Prime Minister, people; it, life, things ◻ *Well, I'm sorry. I have to say what I think. You must* ***take*** *me* ***as you find me****.* AITC ◻ *He thought what a nice wife he had, and that she would be perfect if she would only* ***take*** *him* ***as she found him****.* ILIH ◻ *'Well, she's never shown that side of her character to me.' 'I'm sorry—I don't mean to turn you against her.' 'You haven't. It's always best to* ***take*** *people* ***as you find them****, don't you think?'* ◻ (NONCE) *I always try to get on with everyone.* ***Take as you find****, as my dad always says.* RT

take etc sth as/for gospel etc [V + O + A pass] believe sth unquestioningly or too credulously **V:** take ⚠ accept, receive. **O:** it; what he says, their pronouncements. **o:** gospel, (the) ⚠ gospel-truth, holy writ/scripture ◻ *But I wish they didn't think they were getting away with making you* ***take*** *it all* ***as gospel****.* L ◻ *Not only are the doctors themselves convinced of their own infallability; they also impart this notion to the patients. Whatever a medical man says or does is* ***taken as gospel-truth****, and woe be to any who criticise.* RT ◻ *He wasn't out of my sight for one minute: please* ***accept*** *that* ***as the gospel truth****.*

take sb/sth as he/it is/comes [V + O + A] accept, be willing to tolerate or welcome, sb/sth without wishing him/it to be different; take sb/sth as one finds him/it (qv) **O:** him, the Pope, people; it, life, things ◻ *'I'm not dressed for getting up,' I said. Perhaps after coffee I might find a razor Waterman had left, but for now Miss Miles must* ***take*** *me* ***as I was****.* PP ◻ *I said to him: 'My man, your* property *is ready for display to anyone. But* I *have been cooking, cleaning, and digging for three days and I'm tired. Mr Stent will have to* ***take*** *me* ***as I come****.'* EHOW ◻ *No longer is he sharp or pushful. He just* ***takes*** *things* ***as they come****.* NS

take a back seat [V + O] (informal) change to, or be relegated to, a less important role or function ◻ *It is highly unlikely that Slater intends to move out of the scene or even* ***take a back seat*** *for long.* ST ◻ (astrological prediction) *Someone you love will be obsessed with something other than romance—so you* ***take a back seat*** *for a while.* TVT ◻ *After forty years in the business it's time for me to* ***take a back seat*** *and make room for younger men and new ideas.*

take sb/sth to be sth understand, deduce, that sb/sth is as named or described ◻ *A middle-aged woman whom I* ***took to be*** *his housekeeper was talking to a tradesman at the back-door.* ◻ *The victim is a spinster bombed out from London to a boarding house in 'Thames Lockdon' (which I* ***take to be*** *Henley, where Patrick Hamilton* *spent the war).* L ▫ *There was a brilliant aurora-type display that night, which the Nortonstowe scientists* ***took to be*** *associated with the sudden burst of ionization high in the atmosphere.* TBC ▫ *The best man was wrongly* ***taken to be*** *the bridegroom by the photographers.* ▫ pass as in last example.

take a beating etc [V + O] (informal) bring defeat, heavy criticism, loss of credit on oneself **S:** team, side; government, company; idea, notion; reputation. **o:** a beating, ⚠ pounding, hammering, pummelling, thrashing ▫ *The team has a good record for the season in spite of* ***the beating*** *it* ***took*** *at Hampden last Saturday.* ▫ *Eton, being an ancient institution, is also of necessity an Aunt Sally. It has* ***taken a beating*** *for long enough with fearful exposés of sadism, homosexuality and the like.* SC ▫ *The argument that the public is interested in visiting stars and not the home team has already* ***taken*** *quite* ***a beating*** *this season with the great popular success of 'Peter Grimes' and 'Wozzeck', both sung in English by company singers.* T ▫ *The survivors seemed mostly concerned to challenge each other's credentials or recollections. Martin Gray* ***took a pummelling*** *from almost everyone.* L ⇨ ⚠ take some beating.

take the biscuit/cake [V + O] (informal) be extremely or specially amusing, foolish, annoying, astonishing, outrageous etc ▫ *Pop thought this milord lark* (ie having been thought to be a titled person) *just about* ***took the biscuit*** *and he told Ma all about it as he uncorked the champagne in the bedroom.* BFA ▫ *'Man Alive' and 'The Money Programme' were, no doubt, worthy attempts to present their topics economically within a studio setting. Both were as dull as ditch-water, with Money* ***taking the biscuit.*** L ▫ *You may think your husband is forgetful but John really* ***takes the cake*** *in that respect.*

take a bow/curtain [V + O] acknowledge applause by bowing **S:** cast, company; principal dancer, conductor ▫ *The title describes it as 'a play by Neil Simon'—it is, in fact, a trio of one-acters — and the final credits permit the players to* ***take a*** *well-earned* ***bow.*** NS ▫ *It was a delicious meal, Sheila. You must come and* ***take a bow.*** ▫ *'A fish-witted imbecile like you ought not to be allowed to be a doctor. There should be a law against it.' This was his exit line, and as he turned and walked out, with the patients clustering eagerly at the doors of the waiting-rooms, he had something of the feeling of an actor* ***taking a*** *triumphant* ***curtain.*** PE ▫ lit or fig.

take care (not) to do sth be careful (not) to do sth; make certain/sure[2] (qv) that one does (not) do sth ▫ (astrological prediction) ***Take care not to*** *let a family upset interfere in any way with your usual working routine and concentration.* WI ▫ *He wouldn't suffer half as much as he does with his stomach if he* ***took care to*** *eat properly.* ▫ *'You don't seem to run across our old acquaintance, Smith, these days.' 'That's largely because I* ***take care not to.****'* ▫ *It wasn't that we* (as children) *were harshly treated. It was just that adults seemed to dislike us, and we feared them, and* ***took care to*** *maintain a low profile in front of them.* G

take the cash (in hand) and let the credit go (saying) put immediate financial or material advantage above other considerations, eg honour, fame, prestige, future well-being ▫ (source) *Ah,* ***take the Cash, and let the Credit go,****/Nor heed the rumble of a distant Drum!* THE RUBAIYAT OF OMAR KHAYAM (E FITZGERALD 1809-83) ▫ *'You practically wrote that book for him, yet your name doesn't appear anywhere, inside or out.' 'It's a work of no importance. I was quite content to* ***take the cash and let the credit go.****'* ▫ *People nowadays don't have too much confidence in rewards in heaven. They prefer to* ***take the cash in hand and let the credit go.***

take a chance/chances (on sth) [V + O pass] attempt to do things knowing that one may incur injury, loss, disgrace etc; take risks (qv); run a risk (of sth) (qv) **det:** no, (not) any; a lot of, too many ▫ *He said people should be ready to* ***take chances.*** *He said people shouldn't be afraid.* EHOW ▫ *Oxford's a wonderful driver. He'd have been prepared to* ***take chances*** *that no other driver would take.* PE ▫ *Johnnie thinks he's smart, but he's* ***taking*** *a lot of* ***chances.*** *He'll end up in court yet.* ▫ *The thieves* ***took a chance*** *on the owner of the house staying away all day—a chance that paid off handsomely.*

take etc the consequences (of sth) [V + O pass] accept the result(s) of error, folly etc **V:** take, ⚠ accept, suffer, face ▫ *I have to come out in the open and print my information. And* ***take the consequences*** *if I make a mistake.* PP ▫ *I'm sorry you feel bad, but if you will eat things you're not supposed to you have to* ***suffer the consequences of*** *your greed.* ▫ *I've had enough of your excuses. You pay what you owe by the end of this week or* ***accept the consequences.*** ▫ often with *should, must, have to.*

take the count [V + O] be (knocked) unconscious or helpless; be overcome or defeated (from boxing where the referee counts from one to ten when a boxer has been knocked down) **S:** fighter; politician, businessman ▫ *Jean-Jacques Servan-Schreiber has the resilience of those Russian dolls which when pushed over always bob up again. In September of last year he* ***took the count*** *in Bordeaux, having picked an election fight with the Prime Minister on the latter's home ground. Last Sunday, at Suresnes, he stood triumphant.* NS ▫ *But the extraordinary thing about Nixon, of course, is that though he* ***takes the count*** *of nine each time, he won't stay down.* L

(let sth) take its course [V + O] (let sth) happen, or be done, without interference **S:** fate, matters, the seasons, her grief, the conversation. **adj:** own, ordinary, natural, uninterrupted ▫ *The minds of a Government and a mighty corporation can be changed. But the steel workers have so far chosen to* ***let*** *fate* ***take its course*** *rather than use direct action.* ST ▫ *'I hope we don't have a long winter like last year's.' 'Long or short, it'll* ***take its*** *own* ***course.****'* ▫ *The bulk of investigative work has been done, and they say, therefore, that those detective reporters should sit back and* ***let*** *justice* ***take its course.*** L ▫ *It's economic permissiveness he's under fire for — that is, for* ***letting*** *the forces of the market-place* ***take their*** *natural and painful* ***course,*** *rather than intervening to try to put things right.* L ⇨ ⚠ run its course.

take a decision [V + O pass] decide about sth

□ *They had* ***taken the decision*** *without consulting me — which they had no right to do.* □ ***Decisions*** *to depart from the rules should not be* ***taken*** *lightly, nor should they be taken by individual police officers.* NS □ *First, this Bill blatantly provides that all European Community law and* ***decisions*** *already* ***taken****, or taken at any time in the future, automatically become the law of Britain, without due Parliamentary process.* ST □ often pass; n compound decision-taking.

take/get sb's drift/meaning [V + O] understand what sb means (even if this is indirectly, obscurely or inadequately expressed) □ *Oh, I* ***took her drift*** *all right, though I pretended not to. She's hoping her mother can come to us from hospital to convalesce, but I didn't want to commit myself to anything till I'd discussed it with you.* □ *'You don't want us to launch out at all?' 'Well,'—she was terribly embarrassed* (thinking he meant they should have another child) *—'not perhaps in that way.' The hated red began to stain her cheeks. 'In what way?' asked Harold, and then he* ***took her meaning*** *and her colour.* PW □ *I* ***get your drift*** *now, I think. If you mean by 'integrity' what I would call 'consistency' then we've been arguing at cross-purposes.*

take one's ease [V + O] relax, and enjoy (a period of) comfort and leisure □ *Not more than a dozen guests stood around,* ***taking their ease*** *and watching the latest arrivals.* PP □ *It's your dog, Elsie. Why should your father have to be walking it out on a cold night while you* ***take your ease*** *by the fire?*

take effect[1] [V + O] actually occur; be enforced or become law **S:** increase, levy; regulation, legislation. **A:** on May 1st; from now; when? □ *The price of paraffin is to go up by 10p a gallon,* ***taking effect*** *from midnight, 8th January.* □ *It's definitely been decided that the Upton branch will close down but I don't know yet when this is due to* ***take effect****.*

take effect[2] [V + O] have, produce, an intended or expected effect (on sb/sth) **S:** drug, anaesthetic; alcohol; spell □ *I'm going to give you a pain-killing injection. In a minute or two, when it* ***takes effect****, you'll feel much more comfortable.* □ *But the mixture of whisky and beer, coming as it did on an empty stomach, was beginning to* ***take effect****, and he sat with half-closed eyes, oblivious of their angry gestures and comments.* HD □ *Braking, I nearly sent Lesley through the wind-screen. In my own car I was accustomed to a full inch of play on the pedal before the brakes* ***took effect.***

take a firm etc line [V + O pass] adopt a firm etc method of dealing with sb, a matter or situation **adj:** firm, strong, conciliatory; similar, different □ *School regulations still included the wearing of a uniform and the headmaster* ***took a*** *very firm* ***line*** *on this.* RT □ *'I've no use for that kind of woman,' Harold said. 'If he had to have her around, he should have* ***taken a*** *strong* ***line*** *with her from the first. Thank goodness, darling, you don't go on like that.'* PW □ *In the coal-producing member countries, governments have had to take special measures to assist that industry and the Commission have adopted a sympathetic attitude. We can expect them to* ***take a*** *similar* ***line*** *on measures to assist the industry here.* SC □ *'I don't like you going behind my back like that,' she began. Then she remembered Spenser, who was standing solidly on the carpet, taking it all in, appraising. 'But of course,' Helen added swiftly, and her body relaxed a little as she decided* ***what line*** *to* ***take****, 'since it is all settled, I naturally could not be more delighted.'* AITC

take first/second place [V + O pass] be the most/less important priority amongst one's duties, loyalties, interests, affections etc **A:** with my mother; in her affections, in their list of priorities □ *Her* (my mother's) *method of dealing with the problem was to impose rigid discipline on the family and thus have time for her duties in the parish or diocese — duties which* ***took first place****.* MFM □ *He's set his mind on defining 'consanguinity' and there's no shifting him. Everything else has to* ***take second place*** *when he's in this mood.* ART □ *Finn is a humble and self-effacing person and so automatically* ***takes second place****. When we are short of beds it is always Finn who sleeps on the floor, and this seems thoroughly natural.* UTN □ take second place = 'not take first place'—a further extended scale to third etc place is not implied.

take the floor [V + O pass] rise to address a meeting □ *There was some dispute with the anti-semitic doctors on the staff, as a result of which Schnitzler's chief adversary* ***took the floor*** *at a meeting and proposed a vote of no-confidence in him.* NS □ *Almeyda, opening the Friday afternoon session of the United Nations Conference on Trade and Development here in Santiago, invited the former American Defence Secretary, Robert McNamara, to* ***take the floor****.* NS ⇨ ⚠ hold the floor.

take fright/alarm [V + O] become frightened □ *They shot at another of our agents in the street and he's* ***taken fright****. A third's gone underground.* OMIH □ *Perish the thought that Scotland with so many glorious links with Europe should* ***take fright*** *at the prospect of moving in with the Six* (countries of the EEC). SC □ *Over seven hundred animals quietly queued up to drink and* ***took alarm*** *only when flocks of Quelea finches and sandgrouse gave warning of the approach of predators, man or lion.* NSC

take sth hard/lightly [V + O + A pass] be greatly/little grieved, disturbed, disappointed or inconvenienced by sth **O:** it; his wife's death, her dismissal, the additional burdens; failing his exam. **adv mod:** (much) too, so, very □ *Try not to* ***take*** *it too* ***hard*** *if you don't get anywhere* (with Jenny). *After all, there are plenty of fish in the sea, aren't there?* TGLY □ *She* ***took*** *everything too* ***hard****, that was the trouble, her imagination was fearsome.* TSMP □ *You must have plenty of money that you can* ***take*** *losing £50 so* ***lightly****.* □ take sth hard often preceded by *try not to, (please) don't, I hope you won't, I'm afraid he will* and similar expressions meant to comfort or forewarn sb. ⇨ ⚠ take sb/sth seriously/lightly.

take a hint [V + O pass] understand and do what has been indirectly suggested □ *'I don't know what you're talking about,' he muttered, in a tone that was clearly intended to put an end to the discussion. But Dr Bottwink seemed incapable of* ***taking a hint****.* EM □ *She wanted to be dressed right for the part, and once or twice she* *had asked him, 'Do you like me in this?', hoping he would* ***take the hint*** *and so describe her.* PW □ *She yawned and stretched her arms. 'Time for me to go,' said Peter. 'I can* ***take a hint****.'* □ *I think he'll move out. I'm sure* ***the hint*** *has been* ***taken****.* □ often preceded by modals or by phrases expressing (in)ability eg *can/can't, not seem able to, be capable of*; cf *I thought he would never* ***take the hint****.* ⇨ drop a hint.

(you can) take etc a horse to the water, but you can't make him drink (saying) giving sb the opportunity to do sth becomes useless if he is not willing **V:** take, ⚠ lead, bring □ *'I'm not pleased with her,' said Dr Ford. 'I have suggested that she should go into the Barchester General* (Hospital) *for a good overhaul and a rest. But it's one thing to* ***take a horse to the water*** *and another to* ***make her drink****.'* WDM □ *New College remained largely the haunt of the well-to-do, their sons and their sons' sons, and the desire or ability to learn was a minor consideration. Even today* ***you can take a*** *dead* ***horse to the water, but you can't make him drink****.* L □ (NONCE) *The key to every dispute, he insists, lies in the personalities involved, in getting determined men into amicable agreement. Heron thinks it will be some time before* ***the*** *trade union* ***carthorse can be made to drink*** *Carr's bitter potion.* OBS

take the initiative [V + O pass] be the first person, group etc to act in an undertaking that involves another or others; make an opponent adjust to, or defend himself against, one's own moves □ *He was very sympathetic but he said I placed him in a constitutional difficulty; if he* ***took the initiative*** *and asked the local authority to grant a licence in my particular case,...* MFM □ *There is an imaginary line in draughts, as every player knows, that crosses the board diagonally from corner to corner. It is the line of defence. Whoever gains control of that line* ***takes the initiative****.* OMIH □ *Whitehall is still on the defensive, preferring to react to whatever might emerge from Brussels, or other EEC capitals come to that, rather than* ***take initiatives*** *of its own.* NS □ occas take an initiative, take initiatives.

take it (informal) tolerate or withstand, hardship, pain, stress, criticism, contempt etc **modal:** can, be able to, have to □ *To go on living for me is to go on learning about life — and everything that makes life. Wanting to go on learning makes one vulnerable, of course; you are always exposing yourself to risk. I hope I can* ***take it****.* OBS □ *'Well, there's no need to provoke her, is there?' she said. 'Why, it's only a bit of fun — she can't* ***take it****, that's all; not so well as she can dish it out to the kids.'* TT □ *It means every time I write a play the army takes a caning. It isn't terribly fair. But at the same time it's honest; and they're tough enough to* ***take it****.* G □ *He's a sloppy, irritating bastard, but he's got a big heart. You can forgive somebody almost anything for that. He's had to learn how to* ***take it****, and he knows how to hand it out.* LBA □ preceded by modal or by *be man/strong enough to, know/learn how to.*

take it (that) assume (that) □ *And now this fog! The English climate is certainly unpredictable. I* ***take it that*** *we are still cut off from the outside world?* EM □ *I* ***take it*** *your mother has gone to America, or you wouldn't be in London.* AITC □ *If you walk in with enough confidence people will* ***take it that*** *you have a right to do so.* □ *You'll be joining us later, I* ***take it****?*

take it easy (informal) go, or do, sth (more) slowly; not become (so) flustered, angered, excited etc □ *'If you leave at 10 you should get there by midday all right.' 'I'd rather leave earlier and* ***take it easy****.'* □ *Then his ears began to fill with the phantom buzzing of planes. He kept looking up* (as he climbed) *and fell once, cutting himself. 'Don't be a fool.* ***Take it easy****. There's no point in looking up because you can do nothing to attract attention.'* PM □ *You make a mistake in answering him back, though, mate. He doesn't like that, old Frank doesn't. Just* ***take it easy****. He'll soon lay off you then.* AITC □ MYRA: *There's such satisfaction in behaving well. Not that one's more subtle forms of insult don't escape them entirely.* (She laughs shrilly, almost breaks down.) MILLY (quiet and shrewd): *Myra, love, you'd better* ***take it easy****.* EHOW □ often imper.

take it etc easy (informal) live, or spend a period of time, in a relaxed or restful way **O:** it, ⚠ life, things □ *Children need excitement and activity on holiday as much as adults need to* ***take it easy****.* ST □ PAMELA: *Why not come riding with me then?* STANLEY: *No—not today. I—just want to* ***take things easy*** *today.* FFE □ *Carson had looked a good thing for the championship ever since the day late last year that Lester Piggott said that he would be* ***taking life*** *much* ***easier*** *in future.* SC

take it or leave it [v + v non-rev] (informal) accept or reject sb/sth offered, no other choice being allowed or possible □ *Malouel bought the* (model of a) *shrine, but would not pay a centime more than twenty-five francs. Daniel cursed him. He danced with rage. '****Take it or leave it****,' Malouel said. 'It's an off-season.'* US □ *'What this station will need,' Hawthorne said, 'is someone who speaks Spanish.' 'She speaks French.' 'I said Spanish.' A file drawer slammed shut. '****Take it or leave it****,' Miss Jenkinson said.* OMIH □ *...old-guard (and sometimes young-guard) doctors who loathe the idea of anyone interfering with the almost divine right of the profession to practise a* ***take-it-or-leave-it*** *philosophy on its patients.* OBS □ attrib use *a* ***take-it-or-leave-it*** *attitude.*

take a joke [V + O] accept with good humour teasing, facetious remarks, playful or disconcerting tricks, etc **modal:** can, can't, could(n't), be able to □ *He danced and rode well; and was courteous to ladies; he could* ***take a joke****, and make one.* NS □ *Young Wormersly in the sales department has written a humorous ditty about the sales director to the tune of 'I Who Have Nothing', and believes — quite erroneously — that the sales director can* ***take a joke****.* TVT □ preceded by modal or by *learn to, know how to.* ⇨ ⚠ (not) see the joke.

take the King's/Queen's shilling [V + O pass] enlist as a regular in one of the armed forces (formerly, receipt of a shilling from a recruiting officer made the contract binding) □ *Tired of monotonous work as a farm labourer he* ***took the Queen's shilling*** *and his known history begins with the Boer War.*

take a knock [V + O] suffer a disappointment or a set-back **S:** industry, agriculture; production, output; hopes, expectations. **adj:** bad; severe, sharp, hard □ *Industry* ***took a*** *bad* ***knock*** *in the Cultural Revolution. China was very short of raw materials because of trouble in the mines and on the railways.* OBS □ *The British Government's hope of wooing back Ulster Catholics to cheerful conformity* ***took another knock*** *yesterday from two of Northern Ireland's most thoughtful Catholic politicians.* ST □ *He certainly* ***took a knock*** *when he wasn't re-elected, but he's probably done better for himself in business than he would have in politics.* □ *You must be able to* ***take*** *hard* ***knocks*** *in this business.*

take leave to doubt etc it etc (claim a right to) doubt the truth of sth stated or suggested **Inf:** to doubt, ⚠ to question, to query. **O:** it, that; the story; whether he will □ *But the point of much recent work is that in essence nothing has changed since the Butler Education Act of 1944. I* ***take leave to doubt this****, but...* L □ *Even if a solid fuel heating system were more economical to run—* ***which I take leave to question*** *anyway—we simply don't have storage space.* □ usu first person.

take life[1] [V + O pass] (formal) kill sb **det:** one's (own), another's, a □ *Some people adopt a vegetarian diet because they believe it to be more health-giving, and some from an aversion to* ***taking life****.* □ *And it seems to have been this idealism, coupled with ill-health and depression, that finally brought him to* ***take*** *his own* ***life****.* L □ *Without rivals, she argued wildly, there could be no danger. Her words suggested to Henry that no* ***life*** *was too sacred to be* ***taken****.* WI

take life[2] [V + O] (begin to) acquire positive form, identity, significance; become animated, interesting; come alive (qv); come to life (Vol 1) (qv) **S:** sculpture, language, details; performance, debate, party □ *It was fascinating to watch the lump of clay* ***take life*** *beneath the sculptor's hands.* □ *Presently, that smudge in the distance* ***took life*** *in the shape of a horse and rider pounding along in a cloud of red dust.* □ *Usually a rousing piece, on this recording it never really* ***takes life****.* ⇨ ⚠ bring to life (Vol 1).

take the long view reach decisions, or form opinions, taking into account future developments □ *Only humiliations seemed left, but even here Smith* ***took a long view****, foreseeing as he did the eventual dominance of America.* SC □ *In this situation it is common to say that nothing can be done until law and order are restored. But intransigence in Northern Ireland on both sides makes it necesary to* ***take the long view****.* SC □ *'It would pay you to buy this house if it suits you.' '****In the long view****, yes. But in our present circumstances £120 a month rent is possible and £230 mortgage is not.'* □ variant in the long view.

take etc a lot of stick [possess] (informal) suffer a lot of (unfair) criticism, blame, punishment, exposure to physical risk **V:** take, ⚠ get; give sb. **det:** a lot of, a good/great deal of, a fair amount of, more than enough □ *Yet her native intelligence was often patronised by cultural superiors who treated her humility as synonymous with stupidity. She* ***took a great deal of stick*** *at the Actor's Studio and continued, humbly, to believe that they always knew better than she did.* RT □ (football) *The central striker today must be more adaptable, but must still* ***take a lot of stick*** *without anything like the same scoring opportunities or rewards as before.* TVT □ *Why did it have to happen to her? That woman has* ***taken more stick*** *in the last two years than anyone could deserve.* □ *'I had about 1,000 National Service men go through their training with me,' he said. 'They always seemed so cheerful in spite of all the "****stick****" they* ***took****.'* TVT □ *I'm going to meet my sister at Barker's and she won't half* ***give*** *me* ***stick*** *if I'm delayed.* AITC

take etc sb's measure [possess] know, or estimate fairly accurately, sb's character, importance or abilities **V:** take, ⚠ have, get, □ *Did* (= should) *I stand to attention and ask for the honour of the hand of his daughter? Or did I just make some sort of joke about adding Nikki to my income-tax? Either approach would not only make me look foolish but—as I hadn't* ***taken the measure of*** *the Commander yet—might land me in the Thames.* DIL □ *He detested Aneurin Bevan, largely because Bevan had* ***got his measure*** *and once remarked that he was not a man with whom one should go shooting tigers.* L.

take one's medicine [V + O pass] submit to sth unpleasant □ *When the other boys were caught he owned up and* ***took his medicine*** *with the rest of them.* □ *I think that if we felt that price increases were to affect everybody equally, then most of us would be prepared to* ***take our medicine*** *without squealing.* □ take one's medicine like a man = 'accept physical punishment without complaining or flinching'.

take occasion to do sth [V + O] (formal) make use of a suitable time or situation in order to do sth □ *Marshal Tito delivered a report on the tasks before the alliance in regard to the further development of Socialism in Yugoslavia, but he* ***took occasion to*** *make some references to international affairs.* SC ⇨ ⚠ have etc occasion to do sth.

take my tip [V + O pass] accept my advice □ *Pete is always dreaming up some money-making scheme or other.* ***Take my tip*** *and have nothing to do with them.* □ *It's easy to get carried away at auction sales. You should* ***take a tip from me*** *and carry only as much money as you mean to spend.* □ often imper; variant take a tip from me.

take one look (at sb/sth) [V + O] do no more than look (at sb/sth) for an immediate result □ *I ran into Anna through Sadie, and she* ***took one look****. At first she pursued me. She stopped doing everything else and simply pursued me.* UTN □ *'If he wants an old van, I'll sell him mine for £200.' 'You're an optimist! If he had any sense he'd* ***take one look at*** *it and tell you to get lost.'* □ *The third applicant was the permanently discontented type. You had only to* ***take one look*** *to see that.*

take sth/sb or leave sth/sb take (esp consume) or do without sth, with indifference or equanimity **O:** it, parties; him, Mike; smoking □ *Young people often start experimenting with one of the more innocuous drugs thinking they can* ***take or leave*** *the effects.* □ *The best kind of relationship to have with a neighbour is one where you can* ***take or leave*** *each other without offence.* □ *Yet Mark, I knew, didn't care much for the bright lights, the smarty life; he* ***took or left*** *it.* YWT. □ pron O (*him, it, them, us*) usu repeated after leave; patterns with n O are *I can* ***take***

smoking ***or leave*** *it* or *I can* ***take or leave*** *smoking.*

take pains [V + O pass] be very careful; involve oneself in a great deal of work or trouble **det/adj:** such, (not) many, great, endless. **A:** over her garden, over preparing a meal; to explain sth clearly, to make the guests comfortable; in getting his facts right, in cleaning the carpet. □ *Her garden is her great passion — she* ***takes*** *more* ***pains*** *over it than she does over bringing up her children.* □ *Instead of falling on* (the food) *with joy, as we had expected, the beasts seemed positively afraid of the worms, caterpillars, and beetles that we had* ***taken*** *such* ***pains*** *to collect.* DF □ (golf) *In order to swing a carefully-designed clubhead quietly and consistently along a reasonably straight and very short path, endless* ***pains*** *are* ***taken***. SC □ *In writing, as well as in research, he was a perfectionist; his* ***painstaking*** *efforts in committing himself to print consumed much time, which he did not always possess.* NS □ adj compound painstaking.

take/grab a pew [V + O] (informal) sit down □ *He put a hand on Wormold's shoulder and pushed him through the door. '****Take a pew****, old man,' the stranger said, 'while I turn on a tap.'* OMIH □ *'Do* ***take a pew*** *if you can find room, won't you?' It was difficult, if not impossible* (the chairs being covered with household articles). DBM □ *'Where are the others?' 'Gone to* ***grab a pew*** *before the bar fills up. I said we'd bring over the drinks.'* □ rather dated middle-class usage; usu imper; always sing.

take/have one's pick [possess] choose; select **A:** from the objects on display; of half a dozen suitors □ (advertisement) *Ask your chemist for the 'Spinet', and* ***take your pick*** *from eight romantic shades.* H □ *Three pretexts or justifications (you can* ***take your pick****) have been presented to Mrs Thatcher.* NS □ *The girls were mad for Tom when he was a young man and why, when he could have* ***had his pick*** *of so many, he should have married my Aunt Minnie I never could tell.*

take place [V + O] happen; occur **S:** the sports meeting, an interview; change, improvement, the action. **A:** on Feb 16th; in a London hotel; long ago, soon □ *Also last week the United States announced that its first nuclear test since October 1958 would* ***take place*** *next year in New Mexico.* OBS □ *But even if a similar creation of life did* ***take place*** *on any other planet, Pringle thinks it would not have developed beyond the earliest, simple forms.* TO □ *Both believed all their lives (and so, apparently, did Marx) that no revolution was justified which was not the work of the people for whose benefit it was supposed to* ***take place***. NS □ *...alleged that intimacy (=* sexual relations) *had* ***taken place*** *between his wife and the butler on several occasions.*

take the plunge [V + O] (informal) finally do sth which one has been undecided, or hesitant, about (esp get married or propose marriage) □ *The question is whether I'm good enough to make a living at it. I think I am and so does my wife. If I* ***take the plunge*** *and do it, Valerie will give me her support.* TVT □ *Members of Parliament have been reluctant to let the cameras and microphones in on Parliamentary debates. But my guess is that when the issue is debated again, very shortly, the mood will have tipped in favour of* ***taking the plunge***. L □ *Fred and I had been going together for over two years before he asked me to marry him. I thought he was never going to* ***take the plunge***.

take etc sb's point [V + O pass] understand and appreciate (though not necessarily agree with) sb's reasons or argument **V:** take, ⚠ get, see. **det:** sb's; the, this, that □ *'But here I am, telling you—I am sorry.' 'No, no,' he said, 'no need at all. I* ***take your point****, which seems, if you'll forgive me, that Mr Golding relies too much on the one to the, er, detriment of other aspects.'* TT □ *'It seems to me hard to talk about a bourgeois revolution if it's bourgeois outsiders trying to overthrow established bourgeois.' 'I tried to answer some of that in my last comment but obviously* ***the point*** *wasn't* ***taken***.*'* L □ *Andrew Boyle, Editor, 'World at One' and 'PM' replies:* ***Point taken***. *But a reminder is necessary.* RT □ *Roman patiently explained to the young actresses that there was no need to* thunder *Macbeth like the conventional stage gorgon. They all nodded, and proceeded to thunder* quietly. *Only Francesca Annis* ***got the point*** *and worked on Macbeth like a tearful, disappointed little girl.* ST □ ALISON: *He made up his mind to marry me.* (My parents) *did just about everything they could think of to stop us.* HELENA: *Yes, it wasn't a very pleasant business. But you can* ***see their point***. LBA □ point (already) taken short reply to, or comment on, argument or recommendation. ⇨ ⚠ make one's point; miss the point (of sth).

take pot-luck [V + O] (informal) accept, share, whatever meal is prepared, whatever commodity, entertainment or activity is available at a particular place or time (no choice or alternative being offered) □ *Drop in any evening and* ***take pot-luck***. *We usually eat between 6 and 7.* □ *'I've mislaid the Film Society programme. I can't say I feel like driving fifteen miles to* ***take pot-luck***.*' 'Phone Jack then. He'll be able to tell you what's on.'*

take a powder [V + O] (slang) leave quickly to escape danger, unwanted company, etc □ *'Do me a favour, Baxter,' said Robert, jigging the cup up and down in his hand. 'Scrub off.* ***Take a powder***.*'* CON □ *He's not the first, and won't be the last, to* ***take a powder*** *after getting a young woman pregnant.* □ *'We'll have a story ready in case anyone comes by and asks what we're doing.' 'No fear. If anyone comes by that's when I* ***take a powder***.*'* □ probably a translation (in part) of the French *prendre de la poudre d'escampette* = 'take to one's heels'.

take the rap [V + O] (informal) (be made to) accept the blame and/or penalty for a mistake, misdemeanour, crime etc □ *Years ago ministers* (in government departments) *accepted the blame for mistakes and errors made by their officials. The answerable minister simply* ***took the rap*** *and left.* NS □ *'I don't want your friend and I don't want his cheques.' 'Ah, now, don't be that way, Mr Mazzolini,' Tillie said coaxingly. 'He's all right, and if his cheque isn't, I'll* ***take the rap***.*'* PE □ *I'd confess if I thought someone else was going to have to* ***take the rap*** *for what I had done.*

take risks [V + O pass] knowingly risk the possibility of death, injury, loss etc; take a chance/chances (qv); run a risk (of sth) (qv) **det:** (not) any, no; a lot of, too many □ *The Eskimos **take risks** with their lives, of course, just because they live in such a difficult and hostile environment, but the whole concept of going out to look for an adventure is totally alien to them.* OBS □ *You mean you've never seen this house you've bought? Aren't you **taking** rather **a risk**?* □ *Abdullah was inclined to **take** more **risks** than the other crew members.* L □ *The Labour Party and several members of his own party have in effect served notice on the Prime Minister that they will vote against any terms whatever if they are presented to Parliament before the summer recess. Does he **take the risk** of a defeat? Or wait until the autumn?* NS

take/strike root [V + O] grow roots; (fig) become rooted or firmly fixed **S:** seeds; the idea, his words. **A:** in the soil, in their minds □ *And experience proves that such an institution will die. It is choked by its own perfection. It cannot **take root** for lack of soil.* PL □ *You seem to have given them good advice. I only hope your words of wisdom will **take root**.* □ *It's a mistake to believe that superstitions **strike root** only in ignorant minds.* □ strike root rare.

take sb/sth seriously/lightly [V + O + A pass] have a serious or respectful/flippant or careless attitude towards sb/sth **O:** me, such people; ghosts; his studies, life, the threat, his prophecies. **adv mod:** (much) too, very, more, less, so □ *He was an earnest person, who always appeared to **take** life too **seriously**, though he was capable of being tempted into some fun from time to time.* ST □ *I was what was termed an orderly. My tasks were simple. I noticed with interest that none of them* (ie the nurses) ***took** me **seriously** as a male.* UTN □ *As for the Calcutta Cup game, Dickinson is well aware of the danger of Scottish complacency. 'It's the fact that we are going for a fourth win in a row over England that makes it important for us not to **take** them **lightly**.'* RT □ *Reading to his four children is a pleasure he can only enjoy three nights a week when he isn't on duty in the studio, but it's a job he doesn't **take lightly**.* TVT □ *The article on the cosmic ray threat is not to be **taken** too **seriously**.* ⇨ ⚠ take sth hard/lightly.

take shape [V + O] acquire, or be given, a recognizable or ordered form **S:** the garden, his novel; the new project, a plan □ *Two miles ahead outside Munich the site is beginning to **take shape**.* OBS □ *Once on shore and firmly established, I began to get this strategy working and soon it began to **take shape**.* MFM □ *The squirrel decided that the quickest method would be to jump from the porthole on to the Captain's shoulder. I could see this plan **taking shape** in the little brute's head.* BB □ *I would like to see some of your good resolutions **take** concrete **shape**.*

take sb's side [V + O] support sb against another in a fight, argument or difference of opinion □ *'I heard what you said to George, and I think you should be ashamed.' 'Eh—? What —?' demanded Mr Early in a tone of stupefaction. 'Are you **taking his side**?'* PE □ *Peter Lawford plays a gentleman cracksman who specialises in stealing jewels and ladies' hearts. Suspected of being the murderer, he decides to **take the side of** the law for once, and help find the real culprit.* TVT ⇨ ⚠ next entry.

take sides [V + O] favour or support a person or a group in a dispute or debate **A:** with/against sb; in sth □ *If she **took sides** in their* (ie her two children's) *disputes, as she sometimes did, they both resented it.* PW □ *'It's my job to know what goes on in Havana,' said Captain Segura, 'not to **take sides** or to give information.'* OMIH □ *'I don't like the implication of some of your questions — I thought you were on my side.' 'It's not a question of **taking sides** with anyone but of establishing the facts.'* ⇨ ⚠ previous entry.

take silk [V + O] (legal) be appointed King's/Queen's Counsel (KC/QC) and have the right to wear a silk instead of a stiff gown in court □ *The judge is the Hon. Mr Justice Mais, a Manchester barrister who did not **take silk** but became an expert in ecclesiastical law (he has been Chancellor of three dioceses).* NS □ expression applies to England and Wales only.

take some beating (informal) be difficult to improve on (sth specified) **det:** some, a bit of, a lot of □ *For sheer undiluted courage the story of Mrs Peggy Johns, of Surbiton, Surrey, **takes some beating**.* ST □ *As an example of what not to say to a prospective client, that remark would **take a bit of beating**.* □ *Signor Rigoletto said that English country life **took a lot of beating** and he would like to see how the system worked.* ⇨ ⚠ take a beating etc.

take some doing be difficult to perform or accomplish **det:** some, a bit of, a lot of □ *. . .so I left the country on my own; that **takes some doing**, eh? A woman starting life again all on her own, and I was pregnant, seven months gone.* DPM □ *It doesn't seem to have been a great disadvantage to you, being famous. People have accepted you for yourself; this must have **taken some doing**.* L □ SANDY: *Bits of speeches—she smuggled a tape recorder into the House* (ie of Commons). *That **took a bit of doing**.* TONY: *Illegal, of course.* EHOW □ *Plenty of char* (a species of freshwater game fish) *in these lakes but they swim deep and **take a lot of catching**.* ST □ *An old gramophone record of one of those songs would **take a bit of finding**.* □ *-ing* form of a specific v may be substituted for doing, as shown.

take a step [V + O pass] act in a particular way **det:** a, the; this, that; another, such a □ *It was not just to confound their enemies that the company **took this step**. At the back of its mind was the very real fear that if the wine turned out not to be genuine it would face prosecution.* ST □ *'I reported it to the police, sir.' 'You had no right to **take such a step** without first consulting me.'*

take steps (to do sth) [V + O pass] act (in order to achieve a desired result) □ *Nor was I Dr Gruber, who would have **taken steps to** prevent the onset of such affliction.* AH □ *After a few months I came to the conclusion that drastic **steps** would have to be **taken** if we were to organise any sort of defence at all in Western Europe.* MFM

take the strain [V + O pass] endure a force, weight, pressure **S:** guide, climber; rope, chain; economy □ *When lifting weights, the back, legs and shoulders should all **take the strain** rather* *than one set of muscles.* ▫ *We needed 'security'. To obtain this it would be necessary to get our man-power, our production, and our mobilisation plans so organised that the nation could* ***take the strain*** *efficiently and quickly in an emergency.* MFM

take thought [V + O] think; (esp) concentrate one's attention on sth specific **det:** no, (not) any, little, some. **A:** how to do it; whether one is justified; for others. ▫ (source) ***Take*** *therefore no* ***thought*** *for the morrow, for the morrow shall* ***take thought*** *for the things of itself.* MATTHEW VI 34 ▫ *It's difficult to know how far we can alter our styles by* ***taking thought****. To a great extent our styles are us and we had best make the best of them.* L

take time (to do sth/doing sth) [V + O] extend over a (relatively) long period of time ▫ *It was merely a matter of shock to the nerve centres. Such a thing sometimes* ***took time to*** *mend. The important thing was not to worry.* DC ▫ *The safest procedure would be to get written authority from the London office but that* ***takes time*** *coming — during which this fellow may find another buyer.*

take one's time [V + O] not hurry **A:** to do sth; over sth; (in) doing sth ▫ *It's an important decision for you, my dear, so* ***take your time*** *to think it over.* ▫ *He can write as neatly and legibly as the next person if he* ***takes his time*** *over it.*

take the trouble to do sth [V + O pass] devote time and energy, have sufficient interest or concern to do sth **det/adj:** the, a lot of, a little, no end of; considerable, endless, great ▫ *Some of those who live in these earthquake-prone areas have* ***taken*** *a great deal of* ***trouble to*** *construct houses that will resist damage by earthquake waves.* NSC ▫ *'Have one* (= a drink) *with me,' said Simons, thus revealing his hand a little further. It showed that he was willing to* ***take*** *a little* ***trouble to*** *influence Charles.* HD ▫ *Chesterton had noted that the house, garden and slammed front door, which is seen as a middle class privilege, is exactly what any working-class man would like — if only anyone* ***took the trouble to*** *ask him.* OBS ▫ *His parents had* ***gone to*** *no end of* ***trouble to*** *give him a wonderful twenty-first birthday party.* ▫ variant go to the trouble to do/of doing sth.

take a tumble [V + O] (informal) fall; (fig) diminish sharply or suddenly in value, influence, credibility etc ▫ *Anyone can learn to skate. The thing is not to be frightened of* ***taking a tumble*** *occasionally.* ▫ *It hurt him bitterly to have to apologize to this man who drank and came home with lipstick on the side of his mouth. Virtue, which should have been triumphant, had* ***taken a*** *bad* ***tumble****.* PE ▫ *With increasing overheads to be met, dividends are bound to* ***take a tumble****.*

take (it in) turns (to do sth) share a task, duty etc ▫ *We* ***take it in turns****, once a fortnight, my brother and me,* ***to*** *give the place a thorough going over.* TC ▫ *If you can't agree, you'll have to* ***take turns to*** *sleep in the top bunk. Now, no more argument.*

take umbrage (at sth) [V + O] be offended (by sth) ▫ *Are you surprised that she* ***took umbrage****? Didn't you realise that it was her husband you'd described as a cross between a shark and a limpet?* ▫ *It's impossible to have a normal conversation with him — he* ***takes umbrage at*** *every third thing you say to him.*

take the view that [V + O] consider that ▫ *Yet some engineers* ***take the view that*** *since so much effort has been put into making AGR work it would be sensible in the short term to continue the same line rather than start afresh.* ST ▫ *I used to believe that people brought most of their troubles on themselves but now I* ***take a different view****.* ▫ variant take another, a different, the opposite etc view.

take wing [V + O] rise in flight; (fig) become active, lively, interesting; move on or away, disappear, swiftly **S:** bird; production, plot; one's thoughts; time, the hours, days ▫ *Flocks of guira cuckoos would wait until the lumbering car was within six feet of them, and then they would* ***take wing*** *and stream off like a flock of brown-paper darts.* DF ▫ *This duo* (ie writer and producer) *was sadly disappointing. Only when it came to Byron's incestuous relationship with Augusta Leigh did Mr Cleverdon's generous two hours* ***take wing****.* ST ▫ *I didn't realise it was so late. It's extraordinary how the hours* ***take wing*** *when you're enjoying yourself.* ▫ *'You get a good wage — what on earth do you* do *with your money?' 'I don't know, it just seems to* ***take wing****.'*

a tale of woe sb's account of his misfortunes, difficulties, causes for complaint, etc; an instance of any one of these ▫ (the fishermen lose their hook and line) *We returned to the camp with* ***our tale of woe*** *and the fish we had caught before the mishap.* BM ▫ *Before, as a lecturer, I was bombarded by people expressing their difficulties with some form of Church authority. They had* ***tales of woe*** *and ecclesiastical horror stories. None of that happens any more.* ST ▫ often facetious or derogatory, implying self-pity.

talk business etc [V + O] discuss, have a conversation about, business affairs, etc **n:** business, politics, religion, golf, kids and housekeeping ▫ *'I've got to dine with a man in Downhaven.' 'Nasty wretch, why didn't he ask me?' said Isabel. 'We shall only be* ***talking business****. You wouldn't be interested.'* PW ▫ *'Where was Hasselbacher born?' 'Berlin, I think.' 'Sympathies East or West?' 'We never* ***talk politics****.'* OMIH ▫ *I leaned back against the deep cushions, letting the atmosphere of luxury rub against me like a cat. Johnny* ***talked cars*** *with George; he was, of course, going to buy one soon.* RATT

talk (a load/lot of) cock etc [V + O pass] say false or pretentious things (often on a particular occasion) **n:** (taboo) cock; ⚠ (informal) nonsense, garbage, codswollop, rubbish, tripe, rot ▫ *'You ought to rest yourself. To keep them healthy and good to look upon, that's what God gave us bodies for.' 'You do* ***talk cock****, Frank, don't you?' said Vin Salad in his refined drawl.* ASA ▫ *I* ***talked a lot of cock****, you know, about her — Earth Mother and all that. She's only a cheap crook, really.* HAA ▫ *He gate-crashed startled undergraduates at breakfast, haranguing them on 'the hatred of Germans in Eastern Europe and the inevitability of war'. (I thought the fellow was* ***talking rot****.)* NS ▫ *The pundits change their minds every two or three* *years anyway. I bet there's been more* ***rubbish talked*** *about teaching methods than any other subject under the sun.* □ talk rot dated middle-class usage.

(don't) talk daft (don't) talk foolishly □ JENNY: *Mother reckons some people get indigestion so bad that it go through their stomach to the back.* BEATIE: ***Don't talk daft!*** R □ *'If I'm such a nuisance it's time I moved out of here.' 'You're* ***talking daft****, dad. Where would you go? And nobody's wanting you to move out.'* □ non-standard.

talk like a Dutch uncle talk etc seriously and reprovingly **V:** talk (to sb), lecture, admonish, sb; behave, act □ *Stop* ***talking*** *to me* ***like a Dutch uncle*** *about my duty to my family, my school and my country.* □ *Marie's good at keeping her brothers in order. You should hear her* ***lecturing*** *them* ***like a Dutch uncle*** *when they do something wrong.*

talk of the devil (and he appears) (saying) comment on the unexpected presence or arrival of sb just mentioned □ *'Dr Hasselbacher!' Wormold called to him. 'Oh, it's you, Mr Wormold. I was just thinking of you.* ***Talk of the devil****,' he said, making a joke of it, but Wormold could have sworn that the devil had scared him.* OMIH □ *Dusty would be first into the staffroom, as usual, being next door, but what wasn't on the cards was* (him) *putting the kettle on. Steve shoved in the door — and* ***talk of the devil****, there was Dusty at work on the kettle.* TT □ *'Well, well,' said Alice, welcoming him in, '****talk of the devil and he****'s sure to* ***appear****. I was just wondering if you'd be up here for Easter.'*

the talk of the town [Comp (NP)] sb/sth that is the subject, temporarily, of keen local interest **V:** ⚠ be, become; make sth □ *Frank Stella's show at the Hayward Gallery last year was not exactly* ***the talk of the town****. In terms of attendance, our silent majority returned a wordless 'No'.* ST □ (NONCE) *There is the plain speaker who tells his immediate superior that the affair he is having with his secretary is* ***the talk of the office*** *and that he had better be careful.* TVT

talk posh etc (informal) have, or affect, the type of speech that is used by the upper class **adv:** posh, ⚠ well-off, la-di-da □ *'They' are 'the people at the top', 'the higher-ups', the people who give you the dole, call you up, tell you to go to war, fine you, '****talk posh****', 'are all twisters really'.* L □ *Leddersford is a place where they don't like people who put on airs. To speak standard English is in itself suspect; they call it* ***talking well-off****.* RATT

talk sense [V + O pass] talk sensibly; say sth that is correct, relevant, suitable, more acceptable □ *The worst of being 87-88 is that I never can be quite sure whether I am* ***talking sense*** *or old man's drivel.* MFM □ *It was, he felt, too much to expect that she would* ***talk sense*** *about him* (as an author)*, since he did not write for idiot minds like hers.* US □ *'Well, if you want an exciting holiday, instead of lying on a beach for a fortnight in the sun, why don't you go to Greenland?' 'Ah! Now you're* ***talking sense****!'*

talk shop [V + O] discuss (with colleagues) matters connected with one's trade or profession (often in circumstances when general conversation might be more suitable, eg in the presence of others who are not interested) □ *'Well, it's no good trying to cross-examine Julius* (a Cabinet Minister) *about the British constitution,' said Camilla firmly. 'He hates* ***talking shop*** *anyhow.'* EM □ (a doctor) *Also, a tea break with the nurses is immensely valuable. We always* ***talk shop****. It's the only real chance we get to chat about our patients.* NS

talk etc till/until one is black/blue in the face talk etc as much, hard, long, often as is possible or one has strength for (usu with the implication that this is without result or the desired effect) **modal:** can, may, might. **V:** talk, complain, argue, object; try; search □ *The employers may be listening to what the negotiators are saying, but they're also constantly looking over your shoulder to see if there's a unified workforce behind you. Without this support you could* ***talk until you're blue in the face*** *and get nowhere.* RT □ *You may* ***write poetry until you're black in the face****, but unless you're extremely lucky or hit the fancy of a great number of the reading public, you can't make a living outright from poetry.* L □ *'When they pick up a piece of coal with their fancy tongs in Bournemouth, do they ever wonder how it got there?' said a miner contemptuously. 'I could* ***tell*** *you* ***till I was blue in the face*** *and you wouldn't understand.'* NS.

talk turkey (informal) talk seriously; say, propose, sth definite that is important and usually acceptable to the hearer (originally US, the reference being to the main dish of a celebratory dinner eg at Christmas or Thanksgiving) □ *If you're interested in the job, I don't say we couldn't* ***talk turkey*** *over a pot* (= a drink of beer). HD □ *'I don't think I'll come. Fancy-dress parties aren't really my scene.' 'Not even if I tell you Sue will be there?' 'Ah,* now *you're* ***talking turkey****!'*

a talking head a television studio programme consisting of an address, talk, dialogue, interview, discussion, debate etc straightforwardly presented by one or more people □ *For years now, I have suffered from a number of television producers who dismiss certain programme ideas with the contemptuous remark that 'it'll be all* ***talking heads****'. The implication is that unless the screen is filled with a succession of images and animations and visual tricks, the audience will go to sleep or, even worse, switch to the other channel.* RT

a talking point [Comp (NP)] a subject of interest, worthy of discussion **V:** ⚠ be, become; make sth □ *Northcliffe had been very insistent on good news coverage, but he had also stressed the need for what he called '****talking points****', and some of his successors concentrated too much on these and too little on the hard grind of news-gathering.* L □ *Pushkin—the untranslatable: the notion has been in the air ever since the first rumours of a great Russian poet reached early Victorian England. When, of late, Edmund Wilson and Vladimir Nabokov joined issue about it,* ***the*** *famous* ***talking-point*** *was engaging two livelier and more powerful minds than ever before.* L □ *The Church of Scotland has always been less reluctant than the Church of England to remarry the divorced in church, though emphatically it does not subscribe to divorce on* *demand. 'It's not really* ***a*** *major* ***talking point*** *among ministers,' I was told.* SC □ with or without hyphen; stress pattern a 'talking point.

tall, dark and handsome [adj + adj + adj non-rev] a certain ideal type of male beauty □ *An inch or so short of being really* ***tall, dark and handsome****, Dillman has the easy, relaxed ways of a man used to the Hollywood-style good life.* TVT □ *We live with our parents, much to their chagrin. We have new steady boy-friends every week and, to be noticed by us, they must be* ***tall, dark and handsome****, unless they are short and fair.* H

tall etc oaks from little acorns grow (saying) much may come of little **adj:** tall, ⚠ great, big, large □ (source) *Large streams from little fountains flow,/* ***Tall oaks from little acorns grow****.* LINES FOR A SCHOOL DECLAMATION (D EVERETT 1769-1813) □ *The chief problem left by our* (metaphysical) *view is how to explain such things as the way* ***great oaks from little acorns grow****.* NDN □ (a weekly lottery in aid of local charities) *'****From little acorns big oaks grow****,' Mr Whitehead says. 'This organisation started with two or three people and now we're giving away thousands of pounds.'* G □ *This was an excellent documentary to make one think. I was astonished at the extent of the fiddling that goes on. '****Great oaks from little acorns grow****'! I was glad that the jury (just) came down on the side of conscience.* RT

a tall order Comp (NP)] sth asked, expected or demanded of sb that is difficult to do or provide **V:** ⚠ be, seem; find, think, sth □ *People like Edna, he says, don't need much more than a house that they can be confident they'll not be thrown out of. But even that's* ***a tall order****. The play honestly admits that there's nothing easy about trying to look after Edna.* RT □ (advertisement) *Wales in 16 pages. That's* ***a tall order****. Especially when we've included so much information for those planning their own holiday.* OBS □ (a religious sect) *Did none of the young want to leave, I asked, and was quite frankly told that some did, and were not prevented from going. Their leaving, however, meant cutting off all ties with family and community. Surely* ***a tall order*** *for any young person.* SC

a tall story/tale an account of happenings that is or seems improbable, that is either an invention or an exaggeration of facts □ *Do you believe that yarn, Bertie? It sounds to me* ***a*** *pretty* ***tall story****.* RM □ *His male fellow passengers—and among them was a cynical young Frenchman—were tempted to tell him* ***tall stories*** (about Siberia). *Like heartless, teasing boys, we competed to see how much we could make him swallow* (= believe). AH □ (NONCE) *In my rock-climbing days I heard many* ***stories*** *that sounded* ***tall*** *but were usually true.* SC □ (film review) ***This*** *apparently* ***tall tale*** *is, in fact, based on a real wartime mission called Operation Mincemeat.* RT □ *Ziggy is an 11-year-old boy with a vivid imagination. He lives in a lighthouse on a Mediterranean island, where his* ***tall tales*** *and constant scrapes are the despair of his grandfather, a retired colonel, and his teenage sister Pippa.* TVT

tar and feather sb [V + O pass] punish sb by covering him with tar and feathers as an (illegal) act of public disapproval, mob retaliation, etc □ *He had been accepted as overlord by yeomanry and peasantry, who cheated him up to the limits of their conventions, but would have* ***tarred and feathered*** *any outsider who tried to impose on their lord.* WDM □ *As if to illustrate the right as opposed to the wrong way of employing IRA punishment methods, a young man at the weekend in Londonderry was* ***tarred and feathered*** *for looting. Another had his long hair cut for theft.* L □ *As a figure of trust, authority, and kindness, children particularly admired him* (ie a policeman in a TV series). *Why not? This was an era before Authority, as an idea, had been* ***tarred and feathered****.* L □ non-rev.

teach sb to do sth punish sb so that he does *not* do sth again; make sb afraid to do sth again **S:** I, he, it; that. **Inf:** to tell lies, to give your mother cheek, to takes lifts from strangers, to interfere, to come home at one o'clock in the morning □ *Wait till I get hold of him! I'll* ***teach*** *him* ***to*** *tell lies about me!* □ *'So it ended up that I was cheated out of £50.' 'You're far too trusting, but that should* ***teach*** *you* ***to*** *take cheques from strangers.'* □ *It's a good thing for you Sister's not on duty, Mr Brown. She'd* ***teach you to*** *throw medicine on the floor.* □ FATHER: *I'll* ***teach*** *you* ***to*** *tie a tin-can to the cat's tail!* SON: *I wish you would. It keeps slipping off.* OBS □ joke in last example is based on the ambiguity arising from the fact that the *form* of the expression has do sth while the *meaning* is 'not do sth'; usu in constructions with *will/would/should*; usu used to make threats or predictions.

teach one's grandmother to suck eggs tell or show sb how to do sth that he can do perfectly well, and probably better than oneself □ *Tom could never resist the satisfaction of* ***teaching his grandmother to suck eggs****. 'One can be jealous without being in love,' he went on, 'but one can't be in love without being jealous.'* SPL □ *If what follows reads something like a treatise on how to* ***teach your grandmother to suck eggs****, that is because the Conservative Party at the present time is like nothing so much as* (NONCE) ***a grandmother who cannot suck eggs****.* NS □ seldom used now as irritated recommendation (*Oh, go and* ***teach your grandmother to suck eggs***) not to give unwanted advice.

(you can't) teach an old dog new tricks (saying) (you can't) successfully get old people who are set in their ways to change their ideas, methods of work, etc □ *If more women fail driving tests than men, that is because until very recently they have begun to learn much later in life. Taken by age groups, figures show that the difficulty of* ***teaching old dogs new tricks*** *applies equally to both sexes.* □ (NONCE) *'How about bringing your own father round to a Marxist way of thinking?' I asked. Ajit laughed—nervously. '****You can't teach an old monkey new tricks****. Moreover I want to keep peace at home.'* OBS □ (NONCE) *French actors do not seem to take too easily to this piece of elementary Shakespearean drill. Fun though it is to see these* ***new dogs taught*** *to play our* ***old tricks****, the evening should have had more to offer.* OBS □ (NONCE) *'Even if they have two machines instead of 20 audit clerks, they'll need people to run* *them.' 'I know, but I shall retire. I'm too **old a dog to learn new tricks**.'* TVT

(the) team spirit unselfish and co-operative feelings and actions in promoting the good of a team, group, community, work-force etc of which one is a member □ *Dr Bettelheim protests against the word 'subordination' and argues that he created a system of 'social solidarity', by which he clearly means what headmasters of English public schools call '**team spirit**'.* OBS □ *I knew other people who had not allowed graver illness to stop them from doing what they had set themselves to do. Good advice, good medicine, a good constitution, and luck united to display **the team spirit**, and gradually pulled me back.* AH □ *No man did more than Arnold to divert English education from its proper course. By the end of the 19th century, individuality had been crushed by good form and **team spirit**.* NS

tear one's hair [V + O] tug one's hair with both hands as an expression of anxiety, grief, despair or frustration □ *She stamped and raged and **tore her hair**, and swore she'd never been so insulted.* □ *What I had written this time really was just a random jumble of letters and figures. It amused me to think of some high-powered expert **tearing his hair** trying to decode it.* □ usu fig.

tell all [V + O pass] (facetious) confess to, or describe fully, matters (esp concerned with one's own history, habits and activities) that many would prefer to suppress or gloss over □ *It is not often that one finds a film director ready to catalogue his failures, but Claude Lelouche seems beguilingly prepared to **tell all**.* NS □ *Of recent years harlots of both sexes, and the bent of every category, have come forward to **tell all**; but personally risky, true-life stories of illegal sex are still few and far between.* NS □ *Apart from the daily group-therapy meeting and the weekly AA* (Alcoholics Anonymous) *meeting the only other compulsory and important part of the treatment was one's 'life-story'. Every patient had to write about 3,000 words **telling all**.* NS

tell sb different contradict or correct sb □ *He never said he loved me, nor I didn't care, but once he had taken me he seemed to think he was responsible for me and I **told** him no **different**.* R □ *'She's a gossip, but a harmless one.' 'You think that? There's a few folk round here that would **tell** you **different**.'* □ JO (reading from a magazine): *It says here that Sheik Ahmed—an Arabian mystic—will, free of all charge, draw up for you a complete analysis of your character and destiny.* HELEN: *There's two W's in your future: Work or Want — and no Arabian Knight can **tell** you **different**.* TOH □ non-standard.

tell (sb) a lie (about sth) [V + O + O pass] lie, not be truthful (to sb) (about sth) (habitually or at a particular time) **o:** lie, ⚠ fib, story, untruth; (informal) whopper □ *'Not Pamela? What has she done?' Janice thought a moment. She was improvising a sin for Pamela. 'I think she **told a lie**.'* PW □ *'And you know too that you didn't see somebody waving a scarf on a stick. It was a handkerchief caught on a branch. Daddy found it.' 'Yes,' Nicky muttered. 'Then you're a naughty boy to frighten Sarah like that, and to **tell lies**.'* DC □ *I'm afraid he **told** us **a story about** that money. He simply stole it from the old woman's shop round the corner.* □ *If Mr Louw **told** deliberate **untruths** the case would be simpler. But there is no reason to think that. Like his chief and his colleagues, he is blinkered by his ideology.* SC □ sometimes pl form used when only one lie is referred to. ⇨ speak the truth; tell (sb) the truth.

(can) tell/see sth a mile off (can) easily and quickly perceive sth □ *Not that everybody in our yard hadn't been a struggler—and still was—one way or another. But you **could tell a mile off that** she was a struggler, and that was what nobody liked.* LLDR □ *'Do you think these two are in love, then?' 'Do I* think*? Anyone **can see that a mile off**!'*

tell the same story/tale (of sth) [V + O pass] be evidence of the same state of affairs **det:** the same, a similar; a different, another; its own. **o:** neglect, misery, suffering; success; deceit □ *The owner evidently thought his duties ended with collecting the rents, and every dwelling we visited **told the same story of** neglect.* □ *Robinson declared that he was struggling to make ends meet, but his well-fed appearance and suit of fine Scotch tweed **told another tale**.* □ *The ingenious inhabitants of the ranchitos* (shack houses) *have found their own ways of tapping the electricity supply. But on closer inspection the stench **tells its** own **story** of inadequate or non-existent sanitation.* OBS

tell tales [V + O pass] spread information about another's secrets, misdeeds, faults, habits **A:** on his little sister, on her fellow-lodgers, on each other; about colleagues, about what goes on, about me; to mother, to the teacher, to the police □ JENNY: *All we got was what we pinched out* (of) *the larder and then you used to go and **tell tales** to mother.* R □ *'I thought, perhaps, as you'd helped the Townsend boy to get a job—' 'You've no business to know that. Somebody's been **telling tales**.'* □ *Classroom rules are meant to be kept, of course, but I don't encourage **tell-tales**.* □ *You'd have thought he wasn't amused at all but for the **tell-tale** twitch at the corner of his mouth.* □ n compound a tell-tale; attrib use *a **tell-tale** twitch, fragment.*

tell (sb) the truth [V + IO + O] be truthful (to sb) (about sth) (habitually or on a particular occasion); speak the truth (qv) □ *'Daddy hasn't got your letter at all. I took it and tore it up.' Prissie's face grew still. She sank into a chair. 'Nicky! Are you **telling the truth**?'* DC □ JO: *I had to drag it out of her. She didn't want to tell me.* GEOF: *That doesn't mean to say it's the truth. Do people ever **tell the truth** about themselves?* TOH □ *The sergeant said slowly, 'There is something wrong here. I can smell it. You are not **telling the truth**.'* OMIH □ *Before I read it I began to wonder whether at the end I should lie or **tell the truth** to Phuong.* QA ⇨ tell (sb) a lie (about sth).

tell the truth and shame the devil (saying) tell the truth, esp in circumstances where there seem to be good reasons or strong temptations not to do so □ *'Well,' said Canon Joram, 'It is not for me to criticise,' but he was interrupted, though very prettily, by Jessica who said he must **tell the truth and shame the devil**.* WDM □ *'The garden's still a mess, as you can see.' 'I daresay you've been kept too busy with other things.' 'No; I'll **tell the truth and shame the devil**—I've* *been not too busy, but too lazy.'*

tell the world (that etc) make sth known publicly to as many people as possible, or just openly and emphatically **O:** that (he was coming), who (he was), why (he went), what (to expect) □ *Hi-jacking was a way they caught on to of* ***telling the world that*** *it couldn't afford to ignore the rights of minorities.* □ *Granny Barnacle gave notice to the doctor that she refused further treatment, was discharging herself next day, and that she would* ***tell the world why***. MM □ *'Isn't baby needing his next feed?' 'Can't be. When he's hungry he* ***tells the world***.*'*

to tell you the truth [Disj] speaking frankly or more exactly; as a matter of fact (qv) □ ***To tell you the truth****, old man, I was a bit carried away yesterday. I said things I shouldn't have done.* PE □ ***To tell the truth****, these were not experiments at all. There were no defined objectives, little measurement, no agreed time limit.* NS □ *They have a genuinely happy marriage. '****To tell you the truth****, I'm proud of him,' Gwen says, 'rising up from a labourer to a top job.'* OBS □ *This sheet music on the piano is the theme song I wrote for 'Not On Your Nellie', but it's only handwritten so I don't think I can play it for you. I don't know where I put my spectacles,* ***to tell you the truth***. ST □ *I was very surprised when I heard I'd won. I didn't believe it at first* ***to tell you the truth***. *Thought my pals were having me on.* RT □ *Throughout the length and breadth of the land people were shivering, in ill-heated houses, as they read the morning paper, ate their breakfasts, and grumbled about the weather which,* ***truth to tell****, had been appalling of late.* TBC □ usu fairly unemphatic parenthesis and not intended to contradict any assumption to the contrary; less common variant truth to tell.

(one's) temper rises/frays one finds it difficult, and may fail, to control one's bad temper □ ***My temper rose*** *with every word he spoke but I wanted to avoid any kind of show-down for the time being.* □ *Elsie feared that* ***tempers*** *were* ***rising****, and, brave girl, she drew her father's fire upon herself.* RM □ *We caught a glimpse of what film-making often is—a state of near civil war between the people on the two sides of the camera. Now the second series (Wed. 9.10 BBC 2) is under way, watch out for signs of blood boiling and* ***tempers fraying***. RT □ ***Rising tempers*** *all round made further discussion inadvisable.* □ variant frayed temper.

tempt fate/Providence [V + O pass] rely too much on luck in doing or proposing sth and hence risk failure □ *I had no doubt that Martin did not know of the letter* (inviting the speaker to come and watch the success of an experiment)*; it would have seemed to him* ***tempting fate***. *For myself, I felt the same kind of superstition, even a misgiving, about going down to watch.* NM □ *In the meantime, as if* ***tempting Providence*** *to send them another avenging Tempest* (member of the Hospital Board)*, they transferred Sister Burnstead, on the first of January, to another ward.* MM □ *'He paid the £150 deposit so readily I might have asked for more.' 'And then he might have backed out of the deal altogether. £150 is all you need to go ahead and there's no sense in* ***tempting Providence***.*'* □ esp in the inf and continuous tenses.

ten feet tall [Comp (AdjP)] pleased with and proud of oneself **V:** ⚠ be, feel; look, seem □ *You're always getting up to things. It doesn't really matter what—as long as it is you. You must always be* ***ten feet tall*** *imagining yourself doing this or doing that.* YAA □ *It was a small triumph looking back on it now, but I came out of that room absurdly happy and feeling* ***ten feet tall***.

ten to one [Disj] (informal) very probably; almost, though not quite, certainly (from racing, ie odds of ten to one) □ *Young Mr Shrivenham of the British Embassy gazed upwards as the plane zoomed over Baghdad aerodrome. There was a considerable dust-storm in progress. '****Ten to one*** *they can't come down here.'* TBC □ *I shall be told, and* ***10 to one*** *not pleasantly, that this kind of thing costs money.* NS □ (Boys who misbehave) *out of boredom and a sense of frustration should be sent straight out of school to some form of apprenticeship, working with grown men who will stand no nonsense from them (though* ***ten to one*** *there wouldn't be any).* NS □ occas twenty to one, a hundred to one; sometimes preceded by *it's*.

tender loving care loving concern for sb/sth □ *If patients are in an open ward, few nurses will pass them by without doing some little thing for them. It is in a nurse's tradition to give what is called '****TLC****', '****tender loving care****', some constant little service to the sick.* L □ *A farmer told me once that it was a big problem to explain how some small farms were getting higher yields per acre than the big farms. He had come to the conclusion it was the* ***TLC*** *factor—the* ***tender loving care***. L □ whimsical, and occas facetious; can be abbreviated as shown.

thank goodness etc (that/for sth) I am, let us all be, etc glad, relieved, thankful **n:** goodness, ⚠ heaven(s), God, the Lord. **A:** that he is, that he will; for that, for Dr Finlay, for the army □ *'It's only her leg that's hurt.' '****Thank goodness for*** *that.' Brigit's mind sought and then slipped away from a worse horror. 'Oh,* ***thank goodness*** *she's alive.'* DC □ *Holiday time is when wigs come into their own; and wigs,* ***thank heavens****, are so much lighter and cooler to wear these days.* SC □ *'****Thank God*** *the Government's influence is so little.' 'Would you expand on that?' 'The Government can make enormous mistakes and we can still survive.'* L □ ***Thank heaven for*** *little girls,/For little girls get bigger every day'.* A J LERNER b1918 □ front, middle or end position.

thank one's lucky stars that be specially or unexpectedly fortunate (that) □ *In America it is still possible to choose from a fairly large selection of architect-built homes rather than simply taking Hobson's Choice and* ***thanking your lucky stars that*** *you've found anything that's remotely habitable.* ST □ *You should* ***thank your lucky stars that*** *you didn't have to see her at the last. Your memory is pure, you will always remember her as she used to be.* NS □ often preceded by *you/we/they can/ought to*.

thank you (very much) (ironic) expresses polite refusal □ *A woman remarked that the dockers were holding the country to ransom. Her friend said he would vote for Enoch Powell if he got the chance, and the landlord decided that was* *enough of politics,* ***thank you****.* NS □ *Who's talking about good? I don't want to do her good. I just want to keep her out of sight and mind,* ***thank you very much****.* TSMP □ *If Bill Shankly wants to buy a* (football) *player, any player, the money is there for him. Yet it is usually the chairman who has to bring the subject up every now and then. At the last time of asking there was no one that Shankly wanted to buy,* ***thank you very much****.* OBS □ *For better or for worse, the new generation of 'New Statesman' readers does not, I fancy, relish being told what to think. If they are given the facts they will make up their minds for themselves,* ***thank-you-very-much****.* NS □ *I travelled back and forth from about 1963. I loved it here right away. I only ever want to visit New York between Thanksgiving and Christmas; the rest of the time I'll stay in London,* ***thank you****!* RT □ sometimes facetious; end position, added to statement of opinion, preference or intention, expressing polite refusal of offer or choice that is usu only implied.

thanks to sb/sth [A] because of sb/sth; arising from the good or bad influence or actions of that person/thing **o:** you; their efforts, Tom's forgetfulness; the noise you made □ *Five years ago I could have been made into a boring, heartless climber whom everyone ran a mile from. But,* ***thanks to*** *you, I* have *grasped that a certain fundamental decency to others is necessary if one's to get anywhere.* HAA □ *Moreover,* ***thanks to*** *advancing technology, the coloured documentary has proved itself, in skilful hands, a notable new form of popular visionary art.* HAH □ ***Thanks*** *in part* ***to*** *the elaborate accompaniments, in part* ***to*** *the well-known acoustic difficulties of the theatre, and in part* ***to*** *the singers' own failings, much of Geoffrey Dunn's translations remained inaudible.* ST.

that does it[1] (informal) sth (eg a task or undertaking) is now finished; that's (about) it[2] (qv); (and) that's that/it (qv) □ *He threw in the cuts of lamb, the chopped up bits of onion, carrot and potato, covered it all with salted water, and put the casserole into the oven. '****That does it****,' he said. 'Not exactly how my mother would have cooked her Lancashire hotpot, but good enough for me.'* □ usu present tense; stress pattern that 'does it.

that does it[2] (informal) that is as much as I can endure; the limit of my patience has been reached □ ***That does it****! All you can ever do is criticize. If I'm no good to you, then maybe someone else will value my work. I'm leaving!* □ *Every time we were starting to discuss the really important issue, the telephone rang. And about the tenth time it happened,* ***that did it****! I just left the room.* □ stress pattern that 'does it.

that is (to say)[1] [Conj] accompanies a sentence, clause or phrase which re-defines or further explains a previous one; in other words (qv) □ *The next step after preparing the maps is for the engineer to decide on the 'grade line'—* ***that is****, the height of the centre of the road along the whole route.* NSC □ *His father, as a young officer, had fought against the Grande Armée and had been captured by the French. The boy grew up.* ***that is to say****, among elders for whom the battle of Borodino, the burning of Moscow, the triumphal advance to Paris, were only yesterday.* OBS □ *The doctor told her there was always hope,* ***which was to say*** *there was nothing more he could do.* □ usu front or middle position; tense changes that is to which was for past.

that is (to say)[2] [Conj] accompanies a sentence, clause or phrase which limits the truth, applicability etc of a previous one, sometimes as an afterthought □ *'I think, finally, I shall go into the Navy.' 'You!' 'If they'd have me,* ***that is****.'* PM □ *That's how it was; with the women working and the men letting life flow sweetly past, the Buttafava household was happy as could be. All,* ***that is****, except Fiorella.* ARG □ *He told us that he had several scores to settle in Singapore where he had plied his dangerous trade. Now, however, he was working as a photographer.* ***That is to say****, he would be working if only he had a camera.* NS □ *Baghdad was in the sterling area and money therefore presented no difficulties. Not,* ***that is to say****, in the travel clerk's meaning of the word.* TCB □ front, middle or end position.

that is as (it) may be that (ie sth already mentioned) may possibly be true □ *'We* (actors) *have become casual labourers, but still always on the look-out for parts. The stage just gets you after a while.'* ***That is as it may be****, but it seems to us that that something has gone profoundly wrong.* ST □ *'He's trying to make me believe it,' said Steve. 'And he's made himself believe it.' '****That's as may be****. It does seem to be that his principal obstacle is making Myrtle believe it.'* SPL □ *'She can have time off to have the baby and then go back again. Time off,' she repeated emphatically, 'with pay.' I did not argue.* ***That was as might be****.* SML □ usu that's as may be; stress pattern ˌthat is as (it) 'may be; often followed by *but*-cl or second sentence which adds or implies that whether it is true or not is irrelevant. ⇨ ⚠ be that as it may.

that/there is gratitude etc for you that (ie sth already mentioned) is an admirable token or sign of gratitude etc **n:** gratitude, determination, public spirit, ingenuity; the teaching profession, true love, hospitals □ *He kept on sending me £20 every Christmas long after his debt was paid.* ***That's gratitude for you****!* □ *Favourite possibility at the moment for spending the prize money seems to be buying a mobile libary for the housebound, with local organisations chipping in with the extra cash.* ***That's the*** *Luton* ***spirit for you****.* RT □ *It is clear there are fearful risks in transporting plutonium about the world. Yet Mr Benn approves the deal.* ***There is technology*** *responding to social needs* ***for you****.* NS □ use may be literal or ironic; stress pattern ˌthat/ˌthere is 'gratitude etc for you.

that etc is more like it that etc is a better description, way of behaving, action etc; something like (qv) **S:** that; lazy; a saint; a sadistic maniac. **adv mod:** a lot; a bit; rather □ *The kiss started going on and on rather, but he was the one who finally stepped back, saying: '****That was more like it****, eh?'* TGLY □ *I'm not getting up to catch any 7.45 train. When's the next one? 9.45?* ***That's*** *a bit* ***more like it****.* □ *'That new lad seems a bit slow.' 'Downright* ***lazy is more like it****.'* □ forceful or enthusiastic comment on the suitability/unsuitability of sth.

that is not to say (that) that (ie a previous statement) does not mean (that) **pron:** that, this, which. **O:** (that) he won't come, they wouldn't co-operate □ *You certainly made a hash of filleting those fish.* ***That is not to say**, of course, that I'd have done it any better myself.* □ *The media provide precious little insight into the working of science and the minds of the men who manipulate the machine.* ***This is not to say** there is not a place for the kind of science reportage that is current.* NSC □ *I won't have a drink, thank you—* ***which is not to say** I mightn't be very happy to accept the offer on another occasion.*

that is his story and he's sticking to it (catchphrase) that is sb's account of events or circumstances and he won't change it **det:** his, my; John's, the girl's □ *'What was that rubbish about you having a heights-phobia?' he asked his wife afterwards. 'I want a permanent excuse for not going on these trips. Anyway,* ***that's my story and I'm sticking to it**.'* □ *'You haven't been able to shake his testimony?' 'No. He went there, admittedly to make trouble, but he wasn't carrying a gun and he didn't shoot Benson, because Benson was already dead when he got there.* ***That's his story and he's sticking to it**.'* □ (NONCE) *They were polite but firm: the medicine was fine for whites, but it would not work for black people.* ***That was their belief and they were sticking to it**.* BB

that will be the day (catchphrase) that will be a notable day, time, occasion (when sth happens, sb does sth) (the implication usu being that such a day will never come) □ *The four hired donkeys had been tied up in the stable that Pop had built for when all the family, with the possible exception of Ma, would have a pony or a horse to ride.* ***That would be the day**.* DBM □ *'You wait, you'll come crawling back to me in the end, just you see, you'll be begging for mercy.' '**That'll be the day**,' Jenny said, remembering it just in time before the door slammed.* TGLY □ usu that'll be the day; stress pattern 'that'll be the day; usu ironic.

that will do stop it; that is quite enough □ *'For goodness' sake, Mary,* ***that will do**,' he protested as she tried to pile more food on his plate. 'Do you want me to get as fat as a pig?'* □ ***That'll do**, you two. You're getting far too noisy.* □ reproof for undesirable behaviour or speech, instructing sb that it should stop.

that's all[1] just that; nothing more, better, worse etc □ *'How're you feeling?' 'Fine. A little tired,* ***that's all**.'* □ *You don't have to wait for an answer. Just put the note in the letter-box,* ***that's all**.* □ used to emphasize how slight, unimportant, sth is.

that's all[2] there is no more to be said; that's my last word, my final warning on the subject □ *'What are you putting your shoes on again for?' 'Because I'm driving you home,* ***that's all**. There's often a rough crowd on that last bus.'* □ *Uncle Saunders said in his booming voice, 'I won't have my house filled with all the lame and diseased cats in the neighbourhood,* ***that's all**.'* DC □ *'You're not going to tell on me, Mr Lampton?' 'No, you fool. Just don't do it again,* ***that's all**.'* RATT □ emphasizing declaration, protest, warning or threat; usu spoken with low rising tone on *all*.

that's all I can say [Disj] that is what I think; that is my most suitable comment; in my opinion (whether you like it or not) □ JO: *Why are you marrying Helen?* PETER: *Why shouldn't I marry Helen?* JO: *Your generation has some very peculiar ideas,* ***that's all I can say**.* TOH □ *'This is just an average day for us.' 'Then I wouldn't like to be working here on a busy one,* ***that's all I can say**!'* □ *'I'm not inventing these incidents, you know.' 'I don't suppose you are.* ***All I can say is that** he never showed that side of his character to me.'* □ stress pattern usu that's all 'I can say; variant all I can say is (that).

that's all you know about it (informal) (you show that) you know little about the matter in question; your idea or opinion is mistaken **pron:** you, he, she, they □ *'Don't you care about anybody? You don't care if he waits. You don't care if I go.' '**That's all you know about it**.'* SPL □ *'But people think that a painter, or a writer, doesn't really work like somebody who has to turn up at fixed times for a regular job.' '**That's all they know about it**— they should try it sometime.'* □ stress pattern that's all 'you know about it.

that's my boy/girl you are a good child, man, woman; I approve of sth you've done or promised to do □ *'Oh come on, don't be shy. Stay and be introduced to the others.' 'Well, I suppose I could. Just a few minutes, then.' '**That's my boy**.'* □ *'If it makes you happy, of course I'll give it* (my work) *up.' 'Promise?' 'I promise.' 'Good girl.' He lay back on the pillow. '**That's my girl**,' he murmured, and closed his eyes to sleep again.* AITC □ stress pattern 'that's my boy/girl; used to promise or encourage child or (in friendly mockery) adult.

that's done/torn it (informal) that (ie a misfortune, accident or mistake) has spoiled or ruined sth, made a plan or undertaking ineffective □ *'I hear Shirley Williams has just resigned from the Labour Party.' '**That's done it**, then! Now the Party will split in two.'* □ *'Did she say anything about babysitting?' 'No, but I did.' 'I* told *you never to mention it! I knew it!* ***That's done it**!* ***That's torn it**!'* TSMP □ stress pattern that's 'done/'torn it.

that's for certain/sure! [Disj] you can be sure of that □ *Well, now that he's got his money, you won't see him again,* ***that's for certain!*** □ *'Nice for them to have a friend in the building trade.' 'Oh, Bill won't do the job for nothing,* ***that's for sure!**'* □ affirms the speaker's certainty that sth is so; always in final position; stress pattern 'that's for certain/sure.

that's/there's a good boy etc show how good, obliging, sensible etc you are **Comp:** a (good) boy, a (good) girl; a brave boy, a clever girl, a good chap, a fine fellow, a kind friend □ *Stop banging your drum, Billy,* ***that's a good boy**. Your mother's got a headache this morning.* □ *That's right, pet. Hold your glass with both hands,* ***there's a clever girl**.* □ *'Want a drink?' 'I feel I need a little—' 'I'll bring one in to you. Sit down.' 'A stiff one.' 'Sit down.* ***There's a boy**.'* MM □ *I'll feel better if I know someone's in all the time. There's oceans to drink and the fridge is full of salmon and raspberries and things. Don't invite your friends in though,* ***there's an angel**.* UTN □ follows request that sb should do sth or acknowledgement that he has just done so; stress pattern 'that's/'there's a good boy etc.

that's a good one that's an amusing joke, smart trick, clever remark; (ironic) that's a particularly stupid, naive, impudent, presumptuous etc action, request or proposal □ *As Mrs Parker, over-dressed to kill as usual, sailed by, Johnnie murmured, 'What! No tiara?'* '**That's a good one**,' *Fred chuckled.* □ *'I want you to hypnotise me again.' Joe laughed and came over to her slowly.* '**That's a good one**,' *he said. 'What do you think I am — Svengali?'* AITC □ *'Dad says he's tired and will you take him a cup of tea and he'll get up later.'* 'He's *tired?* **That's a good one**. *Who was up and down all night with the baby, him or me?'* □ stress pattern that's a 'good one.

that's (about) it[1] (informal) sth that has been said, suggested etc is a reasonably accurate description or summing up of a situation □ DIXON: *Confidence! That's a laugh!* PSYCHIATRIST: *And you have none?* DIXON: **That's about it**. *I'm no good, doctor!* OBS □ **That's it**! *You've described exactly what* I *felt about the film.*

that's (about) it[2] (informal) a task or undertaking is now finished (apart perhaps from a few final details); that does it[1] (qv); (and) that's that/it (qv) □ *She surveyed the cold supper she had prepared, decided that* **that was it** *and went off to get dressed before the guests came.* □ *So the two men worked on through the night. It was grey dawn when Kingsley said: 'Well,* **that's about it**. *We've got all the results here, but they need a bit of conversion.'* TBC

that's just it/(just) the trouble that (ie sth already mentioned) is the precise nature of the situation, difficulty, problem; this is it (qv) □ *But what a bad show it had been. Not business at all:* **that was just it**, *Harold didn't really mind his client getting away with something he had no right to get away with. But it had been so unprofessional!* PW □ *'I suppose you can't put in an offer for a house in town till you're sure you can sell this one?'* '**That's just it**, *I'm afraid.'* □ *But only a child could be deceived into doing something so clearly against his own interests.'* '**That's just the trouble**. *He is a child, in all but years.'* □ *'Nobody blames you.' I pulled myself away from her abruptly. 'Oh my God,' I said. '* **That's the trouble**.' RATT □ stress pattern that's just 'it/(just) the 'trouble.

that's life (catchphrase) that's the kind of thing that often happens, that one learns, or must learn, to expect or accept; such is life (qv) □ *I've always liked black-haired and dark-eyed men, but I fell in love with a blond, blue-eyed boy. Oh well—***that's life**, *I suppose.* H □ *At first the decision to close was accepted as just another one of those cruel surprises that often emerge when a big business gobbles up a little business. The women were sad, regretful, but, well, what can you do?* **That's life.** ST □ *Take an organisation like the Army, where it is deemed more important for the men to whitewash the stones round the fire-engine shed than make sure the fire-engine is geared up for action. And* **that's life**. TVT

that's rich (informal) that is very amusing, entertaining; (ironic) that is preposterous, ludicrous □ *Mr Blearney exploded with laughter.* '**That's rich**. *I say* **that's rich**. *Here you are, only just in the game, and you start talking like the rest of them.'* HD □ *Robert threw back his head and laughed out loud. 'Protection.' he said.* '**That's rich**! He *needs it: I can tell you this, my man, and you can tell your superiors when you get back to Scotland Yard: when our movement gets into power, fellows like you are going to be out of a job.'* EM

that's the stuff to give the troops (catchphrase) that is just what is wanted or needed □ *'Great!' said Jill as Jack put the dish of pie and chips in front of her.* '**That's the stuff to give the troops**!' □ *Dollie said, 'Why don't you come here for Christmas?' Gerald was silent for a minute, then he said, 'As a matter of fact, I think I shall go abroad.'* '**That's the stuff to give the troops**,' *Dollie cried.* ASA

(and) that's that/it (informal) sth is over or is finally decided, arranged, forbidden etc; that does it[2] (qv); that's (about) it[1] (qv) □ OLD PEOPLE: *Good night, Doctor.* DOCTOR: *Good night.* (Exit Nurse, taking Old People) **And** *for the time being,* **that's that**. THH □ *He said it was silly of her to behave like a housekeeper, and he wanted to introduce his friends to her, so she went to the door, just once, and said good evening* **and that was that**. TSMP □ (a trainee nurse) *I was no good at school really, but I knew I was quite good at looking after people. Anyway, I wrote off to a few London hospitals when I was 16 and I was accepted by Charing Cross,* **and that was it**. RT □ *Most days you got time off to eat, but if he said 'Not till we've finished such-and-such'* **that would be it**. □ *When Geller backed out of a promise he had made to let himself be tested by a 'New Scientist' panel,* **that** *seemed to* **be that**. NSC

that's what I (always) say [Disj] that's my opinion; that's what I agree with; say I/I say (qv) □ JIMMY (in an imitation of a Midlands accent): *After all, it wouldn't do if we was all alike, would it? It'd be a funny world if we was all the same,* **that's what I always say**! LBA □ JENNY: *Mother reckons some people get indigestion so bad that it go right through their stomach to the back.* BEATIE: *Don't talk daft!* JENNY: **That's what I say**. *You don't get indigestion in the back.* R □ *He should be ashamed of himself.* **What I always say is**, *if you have a job to do, do it right.* □ often follows or accompanies fairly trite remark; stress pattern that's what 'I (always) say; variant what I (always) say is (that); in non-standard use, as in these examples.

that's what I want/I'd like to know that is the important question or point; that is what worries me (the reference usu being to a grievance or complaint) **S:** I, he, they; the tenants, purchasers □ *That's the Council for you. Always something new. And who's to pay for it?* **That's what I'd like to know**. AITC □ *The tenants are tired of promises to modernise these houses. Is it ever going to happen?* **That's what they want to know**. □ *You say you didn't tell her, but how else could she have found out?* **That's what I'd like to know**. □ stress pattern that's what 'I want/'I'd like to know.

that's what the man said (catchphrase) that is what I (we, you, they etc) was told (with the implication that either acceptance or scepticism is advisable) □ *'Are you sure you won't stay the night, Jim?' Alice asked for the third time.* '**That's what the man said**,' *put in her sister.*

'Do stop fussing him.' □ (golf) *The ball vanished altogether and then, seconds later, a bump grew up on the green, split open, and out popped the ball three feet from the hole. Well,* ***that's what the man said.*** SC □ *'I can't believe the road is really impassable. What do you think?' 'Why ask me?* ***You heard what the man said.****'* □ variant you heard what the man said.

that's what you think that is only your belief or opinion; that is not so, although you may think it is **S:** you, he, she, they □ DAVID: *Goodbye—I'll take the memory of you everywhere that I go.* SAM: ***That's what you think!*** HSG □ *Tina's going to finish her training while he does his Military Service, then they're going to get married.* ***That's what she thinks*** *anyway. Personally, I wouldn't bet twopence on it.* □ stress pattern that's what 'you think; expresses mocking disbelief.

that's where you are wrong that is a matter/the point on which you are mistaken **S:** you, he, she, they □ *'I wasn't doing a thing except standing watching. You can't keep me here.'* ***'That's where you're wrong****, my lad. You're helping the police with their enquiries, that's what you're doing.'* □ *'Splendid organizer,' the Brigadier said. 'That's what she thinks. She fancies she could organize a stallion into having pups,' Ma said, 'but* ***that's where she's wrong.****'* DBM

them and us (them) upper or governing classes, bureaucrats, employers etc contrasted with (us) ordinary people and wage-earners (usu with the implication that the former are feared, resented or mistrusted) □ *While some local authorities remain reluctant to enter into the full spirit of what is called public participation in planning, the more ambitious have been genuinely attempting to eliminate the old* ***'them' and 'us'*** *attitude.* SC □ (free 'law clinics') *When Mike Reed thinks a client can manage his own case, he will prompt and advise and then let him alone. But a client like that is still rare: most are inarticulate, emotional, unable to stick to the point, likely to irritate magistrates short of time, and heavily imbued with the idea of* ***Them and Us.*** ST □ (early 1950s) *So, when working-class people are asked to become foremen or non-commissioned officers they often hesitate. Whatever their motives, they will be regarded now as on the side of* ***'Them'****.* UL □ usu in order of headphrase.

then/there again [Conj] additionally; alternatively □ *'You yourself said that might avoid the worst of the trouble.' 'It might.* ***Then again****, it might not.'* TBC □ *Of course it had taken some luck to produce these ideal conditions for his introduction to the job* (as private chauffeur). *For one thing Mr Braceweight was taking a holiday after his operation.* ***Then again****, the man had had the sense, at some remote period of his life, to choose a wife who was exactly like himself.* HD □ JO: *You've no need to worry, Helen. He's gone away. He may be back in six months, but* ***there again*** *he may—* HELEN: *Look, you're only young. Enjoy your life. Don't get trapped. Marriage can be hell for a kid.* TOH □ introduces clause in which another consideration or possibility is mentioned.

then and there [adv + adv rev] at the first opportunity □ *He was not in his office and I eventually tracked him down in the lavatory. So we discussed the problem* ***then and there.*** MFM □ *It was the allegedly deliberate deception in hiding his medical record that prompted McGovern's chief advisers to urge their chief to drop Senator Eagleton* ***there and then.*** *But McGovern hesitated.* L

there are etc fairies at the bottom of the/one's garden [possess] there is sth unusual or interesting in one's surroundings or circumstances **V:** there be, ⚠ have (got). **prep:** with □ (source) ***There are fairies at the bottom of our garden.*** FAIRIES (R RYLEMAN 1877-1957) □ *But to children born and brought up in the grey world of Europe's refugee camps, the 175 acres of field and woodland at the Children's International Village at Sedlescombe, Sussex, is a paradise on earth. At Sedlescombe* ***there are fairies****, not soldiers,* ***at the bottom of their garden.*** TO □ (NONCE) *A frilly net skirt, starred headband and wand, and what little girl doesn't feel indistinguishable from something found squatting* ***at the bottom of the garden.*** G □ (NONCE) *Next to the swastika were blown-up articles from the 'Daily Express' and the 'News of the World' about homosexuality, which were indeed fairly unpleasant. It is hard to take Ms Jean Rook, for instance, declaring that* ***any fairy at the bottom of her garden*** *had better come equipped with wings — or else.* NS □ in last quotation there is a play on fairy, a disparaging and offensive term for a homosexual man.

there are (plenty) more (good) fish in the sea (saying) most losses are replaceable by something just as good □ *Try not to take it to hard if you don't get anywhere* (with Jenny). *After all,* ***there are plenty of fish in the sea****, aren't there?* TGLY □ HAVA: *But he doesn't like me. What can I do?* SAM: *Take your time—you're such a lovely girl—he'll fall—be patient.* HAVA: *Do you really think so? Anyway—I'm not that hard up—* ***plenty more fish in the sea.*** HSG □ *Leicester had got in first on one or two matters recently and Marlborough wanted the opportunity to show him that he, Leicester,* ***wasn't the only fish in the sea.*** TBC □ *He might settle out in Australia. People did. It was sad, but something she would have to cope with.* ***There were plenty of other fish in the sea.*** WI □ variants not be the only fish in the sea, there are as good fish in the sea (as ever came out of it), there are plenty of (other) fish in the sea.

there are more things in heaven and earth than are dreamt of in your philosophy strange things do, or may, occur although they are beyond the range of your understanding, experience or imagination □ (source) ***There are more things in heaven and earth****, Horatio,/* ***Than are dreamt of in your philosophy.*** HAMLET I 5 □ *The litter of rab-pigs, apparently the result of an encounter between her pet female guinea-pig and a rabbit, which caused experts to scratch their heads and wonder whether* ***there were more things in heaven and earth than were dreamed of in their*** *professional* ***philosophies****, appears now to have been a hoax.* SC □ *Certainly the experiment has proved that* ***there are more things in earth than are dreamt of in our*** *conventional*

philosophy, *and the author does great service in spelling out precisely the directions in which more research is required.* G ◻ (NONCE) *It's been proved that* ***there are more things in heaven and hell than*** *this world* ***dreams of***. *Loch Ness is mighty deep. There may be three or four monsters down there.* OBS

there are more/easier ways of killing a cat than by choking it with cream (saying) there is more than one way of doing sth; (esp) if you want to get rid of, or exploit, sb you should do so directly and ruthlessly instead of covering your action with flattery, pretending it is for their own good, or by other such devious means ◻ *'We feel your high academic qualifications are being wasted here, Mr Jenkins. Have you ever thought of making a change?' 'If you mean I'm a rotten teacher but not quite bad enough to sack, I'll remind you* ***there are more ways of killing a cat than by choking it with cream***.*'* ◻ (NONCE) *I feel guilty about always letting you take the rough assignments, but you're so much stronger, and more patient and clever than I am.' 'Oh, stop* ***choking me with cream***. *I learned to accept this way of doing things long ago.'*

there and back [adv + adv non-rev] to a destination and back ◻ *A quarter of a million day-trippers will be crossing the Channel this summer on no-passport excursions to Calais, Boulogne, Dieppe, Le Havre and St Malo. Altogether they will spend about a million pounds on getting* ***there and back***, *another £1.5 million during four or five hours ashore.* TO ◻ *He lived a long way out of the city and thought nothing of making the daily journey,* ***there and back***, *throughout the three terms.* TCM

there, but for the grace of God, go I (saying) it might have been me—except for God's grace, my happier circumstances, etc — who committed this crime, sin or folly, and was thus punished or made to suffer ◻ (source—a comment on seeing some criminals being taken to execution) ***But for the grace of God there goes John Bradford***. J BRADFORD 1510-55 ◻ *There is a lot to be said for professional self-government* (ie professions like medicine, the law, having their own disciplinary 'courts'), *if it really works. But can professionals take effective action against one another? Will they not always be held back by the thought that* ***there, but for the grace of God, go I***? NS ◻ *The characters existed in a drama which had no reference to anybody but themselves. So many television plays are like this, self-absorbed and tiny, so that no onlooker could dream of thinking that* ***there, but for the grace of God, went he***. L ◻ *I know her mother drinks and has lovers and things. But her husband's dead and so you really can't blame her, can you?* ***There-but-for-the-Grace-of-God*** *Department.* FFE ◻ unusual attrib usu in last example.

there is etc the devil (and all (hell)) to pay (saying) face trouble, recriminations, hostility etc as a result of some action or of its having been found out **V:** there is, ⚠ have. **prep:** with ◻ *Of course I won't run you to the station in the ambulance!* ***There'd be the devil and all to pay*** *if it was needed in a hurry.* ◻ *I daren't touch your father's desk. The one time I did attempt to tidy it up* ***there was the devil and all to pay***. ◻ *'Anyone that lives the way you do,' warned the doctor, 'is liable to find himself* ***with the devil to pay***.*'* ◻ *The little manicurist with whom he had been living had walked out on him and with her had gone her manicurist's weekly wage, and now* ***there was hell to pay*** *at the lodgings.* HAA

there is always room at the top (catchphrase) there are always too few people who are really outstanding in a profession, art etc or who are really ruthless in their ambition, and therefore there is ample opportunity for such people to be successful, famous, occupy influential positions ◻ (source — in reply to sb advising him not be a lawyer, as it was an overcrowded profession) ***There is always room at the top***. D WEBSTER 1782-1852 ◻ *Most of us don't brood over the inequities fostered and maintained by those who see to it that* ***there's always room at the top*** *for those who are prepared to tread diligently on enough faces to get there.* OBS ◻ *Crowley was probably a humbug, whose vanity, ambition, and intelligence led him to carve out a niche as the wickedest man in the world:* ***there is always room*** *for a sadist* ***at the top***. ST ◻ expression popularized by John Braine's novel Room at the Top (1957).

there is life in the old boy etc yet (catchphrase) sb/sth is still active, interested or interesting, productive etc in spite of age **n:** boy, girl, chap, firm, bus ◻ *'Your father was in good form tonight. I didn't expect such a lively evening.' 'Oh,* ***there's life in the old boy yet*** *when he gets the kind of company he enjoys.'* ◻ *I'll be 60 next birthday, but* ***there's life in the old dog yet***. RT ◻ *Mae West may be 84, but* ***there's life in the old girl yet***. *She was still working on her film 'Sextette' late at night when...* TVT

there is more to it etc than that etc the definition(s), description(s), reason(s) just given are incomplete or inadequate, do not fully account for it **pron/n:** it, him; things, the book, success; running a business. **n:** (than) good looks, factual information, luck ◻ *While they are here individual parents are relieved from the unceasing vigilance necessary for the safety of their* (handicapped) *children; someone is always on hand to cope. But* ***there is more to it than that***. *Here, without any attempt at therapy, analysis or reappraisals, happier family relationships evolve.* ST ◻ *Dorothy Sayers was certainly a Blimp and ludicrously anti-Semitic. But* ***there was more to her than that***. OBS ◻ *'I've had a lot of luck,' says 19-year-old Ann Townsend, last year's champion European show-jumper. But* ***there is*** *much* ***more to her success than luck***. H ◻ *They moved from London to a house on the edge of the Yorkshire Moors. 'I know actors are expected to live in and around London because that makes you more "available", but* ***there's more to life than that***.*'* TVT

there is no denying etc it etc one cannot deny it; it is a fact **V:** denying, ⚠ escaping, gainsaying, getting away from. **O:** it; the fact, his skill, the power of money; that he's talented ◻ *He's bad-tempered and selfish,* ***there's no denying it***, *but he's also a genius.* ◻ *Mercifully, this kind of maniacal violence is still comparatively rare in pubs. But* ***there's no denying***

that *there has been a steady increase in physical violence during recent years.* TVT □ *'Film music', like the films themselves, is big business, and it is mostly very bad, but* ***there is no escaping that*** *it is what almost everyone in modern India likes to hear.* L □ *They were friendly enough in their own style, but they were a funny lot,* ***there was no getting away from it.*** TGLY □ DAVIES: *I'm a capable sort of man. I mean to say, I've had plenty of offers in my time, you know,* ***there's no getting away from that.*** TC

there is no future (for sb) (in sth) there is no prospect of sth continuing, no prospect of sb's success, improvement in position, wealth, health, happiness etc **det:** no, (not) any; a (great) □ *I didn't leave the RAF till 1947. Then I quit Britain at the same time. I didn't feel* ***there was any future for*** *me or for Britain.* TVT □ *The recent promotion of Miss Cunningham at the age of 41 to the rank of Police Superintendent shows that* ***there is a future for*** *women* ***in*** *the Police Force — a career structure which applies to them as well as to men.* □ *You can earn enough to live on, but* ***there's no future in*** *window-cleaning.*

there is no holding/stopping sb sb cannot be prevented from doing sth □ *After that,* ***there was no holding*** *him, and the day came when he felt he could chuck his job and go all out to make a living as a writer.* OBS □ *Charley said again how, very soon, in no time at all, Pop could acquire a* (French) *accent. Mariette actually applauded, so that suddenly* ***there was no holding*** *Pop, who got up smartly from the breakfast table, bowed to Ma, and said: 'Bonjour, madame. Comment ça va? Au revoir! A bientôt!'* BFA □ *Once let this fellow start talking,* ***there was no stopping*** *him. He talked like a book too, not like a human being.* EM

there is no knowing etc what one cannot know or be sure about what will happen etc **V:** knowing, ⚠ saying, telling. **O:** what, why, whether, when, who; how, how many, how far □ *He was now back at the usual game of 'looking around'.* ***There was no knowing what*** *he could do. He might get a job tomorrow. He might stay out of work for weeks.* AITC □ *He was searching for novae, stars that explode with uncanny violence. Within the next year he might hope to find one or two, since* ***there was no telling when*** *an outburst might occur.* TBC

there is no law against it etc (informal) it is allowed **O:** it; private opinions; looking, eating with your fingers □ *'You look hot.' 'I am, and my shoes are killing me.' 'Take them off then,* ***there's no law against it.'*** □ *At last, Jim went over to the man's table. 'You're embarrassing my companion. Is it necessary for you to sit staring at her?' '****There's no law against looking****, is there? I'll do as I please.'* ⇨ ⚠ there should be a law against it etc.

there is no looking back etc one cannot look back etc **V:** looking back, reasoning with sb, turning back, getting near sb, preventing sth □ *The venison that isn't lying in proprietors' deep-freezes all goes to the exporter.* ***There's*** *simply* ***no buying*** *the stuff for the Scottish housewife.* SC □ *Not that the way was not yet an easy one. But from now onwards* ***there was no looking back.*** SD

there is no mistaking sb/sth it is easy to recognize sb/sth **O:** him; her accent, the threat intended; real coffee □ *'Are you sure it was Andrew?' 'Of course I'm sure. With his thatch of red hair* ***there's no mistaking*** *him.'* □ *'Can't you tell me, Mr Lumley, just what it is that you don't like about the rooms?'* ***There was no mistaking*** *the injured truculence in the landlady's voice.* HD

there is no need for sth/(for sb) to do sth[1] it is not necessary (for sb) to do sth; sth is not necessary **A:** for supervision, for an operation; ***(for sb)*** to stay, to go, to have treatment, to pay me; for supervision, for an operation □ ***There's no need for*** *you* ***to*** *stay up to let me in —just lend me a key.* □ *'I'm afraid the news is bad. Guy died half an hour ago.' Now* ***there was no need to*** *pretend shock and grief. She felt both, so keenly that her voice was almost inaudible.* DC □ *You know as much about the affair as I do.* ***There is no need for*** *my presence at the meeting.*

there is no need for sth/(for sb) to do sth[2] (for sb to do) sth is not only unnecessary but also undesirable, silly or wrong **A:** for obscenity, for embarrassment, for talking like that; ***(for sb)*** to get nasty, to take offence, to be frightened, to shout at them □ *'You're speaking as an expert, of course?' 'Now,* ***there's no need to*** *get nasty, Steve. I'm only trying to help.'* TT □ *'All right, mate!* ***No need to*** *show your bloody skill!' came a hoarse shout. Opening his eyes he saw that he had drawn up dead level with the car next to him, and left barely one inch of clearance.* HD □ *Pharmacists often have trouble deciphering prescriptions, and sometimes have to contact a doctor to check. And* ***there's no need for*** *it; anybody can write legibly if they try.* □ *All right —but lower your voice. You'****ve no need to*** *let the whole restaurant know your intentions.* □ variant have no need to do sth.

there is no occasion for sth/(for sb) to do sth (formal) there is no need, cause or pretext for sth/(for sb) to do sth □ *If we had been luckier, if events had not taken hold of us,* ***there*** *might have* ***been no occasion for*** *him* ***to*** *tell me.* NM □ *'And if the condition gets worse, is it operable?' 'Yes, but* ***there*** *should* ***be no occasion for*** *that in your case, unless you choose to disregard doctor's orders.'*

there is no/not any question there is no doubt **A:** about it, about that; of that, of his guilt; that he did it □ ***No question****, the middle class in America has it better than most other nations.* L □ *With Goldwyn, it is sometimes difficult to tell the dividing line between reality and fantasy—as it is with many people. Myself included.* ***No question*** *about it.* RT □ *They came here to play Rugby and, until provoked today, their reputation was untarnished.* ***There is no question*** *that the Lions were less than innocents in the warfare which took place before a baying 50,000 crowd at Lancaster Park.* OBS □ *England's my home,* ***there's no question*** *of that, but there doesn't seem to be any work for me here.* RT □ ***There is no question*** *of their guilt. The only query is whether the punishment was not too severe.* ST □ *there is* may be deleted before *no question.*

there is no room for doubt etc there is no scope or opportunity for doubt or other feeling, attitude or action **det:** no, (not) any; little, some. **o:** doubt, complacency, dispute, slackness, improvization □ *There is also a fatalistic note: the victim of the crime, in her last words, declares, quite unprotestingly, that it is what she expected; and* ***there is no room for doubt*** *that such an end is what she half invited and half desired.* AH □ *The accused was probably guilty, but, on the evidence presented,* ***there was some room for doubt***. □ ***There is****, accordingly,* ***no room for complacency*** *about what is the main cause of misery in our society.* SC □ *A common meeting ground, that's what we all need. Drama, art, poetry—the great things of the spirit—* ***no room*** *there* ***for*** *petty* ***jealousies*** *or hatreds.* TCB □ *What makes acting more difficult than writing is that actors can't hint at possiblities or point out negative characteristics.* ***There's no room for 'perhaps'****. It's the art of embodiment rather than lengthy discretion.* RT

there is nothing/not anything like sth (for doing sth/to do sth) there is nothing that is so effective in achieving a specified result than some particular remedy etc **o:** a good book; a cup of strong tea; an occasional setback; being laughed at; taking a brisk walk. **A:** for passing the time; to revive you; when you're tired; if one is taking oneself too seriously □ *I always say that* ***there's nothing like*** *a good book* ***for*** *taking you out of yourself.* □ (Virginia is pregnant) *'I've made cocoa,' Mrs Benberg went on. '****There's nothing like*** *a mug of cocoa when you're feeding two.'* AITC □ *Ah well, I suppose* ***there's nothing like*** *an occasional setback* ***to*** *make you realize how lucky you usually are.* □ *Who knows what thoughts were passing through that girl's mind while she was deciding to throw me out?* ***There's nothing like*** *a woman's doing you an injury* ***for*** *making her incensed against you.* UTN □ *If you don't sleep well* ***there's nothing like*** *a brisk walk, a warm bath, and a hot milky drink—in that order—before you go to bed.*

there is room for improvement (catchphrase) there is a possibility, a desirability or a real need, for improvement (the implication usu being that sb/sth is not as satisfactory as he/it could or should be) **A:** always, still. **det:** a lot of, much, a great deal of □ *We asked whether the museum's image was as progressive as some of the objects displayed within. Miss Weston said* ***there was*** *always* ***room for improvement****.* OBS □ (a car) *I felt* ***there was room for improvement*** *in the suspension, which did not show up particularly well on the twisting roads.* SC □ (official documents) ***There is*** *a great deal of* ***room for improvement*** *in United Nations' prose, an enormous amount of room.* L

there etc is/lies the rub (catchphrase) that is where the difficulty or drawback is **adv:** there, ⚠ therein, here □ (source) *To die, to sleep;/To sleep: perchance to dream: ay,* ***there's the rub****;/ For in that sleep of death what dreams may come. . .* HAMLET II 3 □ *The occasional anonymous tipster and the eminent autobiographer may each claim to be serving the cause of truth.* ***There's the rub****, for it is a claim that can be neither wholly admitted nor wholly dismissed.* L □ *The concept obviously attracts Cunard because the QE2 gambling tables would have a substantially increased turnover if it could add casual daily visitors to its passenger list. And* ***therein lies the rub****, because, say critics of Cunard's plan, the turnover will be high enough to bring in the mobsters.* ST □ *Most car owners, however, are well aware that while motoring commuting is unavoidable for some, it can be selfish to the point of being anti-social in other circumstances.* ***The rub lies in*** *making the distinction. At some time or other every car is a nuisance except one's own.* SC □ variants that's the rub, the rub is that, the rub lies in doing sth.

there is a sucker/one born every minute (saying) gullible people are numerous—and cannot always be protected, are there to be exploited, etc □ (source) ***There's a sucker born every minute.*** (attributed to F T BARNUM 1810-91) □ *I would be able to square my conscience with such a phrase as: 'Ah well, no-one is forced to buy the stuff I sell and* ***there is*** *always* ***one born every day****.'* SC □ *And in times of lowered circumstances, you simply preyed on the less reputable impulses to which the mass was subject, when its members became plain suckers ('****one born every minute****, you needn't starve').* HD □ *If dealers buy here, then why shouldn't you, and so cut out the profit margin? There is no reason why not, provided you realise* ***a sucker is born every minute*** *and that this is not a place for the unwary with no knowledge of what to look for or what to pay.* TVT □ use of day in second example unusual; variant a sucker is born every minute.

there is that sth previously mentioned is a point to be acknowledged, taken into account, be thankful for, etc □ *'Against the cost of a long-distance flight you have to set what you may have to pay out for hotels, meals, and so on, on an overland journey.' '****There is that****, indeed. Perhaps I should cost my trip more carefully before deciding.'* □ *'It's just queer Nurse Ellen vanishing like this. Do you think she was cross with me for not wanting her to take the children?' 'Prissie, it's nothing to do with you. At least let's be thankful the children are all right.' 'Yes,* ***there is that****.'* DC □ stress pattern there 'is that.

there is a time (and a place) for everything (saying) there are times, (places), circumstances in which doing any particular thing is appropriate or necessary (with the implication that one does not, or should not, therefore do it anytime or anywhere) □ (source) *To everything* ***there is a season, and a time to every purpose*** *under the heaven.* ECCLESIASTES III 1-8 □ *People down here bothered less about* ***there being a time and place for everything*** *than people at home. Anna, with her midnight baths, dressing-gown at tea-time, and chocolates after breakfast, was in the lead on this.* TGLY □ *Today, as she munched meditatively, she was telling herself, not for the first time, that* ***there was a time and place for everything****—and that the office was definitely not the place for imitations of the boss's wife.* TCB

(but) there it is/you are that is the position; those are the facts □ *'I'm awfully sorry, old man,' he said, 'but Eva invited some friends up. Personally, I'd rather go out. They're crashing bores,* ***but there it is****. Some other time, eh?'* RATT □ *'What sort of job is it?' 'Pretty awful. Culture—poetry, all that sort of thing. Still,*

there it is*. It gives me a job so I oughtn't to complain.'* TCB □ *The girl was looking hurt. But suddenly she couldn't endure her in the room. It was absurd, it was neurotic,* ***but there it was****.* DC □ *If it had been invested in my gold shares it would have come back a hundred times.* ***But there you are****!* DC □ comment expressing acceptance of, or resignation to, a situation one does not like and would change if one could.

there should be a law against it etc (informal) it etc should not be allowed **O:** it; women going about half-naked, toothache, people like you □ *'She offered us a cup of cocoa.' He made a face. '****There should be a law against cocoa****.'* □ *The old chap thought the girls playing beach ball looked really pretty but his wife in the deckchair beside him muttered darkly about naked girls flaunting their charms all over the place and said* ***there should be a law against girls going around half-naked****.* □ *A fish-witted imbecile like you ought not to be allowed to be a doctor.* ***There should be some law against it****.* PE ⇨ ⚠ there is no law against it etc.

there was a time when once, formerly (but no longer) □ *You must forgive me then. Ask Mr Wormold—****there was a time when*** *I was not so suspicious. Shall we have some music?* OMIH □ ***There was a time when*** *the small* (TV) *screen seemed to diminish the choreographer's work. But now producers have learned how to translate ballet on to the box.* RT □ *Thought I'd die of shame if I bungled a step. Now I dance like a bull's foot most of the time, but I don't care as long as I can hang on to the job.* ***Time was*** *though,* ***when*** *I—* AITC □ stress pattern there 'was a time when; variant, time was when, has stress pattern time 'was when.

(and) there you/we are a comment marking the (successful) completion of a task, argument or prediction □ *Nail a piece of pegboard on the inside of your wardrobe door. Screw in some hooks — small ones for belts, larger ones for handbags—****and there you are****! Problem neatly solved.* WI □ *He had thought salmon fishing was a case of leasing a length of river, buying the best tackle,* ***and there you were****.* □ *'We've all passed the test!' 'Well,* ***there you are****, then, you pessimists. I told you you would, didn't I?'*

there's (got to be) a first time for everything (saying) because sth has not happened, or been done, before there is no reason to assume that it never will □ *I tell myself* ***there's got to be a first time for everything****, and children can't stay with their parents forever. But Johnnie going away is the first break in the family and I'm absolutely hating it.* □ *'It can't be rheumatism, doctor. I've never had a rheumatic ache or pain in my life.' 'Well,* ***there's a first time for everything****, you know, and you're not so young as you used to be.'*

there's gold in them thar hills (catchphrase) there are opportunites for making a fortune in the places, pursuits, businesses indicated □ *Two unprofitably mild winters followed with the ski-slopes seldom usable. If* ***there there was*** *to be* ***gold in them thar hills*** *for the promoters, the Aviemore Centre would have to offer holiday-makers a great variety of sports and activities all the year round.* □ (NONCE) *Roger Whittaker's series of lunchtime shows on Friday is a singing shop window for Britain's undiscovered song-writers. Each show introduces lyrics by inspired amateurs and, indeed,* ***there's gold in them thar trills****.* TVT □ *'The next big movie boom is going to be space fantasy,' says Samuel Z. Arkoff, head of American International Pictures. It is, indeed, already upon us. 'Star Wars', the box-office wonder of 1977, has shown that* ***there's gold in them thar galaxies****.* OBS □ originally US, referring to 19th c gold prospecting; deliberately ungrammatical, them thar hills = 'those hills there'; often adapted, as shown.

there's many a slip 'twixt (the) cup and (the) lip (saying) any accident or unforeseen obstacle may prevent one from doing or obtaining sth expected □ *'They're bound to win now.' 'Unless one of them breaks an oar or something.* ***There's many a slip 'twixt the cup and the lip****.'* □ *Of course advertising works, and so does public relations: but as Party Political Broadcasts usually show,* ***there's many a slip 'twixt the cup and the*** *curling* ***lip****.* L

there's no business like show business (catchphrase) there is nothing to compare with the profession of popular entertainment □ (source) ***There's no business like show business****/Like no business I know.* I BERLIN b1888 □ *For this old trouper* ***there is*** *still* ***no business like show business****.* OBS □ (NONCE) *The big-time promotion is undertaken with gusto and no cynicism about public taste. One would say if* ***there's no biz like show biz, there's no biz like grow biz****—but as Lew* (Grade) *told an interviewer: 'If I was only in it for the money I'd be living somewhere I only paid 50% Income Tax.'* SC □ (NONCE) ***There's no business like spy business****: Derek Jacobi appears next week on TV as Guy Burgess in a Granada play about the Terrible Three, 'Philby, Burgess and Maclean'.* OBS □ stress pattern there's ˌno business like 'show business.

there's no place like home (saying) home is the best, the most pleasant, place; East (or) West, home's best (qv) □ (source) *Mid pleasures and palaces though we may roam,/Be it ever so humble,* ***there's no place like home****.* HOME, SWEET HOME (J H PAYNE 1791-1852) □ *She drew the curtains and sat down by Harold's side, and took his hand: and when he said, '****There's no place like home****, is there?' her thoughts did not wince at this too obvious remark.* PW □ *I adore seeing the world. But, let's face it,* ***there*** *really* ***is no place*** *quite* ***like*** *your own* ***home****.* TVT □ *They say* ***there's no place like home****. But when Brian and Vera try to put Tommy in one* (ie a 'home' for old people)*, he refuses to go.* TVT

there's nowt so queer/funny as folk (saying — esp Yorkshire) people, human behaviour, can be more unpredictable, extravagant, baffling etc than anything in nature or art □ *Robin Thornber went to the Yorkshire town of Holmfirth, where Monday's new comedy series was filmed, to see if the people there were anything like the characters on the screen. He found that—* ***there's nowt so queer as folk****.* RT □ (NONCE) *This was a good script, perhaps because the target was the British holidaymaker —ourselves. It seemed to grow naturally from scene to scene, was based on characters familiar* *to most of us, and* ***'there's nowt as funny as folk.'*** L □ nowt = 'nothing', folk = 'human beings'.

(and) thereby hangs a tale (and) connected with, or illustrating, that (ie sth already mentioned) there is a story or further information, often of a revealing or surprising nature □ (source) *And so, from hour to hour, we ripe and ripe,/And then from hour to hour, we rot and rot:/* ***And thereby hangs a tale.*** AS YOU LIKE IT II 5 □ *Muscovites have always resented the crafty Georgians minting money out of them by selling commodities they need. But the prospect of no supplies at all is even worse.* ***Thereby hangs a tale*** *and Russians are spellbound by the latest Georgian saga which has been unfolding.* NS

these days [A (NP)] at the present time; now (contrasted with a time in the past before the time referred to) □ *'Don't be so prickly.' Guy smiled, a little shamefacely. 'Sorry, Biddy. I'm touchy* ***these days****.'* DC □ *All the same, being a housewife is no more boring than working in an office. People think so much of money* ***these days*** *that they under-rate women — or themselves—if they're not actually making it.* RT □ ***These days****, the social responsibility of the scientist is a very fashionable topic for discussion.* L □ front, middle or end position.

they don't make etc them like that any more (catchphrase) one does not now meet, see, obtain people or things or the kind of quality described **V:** make, build; breed, grow, write. **O:** them; girls, ships. **o:** that; my grandmother, the Queen Mary □ *She is a soldier's wife: cheerful, resourceful, warmhearted, adaptable, on top of life; a home maker; no theories, all practicality.'* ***They don't make them like that any more.****'* ST □ *Generation-pride immediately overcame personal dislike:* ***they don't make them like that any more****. Whether he deserves to or not Guy Burgess will now take his place in the gallery of immortal English eccentrics.* OBS □ *'I just have to live it up. I'm not the ordinary guy in the street. I want to do everything.'* ***They don't make 'em*** (= them) ***like Bonar Colleano any more.*** TVT □ *When it comes to nostalgia about old movies, it's not the films themselves that I get the reminiscent soppies* (= sentimental feelings) *over, it's the old forgotten advertising slogans. Never mind '****they don't make films like that anymore****';* ***they don't write slogans like that anymore.*** TVT □ variant they don't come like that any more.

they order things better in France etc (saying) hospitality, education, family life, arrangements for travellers, etc are managed better elsewhere □ (source—opening sentence of the book but never fully explained) ***They order****, said I,* ***this matter better in France.*** A SENTIMENTAL JOURNEY (L STERNE 1713-68) □ *A tenacious character will always get his case against a Government Department heard but the timid may shrink from the ordeal of self-assertion.* ***They order things better in Scandinavia.*** *Professor Hurwitz holds an office specially created to protect citizens against the state.* SC □ *Even in those far-off days, we Scots were lamentably ignorant of our national heritage; we are still slow to exploit its commercial value.* ***They order things better in Transylvania.*** *The Romanian tourist board is making big business out of the so-called 'Dracula Country'.* SC

they shall not pass we shall not be defeated (esp, a slogan in defensive warfare, counter-demonstration, (mass) resistance to take-over, eviction, black-leg workers during a strike, etc) □ (source) ***Ils ne passeront pas.*** (MARECHAL PETAIN, about the Germans, when defending Verdun, 1916) □ (a 'blackshirt' march through the streets of London, 1936) (A very distant sound of chanting is heard: '***They shall not pass, they shall not pass, they shall not pass.****'*) MONTY: *The boys! Listen. Hear them? You know, Sarah, that's the same cry the people of Madrid were shouting.* PRINCE: *And they didn't get past either. Imagine it! All those women and children coming out into the streets and making barricades with their beds and chairs.* CSWB

they that live by the sword shall perish/die by the sword (saying) those who live by committing violence must expect violence to be turned upon themselves □ (source) *Put up again thy sword into his place: for all* ***they that take the sword shall perish with the sword.*** MATTHEW XXVI 52 □ (NONCE) ***Those who live in politics by virtue of machination should not perhaps complain over-loudly if they*** *eventually* ***perish by it.*** NS □ (NONCE) *I was particularly struck, with Ulster in mind, by the boy revolutionary rejecting the Christian message of peace and goodwill with the slogan: '****Them that perish by the gun must live by the gun.****'* ST

a thieves' kitchen [Comp (NP)] a place where criminals etc meet to exchange information, make plans, etc **V:** ⚠ be, become, turn into □ *He told me the story in a café in the Socco Chico, which is* ***the*** *'****thieves' kitchen****' of Tangier. It is here that crooks and smugglers and dope-pedlars congregate, and a pretty villainous gang they are.* DS □ *In the UN he finds military gangsters and expert racists, men who have devoted their lives to the destruction of democracy and the courts. More and more, the UN begins to resemble* ***a thieves' kitchen.*** NS

a thin excuse [Comp/O (NP)] an inadequate reason (for doing/not doing sth) **V:** be, seem; have, give, offer □ *After looking at me with rising embarrassment for some seconds he announced, 'Went to the cinema last night.' This seemed* ***a thin excuse*** *for interrupting my evening's work, but I said politely, 'A good film, I hope?'* DIL □ *'She said she didn't come because she'd lost our address.' 'Well, that's* ***a thin excuse****! She knows lots of people who could have told her.'*

the thin red line the heroic resistance of few against many (originally describing the arrangement of a regiment of highland infantry then red-coated, at the battle of Balaclava, 1854, during the Crimean War) □ (source) *The Russians dash on towards* ***that thin red streak*** *topped with a line of steel.* BRITISH EXPEDITION TO THE CRIMEA (W H RUSSELL 1820-1907) □ *And his photograph of the Black Watch firing a 'feu de joie' — the firing of rifles in the air down the lines from right to left and then left to right to create a kind of rippling effect — aptly illustrates the frailty of* ***the thin red line*** *that was the backbone of Queen Victoria's Empire.* OBS □ (NONCE) (teachers' demonstration outside Parliament) *The principals needed their principles to* *keep them warm; it grew minute by minute windier and colder. To one of the press cameramen it was a good joke: 'You've got* ***the thin blue line*** *here all right.'* T □ blue in last example refers to hands and faces going blue from cold.

a thing of beauty is a joy forever (saying) the pleasure that beauty or a beautiful object, person, scene etc gives will last forever □ (source) ***A thing of beauty is a joy for ever****:/ It's loveliness increases; it will never/Pass into nothingness.* ENDYMION (J KEATS 1795-1821) □ *'£1500! You could get a new one for a tenth of that!' he said, with total lack of appreciation of* ***things of beauty*** *that* ***were a joy forever****.* □ *It was a stump pipe affair with gaily coloured keys. It made a noise like a paralysed duck, and my three-year-old son Leo immediately decided it was* ***a thing of beauty*** *and bound to* ***be a*** *musical* ***joy for ever****.* TVT □ use often facetious, as shown here.

a thing of the past [Comp (NP)] an old-fashioned, defunct, or superseded (type of) article, person, activity, belief etc **V:** ⚠ be; think sth, regard sth as □ *Current fashion hats certainly have a strictly functional aspect. And what of the contemporary hatpin? Or are hatpins* ***things of the past****?* SC □ *Clark once said 'I was born bald!' and indeed his hair was already* ***a thing of the past*** *when he made his screen debut at the age of 33.* TVT □ *A major told me that the screaming, tyrannical sergeant-major spreading terror in the ranks was* ***a thing of the past****. Discipline is imposed in different ways now.* ST □ *The Brazilian team manager was asked about the significance of their World Cup victory. He said artistry had been regarded as* ***a thing of the past****—until the Brazilians won the World Cup with it.* L

things fall apart, the centre cannot hold a society, system, creed, philosophy etc breaks up from within □ (source) ***Things fall apart; the centre cannot hold****;/Mere anarchy is loosed upon the world.* THE SECOND COMING (W B YEATS 1865-1939) □ *'Full House' hangs loose.* ***Things fall apart*** *not because* ***the centre cannot hold*** *but because there is no centre to begin with—by which I mean there is no informing concept, no intellectual authority and no adequately defined editorial purpose.* NS □ *They agreed that* ***things*** *in the permissive society were* ***falling apart****, but they were sure that* ***the centre could*** *and would* ***hold*** *if the stranglehold of the progressives could be broken.* L

things that go bump in the night (facetious) strange or supernatural alarms □ (source) *From ghoulies and ghosties* (= ghouls and ghosts) *and long-leggety beasties/And* ***things that go bump in the night****,/Good Lord, deliver us.* ANONYMOUS □ *Over the years the scientific vocabulary of such matters has grown. Today, telepathy is extra-sensory perception. Spoon-bending is psychokinesis.* ***Things that go bump in the night*** *are paranormal activities or, best of all, non-materialist sciences.* TVT □ *Something should have told them, though, about old Mrs Allardyce in the attic who needs three meals a day behind locked doors. Around this point the camera develops blurred vision, and* ***things go bump in the night****.* NS □ ***Things that go bump in the night*** *hold no terrors for Wendy Gifford—she saves her energy for laying into daylight demolishers.* TVT

to think (that)! how suprising, exciting, absurd, distressing or frightening it is (to think that) □ *All I know is that he gave me a month's notice this morning. And* ***to think!*** *All the years I'd been here with Dr McBurney.* DIL □ (advertisement) ***To think that*** *my hair could look so gorgeous simply by whiffing it over with New Perfumer Spray Set!* H □ *I always said that boiler would explode one day. And* ***to think that*** *if your Bert hadn't just stepped outside for a smoke, he'd have been blown up with it!* □ often introduced by *and.*

think big etc have ambitious, self-confident, purposeful ideas about what one can do, what can be achieved **adv:** big, positive, ambitious; young □ *The snow-capped pictures came from 'Worldwide', a new BBC 2 series showing documentaries from different countries.* ***Think big****, someone said, so they started with China.* L □ *You are going to get well. So* ***think positive****, make plans, encourage your friends to keep in touch — and don't be sorry for yourself.* □ *Arthur Askey, after more than half a century in show business, talks about life at 77 and advises: '****Think young****.'* RT

think straight think logically, competently or clearly □ *He could easily get away, and beyond that he found it impossible to* ***think straight*** *about the situation at all.* HD □ *If you'd both shut up for five minutes, I might tell you. I can't* ***think straight*** *with all these interruptions.* □ *The motor car not only gets us increasingly hooked, personally, but its massive and often dominant presence in the fields of employment, exports, and taxation, makes it almost impossible for governments, let alone individuals, to* ***think straight*** *on the subject.* ST □ usu neg or neg implication.

a think tank an advisory body of people engaged in productivity, management, policy, feasibility etc studies □ *...we should again be able to take a leading place. But we haven't space in our factory. We haven't room in our* ***Think-Tanks****.* RALEIGH PROMOTIONAL CIRCULAR (1911) □ *Neither the techniques of show business, nor the theories of* ***the*** *intellectual* ***think-tanks****, are sufficient to cope with the complexities of the globe that we now inhabit.* NS □ *The report, certain to be used as potent propaganda in the coming French elections, has been produced by the Hudson Institute,* ***the 'think tank'*** *of the controversial 'futurologist' Herman Kahn.* ST □ *Now, however, a new inquiry is being launched. By outsiders? Of course not; it will be conducted by Whitehall's own Central Policy Review Staff (****the 'think tank'*** *headed by Sir Kenneth Berrill).* NS

the third degree intensive and prolonged interrogation, possibly including torture, to elicit information or a confession □ *In this there is a very marked difference between lie-detection techniques, and the use of* ***the 'third degree'****, which has caused many subjects to confess to crimes they have not committed in order to escape from the intolerable situation.* SNP □ *'And your employment before that?' 'Look here,' I said, losing patience, 'what's all this* ***third degree*** *stuff in aid of? I'm asking to open an* *account, not to manage the Bank of England.'* ◻ frequently facetious; attrib use, *this* ***third degree*** *stuff*, common.

third time lucky at the third attempt one will be, is, was successful ('3' being thought of as a 'lucky number') ◻ (filming) *'I've had no trouble of this kind and now two jams* (= the film has jammed) *in as many minutes. It's unbelievable. But never mind!* ***Third time lucky****!' He started the third and only spare magazine.* LWK ◻ *If you missed the two previous 'TV Times' pools contests, don't worry. There's a new Star Competition next week. If you have already entered, you can enter again, and it could be your* ***third time lucky*** *to win our bonanza pools entry.* TVT ◻ *Una now has a new man in her life. Marriage again,* ***third time lucky****?* TVT ◻ may be used to console sb for lack of success in past.

(for) thirty pieces/(for) a handful of silver (in exchange for) money given as a bribe or reward for doing sth dishonourable, betraying another, etc ◻ (source) *And* (Judas Iscariot) *said unto them, What will ye give me, and I will deliver him unto you? And they convenanted with him* ***for thirty pieces of silver****.* MATTHEW XXVI 15 ◻ (source) *Just* ***for a handful of silver*** *he left us,/Just for a riband to stick in his coat.* THE LOST LEADER (R BROWNING 1812-89) ◻ *I thought of my father. He was a good workman—too good a workman to be sacked and too outspoken about his Labour convictions to be promoted. My mother knew what was in my mind. 'Your father would starve before he'd sell himself* ***for a handful of silver****.'* RATT ◻ *He has thrown his humanity into the gutter, he had betrayed the trust that men place in one another, and with his* ***thirty pieces of silver*** *he had bought—what had he bought?* HD

this is it that (ie sth already mentioned) is the precise nature of the situation, difficulty, problem etc; that's just it/(just) the trouble (qv) ◻ *'It can't be much fun, sitting by yourself at home most evenings.'* ***'This is it****! I'm pretty well fed up with being married to an MP, I can tell you.'*

this is where we came in (catchphrase) we are back to where we started; we have seen, done, this before (the reference originally being to the moment at which one saw again the material one had first seen in a continuous cinema programme) ◻ (proposal for the European nuclear deterrent) *Who would have the power to fire this hybrid armament? The French President? The British Prime Minister? Possibly a committee of NATO Defence Ministers. Those who sat through the comic opera of the Multilateral Force will realise at once that* ***this is where we came in****.* NS ◻ PETER: *I stole all my mother's money and it all led nowhere. And now I'm a no-one with nothing. This is where we break up. This is the end of the road.* ALEX: *You said it, this is the end of the road.* ***This is where I came in****.* DPM

this (very) minute etc [A (NP)] now; immediately **n:** minute, ⚠ instant, second ◻ *The child did not answer, but stood quite still, staring intently at the visitor. 'Upstairs* ***this minute****!' It seemed that everything Gladys did must be done* ***that minute****. 'Take her up, Rosa dear.'* HD ◻ *'I said we must be going.' 'Yes, I heard you but I didn't know you meant* ***this very minute****.'* ◻ *'When did you get here?' 'I've just* ***this second*** *arrived.'* ◻ *'I know you're there, whoever you are,' the watchman called, 'and if you don't show yourself* ***this instant*** *I'll set the dog on you.'* ◻ middle or end position.

this side (of) the grave/heaven [A (NP)] in this world; in/during one's lifetime ◻ *Education is a continuous process which does not stop short* ***this side of the grave****.* ◻ *I meditated. The conclusion I reached was that* ***this side the grave*** *there is simply no end to anything.* SML ◻ *Naturally if Frank* (her son in Australia) *could have lived next door and Ella* (her dead daughter) *the other side that would have been better, but* ***this side of*** *that kind of* ***heaven*** *she had everything she wanted.* TSMP

this side (of) idolatry etc [A (NP)] less in amount or degree than idolatry etc **adv mod:** just, well. **n:** idolatry, perfection, destitution, slander; worshipping him, taking life ◻ (source) *For I loved the man, and do honour his memory, on* ***this side idolatry****, as much as any.* DISCOVERIES (S JOHNSON 1709-84) ◻ *Even the eighteenth century, which is often supposed to have frowned on Shakespeare's lack of correctness, admired him only just* ***this side of idolatry****.* OBS ◻ *True, they stopped short at a point well* ***this side of idolatry****; but all concurred in assigning to mescalin a position among drugs of unique distinction.* DOP ◻ *In this country we can still say what we like* ***this side of libel****.* ◻ *The majority of men's parents expect a bride* (in India) *to bring a dowry large enough to be just* ***this side of financially crippling her parents****.* L

this and/or that [pron + pron non-rev] a number of, any one of, some things, activities, subjects etc ◻ *'What are you doing these days, Anna?' 'Oh,* ***this and that****,' said Anna.* UTN ◻ *'I'm sorry, dear,' she said, 'but looking after the house will be just as much as I can manage. I can't have the extra responsibility of worrying whether Dodd's doing* ***this or that*** *for the fowls.'* HAA ◻ *He had been spirited away into grim and secret places where the doctors had given him* ***this*** *drug* ***and that*** *and where, in an attempt to control his difficult behaviour, he had been subjected to numerous electric shocks to the brain.* NS ◻ *Once or twice I asked him directly whether he held* ***this or that*** *theory—which he always denied with the air of one who has been affronted by a failure of taste.* UTN ◻ *I don't know how Tom started this habit but whatever he's speaking about it's bloody* ***this and*** *bloody* ***that*** *the whole time.* ◻ also [det + det non-rev] as in ***this*** *man* ***or that****,* ***this and that*** *excuse.*

this, that, and the other [pron + pron + pron non-rev] a number of, several, things, activities etc ◻ MR BUTCHER: *We're afraid.* PETER: *What of?* MR FISH: ***This, that, and the other****.* DPM ◻ *The bill was a blinder* (ie it amazed him). *He doubted very much if he'd ever get over the bill. Percentages for* ***this,*** *taxes for* ***that****, services for* ***the other****.* BFA ◻ *The exchange rate was still favourable and travel agencies were busy booking people for* ***this, that, and the other*** *foreign holiday resort.* ◻ also [det + det + det non-rev] as in last example.

this time last/next year etc [A (NP)] last/next year at this time/date **n:** ***(last/next)*** year,

⚠ week; Thursday; tomorrow, yesterday □ *The students may be a bit wild and woolly when they first arrive, but they'll soon settle down. And if they don't, they'll be gone before* ***this time next year.*** HAA □ *So much has happened I can hardly believe it was only* ***this time yesterday*** *that I was boarding the train to come here.*

this/a vale of tears man's life on earth seen as a time of effort and sorrow □ *To have a character of the stature of Pottinger shoot himself while travelling in a mail coach would diminish him. It was much more fitting to have him depart* ***this vale of tears*** *in the presence of his enemy.* RT □ *A problem can be solved by the brisk application of a little common sense. This is Mr Powell's approach. Sir Keith is quite different. He observes* ***this vale of tears*** *and then starts to cry himself.* NS □ *Circumstances combined early to make him view the world as* ***a vale of tears.*** □ usu ironic or facetious.

this way and that [A (NP)] in all, or various, directions; by all, or various, means or methods □ *Charles had never seen a knuckle-duster* (ie a piece of metal that protects the knuckles against, and adds force to, a blow) *before, but he recognized it. The bald-headed man considerately turned it* ***this way and that****, so that he could get a good look at it.* HD □ *She pushed the bushes aside, and stepped out cautiously, looking* ***this way and that.*** TST □ *I've tried* ***this way and that*** *to please her and to be a help, but the truth is that she'd rather people thought she had a hard time of it.*

this will hurt me more than it hurts you (catchphrase) excuse or justification for punishing, rejecting, disapointing etc sb, usu on the plea that it is unavoidable or for the other's own good □ (asking for the resignation of subordinates) *'Everyone has to make sacrifices; no one more than I who have to part company with colleagues,' said Asquith, and Churchill never stopped pointing out how near that came to the old lie about '****this will hurt me more than it hurts you.****'* L □ *The film about Andy Warhol was not only a colossal bore to watch; it is even deathly tedious to visit on it the criticism it deserves. The old headmaster's saying, '****This will hurt me more than it hurts you****,' becomes literally true.* NS □ (NONCE) ***This is going to hurt you more than it will hurt me****: an investigation into forms of school punishment, by Brian Jackson and Ann Garvey.* ST

this year, next year, sometime, never [A (NP)] answer to 'When?' (from children's counting, using the letters of a name, a row of buttons, string of beads, etc, to predict when an imagined event (esp marriage) will take place) □ *Time slipping by unnoticed leads me to suggest a little parlour game for you to play without recourse to diaries or record books. Was it* ***this year, next year, sometime, never****, that the following occurred:...?* L □ *These winter woollies are still available and, like any highly individual combination of classics, they never go out of fashion: wear them* ***this year, next year, sometime.*** OBS

a thorn in the flesh/side (of sb/sth) [Comp/O (NP)] sb/sth who irks or annoys another person or group, impairs their well-being, complacency or authority **V:** ⚠ be, become, find sb □ (source) *There was given me* ***a thorn in the flesh****, the messenger of Satan to buffet me, lest I should be exalted above measure.* II CORINTHIANS XII 7 □ *When Cobbett founded his Political Register in 1802 he became* ***a thorn in the flesh of*** *Pitt's government.* RT □ *Mrs Ruth Colver is secretary of the Dorset rights of way group of the Ramblers' Association. She gave up teaching to do her footpath work full-time and is* ***a thorn in the side of*** *administrators.* OBS □ *He's a relative of course, but* ***a thorn in*** *our flesh. I wish he could emigrate or something.* □ (NONCE) *One official sign of the programme's success as* ***a thorn in the Establishment*** *came last month.* NS □ also pl thorns in the flesh of sb/sth; used most frequently about people.

thoroughly modern sb/sth (catchphrase) most up-to-date (from the film '***Thoroughly Modern*** *Millie*', 1967) □ *Just what is* ***thoroughly modern*** *Maggie playing at? In order to save a mere £20 a head on the cost of a return ticket Mrs Thatcher's team booked two charter flights for the American beano.* G □ *At the back of the auditorium are control rooms for sound technicians, electricians and stage manager, with projection facilities for closed-circuit video and TV. This* ***thoroughly modern*** *marvel...* TVT □ *Then on to Bedford where we pay* ***thoroughly modern*** *prices for bed and no breakfast in a middle-of-the-road hotel.* SC

those were the days (catchphrase) that was a good, pleasant, interesting, stimulating etc time to be alive □ *Vernon Bartlett, now 80 years old and retired to Tuscany, was the sort of diplomatic correspondent whose name was flashed on the cinema screen if the 'News Chronicle' wanted him.* ***Those were the days****!* L □ *If the film clips of Marie Lloyd and Little Tich were genuine, then I am amazed that we have not had sight of them before. This combination of nostalgia and modern technology is a delight and I look forward to the rest of the run.* ***Those****, indeed,* ***were the days.*** RT □ *'And it was the first attempt ever by a Prime Minister to use the medium. Baldwin went on the Radio and said it wouldn't do, and the TUC was impressed.' Ah,* ***those were the days****—or were they?* RT

those who can, do; those who cannot, teach (catchphrase) the most talented in a skill or art will practise it, so the task of instruction is left to the less talented □ (source) ***He who can, does. He who cannot, teaches.*** MAXIMS FOR REVOLUTIONISTS (G B SHAW 1856-1950) □ '***Those that can, do; those that can't, teach****,' runs the disparaging adage, and there is something of the same feeling about commentators. 'If he knows so much why doesn't he have a go himself?' In fact, commentating, like criticism or teaching, has little to do with one's own ability as a performer.* RT □ a sneering generalization.

(even) though I say it/so myself [Disj] (it is true) though I may seem boastful or may be accused of prejudice □ *You should also on the radio be able to talk, from a few scattered notes maybe, rather than read a piece written out beforehand. This,* ***though I say it myself****, I had no difficulty in doing.* ST □ *I've always been a good runner, the only trouble being that no matter how fast I run, and I did a very fair lick* ***even though I do say so myself****, it didn't stop me getting* *caught by the cops after the bakery job.* LLDR □ □ dependent clause in front, middle or end position relative to main clause.

(in) thought, word and/or deed (in) any way; (in) any manifestation of human intention whatever □ (source) *We acknowledge and bewail our manifold sins and wickedness, Which we, from time to time, most grievously have committed,* ***By thought, word, and deed****, Against thy Divine Majesty.* BOOK OF COMMON PRAYER □ *No* ***thought, word or deed*** *of his life had roused in him any feeling resembling the guilt he experienced as he stood waiting for Mrs Pettigrew to pay the taxi and turn to ask him, 'Where have you been?'* MM □ *The vicar closed the benediction with an appeal to God to 'keep us all pure* ***in thought, word and deed*** *both now and hereafter' and we sallied forth, not much weighed down by the unlikelihood of such a condition.*

three cheers (for sb/sth) an expression of approval; cheering by a crowd to salute sb/sth in the formula 'Hip, hip' (by a cheer-leader) and 'Hurray' (by all), shouted three times **V:** give (sb), get, call for □ *As the car moved off, the sergeant distinctly heard from the other side of the river bank: '****Three cheers for*** *the Skelper: Hip-Hip-Hurray! Hip-Hip-Hurray! Hip-Hip—'* TO □ *'Do you still have that terrible family next door?' 'Yes, but they're moving shortly and* ***three cheers for*** *that.'* □ *Who, giving a moment's thought to what has been done in our own time in the name of 'democracy', would possibly support it or give it* ***two cheers****? E M Forster could. He found it less hateful than other contemporary forms of government.* AH □ *What landscape that is being made today tends to be not by the private rich but by a few lively corporate or public bodies. I would give* ***two cheers for*** *the Forestry Commission.* L □ two cheers suggests only modified approval.

the three Rs (mastery of) 'reading, (w)riting and (a)rithmetic' as first essentials in education □ *Primary schools have caused a fierce debate between traditionalists and progressives. Do we just want* ***the three Rs****, or more self-expression, or more discipline?* L □ *It has been fashionable for far too long in our teacher training colleges to emphasize the 'child-centred' approach and to denigrate proven and successful methods of teaching* ***the Three R's****, and the valuable memory-training processes of 'learning by heart' and 'learning by repetition'.* RT

three score years and ten 70 years as an expected human life span □ (source) *The days of our years are* ***three score years and ten****; and if by reason of strength they be four score years, yet is their strength labour and sorrow.* PSALMS XC 12 □ *The good book, if we are to believe it, says we are entitled to* ***three score years and ten****. Who am I to argue?* OBS □ *The rate at which the human programme goes to pieces with time is constant. If it weren't, the* ***threescore-and-ten*** *rule would not have the wide validity it has in different places and times.* OBS □ score = '20'; attrib use *the* ***threescore-and-ten*** *rule.*

(the) thrills and spills [n + n non-rev] the excitement of taking part in, or watching, sports or entertainments involving hazards of a not-too-serious kind □ *This final programme of the present series pays tribute to all the winners who have emerged in the past three months—a last look at the excitement, the drama,* ***the thrills and spills****.* TVT □ *They would get a start on the local weekly—and begin to fight, and sometimes even write, their way to the top. The top was indisputably Fleet Street. Since then things have changed: Much of* ***the thrills and spills*** *has evaporated into dull routine.* RT

through no (particular etc) fault etc of one's own [A (Prep)] for reasons one cannot be blamed etc for **adj:** particular, special, outstanding. **n:** fault; ⚠ merit, virtue □ *The Palestine Police Force was 50 per cent below strength, and considered as a force to be no more than 25 per cent effective—* ***through no fault of its own****.* MFM □ *I asked him if he thought he was overpaid. 'The answer is yes,' he replied, 'and no. It's a lot of money. I can't get it down any lower On the other hand,* ***through no fault of my own****, I happen to be born into an era where the mass media is king.'* OBS □ *Childhood was the germ of all mistrust. You were cruelly joked upon and then you cruelly joked. You lost the remembrance of pain through inflicting it. But somehow,* ***through no virtue of his own****, he had never taken that course. Lack of character perhaps.* OMIH

through thick and thin [A (PrepP)] through, or despite, everything that happens or that one has to deal with; through good times and bad times; determinedly; faithfully **V:** fight, struggle, go on; support, stick by, accompany, sb; be faithful, loyal; be a staunch friend □ *Determined to do in Parliament what he promised his voters, Brand fights* ***through thick and thin*** *to retain his integrity.* TVT □ *Yet Stilwell was an almost impossible man to work with, and even the small group of American officers who stuck loyally by him* ***through thick and thin*** *were frightened of him.* ST □ *Barmaids were, as she had told Harold, not promiscuous; it didn't mean that they never took a lover, or that they wouldn't be faithful to him—touchingly faithful* ***through thick and thin****.* PW □ thick and thin non-rev.

through and through [A] completely, in every way or detail □ *He's not just a crook. He's mean and rotten* ***through and through****.* PE □ *And she had only been with him once for a week-end; but her thoughts had been so constantly with him that she felt she knew him* ***through and through****.* PW □ may modify preceding adj.

throw/give a party (for sb/sth) [V + O pass] arrange for a party (for sb/sth) to take place **n** (attrib): dinner, children's, birthday, celebration, Welcome-Home □ *With the arrival of yet another stranger, myself, they felt that something had to be done about it. They* ***threw a party****.* SD □ (advice column) ***Throw a*** *small* ***party*** *and make that an excuse for contacting him.* H □ *'Could I come up for a weekend soon and bring my fiancé with me?' 'You do that, and we'll* ***throw a party for*** *you.'* □ occas pl.

thrust and parry [n + n rev] attack and defence; attack and defend; question and answer (in a fight, confrontation, argument or quarrel; from fencing); the cut and thrust of sth (qv); a battle of wits (qv) □ *Ken Hughes directs with lots of dash, and Richard Harris as Cromwell and Alec Guinness as Charles I* ***thrust and***

parry *with grand panache.* RT □ *Counsel rocked back and forth on the balls of his feet — as counsel are wont to do while preparing the next rapier* ***thrust and parry****—and demanded: 'Was that a rare occurrence?'* SC □ *Any hope that a good phoner-in might engage the morning's politician in some nifty* ***parry-and-thrust*** *with real sparks flying was dulled by the necessity to forbid questions relating to specific constituencies.* L □ also [v + v rev].

a thumbnail portrait/sketch (of sb/sth) a brief account or description of sb/sth □ *'It looks like some kind of Toyland,' she said of the trim little housing estate. As* ***a thumbnail sketch of*** *the set-up, that seemed to me just right.* □ *I was disappointed in the article. Any tourist could have written it—just a list of the usual show-places and half a dozen* ***thumbnail portraits of*** *local worthies.*

thump a/the tub/Bible [V + O pass] speak, preach in a (conventionally) forceful or melodramatic style (from banging one's fist on a pulpit, desk, table, book etc to emphasize one's argument) □ (a film) *The hero, after a night on the town and various rebuffs, gets taken on by a stiff-necked preacher (there are a few magnificent chapel scenes, during one of which* ***a bible*** *gets* ***thumped*** *for real* (= in fact) *as the whole congregation goes into a praise-the-Lord jam session).* NS □ *Mauroy has an old-fashioned* ***tub-thumping*** *style of Socialism.* OBS □ *The history of the Yorkshire Dales is filled with the names of famous lay preachers who held large audiences spellbound with their* ***Bible-thumping*** *oratory.* TVT □ usu found as n compounds tub-/Bible-thumping, and a tub-/Bible-thumper = 'proselytizer, preacher, evangelist etc'.

thus/this far and no further [A (AdvP)] to, but not beyond, an allowed degree of closeness, freedom, familiarity, enterprise etc □ *'There's going to be a change, but I'm going to make it and no one else; if anyone else tries to make it, he's going to go to prison.' 'Then how do you suddenly say, right,* ***this far and no further****?'* L □ *People think they have it under control,* ***thus far and no further*** *and so on, but how many people* decide *to be alcoholics, drug-addicts or chain-smokers?* □ often used as comment, prohibition, warning etc.

tickle sb's ribs [V + O pass] (informal) amuse sb □ (film review) *It's British Comedy Time again. Norman Wisdom, Margaret Rutherford and Jerry Desmonde conspire to* ***tickle your ribs*** *and give you the occasional choke.* RT □ *What* ***tickles the ribs of*** *the lads and lasses of Leeds? David Bell takes the cameras to Yorkshire to tour factories and offices and see how workmates there entertain each other.* TVT □ *The paper carries its due quota of riddles and* ***rib-ticklers*** *for children to try out on each other.* □ adj compound rib-tickling = 'amusing'; n compound a rib-tickler = 'a joke'.

tickled pink [Comp (AdjP)] (informal) pleased and flattered **V:** ⚠ be, seem, look □ *Saturday, February the first, two-thirty at the church. Of course, I've told Nikki—that's my fiancée—all about you, and we'd both be* ***tickled pink*** *if you'd come along.* □ *I am naturally* ***tickled pink*** *because these results vindicate my optimism of 4 July last when the shares were a drab 31p. Today they are 71p.* OBS □ *'You don't think there's a deep streak of perversity in your nature?' Michael Dean inquired. Mr Muggeridge was plainly* ***tickled pink*** *by the idea, and his expression took an increasingly seraphic radiance as the insults of his persecutors became less veiled.* L

the tide turns the course of events, trend of opinion of feeling, changes (usu with the implication of improvement) **A:** against the invader; in our favour; decisively; at (long) last □ *While the coalition forces appeared to have the upper hand early this month when the Portuguese gave the country its independence,* ***the tide*** *now seems to have* ***turned****.* G □ *As late as 1964 I was introducing on BBC Television in Belfast a programme which set out to mock the rigid thinking of our parents. Press reviews and public reaction seemed to prove beyond doubt that our views were welcome, that* ***the tide*** *was* ***turning****.* L □ *I told him of my impulse to ask the man* (who had just committed suicide) *to join us in a drink, and my belief that such a gesture, slight as it was, might have* ***turned the tide*** *in him.* LWK □ variant turn the tide = 'cause a change'.

a tidy sum [O (NP)] (informal) a considerable, perhaps large, amount of money **V:** cost; save, put away, put on one side. **n:** sum, ⚠ penny, amount, bit, (little) fortune □ *Have you seen what they've done to their house? That must have cost them* ***a tidy sum****.* □ *Smoking cigars, eh? You bloody miser, how can you afford them on the old age pension? I always suspected that you had* ***a tidy sum*** *stuck away.* HSG

tie sb's hands [V + O pass] restrict sb's activity, sb's power or authority to do sth □ *These rules of procedure, designed to protect the private citizen from undue interference, do however* ***tie the hands of*** *the police in dealing with somebody whom they have very good reason to suspect of carrying a weapon or illicit or stolen goods.* SC □ *They were industrial moderates. They accepted pit closures and they negotiated with* ***their hands tied*** *because they genuinely believed that strikes or irresponsibly high wage demands would mean a rundown of their industry.* NS □ *It was Gardiner's misfortune* (as editor of the 'Daily News') *that he allowed* ***his hands*** *to be* ***tied*** *unnecessarily. It was his primary interest to serve the interests of the Cadbury owners.* L □ variant do sth with one's hands tied; ***my hands are tied*** used as comment on how little freedom of action one has. ⇨ ⚠ bind/tie sb hand and foot.

tighten etc one's belt [V + O pass] eat less food, spend less money, curtail one's use of any accustomed commodities or services (drawing one's belt tight being supposed to alleviate hunger pangs) **V:** tighten, ⚠ pull in, draw in □ *A real social contract has to mean a movement toward equality, throughout the social structure. Nothing can be more absurd than the spectacle of a few fat men exhorting all the thin ones to* ***tighten their belts****.* NS □ *In Emily's own family uncomfortable things are not said, financial problems are real but cloudy,* ***belts are tightened*** *and chins kept up.* ST □ *Food stocks are at the sort of level which makes any immediate* ***belt-tightening*** *or panic-buying look ridiculous.* ST □ *Not that anyone had much chance to indulge themselves, for ration books curbed everybody's appetite in 1945. The war was draw-*

ing to a close and Britain was still **drawing in her belt**. RT □ n compound belt-tightening.

till/until death us do part [A (AdvP)] for as long as each of us lives □ *I...take thee...to my wedded wife/husband, to have and to hold from this day forward...* **till death us do part**... BOOK OF COMMON PRAYER □ *You should have done so* (ie quarrelled and got rid of him), *Gerald said to himself, when he came down to see you at Cambridge. And now you can't because of Stokesay and Dollie. You're tied to him, a comrade in arms, '***until death do us part***'.* ASA □ *Then he meets the lovely Francesca. She is also a confidence trickster—up to the same game. They marry and promise to love each other* **Till Death Do Them Part**. TVT □ note archaic word-order of the original, with O preceding main v; variant till/until death do us part.

time after time [A] very often; repeatedly; next entry (qv) □ *His father was a runaway baker's apprentice from Norfolk, a violent animal who reckoned to be drunk every evening and who* **time after time** *gambled away his money but somehow lasted the course.* NS □ front, middle or end position.

time and (time) again [A (NP)] very often; repeatedly; previous entry (qv) □ *The old belief that one has only to attend a sale and give a pound or two more than the last bid by a dealer to get a lot cheaply has been disproved* **time and time again**. L □ **Time and again** *movements broke down through passes going astray, and much of the play was scrambling in the extreme.* ST □ front, middle or end position.

time flies (saying) time passes very quickly, more quickly than one takes note of □ (source) *But meanwhile it flies, irretrievable* **time flies**. GEORGICS (VIRGIL 70-19 BC) □ *They handled the script with that racy, laconic eloquence which in America is the demotic obverse of mandarin waffle. The two and a half hours of transmission* **time** *simply* **flew**. OBS □ PETER: *Twelve years? But I only left — a few months ago.* JASON: *That's the way* **time flies**. DPM □ *Another how-***time-flies** *note: remember his enormous hit 'Clair', dedicated to his manager's baby daughter? She's nine years old now.* TVT □ exclamatory use *How* **time flies**!; original Latin words tempus fugit sometimes used.

time hangs/lies heavy on one's hands time passes too slowly, the days seem too long, because one does not have enough to do, one is bored □ *Did he think Irma was lonely? Well, he couldn't answer that one; she had not time to be lonely in the bar. Loneliness was a matter of feeling* **time hanging heavy on your hands**, *wasn't it?* PW □ *As J B Yeats, the father of the poet, said in one of his letters: A society of poor gentlemen* **upon whose hands time lies heavy** *is absolutely necessary to art and literature.* AH □ *The late 19th century, when* **time hung heavy on** *so* **many hands**, *is particularly fruitful in diaries.* NS

the time has come (for sb) to do sth it has now become suitable, right or necessary (for sb) to do sth □ '**The time**,' *says Mrs Gandhi,* '**has come to** *abandon the romantic view of Imperial history. The advantages which accrued were hardly intended; the system built by Britain had a narrow purpose in mind.'* RT □ *A love affair cannot end without heartbreak. And as I have already told so much, I think* **the time has come for** *me* **to** *draw a veil.* SPL □ *Ned had been leaning against the wall, listening, with his arms folded; but now he straightened up and came forward, as if* **the time had come for** *him* **to** *take control of the situation.* CON

time is a great healer (saying) with the passing of time, pain, grief, enmity etc come to be less keenly felt □ *Mr Rees is a decent and honourable man, as his predecessors were before him. He thinks, as they thought, that* **time is a great healer**, *that if people can only be brought together for long they will see where their true self-interest lies. This is an error.* NS □ *Here's a thought for Mr Waugh to ponder (he's a clever chap on his own admission):* **time is** *said to be* **a great healer**—*money is undoubtedly therapeutic too.* NS □ *'It seems against nature, Mrs Salad,' he said to me, 'to see those lovely little orbs* (= eyes) *dimmed. But there!* **Time** *takes and it gives, for all it's called* **the Great Healer**.*'* ASA □ *I was in a state of shock, of course, I couldn't accept that I was alone after all those years of marriage. There are all those clichés—people say* **time** *will* **heal** *and it sounds so trite but it is true.* TVT □ variants time, the great healer; time heals.

time is on the side of sb the more time that passes, the longer sth takes to begin or finish, the more sb will be helped, profited, proved right, etc □ *From the beginning,* **time has been on the side of** *the defendants at Dusseldorf: and now the trial is thoroughly bogged down in continual delays resulting from legal squabbles and intrigue.* OBS □ *But Princess Anne knows that* **time isn't on** *her* **side**. *In a recent interview she was asked when a showjumper should quit competitive riding. 'When you lose your nerve, probably,' she replied. 'It shouldn't take too long.'* TVT □ *Have we, the intellectuals, really pressed the case for the vindication of reason and civilised values? We may comfort ourselves by saying that, if we wait,* **time is on our side**. *I have never believed that. Time is neutral.* L

one's time is one's own one is free to arrange one's duties, activities, leisure periods, holidays etc to suit one's own convenience □ *'I could ask her to tea, but it depends on how long you mean to stay.' 'Oh, I expect I could stay as long as that,' said Alec, without specifying how long 'that' was.* '**My time's my own**, *you see.'* PW □ *'You don't seem to be any less busy since your retirement.' 'No, I'm not idle—though* **my time is my own**.*'*

the time etc is ripe for sth/(for sb) to do sth the time is just right for sth to happen or be done; it is not too early or too late to secure the best results **S:** the time, ⚠ moment, hour. **A:** for (making) a move, move; for a settlement, for a revival of his plays, for our return, for us to return; to expand production, to attack, to ask him □ *It may be thought that* **the time is** *never* **ripe for** *a move like raising the school leaving age.* SC □ *My bet is that British Leyland have their spies out and will be ready to take the Wankel engine up when they think* **the time is ripe**. ST □ *The sea was now choppy and one slightly seasick voice suggested that* **the time was ripe to** *return to the warm comfort of the hotel.* RT

time and tide wait for no man (saying) one

cannot make natural processes fit in with one's hopes or plans; putting off a favourable opportunity to do sth may result in never being able to do it □ *'The camera is at the bottom of my rucksack and the light will be better in the morning.' But* ***time and tide wait for no man*** *and when he went back in the morning the greylag geese had gone.* □ stress pattern time and tide wait for 'no man.

time (alone) will tell etc (saying) I do not know, nobody can know, at present; one will know only in the future **V:** tell, ⚠ reveal, show □ *It seems that Christianity is in a ferment of debate: whether these are death throes or evidence of vitality,* ***time will tell.*** OBS □ ***Time alone will reveal*** *whether they were wise decisions—but good or bad I made them, and the full responsibility is mine.* ST □ ***Only time will show*** *whether David Steel is able to preserve his valley of tranquillity in a landscape of hectic activity.* RT □ usu precedes or follows a dependent clause beginning *if/whether*; variant only time will tell etc.

(the) times change (saying) the conditions, values etc that govern or affect people's lives change □ *I have never quite understood the BBC's official line on bad language. The trouble is that* ***the times*** *are constantly* ***changing.*** *Taboos come and go.* L □ *Canada was still regarded in London as a dominion which would always come to the aid of the mother country without asking too many questions, but* ***times*** *had* ***changed.*** NS □ *The pub whose image had sustained us in exile across the Atlantic was soon to disappear.* ***Times*** *had* ***changed,*** *the landlord explained to us. People want comfort, and carpets, and juke-boxes, and fruit-machines.* NS □ *He's human, so show respect but don't exaggerate. Don't go down on your knees. He doesn't enjoy being toadied to.* ***Times*** *have* ***changed.*** ST □ often with present and past perfect tenses, as shown.

a (little) tin god [Comp (NP)] sb/sth that is given misplaced and foolish respect or veneration **V:** ⚠ be, become; make sth □ (source) *Wherefore the* ***Little Tin Gods*** *harried their little tin souls/For the billet* (= job) *of 'Railway Instructor to* ***Little Tin Gods*** *on Wheels'.* PUBLIC WASTE (R KIPLING 1865-1936) □ HELEN: *Heaven must be the hell of a place. Nothing but repentant sinners up there, isn't it? All the pimps, prostitutes and politicians in creation trying to cash in on eternity and* ***their little tin god.*** TOH □ *The place is reasonably clean and nobody'll get poisoned with the food I give them but I'm not one of these women who make* ***tin gods*** *of their homes.* □ often in construction *make* ***a (little) tin god*** *of sb/sth.*

Tin Pan Alley (writing, publication, performance and promotion of) popular music (from the nickname given to a New York district where much of it is published) □ *Hundreds of songs appear with the most unexceptionable lyrics, but they catch on only if the tune is catchy. Songs which do not meet the requirements are not likely to to be taken up, no matter how much* ***Tin Pan Alley*** *plugs them.* UL □ capital or small initial letters.

tinker, tailor, soldier, sailor any or every kind of man (from a children's counting chant, ***tinker, tailor, soldier, sailor,*** *rich man, poor man, beggar-man, thief* used esp with stones or pips from fruit left on a plate, to foretell what a boy will become or whom a girl will marry) □ *The names and inscriptions on the tombs tell us who the local families were and what they did —* ***tinker, tailor, soldier, sailor.*** RT □ ***Tinker, tailor, soldier, sailor*** *— sweet-talking opportunist Mike Upchat could pass himself off as any of these.* TVT

tip/turn the balance/scale(s) [V + O pass] affect, or finally determine, a decision or choice; (cause to) have a disproportionately greater weight, force, importance or value than sth else **A:** in his favour; against going abroad; the other way □ *'We don't need to go to a place like this.' 'What's wrong with it?' he demanded. I might just have managed to* ***tip the balance,*** *but unfortunately at that moment Ned spoke up.* CON □ *He was in Washington towards the end of September 1956, and when he got back his advice to the inner Cabinet concerning likely American reactions must have carried exceptional weight and may have* ***turned the scale*** *in favour of the policy of armed intervention.* L □ *There's no shortage of applicants for primary school teaching, and up here in North Wales* ***the scales are*** *definitely* ***tipped*** *against you if you don't speak Welsh.* □ *But it is possible that the energy released when rock layers are strained and broken produces a great deal of local heating, enough perhaps to* ***tip the*** *heat* ***balance*** *in the region around the junction of the crust and the mantle, and to form the local pockets of melted rock.* NSC

(only) the tip of the iceberg [Comp (NP)] the small, visible or measurable, part of sth known to be much greater **V:** ⚠ be; see, regard, sth as □ *Theirs was one of the biggest tax evasion cases ever prosecuted, although the million dollars involved was described by a Government lawyer as '****only the tip of the iceberg****'.* OBS □ *Having seen the mass of documents (you see* ***only the tip of the iceberg*** *in the book), there's no question in my mind that...* L □ *But this enchanting profile of Sir Ralph* (Richardson) *seemed to me like a series of partly opened doors in the great man's life, showing just enough to tantalise,* ***tips of icebergs*** *glinting everywhere.* RT □ usu sing.

tip sb a wink [V + IO + O pass] (informal) wink at sb, or make some sign to sb, either secretly to affirm partnership or as a pre-arranged signal to do sth □ *Goldy in the corner with his pal and colleague Chadwick. Dusty well in attendance, lapping it up, all three going through the motions of renewing old friendships—and he* ***tipped a wink at*** *Kathie—* TT □ *If he* ***tipped*** *Elsie* ***a wink,*** *she'd drop in that day, all casual-like, he was sure she would.* TSMP □ variant tip a wink at sb. ➪ ⚠ next entry.

tip sb the wink [V + IO + O pass] (informal) pass on to sb a piece of (usu secret or privileged) information □ *...someone from the foot of the staircase calling out 'Tommy', so that Bevill, flushed, still businesslike, said to Martin 'That's* ***tipped*** *you* ***the wink.****'* NM □ *'The minute you feel like an evening out again you let us know. We've missed babysitting* (for you)*.' 'I will, but at the moment—' 'That's right, slow and steady wins the race. You stay in for a while, but when you're* *ready,* ***tip** us **the wink**.'* TSMP ⇨ ⚠ previous entry.

(give) tit for tat [n + n non-rev] (pay back) a trick, injury etc in exchange for one received □ *Tom pushed Polly off her chair. Then she got up and **gave** him **tit for tat** by pushing him off his.* □ *There's nothing so unproductive as **tit-for-tat** exchanges about whose fault something was.* □ (NONCE) *In addition we have had the great stop-the-strike dispute between the two leaders, which is as good an illustration of political **tit-for-tattery** as one has come across for some time.* NS □ attrib use *a **tit-for-tat** exchange.*

to advantage [A (Prep P)] with profitable or pleasing results **V:** use, employ; show, display, sth. **adj:** great, good, better, (the) best; fine, powerful □ *For short distance measurements the surveyor's tachymeter is now widely used **to advantage**.* NSC □ *McGovern has to make himself known, but is prevented from having a direct confrontation on television with Nixon, in which his directness and honesty might appear **to advantage**.* NS □ *She gave her pearls to her granddaughter, round whose young throat she felt they would be displayed **to** greater **advantage**.* □ *On that route are the ports, and on that route we can use our sea power **to** the best **advantage**.* MFM

to sb's advantage/disadvantage [Comp/A (PrepP)] (not) profitable or useful in promoting sb's success, progress, interests **V:** be; work (out), turn out; find out, hear, learn, sth □ *But like all prime ministers, like all ministers, he prefers to do things in secret and make his decisions public only on his own terms and when he considers it so **to his advantage**.* NS □ *'Perhaps we ought to do a bit of market research to find out why "San Bernadino" was liked by the judges and you weren't?' 'I'd rather not.' 'You fear you might learn something **to your disadvantage**?' 'Of course.'* ST □ *In a period of what seems to be irreversible inflation the laws affecting Hire Purchase and mortgage repayments are very much **to the advantage of** the borrower.* □ end position.

to all appearance(s) [Disj (PrepP)] as far one can see; if one can judge by appearances □ *Camilla Prendergast looked out onto a world in which life seemed* (as the result of the snowstorm and fog) *at a standstill — a world featureless, colourless, and, **to all appearance**, boundless.* EM □ *'Did you suspect anything of this yourself?' 'No. **To all appearances**, they were a happily-married couple.'* □ front, middle or end position.

to all intents (and purposes) [Disj (PrepP)] considered practically; in fact, behaviour, function, appearance etc though perhaps not in name; for (all) practical purposes (q v) □ *If railways are expected to pay their way then so must roads be; yet the demand is never made of them, despite their being **to all intents and purposes** a nationalised industry.* ST □ *Although there was no interference with the physiological apparatus of vision, the animals, when brought into the light, behaved **to all intents and purposes** as if they were blind.* SNP □ *He was in fact at fifty-eight **to all intents** the same Paul Waggett who had decided thirteen years ago to abandon chartered accountancy in London for the life of a Highland sportsman.* RM

to the bad/good constituting a loss/gain to sb (of a specified amount) **NP:** several pounds, twenty herd of cattle, a tube of toothpaste. **V:** be; find oneself; leave sb □ *Alec had been put away: he was gibbering in a madhouse: he had passed completely out of their lives, leaving them £150 per annum **to the good**.* PW □ *The Germans lost heavier ships as well. Before Hitler even asked him to consider invading Britain the German Comander-in-Chief, Admiral Raeder, was ten big destroyers **to the bad** and his men were dispirited too.* NS □ end position, following n that is modified.

to the best of one's ability [A (PrepP)] using all one's strength, speed, knowledge, skill etc whether or not this is adequate □ *On the next page of the diary she had totted up her financial situation **to the best of her ability**.* RFW □ *I thought she was about to ask me a question, and I got ready to answer it, **to the** very, very **best of my ability**.* CON □ front, middle or end position.

to the best of one's knowledge etc [Disj (PrepP)] not lying about, or witholding, any information or opinion one has, though one knows that this may be faulty or incomplete **o:** one's knowledge, ⚠ belief, recollection □ *There was a church of our denomination in Kuwait and the parson certified that, **to the best of his knowledge**, we were good and honest Christians.* BM □ ***To the best of my knowledge**, I have seen ghosts. But the human eye-witness is about the most unreliable source of all.* OBS □ *'He wasn't paid by T. Dan. At least not so far as I'm aware.' 'Not **to the best of your recollection**?' 'Not **to the best of my recollection**.'* NS □ front, middle or end position.

to the bitter end [A (PrepP)] (cliché) to the very end; until further action or involvement becomes impossible; till death or final defeat **V:** stay, wait; watch, carry on fight, resist □ *I wanted to see the three-party discussion on the economy, which was postponed half an hour because they kept on with this atrocious show jumping. Then I watched TV **to the bitter end**.* ST □ *I read through **to the bitter end** and some of it I read again for I wished to have as much in me as memory would hold.* PP □ *People began leaving the ground, making a way between those who were determined to see the game **to its bitter end**.* LLDR □ (NONCE) *'If there is another election,' he corrected me—an 'if' which does not reflect the intentions of the governing coalition, the Popular Unity, who are trusted to follow the path of legality even **to a bitter end**.* OBS.

to boot [Conj] also; as well; in addition □ *Perhaps the government will concede that a health service providing totally free help at the time of need is not a charter for spongers, but good medicine, and good business — and a decent thing, **to boot**.* NS □ *It conveys exactly the wrong message, and a message which is untrue, **to boot**, by implying that firms would not choose, if they were shrewd, to start up or expand in Northern Ireland.* T □ end position.

to the contrary [A (PrepP)] in a way that is the opposite (to a meaning, interpretation, piece of information, instruction etc already indicated) **V:** argue, hear, write; have proof; say/know nothing/something/anything □ *Never take An-*

*drew too seriously; whatever viewpoint somebody is trying to put across, Andrew always delights in arguing **to the contrary**.* □ *If you hear me telling Mulligan that I can't see him tomorrow, don't go and say anything **to the contrary**.* □ *You can assume your chest X-ray reveals nothing wrong unless you hear **to the contrary**.* □ end position.

to one's cost [A (PrepP)] because of expense, trouble, pain, loss etc that resulted **V:** know, learn, find out, sth; take part in, consent to, ignore, sth □ *Derek's a sponger, as two or three of us here know **to our cost**, but I'm sure he's not a thief.* □ *When I came upon the myth of objectivity in certain modern thinkers, it made me angry. I had learned **to my cost** how wrong they were.* L □ ***To my** subsequent **cost** I chose to ignore this excellent advice.* G □ front, middle or end position.

to sb's credit [Disj (PrepP)] in a way that shows merit in sb □ *As Robert was talking I could see Ned getting more and more uncomfortable. But, **to his credit**, he didn't say anything.* CON □ (football) *St Etienne, **to their credit**, refused to hide in a defensive corner, and Rangers must have been surprised at the positive approach adopted by the French.* G □ (chess) *Fischer's tantrums and demands are expressions purely of surplus combative will—a quality Spassky was eventually shown to lack, perhaps **to his credit**.* NS □ front, middle or end position.

to a/the day etc [A (PrepP)] to a degree of accuracy measured in units of days etc **V:** know, tell, foretell, predict, sth; last three months, take 25 yards, cost £5. **o:** a/the day, ⚠ minute; inch, penny □ *The leading troops entered Tripoli at 4am on the 23rd January 1943; three months **to a day** since the beginning of the Alamein battle.* MFM □ *'How long will you take to finish?' 'I can't tell you **to a day**, but between two and three weeks should be sufficient.'* □ *It always took an hour and a half, right **to the minute**, to cook and make preparations.* BM □ *He was a familiar figure near the National Square. At the end of the day, like an energetic passenger on a trans-Atlantic liner, he must have known **to a yard** how far he had walked.* OMIH □ *It's either a very poor or a very mean man who knows **to the penny** what he has in his pocket.* □ middle or end position.

to date [A (PrepP)] up to and including the time of speaking/writing □ ***To date**, Pan Am has carried more than a million and a quarter jet passengers—far more than any other air-line.* OBS □ *They've been advertising in all the local papers for a nurse-companion, but with no result **to date**.* □ front, middle or end position.

to a degree very; extremely; in the extreme (qv) **adj:** generous, conceited, complicated, painful □ *She's rather an interfering type, but kind-hearted and generous **to a degree**.* □ *He is invariably in the throes of conflict with some Council or Board or Bishop or Ministry. These battles are involved **to a degree**, and I have never been able to discover the exact origins of any one of them.* BM □ *Parsimonious **to a degree**, Ibsen invested every penny he could in gilt-edged securities.* NS □ modifies a preceding adj, as shown.

to one's/sb's disgust etc [A (PrepP)] causing one/sb to feel disgust etc **o:** disgust, (utter) dismay, delight, relief, (great) joy, astonishment; (deep) sorrow, horror □ *Stan and Ollie work their way on a cattle boat to Scotland, where they expect to inherit a large estate left by Stan's grandfather. **To their disgust**, they learn on their arrival that the bulk of the estate has been left to Stan's distant cousin, a girl.* TVT □ *The doctor began his usual methodical examination. 'Can you feel this? This?' **To** Brigit**'s** complete **dismay** she could feel nothing at all.* DC □ *In this way the view projected by the first lantern was replaced by the view projected by the second—**to the delight and astonishment of** the beholders.* HAH □ *I tried the other doors on the landing and then the doors in the hallway downstairs. **To my** great **exasperation** they were all locked.* UTN □ front, middle or end position.

to each according to his need(s), (from each according to his abilities) (catchphrase) let everyone have what he needs (and everyone give whatever he is able) (a socialist ideal for a state or community) □ (source) ***From each according to his faculties, to each according to his needs.*** M BAKUNIN 1814-76 □ *On the one hand, extremes of wealth and poverty are repellent. On the other hand, a society which presses the slogan '**to each according to his need, from each according to his ability**' to its logical conclusion risks removing all incentives to work harder—or indeed to work at all.* G □ (a Chinese commune) *'To each according to his work' is the theme, not the more radical '**to each according to his need**'—that comes later, we are told, when the ideal Communist society has been achieved.* OBS □ may be slightly adapted, as shown.

to excess [A (PrepP)] too much; excessively **V:** do sth; eat, drink sth; punish, admire, sb □ *Do everything in moderation and nothing **to excess** was his motto for a happy and healthy life.* □ *They call themselves comedians. I'd like to know what's supposed to be comic about drinking **to excess**.* ART □ end position.

to sb's face [A (PrepP)] directly; in the course of personal communication or confrontation with sb **V:** tell him, call her a slut, praise a child, laugh at you □ (architecture) *The patrons and experts of those days were usually identifiable and could therefore be praised or abused almost **to their faces**.* OBS □ *He had in his service a pious, soft-spoken, tip-toeing, unmarried, middle-aged Irishman for whom Guy felt much affection, and whom he called Tony **to his face** and Creeping Jesus behind his back.* MM □ *Wensley's* (the editor's) *black pencil was hovering around my feature, 'Objects and Subjects', my very own feature, as he would undoubtedly tell me **to my face** within a minute.* PP ⇨ behind sb's back²; ⚠ go behind sb's back (Vol 1).

to a fault too; excessively **adj:** conscientious, honest, tidy, frank, obliging □ *'But if the boss said a spot-check would do there's no need for Robert to go through all these figures.' 'You and I would think not, but that's our Robert—conscientious **to a fault**.'* □ *Trenchard, blunt **to a fault**, informed Reith that he didn't much care for the height of the transmitter masts at, I think, Daventry. They constituted, Trenchard claimed, a risk to the lives of his pilots and their machines.* L □ *McGovern's troops* (here = campaign workers) — *young, unseasoned and notoriously idealistic — have been courteous and orderly* ***to a fault***. L □ end position, modifying an adj describing a praiseworthy quality.

to one's/the fingertips completely and characteristically **n:** an artist, a lady, a Cockney. **adj:** aristocratic, puritanical, professional □ *She's an artist* ***to the finger-tips***. *You can see that in her clothes and her house, never mind the paintings that have made her name.* □ *But more important, Shirley Williams is a pragmatist* ***to her fingertips***. *She didn't resign 'because that would have meant leaving the Shadow Cabinet completely to the anti-marketeers.'* OBS □ *Sister Jenkins of Ward 2A projected a more homely image but was, nevertheless, professional* ***to the tips of her fingers***. □ modifies a preceding n or adj; variant to the tips of one's fingers.

to and fro [adv + adv non-rev] from point to point or place to place; back and forth (qv); backward(s) and forward(s) (qv) **V:** walk, run, hasten; swing, sweep □ *The dog had been watching us all the time, its busy tail sweeping* ***to and fro*** *against the bars.* UTN □ *The huge floor was crowded with people walking* ***to and fro***, *and every one of the chairs round the walls was occupied.* HD □ *One has only to contemplate the average four-seater car conveying just one person plus briefcase* ***to and fro*** *for the day's labour, to appreciate the appalling wasted space that we crowd on to our roads.* ST □ *By this time the television team had tested their equipment several times over, the cameras lining up on the military* ***to-ing and fro-ing*** *around Hyde Park Corner.* OBS □ variant to-ing and fro-ing.

to the full [A (PrepP)] as completely, thoroughly or extensively as possible **V:** live (life), enjoy, realize, appreciate, use, sth □ *Ah, these continentals. They live life* ***to the full*** *in a way that we can only—* TGLY □ *You seem to be afraid that life might pass you by without giving you time to enjoy it* ***to the full***. WI □ *'Now look,' Cosmo was companionable. 'I appreciate everything you say* ***to the full***. *But damn it, you're a man of the world.'* US

to good etc effect [A (PrepP)] with a good etc result **V:** display, show off, sth; speak, plead, argue. **adj:** good, excellent; some; no, disastrous, little □ *'Les Fâcheux' is really a series of individual numbers designed to show off the dancers' virtuosity* ***to good effect***. L □ *He is not much of an administrator himself: though he can use statistics* ***to good effect*** *when he wants to, he has no great grasp of figures.* NS □ *You must have argued* ***to some effect*** *for at least he's off making a final decision about closing down the business.* □ *I'm forever tidying the place up, but* ***to little effect***, *I'm afraid, with this crowd of kids around.*

to one's heart's content [A (PrepP)] as much as, or for as long as, one wants **V:** wander around, play, watch, sleep, chat, eat □ *The monastery is in use but you can wander round* ***to your heart's content***. *It's quiet, there aren't many visitors.* ST □ *All the race-courses in Scotland except one have been told to spend almost* ***to their hearts' content***. *The exception, sadly, is Lanark where the Levy Board are not convinced that racing is a viable proposition.* SC □ PETER: *Playing chess? I'll give you a game.* ALEX: *Not on your Nelly—I only play against myself. This way I can cheat* ***to my heart's content*** *and I never lose.* DPM □ *But if we can't disapprove of our friends' sex-lives these days, at least we can discuss them* ***to our hearts' content***. ASA

to him that hath shall be given (saying) it is those who already have wealth, power, happiness etc who tend to have further good fortune — and not those who most need, or would like to have, it □ (source) ***Unto everyone that hath shall be given***, *and he shall have abundance: but from him that hath not shall be taken away even that which he hath.* MATTHEW XXV 29 □ *Luck is a reward, not a chance gift. It's only for those who fight for it.* ***To him that hath shall be given***. AITC □ *'How much is a Resident's Parking Permit?' '£40 a year. You can get half-yearly or monthly permits but they cost you more.'* ***'Unto him that hath shall be given***, *again. If you've £40 in your pocket to spare at one go, that earns you a rebate.'*

to one's knowledge [Disj (Prep)] according to what one knows, has observed or has been told about □ *Léon Goosens will play Mozart's Oboe Concerto in C — music of felicity. Has Goosens ever blown a single insecure note? Not* ***to my knowledge***, *but Sir Thomas Beecham, in one of his naughty moods, maintained that once. . .* RT □ *It's wrong of Annie to say her family never visit her. John and his wife have been up there,* ***to my knowledge***, *at least three times in the last month.* □ often neg or attached to neg clause; front, middle or end position.

to the last [A (PrepP)] continuously, repeatedly or consistently till the last possible moment (esp death) **n:** patriot, quibbler, fighter, criminal, aesthete, clown. **adj:** patriotic, treacherous, defiant, faithful, hopeful □ *Grosvenor's palsied hands holds up an ear-trumpet to catch the mumblings of Macmillan, a patriot* ***to the last***, *with a British-made spittoon at his elbow.* NS □ *'I've made special arrangements with Almighty God. The Baron won't die before my little biography is finished. I want to check it over with him.' 'God or the Baron?' I asked, funny* ***to the last***, *but Wensley pressed the bell.* PP □ *Vyan, apologetic* ***to the last***, *stood on the island bank watching us out of sight.* LWK □ *He died in prison sixteen years later, protesting his innocence* ***to the last***. □ end position after n or adj it modifies — or front or end position with *fight, argue, protest etc.*

to the letter [A (PrepP)] literally; in every particular **V:** carry out, obey, follow, believe sth □ *Some companies protest that the purpose of the small print is purely to protect them from unjustified and time-wasting claims, nor do they normally invoke it strictly* ***to the letter***. ST □ *Each of us was being punctilious. When I next went down to Barford, I set out to obey Rose* ***to the letter***. NM □ *McGovern's victory speech met my ideas of eloquence* ***to the letter***; *it was unornamented, direct and vivid.* L

to the life [A (PrepP)] exactly like the real (type of) person, thing or situation **n:** my father, the president, Bill □ *'That's an excellent portrait of your father.' 'Yes, it's him* ***to the life***, *isn't it?'* □ *There are very good performances all round. Sandy Ratcliff is perfect as Janice the girl, and Bill Dean and Grace Cave are her parents* ***to the***

horrible ***life***. OBS □ *He can imitate a stag bellowing* ***to the life*** *and has often brought one within gunshot that way.* □ modifies a preceding n.

to sb's liking [Comp/A (PrepP)] that/what sb likes **V:** be; seem; find, see, get, sth □ *I don't intend to get carried away by auction excitement. If I don't see anything* ***to my liking*** *I'll leave before the bidding starts.* □ *As Chris Kingsley says, Man'll have to come to terms with his environment. And I guess the terms won't be altogether* ***to his liking***. TBC □ *Instead of carrying out an invasion of North Africa under a Commander-in-Chief whom I barely knew, I was now to serve under one I knew well. This was much more* ***to my liking*** *and I felt I could handle that business, and Rommel.* MFM □ may also modify a preceding pron, as in first example; often preceded by *not, very much* or *(much) more*.

to a man etc [A (PrepP)] including each single person of a group specified **n:** man, ⚠ woman, boy, girl □ *The Eighth Army consisted in the main of civilians in uniform, not of professional soldiers. And they were, of course,* ***to a man***, *civilians who read newspapers.* MFM □ *But some of the best poker players in the country live in Vegas. Almost* ***to a man***, *they are Southerners.* ST □ *Here, in the Lower Broughton area of Salford, the poor Salford children, vandals* ***to a boy***, *it seemed, were shown brightly answering official questions.* L □ *A lot of people are worried about the adult illiterate. Married ladies, ex-teachers* ***to a woman***, *are being recruited to take discreet evening classes.* OBS □ man often used to denote person of either sex or any age.

(as/as if) to the manner born [Comp/A (PrepP)] (as if) accustomed all one's life to, or having a natural aptitude for, a function, way of speaking or behaving, etc □ (source) HORATIO: *Is it a custom?* HAMLET: *Ay, marry, is't,/But to my mind,—though I am native here,/And* ***to the manner born***, *— it is a custom/More honour'd in the breach than the observance.* HAMLET I 4 □ *John F Kennedy was* ***to the manner born***. *Nothing became him so much as the White House. His true métier was to be President of the United States.* OBS □ *And there was Dusty at work on the kettle* ***to the manner born***, *and doing very nicely thank you.* TT □ (the film) *'An Investigation' scarcely allows him* (Walter Matthau) *to be anything except flat-footed and stoop-shouldered, which he does* ***as to the manner born***. L □ usu in the construction *do sth* ***as to the manner born***.

to my mind [Disj (PrepP)] as I understand and/or react to sth; in sb's book (q v); in sb's/one's opinion (q v); in sb's view (qv); to sb's way of thinking (qv) □ ***To my mind***, *Bach is unsurpassed as a composer.* RT □ *The important paragraphs,* ***to my mind***, *were the first four, which ran as follows:...* MFM □ (a vandalized classroom) *'Whoever did it certainly knows the names of some of the members of the Staff.' 'That's putting it mildly—knows their habits very well too.' 'I'm glad you agree on that.' 'Do you?' 'No doubt at all* ***to my mind***. *Somebody in the School.'* TT □ front, middle or end position.

to a nicety [A (PrepP)] using or achieving an exact degree of accuracy **V:** calculate, aim, design, describe, judge, sth □ *The manner in which she received him was calculated* ***to a nicety*** *to seem cool without being uncivil.* □ *We struck the beach fairly and squarely. Spriggs had brought us in* ***to a nicety***. SD □ end position.

(all) to no/little avail [A (PrepP)] without the desired result; without any useful result □ *A large soldier referred to as Private Sponge gets stuck half way across, being unable to shift his rear quarters. A comrade from behind pushes and one in front pulls,* ***to no avail***. *Private Sponge is immovable.* RT □ *Contrary to Ingeborg's expectations, refreshments only seemed to strengthen the determination of the audience to leave. She cajoled and coaxed, but* ***all to no avail***. ASA □ *The statement conceded that one element in the Provisional leadership, that associated with Mr John Kelly, had already tried to call off the bombings but* ***to no avail***. L □ *I tried to persuade him not to resign but it was* ***to little avail***. *Now he's going to have difficulty in finding another job.* □ middle or end position.

to order [A (PrepP)] at any time if ordered or requested **V:** write poems, make jokes, be cheerful, perform somersaults □ *The idea behind the planning of the 'Masquerade' series demonstrates a will to prove that creative people should be made to work* ***to order***: *'Get half a dozen writers to write about a fancy-dress party.'* ST □ *He slipped from the roof, double-somersaulted and landed, safe but shaken, on his feet. 'It's a pity you can't do that* ***to order***,*' said his wife. 'You'd make our fortune on TV.'* □ often with *can/can't*; end position.

to the point [Comp/A (PrepP)] relevant(ly) **V:** be; speak, write. **adv mod:** altogether, wholly, strictly □ *Stocker mechanically put in a few words that weren't strictly* ***to the point*** *but Ned ignored him and ploughed on.* CON □ *It had been the Astronomer Royal's first intention to speak shortly and* ***to the point***. *Now he was unable to resist the temptation to expatiate at length, just for the pleasure of watching Kingsley's face.* TBC □ *It was a flabby piece anybody could have written. Usually he writes well and* ***to the point***. PP

to the pure all things are pure (saying) pure-minded people are less likely than others to be aware of evil, obscenity, coarseness etc □ (source) ***Unto the pure all things are pure***: *but unto them that are defiled and unbelieving is nothing pure.* TITUS I 15 □ *'He was on playground duty Monday,' said Miss Macallister, 'because I was on yesterday—Mr Golding is on today, and I'm always in between those two.' 'Don't say it,' said Miller* (who had seen that her last remark could be interpreted sexually), *'no explanation needed.' 'You make me sick,' said Miss Elliot. '****To the pure***,*' said Miller, '****to the pure***...*'* TT

to sb's (own) satisfaction [A (PrepP)] sufficiently well to satisfy, convince, meet the requirements or expectations of, sb **V:** prove, establish, settle, sth/that; do the job, complete the work, adjust the engine □ *'If you are the culprit the police will get you.' 'They would have to prove the deed. And if they proved it* ***to my satisfaction*** *I should no longer be in doubt.'* MM □ *About a month after Ben Nevis had established* ***to his own satisfaction*** *the probability of the monster's having quitted the dangerous area of Loch Ness,...* RM □ *...doctors who perform the* *function of curing and caring for those who are incapable of functioning either* ***to their own*** *or other****'s satisfaction****.* NS □ front, middle or end position.

to some purpose [Comp/A (PrepP)] with an aim or result that is/is not satisfactorily or wholly achieved **adj:** some, good. **det:** such (that); no, little; not any □ *Gort saved the men. And being saved, they were able to fight again another day: which they did* ***to some purpose****, as the Germans found out.* MFM □ *Their education has been long and expensive and one would hope* ***to some purpose****.* NS □ *Few have pushed through the tangles of the Records Office* ***to such purpose*** *that they come to a given patch of ground armed with all there is to know about it.* RT □ *'Tutankhamun' (Radio 4) had a lot of decent actors breathing excitedly and chanting Pharaonic hymns at every opportunity and* ***to little purpose****.* L □ middle or end position.

to a T/tee [A (PrepP)] exactly in every detail; in all ways **V:** be (like) sb/sth; resemble, imitate, sb/sth; have (got), do, take off (= imitate), sb; show, demonstrate, sth; suit, fit, sb □ *One of the nurses was giving a spirited imitation of Matron on the warpath. It was the old girl* ***to a T****.* □ *By all accounts Mary is as lazy as he is, so they should suit each other* ***to a T****.* □ *It is a complicated piece* (of sculpture) *which invites you to explore round it and under it and even up it. The sculptor's characteristic balance between solemnity and skittishness is held* ***to a tee****.* OBS

to sb's taste [Comp (PrepP)] suited to sb's personal preferences in food, dress, entertainment, art etc **V:** ⚠ be; seem; find, see, get, sth □ *The silence went on and on, broken only by the munching of the horses, who had found something* ***to their taste****.* ARG □ *'Well,' she said, looking around her, 'there are colour schemes more* ***to my taste*** *than purple and green, but the place is clean enough.'* □ *Neither the elaborate whimsy nor the leer were* ***to*** *Sonia****'s taste****, but...* HAA □ *Alan Friedman's first novel is a sort of Trans-Sexual Express, very long, fairly fast-moving, international, but not a form of transport that will be* ***to*** *everyone****'s taste****.* OBS □ also modifies preceding n, as in first two examples; often neg.

to that effect [A (PrepP)] with that meaning **V:** speak, write, advise. **n:** remark(s), words. **det:** that, this, what, the same. □ *It is only too easy from a small safe island to make liberal protests and then renege on them. Mr Bernard Levin has written an angry article in 'The Times'* ***to that effect****.* NS □ *What it is clear must not happen—and there are rumours* ***to this effect*** *—is for Covent Garden to reach out towards the Wells. Those two great institutions have very different roles to play.* OSB □ (slimming) *Judy didn't say a word to me, but she told ten million 'Radio Times' readers I was going to join her because I'd got a bit of a tum* (tummy)*, or words* ***to the same effect****.* RT □ *Koestler takes off with a remark by one of Gandhi's colleagues* ***to the effect that*** *'it takes a great deal of money to keep Bapu* (= Gandhi) *living in poverty—' and shows that it would similarly have taken a great many corpses to keep him in non-violence.* L □ often modifies a preceding n (esp *words, remarks*); variant to the effect that + clause.

to that end [A (PrepP)] with that intention; in order to achieve that purpose **det:** that, this; what, which □ *He added that Britain and France must first agree on the military strategy, and staff talks* ***to that end*** *should therefore take place.* MFM □ *Leasor's original intention had been to become a doctor and he was studying* ***to that end*** *when the war put paid to such ambitions.* OBS □ *He should have asked for full details of Pforzheim's work from Sir Edgar.* ***To what end****? To distract his attention from the work he had taken on?* ASA □ *The question arises whether Leopold intended to avail himself of Stanley's services* during *the expedition, and if so* ***to what end****.* NS □ also modifies a preceding n; front, middle or end position.

to this day [A (PrepP)] from the time sth happened right up to, and including, the present □ *The writer handled this bird, and sent it to the Natural History Museum at South Kensington, where, for all he knows, the skin may be* ***to this day****.* T □ *Still Crozier would not name his accomplices, and* ***to this day*** *he has kept silent about them.* OBS □ (football) *The Hungarians embraced; but the flag of Merfyn Griffiths, the Welsh linesman, was up. Puskas had been given offside, and* ***to this day*** *the decision is argued.* ST □ front, middle or end position.

to sb's trained etc eye(s) [A (Prep)] as sb by training, insight etc sees or understands sth **V:** be, ⚠ seem, look, appear. **adj:** trained, ⚠ Western, sophisticated, untutored □ *The rule under which, in criminal prosecutions, the burden of proof lay throughout on the prosecution (a rule which* ***to Western eyes*** *is a facet of the doctrine of the presumption of innocence) was approved by the Supreme Soviet and was written into the new code.* OBS □ (film review) *...this uncannily real reconstruction of Sweden during the the First World War. Apart from the period feel which seems* ***to my untrained eye*** *to be perfect, the main performance is utterly convincing.* RT

to the tune of sth [A (PrepP)] (informal) at the cost of (a named sum of money, usu large) **V:** assist, subsidize, underwrite, back, sb/sth □ *It was estimated that the Zambian copper wealth subsidised the other two members of the federation* ***to the tune of*** *between £5 million and £8 million a year.* OBS □ *I seemed somehow to have consumed four glasses of pernod* ***to the tune of*** *several hundred francs.* UTN □ *Dickie Davies is a sucker for boat shows and blames himself* ***to the tune of*** *£5,000 for his brand-new 24 ft Relcraft Sapphire cabin cruiser.* TVT □ usu end position; also modifies preceding n (esp *costs, damage*).

to sb's way of thinking [Disj (PrepP)] according to sb's opinion, view, line of reasoning; in sb's book (qv); in sb's/one's opinion (qv); in sb's view (qv); to my mind (qv) □ *Sex doesn't mean a thing to me.* ***To my way of thinking****, love is the most important and beautiful thing in this world and that's got nothing to do with sex.* EGD □ *He should give up the whole idea now. There are far too many difficulties. Not* ***to his way of thinking****, though. Difficulties are there to be overcome, is always his line.* □ stress pattern to 'my way of thinking.

toe the line [V + O] conform with the regulations and conventions of the group etc to which one belongs; obey orders; do as sb expects or requires one to do □ *And a middle-aged scientist* *said apologetically: 'You must understand; I have a family to support, so what else can I do but* ***toe the line****?'* SC ▫ *She said suddenly: 'What about Dr Rathbone? Is he just a figurehead?' Edward's lips curved in cruel amusement. 'Rathbone has got to* ***toe the line****. Oh, yes, Rathbone's completely in our hands—'* TCB ▫ *He has volunteered to bring this, his own constituency, up to scratch as far as* ***toeing the*** *party* ***line*** *is concerned.* ST ▫ the last example conflates toe the line with *the party line* = 'the party's regulations and conventions'.

toil and moil [v + v non-rev] work hard and long; strive laboriously ▫ *Two men with a cross-cut* (saw) *wouldn't do it* (= fell so many trees) *in a week in the old days, sweating and* ***toiling and moiling****.* L ▫ *It will be a lot more expensive to take them out but, on the other hand, I don't like to think of you* ***toiling and moiling*** *in the kitchen all day to produce a dinner for twelve.* ▫ usu *-ing* form or continuous tenses.

(every/any) Tom, Dick and/or Harry all sorts of people; anybody at all (the implication usu being people of a very ordinary or of a quite unsuitable kind) ▫ *If we were to listen to the half-baked ideas of* ***every Tom, Dick and Harry*** *you know what we'd have? I'll tell you. Anarchy.* G ▫ *As for qualified guides here, there is no legislation for giving them a licence, so that* ***any Tom, Dick or Harry*** *can work as a guide and give not only wrong information, but cause further chaos by not knowing his way about.* NS ▫ *I behaved with moral schizophrenia. I wrote Andrew the same lies with my right hand; with my left I clutched the neck of an agreeably scruffy poet called* ***Tom, Dick or Harry****, who whirled me into the society where I, in fact, belonged.* ST ▫ order of names non-rev.

Tom Tiddler's ground a place, area of activity, body of material, that is open to anyone to pick up what wealth, advantages they can (from a children's game where one player, Tom Tiddler, tries to keep others from crossing a boundary line into his base) ▫ *For several years after the introduction of a Driving Test the situation was that of a* ***Tom Tiddler's Ground*** *where anyone who owned a car and held a licence to drive himself could set himself up as a driving instructor and advertise for pupils.* T ▫ *Verdi had one of the most rewarding and successful careers in musical history. Nowadays his music is* ***Tom Tiddler's ground*** *for festival planners, even the rather piffling fodder.* NS ▫ stress pattern Tom 'Tiddler's ground.

Tommy Atkins (dated slang) British private (ie non-ranking) soldier (from a 19th c specimen form made out to 'Thomas Atkins' issued to recruits) ▫ *...saying in August 1914, 'It'll all be over by Christmas.' I had known all the wishful cant about* ***Tommy Atkins*** *and the Russian steam roller, and the war to end war, and making the world safe for democracy.* AH ▫ *It was desirable also to assert and assume that the British working man was a jolly good fellow, had his head screwed on, was unshakably patriotic. In fact he was good old* ***Tommy Atkins*** *in mufti* (= out of uniform). OBS ▫ variant a tommy, the tommies = 'British soldier(s) (without specification of rank)'.

tomorrow is another day (saying) what will happen, or what one will do, tomorrow or in the future is not something to be concerned about today ▫ *'You can run along now, if you like. These few letters will keep until the morning.' 'But there will be a whole heap of new ones by the morning.' 'I know, dear, I know. If the letters didn't come, that would be the time to start worrying. But* ***tomorrow is another day****.'* AITC ▫ *I can't lie and say it's all going to be lovely. But I hope it will. Like Scarlett O'Hara, I always say* ***tomorrow is another day****.* TVT

tomorrow will/can take care of/look after itself (saying) the future will take its own shape, will bring problems and solutions that can't be predicted and pre-arranged ▫ (source) *Take therefore no thought for the morrow; for* ***the morrow shall take thought for the things of itself****. Sufficient unto the day is the evil thereof.* MATTHEW VI 34 ▫ *'Life is no bed of roses,' they assume; but '****tomorrow will take care of itself****': the working-classes have been cheerful existentialists for ages.* UL ▫ (insurance advertisement) *Don't* ***let tomorrow look after itself****. You must consider what would happen to you and your family if your income was suddenly switched off.* TVT ▫ variant let tomorrow take care of/look after itself.

too many cooks spoil the broth (saying) having too many people responsible for, or engaged in doing, sth will result in its not being done properly ▫ MRS BUTCHER: *Work together? You mad?* PETER: *Many hands make light—how does it go?* ALEX: ***Too many cooks spoil the broth****?* PETER: *Oh shut up, Judas. You must pool resources—pull together—work in harmony—share the labour, share the treasure.* DPM ▫ *If everybody was allowed to have his say the things would never get built.* ***Too many cooks spoil the broth****, you know.* G ▫ (NONCE) *The project has been bedevilled by committees of this and that who have, among them, fully succeeded in* ***spoiling the broth****.* ⇨ many hands make light work.

the tools of the/one's trade the tools, implements, utensils or other aids necessary to, or associated with, a trade, profession, or other activity ▫ *Father is designer, chief glassblower and managing director.* ***The tools of the trade*** *are unbelievably primitive: a long, heavy metal tube for blowing, callipers, a pair of huge tweezers and cold water.* OBS ▫ (a writer) *His first-floor study is stocked with seed catalogues and scores of rowing cups, as well as* ***the*** *more obvious* ***tools of his trade****.* ST ▫ *My father was one of those who can effortlessly create about them Pools of Unease. The theatre, if the play was a dud, found him operating freely and* ***the tools of his trade*** *were ready to hand—clearings of the throat, yawns, deep sighs, hurried glances to right and left, shiftings, shufflings, windings of watches.* NS

top the bill [V + O] be the leading actor, act or feature on a theatre bill or advertisement; (fig) be the most important person or item in a range of attractions, scale of values, etc ▫ *One of the nice things about* ***topping the bills*** *for 20 years is that you can do the kinds of things you want to do.* RT ▫ JIMMY: *And those old favourites, your friends and mine: sycophantic, phlegmatic, and, of course,* ***top of the bill****—pusillanimous.* LBA

(the) top brass (informal) people of the highest rank, position, authority, esp in the armed services □ *From the unusual security precautions it was easy to see that a meeting of* ***the top brass*** *was in progress.* □ (The BBC's 50th anniversary) *threw up one television programme of originality, 'Looking In' by Robert Vas. Otherwise* ***top brass*** *were filmed at a round of celebrations.* L

top dog [Comp (NP)] a person, group, country etc enjoying superiority and advantages over another or others **V:** ⚠ be, become; regard sb as □ *. . .but Europe was drained of life and invention after the* (1914-18) *war and eagerly copied America's hectic fads. America was now* ***top dog*** *and was consumed with what Mr Justice Holmes called 'an itch for the superlative'. It worshipped the unbeatable in any field.* L □ *The well-to-do averted their eyes from the poor. They were too busy having a good time. The upper-middle class were* ***top dogs****.* ST □ *In the crisp words of the grammarians, judging the claims of English as a world language, 'by any of the criteria it is prominent, by some it is pre-eminent, and by a combination of the four it is outstanding.' They don't come much more* ***top dog*** *than that.* NS.

the top of the morning (to you) (informal) good morning □ *'****The top of the morning to you****, Johnnie. And to you, my lovely,' he said to Elvira, who again did not answer.* ASA □ *It's like the Scots being supposed to sprinkle their conversation with 'och, aye' all the time. I've been in Dublin two years now and nobody's wished me '****the top of the morning****' yet.* □ used facetiously, in conscious imitation of a supposed Irish greeting.

top of the pops (informal) the pop music recording currently having the highest sales; (fig) sb/sth outdoing others in popularity or in sb's esteem □ *'****Top of the Pops****' (BBC 1) should surely be rechristened 'pick of the flops' after the 16 June programme, which marks the low point in a sadly deteriorating series of boring programmes.* RT □ ***Top of the pops*** *among West Africa's tourist attractions is undoubtedly the Yankari Game Reserve in Nigeria, which opens for tourists in November until June next year.* SC

top and tail [v + v non-rev] mark, take away from, add to, or otherwise deal with, the top and bottom, beginning and end, both ends etc of sb/sth □ *Jenny helped her mother to* ***top and tail*** *the gooseberries for jam.* □ *The symposium is* ***topped and tailed*** *by a short story which puts Christ's case against God, and one which puts a patient's case against his psychoanalyst.* OBS

toss and turn [v + v non-rev] keep turning from one side to the other, moving restlessly instead of lying or sleeping comfortably □ *All night I have been* ***tossing and turning****, racking my brains to think of what could have possessed that poor young man to kill himself.* EM □ *He knew where his heart lay, but where did his duty lie? And so did he* ***toss and turn****, and get up for a drink of water, and knock over a pile of books.* WDM

touch etc one's forelock [V + O pass] raise one's right hand to one's forehead (equivalent to taking off one's hat/cap) when meeting, or speaking to, or in the presence of, sb as a sign of servile respect; act obsequiously **V:** touch, ⚠ tug, pull □ *Cockney Mullard enjoys the joke. 'Whenever I see the snooty little blighter, I really feel like bowing or* ***touching my forelock****,' he says.* TVT □ *Mr Wright is a centralist. For him London is the only possible source of political, economic and social health. And those who don't* ***touch their forelocks*** *at the mention of London, he despises.* G □ *Lower-class characters are included either as comic butts or faithful* ***forelock-touching*** *adjuncts of the main characters.* NS □ *A hundred years ago, the whole of that countryside was dominated by landlords. This is no longer so, but wherever one goes one feels the ghosts of* ***forelock-pulling*** *tenantry flitting round one.* L □ adj compound forelock-touching/tugging/pulling.

touch pitch and be defiled (saying) one is necessarily defiled by contact with, involvement in, crime, vice, dishonesty, indecency etc □ (source) *He that* ***toucheth pitch*** *shall* ***be defiled*** *therewith.* ECCLESIASTICUS XIII 1 □ *You know that the duty of the artist is to see life whole. If he* ***touches pitch and is defiled****, then he must endure the defilement.* US □ *That's what happens. A policeman thinks he'll take the bribe, just this once—to pay off a debt, or pay for a daughter's wedding. But you can't* ***touch pitch*** *without* ***being defiled*** *and the second offer is more easily accepted—and so on until he is found out.* □ (NONCE) (Dennis Wheatley) *took the grim little householders off into a world of black magic and historical daredevilry, warning them not to stray outside the charmed circle of his books, since those who* ***dabble in pitch*** *may* ***be defiled****.* G

touch wood words that are said while touching sth made from wood with one's fingers, in order to bring, or continue, good luck or to avert bad luck □ *They touched or knocked on the wooden side of the boat before they got on board. What they were doing, in fact, was indulging in a superstition as old as mankind itself. They were calling on the god who was thought to live in wood and trees to keep them safe—which is what you do when you '****touch wood****'—although few of them could have realised it.* OBS □ *Fletcher knows he could easily fall out of favour as a freelance* (jockey) *and that he faces the ever-looming chance of crippling injury. He* ***touches wood*** *when he speaks of his hopes.* RT □ *It turned out to be the best move I ever made. From there I worked my way into London and,* ***touch wood****, I haven't been seriously out of work since.* TVT □ *Our task is a very delicate one:* ***touch wood*** *none of us has been sued, but one can be. We have to carry insurance against negligence on our part.* ST □ usu in imper form of headphrase; may, simply mean 'let us hope' as in last two examples; front, middle or end position, when used in parenthesis.

a tough guy/cookie (informal) a determined, ruthless, unfeeling etc person not easily opposed or persuaded □ *He was* ***the tough guy****, the big shot, who gave orders with the crack of a whip.* PE □ *The most intelligent person in such a district usually takes charge of things—that's me—who usually hires* ***tough guys****—that's them—to get rid of scroungers and strangers—that's you.* DPM □ *Now* he *was* ***a tough cookie****!*

At a bridge table, or a chess board, at a word game — the psychological pressure he put on you to lose was usually irresistible. G

tough etc to the point of brutality etc [Comp (AdjP)] so tough etc as to be almost, or to merit being called, brutal etc **V:** ⚠ be, become, seem; make sb. **adj...n:** tough... brutality, careless...folly, curt...rudeness, terrified...hysteria ▫ *The influence of Leinsdorf's American years following on his apprenticeship with Toscanini has left us thinking of him as a conductor* ***tough to the point of brutality****. But now, returning to Europe, he seems newly relaxed.* G ▫ *There is a newspaper cutting from 20 years ago which quotes him as saying: 'I am* ***careless*** *with money* ***to the point of folly****.' 'Still true', says Jeremy Hawk.* TVT ▫ *Formerly* ***cautious to the point of being uncommunicative****, my companions had changed out of recognition.* SC

(the) tower of Babel noisy place or conditions; a situation or occasion where there is more noise, talk etc than sense, communication or understanding (from the story of God's confounding mens' efforts to build a tower that would reach to heaven by causing them to speak different languages instead of one, so that they could not understand each other and work together; see GENESIS XI 1-9) ▫ *Monboddo also believed that no known language was the original human tongue. These views also were heretical. The orthodox view was that God had created man already endowed with language, and that, until the episode of* ***the Tower of Babel****, one language served us all.* L ▫ (of recorded TV programmes) *Sometimes I wonder whether there are any living souls at all in BBC TV's* ***Tower of Babel*** *at White City on any given night.* ST ▫ (of a block of flats) *Alone! My God, no one could be alone in* ***this tower of Babel****. You'll be all right. You know everybody here.* AITC

a tower of strength [Comp (NP)] (cliché) sb who can always be relied upon for support, encouragement, practical ability, etc **V:** ⚠ be; find sb ▫ *I was much helped all this time by my brigade-major, an officer called Major F W Simpson; he was* ***a tower of strength*** *and took from my shoulders everything he could.* MFM ▫ *One by one she unravelled Mrs P's deepest, darkest fears and helped her deal with them. She was* ***a tower of strength*** *and all the time she was counting the days until Mrs P would go.* TSMP ▫ usu sing in reference to two or more people.

town and gown [n + n non-rev] all classes of people (esp those with commercial interests) living in a university town (= town) and the university staff, students, governing bodies, etc (= gown) ▫ *In those days* (late 17th c) *the antagonism between '****town and gown****' sometimes resulted in considerable violence.* OBS ▫ *The first city to be approached* (about an International Arts Festival in Britain) *was not, in fact, Edinburgh, but Oxford. No agreement could be reached, however, between* ***town and gown*** *and so Rudolf Bing transferred his attentions to Edinburgh.* RT ▫ *The rent issue has gathered venom from the conflicts which beset Cambridge. No simple matter of* ***town versus gown****, but so tight a web of interest drawn against interest that...* NS ▫ can be adapted, as shown.

a tract for the/our times [Comp (NP)] a book, speech, article etc from which a relevant contemporary lesson or warning may be taken (from Tracts for the Times, a series of theological pamphlets published in Oxford 1833-41) **V:** ⚠ be, become; make sth ▫ *'The Destruction of the English Country House' is simultaneously a picture book and, in the editor's words,* ***a 'tract for the times'****.* NS ▫ *If Bendixson has never used or felt the need of a car, he must be both very lucky and rather strange. This book is therefore more of a curio than* ***a tract for our times****.* NS ▫ *You could choose almost any text from the New Testament for a sermon and make* ***a tract for our times*** *of it.*

trail one's coat [V + O pass] express one's views, exaggerate one's assessments, in a way deliberately intended to provoke criticism, argument, rebuke, contradiction ▫ *In the hope of making a few other people laugh at themselves no doubt I overdo it a bit, deliberately* ***trailing my coat****, as I did with those notorious brown and white eggs.* NS ▫ *Two emotions are dominant in Hedda* (character in an Ibsen play)*, the fear of scandal and the fear of ridicule, and we know that Ibsen, though willing to* ***trail his coat*** *in print, was privately dominated by these emotions.* ST ▫ (Northern Ireland) *At Easter the Republicans hold their parades, to the fury of the Orange Order who in their turn march about the streets. It falls to the army to keep these remarkable manifestations apart and to prevent their* ***coat-trailing*** *brinkmanship from erupting into physical violence.* NS ▫ n compound coat-trailing; attrib use ***coat-trailing*** *brinkmanship.*

one's train of thought [O (NP)] a sequence of thoughts, fancies, or reasoning (on a subject); one's/a line of thought (qv) **V:** interrupt, check, stop. **det:** one's (own), another, the same; this, that ▫ *When interested, his powers of concentration were those of a burning-glass, but* ***his trains of thought****, as obstinate and as surefooted as mules, seemed often to lead him far from the place where he was and the person or persons he was with.* AH ▫ *Like all self-centred people, Mollie could hear a question, and then answer it with something else from* ***her*** *own* ***train of thought****.* AITC ▫ *At first his thoughts dwelt on Tillie—her expression when she had said, 'You can kiss me goodnight if you like. I don't mind.' He checked* ***this train of thought****.* PE

to travel hopefully is a better thing/is better than to arrive (saying) the anticipation, occupation and interest of a journey, research project, work in progress, etc can be more rewarding than its achievement ▫ (source) ***To travel hopefully is a better thing than to arrive****, and the true success is to labour.* EL DORADO VI (R L STEVENSON 1850-94) ▫ (administrative, commercial or academic paralysis) *British medical specialists are usually content to trace the symptoms, and then define the cause. The French, by contrast, begin by describing the treatment and discuss the diagnosis later, if at all. We feel bound to adhere in this to the British method, which may not help the patient but which is unquestionably more scientific.* ***To travel hopefully is better than to arrive.*** PL ▫ (NONCE) (In his humour) *he relies on the timing, rather than the punch-line. And that* *goes for Allen himself. It is, you might say, the story of his 35 years to date. For he's a fellow who* ***prefers the journey to the destination****.* RT

travel light travel with as little luggage as possible; (fig) conduct one's life so as to avoid as many cares and responsibilities as possible □ *Had we perhaps room in our car for a respectable relative? Relative, yes. Luggage, no. We were already loaded down, and Levantines, as I well knew, rarely* ***travel light****.* BM □ *For Americans, moving westward, across the Atlantic or across the continent, meant learning to* ***travel light****. And that meant separating yourself from the treasures, as well as the land, of your ancestors.* L □ *Bill could not bear to see anything hurt; when anyone he came in contact with got hurt, he made a practice of moving on. He called it '****travelling light*** *through life'.* HAA

a traveller's tale a traveller's story of sth strange or wonderful intended to entertain, inform or amaze those who stay at home (often with the implication of invention or exaggeration) □ *It used to be said, perhaps on no better authority than the notoriously flimsy evidence of* ***travellers' tales****, that the Chinese followed the amiable and eminently civilised custom of postponing their battles if the weather was wet.* SC □ *So extraordinary are the true facts that the traveller in the undiscovered country of the politicians must, until his stories are corroborated by after-investigators, be content to lie under the imputation of telling such* ***tales*** *as* ***travellers*** *are generally supposed to delight in.* NS

tread the boards [V + O pass] (facetious) work as an actor □ *His success in amateur theatricals led him on to think he could* ***tread the boards*** *for a living.* □ *Melina Mercouri had* ***trodden many boards*** *before achieving world fame in 'Never on Sunday'.* ST

tread water [V + O] keep oneself afloat in a more or less upright position by using one's legs as if walking; (fig) maintain one's position, but be helpless (or too lazy, disinterested) to make progress □ *When he had swum about a hundred yards out he paused,* ***treading water****, and saw that the girl who had been beside him was nowhere to be found.* □ *Suzy has been very good for me. Until 18 months ago, I realise that I was just* ***treading water****. Now I've regained my enthusiasm for so many things.* TVT □ *As for Mr Carter's money policies, Wall Street was lying doggo for a while, and the stock market* ***trod water****, until it saw what kind of a wild liberal we had in there.* L

the treason of the clerks the belittlement of, or reluctance to promote, intellectual or moral values, by educated people; lack of integrity on the part of intellectuals (from the French title of a book by J BENDA 1868-1956, La Trahison des Clercs) □ *The fear of intellectuals to be seen as advocates of reason is* ***the*** *final* ***treason of the clerks****. To be cowardly under fire is understandable, but to cower when there is a world to be taught (and to learn from) is contemptible.* L □ *Perhaps the only way is to use with vengeful passion the instrument* (ie TV) *that completed the mechanised passivity of modern culture. It is* ***a*** *contemptible new* ***treason of the clerks*** *to pass the medium by with an aloof sniff.* OBS □ *If the younger generation has not yet found a voice neither have we. Is it we, the intellectuals, who have once again failed? Is this* ***one more trahison des clercs****? Yet have we really pressed the case for the vindication of reason and civilised values?* L

(a) treasure trove treasure (gold, jewels coins, valuables) found buried which, in most countries, if it is above a stated value and there is no known owner, reverts to the State and not to the finder; (fig) sth found, acquired, experienced etc that gives great pleasure or profit □ *One object of the search this time is buried treasure amounting, it is said, to no less than 200 tons of gold. As* ***treasure trove*** *it would automatically become the property of the Jordanian Government.* OBS □ (film review) *The whole affair has very much the character and tone of an elaborate charade played by unusually talented house guests. It is* ***treasure trove*** *for those who care to dig.* NS □ *Somewhere in the BBC archives, there is* ***a treasure trove*** *of cricket history for future reference.* L □ uncountable or countable.

treat sb like dirt [V + O + A pass] treat sb as if he was of no importance or value and not entitled to courtesy, consideration or even notice □ ***Treating*** *me* ***like dirt****. Why'd you invite me here in the first place if you was* (= were) *going to* ***treat*** *me* ***like dirt?*** TC □ *Oh, she'd been quick enough then apologizing, but the damage was done. She'd been* ***treated like dirt****, made to look small.* TSMP □ *Maybe they are overworked at the Job Centre but they should still* ***treat*** *you like a human being instead of* ***like dirt****.*

the tricks of the trade [O/o (NP)] skilled and effective methods of doing sth, developed within a trade or profession **V:** know, learn, acquire; teach sb; hand on □ *One's apprenticeship is so important. I've been learning my craft for 27 years, like a carpenter, taught by masters to pick up* ***the tricks of the trade****.* RT □ *Anyone in a police station is vulnerable to the professional interrogators who know* ***the tricks of the trade****.* ST □ (a newly recruited Intelligence agent) *A light shone under the crack of Dr Hasselbacher's door. Was he alone or was he in conference with the taped voice? He was beginning to learn* ***the*** *caution and* ***tricks of his*** *unreal* ***trade****.* OMIH □ *I watched 'Stalin' transfixed, horrified. Two-and-a-half hours of sheer blatant propaganda from end to end, using* ***every trick of the trade****.* RT

tried and true [adj + adj non-rev] many times tested and always found faithful, able, reliable, effective etc □ *I have* ***tried and true*** *friends here. It would need more than twice the salary you offer to tempt me to move elsewhere.* □ *The girl decides at the last minute to keep her babe and that* ***tried-and-true*** *tear-jerker rounds things off.* NS □ *In hard times they* (recording companies) *cannot take a chance on something new, different, and possibly good—they must go for* ***tried and true*** *trash.* G □ *All his techniques are* ***tried and true****—it is to that that he attributes his success.* □ also Comp, as in last example.

trip etc the light fantastic (facetious) dance **V:** trip, ⚠ dance, tread □ (source) *Come, and* ***trip*** *it as ye go/On* ***the light fantastic*** *toe.* L'ALLEGRO (J MILTON 1608-74) □ *And rumours of retirement surrounded Astaire, who has often gone on* *record as saying that he is more in love with breeding racehorses and writing songs than with* ***tripping the light fantastic****.* TVT □ *A lot of the fellows that went to the Saturday night discos spent more time leaning on the wall or drinking in the bar than* ***tripping the light fantastic*** *and so the girls danced with each other, or got fed up and stopped going.*

the/a triumph of hope over experience an instance of foolish optimism □ (source) *A gentleman who had been very unhappy in marriage, married immediately after his wife died: Johnson said it was* ***the triumph of hope over experience****.* LIFE OF JOHNSON (J BOSWELL 1740-95) □ (the concert piano is out of tune and has keys that don't sound) *'Still, I daresay it will be all right on the night,' which* ***triumph of hope over*** *not only* ***experience*** *but plain hard fact so stunned Miss Pemberton that she said no more and took her place in the front row of seats.* WDM

the trivial round, the common task (usu facetious) everyday life and work □ (source) ***The trivial round, the common task****,/Would furnish all we ought to ask.* ENGLISH HYMNAL 260 □ *'Have you been very busy selling cars?' 'Yes.* ***The trivial round, the common task****. Only it doesn't always furnish all I need to ask.'* PE □ *I do wish the BBC would realise that most of us can only afford two weeks' holiday a year and nothing is more depressing, when the brief suntan is peeling, than to come back to* ***the trivial round, the common task****, and a whole series of repeats of* (broadcast) *programmes you have already seen or heard.* L

a Trojan horse [Comp (NP)] a disguised means of introducing something harmful or disadvantageous (from the story of the large wooden horse, filled with armed men, which, when taken into their city by the Trojans as a gift, enabled the Greeks to complete their siege of Troy) **V:** ⚠ be, appear, make sth □ *The working-classes hold on to the personal because they can understand it; here that part of the world outside which is after their money makes* ***a*** *pretty* ***Trojan horse*** *for them.* UL □ *In very gradual, complex ways, Britain may prove to be, not* ***the Trojan horse*** *of American influence which France has always feared, but, on the contrary, a counterpoise to the American tide.* L

true blue [Comp (AdjP)] consistent, and uncomprising in principles, codes of conduct, loyalties etc **V:** ⚠ be; find sb, regard sb as. **n:** Tory, Englishman, friend, protestant, conservative □ *He came before an audience of* ***true-blue*** *Tories, with a speech of pure corn, such as only speech-writers write.* NS □ *Little has surfaced to remind the average home decorator that the 210-year-old Berger, the third biggest decorative products company in the UK, is anything other than* ***true-blue*** *British.* ST □ esp used of member of British Conservative ('Tory') Party, or sb of conservative opinions; n compound a true blue; attrib use *a* ***true(-)blue*** *Tory.*

(run) true to form (be) consistent with previous experience, practice, sb/sth's character or nature □ *A Saturday afternoon all to myself—unheard of in my new life. And,* ***true to form****, I've been wasting it.* ST □ *The one anecdote he never fails to relate is how he's appeared in 14 flop musicals, mostly West End.* ***True to form****, he tried to tell me. 'For some years I drifted from one disaster to another — 14 flops.'* RT

the truth, the whole truth, and nothing but the truth (catchphrase) the absolute truth (from the oath taken (GB) by those about to give evidence in a court of justice) □ *In short, Bruce told* ***the truth, the whole truth, and nothing but the truth****: but the facts he related were too strong.* BN □ *The presenters really gave only a prosaic explanation of a few easily explained incidents, and tarnished the reputation of the series. The programme showed* ***the truth and nothing but the truth****—but did it show* ***the whole truth****?* RT

try anything once [V + O pass] be interested and open-minded enough to try any experience, activity, method etc whether one decides, or is able, to continue it or not □ (theatre) *A profusion of poor but honest fringe groups play in pubs and cellars, retaining a marvellous student willingness to* ***try anything once****, though being sometimes less good at doing it twice.* OBS □ *'Would you have eaten it if you'd known it was an octopus?' 'Why not? I'll* ***try anything once****.'* □ *Most of us draw the line somewhere, like the man who said he'd* ***try anything once*** *except incest and folk dancing.* □ often introduced by will/would.

try as one may [Disj] (be unable to do sth) however hard one tries to **modal:** may, might, will, would □ *Fear of life and death, and an endless search for a nest of safety, was the underlying theme in everything Wells wrote. For in real life there is no escape,* ***try as we will****.* □ ***Try as I might****, I just could not get the message across.* OBS □ (cricket) *There was almost complete silence as Lawrence ran up for the first ball of his over. By the end of it Skinner,* ***try as he would****, had not managed to hit the ball further than the fielders standing near the wicket.* TGLY □ front, middle or end position.

try one's luck [V + O] try to do or obtain sth with the hope that one may succeed in doing or obtaining it □ *At the suggestion of my Uncle Steve I decided to* ***try my luck*** *as a window cleaner.* □ *Soon Ellington was hiring out four or five bands a night; he owned a car and house and operated a sign-and-poster-printing business. All before he went to* ***try his luck*** *in New York.* NS □ *The system of criminal justice, he said, is not tested until you plead 'Not Guilty' and* ***try your luck****.* ST

try sb's patience [V + O pass] irritate and exasperate sb; make it very difficult for sb to be, or remain, patient **adv:** (front position) sorely; (end position) hard □ (stalking a foe) *He then started to circle the barn, keeping close to the far wall. The circling of the barn* ***tried his patience*** *hard.* ARG □ *There is a danger that* ***his patience*** *might be* ***tried*** *if the SFA were to offer him an extension of the interim period. A decision must be taken this afternoon to offer a full-time appointment.* SC □ (astrological prediction) *Someone will sorely* ***try your patience****, but you won't want to answer back.* TVT

the tumult and the shouting (dies) [n + n rev] the (noisy) excitement, protest, argument, fuss (abates or is forgotten) □ (source) ***The tumult and the shouting dies****;/The Captains* *and the Kings depart.* RECESSIONAL (R KIPLING 1865-1936) □ *The Permissive Society is now absorbed into the society which existed before it happened.* ***The shouting and the tumult*** *took place after the battle was fought, and what was really a sorting out process was taken to be the battle itself.* TVT □ *Board meetings were conducted as if they were public demonstrations. When* ***the shouting and the tumult died****, there were two problems he had to solve: the flagging demand for coal and the well-being of the miners.* NS

turn one's back [V + O pass] be absent; have gone away or turned aside; not be watchful, or in immediate control of sb/sth □ *It seems I can't* ***turn my back*** *without one of you hurting yourself or doing something silly.* □ *Yes, and as soon as* ***my back****'s* ***turned*** *you'll be off with this sailor boy and ruin yourself for good.* TOH □ *It's very badly done. I'll have to put another coat of paint on myself, but I'll wait till* ***his back****'s* ***turned****. He'll never notice if nothing is said.* □ also pl turn their backs; often pass in dependent clause beginning *when(ever), while, as soon as, every time, no sooner, etc.*

turn the corner [V + O pass] come to the end of a time of difficulty, poverty, struggle, dangerous illness, etc and start on a more favourable or prosperous course □ *His temperature is still going down, and he's breathing more easily. I think we can safely say he's* ***turned the corner****.* □ ***The corner*** *was* ***turned****, this time it seemed for ever, and the Albert Hall, freshly cleaned, trimmed and refurbished, had started a new career.* OBS □ *There's no doubt in my mind: this England team under Ron Greenwood has* ***turned the corner****, and is on course again to be a real force in world football.* TVT

(take/be) a turn for the better/worse (show/be) a change that promises improvement/deterioration **S:** patient, weather, things, business, world affairs □ *When her father's mental illness* ***took a turn for the worse****, the Ministry released her on compassionate grounds.* PW □ *However, these effects* (of science on our lives) *appear to have* ***taken a turn for the worse*** *with pollution and weapons of mass destruction.* L □ *Robert had certainly drunk enough. From being very silent he had become extremely talkative. To some extent it* ***was a turn for the better****.* EM □ *The situation can be radically changed in his favour only by a sharp* ***turn for the better*** *in El Salvador.* OBS

turn sb's head [V + O pass] cause sb to become vain, ambitious or infatuated with sb/sth **S:** praise, adulation, success □ *I had never been spontaneously approached by a publisher before and such condescension rather* ***turned my head****.* UTN □ *'I'm glad,' Mavis said later, 'these things, like that letter, happened now, and not when I was 25. I think* ***my head*** *would have been* ***turned*** *then. I wouldn't have been stable enough to fit it all in.'* OBS □ *Mr Beaton's zeal has incomparably enriched a national archive* (ie of photographs), *that will long be around to* ***turn the heads of*** *young dress designers, and to evoke an age when craftsmanship was still remembered.* L □ *But I observe women a lot. Basically I think we are vain. A woman's happiness is how many* ***heads*** *she can* ***turn****—especially the Northern women I know.* RT

turn King's/Queen's Evidence [V + O (GB) give evidence against accomplices in court of justice □ *A year later he* ***turne[d] Queen's Evidence*** *in the £200,000 jewel rob[-]bery at the house of Harry Oppenheimer.* DS [□] King or Queen used depending on the sex of th[e] reigning monarch; used of a convicted or acc[-]used person.

the/a turn of events [Comp (NP)] a chang[e] or development in circumstances, often un[-]foreseen or beyond one's control **V:** ⚠ be seem; think sth. **adj:** strange, unexpected, sur[-]prising, pleasing, happy □ *Brigit realized the[n] that she was misjudging the girl. Her excitemen[t] about* ***the turn of events*** *was superficial[.] Beneath it she was alarmed and frightened.* DC [□] *It was only* ***a*** *fortunate* ***turn of events*** *tha[t] enabled him to be present.*

a turn of phrase a way of expressing, defining or describing sth **adj:** neat, amusing, unusual startling, offensive, interesting □ ALISON (quot[-]ing her husband): *Poor old Daddy—just one o[f] those sturdy old plants left over from the Edwar[-]dian Wilderness that can't understand why the sun isn't shining any more.* (Rather lamely.) *Something like that anyway.* COLONEL: *He ha[s] quite* ***a turn of phrase****, hasn't he?* LBA □ *'My meal was interrupted and now I have an un[-]finished taste in my mouth.' '****A*** *very expressive, i[f] unpolished,* ***turn of phrase****, if I may say so.'* □ [I] *don't often agree with his points of view but* [I] *enjoy reading his articles for their* ***turns o[f] phrase****.* □ *'I'll do it if it kills me.' 'I don't like* ***your turn of phrase****,' said his wife. 'You shouldn't tempt Providence.'*

a turn of the screw [O (NP)] a degree of pressure, cruelty, irony etc added to a situation already difficult to bear or understand **V:** add, give, apply. **det:** a, another, (just) one more □ *Dante never thought up* ***that turn of the screw*** *for his condemned lovers. Paolo was never promoted to Purgatory.* QA □ (house-buying) *Less ethical gazumping occurs. The later it is before exchanging final contracts, the more vulnerable the buyer becomes to* ***a*** *further* ***turn of the screw*** (eg raising the price of the house). ST □ *I've always been puzzled and fascinated by the question of why private soldiers should perform the feats of endurance and heroism that they do. It adds* ***a turn of the screw*** *to think of Indian soldiers who often did the same, but under British officers.* L

a turn of speed [O/o (NP)] a swift, usu temporary, acceleration of movement or progress **V:** display, produce; put on, lay on. **prep:** with □ *He stepped into the lift, but Dr Hasselbacher, putting on* ***a turn of speed****, entered too.* OMIH □ *I thought the guard-dog would grab him but he got over that fence with* ***a turn of speed*** *that amazed me in such a fat man.*

turn the other cheek [V + O pass] not complain or retaliate when attacked, rebuked or punished (and even be ready to accept further humiliation) □ (source) *Resist not evil: but whosoever shall smite thee on thy right* ***cheek, turn*** *to him* ***the other*** *also.* MATTHEW V 39 □ *Jesus said that one should* ***turn the other cheek*** *when attacked. He went so far as to command one to love one's enemies. No State that has so far existed has been run on such lines.* OBS □ *I wondered* *why I seemed determined to be a boor. Then she said, without a smile, 'It was kind of you to come down tonight.' This was certainly* ***turning the other cheek*** *and somehow not like the Miss Miles I knew or thought I knew.* PP □ *But she couldn't endure the thought of even this much communication with him. Besides there are limits, prescribed mathematical limits, to* ***turning the other cheek***. PW

turn one's stomach [V + O pass] cause sb to be revolted, disgusted □ (TV programme) *If viewers want a real good wallow in violence for its own sake, smeared in treacly sentiment, I suggest they try this. It certainly* ***turns my stomach***. RT □ *The story shows Paul Kersey taking the law into his own hands when his wife is killed and his daughter rendered catatonic* (a 'schizophrenic' state) *by three crazy muggers. The scene of assault is* ***stomach-turning***, *as it needs to be if one is in any way to endorse Kersey's subsequent actions.* NS □ also pl; adj compound stomach-turning; variant one's stomach turns.

turn tail (and flee) flee as the result of defeat, timidity or fear (from the behaviour of animals) □ *Then, suddenly, the dogs' courage failed them, and they all* ***turned tail and fled*** *up the hill again, leaving the mongoose on its hind legs in the field of battle.* BB □ *As they walked through a stone archway Mrs Shaw went chalk white and started trembling. After a few seconds she* ***turned tail*** *and ran out of the castle.* RT □ *'Dr Hasselbacher,' Wormold called to him. For a moment Wormold thought he was going to* ***turn tail*** *without a word. 'What's the matter, Hasselbacher?' 'Oh, it's you, Mr Wormold.'* OMIH

turn turtle (cause to) turn right over (and sink); (cause to) be/fall in an upside down position (and be helpless, immobile) **S:** ship, dinghy; car; horse □ *This vessel rolled alarmingly. Indeed, she had* ***turned turtle*** *on being launched, an occurrence that cause the German Kaiser to call her 'the biggest turtle afloat'.* WI

a turning point [Comp (NP)] an incident that causes or marks the beginning of a new trend in sb's life, a project, the course of events **V:** ⚠ be, make sth, regard sth as, rank as □ *The capture of Brill on 1 April 1572 must rank as* ***a turning point*** *not only in Netherlands history but in world history: an event of the order of the fall of the Bastille, or the execution of Charles I, or 'the shot that rang round the world' at Concord, Massachusetts.* L □ *'Now you tell Mr Stravinsky what your teacher said.' So the boy planted his feet in the middle of the rug and said, 'My teacher said that you represent* ***the turning point*** *in the history of music.'* OBS □ *I think we are now at one of* ***the turning points*** *in the human spirit and it enables us to begin to see a way out of the problem of prejudice.* L □ stress pattern a 'turning point.

Tweedledum and Tweedledee contestants, disputants, rivals, representatives of equal (un)importance and scarcely distinguishable from each other □ (source, with onomatopoeic reference to the sound of fiddling, concerning a quarrel between the musicians Handel and Bononcini) *Strange! that such a high dispute should be/'Twixt* ***Tweedledum and Tweedledee***. (J BYROM 1692-1763) □ ***Tweedledum and Tweedledee****/Agreed to have a battle;/For Tweedledum said Tweedledee/Had spoiled his nice new rattle.* THROUGH THE LOOKING-GLASS (L CARROLL 1832-98) □ *Greater principles were at issue than two kinds of bigot playing* ***Tweedledum and Tweedledee*** *and shaking their fists at each other.* NS □ *...so-called middle ground where* ***Tweedledum*** *for ever embraces* ***Tweedledee*** *in a lugubrious excess of moderation.* NS

twice over [A (AdvP)] not just once but twice **V:** pay, say, tell, shave, stretch □ *The tourists gazed into the wishing well; they had flung in enough coins to have paid for their drinks* ***twice over***. OMIH □ *It was stupid of you not to have taken measurements first. You've bought enough paper to cover the walls* ***twice over***. □ emphatic; usu end position.

twiddle one's thumbs [V + O] sit or stand with fingers interlocked and circle one's thumbs round each other; (fig) do any unimportant thing merely in order to pass time □ *Seeing vast fields where sheep seemed to be grazing in their thousands, I imagined the owner* ***twiddling his thumbs*** *or fishing for trout. But these farmers are both hard-working and anxious.* OBS □ *Don't just sit there* ***twiddling your thumbs***. *Do something useful!* □ n compound thumb-twiddling.

twist sb's arm [V + O pass] (informal) earnestly persuade, cajole, unfairly influence, or improperly force sb to do sth he does not want to **A:** to write the letter, to accept his son as a trainee; for a loan □ *She conceded that sometimes the members of the panel were rude to people who had written in. 'It distresses me when the team takes someone apart. But then I don't* ***twist*** *anybody* ***'s arm*** *to write in. After all, they know the way the programme works.'* RT □ *I tried to persuade him to write a book about his wartime experiences. I suppose we met four or five times with me* ***twisting his arm*** *and him saying, No, he couldn't do it.* OBS □ ***His arm*** *has been* ***twisted*** *hard by several MPs. He has undergone a dramatic conversion and now campaigns vigorously for our exit from the Common Market.* NS □ also pl; n compound arm-twisting.

twist sb's tail [V + O pass] tease, torment, satirize, harass etc sb □ *These women's antics are only the product of male permissiveness. However, I get a great deal of amusement* ***twisting*** *both* ***their*** *'advanced'* ***tails***. ASA □ *That bedraggled old institution, the family, has taken quite a pounding lately, and John Hopkins is not the man to stand idly by while there are* ***tails*** *to be* ***twisted*** *and hands to be slapped.* NS

twist(s) and turn(s) [n + n non-rev] various and confusing tactics intended to achieve or evade sth (often with the implication of prevarication or deceit) □ *Probably the least prepossessing quality of A G Gardiner was that he cared too much about the ephemeral in politics: and Mr Koss displays excessive zeal, to my mind, in teasing out these cares to the last* ***twist and turn***. L □ *We are aware that this account of Mr Jenkins's behaviour is very different from the current Fleet Street version which contrasts the* ***twists and turns*** *of Mr Wilson's devious politics with the manly and straightforward honesty of Mr Jenkins's support for the Common Market.* NS □ sometimes used as [v + v non-rev].

two blacks/wrongs do not make a white/right (saying) one cannot justify a wrong action by saying that another has done something similar or by pleading revenge for a wrong done to oneself □ *'And I suppose you're going to say that I am no great shakes as a wife? Is that it?' 'I know that* ***two blacks don't make a white****, but you cannot really complain about your husband, whatever he is or does. At least, I don't think you can.'* TT □ *He said mantraps were illegal. 'So's poaching,' I reminded him. And then he started some dunderheaded argument about* ***two blacks not making a white*** *or two whites not making a black.* RM □ *Well, professor,* ***two wrongs do not make a right****, so should not our wonderful modern technology have done something about quietening down our factories before producing this super-plane?* RT

two can live as cheaply as one (saying) an argument advanced in favour of two people living together (esp from a man's point of view when women were not commonly assumed to be wage-earners too) □ *In spite of what they say,* ***two can****'t* ***live as cheaply as one****. And wives hanker after certain standards, and ought to have them — within reason, of course. The little money I have won't run to them.* TST

two heads are better than one (saying) two people co-operating are likely each to make up for deficiencies in the other's reasoning, memory, methods or plans □ *'What about Edward? Do I tell him?' 'That I must leave to you.* ***Two heads are*** *often* ***better than one****.'* TCB

two minds with but a single thought (catchphrase) two people concerned with the same subject, intent or purpose; (facetious) two people who happen to think of, say or do the same thing simultaneously □ (source) ***Two souls with but a single thought****/Two hearts that beat as one.* MARIA LOVELL 1803-77 □ *They hurried down to the quay,* ***two minds with but a single thought*** *that they shrank from putting into words.* □ *'What a coincidence!' And from Mark a brilliant, '****Two minds with but a single thought****!' — as it transpired that she had chosen today to come here to picnic also.* YWT

(where) two or three (are) gathered together (catchphrase) (where there is) a group, however small, (that is) united in fellowship, interests or purpose □ (source) *For* ***where two or three are gathered together*** *in my name, there am I in the midst of them.* MATTHEW XVIII 20 □ *To speak into a microphone in a studio is a private pleasure, because you do not think of an audience. You think of* ***two or three gathered together****. You picture the family by the fire, the student lighting and relighting his pipe.* L □ *We are in danger of forgetting the community.* ***Two or three gathered together*** *lies at the heart of our Christian tradition.* NS

two and two make etc four (saying) it is a straightforward and simple calculation; it is a matter of fact, a self-evident proposition **V:** make, ⚠ are, add up to, come to □ Anybody with brains enough to know that ***two and two make four*** *could have guessed the outcome of that situation.* □ *Don't talk to me about children! All your life you sweat your kishkers out to give them a good education and everything they want and what happens? Davey turns round and tells me that* ***two and two*** *don't* ***add up to four****, and Lottie joins the Communist party.* HSG

two's company, (three's a crowd) (catchphrase) it is (more) pleasant, easy, relaxing for two people to be together (than it is for three) (the implication often being that two = 'a woman and a man in love with each other' and that no third person wants to intrude on the couple) □*They say that* ***two's company****, but after years of observing my parents together I have very strong doubts on the matter.* □ *'Why didn't you join us?' 'Oh, you know,* ***three's a crowd****—I didn't want to intrude on you two.'* variant two's company, three's not/none.

a twopenny halfpenny/tuppenny ha'penny affair etc a cheap, insignificant, or paltry affair etc **n:** affair, thing, arrangement, gadget □ *Bangladesh has an army, but it is a* ***twopenny halfpenny affair*** *kept deliberately weak, with the security forces split into three separate groups.* G □ *The way she went on you'd think she'd lost the Crown Jewels instead of a* ***tuppenny-ha'penny*** *coloured glass* ***pendant****.* □ *There's no good conversation. All they talk about is football, or their families, or their* ***twopenny halfpenny jobs****.* □ form tuppenny ha'penny reflects pronunciation.

U

U/non-U upper class/non-upper class usage in language and social behaviour (from UPPER CLASS ENGLISH USAGE (A C ROSS b1907) and see also NOBLESSE OBLIGE (ed N MITFORD 1904-73)) □ *'I'm a schoolteacher.' It seemed to him* ***non-U*** *to say 'schoolmaster' here, like 'perspiration' instead of 'sweat'.* TGLY □ *Deep in the English character, there is an instinct for a* ***U*** *and* ***non-U*** *pronunciation as strong as it ever was.* L □ many people feel the distinctions are arbitrary and not to be taken seriously.

an ugly(-looking) customer a person, or animal, that is or might be dangerous, violent, difficult to control or deal with □ *The two deck hands,* ***ugly-looking customers*** *both of them, moved a little nearer.* □ *As far as the general public is concerned, chimps are only lovable up to the age of 6 years or so, and indeed an old male can be* ***an ugly-looking customer****.*

an ugly duckling (becomes etc a swan) a child, chick, puppy etc born less attractive than his brothers and sisters who later surpasses them (from THE UGLY DUCKLING (H C ANDERSEN 1805-75), a story of a swan chick hatched with ducklings and at first compared unfavourably with them) **V:** becomes, changes into, grows into, is transformed into □ *This situation develops into a dictionary of comedy clichés, including a comic politician and* ***an ugly duckling who grows up into a swan****.* L □ *Eleanor*

Roosevelt was throughout her life an awkward person to have around—not merely because she was born and remained ***the*** *classic* ***ugly duckling*** *but also because in her own person she embodied the old-fashioned American Puritan ethic.* NS □ *A long time ago, I was in an awful play where I had to come downstairs transformed from* ***an ugly duckling*** *into a beautiful lady.* TVT

the unacceptable face of capitalism etc (catchphrase) an aspect of capitalism etc, or sth that may happen within the system of capitalism etc, that cannot be accepted **n:** capitalism, trade unionism, local government, law enforcement, patronage □ (source—comment about the conduct of a financial and business company, 1973) *This is* ***the unacceptable face of capitalism.*** EDWARD HEATH (then Prime Minister). □ ***The unacceptable face of public medicine****? Is it true that in some hospitals terminal patients consent to exploratory operations and experimental treatments in the belief that a reasonable chance of cure or alleviation is being offered?* □ *The Poulson case has shown how* ***local government*** *too,* ***has its unacceptable face.*** OBS □ variant capitalism etc has its unacceptable face.

under the aegis of sth/sb [A (PrepP] protected, supported, or sponsored by sth/sb, esp an institution or public body (from aegis, the shield of Zeus or Athene and a symbol of divine protection) **V:** perform, appear; study, work □ *This is the Morse collection of seventeenth-century Chinese painting, which has come to the British Museum* ***under the aegis of*** *the Arts Council.* ST □ *Incidentally, Mr Harrison is now working on his original material* ***under the aegis of*** *Sussex University and may before long be publishing some of it.* L

under cover of sth [A (PrepP)] shielded, or concealed, by sth; (fig) using the excuse, pretext or explanation of sth **V:** move, manoeuvre, assemble, disappear. **o:** darkness, the bushes; the confusion caused, the noise of the bands □ *George Hutchins jammed his chair against hers and surreptitiously took her hand* ***under cover of*** *a newspaper.* HD □ *He leaned forward to pat* (the horse's) *neck and* ***under cover of*** *the movement extracted the Mauser.* ARG □ ***Under cover of*** *the general excitement, he has slipped away unseen.* □ *I heard reports of big military installations under construction, stories of widespread forest clearance* ***under cover of*** *forest fires.* OMIH

under foot [A (PrepP)] on the ground; on the surface where one walks **V:** crush, trample, sth □ *Here the grass ended and there was a loose sandy soil* ***under foot.*** □ *I wish I'd worn my Wellingtons. I didn't realize it would be so muddy* ***underfoot.*** □ often written as underfoot.

under the guise of sth [A (PrepP)] while appearing, or pretending, to be, or do, sth **o:** friendship, entertainment; a trade conference □ *The great issue for their country is the struggle against a slide towards dictatorship. This, they feel, is what the Prime Minister,* ***under the guise of*** *outward democratic forms, is aiming at.* OBS □ *She's an expert at imposing her will on other members of the family* ***under the guise of*** *encouraging them to make their own decisions.*

under sb's nose [Comp/A (PrepP)] (informal) in full view of sb: openly, or defiantly, in sb's presence **V:** be; vanish, disappear, destroy sth, steal sth, remove sth □ *'Have you a match to light the gas with?' 'There's a box of matches right* ***under your nose.****'* □ *In every tense situation that takes place in public there are always one or two people about who don't see what is happening* ***under their noses.*** CON □ *One of Bill's jobs was to swim ashore in the darkness* ***under the noses of*** *the Germans.* RFW □ (reader's letter) *The British public is subject to a barrage of depravity and corruption from so-called progressive writers, while at the same time real social progress is being quietly nibbled away* ***under our*** *very* ***noses.*** L

under one's own etc name [A (PrepP)] using one's own etc name to claim, or accept, identity, ownership, credit, responsibility etc **V:** appear, perform; write. **det:** one's own, another('s), one's father's. **adj:** (replacing ***one's own etc***) a borrowed, a false □ *Quorum were impressed and three weeks ago asked her to design a* (dress) *collection for them* ***under her own name.*** ST □ *The breed* (of dog) *received official recognition by the Kennel Club and was granted a separate register* ***under its present name.*** OBS □ *I've had grave suspicions that you'd planted yourself here* ***under a false name*** *in order to get information out of me.* TCB □ *There is only one who is a recognisably classic artist at all points, and he secretively walks the earth* ***under the name of*** *Randy Newman.* L □ also pl under their own names; variant under the name of sb/sth where person/thing is specified, as in last example.

under one's own steam [A (PrepP)] (informal) by efforts or means of one's own; without help from anybody else **V:** proceed, move; continue, carry on □ PHILIP: *Where's Rosemary? She said she'd get here* ***under her own steam.*** EHOW □ *Oh, he's got the hang of the job now. I'll leave him to carry on* ***under his own steam*** *for a bit.* □ *'Have you made up your mind if you want Myrtle to go with you to America or not?' 'If she likes to go* ***under her own steam,****' I said.* SPL

under par [Comp (PrepP)] unwell **V:** ⚠ be; feel, look, seem □ *'Sue won't be at the meeting this afternoon. She's gone home ill.' 'I'm not surprised. She's been looking a bit* ***under par*** *recently.'* □ par = (golf) 'the number of shots that has been set as a standard for a good player for each individual hole or for all eighteen holes on a particular golf-course'. ⇨ ⚠ be par for the course.

under protest [A (PrepP)] while protesting, objecting **V:** accept sth; comply, obey □ *'Disobeying a superior officer, I remind you, is a serious offence.' 'Very well, but I want it written down that I am carrying out the order* ***under protest.****'* □ *The police claimed a rise of 35 per cent, and their spokesman accepts an average of 16 per cent* ***under protest.*** SC □ *The children, who never went to bed except* ***under protest,*** *were at last got rid of.* □ usu follows v it modifies.

to understand all is to forgive all (saying) when all the facts are known and understood it is possible to forgive a person for anything □ *'She never used to be like this, did she?' 'She has problems, that woman,' he said '****To understand***

all is to forgive all.*'** TT ▫ (TV interviews) *Why doesn't he ever get tough with his guests or subjects? Something in his format or his approach makes Harty the man who* ***understands all and forgives all. NS

union/unity is strength (saying) groups have more power to act, or resist the actions of others, than individuals have **V:** is; gives; means ▫ (reader's letter) *The old saying still holds good —to beat the Tories we must have unity.* ***Unity is strength.*** NS

united we stand (divided we fall) (saying) a group of people acting together can achieve a desired aim which the members of that group will not be able to achieve if each acts alone ▫ *The photograph shows the front ranks of the marchers, with banners aloft, and all of them with* ***united-we-stand*** *expressions on their faces.* ▫ *Well, what's it to be?* ***United we stand*** *—or are there any dissenters?* ▫ (caption) ***United they stand****, a family from a Welsh valley.* RT ▫ attrib use *a* ***united-we-stand*** *expression, attitude etc.*

the (most) unkindest cut of all the worst insult, case of ill treatment, etc among several ▫ (source — referring to Brutus' part in the assassination of Julius Caesar) *Judge, O you gods, how dearly Caesar lov'd him!/This was* ***the most unkindest cut of all.*** JULIUS CAESAR III 2 ▫ *Perhaps* ***the unkindest cut of all*** *comes in a swift interview with an old female classmate of Nixon's, retailing how, a non-dancer himself, he made* (ie got himself elected) *student president by campaigning for dancing on campus.* NS

an unknown quantity (mathematics) a quantity, number not (yet) determined; (fig) sb/sth one has no experience of, or whose actions, performance, mood etc one can never predict ▫ *Test pilots approach each flight circumspectly. They know they are dealing with* ***an unknown quantity****, so they prepare thoroughly and always have a 'contingency plan' at the ready.* TVT ▫ *Thomas continued to be somewhat of* ***an unknown quantity****. To this day, I don't know how he earned his money, or whether he was single, divorced or a widower.* SC

(how) unlike/different from the home/private life of our own dear Queen (catchphrase) (how) unlike some, possibly idealized, standard of civilized home life, behaviour, business practice, etc (from a remark allegedly made by a Victorian woman during a performance of 'Antony and Cleopatra') ▫ *You don't know what it is like to have to run such a disorganized household—* ***not*** *very* ***like the home life of our dear Queen****, I'm afraid.* ▫ (a television series) *On Saturday I got myself hypnotised for a while by 'Face the Music', its unalloyed jollity always so* ***unlike the private life of our dear****, bitching and back-biting* ***profession****.* L ▫ *Your real diarists — something notable seems to happen to them* every *day, be it a publisher's party or a witty encounter with a bank manager, or a quip from Kingsley Amis;* ***how different from the home life of your*** *humble* ***incumbent*** *of this week.* NS ▫ often adapted, as shown.

the unspeakable in (full) pursuit of the uneatable (catchphrase) fox hunting as a sport ▫ (source) *The English country gentleman galloping after a fox —* ***the unspeakable in full pursuit of the uneatable.*** A WOMAN OF NO IMPORTANCE (O WILDE 1854-1900) ▫ *George Millar hunts, or used to, and turned his author's eye on the mores of those whom another author once described as* ***the unspeakable in pursuit of the uneatable****; what matters is the society of the chase not the victory over the quarry.* ST (NONCE) *Many observers consider the Rock Festival to be a dying form. Too often it means* ***the uncomfortable in pursuit of the inaudible.*** N ▫ often adapted, as shown.

unwept, unhonoured and unsung [Comp (AdjP)] the object of nobody's regard, respect or remembrance **V:** ⚠ be, go; die, depart, remain ▫ (source) *And, doubly dying, shall go down/To the vile dust, from whence he sprung,* ***Unwept, unhonour'd, and unsung.*** THE LAY OF THE LAST MINSTREL (W SCOTT 1771-1832) ▫ *Housework provides the daily backdrop to the lives of a social underclass whose members are not only* ***unwept, unhonoured and unsung****, but unpaid into the bargain.* NS ▫ *Why should one goldfish occupy so much valuable space in a serious weekly magazine when hundreds or thousands of goldfish die every week* ***unwept unhonoured and unsung****?* NS

an unwritten law a long established custom that is difficult to break or disobey ▫ *'Your women are forbidden to marry outsiders,' Frank said. 'Or so I have been told.' 'There is* ***an unwritten law****.'* ARG ▫ *There's no caretaker in the block and according to* ***some unwritten law*** *the ground floor tenant is responsible for keeping the common entrance clean.*

up (with) sb/sth exclamation of, or appeal for, support, approval of sb/sth **o:** the Party, the revolution; devolution, free bargaining ▫ *What's the use of '****Up with*** *the Party' and theoretical flag-waving when you can't be bothered to attend branch meetings?* ▫ (Scottish Nationalism) *The throne would serve the same function as in other Commonwealth countries and the Queen's status or place in the affections of her Scottish subjects has nothing to do with the* ***up****-home-rule-and-down-with-Whitehall argument.* SC ▫ *'Such virtues as most people practise are dictated by self-interest.' 'Then* ***up with*** *self-interest, say I.'* ▫ attrib use *the* ***up****-home-rule argument.* ⇨ down with sb/sth.

up and coming (informal) likely to add to the progress, success, popularity one has begun to achieve **n:** generation; architect, doctor, footballer; publishers ▫ *She says he's got a very good reputation as one of the* ***up and coming*** *young doctors.* RFW ▫ *Jolson's health was not good, and he decided he was too old for the part.* ***Up-and-coming*** *Larry Parks was signed, and Jolson dubbed the songs.* RT ▫ *He has to operate under the 1968 Transport Act which was steered through Parliament by an* ***up-and-coming*** *politician named Richard Marsh.* RT ▫ *Davis, from the East End of London, is* ***up and coming****, having turned pro after a successful junior career.* TVT ▫ usu attrib, *an* ***up-and-coming*** *politician*, but also predic, as shown.

up and down the country/land in various places throughout a particular country ▫ *The product itself is prepared in bottling plants* ***up and down the land.*** OBS ▫ (reader's letter) *The* *launching of the lifeboat was the perfect complement to the programme, reminding us of the great debt we owe to that fine body of men* ***up and down the country***. RT □ up and down non-rev; usu prep p modifying a preceding n.

up and down (the) stairs [A (PrepP)] with repetitious (and/or tiring) use of stairs from one level to another **V:** go, run, toil □ *I don't mind living in a top flat. Going* ***up and down stairs*** *will be good exercise for me.* □ DAVIES: *You want to* (= should) *do all the dirty work all* ***up and down*** *them* (= those) ***stairs***. TC □ *The tall Edwardian houses had been built in the Square's palmier days, when servants toiled* ***up and down the*** *many* ***stairs***. AITC □ up and down non-rev.

up hill and down dale [A (PrepP)] everywhere; to, from etc many places; thoroughly; exhaustively; vigorously **V:** run, chase, search; curse, chivvy, harangue, sb □ *I wish you'd say where you're going, and not have people chasing* ***up hill and down dale*** *trying to find you when you're wanted.* □ (That your legs are sore) *is not surprising, the way you've run them up and downstairs and* ***over hill and dale*** *—let them have their rest.* DC □ *'Johnson won't like your taking his best workman away.' 'He'll be cursing me* ***up hill and down dale***, *I've no doubt.'* □ non-rev; variant over hill and dale.

up and leave etc suddenly, unexpectedly, or disconcertingly leave etc **V:** leave, go; say, do, sth □ *His Austrian grandfather was an opera singer who abruptly* ***upped and left*** *his wife in Vienna.* TVT □ *Courting on the sly like that and suddenly* ***upping and saying*** *he was married, without having mentioned a word of it before.* LLDR □ *Barry Brown, as the fellow in this slender tale, is unutterably dull and it is a great relief all round when Daisy* ***ups and takes*** *a fever at the Colosseum.* L □ infin, or present or past simple tenses.

up stakes/sticks [V + O] move (with one's belongings) to another place of residence or work (from *pull* ***up stakes*** (US), originally referring to the formal abandoning of a claim to land for pioneer settlement or prospecting) □ *Then Morris found a job as a book-keeper in Jerusalem, so the family* ***upped stakes*** *and moved once again.* ST □ *Dana left home all right, but not the family. They simply* ***upped sticks*** *and went with her.* RT □ *Everybody from departmental directors to Parliamentary ushers has to* ***up-sticks*** *and move from Luxembourg to Strasbourg when Parliament is in session.* L

up to a point [A (PrepP)] partly; in some degree **V:** agree, approve; tolerate sb/sth; be, seem. **adj:** true, acceptable, tolerable □ ***Up to a point***, *this is true, but the difference is slight and the over-all agreement considerable.* SNP □ *This haul is encouraging, but only* ***up to a point***. ST □ *It was proper for the Judge to encourage the jury* ***up to a point*** *to come to a definite conclusion.* T □ *'We say that the signal saturates. Is that all clear, John?'* ***'Up to a point***. *What I don't see is how the wave-length comes into it.'* TBC □ front, middle or end position.

up yours etc (taboo) be quiet; go away; drop dead² (qv); (taboo) get knotted (qv); get lost (qv); (taboo) get stuffed (qv) **pron:** yours, you. **n:** (replacing ***yours etc***) your arse, the Establishment □ *'And there'll be five pounds for replacing the lock you broke.'* ***'Up yours!'*** *I said, giving him two fingers.* □ *'The Dawsons will be complaining about the noise again.' 'Oh,* ***up them***. *People have to live, haven't they?'* □ *In the 60 days after he retired from Avis* (a business concern), *Townsend wrote a book impishly titled '****Up the Organisation****'.* RT □ exclamation of contempt and/or defiance, with or without the accompanying gesture of a turned-in hand with first and second fingers raised together (not spread as in the V/victory sign).

an uphill task etc [Comp (NP)] a difficult task, undertaking, either in itself or because of opposition met with **V:** ⚠ be, become; find sth. **n:** an. . .task, ⚠ an. . .fight, an. . .struggle; work, going □ *He never has much to say; sustaining a conversation of more than a few minutes with him is* ***uphill work***. □ *So far, I'm finding 'The Long March of Everyman' (Radio 4, Sundays at 10.10)* ***uphill going***. NS □ *At long last it did seem that we might get a dividend from* ***the uphill fight*** *we had been waging with the Government.* MFM □ *The House of Lords is not prone to wasting counsel's time, but the union certainly had* ***an uphill struggle*** *from the first day with Lord Wilberforce.* ST ⇨ ⚠ be downhill all the way¹.

upon my soul/word certainly; truly; my goodness □ *I believe I could earn more money charring* (= cleaning houses, offices etc for payment), ***upon my soul*** *I do.* □ *'In-eff-icient!' Sir Julius let the syllables fall one by one with an air of shocked amusement.* ***'Upon my soul***, *that is about the last epithet I should have expected to hear applied to me, from such a source, Mrs Carstairs!'* EM □ (advertisement) *That pretty frock, too, has surely a special freshness.* ***Upon my word!*** *What a difference starching with 'Robin' makes.* WI □ rather restrained exclamation, associated with older middle-class speakers and emphasizing a comment, promise, threat, or expressing delight, astonishment etc.

the upper crust (informal) the aristocracy; people who think themselves, or are thought by others to be, on a high social level □ *But, on the whole, working-class people, and in particular the men, simply do not include* ***the 'upper crust'*** *in their picture of life nowadays.* UL □ *While such social types in England can move automatically from Eton into the Cabinet, it's a heavy handicap for an American politician to have gone to Harvard and have an* ***upper-crust*** *accent.* L □ *In 'The Millionairess' he's the* ***upper crust*** *handsome idiot who's married to the rich Mrs Fitzfassenden.* RT □ *We were shown* ***the*** *old style* ***upper crust*** *who won the war, naval officers breezing into battle through a barrage of heroic music.* NS □ attrib use *an* ***upper-crust*** *officer, accent, sport etc.*

the ups and downs (of sb/sth) [n + n non-rev] an alternating pattern of good and bad periods in sb's/sth's fortunes, health, spirits etc **o:** life, career, marriage; controlling the economy, running a business □ *People, we assume, are much the same everywhere: personality will out, and* ***the ups and downs of*** *life are much the same everywhere too.* L □ *Since she could not discuss* ***the*** *baby****'s ups and downs*** *with Joe, Virginia discussed them with Lennie, who was always ready to listen.* AITC □ *They needed a security beyond the accidents of their daily life,* *with* ***its ups and downs of*** *feeling and its too intense dependence on each other.* PW □ *And as the Hallé* (Orchestra) *it became the pride and joy of the North, and of course, not without* ***some ups and downs****, to this day.* OBS □ *She had had* ***her ups and downs****, but she had always managed to pull herself together and have a good time.* H □ often in construction *have one's* ***ups and downs****.*

upset the/sb's applecart [V + O pass] spoil a plan or arrangement; disrupt events; disprove a theory □ *Setting the tray down she gave a squeal, 'I say, you do look a sight! Something* ***upset your apple-cart****?'* US □ *'She was in, of course, I knew that.' 'No, she wasn't, she went out, that was what* ***upset the applecart****.'* TSMP □ *Still, in climbing this high George McGovern has* ***upset enough applecarts*** *to choke all the highways in Miami Beach.* NS □ *I think it is roughly true that Swift was the fellow who* ***upset*** *Marlborough****'s apple-cart****, and a very good thing, too.* L

use one's head/loaf [V + O] (informal) (be able to) think effectively, use one's intelligence (from Cockney rhyming slang, loaf = 'loaf of bread' = 'head') □ *He can put things right if he will only* ***use his head*** *and be unselfish.* AH □ *That box will hold all the empty bottles if you stack the top layer upside down. It's just a case of* ***using your head****, you see.* □ (football) *He can cut off a move by* ***using his loaf*** *when a younger player might have to sprint 60 yards to gain the same result.* TVT □ *'Oh,* ***use your loaf****, for Christ's sake!' I shouted. His incomprehension was beginning to get me down.* CON □ also pl use their heads/loaves.

V

the valley of the shadow of death [O (NP)] a place, or circumstances, in which one is in danger of, or has narrowly escaped, dying **V:** be in; go, pass, through □ (source) *Yea, though I walk through* ***the valley of the shadow of death****, I will fear no evil.* PSALMS XXIII 4 □ (reader's letter) *The precise literal meaning of the Hebrew words used by the Psalmist is '****the valley of the shadow of death****'. Nobody has ever taken them otherwise than metaphorically.* T □ (book review) *This life in* ***the valley of the shadow of death*** *is on the whole painfully convincing.* NS

value for money [O (NP)] worth the price paid **V:** give, get; want, expect □ (1971) *Undoubtedly, some people in the trade have cashed in on the inability of British housewives to recognise* ***value for money*** *in decimal currency.* SC □ *They're ordinary working folk who want to enjoy a night out and get* ***value for money****.* TVT □ *Well, I thought, that's three quid* ((slang) = pounds (sterling)) *for adjectives—perhaps the rest of the book will give* ***value for money****. It does.* L

a value judgement [O (NP)] a subjective assessment of sb/sth's value, usefulness, interest etc which is not, or cannot be, based on evidence or experiment **V:** make; offer, deliver □ *One of the great problems is to understand clearly the relative importance in one's life of '****value judgements****' as opposed or compared to 'knowledge' judgements.* L □ *In all the above examples, the tribunal was forced to make* ***a value judgement*** *on the behaviour of working people and employers using simple tests of 'reasonableness'.* ST

variations on the theme (of sth) different forms of an original, or basic, theme, topic or activity (from *theme and variations* as a particular type of formal musical composition) □ *Her devious husband, aiding and abetting her, thought out new* ***variations on the theme of*** *burglary and blackmailing.* DC □ *Before the War more space was given in 'The Times' to obituary notices. There were many* ***variations on the theme*** *that the world 'would be the poorer for his passing'.* AH □ occas sing.

variety is the spice of life (saying) new, or different, things to do or experience, make life interesting, prevent one from becoming bored or dull □ (source) ***Variety's the*** *very* ***spice of life****,/That gives it all its flavour.* THE TASK (W COWPER 1731-1800) □ *I'm just an odd-job man, really, for anybody who needs one. Oh well,* ***variety is the spice of life****, as they say.* □ (NONCE) ***Useless information is the spice of life****, and it is surely nice to know who was the second youngest prime minister.* L

very good, (sir/madam) yes; certainly; that is agreed; I will do as you say □ *'You wish me to undertake this enquiry, sir?' 'Until you can hand it over to the proper authorities—yes.' '****Very good, sir****.'* EM □ *'Those ginger biscuits are as hard to bite as cracking nuts.' '****Very good, madam****,' said Palmer, and she picked up the offending plate.* WDM □ esp used as formally civil reply to an order or request from a superior, employer, customer etc.

very well all right; I agree; I can do that (the implication usu being unenthusiastic or reluctant agreement or consent) □ *'My lord, this juror wishes to affirm* (instead of taking the oath)*.' '****Very well****, then,' says the judge in that world-weary way judges have.* NS □ *'No, no. I insist on paying my own fare.' '****Very well****, if you feel that way. It's not worth argument.'*

the vexed question/subject (of sth) a subject about which there is much argument and variety of opinion; a problem to which no satisfactory solution has yet been found □ *Will the Prime Minister bear in mind that the Chinese government regards* ***the vexed question of*** *Formosa as of much greater importance than a seat on the United Nations?* T □ *Then there is* ***the vexed question of*** *baptism and education of children of mixed marriages.* G □ *Still on* ***the vexed subject of*** *cheap houses for London commuters, this is a sketch of new terraced houses on an estate at East Tilbury (38 minutes from Fenchurch Street).* ST □ *One of* ***the*** *most* ***vexed questions*** *in assessing the dangers of pollution by insecticides such as DDT is the way in which they are distributed worldwide from the places* *where they are used.* T

a vicious circle/spiral a situation in which a reaction, or effect, increases the original cause or makes the whole process continue □ *Debtors were caught in* ***a vicious circle****: they could not be freed until they had paid their debt, and were not able to pay their debt as long as they were in prison.* L □ *It vexed her to feel as she did, and vexation turned to guilt, and guilt increased her unrest: it was* ***a vicious circle****.* PW □ *The lack of a sense of proportion is exemplified by the assumption on the Republican side that any and every action by the Army, whatsoever the provocation that preceded it, justifies the continuation of bombing and shooting. The whole situation is locked in* ***a vicious spiral****.* L

the village idiot a stock example of a simpleton, eccentrically stupid or foolish person □ *Christian Rodska can claim that he made his television debut as* ***a village idiot****. But he's certainly proved he's nobody's fool as an actor.* TVT □ *He's an old rogue. Playing* ***the village idiot*** *is not going to get him out of trouble this time.*

the villain of the piece [Comp (NP)] the villain in a drama; the person, or group, responsible for mishandling, or interfering with, a situation in politics, business, or social life **V:** ⚠ be; regard sb as, think sb □ *Is the company she has been so loyal to for so many years* ***the villain of the piece****?* TVT □ ***The villain of the piece*** *is suspected to be Lord Aldington. Toby Aldington, the story goes, is encouraging Ted in his wilful ways.* NS □ *The original idea for the conference came from the Chancellor of the Exchequer. It's ironic that Mr Barber, as host, is also one of* ***the villains of the piece****.* L

virtue is its own reward (saying) the satisfaction gained from virtuous conduct etc is sufficient, outweighs any other consideration □ *Don't they say that* ***virtue is its own reward****? It had better be: for even where Good Works are concerned, the bingo business* (ie pure luck) *still applies.* TVT □ (NONCE) CLIVE: *Well,* ***poetry's its own reward****, actually—like* ***virtue****. All Art is.* FFE □ often adapted.

one's vital statistics one's body measurements (esp the bust, waist and hip measurements of a woman) □ (Metrication Board advertisement) *Here's how this lady****'s vital statistics*** *are written down in metric: Height: 165 cm (5ft 5 ins) Bust: 91 cm (36 ins) Waist 74 cm (29 in) Hips 97 cm (38 ins).* □ *Soviet girl models, and there are a few, asked by some pushy Western male journalist for* ***their vital statistics****, are as offended as Victorian ladies.* NS

one's voice breaks[1] a boy's voice changes from the higher voice of a child to the lower voice of a man □ *He used to sing in the choir at Eton till* ***his voice broke****.* WDM □ *It is interesting that though Caruso****'s treble*** *appears to have been a deep one, it* ***broke*** *as a baritone.* OBS

one's voice breaks[2] emotion prevents one from speaking evenly or without interruption □ *I don't think I could read these lines without* ***my voice breaking****. Get someone else to do it.*

the voice of conscience the sense, awareness, that one has failed or sinned; the still small voice (of conscience) (qv) □ *A civilised society is one which sees the evil in itself and provides means to eliminate it where* ***the voice of conscience*** *is active.* NS □ (politicians being severely addressed) *The curious thing is that they accept his manner as if they knew that all good Englishmen should be made to listen to* ***the voice of conscience*** *from time to time.* OBS

W

the wages of sin (is death) the inevitable consequence of wrong-doing is punishment and suffering; (facetious) the pleasure and profit that one gets for having sinned □ (source) *For* ***the wages of sin is death****; but the gift of God is eternal life through Jesus Christ our Lord.* ROMANS VI 23 □ *She had enough faith in spiritual values to feel that they would be the better for it* (a blessing). ***The wages of sin*** *did no one any good.* PW □ *Shivering, he thought of the warmth and light of the hotel where Robert Tharkles had taken Betty.* ***The wages of sin****.* HD

waifs and strays [n + n non-rev] homeless people, dogs, cats etc, esp, formerly, orphaned or abandoned children who had to find what shelter and food they could □ *Aunt Annabel* (who fed stray cats as well as her own) *snuggled against the cat in her arms. 'This is Renoir. He's so fat — He's my own treasure. He merely tolerates the* ***waifs and strays****.'* DC □ nouns can be used separately.

wait and see [v + v non-rev] wait to find out what will happen, or be done, before, or instead of, taking action, making a decision, or forming an opinion, oneself □ *It is probably one of those things that are too complicated for direct calculation. We shall have to* ***wait and see****, I'm afraid.* TBC □ *Kate says as far as her future goes, we'll all have to* ***wait and see****.* TVT □ *A breakdown of the Scottish economy is too near to allow continuance of* ***wait-and-see*** *policies.* SC □ often used with *will, would, must, have to*; attrib use a ***wait-and-see*** *policy, philosophy etc.*

wait etc till/until the cows come home wait etc for a very long time, indefinitely **V:** (will/may/can) wait, complain, argue, sit there □ *He'll go on* ***talking*** *about his experiences in Paraguay* ***till the cows come home*** *unless someone stops him.* □ *One can* ***bat*** *the slogan that 'It's Scotland's oil' to and fro across the table* ***until the cows come home*** *(or until the Americans have built all the rigs)—the English have not the slightest intention of letting it become Scotland's oil.* NS □ *A writer should make himself as clear as* reasonably *possible. But he cannot be as clear as possible, just like that, because the idea of clarity* ***is****, as jurists say, infinitely defeasible, or, to put it more loosely,* ***open to*** *stupid objections* ***until the cows come home****.* NS □ stress pattern ˌwait till the ˈcows come home.

wait one's turn [V + O] not (try to) do sth, obtain attention or service, before others who may have prior rights □ *To see the waiter (who knew us) taking our order and making them* ***wait their turn*** *was too much for a formidable matron among them.* AH □ *I had hoped the game would finish in time for me to catch the 4.15 but at 4.15 I was still* ***waiting my turn*** *to bat.*

(would) wake etc the dead [V + O] be rousingly, disturbingly, or excessively loud **V:** wake, ⚠ waken, awake, awaken □ *His voice came echoing down the stairs. 'What's going on down there? Who's prowling about?' Nurse Ellen gave Brigit a resigned glance. 'That foghorn* ***would wake the*** *very* ***dead****.'* DC □ *He goes roaring by fit to* ***waken the dead*** *on that motorbike of his.*

walk before one can run master the first stages of a skill, or study, before risking failure at a more advanced or ambitious level **modal:** must, ought to, need to. **V:** learn to, want to, try to □ *The L.C.C. architects (careful men) say they want to* ***walk before they can run****.* OBS □ *I was in too much of a hurry in those days. I was trying to* ***run before I could walk****.* TVT □ *William Saroyan learned to* ***run before he could walk****. It has been a long run, and a merry one.* SC □ walk and run rev.

one's walk of life one's place in society as determined by profession, trade, occupation, social background, age group, etc **det:** one's, another, all, every □ *I talked with many people in* ***every walk of life****.* MFM □ *Meeting people in '****all walks of life****' is not always the psychological uplift for media professionals that people in* ***all walks of life*** *suppose.* L □ *A man in Ilford had jobs for insurance salesmen. He was saying 'But we have people from* ***all walks of life****' for the third time when I rang off.* NS □ *'Or one could ask someone in* ***another walk of life****. One could ask Mrs Perfect, for instance.' 'Our daily woman?'* PW □ ***All walks of life*** *provide candidates, and the final selection represents a cross-section of the teenage population.* RT □ in constructions *from/ in* ***all walks/every walk of life****.*

walk the plank [V + O] go/be sent to one's death; be destroyed (from pirates making their prisoners walk blindfold along a plank jutting out from the ship, till they fell into the sea) □ *You might as well ask a man to* ***walk the plank*** *as drive in this fog.* □ *I don't know whether* (English language) *standards are going up or down, I just know that 'in terms of' should be made to* ***walk the plank****.* NS

walk a tightrope [V + O] have to act in a situation where there is little scope for manoeuvre or adjustment and where an exact balance must be preserved (from the tightrope on which acrobats perform) □ *As a manager, you* ***walk a tightrope****. The dividing line between success and failure is very, very thin.* L □ *Two young cops* ***walk a tightrope*** *in the world of crime, starring Paul Michael Glaser as 'Starsky' and David Soul as 'Hutch'.* RT □ *Secondly, the law centres* ***walk a*** *precarious* ***tight rope*** *between pure case work and more active involvement in the community's problems.* ST □ *Not since Charles Blondin crossed the Niagara Falls in 1885 can there have been a piece of* ***tight-rope walking*** *to rival Mr Healey's performance yesterday afternoon.* G □ may be tightrope/tight-rope/tight rope; n compounds tight-rope walker, tight-rope walking.

a walking dictionary etc [Comp (NP)] sb who has and uses an extensive vocabulary, or who possesses the qualities or functions of sth specified to an unusual degree **V:** ⚠ be, become, turn into. **n:** dictionary, adding-machine; miracle, disaster; rag-bag □ *He's* ***a walking dictionary****. And by the way he's a great reader of your books.* RM □ *The lady, even her best friends say, is* ***a walking calculator****.* TVT □ *Pooh, for his size, ate more than any other animal I have every come across.* ***This walking stomach*** *had a daily ration of...* DF □ *Even when the actuality was more than good enough to get by on, Ford was compelled to improve the truth: he was* ***a walking credibility gap****.* L □ also pl.

walls have ears [V + O] (saying) sb may be listening surreptitiously □ *'Shall I come to your hotel?' 'Better if we meet in the Park.* ***Walls have ears****.'* □ *You don't know what it is to live in a police state where* ***walls have ears*** *and your own children may be encouraged to inform against you.*

a Walter Mitty a type of day-dreamer who (habitually) imagines himself the hero in dangerous, important or romantic situations (from the title-character in THE SECRET LIFE OF WALTER MITTY (J THURBER 1894-1961)) □ *He's* ***a*** *real* ***Walter Mitty****. With a broken marriage and stuck in a job he hates, I suppose he needs to escape from reality sometimes.* □ *There is a* ***Walter Mitty*** *side to many people, a conviction that, given the opportunity and the self-confidence, they could move unscalable mountains, or a least scale them.* SC □ *He enjoys writing fiction. 'It's a means of escape. You crawl back into a happy womb where you can be anything and do anything. It's the old* ***Walter Mitty*** *thing.'* OBS □ *But it wasn't just a case of a man convicting himself of megalomania out of his own mouth . There was also the ease of the professor's own passage straight into* ***Walter-Mitty****-land.* NS □ often attrib use ***a Walter-Mitty*** *character, existence etc.*

wall-to-wall carpeting etc a covering which extends over the whole floor area; (fig) things or persons that/who are present everywhere, or in large numbers **n:** carpeting; luxury, clutter; women, policemen □ *You can treat yourself to a weekend of* ***wall-to-wall luxury*** *at the London Hilton* (Hotel)*, of course, for a mere £200-£300.* OBS □ *Mae West was still working on her film 'Sextette' late at night when 50 basketball players stopped to watch her. She stopped to watch them, drawling 'Nothing I love more than* ***wall to wall men****, but it's been a long day and I'm a little tired. One of you will have to leave.'* TVT □ *Grenada's* ***wall-to-wall greenery*** *extends right down the steep hillsides to some of the best beaches in the Caribbean.* OBS

a wandering Jew an itinerant, restless, or unsettled person (from the legendary wandering Jew who spurned Christ and was condemned to wander the earth until Christ's second coming) □ CISSIE: *Ronnie met her when he came to work in Norwich.* ESTHER: ***Another wandering Jew****. Another one who can't settle himself. Hopping about all over the country from one job to another.* ITAJ

the war to end war(s) an optimistic slogan

of the First World War 1914-18 when it was believed, or hoped, that such a major war would never occur again □ *'Joined up when I was seventeen,' he said. 'January, nineteen-fifteen. Served four years.' '**The War to End Wars**.'* TT □ *I had known all the wishful cant* (= insincere talk) *about Tommy Atkins* (= the British soldier)*, and the Russian steam roller, and **the war to end war**, and making the world safe for democracy.* AH

a war/battle of nerves a struggle for power, or control, between people, groups or nations which is conducted by means of threats, tactical manoeuvres, psychological pressures, etc □ *The Russian **war of nerves**, or battle of wits, was looked on not as a bluff but as an indication that hostilities would break out at any moment.* MFM □ *The railway carriages containing terrorists and hostages were two hundred yards away, across an open field. Both sides prepared for **a** long drawn-out **battle of nerves**.*

war to the knife [Comp (NP)] bitter and implacably continued fighting, quarrelling, rivalry **V:** ⚠ be; become, turn into □ *Victor's lot tumbled to it that they'd been set up* (by the rival gang) *for the police and after that it was **war to the knife**.* OBS

warm the cockles (of sb's heart) [V + O pass] make sb feel pleased and cheerful □ *For the rest of the day the port presented a scenario of furious productivity, guaranteed to **warm the cockles of** any dock boss**'s heart**.* ST □ *To know one's way around the intellectual history of the 19th century is to be familiar with instances of generosity and friendship that would **warm the cockles of** historians' **hearts**.* NS □ *This tea is very comforting, Briggs. It **warms the cockles**.* EM □ *'You must meet my daughter,' Wormold said, the whisky **warming his cockles**.* OMIH ⇨ raise sb's hackles.

the warp and woof of sth [n + n non-rev] the (two) elements that form the nature and pattern of sth (from weaving) **o:** experience, life; democratic government, Western music □ *Thus **the warp and woof of** my days at San Jose consisted in trying to learn more about the mysterious, fascinating process of teaching.* OBS □ *You cannot teach a child what he cannot learn so that, in a sense, any child is a product of a kind of self-education — imitation and experiment being **the warp and woof of** it.*

warts and all with no defects omitted from a description or judgement □ (referring to source) *Cromwell's instructions to his painter, Sir Peter Lely were, 'to paint my picture truly like me and not flatter me but remark all these ruffness, pimples, **warts and everything** as you see me; otherwise I never will pay a farthing for it.'* RT □ *His portrait is presented in lively style, **warts and all**, by his friend.* NS

waste not, want not (saying) if you never waste anything, eg food, money, resources, you are not likely to lack what you need □ *The jays were inveterate hoarders. Their motto was obviously '**waste not, want not**'.* DF □ (a goldsmith's workshop) *For the same reasons of economy, all washing water is specially filtered, and all the sweepings are burnt and sifted. **Waste not, want not**.* RT

waste (one's/sb's) time [V + O pass] (cause sb to) do nothing, or sth useless, unwanted, unimportant etc, when some necessary or worthwhile action is needed **A:** looking for it; on formalities; in school □ *It's you who are a fool standing there **wasting time** talking when we should be arranging to get away.* DC □ *Equally, Parliament and the Police are **wasting their time** if penalties are so small that it pays people to go on offending.* L □ *There are always a few people who come in and **waste** the agent**'s time** with a hundred and one questions about property.* □ *Bruno has a job waiting for him in an uncle's electro-welding business and sees another year of schooling as **a waste of time**.* □ *The chassis's rotten with rust, sir. It would be **a waste of my time** and your money to try to repair it.* □ variant a waste of (one's/sb's) time; n compound time-wasting. ⇨ lose/waste no time (in) doing sth.

watch the clock [V + O] be careful not to work any longer than the hours stipulated; (habitually) calculate, or check, how soon one will be entitled to take a break, or finish for the day □ *I wouldn't have him on the premises. Chatting up the typists and **watching the clock** is all he's good for.* □ (advertisement) *Believing deeply in what they're doing, almost everybody works the hours that are necessary to produce the results. There is no time or room for **clock-watchers**.* ST □ used esp of an employee; n compounds a clock-watcher, clock-watching.

watch every penny etc [V + O] consider carefully before committing oneself to any item of expenditure, procedure, speech, diet etc **O:** penny (one spends), word (one utters), move (one makes), bite (one eats) □ *Also, he **watches every penny** he spends, which gives him a reputation for meanness.* OBS □ *She is so ready to take offence and to imagine insults or criticism that you've got to **watch every word** you utter.* □ often follows *have to, must, need to.*

watch it (informal) (warning to sb to) be careful about, not go too far or any further with, a course of action, topic, way of behaving, type of comment □ *But recent information indicates that Ponia is working his cops round the clock to spell out a simple lesson. I am in control here, he is saying: so **watch it**.* NS □ *'Look at Clyde. He's so dozy.' '**Watch it**,' said Clyde.* ST □ *Don't take any wooden pesetas or whatever the bloody things are, and **watch it** with the local talent. So long, Taff.* ILIH

watch/mind one's language/tongue [V + O] (informal) not be, or stop being, impudent, indiscreet, blasphemous etc □ ***Watch your tongue**, my lad, and wipe that grin off your face unless you want me to do it for you.* □ *It would pay him to **watch his language** and pull his socks up* (= improve himself). L

watch (sb/sth) like a hawk [V + O + A pass] keep sb/sth under close and constant observation; be purposefully alert for/to do sth □ *You know how unreasonable girls are and she'll be **watching** her sister and me all the time **like a hawk**.* RM □ *'It's true that Ralph is wary about the audience,' Sir John says. 'He **watches** it **like a hawk**.'* OBS □ *Here, Moses. That dog of mine needs **watching like a hawk**. Surprisin'* (= surprising) *he's not been run over long ago.* L □ *He must have been **watching like a hawk** for just such a moment of confusion that would give* *him his chance.* CON ▫ *The Dashes thrive on a diet of porridge, apples, oranges and bananas, two loaves of bread and jam a day — and Billy* ***watches hawk-like*** *to ensure they don't leave the crusts.* TVT ▫ *I don't like living near a busy road when my daughter's so young. She needs to be* ***watched like a hawk*** *to stop her running out into the traffic—she'll get run over one day.* ▫ variant watch hawk-like.

watch and pray [v + v non-rev] be alert, attentive, careful, while seeking God's help and support ▫ (source) ***Watch and pray****, that ye enter not into temptation.* MATTHEW XXVI 41 ▫ *You must* ***watch****, my dear,* ***and pray****. It is the only way to be a scholar, to* ***watch and pray****.* MM ▫ *In those days when anybody caught pneumonia there was little to be done but* ***watch and pray****.*

watch/mind one's step [V + O] (informal) be very careful how one behaves, speaks etc in order to avoid danger, difficulty, criticism etc ▫ *'I'm the chucker-out,' said Charles, 'so* ***watch your step****.'* HD ▫ ***Watch your step*** *with this fellow. He's been around a bit: he maybe knows just as much as you do.* PE

watch this space [V + O] (catchphrase) keep alert because sth to inform, interest or surprise you will appear here/in this connection (from the caption on reserved advertising space when a (full) notice or advertisement is to follow) ▫ *When Johnny got married he wrote '****Watch This Space****' instead of 'None' in the 'Children' section of his Income Tax Return.* ▫ *This week Berkely Petroleum returned to West Dorset — and to parts of Somerset — to start a series of seismographic tests.* ***Watch this space****.* ST ▫ *Thatcher has said she will abolish the rating system.* ***Watch this space****. She won't. No one will. Not ever.* NS

watch (the rest of) the world go by observe the passing scene, what is going on around one; live a self-sufficient, withdrawn, limited life ▫ *The newspaper lay unopened beside him.* ***Watching the world go by*** *was sufficient entertainment on a fine evening.* ▫ *'Of course,' she laughed, 'the problem of staying here permanently is that one would just sit back and* ***watch the world go by****.'* RT

a watched kettle/pot never boils (saying) waiting attentively for sth to happen, a stage to be reached, makes it seem to take longer ▫ *I wonder if you would like a cup of cold consommé now? It won't spoil your appetite for lunch, but it will remove that feeling of* ***the watched pot*** *which* ***never boils****.* RM ▫ *Don't you know* ***a watched kettle never boils****? Whether they're late or early, looking out of the window won't bring them here any quicker.*

(in/through) the watches of the night (formal) (during) night hours when one is on duty, or simply awake, instead of sleeping ▫ *I'm going to economize. Suddenly* ***in the watches of the night*** *I realized what an expense I was to you.* OMIH ▫ (General Election results on television) *The star performers, Burnet, McKenzie and Butler, were on hand to describe how they would keep themselves and us awake* ***through the watches of the night****.* L ▫ *The story was too unbelievable to be really frightening though I admit it's not the sort of reading with which I'd choose to beguile* ***the night watches****.* ▫ variant (in/through) the night watches.

a watching brief [O (NP)] (legal) a commission to be present at, and to protect a client's interests during, court proceedings; (fig) an agreement or understanding to observe, supervise, report etc on sb's behalf in any situation **V:** hold, have, keep; give sb, entrust sb with ▫ *Lord Pomfret and Mr Wickham were now well away about the iniquity of the proposed draining at Starveacres Hatches with Noel holding* ***a watching brief****.* WDM ▫ *The next few months were spent tidying up loose ends and discussing with De Beers the retention of a skeleton staff to keep* ***a watching brief****.* DS ▫ *Eventually, as the situation cooled somewhat, it became what reporters call* ***a watching brief****: nothing much doing, but always the possibility of trouble.* L ▫ *By June 1955 Attlee had broken with precedent by publicly announcing specific* ***watching briefs*** *for each of his 12 elected shadow colleagues.* NS

(meet) one's Waterloo (be faced with, esp after previous success) a final defeat, a difficulty or obstacle one cannot overcome ▫ (source—from the defeat of Napolean at Waterloo 1815) *Every man* ***meets his Waterloo*** *at last.* SPEECHES (W PHILLIPS 1811-84) ▫ (home repairs) *It all went reasonably well until, becoming confident, I tried my new toy on a cupboard door. That cupboard door was* ***my Waterloo****.* SC

wave the flag [V + O] show and/or stir up patriotic, group, or ideological feeling, (the implication often being that those concerned have not examined their beliefs, feelings etc carefully) ▫ *He obviously pictures the National* (Theatre) *as another prestige, an expensive way of* ***waving the flag****.* L ▫ *These memoranda suggested that the President said: 'Well, I've got to give this speech at Philadelphia on the 4th, and I don't want to talk just about patriotic,* ***flag-waving*** *things.'* L ▫ *Nevertheless, it is probably true that any Scots man or woman, however far removed from the ranks of* ***the flag-wavers****, is aware of an identity in no way equivalent to that of the provincial English.* SC ▫ n compounds a flag-waver, flag-waving. ⇨ ⚠ show/fly the flag.

wave a (magic) wand (and do sth) [V + O pass] (try to) find a means of doing, easily and quickly, sth that is difficult or impossible ▫ *I can meet you at the entrance and you can* ***wave your magic wand and*** *get me a pass in.* HD ▫ *An international manager's job is thankless. He has no vital club roots nor regular playing staff, but is still expected to* ***wave a wand and*** *produce the goods three or four times a year.* TVT ▫ *You've got to overcome this yourself. If I could* ***wave a wand and*** *make you better again, I would.* ▫ *'National security' is* ***a magic wand*** *which tends to anaesthetise opposition—and those entrusted with* ***waving*** *it have a power more menacing than can be found in any statute.* NS

wax and wane [v + v non-rev] increase and then decrease ▫ *His Kingdom stretch from shore to shore,/Till moons shall* ***wax and wane*** *no more.* ENGLISH HYMNAL 420 ▫ *The weakness of the Dyak theory is the problem it leaves regarding the nature of the force of things. What is it like? Can it begin working of its own accord? Can it* ***wax and wane****?* NDN ▫ *'Auriculas and Primroses' is a highly informative book devoted to these fascinating flowers which have* ***waxed and***

***waned** in popularity, through the centuries.* ST

the way one's mind works how one tends to think, learn, reason etc; how one is thinking at a particular time □ *According to **the way their minds work**, some will patiently piece evidence together till it points to a conclusion, others will postulate a conclusion and see if the evidence fits it.* □ *It* (a speech) *has been published already but I make no apology for including it here since it shows **the way my mind** was **working** in March 1944.* MFM

a way of life the normal pattern of social, or working, life of an individual or group □ *Dr Bottwink, you are a foreigner. Naturally, you are not altogether familiar with our customs, our habits, **our way of life**.* EM □ *There is evidence that unemployment is becoming a deeply planted cultural phenomenon, not to say **a way of life**.* NS □ *Banking was **a way of life**, a service with its own peculiar satisfactions and excitements.* TO □ occas pl *other **ways of life**.*

the way of the world what many people do (whether we approve or not) and what we are all accustomed to seeing done □ *Neither of them understood or sympathized with my passivity* (about being asked to resign). *To me it seemed **the way of the world**.* SPL □ *'**The way of the world**, rather than a particular time, that's what we are satirising,' he says.* OBS

a way out (of sth) [Comp/O (NP)] a way of avoiding, or solving, a problem, difficulty etc **V:** (it/there) be; see, look for, find, take. **det:** a, no, some, another, no other. **adj:** the only, the best, the easiest □ *...a man who knows he's caught in a trap but is still convinced that somewhere, somehow there is **a way out**.* NS □ *I think we are now at one of the turning-points in the human spirit, and it enables us to begin to see **a way out of** the problem of prejudice.* L □ *You're a spirited chap: you'll come through. If I lend y'* (= you) *money, that will be **the** easy **way out**.* US □ (reader's letter) *Please help me. I can't think straight any more. I'm worried I may lose Joan's friendship if I tell. What is **the** best **way out**?* H □ *The one thing we cannot afford is to take **the** usual **way out**—and cut back investment.* OBS

the way to a man's heart is through his stomach/belly (saying) men enjoy good food, expect to be fed well and a woman, esp, can please them, or gain their affection, by providing this □ *I was holding her hand. 'Men are carnal,' I said, as a more highbrow way of expressing that **the way to a man's heart is through his belly**.* SML □ *The theme of '**the way to a man's heart is through his stomach**' was important in the script, and the cast had to eat enormous meals and drink wine endlessly.* TVT

ways and means [n + n non-rev] methods and/or resources (whereby one can do or obtain sth) **A:** of making a living; getting round the regulations; to make a living, to prevent you □ *'There are **ways and means** of making a living, even in this country,' assures a friend.* NS □ *All the feeling she had started out with had perished in the search for **ways and means** to express it.* PW □ *'How did you get the dollars to come through America?' I grinned. 'There are **ways and means**.'* RFW □ often follows *there are*.

we shall see what we shall see (catchphrase) a particular outcome cannot be foretold □ *Now I see what the trouble is. Ah well, as for the civil servants that's not so serious, and as for the liaison, well **we shall see what we shall see**.* TBC □ *'Dick's going to give up smoking.' 'That wouldn't be a bad idea. **We shall see what we shall see**, however.'* □ often said sceptically about a promise to do sth, or about a statement that sth will happen.

we was/wuz robbed (catchphrase) complaint, esp in sports, that one, or one's team, should have won, but had extraordinary bad luck, or suffered from an umpire's/referee's wrong decision □ *'**We wuz robbed**' is, of course, a famous boxing expression, but the Australians' attitude over the pitch at Headingley has none of the colourful charm of that phrase and seems to be much deeper seated.* NS □ wuz = was.

we're only here for the beer (catchphrase) we don't pretend to be present in order to help, show goodwill, etc but just to get the drink, or other hospitality, offered (from an advertisement for 'Double Diamond' beer) □ *One of the virtues of these old advertisements, quite apart from their wit, was the emphasis on 'brand image'. There is a contrast here with another slogan, part of our folklore—'**We're only here for the beer**.'* NS □ *Already proficient on piano and whistle, he has just added a year's singing training and can be heard around the Manchester pubs with a folk group. 'But **we're only here for the beer**.'* TVT □ *He worked for a while as a stand-up comic in the Northern Clubs. 'That certainly toughened me up. You never know how you're going to go, because basically **they're only there for the beer**.'* RT □ occas with other prons and with there (for here) which breaks the rhyming jingle.

weak at the knees [Comp (AdjP)] (informal) temporarily weak, trembling, perhaps hardly able to stand, from illness, emotion etc **V:** ⚠ be, feel, go □ *'How do you feel?' 'Fine, really. A bit **weak at the knees** but that will soon pass.'* □ *Rudolph Valentino, the Adonis of the silent films, had one great quality—to make women feel **weak at the knees**.* TVT

a weaker vessel a person less able to withstand physical or mental strain, temptation or exploitation, than others □ (source) *Likewise, ye husbands, dwell with them according to knowledge, giving honour unto the wife, as unto **the weaker vessel**, and as being heirs together of the grace of life.* I PETER III 7 □ *There was a danger that the administrative echelons and units might accept the position of being **the weaker vessels** and decide that fighting was not their business.* MFM □ *I'm asking you, as a kindness to **a weaker vessel** than yourself, to make the arrangements.* US

wear one's learning etc lightly [V + O + A pass] not be self-important about, nor try to impress others with, how much one knows **n:** learning, ⚠ wisdom, culture, brightness □ *His considerable erudition keeps cropping up, and this can be disconcerting. He was never one to **wear his learning lightly**.* RT □ *The show is stamped with his **lightly-worn brightness** and real love of reading.* RT □ *The 'Observer's' Sue McHarg jaunted through Tuscany recently **wearing her culture lightly**.* NS □ variant one's lightly-worn learning etc.

wear one's/a legal etc hat [V + O] fill, play, a different role; speak, or act, as a lawyer etc in contrast with other interests or opinions one may have **adj:** legal, official, administrative; doctor's, manager's, referee's; (a) different ▫ *This is not a novel or a new book of stories. Donleavy is* ***wearing a*** *very* ***different hat*** *this time out.* G ▫ *Kidnapping, flight from creditors, a publicity stunt—these theories are widely canvassed—the latter dangerously embarrassing for Larkin,* ***wearing his publicist's hat.*** SC ▫ *Mr Brian Baird, a public relations consultant, is masterminding the proceedings. He, as they say in the PR* (= Public Relations) *business, is* ***wearing a lot of hats.*** ST ▫ *'You are Purdeys, Mr Lawrence?' 'Purdeys,' said Mr Lawrence who, until 1970, had been the firm's Managing Director, 'is one of* ***the hats I wear.'*** TVT

wear and tear [n + n non-rev] deterioration and damage from (continued) use **adj:** fair, normal, general ▫ (advertisement) *The luxurious interior sprung mattress is guaranteed by the manufacturers for 5 years against fair* ***wear and tear.*** OBS ▫ (characters in a Shakespeare play) *Claudio and Hero are less likely to survive what high court judges call the* ***wear and tear*** *of married life than the sparkier Benedick and Beatrice.* G ▫ *Most conditions of the elderly dog or cat are the result of general* ***wear and tear*** *throughout their lives.* SC

wear thin [V + Comp] (begin to) become exhausted, less effective, less interesting or less amusing **S:** idealism, patience; mask, pretence; friendship; style, joke. **adv mod:** a little, a bit, rather, very ▫ *It is the same enthusiasm that made him the youngest Methodist minister in the whole of New York State at 19, and the youngest ex-Methodist minister at 22. That was when the idealism* ***wore*** *a little* ***thin.*** SC ▫ *It was even more imperative to present a smiling face to him. But the mask, she was afraid, was going to* ***wear thin.*** DC ▫ *Indeed the friendship, though never abandoned, did ultimately* ***wear thin.*** SC ▫ *Did the joke, even the music, begin to* ***wear*** *a little* ***thin*** *in Act 2?* ST

wear the trousers/breeches [V + O] be the dominant partner in a marriage ▫ *It would be quite false to call Tom a hen-pecked* (= dominated by his wife) *husband; nevertheless one does gather the impression that she* ***wears the trousers.*** ▫ *I choose his clothes for him. Not that he doesn't* ***wear the trousers*** *in our house. He does what he wants.* TVT ▫ pron S usu stressed.

the weather breaks/holds good weather changes for the worse/weather, of any kind, continues unchanged ▫ *Next day* ***the weather broke.*** *Tantrums of rain burst across the Grand' Place.* US ▫ *After going through the family news Lydia told Eleanor about the plans for the water-party, provided* ***the weather held.*** WDM ▫ *Youngsters enjoy this snowy* ***weather.*** *Ours are praying for it to* ***hold*** *till the weekend so that they can go sledging.*

weather/ride the storm [V + O] (nautical) endure and survive a storm; (fig) surmount opposition, criticism, difficult circumstances, without being seriously affected; ride out (Vol 1) (qv) ▫ *Rural outlets* (shops etc) *though generally small, tend to enjoy higher profitability and will be better able to* ***weather the storm.*** G ▫ *La Scala has had long practice in* ***weathering whatever storm*** *is passing.* RT ▫ (chess) *We'll certainly have to look at that nineteenth game with Spassky's bold sacrifice of two pieces and Fischer calmly* ***weathering the storm.*** NS ▫ *The scale and selectivity of the work recall Winston Churchill's war memoirs, and so does the title of the volume, '****Riding the Storm****'.* L

weave a/one's spell [V + O pass] have a magical effect; charm, interest or influence sb or sth in its own special way ▫ *It's too much expense and effort at my age. If I could* ***weave a spell*** *and have myself carried there, I'd go.* ▫ *We all have to go through it—fresh air, hard training and clean living begin to* ***weave their spell.*** OBS

weigh anchor [V + O] (nautical) raise the anchor(s); prepare to leave the docking berth, or moorings ▫ *He looked over to the L.C.T.* (= landing craft)*; she was* ***weighing anchor*** *to get away before the falling tide left her stranded.* RFW

weigh the consequences (of sth) [V + O pass] consider carefully what will, or may be, the result(s) of doing sth, or of sth happening **o:** disobedience, failure; strike-action; claim, decision; declaring war, resigning from office ▫ *It was precisely because we had* ***weighed*** *and compared* ***the consequences of*** *Mr Wilson remaining Leader of the Labour Party with the consequences of his deciding to go that we published our leading article at all.* NS ▫ *A footballer's mind has to work fast, as well as his feet. He can't stop, like a chess-player, to* ***weigh the consequences of*** *every move.*

weigh the evidence [V + O pass] (try to) assess how much evidence there is, and what value it has; compare evidence for and against sth in order to decide which is the more convincing ▫ *Some believe that a person's political opinions are consciously arrived at after a thorough* ***weighing of the evidence*** *and are modifiable.* SNP ▫ *Lawyers are used to* ***weighing the evidence*** *of witnesses and getting through a lot of it.* L ▫ cf *the weight of evidence* = 'the extent of the evidence', as in *Given* ***the weight of evidence*** *on his side, in any rational, informed debate Wheldon would probably have little to fear.* NS

weigh a ton (informal) be very, or comparatively, heavy, esp to hold or to carry ▫ *That damn suitcase* ***weighs a ton*** *before you start putting anything in it.* ▫ *There was also an eighteenth-century Indian elephant, made of wood though* ***weighing a ton.*** OBS

weigh one's words [V + O pass] speak, or write, with deliberate care in choosing one's words, either for stylistic reasons or to make one's meaning perfectly clear, avoid giving offence, etc ▫ *He was as deliberate in his speech as he was in his work,* ***weighing his words*** *momentously.* AITC ▫ *And a multitude of similar horrors 'helter-skelter development' (a proliferation of fairgrounds?) suggest that Grosvenor and Macmillan are hardly men who* ***weigh each word.*** NS

weight of numbers the combined weight, strength, influence etc of a group which outnumbers another ▫ *In modern warfare, mobility* *and sophisticated weapons are more important than* ***weight of numbers.*** □ (a football match) *Manchester began to dominate, if only by sheer* ***weight of numbers.*** G □ often in prep phrase *by sheer* ***weight of numbers.***

a welfare state a state, country (esp UK from 1946), that makes itself responsible for the welfare of its citizens by providing social and health services, subsistence payments, etc □ *Political minds seemed to be concentrated on the creation of* ***a welfare state.*** MFM □ *What kind of* ***welfare state*** *is it in which a health service simply cannot meet the demands made on it?* □ *Not only in* ***a*** *pre-****Welfare State*** *were they* (children) *an insurance against old age, but a large family in one's prime meant an increase of dignity, influence and wealth.* G

well aware of sth/that [Comp (AdjP)] fully informed, conscious, of sth/that **V:** ⚠ be, appear; make sb. **o:** ***(of)*** that, the fact; my faults, your loyalty. **cl:** ***(that)*** it will be a difficult job, he dislikes me, money doesn't grow on trees □ *Disraeli was* ***well aware of*** *the scepticism which he continually provoked.* NS □ *What this means is that the planners are* ***well aware that*** *in the past more schemes have failed to reach their target profits.* ST □ *He was addressing a committee already* ***well aware of*** *the difficulties.*

well done(!) comment, or exclamation, of approval and congratulation □ *At the final whistle he marches to the dressing room. '****Well done****, lads,' he tells them as they come in.* OBS □ *The boy pianist himself arrived, smiling calmly, to join them in the wings. '****Well done****, mate,' Lew Lewis said, patting him on the back.* ST

well and good that is all right; that is good, or satisfactory □ *If there was no beast—and almost certainly there was no beast — in that case,* ***well and good.*** LF □ *If the labelled diamonds turn up in the day's production at the sort-house,* ***well and good.*** *But if someone picks one up and tries to smuggle it through the turnstiles, a sort of Geiger counter sets off an alarm bell.* DS □ *Some would argue that it is industry which should be fostered, and that if, for various reasons, the traditional tourist business is weakened,* ***well and good.*** SC □ non-rev; usu end position in *if*-cl.

well heeled [Comp (AdjP)] (informal) prosperous in appearance and in fact; having plenty of money **V:** ⚠ be, appear, look □ *The women in particular; they were mainly the sort who are too* ***well-heeled*** *and too idle to take up any sort of work on reaching adult years.* CON □ *Both* (communities) *are reasonably* ***well heeled*** *and comfortably off, and both enjoy a high amenity coefficient.* SC □ *The discriminating and* ***well-heeled*** *tourist can be entertained to lunch and dinner and be the house-guest of some of the most famous princely names of Italy.* L □ sometimes hyphenated; stress pattern well 'heeled; attrib use *a* ***well-heeled*** *tourist.* ⇨ be down at heel (Vol 1).

well I never (did)(!) (informal) exclamation of pleased or displeased surprise □ ***Well, I never did.*** *French or not, you certainly don't look like a schoolmistress.* TGLY □ ***'Well I never!'*** *she exclaimed in the midst of reading her cousin's letter. 'How stories get garbled as they're passed around! You'll be surprised to hear what you've been doing.'*

well met a comment that it is a fortunate, or convenient, occasion of meeting □ *'Fine day for a shoot,' Patrick said. Julian then said to them all: 'Well, this is* ***well met****, what?'* TGLY □ *'General,' he called. 'What can I do for you?' 'Hail,' the Brigadier said. '****Well met****, Larkin.'* DBM

well and truly [adv + adv non-rev] completely; thoroughly □ *Then he manages to get dug in,* ***well and truly*** *dug in, in a publishing business.* PP □ *We made our exodus, determined not to get lost again. Within the hour we were* ***well and truly*** *lost.* OBS □ *A number of relatives might suspect that people like you in your anxiety to get a kidney might wish to take the kidney out before their dear relative is* ***well and truly*** *dead.* L □ modifies adj or pp.

wet the baby's head [V + O pass] have a drink, give or take part in a drinking party, in order to celebrate a birth □ *The night Mark was born, in March 1955, Bonar was out with Bernard Braden and a few of the boys '****wetting the baby's head****,' he said.* TVT □ *The tragedy happened after the crew of the Scottish registered boat visited a quayside pub to '****wet the baby's head.****'* SC

wet/not dry behind the ears [Comp (AdjP)] (informal) immature; inexperienced; naive (from the state of young animals after birth) **V:** ⚠ be, seem, remain. **adv mod:** still; a little, a bit, somewhat □ (reader's letter) *Any bloke that let himself be lumbered with all the different tasks that Mrs Kantypowicz mentions must be a little* ***wet behind the ears.*** RT □ *There seemed to be something wrong about tough old NCOs* (= Non-Commissioned Officers) *having to jump to attention for some rosy-faced kid of an officer* ***not*** *yet* ***dry behind the ears.***

a wet blanket [Comp (NP)] (informal) sb/sth that discourages, reduces pleasure or enthusiasm **V:** ⚠ be, appear, feel □ *I don't drink, smoke or dance and I haven't much light conversation either. I'd just be* ***a wet blanket*** *at your party.* □ *He allows us neither to lose all sympathy for William nor to feel none for* ***the*** *die-hard German* ***wet-blanket*** *he eventually married.* NS □ *The weather cast* ***a wet blanket*** *over Ascot: the Earl Marshal's strictures against the wearing of hot pants in the Royal Enclosure became an academic question.* □ also pl; sometimes hyphenated.

a wet nurse a woman employed, esp formerly, to breast-feed an infant; (fig) someone who gives another person support, encouragement (the implication being that the person receiving the support etc is behaving childishly) □ *'He just needs to be given confidence in himself.' 'Well, somebody else can try. I don't see myself in the role of* ***wet nurse*** *to his deprived little ego.'* □ *He has no strength of character. He's always needing to be* ***wet-nursed.*** □ stress pattern a 'wet nurse; variant (v, used only in fig sense) wet-nurse.

wet or fine [adj + adj non-rev] whatever the weather; come rain, come shine (qv); (in) fair (weather) and/or foul (qv); in any case/event (qv) □ *A warm, sunny day will be nice, but Britain will enjoy the Royal wedding whether the weather's wet or fine for Prince Charles and*

Lady Diana. □ *So I took my umbrella, which I always do,* ***wet or fine****.* RM □ can function adverbially, as in second example.

wet one's whistle [V + O] (dated informal) have an (alcoholic) drink □ *Are you coming out to* ***wet your whistle****, Dad, or do you want to watch the rest of that programme?* □ *John thought of turning down the whisky but the chairman said that, if it was his speech he was worrying about, he'd be all the better for* ***wetting his whistle*** *first.* □ also pl wet their whistles.

what are we waiting for? let us go ahead and do sth just previously indicated □ *'Why not come over to our place instead? We have cold salmon in the fridge and a roast in the oven, and wine to go with both.' '****What are we waiting for?****' said John, rising at once.* □ *'Have you anything really shocking, Reggie? I adore mucky books.' 'I like my pornography in real life,' I said. 'Well,* ***what are we waiting for?****'* RATT □ enthusiastic response to a suggestion etc; often facetious or ironic.

what the butler saw (catchphrase) sth (mildly) improper, or embarrassing because usu not done or seen except in private (from, formerly, penny-in-the-slot peepshows) □ ***What the butler saw*** *when the phone rang in the Rothschild residence in Mayfair in the late 1890s was this superb switchboard, its fittings in gleaming ivory.* OBS □ *Then they set up the round contrivance. It had two eye-holes in it, and as she looked at it Victoria cried: 'It's like things on piers.* ***What the butler saw****.'* TCB

what could be more natural etc (than sth)? nothing could be more natural etc (than sth) **adj:** ***(more)*** natural, suitable, appropriate, beautiful, inviting; nicer, worse □ ***What could be more natural than*** *that everyone should be brought here who might have learned anything from me****?*** TBC □ *It's not good for father to be living alone, and since he's marrying a woman we all like and respect* ***what could be more suitable?*** □ *Now* ***what could be nicer than*** *this simple meal you've just served us****?*** □ refers to sb/sth in a previous clause, or in a following *than* -cl.

what d'you call him (informal) sb/sth whose name one cannot recall, perhaps for the moment **O:** him, her, it □ *'Haven't you got a* ***what d'you call it****?' 'A darning needle? Would I be doing it this way if I had?'* □ *Then I ran into old* ***what d'you call him****. You know, the fellow who keeps the corner shop.* □ usu said to sb who is expected to know who/what one means; n compound a what d'you call it.

what do you know(!) (informal) exclamation introducing, or commenting on, an interesting, or surprising, item of information □ *'And* ***what do you know****, my dear,' continued Mrs Clipp excitedly, 'you know that interesting looking man? I've found out who he is.'* TCB □ *'Bill tells me that he's getting married to Jane next month.' 'Well,* ***what do you know!*** *They've kept it very dark, the pair of them.'*

what do you mean, lazy etc?/! (informal) I don't understand; I question, or contradict, your statement **S:** you, they; the man, his teacher. **adj:** lazy, stupid, crooked, devious □ *'Get up, you lazy thing.' '****What do you mean, lazy?*** *I've done a lot more work today than she has.'* □ *'The petrol tank's nearly empty.' '****What do you mean, nearly empty!*** *I filled up on my way home.'* □ MICK: *Well, you say you're an interior decorator, you'd better be a good one.* DAVIES: *A what?* MICK: ***What do you mean, a what?*** *A decorator. An interior decorator.* TC □ indignant or angry challenge or denial; expression repeats adj used by previous speaker.

what do you think you're doing? (informal) why are you doing this? why are you etc acting, or behaving, in this way? **S:** you, he; the idiots, your mother. **A:** throwing stones at the hens, bursting in here; down there on your hands and knees □ *He picked up a handful of gravel and drew back his arm to throw. 'Stop it, Patrick,' Jenny called. '****What do you think you're doing?*** *For shame, leave them alone.'* TGLY □ ***What*** *the blue blazes* (dated exclamation indicating surprise and, usu, disapproval) ***do you think you're doing*** *slouching across the parade ground like a bag of rags?'* TVT □ usu indicates disapproval, criticism, scorn etc.

what does one/sb (go and/have to) do but do sth (informal) expression of irritation, self-disgust etc when sb unexpectedly, inconveniently, or foolishly does sth **S:** I, you; the silly fellow, the Board of Management. **cl:** fall on my face, forget to lock up, turn down the offer □ *Stepping forward to receive my award* ***what do I do but*** *fall flat on my face.* □ *We had just notified all the parents about the arrangements when* ***what does*** *the Bus Company* ***go and do but*** *change the timetable.* □ *I have more teapots than I'll ever use so* ***what does*** *she* ***have to do but*** *waste money buying me a new one.* □ previous clause or sentence gives circumstances in which foolish action is performed.

what the eye doesn't see (the heart doesn't crave for/grieve over) (saying) you can't, or shouldn't, be troubled about sth you don't know exists □ *'It's a shame not to keep some of these strawberries for the children.' 'Then there wouldn't be enough for everybody —and* ***what the eye doesn't see, the heart won't crave for****.'* □ *When I was very young and first married I was very idealistic. But one changes as one gets older. Fidelity is not all that important.* ***What the eye doesn't see***— ST □ *But it's better they shouldn't know that I was deliberately responsible for their being sent here.* ***What the eye doesn't see, the heart doesn't grieve over****.* TBC

what has sb got that I/we haven't (got)? (informal) why is sb (so much) more popular, successful etc than me? □ *I long to be seductive and tempting.* ***What's*** *Alice* ***got that I haven't got?*** RATT □ *Here they were, regular customers, and she had turned them all down in favour of this comparative stranger. '****What has*** *he* ***got that we haven't got?****' demanded, plaintively, the drunkest of the three.* PW □ plaintive or ironic comment.

(and/or) what have you (informal) (and/or) other person(s), thing(s), or event(s) of a similar kind; and so on; et cetera □ *If you add on rates, insurance, heating* ***and what have you****, that man is paying something approaching half his income just to have a roof over his head.* ST □ *And membership of these castes is advertised by clothes, by house fronts, by cars, by the plethora of modern* *urban dialects—camp, hippy, deb, media-freak, or **what-have-you**.* L □ sometimes hyphenated.

what the hell (informal) an exclamation expressing a defiant 'don't-care' attitude about one's action or about a situation □ *During his time with the Army of Occupation, certain illegal transactions in marks (but **what the hell**, everybody does it) had enabled George to pay off the mortgage on it, and so now the house was his own.* PE □ *'Are you coming on with us, Bill?' 'I shouldn't, but **what the hell**. I'm going to get into trouble when I get home, anyway.'* □ *Then Johnny came up. '**What the hell**, Margot,' he said, and they resumed their quarrel.* H

what the hell etc? (informal) what, which thing? **n:** (flaming/merry) hell, ⚠ devil, blazes, heck, dickens □ *'**What the hell** has it got to do with you where I work?' he would have liked to say.* HD □ *Well, **what the** merry **Ellen** (= merry hell) does he think we're sitting here waiting for?* BFA □ usu expressing speaker's bad temper, hostility, scorn etc. ⇨ ⚠ how the hell etc? where the hell etc? who the hell etc? why the hell etc?

what a hope(!) (informal) an exclamation, emphasizing the improbability of sth just mentioned either happening or being done □ *A French brigade would fall back, leaving the Lothians to hold the line until midnight. We would then withdraw and embark at St Valéry. **What a hope**, thought I.* ST □ *Perhaps she thinks looking at outdoor clothes will bring her nearer to wearing them. **What a hope**, poor thing.* DC ⇨ ⚠ not have a hope (in hell) (of sth).

what if?[1] what will happen, what will we do, if? □ *You make it all sound very easy, but **what if** the idea doesn't come off?* □ *'If I'm not back by the time you arrive, get a key from the people next door.' 'And **what if** they're not in?'* □ *We can't sit here in the first-class. **What if** the ticket collector comes along?* □ if introduces possibility to be considered.

what if?[2] what does it matter, why should we care, if? **cl:** he does, it is, they have □ *'Take your mac. It looks as if it's going to rain.' '**What if** it does? I'm not made of paper.'* □ *'It has a telescopic tube.' '**What if** it has?' 'It might telescope at the wrong moment.'* OMIH □ *'All his life he's been used to giving orders.' '**What if** he has? He'll have to get unused, now that he's retired.'* □ dismisses possibility that has already been mentioned as being of no importance.

what is all this etc in aid of(?) (informal) what is the reason for, or the explanation of, all this etc? **S:** all this, that outburst, these questions □ *'I suspect you're wondering **what all this is in aid of**,' he said. I said yes.* NM □ *'And **what**, may I ask, **is this** song of hate **in aid of**?' 'Fergus, we're going to have a baby.'* DC □ as a question, may express surprise and indignation.

what is one doing, doing sth? (informal) why is one doing this job etc? **S:** you, he; the Council; the old fellow, a nice girl like you; your mucky boots, a photograph of her. **cl:** doing this job, climbing up there, (sitting) here, working in a dump like this, lying on the table, among his papers □ *I meant, of course, **what are you doing doing** this job?* HD □ *'And who the devil may you be?' he asked truculently. '**What are you doing, hanging about** here?'* EM □ *I could be in St Tropez, **what was I doing going** on a week's thrash round mountains?* OBS □ *Complacent manufacturers were apt to chuck Marion Giordan under the chin during factory tours and ask **what was** a nice girl like her **doing** in a place like this?* RT □ □ implies surprise, puzzlement, disapproval, suspicion etc.

what is done cannot be undone (saying) what has already been done cannot be changed □ *But we can't change him, so we must make the best of it. **What's done can't be undone**, no use crying over spilt milk.* AITC □ *I can't forgive so many bad novelists for having written about* (Leonardo da Vinci). *But there you are, **what's done cannot be undone**.* ASA □ often said to console sb who regrets what has happened.

what is eating sb? (informal) why is sb depressed, cross, sulky etc? □ ME: ***What's eating** you?* JENNIFER: *It's That Awful Woman.* ME: *Miss Perkins?* JENNIFER: *Who else?* H □ *'You've no business taking up the whole pavement with your prams,' said a stout woman. '**What's eating** her, I wonder?' said Anne.*

what/that is sb's (little) game(?) (informal) what/that is the scheme, purpose, deception etc sb is trying to effect(?) □ *I don't know **what your game is**, but I assure you we're going to find out.* □ *So **that was your little game**! Get me a temporary transfer and then work yourself into my job.* □ *But this sneaking hotel business is just the way the Campbells would go to work. However, I'll stop **their little game**.* RM □ can be short question; variant spot/spoil/see through/stop sb's (little) game.

what is/was good enough for my father etc is good enough for me/us (saying) if a belief, practice, way of life, method of work, etc satisfied previous generations, other people, etc, that is a good enough reason for retaining it **o:** my father, their mistresses, my doctor; royalty □ *My father was a Liberal, and his father before him, and **what was good enough for my father is good enough for me**.* □ ***What was good enough for our predecessors** can never **be good enough for us**, because we live in different conditions and are different people.* AH

what is the hurry/rush? (informal) why are you hurrying, wanting to do sth immediately; there is no need to hurry, to start now □ *'Let's get it over.' 'Get it over? **What's the hurry?**'* AITC □ *'Have you written that letter yet?' '**What's the rush?**'*

what is it to sb? (informal) it doesn't affect or interest sb **cl:** to come home the other way; that people starve in another country, that I'm worried out of my mind; if I spent twice as much on clothes as I do; whether we're married or not □ ***What's it to** Johnny to carry in a few logs when he's here?* □ *He gets his three meals a day and **what is it to** him if thousands starve elsewhere?* □ *'You're charging a guinea a week, is that right?' '**What's it to** you if I am?'* HD

what etc is the matter/wrong (with sb/sth)(?) what is wrong (with sb/sth)? what is the nature of sb's illness, sb/sth's weakness or failing? **S:** what? whatever? something, (not) anything, nothing. **o:** you; the patient, the invalid; her husband, those young people; the record-player, that car □ ***What's the matter**, Mrs Gaye? Are you feeling sick?* DC □ *'The girl's unusually quiet these days,' said her father. '**Is***

there ***anything the matter****, do you know?'* □ *'Chris!' 'All right, Nat, forget it.' 'There****'s something the matter****.'* PM □ ***What****, for instance,* ***is the matter with*** *Perthshire? Dumbarton county sends twice as many* (students) *as Perth to the universities.* SC □ *'The car's giving trouble.' 'For goodness sake!* ***What's the matter with*** *it now?'*

what etc is the matter/wrong with sb/sth? what can be said against that? how can that be criticized? what objection is there to that? **S:** what? anything, something, nothing. **o:** (going) this afternoon, (seeing him) now, (appointing) Jones □ *'We really must see the Browns while we're here.'* ***'What's the matter with*** *this afternoon, then?'* □ *I only spoke the truth—there****'s nothing wrong with*** *speaking one's mind, is there?*

(and) what is more [Conj] furthermore; as must also be noted; (and) more importantly □ *The difficulties are considerable, for we now have to carry yet another rocket and its fuel.* ***What is more****, we have to make sure that the braking rocket is pointing the right way.* NSC □ *'There's a sight too many folks after a man's money in this town.'* ***'And what's more****, they get it.'* HD □ usu front or middle position.

what is the next step? what should, can one do next? where does one go from here? (qv) □ *'We've arranged for the principal speakers and booked the conference hall.* ***What's the next step?'*** *'We must book hotel rooms—but not until we know how many people will be at the conference.'* □ *If the fight to regain economic stability has created so much unemployment already and that fight has still not been won, it is a little frightening to think* ***what the next step*** *may have to* ***be****.*

what is so special etc about sb/sth? what makes one person/thing any different from another? (the implication being that the speaker expects a negative answer) **adj:** special, wonderful, remarkable, unusual; awful, disgraceful. **o:** him, that; religion, politics; France, Wales □ ***What's so special about*** *motorists?* □ *'You're a wonderful woman: I don't know how you manage.'* ***'What's so wonderful about*** *me?'* □ *'Oh, I couldn't ask him to sleep on the floor.'* ***'What*** *would* ***be so terrible about*** *that?'*

what a life! exclamation of complaint, or exasperation, in not very serious circumstances □ *Now I shall have to write another letter, telling them they've sent the wrong forms. Oh dear,* ***what a life!*** □ *'How many times have you been up and down these stairs with trays, Mary?' 'About the same as you.* ***What a life!****'* □ comments on one's own or another's whole life style usu include adj eg ***What a*** *rotten, tragic, downtrodden, easy, interesting etc* ***life*** *(he has, I lead, etc)!*

what little money etc one has etc the small amount of money etc one has etc **n:** money, time, room; leisure, patience, information; (few) belongings, (few) friends. **cl:** one has, he can spare; they remember; is available, can be got, remain; there is, there are □ *I am not a rich woman but* ***what little money I have*** *will be yours when I die.* □ ***What little space there was*** *below the sloping ceiling was as closely covered with pictures as an Italian votive chapel.* AITC □ *Dicky Torver spends* ***what little time he has*** *left over from the mill-girls in drinking himself to death.* RATT □ *My parents eat little at their age, but* ***what little they do eat*** *they like to be good.* RFW □ few used with pl nouns.

what/that makes sb/sth tick (informal) that which motivates sb/sth and makes him/it live, behave, react as he/it does □ *You're a mysterious little person. I don't know* ***what makes*** *you* ***tick*** *at all.* TGLY □ *Mrs Tuchman's new book provides most of the answers for those who, like myself, have wondered for years* ***what made*** *that astonishing man* ***tick****.* ST □ *'More understanding of capitalism and of* ***what makes*** *industry* ***tick*** *must,' he demanded, 'be got across to the products of higher education.'* NS □ *Where would Mr Goodrich be without his chip on the shoulder, his grievance against women? It was* ***that*** *that* ***made*** *him* ***tick****, to use a vulgarism.* PW

what Manchester says/thinks today, London/the world will say/think tomorrow (dated saying) what starts as an opinion, belief, theory etc held in one small geographical, intellectual, or social field rapidly becomes accepted far more widely □ *It was even said that* ***what Manchester says today, London will say tomorrow****—a pronouncement that is almost unintelligible in this age of centralisation.* L □ ***'What Manchester thinks today the world will think tomorrow,'*** *is an outdated belief. The old parochial outlook has become a world view.* T

what more can one ask etc? surely this is an ideal, or entirely satisfactory, state of affairs, arrangement, lot in life, etc? **V:** ask, ⚠ wish (for), want, desire □ *Happiness with family or friends, and a contented marriage partner.* ***What more can you ask?*** TO □ *An easily-run chalet near a safe beach—****what more can you want*** *for a family holiday?*

what a nerve etc(!) (informal) an exclamation of astonished disapproval or outrage at sb's presumption, impudence; of all the nerve etc(!) (qv) **n:** a nerve, ⚠ a cheek, a neck □ *'Will you be taking a wee dram* (= a small drink of whisky)*?' 'At half past six in the morning?' Mrs Odd exclaimed.* ***'What a nerve!'*** RM □ *We're used to kids stealing our fruit. But* ***what a neck****, coming over the wall with a basket!* ⇨ ⚠ have (got)/with a nerve.

what of it? is it important? does it matter? (the implication being that the speaker doesn't think so) □ *The man was a curious mixture, and besides, Charles had little or no experience of the type he represented. Well,* ***what of it?*** *He needed help, and here it was offered.* HD □ *'You're not having your meal just now, I hope?' the neighbour hesitated. 'Yes, we are,* ***what of it?*** *Come right in.'* □ stress pattern what 'of it?

what on earth/in the world? (informal) what, which thing? □ *And isn't it a blessing we have Prissie.* ***What on earth*** *would we have done without her?* DC □ *'We'll kidnap the dog,' I said. Finn stared at me.* ***'What in the world*** *for?' he said.* UTN □ *I wondered dully* ***what on earth*** *I ought to do about her bank books, for she had considerable sums of money in Seattle and in England.* RFW □ emphasizes questioner's bewilderment, indecision etc. ⇨ ⚠ how on earth/in the world? where on earth/in the world? who on earth/in the world? why on earth/in the world?

what a pity/shame(!) I'm so sorry! **cl:** (that) you can't be there, (that) it had to rain today; for the children to miss it; about your headache □ *Oh, dear—we're leaving for our son's wedding in Germany on the 12th.* ***What a pity!*** *Is that the only time you could come?* □ *Oh, Paul,* ***what a pity*** *you didn't call in to see Mrs Macroon.* RM □ *I hear you had your bike stolen, Patrick.* ***What a shame!*** □ exclamation of regret or sympathetic concern.

what price that etc? (informal) how likely is it that sth will happen or be done? what do you think of sb/sth? how would you value sb/sth (now)? **pron:** that, this, those, these. **cl:** (replacing ***that etc***) (that) he's on the next Honours list, (that) the project never gets off the ground; (this/that) for an excuse; your old man; the rule of law, equality of opportunity □ *Having French lessons now, Ma. Eh?* ***What price that?*** BFA □ *'****What price this*** *for a natty gents' suiting?' Meg laughed, showing him a sample of tweed in large purple and yellow checks.* □ *But if thirty or forty thousand dockers do defy the court, as they have done and probably will do again,* ***what price the rule of law?*** L □ *He was toiling through the night bringing a restraining British influence to bear.* ***What price that influence now?*** *The plain truth of course, is that it never existed.* NS

what (do you) say we etc do sth? (informal) shall we do this? don't you think it would be a good idea to do this? **cl:** we have a party, you have lunch with me, we go swimming □ *He heard Ma agree that the cocktail was a beauty. '****What say we*** *have a cocktail party and give them this one?'* DBM □ *It's a lovely afternoon.* ***What say we*** *skip this lecture and take a walk by the river?*

(and) what sb says goes (informal) (and) people, sb's employees, sb's family etc have to obey, agree with, sb; sb's word is law (qv) □ *'He's the sort of Nero of this region,' said the District Officer, '****and what*** *he* ***says goes****.'* BB □ *Lina Lalandi makes a point of introducing promising newcomers during the festival. It's a one-woman show* ***and what*** *she* ***says goes****.* OBS □ stress pattern (and) what ˌsb says ˈgoes.

what will they think of next?/! (informal) a comment on hearing of an invention, new law, fashion, art form, gadget etc (the implication being that it is astonishing or ridiculous) □ *Innocent bicycle pumps had proved to be plastic bombs and gone off at the stroke of eleven. '****What'll they think of next?****' people said at parties.* QA □ *In one scene Fields peers through the keyhole of an hotel bedroom to ascertain if he is in the right corridor. As he straightens up he murmurs, '****What will they think of next!****'* RT

what with sth (informal) because of sth **o:** the bad weather, the noise and the dirt; being so tired □ ***What with*** *the bad weather this spring I wasn't able to do much gardening.* □ ***What with*** *income tax and alimony—I tell you, it's a dog's life.* PE □ *But nowadays,* ***what with*** *Conservancy Boards and drainage schemes and things, the river runs away much quicker than it used to.* EM □ often precedes list of two, or more, items given as reasons or explanations; the list of items may be followed by *and so on, and whatnot, etc.*

what with one thing and another (informal) because of various duties, burdens, engagements, incidents etc □ *It occurred to him that,* ***what with one thing and another*** *during the day, he had never checked Tillie's information about the warehouse robbery.* PE □ BESSIE: ***What with one thing and another*** *I don't know if I'm coming or going.* HSG □ *'We are a little upset,* ***what with one thing and another****,' said Mrs Pettigrew.* MM □ front, middle or end position.

what's the big idea? (informal) what is the reason for such behaviour, such an action, or arrangement? (the implication being that there is no valid reason) □ *They tell me you've taken a job at the hospital as an orderly. Carrying buckets and emptying bedpans.* ***What*** *the bloody hell****'s the big idea?*** HD □ *'All these particulars* (= details) *are on my application form,' he said, losing patience, 'so* ***what's the big idea*** *of making me go over them all again?'*

what's cooking(?) (informal) what is being planned or done(?) **A:** in here; at the office; down Exeter way (= near Exeter) □ ***What's cooking*** *in television's most star-studded quiz game? Find out as Bob Monkhouse fires the questions.* TVT □ *The club usually has something special on, on a Friday night. We'll drop in a see* ***what's cooking****, anyway.* □ *Tony Marchant may have met the girl of his dreams. But Mum mustn't know* ***what's cooking****.* TVT

what's in a name? a name is no reflection of its owner's worth or merit □ (source) ***What's in a name?*** *that which we call a rose/By any other name would smell as sweet.* ROMEO AND JULIET II 2 □ *She's not ashamed of the name Bloggs—after all, Mozart might have been called Bloggs, if God or Nature or whoever hadn't decided otherwise.* ***What's in a name?*** L

what's the odds? (informal) what does it matter? one action, choice, result etc will be as good, or as bad, as another; make no odds (qv) □ SAM: *I've been poisoned by someone or something.* ***What's the odds?*** *By my life or my wife.* HSG □ *'Do it tomorrow instead if you'd rather.' '****What's the odds?*** *I shall be just as busy tomorrow.'*

whatever happened to sb/sth? (catchphrase) where is sb and what is he doing now? is sb/sth that we used to know, hear about, talk about still in existence? **o:** him, her, them; the traditional granny; romantic love, student revolt □ *As a postscript to 'People' we also begin a series entitled '****Whatever Happened To****—', devoted to personalities whose names used regularly to hit the headlines and are still remembered.* OBS □ *This week's movie aspirant is Simon Ward of the super-colossal 'Young Churchill'. Will we ever be saying* ***whatever-happened-to-him?*** ST □ *There are two things that a discussion series like Radio Three's '****What Happened to*** *Equality?' can hope to achieve.* OBS

whatever is, is right (saying) nothing in nature can be said to be unnatural; (the belief that) one should not question, or rebel against, established practice or conditions □ (source) *All discord, harmony not understood;/All partial evil, universal good;/And, spite of pride, in erring reason's spite,/One truth is clear,* ***Whatever 'IS, is RIGHT****.'* AN ESSAY ON MAN (A POPE 1688-1744) □

My contention is that most people are subjected to a sustained and ever-increasing bombardment of invitations to assume that ***whatever is, is right****, so long as it is widely accepted and can be classed as entertaining.* UL

whatever you do, (don't do sth) [Conj] whatever the circumstances may be (don't do sth specified by the speaker) **cl:** don't tell Mary, don't forget to switch off, don't let him get away □ *Now,* ***whatever you do, don't*** *tell Mary. She's always saying I can't look after myself.* □ *That's the only key I have.* ***Don't*** *lose it,* ***whatever you do****.* □ front, middle or end position; two parts of expression can be reversed, as in second example.

wheeling and dealing (informal) intense, and often unscrupulous, bargaining and intrigue to win commercial, or political, advantage □ ***Wheeling and dealing*** *was taking place on a level which made the English attempts at trading look like a church charity sale.* ST □ *This week's 'Man Alive' shows how glamour has taken a back seat to the* ***wheeling and dealing****.* RT □ *People want to be nominated for the Nobel Prize, even if they have no chance of getting it. It is the nature of human beings that there must be a certain amount of* ***wheeling and dealing****: 'I'll back your chap if you back mine.'* L □ *He was one of those fringe personalities, on first-name terms with the Hollywood barony, who had never seemed able to find a continuing niche for his own talents—a* ***wheeler-dealer*** *whose deals kept coming unstuck.* ST □ (General Robert E Lee, USA) *He had an extraordinary sense of the humanity of quite inhuman people, and tolerated them long enough to win them over: powerful men, who were really the scum of the Republic, gun contractors, war profiteers,* ***wheeler-dealers*** *of every stripe.* L □ *I don't like these business conferences—the drinking goes on late into the night as everyone* ***wheels and deals*** *and fixes big contracts.* □ non-rev; n compound wheeler-dealer; variant wheel and deal.

the wheels of industry etc that which enables industry to function **o:** industry, society, the Parliamentary system, higher education □ *There would be a thriving tourist trade and* ***the wheels of industry*** *would be turning.* OBS □ *Courtesy, and even a little hypocrisy at times, will help* ***the wheels of any*** *community* ***system*** *to run smoothly.*

wheels within wheels a complex arrangement of influences, or centres of power and decision-making, which make quick settlements difficult and which often baffle the onlooker □ (source) *And they four had one likeness: and their appearance and their work was as it were a* ***wheel in the middle of a wheel****.* EZEKIEL I 16 □ *The ordinary citizen often feels that, with a little good-will, some matter of international politics could be easily settled, but there are always* ***wheels within wheels****.* □ *There are some people quite high up in Admin who don't know everything that's going on. It's a great place for* ***wheels within wheels****.*

when all is said and done when one has considered all the circumstances and facts; after all (qv) □ (advertisement) ***When all's said and done*** *oil's cheaper to run.* RT □ *But* ***when all is said and done****, my mother was a most remarkable woman, with a strong and sterling character.* MFM □ ***When all's said and done****, exterminating one's enemies is still the most satisfying occupation.* L □ accompanies a statement of what sb believes to be a fact; said and done non-rev; usu front or middle position.

when/while the cat's away, the mice will play (saying) people will take advantage of the absence of authority, supervision, to do as they like, enjoy themselves, etc □ *'The hotel is run by a Miss Dupont. But it seems she's away in Brest for the day.' '****When the cat's away****,' Ma said.* BFA □ *Play up to her, won't you? Be the husband who's taking a holiday —* ***playing while the cat's away****.* PW □ often adapted, as shown.

when Greek meets Greek (then is/comes the tug of war) (saying) when two people of equal calibre, strength, determination, cunning etc oppose each other (then there is a real struggle) □ (source) ***When Greeks joined Greeks, then was the tug of war****!* THE RIVAL QUEENS (N LEE 1655-92) □ ***Greek meets Greek****. It's a match worthy of Greek legend: Archbishop Makarios versus General Grivas—the wily, subtle prelate seeking to outmatch one of the most practised exponents of urban guerrilla warfare.* L

when in Rome, do as the Romans do (saying) adjust your habits to suit the customs of the place you are living in, or of the people you are living with (from the Latin of St Ambrose (4th c)) □ *Taking opium in China is totally different from taking it in Berwick-on-Tweed. One is, I think, an experience—'****do in Rome as the Romans do****.' The other is a violation of the laws of the country.* L □ *'Just tell your friends you can't eat three enormous meals a day.' 'I wouldn't like to offend them.* ***In Rome****, better* ***do as the Romans do****—especially as it's only for a week.'*

when etc she is good she is very, very good (but when she is bad she is horrid) sb/sth can, at his/its best, be charming, talented, helpful, outstanding etc (but can, at his/its worst, be rude, obtuse, unhelpful, mediocre etc) **S:** she, it; Mary, ducal families; it, that magazine □ (source) *There was a little girl/Who had a little curl/Right in the middle of her forehead./****When she was good/She was very, very good,/But when she was bad she was horrid****.* H W LONGFELLOW 1807—82 □ (a tennis player) *They accept that* ***when she is good she is very, very good and when she is bad she is horrid****—capable of being beaten by the lowliest player on the circuit.* RT □ *It is nice to read in these pages that, sometimes* ***when ducal families were good, they were very very, good*** *and were even praised by American journalists.* L □ ***When 'Hers' is good, it is very, very good but when it is bad it is*** *surprisingly* ***flat and banal*** *for a poet's novel.* L □ often adapted to criticize people or things.

where the action is (informal) where people are doing things and there are things to be done; a busy centre of work, amusement etc **V:** be: look for; find out □ *Pug claims they still miss the hills and streams of Tennessee. But Vegas is* ***where the action is*** *and his wife accepts his way of life.* ST □ *Friends fly in from London sometimes and ask* ***where's the action*** *and I have to ring* *another friend to find out.* OBS

where does one go from here? (catchphrase) what (more) can one do now? what is the next step? (qv) □ *One question becomes increasingly disturbing:* ***where do we go from here?*** *August will see the end of the scheme and of government subsidies.* RT □ *All the time it* (my mind) *wandered back to Phuong and the one thought—suppose Pyle is right and I lose her:* ***where does one go from here?*** QA

where the hell etc? (informal) where? whereabouts? **n:** hell, ⚠ devil, blazes, heck, dickens □ *We searched the other rooms, but without much hope. '**Where the hell** else can we look?' asked Finn.* UTN □ usu indicates speaker's bad temper, hostility, scorn etc. ⇨ ⚠ how the hell etc? what the hell etc? who the hell etc? why the hell etc?

where is sb/sth going to stop? is there any point beyond which sb/sth will not go? (usu a reference to behaviour, conditions etc that is/are regarded with disapproval) □ *If a man is going to be able to walk through a girl's bathroom wall,* ***where is*** *he* ***going to stop?*** TST □ *It was petty theft and, however trivial in this case, once you let that kind of thing pass in a business* ***where is*** *it* ***going to stop?*** □ often follows *if*-cl.

where is our wandering boy/girl tonight? (catchphrase) said of anybody who is not where he/she is expected to be or ought to be □ (source) *Oh!* ***Where is my wandering boy tonight?****/The boy who was bravest of all.* ANONYMOUS SONG □ *'**Where is our wandering girl tonight?**' Hanna looked away, but Emma was hard to stop. 'I wonder,' she whispered, 'if T—' (a man I hardly knew) 'is on his lonesome.'* NM □ usu facetious.

where on earth/in the world? (informal) where? whereabouts? □ JIMMY: *Going out? On a Sunday evening in this town?* ***Where on earth*** *are you going?* □ emphasizes questioner's bewilderment, indecision etc. ⇨ ⚠ how on earth/in the world? what on earth/in the world? who on earth/in the world? why on earth/in the world?

where/while there's life there's hope (saying) as long as I breathe, I hope (from the Latin dum spiro, spero) □ *You never feel squeamish. Nurses don't. You don't mind what you're having to do because* ***where there's life there's hope.*** TVT □ MR FISH: ***Where there's life there's hope.*** MRS FISH: *Will hope light the gas? Will it fill the belly?* DPM □ *I'm sure my other niece wouldn't mind my mentioning it* (ie childlessness), *for even if they have been married for nearly ten years* ***while there's life there's hope****, as they say.* WDM

where there's muck there's money (saying) dirty work means profitable work; slagheaps, mill-chimneys etc are signs of wealth for somebody □ *This incident gives me a picture of a shrewd movie mogul.* ***Where there's muck there's money.*** DM □ *Best slate was so plentiful that any piece that was not almost perfect went on to the scrap-heaps, which grew prodigiously —* ***muck begetting money*** *in copybook style.* OBS □ variants muck and money go together, muck means/begets money.

where there's a will there's a way (saying) if one is sufficiently willing or determined, a way to do or obtain sth can usu be found □ *'I don't see how you can put them all up for the night.' 'Oh,* ***where there's a will there's a way****. We'll manage.'*

where would one be/what would one do without sb/sth? one's life or work would be almost impossible, very difficult, greatly diminished in quality, etc without sb/sth **S:** I, you, she, he, they; the country, your boss; working mothers. **o:** you, her, him, them, me; the voluntary services, your help; convenience foods, something to complain about □ *Thank God for the mobile shop. I don't know* ***what I would do without*** *it.* □ *And isn't it a blessing we have Prissie.* ***What would we*** *have* ***done without*** *her?* DC □ *When I applied for a posting they told me, 'No, you're doing important work.* ***Where would our boys be without*** *you? Their teeth would fall out.'* ST

which/that is not saying much which is no great praise; which indicates very little difference **s:** which, that, it; to say that □ *Indeed French* (rugby) *selectors receive just about the same respect from their Press and public as do French politicians,* ***which****, of course,* ***isn't saying much****.* RT □ *The* (Women's Liberation) *movement emerges with more sympathy than almost anything else in the book,* ***which is not saying much****. Nobody, in this world of petty manoeuvres and skirmishes, is particularly admirable: nobody is particularly bad.* NS □ *'She's a better cook than the last one, though.' '**That's not saying much**, is it? Anybody would have to be.'*

a whiff of grapeshot gunfire, as a swift means of suppressing disorder, rebellion etc □ (source) *. . . and as far as this which you call Third Estate* (ie the common people) *brave Broglie* (commanding the army) *with* ***a whiff of grapeshot****, if need be, will give quick account of it.* ***The whiff of grapeshot*** *can, if needful, become a blast and tempest.* THE FRENCH REVOLUTION I V 3 (T CARLYLE 1795-1881) □ *My only quarrel* (with the plot of the novel) *is that* ***a whiff of grapeshot*** *is more likely to move the electorate in favour of the Government in power than against it, especially if it is a Conservative Government.* ST

the while [A (NP)] at the same time (that one is doing sth else) □ *When he had done that he thought he would try a gin and tonic. He did, reading some book or other* ***the while****.* TGLY □ *He's also given to elaborating anxieties about his commitment, or lack of it, to revolutionary causes — sipping champagne in the Ritz* ***the while****.* □ end position; usu pres p phrase; equivalent to *while* + clause, eg ***while*** *he sipped champagne in the Ritz.*

a whipping boy [Comp (NP)] a scapegoat; sb/sth that is blamed, punished etc instead of others (from, formerly, a boy kept to be whipped for the misbehaviour of a young prince) **V:** ⚠ be, become; treat sb as □ *'Imperialists' are treated as before—as handy* ***whipping boys****.* T □ *Communism became* ***a*** *good* ***whipping boy*** *for Lewis from his earliest days in power.* ST □ (dental decay) *Manufacturers felt that nobody had yet proved that chocolate or confectionery was the real villain—although it was certainly* ***the whipping boy****.* OBS □ stress pattern a 'whipping boy.

whistle stop(s) short stop(s) on a journey, esp to meet and talk to an electorate, business associates, prospective customers, etc (from US, where politicians on tour used to address rural voters from the observation platforms of trains, the 'stops' having been previously advertised) □ *In spite of a physically exacting winter election campaign — much of it by train with frequent '**whistle stops**' — the Prime Minister appears to be well.* T □ *Mostly because she was too busy with **whistle-stop** tours to Australia and the Continent to have settled at home at all, Cilla is glad that she and Bobby didn't marry until 1968.* RT □ attrib use *a **whistle-stop** tour.*

a white Christmas snow at Christmas time □ *There seems to be snow in the air. To judge from the forecast, we may expect **a white Christmas**.* EM □ *The woman rubbed her hands and observed that it was cold enough to have **a white Christmas** yet.* AITC □ *And may all **your Christmases** be **white**.* WHITE CHRISTMAS (I BERLIN b1942)

a white-/blue-collar job etc professional, business and clerical employment/manual work, or skilled, semi-skilled or unskilled labour **n:** job, worker; home, district; demands, attitudes □ *The expansion of higher education on Oxbridge lines led increasing numbers to expect well-paid **white-collar jobs**.* NS □ *Boys from **blue-collar homes** are still 4 times less likely to get to a university (and girls 10 times less likely) than the children of parents in non-manual work.* SC □ *In America there is now a phenomenon familiarly called '**blue-collar blues**'. It is an expression of individual revolt which takes the form of widespread absenteeism.* L □ *He was the **white-collar** one of the family, the one who was going to make good and redeem all their fortunes.* CON □ white collar, blue collar sometimes without hyphen.

a white elephant sth useless, seldom used, or too costly to be worth maintaining □ *'Crux' in the 'New Statesman' subsequently described the Land Commission as '**a white elephant**'.* NS □ *It is something of a surprise to come across a compact, well-sited and sheltered outdoor sports stadium neglected, moss-grown, decrepit. **This** sporting **white elephant** lies within the Royal and Ancient Burgh of Linlithgow.* SC □ *The recent Budget has offered hundreds of millions of pounds to shore up private enterprise and to finance such **white elephants** as Concorde and the Channel Tunnel.* NS □ *There's a **white-elephant** stall at the Charity Sale.* You know, *people donate some household article they don't want that someone else may have a use for.* □ attrib use *a **white-elephant** stall.*

the white feather a symbol of fear, cowardice, or timidity (from cock-fighting, where a game cock displaying the white rim of feather under his hackle acknowledges defeat, wants to give up) □ *The early attacks* (on Britain) *from the air were noticeable enough for a naval officer to be heard saying playfully to another. 'What! Going to sea, are you? So you're showing **the white feather**!'* AH

a (great) white hope a talented person who is thought likely to bring success or victory (eg in sport) □ ***Our white hope** wrecked his knee on the eve of the match—so we were doomed from the start.* BM □ *Still only thirty-two, Kubrick is one of **the great white hopes** of the commercial film industry.* OBS □ *I'm going to go and look at some of his other works before trying to guess whether we really do have **a** new UK **white hope** shaping up in the gym.* NS

a white lie a lie that does no harm and is merely more convenient, or polite, than telling the truth □ *'Have you ever told **a white lie**?' Certainly, to have to admit to having told lies is to put oneself in a poor light, yet very few people could truthfully answer 'No'.* SNP □ *I said there was no more drink in the house — **a white lie** amply justified by the need to get him sobered up.* □ also pl.

the white man's burden the former concept (justifying colonization etc) of the European's duty to advance civilization, education, trade, public health, etc in underdeveloped parts of the world □ (source) *Take up **the White Man's burden**— /Send forth the best ye breed— /Go, bind your sons to exile/To serve your captives' need.* THE WHITE MAN'S BURDEN (R KIPLING 1865-1936) (reader's letter) *If we look back to the bad old days of exploration, colonisation and empire building—and, remember, at the time, all these were considered most commendable, '**the white man's burden**' in fact — we had one enviable reputation.* SC □ *In shuttered rooms were stored the littered remains of **the white man's burden**: scouting staffs, punchbags, dumb-bells, chest-expanders, smashed cricket bats.* L □ *His belief in the Greater Britain and the modern version of **the white man's burden** (the peace-keeping role in Asia) is to be found in that speech.* NS

the white man's grave the name formerly given to various (tropical) regions with climates and/or endemic diseases to which white men could not easily adjust □ *The malaria-carrying mosquito is honoured in Sierra Leone today for making the country **the** '**white man's grave**' in the past and preventing Europeans settling here.* T

a white night a sleepless night (from French nuit blanche with the same meaning) □ *I didn't feel particulary tired, or sleepy, after **my white night**. It was the day after that again, that it hit me.* SC □ *Isabel didn't sleep at all that night: it was **a nuit blanche**, the first she had ever had.* PW □ also pl.

a white slave a white-skinned prostitute, esp one inveigled into a foreign country by the promise of other employment □ *It has never been suggested that the employment agencies engage in what used to be called, a generation or two before the permissive age, the **white slave** traffic.* OBS □ *People say that Earl's Court is the centre of the **white slave** trade, and I wouldn't doubt it. There's a continual sexual electricity in the air.* L □ *'And would she then be shipped off to St Milo's like **a white slave**?' Isabel smiled. 'It wouldn't be done like that, of course. You're so uncivilised, Harold!'* PW □ also pl; attrib use, *the **white-slave** traffic, trade*, often found and may be hyphenated or not.

white trash any person(s) of European or American extraction who is/are thought (by sb or by another group) worthless or despicable (from, formerly, the description used about members of the poor white population in the

Southern States of the US) □ *Cosmo and Dorothy where shown up for what they were:* ***white trash****, on the other side of the line, irretrievably 'petit-bourgeois'.* US

a whited sepulchre [Comp (NP)] a hypocrite; sb who pretends to be pious, righteous, although he is not **V:** ⚠ be; think sb, regard sb as □ (source) *For ye are like unto* ***whited sepulchres****, which indeed appear beautiful outward, but are within full of dead men's bones, and of all uncleanness.* MATTHEW XXIII 27 □ *The revelation not only shocked Mary, but made her wonder how many more of her hitherto respected elders might be* ***whited sepulchres****.*

a whiter shade of pale [Comp (NP)] (facetious) become extremely pale in the face etc as a result of illness, shock, fear **V:** ⚠ be, turn, become □ *There was no need to add the gory details except for the malicious pleasure of watching his audience turn* ***a whiter shade of pale****.* □ *Although I was called the lady in white, a lot of my clothes were verging on cream. Anyway, it's very difficult to find two whites the same —I just used to wear* ***a whiter shade of pale*** *and hope for the best.* TVT

(wash) whiter than white (make sth be/seem) unusually, unnaturally, or exaggeratedly white, pure, holy, perfect etc (from the advertising claims of soap and detergent manufacturers) □ *Success in life appears to be measured by the horse-power of your car and whether you have the ability to overtake at 200 km.p.h., the* ***whiter-than-white****ness of your wash and the degree to which your possessions are brand-new.* L □ *At such a difficult time it is particularly obvious that the Government must* ***wash whiter than white****. But at any time it is essential that confidence should be maintained in the standards of public figures.* ST □ *I suggested to Steiger that it was a pity that the characters his co-star, Sidney Poitier, usually depicted were, morally, so much* ***whiter than white****.* RT □ *There was Dick, centre-stage. Behind him, a large choir dressed in* ***whiter than white*** *raiment.* NS □ n compound (the) whiter-than-whiteness (of sth); attrib use ***whiter than white*** *raiment.*

who am I to argue etc? what authority, moral strength, etc have I that entitles me to argue etc? **S:** I, he, she, you, they. **Inf:** to argue, to object, to interfere; to decide (what's best), to pass (judgment) □ *The good book, if we are to believe it, says we are entitled to three score years and ten.* ***Who am I to argue?*** OBS □ *Alice is a woman now with her own rights.* ***Who am I to say*** *what's best for her?* TST □ ***Who are they to tamper*** *with the sacred Rules of Golf?* ST

who cares? (informal) nobody cares; I, at least, don't care **O:** what he wants; whether they come or not; how it ends □ *About 'Buchanan Dying', John Updike's long play dealing with the last days of America's fifteenth president, the reader will probably also ask the one truly fatal question:* ***who cares?*** NS □ *'If you're really so kind as to buy a drink for us, I'll have a dry Martini.'* ***Who cares*** (Charles thought) *what he wants? A gentleman would have asked the girl what she wanted first.* HD □ often contradicts suggestion, or assumption, that sth matters or is important.

who does he think he is? (informal) why does he etc behave, talk so pretentiously, authoritatively? (the implication being that he has no right or reason to do so) **S:** he, she, they; the Joneses, the Council. **pron:** he, she, they. □ *'What pretensions!' I kept repeating. '****Who on earth does he think he is?****'* DOP □ (reader's letter) ***Who does Christopher Headington think he is*** *when he complains that the audiences were not in the right frame of mind?* RT □ *'****Who does he think he is****, then?' asked the holidaymaker, 'The Archbishop of Canterbury or something?'* RT

who the hell etc? (informal) who? which person? **n:** hell, ⚠ devil, blazes, heck, dickens □ *The presence of yet another unexpected guest was the last straw. 'And* ***who the devil*** *may you be?' he asked truculently.* EM □ usu indicates speaker's bad temper, hostility, scorn etc. ⇨ ⚠ how the hell etc? what the hell etc? where the hell etc? why the hell etc?

who/what is he/that he's/it's when sb's/sth's at home? (facetious) who/what is sb/sth? **cl:** ***(who)*** he. . .he's, Claire. . .she's; ***(what)*** that. . .it's, a palaeontologist. . .it's □ *'A master to whom all we poor novelists bow the knee,' said Goodrich. Harold sniffed: '****What is he, when he's at home?****'* PW □ *'I haven't got my first degree yet but I'm very interested in endocrinology.' 'Will you listen to the boy!* ***What's that when it's at home?****'*

who on earth/in the world? (informal) who? which one? □ *Now* ***who on earth*** *is going to break the news to his mother?* □ ***Who in the world*** *could have guessed that he'd turn up?* ⇨ ⚠ how on earth/in the world? what on earth/in the world? where on earth/in the world? why on earth/in the world?

the whole/full bag of tricks (informal) all the articles, items, procedures, manoeuvres etc that are relevant and possible □ *He talked to me as if I was his equal in knowledge and understanding of gynaecology and* ***the whole bag of tricks****.* AH □ *'The Vardons were the darlings of the gods — wild, lawless, and proud as the devil,' his invention ran ahead as he spoke, 'murder, rape, incest,* ***the whole bag of tricks****.'* HAA □ *He has made no attempt to prevent the top brass of the civil service from resorting to* ***the full bag of tricks*** *to head off any serious investigation into their privileges and powers.* NS

the whole caboodle (informal) the whole amount or number □ *The answer, of course, is a terrible disappointment for all those who imagined little Dickie dreaming one day of being in the driving seat, not just of one engine, but* ***the whole caboodle****.* RT □ *I knew there was a Mrs Wiggins and seven little Wigginses but he never indicated he was bringing* ***the whole caboodle*** *with him.* ⇨ ⚠ next entry.

the whole shooting match (informal) every member, item, event, aspect □ *What he'd have liked to do was sack* ***the whole shooting-match*** *and recruit a work force of his own.* SC □ *No conceivable writer or painter (especially painter) could have been trusted to render the scene honestly:* ***the whole shooting match*** *would have sunk without trace under the assaults of their 'personal vision'.* ILIH □ *It contained the gist of the whole debate and it's worth quoting, because it will be fed to the Communist millions* *as the only true report of what* ***the whole shooting match*** *was about.* L □ with or without hyphen. ⇨ ⚠ previous entry.

(those) whom the gods love, die young (saying) the only consolation for the death of good, talented, beautiful etc young people is that their presence is wanted in 'heaven' □ (source) *'**Whom the gods love die young**' was said of yore.* DON JUAN (G GORDON, LORD BYRON 1788-1824) □ *You have only got to read books about that time* (1914-18) *to read about the marvellous people who were killed then; the very best seemed to go. Yes,* ***those whom the gods love die young****.* L □ *After the war Eric became MP for Grantham and a year or two later suddenly fell dead in his garden, only in his early forties—a case, if ever there was one, of '**Those whom the gods love, die young**.'* ST

why the hell etc? (informal) why? **n:** (flaming/merry) hell, ⚠ devil, blazes, heck, dickens □ ***Why the hell*** *did you have to tell James that I'm taking Mary out to dinner tonight —don't you know he's keen on her, too**?*** □ ***Why the blazes*** *has Jack resigned**?** He's just been promoted, even if he doesn't like his new boss very much.* □ usu expresses speaker's exasperation and/or perplexity. ⇨ ⚠ how the hell etc? what the hell etc? where the hell etc? who the hell etc?

why on earth/in the world? (informal) why? for what reason? □ ***Why on earth*** *did she have to go all the way to London Airport for dinner**?*** WI ⇨ ⚠ how on earth/in the world? what on earth/in the world? where on earth/in the world? who on earth/in the world?

why and wherefore(?) for what reason(s)(?) □ *Any intelligent child will want to know* ***why and wherefore*** *he is being ordered, or forbidden, to do this or that.* □ *A trip from Wales to London was nothing to them; and no one asked them* ***the why and the wherefore****—and if they did, business, the sacred word business, covered it all.* PW □ *I learned not only secrets of reviving flagging flowers, drying leaves and blooms without loss of colour but* ***the whys and wherefores*** *as well.* ST □ *I found, when I was about 16 years old, that I didn't sleep and I was able to do without it. I've never looked into* ***the whys and wherefores of*** *it. It's just a simple fact.* L □ non-rev; variant the why(s) and (the) wherefore(s) (of sth).

wide awake [Comp (AdjP)] fully awake, not half-sleeping or drowsy; (fig) aware and alert, understanding and/or taking advantage of events or circumstances **V:** ⚠ be, look, feel □ *Instantly, realizing what had happened, she was* ***wide awake****. In her dream she had walked, and her legs, obeying the fantasy in her mind had disturbed the bedclothing.* DC □ *I am sure the* ***wide awake*** *people of this country will participate in the debate.* SC □ *This new secretary of his, Simpson realized, was too* ***wide awake*** *by half. He'd have to see about getting rid of her.* □ attrib use *a* ***wide-awake*** *mind, a* ***wide-awake*** *person.*

a wide boy (dated slang) sb who is shrewd and unscrupulous in business, or who tries, or manages, to impress and outwit others in small dealings □ *The idea of himself as* ***a 'wide boy'****, so dear to many men, was foreign to Harold. But he believed himself to be a man of the world.* PW □ *And of course the speakers attacked advertising trends: 'This is the first generation of mugs with money, and* ***the wide boys*** *are after it.'* L □ *The barman grinned at the man at the other end of the bar. 'Three of* ***the wide boys****,' he observed. 'We don't want their sort in here.'* PE

wide of the mark [Comp (AdjP)] off target (eg in shooting); (fig) inaccurate as an estimate, description, definition **S:** it; the shot, his suggestion. **V:** ⚠ be, go □ *In their valuation of collectors' items, the amateurs' team sometimes went as* ***wide of the mark*** *as £500 or more.* RT □ *Actually the drawing is like the work of a minor illustrator of children's books, and the suggestion that it's like a Klee is very* ***wide of the mark****.* NS

the widow's cruse a small store or supply of sth that seems self-renewing or inexhaustible (in allusion to the miracle described in 2 KINGS IV 1-7) □ *I've never known a gas cylinder last so long. I was beginning to think I'd got hold of some kind of* ***widow's cruse****.*

the widow's mite a small contribution, esp of money, that is as much as, or more than, the giver can afford (in allusion to MARK XII 41-44) □ *Don't feel ashamed—we don't despise* ***the widow's mite****, and, as they say, every penny helps.*

a widow's peak hair growth, or styling, which slopes back at each side from the centre of the forehead □ *He was a tall, colourless man, with hair that receded from* ***a*** *thinning* ***widow's peak****.* AITC

widow's weeds black mourning clothes, including a hat with black veil (from what was, formerly, conventional wear for a widow for a period following her husband's death) □ *I often saw women in* ***widow's weeds****. By 1918 the anonymous slaughter had created a grief too vast for dressing up.* NS

a wild goose chase a search for sb/sth who/that can, or will, not be found; a useless investigation or enterprise; a fool's errand (qv) □ *'On* ***this wildgoose chase*** *after an imaginary monster, eh?' he asked.* RM □ *No, I can't explain now. But I'll tell you what, if you think by lunch-time tomorrow that I've got you out on* ***a wild-goose chase****, I'll stand you a crate of Scotch.* TBC □ *I spent a pleasant evening with a man who had quit* ***the wild goose chase*** *of journalism to catch lobsters in North Wales and who had come over to buy a good second-hand boat.* L □ often follows *be on/be sent on*; stress pattern a wild 'goose chase; may be wild goose/wild-goose/ wildgoose.

wild horses couldn't/wouldn't drag him there etc (informal) no power, or persuasion, would make sb say or reveal sth, or make him leave etc **cl:** drag the information out of me, drag him to church, keep her at home, make me do otherwise □ MR PARADOCK: *Middie's coffee is made by a secret process, Bug.* ***Wild horses wouldn't drag it*** *out of her.* ART □ ***Wild horses will not drag from me*** *the name of the extremely grand and prosperous Sunday newspaper that had someone going around London last week.* NS □ *As soon as I read about the monster in the 'Daily Tale'* ***wild horses couldn't have kept me*** *in Nottingham and I came to Little Todday.* RM □ *'You sweet idiot,' thought Victoria, 'don't you know* ***wild horses wouldn't drive me*** *away* *from Baghdad!'* TCB

a wild man an extremist in a political party, creed or profession, uncompromising in his views or actions □ *'We want Lewis Eliot in on this,' he said. 'Why?' asked Mounteney. 'Because you're* ***a wild man****, Arthur, and he's a cunning old dog.'* NM □ also pl.

the Wild West the western territories of the US around the middle of the 19th c, while they were still not developed nor under stable government □ ***The Wild West*** *was exactly that: even in a sheriff's posse the difference between the good man and the bad and the lucky was very blurred.* L □ *He was reading a* ***Wild West*** *story.* □ *It sells papers in various languages, and women's magazines, and* ***Westerns*** *and Science Fiction and Amazing Stories.* UTN □ attrib use, *a* ***Wild West*** *story*, now rare—books, films etc dealing with life in this area (esp during 19th c) usu described as *Westerns*; variant the wild and woolly west (next entry (qv)).

wild and woolly [adj + adj non-rev] (informal) rough, uncivilized, or uncultured (from the '***wild and woolly*** *West'*, facetious variant of previous entry (qv)) □ *I like to spend my holidays where there's a bit of life and entertainment. I wouldn't fancy these* ***wild and woolly*** *places in the north of Scotland that you favour.* □ (opening of a residential college for young writers) *They may be a bit* ***wild and woolly*** *when they first arrive, but they'll soon settle down.* HAA

a wildcat scheme etc a rash, hazardous and, probably, impractical scheme, esp for making money **n:** scheme, ⚠ venture; speculation □ *When it came to deciding which troops would carry out* ***these wild-cat schemes****, the answer was always the same.* MFM □ *The lawyer might have seen it as his business* not *to be too efficient if he thought a young client was launching out on* ***a wildcat venture****.*

a wildcat strike a strike suddenly, or irresponsibly, decided upon by a group of workers, esp one not authorized or backed by a Trade Union □ *Frantic mobs of native workers gathered around the water points each night when the rations were doled out, and* ***wildcat strikes*** *were breaking out among the unloading parties.* BN

the wilder shores of love etc (catchphrase) the extreme, most extravagant, unusual, unrestrained etc forms of love etc (source probably the book title THE WILDER SHORES OF LOVE (L BLANCH b1907)) **o:** love, farce, tastelessness, bigotry, popular journalism □ *Barker is actually, by training and instinct, a traditional actor shipwrecked on* ***the wilder shores of farce****.* RT □ *The Tribunites* (ie British left-wing Labour MPs and supporters) *are remounting the old barricades.* ***The wilder shores of trade unionism*** *are lapped by similar rhetoric.* G □ *John Heilpern reports on an explosive dispute on* ***the wilder shores of psychiatry*** *which, he says, points up conflicting attitudes to madness.* OBS □ *I'd make it* (Professor Randolph Quirk's 'The Use of English') *compulsory reading for anyone engaged with words, and particularly for those of my fellow Scots who have got stranded on* ***the wilder shores of*** *linguistic* ***nationalism****.* L

a will o' the wisp [O (NP)] a flicker of light from marsh-gas; (fig) a fanciful or imprecise idea, belief, ambition etc that is either an illusion, or is difficult to define or substantiate **V:** follow, pursue, chase □ *Apart from this, the poor fellow's following* ***the will-o'-the-wisp*** *of surgical specialization struck sympathy from my bosom.* DIL □ *If John had been in his place, he would have been pursuing* ***a*** *wild* ***will-o'-the-wisp*** *half his life, upsetting the balance of the English historical profession.* ASA □ o' = 'of'; can be hyphenated or unhyphenated.

will/would (not) wash (informal) (not) be acceptable as valid, true, reasonable, likely etc **S:** it, that; the story, his explanation, that theory □ *Bacon's own defence of his actions is rather more interesting and illuminating, although how far it* ***would wash*** *in a modern court I could not presume to guess.* SC □ *Then there is the military cost. We are told that this is irrelevant, that the troops 'have to be stationed somewhere'. But this* ***will not wash****.* NS □ *'Perhaps he wore a monocle because he had something wrong with one eye,' Charles said. Burge turned to face him.* ***'Won't wash****,' he said curtly.* HD □ a terse comment on the unreasonableness etc of sth.

a willing horse a willing worker (contrasted with sb who complains or resists) □ *In Ted Heath's place* ***a willing horse*** *was eventually found in Willie Whitelaw; and it was he who had to perform tirelessly throughout.* NS □ *You're too obliging for your own good. Remember, it's* ***the willing horse*** *who gets the load.* □ *'The others don't do much to help, do they?' 'Well, that's partly my own fault—****the willing horse****, you know.'* □ also pl; sometimes used in expression *lay the load on* ***the willing horse****.*

win/lose by a (short) neck (horse racing) win/lose by the length of a horse's neck; (fig) succeed/fail by a (very) narrow margin □ (a horse race) *Golden Pleasure, a filly that has run well this season, was expected to romp home* (= win with ease) *in this afternoon's race. But some of the other runners gave her stiff competition and she* ***won*** *only* ***by a short neck****.* □ *There were many very well qualified people interviewed for that job. You* ***lost*** *it only* ***by a neck****—and that's no disgrace.* ⇨ ⚠ neck and neck (with sb/sth).

win etc the hand (and heart) of sb [V + O pass] (formal) become sb's husband or wife **V:** win, ⚠ gain; seek □ *Anyone who hopes to* ***win the hand of*** *the fair Gillian would need to have a lot more money than Ian.* □ *Their father had been surprised that neither of them had* ***won the heart and hand of*** *an officer in the RAF.* RM □ *She was a Jewess* ***whose hand*** *had been* ***sought*** *in marriage a year earlier by a Protestant, whose feelings she returned fully.* SNP □ hand and heart rev. ⇨ ⚠ win the heart of sb.

win hands down win without effort or by a clear lead (from horse-racing where a jockey lowers his hands to a relaxed position when he knows he is winning easily) □ (advertisement) *In the unanimous opinion of the judges Helen* ***wins hands down*** *on the value she got and the comfortable energy-saving way she did it.* ST □ *It's hardly surprising that when they come to the 11 plus, the middle-class children* ***win hands down*** *and that they win most of the places in the academic streams at the comprehensive schools.*

L □ *As far as having influence* (was concerned), *Sir Harold Johnson* ***had*** *the edge over Annette's father,* ***hands down****.* SML □ (film review) *The Americans* ***have*** *it* ***hands down*** *this week, or maybe hands up.* NS □ variant have sth hands down.

win the heart of sb [V + O pass] endear oneself to sb; engage sb's affection □ ...*Olga Korbut, the 17-year-old little Russian girl who* ***won the hearts of*** *everyone in the gymnastic hall.* RT □ *The child has quite* ***won*** *the old man****'s heart****.* □ *Both my parents who, as I have indicated elsewhere, led nomadic lives, used to* ***win the hearts of*** *their servants.* AH ⇨ ⚠ win etc the hand (and heart) of sb.

win or lose [v + v non-rev] whether one wins or loses, succeeds or fails □ *Full of doubts about the German war, knowing what it meant for them,* ***win or lose****, they nevertheless fought it.* NM □ ***Win or lose****, Docherty's team will provide England with a further opportunity to study some of the difficulties which are likely to be encountered against Italy in the World Cup.* G □ front, middle or end position.

the wind of change (catchphrase) signs of change, esp in political, or social, conditions (first used by Prime Minister Harold Macmillan in 1960 with reference to (the need for) constitutional reforms in Africa and its gradual decolonization) □ *But his warning that* ***the*** *'****wind of change****' should not become a 'howling tempest' comes a little late: the storm has already broken across Central Africa.* OBS □ *Nobody prepared them for* ***the*** *'****winds of change****'. The Fourth Republic allowed the myth that Algeria would remain French forever to take root.* NS □ (reader's letter) *Perhaps the party system itself requires a waft of* ***the wind of change****.* T

wind and weather [n + n non-rev] varying weather of all kinds, esp weather that one is exposed to, or that affects natural or man-made objects □ *The seamen who could to a certain extent laugh at* ***wind and weather*** *had made a joke of the rock.* PM □ *It wasn't merely its ten rooms, its raw newness, its glaring red brick of the type which is supposed to mellow with* ***wind and weather****...* RATT

wine and dine [v + v rev] have, or share, or entertain sb to, a set meal with wine, as a social or formal occasion □ *So we* ***dined and wined*** *and walked and talked, and when I stopped to think, as occasionally I did, I thought, 'Well, it won't last.'* PP □ (astrologist's forecast) *A perfect week for the happy-go-lucky Piscean. Plenty of opportunities for* ***wining and dining*** *and flirting outrageously.* TO □ *But there is no evidence that advisory councils have ever been taken seriously, after their* ***wining and dining*** *was done.* L

wine, woman/women and song (symbols of) social pleasures or indulgences □ (source—translated from German—attributed to M LUTHER 1483-1546) Who loves not ***wine, woman, and song****/Remains a fool his whole life long.* □ (NONCE) *If he was wondering how much of his fifty pounds Robert had drawn out to squander on* ***wine, women and drugs****, instead of using it to finance his exhibition, he was keeping the question to himself.* CON □ (NONCE) *'Bang went a pun' note* (= £1) —*maistly* (= mostly) *on* ***wine, weemen*** (= women) ***and seegars*** (= cigars). BBCTV

a winter of discontent (catchphrase) a period during the winter months made additionally unpleasant by strikes in key public services, eg hospitals and the water supply industry (used esp with reference to the winter of 1978 in Great Britain) □ (source) *Now is* ***the winter of*** *our* ***discontent****/Made glorious summer by this sun of York.* RICHARD THE THIRD I 1 □ *The spectre of* ***a winter of*** *industrial* ***discontent*** *nagged at investors.* BBCR □ *Once more the people of Britain are experiencing* ***a winter of discontent****.* BBCR □ (interview with hospital worker's leader) *Do you think there is a likelihood that that winter—* ***the winter of discontent*** *as it was called — could be repeated?* BBCR □ *Do you envisage* ***a winter of discontent*** *owing to the Government's 6% pay limit on the public sector?* BBCR

wise after the event [Comp (AdjP)] know, realize, what should have been done, thought, or provided for, in connection with an event, but only after it has happened **V:** ⚠ be, appear □ MR PARADOCK: *I could see it coming.* MRS PARADOCK: *You mean you think you could see it coming. You're being* ***wise after the event*** *again.* ART □ *It is difficult to imagine a time when Mozart's 'The Marriage of Figaro' did not exist and,* ***wise after the event****, we cannot conceive of it being accepted as anything else but a masterpiece.* RT □ GILL: *Old Mr* ***Wise-after-the-event****, who's always read the reviews and then chastises the other reviewers before he lays himself on the line.* ST □ *I do not want to trouble a picture of the beginning with* ***wisdom after the event****.* LWK □ unusual variant wisdom after the event. ⇨ ⚠ with (the wisdom/ease of) hindsight.

a wise guy (US informal) a sharp and knowing person, esp one who is, or thinks himself, witty, good at repartee, etc □ *David Frost goes down frightfully well in the States. The Americans like* ***wise guys****, whereas we love our failures.* RT □ stress pattern a 'wise guy.

a wise/foolish virgin a provident/ improvident person (in allusion to MATTHEW XXV 1-12) □ *At the rare stations boiling water was on tap, and the overcoated passengers queued with teapots: my Czech, like* ***a wise virgin****, had provided us with one before leaving Harbin.* AH □ also pl.

wish etc (that) the ground would (open and) swallow one be so embarrassed, or ashamed, that all one wishes to do is to disappear from sight **V:** wish, ⚠ hope, pray □ *'An awkward moment?' 'I'll say it was. All I* ***wished*** *was for* ***the ground*** *to* ***open and swallow me****.'* □ *Houseman was clearly* ***hoping that the ground might swallow him*** *at that second and there were few among the Chelsea* (football) *following who wouldn't have gladly dug the hole.* ST

wish one had a pound etc for every book etc an exclamatory comment on a great number of items, or on how frequently sth occurs **O:** pound, ⚠ (slang) quid (= pound), shilling (former unit of GB currency), dollar. **o:** every book on these shelves, every mile you've travelled, every time I've heard him say that □ *'I* ***wish I had a shilling****,' said Derek looking round the room, '****for every book*** *on these shelves.'* □ *My* *grandfather often said he* ***wished he had a dollar for every mile*** *he led his span* (of oxen) *by the head through the veld.* LWK

the wish is father to/of the thought (saying) one thinks that sth is true, or likely, because one wishes it to be so; wishful thinking (qv) □ (source — the King is ill and old) PRINCE HENRY: *I never thought to hear you speak again.*/KING HENRY: ***Thy wish was father****, Harry,* ***to that thought****./I stay too long by thee, I weary thee.* 2 HENRY IV 5 □ *He tends to avoid painful choices of policies by making* ***the wish the father of the thought****. As he sees it, the British policies towards the underdeveloped world that are morally right are also profitable.* ST □ *Her parents say, though there* ***the wish*** *may* ***be father to the thought****, that Annette is not seriously interested in this young man.*

wish/hope to God (that) (informal) wish/hope emphatically, or earnestly (that) **cl:** (that) they would leave soon, (that) you had, (that) it would stop raining □ *'I nearly came to see you yesterday evening.' 'I* ***wish to God*** *you had, for then I wouldn't have been cleaning the windows and so I wouldn't have fallen off the step-ladder.'* □ (They) *shuffled in and out of the Ministry under Mr Healey's awful eye, opening new Warrant Officers' Messes at Devonport and* ***hoping to God that*** *they would move on soon to a post where there was a real job of work to be done.* ST

wish sb well/ill give sb one's good wishes for success, health, happiness/hope that sb will not achieve success etc; hope that sb will have good/bad luck in his life or dealings □ *Show-business agents come and go in his London hotel room, talking of Dusty Hoffman and* ***wishing*** *each other* ***well****.* OBS □ *Pritchett will be working with a new secretary. I* ***wish*** *them both* ***well****.* NS □ *It's becoming increasingly difficult not to* ***wish*** *that old lady* ***ill****. She's tyrannizing her whole family.* □ *It's not that I* ***wish*** *Johnston any* ***ill****—we just don't see eye to eye about anything.*

wish you were here (catchphrase) I would enjoy your company and you would enjoy the scenery, circumstances etc if you were where I am now (in allusion to the shortened greeting or message sent on a holiday postcard to a relative or friend) □ *The card just said 'Having wonderful time.* ***Wish you were here****,' or some such thing.* CON □ *In Radio 4's study of tourism, '****Wish You Were Here****', he described Blackpool as 'a resort in which people can come along and forget their inhibitions.'* L

wishful thinking persuading oneself that sth is true, or will or could happen, because it is what one would like; the wish is father to/of the thought (qv) □ *When Ministers predict that we are on the verge of a boom, they are naturally suspected of* ***wishful thinking****.* SC □ *In the event of an emergency! What had given rise to such a phrase? Refinement?* ***Wishful thinking****? Hypocrisy? War was now a certainty.* AH □ (reader's letter) *Let's not waste a precious second on* ***wishful thinking*** *or useless regrets. Life really is too short.* TVT

to wit [Conj (PrepP] (formal) that is; namely; (more) specifically □ *There were plainly hopes in the family that a more intimate tie would develop between landlord and tenants,* ***to wit****, through the marriage of his lordship to Marcus's sister, Marian.* RT □ *'They should have appointed a more responsible person.' '****To wit*** *yourself, I suppose.'* □ *It seemed fair to assume that such objectives occupied the same place in Mr Arblaster's thinking as in his book:* ***to wit****, none.* NS □ often facetious, as in second and last examples; usu front position, preceding the n or pron denoting the thing(s) or person(s) named.

wit and wisdom [n + n non-rev] quickness of mind and sagacity, esp seen as an ideal combination of qualities in a speaker or writer □ *I would not have traded one minute of his* ***wit and wisdom*** *for an evening's local news and views.* L □ *All in all, then, a rattling good Celtic yarn with a few fragments of* ***wit-and-wisdom*** *thrown in.* NS □ *One of the great space-fillers of this time of year for newspapers is the 'Sayings of the Year' feature, in which we are reminded of all the* ***wise and witty*** *things that our political masters have uttered in the past year.* L □ variant witty and wise [adj + adj rev].

the witching hour/time (of night) midnight (when witches were once supposed to be specially active and powerful) □ (source) *'Tis now* ***the*** *very* ***witching time of night****,/When churchyards yawn and hell itself breathes out/Contagion to this world.* HAMLET III 2 □ (changing watch at sea) *'She's all yours and the Old Man* ((slang) = captain of the ship) *is in one of his moods, so watch out for sparks.' 'See you again at* ***the witching hour****.'* PM

with all one's might [A (PrepP)] using all one's physical strength, mental or nervous energy, powers of concentration, powers of persuasion, etc; with might and main (qv) □ *He looked, and saw Bullivant on his feet thumping the boy at the desk in front* ***with all his might****.* LLDR □ *Don't blame me. I tried* ***with all my might*** *to make her change her mind.*

with bated breath [A PrepP)] scarcely breathing because one is tense with excitement, expectation, anxiety etc; excitedly; anxiously; expectantly **V:** wait; watch, listen; proceed □ *I waited* ***with 'bated breath'****, as you would say, for the solution, but once again none came.* TBC □ *Carefully we undid the door and stood watching* ***with bated breath*** *as the tiny animals scuttled into their new home.* BB

with the best (of them) [A (PrepP)] (do sth) as ably, efficiently, as the best practitioners of an art, skill or trade **V:** argue, haggle, do battle; gamble □ *Of course he can give a course of lectures and contribute an essay to an academic volume* ***with the best of them****.* ST □ (rugby) *Now 21 boys began playing with an unbridled ferocity which I found infectious. Within a short time I found myself hacking and charging* ***with the best of them****.* OBS

with the best will in the world [Disj (PrepP)] however good one's intentions are; even if one is as well disposed as possible □ ***With the best will in the world****,* (the job is) *too much for one pair of hands.* DIL □ *The established museums by the nature of things can never,* ***with the best will in the world****, be expected to cater indefinitely for the individual student.* SD □ *Strawberry plants from one's garden are not the kind of presents to give or receive.* ***With the best will in the world****, one can spread disease and trouble.* SC □ usu accompanies a statement of what cannot be done or allowed; usu front or middle position.

(spelt) with a capital S etc [A (PrepP)] using a capital initial letter to emphasize the importance, for the speaker and/or in a particular context, of a word usually spelt without a capital S etc **o:** A, B,. . .X, Y, Z □ *There's a very great oversimplification in thinking that there is something called Science, **with a capital 'S'**.* L □ *'I've been thinking about us,' I said, trying to make it sound as if 'us' was **spelt with a capital U**.* SML □ *'This is St Clair Road,' she said. 'We live at the top. It's T' Top* (= The Top) *in Warley, though, **with a capital T**.'* RATT

with a difference having an individual quality; (doing sth) in a individual way that distinguishes sb/sth from others of the same kind **n:** hotel, memorial; performance, pop-singer. **cl:** wear the uniform, sings her mother's song, gets drunk, practises medicine ☞ (source) OPHELIA: *There's rue for you; and here's some for me; we may call it herb of grace o' Sundays. O! you must wear your rue **with a difference**.* HAMLET IV 5 □ *But the deepest pleasure is that of raising up, for the first time for all to see, the 'monument **with a difference**'.* ST □ *You can't judge by appearances in 'The Norman Conquests': a domestic comedy **with a** devastating **difference**.* TVT □ modifies preceding n or clause.

with flying colours [A (PrepP)] with conspicuous success (from a fighting ship with all her flags still flying after defeating an enemy) **V:** come through, emerge, pass (the test) □ *Well, you've come through the ordeal, if ordeal it was, **with flying colours**.* □ *My son is convinced that if he had been interviewed by a high-qualified chemist like his professor he would have got through **with flying colours**.* SML □ *There are circumstantial accounts of two Cabinet crises out of which the author emerges **with flying colours**.* L □ *On these grounds there is little doubt that the lie-detection technique emerges **with flying colours**.* SNP

with (a) good grace [A (PrepP)] good-temperedly; without anger or resentment **V:** accept, take, sth; lose, surrender; join in □ *Waldegaard's team seemed prepared to accept the decision **with good grace**.* G □ *This was not a question of accepting the inevitable **with as good a grace as possible**. A free vote offered a likely advantage to the government.* NS □ *Brian, I noticed, put up his hand last of all. He said: 'I think it should be unanimous, Mr Chairman. That's the way we like it,' losing on behalf of his friends **with** very **good grace**.* ST □ *MPs should remember that membership is a privilege worth having and that if we go in we should go in **with a good grace**.* SC □ variant with as good a grace as possible.

with gusto [A (PrepP)] with obvious enjoyment of what one is doing **V:** devour, attack; sing, perform. **adj:** great, such, tremendous □ *Elbows up and heads down, they demolished the platefuls of steaming meat and vegetables **with gusto**.* □ *In the film's battle scenes Berber tribesmen played themselves **with** great **gusto** and US Marines from a nearby base stood in for the Foreign Legion.* OBS □ often in expression ***with** great **gusto***.

with (the wisdom/ease of) hindsight [A (PrepP)] with, helped by, understanding of the nature of events only possible after they have occurred □ *Without this incident, their relationship would have broken up anyway though perhaps a little later — and **with hindsight** we think we can see why.* OBS □ *Of course it can be argued that Guthrie wrote **with the ease of hindsight** a century after the events he describes.* NS ⇨ ⚠ wise after the event.

with knobs on (informal) in an extreme form; to an extreme degree □ *'I think you're being a selfish pig!' 'The same to you **with knobs on**.'* □ *I have still to see anything better than the shoe-shop routine in 'The Barkleys of Broadway'; that was trick photography **with knobs on**.* RT □ *'Was it a tough interview?' '**With knobs on**! They had me on the line all right.'* □ can follow (and modify) a n, or be used independently.

with/without the knowledge and consent of sb [A (PrepP)] (formal) with the full permission of sb/without sb, who ought to be informed, knowing anything about it **V:** move, arrive; occupy, take over, sth; enlarge, extend, build, sth □ *The subsequent decision to abandon convertibility and later the decision to devalue the £1 were both taken **with the knowledge and consent of** the US authorities.* SC □ *Your insurance policy doesn't cover theft by somebody occupying the flat **with your knowledge and consent**.* □ *If you build an extension to your house **without the knowledge and consent of** the local planning authorities, you may have to demolish what has just been built.* □ knowledge and consent non-rev.

with malice aforethought [A (PrepP)] (legal) with premeditated intention to commit a crime; with deliberate intention to harm, obstruct, annoy or embarrass sb □ *On radio discussion programmes premeditated oaths are out, a ruling which strikes me as both sensible and well-mannered. I have no wish to spit in the ear of any listener **with malice aforethought**.* L

with might and main [A (PrepP)] using all one's physical strength, mental or nervous energy, etc; with all one's might (qv) **V:** strive, struggle, fight □ *I'm sure I've striven **with might and main** to bring these children up properly, but sometimes I think I haven't made a very good job of it.* □ *Three of the local lads have formed a group. They play **with** more **might and main** than musicianship but they're all right for dancing to.*

with one hand/both hands tied behind one's back [A (PrepP)] (try to do sth) when severely restricted; (be able to do sth) even though restricted **V:** fight, beat, sb; achieve, win, sth □ *Mr Nixon told us that 'the time is past for the United States to compete **with one hand tied behind her back**.'* NS □ *Nothing to it. I can run this pub **with one hand tied behind my back**.* AITC □ *But the real problem in tackling the story of the Whitechapel murders is that most listeners will be in no doubt that they could have written a better script **with** their eyes shut and **both hands tied behind their backs**.* RT

with one voice [A (PrepP) unanimously; expressing the agreement of all concerned **V:** speak, say; agree, consent to, approve, sth; decry, oppose, sth □ *They said **with one voice***

that they have been hoping and waiting for such an approach for a long time. MFM □ *It is rare to find the three teachers' organisations in Scotland speaking* ***with one voice***. SC

with respect (to sb) [Disj (PrepP)] respectfully; not insolently, nor dismissing another's authority, opinion, knowledge, experience etc **adj:** all, due, the greatest □ *'Well, what are you hanging about for?' '****With respect****, sir, wouldn't it be better to send a policewoman?'* □ *I would suggest,* ***with*** *all* ***respect to*** *the parents, that they are not always the best judges of a child's capabilities.* □ front or middle position. ⇨ ⚠ previous entry; in respect of sth; in terms of sth.

with respect to sth (formal) with reference to sth; in/with regard to sth (qv) □ *Some people, harking back to Locke's distinction between primary and secondary qualities, are willing to concede the force of this argument* ***with respect to*** *colour, but balk at its extension to shape.* SNP □ ***With respect to*** *your other enquiry, about pension rights, I enclose an explanatory leaflet.* ⇨ ⚠ in respect of sth, previous entry.

with etc (no) strings (attached/binding its use) [possess] with (no) special conditions which limit the use, or enjoyment, of sth **prep:** with, ⚠ without. **V:** have, (there) be □ *I don't think the Government should give an increase* ***with no strings attached*** *to doctors while they give dentists a possible increase* ***with strings attached***. SC □ *The* (Polish) *Ministry of Culture lent us a car, chauffeur and a pretty and wildly energetic guide-interpreter.* ***There were no*** *party* ***strings attached***. OBS □ *They are the UN special agencies, the one undoubted success which the United Nations can claim. No other dispenser of aid* ***without strings*** *is in sight.* SC □ (Rockefeller) *He's the only philanthropist I can think of who gave away his fortune* ***with*** *absolutely* ***no strings binding its use***. L □ attached almost always used.

with a vengeance [A (PrepP)] to an extreme degree □ *I was warned it would be hard work, and hard work* ***with a vengeance*** *it was.* □ *I'm afraid* our *ways have diverged* ***with a vengeance****! Never mind, we'll try and forget sore subjects, just for Christmas, shall we?* EM □ *Under Albert and Victoria,* (the concept of) *House, Hearth and Virtue took root* ***with a vengeance***. NS □ can also modify a preceding n, as shown in first example.

with a view to doing sth with the intention and hope of doing sth, either soon or later **cl:** being called to the Bar, settling there, becoming a teacher, improving conditions, opening another branch □ *I went to Mr A N Seligman's chambers in Lincoln's Inn* ***with a view to*** *getting called to the Bar* (= qualifying as a barrister). RFW □ *Attempts are being made to organise a conference* ***with a view to*** *setting up an international convention on adoption law.* L □ *13 Corps was to break into the enemy positions and operate with 7th Armoured Division* ***with a view to*** *drawing enemy armour in that direction.* MFM

with a will [A (PrepP)] with willingness and determination **V:** set to, go to it; work, dig, promote □ *Having been promised £1 each if they made a good job of it, the boys set to* ***with a will***. □ *She tried to throw herself* ***with a will*** *into life among the deck-chairs, spades, buckets and thermos flasks.* PW □ *Top soloists can be capricious and eccentric in the extreme. But youthful conductor Christopher Seaman takes on the job of 'backing' any soloist* ***with a will*** *and rare skill.* RT

one's withers are unwrung (formal) one does not feel any distress, sorrow or pity (when one might possibly be expected to feel such distress etc) □ (source) *We that have free souls, it* (a play) *touches us not. Let the galled jade wince,* ***our withers are unwrung***. HAMLET III 2 □ *Since nothing we learn about Chinaski suggests that he could ever have done anything more than deliver letters, and that isn't exactly the world's worst job,* ***our withers remain unwrung***. L □ *Miss Stassinopoulos hopes that her book will destroy the Women's Liberation movement. We jaded* (Lib) *writers may be galled by malicious misrepresentation, and even more by the unsympathetic depiction of our own sillinesses, but* ***the withers of*** *the movement* ***are unwrung***. L □ (NONCE) *Bill Douglas has magnificently retained the child's sense of confusion and mystery.* ***Our withers are wrung*** *precisely because we understand so much more than the child can.* NS

within/in living memory [A (PrepP)] at, or during, a time that people still living can recall □ *Langham* (Hotel) *managed to be raffish and highly respectable at the same time.* ***Within living memory****, Haile Selassie, Mrs Simpson and Aleister Crowley could have been found there.* L □ *The country was occupied* ***within living memory*** *by whites through a combination of force and deceit.* SC □ *Never write a biography of a 'character' who has died* ***within living memory***. NS □ *Prices have been going up faster for longer than at any time* ***in living memory***. OBS

within reason [Comp/A (PrepP)] reasonable; to a reasonable degree; not immoderate(ly), extravagant(ly) or ridiculous(ly) **V:** be; spend, eat, smoke, exercise □ *'Do me a favour.' 'Of course. Anything you like.' He smiled at her. '****Within reason****.'* PE □ *Name a price* ***within reason*** *and I'll take the house off your hands.* □ *A husband with a family should drink '****within reason****', that is, should know when he has had enough, and should always 'provide'.* UL □ *He would spend as much time in the constituency as was* ***within reason***. ST

without benefit of clergy etc [A (PrepP)] without the professional services of the Church or a minister of religion, etc (benefit of clergy originally = 'benefit to clergy', ie a right, abolished in 1827, that clergy should not be tried for crime in a secular court) **o:** clergy, law, medicine; Press, schooling □ *War overtook them and closed churches so they 'married'* ***without benefit of clergy***. □ *So this time the City establishment is determined to show that they can run their own ship on tighter lines* ***without benefit of law***. G □ *From this picture of violence and passion and love the victims of Captain Segura were alone excluded — they suffered and died* ***without benefit of Press***. OMIH

without fail [A (PrepP)] with absolute and dependable certainty **V:** return, start; pay □ *'I'll be back by 7.30,* ***without fail****.' 'See and remember that, then — for I won't wait for you.'* □ JENNY: *Every time there's bin* (= been) *a rise* *someone gets sacked.* ***Without fail.*** R

without fear or favour [A (PrepP)] (formal) impartially, according to one's understanding of the truth or of one's duty □ *The Northern Ireland Secretary, Mr William Whitelaw, proclaimed to the people of Ulster 'We will not desert you. We will do our duty to you all* ***without fear or favour****.'* L □ (a non-commercial radio-station) *Names are named in all their programmes,* ***without fear or favour*** *to the limit allowed by American law.* L

without a hitch [A PrepP)] (informal) successfully; without interruptions, mishaps or obstructions **V:** go, work; carry through, operate, sth □ *The removal van was quite prepared to come in the evening when it was dark, and the whole operation went* ***without a hitch****.* TSMP □ *The first of the units to be used privately in Britain has been working for more than three months '****without a hitch****' at Dalreagh nursing home, Stockport.* G □ *And if the meeting comes off* ***without a hitch****—well, it might be the saving of everything.* TCB

without more/further ado [A (PrepP)] without delay, fuss, or hesitation **V:** begin, set out; leave, depart □ *She was working at an oil painting upon an easel, and she went back to this* ***without more ado****.* RFW □ *Another legal conundrum that needs to be sorted out,* ***without more ado****, is the apparent failure of the authorities to make it possible for people to be tried in Welsh in the Crown Court.* NS □ *The stage has thus been cleared for his songs, and they are performed* ***without further ado*** *by a cast of ten.* L □ comparative, more/further, does not necessarily imply there has been earlier delay.

without prejudice (to sth) [A (PrepP) (legal) without any negative, harmful or restricting effect (on sth) **o:** one's case, a ruling, a benefit □ *It was finally agreed that the British and Americans would provide food for one month for the population in their sectors of Berlin,* ***without prejudice to*** *any future decision on the question of principle.* MFM □ *The judge overruled the objection, saying that the defendant could answer prosecuting counsel's question* ***without prejudice*** . □ *Cover claims made on Policy B were* ***without prejudice to*** *any claims lodged in respect of Policy A.*

without a/one word [A (PrepP)] without making any comment, explanation, or complaint □ *I recognized it as the parcel containing my manuscripts. I reached out for it and she passed it over* ***without a word****.* UTN □ *Who was this dark-haired dark-eyed girl? Why had Fergus decided to bring her here* ***without one word*** *to her first?* DC □ *The old man looked up. For a moment Wormold thought he was going to turn tail* ***without a word****.* OMIH □ front, middle or end position.

without a word of a lie [Disj (PrepP)] (informal) what I'm telling you, describing, is absolutely true, however unlikely it seems □ ***Without a word of a lie****, I sat there for an hour and a half before they even came to take my name.* □ front, middle or end position.

woe betide sb the person mentioned will/would surely be punished, reprimanded etc □ *He knew that many of the men had to hand theirs* (paypackets) *over as soon as they came home on Friday, and* ***woe betide*** *them if the seal was not intact.* AITC □ *Judge Maude said: '****Woe betide*** *anyone who should injure Mr Gardiner as a result of this case.'* T □ *He would throw at me a great tome on money matters and question me on Monday morning about it.* ***Woe betide me*** *if I hadn't done my homework over the weekend.* L □ almost always precedes *if*-cl.

a wolf in sheep's clothing a person who appears to be friendly, or harmless, but is really an enemy or evil-doer □ (source) *Beware of false prophets, which come to you* ***in sheep's clothing****, but inwardly they are ravening* ***wolves****.* MATTHEW VII 15 □ *Stevenson hadn't been an innocent dupe of anyone: he too was* ***a wolf in sheep's clothing****.* □ (NONCE) *It is true, as Elizabeth Longford says, that Churchill described Attlee as '****a sheep in sheep's clothing****'. Yet when Colville asked him which of his Labour colleagues he respected most, he replied, 'Attlee'.* L

wolf whistle(s) loud whistling directed at a woman, esp in the street or other public places, to show that men find her physically attractive □ (He) *gave a* ***wolf whistle*** *when he saw her in the dazzling white dress.* AITC □ *Then he would retire with Milly to England, where there would be no Captain Seguras and no* ***wolf-whistles****.* OMIH □ stress pattern 'wolf whistle(s).

a woman's/wife's place is in the home (saying) a woman's role in life is to manage a home and bring up children □ *In 1952* ***a woman's place was*** *widely regarded—dare I say it—as* ***in the home****.* L □ *The opinions of past generations that '****a woman's place is in the home****' and that 'a man should be the breadwinner' still linger on.* OBS □ *Beryl's male chauvinist neighbours are up in arms. According to them,* ***a woman's place is in the home****—not in the library.* TVT □ *I've got some very old-fashioned ideas about matrimony because I really believe that* ***a wife's place is in the home****. If I ever married I would certainly give up my career.* TVT □ a maxim now widely contested.

a woman's touch the handling of (domestic) arrangements, of a delicate situation, etc that a woman may be supposed to be better at than a man □ *His London flat near High Street, Kensington, is the sort of mess of books, records and empty wine bottles that cries out for* ***a woman's touch****.* TVT □ *'I suppose we shall have to soothe the fellow down.' 'Perhaps you should go;* ***a woman's touch*** *might do the trick.'*

(in) the womb of time (in) the period before sth happens, becomes known or reveals itself □ (source) *There are many events* ***in the womb of time*** *which will be delivered.* OTHELLO I 3 □ *Mammal fossils exist from this period, but man himself, as we know him, was still* ***in the womb of time****.* □ *'And I don't just mean that as a competitor with Robin, or almost any other man living, I'm in a grotesque position.' What he did mean remained unuttered so long that Patrick felt it might never leave* ***the womb of time****.* TGLY

women and children first (catchphrase) the accepted order of precedence in rescue or relief work, esp evacuation of a sinking ship □ *If the police are not there before us, they are obviously making a sweep tonight.* ***Women and children***

first. *The professor can wait.* OMIH □ *He preferred to sail in ships of a nationality that shall be nameless because in the event of a disaster there would be no nonsense about* ***women and children first***.

wonders will never cease a comment when sth, perhaps comparatively trivial, happens to surprise and please one □ *'I've got it, Minnie!' 'No!' said Mrs Paxon, 'Well,* ***wonders will never cease***.*'* WDM □ *'Where's Johnny?' 'Round the back, washing the car.' 'What!* ***Wonders will never cease***.*'*

word for word with exact repetition of everything said, or written; verbatim □ *I suppose you'll be wondering how it is that I'm able to tell you* ***word for word*** *what Jim's man said to him.* LLDR □ *If you just listen to Walter Pigeon's speech* (in 'Forbidden Planet') *you'll notice it is an almost* ***word-for-word*** *adaptation of 'The Tempest' Act IV Scene I: 'The cloud-capped towers, the gorgeous places...'* RT □ attrib use *a* ***word-for-word*** *adaptation.*

a word in season [O (NP)] sth that is said to sb, esp as advice, sympathy, warning etc at the time when circumstances make it appropriate **V:** ⚠ offer, ⚠ give, utter □ (source) *The Lord God hath given me the tongue of the learned, that I should know how to speak* ***a word in season*** *to him that is weary.* ISAIAH L 4 □ *But you will admit that I tried, however obliquely, to give you* ***a word in season***. US □ *Sometimes it is only sensible to interfere.* ***A word in season*** *might have saved Paterson from his own folly.*

sb's word is (as good as) his/her bond sb's promise is as much to relied upon as if it were legally binding □ *The qualities that he stands for are the old-fashioned mahogany ones: that a man****'s word should be his bond****, that bargains should be honoured, that there comes a time when you have to trust even your opponents.* NS □ *People long for the days of fair play, when an Englishman****'s word was his bond****, he says.* OBS □ *But we've got Adam's word on paper—though far be it from me not to remember that* ***his word is as good as his bond***. WDM ⇨ ⚠ as good as one's word.

sb's word is law sb must be, or always is, obeyed, agreed with; (and) what sb says goes (qv) □ *The Decca supporters made out a strong enough case to cause the Federal Aviation Agency—* ***whose word is law*** *where US air traffic control is concerned—to offer to make a full-scale trial of Decca under American conditions.* NSC □ *Dad was just being a big show-off. He likes to think* ***his word is law*** *at home.*

(the) word is that it is said, reported, that **cl:** that Mark's been sacked, that the house will be sold □ *I don't know if it's true but* ***word is that*** *Mark's been sacked for embezzing company funds.* □ ***The word*** *in the City* (= London's financial centre) ***is that*** *one of the major oil multinationals will sell off its interests in textiles.*

a word of warning (to sb) a warning statement, remark (made to sb) □ *It is unlikely that professional historians or students of history will need* ***this word of warning***. L □ *Today there are still dotted round the world powerful criminals living beneath a cloak of sunny respectability.* ***A word of warning to*** *these far from gentle readers. It is most unlikely that the name of any one of them was not on the files of IDSO in London or Johannesburg.* DS □ also pl *two* ***words of warning***.

(by) word or sign [n + n non-rev] (formal) (by) saying sth, or by gesture/facial expression □ *The historian was too well versed in the customs of the English to be surprised at the fact that his companions preferred to breakfast without acknowledging* ***by word or sign*** *that he was not alone.* EM □ *'I heard you the first time.' 'Well if you give neither* ***word nor sign*** *that you did, how am I supposed to know?'* □ often neg, as in second example.

word perfect [Comp (AdjP)] able to repeat a passage of verse or prose, a part in a play, etc without mistakes or hesitations **V:** ⚠ be, become, get; make oneself □ *By Friday, when the show is recorded, we are all expected to be* ***word perfect***. TVT □ *With each repetition, he* (a young child) *takes renewed delight in the rhythmic, euphonic, reduplicated sounds and soon becomes* ***word*** *(or rather sound)* ***perfect***. MFF

a word to the wise a word is enough for the wise; an intelligent person can take a hint, draw his own conclusions without a lot of explanation (translation of Latin Dictum (later Verbum) sapienti sat est. PERSA (PLAUTUS ?-184 BC) often abbreviated in English speech or writing to verb sap) □ *When the one thing that can be said in a man's favour is 'I know nothing against him' I take that as* ***a word to the wise***. □ ***Verb Sap*** *means—well, it's short for something. I don't exactly remember what, but it's the same as 'Amen' or 'Enough said'.* RM

words fail one/sb one cannot (continue to) express, or describe, sth, either because one feels any attempt would be inadequate, or because one is overcome by embarrassment, anger, astonishment etc □ *People who take an active part in war aren't given to writing about the experience. It is not that they lack impressions, but* ***words fail them***. L □ *Here* ***words failed*** *his lordship who went red in the face and said no more.* WDM □ ***Words*** *do not* ***fail me*** *about this pitiful travesty: contempt cuts them short.* NS

words of wisdom wise or sensible remarks, advice **V:** offer, give, proffer, utter □ *With tension mounting on the borders of Israel, and European economies half-crippled by the Arab oil policy, these* ***words of wisdom*** *seem doomed to fall on stony ground.* SC □ *And the rest of the fellers* (= fellows) *fell for the press gang's* (here = Youth Employment Officer's) ***words of wisdom***. *The idea was: go and work at the factories which are on your doorstep.* L □ *Since he's known and grown up with some of the vintage villains of our time and has himself been done* (= convicted) *three times, he was worth a visit for some modern* ***words of wisdom*** *on that other world.* ST □ often ironic.

work it/things (so) that etc (informal) arrange affairs, a situation, to suit a particular purpose **A:** (so) that...; ⚠ better; that way, another way □ *I wanted to* ***work it so that*** *I didn't get asked in, or at any rate no further than the hall.* CON □ *We'll try it to* ***work it that*** *we travel down to London together.* □ *Why the devil can't they* ***work things so that*** *a candidate gets his medical* before *the interview?* □ *'He might* *accept help if he thought it was a grant from some trust or public body.' 'Well, we'll see if we can* ***work it that way****.'* □ *Maybe, if she had* ***worked things better****, she might have had more time with David.*

work like a charm be quickly and easily successful; have an immediate effect □ *The shrewd scheme was about to* ***work like a charm*** *when unfortunately the authorities wouldn't allow him to fly his planes over the planned route.* OBS □ *'There,' he said. 'Drink that, it'll help you to pull yourself together.' I don't know what was in it but it* ***worked like a charm****.*

work like a Trojan etc work very hard; work harder and longer than is normally expected of anyone **n:** Trojan, ⚠ black, slave; horse □ *To do the battery full justice, both officers and men appreciated the situation and* ***worked like slaves****.* SD □ *My husband left a fortune of over a million pounds, all made by his own efforts. He worked* ***like a black*** *from the time he was twelve.* PP □ *The 14th is too soon. Even if we all* ***worked like horses*** *from now till then the exhibition couldn't be got ready.* □ *Army teams* ***did Trojan work*** *rescuing people and animals trapped by the floods.* □ use of black (= 'negro') in this context now considered offensive; variant (do) Trojan work.

work a miracle/wonders [V + O] have an unusually, or marvellously, beneficial effect; do etc wonders/miracles (for/with sb/sth) (qv) **A:** for the industry, for these patients; in bringing on backward pupils, in increasing circulation figures □ *She had thought that being happy would* ***work a miracle*** *in him and turn him into a normal confident person.* DC □ (advertisement) *For many years Trill developed by L'Oreal of Paris in the world's greatest hair beauty laboratory, has been* ***working*** *near* ***miracles*** *for dry hair sufferers.* WI □ *But the Japanese hope that the success of their small-sized, low-fuel-consumption cars will* ***work wonders****.* G □ n compound a miracle-worker.

work or want [v + v non-rev] work hard or suffer a life of poverty; earn what one needs or do without it □ HELEN: *Listen Jo, don't bother your head about Arabian mystics. There's two w's in your future.* ***Work or want****, and no Arabian Knight can tell you different.* TOH □ *It was* ***work or want*** *in those days and our father applied the rule to us boys as well as to himself.*

work the oracle [V + O] produce the desired result or decision (esp by cunning, influence or bribery) □ *If you can't persuade him to lend us the money, how do you expect me to* ***work the oracle****?* □ *And then from the end of the corridor came this blast of music. 'I think it must be the Supply* (teacher) ***working the oracle****—nothing like a nice bit of music for an easy half-hour.'* TT

work etc till/until one drops continue (working etc) until one collapses **V:** work, walk, keep on, practise □ *She shops in the chain stores and claims that the clothes that she buys 'have to* ***work till they drop****.'* OBS □ *But there was tremendous competition, and the only way to get on was to practise and* ***practise till you dropped****, and then get up and practise again.* TVT

work etc a treat (informal) work (= 'function') etc well, so as to give pleasure or satisfaction **V:** work, (roses) grow, (sun shine, (drink) go down, (colour) suit sb, (sb) look □ *Earlier, bush telegraph* ***worked a treat****. There were back-to-work announcements in the local bingo halls, in pubs and clubs and a power of telephoning and a door-knocking.* ST □ *And, yes please, a little more of the wild boar with Satzle* (home-made-pasta) *and another glass of wine would* ***go down a treat****.* SC □ *Effie Bunce's sister Ruby undertook to clean all the silver, saying she'd make the brights* ***shine a treat****; an expression at which Palmer shuddered and drew in her breath.* WDM

a world away from sth very different from, widely separated from, sth in space or time □ *It was* ***a world away from*** *the ordinary presentation of politics: the prepared public appearances.* L □ *This is all* ***a world away from*** *the day just over 20 years ago when Gordon Parker, who is the chairman of the company, bought a derelict and silted up dock.* ST □ *Indeed his interests are* ***a world away from*** *Hollywood. He says he feels sorry for friends who are caught up in the film world with no other means of work.* RT □ also pl worlds away from sth.

the world, the flesh, and the devil all that is not holy; all that tempts mankind to wickedness or imperfection □ (source) *From the deceits of* ***the world, the flesh, and the devil****, Good Lord, deliver us.* BOOK OF COMMON PRAYER □ *There are a lot of irritating things about 'Any Questions'* (a radio programme). *First, there's an immaculate attention to balance—the political, the social, male and female,* ***the world, the flesh and the*** *odd* ***devil****.* L

(all) the world and his wife all, or most, people; a very large company of people □ *Across the room was a tall and languid citizen and* ***the world and his wife*** *knew him for an actor, a Man of the Theatre with an international name.* PP □ *It's to be a very grand fête.* ***All the world and his wife*** *will be there.*

the world is/remains one's oyster one is fortunate enough to do in life, or get from life, whatever one wants or enjoys □ (source) FALSTAFF: *I will not lend thee a penny.* PISTOL: *Why, then* ***the world's mine oyster****/Which I with sword will open.* MERRY WIVES OF WINDSOR II 2 □ ***The world remains*** *very much a young people****'s oyster****. How well they use it depends on the skill and judgement with which they open the shell.* G □ *I used to lie in bed, listening to the sirens of ships as they dropped down the London river. I knew* ***the world would be my oyster*** *while I was still a snotty-nosed* ((slang) = supercilious) *kid.* L □ (crime detectives on radio and television) *The rat is bound to be cornered in penthouse apartment, dockside dive* (= disreputable bar), *luxury yacht, Amsterdam night-club or airport lounge.* ***The world is their oyster****—how they get about!* RT □ is almost always used.

the world is one's parish one's interests and activities are very wide; one travels widely, is knowledgeable about many peoples and places □ (source) *I look upon all* ***the world*** *as* ***my parish****.* JOURNAL (J WESLEY 1703-91) □ *Their forbears protected dependants and servants and poor neighbours; they themselves were displaced and migrant, and* ***the world was their parish****.* AH

the world is so full of a number of things life is so interesting, so full of things to see and do □ (source) ***The world is so full of a number of things,****/I'm sure we should all be as happy as kings.* A CHILD'S GARDEN OF VERSES (R L STEVENSON 1850-94) □ *Indeed the rhapsodies of Ruskin, like 'The Princess' and 'The Ring and the Book', down to the notes and poems of Hopkins, and even Kipling, all share something of enthusiastic accumulation. If* ***the world is so full of a number of things****, they are all kept happily busy recording the fact.* L

a/the world of difference a very great difference, disparity (between X and Y) □ (advertisement) *When you buy it you'll see what* ***a world of difference*** *there is in a margarine made only from the best ingredients.* WI □ *There was* ***a world of difference*** *between these people and the couple in the loft; they were harder, more brutal, less absorbed in pursuits outside themselves.* HD

the (whole) world over everywhere; in any place in the world; all over the world □ *It would appear that the direction the world should take ought to depend, not on politicians, but on the co-operation of scientists* ***the world over****.* L □ *Wherever the young and impatient saunter down the street, the transistor rocking from their wrist, the American language envelops them.* ***The world over****, a Basic American is now the jargon of hope —or, to put it more dubiously, of zestful greed.* L

(think/consider) the world owes one a living (think that) one is entitled to be well supported, or provided for, either on account of one's merits or simply because one exists □ *So many people* ***think the world owes them a living*** *and they don't go and do anything about it.* OBS □ STANLEY (raging): *Just who the hell do you think you are? So* ***the world owes you a living****; is that it?* FFE □ *For the simple reason that we have no natural resources to speak of,* ***the world*** *doesn't* ***owe us a living****.* L □ (NONCE) *Winning the Bardic crown is a tremendous thrill. You get mistaken ideas about yourself, that you're a genius and that* ***Wales owes you a living****.* RT

(think etc) the world well lost (think that) the loss of many of life's advantages and rewards is either not regrettable, or is amply compensated for (by sth specified by the context) **V:** think, ⚠ count, consider. **A:** for love, for Christ; in such a cause, in each other's company □ (source) *All For Love or* ***The World Well Lost****.* (title of a play by J DRYDEN 1631-1700) □ *So many of his heroes and heroines find happiness as comrades bravely challenging society, or* ***considering the world well lost*** *by going into retreat in Labrador or France or Italy.* L

the world will/would be a poorer place/ the poorer the quality of life for all, or for an individual, will/would be diminished **A:** for his death; without the much-maligned do-gooders, without her kindly presence. **cl:** if we forget the old values, if we couldn't have a good laugh sometimes □ ***The the world will be a poorer place*** *if the younger musicians aren't given a proper hearing, perhaps on Radio 3.* L □ (obituary notices) *There were many variations on the theme that '****the world would be the poorer*** *for his passing', that 'his death has cast a gloom over a wide circle', or that 'he has left a gap which can never be filled'.* AH

world without end [A (NP)] (formal) eternally; for ever; incessantly, without respite; too long or too frequently □ *As it was in the beginning, is now, and ever shall be:* ***world without end****. Amen.* BOOK OF COMMON PRAYER □ *They're right to question at least the wisdom of their elders as intelligent young people always have and I hope,* ***world without end****, always will.* □ *In my job I get the occasional word of praise, some useful suggestions, and complaints* ***world without end****.* □ usu end position.

worldly wise [Comp (AdjP)] experienced and shrewd in worldly affairs, business, social behaviour, current trends, etc (in allusion to Mr Worldly Wise, a character in THE PILGRIM'S PROGRESS (J BUNYAN 1628-88)) **V:** ⚠ be, become, appear □ *I shut away the sense of outrage, my own sense of outrage as well as his, and brought out the* ***worldly wise****, official's argument.* NM □ (references to dirty jokes in comedians' scripts) *All comics do it. You get a big laugh because the ones that know the joke feel flattered at being told how* ***worldly wise*** *they are, and the rest of them laugh because the others do.* HD □ *Morton, for all his* ***worldly wisdom****, was as susceptible to flattery as the next man.* □ n compound worldly wisdom.

the worm turns a humble, timid or dominated person rebels, retaliates, asserts himself □ *The 70s will surely be the decade in which* ***the worm turned****. Through a whole network of agencies the 'little man' turned on those who oppress and abuse him, and answered back.* RT □ *Women were on the move. Boatloads of them emigrated: governessing* ***worms turned****; doves became hawks.* L

the worse for wear [Comp (AdjP)] worn or damaged (by use, misuse, age, temporary stress, etc) **V:** ⚠ be, seem, feel, look. **adv mod:** somewhat, a bit, a little, (not too) much, none, (not) any □ *Perhaps in five years people will have forgotten me, perhaps not. I'll be 46. I won't be too much* ***the worse for wear****. And I'll finally be able to live like everyone else.* OBS □ *Carefully we undid the door and the tiny animals scuttled into their new home. None appeared to have got wet, which relieved me, though one or two of them looked a bit* ***the worse for wear*** *after the journey.* BB □ *The book's out of print, but I have a copy somewhat* ***the worse for wear*** *I could lend you.*

worse luck (informal) which is a pity, a misfortune □ *We'll see you at Robin's party, I hope?' 'I'm on duty that night,* ***worse luck****.'* □ *I suppose that's why my old man would never hang himself,* ***worse luck****, because he never gets a look into his clock* ((slang) = a look on his face) *like this bloke* ((slang) = man) *had.* LLDR □ comment on sth previously mentioned by speaker or by another person; middle or end position.

worse than useless [Comp (AdjP)] positively harmful; a positive hindrance or drawback; absolutely no use, good or help at all **V:** ⚠ be, become make sth □ *Again, excavations if not properly conducted were* ***worse than useless*** *in that they involved the destruction of historic evidence.* SD □ *The road map he lent me, which I subsequently discovered had been published in*

1972, was ***worse than useless.***

worse things happen at sea (saying) our lot could be worse; worse things happen every day, to other people, in other places, etc □ *But the really flat ones* (phrases) *are a minority; in most the note is of a cheerful patience: 'grin and bear it', 'we're short o' nowt* (= of nothing) *we've got'; '**worse things 'appen** (= happen) **at sea**'.* UL

worship the ground sb walks/treads on be completely devoted to, or infatuated with, sb □ *I am not one of these mothers who* ***worship the ground*** *their sons* ***walk on*** *but John's got a lot more to him than you've ever given him credit for.* □ *And my daughter Janice—you made a big hit with her. Do you think that's too colloquial? I could say '**worships the ground** you **tread on**'.* PW

(well) worth doing etc [Comp (AdjP)] certain, or very likely, to repay the effort, time, sacrifice etc given; next entry (qv) **V:** ⚠ be, seem; make sth. **pres p:** doing, making, looking at □ *I had no intention of looking for Anna, but by the time I was passing Bond Street it really seemed that there was nothing else in the world that was* ***worth doing.*** UTN □ *Such detours are* ***well worth*** *making and can greatly reduce the soporific boredom of motorway driving.* SC □ *She was* ***worth*** *looking at. A tall, beautifully proportioned figure, with brown hair caught back by a ribbon.* TST

(well) worth it etc [Comp (AdjP)] certain, or very likely, to repay the effort, time etc, given; previous entry (qv) **V:** ⚠ be, seem; make sth **n:** a visit, a drive, a second showing; the trouble □ *I've cut smoking to a packet a week in order to pay the bill, but it's* ***worth it.*** OBS □ *The Surrealist Art Centre at 31 Brook Street is* ***well worth a visit.*** □ *As there would not have been the slightest question of getting them to agree to the proposal once you had driven it into their heads, it would hardly have been* ***worth the trouble.*** CON

(not) worth a row of beans [Comp (AdjP)] (informal) (not even) of slight value, importance, or significance **V:** ⚠ be, seem; make sth □ *I'm perfectly aware I haven't any influence on him that's* ***worth a row of beans.*** NM □ *Your assurances are**n't worth a row of beans**, never have been. What I want to see is results.*

worth one's salt [Comp (AdjP)] deserving what one earns; fulfilling one's function, or performing one's work, competently (a reference to a ration of salt included in forms of payment given to Roman soldiers) **V:** ⚠ be, seem; think sb. **n:** anybody; youngster, teacher, journalist, editor □ *These have ambition, as every man who is* ***worth his salt*** *should have.* MFM □ *She hoped, being quite humble inside, that they would feel she was* ***worth her salt.*** WDM □ (hitch-hiking) *As long as there is the possibility of keeping holiday funds for necessities like food and souvenir buying, no youngster* ***worth his salt*** *is going to squander money on travel.* ST □ *Any journalist* ***worth his salt*** *will naturally welcome the opportunity for a really good bit of investigative reporting.* L □ often modifies a preceding n.

worth a try [Comp (AdjP)] sufficiently likely to achieve a successful result to justify one's trying it; give it/sb a try[1] (qv); give sb/sth etc a trial (qv) **S:** plan, project, procedure; request; remedy. **V:** ⚠ be, seem, find sth □ HELEN (thinking patient reasonableness may be **worth a try**): *She simply said that she's going to church with me. I don't see why that calls for this incredible outburst.* LBA □ *It would be such good publicity if he agreed to speak. It seems* ***worth a try.***

worth one's/its weight in gold (to sb) [Comp (AdjP)] unusually valuable or useful (to sb) **V:** be, ⚠ seem; find sth □ *Hotel managers are ten a penny but a good cook is* ***worth his weight in gold.*** □ *Add to this that he was a born exhibitionist and we had the kind of person* ***worth his weight in gold to*** *a skilled biographer.* SC □ (reader's letter) *May I thank the BBC for the two words often seen in musical programmes in brackets ('First performance'). They are* ***worth their weight in gold*** *to the real music-lover.* RT □ *I ask you what sort of an inflated woman is that? She's got bosom, bosom and still more bosom. I bet every inch of her chest is* ***worth its weight in gold.*** TOH

worth while [Comp (AdjP)] worthy; having value in itself; sufficiently important, interesting, profitable etc to give a good return for time, effort, attention spent **V:** ⚠ be, become sth □ *In practice, however, to do one's duty is* ***worth while,*** *and it is possible to get real happiness out of trying to do it.* WI □ *'But since we are among friends,' he continued, conscious now that he had among his audience someone whom it might conceivably be* ***worth while*** *to impress.* EM □ *That's what made the* (illicit) *traffic really* ***worth while.*** DS □ (police recruitment advertisement) *You'll be well-paid for doing a* ***worthwhile*** *job.* OBS □ *It's* ***worth-while*** *noting that this year the negotiations for British entry were conducted by the Council of Ministers.* L □ sometimes spelt as one word, or hyphenated, even when used as Comp as in the last example; attrib use *a* ***worthwhile*** *job*; stress patterns it's ˌworth ˈwhile, a ˈworthwhile job. ⇨ ⚠ next entry.

worth sb's while [Comp (AdjP)] profitable, or interesting, to sb **S:** gamble, investment; examination, trail. **V:** ⚠ be; think sth, make sth. **A:** coming; to love me □ *He stayed so short a time it was hardly* ***worth his while*** *coming.* □ *The trouble is I am an old man. You do not think it* ***worth your while*** *to love me.* OBS □ *Gangs would approach an Export Express driver and make it substantially* ***worth his while*** *to leave his car unattended in a moment of carelessness.* HD □ *He wasn't convinced that attendance was* ***worth his while.*** ⇨ ⚠ previous entry.

worthy of the name deserving to be named, or defined, as sth (which is specified by context) **n:** nurse, doctor; training, education; entertainment, spectacle; religion □ *All theatre* ***worthy of the name*** *is a form of education, and deserves official encouragement for that reason alone.* NS □ *Most designers* ***worthy of the name*** *can be witty without too much tongue in cheek, producing clothes for a giggle that are clever as well.* SC □ *I realised that Sartre's work was a lifelong dialogue with Marx, and that the same could still be said of any French intellectual* ***worthy of the name.*** L □ *No taxpayer* ***worthy of the name*** *would have grudged Elkin and his guest their dinner in the Mother of Parliaments.* PP □ almost always modifies a preceding n.

would as soon do A (as B) (informal) would as willingly, or more willingly, do sth (as sth else) ▫ *Let Susan have my ticket since she's keen to see the show. I'm so tired* ***I'd as soon*** *stay at home anyway.* ▫ *I'll tell you this—I* ***would as soon*** *cook for people* ***as*** *make beds.* ▫ *'Let me ring for a taxi to take you home.' 'No thanks.* ***I'd sooner*** *walk, really I would.'* ▫ HELEN: ***Would*** *you* ***sooner*** *I stayed here with you?* JO: *No, thanks.* TOH ▫ variant would sooner do A (than B).

would you believe (it)(?) (informal) exclamatory comment expressing, or inviting, astonishment or dismay ▫ *What we didn't need was the heavens to open* (= a very heavy rain) *—and,* ***would you believe,*** *come straight through the roof.* TVT ▫ (preparing a film set) *Peter Graham Scott is harassed. 'They've knocked the skull off the skeleton,' he says. '****Would you believe it?*** *We've got to find another.'* RT ▫ (advertisement) *D.I.Y.* (= do it yourself) *double glazing?* ***Would you believe?*** *Crittall factory-made-to-measure panels can cost less than kits that leave you to do all the work yourself!* TVT ▫ stress pattern would you be'lieve (it)(?).

wouldn't be seen dead (in a ditch) with sb/in sth (informal) strongly dislike, despise sb/sth **A:** with him, with any of them; wearing one of her hats, carrying a shopping-bag; in such clothes, in his company, in a car that cost less than £5000 ▫ *'I* ***wouldn't be seen dead in*** *the clothes Wally wears,' he said.* TVT ▫ *Every pedlar finds customers ready to buy everything, from shawls the fans* ***wouldn't be seen dead in*** *back home, to keyrings of footballers passing balls.* OBS ▫ *And I think they regard it* ('The Red Flag') *as some deviationist song and tune that they* ***would not be seen dead with.*** L ▫ *'Most people favour one or the other party.' 'Well I* ***wouldn't be seen dead in a ditch with*** *either of them.'* ▫ *'As for doing commercial television adverts,' Patrick concludes, 'I should infinitely prefer to* ***be seen dead in a ditch.'*** RT ⇨ ⚠ die in a ditch.

wouldn't know/recognize sth if one saw one (informal) not even know what a particular object, animal etc is; know nothing about an activity, skill, trade etc indicated by a specific object etc ▫ *He hoped Cosmo would not glance in that direction or, if he did so, that he might be one of those untroubled by dental caries, who* ***would not recognize*** *a drill* ***if he saw one.*** ▫ *I* ***wouldn't know*** *a nasturtium* ***if I saw one.*** ▫ *Fisheries experts! They* ***wouldn't know*** *a sole* ***if they saw one,*** *unless it was fried and lying on a plate.*

(flee from) the wrath to come (formal) (try to escape from) the threat of anger, punishment, revenge or persecution foreseen as threatening one ▫ (source) *O generation of vipers, who hath warned you to* ***flee from the wrath to come?*** MATTHEW III 7 ▫ (New Zealand) *We don't realise here that there are a fair number of American expatriates,* ***fleeing from the wrath to come.*** OBS ▫ *The Commandant of the Loyal Citizens of Ulster can be depended upon to warn of* ***the wrath to come.*** *He* knows *the Lord supports his cause.* ST

wreak havoc [V + O pass] cause disruption or destruction **A:** in the ranks; with their prospects; among the crops ▫ *Just when the face of London was being changed by Nash and those who followed him, Cubitt and Peto and Ladbroke, the railways came and* ***wrought*** *even greater* ***havoc.*** L ▫ *'It's genuine quick bowlers that win matches, and at the moment England just don't have one.' The moment we do, presumably, we shall once more be in a position to* ***wreak havoc*** *among the Australian ranks.* RT ▫ *His business agility and restlessness* ***wreak havoc*** *in his personal life.* TVT ▫ *As in his great days, Nielsen's lightning services* ***wreaked havoc*** *with his opponents's leads.* DM ▫ past tense form is wrought, but cf last example.

wring one's hands [V + O] squeeze and twist one's hands together as a sign of anxiety, distress or despair ▫ *The congratulations drove Sir Derek Walker-Smith, one of the leading Conservative opponents of* (Common Market) *entry, to quote Sir Robert Walpole: 'They are ringing their bells now: soon they will be* ***wringing their hands.'*** L ▫ *Stop* ***wringing hands*** *and bandying insults. Men do not, alas, become wiser by being told they are stupid.* OBS ▫ *Congress heard that the Carter staff was doing an exhaustive study on reforming welfare, but the leaders in Congress and the leaders of Mr Carter's own party started to* ***wring their hands*** *and shout: 'Promises, promises! Studies, studies! But where are the bills?'* L

wring sb's neck [V + O pass] strangle, throttle, sb (a reference to the usual method of killing hens) ▫ *'Of course he has to come in to our office.' 'To see you, no doubt. If he ever makes a pass at you, I'll* ***wring his neck.'*** AITC ▫ *Daniel could have* ***wrung*** *both* ***their necks.*** ▫ *He was certain the man had marked him down, was out to* ***wring his neck*** *before pitching the dead chicken that remained over the heads of the crowd.* LLDR ▫ usu expression of anger or exasperation, or a form of threat; often with *will/would/could.*

writ large/small in enlarged/reduced form; made more/less obvious, conspicuous ▫ (source) *New Presbyter is but old Priest* ***writ large.*** ON THE NEW FORCERS OF CONSCIENCE UNDER THE LONG PARLIAMENT (J MILTON 1608-74) ▫ *As I saw it, a chase for power had probably brought them together.* They *might use other other words for it, words* ***writ large*** *in flowering script.* PP ▫ *Glasgow has cities' problems* ***writ large.*** NS ▫ *Disappointment was* ***writ large*** *on the faces of the British team.* G ▫ *They are the lessons of the concentration camps* ***writ small;*** *and it is typical of Lewin's integrity that we are never allowed to forget either that black prisoners were worse off than he is.* ST ▫ often modifies a preceding n, as shown.

the writing (is) on the wall there are unmistakeable signs that warn of failure, disaster, defeat (in allusion to DANIEL V) ▫ *Miss Todd's view* (is) *that no British-sponsored political solution is possible, on just terms. As with Ulster, the question is whether* ***the writing on the wall*** *can be read in time.* OBS ▫ *I destroyed the only source of income my family had. Though they survived the initial disaster,* ***the writing was on the wall.*** ST ▫ *The 'Daily Sketch's' death sentence all too starkly underlines* ***the writing*** *that*

has been on the *Fleet Street* ***wall****, for all to see, since 1966.* NS □ (young players) When their optimism and defensive shortcomings were exposed ***the writing was on the wall****.* G

a wrong 'un [Comp (NP)] (dated slang) a dishonest, or criminal, person; an unreliable, or untrainable, domestic or sporting animal; a counterfeit coin, or note, or other false article **V:** ⚠ be, look; find sb/sth to be □ *He sent me some business without knowing me from Adam; I might have been a complete crook for all he knew. If I'd been* ***a wrong 'un*** *where would he have been?* PW □ *I sometimes think the only thing to do with my car is to push it over a cliff. It's been* ***a wrong 'un*** *from the start.* □ 'un = 'one'; also pl wrong 'uns.

the wrong way round [A (NP)] in the wrong direction; with the correct sequence or relation of parts, items, priorities etc reversed **V:** be; go, point, face; place, put, sth; get it, tell it □ *'Anna loves you,' I said. 'Yes, of course,' said Hugo. 'She's as crazy about me as I am about Sadie. But I thought you were in on all this, Jake?' 'I was in on it,' I said. 'I got it all* ***the wrong way round****, that's all!'* UTN □ *Most Britons over 30 were taught foreign languages* ***the wrong way round****: first to read them, then to write them, third to speak and fourth to hear and understand.* OBS □ *Now all the journalists want to become tycoons. I think it is* ***the wrong way round****.* L

X

x marks the spot (catchphrase) a cross indicates the exact location (from, originally, an explanatory caption to a newspaper photograph or drawing of 'the scene of the crime', in which a cross showed the position of the victim's body, etc) □ (postcard message) *Mother's house is white blob half hidden by large tree in top right-hand corner — but* ***x marks*** *exact* ***spot****.* □ *We managed to get this photo of Philip's boat moving out ahead of the leader as they both rounded the lighthouse.* ***X marks the spot****!* □ now used facetiously on holiday postcards or snapshots with reference to a cross indicating one's hotel bedroom, a favourite meeting-place, etc.

Y

(from) the year dot (informal) (from) a starting point far back in the past; (at) some distant time in the future □ *You know the fascination now of old and yellowed press cuttings* ***from the year dot****. For your great grand-children,* ***the year dot*** *is now.* ST □ (fuel shortage) *. . . trying to get people to realise that this isn't something that's going to happen in* ***the year dot*** *but within the lifetime of the youngest of us.* SC □ PRINCESS ANNE: *Any wedding list, let's face it, is going to have omissions. We've tried very hard to think of people who've helped us — especially from my point of view —* ***from the year dot*** *onwards.* L

the Yellow Peril fear (first raised, esp in Germany and North America, in the 1890s and whipped up from time to time since then) that the Chinese and/or Japanese nations will overrun the world □ *We were scornful of messmates who held that if war in the Far East did come it would not be between European Nations but between Whites and Yellows: had not the German Emperor spoken of* ***the Yellow Peril****? 'Nonsense!' we scoffed.* BM □ *In Lyndon Johnson's final days in the White House his own Secretary of State publicly defended the Vietnam War by evoking the spectre of '****the Yellow Peril****'.* NS □ *The other myth that's now quite abandoned is that of the Chinese as* ***a 'yellow peril'*** *wanting to flood through Asia with invading hordes.* L

the yellow press newspapers, journalism, specializing in sensational items of news, or in presenting any items as sensationally as possible □ (news coverage of an air crash) *The gratuitous film reports of the Hong Kong and French disasters were in the worst traditions of* ***the yellow press****.* L

yes and no one cannot agree, consent, report success etc in every respect □ *'Would you say Andrew was a good teacher?' '****Yes and no****. He gets marvellous results from his pupils in exams, but few of them seem to be able to think for themselves once they have left school.'* □ *'Well?' said the Prime Minister. '****Yes and no****,' was Parkinson's answer. 'I've had to promise to fit the place up as a regular scientific establishment.'* TBC □ non-rev.

yet awhile (not) until a little/some time later □ *Oh, someone'll be going our way to drop us off, sure to. Don't want to start making tracks (=* leaving) ***yet awhile****, though, do we?* TGLY

you ain't seen nothing yet (catchphrase) there is much better/worse to follow □ *It's really true — as Jolson would say: '****You ain't seen nothing yet****.' Prepare for Hughie Green as you've never seen.* TVT □ *'Is this the kind of food they give you here?' 'Boy,* ***you ain't seen nothin' yet****. This is high class for here, this is.'* □ *'Conditions aren't as bad as they expected. Let them hang on —* ***they haven't seen anything yet****.'* □ usu second person, but can be third person, as in last example; ain't here = 'haven't'.

you (can) bet your (sweet) life (that) [Disj] (informal) I confirm to you (that); it is certain (that); I'll/you bet (that) (qv) □ *All my life I worked in the open air and* ***you bet your life*** *I'm going to die there — come on, Mr Segal, push me into the garden.* HSG □ *'Will I ever learn to speak French well?' '****You can bet your sweet life*** *you will, and very soon, too.'* □ *If you* *do that again, out you go—**you can bet your sweet life on** that.* □ front or end position; variant you (can) bet your sweet life on sth. ⇨ ⚠ I'll bet.

you can keep sth/sb (informal) I don't like, I have a poor opinion of, sth/sb **O:** it, him; city life, foreign cuisine, Italian opera □ *'**You can keep** the city life,' says Ern Gray's partner and girlfriend, Judy Bateson, a physiotherapist from Liverpool who originally came to Wales to convalesce after a car accident.* TVT □ *Why should it be considered such a virtue to be 'good with children'? **You can keep** children as far as I'm concerned.* □ abrupt dismissed of sth or sb.

you can prove anything with/by statistics/figures (catchphrase) it is possible to use statistical, numerical, information to support any argument, esp if a set of figures is quoted without balancing them against another relevant set or against other information □ (source) *A witty statesman said, **you might prove anything by figures.*** CHARTISM (T CARLYLE 1795-1881) □ *When the psychologist attempts to employ statistical methods he encounters the usual obscurantist notion that **you can prove anything with statistics.*** SNP □ *Don't quote that sort of stuff at me. We all know **you can use figures to prove anything**, and they need to be construed in the context of the individual programmes.* T □ variants you can use statistics/figures to prove anything, statistics/figures can (be made to) prove anything.

you can say that again (informal) you are undeniably correct; that is absolutely true; you said it (qv); you're telling me! (qv) **S:** you, he, she, they □ MARY: *I'm worried about Dad, Andy. He's gone to bits. Andy, it's serious!* ANDY: ***You can say that again**!* OBS □ *'Day and night I roamed Los Angeles gathering data. I became a data addict.' **He can say that again** (and does, incidentally).* L □ *The local* (ie man) *tugs on his cap* (and says) *'Mind you, you'd never know it was a brewery.' **He can say that again.** It's hard to find the brewery down the meandering country lane.* RT □ used to express emphatic, and often ironic, agreement; stress pattern you can say 'that again.

you can/can't take sb/sth anywhere (catchphrase) a child, animal, dependant etc can/can't be trusted to behave well, be found acceptable, anywhere □ *If a dog has been properly trained **you can take** him **anywhere.*** □ *When our second daughter was three years old she was so badly behaved **you couldn't take** her **anywhere.*** □ (advertisement for whisky) ***You can take** a White Horse **anywhere.*** OBS □ ***You couldn't take** Ursula **anywhere**, but it was no fun going without her.* L

you can't win (catchphrase) whatever one chooses to do has an unhappy conclusion, does not please or satisfy □ *Love is in the mind, in the past, round the corner, slipping through the fingers. **You can't win.*** NS □ *She would ladle fresh supplies* (of food) *on to his pile so that he eventually refused any more. 'Wassamatta* (= what's the matter) *you don't like my food no more?' This is what is known as the '**Can't Win**' situation wherein whatever the child does, the mother has left herself an opening to feel aggrieved.* TVT

you could have fooled me (informal) I wouldn't have thought so (and still don't, or am still not sure) □ *'What a nice hair-do you've had.' 'Oh don't pretend you don't know it's a wig.' 'No! Well, **you could have fooled me.**'* □ *'A triumph of naturalism and human values over aesthetic pretensions,' one reviewer described his work. **You could have fooled me.*** □ stress pattern you could have ˌfooled 'me.

you could say (that) it is fairly true or correct (that); it is a possible opinion (that) □ ***You could say** I have a fair amount of responsibility—if neglected, a machine could grind to a halt.* ST □ *Neil has been slimming. **You could say** he was blackmailed into it.* RT □ ***You could say that** this triangle is the geometric hub of the West Midlands, maybe of England too. A distribution corridor for anything on wheels and much else beside.* G □ stress pattern you 'could say (that).

you don't mean to tell me/say (that)? can it really be true that? **S:** you, he, she, they □ *'You've heard of—of Jehovah's Witnesses?' Her head swivelled round. She was trying to keep her startled eyes on his. '**You don't mean to say** you're one of them?'* HD □ HELEN: ***You don't mean to tell me** he's gone?* JO: *Now that you've been rude to my friend.* HELEN: *What an arty little freak!* TOH □ ***He doesn't mean to tell us**, I hope, that Mike's been cheating him?* □ expresses surprised disbelief; neg and/or interrog; usu second person; variant do you mean to tell me/say (that)?

you don't say (so)! (catchphrase) can that be true! I'm surprised to hear that! □ (advice from an Income Tax consultant) *'Do you claim for the room you work in, for instance?' 'Good Lord, no. Could I?' 'Yes, and for your stationery and typing and for a proportion of your telephone calls—' '**You don't say so!**'* PW □ *'I've a touch of indigestion.' 'Comes from eating too much.' '**You don't say!**'* □ often genuinely astonished response to information but sometimes ironic as in last example; stress pattern you don't 'say (so)!

you have (got) to be/must be joking/kidding (informal) you must be, can only be, joking □ *'Turn the volume down?' said one disco manager. '**You have to be joking.** The kids want it loud enough to go right through them, and if we lowered the level, they'd go somewhere else tomorrow night.'* OBS □ *He decides to move from Manhattan to Brooklyn in order to come to grips with 'real life and the significant issues of our time'. '**You've got to be kidding,**' says his wife.* L □ *Then one of the strangers stepped forward: 'You're under arrest.' The charge was armed robbery of the Mercury Savings and Loan Association in nearby Buena Park. De Palma laughed shakily: '**You must be kidding.**'* OBS □ joking esp GB, kidding esp US; said to or about sb, almost always to express disbelief or scepticism.

you know¹ you know or understand very well; you are a person I don't need to tell, explain, things to □ *I've never really noticed anybody. Not noticed what kind of person he was: just whether he was a good businessman, a sound employee, or a serious rival—**you know.*** HD □ *'What sort of girl is she?' 'Well, **you know**, old man. The sort of girl one runs into in London.'* TGLY □ *I'm hopeless at explaining myself, **you***

***know**, so why didn't you speak up for me?* □ often preceded by short pause; fall-rise tone on know.

you know² I am informing, or reminding, you □ *'**You know** I didn't ask you to the party, Wicks,' said Lydia, 'but you're always welcome.'* WDM □ *You'll never catch that train. It's half past three now, **you know**.* □ *'That's good jam.' 'Well, my wife makes her own **you know**.'* □ usu front or end position; low tones on you and know.

you know³ I am giving you my opinion, or advice □ ***You know**, Elsie, it's a most frightful thing to say, but I think Daddo is getting old.* RM □ *She ought to have dancing lessons, **you know**, she's crazy about dancing.* DC □ usu front or end position; low tones on you and know.

you know⁴ I am correcting, or contradicting, you □ *'Bill's a good husband.' 'He isn't, **you know**.'* □ *If you don't give it to me, I'll take it from you.' 'You won't, **you know**. But try if you like.'* □ usu end position; mid tone on you, fall-rise tone on know.

you know what etc (informed) sth etc that is known by the speakers but is not named for any of a variety of reasons, eg prudery, a wish to keep sth secret, a fear of being overheard, etc **pron/adv:** what, ⚠ where, who □ *'Shall I go on about **you know what**?' Chadwick said to Dusty. 'Listen,' said Dusty, 'this bloke* ((slang) = man) *was at College with Goldilocks. Make with the dirt* (= provide the information).*'* TT □ *'Good luck with your plans,' she finished off the letter, 'and don't let **you know who** bully you.'*

you know what you can do (with it/sth) (informal)I don't want sth, will have nothing to do with it, refuse to accept it, etc; next entry (qv) **S:** you, they; Jane, Mr Ashton. **o:** it, that; your apology, your lawyer's letter; his £5, their free gifts □ *He has been taken into their confidence, and cannot decently tell them that **they know what they can do with** their typescript.* AH □ *'Another 75p a week is all I can offer.' 'I suppose **you know what you can do with** that.'* □ *I'll **tell** her **what** she **can do with** her rules if she quotes them at me any more.* □ euphemism, abruptly and discourteously rejecting a suggestion; variant tell sb what he can do with sth.

you know where you can put sth (informal) I am not interested in, refuse to accept, sth; previous entry (qv) **S:** you, she, he, they; Jack; the County Council **O:** it; that idea, Aunt Mary's plans □ ***You know where you can put** that idea. I've never heard anything so stupid in my life* □ *I'm not interested in Jack's sales report —it's rubbish. **He knows where he can put** it.* □ *I don't care if your Aunt Mary wants to go to Spain this summer. If she doesn't stop interfering, I'll **tell** her **where** she **can put** her ideas.* □ euphemism, abruptly and discourteously rejecting a suggestion; variant tell sb where he can put sth.

you and your meetings etc (informal) teasing, impatient, or contemptuous remark about sth that sb often does, says, suggests etc **pron:** you, her, him, them. **adj:** your, ⚠ her, his, their. **n:** meetings, fishing, football; friendships, love; dog □ *Oh, **you and your** committee **meetings**! I think that's all you live for!* □ (to Peter who has given his food to a tramp) *Ah, get out of it, **you and your** high and bloody mighty **gestures**. I work for my living. Fool!* TK □ *'Uncle Fred has to take care of his health now.' '**Him and his health**! He'll probably outlive the lot of us.'* □ usu second person.

you name it (they have it etc) every person, thing, place, you care to name or think of (we have met, enjoyed, visited etc) **cl:** they have it, he's done it, we've seen it □ *In the New Philharmonia Chorus we get around — Parma, Florence, Lisbon, Coventry, Gothenburg, Paris, Edinburgh, **you name it**; one gets to be quite a connoisseur of audiences.* RT □ *Fund-raising is as much a part of American life as baseball; for museums, public television, deprived children—**you name it, a group is supporting it**.* NS □ (He) *has sounded off about everything on television and in papers and magazines. '**You name it**,' he actually says '**I've written it**.'* TVT □ *Broken bones, torn muscles, displaced vertebrae, multiple bruises—**you name it and these men get it**.* TVT

you/we only live once (saying) let people enjoy themselves while they can; life is short so why should people spend time doing what they dislike when they could be enjoying themselves □ *Forget your diet and have another chocolate. **You only live once**, and you can starve yourself tomorrow.* □ *The barmaid looked at him and said: 'Well, **we only live once**, don't we? What I say is, why not have a good time while we can.'* PE □ *'**We live only once**,' said Aznavour. 'We are going to have plenty of time to rest so why rehearse?'* TVT □ S usu you.

you and the other (ninety-)nine (catchphrase) I don't believe you can; you and who else? (qv); you and whose army? (qv) □ *'I would build a better wall myself.' 'I daresay you could, **you and the other nine**.'* □ *'I'm gonna thump* (= going to hit) *you.' '**Where's the other ninety-nine**?'* □ variant where are the other (ninety-) nine? □ derisive reply to a boast or threat.

you pays your money and (you) takes your choice (catchphrase) you choose whatever alternative course, explanation etc you like (from a cockney stallholder's cry to prospective customers) □ *Could Blake and Philby be the greatest triple agents of all time? Could Blake really have escaped from the Scrubs without an official blind eye? **You pays your money and takes your choice**.* OBS □ *For the city is a dressing-up box, a dime store of identities. **You pays your money and you takes your choice**.* L □ *Today's set-to in the Commons on housing, land prices and the environment was once again a matter of '**you pays your money and you takes your choice**.'* T

you said it (informal) I agree wholeheartedly; you are absolutely right; you can say that again (qv); you're telling me! (qv) □ GEOF: *She likes to make an effect.* JO: *Like me?* GEOF: ***You said it**.* TOH □ ALEX: *Isn't she fat?* PETER: ***You said it**. I'm sure one day she'll just float away.* DPM □ expresses emphatic agreement; stress pattern you 'said it.

you scratch my back and I'll scratch yours (informal) you help me, bring me business, get me into office, etc and I'll do the same for you □ *These 'Americans of a certain class' stick together. For the marrieds, it's **you scratch my back, I'll scratch yours**.* NS □ *Our* *nerve has failed and we are implicitly saying to the reader: 'Don't hit me and I won't hit you', or '**you scratch my back and I'll scratch yours**'.* L □ often suggests unfair arrangements for mutual help between privileged persons.

you what! (informal) an exclamation of disbelief, shock, anger etc about sth reported to one □ JO: *My baby may be black.* HELEN: ***You what**, love?* JO: *My baby will be black.* TOH □ *'Joe was bulldozing down the orchard wall, as I was passing.' '**He was what!**—Oh my God!'* □ *'Where did you get that doll?' 'I swapped the kitten for her.' '**You what!**'* □ usu second person; variants he was (doing) what! you did what!

you and who else? (catchphrase) you can't, are not able to—not without help anyway; you and the other (ninety-)nine (qv); next entry (qv) **pron:** you, her, him, them □ *'Come on, I'll race you.' 'You blinkin'* ((slang) = (taboo) bloody) *won't mate.' 'I blinkin' well will.' '**You an'**(= and) **who else?**'* TT □ *'Pete won't let you go. He'd tie you up first.' 'Oh yes, **him and who else?**'* □ usu second person; derisive reply to boast or threat.

you and whose army? (informal) you can't, are not able to—not without help anyway; you and the other (ninety-)nine (qv); previous entry (qv) □ *'If you leave the bathroom untidy again, I'll* make *you clear it up.' 'Oh yes? **You and whose army?**'* □ *'If you won't stop Mother making a fool of herself, I will.' '**You and whose army?**'* □ usu second person; derisive reply to a boast or threat.

you're the boss (informal) you decide; I am prepared to do as you say **pron:** you, he, she □ JO: *I'll meet you down by that ladies' hairdressing place.* BOY: *Okay, **you're the boss**.* TOH □ *'I think we should drive straight home.' 'Carry on then, **you're the boss**.'* □ ironic, often good-humoured, acknowledgement that sb is in charge; stress pattern ˌyou're the ˈboss; usu second person.

you're a long time dead (saying) life is short, so enjoy yourself, make yourself useful, happy, experience all you can, etc while you have the chance □ DAVID: *Look, just leave me alone. I don't think we want any today.* SAM: *Oh, cheer up, Davey, **you're a long time dead**.* HSG

you're only young once (saying) let young people have what freedom and fun they can get, because they'll have enough work and worry later □ *It is a selfishness which the parents condone and support; there is all the rest of life to come and you cannot do much about that; you must let them ''ave* (= have) *a good time while they can'; after all, '**yer**(*= you are) ***only young once**'.* UL □ MR BUTCHER *So we'll all forget for a few hours and enjoy ourselves. A few drinks? **You're only young once**?* DPM

you're telling me! (informal) I already know, and emphatically agree with what you say; you can say that again (qv); you said it (qv) □ *'By God it's cold!' '**You're telling me!**'* □ *'How can I help worrying* (about the baby). *If she just wouldn't cry so much it wouldn't be so bad.' '**You're telling me**,' Joe said bitterly.* AITC □ stress pattern you're ˌtelling ˈme.

you're welcome (esp US informal) it's a pleasure; it's no trouble at all; don't mention it (qv) □ *'Cheerio, then and thanks for the lift.' '**You're welcome**.'* □ *'You've been most helpful.' '**You're welcome**. That's what we're here for.'* □ reply after being thanked for a service, information etc given.

you've said it all (informal) you've summed up the situation pefectly □ *'A decision might have to be taken within a matter of weeks, because the opportunity suddenly recurred.' 'Jack, **you've said it all**.'* □ emphatic form of agreement.

a young hopeful a boy or girl who has hopes for the future, or for whom hopes are felt □ *That was a long time ago. Jack's a married man with four **young hopefuls** now.* □ *Eliot's identification of London office-workers with the occupants of Dante's hell, must have persuaded many **a young hopeful** that it would be not merely tiring but downright uncultured to get a job of work.* L

the young idea young people, esp schoolboys or schoolgirls and students □ (source) *Delightful task! to rear the tender thought,/To teach **the young idea** how to shoot.* THE SEASONS (J THOMSON 1700-48) □ (archaeological excavation) *Alcock and I took it in turns to instruct **the younger idea**. And to do it justice, **the young idea** took the somewhat strenuous ordeal exceedingly well.* SD □ *We were a tame lot, really—ours not to question why. **The young idea** is a little more sure of itself today.*

young and old [n + n rev] (people) of all ages □ *Letters of complaint poured into 'The Sunday Times' by the hundreds. **Young and old**, town and country, home and abroad were in a state of fury.* ST □ *I managed to cover eight cities and met enough Germans, **young and old**, to bring my opinions up to date a bit.* L

your best friend won't tell you (catchphrase) even friends don't like to inform you (of an embarrassing thing about yourself) (from a former caption for 'Lifebuoy' soap, which was advertised as a safeguard against BO = body odour) □ *Now **your best friends won't** have to **tell you**. Surgeons in Denmark have come to the rescue of people who have serious problems with underarm sweating.* ST □ (NONCE) *Whatever subjects are or are not taboo, that you are getting a bit thin on top or have developed a bald spot is something that even **your best friends** delight to **tell you**.* SC

your guess is as good as mine (catchphrase) don't ask me because I don't know the answer either (the implication often being that perhaps nobody does) □ *'Do you believe they intend war eventually?' the Chief asked. '**Your guess is as good as mine**.'* OMIH □ DAVID (to his father): *I wish I really knew what you really wanted of me.* SAM (shrugs): *I wish you knew what you wanted of yourself. Anyway, **your guess is as good as mine**.* HSG □ usu second person, though meaning may be 'any person's guess is as good as another's'.

your humble servant (dated) I; me; myself; a way of acknowledging an order or request from a superior; an expression which precedes the signature of a letter on petition from an inferior to a superior □ *'And do you do all this extra work for the same salary?' 'They expected me to, but that's where **your humble servant** dug her toes in.'* □ usu facetious as in example.

your need is greater than mine (catchphrase) you may, or must, have sth because you need it more than I do **adj** [1]: your, my, his; Jack's. **adj** [2]: mine, yours, hers; Jane's □ (source —said on giving his water-bottle to a dying soldier on the battle-field at Zutphen, 1586) ***Thy necessity is*** *yet* ***greater than mine***. SIR PHILIP SIDNEY 1554-86 □ *We all enjoyed the story. When it was done, I offered Raseh the ten dollars. He refused it. He did not say that* ***my need was greater than his****, because that would have been manifestly untrue.* NDN □ *Carter said, 'I drank most of it in the plane. There's only one glass left in the flask.' 'Obviously our friend here must have it,' Mr MacDougall said. '****His need is greater than ours****.'* OMIH

yours to command (formal) ready to obey your orders, to do what you want **adj:** yours, hers, his, theirs □ CLIVE: *What is your wish, Madam? I am* ***yours to command****.* LOUISE: *I've told you already, my little Cossack. Be happy.* FFE □ *If that is what the readers want, I am* ***theirs to command****; and after all who is fool enough to kill off a golden goose?* G □ usu second person; often facetious.

yours truly (informal) I, me, myself (from the use of 'yours truly' before putting one's signature to a letter) □ DIXON: *Y'know* (= you know)*, it's a funny thing but even the best of us can fall by the wayside and* ***yours truly*** *is no exception.* OBS □ PRINCESS ANNE: *Pressmen were all over the place, just trying to get a picture of* ***yours truly*** *in tears.* BBCTV □ *And guess who's taking the sixth form party to the Motor Show? That's right. Little old* ***yours*** *bloody* ***truly****.* TGLY

Z

the zero option a proposal made by President Reagan's administration on 19 November 1981 that, in return for the removal of certain Soviet medium-range missiles aimed at European targets, the US and its allies would cancel their 1979 agreement to install new types of American missiles in various European countries □ ***The zero option*** *calls on the Soviet Union to remove all its SS20 missiles aimed at Europe. In return NATO would not deploy new Cruise and Pershing II missiles.* BBCR □ *The official* (West German) *line is that the missiles will go in unless Reagan first attains his negotiating target of* ***the 'Zero Option'****, the elimination of the Soviet SS20 missiles in return for abandoning the Nato programme.* ST

Index of headphrases

This index lists the verbs, adverbs, nouns, pronouns, adjectives and prepositions which appear in the headphrases in this volume of the dictionary, whether as part of an entirely fixed expression (eg *feet* in *find one's feet*), or as an optional part of an expression which is otherwise fixed (eg *own* in *on sb's/one's (own) head be it*), or as alternative elements in an expression (e g *finish, play-off* in *a sudden death finish/play-off*). Also listed are the less fixed, but still 'restricted', elements of an expression which can be substituted at one specific point in the headphrase. These are listed in the body of the entry (after **S:**, **n:**, **V:**, etc) beginning with the word given in the headphrase. For example, below the headphrase *a close etc thing* is found the list **adj:** *close*, ⚠ *close-run, near*. Each adjective appears in the index, with both the alternative form of the idiom and the form given in the main text being shown where appropriate.

Where two classes of expressions are concerned, not all the restricted alternative elements of a headphrase are indexed. The classes [possess] and [V + Comp] regularly show limited sets of collocating verbs (➪ Introduction, 3.1, 3.2). For example, the occurrence of *have (got), get, give sb, there be* in [possess] entries, and *be, become, get, make sb/sth* in [V + Comp] entries, is so frequent that, in order to avoid confusing the user with a dauntingly long index, these commonly occurring verbs are not indexed. All such idioms can, of course, be found via other significant words which are indexed.

The index will help the user find an entry by means of any of the significant words of the idiomatic expression when he is unsure of the precise form given in the dictionary.

The arrangement of the index is as follows:

1 Each index word (printed in **bold** type) is listed alphabetically and followed by the headphrase(s) (printed in light type) in the form in which it appears in this dictionary, a tilde (~) being used for the indexed word:

The headphrases themselves are arranged in the order in which they appear in the dictionary and the user will be able to find the main entries by following the alphabetical order of the first important word in the expression (e g *gentleman's* in *a gentleman's agreement*). ➪ Introduction, 2.

2 Only words that appear in the headphrase are indexed. Where an idiom as a whole collocates regularly with a limited set of verbs, for example, the collocates are listed in the entry but are not indexed. For example, in the entry *child's play* the list **V:** ⚠ *be, seem, appear* is given. This tells the user that the idiom is used with one of the three verbs shown. However, none of the verbs is indexed because none is an essential part of the idiom itself. The expression is listed in the main text under *child's* and in the index under *play*.

3 Although certain words can function as different parts of speech (e g *bear* can be a verb or a noun), there has been no attempt to show such differences in the index. Foreign users especially will be more interested in the form of a word than in its function when they are trying to find a particular idiom.

A

B

C

index of headphrases

D

E

F

G

H

J

M

N

O

P

Q

R

S

T

U

V

W

Z

Index of variant and derived forms

This index covers both the structural variants of headphrases and the noun, adjective, and adverb compounds derived from headphrases recorded in the main part of the Dictionary. For a full treatment of these variants and derivatives ⇨ Introduction, 8.

Each variant and derived compound is listed alphabetically and is followed by the headphrase(s) of the entry (or entries) in which it appears in the main text:

(do) Trojan work work like a Trojan
a pickpocket pick sb's pocket

Hyphenation or lack of it tends to be a matter of printing convention or individual usage. Noun and adjective compounds may be printed as one word, or as two (or more) words with or without a hyphen (or hyphens). The entries in this Dictionary and in this index generally show the most accepted form in British usage, but variations are recorded where appropriate, eg *a show-stopper/showstopper*.

can't/can hardly hear oneself speak can't hear oneself think
capitalism etc has its unacceptable face the unacceptable face of capitalism etc
change for the better/worse a change for the better/worse
the changing/changed face of sth change the face of sth
characterized, typified etc by nothing if not by sth nothing if not sth
a Cheshire-cat grin/smile grin like a Cheshire cat
chock(-)full (of/with sb/sth) chock-a-block (full) (with sb/sth)
a choice of (two) evils the lesser of two evils
clean-handed have clean hands
clear-headed have a clear head[1,2]
a clock-watcher watch the clock
clock-watching watch the clock
close-run run sb/sth close
coal-black (as) black as coal
coat-trailing trail one's coat
a coffin nail a nail in sb's/sth's coffin
come rain or shine come rain, come shine
come storm or shine come rain, come shine
come sun or shower come rain, come shine
(have sth) coming out of one's ears eat/drink (sth) till/until it comes out of one's ears
a confidence trickster/man a con(fidence) trick
the confirmation of one's worst fears confirm one's worst fears
a conman a con(fidence) trick
conspicuously absent conspicuous/distinguished by one's/its absence
corner-cutting cut corners
(a) counting of heads count heads
crystal-clear (as) clear as crystal
cut more ways than one cut both/two ways
cut several ways cut both/two ways
DV God willing
the dark continent darkest Africa
one's darkest hour the darkest hour is that/comes before the dawn
the day/time is approaching when the day/time is not (so) far off/distant when
daybreak dawn/day breaks
dead-certain/-sure dead certain/sure (of/about sth)
dead on two o'clock etc dead on time
a deadbeat dead beat
dear to the soul of sb dear to sb's heart
a death agony one's death agony/throes
the death throes one's death agony/throes
decision-taking take a decision
a declaration of interest declare an/one's interest
die in one's boots die in harness
dirty deeds dirty work
display the wisdom of Solomon (as) wise as Solomon
a disturbance of the peace disturb/keep the peace
do sb all the good in the world do sb a power/world of good
do as/what sb says/tells one do as/what one is told
do the best one can do/try one's best
do sb's bidding at sb's bidding
a do-gooder do good
do-gooding do good
do sb/sth the injustice do sb/sth justice
do x months/years do time etc
do one's rounds do/go the rounds
do sth too often etc for one's own good have too much money etc for one's own good
do sth with one's hands tied tie sb's hands
do you mean to tell me/say (that)? you don't mean to tell me/say (that)?
dog does not eat dog dog eat dog
Don Juanism a Don Juan
don't cross your bridges before/until you come to them cross one's bridges when one comes to them
a double-dyed reactionary etc a dyed-in-the-wool reactionary etc
a drawer of morals draw/point a moral
the dreaded moment dread the moment (when)
drink a bitter cup drink/drain the cup of sorrow etc
dry-as-dust (as) dry as dust
(in) every nook and cranny nooks and crannies
every virtue/quality has its vice/defect have the vices/defects of one's virtues/qualities
eye-catching catch sb's eye
face downward(s)/upward(s) face down/up
face the fact that face (the) facts
one's face is red have a red face
face-lifting have a face-lift
face-saving lose/save face
a faint-heart faint heart ne'er/never won fair lady
fair shares (for all) get etc a/one's fair share
fair weather (in) fair (weather) and/or foul
fairly and squarely fair (and) square
fairly and squarely fair and square[1,2]
a far remove from sth (not) far removed from sth
feel one's heart sink(ing) one's heart sinks
one's feelings are mixed have etc mixed feelings
fellow-travelling a fellow traveller
a few go a long way a little (sth) goes a long way
fight hand-to-hand hand-to-hand fighting etc
fight like cat and dog (have/lead) a cat-and-dog life
find the going heavy etc heavy etc going
finders keepers finding is keeping
findings keepings finding is keeping
fine-feathered fine feathers make fine birds
fitness for human consumption fit for human consumption
a flag-waver wave the flag
flag-waving wave the flag
fleetness of foot fleet of foot
(cause) a flutter in the dovecote(s) flutter the dovecotes
follow my leader follow sb's lead
fool enough etc (to do sth) enough of a fool etc (to do sth)
foot-stamping stamp one's foot
football-crazy mad etc about sb/sth

(just) for the fun of it (just) for fun
for good or ill for better or (for) worse
for the sake of argument (just) for argument's sake
for those who like that sort of thing if one likes that kind/sort of thing
for want of anything better to do (than) have nothing better to do (than)
forelock-touching/-tugging/-pulling touch etc one's forelock
frayed temper (one's) temper rises/frays
free-load a free loader
free-loading a free loader
freedom of speech free speech
from one job etc to another/the next from job etc to job etc
fuck all damn all
full marks to sb (for sth) give sb etc full marks (for sth)
fund-raising raise (the) money etc
fussing and bothering fuss and bother
gain on the swings what one loses on the roundabouts swings and roundabouts
a game of cat and mouse (play) a cat-and-mouse game
generate less light than heat generate more heat than light
generate a lot of heat generate more heat than light
get one's fingers burnt burn one's fingers
get a lucky strike strike lucky
the gilded pill gild/sugar the pill
give sb a box on the ear box sb's ear(s)
give sb's memory a jog jog one's/sb's memory
give a shrug of one's/the shoulders shrug one's shoulders
give sb a swelled/swollen head one's head swells
gnash one's teeth gnashing of teeth
go Dutch a Dutch treat
go the same way (as sb/sth) go the way of sb/sth
a go-slow go slow
go through hell and/or high water come hell or high water
go to the trouble to do/of doing sth take trouble to do sth
the going is heavy etc heavy etc going
a good-for-nothing good for nothing
(and) a good time was had by all have a good time
sb's got a hope! not have a hope (in hell) (of sth)
grapple hand-to-hand hand-to-hand fighting etc
a Greek gift fear the Greeks, bearing gifts
green-fingered have green fingers
grin broadly give (sb)/get a broad grin/smile
(feel/make) one's/sb's hackles rise raise sb's hackles
had it not been for sb/sth if it wasn't for sb/sth (doing sth)
hair-splitting split hairs
sb's hands are clean have clean hands
one's hands are full have one's hands full
have any/no idea of what it is to be/do sth know what it is to be/do sth
have etc a better than even/fifty-fifty chance have etc an even/a fifty-fifty chance (of doing sth)
have etc better than an even/a fifty-fifty chance have etc an even/a fifty-fifty chance (of doing sth)
have better things/something better to do (than) have nothing better to do (than)
have come to stay be here to stay
have a cowardly etc streak (in one) have a streak of cowardice etc (in one)
have/get one's face lifted have a face-lift
have gone (quite) far enough go too etc far
have/be a good etc day have/be one of one's good etc days
have one's good etc days have/be one of one's good etc days
have got it bad have got it badly
have/with a grin (on one's face) like a Cheshire cat grin like a Cheshire cat
have sth hands down win hands down
have a heavy cross to bear/carry bear/carry one's cross
have etc the luck of the devil have the devil's own luck
have nine lives (like a cat) like a cat with nine lives
have no earthly chance (of achieving sth) haven't an earthly (chance) (of achieving sth)
have no/not have any idea of what it is to be/do sth know what it is to be/do sth
have no need to do sth there is no need for sth/(for sb) to do sth[1,2]
have only (got) to say the word (just) say the word
have a swelled/swollen head one's head swells
have wisdom/understanding/appreciation beyond one's years old etc beyond one's years
have sb's word (of honour) (that) give (sb) one's word (of honour) (that)
he was (doing) what! you what!
he who laughs last laughs longest/loudest have the last laugh
a head-count count heads
head-counting count heads
head-scratching scratch one's head
head-shaking shake one's head[2]
a head-shrinker shrink heads
heart-breaking break one's/sb's heart
one's heart gets the better of one's head one's head rules/governs one's heart
one's heart runs away with one's head one's head rules/governs one's heart
heart-searching search one's heart/soul
one's heart's desire everything/all (that) the heart (of a man) could desire
heavy-hearted have a heavy/light heart
a hell-raiser raise Cain/(merry) hell[1]
a high-flyer fly high
high-flying fly high
a hole in (the) corner business etc (a) hole and corner business etc
hollow laughter a hollow laugh
hopes are high have high hopes
hopes run high have high hopes
sb's hunch is (that) have a hunch (that)
I don't know how to put it put it etc differently etc

I'll give you a penny for your thoughts a penny for your thoughts
ice-cold (as) cold as ice etc
if/whether any living soul(s) not a (living) soul
if ever I/if I ever saw one if ever there was one
if sth is (not) so, (then) I'm a Dutchman or I'm a Dutchman
if it kills one if one dies in the attempt
if it's the last thing one does if one dies in the attempt
if pigs had wings they might be taught to fly pigs may/might fly
if that day should ever dawn dawn/day breaks
if you get my meaning/drift if you know etc what I mean
in sb's/sth's absence in the absence of sb/sth
in bare outline a bare outline (of sth)
in one's capacity as sth in an advisory etc capacity
in the long view take the long view
in more than one case/instance more than once
in order that sb may do sth in order to do sth
in sb's/sth's palmy days in/during the palmy days
in the parlance of sb in common etc parlance
in sober fact/truth sober fact etc
in spirit and/as well as in letter the letter of the law etc
in the spirit in which sth is intended/meant/offered in the right etc spirit
in this/that/another/a different light in the light of sth
in this/that regard in/with regard to sth
in the vein of sb/sth in a similar etc vein
in war/peace time in time of war etc
the injured innocent injured innocence
ink black as black as ink etc
invention is born of necessity necessity is the mother of invention
it can happen here it can't happen here etc
it comes to us all death/old age comes to us all
it is all part of the day's work it is all in the day's work
it is a funny thing (but) the funny thing is
it is just as well that it/that is just as well
it takes a thief to catch a thief set a thief to catch a thief
it would be better doing/to do sth do better to do sth
it's/he's the exception that proves the rule the exception proves the rule
it's odds on (that) the odds are (that)
its vices/defects are those of its virtues/qualities have the vices/defects of one's virtues/qualities
a jet-setter the jet set
just one pebble on the beach not the only pebble on the beach
just then just now[1]
keep one's conscience clear have a clear conscience
keep dead silent dead silence
keep an ear/an eye/a weather eye open keep one's ears/eyes open
keep one's face straight keep a straight face
keep one's hands clean have clean hands
keep one's head clear have a clear head[2]
keep (sb's) memory green sb's memory is green
keep one's/the mind a blank one's/the mind goes blank
keep the pot on the boil keep the pot boiling[2]
the King is dead, long live the King long live the King
know right from wrong right and wrong
know what one doesn't like not know anything about sth but know what one likes
(you) know what I mean? if you know etc what I mean
know/be aware of who's who know etc what's what
(all) labour/work/toil in the vineyard (all) labourers etc in the vineyard
the land of milk and honey a land flowing with milk and honey
the land of promise a/the promised land
a last ditcher the last ditch
laughter-prone prone to sth[2]
the law etc has a long arm the long arm of the law
the law's etc arm is long the long arm of the law etc
lay waste to sth lay sth waste
a lead-swinger swing the lead
leave no avenue unexplored explore every avenue
leave sth till/until the eleventh hour at the eleventh hour
leave sth till/until the last minute at the last minute
a leg-pull pull sb's leg
a leg-puller pull sb's leg
let the cobbler stick to his last the cobbler should stick to his last
let a man etc have enough rope (and he'll hang himself) give a man etc enough rope (and he'll hang himself)
let tomorrow take care of/look after itself tomorrow will/can take care of/look after itself
lie possum play possum
one's life expectancy the expectation of life
life is hard a hard life
a life-saver save sb's/one's life etc
life-saving save sb's/one's life etc
light-hearted have a heavy/light heart
one's lightly-worn learning etc wear one's learning etc lightly
(when) the lights go on the lights are going out all over Europe
(like) a Cheshire cat's grin/smile grin like a Cheshire cat
like cutting butter with a hot knife like a (hot) knife through butter/margarine
like the proverbial bad penny like a bad penny
like a rudderless ship like a ship without a rudder
a little fish in a big pond a big fish in a little pond

a little of sb/sth goes a long way a little (sth) goes a long way
look as if/though sb has been dragging one backwards through hedges look as if/though one has been dragged through a hedge backwards
look as if/though one has been feeding hens in the rain look as if/though one has slept in that suit etc for a week
look at sb (in an) old-fashioned way give sb/get an old-fashioned look
look blank give sb/get a blank look
look like a ghost look as if/though one has seen a ghost
lose no time (in) doing sth waste (one's/sb's) time
loss-making make a loss/profit
a loss of face lose/save face
(a) loss of life lose one's life
a lucky strike strike lucky
maintáin the spirit as much/as well as the letter of the law etc the letter of the law etc
make certain/sure about/of sth make certain/sure[1]
make certain/sure of sth make certain/sure[2]
a make-do-and-mend make do and mend
make one's gorge rise one's gorge rises
make sb's heart sink one's heart sinks
make a laughing stock of sb/sth make etc (sb/sth) a laughing stock
make life hell for sb life is hell
make life worth living life is (not) worth living
make oneself look foolish/silly/ridiculous etc make oneself/sb look etc a fool etc
make a lucky strike strike lucky
make one's/the mind a blank one's/the mind goes blank
make one's/the mind go blank one's/the mind goes blank
make one's mouth water one's mouth waters
make a new man/woman of sb (like) a new man/woman
make-or-break make or break etc
make so bold as to do sth make bold to do sth
male chauvinism a male chauvinist (pig/swine)
marry for convenience a marriage of convenience
master of the house the man/lady of the house
a matchmaker make a match
matchmaking make a match
the matter etc is (purely etc) academic (a matter etc) of academic interest/concern
matter-of-çourse (as) a matter of course
matter-of-fact a matter of fact
matter-of-factly a matter of fact
matter-of-factness a matter of fact
sb/sth may/can go hang let sb/sth go hang
a/the meeting of extremes extremes meet
a merrymaker make merry
merrymaking make merry
mind-blowing blow one's/sb's mind
a mind-boggler one's/the mind/imagination boggles
mind-boggling one's/the mind/imagination boggles
one's/the mind is a blank one's/the mind goes blank
sb's mind is open have an open mind
mind other people's business mind one's own business
a mind-reader read sb's mind/thoughts
mind your own business mind one's own business
a miracle-worker work a miracle/wonders
a mischief-maker make etc mischief
mischief-making make etc mischief
mistress of the house the man/lady of the house
a mixture of motives have etc mixed motives
money-mad mad etc about sb/sth
money-making make money
money marries money marry money
more changeable than a weathercock (as) changeable as a weathercock
more harm than good comes of doing sth do more harm than good
the more the pity more's the pity
more than one can claim/say for sb/sth more than one can say for/of sb/sth
more than meets the eye in it etc more in it etc than meets the eye
a morning-after the morning after (the night before)
one's motives are mixed have etc mixed motives
mouth-watering one's mouth waters
muck means/begets money where there's muck there's money
muck and money go together where there's muck there's money
muck rake rake muck
a muck-raker rake muck
muck-raking rake muck
a mummy's boy a mother's boy
muscle flexing flex one's muscles
(if sb doesn't like it,) sb must lump it like it or lump it
nail-picking pick one's nose etc
name-calling call sb names
name-dropping drop names
nature's abhorrence of a vacuum nature abhors a vacuum
need the wisdom of Solomon (as) wise as Solomon
neither of them grows/gets any younger/thinner not grow/get any younger/thinner
never see hide nor hair of sb/sth neither hide nor hair of sb/sth
never think to see/one would see the day live to see the day
a new high/low an all-time high/low
a night on the town a (big) night out
(in/through) the night watches (in/through) the watches of the night
a nine-to-fiver a nine to five job etc
no/not any better etc than the next (one) as good etc as the next (one)
no/not any better etc than the next man as good etc as the next man
sb/sth, no less no less (a person/place) (than sb/sth)

(with) no/some etc loss of cool keep/lose one's cool
no price is too high to pay pay a/the price (for sth)
no/small/little wonder it is no wonder (that)
none of them grows/gets any younger/thinner not grow/get any younger/thinner
nose-picking pick one's nose etc
not be the only fish in the sea there are (plenty) more (good) fish in the sea
not feel (so) good feel good
not know if/whether one is on one's arse or one's elbow not know if/whether one is on one's head or one's heels
not know where to put oneself not know what to do with oneself
not let one's left hand know what one's right hand is doing one's left hand does not know what one's right hand is doing
not (just/quite) right (for sb/sth) just right (for sb/sth)
not a schoolmaster etc for nothing not for nothing[2]
not that I'm any judge if I'm any judge (of sb/sth)
a not unmixed blessing a mixed blessing
noted, renowned etc for nothing if not for sth nothing if not sth
nothing happens to sb if anything happens to sb
observe the spirit as much/as well as the letter of the law etc the letter of the law etc
of every shape and size of all shapes and sizes
of sorts of a kind/sort
of tender age at a tender age
the old(-)boy net(work) an old boy
old-fogeyish an old fogey
old-fogeyism an old fogey
old-maidish an old maid
old maidishness an old maid
on sb's account on account of sb/sth
(be) on the crest of the wave ride (the crest of) the wave
on the footing of sth/that on a firm etc footing
on form on present etc form
on the lines of sth on these lines
on merit on sb's merits
on more than one occasion more than once
on a note of optimism etc on an optimistic etc note
on one/this/that condition on (the) condition that
on the score of sth on that score
on second thoughts have second thoughts
on the terms agreed on these terms
on the terms on which on these terms
on the terms proposed on these terms
on that basis on the basis of sth
on that front on the home etc front
on these/those conditions on (the) condition that
on this/that ground on the ground(s) that
on this/that scale on a large etc scale
on this/that understanding on the understanding that
on those/other/all kinds of grounds on the ground(s) that
(be) on time dead on time
on what conditions on (the) condition that
once a certain point is reached beyond a certain point
only half the story not the whole etc story
only time will tell etc time (alone) will tell etc
open-minded have an open mind
the opening of Pandora's box open Pandora's box
or however or whatever
or whenever or whatever
an ounce of prevention is worth a pound/ton of cure prevention is better than cure
over hill and dale up hill and down dale
a pace-setter set the pace
a packed house pack the house
painstaking take pains
a Pandora's box open Pandora's box
parish-pumpery the parish pump
parish-pumping the parish pump
one's/sb's paths cross cross sb's path
pay sb the compliment of doing sth pay (sb) a compliment
pay (sb) compliments pay (sb) a compliment
peace(-)keeping keep the peace
(how/which way) the pendulum swings the swing of the pendulum
(a) penny for them/'em a penny for your thoughts
a pickpocket pick sb's pocket
pit black as black as ink etc
pitch black as black as ink etc
plough one's own furrow plough a lone/lonely furrow
a plougher of a lonely furrow plough a lone/lonely furrow
point (already) taken take etc sb's point
poker-faced a poker face
poker-stiff (as) stiff as a poker
a pot-boiler keep the pot boiling[1]
a pound etc here and a pound etc there here and there
a practical joker a practical joke
a precious lot (of sth) precious few/little
prefer the devil one knows to the devil one doesn't the devil one knows is better than the devil one doesn't
the pricks/prickings of conscience one's conscience pricks one
probably sooner than later sooner or later
profit-making make a loss/profit
a pub-crawler a pub crawl
pub-crawling a pub crawl
a puff-puff a puffing billy
a puffer a puffing billy
pursed-lipped purse one's lips
put sb wise (to sb/sth) get wise (to sb/sth)
question-begging beg the question
the question is/remains open an open question
a queue jumper jump the queue
queue-jumping jump the queue
raise eyebrows raise one's/sb's eyebrows
raise some/certain eyebrows raise one's/sb's eyebrows
a raiser of hackles raise sb's hackles
ramrod-stiff/-straight (as) stiff/straight as a ramrod
rather the devil one knows than the devil

one doesn't the devil one knows is better than the devil one doesn't
a **reactionary etc of the deepest dye** a dyed-in-the-wool reactionary etc
a rib-tickler tickle sb's ribs
rib-tickling tickle sb's ribs
rightly or wrongly right and/or wrong
the rise and fall (of sb/sth) rise and fall[1]
the rise and fall of sb/sth rise and fall[2]
a risk/threat/danger to life and limb life and/or limb
the rot starts/sets in start the rot
rough-house sb a rough house
the rub is that there etc is/lies the rub
the rub lies in doing sth there etc is/lies the rub
rules are made to be broken break the rules
(cause) a rustle in the dovecote(s) flutter the dovecotes
a scene-stealer steal the show/scene
searching of heart search one's heart/soul
searching of soul search one's heart/soul
see etc the lie of the land see how the land lies
set too hot a pace (for sb) the pace is etc too hot (for sb)
shame on you! for shame(!)
a short-fall fall short (of sth)
a short haul a long haul
short of sth (nothing can/will do sth) nothing short of sth (can/will do sth)
should the worst come to the worst if the worst/it comes to the worst
show scant respect for persons be no/not any respecter of persons
a show-stopper/showstopper stop the show
show wisdom/understanding/appreciation beyond one's years old etc beyond one's years
a sigh of relief arose breathe etc a sigh of relief
sight-seeing see the sights
a sightseer see the sights
a skeleton outline (of sth) the bare bones (of sth)
slap bang in the middle (of sth) bang etc in the middle (of sth)
a small fish in a big pond a big fish in a little pond
smart aleckry a smart alec(k)
smart-alecky a smart alec(k)
smile broadly give (sb)/get a broad grin/smile
soft-soaping soft soap
(at) some or other time (at) some time or other
something happens to sb if anything happens to sb
sooner rather than later sooner or later
soul-searching search one's heart/soul
soundness in wind and limb sound in wind and limb
a special pleader special pleading
a speech-maker make etc a speech
speech-making make etc a speech
a spent force spend one's/its force
a spine-chiller chill sb's/the spine etc
spine-chilling chill sb's/the spine etc
(be) spit-and-polished spit and polish
spot etc sb's (little) game what/that is sb's (little) game
a spring clean spring clean
spring cleaning spring clean
(stars of) stage, screen and television stage and screen
statistics/figures can (be made to) prove anything you can prove anything with/by statistics/figures
a steady (boy-friend/girl-friend) go steady (with sb)
stomach-turning turn one's stomach
one's stomach turns turn one's stomach
stone-cold (as) cold as ice etc
stop sb short stop short (at sth)
stops and starts stop and start
strike the iron while it is hot strike while the iron is hot
a string-puller pull (the) strings/wires
string pulling pull (the) strings/wires
the stuff of which dreams etc are made the stuff that dreams etc are made of
a sucker is born every minute there is a sucker/one born every minute
suffer from a swelled/swollen head one's head swells
(the) sugar on the pill gild/sugar the pill
suspend (one's) disbelief the suspension of disbelief
the sweet taste of stolen fruit stolen sweets etc are sweeter/the sweetest
swollen-headed one's head swells
take another/a different/the opposite etc view take the view that
take one's ease at one's ease
take a tip from me take my tip
talk etc for the sake of it art etc for art's etc sake
teach sb a lesson learn a/one's lesson
a tell-tale tell tales
tell sb what he can do with sth you know what you can do (with it/sth)
tell sb where he can put sth you know where you can put sth
and that and all that
that/this is all I need all one needs is sth
that/this is the funny thing the funny thing is (that)
that's the best/worst of sth the best/worst of it/sth is (that)
that's the rub there etc is/lies the rub
there are as good fish in the sea (as ever came out of it) there are (plenty) more (good) fish in the sea
there are plenty of (other) fish in the sea there are (plenty) more (good) fish in the sea
there's no harm in doing sth do no/not do any harm
they don't come like that any more they don't make etc them like that any more
thick-skinned have a thick/thin skin
thin-skinned have a thick/thin skin
think positive(ly) positive thinking
the throes of death one's death agony/throes
thumb-twiddling twiddle one's thumbs
a tightrope walker walk a tightrope
tightrope walking walk a tightrope
till death do us part till/until death us do part

time, the great healer time is a great healer
time heals time is a great healer
time was when there was a time when
tip a wink at sb tip sb a wink
to the effect that to that effect
to the tips of one's fingers to one's/the fingertips
a tommy Tommy Atkins
touch-and-go be touch and go
a trail-blazer blaze a trail
trail-blazing blaze a trail
transform geese into swans (all) sb's geese are swans
treble crossing a double cross
(do) Trojan work work like a slave etc
a trouble-maker make/cause trouble
a true blue true blue
trumpet-blowing blow one's own trumpet
truth to tell to tell you the truth
a tub-thumper thump a/the tub/Bible
tub-thumping thump a/the tub/Bible
turn geese into swans (all) sb's geese are swans
turn the tide the tide turns
a turncoat change/turn one's coat
two can play at that game the game is (not) worth the candle
two's company, three's not/none two's company, (three's a crowd)
um and ah hum and ha(w)
under the name of sb/sth under one's own etc name
unlucky at cards lucky at cards, unlucky in love
until death do us part till/until death us do part
velvet-smooth (as) smooth as velvet
the very thing just the thing
a viewpoint a/one's point of view
one's voice has an edge to it have an edge to one's voice
want no part of it not want any part of sth
was my face red! have a red face
a waste of (one's/sb's) time waste (one's/sb's) time
waste no time (in) doing sth waste (one's/sb's) time
waste no words not waste words
watch hawk-like watch (sb/sth) like a hawk
wave a red rag at a bull (like) a red rag to a bull
the weak(est) link in the chain a chain is (only) as strong as its weakest link
well-meaning mean well
were it not for sb/sth if it wasn't for sb/sth (doing sth)
wet-nurse a wet nurse
a what-d'you-call-it what d'you call him
what one gains on the swings one loses on the roundabouts swings and roundabouts
what hope does sth/sb have? not have a hope (in hell) (of sth)
what I (always) say is (that) that's what I (always) say
what's the world coming to? I don't know what the world's coming to
wheel and deal wheeling and dealing
a wheeler-dealer wheeling and dealing
when the great day dawns dawn/day breaks
where are the other (ninety-)nine? you and the other (ninety-)nine
(the) whiter-than-whiteness (of sth) (wash) whiter than white
the why(s) and (the) wherefore(s) (of sth) why and wherefore?
the wild and woolly west the Wild West
one will cross that bridge when one comes to it cross one's bridges when one comes to them
a wire-puller pull (the) strings/wires
wire pulling pull (the) strings/wires
wisdom after the event wise after the event
with as good a grace as possible with (a) good grace
with clockwork regularity (as) regular as clockwork
with/having eyes as big as saucers (as) big/round as saucers
with one's hand on one's heart hand over heart
with/and no expense etc spared spare no expense etc
with pursed lips purse one's lips
with a shake of one's head shake one's head
with a shrug of one's/the shoulders shrug one's shoulders
with a sinking heart one's heart sinks
with a wisdom/an understanding beyond one's years old etc beyond one's years
within a stone's throw (of sth) a stone's throw ((away) from sth)
without a hope in hell not have a hope (in hell) (of sth)
without turning a hair not turn a hair
witty and wise wit and wisdom
word-eating eat one's words
(on sb's) word of honour give (sb) one's word (of honour) (that)
worldly wisdom worldly wise
would sooner do A (than B) would as soon do A (as B)
you (can) bet your sweet life on sth you (can) bet your (sweet) life (that)
you can use statistics/figures to prove anything you can prove anything with/by statistics/figures
you can't have your bread buttered on both sides know which/what side one's bread is buttered (on)
you did what! you what!
you heard what the man said that's what the man said
you know something(?) do you know
you've never had it so good have it good